India

Jammu & Kashmir (including Ladakh) p225
Himachal Pradesh p282
Punjab & Haryana p201
Uttarakhand p412
Delhi p56
Sikkim p535
Northeast States p559
Uttar Pradesh p376
Agra & the Taj Mahal p352
Rajasthan p104
Bihar & Jharkhand p516
West Bengal & Darjeeling p483
Gujarat p686
Madhya Pradesh & Chhattisgarh p621
Kolkata (Calcutta) p452
Odisha p593
Mumbai (Bombay) p734
Maharashtra p772
Telangana & Andhra Pradesh p911
Goa p809
Karnataka & Bengaluru p851
Tamil Nadu & Chennai p1002
Kerala p941

THIS EDITION WRITTEN AND RESEARCHED BY

Abigail Blasi, Lindsay Brown, Anirban Mahapatra, Isabella Noble, John Noble, Kevin Raub, Sarina Singh, Michael Benanav, Mark Elliott, Paul Harding, Anna Kaminski, Bradley Mayhew, Iain Stewart

PLAN YOUR TRIP

TEA PLANTATION, MUNNAR P972

INSTANTS /GETTY IMAGES ©

PANGONG TSO P253

SUTTIPONG SUTIRATANACHAI/ GETTY IMAGES ©

ON THE ROAD

Contents

ON THE ROAD

Contents

Welcome to India

A land of remarkable diversity – from ancient traditions and artistic heritage to magnificent landscapes and culinary creations – India will ignite your curiosity, shake your senses and warm your soul.

Natural Splendour

From the towering icy peaks of the northern mountains to the sun-washed beaches of the southern coast, India's dramatic terrain is breathtaking. Along with abundant natural beauties, exquisite temples rise majestically out of pancake-flat deserts and crumbling fortresses peer over plunging ravines. Aficionados of the great outdoors can scout for big jungle cats on wildlife safaris, paddle in the shimmering waters of beautiful beaches, take blood-pumping treks high in the Himalaya, or simply inhale pine-scented air on a meditative forest walk.

Glorious Gastronomy

Brace yourself – you're about to take one of the wildest culinary trips of your travelling life. Here you'll fry, simmer, sizzle, knead, roast and flip across a deliciously diverse repertoire of dishes. The hungry traveller can look forward to a tasty smorgasbord of regionally distinct recipes, all with their own traditional preparation techniques and presentation styles – from the competing flavours of masterfully marinated meats and thalis to the simple splendour of vegetarian curries and deep-sea delights.

Explore the Unexpected

India tosses up the unexpected. This can be challenging, particularly for the first-time visitor: the poverty is confronting, Indian bureaucracy can be exasperating and the crush of humanity may turn the simplest task into a frazzling epic. Even veteran travellers find their nerves frayed at some point; yet this is all part of the India ride. With an ability to inspire, frustrate, thrill and confound all at once, adopting a 'go with the flow' attitude is wise if you wish to retain your sanity. Love it or loathe it – and most travellers see-saw between the two – to embrace India's unpredictability is to embrace its soul.

Sacred Celebrations

Spirituality is the common characteristic painted across the vast and varied canvas that is contemporary India. The multitude of sacred sites and rituals are testament to the country's long, colourful, and sometimes tumultuous, religious history. And then there are its festivals! India hosts some of the world's most divine devotional celebrations – from formidable city parades celebrating auspicious events on the religious calendar to simple village harvest fairs that pay homage to a locally worshipped deity.

Why I Love India

By Sarina Singh, Writer

The moment I start to think I'm right on the precipice of unravelling one of India's deep mysteries, it has an uncanny way of reminding me that it would take more than just a few lifetimes to do so. Indeed, demystifying India is a perpetual work in progress. And that is precisely what makes the country so deeply alluring for me. The constant exploration. The playful unpredictability. And knowing that, just when it's least expected, you can find yourself up close and personal with moments that have the power to alter the way you view the world and your place in it.

For more about our writers, see p1248

Above: Taj Mahal (p354)

India

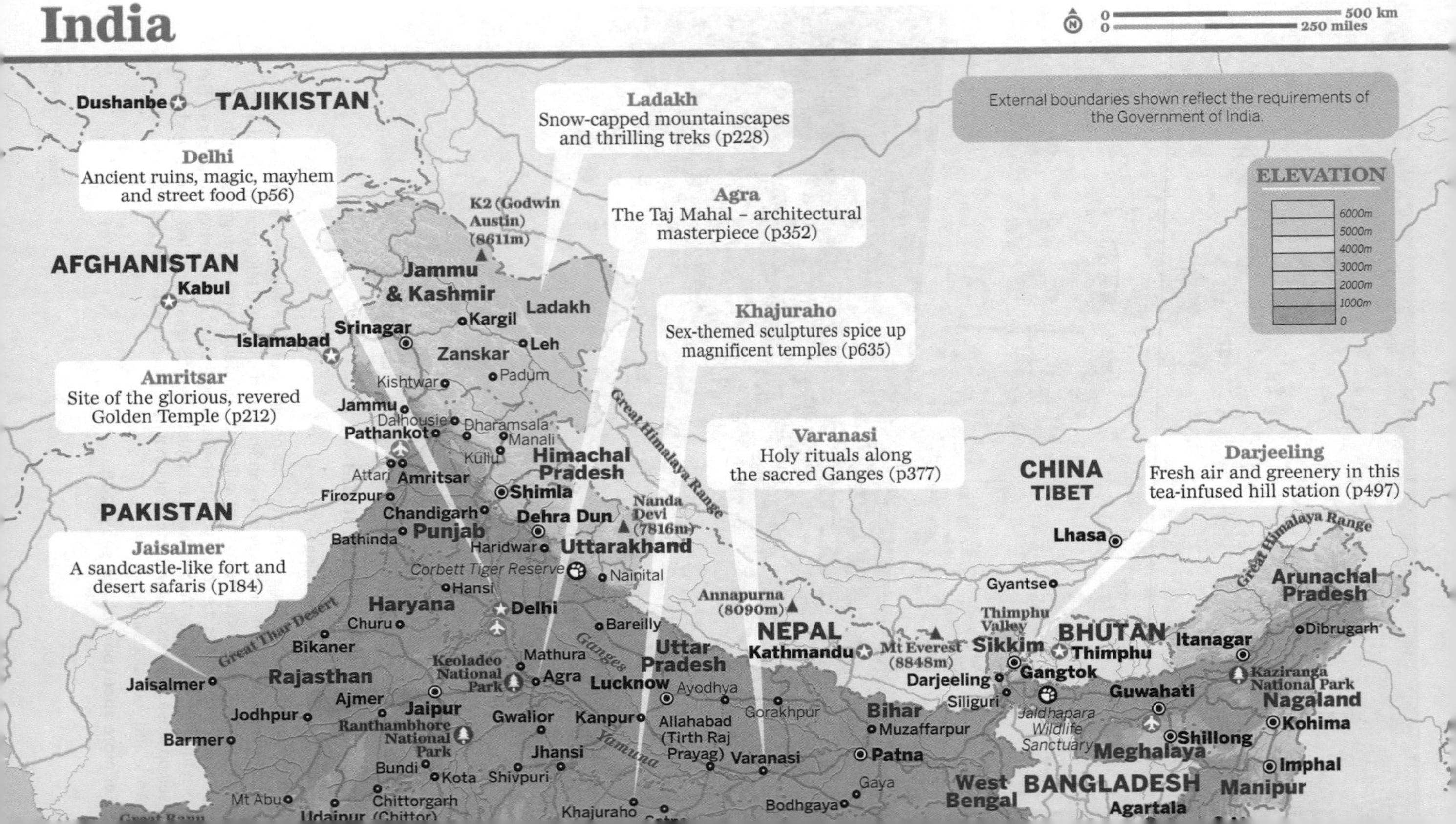
0 500 km
0 250 miles
External boundaries shown reflect the requirements of the Government of India.
ELEVATION
6000m
5000m
4000m
3000m
2000m
1000m
0
Ladakh
Snow-capped mountainscapes and thrilling treks (p228)
Delhi
Ancient ruins, magic, mayhem and street food (p56)
Agra
The Taj Mahal – architectural masterpiece (p352)
Khajuraho
Sex-themed sculptures spice up magnificent temples (p635)
Amritsar
Site of the glorious, revered Golden Temple (p212)
Varanasi
Holy rituals along the sacred Ganges (p377)
Darjeeling
Fresh air and greenery in this tea-infused hill station (p497)
Jaisalmer
A sandcastle-like fort and desert safaris (p184)
Dushanbe
TAJIKISTAN
AFGHANISTAN
Kabul
Islamabad
PAKISTAN
K2 (Godwin Austin) (8611m)
Jammu & Kashmir
Srinagar
Kargil
Ladakh
Leh
Zanskar
Padum
Kishtwar
Jammu
Dalhousie
Dharamsala
Manali
Pathankot
Kullu
Himachal Pradesh
Attari
Amritsar
Firozpur
Shimla
Chandigarh
Punjab
Bathinda
Dehra Dun
Haridwar
Uttarakhand
Nanda Devi (7816m)
Great Himalaya Range
Corbett Tiger Reserve
Nainital
Hansi
Haryana
Delhi
Churu
Bareilly
Great Thar Desert
Bikaner
Rajasthan
Jaisalmer
Keoladeo National Park
Mathura
Agra
Ganges
Uttar Pradesh
Lucknow
Ayodhya
Ajmer
Jaipur
Jodhpur
Ranthambhore National Park
Gwalior
Kanpur
Allahabad (Tirth Raj Prayag)
Barmer
Jhansi
Yamuna
Bundi
Kota
Shivpuri
Mt Abu
Chittorgarh (Chittor)
Udaipur
Khajuraho
Annapurna (8090m)
NEPAL
Kathmandu
Mt Everest (8848m)
Gorakhpur
Varanasi
Bihar
Muzaffarpur
Patna
Gaya
Bodhgaya
CHINA
TIBET
Lhasa
Gyantse
Thimphu Valley
Sikkim
BHUTAN
Thimphu
Darjeeling
Gangtok
Siliguri
Jaldhapara Wildlife Sanctuary
Guwahati
Itanagar
Arunachal Pradesh
Dibrugarh
Kaziranga National Park
Nagaland
Kohima
Shillong
Meghalaya
Imphal
Manipur
West Bengal
BANGLADESH
Agartala

Mumbai
Bollywood, big city dazzle and grandiose architecture (p734)
Ajanta Caves
Ancient caves along a horseshoe-shaped cliff (p787)
Goan Beaches
The Arabian sea laps golden sands (p809)
Hampi
Ruins pepper a boulder-strewn landscape (p896)
Keralan Backwaters
Houseboats and canoes on palm-fringed rivers (p941)
Wildlife Sanctuary
Ahmedabad
Ujjain
Dewas
Bhopal
Dindori
Jamshedpur
(Calcutta)
Mizoram
MYANMAR (BURMA)
Jamnagar
Rajkot
Dwarka
Porbandar
Bhavnagar
Junagadh
Sasan Gir Wildlife Sanctuary
Diu
Porbandar Coast
Vadodara (Baroda)
Mandu
Indore
Khandwa
Kanha National Park
Seoni
Chhattisgarh
Bilaspur
Sambalpur
Similipal National Park
Kharagpur
Sunderbans Tiger Reserve
Digha
Balasore
Surat
Dhule
Jalgaon
Nagpur
Raipur
Odisha (Orissa)
Cuttack
Paradip
Daman
Dahanu
Ajanta
Maharashtra
Bhubaneswar
Konark
Puri
Berhampur
Ranipur-Jharial
Nasik
Aurangabad
Kalyan
Upper Godavari Valley
Mumbai (Bombay)
Pune
Telangana
Mahabaleshwar
Konkan Hills
Sholapur
Warangal
Hyderabad
Bheemunipatnam
Visakhapatnam
Vijapura (Bijapur)
Kakinada
Belgaum (Belagavi)
Vijayawada
Machilipatnam
Arabian Sea
Panaji (Panjim)
Goa
Gadag
Hampi
Hubli (Hubballi)
Hospet (Hosapete)
Andhra Pradesh
Eastern Ghats
Ongole
Bay of Bengal
Karnataka
Nellore
Nandi Hills
Hassan
Chittoor
Chennai (Madras)
Mangaluru (Mangalore)
Mysuru (Mysore)
Bengaluru (Bangalore)
Mamallapuram
Andaman Islands
Ooty (Udhagamandalam)
Puducherry (Pondicherry)
Port Blair
Andaman Sea
Thalasseri (Tellicherry)
Kozhikode (Calicut)
Chidambaram
Coimbatore
Lakshadweep Islands
Tamil Nadu
Trichy (Tiruchirappalli)
Lakshadweep Sea
Kochi (Cochin)
Western Ghats
Madurai
Kerala
Periyar Wildlife Sanctuary
Rameswaram
Kollam
Thiruvananthapuram (Trivandrum)
Kovalam
Kanyakumari
Gulf of Mannar
SRI LANKA
Nicobar Islands
INDIAN OCEAN
Colombo

India's Top 17

1

Taj Mahal

1 Exquisite tomb that's as much a monument to love as it is to death, the Taj Mahal (p354) is arguably the world's most beautiful building, and has been enshrined in the writings of Tagore and Kipling. Built by Emperor Shah Jahan in adoration of his third wife, Mumtaz Mahal, this milky-white marble mausoleum is inlaid with calligraphy, precious and semiprecious stones and intricate floral designs representing eternal paradise, and is the pinnacle of Mughal architecture as well as romance.

Otherworldly Hampi

2 Magnificent, even in ruins, Hampi (p896) was once the cosmopolitan Vijayanagar, capital of a powerful Hindu empire, spread across an emerald-green and terracotta-red landscape. Its temples and royal structures combine sublimely with the terrain: giant rocks balance on slender pedestals near an ancient elephant garage; temples tuck into crevices between boulders; and wicker coracles float by rice paddies and bathing buffalo near a gargantuan bathtub for a former queen. As the sunset casts a rosy glow over the dreamy landscape, you might just forget what planet you're on.

ELENA-STUDIO / GETTY IMAGES ©

2

PIKOSO.KZ / SHUTTERSTOCK ©

Ladakh's Moonscapes

3 As you head north, the air grows cooler and crisper, and you reach quaint, historic hill stations, summer escapes that are ringed by snow-capped peaks. In Ladakh (p228) cultural influences came not by coasts but via mountain passes. Tibetan Buddhism thrives, and multilayered monasteries emerge from the forest or steep cliffs as vividly and poetically as the sun rises over Khangchendzonga. Weathered prayer flags flutter in the wind and the soothing sound of monks chanting reverberates in meditation halls, all in the shadow of the mighty Himalaya. Shanti Stupa (p230)

Caves of Ajanta

4 They may have been ascetics, but the 2nd-century-BC monks who created the Ajanta caves (p787) certainly had an eye for the dramatic. The 30 rock-cut forest grottoes punctuate the side of a horseshoe-shaped cliff, and originally had individual staircases leading down to the river. The architecture and towering stupas made these caves inspiring places to meditate and live, but the real bling came centuries later, in the form of exquisite carvings and paintings depicting the Buddha's former lives. Renunciation of the worldly life was never so serenely sophisticated.

3

4

SNEHAL JEEVAN PAILKAR / SHUTTERSTOCK ©

VINOD V CHANDRAN / SHUTTERSTOCK ©

Backwaters of Kerala

5 It's like heading into a dream, lazily navigating the tropically radiant backwaters of Kerala (p964): what is probably India's most laid-back state has 900km of interconnected rivers, lakes, canals and lagoons lined with the swaying palms of thick coconut groves and picturesque villages. One of the most popular and scenic ways to peruse these parts is by cruising on a teak-and-palm-thatch houseboat. Drift along the waterways – as the sun sinks behind the trees, while snacking on succulent Keralan seafood – and forget all about life on land for a while.

Architectural Mumbai

6 In a way that is quintessentially Indian, Mumbai (p734) absorbs influences into its midst and inventively makes them its own. The result is a heady architectural melange of buildings with a raft of design influences. The art deco and modern towers lend the city its cool, but it's the eclectic Victorian-era structures – the neo-Gothic, Indo-Saracenic and other old flourishes – that have significantly added to Mumbai's magic. All those spires, gables, arches and onion domes, set off by lofty palms and leafy banyans, are apt embellishments for this movie star city.

Safaris

7 Tiger and leopard spotting in India is very much a matter of luck and timing, but thousands do. Even if you don't, it's a pleasure to simply wander through one of India's many beautiful forest reserves (p1173) observing chital (spotted deer), peacocks and langur monkeys while colourful birds and butterflies flit overhead. Or for a completely different safari experience, hop aboard a 'ship of the desert'. At towns such as Jaisalmer or Bikaner, you can ride on camelback through desert scrub, stopping at night to camp among a ocean of sand dunes and under a shedload of stars. Chital at Bandipur National Park (p878)

JANE SWEENEY / GETTY IMAGES ©

Cuppa in a Hill Station

8 India's valleys, deserts and palm-lined beaches are full of wonders, but come summer it can get darn hot down there. India's erstwhile princes and British colonials used to escape the heat by heading to the cool mountain refuges, such as Darjeeling (p497; pictured above left), and the hill stations still serve up lush forests and crisp mountain air. So, curl up under a blanket with a steaming cup of local tea and watch birds swooping across misty hillsides, broody clouds drifting over bulbous tea trees and village kids running through mountain fog and meadow wildflowers.

Holy Varanasi

9 Welcome to Varanasi (p377), a city full of life and death, and one of India's most revered sacred cities. Pilgrims flock here to worship, take a holy dip in the Ganges River, or cremate loved ones. Hindus believe the waters of the Ganges cleanse away sins, while dying here is deemed particularly propitious as it offers emancipation from the arduous life-and-death cycle. Varanasi will swiftly sweep you into its dizzying spiritual whirlwind – just take a deep breath and immerse yourself in pondering the meaning of life, death...and beyond. Dashashwamedh Ghat (p382)

Goan Beaches

10 With nodding palms on one side of the sugar-white sands and lapping powder-blue waves on the other, Goa's coastline is lined by beautiful beaches (p809) and has an easy-going hedonistic atmosphere that's like nowhere else in India. It's not an undiscovered paradise: this cool coastal strip bustles with fellow travellers, vendors and beach-shack eateries. It's a slice of paradise that appeals to social creatures and fans of creature comforts who like their seafood fresh and their holidays easy. Palolem Beach (p846)

Jaisalmer's Desert Mirage

11 A gigantic, golden sandcastle that rises like a mirage from the desert of Rajasthan, the 'Land of Kings', Jaisalmer's 12th-century citadel (p184; pictured below) is romantically picturesque. This sandstone fort, with its crenellated ramparts and undulating towers, is a fantastical structure, elegantly blending in with the toffee-gold hues of its desert environs. Inside, a royal palace, atmospheric old *havelis* (traditional residences), delicately chiselled Jain temples and skinny lanes all conspire to create one of the country's best places to get lost.

Cheeky Khajuraho

12 Care to see a nine-person orgy? Couples imaginatively intertwined? Hot nymphs? Khajuraho is the place! Some say the sensuous carvings on Khajuraho's temples (p635) depict the Kama Sutra, or Tantric practices for initiates; others, that they're educational models for children or allegories for the faithful. But pretty much everyone agrees that they're delightfully mischievous. Once the initial titillation wanes, you'll notice that the carving and architecture of these historic temples are remarkably skilled and multifariously mind stirring.

11

12

Epic Rail Journeys

13 A long train journey (p34) across India, from sun-baked plains to lime-green rice paddies, is an epic experience. Domestic flights are increasingly popular, but as the estimated 25 million daily train passengers can attest, you can't soak up India's dramatically diverse landscape and mingle with so many people on a plane. It's a chance to leisurely chit-chat over a hot cup of chai, or gaze out of the window at the passing land and people, listening to the click-clacking soundtrack of the rattling rails. Nilgiri Mountain Railway (p1084)

Delhi

14 India's capital (p56) bears the mighty remnants of former empires, from great Mughal tombs to the grandiose British-era mansions. There's so much to see here: the crumbling splendour of Old Delhi – with the Jama Masjid, Red Fort and its havelis, the ancient forts of Tughlabad and Purana Qila, and the wonders of Qutb Minar and Mehrauli Archaeological Park. Add to this the city's many fine eateries, with offerings from street food to modern Indian, superb museums and amazing shopping, and it's easy to see why Delhi mesmerizes many. Jama Masjid (p66)

MARTCHAN / SHUTTERSTOCK ©

SAIKO3P / SHUTTERSTOCK ©

Amritsar's Golden Temple

15 The Golden Temple (p212) in Amritsar, is the Sikhs' holiest of shrines, and has a magical atmosphere. Seeming to float atop a glistening pool named for the 'nectar of immortality', the temple is truly golden (the lotus-shaped dome is gilded in the real thing). Even when crowded with pilgrims it has a graceful tranquillity, with the sounds of *kirtan* (Sikh devotional singing) and birds chirping outside, and the mirror-like sacred pool that surrounds it.

French-Flavoured Puducherry

16 A place where you can gorge on yoga, *pain au chocolat*, Hindu gods and colonial-era architecture all at once is a *très bien* proposition. In this former French colony (p1037), yellow houses line cobblestone streets, grand cathedrals are adorned with architectural frou-frou, and the croissants are the real deal. But Puducherry's also a Tamil town – with all the history, temples and hustle and bustle that go along with that – and a classic retreat town, too, with the Sri Aurobindo Ashram at its heart. Notre Dame des Anges (p1040)

Mighty Mehrangarh

17 India has many inconceivably magnificent fortresses, but Jodhpur's Mehrangarh (p175) is among the finest, rearing up from its rocky outcrop. Like others, its huge doorways were built to accommodate elephants and its entryways designed to confuse invaders, but this is one of the most imposing settings of them all (though there's a lot of competition). India's forts typically tower above their surroundings like fantastical story-book visions, but Mehrangarh has the added glory of mesmerising views down to Jodhpur, Rajasthan's magical-looking blue city.

Need to Know

For more information, see Survival Guide (p1177)

Currency
Indian rupees (₹)

Languages
Hindi, English

Visas
More than 100 nationalities can obtain a 30-day e-Tourist visa (p1194); this is valid from the day you arrive. For longer trips, you'll need to obtain a six-month tourist visa, valid from the date of issue.

Money
There are ATMs in most towns; carry cash as backup. Mastercard and Visa are the most widely accepted credit cards.

Mobile Phones
Roaming connections are excellent in urban areas, poor in the countryside and the Himalaya. Local prepaid SIMs are widely available; they involve some straightforward paperwork and sometimes a wait of up to 24 hours for activation.

Time
India Standard Time (GMT/UTC plus 5½ hours)

When to Go

High Season
(Dec–Mar)

- Pleasant weather – warm days, cool nights. Peak tourists. Peak prices.
- December and January bring chilly nights in the north.
- Temperatures climb steadily from February.

Shoulder
(Jul–Nov)

- Passes to Ladakh and the high Himalaya open from July to September.
- Monsoon rain-showers persist through to September.
- The southeast coast and southern Kerala see heavy rain from October to early December.

Low Season
(Apr–Jun)

- April is hot; May and June are scorching. Competitive hotel prices.
- From June, the monsoon sweeps from south to north, bringing draining humidity.
- Beat the heat (but not the crowds) in the cool hills.

Useful Websites

Lonely Planet (www.lonelyplanet.com/india) Destination information, the Thorn Tree Travel Forum and more.

Incredible India (www.incredibleindia.org) Official India tourism site.

Templenet (www.templenet.com) Temple talk.

Rediff News (www.rediff.com/news) Portal for India-wide news.

World Newspapers (www.world-newspapers.com) Links to India's English-language publications.

Important Numbers

From outside India, dial your international access code, India's country code (91), then the number (minus the initial '0').

Country code	91
International access code	00
Emergency (Ambulance/Fire/Police)	112

Exchange Rates

Australia	A$1	₹51
Canada	C$1	₹51
Euro zone	€1	₹73
Japan	¥100	₹61
New Zealand	NZ$1	₹48
UK	UK£1	₹85
US	US$1	₹69

For current exchange rates see www.xe.com

Daily Costs

Budget: Less than ₹3000

- Dorm bed: ₹400–600
- Double room in a budget hotel: ₹400–700
- All-you-can-eat thalis (plate meals): ₹120–300
- Bus and train tickets: ₹300–500

Midrange: ₹4000–9000

- Double hotel room: ₹1500–5000
- Meals in midrange restaurants: ₹600–1500
- Admission to historic sights and museums: ₹500–1000
- Local taxis/autorickshaws: ₹500–2000

Top End: More than ₹9000

- Deluxe hotel room: ₹5000–22,000
- Meals at superior restaurants: ₹2000–5000
- First-class train travel: ₹1000–8000
- Renting a car and driver: ₹1800 upwards per day

Opening Hours

Opening hours are year-round for banks, offices and restaurants; many sights keep summer and winter opening hours.

Banks (nationalised) 10am–2pm/4pm Monday to Friday, to noon/1pm/4pm Saturday; closed second and fourth Saturday of month.

Restaurants 8am–10pm or lunch noon–3pm, dinner 7pm–10pm or 11pm

Bars & Clubs noon–12.30am

Shops 10am–7pm or 8pm, some closed Sunday

Arriving in India

Indira Gandhi International Airport (p1195) Prepaid taxis cost from ₹450 to the centre; express buses every 20 minutes (₹100); airport express metro trains (₹60/100 Sunday/Monday to Saturday) link up with the metro system. If you're transferring from terminal 1 to 3 allow at least three hours; the shuttle bus can take an hour.

Chhatrapati Shivaji International Airport (p1195) Prepaid taxis cost ₹680/820 (non-AC/AC) to Colaba and Fort and ₹400/480 to Bandra. From Colaba, an UberGo is around ₹385 off-peak.

Kempegowda International Airport (p1195) Metered AC taxis to the centre cost ₹750 to ₹1000. Air-conditioned Vayu Vajra buses run very regularly to/from the airport to destinations around the city; fares start at ₹180.

Chennai International Airport (p1195) Suburban trains to central Chennai run every 15 minutes (₹10) from 4.53am to 11.43pm from Tirusulam station at the airport. Prepaid taxis cost ₹450 to ₹600.

Getting Around

Transport in India is frequent and inexpensive, though not always fast. Consider domestic flights or sleeper trains as an alternative to long, uncomfortable bus rides.

Air Flights available to most major centres and state capitals; cheap flights with budget airlines.

Train Frequent services to most destinations; inexpensive tickets available, even on sleeper trains.

Bus Buses go everywhere; some destinations are served 24 hours but longer routes may have just one or two buses a day.

For much more on **getting around**, see p1197

If You Like...

Cycling

Bengaluru & Karnataka Go for a peaceful roll around the ruins of Bidar Fort and nearby Bahmani tombs. (p851)

Odisha Bike around the beautiful scenery, with good roads and very little traffic in Odisha's tribal country, around Koraput. (p593)

Padum Valley Mountain bikes are now available to rent through ZAP in Zanskar. (p263)

Forts & Palaces

India's architecture tells a tale of conquest, domination and inordinate riches.

Rajasthan Nowhere matches the Land of Kings for romantic splendour, with Jaisalmer, Jodhpur, Amber and lace-like Udaipur. (p104)

Maharashtra The land of Shivaji has defensive masterpieces including Daulatabad, and Janjira, an island fortress. (p772)

Hyderabad The rugged Golconda Fort complements the many ethereal palaces of the City of Pearls. (p913)

Delhi This historically strategic city has imperial forts like other places have traffic islands. (p56)

Ladakh Leh and Stok palaces are like mini versions of Tibet's fantastical Potala Palace. (p228)

Mysuru The majestic Mysuru Palace is the former residence of Mysuru's maharajas. (p867)

Grand Temples

No one does temples like India – from psychedelic Technicolor Hindu towers to silently grand Buddhist cave temples and Amritsar's gold-plated fairy-tale Sikh shrine.

Tamil Nadu A temple wonderland, with towering, fantastical structures that climb to the sky in busy rainbows of sculpted deities. (p1002)

Golden Temple The queen of Sikh temples rises like a shining gem over a pool in Amritsar. (p212)

Rajasthan Jain temples at Jaisalmer, Ranakpur and Mt Abu offer some of India's most mind-blowingly intricate carvings. (p104)

Khajuraho Exquisite carvings of deities, spirits, musicians, regular people, mythological beasts – and sex. Lots of sex. (p635)

Tawang Gompa The world's second-largest Buddhist monastery, in Arunachal Pradesh, is set against snowy peaks. (p578)

South Sikkim Gigantic Buddhist and Hindu sculptures rise unforgettably above three forested foothill ridges at Namchi (p549) and Ravangla (p550), backed by a horizon of white-topped Himalayan peaks.

Ajanta Ancient, vast, sculpted caves. Because monks like beautiful sculpture, too. (p787)

Delhi The almost-psychedelic structure of Akshardham versus the simplicity of the all-faith Bahai House of Worship. (p56)

Odisha The Sun Temple at Konark, with a vast, splendid stone chariot of the sun god Surya that features intricate erotic imagery. (p608)

Ancient Ruins

You can wander back through time throughout India, with the legacy of countless cultures and empires scattered across cities and countryside: you don't get to be a 5000-year-old civilisation without having lots of these around.

Hampi Rosy-hued temples and palaces of the mighty capital of Vijayanagar are scattered among otherworldly looking boulders and hilltops. (p896)

Mandu Many of the tombs, palaces, monuments and mosques on Mandu's 20-sq-km green plateau are among India's finest Afghan architecture. (p665)

Nalanda This Unesco-listed, 1600-year-old university once

Top: Buddhist stupa in Padum (p263)

Bottom: Kailasa Temple (p784), Ellora

enrolled 10,000 monks and students. Its monasteries, temples and stupas are still elegant in ruins. (p531)

Delhi Conquered and built up repeatedly over the past 3000 years, Delhi is packed full of the monumental ruins of ancient powerhouses. (p56)

Fatehpur Sikri A ghostly abandoned Mughal city, close to Agra and the Taj Mahal. (p371)

Maharashtra Magnificent rock-cut Buddhist temple caves. (p772)

City Sophistication

India's cities are a world away from life in small towns or the countryside. With booming economies and millennia of sophistication under their belts, India's cities have vibrant arts scenes, excellent restaurants and heaps of style.

Mumbai Home of Bollywood, Mumbai has it all: fashion, film stars, fine dining, glamorous bars and (along with Delhi) the country's best art galleries. (p734)

Delhi Urban sophisticate Delhi is famous for its cultural life, with regular festivals, plus exceptional shopping, museums, street food and swish restaurants. (p56)

Kolkata (Calcutta) Renowned for its poetry and poetics, Kolkata also has fabulous colonial-era architecture and a lively arts scene. (p452)

Bengaluru (Bangalore) This IT hub has a boozy nightlife with microbreweries, gastropubs and rock bars full of locals looking to party. (p853)

Chennai (Madras) Towering temples, elegant bars, swish hotels, fabulous shopping and a booming restaurant scene. (p1005)

Bazaars

Indian megamalls are popping up like monsoon frogs, but the bazaar – with its spices and gold, garbage and flowers – is still where it's at.

Old Delhi The Mughal-era bazaars feel like a direct link with the past, selling everything from gold to ball bearings, plus some of India's finest street food. (p60)

Goa Tourist flea markets are huge on the north coast, while Panaji (Panjim) and Margao bazaars make for excellent wandering. (p809)

Mumbai The megalopolis's old, characterful markets are firmly divided: Mangaldas (fabric), Zaveri (jewellery), Crawford (produce) and Chor (random antique bits). (p734)

Hyderabad The colourful, swarming streets around the Charminar sell bangles, birds, vegetables, wedding saris, antiques and much more. (p913)

Mysuru Devaraja Market is about 125 years old and filled with about 125 million flowers, fruits and vegetables. (p867)

Ahmedabad Manek Chowk proffers fresh-produce market by day and heaving night market by night, with copperware and textiles sold in the streets around it. (p688)

Beaches

India has some stunning stretches of paradisiacal coast, with tall palms and powdery white sand, while elsewhere the shoreline is more tinselled, with plenty of personality, people-watching and snack carts.

Kerala Varkala is backed by beautiful sea-cliffs and has a busy backpacker scene, Kovalam (p949) is a pretty resort with a golden bay. (p953)

Goa Even when overrun with travellers, the beaches are still lovely somehow. Mandrem and Palolem are two of the prettiest. (p809)

Havelock Island In the Andaman Islands, one of the world's most gorgeous beaches has clear, aquamarine water lapping against white powder. (p1095)

Gokarna Originally for Goa overflow, Gokarna's beautiful beaches are part of a sacred ancient village. (p893)

Boat Tours

India's waterways are a wonderful escape, and from canoes to steamships to houseboats, there are lots of ways to experience India's aquatic side.

Kerala Languorous drifting on the backwaters around Alappuzha (Alleppey; p960), canoe tours from Kollam (Quilon; p957) and bamboo-raft tours in **Periyar Wildlife Sanctuary** (p968).

Goa Dolphin- and croc-spotting tours on the Mandovi River; cruise to a secluded beach by outrigger fishing boat. (p809)

Andaman Islands See mangroves, rainforest and reefs with 50 types of coral at Mahatma Gandhi Marine National Park. (p1086)

Uttar Pradesh Navigate UP's chaotic holiness with dawn tours of Varanasi's ghats and sacred river cruises in Chitrakut, Mathura and Allahabad. (p376)

Assam Four- to 10-night steamboat cruises are offered along the mighty Brahmaputra River as it meanders through the Northeast. (p561)

Odisha Spot rare Irrawaddy dolphin as you tour Chilika Lake, Asia's largest brackish lagoon. (p609)

Traveller Enclaves

Sometimes you just want to find the like-minded, exchange stories and discuss strange bowel events. There are places for that.

Hampi The stunning beauty of Hampi's landscape and architecture makes everyone want to stay for a while. (p896)

Goa Traveller magnet and beach haven, with Palolem (p846) and (cheaper) Arambol (p838) as its chief enclaves.

Rishikesh In the mountains, this is a major international traveller yoga centre, whether you're a devotee or a newbie. (p414)

Sudder St, Kolkata The accommodation on Kolkata's tourist lane is grungy but great for meeting fellow travellers. (p452)

McLeod Ganj Because who doesn't want to be near the Dalai Lama? (p319)

Pushkar Travellers, pilgrims, camels: everyone converges on this Rajasthan town for the Camel Fair, but pilgrims and travellers head to its picture-perfect lake year-round. (p136)

Delhi Love it or hate it, almost every India traveller passes through Delhi's Paharganj at some point, and the capital's hostels are the newest traveller hot spots. (p56)

Puducherry Ex-French, popular yoga-ashram hangout with a refreshing European feel, boho boutiques and chilled cafes. (p1037)

Parvati Valley People hang out for weeks or months enjoying the laidback pleasures and ethe-

Elephant walking along the beach on Havelock Island (p1095)

real beauty of this Himalayan valley. (p302)

Yoga, Ayurveda & Spiritual Pursuits

Bihar Bodhgaya is the place of Buddha's enlightenment, with temples from across the globe and Buddhist meditation courses. (p518)

Kerala The southern state is where ayurveda originated, and there's a herbal-oil-based treatment on almost every corner. (p941)

Rishikesh One of India's most popular places to salute the sun, with lessons for every level. (p414)

McLeod Ganj Home of the Dalai Lama and India's capital of Tibetan Buddhism, with a big meditation, yoga, philiosophy and holistic medicine scene. (p320)

Mysuru K Pattabhi Jois developed Ashtanga yoga here, and this is still a great centre for taking long or short courses, whatever your experience. (p867)

Puducherry A big yoga and ashram hangout, there are various schools, teacher training and a yoga festival. (p1037)

Ladakh Many places do meditation courses or drop-ins and anyone can join in at a Buddhist monastery. (p228)

Arts & Crafts

Practically every town, village and neighbourhood here has its own tradition of devotional painting, silk weaving, camel-hide decorating, mirrored embroidering, or other art you won't find anywhere else.

Gujarat Some of India's finest textiles and embroidery are found in the tribal villages of Kachchh, where traditional craft has been practised for centuries. (p686)

Rajasthan India's textile traditions are legion. Villages in Rajasthan specialise in embroidery with tiny mirrors: like jewellery for your clothes. (p104)

Bihar Folk paintings known as Mithila (or Madhubani) colourfully depict village scenes; more readily available in Delhi than locally. (p518)

Tamil Nadu The Tamil tradition of sculpting bronze figures of Nataraja, the cosmic dancer, is about 1000 years old, and the silks and saris from Kanchipuram are renowned too. (p1002)

Kashmir Famous for its hand-woven carpets and jewel-bright papier mâché. (p225)

Month by Month

TOP EVENTS

Holi, February or March

Ganesh Chaturthi, August or September

Onam, August or September

Navratri & Dussehra, September or October

Diwali, October or November

January

Post-monsoon cool lingers throughout the country, with downright cold in the mountains. Pleasant weather and several festivals make it a popular time to travel, while Delhi hosts big Republic Day celebrations.

Free India

Republic Day commemorates the founding of the Republic of India on 26 January 1950; the biggest celebrations are in Delhi, which holds a huge military parade along Rajpath, and the Beating of the Retreat ceremony three days later. There are pigeon races in Old Delhi. (p57)

Kite Festival

Sankranti, the Hindu festival marking the sun's passage into Capricorn, takes place on either 14 or 15 January, and is celebrated in many ways across India – from banana-giving to cockfights. But it's the mass kite-flying in Gujarat, Andhra Pradesh, Uttar Pradesh and Maharashtra that's most spectacular.

Southern Harvest

The Tamil festival of Pongal, equivalent to Sankranti, marks the end of the harvest season. Families prepare pots of *pongal* (a mixture of rice, sugar, dhal and milk), symbolic of prosperity and abundance, then feed them to decorated and adorned cows.

Pilgrimage, Size: Extra-Large

The huge Hindu pilgrimage, Kumbh Mela, takes place every three years, rotating between four different locations. All involve mass devotion – mass as in tens of millions of people. The next ritual group bathings are in Prayag (2019) and Haridwar (2021/22). (p1129)

February

This is a good time to be in India, with balmy weather in most non-mountainous areas. It's still peak travel season; sunbathing and skiing are still on.

Celebrating Saraswati

On Vasant Panchami, Hindus dress in yellow and place books, musical instruments and other educational objects in front of idols of Saraswati, the goddess of learning, to receive her blessing. The holiday sometimes falls in February.

Tibetan New Year

Losar is celebrated by Tantric Buddhists all over India – particularly in Himachal Pradesh, Sikkim, Ladakh and Zanskar – for 15 days. Losar is usually in February or March, though dates can vary between regions.

Skiing the Northern Slopes

Jammu and Kashmir, Himachal Pradesh and Uttarakhand have some fine skiing and snowboarding for all levels. Snow season tends to be January to March; February's a safe bet.

Shivaratri

This day of Hindu fasting recalls the *tandava* (cosmic victory dance) of Lord

Shiva. Temple processions are followed by the chanting of mantras and anointing of linga (phallic images of Shiva). Shivaratri can also fall in March.

Taj Mahotsav

This 10-day carnival of culture, cuisine and crafts is Agra's biggest and best party. Held at Shilpgram, the festival features more than 400 artisans from all over India, a potpourri of folk and classical music, and dances from various regions and enough regional food to induce a curry coma.

March

The last month of the travel season, March is full-on hot in most of the country, with rains starting in the northeast. Wildlife is easier to spot as animals come out to find water.

Holi

One of North India's most ecstatic festivals; Hindus celebrate the beginning of spring according to the lunar calendar, in February or March, by throwing coloured water and *gulal* (powder) at anyone within range. Bonfires the night before symbolise the demise of demoness Holika. (Upcoming dates: 2 March 2018, 21 March 2019, 10 March 2020.)

Wildlife-Watching

When the weather warms up, water sources dry out and animals venture into the open to find refreshment: your chance to spot elephants, deer and, if you're lucky, tigers and leopards. Visit www.sanctuaryasia.com for detailed info.

Rama's Birthday

During Rama Navami, which lasts anywhere from one to nine days, Hindus celebrate Rama's birth with processions, music, fasting and feasting, enactments of scenes from the Ramayana and, at some temples, ceremonial weddings of Rama and Sita idols. (Upcoming dates: 26 March 2018, 14 April 2019, 2 April 2020.)

Mahavir's Birthday

Mahavir Jayanti commemorates the birth of Jainism's 24th and most important *tirthankar* (teacher and enlightened being). Temples are decorated and visited, Mahavir statues are given ritual baths, processions are held and offerings are given to the poor. (Upcoming dates: 29 March 2018, 17 April 2019, 6 April 2020.)

April

The heat has officially arrived in most places, which means you can get deals and avoid tourist crowds. The Northeast, meanwhile, is wet, but it's peak time for visiting Sikkim and upland West Bengal.

Easter

The Christian holiday marking the Crucifixion and Resurrection of Jesus Christ is celebrated simply in Christian communities with prayer and good food. (Upcoming dates: 1 April 2018, 21 April 2019, 12 April 2020.)

May

It's hot almost everywhere. Really hot. Festivals take a back seat as humidity builds up, awaiting the release of the rain. Hill stations are hopping, though, and in the mountains it's pre-monsoon trekking season.

Buddha's Birthday

The celebration of Buddha's birth, nirvana (enlightenment) and parinirvana (total liberation from the cycle of existence, or passing away), Buddha Jayanti is quiet but moving: devotees dress simply, eat vegetarian food, listen to dharma talks and visit monasteries or temples. (Upcoming dates: 22 May 2018, 12 May 2019, 30 April 2020.)

Ramadan (Ramazan)

Thirty days of dawn-to-dusk fasting mark the ninth month of the Islamic calendar. Muslims traditionally

LUNAR CALENDAR

Many festivals follow the Indian lunar calendar (a complex system based on astrology) or the Islamic calendar (which falls about 11 days earlier each year), and therefore change annually relative to the Gregorian calendar. Contact local tourist offices for festival dates.

turn their attention to God, with a focus on prayer and purification. Ramadan begins around 16 May 2018, 6 May 2019 and 24 April 2020.

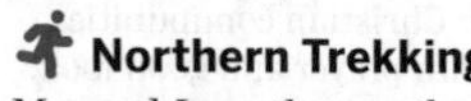

Northern Trekking

May and June, the months preceding the rains in the northern mountains, are good times for trekking, with sunshine and temperate weather. Consider Himachal Pradesh, Kashmir (but not Ladakh) and Uttarakhand.

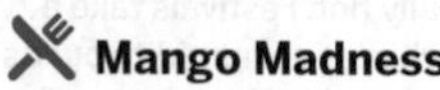

Mango Madness

Mangoes are indigenous to India, which is why they're so ridiculously good here (seriously, it's ridiculous). The season starts in March; in May the fruit is sweet, juicy and everywhere.

June

June is low, low season for travellers in India on account of the heat, but a good time to trek up north. The rainy season, or pre-monsoon extreme heat, has started just about everywhere else.

Eid al-Fitr

Muslims celebrate the end of Ramadan with three days of festivities. Prayers, shopping, gift-giving and, for women and girls, *mehndi* (henna designs) may all be part of the celebrations. (Upcoming dates: 15 June 2018, 5 June 2019, 24 May 2020.)

July

All going well, it should be raining almost everywhere now, with many remote roads being swept away. Consider visiting Ladakh, where the weather's surprisingly fine, or do a rainy-season meditation retreat, an ancient Indian tradition.

Odisha Festival of Chariots

Rath Yatra (Chariot Festival) sees effigies of Lord Jagannath (Vishnu incarnated as lord of the world) and his siblings carried through towns on vast, colourful chariots, most famously in Puri, Odisha (Orissa). Millions come to see them. (Upcoming dates: 14 July 2018, 4 July 2019, 23 June 2018.)

August

Monsoon should be still going strong, but this is prime time to visit Ladakh. Some travellers love tropical areas, such as Kerala or Goa, this time of year: the jungles are lush, green and glistening in the rain, and rainfall is sometimes only a few hours a day.

Independence Day

This public holiday on 15 August celebrates India's independence from Britain in 1947. Celebrations include flag-hoisting ceremonies and parades. The biggest celebrations are in Delhi, where the Prime Minister addresses the nation from the Red Fort and there's pigeon racing and kite flying in Old Delhi.

Krishna's Birthday

Janmastami celebrations can last a week in Krishna's birthplace, Mathura; elsewhere the festivities range from fasting to *puja* (prayers) and offering sweets, to drawing elaborate *rangoli* (rice-paste designs) outside the home. Janmastami is held August/September. (Upcoming dates: 15 August 2018, 3 September 2019, 23 August 2020.) (p410)

Parsi New Year

Parsis celebrate Pateti, the Zoroastrian new year, especially in Mumbai. Houses are cleaned and decorated with flowers and *rangoli,* the family dresses up and eats special fish dishes and sweets, and offerings are made at the Fire Temple.

Eid al-Adha

Muslims commemorate Ibrahim's readiness to sacrifice his son to God by slaughtering a goat or sheep and sharing it with family, the community and the poor. (Upcoming dates: 22 August 2018, 12 August 2019, 31 July 2020.)

Onam

In August or September, Onam is Kerala's biggest cultural celebration, when the entire state celebrates the golden age of mythical King Mahabali for 10 days. (Upcoming dates: 24 August 2018, 10 September 2019, 30 August 2020.)

Snake Festival

The Hindu festival Naag Panchami venerates snakes as totems against flooding and other evils. It's dedicated to Ananta, the serpent upon whose coils Vishnu rested between universes. Women return to their family homes and fast.

(15 August 2018, 5 August 2019, 25 July 2020).

Brothers & Sisters

On Raksha Bandhan (Narial Purnima), which means 'protective tie', girls tie amulets known as *rakhis* to the wrists of brothers and close male friends to protect them in the coming year. Brothers reciprocate with gifts and promises to take care of their sisters. (Upcoming dates: 26 August 2018, 15 August 2019, 3 August 2020.)

September

The rain is now petering out (with temperatures still relatively high), and the monsoon is usually finished in places such as Rajasthan. The second trekking season begins mid-month in the Himalaya and runs through October.

Ganesh Chaturthi

Hindus celebrate the 10-day Ganesh Chaturthi, the celebration of the birth of the much-loved elephant-headed god, with verve, particularly in Mumbai, Hyderabad and Chennai. Clay idols of Ganesh are paraded through the streets before being ceremonially immersed in rivers, tanks (reservoirs) or the sea. (Upcoming dates: 13 September 2018, 2 September 2019, 22 August 2020.)

Muharram

Shiite Muslims commemorate the martyrdom of the Prophet Mohammed's grandson Imam Hussain, an event known as Ashura, with fasting, beautiful processions and a month of grieving and remembrance. Sunni Muslims also mark this, but with fasting and celebrations marking when Moses (Moosa) fasted because Allah saved the Israelites from their enemy in Egypt. (Upcoming dates: 21 September 2018, 10 September 2019, 29 August 2020.)

October

This is when the travel season starts to kick off in earnest. October, aka shoulder season, brings festivals, mostly good weather with reasonably comfy temperatures, and lots of post-rain greenery and lushness.

Gandhi's Birthday

The national holiday of Gandhi Jayanti is a solemn celebration of Mohandas Gandhi's birth, on 2 October, with prayer meetings at his cremation site in Delhi, Raj Ghat. (p67)

Let it Rain

Water bodies are full up after the rains, making for spectacularly thundering white-water falls. This is also the season for rafting in some areas; visit www.indiarafting.com.

Durga Puja

The conquest of good over evil is exemplified by the goddess Durga's victory over buffalo-headed demon Mahishasura. Celebrations occur around the time of Dussehra, particularly in Kolkata, where thousands of images of the goddess are displayed then ritually immersed in rivers and water tanks.

Navratri

The exhuberant Hindu 'Festival of Nine Nights' leading up to Dussehra celebrates the goddess Durga in all her incarnations. Festivities, in September or October, are particularly vibrant in West Bengal, Maharashtra and Gujarat; in Kolkata, Durga images are ritually immersed in rivers and tanks. (Upcoming dates: 9 October 2018, 29 September 2019, 17 October 2020.) (p694)

Dussehra

Colourful Dussehra celebrates the victory of the Hindu god Rama over the demon-king Ravana and the triumph of good over evil. Dussehra is big in Kullu, where more than 200 village deities are carried into the town on palanquins and festivities go on for a week. (Upcoming dates: 19 October 2018, 8 October 2019, 25 October 2020.) (p306)

Pushkar Camel Fair

Held during Kartika (the eighth Lunar month, usually October or November), this fair attracts around 200,000 people, bringing some 50,000 camels, horses and cattle. It's a swirl of colour, magic and mayhem, thronged with musicians, mystics, tourists, camera crews, traders, devotees and animals. (p138)

November

The climate is blissful in most places, still hot but not uncomfortably so, but the southern monsoon is sweeping Tamil Nadu and Kerala.

Snowboarding in Gulmarg (p276), Kashmir

Diwali

In the lunar month of Kartika, Hindus celebrate Diwali (Festival of Lights) for five days. There's massive build up to this, and on the day people exchange gifts, light fireworks, and light lamps to lead Lord Rama home from exile. One of India's prettiest and noisiest festivals. (Upcoming dates: 7 November 2018, 27 October 2019, 14 November 2020.)

Guru Nanak's Birthday

Nanak Jayanti, birthday of Guru Nanak, founder of Sikhism, is celebrated with prayer, *kirtan* (devotional singing) and processions for three days, especially in Punjab and Haryana. The festival may also be held on 14 April, possibly Nanak's actual 1469 birth date.

December

December is peak tourist season for a reason: it's an escape from the cold elsewhere, you're guaranteed glorious weather (except for the chilly mountains), the humidity's low, the mood is festive and the beach rocks.

The Prophet Mohammed's Birthday

The Islamic festival of Eid-Milad-un-Nabi celebrates the birth of the Prophet Mohammed with prayers and processions, especially in Jammu and Kashmir. It falls around 1 December 2017, 21 November 2018, and 10 November 2019.

Birding

Many of India's 1250-plus bird species perform their winter migration from November to January or February, and excellent birdwatching spots are peppered across the country; www.birding.in is an excellent resource.

Camel Treks in Rajasthan

The cool winter (November to February) is the time to mount a camel and ride through the Rajasthani desert. Setting out from Jaialmer or Bikaner, you can explore the Thar Desert and sleep under a shedload of stars.

Christmas

Christian Goa comes alive in the lead-up to Christmas, midnight Masses are held on 24 December, and Christmas Day is celebrated with feasting and fireworks.

Itineraries

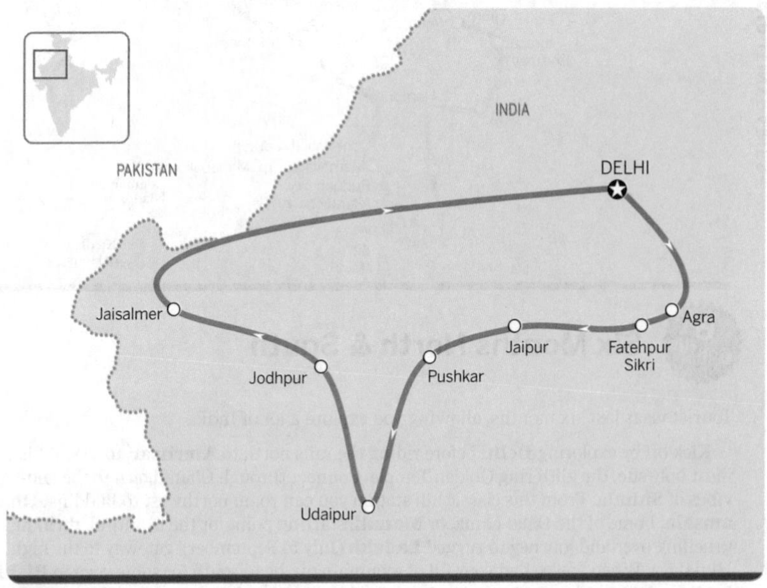

Golden Triangle & the Land of the Kings

This might be a well-worn trail, but there's a reason for that. The Golden Triangle of Delhi, Agra and Jaipur combines some of India's most jaw-dropping sights.

Kick off in **Delhi**, visiting the tumult of Old Delhi with its Mughal-era Red Fort and Jama Masjid, and taking it easy wandering Lodi Gardens, and Humayun's Tomb. Next, catch a train to **Agra** and see how beautiful the Taj Mahal, the world's most extravagant monument to love, really is. Explore Agra Fort and devote a day to nearby **Fatehpur Sikri**, a ghostly Mughal city. Continue on to the Pink City **Jaipur**, and devote several days to its whirlwind of bazaars, the City Palace, Hawa Mahal, and the Amber Fort.

Loop back to Delhi, or travel on to **Pushkar** for a few days of chilling out around lake-side temples, then take time to stay lakeside, go boating and explore elegant **Udaipur**. Next visit magnificent hilltop Kumbhalgarh and the temple at Ranakpur, en route to **Jodhpur**. See the Blue City unfurled beneath you from the mighty battlements of Mehrangarh Fort. Finish off in fortified **Jaisalmer** and go all Lawrence of Arabia on camel-back through the dunes, sleeping under a firmament of stars. Finally, loop back to Delhi, with one last cycle ride through Old Delhi, an early morning trip to the ruins of Qutb Minar, or shopping in its amazing emporiums, markets and boutiques.

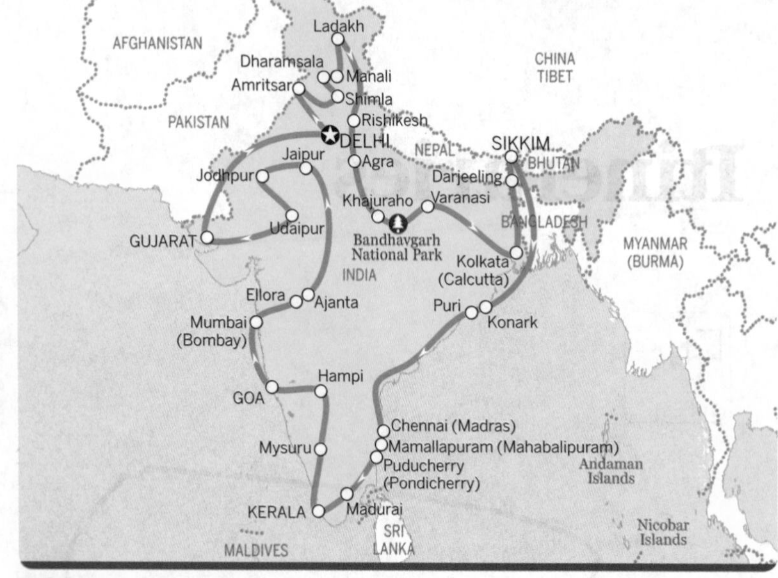

Six Months North & South

Tourist visas last six months, allowing you explore a lot of India.

Kick off by exploring **Delhi** before riding the rails north to **Amritsar**, to see Sikhism's most holy site, the glittering Golden Temple. Connect through Chandigarh to the laid-back vibes of **Shimla**. From this classic hill station you can roam northwest to Buddhist **Dharamsala**, home of the Dalai Lama, or **Manali**, starting point for the beautiful, thrilling but gruelling overland journey to rugged **Ladakh** (July to September), gateway to the high Himalaya. When you've had your fill of mountain air, head south for some yoga in **Rishikesh**, and descend to **Agra**, to see the vision-like Taj Mahal. Next go south **Khajuraho**, with its risque temples, and scan the jungle for tigers in **Bandhavgarh National Park**. Continue to the holy city of **Varanasi** for a boat trip along the sacred Ganges.

You can meander on detours as you train it eastwards to **Kolkata** (Calcutta), bustling capital of West Bengal. Swing north as far as **Darjeeling** or **Sikkim** for sweeping Himalayan views, then drift down the coast to the temple towns of **Konark** and **Puri** in Odisha (Orissa). Fly south to **Chennai** (Madras) for a different kind of India.

From here you have a chance to visit the wonders of **Mamallapuram** (Mahabalipuram), for temple carvings; **Puducherry** (Pondicherry), for colonial-era heritage combined with contemporary charm; and **Madurai**, for deity-encrusted temple towers. At this point, you've more than earned a long stay at **Kerala's** beaches, before taking a trip inland to nostalgic **Mysuru** to see how maharajas lived.

Continuing north, head to **Hampi**, where temples and ruined cities are strewn among the boulders, then get a second dose of beach life on the coast of **Goa**. Wine, dine and go Bollywood-crazy in **Mumbai** (Bombay), fast-paced capital of the west coast; then admire the glory of the cave paintings and carvings at **Ajanta** and **Ellora**.

Finish on a high in Rajasthan with its the coloured-city triple – pink **Jaipur**, blue **Jodhpur** and white **Udaipur**. There might just be time to detour to the fascinating temples, exquisite embroidery villages and nature reserves of **Gujarat**, before closing the circle with a last train ride to Delhi.

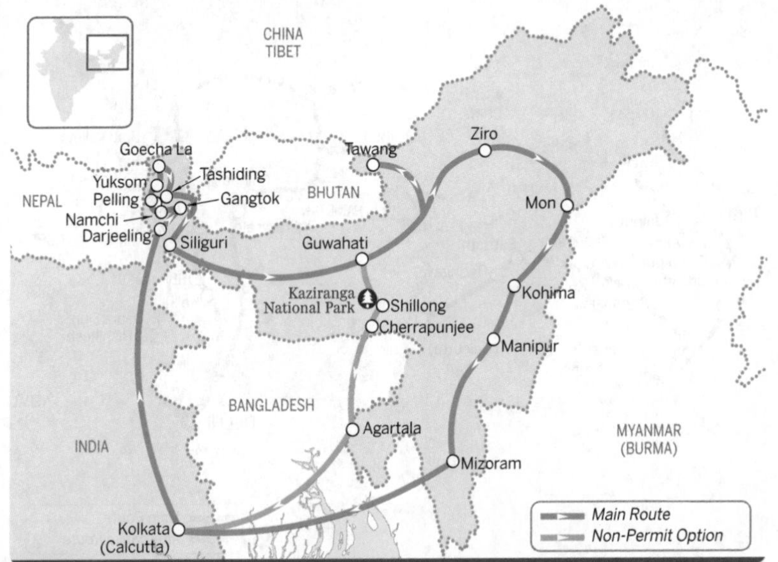

Mountains & Tribal Culture

Sikkim and the Northeast States, with their incredible mountain scenery, are still a well-kept secret for many travellers. Insurgencies and permit restrictions have long put off visitors, but India's last frontier is slowly opening up to the outside world. From Kolkata, you can go north to Darjeeling, see astounding Himalayan vistas in Sikkim then visit the world of India's hill tribes. Advance planning is essential – permits are mandatory and there are security risks to consider.

Starting in **Kolkata**, make your first stop genteel **Darjeeling** – here you can sample India's finest teas and pick up a permit for Sikkim, one of India's most serene quarters. **Gangtok**, the Sikkimese capital, is the starting point for jeep rides to historic Buddhist temples set amid dramatic scenery. Veer to **Namchi** to see the giant statues of Shiva and Padmasambhava, and to **Pelling** for inspiring views of the white-peaked Khangchendzonga and the beautiful Pemayangtse Gompa, ringed by gardens and monks' cottages. Take the weeklong trek from **Yuksom** to **Goecha La**, a 4940m pass with incredible views, then exit Sikkim via **Tashiding**, with more wonderful views and another stunning gompa, before travelling to **Siliguri** for the journey east.

Arrange tours for the Northeast States (including permits for Arunachal Pradesh) in **Guwahati** or online. Then head from Guwahati to **Arunachal Pradesh** to pay your respects at the stunning Buddhist monastery at **Tawang**, before exploring the tribal villages around **Ziro**, where the elders have dramatic facial tattoos and piercings. A visit to Nagaland opens up fascinating tribal villages around **Mon** – featuring a rugged countryside dotted by traditional longhouses and remote settlements – and the capital **Kohima**, with its WWII relics. Going south, there's a fair chance of encountering Meitei culture in **Manipur** and Mizo culture in **Mizoram**, before you fly back to Kolkata.

Alternately, you could also try this classic loop (Arunachal permits not required): from Guwahati, head to **Kaziranga National Park** to spot rare rhinos. Detour to sleepy **Shillong**, and hike to the waterfalls and incredible living root bridges of **Cherrapunjee**. Drive on to **Agartala**, the capital of Tripura, before returning to Kolkata by air or overland through Bangladesh.

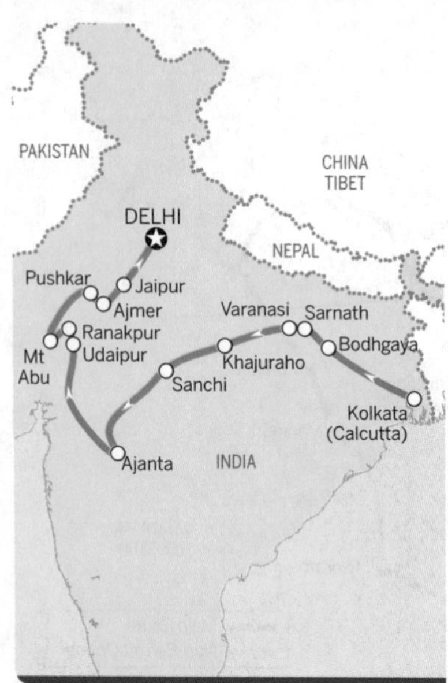

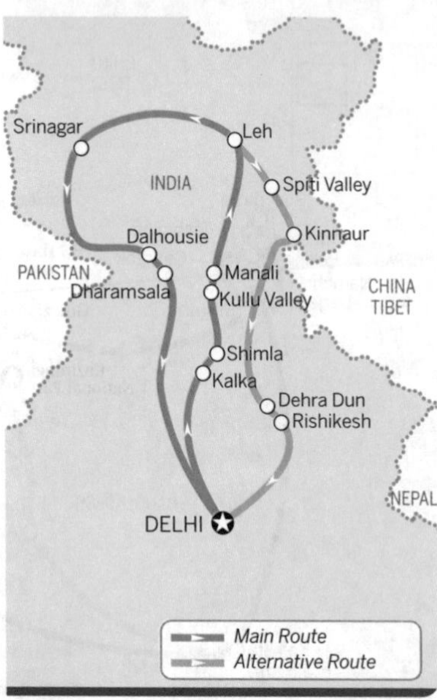

3 WEEKS The Spiritual Centre

Take in some of India's most fabulous temples in this temple-hopping trip around the central plains.

Start amid the chaos and rich cultural life of **Kolkata**, then swap the big-city bustle for the peace and spirituality of **Bodhgaya**, where the Buddha attained enlightenment. Roll across the plains to **Sarnath**, where the Buddha first taught the dharma.

Move onto the sacred city of **Varanasi**. See the rituals on the banks of the River Ganges, then ramble to the Hindu temples of **Khajuraho**, which seethe with erotic carvings. Head southwest to **Sanchi**, where Emperor Ashoka first embraced Buddhism, then zip through Bhopal to Jalgaon, jumping-off point for the carving-filled caves of **Ajanta**.

Next, detour into Rajasthan; stop off in whimsical **Udaipur**, with its lakes and palaces, then explore the Jain temples of **Ranakpur** or **Mt Abu**. Continue to **Pushkar**, curled around its sacred lake, then make a trip to nearby **Ajmer**, one of India's key Islamic pilgrimage sites. Take a final stop in atmospheric **Jaipur**, then end the trip in **Delhi**, with its magnificent Islamic ruins and the shrine of Hazrat Nizamuddin.

4 WEEKS Himalayan Adventures

See soul-feeding Himalayan views on this mountainous loop.

Start by riding the rails from **Delhi** to **Kalka**, to board the narrow-gauge train to colonial-era **Shimla**. From here you can ramble around the hills, then join the traveller pilgrimage north to the **Kullu Valley**, stepping up a gear with some adventurous mountain activities.

From the hill resort of **Manali**, embark on the thrilling, winding, two-day journey to **Leh** in Ladakh (July to September), to hike to dramatic Buddhist monasteries and trekking peaks. For a short loop, continue from Leh to Kargil and on to Kashmir (checking first that it's safe to travel). Stay on a **Srinagar** houseboat, then loop through Jammu to elegant **Dalhousie**, and soak up Buddhist culture in nearby **Dharamsala**, before returning to Delhi.

With more time to spare, head southeast from Leh into the dramatic **Spiti Valley**, where ancient monasteries blend into the arid landscape. Ride the rattletrap bus to rugged **Kinnaur**, with its plunging landscapes, and make stops in **Dehra Dun** and **Rishikesh** to soak up some Hindu culture, before finishing in Delhi.

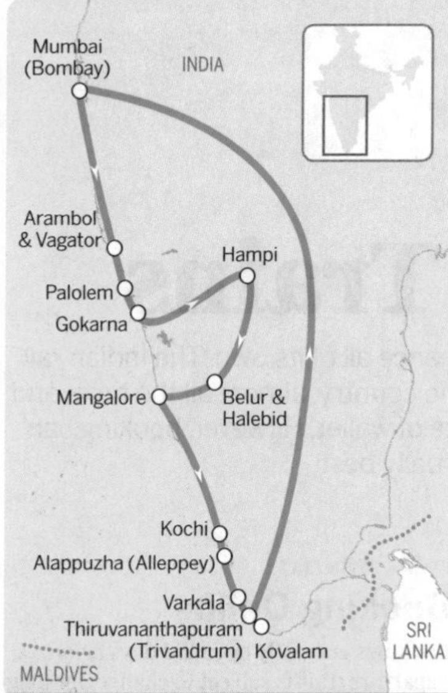

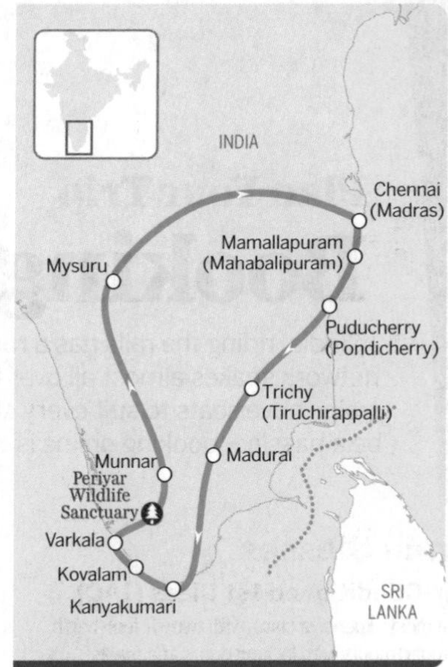

2 WEEKS Southern Beaches

This route meanders to some of India's finest beaches and charismatic coastal towns.

Start in **Mumbai** and people-watch, amble and sample *bhelpuri* (crisp noodle salad) at Girgaum Chowpatty beach. Take a boat trip to the rock-cut temples on Elephanta Island, then travel south by train to beach-blessed **Goa**.

Take your pick from tropical sandy stretches of **Arambol**, **Vagator** and **Palolem**, then continue along the coast to the sacred town of **Gokarna**. Now for a change of pace; head inland to **Hampi**, with its serene Vijayanagar ruins, and witness the zenith of medieval stone carving in the Hoysala temples of **Belur** and **Halebid**. Return by train to **Mangalore** to dine on spectacular seafood, then chug south to the lovely, laid-back town of **Kochi** (Cochin), a melting-pot mix of influences from as far afield as China and the Middle East.

Cruise Kerala's backwaters from **Alappuzha** (Alleppey), before dipping your toes in the warm waters around beach resorts **Varkala** or **Kovalam**. Make your last stop **Thiruvananthapuram** (Trivandrum), home to fascinating, often-overlooked museums, before flying back to Mumbai.

3 WEEKS A Southern Loop

Chennai is the easiest starting point for exploring India's southern tip. Ideal timing weatherwise is from October to February, when the weather is balmy and neither too hot or hitting the monsoon.

Kick off with some firey thalis in **Chennai**, then see intricate temple carvings in **Mamallapuram**, one-time home of the Pallava kings.

Next, head for French-flavoured **Puducherry**, before leaving the coast behind and heading inland to the temple towns of Tamil Nadu: take in the boulder-covered **Trichy** (Tiruchirappalli), and **Madurai**, with its soaring, deity-covered *gopurams* (temple towers). From here, it's easy to zip down to **Kanyakumari**, the southernmost point of India.

Kick back on the coast at **Kovalam** or **Varkala**, then trade the sand for jungle fronds in steamy **Periyar Wildlife Sanctuary**, home to tigers and elephants, or take a trip up to **Munnar**, Kerala's centre of tea plantations, for tranquil rambles in the hills. En route back to Chennai visit colourful **Mysuru**, with its fabulously flamboyant maharaja's palace and giant stone Nandi (bull statue).

Plan Your Trip

Booking Trains

In India, riding the rails has a romance all of its own. The Indian rail network snakes almost all over the country, almost all the time, and trains have seats to suit every size of wallet. However, booking can be a hassle – booking online is usually best.

Train Classes

Air-Conditioned 1st Class (1AC)

The most expensive class, with two- or four-berth compartments with locking doors and meals included.

Air-Conditioned 2-Tier (2AC)

Two-tier berths arranged in groups of four and two in an open-plan carriage. Bunks convert to seats by day and there are curtains, offering some privacy.

Air-Conditioned 3-Tier (3AC)

Three-tier berths arranged in groups of six in an open-plan carriage with no curtains; popular with Indian families.

AC Executive Chair (ECC)

Comfortable, reclining chairs and plenty of space; usually on Shatabdi express trains.

AC Chair (CC)

Similar to the Executive Chair carriage but with less-fancy seating.

Sleeper Class (sl)

Open-plan carriages with three-tier bunks and no AC; the open windows afford great views.

Unreserved/reserved 2nd Class (II/SS or 2S)

Wooden or plastic seats and a lot of people – but cheap!

Booking Online

Bookings currently open 120 days before departure (this is subject to change) for long-distance trains, sometimes less for short-haul trips. Seats fill up quickly – reserve at least a week ahead where possible, though shorter journeys are usually easier to obtain.

Express and mail trains form the mainstay of Indian rail travel. Not all classes are available on every train, but most long-distance services have general (2nd-class) compartments with unreserved seating and more comfortable reserved compartments, usually with the option of sleeper berths for overnight journeys. Sleeper trains offer the chance to travel huge distances for not much more than the price of a midrange hotel room.

Shatabdi express trains are same-day services with seating only; Rajdhani express trains are long-distance overnight services between Delhi and state capitals with a choice of 1AC, 2AC, 3AC and 2nd class. More expensive sleeper categories provide bedding. In all classes, a padlock and a length of chain are useful for securing your luggage to baggage racks.

These websites are useful for online international bookings.

Cleartrip (www.cleartrip.com) A reliable private agency and the easiest way to book; accepts international MasterCard and Visa credit cards. Can only book direct journeys. If booking from outside India before you have a local mobile number, a work-around is to enter a random number, and use email only to communicate.

RAILWAY RAZZLE DAZZLE

You can live like a maharaja on one of India's luxury train tours, with accommodation on board, tours, admission fees and meals included in the ticket price.

Palace on Wheels (www.palaceonwheels.net) Eight- to 10-day luxury tours of Rajasthan, departing from Delhi. Trains run on fixed dates from September to April; the fare per person for seven nights starts at US$6500/4890/4325 (in a single/double/triple cabin). Try to book 10 months in advance.

Royal Rajasthan on Wheels (www.royalrajasthanonwheels.co.in) Runs lavish one-week trips from October to March, starting and finishing in Delhi. The fare per person per night starts from US$875/625 for single/twin occupancy in deluxe suites.

Deccan Odyssey (www.deccan-odyssey-india.com) Seven nights covering the main tourist spots of Maharashtra and Goa. Fares per person start at US$5810/4190 (Indian tourists ₹371,900/268,360) for single/double occupancy. There are also several other shorter luxurious trips on offer.

Golden Chariot (www.goldenchariottrain.com) Seven-night tours seeing the south in sumptuous style from October to March, starting in Bengaluru (Bangalore). Fares per person start at single/double US$5530/4130 (Indian tourists ₹182,000/154,000).

Mahaparinirvan Express (aka Buddhist Circuit Special; www.railtourismindia.com) Running September to March to Buddhist sites over eight days, starting in Delhi, with overnight stays in hotels. Rates start from US$1155/945 per person in 1st class/AC 2 Tier class.The trip includes Nepal (the visa fee is not included in the price).

IRCTC (www.irctc.co.in) Government site offering bookings for regular trains and luxury tourist trains; Mastercard and Visa are accepted.

Make My Trip (www.makemytrip.com) Reputable private agency; accepts international cards. Again, you'll need an Indian mobile number. You'll then need to create an IRCTC User ID: choose a User ID (username), put in your name, birth date and address. For the 'Pincode' (postcode) '123456' will work. For the State choose 'Other'.

Yatra (www.yatra.com) Books flights and trains; accepts international cards.

Reservations

You must make a reservation for all chair-car, executive chair-car, sleeper, 1AC, 2AC and 3AC carriages. No reservations are required for general (2nd-class) compartments. Book well ahead for overnight journeys or travel during holidays and festivals. Waiting until the day of travel to book is not recommended.

Train Passes

IndRail passes permit unlimited rail travel for a fixed period, ranging from half a day to 90 days, but offers limited savings and you must still make reservations. Sample prices are US$19/43/95 (sleeper/2AC, 3AC & chair car/1AC) for 24 hours. The easiest way to book these is through the IndRail pass agency in your home country – click on the Passenger Info/Tourist Information link on www.indianrailways.gov.in/railwayboard for further details.

Plan Your Trip

Trekking

India has world-class trekking opportunities, particularly in the Himalaya, where staggering snow-clad peaks, traditional tribal villages, sacred Hindu sites, ancient Buddhist monasteries and blazing fields of wildflowers are just some of the features that create extraordinary mountain experiences. Hit the trails for easy half-day jaunts or strenuous multiweek expeditions.

Best Treks

The Himalaya

Jammu & Kashmir The moonscape ranges rising in Ladakh offer some incredible trails, including routes through the popular Markha Valley and wildly beautiful Zanskar region (p258).

Himachal Pradesh Alpine adventures are easily accessible, including on treks from McLeod Ganj to Bharmour (p330), between the Parvati and Pin Valleys (p304), and on the Buddhist-infused Homestay Trail in the Spiti region (p348).

Uttarakhand Enjoy the pristine splendour of the Kauri Pass, Milam Glacier and Har-ki-Dun treks (p434) or join pilgrims en route to sacred religious sites such as Kedarnath Temple (p435) or Hem Kund (p439).

Sikkim Gaze at Khangchendzonga (8598m), the world's third-highest mountain, on the Goecha La trek (p556).

South India

Karnataka Explore the serene hills and forests of Kodagu (p881).

Kerala Go in search of tigers, elephants and deer at Periyar Wildlife Sanctuary (p968).

Tamil Nadu Head to Kodaikanal (p1072), which has some lovely forest hikes along misty trails, prettier and more laid-back hiking hill-station base than Ooty.

Trail Tips

The commercial trekking industry is much less developed in India than in neighbouring Nepal. Thus many places still feel wild and relatively unspoilt. Still, on most routes, you can hire porters or pack animals to haul your gear. If you go with a trekking company, some gear may be supplied. Specify *everything* that's included beforehand, and get it in writing if possible.

Wherever you go, make sure you have any permits you may need.

Monitor your health – Acute Mountain Sickness (p1211) is a serious risk on trails over 3000m.

And beware of herding dogs; they're famously aggressive.

Route Planning

Detailed maps of the Indian Himalaya are difficult to buy in-country. Some maps found online are good enough for planning, and even navigating if you're experienced at reading them. For Ladakh, pricey 1:300,000 scale maps can be bought in Leh; some maps from the 1:200,000 Leomann series are often available in Manali and McLeod Ganj.

On popular pilgrims' trails, it's impossible to get lost, but less-travelled tracks can fork or vanish altogether, so hiring a local guide can be wise.

For information on climbing Himalayan summits over 6000m, check the website of the Indian Mountaineering Foundation (www.indmount.org).

Getting High Safely

Throughout the Himalaya, plan in some extra days to acclimatise while en route to high-altitude destinations. These mountains deserve your respect – don't try to trek beyond your physical or technical abilities.

Peak Bagging

Mountaineers need permission from the **Indian Mountaineering Foundation** (☎011-24111211; www.indmount.org; 6 Benito Juarez Rd, New Delhi) in Delhi to climb most peaks over 6000m. Expedition fees vary, rising with the height of the peak and number of people on your team. Fortunately, permits for quite a few high 'trekking' summits cost only US$30 to US$100, particularly in Ladakh, Lahaul, Spiti and Sikkim; among them is Stok Kangri (6120m), an affordable but rewarding taste of high-altitude mountaineering.

Packing

- Bring gear and clothing that are appropriate for the conditions you expect to encounter.
- On well-established trails, heavy hiking boots are overkill, but on remote mountain tracks they can be lifesavers.
- First-aid and water-purification supplies are often essential.
- Rain gear is a must, and warm layers are crucial for comfort at altitude.
- Remember sunscreen!

Trekking Ethics

- Follow low-impact trekking practices (you know the mantra – take only photographs, leave only footprints).
- Cook over stoves, since local people rely on limited fuel-wood sources.

MOST ADVENTUROUS TREKS

The isolated, northeast mountain state of Arunachal Pradesh is an adventurous destination for experienced trekkers. One of the top spots to check out is Namdapha National Park (p574), which is bogglingly rich in biodiversity.

- Respect local cultural sensibilities by dressing modestly; ask permission before snapping photos; remember that while locals' hospitality may be endless, their food supply might not be; and refrain from giving gifts to children.

When to Go

With India's diverse topography, the best trekking times depend on the region.

May–June This is a good time for mountain trekking, but also high season for domestic Indian travellers. Trails to holy Hindu sites can be packed.

Mid-July–mid-September During monsoon, trekking in the wrong place can be deadly. Ladakh and Spiti stay pretty dry. Uttarakhand's famous Valley of Flowers National Park (p439) unfurls a dazzling botanical carpet.

Mid-September–mid-November Post-monsoon, searing blue skies usually bless the Himalaya. While nights may dip below freezing, days are usually sunny and warm. Facilities often close for winter, so check in advance to see what will be open.

December–March February is the only month where you can attempt the hazardous Chadar Trek (p264), walking along a frozen river to the Zanskar region.

April Head for the hill stations, as it's ripping hot down low and usually still snow-packed up high.

Plan Your Trip

Yoga, Spas & Spiritual Pursuits

India offers a profound spiritual journey for those so inclined, and even sceptical travellers can enjoy the benefits of trips to spas and yoga centres.

What to Choose

Ashrams

India has plentiful ashrams – places of communal living established around the philosophies of a guru (spiritual guide or teacher). You can arrange to stay for an extended period, living by the rules of particular organisation.

Ayurveda

Ayurveda is the ancient science of Indian herbal medicine and holistic healing, based on natural plant extracts, massage and therapies to treat body and mind.

Meditation

Many centres in Buddhist areas offer training in *vipassana* (mindfulness meditation) and Buddhist philosophy; many require a vow of silence and abstinence from tobacco, alcohol and sex.

Spa Treatments

India's spas offer an enticing mix of international therapies and local techniques based on ancient ayurvedic traditions.

Yoga

Yoga's roots lie in India and you'll find hundreds of schools following different disciplines to suit all levels of skill and commitment.

Yoga

You can practise yoga almost everywhere, from beach resorts to mountain retreats. In 2014, at India's initiative, the UN adopted a resolution declaring 21 June International Yoga Day.

Karnataka

Mysuru (p874) The birthplace of Ashtanga yoga; there are centres all over the state.

Kerala

Sivananda Yoga Vedanta Dhanwantari Ashram (p948) Renowned for longer courses; near Trivandrum.

Maharashtra

Kaivalyadhama Yoga Hospital (p798) Yogic healing in Lonavla.

Ramamani Iyengar Memorial Yoga Institute (p803) Advanced courses; in Pune.

Mumbai

Yoga Institute (p751) Daily and longer-term programs.

Yoga House (p750) Hatha yoga in a lovely setting.

Yogacara (p749) More hatha yoga.

Tamil Nadu

International Centre for Yoga Education & Research (p1040) Has 10-day introductory courses and advanced training in Puducherry.

Krishnamacharya Yoga Mandiram (p1011) Chennai-bsed yoga courses, therapy and training.

Andaman Islands

Flying Elephant (p1098) Yoga and meditation in tropical surroundings on Havelock Island.

Goa

Himalaya Yoga Valley (p838) Popular training school; Mandrem.

Swan Yoga Retreat (p833) Retreat in a soothing jungle location; Assagao.

Himalayan Iyengar Yoga Centre (p838) Courses in Arambol.

Bamboo Yoga Retreat (p850) Beachfront yoga; Patnem.

Uttarkhand

Rishikesh (p415) Take your pick from centres and ashrams offering yoga for all levels.

Ashrams

Many ashrams ('places of striving') are headed by charismatic gurus. Some tread a fine line between spiritual community and personality cult. Many gurus have amassed fortunes collected from devotees, and others have been accused of sexually exploiting their followers. Always check the reputation of any ashram you wish to join.

Most ashrams offer philosophy, yoga or meditation courses, and visitors are usually required to adhere to strict rules. A donation is appropriate to cover your expenses.

Kerala

Matha Amrithanandamayi Mission (p960) Amrithapuri-based; famed for its female guru Amma, 'The Hugging Mother'.

Maharashtra

Brahmavidya Mandir Ashram (☎07152-288388; shared r ₹150; ⏲6am-noon & 2-7pm) Established by Gandhi's disciple Vinoba Bhave; in Sevagram.

Sevagram Ashram (p792) Founded by Gandhi; in Sevagram.

Osho International Meditation Resort (p802) Follows the sometimes controversial teachings of Osho; based in Pune.

Tamil Nadu

Sri Aurobindo Ashram (p1038) Puducherry ashram founded by Sri Aurobindo.

Sri Ramana Ashram (p1035) Founded by Sri Ramana Maharshi; in Tiruvannamalai.

Kolkata

Belur Math (p464) Ramakrishna Mission headquarters, founded by Swami Vivekananda.

Ayurveda

Ayurveda – Indian herbal medicine – aims to restore balance in the body.

Goa

Shanti Ayurvedic Massage Centre (p838) A centre in Mandrem.

Karnataka

Ayurvedagram (p858; Bengaluru) In a garden setting.

Soukya (p858; Bengaluru) Ayurveda and yoga.

Indus Valley Ayurvedic Centre (p869; Mysuru) Therapies from ancient scriptures.

Swaasthya (p882; Coorg) Retreats and therapies.

Kerala

Dr Franklin's Panchakarma Institute (p952) (Chowara) South of Kovalam.

Eden Garden (p955; Varkala) Treatments and packages.

Santhigiri Ayurveda Centre (p959; Kollam) Seven- to 21-day packages and day treatments. Branch at Kumily (p969).

Ayur Dar (p980; Kochi) Treatments of one to three weeks.

Himachal Pradesh

Men-Tsee-Khang (Tibetan Medical & Astrological Institute; p324) The primary authority on Tibetan medicine and has its HQ and two clinics in McLeod Ganj, plus nearly 50 other clinics across India.

Ayuskama Ayurvedic Clinic (p331; Bhagsu) Dr Arun Sharma gives highly rated treatments and courses for would-be practitioners.

Tamil Nadu

Sita (p1040; Puducherry) Ayurveda and yoga.

Sivananda Yoga Vedanta Centre (p1061; Madurai) Classes and training in central Madurai, plus courses and teacher training at its ashram.

Mamallapuram (p1027) Lots of yoga classes (of varying quality). In Kovalam village nearby; has beach yoga and annual surf and yoga festival (p1025).

Uttar Pradesh

Swasthya Vardhak (p383; Varanasi) Ayurveda.

Madhya Pradesh

Kairali Spa (p632) Ayurveda in Orchha.

Ayur Arogyam (p642) Expert ayurvedic treatments in Khajuraho.

Maharashtra

Yogacara (p749) Ayurveda and massage.

Buddhist Meditation

Whether for an introduction or more advanced study, there are India-wide courses and retreats. McLeod Ganj is the main centre for the study of Tibetan Buddhism; public teachings or audiences are given by both the Dalai Lama and the 17th Karmapa.

Himachal Pradesh

Library of Tibetan Works & Archives (p326) Serious Buddhist philosophy courses in McLeod Ganj.

Himachal Vipassana Centre (Map p320; ☎9218414051; www.sikhara.dhamma.org; Dharamkot; ⏰Apr–mid-Nov) Strict 10-day retreats in Dharamkot, near McLeod Ganj.

Tushita Meditation Centre (p331) Ten-day silent retreat courses and drop-in meditation sessions; Dharamkot.

Deer Park Institute (p334) Courses and workshops on Buddhist and Indian philosophy, and meditation retreats led by Buddhist masters; in Bir.

Jammu & Kashmir

Mahabodhi Centre (p232) Various *vipassana* courses and drop-in sessions in Leh.

Bihar

Root Institute for Wisdom Culture (p527) Courses from two to 21 days; in Bodhgaya.

International Meditation Centre (Map p526; ☎0631-2200707; bsatyapala@gmail.com; per day incl accommodation & food ₹500) Informal 10-day courses; Bodhgaya.

Mumbai

Global Pagoda (p748) *Vipassana* courses from one to 10 days; on Gorai Island.

Maharashtra

Vipassana International Academy (p779) Holds 10-day *vipassana* courses in Igatpuri.

Andhra Pradesh

Numerous Burmese-style *vipassana* courses, including the Vipassana International Meditation Centre (p920) near Hyderabad, Dhamma Vijaya (p934) near Eluru, and Dhamma Nagajjuna (p934; Nagarjuna Sagar).

Spa Treatments

From solo practitioners to opulent spas, there are choices nationwide. Be cautious of dodgy one-on-one massages by private (often unqualified) operators – seek recommendations and trust your instincts.

Madhya Pradesh & Chhattisgarh

Jiva Spa (p627) Massages, scrubs and wraps in beautiful surrounds in Gwalior.

Mumbai

Antara Spa (☎022-66939999; www.theclubmumbai.com; 197 DN Nagar, Andheri West; 1hr massage ₹2975-3320; ⏰10am-7.30pm) International treatments.

Palms Spa (p751) Renowned Colaba spa.

Top: Global Pagoda (p748), Mumbai

Bottom: Ayurvedic treatment

MILA SUPINSKAYA GLASHCHENKO / SHUTTERSTOCK©

Woman practising yoga

Uttarkhand

Haveli Hari Ganga (p423) In Haridwar, overlooking the Ganges.

Kolkata

Vedic Village (p489) Touted to have the finest medical spa in the country; near Kolkata.

Karnataka

Emerge Spa (p869) Pampering Asian-influenced treatments near Mysuru.

Goa

Humming Bird Spa (p846) For all kinds of pampering; in Palolem.

Uttar Pradesh

Aarna Spa (p383) Ayurveda, aromatherapy and pampering in Varanasi.

Kerala

Neeleshwar Hermitage (p1000) Beachfront ecoresort near Bekal.

Plan Your Trip
Volunteering

India may be beautiful, rich in culture and history, but poverty and hardship are the harsh reality for many people. Many travellers want to try to do something to help, and charities and aid organisations across the country welcome committed volunteers.

Aid Programs

There are numerous opportunities for volunteers in India. It may be possible to find a placement after you arrive, but charities and nongovernment organisations (NGOs) generally prefer volunteers who have applied in advance and been approved for the kind of work involved. Reputable organisations may insist on a criminal background check for working with children. **Ethical Volunteering** (www.ethicalvolunteering.org) provides useful guidelines for choosing an ethical sending agency.

As well as international organisations, local charities and NGOs often have opportunities, though it can be harder to assess the work that these organisations are doing. For listings of local agencies, check www.ngosindia.com or contact the Delhi-based **Concern India Foundation** (Map p76; ☎011-64598584; www.concernindiafoundation.org; A-52 Amar Colony, Lajpat Nagar IV; Ⓜ Lajpat Nagar).

The following programs are just some of many that may have opportunities for volunteers; contact them in advance to arrange a placement. Note that Lonely Planet does not endorse any organisations that we do not work with directly, so it is essential that you do your own thorough research before agreeing to volunteer with any organisation.

Caregiving

If you have medical experience, there are numerous opportunities to provide health

How to Volunteer

Choosing an Organisation

Choose an organisation that can specifically benefit from your abilities and skills.

Time Required

How much time you can devote to a project? You're more likely to be of help if you commit for at least a month, ideally more.

Money

Giving your time for free is only part of the story; most organisations expect volunteers to cover their accommodation, food and transport.

Working 9 to 5

Make sure you understand what you are signing up for; many organisations expect volunteers to work full-time, five days a week.

Transparency

Ensure that the organisation you choose is reputable and transparent about how it spends its money. Where possible, get feedback from former volunteers.

care and support for the most vulnerable in Indian society.

Kolkata

Missionaries of Charity (p467) St Teresa's charity (Mother Theresa's Motherhouse) places volunteers in hospitals and homes for impoverished children and adults.

Calcutta Rescue (☎033-22175675; www.calcuttarescue.org; 4th fl, 85 Collin St) Placements for medical and health professionals in Kolkata and other parts of West Bengal.

Maharashtra

Sadhana Village (☎020-25380792; www.sadhana-village.org; 1, Priyankit, Lokmanya Colony, Paud Rd) Pune residence for disabled adults; has a minimum commitment of two months for volunteers.

Rajasthan

Marwar Medical & Relief Society (☎0291-2545210; www.mandore.com; Dadwari Lane, c/o Mandore Guesthouse) NGO running educational, health, environmental and other projects in villages in the Jodhpur district. Short- or long-term volunteers are welcome.

Community

Many community volunteer projects work to provide health care and education to villages.

Bihar & Jiharkhand

Root Institute for Wisdom Culture (p527) Occasional placements to train local Bodhgaya health workers.

Delhi

Hope Project (p79) A broad-based community project, welcoming short- or long-term volunteers who can offer childcare, medical, ELT, IT or other skills.

HELPING TIBETAN REFUGEES

Since 1959, more than 100,000 Tibetan refugees have fled to India to escape persecution. Newly arrived refugees require extensive support and there are often volunteering opportunities in McLeod Ganj, and other areas with large Tibetan populations.

Karnataka

Kishkinda Trust (p903) Volunteers needed to assist with sustainable community development in Hampi.

Madhya Pradesh & Chhattisgarh

Orchha Home-Stay (p634) Offers volunteer placements in varied roles to help rural villagers.

Mumbai

Slum Aid (www.slumaid.org) Working in Mumbai slums to improve lives; placements from two weeks to six months.

Rajasthan

URMUL Trust (☎0151-2523093; www.urmul.org; Ganganagar Rd, Urmul Bhawan, Bikaner) Provides primary health care and education to desert dwellers in arid western Rajasthan. Volunteer placements (minimum one month) are available in English teaching, health care and other work.

Seva Mandir (☎0294-2451041; www.sevamandir.org; Old Fatehpura, Udaipur) NGO working in southern Rajasthan on projects including afforestation, water resources, health, education, and empowerment of women and village institutions.

Himachal Pradesh

Lha (p325) Arranges placements at a host of projects with the Tibetan community, including for language teachers and healthcare or IT professionals; in McLeod Ganj.

West Bengal

Human Wave (☎033-26854904; www.humanwaveindia.org; Mankundu) Short-term placements on community development and health schemes.

Makaibari Tea Estate (p496) Kurseong-based; volunteers assist with primary school teaching, health work and organic farming.

Teaching

Many Buddhist schools need teachers of English for long-term placements; enquire locally in Sikkim, Himachal Pradesh, West Bengal and Ladakh. Teaching experience is preferred. Ask questions if organisations do not require safety checks for adults working with children.

Himachal Pradesh

Learning & Ideas for Tibet (p325) Based in McLeod Ganj; current needs are for teachers of

English, French, German, Mandarin, Japanese and computer skills, to work with Tibetan refugees.

West Bengal & Darjeeling

Hayden Hall (p505) Offers minimum two-month opportunities for volunteers with medical, teaching and business experience; in Darjeeling.

Jammu & Kashmir

Druk Padma Karpo School (p245) Buddhist monastery school in Ladakh (Shey) with long-term placements (May to September only) for English teachers.

Phuktal Gompa (p266) Accepts short-term EFL teaching volunteers; Zanskar.

Csoma's Room (http://csomasroom.kibu.hu) This Hungarian outfit takes teachers (as well as restorers) in Zangla.

Working with Children

Various charities provide support for disadvantaged children. Travellers should ask questions if organisations do not require safety checks for adults working with children.

Delhi

Salaam Baalak Trust (p79) Volunteer English teachers, doctors, counsellors and computer experts provide education and support for street children.

Reality Tours & Travel (p79) Slum education projects; volunteers should have relevant professional or academic qualifications. Minimum three months.

Torch (Map p72; torchdelhi.wixsite.com/torch; 30D Nizamuddin Basti, Nizamuddin West; M JLN Stadium) Works with homeless children, and looks for volunteers who can help with art activities, music and writing.

Goa

Mango Tree Goa (p822) Opportunities in Mapusa for volunteer nurses and teaching assistants to help impoverished children.

El Shaddai (p833) Placements helping impoverished and homeless children; one-month minimum commitment; Assagao.

Uttar Pradesh

Learn for Life Society (p383) Volunteer opportunities at a small Varanasi school for disadvantaged children.

Himachal Pradesh

Kullu Project (☎9418102083; www.kulluproject.org) Places volunteers in schools, orphanages and other organisations working with disadvantaged kids in the Kullu Valley.

Rogpa (Map p322; ☎9857973026; www.tibetrogpa.org; Mithanala Rd, off Bhagsu Rd; ⊙9am-5pm Mon-Sat) Volunteers provide childcare for Tibetan families; McLeod Ganj.

Working with Women

India has a range of local charities working to empower and educate women.

Rajasthan

Sambhali Trust (p181) In Jodhpur; volunteers needed to teach and help organise workshops for disadvantaged women.

Tamil Nadu

RIDE (p1032) Works to empower village women and welcomes volunteers; Kanchipuram.

Environment & Conservation

To help with environmental education and sustainable development, there are a range of local organisations.

Andaman Islands

ANET (p1094) Volunteers assist with environmental activities from field projects to general maintenance.

Reef Watch Marine Conservation (p1094) Marine conservation non-profit organisation accepts volunteers for anything from beach clean-ups to fish surveys. Contact them directly to discuss possibilities.

Himachal Pradesh

Ecosphere (p348) This multifaceted sustainable-development NGO in Kaza has openings for short- and long-term volunteers including clean-energy projects and cafe work.

Kullu Project Places volunteers with Great Himalayan National Park community groups developing organic farming and local products.

Karnataka

Rainforest Retreat (p882) Organic farming, sustainable agriculture and waste management are catchphrases at this lush hideway amid spice plantations; check the website for volunteering options; in Coorg.

AGENCIES OVERSEAS

International volunteering agencies abound, and it can be tricky trying to assess which ones are worthwhile. Agencies offering the chance to do whatever you want, wherever you want, are almost always tailoring projects to the volunteer rather than finding the right volunteer for the work that needs to be done. Look for projects that will derive real benefits from your skills. To find agencies in your area, read Lonely Planet's *Volunteer: A Traveller's Guide*, or try one of the following:

Himalayan Education Lifeline Programme (HELP; www.help-education.org) British-based charity organising placements for volunteer teachers at schools in Sikkim.

Indicorps (www.indicorps.org) Matches volunteers to projects across India, particularly in social development.

Jamyang Foundation (www.jamyang.org) Arranges volunteer placements for experienced teachers in Buddhist nunneries in Zanskar and Himachal Pradesh.

Voluntary Service Overseas (VSO; www.vso.org.uk) British organisation offering long-term professional placements in India and worldwide.

Workaway (www.workaway.info) Connects people with hotels, guesthouses, organic farms, restaurants and more, where they will get free accommodation and food in return for working five days a week.

Maharashtra

Nimbkar Agricultural Research Institute (☎02166-220945; www.nariphaltan.org; Phaltan-Lonand Rd, Tambmal, Phaltan) Offers internships in sustainable agriculture lasting two to six months for agriculture, engineering and science graduates.

Tamil Nadu

Keystone Foundation (p1078) Kotagiri-based, offers occasional opportunities to help improve environmental conditions, working with Indigenous communities.

Working with Animals

Seeing all those stray dogs can make you want to help out: you're in luck, opportunities for animal lovers are plentiful.

Andhra Pradesh

Blue Cross of Hyderabad (p920) A shelter with more than 1300 animals; volunteers help care for animals or work in the office.

Goa

International Animal Rescue (p832) Rescues and looks after dogs, cats and other animals; volunteers are welcome, but must have evidence of rabies vaccination.

Mumbai

Welfare of Stray Dogs (☎022-64222838; www.wsdindia.org; Yeshwant Chambers, B Bharucha Marg, Kala Ghoda) Volunteers can work with the animals, manage stores or educate kids in school programs.

Rajasthan

Animal Aid Unlimited (p157) In Udaipur, accepts volunteers to help injured, abandoned or stray animals.

Tamil Nadu

Madras Crocodile Bank (p1024) A reptile conservation centre in Vadanemmeli with openings for volunteers (minimum two weeks).

Arunachala Animal Sanctuary (p1036) Travellers are welcome to help; just show up. Potential openings for longer-term volunteers; in Tiruvannamalai.

Design & Restoration

There are various places where those with architectural and building skills can help.

Tamil Nadu

ArcHeS (p1058) Aims to preserve the architectural and cultural heritage of Chettinadu; openings for historians, geographers and architects, usually for around three to four months; Kothamangalam.

Jammu & Kashmir

Csoma's Room (p45) Volunteers restore and preserve traditional architecture in Zanskar.

Plan Your Trip

Travel with Children

Fascinating and thrilling; India will be even more astounding for children than for their wide-eyed parents. The scents, sights, and sounds of India will make for an unforgettable adventure and one that most kids will take in their stride.

India for Kids

Travel with children in India is usually a delight, though you (and your kids) may have to get used to being the centre of attention. Locals will thrill at taking a photograph or two beside your bouncing baby. This may prove tiring and disconcerting, but you can always politely decline.

As a parent on the road in India, the key is to remain firm, even if you feel you may offend a well-meaning local by doing so. The attention your children will inevitably receive is almost always good-natured; kids are the centre of life in many Indian households, and your own will be treated just the same. Hotels will almost always come up with an extra bed or two, and restaurants with a familiar meal.

Children's Highlights

Best Fairy-Tale Splendours

Jaisalmer Enjoy playing knights around the world's biggest sandcastle, Jaisalmer's centuries-old fort (p184), and take a camel ride in the Thar Desert.

Delhi Run around magnificent forts, explore Lodi Gardens (p70) and Mehrauli (p101), or try hands-on exhibits and ride in a toy train at the National Rail Museum (p74).

Best Regions for Kids

Rajasthan

Vibrant festivals, medieval forts, fairy-tale palaces, camel rides across desert dunes and a well-oiled tourist infrastructure for hassle-free travel. For older kids there's the thrill of the incredible Flying Fox (zip wires) at Jodhpur.

Goa

Palm-fringed, white-sand beaches and inexpensive exotic food; an ideal choice for family holidays, whatever the budget.

Uttar Pradesh

The picture-perfect Taj Mahal and the nearby abandoned city of Fatehpur Sikri will set young imaginations ablaze.

Kerala

Canoe and houseboat adventures, surf beaches, Arabian Sea sunsets, snake boat races, wildlife-spotting and elephant festivals.

Himachal Pradesh

Pony and yak rides around colonial-era hill stations, rafting, horse riding, tandem paragliding (kids can do it), walks and canyoning around Manali.

Ranthambhore National Park Step into a *Jungle Book* world (p141), home to a monkey kingdom, and hop aboard a jeep to scout for Shere Khan.

Udaipur Go boating on the lake (p154), take a horse-riding excursion, and explore fairy-tale palaces.

Orchha Wander the crumbling palaces and battlements of little-known Orchha (p630).

Madhya Pradesh The land of Kipling's *Jungle Book*, with jungles, and tiger-spotting safaris (p657).

Best Natural Encounters

Tiger parks, Madhya Pradesh Delve deep into the jungle or roam the plains at the tiger parks of Kanha (p676), Pench (p680) or Bandhavgarh (p678). You might not see a tiger, but there's plenty of other wildlife worth spotting.

Elephants, Kerala In Periyar (p968), kids can spot wild elephants.

Dolphins, Goa Splash out on a dolphin-spotting boat trip from almost any Goan beach to see them cavorting among the waves (p823).

Hill-station monkeys Head up to Shimla (p288) (Himachal Pradesh) or Matheran (p797; Maharashtra) for close (but not too close...they can be vicious!) encounters with cheeky monkeys.

Lions, Gujarat Go on safari through Gir National Park (p714) at dusk or dawn and spot the only Asiatic lions in existence.

Keoladeo National Park, Rajasthan Take a bike ride to spot myriad multi-hued birdlife in this reserve (p127).

Mudumalai Tiger Reserve, Tamil Nadu Visit an elephant camp (p1084) where the park's working elephants (many rescued and unfit to return to the wild) are fed and washed.

Funnest Forms of Transport

Autorickshaw, anywhere Bump thrillingly along at top speed in these child-scale vehicles (p1201).

Bike, Delhi Pedal around on a DelhiByCycle tour (p79); for older children who are competent riders, or toddlers who can fit in a child seat.

Toy Train, Darjeeling Ride the cute-as-a-button steam toy train between Kurseong and Darjeeling, past colourful mountain villages and rushing waterfalls (p507).

Hand-pulled rickshaw, Matheran From this monkey-infested hill station, you can continue to the village on horseback or in a hand-pulled rickshaw (p797).

Houseboat, Alappuzha (Alleppey) Go boating on Kerala's beautiful backwaters (p960), with lots of interesting stops en route. If you hit town on the second Saturday in August, take the kids along to see the spectacular Nehru Trophy boat race.

Best Coastal Kickbacks

Palolem, Goa Plump for a beachfront palm-thatched hut and take it easy at beautiful Palolem beach (p846), with Goa's shallowest, safest waters.

Patnem, Goa Kick back at peaceful Patnem (p849), with its nice sand beach and cool, calm, child-friendly beach restaurants.

Havelock Island Splash about in the shallows at languid Havelock Island (p1095), part of the Andaman Island chain, where there's also sensational diving possibilities.

Planning

Before you Go

- Look at climate charts; choose your dates to avoid the extremes of temperature that may put younger children at risk.
- Visit your doctor to discuss vaccinations, health advisories and other heath-related issues involving your children well in advance of travel.
- For more tips on travel in India, and firsthand accounts of travels in the country, pick up Lonely Planet's *Travel with Children* or visit the Thorn Tree Forum at lonelyplanet.com.

What to Pack

You can get these items in many parts of India too:

- Disposable or washable nappies, nappy rash cream (Calendula cream works well against heat rash too), extra bottles, wet wipes, infant formula and canned, bottled or rehydratable food.
- A fold-up baby bed or the lightest possible travel cot you can find (companies such as KidCo make excellent pop-up tent-style beds), since hotel cots may prove precarious. Don't take a stroller/pushchair, as this will be impractical to use as pavements are often scarce. A much better option is a backpack, for smaller kids, so

they're lifted up and out of the daunting throng, plus with a superb view.

- A few less-precious toys that won't be mourned if lost or damaged.
- A swimming jacket, life jacket or water wings for the sea or pool.
- Good sturdy footwear.
- Audiobooks, for whiling away long journeys.
- Insect repellent, mosquito nets, hats and sun lotion.

Eating

- If you're travelling in the regions of India, such as Rajasthan, Himachal Pradesh, Goa, Kerala, or the big cities, you'll find it easy to feed your brood. In major cities and more touristy towns there's always a wide range of international cuisines on offer.
- While on the road, easy portable snacks such as bananas, samosas, *puri* (puffy dough pockets), white-bread sandwiches and packaged biscuits (Parle G brand are a perennial hit) are available.
- Many children will delight in paneer (unfermented cheese) dishes, simple dhals (mild lentil curries), creamy kormas, buttered naans (tandoori breads), pilaus (rice dishes) and Tibetan *momos* (steamed or fried dumplings).
- Few children, no matter how culinarily unadventurous, can resist the finger-food fun of a vast South Indian dosa (paper-thin lentil-flour pancake).

Accommodation

- India offers such an array of accommodation options – from beach huts to five-star bubbles – that you're bound to be able to find something that will appeal to the whole family.
- The swish upmarket hotels are almost always child-friendly, but so are many upper midrange hotels, whose staff will usually rustle up an extra mattress or two; some places won't mind cramming several children into a regular-sized double room along with their parents.
- The very best five-stars come equipped with children's pools, games rooms and even children's clubs, while an occasional night with a warm bubble bath, room service, macaroni cheese and a banquet of satellite TV will revive even the most disgruntled young traveller's spirits.

On the Road

- Travel in India, be it by taxi, local bus, train or air, can be arduous for the whole family. Concepts such as clean public toilets, changing rooms and safe playgrounds are rare in much of the country. Public transport is often extremely overcrowded so plan fun, easy days to follow longer bus or train rides.
- Pack plenty of diversions (iPads or laptops with a stock of movies downloaded make invaluable travel companions, as do audiobooks, plus the good old-fashioned story books, cheap toys and games available widely across India).
- If you are hiring a car and driver – a sensible and flexible option – and you require safety capsules, child restraints or booster seats, bring these with you or make this absolutely clear to the hiring company as early as possible. Don't expect to find these items readily available. And finally, don't be afraid to tell your driver to slow down and drive responsibly.

Health

- The availability of a decent standard of health care varies widely in India. Talk to your doctor at home about where you will be travelling to get advice on vaccinations and what to include in your first-aid kit.
- Access to health care is better in traveller-frequented parts of the country where it's almost always easy to track down a doctor at short notice (most hotels will be able to recommend a reliable one).
- Prescriptions are quickly and cheaply filled over the counter at numerous pharmacies, often congregating near hospitals.
- Diarrhoea can be very serious in young children. Seek medical help if it is persistent or accompanied by fever; rehydration is essential. Heat rash, skin complaints such as impetigo, insect bites or stings can be treated with the help of a well-equipped first-aid kit or resources from a local pharmacy.

Regions at a Glance

From 21st-century chic to remote tribal villages, from palm-fringed backwaters to knife-edge mountain ranges, and from ancient temples to jungle-tangled fortresses, India's regions are an astounding cocktail of contrasts, colour and experiences.

Delhi

Food
Shopping
Ruins

Delhi is a city where you can travel back in time, from the magnificent ruins of imperial cities to the futuristic satellite city of Gurgaon, while feasting on everything from modern Indian to street food and experiencing shopping heaven in Delhi's bazaars and emporiums.

p56

Rajasthan

Palaces & Forts
Arts & Crafts
Wildlife

Rajasthan's forts and palaces are the epic riches of this 'Land of Kings', while their royal hunting reservations are now national parks, ripe for spotting tigers and other wildlife. You'll also find princely legacies in Rajasthan's bazaars, from miniature paintings to traditional puppets.

p104

Punjab & Haryana

Architecture
Borders
Food

Besides the stunning Golden Temple, the Punjab has palaces and follies, and the region is also home of butter chicken, basmati rice, naan, tarka dhal, and the tandoor (clay oven). The Attari-Wagah border crossing is worth a trip for its fabulous transborder pomp.

p201

Jammu & Kashmir (including Ladakh)

Landscapes
Trekking
Religion

From alpine Kashmir to the moonscapes of Ladakh and Zanskar, be humbled by the scale of nature and take hikes through Buddhist villages. Mantras fill Ladakh's gompas, pilgrims converge on Amarnath's ice lingam and Sufi spirituality suffuses Srinagar.

p225

Himachal Pradesh

Adventure
Scenery
Cultures

High Himalayan passes and plunging valleys make for great trekking, climbing, motorcycling, paragliding and skiing. The scenery is consistently awe-inspiring, and the cultural variety huge, from colourful Hindu festivals to ancient Buddhist monasteries.

p282

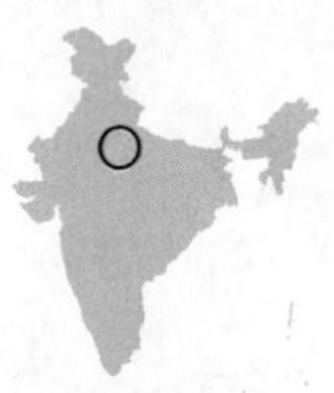

Agra & the Taj Mahal

Architecture
Tombs
Forts

Agra's Mughal architecture is the height of imperial virtuosity. The Taj Mahal is so famous that it's as familiar, yet its ethereal beauty will make you catch your breath. And don't miss out on other local masterpieces, such as Akbar's Mausoleum or the mighty Agra Fort.

p352

Uttar Pradesh

Architecture
Religion
Ghats

Uttar Pradesh contains ancient Islamic cities, two of Buddhism's most sacred pilgrimage centres, and two of the seven sacred cities of Hinduism. The Ganges River and its tributaries flow across UP, lined with holy ghats (ceremonial steps).

p376

Uttarakhand

Trekking
Yoga
Wildlife

Trekkers can take their pick from temples, sacred lakes, remote glaciers and rolling alpine meadows. Head to Rishikesh for a spiritual tune-up, and seek snow leopards, Asiatic black bears, brown bears and blue sheep in the national parks.

p412

Kolkata (Calcutta)

Culture
Food
Architecture

Once the British Indian capital, Kolkata is full of colonial-era architecture, but the modern city mingles chaos and culture in an enticing and very Indian mix. Cuisine here is renowned across the subcontinent, with the focus on fresh fish and prawns.

p452

West Bengal & Darjeeling

Hill Stations
Wildlife
Hotels

Darjeeling is the quintessential Indian hill station, offering spectacular Himalayan views, and historic accommodation. Take a trip to West Bengal to spot an awesome Royal Bengal tiger.

p483

Bihar & Jharkhand

Religion
Ruins
Wildlife

Bodhgaya, where Buddha attained enlightenment, is a magnet for pilgrims, while the Unesco-listed ruins of the ancient Nalanda university are one of many early Buddhist relics. Jharkhand's serene Betla (Palamau) National Park is famous for its wild pachyderms.

p516

Sikkim

Views
Monasteries
Trekking

Sikkim pimples its forested ridges with Buddhist monasteries, surreal Hindu temples and the odd gleaming mega-statue. Behind rises a thrilling panorama of Himalayan peaks, the mesmerising presence of Khangchendzonga the focus of photographers and the energies of energetic trekkers.

p535

Northeast States

Tribes
Wildlife
Adventure

This area is home to some of India's most enigmatic tribes, and the one-horned Indian rhino is just one of the local roll-call of exotic animals on this wild frontier.

p559

Odisha

Temples
Tribes
Wildlife

Odisha's dazzling temples tell a captivating tale of rulers who spared no expense in their veneration of the divine. The tribal markets of Onkadelli and Chatikona offer fascinating opportunities to mingle, and there are tiger reserves, crocodile-filled mangrove forests and coastal wetlands.

p593

Madhya Pradesh & Chhattisgarh

Wildlife
Monuments
Tribes

Madhya is home to some of India's top tiger habitats, with good prospects of sightings. And while you're looking for tigers you'll see plenty of other wildlife too.

p621

Gujarat

Wildlife
Crafts
Treks

Here you can see Asia's only wild lions and India's only wild asses, as well as Gujarati embroiderers, weavers, printers and dyers producing some of India's finest textiles. Or join Hindu and Jain pilgrims on treks up stunning, temple-topped peaks.

p686

Mumbai (Bombay)

Architecture
Food
Nightlife

Blending British grandeur and Indian flamboyance, Mumbai's architecture is a fabulous fusion of styles. Flavours from India and beyond mingle here, from local snacks to global flavours. Spot Bollywood stars and beautiful people as you dance till dawn in sleek bars and neon-filled nightclubs.

p734

Maharashtra

Caves
Beaches
Wine

Ajanta and Ellora hide exquisite cave paintings and rock sculptures, while the Konkan Coast has some of the most secluded beaches in India. Nasik is the epicentre of India's burgeoning wine industry, producing exciting vintages that are starting to cause a real stir.

p772

Goa

Beaches
Food
Architecture

Goa's beaches are no secret, but with palms swaying overhead and golden sand under your feet, it doesn't matter; there are still spots to escape the crowds. Add fresh seafood, and beautiful colonial-era architecture, and you can see what all the fuss is about.

p809

Karnataka & Bengaluru

Temples
Wildlife
Food

The temples of Karnataka overflow with carved embellishments, while the Nilgiri Biosphere Reserve is home to one of Asia's biggest populations of elephants. The table is laden too, with everything from Udupi vegetarian thalis to Mangalorean seafood.

p851

Telangana & Andhra Pradesh

Religion
Food
Beaches

Hyderabad's past splendours and contemporary style make it one of India's most engaging cities, while its famed biryani and spicy veggie dishes provide a rich cuisine. Ancient Buddhist remains are dotted throughout the region, and Tirumala is a major pilgrimage site.

p911

Kerala

Backwaters
Food
Wildlife

The inlets and lakes of Kerala's backwaters are a peaceful retreat from the modern age. Back on land is a fine assortment of wildlife-filled national parks, while the Keralan kitchen offers delicate dishes flavoured with coconut and spices.

p941

Tamil Nadu & Chennai

Temples
Hill Stations
City Life

Age-old tradition collides with cosmopolitan flair in Chennai, while Tamil Nadu's intricately carved, colour-bursting temples attract pilgrims from all over India. Escape into the Western Ghats' cool, Raj-era hill stations, or in Puducherry's pretty French Quarter.

p1002

Andaman Islands

Diving
Beaches
Tribes

With lush greenery, pristine waters and golden coastline, the Andaman Islands are an ideal place to chillout on sun-warmed sands. This prime snorkelling and diving destination is excellent for first-timers and veterans, and is culturally fascinating, with many tribal groups.

p1086

On the Road

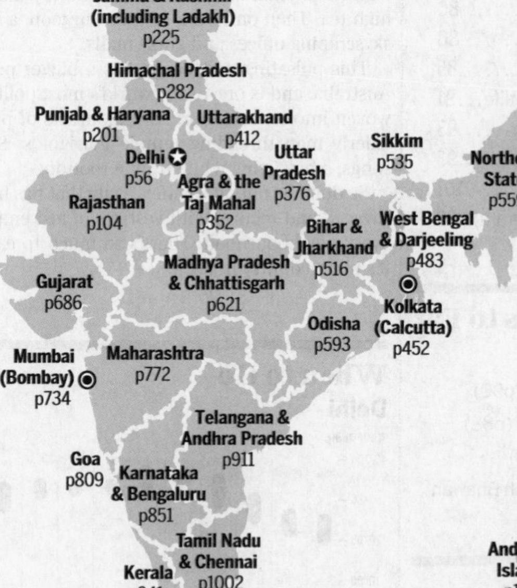

Jammu & Kashmir (including Ladakh)
p225
Himachal Pradesh
p282
Punjab & Haryana
p201
Uttarakhand
p412
Delhi
p56
Uttar Pradesh
p376
Sikkim
p535
Northeast States
p559
Agra & the Taj Mahal
p352
Rajasthan
p104
Bihar & Jharkhand
p516
West Bengal & Darjeeling
p483
Madhya Pradesh & Chhattisgarh
p621
Gujarat
p686
Kolkata (Calcutta)
p452
Odisha
p593
Mumbai (Bombay)
p734
Maharashtra
p772
Telangana & Andhra Pradesh
p911
Goa
p809
Karnataka & Bengaluru
p851
Tamil Nadu & Chennai
p1002
Kerala
p941
Andaman Islands
p1086

Delhi

011 / POP 25.7 MILLION / ELEV 293M

Includes ➡

Best Places to Eat

- Bukhara (p89)
- Indian Accent (p90)
- Masala Library (p88)
- Cafe Lota (p89)
- Andhra Pradesh Bhawan Canteen (p88)

Best Places to Sleep

- Lodhi (p84)
- Manor (p85)
- Madpackers Hostel (p84)
- Stops @ The President (p80)

Why Go?

Delhi is a city where time travel is feasible. Step aboard your time machine (the sleek and efficient metro) and you can go from Old Delhi, where labourers haul sacks of spices and jewellers weigh gold on dusty scales, to modern New Delhi, with its colonial-era parliament buildings and penchant for high tea. Then on to the future: Gurgaon, a satellite city of skyscraping offices and glitzy malls.

This pulsating metropolis has a bigger population than Australia, and is one of the world's most polluted cities. But woven into its rich fabric are moments of pure beauty: an elderly man threading temple marigolds; Sufi devotional songs; a boy flying a kite from a rooftop.

So don't be put off. Delhi is a city that has been repeatedly ravaged and reborn, with vestiges of lost empires in almost every neighbourhood. There's so much to experience here, it's like a country in itself.

When to Go

Delhi

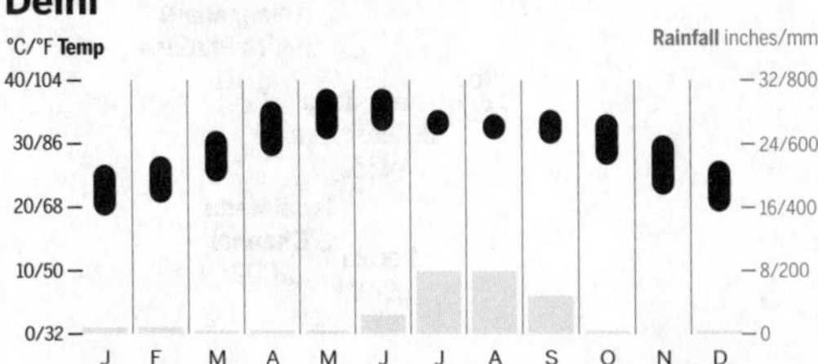

Oct–Mar Delhi at its best: it's warm with clear skies. Morning fog can play havoc with flight schedules.

May–Aug The months to avoid – hot, humid and uncomfortable.

Jun–Sep Monsoon season sees high temperatures and regular rain – a sticky combination.

History

Delhi is said by Hindus to be the site of ancient Indraprastha, home of the Pandavas in the Mahabharata. Excavations near the Purana Qila have revealed evidence of human habitation dating back 3000 years. The name Delhi is linked to the Maurya king Dhilu, who ruled the region in the 1st century BC, but for most of its existence, the city has been known by the multiple different names given to it by its conquerors.

The first city for which clear archaeological evidence remains was Lal Kot, or Qila Rai Pithora, founded by the Hindu king Prithviraj Chauhan in the 12th century. The city fell to Afghan invaders in 1191, and for the next 600 years, Delhi was ruled by a succession of Muslim sultans and emperors. The first, Qutub-ud-din Aibak, razed the Hindu city and used its stones to construct Mehrauli and the towering Qutb Minar.

Qutub-ud-din Aibak's 'Mamluk' (Slave) dynasty was quickly replaced by the Khilji dynasty, following a coup. The Khiljis constructed a new capital at Siri, northeast of Mehrauli, supplied with water from the royal tank at Hauz Khas. Following another coup, the Tughlaq sultans seized the reins, creating a new fortified capital at Tughlaqabad, and two more cities – Jahanpurah and Firozabad – for good measure.

The Tughlaq dynasty fell after Tamerlane stormed through town in 1398, opening the door for the Sayyid and Lodi dynasties, the last of the Delhi sultanates, whose tombs are scattered around the Lodi Gardens. The scene was set for the arrival of the Mughals. Babur, the first Mughal emperor, seized Delhi in 1526, and a new capital rose at Shergarh (the present-day Purana Qila), presided over by his son, Humayun.

Frantic city building continued throughout the Mughal period. Shah Jahan gained the Peacock Throne in 1627 and raised a new city, Shahjahanabad, centred on the Red Fort. The Mughal city fell in 1739, to the Persian Nadir Shah, and the dynasty went into steep decline. The last Mughal emperor, Badahur Shah Zafar, was exiled to Burma (Myanmar) by the British for his role in the 1857 First War of Independence; there were some new rulers in town.

When the British shifted their capital to Delhi from increasingly rebellious Calcutta in 1911, it was time for another bout of construction. The architect Edwin Lutyens drew up plans for a new city of wide boulevards and stately administrative buildings to accommodate the colonial government – New Delhi was born.

In 1947 Partition – the division of India and Pakistan – saw Delhi ripped apart as many inhabitants fled to the north and migrants flooded inwards, a trauma from which some say the city has never recovered. The modern metropolis certainly faces other challenges too – traffic, population, crime and the deepening chasm between rich and poor. However, the city on the Yamuna River continues to flourish, with its new satellite cities spreading Delhi further and further outwards.

Sights

Most sights in Delhi are easily accessible by metro, though to reach some you'll have to take a rickshaw or taxi from the stop, even though it bears the same or similar name

DELHI'S TOP FESTIVALS

To confirm exact dates contact India Tourism Delhi (p97).

Republic Day (26 Jan) A spectacular military parade in Rajpath.

Beating of the Retreat (29 Jan) More military pageantry in Rajpath.

St.Art (Dec-Mar) Street art festival.

Independence Day (15 Aug) India celebrates its Independence from Britain.

Dussehra (Durga Puja; Sep/Oct) Hindu celebration of good over evil with parades of colourful effigies.

Qutb Festival (Oct/Nov) Sufi singing and classical music and dance at the Qutb Minar complex.

Diwali (Festival of Light; Oct/Nov) Fireworks across the city for the Festival of Light.

Delhi International Arts Festival (DIAF; www.diaf.in; Nov/Dec) Exhibitions, performing arts, film, literature and culinary events.

Delhi Highlights

1. **Red Fort** (p60) Exploring this Mughal masterpiece, imagining its former traumas and splendours.
2. **Humayun's Tomb** (p69) Enjoying the architectural virtuosity and mirror-image gardens of Delhi's most spectacular resting place.
3. **Jama Masjid** (p66) Experiencing the serenity of the 'Friday Mosque', with its wide open courtyard.
4. **Qutb Minar Complex** (p101) Visiting Delhi's first Islamic city at sunrise.
5. **Hazrat Nizam-ud-din Dargah** (p69) Drinking in the mystical, magical atmosphere and hearing *qawwali*

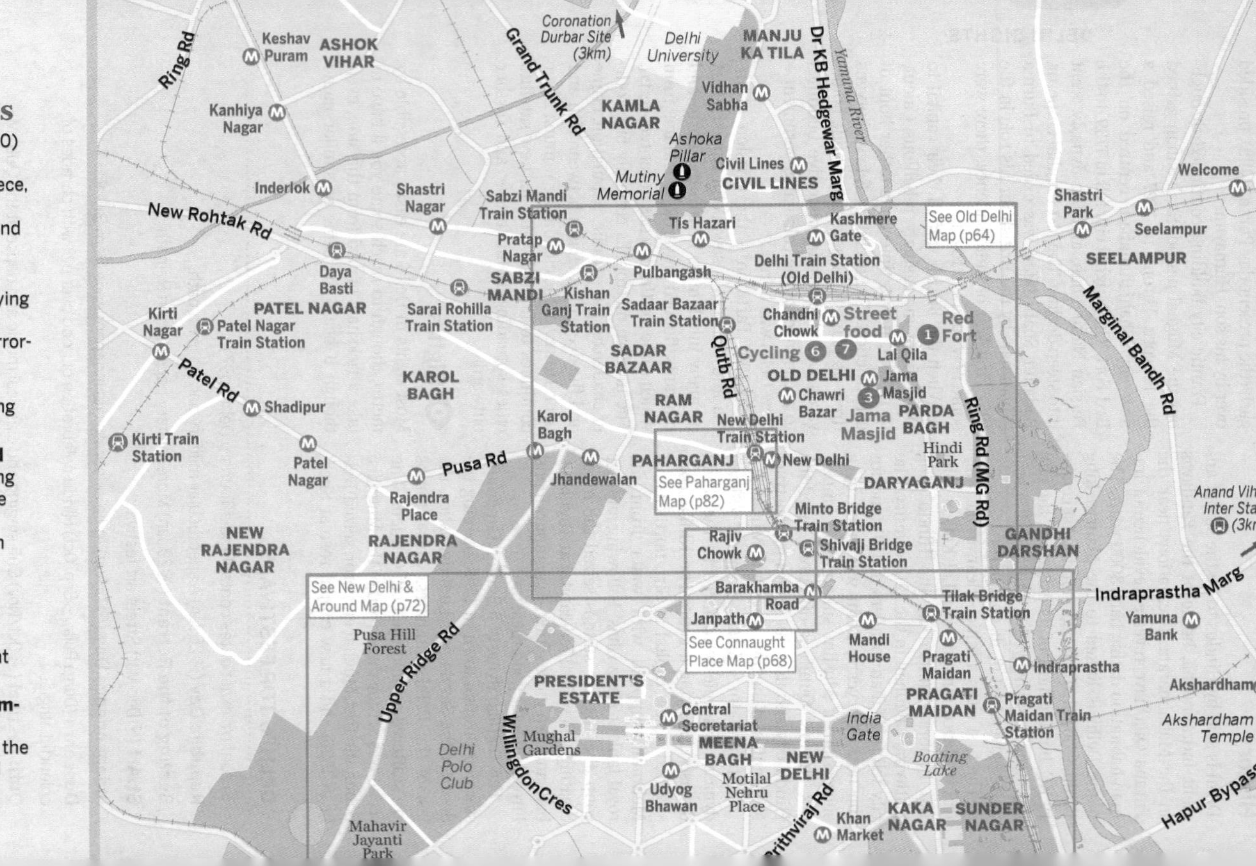

(Islamic devotional singing) at this hallowed Sufi shrine.

6 Cycling (p79) Taking a rollicking, eye-opening bike ride through Old Delhi at dawn.

7 Street food (p86) Sampling some of Old Delhi's flavour-packed street food, such as Gali Paratha Wali's stuffed breads with attitude.

8 Lodi Gardens (p70) Roaming around Delhi's favourite tree-shaded, tomb-dotted park.

9 Shahpur Jat (p96) Browsing contemporary Indian fashion designs at this independently minded village.

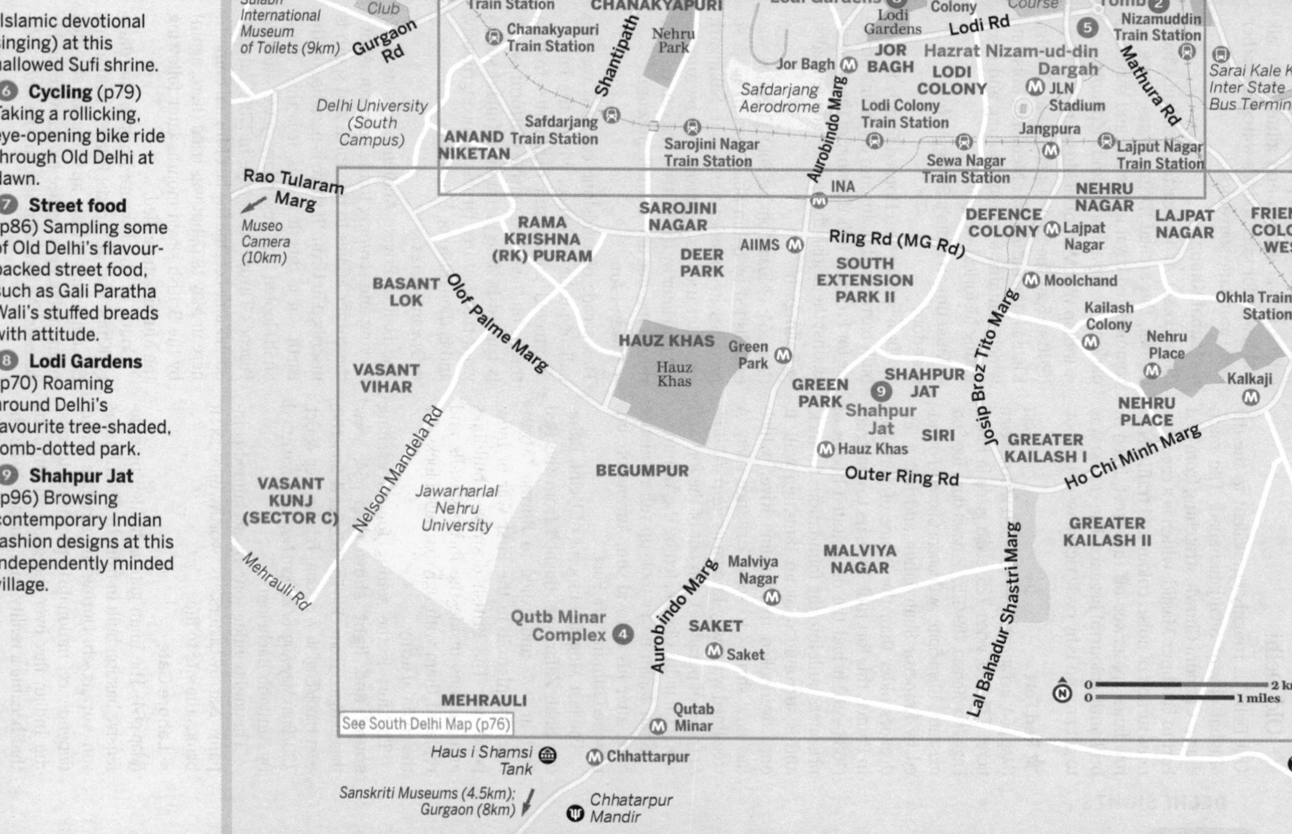

to the sight, eg Qutb Minar and Tughlaqabad. Note that many places are closed on Monday.

Old Delhi

'Old Delhi' is roughly equivalent to the the Mughal city of Shahjahanabad. The main drag is Chandni Chowk, stretching from Red Fort to Fatehpur Masjid, which is a cacophonous tumult of noise, colour and traffic. Narrow lanes spiderweb off the street, lined by brilliantly colourful bazaars. The easiest way to get around is by cycle rickshaw or on foot.

★ Red Fort FORT

(Map p64; Indian/foreigner ₹30/500, with museum ticket ₹35/500, video ₹25, audio guide in Hindi/English or Korean ₹69/115; dawn-dusk Tue-Sun, museums 10am-5pm; M Chandni Chowk) Founded by Emperor Shah Jahan and just a few decades older than the Palace of Versailles in France, this fort took 10 years to construct (1638–48). It had the decapitated bodies of prisoners built into the foundations for luck, and is surrounded by an 18m-high wall. It once overlooked the Yamuna River, which has now shrunk to some distance away. A tree-lined waterway, known as *nahr-i-bihisht* (river of paradise), ran out of the fort and along Chandni Chowk, fed by the Yamuna.

Shah Jahan never took up full residence here, after his disloyal son, Aurangzeb, imprisoned him in Agra Fort.

The last Mughal emperor of Delhi, Bahadur Shah Zafar, was flushed from the Red Fort in 1857 and exiled to Burma (Myanmar) for his role in the First War of Independence. The British destroyed buildings and gardens inside the fortress walls and replaced them with ugly barrack blocks for the colonial army.

The fort is the setting for an evening **sound and light show** (Map p64; www.theashokgroup.com; Tue-Fri ₹60, Sat & Sun ₹80; in Hindi/English 7/8.30pm Feb-Apr, Sep & Oct, 7.30/9pm May-Aug, 6/7.30pm Nov-Jan), narrated by Amitabh Bachchan.

The audio guide tour, by acclaimed company Narrowcasters, is worthwhile as it brings the site to life.

➡ Lahore Gate

(Map p64) The main gate is hidden by a defensive bastion built in front by Shah Jahan's son Aurangzeb. During the struggle for independence, nationalists promised to raise the Indian flag over the gate, an ambition that became a reality on 15 August 1947. The Prime Minister makes a speech here every Independence Day.

➡ Chatta Chowk

(Covered Bazaar) This imperial bazaar used to cater to royal women and glitter with silk and jewels for sale. Today's wares are rather more mundane souvenirs.

➡ Naubat Khana

(Drum House) At the eastern end of Chatta Chowk, the arched 'Drum House' once accommodated royal musicians and served as parking for royal horses and elephants.

➡ Indian War Memorial Museum

(10am-5pm Tue-Sun) Upstairs at Naubat Khana is the Indian War Memorial Museum, which contains ferocious-looking and fascinating historical weaponry.

➡ Museum on India's Struggle for Freedom

(10am-5pm Tue-Sun) Housed in ugly British-built barracks, the Museum on India's Struggle for Freedom tells the story of the struggle against the British that led to Independence.

➡ Salimgarh

(Map p64; 10am-5pm Tue-Sun) This fort was established by Salim Shah Suri in 1546, so predates its grander neighbour. Salimgarh was later used as a prison, first by Aurangzeb and later by the British; you can visit the ruined mosque and a small museum.

➡ Diwan-i-Am

This arcade of sandstone columns was the hall of public audience, where the emperor greeted guests and dignitaries from a throne on the raised marble platform, which is backed by fine pietra-dura (inlaid stone) work that features Orpheus, incongruously, and is thought to be Florentine.

➡ Diwan-i-Khas

The Hall of Private Audience was used for bowing and scraping to the emperor. Above the corner arches to the north and south is inscribed in Urdu, 'If there is paradise on the earth – it is this, it is this, it is this'. Nadir Shah looted the legendary jewel-studded Peacock Throne from here in 1739. Bahadar Shah Zafar became the last Mughal emperor here in May 1857, but was tried (here, again) by the British seven months later following the Mutiny, and exiled.

South of the Diwan-i-Khas is the dainty **Khas Mahal** (Special Palace), containing the emperor's private apartments, shielded from prying eyes by lace-like carved marble screens. An artificial stream, the *nahr-i-bi-*

hisht (river of paradise), once flowed through the apartments to the adjacent **Rang Mahal** (Palace of Colour), home to the emperor's chief wife. The exterior of the palace was once lavishly painted; inside is an elegant lotus-shaped fountain.

➡ Mumtaz Mahal

South of the Rang Mahal is this pavilion, thought to have been built for Arjumand Banu Begum (also known as Mumtaz Mahal) – the Taj Mahal is her mausoleum. Today it houses the **Museum of Archaeology** (⌚10am-5pm Tue-Sun), with imperial objects from those of Akbar to the rose-water sprinklers and calligraphy of the last emperor, Badapur Shah.

➡ Royal Baths

Closed to the public, the royal *hammams* once contained a sauna and hot baths for the royal family.

➡ Moti Masjid

(Pearl Mosque) This small white mosque was built by Aurangzeb as his private place of worship. The outer walls align with the fort walls, while the inner walls are askew to align with Mecca. It is closed to visitors.

➡ Shahi Burj

The Shahi Burj is a three-storey octagonal tower that was Shah Jahan's favoured workplace. From here he planned the running of his empire. In front of the tower is what remains of an elegant formal garden, centred on the Zafar Mahal, a sandstone pavilion surrounded by a deep, empty water tank.

Chandni Chowk AREA

(Map p64; Ⓜ Chandni Chowk) Old Delhi's main drag is lined by Jain, Hindu and Sikh temples, plus a church, with the Fatehpuri Masjid at one end. Tree-lined and elegant in Mughal times, the thoroughfare is now mind-bendingly chaotic, with tiny little ancient bazaars tentacling off it. In the Mughal era, Chandni Chowk centred on a pool that reflected the moon, hence the name, 'moonlight place'. The main street is almost impossible to cross, full as it is of cars, hawkers, motorcycles, rickshaws and porters.

Digambara Jain Temple JAIN TEMPLE

(Map p64; Chandni Chowk; ⌚6am-noon & 6-9pm; Ⓜ Chandni Chowk) Opposite the Red Fort is the red sandstone Digambara Jain Temple, built in 1658. It houses a fascinating **bird hospital** (Map p64; donations appreciated; ⌚10am-5pm) established in 1956 to further the Jain principle of preserving all life, treating 30,000 birds a year. Squirrels and vegetarian birds are admitted; predators are treated as outpatients. Remove shoes and leather items before entering the temple.

Sunehri Masjid MOSQUE

(Golden Mosque; Map p64; ⌚dawn-dusk; Ⓜ Chandni Chowk) Built in 1721, this mosque has gilded domes, hence its name. In 1739, the Persian invader Nadir Shah stood on the roof and watched his soldiers massacre thousands of Delhi's inhabitants.

Sisganj Gurdwara SIKH TEMPLE

(Map p64; Chandni Chowk) The icing-sugar-white 18th-century Sisganj Gurdwara marks the martrydom site of the ninth Sikh guru, Tegh Bahadur, executed by Aurangzeb in 1675 for resisting conversion to Islam. A banyan tree marks the spot where he was killed.

Fatehpuri Masjid MOSQUE

(Map p64; Chandni Chowk; ⌚5am-9.30pm; Ⓜ Chandni Chowk) Built by Fatehpuri Begum, one of Shah Jahan's wives, this 17th-century mosque is a haven of tranquillity after the frantic streets outside. The central pool was taken from a noble house, hence the elaborate shape. After the 1857 uprising the mosque was sold to a Hindu nobleman by the British for ₹19,000 and returned to

THE PIGEONS OF OLD DELHI

Pigeon rearing *(kabootar bazi)* is a popular hobby in Old Delhi, among those who can afford it – it costs from ₹5000 per bird. Some pigeons are trained to fight, some are fast, some are noted for their endurance. The practice first gained popularity during Mughal rule, when the birds were used for communication, and when Shahjahanabad was first built there were rival pigeon clubs all over the city. It's said that Nadir Shah's Delhi massacre was sparked after a row over the sale of a pigeon between one of his soldiers and a local fancier. Today there are still so many keepers that flying has to follow a timetable so that flocks don't clash. There are strict hierarchies among the owners; it takes more than 20 years to become a Khalifa (master pigeon keeper). The most spectacular event, of pigeon racing *(haqaana)*, takes place on Republic Day.

Red Fort

HIGHLIGHTS

The main entrance to the Red Fort is through 1 **Lahore Gate** – the bastion in front of it was built by Aurangzeb for increased security. You can still see bullet marks on the gate, dating from 1857, the First War of Independence, when the Indian army rose up against the British.

Walk through the Chatta Chowk (Covered Bazaar), which once sold silks and jewellery to the nobility; beyond it lies 2 **Naubat Khana**, a russet-red building, which houses Hathi Pol (Elephant Gate), so called because visitors used to dismount from their elephants or horses here as a sign of respect. From here it's straight on to the 3 **Diwan-i-Am**, the Hall of Public Audiences. Behind this are the private palaces, the 4 **Khas Mahal** and the 5 **Diwan-i-Khas**. Entry to this Hall of Private Audiences, the fort's most expensive building, was only permitted to the officials of state. The artificial stream the Nahr-i-Behisht ('stream of paradise') used to run a cooling channel of water through all these buildings. Nearby is the 6 **Moti Masjid (Pearl Mosque)** and south is the 7 **Mumtaz Mahal**, housing the Museum of Archaeology, or you can head north, where the Red Fort gardens are dotted by palatial pavilions and old British barracks. Here you'll find the 8 **baoli**, a spookily deserted water tank. Another five minutes' walk – across a road, then a railway bridge – brings you to the island fortress of 9 **Salimgarh**.

TOP TIPS

➡ To avoid crowds, get here early or late in the day; avoid weekends and public holidays.

➡ An atmospheric way to see the Red Fort is by night; you can visit after dark if you attend the nightly Sound & Light Show.

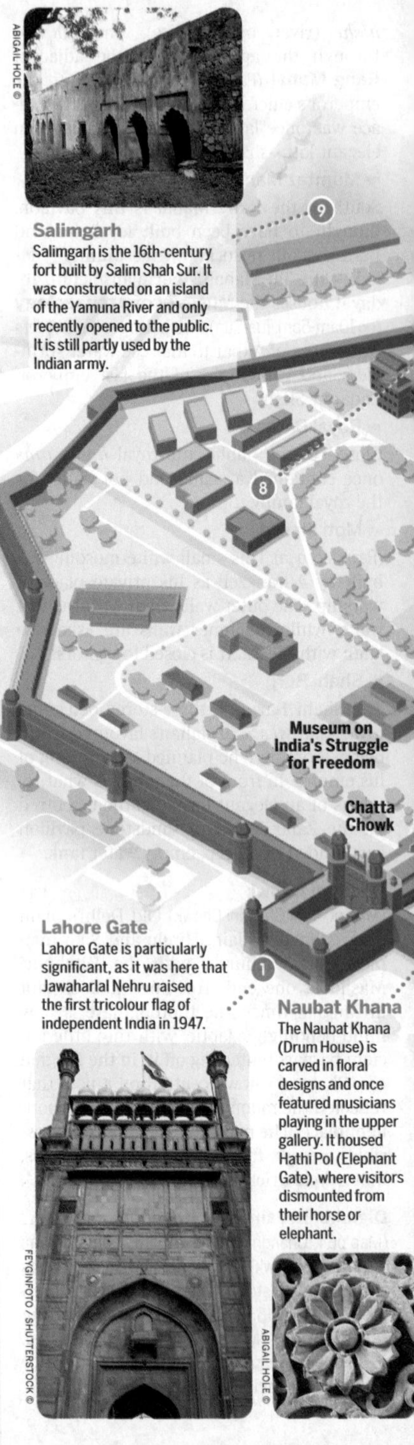

Salimgarh
Salimgarh is the 16th-century fort built by Salim Shah Sur. It was constructed on an island of the Yamuna River and only recently opened to the public. It is still partly used by the Indian army.

ABIGAIL HOLE ©

Lahore Gate
Lahore Gate is particularly significant, as it was here that Jawaharlal Nehru raised the first tricolour flag of independent India in 1947.

FEYGINFOTO / SHUTTERSTOCK ©

Naubat Khana
The Naubat Khana (Drum House) is carved in floral designs and once featured musicians playing in the upper gallery. It housed Hathi Pol (Elephant Gate), where visitors dismounted from their horse or elephant.

ABIGAIL HOLE ©

CARLOS NETO / SHUTTERSTOCK ©

KIMBERLEY COOLE/GETTY IMAGES ©

Baoli

The Red Fort step well is seldom visited and is a hauntingly deserted place, even more so when you consider its chambers were used as cells by the British from August 1942.

Moti Masjid

The Moti Masjid (Pearl Mosque) was built by Aurangzeb in 1662 for his personal use. The domes were originally covered in copper, but the copper was removed and sold by the British.

Diwan-i-Khas

This was the most expensive building in the fort, consisting of white marble decorated with inlay work of cornelian and other stones. The screens overlooking what was once the river (now the ring road) were filled with coloured glass.

Baidon Pavilion

Zafar Mahal

Hammam

5

6

Rang Mahal

4

Mumtaz Mahal

7

3

2

PIT STOP

To refuel, head to Gali Paratha Wali, a foodstall-lined lane off Chandni Chowk noted for its many varieties of freshly made paratha (traditional flat bread).

NORTH

Delhi Gate

Diwan-i-Am

These red sandstone columns were once covered in shell plaster, as polished and smooth as ivory, and in hot weather heavy red curtains were hung around the columns to block out the sun. It's believed the panels behind the marble throne were created by Florentine jeweller Austin de Bordeaux.

ABIGAIL HOLE ©

Khas Mahal

Most spectacular in the Emperor's private apartments is a beautiful marble screen at the northern end of the rooms; the 'Scales of Justice' are carved above it, suspended over a crescent, surrounded by stars and clouds.

Old Delhi

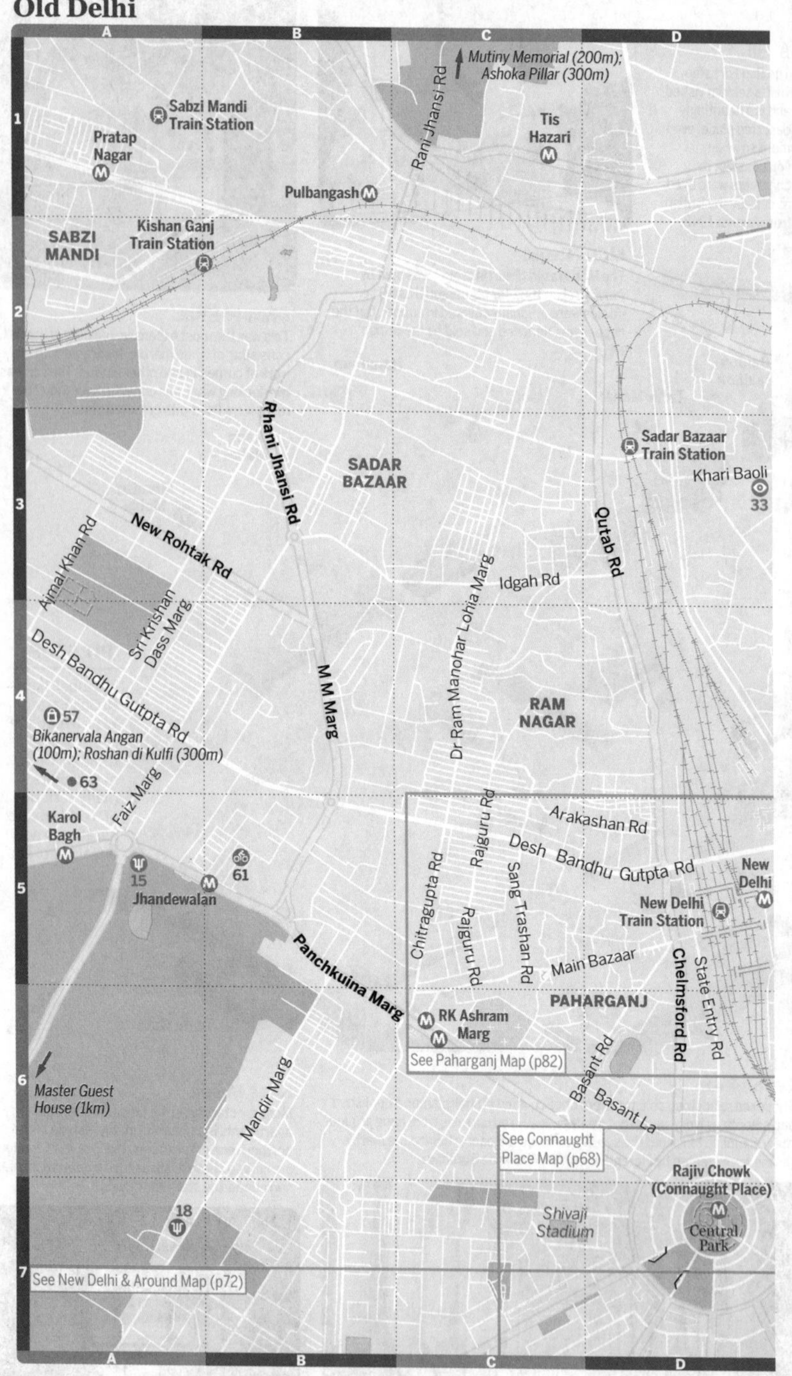

A
B
C
D
1
2
3
4
5
6
7
Mutiny Memorial (200m); Ashoka Pillar (300m)
Rani Jhansi Rd
Sabzi Mandi Train Station
Pratap Nagar
Tis Hazari
Pulbangash
SABZI MANDI
Kishan Ganj Train Station
Rhani Jhansi Rd
SADAR BAZAAR
Sadar Bazaar Train Station
Khari Baoli
33
New Rohtak Rd
Ajmal Khan Rd
Qutab Rd
Idgah Rd
Dr Ram Manohar Lohia Marg
Sri Krishan Dass Marg
Desh Bandhu Gutpta Rd
M M Marg
RAM NAGAR
57
Bikanervala Angan (100m); Roshan di Kulfi (300m)
63
Faiz Marg
Karol Bagh
Rajguru Rd
Arakashan Rd
Desh Bandhu Gutpta Rd
15
61
Jhandewalan
Chitragupta Rd
Sang Trashan Rd
New Delhi
New Delhi Train Station
Main Bazaar
Panchkuina Marg
Chelmsford Rd
State Entry Rd
PAHARGANJ
RK Ashram Marg
See Paharganj Map (p82)
Basant Rd
Basant La
Master Guest House (1km)
Mandir Marg
See Connaught Place Map (p68)
Rajiv Chowk (Connaught Place)
Central Park
Shivaji Stadium
18
See New Delhi & Around Map (p72)

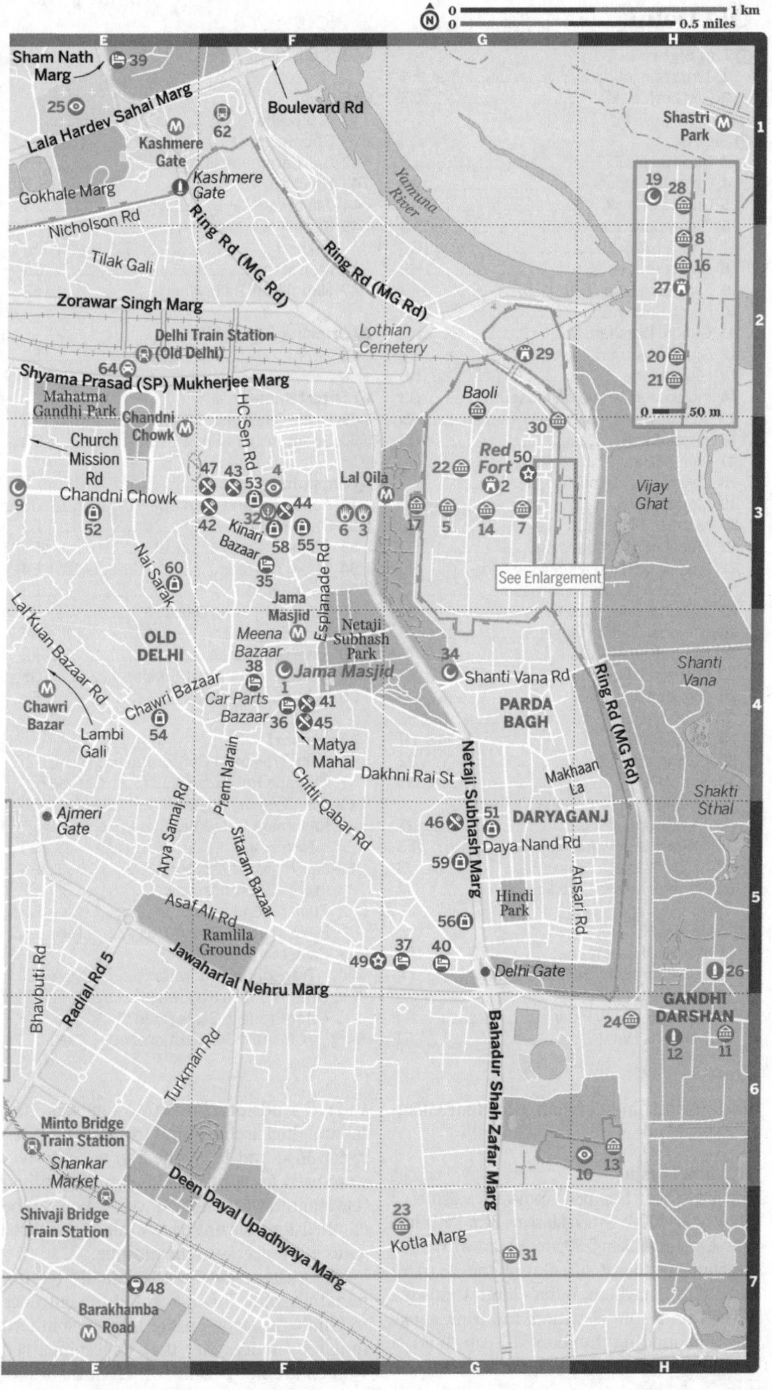

0 1 km
0 0.5 miles
Sham Nath Marg
Lala Hardev Sahai Marg
Boulevard Rd
Kashmere Gate
Gokhale Marg
Nicholson Rd
Ring Rd (MG Rd)
Yamuna River
Shastri Park
Tilak Gali
Zorawar Singh Marg
Delhi Train Station (Old Delhi)
Lothian Cemetery
Shyama Prasad (SP) Mukherjee Marg
Mahatma Gandhi Park
Chandni Chowk
HC Sen Rd
Baoli
Church Mission Rd
Red Fort
Lal Qila
Vijay Ghat
Kinari Bazaar
Esplanade Rd
See Enlargement
Nai Sarak
Lal Kuan Bazaar Rd
Jama Masjid
Meena Bazaar
Netaji Subhash Park
OLD DELHI
Shanti Vana Rd
Shanti Vana
Chawri Bazaar
Car Parts Bazaar
PARDA BAGH
Chawri Bazar
Lambi Gali
Matya Mahal
Prem Narain
Chitli Qabar Rd
Dakhni Rai St
Netaji Subhash Marg
Makhaan La
Shakti Sthal
Ajmeri Gate
Arya Samaj Rd
DARYAGANJ
Daya Nand Rd
Sitaram Bazaar
Hindi Park
Ansari Rd
Asaf Ali Rd
Ramlila Grounds
Radial Rd 5
Jawaharlal Nehru Marg
Delhi Gate
Bhavbuti Rd
GANDHI DARSHAN
Turkman Rd
Bahadur Shah Zafar Marg
Minto Bridge Train Station
Shankar Market
Deen Dayal Upadhyaya Marg
Shivaji Bridge Train Station
Kotla Marg
Barakhamba Road
0 50 m

Old Delhi

Top Sights

1 Jama Masjid F4
2 Red Fort G3

Sights

3 Bird Hospital F3
4 Chandni Chowk F3
5 Chatta Chowk G3
6 Digambara Jain Temple F3
7 Diwan-i-Am G3
8 Diwan-i-Khas H2
9 Fatehpuri Masjid E3
10 Feroz Shah Kotla H6
11 Gandhi Darshan H6
12 Gandhi Memorial H6
13 Hawa Mahal H6
14 Indian War Memorial Museum G3
15 Jhandewalan Hanuman Temple A5
16 Khas Mahal H2
17 Lahore Gate G3
18 Lakshmi Narayan Temple A7
19 Moti Masjid H1
20 Mumtaz Mahal H2
21 Museum of Archaeology H2
22 Museum on India's Struggle for Freedom G3
23 National Bal Bhavan G7
24 National Gandhi Museum H6
Naubat Khana (see 14)
25 Nicholson Cemetery E1
26 Raj Ghat H5
27 Rang Mahal H2
28 Royal Baths H1
29 Salimgarh G2
30 Shahi Burj G3
31 Shankar's International Dolls Museum G7
32 Sisganj Gurdwara F3
33 Spice Market D3
34 Sunehri Masjid G4

Sleeping

35 Haveli Dharampura F3
36 Hotel Bombay Orient F4
37 Hotel Broadway G5
38 Hotel New City Palace F4
39 Maidens Hotel E1
40 Stops @ The President G5

Eating

41 Al-Jawahar F4
Chor Bizarre (see 37)
42 Gali Paratha Wali F3
43 Haldiram's F3
44 Jalebiwala F3
45 Karim's F4
Lakhori (see 35)
46 Moti Mahal G5
47 Natraj Dahi Balle Wala F3

Drinking & Nightlife

48 24/7 E7

Entertainment

49 Delite Cinema F5
50 Sound & Light Show G3

Shopping

51 Aap Ki Pasand (San Cha) G5
52 Ballimaran E3
53 Chandni Chowk F3
54 Chawri Bazaar E4
55 Dariba Kalan F3
56 Daryaganj Kitab Bazaar G5
57 Karol Bagh Market A4
58 Kinari Bazaar F3
59 Musical Instrument Shops G5
60 Nai Sarak E3

Transport

Delhi Transport Corporation (see 62)
Haryana Roadways (see 62)
61 Jhandewalan Cycle Market B5
62 Kashmere Gate Inter State Bus Terminal F1
63 Lalli Motorbike Exports A4
64 Prepaid Autorickshaws E2
Punjab Roadways (see 62)
Rajasthan Roadways (see 62)
Rajasthan State Road Transport Corporation (see 62)
Uttar Pradesh Roadways (see 62)
Uttar Pradesh State Road Transport Corporation (see 62)

Muslim worship in exchange for four villages 20 years later.

★ Jama Masjid MOSQUE

(Friday Mosque; Map p64; camera & video each ₹300, tower ₹100; ⊙non-Muslims 8am-1hr before sunset, minaret 9am-5.30pm; M Chawri Bazaar)
A beautiful pocket of calm at the heart of Old Delhi's mayhem, India's largest mosque is built on a 10m elevation, towering above the surrounding hubbub. It can hold a mind-blowing 25,000 people. The marble and red-sandstone 'Friday Mosque' was Shah Jahan's final architectural triumph, built between 1644 and 1658. The four watchtowers were used for security. There are two minarets standing 40m high, one of which can be climbed for amazing views. All of the three gates allow access to the mosque.

The eastern gate was originally for imperial use only. Buy a ticket at the entrance to climb 121 steps up the narrow southern minaret (notices say that unaccompanied women are not permitted). From the top of the minaret, you can see how architect Edwin Lutyens incorporated the mosque into his design of New Delhi – the Jama Masjid, Connaught Place and Sansad Bhavan (Parliament House) are in a direct line.

Visitors should remove their shoes at the top of the stairs. There's no charge to enter the mosque, but you'll have to pay the camera charge whether you want to use your camera or not.

Raj Ghat MONUMENT

(Map p64; ⏲10am-8pm; M Jama Masjid) FREE On the banks of the Yamuna River, this peaceful park contains a simple black-marble platform marking the spot where Mahatma Gandhi was cremated following his assassination in 1948. This **memorial** (Map p64) is a thought-provoking spot, inscribed with what are said to have been Gandhi's final words, *Hai Ram* (Oh, God). Every Friday (the day he died) commemorative prayers are held here at 5pm, as well as on 2 October and 30 January, his birth and death anniversaries.

Across Kisan Ghat Rd is the **Gandhi Darshan** (Map p64; ⏲10am-5pm Mon-Sat; M Indraprastha) FREE, a pavilion displaying photos relating to the Mahatma. Nearby memorials commemorate where Jawaharlal Nehru, Indira Gandhi and Rajiv Gandhi were cremated.

National Gandhi Museum MUSEUM

(Map p64; ☎011-23310168; http://gandhimuseum.org; Raj Ghat; ⏲9.30am-5.30pm Tue-Sun; M Jama Masjid) FREE An interesting museum preserving some of Gandhi's personal belongings, including his spectacles and even two of his teeth. Movingly and somewhat macabrely, also here are the dhoti, shawl and watch he was wearing when he was assassinated, and one of the bullets that killed him.

Feroz Shah Kotla HISTORIC SITE

(Map p64; Bahadur Shah Zafar Marg; Indian/foreigner ₹15/200, video ₹25; ⏲dawn-dusk; M ITO) Firozabad, the fifth city of Delhi, was built by Feroz Shah Tughlaq in 1354, the first city here to be built on the river. Only the fortress remains, with crumbling walls protecting the Jama Masjid (Friday mosque), a *baoli* (step-well), and the pyramid-like **Hawa Mahal** (Map p64), topped by a 13m-high sandstone **Ashoka Pillar** inscribed with 3rd-century-BC Buddhist edicts. There's an otherworldly atmosphere to the ruins.

On Thursday afternoon, crowds gather at the mosque to light candles and incense and leave bowls of milk to appease Delhi's djinns (invisible spirits), who are said to occupy the underground chambers beneath the mosque. Shoes should be removed when entering the mosque and Hawa Mahal.

Shankar's International Dolls Museum MUSEUM

(Map p64; ☎011-3316970; www.childrensbooktrust.com; Nehru House, 4 Bahadur Shah Zafar Marg; adult/child ₹17/6; ⏲10am-6pm Tue-Sun; M ITO) Set up by K Shankar Pillai, a political cartoonist, who started collecting dolls in 1950, this museum has an impressive if quirky collection of 6500 costumed dolls from 85 countries.

National Bal Bhavan MUSEUM

(Map p64; www.nationalbalbhavan.nic.in; Kotla Marg; adult/child ₹20/free; ⏲9am-5.30pm Tue-Sat; M Mandi House) Delhi's children's museum is a charming hodgepodge, with a polychrome-painted toy train ride, parrots, guinea pigs, rabbits and a small aquarium.

Nicholson Cemetery CEMETERY

(Map p64; Lala Hardev Sahai Marg; ⏲8am-6pm Apr-Sep, 9am-5pm Oct-Mar; M Kashmere Gate) Close to Kashmere Gate, this fascinating, forgotten cemetery is the last resting place for hundreds of Delhi's colonial-era residents, many of whom perished in childhood. The most famous (ex)-resident is the eponymous Brigadier General John Nicholson, who died from injuries sustained during the 1857 First War of Independence. He had a formidable reputation, and was so admired by some of his troops that he inspired a religious cult, but he was also contemptuous of the 'natives' and sadistically violent towards his adversaries.

Take the metro to see the British-erected **Mutiny Memorial** (Rani Jhansi Rd; M Pulbangash) and **Ashoka Pillar** (Rani Jhansi Rd; M Kashmere Gate), transported here by Feroz Shah.

Coronation Durbar Site MONUMENT

(Shanti Swaroop Tyagi Marg; M Model Town) This historical oddity is worth seeking out if you like exploring forgotten corners. Around 10km north of Old Delhi, a lone obelisk marks the site where King George V was declared emperor of India in 1911, and where the great durbars (fairs) were held to honour India's British overlords in 1877 and 1903. A few marble busts of British officials and a mammoth statue of George V decorate the neighbouring park. Take an autorickshaw from the metro.

Lakshmi Narayan Temple HINDU TEMPLE

(Birla Mandir; Map p64; Mandir Marg; ⏲4.30am-1.30pm & 2.30-9pm; M Ramakrishna Ashram Marg) This Orissan-style temple was erected by

Connaught Place

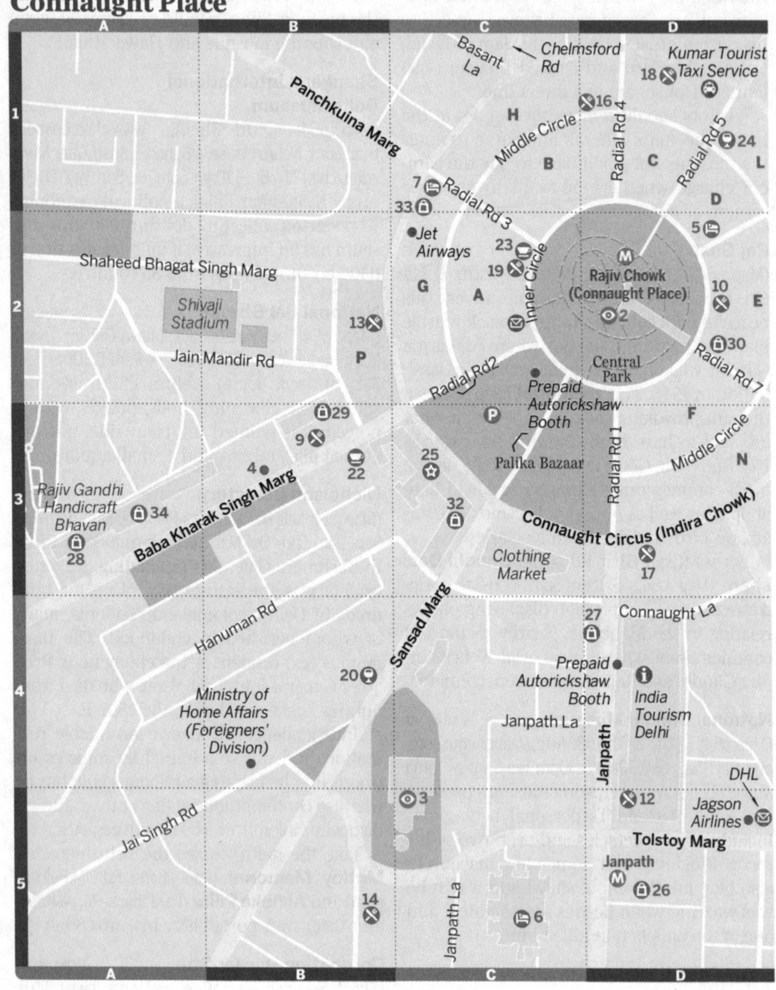

the wealthy industrialist BD Birla in 1939; the main shrine honours Lakshmi, goddess of wealth. Gandhi inaugurated the complex as a temple for all castes; a sign on the gate says 'Everyone is Welcome'.

Jhandewalan Hanuman Temple HINDU TEMPLE

(Map p64; Link Rd, Jhandewalan; dawn-dusk; M Jhandewalan) This temple is not to be missed (it's actually hard to miss) if you're in Karol Bagh. Take a short detour to see the 34m-high Hanuman statue that soars above the train tracks. Getting up close, there are passageways through the mouths of demons to a series of atmospheric, deity-filled chambers.

Connaught Place Area

Connaught Place AREA

(Map p68; M Rajiv Chowk) This confusing circular shopping district was named after George V's uncle, the Duke of Connaught, and fashioned after the Palladian colonnades of Bath. Greying, whitewashed, colonadded streets radiate out from the central circle of Rajiv Chowk, with blocks G to N in the outer circle and A to F in the inner circle. Today they mainly harbour brash, largely in-

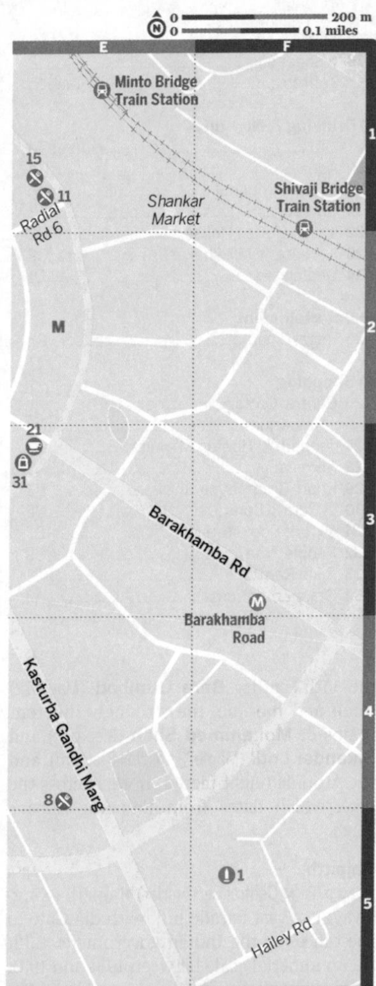

terchangeable but popular bars, and international chainstores, plus a few good hotels and restaurants. Touts are rampant.

Jantar Mantar HISTORIC SITE
(Map p68; Sansad Marg; Indian/foreigner ₹25/200, video ₹25; ⊙dawn-dusk; Ⓜ Patel Chowk) This is one of five observatories built by Maharaja Jai Singh II, ruler of Jaipur. Constructed in 1725, Jantar Mantar (derived from the Sanskrit word for 'instrument', but which has also become the Hindi word for 'abracadabra') is a collection of curving geometric buildings that are carefully calibrated to monitor the movement of the stars and planets.

Agrasen ki Baoli MONUMENT
(Map p68; Hailey Lane; ⊙dawn-dusk; Ⓜ Janpath) This atmospheric 14th-century step-well was once set in the countryside, till the city grew up around it; 103 steps descend to the bottom, flanked by arched niches. It's a remarkable thing to discover among the office towers southeast of Connaught Place. It's garnered more attention since it was used as a shelter by Aamir Khan in the 2015 movie *PK*.

New Delhi & Around

★Humayun's Tomb HISTORIC BUILDING
(Map p72; Mathura Rd; Indian/foreigner/under 15 ₹30/500/free, video ₹25; ⊙dawn-dusk; Ⓜ JLN Stadium) Humayun's tomb is sublimely well proportioned, seeming to float above its symmetrical gardens. It's thought to have inspired the Taj Mahal, which it predates by 60 years. Constructed for the Mughal emperor in the mid-16th century by Haji Begum, Humayun's Persian-born wife, the tomb marries Persian and Mughal elements, with restrained decoration enhancing the architecture. The arched facade is inlaid with bands of white marble and red sandstone, and the building follows strict rules of Islamic geometry, with an emphasis on the number eight.

The tomb has had six years of restoration, and a new visitor centre is due to open at the site. The surrounding gardens contain the tombs of the emperor's favourite barber – an entrusted position given the proximity of the razor to the imperial throat – and Haji Begum. This was where the last Mughal emperor, Bahadur Shah Zafar, took refuge before being captured and exiled by the British in 1857.

To the right as you enter the complex, **Isa Khan's tomb** (Map p72; ⊙dawn-dusk) is a fine example of Lodi-era architecture, constructed in the 16th century. Further south is the monumental Khan-i-Khanan's tomb (p75), plundered in Mughal times to build Safdarjang's tomb.

★Hazrat Nizam-ud-din Dargah SHRINE
(Map p72; off Lodi Rd; ⊙24hr; Ⓜ JLN Stadium) Visiting the marble shrine of Muslim Sufi saint Nizam-ud-din Auliya is Delhi's most mystical, magical experience. The dargah is hidden away in a tangle of bazaars selling rose petals, attars (perfumes) and offerings, and on Thursday evenings from sunset you can hear Sufis singing *qawwali* (Islamic de-

Connaught Place

Sights

1 Agrasen ki Baoli F5
2 Connaught Place D2
3 Jantar Mantar C5

Activities, Courses & Tours

4 Delhi Tourism & Transport Development Corporation Booth B3

Sleeping

5 Hotel Palace Heights D2
6 Imperial C5
7 Radisson Blu Marina C1

Eating

8 Caara Cafe E4
9 Coffee Home B3
10 Farzi Cafe D2
11 Haldiram's E1
12 Hotel Saravana Bhavan D5
13 Hotel Saravana Bhavan B2
14 Kerala House B5
15 Naturals E1
16 Nizam's Kathi Kabab D1
17 Rajdhani D3
18 Sagar Ratna D1
19 Wenger's C2
Zäffrān (see 5)

Drinking & Nightlife

1911 (see 6)
20 Aqua B4
Atrium, Imperial (see 6)
21 Cha Bar E3
22 Indian Coffee House B3
23 Keventer's Milkshakes C2
24 Unplugged D1

Entertainment

25 Regal Cinema C3

Shopping

26 Central Cottage Industries Emporium D5
27 Janpath & Tibetan Markets D4
28 Kamala A3
29 Khadi Gramodyog Bhawan B3
30 M Ram & Sons D2
31 Oxford Bookstore E3
32 People Tree C3
33 Rikhi Ram C1
34 State Emporiums A3

votional singing), amid crowds of devotees. The ascetic Nizam-ud-din died in 1325 at the ripe old age of 92. His doctrine of tolerance made him popular not only with Muslims, but with Hindus, Sikhs and Buddhists as well.

Later kings and nobles wanted to be buried close to Nizam-ud-din, hence the number of nearby Mughal tombs. Other tombs in the compound include the graves of Jahanara (daughter of Shah Jahan) and the renowned Urdu poet Amir Khusru. Scattered around the surrounding alleyways are more tombs and a huge *baoli* (step-well). Entry is free, but visitors may be asked to make a donation.

A tour with the Hope Project (p79), which ends at the shrine, is recommended for some background.

Lodi Gardens PARK
(Map p72; Lodi Rd; ⏲6am-8pm Oct-Mar, 5am-8pm Apr-Sep; Ⓜ Khan Market or Jor Bagh) Delhi's loveliest escape was originally named after the wife of the British Resident, Lady Willingdon, who had two villages cleared in 1936 in order to landscape a park to remind her of home. Today named after their Lodi-era tombs, the gardens, favoured getaway for Delhi's elite and courting couples, contain the 15th-century **Bara Gumbad** (Map p72) tomb and mosque, the strikingly different tombs of **Mohammed Shah** (Map p72) and **Sikander Lodi** (Map p72; Ⓜ JLN Stadium), and the Athpula (eight-piered) bridge across the lake, which dates from Emperor Akbar's reign.

Rajpath AREA
(Map p72; Ⓜ Central Secretariat) Rajpath (Kingsway) is a vast parade linking India Gate to the offices of the Indian government. Built on an imperial scale between 1914 and 1931, this complex was designed by Edwin Lutyens and Herbert Baker, and underlined the ascendance of the British rulers. Yet just 16 years later, the Brits were out on their ear and Indian politicians were pacing the corridors of power.

At the western end of Rajpath, the official residence of the president of India, Rashtrapati Bhavan (p71), now partially open to the public via guided tour, is flanked by the mirror-image dome-crowned **North Secretariat** (Map p72) and **South Secretariat** (Map p72), housing government ministries. The Indian parliament meets nearby at the **Sansad Bhavan** (Parliament House; Map p72; Sansard Marg), a circular, colonnaded edifice at the end of Sansad Marg.

At Rajpath's eastern end is mighty **India Gate** (Map p72; 24hr). This 42m-high stone memorial arch, designed by Lutyens, pays tribute to around 90,000 Indian army soldiers who died in WWI, the Northwest Frontier operations and the 1919 Anglo-Afghan War.

Rashtrapati Bhavan HISTORIC BUILDING

(President's House; Map p72; 011-23015321; www.presidentofindia.nic.in/visit-to-rashtrapati-bhavan.htm; ₹50, online reservation required; 9am-4pm Fri-Sun; M Central Secretariat) Formerly home to the British Viceroy, the President's House has 340 rooms, with 2.5km of corridors, and it's fascinating to take a peek inside. Your guided visit takes in the domed Durbar Hall, the intimate presidential library and the gilded Ashoka Hall.

Rashtrapati Bhavan Museum MUSEUM

(Map p72; 011-23792177; www.presidentofindia.nic.in; gate 30, Mother Theresa Crescent Rd; tour ₹50; 9am-4pm Fri-Sun; M Patel Chowk) Occupying the presidential stables and garages, this swish museum has state-of-the-art displays including a virtual-reality walk with Gandhi and 3D images of presidential speeches, plus vehicles, such as a Mercedes given to Rajiv Gandhi by the King of Jordan. Book ahead online.

Mughal Gardens GARDENS

(Map p72; usually 9.30am-4pm Tue-Sun mid-Feb–mid-Mar; M Central Secretariat) FREE The extravagance of these glorious gardens is such that Mountbatten, India's last viceroy, was said to have employed 418 gardeners. There are fountains, cypress, bougainvillea, climbing roses, symmetrical lawns and wandering peacocks. If you're in town when the gardens are in flower (the same months they're open), they're not to be missed.

National Museum MUSEUM

(Map p72; 011-23019272; www.nationalmuseumindia.gov.in; Janpath; Indian/foreigner ₹20/650, camera Indian/foreigner ₹20/300; 10am-5pm Tue-Sun, free guided tour 10.30am & 2.30pm Tue-Fri, 10.30am, 11.30am & 2.30pm Sat & Sun; M Central Secretariat) This glorious if dusty museum is full of treasures. Mind-bogglingly ancient, sophisticated figurines from the Harappan civilisation, almost 5000 years old, include the remarkable Dancing Girl, and there are also some fine ceramics from the even older Nal civilisation. Other items include Buddha relics, exquisite jewellery, miniature paintings, medieval woodcarvings, textiles and musical instruments.

Allow at least two hours. Bring identification to obtain an audio guide (included in the foreigner ticket price; ₹150 extra for Indian tourists). There's also a cafe.

National Gallery of Modern Art GALLERY

(Map p72; 011-23386111; www.ngmaindia.gov.in; Jaipur House, Dr Zakir Hussain Marg; Indian/foreigner ₹20/500; 10am-5pm Tue-Sun; M Khan Market) Housed in the Maharaja of Jaipur's domed former palace (built in 1936), Delhi's flagship art gallery displays collections tracing the development of Indian art from the mid-19th century to the present day, from 'Company Paintings' created by Indian artists to please their British rulers to the artworks of Nobel Prize–winner Rabindranath Tagore. Photography is prohibited.

Gandhi Smriti MUSEUM

(Map p72; 011-23012843; 5 Tees Jan Marg; 10am-5pm Tue-Sun, closed every 2nd Sat of month; M Racecourse) FREE This poignant memorial to Mahatma Gandhi is in Birla House, where he was shot dead on the grounds by a Hindu zealot on 30 January 1948, after campaigning against intercommunal violence.

The house itself is where Gandhi spent his last 144 days. The exhibits include rooms preserved just as Gandhi left them, a detailed account of his life and last 24 hours, and vivid miniature dioramas depicting scenes from his life.

Indira Gandhi Memorial Museum MUSEUM

(Map p72; 011-23010094; 1 Safdarjang Rd; 9.30am-4.45pm Tue-Sun; M Racecourse) FREE In the residence of controversial former prime minister Indira Gandhi is this interesting museum devoted to her life and family, India's Kennedys. It displays her personal effects, including the blood-stained sari she was wearing when she was assassinated in 1984. Many rooms are preserved as they were, providing a window into the family's life. An exhibit at the rear charts the life of Indira's son, Rajiv, who met a similarly violent end and was assassinated in 1991.

Nehru Memorial Museum MUSEUM

(Map p72; 011-23016734; www.nehrumemorial.nic.in; Teen Murti Rd; 9am-5.30pm Tue-Sun; M Udyog Bhawan) FREE Built for the British commander-in-chief and previously called 'Flagstaff House', the stately Teen Murti Bhavan was later the official residence of

New Delhi & Around

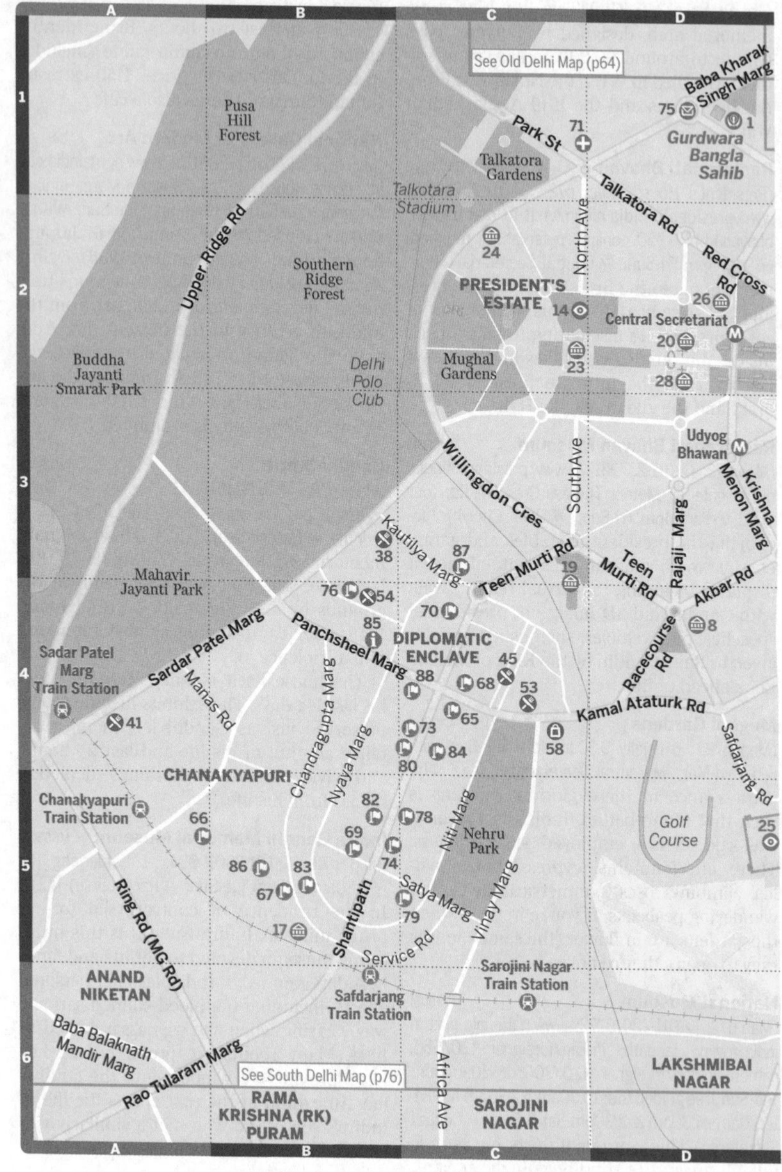

Jawaharlal Nehru (India's first prime minister). It's now a museum devoted to Nehru's life and work; the bedroom, study and drawing room are preserved as if he'd just popped out.

On the grounds is a 14th-century hunting lodge, built by Feroz Shah, and a more recent **planetarium** (Map p72; ☎011-23014504; www.nehruplanetarium.org; 45min show adult/child ₹60/40; ⊙shows English 11.30am & 3pm, Hindi 1.30pm & 4pm), which has shows about the stars in Hindi and English.

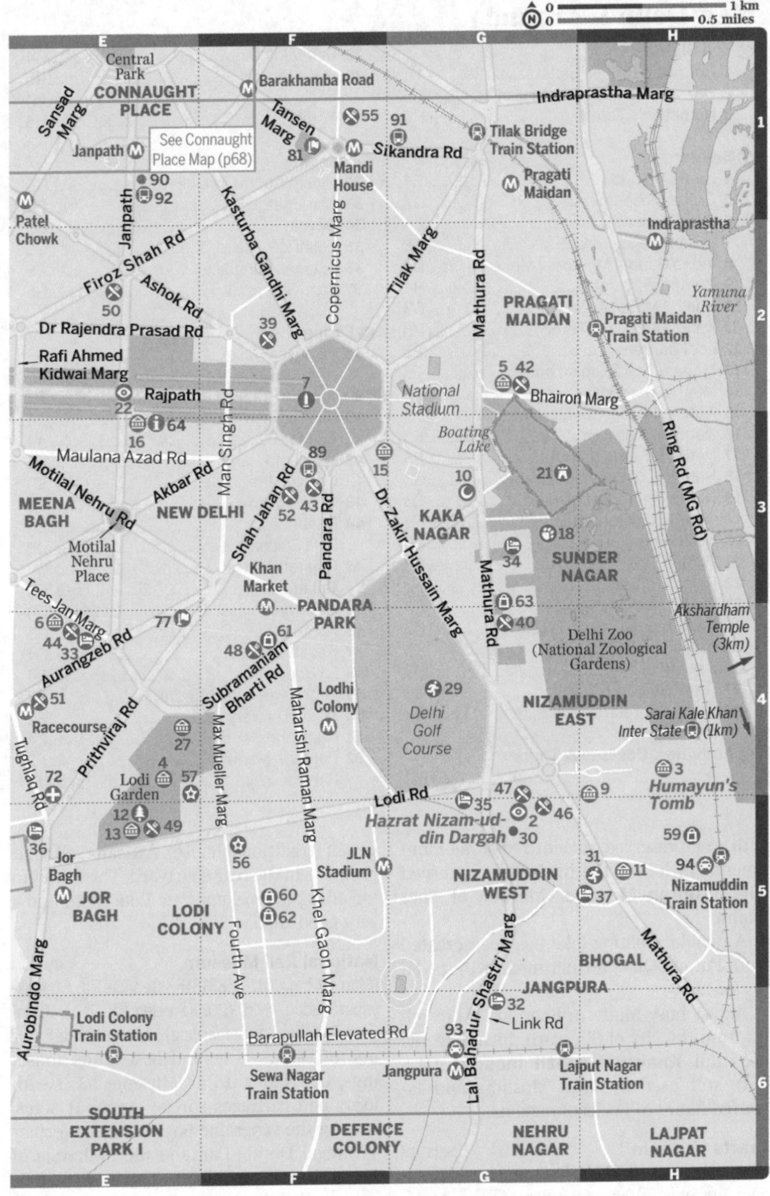

Purana Qila FORT

(Old Fort; Map p72; ☎011-24353178; Mathura Rd; Indian/foreigner ₹5/200, video ₹25, sound & light show adult/child ₹100/50; ⊙dawn-dusk; Ⓜ Pragati Maidan) The unimaginatively named 'Old Fort' is where Mughal Emperor Humayun met his end in 1556, tumbling down the steps of the **Sher Mandal**, which he used as a library. The fort had been built by Afghan ruler Sher Shah (1538–45), during his brief ascendancy over Humayun. It's well worth a visit, with its peaceful garden studded

New Delhi & Around

Top Sights
1 Gurdwara Bangla Sahib D1
2 Hazrat Nizam-ud-din Dargah G5
3 Humayun's Tomb H4

Sights
4 Bara Gumbad E4
5 Crafts Museum G2
6 Gandhi Smriti E4
7 India Gate F2
8 Indira Gandhi Memorial Museum D4
9 Isa Khan's Tomb H4
10 Khairul Manazil G3
11 Khan-i-Khanan's Tomb H5
12 Lodi Gardens E5
13 Mohammed Shah's Tomb E5
14 Mughal Gardens C2
15 National Gallery of Modern Art F3
16 National Museum E3
17 National Rail Museum B5
18 National Zoological Gardens G3
19 Nehru Memorial Museum C3
Nehru Planetarium .... (see 19)
20 North Secretariat D2
21 Purana Qila G3
22 Rajpath E2
23 Rashtrapati Bhavan C2
24 Rashtrapati Bhavan Museum C2
25 Safdarjang's Tomb D5
26 Sansad Bhavan D2
27 Sikander Lodi's Tomb E4
28 South Secretariat D2

Activities, Courses & Tours
Aura .... (see 61)
29 Delhi Golf Club G4
30 Hope Project G5
Lodhi Spa .... (see 35)
31 Torch H5

Sleeping
32 Bloom Rooms @ Link Rd G6
33 Claridges E4
34 Devna G3
35 Lodhi G5
36 Lutyens Bungalow E5
37 Zaza Stay H5

Eating
38 Alkauser B3
Altitude Cafe .... (see 62)
39 Andhra Pradesh Bhawan Canteen F2
40 Basil & Thyme G4
41 Bukhara A4
42 Cafe Lota G2
Chicken Inn .... (see 52)
43 Chor Bizarre F3
44 Dhaba E4
Diva Spiced .... (see 62)
45 Gujarat Bhawan C4
Gulati .... (see 52)
Havemore .... (see 52)
46 Karim's G5
47 Kebab Stands G4
48 La Bodega F4
49 Lodi Garden Restaurant E5
50 Masala Library E2
51 Nagaland House E4
52 Pandara Market F3
Perch .... (see 48)

with well-preserved ancient red-stone monuments, including the intricately patterned **Qila-i-Kuhran Mosque** (Mosque of Sher Shah).

A popular boating lake has been created from Purana Qila's former moat, with pedalos for hire.

Across busy Mathura Road are more relics from the city of Shergarh, including the beautiful **Khairul Manazil mosque** (Map p72), still used by local Muslims and favoured haunt of flocks of pigeons.

Crafts Museum MUSEUM

(Map p72; ☎011-23371641; Bhairon Marg; ⏰10am-5pm Tue-Sun; Ⓜ Pragati Maidan) **FREE** Much of this lovely museum is outside, including tree-shaded carvings and buildings. Displays celebrate the traditional crafts of India, with some beautiful textiles on display indoors, such as embroidery from Kashmir and cross-stitch from Punjab. Highlights include an exquisite reconstructed Gujarati *haveli* (traditional house). Artisans sell their products in the rear courtyard. The museum includes the excellent Cafe Lota (p89) and a very good shop.

National Rail Museum MUSEUM

(Map p72; ☎011-26881816; Service Rd, Chanakyapuri; adult/child ₹20/10, video ₹100; ⏰10am-5pm Tue-Sun; Ⓜ Safdarjung) A contender for one of Delhi's best (and best-value) museums, the National Rail Museum has steam locos and carriages spread across 11 acres. Among the venerable bogies are the former Viceregal Dining Car, and the Maharaja of Mysore's rolling saloon. The new indoor gallery includes some hands-on exhibits, a miniature railway, and three simulators (weekends only). A toy train (adult/child ₹20/10) chuffs around the grounds.

National Zoological Gardens ZOO

(Map p72; ☎011-24359825; www.nzpnewdelhi.gov.in; Mathura Rd; adult/child Indian ₹40/20, foreigner

Pindi ....(see 52)
53 Sagar Ratna C4
54 Sana-di-ge B4
Sodabottleopenerwala ....(see 61)
55 Triveni Terrace Cafe F1

Drinking & Nightlife
Café Turtle ....(see 59)
Café Turtle ....(see 61)

Entertainment
56 Habitat World F5
57 India International Centre E4

Shopping
58 Aap Ki Pasand (San Cha) C4
Anand Stationers ....(see 61)
Anokhi ....(see 58)
Anokhi ....(see 61)
59 Anokhi H5
Bahrisons ....(see 61)
Fabindia ....(see 61)
60 Fabindia F5
Full Circle Bookstore ....(see 61)
Kama ....(see 61)
61 Khan Market F4
62 Meharchand Market F5
Mehra Bros ....(see 61)
OCM Suitings ....(see 61)
63 Sunder Nagar Market G3
The Shop ....(see 60)

Information
64 Archaeological Survey of India E3
65 Australian High Commission C4
66 Bangladeshi High Commission A5
67 Bhutanese Embassy B5
68 British High Commission C4
69 Canadian High Commission B5
70 Chinese Embassy C4
71 Dr Ram Manohar Lohia Hospital C1
72 East West Medical Centre E4
73 French Embassy C4
74 German Embassy B5
75 India Post D1
76 Irish Embassy B4
77 Israeli Embassy E4
78 Japanese Embassy C5
79 Malaysian High Commission C5
80 Myanmar Embassy C4
81 Nepali Embassy F1
82 Netherlands Embassy B5
83 New Zealand High Commission B5
84 Pakistani Embassy C4
85 Sikkim House B4
86 Singaporean High Commission B5
87 Sri Lankan High Commission C3
88 US Embassy C4

Transport
89 Bikaner House F3
90 Chanderlok House E1
91 Himachal Bhawan G1
92 Himachal Pradesh Tourism Development Corporation E1
93 Metropole Tourist Service G6
94 Prepaid Autorickshaws H5
Rajasthan Tourism ....(see 89)

₹200/100, camera/video ₹50/200, battery-operated vehicle adult/child ₹67/34; 9am-4.30pm Sat-Thu, to 4pm Oct-Mar; M Pragati Maidan) Founded in 1952, this is a vast green space in the city, covering 86 hectares. Kept in reasonable conditions are lions, tigers, elephants, hippos, rhinos, spectacular birds and monkeys. You can hire battery-operated vehicles to get around.

Safdarjang's Tomb TOMB
(Map p72; Aurobindo Marg; Indian/foreigner ₹15/200, video ₹25; dawn-dusk; M Jor Bagh) Built by the Nawab of Avadh for his father, Safdarjang, this grandiose, highly decorative mid-18th-century tomb is an example of late Mughal architecture. There were insufficient funds for all-over marble, so materials to cover the dome were taken from the nearby mausoleum of Khan-i-Khanan, and it was finished in red sandstone.

Khan-i-Khanan's Tomb HISTORIC BUILDING
(Map p72; Indian/foreigner ₹15/200; dawn-dusk; M Jangpura) This is the monumental tomb of a poet and minister in Akbar's court. Khan-i-Khanan had it built for his wife in 1598, and was buried here himself in 1627. It was later plundered to build nearby Safdarjang's tomb, and more of its decoration was stripped in the 19th century.

★ **Gurdwara Bangla Sahib** SIKH TEMPLE
(Map p72; Ashoka Rd; 4am-9pm; M Patel Chowk) This magnificent, huge, white-marble gurdwara, topped by glinting golden onion domes, was constructed at the site where the eighth Sikh guru, Harkrishan Dev, stayed before his 1664 death. Despite his tender years, the six-year-old guru tended to victims of Delhi's cholera and smallpox epidemic, and the waters of the large tank are said to have healing powers. It's full of colour and life, yet tranquil, and live devotional songs waft over the compound.

South Delhi

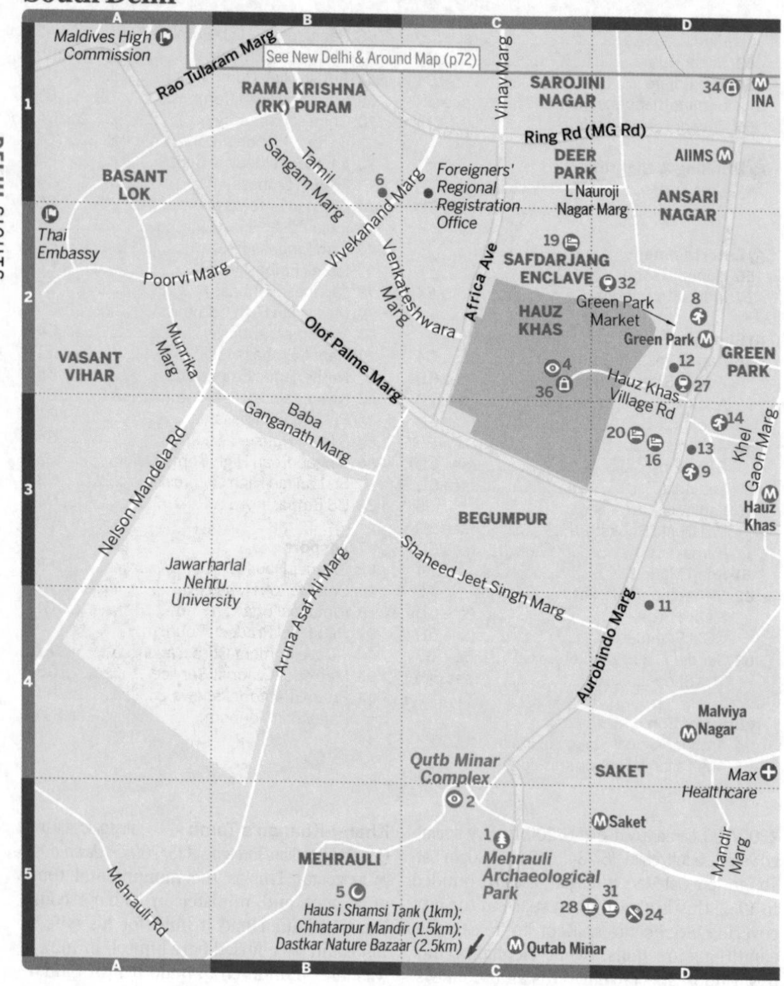

South Delhi

Hauz Khas AREA

(Map p76; dawn-dusk; Green Park) Built by Sultan Ala-ud-din Khilji in the 13th century, Hauz Khas means 'noble tank', and its reservoir once covered 28 hectares. It collected enough water during the monsoon to last Siri Fort throughout the dry season. Today it's much smaller, but still a beautiful place to be, thronged by birds and surrounded by parkland. Alongside it are the ruins of Feroz Shah's 14th-century madrasa (religious school) and **tomb** (Map p76), which he had built before his death in 1388.

To reach the lake shore, cut through the adjacent **Deer Park** (daylight hours), which has more ruined tombs and a well-stocked deer enclosure. There are numerous Lodi-era tombs scattered along the access road to Hauz Khas Village, and in nearby Green Park.

Bahai House of Worship TEMPLE

(Lotus Temple; Map p76; 011-26444029; www.bahaihouseofworship.in; Kalkaji; 9am-7pm Tue-Sun Apr-Sep, to 5.30pm Oct-Mar; Kalkaji Man-

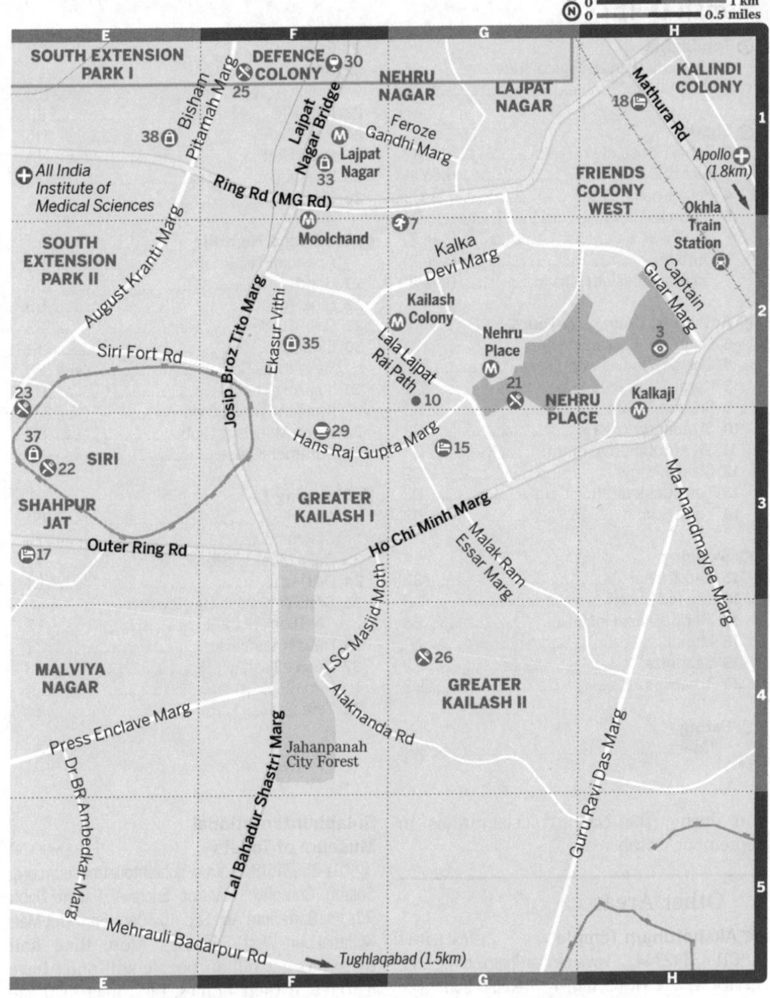

dir) Designed for tranquil worship, Delhi's beautiful Lotus Temple offers a rare pocket of calm in the hectic city. This architectural masterpiece was designed by Iranian-Canadian architect Fariburz Sahba in 1986. It is shaped like a lotus flower, with 27 delicate-looking white-marble petals. The temple was created to bring faiths together; visitors are invited to pray or meditate silently according to their own beliefs. The attached visitor centre tells the story of the Bahai faith. Photography is prohibited inside the temple.

Chhatarpur Mandir HINDU TEMPLE

(Shri Adya Katyayani Shakti Peeth Mandir; ☎011-26802360; www.chhattarpurmandir.org; Main Chhatarpur Rd; ⏰4am-midnight; Ⓜ Chhatarpur) India's second-largest temple (after Akshardham), this impressive sandstone and marble complex dates from 1974, and is dedicated to the goddess Katyayani (one of the nine forms of Parvati). There are dozens of shrines with towering South Indian *gopurams* (temple towers), and an enormous statue of Hanuman stands guard over the compound. Weekdays tend to be fairly sedate, but it gets crowded at weekends

South Delhi

Top Sights

1 Mehrauli Archaeological Park C5
2 Qutb Minar Complex C5

Sights

3 Bahai House of Worship H2
Feroz Shah's Tomb .... (see 4)
4 Hauz Khas C2
5 Hijron ka Khanqah B5
Iron Pillar .... (see 2)
Qutb Minar .... (see 2)
Quwwat-ul-Islam Masjid .... (see 2)

Activities, Courses & Tours

6 Central Hindi Directorate B1
7 Concern India Foundation G2
8 Kerala Ayurveda D2
9 Saffron Palate D3
10 Sivananda Yoga G2
11 Sri Aurobindo Ashram D4
12 Studio Abhyas D2
13 Tushita Meditation Centre D3
14 Yoga Studio D3

Sleeping

15 Bed & Chai G3
16 Jugaad Hostel D3
17 Madpackers Hostel E3
18 Manor H1
19 Scarlette C2
20 Treetops D3

Eating

Coast .... (see 36)
21 Epicuria G2
22 Greenr E3
Indian Accent .... (see 18)
23 Potbelly E2
24 Rose Cafe D5
Sagar Ratna .... (see 25)
25 Swagath F1
26 Swagath G4

Drinking & Nightlife

Anandini Tea Room .... (see 37)
27 Bandstand D2
28 Blue Tokai C5
29 Café Turtle F3
30 Ek Bar F1
Hauz Khas Social .... (see 36)
31 Jugmug Thela D5
Kunzum Travel Cafe .... (see 36)
32 Piano Man Jazz Club D2
Summer House .... (see 27)

Shopping

Anokhi .... (see 35)
Claymen .... (see 36)
33 Delhi Musical Stores F1
34 Dilli Haat D1
35 Greater Kailash I: M-Block & N-Block Markets F2
36 Hauz Khas Village C2
37 NeedleDust E3
Nimai .... (see 22)
38 Timeless E1

and during the Navratri celebrations in September/October.

Other Areas

★Akshardham Temple — HINDU TEMPLE

(☎011-43442344; www.akshardham.com; National Hwy 24, Noida turning; temple admission free, exhibitions ₹170, water show ₹80; ⊙temple 9.30am-6.30pm Tue-Sun, exhibitions 9.30am-5pm, water show after sunset; Ⓜ Akshardham) In the eastern suburbs, the Gujarati Hindu Swaminarayan Group's Akshardham Temple was built in 2005, and is breathtakingly lavish. Artisans used ancient techniques to carve the pale red sandstone into elaborate reliefs, including 20,000 deities, saints and mythical creatures. The centrepiece is a 3m-high gold statue of Bhagwan Shri Swaminarayan.

The complex includes a boat ride through 10,000 years of Indian history, animatronics telling stories from the life of Swaminarayan, and musical fountains.

Sulabh International Museum of Toilets — MUSEUM

(☎011-25031518; www.sulabhtoiletmuseum.org; Sulabh Complex, Mahavir Enclave, Palam Dabri Rd; ⊙10am-5pm Apr-Sep, 10.30am-5pm Oct-Mar; Ⓜ Janakpuri West) FREE More than half of India's 1.2 billion people still don't have a toilet in their homes, but since 1970 the Sulabh NGO has worked to address India's sanitation issues, constructing new public toilets and developing 'scavenger-free' pour-flush toilets – it's long been illegal for people to work as manual scavengers in order to empty untreated waste, but this caste-defined task is still prevalent in many areas. The organisation also educates, and their small, quirky museum traces the history of the water closet from 2500 BC to modern times. Take a rickshaw from the metro stop.

Sanskriti Museums — MUSEUM

(www.sanskritifoundation.org; Anandagram, Mehrauli Gurgaon Rd; ⊙10am-5pm Tue-Fri; Ⓜ Arjangarh) FREE On the way to Gurgaon, this little-known, well-kept place contains museums devoted to 'everyday art' and Indian terracotta and textiles. Much of the museum is outside and covers 7 acres. Objects such as kitchenware and hookahs are works of art, and there are expressive terracotta sculptures and intricate textiles from Gujarat, Rajasthan, Kashmir and Bengal.

Activities

Delhi Golf Club GOLF

(Map p72; ☎011-24307100; www.delhigolfclub.org; Dr Zakir Hussain Marg; 18 holes weekdays/weekends Indian ₹6000/8000, foreigner US$100/150; ⏲dawn-dusk; Ⓜ Khan Market) Carved out of the undergrowth in 1931, this golf club now covers 220 acres and is a spectacular place to tee off, with beautiful, well-tended fairways, peacocks and Mughal tombs. Weekends are busy.

Kerala Ayurveda AYURVEDA

(Map p76; ☎011-41754888; www.ayurvedancr.com; E-2 Green Park Extn; 1hr synchronised massage with steam ₹1500, sirodhara ₹3000; ⏲8am-8pm; Ⓜ Green Park) Treatments from *sarvang ksheerdhara* (massage with buttermilk) to *sirodhara* (warm oil poured on the forehead).

Aura SPA

(Map p72; ☎8800621206; www.aurathaispa.com; Middle Lane, Khan Market; 1hr dry/oil massage ₹1400/2800; ⏲10am-9pm; Ⓜ Khan Market) Glitzy spa offering Thai-inspired massages and treatments. There are also branches at Karol Bagh, GK1, GK2 and Green Park.

Tours

★Reality Tours & Travel TOURS

(☎9818227975; http://realitytoursandtravel.com; 2hr tour ₹850; ⏲10am-6pm) Long-established in Mumbai, the highly professional Reality Tours are now offering tours of Delhi, including the excellent Sanjay Colony tour – a visit to a slum area of Delhi (no photographs permitted out of respect for locals' privacy). The tour guides are knowledgable and friendly, and 80% of profits go to supporting development projects in the colony.

★DelhiByCycle CYCLING

(☎9811723720; www.delhibycycle.com; per person ₹1850; ⏲6.30-10am) Founded by a Dutch journalist, these cycle tours are the original and the best, and a thrilling way to explore Delhi. Tours focus on specific neighbourhoods – Old Delhi, New Delhi, Nizamuddin, and the banks of the Yamuna – and start early to miss the worst of the traffic. The price includes chai and a Mughal breakfast. Child seats are available.

★Salaam Baalak Trust WALKING

(SBT; Map p82; ☎011-23584164; www.salaambaalaktrust.com; Gali Chandiwali, Paharganj; suggested donation ₹200; Ⓜ Ramakrishna Ashram Marg) Founded on the proceeds of Mira Nair's 1988 film about the life of street children, *Salaam Bombay!*, this charitable organisation offers two-hour 'street walks' guided by former street children, who will show you firsthand what life is like for Delhi's homeless youngsters. The fees help the Trust assist street children.

Intach WALKING

(☎011-41035557; www.intachdelhichapter.org; tour ₹200) Intach runs walking tours with expert guides, exploring different areas, such as Chandni Chowk, Nizamuddin, Hauz Khas and Mehrauli. Custom walks can also be arranged.

Delhi Heritage Walks WALKING

(www.delhiheritagewalks.com; 3hr walk ₹500) Fascinating walks led by knowledgable guides around Mehrauli, Old Delhi, Tughlaqabad and more.

Delhi Metro Walks WALKING

(www.delhimetrowalks.com; half- to full-day group walks per person ₹300-600) Delhi-wallah Surekha Nurain shares her extensive knowledge about architecture, history and culture on recommended group or private tours, visiting both mainstream sights and off-the-beaten-track locations. She has several specially themed walks for families.

Street Connections WALKING

(www.walk.streetconnections.co.uk; 3hr walk ₹500; ⏲9am-noon Mon-Sat) This fascinating walk through Old Delhi is guided by former street children who have been helped by the Salaam Baalak Trust (p79). It explores the hidden corners of Old Delhi, starting at Jama Masjid and concluding at one of the SBT shelters.

Hope Project WALKING

(Map p72; ☎011-24357081; www.hopeprojectindia.org; 127 Hazrat Nizamuddin; 1½hr walk suggested donation ₹300; Ⓜ JLN Stadium) The Hope Project guides interesting walks around the Muslim basti (slum) of Nizamuddin. Take the walk in the afternoon to end at the *qawwali* (Islamic devotional singing) at the

Hazrat Nizam-ud-din Dargah, or at the more intimate session at the shrine of Hazrat Inayat Khan on Friday. Wear modest clothing.

Peteindia WALKING
(www.peteindia.org; 2hr tour ₹750) An NGO offering guided walks around the central area that's home to Delhi's magicians, puppeteers and circus performers, also known as the tinsel slum (the 'Kathputli Colony'). It's not the best organised tour but nonetheless a unique opportunity to see some of the performers, subject of the 2015 documentary *Tomorrow We Disappear*, and discover more about their communities.

Ho Ho Bus Service TOURS
(Hop-on, Hop-off; ☎1280; http://hohodelhi.com; Indian/foreigner ₹350/700, two-day ticket ₹600/1200; ⏲departures 8.30am-2.40pm Tue-Sun) The Delhi Tourism & Transport Development Corporation runs the air-conditioned Ho Ho Dilli Dekho bus service, which circuits the major sights every 45 minutes or so from 8.30am to 6.30pm, with the last stop at Jantar Mantar at 6.45pm (last departure at 2.40pm). Buy tickets from the **booth** (Map p68) near the DTTDC office.

Courses

Sivananda Yoga HEALTH & WELLBEING
(Map p76; www.sivananda.org.in; A41 Kailash Colony; suggested donation per class ₹400; Ⓜ Kailash Colony) This excellent ashram offers courses and workshops for both beginners and the advanced, plus drop-in classes ranging from one to two hours. On Sunday there is a free introductory drop-in class.

Yoga Studio YOGA
(Seema Sondhi; Map p76; www.theyogastudio.info; 43 D-Block Hauz Khas; 4/8/12 classes ₹2200/3200/3700, drop in ₹800; Ⓜ Hauz Khas) Seema Sondni's 75-minute classes practise various forms of Ashtanga Vinyasa. From beginners to advanced practioners: contact in advance so you can attend an appropriate class.

Studio Abhyas MEDITATION, YOGA
(Map p76; ☎011-26962757; www.abhyastrust.org; F-27 Green Park; Ⓜ Green Park) Yoga and meditation classes and Vedic chanting, for practitioners at any level; also offer children's classes.

Sri Aurobindo Ashram MEDITATION, YOGA
(Map p76; ☎011-26567863; www.sriaurobindoashram.net; Aurobindo Marg; Ⓜ Hauz Khas) Ashram offering free yoga and meditation classes for serious practitioners.

Tushita Meditation Centre MEDITATION
(Map p76; ☎011-26513400; www.tushitadelhi.com; 9 Padmini Enclave; by donation; ⏲6.30-7.30pm Mon & Thu; Ⓜ Hauz Khas) Guided Tibetan/Buddhist meditation sessions.

Saffron Palate COOKING
(Map p76; ☎9971389993; www.saffronpalate.com; R21 Hauz Khas Enclave; cooking class without/with market visit ₹6000/8000; ⏲varies; Ⓜ Hauz Khas) Recommended 2½-hour Indian cookery classes, where you eat the food afterwards, are run by Neha Gupta in her family home. You can also arrange a 4½-hour course including a market visit.

Central Hindi Directorate LANGUAGE
(Map p76; ☎011-26178454; http://hindinideshalaya.nic.in/english; West Block VII, RK Puram, Vivekanand Marg; 60hr basic course ₹6000) Runs certificate and diploma courses in Hindi; basic courses last 60 hours, with three classes a week.

Sleeping

Delhi hotels range from wallet-friendly dives to lavish five-stars; wherever you are on the scale, it's wise to book ahead, and reconfirm 24 hours before arrival. Most places offer airport pick-up, arranged in advance.

Hotel rooms above ₹1500 per night attract a 8.4% service tax, a 15% luxury tax and nominal Krishi Kalyan Cess (a national agriculture initiative) and Swaccha Bharat Abhiyan Cess (a national sanitation and infrastructure initiative) charges of 0.05% each.

Old Delhi

★ **Stops @ The President** HOSTEL $
(Map p64; ☎011-41056226; www.gostops.com; 4/23B Asaf Ali Rd; dm ₹500-800, d ₹3000; ❄@📶; Ⓜ New Delhi) This is one of the best of Delhi's new breed of hostels, in a great location on the edge of Old Delhi, with a brightly tiled kitchen, lounge areas, three friendly dogs, and comfortable, clean dorms and rooms.

Hotel New City Palace HOTEL $
(Map p64; ☎011-23279548; www.hotelnewcitypalace.in; 726 Jama Masjid; r ₹700; ❄; Ⓜ Chawri Bazaar) A palace it's not, but this mazelike hotel has an amazing location overlooking the Jama Masjid. Rooms aren't big, and have

small, hard beds with greying sheets, but some have windows and views. The bathrooms (squat toilets) could do with a good scrub, but staff are friendly.

Hotel Bombay Orient HOTEL **$$**
(Map p64; ☎011-43101717; Matya Mahal; s/d from ₹970/1430, with AC ₹1370/1830; ❄; Ⓜ Jama Masjid) Opposite famous restaurant Karim's in Old Delhi, this is a friendly place to stay and you'll be in the thick of it. Rooms are clean and tidy, but ask to see a few before you commit. Bookings are recommended.

Hotel Broadway HOTEL **$$**
(Map p64; ☎011-43663600; www.hotelbroadwaydelhi.com; 4/15 Asaf Ali Rd; s/d incl breakfast from ₹3250/4805; ❄@📶; Ⓜ New Delhi) The Broadway was Delhi's first high-rise when it opened in 1956. Today it's comfortable, quirky, and in a great Old Delhi location. It's worth staying here for the restaurant Chor Bizarre (p86) and Thugs bar. Some rooms have old-fashioned wood panelling, while others have been quirkily kitted out by French designer Catherine Lévy. Ask for one with views over Old Delhi.

★**Haveli Dharampura** HERITAGE HOTEL **$$$**
(Map p64; ☎011-23263000; www.havelidharampura.com; 2293 Gali Guliyan; d from ₹13,640; ❄📶; Ⓜ Jama Masjid) This is a beautiful restored *haveli*, full of Mughal atmosphere and centred around a courtyard. Rooms have grandiose polished-wood beds, but it's worth paying for a larger room, as the smallest are a little cramped. The excellent restaurant, Lakhori (p86), serves historic Mughal recipes, and there's *kathak* dancing Friday to Sunday evenings.

Maidens Hotel HOTEL **$$$**
(Map p64; ☎011-23975464; www.maidenshotel.com; 7 Sham Nath Marg; r from ₹19,840; ❄@📶🏊; Ⓜ Civil Lines) Oberoi-owned Maidens is a grand heritage hotel dating from 1903 – a creamy neoclassical confection fronted by pea-green lawns. Lutyens stayed here while supervising the building of New Delhi, and the high-ceilinged rooms have a colonial-era charm but contemporary comforts. There are two restaurants, a pool and a bar.

Paharganj & Around

Love it or hate it, this hectic traveller hub is no oasis of serenity. But it is packed with hotels, trinket shops, and restaurants of every cuisine, and is convenient for New Delhi Railway Station/Airport metro.

> **PRICE RANGES**
>
> The following price ranges refer to a double room with private bathroom and are inclusive of tax.
>
> **$** less than ₹1500
>
> **$$** ₹1500–5000
>
> **$$$** more than ₹5000

If your hotel is on the the Main Bazaar or Arakashan Rd, taxi drivers can make it all the way to the door, though they may be reluctant as it's so congested. If you're having issues, ask to be dropped at Chhe Tooti Chowk and complete your journey on foot.

You can walk to the Main Bazaar in minutes from Ramakrishna Ashram Marg metro. The New Delhi metro is more convenient for Arakashan Rd, which is around 10 minutes' walk from the stop, over a bridge.

★**Backpacker Panda** HOSTEL **$**
(Map p82; http://backpackerpanda.com; dm 8-bed ₹400, 6-bed ₹450; 📶; Ⓜ Ramakrishna Ashram Marg) A great alternative to Paharganj's less-than-fancy cheap hotels, Panda offers bright, clean dorms (one is female only) with attached bathrooms, charge points, lockers, windows, clean linen and comfortable mattresses. It's close to the metro. Win-win!

★**Hotel Amax Inn** HOTEL **$**
(Map p82; ☎011-23543813; www.hotelamax.com; 8145/6 Arakashan Rd; s/d/tr from ₹850/950/1350; ❄@📶; Ⓜ New Delhi) In a lane off chaotic Arakashan Rd, the Amax is a long-running traveller favourite, with clean, occasionally stuffy, good-value budget rooms. Staff are friendly, and clued up about traveller needs, and there's a small greenery-fringed terrace. The triple (Room 403) opening onto the rooftop has the added advantage of a window and a nicely stencilled wall.

Zostel HOSTEL **$**
(Map p82; ☎011-39589005; www.zostel.com/zostel/Delhi; 5 Arakashan Rd; 6-8-bed dm ₹549, d ₹1499; 📶; Ⓜ New Delhi) Part of the Zostel chain, this place is shabbier than some of Delhi's other backpacker hostels. However, it's got the obligatory cheerful murals, the dorms are a pretty good deal, and it's a friendly place to meet other backpackers.

Paharganj

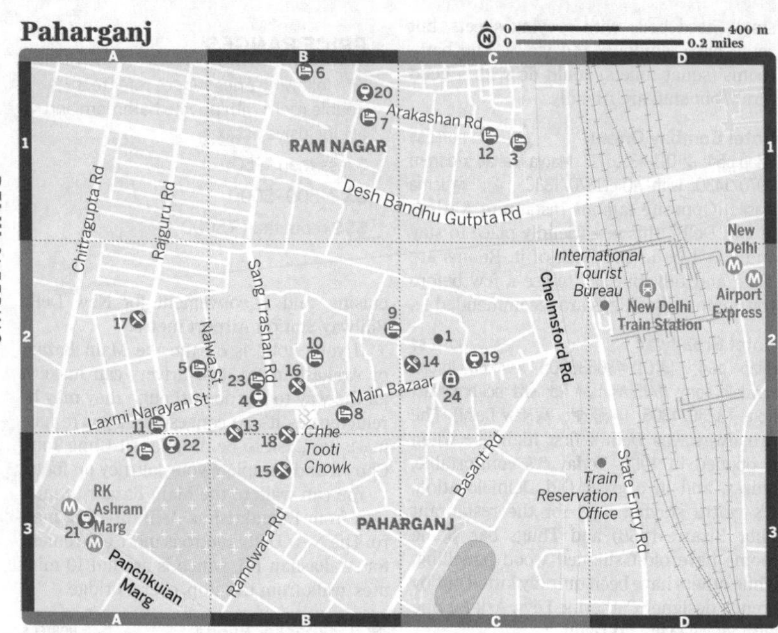

Paharganj

Activities, Courses & Tours
1 Salaam Baalak Trust C2

Sleeping
2 Backpacker Panda A3
3 Bloom Rooms @ New Delhi C1
4 Cottage Ganga Inn B2
5 Diya A2
6 Hotel Amax Inn B1
7 Hotel Godwin Deluxe B1
8 Hotel Hari Piorko B2
9 Hotel Namaskar B2
10 Hotel Rak International B2
11 Metropolis Tourist Home A2
12 Zostel C1

Eating
13 Brown Bread Bakery B2
Cafe Fresh .... (see 11)
14 Everest Bakery C2
Malhotra .... (see 11)
15 Narula Bakery B3
16 Shimtur B2
17 Sita Ram Dewan Chand A2
18 Tadka B3

Drinking & Nightlife
19 Gem C2
20 Karen Cafe B1
21 Metro Bar A3
22 My Bar A3
23 Sam's Bar B2

Shopping
24 Main Bazaar C2

Hotel Namaskar HOTEL $
(Map p82; ☎011-23583456; www.namaskarhotel.com; 917 Chandiwalan, Main Bazaar; r ₹400-650, with AC ₹700; ❄☜) Up a narrow alley opposite the Dayal Boot House, this long-running traveller cheapo is run by two amiable brothers and offers a friendly welcome. It may be humid and noisy, but the rooms get a fresh coat of powder-pink paint annually, which gives it a fresher feel than many of its peers.

Cottage Ganga Inn HOTEL $
(Map p82; ☎011-23561516; www.cottagegangainn.com; 1532 Bazar Sangtrashan; s/d from ₹1000/1300; ❄@☜; Ⓜ Ramakrishna Ashram Marg) Quieter than most Paharganj choices, this place is tucked in a courtyard off the Main Bazaar, next to a nursery school. It's clean, calm, comfortable and good value. Rooms at the front have windows and cost more.

Hotel Rak International HOTEL $

(Map p82; 011-23562478; www.hotelrakinternational.com; 820 Main Bazaar, Chowk Bawli; s/d ₹650/750, with AC ₹850/950; ; Ramakrishna Ashram Marg) Hotel Rak International is off the Main Bazaar (so it's quieter) and overlooks a little square and temple. The modest rooms at this popular place are a good choice in this price range, with marble floors and bathrooms, plus, unusually, twin rooms and…windows! The pricier rooms overlook the square.

★ **Bloom Rooms @ New Delhi** HOTEL $$

(Map p82; 011-40174017; http://bloomrooms.com; 8591 Arakashan Rd; s/d incl breakfast from ₹2200/2900; ; New Delhi) Bloom Rooms' white-and-yellow, pared-down designer aesthetic is unlike anything else in the 'hood. Plus there are soft pillows, comfortable beds, good wi-fi and free mineral water. Its Re restaurant is a bit gloomy but the food is tasty.

Diya B&B $$

(Map p82; 9811682348; http://stay.streetconnections.co.uk; Tilak St; s/d incl breakfast ₹2000/2750; ; Ramakrishna Ashram Marg) The kind of place you'd really like kept secret, this is like a South Delhi guesthouse, but on a Paharganj backstreet, and has three lovely, well-cared-for rooms, one with a balcony. There's also a shared kitchen. It's run by Street Connections, and the staff and management are former street kids from the Salaam Baalak Trust. Reservations are essential. Great for solo women.

Hotel Hari Piorko HOTEL $$

(Map p82; Main Bazaar; r ₹1450-1850; ; Ramakrishna Ashram Marg) It's worth paying just that bit extra to have a fish tank in your room – this is the only hotel in Delhi, to our knowledge, with this option. Even without the fish tanks, this is a good choice – the pricier rooms are also more spacious. There's the Fire & Ice restaurant too, with a balcony overlooking the Main Bazaar.

Hotel Godwin Deluxe HOTEL $$

(Map p82; 011-23613797; www.godwinhotels.com; 8501 Arakashan Rd; s/d incl breakfast ₹3000/3250; ; New Delhi) Run by the same owners as the Grand Godwin next door, Godwin Deluxe offers similar good service, and comfortable, spacious, clean rooms.

Metropolis Tourist Home HOTEL $$

(Map p82; 011-23561794; www.metropolistouristhome.com; 1634-5 Main Bazaar; r from ₹2000; ; Ramakrishna Ashram Marg) A long-standing favourite in the backpacking district, this hotel has comfortable, renovated rooms decorated in a hundred shades of brown. The slightly pricey rooftop restaurant feels almost European, with its greenery, low lights and foreign clientele.

Connaught Place & Around

★ **Imperial** HOTEL $$$

(Map p68; 011-23341234; www.theimperialindia.com; Janpath; r from ₹24,300; ; Janpath) Classicism meets art deco at the Imperial, which dates from 1931 and was designed by FB Blomfield, an associate of Lutyens. Rooms have high ceilings, flowing curtains, French linen and marble baths. There's the temple-like Thai restaurant Spice Route; the 1911 bar (p91) is highly recommended; and the Atrium cafe (p91) serves the perfect high tea.

The hallways and atriums are lined with the hotel's venerable 18th- and 19th-century art collection.

Hotel Palace Heights HOTEL $$$

(Map p68; 011-43582610; www.hotelpalaceheights.com; 26-28 D-Block; s/d ₹8100/8650; ; Rajiv Chowk) This small-scale boutique hotel offers some of busy Connaught Place's nicest rooms, with gleaming white linen, and caramel and amber tones. There's an excellent restaurant, **Zāffrān** (Map p68; 011-43582610; Hotel Palace Heights, 26-28 D-Block; mains ₹350-650; noon-3.30pm & 6.30-11.30pm; Rajiv Chowk).

Radisson Blu Marina HOTEL $$$

(Map p68; 011-46909090; www.radisson.com/hotels/indnedl; 59 G-Block; s/d ₹10,000/11,000; ; Rajiv Chowk) Connaught Place's swishest choice, the Radisson feels pleasingly luxurious, with sleek, stylish, all-mod-con rooms, the Great Kebab Factory, and a cool bar, the Connaught, where you can sip drinks under hanging red lamps.

West Delhi

Master Guest House GUESTHOUSE $$

(011-28741089; www.master-guesthouse.com; R-500 New Rajendra Nagar; s/d incl breakfast from ₹2071/3270; ; Rajendra Place) In a quiet suburban area, this smart and polished home is a tight ship run by the knowledgable Ushi and Avnish, and has three tastefully furnished rooms with spotless bathrooms. There's a leafy rooftop terrace.

Shanti Home HOTEL $$$
(☎011-41573366; www.shantihome.com; A-1/300 Janakpuri; s/d incl breakfast from ₹5500/6500; ❄@📶; Ⓜ Uttam Nagar East) In west Delhi, this small boutique place is close to the metro and offers beautifully decorated rooms that get gradually swisher the more you spend. There are spacious lounge areas, an excellent, lantern-lit rooftop restaurant, a gym, cooking classes and spa service.

New Delhi

Bloom Rooms @ Link Rd HOTEL $$
(Map p72; ☎011-41261400; bloomrooms.com; 7 Link Rd; s/d incl breakfast from ₹2900/3700; ❄@📶; Ⓜ Jangpura) A few minutes' walk from the metro, this is a quiet and convenient spot for Khan Market, Humayun's Tomb and Lodi Gardens. Bloom Rooms' designer white-and-yellow aesthetic is pleasingly Scandi-esque. Pillows are soft, wi-fi is fast, and there's a branch of Amici, a respected local Italian restaurant.

★ **Lodhi** HOTEL $$$
(Map p72; ☎011-43633333; www.thelodhi.com; Lodi Rd; r from ₹21,800; ❄📶🏊; Ⓜ JLN Stadium) The Lodhi is one of Delhi's finest luxury hotels, with huge, lovely rooms and suites. Each room has a balcony with private plunge pool, and those on the upper floors have great views, some over to Humayun's Tomb. Attention to detail is superb. There's also a top-notch **spa** (Map p72; ☎011-43633333; www.thelodhi.com; Lodhi Hotel, Lodi Rd; 1hr massage from ₹3800; Ⓜ JLN Stadium).

Claridges HOTEL $$$
(Map p72; ☎011-39555000; www.claridges.com; 12 Aurangzeb Rd; d from ₹13,050; ❄@📶🏊; Ⓜ Racecourse) Fronted by manicured green lawns, elegant Claridges was built in 1952. Colonial-era-styled rooms have all comforts, and there are some excellent dining options, including romantic Mediterranean Sevilla, with its curtained pavilions, and imagine-you're-on-the-highway **Dhaba** (Map p72; ☎011-39555000; The Claridges, 12 Aurangzeb Rd; dishes ₹700-2000; ⏲12.30-2.30pm & 7-11.30pm; Ⓜ Racecourse), with traditional Punjabi food.

Zaza Stay GUESTHOUSE $$$
(Map p72; ☎011-47373450; www.zaza.co.in; G54, Nizamuddin West; s/d incl breakfast ₹4000/5000) Owned by a couple who have their own homewares brand, this guesthouse has beautifully decorated rooms with leafy outlooks in Nizamuddin; a quiet and restful area, but still close to the Dargah and Humayun's Tomb.

Lutyens Bungalow GUESTHOUSE $$$
(Map p72; ☎011-24611341; www.lutyensbungalow.co.in; 39 Prithviraj Rd; s/d incl breakfast from ₹6500/8000; ❄@📶🏊; Ⓜ Racecourse) A rambling bungalow with a colonial feel, surrounded by verandahs and hanging lamps, this family-run guesthouse has a wonderful garden, with lawns, flowers and fluttering parakeets. Rooms are pleasant, with wooden furnishings and an old-fashioned vibe, and it's a particularly good place to stay with kids because of the unusual amount of rambling space.

South Delhi

★ **Madpackers Hostel** HOSTEL $
(Map p76; S39-A 3rd fl, Panchsheel Park Sth; 6-14-bed dm ₹650-850; ❄📶; Ⓜ Hauz Khas) A friendly, relaxed hostel with a bright and airy sitting room that's one of the best places in town to hang out and meet like-minded travellers. It has mixed dorms (with one female-only) and graffitied walls, and it's in a leafy area of south Delhi.

Jugaad Hostel HOSTEL $
(Map p76; Mohamed Pur; dm ₹600-800, r ₹2400) In a nicely untouristed if out-of-the-way area, this is a great hostel close to a huge Friday market. There are dorms including a women-only dorm, private rooms, swing chairs on the rooftop and a friendly, helpful welcome.

Bed & Chai HOSTEL $$
(Map p76; www.bedandchai.com; R55 Hans Raj Gupta Marg; dm ₹850, d without/with bathroom from ₹2500/3100) For a quiet stay, this French-owned guesthouse has simple rooms, decorated with flashes of colour and some quirky, original design touches. There's a dorm, a roof terrace and, of course, excellent chai.

Treetops GUESTHOUSE $$
(Map p76; ☎9899555704; baig.murad@gmail.com; R-8B Hauz Khas Enclave; s/d from ₹2500/3500; ❄📶; Ⓜ Hauz Khas) Motor-journalist-novelist-philosopher Murad and his hobby-chef wife Tannie have a gracious home. To stay here feels rather like visiting some upper-crust relatives from another era. There are two large rooms opening onto a leafy rooftop terrace; the smaller room downstairs is cheaper but can feel less private. Evening meals are available.

MAJNU-KA-TILLA

Majnu-ka-Tilla is an enclave that has served as a base for Tibetan refugees since around 1960. It's a popular alternative traveller hub for those who prefer something more relaxed than Paharganj, with a laid-back, little Lhasa vibe. It's named after a local hermit boatman who was nicknamed 'crazy' *(majnu)* and who met Guru Nanak, the founder of Sikhism, here on a small hill *(tilla)*; the nearby 18th-century Majnu-ka-Tilla Gurdwara was built to commemorate the Guru's soujourn here.

Majnu-ka-Tilla's streets are too narrow for traffic, and it's close to the Yamuna River. There's a monastery here, and plenty of maroon-robed Buddhist monks and Tibetans. There are also rather a lot of beggars, but the streets have a small-town, safe-feeling vibe.

Cheapie **Ga-Kyegu House** (011-23815196; gakyeguhouse@hotmail.com; H-158, Block 7, Tibetan Colony; r ₹700, without bathroom ₹550; ; Vidhan Sabha) has some bargain rooms with Yamuna River views. Friendly **Wongdhen House** (011-23816689; 15-A New Tibetan Colony; r ₹800-1000, without bathroom ₹500; ; Vidhan Sabha) has simple, shabby rooms and a good restaurant; next-door **Lhasa House** (011-23939888; lhasahouse@rediffmail.com; 16 New Aruna Nagar; r ₹500-1000; Vidhan Sabha) is better value. **Ama** (H40, New Aruna Nagar; 7am-9.30pm; ; Vidhan Sabha) and **Kham Cafe** (New Aruna Nagar; 7am-7.30pm; Vidhan Sabha) are splendid places to chill over coffee, and below Ama is good-value **Akama** (9am-7.30pm; Vidhan Sabha), selling Tibetan artefacts. Two good eating options are **Tee Dee** (32 New Aruna Nagar; dishes ₹60-210; 8.30am-10.30pm; Vidhan Sabha) and long-running and popular **Dolma House** (Block 10, New Tibetan Colony; dishes ₹70-180; 7am-10pm). For a refreshing change, try Korean **Kori's** (Tsampa Café; Tsampa House, 18-19 New Camp; dishes ₹80-290; 7.30am-10pm;).

To reach here, take the metro to Vidhan Sabha, from where shared auto-/cycle-rickshaws (₹40/20) will take you to the enclave on KB Hedgewar Marg. Ask for the 'wrong side'.

★Manor HOTEL $$$

(Map p76; 011-26925151; www.themanordelhi.com; 77 Friends Colony (West); d incl breakfast from ₹11,000;) With only 16 rooms, this boutique hotel oozes privacy and elegance. Set amid manicured lawns off Mathura Rd, the Manor has large rooms with contemporary furnishings in soothing earth colours and offering the utmost comfort. The restaurant, Indian Accent (p90), is one of Delhi's best.

★Devna GUESTHOUSE $$$

(Map p72; 011-41507176; www.tensundernagar.com; 10 Sunder Nagar; s/d ₹5450/5800;) Devna has lots of charm, with antique wooden furniture, photographs of maharajas, and works of art. The upstairs rooms open onto small terraces, with views over the pretty courtyard garden, and it's close to the expansive grounds of Delhi's zoo.

Scarlette GUESTHOUSE $$$

(Map p76; 011-41023764; www.scarlettenewdelhi.com; B2/139 Safdarjung Enclave; d from ₹7000;) In serene, leafy Safdarjung Enclave, close to Hauz Khas Village and the Deer Park, Scarlette is a *maison d'hôtes* (guesthouse) with four rooms, plus an apartment, decorated with beautiful artistic flair by the French textile-designer owner. It's a good choice for solo women.

Airport Area & Beyond

Delhi's Aerocity is a convenient area of big hotels, only 4km from the airport – ideal if you're only stopping over for a night. It's served by the Delhi Aerocity metro stop. Take your pick from brands such as Hotel Pullman, Lemon Tree, and the super-luxurious Hilton-run Andaz Delhi; the cheapest option is the Hotel Delhi Aerocity. There are also a few choices in nearby Vasant Kunj.

See www.newdelhiairport.in for details of several sleeping options at the airport..

Eating

Old Delhi

★Jalebiwala SWEETS $

(Map p64; Dariba Corner, Chandni Chowk; jalebis per 100g ₹50; 8am-10pm; Lal Qila) Century-old Jalebiwala does Delhi's – if not India's – finest *jalebis* (deep-fried, syrupy dough), so pig out and worry about the calories tomorrow.

★ Gali Paratha Wali STREET FOOD $

(Map p64; Gali Paratha Wali; parathas ₹15-35; ⏰7am-11pm; Ⓜ Jama Masjid) This lane off Chandni Chowk has been serving up delectable *parathas* (traditional flat bread) fresh off the *tawa* (hotplate) for generations, originally serving pilgrims at the time of the Mughals. Choose from a spectacular array of stuffings, from green chilli and paneer to lemon and banana.

Natraj Dahi Balle Wala STREET FOOD $

(Map p64; 1396 Chandni Chowk; plates ₹50; ⏰10.30am-11pm; Ⓜ Chandni Chowk) This tiny place with the big red sign and the big crowds is famous for its *dahi bhalle* (fried lentil balls served with yoghurt and garnished with chutney) and deliciously crispy *aloo tikki* (spiced potato patties).

Haldiram's FAST FOOD $

(Map p64; 1454/2 Chandni Chowk; mains ₹70-180; ⏰10am-10.30pm; Ⓜ Chandni Chowk) This clean, bright cafeteria-cum-sweet-shop is a popular stop for its top-notch dosas (large South Indian savoury crêpes), and thalis, and it also sells *namkin* (savouries) and *mithai* (sweets) to eat on the hoof. There's a popular branch at **Connaught Place** (Map p68; 6 L-Block, Connaught Place; snacks ₹70-230; ⏰8.30am-10.30pm; Ⓜ Rajiv Chowk).

★ Karim's MUGHLAI $$

(Map p64; Gali Kababyan; mains ₹120-400; ⏰9am-12.30am; Ⓜ Jama Masjid) Just off the lane leading south from Jama Masjid, Karim's has been delighting carnivores since 1913. Expect meaty Mughlai treats such as mutton *burrah* (marinated chops), delicious mutton Mughlai, and the breakfast mutton and bread combo *nahari*. There are branches all over town, including at **Nizamuddin West** (Map p72; 168/2 Jha House Basti; dishes ₹120-400; ⏰8am-10pm Tue-Sat; Ⓜ JLN Stadium), but this location is the oldest and best.

FOOD & DRINK TAXES

Drinks taxes ratchet your bill up by 20% (alcoholic) or 12.5% (nonalcoholic), and restaurants also levy 12.5% VAT on food, plus AC places have to charge a 14% service tax on the 'service' element of your bill. Many also add a 10% service charge. So be aware that all up you may have to pay around 30% or more above what's shown on the menu.

Al-Jawahar MUGHLAI $$

(Map p64; Matya Mahal; mains ₹60-350; ⏰7am-midnight; Ⓜ Jama Masjid) Although overshadowed by its famous neighbour, Karim's (p86), Al-Jawahar is also fantastic, serving up tasty Mughlai cuisine at formica tables in an orderly dining room, and you can watch breads being freshly made at the front. Kebabs and mutton curries dominate the menu, but it also does good butter chicken and korma.

Lakhori INDIAN $$$

(Map p64; Haveli Dharampura, 2293 Gali Guliyan; tasting menus veg/non-veg ₹1800/2200, other dishes around ₹400-600; ⏰10am-10.30pm; 📶; Ⓜ Jama Masjid) A different experience in the old city, this restored *haveli* is a labour of love by politician Vijay Goel, and it's good to see one of Old Delhi's grand *havelis* finally get some TLC. The restaurant is especially atmospheric in the evening, with tables in the courtyard and Mughlai and local recipes on the menu.

Moti Mahal MUGHLAI $$$

(Map p64; ☎011-23273661; 3704 Netaji Subhash Marg; mains ₹290-620; ⏰noon-midnight) There's only one true Moti Mahal, and this been open for six generations – it's full of charm, with a stuck-in-time atmosphere; it'd make a perfect film set for Wes Anderson. Delhi-ites rate the place for its superior butter chicken and *dhal makhani*. There's live *qawwali* (Islamic devotional singing) Wednesday to Monday from 8pm to 11.30pm.

Chor Bizarre KASHMIRI $$$

(Map p64; ☎011-23273821; Hotel Broadway, 4/15 Asaf Ali Rd; mains ₹325-500; ⏰noon-3pm & 7.30-11pm; Ⓜ New Delhi) A dimly lit cavern filled with bric-a-brac, including a vintage car, Chor Bizarre (meaning 'thieves market') offers delicious and authentic Kashmiri cuisine, including *wazwan,* the traditional Kashmiri feast.

Paharganj & West Delhi

Paharganj is the main backpacker hub, and its restaurants proffer a wide-ranging mishmash of global cuisine ranging from pizza to banana pancakes. There are more cheap eats in the bazaars at Karol Bagh.

★Sita Ram Dewan Chand INDIAN $
(Map p82; 2243 Chuna Mandi; half-/full plate ₹30/55; ⏲8am-5pm; Ⓜ Ramakrishna Ashram Marg) A family-run hole-in-the-wall serving inexpensive portions of just one dish – *chole bhature* (spicy chickpeas), accompanied by delicious, freshly made, puffy, fried bread. It's a traditional breakfast but many people are partial to some at any time of day.

Narula Bakery BAKERY $
(Map p82; sandwiches ₹15-25; ⏲9am-10pm; Ⓜ Ramakrishna Ashram Marg) A tip-top takeaway bakery if you're looking for a bargain lunch, this place has veg, cheese and corn or paneer *kulcha* sandwiches.

Everest Bakery NEPALI $
(Map p82; Chandiwalan; dishes ₹50-250; ⏲8am-11pm; Ⓜ Ramakrishna Ashram Marg) This chilled little fan-cooled place off the Paharganj main drag offers the usual every-sort cuisine, but including *momos* and impressive salads. There's also a real Italian coffee machine, a rare beast in Paharganj.

Brown Bread Bakery BAKERY $
(Map p82; Ajay Guest House, 5084-A, Main Bazaar; snacks ₹65-150; ⏲7am-11pm; 📶; Ⓜ Ramakrishna Ashram Marg) A popular traveller hang-out, with a rustic, wicker-heavy interior, organic Brown Bread has simple food that hits the spot, with omelettes, pizzas, lots of different breads and very good chips.

Bikanervala Angan FAST FOOD $
(82 Arya Samaj Rd, Karol Bagh; mains ₹35-170; ⏲11am-10.30pm; Ⓜ Karol Bagh) This small but buzzing Karol Bagh canteen is a useful pit-stop for South Indian treats, fast food and snacks. Thalis start at ₹165.

Roshan di Kulfi ICE CREAM $
(Ajmal Khan Rd, Karol Bagh; kulfi around ₹70; ⏲8.30am-9.30pm; Ⓜ Karol Bagh) A Karol Bagh institution for its scrumptious special *pista badam kulfi* (frozen milk dessert with pistachio, almond and cardamom). It's around 500m northwest of Karol Bagh metro.

★Shimtur KOREAN $$
(Map p82; 3rd fl, Navrang Guesthouse, Tooti Galli; meals ₹240-500; ⏲10am-11pm; Ⓜ Ramakrishna Ashram Marg) It takes determination to find this place: take the turning for the Hotel Rak International, opposite which is the grotty, unsigned Navrang Guesthouse. Follow the stairs to its rooftop and you'll find a small, bamboo-lined, softly lit terrace. The Korean food is fresh and delicious here. Try the *bibimbap* (rice bowl with a mix of vegetables, egg and pickles; ₹240). Beer is available (₹170).

Cafe Fresh VEGETARIAN $$
(Map p82; Laxmi Narayan St; dishes ₹115-240; ⏲8am-11pm; 📶; Ⓜ Ramakrishna Ashram Marg) This cafe has veg appeal, catering to a mix of Indians and foreigners; it's an attractively calm place to retreat (down a few steps) from the busy street.

Tadka INDIAN $$
(Map p82; 4986 Ramdwara Rd; mains ₹150-190; ⏲8.30am-10.30pm; Ⓜ Ramakrishna Ashram Marg) Named for everyone's favourite dhal, Tadka is a reliable vegetarian choice, serving up perfectly fine paneer dishes and other veg treats (ordinary/special thali ₹200/280) under whirring fans.

Malhotra MULTICUISINE $$
(Map p82; 1833 Laxmi Narayan St; mains ₹80-425; ⏲7am-11pm; 📶) One street back from the Main Bazaar chaos, Malhotra is a reliable local choice, popular with locals and foreigners, with a good menu of set breakfasts and North Indian standards, such as *mattar paneer* (pea and cottage cheese curry).

Connaught Place

★Naturals ICE CREAM $
(Map p68; 8 L-Block, Connaught Place; cup/cone ₹65, double scoop ₹130; ⏲11am-midnight; Ⓜ Rajiv Chowk) Founder Mr Kamath's dad was a mango vendor in Bangalore, which apparently inspired his love of fruit. He went on to start Naturals, with its wonderfully creamy, fresh flavours, such as watermelon, coconut, (heavenly) mango and roasted almond.

★Hotel Saravana Bhavan SOUTH INDIAN $$
(Map p68; 46 Janpath; dishes ₹95-210, thali ₹210; ⏲8am-11pm; Ⓜ Janpath) Fabulous dosas, *idlis* and other South Indian delights. This is the biggest and the best of Delhi's Saravana Bhavan branches, and you can see dosas being made in the back. Also offers great South Indian coffee.

Kerala House SOUTH INDIAN $
(Map p68; 3 Jantar Mantar Rd; meals ₹50; ⏲8-10am, 12.30-3pm & 7-9.45pm; Ⓜ Patel Chowk) The Kerala staff canteen is open to the public and tasty meals here are a lip-smacking bargain, including unlimited rice, fish curry, fish fry, *sambar*, a couple of veg dishes and pickle.

Coffee Home INDIAN $

(Map p68; Baba Kharak Singh Marg; meals ₹50-150; ⏲11am-8pm; Ⓜ Shivaji Stadium) With a shaded garden eating area, and a spacious interior under whirring fans, Coffee Home is always busy with office workers lingering over chai and feasting on South Indian snacks such as *masala dosa*. It is handily located next to the government emporiums.

Hotel Saravana Bhavan SOUTH INDIAN $

(Map p68; 15 P-Block, Connaught Place; mains ₹95-210; ⏲8am-11pm; Ⓜ Rajiv Chowk) Delhi's best thali is served up in unassuming surroundings – a simple Tamil canteen on the edge of Connaught Place. There are queues every meal time to sample the splendid array of richly spiced veg curries, dips, breads and condiments that make it onto every thali plate.

Wenger's BAKERY $

(Map p68; 16 A-Block, Connaught Place; snacks ₹30-100; ⏲10.45am-7.45pm; Ⓜ Rajiv Chowk) Legendary Wenger's was opened by a Swiss couple in 1926, and has been baking up a storm ever since. Come for cakes, sandwiches, biscuits and savoury patties.

Nizam's Kathi Kabab FAST FOOD $

(Map p68; 5 H-Block, Connaught Place; kebabs ₹80-270; ⏲11.30am-11pm; Ⓜ Rajiv Chowk) This takeaway eatery creates masterful kebabs, biryani and *kati* rolls (kebabs wrapped in a hot *paratha*). It's always busy with meat-loving hoards, but there are also paneer, mushroom and egg options available so vegies don't have to miss out.

★ **Masala Library** MODERN INDIAN $$$

(Map p72; 21A Janpath; tasting menu ₹2600; ⏲noon-2.45pm & 7pm-1am; Ⓜ Janpath) Restaurateur Zorawar Kalra has brought his Masala Library to Delhi (the first was in Mumbai), with creative cooking that adds a dash of magic to your meal, with molecular cuisine and dishes such as coconut and mango *amuse-bouche* disguised as a bird's nest and levitating chocolate balls. Arrive hungry and try the 19-course tasting menu.

★ **Rajdhani** INDIAN $$$

(Map p68; ☎011-43501200; 1/90 P-Block, Connaught Place; thalis ₹475; ⏲noon-3.30pm & 7-11pm; Ⓜ Rajiv Chowk) Thalis fit for a king. Treat yourself with food-of-the-gods vegetarian thalis that encompass a fantastic array of Gujarati and Rajasthani dishes.

Farzi Cafe MODERN INDIAN $$$

(Map p68; ☎9599889700; 38 E-Block, Connaught Place; mains ₹360-560; ⏲noon-12.30am; Ⓜ Rajiv Chowk) This buzzy CP joint signifies the Delhi foodie penchant for quirkiness, with all sorts of 'molecular gastronomy' and unusual fusion dishes such as butter chicken *bao* (in a bun). It's only ₹85 for Kingfisher beer, and there are *banta* (traditional homemade fizzy pop) cocktails. There's live Sufi, Hindi and pop music on Friday and Saturday nights from 10pm.

Chor Bizarre KASHMIRI $$

(Map p72; ☎011-23071574; Bikaner House, Pandara Rd; mains ₹325-500; ⏲12.30-3pm & 7.30-11pm; Ⓜ Khan Market) In the beautifully restored colonial-era Bikaner House, Chor Bizarre ('Thieves' Market') is a new branch of the famous Old Delhi restaurant. The interior is full of quirky old-fashioned charm, and the menu includes authentic, delicious dishes such as Kashmiri *haaq* (spinach with chilli).

New Delhi & Around

New Delhi, with its dazzlingly opulent five-star hotels, malls and upmarket enclaves around Khan Market, Lodi Rd and Mathura Rd, is where to head if you feel like a swanky meal, with a fabulously wide mix of cuisines.

★ **Andhra Pradesh Bhawan Canteen** SOUTH INDIAN $

(Map p72; 1 Ashoka Rd; dishes ₹130-160, thalis ₹110; ⏲8-10.30am, noon-3pm & 7.30-10pm; Ⓜ Patel Chowk) A hallowed bargain, the canteen at the Andhra Pradesh state house serves cheap and delicious unlimited South Indian thalis to a seemingly unlimited stream of patrons. Come on Sunday for the fabled Hyderabadi biryani (₹200).

★ **Triveni Terrace Cafe** CAFE $

(Map p72; 205 Tansen Marg, Mandi House; dishes ₹55-220; ⏲10am-7.30pm; Ⓜ Mandi House) Run by the same folks in charge of the Craft Museum's Cafe Lota, this is a focus for Delhi's arty set, with good-value tasty Indian meals and snacks, such as chilli toast, and nice seating on a leafy terrace overlooking a grassy amphitheatre or inside in a fan-cooled room.

Gujarat Bhawan GUJARATI $

(Map p72; 11 Kautilya Marg, Chanakyapuri; breakfast ₹60, thali ₹110-140; ⏲8-10am, 12.30-2.30pm &

7.30-10pm; M Racecourse) The Gujarat Sterun canteen is nothing fancy, but serves up nourishing, plentiful, cheap-as-chips vegetarian home-style Gujarati thalis.

Kebab Stands STREET FOOD $
(Map p72; Hazrat Nizam-ud-din Dargah; kebabs from ₹30; ⊙noon-11pm; M JLN Stadium) The alley in front of Hazrat Nizam-ud-din Dargah becomes a hive of activity every evening as devotees leave the shrine in search of sustenance. Canteen-style kebab houses cook up lip-smacking beef, mutton and chicken offerings at bargain prices, with biryani and roti as filling side orders.

Nagaland House INDIAN $
(Map p72; 29 Dr APJ Abdul Kalam Rd; thalis ₹120-200; ⊙noon-2pm & 7.30-10pm; M Racecourse) The Nagaland canteen is a simple room overlooking a tangle of palm trees and is worth seeking out for punchy pork offerings, with dishes such as pork with bamboo shoots and a Naga-style pork thali. Veg and chicken thalis are also available.

★Cafe Lota MODERN INDIAN $$
(Map p72; Crafts Museum; dishes ₹215-415; ⊙8am-10pm; M Pragati Maidan) Bamboo slices the sunlight into flattering stripes at this outdoor restaurant offering delicious cooking with a twist. Sample their take on fish and (sweet potato) chips, or *palak patta chaat* (crispy spinach, potatoes and chickpeas with spiced yoghurt and chutneys), as well as amazing desserts and breakfasts. It's great for kids.

Caara Cafe CAFE $$
(Map p68; ☎1204569000; British Council, 17, Kasturba Gandhi Marg; mains ₹160-350; ⊙8am-8pm Mon-Sat, 8am-6pm Sun) In the British Council is this most serene, light-filled cafe, hung with Brit art from their collection, so you can sip tea and coffee and nibble on healthy-looking cakes, vegetable curry and salads against the backdrop of a few Damian Hirsts.

★Sodabottleopenerwala PARSI $$
(Map p72; Khan Market; dishes ₹85-900; ⊙noon-11pm; M Khan Market) The name is like a typical trade-based Parsi surname, the place emulates the Iranian cafes of Mumbai, and the food is authentic Persian, including vegetable berry *pulav*, mixed-berry trifle and *lagan nu custer* (Parsi wedding custard).

★Alkauser STREET FOOD $$
(Map p72; www.alkausermughlaifood.com; Kautilya Marg; kebabs from ₹170, biryani from ₹280; ⊙6-10.30pm) The family behind this hole-in-the-wall takeaway earned their stripes cooking kebabs for the Nawabs of Lucknow in the 1890s. The house speciality is the *kakori* kebab, a pâte-smooth combination of lamb and spices, but other treats include biryani and perfectly prepared lamb *burra* (marinated chops) and *murg malai tikka* (chicken marinated with spices and paneer).

Epicuria FOOD HALL $$
(Map p76; Nehru Place; fast-food dishes ₹100-300; M Nehru Place) This is a food court where you can select fast food from a variety of outlets, including Karim's, Khanchacha, Sagar Ratna and more. You buy a card for ₹500 then pay with it at any outlet – if there's change you can get the money back from the cashier. It also houses some more formal restaurants, including Italian Fio and Dhaba by Claridges.

Sagar Ratna SOUTH INDIAN $$
(Map p72; The Ashok, 50B, Diplomatic Enclave; dishes ₹240-350; ⊙8am-11pm) Considered the best of all the Sagar Ratna locations around town, this venerable South Indian restaurant is always buzzing with families, couples and kitty parties, and does a great line in dosas, *idlis, uttapams* (savoury rice pancakes) and thalis. There are other branches in **Connaught Place** (Map p68; 15-K Block, Connaught Place; dishes ₹115-170; ⊙8am-11pm; M Rajiv Chowk) and **Defence Colony** (Map p76; Defence Colony Market; dishes ₹115-170; ⊙8am-11pm; M Lajpat Nagar).

★Sana-di-ge MANGALOREAN $$$
(Map p72; ☎011-40507777; 24/48 Commercial Centre, Malcha Marg; mains ₹345-900; ⊙noon-3.45pm & 7-11.30pm) Fresh fish is flown in daily from Mangalore to this buzzing restaurant in the diplomatic district. There are an intimate three levels, decorated with geometric screens and with a terrace and bar. Food is wonderful and authentic, so head here for *anjal* fry, crab pepper fry, *marvai* (clams) or the signature *elaneer payasam*.

★Bukhara INDIAN $$$
(Map p72; ☎011-26112233; ITC Maurya, Sardar Patel Marg; mains ₹800-2600; ⊙12.30-2.45pm & 7-11.45pm) One of Delhi's best restaurants, this hotel eatery with low seating and crazy-paving walls serves wow-factor Northwest Frontier–style cuisine, with silken kebabs

and its famous Bukhara dhal. Reservations are essential.

Perch INTERNATIONAL $$$
(Map p72; Khan Market; snacks & dishes ₹110-950, wine by the glass ₹300-650, cocktails ₹450-650; 11.30am-1am; ; M Khan Market) The coolification of upscale shopping enclave Khan Market continues apace with Perch, a wine bar–cafe that's all pared-down aesthetic, waiters in pencil-grey shirts, soothing music, international wines and pleasing international snacks such as Welsh rarebit and tiger prawn with soba noodles.

La Bodega MEXICAN $$$
(Map p72; 011-43105777; 29, 1st fl, Middle Lane, Khan Market; dishes ₹325-925; noon-midnight; M Khan Market) This chic-yet-cool restaurant has big windows over leafy views, and offers interesting Mexican street food in small plates such as duck tacos with refried beans, *pico de gallo* and guacamole, as well as quesadillas or burritos with chicken and interesting salads.

Basil & Thyme ITALIAN $$$
(Map p72; Sundar Nagar Market; mains ₹465-745; 11am-11pm; M Khan Market) This elegant icon has shifted locales but still buzzes with expats and locals, who flock to dine on delicate Mediterranean flavours (no alcohol), in a serene, leafy setting.

Lodi Garden Restaurant MEDITERRANEAN $$$
(Map p72; 011-24652808; Lodi Rd; mains ₹600-1400; 12.30pm-12.30am; M Jor Bagh) This garden restaurant is mostly about ambience: there are lanterns dangling from the trees, tables in curtained pavilions and wooden carts. Although not quite as impressive as the surroundings, the menu traverses Europe and the Middle East, and there's a popular Sunday brunch.

Pandara Market INDIAN $$$
(Map p72; Pandara Rd; mains ₹400-800; noon-1am; M Khan Market) This is the enduring go-to place for excellent Mughlai and Punjabi food. Prices, standards and atmosphere are high along the strip. For quality food, try **Gulati** (Map p72; Pandara Market; mains ₹385-685; noon-midnight; M Khan Market), **Havemore** (Map p72; Pandara Market; mains ₹375-725; noon-2am; M Khan Market), **Pindi** (Map p72; Pandara Market; mains ₹330-570; noon-midnight; M Khan Market) or **Chicken Inn** (Map p72; Pandara Market; mains ₹380-700; noon-midnight; M Khan Market).

South Delhi

There are some fantastic independent restaurants tucked into the southern suburbs of Hauz Khas, Shahpur Jat, Saket and Mehrauli.

Potbelly NORTH INDIAN $$
(Map p76; 116C Shahpur Jat Village; mains ₹250-420, thalis ₹250; 12.30-11pm; M Hauz Khas) It's a rare treat to find a Bihari restaurant in Delhi, and this artsy, shabby-chic place with fabulous views has authentic thalis and dishes such as *litti* chicken (whole-wheat balls stuffed with *sattu* and served with *khada masala* chicken).

★**Indian Accent** INDIAN $$$
(Map p76; 011-26925151; Manor, 77 Friends Colony (West); dishes ₹725-1425, tasting menu non-veg/veg ₹2995/3095) In the boutique hotel Manor (p85), chef Manish Mehrotra creates inspired modern Indian cuisine, where seasonal ingredients are married in surprising and beautifully creative combinations. The tasting menu is astoundingly good, with wow-factor combinations such as tandoori bacon prawns or paper dosa filled with wild mushroom and water chestnuts. Book well ahead.

Rose Cafe CAFE $$$
(Map p76; 011-29533186; 2 Westend Marg, Saidullajab; dishes ₹299-520; noon-9pm; M Saket) Almost opposite the fake Dilli Haat market, 'Delhi Haat', an unprepossessing building harbours the Rose Cafe, prettily pale blue and pink. It's all cake stands and freshly prepared Mediterranean and comfort food, with heart-warming dishes such as shepherd's pie, pancakes and all-day breakfasts.

Swagath SOUTH INDIAN $$$
(Map p76; M9 M-Block Market; dishes ₹300-1300; noon-11.45pm; M Kailash Colony) Serving supremely scrumptious Indian seafood (especially crab, prawns, lobster and fish), Swagath will take you on a culinary tour through the fishing villages of South India in inauthentically smart surroundings. There are several branches, including at **Defence Colony Market** (Map p76; 14 Defence Colony Market; dishes ₹365-1300; 11.30am-11.30pm; M Lajpat Nagar).

Coast SOUTH INDIAN $$$
(Map p76; above Ogaan, Hauz Khas; dishes ₹360-580; noon-midnight; M Green Park) A light, bright restaurant on several levels, with

views over the parklands of Hauz Khas, chic Coast serves light South Indian dishes, such as *avial* (vegetable curry) with pumpkin *erisheri* (with black lentils), plus tacos, salads and hit-the-spot mustard-tossed fries.

Drinking & Nightlife

Delhi's ever-growing cafe scene has given rise to some cafes with artisanal coffee beans, coffee menus and Turkish pastries. The city's bar and live-music choices are also burgeoning, though licences rarely extend later than 12.30am. For the latest places to go at night, check the hip and informative Little Black Book (http://littleblackbookdelhi.com) or Brown Paper Bag (http://bpbweekend.com/delhi). For gigs, check Wild City (thewildcity.com).

Cafes

★Blue Tokai CAFE
(Map p76; Khasra 258, Lane 3 West End Marg, Saidulajab; ⌚9am-8.30pm; Ⓜ Saket) In an unlikely, tiny lane behind the fake Dilli Haat shopping centre ('Delhi Haat'), Blue Tokai produces and grinds its own amazing coffee; you can get serious caffeine hits such as nitrogen-infused cold brew – there's even a tasting menu. Snacks include 'no leaf salad with pumpkin'.

Feeling more like San Francisco than a dusty Mehrauli lane, it's full of hipster Delhi-ites saying things like 'that is so millennial!'

★Atrium, Imperial CAFE
(Map p68; Janpath; ⌚8am-11.30pm; Ⓜ Janpath) Is there anything more genteel than high tea at the Imperial? Sip tea from bone-china cups and pluck dainty sandwiches and cakes from tiered stands, while discussing the latest goings-on in Shimla and Dalhousie. High tea is served in the Atrium from 3pm to 6pm daily (weekday/weekend ₹1200/1500 plus tax).

Indian Coffee House CAFE
(Map p68; 2nd fl, Mohan Singh Place, Baba Kharak Singh Marg; ⌚9am-9pm; Ⓜ Rajiv Chowk) Indian Coffee House has faded-to-the-point-of-dilapidated charm, with the waiters' plummage-like hats and uniforms giving them a rakish swagger. You can feast on finger chips and sandwiches like it's 1952, and the roof terrace is a tranquil spot to linger.

Jugmug Thela TEAHOUSE
(Map p76; Khasra 258, Westend Marg, Saidulajab; ⌚10am-8.30pm; Ⓜ Saket) A hidden surprise in a tiny back lane, this is an artisanal tea specialist styled as a streetside tea stall. They have more than 180 herbs and spices to work with, and serve delicious ayurvedic teas and fine blends such as Kinnow and Rose Earl Grey, iced teas and coffees, plus organic coffee and homebaked cookies.

Keventer's Milkshakes CAFE
(Map p68; 17 A-Block, Connaught Place; ⌚9am-11pm; Ⓜ Rajiv Chowk) Keventer's has a cult following for its legendary creamy milkshakes (₹100), slurped out of milk bottles on the pavement in front of the stand.

Café Turtle CAFE
(Map p72; Full Circle Bookstore, Khan Market; ⌚9.30am-8.30pm; Ⓜ Khan Market) Allied to the Full Circle Bookstore (p95), this brightly painted boho cafe gets busy with chattering bookish types, and is ideal when you're the mood for coffee and cake in cosy surroundings, with a leafy outdoor terrace as well. There are branches in GK1's **N-Block Market** (Map p76; N-Block Market, Greater Kailash I; ⌚8.30am-8.30pm; Ⓜ Kailash Colony) and **Nizamuddin East** (Map p72; 8 Nizamuddin East Market, Full Circle Bookstore; ⌚8.30am-8.30pm; Ⓜ Jangpura).

Kunzum Travel Cafe CAFE
(Map p76; www.kunzum.com; T49 Hauz Khas Village; ⌚11am-7.30pm Tue-Sun; 📶; Ⓜ Green Park) Quirky Kunzum has a pay-what-you-like policy for the self-service French-press coffee and tea, and sells its own brand of travel guides to Delhi. There's free wi-fi and travel books and magazines to browse.

Bars

★1911 BAR
(Map p68; Imperial Hotel, Janpath; ⌚11am-12.45am; Ⓜ Janpath) The Imperial, built in the 1930s, resonates with bygone splendour. This bar is a more recent addition, but still riffs on the Raj. Here you can sip the perfect cocktail (around ₹900) amid designer-clad clientele, against a backdrop of faded photos and murals of maharajas.

★Piano Man Jazz Club CLUB
(Map p76; http://thepianoman.in; B 6 Commercial Complex, Safdarjung Enclave; ⌚noon-3pm & 7.30pm-12.30am) The real thing, this popular, atmospheric place with proper-musos is a

dim-lit speakeasy with some excellent live jazz performances.

★**Bandstand** BAR

(Map p76; Aurobindo Market; noon-1am; ; Green Park) This popular place is near Hauz Khas and has a great glass-covered terrace with views over the tombs of Green Park. It's also one of Delhi's live-music venues, with gigs from 9pm on Thursday and Sunday.

★**Ek Bar** BAR

(Map p76; D17, 1st fl, Defence Colony; noon-3.30pm & 6pm-12.30am; Lajpat Nagar) On the upper floors of a building in the exclusive area of the Defence Colony, this place has stylish, kooky decor in deep, earth-jewel colours, serious mixology (drinks ₹250 to ₹800) showcasing Indian flavours (how about a gin and tonic with turmeric?), modern Indian bar snacks, nightly DJs, and a see-and-be-seen crowd.

★**Unplugged** BAR

(Map p68; 011-33107701; 23 L-Block, Connaught Place; noon-midnight; Rajiv Chowk) There's nowhere else like this in Connaught Place. You could forget you were in CP, in fact, with the big garden, wrought-iron chairs and tables, and swing seats, all under the shade of a mother of a banyan tree hung with basket-weave lanterns. In the evenings there are regular live gigs, anything from alt-rock to electro-fusion. A Kingfisher costs ₹100.

Hauz Khas Social BAR

(Map p76; 9A & 12 Hauz Khas Village; 10.30am-midnight; Green Park) This chilled-out place is a Hauz Khas hub, and has large rooms with plate-glass windows overlooking lush greenery. There are cocktails and snacks, and a busy smokers' terrace. There's also regular live music and DJs.

Summer House BAR

(Map p76; 1st fl, Aurobindo Place Market; 11am-1am; Green Park) Close to Hauz Khas, this roomy, rustic 1st-floor bar has a spacious terrace and is a popular, lively evening haunt for a mixed crowd of men and women. There's regular live music. A Kingfisher costs ₹175.

24/7 BAR

(Map p64; Lalit Hotel, Maharaja Rajit Singh Marg; 24hr; Barakhamba Rd) The 24-hour lobby bar at the Lalit Hotel is the perfect spot for a welcome-to-Delhi drink after a long flight.

Aqua BAR

(Map p68; Park Hotel, 15 Sansad Marg; 11am-midnight; ; Janpath) If you feel the need for some five-star style after visiting Jantar Mantar or shopping in Connaught Place, Aqua is an ideal place to flop, forget the world outside, and sip cocktails by the pool.

Karen Cafe BAR

(Map p82; Arakashan Rd; 9am-11pm; New Delhi) An escape from the fraught street level, this tiny rooftop cafe has a few tables and a good viewpoint for overlooking the street. It's decorated with Bob Marley posters, wicker chairs and hanging lamps, and, while the service is slow and the food basic, it's as chilled as you'll get on this strip.

Sam's Bar BAR

(Map p82; Main Bazaar; 11am-1am; Ramakrishna Ashram Marg) Sam's Bar is more laid-back than most Paharganj bars, and a good choice for a drink and a chat, with a mixed crowd of men and women, locals and foreigners. There are snacks and a range of local (₹150 Kingfishers) and international beers and spirits.

Gem BAR

(Map p82; 1050 Main Bazaar, Paharganj; 11am-12.30am; Ramakrishna Ashram Marg) This wood-panelled dive is the kind of place you can forget what time of day it is – a dark, long-standing Paharganj hang-out that's popular with (male) locals and other travellers; bottles of local beer cost from ₹140. The upstairs area has more atmosphere.

My Bar BAR

(Map p82; Main Bazaar, Paharganj; 11am-12.30pm; Ramakrishna Ashram Marg) A dark and dingy bar, this place is lively, loud and fun, with a cheery, mixed crowd of backpackers and locals, who may even start dancing... There are several other branches, in CP and Hauz Khas. Drinks are ₹70 to ₹300 (beer from ₹85).

Metro Bar BAR

(Map p82; 19 Panchkuian Rd; 11am-1am; Ramakrishna Ashram Marg) Tucked around the corner from the Ramakrishna Ashram Marg metro station is a row of much-of-a-muchness bars that are favoured by local businessmen, with not particularly talented female singers belting out requests from the clientele. Metro Bar is the pick of the bunch – fun and friendly, with good Indian food.

Entertainment

Music & Cultural Performances

Habitat World LIVE PERFORMANCE

(Map p72; 011-43663333; www.habitatworld.com; India Habitat Centre, Lodi Rd; M Jor Bagh) This is an important Delhi cultural address, with art exhibitions, performances and concerts, mostly free. They also arrange regular Delhi walks.

India International Centre LIVE PERFORMANCE

(Map p72; 011-24619431; www.iicdelhi.nic.in; 40 Max Mueller Marg; M Khan Market) The IIC is a key location for a sector of Delhi society, usually elderly intellectuals. Although the club is for members only, the public is welcome to the regular, quality, free exhibitions, talks and concerts.

Cinemas

Delite Cinema CINEMA

(Map p64; 011-23272903; www.delitecinemas.com; 4/1 Asaf Ali Rd; M New Delhi) Founded in 1954 as the tallest building in Delhi, the Delite was renovated in 2006 and it's no ordinary cinema, with a painted dome and Czech chandeliers. It's a great place to see a masala picture (full-throttle Bollywood, a mix of action, comedy, romance and drama), with famous extra-large samosas available in the interval.

Regal Cinema CINEMA

(Map p68; front/back stalls ₹80/100, balcony ₹100/120; M Rajiv Chowk) With a regular turnaround of Bollywood hits, this Connaught Place cinema, open since 1932, is a popular place to catch the latest releases. As of 2017 it also includes the Delhi branch of Madame Tussauds.

Shopping

Meharchand Market MARKET

(Map p72; Lodi Colony; M Lodhi Colony) Across the road from the government housing of the Lodi Colony, this is a long strip of small boutiques selling homewares and clothes. Shops include **Fabindia** (Map p72; 11am-8pm), **the Shop** (Map p72; 10am-8pm Mon-Sat, 11am-6pm Sun), and stand-out eateries are the organic **Altitude Cafe** (Map p72; mains ₹340-580; 8am-5pm;) and Asian-tapas restaurant **Diva Spiced** (Map p72; tapas ₹320-560, mains ₹390-1200; 11.30am-11.30pm).

Timeless BOOKS

(Map p76; 011-46056198; 46 Housing Society, Part I, South Extension; 10am-7pm Mon-Sat) Hidden in a back lane (ask around), Timeless has a devoted following for its quality coffee-table books on topics from Indian textiles to architecture.

Delhi Musical Stores MUSIC

(Map p76; 23276909; www.indianmusicalinstruments.com; C99 Lajpat Nagar; 11am-8pm Mon-Sat; M Lajpat Nagar) Delhi Musical Stores has a fine choice of tablas, harmoniums, sitars and more.

KUSHTI

Wander the districts north of Kashmere Gate in Old Delhi and you may notice a disproportionately high number of muscular men. No, it's not your imagination. This dusty quarter is the favoured stomping ground for Delhi's traditional mud wrestlers. *Kushti*, or *pehlwani*, is a full-contact martial art, fusing elements of yoga and philosophy with combat and intense physical training.

Young men enrol at *akharas* (training centres) in their early teens, and follow a strict regimen of daily exercise, climbing ropes, lifting weights and hauling logs to build up the necessary muscle bulk for this intensely physical sport. Even diet and lifestyle is strictly controlled; sex, tobacco and alcohol are forbidden, and wrestlers live together in rustic accommodation under the supervision of a coach who doubles as spiritual guide.

Bouts take place on freshly tilled earth, adding an extra element of grit to proceedings. As with other types of wrestling, the aim is to pin your opponent to the ground, but fights often continue until one wrestler submits or collapses from exhaustion. At regional championships, wrestlers compete for golden *gadas* (ceremonial clubs), a tribute to the favoured weapon of Hanuman, patron deity of wrestling.

Most *akharas* welcome spectators at the daily dawn and dusk training sessions, so long as this doesn't interfere with training. Seek permission first to avoid offending these muscle-bound gents – the blog http://kushtiwrestling.blogspot.com is a good introduction to the sport and the main *akharas*.

Aap Ki Pasand (San Cha) DRINKS
(Map p64; 15 Netaji Subhash Marg; ⏲10am-7pm Mon-Sat) Specialists in the finest Indian teas, from Darjeeling and Assam to Nilgiri and Kangra. You can try before you buy, and teas come lovingly packaged in drawstring bags. There's another branch at **Santushti Shopping Complex** (Map p72; ☎011-264530374; www.sanchatea.com; Racecourse Rd; ⏲10am-6.30pm Mon-Sat; Ⓜ Racecourse).

Daryaganj Kitab Bazaar MARKET
(Book Market; Map p64; ⏲8am-6pm Sun) Come Sunday, books spread across the pavements for around 2km from Delhi Gate northwards to the Red Fort, and a shorter distance west along Jawaharlal Nehru Marg. Rummage for everything from Mills & Boon to vintage children's books. It's best to arrive early, as it gets busy.

Anokhi CLOTHING
(Map p72; www.anokhi.com; 32 Khan Market; ⏲10am-8pm; Ⓜ Khan Market) Anokhi specialises in block-print clothes and homewares, showcasing traditional designs with a modern design sensibility. There are branches at the **Santushti Shopping Complex** (Map p72; ⏲10am-7pm Mon-Sat; Ⓜ Racecourse) and **N-Block Market** (Map p76; Greater Kailash I; ⏲10am-8pm; Ⓜ Kailash Colony), with a discount store in **Nizamuddin East** (Map p72; ⏲10am-8pm Mon-Sat).

OCM Suitings CLOTHING
(Map p72; ☎011-24618937; Khan Market; ⏲11am-8pm Mon-Sat; Ⓜ Khan Market) Men's wool suits from ₹9500 (including material) and ankle-length skirts from ₹550 (excluding material). Suits are ready in around seven to 10 days.

Musical Instrument Shops MUSICAL INSTRUMENTS
(Map p64; Netaji Subhash Marg; ⏲approx 10am-8pm Mon-Sat) For competitively priced instruments, inspect the instrument shops along Netaji Subhash Marg in Daryaganj.

Rikhi Ram MUSIC
(Map p68; ☎011-23327685; www.rikhiram.com; 8A G-Block, Connaught Place; ⏲noon-8pm Mon-Sat; Ⓜ Rajiv Chowk) A beautiful old shop selling professional classic and electric sitars, tablas and more.

Old Delhi

Main Bazaar HANDICRAFTS, CLOTHING
(Map p82; Paharganj; ⏲10am-9pm Tue-Sun; Ⓜ Ramakrishna Ashram Marg) The backpacker-oriented bazaar that runs through Paharganj sells almost everything you want, and a whole lot more. It's great for buying presents, clothes, inexpensive jewellery bits and bobs, and luggage to put everything in as you're leaving India, or for hippy-dippy

OLD DELHI'S BAZAARS

Old Delhi's bazaars are a bamboozling, sensual whirlwind, combining incense, spices strong enough to make you sneeze, rickshaw fumes, brilliant colours, and hole-in-the-wall shops packed with goods that shimmer and glitter. This is less retail therapy, more heightened reality. The best time to visit is midmorning or later in the day, when the streets are less busy.

Whole districts here are devoted to individual items. **Chandni Chowk** (Map p64; ⏲10am-7pm Mon-Sat; Ⓜ Chandni Chowk) is all clothing, electronics and break-as-soon-as-you-buy-them novelties. For silver jewellery, head for **Dariba Kalan** (Map p64; ⏲approx 10am-8pm; Ⓜ Chawri Bazaar), the alley near the Sisganj Gurdwara. Off this lane, the **Kinari Bazaar** (Map p64; Kinari Bazaar; ⏲11am-8pm; Ⓜ Jama Masjid), literally 'trimmings market', is famous for *zardozi* (gold embroidery), temple trim and wedding turbans. Running south from the old Town Hall, **Nai Sarak** (Map p64; ⏲approx 10am-8pm; Ⓜ Jama Masjid) is lined with stalls selling saris, shawls, chiffon and *lehanga,* while nearby **Ballimaran** (Map p64; Ballimaran; ⏲10am-8pm; Ⓜ Chandni Chowk) has sequined slippers and fancy, curly-toed jootis (traditional slip-on shoes). For gorgeous wrapping paper and wedding cards, head to **Chawri Bazaar** (Map p64; ⏲10am-7pm), leading west from the Jama Masjid.

Beside the Fatehpuri Masjid, on Khari Baoli, is the nose-numbing **Spice Market** (Gadodia Market; Map p64; Khari Baoli; Ⓜ Chandni Chowk), ablaze with piles of scarlet-red chillis, ginger and turmeric roots, peppercorns, cumin, coriander seeds, cardamom, dried fruit and nuts. There's a constant trail of workers carrying huge sacks on their heads, and the spices in the air are so strong that everyone keeps sneezing.

clothes to wear on your trip. Haggle with purpose.

Karol Bagh Market MARKET
(Map p64; approx 10am-7pm Tue-Sun; M Karol Bagh) Favoured for clothes and wedding shopping, this market shimmers with all things sparkly, from dressy *lehanga choli* (skirt-and-blouse sets) to princess-style shoes. There are also electronics at Gaffar market (head here if you need a cracked phone screen replaced) and chrome motorcycle parts.

Connaught Place

★Central Cottage Industries Emporium ARTS & CRAFTS
(Map p68; 011-23326790; Janpath; 10am-7pm; M Janpath) This government-run multilevel store is a wonderful treasure trove of fixed-price, India-wide handicrafts. Prices are higher than in the state emporiums, but the selection of woodcarvings, jewellery, pottery, papier mâché, stationery, brassware, textiles (including shawls), toys, rugs, beauty products and miniature paintings makes it a glorious one-stop shop for beautiful crafts. Downstairs there's the Smoothie Factory cafe.

★Kamala ARTS & CRAFTS
(Map p68; Baba Kharak Singh Marg; 10am-7pm Mon-Sat; M Rajiv Chowk) Crafts, curios, textiles and homewares from the Crafts Council of India, designed with flair and using traditional techniques but offering some contemporary, out-of-the-ordinary designs.

★People Tree HANDICRAFTS, CLOTHING
(Map p68; Regal Bldg, Sansad Marg; 11am-7pm; M Rajiv Chowk) This hole-in-the-wall shop sells fixed-price, fair-trade, ubercool T-shirts with funky Indian designs and urban attitude, as well as bags, jewellery and Indian-god cushions.

★State Emporiums HANDICRAFTS, CLOTHING
(Map p68; Baba Kharak Singh Marg; 11am-1.30pm & 2-6.30pm Mon-Sat; M Shivaji Stadium) Handily in a row are these regional treasure-filled emporiums. They may have the air of torpor that often afflicts governmental enterprises, but shopping here is like travelling around India – top stops include Kashmir, for papier mâché and carpets; Rajasthan, for miniature paintings and puppets; Uttar Pradesh, for marble inlay work; Karnataka, for sandalwood sculptures; Tamil Nadu, for metal statues; and Odisha, for stone carvings.

Janpath & Tibetan Markets ARTS & CRAFTS
(Map p68; Janpath; 11.30am-7pm Mon-Sat; M Rajiv Chowk) These twin markets sell shimmering mirrorwork embroidery, colourful shawls, Tibetan bric-a-brac, brass Oms and dangly earrings. There are some good finds if you rummage through the junk, and if you haggle you can get some excellent bargains.

Khadi Gramodyog Bhawan CLOTHING
(Map p68; Baba Kharak Singh Marg; 10.30am-8pm; M Rajiv Chowk) Known for its excellent *khadi* (homespun cloth), including good-value shawls, plus handmade paper, incense, spices, henna and lovely natural soaps.

M Ram & Sons CLOTHING
(Map p68; 011-23416558; 21 E-Block, Connaught Place; 10.30am-8pm; M Rajiv Chowk) A popular Delhi tailor, offering suits from ₹8000. Tailoring is possible in 24 hours.

Oxford Bookstore BOOKS
(Map p68; N81 Connaught Place; 10am-9.30pm Mon-Sat, 11am-9.30pm Sun; M Rajiv Chowk) A swish but somewhat soulless bookstore, where you could nevertheless browse for hours. Staff are not as knowledgable as at other Delhi bookshops, although it sells good gifts, such as handmade paper notebooks. The attached **Cha Bar** (Map p68; Oxford Bookstore, N81 Connaught Place; 10am-9.30pm Mon-Sat, 11am-9.30pm Sun; M Rajiv Chowk) is a buzzing meeting spot.

New Delhi

★Khan Market MARKET
(Map p72; approx 10.30am-8pm Mon-Sat; M Khan Market) Khan Market is Delhi's most upmarket shopping enclave, the most expensive place to rent a shop in India, and is favoured by the elite and expats. Its boutiques focus on fashion, books and homewares, and it's also a good place to eat and drink.

For handmade paper, check out **Anand Stationers** (Map p72; 10am-8pm Mon-Sat, noon-6pm Sun), or try **Mehra Bros** (Map p72; 10am-7pm Mon-Thu & Sat, 10am-8pm Fri, 11am-6pm Sun) for cool papier-mâché ornaments. Literature lovers should head to **Full Circle Bookstore** (Map p72; www.fullcirclebooks.in; 9.30am-8.30pm) and **Bahrisons** (Map p72; www.booksatbahri.com; 10.30am-7.30pm Mon-

WORTH A TRIP

SHAHPUR JAT

A 1km rickshaw ride northeast from Hauz Khas metro, the urban village of Shahpur Jat is one of the best places in Delhi to buy upmarket independent designer threads. Stores to seek out include **Nimai** (Map p76; ☎011-64300113; 416 Shahpur Jat Village; ⊙11am-7.30pm; MHauz Khas) for one-of-a-kind costume jewellery and **NeedleDust** (Map p76; www.needledust.com; 40B, ground fl, Shahpur Jat; ⊙10.30am-7.30pm Mon-Sat, 11am-6.30pm Sun; MHauz Khas) for embroidered leather shoes, and there are some choice independent restaurants, such as artsy Bihari Potbelly (p90), and vegan organic **Greenr** (Map p76; ☎7042575339; mains ₹250-375; ⊙11am-7.30pm; ; MHauz Khas). For superb fine tea tastings head to **Anandini Tea Room** (Map p76; 12A, DDA Flats; ⊙11am-7pm; MHauz Khas).

Sat, 11.30am-7.30pm Sun). For Indian clothes and homewares, hit **Fabindia** (Map p72; ⊙10.30am-9.30pm) and Anokhi (p94), and for elegantly packaged ayurvedic remedies, browse **Kama** (Map p72; ⊙10.30am-8.30pm).

Sunder Nagar Market ARTS & CRAFTS
(Map p72; Mathura Rd; ⊙approx 10.30am-7.30pm Mon-Sat) Long-time genteel and sleepy Sundar Nagar has turned increasingly chic. It's long specialised in Indian and Nepali handicrafts, replica 'antiques', furniture and fine Indian teas, but much-loved restaurant Basil & Thyme (p90) has moved here, and there's the cool watering hole, No 8.

South Delhi

★Dilli Haat ARTS & CRAFTS
(Map p76; Aurobindo Marg; foreigner/Indian ₹100/20; ⊙10.30am-10pm; MINA) This open-air food-and-crafts market is a cavalcade of colour and sells regional handicrafts from all over India; bargain hard. With lots of food stands, it's also a good place to sample cheap, delicious regional specialities – try food from Nagaland or Tamil Nadu (dishes are around ₹70 to ₹100).

★Hauz Khas Village HANDICRAFTS, CLOTHING
(Map p76; ⊙11am-7pm Mon-Sat; MGreen Park) It's not as hip as it was a few years ago, but still well worth a browse. This arty little enclave has narrow lanes crammed with boutiques selling designer Indian clothing, handicrafts, contemporary ceramics, handmade furniture and old Bollywood movie posters. Shops to seek out include **Claymen** (Map p76; ⊙hours vary), Maarti, Ogaan and Bodice.

Dastkar Nature Bazaar MARKET
(http://dastkar.org; Andheria Modh; ⊙10am-7pm Tue-Sun; MChhatarpur) Not-for-profit NGO Dastkar promotes regional crafts, and its outdoor craft bazaar holds monthly themed events, showcasing cutting-edge regional culture, craft and food.

Greater Kailash I: M-Block & N-Block Markets MARKET
(Map p76; ⊙approx 10am-8pm Wed-Mon; MKailash Colony) A two-part midrange shopping enclave with swanky boutiques and posh eateries, best known for Fabindia, which has several branches here. Also check out clothes store Anokhi.

Information

DANGERS & ANNOYANCES

Delhi is relatively safe in terms of petty crime, though pickpocketing can be a problem in crowded areas so keep your valuables safe.

Train Station Hassle

Touts at New Delhi train station endeavour to steer travellers away from the legitimate International Tourist Bureau and into private travel agencies where they earn a commission. Touts often tell people that their tickets are invalid, there's a problem with the trains, or say they're not allowed on the platform. They then 'assist' in booking expensive taxis or 3rd-class tickets passed off as something else. You're particularly vulnerable when arriving tired at night. As a rule of thumb: don't believe anyone who approaches you trying to tell you anything at the train station, even if they're wearing a uniform or have an official-looking pass.

Women Travellers

Delhi has, unfortunately, a deserved reputation as being unsafe for women. Precautions include never walking around in lonely, deserted places, even during daylight hours, keeping an eye on your route so you don't get lost (download a map that you can use offline) and taking special care after dark – ensure you have a safe means of transport home with, for example, a reputable cab company or driver.

Touts

Taxi-wallahs at the airport and around tourist areas frequently act as touts for hotels, claiming that your hotel is full, poor value, dangerous, burnt down or closed, or that there are riots in Delhi. Any such story is a ruse to steer you to a hotel where they will get a commission. Insist on being taken to where you want to go – making a show of writing down the registration plate number, and phoning the autorickshaw/taxi helpline may help. Men who approach you at Connaught Place run similar scams to direct you to shops and tourist agents, often 'helpfully' informing you that wherever you're headed is closed.

INTERNET ACCESS

Almost all hotels and many cafes offer free wi-fi access these days.

MEDIA

➡ For printed listings see the weekly calendar pamphlet *Delhi Diary* (₹30), which is available at local bookshops. *Motherland* (www.motherlandmagazine.com) is a stylish bi-monthly cultural magazine.

➡ To check out what's on, see the ubercool Little Black Book (www.littleblackbookdelhi.com) or Brown Paper Bag (brownpaperbag.in/delhi). Don't miss the Delhi Walla blog (www.thedelhiwalla.com), a wonderful window into Delhi's daily life.

MEDICAL SERVICES

Pharmacies are found on most shopping streets and in most suburban markets. Hospitals:

All India Institute of Medical Sciences (AIIMS; Map p76; ☎011-65900669; www.aiims.edu; Ansari Nagar; Ⓜ AIIMS)

Apollo Hospital (☎011-29871090; www.apollohospdelhi.com; Mathura Rd, Sarita Vihar; Ⓜ Sarita Vihar)

Dr Ram Manohar Lohia Hospital (Map p72; ☎011-23365525; www.rmlh.nic.in; Baba Kharak Singh Marg; Ⓜ Patel Chowk)

East West Medical Centre (Map p72; ☎011-24690429; www.eastwestrescue.com; 37 Prithviraj Rd; Ⓜ Racecourse)

Max Healthcare (Map p76; ☎011-26515050; Press Enclave Rd, Saket; Ⓜ Saket)

POST

There are post offices all over Delhi that can handle letters and parcels (most with packing services nearby). Poste restante is available at the New Delhi office of **India Post** (Map p72; ☎011-23743602; Gole Dakhana, Baba Kharak Singh Marg; ⏲10am-5pm Mon-Sat); ensure mail is addressed to GPO, New Delhi – 110001. There is a convenient India Post branch at **Connaught Place** (Map p68; 6 A-Block, Connaught Place; ⏲8am-7.30pm Mon-Sat; Ⓜ Rajiv Chowk).

Courier services may be arranged through **DHL** (Map p68; ☎011-23737587; ground fl, Mercantile Bldg, Tolstoy Marg; ⏲8am-8pm Mon-Sat; Ⓜ Rajiv Chowk) at Connaught Place.

TOURIST INFORMATION

Archaeological Survey of India (Map p72; ☎011-23010822; www.asi.nic.in; Janpath; ⏲9.30am-1pm & 2-6pm Mon-Fri; Ⓜ Central Secretariat) Next door to the National Museum, the Archaeological Survey of India stocks publications about India's main archaeological sites.

India Tourism Delhi (Government of India; Map p68; ☎011-23320005, 011-23320008; www.incredibleindia.org; 88 Janpath; ⏲9am-6pm Mon-Fri, to 2pm Sat; Ⓜ Janpath) This is the only official India Tourism office, apart from the booth at the airport. Ignore touts who (falsely) claim to be associated with this. It's a useful source of advice on Delhi, getting out of Delhi, and visiting surrounding states. Has free Delhi maps and brochures, and publishes a list of recommended agencies and B&Bs. Come here to report tourism-related complaints.

ℹ Getting There & Away

AIR

Indira Gandhi International Airport (p1195) is about 14km southwest of the centre. International and domestic flights use gleaming Terminal 3. Terminal 1 is reserved for low-cost carriers. Free shuttle buses (present your boarding pass and onward ticket) run between the two terminals every 20 minutes, but can take much longer. Leave at least three hours between transfers to be safe.

The arrivals hall at Terminal 3 has 24-hour foreign exchange, ATMs, prepaid taxi and car-hire counters, tourist information, a pharmacy, bookshops, cafes and a **Plaza Premium Lounge** (☎011-61233922; s/d 3 hr US$37/52, 6 hr 52/66) with short-stay rooms (there's another of these at Terminal 1 arrivals).

You'll need to show your boarding pass to enter the terminal. At check-in be sure to collect tags for all your carry-on bags and ensure these are stamped as you go through security.

Delhi's airport can be prone to thick fog from November to January (often disrupting airline schedules) – it's wise to allow a day between connecting flights during this period.

Air India (☎1800 1801407; www.airindia.com)

Jagson Airlines (Map p68; ☎011-23721593; www.jagsongroup.in; Vandana Bldg, 11 Tolstoy Marg; ⏲10am-6pm Mon-Sat; Ⓜ Janpath)

Jet Airways (Map p68; ☎011-39893333; www.jetairways.com; 11/12 G-Block, Connaught Place; ⏲9.30am-6pm Mon-Sat; Ⓜ Rajiv Chowk)

SpiceJet (☎1800 1803333; www.spicejet.com)

BUS

Most travellers enter and leave Delhi by train, but buses are a useful option to some destinations and if the trains are booked up.

Most state-run services leave from the large **Kashmere Gate Inter State Bus Terminal** (ISBT; Map p64; ☎ 011-23860290; Ⓜ Kashmere Gate) in Old Delhi, accessible by metro. Offices at the terminal:

Delhi Transport Corporation (Map p64; ☎ 011-23370210; www.dtc.nic.in)

Haryana Roadways (Map p64; ☎ 011-23868271; www.hartrans.gov.in)

Punjab Roadways (Map p64; ☎ 011-44820000; www.punbusonline.com)

Rajasthan Roadways (Map p64; ☎ 011-23386658, 011-23864470; Counter 36, Kashmere Gate Inter State Bus Terminal)

Rajasthan State Road Transport Corporation (Map p64; ☎ 011-23864470; http://rsrtc.rajasthan.gov.in)

Uttar Pradesh Roadways (Map p64; ☎ 011-23868709)

Uttar Pradesh State Road Transport Corporation (Map p64; ☎ 011-2622363; www.upsrtc.com)

The **Anand Vihar Inter State Bus Terminal** (ISBT) has some services to Nainital and Kumaun in Uttarakhand. Some cheaper buses to destinations in Uttar Pradesh, Madhya Pradesh and Rajasthan leave from the **Sarai Kale Khan Inter State Bus Terminal** (ISBT) on the ring road near Nizamuddin train station.

Arrive at least 30 minutes ahead of your departure time. You can avoid the hassle by paying a little more for private deluxe buses that leave from locations in central Delhi – enquire at travel agencies or your hotel for details.You can also book tickets or check information on **Cleartrip** (www.cleartrip.com), **Make My Trip** (www.makemytrip.com) or **Goibibo** (www.goibibo.com).

There are buses to Agra, but considering the traffic at either end, you're better off taking the train. **Himachal Pradesh Tourism Development Corporation** (HPTDC; Map p72; hptdc.gov.in; Chanderlok Building, 36 Janpath; Ⓜ Janpath) runs buses from **Himachal Bhawan** (Map p72; ☎ 011-23716689; Sikandra Rd; Ⓜ Mandi House) to Manali (₹1300, nine hours) and Shimla (₹900, 10 hours) at 6.30pm. Tickets are sold at Himachal Bhawan and **Chanderlok House** (Map p72; ☎ 011-23325320; 36 Janpath).

Himachal Road Transport Corporation (HRTC; ☎ 011-23868694; www.hrtc.gov.in) also has AC buses starting from Himachal Bhawan, to Shimla (₹935, seven daily) and to Manali (₹1430, 7pm). These stop at the ISBT Kashmiri Gate an hour later.

Rajasthan Tourism (Map p72; ☎ 011-23381884; www.rtdc.com; Bikaner House, Pandara Rd; Ⓜ Khan Market) runs deluxe buses from **Bikaner House** (Map p72; ☎ 011-23383469; Pandara Rd; Ⓜ Khan Market), near India Gate, to the following destinations:

Ajmer Volvo ₹1200, nine hours, three daily

Jaipur non AC/super deluxe/Volvo ₹400/625/900, six hours, every one to two hours

Jodhpur Volvo ₹1625, 11 hours, two daily

Udaipur Volvo ₹1800, 15 hours, one daily

Women receive a discount of 30% on all Rajasthan Tourism bus prices.

TRAIN

There are three main stations in Delhi: (Old) Delhi train station (aka Delhi Junction) in Old Delhi, New Delhi train station near Paharganj, and Nizamuddin train station, south of Sunder Nagar. Make sure you know which station your train is leaving from.

The best option for foreign travellers is to visit the helpful **International Tourist Bureau** (ITB; Map p82; ☎ 011-23405156; 1st fl, New Delhi Train Station; ⊙ 24hr). The entrance to the ITB is before you go onto platform 1 (on the Paharganj side of New Delhi train station), via a staircase just to the right of the entrance to the platform. Do *not* believe anyone who tells you it has shifted, closed or burnt down – this is a scam to divert you elsewhere. Walk with confidence and ignore all 'helpful' or 'official' approaches. The ITB is a large room with about 10 or more computer terminals – don't be fooled by other 'official' offices.

When making reservations here, you can pay in cash (rupees) only. Bring your passport.

When you arrive, take a ticket from the machine that gives you a place in the queue. Then complete a reservation form – ask at the information counter to check availability. You can then wait to complete and pay for your booking at the relevant counter. This is the best place to get last-minute bookings for quota seats to popular destinations, but come prepared to queue.

There's also a public **Train Reservation Office** (Map p82; Chelmsford Rd; ⊙ 8am-8pm Mon-Sat, to 2pm Sun) closer to Connaught Place, but touts here are notorious for targetting travellers.

ℹ Getting Around

TO/FROM THE AIRPORT

Whatever time your flight arrives, it's a good idea to book a hotel in advance and notify staff of your arrival time – some places may allow you to check in early. Organised city transport runs to/from Terminal 3; a free shuttle bus runs every 20 minutes between Terminal 3 and Terminal 1.

Pre-arranged Pick-ups Hotels offer pre-arranged airport pick-up, but these are usually more expensive than arranging a taxi yourself – however, it may be worth it to ease your arrival.

You'll pay extra to cover the airport parking fee (up to ₹220) and ₹100 charge to enter the arrivals hall. To avoid the entry fee, drivers may wait outside Gates 4 to 6.

Metro The Airport Express line (www.delhimetrorail.com) runs every 10 to 15 minutes from 5.15am to 11.40pm, completing the journey from Terminal 3 to New Delhi train station in around 20 minutes (International/domestic terminal–New Delhi, ₹60/50). It's usually empty because it's a separate line from the rest of the metro. You can use a smart card, or buy a token

MAJOR TRAINS FROM DELHI

DESTINATION	TRAIN NO & NAME	FARE (₹)	DURATION (HR)	FREQUENCY	DEPARTURES & TRAIN STATION
Agra	12280 Taj Exp	100/370 (A)	3	1 daily	7am NZM
	12002 Bhopal Shatabdi	515/1010 (B)	2	1 daily	6am NDLS
Amritsar	12029/12013 Swarna/Amritsar Shatabdi	790/1620 (B)	6	1-2 daily	7.20am/4.30pm NDLS
Bengaluru	22692 Bangalore Rajdhani	2960/4095/6775 (C)	34	4 weekly	8.50pm NZM
Chennai	12434 Chennai Rajdhani	2795/3860/6355 (C)	28	2 weekly	3.55pm NZM
	12622 Tamil Nadu Exp	780/2040/2990 (D)	33	1 daily	10.30pm NDLS
Goa (Madgaon)	12432 Trivandrum Rajdhani	3385/4730/7815 (C)	26	3 weekly	10.55am NZM
	12780 Goa Exp	170/540/740 (D)	27	1 daily	3pm NZM
Haridwar	12017 Dehradun Shatabdi	595/1190 (B)	4½	1 daily	6.45am NDLS
Jaipur	12958 ADI Swama Jayanti Rajdani	1210/1660/2755 (C)	4½	1 daily	7.55pm NDLS
	12916 Ashram Exp	235/590/825 (D)	5	1 daily	3.20pm DLI
	12015 Ajmer Shatabdi	355/740 (B)	4½	1 daily	6.05am NDLS
Kalka (for Shimla)	12011 Kalka Shatabdi	640/1295 (B)	4	2 daily	7.40am NDLS
Khajuraho	12448 UP Sampark Kranti Exp	365/955/1350 (D)	10½	1 daily	8.10pm NZM
Lucknow	12004 Lucknow Swran Shatabdi	885/1850 (B)	6½	1 daily	6.10am NDLS
Mumbai	12952 Mumbai Rajdhani	2085/2870/4755 (C)	16	1 daily	4.45pm NDLS
	12954 August Kranti Rajdani	2085/2870/4755 (C)	17½	1 daily	4.50pm NZM
Udaipur	12963 Mewar Exp	415/1095/1555 (D)	12½	1 daily	7pm NZM
Varanasi	12560 Shivganga Exp	415/1100//1565 (D)	12½	1 daily	6.55pm NDLS

Train stations: NDLS – New Delhi; DLI – Old Delhi; NZM – Hazrat Nizamuddin

Fares: (A) 2nd class/chair car; (B) chair car/1st-class AC; (C) 3AC/2AC/1st-class AC; (D) sleeper/3AC/2AC

for the other lines at Airport station; check with customer services.

Bus Air-conditioned buses run from outside Terminal 3 to Kashmere Gate ISBT every 10 minutes, via the Red Fort, LNJP Hospital, New Delhi Station Gate 2, Connaught Place, Parliament St and Ashoka Rd.

Taxi In front of the arrivals buildings at Terminal 3 and Terminal 1 are **Delhi Traffic Police Prepaid Taxi counters** (✆ complaints 56767, women's helpline 1091; www.delhitrafficpolice.nic.in) offering fixed-price taxi services. You'll pay about ₹350 to New or Old Delhi, and ₹450 to the southern suburbs in a battered old black-and-yellow taxi. There's a 25% surcharge between 11pm and 5am. Travellers have reported difficulty in persuading drivers to go to their intended hotel. Firmly insist that the driver takes you to your chosen destination and only surrender your voucher when you arrive where you want.

You can also book a prepaid taxi at the **Megacabs counter** (✆ 011-41414141; www.megacabs.com) at both the international and domestic terminals. It costs ₹600 to ₹700 to the centre, but you get a cleaner car with air-con.

AUTORICKSHAW & TAXI

Local taxis (recognisable by their black and yellow livery) and autorickshaws have meters but these are effectively ornamental as most drivers refuse to use them. Delhi Traffic Police run a network of prepaid autorickshaw booths, where you can pay a fixed fare, including 24-hour stands at the New Delhi, **Old Delhi** (Map p64; ⏲24hr) and **Nizamuddin** (Map p72) train stations; elsewhere, you'll need to negotiate a fare before you set off.

Other booths are **outside the India Tourism Delhi office** (Map p68; 88 Janpath; ⏲11am-8.30pm) and at **Central Park** (Map p68), Connaught Place.

Fares are invariably elevated, especially for foreigners, so haggle hard, and if the fare sounds too outrageous, find another cab. For an autorickshaw ride from Connaught Place, fares should be around ₹30 to Paharganj, ₹60 to the Red Fort, ₹70 to Humayun's Tomb and ₹100 to Hauz Khas. However, it will be a struggle to get these prices. Visit www.taxiautofare.com for suggested fares for these and other journeys. To report overcharging, harassment, or other problems take the licence number and call the Auto Complaint Line on 011-42400400/25844444.

Taxis typically charge twice the autorickshaw fare. Note that fares vary as fuel prices go up and down. From 11pm to 5am there's a 25% surcharge for autorickshaws and taxis.

Kumar Tourist Taxi Service (Map p68; ✆ 011-23415930; www.kumarindiatours.com; 14/1 K-Block, Connaught Place; ⏲9am-9pm) is a reliable company; a day of Delhi sightseeing costs from ₹2000 (an eight-hour and 80km limit applies).

Metropole Tourist Service (Map p72; ✆ 011-24310313; www.metrovista.co.in; 224 Defence Colony Flyover Market; ⏲7am-7pm) is another reliable and long-running taxi service, and good value, charging ₹1500 for up to 80km for one day's car and driver hire, plus ₹100/15 per hour/kilometre thereafter.

Shared electric rickshaws are also a possibility, which means cheaper fares, but only if you're going in the same direction as other passengers.

Radiocabs

You'll need a local mobile number to order a radiocab, or ask a shop or hotel to assist you. These air-conditioned cars are clean, efficient, and use reliable meters, usually charging ₹23 at flagfall then ₹23 per kilometre. Try **Easycabs** (✆ 011-43434343; www.easycabs.com) or **Quickcabs** (✆ 011-45333333; www.quickcabs.in).

Taxi & Auto Apps

Car-sharing services **Uber** (www.uber.com) and **Ola Autos & Cabs** (www.olacabs.com) have transformed travel around Delhi. If you have a local number and a smartphone, download these apps and you can arrange pick-ups from your exact location (though the car/auto will sometimes stop a little way away), then pay the electronically calculated fee in cash when you complete the journey and thus side-stepping much haggling. Uber was banned in 2014 following an assault by one of its drivers but checks have been improved since.

BUS

With the arrival of the metro, travellers rarely use Delhi's public buses, which can get crowded, but there are several useful routes, including the Airport Express bus (₹75) and Bus GL-23, which connects the Kashmere Gate and Anand Vihar bus stations. AC fares are ₹10 to ₹25.

CYCLE-RICKSHAW

Cycle-rickshaws are useful for navigating Old Delhi and the suburbs, but are banned from many parts of New Delhi, including Connaught Place. Negotiate a fare before you set off – expect to pay around ₹10 per kilometre.

METRO

Delhi's **metro** (✆ 011-23417910; www.delhimetrorail.com) is superb: fast and efficient, with signs and arrival/departure announcements in Hindi and English. Trains run from around 6am to 11pm and the first carriage in the direction of travel is reserved for women only. Trains can get insanely busy at peak commuting times (around 9am to 10am and 5pm to 6pm) – avoid travelling with luggage during rush hour if at all possible (however, the Airport Express is always empty, as it's separate from the other lines).

Tokens (₹8 to ₹50) are sold at metro stations. There are also one-/three-day 'tourist cards' (₹150/300, ₹50 deposit, ₹30 refundable when you return it) for unlimited short-distance travel, and a Smart Card (₹150, ₹50 deposit, ₹30 refundable), which can be recharged for amounts from ₹200 to ₹1000 – these make fares 10% cheaper than paying by token.

Because of security concerns, all bags are X-rayed and passengers must pass through an airport-style scanner.

GREATER DELHI

★Qutb Minar Complex HISTORIC SITE

(Map p76; ☎011-26643856; Indian/foreigner ₹30/500, video ₹25, Decorative Light Show Indian/foreigner ₹20/250, audio guide ₹100; ⊙dawn-dusk; M Qutab Minar) If you only have time to visit just one of Delhi's ancient ruins, make it this. The first monuments here were erected by the sultans of Mehrauli, and subsequent rulers expanded on their work, hiring the finest craftsmen and artisans to set in stone the triumph of Muslim rule. The Qutb Festival (p57) of Indian classical music and dance takes place here every October/November. To reach the complex, take the metro to Qutab Minar station, then take an autorickshaw for the 1km to the ruins.

➡ Qutb Minar

(Map p76) The Qutb Minar that gives the complex its name is an unmissable, soaring Afghan-style victory tower and minaret, erected by sultan Qutb-ud-din in 1193 to proclaim his supremacy over the vanquished Hindu rulers of Qila Rai Pithora. Ringed by intricately carved sandstone bands bearing verses from the Quran, the tower stands nearly 73m high and tapers from a 15m-diameter base to a mere 2.5m at the top.

➡ Quwwat-ul-Islam Masjid

(Might of Islam Mosque; Map p76) At the foot of the Qutb Minar stands the first mosque to be built in India. An inscription over the east gate states that it was built with materials obtained from demolishing '27 idolatrous temples'. As well as intricate carvings that show a clear fusion of Islamic and pre-Islamic styles, the walls of the mosque are studded with sun disks, *shikharas* and other recognisable pieces of Hindu and Jain masonry. This was Delhi's main mosque until 1360.

➡ Iron Pillar

(Map p76) In the courtyard of the Quwwat-ul-Islam Masjid is a 6.7m-high iron pillar that is much more ancient than any of the surrounding monuments. It hasn't rusted over the past 1600 years, due to both the dry atmosphere and its incredible purity. A six-line Sanskrit inscription indicates that it was initially erected outside a Vishnu temple, possibly in Bihar, in memory of Chandragupta II, who ruled from AD 375 to 413. Scientists are at a loss as to how the iron was cast using the technology of the time.

★Mehrauli Archaeological Park PARK

(Map p76; ⊙dawn-dusk; M Qutab Minar) FREE There are extraordinary riches scattered around Mehrauli, with more than 440 monuments – from the 10th century to the British era – dotting a forest and the village itself. In the forest, most impressive are the time-ravaged tombs of Balban and Quli Khan, his son, and the Jamali Khamali mosque, attached to the tomb of the Sufi poet Jamali. To the west is the 16th-century Rajon ki Baoli, Delhi's finest step-well, with a monumental flight of steps.

At the northern end of Mehrauli village is Adham Khan's Mausoleum, which was once used as a British residence, then later as a police station and post office. Leading northwards from the tomb are the pre-Islamic walls of Lal Kot.

To the south of the village are the remains of the Mughal palace, the Zafar Mahal, once in the heart of the jungle. Next door to it is the Sufi shrine, the Dargah of Qutb Sahib. There is a small burial ground with one empty space that was intended for the last king of Delhi, Bahadur Shah Zafar, who died in exile in Burma (Myanmar) in 1862. South of here is a Lodi-era burial ground for *hijras* (tranvestites and eunuchs), **Hijron ka Khanqah** (Map p76; Kalka das Marg; ⊙dawn-dusk). The identity of those buried here is unknown, but it's a well-kept, peaceful place, revered by Delhi's *hijra* community. A little further south are Jahaz Mahal ('ship palace', also built by the Mughals) and the **Haus i Shamsi tank** (off Mehrauli-Gurgaon Rd).

You can reach the forested part of the park by turning right from the metro station onto Anuvrat Marg and walking around 500m. A good way to explore the ruins is by guided walking tour.

★Tughlaqabad FORT

(Indian/foreigner ₹15/200, video ₹25; ⊙dawn-dusk; M Tughlakabad) This magnificent 14th-century ruin, half reclaimed by jungle and gradually being encroached on by villages, was Delhi's third incarnation, built by Ghiyas-ud-din Tughlaq. The sultan poached workers from the Sufi saint Nizam-ud-din, who issued a curse that shepherds would inhabit the fort. However, it's monkeys rather than shepherds that have taken over. There are fantastic emerald-green views. Interlinking underground rooms were used as storehouses. To reach the fort, take an autorickshaw from the Tughlakabad metro (one way/return ₹80/160).

Gurgaon (Gurugram)

The area of Gurgaon (Gurugram) is said to have been presented to Guru Dronacharaya in gratitude for his teaching by its rulers, the Kaurava and Pandava, hence its recent Mahabharata-inspired name change to Gurugram. Delhi's foremost satellite city was once a collection of villages and farmland, but its fortunes changed when the car company Maruti Suzuki India Limited set up a manufacturing base here in the 1970s. Change accelerated in the 1990s, and Gurgaon is now a booming new town, a concrete-laden development of telecommunications companies, call centres, malls, office blocks and hotels, with India's third-highest income per capita.

Sights

Sultanpur National Park NATIONAL PARK

(http://haryanaforest.gov.in/SultanpurNationalPark.aspx; Sultanpur; foreigner/Indian ₹40/5, camera/video ₹25/500; 7am-4.30pm) It's incredible to think that Gurgaon is only 15km away from Sultanpur National Park. These wetlands shimmer with local and visiting migratory birds, including kingfishers, flamingoes, geese, teal and storks. It's best to get here in early morning, and you can stay overnight at government-run **Rosy Pelican Tourist Complex** (0120-4355020; r from ₹2175). The easiest way to get here is by taxi from Gurgaon.

Museo Camera MUSEUM

(9810009099; www.indiaphotoarchive.org; T-23/5, DLF Phase III; requested donation per person ₹300; Rapid Metro Phase III) This wonderful museum grew out of the collection of Indian photographer Aditya Arya, with the oldest photographs here dating to the 1880s. Meet the Sinar – the Rolls-Royce of cameras – and the same model of Hasselblad that went to the moon and back. You can also see some incredible early photos, dating to the 1850s.

Sleeping

Gurgaon is full of five-star and luxury business hotels, catering to the many business travellers who stay here, as well as to holidaymakers who fancy luxurious accommodation that's less expensive than in Delhi's city centre, and close to the area's many luxury malls. There is also a smattering of guesthouses and humbler hotels.

Harry's Bed & Breakfast B&B **$$**

(9871699996, 9810158515; www.harrysbedandbreakfast.com; Plot 40, Silver Oaks Avenue, DLF 1; s/d ₹2300/2800; ; M Sikanderpur) The unmistakable aromas of southern spices welcome you into this Tamil-owned B&B in a quiet corner of Gurgaon. Spacious, well-lit rooms have plush interiors and en suite bathrooms, and there's complimentary wi-fi and a sumptuous breakfast. One room comes kitted out with its own tiny garden. With notice, the hosts can rustle up a full Tamil meal.

★ **Tikli Bottom** HOTEL **$$$**

(www.tiklibottom.com; Manender Farm, Gairatpur Bas; s/d incl full board ₹12,000/21,000;) Around 50km south of central Delhi, this peachy Lutyens-style bungalow surrounded by wooded hills, run by a British couple, seems to come from another era, one of toasted teacakes, lawns and chintz. There are four high-ceilinged guest rooms and spacious lounges, plus a beautiful pool with hill views overlooked by a pagoda.

You can also come here for a day, hang out for lunch (adult/aged 12 to 18/under 12 ₹1750/800/300) and explore the countryside with its rambling chickens and emus. For day visitors wanting to swim, the day charge for a room is ₹4500.

Trident HOTEL **$$$**

(www.tridenthotels.com; 443, Udyog Vihar, Phase V, Sector 19; r from ₹15,500; ; M IFFCO Chowk) A contemporary palace, with Mughal-style domes and reflection pools, this has huge rooms and all facilities, and offers good value compared with city-centre five stars. There are excellent eating options and a separate Sunday brunch for kids as well as adults.

Eating

Gurgaon has many great places to eat, though only in the midrange to top-end price brackets, and as it's all so new, places can feel rather soulless. However, not only are there some great hotel restaurants, but there's also DLF Cyber Hub, which is dedicated entirely to gastronomy.

Fat Lulu's PIZZA **$$**
(0124-4245497; Cross Point DLF City IV, DLF Galleria Rd, Gurgaon; pizzas from ₹425; 11.30am-11pm) A delightful little eatery opposite the popular Galleria Market, Fat Lulu's has thin-crust pizzas loaded with toppings, from classic Italian to those with an Indian twist (chicken tikka masala). It has a quirky and colourful dining room that will appeal to those who like a bit of ambience on the side.

DLF Cyber Hub INTERNATIONAL **$$**
(www.dlfcyberhub.com; DLF Cyber City, Phase II, NH8; mains from ₹200; most restaurants 11am-midnight; Rapid Metro DLF Cyber City) This is a food court par excellence, and you'll find any type of cuisine you fancy here. Standouts include **Sodabottleopenerwala**, for Parsi cusine; the cool **Gurgaon Social**, with private rooms; **Farzi Cafe**, for molecular cuisine and cheap beer; the **People & Co** for live comedy; **Yum Yum Cha** for funky decor and pan-Asian food; and **Sion 7** for craft beer brewed on site.

★**Amaranta** SEAFOOD, INDIAN **$$$**
(0124-2451234; The Oberoi, 443 Udyog Vihar, Phase V; mains ₹1900-2100; 12.30-3pm & 7pm-midnight; M IFFCO Chowk) The Oberoi Gurgaon's swish restaurant wins plaudits for its creative Indian cuisine. Its seafood is outstanding, flown in daily from the coast, but for the full experience try a seven- or nine-course tasting menu (veg/non-veg ₹4000/5900).

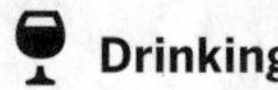

Drinking

Gurgaon has lots of drinking and nightlife options, particularly at DLF Cyber Hub and along Golf Course Rd, and is popular with middle-class locals for a night out, with plenty of bars and restaurants offering live music. DLF Cyber Hub also includes a popular comedy club, the People & Co. As in Delhi, most places only open until 12.30am.

☆ Entertainment

Kingdom of Dreams THEATRE
(0124-4528000; www.kingdomofdreams.in; Auditorium Complex, Sector 29; Culture Gully ₹599 refundable on a purchase, shows from ₹1099 Tue-Fri, ₹1199 Sat & Sun; 12.30pm-midnight Tue-Fri, noon-midnight Sat & Sun, showtimes vary; M IFFCO Chowk) An entertainment extravaganza for lovers of Bollywood cinema, Kingdom of Dreams offers an out-and-out sensory assault. You can take in one of three musicals at the Nautanka Mahal, supported by world-class techno-wizardry, as the cast swing, swoop and sing from the rafters. There's a free shuttle here from the metro every 15 minutes.

Shopping

Gurgaon offers a certain kind of shopping heaven, whole streets lined by flashy malls, with lots of big-name labels and chainstores, plus a few local independent names to spice up the mix, such as **Atelier Mon** (www.ateliermon.com; 27/4, Deodar Marg, Block A, Sector 26A; 11am-6pm Mon-Sat; M Sikanderpur).

Transport

Rapid Metrorail Gurgaon (http://rapidmetrogurgaon.com/home; fare ₹20) This 5km circular track has trains running every five minutes, and connects Sikanderpur with DLF Cyber City.

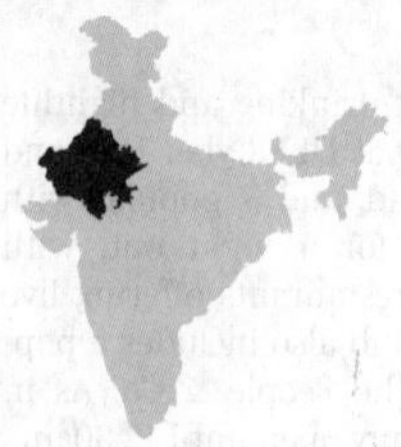

Rajasthan

Includes ➡

Best Forts & Palaces

- ➡ Jaisalmer (p184)
- ➡ Jodhpur (p174)
- ➡ Bundi (p143)
- ➡ Chittorgarh (p149)

Best Heritage Hotels

- ➡ Rambagh Palace (p117)
- ➡ Pal Haveli (p179)
- ➡ Taj Lake Palace (p159)
- ➡ Bundi Vilas (p146)
- ➡ Laxmi Niwas Palace (p198)

Why Go?

It is said there is more history in Rajasthan than in the rest of India put together. Welcome to the Land of the Kings – a realm of maharajas, majestic forts and lavish palaces. India is littered with splendid architecture, but nowhere will you find fortresses quite as magnificent as those in Rajasthan, rising up imperiously from the landscape like fairy-tale mirages or adventure movie sets.

As enchanting as they are, though, there is more to this most royal of regions than its architectural wonders. This is also a land of sand dunes and jungle, of camel trains and wild tigers, of glittering jewels, vivid colours and vibrant culture. There are enough colourful festivals here to fill a calendar, while the shopping and cuisine are nothing short of spectacular. In truth, Rajasthan just about has it all – it is the must-see state of India, brimming with startling, thought-provoking and, ultimately, unforgettable attractions.

When to Go

Jaipur

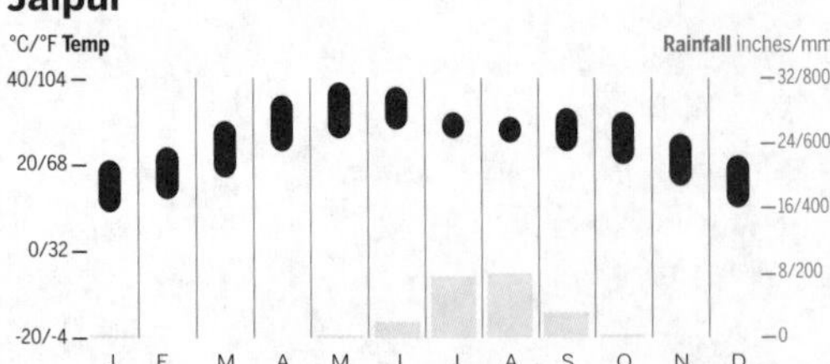

Dec–Feb Pleasant daytime temperatures, but can get cold at night. Peak tourists, peak prices.

Sep–Nov, Feb & Mar Warm nights suit many visitors fleeing colder climes.

Apr–Aug April and June are hot awaiting the monsoon, which brings the rain in July and August.

History

Rajasthan is the ancestral home of the Rajputs, warrior clans who claim to originate from the sun, moon and fire, and who have controlled this part of India for more than 1000 years. While they forged marriages of convenience and temporary alliances, pride and independence were always paramount, and this lack of unity led to the Rajputs becoming vassals of the Mughal empire.

Mughal rule of Rajasthan was marked by rebellion, uprisings and tragedy, as whole cities committed *jauhar* (ritual mass suicide) rather than submit to the Mughals. Nevertheless, As the Mughal empire declined, the Rajputs clawed back their independence and signed treaties with the British allowing individual Rajput kingdoms to operate as independent princely states under the umbrella of British rule.

At Independence, Rajasthan's many maharajas were allowed to keep their titles and property holdings and were paid an annual stipend commensurate with their status to secure their participation in the union. However, this favourable arrangement lapsed in the 1970s and Rajasthan submitted fully to central control.

EASTERN RAJASTHAN

Jaipur

☎0141 / POP 3.05 MILLION

Enthralling, historical Jaipur, Rajasthan's capital, is the gateway to India's most flamboyant state.

The city's colourful, chaotic streets ebb and flow with a heady brew of old and new. Careering buses dodge dawdling camels, leisurely cycle-rickshaws frustrate swarms of motorbikes, and everywhere buzzing autorickshaws watch for easy prey. In the midst of this mayhem, the splendours of Jaipur's majestic past are islands of relative calm evoking a different pace and another world.

At the city's heart, the City Palace continues to house the former royal family; the Jantar Mantar, the royal observatory, maintains a heavenly aspect; and the honeycomb Hawa Mahal gazes on the bazaar below. And just out of sight, in the arid hill country surrounding the city, is the fairy-tale grandeur of Amber Fort, Jaipur's star attraction.

History

Jaipur is named after its founder, the great warrior-astronomer Jai Singh II (1688–1743), who came to power at age 11 after the death of his father, Maharaja Bishan Singh. Jai Singh could trace his lineage back to the Rajput clan of Kachhwahas, who consolidated their power in the 12th century. Their capital was at Amber (pronounced 'amer'), about 11km northeast of present-day Jaipur, where they built the impressive Amber Fort.

The kingdom grew wealthier and wealthier, and this, plus the need to accommodate the burgeoning population and a paucity of water at the old capital at Amber, prompted the maharaja in 1727 to commence work on a new city – Jaipur.

Northern India's first planned city, it was a collaborative effort using Singh's vision and the impressive expertise of his chief architect, Vidyadhar Bhattacharya. Jai Singh's grounding in the sciences is reflected in the precise symmetry of the new city.

In 1876 Maharaja Ram Singh had the entire Old City painted pink (traditionally the colour of hospitality) to welcome the Prince of Wales (later King Edward VII). Today all residents of the Old City are compelled by law to preserve the pink facade.

Sights

Old City (Pink City)

The Old City (often referred to as the Pink City) is both a marvel of 18th-century town planning, and a place you could spend days exploring – it's the beating heart of Jaipur.

Avenues divide the Pink City into neat rectangles, each specialising in certain crafts, as ordained in the Shilpa Shastra (ancient Hindu texts). The main bazaars in the Old City include Johari Bazaar, Tripolia Bazaar, Bapu Bazaar and Chandpol Bazaar.

The whole is partially encircled by a crenellated wall punctuated at intervals by grand gateways. The major gates are Chandpol (*pol* means 'gate'), Ajmer Gate and Sanganeri Gate.

★City Palace PALACE

(☎0141-4088888; www.royaljaipur.in; Indian/foreigner incl camera ₹130/500, guide from ₹300, audio guide free, Royal Grandeur tour Indian/foreigner ₹2000/2500; ⏲9.30am-5pm) A complex of courtyards, gardens and buildings, the impressive City Palace is right in the centre of the Old City. The outer wall was built by Jai

Rajasthan Highlights

❶ **Jaisalmer** (p184) Wandering the bustling alleys of the honey-coloured fort, then riding a camel among desert dunes.

❷ **Pushkar** (p136) Making a lakeside pilgrimage to Rajasthan's holiest town.

❸ **Ranthambhore National Park** (p141) Searching for tigers in the ravines and forests.

❹ **Mehrangarh** (p175) Taking in the views of the Blue City from the imposing ramparts of Jodhpur's mighty fortress.

❺ **Udaipur** (p152) Kicking back in Rajasthan's romantic idyll with palaces and a picturesque lake.

❻ **Pink City** (p105) Wandering the colourful bazaars of Jaipur and the marvellous Amber Fort.

❼ **Bundi** (p143) Resting up in this town with its low-key backpacker vibe, fairy-tale palace and a solemn fort.

❽ **Shekhawati** (p173) Admiring the whimsical frescos adorning the crumbling havelis.

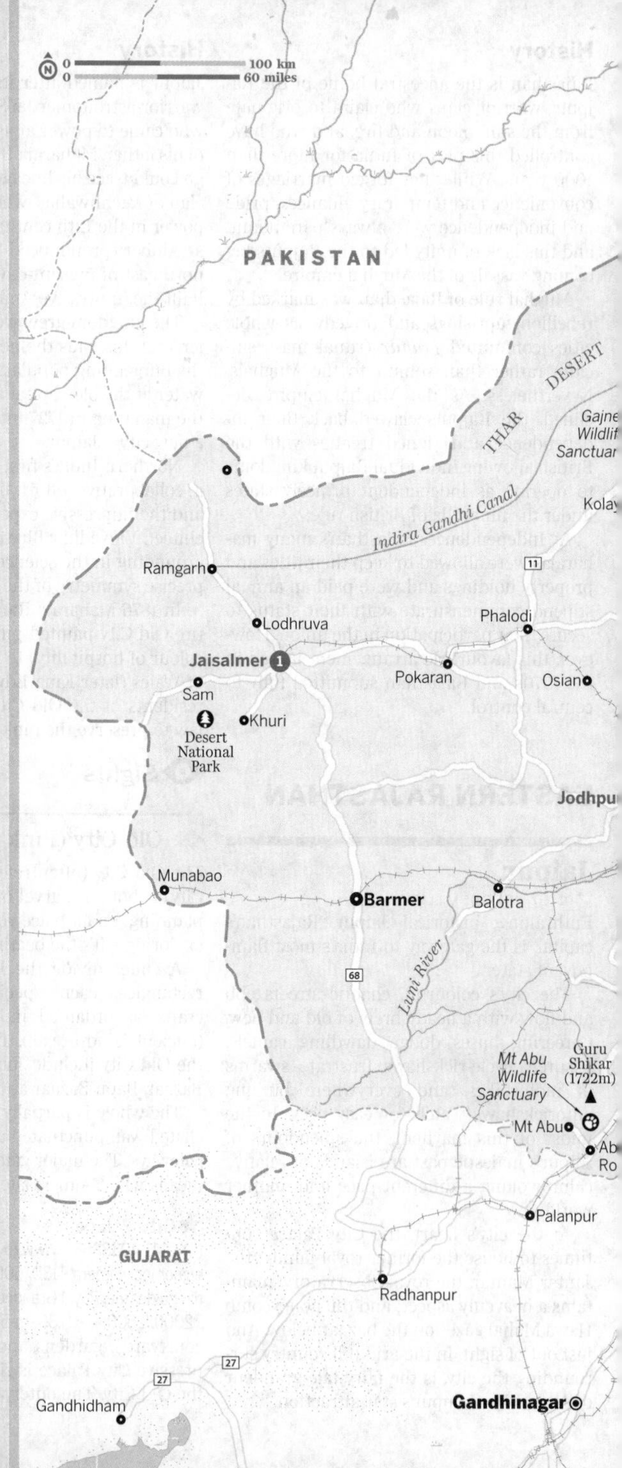

Ganganagar
Sirsa
HARYANA
UTTAR PRADESH
Yamuna River
Suratgarh
Anupgarh
Hisar
Rajgarh
DELHI
Churu
Shekhawati
8
Rewari
Ratangarh
Ramgarh
Jhunjhunu
Bikaner
Mandawa
Fatehpur
Neemrana
Deshnok
Tal Chhapar Wildlife Sanctuary
Nawalgarh
Patan
Udaipurvati
Kotputli
Nokha
Sikar
Alwar
Deeg
Mathura
Shahpura
Nagaur
Sariska Tiger Reserve & National Park
Bharatpur
Agra
Amber
Abhaneri
Fatehpur Sikri
Keoladeo National Park
Jaipur
6
Dausa
Sambhar Salt Lake
Bagru
Sanganer
Dholpur
Pushkar
2
Kishangarh
Ajmer
Karauli
Ranthambhore National Park
3
Saraswati River
Tonk
Beawar
Sawai Madhopur
Kekri
Pali
Deoli
Deogarh
7
Bundi
Shivpuri
Bhilwara
Kumbhalgarh
Rajsamand
Bijolia
Kota
Saira
Baroli
Chittorgarh
Bijaipur
Udaipur
5
Jhalawar
Jhalrapatan
Gandhi Sagar
Jaisamand Lake
MADHYA PRADESH
Dungarpur
Banswara
Ratlam
Bhopal
Ujjain
9
44
48
19
52
21
46

Jaipur

Singh II, but within it the palace has been enlarged and adapted over the centuries. There are palace buildings from different eras, some dating from the early 20th century. It is a striking blend of Rajasthani and Mughal architecture.

The price of admission includes entry to Royal Gaitor and the Cenotaphs of the Maharanis, as well as to Jaigarh, a long climb above Amber Fort. This composite ticket is valid for two days and costs Indians an extra

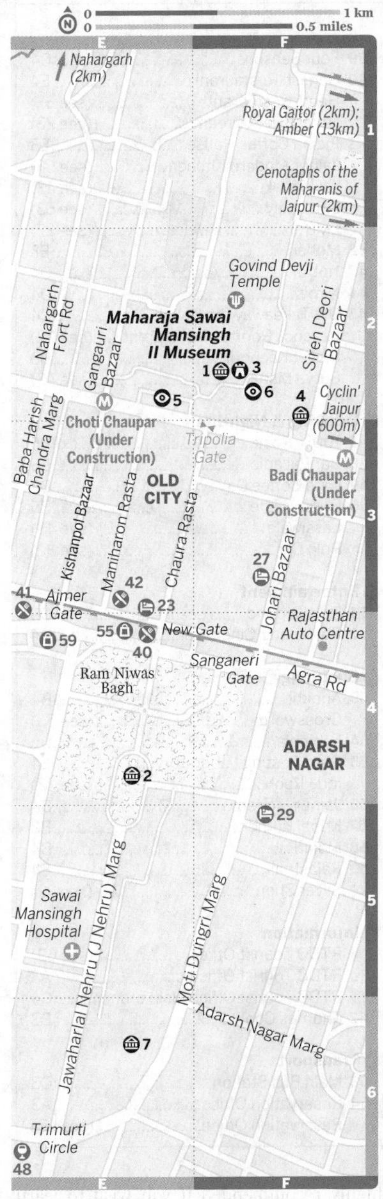

₹60 on top of City Palace entry (no extra cost for foreigners).

➡ **Mubarak Mahal**

Entering through Virendra Pol, you'll see the Mubarak Mahal (Welcome Palace), built in the late 19th century for Maharaja Madho Singh II as a reception centre for visiting dignitaries. Its multiarched and colonnaded construction was cooked up in an Islamic, Rajput and European stylistic stew by the architect Sir Swinton Jacob. It now forms part of the **Maharaja Sawai Mansingh II Museum**, containing a collection of royal costumes and superb shawls, including Kashmiri pashmina. One remarkable exhibit is Sawai Madho Singh I's capacious clothing; it's said he was a cuddly 2m tall, 1.2m wide and 250kg.

➡ **The Armoury**

The Anand Mahal Sileg Khana – the Maharani's Palace – houses the Armoury, which has one of the best collections of weapons in the country. Many of the ceremonial items are elegantly engraved and inlaid, belying their grisly purpose.

➡ **Diwan-i-Khas (Sarvatobhadra)**

Set between the Armoury and the Diwan-i-Am art gallery is an open courtyard known in Sanskrit as Sarvatobhadra. At its centre is a pink-and-white, marble-paved gallery that was used as the Diwan-i-Khas (Hall of Private Audience), where the maharajas would consult their ministers. Here you can see two enormous silver vessels, each 1.6m tall and reputedly the largest silver objects in the world.

➡ **Diwan-i-Am Art Gallery**

Within the lavish Diwan-i-Am (Hall of Public Audience) is this art gallery. Exhibits include a copy of the entire Bhagavad Gita (scripture) handwritten in tiny script, and miniature copies of other holy Hindu scriptures, which were small enough to be easily hidden in the event that zealot Mughal armies tried to destroy the sacred texts.

➡ **Pitam Niwas Chowk & Chandra Mahal**

Located towards the palace's inner courtyard is Pitam Niwas Chowk. Here four glorious gates represent the seasons – the **Peacock Gate** depicts autumn, the **Lotus Gate** signifies summer, the **Green Gate** represents spring, and finally the **Rose Gate** embodies winter.

Beyond this *chowk* (square) is the private palace, the Chandra Mahal, which is still the residence of the descendants of the royal family and where you can take a 45-minute **Royal Grandeur guided tour** of select areas.

★ **Jantar Mantar** HISTORIC SITE
(Indian/foreigner ₹50/200, guide ₹200, audio guide ₹100; 9am-4.30pm) Adjacent to the

Jaipur

Top Sights

1 Maharaja Sawai Mansingh II Museum ... F2

Sights

2 Central Museum ... E4
3 City Palace ... F2
4 Hawa Mahal ... F2
5 Iswari Minar Swarga Sal ... E2
6 Jantar Mantar ... F2
7 SRC Museum of Indology ... E6

Activities, Courses & Tours

8 Charak Ayurveda ... B2
9 Kerala Ayurveda Kendra ... A1
10 Kripal Kumbh ... B2
11 Madhavanand Girls College ... A2
12 Mansingh Hotel ... C3
RTDC ... (see 60)
Vintage Jeep Tour ... (see 31)

Sleeping

13 All Seasons Homestay ... B4
14 Alsisar Haveli ... C3
15 Atithi Guest House ... B3
16 Dera Rawatsar ... C2
17 Hotel Anuraag Villa ... A2
18 Hotel Arya Niwas ... C3
19 Hotel Bissau Palace ... D1
20 Hotel Diggi Palace ... D5
21 Hotel Meghniwas ... A2
22 Hotel Pearl Palace ... B4
23 Hotel Sweet Dream ... E3
24 Jaipur Inn ... B2
25 Jas Vilas ... A2
26 Karni Niwas ... C3
27 LMB Hotel ... F3
28 Madhuban ... A2
29 Nana-ki-Haveli ... F5
30 Narain Niwas Palace Hotel ... D6
31 Pearl Palace Heritage ... B4
32 Rambagh Palace ... D6
33 Roadhouse Hostel Jaipur ... B4
34 Shahpura House ... A2
35 Tony Guest House ... B3
36 Vinayak Guest House ... A3

Eating

Anokhi Café ... (see 53)
37 Copper Chimney ... C4
38 Dãsaprakash ... D4
39 Four Seasons ... C4
40 Ganesh Restaurant ... E4
Handi Restaurant ... (see 37)
Hotel Sweet Dream ... (see 23)
41 Indian Coffee House ... E3
Jaipur Modern Kitchen ... (see 56)
Jal Mahal ... (see 43)
Little Italy ... (see 53)
LMB ... (see 27)
42 Mohan ... E3
43 Natraj ... D4
44 Niro's ... D4
45 Old Takeaway the Kebab Shop ... C4
Peacock Rooftop Restaurant ... (see 22)
46 Rawat Kachori ... B3
Surya Mahal ... (see 43)

Drinking & Nightlife

47 100% Rock ... B5
48 Bar Palladio ... E6
49 Café Coffee Day ... B3
50 Curious Life ... B5
Lassiwala ... (see 43)
Polo Bar ... (see 32)

Entertainment

51 Polo Ground ... C6
52 Raj Mandir Cinema ... D4

Shopping

53 Anokhi ... B4
Crossword ... (see 53)
54 Fabindia ... D5
55 Gem-Testing Laboratory ... E4
Inde Rooh ... (see 22)
56 Jaipur Modern ... B4
57 Kripal Kumbh ... B2
58 Mojari ... B4
59 Rajasthali ... E4
Silver Shop ... (see 22)

Information

RTDC Tourist Office ... (see 63)
60 RTDC Tourist Office ... A3
61 RTDC Tourist Office Main branch ... C4
62 Thomas Cook ... B3

Transport

63 Main Bus Station ... C3
64 Reservation Office ... A3
Reservation Office ... (see 63)

City Palace is Jantar Mantar, an observatory begun by Jai Singh II in 1728 that resembles a collection of bizarre giant sculptures. Built for measuring the heavens, the name is derived from the Sanskrit *yanta mantr,* meaning 'instrument of calculation', and in 2010 it was added to India's list of Unesco World Heritage Sites. Paying for a local guide is highly recommended if you wish to learn how each fascinating instrument works.

Jai Singh liked astronomy even more than he liked war and town planning. Before constructing the observatory he sent scholars abroad to study foreign constructs. He built five observatories in total, and this is the largest and best preserved (it was restored in 1901). Others are in Delhi, Varanasi and Ujjain. No traces of the fifth, the Mathura observatory, remain.

A valid Amber Fort/Hawa Mahal composite ticket will also gain you entry.

★**Hawa Mahal** HISTORIC BUILDING
(Sireh Deori Bazaar; Indian/foreigner incl camera ₹50/200, guide ₹200, audio guide Hindi/English ₹115/170; ⏲9am-5.30pm) Jaipur's most distinctive landmark, the Hawa Mahal is an extraordinary pink-painted delicately honeycombed hive that rises a dizzying five storeys. It was constructed in 1799 by Maharaja Sawai Pratap Singh to enable ladies of the royal household to watch the life and processions of the city. The top offers stunning views over Jantar Mantar and the City Palace in one direction and over Sireh Deori Bazaar in the other.

There's a small **museum** (open Saturday to Thursday), with miniature paintings and some rich relics, such as ceremonial armour, which help evoke the royal past.

Claustrophobes should be aware that the narrow corridors can sometimes get extremely cramped and crowded inside the Hawa Mahal.

Entrance is from the back of the complex. To get here, return to the intersection on your left as you face the Hawa Mahal, turn right and then take the first right again through an archway. Shopkeepers can show you another way – past their shops!

A valid Amber Fort composite ticket will also gain you entry.

DON'T MISS

HEAVEN-PIERCING MINARET

Piercing the skyline near the City Palace is this unusual minaret, **Iswari Minar Swarga Sal** (Heaven-Piercing Minaret; Indian/foreigner ₹50/200; ⏲9am-4.30pm) erected in the 1740s by Jai Singh II's son and successor Iswari. The entrance is around the back of the row of shops fronting Chandpol Bazaar – take the alley 50m west of the minaret along the bazaar or go via the Atishpol entrance to the City Palace compound, 150m east of the minaret. You can spiral to the top of the minaret for excellent views.

Iswari ignominiously killed himself by snakebite (in the Chandra Mahal) rather than face the advancing Maratha army – his 21 wives and concubines then did the necessary noble thing and committed *jauhar* (ritual mass suicide by immolation) on his funeral pyre.

A valid Amber Fort/Hawa Mahal composite ticket will also gain you entry.

New City

By the mid-19th century it became obvious that the well-planned city was bulging at the seams. During the reign of Maharaja Ram Singh (1835–80) the seams ruptured and the city burst out beyond its walls. Civic facilities, such as a postal system and piped water, were introduced. This period gave rise to a part of town very different from the bazaars of the Old City, with wide boulevards, landscaped grounds and grand European-influenced buildings.

Central Museum MUSEUM
(Albert Hall; J Nehru Marg; Indian/foreigner ₹40/300, audio guide Hindi/English ₹115/175; ⏲9am-6pm) This museum is housed in the spectacularly florid Albert Hall, south of the Old City. The building was designed by Sir Swinton Jacob, and combines elements of English and North Indian architecture, as well as huge friezes celebrating the world's great cultures. It was known as the pride of the new Jaipur when it opened in 1887. The grand old building hosts an eclectic array of tribal dress, dioramas, sculptures, miniature paintings, carpets, musical instruments and even an Egyptian mummy.

SRC Museum of Indology MUSEUM
(24 Gangwell Park, Prachyavidya Path; Indian/foreigner incl guide ₹40/100; ⏲8am-6pm) This ramshackle, dusty treasure trove is an extraordinary private collection. It contains folk-art objects and other pieces – there's everything from a manuscript written by Aurangzeb and a 200-year-old mirror work swing from Bikaner to a glass bed (for a short queen). The museum is signposted off J Nehru Barg.

City Edge

Surrounding the city are several historic sites including forts, temples, palaces and gardens. Some of these can be visited on the way to Amber Fort.

Nahargarh FORT
(Tiger Fort; Indian/foreigner ₹50/200; ⏲10am-5pm) Built in 1734 and extended in 1868, this sturdy fort overlooks the city from a sheer ridge to the north. The story goes that the

fort was named after Nahar Singh, a dead prince whose restless spirit was disrupting construction. Whatever was built in the day crumbled in the night. The prince agreed to leave on condition that the fort was named for him. The views are glorious and there's a restaurant that's perfect for a beer.

The best way to visit is to walk or take a cycle-rickshaw (₹50 from MI Rd) to the end of Nahargarh Fort Rd, then climb the steep, winding 2km path to the top. To drive, you have to detour via the Amber area in a circuitous 8km round trip.

A valid Amber Fort/Hawa Mahal composite ticket will also gain you entry.

Royal Gaitor HISTORIC SITE
(Gatore ki Chhatriyan; Indian/foreigner ₹40/100; ⌚9am-5pm) The royal cenotaphs, just outside the city walls, beneath Nahargarh, are an appropriately restful place to visit and feel remarkably undiscovered. The stone monuments are beautifully and intricately carved. Maharajas Pratap Singh, Madho Singh II and Jai Singh II, among others, are honoured here. Jai Singh II has the most impressive marble cenotaph, with a dome supported by 20 carved pillars.

Jal Mahal HISTORIC BUILDING
(Water Palace; ⌚closed to the public) Near the cenotaphs of the maharanis of Jaipur, and beautifully situated in the watery expanse of Man Sagar, is this dreamlike palace. It's origins are uncertain, but it was believed to have been extensively restored if not built by Jai Singh II (1734). It's accessed via a causeway at the rear, and is undergoing restoration under the auspices of the Jal Tarang (www.jaltarang.in) project.

Cenotaphs of the Maharanis of Jaipur HISTORIC SITE
(Maharani ki Chhatri; Amber Rd; Indian/foreigner ₹40/100; ⌚9am-5pm) Located between Jaipur and Amber, 5km from the centre, the cenotaphs of the maharanis of Jaipur are worth a visit for a stroll.

Galta HINDU TEMPLE
Squeezed between cliffs in a rocky valley, Galta is a desolate, if evocative, place. The temple houses a number of sacred tanks, into which some daring souls jump from the adjacent cliffs. The water is claimed to be several elephants deep and fed from a spring that falls through the mouth of a sculpted cow.

There are some original frescos in reasonable condition in a chamber at the end of the bottom pool, including those depicting athletic feats, the maharaja playing polo, and the exploits of Krishna and the *gopis* (milkmaids).

It is also known as the Monkey Temple and you will find hundreds of monkeys living here – bold and aggressive macaques and more graceful and tolerable langurs. You can purchase peanuts at the gate to feed to them, but be prepared to be mobbed by teeth-barring primates.

Although only a few kilometres east of the City Palace, Galta is about 10km by road from central Jaipur. An autorickshaw should charge around ₹300 return with waiting time, a taxi will charge at least ₹600.

TOP STATE FESTIVALS

Jaisalmer Desert Festival (⌚Jan/Feb) A chance for moustache twirlers to compete in the Mr Desert contest.

Gangaur (⌚Mar/Apr) A festival honouring Shiva and Parvati's love, celebrated statewide but with fervour in Jaipur.

Mewar Festival (p157) Udaipur's version of Gangaur, with free cultural events and a colourful procession down to the lake.

Teej (⌚Jul/Aug) Jaipur and Bundi honour the arrival of the monsoon and Shiva and Parvati's marriage.

Dussehra Mela (⌚Oct/Nov) Commemorates Rama's victory over Ravana (the demon king of Lanka). It's a spectacular time to visit Kota – the huge fair features 22m-tall firecracker-stuffed effigies.

Marwar Festival (p178) Celebrates Rajasthani heroes through music and dance; one day is held in Jodhpur, the other in Osian.

Pushkar Camel Fair (p138) The most famous festival in the state; it's a massive congregation of camels, horses and cattle, pilgrims and tourists.

On the ridge above Galta is the **Surya Mandir** (Temple of the Sun God), which rises 100m above Jaipur and can be seen from the eastern side of the city. A 2.5km-long walking trail climbs up to the temple from Suraj Pol, or you can walk up from the Galta side. There are hazy views over the humming city.

Activities

Several hotels will let you use their pool for a daily fee; try those at Narain Niwas Palace Hotel (p117) and **Mansingh Hotel** (Sansar Chandra Marg; nonguests ₹350; 7am-8pm).

Kerala Ayurveda Kendra AYURVEDA
(0141-4022446; www.keralaayurvedakendra.com; 32 Indra Colony, Bani Park; 9am-9pm) Is Jaipur making your nerves jangle? Get help through ayurvedic massage and therapy. Treatments include *sirodhara* (₹1500/2400 for 50/90 minutes), where medicated oil is steadily streamed over your forehead to reduce stress, tone the brain and help with sleep disorders. Massages (male therapist for male clients and female for female clients) cost from ₹500 for 55 minutes.

It offers free transport to/from your hotel.

Charak Ayurveda AYURVEDA
(0141-2205628; www.charakayurveda.com; E-7 Kantichandra Marg, Bani Park; 9am-2pm & 3-7pm Mon-Sat, 9am-1pm Sun) A full range of ayurvedic treatments are available. Massages start at ₹500.

Yog Sadhna Ashram YOGA
(9314011884; www.yogsadhnaindia.org; Bapu Nagar; Wed-Mon) Free classes take place among trees off University Rd (near Rajasthan University) and incorporate breathing exercises, yoga asanas (postures) and exercise. Most of the classes are in Hindi, but some English is spoken in the 7.30am to 9.30am class. You can visit for individual classes, or register for longer courses.

Madhavanand Girls College YOGA
(C19 Behari Marg, Bani Park; 6-7am) This college runs free casual yoga classes every day in both Hindi and English. Very convenient if you happen to be lodging in Bani Park – the college is next door to Madhuban hotel.

Courses

Jaipur Cooking Classes COOKING
(9928097288; www.jaipurcookingclasses.com; 33 Gyan Vihar, Nirman Nagar, near Ajmer Rd; class veg/nonveg from ₹2000/3700) Popular cooking classes with chef Lokesh Mathur, who boasts more than 25 years' experience working in the restaurant and hotel business. Classes cover both classic dishes and Rajasthani menus and can be veg or nonveg. After a three-hour lesson, you sit down for a lunch or dinner of what you've prepared. Lokesh's kitchen is outside the western outskirts of Jaipur.

Call ahead for exact directions for your autorickshaw driver.

Kripal Kumbh ART
(0141-2201127; B18A Shiv Marg, Bani Park) Advance bookings are essential for these free lessons in blue pottery. Lessons aren't possible during the monsoon, from late June to mid-September. There's also a **showroom** (www.kripalkumbh.com; 9.30am-6pm Mon-Sat).

Dhamma Thali Vipassana Meditation Centre HEALTH & WELLBEING
(0141-2680220; www.thali.dhamma.org; courses by donation) This serene *vipassana* meditation centre is tucked away in the hilly countryside near Galta, a 12km drive east of the city centre. It runs courses in meditation for both beginners and more advanced students throughout the year. Courses are usually for 10 days, during which you must observe noble silence – no communication with others.

Tours

Cyclin' Jaipur CYCLING
(7728060956; www.cyclinjaipur.com; 4hr tour ₹2000; tour 6.45am) Get up early to beat the traffic for a tour of the Pink City by bike, exploring the hidden lanes, temples, markets and food stalls of Jaipur. It's a unique and fun way to learn about the workings and culture of the city. Breakfast and refreshments during the tour are included, and helmets are provided on demand.

Tours start at Karnot Mahal, on Ramganj Chaupar in the Old City. Tailor-made walking and food tours are also available.

Vintage Jeep Tour SIGHTSEEING
(9829404055, 0141-2373700; www.pearlpalaceheritage.com/exclusive-vintage-jeep-tour-jaipur; Lane 2, 54 Gopal Bari; per person ₹2500; 9am-5.30pm) A fun way to explore Jaipur's major sights (including Amber and the City Palace) is by jeep – a genuine US Army 1942 Ford Jeep. With a dedicated driver and a guide on board, you are guaranteed to be part of a small tour group (maximum three guests), giving great flexibility. Admission prices and lunch costs are not included.

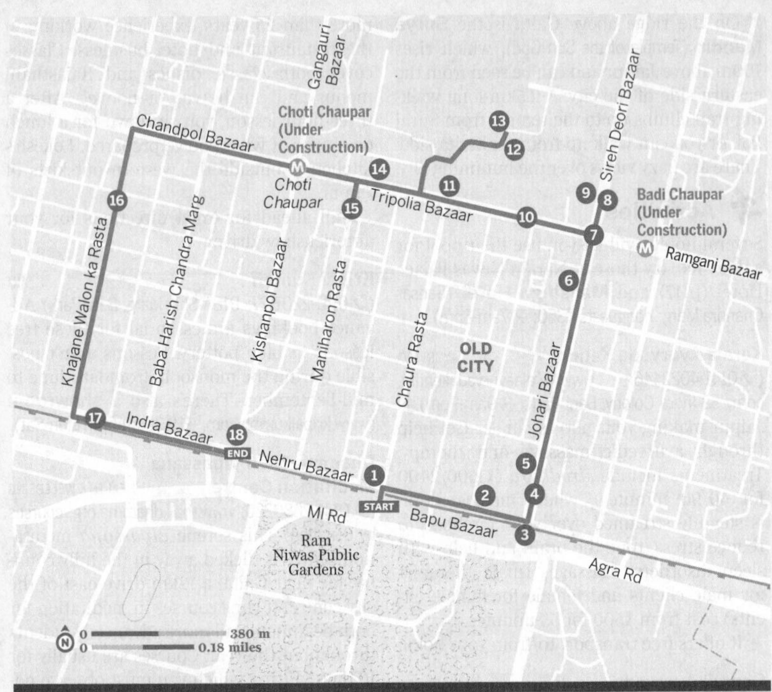

Walking Tour Pink City

START NEW GATE
END AJMER GATE
LENGTH 4.5KM; THREE TO FIVE HOURS

Entering the old city from **1 New Gate**, turn right into **2 Bapu Bazaar**, inside the city wall. Brightly coloured bolts of fabric, jootis (traditional shoes) and aromatic perfumes make the street a favourite destination for Jaipur's women. At the end of Bapu Bazaar you'll come to **3 Sanganeri Gate**. Turn left into **4 Johari Bazaar**, the jewellery market, where you will find jewellers, goldsmiths and artisans doing highly glazed meenakari (enamelwork), a speciality of Jaipur.

Continuing north you'll pass the famous **5 LMB Hotel**, the **6 Jama Masjid**, with its tall minarets, and the bustling **7 Badi Chaupar**. Be very careful crossing the road here. To the north is **8 Sireh Deori Bazaar**, also known as Hawa Mahal Bazaar. The name is derived from the spectacular **9 Hawa Mahal** (p111), a short distance to the north. Turning left on **10 Tripolia Bazaar**, you will see a lane leading to the entrance to the Hawa Mahal. A few hundred metres west is the **11 Tripolia Gate**. This is the main entrance to the **12 Jantar Mantar** (p109) and **13 City Palace** (p105), but only the maharaja's family may enter here. The public entrance is via the less ostentatious Atishpol (Stable Gate), a little further along.

After visiting the City Palace complex, head back to Tripolia Bazaar and resume your walk west past **14 Iswari Minar Swarga Sal** (p111), which is well worth the climb for the view. Cross the bazaar at the minaret and head west. The next lane on the left is **15 Maniharon Rasta**, the best place to buy colourful lac (resin) bangles.

Back on Tripolia Bazaar, continue west to cross Choti Chaupar to Chandpol Bazaar until you reach a traffic light. Turn left into **16 Khajane Walon ka Rasta**, where you'll find marble and stoneware carvers at work. Continue south until you reach a broad road just inside the city wall, **17 Indra Bazaar**. Follow the road east towards **18 Ajmer Gate**, which marks the end of the tour.

RTDC TOURS

(☎2200778; tours@rtdc.in; RTDC Tourist Office, Platform 1, Jaipur Train Station; half-/full-day tour ₹400/500; ⏲8am-6.30pm Mon-Sat) Full-day tours (9am to 6pm) take in all the major sights of Jaipur (including Amber Fort), with a lunch break at Nahargarh. The lunch break can be as late as 3pm, so have a big breakfast. Rushed half-day tours (8am to 1pm, 11.30am to 4.30pm, and 1.30pm to 6.30pm) still squeeze in Amber. The tour price doesn't include admission charges.

Departing at 6.30pm, the **Pink City by Night tour** (₹700) explores several well-known sights and includes dinner at Nahargarh.

Tours depart from Jaipur train station; the company also picks up and takes bookings from the RTDC Hotel Teej, RTDC Hotel Gangaur and the tourist office at the main bus station.

Sleeping

Jaipur accommodation pretty much covers all bases, and travellers are spoiled for choice in all budget categories. From May to September, most midrange and top-end hotels offer bargain rates, dropping prices by 25% to 50%.

Around MI Road

★Hotel Pearl Palace HOTEL $

(☎0141-2373700, 9414236323; www.hotelpearlpalace.com; Hari Kishan Somani Marg, Hathroi Fort; dm ₹400, r with AC ₹1310-1910; ❄@📶) The dependable Pearl Palace continues to surprise. Ongoing renovations means many excellent rooms simply defy their ordinary tariffs. There's quite a range of rooms to choose from – small, large, some with AC or fan cooling, and all are spotless. Services include money changing, city tours and travel arrangements, and the hotel boasts the excellent Peacock Rooftop Restaurant (p118). Advance booking is recommended.

Karni Niwas GUESTHOUSE $

(☎0141-2365433, 9929777488; www.hotelkarniniwas.com; C5 Motilal Atal Marg; r ₹1000, with AC ₹1500; ❄@📶) This friendly hotel has clean, cool and comfortable rooms, often with balconies. There's no restaurant, but there are relaxing plant-decked terraces to enjoy room service on. And being so central, restaurants aren't far away. The owner shuns commissions for rickshaw drivers; free pick-up from the train or bus station is available.

Roadhouse Hostel Jaipur HOSTEL $

(☎9945522299; www.roadhousehostels.com; D-76 Shiv Heera Path; dm/s/d ₹300/1000/1200; ❄📶) This bright and friendly hostel is in a quiet residential part of town, but it's not too far from all the restaurants on MI Rd. Six- and eight-bed dorms are spotless and air-conditioned and there are a couple of private rooms. There is a free-use kitchen and games room, and management will help with transport tickets.

There's a handy rickshaw stand at the end of the road.

Tony Guest House GUESTHOUSE $

(☎9928871717; www.facebook.com/tonyguesthousejaipur; 11 Station Road; dm/s/d ₹180/280/340, r with bathroom ₹600; ⊖@📶) This friendly choice on a busy road is well set up for travellers and backpackers on a tight budget, with a rooftop garden, honest travel advice, internet and free-flowing chai. Rooms are extremely basic, some with plywood partition walls, and only one has a private bathroom, although it's with a cold-water shower. The common shower is hot.

★Atithi Guest House GUESTHOUSE $$

(☎0141-2378679; www.atithijaipur.com; 1 Park House Scheme Rd; s/d ₹1200/1310, with AC ₹1530/1750; ❄@📶) This nicely presented modern guesthouse, well situated between MI and Station Rds, offers strikingly clean, simple rooms dotted around a quiet courtyard. It's central but peaceful, and the service is friendly and helpful. Meals are available (the thali is particularly recommended) and you can have a drink on the very pleasant rooftop terrace.

Pearl Palace Heritage HOTEL $$

(☎0141-4106599, 9772558855; www.pearlpalaceheritage.com; Lane 2, 54 Gopal Bari; r ₹3260-3815; ❄📶) The second hotel for the successful Pearl Palace team is a midrange property boasting some very special characteristics. Stone carvings adorn the halls and each spacious room vibrantly recreates an individual cultural theme, such as a village hut, a sandstone fort, or a mirror-lined palace boudoir. Modern luxuries and facilities have been carefully integrated into the appealing traditional designs.

Dera Rawatsar HOTEL $$

(☎0141-2200770; www.derarawatsar.com; D194 Vijay Path; r incl breakfast ₹4500-5500, ste ₹8000; ❄@📶🏊) Situated in a quiet suburban street and yet close to the bus station, this tranquil hotel is managed by three generations of women of a gracious Bikaner noble family. The hotel has a range of lovely decorated rooms, sunny courtyards, and offers home-style Indian meals. It is an excellent choice for young families and solo female travellers.

All Seasons Homestay HOMESTAY $$
(☎0141-2369443, 9460387055; www.allseasonshomestayjaipur.com; 63 Hathroi Fort; s/d from ₹1600/1700, deluxe ₹2000;) Ranjana and her husband Dinesh run this welcoming homestay in their lovely bungalow on a quiet backstreet behind Hathroi Fort. There are 10 pristine guest rooms, two of which have small kitchens for longer stays. There's a pleasant lawn, home-cooked meals and cooking lessons. Advance booking is recommended.

Nana-ki-Haveli HERITAGE HOTEL $$
(☎0141-2615502; www.nanakihaveli.com; Fateh Tiba; r ₹1800-3000;) Tucked-away off Moti Dungri Marg is this tranquil place with attractive, comfortable rooms decorated with traditional flourishes (discreet wall painting, wooden furniture). It's hosted by a lovely family and is a good choice for solo female travellers. It's fronted by a relaxing lawn and offers home-style cooking and discounted rooms in summer.

Hotel Arya Niwas HOTEL $$
(☎0141-4073456; www.aryaniwas.com; Sansar Chandra Marg; s ₹1635-2725, d ₹2350-3110;) Just off Sansar Chandra Marg, behind a high-rise tower, this very popular travellers' haunt has a travel desk, bookshop and yoga lessons. For a hotel of 92 rooms it is very well run, though its size means it's not as personal as smaller guesthouses. The spotless rooms vary in layout and size so check out a few.

Outside, there's an extensive terrace facing a soothing expanse of lawn. The self-service vegetarian restaurant doesn't sell beer, but you can bring your own.

Alsisar Haveli HERITAGE HOTEL $$$
(☎0141-2368290; www.alsisar.com; Sansar Chandra Marg; s/d from ₹7605/10,530;) This genuine heritage hotel housed in a gracious 19th-century mansion is set in beautiful green gardens, and boasts a lovely swimming pool and grand dining room. Its bedrooms don't disappoint either, with elegant Rajput arches and antique furnishings. Though a little impersonal, perhaps because it hosts many tour groups, occasional discounts can be found by booking directly online.

Hotel Diggi Palace HERITAGE HOTEL $$$
(☎0141-2373091; www.hoteldiggipalace.com; off Sawai Ram Singh Rd; s/d incl breakfast from ₹4000/5000;) About 1km south of Ajmer Gate, this former residence of the *thakur* (nobleman) of Diggi is surrounded by vast shaded lawns. Once a budget hotel, the more expensive rooms are substantially better than the cheaper options. Management prides itself on using organic produce from the hotel's own gardens and farms in the restaurant.

Bani Park

The Bani Park area is relatively peaceful, away from the main roads, about 2km west of the Old City (northwest of MI Rd).

Vinayak Guest House HOTEL $
(☎0141-2205260; vinayakguesthouse@yahoo.co.in; 4 Kabir Marg, Bani Park; r ₹500-1100;) This welcoming guesthouse is actually in a small, quiet street behind busy Kabir Marg, very convenient to the train station. There is a variety of different rooms and tariffs; those with air-con also have great renovated bathrooms and are your best option. The vegetarian restaurant on the rooftop gets good reports.

★Madhuban HOTEL $$
(☎0141-2200033; www.madhuban.net; D237 Behari Marg; s/d/ste from ₹2290/2615/3865;) Madhuban has bright, antique-furnished, spotlessly clean rooms, plus a private enclosed garden for alfresco meals. The vibrantly frescoed restaurant serves Rajasthani specialities in addition to Continental and North Indian dishes, and sits beside the courtyard plunge pool. The relatively peaceful locale of Bani Park makes this place a comfortable stay. Bus and train station pick-up available.

Hotel Anuraag Villa HOTEL $$
(☎0141-2201679; www.anuraagvilla.com; D249 Devi Marg; s/d ₹1080/1310, with AC from ₹1800/1970;) This quiet and comfortable option has no-fuss, spacious rooms and an extensive lawn where you can find some quiet respite from the hassles of sightseeing. It has a highly commended vegetarian restaurant with its kitchen on view, and efficient, helpful staff.

Jaipur Inn HOTEL $$
(☎9829013660, 0141-2201121; www.jaipurinn.com; B17 Shiv Marg, Bani Park; r from ₹1500-2000; ❄@📶) Once a budget travellers' favourite, this is now a midrange hotel offering an assortment of eclectic and individual rooms. Inspect a few before settling in. Plus points include the helpful manager and several common areas where travellers can make a coffee, use the wi-fi, or grab a meal. Yoga and Bollywood dance lessons can be had on the rooftop.

Hotel Meghniwas GUESTHOUSE $$$
(☎0141-4060100; www.meghniwas.com; C9 Sawai Jai Singh Hwy; r/ste ₹5760/8220; ❄@📶🏊) In a building erected by Brigadier Singh in 1950 and run by his gracious descendants, this very welcoming hotel has comfortable and spotless rooms, with traditional carved-wood furniture and leafy outlooks. The standard rooms are spacious, and although it's on a major road it is set well back behind a leafy garden. There's a first-rate restaurant and an inviting pool.

Jas Vilas GUESTHOUSE $$$
(☎0141-2204638; www.jasvilas.com; C9 Sawai Jai Singh Hwy; s/d incl breakfast from ₹6250/6960; ❄@📶🏊) This small but impressive hotel was built in 1950 and is still run by the same charming family. It offers spacious rooms, most of which face the large sparkling pool set in a romantic courtyard. Three garden-facing rooms are wheelchair accessible. In addition to the relaxing courtyard and garden, there is a cosy dining room and helpful management.

Shahpura House HERITAGE HOTEL $$$
(☎0141-2203069; www.shahpura.com; D257 Devi Marg; s/d/ste from ₹7140/8330/9520; ❄@📶🏊) Elaborately built and decorated in traditional style, this heritage hotel offers immaculate rooms, some with balconies, featuring murals, coloured-glass lamps, flat-screen TVs, and even ceilings covered in small mirrors (in the suites). This rambling palace boasts a durbar hall (royal reception hall) with a huge chandelier, and a cosy cocktail bar.

There's also an inviting swimming pool and an elegant rooftop terrace restaurant that stages cultural shows.

Old City

Hotel Sweet Dream HOTEL $
(☎0141-2314409; www.hotelsweetdreamjaipur.in; Nehru Bazaar; s/d ₹900/1150, with AC from ₹1600/1850; ❄📶) Probably the best option right inside the Old City, and one of Jaipur's better budget hotels. Several of the rooms have been renovated and enlarged (reducing the overall room count). There are increasing amenities the higher up the price scale (and rickety elevator) you go. There's a bar plus an excellent rooftop terrace restaurant.

Hotel Bissau Palace HERITAGE HOTEL $$
(☎0141-2304391; www.bissaupalace.com; outside Chandpol; r ₹3270-6540; ❄@📶🏊) This is a worthy choice if you want to stay in a palace on a budget. It's actually just outside the city walls, less than 10 minutes' walk from Chandpol (a gateway to the Old City). There's a swimming pool, a handsome wood-panelled library and three restaurants. The hotel has oodles of heritage atmosphere, with antique furnishings and mementos.

Rambagh Environs

Rambagh Palace HERITAGE HOTEL $$$
(☎0141-2385700; www.tajhotels.com; Bhawani Singh Marg; r from ₹43,560; ❄@📶🏊) This splendid palace was once the Jaipur pad of Maharaja Man Singh II and his glamorous wife Gayatri Devi. Veiled in hectares of manicured gardens, the hotel – run by the luxury Taj Group brand – has fantastic views across the immaculate lawns. More expensive rooms are naturally the most sumptuous.

Nonguests can join in the magnificence by dining in the lavish restaurants or drinking tea on the gracious verandah. At least treat yourself to a drink at the spiffing Polo Bar (p120).

Narain Niwas Palace Hotel HERITAGE HOTEL $$$
(☎0141-2561291; www.hotelnarainniwas.com; Narain Singh Rd; s/d incl breakfast from ₹8425/10,530, deluxe d ₹13,455; ❄@📶🏊) In Kanota Bagh, just south of the city, this genuine heritage hotel has wonderful ramshackle splendour. There's a lavish dining room with liveried staff, an old-fashioned verandah on which to drink tea, and antiques galore. The standard rooms are in a garden wing and aren't as spacious as the high-ceilinged deluxe rooms, which vary in atmosphere and amenities.

Out back you'll find a large secluded pool (nonguests ₹300 for two hours between 8am and 4pm), a heavenly spa, and sprawling gardens complete with peacocks.

Eating

Around MI Rd

Indian Coffee House CAFE $
(MI Rd; coffee ₹20-40, snacks ₹35-60; 6am-9pm) Set back from the street, down an easily missed alley, this traditional coffee house (a venerable co-op–owned institution) offers a pleasant cup of filtered coffee in very relaxed surroundings. Aficionados of Indian Coffee Houses will not be disappointed by the fan-cooled, pale-green ambience. Inexpensive *pakoras* (deep-fried battered vegetables) and dosas grace the menu.

Jal Mahal ICE CREAM $
(MI Rd; cups & cones ₹30-120; 10am-11pm) This great little ice-cream parlour has been going since 1952. There are around 50 flavours to choose from, but if it's hot outside, it's hard to beat mango. There are also plenty of other ice-cream concoctions, including sundaes and banana splits, many with fanciful names.

Old Takeaway the Kebab Shop KEBAB $
(151 MI Rd; kebabs ₹90-180; 6-11pm) One of several similarly named roadside kebab shops on this stretch of MI Road, this one (next to the mosque) is the original (so we're told) and the best (we agree). It knocks up outstanding tandoori kebabs, including paneer *sheesh*, mutton *sheesh* and tandoori chicken. Like the sign says: a house of delicious nonveg corner.

Rawat Kachori SWEETS $
(Station Rd; kachori ₹30, lassi ₹50, sweets per kg ₹350-850; 6am-10pm) Head to this popular takeaway with an attached restaurant for delicious Indian sweets and famous kachori (potato masala in a fried pastry case), a scrumptious savoury snack. A salty or sweet lassi or a delicious milk crown (fluffy dough with cream) should fill you up for the afternoon.

★ **Peacock Rooftop Restaurant** MULTICUISINE $$
(0141-2373700; Hotel Pearl Palace, Hari Kishan Somani Marg; mains ₹175-340; 7am-11pm) This multilevel rooftop restaurant at the Hotel Pearl Palace gets rave reviews for its excellent yet inexpensive cuisine (Indian, Chinese and Continental) and fun ambience. The attentive service, whimsical furnishings and romantic view towards Hathroi Fort make it a first-rate restaurant. In addition to the dinner menu, there are healthy breakfasts and great-value burgers, pizzas and thalis for lunch.

It's wise to make a booking for dinner.

Four Seasons MULTICUISINE $$
(0141-2375450; D43A Subhash Marg; mains ₹125-295; 11am-3.30pm & 6.30-11pm;) Four Seasons is one of Jaipur's best vegetarian restaurants. It's a popular place with dining on two levels and a glass wall to the busy kitchens. There's a great range of dishes on offer, including tasty Rajasthani specialities, South Indian dosas, Chinese fare, and a selection of thalis and pizzas. No alcohol.

Anokhi Café INTERNATIONAL $$
(0141-4007245; 2nd fl, KK Square, C-11 Prithviraj Marg; mains ₹250-350; 10am-7.30pm;) This relaxing cafe with a fashionable organic vibe is the perfect place to come if you're craving a crunchy, well-dressed salad, a quiche or a thickly filled sandwich – or just a respite from the hustle with a latte or an iced tea. The delicious organic loaves of bread are made to order and can be purchased separately.

Handi Restaurant NORTH INDIAN $$
(MI Rd; mains ₹220-440; noon-3.30pm & 6-11pm) Handi has been satisfying customers since 1967, with scrumptious tandoori and barbecue dishes and rich Mughlai curries. In the evenings it sets up a smoky kebab stall at the entrance to the restaurant. Good vegetarian items are also available. No beer.

It's opposite the main post office, tucked at the back of the Maya Mansions.

Surya Mahal SOUTH INDIAN $$
(0141-2362811; MI Rd; mains ₹130-310, thalis ₹240-350; 8am-11pm;) This popular option near Panch Batti specialises in South Indian vegetarian food; try the delicious *masala dosa* and the tasty *dhal makhani* (black lentils and red kidney beans). There are also Chinese and Italian dishes, and good ice creams, sundaes and cool drinks.

Natraj INDIAN $$
(0141-2375804; MI Rd; mains ₹150-250, thalis ₹250-520; 9am-11pm;) Not far from Panch Batti is this classy vegetarian place, which has an extensive menu featuring North Indian, Continental and Chinese cuisine. Diners are blown away by the potato-encased 'vegetable bomb' curry. There's a good selection of thalis and South Indian food – the *paper masala dosa* is delicious – as well as a great array of Indian sweets.

Dãsaprakash SOUTH INDIAN $$
(☎0141-2371313; 5 Kamal Mansions, MI Rd; mains ₹115-240, thalis ₹310-345; ⏰9am-10.30pm; ❄✍) Part of a renowned chain established in 1921, Dãsaprakash specialises in vegetarian South Indian cuisine, including thalis and several versions of dosa and *idli* (spongy, round, fermented rice cake). Afterwards you can choose from a wonderful selection of cold drinks and over-the-top ice-cream sundaes.

★**Niro's** INDIAN $$$
(☎0141-2374493; MI Rd; mains ₹250-500; ⏰10am-11pm; ❄) Established in 1949, Niro's is a long-standing favourite on MI Rd that, like a good wine, only improves with age. Escape the chaos of the street by ducking into its cool, clean, mirror-ceilinged sanctum to savour veg and nonveg Indian cuisine with professional service. Classic Chinese and Continental food are available, but the Indian menu is definitely the pick.

Even locals rave about the butter chicken and rogan josh. Beer and wine are served.

Copper Chimney INDIAN $$$
(☎0141-2372275; Maya Mansions, MI Rd; mains ₹300-475, thali veg/nonveg ₹490/575; ⏰noon-3.30pm & 6.30-11pm; ❄) Copper Chimney is casual, verging on elegant, and is definitely welcoming, with the requisite waiter army and a fridge of cold beer. It offers excellent veg and nonveg Indian cuisine (with generous servings), including aromatic Rajasthani specials. Continental and Chinese food is also on offer, as is a small selection of Indian wine, but the curry-and-beer combos are hard to beat.

Little Italy ITALIAN $$$
(☎0141-4022444; 3rd fl, KK Square, Prithviraj Marg; mains ₹300-500; ⏰noon-10pm; ❄) The best Italian restaurant in Jaipur, Little Italy is part of a small national chain that offers excellent vegetarian pasta, risotto, and wood-fired pizzas in cool, contemporary surroundings. The menu is extensive and includes some Mexican items, plus first-rate Italian desserts. It's licensed and there's an attached sister concern, Little India, with an Indian and Chinese menu.

Jaipur Modern Kitchen MEDITERRANEAN $$$
(☎0141-4113000; www.jaipurmodern.com; 51 Sardar Patel Marg, C-Scheme; mains ₹300-550; ⏰11am-11pm; ❄✍) 🍃 In addition to the homewares and fashion, Jaipur Modern boasts this super Mediterranean cafe showcasing organic ingredients and supporting local sustainable agriculture. The tasty pizzas, pasta, *momos* and wraps are all made in-house. There's even a special emphasis on locally grown quinoa; the Q menu features soups, appetisers, mains and desserts, all containing the versatile seed.

Old City

Ganesh Restaurant NORTH INDIAN $
(Nehru Bazaar; mains ₹100-160; ⏰9am-11.30pm; ✍) This pocket-sized outdoor restaurant is in a fantastic location on the top of the Old City wall near New Gate. The chef is in a pit on one side of the wall, so you can check out your pure vegetarian food being cooked. If you're looking for a local eatery with fresh tasty food such as paneer butter masala, you'll love it.

There's an easy-to-miss signpost, but no doubt a stallholder will show you the narrow stairway.

Mohan INDIAN $
(144-5 Nehru Bazaar; mains ₹25-150, thali ₹80; ⏰9am-10.30pm; ✍) Tiny Mohan is easy to miss: it's a few steps down from the footpath on the corner of the street. It's basic, cheap and a bit grubby, but the thalis, curries (half-plate and full plate) and snacks are freshly cooked and very popular.

LMB INDIAN $$
(☎0141-2560845; Johari Bazaar; mains ₹210-320; ⏰8am-11pm; ❄✍) Laxmi Misthan Bhandar, LMB to you and me, is a vegetarian restaurant in the Old City that's been going strong since 1954. A welcoming air-conditioned refuge from frenzied Johari Bazaar, LMB is also an institution with its singular decor, attentive waiters and extensive sweet counter. Now it is no longer purely *sattvik* (pure vegetarian), you can now order meals with onion and garlic.

Popular with both local and international tourists, try the Rajasthan thali (₹540) followed by the signature *kulfa* (₹100, a fusion of *kulfi* and *falooda* with dry fruits and saffron).

Hotel Sweet Dream MULTICUISINE $$
(☎0141-2314409; www.hotelsweetdreamjaipur.in; Nehru Bazaar; mains ₹130-285; ❄) This hotel in the Old City has a splendid restaurant on the roof with views down to bustling Nehru Bazaar. It's a great place to break the shopping spree and grab a light lunch or a refreshing *makhania* lassi (₹140) made with fresh fruits and curd. The menu includes pizza and Chinese, but the Indian is best.

Drinking & Nightlife

★Lassiwala CAFE

(MI Rd; lassi small/large ₹25/50; ⏲7.30am until sold out) This famous, much-imitated institution is a simple place that whips up fabulous, creamy lassis in clay cups. Get here early to avoid disappointment! Will the real Lassiwala please stand up? It's the one that says 'Shop 312' and 'Since 1944', directly next to the alleyway. Imitators spread to the right as you face it.

★Curious Life CAFE

(☎0141-2229877; www.facebook.com/curiouslifecoffeeroasters; P25 Yudhisthira Marg, C-Scheme; coffees from ₹75; ⏲9am-10pm; 📶) The latest coffee trends brew away in this showcase of Indian hipster-hood. Single-origin, espresso, French press, AeroPress, V60 pour over – you name it, and you'll find it brewing here among the predominantly 20-something crowd. There are also cold brews, smoothies, shakes and muffins, all underscored by a curiously retro soundtrack.

★Bar Palladio BAR

(☎0141-2565556; www.bar-palladio.com; Narain Niwas Palace Hotel, Narain Singh Rd; cocktails ₹500-700; ⏲6-11pm) This cool bar-restaurant boasts an extensive drinks list and an Italian food menu (mains ₹350 to ₹400). The vivid blue theme of the romantic Orientalist interior flows through to candlelit outdoor seating, making this a very relaxing place to sip a drink, snack on bruschetta and enjoy a conversation. Il Teatro is an occasional live-music event at the bar – see the website for dates.

100% Rock BAR

(Hotel Shikha, Yudhishthir Marg, C-Scheme; pint of beer/cocktails from ₹190/300; ⏲11am-12.30am; 📶) Attached to, but separate from Hotel Shikha, this is the closest thing there is to a beer garden in Jaipur, with plenty of outdoor seating as well as air-conditioned side rooms and a clubby main room with a small dance floor. Two-for-one beer offers are common, making this popular with local youngsters.

Polo Bar BAR

(Rambagh Palace Hotel, Bhawan Singh Marg; ⏲noon-midnight) This spiffing watering hole adorned with polo memorabilia boasts arched, scalloped windows framing the neatly clipped lawns. A bottle of beer costs from ₹400 according to the label, a glass of wine starts at ₹550, and cocktails cost from ₹600. Delicious snacks are also available throughout the day.

Café Coffee Day CAFE

(Country Inn & Suites, MI Rd; coffees ₹80-150; ⏲10am-10pm) The franchise that successfully delivers espresso to coffee addicts, as well as the occasional creamy concoction and muffin, has several branches in Jaipur. In addition to this one, sniff out the brews at Paris Point on Sawai Jai Singh Hwy (aka Collectorate Rd), at the central museum, and near the exit point at Amber Fort.

☆ Entertainment

Jaipur isn't a big late-night party town, though many of its hotels put on some sort of evening music, dance or puppet show. English-language films are occasionally screened at some cinemas – check the cinemas and local press for details.

Raj Mandir Cinema CINEMA

(☎0141-2379372; www.therajmandir.com; Baghwandas Marg; tickets ₹120-400; ⏲reservations 10am-6pm, screenings 12.30pm, 3pm, 6.30pm & 10pm) Just off MI Rd, Raj Mandir is *the* place to go to see a Hindi film in India. This opulent cinema looks like a huge pink cream cake, with a meringue auditorium and a foyer somewhere between a temple and Disneyland. Bookings can be made one hour to seven days in advance at windows 9 and 10.

Advance booking is your best chance of securing a seat, but forget it in the early days of a new release. Alternatively, sharpen your elbows and join the queue when the current booking office opens 45 minutes before curtain up. Avoid the cheapest tickets, which seat you very close to the screen.

Chokhi Dhani LIVE PERFORMANCE

(☎0141-5165000; www.chokhidhani.com; Tonk Rd; adult/child incl Rajasthani thali from ₹600/350; ⏲6-11pm) Chokhi Dhani, meaning 'special village', is a mock Rajasthani village 20km south of Jaipur, and is a fun place to take kids. There are open-air restaurants, where you can enjoy a tasty Rajasthani thali, plus a bevy of traditional entertainment – dancers, acrobats, snack stalls – and adventure-park-like activities for kids to swing on, slide down and hide in.

There are more expensive tickets depending on which dining experience you opt for. A return taxi from Jaipur, including waiting time, will cost about ₹800.

Polo Ground SPECTATOR SPORT

(ticket info 0141-2385380; Ambedkar Circle, Bhawan Singh Marg) Maharaja Man Singh II indulged his passion for polo by building an enormous polo ground next to Rambagh Palace, which is still a polo-match hub today. A ticket to a match also gets you into the lounge, which is adorned with historic photos and memorabilia. The polo season extends over winter. Contact the Rajasthan Polo Club for info about tickets.

Shopping

Jaipur is a shopper's paradise. Commercial buyers come here from all over the world to stock up on the amazing range of jewellery, gems, textiles and crafts that come from all over Rajasthan. You'll have to bargain hard, particularly around major tourist sights.

Many shops can send your parcels home for you – often cheaper than if you do it yourself.

The city is still loosely divided into traditional artisans' quarters. **Bapu Bazaar** is lined with saris and fabrics, and is a good place to buy trinkets. **Johari Bazaar** and **Sireh Deori Bazaar** are where many jewellery shops are concentrated, selling gold, silver and highly glazed enamelwork known as meenakari, a Jaipur speciality. You may also find better deals for fabrics with the cotton merchants of Johari Bazaar.

Kishanpol Bazaar is famous for textiles, particularly *bandhani* (tie-dye). **Nehru Bazaar** also sells fabric, as well as jootis (traditional shoes), trinkets and perfume. The best place for bangles is Maniharon Rasta.

Plenty of factories and showrooms are strung along the length of the road to Amber, between Zorawar Singh Gate and the Park Regis Hotel, to catch the tourist traffic. Here you'll find huge emporiums selling block prints, blue pottery, carpets and antiques. Note that these shops are used to busloads of tourists swinging in to blow their cash, so you'll need to wear your bargaining hat.

Rickshaw-wallahs, hotels and travel agents will be getting a hefty cut from any shop they steer you towards. Many unwary visitors get talked into buying things for resale at inflated prices, especially gems. Beware of these get-rich-quick scams.

Jaipur Modern FASHION & ACCESSORIES

(0141-4112000; www.jaipurmodern.com; 51 Sardar Patel Marg, C-Scheme; 11am-11pm) This contemporary showroom offers local arts and crafts, clothing, homewares, stationary and fashion accessories. The staff are relaxed (no hard sell here) and if you are not in the mood to shop, there's a great cafe serving Lavazza coffee and Mediterranean snacks.

SHOPPING FOR GEMS

Jaipur is famous for precious and semi-precious stones. There are many shops offering bargain prices, but you do need to know your gems. The main gem-dealing area is around the Muslim area of Pahar Ganj, in the southeast of the Old City. Here you can see stones being cut and polished in workshops tucked off narrow backstreets.

One of the oldest scams in India is the gem scam, where tourists are fooled into thinking they can buy gems to sell at a profit elsewhere. To receive an authenticity certificate, you can deposit your gems at the **gem-testing laboratory** (0141-2568221; www.gtljaipur.info; Rajasthan Chamber Bhawan, MI Rd; 10am-4pm Mon-Sat) between 10am and 4pm, then return the following day between 4pm and 5pm to pick up the certificate. The service costs ₹1050 per stone, or ₹1650 for same-day service, if deposited before 1pm.

Inde Rooh CLOTHING

(9829404055, 9929442022; www.inderooh.com; Hotel Pearl Palace, Hari Kishan Somani Marg; 10.30am-10.30pm) This tiny outlet in the Hotel Pearl Palace highlights the talents of Jaipur's traditional block printers blended with contemporary design. Handmade and stitched, the quality and value of the women's and menswear compares well with Jaipur's more famous fashion houses. Homewares are also available.

Rajasthali ARTS & CRAFTS

(MI Rd; 11am-7.30pm Mon-Sat) This state-government-run emporium, opposite Ajmer Gate, is packed with quality Rajasthani artefacts and crafts, including enamelwork, embroidery, pottery, woodwork, jewellery, puppets, block-printed sheets, miniatures, brassware, mirrorwork and more. Scout out prices here before launching into the bazaar; items can be cheaper at the markets, but the quality is often higher at the state emporium for not much more money.

Anokhi CLOTHING, TEXTILES
(www.anokhi.com; 2nd fl, KK Square, C-11 Prithviraj Marg; ⏲9.30am-8pm Mon-Sat, 11am-7pm Sun) Anokhi is a classy, upmarket boutique selling stunning high-quality textiles such as block-printed fabrics, tablecloths, bed covers, cosmetic bags and scarves, as well as a range of well-designed, beautifully made clothing that combines Indian and Western influences. There's a wonderful little cafe on the premises and an excellent bookshop in the same building.

Fabindia CLOTHING
(☎0141-4015279; www.fabindia.com; B 4 E- Prithviraj Road; ⏲11am-9pm) A great place to coordinate colours with reams of rich fabrics, plus furniture and home accessories. You can also find organically certified garments, beauty products and condiments. Located opposite Central Park, gate number 4.

Silver Shop JEWELLERY
(Hotel Pearl Palace, Hari Kishan Somani Marg; ⏲6-10pm) A trusted jewellery shop backed by the hotel management that hosts the store. A money-back guarantee is offered on all items. Find it under the peacock canopy in the hotel's Peacock Rooftop Restaurant.

Crossword BOOKS
(1st fl, KK Square, Prithvirag Marg; ⏲11am-9pm) Crossword is an excellent bookshop with all sorts of fiction and nonfiction, including the latest best sellers, pictorial books and books on Indian history. Music CDs and DVDs are also available. There is a cafe and restaurant in the same building.

Mojari CLOTHING
(☎0141-2377037; D-67 Shiv Heera Marg; ⏲10am-6.30pm) Named after the traditional decorated shoes of Rajasthan, Mojari is a UN-supported project that helps rural leatherworkers, traditionally among the poorest members of society. A wide variety of footwear (₹300 to ₹1000) is available, including embroidered, appliquéd and open-toed shoes, mules and sandals. There's a particularly good choice for women, plus a small selection of handmade leather bags and purses.

ℹ Information

INTERNET ACCESS

Internet cafes are thin on the ground, but almost all hotels and guesthouses provide wi-fi and/or internet access.

Mewar Cyber Café (Station Rd; per hr ₹30; ⏲7am-11pm) Near the main bus station.

MEDICAL SERVICES

Most hotels can arrange a doctor on-site.

Santokba Durlabhji Memorial Hospital (SDMH; ☎0141-2566251; www.sdmh.in; Bhawan Singh Marg) Private hospital, with 24-hour emergency department, helpful staff and clear bilingual signage. Consultancy fee ₹400.

Sawai Mansingh Hospital (SMS Hospital; ☎0141-2518222, 0141-2518597; Sawai Ram Singh Rd) State-run, but part of Soni Hospitals group (www.sonihospitals.com). Before 3pm, outpatients go to the CT & MRI Centre; after 3pm, go to the adjacent Emergency Department.

MONEY

There are plenty of places to change money, including numerous hotels, and masses of ATMs, most of which accept foreign cards.

Thomas Cook (☎0141-2360940; Jaipur Towers, MI Rd; ⏲9.30am-6pm) Changes cash and travellers cheques.

POST

DHL Express (☎0141-2361159; www.dhl.co.in; G8, Geeta Enclave, Vinobha Marg; ⏲10am-8pm) Look for the sub-branch on MI Rd then walk down the lane beside it to find DHL Express. For parcels, the first kilogram is expensive, but each 500g thereafter is cheap. All packaging is included in the price. Credit cards and cash accepted.

Main Post Office (☎0141-2368740; MI Rd; ⏲8am-7.45pm Mon-Fri, 10am-5.45pm Sat) A cost-effective and efficient institution, though the back-and-forth can infuriate. Parcel-packing-wallahs in the foyer must first pack, stitch and wax seal your parcel for a small fee before sending.

TOURIST INFORMATION

Jaipur Vision and *Jaipur City Guide* are two useful, inexpensive booklets available at bookshops and some hotel lobbies (where they are free). They feature up-to-date listings, maps, local adverts and features.

RTDC Tourist Office (☎0141-5155137; www.rajasthantourism.gov.in; former RTDC Tourist Hotel, MI Rd; ⏲9.30am-6pm Mon-Fri) has maps and brochures on Jaipur and Rajasthan. Additional branches at the **airport** (☎0141-2722647; ⏲9am-5pm Mon-Fri), **Amber Fort** (☎0141-2530264; ⏲9.30am-5pm Mon-Fri), **Jaipur train station** (☎0141-2200778; platform 1; ⏲24hr) and the **main bus station** (☎0141-5064102; platform 3; ⏲10am-5pm Mon-Fri).

ℹ Getting There & Away

AIR

Jaipur International Airport (☎0141-2550623; www.jaipurairport.com) is located 12km southeast of the city.

It's possible to arrange flights to Jaipur from Europe, the US and other places, via Delhi. A few direct flights run to Bangkok and Singapore and the Gulf.

Air India (☎ 0141-2743500, airport 0141-2721333; www.airindia.com; Nehru Place, Tonk Rd) Daily flights to Delhi and Mumbai.

IndiGo (☎ 9212783838; www.goindigo.in; Terminal 2, Jaipur International Airport) Flights to Ahmedabad, Bengaluru (Bangalore), Chennai (Madras), Delhi, Hyderabad, Kolkata (Calcutta), Mumbai and Pune.

Jet Airways (☎ 0141-2725025, 1800 225522; www.jetairways.com; ⊙ 5.30am-9pm) Flights to Delhi and Mumbai.

SpiceJet (☎ 9871803333; www.spicejet.com; Terminal 2, Jaipur International Airport; ⊙ 6am-7pm) Daily flights to Delhi.

Scoot (☎ 8000016354; www.scoot.com) Three weekly flights to Singapore.

Thai Smile (☎ Thailand +662-1188888; www.thaismileair.com) Three weekly flights to Bangkok.

BUS

Rajasthan State Road Transport Corporation (RSRTC, aka Rajasthan Roadways) buses all leave from the **main bus station** (Station Rd; left luggage per bag per 24hr ₹10), picking up passengers at Narain Singh Circle (where you can also buy tickets). There's a left-luggage office at the main bus station, as well as a prepaid autorickshaw stand.

Ordinary buses are known as 'express' buses, but there are also 'deluxe' buses (coaches, really, but still called buses), which vary a lot but are generally much more expensive and comfortable (usually with air-con but not always) than ordinary express buses. Deluxe buses leave from Platform 3, tucked away in the right-hand corner of the bus station. Unlike ordinary express buses, seats can be booked in advance from the **reservation office** (☎ 0141-5116032; Main Bus Station).

With the exception of those going to Delhi (half-hourly), deluxe buses are much less frequent than ordinary buses.

CAR & MOTORCYCLE

Most hotels and the RTDC tourist office can arrange a car and driver. Depending on the vehicle, costs are ₹9 to ₹12 per kilometre, with a minimum rental rate equivalent to 250km per day. Also expect to pay a ₹200 overnight charge, and note that you will have to pay for the driver to return to Jaipur even if you are not returning.

Rajasthan Auto Centre (p1203) You can hire, buy or fix a Royal Enfield Bullet (and lesser motorbikes) at Rajasthan Auto Centre, the cleanest little motorcycle workshop in India. To hire a 350cc Bullet costs ₹600 per day (including helmet) within Jaipur.

TRAIN

The **reservation office** (☎ enquiries 131, reservations 135; ⊙ 8am-2pm & 3-8pm) is to your left as you enter Jaipur train station. It's open for advance reservations only (more than five hours before departure). Join the queue for 'Freedom Fighters and Foreign Tourists' (counter 769).

For same-day travel, buy your ticket at the northern end of the train station at Platform

MAIN BUSES FROM JAIPUR

DESTINATION	FARE (₹)	DURATION (HR)	FREQUENCY
Agra	261-289, AC 470-573	5½	11 daily
Ajmer	150, AC 316	2½	at least hourly
Bharatpur	195, AC 410	4½	at least hourly
Bikaner	334, AC 596	5½-7	hourly
Bundi	216	5	5 daily
Chittorgarh	339, AC 585	7	6 daily
Delhi	273, AC 800	5½	at least hourly
Jaisalmer	593	14	2 daily
Jhunjhunu	181, AC 321	3½-5	half-hourly
Jodhpur	340, AC 741	5½-7	every 2 hours
Kota	252	5	hourly
Mt Abu (Abu Road)	486, AC 866	10½-13	6 daily
Nawalgarh	145, AC 258	2½-4	hourly
Pushkar	161	3	daily
Udaipur	420, AC 914	10	6 daily

1, window 10 (closed 6am to 6.30am, 2pm to 2.30pm and 10pm to 10.30pm).

Station facilities on Platform 1 include an RTDC tourist office, Tourism Assistance Force (police), a cloakroom for left luggage (₹16 per bag per 24 hours), retiring rooms, restaurants and air-con waiting rooms for those with 1st-class and 2AC train tickets.

There's a prepaid autorickshaw stand and local taxis at the road entrance to the train station.

Services include the following:

Agra sleeper ₹185, 3½ to 4½ hours, nine daily

Ahmedabad sleeper ₹350, nine to 13 hours, seven daily (12.30am, 2.20am, 4.25am, 8.40am, 11.45am, 2.20pm and 8.35pm)

Ajmer (for Pushkar) sleeper ₹90, two hours, 21 daily

Bikaner sleeper ₹275, 6½ to 7½ hours, three daily (12.45am, 4.15pm, 9.45pm)

Delhi sleeper ₹245, 4½ to six hours, at least nine daily (1am, 2.50am, 4.40am, 5am, 6am, 2.35pm, 4.25pm, 5.50pm and 11.15pm), more on selected days

Jaisalmer sleeper ₹350, 12 hours, three daily (11.10am, 4.15pm and 11.45pm)

Jodhpur sleeper ₹250, 4½ to six hours, 10 daily (12.45am, 2.45am, 6am, 9.25am, 11.10am, 11.25am, 12.20pm, 5pm, 10.40pm and 11.45pm)

Ranthambhore NP (Sawai Madhopur) sleeper ₹180, two to three hours, at least nine daily (12.30am, 5.40am, 6.40am, 11.05am, 2pm, 4.50pm, 5.35pm, 7.35pm and 8.45pm), more on selected days

Udaipur sleeper ₹270, seven to eight hours, three daily (6.15am, 2pm and 11pm)

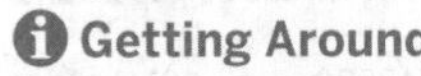

Getting Around

TO/FROM THE AIRPORT

There are no bus services from the airport. An autorickshaw/taxi costs at least ₹350/450. There's a prepaid taxi booth inside the terminal.

AUTORICKSHAW

Autorickshaw drivers at the bus and train stations might just be the pushiest in Rajasthan. Use the fixed-rate prepaid autorickshaw stands instead. Keep hold of your docket to give to the driver at the end of the journey. In other cases be prepared to bargain hard – expect to pay at least ₹80 from either station to the Old City.

CYCLE-RICKSHAW

You can do your bit for the environment by flagging down a lean-limbed cycle-rickshaw rider. Though it can be uncomfortable watching someone pedalling hard to transport you, this *is* how they make a living. A short trip costs about ₹50.

PUBLIC TRANSPORT

Jaipur Metro (0141-2385790; www.jaipurmetrorail.info) operates about 10km of track, known as the Pink Line, and nine stations. The track starts southwest of the Pink City in Mansarovar, travels through Civil Lines, and currently terminates at Chandpole. At the time of writing, the continuation of this track

MAJOR TRAINS FROM JAIPUR

DESTINATION	TRAIN	DEPARTURE TIME	ARRIVAL TIME	FARE (₹)
Agra (Cantonment)	19666 Udaipur-Kurj Exp	6.15am	11am	185/510 (A)
Agra (Fort)	12035 Jaipur-AF Shatabdi	7.05am	10.35am	505/1050 (D)
Ahmedabad	12958 Adi Sj Rajdhani	12.30am	9.40am	1130/1580 (B)
Ajmer (for Pushkar)	12195 Ajmer-AF Intercity	9.40am	11.50am	100/325 (C)
Bikaner	12307 Howrah-Jodhpur Exp	12.45am	8.15am	275/705 (A)
Delhi (New Delhi)	12016 Ajmer Shatabdi	5.50pm	10.40pm	570/1205 (D)
Delhi (S Rohilla)	12985 Dee Double Decker	6am	10.30am	505/1205 (D)
Jaisalmer	14659 Delhi-JSM Exp	11.45pm	11.40am	350/935 (A)
Jodhpur	22478 Jaipur-Jodhpur SF Exp	6am	10.30am	515/625 (E)
Sawai Madhopur	12466 Intercity Exp	11.05am	1.15pm	180/325/560 (F)
Udaipur	19665 Jaipur–Udaipur Exp	11pm	6.45am	270/715 (A)

Fares: (A) sleeper/3AC, (B) 3AC/2AC, (C) 2nd-class seat/AC chair, (D) AC chair/1AC, (E) AC chair/3AC, (F) sleeper/AC chair/3AC

through the Pink City from Chandpole to Badi Chaupar was under construction. Fares are between ₹5 and ₹15.

TAXI

There are unmetered taxis available, which will require negotiating a fare.

Metro Cabs (☎0414-4244444; www.metro-cabs.in; flagfall incl 2km ₹50, then per km ₹10-12, plus per min ₹1, night surcharge 10pm-6am 25%; ⏲24hr) Taxis can be hired for sightseeing for four-/eight-hour blocks for ₹700/1350.

Around Jaipur

Amber

The magnificent, formidable, honey-hued fort of Amber (pronounced 'amer'), an ethereal example of Rajput architecture, rises from a rocky mountainside about 11km northeast of Jaipur, and is the city's must-see sight.

Amber was the former capital of Jaipur state. It was built by the Kachhwaha Rajputs, who hailed from Gwalior, in present day Madhya Pradesh, where they reigned for over 800 years. The construction of the fort, which was begun in 1592 by Maharaja Man Singh, the Rajput commander of Akbar's army, was financed with war booty. It was later extended and completed by the Jai Singhs before they moved to Jaipur on the plains below.

The town of Amber, below the fort, is also worth visiting, especially the Anokhi Museum of Hand Printing. From the museum you can walk around the ancient town to the restored **Panna Meena Baori** (step-well) and **Jagat Siromani Temple** (known locally as the Meera Temple).

Sights

★Amber Fort FORT

(Indian/foreigner ₹100/500, night entry ₹100, guide ₹200, audio guide ₹200-250; ⏲8am-6pm, last entry 5.30pm, night entry 7-9pm) This magnificent fort comprises an extensive palace complex, built from pale yellow and pink sandstone, and white marble, and is divided into four main sections, each with its own courtyard. It is possible to visit the fortress on elephant-back, but animal welfare groups have criticised the keeping of elephants at Amber because of reports of abuse, and because carrying passengers can cause lasting injuries to the animals.

WORTH A TRIP

ABHANERI

Abhaneri is home to one of Rajasthan's most spectacular step-wells. With around 11 visible levels (depending on groundwater level) of zigzagging steps, the 10th-century **Chand Baori** (⏲dawn-dusk) FREE is an incredible geometric wonder. Flanking the well is a small crumbling palace, where royals used to picnic and bathe in private rooms (water was brought up by ox-power).

Abhaneri is about 95km from Jaipur and about 10km from National Hwy 21, the main Agra–Jaipur highway. From Jaipur catch a bus to Sikandra (₹70, 1½ hours), from where you can hop in a crowded share taxi (₹10) for the 5km trip to Gular. From Gular catch a share taxi or minibus to Abhaneri (another 5km and ₹10). If you have your own transport, Abhaneri and its step-well is a worthwhile stop between Jaipur and Agra/Bharatpur.

As an alternative, you can trudge up to the fort from the road in about 10 minutes, or take a 4WD to the top and back for ₹400 (good for up to five passengers), including a one-hour wait time. For night entry, admission for foreigners drops to the Indian price.

However you arrive, you will enter Amber Fort through the **Suraj Pol** (Sun Gate), which leads to the **Jaleb Chowk** (Main Courtyard), where returning armies would display their war booty to the populace – women could view this area from the veiled windows of the palace. The ticket office is directly across the courtyard from the Suraj Pol. If you arrive by car you will enter through the **Chand Pol** (Moon Gate) on the opposite side of Jaleb Chowk. Hiring a guide or grabbing an audio guide is highly recommended, as there are very few signs and many blind alleys.

From Jaleb Chowk, an imposing stairway leads up to the main palace, but first it's worth taking the steps just to the right, which lead to the small **Siladevi Temple**, with its gorgeous silver doors featuring repoussé (raised relief) work.

Heading back to the main stairway will take you up to the second courtyard and the **Diwan-i-Am** (Hall of Public Audience), which has a double row of columns, each topped by a capital in the shape of an elephant, and latticed galleries above.

The maharaja's apartments are located around the third courtyard – you enter through the fabulous **Ganesh Pol**, decorated with beautiful frescoed arches. The **Jai Mandir** (Hall of Victory) is noted for its inlaid panels and multimirrored ceiling. Carved marble relief panels around the hall are fascinatingly delicate and quirky, depicting cartoon-like insects and sinuous flowers. Opposite the Jai Mandir is the **Sukh Niwas** (Hall of Pleasure), with an ivory-inlaid sandalwood door and a channel that once carried cooling water right through the room. From the Jai Mandir you can enjoy fine views from the palace ramparts over picturesque **Maota Lake** below.

The **zenana** (secluded women's quarters) surrounds the fourth courtyard. The rooms were designed so that the maharaja could embark on his nocturnal visits to his wives' and concubines' respective chambers without the others knowing, as the chambers are independent but open onto a common corridor.

The **Amber Sound & Light Show** (☎0141-2530844; Kesar Kiyari complex; Indian/foreigner ₹100/200; ⏲English 7.30pm, Hindi 8.30pm) takes place below the fort in the complex near Maota Lake.

Jaigarh FORT

(Indian/foreigner ₹50/100, car ₹50, Hindi/English guide ₹200/300; ⏲9am-5pm) A scrubby green hill rises above Amber and is topped by the imposing Jaigarh, built in 1726 by Jai Singh. The stern fort, punctuated by whimsical-hatted lookout towers, was never captured and has survived intact through the centuries. It's an uphill walk (about 1km) from Amber and offers great views from the Diwa Burj watchtower. The fort has reservoirs, residential areas, a puppet theatre and the world's largest wheeled cannon, Jaya Vana.

During the Mughal empire, Jaipur produced many weapons for the Mughal and Rajput rulers. The cannon, a most spectacular example, was made in the fort foundry, which was constructed in Mughal times. The huge weapon dates from 1720, has a barrel around 6m long, is made from a mix of eight different metals and weighs 50 tonnes. To fire it requires 100kg of gunpowder, and it has a range of 30km. It's debatable how many times this great device was used.

A sophisticated network of drainage channels feed three large tanks that used to provide water for all the soldiers, residents and livestock living in the fort. The largest tank has a capacity for 22.8 million litres of water. The fort served as the treasury of the Kachhwahas, and for a long time people were convinced that at least part of the royal treasure was still secreted in this large water tank. The Indian government even searched it to check, but found nothing.

Within the fort is an armoury and museum, with the essential deadly weapons collection and some royal knick-knacks, including interesting photographs, maps of Jaigarh, spittoons, and circular 18th-century playing cards. The structure also contains various open halls, including the Shubhat Niwas (Meeting Hall of Warriors), which has some weather-beaten sedan chairs and drums lying about.

Admission is free with a valid ticket from the Jaipur City Palace that is less than two days old.

Anokhi Museum of Hand Printing MUSEUM

(☎0141-2530226; Anokhi Haveli, Kheri Gate; adult/child ₹80/25; ⏲10.30am-4.30pm Tue-Sat, 11am-4.30pm Sun, closed May–mid-Jul) This interesting museum in a restored *haveli* documents the art of hand-block printing, from old traditions to contemporary design. You can watch masters carve unbelievably intricate wooden printing blocks and even have a go at printing your own scarf or T-shirt. There's a cafe and gift shop, too.

Sleeping

★ Mosaics Guesthouse GUESTHOUSE $$

(☎0141-2530031, 8875430000; www.mosaics-guesthouse.com; Siyaram Ki Doongri; s/d incl breakfast ₹3300/3800; ❄@🛜) Get away from it all at this gorgeous arty place (the French owner is a mosaic artist and will show off his workshop) with four lovely rooms and a rooftop terrace with beautiful fort views. Set-price Franco-Indian meals cost ₹800/1000 for veg/nonveg. It's about 1km past the fort near Kunda Village – head for Siyaram Ki Doongri, where you'll find signs.

Bharatpur & Keoladeo National Park

☎05644252,350 / POP 252,350

Bharatpur is famous for its wonderful Unesco-listed Keoladeo National Park, a wetland and significant bird sanctuary. Apart from the park, Bharatpur also has a few historic vestiges, though it wouldn't be worth making the journey for these alone. The town is dusty, noisy and not particularly visitor-

Bharatpur

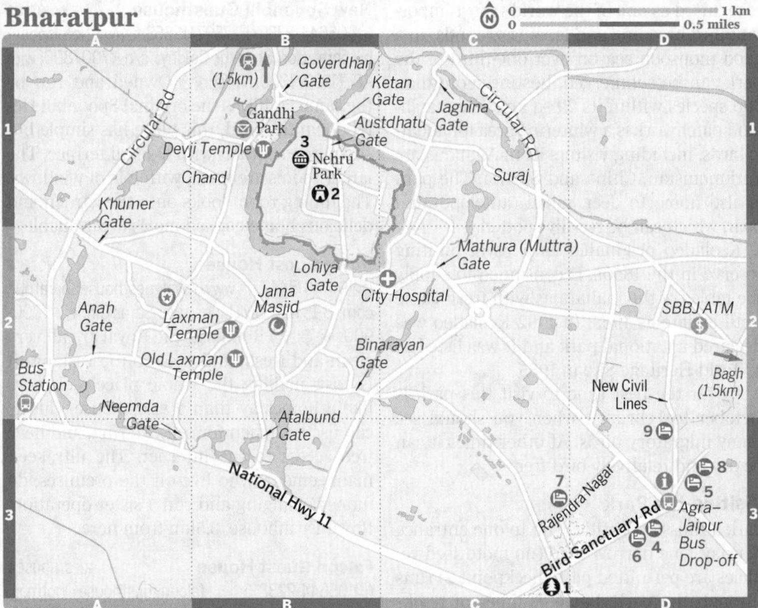

friendly. Bharatpur hosts the boisterous and colourful **Brij Festival** just prior to Holi celebrations.

Sights

Lohagarh FORT

FREE The still-inhabited, 18th-century Lohagarh, or Iron Fort, was so named because of its sturdy defences. Despite being somewhat forlorn and derelict, it is still impressive, and sits at the centre of town, surrounded by a moat. There's a northern entrance, at **Austdhatu (Eight-Metal) Gate** – apparently the spikes on the gate are made of eight different metals – and a southern entrance, at **Lohiya Gate**.

Maharaja Suraj Mahl, constructor of the fort and founder of Bharatpur, built two towers, the **Jawahar Burj** and the **Fateh Burj**, within the ramparts to commemorate his victories over the Mughals and the British. The fort also contains three much decayed palaces within its precincts.

One of the palaces, centred on a tranquil courtyard, houses a **museum** (Indian/foreigner ₹20/100, photography prohibited inside museum; ⌚9.45am-5.15pm Tue-Sun). Upstairs is a ragtag display of royal artefacts, including weaponry. More impressive is the Jain sculpture gallery, which includes some beautiful 7th- to 10th-century pieces. The most spectacular feature of the museum, however, is the palace's original *hammam* (bathhouse), which retains some fine carvings and frescos.

Bharatpur

Top Sights
1 Keoladeo National Park ...C3

Sights
2 Lohagarh ...B1
3 Museum ...B1

Sleeping
4 Birder's Inn ...D3
5 Falcon Guest House ...D3
6 Hotel Sunbird ...D3
7 Kiran Guest House ...C3
8 New Spoonbill Guesthouse ...D3
9 Royal Guest House ...D3

Flexible category 3
State Bank of India ATM ...(see 5)

Keoladeo National Park

This tremendous bird sanctuary and **national park** (Indian/foreigner ₹75/500, video ₹600/900, guide per hr ₹150, bike/mountain-bike/binoculars rental per day ₹25/40/100; ⌚6am-6pm Apr-Sep, 6.30am-5pm Oct-Mar) has long been recognised as one of the world's most important bird breeding and feeding grounds. In a good monsoon season over one-third of the park can be submerged, hosting more than 360 species within its 29 sq km. The marshland patchwork is a wintering area for aquatic birds, including visitors from Afghanistan, Turkmenistan, China and Siberia. The park is also home to deer, nilgai (antelope) and boar, which can be readily spotted.

Keoladeo originated as a royal hunting reserve in the 1850s. It continued to supply the tables of the maharajas with fresh game until as late as 1965. In 1982 Keoladeo was declared a national park and it was listed as a World Heritage Site in 1985.

By far the best time to visit this park is October to February, when you should see many migratory birds. At other times it can be dry and relatively bird-free.

Visiting the Park

Park admission entitles you to one entrance per day. One narrow road (no motorised vehicles are permitted past checkpoint 2) runs through the park, but a number of tracks and pathways fan out from it and thread their way between the shallow wetlands. Generally speaking, the further away from the main gate you go, the more interesting the scenery, and the more varied the wildlife becomes.

Only the government-authorised cycle-rickshaws (recognisable by the yellow license plate) are allowed beyond checkpoint 2, and they can only travel along the park's larger tracks. You don't pay an admission fee for the drivers, but they charge ₹100 per hour; some are very knowledgeable.

An excellent way to see the park is by hiring a bicycle at the park entrance. Having a bike is a wonderfully quiet way to travel, and allows you to avoid bottlenecks and take in the serenity on your own. However, we recommend that lone female travellers who wish to cycle do so with a guide (who will cycle alongside you), as we've had more than one report of lone women being harassed by young men inside the park in recent years.

You get a small map with your entrance ticket, though the park isn't big, so it's difficult to get lost.

Sleeping

There are plenty of sleeping options, suiting all budgets, near the park on Bird Sanctuary Rd, so don't feel pressured by touts at Bharatpur's train or bus stations.

New Spoonbill Guesthouse HOTEL **$**
(05644-223571, 7597412553; www.hotelspoonbill.com; Gori Shankur Colony; s/d ₹700/800, with AC ₹1100/1200;) Owned and run by the same family as the original Spoonbill Hotel down the road, this place has simple but smart rooms, each with a small terrace. The larger rooms are great, with lots of windows. The dining room looks onto the garden and delicious home-cooked meals are available.

Royal Guest House HOTEL **$**
(9414315457; www.royalguesthousebharatpur.com; B-15 New Civil Lines, near Saras Circle; r ₹300-900;) Rooms at the Royal are all very clean and fresh, and the rooftop restaurant is cosy, making the whole place feel more like a homestay than a guesthouse. Guests can use a kitchen for self-catering, and have free access to the internet. The ultrakeen management, who live on the premises, do money changing and run a sister operation, Royal Farmhouse, 3.5km from here.

Falcon Guest House GUESTHOUSE **$**
(05644-223815; falconguesthouse@hotmail.com; Gori Shankur Colony; s/d from ₹600/800, r with AC ₹1200-1500;) The Falcon may well be the pick of a bunch of hotels all in a row and all owned by the same extended family. It's a well-kept, snug place to stay, run by the affable Mrs Rajni Singh. There is a range of comfortable, good-sized rooms at different prices, including a family room. The best rooms have balconies.

Kiran Guest House GUESTHOUSE **$**
(05644-223845; www.kiranguesthouse.com; 364 Rajendra Nagar; r ₹400-800, with AC ₹1100;) Managed by eager-to-please brothers, this guesthouse delivers great value, with seven simple, clean and spacious rooms and a pleasant rooftop where you can eat tasty home cooking. It's on a quiet road not far from Keoladeo park. Nature guiding and free pick-up from the Bharatpur train and bus stations are offered.

★**Hotel Sunbird** HOTEL **$$**
(05644-225701; www.hotelsunbird.com; Bird Sanctuary Rd; s/d from ₹2100/2550, ste ₹2950;) This popular, well-run place close to the Keoladeo park entrance may look modest from the road, but out back boasts a lovely garden (with bar) and spacious rooms with balconies. Rooms are clean and comfortable and the restaurant dishes up a good range of tasty veg and nonveg dishes. Packed lunches and guided tours for the park are available.

★Birder's Inn HOTEL **$$**
(☎05644-227346; www.birdersinn.com; Bird Sanctuary Rd; r incl breakfast from ₹3500;) The Birder's Inn is a popular, long-standing base for exploring the national park. There is a multicuisine restaurant and a small pool to cool off in. The rooms are airy, spacious and nicely decorated, and are set far back from the road in well-tended gardens. Guides from the hotel are available for Keoladeo.

Information

Main Post Office (⏲10am-1pm & 2-5pm Mon-Sat) Near Gandhi Park.

Tourist Office (☎05644-222542; Saras Circle; ⏲9am-5pm) On the crossroads about 700m from the national park entrance; has a free map of Bharatpur and Keoladeo National Park.

Getting There & Away

BUS

Buses running between Agra and Jaipur will drop you by the tourist office or outside the Keoladeo park entrance if you ask.

Services from Bharatpur **bus station** include the following:

Agra non-AC/AC ₹68/171, 1½ hours, half-hourly around the clock

Alwar ₹136, four hours, hourly until 8pm

Deeg ₹39, one hour, hourly until 8pm

Delhi ₹192, five hours, half-hourly from 6am to 7pm, then hourly until 11pm

Fatehpur Sikri ₹28, 45 minutes, half-hourly around the clock

Jaipur ₹195, 4½ hours, half-hourly around the clock

TRAIN

The **train station** is about 4km from Keoladeo and the main hotel area; a rickshaw should cost around ₹70.

Agra 2nd-class seat/sleeper/3AC ₹60/150/510, 1½ to two hours, nine daily between 4.45am and 8.10pm

Delhi 2nd-class seat/sleeper/3AC ₹95/180/510, three to four hours, 12 trains daily, plus three other services on selected days

Jaipur 2nd-class seat/sleeper/3AC ₹110/150/510, three to four hours, nine daily between 2am and 10pm

Ranthambhore NP (Sawai Madhopur) 2nd-class seat/sleeper/3AC ₹135/180/560, two to three hours, 10 daily between 1am and 9.40pm. These trains all continue to Kota (four hours) from where you can catch buses to Bundi.

Getting Around

A cycle- or autorickshaw from the bus station to the main hotel area should cost around ₹40 (add an extra ₹30 from the train station).

Alwar

☎0144 / POP 341,430

Alwar is perhaps the oldest of the Rajasthani kingdoms, forming part of the Matsya territories of Viratnagar in 1500 BC. It became known again in the 18th century under Pratap Singh, who pushed back the rulers of Jaipur to the south and the Jats of Bharatpur to the east, and who successfully resisted the Marathas. It was one of the first Rajput states to ally itself with the fledgling British empire, although British interference in Alwar's internal affairs meant this partnership was not always amicable.

Alwar is the nearest town to Sariska Tiger Reserve and National Park and boasts a fascinating museum, but it sees relatively few tourists.

Sights

City Palace HISTORIC BUILDING
(Vinay Vilas Mahal) Under the gaze of Bala Quila fort sprawls the colourful and convoluted City Palace complex, with massive gates and a tank reflecting a symmetrical series of ghats and pavilions. Today most of the complex is occupied by government offices, overflowing with piles of dusty papers and soiled by pigeons and splatters of *paan* (a mixture of betel nut and leaves for chewing).

MAJOR TRAINS FROM BHARATPUR

DESTINATION	TRAIN	DEPARTURE	ARRIVAL	FARE (₹)
Agra (Cantonment)	19666 Udz-Kurj Exp	9.46am	10.55am	150/510 (A)
Delhi (Hazrat Nizamuddin)	12059 Kota-Jan Shatabdi	9.25am	12.30pm	135/415 (B)
Jaipur	19665 Kurj-Udaipr Exp	6.55pm	10.50pm	150/510 (A)
Sawai Madhopur	12904 Golden Temple Mail	10.30am	12.55pm	180/560 (A)

Fares: (A) sleeper/3AC, (B) 2nd-class/AC chair

WORTH A TRIP

SURAJ MAHL'S PALACE, DEEG

At the centre of Deeg – a small, rarely visited, dusty tumult of a town about 35km north of Bharatpur – stands the incongruously glorious **Suraj Mahl's Palace** (Indian/foreigner ₹15/200; ⏲9.30am-5.30pm Sat-Thu), edged by stately formal gardens. It's one of India's most beautiful and carefully proportioned palace complexes. Pick up a map and brochure at the entrance; photography is not permitted in some of the bhavans (buildings).

Built in a mixture of Rajput and Mughal architectural styles, the 18th-century **Gopal Bhavan** is fronted by imposing arches to take full advantage of the early-morning light. Downstairs is a lower storey that becomes submerged during the monsoon as the water level of the adjacent tank, **Gopal Sagar**, rises. It was used by the maharajas until the early 1950s, and contains many original furnishings, including faded sofas, huge punkas (cloth fans) that are over 200 years old, chaise longues, a stuffed tiger, elephant-foot stands, and fine porcelain from China and France.

In an upstairs room at the rear of the palace is an Indian-style marble dining table – a stretched oval-shaped affair raised just 20cm off the ground. Guests sat around the edge, and the centre was the serving area. In the maharaja's bedroom is an enormous 3.6m by 2.4m wooden bed with silver legs.

Two large tanks lie alongside the palace, the aforementioned Gopal Sagar to the east and **Rup Sagar** to the west. The well-maintained gardens and flowerbeds, watered by the tanks, continue the extravagant theme with over 2000 fountains. Many of these fountains are in working order and coloured waters pour forth during the monsoon festival in August.

The **Keshav Bhavan** (Summer or Monsoon Pavilion) is a single-storey edifice with five arches along each side. Tiny jets spray water from the archways and metal balls rumble around in a water channel imitating monsoon thunder. Deeg's massive walls (which are up to 28m high) and 12 vast bastions, some with their cannons still in place, are also worth exploring. You can walk up to the top of the walls from the palace.

Other bhavans (in various states of renovation) include the marble **Suraj Bhavan**, reputedly taken from Delhi and reassembled here, the **Kishan Bhavan** and, along the northern side of the palace grounds, the **Nand Bhavan**.

Deeg is an easy day trip (and there's nowhere good to stay) from Bharatpur or Alwar by car. All the roads to Deeg are rough and the buses crowded. Frequent buses run to and from Alwar (₹60, 2½ hours) and Bharatpur (₹28, one hour).

Hidden within the City Palace is the excellent **Alwar Museum** (Indian/foreigner ₹50/100; ⏲9.45am-5.15pm Tue-Sun).

The museum's eclectic exhibits evoke the extravagance of the lifestyle of the maharajas: stunning weapons, stuffed Scottish pheasants, royal ivory slippers, erotic miniatures, royal vestments, a solid silver table, and stone sculptures, such as an 11th-century sculpture of Vishnu.

Somewhat difficult to find in the Kafkaesque tangle of government offices, the museum is on the top floor of the palace, up a ramp from the main courtyard. There should be plenty of people around to point you in the right direction and from there you can follow the signs.

Cenotaph of Maharaja Bakhtawar Singh HISTORIC BUILDING

This double-storey edifice, resting on a platform of sandstone, was built in 1815 by Maharaja Vinay Singh, in memory of his father. To gain access to the cenotaph, take the steps to the far left when facing the palace. The cenotaph is also known as the Chhatri of Moosi Rani, after one of the mistresses of Bakhtawar Singh who performed *sati* (self-immolation) on his funeral pyre – after this act she was promoted to wifely status.

Bala Quila FORT

This imposing fort stands 300m above Alwar, its fortifications hugging the steep hills that line the eastern edge of the city. Predating the time of Pratap Singh, it's one of the few forts in Rajasthan built before the rise of the Mughals, who used it as a base for attacking Ranthambhore. Mughal emperors Babur and Akbar have stayed overnight here, and Prince Salim (later Emperor Jehangir) was exiled in Salim Mahal for three years.

Now in ruins, the fort houses a radio transmitter station and parts can only be visited with permission from the superintendent of police. However, this is easy to get: just ask at the superintendent's office in the City Palace complex. You can walk the very steep couple of kilometres up to the fort entrance or take a 7km rickshaw ride.

Sleeping & Eating

★Aravali Clarks Inn HOTEL **$$**
(☎0144-2332316; www.clarksinn.in; Nehru Rd; s/d incl breakfast from ₹2500/3000, ste ₹6000;) One of the town's best choices, this conveniently located hotel has recently come under the patronage of Clarks Inn and is undergoing refurbishment. Rooms are large and well furnished and boast big bathrooms. The multicuisine Bridge restaurant is one of the best in town, and there's a bar. The pool is summer only.

Turn left out of the train station and it's about 300m down the road.

Hotel Hill View HOTEL **$$**
(☎0144-2700989; www.hillviewalwar.com; 19 Moti Dungri Rd; r from ₹2100;) Rooms at this centrally located hotel vary so much that you may prefer a cheaper 'deluxe' to a pricier 'super deluxe'; inspect a few before deciding. The same management runs three Inderlok restaurants in town, including one here, so the food is good. The attached bar may or may not be an advantage depending on the clientele.

It is found south of the city centre on the road that encircles Moti Dungri.

RTDC Hotel Meenal HOTEL **$$**
(☎0144-2347352; meenal@rtdc.in; Topsingh Circle; s/d ₹900/1100, with AC ₹1100/1300;) A respectable option with tidy yet bland rooms typical of the chain. It's located about 1km south of town on the way to Sariska, so it's quiet and leafy, though a long way from the action.

Prem Pavitra Bhojnalaya INDIAN **$**
(☎9314055521; near Hope Circle; mains ₹75-100; ⊙10.30am-4pm & 6.30-10pm;) Alwar's renowned restaurant has been going since 1957. In the heart of the old town, it serves fresh, tasty pure-veg food – try the delicious *aloo parathas* (bread stuffed with spicy potato) and *palak paneer* (unfermented cheese cubes in spinach puree). The servings are big; half-serves are available. Finish off with the famous *kheer* (creamy rice pudding).

You have to pay 10% extra to eat in the air-conditioned section – but it is worth it. Turn right out of the bus station, take the first left (towards Hope Circle) and it's on your left after 100m.

Information

State Bank of Bikaner & Jaipur (Company Bagh Rd; ⊙9.30am-4pm Mon-Fri, to 12.30pm Sat) Changes major currencies and travellers cheques and has an ATM. Near the bus stand.

Tourist Office (☎0144-2347348; Nehru Rd; ⊙10am-5pm Mon-Sat) Helpful centre (if actually open when it should be) offering a map of Alwar and information on Sariska. Near the train station.

Getting There & Around

A cycle-rickshaw between the bus and train stations costs ₹80. Look out for the shared taxis (₹10) that ply fixed routes around town. They come in the form of white minivans and have the word 'Vahini' printed on their side doors. One handy route goes past Aravali Clarks Inn, the tourist office and the train station before continuing on to the bus station and terminating a short walk from the City Palace complex.

A return taxi to Sariska Tiger Reserve will cost you around ₹1500.

BUS

The Alwar **bus station** is on Old Bus Stand Rd, near Manu Marg. Services:

Bharatpur ₹128, four hours, hourly from 5am to 8.30pm

Deeg ₹87, 2½ hours, hourly from 5am to 8.30pm

Delhi ₹176, four hours, every 20 minutes from 5am to 9pm

Jaipur ₹160, four hours, half-hourly from 6am to 10.30pm

Sariska ₹35, one hour, half-hourly from 6am to 10.30pm

TRAIN

The **train station** is fairly central, on Naru Marg. Around a dozen daily trains leave for Delhi (sleeper/3AC ₹180/560, three to four hours) throughout the day.

It's also three to four hours to Jaipur (sleeper/3AC ₹180/510) from here. Sixteen trains depart daily and prices are almost identical to those for Delhi.

Sariska Tiger Reserve & National Park

☎0144

Enclosed within the dramatic, shadowy folds of the Aravalli Hills, the **Sariska Tiger Reserve & National Park** (☎0144-2841333; www.rajasthanwildlife.in; Indian/foreigner ₹105/570, vehicle ₹250; ⏲ morning safari 7-10.30am, evening safari 2-5.30pm Nov-Feb, timings vary by 30min Mar-Jun & Oct, no safaris Jul-Sep, tickets on sale an hour before entry time) is a tangle of remnant semideciduous jungle and craggy canyons sheltering streams and lush greenery. It covers 866 sq km (including a core area of 498 sq km), and is home to peacocks, monkeys, majestic sambars, nilgai, chital, wild boars and jackals.

Unfortunately, despite its name, you're unlikely to spot a tiger in Sariska. It is, however, still a fascinating sanctuary. The best time to spot wildlife is November to March, and you'll see most wildlife in the evening. The park is closed to safaris from 1 July to 30 September. Your chances of spotting wildlife at this time is minimal, in any case, and the park is only open for temple pilgrimage.

Sights

Besides wildlife, Sariska has some fantastic sights within the reserve or around its peripheries, which are well worth seeking out. If you take a longer tour, you can ask to visit one or more of these. Some are also accessible by public bus.

Kankwari Fort FORT

Deep inside the sanctuary, this imposing small jungle fort, 22km from Sariska, offers amazing views over the plains of the national park, dotted with red mud-brick villages. A four- to five-hour 4WD safari (one to five passengers plus mandatory guide) to Kankwari Fort from the Forest Reception Office near the reserve entrance costs ₹2600, plus guide fee (₹300).

This fort is the inaccessible place that Aurangzeb chose to imprison his brother, Dara Shikoh, Shah Jahan's chosen heir to the Mughal throne, for several years before he was beheaded.

Bhangarh HISTORIC SITE

Around 55km from Sariska, beyond the inner park sanctuary and out in open countryside, is this deserted, well-preserved and notoriously haunted city. Founded in 1631 by Madho Singh, it had 10,000 dwellings, but was suddenly deserted about 300 years ago for reasons that remain mysterious. Bhangarh can be reached by a bus (₹39) that runs twice daily through the sanctuary to nearby Golaka village. Check what time the bus returns, otherwise you risk getting stranded.

Tours

Private cars, including taxis, are limited to sealed roads heading to the temple and are allowed only on Tuesday and Saturday. The best way to visit the park is by gypsy (open-topped, six-passenger 4WD), which can explore off the main tracks. Gypsy safaris start

SARISKA'S TIGER TALE

Sariska Tiger Reserve took centre stage in one of India's most publicised wildlife dramas. In 2005 an Indian journalist broke the news that the tiger population here had been eliminated, a report that was later confirmed officially after an emergency census was carried out.

An inquiry into the crisis recommended fundamental management changes before tigers be reintroduced to the reserve. Extra funding was proposed to cover relocation of villages within the park as well as increasing the protection force. But action on the recommendations has been slow and incomplete despite extensive media coverage and a high level of concern in India.

Nevertheless, a pair of tigers from Ranthambhore National Park were moved by helicopter to Sariska in 2008. By 2010, five tigers had been transferred. However, in November 2010 the male of the original pair was found dead, having been poisoned by local villagers, who are not supportive of the reintroduction. The underlying problem: the inevitable battle between India's poorest and ever-expanding village populace with the rare and phenomenally valuable wildlife on their doorstep. Plans to relocate and reimburse villagers inside the park have largely failed to come to fruition, and illegal marble mining and clashes between cattle farmers and park staff have remained a problem.

In early 2012 the first cubs were sighted. At the time of writing, Sariska's tiger population was thought to be 14.

Only time will tell if this reintroduction is successful – inbreeding in the small population is an understandably high concern. Despite much vaunted successes for Project Tiger (www.projecttiger.nic.in) at a national level, Sariska remains a sad indictment of tiger conservation in India, from the top government officials down to the underpaid forest guards.

at the park entrance, and vehicle plus driver hire is ₹2100 for a three-hour safari; the vehicles can take up to five people (including guide). The bigger 20-seat canters cost ₹5000 for the vehicle and driver, but offer a much diminished experience. Guides are mandatory (₹300 for three hours).

Bookings can be made at the **Forest Reception Office** (☎0144-2841333; www.rajasthanwildlife.in; Jaipur Rd; ⊙ticket sales 6.55-7.30am & 1-3pm Nov-Jan, timings vary by 30min Mar-Jun & Oct), where buses will drop you.

Sleeping

RTDC Hotel Tiger Den HOTEL $$

(☎0144-2841342; tigerden@rtdc.in; s/d incl breakfast ₹1860/2645, with AC ₹2505/3290, ste ₹4780; ❄) Hotel Tiger Den isn't fancy – a cement block fronted by a lawn and backed by a rambling garden. It's best feature is that it is very close to the reserve entrance. On the plus side the management is friendly, there is a bar, and the rooms have balconies with a pleasant outlook. Bring a mosquito net or repellent.

Hotel Sariska Palace HERITAGE HOTEL $$$

(☎7073474870; www.thesariskapalace.in; r incl breakfast ₹8400, ste from ₹13,500; ❄📶🏊) Near the reserve entrance is this imposing former hunting lodge of the maharajas of Alwar. There's a driveway leading from opposite the Forest Reception Office. Rooms have soaring ceilings and soft mattresses, and those in the annexe by the swimming pool have good views. The Fusion Restaurant here serves expensive Indian and Continental dishes, as well as hosting a buffet (lunch/dinner ₹750/900).

Sariska Tiger Heaven HOTEL $$$

(☎9251016312; www.sariskatigerheaven.com; r incl all meals from ₹7500; ❄📶🏊) This isolated place about 3km west of the bus stop at Thanagazi village has free pick-up on offer. Rooms are set in stone-and-tile cottages and have big beds and windowed alcoves. It's a tranquil, if overpriced, place to stay. Staff can arrange 4WDs and guides to the reserve.

Getting There & Away

Sariska is 35km from Alwar, a convenient town from which to approach the reserve. There are frequent (and crowded) buses from Alwar (₹35, one to 1½ hours, at least hourly) and on to Jaipur (₹129, four hours). Buses stop in front of the Forest Reception Office.

Ajmer

☎0145 / POP 542,330

Ajmer is a bustling, chaotic city, 130km southwest of Jaipur and just 13km from the Hindu pilgrimage town of Pushkar. It surrounds the expansive lake of Ana Sagar, and is itself ringed by rugged Aravalli Hills. Ajmer is Rajasthan's most important site in terms of Islamic history and heritage. It contains one of India's most important Muslim pilgrimage centres, the shrine of Khwaja Muin-ud-din Chishti, who founded the Chishtiya order, the prime Sufi order in India. As well as some superb examples of early Muslim architecture, Ajmer is also a significant centre for the Jain religion, possessing an amazing golden Jain temple. However, with Ajmer's combination of high-voltage crowds and traffic, especially during Ramadan and the anniversary of the saint's death, most travellers choose to use Ajmer as a stepping stone to laid-back Pushkar.

Sights

Dargah of Khwaja Muin-ud-din Chishti ISLAMIC SHRINE

(www.dargahajmer.com; ⊙4am-9pm summer, 5am-9pm winter) This is the tomb of Sufi saint Khwaja Muin-ud-din Chishti, who came to Ajmer from Persia in 1192 and died here in 1236. The tomb gained its significance during the time of the Mughals – many emperors added to the buildings here. Construction of the shrine was completed by Humayun, and the gate was added by the Nizam of Hyderabad. Mughal emperor Akbar used to make the pilgrimage to the dargah from Agra every year.

You have to cover your head in certain parts of the shrine, so remember to take a scarf or cap – there are plenty for sale at the colourful bazaar leading to the dargah, along with floral offerings and delicious toffees.

The main entrance is through **Nizam Gate** (1915). Inside, the green and white mosque, **Akbari Masjid**, was constructed in 1571 and is now an Arabic and Persian school for religious education. The next gate is called the **Shahjahani Gate**, as it was erected by Shah Jahan, although it is also known as 'Nakkarkhana', because of the two large *nakkharas* (drums) fixed above it.

A third gate, **Buland Darwaza** (16th century), leads into the dargah courtyard.

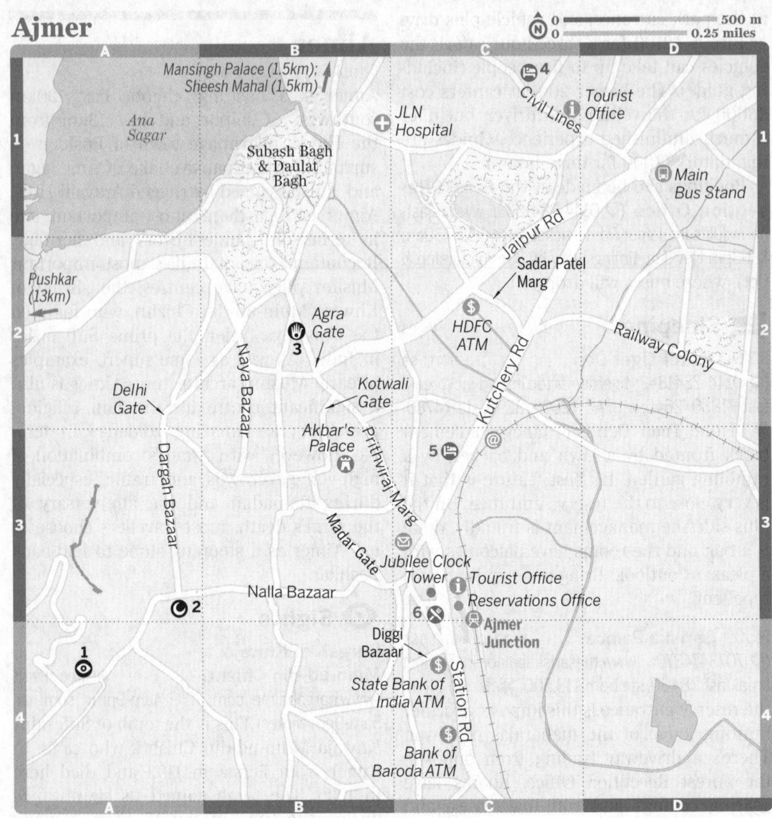

Ajmer

Sights

1 Adhai-din-ka-Jhonpra A4
2 Dargah of Khwaja Muin-ud-din Chishti A3
3 Nasiyan (Red) Temple B2

Sleeping

4 Badnor House C1
5 Haveli Heritage Inn C3

Eating

6 Madina Hotel C3

Flanking the entrance of the courtyard are the *degs* (large iron cauldrons), one donated by Akbar in 1567, the other by Jehangir in 1631, for offerings for the poor.

Inside this courtyard, the saint's domed tomb is surrounded by a silver platform. Pilgrims believe that the saint's spirit will intercede on their behalf in matters of illness, business or personal problems, so the notes and holy string attached to the railings around are thanks or requests.

Pilgrims and Sufis come from all over the world on the anniversary of the saint's death, the Urs, in the seventh month of the Islamic lunar calendar. Crowds can be suffocating.

Bags must be left in the cloakroom (₹10 each, with camera ₹20) outside the main entrance.

Nasiyan (Red) Temple JAIN TEMPLE

(Prithviraj Marg; ₹10; ⏲8.30am-5.30pm) This marvellous Jain temple, built in 1865, is also known as the Golden Temple, due to its amazing golden diorama in the double-storey temple hall. The intricate diorama depicts the Jain concept of the ancient world, with 13 continents and oceans, the golden city of Ayodhya, flying peacock and elephant gondolas, and gilded elephants with many tusks. The hall is also decorated with gold, silver and precious stones. It's unlike any other temple in Rajasthan and is well worth a visit.

Adhai-din-ka-Jhonpra HISTORIC SITE
(Two-and-a-Half-Day Building; ⌚dawn-dusk) Beyond the Dargah of Khwaja Muin-ud-din Chishti, on the town outskirts, are the extraordinary ruins of the Adhai-din-ka-Jhonpra mosque. According to legend, construction in 1153 took only 2½ days. Others say it was named after a festival lasting 2½ days. It was originally built as a Sanskrit college, but in 1198 Mohammed of Ghori seized Ajmer and converted the building into a mosque by adding a seven-arched wall covered with Islamic calligraphy in front of the pillared hall.

Sleeping & Eating

Haveli Heritage Inn HOTEL $$
(☎0145-2621607; www.haveliheritageinn.com; Kutchery Rd; r ₹1340-3000; ❄@) Set in a 140-year-old *haveli,* this welcoming city-centre oasis is arguably Ajmer's best midrange choice. The high-ceilinged rooms are spacious (some are almost suites), simply decorated, air-cooled and set well back from the busy road. There's a pleasant, grassy courtyard and the hotel is infused with a family atmosphere, complete with home-cooked meals.

Badnor House GUESTHOUSE $$
(☎0145-2627579; www.badnorhouse.com; Savitri Girl's College Rd, Civil Lines; s/d incl breakfast ₹2600/3000; ❄) This guesthouse provides an excellent opportunity to stay with a delightful family and receive down-to-earth hospitality. There are three heritage-style doubles and an older-style, spacious and comfortable self-contained suite with private courtyard. The host is also an occasional travel photographer.

Mansingh Palace HOTEL $$$
(☎0145-2425956; www.mansinghhotels.com; Circular Rd; r from ₹4200, ste ₹7000; ❄@) This modern place, on the shores of Ana Sagar about 3km from the centre, is rather out of the way, but has attractive and comfortable rooms, some with views and balconies. The hotel has a shady garden, a bar and a good restaurant, the Sheesh Mahal.

Madina Hotel NORTH INDIAN $
(Station Rd; mains ₹30-100; ⌚9am-11pm) Handy if you're waiting for a train (it's opposite the station), this simple, open-to-the-street eatery cooks up cheap veg and nonveg fare, with specialities such as chicken Mughlai and *rumali roti* (huge paper-thin chapati).

Sheesh Mahal MULTICUISINE $$
(Circular Rd; mains ₹150-375; ⌚noon-3pm & 7-10.30pm) This upmarket restaurant, located in Ajmer's top hotel, the Mansingh Palace (p135), offers excellent Indian, Continental and Chinese dishes, as well as a buffet when the tour groups pass through. The service is slick, the air-con is on the chilly side, and the food is very good; it also boasts a bar.

Information

JLN Hospital (☎0145-2625500; Daulat Bagh; ⌚24hr)
Main Post Office (Prithviraj Marg; ⌚10am-1pm & 1.30-6pm Mon-Sat) Less than 500m from the train station.
Satguru's Internet (60-61 Kutchery Rd; per hr ₹30; ⌚9am-10pm)
Tourist Office Ajmer Junction Train Station (⌚9am-5pm); RTDC Hotel Khadim (☎0145-2627426; ⌚9am-5pm Mon-Fri)

Getting There & Away

For those pushing on to Pushkar, haggle hard for a private taxi – ₹350 is a good rate.

BUS

Government-run buses leave from the **main bus stand** in Ajmer, from where buses to Pushkar (₹14, 30 minutes) also leave throughout the day. In addition to these buses, there are less-frequent 'deluxe' coach services running to major destinations such as Delhi and Jaipur. There is a 24-hour cloakroom at the bus stand (₹10 per bag per day).

DESTINATION	FARE (₹)	DURATION (HR)
Agra	392	10
Ahmedabad	543	13
Bharatpur	330	7
Bikaner	267	7
Bundi	184	5
Chittorgarh	195, AC 348	5
Delhi	404, AC 1096	8½
Jaipur	148, AC 314	2½
Jaisalmer	458	11
Jodhpur	205, AC 445	6
Udaipur	285, AC 542	9

TRAIN

Ajmer is a busy train junction. To book tickets, go to booth 5 at the train station's **reservations office** (⌚8am-8pm Mon-Sat, to 2pm Sun). Services include the following:

Agra (Agra Fort Station) sleeper/AC Chair ₹275/570, 6½ hours, three daily (2.10am, 12.50pm and 3pm)
Chittorgarh sleeper/3AC ₹180/560, three hours, at least six daily (1.25am, 2.15am, 1pm, 4.10pm, 8.30pm and 9.05pm)
Delhi (mostly to Old Delhi or New Delhi stations) 2nd-class seat/sleeper ₹165/300, eight hours, 11 daily around the clock
Jaipur 2nd-class seat/sleeper/AC chair ₹100/150/325, two hours, at least 24 throughout the day
Jodhpur sleeper/3AC ₹185/510, four to five hours, two direct daily (1.40pm and 2.25pm)
Mt Abu (Abu Road) sleeper ₹245, five hours, 12 daily
Mumbai sleeper ₹495, around 19 hours, three daily (6.35am, 9.20am and 12.40pm)
Udaipur sleeper ₹245, five hours, four daily (1.25am, 2.15am, 8.25am and 4.10pm)

Pushkar

☎0145 / POP 21,630

Pushkar has a magnetism all of its own – it's quite unlike anywhere else in Rajasthan. It's a prominent Hindu pilgrimage town and devout Hindus should visit at least once in their lifetime. The town curls around a holy lake, said to have appeared when Brahma dropped a lotus flower. It also has one of the world's few Brahma temples. With 52 bathing ghats and 400 milky-blue temples, the town often hums with *puja* (prayers), generating an episodic soundtrack of chanting, drums and gongs, and devotional songs.

The result is a muddle of religious and tourist scenes. The main street is one long bazaar, selling anything to tickle a traveller's fancy, from hippy-chic tie-dye to didgeridoos. Despite the commercialism and banana pancakes, the town remains enchantingly small and authentically mystic.

Pushkar is only 11km from Ajmer, separated from it by rugged Nag Pahar (Snake Mountain).

Sights

Fifty-two bathing ghats surround the lake, where pilgrims bathe in the sacred waters. If you wish to join them, do so with respect. Remember, this is a holy place: remove your shoes and don't smoke, kid around or take photographs.

Some ghats have particular importance: Vishnu appeared at **Varah Ghat** in the form of a boar, Brahma bathed at **Brahma Ghat**, and Gandhi's ashes were sprinkled at **Gandhi Ghat**, formerly Gau Ghat.

Pushkar boasts hundreds of temples, though few are particularly ancient, as they were mostly desecrated by Aurangzeb and subsequently rebuilt.

Old Rangji Temple HINDU TEMPLE
Old Rangji Temple is close to the bazaar and is often alive with worshippers.

Savitri Mata Temple HINDU TEMPLE
(Saraswati Temple; ropeway return trip ₹92; ⏲ ropeway 9.30am-7.30pm) The ropeway makes the ascent to the hilltop Saraswati Temple a breeze. The temple overlooks the lake and the views are fantastic at any time of day. Alternatively, you could take the one-hour trek up before dawn to beat the heat and capture the best light.

Brahma Temple HINDU TEMPLE
Pushkar's most famous temple is the Brahma Temple, said to be one of the few such temples in the world as a result of a curse by Brahma's consort, Saraswati. The temple is

MAJOR TRAINS FROM AJMER

DESTINATION	TRAIN	DEPARTURE	ARRIVAL	FARE (₹)
Agra (Agra Fort Station)	12988 Ajmer-SDAH Exp	12.50pm	6.50pm	275/695 (A)
Delhi (New Delhi)	12016 Ajmer Shatabdi	2.05pm	10pm	720/1530 (B)
Jaipur	12991 Udaipur-Jaipur Exp	11.30am	1.30pm	100/325/440 (C)
Jodhpur	15014 Ranighat Exp	1.40pm	5.35pm	185/510 (A)
Udaipur	09721 Jaipur-Udaipur SF SPL	8.25am	1.15pm	140/245/490/560 (D)

Fares: (A) sleeper/3AC, (B) AC chair/1AC, (C) 2nd-class seat/AC chair/1AC, (D) 2nd-class seat/sleeper/AC chair/3AC

Pushkar

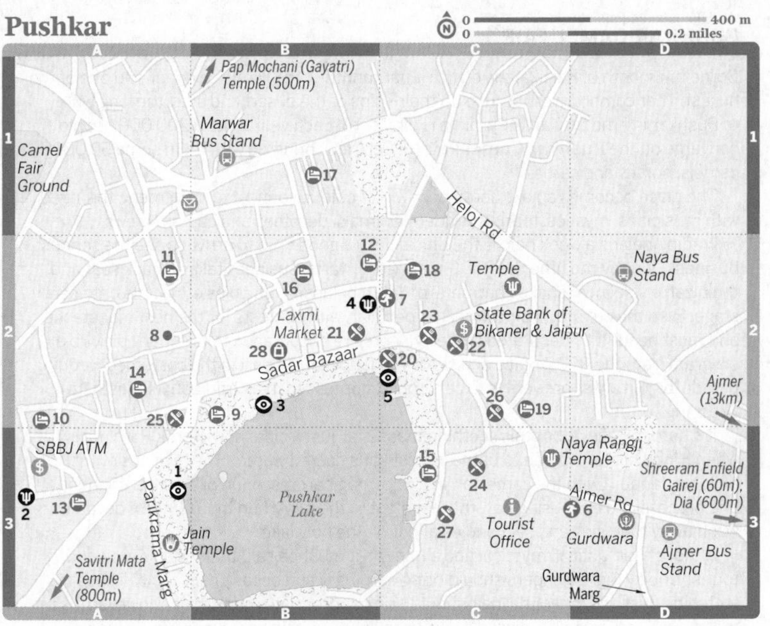

Pushkar

Sights
1 Brahma Ghat A3
2 Brahma Temple A3
3 Gandhi Ghat B2
4 Old Rangji Temple B2
5 Varah Ghat C2

Activities, Courses & Tours
Cooking Bahar .... (see 8)
6 Government Homeopathic Hospital D3
7 Roshi Hiralal Verma C2
8 Saraswati Music School A2

Sleeping
9 Bharatpur Palace B2
10 Hotel Akash A2
11 Hotel Everest A2
12 Hotel Kanhaia Haveli B2
13 Hotel Navaratan Palace A3
14 Hotel Paramount Palace A2
15 Hotel Pushkar Palace C3
16 Hotel Tulsi Palace B2
17 Hotel White House B1
18 Inn Seventh Heaven C2
19 Shyam Krishna Guesthouse C2

Eating
20 Falafel Wrap Stalls C2
21 Honey & Spice B2
22 Naryan Café C2
23 Om Baba Restaurant C2
24 Om Shiva Garden Restaurant C3
25 Out of the Blue A2
26 Shri Vankatesh C2
Sixth Sense .... (see 18)
27 Sunset Café C3

Shopping
28 Sadar Bazaar B2

marked by a red spire, and over the entrance gateway is the *hans* (goose symbol) of Brahma. Inside, the floor and walls are engraved with dedications to the dead.

Pap Mochani (Gayatri) Temple HINDU TEMPLE
The sunrise views over town from Pap Mochani (Gayatri) Temple, reached by a track behind the Marwar bus stand, are well worth the 30-minute climb.

Activities

Government Homeopathic Hospital AYURVEDA
(Ajmer Rd; 1hr full-body massage ₹500; 9am-1pm & 4-6pm) For a noncommercial massage-treatment experience, try the ayurvedic

PUSHKAR CAMEL FAIR

Come the month of Kartika, the eighth lunar month of the Hindu calendar and one of the holiest, Thar camel drivers spruce up their ships of the desert and start the long walk to Pushkar in time for Kartik Purnima (Full Moon). Each year around 200,000 people converge on the **Pushkar Camel Fair** (Oct/Nov), bringing with them some 50,000 camels, horses and cattle.

The place becomes an extraordinary swirl of colour, sound and movement, thronged with musicians, mystics, tourists, traders, animals, devotees and camera crews.

Trading begins a week before the official fair (a good time to arrive to see the serious business), but by the time the RTDC mela (fair) starts, business takes a back seat and the bizarre sidelines (snake charmers, children balancing on poles etc) jostle onto centre stage. Even the cultural program seems peculiar, with contests for the best moustache, and most beautifully decorated camel. Visitors are encouraged to take part: pick up a program from the RTDC office and see if you fancy taking part in the costumed wedding parade, or join a Visitors versus Locals sports contest such as traditional Rajasthani wrestling.

It's hard to believe, but this seething mass is all just a sideshow. Kartik Purnima is when Hindu pilgrims come to bathe in Pushkar's sacred waters. The religious event builds in tandem with the camel fair in a wild, magical crescendo of incense, chanting and processions to dousing day, the last night of the fair, when thousands of devotees wash away their sins and set candles afloat on the holy lake.

Although fantastical, mystical and a one-off, it must be said that it's also crowded, touristy, noisy (light sleepers should bring earplugs) and occasionally tacky. Those affected by dust and/or animal hair should bring appropriate medication. However, it's a grand epic, and not to be missed if you're anywhere within camel-spitting distance.

The fair usually takes place in November, but dates change according to the lunar calendar.

department at the small and basic Government Homeopathic Hospital.

Roshi Hiralal Verma REIKI, YOGA
(9829895906; Ambika Guest House, Laxmi Market) Offers reiki, yoga and shiatsu; costs depend on the duration and nature of your session.

Courses

Saraswati Music School MUSIC
(Birju 9828297784, Hemant 9829333548; saraswati_music@hotmail.com; Mainon ka Chowk) Teaches tabla (drums), flute, harmonium, singing, and *kathak* (classical dance) and Bollywood dance. For music, contact Birju, who's been playing for around 20 years, and charges from ₹350 for two hours. He often conducts evening performances (7pm to 8pm), and also sells instruments. For dance, contact Hemant.

Cooking Bahar COOKING
(0145-2773124; www.cookingbahar.com; Mainon ka Chowk; 2-3hr class ₹1100) Part of the Saraswati Music School family, Deepa conducts cooking classes that cover three vegetarian courses.

Sleeping

Owing to Pushkar's star status among backpackers, there are far more budget options than midrange, though many budget properties have a selection of midrange-priced rooms. At the time of the camel fair, prices multiply up to three-fold or more, and it's essential to book several weeks ahead.

★**Hotel Everest** HOTEL $
(9414666958, 0145-2773417; www.pushkarhoteleverest.com; off Sadar Bazaar; r ₹300-850, with AC ₹1000-1150;) This welcoming budget hotel is nestled in the quiet laneways north of Sadar Bazaar. It's run by a friendly father-and-son team who can't do too much for their appreciative guests. The rooms are variable in size, colourful and spotless, and the beds are comfortable. The rooftop is a pleasant retreat for meals or just relaxing with a book.

Hotel Tulsi Palace HOTEL $
(8947074663; www.hoteltulsipalacepushkar.com; VIP Rd, Holika Chowk; r ₹500-700, with AC ₹1000-1500;) Tulsi Palace is a great budget choice with a variety of bright and

airy rooms around a central courtyard. The attached Little Prince Cafe on the 1st-floor verandah serves Continental breakfasts and Indian lunch and dinner, and boasts prime street-life views. The friendly staff will help with your transport needs.

Hotel White House GUESTHOUSE $

(☎0145-2772147; www.pushkarwhitehouse.com; off Heloj Rd; r ₹350-950, with AC ₹1000-1500; ❄@📶) This place is indeed white, with spotless rooms. Some are decidedly on the small side, but the nicest are generous and have balconies to boot. There is good traveller fare and green views from the plant-filled rooftop restaurant. It's efficiently run by a woman and her two sons. Yoga is offered, as is a welcome brew of mango tea for every guest.

Hotel Akash HOTEL $

(☎0145-2772498; filterboy21@yahoo.com; Badi Basti; d ₹600, s/d without bathroom ₹300/500; 📶) A simple budget place with keen young management and a large tree sprouting up from the courtyard to shade the rooftop terrace. Rooms are basic fan-cooled affairs that open out to a balcony restaurant good for spying on the street below.

Bharatpur Palace HOTEL $

(☎0145-2772320; bharatpurpalace_pushkar@yahoo.co.in; Sadar Bazaar; r ₹400-1000, without bathroom ₹250-600; ❄) This rambling building occupies one of the best spots in Pushkar, on the upper levels adjacent to Gandhi Ghat. It features aesthetic blue-washed simplicity: bare-bones rooms with unsurpassed views of the holy lake. The rooftop terrace (with restaurant) has sublime vistas, but respect for bathing pilgrims is paramount for intended guests.

Room 1 is the most romantic place to wake up: it's surrounded on three sides by the lake. Rooms 9, 12, 13 and 16 are also good.

Shyam Krishna Guesthouse GUESTHOUSE $

(☎0145-2772461; skguesthouse@yahoo.com; Sadar Bazaar; s/d ₹400/700, without bathroom ₹300/500; 📶) Housed in a lovely old blue-washed building with lawns and gardens, this guesthouse has ashram austerity and genuinely friendly management. Some of the cheaper rooms are cell-like, though all share the simple, authentic ambience. The outdoor kitchen and garden seating are a good setting for a relaxing meal of hearty vegetarian fare, but watch out for passing troops of monkeys.

Hotel Paramount Palace HOTEL $

(☎0145-2772428; www.pushkarparamount.com; r ₹200-1000; 📶) Perched on the highest point in Pushkar overlooking an old temple, this welcoming hotel has excellent views of the town and lake (and lots of stairs). The rooms vary widely; the best (106, 108, 109) have lovely balconies, stained-glass windows and are good value, but the smaller rooms can be dingy. There's a dizzyingly magical rooftop terrace.

Hotel Navaratan Palace HOTEL $

(☎0145-2772145; www.navratanpalace.com; s/d incl breakfast ₹800/900, with AC ₹1000/1200; ❄📶🏊) Located close to the Brahma Temple, this hotel has a lovely enclosed garden with a fabulous pool (₹100 for nonguests), children's playground and pet tortoises. The rooms, crammed with carved wooden furniture, are clean and comfortable but small.

★**Inn Seventh Heaven** HERITAGE HOTEL $$

(☎0145-5105455; www.inn-seventh-heaven.com; Choti Basti; r ₹1350-3300; ❄@📶) Enter this lovingly converted *haveli* through heavy wooden doors into an incense-perfumed courtyard, with a marble fountain in the centre and surrounded by tumbling vines. There are just a dozen individually decorated rooms situated on three levels, all with traditionally crafted furniture and comfortable beds. Rooms vary in size, from the downstairs budget rooms to the spacious Asana suite.

On the roof you'll find the excellent Sixth Sense restaurant (p140), as well as sofas and swing chairs for relaxing with a book. Early booking (two-night minimum, no credit cards) is recommended.

Hotel Kanhaia Haveli HOTEL $$

(☎0145-2772146; www.pushkarhotelkanhaia.com; Choti Basti; r ₹400-600, with AC ₹1500-1800; ❄📶) Boasting a vast range of rooms, from budget digs to suites, you are sure to find a room and price that suits. Rooms get bigger and lighter, with more windows, the more you spend. Some rooms have balconies, while all have cable TV. There is a multicuisine restaurant with views on the rooftop.

Dia B&B $$

(☎0145-5105455; www.diahomestay.com; Panch Kund Marg; r incl breakfast ₹3550-4950; ❄@📶) This beautifully designed B&B by the folks at Inn Seventh Heaven has five very private doubles a short walk from town. The rooms are straight out of a design magazine and will have you swooning (and extending your booking). You can dine here at the cosy rooftop restaurant or head to the Sixth Sense restaurant at Inn Seventh Heaven.

Hotel Pushkar Palace HERITAGE HOTEL **$$$**
(☎0145-2772001; www.hotelpushkarpalace.com; s/d/ste incl breakfast ₹7715/8310/17,805; ❄@) Once belonging to the maharaja of Kishangarh, the top-end Hotel Pushkar Palace boasts a romantic lakeside setting. The rooms have carved wooden furniture and beds, and all rooms above the ground floor, and all the suites, look directly out onto the lake: no hotel in Pushkar has better views. A pleasant outdoor dining area overlooks the lake.

Ananta Spa & Resort RESORT **$$$**
(☎0145-3054000; www.anantahotels.com; Leela Sevri, Ajmer Rd; r incl breakfast from ₹6000; ❄@📶🏊) The arrival of Ananta, an (almost) five-star resort sprawling on 3.5 hectares in the rugged ranges 4km from Pushkar, heralds a new era in pilgrimages. Lucky pilgrims zip from reception to the Balinese-style cottages on golf buggies. Rooms are spacious and fully appointed, but most guests will gravitate to the luscious pool, spa, games room, restaurant, lounge or bar.

Eating

Pushkar has plenty of atmospheric eateries with lake views, and menus reflecting backpacker preferences. Strict vegetarianism, forbidding even eggs, is the order of the day.

Naryan Café CAFE **$**
(Mahadev Chowk, Sadar Bazaar; breakfast from ₹100; ⏲7.30am-10pm) Busy any time of day, this is particularly popular as a breakfast stop: watch the world go by with a fresh coffee (from ₹40) or juice (from ₹80) and an enormous bowl of homemade muesli, topped with a mountain of fruit.

Shri Vankatesh INDIAN **$**
(Choti Basti; mains ₹60-100; ⏲9am-10pm) Head to this no-nonsense local favourite and tuck into some dhal, paneer or kofta, before mopping up the sauce with some freshly baked chapatis and washing it all down with some good old-fashioned chai. The thalis (₹70 to ₹150) are excellent value, too. Watch your food being cooked or head upstairs to people-watch the street below.

Falafel Wrap Stalls MIDDLE EASTERN **$**
(Sadar Bazaar; wraps ₹70-130; ⏲7.30am-10.30pm) Perfect for quelling a sudden attack of the munchies, and a big hit with Israeli travellers, these adjacent roadside joints knock up a choice selection of filling falafel-and-hummus wraps. Eat them while sitting on stools on the road or devour them on the hoof.

Out of the Blue MULTICUISINE **$$**
(Sadar Bazaar; mains ₹170-280; ⏲8am-11pm; 📶) Distinctly a deeper shade of blue in this sky-blue town, Out of the Blue is a reliable restaurant. The menu ranges from noodles and *momos* (Tibetan dumplings) to pizza, pasta, falafel and pancakes. A nice touch is the street-level espresso coffee bar (coffees ₹60 to ₹80) and German bakery.

Sixth Sense MULTICUISINE **$$**
(Inn Seventh Heaven, Choti Basti; mains ₹100-200; ⏲8.30am-4pm & 6-10pm; 📶) This chilled rooftop restaurant is a great place to head to even if you didn't score a room in the popular hotel. The pizza and the Indian seasonal vegetables and rice are all serviceable, as is the filter coffee and fresh juice. Its ambience is immediately relaxing and the pulley apparatus that delivers food from the ground-floor kitchen is very cunning.

Save room for the desserts, such as the excellent homemade tarts.

Om Shiva Garden Restaurant MULTICUISINE **$$**
(☎0145-2772305; www.omshivagardenrestaurant.com; mains ₹140-250; ⏲8am-11pm; 📶) This traveller stalwart near Naya Rangji Temple continues to satisfy, with wood-fired pizzas and espresso coffee featuring on its predominately Italian and North Indian menu. It's hard to pass on the pizzas, but there are also some Mexican and Chinese dishes and 'German bakery' items to try.

Honey & Spice MULTICUISINE **$$**
(Laxmi Market, off Sadar Bazaar; mains ₹90-250; ⏲8am-5.30pm; 🖉) 🍃 Run by a friendly family, this tiny wholefood breakfast and lunch place has delicious South Indian coffee and homemade cakes. Even better are the salads and hearty vegetable combo stews served with brown rice – delicious, wholesome and a welcome change from frequently oil-rich Indian food.

Sunset Café MULTICUISINE **$$**
(mains ₹80-250; ⏲7.30am-midnight; 📶) Right on the eastern ghats, this cafe has sublime lake views. It offers the usual traveller menu, including curries, pizza and pasta, plus there's a German bakery serving reasonable cakes. The lakeside setting is perfect at sunset and gathers a crowd.

Om Baba Restaurant MULTICUISINE $$
(☎0145-2772858; off Sadar Bazaar; mains ₹130-220; ⌚8.30am-11pm) Om Baba Rooftop Restaurant serves all the traveller favourites so common in the neighbourhood (pizza, pasta, falafel, hummus), but it's the views from the rooftop that sets this place apart.

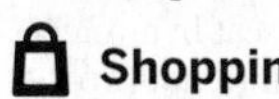

Shopping

Sadar Bazaar MARKET
Pushkar's Sadar Bazaar is lined with enchanting little shops and is a good place for picking up gifts. Many of the vibrant Rajasthani textiles originate from Barmer, south of Jaisalmer. There's plenty of silver and beaded jewellery catering both to local and foreign tastes, including some heavy tribal pieces. As Pushkar is touristy, you'll have to haggle.

The range of Indian-music CDs makes this market an excellent place to sample local tunes.

Information

Foreign-card-friendly ATMs and unofficial money changers are dotted around Sadar Bazaar.

Post Office (off Heloj Rd; ⌚9.30am-5pm Mon-Fri) Near the Marwar bus stand.

State Bank of Bikaner & Jaipur (SBBJ; Sadar Bazaar; ⌚10am-4pm Mon-Fri, to 12.30pm Sat) Changes travellers cheques and cash. The SBBJ ATM accepts international cards.

Tourist Office (☎0145-2772040; Hotel Sarovar; ⌚10am-5pm) Free maps and camel fair programs.

DANGERS & ANNOYANCES

Beware of anyone giving you flowers to offer a *puja* (prayer): before you know it you'll be whisked to the ghats in a well-oiled hustle and asked for a personal donation of up to ₹1000. Other priests do genuinely live off the donations of others and this is a tradition that goes back centuries – but walk away if you feel bullied and always agree on a price before taking a red ribbon (a 'Pushkar passport') or flowers.

During the camel fair, Pushkar is besieged by pickpockets working the crowded bazaars. You can avoid the razor gang by not using thin-walled day packs and by carrying your pack in front of you. At any time of year, watch out for rampaging motorbikes ridden by inconsiderate youths in the bazaar.

Getting There & Away

Pushkar's tiny train station is so badly connected it's not worth bothering with. Use Ajmer junction train station instead.

A private taxi to Ajmer costs around ₹300 (note that it's almost always more expensive in the opposite direction). When entering Pushkar by car there is a toll of ₹20 per person.

BUS

Frequent buses to/from Ajmer (₹14, 30 minutes) depart from the **Naya Bus Stand**, and also from the **Ajmer Bus Stand** on the road heading eastwards out of town. Most other buses leave from the Naya Bus Stand, though some may still use the old **Marwar Bus Stand** (but not RSRTC buses).

Local travel agencies sell tickets for private buses – you should shop around. These buses often leave from Ajmer (p135), but the agencies should provide you with free connecting transport. Check whether your bus is direct, as many services from Pushkar aren't. And note, even if they are direct buses they may well stop for some time in Ajmer, meaning it's often quicker to go to Ajmer first and then catch another bus from there.

Getting Around

There are no autorickshaws in central Pushkar, but it's a breeze to get around on foot. If you want to explore the surrounding countryside, you could try hiring a motorbike (₹400 per day) from one of the many places around town. For something more substantial, try **Shreeram Enfield Gairej** (Ajmer Rd; Enfield Bullet hire per day ₹700, deposit ₹50,000), which hires Enfield Bullets and sells them.

Ranthambhore National Park

☎07462

This famous **national park** (www.rajasthanwildlife.in; ⌚Oct-Jun) is the best place to spot wild tigers in Rajasthan. Comprising 1334

BUSES FROM PUSHKAR (NAYA BUS STAND)

DESTINATION	FARE (₹)	DURATION (HR)	FREQUENCY
Bikaner	225	6	hourly
Bundi	200	6	daily (11am)
Jaipur	160	4	7 daily (7.15am, 7.45am, 8am, 8.30am, 9.30am, 2pm & 4pm)
Jodhpur	185	5	3 daily (8am, 10.30am & 12.30pm)

sq km of wild jungle scrub hemmed in by rocky ridges, at its centre is the 10th-century Ranthambhore Fort. Scattered around the fort are ancient temples and mosques, hunting pavilions, crocodile-filled lakes and vine-covered *chhatris* (burial tombs). The park was a maharajas' hunting ground until 1970, a curious 15 years after it had become a sanctuary.

Seeing a tiger (around 52 to 55 in 2016) is partly a matter of luck; leave time for two or three safaris to improve your chances. But remember there's plenty of other wildlife to see, including more than 300 species of birds.

It's 10km from Sawai Madhopur (the gateway town for Ranthambhore) to the first gate of the park, and another 3km to the main gate and Ranthambhore Fort.

Sights

Ranthambhore Fort FORT

(6am-6pm) FREE From a distance, the magical 10th-century Ranthambhore Fort is almost indiscernible on its hilltop perch – as you get closer, it seems almost as if it is growing out of the rock. It covers an area of 4.5 sq km, and affords peerless views from the disintegrating walls of the Badal Mahal (Palace of the Clouds), on its northern side. The ramparts stretch for more than 7km, and seven enormous gateways are still intact.

To visit the on the cheap, join the locals who go there to visit the temple dedicated to Ganesh. Shared 4WDs (₹40 per person) go from the train station to the park entrance – say 'national park' and they'll know what you want. From there, other shared 4WDs (₹20 per person) shuttle to and from the fort, which is inside the park. Alternatively hire your own gypsy (and driver) for about ₹1000 for three hours through your hotel.

Activities

Safaris take place in the early morning and late afternoon, starting between 6am and 7am or between 2pm and 3.30pm, depending on the time of year. Each safari lasts for around three hours. The mornings can be exceptionally chilly in the open vehicles, so bring warm clothes.

The best option is to travel by **gypsy** (six-person, open-topped 4WD; Indian/foreigner ₹730/1470). You still have a chance of seeing a tiger from a **canter** (20-seat, open-topped truck; ₹510/1250), but other passengers can be very rowdy.

Be aware that the rules for booking safaris (and prices) are prone to change. You can book online through the park's official website (www.rajasthanwildlife.in), or go in person to the safari booking office, which is inconveniently located 1.5km from Hammir Circle, in the opposite direction to the park. And to be sure of bagging a seat in a vehicle, start queuing at least an hour (if not two) before the safaris are due to begin – meaning a very early start for morning safaris! Booking with hotels is much simpler, but be aware that they add commission to the rates.

Sleeping

Hotel Aditya Resort HOTEL $

(9414728468; www.hoteladityaresort.com; Ranthambhore Rd; r ₹400-700, with AC ₹900;) This friendly place is one of the better of the few ultracheapies along Ranthambhore Rd. There are just six simple, unadorned rooms (get one with an outside window; only a couple have air-conditioning), and a basic rooftop restaurant. The staff will help with safari bookings, but be sure to ask how much they are charging for the service.

★ **Hotel Ranthambhore Regency** HOTEL $$

(07462-221176; www.ranthambhor.com; Ranthambhore Rd; s/d incl all meals from ₹6500/7500;) A very professional place that caters to tour groups but can still provide great service to independent travellers. It has immaculate, well-appointed rooms (think marble floors, flat-screen TVs etc), which would rate as suites in most hotels. The central garden with an inviting pool is a virtual oasis, and there's a pampering spa next to the restaurant.

Tiger Safari Resort HOTEL $$

(07462-221137; www.tigersafariresort.com; Ranthambhore Rd; r incl breakfast ₹1800-2200;) A reasonable midrange option, with spacious doubles and 'cottages' (larger rooms with bigger bathrooms) facing a garden and small pool. The management is adept at organising safaris, wake-up calls and early breakfasts before the morning safari. As per the other hotels, a commission is added for this service, so ask for a breakdown of the costs.

Ankur Resort HOTEL $$

(07462-220792; www.ankurresorts.com; Ranthambhore Rd; s/d incl all meals ₹3500/4000, cottages ₹4000/5000;) Ankur Resort is good at organising safaris, wake-up calls and early breakfasts for tiger spotters. Standard rooms are fairly unadorned, but clean and comfortable with TVs. The cottages boast better beds, a fridge and settee, and overlook the surrounding gardens and pool.

★**Khem Villas** BOUTIQUE HOTEL **$$$**
(☎07462-252099; www.khemvillas.com; Khem Villas Rd; s/d incl all meals ₹12,000/14,000, tents ₹19,000/23,000, cottages ₹21,000/25,000; ❄@📶) Set in 9 hectares of organic farmland and reforested land, this splendid ecolodge was created by the Singh Rathore family, the driving force behind the conservation of tigers at Ranthambhore. The accommodation ranges from colonial-style bungalow rooms to luxury tents and sumptuous stone cottages. Privacy is guaranteed – you can even bathe under the stars.

In addition to jungle safaris, Khem Villas runs a river safari (₹5000 for two people) on the Chambal river where you can see gharial and mugger crocodiles plus numerous bird species.

ℹ Information

There's an ATM just by Hammir Circle, as well as others by the train station.

Ranthambore Adventure Tours (☎9414214460; ranthambhoretours@rediff.mail.com; Ranthambhore Rd) Safari agency that gets good reviews.

Tourist Office (☎07462-220808; Train Station; ⏰9.30am-6pm Mon-Fri) Has maps of Sawai Madhopur, and can offer suggestions on safaris.

Safari Booking Office (www.rajasthanwildlife.com; ⏰5.30am-3.30pm) Seats in gypsies and canters can be reserved on the website, though a single gypsy (with a premium price) and five canters are also kept for direct booking at the Forest Office. Located 500m from the train station.

ℹ Getting There & Away

There are very few direct buses to anywhere of interest, so it's always preferable to take the train.

TRAIN

Sawai Madhopur junction station is near Hammir Circle, which leads to Ranthambhore Rd.

Agra (Agra Fort Station) sleeper ₹210, six hours, three daily (11.10am, 4.10pm, 11.15pm)

Delhi 2nd-class/sleeper/3AC ₹190/260/660, 5½ to eight hours, 13 daily

Jaipur 2nd-class seat/sleeper/3AC ₹100/180/560, two hours, 11 to 13 daily

Keoladeo NP (Bharatpur) 2nd-class/sleeper/3AC ₹95/180/560, 2½ hours, 12 to 13 daily

Kota (from where you can catch buses to Bundi) 2nd-class/sleeper/3AC ₹90/180/560, one to two hours, hourly

ℹ Getting Around

Bicycle hire (around ₹40 per day) is available in the main bazaar. Autorickshaws are available at the train station; it's ₹50 to ₹100 for an autorickshaw from the train station to Ranthambhore Rd, depending on where you get off. Many hotels will pick you up from the train station for free if you call ahead.

If you want to walk, turn left out of the train station and follow the road up to the overpass (200m). Turn left and cross the bridge over the railway line to reach a roundabout (200m), known as Hammir Circle. Turn right here to reach the safari booking office (1.5km) or left to find accommodation.

UDAIPUR & SOUTHERN RAJASTHAN

Bundi

☎0747 / POP 103,290

A captivating town with narrow lanes of Brahmin-blue houses, lakes, hills, bazaars, and a temple at every turn, Bundi is dominated by a fantastical palace of faded parchment cupolas and loggias rising from the hillside above the town. Though an increasingly popular traveller hang-out, Bundi attracts nothing like the tourist crowds of places such as Jaipur or Udaipur. Few places in Rajasthan retain so much of the magical atmosphere of centuries past.

Bundi came into its own in the 12th century when a group of Chauhan nobles from Ajmer were pushed south by Mohammed of Ghori. They wrested the Bundi area from the Mina and Bhil tribes and made Bundi the capital of their kingdom, known as Hadoti. Bundi was generally loyal to the Mughals from the late 16th century on, but it maintained its independent status until incorporated into the state of Rajasthan after 1947.

👁 Sights

Bundi has around 60 beautiful *baoris* (stepwells), some right in the town centre. The majesty of many of them is unfortunately diminished by their lack of water today – a result of declining groundwater levels – and

Bundi

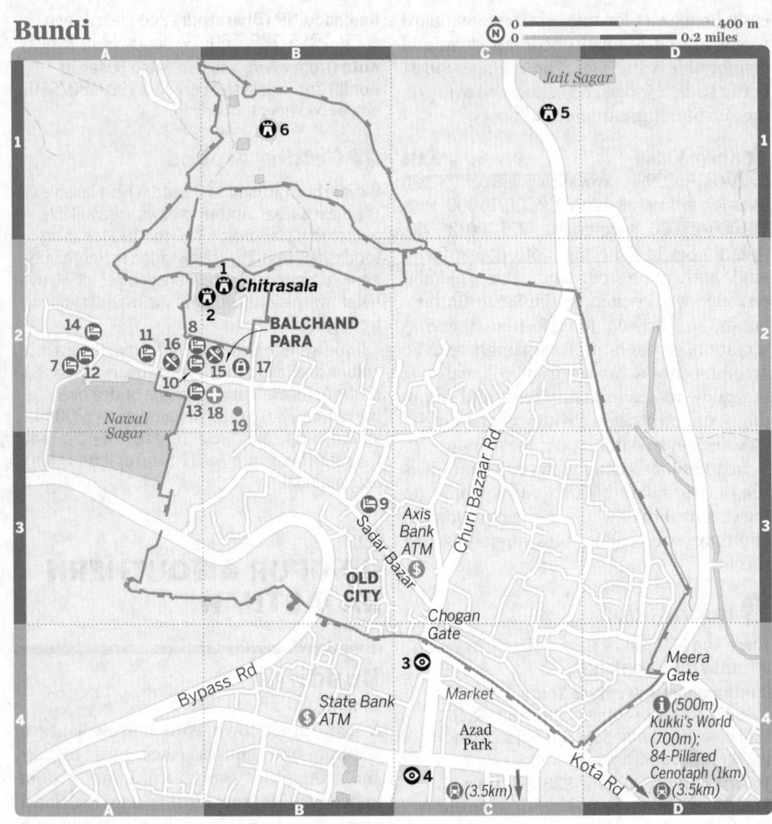

Bundi

Top Sights

1 Chitrasala B2

Sights

2 Bundi Palace B2
3 Nagar Sagar Kund C4
4 Raniji-ki-Baori C4
5 Sukh Mahal C1
6 Taragarh B1

Sleeping

7 Annpurna Haveli A2
8 Bundi Vilas A2
9 Dev Niwas B3
10 Haveli Braj Bhushanjee A2
11 Haveli Katkoun A2
12 Hotel Bundi Haveli A2
13 Kasera Heritage View A2
14 Shivam Tourist Guest House A2

Eating

Bundi Vilas .... (see 8)
15 Morgan's Place B2
16 Rainbow Cafe A2

Shopping

17 Yug Art B2

Information

18 Ayurvedic Hospital B2
19 Roshan Tour & Travel B2

by the rubbish that collects in them which no one bothers to clean up. The most impressive, **Raniji-ki-Baori** (Queen's Step-Well; Indian/foreigner ₹50/200; ⏲9.30am-5pm), is 46m deep and decorated with sinuous carvings, including the avatars of Lord Vishnu. The **Nagar Sagar Kund** is a pair of matching step-wells just outside the old city's Chogan Gate.

Three sights around town, the Rani-ji-ki-Baori, **84-Pillared Cenotaph** (Indian/foreigner ₹50/200; ⌚9.30am-5pm) and Sukh Mahal (p145), can be visited using a composite ticket (Indian/foreigner ₹75/350) – a great saving if you plan to visit two or more of these sights.

Bundi Palace PALACE
(Garh Palace; Indian palace/fort/camera ₹80/100/50, foreigner palace, fort & camera ₹500; ⌚8am-6pm) This extraordinary, partly decaying edifice – described by Rudyard Kipling as 'the work of goblins rather than of men' – almost seems to grow out of the rock of the hillside it stands on. Though large sections are still closed up and left to the bats, the rooms that are open hold a series of fabulous, fading turquoise-and-gold murals that are the palace's chief treasure. The palace is best explored with a local guide (₹700 half-day), who will be charged ₹100 to enter.

The palace was constructed during the reign of Rao Raja Ratan Singh (r 1607–31) and added to by his successors. Part of it remained occupied by the Bundi royals until 1948.

If you are going up to Taragarh as well as the palace, get tickets for both at the palace entrance. Once inside the palace's **Hathi Pol** (Elephant Gate), climb the stairs to the Ratan Daulat or **Diwan-e-Aam** (Hall of Public Audience), with a white marble coronation throne. You then pass into the **Chhatra Mahal**, added by Rao Raja Chhatra Shabji in 1644, with some fine but rather weathered murals. Stairs lead up to the **Phool Mahal** (1607), the murals of which include an immense royal procession, and then the **Badal Mahal** (Cloud Palace; also 1607), with Bundi's very best murals, including a wonderful Chinese-inspired ceiling, divided into petal shapes and decorated with peacocks and Krishnas.

★**Chitrasala** PALACE
(Umaid Mahal; ⌚8am-6pm) Within the Bundi Palace complex is the Chitrasala, a small 18th-century palace built by Rao Ummed Singh. To find it, exit through the palace's Hathi Pol (Elephant Gate) and walk round the corner uphill. Above the palace's garden courtyard are several rooms covered in beautiful paintings. There are some great Krishna images, including a detail of him sitting up a tree playing the flute after stealing the clothes of the *gopis* (milkmaids).

The back room to the right is the **Sheesh Mahal**, badly damaged but still featuring some beautiful inlaid glass, while back in the front room there's an image of 18th-century Bundi itself.

Taragarh FORT
(Star Fort; ₹100, camera/video ₹50/100; ⌚8am-5pm) This ramshackle, partly overgrown 14th-century fort, on the hilltop above Bundi Palace, is a wonderful place to ramble around – but take a stick to battle the overgrown vegetation, help the knees on the steep climb and provide confidence when surrounded by testosterone-charged macaques. To reach it, just continue on the path up behind the Chitrasala.

Jait Sagar LAKE
Round the far side of the Taragarh hill, about 2km north from the centre of town, this picturesque, 1.5km-long lake is flanked by hills and strewn with pretty lotus flowers during the monsoon and winter months. At its near end, the **Sukh Mahal** (Indian/foreigner ₹50/200; ⌚9.30am-5pm) is a small summer palace surrounded by terraced gardens where Rudyard Kipling once stayed and wrote part of *Kim*.

Tours

Keshav Bhati TOURS
(☎9414394241; bharat_bhati@yahoo.com) Keshav Bhati is a retired Indian Air Force officer with a passion for Bundi. He is also an official tour guide with an encyclopaedic knowledge of the region and is highly recommended. Tour prices are negotiable.

Kukki's World TOURS
(☎9828404527; www.kukkisworld.com; 43 New Colony; half-/full-day tour for 2 people US$56/78) OP 'Kukki' Sharma is a passionate amateur archaeologist who has discovered around 70 prehistoric rock-painting sites around Bundi. His trips get you out into the villages and countryside, which he knows like the back of his hand. You can visit his collection of finds and select sites from his laptop at his house (about 300m south of the tourist office) beforehand.

Sleeping

Shivam Tourist Guest House GUESTHOUSE $
(☎9460300272, 0747-2447892; Balchand Para; s/d ₹450/500, r with AC ₹800-1000) This guesthouse is run by an energetic young couple who are keen to help travellers get the most from their stay in Bundi. Rooms are simple but comfortable and spotless; the better

rooms are upstairs. There is an all-veg rooftop restaurant, cooking and henna-design classes are offered, plus they can help with booking transport.

Annpurna Haveli GUESTHOUSE $
(☎0747-2447055, 9602805455; www.annpurnahavelibundi.com; Balchand Para; r ₹800, r with breakfast & AC ₹1200; ❄📶) Annpurna is a very peaceful family-run guesthouse of just six rooms opposite Nawal Sagar. The simple and clean rooms are a great budget choice, and the best rooms have lake views. Home-cooked meals are enjoyed either in the dining room or on the roof in fine weather.

★**Haveli Braj Bhushanjee** HERITAGE HOTEL $$
(☎0747-2442322, 9783355866; www.kiplingsbundi.com; Balchand Para; r ₹1500-6000; ❄📶) This rambling 200-year-old *haveli* is run by the very helpful and knowledgeable Braj Bhushanjee family, descendants of the former prime ministers of Bundi. It's Bundi's first guesthouse and an enchanting place with original stone interiors, a private garden, splendid rooftop views, beautiful, well-preserved murals, and all sorts of other historic and valuable artefacts.

The terrific range of accommodation includes some lovely, modernised rooms that are still in traditional style. It's a fascinating living museum where you can really get a feel for Bundi's heritage. The *haveli* is opposite the Ayurvedic Hospital, though the main entrance is around the corner.

★**Hotel Bundi Haveli** HOTEL $$
(☎9929291552, 0747-2447861; www.hotelbundihaveli.com; Balchand Para; r ₹1300-4750; ❄📶) The exquisitely renovated Bundi Haveli leads the pack in terms of contemporary style and sophistication. Spacious rooms, white walls, stone floors, colour highlights and framed artefacts are coupled with modern plumbing and electricity. Yes, it's very comfortable and relaxed and there's a lovely rooftop dining area boasting palace views and an extensive, mainly Indian menu (mains ₹100 to ₹280).

Dev Niwas HERITAGE HOTEL $$
(☎0747-2442928, 8233345394; www.jagatcollection.com; Maaji Sahib-ki-Haveli; r ₹870-1300, with AC ₹3050, ste ₹4350; ❄📶) 🍃 Dev Niwas is a fine *haveli,* just off the busy Sadar Bazaar. Inside is a peaceful oasis with courtyards and open-sided pavilions. Rooms are all very different, yet they are all comfortably furnished and fitted with modern bathrooms. The open-sided restaurant has cushion seating and there are great views of the fort.

Bundi Vilas HERITAGE HOTEL $$
(☎0747-2444614, 9214803556; www.bundivilas.com; r incl breakfast ₹4000-5000; ❄@📶) This 300-year-old *haveli* up a side alley has been tastefully renovated with golden Jaisalmer sandstone, earth-toned walls and deft interior design. The five deluxe and two suite rooms exude period character yet boast excellent bathrooms. Set in the lee of the palace walls, this guesthouse has commanding views of the town below and palace above from the rooftop terrace restaurant.

Kasera Heritage View GUESTHOUSE $$
(☎9983790314, 0747-2444679; www.kaseraheritageview.com; s/d from ₹800/1000, r with breakfast & AC from ₹2000; ❄@📶) A revamped *haveli,* Kasera has an incongruously modern lobby, but offers a range of slightly more authentic rooms. The welcome is friendly, it's all cheerfully decorated, the rooftop restaurant has great views, and discounts of 20% to 30% are offered in summer. The owners' sister *haveli,* Kasera Paradise, just below the palace, has the same contact details and rates.

Haveli Katkoun GUESTHOUSE $$
(☎0747-2444311, 9414539146; www.katkounhavelibundi.com; s/d ₹700/1200, r incl breakfast & AC ₹2400; ❄📶) Just outside the town's western gate, Katkoun is a completely revamped *haveli* with friendly family management who live downstairs. It boasts large, spotless rooms offering superb views on both sides, to either the lake or palace, and has a good rooftop restaurant (mains ₹65 to ₹200), known for its Indian nonveg dishes.

✖ Eating

★**Bundi Vilas** INDIAN $$
(☎0747-2444614; www.bundivilas.com; Balchand Para; mains ₹210-250, set dinners ₹700; ⊙7.30-10am, 1-3pm & 7-10pm; 📶📋) The most romantic restaurant in Bundi welcomes visitors from other hotels. Dine in the sheltered yet open-sided terrace, or on the rooftop with uninterrupted views of the fort. It's wise to book for dinner as spots are limited for the candlelit experience beneath the floodlit palace. The set dinner offers several courses of exquisite food and wine is available.

Bundi Vilas has its own farm on the outskirts of Bundi that supplies much of its fresh fruit and vegetables. Do try the home-made jams if you get the chance.

Morgan's Place MULTICUISINE $$
(Kasera Paradise Hotel; mains ₹130-240; ⏲9am-10pm; ☎) Morgan's Place is a relaxed (possibly overly relaxed) rooftop restaurant with good espresso (coffees ₹60 to ₹100). If you're in the mood for caffeine, don't mind climbing lots of stairs, and aren't in a hurry, then it delivers. It also serves fresh juice, respectable pizza and pasta, and falafel.

Rainbow Cafe MULTICUISINE $$
(☎9887210334; mains ₹120-260, thalis ₹250-500; ⏲7am-11pm; ☎) Bohemian ambience with chill-out tunes, floor-cushion seating, good snacks and special lassis. You need to be patient, but food eventually emerges from the tiny kitchen. Located on the rooftop of the town's western gate and caged off from marauding macaques with a bamboo trellis.

Shopping

Yug Art ART
(www.yugartbundi.com; near Surang Gate; portrait postcard ₹800-1600, comics from ₹3000; ⏲10am-7.30pm) Many art shops will offer you Rajasthani miniatures, but Yug Art offers to put you into one. Provide a photo and you can be pictured on elephant-back or in any number of classical scenes. Alternatively, Yug will record your India trip in a unique travel comic – you help with the script and he'll provide the artwork.

Information

Head to Sadar Bazar to find ATMs.

Ayurvedic Hospital (☎0747-2443708; Balchand Para; ⏲9am-1pm & 4-6pm Mon-Sat, 9-11am Sun) This charitable hospital prescribes natural plant-based remedies. There are medicines for all sorts of ailments, from upset tummies to arthritis, and many of them are free.

Roshan Tour & Travel (internet per hr ₹40; ⏲8am-10pm) Travel agency that books train tickets, exchanges currency and has an internet cafe. Located 300m south of the palace.

Tourist Office (☎0747-2443697; Kota Rd; ⏲9.30am-6pm Mon-Fri) Offers bus and train schedules, free maps and helpful advice.

Getting There & Away

BUS

For Ranthambhore, it's quicker to catch the train or a bus to Kota, then hop on a train to Sawai Madhopur.

Direct services from **Bundi bus stand**:

Ajmer ₹186, four hours, hourly

Jaipur ₹216, five hours, hourly

Jodhpur ₹376, eight hours, five per day

Kota ₹39, 40 minutes, every 15 minutes

Pushkar ₹200, 4½ hours, two daily

Sawai Madhoper ₹120, five hours, three daily

TRAIN

Bundi station is 4km south of the old city. There are no daily trains to Jaipur, Ajmer or Jodhpur. It's better to take a bus, or to catch a train from Kota or Chittorgarh.

Agra (Agra Fort Station) sleeper ₹160, 12½ hours, daily (5.35pm)

Chittorgarh sleeper ₹180, 2½ to 3½ hours, three to five daily (2.08am, 2.24am, 7.05am, 9.16am and 11pm)

Delhi (Hazrat Nizamuddin) sleeper ₹325, eight to 12 hours, two daily (5.48pm and 10.35pm)

THE MINI-MASTERPIECES OF KOTA & BUNDI

Some of Rajasthan's finest miniature and mural painting was produced around Bundi and Kota, the ruling Hada Rajputs being keen artistic patrons. The style combined the dominant features of folk painting – intense colour and bold forms – with the Mughals' concern with naturalism.

The Bundi and Kota schools were initially similar, but developed markedly different styles, though both usually have a background of thick foliage, cloudy skies and scenes lit by the setting sun. When architecture appears it is depicted in loving detail. The willowy women sport round faces, large petal-shaped eyes and small noses – forerunners of Bollywood pin-ups.

The Bundi school is notable for its blue hues, with a palette of turquoise and azure unlike anything seen elsewhere. Bundi Palace (p145) in particular hosts some wonderful examples.

In Kota you'll notice a penchant for hunting scenes with fauna and dense foliage – vivid, detailed portrayals of hunting expeditions in Kota's once thickly wooded surrounds. Kota's City Palace (p148) has some of the best-preserved wall paintings in the state.

Sawai Madhopur sleeper ₹180, 2½ to five hours, three daily (5.35pm, 5.48pm and 10.35pm; the last train is the fastest)

Udaipur sleeper ₹220, five hours, daily (12963 Mewar Express; 2.08am)

Getting Around

An autorickshaw from town to the train station costs ₹70 by day and ₹100 to ₹120 at night.

Kota

0744 / POP 1 MILLION

An easy day trip from Bundi, Kota is a gritty industrial and commercial city on the Chambal, Rajasthan's only permanent river. You can take boat trips on the river here, for bird- and crocodile-watching, or explore the city's old palace.

Sights

City Palace PALACE, MUSEUM

(Kotah Garh; www.kotahfort.com; Indian/foreigner ₹100/300; 10am-4.30pm) The City Palace, and the fort that surrounds it, make up one of the largest such complexes in Rajasthan. This was the royal residence and centre of power, housing the Kota princedom's treasury, courts, arsenal, armed forces and state offices. The palace, entered through a gateway topped by rampant elephants, contains the offbeat **Rao Madho Singh Museum**, where you'll find everything for a respectable Raj existence, from silver furniture to weaponry, as well as perhaps India's most depressingly moth-eaten stuffed trophy animals.

The oldest part of the palace dates from 1624. Downstairs is a durbar (royal audience) hall with beautiful mirrorwork, while the elegant, small-scale apartments upstairs contain exquisite, beautifully preserved paintings, particularly the hunting scenes for which Kota is renowned.

To get here, it's around ₹40 in an autorickshaw from the bus stand, and at least ₹70 from the train station.

Activities

Boat Trips BOATING

(per person 5min/1hr ₹60/1300, max 6 people; 10.30am-dusk) A lovely hiatus from the city is a Chambal River boat trip. The river upstream of Kota is part of the **Darrah National Park** and once you escape the city it's beautiful, with lush vegetation and craggy cliffs on either side. Boats start from **Chambal Gardens** (Indian/foreigner ₹2/5), 1.5km south of the fort on the river's east bank.

Trips provide the opportunity to spot a host of birds, as well as gharials (thin-snouted, fish-eating crocodiles) and muggers (keep-your-limbs-inside-the-boat crocodiles).

Sleeping

Palkiya Haveli HERITAGE HOTEL $$

(0744-2387497; www.palkiyahaveli.com; Mokha Para; s/d ₹2725/3315;) This exquisite *haveli* has been in the same family for 200 years. Set in a deliciously peaceful corner of the old city, about 800m east of the City Palace, it's a lovely, relaxing place to stay, with welcoming hosts, a high-walled garden and a courtyard with a graceful neem tree.

There are impressive murals and appealing heritage rooms, and the food is top-notch.

Information

Tourist Office (0744-2327695; RTDC Hotel Chambal; 9.30am-6pm Mon-Sat) Has free maps of Kota and helpful staff. Turn left out of the bus stand, right at the second roundabout and it's on your right.

Getting There & Away

BUS

Services from the main bus stand (on Bundi Rd, east of the bridge over the Chambal River) include the following:

Ajmer (for Pushkar) ₹230, four to five hours, at least 10 daily

Bundi ₹35, 40 minutes, every 15 minutes throughout the day

Chittorgarh ₹184, four hours, half-hourly from 6am

Jaipur ₹240, five hours, hourly from 5am

Udaipur ₹350 to ₹400, six to seven hours, at least 10 daily

TRAIN

Kota is on the main Mumbai–Delhi train route via Sawai Madhopur, so there are plenty of trains to choose from, though departure times aren't always convenient.

Agra (Fort) sleeper ₹225, five to nine hours, three to four daily (7.30am, 9.50am, 2.40pm and 9pm)

Chittorgarh sleeper ₹150, three to four hours, three to four daily (1.10am, 1.25am, 6.05am and 8.45am)

Delhi (New Delhi or Hazrat Nizamuddin) sleeper ₹315, five to eight hours, almost hourly

Jaipur sleeper ₹225, four hours, six daily (2.55am, 7.40am, 8.55am, 12.35pm, 5.35pm and 11.50pm), plus other trains on selected days

Mumbai sleeper ₹490, 14 hours, five daily fast trains (7.45am, 2.25pm, 5.30pm, 9.05pm and 11.45pm)

Sawai Madhopur 2nd-class seat/sleeper ₹125/180, one to two hours, more than 24 daily

Udaipur sleeper ₹245, six hours, one or two daily (1.10am and 1.25am)

Getting Around

Minibuses and shared autorickshaws link the train station and main bus stand (₹10 per person). A private autorickshaw costs around ₹50.

Chittorgarh (Chittor)

☎01472 / POP 116,410

Chittorgarh (the fort, *garh,* at Chittor) is the largest fort complex in India, and a fascinating place to explore. It rises from the plains like a huge rock island, nearly 6km long and surrounded on all sides by 150m-plus cliffs.

Its history epitomises Rajput romanticism, chivalry and tragedy, and it holds a special place in the hearts of many Rajputs. Three times (in 1303, 1535 and 1568) Chittorgarh was under attack from a more powerful enemy; each time, its people chose death before dishonour, performing *jauhar.* The men donned saffron martyrs' robes and rode out from the fort to certain death, while the women and children immolated themselves on huge funeral pyres. After the last of the three sackings, Rana Udai Singh II fled to Udaipur, where he established a new capital for Mewar. In 1616, Jehangir returned Chittor to the Rajputs. There was no attempt at resettlement, though it was restored in 1905.

Sights

★Chittorgarh — FORT

(Indian/foreigner ₹15/200, Sound & Light Show (in Hindi) ₹100; ⊙dawn-dusk, Sound & Light Show dusk) A zigzag ascent of more than 1km starts at **Padal Pol** and leads through six gateways to the main gate on the western side, the **Ram Pol** (the former back entrance). Inside Ram Pol is a still-occupied village (turn right here for the ticket office). The rest of the plateau is deserted except for the wonderful palaces, towers and temples that survive from the fort's heyday, along with a few recent temples. A loop road runs around the plateau.

A typical vehicular exploration of the fort takes two to three hours. Licensed guides charging around ₹400 for up to four hours are available for either walking or autorickshaw tours, usually at the ticket office.

➡ Meera & Kumbha Shyam Temples

Both of these temples southeast of the **Rana Kumbha Palace** were built by Rana Kumbha in the ornate Indo-Aryan style, with classic, tall *sikharas* (spires). The **Meera Temple**, the smaller of the two, is now associated with the mystic-poetess Meerabai, a 16th-century Mewar royal who was poisoned by her brother-in-law but survived due to the blessings of Krishna. The **Kumbha Shyam Temple** (Temple of Varah) is dedicated to Vishnu and its carved panels illustrate 15th-century Mewar life.

MAJOR TRAINS FROM KOTA

DESTINATION	TRAIN	DEPARTURE	ARRIVAL	FARE (₹)
Agra	19037/19039 Avadh Exp	2.40pm	9.50pm	225/600/850 (A)
Chittorgarh	29020 Dehradun Exp	8.45am	11.35am	150/715/1180 (C)
Delhi (Hazrat Nizamuddin)	12903 Golden Temple Mail	11.05am	6.45pm	315/805/1115/1855 (E)
Jaipur	12955 Mumbai–Jaipur Exp	8.55am	12.40pm	225/580/780/1275 (E)
Mumbai	12904 Golden Temple Mail	2.25pm	5.20am	490/1275/1805/3035 (E)
Sawai Madhopur	12059 Shatabdi	5.55am	7.03am	125/370 (D)
Udaipur	12963 Mewar Exp	1.25am	7.15am	245/580/780/1275 (E)

Fares: (A) sleeper/3AC/2AC, (B) sleeper, (C) sleeper/2AC/1AC, (D) 2nd class/AC chair, (E) sleeper/3AC/2AC/1AC

Chittorgarh (Chittor)

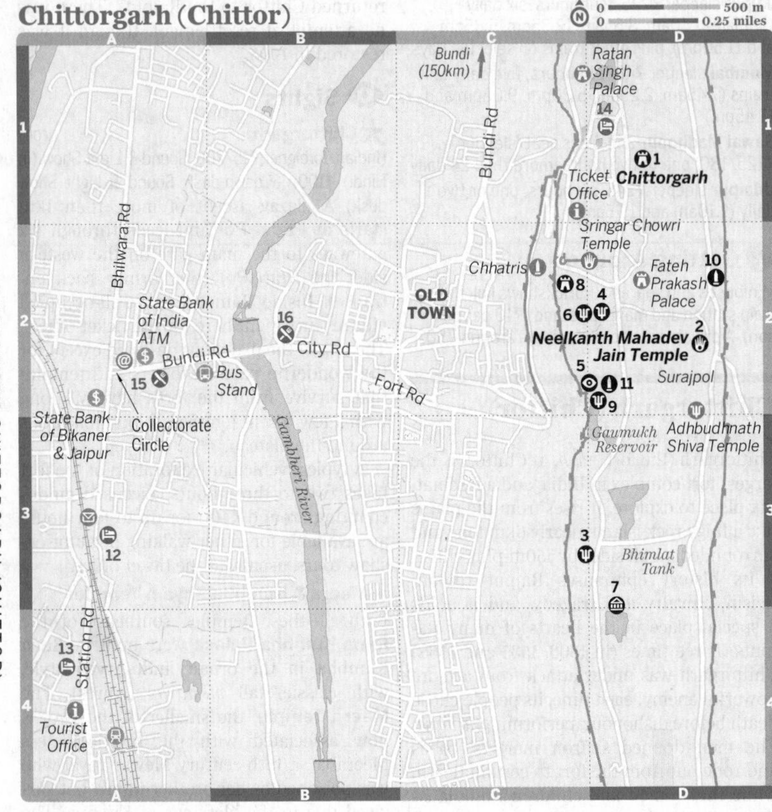

Chittorgarh (Chittor)

Top Sights

1 Chittorgarh....D1
2 Neelkanth Mahadev Jain Temple....D2

Sights

3 Kalika Mata Temple....C3
4 Kumbha Shyam Temple....D2
5 Mahasati....D2
6 Meera Temple....C2
7 Padmini's Palace....D3
8 Rana Kumbha Palace....C2
9 Samidheshwar Temple....D2
10 Tower of Fame....D2
11 Tower of Victory....D2

Sleeping

12 Hotel Pratap Palace....A3
13 Hotel Shree Ji....A4
14 Padmini Haveli....D1

Eating

15 Chokhi Dhani Garden Family Restaurant....A2
16 Saffire Garden Restaurant....B2

➡ Tower of Victory

The glorious **Tower of Victory** (Jaya Stambha), symbol of Chittorgarh, was erected by Rana Kumbha in the 1440s, probably to commemorate a victory over Mahmud Khilji of Malwa. Dedicated to Vishnu, it rises 37m in nine exquisitely carved storeys, and you can climb the 157 narrow stairs (the interior is also carved) to the 8th floor, from where there's a good view of the area.

Below the tower, to the southwest, is the **Mahasati** area, where there are many *sati* (self-immolation) stones – this was the royal cremation ground and was also where 13,000 women committed *jauhar* in 1535. The **Samidheshwar Temple**, built in the

6th century and restored in 1427, is nearby. Notable among its intricate carving is a Trimurti (three-faced) figure of Shiva.

➡ Gaumukh Reservoir

Walk down beyond the Samidheshwar Temple and at the edge of the cliff is a deep tank, the Gaumukh Reservoir, where you can feed the fish. The reservoir takes its name from a spring that feeds the tank from a *gaumukh* (cow's mouth) carved into the cliffside.

➡ Padmini's Palace

Continuing south, you reach the **Kalika Mata Temple**, an 8th-century sun temple damaged during the first sacking of Chittorgarh and then converted to a temple for the goddess Kali in the 14th century. **Padmini's Palace** stands about 250m further south, beside a small lake with a central pavilion. The bronze gates to this pavilion were carried off by Akbar and can now be seen in Agra Fort.

➡ Surajpol & Tower of Fame

Surajpol, on the fort's east side, was the main gate and offers fantastic views across the cultivated plains. Opposite is the **Neelkanth Mahadev Jain Temple**. A little further north, the 24m-high **Tower of Fame** (Kirtti Stambha), dating from 1301, is smaller than the Tower of Victory. Built by a Jain merchant, the tower is dedicated to Adinath, the first Jain *tirthankar* (one of the 24 revered Jain teachers) and is decorated with naked figures of various other *tirthankars,* indicating that it is a monument of the Digambara (sky-clad) order. A narrow stairway leads up the seven storeys to the top. Next door is a 14th-century Jain temple.

Sleeping & Eating

★Padmini Haveli HERITAGE HOTEL **$$**

(9414734497, 9414110090; www.thepadminihaveli.com; Annapoorna Temple Rd, Shah Chowk, Village, Chittorgarh Fort; r/ste incl breakfast ₹4000/5000;) This fabulous guesthouse with charming, enthusiastic and well-informed hosts is the only accommodation within the fort. Stylish rooms boast granite bathrooms and traditional decoration, and open onto the communal courtyard of the *haveli*. The hosts are official Chittorgarh guides and they live on-site, providing Italian coffee and homemade meals and jams.

There are only six rooms, three standard and three suites, so booking is advised. This white-washed *haveli* with a large black door can be hard to find in the labyrinthine laneways of the village, so call first.

Hotel Shree Ji HOTEL **$$**

(9413670931, 01472-249131; hotelshreeji@gmail.com; Station Rd; s/d from ₹1800/2000;) A cheerful and efficient business hotel, just 300m from the train station, and a world away from the lacklustre hotels near the bus station. Rooms are bright and spotless and come with complimentary morning tea, newspaper and bottle of water. The restaurant serves an inexpensive thali in the evening.

Hotel Pratap Palace HOTEL **$$**

(01472-240099; www.hotelpratappalacechittaurgarh.com; off Maharana Pratap Setu Marg; r ₹1500, with AC ₹1800-4500;) This hotel has a wide range of rooms, though its business as a lunch stop for bus groups takes precedence over its accommodation enterprise. Even the more expensive rooms suffer from poor maintenance, and cleanliness standards could be higher. There's a large multicuisine restaurant that produces buffets for tour groups. Try and order à la carte if you can.

The owners also run village tours, horse rides and the upmarket Hotel Castle Bijaipur out of town.

Hotel Castle Bijaipur HERITAGE HOTEL **$$$**

(01472-240099; www.castlebijaipur.co.in; r from ₹8700;) This fantastically set 16th-century palace is an ideal rural retreat 41km by road east of Chittorgarh. It's a great place to settle down with a good book, compose a fairy-tale fantasy or just laze around. Rooms are romantic and luxurious, and there's a pleasant garden courtyard and an airy restaurant serving Rajasthani food. It's popular with tour groups.

Reservations should be made through the website or through Chittorgarh's Hotel Pratap Palace. The owners can arrange transfer from Chittor as well as horse and 4WD safaris, birdwatching, cooking classes, massage and yoga.

Chokhi Dhani Garden Family Restaurant INDIAN **$**

(9413716593; Bundi Rd; mains ₹80-150, thalis ₹110-290; 9am-10.30pm;) This fan-cooled roadside *dhaba* (snack bar) with extra seating in the back does a good-value selection of vegetarian dishes, including filling thalis and a variety of North and South Indian dishes.

Saffire Garden Restaurant MULTICUISINE $
(City Rd; mains ₹100-170; ⌚8am-10pm; ❄) Sit at tables on the small, tree-shaded lawn or inside the air-conditioned room at the back, and tuck into a variety of standard, but tasty enough, Indian and Chinese dishes.

Information

ATMs can be found near Collectorate Circle.

State Bank of Bikaner & Jaipur (SBBJ; Bhilwara Rd; ⌚9.30am-4pm Mon-Fri, to noon Sat) ATM and money changing.

Mahavir Cyber Cafe (Collectorate Circle; per hour ₹40; ⌚8am-10pm)

Tourist Office (☎01472-241089; Station Rd; ⌚10am-1.30pm & 2-5pm Mon-Sat) Friendly and helpful, with a town map and brochure.

Getting There & Away

BUS

There are no direct buses to Bundi; take the train instead. Services from the Chittorgarh **bus stand** include the following:

Ajmer (for Pushkar) ₹197, AC ₹350, four hours, hourly until mid-afternoon

Jaipur ₹339, AC ₹667, seven hours, around every 1½ hours

Kota ₹184, four hours, half-hourly

Udaipur ₹120, with AC ₹255, 2½ hours, half-hourly

TRAIN

Ajmer (for Pushkar) sleeper ₹150, three hours, five to seven daily (12.35am, 2.50am, 8.20am, 10.10am, 7.30pm, 7.45pm and 11.30pm)

Bundi sleeper ₹150, two to 3½ hours, three daily (1.50pm, 3.35pm and 8.50pm)

Delhi (Delhi Sarai Rohilla or Hazrat Nizamuddin) sleeper ₹380, 10 hours, two daily fast trains (7.30pm and 8.50pm)

Jaipur sleeper ₹220, 5½ hours, four daily (12.35am, 2.45am, 8.20am and 8.35am)

Sawai Madhopur sleeper ₹210, four to nine hours, three daily (1.50pm, 3.35pm and 8.50pm; the latest is the quickest)

Udaipur sleeper ₹150, two hours, six daily (4.25am, 5.05am, 5.33am, 6.35am, 4.50pm and 7.25pm)

Getting Around

A full tour of the fort by autorickshaw should cost around ₹400 return. You can arrange this yourself in town.

Udaipur

☎0294 / POP 451,735

Beside shimmering Lake Pichola, with the ochre and purple ridges of the wooded Aravalli Hills stretching away in every direction, Udaipur has a romance of setting unmatched in Rajasthan and arguably in all India. Fantastical palaces, temples, *havelis* and countless narrow, crooked, timeless streets add the human counterpoint to the city's natural charms. For the visitor there's the tranquillity of boat rides on the lake, the bustle and colour of ancient bazaars, a lively arts scene, the quaint old-world feel of its better hotels, endless tempting shops and some lovely countryside to explore on wheels, feet or horseback.

Udaipur's tag of 'the most romantic spot on the continent of India' was first applied in 1829 by Colonel James Tod, the East India Company's first political agent in the region. Today the romance is wearing slightly thin as ever-taller hotels compete for the best view and traffic clogs ancient thoroughfares.

Udaipur was founded in 1568 by Maharana Udai Singh II following the final sacking of Chittorgarh by the Mughal emperor Akbar. This new capital of Mewar had a much less vulnerable location than Chittorgarh. Mewar still had to contend with repeated in-

MAJOR TRAINS FROM CHITTORGARH

DESTINATION	TRAIN	DEPARTURE	ARRIVAL	FARE (₹)
Ajmer (for Pushkar)	12991 Udaipur-Jaipur Exp	8.20am	11.25am	120/410/550 (A)
Bundi	29019 MDS-Kota Exp	3.35pm	5.45pm	160/735/1200 (B)
Delhi (Hazrat Nizamuddin)	12964 Mewar Exp	8.50pm	6.35am	370/975/1380/2325 (C)
Jaipur	12991 Udaipur-Jaipur Exp	8.20am	1.30pm	160/545/750 (A)
Sawai Madhopur	29019 MDS-Kota Exp	3.35pm	9.25pm	210/735/1200 (B)
Udaipur	19329 Udaipur City Exp	4.50pm	7.15pm	160/530/735/1200 (C)

Fares: (A) 2nd-class seat/AC chair/1st-class seat, (B) sleeper/2AC/1AC, (C) sleeper/3AC/2AC/1AC

vasions by the Mughals and, later, the Marathas, until British intervention in the early 19th century. This resulted in a treaty that protected Udaipur from invaders while allowing Mewar's rulers to remain effectively all-powerful in internal affairs. The ex-royal family remains influential and in recent decades has been the driving force behind the rise of Udaipur as a tourist destination.

Sights

★City Palace PALACE

(www.eternalmewar.in; adult/child ₹30/15; 9am-11pm) Surmounted by balconies, towers and cupolas towering over the lake, the imposing City Palace is Rajasthan's largest palace, with a facade 244m long and 30.4m high. Construction was begun in 1599 by Maharana Udai Singh II, the city's founder, and it later became a conglomeration of structures (including 11 separate smaller palaces) built and extended by various maharanas, though it still manages to retain a surprising uniformity of design.

You can enter the complex through **Badi Pol** (Great Gate) at the northern end, or the **Sheetla Mata Gate** to the south. Tickets for the City Palace Museum are sold at both entrances. Note: you must pay the ₹30 City Palace entrance ticket in order to pass south through **Chandra Chowk Gate**, en route to the Crystal Gallery or Rameshwar Ghat for the Lake Pichola boat rides, even if you have a City Palace Museum ticket.

Inside Badi Pol, eight arches on the left commemorate the eight times maharanas were weighed here and their weight in gold or silver distributed to the lucky locals. You then pass through the three-arched **Tripolia Gate** into a large courtyard, **Manek Chowk**. Spot the large tiger-catching cage, which worked rather like an oversized mousetrap, and the smaller one for leopards.

★City Palace Museum MUSEUM

(adult/child ₹250/100, camera or video ₹250, guide ₹250, audio guide ₹200; 9.30am-5.30pm, last entry 4.30pm) The main part of the City Palace is open as the City Palace Museum, with rooms extravagantly decorated with mirrors, tiles and paintings, and housing a large and varied collection of artefacts. It's entered from **Ganesh Chowk**, which you reach from Manek Chowk.

The City Palace Museum begins with the **Rai Angan** (Royal Courtyard), the very spot where Udai Singh met the sage who told him to build a city here. Rooms along one side contain historical paintings, including several of the Battle of Haldighati (1576), in which Mewar forces under Maharana Pratap, one of the great Rajput heroes, gallantly fought the army of Mughal emperor Akbar to a stalemate.

As you move through the palace, highlights include the **Baadi Mahal** (1699), where a pretty central garden gives fine views over the city. **Kishan (Krishna) Vilas** has a remarkable collection of miniatures from the time of Maharana Bhim Singh (r 1778–1828). The story goes that Bhim Singh's daughter Krishna Kumari drank a fatal cup of poison here to solve the dilemma of rival princely suitors from Jaipur and Jodhpur who were both threatening to invade Mewar if she didn't marry them. The **Surya Choupad** boasts a huge, ornamental sun – the symbol of the sun-descended Mewar dynasty – and opens into **Mor Chowk** (Peacock Courtyard) with its lovely mosaics of peacocks, the favourite Rajasthani bird.

The southern end of the museum comprises the **Zenana Mahal**, the royal ladies' quarters built in the 17th century. It now contains a long picture gallery with lots of royal hunting scenes (note the comic-strip-style of the action in each painting). The Zenana Mahal's central courtyard, **Laxmi Chowk**, contains a beautiful white pavilion and a stable of *howdahs*, palanquins and other people-carriers.

Crystal Gallery GALLERY

(City Palace Complex; adult/child incl audio guide & drink ₹550/350, photography prohibited; 9am-7pm) The Crystal Gallery houses rare crystal that Maharana Sajjan Singh (r 1874–84) ordered from F&C Osler & Co in England in 1877. The maharana died before it arrived, and all the items stayed forgotten and packed up in boxes for 110 years. The extraordinary, extravagant collection includes crystal chairs, sofas, tables and even beds. The rather hefty admission fee also includes entry to the grand **Durbar Hall**. Tickets are available at the City Palace gates or the Crystal Gallery entrance.

Government Museum MUSEUM

(Indian/foreigner ₹20/100; 10am-5pm Tue-Sun) Entered from Ganesh Chowk, this museum has a splendid collection of jewel-like miniature paintings of the Mewar school and a turban that belonged to Shah Jahan, creator of the Taj Mahal. Stranger exhibits include

Udaipur

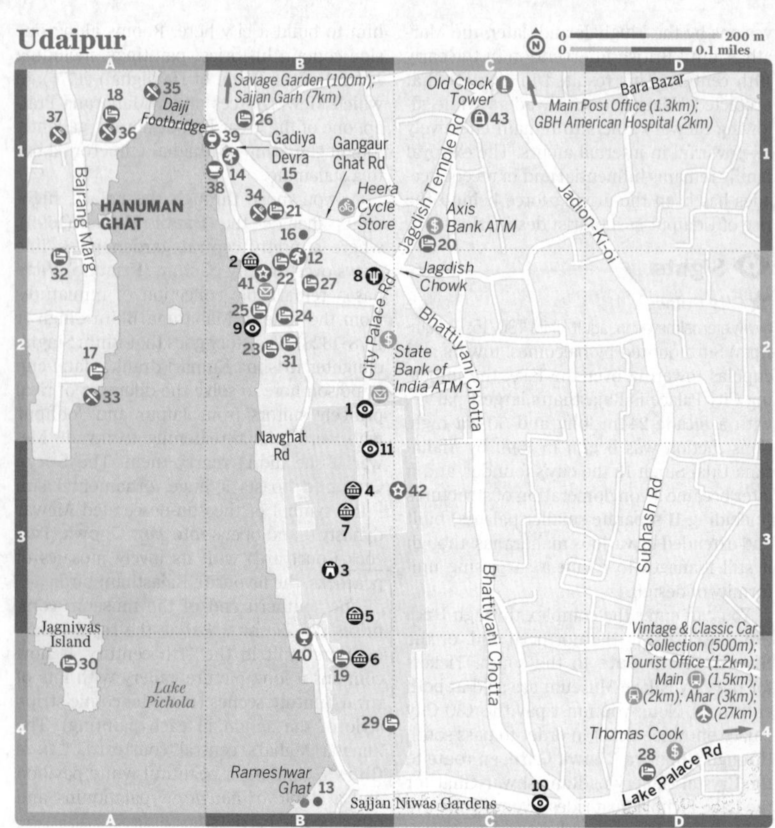

a stuffed monkey holding a lamp. There are also regal maharana portraits in profile, documenting Mewar's rulers along with the changing fashions of the moustache.

★Lake Pichola

LAKE

Limpid and large, Lake Pichola reflects the grey-blue mountains on its mirror-like surface. It was enlarged by Maharana Udai Singh II, following his foundation of the city, by flooding Picholi village, which gave the lake its name. The lake is now 4km long and 3km wide, but remains shallow and dries up completely during severe droughts. The City Palace complex, including the gardens at its southern end, extends nearly 1km along the lake's eastern shore.

Boat trips (adult/child 10am-2pm ₹400/200, 3-5pm ₹700/400; ⏲10am-5pm) leave roughly hourly from Rameshwar Ghat, within the City Palace complex (note, you have to pay ₹30 to enter). The trips make a stop at Jagmandir Island, where you can stay for as long as you like before taking any boat back. Take your own drinks and snacks, though, as those sold on the island are extortionately expensive. You can also take 25-minute boat rides from **Lal Ghat** (₹250 per person) throughout the day without the need to enter the City Palace complex: it's worth checking in advance what time the popular sunset departure casts off.

Jagmandir Island

ISLAND

The palace on Jagmandir Island, about 800m south of Jagniwas, was built by Maharana Karan Singh II in 1620, added to by his successor Maharana Jagat Singh, and then changed very little until the last few years when it was partly converted into another (smaller) hotel. When lit up at night it has more romantic sparkle to it than the Lake Palace. As well as the seven hotel rooms, the island has a restaurant, bar and spa, which are open to visitors.

Udaipur

Sights

1	Badi Pol	B2
2	Bagore-ki-Haveli	B2
3	City Palace	B3
4	City Palace Museum	B3
5	Crystal Gallery	B3
6	Durbar Hall	B4
7	Government Museum	B3
8	Jagdish Temple	B2
9	Lal Ghat	B2
10	Sheetla Mata Gate	C4
11	Tripolia Gate	B3

Activities, Courses & Tours

	Art of Bicycle Trips	(see 14)
	Ashoka Arts	(see 21)
12	Ayurvedic Body Care	B2
13	Lake Pichola Boat Trips	B4
	Millets of Mewar	(see 36)
14	Prakash Yoga	B1
15	Prem Musical Instruments	B1
16	Shashi Cooking Classes	B1
	Sushma's Cooking Classes	(see 22)

Sleeping

17	Amet Haveli	A2
18	Dream Heaven	A1
19	Fateh Prakash Palace Hotel	B4
20	Hotel Baba Palace	C1
21	Hotel Gangaur Palace	B1
22	Hotel Krishna Niwas	B2
23	Jagat Niwas Palace Hotel	B2
24	Jaiwana Haveli	B2
25	Lal Ghat Guest House	B2
26	Nukkad Guest House	B1
	Poonam Haveli	(see 22)
27	Pratap Bhawan	B2
28	Rangniwas Palace Hotel	D4
29	Shiv Niwas Palace Hotel	B4
30	Taj Lake Palace	A4
31	Udai Garh	B2
32	Udai Kothi	A2

Eating

33	Ambrai	A2
34	Cafe Edelweiss	B1
	Charcoal	(see 27)
	Jagat Niwas Palace Hotel	(see 23)
35	Little Prince	A1
	Mayur Rooftop Cafe	(see 20)
36	Millets of Mewar	A1
37	Queen Cafe	A1

Drinking & Nightlife

	Jaiwana Bistro Lounge	(see 24)
38	Jheel's Ginger Coffee Bar	B1
39	Paps Juices	B1
40	Sunset Terrace	B4

Entertainment

41	Dharohar	B2
42	Mewar Sound & Light Show	C3

Shopping

43	Sadhna	C1

With its entrance flanked by a row of enormous stone elephants, the island has an ornate 17th-century tower, the **Gol Mahal**, carved from bluestone and containing a small exhibit on Jagmandir's history, plus a garden and lovely views across the lake.

Boat trips (p154) leave roughly hourly from Rameshwar Ghat, within the City Palace complex (note, you have to pay ₹30 to enter). The trips make a stop at Jagmandir Island, where you can stay for as long as you like before taking any boat back. Take your own drinks and snacks, though, as those sold on the island are extortionately expensive.

Jagdish Temple HINDU TEMPLE

(⌚5.30am-2pm & 4-10pm) Reached by a steep, elephant-flanked flight of steps, 150m north of the City Palace's Badi Pol, this busy Indo-Aryan temple was built by Maharana Jagat Singh in 1651. The wonderfully carved main structure enshrines a black stone image of Vishnu as Jagannath, Lord of the Universe. There's also a brass image of the Garuda (Vishnu's man-bird vehicle) in a shrine facing the main structure.

Bagore-ki-Haveli MUSEUM

(Indian/foreigner ₹40/80, camera ₹50; ⌚9.30am-5.30pm) This gracious 18th-century *haveli*, set on the water's edge in the Gangaur Ghat area, was built by a Mewar prime minister and has since been carefully restored. There are 138 rooms set around courtyards, some arranged to evoke the period during which the house was inhabited, while others house cultural displays, including – intriguingly enough – the world's biggest turban.

The *haveli* also houses a gallery featuring a fascinating collection of period photos of Udaipur and a surreal collection of world-famous monuments carved out of polystyrene.

Sajjan Garh PALACE

(Monsoon Palace) Perched on top of a distant hill like a fairy-tale castle, this melancholy, neglected late-19th-century palace was constructed by Maharana Sajjan Singh. Originally an astronomical centre, it became a monsoon palace and hunting lodge. Now government owned, it's in a sadly dilapidated state, but visitors stream up here for the marvellous views, particularly at sunset. It's 5km west of the old city as the crow flies, about 9km by the winding road.

At the foot of the hill you enter the 5-sq-km **Sajjan Garh Wildlife Sanctuary** (Indian/foreigner ₹50/300, car ₹200). A good way to visit is with the daily sunset excursion in a minivan driven by an enterprising taxi driver who picks up tourists at the entrance to Bagore-ki-Haveli at Gangaur Ghat every day at 5pm. The round trip costs ₹300 per person, including waiting time (but not the sanctuary fees). His minivan has 'Monsoon Palace–Sajjangarh Fort' written across the front of it. Alternatively, autorickshaws charge ₹400 including waiting time for a round trip to the sanctuary gate, which they are not allowed to pass. Taxis ferry people the final 4km up to the palace for ₹150 per person.

Vintage & Classic Car Collection MUSEUM
(Garden Hotel, Lake Palace Rd; adult/child ₹250/150, lunch or dinner ₹230; 9am-9pm) The maharanas' car collection makes a fascinating diversion, for what it tells about their elite lifestyle and for the vintage vehicles themselves. Housed within the former state garage are 22 splendid vehicles, including a seven-seat 1938 Cadillac complete with purdah system, the beautiful 1934 Rolls-Royce Phantom used in the Bond film *Octopussy,* and the Cadillac convertible that whisked Queen Elizabeth II to the airport in 1961. The museum is a 10-minute walk east along Lake Palace Rd.

Activities

Krishna Ranch HORSE RIDING
(9828059505; www.krishnaranch.com; full day incl lunch ₹1200) Situated in beautiful countryside near Badi village, 7km northwest of Udaipur, and run by the owners of Kumbha Palace guesthouse. Experienced owner-guide Dinesh Jain leads most trips himself, riding local Marwari horses through the surrounding hills. There are also attractive cottages (p159) at the ranch.

Prakash Yoga YOGA
(0294-2524872; inside Chandpol; class by donation; classes 8am & 7pm) A friendly hatha yoga centre with hour-long classes. The teacher has more than 20 years' experience. It's tucked inside Chandpol, near the footbridge, but well signed.

Ayurvedic Body Care AYURVEDA, MASSAGE
(0294-2413816; www.ayurvedicbodycare.com; 38 Lal Ghat; 9.30am-8.30pm) A small and popular old-city operation offering ayurvedic massage at reasonable prices, including a 20-minute head or back massage (₹350) and a 50-minute full-body massage (₹850). It also sells ayurvedic products such as oils, moisturisers, shampoos and soaps.

Courses

Shashi Cooking Classes COOKING
(9929303511; www.shashicookingclasses.blogspot.com; Sunrise Restaurant, 18 Gangaur Ghat Rd; 4hr class ₹1500; classes 10.30am & 5.30pm) Readers rave about Shashi's high-spirited classes, teaching many fundamental Indian dishes. Classes go for 3½ to four hours and include a free recipe booklet.

Sushma's Cooking Classes COOKING
(7665852163; www.cookingclassesinudaipur.com; Hotel Krishna Niwas, 35 Lal Ghat; 2hr class ₹1000) A highly recommended cooking class run by the enthusiastic Sushma. Classes offer up anything from traditional Rajasthani dishes and learning how to make spice mixes, through bread-making to the all-important method of making the perfect cup of chai.

Prem Musical Instruments MUSIC
(9414343583; 28 Gadiya Devra; per hr ₹700; 10.30am-6pm) Rajesh Prajapati (Bablu) is a successful local musician who gives sitar, tabla and flute lessons. He also sells and repairs those instruments and can arrange performances.

Ashoka Arts ART
(Hotel Gangaur Palace, Ashoka Haveli, Gangaur Ghat Rd; per hr ₹200) Learn the basics of classic miniature painting from a local master.

Tours

Art of Bicycle Trips CYCLING
(8769822745; www.artofbicycletrips.com; 27 Gadiya Devra, inside Chandpol; half-day tour ₹1950) This well-run outfit offers a great way to get out of the city. The Lakecity Loop is a 30km half-day tour that quickly leaves Udaipur behind to have you wheeling through villages, farmland and along the shores of Fateh Sagar and Badi Lakes. Other options include a vehicle-supported trip further afield to

Kumbhalgarh and Ranakpur. Bikes are well maintained and all come with helmets.

Millets of Mewar WALKING

(☎8890419048; www.milletsofmewar.com; Hanuman Ghat; per person ₹1000, min 2 people) Health-food specialists Millets of Mewar (p160) organises 2½-hour city tours on which you can meet local artisans who live and work in Udaipur. Tours should be booked a day in advance; they leave from the restaurant at 10am.

Festivals & Events

Holi RELIGIOUS

(⏲Feb/Mar) If you're in Udaipur in February/March, you can experience the festival of Holi, Udaipur-style, when the town comes alive in a riot of colour.

Mewar Festival RELIGIOUS

(⏲Mar/Apr) Holi is followed in March/April by the procession-heavy Mewar Festival – Udaipur's own version of the springtime Gangaur festival.

Sleeping

Many budget and midrange lodgings cluster close to the lake, especially on its eastern side in Lal Ghat. This area is a tangle of streets and lanes close to the City Palace. It's Udaipur's tourist epicentre and boasts numerous eateries and shops. Directly across the water from Lal Ghat, Hanuman Ghat has a slightly more local vibe and often better views, though you're certainly not out of the touristic zone.

Lal Ghat

Lal Ghat Guest House GUESTHOUSE $

(☎0294-2525301; lalghat@hotmail.com; 33 Lal Ghat; dm ₹200, r ₹1000, without bathroom ₹750, with AC ₹2000; ❄@📶) This mellow guesthouse by the lake was one of the first to open in Udaipur, and it's still a sound choice, with an amazing variety of older and newer rooms. Accommodation ranges from a spruce, non-smoking dorm (with curtained-off beds and lockers under the mattresses) to the best room, which sports a stone wall, a big bed, a big mirror and air-con.

Most rooms have lake views and those in the older part of the building generally have more character. There's a small kitchen for self-caterers.

Nukkad Guest House GUESTHOUSE $

(☎0294-2411403; nukkad_raju@yahoo.com; 56 Ganesh Ghati; s/d without bathroom ₹100/200, r ₹300-500; @📶) Nukkad has clean and simple fan-cooled good-value rooms, plus a sociable, breezy, upstairs restaurant with very good Indian and international dishes. You can join afternoon cooking classes and morning yoga sessions (by donation) without stepping outside the door – just don't stay out past curfew or get caught washing your clothes in your bathroom.

★Jagat Niwas Palace Hotel HERITAGE HOTEL $$

(☎0294-2420133, 0294-2422860; www.jagatniwaspalace.com; 23-25 Lal Ghat; r ₹2000-3185, with lake view ₹4860-8100; ❄@📶) This leading midrange hotel set in two converted lakeside *havelis* takes the location cake, and staff are efficient and always courteous. The lake-view rooms are charming, with carved wooden furniture, cushioned window seats and pretty prints. Rooms without a lake view are almost as comfortable and attractive, and considerably cheaper.

The building is full of character, with lots of pleasant sitting areas, terraces and courtyards, and it makes the most of its position with a picture-perfect rooftop restaurant

Jaiwana Haveli HOTEL $$

(☎0294-2411103, 9829005859; www.jaiwanahaveli.com; 14 Lal Ghat; r from ₹3265; ❄@📶) Professionally run by two helpful, efficient brothers, this smart midrange option has spotless, unfussy rooms with good beds, TVs and attractive block-printed fabrics. Book a corner room for views. The rooftop restaurant has great lake views and Indian food (mains ₹140 to ₹300), plus there's a mod cafe (p160) on the ground floor.

ANIMAL AID UNLIMITED

The spacious refuge of **Animal Aid Unlimited** (☎9352511435, 9602055895; www.animalaidunlimited.com; Badi Village) treats around 200 street animals a day (mainly dogs, donkeys and cows) and answers more than 3000 emergency rescue calls a year. The refuge welcomes volunteers and visitors: you can visit between 9am and 4pm without needing to call first, though avoid lunchtime (1pm to 2pm). The refuge is in Badi village, 7km northwest of Udaipur.

A round trip by autorickshaw, including waiting time, costs around ₹350 to ₹400. Call Animal Aid Unlimited if you see an injured or ill street animal in Udaipur.

Hotel Baba Palace HOTEL $$
(☎0294-2427126; www.hotelbabapalace.com; Jagdish Chowk; r/deluxe r incl breakfast ₹2250/2750; ❄📶) This slick hotel has sparkling, fresh rooms with decent beds behind solid doors and there's a lift. It's eye to eye with Jagdish Temple, so many of the rooms have interesting views; all have air-conditioning and TVs, some have delightfully canopied beds. On top there's the popular Mayur Rooftop Cafe (p160). Free train station or airport pick-ups available.

Hotel Krishna Niwas HOTEL $$
(☎0294-2420163, 9414167341; www.hotelkrishnaniwas.com; 35 Lal Ghat; d ₹1500-2000; ❄@📶) Run by an artist family, Krishna Niwas has smart, clean, all air-con rooms; those with views are smaller, and some come with balconies. There are splendid vistas from the rooftop, and a decent restaurant. You can also try your own cooking after taking one of the popular cooking lessons (p156) here.

Pratap Bhawan HOTEL $$
(☎0294-2560566; www.pratapbhawanudaipur.com; 12 Lal Ghat; r ₹1450-2250; ❄📶) A curving marble staircase leads up from the wide lobby to large rooms with good, big bathrooms and, in many cases, cushioned window seats. A deservedly popular place, even if recent price hikes have spun the place slighlty out of the budget category. The rooftop Charcoal restaurant is nice for sitting out at night.

Poonam Haveli HOTEL $$
(☎0294-2410303; www.hotelpoonamhaveli.com; 39 Lal Ghat; r incl breakfast ₹3215; ❄@📶) A fairly modern place decked out in traditional style, friendly Poonam has 16 spacious, spotlessly clean rooms with marble floors, big beds, TVs and spare but tasteful decor, plus pleasant sitting areas. None of the rooms enjoy lake views, but the rooftop restaurant does, and also boasts wood-fired pizzas among the usual Indian and traveller fare.

Hotel Gangaur Palace HERITAGE HOTEL $
(☎0294-2422303; www.ashokahaveli.com; Ashoka Haveli, 339 Gangaur Ghat Rd; s ₹400-2000, d ₹500-2500; ❄@📶) This elaborate, faded *haveli* is set around a stone-pillared courtyard, with a wide assortment of rooms on several floors. It's gradually moving upmarket and rooms range from windowless with flaking paint to bright and recently decorated with lake views. Many have wall paintings and window seats.

The hotel also boasts an in-house palm reader, art shop, art school (p156), and a rooftop restaurant.

Udai Garh HOTEL $$
(☎9660055500, 0294-2421239; www.udaigarhudaipur.in; 21 Lal Ghat; r incl breakfast ₹2600-3400; ❄📶🏊) Set just back from the lakeshore, Udai Garh is an oasis of peace, with a central courtyard and spacious rooms. Unfortunately the rooms don't quite capture a lake view, but the wonderful rooftop, with a neat swimming pool and delightful restaurant, certainly does.

Hanuman Ghat

Dream Heaven GUESTHOUSE $
(☎0294-2431038; www.dreamheaven.co.in; Hanuman Ghat; r ₹400-1200; ❄@📶) This higgledy-piggledy building boasts clean rooms with wall hangings and paintings. Bathrooms are smallish, though some rooms have a decent balcony and/or views. The food at the rooftop restaurant (dishes ₹100 to ₹150), which overlooks the lake, is fresh and tasty; it's the perfect place to chill out on a pile of cushions and the only place to pick up wi-fi.

Amet Haveli HERITAGE HOTEL $$$
(☎0294-2431085; www.ametheveliudaipur.com; Hanuman Ghat; s/d from ₹4165/4760; ❄@📶🏊) A 350-year-old heritage building on the lakeshore, with delightful rooms featuring cushioned window seats, coloured glass and little shutters. They're set around a pretty courtyard and pond. Splurge on one with a balcony or giant bath tub. One of Udaipur's most romantic restaurants, Ambrai (p160), is part of the hotel.

Udai Kothi HOTEL $$$
(☎0294-2432810; www.udaikothi.com; Hanuman Ghat; r ₹6500-10,000; ❄@📶🏊) A bit like a five-storey wedding cake, Udai Kothi is a glittery, modern building (there's an elevator) with lots of traditional embellishments – cupolas, interesting art and fabrics, and window seats in some rooms, marble bathrooms and carved-wood doors in others – and thoughtful touches such as bowls of floating flowers throughout. Rooms are pretty, individually designed and well equipped.

The apex is the rooftop terrace, where you can dine well at the restaurant and swim in Udaipur's best rooftop pool (nonguests ₹500).

City Palace

Shiv Niwas Palace Hotel HERITAGE HOTEL $$$
(☎0294-2528016; www.hrhhotels.com; City Palace Complex; r ₹18,000-103,000; ❄@📶🏊) This hotel, in the former palace guest quarters, has opulent common areas such as its pool courtyard, bar and lawn garden. Some of the suites are truly palatial, filled with fountains and silver, but the standard rooms are poorer value. Go for a suite, or just for a drink, meal or massage. Rates drop dramatically from April to September.

Fateh Prakash Palace Hotel HERITAGE HOTEL $$$
(☎0294-2528016; www.hrhhotels.com; City Palace Complex; r/premier ste ₹23,000/45,000; ❄@📶🏊) Built in the early 20th century for royal functions, the Fateh Prakash has luxurious rooms and gorgeous suites, all comprehensively equipped and almost all looking straight out onto Lake Pichola. Views aside, the general ambience is a little less regal than at Shiv Niwas Palace Hotel – although the Sunset Terrace bar (p160) is a great place for an evening drink.

Taj Lake Palace HERITAGE HOTEL $$$
(☎0294-2428800; www.tajhotels.com; r from ₹38,250; ❄@📶🏊) The icon of Udaipur, this romantic white-marble palace seemingly floating on the lake is extraordinary, with open-air courtyards, lotus ponds and a small, mango-tree-shaded pool. Rooms are hung with breezy silks and filled with carved furniture. Some of the cheapest overlook the lily pond rather than the lake; the mural-decked suites will make you truly feel like a maharaja.

Other Areas

★**Krishna Ranch** COTTAGE $$
(☎9828059505, 9828059506; www.krishnaranch.com; s/d incl meals from ₹2000/2500; 📶) 🌿 This delightful countryside retreat has five cottages set around the grounds of a small farm. Each comes with attached bathroom (with solar-heated shower), tasteful decor and farm views. All meals are included and are prepared using organic produce grown on the farm. The ranch is 7km from town, near Badi village, but there's free pick-up from Udaipur.

It's an ideal base for the hikes and horse treks (p156) that the management – a Dutch-Indian couple – organises from here, though you don't have to sign up for the treks to stay here.

Rangniwas Palace Hotel HERITAGE HOTEL $$
(☎0294-2523890; www.rangniwaspalace.com; Lake Palace Rd; s ₹1090-1420, d ₹1310-1635, ste ₹3050-4360; ❄📶🏊) This 19th-century palace boasts plenty of heritage character and a peaceful central garden with a small pool shaded by mature palms. The quaint rooms in the older section are the most appealing, while the suites – full of carved wooden furniture and boasting terraces with swing seats or balcony window seats overlooking the garden – are a delight.

Eating

Udaipur has scores of sun-kissed rooftop restaurants, many with mesmerising lake views. The fare is not always that inspiring or varying, but competition keeps most places striving for improvement.

Lal Ghat

Cafe Edelweiss CAFE $
(73 Gangaur Ghat Rd; coffee from ₹60, sandwiches from ₹140; ⏰8am-8pm; 📶) The Savage Garden restaurant folks run this itsy cafe with baked goods and coffee. Offerings included sticky cinnamon rolls, blueberry chocolate cake, spinach-and-mushroom quiche or apple strudel, muesli or eggs for breakfast, and various sandwiches.

★**Jagat Niwas Palace Hotel** INDIAN $$
(☎0294-2420133; 23-25 Lal Ghat; mains ₹250-325; ⏰7am-10am, noon-3pm & 6-10pm) A wonderful, classy, rooftop restaurant with superb lake views, delicious Indian cuisine and excellent service. Choose from an extensive selection of mouth-watering curries (tempered for Western tastes) – mutton, chicken, fish, veg – as well as the tandoori classics. There's a tempting cocktail menu, Indian wine and the beer is icy cold. Book ahead for dinner.

Charcoal MULTICUISINE $$
(☎8769160106; www.charcoalpb.com; Pratap Bhawan, 12 Lal Ghat; mains ₹140-480; ⏰8am-11pm; 📶) As the name implies, barbecue and tandoor specials feature at this innovative rooftop restaurant. There are plenty of vegetarian and juicy meat dishes on offer and the homemade soft corn tacos with a variety of fillings are deservedly popular.

Mayur Rooftop Cafe MULTICUISINE **$$**
(Hotel Baba Palace, Jagdish Chowk; mains ₹150-290; 7am-10pm;) This delightful rooftop restaurant has a great view of the multihued light show on the Jagdish Temple. You can choose the air-con room or the breezy open section. The usual multicuisine themes fill out the menu, and the quality is top-notch. The thali is great value and vegetarians will love the choice of nine paneer dishes.

Savage Garden MEDITERRANEAN **$$$**
(8890627181; inside Chandpol; mains ₹280-520; 11am-11pm) Tucked away in the backstreets near Chandpol, Savage Garden does a winning line in soups, chicken, and homemade pasta dishes. Try ravioli with lamb ragu, and the sweet-savoury stuffed chicken breast with nuts, cheese and carrot rice. The setting is a whitewashed 250-year-old *haveli* with bowls of flowers, tables in alcoves and a pleasant courtyard. Indian wine is also served.

Hanuman Ghat

Millets of Mewar INDIAN **$**
(www.milletsofmewar.com; Hanuman Ghat; mains ₹110-180; 8.30am-10.30pm;) Local millet is used where possible instead of wheat and rice at this environmentally aware, slow-food restaurant. There are vegan options, gluten-free dishes, fresh salads, and juices and herbal teas. Also on the menu are multigrain sandwiches and millet pizzas, plus regular curries, Indian snacks, pasta and pancakes.

Little Prince MULTICUISINE **$**
(Daiji Footbridge; mains ₹100-160; 8.30am-11pm) This lovely open-air eatery looking towards the quaint Daiji Footbridge dishes up delicious veg and nonveg meals. There are plenty of Indian options, along with pizzas, pastas and some original variations on the usual multicuisine theme, including Korean and Israeli dishes. The ambience is super-relaxed and the service friendly.

Queen Cafe INDIAN **$**
(14 Bajrang Marg; mains ₹70-80; 8am-10pm) This restaurant is like a family's front room, serving up good home-style Indian vegetarian dishes. Try the pumpkin curry with mint and coconut, and the Kashmir *pulao* with fruit, vegies and coconut. Host Meenu also offers cooking classes and walking tours that start with a home-cooked breakfast.

★ **Ambrai** NORTH INDIAN **$$$**
(0294-2431085; www.amethaveliudaipur.com; Amet Haveli, Hanuman Ghat; mains ₹315-515; 12.30-3pm & 7.30-10.30pm) Set at lake-shore level, looking across the water to the floodlit City Palace in one direction and Jagniwas in the other, this is one highly romantic restaurant at night with candlelit, white-linen tables beneath enormous trees. And the service and cuisine do justice to its fabulous position, with terrific tandoor and curries and a bar to complement the dining.

Drinking & Nightlife

Jaiwana Bistro Lounge CAFE
(9829005859; Jaiwana Haveli, 14 Lal Ghat; coffees from ₹100; 7am-10.30pm;) This modern, cool and clean cafe has espresso coffee and fresh healthy juices to help wash down the tasty bakery items and other main meals.

Paps Juices JUICE BAR
(inside Chandpol; juices ₹60-180; 9am-8pm) This bright-red spot is tiny but very welcoming, and a great place to refuel during the day with a shot of Vitamin C from a wide range of delicious juice mixes. If you want something more substantial, the muesli mix is pretty good, too.

Jheel's Ginger Coffee Bar CAFE
(Jheel Palace Guest House, 56 Gangaur Ghat Rd; coffees ₹80-110; 8am-8pm;) This small but slick cafe by the water's edge is on the ground floor of Jheel Palace Guest House. Large windows afford good lake views, and the coffee is excellent. It also does a range of cakes and snacks. Note, you can take your coffee up to the open-air rooftop restaurant if you like.

Sunset Terrace BAR
(Fateh Prakash Palace Hotel; beer/cocktails from ₹400/650; 7am-10.30pm) On a terrace overlooking Lake Pichola, this bar is perfect for a sunset gin and tonic. It's also a restaurant (mains ₹400 to ₹950), with live music performed every night.

☆ Entertainment

Dharohar DANCE
(0294-2523858; Bagore-ki-Haveli; Indian/foreigner ₹90/150, camera ₹150; 7-8pm) The beautiful Bagore-ki-Haveli (p155) hosts the best (and most convenient) opportunity to see Rajasthani folk dancing, with nightly shows of colourful, energetic Marwari, Bhil

and western Rajasthani dances, as well as traditional Rajasthani puppetry.

Mewar Sound & Light Show LIVE PERFORMANCE
(Manek Chowk, City Palace; adult/child ₹150/100; ⏲7pm Sep-Mar, 7.30pm Apr, 8pm May-Aug) Fifteen centuries of intriguing Mewar history are squeezed into one atmospheric hour of commentary and light switching – in English from September to April, in Hindi other months.

Shopping

Tourist-oriented shops – selling miniature paintings, wood carvings, silver jewellery, bangles, spices, camel-bone boxes, and a large variety of textiles – line the streets radiating from Jagdish Chowk. Udaipur is known for its local crafts, particularly miniature painting in the Rajput-Mughal style, as well as some interesting contemporary art.

The local market area extends east from the old clock tower at the northern end of Jagdish Temple Rd, and buzzes loudest in the evening. It's fascinating as much for browsing and soaking up local atmosphere as it is for buying. Bara Bazar, immediately east of the old clock tower, sells silver and gold, while its narrow side street, Maldas St, specialises in saris and fabric. A little further east, traditional shoes are sold on Mochiwada.

Foodstuffs and spices are mainly found around the new clock tower at the east end of the bazaar area, and Mandi Market, 200m north of the tower.

Sadhna CLOTHING
(☎0294-2454655; www.sadhna.org; Jagdish Temple Rd; ⏲10am-7pm) This is the crafts outlet for Seva Mandir, a long-established NGO working with rural and tribal people. The small, hard-to-see shop sells attractive fixed-price textiles; profits go to the artisans and towards community development work.

Information

EMERGENCY

Police (☎0294-2414600, emergency 100) There are police posts at Surajpol, Hatipol and Delhi Gate, three of the gates in the old-city wall.

INTERNET ACCESS

You can surf the internet at plenty of places, particularly around Lal Ghat, for ₹40 per hour. Many places double as travel agencies, bookshops, art shops etc.

MEDICAL SERVICES

GBH American Hospital (☎24hr enquiries 0294-2426000, emergency 9352304050; www.gbhamericanhospital.com; Meera Girls College Rd, 101 Kothi Bagh, Bhatt Ji Ki Bari) Modern, reader-recommended private hospital with 24-hour emergency service, about 2km northeast of the old city.

MONEY

There are lots of ATMs, on City Palace Rd near Jagdish Temple, near the bus stand and outside the train station.

Thomas Cook (Lake Palace Rd; ⏲9.30am-6.30pm Mon-Sat) Changes cash and travellers cheques.

POST

DHL (1 Town Hall Rd; ⏲10am-7pm Mon-Sat) Has a free collection service within Udaipur.

DHL Express (☎0294-2525301; Lal Ghat Guesthouse, Lal Ghat) Conveniently situated inside Lal Ghat Guesthouse.

Main post office (Chetak Circle; ⏲10am-1pm & 1.30-6pm Mon-Sat) North of the old city.

RSRTC BUSES FROM UDAIPUR

DESTINATION	FARE (₹)	DURATION (HR)	FREQUENCY
Ahmedabad	236, AC 585	5	hourly from 5.30am
Ajmer (for Pushkar)	296	7	hourly from 5am
Bundi	328	6	daily (7.45am)
Chittorgarh	120	2½	half-hourly from 5.15am
Delhi	672, AC 1685	15	4 daily
Jaipur	424, AC 903	9	hourly
Jodhpur	273, AC 604	6-8	hourly
Kota	291	7	hourly
Mt Abu (Abu Road)	166	4	10 daily from 5.30am

Post office (City Palace Rd; ⊙10am-4pm Mon-Sat) Tiny post office that sends parcels (including packaging them up), and there are virtually no queues. Beside the City Palace's Badi Pol ticket office.

TOURIST INFORMATION

Small tourist offices operate erratically at the train station and airport.

Tourist office (☎0294-2411535; Fateh Memorial Bldg; ⊙10am-5pm Mon-Sat) Not situated in the most convenient position, 1.5km east of the Jagdish Temple (though only about 500m from the bus stand), this place dishes out a limited amount of brochures and information.

 Getting There & Away

AIR

Udaipur's airport, 25km east of town, is served by flights from Delhi, Mumbai and other hubs. A prepaid taxi from the airport to the Lal Ghat area costs ₹450.

Air India (☎0294-2410999, airport office 0294-2655453; www.airindia.com; 222/16 Mumal Towers, Saheli Rd) Flies daily to Mumbai and Delhi (via Jodhpur).

IndiGo (☎9212783838; www.goindigo.in) Three flights daily to Delhi and two flights daily to Mumbai.

Jet Airways (☎0294-5134000; www.jetairways.com; Maharana Pratap Airport, Dabok) Flies direct to Delhi and Mumbai daily.

Spice Jet (☎9871803333; www.spicejet.com) Flies twice daily to Delhi and daily to Mumbai.

BUS

RSRTC and private buses run from the **main bus stand**, 1.5km east of the City Palace. Turn left at the end of Lake Palace Rd, take the first right then cross the main road at the end, just after passing through the crumbling old Surajpol Gate. It's around ₹40 in an autorickshaw.

If arriving by bus, turn left out of the bus stand, cross the main road, walk through Surajpol Gate then turn left at the end of the road before taking the first right into Lake Palace Rd.

Private bus tickets can also be bought at any one of the many travel agencies lining the road leading from Jagdish Temple to Daiji Footbridge.

TRAIN

The train station is about 2.5km southeast of the City Palace, and 1km directly south of the main bus stand. An autorickshaw between the train station and Jagdish Chowk should cost around ₹50. There's a prepaid autorickshaw stand at the station.

There are no direct trains to Abu Road, Jodhpur or Jaisalmer.

Agra sleeper ₹370, 13 hours, daily (10.20pm)

Ajmer (for Pushkar) seat/sleeper ₹145/215, five hours, four daily (6am, 3.05pm, 5.15pm and 10.20pm), via Chittorgarh (seat/sleeper ₹95/150, two hours)

Bundi sleeper ₹220, 4½ hours, daily (6.15pm)

Delhi sleeper ₹425, 12 hours, two daily (5.15pm and 6.15pm)

Jaipur seat/sleeper ₹180/270, around seven hours, three daily (6am, 3.05pm and 10.20pm)

 Getting Around

AUTORICKSHAW

These are unmetered, so you should agree on a fare before setting off – the normal fare anywhere in town is around ₹40. You will usually have to go through the rigmarole of haggling, walking away etc to get this fare. Some drivers ask tourists for ₹100 or more. It costs around ₹350 to hire an autorickshaw for a day of local sightseeing.

The commission system is in place, so tenaciously pursue your first choice of accommodation.

MAJOR TRAINS FROM UDAIPUR

DESTINATION	TRAIN	DEPARTURE	ARRIVAL	FARE (₹)
Agra (Cantonment)	19666 Udaipur-Kurj Exp	10.20pm	11am	370/995 (A)
Ajmer (for Pushkar)	Udaipur-Jaipur SF SPL	3.05pm	8pm	140/490 (B)
Bundi	12964 Mewar Exp	6.15pm	10.33pm	220/560 (A)
Chittorgarh	12982 Chetak Exp	5.15pm	7.10pm	180/560 (A)
Delhi (Hazrat Nizamuddin)	12964 Mewar Exp	6.15pm	6.35am	425/1115 (A)
Jaipur	12991 Udaipur-Jaipur Exp	6am	1.30pm	180/625 (B)

Fares: (A) sleeper/3AC, (B) 2nd-class seat/AC chair

OFF THE BEATEN TRACK

KUMBHALGARH WILDLIFE SANCTUARY

Ranakpur is a great base for exploring the hilly, densely forested **Kumbhalgarh Wildlife Sanctuary** (Indian/foreigner ₹50/300, 4WD or car ₹200, camera/video free/₹400; ⏲ safaris 6-9am & 3-4.30pm), which extends over some 600 sq km. It's known for its leopards and wolves, although the chances of spotting antelopes, gazelles, deer and possibly sloth bears are higher, especially from March to June. You will certainly see some of the sanctuary's 200-plus bird species.

Beside the park office, near the Ranakpur Jain temples, is the recommended tour company **Evergreen Safari** (☎7568830065; gypsy safari ₹2500). There are also several safari outfits on the road leading up to Kumbhalgarh Fort, including **A-one Tour & Safari** (☎8003854293; Pratap Circle; 2/6 people ₹3000/4500; ⏲ safaris 6-9am & 3-4.30pm). Most hotels will use these or similar outfits to organise your safari.

There's a ticket office for the sanctuary right beside where the bus drops you off for the Jain temples, but the nearest of the sanctuary's four entrances is 2km beyond here.

BICYCLE & MOTORCYCLE

A cheap and environmentally friendly way to buzz around is by bicycle (around ₹200 per day), although motorcycle traffic and pollution make it very tiresome if not dangerous. Scooters and motorbikes, meanwhile, are great for exploring the surrounding countryside.

Heera Cycle Store (☎9950611973; off Gangaur Ghat Rd; ⏲7.30am-8pm) Hires out bicycles/scooters/Bullets for ₹200/500/800 per day (with a deposit of US$200/400/500); you must show your passport and driver's licence.

Around Udaipur

Kumbhalgarh

☎02954

About 80km north of Udaipur, Kumbhalgarh is a fantastic, remote fort, fulfilling romantic expectations and vividly summoning up the chivalrous, warlike Rajput era.

The large and rugged Kumbhalgarh Wildlife Sanctuary can also be visited from Kumbhalgarh.

Sights

Kumbhalgarh FORT

(Indian/foreigner ₹15/200, Light & Sound Show (in Hindi) ₹100/200; ⏲9am-6pm, Light & Sound Show 6.30pm) One of the many forts built by Rana Kumbha (r 1433–68), under whom Mewar reached its greatest extents, this isolated fort is perched 1100m above sea level, with endless views melting into blue distance. The journey to the fort, along twisting roads through the Aravalli Hills, is a highlight in itself.

Kumbhalgarh was the most important Mewar fort after Chittorgarh, and the rulers, sensibly, used to retreat here in times of danger. Not surprisingly, Kumbhalgarh was only taken once in its entire history. Even then, it took the combined armies of Amber, Marwar and Mughal emperor Akbar to breach its strong defences, and they only managed to hang on to it for two days.

The fort's thick walls stretch about 36km; they're wide enough in some places for eight horses to ride abreast and it's possible to walk right round the circuit (allow two days). They enclose around 360 intact and ruined temples, some of which date back to the Mauryan period in the 2nd century BC, as well as palaces, gardens, step-wells and 700 cannon bunkers.

If you're staying here and want to make an early start on your hike around the wall, you can still get into the fort before 9am, although no one will be around to sell you a ticket.

There's a **Light & Sound Show** (in Hindi) at the fort every evening.

Sleeping

Kumbhal Castle HOTEL $$

(☎02954-242171; www.thekumbhalcastle.com; Fort Rd; r from ₹3130; ❄📶🏊) The modern Kumbhal Castle, 2km from the fort, has plain but pleasant white rooms featuring curly iron beds, bright bedspreads and window seats, shared balconies and good views. The super-deluxe rooms are considerably bigger and worth considering for the few hundred extra rupees. There's an in-house restaurant.

Aodhi HOTEL $$$

(☎8003722333, 02954-242341; www.eternalmewar.in; r from ₹8775; ❄@📶🏊) Just under

2km from the fort is this luxurious and blissfully tranquil hotel with an inviting pool, rambling gardens and winter campfires. The spacious rooms, in stone buildings, all boast their own palm-thatched terraces, balconies or pavilions, and assorted wildlife and botanical art and photos.

Nonguests can dine in the restaurant, where good standard Indian fare is the pick of the options on offer, or have a drink in the cosy Chowpal Bar. Room rates plummet from April to September.

Getting There & Away

From Udaipur's main bus stand, catch a Ranakpur-bound bus as far as Saira (₹78, 2¼ hours, hourly), a tiny crossroads town where you can change for a bus to Kumbhalgarh (₹41, one hour, hourly). That bus, which will be bound for Kelwara, will drop you at the start of the approach road to the fort, leaving you with a pleasant 1.5km walk to the entrance gate.

The last bus back to Saira swings by at 5.30pm (and is always absolutely jam-packed). The last bus from Saira back to Udaipur leaves at around 8pm. To get to Ranakpur from Kumbhalgarh, head first to Saira then change for Ranakpur (₹20, 40 minutes, at least hourly).

A day-long round trip in a private car from Udaipur to Kumbhalgarh and Ranakpur will cost around ₹2000 per car.

Ranakpur

02934

On the western slopes of the Aravalli Hills, 75km northwest of Udaipur, and 12km west of Kumbhalgarh as the crow flies (but 50km by road, via Saira), the village of Ranakpur hosts one of India's biggest and most important Jain temple complexes.

The village also makes a great base for exploring the impressive Kumbhalgarh Wildlife Sanctuary (p163) or for taking a day trip to visit the fort at Kumbhalgarh (p163).

Sights

Ranakpur JAIN TEMPLE

(Indian/foreigner incl audio guide free/₹200, camera/tablet ₹100/200; Jains 6am-7pm, non-Jains noon-5pm) Built in the 15th century in milk-white marble, the main temple of Ranakpur, **Chaumukha Mandir** (Four-Faced Temple), is dedicated to Adinath, the first Jain *tirthankar* (depicted in the many Buddha-like images in the temple). An incredible feat of Jain devotion, the temple is a complicated series of 29 halls, 80 domes and 1444 individually engraved pillars. The interior is completely covered in knotted, lovingly wrought carving, and has a marvellously calming sense of space and harmony.

Shoes, cigarettes, food and all leather articles must be left at the entrance; women who are menstruating are asked not to enter.

Also exquisitely carved and well worth inspecting are two other Jain temples, dedicated to **Neminath** (the 22nd *tirthankar*) and **Parasnath** (the 23rd *tirthankar*), both within the complex, and a nearby **Sun Temple**. About 1km from the main complex is the **Amba Mata Temple**.

Sleeping

★ **Aranyawas** HOTEL $$

(02956-293029; www.aranyawas.com; r incl dinner & breakfast ₹5000;) In secluded, tree-shaded grounds off Hwy 32, 12km south of the temple, Aranyawas has 28 attractive rooms in two-storey stone cottages. They aren't fancy, but are spacious, neat and tasteful, with pine furnishings and, in most cases, balconies overlooking a river and jungle-clad hills. There's a large *baori*-inspired pool surrounded by trees and a bonfire for evening drinks in winter.

The restaurant (mains ₹150 to ₹250, buffet lunch/dinner ₹450/500) is a lovely place to stop for a meal even if you're not staying here.

Ranakpur Hill Resort HOTEL $$$

(02934-286411; www.ranakpurhillresort.com; Ranakpur Rd; s/d from ₹5850/6435;) This is a well-run hotel with a nice pool and gardens, around which are arranged the attractive cottages sporting marble floors, stained glass, floral wall paintings and touches of mirrorwork. There is also a good multicuisine restaurant, and horse-riding packages can be arranged. Check for discounts on the website. It's 3.5km north of the temple complex, along Hwy 32.

Getting There & Away

There are direct buses to Ranakpur leaving roughly hourly from the main bus stands in both Udaipur (₹93, three hours) and Jodhpur (₹189, four to five hours). You'll be dropped outside the temple complex unless you state otherwise. Return buses stop running around 7pm. Buses departing for Udaipur can drop you at Saira (₹20, 40 minutes, hourly), about 25km south of Ranakpur, to connect with a bus to Kumbhalgarh (₹41, one hour, hourly).

A day-long round trip in a private car from Udaipur to Ranakpur and Kumbhalgarh costs around ₹2000.

Mt Abu

☎02974 / POP 22,950 / ELEV 1200M

Rajasthan's only hill station nestles among green forests on the state's highest mountain at the southwestern end of the Aravalli Hills and close to the Gujarat border. Quite unlike anywhere else in Rajasthan, Mt Abu provides Rajasthanis, Gujaratis and a steady flow of foreign tourists with respite from scorching temperatures and arid terrain elsewhere. It's a particular hit with honeymooners and middle-class families from Gujarat.

Mt Abu town sits towards the southwestern end of the plateau-like mountain, which stretches about 19km from end to end and 6km from east to west. The town is surrounded by the 289-sq-km Mt Abu Wildlife Sanctuary, which extends over most of the mountain.

The mountain is of great spiritual importance for both Hindus and Jains and has over 80 temples and shrines, most notably the exquisite Jain temples at Delwara, built between 400 and 1000 years ago.

Be mindful that if you arrive during Diwali (October or November), or the following two weeks, prices soar and the place is packed. Mt Abu also gets pretty busy from mid-May to mid-June, before the monsoon. In the cooler months, you'll find everyone wrapped up in shawls and hats; pack something woolly to avoid winter chills in poorly heated hotel rooms.

Sights

The white-clad people you'll see around town are members of the **Brahma Kumaris World Spiritual University** (www.bkwsu.com), a worldwide organisation that has its headquarters here in Mt Abu. The university's **Universal Peace Hall** (Om Shanti Bhawan; 8am-6pm), just north of Nakki Lake, has free 30-minute tours that include an introduction to the Brahma Kumaris philosophy (be prepared for a bit of proselytising). The organisation also runs the **World Renewal**

DON'T MISS

DELWARA TEMPLES

The **Delwara Temples** (donations welcome; Jains 6am-6pm, non-Jains noon-6pm) are Mt Abu's most remarkable attraction and feature some of India's finest temple decoration. They predate the town of Mt Abu by many centuries and were built when this site was just a remote mountain wilderness. It's said that the artisans were paid according to the amount of dust they collected, encouraging them to carve ever more intricately. Whatever their inducement, there are two temples here in which the marble work is dizzyingly intense.

The older of the two is the **Vimal Vasahi**, on which work began in 1031 and was financed by a Gujarati chief minister named Vimal. Dedicated to the first *tirthankar*, Adinath, it took 1500 masons and 1200 labourers 14 years to build, and allegedly cost ₹185.3 million. Outside the entrance is the **House of Elephants**, featuring a procession of stone elephants marching to the temple, some of which were damaged long ago by marauding Mughals. Inside, a forest of beautifully carved pillars surrounds the central shrine, which holds an image of Adinath himself.

The **Luna Vasahi Temple** is dedicated to Neminath, the 22nd *tirthankar*, and was built in 1230 by the brothers Tejpal and Vastupal for a mere ₹125.3 million. Like Vimal, the brothers were both Gujarati government ministers. The marble carving here took 2500 workers 15 years to create, and its most notable feature is its intricacy and delicacy, which is so fine that, in places, the marble becomes almost transparent. The many-layered lotus flower that dangles from the centre of the dome is a particularly astonishing piece of work.

As at other Jain temples, leather articles (including belts and shoes), cameras and phones must be left at the entrance, and menstruating women are asked not to enter.

Delwara is about 3km north of Mt Abu town centre: you can walk there in less than an hour, or hop aboard a shared taxi (₹10 per person) from up the street opposite Chacha Cafe. A taxi all to yourself should be ₹200 round trip, with one hour of waiting time.

Mt Abu

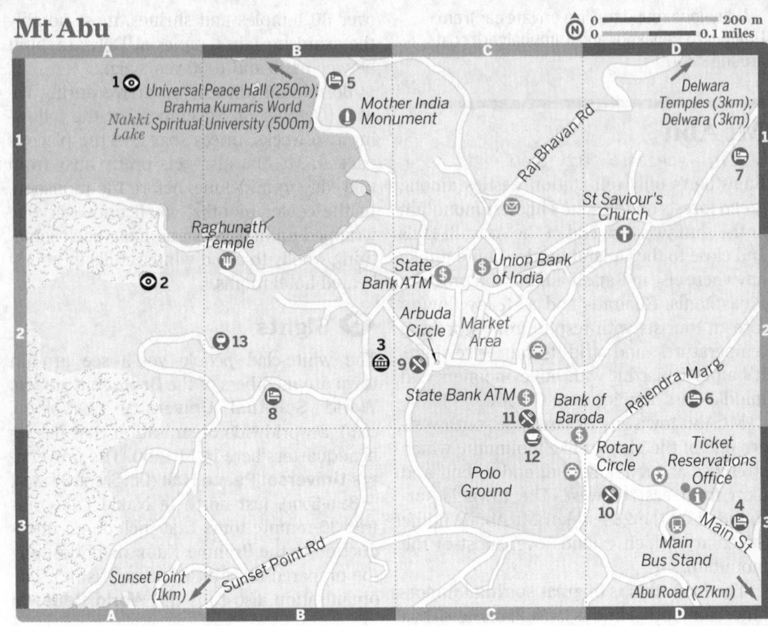

Mt Abu

Sights

1 Nakki Lake ... A1
2 Toad Rock ... A2
3 World Renewal Spiritual Museum ... B2

Activities, Courses & Tours

Mt Abu Treks ... (see 5)
Shri Ganesh Hotel ... (see 8)

Sleeping

4 Hotel Hilltone ... D3
5 Hotel Lake Palace ... B1
6 Kishangarh House ... D2
7 Mushkil Aasan ... D1
8 Shri Ganesh Hotel ... B2

Eating

9 Arbuda ... C2
10 Kanak Dining Hall ... D3
Mulberry Tree Restaurant ... (see 4)
11 Sankalp ... C2

Drinking & Nightlife

12 Cafe Coffee Day ... C3
13 Polo Bar ... B2

Spiritual Museum (8am-8pm) FREE in the town centre.

Nakki Lake LAKE

Scenic Nakki Lake, the town's focus, is one of Mt Abu's biggest attractions. It's so named because, according to legend, it was scooped out by a god using his *nakh* (nails). Some Hindus thus consider it a holy lake. It's a pleasant 45-minute stroll around the perimeter – the lake is surrounded by hills, parks and strange rock formations. The best known, **Toad Rock**, looks like a toad about to hop into the lake.

Sunset Point VIEWPOINT

Sunset Point is a popular place to watch the brilliant setting sun. Hordes stroll out here every evening to catch the end of the day, the food stalls and all the usual hill-station entertainment. To get there, follow Sunset Point road west of the Polo Ground out of town.

Mt Abu Wildlife Sanctuary WILDLIFE RESERVE

(Indian/foreigner ₹50/300, vehicle ₹200; 8am-5pm) This 289-sq-km sanctuary covers much of the mountain plateau and surrounds the town of Mt Abu. It is home to leopards, deer, foxes and bears. Contact Mt Abu Treks to arrange an overnight stay.

Guru Shikhar MOUNTAIN

At the northeast end of the Mt Abu plateau, 17km by the winding road from the town, rises 1722m-high Guru Shikhar, Rajasthan's highest point. A road goes almost all the way to the summit and the **Atri Rishi Temple**, complete with a priest and fantastic, huge views. A popular spot, it's a highlight of the RSRTC tour; if you decide to go it alone, a 4WD from Mt Abu will cost ₹600 return.

Tours

Mt Abu Treks TREKKING

(9414154854; www.mount-abu-treks.blogspot.com; Hotel Lake Palace; 3-4hr trek per person ₹500, full day incl lunch ₹1200) Mahendra 'Charles' Dan arranges tailor-made treks ranging from gentle village visits to longer, wilder expeditions into Mt Abu Wildlife Sanctuary. He's passionate and knowledgeable about the local flora and fauna. Short treks are available as well as an overnight village trek including all meals (₹2000). The sanctuary entrance fee (₹50/300 Indian/foreigner) is not included.

Shri Ganesh Hotel TREKKING

(02974-237292; lalit_ganesh@yahoo.co.in; per person 1hr ₹200, 4hr ₹1000) Organises good short hikes starting at 7am or 4pm.

RSRTC TOURS

(half-/full-day tours ₹50/110; half-day tour 1pm, full day 9.30am) The RSRTC runs bus tours of Mt Abu's main sights, leaving from the bus stand where reservations can be made. Both tours visit Achalgarh, Guru Shikhar and the Delwara temples and end at Sunset Point. The full-day tour also includes Adhar Devi, the Brahma Kumaris Peace Hall and Honeymoon Point. Admission and camera fees and the ₹20 guide fee are extra.

Sleeping

Room rates can double, or treble, during the peak seasons – mid-May to mid-June, Diwali and Christmas/New Year – but generous discounts are often available at other times at midrange and top-end places. If you have to come here during Diwali, you'll need to book way ahead and you won't be able to move for the crowds. Many hotels have an ungenerous 9am checkout time.

Shri Ganesh Hotel HOTEL $

(02974-237292; lalit_ganesh@yahoo.co.in; dm ₹250, s/d ₹500/600, r with bathroom ₹700-1500;) A fairly central and popular budget spot, Shri Ganesh is well set up for travellers, with an inexpensive cafe and plenty of helpful travel information. Rooms are well used but kept clean. Some have squat toilets and limited hours for hot water. Daily forest walks and cooking lessons are on offer.

Mushkil Aasan GUESTHOUSE $

(9426057837, 02974-235150, 9429409660; mushkilaasan.abu@gmail.com; s/d/q ₹1000/1300/1650;) A lovely guesthouse nestled in a tranquil vale in the north of town (near Global Hospital), with nine homely decorated rooms and a delightfully planted garden. Home-style Gujarati meals are available, and checkout is a civilised 24 hours. Rooms next to the reception area can be noisy.

Hotel Lake Palace HOTEL $$

(02974-237154; www.savshantihotels.com; r incl breakfast from ₹4165;) Spacious and friendly, Lake Palace has an excellent location, with small lawns overlooking the lake. Rooms are simple, uncluttered, bright and clean. All have air-conditioning and some have semiprivate lake-view terrace areas. There are rooftop and garden multicuisine restaurants, too.

Kishangarh House HERITAGE HOTEL $$$

(02974-238092; Rajendra Marg; cottages incl breakfast ₹4950, r incl breakfast from ₹6500;) The former summer residence of the maharaja of Kishangarh is now a plush heritage hotel. The deluxe rooms in the main building are big, with extravagantly high ceilings. The cottage rooms at the back are smaller but cosier. There's a delightful

TREKKING AROUND MT ABU

Getting off the well-worn tourist trail and out into the forests and hills of Mt Abu is a revelation. This is a world of isolated shrines and lakes, weird rock formations, fantastic panoramas, nomadic villagers, orchids, wild fruits, plants used in ayurvedic medicine, sloth bears (which are fairly common), wild boars, langurs, 150 bird species and even the occasional leopard.

A warning from the locals before you set out: it's very unsafe to wander unguided in these hills. Travellers have been mauled by bears and, even more disturbing, have been mugged (and worse) by other people.

sun-filled drawing room and lovely terraced gardens.

Hotel Hilltone HOTEL $$$
(☎02974-238391; www.hotelhilltone.com; Main St; s/d incl breakfast from ₹5355/6545; P ❄ 📶 ≋) A modern, well-run hotel in spacious grounds, the punningly named Hilltone takes a leaf out of the more famous hospitality brand with stylishly comfortable and modern rooms that punch above the price tag. The in-house Mulberry Tree Restaurant serves alcohol and nonveg Indian food – a rarity in Mt Abu.

Eating

Kanak Dining Hall INDIAN $
(Lake Rd; thali Gujarati/Punjabi ₹110/140; ⏲8.30am-3.30pm & 7-11pm) The excellent all-you-can-eat thalis are contenders for Mt Abu's best meals. There's seating indoors in the busy dining hall or outside under a canopy. It's conveniently located near the bus stand for the lunch break during the all-day RSRTC tour.

Arbuda INDIAN $
(Arbuda Circle; mains ₹100-150; ⏲7am-10.30pm; 🖉) This big restaurant is set on a sweeping open terrace filled with chrome chairs. It's very popular for its vegetarian Gujarati, Punjabi and South Indian food, and does fine Continental breakfasts and fresh juices.

Sankalp SOUTH INDIAN $$
(Hotel Maharaja, Lake Rd; mains ₹90-250; ⏲9am-11pm) A branch of a quality Gujarat-based chain serving up excellent South Indian vegetarian fare. Unusual fillings such as pineapple or spinach, cheese and garlic are available for its renowned dosas and *uttapams* (savoury South Indian rice pancake), which come with multiple sauces and condiments. Order *masala pappad* (wafer with spicy topping) for a tasty starter.

Mulberry Tree Restaurant MULTICUISINE $$
(Hilltone Hotel, Main St; mains ₹250-350) Mt Abu's Gujarati tourists make veg thalis the order of the day in the town, so if you're craving a bit of nonveg, the smart Mulberry Tree Restaurant at the Hilltone Hotel is the place to go. There are plenty of meaty Indian options on the menu and alcohol is available to wash it down.

Drinking & Nightlife

Polo Bar BAR
(☎02974-235176; Jaipur House; ⏲11.30am-3.30pm & 7.30-11pm) The terrace at the Jaipur Hotel, formerly the maharaja of Jaipur's summer palace, is a dreamy place for an evening tipple, with divine views over the hills, lake and the town's twinkling lights.

Cafe Coffee Day CAFE
(Main St; coffee from ₹110; ⏲9am-11pm) A branch of the popular caffeine-supply chain. The tea and cakes aren't bad either.

Information

There are ATMs on Raj Bhavan Rd, including one outside the tourist office, as well as on Lake Rd.

Bank of Baroda (Main St; ⏲10am-3pm Mon-Fri, to 12.30pm Sat) Changes currency and travellers cheques, and does credit-card advances.

Union Bank of India (Main Market; ⏲10am-3pm Mon-Fri, to 12.30pm Sat) Changes travellers cheques and currency.

Main Post Office (Raj Bhavan Rd; ⏲9am-5pm Mon-Sat)

Tourist Office (⏲9am-5.30pm Mon-Fri) Opposite the main bus stand, this centre distributes free maps of town.

Getting There & Away

Access to Mt Abu is by a dramatic 28km-long road that winds its way up thickly forested hillsides from the town of Abu Road, where the

MAJOR TRAINS FROM ABU ROAD

DESTINATION	TRAIN	DEPARTURE	ARRIVAL	FARE (₹)
Ahmedabad	19224 Jammu Tawi-Ahmedabad Exp	10.50am	3pm	150/510 (A)
Delhi (New Delhi)	12957 Swarna J Raj Exp	8.50pm	7.30am	1265/1775 (B)
Jaipur	19707 Aravali Exp	10.07am	6.55pm	270/715 (A)
Jodhpur	19223 Ahmedabad-Jammu Tawi Exp	3.30pm	7.55pm	195/510 (A)
Mumbai	19708 Aravali Exp	4.50pm	6.35am	365/985 (A)

Fares: (A) sleeper/3AC, (B) 3AC/2AC

nearest train station is located. Some buses from other cities go all the way up to Mt Abu, others only go as far as Abu Road. Buses (₹30, one hour) run between Abu Road and Mt Abu half-hourly from about 6am to 7pm. A taxi from Abu Road to Mt Abu is ₹350 by day or ₹450 by night. Vehicles are charged when entering Mt Abu (small/large car ₹100/200).

BUS

Services from Mt Abu's **main bus stand**:

Ahmedabad ₹182, seven hours, four daily (6am, 7.30am, 10.15am and 2.45pm)

Jaipur AC ₹924, 11 hours, daily (6.30pm)

Udaipur ₹198, 4½ hours, four daily (8am, 9.15am, 12.45pm and 7pm)

TRAIN

Abu Road station is on the line between Delhi and Mumbai via Ahmedabad. An autorickshaw from Abu Road train station to Abu Road bus stand costs ₹20. Mt Abu has a train **reservations office** (8am-2pm Mon-Sat), above the tourist office, with quotas on most of the express trains.

Getting Around

To hire a jeep or taxi for sightseeing costs about ₹650/1200 per half-day/day. Many hotels can arrange a vehicle, or you can hire your own vehicle with driver in the town centre.

NORTHERN RAJASTHAN (SHEKHAWATI)

Far less visited than other parts of Rajasthan, the Shekhawati region is renowned for its extraordinary painted *havelis* (ornately decorated residences), highlighted with dazzling, often whimsical, murals. Part of the region's appeal is that these works of art are found in tiny towns connected by single-track roads that run through desolate countryside north of Jaipur. Today it seems curious that such attention and money were lavished on these out-of-the-way houses, but these were once the homelands of wealthy traders and merchants.

From the 14th century onwards, Shekhawati's towns were important trading posts on caravan routes from Gujarati ports to the fertile and booming cities of the Ganges plain. The expansion of the British port cities of Calcutta (now Kolkata) and Bombay (Mumbai) in the 19th century could have been the death knell for Shekhawati, but the merchants moved to these cities, prospered, and sent funds home to construct and decorate their extraordinary abodes.

Nawalgarh

01594 / POP 63,950

Nawalgarh is a small nontouristy town almost at the very centre of the Shekhawati region, and makes a great base for exploring. It boasts several fine *havelis*, a colourful, mostly pedestrianised bazaar and some excellent accommodation options.

Sights

Dr Ramnath A Podar Haveli Museum MUSEUM

(www.podarhavelimuseum.org; Indian/foreigner ₹75/100, camera ₹30; 8.30am-6.30pm) Built in 1902 on the eastern side of town, and known locally as 'Podar Haveli', this is one of the region's few buildings to have been thoroughly restored. The paintings of this *haveli* are defined in strong colours, and are the most vivid murals in town, although purists point to the fact that they have been simply repainted rather than restored.

On the ground floor are galleries on Rajasthani culture, including costumes, turbans, musical instruments and models of Rajasthan's forts.

Morarka Haveli Museum MUSEUM

(₹70; 8am-7pm) This museum has well-presented original paintings, preserved for decades behind doorways blocked with cement. The inner courtyard hosts some gorgeous Ramayana scenes; look out for the slightly incongruous image of Jesus on the top storey, beneath the eaves in the courtyard's southeast corner.

Bhagton ki Choti Haveli HISTORIC BUILDING

(Bhagat Haveli; ₹70) On the external western wall of Bhagton ki Choti Haveli is a locomotive and a steamship. Above them, elephant-bodied *gopis* (milkmaids) dance. Adjacent to this, women dance during the Holi festival. Inside you'll find a host of other murals, including one strange picture (in a room on the western side) of a European man with a cane and pipe, and a small dog on his shoulder.

Tours

Ramesh Jangid's Tourist Pension TOURS

(01594-224060; www.touristpension.com; guided hikes 2-3 days per person from ₹2250) Ramesh Jangid organises guided hiking trips, guided camel-cart rides (half-day ₹2000 for two people) to outlying villages, and guided tours by car (full day ₹3500 for up to four

Shekhawati

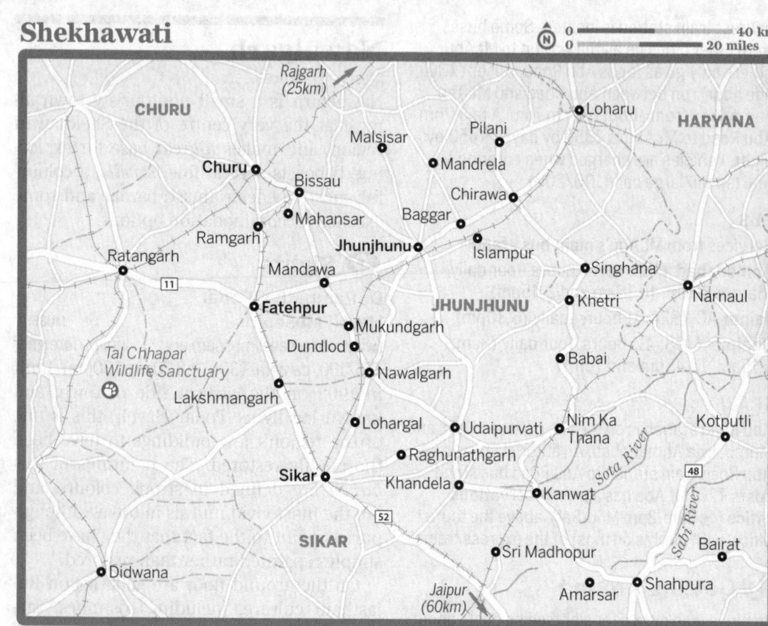

people) to other towns in the region. Lessons in Hindi, tabla, cooking and local crafts such as *bandhani* (tie-dyeing) can also be arranged.

Sleeping

Ramesh Jangid's Tourist Pension GUESTHOUSE $
(☎01594-224060; www.touristpension.com; s/d/tr from ₹800/1050/1350; @ 📶) This guesthouse, run by genial Rajesh, son of Ramesh at Apani Dhani, offers homely, clean accommodation in spacious, cool rooms with big beds. Some rooms have furniture carved by Rajesh's grandfather, and the more expensive rooms also have murals created by visiting artists. Pure veg meals, made with organic ingredients, are available, including a delectable vegetable thali for ₹250.

The family also arranges all sorts of tours (p169) around Shekhawati.

On the western edge of town, near the Maur Hospital, this pension is well known, so if you get lost, just ask a local to point you in the right direction.

DS Bungalow GUESTHOUSE $
(☎9983168916; r ₹400-500) Run by a friendly, down-to-earth couple, this simple place with boxy air-cooled rooms is a little out of town on the way to Roop Niwas Kothi. It's backed by a garden with a pleasant outdoor mud-walled restaurant serving delicious home-cooking. The more energetic can arrange camel tours here.

Shekhawati Guesthouse GUESTHOUSE $
(☎01594-224658; www.shekhawatiguesthouse.com; r incl breakfast ₹600/800, r with AC ₹1000-1500; ❄ @ 📶) This corner of rural loveliness is more like a homestay run by a very friendly couple. There are six rooms in the main building plus five lovely, mud-walled thatched cottages in the garden. The organic garden supplies most of the hotel's produce needs, which can be enjoyed in the lovely outdoor restaurant.

It's 4km east of the bus stand (₹70 by taxi). Pick-up from the bus or train station can be arranged, as can cooking lessons.

★ Apani Dhani GUESTHOUSE $$
(☎01594-222239; www.apanidhani.com; s/d from ₹1080/1420, r with AC from ₹2500; ❄ 📶) This award-winning ecotourism venture is a delightfully relaxing place. Rooms with comfortable beds are in cosy mud-hut, thatched-roof bungalows set around a bougainvillea-shaded courtyard. The adjoining organic farm supplies food, and there are

solar lights, water heaters and compost toilets. It's on the western side of the Jaipur road. Five per cent of the room tariff goes to community projects.

Tours around the area, via bicycle, car, camel cart or on foot, can be arranged.

Getting There & Away

BUS

The **main bus stand** is little more than a dusty car park accessed through a large yellow double-arched gateway. Services run roughly every hour to Jaipur (₹145 to ₹258, 3½ hours), Jhunjhunu (₹40, one hour) and Mandawa (₹35, 45 minutes).

TRAIN

Nawalgarh is on the route of the biweekly Sikar Dee Express. The train departs Dehli Sarai Rohilla station at 6.50am (on Wednesday and Friday) and arrives at Nawalgarh station at 12.15pm (sleeper/3AC ₹195/510, other classes available). The train continues to Sikar (arrives 1.10pm) on broad gauge, but beyond Sikar to Jaipur work is ongoing to convert the old metre-gauge track. In the opposite direction, the train departs Nawalgarh at 2.45pm (also on Wednesday and Friday) and arrives at Delhi at 9pm (via Jhunjhunu; 2nd class ₹55).

Jhunjhunu

01592 / POP 118,470

Shekhawati's most important commercial centre has a different atmosphere from the smaller towns, with lots of traffic and concrete, and the hustle and bustle that befits the district capital. It does, on the other hand, have some appealing *havelis* and a colourful bazaar.

Sights

Mohanlal Ishwardas Modi Haveli HISTORIC BUILDING

(Nehru Bazaar; ₹50) On the northern side of Nehru Bazaar is Mohanlal Ishwardas Modi Haveli (1896). A train runs merrily across the front facade. Above the entrance to the outer courtyard are scenes from the life of Krishna. On a smaller, adjacent arch are British imperial figures, including monarchs and robed judges. Facing them are Indian rulers, including maharajas and nawabs.

Around the archway, between the inner and outer courtyards, there are some glass-covered portrait miniatures, along with some fine mirror-and-glass tilework.

Khetri Mahal HISTORIC BUILDING

(₹50) A series of small laneways at the western end of Nehru Bazaar (a short rickshaw drive north of the bus station) leads to the imposing Khetri Mahal, a small palace dating from around 1770 and once one of Shekhawati's most sophisticated and beautiful buildings. It's believed to have been built by Bhopal Singh, Sardul Singh's grandson, who founded Khetri. Unfortunately, it now has a desolate, forlorn atmosphere, but the architecture remains a superb open-sided collection of intricate arches and columns.

Modi Havelis HISTORIC BUILDING

(Nehru Bazaar; ₹50) The Modi Havelis face each other and house some of Jhunjhunu's best murals and woodcarving. The *haveli* on the eastern side has a painting of a woman in a blue sari sitting before a gramophone; a frieze depicts a train, alongside which soldiers race on horses. The spaces between the brackets above show the Krishna legends. The *haveli* on the western side has some comical pictures, featuring some remarkable facial expressions and moustaches.

Sleeping

Hotel Jamuna Resort HOTEL $$

(9414255035, 01592-232871; www.hoteljamunaresort.in; near Nath Ka Tilla; r ₹1500-3500;) Hotel Jamuna Resort has everything the traveller needs. The rooms in the older wing are either vibrantly painted with murals or decorated with traditional mirrorwork, while the rooms in the newer wing are modern and airy. There's an inviting pool (₹100 for nonguests) set in the garden, plus purpose-built kitchens set up for in-house cooking courses.

The affable owner, Laxmi Kant Jangid has a wealth of knowledge on the villages of Shekhawati and tours can be organised here. Free pick-up from the train or bus stations can be arranged.

Getting There & Away

BUS

There are two bus stands: the **main bus stand** and the **private bus stand**. Both have similar services and prices, but the government-run buses from the main bus stand run much more frequently. Shared autorickshaws run between the two (₹8 per person).

Services from the main bus stand:

Bikaner ₹226, five to six hours, hourly

Delhi ₹230, five to six hours, hourly

Fatehpur ₹45, one hour, half-hourly
Jaipur ₹183, four hours, half-hourly
Mandawa ₹25, one hour, half-hourly
Nawalgarh ₹40, one hour, half-hourly

TRAIN

Jhunjhunu is on the route of the biweekly Sikar Dee Express. The train departs Delhi Sarai Rohilla station at 6.50am (on Wednesday and Friday) and arrives at Jhunjhunu station at 11.30am (sleeper/3AC ₹180/510, other classes available). In the opposite direction, the train departs Jhunjhunu at 3.30pm (also on Wednesday and Friday) and arrives at Delhi at 9pm. The train line to Sikar via Nawalgarh (2nd class ₹55) is broad gauge, but beyond Sikar to Jaipur work is ongoing to convert the old metre-gauge track.

Fatehpur

☎01571 / POP 92,600

Established in 1451 as a capital for nawabs (Muslim ruling princes), Fatehpur was their stronghold for centuries before it was taken over by the Shekhawati Rajputs in the 18th century. It's a busy little town, with plenty of *havelis*, many in a sad state of disrepair, but with a few notable exceptions.

Sights

Apart from the magnificent Le Prince Haveli, other sights include the nearby **Chauhan Well**; **Jagannath Singhania Haveli**; the **Mahavir Prasad Goenka Haveli**, which is often locked but has superb paintings; the **Geori Shankar Haveli**, with mirrored mosaics on the antechamber ceiling; and south of the private bus stand, **Vishnunath Keria Haveli**, and **Harikrishnan Das Saraogi Haveli**, with a colourful facade and iron lacework.

Le Prince Haveli HISTORIC BUILDING
(☎01571-233024; www.cultural-centre.com; incl guided tour ₹200; ⏲9am-6pm) This 1802 *haveli* has been stunningly restored by French artist Nadine Le Prince and is one of the most exquisite *havelis* in Shekhawati. Family and visiting artists help to manage the building and conduct the detailed guided tours (30 to 45 minutes). There's a restaurant (bookings required) plus a small gallery. Many of the rooms have been converted into beautifully decorated guest rooms.

The *haveli* is around 2km north of the two main bus stands, down a lane off the main road. Turn right out of the bus stands, and the turn-off will eventually be on your right, or hop into an autorickshaw.

Tours

Shekhawati Bikers TOURS
(☎01571-233024; per person per day from ₹3600) Le Prince Haveli can get you on a classic Royal Enfield Bullet for a guided tour around the relatively traffic-free roads of Shekhawati.

Sleeping

★**Le Prince Haveli** BOUTIQUE HOTEL **$$**
(☎8094880977, 01571-233024; www.leprincehaveli.com; near Chauhan Well; r from ₹1500, with bathroom from ₹2200, with AC ₹3500-6000; ❄📶🏊) The beautifully restored Le Prince Haveli has opened its artists' residence rooms to travellers. There are 18 highly variable, traditional-style rooms overlooking the central courtyard. The alfresco bar and pool area are great places to unwind, and the adjacent restaurant on the terrace serves buffet meals (Indian and French cuisine) and Italian coffee.

There's a 20% discount in summer.

Getting There & Away

At the **private bus stand**, on the Churu–Sikar road, buses leave for the following Shekhawati destinations throughout day, departing as they fill with passengers:

Churu ₹39, one hour
Jhunjhunu ₹45, one hour
Mandawa ₹34, one hour
Ramgarh ₹25, 45 minutes

From the **RSRTC bus stand**, further south down the same road, buses leave for the following:

Bikaner ₹195, 3½ hours, hourly
Delhi ₹288, seven hours, five daily
Jaipur ₹157, 3½ hours, two daily

Mandawa

☎01592 / POP 23,350

Of all the towns in the Shekhawati region, Mandawa is the one best set up for tourists, with plenty of places to stay and some decent restaurants. It's a little touristy (a relative term compared to other parts of Rajasthan), but this small 18th-century settlement is still a pleasant base for your *haveli* explorations.

There is only one main drag, with narrow lanes fanning off it. The easy-to-find Hotel Mandawa Haveli is halfway along this street

SHEKHAWATI'S OUTDOOR GALLERIES

In the 18th and 19th centuries, shrewd Marwari merchants lived frugally and far from home while earning money in India's new commercial centres. They sent the bulk of their vast fortunes back to their families in Shekhawati to construct grand *havelis* (traditional, ornately decorated mansions) to show their neighbours how well they were doing and to compensate their families for their long absences. Merchants competed with one another to build ever more grand edifices – homes, temples, step-wells – which were richly decorated, both inside and out, with painted murals.

The artists responsible for these acres of decoration largely belonged to the caste of *kumhars* (potters) and were both the builders and painters of the *havelis*. Known as *chajeras* (masons), many were commissioned from beyond Shekhawati – particularly from Jaipur, where they had been employed decorating the new capital's palaces – and others flooded in from further afield to offer their skills. Soon, there was a cross-pollination of ideas and techniques, with local artists learning from the new arrivals.

The early paintings are strongly influenced by Mughal decoration, with floral arabesques and geometric designs. The Rajput royal courts were the next major influence; scenes from Hindu mythology are prevalent, with Krishna particularly popular.

With the arrival of Europeans, walls were embellished with paintings of the new technological marvels to which the Shekhawati merchants had been exposed in centres such as Calcutta. Pictures of trains, planes, telephones, gramophones and bicycles featured, often painted direct from the artist's imagination. Krishna and Radha are seen in flying motorcars, while the British are invariably depicted as soldiers, with dogs or holding bottles of booze.

These days most of the *havelis* are still owned by descendants of the original families, but not inhabited by their owners, for whom small-town Rajasthan has lost its charm. Many are occupied just by a single *chowkidar* (caretaker), while others may be home to a local family. Though they are pale reflections of the time when they accommodated the large households of the Marwari merchant families, they remain a fascinating testament to the changing times in which they were created. Only a few *havelis* have been restored; many more lie derelict, slowly crumbling away.

For a full rundown on the history, people, towns and buildings of the area, track down a copy of the excellent *The Painted Towns of Shekhawati* by Ilay Cooper, which can be picked up at bookshops in the region or in Jaipur.

and makes a handy point of reference. Most buses drop passengers off on the main street as well as by the bus stand.

Sights

Binsidhar Newatia Haveli HISTORIC BUILDING
This 1920s *haveli* on the northern side of the Fatehpur–Jhunjhunu road houses the State Bank of Bikaner & Jaipur. There are fantastically entertaining paintings on the external eastern wall, including a European woman in a chauffeur-driven car, the Wright brothers in flight watched by women in saris, a strongman hauling along a car, and a bird-man flying in a winged device.

Murmuria Haveli HISTORIC BUILDING
The Murmuria Haveli dates back to the 1930s. From the sandy courtyard out front, you can get a good view of the southern external wall of the adjacent double *haveli:* it features a long frieze depicting a train and a railway crossing. Nehru is depicted on horseback holding the Indian flag. Above the arches on the southern side of the courtyard are two paintings of gondolas on the canals of Venice.

Sleeping

Hotel Shekhawati HOTEL $
(☎01592-223036, 9314698079; www.hotelshekhawati.com; r ₹400-2800; ❄@📶) Near Mukundgarh Rd, the only real budget choice in town is run by a retired bank manager and his son (who's also a registered tourist guide). Bright, comically bawdy murals painted by artistic former guests give the rooms a splash of colour. Tasty meals are served on the peaceful rooftop.

Competitively priced camel, horse and 4WD tours can also be arranged.

Hotel Mandawa Haveli HERITAGE HOTEL **$$**
(☎01592-223088, 8890841088; www.hotelmandawahaveli.com; s/ste from ₹1750/5500, d ₹2200-2800; ❄📶) Close to Sonathia Gate, on the main road, this hotel is set in a glorious, restored 1890s *haveli* with rooms surrounding a painted courtyard. The cheapest rooms are small, so it's worth splashing out on a suite, filled with arches, window seats and countless small windows.

There's a rooftop restaurant serving delicious food; it's especially romantic at dinner time, when the lights of the town twinkle below. A set dinner costs ₹550.

Hotel Radhika Haveli Mandawa HERITAGE HOTEL **$$**
(☎01592-223045, 9784673645; www.hotelradhikahavelimandawa.com; s/d/ste incl breakfast ₹1800/2800/3600; ❄📶) This lovely restored *haveli* sits in a quiet part of town with a lawn (and pet rabbit) and boasts comfortable and tasteful rooms that are traditional but without garish murals. There's a good vegetarian restaurant in-house, but it's very close to Monica Rooftop Restaurant should you crave a chicken dish.

Hotel Heritage Mandawa HERITAGE HOTEL **$$**
(☎01592-223742, 9414647922; www.hotelheritagemandawa.com; r ₹1635-6215; ❄📶) South of the Subash Chowk is this gracious old *haveli* with traditionally decorated rooms. The eclectic suites have small mezzanine levels either for the bed or the bathroom. Rooms are highly variable, so check a few. Music performances and puppet shows are held in the small garden.

Hotel Castle Mandawa HERITAGE HOTEL **$$$**
(☎01592-223124; www.castlemandawa.com; r incl breakfast from ₹10,230; ❄@📶🏊) Mandawa's large upmarket hotel in the town's converted fort is a swish and generally comfortable choice. Some rooms are far better appointed than others (the best are the suites in the tower, with four-poster and swing beds), so check a few before you settle in. The gardens and grounds boast restaurants, a coffeeshop and cocktail bar, a pool and an ayurvedic spa.

✕ Eating

Monica Rooftop Restaurant INDIAN **$$**
(☎01592-224178; mains ₹180-400; ⏲8am-9pm) This delightful rooftop restaurant, in between the fort gate and main bazaar, serves tasty Indian and Chinese meals and cold beer. It's in a converted *haveli,* but only the facade, rather than the restaurant itself, has frescos.

Bungli Restaurant INDIAN **$$**
(☎9929439846; Goenka Chowk; mains ₹140-220, thalis ₹260-360; ⏲5am-11pm) A popular outdoor travellers' eatery near the Bikaner bus stand, Bungli serves piping-hot tandoori and cold beer from a down-at-heel setting. The food is cooked fresh by a chef who hails from Hotel Castle Mandawa. Early risers can enjoy an Indian breakfast and yoga class (5.30am, 6am, 6.30am) for a total of ₹400.

ℹ Getting There & Away

The **main bus stand**, sometimes called Bikaner bus stand, has frequent services (roughly half-hourly), including those listed below. Note, there is also a separate **Nawalgarh bus stand**, just off the main drag, with services to Nawalgarh only. Both bus stands are so small they are unrecognisable as bus stands unless a bus is waiting at them. Look for the chai stalls that cluster beside them and you should have the right spot. The main bus stand is at one end of the main street, on your left as the road bears right.

Bikaner ₹223, five hours
Fatehpur ₹34, one hour
Jhunjhunu ₹25, one hour
Nawalgarh ₹35, 45 minutes

JAISALMER, JODHPUR & WESTERN RAJASTHAN

Jodhpur

☎0291 / POP 1,033,900

Mighty Mehrangarh, the muscular fort that towers over the Blue City of Jodhpur, is a magnificent spectacle and an architectural masterpiece. Around Mehrangarh's base, the old city, a jumble of Brahmin-blue cubes, stretches out to the 10km-long, 16th-century city wall. The Blue City really is blue! Inside is a tangle of winding, glittering, medieval streets, which never seem to lead where you expect them to, scented by incense, roses and sewers, with shops and bazaars selling everything from trumpets and temple decorations to snuff and saris.

Modern Jodhpur stretches well beyond the city walls, but it's the immediacy and buzz of the old Blue City and the larger-than-life fort that capture travellers' imaginations. This crowded, hectic zone is also Jodhpur's main tourist area. Areas of the old city further west, such as Navchokiya, are just as atmospheric, with far less hustling.

History

Driven from their homeland of Kannauj, east of Agra, by Afghans serving Mohammed of Ghori, the Rathore Rajputs fled west around AD 1200 to the region around Pali, 70km southeast of Jodhpur. They prospered to such a degree that in 1381 they managed to oust the Pratiharas of Mandore, 9km north of present-day Jodhpur. In 1459 the Rathore leader Rao Jodha chose a nearby rocky ridge as the site for a new fortress of staggering proportions, Mehrangarh, around which grew Jodha's city: Jodhpur.

Jodhpur lay on the vital trade route between Delhi and Gujarat. The Rathore kingdom grew on the profits of sandalwood, opium, dates and copper, and controlled a large area, which became cheerily known as Marwar (the Land of Death) due to its harsh topography and climate. It stretched as far west as what's now the India–Pakistan border area, and bordered with Mewar (Udaipur) in the south, Jaisalmer in the northwest, Bikaner in the north, and Jaipur and Ajmer in the east.

Sights & Activities

★Mehrangarh FORT

(www.mehrangarh.org) Rising perpendicular and impregnable from a rocky hill that itself stands 120m above Jodhpur's skyline, Mehrangarh is one of the most magnificent forts in India. The battlements are 6m to 36m high, and as the building materials were chiselled from the rock on which the fort stands, the structure merges with its base. Still run by the Jodhpur royal family, Mehrangarh is packed with history and legend. You don't need a ticket to enter the fort itself, only the museum section.

Mehrangarh's main entrance is at the northeast gate, **Jai Pol**. It's about a 300m walk up from the old city to the entrance, or you can take a winding 5km autorickshaw ride (around ₹120).

Jai Pol was built by Maharaja Man Singh in 1808 following his defeat of invading forces from Jaipur. Past the museum ticket office and a small cafe, the 16th-century **Dodh Kangra Pol** was an external gate before Jai Pol was built, and still bears the scars of 1808 cannonball hits. Through here, the main route heads up to the left through the 16th-century **Imritia Pol** and then **Loha Pol**, the fort's original entrance, with iron spikes to deter enemy elephants. Just inside the gate are two sets of small hand prints, the *sati* (self-immolation) marks of royal widows who threw themselves on their maharajas' funeral pyres – the last to do so were Maharaja Man Singh's widows in 1843.

Past Loha Pol you'll find a restaurant and **Suraj Pol**, which gives access to the museum. Once you've visited the museum, continue on from here to the panoramic **ramparts**, which are lined with impressive antique artillery. The ramparts were fenced off in 2016 after a fatal selfie accident. Hopefully a temporary measure, as the views are spectacular.

Also worth exploring is the right turn from Jai Pol, where a path winds down to the **Chokelao Bagh**, a restored and gorgeously planted 18th-century Rajput garden (you could lose an afternoon here lolling under shady trees reading a book), and the **Fateh Pol** (Victory Gate). You can exit here into the old city quarter of Navchokiya.

★Mehrangarh Museum MUSEUM

(www.mehrangarh.org; Indian/foreigner incl audio guide ₹100/600, camera/video ₹100/200, Indian/foreign-language guide ₹170/225; ⌚9am-5pm) The fort's museum encompasses the fort's former palace, and is a superb example of Rajput architecture. The network of courtyards and halls features stone-lattice work so finely carved that it often looks more like sandalwood than sandstone. The galleries around **Shringar Chowk** (Anointment Courtyard) display India's best collection of elephant *howdahs* and Jodhpur's royal palanquin collection. The superb audio guide (available in 11 languages) is included with the museum ticket, but bring ID or a credit card as deposit.

One of the two galleries off **Daulat Khana Chowk** displays textiles, paintings, manuscripts, headgear and the curved sword of the Mughal emperor Akbar; the other gallery is the armoury. Upstairs is a fabulous **gallery of miniature paintings** from the sophisticated Marwar school and the beautiful 18th-century **Phul Mahal** (Flower Palace), with 19th-century wall paintings depicting the 36 moods of classical ragas as well as royal portraits; the artist took 10

Jodhpur

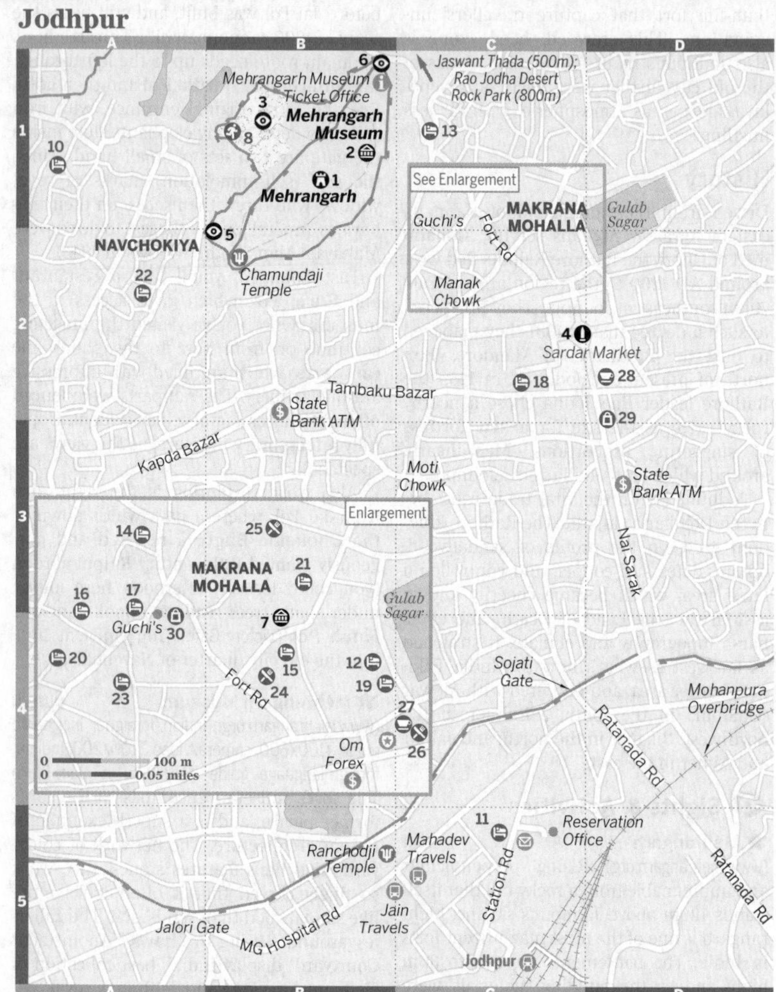

years to create them using a curious concoction of gold leaf, glue and cow's urine.

Takhat Vilas was the bedchamber of Maharaja Takhat Singh (r 1843–73), who had just 30 maharanis and numerous concubines. Its beautiful ceiling is covered with Christmas baubles. You then enter the extensive *zenana*, the lovely latticed windows of which are said to feature over 250 different designs (and through which the women could watch the goings-on in the courtyards). Here you'll find the **Cradle Gallery**, exhibiting the elaborate cradles of infant princes, and the 17th-century **Moti Mahal** (Pearl Palace), which was the palace's main durbar hall (royal reception hall) for official meetings and receptions, with gorgeously colourful stained glass.

Rao Jodha Desert Rock Park PARK

(☎9571271000; www.raojodhapark.com; Mehrangarh; ₹100, guide ₹200; ⏰7am-7pm Apr-Sep, 8am-6pm Oct-Mar) This 72-hectare park – and model of ecotourism – sits in the lee of Mehrangarh. It has been lovingly restored and planted with native species to show the natural diversity of the region. The park is crisscrossed with walking trails that take you up to the city walls, around Devkund Lake,

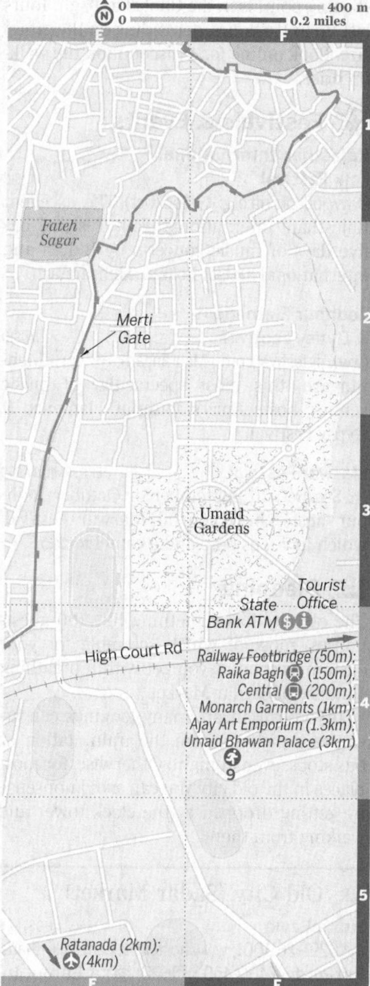

Jodhpur

Top Sights

1	Mehrangarh	B1
2	Mehrangarh Museum	B1

Sights

3	Chokelao Bagh	B1
4	Clock Tower	C2
5	Fateh Pol	B2
6	Jai Pol	B1
7	Tunwarji ka Jhalra	B4

Activities, Courses & Tours

8	Flying Fox	B1
9	Sambhali Trust	F4

Sleeping

10	Cosy Guest House	A1
11	Govind Hotel	C5
12	Haveli Inn Pal	B4
13	Hill View Guest House	C1
14	HosteLavie	A3
15	Hotel Haveli	B4
16	Kesar Heritage Hotel	A3
17	Krishna Prakash Heritage Haveli	A3
18	Nirvana Home	C2
19	Pal Haveli	B4
20	Pushp Paying Guest House	A4
21	Raas	B3
22	Singhvi's Haveli	A2
23	Yogi Guest House	A4

Eating

	Indique	(see 19)
24	Jhankar Choti Haveli	B4
25	Jharokha	B3
	Nirvana	(see 18)
26	Omelette Shops	C4

Drinking & Nightlife

27	Cafe Sheesh Mahal	C4
	Govind Hotel	(see 11)
28	Shri Mishrilal Hotel	D2
	Stepwell Cafe	(see 7)

Shopping

29	MV Spices	D2
30	Sambhali Boutique	A4

spotting local birds, butterflies and reptiles. For an extra insight into the area's native flora and fauna, take along one of the excellent local guides.

Walks here are the perfect restorative if the Indian hustle has left you in need of breathing space. Visit in the early morning or late afternoon for the most pleasant temperatures. The visitors centre is thoughtfully put together, and there's a small cafe, too.

Jaswant Thada HISTORIC BUILDING
(Indian/foreigner ₹15/50, camera/video ₹25/50, guide ₹50; 9am-5pm) This milky-white marble memorial to Maharaja Jaswant Singh II, sitting above a small lake 1km northeast of Mehrangarh, is an array of whimsical domes. It's a welcome, peaceful spot after the hubbub of the city, and the views across to the fort and over the city are superb. Built in 1899, the cenotaph has some beautiful *jalis* (carved-marble lattice screens) and is hung with portraits of Rathore rulers going back to the 13th century.

Look out for the memorial to a peacock that flew into a funeral pyre.

Umaid Bhawan Palace PALACE
(museum Indian/foreigner ₹50/100; museum 9am-5pm) Take an autorickshaw to this hilltop palace, 3km southeast of the old city. The royal incumbent, Gaj Singh II, still lives in part of the building. Built in 1929, the 365-room edifice was designed by the British architect Henry Lanchester for Maharaja Umaid Singh. It took more than 3000 workers 15 years to complete, at a cost of around ₹11 million.

The building is mortarless, and incorporates 100 wagon loads of Makrana marble and Burmese teak in the interior. Apparently its construction began as a royal job-creation program during a time of severe drought. Much of the building has been turned into a suitably grand hotel.

Casual visitors are not welcome at either the royal residence or the hotel, but you can visit the **museum**, housed in one side of the building. It includes photos showing the elegant art-deco design of the palace interior, plus an eccentric collection of elaborate clocks. Don't miss the maharaja's highly polished classic cars, displayed in front of the museum, by the entrance gate.

Tunwarji ka Jhalra HISTORIC BUILDING
(Step-well; Makrana Mohalla) FREE This geometrically handsome step-well (also known as a *baori* or *wav*) has been rejuvenated after decades as a rubbish dump. It's clean lines and clear, fish-filled water will leave you mesmerised. It's a great place to just sit and watch, but the attached cafe (p181) adds further incentive for a visit.

Clock Tower MONUMENT
The century-old clock tower is an old city landmark surrounded by the vibrant sounds, sights and smells of Sardar Market, which is marked by triple gateways at its northern and southern ends. The narrow, winding lanes of the old city spread out in all directions from here. Westward, you plunge into the old city's commercial heart, with crowded alleys and bazaars selling vegetables, spices, sweets, silver and handicrafts.

Flying Fox ADVENTURE SPORTS
(www.flyingfox.asia; adult/child ₹1900/1600; 9am-5pm) This circuit of six zip lines flies back and forth over walls, bastions and lakes on the northern side of Mehrangarh. A brief training session is given before you start and safety standards are good: 'awesome' is the verdict of most who dare. Flying Fox has a desk near the main ticket office and its starting point is in the Chokelao Bagh. Tours last up to 1½ hours, depending on the group size. Book online for a discount on the walk-up price.

Festivals & Events

Rajasthan International Folk Festival MUSIC
(www.jodhpurriff.org; Sep/Oct) The excellent Rajasthan International Folk Festival has five days of music concerts by Indian and international artists held at Mehrangarh.

Jodhpur Flamenco & Gypsy Festival MUSIC
(www.jfgfestival.com; Mehrangarh; Apr) Mehrangarh, this most spectacular of music venues, hosts April's Jodhpur Flamenco & Gypsy Festival.

Marwar Festival PERFORMING ARTS
(Sep/Oct) In September or October Jodhpur hosts the colourful Marwar Festival, which includes polo and a camel tattoo.

Sleeping

The old city has something like 100 guesthouses, most of which scramble for your custom as soon as you get within breathing distance of Sardar Market.

If you call ahead, many lodgings can organise a pick-up from the train station or bus stops, even at night. Otherwise, for most places in the old city you can avoid nonsense by getting dropped at the clock tower and walking from there.

Old City (Sadar Market)

HosteLavie HOSTEL $
(0291-2611001; www.hostelavie.com; Killi Khana, Fort Rd; dm ₹400-450, r ₹1600;) A European-style hostel with clean air-con dorms, where each bed sports a lockable locker and mobile charging point. The dorms are four- and six-bed and each one has its own bathroom. There are also double rooms, making this a good budget option between the fort and the clock tower. It has the obligatory rooftop terrace restaurant.

Rooms are simple and those facing inside are darker but quieter, compared to the airier rooms facing the busy thoroughfare.

Hill View Guest House GUESTHOUSE $
(0291-2441763; hill_view2004@yahoo.com; Makrana Mohalla; dm ₹150, r ₹300-700;) Perched above town and just below the fort

walls, this hotel is run by a friendly, enthusiastic Muslim family, who'll make you feel right at home. Rooms are basic, clean and simple, all with bathrooms (but not all with decent windows), and the terrace has a great view over the city. Good, home-cooked veg and nonveg food is on offer.

Village and camel tours can be arranged here.

Kesar Heritage Hotel GUESTHOUSE $
(☎9983216625; www.kesarheritage.com; Makrana Mohalla; r ₹900-1800; ❄📶) A popular budget choice, Kesar plays a good hand with large airy rooms (a few have balconies, air-con and flat-screen TVs) and friendly, helpful management. The sidestreet location puts noisily sputtering rickshaws out of earshot of light sleepers. The rooftop restaurant looks up to Mehrangarh.

Pushp Paying Guest House GUESTHOUSE $
(☎0291-2648494; www.pushpguesthouse.com; Pipli-ki-Gali, Naya Bass, Manak Chowk; r ₹600, with AC ₹900; ❄@📶) A small family-run guesthouse with five clean, colourful rooms with windows. It's tucked down the narrowest of alleys, but you get an up-close view of Mehrangarh from the rooftop restaurant, where owner Nikhil rustles up great vegetarian fare (dishes ₹30 to ₹90). Nikhil will send a rickshaw to the railway station to pick you up for ₹60 to ₹100.

Yogi Guest House GUESTHOUSE $
(☎0291-2643436; www.yogiguesthouse.com; r ₹800, with AC ₹1500-1900; ❄📶) Yogi's is a venerable travellers' hang-out, with budget and midrange rooms in a 500-year-old blue-washed *haveli* just below the fort walls. It's a friendly place with well-kept, clean rooms. There's also a lovely rooftop restaurant with great views.

★Krishna Prakash Heritage Haveli HERITAGE HOTEL $$
(☎0291-2633448; www.kpheritage.com; Nayabas; r incl breakfast ₹1550-3850; ❄@📶🏊) This multilevel heritage hotel right under the fort walls is great value and a peaceful choice. It has decorated carved furniture and colourful murals, and rooms are well proportioned; the deluxe ones are a bit more spruced up, generally bigger, and set on the upper floors, so airier. There's a shaded swimming pool and a relaxing terrace restaurant.

Free bus and train station pick-ups are offered and there are facilities for drivers.

Haveli Inn Pal HERITAGE HOTEL $$
(☎0291-2612519; www.haveliinnpal.com; Gulab Sagar; r incl breakfast ₹3500-4680; ❄@📶) This smaller sibling of Pal Haveli is accessed through the same grand entrance, but is located around to the right in one wing of the grand *haveli*. It's a simpler heritage experience, with comfortable rooms, and lake or fort views from the more expensive ones. It has its own very good rooftop restaurant, Panorama 360, a mere chapati toss from Indique.

Free pick-ups from Jodhpur transport terminals are offered, and discounts are often available for single occupancy.

Hotel Haveli HOTEL $$
(Haveli Guesthouse; ☎0291-2614615; www.hotel-haveli.net; Makrana Mohalla; s/d from ₹1465/1815; ❄@📶) This 250-year-old building inside the walled city is a popular, efficient and friendly place. Rooms vary greatly and are individually decorated with colour themes and paintings; many have semibalconies and fort views. The rooftop restaurant, Jharokha (p180), has excellent views and nightly entertainment. It's opposite the restored and beautiful Tunwarji ka Jhalra step-well.

Nirvana Home HOTEL $$
(☎0291-5106280; www.nirvana-home.com; 1st fl, Tija Mata ka Mandir, Tambaku Bazaar; s/d from ₹1200/1600, ste ₹3000; ❄📶) It's not often you get to lay your head down in a converted Hindu temple, but Nirvana Home gives you the chance. The hotel is in a busy bazaar, but rooms run off a lovely internal courtyard thick with pot plants. Windows face inside, with views of original 300-year-old temple frescos (fixtures are thankfully newer).

★Pal Haveli HERITAGE HOTEL $$$
(☎0291-3293328; www.palhaveli.com; Gulab Sagar; r incl breakfast ₹5935-11,115; ❄@📶) This stunning *haveli*, the best and most attractive in the old city, was built by the Thakur of Pal in 1847. There are 21 charming, spacious rooms, mostly large and elaborately decorated in traditional heritage style, surrounding a central courtyard. The family retain a small museum here. The rooftop restaurant, Indique (p180), is one of the city's finest and boasts unbeatable views.

Raas BOUTIQUE HOTEL $$$
(☎0291-2636455; www.raasjodhpur.com; Tunwarji ka Jhalara; r incl breakfast ₹19,000-41,000; ❄@📶🏊) Developed from a 19th-century city mansion, Jodhpur's first contempo-

rary-style boutique hotel is a splendid retreat of clean, uncluttered style, hidden behind castle-like gates. The red-sandstone-and-terrazzo rooms come with plenty of luxury touches. Most have balconies with great Mehrangarh views – also to be enjoyed from the lovely pool in the garden-courtyard. There are two restaurants and a highly indulgent spa.

Old City (Navchokiya)

Cosy Guest House GUESTHOUSE $
(9829023390, 0291-2612066; www.cosy-guesthouse.com; Chuna Ki Choki, Navchokiya; r ₹400-1550, without bathroom ₹250;) A friendly place in an enchanting location, this 500-year-old glowing blue house has several levels of higgledy-piggledy rooftops and a mix of rooms, some monastic, others comfortable. Ask the rickshaw driver for Navchokiya Rd, from where the guesthouse is signposted, or call the genial owner, Mr Joshi.

★ **Singhvi's Haveli** GUESTHOUSE $$
(0291-2624293; www.singhvihaveli.com; Ramdevji-ka-Chowk, Navchokiya; r ₹700-2800;) This 500-odd-year-old, family-run, red-sandstone *haveli* is an understated gem. Run by two friendly brothers, Singhvi's has 13 individual rooms, ranging from simple places to lay your head to the magnificent Maharani Suite, with its 10 windows and fort view. The relaxing vegetarian restaurant is a great place to sample a Rajasthani thali and is decorated with sari curtains and floor cushions.

Train Station Area

Govind Hotel HOTEL, HOSTEL $
(0291-2622758; www.govindhotel.com; Station Rd; dm ₹250, s/d from ₹800/900, s/d with AC from ₹1400/1600;) Well set up for travellers, with helpful management, an internet cafe, and a location convenient to the Jodhpur train station. All rooms are clean and tiled, with fairly smart bathrooms. There's a rooftop restaurant and a **coffeeshop** (Govind Hotel, Station Rd; 10am-10pm) with excellent espresso and cakes.

Eating

Omelette Shops STREET FOOD $
(omelettes from ₹25; 10am-10pm) On your right and left as you leave Sadar Market through its northern gate, these two omelette stalls compete for the attentions of passing travellers by knocking up seemingly endless numbers and varieties of cheap, delicious omelettes. Both do a decent job, and are both run by characters worth spending a few minutes with.

Three tasty, spicy boiled eggs cost ₹15, and a two-egg masala and cheese omelette with four pieces of bread is ₹30.

★ **Indique** INDIAN $$
(0291-3293328; Pal Haveli Hotel; mains ₹250-400; 11am-11pm) This candlelit rooftop restaurant at the Pal Haveli hotel is the perfect place for a romantic dinner, with superb views to the fort, clock tower and Umaid Bhawan. The food covers traditional tandoori, biryanis and North Indian curries, but the Rajasthani *laal maas* (mutton curry) is a delight. Ask the barman to knock you up a gin and tonic before dinner.

Nirvana INDIAN $$
(0291-5106280; 1st fl, Tija Mata ka Mandir, Tambaku Bazar; mains ₹130-200; 9am-10pm) Sharing premises with a Rama temple and a hotel, Nirvana has both an indoor cafe, covered in ancient Ramayana wall paintings, and a rooftop eating area with panoramic views. The Indian vegetarian food is among the most delicious you'll find in Rajasthan. The special thali is enormous and easily enough for two. Continental and Indian breakfasts are served in the cafe.

Jhankar Choti Haveli MULTICUISINE $$
(9828031291; Makrana Mohalla; mains ₹130-360; 8am-10pm;) Stone walls and big cane chairs in a leafy courtyard, along with prettily painted woodwork and whirring fans, set the scene at this semi-open-air travellers' favourite. It serves up good Indian vegetarian dishes, plus pizzas, burgers and baked-cheese dishes. There's also an air-con section and a rooftop for meals with a view.

On the Rocks NORTH INDIAN $$
(0291-5102701; Circuit House Rd; mains ₹130-375; 12.30-3.30pm & 7.30-11pm) This leafy garden restaurant, 2km southeast of the old city, is very popular with locals and tour groups. It has tasty Indian cuisine, including lots of barbecue options and rich and creamy curries, plus a small playground and a cavelike bar (open 11am to 11pm) with a dance floor (for couples only).

Jharokha INDIAN $$$
(0291-2614615; www.hotelhaveli.net; Hotel Haveli, Makrana Mohalla; mains ₹225-355; 8am-11pm) The rooftop terrace of the Hotel Haveli

hosts this classy restaurant, with uniformed staff, Indian wine and Spanish *cerveza*. The excellent veg and nonveg dishes include Rajasthani specialities, such as *govind gatta* (cottage cheese and gram-flour dumplings in a yoghurt curry), plus other North Indian curries; try the *aloo Simla mirch* (green bell peppers and potatoes in a spicy gravy).

Drinking & Nightlife

★Shri Mishrilal Hotel CAFE
(Sardar Market; lassi ₹30; ⌚8.30am-10pm) Just inside the southern gate of Sardar Market, this place is nothing fancy, but whips up the most superb creamy *makhania* lassis. These are the best in town, probably in all of Rajasthan, possibly in all of India.

★Cafe Sheesh Mahal CAFE
(Pal Haveli Hotel; coffee from ₹100; ⌚9.30am-9pm) Coffee drinkers will enjoy the precious beans and the care that is bestowed on them at the deliciously air-conditioned Cafe Sheesh Mahal. And if you're feeling hungry the pancakes here are gaining legendary status.

Stepwell Cafe CAFE
(☎0291-2636455; Tunwarji ka Jhalra; coffee from ₹120; ⌚noon-10.30pm; 📶) This delightful modern cafe with espresso coffee, cakes and Italian dishes sits on one side of the wonderfully restored step-well, Tunwarji ka Jhalra. It's a great place to relax and contemplate the time when step-wells such as these kept the city alive. Or you can just watch the kids jump into the water with an impressive booming splash.

Shopping

Plenty of Rajasthani handicrafts are available in Jodhpur, with shops selling textiles and other wares clustered around Sardar Market and along Nai Sarak. You'll need to bargain hard. The town is known for antiques.

MV Spices FOOD
(www.mvspices.com; 107 Nai Sarak; ⌚9am-9pm) The most famous spice shop in Jodhpur (and believe us, there are lots of pretenders!), MV Spices has several small branches around town, including one at Meherangarh, that are run by the seven daughters of the founder of the original stall. It will cost around ₹100 to ₹500 for 100g bags of spices, and the owners will email you recipes so you can use your spices correctly when you get home.

JODHPUR'S JODHPURS

A fashion staple for self-respecting horsey people all around the world, jodhpurs are riding breeches – usually of a pale cream colour – that are loose above the knee and tapered from knee to ankle. It's said that Sir Pratap Singh, a legendary Jodhpur statesman, soldier and horseman, originally designed the breeches for the Jodhpur Lancers. When he led the Jodhpur polo team on a tour to England in 1897, the design caught on in London and then spread around the world.

If you fancy taking home an authentic pair of jodhpurs from the city they originated in, head to **Monarch Garments** (☎9352353768; www.monarch-garments.com; A-13 Palace Rd; ⌚10.30am-8.45pm), opposite the approach road leading up to Umaid Bhawan Palace. Here you can buy ready-made jodhpurs or have a pair tailored for you within two days. Prices are polo club–worthy, starting at around ₹9000.

Sambhali Boutique FASHION & ACCESSORIES
(Killi Khana; ⌚10am-7pm) This small but interesting shop sells goods made by women who have learned craft skills with the **Sambhali Trust** (☎0291-2512385; www.sambhali-trust.org; c/o Durag Niwas Guest House, 1st Old Public Park, Raika Bagh, Jodhpur), which works to empower disadvantaged women and girls. Items include attractive *salwar* trousers, cute stuffed silk or cloth elephants and horses, bracelets made from pottery beads, silk bags, and block-printed muslin curtains and scarves.

Ajay Art Emporium ANTIQUES
(Palace Rd; ⌚10am-7pm) Good quality replica Rajasthani antiques and furniture.

Information

There are foreign-card-friendly ATMs dotted around the city, though fewer are in the old city.

Om Forex (Sardar Market; internet per hr ₹30; ⌚9am-10pm) Exchanges currency and also has an internet facility.

Guchi's (Killikhana, Naya Bass, Makrana Mohalla; internet ₹50 per hr; ⌚8am-10pm)

As well as all forms of ticketing and vehicle hire, Guchi's has fast broadband internet and a wealth of knowledge on what to do and where to go, including how to do an excursion to Osian.

Main Post Office (Station Rd; ⊙9am-4pm Mon-Fri, to 3pm Sat, stamp sales only 10am-3pm Sun)

Tourist Office (☎0291-2545083; High Court Rd; ⊙9am-6pm Mon-Fri) Offers a free map and willingly answers questions.

Getting There & Away

AIR

The airport is 5km south of the city centre, about ₹400/150 by taxi/autorickshaw.

Jet Airways (☎0291-2515551; www.jetairways.com; Jodhpur Airport) and **Indian Airlines** (☎0291-2510758; www.indian-airlines.nic.in; 2 West Patel Nagar, Circuit House Rd, Ratanader) both fly daily to Delhi and Mumbai.

BUS

Government-run buses leave from the **central bus stand** (Raika Bagh), directly opposite Raika Bagh train station. Walk east along High Court Rd, then turn right under the small tunnel. Services include the following:

Ajmer (for Pushkar) ₹207, AC ₹447, five hours, hourly until 6.30pm

Bikaner ₹243, 5½ hours, frequent from 5am to 6pm

Jaipur ₹336, AC ₹730, seven hours, frequent from 4.45am to midnight

Jaisalmer ₹266, 5½ hours, 10 daily

Mt Abu (Abu Road) ₹271, 7½ hours, nine daily until 9.30pm

Osian ₹62, 1½ hours, half-hourly until 10pm

Rohet ₹47, one hour, every 15 minutes

Udaipur ₹273, AC ₹604, seven hours, 10 daily until 6.30pm

For private buses, you can book through your hotel, although it's cheaper to deal directly with the bus operators on the road in front of Jodhpur train station. **Jain Travels** (☎0291-2643832; www.jaintravels.com; MG Hospital Rd; ⊙7am-11pm) and **Mahadev Travels** (☎0291-2633927; MG Hospital Rd; ⊙7am-10pm) are both reliable. Buses leave from bus stands out of town, but the operator should provide you with free transport (usually a shared autorickshaw) from their ticket office. Example services:

Ajmer (for Pushkar) ₹180, five hours, at least six daily

Bikaner seat/sleeper ₹220/320, five hours, at least five daily

Jaipur seat/sleeper ₹260/380, 7½ hours, five daily

Jaisalmer ₹300, 5½ hours, hourly

Mt Abu (direct) seat/sleeper ₹315/550, 7½ hours, daily

TAXI

You can organise taxis for intercity trips, or longer, through most accommodation places; otherwise, you can deal directly with drivers. There's a taxi stand outside Jodhpur train station. A reasonable price is ₹12 per kilometre (for a non-AC car), with a minimum of 250km per day. The driver will charge at least ₹100 for overnight stops and will charge for his return journey.

TRAIN

The computerised **reservation office** (Station Rd; ⊙8am-8pm Mon-Sat, to 1.45pm Sun) is 300m northeast of Jodhpur train station. Window 786 sells the tourist quota. Services:

Ajmer (for Pushkar) sleeper/3AC ₹185/510, 5½ hours, two daily (6.35am and 7am)

Bikaner sleeper/3AC ₹210/530, 5½ to seven hours, five to eight daily (7.25am, 7.40am, 9.50am, 10.30am, 10.55am, 2.25pm, 4.35pm and 8.10pm)

Delhi sleeper/3AC ₹380/986, 11 to 14 hours, four daily (6.35am, 11.15am, 7.50pm and 9.15pm)

MAJOR TRAINS FROM JODHPUR

DESTINATION	TRAIN	DEPARTURE	ARRIVAL	FARE (₹)
Ajmer (for Pushkar)	54801 Jodhpur-Ajmer Fast Passenger	7am	12.35pm	185/510
Bikaner	14708 Ranakpur Exp	9.50am	3.35pm	210/530
Delhi	12462 Mandor Exp	7.50pm	6.40am	380/986
Jaipur	14854 Marudhar Exp	9.45am	3.30pm	250/625
Jaisalmer	14810 Jodhpur-Jaisalmer Exp	11pm	6am	215/565
Mumbai	14707 Ranakpur Exp	2.45pm	9.40am	485/1270

Fares: sleeper/3AC

Jaipur sleeper/3AC ₹250/625, five to six hours, six to 12 daily from 6.10am to midnight

Jaisalmer sleeper/3AC ₹215/565, five to seven hours, three daily (5.20am, 7.25am, 5.50pm and 11pm)

Mumbai sleeper/3AC ₹485/1270, 16 to 19 hours, two to six daily (5.35am, 2.45pm, 6.20pm, 6.45pm, 7.20pm and 11.55pm); all go via Abu Rd for Mt Abu (4½ hours)

Udaipur There are no direct trains; change at Marwar Junction.

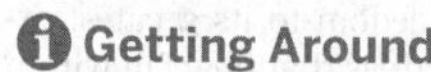

Despite the absurd claims of some autorickshaw drivers, the fare between the clock tower area and the train stations or central bus stand should be around ₹60 to ₹80. A couple of companies have reliable fixed-price taxis that can be pre-booked.

BORDER CROSSING: JODHPUR TO KARACHI

For Karachi (Pakistan), the 14889 Thar Express, alias the Jodhpur–Munabao Link Express, leaves Bhagat Ki Kothi station, 4km south of the Jodhpur train station, at 1am on Saturday only. You need to arrive at the station six hours before departure – the same time it takes to reach Munabao (about 7am) on the border. There you undergo lengthy border procedures before continuing to Karachi (assuming you have a Pakistan visa) in a Pakistani train, arriving about 2am on Sunday. Accommodation is sleeper only, with a total sleeper fare of around ₹500 from Jodhpur to Karachi. In the other direction the Pakistani train leaves Karachi at about 11pm on Friday, and Indian train 14890 leaves Munabao at 7pm on Saturday, reaching Jodhpur at 11.50pm. It is currently not possible to book this train online; you will need to go to the station.

Around Jodhpur

Southern Villages

A number of traditional villages are strung along and off the Pali road southeast of Jodhpur. Most hotels and guesthouses in Jodhpur offer tours to these villages, often called Bishnoi village safaris. The Bishnoi are a Hindu sect who follow the 500-year-old teachings of Guru Jambheshwar, who emphasised the importance of protecting the environment. Many visitors are surprised by the density – and fearlessness – of wildlife such as blackbuck, nilgai (antelope), chinkara (gazelle) and desert fox around the Bishnoi villages.

The 1730 sacrifice of 363 villagers to protect khejri trees is commemorated in September at **Khejadali village**, where there is a memorial to the victims fronted by a small grove of khejri trees.

At **Guda Bishnoi**, the locals are traditionally engaged in animal husbandry. There's a small lake (full only after a good monsoon) where migratory birds, such as demoiselle cranes, and mammals such as blackbucks and chinkaras, can be seen, particularly at dusk when they come to drink.

The village of **Salawas** is a centre for weaving beautiful *dhurries* (rugs), a craft also practised in many other villages. A cooperative of 42 families here runs the **Roopraj Dhurry Udyog** (☎0291-2896658; rooprajdurry@sify.com; ⏰dawn-dusk), through which all profits go to the artisans. A 3ft by 5ft *dhurrie* costs a minimum of ₹3000, a price based on two weavers working several hours a day for a month at ₹50 per day each. Other families are involved in block-printing.

Bishnoi village tours tend to last four hours in total and cost around ₹800 per person. Those run by Deepak Dhanraj of **Bishnoi Village Safari** (☎9829126398; www.bishnoivillagesafari.com; half-day tour per person ₹800) get good feedback, but many other places do them.

Osian

☎02922 / POP 12,550

The ancient Thar Desert town of Osian, 65km north of Jodhpur, was an important trading centre between the 8th and 12th centuries. Known as Upkeshpur, it was dominated by the Jains, whose wealth left a legacy of exquisitely sculpted, well-preserved temples. The **Mahavira Temple** (Indian/foreigner free/₹10, camera ₹100; ⏰6am-8.30pm) surrounds an image of the 24th *tirthankar* (great Jain teacher), formed from sand and milk. **Sachiya Mata Temple** (⏰6am-7.15pm) is an impressive walled complex where both Hindus and Jains worship.

Osian, along with Jodhpur, co-hosts the Marwar Festival (p178), a colourful display of Rajasthani folk music, dance and costume held every September/October.

Prakash Bhanu Sharma, a personable Brahmin priest, has an echoing **guesthouse** (☎9414440479, 02922-274331; s/d without bathroom ₹400/600) geared towards pilgrims, opposite the Mahavira Temple. **Safari Camp Osian** (☎9928311435; www.safaricamposian.com; d tent incl dinner, breakfast & camel ride from ₹9000) is a fancier tented-camp option.

Tours

Gemar Singh SAFARI
(☎9460585154; www.hacra.org; per person per day around ₹2050, min 2 people) Gemar Singh arranges popular camel safaris, homestays, camping, desert walks and 4WD trips in the deserts around Osian and its Rajput and Bishnoi villages. Pick-up from Osian bus station, or from Jodhpur, can be arranged.

Getting There & Away

Frequent buses depart from Jodhpur to Osian (₹62, 1½ hours). Buses also run from Phalodi (₹83, two hours). Trains between Jodhpur and Jaisalmer also stop here. A return taxi from Jodhpur costs about ₹1500.

Jaisalmer

☎02992 / POP 65,480

The fort of Jaisalmer is a breathtaking sight: a massive sandcastle rising from the sandy plains like a mirage from a bygone era. No place better evokes exotic camel-train trade routes and desert mystery. Ninety-nine bastions encircle the fort's still-inhabited twisting lanes. Inside are shops swaddled in bright embroideries, a royal palace and numerous businesses looking for your tourist rupee. Despite the commercialism, it's hard not to be enchanted by this desert citadel. Beneath the ramparts, particularly to the north, the narrow streets of the old city conceal magnificent *havelis,* all carved from the same golden-honey sandstone as the fort – hence Jaisalmer's designation as the Golden City.

A city that has come back almost from the dead in the past half-century, Jaisalmer may be remote, but it's certainly not forgotten – indeed it's one of Rajasthan's biggest tourist destinations.

History

Jaisalmer was founded way back in 1156 by a leader of the Bhati Rajput clan named Jaisal. The Bhatis, who trace their lineage back to Krishna, ruled right through to Independence in 1947.

The city's early centuries were tempestuous, partly because its rulers relied on looting for want of other income, but by the 16th century Jaisalmer was prospering from its strategic position on the camel-train routes between India and Central Asia. It eventually established cordial relations with the Mughal empire. In the mid-17th century, Maharawal Sabal Singh expanded the Jaisalmer princedom to its greatest extents by annexing areas that now fall within the administrative districts of Bikaner and Jodhpur.

Under British rule the rise of sea trade (especially through Mumbai) and railways saw Jaisalmer's importance and population decline. Partition in 1947, with the cutting of trade routes to Pakistan, seemingly sealed the city's fate. But the 1965 and 1971 wars between India and Pakistan gave Jaisalmer new strategic importance, and since the 1960s, the Indira Gandhi Canal to the north has brought revitalising water to the desert.

Today, tourism, wind-power generation and the area's many military installations are the pillars of the city's economy.

Sights

★Jaisalmer Fort FORT
Jaisalmer's fort is a living urban centre, with about 3000 people residing within its walls. It is honeycombed with narrow winding lanes, lined with houses and temples – along with a large number of handicraft shops, guesthouses and restaurants. You enter the fort from the east, near Gopa Chowk, and pass through four massive gates on the zigzagging route to the upper section. The final gate opens into the square that forms the fort's centre, **Dashera Chowk**.

Founded in 1156 by the Rajput ruler Jaisal and reinforced by subsequent rulers, Jaisalmer Fort was the focus of a number of battles between the Bhatis, the Mughals of Delhi and the Rathores of Jodhpur. In recent years, the fabric of the fort has faced increasing conservation problems due to unrestricted water use caused, in the most part, by high tourist numbers.

★Fort Palace PALACE
(Indian/foreigner incl compulsory audio guide ₹100/500, camera ₹100; ⊙8am-6pm Apr-Oct, 9am-6pm Nov-Mar) Towering over the fort's main square, and partly built on top of

ARRIVAL IN JAISALMER

Touts work the buses heading to Jaisalmer from Jodhpur, hoping to steer travellers to guesthouses or hotels in Jaisalmer where they will get a commission. Some may even approach you before the bus leaves Jodhpur; others ride part or all of the way from Jodhpur, or board about an hour before Jaisalmer. On arrival in Jaisalmer, buses can be surrounded by touts baying for your attention. Don't believe anyone who offers to take you anywhere you like for just a few rupees, and do take with a fistful of salt any claims that the hotel you want is full, closed or no good any more. Many hotels will offer pick-ups from the bus or train station.

Also be very wary of offers of rooms for ₹100 or similar absurd rates. Places offering such prices are almost certainly in the camel-safari hard-sell game with the objective of getting you out of the room and on to a camel as fast as possible. If you don't take up their safari offers, the room price may suddenly increase or you might be told there isn't a room available any more.

Touts are less prevalent on the trains, but the same clamour for your custom ensues outside the station once you have arrived.

the Hawa Pol (the fourth fort gate), is the former rulers' elegant seven-storey palace. Highlights of the tour include the mirrored and painted Rang Mahal (the bedroom of the 18th-century ruler Mulraj II), a gallery of finely wrought 15th-century sculptures donated to the rulers by the builders of the fort's temples, and the spectacular 360-degree views from the rooftop.

One room contains an intriguing display of stamps from the former Rajput states. On the eastern wall of the palace is a sculpted pavilion-style balcony. Here drummers raised the alarm when the fort was under siege. You can also see numerous round rocks piled on top of the battlements, ready to be rolled onto advancing enemies. Much of the palace is open to the public – floor upon floor of small rooms provide a fascinating sense of how such buildings were designed for spying on the outside world. The doorways connecting the rooms of the palace are quite low. This isn't a reflection on the stature of the Rajputs, but was a means of forcing people to adopt a humble, stooped position in case the room they were entering contained the maharawal.

The last part of the tour moves from the king's palace (Raja-ka-Mahal) into the queen's palace (Rani-ka-Mahal), which contains an interesting section on Jaisalmer's annual Gangaur processions in spring. The worthwhile 1½-hour audio-guide tour (available in six languages) is included with the entry fee, but you must leave a ₹2000 deposit, or your passport, driver's licence or credit card.

Jain Temples JAIN TEMPLE

(Indian/foreigner ₹50/200, camera ₹50; Chandraprabhu, Rikhabdev & Gyan Bhandar 8am-noon, other temples 11am-noon) Within the fort walls is a maze-like, interconnecting treasure trove of seven beautiful yellow sandstone Jain temples, dating from the 15th and 16th centuries. Opening times have a habit of changing, so check with the caretakers. The intricate carving rivals that of the marble Jain temples in Ranakpur and Mt Abu, and has an extraordinary quality because of the soft, warm stone. Shoes and all leather items must be removed before entering the temples.

Chandraprabhu is the first temple you come to, and you'll find the ticket stand here. Dedicated to the eighth *tirthankar,* whose symbol is the moon, it was built in 1509 and features fine sculpture in the *mandapa,* the intensely sculpted pillars of which form a series of *toranas.* To the right of Chandraprabhu is the tranquil **Rikhabdev** temple, with fine sculptures around the walls, protected by glass cabinets, and pillars beautifully sculpted with *apsaras* and gods.

Behind Chandraprabhu is **Parasnath,** which you enter through a beautifully carved *torana* culminating in an image of the Jain *tirthankar* at its apex. A door to the south leads to small **Shitalnath**, dedicated to the 10th *tirthankar,* whose image is composed of eight precious metals. A door in the northern wall leads to the enchanting, dim chamber of **Sambhavanth** – in the front courtyard, Jain priests grind sandalwood in mortars for devotional use. Steps lead down to the **Gyan Bhandar**, a fascinating

Jaisalmer

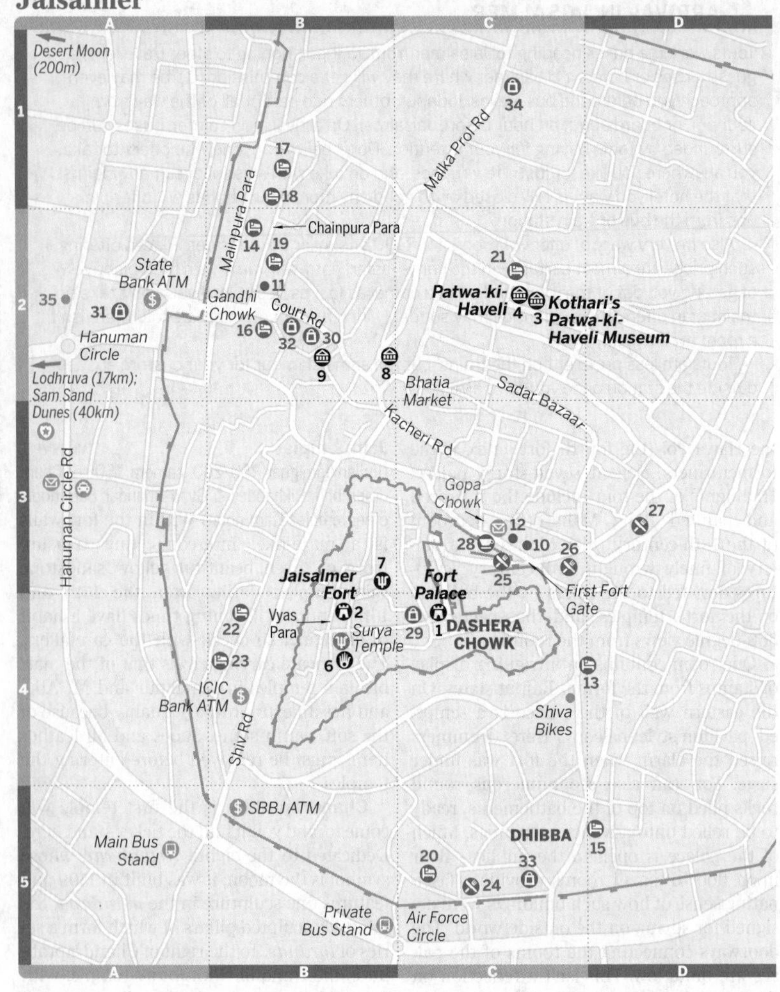

tiny underground library founded in 1500, which houses priceless ancient illustrated manuscripts. The remaining two temples, **Shantinath** and **Kunthunath**, were built in 1536 and feature plenty of sensual carving. Note, the restrictive visiting times are for non-Jains. The temples are open all day for worshippers.

Laxminarayan Temple — HINDU TEMPLE

The Hindu Laxminarayan Temple, in the centre of the fort, is simpler than the Jain temples here and has a brightly decorated dome. Devotees offer grain, which is distributed before the temple. The inner sanctum has a repoussé silver architrave around its entrance, and a heavily garlanded image enshrined within.

★ Patwa-ki-Haveli — HISTORIC BUILDING

(Government sections Indian/foreigner ₹50/200; ⏲9am-6pm) The biggest fish in the *haveli* pond is Patwa-ki-Haveli, which towers over a narrow lane, its intricate stonework like honey-coloured lace. Divided into five sections, it was built between 1800 and 1860 by five Jain brothers who made their fortunes in brocade and jewellery. It's all very

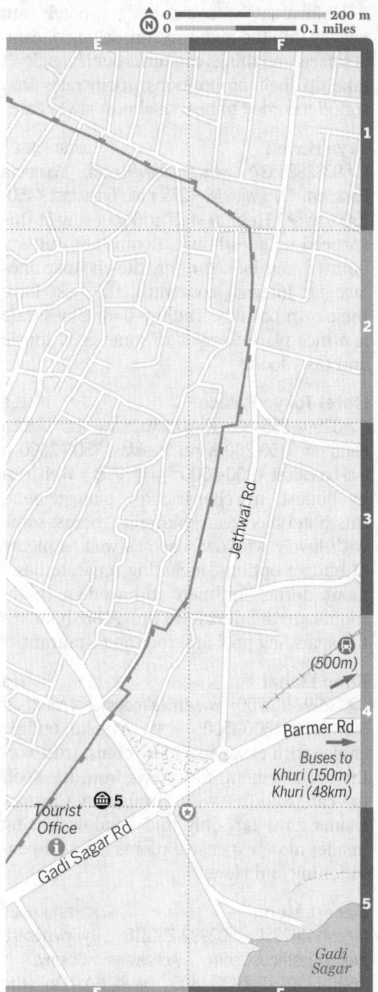

Jaisalmer

impressive from the outside; however, the first of the five sections, the privately owned **Kothari's Patwa-ki-Haveli Museum** (Indian/foreigner ₹100/250; 9am-6pm), richly evokes 19th-century life and is the only one worth paying entry for.

Other sections include two largely empty government-owned 'museums' and two private sections containing shops.

Nathmal-ki-Haveli HISTORIC BUILDING
(donation requested; 8am-7pm) This late-19th-century *haveli,* once used as the prime minister's house, is still partly inhabited. It has an extraordinary exterior, dripping with carvings, and the 1st floor has some beautiful paintings using 1.5kg of gold leaf. The left and right wings were the work

of two brothers, whose competitive spirits apparently produced this virtuoso work – the two sides are similar, but not identical. Sandstone elephants guard the entrance.

Desert Cultural Centre & Museum MUSEUM
(Gadi Sagar Rd; museum ₹50, camera ₹50, combined museum & puppet show ₹100; ⏲museum 10am-6pm, puppet show 6.30-8.30pm) This interesting little museum tells the history of Rajasthan's princely states and has exhibits on traditional Rajasthani culture. Features include Rajasthani music (with video), textiles, a *kavad* mobile temple, and a *phad* scroll painting depicting the story of the Rajasthani folk hero Pabuji, used by travelling singers as they recite Pabuji's epic exploits. It also hosts nightly half-hour **puppet shows** with English commentary. The ticket includes admission to the Jaisalmer Folklore Museum.

Thar Heritage Museum MUSEUM
(off Court Rd; ₹40, camera ₹20; ⏲10am-8pm) This private museum has an intriguing assortment of Jaisalmer artefacts, from turbans, musical instruments, fossils and kitchen equipment to displays on birth, marriage, death and opium customs. It's brought alive by the guided tour you'll get from its founder, local historian and folklorist LN Khatri. Look for the snakes and ladders game that acts as a teaching guide to Hinduism's spiritual journey. If the door is locked you'll find Mr Khatri at his shop, Desert Handicrafts Emporium, nearby on Court Rd.

Tours

The tourist office (p192) runs sunset tours to the Sam Sand Dunes (₹200 per person, minimum four people). Add ₹100 if you'd like a short camel ride, too. Other tours visit Amar Sagar, Lodhruva and Bada Bagh by car.

Sleeping

While staying in the fort might appear to be Jaisalmer's most atmospheric choice, habitation inside the fort – driven in no small part by tourism – is causing irreparable damage to the monument. As a result, we don't recommend staying inside. Fortunately, there's a wide choice of good places to stay outside the fort. You'll get massive discounts between April and August, when Jaisalmer is hellishly hot.

Unfortunately, some budget hotels are heavily into the high-pressure selling of camel safaris and things can turn sour if you don't take up their propositions; room rates that sound too good to be true almost always are.

Arya Haveli GUESTHOUSE $
(☎9782585337; www.aryahaveli.com; Mainpura Para; dm ₹175, with AC ₹275, r incl breakfast ₹450-1500; ❄📶) Helpful staff add to a stay at this spruced-up guesthouse. Rooms are well appointed and looked after; the cheaper ones face an internal courtyard, the best have their own balcony. The top-floor Blues Cafe is a nice place to relax to some good music and tasty food.

Hotel Tokyo Palace HOTEL $
(☎02992-255483; www.tokyopalace.net; Dhibba Para; dm ₹150-200, s incl breakfast ₹500-2000, d incl breakfast ₹900-3000; ❄@📶🏊) Well run by honest, traveller-friendly management, this hotel has clean midrange rooms, some with lovely window seats, as well as plenty of budget options, including separate basement dorms for men and women (bathrooms are the next level up). A big bonus is the sparkling pool and rooftop restaurant.

Roop Mahal HOTEL $
(☎02992-251700; www.hotelroopmahal.com; off Shiv Rd; r ₹600-1500; ❄📶) A solid budget choice with clean spacious rooms, trustworthy management, fort views from the rooftop cafe, and free wi-fi throughout. Cheaper rooms have fan only and windows facing inside; more expensive rooms have air-conditioning and views.

Desert Moon GUESTHOUSE $
(☎9414149350, 02992-250116; www.desertmoonguesthouse.com; Achalvansi Colony; s ₹600-1200, d ₹900-1800; ❄@📶) On the northwestern edge of town, 1km from Gandhi Chowk, Desert Moon is in a quiet location beneath the Vyas Chhatri sunset point. The guesthouse is run by a friendly Indian-Kiwi couple who offer free pick-up from the train and bus stations. The 11 rooms are cool, clean and comfortable, with polished stone floors, tasteful decorations and sparkling bathrooms.

Hotel Renuka HOTEL $
(☎02992-252757; www.hotelrenuka.net; Chainpura Para; s/d ₹450/550, with AC ₹850/950; ❄@📶) Spread over three floors, Renuka has squeaky-clean rooms – the best have balconies, bathrooms and air-conditioning. It's

been warmly accommodating guests since 1988, so management knows its stuff. The roof terrace has great fort views and a good restaurant, and the hotel offers free pick-up from the bus and train stations.

Hotel Swastika HOTEL $

(☎ 02992-252483; swastikahotel@yahoo.com; Chainpura Para; dm ₹100, s/d/tr ₹200/300/400, r with AC ₹600; ❄📶) In this well-run place, the only thing you'll be hassled about is to relax. Rooms are plain, quiet, clean and very good for the price; some have little balconies. There are plenty of restaurants nearby.

★ **Hotel Nachana Haveli** HERITAGE HOTEL $$

(☎ 02992-252110; www.nachanahaveli.com; Goverdhan Chowk; r/ste incl breakfast ₹3950/4950; ❄@📶) This 280-year-old royal *haveli,* set around three courtyards – one with a tinkling fountain – is a fascinating hotel with a highly regarded restaurant, Saffron. The raw sandstone rooms have arched stone ceilings and the ambience of a medieval castle. They are sumptuously and romantically decorated. The common areas come with all the Rajput trimmings, including swing chairs and bearskin rugs.

Although centrally located, the hotel is set back from the road and the stone walls ensure a peaceful sleep.

Hotel Gorakh Haveli HOTEL $$

(☎ 02992-252978; www.hotelgorakhhaveli.com; Dhibba Para; s/d ₹1000/1500, with AC ₹1500/2500; ❄📶) A pleasantly low-key spot south of the fort, Gorakh Haveli is a modern place built with traditional sandstone and some attractive carving. Rooms are comfy and spacious, staff are amiable, and there's a reasonable all-veg, multicuisine rooftop restaurant (mains ₹30 to ₹150), with fort views, of course. A 30% discount on rooms is offered in summer.

Hotel Pleasant Haveli HOTEL $$

(☎ 02992-253253; www.pleasanthaveli.com; Chainpura Para; r from ₹2450; ❄📶) This welcoming place has lots of lovely carved stone, a beautiful rooftop (with restaurant) and just a handful of spacious and attractive colour-themed rooms, all with modern, well-equipped bathrooms and air-con. Complimentary water bottle and free pick-ups from transport terminals are available.

Shahi Palace HOTEL $$

(☎ 02992-255920; www.shahipalacehotel.com; off Shiv Rd; r ₹350-2000; ❄@📶) Shahi Palace is a deservedly popular option. It's a modern building in the traditional style with carved sandstone. It has attractive rooms with raw sandstone walls, colourful embroidery, and carved stone or wooden beds. The cheaper rooms are mostly in two annexes along the street, **Star Haveli** and **Oasis Haveli**. The rooftop restaurant (mains ₹80 to ₹200) is excellent.

Indian veg and nonveg dishes are available, plus some European fare, cold beer and a superb evening fort view.

★ **1st Gate Home Fusion** BOUTIQUE HOTEL $$$

(☎ 02992-254462, 9462554462; www.1stgate.in; First Fort Gate; r incl breakfast from ₹8190; ❄@📶) Italian-designed and super-slick, this is Jaisalmer's most sophisticated hotel and it is beautiful throughout, with a desert-meets-contemporary-boutique vibe. The location lends it one of the finest fort views in town, especially from its split-level, open-air restaurant-cafe area. Rooms are immaculate with complimentary minibar (soft drinks), fruit basket and bottled water replenished daily.

Killa Bhawan Lodge HOTEL $$$

(☎ 02992-253833; www.killabhawan.com; Patwa-ki-haveli Chowk; r incl breakfast from ₹4165; ❄📶) Near Patwa-ki-Haveli, this small hotel is a delight. There are five big and beautifully decorated rooms, a pleasant rooftop restaurant, KB Cafe, that looks up to the fort, and free tea and coffee all day.

★ **Suryagarh** HOTEL $$$

(☎ 02992-269269; www.suryagarh.com; Kahala Fata, Sam Rd; r/ste incl breakfast from ₹18,000/23,000; ❄@📶🏊) The undisputed king in this category, Suryagarh rises like a fortress beside the Sam road, 14km west of town. It's a brand-new building in traditional Jaisalmer style centred on a huge palace-like courtyard with beautiful carved stonework. Features include a fabulous indoor pool and a multicuisine restaurant, Nosh (mains ₹650 to ₹800; nonguests welcome). Rooms follow the traditional/contemporary theme.

It's a spectacular place, but it doesn't stop there. A great range of activities and excursions are on offer plus nightly entertainment.

Eating & Drinking

★ **1st Gate Home Fusion** ITALIAN, INDIAN $$

(☎ 02992-254462, 9462554462; First Fort Gate; mains ₹220-460; ⏰7.30-10.30am, noon-3pm &

JAISALMER CAMEL SAFARIS

Trekking around by camel is the most evocative and fun way to sample Thar Desert life. Don't expect dune seas, however – the Thar is mostly arid scrubland sprinkled with villages and wind turbines, with occasional dune areas popping out here and there. You will often come across fields of millet, and children herding flocks of sheep or goats, the neck bells of which tinkle in the desert silence.

Most trips now include 4WD rides to get you to less frequented areas. The camel riding is then done in two two-hour batches, one before lunch, one after. It's hardly camel *trekking*, but it's a lot of fun nevertheless. A cheaper alternative to arranging things in Jaisalmer is to base yourself in the small village of Khuri (p193), 48km southwest, where similar camel rides are available, but where you're already in the desert when you start.

Before You Go

Competition between safari organisers is cut-throat and standards vary. Most hotels and guesthouses are very happy to organise a camel safari for you. While many provide a good service, some may cut corners and take you for the kind of ride you didn't have in mind. A few low-budget hotels in particular exert considerable pressure on guests to take 'their' safari. Others specifically claim 'no safari hassle'.

You can also organise a safari directly with one of the several reputable specialist agencies in Jaisalmer. Since these agencies depend exclusively on safari business it's particularly in their interest to satisfy their clients. It's a good idea to talk to other travellers and ask two or three operators what they're offering.

A one-night safari, leaving Jaisalmer in the afternoon and returning the next morning, with a night on some dunes, is a minimum to get a feel for the experience: you'll probably get 1½ to two hours of riding each day. You can trek for several days or weeks if you wish. The longer you ride, the more understanding you'll gain of the desert's villages, oases, wildlife and people.

The best-known dunes, at Sam (p193), 40km west of Jaisalmer, are always crowded in the evening and are more of a carnival than a back-to-nature experience. The dunes near Khuri are also quite busy at sunset, but quiet the rest of the time. Operators all sell trips now to 'nontouristy' and 'off-the-beaten-track' areas. Ironically, this has made Khuri quieter again, although Sam still hums with day-tripper activity.

With 4WD transfers included, typical rates are between ₹1200 and ₹2500 per person for a one-day, one-night trip (leaving one morning and returning the next). This should include meals, mineral water, blankets and sometimes a thin mattress. Check that there will be one camel for each rider. You can pay for greater levels of comfort (eg tents, better food), but *always* get it all down in writing.

You should get a cheaper rate (₹1000 to ₹1500 per person) if you leave Jaisalmer in the afternoon and return the following morning. A quick sunset ride in the dunes at Sam costs around ₹600 per person, including 4WD transfer. At the other end of the scale, you can arrange for a 20-day trek to Bikaner. Expect to pay between ₹1200 and ₹2000 per person per day for long, multiday trips, depending on the level of support facilities (4WDs, camel carts etc).

7-11pm; 📶 🌱) Sitting atop the boutique hotel of the same name, this split-level, open-air terrace boasts dramatic fort views and a mouth-watering menu of authentic vegetarian Italian and Indian dishes. Also on offer are excellent wood-fired pizzas and good strong Italian coffee. Snacks and drinks are available outside meal times (7.30am to 11pm).

★ Saffron MULTICUISINE $$

(Hotel Nachana Haveli, Goverdhan Chowk; mains ₹195-415; ⏲7am-11pm) On the spacious roof terrace of Hotel Nachana Haveli, the veg and nonveg food here is excellent. It's a particularly atmospheric place in the evening, with private and communal lounges and more formal seating arrangements. The Indian food is hard to beat, though the Italian isn't too bad either. Alcohol is served.

What to Take

A wide-brimmed hat (or Lawrence of Arabia turban), long trousers, a long-sleeved shirt, insect repellent, toilet paper, a torch (flashlight), sunscreen, a water bottle (with a strap), and some cash (for a tip to the camel men, if nothing else) are recommended. Women should consider wearing a sports bra, as a trotting camel is a bumpy ride. It can get cold at night, so if you have a sleeping bag bring it along, even if you're told that lots of blankets will be supplied. During summer, rain is not unheard of, so come prepared.

Which Safari?

Recommendations shouldn't be a substitute for doing your own research. Whichever agency you go for, insist that all rubbish is carried back to Jaisalmer.

Sahara Travels (☎02992-252609; www.saharatravelsjaisalmer.com; Gopa Chowk; ⏱6am-8pm) Run by the son of the late LN Bissa (aka Mr Desert), this place is very professional and transparent. Trips are to 'nontouristy' areas only. Prices for an overnight trip (9am to 11am the following day) are ₹1900 per person, all inclusive. A cheaper overnight alternative that avoids the midday sun starts at 2pm and finishes at 11am for ₹1500.

Trotters (☎9828929974; www.trottersjaisalmer.net; Gopa Chowk; ⏱5.30am-9.00pm) This company is transparently run with a clear price list showing everything on offer, including trips to 'off-the-beaten-track' areas as well as cheaper jaunts to Sam or Khuri. Prices for an overnight trip (6.30am to 11am the following day) are ₹1950 to ₹2450 per person, all inclusive.

Thar Desert Tours (☎91-9414365333; www.tharcamelsafarijaisalmer.com; Gandhi Chowk; ⏱8.30am-7.30pm) This well-run operator charges ₹1200 per person per day including water and meals, adjusting prices depending on trip times. It limits tours to five people maximum, and we also receive good feedback about them. Customers pay 80% upfront.

In the Desert

Camping out at night, huddling around a tiny fire beneath the stars and listening to the camel drivers' songs, is magical.

There's always a long lunch stop during the hottest part of the day. At resting points the camels are unsaddled and hobbled; they'll often have a roll in the sand before limping away to browse on nearby shrubs, while the camel drivers brew chai or prepare food. The whole crew rests in the shade of thorn trees.

Take care of your possessions, particularly on the return journey. Any complaints you do have should be reported, either to the **Superintendent of Police** (☎02992-252233), the **tourist office** (p192) or the intermittently staffed **Tourist Assistance Force** (Gadi Sagar Rd) posts inside the First Fort Gate and on the Gadi Sagar access road.

The camel drivers will expect a tip (up to ₹100 per day is welcomed) at the end of the trip; don't neglect to give them one.

Monica Restaurant MULTICUISINE **$$**
(Amar Sagar Pol; mains ₹100-300, veg/nonveg thali ₹175/375; ⏱8am-3pm & 6-11pm) The airy open-air dining room at Monica just about squeezes in a fort view, but if you end up at a non-view table, console yourself with the excellent veg and nonveg options. Meat from the tandoor is particularly well-flavoured and succulent, the thalis varied, and the salads fresh and tasty.

Jaisal Italy ITALIAN **$$**
(First Fort Gate; mains ₹180-290; ⏱7.30am-11pm; ❄📶) Just inside First Fort Gate, Jaisal Italy has a decent vegetarian Italian menu, including bruschetta, antipasti, pasta, pizza, salad and desserts, plus Spanish omelettes. All this is served up in an exotically decorated indoor restaurant (cosy in winter, deliciously air-conditioned in summer) or on a delightful terrace atop the lower fort walls, with cinematic views. Alcohol is served.

Desert Boy's Dhani INDIAN $$
(Dhibba Para; mains ₹120-250, thali ₹400; ⏲11am-4pm & 7-11pm; ❄📶✍) A walled-garden restaurant where tables are spread around a large, stone-paved courtyard shaded by a big tree. There's also traditional cushion seating undercover and in an air-con room. Rajasthani music and dance is performed from 8pm to 10pm nightly, and it's a very pleasant place to eat excellent, good-value Rajasthani and other Indian veg dishes.

Natraj Restaurant MULTICUISINE $$
(Aasani Rd; mains ₹120-180; ⏲10am-10pm; 📶✍) This rooftop restaurant has a satisfying view of the upper part of the Salim Singh-ki-Haveli next door. The pure veg food is consistently excellent and the service is great. The delicious South Indian dosas (large savoury crêpes) are fantastic value.

Bhang Shop CAFE
(Gopa Chowk; lassi from ₹150) Jaisalmer's licensed Bhang Shop is a simple, unpretentious place. The magic ingredient is *bhang:* cannabis buds and leaves mixed into a paste with milk, ghee and spices. As well as lassi, it also does a range of *bhang*-laced cookies and cakes – choose either medium or strong. *Bhang* is legal, but it doesn't agree with everyone, so go easy.

Shopping

Jaisalmer is famous for its stunning embroidery, bedspreads, mirrorwork wall hangings, oil lamps, stonework and antiques. Watch out when purchasing silver items: the metal is sometimes adulterated with bronze.

There are several good *khadi* (homespun cloth) shops where you can find fixed-price tablecloths, rugs and clothes, with a variety of patterning techniques including tie-dye, block printing and embroidery. Try **Zila Khadi Gramodan Parishad** (Malka Prol Rd; ⏲10am-6pm Mon-Sat), **Khadi Gramodyog Bhavan** (Dhibba; ⏲10am-6pm Mon-Sat) or **Gandhi Darshan Emporium** (near Hanuman Circle; ⏲11am-7pm Fri-Wed).

Bellissima ARTS & CRAFTS
(Dashera Chowk; ⏲8am-9pm) This small shop near the fort's main square sells beautiful patchworks, embroidery, paintings, bags, rugs, cushion covers and all types of Rajasthani art. Proceeds assist underprivileged women from surrounding villages, including those who have divorced or been widowed.

Jaisalmer Handloom ARTS & CRAFTS
(www.jaisalmerhandloom.com; Court Rd; ⏲9am-10pm) This place has a big array of bedspreads, tapestries, clothing (ready-made and custom-made, including silk) and other textiles, made by its own workers and others. If you need an embroidered camel-saddle-cloth (and who doesn't?), try for one here.

Desert Handicrafts Emporium ARTS & CRAFTS
(Court Rd; ⏲9.30am-9.30pm) With some unusual jewellery, paintings, and all sorts of textiles, this is one of the most original of numerous craft shops around town.

Information

MONEY

There are ATMs near Hanuman Circle, on Shiv Rd, and outside the train station. Lots of licensed money changers are in and around Gandhi Chowk.

POST

Main post office (Hanuman Circle Rd; ⏲10am-5pm Mon-Sat) West of the fort.

Post office (Gopa Chowk; ⏲10am-5pm Mon-Fri, to 1pm Sat) Just outside the fort gate; sells stamps and you can send postcards.

TOURIST INFORMATION

Tourist office (☎02992-252406; Gadi Sagar Rd; ⏲9.30am-6pm) Friendly office with a free town map.

Getting There & Away

AIR

Jaisalmer's new airport, 5km south of town, has been lying mothballed for a few years, but there have been signs that regular domestic flights would soon resume. Meanwhile, **Supreme Airlines** (☎9820588749; www.supremeairlines.com) was planning to fly a small plane from Delhi to Jaisalmer via Bikaner. Check locally to see if the route is currently operating.

BUS

RSRTC buses leave from the **main bus stand** (Shiv Rd). There are services to Ajmer (₹430, 9½ hours) and Jodhpur (₹266, 5½ hours) throughout the day. Buses to Khuri (₹39, one hour) depart from a **stand** just off Gadi Sagar Rd on Barmer Rd.

A number of private bus companies have ticket offices at Hanuman Circle. **Hanuman Travels** (☎9413362367) and **Swagat Travels** (☎02992-252557) are typical. The buses themselves leave from the **private bus stand** (Air Force Circle). Typical services:

Ajmer (for Pushkar) seat/sleeper ₹300/450, nine hours, two or three daily

Bikaner seat/sleeper ₹200/400, 5½ hours, three to four daily

Jaipur seat/sleeper ₹400/500, 11 hours, two or three daily

Jodhpur seat/sleeper ₹200/400, five hours, half-hourly from 6am to 10pm

Udaipur sleeper ₹350/450, 12 hours, one or two daily

TAXI

One-way taxis should cost about ₹4500 to Jodhpur, ₹5000 to Bikaner or ₹8000 to Udaipur. There's a **taxi stand** on Hanuman Circle Rd.

TRAIN

The **train station** (⏲ ticket office 8am-8pm Mon-Sat, to 1.45pm Sun) is on the eastern edge of town, just off the Jodhpur road. There's a reserved ticket booth for foreigners.

Bikaner sleeper/3AC ₹250/625, around six hours, one or two daily (1.10am and 11.55pm)

Delhi sleeper/3AC ₹450/1205, 18 hours, two or three daily (12.45am, 1.10am, 5pm) via Jaipur (12 hours)

Jaipur sleeper/3AC ₹350/935, 12 hours, three daily (12.45am, 5pm, 11.55pm)

Jodhpur sleeper/3AC ₹215/565, five to six hours, three daily (12.45am, 6.45am and 5pm)

ℹ Getting Around

AUTORICKSHAW

It costs around ₹40 from the train station to Gandhi Chowk.

CAR & MOTORCYCLE

It's possible to hire taxis or 4WDs from the stand on Hanuman Circle Rd. To Khuri, the Sam Sand Dunes or Lodhruva, expect to pay ₹1000 to ₹1200 return including a wait of about an hour or so.

Shiva Bikes (First Fort Gate; motorbike per day ₹500-2000; ⏲8am-9pm) A licensed hire place with motorbikes (including Royal Enfield Bullets) and scooters for exploring town and nearby sights. Helmets and area maps are included.

Around Jaisalmer

Sam Sand Dunes

Sam Sand Dunes AREA

(vehicle/camel ₹50/80) The silky Sam Sand Dunes, 41km west of Jaisalmer along a good sealed road (maintained by the Indian army), are one of the most popular excursions from the city. The band of dunes is about 2km long and is undeniably one of the most picturesque in the region. Some camel safaris camp here, but many more people just roll in for sunset, to be chased across the sands by tenacious camel owners offering short rides. Plenty more people stay overnight in one of the several tent resorts near the dunes.

The place acquires something of a carnival atmosphere from late afternoon till the next morning, making it somewhere to avoid if you're after a solitary desert experience.

If you're organising your own camel ride on the spot, expect to pay ₹300 for a one-hour sunset ride, but beware tricks from camel men such as demanding more money en route.

Khuri

☎03014

The village of Khuri, 48km southwest of Jaisalmer, has quite extensive dune areas attracting their share of sunset visitors, and a lot of mostly smallish 'resorts' offering the same sort of overnight packages as Sam. It also has a number of low-key guesthouses where you can stay in tranquillity in a traditional-style hut with clay-and-dung

MAJOR TRAINS FROM JAISALMER

DESTINATION	TRAIN	DEPARTURE	ARRIVAL	FARE (₹)
Bikaner	12467 Leelan Exp	11.55pm	5.20am	250/625
Delhi	14660 Jaisalmer-Delhi Exp	5pm	10.55am	450/1205
Jaipur	14660 Jaisalmer-Delhi Exp	5pm	4.50am	350/935
Jodhpur	14809 Jaisalmer-Jodhpur Exp	6.45am	1pm	215/565

Fares: sleeper/3AC

walls and thatched roof, and venture out on interesting camel trips in the relatively remote and empty surrounding area.

Khuri is within the **Desert National Park**, which stretches over 3162 sq km southwest of Jaisalmer to protect part of the Thar ecosystem, including wildlife such as the desert fox, desert cat, chinkara (gazelle), nilgai (antelope), and some unusual bird life including the endangered great Indian bustard.

Be aware that the commission system is entrenched in Khuri's larger accommodation options. If you just want a quick camel ride on the sand dunes, expect to pay around ₹150 per person.

Sleeping

★Badal House HOMESTAY $
(☎8107339097; r or hut per person incl full board ₹400) Here you can stay in a family compound in the centre of the village with a few spotlessly clean, mud-walled, thatch-roofed huts and equally spotless rooms (one with its own squat toilet), and enjoy good home-cooking. Former camel driver Badal Singh is a charming, gentle man who charges ₹600 for a camel safari with a night on the dunes.

He doesn't pay commission so don't let touts warn you away.

Getting There & Away

You can catch local buses from Jaisalmer to Khuri (₹30, one hour) from a road just off Gadi Sagar Rd. Walking from Jaisalmer Fort towards the train station, take the second right after the tourist office, then wait by the tree on the left, with the small shrine beside it. Buses pass here at around 10am, 11.30am, 3.30pm and 4pm.

Return buses from Khuri to Jaisalmer leave at roughly 8am, 9am, 10.30am, 11.30am and 2.30pm.

A taxi from Jaisalmer will cost at least ₹1200 to ₹1500. Even if you are staying here you will be paying for the return trip.

Bikaner

☎0151 / POP 644,400

Bikaner is a vibrant, dust-swirling desert town with a fabulous fort and an energising outpost feel. It's less dominated by tourism than many other Rajasthan cities, though it has plenty of hotels and a busy camel-safari scene, which attracts travellers looking to avoid the Jaisalmer hustle.

History

The city was founded in 1488 by Rao Bika, a son of Rao Jodha, Jodhpur's founder, though the two Rathore ruling houses later had a serious falling out over who had the right to keep the family heirlooms. Bikaner grew quickly as a staging post on the great caravan trade routes from the late 16th century onwards, and flourished under a friendly relationship with the Mughals, but declined as the Mughals did in the 18th century. By the 19th century the area was markedly backward, but managed to turn its fortunes around by hiring out camels to the British during the First Anglo-Afghan War. In 1886 it was the first desert princely state to install electricity.

Sights

★Junagarh FORT
(Indian/foreigner ₹50/300, video ₹150, audio guide ₹50, ID required; ⏲10am-5.30pm, last entry 4.30pm) This most impressive fort was constructed between 1589 and 1593 by Raja Rai Singh, ruler of Bikaner and a general in the army of the Mughal emperor Akbar. You enter through the **Karan Prole** gate on the east side and pass through three more gates before the ticket office for the palace museum. An audio guide (requiring an identity document as a deposit), is available in English, French, German and Hindi, and is very informative.

The beautifully decorated **Karan Mahal** was the palace's Diwan-i-Am (Hall of Public Audience), built in the 17th and 18th centuries. **Anup Mahal Chowk** has lovely carved *jarokhas* (balcony windows) and *jali* screens, and was commissioned in the late 17th century by Maharaja Anup Mahal. Rooms off here include the sumptuous **Anup Mahal**, a hall of private audience with walls lacquered in red and gold, and the **Badal Mahal** (Cloud Palace), the walls of which are beautifully painted with blue cloud motifs and red and gold lightning.

The **Gaj Mandir**, the suite of Maharaja Gaj Singh (r 1745–87) and his two top wives, is a fantastic symphony of gold paint, colourful murals, sandalwood, ivory, mirrors, niches and stained glass. From here you head up to the palace roof to enjoy the views and then down eventually to the superb **Ganga Durbar Hall** of 1896, with its pink stone walls covered in fascinating relief carvings. You then move into **Maharaja Ganga Singh's office** and finally into the

BIKANER CAMEL SAFARIS

Bikaner is an excellent alternative to the Jaisalmer camel-safari scene. There are fewer people running safaris here, so the hassle factor is quite low. Camel trips tend to be in the areas east and south of the city and focus on the isolated desert villages of the Jat, Bishnoi, Meghwal and Rajput peoples. Interesting wildlife can be spotted here, such as nilgais (antelope), chinkaras (gazelle), desert foxes, spiny-tailed lizards and plenty of birds including, from September to March, the demoiselle crane.

Three days and two nights is a common camel-safari duration, but half-day, one-day and short overnight trips are all possible. If you're after a serious trip, Jaisalmer is a two-week trek. The best months to head into the desert are October to February. Avoid mid-April to mid-July, when it's searingly hot.

Typical costs are ₹1800 to ₹2500 per person per day including overnight camping, with tents, mattresses, blankets, meals, mineral water, one camel per person, a camel cart to carry gear (and sometimes tired riders), and a guide in addition to the camel men.

Many trips start at Raisar, about 8km east of Bikaner, or Deshnok, 30km south. Travelling to the starting point by bus rather than 4WD is one way of cutting costs.

Vikram Vilas Durbar Hall, where pride of place goes to a WWI De Havilland DH-9 biplane bomber: General Maharaja Sir Ganga Singh commanded the Bikaner Camel Corps during WWI and was the only non-white member of Britain's Imperial War Cabinet during the conflict.

Prachina Cultural Centre & Museum MUSEUM
(Junagarh; Indian/foreigner ₹30/100; ⏲9am-6pm) Across the fort's main courtyard from the palace entrance, this museum is fascinating and well labelled. It focuses on the Western influence on the Bikaner royals before Independence, including crockery from England and France and menu cards from 1936, as well as some exquisite costumes, jewellery and textiles, and exhibits on contemporary Bikaner crafts.

Old City AREA
The old city still has a medieval feel despite the motorbikes and autorickshaws. This labyrinth of narrow, winding streets conceals a number of fine *havelis,* and a couple of notable Jain temples just inside the southern wall, 1.5km southwest of Bikaner Junction train station. It makes for an interesting wander – we guarantee you'll get lost at least once. The old city is encircled by a 7km-long, 18th-century wall with five entrance gates, the main entrance being the triple-arched Kothe Gate.

★Bhandasar Temple JAIN TEMPLE
(⏲5am-1pm & 5.30-11.30pm) Of Bikaner's two Jain temples, Bhandasar is particularly beautiful, with yellow-stone carving and vibrant paintings. The interior of the temple is stunning. The pillars bear floral arabesques and depictions of the lives of the 24 *tirthankars* (great Jain teachers). It's said that 40,000kg of ghee was used instead of water in the mortar, which locals insist seeps through the floor on hot days. The priest may ask for a donation for entry, although a trust pays for the temple upkeep.

Tours

Camel Man TOURS
(☎9799911117, 9829217331, 0151-2231244; www.camelman.com; Vijay Guest House, Jaipur Rd; half-/full-/multiday trip per person per day from ₹800/1200/1800) The standout Bikaner safari operator in terms of quality, reliability and transparency of what's on offer is Vijay Singh Rathore, aka Camel Man, who operates from Vijay Guest House.

Vino Desert Safari TOURS
(☎0151-2270445, 9414139245; www.vinodesertsafari.com; Vino Paying Guest House; 1 day, 1 night per person ₹2500, multiday trek per person per day ₹1500-2000) A popular and long-established outfit, Vino Desert Safari is run by Vinod Bhojak, of Vino Paying Guest House.

Vinayak Desert Safari TOURS
(☎0151-2202634, 9414430948; www.vinayakdesertsafari.com; Vinayak Guest House; half-day 4WD safari per person ₹500, full- or multiday 4WD safari per person ₹900-2000) Vinayak Desert Safari runs 4WD safaris with zoologist Jitu Solanki. This safari focuses on desert animals and

Bikaner

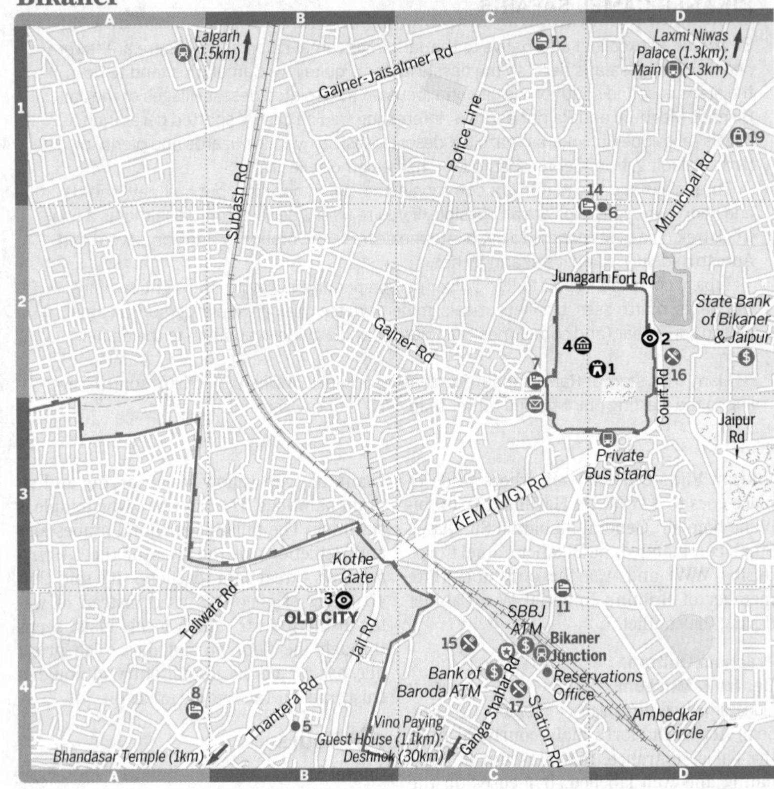

birds including the impressive cinereous vulture, with its 3m wingspan, which visits the area in numbers from November to March.

Gouri Guide TOURS
(☎0151-2543306, 9461159796; gouriguide@yahoo.in; Shanti House, New Well, Old City; per person per hr ₹50) Gouri is a knowledgeable and personable guide based in the Old City who can show all the well-known sights and many of the lesser-known sights of Bikaner. He also runs a small guesthouse.

Sleeping

★Vijay Guest House GUESTHOUSE $
(☎0151-2231244, 9829217331; www.camelman.com; Jaipur Rd; r ₹500-1000, with AC ₹1200-1500, ste ₹1800; ❄📶) About 4km east of the centre, this is a home away from home, with spacious, light-filled rooms, a warm welcome and good home-cooked meals. Owner Vijay is a camel expert and a recommended safari operator (p195). Free pick-up and drop-off from rail and bus stations.

As well as camel trips, 4WD outings to sights around Bikaner, and tours to the owner's house in the village of Thelasar, Shekhawati, are offered.

Vino Paying Guest House GUESTHOUSE $
(☎9414139245, 0151-2270445; www.vinodesertsafari.com; Ganga Shahar; s ₹250-300, d ₹350-400; @🏊) This guesthouse, in a family home 3km south of the main train station, is a cosy choice and the base of a good camel-safari operator (p195). It has six rooms in the house and six in cool adobe huts around the garden, where there's also a plunge pool. It's excellent value, and the family is helpful and welcoming.

Home-cooked food is served and cooking classes are on offer. It's opposite Gopeshwar Temple; free pick-ups are offered.

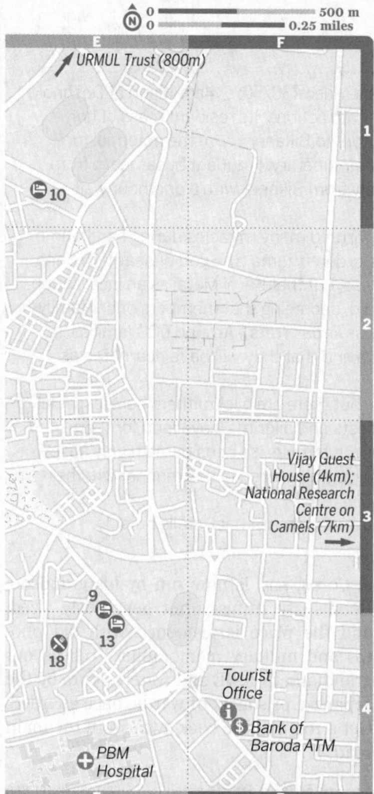

Bikaner

Top Sights
1 Junagarh ... D2

Sights
2 Karan Prole ... D2
3 Old City ... B4
4 Prachina Cultural Centre & Museum ... C2

Activities, Courses & Tours
5 Gouri Guide ... B4
6 Vinayak Desert Safari ... D2

Sleeping
7 Bhairon Vilas ... C2
8 Bhanwar Niwas ... A4
9 Chandra Niwas Guest House ... E3
10 Hotel Harasar Haveli ... E1
11 Hotel Jaswant Bhawan ... C4
12 Hotel Kishan Palace ... C1
13 Udai Niwas ... E4
14 Vinayak Guest House ... D2

Eating
15 Amberwalla ... C4
Café Indra ... (see 13)
16 Gallops ... D2
17 Heeralal's ... C4
18 Road Runner Cafe ... E4
Shakti Dining ... (see 18)

Shopping
19 Bikaner Miniature Arts ... D1

Vinayak Guest House GUESTHOUSE $
(☎0151-2202634, 9414430948; vinayakguesthouse@gmail.com; r ₹400-800, with AC ₹1000; ❄@📶) This place offers six varied and clean rooms in a quiet family house with a little sandy garden (hot water only by bucket in some rooms). On offer are a free pick-up service, good home-cooked food, cooking lessons, bicycles (₹25 per day), and camel safaris and wildlife trips with Vinayak Desert Safari (p195). It's about half a kilometre north of Junagarh.

Chandra Niwas Guest House HOTEL $
(☎0151-2200796, 9413659711; chandraniwas@yahoo.in; Rangmanch Rd, Civil Lines; r ₹500, with AC ₹800-1500; ❄📶) This small and welcoming guesthouse is in a relatively quiet location, though still handy to Bikaner's sights. The rooms are clean, comfortable and tidy, and there is a lovely terrace restaurant where you can get a veg/nonveg thali for ₹180/250, plus there's a coffeeshop next door.

Hotel Jaswant Bhawan HOTEL $
(☎9001554746, 0151-2548848; www.hoteljaswantbhawan.com; Alakh Sagar Rd; r ₹1000-1600; ❄@📶) This is a quiet, welcoming place run by descendants of Bikaner prime ministers. It has a small garden and a comfy, old-fashioned sitting room with historic family photos. The air-conditioned rooms are spacious, plain and airy. Good meals are available (as are cooking lessons). It's a two-minute walk from the main train station, via the station's 'foot over bridge'.

★**Bhairon Vilas** HERITAGE HOTEL $$
(☎9928312283, 0151-2544751; www.bhaironvilas.com; r from ₹1500-2000; ❄@📶🏊) This hotel on the western side of Junagarh is run by a former Bikaner prime minister's great-grandson. Rooms are mostly large and are eclectically and elaborately decorated with antiques, gold-threaded curtains and old family photographs. There's a bar straight out of the Addams Family, a garden restaurant, a coffeeshop, and a boutique that

DON'T MISS

THE TEMPLE OF RATS

The extraordinary **Karni Mata Temple** (camera/video ₹30/50; ⌚4am-10pm) at Deshnok, 30km south of Bikaner, is one of India's weirder attractions. Its resident mass of holy rodents is not for the squeamish, but most visitors to Bikaner brave the potential for ankle-nipping and put a half-day trip here on their itinerary. Frequent buses leave from Bikaner's main bus stand. A return autorickshaw from Bikaner with a one-hour wait costs ₹400 to ₹450.

Karni Mata lived in the 14th century and performed many miracles during her lifetime. When her youngest son, Lakhan, drowned, she ordered Yama (the god of death) to bring him back to life. Yama said he was unable to do so, but that Karni Mata, as an incarnation of Durga, could restore Lakhan's life. This she did, decreeing that members of her family would no longer die but would be reincarnated as *kabas* (rats). Around 600 families in Deshnok claim to be descendants of Karni Mata and that they will be reincarnated as *kabas*.

The temple isn't, in fact, swarming with rats, but there are a lot of them here, especially in nooks and crannies and in areas where priests and pilgrims leave food for them. And yes, you do have to take your shoes off to enter the temple: it's considered highly auspicious to have a *kaba* run across your feet – you may be graced in this manner whether you want it or not.

You can find food and drinks for yourself at the numerous snack stalls outside.

specialises in beautiful, original wedding saris.

Camel safaris and local guides can be arranged here.

Hotel Harasar Haveli HOTEL **$$**
(☎0151-2209891; www.harasar.com; r ₹1800-2800; ❄📶) At this modern hotel with the frontage of an old sandstone *haveli* you'll find unexpectedly grand accommodation. The decor is stylish: that's not fancy blue and gold wallpaper in your room, but exquisitely hand-painted floral patterns. Old dark-wood furniture continues the classy character. Service is great, and the in-house restaurant on the terrace serves alcohol.

Located opposite Karni Singh Stadium, about 1km northeast of Junargarh.

Udai Niwas HOMESTAY **$$**
(☎9971795447, 0151-2223447; Rangmanch Rd, Civil Lines; s/d ₹2000/2500; ❄) This friendly and relaxed homestay is set behind its cheerful associated Café Indra. The rooms are large and comfortable, and you can choose to eat the delicious home-cooked meals with the family in the dining room or not. There's even a laundry to do your own washing.

Hotel Kishan Palace HOTEL **$$**
(☎9829512610, 0151-2527762; www.hotelkishanpalaceheritage.com; 8B Gajner-Jaisalmer Rd; r with fan ₹750, r incl breakfast with AC ₹1500; ❄📶) An old Bikaner house, this hotel was once the home of a colonel of the Bikaner Camel Corps, and is now run by his grandson. Rooms are unfussy but generously sized, and the place is festooned with old photos and military memorabilia – check out grandfather's MBE and watercolours by the Japanese prisoners of war he once guarded. Get a room at the back away from the main road.

Laxmi Niwas Palace HERITAGE HOTEL **$$$**
(☎0151-2202777; www.laxminiwaspalace.com; r ₹10,500-14,500, ste ₹22,000-31,000; ❄@📶🏊) Located 2km northeast of the city centre, this pink-sandstone hotel is part of the royal palace, dating from 1902. It has opulent interiors with stone carvings, and is set in large lovely grounds. Rooms are mostly large, elegant and evocative, while the bar and billiards room contain more trophy skins from tigers than are probably still alive in Rajasthan.

Bhanwar Niwas HERITAGE HOTEL **$$$**
(☎0151-2529323; www.bhanwarniwas.com; Rampuria St; r ₹6000; ❄@📶) This superb hotel has been developed out of the beautiful Rampuria Haveli – a gem in the old city, 300m southwest of the City Kotwali police station. It has 26 all-different, spacious and delightfully decorated rooms, featuring stencil-painted wallpaper, marble or mosaic floors and antique furnishings. Comfortable common rooms drip with antiques and are arranged around a large courtyard.

Eating & Drinking

Café Indra CAFE $
(☎8287895446; Rangmanch Rd, Civil Lines; mains ₹120-170; ⏲11.30am-10.30pm; ❄) This bright and clean cafe is a great place to relax with a coffee or a cool drink, and equally good as a place for lunch or dinner, with an array of pizzas, burgers and wraps.

Amberwalla MULTICUISINE $
(☎0151-2220333; Station Rd; mains ₹60-120, thalis ₹190-200; ⏲7am-11pm; ❄✎) This large bright and airy 'diner' caters for everyone with Continental, Chinese, North Indian and South Indian mains, plus sweets, ice cream and a large bakery.

★ **Gallops** MULTICUISINE $$
(☎0151-3200833; www.gallopsbikaner.com; Court Rd; mains ₹200-350; ⏲10am-10pm; ❄📶) This contemporary cafe and restaurant close to the Junagarh entrance is known as 'Glops' to rickshaw-wallahs. There are snacks such as pizzas, wraps and sandwiches, and a good range of Indian and Chinese veg and non-veg dishes. You can sit outside or curl up in an armchair in the air-conditioned interior with a cold beer or an espresso (coffees from ₹100).

Shakti Dining INDIAN $$
(☎9928900422; Prithvi Niwas, Civil Lines; mains ₹150-260; ⏲11am-11pm; ❄📶) Central and modern, Shakti's serves good Indian classics in a garden setting or in air-conditoned comfort. Also here is the funky **Road Runner Cafe** (☎0151-2545033, 9928900422; mains ₹150-260; ⏲11am-11pm; ❄📶) for a more casual dining experience.

Heeralal's MULTICUISINE $$
(☎0151-2205551; Station Rd; mains ₹150-210, thalis ₹165-270; ⏲7.30am-10.30pm; ❄✎) This bright and hugely popular 1st-floor restaurant serves up pretty good veg Indian dishes, plus a few Chinese mains and pizzas (but unfortunately no beer), amid large banks of plastic flowers. It's a good place to sit and relax if waiting for a train. The ground-floor fast-food section is less appealing, but it does have a good sweets counter.

Shopping

Bikaner Miniature Arts ART
(☎9829291431; www.bikanerminiturearts.com; Municipal Rd; ⏲9am-8pm) The Swami family has been painting miniatures in Bikaner for four generations, and now run this art school and gallery. The quality of work is astounding, and cheaper than you'll find in some of the bigger tourist centres. Art classes can be arranged.

Information

Main Post Office (⏲9am-4pm Mon-Fri, to 2pm Sat) Near Bhairon Vilas hotel.

PBM Hospital (☎0151-2525312; Hospital Rd) One of Rajasthan's best government hospitals, with 24-hour emergency service.

Tourist Office (☎0151-2226701; ⏲9.30am-6pm Mon-Fri) This friendly office (near Pooran Singh Circle) can answer most tourism-related questions and provide transport schedules and maps.

Getting There & Away

AIR

Supreme Airlines (p192) flies a small plane (one way from ₹560) Monday to Saturday from Jaipur to Bikaner (departing 7am) and Bikaner to Jaipur (departing 8.45am). These schedules are likely to change.

BUS

There's a **private bus stand** outside the southern wall of Junagarh with similar services (albeit slightly more expensive and less frequent) to the government-run services from the **main bus stand**, which is 2km directly north of the fort (autorickshaw ₹20).

Services from the main bus stand:

Ajmer (for Pushkar) ₹269, six hours, half-hourly until 6pm

MAJOR TRAINS FROM BIKANER JUNCTION

DESTINATION	TRAIN	DEPARTURE	ARRIVAL	FARE (₹)
Delhi (Sarai Rohilla)	22471 Dee Intercity SF Exp	9.30am	5.25pm	305/785
Jaipur	12467 Leelan Exp	6am	12.35pm	275/705
Jaisalmer	12468 Leelan Exp	11.15pm	4.50am	250/625
Jodhpur	14887 KLK-BME Exp	11am	4pm	200/510

Fares: sleeper/3AC

Delhi ₹445, 11 hours, at least four daily

Deshnok ₹35, one hour, half-hourly until 4.30pm

Fatehpur ₹136, 3½ hours, half-hourly until 5.45pm

Jaipur ₹334, with AC ₹596, seven hours, hourly until 5.45pm

Jaisalmer ₹309, 7½ hours, noon daily

Jhunjhunu ₹226, five hours, four daily (7.30am, 8.30am, 12.20pm and 6.30pm)

Jodhpur ₹243, five hours, half-hourly until 6.30pm

Pokaran ₹211, five hours, hourly until 12.45pm

For Jaisalmer, it's sometimes faster to head to Pokaran (which has more departures) and change there.

TRAIN

The main train station is Bikaner Junction, with a computerised **reservations office** (⌚8am-10pm Mon-Sat, to 2pm Sun) in a separate building just east of the main station building. The foreigner's window is 2931. A couple of other useful services go from Lalgarh station in the north of the city (autorickshaw ₹50).

Delhi (Delhi Sarai Rohilla) sleeper/3AC ₹305/785, eight to 14 hours, three to five daily, 6.30am, 9.30am, 4.45pm, 5.05pm and 11.30pm

Jaipur sleeper/3AC ₹275/705, 6½ hours, five daily, 12.05am, 6am, 6.45pm, 11.05pm and 11.55pm

Jaisalmer sleeper/3AC ₹250/625, 5½ hours, one or two daily, 6.30pm and 11.15pm

Jodhpur sleeper/3AC ₹200/510, five hours, six to seven daily, 12.45am, 6.35am, 9.30am, 11am, 1.40pm, 9.40pm and 10.10pm

No direct trains go to Ajmer for Pushkar.

Getting Around

An autorickshaw from the train station to Junagarh palace should cost ₹30, but you'll probably be asked for more.

Around Bikaner

National Research Centre on Camels

MUSEUM

(☎0151-2230183; www.nrccamel.res.in; Indian/foreigner ₹30/100, camera ₹50, rides ₹50; ⌚2-6pm) The National Research Centre on Camels is 8km southeast of central Bikaner, beside the Jodhpur–Jaipur Bypass. While here you can visit baby camels, go for a short ride and look around the small museum. There are about 400 camels, of four different breeds. The British Army had a camel corps drawn from Bikaner during WWI. Guides are available for ₹50-plus. The on-site Camel Milk Parlour offers samples to try including *kulfi* and lassi.

The round trip from Bikaner, including a half-hour wait at the camel farm, is around ₹150/₹400 for an autorickshaw/taxi.

Punjab & Haryana

Includes ➡

Best Places to Eat

- Kesar Da Dhaba (p216)
- Bharawan Da Dhaba (p217)
- Makhan Fish (p217)
- Virgin Courtyard (p208)
- Gopal's (p208)

Best Places to Sleep

- Baradari Palace (p220)
- Ramada Amritsar (p216)
- Mrs Bhandari's Guesthouse (p216)
- Vivanta By Taj (p224)
- Hotel Icon (p207)

Why Go?

The neighbouring states of Punjab and Haryana were carved from the Indian half of Punjab province in the aftermath of Partition in 1947. Since then, Punjab has grown from strength to strength as the homeland of India's fabulously welcoming Sikh community, while Haryana has emerged as a dynamic hub for business and industry. Both share the same capital city, Chandigarh, which is geographically seated between the two states.

Studded with gleaming gurdwaras (Sikh temples) – including the overwhelming Golden Temple in Amritsar – Punjab has become a popular stop on the traveller circuit. Haryana, on the other hand, is more of a touristic mystery. The hinterland around the two states is dotted with fascinating, rarely visited historical towns that tell tales of battling empires and playboy maharajas, while some of India's most alluring abandoned forts hide among their dusty bazaars.

When to Go

Chandigarh

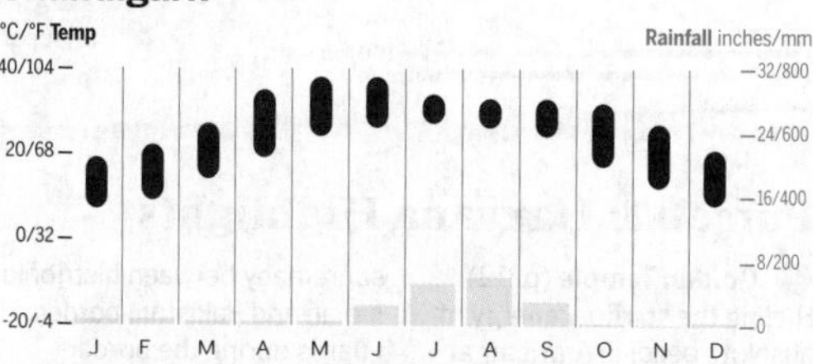

Mar Three days of Sikh celebrations for Holla Mohalla unravel at Anandpur Sahib.

Apr Punjab's largest festival, Baisakhi, marks the Sikh New Year and the founding of the Khalsa.

Oct Diwali means lights, candles and fireworks everywhere; it's particularly magical at the Golden Temple.

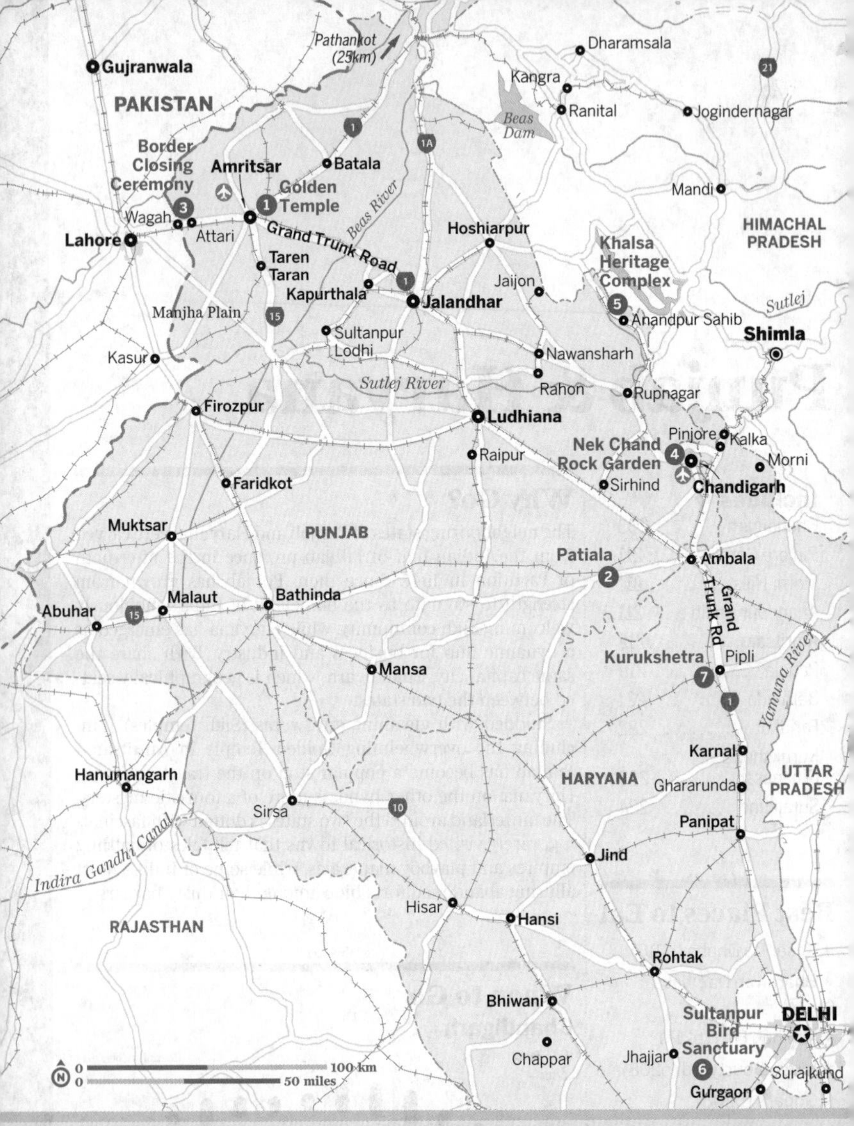

Punjab & Haryana Highlights

1 Golden Temple (p212) Feeling the spiritual energy of absolute belief in Amritsar at Sikhism's holiest site.

2 Qila Mubarak (p219) Sizing up Patiala's impossibly charming 18th-century fort.

3 Attari-Wagah Border Checkpost (p221) Watching the theatrical battle for supremacy between histrionic Indian and Pakistani border guards during the border-closing ceremony.

4 Nek Chand Rock Garden (p203) Tumbling into an alternative reality in Chandigarh's unique rock garden.

5 Khalsa Heritage Complex (p212) Visiting this lotus flower–shaped museum of Sikh history.

6 Sultanpur Bird Sanctuary (p224) Spying on migratory bird species that come to roost at this sanctuary.

7 Brahmasarovar (p223) Brushing up on India's epic and mythological history in Kurukshetra.

CHANDIGARH

0172 / POPULATION 1,055,000

Chandigarh shows itself off to global travellers much like greater India would wish to be seen – prosperous, comfortable and cosmopolitan. Officially a union territory controlled by the central government, Chandigarh is the joint capital of Punjab and Haryana. It is also the first planned city of independent India.

When the Swiss architect Le Corbusier was commissioned with the job of designing Chandigarh in 1950, he conceived a people-oriented city of sweeping boulevards, lakes, gardens and grand civic buildings, executed in his favourite material: reinforced concrete. And thus Chandigarh came into being: turn the clocks forward and the parks, monuments and civic squares are still here, albeit somewhat aged.

Each sector of the city is self-contained and pedestrian-friendly. Most visitors concentrate their attention on Sector 17 (for shops and restaurants) and Sector 22 (for hotels).

Sights

★Nek Chand Rock Garden GARDENS

(www.nekchand.com; Sector 1; adult/child ₹20/10; 9am-6pm Oct-Mar, to 7.30pm Apr-Sep) Nek Chand Rock Garden is unique: it's the surreal fantasy of a local transport official who, starting in 1957, spent almost 20 years personally creating more than 2000 sculptures using stones, debris and other discarded junk that was left over from the 50-odd villages destroyed in order to build the city of Chandigarh. Now, entering this fantastical, 10-hectare sculpture garden is like falling down a rabbit hole into the labyrinthine interior of one man's imagination.

★Capital Complex NOTABLE BUILDING

(10am-5pm Mon-Fri) FREE At the epicentre of Le Corbusier's planned city are the imposing concrete **High Court**, **Secretariat** and **Vidhan Sabha** (Legislative Assembly), shared by the states of Punjab and Haryana. All three are classic pieces of 1950s architecture from the proto-brutalist school, with bold geometric lines and vast sweeps of moulded concrete. To visit the complex, you must first register with your passport at the **High Court Tourist Office** (High Court Complex; 10am-6pm Mon-Sat). You will then be given a free guided tour, which lasts for around 1½ hours.

Sukhna Lake LAKE

(Sector 1; 8am-10pm) Fulfilling the leisure objective of Le Corbusier's urban master plan, this landmark artificial lake is a popular rest and recreation stop for Chandigarh's resident families. It has ornamental gardens, a children's fairground, places to eat and drink, and pedal boats (p206) to hire for leisure rides on the still waters of the lake. Electric carts (₹10 per person) shuttle passengers between here and Nek Chand Rock Garden.

Le Corbusier Centre MUSEUM

(Madhya Marg, Sector 19-B; 10am-5pm Tue-Sun) FREE One for fans of 20th-century avant-garde architecture and design, this fascinating museum displays documents, sketches and photos of Le Corbusier, along

TOP STATE FESTIVALS

Kila Raipur Sports Festival (Rural Olympics; www.ruralolympic.net; Feb) Three days of traditional games and contests including bullock-cart races, kabaddi, strongman contests and folk dancing in Kila Raipur near Ludhiana.

Surajkund Crafts Mela (1-15 Feb) This fair features a splendid congregation of folk artists, artisans, musicians and dancers from across North India in Surajkund (p224).

Holla Mohalla (Mar) Sikhs celebrate the foundation of the Khalsa (Sikh brotherhood) with martial-arts demonstrations and battle re-enactments in Anandpur Sahib.

Baisakhi (13-14 Apr) Sikhs across Punjab head to gurdwaras to celebrate the Punjabi New Year, and revel in colourful celebrations, music, dance and feasting.

Pinjore Heritage Festival (late Dec) This two-day cultural bash features music and dance performances, handicrafts and food stalls at Pinjore Gardens, near Chandigarh.

Harballabh Sangeet Sammelan (www.harballabh.org; late Dec) This 140-year-old music festival in Jalandhar showcases Indian classical music over three days.

Gita Jayanti (Nov/Dec) One week of cultural events takes place in Kurukshetra to commemorate the anniversary of the Bhagavad Gita sermons as cited in the Mahabharata.

Chandigarh

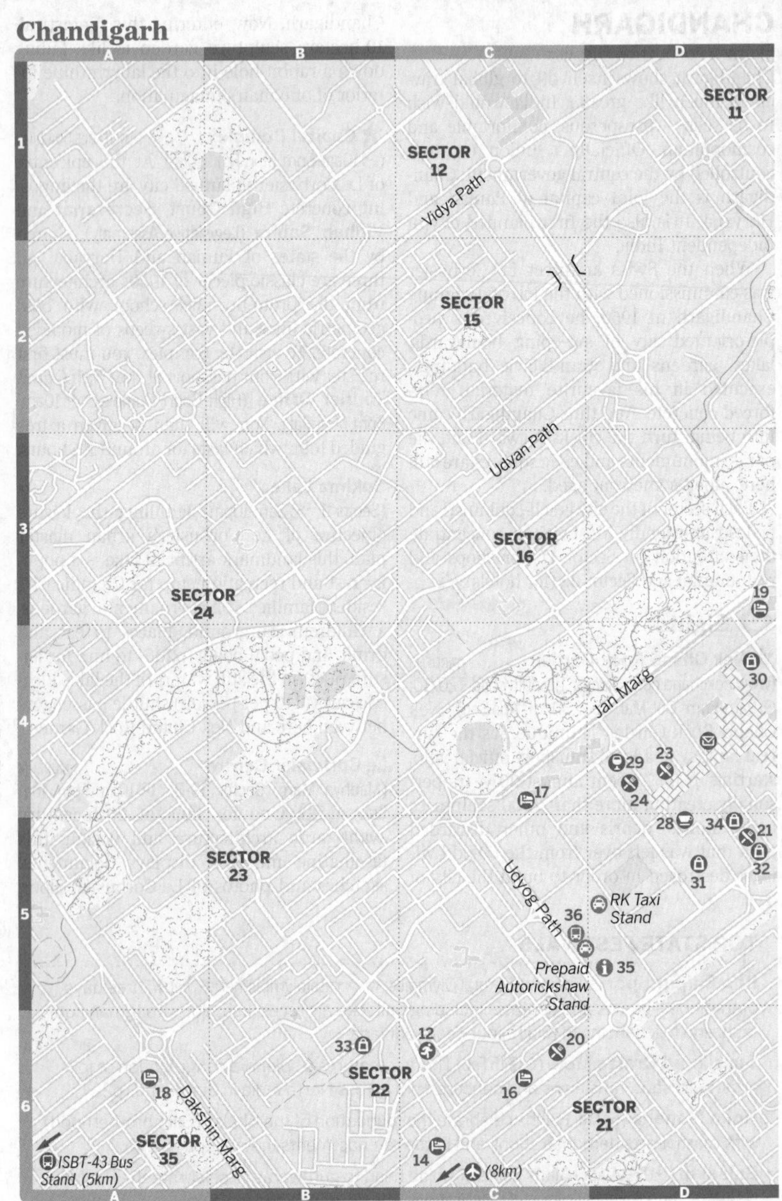

with letters revealing the politics behind the Chandigarh project, including one from Jawaharlal Nehru to the Punjab Chief Minister recommending Corbusier for the project. Also interesting are some sketches, paintings and a model for a proposed Governor's House that was eventually rejected because Nehru found it too extravagant.

Government Museum & Art Gallery GALLERY
(Jan Marg, Sector 10-C; admission ₹10, camera ₹5; ⏲10am-4.30pm Tue-Sun) You'll find a fine

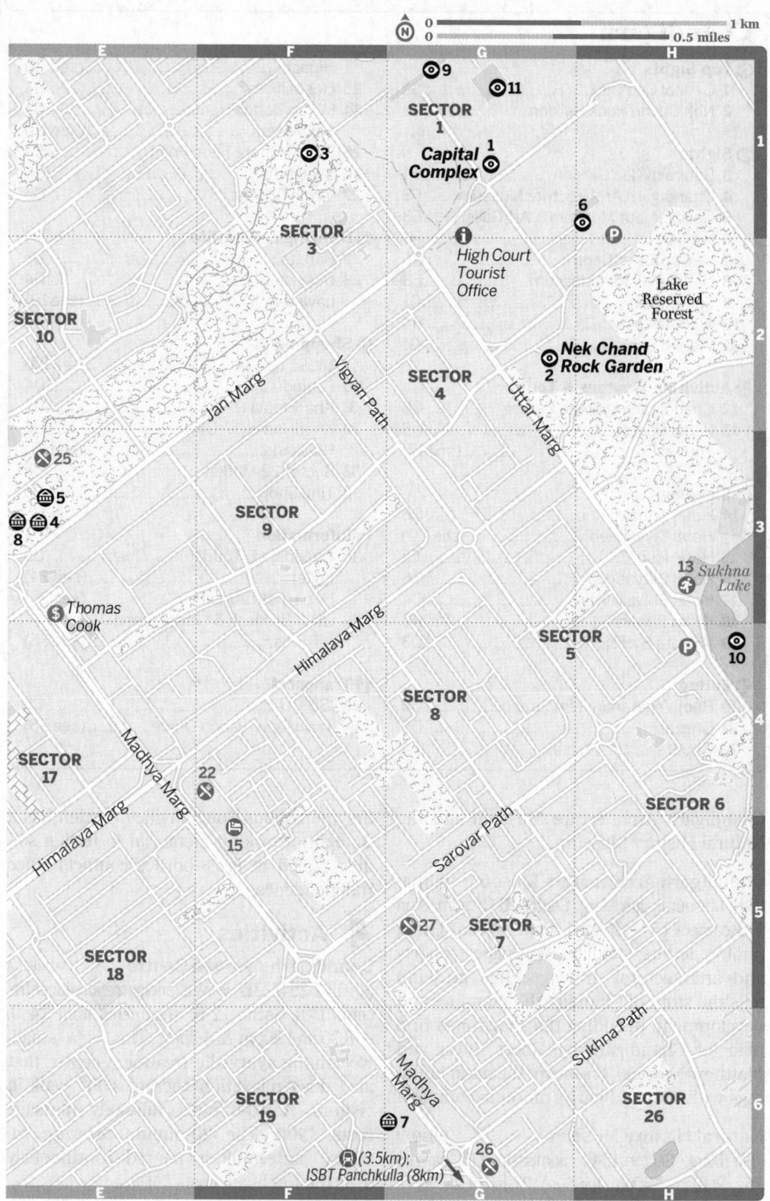

collection of artworks and treasures at this impressive state museum, including trippy paintings of the Himalayas by Russian artist Nicholas Roerich, elegant carvings from the Buddhist Ghandara civilisation, *phulkari* (embroidery work) and Sobha Singh's much-reproduced portrait of Guru Gobind Singh. At one end, through a separate entrance, is the **Child Art Gallery**, with colourful artworks from local schoolchildren. The ₹10-ticket covers entrance to the Government Museum & Art Gallery, the

Chandigarh

Top Sights
1 Capital Complex.....G1
2 Nek Chand Rock Garden.....G2

Sights
3 Bougainvillea Garden.....F1
4 Chandigarh Architecture Museum.....E3
5 Government Museum & Art Gallery.....E3
6 High Court.....H1
7 Le Corbusier Centre.....G6
8 Natural History Museum.....E3
9 Secretariat.....G1
10 Sukhna Lake.....H4
11 Vidhan Sabha.....G1

Activities, Courses & Tours
12 Chandigarh Ayurved Centre.....C6
13 Pedal Boats.....H3
Tourist Bus.....(see 17)

Sleeping
14 Hotel Aquamarine.....C6
Hotel Divyadeep.....(see 20)
15 Hotel Icon.....F5
16 Hotel Satyadeep.....C6
17 Hotel Shivalikview.....C4
18 Kisan Bhawan.....A6
19 Vivanta By Taj.....D3

Eating
20 Bhoj Vegetarian Restaurant.....C6
21 Ghazal.....D5
22 Gopal's.....F4
Hibachi.....(see 15)
23 Hot Millions.....D4
24 Indian Coffee House.....D4
Sai Sweets.....(see 16)
25 Stop 'N Stare Food Point.....E3
26 Swagath.....G6
27 Virgin Courtyard.....G5

Drinking & Nightlife
28 Barista.....D5
29 Blue Ice.....D4
Lava Bar.....(see 19)

Shopping
1469.....(see 23)
30 Fabindia.....D4
31 Khadi India (17-E).....D5
32 Khadi India (17-G).....D5
Phulkari.....(see 31)
33 Sector 22 Market.....B6
34 Tiny Shop.....D5

Information
35 Chandigarh Tourism.....D5
E-Net.....(see 24)
Himachal Tourism.....(see 35)
Uttar Pradesh & Uttarakhand Tourism.....(see 35)

Transport
36 ISBT 17.....C5
Train Reservation Office.....(see 35)

Chandigarh Architecture Museum and the Natural History Museum.

Chandigarh Architecture Museum MUSEUM
(City Museum; Jan Marg, Sector 10-C; admission ₹10, camera ₹5; ⏲10am-4.30pm Tue-Sun) Using photos, letters, models, newspaper reports and architectural drawings, this museum tells the story of Chandigarh's planning and development, including the abandoned first plan for Chandigarh by Albert Mayer and Matthew Nowicki. It's one of the main buildings within Chandigarh's museum complex.

Natural History Museum MUSEUM
(Jan Marg, Sector 10-C; admission ₹10, camera ₹5; ⏲10am-4.30pm Tue-Sun) This place is a must-visit for those travelling with children, and has exhibits featuring fossils, model dinosaurs, exquisite hand-embroidered pictures of birds and a diorama with a caveman using an electric torch to illuminate his cave art!

Bougainvillea Garden GARDENS
(Sector 3; ⏲8am-5pm) FREE Home to an overwhelming population of bougainvilleas, the eponymous Bougainvillea Garden has a thought-provoking memorial to Indian soldiers killed in cross-border conflicts since Independence.

Activities

Chandigarh Ayurved Centre AYURVEDA
(☎0172-2542231; www.chandigarhayurvedcentre.com; 1701, Sector 22-B; treatments from ₹450; ⏲8.30am-1.30pm & 4-8pm) This is a small, welcoming ayurvedic treatment centre that also does relaxation therapies for walk-in visitors. A 40-minute, full-body massage costs ₹900. The 20-minute *takradhara*, where buttermilk is poured continuously over the forehead, costs ₹500.

Pedal Boats BOATING
(Sukhna Lake; 2-/4-seater per 30min ₹100/200; ⏲8.30am-5.30pm) Brightly coloured boats are available through the day for some carefree boating on the still waters of the Sukhna Lake (p203). The ticket counter is on the approach to the quay, across a courtyard from a bunch of snack and juice stalls.

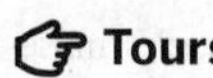

Tours

Tourist Bus BUS
(☎0172-2703839; 1 stop ₹10, half-day tour ₹50; ⏲10am & 2.30pm) Chandigarh Tourism runs an open-top, hop-on hop-off double-decker tourist bus leaving from outside Hotel Shivalikview. Buy a ticket at the time of boarding the vehicle. There are two half-day trips daily, visiting the Rose Garden, Government Museum & Art Gallery, Nek Chand Rock Garden and Sukhna Lake.

Sleeping

Chandigarh's hotels are pricier than elsewhere in Punjab and Haryana. Very few budget addresses are willing to accept foreign tourists.

Kisan Bhawan GUESTHOUSE $
(☎0172-5039153; Dakshin Marg, Sector 35-A; dm/d ₹80/1200; ❄) Large and easy-to-spot Kisan Bhawan is a sound choice, but only if you can get in. It's a subsidised rest house where priority is given to farmers and other agricultural industry personnel visiting Chandigarh. However, it's open to the general public too, and has simple but well-kept AC rooms and dorm beds suited to those travelling on a budget.

Hotel Satyadeep HOTEL $
(☎0172-2703103; hddeepsdeep@yahoo.com; SCO 1102-3, Sector 22-B; d from ₹1750; ❄@) Run by a management comprising courteous Sai Baba devotees, Satyadeep has wood-panelled corridors leading to simple, well-kept, bright and breezy rooms that open out onto shared balconies. It's upstairs from Sai Sweets, which meets your craving for post-dinner desserts.

Hotel Shivalikview HOTEL $$
(☎0172-4672222; www.citcochandigarh.com/shivalikview; Sector 17-E; d incl breakfast & dinner ₹4550; ❄@🛜🏊) Operated by the state tourism board, this hulk of a building is much more pleasant inside than it looks from the outside. Rooms are unexciting but large, clean and comfortable. The hotel has friendly staff, an outdoor pool, a gym, an Indian restaurant and a rooftop Chinese restaurant. It's a five-minute walk from the Sector 17 commercial area.

★ **Hotel Icon** BOUTIQUE HOTEL $$$
(☎9501113920; www.iconhotels.asia; SCO 58-61, Madhya Marg, Sector 8-C; d incl breakfast from ₹5200; ❄@🛜) Undoubtedly one of Chandigarh's best boutique addresses, the Icon justifies every penny it charges in the form of elegant wood-floored, satin-upholstered rooms, a bakery with good coffee and one of the best fine-dining restaurants in town. There are a few spas located within the same shopping complex, where the reception can book you a therapy session.

Hotel Divyadeep HOTEL $$
(☎0172-2705191; hddeepsdeep@yahoo.com; SCO 1090-1, Sector 22-B; d ₹3100; ❄) Run by a group of Sai Baba devotees, Divyadeep has smart but austere rooms, and welcoming staff. It's above Bhoj Vegetarian Restaurant.

Vivanta By Taj HOTEL $$$
(Taj Chandigarh; ☎0172-6613000; www.vivanta.tajhotels.com; Sector 17-A; d from ₹10,600; ❄@🛜🏊) Not as grand as some of the Taj Group's other properties, this hotel still offers luxurious, flawless service and rooms with floor-to-ceiling windows, minibars, flatscreen TVs, electronic safes and all the other

JUNK ART GENIUS

Surprising as it may seem, Chandigarh's most popular tourist attraction, Nek Chand Rock Garden (p203), was never intended for public display. When road inspector Nek Chand Saini, a recently arrived refugee from the Pakistan side of Punjab, started building his surreal rock garden using recycled material left over from the construction of Le Corbusier's model city, it was just a hobby. However, it soon became an obsession: working in secret on a patch of waste ground mostly at night, Chand unleashed legions of pottery-mosaic animals and armies of broken-bangle dancing girls. Cast-concrete canyons appeared from nowhere, and cascading waterfalls burst forth from the jungle. Chand's efforts were finally discovered by a government survey crew 15 years after work began, and came perilously close to being demolished. Fortunately, the city council saw the cultural merits of the rock garden, and Chand was granted a government salary and his own work crew to complete the project. Today, the Nek Chand Rock Garden covers more than 10 hectares, with nearly 5000 figures of humans, animals and mythical beasts. For more on the Nek Chand story, visit www.nekchand.com.

mod cons you'd expect at this price. There are several restaurants, a pleasant pool, the slick Lava Bar (p209), a spa and a 24-hour business centre.

Hotel Aquamarine BOUTIQUE HOTEL $$$
(☎0172-5014000; www.hotelaquamarine.com; Himalaya Marg, Sector 22-C; d incl breakfast from ₹5200; ❄@📶) This is one of Chandigarh's proper boutique hotels, shielded from the road by a leafy terrace and featuring rooms full of luscious fabrics and framed artworks. There's a good restaurant and coffee shop, but no pool or gym.

Eating

The gastronomic connoisseur is well catered for in Chandigarh, with a growing selection of fine-dining restaurants supplementing the abundant fast-food joints year after year.

★**Gopal's** NORTH INDIAN $
(SCO 20-21, Sector 8-C; snacks ₹80-100; ⏲8am-11pm; ❄✍) Every Indian city or town should have a restaurant like Gopal's – an air-conditioned, clean and smart diner that churns out cheap, utterly delicious platters of dosas, *puris* and *chhole bhature* (deep-fried flat-bread served with spicy chickpea curry) for hungry patrons through the day. The ground-floor sweet shop has a divine selection of Indian desserts that you can take away.

Sai Sweets SWEETS $
(SCO 1102-3, Sector 22-B; snacks ₹60-80; ⏲7.30am-8.30pm; ✍) This clean and wholesome sweet shop below Hotel Satyadeep serves tasty *mithai* (Indian sweets) by the kilogram. Also on offer are substantial snacks such as *tikki chaat* (potato cutlets), *panipuri* (round, hollow *puri* fried crisp and filled with a mixture of chutney, chilli, potato, onion and chickpea) and *pav bhaji* (tomato-based dish served with bread rolls).

Stop 'N Stare Food Point CAFE $
(Sector 10, behind Government Museum & Art Gallery; snacks ₹40-60; ⏲10am-6pm; ✍) Perfect for a pit stop after a tour of Chandigarh's museums, this simple cafe with shaded garden seating serves lassi, tea and instant coffee as well as Indian snacks such as patties, *paratha* (Indian-style flaky bread) and *kulcha* (soft-leavened bread eaten with a chickpea masala).

SLEEPING PRICE RANGES

Accommodation price ranges refer to a double room with bathroom and include taxes:

$ below ₹2000

$$ ₹2000 to ₹4000

$$$ above ₹4000

★**Virgin Courtyard** ITALIAN $$
(☎0172-5070045; SCO 1A, Sector 7; mains ₹250-400; ⏲11.30am-11.30pm; ❄📶) This fantastic alfresco dining address, spread across an ivory-white villa and a shaded courtyard, is arguably the closest you'll get to Italian cuisine in Chandigarh – albeit with an Indian twist. Try the arancini, served with a tangy tomato-based sauce and radish shavings, or the subtly flavoured panna cotta with meringues on the side. Chilled beers (₹300) are available too.

★**Hibachi** MULTICUISINE $$
(SCO 58-61, Madhya Marg, Sector 8-C; mains ₹250-400; ⏲11.30am-11.30pm; ❄📶) On the ground floor of Hotel Icon, Hibachi is the place to go if you're craving some Japanese or Southeast Asian food. There's some imaginative sushi on offer here, along with Burmese *khao suey*, pad thai, Chinese *kung pao* chicken with peanuts and even Malay-style laksa. There's also a well-stocked bar serving chilled beers (₹250) and premium Scottish malts.

Indian Coffee House SOUTH INDIAN $
(SCO 12, Sector 17; mains ₹40-60; ⏲9am-10pm; ✍) Always busy with locals, this 40-year-old institution is a great place for breakfast or lunch, with egg, toast and fabulously affordable filter coffee (₹30) sharing a menu of South Indian favourites such as *idli* (spongy, fermented rice cake), *vada* (doughnut-shaped, deep-fried lentil savoury) and dosa (large savoury crêpe). You can also buy good Indian coffee powder here (per kilogram ₹700).

Bhoj Vegetarian Restaurant INDIAN $
(SCO 1090-1, Sector 22-B; thali ₹140-170; ⏲7.30am-10.30pm; ❄✍) Contiguous to Hotel Divyadeep and run by Sai Baba devotees, this cosy haven serves a house thali with artfully spiced curries that change throughout the day. Thalis come in large or small portions. The restaurant also has a good selection of Indian deserts.

Hot Millions MULTICUISINE $$
(SCO 73-4, Sector 17-D; snacks ₹100-150, mains ₹200-300; ⏲11.30am-11pm; ❄) This popular eatery is set in Chandigarh's shopping central, serving fast food downstairs and posh

sit-down meals upstairs (accessed through a door on the side of the block). The Indianised pizzas in different pidgin avatars seem to have a loyal following. The eatery has branches all over town.

★Ghazal MUGHLAI $$$

(☎0172-2704448; SCO 189-91, Sector 17-C; mains ₹350-550; ⊙11.30am-11.30pm; ❄) A Chandigarh stalwart and still going strong, Ghazal has a dignified air and a fine menu of Mughlai classics including chicken and mutton, plus some well-prepared Continental and Chinese dishes. The vegetable *jalfrezi* (₹275) is a fiery sensation. At the back of the restaurant, a suited bartender guards a long line of imported single malts and beers (₹300).

Swagath INDIAN $$$

(☎0172-5002626; SCO 128, Madhya Marg, Sector 26; mains ₹250-550; ⊙11am-midnight; ❄) One of a string of swanky restaurants along Madhya Marg in Sector 26, this South Indian–themed place specialises in Mangalorean and Chettinad seafood – from prawns, squid and crab to tandoori pomfret and fish *gassi* (coconut-based curry). However, it also has an impressive North Indian menu, with some tasty Mughlai and Punjabi treats from the tandoor.

Drinking & Nightlife

Chandigarh's abundant wine and liquor stores turn into pavement bars every evening, but there are also plenty of salubrious, upscale watering holes. Women are far less likely to get hassled if they're with a male companion.

Lava Bar BAR

(Vivanta By Taj, Sector 17-A; beers/cocktails ₹450/600; ⊙noon-11.30pm) Considering it's housed inside the plush Taj hotel, this small bar is relatively laid-back, with a cosy atmosphere and live bands or a DJ playing most nights. Despite the steep prices, it's a good place for a drink, especially for solo and women travellers.

Blue Ice BAR

(SCO 7, Sector 17-E; beers/cocktails ₹400/500; ⊙noon-midnight) This slick, split-level restaurant-bar appeals to smartly dressed drinkers. There's a straightforward snacks menu and live music over the weekends to accompany your drink of choice.

Barista CAFE

(1st fl, SCO 63-4, Sector 17; coffee ₹90, snacks ₹90-200; ⊙9am-10pm) This chain coffee shop is a handy retreat from the orgy of consumerism in the Sector 17 area. Besides pressing out strong and aromatic Lavazza coffee, it also offers a few sandwiches, puffs and muffins.

Shopping

The spacious, pedestrianised shopping area of Sector 17 is a cathedral to consumerism, and could well be your reason to stay an extra day in Chandigarh.

★1469 GIFTS & SOUVENIRS

(www.1469workshop.com; SCO 81, Sector 17-D; ⊙11am-8pm) Named after the birth year of Guru Nanak (the founder of the Sikh faith), this funky independent clothing store sells fabulously colourful scarves, shawls and traditional Punjabi clothing, as well as modern T-shirts with an irreverent Punjabi twist. It also stocks some lovely jewellery, including the steel *kara* bracelets worn by Sikhs.

Fabindia CLOTHING

(www.fabindia.com; SCO 50-1, Sector 17-A; ⊙11am-8pm) This premium Indian chain store sells gorgeous garments fusing Indian and Western designs and motifs. It also stocks a superb selection of homewares such as table mats, cushion covers, bedspreads and rugs that make for great souvenirs and gifts.

Khadi India (17-E) CLOTHING

(SCO 28, Sector 17-E; ⊙10am-7pm Mon-Sat) This non-government operation has good-value, homespun textiles and herbal beauty products of premium quality, the sale of which directly supports small community producers in rural India. There's another **outlet** (SCO 192-193, Sector 17-G; ⊙10am-7pm Mon-Sat), a few minutes' walk east.

Phulkari ARTS & CRAFTS

(SCO 27, Sector 17-E; ⊙11am-8pm Mon-Sat) This official Government of Punjab emporium stocks everything from inlaid wooden tables and brightly embroidered *phulkari* textiles to dupattas (ladies' scarves) and jootis (traditional embroidered slip-on shoes).

Sector 22 Market MARKET

(off Sector 22 Market Rd; ⊙10am-10pm) This bustling, sprawling street market sells a mind-boggling array of household goods and clothing, and is sprinkled with pop-up street-food stalls selling yummy local treats.

Tiny Shop ARTS & CRAFTS

(Basement SCO 186-188, Sector 17-C; ⊙11am-8pm Mon-Sat) As cute as the name suggests, this basement boutique opened in 1980 and is secretly tucked away underneath a row of shops and restaurants in the busy Sector 17 market area. It sells artistic knick-knacks and household goods that make unique souvenirs to take back home.

Information

INTERNET ACCESS

Each of the central sector markets has at least one internet cafe with reliable and fast connections. Rates are around ₹30 per hour, and places are usually open between 10am and 7pm, excluding Sundays.

E-Net (2nd fl, SCO-12, Sector 17; per hr ₹30; 10.30am-8pm) Up the steps beside Indian Coffee House, this place has fast connections. A photo ID is required to access the internet.

MEDICAL SERVICES

Silver Oaks Hospital (0172-5097112; www.silveroakshospital.com; Phase 9, Sector 63, Mohali) This state-of-the-art, world-class hospital is about 7km southwest of Chandigarh's centre. It is well set up to treat foreign visitors.

MONEY

Most sector markets have ATMs accepting foreign cards. Sector 17 has the highest concentration of ATMs as well as local bank branches.

Thomas Cook (0173-6610901; SCO 17, Sector 9-D; 10am-7pm Mon-Fri, to 4pm Sat) can help with foreign exchange.

POST

Chandigarh's **main post office** (Sector 17; 10am-4pm Mon-Sat) has international parcel and express post services.

TOURIST INFORMATION

Several book stands and kiosks sell Vardhman's better-than-average *Chandigarh Tourist & Road Map* (₹50).

Chandigarh Tourism (0172-2703839; 1st fl, ISBT 17; 9am-5pm Mon-Sat)

Himachal Tourism (0172-2708569; 1st fl, ISBT 17; 10am-5pm Mon-Sat, closed 2nd Sat of month)

Uttar Pradesh & Uttarakhand Tourism (0172-2713988; 2nd fl, ISBT 17; 10am-5pm Mon-Sat, closed 2nd Sat of month)

Getting There & Away

AIR

Chandigarh airport is about 9km southeast of the centre. AC bus 201 runs from both main bus stands to the airport from 7.30am to 6pm (₹30). Alternatively, take an autorickshaw for around ₹200 or a taxi for around ₹500.

There are daily domestic flights operated by **Air India** (1800-1801407; www.airindia.in), **GoAir** (9223222111; www.goair.in), **IndiGo** (9910383838; www.goindigo.in), **Jet Airways** (1800-225522; www.jetairways.com) and **SpiceJet** (9654003333; www.spicejet.com) to Delhi, Mumbai, Bengaluru and Srinagar.

There are two international flights to Dubai, operated by Air India and IndiGo.

BUS

Chandigarh has two main Inter State Bus Terminals (ISBT) – one in Sector 17 and one in Sector 43. Numerous red AC buses run between the two terminals (₹20).

ISBT Panchkulla is further from the centre and has buses to Morni. Local buses 2F and 30B link ISBT 17 and ISBT Panchkulla (₹30).

TRAIN

The train station is 7km southeast of the city centre, though there's a handy **train reservation office** (8am-8pm Mon-Sat, to 2pm Sun) on the 1st floor of ISBT 17. There's no prepaid autorickshaw fee from the centre to the train station, but expect to pay around ₹100.

Several fast trains go to New Delhi daily. The quickest and slickest is the twice-daily Kalka Shatabdi (AC chair/1AC ₹605/1205, 3½ hours), which leaves at 6.53am and 6.23pm. To get to Delhi for less, buy an unreserved 'general' ticket (₹110) when you turn up at the station, and then just pile into the 2nd-class carriage of the next available train.

More than half a dozen trains go to Kalka (2nd class ₹45, 35 minutes), from where narrow-gauge trains rattle up the hills to Shimla.

Two daily trains go to Amritsar (2nd class/AC chair ₹120/435, 4½ hours), at 7am and 5.10pm.

Getting Around

Expect to pay about ₹50 for a short hop in an autorickshaw. Hiring one for half a day (up to four hours) to take in sights such as Nek Chand Rock Garden and Sukhna Lake will cost around ₹500. Bicycles (₹200 per eight hours, ₹500 refundable deposit) are available at the entrance to Sukhna Lake.

Numerous local buses, including 203 and 22, link ISBT 17 with the train station (₹10). There's a prepaid autorickshaw stand outside ISBT 17, but it only does fares within the city centre, such as to ISBT 43 (₹60). For places further afield, such as the train station (about ₹100) or the airport (about ₹200), you'll have to negotiate with the driver directly.

RK Taxi Stand is behind ISBT 17 and charges ₹500 for the airport, ₹1500 return for Morni and ₹1000/1500 for a half-/full-day city tour.

AROUND CHANDIGARH

Pinjore Gardens

The beautifully restored, 17th-century Mughal-era **Pinjore Gardens** (Yadavindra Gardens; ☎01733-230759; Pinjore; ₹20; ⏲7am-10pm), on the edge of the small town of Pinjore, are built on seven levels with water features and serene views of the Shivalik Hills.

Within the grounds there's a **restaurant** (mains ₹80-180; ⏲10am-7pm; ❄) in the Rang Mahal pavilion, which also has a bar. Come in December for regional delicacies and cultural performances as part of the Pinjore Heritage Festival (p203).

Should you fancy an overnight stay, there are pleasant rooms with Mughal-style flourishes and views of the gardens at the **Budgerigar Motel** (☎01733-231877; pinjore@hry.nic.in; d from ₹2350; ❄). Its main entrance is just outside the garden walls, to the right as you face the entrance, but it can also be accessed from inside the gardens through the restaurant.

Nearby is the **Bhima Devi Museum** (⏲10am-5pm) FREE, made up of a collection of small artefacts in the grounds of the scattered ruins of the ornate, 10th-century **Bhima Devi Temple**, which was torn down when the gardens were originally constructed. To get here, turn left as you exit the gardens and walk past the water park.

Frequent buses leave from Chandigarh's ISBT 43 to Pinjore (₹30, one hour). The gardens are on your left as you drive into the town. Less frequent services depart from ISBT 17.

Morni Hills

Perched at 1220m, **Morni Hills** is Haryana's only hill station, set amid monkey-filled forests on a spur running west from the Shivalik Hills. Here you'll find a handful of rustic resorts, the village of Morni and – 7km downhill from the village – **Tikkar Taal**, a pair of pretty lakes with boats for rent (from ₹200).

With a pleasant location on the shore of the second lake, **Tikkar Taal Tourist Complex** (☎01733-250166; Tikkar Taal; d ₹3500; ❄) has clean, comfortable rooms with private bathrooms and views of the lake. There's a restaurant with terraced seating and gardens leading down to the lake. There's nothing much to do here, but it's a wonderfully peaceful place to stay if you want to escape the urban frenzy for a day or two.

There are daily buses to Morni (₹30, two hours) from Chandigarh's **ISBT Panchkulla** (Panchkulla) bus station. From Morni village, there are three minibuses to Tikka Taal (₹20; 6.30am, 7.30am and 3.30pm). They return from outside Tikkar Taal Tourist Complex at 7.30am, 8.30am and 4.15pm. The 4.15pm connects with the last bus back to Chandigarh, which leaves Morni village at 5pm.

Private cars from Morni village to Tikka Taal cost about ₹700 return, including waiting time. Alternatively, it's a lovely two-hour, 7km downhill walk. When returning, hike back up the road towards Chandigarh, then turn left as the road bears sharp right (after less than 1km).

PUNJAB

Forged from the Indian half of Punjab province after Partition, Punjab is the homeland of India's Sikh population. Irrigated by mighty Himalayan rivers such as the Beas, the Ravi and the Sutlej, it is an expanse of fertile land that supplies a bulk of India's demand for wheat and rice, while also doubling as a nerve centre of India's textile and manufacturing industries. A particularly tourist-friendly region, thanks to its strong expatriate connections with the UK and Canada, Punjab provides a wonderful opportunity to go traipsing into the backyards of North India.

Must-try Punjabi dishes include *kulcha* (fried bread), *chhole* (spicy chickpea curry), char-grilled tandoori mutton, *dhal makhani* (black lentils and red kidney beans in a cream and butter gravy), tandoori chicken, *rajma chawal* (kidney bean curry with basmati rice), Amritsari fried fish and the iconic butter chicken, the prototype for chicken tikka masala.

Anandpur Sahib

☎01887 / POPULATION 16,500

The second most important pilgrimage site for Sikhs after the Golden Temple in Amritsar, Anandpur Sahib was founded in 1664 by the ninth Sikh guru, Guru Tegh Bahadur, some years before he was beheaded by the Mughal emperor Aurangzeb. To resist the persecution of the Sikhs, his son, Guru Gobind Singh, founded the Khalsa (Sikh brotherhood) here in 1699, an event celebrated during the Holla Mohalla (p203) festival.

Sights

Kesgarh Sahib SIKH TEMPLE

The largest and most dramatic gurdwara in Anandpur Sahib is the Kesgarh Sahib, set back from the main highway on the edge of the old town. An elegant white structure with a domed central spire, it marks the spot where the Khalsa was inaugurated, and enshrines an armoury of sacred Sikh weapons.

Anandpur Sahib Fort FORT

(Kesgarh; dawn-dusk) FREE Behind the Kesgarh Sahib gurdwara, a broad paved path climbs the hillside to the small Kesgarh fort, which affords glorious views over a sea of gurdwara domes. Kesgarh is the most prominent of Anandpur Sahib's five forts, all of which were built by Guru Gobind Singh as defensive battlements.

Khalsa Heritage Complex MUSEUM

(Virasat-e-Khalsa; www.virasat-e-khalsa.net; 8am-8pm Tue-Sun) FREE The striking five-petal form (inspired by the five warrior-saints in the Khalsa) of the Khalsa Heritage Complex, which opened in 2011, is one of India's most impressive modern buildings. This fascinating museum complex uses elaborate murals and friezes to bring Sikh history to life.

Sleeping & Eating

Hotel Holy City Paradise HOTEL $

(9815135800; Academy Rd; d ₹1780;) Clearly the best among Anandpur Sahib's limited staying options, this small but well-run place has clean and comfy rooms, a good restaurant serving local food and an excellent location in the heart of town.

Hotel Paramount Residency HOTEL $

(01887-233619; Academy Rd; r from ₹1050;) Above the road linking Kesgarh Sahib to the fort, Hotel Paramount Residency has austere, spartan rooms but a friendly welcome and a good location close to the Khalsa Heritage Complex.

Pal Restaurant INDIAN $

(mains ₹50-100; 7.30am-11pm) Pal Restaurant, above Pal Sweetshop, is close to the bus station and serves good-value Indian cuisine, including local thalis. Turn left out of the bus stand, left again, and it's on your left.

Information

About 2km from the centre, **Mata Nanki Charitable Hospital** (01887-230284; Ropar Rd, near Khalsa College) is a small but reputable general hospital run by a British-based charity.

Getting There & Away

The bus and train stations are 300m apart on the main road outside town. Buses leave frequently for Chandigarh (₹100, two hours), Amritsar (₹190, 4½ hours) and Patiala (₹120, three hours).

Five daily trains go to Chandigarh (2nd class/sleeper/3AC ₹95/170/540, two to three hours) between 5.45am and 4.40pm. The overnight 14554 Himachal Express (sleeper/3AC ₹215/580, 7½ hours, 10.05pm) goes to New Delhi.

Amritsar

0183 / POPULATION 1.13 MILLION

Founded in 1577 by the fourth Sikh guru, Guru Ram Das, Amritsar is home to the spectacular Golden Temple, Sikhism's holiest shrine and one of India's most serene and humbling sights. The same cannot be said for the hyperactive streets surrounding the temple, but they're a delight to walk through for a sensory overload of sights, sounds and smells.

Sights

★Golden Temple SIKH TEMPLE

(Golden Temple Complex; 24hr) FREE The legendary Golden Temple is actually just a small part of this huge gurdwara complex, known to Sikhs as Harmandir Sahib. Spiritually, the focus of attention is the tank that surrounds the gleaming central shrine – the **Amrit Sarovar** (Pool of Nectar; Golden Temple Complex), from which Amritsar takes its name, excavated by the fourth Sikh guru, Ram Das, in 1577. Ringed by a marble walkway, the tank is said to have healing powers, and pilgrims come from across the world to bathe in its sacred waters.

Floating at the end of a long causeway, the Golden Temple itself is a mesmerising blend of Hindu and Islamic architectural styles, with an elegant marble lower level adorned with flower and animal motifs in pietra dura work (as seen on the Taj Mahal). Above this rises a shimmering second level, encased in intricately engraved gold panels, and topped by a dome gilded with 750kg of gold. In the gleaming inner sanctum (photography prohibited), priests and musicians keep up a continuous chant from the Guru Granth Sahib (the Sikh holy book), adding to the already intense atmosphere. Given the never-ending beeline of devotees, you will likely get a few minutes within the sanctum before you are gently urged to exit and make way for other devotees. Entry and exit are both via the causeway.

The **Guru Granth Sahib** is installed in the temple every morning and returned at night to the **Akal Takhat** (Timeless Throne), the temporal seat of the Khalsa brotherhood. The ceremony takes place at 5am and 9.30pm in winter, and 4am and 10.30pm in summer. Inside the Akal Takhat, you can view a collection of sacred **Sikh weapons**. The building was heavily damaged when it was stormed by the Indian army during Operation Blue Star in 1984. It was repaired by the government but Sikhs refused to use the tainted building and rebuilt the tower from scratch.

More shrines and monuments are dotted around the edge of the compound. Inside the main entrance clock tower, the **Sikh Museum** (7am-7pm summer, 8am-6pm winter) FREE shows the persecution suffered by the Sikhs at the hands of Mughals, the British and Indira Gandhi. At the southeast end of the tank is the **Ramgarhia Bunga**, a protective fortress topped by two Islamic-style minarets; inside is a stone slab once used for Mughal coronations, seized from Delhi by Ranjit Singh in 1783.

★Guru-Ka-Langar SIKH SITE

(Golden Temple Complex; 24hr) FREE At the southeast end of the Golden Temple Complex is the Guru-Ka-Langar, an enormous dining room where an estimated 100,000 pilgrims come to eat every day after praying at the Golden Temple. There's no charge to eat here, but a donation is appropriate, and voluntary help with the staggering pile of washing up is always appreciated. Catering equally to everyone from paupers to millionaires, it's a humbling demonstration of the Sikh principles of hospitality, community service and charity.

Jallianwala Bagh HISTORIC SITE

(Golden Temple Rd; 6am-9pm summer, 7am-8pm winter) FREE Reached through a narrow gatehouse leading to an enclosed courtyard, this poignant park commemorates the 1500 Indians killed or wounded when a British officer ordered his soldiers to shoot unarmed protesters in 1919. Some of the bullet holes are still visible in the walls, as is the well into which hundreds desperately leapt to avoid the bullets. There's an eternal flame of remembrance, an exhibition telling stories of victims, and a Martyrs' Gallery, with portraits of Independence heroes.

GOLDEN TEMPLE ETIQUETTE

Before entering the compound, remove your shoes and socks (there are *chappal* (sandal) stands at the entrances), wash your feet in the shallow foot baths and cover your head; scarves can be borrowed (no charge) or bought from nearby souvenir hawkers for ₹10. Tobacco and alcohol are strictly prohibited within the premises. If you want to sit beside the tank, sit cross-legged and do not dangle your feet in the water. Photography is permitted from the walkway surrounding the pool, but not inside the Golden Temple itself. Staff-wielding, blue-robed temple guards called *jathhedars* patrol the compound around the clock; approach them for any assistance or query regarding etiquette.

Ram Bagh PARK

(MMM Rd; dawn-dusk) FREE Located about a kilometre east of the train station, Ram Bagh was the former palace grounds of Maharaja Ranjit Singh and now serves as a public park. In the heart of the well-tended and manicured greenery, you'll find the **summer palace** of the former maharaja, in commission between 1818 and 1837. It's a modest structure in comparison to some of India's other palaces but a very atmospheric building nonetheless.

Baba Atal Tower SIKH TEMPLE

FREE Just outside the Golden Temple Complex, to the south, is the octagonal Baba Atal Tower, constructed in 1784 to commemorate Atal Rai, the son of sixth Sikh guru Har Gobind, who, according to legend, revived a playmate from the dead, then gave his own life as penance for interfering in God's designs. The nine storeys each represent one year of Atal's short life.

Khalsa College HISTORIC BUILDING

(www.khalsacollegeamritsar.org; GT Rd; dawn-dusk) FREE This vast, sprawling castle of a college, on your right as you head west of town along GT Rd, was founded in 1890 to educate

Amritsar

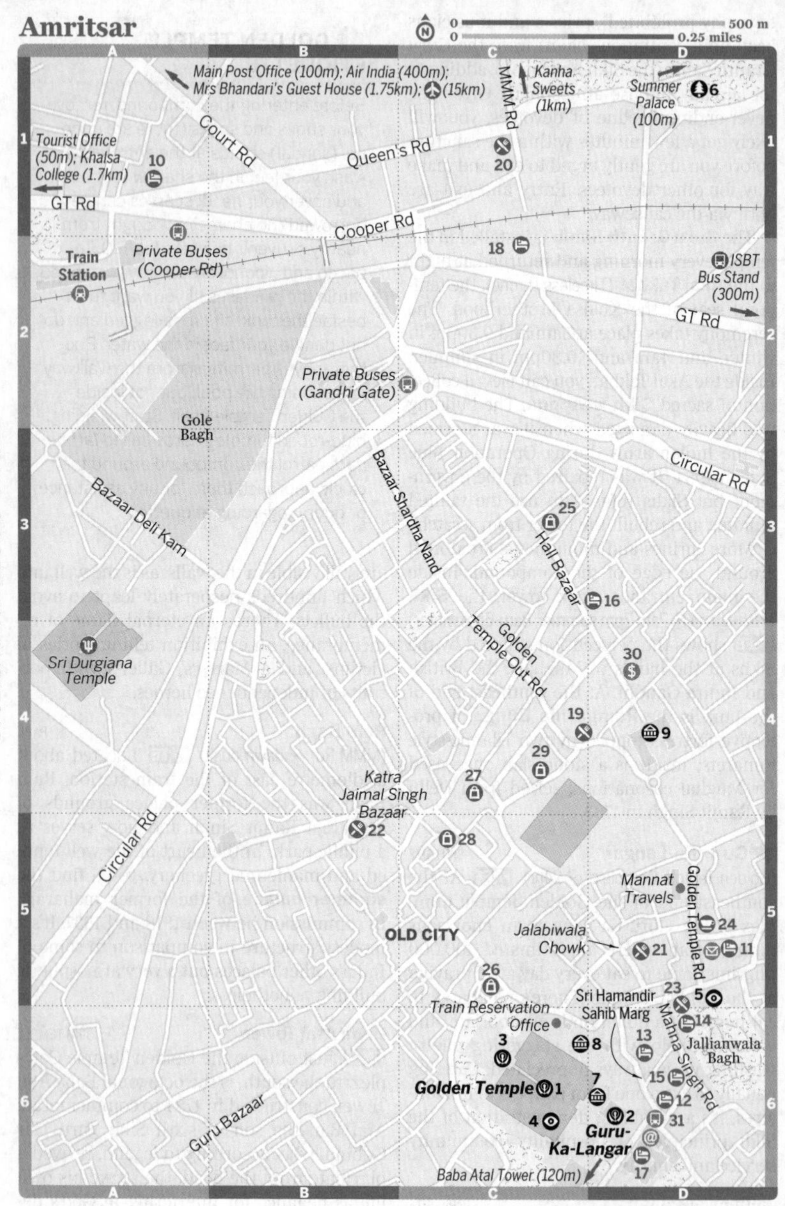

the cream of Punjabi society. It's a glorious example of the Indo-Saracenic style of architecture, with an imposing domed red-sandstone facade fronted by grassy fields. You can't enter the academic and administrative wings of the college, but exploring the campus is okay.

Town Hall HISTORIC BUILDING

(Golden Temple Rd) A gorgeous 19th-century mansion north of the Golden Temple, the Town Hall often doubles as a venue for art exhibitions, meetings and public events. In 2017 it became home to a permanent exhi-

Amritsar

Top Sights
1 Golden Temple C6
2 Guru-Ka-Langar D6

Sights
3 Akal Takhat C6
4 Amrit Sarovar C6
5 Jallianwala Bagh D5
6 Ram Bagh D1
7 Ramgarhia Bunga D6
8 Sikh Museum C6
9 Town Hall D4

Sleeping
10 Grand Hotel A1
11 Hotel Golden Tower D5
12 Hotel Grace D6
13 Hotel Indus D6
14 Lucky Guest House D6
15 MK Sood Guesthouse D6
16 Ramada Amritsar D3
17 Sri Guru Ram Das Niwas D6
18 Tourist Guesthouse C2

Eating
Bharawan Da Dhaba .... (see 19)
19 Brothers' Dhaba C4
20 Crystal Restaurant C1
21 Gurdas Ram D5
22 Kesar Da Dhaba B5
23 Neelam's D5

Drinking & Nightlife
Bottoms Up Pub .... (see 10)
24 Café Coffee Day D5

Shopping
25 Booklovers Retreat C3
26 Kathian Bazaar C5
27 Katra Jaimal Singh Bazaar C4
28 Shashtri Bazaar C5
29 Tahali Sahib Bazaar C4

Information
30 HDFC Bank D4
ICICI Bank .... (see 30)

Transport
31 Free Yellow Buses D6
Prepaid Taxi Booth .... (see 31)

bition chronicling the tumultuous history of Amritsar and Punjab in the years since the Partition of India.

Tours

The Grand Hotel runs day tours of the main sights (per person ₹500) and evening tours (per person ₹800, starting at 3pm) to the Attari-Wagah border-closing ceremony, Mata Temple and Golden Temple.

The tourist office (p219) runs an interesting two-hour Heritage Walk (Indian/foreigner ₹25/75), covering the old-city bazaars. It starts from the Town Hall at 8am daily (9am December to February) and finishes outside the Golden Temple. Just turn up at the Town Hall 10 minutes before start time.

Sleeping

Most of Amritsar's budget digs suffer from deafening traffic noise – bring earplugs. The more pleasant addresses are either pricey or far removed from the action.

Grand Hotel HOTEL $
(☎0183-2562424; www.hotelgrand.in; Queen's Rd; d from ₹1510; ❄@☎) Across the road from the train station, but far from grungy, the Grand is an oasis of calm amid an otherwise chaotic location. Rooms are spacious – if not exactly grand – and surround a wonderfully charming courtyard garden. The restaurant, with seating overlooking the garden, and the inviting bar serving chilled beers are also highly recommended. The hotel management organises tours.

Sri Guru Ram Das Niwas GUESTHOUSE $
(Golden Temple Complex; dm free but donations appropriate, d without/with AC ₹300/₹500; ❄@) Inexpensive rooms are available in this *niwas* (pilgrims' hostel) at the southeast end of the Golden Temple Complex. Foreigners are generally accommodated in the dorm at Sri Guru Ram Das Niwas, or at rooms in the other buildings in the vicinity. Check in at the nearby Guru Arjan Dev Niwas to see what is available.

Staying here is a fascinating experience but rooms and dorms are basic, with shared bathrooms, and there's a three-day maximum stay. Each person gets use of a locker in the dorms, but you need your own padlock.

Tourist Guesthouse GUESTHOUSE $
(☎9356003219; www.touristguesthouse.com; 1355 GT Rd; dm/d ₹200/600; @☎) This good-value backpacker stalwart offers pocket-friendly prices and humble rooms with high ceilings

and fans. There's a garden restaurant, rooftop seating and an overall traveller-oriented vibe. On the downside, this is one of the few places in town that charges for wi-fi (per day ₹100) and the location, between a busy flyover and the railway line, is hardly the quietest.

MK Sood Guesthouse HOTEL $
(☎0183-5093376; Braham Buta Bazaar; r ₹1100; ❄📶) Small, quaint and clean, this place benefits from a quieter location than most old-city hotels in the vicinity of the Golden Temple area. All rooms have AC, but some are more spacious and comfortable than others, so ask to see a few before deciding. Wi-fi is available free of charge, but in the lobby only.

★Mrs Bhandari's Guesthouse GUESTHOUSE $$
(☎0183-2228509; www.bhandariguesthouse.wordpress.com; 10 Cantonment; d from ₹2570; ❄@📶🏊) Founded by the much-missed Mrs Bhandari (1906–2007), this slightly mothballed but friendly guesthouse is set in spacious grounds in Amritsar cantonment, about 2km from the centre. The large rooms have a hint of colonial-style charm about them, and the welcome is warm. The well-kept gardens are vast, and include swings, see-saws, plenty of seating and a small swimming pool.

Budget travellers can camp here for ₹300 per person if they bring their own gear. Pick-up is free from the train station and meals are available (breakfast/lunch/dinner ₹350/600/600). It's about ₹70 in a cycle-rickshaw from the old city. The gate shuts at 9pm; you'll have to leave a word at the office if you intend to return late at night.

Hotel Grace HOTEL $
(☎0183-2559355; www.hotelgrace.net; 35 Braham Buta Bazaar; d without/with AC from ₹800/1200; ❄@📶) This low-profile hotel in a market area to the east of Golden Temple has a fair mix of rooms that are hard to beat in terms of affordability. The best are at the front, with plenty of natural light, while the smaller and more modest rooms to the rear promise great value for money.

Hotel Golden Tower HOTEL $
(☎0183-2534446; off Golden Temple Rd, Fuwara Chowk; d from ₹1650; ❄@📶) More glam outside than in, the Golden Tower is a reasonable choice in a good location. The sparsely decorated but large, clean rooms come with TV, mini-fridge and wi-fi. It's a good place to stay, especially if you plan to visit the Golden Temple late at night or early in the morning.

Lucky Guest House HOTEL $
(☎0183-2542175; Mahna Singh Rd; r from ₹650; ❄) This solid, old-city budget option has basic rooms that are a bit pokey, but the location is good and the market nearby provides ample opportunities for shopping and sightseeing excursions. Not all rooms have a window, so ask to see a few before checking in.

Hotel Indus HOTEL $$
(☎0183-2535900; www.hotelindus.com; 211/3 Sri Hamandir Sahib Marg; d from ₹2100; ❄@📶) The dramatic million-dollar view of the Golden Temple from the rooftop is reason enough to stay at this modern hotel. Rooms are compact but comfy, and suitably appointed for the price. Book well ahead to secure one of the two rooms with temple vistas.

★Ramada Amritsar HOTEL $$$
(☎0183-5025555; www.ramadaamritsar.com; Hall Bazaar; d incl breakfast from ₹4700; ❄@📶🏊) This grand-looking hotel is the best (and only) top-end option in the old city. The lobby is somewhat chintzy, but rooms are smart and modern, and the service is excellent. It's walking distance from the Golden Temple, the glass-walled rooms have wonderful views of the old city, and there's a small but cosy pool on the terrace.

Eating

Amritsar is famous for its *dhabas* (casual eateries serving snacks and basic meals) serving yummy Punjabi treats such as *kulcha* (deep-fried flatbread), stuffed *parathas*, spicy variants of lentils and Amritsari deep-fried fish tikkas garnished with lemon, chilli, garlic and ginger. Hotels and restaurants in the Golden Temple area are usually vegetarian and don't serve alcohol.

★Kesar Da Dhaba PUNJABI $
(Shastri Market, Chowk Passian; mains ₹70-130; ⏱11am-5pm & 7-11pm; 🌱) Originally founded in Pakistan's Punjab province, this 100-year-old eatery relocated to Amritsar after Partition. Since then, it has been serving up delicious *paratha* thalis (₹200 to ₹250) and silver-leaf-topped *firni* or ground rice pudding (₹20) in small clay bowls, as well as arguably the best lassi in town (₹50). Kitchen tours are available for diners; just ask at the reception.

★Bharawan Da Dhaba PUNJABI **$$**

(Town Hall Chowk; meals ₹160-190; ⊙8am-midnight; ❄✍) Pronounced 'praa-waan', this down-to-earth Amritsar institution has been serving lip-smacking Punjabi treats since 1912. Order yourself a regional thali here, and you'll be treated to a delectable platter comprising dhal and paneer (cottage cheese), served with naan, roti or rice (or all of them). The eatery has pleasant views of the Town Hall area through its glassy shopfront.

Kanha Sweets NORTH INDIAN **$**

(Lawrence Rd; sweets ₹20-40; ⊙breakfast 8am-10pm; ✍) Apart from being a top-notch confectionery, this small but incredibly popular takeaway joint is known for the best *puri* platters (₹70) in Amritsar, comprising balloon-like *puris*, sharply flavoured potato curry and pickles. It's only served for breakfast between 8am and 2pm, but the sweets counter remains opens to 10pm.

Gurdas Ram INDIAN **$**

(Jalebiwala Chowk; jalebi per serving ₹20; ⊙9.30am-10.30pm; ✍) Get your fingers sticky at this 60-year-old *jalebi* joint, serving up the delicious Indian dessert consisting of saffron-coloured coils of deep-fried batter dunked in sugar syrup. The place is so famous they even named the street crossing after it (Jalebiwala Chowk).

Neelam's MULTICUISINE **$**

(Golden Temple Rd, Jallianwala Bagh; mains ₹70-170; ⊙9am-11pm; ❄✍) Not far from the Golden Temple, this tiny two-tone eatery is a convenient spot to recharge your batteries. It does some quick-and-easy multicuisine dishes, including a backpacker breakfast and some South Indian staples, but don't miss the great-value *kulcha* (₹50), served with a chickpea side dish and a spicy chutney.

★Makhan Fish PUNJABI **$$**

(Old Jail Rd, near Trillium Mall; mains ₹150-350; ⊙11am-11pm; ❄) This no-frills restaurant does the definitive version of Amritsar's legendary fried fish and oven-baked fish tikkas, as well as a number of local preps featuring chicken, mutton and fish. Note that the signature fish dishes are made and served by weight – 250g serves approximately two. Curiously, there's a Chinese menu on offer too, featuring a list of generic impersonations.

Brothers' Dhaba PUNJABI **$$**

(Bade Bhai Ka; Town Hall Chowk; meals ₹140-180; ⊙8am-midnight; ❄✍) This fast and friendly upmarket *dhaba* serves some of Amritsar's tastiest *parathas* stuffed with herbs, potato and pomegranate seeds that burst in the mouth as tiny explosions of taste. It also

THE JALLIANWALA BAGH MASSACRE

Following the introduction of the *Rowlatt Act 1919*, which gave British authorities the power to imprison Indians suspected of sedition without trial, Amritsar became a focal point for the Independence movement. After a series of hartals (strikes) in which many protesters and three British bank managers were killed, Brigadier-General Reginald Dyer was called upon to return order to the city.

On 13 April 1919 (Baisakhi Day), more than 5000 Indians convened for a peaceful protest in Jallianwala Bagh (p213), a public courtyard surrounded by high walls on all sides, with only a narrow lane on the northern side for entry and exit. Under orders to make an example of the protesters, Dyer arrived with 150 troops and ordered his soldiers to open fire. When the barrage of bullets ceased, nearly 400 protesters were dead, according to the British authorities (although Indian National Congress placed the figure at more than 1000), and around 1500 were wounded, including many women and children.

Dyer's action was supported by the British establishment but described as 'monstrous' by Winston Churchill, and as 'a savage and inappropriate folly' by Edwin Montagu, the Secretary of State for India. The Nobel Prize–winning poet Rabindranath Tagore renounced his knighthood in protest against the massacre. The incident galvanised Indian nationalism – Gandhi responded with a program of civil disobedience, announcing that 'cooperation in any shape or form with this satanic government is sinful'.

Reginald Dyer died in retirement in England in 1927. Michael O'Dwyer, governor of the Punjab at the time of the massacre, was assassinated by the Sikh revolutionary Udham Singh in London in 1940. Richard Attenborough's acclaimed film *Gandhi* (1982) dramatically re-enacts the events at Jallianwala Bagh.

AMRITSAR'S BAZAARS

The Golden Temple sits on the edge of a mesmerising maze of crowded market streets, where anything and everything can be found, from ceremonial swords to wedding suits. Start your explorations at the main entrance to the Golden Temple. From here, stroll northwest (so, to your left if you have your back to the Golden Temple) to the end of the temple compound and duck into the atmospheric **Kathian Bazaar** for blankets, stationery, tin pots and red-and-silver wedding bangles. At the far end, turn right onto bustling Guru Bazaar Rd, past shops full of glittery womenswear, then take the first left into **Shashtri Bazaar**, where dupattas give way to fancy woollen shawls. At the end of the bazaar, turn right and continue past a string of food and fruit stalls to frenetic **Katra Jaimal Singh Bazaar**, crammed with tailors and fashion stores. At the T-junction, turn left into **Tahali Sahib Bazaar**, piled high with glittering *juttis* (shoes) and satin dupattas (scarves).

On a less chaotic note, if you want to indulge in crowd-free shopping, the tourist corridor from Town Hall to Golden Temple is lined with several shops selling good-quality souvenirs at negotiable prices.

does hot and yummy breakfast platters featuring curried potato and deep-fried *kulcha*.

Crystal Restaurant MULTICUISINE **$$$**
(Crystal Chowk; mains ₹300-450; ⏲11am-11.30pm; ❄) Worth the splurge, this classy, ground-floor restaurant has a fin-de-siècle air, with mirror-lined walls and ornate stucco trim. The menu is dominated by Mughlai favourites – the house speciality is the delicious *murgh tawa frontier* (₹390), morsels of chicken in dense onion gravy. The place also has a decent European menu featuring the usual range of grills, steaks, roasts and bakes.

Drinking & Nightlife

Bottoms Up Pub BAR
(Queen's Rd, Grand Hotel; beers ₹120; ⏲11am-11pm) The congenial bar at the Grand Hotel serves icy cold, glycerine-free, draught Kingfisher beer and some tasty meals from the hotel's common kitchen.

Café Coffee Day CAFE
(Golden Temple Rd; coffees from ₹80; ⏲9am-11pm) An air-conditioned oasis with fresh coffee, this chain cafe is conveniently located within shouting distance from the Golden Temple area. There's tasty cakes, puffs, wraps and street-view seating to go with your latte or espresso.

Shopping

Booklovers Retreat BOOKS
(Hall Bazaar; ⏲9am-8pm Mon-Sat) Booklovers is an old-school store laden with interesting tomes spanning diverse genres, including the latest Indian and international English best sellers.

Information

INTERNET ACCESS

Free in-room wi-fi is widely available at Amritsar's hotels.

Guru Arjun Dev Niwas Net Cafe (Guru Arjun Dev Niwas; per hr ₹30; ⏲6am-1am) This is a handy internet cafe close to the Golden Temple complex.

MEDICAL SERVICES

Fortis Escorts Hospital (☎0183-3012222, 9915133330; www.fortishealthcare.com; Majitha Verka Bypass) This international-standard hospital is in Amritsar's suburbs, about 7km northeast of the old city.

MONEY

Amritsar has an ever-mushrooming supply of ATMs, though there are no moneychangers at the airport. **Mannat Travels** (☎0183-5006006; 5 Dharam Singh Market, Fuwara Chowk; ⏲10am-7pm Mon-Sat) is a trustworthy moneychanger in the old city.

HDFC (ground fl, RS Towers, Hall Bazaar; ⏲10am-4pm Mon-Sat) and **ICICI** (ground fl, RS Towers, Hall Bazaar; ⏲9am-6pm Mon-Sat) deal in foreign exchange and have ATMs that accept foreign cards.

POST

At the junction of Court Rd with Albert Rd is the **main post office** (Court Rd; ⏲10am-4pm Mon-Fri, to 2pm Sat), with fast post and parcel facilities. There is also a handy **post office** (Golden Temple Rd, Fuwara Chowk; ⏲10am-4pm Mon-Fri, to 2pm Sat) near the Golden Temple with similar facilities.

TOURIST INFORMATION

By the entrance to the train station is a **tourist office** (☎ 0183-2402452; www.punjabtourism.gov.in; Train Station exit, Queen's Rd; ⏲10am-5pm Tue-Sun) with brochures and free maps covering Punjab, including detailed street maps of Amritsar, Patiala and Kapurthala.

Getting There & Away

AIR

About 11km northwest of the centre, Amritsar's Sri Guru Ram Dass Jee International Airport has connections to major Indian cities such as Delhi and Mumbai, courtesy of **Air India** (☎ 0183-2214062; www.airindia.in; ⏲10am-5pm), **Jet Airways** (☎ 1800-225522; www.jetairways.com) and **SpiceJet** (☎ 1800-1803333; www.spicejet.com). It also has a few international flights (to the Middle East mostly, but Air India also flies to Birmingham).

BUS

Companies running private buses operate from near **Gandhi Gate**, and from **Cooper Rd**, near the train station. Evening AC buses run to Delhi (₹800, 10 hours) and Jaipur (seat/sleeper ₹700/900, 16 hours), while non-AC ones run to Jammu (₹250, four hours). AC buses also run through the day to Chandigarh (₹600, four hours).

The main **Inter State Bus Terminal** (ISBT; GT Rd) is about 3km north of the Golden Temple, near Mahan Singh Gate. There's at least one daily bus to Chamba (₹260, six hours), Dharamsala (₹280, seven hours) and Manali (₹600, 12 hours).

Frequent buses also serve Attari (₹30, one hour), Faridkot (₹120, three hours), Pathankot (₹120, three hours) and Patiala (₹230, five hours).

TRAIN

Apart from the train station, there's a less busy **train reservation office** (Golden Temple; ⏲8am-8pm Mon-Sat, to 2pm Sun) at the Golden Temple.

The fastest train to Delhi is the twice-daily Amritsar Shatabdi (AC chair/1AC ₹790/1620, six hours, 5am and 4.50pm). From New Delhi train station, the same trains make the return trip at 7.20am and 4.30pm. There are around a dozen other daily trains to Delhi (sleeper/3AC/2AC ₹290/760/1060), taking seven to nine hours.

Four daily trains go to Chandigarh (2nd class/AC chair ₹120/440, five hours) between 5.15am and 5.50pm. Ten daily trains go to Pathankot (sleeper/3AC ₹140/490, three hours), leaving between 4.40am and 8.30pm.

The daily 6.40pm Amritsar-Howrah Mail links Amritsar with Varanasi (sleeper/3AC/2AC ₹500/1350/1965, 22 hours) and Kolkata's Howrah train station (sleeper/3AC/2AC ₹695/1860/2740, 37 hours).

Getting Around

Free yellow buses (Sri Harmandir Sahib Marg) run between the train station and the Golden Temple from 4am to 9pm. Otherwise, from the train station to the Golden Temple, a rickshaw/autorickshaw will cost around ₹50/100 but you'll have to haggle hard for a fair price. Taxis loiter around the station and at the **prepaid taxi booth** (Sri Harmandir Sahib Marg) to the east of Golden Temple, while **Ola Cabs** (☎ 0183-3355335) has smart and swift radio taxis plying Amritsar round the clock. To the airport, an autorickshaw costs around ₹250 and a taxi about ₹500.

Taxis taking you to the Golden Temple area will often drop you at Fuwara (Fountain) Chowk or the Town Hall, from where you can walk the last few hundred metres through a pedestrianised tourist corridor and souvenir market, flanked by graceful red-sandstone shopping arcades on both sides.

Patiala

☎ 0175 / POPULATION 405,200

Punjab's best-kept secret, Patiala was once the capital of an independent Sikh state, ruled by an extravagant family of maharajas. As the Mughal empire declined, the rulers of Patiala curried favour with the British and filled their city with lavish palaces and follies. After Independence and the subsequent abolition of privy purses, royal fortunes began to decline, and the once regal city slowly became a shadow of its former self. Today, the grand monuments are all crumbling, but the old city, ringed by 10 historic gates, is still swooningly atmospheric. In mid-January, the skies above Patiala burst into life for the Basant kite festival.

Sights

Qila Mubarak FORT

(Adalat Bazar; museum ₹10; ⏲museum 10.15am-4.45pm Tue-Sun) The ancestral home of the maharajas of Patiala, this richly ornamented 18th-century fort is an *Arabian Nights* fantasy of soaring buttresses and latticed balconies. You can't enter the interior of the fort, but you are allowed to walk between the hugely impressive inner and outer walls, surrounded by crumbling masonry and flocks of parakeets. Inside, to your right, the 1859 **Durbar Hall museum** has a wonderful collection of weaponry, royal portraits, outrageous chandeliers and other treasures rescued from decaying palaces.

Sheesh Mahal MUSEUM
(Sheesh Mahal Rd; ₹10; ⏰10.30am-5pm Tue-Sun) The totally over-the-top Sheesh Mahal, graced by two wedding-cake towers and an ornamental suspension bridge, is arguably one of the prettiest buildings in Punjab. Inside the lavishly decorated interior is a gallery displaying royal treasures including paintings, coins, medallions and various finely crafted objects of art. The tree-shaded parks fronting the mansion boast some exquisite marble statues of kings and queens, including a larger-than-life 1903 sculpture of Queen Victoria by noted British sculptor Francis Derwent Wood.

Sleeping & Eating

★ **Baradari Palace** HERITAGE HOTEL $$$
(☎0175-2304433; www.neemranahotels.com; Baradari Gardens; d from ₹6440; ❄📶) Built as a garden palace for Maharaja Rajinder Singh, this nostalgic heritage hotel is undoubtedly Punjab's most graceful place to spend a night. The artfully restored rooms are an exercise in luxury and classy aesthetics, while the mansion's stately terraces and grand patios overlook elegant gardens. It's a 20-minute walk west from the bus stand, or a ₹50 cycle-rickshaw ride.

Gopal's NORTH INDIAN $
(Lower Mall Rd; mains ₹60-120; ⏰8am-10pm; 🌿) This popular vegetarian eatery prides itself on delicious servings of *chhole bhature*, thalis and sweetmeats that are wolfed down by eager diners through the day. There's some passable pan-Indian and quasi-Chinese stuff also served on the side, but you're better off sticking to the signature dishes.

Getting There & Away

Frequent buses run from Patiala to Chandigarh (₹70, two hours), Amritsar (₹230, five hours), Sirhind (₹40, one hour) and Anandpur Sahib (₹120, three hours). A reserved taxi from Amritsar will do a day trip to Patiala for ₹2500.

Sirhind

An easy day trip from Chandigarh, Sirhind (surr-hind) is famous for the **Gurdwara Fatehgarh Sahib**, which commemorates the 1704 martyrdom of the two youngest sons of the 10th Sikh guru, Gobind Singh, entombed alive by the Mughals for refusing to convert to Islam. The gurdwara hosts the three-day **Shaheedi Jor Mela** held every December. Remove your shoes and cover your hair when visiting.

Sirhind also has several forlorn relics from Mughal times. The **Rauza Sharif**, mausoleum of Sufi saint Shaikh Ahmad Faruqi Sirhindi, draws pilgrims during the **Urs** festival in August. Down a lane closer to the bus stand, the dilapidated **Aam Khas Bagh** was once a grand Mughal garden with an enormous *baoli* (step-well) and offers some interesting photo ops and pleasant encounters with local people.

Getting There & Away

Buses connect Sirhind with Patiala (₹40, one hour) and Chandigarh (₹50, 1½ hours), although they leave from different parts of town. Shared autorickshaws link Gurdwara Fatehgarh Sahib with Sirhind's Chandigarh bus stand (per person ₹10) and its Patiala bus stand (per person ₹10).

India-Pakistan Border At Attari-Wagah

Because of the tense relations between India and Pakistan, few foreigners actually cross the border between Attari and Wagah, 30km west of Amritsar. However, plenty of people come to watch the curious border-closing ceremony every evening at the Attari-Wagah Border Checkpost.

Sights

Border-Closing Ceremony GATE
(Attari-Wagah) Every afternoon, just before sunset, members of the Indian and Pakistani border guards meet at the border post between Attari and Wagah to engage in a 30-minute display of military showmanship that verges on pure theatre. Officially, the purpose of the ceremony is to lower the national flag and formally close the border for the night, but what actually occurs is a bizarre mix of pseudo-formal and competitive marching, flag-folding, chest beating, forceful stomping and almost comical high-stepping.

Getting There & Away

Buses run from Amritsar to Attari (₹30), from where it's a 2km walk to the customs post (or ₹10 in a shared autorickshaw). The border ceremony is held a few hundred metres beyond the

BORDER CROSSING – PAKISTAN

Border Hours

Despite official opening hours, you should confirm the **border** (Attari-Wagah; ⊙10am-3.30pm) is open at all before you leave Amritsar. Also, arrive at least an hour before the border closes.

Foreign Exchange

There are banks with moneychanging facilities and ATMs on both sides of the border, but it's wise to also change some money in Amritsar first.

Onward Transport

From Wagah in Pakistan, there are frequent buses and taxis to Lahore, 30km away.

Visas

Visas are theoretically available at the Pakistan embassy in Delhi. However, it is almost always easier to obtain a Pakistan visa in your home country.

customs post. Note that for spectators, cameras are permitted but bags, large and small, are banned. Lockers (₹50) are available beside the entrance gate.

Most people arrange a taxi with their hotel in Amritsar, which can be chartered for ₹1500. Alternately, you can take a shared taxi from the southeast gate of the Golden Temple (₹250 per person). Just hang out around the prepaid taxi booth sometime before 3pm and drivers will find you.

Pathankot

☎0186 / POPULATION 148,500

The dusty frontier town of Pathankot is merely a transport hub for the neighbouring states of Himachal Pradesh and Jammu & Kashmir, and there's little here to make you linger.

The Pathankot bus station has a **guesthouse** (r ₹500) featuring very basic rooms and a common shower room. Just outside the bus station, **Hotel Comfort** (☎0186-2226403; Gurdaspur Rd; d from ₹1890; ❄) is perhaps the best place to stay if you're planning a quick and convenient exit from Pathankot the following morning.

The Pathankot bus station has a few simple restaurants catering to passengers in transit that serve cheap but tasty local North Indian fare through the day. Expect to pay between ₹60 and ₹100 for a quick meal.

There's a **Himachal Tourism booth** (☎0186-2220316; ⊙10am-5pm Mon-Sat) at Pathankot Junction train station, with relevant tourist information on the neighbouring state.

Getting There & Away

From Pathankot Junction train station on Gurdaspur Rd there are 12 daily trains to Amritsar (2nd class/AC chair ₹65/260, two to three hours) from 4.15am to 11.50pm. Ten daily trains leave for New Delhi (sleeper/3AC/2AC ₹285/765/1095, eight hours) between 2.20am and 8.05pm.

For Dharamsala and McLeod Ganj, four daytime trains run along the narrow-gauge line to Kangra Mandir (seat ₹35, five hours), leaving at 6.45am, 10am, 1.20pm and 3.50pm.

From the bus station, also on Gurdaspur Rd, there are three or four direct buses for McLeod Ganj (₹170, 4½ hours) each morning, or you could go via Dharamsala (₹150, four hours). There are frequent bus services through the day to Amritsar (₹100, three hours), Chandigarh (₹280, six hours), Dalhousie (₹110, 3½ hours), Delhi (ordinary/Volvo AC ₹520/1140, 11 hours), Jammu (₹100, three hours) and Manali (₹390, 11 hours).

Bathinda

☎0164 / POPULATION 218,000

Bathinda is a quiet, friendly town that sees few foreign tourists (or even domestic tourists for that matter). However, the bazaars around the bus station are fun to wander through, and you can also stop by at the auction centres where farmers gather on select days to sell their agricultural produce.

Sights

Govindgarh FORT

(⊙dawn-dusk) FREE Of all the ruined forts in Punjab, Bathinda's Govindgarh is the mightiest and most impressive. It's also one of the oldest, dating way back to the 7th century, although rebuilt in its current red-brick form during the 12th century. It's an enormous structure, located bang in the middle of the city, and an unexpected highlight of a visit to this region. The fort's 36m-tall, 6m-thick walls tower over the old city bazaars and – best of all – can be freely explored.

Unlike other ancient forts in the region, Govindgarh has two gurdwaras and is thus always open to the public. Besides visiting the gurdwaras themselves, you can wander the lawned gardens within the walls and even climb up to a spot on the ramparts for magnificent views of the city. Don't miss walking around the outside of the fort to the western face, where the immense walls are at their most impressive, towering above dhobi-wallahs (clothes washers) and cotton-loomers working on the dusty streets below.

To get to the fort, turn left out of the bus station, then left at the roundabout and keep walking straight for about 1km.

Sleeping

Hotel Appreciate HOTEL $
(0164-3201875; d from ₹1650;) Hotel Appreciate promises the best value among a bunch of hotels near the bus station. Behind the property's Lego-like facade are simple AC rooms with hot showers and clean sheets.

Hotel Stella BUSINESS HOTEL $$$
(0164-5015000; Barnala Bypass Rd; d incl breakfast from ₹4600;) Very upscale by Bathinda's standards, this fancy business hotel offers new-age creature comforts in its smartly appointed rooms, while the terrace pool and bar are definite draws on idle evenings. There's a good restaurant serving delicious Punjabi and pan-Indian food. It's located about 2km north of the bus stand.

Eating

Sagar Ratna SOUTH INDIAN $
(GT Rd; mains ₹80-120; 11am-10pm;) For a pleasant departure from local Punjabi flavours, try one of the many dosas at this authentic South Indian restaurant located on the main drag. There's good South Indian coffee to go with your meal of choice.

Yellow Chilli MODERN INDIAN $$
(Barnala Bypass Rd; mains ₹150-300; noon-3pm & 7-11pm;) New-age Indian cuisine comes to Bathinda in the form of imaginative dishes designed by a celebrity chef at this stylish restaurant. It's a good place to order fish and meat dishes in town.

Getting There & Away

Ten daily trains leave for New Delhi (sleeper/3AC ₹200/490, 5½ to seven hours) round the clock. Five daytime trains go to Patiala (2nd class/AC chair ₹80/260, three hours) between 6.30am and 5.50pm.

Frequent buses go to Amritsar (₹180, four hours), Chandigarh (non-AC/AC ₹250/480, five hours), Faridkot (₹70, 1½ hours) and Patiala (₹170, three hours).

Faridkot

Faridkot was the capital of a once glorious Sikh state that has all but vanished over time. It's one of Punjab's least visited towns, and remains well off the beaten tourist track.

Today, peacocks stalk the faded battlements of the once mighty **Qila Mubarak**, a fort protected by 15m-high walls, which was the ancestral home of the maharajas of Faridkot. Nearby, the **Tilla Baba Farid Ji** is a recent rebuild of an age-old gurdwara, dedicated to the 13th-century Sufi poet Baba Sheikh Farid, whose poems were an inspiration for Guru Nanak, founder of Sikhism. Also in town is the **Raj Mahal**, the current residence of the former royal family, who moved here from the fort in the 1880s. There's also the beautiful, 30m-tall, French-designed **Victoria Clock Tower** (c 1902), as well as the attractive pastel-green **District Library**.

There are a few hotels about a 750m walk from the bus station. Turn left out of the bus station, left at the roundabout, then first right and you'll soon reach them all.

You'll find a few around-the-clock eateries serving *parathas* and local fare on the crowded streets around the bus station, as well as restaurants at both **Hotel Trump Plaza** (9216800789; Kotkapura Rd; d from ₹1650;) and **Sangam Hotel & Restaurant** (01639-252144; Kotkapura Rd; d from ₹1420;).

There's a beer bar at the Hotel Trump Plaza.

Getting There & Away

Frequent buses run from Faridkot to Amritsar (₹120, three hours), Bathinda (₹70, 1½ hours), Chandigarh (₹240, five hours) and Patiala (₹120, two hours).

Kapurthala

Once the capital of a wealthy independent state, Kapurthala is an unusual place to explore. The resident maharaja, Jagatjit Singh, was a travel junkie – he married Spanish flamenco dancer Anita Delgado and constructed numerous buildings inspired by his travels.

The **Jagatjit Palace** (now the exclusive Sainik School) was modelled on Versailles, while the **Moorish Mosque** copies the Grand Mosque in Marrakesh (Morocco). Other buildings of note include the British-style **Jagatjit Club** and **Jubilee Hall**, and the **Shalimar Gardens** (containing the cenotaphs of the Kapurthala royal dynasty).

Located on Sultanpur Rd, **Hotel Ramneek** (☎9781322478; Sultanpur Rd; d from ₹1650) ranks a few notches above Kapurthala's other budget hotels. There are some decent AC rooms at **Hotel Royal** (☎01822-505110; Jallandhar Rd; d from ₹1100; ❄), 200m from the bus stand.

There are several proletarian eateries in town serving tasty *paratha*-yoghurt breakfasts and dhal-roti-pickle meals, as well as the restaurants found at Hotel Ramneek and Hotel Royal.

There's a beer bar at Hotel Ramneek.

Getting There & Away

To get to Amritsar from Kapurthala, you need to take a bus to Subhanpur (₹10, 30 minutes) then change for Amritsar (₹60, 1½ hours). There are four morning buses to Faridkot (₹120, 2½ hours) between 6am and 10.30am.

HARYANA

Bordering India's national capital of Delhi to the west and northwest, burgeoning Haryana was the setting for several pivotal events through the history of northern India. Nonetheless, between its vast agricultural expanses and booming industrial hot spots, modern Haryana is home to very few sights that truly appeal to foreign tourists. Barring a few destinations of specific interest, most of the state lies beyond the tourism radar.

Kurukshetra (Thanesar)

☎01744 / POPULATION 964,200

According to Hindu legend, Kurukshetra (formerly Thanesar) was where Lord Brahma created the universe, and where Lord Krishna delivered his Bhagavad Gita sermon before the epic 18-day Mahabharata battle, an event commemorated by the Gita Jayanti (p203) festival. Given its religious and mythological significance, the town is mobbed by pilgrims, sadhus and educational tour groups, who vastly outnumber the few tourists.

English maps of the area are available at the ticket counter of the Sri Krishna Museum and are available for free with every purchased museum ticket.

Sights

Brahmasarovar HISTORIC SITE

FREE The focus of attention at Kurukshetra is the sacred Brahmasarovar, India's largest ceremonial tank. According to Hindu holy texts, the ghat-flanked tank was created by Lord Brahma. Sadhus crowd the ghats through the day, while the ashrams beside the tank feature scenes from Hindu epics and walk-through models of sacred sites. A giant modern sculpture, depicting Lord Krishna imparting the Bhagavad Gita sermons to Arjuna in the Mahabharata, stands tall in a park central to the complex.

Sheikh Chehli's Tomb TOMB

(Indian/foreigner ₹5/100; ⊙9am-5pm) The impressive mausoleum of 17th-century Sufi mystic Sheikh Chehli, who provided spiritual guidance for the Mughal prince Dara Shikoh, lies in a quaint neighbourhood about 2km northwest of the town centre. Behind the brick and sandstone tomb, and predating it by more than a thousand years, is a raised mound known as **Harsh Ka Tilla**, where you can view excavated, 7th-century ruins from historical Thanesar. The ruins stretch for about 1km.

Sri Krishna Museum MUSEUM

(Pehowa Rd; ₹30; ⊙10am-5pm) The Sri Krishna Museum features an impressive collection of sculptures, carvings and paintings, and a low-tech multimedia exhibition with dioramas, giant statues, surreal sounds and a walk-through maze. Look out for some rare exhibits, such as palm-leaf etchings from Orissa and excavated artefacts from ancient Indus Valley settlements. There's a simple canteen (veg thali ₹80, chai ₹10) with alfresco seating in the museum gardens.

Sleeping & Eating

Yatri Niwas HOTEL $$

(☎01744-291615; Pipli-Jyotisar Rd; d from ₹1750; ❄) Fronted by a grassy lawn, this whitewashed standard-issue government complex has unimaginative but well-appointed rooms assuring adequate value for money, as well as service and security to match. Food (veg thalis ₹130) at the in-house restaurant is recommended, and day trippers can also step in for meals. The property is a five-minute walk north of Brahmasarovar.

Getting There & Around

Local buses between Chandigarh (₹90, two hours) and Delhi (₹160, four hours) stop at Pipli on the national highway, about 6km outside Kurukshetra. From here, shared autorickshaws (₹20) shuttle passengers between the bus stand and Brahmasarovar.

You can hire a rickshaw for about ₹300 to show you the major sights in town.

Sultanpur Bird Sanctuary

About 48km southwest of Delhi, thrown around scattered wetlands, the Sultanpur Bird Sanctuary is a 145-hectare national park that plays host to more than 250 resident and migratory bird species.

Sights

Sultanpur Bird Sanctuary NATURE RESERVE
(Indian/foreigner ₹5/40, camera/video ₹25/500; 7am-4.30pm Wed-Mon) Many of the bird species that frequent this park come from faraway countries such as Russia, China and Afghanistan. The more recognisable ones include the Siberian crane, painted and black-necked storks, greater and lesser flamingos, common teal, yellow parakeet and black-headed ibis. The best season to view these feathered creatures is from October to March. A relaxed birdwatching tour of the sanctuary can take up to three hours.

Sleeping

Bird Sanctuary Tourist Complex HOTEL $$
(0124-2375242; d from ₹1750;) Adjacent to the park fence and set in a quasi-forested landscape, this tourist complex operated by Haryana Tourism features a mix of decent to pleasant rooms and can be a quiet and relaxed place to spend a night. The complex has an in-house restaurant that serves snacks and meals, including to day visitors with prior notice.

Getting There & Around

Public transport is limited in the area. From Delhi, it's much easier to hire a taxi for a day trip (around ₹1800). Leave early to escape the insufferable traffic that builds up along the way during rush hour.

Surajkund

Some 20km south of downtown Delhi, Surajkund is named after the 10th-century **sun pool** that was built here by Raja Surajpal, leader of the sun-worshipping Tomar clan. The village is mobbed for the annual two-week Surajkund Crafts Mela in February, but sees few visitors at other times.

Festivals & Events

Surajkund Crafts Mela FAIR
(1-15 Feb) A splendid congregation of folk artists, artisans, musicians and dancers from across North India, this vibrant crafts fair is a great place to acquaint yourself with the region's living artistic and folk traditions. It's also a convenient place to shop for good-quality handicrafts and other souvenirs. Food stalls and cultural performances only add to the variety of entertainment available.

Sleeping

★ **Vivanta By Taj** HOTEL $$$
(0129-4190000; www.vivanta.tajhotels.com; Shooting Range Rd; d from ₹8400;) A clear favourite among the few luxury addresses in close proximity to the Surajkund fairground, this smart and stylish hotel has ultra-comfortable rooms overlooking ample manicured greenery. The infinity pool could easily rank among India's best, while the lavish spa is the perfect place to spend the lazy afternoon hours.

Getting There & Around

Special buses operated by **Haryana Tourism** (011-23324911; www.haryanatourism.gov.in; 36 Chander Lok Building, Janpath) run to Surajkund from Delhi through the duration of the crafts fair. At other times, local buses (₹10) run from Badarpur, accessible from Delhi by metro. A day trip from Delhi by taxi costs around ₹1000.

Jammu & Kashmir (including Ladakh)

Includes ➡

Best Places to Eat

- Alchi Kitchen (p257)
- Bon Appetit (p240)
- Food Planet (p239)
- Falak (p280)
- Café Cloud (p247)

Best Places to Sleep

- Stok Palace Heritage Hotel (p244)
- Srinagar Houseboats (p270)
- Nimmu House (p256)
- Khyber Himalayan Resort & Spa (p276)
- Hidden North Guest House (p255)

Why Go?

The state of Jammu & Kashmir (J&K) brings together three incredibly different worlds. Hindu Jammu and Katra, in the south, are the state's rail hubs and a major draw for domestic pilgrims. Muslim Kashmir is India's Switzerland, attracting hordes of local tourists seeking cool summer air, alpine scenery and Srinagar's romantic houseboat accommodation. And then there's the Himalayan land of Ladakh, which for most foreigners is J&K's greatest attraction. Its disarmingly friendly, ethno-linguistically Tibetan people are predominantly Buddhist; their timeless monasteries are set between arid canyons and soaring peaks, while emerald-green villages nestle photogenically in highland deserts.

Kashmir is politically volatile, with July and August often the 'season' for shutdowns, demonstrations and curfews. Indeed, arguments over Kashmir's status caused three 20th-century wars. Ladakh is altogether different, a calm place where your main concern will be high-altitude acclimatisation.

When to Go

Leh

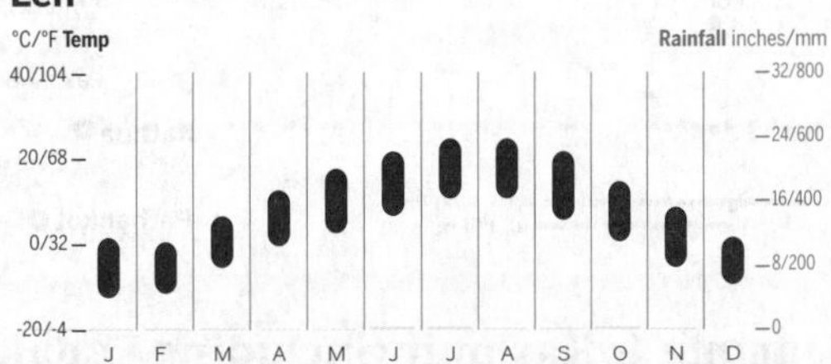

Apr–Jun Kashmir is in full bloom but overloaded with domestic tourists. Prices peak.

Jul–Aug Perfect for Ladakh; rain drenches Jammu. Pilgrims flood to Amarnath.

Dec–Mar Ski season at Gulmarg. Ladakh has festivals but no road access or tourists.

Jammu & Kashmir (including Ladakh) Highlights

❶ **Indus Valley monasteries** (p245) Murmuring meditative mantras in mural-decked gompas (Tibetan Buddhist monasteries) such as Chemrey or Thiksey.

❷ **Markha Valley** (p248) Experiencing the stark magnificence of Ladakh with a hassle-free (and traffic-free) homestay trek.

❸ **Srinagar** (p270) Enjoying an amusingly caricatured Raj-type experience relaxing on a deluxe Dal Lake houseboat.

❹ **Pangong Tso** Gawking at the mountain scenery backing this surreally blue lake.

❺ **Yapola Gorge** (p257) Discovering a thrillingly dramatic canyon en route to the breathtaking Sengge La.

❻ **Leh** (p229) Escaping India's humid summer heat in the dusty medieval backstreets and Potala-style palace of this entrancing traveller hub.

❼ **K3** (p280) Trailblazing the 'world's most dangerous road', the route from Kishtwar to Keylong.

LADAKH

Spectacularly jagged, arid mountains enfold this magical Buddhist ex-kingdom. Picture-perfect gompas (Tibetan Buddhist monasteries) dramatically crown rocky outcrops amid whitewashed stupas and *mani* walls. Colourful fluttering prayer flags share their spiritual messages metaphorically with the mountain breeze. Prayer wheels spun clockwise release more merit-making mantras. Gompa interiors are colourfully awash with the murals and statuary of countless bodhisattvas.

Though threatened by a rapidly increasing number of visitors, Ladakh has much to teach the West regarding ecological awareness. Most Ladakhis are cash poor yet their traditional mudbrick homesteads are large and virtually self-sufficient in fuel and dairy products, organic vegetables, and barley used to make *tsampa* (roast barley flour) and *chhang* (barley beer).

The walls of dramatic mountains that hem in Ladakh make for an unforgettable landscape, but be aware that road access requires crossing tortuous high passes, which close from around October to May (or longer when snows are heavy).

History

Ladakh's (now-deposed) royal family traces its dynasty back 39 generations to AD 975. They took the name Namgyal (Victorious) in 1470 when their progenitor Lhachen Bhagan, ruling from Basgo (p256), conquered a competing Ladakhi kingdom based at Shey (p245). Although Ladakh had been culturally 'Tibetanised' in the 9th century, Buddhism originally arrived in an Indian form that's visible in ancient temple artisanship at Alchi (p257). Over time, however, different Buddhist sects struggled for prominence, with the Tibetan Gelukpa order eventually becoming the majority philosophy after its introduction in the 14th century by Tibetan pilgrim Tsongkhapa, who left a curious relic at Spituk (p231).

Ladakh's great 'lion king', Sengge Namgyal (r 1616–42) gained riches by plundering gold reserves from western Tibet and re-established a capital at Leh. Ladakh remained an independent kingdom until the 1840s when the region was annexed by the Jammu maharajas. The Namgyals eventually passed Leh Palace to the Indian Archaeological Survey and retired to their summer palace at Stok (p244).

Ladakh is now a pair of sub-districts within Jammu and Kashmir. That's a culturally odd situation for this 'little Tibet', which is one of the last Tantric Buddhist societies on Earth. When tourism was first permitted in 1974 commentators feared that the area would quickly lose its identity. But for decades the traditional lifestyle of the Ladakhis proved unexpectedly robust to outside influences, aided partly by the area's seasonal inaccessibility. Meanwhile, locally relevant technologies, such as solar energy and Trombe thermal-storage walls, have helped to improve rural living standards.

In the last decade, change has accelerated as road construction brings accessibility to once isolated villages. In 2010 Ladakh was ravaged by an unseasonable cloudburst.

TOP STATE FESTIVALS

Western J&K has numerous Hindu pilgrimages. In Ladakh and Zanskar, Buddhist temple festivals abound; www.reachladakh.com has a detailed festival calendar.

Dosmoche (Feb-early Mar; Leh, Diskit, Likir) Buddhist New Year. Masked dances; effigies representing the evil spirits of the old year are burnt or cast into the desert.

Matho Nagrang (p245; Feb-Mar; Matho) Monastery oracles perform blindfolded acrobatics and ritual mutilations.

Amarnathji Yatra (p277; Jul–mid-Aug; Amarnath) Hindu pilgrims' mountain trek to Armanath.

Ladakh Festival (20-24 Sep; Leh) Events include a carnivalesque opening parade, Buddhist dances, polo, music and archery.

Losar (Dec; Ladakh, Zanskar) Tibetan New Year is celebrated two months earlier in Ladakh.

Chandi Mata Yatra (Aug) Tens of thousands make the scenic two-day hike (or seven-minute helicopter ride) to Machail.

Flash floods washed away whole sections of Leh, graphically illustrating Ladakh's vulnerability to climate change.

Climate

Ladakh's short tourist season (July to early September) typically sees mild to hot T-shirt weather by day and pleasant, occasionally chilly nights. Early July is great for flowers and peaks are still dusted with snow, but August is better for high passes, which can still be snowbound into mid-July. On higher treks night-time temperatures can dip below 0°C even in midsummer. By September snow is likely on higher ground although major passes usually stay open until October. Access roads close entirely in winter when temperatures can fall below -20°C and most tourist infrastructure shuts down.

Ladakh enjoys sunshine an average of 300 days a year, but storms can brew suddenly.

Language

Though they use the same script, the Tibetan and Ladakhi languages are significantly different. The wonderfully all-purpose word *jule* (pronounced '*joo*-lay') means 'hello', 'goodbye', 'please' and 'thanks'. To the greeting *khamzang*, simply reply *khamzang*. *Zhimpo-rak* means 'It's delicious'.

Rebecca Norman's excellent *Getting Started in Ladakhi* (₹200) has plenty more phrases and useful cultural tips.

Leh

☎01982 / POP 46,300 / ELEV 3520M

Few places in India are at once so traveller-friendly and yet so enchanting and hassle-free as mountain-framed Leh. Dotted with stupas and crumbling mudbrick houses, the Old Town is dominated by a dagger of steep rocky ridge topped by an imposing Tibetan-style palace and fort. Beneath, the bustling bazaar area is draped in a thick veneer of tour agencies, souvenir shops and tandoori-pizza restaurants, but a web of lanes quickly fans out into a green suburban patchwork of irrigated barley fields. Here, gushing streams and narrow footpaths link traditionally styled Ladakhi homes and hotels that feature flat roofs, sturdy walls and ornate wooden window frames. Leh's a place that's all too easy to fall in love with – but take things very easy on arrival as the altitude requires a few days' acclimatisation before you can safely start enjoying the area's gamut of adventure activities.

Sights

Central Leh

★Leh Palace PALACE

(Map p230; Indian/foreigner ₹10/200; ⌚dawn-dusk) Bearing a passing similarity to the Potala Palace in Lhasa (Tibet), this nine-storey dun-coloured edifice is Leh's dominant structure and architectural icon. It took shape under 17th-century king Singge Namgyal but has been essentially unoccupied since the Ladakhi royals were stripped of power and shuffled off to Stok in 1846. Today the sturdy walls enclose some exhibition spaces and a small prayer room, but the most enjoyable part of a visit is venturing to the uppermost rooftops for the view.

Interesting structures ranged around the palace's base include the prominent **Namgyal Stupa** (Map p230), the colourfully muralled **Chandazik Gompa** (Chenrezi Lhakhang; Map p230; ₹30; ⌚approx 8am-6pm) and the 1430 **Chamba Lhakhang** (Map p230) with medieval mural fragments between the inner and outer walls. Don't count on any of these being open though.

Leh Old Town AREA

Behind Leh's fanciful Sunni men's mosque, **Jamia Masjid** (Map p230; Main Bazaar), winding alleys and stairways burrow between and beneath a series of old mudbrick Ladakhi houses and eroded chortens. The alleys themselves are a large part of the attraction, but some buildings have been particularly well restored, notably the pair of 17th-century mansions now housing **LAMO** (Ladakh Arts & Media Organisation; Map p230; ☎01982-251554; www.lamo.org.in; with/without tour ₹100/50; ⌚11am-5pm Mon-Sat) arts centre.

Central Asian Museum MUSEUM

(Map p230; www.tibetheritagefund.org; suggested donation ₹50; ⌚hours vary) One of Leh's most remarkable buildings, this tapered four-storey stone tower is a 21st-century construction based on a historic Lhasa mansion, with the added flourish of a fortress-style drawbridge. Inside, exhibits are relatively limited but the top floor Faces of Ladakh mini-photoessays are thought-provoking.

Chokhang Vihara BUDDHIST TEMPLE

(Map p230; Main Bazaar; ⌚approx 5am-8pm) With its coppiced willows, the large courtyard of this 20th-century temple offers an oasis of relatively meditative calm just steps from the bustle of Main Bazaar. Inside, a

Central Leh

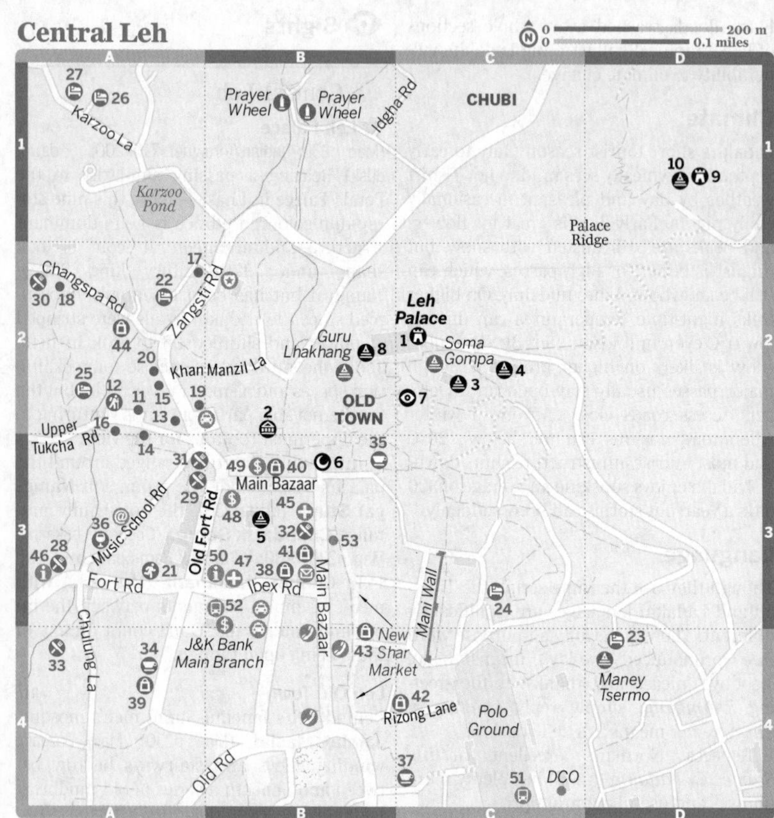

monk keeps up his high-speed chant while blessing the prayer flags and pennants of arriving supplicants.

Tsemo Fort CASTLE

(Map p230; ₹20; ⏲10am-6pm) Visible from virtually everywhere in Leh, 16th-century Tsemo (Victory) Fort is a defining landmark that crowns the top of Palace Ridge, though there's little to see inside apart from a tiny Buddhist shrine. Directly beneath, **Tsemo Gompa** (Map p230; ₹30; ⏲7.30am-6pm) consists of two little 15th-century temple buildings. One enshrines an 8m-tall gold-faced Maitreya. The other is an atmospheric *gonkhang,* home of protector deities.

Greater Leh

Gomang Stupa BUDDHIST MONUMENT

(Map p234) This 9th-century whitewashed stupa rises in concentric serrated layers flanked by numerous chortens. Recent restoration masks its aura of great antiquity but its peaceful, shady setting remains a refreshingly spiritual escape from the tourist-centric developments of surrounding Changspa.

Shanti Stupa BUDDHIST MONUMENT, VIEWPOINT

(Map p234; ⏲dawn-9pm) Dominating Leh from a high, rocky ridge, this gigantic white spired pudding of a stupa was built between 1983 and 1991 by Japanese monks to promote world peace.

Sankar AREA

(Map p234) For a charming wander, follow canal streams in the captivating yet relatively accessible area around little **Sankar Gompa** (₹30) and the one-room **geological museum** (☎9419178704; www.ladakhrocksminerals.com; ₹50; ⏲10.30am-1pm & 2-7pm May-Aug). For memorable views, continue about 1km uphill to the laudable **Donkey Sanctuary** (☎Tsering Motup 8492812133; www.donkeysanctuary.in; Korean Temple Rd) or the nearby 11th-century **Tisseru**

Central Leh

Top Sights

1 Leh Palace C2

Sights

2 Central Asian Museum B2
3 Chamba Lhakhang C2
4 Chandazik Gompa C2
5 Chokhang Vihara B3
6 Jamia Masjid B3
7 LAMO C2
8 Namgyal Stupa B2
9 Tsemo Fort D1
10 Tsemo Gompa D1

Activities, Courses & Tours

11 Gesar Travel A2
GraviT ..... (see 28)
12 Hemis National Park Guide Service A2
Hidden North Adventures ..... (see 31)
13 Higher Himalaya A2
Ladakh Mitra ..... (see 14)
14 Ladakhi Women's Travel Company A3
15 Luna Ladakh A2
16 Open Ladakh A2
17 Rimo A2
18 Shayok Tours & Travels A2
19 Splash Adventures A2
20 Summer Holidays A2
21 Wet'n'Wild A3
Wild East Adventure ..... (see 11)

Sleeping

22 Kang-Lha-Chen A2
23 Namgyal Guest House D4
24 Palace View Guest House C3
25 Saiman Guest House A2
26 Saser A1
27 Travellers' House A1

Eating

28 Chopsticks A3
29 Il Forno A3
30 La Piazzetta A2
31 Ladakh Café A3
Ladakhi Food ..... (see 16)
32 Neha Snacks B3
33 Penguin Garden A4

Drinking & Nightlife

34 Ja Khang A4
35 Lala's Art Cafe B3
36 Lehchen A3
37 Tololing Tea Stall C4

Shopping

Dzomsa ..... (see 31)
38 Indus Wine Shop B3
39 Jigmat Couture A4
40 Ladakh Bookshop B3
41 Lehling Bookshop & Cafe B3
42 Norbulingka C4
43 Nowshera Bazaar B4
Tibetan Refugee Market ..... (see 15)
44 Venture Ladakh A2

Information

45 Het Ram Vinay Kumar Pharmacy B3
46 Mantra Travel Lounge A3
47 Oxygen Bar B3
48 Paul Merchant B3
49 SBI ATM B3
50 Tourist office B3

Transport

51 Buses to Kargil C4
HPTDC ..... (see 21)
52 HPTDC Buses Departure Point B3
53 Jet Airways B3

Stupa (Tisuru Rd, Upper Leh) FREE, a bulky, partly restored mudbrick ruin that looks like a half-built ziggurat (stepped pyramid).

Out of Town

Spituk Gompa BUDDHIST MONASTERY

(Pethub Galdan Targailing Monastery; 01982-260036; www.spitukmonastery.org; Spituk; suggested donation ₹30-50; 7am-6.30pm) Founded in the late 14th century as See-Thub ('Exemplary') Monastery, impressive Spituk Gompa surveys the Indus Valley with multiple mudbrick buildings tumbling merrily down a steep hillock towards Spituk village. For fine views, it's worth climbing the exterior stairway to the three-tiered *latho* (spirit shrine) and **gonkhang** (7am-6.30pm), which holds the monastery's guardian deities.

Hall of Fame MUSEUM

(Leh-Spituk hwy Km428; Indian/foreigner/camera ₹25/50/50; 9am-1pm & 2-7pm) Two rooms of this extensive, well-presented museum look at Ladakhi history and culture. But mostly it commemorates the Indian Army's role in Ladakh, from helping with cloudburst relief in 2010 to the high-altitude battles fought with Pakistan during the 20th century. A 30-minute film introduces the 1999 Kargil War.

3D Mandala BUDDHIST SITE

(Trans Himalayan Cultural Centre) A truly vast Wheel-of-Life mandala, the size of a football pitch, is under fitful construction at the northern edge of town. Site access is off the road that leads to pretty, unspoilt Gonpa Village (p232). But for a better view, look down from the Nubra Hwy at around Km6.

Gonpa Village VILLAGE

Almost entirely off the radar of visitors, this photogenic knot of traditional houses and minor Buddhist monuments is around 4km north of central Leh. There is a small gompa above the TV tower and a chorten on the cairn-speckled ridge-top above that. Excellent views.

Activities

Cycling

An exhilarating yet almost effortless way to enjoy the fabulous scenery around Leh is the **Khardung La roll-down**, where a jeep takes you and a bicycle up to the 'world's highest road pass' and gravity brings you back down. Potholes and streams in the uppermost 14km (above South Pullu army camp) mean it's (arguably) better to skip the top section and simply whizz down the last 25km to Leh on smoothly paved new asphalt. Depending on group size, packages cost between ₹1000 and ₹1500 per person including bicycle hire and support vehicle.

A permit is technically required for the upper section of the pass but occasionally companies talk their way round this and we were never asked for paperwork. Book one day ahead through **Summer Holidays** (Map p230; 9906985822; www.mtbladakh.com; Zangsti Rd) or **Himalayan Bikers** (Map p234; 9469049270, 9906989109; www.himalayan-bikers.com; Changspa; 7.30am-9.30pm late-May–mid-Sep). Both also rent mountain bikes (₹500 to ₹700 per day).

Meditation & Yoga

Various yoga, reiki and meditation places pop up each summer: look along Changspa Rd for fliers. The **Mahabodhi Centre** (Map p234; 01982-251162; www.mahabodhi-ladakh.org; Changspa Rd; Mon-Sat May–mid-Sep) is longer established and has a range of drop-in sessions. It and **Open Ladakh** (Map p230; 9419983126, 9906981026; www.openladakh.com; unit 23-24, Hemis Complex, Upper Tukcha Rd) offer longer retreats at Choglamsar and Stok respectively.

Mountaineering

Ladakh has 118 'open' peaks above 6000m, many of which are rarely, if ever, scaled. For a list, see www.indmount.org/openpeaks-jandk.aspx. A popular destination is 6121m **Stok Kangri** (Kanglha-jhal; Jun-Aug), the triangular snowcapped 'trekking peak' usually visible straight across the valley from Leh. Although accessible to those with minimal climbing experience, scaling its uppermost slopes requires ice axes, ropes, crampons, considerable fitness and an experienced guide. Pre-climb acclimatisation is essential as AMS can be a serious worry. Permits are required (Indian/foreigner free/US$50). From Stok, the well-organised agency **Ladakh Mitra** (Map p230; 9419999830, 9596929195; www.ladakhmitra.com; 1st, fl, unit 17, Hemis Complex, Upper Tukcha Rd; 10am-7pm May–mid-Oct) runs a series of tent camps en route, so you can ascend with minimal baggage. Assuming at least four in a group, six-day packages typically start at ₹16,000/19,000 for Indians/foreigners including permits, food, sleeping, climbing gear and transport. Climbing alone with a personal guide costs ₹27,000/30,000, and not much less for a group of two or three. Bring your own gloves, head torch and sunglasses.

A good place to meet fellow climbers or to exercise your grips is the small bouldering-cafe **GraviT** (Map p230; www.facebook.com/GraviT.Leh; 2nd fl, Raku Complex, Fort Rd; climbing wall per hr ₹80, excursions per day ₹2000; 4-8.30pm), which also organises Sunday expeditions to local climbing spots near Shey plus the annual **Suru Boulder Fest** (www.facebook.com/Suru.boulder; late Aug).

Rafting & Kayaking

In summer, numerous agencies offer daily rafting excursions through glorious canyon scenery. Experienced paddlers can follow in a kayak for around 50% extra. Expect to get very wet. Relatively easy Phey–Nimmu (grade II, beginners, mid-July to late August) typically costs ₹1200; while tougher and more picturesque Chilling–Nimmu (grade III, late June to early September) generally costs around ₹1600 including equipment and lunch (bring extra drinking water). Reliable specialist companies include **Rimo** (Map p230; 01982-253348; www.rimoriver-expeditions.com; Zangsti Rd; 5.30am-9pm Jul & Aug, 9am-5pm May, Jun & Sep), **Wet'n'Wild** (Map p230; 01982-255122, 9419819721 9622967631; www.wetnwildexplorations.com; Fort Rd; mid-May–late-Sep) and **Splash Adventures** (Map p230; 9622965941; www.splashladakh.com; Zangsti Parking), while **Luna Ladakh** (Map p230; 9419977732; www.luna-ladakh.com; Zangsti Rd; Jun-Aug) adds rafting as the finale to a package including mountain biking (Spituk–Zingchen) and trekking (Zingchen–Chilling with homestays) costing ₹16,000/20,000 for two people on a three-/four-day package. Cheaper for bigger groups.

Given enough interest, Wet'n'wild and Rimo offer group expeditions that descend the Zanskar River from Zangla to Nimmu (three days rafting, three days travel). Renowned British Himalayan river veteran Darren Clarkson-King runs full Zanskar raft packages with **Pureland Expeditions** (www.purelandexpeditions.com).

Trekking & Jeep Safaris

The range of possible treks is phenomenal. The classic multiday trek follows the utterly delightful roadless Markha Valley (p248). A one-day taster that's hard to beat is the Rumbak and Yurutse day hike (p250). Both are perfectly feasible without a guide and carrying only minimal baggage.

The most popular jeep safaris are to the high-altitude mountain lake of Pangong Tso (p253) and through beautiful Nubra Valley. You'll need an agency, if only to organise the permit, which is required by foreign visitors for many areas in northern Ladakh.

Countless agencies offer trekking packages, jeep tours, rafting, biking and permit procurement. Few are systematically bad but many are very inconsistent. A deciding factor is often which agent happens to have a group leaving on the day you need to depart. Ask fellow travellers for recent recommendations and look along Changspa Rd and the eastern end of Upper Tukcha Rd where there is a high concentration of agencies. We have found small operators **Higher Himalaya** (Map p230; ☎9419333393; www.higherhimalaya.com; Zangsti Rd), Hidden North and **Shayok** (Map p230; ☎9419342346, 9419888902; www.shayok-tours.com; Changspa Rd) to be especially honest, competitive and helpful with trekking information and as short-notice jeep-tour fixers. If you're making advance group bookings, reliable, well-established upper-market options include **Yama** (Map p234; ☎01982-257833, 9419178763, 9406228456; www.yamatreks.com; Fort Rd), **Wild East** (Map p230; ☎01982-257939; www.wildeastadventure.com; Hemis Complex, Upper Tukcha Rd) and **Gesar** (Map p230; ☎01982-251684; Hemis Complex 16, Upper Tukcha Rd).

Hidden North Adventures TREKKING
(Map p230; ☎01982-258844, 9419218055; www.hiddennorth.com; LBA Shopping Complex, Zangsti Rd DB2; ⏲mid-Mar–mid-Oct) Tashi has two decades of guiding experience and offers loads of interesting alternative trekking ideas to get you away from the typical hiking routes. Some routes start from his own guesthouse in Phyang.

Ladakhi Women's Travel Company TREKKING
(Map p230; ☎9469158137, 01982-257973; www.ladakhiwomenstravel.com; unit 22, Hemis Complex, Upper Tukcha Rd; ⏲10am-6pm) This small, highly reputable female-run operation specialises in Markha and Sham homestay trek packages. In winter it offers snow leopard-seeking trips based in Rumbak. Trips are full packages for female or mixed groups, ie male customers are only accepted if their group also includes women.

Sleeping

The choice is phenomenal and few options are dire, so don't panic if our suggestions are full. Booking ahead through online agencies is usually a bad idea as you'll likely pay double and room standards can vary significantly within each property. When possible it's worth looking at a few before checking in.

In winter the majority of accommodation closes down.

LEH – WATER & ECO-AWARENESS

Water is precious – those streams you see cascading beside virtually every lane aren't a sign of plenty but an elaborate network of irrigation channels that keep Leh from reverting to a dusty mountain desert. Anything you can do to save water is a positive step. Bucket baths save a lot compared to showers, and a few guesthouses offer traditional water-free Ladakhi long-drop toilets that recycle human waste into compost. Don't put anything nonbiodegradable down the hole: whatever goes in will end up on a farmer's field in a year or two.

Guesthouses rarely provide toilet paper (buy your own) and generally it should not be flushed: when there's a plastic bin, use it.

To save Leh from vanishing under a sea of plastic bottles, refills of purified, pressure-boiled water are provided for ₹7 per litre by environmental organisation **Dzomsa** (p241). It also has an ecofriendly laundry service (₹95 per kg) and serves locally sourced *tsestalulu* (sea buckthorn) and apricot juices that are free of packaging.

Leh

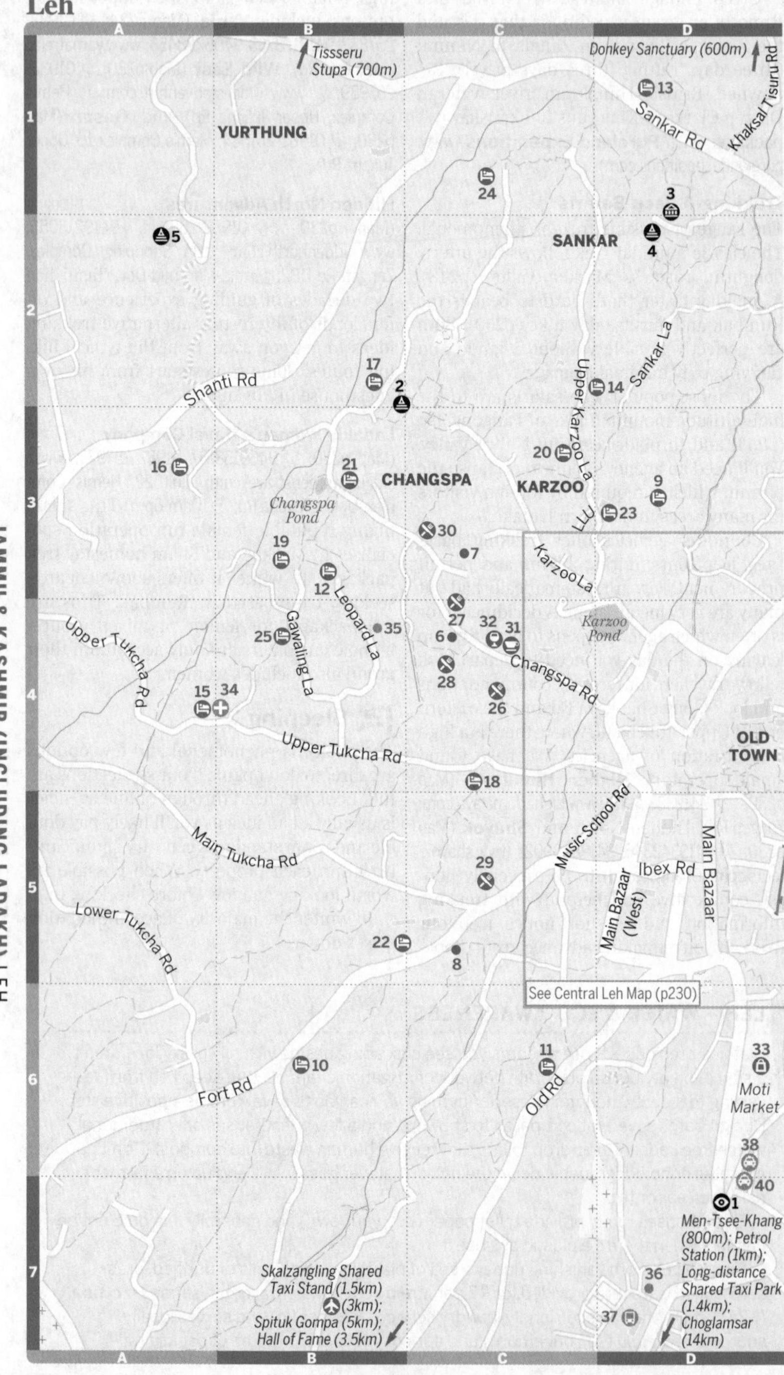

A
B
C
D
1
2
3
4
5
6
7
Tisseru Stupa (700m)
Donkey Sanctuary (600m)
Khaksal Tisuru Rd
Sankar Rd
YURTHUNG
SANKAR
Sankar La
Upper Karzoo La
Shanti Rd
CHANGSPA
KARZOO
Changspa Pond
Karzoo La
Karzoo Pond
Upper Tukcha Rd
Gawaling La
Leopard La
Changspa Rd
OLD TOWN
Music School Rd
Main Tukcha Rd
Ibex Rd
Main Bazaar (West)
Main Bazaar
Lower Tukcha Rd
See Central Leh Map (p230)
Fort Rd
Old Rd
Moti Market
Skalzangling Shared Taxi Stand (1.5km)
(3km);
Spituk Gompa (5km);
Hall of Fame (3.5km)
Men-Tsee-Khang (800m); Petrol Station (1km); Long-distance Shared Taxi Park (1.4km); Choglamsar (14km)

Try the back alleys of Upper Changspa for ultra-budget places, Upper Karzoo for garden homestay-guesthouses around the ₹800 mark, and Upper Tukcha for slightly plusher family guesthouses costing around ₹1200 with en suite. Many areas have a rash of new hotels, mostly much alike and catering predominantly to Indian tourist groups. These cost around ₹3500 to ₹5000 but in many cases, other than the spontaneous provision of towels and toilet paper, rooms aren't much better than a good guesthouse, and several are down dusty Fort Rd or inconveniently out in Skara, some 3km from the centre.

Sankar and Yurthung areas are often idyllically peaceful but are a fairly long, dark walk home from town. Taxis cost ₹150 to ₹200 by day, but disappear later at night.

Central Leh

Saiman Guest House GUESTHOUSE $
(Map p230; off Upper Tukcha Rd; r ₹700-1200, without bathroom ₹600-700; wi-fi) This outwardly unremarkable family home is a great choice thanks to spacious, sparkling-clean rooms, parasol tables on the flower-edged lawn and a small guest lounge where travellers sit to chat and use the wi-fi over thermos flasks of cardamom tea. English-speaking hostess Shahida is a mine of local information.

Namgyal Guest House GUESTHOUSE $
(Map p230; ☎01982-253307, 9906973364; r ₹700, without bathroom ₹400-500) Backing onto the mysterious Maney Tsermo Buddhist monument, this delightful budget guesthouse is run by ever-laughing Dolkar. She lives in the new annexe, where three en suite rooms have sit-down toilets and geyser showers. In the traditional Ladakhi main house, upstairs rooms are worth the ₹100 extra for higher ceilings and more light. All rooms share three toilets, one of which is sit-down but seatless.

Travellers' House GUESTHOUSE $
(Map p230; ☎01982-252048; thetravellershouse@gmail.com; Karzoo Lane; d ₹900-1200; ⊙May-early Oct; wi-fi) Eight well-kept, no-nonsense guest rooms with geyser-equipped bathrooms and well-chosen art photography face the home of the inspiringly international-minded family owners and their pet poodle. Ladakhi breakfast with homemade *khambir* (bread) is available (from ₹150).

Saser GUESTHOUSE $
(Map p230; ☎9596967447, 01982-250162; Karzoo Lane; d ₹600-800; ⊙Apr-Oct) This attractive,

Leh

Sights
1 Friendship Gate....D7
2 Gomang Stupa....B2
3 Ladakh Rocks & Minerals Museum....D1
4 Sankar Gompa....D2
5 Shanti Stupa....A2

Activities, Courses & Tours
6 Himalayan Bikers....C4
7 Mahabodhi Centre....C3
8 Yama Adventures....C5

Sleeping
9 All View....D3
10 Almighty Guesthouse....B6
11 Chonjor Residency....C6
12 Chow Guest House....B3
13 Deskit Villa....D1
14 Destination Guesthouse....D2
15 Gangs-Shun....A4
16 Goba Guest House....A3
17 Gomang Boutique Hotel....B2
18 Haldupa Guest House....C4
19 Kunzang....B3
20 Kurja Garden House....C3
21 Ladakh Residency....B3
22 Lha-Ri-Mo....B5
23 Lotus Hotel....D3
24 Tsetan Guest House....C1
25 Zaltak Guesthouse....B4

Eating
26 Bon Appetit....C4
27 Food Planet....C4
28 KH Restaurant....C4
29 Tibetan Kitchen....C5
30 Wonderland Restaurant & Coffee Shop....C3

Drinking & Nightlife
31 Bikers' Café....C4
32 Elements....C4

Shopping
33 Moti Market....D6

Information
34 Dr Morup....B4
35 Snow Leopard Conservancy India Trust....B4

Transport
36 Ladakh Maxicab Union....D7
37 Main Bus Station....D7
38 Market Taxi Stand....D6
39 Shared Jeep-Taxis to Diskit....E6
40 Shared Taxis to Choglamsar & Skalzangling....D7

low-key guesthouse has rooms with log beams and framed photos. The better, upper ones share a balcony from which there are lovely views towards Tsemo Fort across the sweet little flower-edged lawn. There's a small library of English books on an ornate Tibetan cabinet in the cosy breakfast room.

Palace View Guest House GUESTHOUSE $
(Map p230; ☎01982-257773, Wasim 9906991786; palace.view@hotmail.com; d ₹500-1000;) Just north of the polo ground, this fine-value family place keeps its promises with stupendous views across the Old Town and palace from rooftop sitting areas and some of the neat en suite rooms. Showers run very hot.

Kang-Lha-Chen HOTEL $$
(Map p230; ☎01982-252144, 01982-202289; www.hotelkanglhachen.com; Zangsti; s/d ₹2950/4150; May–mid-Oct;) Central, yet set around a peaceful garden-courtyard with seating beneath apricot trees, this long-standing favourite has old-fashioned but well-maintained rooms with excellent box-spring mattresses, Tibetan-style bedside tables and wicker-weave ceilings. The restaurant feels somewhat temple-like, and an oft-missed highlight is the delightful sitting room designed like an antique Ladakhi kitchen.

Almighty Guesthouse GUESTHOUSE $$
(Map p234; ☎9419179501, 9419345817; www.almightyladakh.com; Shagaran Leh; ₹1000-3000; mid-Apr–Oct;) This luxurious family guesthouse has six capacious rooms with standards better than most hotels. It's slightly hemmed in by bigger buildings but from the rooftop you can glimpse Stok Kangri, the palace and Shanti Stupa. There's patio seating in the small yard. It's near Pangong Hotel.

Greater Leh

★**Destination Guesthouse** GUESTHOUSE $
(Map p234; ☎9419179922; phuntsog.angmo@yahoo.com; Upper Karzoo Lane; d ₹800-1000; Jun–mid-Oct;) Excellent-value modern home with elements of chinoiserie, traditional ceilings and superb views from a communal semicircular balcony off the guest lounge, which has free tea and info leaflets.

All View GUESTHOUSE $
(Map p234; ☎9419178854, 01982-252761; Chubi; d ₹500) Remarkable value en suite rooms are arranged off communal balconies that wrap around a peaceful lawn shaded by apple trees. The guesthouse is hidden away at the end of a quiet, dead-end footpath. Many of the guests who manage to find it seem to stay all season.

Tsetan Guest House GUESTHOUSE $
(Map p234; ☎9469049131, 9622249125; http://tsetanguesthouse.com; Upper Changspa; d ₹1000-1200, s/d without bathroom ₹300/600; ⊙May-Oct) The young, eponymous owner, Tsetan, has a polite but unquenchable enthusiasm that transforms this simple, back-lane guesthouse into a community brimming with traveller camaraderie. Three new, en suite rooms are particularly impressive. Organic garden dinners can be ordered and there are occasional opportunities to join the family making *momos* (Tibetan dumplings).

Zaltak Guesthouse GUESTHOUSE $
(Map p234; Gawaling Rd; d ₹1200, r without bathroom ₹400-600, dm ₹250; P wifi) The old block is an upgraded standard Ladakhi house with some of the cleanest budget rooms in Leh. The new back building has excellent-value en suite rooms with sitting areas, large beds and hotel-standard bathrooms.

Chow Guest House GUESTHOUSE $
(Map p234; ☎01982-252399; d ₹600-800, without bathroom ₹400-500; wifi) This excellent-value family-run guesthouse has sparkling-clean, airy budget rooms with log ceilings. It's set behind a flower-filled, walled garden accessed by vehicle off Upper Tukcha Rd or on foot via a narrow path from Changspa Rd.

Gangs-Shun HOMESTAY $
(Map p234; ☎9419218657, 9858060706, 01982-252603; www.gangsshunhomestay.com; Upper Tukcha Rd; d/tr ₹1200/1500; wifi) With box-spring mattresses and towels provided in the mostly spacious rooms, the experience here is more comfortable than certain mid-market hotels, but the English-speaking doctor-host is keen that you have a genuinely interactive experience – hence the lack of TVs.

Kurja Garden House GUESTHOUSE, HOTEL $
(Map p234; ☎01982-251134, 9419177344; kurjagarden@gmail.com; Upper Karzoo Lane; guesthouse d ₹800-1200, without bathroom ₹500, hotel s/d ₹2300/2700; ⊙mid-May–Oct; P wifi) Six mostly large, superclean guest rooms sit above a friendly family home. The rooftop offers memorable views and occasional t'ai chi lessons. Across the chrysanthemum-edged vegetable garden is an eight-room hotel section with smart new facilities (but without the guesthouse's views). Excellent value.

Haldupa Guest House GUESTHOUSE $
(Map p234; ☎01982-251374; Upper Tukcha Rd; r upstairs/downstairs ₹1200/1000, without bathroom ₹400-800; wifi) A handful of cheaper rooms are inside the enchanting owners' wonderfully authentic original house that is dominated by a splendid shrine room. The rest are modern with decent bathrooms, hot showers and poplar-willow ceilings in a separate block overlooking the peaceful vegetable garden.

Goba Guest House GUESTHOUSE $
(Map p234; ☎01982-253670; gobaguesthouse@gmail.com; Goba Lane; r ₹1000, s/d without bathroom from ₹300/500; P nonsmoking wifi) There's a great spirit to the traditional main house, open year-round and topped with a prayer room and lovely rooftop panoramas. A more neutral hotel-style block (open April to September) has 15 spacious en suite rooms. The garden is a veritable field from which home-grown organic vegetables form the mainstay of family-cooked dinners (book by 4pm).

★**Deskit Villa** BOUTIQUE HOTEL $$
(Map p234; ☎9622988836, 9419178998, 01982-253498; www.deskit-villa.com; Sankar; guesthouse s/d ₹1750/2000, hotel ₹3400/3700; air-con wifi) Hidden behind a family garden guesthouse that's delightful in itself, a 'secret' eight-room boutique hotel offers some of the best pampering in Leh, with supercomfortable beds, a stupendous rooftop panorama and lots of public space in which to unwind. The dining room is designed like a traditional Ladakhi kitchen.

★**Chonjor Residency** HOTEL $$
(Map p234; ☎01982-253165, 9906977774; chonjorresidencyleh@gmail.com; Old Rd; s/d ₹2500/3100; wifi) Tucked discreetly onto Old Rd, this stylish 2016 hotel has elegant pine furnishings, heavy fabrics, personalised toiletries, coffee-makers in each room and excellent beds – all a notch more impressive than most hotels at this price. A lift takes you to the astroturf roof garden, which has views of Tsemo Fort.

Lotus Hotel HOTEL $$
(Map p234; ☎01982-257265; www.lotushotel.in; Upper Karzoo Lane; s/d ₹4000/4100; ⊙Mar-Nov; wifi) Apart from the parasol tables out the

SLEEPING PRICE RANGES

Accommodation price ranges for Kashmir and Ladakh:

$ less than ₹1500

$$ ₹1500–₹5000

$$$ more than ₹5000

Beware that at virtually any accommodation you'll pay far more by booking ahead than if you just show up. Outside of the May and June peak season, there's almost always some space available.

front you might think you'd arrived at a colourful Tibetan monastery as you enter this photogenic two-storey feast of Ladakhi detail.

Rooms continue the theme, with ornately carved bedheads and *chokse* (low, colourfully painted tables). Mattresses are comfy, but some bathrooms are cramped, with water from the new, large shower heads flowing onto a small curtained area of floorspace. A great delight is sipping tea amid the rose bushes and apple trees in the paved garden that has fine views of Tsemo Fort hill.

Very limited parking,

Kunzang BOUTIQUE HOTEL **$$**

(Map p234; 9419657123; www.hotelkunzangleh.com; Western Changspa; s/d ₹2750/3500; P) The Kunzang's 12 rooms have an understated boutique quality, with fresh, pale decor, large shower heads, excellent beds, fine linens and piled cushions with stylised tree motifs. Balconies look across the veggie garden, which supplies the restaurant's organic kitchen, towards the co-owned, basic Kunzang Guesthouse in one of Changspa's more archetypal old farmhouses.

Lha-Ri-Mo HOTEL **$$**

(Map p234; 01982-252101, 9419178233; www.lharimo.com; Fort Rd; s/d ₹2670/3690; May–mid-Oct; P) Magenta window frames set in whitewashed walls create a magical monastery-like impression, and enclose a willow-shaded lawn-garden. The restaurant and neo-Tibetan lounge are also impressive. Guest rooms aren't quite as delightful but they're neatly appointed with brass-effect lamps and the odd wrought-iron mirror.

★Gomang Boutique Hotel BOUTIQUE HOTEL **$$$**

(Map p234; 01982-253536; www.gomanghotelleh.com; Upper Changspa; s/d/ste ₹10,000/10,500/13,000; mid-Mar–mid-Nov; P) Leh abounds with new hotels, but the award-winning Gomang stands out for the loving care of its management, the gliding service and the attention to detail. Boutique features include Gomang-branded toiletries, tab-folded toilet-paper rolls and fine bed sashes, but what really impresses are the swish yet homely public spaces with heaped colourful cushions on black leather sofas.

★Ladakh Residency HOTEL **$$$**

(Map p234; 01982-254111, 9419178039; www.ladakhresidency.com; Changspa Rd; s/d/ste ₹5120/6590/8785; mid-Apr–mid-Oct;) Decorated with *thangka* (Tibetan cloth painting) and Nicholas Roerich prints, this layered collage of wooden balconies and marble floors has proper king-size beds, bathrooms with branded toiletries and Stok Kangri views from many rooms. Furniture is classily unfussy; kettles are provided; and there's a working elevator. Management has a perfect blend of personal care and professional attentiveness.

Eating

From June to September, traveller cafes abound, and European, Israeli and Chinese options supplement curries, banana pancakes, tandoori pizzas and Tibetan favourites. Competition keeps standards generally high, especially in the garden and rooftop restaurants of Changspa. Food options around Main Bazaar tend to get mixed reviews.

Most places close by 11pm in tourist season. From October to May it's wise to assume that almost none will open at all.

Central Leh

Ladakhi Food LADAKHI **$**

(Map p230; Unit 34, Hemis Complex, Upper Tukcha Rd; mains ₹70-100, tea ₹10; 6am-10.30pm) If you don't mind sitting at unvarnished plank benches in a bare box room, this is one central Leh eatery where you can taste authentic Ladakhi food made predominantly for locals. The lunch plate is a bargain, ideally washed down with salt-butter tea.

Ladakh Café VEGAN **$**

(Map p230; Music School Lane; mains ₹80-160, juices ₹150; 8.30am-9pm Apr-Nov;) Leh's first vegan cafe is squeezed into a cute little corner, and features bananas hanging on chains and carafes of free, mint-infused drinking water at the tables. The spicy 'power bowl' makes a delicious lunch; traditional Ladakhi *skyu* (flat barley pasta shapes in vegetable stew) costs only ₹80; and there's a superb range of freshly squeezed juices.

Neha Snacks INDIAN $

(Map p230; Main Bazaar; snacks ₹15-80, thali ₹200; ⏰9.30am-9pm) Attractive if minimalist snack shop that's so popular you'll have to squeeze together with strangers at one of the handful of tables. This is fast food Punjabi style, with particularly good *samosa chaat* (₹60) – dhal, yoghurt and spicy sauce ladelled over a crumbled samosa.

Penguin Garden MULTICUISINE $$

(Map p230; www.penguin.co.in; Chulung Lane; mains ₹110-280, half/whole tandoori chicken ₹270/540, rice ₹60, beer ₹150; ⏰8am-10.30pm; 📶) Strung with subtle lights and dotted with masks, it's well worth seeking out this slightly hidden garden restaurant where you can sit beneath apricot trees and listen to a gushing stream. If the fresh-cooked tandoori chicken has run out (typical by mid-evening) there is still a world of cuisine to explore.

Chopsticks ASIAN $$

(Map p230; ☎9622378764; Raku Complex, Fort Rd; mains ₹190-385, rice ₹77; ⏰noon-10.30pm) Though it also does curries and traditional Ladakhi *skyu* (flat barley pasta shapes in vegetable stew), this modern pan-Asian restaurant has built its solid reputation on quality wok dishes and Thai curries. Enter via the outdoor terrace, raised above the melee of Fort Rd.

La Piazzetta MULTICUISINE $$

(Map p230; ☎9419046476; Changspa Rd; mains ₹170-350, rice ₹90, pizzas ₹270-380; ⏰9.30am-11.30pm mid-Apr–late Sep; 📶) Candles, lanterns, muralled walls and an open fire (on colder nights) create a warm, dimly lit appeal that keeps this garden restaurant buzzing well after most others have closed – it's one of few places you may get food after 11pm. The menu includes Indian, Ladakhi, Kashmiri, tandoori and European dishes, and a brave if rather un-Thai stab at green curry.

Tibetan Kitchen ASIAN $$

(Map p234; ☎9622273505; off Fort Rd; mains ₹140-350 half/whole tandoori chicken ₹250/500) Local families tend to eat at home, but for a special treat this is one of the few tourist-area restaurants they are likely to come to, thanks to ever-reliable Chinese, tandoori, Indian and especially Tibetan cuisine. The chicken *thukpa* (Tibetan noodle soup) is beautifully balanced. Try *sabagleb*, essentially a crispy circular pie with *momo*-stuffing inside.

Il Forno ITALIAN, INDIAN $$

(Map p230; Zangsti Rd; mains ₹170-300, rice ₹100, beer ₹200; ⏰8.30am-11.30pm; 📶) Part enclosed, part shaded, part open, Il Forno's rooftop offers remarkable views of the Leh Palace and Tsemo Fort across Main Bazaar. Reliable for years, the menu covers many bases but its speciality remains the thin-crust wood-oven pizza (₹250 to ₹300; noon to 11pm) simply smothered with cheese. There's also a fairly reliable supply of cold beer.

Changspa

★Food Planet MULTICUISINE $$

(Map p234; ☎9837943385; Changspa Rd; mains ₹100-260, tea/coffee ₹15/45, beer/hookah ₹180/250; ⏰8am-11pm) A Russian–Indian couple has created a menu that really covers the globe. Although some of the more untraditional items were unavailable when we visited (guacamole, Uzbek *shurpa* soup, stuffed mushrooms), they still had a wide range of novelties including Hawaiian salad,

LADAKHI FOOD

Ladakh's Tibetan favourites include *momo* (dumplings wrapped ravioli-style in thin pasta) and *thukpa* (noodle soup). A more genuinely Ladakhi dish is *skyu*, a vegetable stew containing something like a barley version of Italian *orecchiette* (pasta 'ears'). Harder to find is *paba*, pea-and-barley meal that is often dunked in *tangtur* (boiled vegetables in curd). Also used for dunking are *tingmo* (pronunced tee-mo), steamed, unsweetened buns that are typically made in flower-like form with bready 'petals'. *Namthuk* is a barley 'soup', like a thin porridge, that sometimes acts as a drink with meals. Ladakh's barley beer, *chhang*, is available at rural homestays but not for general sale. *Namkin chai* (*nun chai* in Kashmiri) is pink, salted milk tea *(nimak chai)* with added yak's butter. Traditionally the butter is blended into the tea by vigorous use of a plunger in a long cylindrical churning vessel called a *gurgur*, causing the tea to be commonly nicknamed *gurgur chai*.

tom yam soup and an utterly divine chicken breast with mango salsa. Plus all the usuals.

Wonderland Restaurant & Coffee Shop MULTICUISINE **$$**
(Map p234; ☎9622972826; pemawangchen67@gmail.com; Changspa Rd; mains ₹110-300; ⌚6.30am-10.30pm) Of several long-established rooftop restaurants on Changspa Rd, ever-popular Wonderland has neither the best view nor the snazziest decor but the food is consistently reliable (especially the Indian and Tibetan); the coffee is excellent, and fine value; and the place opens well before most others, making it ideal for breakfast when you want an early start.

KH Restaurant MULTICUISINE, KOREAN **$$**
(Map p234; Changspa Rd; mains ₹150-500, rice ₹90, beer ₹180; ⌚approx 10am-11pm; 📶) This is the most low-key of Changspa's garden restaurants and the place where we've most often stumbled across folks sitting round the bonfire pit, informally jamming acoustic music and rolling mixed herbs. Food covers all bases but Korean is the speciality.

★**Bon Appetit** MULTICUISINE **$$$**
(Map p234; ☎01982-251533; mains ₹220-440, beer/cocktails from ₹200/250; ⌚11am-11pm; 📶) Hidden down unlikely footpaths south of Changspa Rd, Bon Appetit maintains a cuisine that has far more finesse than anything else in Leh, so consider booking. Much on the eclectic menu has an Italian feel, but you'll also find delightfully light veggie tempura, sublime cashew chicken and succulent tandoori grills. Ask about wine and cocktails.

Drinking & Nightlife

Recently remodelled **Lehchen** (Map p230; Music School Rd; cocktails ₹300-330, small/large beers ₹180/250, wine ₹600; ⌚noon-11pm; 📶) is Leh's first genuinely appealing cocktail bar. Classy Bon Appetit (p240) serves beer legally and is applying for a cocktail licence. Many rooftop and Changspa-garden places unofficially serve 'pop juice' (ie beer) on request; good bets include La Piazzetta (p239), **Bikers' Café** (Map p234; Changspa Rd; small beers ₹150; ⌚8am-2am, kitchen to midnight) and Il Forno (p239). **Elements** (Map p234; Changspa Rd; beer/rum from ₹150/180; ⌚11am-late) is typically open far later than most, though how long it will be allowed to do so remains to be seen. For takeaway booze, there's **Indus Wine Shop** (Map p230; Ibex Rd; beer/wine ₹105/850; ⌚10am-1pm & 3-9.30pm); it closes on 'dry days' (eighth, 15th and last days of the Tibetan month) as do all legal bars.

Barista coffee has only recently hit Leh but there are already many excellent choices. Top contenders include bookshop-cafe Lehling, old faithful Wonderland Restaurant and the brilliant if easily missed **Ja Khang** (Map p230; Main Bazaar, West; coffee ₹60-90; ⌚8.30am-9pm; 📶), which has great macchiato and a very special interior.

For a good cheap cup of Ladakhi *nimak chai* (salt tea), visit Ladakhi Food (p238) or join the locals at basic **tea stalls** (Map p230; Chandu Market; tea/bread ₹10/10; ⌚6am-7pm) in dusty Chandu Market.

★**Lala's Art Cafe** CAFE
(Leh Heritage House; Map p230; www.tibetheritagefund.org; Old Town; coffee from ₹50; ⌚9.30am-7pm Mon-Sat) Entered beside a 2000-year-old Buddha stela, this tiny, mudbrick house with a historic ground-floor shrine was saved from demolition and brilliantly restored in 2006. Stone steps lead to a cafe with floor seating and a small art display; a ladder stairway continues to an open roof terrace. Serves French-press coffee (₹50), *khambir* (Ladakhi bread) sandwiches (₹70), apricot pudding (₹60), local juices, and fruit or mint lassis.

Shopping

Dozens of colourful little shops, street vendors and **Tibetan Refugee Markets** (Map p230; ⌚10am-9pm May-Sep) sell wide selections of *thangkas,* Ladakhi hats, 'antiques' and heavy turquoise jewellery, as well as Kashmiri shawls and various Nepali, Tibetan and Chinese knick-knacks. Compare prices in fascinating, very local-focused **Moti Market** (Map p234), the little family shops of **Nowshera Bazaar** (New Shar Market; Map p230) or the upmarket Tibetan outlet **Norbulingka** (Map p230; www.norbulingkashop.org; Rizong Complex; ⌚9am-7pm Jul-Sep). Suavely mod-trad **Jigmat Couture** (Map p230; ☎9697000344, 01982-255065; www.jigmat.com; Tsaskan Complex, Main Bazaar, West; ⌚10.30am-7.30pm Mon-Sat, 3.30-7.30pm Sun) is Leh's first designer-fashion boutique.

Lehling (Map p230; Main Bazaar; ⌚9am-10pm; 📶) and Ladakh Bookshop are particularly well stocked with postcards, novels, spiritual works and books on Ladakh, Kashmir and Tibet.

ALTITUDE PROBLEMS

Leh's altitude, above 3500m, means that many visitors will suffer from headaches and dizziness on arrival. Mild symptoms can be partly relieved by resting and drinking plenty of fluids. If that doesn't help, or if you have inadvertently overexercised, either breathe oxygen at the oxygen bar or, as long as it's combined with rest, take one Diamox tablet morning and evening for three days. Tablets are available from **Het Ram Vinay Kumar Pharmacy** (Map p230; 01982-252160; Main Bazaar; 10am-9pm). Should symptoms become severe, you risk developing potentially fatal Acute Mountain Sickness (AMS), but the condition is eminently treatable if you act promptly. The best option is to call English-speaking specialist **Dr Morup** (Map p234; 9419883851; Upper Tukcha Rd; consultation ₹1000; on call), who can assist you at your hotel and/or help you find appropriate treatment.

Old Fort Rd, Main Bazaar and Changspa Rd have several outdoor-equipment stores. Some, including **Venture Ladakh** (Map p230; 9858323091; www.ventureladakh.in; Changspa Rd; 9am-9pm Jun-Sep), rent climbing and trekking gear.

★**Dzomsa** FOOD & DRINKS
(Map p230; Zangsti; 8.30am-9.30pm) Fill up drinking-water bottles here (₹7 per litre). Dzomsa also offers an environmentally friendly laundry service (₹95 per kg), fresh apricot and buckthorn juices (₹20/80 per glass/litre), and a range of local products and secondhand books.

Ladakh Bookshop BOOKS
(Map p230; 9868111112; hanishbooks@yahoo.co.in; Main Bazaar; 9am-9pm) Hidden upstairs opposite the entrance to Chokhang Vihara, this excellent bookshop publishes locally relevant works and stocks the updated 2013 edition of Olizane's indispensible *Ladakh Trekking Maps* (₹1500 per sheet).

Information

INTERNET ACCESS

The best wi-fi in Leh is at the **Mantra Travel Lounge** (p241) – pay by donation.

MEDICAL SERVICES

Oxygen Bar (Map p230; Tourist Office, Ibex Rd; examination ₹10, oxygen per 30min ₹50; 10.30am-7pm Mon-Sat, to 4pm Sun) If you fear that you're suffering from altitude sickness, this comfy room above the tourist office will give you a brief examination and, if they think it's necessary, you can breathe almost-pure oxygen as a makeshift remedy.

Men-Tsee-Khang (01982-253566; www.men-tsee-khang.org; consultation ₹100; 9am-1pm & 2-5pm Mon-Fri, plus 1st & 3rd Sat of month) Charitable foundation with an *Amchi* (Tibetan herbal medicine) centre and dispensary. Consultations available without appointment. Physio-therapeutic massages available.

MONEY

There are numerous moneychangers on Changspa Rd, Upper Fort Rd and around Main Bazaar.

Paul Merchant (Map p230; Main Bazaar; 9.30am-8pm) gives reliably fair rates for cash and travellers cheques.

On rare occasions almost all Leh's ATMs have been known to temporarily stop functioning; it's wise to keep a stock of cash available.

TELEPHONE

AirCel (Map p230; Main Bazaar; 10am-6pm) and **AirTel** (Map p230; off Main Bazaar; 10am-5.30pm) sell inexpensive pay-as-you-go SIM cards for use within the Kashmir Valley, Jammu, Kishtwar, Bhadarwah and within 20km of Leh. You'll need four photographs plus photocopies of your passport and visa.

Some internet cafes, including **Sky Cyber** (Map p230; Samkar Complex, Main Bazaar; international calls per min ₹14-24, internet per hr ₹60; 9am-9.30pm) and **Peace Internet** (Map p230; Music School Rd; per hr ₹90; 9.30am-9pm), allow you to make domestic and international landline calls from small booths.

TOURIST INFORMATION

Tourist office (Map p230; 01982-257788; Ibex Rd; 9am-8pm Mon-Sat, 10am-4pm Sun) Recently revamped and helpful with festival dates and bus timetables. Has a couple of interesting exhibitions. Free city maps are almost useless.

Mantra Travel Lounge (Map p230; 9419219783; www.facebook.com/mantrathetravellounge; Raku Complex, Fort Rd; 10am-9.30pm;) A youthful cafe-style alternative, designed as an info and exchange centre; meet fellow travellers or use free wi-fi.

Noticeboards at Mantra, outside **Dzomsa**, in agencies and pasted over town have adverts for tours, treks and activities. There's an active forum for Ladakh travellers on www.indiamike.com.

REACHING LADAKH

Only two road routes, both beautiful but seasonal, link Ladakh to the rest of India: the route to Manali (p249) is spectacular but long and rather arduous, while crossing the perilous **Zoji La** (Srinagar-Kargil Rd; ⊙often closed for maintenance 11am-3pm Mon-Sat Apr–mid-Nov) to Srinagar scares the *momos* out of many first-time travellers. Both roads close altogether from October or November until May, leaving flying as the only option for reaching Leh. Allow at least a couple of spare days in case of delays.

ℹ Getting There & Away

AIR

Flights are dramatically scenic, but can be cancelled at short notice during bad weather. **Jet Airways** (Map p230; ☎01982-251512, 01982-257444; www.jetairways.com; Main Bazaar; ⊙10am-1.30pm & 2-4pm, to 5pm summer), **Air India** (☎01982-252076; Airport; ⊙6am-noon) and **GoAir** (☎01982-253940; Airport) fly to Delhi; the latter uses Delhi's old Terminal 1 so is worth avoiding if you plan a quick transfer to/from an international flight.

GoAir flies daily to Jammu and to Srinagar but not back, as part of Mumbai–Leh–Srinagar–Mumbai and Delhi–Leh–Jammu–Delhi loop flights.

Air India flies each way to/from Srinagar (Wednesdays) and Jammu (thrice weekly). For Dharamsala, connect through Jammu.

Almost all flights fly early morning and the airport closes by 10am.

BUS

Main Bus Station (Map p234) The main bus station is 700m south of the town centre via the Kigu-Tak stepped bazaar from Friendship Gate. The large site is divided into sub-areas for local minibuses, private (LBOC) buses and state services (J&K SRTC).

MOTORCYCLE

Touring Ladakh by motorcycle has become a major fad in the last few years. Leh has countless rental companies, especially along Music School Rd and Changspa Rd, with more than 8000 bikes reckoned to be available, yet in June (peak Indian holiday season) there may still be excess demand. Hiring an Enfield Bullet typically costs ₹1000 to ₹1500 per day; a 'Scooty' (moped) just ₹700.

Double-check fittings and brakes, and check insurance (rarely included or even available). You'll need to show your licence (though a few agencies will quietly rent to unlicensed riders) and leave some sort of ID.

Carry spare fuel for longer trips: Ladakh's only petrol stations are at Leh, Choglamsar, Serthi (near Karu; NH1 Km440.5), Diskit (opening unreliable), Spituk, Padum (unreliable), Phyang junction, Khalsi (NH1 Km338.7), Wakha and Kargil (two).

SHARED JEEP & SHARED TAXI

From the **Long-distance Shared-Taxi Park** (Leh-Choglamsar Rd), 400m south of the main petrol pump:

Kargil (per seat ₹900 to ₹1000, seven hours) Throughout the morning, but mainly 8am to 10am.

Manali (front/middle/back seats ₹3000/2500/2000, 19 to 22 hours) Departures approximately 4pm to 6pm.

Srinagar (front/back seats ₹2500/2000, 15 hours) Departures approximately 4pm to 6pm.

From **outside Zaika Restaurant** (Map p234) at the entrance to the polo ground (no bookings):

Nubra Valley Most jeeps to Diskit (₹400) depart before 8am but we have found cars here as late as 3pm. Remember that foreigners need a permit. Possibly also jeeps for Sumur or other Nubra destinations.

From the **Old Bus Stand** (Map p234; Old Bus Stand; ₹20) (southern end of Moti Market):

Indus Valley Shared taxis depart relatively frequently to Choglamsar (₹20). Change there for Thiksey, Shey, Karu, Matho and Stok.

Spituk Take a shared minivan (₹10) to **Skalzangling** (NH1) near the airport and change.

TAXIS & CHARTER JEEPS

Given irregular bus services, chartering a vehicle makes sense for visiting rural Ladakh. Fares are set by the **Ladakh Taxi Operator Cooperative** (Map p230; Ibex Rd; ⊙10am-1pm & 2-4pm), which publishes an annually updated booklet (₹25), sold at its office. The great news is there's no haggling, though booking via a small local agency can sometimes get a minor discount (and a reliable driver).

We quote the lowest standard rates, ie for taxi-vans or Sumo charter jeeps. Prices are 5% higher for Xylo, Scorpio and Qualis vehicles, 10% higher for Innova and Aria. Rates assume reasonable photo and visit stops; longer waits are officially chargeable (per hour/half-day/full day ₹286/1195/2391). Extra overnight stops add a further ₹350.

Requesting unplanned diversions from the agreed route once underway can cause unexpected difficulties, so plan carefully.

BUSES FROM LEH

Unless noted, departures are from the main bus station area. Some services depart earlier in winter. Durations very approximate.

DESTINATION	COST (₹)	DURATION	DEPARTURES
Alchi	107	2¼hr	4pm (returns 7.30am)
Chemrey	60	1½hr	use Sakti buses
Chiktan (A)	278	8hr	8am Tue, Thu, Sun (returns Wed, Sat, Mon)
Chilling	100	2½hr	9am Sun (returns 1pm)
Choglamsar (E)	20	25min	as full
Dha (A)	245	7hr	9am. Diverts Fri to Hanu Gongma.
Fokha via Shargol & Mulbekh (A)	384	8hr	7am Sat
Hemis Shukpachan (A)	131	4hr	2pm alternate days (returns 8.30am)
Kargil (C)	400	8-10hr	5am
Keylong (D)	550	14hr	5am
Hanle (B) [no foreigners]	495	11	6.30am Sat
Lamayuru	195	5hr	9am summer. Or use Chiktan, Fokha, Kargil or Srinagar buses.
Likir Gompa	80	2hr	4pm (returns 7.30am)
Manali			seasonal (p249)
Manggyu (A)	128	3hr	1pm Wed
Matho	30	50min	4.40pm
Ney (via Basgo)	95	2hr	4pm (returns 7.30am)
Phyang	35	45min	7.30am, 2pm
Sakti	50	1¾hr	8.30am, 1.30pm, 3.30pm, 4.30pm (returns 7.30am, 8am, 9am, 3pm)
Saspol	90	2	3pm (returns 7.30am)
Shey (E)			use shared taxis changing at Choglamsar
Spangmik (Pangong Tso)	270	8hr	6.30am Tue, Thu, Sat (returns 8am next day)
Spituk (E)			use shared taxis changing at Skalzangling
Srinagar (B)	1060	18-20hr	2pm
Stakna	41	40min	4.30pm (returns 8.45am)
Stok			use shared taxis changing at Choglamsar
Tangtse (B)	118	4hr	6.30am Wed, Sat, Sun
Thiksey	30	40min	8.30am
Tia & Timishgan (A)	143	4hr	1pm (returns 8am)
Turtuk (B)	370	10-11hr	6am Sat (returns Sun)
Zanskar	800		call 9469562036

(A) LBOC Bus (01982-252792); (B) J&K SRTC (01982-252085); (C) Kargil Bus Operators Union; departs from the **polo ground** (Map p230); buy tickets the afternoon before departure from driver; (D) HRTC; (E) Shared taxi from Old Bus Stand.

All other services (except Manali) are local minibuses, mostly working with the **Mazda Bus Operators' Cooperative** (Map p234; ☎9906995889, 01982-253262); no prebooking.

Getting Around

TO/FROM THE AIRPORT

The airport (Km430, Leh–Spituk Hwy) is 4km south of the centre. Taxi transfers cost ₹230/300 to central Leh/Changspa.

TAXI

Leh's little micro-van taxis charge from ₹100 per hop. Flagging down rides rarely works; to make arrangements go to a taxi stand, most centrally at **Zangsti** (Map p230; Zangsti Parking), **Moti Market** (Map p234; Old Bus Stand) or the **central taxi stand** (Map p230; Ibex Rd) near the tourist office.

Around Leh – Southeast

☎01982

The main day trips around Leh are the monastery and palace villages of the Indus Valley. You can combine several of the destinations to make a full-day taxi trip, or visit one or two as part of a longer jeep excursion to Pangong, Tso Moriri or Nubra via Wari La.

The most popular choices are Shey, Thiksey and Hemis, but you can avoid the main tourist rush by picking lesser-known villages like Matho and Sakti (p248). Several other villages are starting points for great hikes, notably to the Markha Valley, where you can walk for days between village homestays.

Stok

POP 1640 / ELEV 3490M

Across the valley from Leh, Stok's main drawcards are its 19th-century royal palace, its collection of older Ladakhi houses and its role as a possible starting point for hikes to Rumbak (p250) and the Markha Valley (p248) and for climbing Stok Kangri (p232). Stok also makes a quiet alternative to Leh as a Ladakh touring base thanks to its small but excellent choice of accommodation.

Sights

Stok's primary attraction is its three-storey **palace** (☎01982-242003; ₹70; ⏰8am-1pm & 2-6pm May-Sep). A smaller and more intimate version of Leh Palace, it is the summer home of Ladakh's former royal family, but it also doubles as a museum and as one of the region's most exclusive guesthouses.

Bring a torch to visit **Stok Abagon** (☎9906988325; suggested donation ₹50), a ruinous 350-year-old house and kitchen down a short alley from Stok Palace. Or cross town to **Gyab-Thago Heritage House** (☎9622966413, 9797310988, 9419218421; Village Rd; suggested donation ₹100; ⏰10am-5pm May-Sep), a far more complete and better organised historic home: most of the interior furnishings and fittings are carefully maintained by the original owners, who now live at the homestay next door.

The easiest way to travel between the two is on a 5km loop via the Trekking Point, passing modest **Stok Gompa**, which sits beneath a golden Buddha statue that's visible for miles.

There are plenty more old buildings and assorted stupas to discover by wandering.

Sleeping & Eating

Gyab-Thago Homestay GUESTHOUSE $

(☎9419218421; www.ladakhmitra.com; r without bathroom incl half board per person ₹1000; ⏰May-Sep) Thoroughly traditional but markedly more comfortable than many homestays, Gyab Thago's rooms are airy and clean, sharing a spick-and-span bathroom. Meals in the impressive Ladakhi kitchen-dining room are so authentic that groups come here from Leh specially for the experience, though you won't get quite as full a spread if you pay standard homestay rates.

Stok Palace Heritage Hotel HERITAGE HOTEL $$$

(☎9650207467; www.stokpalaceheritage.com; Stok Palace; ste ₹16,100-34,000, cottages ₹32,000) Sleep in a genuine, functioning Ladakhi royal palace; the suites of old rooms have been redecorated (and have impressive bathrooms), but maintain plenty of traditional design features. The very special 'Queen's Room' retains darkly brooding original murals, almost 200 years old. There's also a trio of new, supercomfortable Ladakhi-style cottages in an apricot orchard nearby.

Each cottage sleeps four and has a fully equipped kitchen, underfloor heated bathrooms and wood stoves for winter heating. Suite rates include dinner. You will probably get to dine with the royals at least once during your stay.

Woody Vu BOUTIQUE HOTEL $$$

(☎9797643532; www.woodyvu.com; Village Rd; r ₹10,000; ⏰mid-Feb–Oct) Woody Vu has five rustic-luxury rooms with superb mattresses and boutique features while maintaining the spirit of an old Ladakhi house. Meals are taken in a traditional kitchen-dining room, and views are magnificent, especially from the four-poster Khardungla Room. Bookings (via Delhi) required. There's wi-fi, but, to encourage social interaction, there are no TVs.

Getting There & Away

From Leh's old bus stand, shared taxis run to Choglamsar, where you can switch to a Stok-bound minivan (₹30 to ₹50 per seat, ₹300 per vehicle). Vans leave Stok for Leh when full – typically once or twice an hour – from the Trekking Point using Main Rd.

A taxi from Leh costs ₹574/744 one-way/return.

Matho

POP 1240 / ELEV 3485M

Matho's large Sakya Buddhist **monastery** (☎01982-246085; www.mathomuseumproject.com) is perched above the bucolic village with dreamy views across the Indus Valley's patchwork of emerald-green fields, sandy deserts and mountain horizons. The dynamic gompa has impressive architecture, a new museum under construction and an interesting *thangka*-restoration workshop.

Matho Nagrang RELIGIOUS
(Matho Gompa; ⏲Feb-Mar) During this famous festival, Matho monastery oracles perform daring acrobatics while effectively blindfolded, 'seeing' only through the fearsome 'eyes' painted on their chests. They also engage in ritual acts of self-mutilation and make predictions for the coming year.

Shey

POP 2490 / ELEV 3240M

Shey is an attractive, pond-dappled oasis from which rises a central dry rocky ridge dominated by extensive fortress ruins and a former palace containing Ladakh's most celebrated Buddha statue. Around 700 whitewashed stupas dot the village, some dating back to the 11th century. But Shey's biggest tourist draw is none of the above: Indian tourists flock here to see the school (p245) that featured in the 2009 Bollywood movie *3 Idiots*.

Naropa Royal Palace PALACE
Along the top of Shey's ridge, a series of fortress ruins bracket the three-storey, 17th-century Naropa Royal Palace, which has enjoyed a wholesale reconstruction in recent years. The **palace temple** (₹20; ⏲8am-6pm) contains a 7.5m-tall gilded copper Buddha that dates to 1645. The upper door opens to his inscrutably smiling face.

Druk Padma Karpo School FILM LOCATION
(Druk White Lotus School; www.dwls.org; Km457.9, Leh-Karu Hwy; donation appreciated; ⏲9am-1pm & 2-6pm Apr-Aug; P) Though best known for its cameo role in *3 Idiots*, this school of more than 700 students has a fascinating campus of prize-winning modern buildings incorporating the latest in sustainable technological engineering. It was essentially rebuilt following devastation in the August 2010 cloudburst. In season, 'briefing' talks followed by tours of the site depart several times an hour.

Thiksey

POP 2490 / ELEV 3260M

Glorious **Thiksey Gompa** (☎01982-267011; www.thiksey-monastery.org; admission ₹30, video ₹100; ⏲6am-1pm & 1.30-6pm, festival Oct/Nov)

THE ELUSIVE SNOW LEOPARD

Much celebrated but rarely seen, the snow leopard is one of Ladakh's most iconic mammals. There are thought to be less than 300 left, and possibly as few as 100. Hoteliers still talk of an American photographer who spent a whole summer criss-crossing the mountains, hoping in vain to snap a single shot of a leopard – he chose the wrong season. February and March is when the big cats follow their prey (ibex and blue sheep) to lower altitudes, and the snowy terrain at this time makes their tracks easier to discern.

Campaigns to save the animal and its ecosystem have been relatively successful over the last decade, persuading villagers that the leopards can be a boon rather than a threat to their livelihoods. In part this has been achieved by encouraging homestays for leopard-watchers in places such as **Rumbak** (p250) (₹1500; **Hemis National Park permit** (p248) required), Phyang, Uley (9km from **Yangthang**) and the Rong region (between Upshi and Tso Moriri). Such tours are operated by the **Ladakhi Women's Travel Company** (p233) and **Hidden North** (p233), among others.

The **Snow Leopard Conservancy Office** (Map p234; ☎01982-257953; www.snowleopardhimalayas.in; Leopard Lane, Leh; ⏲4pm Fri or by appointment) screens a related documentary on Friday afternoons; avoid dropping in at other times without an appointment as staff have limited time to spare.

Around Leh

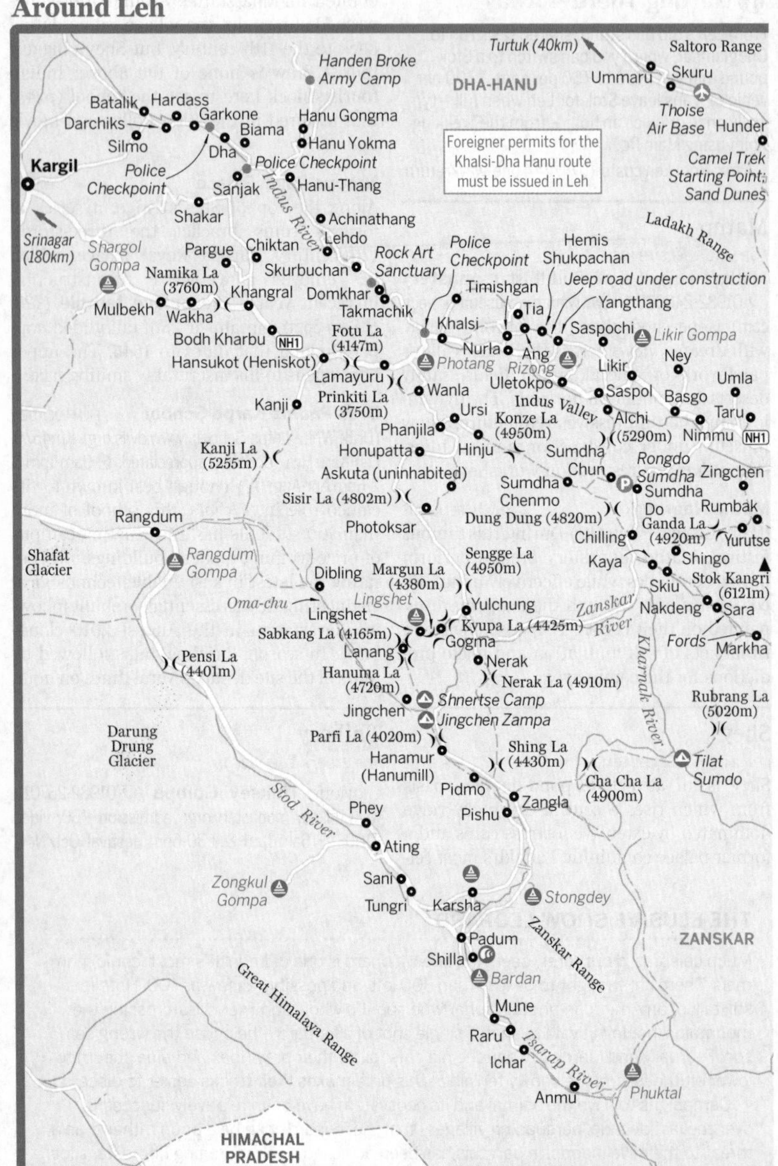

is one of Ladakh's biggest and most recognisable monasteries, photogenically cascading its assorted Tibetan-style buildings down a raised rocky promontory. At its heart, the main *dukhang* (prayer hall) oozes atmosphere, and a Maitreya temple contains a giant 'future' Buddha whose expression is simultaneously peaceful, smirking and vaguely menacing. Smaller but much more obviously ancient is the *gonkhang* and the tiny old library up on the rooftop (often closed).

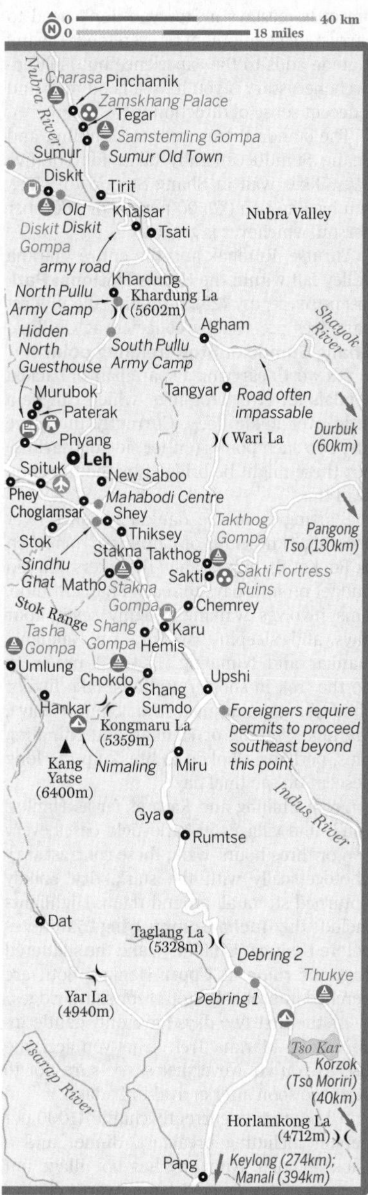

The Thiksey entrance ticket includes entry to a fascinating **museum** (hours vary) – if anyone's there to open it; it's hidden away beneath the monastery restaurant.

Virtually any Ladakhi monastery will start the day with chanted prayers, and respectful visitors are usually welcome to join or watch. Thiksey's impressive prayer hall and the large number of monks who participate make the experience particularly memorable here. However, it has become so popular that tourists often outnumber monks. Prayers take place between 6am and 7.30am most days.

Sleeping & Eating

To be ready for the start of morning prayers, some visitors stay in the monastery's plain guest rooms or the more comfortable **Chamba Hotel** (01982-267385, 9419178381; www.thiksay.org; Km454.2, Leh-Karu Hwy; s/d ₹2760/3640) at the base of the gompa hill. For longer, more meditative stays, try the small, charming guesthouse of the **Nyerma Nunnery** (The Taras; 9906985911; www.ladakhnuns.com; r incl half board per person ₹950; May-Sep).

★**Café Cloud** MULTICUISINE $$$
(9419983021, 01982-267100; Km453.3, Leh-Karu Hwy; mains ₹250-575; 9am-8pm mid-May–Sep;) Tucked away behind adobe walls, this upmarket garden restaurant is essentially the only choice for quality European food east of Leh. A great choice is pan-seared sea bass (₹599), served on mustard-flavoured potatoes with al dente vegetables. The restaurant also does an excellent Indian vegetarian lunch buffet (₹605) and a veg/nonveg meal of the day (₹390/435).

Hemis

POP 350 / ELEV 3670M

Unlike most Ladakhi monasteries, the 17th-century **Hemis Gompa** (www.drukpa-hemis.org; ₹100; 8am-1pm & 2-6pm), spiritual centre of Ladakh's Drukpa Buddhists, is set discreetly into a cliff-backed valley rather than on top of a crag, but it's arguably Ladakh's most famous Buddhist monastic complex. The central courtyard and main temple buildings have lots of colour, the **museum** (Hemis Gompa; free with monastery admission; 8am-1pm & 2-6pm mid-Apr–mid-Oct) is fascinating, and there's plenty more to explore amid the atmospheric upper shrines.

To escape the tourist hordes, stroll beyond the new school construction along a lovely stream-side path, then take the concrete stairway that leads up to the **Gotsang Hermitage** (dawn-dusk), with two attractive main temple buildings and also containing the cave where Tantric master Gyalwang Gotsang (1189–1258) meditated. Also known as Golsangapa, he was the enlightened Tibetan lama who charted the pilgrim path around Mt Kailash and to whom Ladakh's Drukpa Buddhists cast back their lineage. Allow nearly an hour for the trip up, half that back.

Near the main monastery, the compact and timeless **Hemis village** is also worth a stroll, with narrow alleys running between tightly packed homes.

Ever popular, the annual **Tse-Chu festival** (Hemis Gompa; ⌚Jul) sees three days of masked dances that artfully tell the story of Padmasambhava's life.

You can go to Karu by shared taxi from Choglamsar (₹50). From Karu, Hemis is 7km up a winding lane (taxi one-way/return ₹300/500).

Chemrey & Takthog

POP 6920 / ELEV 3660M

Less popular with travellers than Thiksey but every bit as spectacular, **Thekchhok Gompa** (Chemrey Monastery; Karu-Pangong road, Km7.3; museum ₹50; ⌚museum 8.30am-1pm & 2-6pm, festival Nov) sits high on a hillock above waving fields of ripening barley. It's the perfect Ladakhi postcard view. Around 3km further north, at the third of three junctions (Km10.4), a road leads towards the Wari La pass through **Sakti**, a charming village of gently terraced fields, waterlogged meadows and stone walls. The lane skirts Sakti's shattered stone **fortress ruins** (Km1.5, Wari La Rd, Sakti) FREE and several Buddhist monuments, the most famous of which is **Takthog (Dakthok) Gompa** (Km4.6, Wari La Rd, Sakti; donation appropriate; ⌚festival Jul).

The charming homestay **Solpon** (☎9906304067; Km2.3, Wari La Rd; per person with half board ₹800; wi-fi), 2km from Takthog Gompa, has great views of Sakti Castle, while the area's best hotel is **Sakti Villa** (☎01982-251063; www.saktivilla.com; Km4.3, Wari La Rd; s/d ₹2600/2900), 300m before Takthog Gompa.

Chemrey and Takthog are short diversions off the Karu–Pangong road and are generally visited as add-ons to a two-day Pangong jeep excursion. Alternatively, you can visit both monasteries as a day trip from Leh by taxi (around ₹2500 return).

Markha Valley & Rumbak

Ladakh's most celebrated trekking route follows a relatively straightforward and scenically glorious route through timeless villages in the roadless Markha Valley before crossing the Kongmaru La (5260m). A plethora of homestays means you don't need to carry much equipment or even food. Having a guide adds to the experience but isn't entirely necessary if you have a good map and a decent sense of direction.

The standard trek between Chilling and Shang Sumdo generally takes four or five days. Taxis wait at Shang Sumdo to whisk you back to Leh (₹2500 per car or ₹600 per person, whichever is greater).

Yurutse, Rumbak and the entire Markha Valley fall within the **Hemis National Park** (per person per day ₹20), for which the modest park fees are usually collected at Chilling, **Shang Sumdo** or **Stok trekking point**.

It's worth carrying a spare pair of backed sandals for river crossings, which can be a little over ankle deep. Currently there are just two such points (either side of Markha) but these might be bridged by the time you read this.

Starting from the dangling-basket river crossing 4km south of **Chilling** (Nimmu-Nerak Rd, Km28), reasonably fit hikers should budget on four days to reach Shang Sumdo. This involves walking roughly seven-hour days and sleeping at Sara or Nakdeng, Hankar and Nimaling. If you'd prefer to do the trek in shorter sections, take five or six days, stopping instead at Skiu or Kaya, Markha, Umlung or Hankar, and Nimaling plus, perhaps, Chokdo to break up the long descent on the final day.

From Chilling and Kaya as far as Hankar you'll find villages in barleyfield oases every two or three hours' walk; these contrast very photogenically with the stark, dry, spikily upturned strata all around them. Highlights include tiny **Tacha Gompa**, lying 25 minutes before Umlung (Umblung), and the shattered **fortress ruins** at Upper Hankar. Both are perched improbably atop razor-sharp ridges.

As the first two days have only gentle inclines, the Markha Trek helps you acclimatise as you go. Nevertheless, be sure not to start too soon after arrival in Ladakh.

All homestays currently charge ₹1000 per person including breakfast, dinner and a packed lunch. Nimaling has no village but a camp of pre-erected tents (warm clothes are essential here) charges ₹1200 per head including meals.

If you're well pre-acclimatised, you could add two or three beautiful extra days by starting from Zingchen (₹1650 by taxi from Leh, with a homestay and campsite). From there it's three to four hours' walk to the

LEH TO MANALI

Beautiful but exhausting and occasionally spine-jangling, this is a ride you won't forget. The Upshi–Keylong section crosses four passes over 4900m, and then there's the infamously unpredictable Rohtang Pass before Manali. Although the road is 'normally' open from June to late September, unseasonable snow or major landslides can close it for days (or weeks). BCM (www.bcmtouring.com), LAHDC (http://leh.nic.in) and High Road (http://vistet.wordpress.com) report the road's current status.

Transport Options

BUS & MINIBUS

The cheapest option is to take the 5am HRTC bus to Keylong (₹540, 14 hours) and change there. Buy tickets from the driver's assistant the evening before; the incoming bus should arrive around 7pm (look for the HP number plate).

Marginally more comfortable **HPTDC** (Map p230; ☎9418691215, 9906229196; Fort Rd; ⊙10am-1.30pm & 2.30-7pm, Jul-early Sep) buses (₹2700, two days) leave every second day in July and August plus a couple of times in early September. Departures are at 5am from opposite the **tourist office** (Map p230; Ibex Rd). Prebook upstairs in the small office beside Wet'n'Wild (p232). Fares include basic overnight accommodation in dorms at Keylong plus one breakfast and dinner.

Nonstop 11-seater Tempo minibuses leave around 1am (15 to 21 hours). Tickets cost ₹2000 through agencies or ₹1800 direct from **Ladakh Maxicab Union** (Map p234; ☎01982-253192). Book two days ahead for a decent seat and double-check the departure point, which is often Zangsti Taxi Stand (p244). The route will be far quicker once the Rohtang Tunnel opens, hopefully in 2018.

JEEP

HP-registered jeeps at the Long-distance Shared-Taxi Park (p242) ask ₹2000/2500/3000 back/middle/front seat to Manali; they generally depart between 4pm and 6pm. These folks are sometimes in a hurry to leave, so you may be able to rent the whole vehicle for considerably less than the official charge (from ₹19,500 including one overnight stop en route).

CAR & MOTORCYCLE

There's no petrol station for 365km between Karu and Tandi (8km south of Keylong). Driving northbound, the Rohtang Pass requires permits (p252), and on Tuesdays after 6am northbound private traffic is not allowed beyond Gulaba towards the pass. Southbound traffic is unaffected.

Which Overnight Stop?

The Leh–Manali trip can take anywhere from 15 to 22 hours. Overnighting in Sarchu breaks the journey into two roughly equal sections, but the altitude (around 4000m) can cause problems (especially if heading northbound, as you're unlikely to be acclimatised). Note that there are essentially two Sarchus: a 500m strip of cheap, ugly metal-shack cafes just north of the Km222 bridge, and a dozen bedded tent-camps mostly dotted between Km214 and Km217.4 on an attractive raised riverside plateau. There's also a series of metal huts at Km205.8.

Stopping at Keylong, Jispa (Km138 to Km139) and Gemur (Km134) is more comfortable, with better accommodation at significantly lower altitudes, but Leh–Keylong is a very long day's ride.

To make Leh–Manali a three-day ride you might stop in Pang (Km298) and then Keylong. Pang has an altitude of 4634m, so the unacclimatised might need to use the army camp's free oxygen if altitude sickness hits. Pang's parachute cafes and mud-walled hostel rooms are very basic.

Lonely parachute cafes are also available at Debring (Km343 and Km340), Whisky Nallah (Km270), Bharatpur (Km197), Zingzingbar (Km174) and Darcha Bridge (Km143). There's generally one midsummer tent at Taglang La, too.

single lonely homestay at Yurutse; should that be full you might have to backtrack to Rumbak. Start early the next morning; cross the Ganda La (4920m) and descend to tiny Shingo (six to seven hours), where there are three homestays.

Rumbak VILLAGE

Rumbak's compact old core has an architectural coherence that makes it one of the most appealing of Ladakh's roadless villages. A fine saw-toothed mountain horizon adds to the scene. Barely three hours' walk from Zingchen (and an easy taxi hop from Leh), Rumbak (along with Yurutse) makes a good one- or two-day hiking escape from the capital, and nine families here offer homestays.

In March, Rumbak is a popular starting point for snow leopard-watching treks. In summer you can hike to Stok, in a strenuous seven to eight hours, via the 4900m Stok La (Namling La) pass: turn left and descend at the second mini-pass. (If there's cloud on the pass, don't attempt this without a guide.) You might also stay in Rumbak before scaling 6121m Stok Kangri, or as you hike the longer variant of the Markha Valley Trail.

Rumbak & Yurutse Day Hike HIKING

For a satisfying one-day hike, prebook a return taxi to **Zingchen** (Jingchan) (around ₹3000 for up to six people), starting around 7am, returning 5.30pm. Walk up a lovely river valley for 3½ to four hours to mysterious one-house village **Yurutse** via a parachute tent (around halfway), which serves Maggi noodle breakfasts. Return via brilliant, old-world Rumbak village (1¼ hours) using a short-cut high trail with great views. Perhaps sample *chhang* (barley beer) in a traditional home before strolling back to Zingchen.

Though constantly uphill, the route to Yurutse is never seriously steep and has no high passes. The path is easy to follow except just after the parachute tent: essentially stay on the left (true right) bank until the next side valley where you cross the main river on a double tree-trunk 'bridge'. Opposite the next side valley keep right and take the rising path (rather than the riverside) to climb to Yurutse.

On return the side path to Rumbak is very obvious, contouring round the hillside immediately after you cross back across the twin-trunk bridge.

Friendly families at Yurutse and Rumbak will serve tea to visitors, but naturally you are expected to pay.

Nubra Valley

☎01980

The deep-cut Shayok and Nubra River Valleys offer tremendous scenery on a grand scale, with green oasis villages surrounded by thrillingly stark scree slopes, boulder fields and harsh arid mountains. There are sand dunes, monasteries, a ruined palace and – at Turtuk and Bogdang – a whole different culture (Balti) to discover. Permits are required by foreigners.

ℹ Getting There & Away

The majority of visitors explore the Nubra Valley using a chartered jeep from Leh. There are many variants. Leh–Diskit–Hunder return in two days costs from ₹7800 per vehicle. One day is far too rushed to really enjoy the experience. A Leh–Turtuk three-day return costs ₹13,872. To add Sumur/Panamik costs around ₹1500/2500 extra.

Alternatively, as long as you have Nubra permits, it's easy enough to travel by shared jeep to Diskit, where there is a taxi stand to organise local excursions and from which Turtuk is reachable by bus (daily except Sundays). It's possible to visit Hunder on the way back from Turtuk, taking a cheap taxi back to Diskit after you've explored.

While most visitors access Nubra via Khardung La, a narrow road across the remote Wari La has been upgraded and allows an alternative loop returning via Agham and Shakti/Takthog.

Leh to Diskit

The Nubra road zigzags up stark bare-rock mountains for around 1½ hours to **Khardung La** (Leh-Diskit Rd Km39), which at 5602m is claimed (disputably) to be the world's highest motorable pass. Descending again, look for marmot and *dzo* (a cow and yak cross-breed) around the pretty pond known rather misleadingly as **Tsolding Buddha Park** (Leh-Diskit Rd Km50.5). Army posts check permits and passports at Km24 and Km53. After **Khardung** village (Km71 to Km72), the scenery takes on a Grand Canyon grandeur. There are splendid Shayok Valley views at Km86, with the green fields of **Tsati** village far below fading into the grey-white river sands. **Khalsar** (Km95) was ravaged in 2015 by floods but there are still a couple of small restaurants; one 2km beyond Khalsar offers free archery and various **rafting** (☎9419300811, 9818983983; rsrkhalsar@gmail.com; Khalsar-Diskit Rd Km3.5; per person ₹800-1800; ⊙May–mid-Sep) opportunities on the

Shayok River. Some 10km after Khalsar, the river plain has a series of modest sand dunes on which you can **ride quad bikes** (☎9419834983; Leh-Diskit Rd Km103.5, Khalsar sand dunes; ₹1200; ⏰7.30am-7pm May-Sep).

The latter route is seriously landslide-prone and crosses major fords (at Km20.6, Km25.5 and Km28.3 from Agham) that can be very hard to cross on a summer's afternoon, so leave early in the morning.

Diskit

POP 1850 / ELEV 3125M

Diskit is centred around a brash bazaar street that leads down from Nubra's only bus/taxi station, perpendicular to the Leh–Turtuk road. From the bottom of the bazaar, swing right past the Spangla Guesthouse to find an altogether softer Diskit along a lane that leads 1.5km to the Old Diskit area of stupas, a big *mani* wall and a crumbling old Ladakhi mansion. Where the Old Town lane rejoins the main Leh–Hunder road, a 2km spaghetti of hairpins winds up to splendid **Diskit Gompa** (Ganden Tashi Chosling Gompa; ₹30; ⏰7am-7pm) passing a gigantic (32m) full-colour **Chamba (Maitreya Buddha) statue** (Diskit Gompa Rd) on an intermediate hill.

In the bazaar area, **Sand Dune Hotel** (☎01980-220022, 9419568208; r standard/luxury ₹1200/2000, s/d without bathroom ₹400/500) has the prettiest garden of six decent options. For bargain deals, look across town near the base of the Diskit Gompa access lane, notably upstairs rooms at stream-serenaded **Kharyok Deluxe Guest House** (☎9469176131, 01980-220050, 9419538846; kharyokguesthouse@gmail.com; Diskit bypass; r downstairs/upstairs ₹600/800; P 📶) or the newest rooms at old faithful **Sunrise Guest House** (☎01980-220011, 9469261853; sunrise.guest66@gmail.com; Old Diskit; s/d ₹500/600, d/tr without bathroom ₹300/350; ⏰May-Sep). There are several additional choices in between.

ℹ Getting There & Away

Shared jeeps to Leh (₹400, 4½ hours) depart when full from Diskit bus station between 6.45am and approximately 9am. There are also overloaded afternoon minibuses to virtually every main Nubra village (including Panamik 3pm and Turtuk 2.30pm, except Sundays) returning early morning.

For charter jeeps, ask at the **Nubra Taxi Union** (☎9469727786, 01980-220339; ⏰7am-6pm). Useful fares include:

Diskit Gompa ₹200 return
Hunder direct/via camel point ₹300/400
Tegar & Sumur ₹2000 return
Turtuk ₹3474/4517 one way/return
Spangmik (Pangong Tso) via Agham ₹8900.

Hunder

POP 1240 / ELEV 3085M

Lost in greenery and closely backed by soaring valley cliffs, Hunder village is far and away Nubra's top attraction for Indian visitors, who settle into relatively comfy guesthouses and tent camps, and then spend the late afternoon riding **Bactrian camels** (Hunder sand dunes; per 15min/hr ₹200/600; ⏰May-Sep) through a series of photogenic sand dunes. The riding point is nearly 3km from Old Hunder, where a precarious little ridge-top **fort ruin** rises high above the main road near the modest **gompa** (⏰6-8am) and a fascinating series of *mani* walls, stupas and sub-shrines.

Increasingly, foreign backpackers who don't require the relative comfort of Hunder's accommodation options tend to make their way to less-commercial Turtuk or visit Hunder from nearby Diskit, which has better transport connections.

Hidden in pretty, semi-rural settings, accommodation comprises around 20 garden guesthouses, a handful of slightly larger 'hotels', a cottage resort and a dozen 'luxury' camps. Most of the latter seem overpriced, but **Kora Valley** (☎9469517223, 01980-221339; www.thakora.in; Umbey Rd; d tent ₹2000, incl full board ₹3000; ⏰May-Sep; P 📶) 🍃 offers decent value. You can usually turn up and find something without booking ahead if you're not too fussy, but you might need to search around a bit during peak season.

Most Hunder guesthouses charge in the ₹1000 to ₹1500 range, such as the pleasant **Goba Guest House** (☎01980-221083, 9419827912; rkkhadka2805@gmail.com; d ₹1000-1200; ⏰Apr-Sep). There's very little in the sub-₹600 range, but ever-helpful Gulam's **Himalayan Guest House** (☎01980-221131, Ghulam 9469177470; www.facebook.com/himalayanhunder; d/tr from ₹600/800, s/d/tr without bathroom ₹400/450/500; ⏰Apr-Oct) (note, *not* Himalayan Eco Resort) remains a reliable backpacker choice, and the small, family-run **Galaxy Guest House** (☎01980-221054, 9419585450; dm/d/q ₹300/1000/1200, incl half-board ₹500/1500/2000; ⏰Apr-Nov; P 📶) 🍃 has one four-bed dormitory along with its very clean, fair-value en suite rooms.

Turtuk

POP 3750 / ELEV 2790M

The turbulent Shayok valley between Hunder and Turtuk is 80km of scenic magnificence marred only very occasionally by military installations. The grand raw-rock valley briefly narrows near tiny **Changmar**, the western limit of Ladakhi-Buddhist culture. Thereafter, the rare green splashes of village are culturally and linguistically Muslim Balti. The main centres of Turtuk and less-visited **Bogdang** villages are raised patchworks of fields and houses on terrace ledges above the main road. Summer sees locals carting huge bundles of barley straw on their backs between the apricot trees. Upper Turtuk has unforgettable views towards serrated high peaks in Pakistan: the frontline is only 7km away. Indeed Turtuk itself was part of Pakistan until the 1971 war.

Note that while many travellers find Turtuk a Ladakh highlight, some others consider its quiet simplicity doesn't quite justify the long journey.

The village has three distinct sections. The main road passes through the lower part known as Turtuk Chutang. Most guesthouses and homes are in the pretty village area on the raised plateau above, which is divided by a side river into older Turtuk Youl and more open, green Turtuk Farol. The two upper areas are connected by a suspension footbridge.

The main delight is simply watching Turtuk village life and wandering between the beautiful field-hemmed viewpoints. The old houses of Turtuk Youl are being upgraded rapidly but many retain 'coolers' – stone block mini-buildings through which ice-cold streams are funnelled to form natural refrigerators.

The town's **Old Mosque** (Turtuk Youl) has a distinctive wooden minaret with spiral staircase, and the modest little **Pon Khar** (Yabgo Royal House; ☎01980-248114; Turtuk Youl; by donation; ⌚7-9.30pm, hours vary) 'palace' is still home to the raja, who traces the royal family's once-magnificent dynasty in his one-room museum.

For a slightly longer hike you could wander up to the small Buddhist monastery at the Bogdang end of Farol.

Sleeping & Eating

The best views are in Turtuk Farol where the long-term travellers' favourite is **Kharmang Guest House** (☎9596476308, 9469006200, 01980-248104; www.kharmangguesthouse.yolasite.com; Turtuk Farol; d incl half-board summer/winter ₹1800/3000, r without bathroom per person ₹400-700). **Khan Guest House** (☎9469232578, 01980-248130; Turtuk Farol; r per person incl half-board ₹500) is also attractively located, while the rather tatty **Kashmiri Homestay** (☎01980-248117; Turtuk Farol; r per person incl half-board ₹300) has Turtuk's cheapest beds.

LADAKH PERMITS

To visit Nubra Valley, Pangong Tso, Dha Hanu, Tso Moriri and the Upper Indus (beyond Upshi) foreigners require a permit (Indian citizens simply fill in a self-declaration form). Applications must be processed through an approved travel agency, though in 2016 it was possible to start the process online. One minor hitch, for single travellers, is that there must be at least two applicants at the time of application, but agencies can usually fudge this and once you have the permit, travelling alone seems – for now at least – perfectly OK.

Applications must be made before 6pm (or 4pm Sunday) to be valid for next day use, but it's wise to leave a couple of hours' leeway. Before departure, it's a good idea to make several extra copies of your permit.

Permits are valid for up to seven days. On top of the variable agency fee (typically ₹150 to ₹200), the permit cost is composed of three elements: a ₹100 Red Cross contribution; a ₹20 per day 'wildlife fee' (not required for Dha Hanu permits); and a ₹300 ecological tax. The ecological tax is valid for a year, so you won't pay it a second time if you later require another permit, assuming you apply with the same agency.

Foreigners are not generally allowed to visit Hanle village nor to drive the road between Pangong and Tso Moriri via Chushul, Loma and Mahe. For Indian citizens the situation seems to vary year by year; at the time of research, Hanle permits were being given fairly easily by the **DCO** (Deputy Commissioner's Office; Map p230; Polo Ground; ⌚10am-3pm Mon-Sat) in Leh in less than an hour.

On the main road, **Ashoor Guest House** (☎9419800776, 01980-248153; ashoor.turtuk@yahoo.com; Main Rd, Turtuk Chutang; r ₹700-1200, without bathroom from ₹600; ⊙Apr-Oct; P) is great value, and **Turtuk Holiday** (☎9906993123; www.turtukholiday.com; Main Rd, Turtuk; d tent incl half-board ₹4350; ⊙Apr-Oct; P) , currently a garden tent camp, is building a full hotel.

Balti Farm (☎01980-248103; www.turtukholiday.com; Turtuk Holiday, Main Rd, Turtuk; mains ₹200; ⊙8am-10pm) at Turtuk Holiday does imaginative takes on Balti cuisine, with a choice of garden or indoor seating. **Ashoor Restaurant** (Main Rd, Turtuk Chutang; mains ₹80-200, rice ₹90; ⊙7.30am-11pm;) opens late and serves a surprising range of delicious vegetarian curries. Most other 'restaurants' offer little more than chow mein or Maggi instant noodles. If that suits, or if you just fancy nursing a mint tea while listening to the sound of the river, **Friends' Cafe** (Turtuk Farol; mains ₹100, tea ₹20; ⊙7am-9pm May-Sep) is a congenial choice.

Getting There & Away

Bring spare photocopies of your permit.

Shared jeeps (₹200, three hours) and overloaded minibuses (₹100, four hours) leave Turtuk at 6am for Diskit (buses return at 2.30pm, except Sundays) on a mostly well-paved lane. On Saturday mornings a bus departs Leh at 6am for Turtuk (₹370, 10 to 11 hours), returning from Turtuk to Leh at 6am the next morning.

Sumur, Tegar & Panamik

POP 3240 / ELEV 3130M

If you have your own transport, Sumur-Tegar is worth considering as a laid-back Nubra base with a shady orchard environment. Like busier alternative Hunder, **Sumur** even has its own sand dunes with the opportunity for quick **camel-riding** (Khalsar-Panamik Rd Km22; per 15min ₹200; ⊙May-Sep) jaunts. Don't expect much of **Panamik** (Km44), whose sometimes-touted hot springs are pitifully underwhelming. Much more interesting is **Tegar** (Tiger) village, where the **Zimskang Museum** (by donation ₹50; ⊙by request, best evening) is an unmarked historic house, found by descending a footpath alongside chortens and a *mani* wall from the ancient little Manekhang Gompa. High on an unstable hillside above the gompa, the three-storey shell of **Zamskhang Palace** (Khalsar-Panamik Rd Km25) sits above the crumbling rubble of Nubra's former royal citadel (Km25). And an appealing if steep back lane loops back to Sumur via the colourfully rebuilt **Samstemling Gompa** (by donation; ⊙6am-noon & 1.30-6pm).

Sleeping

AO Guesthouse GUESTHOUSE $

(☎9469731976, 9469263966; Sumur Link Rd; r ₹500-1000; ⊙May-Oct) This friendly place has a pleasant garden courtyard, a shared upper terrace and fine views from the best upstairs rooms. The helpful owner has a vehicle if you need transfers, and the guesthouse's proximity to the main junction (Km99.7) also makes it better than most Sumur options for public transport.

Yarab Tso HOTEL $$

(☎9419977423, 01980-223544; www.hotelyarabtso.com; Main Rd Km24.5, Tegar; d ₹1800-2600, incl half-board ₹3100-4300; P) From the outside this is an impressive traditional-style Ladakhi building set in farm-size grounds. Inside, there's an appealing family-style sitting room, but guest room interiors vary substantially, and some have lurid pink trim. Look at a few before choosing (the upper rooms are best).

Getting There & Away

Buses to Diskit depart between 8am and 8.30am, returning about 3pm. A shared jeep-taxi to Leh leaves at 7.30am most mornings.

Pangong Tso

ELEV 4250M

Stretching around 150km (with the eastern two-thirds in China), this mesmerising lake plays artist with a surreal palette of vivid blues, which contrasts magically with the surrounding colourful mineral swirls of starkly arid, snow-brushed mountains. The scene is also striking for the almost total lack of habitation along shores whose turquoise waters can look Caribbean. Visitor activities don't stretch much beyond ogling the ever-changing lake, but one 'sight' is a sand spit nicknamed **'Shooting Point'** since its use as a filmset for the 2009 Bollywood hit *3 Idiots*.

A Leh–Pangong jeep safari is a joy in itself, scenically magnificent and constantly varied with serrated peaks, trickling streams, horse meadows, reflective ponds, drifting sands and a 5369m pass. It's a long drive, so plan on sleeping at least one night (ideally in Spangmik or Man, then drive next morning on unpaved lakeside trails to end-of-the-world Merak). Foreigners require permits (p252) and may not loop to Tso Moriri via Loma Bend (Indians with Chushul permits may do so).

Sleeping

Spangmik

A victim of its own success, pretty Spangmik now has dozens of summer tent camps (typically ₹3000 to ₹5600, walk-in from ₹1500) marring the once-picturesque, dry-stone-walled meadows. But it doesn't take much effort to escape the crowds, especially if you stay at one of the old-fashioned, basic homestays (typically ₹500 including half-board) at the top of the village. Our favourite is the three-room **Gongma** (9469534270; r per person incl half-board ₹500-600).

Right in central Spangmik, overpriced **Ser Bhum Tso Resort** (9419176660, 9469718862; serbhumtso@gmail.com; s/d ₹3543/3665, incl half-board ₹4130/4720; mid-Apr–late Oct) is the nearest approximation to a hotel, with dusty corridors and wind-rattled picture-windows but good beds and en suite facilities. Somewhat more indulgent are the pine-fresh, luxuriously appointed bungalows of **Changla Queen** (01981-201122, 99419818253; changlaqueen17580@gmail.com; s/d ₹2800/3000, incl half-board ₹5000/3500; Mar-late Oct), though they suffer from a slightly isolated, arid location 3km west.

Man

A maze of dry-stone walls and trickling brooks, Man is a quiet and lived-in village. You might be met by helpful, English-speaking **Naga Nurbu** (9469587150; r per person incl half-board ₹500) who runs a small parachute cafe and has a homestay room (four mats on a floor). There are several other simple homestay choices, including **Yokma** (r per person incl half-board ₹500-700), which has views from a small garden sitting area. At the opposite end of the scale, the eight circular units of **Pangong Hermitage** (9419863755; www.wildexp.com; d incl full board ₹10,000-15,000; May-Oct) are astoundingly luxurious for such a remote place – but prices are steep.

Getting There & Away

In summer a bus runs from Leh to Spangmik, departing at 6.30am on Tuesdays, Thursdays and Saturdays (₹270), returning next morning at 8am.

One-/two-day return jeep tours from Leh cost ₹6811/8108 to Spangmik, or ₹7867/9636 to Man and Merak. The road to Spangmik is paved but the 10km onwards to Man is rough. Reaching Merak is essentially impossible on summer afternoons, when the fords become impassably strong.

It's also possible to combine Nubra and Pangong into a single loop, running Leh–Diskit–Pangong–Leh in three days (from ₹20,476), but before booking, check whether the landslide-prone Agham–Shayok road is open.

Tso Moriri Loop

ELEV 4540M (TSO MORIRI)

One of Ladakh's magical great lakes, **Tso Moriri** shimmers with an ever-changing series of reflections in its vivid blue waters. However, the long drive from Leh, while impressive in places, is neither as varied nor as photogenic as the Pangong (p235) route.

In compensation, few tourists come to Tso Moriri, and you'll have a fair chance of encountering nomadic shepherds. The easiest way to visit is on a two- or three-day loop from Leh, overnighting at **Korzok**.

Trips loop back to Leh via Puga's minor salt-crusted springs and mini-geysers then pass close to **Tso Kar**, a large briny lake whose main attraction is for birdwatchers spotting elusive black-necked cranes. Seasonal accommodation is available in nearby **Thukye**, a tiny shepherd's hamlet.

To visit Tso Moriri and the Indus Valley beyond Upshi, foreigners need at least three copies of the relevant permits, issued in Leh. They're checked at Upshi, Mahe Bridge and Korzok. Indian citizens need three self-declaration forms. Permits are not needed for Tso Kar if you visit from the Manali highway.

Sleeping & Eating

Korzok

The best deals are in basic but acceptable homestays. Cheapest options include **Rosefinch** (d without bathroom ₹500-700) and more attractively located **Goose** (9469591231; tr with/without bathroom ₹1200/700), which has lake views from its two best rooms. Marginally more comfortable with simple en suite booth-bathrooms are **Dolphin** (9419856244, 9906995628; d with/without bathroom ₹1500/1000) and **Crane** (9469534654, 9419673332; d ₹1500, incl half-board ₹2000), the latter with views and an English-speaking host.

Rooms at **Hotel Lake View** (☎9419345362, 9469457025; www.tsomoririhotellakeview.com; Korzok; s/d ₹2992/3850; ⊙May–mid-Oct) are pleasantly appointed once you get to them. However, the public areas are tatty.

Korzok has half-a-dozen tiny eateries, including a one-room 'organic cafe' that offers ₹10 water-bottle refills.

Thukye (Tso Kar)

Overlooking the crane breeding grounds at Thukye, rooms 107 to 112 of motel-like **Tsokar Eco Resort** (☎Leh 9419643478; tsokarresort@yahoo.com; s/d/tr ₹2200/2850/3000, s/d without bathroom ₹1600/1800) are the area's only en suite rooms, though there are bedded tents with attached bathrooms at next door **Lotus Camp** (☎9419819078; chotsering100@yahoo.com; d incl half-board ₹4650; ⊙Jun–mid-Sep) and at cheaper, simpler two-tent **Tsepal Guest House** (☎9419851995; tent/room ₹1500/1000; ⊙Jun-Sep).

Getting There & Away

Unless you're prepared to wait for the Korzok public bus (thrice monthly), the only realistic way to reach Tso Moriri is by chartered jeep from Leh, where foreigners will need to apply for a permit. Alternatively, you could continue by hiking to Kibber in Spiti (Himachal Pradesh; one week including a 5500m pass with some glacier walking) or driving to Manali (two nights, three days).

A two-day jeep charter looping Leh–Korzok–Thukye then returning to Leh across Taglang La costs ₹12,890 by Sumo and ₹14,283 by Innova jeep. A three-day, one-way excursion doing the same but then continuing south to Keylong and Manali costs from ₹22,347 and ₹26,223 respectively.

Leh to Kargil

There are many fascinating sights close to the Leh–Srinagar road. You'll need a vehicle to make the most of numerous short diversions, for example to Basgo, Likir and Alchi. The most popular stops en route are Mulbekh (for its castle and ancient carved Buddha statue) and the village of Lamayuru, where there's a memorable monastery and curious 'Moonland' erosion formations. With more time consider canyon-land side trips to Chilling (30km) and/or Wanla-Honupatta.

Hopping by very limited public transport is slow going: other than Leh–Kargil and Leh–Srinagar through buses, the only options west from Khalsi are Leh–Dha buses (daily), Leh–Lamayuru (summer only) and four other weekly services to Chiktan or Fokha. Lamayuru and Khalsi both have a couple of taxis but tracking them down can be difficult. Khalsi also has a daily bus to Wanla.

It makes sense to get a group together in Leh and arrange a shared jeep with side trips, at least as far as Mulbekh or Shargol from where there are buses to Kargil.

Phyang

☎01982 / POP 2160 / ELEV 3580M

Pretty Phyang village is a large, green expanse of layered, tree-hemmed barley fields, 20km from Leh in the next parallel valley west. There's a big **gompa**, a **fortress ruin** and an ancient **Guru Lakhang** (Guru Gonpa; ☎Lobsang Chospal 9596834460, Tsering Norboo 9469728179; gurulakhang@gmail.com; by donation; ⊙on request), but it's almost entirely uncommercialised, with neither hotel nor restaurant. You're most likely to come here to unwind at the Hidden North Guest House, but there are also **farmstays** (☎01982-226117; www.icestupa.org/farmstays; per day approx ₹750) in several local homes.

★**Hidden North Guest House** GUESTHOUSE $
(☎01982-226007, 9419218055; www.hiddennorth.com; Phyang Tsakma; r ₹1000, without bathroom ₹600-800; ⊙May-Sep or by arrangement; P 🛜)
A young Ladakhi–Italian family has created this delightfully relaxing getaway where panoramic views encompass a spiky mountain horizon and Phyang's large, restored gompa, all viewed across a wide green terraced foreground. Meals, guided treks and **animal-watching** (⊙Feb & Mar) trips are available. Free filtered water. Wi-fi after 6pm.

Getting There & Around

From Leh there are buses to the gompa area at 8am and 2.30pm. For the Hidden North Guest House ask for Phyang Tsakma. There's also a 9am 'teachers' bus'. On Saturdays at 4.30pm a minibus runs all the way from Leh to Murabak, returning Monday morning at 8am.

Without your own transport, getting around the village will involve a considerable amount of walking. Fortunately, **Hidden North** (p255) rents a couple of mountain bikes to make things easier.

Nimmu & Chilling

West of Phyang, shortly past the confluence of the Indus and Zanskar Rivers, you'll reach the pretty village of Nimmu, which has several older farmhouses and some appealing accommodation.

Around 30km up the Zanskar from Nimmu, idyllic Chilling is famed for its coppersmiths, but is used mostly as a starting point for rafting (p232) back to Nimmu, or as the trailhead for the Markha Valley Trek (p248), which starts by crossing the river 4km south of town in a dangling basket contraption.

The 90-minute canyon drive from Nimmu to Chilling is worth the effort for the views alone, which stretch over the confluence of the olive-green Indus River and the turbid brown Zanskar. At first glance Chilling seems little more than a teahouse (Km28.6), but hidden above, the village proper is a fascinating place, set on a fertile green plateau, more easily accessed from a low-profile path starting at Km27.9.

Sleeping & Eating

Surprisingly, there's a choice of high-quality accommodation in Nimmu, notably the very characterful Nimmu House. Far more affordable are the good-value roadside properties **Nilza Guest House** (01982-225654, 9622971571; raftanimo@gmail.com; Kargil-Leh Hwy Km387.4, Nimmu; r ₹1200, without bathroom ₹600-800; Jun–mid-Sep) and similarly decent **Takshos Hotel** (01982-225064, 9419815233; Leh-Srinagar Hwy, Nimmu; r ₹1500-2000; Jun-Sep; P, wi-fi).

Five families in Chilling offer ₹1000-per-person homestays.

★ **Nimmu House** HERITAGE HOTEL $$$
(8826293261; http://ladakh.nimmu-house.com; off NH1 at Km387.6, Nimmu; s/d incl full board ₹10,950/12,100; late Apr-late Sep; P, wi-fi) A fabulous three-storey mansion and palace, once belonging to cousins of the Ladakhi royals. It's at once supercomfortable, with memory-foam beds and light-touch luxurious interiors, while maintaining the spirit of the old building, with wobbly old floors, antique pillars and several unrestored elements including the upper-floor shrine rooms where the octogenarian owner still perambulates most evenings to say her prayers.

Getting There & Away

Chilling is 28km south of Nimmu and is served by a bus from Leh that leaves 9am Sundays (plus Wednesdays in winter), continues to the Markha Valley trekking point, then returns around 1pm the same afternoon.

Basgo & Ney

POP 1680 / ELEV 3650M

Basgo was once a capital of lower Ladakh, and the shattered remnants of its former **citadel and palace** (Basgo; per temple ₹30) form a remarkable sight above the NH1 highway. It's worth the 1.6km detour to the top of the stabilised ruins to enjoy unusual views and to visit two enclosed two-storey medieval Maitreya statues, one of bronze, the other of painted clay. Driving another 8km north through the verdant oasis village of Ney brings you to the gleaming golden form of a new **giant Buddha statue**, claimed to be nearly 26m tall, though that includes the three-storey building that forms his 'stool'.

Sham (Likir, Yangthang, Hemis Shukpachan & Timishgan)

01982

The 'Sham baby trek' is popularly used as a three-day acclimatisation warm-up hike. Its big advantages are a lack of high passes, ample homestays and the fact that you can choose to stop at any stage and still have a relatively painless way to get back to Leh. Downsides include lack of shade and the fact that the route parallels, and partly follows, the Likir–Yangthang–Hemis Shukpachan road, which will soon extend to Timishgan. Although typically started from Likir, the longer Likir–Yangthang leg could easily be skipped without great loss. In fact an interesting alternative is to walk Timishgan–Hemis Shukpachan–Yangthang then descend via **Rizong Gompa** (7am-1pm & 1.30-6pm) to the NH1 at Uletokpo.

Likir has the comfortable and inviting **Hotel Lhukhil** (9419214715; sonam.yasmin@yahoo.com; s/d ₹1530/2060, incl half-board ₹2190/2700; mid-May–mid-Sep; P), plus a few good-value if very simple budget options in the scenic area up by the photogenic **Likir Gompa** (Upper Likir; museum ₹20; 8am-1pm & 2-6pm), which is backed by a giant, gleaming, gold-painted 20th-century Maitreya statue.

The magical little hamlet of **Yangthang** has four traditional if basic homestays with floor mattresses and meals included. In **Hemis Shukpachan** are nearly a dozen widely scattered homestays and a small tent resort/guesthouse.

In **Timishgan**, a former Ladakhi capital that is a particularly worthy destination in its own right, you'll find numerous homestays, several also offering camping facilities in their yards, plus **Namra Hotel** (☎9419178324, 01982-229033; www.namrahotel.com; Ang Rd; s/d/ste ₹2915/3465/4785, incl half-board ₹4015/4565/5885), an oasis of comfort for arriving trekkers. Five kilometres from central Timishgan, **Tia** is one of Ladakh's most delightful village ensembles.

Getting There & Away

A daily bus runs from Leh to Timishgan and Tia at 1pm, returning at 8am. On alternate days, there's a Leh–Hemis Shukpachan bus on a similar schedule driving via Likir and Yangthang. There's also a daily Leh–Likir bus. The daily bus from Likir Gompa to Leh leaves around 7.30am. If you want to leave later, walk down to the NH1 (around 1.5km from lower Likir) and pick up the (summer-only) bus from Lamayuru that should pass through some time between 4pm and 5.30pm.

Alchi & Saspol

POP 2380 / ELEV 3100M

The rural village of Alchi has become a regional tourism magnet thanks to the special murals and carvings of the world-famous **Choskhor temple complex** (foreigner/Indian ₹50/20; ⌚8am-1pm & 2-6pm), founded in the early 11th century by 'Great Translator' Lotsava Ringchen Zangpo. The complex comprises four main temple buildings. Each one is small and unobtrusive from outside but their design and millennium-old murals are rare archetypes of Ladakh's first wave of Indo-Tibetan Buddhist art.

If you want more in the same genre, don't miss the **triple chamba** (Chamchen Choskorling; NH1 Km371.5) at nearby Saspol, which also has Zangpo-era **cave paintings** (Gon Nila-Phuk) cut into the cliff beneath its ruined fortress. Or escape the crowds altogether by visiting the 10th-century **temple complex** (Manggyu) at Manggyu, some 15km from the Alchi Bridge.

In the the temple area, Alchi has around a dozen accommodation options, though several offer lacklustre rooms behind misleadingly tempting facades. Walk-in bargains are often available. In a sizeable garden 800m back towards Leh, the friendly, all-en suite **Choskor Guest House** (☎9419826363; Alchi; s ₹300-500, d ₹500-700; P 📶) charges homestay prices for decent, if older, guesthouse rooms. Another alternative is to sleep across the river in Saspol which has three homestays; the super-obliging **Thongyok** (☎9419001904, 9419177523; thongyok.guesthouse@gmail.com; NH1 Km371.3; dm ₹300, r with/without bathroom ₹1500/700; P 📶) is especially recommended.

★ **Alchi Kitchen** LADAKHI $

(☎9419438642; alchikitchen@gmail.com; Alchi; mains ₹100-250; ⌚7.30am-10pm May-Sep, closed 11am-2pm Wed & Sat) If you thought Ladakhi food a little bland, think again. Alchi Kitchen's flavoursome *skyu* and *chhutagi* (both barley-pasta shapes in vegetable stew) are laboriously made to order in the open kitchen, where cooking lessons are held on Wednesday and Saturday lunchtimes (half-hour sessions ₹300; call one day ahead). Tangy chutneys, salads, breakfasts and apricot desserts are also served in the striking, mod-trad restaurant.

Getting There & Away

Central Alchi is 4km down a dead-end spur lane that leaves the Leh–Kargil road at Km370, immediately crossing a bridge over the Indus. Direct buses to Leh depart daily at 7.30am from both Alchi (₹100, 2¼ hours) and Saspol (₹90, two hours), returning at 4pm and 3pm respectively. A return taxi from Alchi to Mangyyu would cost around ₹2500 – if you could find one to take you.

Yapola Valley

The lane running south from Km317.8 on the NH1 (8km east of Lamayuru) links several fascinating, unspoilt villages, a superb canyon and some of Ladakh's most impressive mountain landscapes. **Wanla** alone is worth the brief diversion from the Leh–Kargil road to see its tiny medieval **gompa** (www.achiassociation.org; ₹20; ⌚dawn-dusk) perched on a knife-edge ridge above town. At minuscule **Phanjila**, a spur road diverges to appealing **Hinju**, where homestays can arrange horses for the trek to Sumdha Do (two days) and Chilling (three days), crossing the 4950m **Konze La** (strenuous).

South of Phanjila, a newly improved road passes through utterly spectacular **Yapola Gorge** beside traditional, closely clumped **Honupatta** village, then across the magnificent **Sisir La** and **Sengge La** passes (rougher, summer only), descending in between to **Photoksar**, a cliff-knoll village at over 4100m. Jeeps can now reach the 4425m **Kyupa La** pass, from which Lingshet, trekking base for reaching Zanskar, is a half-day walk.

Wanla has four homestays and guesthouses, of which the most tempting is the **Rongstak** (☎9419982366, 9419371005; Phanjila Rd Km6.3, Wanla; per person incl full board ₹1100;

TREKKING IN LADAKH & ZANSKAR

Bargain-value, thrillingly scenic treks can take you into magical roadless villages, through craggy gorges and across stark, breathless mountain passes flapping with prayer flags.

Seasons

The main trekking season is from late June to late August, though in the Markha and Sham areas routes can be feasible from May to early October. Late August is usually preferable for trails with significant river crossings due to lower water levels.

Preparation

Most trekking routes start around 3500m, often climbing above 5000m, so proper acclimatisation is essential to avoid Acute Mountain Sickness (AMS). You could acclimatise with 'baby' treks or by adding extra (if less interesting) days to the core treks – for instance starting from Lamayuru or Martselang rather than Hinju/Photoksar or Shang Sumdo – but this often means walking along roads or jeep tracks. Other tips:

- Consider prebooking a jeep transfer back from your finishing point.
- Carry a walking stick and backed sandals for wading rivers.
- Use water-filtering bottles for convenience.

Horse Treks

At these altitudes, carrying heavy packs is much more exhausting than many walkers anticipate. For wilder routes, engaging packhorses reduces the load and the accompanying horseperson can often double as a guide. Agencies will very happily arrange all-inclusive packages with horses, guides, food and (often old) camping gear. If you're self-sufficient and patient it's often possible to find your own horseperson from around ₹700 per horse or donkey per day. Note that you will almost always need to engage more than one horse as the animals need 'company' and the horseperson might not want to leave others behind. You'll also pay for any extra days needed for them to return to their next starting point. During harvest season (August) availability drops and prices rise.

Homestay Treks

Almost all rural villages along well-trodden trekking routes offer very simple but wonderfully authentic homestays. The cost is typically fixed at ₹1000 per person (less in Zanskar) including simple meals that are often taken in the traditional family kitchen. Mudbrick rooms generally have rugs, blankets and solar-battery electric lamps.

Smaller villages occasionally run out of homestay beds but you can usually find floor space in kitchens or dining rooms. Bigger villages such as Rumbak, Hinju and Skiu/Kaya can generally handle all comers, but they work on a rota system, meaning sometimes one homestay will be full while others remain empty.

May-Oct) at the northern edge of town. There's also camping here and at Phanjila, a single homestay at Ursi and many more in Hinju. Honupatta and Photoksar have homestays.

Mid-sized buses run each morning from Wanla to Khalsi, returning at 3.30pm.

Lamayuru

01982 / POP 700 / ELEV 3390M

Slow-paced Lamayuru is one of Ladakh's most memorable villages and an ideal place to break the journey from Kargil to Leh. Set among mountain-backed badlands, picturesque homes huddle around a crumbling central hilltop that's a Swiss cheese of caves and erosion pillars topped by a photogenic gompa.

Yungdrung Gompa BUDDHIST MONASTERY
(Lamayuru Monastery; NH1 Km310.1; ₹50; 7am-1pm & 1.30-6pm) Lamayuru's gompa is one of the most photogenic Buddhist monasteries in Ladakh. It caps the village's central hill, whose eroded slopes are huddled with picturesque homes and pitted with caves.

You might also find seasonal parachute cafes, so named as they are tents made from old army parachutes. These provide tea and simple snacks, and sometimes offer very basic lodging.

Having an experienced local guide is not only useful for route finding but also for making social interactions more meaningful at homestays. With a couple of days' notice you can engage a guide through **Hemis National Park Guide Service** (Map p230; ☎9906975427; hemis_npark@yahoo.co.in; 1st fl, unit 11, Hemis Complex, Upper Tukcha Rd, Leh; ⏲10am-6pm) or through trekking agencies. Costs average around ₹2000 per day including food.

Which Trek?

Popular options:

DAYS	ROUTE	HOMESTAYS	HIGH PASSES
2	Zingchen-Rumbak-Stok	plenty	4900m
2 (3)	Hinju-Sumdha Chenmo-(Sumdha Chun)-Sumdha Do	limited	4950m
2	Anmu-Phuktal-Anmu	yes	no
3	Zingchen-Yurutse-Skiu-Chilling	yes	4920m
4+	Chilling-Kaya-Markha-Hankar-Nimaling-Shang Sumdo	yes (or tent-camp)	5260m
5 (8)	(Rumtse)-Tso Kar-Korzok	no	4 (7)
5 (8)	(Padum)-Anmu-Phuktal-Ramjak (Darcha)	some days	5090m
4 (9)	(Lamayuru-Photoksar)-Kyupa La-Lingshet-Pidmo-(Padum)	limited	2 (5)

For a relatively easy trek, Zingchen–Rumbak–Yurutse–Zingchen makes a great one- or two-day sampler from Leh.

For a link to Spiti, try the six-night Korzok–Kibber trek, which has just one major pass and a river crossing.

Further Information

- Lonely Planet's *Trekking in the Indian Himalaya*
- *Ladakh Zanskar* (http://ladak.free.fr) by Jean Louis Taillefer. Excellent if you read French.
- Cicerone's *Trekking in Ladakh*
- My Himalayas (www.myhimalayas.com/travelogues/ladakh.htm) Info on trekking routes for Ladakh, dating predominantly from 2006 to 2007 but mostly still relevant.

Sleeping & Eating

Lamayuru has around a dozen small, budget guesthouses.

Tharpaling Guest House GUESTHOUSE $
(☎9419343917, 01982-224516; NH1 Km310.9; d ₹500) Ever-smiling matriarch Tsiring Yandol gives this roadside place a jolly family feel, serving dinners in a particularly homely communal dining room. All but two rooms have en suite bathrooms.

Lion's Den GUESTHOUSE $
(☎9419880499, 01982-224542; liondenhouse@gmail.com; NH1 Km311.7; d ₹900-1000, r without bathroom ₹600; 📶) At the very eastern edge of town (towards Leh), Lion's Den has fair-value standard rooms, but its big hit is room 101, which has excellent views of the 'moonland' erosion zone from box windows and an unfenced balcony. Towels and toilet paper provided. Appealing Ladakhi dining room downstairs.

Dragon Hotel GUESTHOUSE **$$**
(Tashi Homestay; 01982-224501, 9469294037; https://dragonhotellamayuru.wordpress.com; r ₹2000, s/d without bathroom ₹400/500; hotel May-Sep, homestay year-round;) Accessed through a garden restaurant directly behind the bus stop, the Dragon Hotel's upper rooms (103, 104, 107 and 108) are attractively appointed with new geyser bathrooms. The homestay section is spartan in contrast but clean, and the rooftop has great views.

Hotel Moonland HOTEL **$$**
(9419888508, 01982-224576; www.hotelmoonland.in; NH1 Km310.5; s/d ₹1200/1500; late Apr-Sep;) Set in a pretty garden at the first hairpin, 400m beyond the bus stop, Moonland's rooms have droopy curtains and offer little in terms of decor, but all come with tiled hot-shower bathrooms. The agreeable restaurant has postcard-perfect views across barley fields towards the monastery complex. Dinner costs ₹330 and beer is available for ₹200.

Getting There & Away

Most buses stop only briefly in passing, and times can be plus or minus an hour:

Chiktan Departs around 1pm Tuesday, Thursday and Sunday.

Fokha via Shargol and Mulbekh Departs around lunchtime on Saturday.

Kargil Departs between 9am and 10am.

Leh Departs daily at 2pm in summer. The Kargil–Leh bus passes through between 8.30am and 9.30am daily but is often full on arrival. Other services stop at around 11am four days a week.

Srinagar Early evening. Hopefully.

Mulbekh, Wakha & Shargol

01985 / POP 4060 / ELEV 3270M

The Wakha–Mulbekh Valley looks like a calm grass-green sea over which a vast tsunami of frothing red mountains is about to crash. It's breathtaking at sunset, especially when viewed from the former castle site.

This is the last predominantly Buddhist area on the route west from Leh, a role Mulbekh flaunts with its famous roadside Buddha Relief and two small but intriguing little monasteries, Rgyal Gompa near Wakha and Shargol Gompa some 10km to the west.

The area's best accommodation is **Horizon Camp** (9469045459; horizonladakhcamp@gmail.com; NH1 Km245, Wakha; d ₹1500, incl half-board ₹2300; May-Sep; P), an unusually fair-value bedded tent camp in a beautiful roadside flower garden, 150m from Wakha's petrol station. Central Mulbekh has several inexpensive, friendly homestay-guesthouses.

Mulbekh Chamba BUDDHIST MONUMENT
(NH1 Km243.3) Mulbekh's foremost sight is a 1000-year-old Maitreya Buddha relief, carved into an 8m fang of rock. It's right by the roadside, rising through the middle of the minuscule Chamba Gompa and partly shaded by a tree flapping with prayer flags.

Mulbekh Castle Site VIEWPOINT
Mulbekh is overlooked by the impregnable site of King Tashi Namgyal's 18th-century castle, high high above. Burnt during an 1835 raid, the castle has only two tower stubs remaining, but the site sports a small gompa, and a new one is under construction. There are symphonic views across the green valley to the highly sculpted rocky mountains behind.

Getting There & Away

Several overloaded Kargil-bound buses (from Chiktan, Shakar etc) pass through between 7am and 8.30am, returning ex Kargil around 3pm. In the afternoon, a J&K SRTC bus leaves Shargol for Kargil at 3pm (returning 7am).

A Kargil–Fokha bus departs Kargil at 2.30pm returning the next morning, and on Saturdays there's a Leh–Fokha bus returning Sunday morning.

Towards Lamayuru the Kargil bus passes through Mulbekh between 6am and 7am, usually making a breakfast stop at Wakha. To reserve a seat, flag down the Leh–Kargil bus the day before and leave a deposit.

KARGIL & ZANSKAR

Ladakh's less visited 'second half' comprises remote, sparsely populated Buddhist Zanskar and the slightly greener Suru Valley. Residents of the Suru Valley, and its regional capital, Kargil, predominantly follow Shia Islam. Scenery reaches some truly majestic mountain climaxes.

Kargil

01985 / POP 18,200 / ELEV 2690M

If you're arriving from Srinagar, Ladakh's proudly Muslim second city seems quaint, with its vibrant workshops and old merchant stores cramming the packed, ramshackle central area. Coming from Padum or Leh, however, Kargil can feel grimy, male-dominated and a tad chaotic.

The city is deep within a high-sided river valley. The landscape looks more attractive if you climb to the little **Central Asian Museum** (Munshi Aziz Bhat Museum; ☎9419289275, 9469730109; www.kargilmuseum.org; 147 Munshi Enclave; admission/camera ₹50/50; ⊙8am-8pm Apr-Nov, 10am-5pm Dec-Mar), which celebrates Kargil's former glory as a trading post on caravan routes. It's up the stairway that starts around three minutes' walk along Main Bazaar from Roots Cafe (p262), which is Kargil's most traveller-friendly address. The cafe is a sensible first stop to get inspired for treks, excursions, rafting or other activities in the fascinating but little-visited region around the city. Don't miss an excursion to Hundarman.

Kargil's central junction is Lal Chowk where north–south Main Market intersects with Hospital Rd around 300m uphill from Poyen Bridge.

★Hundarman VILLAGE

(www.rootscollectiveindia.org; admission without/with guide ₹100/250; ⊙10am-5pm Sat-Thu or by arrangement) Set in a sharp mountain gully 11km from Kargil, the tumbledown ghost village of Hundarman is a remarkable sight. Rocky crags tower above, a steeply raked arc of stone-walled terraces sits below and virtually all of the low-ceilinged homes are stacked on top of one another, forming a fascinating core that has been (somewhat) preserved as a unique time capsule.

A guided visit organised through Roots Cafe (₹250 per person plus ₹700 taxi return) is recommended, as it gets you into two museum rooms displaying aged utensils, touching personal mementos of former residents and projectiles that hit the village in the various Indo-Pakistan wars. En route there's the curiosity of passing through the minefield area that once formed the Indo-Pakistan border. And at a lonely tea shack (Km7), binoculars are rented (₹20) for better glimpses of the current Line of Control at the ruined village of Brolma.

While some of Hundarman's former population now live in Pakistan, the upper village 1km beyond is still populated and is a fascinating place to wander as well, though you'll need your passport and a local guide to get past the army checkpoint.

Sleeping

If your budget is really tight, try the ragged but survivable **Tourist Bungalow II** (d ₹400), hidden behind Hussaini Park, or gloomy **Kacho Guesthouse** (☎9469562070; Hospital Rd; d ₹500), with its cheery apricot garden. But when occupancy is low, far better hotels often slash their rates, and you can find good deals at around ₹1000.

Several hotels claim to offer wi-fi, but none actually worked in our experience. (Main Bazaar has several internet cafes that are far from reliable.)

New International Guest House GUESTHOUSE $

(☎01985-233044, 9419176568; 73murtaza@gmail.com; Hussaini Park; r ₹1200-1500, walk-in ₹800-1200; ⊙May-Oct) Contrasting vividly with most of the other bus station dives, this guesthouse has rooms that are unusually airy and well kept despite the difficulty of cleaning the carpeted floors. Owner Mohammad Murtaza is charming and helpful.

Tourist Facilitation Centre GUESTHOUSE $

(TFC; ☎Manzoor 9469464964; d/ste ₹820/1500; ⊙Apr-Oct) Up a theatrical spiral staircase in a still-fresh 2012 building, great-value double rooms are hotel-standard, with fan, geyser and carved wooden bedsteads – many with Suru views. 'VIP' rooms come with ludicrously oversized lounges containing up to a dozen sofas apiece.

The hotel is in Bemathang's riverside park, 1.5km south of the centre towards Baroo. Book through the Tourist Reception Centre (p262).

★Hotel Jan Palace HOTEL $$

(☎9419504904, 01985-234135; www.janpalacekargil.com; Bus Station Approach; r ₹2300-4000, walk-in ₹1000-1500, mains ₹165-430) Management changed in 2016, but the Jan Palace's spacious rooms remain among the brightest and most reliably clean in central Kargil. Bedrooms offer little decorative style, but modern bathrooms are spotless and come with towels, toiletries and super-hot solar showers. Interesting rooftop views, too.

★Zojila Residency HOTEL $$

(☎9419176249, 01985-232281; www.zojilaresidency.com; Bemathang; s/d/ste ₹2420/3260/5860; ⊙Apr-Oct; 📶) A professional lobby leads to fresh rooms that have high ceilings, stylish white, olive and purple colour schemes and slightly art deco wooden furniture. Many rooms face the river across a waterside garden with ample (albeit unshaded) seating.

Around 300m beyond Iqbal (Bardo) bridge, it's the best of several choices in the Bemathang neighbourhood, 1km south of central Kargil.

Eating

Charming little **Roots Cafe** (9419289275; www.rootscollectiveindia.org; Main Bazaar; 8am-10pm) is popular for snacks. Of numerous Main Bazaar options, our favourite is the **PC Palace Restaurant** (PC Palace Hotel, Main Bazaar; mains ₹110-385; 7.30am-10pm). Along the lane descending to Poyen Bridge from Lal Chowk, a series of snack carts appears from early afternoon. At least four bakeries operate in the central area.

Information

Tourist Reception Centre (01985-232721; 10am-4pm Mon-Sat) Follow signs from Main Bazaar to this vine-draped governmental building and head upstairs to get a free copy of the very useful *Exploring Kargil* guide-map. You can also book Suru Valley tourist bungalows here.

Getting There & Away

Charter and shared jeeps to Leh and Srinagar leave from the **Jeep Drivers' Cooperative** (01985-232079; Lal Chowk) just off Main Market.

For Zanskar, shared jeeps depart from the 'old bus station', now called 'Hussaini Park', just east of Khomeini Chowk, a block south of Lal Chowk. A **ticket office** (Hussaini Park; 7am-7pm) here sells tickets for private buses to Leh and Srinagar, which leave from outside.

A **J&K SRTC bus ticket booth** (9469530271; Hussaini Park; 9am-4pm) is hidden away at the back of Hussaini Park. Private services for Kargil-region destinations mostly use the large **local bus station**, around 1km southeast.

Leh Buses (private/J&K SRTC ₹400/550, 10 hours, one to two daily) depart Hussaini Park around 4.30am, passing Mulbekh (two hours) and Lamayuru (five hours). You might still find a shared jeep (₹900 to ₹1000) as late as 7am. Charters cost ₹7100.

Mulbekh Minibuses (₹60) leave at 2pm and 3pm from the local bus station, returning next morning.

Srinagar Private buses (₹400, 10 hours, one to two daily) depart Hussaini Park at 10pm, driving overnight to reach the hair-raising Zoji La Pass before the one-way system for large vehicles reverses. Shared jeeps (₹900, seven hours) can leave any time. Road conditions permitting, it's worth hiring your own taxi (₹6400) to experience the scenery, which is especially memorable between Drass and Kangan.

Suru Valley For Sanku and nearer villages, red-and-white minibuses depart sporadically from the local bus station. For Panikhar (₹80), the 7.30am J&K SRTC bus loads up on Main Bazaar at Lal Chowk. The 11.30am bus for Parkachik and the 12.30pm service to Barsoo (for Khartse Khar) leave from a small area between Hussaini Park and the river. Between noon and 2pm you might find shared Omni micro-vans to Panikhar from Poyen Bridge; chartering to Panikhar/Parkachik costs ₹2100/2800.

Zanskar Kargil–Padum buses are sporadic. Shared jeeps (₹1000 to ₹2000, 10 to 12 hours) park in the old bus station and depart at dawn or earlier. Chartering costs ₹13,400, with a ₹2275 supplement if you want to overnight en route at Rangdum or Parkachik. Book through the central Jeep Drivers' Cooperative or via **Roots Cafe** (p262).

Getting Around

By day, micro-vans (₹10) shuttle down the riverside from Poyen Bridge via the main bus station to Bemathang and Baroo.

Suru Valley

01985

Potentially as big an attraction as better-known Zanskar, to which it is the main access route, the Suru Valley's semi-alpine Muslim villages are dotted among wide green valleys with fabulous snow-topped mountainscapes rising above. These are most apparent between **Purtikchay** and **Damsna** and again from **Parkachik**. If you're driving, consider a 5km detour east of busy little Sanku towards Barsoo/Bartoo to see the **Khartse Khar Buddha** (Barsoo Rd, Khartse Khar) carving.

The valley has little tourist infrastructure, but English-speaking guide Gulam Ali is a helpful contact should you want trekking ideas. He runs the homestay-style Hotel Khayoul, hidden away near the tourist bungalow in the upper west area of **Panikhar**; call ahead as he also works in Kargil.

Sleeping

Good budget options include the unpretentious but decently maintained J&K Tourist Bungalows at several Suru locations. The best are at Purtikchay, Tangole and Parkachik, but there are also bungalows at Sanku,

Panikhar and Rangdum; book at the Tourist Reception Centre in Kargil. There are four guesthouse/homestays between Sanku and Panikhar, of which the most interesting is the **Hotel Khayoul** (☎9469192810, 9419864611; khayoulhotel@gmail.com; Panikhar; r ₹500-600).

Getting There & Away

Private buses run fairly regularly between Kargil and Sanku. J&K SRTC buses to Kargil leave Panikhar around 8am and noon (₹80), and Parkachik (₹112) around 7am.

Share taxis (₹100) are occasionally available on the Panikhar–Kargil route. For Zanskar, onward transport is generally limited to highly uncertain hitching. Panikhar's **Hotel Khayoul** (p263) can organise vehicles with advance notice.

Zanskar

☎01983

Majestically rugged, the greatest attraction of this mountain-hemmed Ladakhi Buddhist valley is simply getting there, preferably on a trek. As in Ladakh, the main sights are timeless monasteries, notably at Karsha, Stongdey, Sani and Phuktal, the latter only accessible on foot. The area's tiny capital, Padum, is not much more than a village with a few shops. It is not a major attraction in itself but is a key transit point if you want to drive in or out on what remains, for now, the only access route (via Kargil). While days can be scorching hot, come prepared for cold nights, even in summer.

Rangdum

POP 280 / ELEV 3980M

Wind-scoured little Rangdum is typically where shared jeeps take a meal break on the 11-hour Kargil–Padum ride. But if the weather is fine and time is short, it's worth forgoing or rushing your snack and using the time to photograph the **village** (away from the uglier restaurant area). **Rangdum Gompa** (₹50) is 5km away, while scenic **Shakmak Kharpo** is worth a trip for a pretty picture.

With its relatively fresh look and open-air terrace, **La Himalaya 3800** (☎9469735834, 9419177627; r without/with bathroom ₹1000/1500, mains ₹40-120; ⏰May-Aug) attracts much of the passing lunch trade, and its guest rooms are Rangdum's neatest. Hidden behind, the outwardly grungy Alpine Hut actually does a very good, cheap *aloo mattar* (potato and pea curry).

Padum

☎01983 / POP 1710 / ELEV 3570M

Zanskar's dusty little capital village is a useful hub with an impressive mountain backdrop, though it lacks much architectural character. Within a block of the central crossroads you'll find the bus/share taxi stand, shops, an unreliable phone/internet cafe, the majority of Padum's dozen hotel-guesthouses and restaurants plus the **helipad**. Older, more atmospheric areas are at **Pibiting**, **Padum Khar** (Old Padum) and across the valley at Karsha (p265). Central Padum is primarily useful as a place to organise or relax after a long trek. Cafe-agency ZAP (p263) is a very useful spot for meeting fellow walkers or arranging excursions.

Unlike most of Zanskar, central Padum has mains electricity for much of the day, and better hotels have generators as backup.

Activities

Multiday trekking remains a popular way to reach the Yapola Valley (north) or Ramjak (south) for connections to Lamayuru or Keylong, respectively. Tents and provisions are needed for some sections, and guides/horses can sometimes be organised on the spot. Ask at your guesthouse, at one of several agencies, or at ZAP, which is unusually active in helping travellers meet companions.

★ZAP ADVENTURE SPORTS
(Zanskar Adventure Point; www.zapladakh.com; Main Bazaar; ⏰8.30am-10pm) ZAP is the go-to centre in Padum for information about Zanskar travel, trekking help and shared transport (sign-up lists for Pidmo, Ichar etc) – and the satellite wi-fi (₹4 per minute) even works occasionally. It's the best place in Padum to rent quality mountain bikes (motorbikes should follow), and with advance notice they can organise kayaking and rafting trips.

Sleeping & Eating

Most hotels close from late October to June, except when prebooked for winter trekking groups.

Mont-Blanc Guest House HOMESTAY $
(☎9469239376, 9419177627; tenzinpalkit@yahoo.co.in; s/d ₹700/1000, without bathroom ₹500/800) Slightly removed from the main market, 200m before the mosque, this friendly four-room guesthouse has some of Padum's most attractively appointed rooms. There are fine views, especially from the

TREKKING TO ZANSKAR

The Ladakh–Zanskar trek is most often undertaken as an agency-arranged group expedition with packhorses and full camping gear, starting at Photoksar village and being met at the other end by a vehicle at Pidmo Bridge.

If you prefer to organise your trek independently, the jeep road now extends as far as the Kyupa La pass, which is around ₹9000 by chartered taxi from Leh. If you can find Lingshet-bound locals you'll pay around ₹2000 per seat (jeeps run a few times a week, departing Leh around 2am to arrive at road's end by mid-morning).

Horses or donkeys and local guides are usually available in Lingshet at short notice. With a few days' notice, Tundup (☎9469731079) at **Lala's Art Cafe** (p240) in Leh can make arrangements so your horseperson is waiting for you at Kyupa La.

The main route can be done without camping in midsummer, but homestays and tea tents are very limited, so carrying a tent and sleeping bag for emergencies is advised in case there is no space.

Day 1 Drive to Kyupa La (depart Leh by 2am or Lamayuru before dawn). Walk five hours to the sprawling, very diffuse village of Lingshet whose large, welcoming gompa is at the settlement's upper north edge. Lingshet has plenty of widely dotted homestay options (mostly on partly disconnected sub-ridges) but none is signed so you'll need to ask around. If you have enough energy, it's possible to continue three hours further to a campsite at Lanang. A single building here has two small, ultra-basic rooms where you can overnight (₹300), assuming the caretaker turns up. If he doesn't appear, there's also a doorless shelter where you could shiver the night away should your tent fail.

Day 2 Hike 10 hours from Lingshet or seven from Lanang, including three hard, steep hours up the Hanuma La (4720m). Sleep at Shnertse, which has camping and a hard-based tea tent. Or continue around two hours further, descending to the bridge where there's camping and a single hut (often used by groups as a kitchen). More reliable for a homestay bed is Jingchen, a lonely farmhouse 40 minutes' walk up the side valley.

Days 3 and 4 Hike seven hours including over the steep Parfila La to Hanamur (Hanumil) village (one homestay, two camps). Most people sleep here but less attractive Pidmo (with a very basic homestay) is just two hours further. A prebooked car can collect you at Pidmo Bridge. Otherwise walk on a further two hours to Zangla.

Winter: The Chadar Trek

In winter, snow cuts off Zanskar's tenuous road links altogether. But in February it is possible to walk in from Chilling following an ancient seasonal trade trail that essentially follows the frozen Zanskar River – often on the ice, crossing side streams on precarious snow bridges and camping in caves en route. This hazardous 'Chadar Trek' was once seen as an 'ultimate adventure', but, while it remains hazardous (don't attempt it without serious equipment and experienced guides), increased popularity with Indian domestic tourists means that of late the trek can feel oddly overcrowded. Also, climate change has made the ice less stable than in previous decades, adding to the risk of falling through into the frozen waters. If you attempt the trek, allow around six days each way, and when selecting a support company don't seek out the cheapest (which often have too few guides and porters per client).

rooftop and front-facing windows. A small trekking agency is attached.

Hotel Ibex GUESTHOUSE $
(☎9419803731, 01983-245214; ibexpadumzanskar@gmail.com; Main Market; s ₹600-1000, d ₹1000-1300, mains ₹80-240) At the centre of Padum, this perennial backpacker favourite has aging but fair-priced rooms with solar-heated showers set around a garden courtyard. Brutal tree-cutting and new corrugate rooftops have diminished the place's charm, but it remains something of an oasis from the nearby market street.

Zambala Hotel HOTEL $
(☎9469658121, 9469629336; Zambala Rd; r ₹800-1000, prebooked ₹3800) Two minutes' walk from the bazaar, the Zambala has 13 pleasant rooms wrapped around a small grassy central

space. There's no real reception; ask for assistance at the guest-only dining room upstairs.

Chumathang Restaurant MULTICUISINE **$**
(Main Market; mains ₹70-160; ⏲9am-10.30pm) With Chinese lamps and sturdy furniture, this pleasant upstairs eatery offers a fairly wide-ranging menu that's cooked with reasonable skill and can be served with good naan (tandoor-cooked flat bread) and ₹200 beers.

ℹ Information

The J&K Bank has an ATM (open 10am to 5pm), but in case that isn't functioning, you'd be wise to bring an ample wad of rupees with you to Zanskar. In an emergency, **ZAP** (p263) will change small sums of Euro or US dollars (up to around $100) at understandably mediocre rates.

ℹ Getting There & Away

Transport options to Padum remain limited, all going via Kargil and available in summer only.

A few times monthly, a **KT Dorje** (☎9419513392) bus bound for Leh (₹800) departs around 3.30am, stopping the night at Kargil (₹550).

Jeeps run to Kargil (per person/vehicle ₹1500/13,400, around 12 hours). Bargaining might be possible with returning Kargil drivers. To Leh, front/back seats in shared jeeps cost ₹3000/2500 (nearly 24 hours). Contact the drivers the evening before – their vehicles are generally parked along Zambala Rd with destination signs in windows.

Other one-way/return jeep rates from Padum:

Anmu ₹3000/3500
Ichar ₹2000/2700
Karsha ₹1200/1500
Pidmo Bridge ₹2500/3000
Rangdum ₹7000/9000
Stongdey Gompa ₹1000/1500
Zangla ₹2000/2700

To find a shared ride to such destinations, particularly to the trekking trailheads, ask at **ZAP** (p263).

The only petrol station in Zanskar is at Km3.3 of the Padum–Karsha road. In summer it usually has supplies but can't be fully relied upon.

Karsha

POP 1080 / ELEV 3663M

Across the valley from Padum, Karsha is Zanskar's most striking village, full of photogenic old-fashioned homes, barley fields and threshing circles worked by *dzo* (yak-cow half breeds). Rising directly above is a near-vertical red rock mountainside, sliced in half by a deep chasm. Whitewashed monastic buildings cascading down one side form Zanskar's biggest Buddhist **monastery complex**, with an **upper prayer hall** (Karsha Gompa; ₹100) that contains the mummified body of its 14th-century founder. Climbing the other side of the chasm is a Buddhist **nunnery**, an ancient **citadel site** and a remarkable yet little-visited Alchi-style **temple** (⏲by request) featuring a splendid 11th-century carved figure.

There are three campsites and several homestay-guesthouses in Karsha. The latter are simple family places in appealing traditional buildings. **Grand Leopard** (☎9469290976; schosgyalpali@yahoomail.co.in; per person incl full board ₹800) is particularly great for food and for its very knowledgeable, hospitable owners; **Theiur** (☎9469407411, 9469846715; r ₹600, meals ₹150) is unusual for its large garden and for having an indoor toilet.

Zangla

POP 1070 / ELEV 3500M

Forming an arc of traditional homes around a wide circle of terraced barley fields, Zangla is the last major road-linked Zanskar village east of Padum. On a bare crag at its southwestern corner is the small hilltop **fortress palace**, and at the far end of the village, there's a small, friendly Buddhist **nunnery** from which an alternative trail leads north to Km33 on the road to Pidmo Bridge (5km beyond).

Zangla makes a fine if bumpy half-day jeep excursion from Padum. En route, admire scenes of geological strata and make the winding trip 2.6km up to **Stongdey Gompa** (Padum-Zangla Rd, Km13.3) for morning views of the superbly jagged mountain horizon.

There are several homestays in the upper village near the junction for the palace lane. The well-kept Pami Homestay is easy to spot with its distinctive lavender-pink window frames.

South of Padum

The road south from Padum passes **Bardan Gompa** (Padum-Raru Rd, Km10.4; ₹50), spectacularly set on a rocky outcrop high above the river. Some 7km further, **Muney Gompa** is less dramatic despite its own riverside crag setting, but its five-room **Shanti Guesthouse** (www.shanti-house.net; Muney Gompa, Padum-Raru

Rd, Km17; r per person per 2-night/1-week incl full board €50/170) is managed with great flair as a place to spend a few days unwinding and soaking up monastic and local culture. **Ichar** is one of the valley's most intriguing villages, with a looming gompa and, on slightly higher ground, a small reflective pond and a knot of very evocative old-town homes.

ANMU TO PHUKTAL TREK

The 2015 floods made the Ichar–Anmu road impassable to vehicles, but by the time you read this, **Anmu** should once again be the trailhead for the scenically impressive five-hour hike to Phuktal Gompa (also practicable in eight hours from Ichar).

Trekking from Anmu, follow the obvious, gently undulating trail to Cha (2½ hours). Then head through the centre of that relatively large village and follow the arc of walls around the back of the extensive green area to find the path to Phuktal. That gently climbs a low pass then descends steadily to the river (after passing, but not crossing, a bridge). Just two minutes later a last short climb brings you to Phuktal's monastery **guesthouse** (Phuktal; per person ₹400). Visible impressively ahead, as though tumbling out of a cliff cave, is **Phuktal Gompa** (http://phuktalmonastery.com; ⏲ prayers 4.30am, noon & 7pm in summer), a 15-minute stroll away.

If the guesthouse's four rooms are full, the nearest accommodation involves crossing the bridge and walking 1½ hours to the village of **Purney**. Each of the three farmsteads there offers rooms and camping places, and they run two basic shop-teahouses.

To continue on, directly below lower Purney where two rivers meet, cross another bridge. Turning left here would take you eventually to Darcha in Himachal Pradesh (a trip that requires pre-planning – four days, a guide and gear for the 5090m Shingo La). Or turn right to return to Anmu in around three hours via the pretty flower-filled, one-homestead village of **Gyalbok** (1¼ hours).

The Anmu–Phuktal route doesn't require a guide if you have a map and hiking experience, but be sure to ask for recent updates on path and bridge conditions.

ZANSKAR TO DARCHA TREK

Continuing south from the Phuktal trek at Purney, you can hike on to meet the main Leh–Manali road at Darcha, north of Keylong. Traditionally that took around a week, but it's no longer necessary to walk the last two or three days as there's a twice-daily bus from Chika to Keylong (₹60, two hours). Indeed the road extends far further north – currently to the top of the Shingo La, where you can book a taxi to meet you. By 2018 the road is supposed to reach **Kargyak** village, which will reduce the trek to a three- or four-day homestay hike, as there are several tiny settlements in the valley between Purney and Kargyak.

THE KASHMIR VALLEY

Rimmed by layers of alpine peaks, the 140km-long Kashmir Valley opens up as a giant, flat upland bowl of lakes and orchards. Tin-roofed villages guard terraced paddy fields delineated by apple groves and pin-straight poplars. Proudly independent-minded Kashmiris mostly follow a Sufi-based Islamic faith, worshipping in distinctive box-shaped mosques with central spires. The region is also known for its Amarnathji Yatra (p277).

History

Geologists and Hindu mystics agree that the Kashmir Valley was once a vast lake. Where they disagree is whether it was drained by a post–ice age earthquake or by Lord Vishnu and friends as a ploy to kill a water demon.

In the 3rd century BC the Hindu kingdom of Kashmir became a major centre of Buddhist learning under Emperor Ashoka. In the 13th and 14th centuries, Islam arrived through the inspiration of peaceable Sufi mystics. Later, some Muslim rulers such as Sultan Sikandar 'Butshikan' (r 1389–1413), set about the destruction of Hindu temples and Buddhist monasteries. However, others such as the great Zain-ul-Abidin (r 1423–74) encouraged such religious and cultural tolerance that medieval visitors reported finding it hard to tell Hindus and Muslims apart. Mughal emperors including Akbar (1556–1605), whose troops took Kashmir in 1586, saw Kashmir as their Xanadu and developed a series of extravagant gardens around Srinagar.

When the British arrived in India, Jammu and Kashmir were a loose affiliation of independent kingdoms, nominally controlled by the Sikh rulers of Jammu. In 1846, after the British defeated the Sikhs, they handed Kashmir to Maharaja Gulab Singh in return for a yearly tribute of six shawls, 12 goats and a horse. Singh's autocratic Hindu-Dogra dynasty ruled until Independence, showing an infamous disregard for the welfare of the Muslim majority.

Partition & Conflict

As Partition approached in 1947, Maharaja Hari Singh favoured Kashmiri independence rather than joining either India or Pakistan, but he failed to make a definitive decision. Finally, to force the issue, Pashtun tribespeople backed by the new government in Pakistan attempted to grab the state by force, setting off the first India–Pakistan war. The invaders were pushed out of the Kashmir Valley, but Pakistan retained control of Baltistan, Muzaffarabad and the valley's main access routes. Kashmir has remained divided ever since along a tenuous, UN-demarcated border known as the Line of Control. A proposed referendum to let Kashmir's people decide (for Pakistan or India) never materialised, and Pakistan invaded again in 1965, triggering another protracted conflict.

In the 1970s, a generation of visitors rediscovered Indian Kashmir as an idyllic summer getaway. But armed rebellion became intense during the later 1980s, and Kashmir was placed under direct rule from Delhi in 1990. For several bloody years massacres and bomb attacks were countered by brutal counter-insurgency tactics from the Indian armed forces. Significant human-rights abuses were reported on both sides.

After the brief India–Pakistan 'Kargil War' of 1999, a ceasefire and increasing autonomy for Kashmir were matched by a significant reduction in tensions. Coordinating relief after a tragic 2005 earthquake also helped bring the Indian and Pakistani governments a little closer. Militant attacks dwindled, and domestic tourism blossomed anew despite disturbances in 2008 (over an arcane land dispute at Amarnath) and 2010 (after the shooting of juvenile stone-throwers).

But in July 2016, months of unrest were ignited by the army's killing of Burhan Wani, a prominent pro-independence social media activist and 'commander' of Hizbul Mujahideen, considered to be a terrorist organisation. Dozens of people died and thousands were injured, many blinded by pellet guns.

SAFETY IN KASHMIR

Check the security situation before heading to the Kashmir Valley: serious troubles can flare up suddenly in Srinagar and Anantnag. However, even when tensions in the valley run high, don't be deterred from visiting ever-calm Ladakh.

For information before you travel, the Jammu and Kashmir travellers' forum at www.indiamike.com can be useful, and it's always worth keeping an eye on at least one of the local news outlets, such as *Greater Kashmir* (www.greaterkashmir.com), *Daily Excelsior* (www.dailyexcelsior.com), *Kashmir Monitor* (www.kashmirmonitor.in), and *Kashmir Times* (www.kashmirtimes.com).

Srinagar

0194 / POP 1,405,000 / ELEV 1583M

Ringed by an arc of green mountains, Srinagar's greatest drawcard is mesmerisingly placid Dal Lake, on which a bright array of stationary houseboats form a colourful scene and a unique opportunity for romantic chill-outs. Famous Mughal gardens are strung out over several kilometres around the lake's less urbanised eastern shore; these contrast with a fascinatingly chaotic old city centre that is topped by a fortress and dotted with historic wooden mosques. Add in a mild summer climate, feisty Kashmiri cuisine and the (highly disputed) tomb of Jesus Christ, and you have one of India's top domestic tourist draws.

Except, that is, when communal tensions paralyse the city. Sadly that happens all too regularly, leaving a chance that you'll be stuck in strikes, pro-independence demonstrations and partial curfews. Although foreign tourists themselves have never been seen as targets, it's always worth checking the latest situation before you visit.

Sights

Dal Lake & Around

★Dal Lake LAKE

Over 15km around, Dal Lake is Srinagar's jewel, a vast sheet of water reflecting the carved wooden balconies of the houseboats and the misty peaks of the Pir Panjal mountains. Flotillas of gaily painted *shikaras* (gondola-like taxi boats) skiff around the lake, transporting goods to market, children to school and travellers to delightful houseboats inspired by originals from the Raj era.

If you get up early, you can paddle out to see the floating flower and **vegetable market** (5-6.30am): a colourful spectacle, but

Srinagar

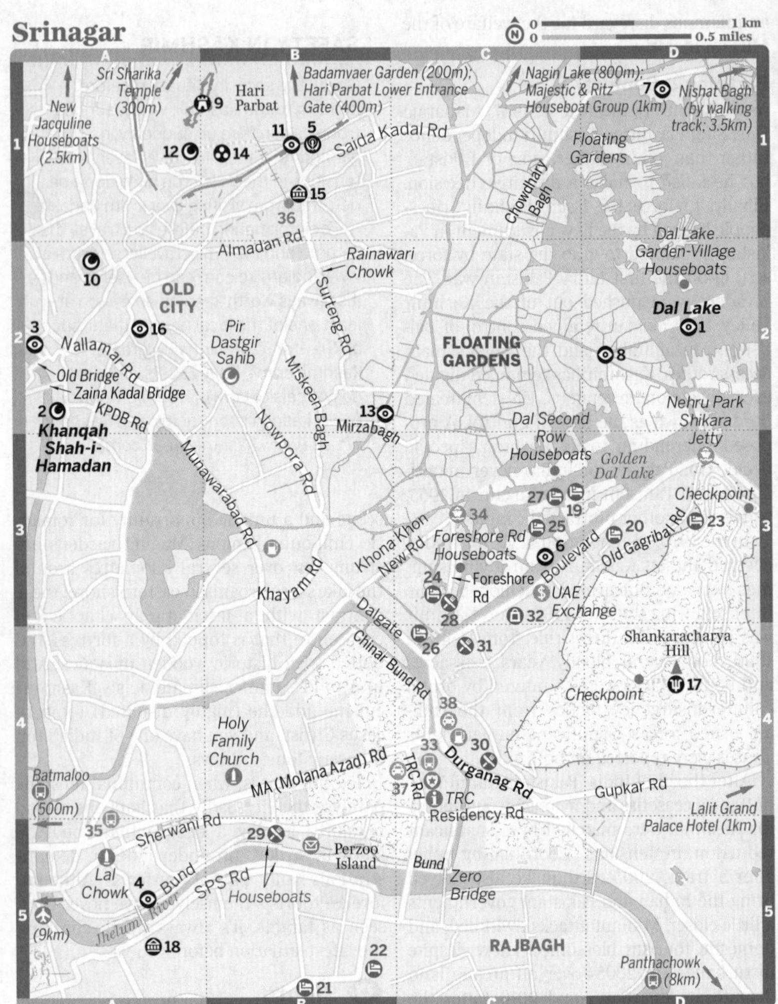

one where you can expect plenty of attention from souvenir vendors.

For a visual portrait of Dal Lake life, watch the prize-winning 2012 movie *Valley of Saints*.

First Row Houseboats LANDMARK
(Dal Lake) For guests, the first-row houseboats can prove noisy and lacking in privacy. However, as an attraction they collectively form Srinagar's signature image.

Floating Gardens & Lake Villages GARDENS
Much of Dal Lake is thick with foliage, lotus patches and large areas of cultivated vegetable gardens linked by channels and served by villages of stilted walkways. Before the 2014 floods, a great way to see these areas was by walking along Chowdhary Bagh to a footbridge and causeway leading to the pumping station near Nishat Bagh Mughal Garden. However, the route has yet to be fully repaired so ask before setting out this way.

Mirzabagh Veg Boat Dock HARBOUR
Much of Srinagar's fresh produce is brought in from 'floating gardens' and landed at this tiny dock, making for photogenic scenes.

Srinagar

Top Sights
1 Dal Lake ... D2
2 Khanqah Shah-i-Hamadan ... A2

Sights
3 Badshah Tomb ... A2
4 Bund ... A5
5 Chetipacha Gurdwara ... B1
6 First Row Houseboats ... C3
7 Floating Gardens & Lake Villages ... D1
8 Floating Vegetable Market ... D2
9 Hari Parbat Fort ... B1
10 Jama Masjid ... A2
11 Kathi Darwaza ... B1
12 Makhdoom Sahib Shrine ... A1
13 Mirzabagh Veg Boat Dock ... B2
14 Mosque of Akhund Mulla Shah ... B1
15 Naagar-Nagar Interpretation Centre ... B1
16 Naqshband Sahib ... A2
17 Shankaracharya Mandir ... D4
18 Sri Pratap Singh Museum ... A5

Sleeping
19 Chicago Group of Houseboats ... C3
20 Chocolate Box ... D3
21 Comrade Inn ... B5
22 Green Acre ... B5
23 Hotel Swiss ... D3
24 John Friends Guesthouse ... C3
25 Moon of Kashmir ... C3
26 Noor Guest House ... C4
27 Young Beauty Star ... C3

Eating
28 Crescent Lake View Restaurant ... C3
29 Mughal Darbar ... B5
30 New Krishna Vaishno Bhojnalay ... C4
31 Stream ... C4

Shopping
32 Wine Shop ... C3

Transport
33 J&K SRTC Bus Station ... C4
34 Khona Khon New Rd Shikaras ... C3
35 Lal Chowk City Minibus Stand ... A5
36 Makhdoom Sahib Ropeway ... B1
37 Tourist Taxi Stand 1 ... C4
38 Tourist Taxi Stand 7 (Anantnag sumos) ... C4

Shankaracharya Mandir HINDU TEMPLE
On top of thickly forested Shankaracharya Hill, this small Shiva temple is built from hefty blocks of visibly ancient grey stone. Previously known as Takht-i-Sulaiman (Throne of Solomon), it's now named for a sage who reached enlightenment here in AD 750, but signs date the octagonal structure as 5th century and the site is even older. Some claim, very controversially, that a previous temple here was once renovated by Jesus and St Thomas.

Access is by a winding 5.5km road from a checkpoint near Nehru Park (₹300 return by autorickshaw). Walking up is not recommended as there are bears living in the intermediate forest. The road ends at another police checkpoint, where you must leave phones and cameras before climbing five minutes up a stairway to the temple and its panoramic views of Srinagar and Dal Lake.

Mughal Gardens

Srinagar's famous gardens date to the Mughal era. Most have a fundamentally similar design, with terraced lawns, fountain pools and carefully manicured flowerbeds interspersed with mighty *chinar* (plane) trees, pavilions and mock fortress facades.

The most famous garden is **Shalimar Bagh** (adult/child ₹20/10; 10am-7pm), built for Nur Jahan by her husband, Jehangir. However, **Nishat Bagh** (adult/child ₹20/10; 9am-dusk) is more immediately impressive, with steeper terracing and a lake-facing panorama.

Pari Mahal (adult/child ₹20/10; 9am-7.30pm) is set amid palace ruins high above the lakeshore. The ensemble looks most intriguing at night from afar. En route to Pari Mahal are the petite **Cheshmashahi Garden** (Pari Mahal Rd; adult/child ₹20/10; 8.30am-7.30pm) and the extensive, less formal **Botanical Garden** (adult/child ₹20/10; 8.30am-6.30pm), behind which, in March and April, a 12-hectare **Tulip Garden** (adult/child ₹100/50; Mar & Apr) blooms colourfully.

Old City

The main points of interest in Old Srinagar are distinctive Kashmiri mosques. When visiting, follow normal Islamic formalities (dress modestly, remove shoes), and ask permission before entering or taking interior photos. Women will usually be expected to cover their hair and use a separate entrance. South of the Old City area, the **Bund** (Jhelum Riverfront) retains a few colonial-era buildings.

★Khanqah Shah-i-Hamadan MOSQUE
(Khanqah-e-Muala; Khawaja Bazaar area; ⏲4.30am-9pm) This distinctively spired 1730s Muslim meeting hall is one of Srinagar's most beautiful mosques. It was constructed without any nails, and both frontage and interiors are covered in painted papier-mâché reliefs and elaborately coloured *khatamband* (faceted wood panelling). Non-Muslim visitors can peek through the door but may not enter.

★Badshah Tomb ARCHITECTURE
(Old City; ⏲9am-6pm) Looking more Bulgarian than Kashmiri, the multi-domed 15th-century brick tomb of King Zeinalabdin's mum was built on the plinth of a much older former Buddhist temple. It's within an ancient graveyard hidden in Gadu Bazaar's

HOUSEBOATS

Srinagar's signature houseboats first appeared in colonial times when the British were prohibited from owning land. The best 'Deluxe' boats are palatial, with chandeliers, carved walnut panels, ceilings of *khatamband* (faceted wood panelling) and chintzy sitting rooms redolent of the late Raj era. Category A boats are comfy but less grand. Lower categories (C, D) can be pretty ropey and might lack interior sitting areas.

Be aware that unlike those in Kerala, these boats never move. The Srinagar houseboat experience is more like staying in a romantic, floating mini-guesthouse complete with cook and waiter. Most are moored in sizeable groups, so you have excellent people-watching on the one hand; on the other, don't expect quiet seclusion unless you pick one way out of the central area.

Better houseboats typically have three or four en suite double bedrooms, the back one usually bigger and sometimes better appointed than the rest.

Choosing from 1400 boats is challenging. Some owners are superfriendly families; others are crooks. Ask fellow travellers for recent firsthand recommendations. Outside the busiest seasons (May, June and October) and especially when the political climate drives tourists away, look carefully at a selection and pick one that suits your taste. Many owners will offer a free, no-strings *shikara* (gondola-like boat) ride to come and check out their boat.

Houseboat Tips

For most visitors, staying on a houseboat is a relaxing Srinagar highlight. But a few have reported feeling cheated, being held virtual hostage or suffering inappropriate advances from houseboat staff. Some tips:

- Beware of houseboat packages and *never book in Delhi*.
- Check out houseboats in person or via trusted websites before agreeing to anything.
- Get a clear, possibly written, agreement stating what the fees cover (tea? drinking water? *shikara* transfer? canoe usage? second helpings at dinner?).
- Check whether the boat really is the category that the owner claims (certificates should be posted) or risk paying Deluxe prices for a B-grade boat.
- Don't be pressured into giving 'charity' donations or signing up for overpriced treks.
- Don't leave valuables unattended: boat-borne thieves work rapidly.
- Don't leave your passport with the houseboat owner.
- Tell a friend or trusted hotelier where you're staying.
- Trust your instincts.

Choosing the Area

There are boats dotted along the banks of the Jhelum River, but most options are on Dal and Nagin Lakes. Nagin Lake is generally quieter than Dal Lake, but it's rather far from the city centre. In almost any location, visits from *shikara*-riding souvenir sellers are common.

Dal Lake options:

Dal First Row (p268) Facing the Boulevard, easy to-and-fro by *shikara* (gondola-like boat; ₹50 per hop), but busy and noisy in season. In many cases these boats are better to look at than to stay in.

maze of copperware, spice and cloth vendors' shops. To view the interior, you will need to find the caretaker; ask at the shops in front of the cemetery.

★ **Jama Masjid** MOSQUE

(Nowhatta; ⏲8am-9pm) Looking like the movie set for an imagined Central Asian castle, this mighty 1672 mosque forms a quadrangle around a large garden courtyard with fountain and monumental spired gatehouses marking the four cardinal directions. There's room for thousands of devotees among the 378 roof-support columns, each fashioned from the trunk of a single deodar tree.

Naqshband Sahib RELIGIOUS SITE

(Khanyar Chowk area; ⏲6.30am-8.30pm) This beautifully proportioned if uncoloured

Dal Second Row (Golden Dal Lake) Though only slightly further back, boats here are invisible from the Boulevard and better placed for sunset views. There's plenty of colourful bustle, yet it's only ₹80 to reach here by *shikara* from Ghats 9 or 12. The location has a good balance of movement and peace. Our Deluxe favourite is **Young Beauty Star** (☎9419060790; www.dallakehouseboat-raga.com; s ₹2000-2250, d ₹3000-3700; Ghat 9), with a junction location that's ideal for watching life go by. Similarly comfortable but without the same perfect location, **Chicago's** (☎0194-2502558, Ajaz Khar 9419061430; chicagohouseboats.com; s/d mid-Apr–mid-Oct ₹2250/3300, mid-Oct–mid-Apr ₹1800/2700) three boats have reliably friendly English-speaking owners and once hosted Indira Gandhi.

Dal Lake Garden-Village Many more boats lie in village-like clusters further back: peaceful except during prayers, but somewhat trickier to 'escape' from should you go stir-crazy. Low-key **Moon of Kashmir** (☎9906686454; www.moonofkashmir.com; Dal Lake Garden Village; d ₹1200-1800, incl half-board ₹2000-3500; Ghat 7) is very welcoming.

Foreshore Road Easy access, but less romantic than being on the open lake. Boats are often basic but inexpensive (under ₹1000). Security is a minor concern, as thieves can easily slip aboard.

Butts Clermont (☎9419056761, 0194-2415325; www.buttsclermonthouseboat.com; Naseem Bagh, Hazratbal; d from ₹6000) Way up above Hazratbal, this lonely gaggle of houseboats is moored beside its own private Mughal garden. It's long been a VIP favourite but they're not quite worth the high price.

Nagin Lake options:

Nagin East Bank Boats are easily accessible by road and have views of Hari Parbat. Houseboat group **Majestic & Ritz** (☎9906874747, 9858004462; http://majestichouseboat.com; south of Nagin Club; s/d from ₹3100/3500) are friendly and reliable, and **Butterfly** (☎0194-2429889, 0194-2420212; r ₹3000-5000) is funky. Drop-in bargains are possible at several boat groups.

Nagin West Bank Boats have glorious sunset views with wooded mountain scarps reflected in the lake. They are usually approached by *shikara* from the east bank, but most also have laneway access via a wealthy, visibly religious residential area. Getting into town is a pain, so plan to spend your days relaxing aboard if you pick this area. **New Jacquline** (☎0194-2421425, 9419001785; www.newjacqulinehouseboats.com; d ₹3400-8000) is a particularly comfortable choice here.

Prices

Officially, prices are 'set' by the Houseboat Owners Association and range from ₹600/800 for a category-D single/double to ₹3800/4800 for a Deluxe single/double (or ₹900/1300 to ₹5000/6500 including half-board). In reality, however, that's only a vague guide. Some places openly ask more, many ask less, and when occupancy is low, it's often possible to find great bargains.

17th-century shrine was built in Himachal Pradesh style, with alternating layers of wood and brick to dissipate the force of earthquakes.

Hari Parbat Hill

Visible from all over Srinagar, this hilltop was once an island in a giant lake. It's now home to the **Sri Sharika Temple** (Chakreshwar; www.hariparbat.org; Hari Parbat) and is crowned by Hari Parbat Fort, which is entered via a lane starting north of Badamvaer gardens. The **Naagar-Nagar Interpretation Centre** (Ropeway Gardens; 10am-4pm Sat-Thu) provides interesting historical context to the area. Beside it, a cable car runs to the hill's southern mid-slopes, near the **Akhund Mulla Shah Mosque** ruins and the **Makhdoom Sahib Shrine**. Three step routes lead to the same area: the most easterly starts near **Kathi Darwaza**, a historical gateway close to **Chetipacha Gurdwara** (Chattipatshahi Gurudwara).

Hari Parbat Fort FORTRESS
(Koh-e-Maran Fort; permission note for foreigner/Indian ₹100/50; 10am-3pm Sat-Thu) On the strategically and spiritually significant Hari Parbat, north of the city centre, is this fortress, which dates to the 6th century. The hill was also fortified by Emperor Akbar in 1590, but most of the upper fortress dates from the 1808 constructions of Pathan governor Atta Mohammad Khan. To visit, first apply for a stamped permissory note from the TRC (p274) or Naagar-Nagar Interpretation Centre (passport copy required).

Badamvaer GARDENS
(Badanwari; Hari Parbat Rd; adult/child ₹10/5; 8am-8.30pm) Created in the 16th century, then planted with almond trees in 1876, this orchard garden fell apart during Kashmir's 1990s troubles but has been beautifully restored since 2007. The main attraction, other than the spring blossoms and summer shade of the fruit trees, is the circular Warishkhanshah covered well in the park's centre.

Central Srinagar

Sri Pratap Singh Museum MUSEUM
(0194-2312859; SPS Rd; Indian/foreigner ₹10/50, photography per gallery ₹100/200; 10am-4pm Tue-Sun) It's worth visiting this richly endowed historical museum for Mughal papier-mâché work, 4th-century tiles, 8th-century god-statues, stuffed birds, mammoth bones, weaponry and traditional Kashmiri costumes. The collection is being gradually relocated from the touchingly unkempt 1872 Lalmandi Palace of Maharaja Pratap Singh to a purpose-built new museum building behind.

Activities

The alpine lakes, meadows and uplands of Kashmir offer some stunning hiking opportunities, but unlike in Ladakh, it can be hard to find fellow walkers to join a group. Virtually every houseboat owner will have a 'brother' who can take you and there are ever more online sites offering trek packages, but you may be able to get a better deal simply by heading to Aru, Pahalgam, Sonamarg or Naranag and organising things for yourself. If you do that, consider pre-renting camping equipment from the Mountaineering Information Office in the same compound as Srinagar TRC (p274).

Sleeping

Staying on a houseboat (p270) is one of Srinagar's main attractions, but choose carefully. Budget hotel options are relatively limited (try Dalgate or Old Gagribal Rd), while there are midrange hotels in profusion. Many, however, are unkempt and rely on noisy, large groups. Ask to see a few rooms before making a decision. Note that when there's no civil unrest, prices can rise very steeply during Indian holiday seasons (typically May, June and October).

John Friends Guesthouse GUESTHOUSE $
(0194-2458342; off Foreshore Rd; dm ₹200, d without/with bathroom ₹300/500;) Reached from Foreshore Rd by a plank-and-stilt walkway, John Friends' signature attraction is its apple-tree garden and direct access to backwater canals (although they're somewhat stagnant and mosquito-nibbled here). The 12 bargain-value rooms have been entirely rebuilt since the 2014 floods, and there's a mat-on-floor dorm. Self-paddled boat hire costs just ₹30 per hour.

Noor Guest House GUESTHOUSE $
(9491034268, 0194-2450872; noorguesthouse@ymail.com; off Dalgate; d ₹500-1000;) Largely rebuilt in 2015, this popular if slightly cramped little backpacker favourite has a small yard, two narrow communal balconies with partial lake views, and helpful extras such as a shared kitchen, laundry service and bicycle rental. Wi-fi ₹100 per day.

★Hotel Swiss GUESTHOUSE $$
(☎0194-2500115, Rouf 9906519745; www.swisshotelkashmir.com; 172 Old Gagribal Rd; d ₹850-3000; @📶) One of India's friendliest family guesthouses, the Swiss isn't showy but offers high-quality hotel rooms with fresh, varnished pine walls at foreigner walk-in prices that are vastly cheaper than their nominal web-advertised rates. It's handy for the lake yet set back far enough to avoid traffic noise in an area that generally stays safe during periods of unrest.

★Green Acre HOTEL $$
(☎9419213145, 0194-2453859; www.wazirhotels.com; Rajbagh; s/d ₹4500/5500, ste ₹9500-40,000; ❄📶) Set amid the lawns of a glorious rose garden, Green Acre's centrepiece is a 1942 classic-Raj mansion with a perfect reading perch on the 1st-floor common balcony. The property has been entirely refurbished since the 2014 floods, with plenty of period touches retained in the heritage rooms.

Chocolate Box BOUTIQUE HOTEL $$
(☎0194-2500298, 9796577334; www.chocolateboxsrinagar.com; Boulevard; d ₹5000-6500, walk-in ₹3500-4500) Well-chosen elements of designer style make this 13-room boutique hotel one of the Boulevard's most appealing options. Rooms 107 and 108 have private lake-facing balconies. Walk-in rates are significantly reduced.

Comrade Inn HOTEL $$$
(☎0194-2313440; www.comradeinn.com; Rajbagh; d ₹6000, walk-in ₹4000; ❄📶) Well-trained staff lead you through corridors richly decked in modern art to the fully equipped rooms, which have excellent box-spring beds, crisp cotton sheets, rainforest showers, fridge, kettle and stylish lighting.

Lalit Grand Palace Hotel HERITAGE HOTEL $$$
(☎0194-2501001; www.thelalit.com; Gupkar Rd; r/ste from ₹20,500/24,150; 📶🏊) This 1910 former Maharaja's palace is set in hectares of manicured lawns with many historical heirlooms dotted about the suave interior. Only suites occupy the original palace building, but rooms in the long new wing are effortlessly stylish; those on the ground floor have walk-out garden balconies.

Eating & Drinking

Srinagar's Muslim mores mean that alcohol isn't served in restaurants, though a few upmarket hotels have bars. For takeaway alcohol there's an entirely unadvertised **wine shop** (Boulevard, Heemal Hotel Shopping Complex; ⏲10am-8pm Sat-Thu, closed during Ramadan) off the Boulevard. For nonalcoholic refreshment, there are a couple of quirky tea shops on The Bund (p269).

KASHMIRI FOOD

Kashmir has a distinct cuisine all of its own. A full traditional *wazwan* (banquet) can have dozens of courses, notably *goshtaba* (pounded mutton balls in saffron-yoghurt curry), *tabak maaz* (fried lamb's ribs) and rogan josh (rich, spicy lamb curry). Kashmiri chefs also serve deliciously aromatic cheese-based curries and seasonal *nadir* (lotus stems), typically served in *yakhni* (a curd-based sauce made with fennel). Kashmiri kahwa is a luxurious golden tea flavoured with saffron, cinnamon and crushed almonds.

New Krishna Vaishno Bhojnalay DHABA $
(Durganag Rd; mains ₹50-100; ⏲8am-4pm & 7-10.30pm) Crowds clamour for the tasty, inexpensive vegetarian meals, dosas and South Indian breakfasts at Srinagar's small, 'original' *dhaba* (casual eatery serving snacks and basic meals). Pre-pay at counter.

Crescent Lake View Restaurant MULTICUISINE $$
(Ama Tours; Foreshore Rd; mains ₹120-250; ⏲8am-10.30pm; 📶) With four modernist tables with settees, computers for customer use, money-changing facilities and a tour/trekking agency in-house, this backpacker-oriented business covers many bases. The percolated coffee is good, and food ranges from banana pancakes to *wazwan* (traditional Kashmiri multicourse meal).

Stream MULTICUISINE $$
(Boulevard; mains ₹170-350; ⏲11am-10pm; ❄) Comfortably air-conditioned, this reliable, smart eatery is slightly set back from the Boulevard and serves a particularly good range of pan-Indian options, plus pizza, coffee and ice cream.

Mughal Darbar KASHMIRI $$$
(☎0194-2476998; Residency Rd; mains ₹105-340, 1-/4-person wazwan ₹640/2875; ⏲10.30am-10.30pm; ❄) This upstairs restaurant is a great place to try a full spread of Kashmir's mutton-based cuisine, though good Indian

veg dishes are also served. A special room with carpet seating and copper serving dishes is available if booking ahead for a full *wazwan* (traditional Kashmiri multi-course meal). The main dining room features an engrossing 'Where is heaven?' oriental mural.

Shopping

The Boulevard's various emporia sell Kashmiri souvenirs including elegantly painted papier-mâché boxes and carved walnut woodwork, plus cashmere and pashmina shawls. Chain-stitched *gabbas* (Kashmiri rugs with appliqué), crewel embroidery work or floral *namdas* (felted wool carpets) also make good souvenirs. Saffron, cricket bats and dried fruits are widely sold around Lal Chowk.

Information

TRC (Tourism Reception Centre; ☎0194-2502270, 0194-2456291; www.jktourism.org; TRC Rd; ⏲24hr, permit applications 10am-3pm) Expect a mixture of help and eliptical musings from this information office, which should soon move into a large neo-traditional building if construction proceeds to plan. Apply here for permits for visiting Hari Parbat fort and for trekking the Naranag–Sonamarg Seven Lakes route. The 'recreation department' rents camping and hiking equipment.

UAE Exchange (Boulevard; ⏲9.30am-1.30pm & 2-6pm Mon-Fri, 10am-2pm Sat) Hidden down the driveway directly east of Hotel Sunshine, this money changer offers good cash rates and exchanges travellers cheques with commission.

Getting There & Away

AIR

Served by several daily flights from Delhi and Jammu and at least one from Mumbai and Leh (inbound, GoAir), Srinagar's airport is 1.2km behind a security barrier where there can be long queues for baggage and body screening. To get through you'll need to show an air ticket or e-ticket confirmation printout. Allow at least two hours' leeway. In times of turmoil it might be necessary to travel to the airport before dawn to avoid curfews – the airport keeps functioning, but road access might be closed all day.

On arrival by air, foreigners must fill a J&K entry form which demands you give the name of your hotel. If you don't know where you'll be staying, write 'TRC' (Tourist Reception Centre).

BUS & JEEP

Anantnag Shared Sumo (₹80, 90 minutes) from **Tourist Taxi Stand 7** (Dalgate). Change in Anantnag for Pahalgam and Vailoo.

Jammu The well-paved Srinagar–Jammu road has many scenic points and snow is cleared year-round, but jams are common and landslides and strikes can cause delays.

Private buses (mostly overnight) start from Panthachowk bus station, 8km south of the centre. Rickety J&K SRTC buses (class B/A/18-seater bus ₹300/420/510, 10 to 13 hours) depart at 6.30am, 7.30am and (some evenings) 7.30pm from the far more convenient **J&K SRTC bus station** (☎0194-2455107; TRC Rd). Shared jeeps (per person/vehicle ₹700/4950) leave from across the road; finding a ride is easiest from 6.30am to 9am.

Kargil Shared jeeps (per person/vehicle ₹900/6400) depart before 9am from **Tourist Taxi Stand 1** (TRC Rd) and from Kaksarai near SMHS hospital in Karan Nagar (western Srinagar), where there are also private buses leaving around 5am (₹400).

Kishtwar There's reportedly a daily through bus, but normally the route is done in hops via Anantnag and Vailoo. You'll have to stay overnight in Vailoo (or nearby Kokernag): Kishtwar shared jeeps (per person/vehicle ₹300/3500, six hours) depart from there between 6am and 10am.

Leh The J&K SRTC typically departs at 7.30am (₹1060, two days) and makes a night stop en route in Kargil; book one day ahead. In times of turmoil, if the bus runs at all, it departs at 11.30pm to avoid trouble.

From Tourist Taxi Stand 1, most shared jeeps (per person ₹2100, 14 hours) leave before 7am. Book at least a day ahead to score good seats.

Delhi J&K SRTC (seat/sleeper ₹1490/1670, around 24 hours, 7.30am).

J&K SRTC also advertises ₹420 return bus excursions to tourist destinations including Sonamarg, Gulmarg, Yusmarg and Pahalgam, all departing between 7.30am and 9am. However, few actually run outside the peak May/June period. Before paying the ticket, ask fellow potential passengers whether they might prefer to share a Sumo from the taxi stand opposite.

Batmaloo bus station, west of centre, has services to Kangan for Sonamarg or Naranag and frequent sumos to Tangmarg for Gulmarg.

Dozens of stands offer jeep rental. Approximate return prices include Pahalgam (₹3000), Sonamarg (₹2700) and Gulmarg (₹2500). Your hotel might offer better deals.

TRAIN

The nearest train station is at Nowgam, around 10km south of the Old City. Trains currently only run Banihal–Qazigund–Anantnag–Nowgam–Baramulla. Theoretically the Jammu–Katra–Nowgam–Baramulla line should be complete by 2018, but that's not considered likely.

Getting Around

Autorickshaws cost ₹50 for short hops, around ₹250 per hour for tours.

Shikaras, colourful gondola-like boats, officially charge ₹500 per hour, or ₹50/80 for hops from the shore to front/mid-row houseboats. In reality some *shikara*-wallahs (notably from **Khona Khon New Rd**) accept as little as ₹200 per hour, but the less you pay the more likely you'll be to encounter some alternative sales pressure. Pay only ₹20 to nip across to Nehru Park from the nearest **jetty**.

Overcrowded minibuses ply the main routes, including Lal Chowk–Hazratbal and Lal Chowk–Shalimar Bagh via Dal Lake's south bank.

If you can handle the manic traffic, you can sightsee by bicycle in the relatively flat Old City and lakefront areas. Rental opportunities are limited, but a few bikes are occasionally available (usually for guests only) from **Hotel Swiss** (p273) and **Noor Guest House** (p272) (₹250 per day).

TO/FROM THE AIRPORT

Srinagar International Airport Prepaid taxis from the airport cost ₹610/710/710 to Lal Chowk/Dalgate/Nehru Park. Alternatively, walk (1.2km) or take the free shuttle bus to the outer security gate and try to find an auto from there. The shuttle claims to run every 20 minutes, but it actually operates irregularly.

In curfew times, getting to the airport can cost as much as ₹1000, and you'll probably have to get there at dawn whatever time your flight is. The terminal building only allows passenger access three hours before a scheduled departure, so you may be stuck waiting outside.

Pahalgam & Aru

☎01936 / POP 10,300 / ELEV 2150M

Surrounded by alpine peaks, the Lidder and Seshnag Rivers tumble down picturesque, deep-cut mountain valleys covered with giant conifers. The surrounding mountains contain many beauty spots and more than 20 lakes, to which countless guides and horsemen are more than keen to take you.

Not quite spoiling this great natural beauty is Pahalgam, sprawling 4km around the river junction. It's a major resort town offering golf and rafting and is a staging point for the midsummer Amarnathji pilgrimage.

Hotels are likely to urge you to try a donkey hike or full-blown trek. In fact the best hiking often starts 12km away in **Aru**, a tiny village set in magical upland landscapes amid the foothill peaks. Aru (elevation 2440m) is increasingly used as a starting base by backpackers who blow straight through Pahalgam with just a change of vehicle.

Pahalgam's 200-plus hotels range from the vaguely Scandinavian-styled **Himalaya House** (☎01936-243072; www.himalayahouse.in; Laripora Rd, Pahalgam; r ₹3750-5625; wifi) and fashion-conscious **Pine Spring** (☎01936-243386; http://pahalgam.hotelpinespring.com; Laripora Rd, Pahalgam; s/d/ste ₹6500/7500/11,000) to old-fashioned chocolate-box cottage-style **Alpine Inn** (☎9906756030, 01936-243065; www.alpineinnpahalgam.com; Heevan Link Rd, Pahalgam; s/d ₹2800/4200; wifi) and the aging but peacefully secluded **Ramba Palace** (Bentes Lodge; ☎01936-243296, 9419727379; rambapalace@yahoo.com; Mamal; d ₹500-1000, without bathroom ₹400-600) – basic but with breathtaking views.

Prices can fluctuate by 600%, peaking in May and June. Better options tend to be set close to the river road that runs behind the golf course to the 'second bridge' near the Laripura bus stand.

Western visitors who can forgo luxury tend to ignore Pahalgam's resort melee and head straight for Aru. Budget options predominate here, including the welcoming **Friends Guesthouse** (☎01936-210928; www.friendsguesthousepahalgam.com; Aru; d ₹500-1400); **Rohella Guesthouse** (☎01936-211339, 9622761355; www.rohella.brinkster.net; Aru; s/d ₹500/600; Apr-Oct), a firm favourite with the dreadlock crowd; and **Milky Way Hotel** (☎01936-210899, 9419435832; www.milkywaykashmir.com; Aru; r ₹2500-3200, without bathroom ₹800), which is a slight cut above, with an OK restaurant.

Getting There & Around

During tourist season, J&K SRTC buses make day return trips from Srinagar (₹420, 2½ hours), departing Srinagar around 7.30am and departing Pahalgam at 4.30pm. However, the service can be cancelled at short notice.

Alternatively, from Srinagar, head first to Anantnag by shared jeep (₹80, one hour) or by (rare) local bus (₹50, 1½ hours), then swap vehicle at the same Sumo stand.

The only vehicles permitted to go to Aru (from ₹600) and Chandawari (from ₹700, 19km) start from the **tourist taxi stand** (☎01936-243126; www.taxistandpahalgam.com; Pahalgam), 10 minutes' walk up the main road from the Pahalgam **jeep stand & bus station** (Pahalgam Bazaar). Prices are dependent on your choice from four vehicle classes.

Gulmarg

☎01954 / ELEV BASE/TOP STATION 2600M/3750M

Foreigners who have seen mountaintops and snow before might find Gulmarg's double-shot **gondola** (www.gulmarggondola.com; cable car first stage/both stages ₹700/1600, ski pass per day/week for foreigners ₹1800/9050, for Indians ₹1150/6800; ⏰9am-3pm, last return around 5pm) overrated due to gruelling queues at the cable car.

But in winter Gulmarg comes into its own as a ski centre, famed for its perfect high-altitude powder. Although a chair lift partially paralleling the gondola's second stage does offer an easy way up, this is really a venue for extreme skiers. The basin enfolding the gondola is patrolled and blasted for avalanche prevention, but the vast majority of other couloirs and forest tracks are unsecured, so it's essential to be snow-savvy and to check conditions carefully. **Gulmarg Avalanche Advisory** (http://gulmarg-avalanche-advisory.com) gives detailed updates throughout the season, which runs December to March, with the best conditions usually from mid-January to late February.

GM Ahanger (☎9596295371, 9697767268; ahangergm@gmail.com) has been recommended as a ski guide, and several outlets rent decent gear. Swiss **FSH** (Free Ski Himalaya; ☎+41-33-5349301; www.freeskihimalaya.com) and Australia-based **Bills Trips** (☎+61-409-161978; www.billstrips.com) offer complete ski packages, and **Kashmir Heli-Ski** (www.kashmirheliski.in) can get you even further off-piste.

Gulmarg is only 1½ hours' drive from Srinagar, but stay overnight to get a head start onto the pistes. Modest but switched-on **Raja Hut** (☎9797297908, 9596245006; rk5536058@gmail.com; d from ₹2500) is run by a genial snowboarder and is favoured by many budget-minded international adventure folk. Other decent choices include the cheery if slightly worn, pine-decor **Heevan Retreat** (☎01954-254455; www.ahadhotelsandresorts.com; r/ste from ₹6700/14,375; 📶), plain family-style **Shaw Inn** (☎01954-254532; s/d ₹7000/7500) or the dauntingly suave palace-hotel Khyber Himalayan (p276).

Khyber Himalayan Resort & Spa HOTEL **$$$**
(☎9596780653; www.khyberhotels.com; Khyber Rd; d ₹13,500-21,500, cottage ₹40,000-150,000; 📶🏊) Gulmarg's only true luxury resort is almost intimidating in its grandeur, the public areas feeling like an emir's palace reinvented with a 21st-century twist. Complete with indoor pool, spa and unexpectedly impressive views from the tea shop terrace behind.

ℹ Getting There & Away

A day-return jeep hire from Srinagar costs ₹2200 per vehicle (around two hours each way). Alternatively, from Srinagar's Batmaloo bus station, take a shared jeep to Tangmarg (₹80), then change for the last 13km of hairpins to Gulmarg (₹40).

In summer a barrier is closed beside the **jeep stand**, forcing you to walk the last 15 minutes to the gondola.

Naranag & Lake Gangabal

☎01942 / POP 450 /
ELEV NARANAG/GANGABAL 2280M/3575M

Home to seminomadic Gujar people and a pair of remarkable 8th-century **Shiva temple ruins** (Naranag), little Naranag sits in a deep-cut river valley thick with mature conifer forests. For most visitors, however, it's best known as the trailhead for multiday treks in Kashmir's 'Great Lakes' uplands.

The prime two-day destination for hikers is beautiful **Lake Gangabal**, which can be accessed in around seven strenuous hours' hike from Naranag village.

It's possible to trek in five or six days between Naranag and Sonamarg via the classic '**Seven Lakes**' route, but beware that certain passes can be impassably snowy till late July. There are several route variations, but all require a permit that's checked near Vishansar Lake. Some guides claim they can talk their way around this requirement or that they can apply at Manigal camp near Kangan, but it's wise to play safe and get the paperwork done at the TRC (p274) in Srinagar, where the process should be a quick formality (bring visa/passport copy, photo and planned itinerary).

Prospective guides will likely find you on arrival in Naranag and will happily arrange packhorses, but standards of English aren't great and pricing can be very sketchy. Most local guides have tents and sleeping bags available, but quality is often poor and bringing your own would be wise (rentable from Srinagar TRC).

The attractive **Swiss Retreat** (swissretreatkashmir@gmail.com; Naranag; r ₹850-1350) should eventually be Naranag's nicest option. Till its completion, choose between eight scruffy homestay-guesthouses, most of them in a state of disarray. The best of a bad lot are **Khan Guesthouse** (☎Imtiaz

9697559256; d without bathroom ₹400-600) and **Gulshan Lodge** (Naranag; r ₹500-1200). On Gangabal's upland meadows there's a tourist hut; it's rarely if ever manned, but you might find it open if you need to take refuge from inclement weather.

Getting There & Away

A once-daily bus service leaves Naranag at 8am for Kangan (₹20, 80 minutes), returning at 3pm. There are Kangan–Srinagar shared Sumos (₹70, one hour) and cheaper buses serving Srinagar's Batmaloo bus station.

A charter jeep from Srinagar costs ₹2500 (two hours).

Sonamarg

0194 / POP 800 (SUMMER ONLY) / ELEV 2670M

For trips between Kargil and Srinagar, Sonamarg is a popular meal stop, less for its culinary reputation than as a way to recover from and prepare for the nerve-jangling 3529m pass, Zoji La (p242). The main bazaar strip has many refuelling stop *dhabas* for passing motorists. There's a tandoor bakery at the back of the Sumo stand.

The name Sonamarg means 'Golden Meadow', suitably enticing for an upland valley surrounded by soaring, sharpened peaks and *Sound of Music* scenery. The main, seasonal settlement, at Km85 of the Srinagar–Leh highway, is an uninteresting strip of hotels and simple restaurants. But that's easy to escape by walking for around an hour into a parallel valley to admire the multiple fingertips of **Thajiwas Glacier**. If you want to hike much further, Sonamarg is the end (or possible start) of the **Seven Lakes Trek** from Narang. Or, with suitable documentation, join the seasonal pilgrims on the Amarnathji Yatra that starts just 15km east of Sonamarg at Baltal.

Sleeping

Poorly maintained rooms above Sonamarg's jerry-built restaurants cost ₹1500 to ₹4000 in May and June but as little as ₹400 at other times. **Hotel Royal** (Sonamarg Bazaar; r ₹1500-2000; May-Oct) is the best of this dreary lot; better options across the road include **Hotel Kongposh** (r ₹4000). The aging but beautifully located **Tourist Dormitories** (Thajiwas Meadow; dm ₹200) and **Alpine Hut** (Thajiwas Meadow; r ₹3000) are 15 minutes' walk from Km83 towards Thajiwas Glacier. Many of the better hotels are between Km83 and Km84.

Getting There & Away

Srinagar Direct buses are appallingly slow (₹120, over five hours) so most locals take a shared Sumo to Kangan (₹80, 90 minutes) and another from there to Srinagar (₹70, one hour).

Kargil Chartered jeeps ask ₹6000. Kargil- and Leh-bound buses pass through at around 8am and 10.30am, respectively, but are often full on arrival. So, too, are most shared jeeps from Srinagar, but it's worth looking for JK07 number plates at the restaurant strip or bus stand. If space is available, pay ₹600 per person to

THE AMARNATHJI YATRA

Amarnath's unique attraction is a natural stone lingam, seen as symbolising Lord Shiva, in a holy mountain cave at an altitude of 3888m. Joining the scenic *yatra* (pilgrimage) to behold it, in mid-July to mid-August, is an unforgettable experience. But with around 20,000 pilgrims a day, it's certainly not a meditative country hike.

There are two routes. From the vast **Baltal Camp**, 15km east of Sonamarg, Amarnath is just 14km away (two days, one night). Wealthier pilgrims complete the journey by pony, dandy (palanquin) or in part by helicopter. The longer approach starts from Pahalgam with a 16km taxi ride to Chandanwari (₹700), then a 36km, three-day/two-night hike. Either way, camps en route provide all the essentials, so you don't need to carry much more than spare warm clothes.

Beware that both blizzards and Kashmiri militants have killed pilgrims in the past, and prospective *yatri* (pilgrims) must apply for a permit through the official pilgrimage organisation, the **Sri Amarnath Shrine Board** (SASB; 0194-2468250, 0194-2501679, winter enquiries 0191-2503399; www.shriamarnathjishrine.com; mid-Jul–mid-Aug). You can download the form online, but you'll need to present it, along with photos, passport/visa copy, a medical certificate and a ₹150 fee, in either Jammu or at the TRC in Nowgam, 12km from Srinagar. Those under 13 or over 75 years old are not permitted to do the *yatra*.

Kargil. An alternative is to have a friendly hotelier phone-reserve a seat in a jeep ex-Srinagar, but you'll need to pay the fare up front (plus his commission).

JAMMU & SOUTHERN KASHMIR

Jammu, the hub of J&K's predominantly Hindu southern region, swelters at the edge of the plains. Its self-billing as the 'city of temples' is somewhat overblown, and the floods of *yatri* (Hindu pilgrims) who constitute the vast majority of the region's tourists pass quickly through en route to Katra (April to June and October to December), Gulabgarh (August) or Amarnath (July) via Pahalgam.

But the region has several lesser-known attractions, including the launch point, at Kishtwar, for the remarkable K3 route. The road heads via Killar to Keylong in Himachal Pradesh, following the dramatic Chenab River canyons and navigating one section of narrow jeep road that has been dubbed the 'world's most dangerous'.

Jammu

0191 / POP 560,000 / ELEV 330M

Steaming hot compared to the rest of the state, Jammu is J&K's winter capital. Pre-Independence the city was the seat of the powerful Dogra dynasty, whose palaces remain the city's most appealing sights. Religiously Hindu, Jammu dubs itself as the 'city of temples'. Few of these temples are historically significant, and for foreign tourists there's little pressing need to hang around after making transport connections to Amritsar, Srinagar or Dharamsala.

But if you've got time to kill, consider one of the set three- to four-hour sightseeing circuits offered by certain autorickshaw drivers (₹350 to ₹500), typically starting from near the central, army-fortified Raghunath Mandir.

Sights

Raghunath Mandir HINDU TEMPLE

(Raghunath Bazaar; donations accepted; 6am-8.30pm) The large, 19th-century Raghunath Mandir marks the heart of older Jammu and features several pavilions containing thousands of what look like grey pebbles set in concrete. In fact, these are *saligrams* (ammonite fossils) symbolically representing the myriad deities of the Hindu pantheon.

Central Gurdwara SIKH TEMPLE

Giving new definition to the lower city centre area, this large, new, classically designed Sikh complex has a light, airy feel, and its gilded domes make it look, to many foreign visitors, like the very archetype of an Indian temple.

Mubarak Mandi PALACE

(Durbagarh Rd) Started in 1710 and vastly expanded after 1824 under the Dogras, this extensive complex of palace buildings is fascinating for both its scale and its startling state of semi-collapse. The only part that's accessible is the former durbar hall containing the **Dogra Art Gallery** (0191-2561846; kirpal_308@rediffmail.com; foreigner/Indian ₹50/10, photography ₹240/120; 10am-5pm Tue-Sun).

Amar Mahal PALACE

(standard/special entry ₹20/200, photography ₹50; 9am-1pm & 2-6pm Tue-Sun Apr-Sep, to 5pm Oct-Mar) In the 1890s, the Dogra maharajas moved from Mubarak Mandi (p278) to this very European brick mansion a few kilometres from town, with castle-style mini-turrets and wide clifftop views. It's now a museum whose star exhibit is a canopied royal throne made from over 100kg of gold. Other rooms introduce the characters who once lived here, and with the 'special' ticket you can visit the upstairs maharani's chambers, which feature a Queen Victoria portrait and a bathroom complete with perfume collection.

Sleeping

Green View Hotel GUESTHOUSE $

(0191-2573906, 9419198639; 69 Chand Nagar; s/d/tr/q ₹200/600/800/1000, with AC ₹1000/1200/1600/1800;) Hidden down an unprepossessing lane off Vinaik Bazaar, this backpacker fallback has regularly repainted rooms that are considerably better than you'd guess from their padlocked grey doors. The mini box singles share OK bathrooms and are about the cheapest rooms for foreigners in Jammu. Good views of the Central Gurdwara from the rooftop.

Hotel Natraj HOTEL $$

(0191-2547450; www.natrajhoteljammu.com; Residency Rd; s/d ₹1400/1800, with view ₹2000/2500;) Stylish chocolate-and-cream rooms have good air-con and, in the smallish bathrooms, piping-hot showers. Reception is hid-

Jammu

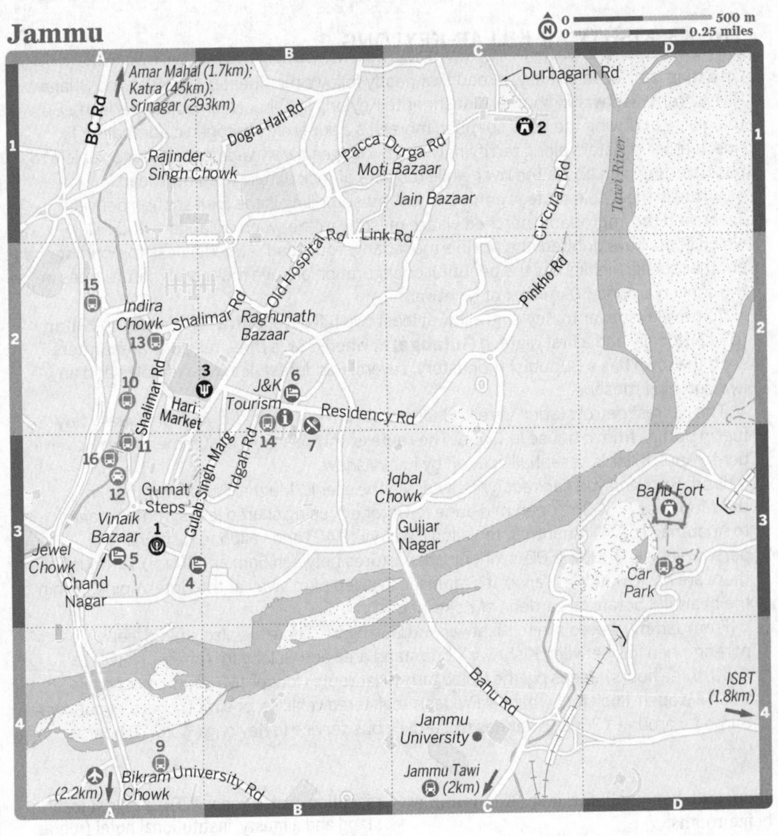

Jammu

Sights
1 Central Gurdwara A3
Dogra Art Gallery .... (see 2)
2 Mubarak Mandi C1
3 Raghunath Mandir B2

Sleeping
4 Fortune Riviera A3
5 Green View Hotel A3
6 Hotel Natraj B2

Eating
7 Falak B2

Transport
Air India .... (see 14)
8 Bahu Fort Matador Stop D3
9 Bikram Chowk Matador Stop A4
10 Bus company ticket stalls A2
11 Bus Station A3
12 Bus Station Ramp (Srinagar jeeps) A3
13 Indira Chowk A2
14 J&K SRTC Srinagar Bus booking office B2
15 Matadors to Nagrota & Buses to Udhampur A2
16 Private Bus Offices A3

den away in a compact, modern vegetarian restaurant on Panj Bakhtar Rd. A couple of rooms face out across Residency Rd, which is its official address.

On the website, only the photos in 'Gallery' actually show the hotel.

Fortune Riviera HOTEL $$$
(☎0191-2561415; www.fortunehotels.in; Gulab Singh Marg; s/d from ₹6600/7150; ❄📶) Central Jammu's most stylish and attentively businesslike hotel has a glass elevator in the four-storey atrium, two restaurants, a coffee

THE K3: KISHTWAR-KILLAR-KEYLONG

On a map it all looks so easy: a road that neatly follows the Chenab, Chandra and Bhaga Rivers from Kishtwar in southern Kashmir to Keylong in Lahaul (Himachal Pradesh). But the reality of driving the K3 is so much more: it's a superbly photogenic adrenaline-fix ride. It roller-coasters along terrifyingly narrow ledges barely wide enough for a vehicle to pass, skirting high above the river while daggers of rock dangle from overhead.

Virtually the whole route is gorgeous, but most thrilling is the 5km section between Tayari and the improbably perched village of Ishtiyari (between Gulabgarh and Killar), which some have dubbed 'the world's most dangerous road'. Although less toe-curling, another scenic highlight is the beautiful configuration of huge rocks and mature trees in the canyon around 50km east of Kishtwar.

To travel Kishtwar to Keylong, allow at least two full days, with a night's stop in **Killar** (p343). Ideally add a first night in **Gulabgarh**, where J&K's three religious areas intersect; the town has a Buddhist monastery, several Paddari-style Hindu temples and an eye-catching mosque.

The nearest petrol stations are in Bhadarwah and Kishtwar, but you can usually buy fuel in bottles from a house in Tayari. The route is only passable in summer; from November to April, Killar is essentially cut off by heavy snow.

From Srinagar, you can reach Kishtwar via the scenic 'Mughal Road' over the Sinthan Top pass (3800m; open mid-June to October), using shared jeeps from Srinagar to Anantnag (p274), Anantnag to Vailoo ('Wai-yil'; ₹40) and Vailoo to Kishtwar (per person/vehicle ₹300/3500, six hours, departures between 6am and 10am). Although there are basic hotels in Vailoo, it's far nicer to sleep 6km away at the Hotel Alpine, within the beautiful botanical gardens of Kokernag.

From Jammu, buses run to Kishtwar and Gulabgarh. There are also shared jeeps, departing when full, between Kishtwar's bus stand area and Gulabgarh (per seat ₹100 to ₹150, three hours). Jeeps ply the Gulabgarh-Killar route (four or five hours) most days when it's open. Look for Himachal Pradesh-registered vehicles, or simply charter your own Sumo for around ₹3000. Killar has twice-daily bus service to Keylong (₹210, 10 hours).

shop and bar – all for just 29 soothingly beige rooms.

Eating

The Residency Rd area has a fairly wide range of options, including vegetarian restaurants, fast food, a Café Coffee Day opposite KC Plaza, and good cheap street food outside the Hotel Natraj.

★Falak INDIAN **$$$**
(0191-2520770; www.kcresidency.com; 7th fl, KC Residency Hotel, Residency Rd; mains veg/nonveg from ₹455/630; noon-11pm) This revolving restaurant serves superb pan-Indian cuisine and offers 360-degree views of the crowded Jammu cityscape. Try the Jammu speciality *khatta gosht dhoonidar* (smoked lamb flavoured with pomegranate paste).

Information

J&K Tourism (0191-2548172; www.jktdc.org; Residency Rd; 8am-8pm Mon-Sat May-Sep, reduced hours Oct-Apr) The J&K Tourism complex includes a refreshingly air-conditioned reception centre (maps ₹10), a tourist jeep stand and a musty, institutional hotel (rooms from ₹500) hiding an attractive Kashmiri restaurant and typical old-school Indian bar.

Getting There & Away

AIR

Airlines flying domestically out of Jammu:

Air India (0191-2456086; www.airindia.com; J&K Tourism complex; 10am-1pm & 2-4.45pm Mon-Sat) Delhi, Srinagar, Leh (Monday & Friday).

GoAir (www.goair.in) Delhi, Srinagar, Mumbai (via Delhi).

IndiGo (0191-2430439; www.goindigo.in) Delhi, Mumbai (via Srinagar).

Jet Airways (0191-2453888; www.jetairways.com) Delhi, Srinagar.

SpiceJet (www.spicejet.com) Delhi, Srinagar.

Vistara (www.airvistara.com) Srinagar

BUS & JEEP

Most public buses still use the big, rotting concrete **bus station** (General Bus Stand; BC Rd) complex, which has dozens of **private bus**

offices and agencies, especially along the chaotic strip on BC Rd in the shadow of a highway overpass. Many private buses wait along that road rather than use the big new **ISBT** (New Interstate Bus Terminal; Transport Nagar Rd, Narwal) – at least for now.

Amritsar Daily buses (₹175, six hours, frequent) via Pathankot in Punjab (₹90, 2½ hours).

Bani (₹240, 8½ hours, four daily) via Basohli.

Chamba HRTC bus (₹280, one daily in morning).

Chandigarh Private buses (seat/AC/sleeper from ₹350/450/600, eight hours, frequent in early morning and late evening).

Delhi Public buses (₹580, 13 hours, 13 daily) and private services (seat/sleeper/recliner from ₹800/1000/1500, several in evening). Departures are from outside the (old) bus station but may move to the ISBT; double-check departure location when booking.

Dharamsala There's a direct bus (₹260, six hours, one in morning); otherwise change at Pathankot. Several private bus companies say they go to Dharamsala but will drop you at Gaggal (AC ₹750).

Gulabgarh Buses marked 'Paddar' (₹350, 10 hours) leave before dawn from **Indira Chowk**.

Katra Buses (₹50, 1¾ hours, half-hourly) depart from both the bus and train stations. Minibuses and taxis are frequent, too, in pilgrimage season.

Kishtwar Buses (₹260, seven hours, nine daily in early morning) depart from the northeast corner of the bus station or from Indira Chowk.

Manali Private buses (AC ₹850, 12 hours) ply this route in evenings, plus there's one morning service. Ask at the **bus company ticket stalls** north of Lords Inn.

Srinagar Most services are cancelled when Kashmir experiences turmoil. Journey time is 11 hours, but traffic jams can extend that considerably. Pre-purchase tickets for the J&K SRTC bus (lower/upper class ₹418/520, one in morning) at a **special booking office** (Idgah Rd). Several private companies on the bus station strip have overnight services. Jeeps offering shared rides (from ₹600 to ₹800, depending on occupancy) gather along the **bus station ramp** (Shalimar Rd) and near Jewel Chowk; although they're quicker than buses, departure times are highly uncertain.

TRAIN

Jammu Tawi, Jammu's main train station, is south of the river, 5km from the bus station. The new northbound railway should one day reach Srinagar.

Amritsar Jat TataMuri Express (18110; sleeper/3AC/2AC ₹184/485/690, five hours, 2.20pm).

Delhi Uttar Sampark Kranti Express (12446; sleeper/3AC/2AC ₹355/920/1300, 10 hours, 9pm). The slower Jhelum Express (11078) departs at 9.45pm and continues to Agra (sleeper/3AC/2AC ₹395/1060/1498, 14 hours).

Getting Around

For local transport into town from the airport, turn left on exiting the airport grounds and wait at the Durga Petrol Station. To the airport from Residency Rd, autorickshaws/taxis cost around ₹150/250, or use 'Satwari'-bound minibuses.

Locals call the little local buses 'matadors' (the trade name of the vehicles that originally served this purpose). Matadors charge ₹10 for most rides, less for shorter hops.

Although there's a specific service that runs between the bus and train stations, 'Panjtirthi Railway Station' services are more frequent and follow the same route, often terminating near **Indira Chowk** (p281).

From the bus station, 'Janipur Fort' matadors take BC Rd to **Bikram Chowk** to **Bahu Fort**. **'Nagrota' matadors** (BC Rd) pass within 300m of the Amar Mahal.

Short autorickshaw hops start at ₹50.

Around Jammu

Just an hour by bus from Jammu, appealing **Akhnoor** features a sturdy fortress ruin, a gurdwara (Sikh temple) and a three-*vihara* Hindu temple rising in concert on the western river bank of the powerful Chenab. Along the fort's base, an arcaded promenade passes the 1822 coronation point of the Dogra ruler Gulab Singh.

Accessed by foot, palanquin or helicopter from **Katra**, the latter-day **Vaishno Devi Shrine** is one of India's busiest pilgrim sites. It attracts millions of domestic visitors, but it's less of a draw for most non-Hindus.

Further afield, fort town **Bhadarwah** (pronounced Badra-wa) markets itself as Chota (Little) Kashmir, with a wide, fertile valley that's hemmed by appealing, forested slopes and peppered with villages. Around 1km north of the town centre is the garish pink Chandi Mata Temple, starting point of the annual pilgrimage to **Machail** in Paddar (via more accessible Gulabgarh). **Gulabgarh** has classic Paddari shrines of its own and is a good launch point for the most exciting section of the **K3 route** to Killar in Himachal Pradesh.

Himachal Pradesh

Includes ➡

Best Places to Eat

- La Plage (p315)
- Cecil Restaurant (p290)
- Hotel Deyzor Restaurant (p346)
- Moonpeak (p328)
- Evergreen (p305)

Best Places to Sleep

- Orchard Hut (p338)
- Wildflower Hall (p292)
- Hotel Deyzor (p345)
- Alliance Guesthouse (p308)
- Tashi Khangsar Hotel (p350)

Why Go?

With spectacular snowy peaks and plunging river valleys, beautiful Himachal is India's outdoor adventure playground. From trekking and climbing to rafting, paragliding and skiing, if it can be done in the mountains, it can be done here. A convoluted topography of interlocking mountain chains also makes Himachal a spectacular place simply to explore, by bus, car, motorbike, jeep or foot. Every pass crossing into a new valley brings you into a different world, with its own culture, deities and even language. Villages perched on staggering slopes enchant with fairy-tale architecture and their people's easygoing warmth.. Hill stations appeal with a holiday atmosphere and colonial echoes, while backpacker magnets lure with their blissed-out vibe and mountain beauty. Such is the richness of the Himachali jigsaw that in McLeod Ganj, the Dalai Lama's home-away-from-home, and in Lahaul and Spiti, with their centuries-old Buddhist cultures, you might even think you've stumbled into Tibet.

When to Go

Manali

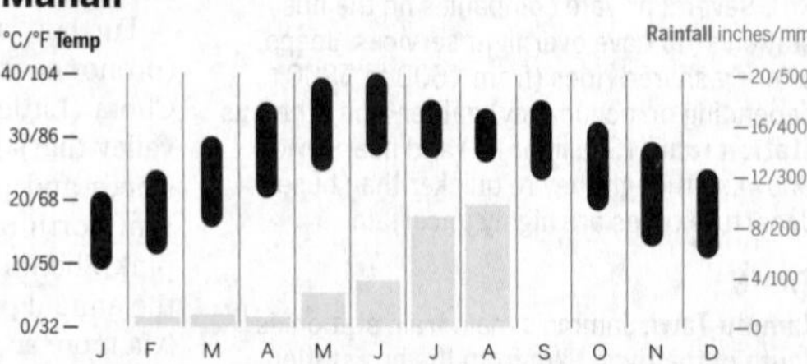

May–Jun & early Sep–Oct Outside the monsoon season; perfect for trekking and other activities.

Mid-Jul–early Sep The monsoon: visit Lahaul and Spiti, which stay dry.

Nov–Apr Good for snow-lovers, but the high passes to Lahaul and Spiti are blocked.

SOUTHERN HIMACHAL PRADESH

As soon as you cross the state line from Haryana, the landscape starts to crinkle and fold in steep, forest-covered ridges – the foothills that herald the grand Himalayan ranges further north. The main travel destination in the south is the popular hill station Shimla, the former summer capital of British-ruled India.

Shimla

0177 / POP 170,000 / ELEV 2205M

Strung out along a 12km ridge, with steep forested hillsides falling away in all directions, the Himachal capital is a good appetite-whetter for the awe-inspiring mountain tracts of the state's interior. Shimla is one of India's most popular hill resorts, buzzing with a happy flow of Indian vacationers and full of relics of its previous life as the summer capital of British India. Traffic is banned from the central part of town, so walking is pleasant – even when huffing and puffing uphill. The long, winding main street, the Mall, runs east and west just below the spine of the hill. South of it, the maze-like alleys of the bustling bazaar cascade steeply down to traffic-infested Cart Rd.

From mid-July to mid-September, Shimla is frequently wreathed in cloud, and in winter it often gets a carpeting of snow.

History

Until the British arrived, there was nothing at Shimla but a sleepy forest glade known as Shyamala (a local name for Kali – the Hindu destroyer-of-evil goddess). Then the new British political officer for the Hill States, Charles Kennedy, built a cottage here in 1822 and nothing was ever the same again. In 1864, Simla (its colonial-era name) became the official summer capital of the Raj, and from then until 1939 the entire government of India fled here for half of every year from the sweltering heat of the lowlands, bringing with them hundreds of muleloads of files, forms and other paraphernalia of government.

When the Kalka–Shimla railway was opened in 1906, Shimla's status as India's premier hill station was assured. The town became a centre not only of government but also of social frolics for the elite of the Raj. Maharajas as well as colonial grandees built mansions here, and the season was filled with grand balls at the Viceroy's lodge, picnics in the woods, amateur dramatics at the Gaiety Theatre and much flirtation and frivolity. Rudyard Kipling, who spent several summers here, used Shimla as the setting for parts of *Kim* and his short-story collection *Plain Tales from the Hills*.

Sights

★The Ridge STREET

The broad esplanade extending east from Scandal Point is called the Ridge and it's thronged with strolling locals and tourists all day. In clear weather a jagged line of distant snowy peaks is clearly visible to the north.

Christ Church CHURCH

(0177-2652953; the Ridge; 10.30am-1pm & 2-5.30pm, services in English 9am Sun) At the Ridge's east end, the very English Christ Church, opened in 1846, is one of the oldest surviving churches in northern India and

TOP STATE FESTIVALS

Losar (Tibetan New Year; late Jan, Feb or early March) Tibetans across Himachal, including in McLeod Ganj and Spiti, celebrate their New Year with processions, music, dancing and *chaams* (ritual masked dances by monks).

Minjar Festival (last Sun Jul-1st Sun Aug) A week of processions, music, dance and markets at Chamba.

Ki Chaam Festival (Jul/Aug) A week of rituals at Ki Gompa culminates in a day of whirling dances by brightly costumed and masked lamas.

Manimahesh Yatra (late Aug/early Sep) Hundreds of thousands of Shaivites trek up to 4200m to bathe in Manimahesh Lake near Bharmour, one of Shiva's mythical abodes.

Phulech Festival (Sep/Oct) Villagers in Kalpa and throughout Kinnaur fill temple courtyards with flowers; oracles perform sacrifices and make predictions for the coming year.

Dussehra (Oct; variable dates) Intense and spectacular weeklong celebration of the defeat of the demon Ravana, at Kullu (p306).

Himachal Pradesh Highlights

❶ **Kinnaur-Spiti loop** (p344) Daring the hair-raising passes, gorges and cliff-ledge roads of one of Asia's great road-trips.

❷ **Trekking** (p330) Choosing from dozens of spectacular mountain crossings – easy, demanding, or moderate such as the Indrahar La.

❸ **McLeod Ganj** (p320) Immersing yourself in Tibetan culture or yoga, volunteering with refugees or just chilling out in the mountains.

❹ **Manali** (p309) Skiing, trekking, climbing, paragliding, rafting or just enjoying the traveller scene in Himachal's backpacker playground.

❺ **Spiti** (p344) Exploring the ancient rock-perched Buddhist monasteries, high-altitude villages and starkly spectacular landscapes of this stunningly beautiful, remote region.

❻ **Shimla** (p283) Riding the toy train up from the plains and exploring relics of the British Raj in its former summer capital, still one of India's favourite hill stations.

❼ **Parvati Valley** (p302) Blissing out on the hippie trail in this hauntingly beautiful valley.

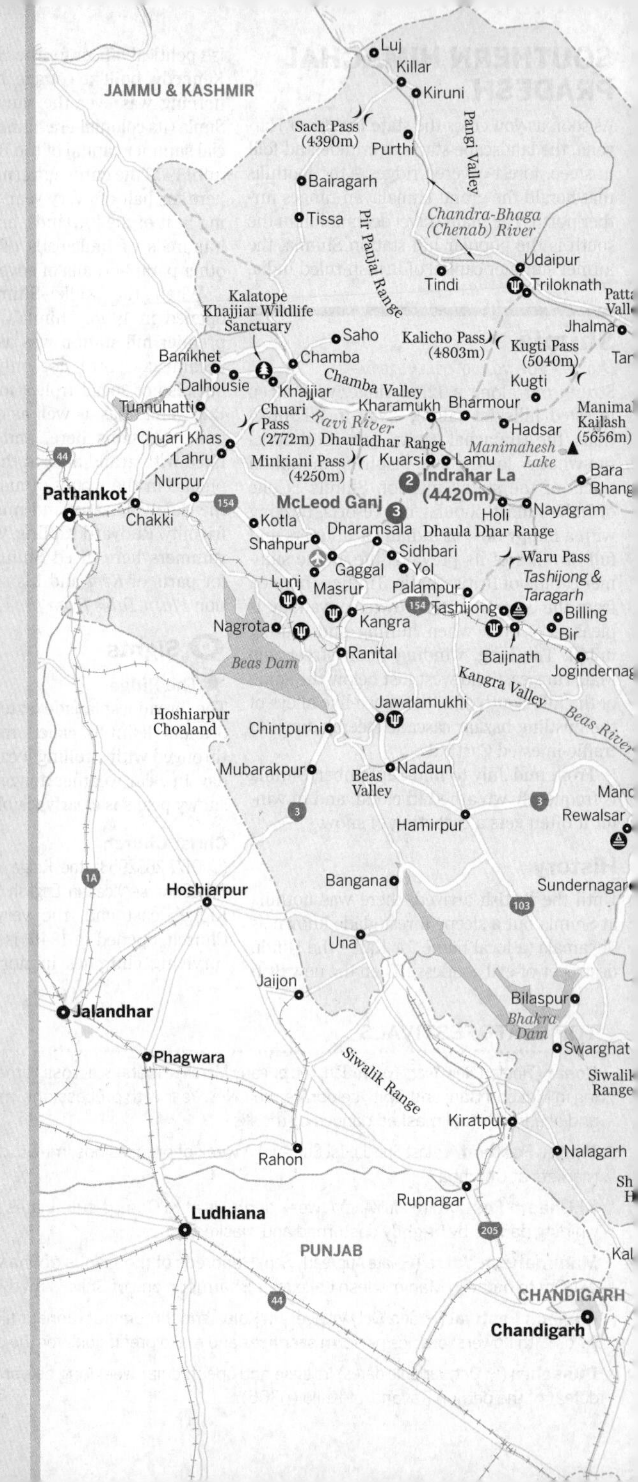

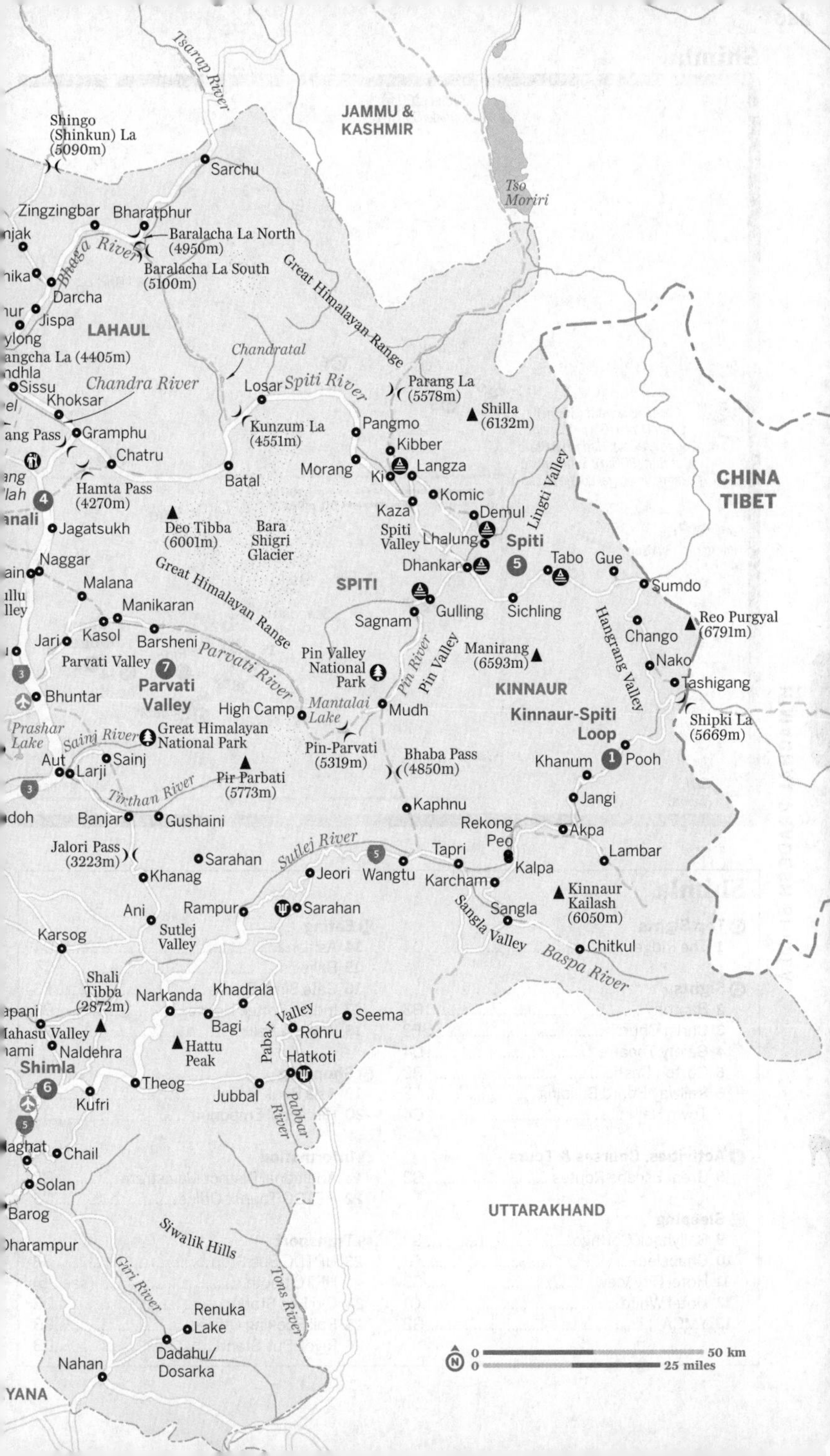

JAMMU & KASHMIR
Tsarap River
Tso Moriri
Shingo (Shinkun) La (5090m)
Sarchu
Zingzingbar
Bharatphur
Baralacha La North (4950m)
Baralacha La South (5100m)
Bhaga River
Darcha
Jispa
LAHAUL
Great Himalayan Range
Chandratal
Chandra River
Sissu
Khoksar
Losar
Spiti River
Parang La (5578m)
Shilla (6132m)
Gramphu
Kunzum La (4551m)
Pangmo
Kibber
Chatru
Hamta Pass (4270m)
Batal
Morang
Ki
Langza
Komic
Kaza
Demul
Lingti Valley
CHINA TIBET
Jagatsukh
Deo Tibba (6001m)
Bara Shigri Glacier
Spiti Valley
Lhalung
Spiti
Naggar
Malana
Dhankar
Tabo
Gue
SPITI
Sumdo
Manikaran
Gulling
Sagnam
Sichling
Hangrang Valley
Reo Purgyal (6791m)
Chango
Jari
Kasol
Barsheni
Parvati River
Pin Valley National Park
Pin River
Pin Valley
Manirang (6593m)
Nako
Parvati Valley
Parvati Valley
KINNAUR
Tashigang
Bhuntar
High Camp
Mantalai Lake
Mudh
Kinnaur-Spiti Loop
Shipki La (5669m)
Prashar Lake
Sainj River
Great Himalayan National Park
Pin-Parvati (5319m)
Bhaba Pass (4850m)
Khanum
Pooh
Aut
Larji
Sainj
Pir Parbati (5773m)
Jangi
Tirthan River
Kaphnu
Banjar
Gushaini
Rekong Peo
Akpa
Jalori Pass (3223m)
Sarahan
Sutlej River
Tapri
Lambar
Khanag
Jeori
Wangtu
Karcham
Kalpa
Kinnaur Kailash (6050m)
Ani
Rampur
Sarahan
Sangla
Sutlej Valley
Sangla Valley
Karsog
Chitkul
Baspa River
Shali Tibba (2872m)
Narkanda
Khadrala
Bagi
Pabar Valley
Seema
Rohru
Mahasu Valley
Naldehra
Hattu Peak
Hatkoti
Shimla
Theog
Jubbal
Pabbar River
Kufri
Chail
Solan
Barog
UTTARAKHAND
Siwalik Hills
Giri River
Toms River
Renuka Lake
Dadahu/ Dosarka
Nahan
0 50 km
0 25 miles

Shimla

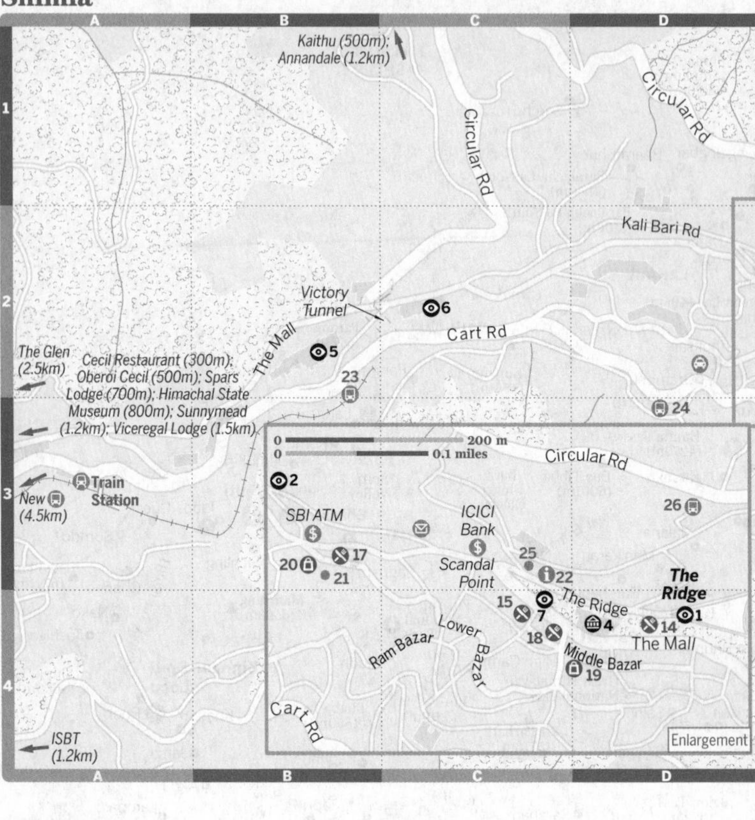

Shimla

Top Sights

1 The Ridge D4

Sights

2 Bantony B3
3 Christ Church F2
4 Gaiety Theatre D4
5 Gorton Castle B2
6 Railway Board Building C2
7 Town Hall C4

Activities, Courses & Tours

8 Great Escape Routes G2

Sleeping

9 Ballyhack Cottage G2
10 Chapslee G1
11 Hotel City View G3
12 Hotel White G1
13 YMCA G2

Eating

14 Ashiana D4
15 Baljee's C4
16 Café Simla Times F3
17 Indian Coffee House B3
18 Wake & Bake C4

Shopping

19 Asia Book House D4
20 Himachal Emporium B3

Information

21 Additional District Magistrate B3
22 HPTDC Tourist Office C3

Transport

23 HPTDC Bus Stop B2
HRTC booth .... (see 25)
24 Old Bus Station D3
25 Rail Booking Office C3
26 Rivoli Bus Stand D3

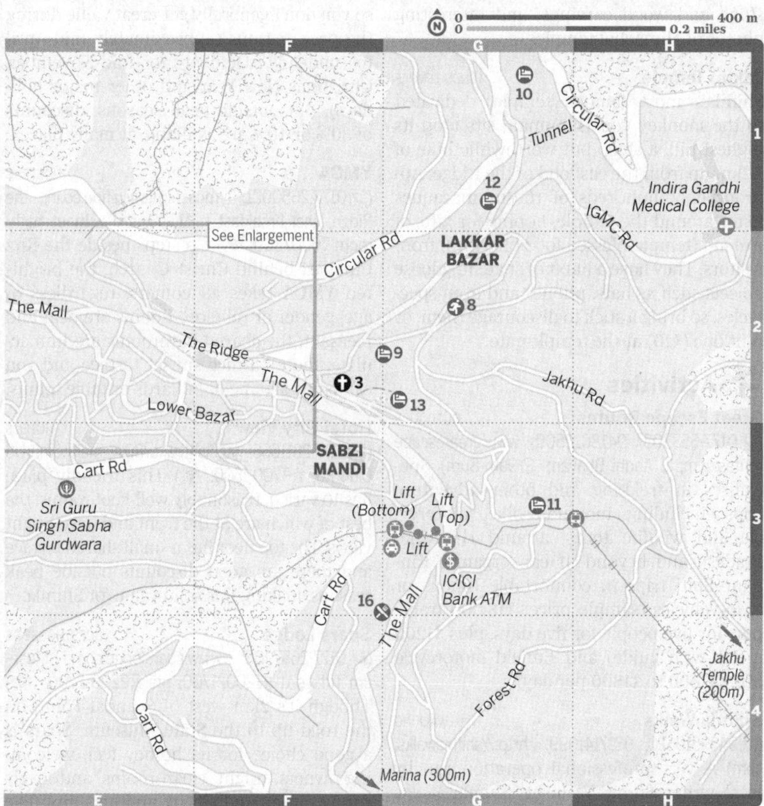

Shimla's most famous landmark. It contains some touching Raj-era memorials and typical Victorian stained glass.

Gaiety Theatre HISTORIC BUILDING
(☎0177-2650173; www.gaiety.in; the Mall; Indian/foreigner ₹10/25, camera ₹15/25; ⏲tours 11am-1.30pm & 2-5.30pm Tue-Sun) This lovely Victorian theatre, opened in 1877 and now splendidly restored, has long been a focus of Shimla social life. Rudyard Kipling, Shashi Kapoor and various viceroys are among those who have trodden its Burmese teak boards. Today it hosts visiting theatre companies as well as 15 local dramatic societies, plus concerts and exhibitions. Mr R Gautam gives excellent guided tours, explaining its history as you appreciate the view from the viceroy's private box.

★Viceregal Lodge HISTORIC BUILDING
(Indian Institute of Advanced Study; www.iias.org; tour Indian/foreigner ₹40/85, grounds only ₹20; ⏲9.30am-5.30pm Tue-Sun, to 7pm mid-May–mid-Jul, tours every 45min 10am-4.45pm) The official summer residence of the British viceroys was completed in 1888 and the entire Indian subcontinent was ruled from here for just over half of every year (usually early April to late October) from then till WWII. Henry Irwin's grand, grey sandstone creation resembles a cross between Harry Potter's Hogwarts and a Scottish baronial castle. Half-hour building tours visit three rooms with interesting photo exhibits (one was the billiards room) and the three-storey entrance hall lined in Burmese teak.

Himachal State Museum MUSEUM
(Indian/foreigner ₹20/100, camera ₹50/100; ⏲10am-5pm Tue-Sun) About 2.5km west of Scandal Point, up near the telecommunications mast, the state museum occupies an 1860s mansion and houses an impressive collection of Himachali, Rajasthani and Punjabi miniatures, as well as colourful traditional costumes and jewellery, delicate

stone and wood carvings, and interesting photos of Himachal temples.

Jakhu Temple HINDU TEMPLE

Shimla's most famous temple, dedicated to the monkey god Hanuman, sits atop its highest hill, a steep but worthwhile hike of 1.2km up from the east end of the Ridge. Appropriately, hundreds of rhesus macaques loiter around the temple, hoping for gifts of *prasad* (temple-blessed food offerings) from visitors. They have a habit of snatching loose objects such as hats, phones and even spectacles, so bring a stick to discourage them, or rent one (₹10) at the temple gate.

Activities

Great Escape Routes OUTDOORS

(☎0177-6533037, 9418012500; www.greatescaperoutes.com; 6 Andhi Bhavan; ⌚9am-8pm) Specialises in trekking and other adventure trips, including mountain-bike, motorcycle and wildlife tours, around Himachal Pradesh and beyond. It can organise Kinnaur–Spiti trips in comfortable Innova or Xylo vehicles (sample price: ₹18,000 transport for five people for five days, plus ₹1200 a day with guide) and Enfield motorcycle hire (₹1600 to ₹1800 per day).

Shimla Walks WALKING

(☎9459519620, 9817141099; http://shimlawalks.com) A very professional operation run by local writer Sumit Vashisht, Shimla Walks offers excellent guided walks on and off the beaten track. Day or half-day trips (₹2000 to ₹3500 for up to four people) provide rare insights along the popular route to the Viceregal Lodge, or take you to writers' and artists' houses or Shimla's hidden Raj-era cemeteries.

Sleeping

Shimla has a lot of hotels but many of them are a long way from the centre. The town's popularity with domestic tourists keeps room rates high in the better-located places, so you don't generally get great value during the peak seasons (approximately mid-April to mid-July, October to mid-November, Christmas/New Year and other major holidays). But outside peak seasons, discounts of 30% or 40% are available at many places.

SLEEPING PRICE RANGES

Accommodation price ranges for this chapter (referring to accommodation for two people, including taxes, without any meals):

$ below ₹1200

$$ ₹1200–₹3500

$$$ above ₹3500

YMCA HOSTEL **$**

(☎0177-2650021; ymcashimla@yahoo.co.in; the Ridge; incl breakfast r ₹1500, s/d without bathroom ₹600/800; 📶) Up steps beside the Ritz Cineplex behind Christ Church, the bright-red YMCA takes all comers, regardless of age, gender or religion. Rooms are neat and pleasant, the shared bathrooms are immaculate, there's a nice sunset terrace and you can enjoy a game of billiards or table tennis.

Hotel City View HOTEL **$**

(☎0177-2811666; jagdishthakur80@gmail.com; US Club Rd; r ₹700-1500; 📶) This friendly place has 10 varied, reasonably well-kept rooms, the best of which are at the front and have bright views. The top floor has a small shared terrace and there are good discounts outside peak seasons, making this solid value for Shimla.

Spars Lodge GUESTHOUSE **$$**

(☎0177-2657908; www.sparslodge.com; Museum Rd; s/d ₹1200/1700, ste ₹2200-2700; 📶) Though it's 2km west of Scandal Point, on the road up to the State Museum, Spars is a good choice for its homey feel, welcoming owners, bright, clean rooms, and lovely sunny dining and sitting area upstairs. The restaurant (mains ₹160 to ₹420) serves great food, including local trout and all-day English breakfasts, and has wi-fi.

Hotel White HOTEL **$$**

(☎0177-2656136; www.hotelwhitesimla.com; Lakkar Bazar; d ₹2150-2740, ste ₹3570-5360; 📶) Northeast of the Ridge through a bustling bazaar, the White is well run and rates are fixed all year. Rooms are clean, large and well kept, with good beds, and nearly all of them have a balcony or terrace looking over the valley below.

★ **Sunnymead** B&B **$$$**

(☎9736584045, 0177-2801436; http://sunnymeadestate.com; Sunnymead Estate, below Cart Rd, near Old MLA Quarters & Hotel Blossom; s/d incl breakfast ₹5000/6500; 📶) You could imagine yourself in the English countryside in this wonderfully cosy 1890s cottage full of interesting art, books and furnishings, with a couple of dogs, a cat and a lovely flower garden. The four rooms are comfy and char-

THE MALL, SHIMLA'S 7KM STROLL

The largely traffic-free Mall is the heartbeat of Shimla life, strung with hotels, shops, eateries, colonial-era buildings in assorted states of repair, and people everywhere. It runs up from Chotta Shimla, southeast of the centre, to Scandal Point, the official centre of town, then continues west to the Viceregal Lodge.

The top landmarks you'll pass in an east–west walk along the Mall include the handsome half-timbered **Clarkes Hotel**, dating from the 1890s; the Gaiety Theatre (p287), in action since 1877; and the **Town Hall**, almost beside Scandal Point, dating from 1910 and oddly reminiscent of the mansion in Hammer Horror films.

West of Scandal Point, just above the Mall, a pretty 1883 quasi-Tudor folly houses the post office (p291). Also just above the Mall, the wonderfully whimsical **Bantony** (Kali Bari Rd) is a turreted red-brick mansion from 1880 that was once home to the Maharajah of Sirmaur. Bantony is now sadly the epitome of Shimla picturesque decay.

Another 500m west, the turreted **Railway Board Building**, built in 1897 with fire-resistant cast iron and steel, now houses government and police offices. Just past here is the austere grey-stone **Gorton Castle** from 1904, formerly the colonial government secretariat and now the Himachal Pradesh Accountant-General's Office (visitors can walk round the outside only). A further 1km brings you to Shimla's most famous luxury hotel, the Oberoi Cecil, founded in 1902 and radically refurbished in the 1990s but century-old half-timbering on its western end. From the Oberoi, it's 1.4km on westward to the most splendiferous of all Shimla's Raj-era edifices, the Viceregal Lodge (p287).

acterful, and good Indian or English dinners (₹1200) are available as well as the excellent and generous breakfast.

Although it's 3km west of the heart of town, down a short path from busy Cart Rd, Sunnymead is only about 10 minutes' walk below the Viceregal Lodge, which is linked to the centre by the largely traffic-free Mall. The original mud-plastered wood-and-stone structure was maintained when the house was fully renovated a few years ago.

Ballyhack Cottage B&B $$$

(☎8091300076; www.ballyhackcottage.com; Sidhowal Lodge Estate, the Ridge; d incl breakfast ₹4500; wi-fi) A new building on one of Shimla's oldest properties, in a superb central location just off the Ridge, five-room Ballyhack combines an evocatively colonial ambience (polished-wood floors and furniture, old prints, tiled floors, rugs) with current amenities including comfy beds, tea/coffee equipment and good contemporary bathrooms. The garden terraces have views to the distant Himalaya in good weather.

★**Oberoi Cecil** HOTEL $$$

(☎0177-2804848; www.oberoicecil.com; the Mall, Chaura Maidan; s/d incl breakfast & wi-fi from ₹16,000/17,250; air-con, internet, wi-fi, pool) This grand high-rise, 2km west of Scandal Point, is Shimla's glitziest hotel. Discreet colonial-era charm combines happily with modern, wood-clad luxury in the plush rooms, with their tastefully trad furnishings, and the spacious common areas. The hotel has a lovely indoor pool and fine restaurant and service is polished but friendly.

★**Chapslee** HERITAGE HOTEL $$$

(☎0177-2658663; www.chapslee.com; Elysium Hill; r incl half-board ₹20,800-30,200, B&B ₹14,250; wi-fi) For the full Raj treatment, you can't beat this lavish mansion where the Raja of Kapurthala's grandson lovingly maintains an aristocratic lifestyle of bygone days. From its huge gold-toned drawing room to the five super-comfortable bedrooms, the exclusive retreat is crammed with chandeliers, tapestries, antiques and family portraits. Impeccable service and fine meals add up to a memorable experience.

Eating

Baljee's INDIAN $

(26 the Mall; snacks & mains ₹85-235; ⏲9am-10.30pm) Clean, cosy and air-conditioned, with bow-tied waiters, Baljee's gets packed with Indian families, many of whom come for the snacks and South Indian specialities. Breakfasts of omelettes, toast and dosas are good, too.

Indian Coffee House CAFE $

(the Mall; dishes ₹25-80; ⏲8am-8.30pm) This Shimla institution is like an old boys' club with its ageing leather seats, uniformed waiters and blackboard menu. Packed with chattering locals (not quite all men) for much of the day, it's the most atmospheric place in town for breakfast, cheap dosas and coffee (don't even ask for tea!).

Wake & Bake MULTICUISINE **$$**
(34/1 the Mall; dishes ₹120-320; 9.30am-10pm;) This upstairs cafe is about the hippest eatery in Shimla (which isn't saying too much), serving up organic South Indian coffee, breakfasts, pizza by the slice, hummus, falafel, toasties, veg stir-fry, pasta and excellent crêpes. Wi-fi is free.

Ashiana INDIAN **$$**
(the Ridge; mains ₹115-275; 9am-10pm) In a fanciful circular building, Ashiana is an almost-elegant restaurant and good people-watching spot, with a delightful sunny terrace. As well as tasty North Indian dishes there are Chinese and a few Thai and South Indian favourites.

★ **Cecil Restaurant** MULTICUISINE **$$$**
(0177-2804848; Oberoi Cecil, the Mall, Chaura Maidan; mains ₹1000-1700; 7.30-10.30pm) For a special dinner, look no further than the colonial-era elegance of the Cecil Restaurant at the Oberoi. The menu is strong on curries from all over India and Thailand too, but there are plenty of Continental options as well, including Kullu Valley trout. Book ahead in high season.

Drinking & Nightlife

The most stylish places for a drink are the lounge bars at top-end hotels such as the Oberoi Cecil (p289) or (if you like a DJ soundtrack) the **Marina** (0177-6629999; www.marinashimla.com; the Mall). Cheaper drinks are available at restaurants such as Ashiana and **Café Simla Times** (the Mall; mains ₹245-445; noon-10.30pm;), both of which have panoramic terraces too.

Shopping

Indian tourists browse fashionable shops along the Mall for Himachali and Kashmiri shawls and other apparel. For a slice of more traditional commerce, wander the bazaar labyrinth below the Mall. You can buy anything here from peacock feathers and henna kits to bangles and bicycles. Different zones are devoted to vegetables (the Sabzi Mandi), spices, fabrics and other goods.

Asia Book House BOOKS
(the Mall; 10.30am-8.30pm Mon-Sat, 1-7.30pm Sun) Novels, guides and other books on India.

Himachal Emporium ARTS & CRAFTS
(0177-2011234; www.himcrafts.com; the Mall; 10am-1pm & 2.30-7.30pm Mon-Sat) Kullu and Kinnauri shawls, thick Lahauli wool socks and other appealing Himachal crafts are sold at reasonable prices at this state-government crafts enterprise.

Information

HPTDC Tourist Office (Himachal Pradesh Tourist Development Corporation, Himachal Tourism; 0177-2652561; www.hptdc.gov.in; Scandal Point; 9am-7pm, to 8pm mid-Apr–Jun & mid-Sep–mid-Nov) Very helpful for local information and advice; also books HPTDC buses, hotels and tours.

ICICI Bank (Scandal Point; 10am-4pm Mon-Sat, closed 2nd & 4th Sat each month) Exchanges foreign currency and has a 24-hour ATM.

BUSES FROM SHIMLA ISBT

DESTINATION	FARE (₹)	DURATION (HR)	DEPARTURES
Chandigarh	172-229	4	every 15-30min, 4am-10pm
Dehra Dun	322-517	8	3 daily
Delhi	414-915	10	17 daily
Dharamsala	360-497	8-10	7 daily
Kalpa	400	11	6.15am
Kullu	319-740	7-8	8 daily
Manali	377-871	8-9	7 daily
Mandi	218-502	6	15 daily
Rekong Peo	355	10	approximately hourly 4-11.15am & 6.30-11.15pm
Sangla	350	10	7.15am
Sarahan	300	7	9.30am & 10.30am

Indira Gandhi Medical College (☎ 0177-2803073; IGMC Rd) Large public hospital with 24-hour outpatient department.

Getting There & Away

BUS

The Himachal Road Transport Corporation (HRTC) runs seven comfortable Volvo AC buses to Delhi (₹915, 10 hours) each day, as well as 10 cheaper AC and non-AC services (₹414 to ₹684). Other HRTC AC buses head to Manali (nine hours), via Mandi and Kullu, at 9.30am (₹544, non-Volvo) and 7.30pm (₹871, Volvo), and to Dharamsala (₹475, eight hours, non-Volvo) at 4.30pm. All HRTC buses leave from the **ISBT** (Inter State Bus Terminus, New Bus Station; Tutikandi), a 5km trip west from the town centre: you can make reservations at the **HRTC booth** (Scandal Point; ⏲8am-7.30pm) at Scandal Point or at the **main post office** (Scandal Point; ⏲9.30am-5.30pm Mon-Sat, 10am-5pm Sun).

The Himachal Pradesh Tourism Development Corporation (HPTDC) runs a Volvo AC bus to Delhi (₹900, 10 hours) at 8.30pm, and a non-AC deluxe bus to Manali (₹550, nine hours) at 8.30am, both starting from a **stop** (Cart Rd) on Cart Rd west of Victory Tunnel: get tickets at the HPTDC Tourist Office.

TAXI

The **Kalka-Shimla Himachal Taxi Union** (☎ 0177-2658225; Cart Rd) has its office near the Old Bus Station, while **Vishal Himachal Taxi Operators Union** (☎ 0177-2805164; Cart Rd) operates from the bottom of the passenger lift. Most hotels and travel agencies can organise car transfers to other towns, or a car and driver for an extended tour. A non-AC cab for up to four people to Manali costs around ₹5200, to Chandigarh ₹2100 and to Delhi around ₹6200. You pay between ₹300 and ₹1000 more for AC, depending on distance.

Vishal charges ₹1550 for day trips up to 80km, plus ₹12 for each extra kilometre.

TRAIN

One of the little joys of Shimla is getting to it by the narrow-gauge Kalka–Shimla Railway from Kalka, just north of Chandigarh. This 'toy train' has been operating since 1906 and is one of the World Heritage–listed Mountain Railways of India. Although the steam trains are long gone, it's a scenic five to six-hour trip, with 102 tunnels and 988 bridges on its winding 96km route. Shimla station is 1.5km west of Scandal Point on Cart Rd – a 20- to 30-minute uphill walk to town.

Trains leave Kalka for Shimla at 3.30am, 5am, 5.20am, 6am and 12.10pm, and start the return trip at 10.25am, 2.25pm, 4.55pm, 5.50pm and 6.30pm. The most comfortable option is the Shivalik Express (train 52451 from Kalka at 5.20am, train 52452 from Shimla at 5.50pm) with AC chair cars only, costing ₹420/510 uphill/downhill including food. Other trains have fairly spartan 1st-class coaches (₹270 to ₹320) and usually 2nd-class coaches (₹25 unreserved, ₹40 to ₹65 reserved).

The **Himalayan Queen** service runs from/to Delhi Sarai Rohilla, with comfortable connection times at Kalka and total fares of ₹700/135 (AC chair/2nd class) for the Delhi–Shimla (or vice-versa) trip. A quicker alternative for the Delhi–Kalka (or vice-versa) leg is the Kalka Shatabdi: train 12011 departs New Delhi station for Kalka (AC chair car ₹640) at 7.40am and train 12012 leaves Kalka for New Delhi (₹725) at 5.45pm.

There's a **rail booking office** (Scandal Point; ⏲9am-1pm & 2-4pm Mon-Sat).

Getting Around

The only way to get around central Shimla is on foot. Vehicles, including taxis, are banned from the Ridge and much of the Mall. Fortunately a two-part **lift** (per person ₹10; ⏲8am-9pm Jul-Apr, 8am-10pm May & Jun) connects **Cart Rd** with the **Mall** about 600m east of Scandal Point. Taxis from the train station/ISBT to the bottom of the lift cost ₹150/250. Green-and-white local buses (₹7) run every few minutes between the ISBT and the **Old Bus Station** (☎ 0177-2656326; Cart Rd).

Porters will carry your luggage uphill (about ₹100 from Cart Rd to the Mall) but many double as hotel touts.

Naldehra & Around

☎ 0177

The hill country in every direction from Shimla is beautiful, with plunging green river valleys and vistas over distant mountain ranges – best enjoyed away from the traffic-infested main roads. Some scruffy towns attract crowds of day-trippers for amusement parks, pony rides or the modest winter skiing at Narkanda, but there are a few out-of-the-ordinary places to stay scattered around the region.

TIMINGS FOR HIMALAYAN QUEEN

DEPART	ARRIVE/DEPART KALKA	ARRIVE	TRAIN NOS
Delhi Sarai Rohilla 5.35am	11.10am/12.10pm	Shimla 5.30pm	14095 & 52455
Shimla 10.25am	4.10pm/4.55pm	Delhi Sarai Rohilla 10.40pm	52456 & 14096

Naldehra Golf Club (☎0177-2747656; http://naldehragolfclub.com; green fees Indian/foreigner ₹575/863, club hire ₹288; ⊙7am-7pm Apr-Sep, 9am-5pm Oct-Mar), 25km northeast of Shimla, was founded in 1905 by viceroy Lord Curzon (who loved Naldehra so much he named his daughter after it). The course, set on a ridge among tall cedars, is a challenging one with the quirk that many holes share one fairway, criss-crossing it at different angles. Hire a caddy (₹150 per nine holes) or you won't know where you're going. You can have a drink in the clubhouse whether you're playing or not.

★ **Wildflower Hall** HERITAGE HOTEL $$$
(☎0177-2648585; www.oberoihotels.com; s/d from ₹28,560/29,750; ❄@🛜≋) The most regal lodgings in Himachal Pradesh, Wildflower Hall looms above the hamlet of Chharabra, 14km east of Shimla, exuding wealth from its teak-panelled lobby to its chandelier-lit indoor pool and its opulent colonial-style rooms with marble bathrooms. Rates fluctuate madly.

The **restaurant** (☎0177-2648686; mains ₹1150-2700; ⊙12.30-3.30pm & 7-10.30pm), with a lovely panoramic terrace, serves a daily changing menu of Indian, Continental and Asian fare and is open to nonguests.

ℹ Getting There & Around

There are bus services from Shimla to most places of any size, including 11 daily buses to Naldehra (₹34, one hour) from Shimla's small **Rivoli bus stand** (Circular Rd). Shimla taxi operators (p291) offer reasonably priced drop-offs and day trips.

KINNAUR

The district of Kinnaur, stretching up to the border with Tibet in southeastern Himachal, is blessed with magnificent mountain and valley scenery and a distinctive cultural and ethnic mix that mutates from Aryan Hindu to Tibetan Buddhist as you progress eastward. The Kinnauris are proud but friendly people, recognisable anywhere in India by their green felt *basheri* hats.

Hwy 05 (formerly Hwy 22) threads a spectacular route up the Sutlej (Satluj) valley, following or paralleling the course of the historic Hindustan–Tibet Road, a track constructed by the British in the 19th century in the hope of providing access to Tibet. The main valley is scarred by multiple dam projects that are turning the powerful Sutlej River into a generator, so to best appreciate Kinnaur you need to get up into the hills and side valleys.

Check road conditions beforehand, as monsoon landslides, floods or winter snows can block the roads for days or even weeks.

Beyond Kinnaur lies remote Spiti, which combines with Kinnaur into a loop from Shimla to Manali or Keylong that is an unending sequence of hair-raising roads through breathtaking scenery.

Lower Kinnaur gets monsoon rains in July and August, but east of Rekong Peo the landscape quickly becomes much more arid as you pass through a gap in the Great Himalayan Range and into the range's rain shadow. During Kinnaur's peak domestic tourist seasons – mid-April to June and mid-September to mid-October – it's worth booking ahead for rooms in popular spots including Sarahan, the Sangla Valley, Kalpa and Nako. At other times you may well get discounts.

Rampur

☎01782 / POP 10,300 / ELEV 1005M

The gateway to Kinnaur, this bustling bazaar town was the winter capital of the Bushahr rajas who ruled Kinnaur from the 18th to mid-20th centuries. Most travellers coming from Shimla push on to Sarahan or beyond, but if you have time here, check out the very handsome **Padam Palace**, built for the Raja of Bushahr in the 1920s; only the garden is open to visitors but from there you can fully admire the building's stone arches, carved-wood upper storey, turreted towers and multi-gabled bandstand. Rampur's **Lavi Fair**, a huge commercial and cultural get-together in the second week of November, attracts traders and pilgrims from all over northwest India.

Rampur now has one of Kinnaur's best hotels, the **Nau Nabh** (☎01782-234405; www.hotelnaunabh.com; r ₹2975-6545; ❄🛜), with good-sized, beautifully kept rooms in a renovated 200-year-old section of the Padam Palace, and easily the town's best **restaurant** (mains ₹180-350; ⊙7am-11pm). Cheaper town-centre options include **Hotel Satluj View** (☎01782-233924; hotelsatlujview@yahoo.in; r ₹550-2380; ❄🛜), with rooms ranging from dingy but clean to large and air-conditioned.

ℹ Getting There & Away

Rampur's bus station is 2km east of the centre but many people jump on through buses at the rather chaotic Old Bus Stand in the centre. From the bus station there are services to Rekong Peo (₹160, five hours) at least hourly till 4.30pm, to Shimla (₹205, five hours) every half-hour till 9.30pm, to Sarahan (₹65, two hours) about every 20 minutes till 5.45pm, to Sangla (₹160, four hours) at 6am and 12.30pm, and to the Jalori Pass (₹123, four hours), Banjar (₹157, six hours) and Kullu (₹237, 10 hours) at 9.40am.

Sarahan

01782 / POP 1700 / ELEV 1920M

The former summer capital of the Bushahr kingdom, Sarahan is dominated by the fabulous two-towered **Bhimakali Temple** (6am-8pm), dedicated to a local version of the goddess Kali and built in the traditional Kinnauri manner from layers of stone and timber to absorb the force of earthquakes.

The right-hand tower (as viewed from the entrance) was recently rebuilt after the 12th-century original collapsed. The left-hand tower dates from the 1920s and contains the highly revered Bhimakali shrine beneath a beautiful silver-filigree canopy on its top floor.

The towers' curved, peaked roofs suggest the Tibetan influence on Kinnauri architecture, which becomes more marked as you move up the valley.

For entry to the innermost courtyard with the towers, male visitors must wear a cap (available on the spot), and cameras, mobile phones and leather items must be left in lockers.

Most lodgings will provide meals, or you can choose from a handful of *dhabas* in the bazaar area below the temple.

There's a **State Bank ATM** (Main Bazar) opposite the Civil Hospital.

Temple Resthouse GUESTHOUSE **$**
(01782-274248; dm ₹70, r ₹350-550) Rooms here, within the ancient temple precinct itself, are plain and simple but, unlike most temple accommodation, far from gloomy. The upper-storey rooms in particular are bright, spacious and airy, with hot water.

Hotel Trehan's HOTEL **$**
(9816687605; www.hoteltrehansarahan.com; r ₹600-1000;) Run by a friendly family, this rambling budget establishment has rooms with ornate ceilings, big windows and chintzy tapestries of Indian epics that give it a touch of character. Shared terraces have great views over the valley and there's a restaurant for all meals.

Hotel Srikhand HOTEL **$$**
(01782-274234; www.hptdc.gov.in; s ₹1430-2860, d ₹1900-3810) The most popular and just about the best place in town at research time, though that's lukewarm praise. Rooms are carpeted and have mountain views, and in most cases balconies, but are in serious need of some TLC. There's a reasonable **restaurant** (mains ₹100-275; 7.30am-10pm) but really the best thing about the hotel is the panoramic terrace of the bar.

Getting There & Away

There are buses to Shimla (₹300, seven hours) at 4am, 6.30am, 8am and noon, but you can also get one of the frequent services to Rampur (₹65, two hours) and change there. To head on eastward into Kinnaur, take any bus as far as Jeori (₹30, 45 minutes) on Hwy 05 below Sarahan,

INNER LINE PERMITS

Foreigners planning to travel the spectacular Kinnaur–Spiti loop, in either direction, need an inner line permit for the section between Rekong Peo in Kinnaur and Sumdo in Spiti. This is easily and quickly obtained, any day except Sunday or the second Saturday of the month, in Rekong Peo (p295) or Kaza (p345). If necessary, you can also get the permit at the office of the **Additional District Magistrate** (ADM; 0177-2657005; Room 207/208, Block B, Collectorate Building; 10am-1.30pm & 2-5pm Mon-Sat, closed 2nd Sat each month) in Shimla (down a lane off the Mall 300m west of Scandal Point), though the process here is slightly more complicated: there must be at least two people applying together and you first need a sponsorship letter from an authorised travel agency (costing up to ₹200). Take this and copies of your passport's identity and visa pages to the ADM office. You'll be sent to the Sugam Centre, in the same governmental complex, to fill in a form, have your photo taken and pay ₹300 per person. You then return to the ADM office, where permits are usually issued within 30 minutes.

Note that a few Asian nationalities, including Chinese and Taiwanese, cannot get inner line permits but must apply for a special permit from the Home Affairs Ministry in Delhi.

and catch an eastbound bus there. The last bus from Jeori up to Sarahan leaves around 6.30pm. Taxis are about ₹350.

Sangla Valley

The Sangla, or Baspa, Valley is a deeply carved cleft between burly mountain slopes, where evergreen forests rise to alpine meadows crowned by snowy summits. Villages here feature houses and temples built in traditional Kinnauri timber-and-stone style. The road up the valley leaves Hwy 05 at Karcham, passing the gushing outflow pipes from a big hydroelectric plant: the first 15km, up to the dam just below the valley's only town, Sangla, are truly hair-raising.

Sangla & Around

☎ 01786

The largest settlement in the valley, the small town of Sangla is a place where you might stop for lunch, change buses or stay overnight if you can't find onward transport further up the valley. It has a couple of cybercafes and a State Bank ATM on the main street.

Kamru Fort FORT

(⏲5am-6pm) Clinging to a rocky spur 2km north of Sangla (about 30 minutes' walk), Kamru village was the original capital of the kingdom of Bushahr. The old Kamru Fort, a 329-step climb up from the foot of the village, contains several handsome wood-and-stone buildings with curved, peaked roofs, notably its main tower with its shrine to the goddess Kamakhya Devi. On the way up is the **Badrinath Temple**, a classic example of Kinnauri religious syncretism with both Hindu and Buddhist shrines.

Baspa Guest House GUESTHOUSE $

(☎9816385065; Sangla; d ₹600-700, tr & q ₹1200-1400) Just down the street from the bus stand, the bare-bones but adequately clean Baspa is a popular budget option. Rooms vary, so look at a few: those on the top floor have showers in their bathrooms, while others have a hot tap and a bucket and scoop.

★ **Banjara Camps** TENTED CAMP $$$

(☎011-65152334; www.banjaracamps.com; Batseri; incl full board s ₹7000-11,500, d ₹8000-12,500; ⏲closed Nov–mid-Mar) Banjara's comfortable, large tents, with beds, furniture and proper bathrooms, are spaced around a flower-strewn apple orchard on a scenic river bend 6km up the valley from Sangla. There are also two riverbank cottages and 14 beautifully crafted rooms in a handsome stone building, the Retreat. It's excellent accommodation, with good multicuisine food, in a near-idyllic setting.

ℹ Getting There & Away

Buses from Sangla (times approximate):

Chitkul (₹35, 1½ hours) 11am, 1.30pm, 5.30pm

Rampur (₹160, four hours) 6.30am, 11.30am, 12.30pm, 5.30pm

Rekong Peo (₹65, 2½ hours) 7am, 1pm, 2.45pm

Shimla (₹350, 10 hours) 6.30am, 5.30pm (or go to Rampur and change buses there)

Taxis ask ₹1500 to Chitkul and ₹800 to Karcham.

Chitkul

POP 600 / ELEV 3450M

The last stop on an old trade route to Tibet and at the junction of several trekking routes, Chitkul is easily the most scenic settlement along the Sangla. It sees a steady flow of international and domestic tourists, but villagers maintain a pretty traditional lifestyle and a somewhat reserved attitude to outsiders.

Sights & Activities

A good number of traditional Kinnauri-style wooden houses topped with slate roofs survive despite the encroachment of concrete and tin. The **Mohatmin Mandir** temple in the middle of the village, dedicated to the local god Mathi, has some excellent carving in wood and stone.

Walks & Treks

A short walk up the hillside above the village opens up some great views; even better is the 3km track up the beautiful valley to the **Indo-Tibetan Border Police Post** at Nagasti. The high white peak of Tholla beckons ahead, but civilians are not allowed past the border post even though Tibet is still about 40km away. For longer day walks you can head up the Baspa's side valleys.

Chitkul is also where the three-day trekking trail circumambulating Kinner Kailash descends into the Sangla Valley. Trekking routes to the Pabbar Valley and Uttarakhand's Garhwal region head over passes on the south side of the valley (it's eight to 10 days to Harsil near Gangotri).

Banjara Camps, among others, organises treks in this region. Baabe at Kinner Heights guesthouse can help organise guides, porters, food and equipment.

Sleeping & Eating

Several guesthouses and a couple of larger but not very inviting hotels are set at the foot of the village. Among the best guesthouses is **Kinner Heights** (☎8988238129; s ₹500-550, d ₹750-1200; ⏰closed Dec-Mar), with good clean rooms. Owner Baabe makes good meals and can give tips on walks and treks. Also dependable is the long-running **Thakur Guest House** (☎8988209604; r ₹500-900; ⏰closed Nov-Mar), with decent clean rooms and an upstairs restaurant.

Getting There & Away

Buses leave Chitkul for Rekong Peo (₹100, four hours) at around 6am and 1.30pm, and for Shimla (₹380, 11 hours) at 3.30pm, all going through Sangla.

Rekong Peo

☎01786 / POP 2400 / ELEV 2290M

Rekong Peo is the main administrative and commercial centre for Kinnaur and a transport hub, but the main reason to visit is as a stepping stone to the pretty village of Kalpa, or to obtain an inner line permit for onward travel to upper Kinnaur and Spiti. Known locally as 'Peo', the town spreads along a looping road about 10km above Hwy 05. Most hotels, and an SBI ATM, are in the main bazaar below the bus stand.

Hotel Fairyland (☎9459700037; Main Bazar; r ₹550-650) is the best of an otherwise grotty bunch of budget hotels in the main bazaar.

Head to **Little Chef's Restaurant** (Main Bazar; mains ₹130-260; ⏰8am-10pm) for the most salubrious surroundings and a decent range of Indian dishes.

Information

Several agencies in the Tourist Information Centre building, 200m down the main road from the roundabout in the main bazaar, are good for arranging inner line permits. **Monk Travels** (☎9805530056; www.themonktravels.com; Office 201, TIC Bldg) will obtain your permit for ₹400 within about an hour if you bring your passport between 10am and 4pm (best in the morning) – except on Sundays and the second Saturday of each month, when the permit-issuing office is closed. All travellers must come in person to be photographed. The permits are valid for 14 days.

Getting There & Away

The bus stand is 2km uphill from the main bazaar by road, or 500m if you take the steps starting next to the police compound at the top of ITBP Rd (which runs up off Main Bazar at Little Chef's restaurant).

Buses run roughly hourly, 4.30am to 6.30pm to Shimla (₹355, 10 hours), with deluxe services (₹435) at 5.30am and 1.30pm. For Sarahan, change at Jeori (₹135, 3½ hours). Buses to Sangla (₹65, 2½ hours) and Chitkul (₹100, four hours) leave at 9.30am and 2.30pm, and there are noon and 4pm buses just to Sangla.

For Spiti, there's a 7am bus to Kaza (₹355, 11 hours) via Nako (₹175, five hours) and Tabo (₹270, eight hours). A second bus heads to Nako at noon. Both these depart Rekong Peo 30 minutes earlier from November to March.

Taxi rates are ₹3500 to Chitkul, ₹7000 to Shimla and ₹8000 to Kaza.

Kalpa

☎01786 / POP 1250 / ELEV 2960M

Reached by a winding 7km road up through pine woods and apple orchards from Rekong Peo, Kalpa is a little gem of a village. Majestic views of the Kinner Kailash massif, especially Kinner Kailash (6050m) and Jorkanden (6473m), grab your eyeballs and don't let go.

Kalpa's central temple group encompasses the colourful Buddhist monastery **Lochawa La-Khang** (Samdub Choeling); a recently rebuilt, tower-style **fort** just above it; and the Hindu **Narayan-Nagini temple** about 50m along the path past the Lochawa La-Khang. The Narayan-Nagini's ornate sculptures include tigers (a vehicle of Durga, to whom it's dedicated) and dragons (evidence of the strong Tibetan influence in this region).

For an ambitious full-day hike, ask locals about the trail up to the meadows and ponds of **Chakkha**, starting from Hotel Kinner Kailash on Roghi Rd.

Sleeping & Eating

Kalpa has a good range of accommodation, with several guesthouses in Chini, the main part of the village, plus a number of modern hotels on Roghi Rd, a 500m walk (or longer drive) above the centre.

Hotel Blue Lotus HOTEL $
(☎01786-226001; khokanroy.bluelotus@gmail.com; r ₹800-1200; 📶) Only 100m from the bus stand, this friendly, concrete place is hard to beat for sheer convenience. Rooms are a touch shabby but not bad value, and

the wide, sunny terraces face directly across to the mountains – ideal for meals with a view (mains ₹60 to ₹250).

Chini Bungalow Guest House GUESTHOUSE $
(☎9805495656; r ₹1200) Just 100m up a path from the centre of Kalpa, this is a friendly little place with five clean, cosy rooms and great temple and mountain views from its balconies and flowery garden. The two upstairs rooms are best but all are fine. No meals, but you can eat at Hotel Blue Lotus, nearby. Off-season discounts are around 50%.

★**Grand Shamba-La** HOTEL $$$
(Grand Shangri-La; ☎9805695423, 01786-226134; http://thegrandshambala.com; Roghi Rd; r ₹3850-4950; 📶) The very comfortable rooms here are beautifully pine-panelled and decked with Tibetan-design fabrics, and the best enjoy stupendous views from picture windows. Beds are soft, the bathrooms have great hot showers, and Indian, Tibetan and Chinese food (mains ₹120 to ₹300) is excellent. There's also a good library with books on India and Tibet.

ℹ Getting There & Away

Buses run at least hourly from 7am to 7pm between the roundabout in Rekong Peo's main bazaar and Kalpa (₹15, 30 minutes), or you can take a taxi (₹400/500 from Rekong Peo to lower/upper Kalpa). First bus down from Kalpa leaves at 6.30am. For walkers, a well-worn stepped path of about 3km short-cuts the winding 7km road.

Buses depart for Shimla (₹400, 11 hours) at 6.30am, 10.30am and 2.30pm, and for Sangla (₹60, three hours) and Chitkul (₹90, 4½ hours) at around 8.30am. More buses run from Rekong Peo.

Rekong Peo to Sumdo

The road from Kinnaur into Spiti is a procession of awe-inspiring vistas, often clinging precariously to cliffsides, the river flashing hundreds of metres below. Foreigners must show their inner line permits at the **Akpa checkpoint** on Hwy 05, 17km east of the Rekong Peo turn-off.

Near Khab, Hwy 05 heads off up to the Chinese border at the Shipki La (off-limits to foreigners). The valley road (now Hwy 505) continues 2km to the confluence of the Sutlej and Spiti Rivers, then threads the dramatic Spiti gorge upstream. High above the Spiti River, Nako village is an interesting place to break the journey. North of Nako the road descends to the river again at Chango. Sumdo, 14km further on, marks the administrative border between Kinnaur and Spiti: foreigners must show their inner line permits again here.

Nako

POP 570 / ELEV 3660M

High above the Hangrang Valley (as the lower Spiti valley is called), this almost medieval-feeling village of stone and mud-brick houses is a great place to break the journey for a day or two. Administratively part of Kinnaur but culturally in Buddhist Spiti, Nako is centred on a small sacred lake, behind which rise towering rock-strewn mountains dotted by chortens.

On the western edge of Nako you'll find the four 11th-century chapels of **Nako Gompa**, containing some fine murals and sculptures in similar styles to those of Spiti's famous Tabo Gompa.

Activities

For fine vistas, walk up to the **prayer wheel** on the hill above the lake (about 500m from the village centre). For even better vistas, continue about 800m (more steeply upward) to the 3900m **Nako Pass**, a noticeable cleft in the rocky ridge to the south.

Beyond Nako Pass a scenic pilgrimage and hiking trail continues to the historic monastery at the remote hamlet **Tashigang** – about three hours, fairly level, from the pass. Guru Padmasambhava is believed to have meditated and taught at Tashigang. Hard-core hikers can continue for about two hours further to caves and a tiny monastery at Tsomang (or Somang).

It's possible to sleep and eat at the Tashigang monastery: take a gift for the monks by way of donation (sugar is one thing they appreciate). The Nako authorities like tourists to go with a guide (₹500 to ₹1500), though the path is clear and many people go without one.

Sleeping

Nako has simple homestays and guesthouses such as **Amar Home Stay** (☎9418629453; s/d ₹500/550), signposted down steps 20m from the bus stop, where clean rooms with hot-water bathrooms open onto a pretty garden. Better, though sometimes busy with groups, are the excellent **Knaygoh Kinner Camps** (☎9418440767; www.knaygohkinnercamps.com; d tent incl half-board ₹4500-5500, r ₹3500; ⏲late Apr-late Oct), a short walk above the lake, with cosy en-suite tents and four clean rooms, and the ugly but quite comfy **Hotel Reo Purguil**

(☎9459494111; vjneginawa69@gmail.com; r ₹700-2000; ⌚May-Oct), next to the bus stop.

Getting There & Away

Buses to Rekong Peo (₹175, five hours) leave Nako at about 8am and noon. A bus to Tabo (₹105, three hours) and Kaza (₹177, 5½ hours) stops here about noon, and there's a bus around 4pm or 5pm just to Sumdo.

CENTRAL HIMACHAL PRADESH

Central Himachal is focused on the Kullu Valley, a green vale between high mountains, watered by the Beas River flowing south from the Rohtang La pass. Manali, below the Rohtang, is one of northern India's most popular travel destinations, a centre for all types of Indian and foreign travellers – hippies, hikers, honeymooners, weekenders and adrenaline junkies.

The Kullu Valley is known as Dev Bhumi (Valley of Gods) either because of its many sacred sites or simply because of its exceptional beauty. It's also famous for, among other things, its warm woollen shawls and its charas (hashish). Side valleys like the Parvati and Tirthan Valleys are, if anything, even more beautiful. In the hundreds of mountain villages, life still goes on in a pretty traditional way, and the chance to get away from the towns amid the spectacular landscape shouldn't be missed.

Mandi

☎01905 / POP 26,500 / ELEV 800M

The rambunctious bazaar town of Mandi (its name means 'market'), at the junction of main roads from Kullu, Shimla and Dharamsala, is no tourist town, and it has a sticky air reminiscent of the plains. But it's dotted with (according to official figures) 81 temples, many of them ancient Shaivite shrines, and it's fun tracking these down in the bazaars and along the banks of the Beas River.

Mandi is centred on a sunken-garden-cum-shopping-complex called Indira Market, with steps on the north side up to the Raj Mahal Palace. East of Mandi, Hwy 3 threads a dramatic gorge along the Beas River before turning north into the Kullu Valley.

Sights

Bhootnath Mandir HINDU TEMPLE

At the entrance to Bhootnath Bazar, 100m northwest of Indira Market, this 16th-century temple recently had its garish paintwork removed, showing off its fine stone carving to much better effect. It's the focal point for the animated Shivaratri Festival honouring Lord Shiva in February/March.

River Temples

If you follow Bhootnath Bazar to the Beas River you'll find the very colourful **Ekardash Rudra Mandir**, the British-built Victoria Bridge, some cremation ghats and several carved stone *sikhara* (corncob- or beehive-shaped) temples. Most impressive of these, facing each other across the Beas 150m east of the ghats, are the intricately sculpted, centuries-old **Panchvaktra Mandir** on the south bank and **Triloknath Mandir** on the north.

Sleeping & Eating

Hotel Krishna HOTEL $

(☎01905-223088; Facing Indira Market; s/d ₹400/550) The Krishna has adequate, medium-sized, clean-enough rooms with ceiling fans, and may have vacancies when other hotels on the same street are full.

Raj Mahal Palace HERITAGE HOTEL $$

(☎01905-222401; www.rajmahalpalace.com; District Court Gate; r ₹1600-4300; ❄📶) The Raj

BUSES FROM MANDI

DESTINATION	FARE (₹)	DURATION (HR)	DEPARTURES
Delhi	525-1072	13	20 daily
Dharamsala	197	6	5 daily
Kullu	106	2½	half-hourly
Manali	170-340	4	half-hourly
Palampur	160	4	hourly
Rekong Peo	218-295	12	7 daily
Shimla	218-250	6	16 daily

Mahal occupies part of the palace of Mandi's ex-royal family, who are still in residence. It has a degree of olde-worlde charm, though maintenance is lagging. 'Standard' rooms are nothing fancy, but the large deluxes and super-deluxes still have an aristocratic touch.

The **Copacabana Bar & Restaurant** (mains ₹160-350; ⏰7am-10pm) here, with the option of eating out on a large, tree-shaded lawn, is part of the appeal – peaceful for breakfast, animated for dinner.

ℹ Getting There & Away

The bus stand is 500m east of the centre across the Suketi Khad stream, a ₹30 autorickshaw ride. For Dharamsala, if there are no immediate buses, head to Palampur and change there.

Rewalsar Lake

☎01905 / ELEV 1350M

Hidden in the hills 24km southwest of Mandi, the sacred lake of Rewalsar is revered by Buddhists, Hindus and Sikhs. Tibetan Buddhists know it as Tso-Pema (Lotus Lake) and believe it was created when the king of Mandi tried to burn alive the revered Buddhist sage Padmasambhava (Guru Rinpoche), to prevent his daughter Mandarava running off with the long-haired Tantric master. The lake's 800m perimeter is surrounded by a collection of mostly modern temples, monasteries and monuments, in which all three faiths are represented.

Sights & Activities

Immediately in front of the entrance arch on the lake's east side is the **Fish Feeding Point**, where a seething mass of holy carp gobbles up flour balls or puffed rice thrown by visitors. The Tibetan-style **Drikung Kagyu Gompa** (www.dk-petsek.org), with its academy for Buddhist monks, stands immediately to the right here. Its temple features a large, central Sakyamuni statue, with Padmasambhava to the left.

Moving clockwise around the lake, you pass a colourful lakeshore **shrine to Padmasambhava** and then the **Tso-Pema Ogyen Heruka Nyingmapa Gompa**, with artful murals and atmospheric afternoon and morning *pujas* (prayer sessions). A few minutes' detour uphill from the lake, passing the **Zigar Drukpa Kargyud Institute**, with outsized statues of Tantric protectors in its temple, takes you to Rewalsar's signature monument, a giant 12m-high **statue of Padmasambhava**, with his trademark fiercely staring eyes and right hand in the warding-off-evil *mudra* (gesture). Inaugurated by the Dalai Lama in 2012, it affords grand views over the lake.

Continuing clockwise around the lake, you pass a small **Hindu temple group** before reaching a grassy little **lakeside park** with a couple of benches where you can enjoy the view and atmosphere. On the far side of the lake is the gold-domed **Guru Gobind Singh Gurdwara**, a Sikh temple built in the 1930s. Rewalsar is of special significance to Sikhs as the place where, in 1701, Guru Gobind Singh, the 10th Sikh guru, issued a call to the Hindu rajas of the Punjab hills for joint resistance against the Mughals.

The other main Buddhist site is the **Padmasambhava Cave**, high above the lake, where Padmasambhava allegedly meditated. It's a climb of about 1.5km from behind the big Padmasambhava statue – or take a taxi (one way/return ₹500/600), or jump on one of the buses departing Rewalsar bus stand at 9.30am, 10.30am, 11.30am, 2pm and 5pm for Naina Devi Temple (₹30) and get off 1km before the temple.

Sleeping & Eating

Hotel Lotus Lake HOTEL $

(☎01905-240239; hlotuslake@yahoo.com; r ₹500-700) The best rooms at this Buddhist-run place, near the lakeshore Padmasambhava shrine, are bright, with lake views. The cheapest are shabbier and viewless. All are adequately clean, with hot-water bathrooms.

Drikung Kagyu Gompa Guesthouse GUESTHOUSE $

(☎01905-240243; www.dk-petsek.org; r ₹500, without bathroom ₹200) Of several monastery guesthouses this is probably the best, offering a shared terrace with peaceful lake views.

Emaho Bistro CAFE $

(Drikung Kagyu Gompa; dishes ₹40-120, breakfast ₹150; ⏰8am-8pm; wi-fi) Has good coffee, good wi-fi, views across the lake and excellent all-day breakfasts, cakes, juices, teas and other snacks and light dishes. What more could you ask for?

ℹ Getting There & Away

Buses from Mandi to Rewalsar (₹35, 1¼ hours) leave frequently until late afternoon from the street between Indira Market and the Suketi Khad bridge. The last one back leaves about 6pm. A taxi is ₹600/1000 one way/return.

Tirthan & Banjar Valleys

From the south end of the Kullu Valley, the Tirthan Valley leads up southeast into the region known as Inner Seraj. This is an area of exceptional valley and mountain scenery, unspoiled villages and nature, great walks and inviting guesthouses. It's becoming known among Indians seeking a low-key escape from the plains, but is still off most foreign visitors' radar. It's the gateway to the spectacular, World Heritage–listed Great Himalayan National Park, 754 pristine square kilometres of steep-sided river valleys and mountains reaching right up to the 6000m-plus peaks of the Great Himalayan Range.

Inner Seraj has two main valleys – that of the Tirthan River itself, and the Banjar Valley which rises southward from the small town of Banjar. The Banjar Valley climbs to the 3132m Jalori Pass, which leads over to the Sutlej valley and thus forms the most direct route linking the Kullu Valley with Kinnaur.

Sights & Activities

Access to the core zone of the Great Himalayan National Park requires some preparation and paperwork, which is worthwhile only if you have at least two full days, preferably several more. But there are also good hikes in the buffer zone along the park's western edge, called the Ecozone, and even outside the park completely, such as from the Jalori Pass. The Tirthan Valley is also tops for birdwatching (best in April, May, October and November) and trout fishing (best from about April to June and August to October).

★ Jalori Pass VIEWPOINT

At the top of the Banjar Valley, Hwy 305 climbs over the panoramic 3223m Jalori Pass, marked by a couple of *dhabas* and a Mahakali temple. In calm weather this is a great spot for observing Himalayan griffon vultures, the biggest birds in the Indian Himalaya. From the pass you can walk 6km east (pretty level) to the small, holy **Saryolsar Lake**, or 3km west (uphill) to the scanty ruins of **Raghupur Fort**, through evergreen oak forests in both cases.

A taxi round trip from Jibhi to the pass, including time for you to walk to Saryolsar or Raghupur, costs ₹1800. The road over the pass is unpaved for the 16km from Ghiyagi on the north side to Khanag on the south, and the pass is normally closed by snow from approximately mid-December to early March.

From Saryolsar Lake trekkers can continue to Lambhari (or Lambri) Top, a ridge at about 3600m with spectacular mountain vistas (two or three days there and back).

Great Himalayan National Park

The **park** (GHNP; www.greathimalayannationalpark.org) embraces four river valleys descending westward from the Great Himalayan Range, easily the most visited of which is the Tirthan Valley. Coming up the Tirthan from the west, you enter the Ecozone at Gushaini village and the core zone 8km upstream from there. The

TOP WALKS & TREKS IN THE GREAT HIMALAYAN NATIONAL PARK

Ecozone

GUSHAINI TO PARK GATE

This lovely day hike takes you 8km from the bridge in Gushaini to the gate of the national park's core zone, following the steep-sided, thickly forested Tirthan Valley, with the river a constant presence below and some beautiful waterfalls en route. Total ascent is about 500m and it takes about three hours to go up, a bit less coming down.

RANGTHAR TREK

A two- or three-day moderate-level trek at altitudes between about 2100m and 2800m, with great mountain vistas, starting from Pekhri village, reachable by 4WD north from Gushaini.

Core Zone

RAKHUNDI TREK

Easy to moderate trek to panoramic high meadow at about 3600m on north side of Tirthan Valley in the national park core zone; four or five days from Gushaini and back.

THIRAT (TIRTH) TREK

One of the finest core zone treks: from Gushaini to the head of the Tirthan River at about 4000m, and back; six to nine days, moderate to strenuous.

Kullu, Parvati & Tirthan Valleys

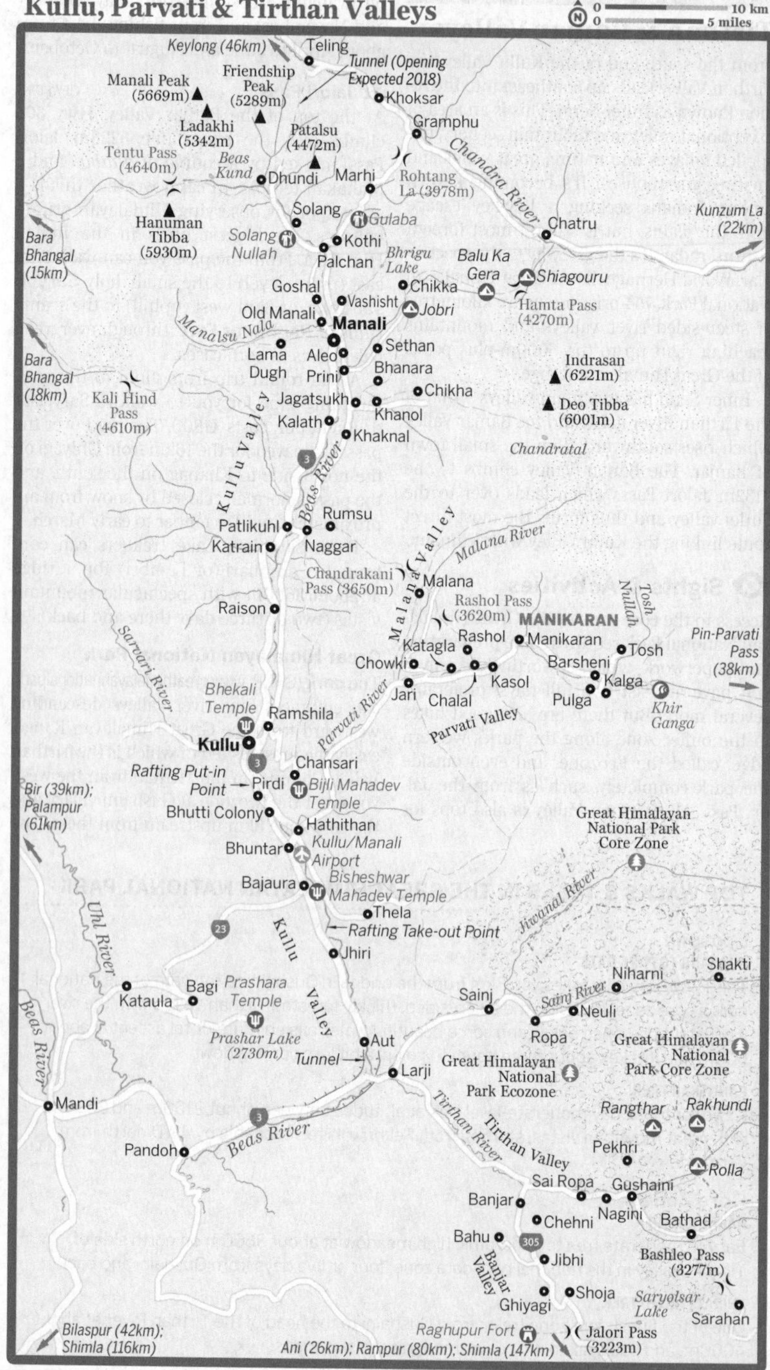

glaciers, snow and alpine meadows of the park's higher altitudes give way to lush forests lower down, and park is home to a great variety of wildlife including snow leopards, bears and more than 200 bird species.

For any overnight stays in the core zone, you must obtain a permit (Indian/foreigner per day ₹100/400) and hire a certified local guide and porters. It's easiest to organise things with the help of a local agency such as **Sunshine Himalayan Adventures** (☎01902-225182, 9418102083; www.sunshineadventure.com; Akhara Bazar, Kullu), with a base near Gushaini, or Banjar-based **Himalayan Ecotourism** (☎9816091093; http://himalayanecotourism.in; Banjar), both of which are closely involved with the local community and offer birdwatching and wildlife tours as well as treks. Costs for equipped, staffed and guided treks range between about ₹2000 and ₹4000 per person per day depending on group size, length of trek and other variables.

The best hiking and trekking months are April to June and September to November. Many routes are closed by snow from December to March.

Sleeping & Eating

Doli Guest House GUESTHOUSE $
(Rana Swiss Cottage; ☎01903-228234; www.kshatra.com; Jibhi; s/d/tr ₹660/770/880, cottages d/tr ₹1650/2200;) In business since 1992, Doli is one of the area's best-value stays. The 50-year-old wooden house has six simple en-suite rooms with colourful textiles, and its cafe, opening into a pretty garden overlooking the Jibhi Nala stream, serves Indian, Continental and Israeli food, with an emphasis on organic ingredients (mains ₹100 to ₹250, thali ₹200).

★**Raju Bharti's Guest House** GUESTHOUSE $$
(☎9459833124; www.facebook.com/Rajubhartiguesthouse; Gushaini; per person incl full board ₹1800) The Tirthan Valley's best known guesthouse, wood-built Raju's has a perfect riverbank location 400m downstream from Gushaini bridge. Access is by an exciting basket-on-a-cable affair across the rushing river. The two doubles and six 'family suites' (one double and one twin room each) are all cosy and clean. It's very popular and gets fully booked about three months ahead for the April to June season.

Leena's Place GUESTHOUSE $$
(☎9816057101; www.jibhiadventure.com; Jibhi; d incl breakfast ₹1600-2500;) A friendly and well-run place 500m down Hwy 305 from Jibhi village in the Banjar Valley, Leena's has five bright, comfortable rooms in pine and mud-covered brick, with home-cooked, vegetarian meals available. Guests can do their own cooking if preferred.

Owner Lalit offers treks, bike tours and other activities.

Bisht Niwas Home Stay HOMESTAY $$
(☎9816650262; http://tirthanstay.com; Nagini; d ₹1200, incl breakfast ₹1500) With six almost new and spotlessly clean rooms and a great riverside location, Bisht offers some of the best value in the area. It's 2.7km west down the valley road from Gushaini.

Khem Bharti Guest House GUESTHOUSE $$
(Hotel Trout Valley; ☎9459101113; www.troutvalley.co.in; Nagini; r incl full board ₹2800-3800) Provides good wood-panelled rooms, excellent home-cooked meals and plenty of local information and help, in a handsome 50-year-old house, 2.8km down the valley road from Gushaini.

Getting There & Away

The road up the Tirthan Valley (Hwy 305) leaves the Kullu–Mandi road (Hwy 3) at the south end of the 3km-long Aut Tunnel, south of Aut town. Buses running between Mandi and Kullu (or vice-versa) will drop you at Aut. Taxis from Aut to Gushaini or Jibhi cost ₹1000: to arrange one in advance you can call English-speaking Aut-based driver **Bharat** (☎9816610023).

Buses from Aut to Banjar (₹37, 1½ hours), some of them originating in Kullu, leave Aut at least hourly from 8am to 4pm or later. The last Banjar–Aut bus leaves at 5.30pm. From Banjar, nine buses run to Gushaini (₹7, 30 minutes) and Bathad (₹15, one hour) between 7.30am and 5pm. Returning, the first and last buses from Bathad are at 7.30am and about 4.30pm. The 7.30am, 8am and 3pm departures continue to Aut and Kullu.

At least four buses depart Banjar between 7.30am and 12.30pm for Jibhi (₹12, 30 minutes) and, from about March to mid-December, the Jalori Pass (₹31, 1½ hours) and various destinations beyond it including Rampur (₹158, six hours, departing Banjar at 7.30am and 11.30am). Further buses head up from Banjar to Jibhi until at least 4.30pm.

Bhuntar

☎01902 / POP 4500

This market town is the location of the Kullu Manali airport, and the main junction for transport to the Parvati Valley. At Bajaura, 5km south of Bhuntar, the 9th-century **Bisheshwar**

Mahadev Temple is well worth a stop. A rare and outstandingly handsome Kullu Valley example of the classic stone *sikhara* temples of the North Indian plains, it's dedicated to Shiva as Lord of the Universe. The temple is covered all over with ornate carving, and niches on the outside contain superb reliefs of Vishnu (west side), Ganesh (south) and Durga (north). It's 200m east of Hwy 3.

Sleeping & Eating

The best hotel is **Hotel Malabar** (01902-266199; www.hotelmalabarkullu.com; r ₹2380-3340;), 500m north of the airport, with cosy, pine-panelled rooms and a good multicuisine restaurant (mains ₹180 to ₹300). About 500m further up the main street, **Hotel Amit** (01902-265123; www.hotelamitkullu.com; r non-AC ₹1780-2380, AC ₹3090-3680;) has some cheaper non-AC rooms but is a lot less appealing. Discounts of around 30% are often offered at both places. **Hotel Sunbeam** (9418641908; d ₹500-1000), next to the Amit, is an adequately clean budget option.

Getting There & Away

The airport is at the southern end of town, 600m from the bus stand. Air India flies to/from Delhi daily, though flights are sometimes cancelled in bad weather.

Frequent buses run until about 10pm to Kullu (₹15, 30 minutes) and Mandi (₹90, two hours). For Manali (₹70, 2½ hours), flag down a bus on the main road or change in Kullu. Buses up the Parvati Valley run about half-hourly from about 5.30am to 6pm. Buses to Dharamsala, Shimla and Delhi pass through Bhuntar two to 2½ hours after leaving Manali: you'll normally have to flag them down on the main road. The taxi stand is opposite the bus stand: fares are ₹950 to Kasol, ₹1550 to Barsheni and ₹1400 to Manali.

Parvati Valley

The Parvati River enters the Beas just above Bhuntar and its ethereally beautiful valley stretches back up to the hot springs at Manikaran and beyond into the 5000m heights of the Great Himalayan Range. The valley has a well-deserved reputation for its charas (hashish), and several villages have been transformed into hippie/backpacker hangouts, offering cheap accommodation, international food and nonstop music to crowds of international travellers. Like Manali, the Parvati is a favourite destination along the 'hummus trail' followed by post-military service Israeli travellers. It's also increasingly popular among young Indians. Police sometimes set up checkpoints along the roads to search for charas.

There are some excellent treks in the area, including over the Chandrakani Pass to/from Naggar, or the Pin-Parvati Pass to/from Spiti. For safety reasons, solo trekking is not recommended.

Accommodation is plentiful and cheap, with backpacker-oriented guesthouses clustering especially in and around Kasol but also at Jari and places beyond Manikaran, such as Pulga, Kalga, Tosh and Khir Ganga. Prices are very negotiable and in the smaller places rooms for ₹300 or less can often be found.

Buses up the valley start from Bhuntar about half-hourly from about 5.30am to 6pm, going to Jari (₹30, 1¼ hours), Kasol (₹40, 1¾ hours) and Manikaran (₹50, two hours); about half of them continue to Barsheni (₹75, three hours). A few buses run from Manali or Kullu all the way to Manikaran (and back), but more likely you'll have to change in Bhuntar.

Plentiful taxis are available for travel into and around the valley. Typical fares include ₹300 from Jari to Kasol, ₹150 from Kasol to Manikaran, ₹1000/1500 one way/return from Kasol to Nerang (for Malana), ₹2200 from Kasol to Manali, and ₹550 from Manikaran to Barsheni.

CHARAS

Many travellers are attracted to the Parvati Valley and the Manali area by the famous local charas (hashish), which is seriously potent stuff. Though it's smoked fairly openly in the Parvati Valley, Old Manali and Vashisht, it's still illegal and police do arrest people for possession (or hit them for hefty bribes).

Jari

Jari is a ramshackle roadside bazaar village 20km up the Parvati Valley from its mouth. Travellers head for the peaceful hillside hamlet of Mateura Jari, with its cheap accommodation and several traditional wood-and-stone temples, a 700m uphill hike from Jari bus stop (follow the 'Village Guest House' signs).

For guide services to Malana or trekking anywhere in the Parvati Valley, contact **Negi's Himalayan Adventure** (9418281894,

9816081894; www.negis-kasol-malana-parvati.com; Hotel Negi's Nest II, Chowki) at Hotel Negi's Nest II, across the river from Jari (a ₹150 taxi ride). Owner Chapu Negi is head of the area's mountain rescue team, so he's as reliable as it gets. A guide for a day costs ₹2000, and trekking is around ₹3000 per person per day, plus transport. The **hotel rooms** (☎9418281894; www.negis-kasol-malana-parvati.com; d ₹2500-3000, tr ₹3500, tr tent ₹1500; 📶) are comfortable and pine-panelled with good clean bathrooms, and there's a restaurant and kitchen for guests, plus tents for lower budgets.

Sleeping & Eating

In addition to places in Mateura Jari, you'll find a few more homestays and guesthouses tucked away along the pathways and in Punthal, 1km further.

Village Guest House GUESTHOUSE $
(☎9816594249; www.facebook.com/village-guest-house-kasol-jari-205081383167806; r ₹500, without bathroom ₹300; 📶) This large-ish, welcoming property is the first you come to in Mateura Jari and has the most comfortable rooms, especially those with attached bathroom ranged along the pretty garden. The family here are charming and they serve up good Indian and traveller food, too (mains ₹100 to ₹350).

Malana

Remote Malana, high on a hillside 20km up a side valley north of Jari, is one strange village. Its people – descended, according to legend, from deserters from Alexander the Great's army – speak their own unique language, operate what's called the world's oldest democracy, consider outsiders unclean and step aside if you pass them to avoid being touched. Malana's famous charas (hashish), known as 'cream', is the backbone of its economy, and is what many visitors mainly come for. A rough road now reaches within striking distance of Malana, but for centuries it was one of the most isolated spots in the region. Be ready for random police checkpoints on the road, and bring your passport because security at the hydroelectric station en route may want to see it.

Sights & Activities

More than half of Malana's traditional wood-and-stone houses were burned in a fire in 2008 and some have been replaced by cinderblock boxes, but the temples were rebuilt in traditional wood and stone, with intricately carved balconies. They are dedicated to the local deity Jamdagni (Jamlu) Rishi, and attract pilgrims from around the region, especially during Malana's main festival, which starts on 15 August and continues for four or five days, with flowery costumes, processions, music, dancing and, of course, plenty of charas. One of the two main temples stands on the village's central open space, facing a stone platform and stepped seating for village assemblies (Malana's 'parliament').

In the village, you must obey a litany of esoteric rules or face fines of up to ₹3500. Don't step off the main path, don't touch the temples or photograph them without permission, don't stray on to any sacred spots (even though there's nothing obvious to identify them), and don't touch any villagers or their belongings. To get the most out of the cultural experience and avoid breaking rules, it's worthwhile to visit with a knowledgeable guide.

There are some good walks in the area. Trekkers can head over the Chandrakani Pass, a steep two-hour hike up from Malana, and on to Naggar in two or three days, or venture southeast over the Rashol Pass to Kasol (17km), staying in a homestay in Rashol en route.

WARNING – DEADLY VACATIONS

Since the mid-1990s, more than two dozen foreign tourists have disappeared from the Kullu and Parvati Valleys. While some got too deep into the local drug trade and crossed the wrong people, others became lost or fatally injured while trekking alone through the confusing and rugged mountain terrain.

If you plan to head into the hills, we recommend going with a guide who can steer you away from natural – and human – hazards. It's a good idea to let your guesthouse know where you are going and when you plan to return. Avoid walking alone, and be cautious about befriending sadhus (holy people) or others wandering in the woods. So go, hike, and enjoy this incredible area – just be smart about it, for your family's sake!

Sleeping

Malana has a half-dozen pretty basic guesthouses, mostly at the top of the village, run by outsiders and with poor sanitation. **Dragon Guest House** (9805105400; r without bathroom ₹300-600) is one of the most popular, with tolerably clean wood-walled rooms. Its kitchen cooks up Israeli, Indian and Italian food (mains ₹80 to ₹200). **Chand View Guest House** (9805261446; r ₹250-500) has some attached bathrooms.

Getting There & Away

The easy way to reach Malana is by taxi from Jari to Nerang (₹800 one way, ₹1500 return with a three-hour wait), a collection of trackside shacks from which it's a 30- to 45-minute walk up to the village.

One daily bus to Jari and Kullu (three hours) leaves Nerang at 9am, starting back from Kullu about 3pm.

Kasol

01902 / POP 750 / ELEV 1600M

Stretched along the lovely Parvati River with mountains rising all around, Kasol is the main traveller hang-out in the valley. It's a small village, but almost overrun with reggae bars, bakeries and cheap guesthouses catering to a largely backpacker crowd, nowadays including growing numbers of Indians. It's also a summertime venue for trance parties transplanted from Goa, and at any time an easy base for exploring the forested valley or just chilling out. The village divides into Old Kasol on the Bhuntar side of its bridge, and New Kasol on the Manikaran side.

Sleeping

Royal Orchard GUESTHOUSE $

(9459342032; r ₹600-1000; wi-fi) These 21 spacious, clean rooms in a recently constructed three-storey building in an apple orchard are in high demand. The upper two floors have private balconies, and all rooms have international TV and wi-fi. There's a cafe too. It's 100m down a lane running towards the river, 80m past Evergreen restaurant in New Kasol.

Taji Place GUESTHOUSE $

(9816461684; chetanthakurkasol@gmail.com; d ₹1500-3500, without bathroom ₹500, cottage for 3 ₹3000; wi-fi) On a sweet riverside property with a big lawn and apple trees, Taji has a range of tidy rooms, and the four ₹3500 options are quality pine-panelled abodes with new bathrooms. There's no sign: it's at the end of

PIN-PARVATI TREK

Only accessible from late June to late September/early October, this strenuous but rewarding six- to nine-day wilderness trek crosses the snow-bound Pin-Parvati Pass (5319m) from the Parvati Valley to the Pin Valley in Spiti. July and August can be pretty wet and September is the best month. There is accommodation at Khir Ganga, which has a hot-spring bathing area, and Mudh, but none in between, so you need to be self-sufficient or go with a trekking agency. Organised treks are relatively pricey because pack animals cannot get across the pass so you need porters (often three per person because of the trek's length) and the crew need to be transported back to their starting point.

From Barsheni (or Pulga or Kalga), the route ascends through forest and pasture to Khir Ganga hot springs and Thakur Khan. Two more days through a more arid alpine zone takes you via Pandupul rock bridge (which can be tricky when wet) and Mantalai Lake to High (or Plateau) Camp. A challenging tramp over scree and snow, requiring ropes, leads over the pass then down into the Pin Valley. A day or two extra for acclimatisation, rest or shorter stages on the way up is beneficial, and the final stage could easily be broken into two days of hiking through the Pin Valley National Park to Mudh.

The trek can also be done in the east–west direction.

STAGE	ROUTE	DURATION (HR)	DISTANCE (KM)
1	Barsheni to Khir Ganga	3-4	12
2	Khir Ganga to Thakur Khan	6	15
3	Thakur Khan to Mantalai Lake	7	16
4	Mantalai Lake to High Camp	4	12
5	High Camp to Pin Valley Camp via Pin-Parvati Pass	5-6	12
6	Pin Valley Camp to Mudh	8	20

WORTH A TRIP

KHIR GANGA

This sloping alpine meadow is a beautiful three- to four-hour walk up the Parvati Valley from **Barsheni**, which is 13km up from Manikaran. The meadow is home to delectable hot springs and a shabby collection of shack guesthouses (rooms ₹200 to ₹500) and cafe-restaurants, open from about April to October – it's a popular spot to drop out for a few days. A day trip to Khir Ganga and back is also well worthwhile. The walk from Barsheni, in which you ascend about 800m, is also the first stage of the Pin-Parvati trek. Paths run along both sides of the valley, through **Nakthan** village on the north side, and **Kalga** village on the south side, meeting about 45 minutes before Khir Ganga. The Nakthan route is prettier, sunnier and more frequented.

The **hot springs** (dawn-dusk) FREE, at the top of the meadow, are the perfect temperature – hot but not too hot – and feature a large men's pool with fantastic views and a smaller, enclosed women's pool from which you can at least see the sky. The pools are part of a temple, so decorum is required – no mixed bathing, nudity or smoking!

Buses to Barsheni (₹30, one hour), some of them coming from Bhuntar, leave from the road above Manikaran bus station, roughly half-hourly from about 7.30am to noon, then about hourly till 5.30pm. The last bus back down leaves Barsheni at 5pm.

a lane running down towards the river, 80m past Evergreen restaurant in New Kasol.

Alpine Guest House HOTEL **$$**
(9418400328; alpinehimachal@gmail.com; r ₹1000-2500) Rooms at this place among pines in Old Kasol are spacious and reasonably well kept (the bigger, brighter ones are upstairs), but the great plus is the expansive terrace with its open-air restaurant, right on the bank of the rushing, tumbling, beautiful river.

Eating

★Evergreen MULTICUISINE **$$**
(New Kasol; mains ₹200-400; 10am-11pm) A perennial favourite for pizza, lasagne, homemade tofu, Turkish kebabs, lamb and chicken dishes and good Israeli specials – the chicken *sipoodim* (barbecue), served with chips and hummus, is an excellent meal. You can eat at tables in the front room or head into the smoky cushioned area inside.

Moon Dance Café & German Bakery MULTICUISINE **$$**
(mains ₹180-400; 9am-11pm) Moon Dance, just west of the bridge, stands tall among the numerous traveller restaurants for its great baked goods, strong coffee, baguettes, waffles, crêpes, shakes, juices and good-value breakfasts (₹200 to ₹300) in the sunny courtyard.

Information

Kasol has a few internet cafes, charging ₹40 per hour. The **Central Bank of India ATM**, in the side street just east of the bridge, accepts some international cards.

Manikaran

01902 / POP 6100 / ELEV 1730M

With steam continually issuing from the river bank beneath its large temple, the busy little pilgrim town of Manikaran, 4km east of Kasol, is famous for its hot springs and is sacred for both Sikhs and Hindus. According to legend, a giant snake stole goddess Parvati's earrings while she was bathing (during an 11,000-year meditation session with Shiva), then snorted them out from underground, along with various other jewels, which released the hot springs. The water emerging from the ground is hot enough to boil rice and has to be cooled with river water for bathing. Locals say it can cure everything from rheumatism to bronchitis.

Sights

The five-storey **Sri Guru Nanak Ji Gurdwara** (Gurdwara Sahib), on the north bank of the foaming river, was built in 1940. The main prayer hall, with its carpets and glittering glass columns, is on the top floor (shoes off, head-coverings on, for men and women). One level down is the eating hall where free rice, dahl, curry, chapatis and tea are served round the clock to all comers (these meals are as good as any in town). Below that are men's and women's indoor bathing pools and, to one side, a sauna-like 'hot cave'. Across the footbridge are a more inviting open-air men's pool and another enclosed women's pool. Bring a swimming costume, towel and flip-flops if you want to bathe.

Next to the gurdwara is a **Shiva temple** where the rice for the gurdwara cooks in big pots in pools of boiling hot-spring water. A happy, quite light-hearted atmosphere prevails in both temples.

Along the esplanade of the traffic-free north side of town, you'll find the ornate wood-and-stone, chalet-style **Naina Bhagwati Temple**, dedicated to the goddess, born from Shiva's third eye, who located Parvati's missing earrings.

Sleeping

Fateh Paying Guesthouse GUESTHOUSE $
(9816894968; r ₹300; @) Signposted up an alley in the old part of town, this big green house has just five simple but pleasant rooms, with welcoming owners, a sunny rooftop terrace and a tiny hot spring pool. Unlike many places, Fateh keeps the same rates all year. Local meals are available.

Kullu

01902 / POP 18,500 / ELEV 1220M

The bustling administrative capital of the Kullu Valley is a return to Indian normality from the valley's hippie holiday resorts. Few travellers stop here for long but it's a likeable enough place, and in October it stages the area's biggest and most colourful festival, the Kullu Dussehra.

The Beas River runs down the east side of Kullu, and its tributary the Sarvari River runs across the middle of town, dividing Kullu into southern and northern halves. The southern part (Dhalpur) has the taxi stand, tourist office, Dussehra grounds (two large, adjoining, open spaces) and most restaurants and hotels. The bus station and Raghunath Temple are north of the Sarvari. A footbridge across the Sarvari near the bus station crosses to a bazaar street, which brings you out near the Hotel Shobla International.

Sights

Raghunath Temple HINDU TEMPLE
(7am-8.30pm) Kullu's pre-eminent temple enshrines the Kullu Valley's major deity, a tiny bronze idol of Raghunath Ji (Rama) that lords it over the Dussehra celebrations. The 17th-century temple is in the Sultanpur area on the hill above the bus station and near the Raja Rupi, the palace of the former Kullu rajas; the main shrine closes for several hours in the middle of the day, but you'll probably still be able to peer through its window.

★**Bijli Mahadev Temple** HINDU TEMPLE
There are several important temples in Kullu's surrounding hills. The Shaivite Bijli Mahadev, a 20km uphill drive southeast to Chansari followed by a 2.5km uphill hike, commands spectacular panoramas over the Kullu and Parvati Valleys from its 2460m hilltop location. Beside the temple stands a 20m wooden pole, which attracts occasional divine blessings in the form of lightning: the surge of power shatters the stone Shiva lingam inside the temple, which is then glued back together with butter.

Bijli Mahadev attracts crowds of pilgrims during the Shaivite Sawan Kamaina festival from mid-July to mid-August. A few daily

KULLU DUSSEHRA

Kullu town and valley's most important god, Raghunath Ji, is a version of Rama, the hero god of the Ramayana, so you might expect **Dussehra** (Oct; variable dates), the October festival that celebrates Rama's victory over the demon-king Ravana, to be something special here. The one day on which Dussehra is celebrated elsewhere is just the first of seven days in Kullu. The opening day is the most exciting, with more than 200 village deities *(devtas)* arrriving in Kullu on palanquins, then parading to the Dussehra grounds in a wonderful cavalcade, with drums beating and giant trumpets blaring, decked in gorgeous garlands and draperies studded with silver masks. Here the tiny Raghunath Ji idol is placed in a large chariot and pulled to its allotted place by teams of rope-hauling devotees amid excited crowds.The village *devtas* 'dance' – tilting from side to side and charging backwards and forwards – before settling down in their allotted positions around the grounds, where they and their attendants camp for the week of the festival.

The rest of the week is focused mainly on a huge retail fair spread over the Dussehra grounds, outbreaks of music and dancing around the devta tents, and colourful evening folk dance, music and other performances in the adjacent auditorium. On the seventh day there are more processions and everyone starts for home.

SHOPPING FOR SHAWLS

The Kullu Valley is famous for its traditional wool shawls – lightweight but wonderfully warm and attractively patterned – and the highway between Bhuntar and Manali is lined with scores of shops and showrooms. Kullu shawls are woven on wooden hand-looms using wool from sheep or hair from pashmina goats or angora rabbits. This industry provides an income for thousands of local women, many of whom have organised themselves into shawl-weaving cooperatives.

For high quality without the hard sell, head to the nearest branch of **Bhuttico** (www.bhutticoshawl.com), the Bhutti Weavers' Cooperative, which was established in 1944 and has showrooms in every town in the valley and several beyond, plus a large **factory showroom** (Bhutti Colony; ⏲9am-7pm) 8km south of Kullu. Bhuttico charges fixed prices, so it's a good place to gauge price and quality. Expect to pay upwards of ₹700 for a lambswool shawl, ₹1200 to ₹1600 for an angora-lambswool blend, ₹3500 for pashmina-lambswool and ₹6000 for pure pashmina. Bhuttico also makes scarves, topis, jackets, bags, gloves, *pullas* (slippers made from cannabis stalks), and *pattus*, the wonderfully patterned wraparound wool garments that are Kullu women's traditional clothing.

buses from Kullu bus station run as far as Chansari (₹28, 1¼ hours). A taxi from Kullu to Chansari costs ₹1300 round trip.

Sleeping & Eating

Hotel Aaditya HOTEL $
(☎9418001244, 01902-224263; Lower Dhalpur; d ₹660-2640; 📶) Just across the footbridge from the bus station, Aaditya tries harder than most in this price range, with friendly service, comfy beds, and a range of rooms, many with balconies overlooking the Sarvari River.

Hotel Vikrant HOTEL $
(☎9816438299; vikramrashpa@gmail.com; Dhalpur; d ₹400-1200) Up a tiny path behind the HPTDC office, Vikrant is a backpacker-friendly place where wood panelling and shared balconies give the rooms a simple charm. Those upstairs are bigger and brighter, but all have fans and hot showers.

Hot Spice MULTICUISINE $$
(Dhalpur; mains ₹120-250; ⏲9am-10pm) For good-value thalis and breakfasts, or a tasty tandoori trout, head for this pleasant open-air cafe up the lane behind the tourist office.

Getting There & Away

A mixture of HRTC and private buses runs about every 15 minutes to Bhuntar (₹15, 30 minutes), Manali (₹60, 90 minutes) and Mandi (₹106, two hours), until 9pm or 10pm. Buses to Naggar (₹30, one hour) go every half-hour, 7am to 6pm. A few buses go to destinations in the Parvati Valley, but usually you have to go to Bhuntar and change. Buses from Manali to destinations beyond the Kullu Valley stop in Kullu about 1½ hours after departure.

Naggar

☎01902 / POP 550 / ELEV 1710M

High on the east side of the Kullu Valley, sleepy Naggar was once capital of the Kullu kingdom and is perhaps the most charming village in the valley today. Russian painter and explorer Nicholas Roerich (Nikolai Rerikh) liked it so much he settled here in the early 20th century. It's an easy day trip from Manali, but with interesting sights and fine walks (including the Chandrakani Pass trek to Malana in the Parvati Valley), and some good guesthouses and restaurants, it's a fine place for a few days' relaxing stay.

Naggar's sights and accommodation are in the upper part of the village, 1km to 2km uphill from the bus stop, which is in the bazaar area on the main road.

Sights

Naggar Castle FORT
(₹30; ⏲9am-6pm) Built by the rajas of Kullu around 1500, this fort-cum-mansion is a fine example of the earthquake-resistant, alternating-stone-and-timber style of Himachali architecture. Sold to the British assistant commissioner in 1846, it later became a courthouse and then, in 1976, a hotel.

★ International Roerich Memorial Trust MUSEUM
(☎01902-248590; http://irmtkullu.com; Indian/foreigner/camera/video ₹50/100/30/60; ⏲10am-1pm & 1.30-6pm Tue-Sun, to 5pm Nov-Mar) This

fascinating memorial and museum complex 1km above the castle focuses on the former home of Russian painter, writer and Inner Asian explorer Nicholas Roerich and his wife Elena Roerich, a philosopher, writer and translator. They settled here in 1928 and stayed until his death in 1947. The couple's semi-mystical, aesthetico-orientalist philosophising had an international following in their lifetimes, but it is Nicholas' art that has had the most enduring appeal.

The house's lower floor displays some of Nicholas' landscape paintings (many depicting Himalayan mountains) and paintings by the couple's son Svyatoslav, while the upper floor preserves some of the private rooms (you can only look in through the windows). In the scenic hillside gardens are Nicholas' *samadhi* (tomb) and an exhibit on Svyatoslav and his wife, the Indian film star Devika Rani.

Down the road there's a good little book, print and postcard shop, while a five-minute uphill walk takes you to the **Urusvati Himalayan Research Institute** (incl in Roerich Trust admission; ⏲10am-1pm & 1.30-6pm Tue-Sun, to 5pm Nov-Mar), with further exhibits on the work of the Roerichs and their associates.

Temples

Naggar is home to several intriguing and beautiful small temples. Down the street beside the castle, the 11th-century *sikhara*-style **Vishnu Mandir** is relatively plain and squat. Turn left just past this, then left at the next fork, to the lovely little **Gauri Shankar Temple**, of similar style and date but more finely proportioned and carved. It's dedicated to Shiva.

About 400m up the road from the castle, the pagoda-style **Tripura Sundari Temple** is sacred to the local earth/mother goddess. The existing building is only about 35 years old, but the site has probably been sacred since pre-Hindu times. The track leading uphill off the road here leads 1km to a junction where a right turn takes you 150m to the **Murlidhar Temple**, honouring Krishna the flute-player. It dates from about the 11th century, and stands on the site of the ancient town of Thawa, which predated Naggar by around 1000 years.

Activities

Ragini Treks & Tours TREKKING
(☎9817076890; raginitours@hotmail.com; Hotel Ragini) Ragini Treks & Tours, just above Naggar Castle, is an experienced operator for the Chandrakhani Pass and other treks in the area.

Chandrakani Pass Trek

The excellent and popular trek from Naggar to Malana, via the 3650m Chandrakani Pass, is accessible between late May and October. It's basically a two-day trek with six to eight hours' actual walking up to the pass, then two to three hours down to Malana. Reputable agencies in Naggar charge around ₹3000 per person per day for guided and equipped treks with porters.

The way is not always obvious, and dangerously bad weather can occur at almost any time, so don't go without a guide (except perhaps in June when the route is busiest). The ideal season is mid-September to mid-October, without both crowds and snow. July and August can both see heavy rain.

As always, agree to the full final price for a trek beforehand, including items such as any return transport for guides and porters, and their and your food.

If you want to go more independently, at least take a local guide recommended by your guesthouse. This will cost a minimum ₹1000 per day, and porters are at least ₹600. Go prepared for overnight camping and with enough food.

Sleeping & Eating

★ **Alliance Guesthouse** GUESTHOUSE $
(☎9418025640, 9817097033; www.alliancenaggar.com; Roerich Marg; r ₹440-1800, tr & q ₹2200; @📶) Peacefully located on the road up to the Roerich Museum, this friendly place run by a French/Indian family has a range of spotless rooms with comfy beds, from shared-bathroom cheapies to duplexes perfect for families. Much thought has gone into guests' comfort and convenience, with touches including kettles, tea, coffee, reading lamps and even cotton buds in the rooms.

Excellent Indian and Continental food, including local trout and a few specialities with a French touch, is available for guests (mains ₹100 to ₹400). Room rates can be flexible, especially if you stay a few days. Alliance also offers a library, plentiful sitting areas, transport bookings and information on the area and treks; everything you could want.

Mannat Home GUESTHOUSE $$
(☎9816048116; www.mannathome.com; r ₹1200-3000, per month ₹14,000-35,000; @📶) Opposite the castle, Mannat offers seven different,

clean, parquet-floored and mostly spacious rooms. The majority have views and some have a balcony and/or kitchen. Meals are available, your hosts are friendly, and it has excellent monthly rates for long-stayers.

The Castle HERITAGE HOTEL **$$**
(☎01902-248316; www.hptdc.gov.in; incl breakfast s ₹1800-3510, d ₹2400-4680; 📶) The HPTDC hotel occupying the castle has historical atmosphere and traditional stone-and-wood construction but decor and furnishings are rather spartan. Prices depend mainly on room size and views (which are superb from some rooms). There's an affordable **restaurant** (mains ₹170-440; ⏲8am-10pm) with a terrace overlooking the valley.

Getting There & Away

Buses run about hourly to and from Manali between 8am and 6pm (₹30, one hour), and to Kullu (₹30, one hour) about half-hourly, 7.30am to 7pm. A taxi from Manali to Naggar costs about ₹800. An autorickshaw/taxi up to the castle from the bus stop (1km uphill) is around ₹70/100.

Manali

☎01902 / POP 8100 / ELEV 1900M

Surrounded by high peaks in the beautiful green Beas valley, with mountain adventures beckoning from all directions, Manali is a year-round magnet. Backpackers come to hang out in the hippie villages around the main town; adventurers come for trekking, climbing, rafting and skiing; Indian families and honeymooners come for the mountain air and a taste of snow on the 3978m Rohtang La pass. It makes sense to unwind and feed up here for a few days while organising your trip into the mountains.

So popular has Manali become among Indian tourists that this once bucolic retreat now has an estimated 800 to 1000 hotels and guesthouses in the town and outskirts, and from mid-April to mid-July, mid-September to mid-October, and over Christmas–New Year it gets pretty well overrun, with dire traffic jams along its narrow lanes and the main roads approaching town.

Sights

★Hadimba Temple HINDU TEMPLE
(Map p310) This much-revered wood-and-stone mandir, constructed in 1553, stands in a clearing in the cedar forest about 2km west of central Manali. Pilgrims come from across India to honour Hadimba, the demon wife of the Pandava Bhima from the Mahabharata. The temple's wooden doorway, under a three-tier pagoda-style roof, is richly carved with figures of gods, animals and dancers; antlers and ibex horns adorn the outside walls.

Old Manali
Old Manali, about 2km northwest of the Mall on the far side of the Manalsu Nala stream, existed long before the modern town. Today it's the hub of the backpacker scene but still has some of the feel of an Indian mountain village once you get up past the core backpacker zone. There are some remarkable old houses of wood and stone, and the towered **Manu Maharishi Temple** (Map p310) is built on the site where, legend says, the ark of the Noah-like Manu, the creator of civilisation, landed after the great flood.

Buddhist Monasteries
There's a small Tibetan community south of the town centre. The much-visited **Himalayan Nyinmapa Buddhist Temple** (Map p314; ⏲6am-6pm) contains a two-storey statue of Sakyamuni, the historical Buddha. Just west is the more traditional **Von Ngari Monastery** (Map p314; ⏲6am-7pm), with an atmospheric juniper-scented prayer room crammed with statues of bodhisattvas (enlightened beings) and revered lamas.

Activities

Himalayan Extreme Centre OUTDOORS
(Map p310; ☎9816174164; www.himalayan-extreme-centre.com; Old Manali; ⏲9am-8pm) This long-running, professional and friendly outfit – also with a branch in Vashisht– can arrange almost any activity you fancy. Drop in and browse the catalogue.

Himalayan Caravan OUTDOORS
(Map p310; ☎9816316348; www.himalayancaravan.com; Old Manali; ⏲office 9am-10pm mid-Mar–mid-Dec) Professional operator good for trekking, rock climbing, mountaineering, snowboarding and skiing.

Himalayan Trails OUTDOORS
(Map p310; ☎9816828583; www.himalayantrails.in; Dragon Market, Old Manali; ⏲9.30am-10pm) Energetic young company doing trekking, day hikes, mountain biking, rock climbing and more; runs open-group treks that individuals can join and has mountain bikes for rent.

Manali & Vashisht

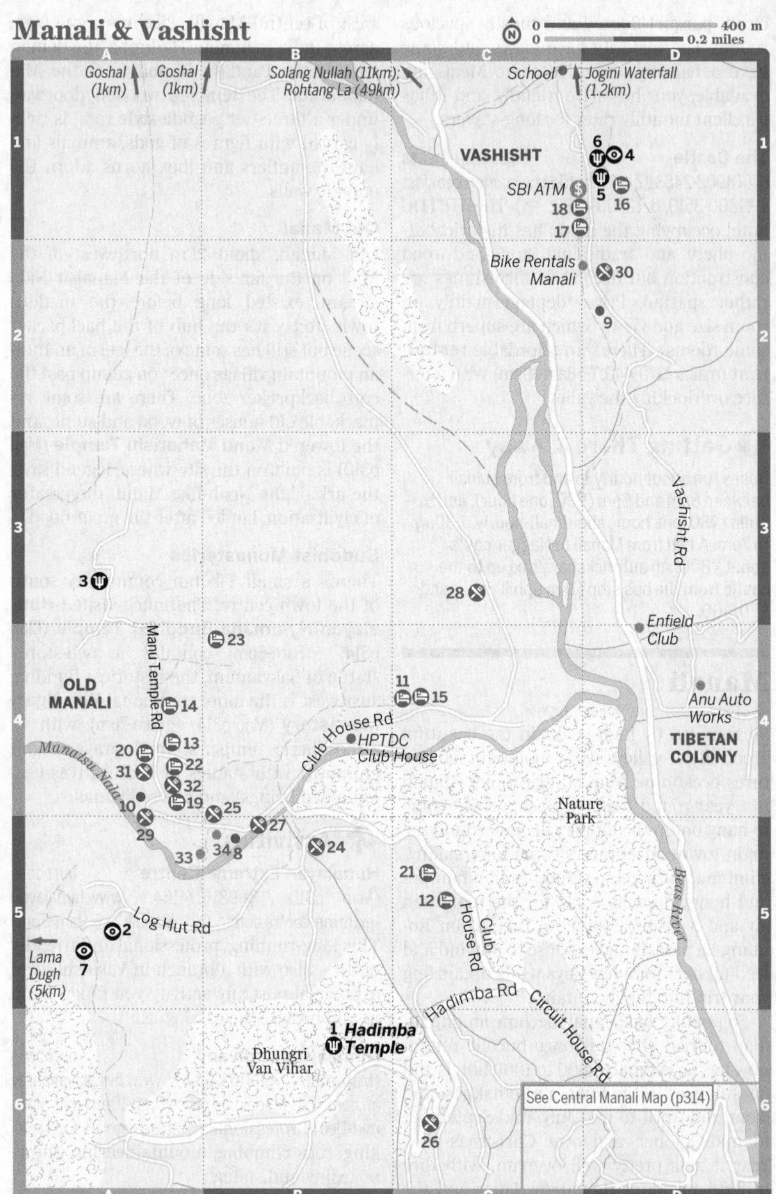

Sleeping

Many midrange and top-end hotels slash prices dramatically outside the peak seasons. Manali town is chock-full of budget and midrange hotels but the best budget places, by far, are a couple of kilometres north in the villages of Old Manali and Vashisht. The best upmarket hotels are between the town centre and Old Manali along Circuit House and Club House Rds, on spacious, still-green properties that once belonged to early British residents.

Manali & Vashisht

Manali

★Banon Resorts HOTEL $$$
(Map p310; ☎01902-253026; www.banonresortmanali.com; Club House Rd; d ₹7140, ste ₹8330-10,710, cottage ₹21,420; ❄📶) This quiet, luxury hotel is a little slicker than its competition. The spacious, centrally heated rooms in the main building have an uncluttered, contemporary feel with pine, white paint and modern art – and huge bathrooms. The two-bedroom cottages are the last word in luxurious peace and privacy.

Johnson Hotel HOTEL $$$
(Map p314; ☎01902-253764; http://johnsonhotel.in; Circuit House Rd; r/apt ₹5330/10,900; ❄📶) One of a few places belonging to descendants of a prominent Raj-era landowner, the Johnson is a classy wood-and-stone hotel with 12 good-sized rooms whose rugs and bedspreads lend them a mildly folksy air. It also has five two-bedroom apartments ('cottages') in the original 1900 lodge, and lovely gardens, plus an excellent restaurant (p314). Everything's in immaculate shape.

Johnson Lodge HOTEL $$$
(Map p314; ☎01902-251523; www.johnsonlodge.com; Circuit House Rd; d ₹5935, cottage for 4 ₹13,650; ❄📶) Four-storey Johnson Lodge offers big, bright pastel-hued rooms with a contemporary air, as well as luxurious two-bedroom duplex apartments ('cottages'). The modern bar and multicuisine restaurant (mains ₹265 to ₹485 and an excellent drinks list) hosts live music (could be Sufi, Indian indie, blues...) a few nights a week.

Sunshine Heritage HERITAGE GUESTHOUSE $$$
(Sunshine Guest House; Map p310; ☎01902-252320; www.thesunshineheritage.com; Club House Rd; r ₹3990; 📶) Authentically colonial, the Sunshine is set in delightfully peaceful, secluded grounds off busy Club House Rd. It has large triples and quads in its original 1921 wood-and-stone building, where rooms have polished walnut-and-pine floors and recently modernised bathrooms. There are also four spacious doubles in a slightly less venerable building next door.

Old Manali

Old Manali has many, mostly budget, guesthouses along its one street, Manu Temple Rd, and on various lanes and pathways off it. Some of them close from about December to April.

OUTDOOR ACTIVITIES AROUND MANALI

Manali is the adventure sports capital of Himachal Pradesh, and all kinds of activities can be organised through operators here.

Mountain Biking

Agencies offer bike hire for ₹400 to ₹800 per day (and can give current info on routes) or will take you on guided rides – ranging from day outings to two-week trips to Ladakh or Spiti costing around ₹3000 per person per day with vehicle support. **Himalayan Bike Bar** (Map p314; www.facebook.com/himalayanbikebar; Mission Rd; ⌚10am-8pm Mon-Sat) is an MTB specialist renting and selling bikes: new bikes cost from around ₹22,000 to ₹72,000.

Mountaineering

Agencies such as Himalayan Caravan (p309) and Himalayan Extreme Centre (p309) arrange expeditions of 10 to 14 days to peaks around the head of the Solang valley, including Friendship Peak (5289m) and Ladakhi (5342m), which are suitable for those with limited experience (training is available), and the more difficult Hanuman Tibba (5930m) and Manali Peak (5669m). Deo Tibba (6001m), above the east side of the Kullu Valley, is another exciting peak for experienced climbers. Typical prices are ₹4500 to ₹5000 per person per day including instructor/guides, equipment, transport, food and camping. The season runs from April to November and conditions tend to be best in the last couple of months.

Paragliding

Paragliding is popular at Solang Nullah and at Gulaba and Marhi (below the Rohtang La, less crowded than Solang) from April to October (except during the monsoon). September and October generally have the best thermals, though May and June can be good at Gulaba and Marhi. Tandem flights at Solang Nullah cost around ₹900 for a one- to two-minute flight, or ₹2000 to ₹3000 for five to 10 minutes from the top of the cable car. Pilots should have a licence issued by the Himachal Pradesh Department of Tourism. Adventure-tour operators can organise tandem flights at Gulaba and Marhi for ₹1000 to ₹4000 depending on duration.

Rafting

There is 14km of Grade II and III white water between Pirdi, on the Beas River 3km south of Kullu, and the take-out point at Jhiri; trips with adventure agencies from Manali cost any-

Zostel HOSTEL $
(Map p310; ☎9816655763; www.zostel.com; dm ₹450-500, r ₹2000; ⓦ) Well-run Zostel has a good, friendly, backpacker atmosphere with welcoming, helpful management and staff. There's a good garden cafe with Indian and Continental food (mains ₹110 to ₹250), and the accommodation has a few above-average touches such as reading lights and electric sockets for every bunk, and king-size beds in the private rooms.

Apple View Guest House GUESTHOUSE $
(Map p310; ☎9816887844; www.appleview-manali.com; r ₹300, without bathroom ₹300; ⓦ) Up steps signposted 'Red House Cafe' opposite the HPTDC Club House, this homey family-run guesthouse is one of the best deals in Manali. It has 12 plain, well-kept rooms and a pleasant little patio, and offers a simple but good menu of Indian and Continental food (mains ₹60 to ₹80).

If it's full, try the **Eagle Guest House** (Map p310; ☎9816397788; liatasher@hotmail.com; r ₹400-600, incl breakfast ₹600-800; ⌚closed Jan & Feb; ⓦ) 50m along the path.

Mountain Dew Guesthouse GUESTHOUSE $
(Map p310; ☎9816446366; Manu Temple Rd; s ₹500-600, d ₹600-900; ⓦ) This good-value, three-storey place offers good-sized, decently maintained rooms with east-facing shared terraces. The top floor is best: new rooms and the finest views.

Tourist Nest Guest House GUESTHOUSE $
(Map p310; ☎01902-252383; touristnest@gmail.com; r ₹700-1000; ⓦ) In the heart of Old Manali, Tourist Nest has bright, clean, tiled, well-kept rooms with private balconies.

where between ₹650 and ₹1150 per person, plus transport (around ₹2000 to ₹2500 per van). May, June, late September and October are the best times (it's banned from 15 July to 15 August because of the monsoon).

Skiing & Snowboarding

From January to mid-March, Solang Nullah transforms into Himachal's main ski and snowboarding resort. Equipment can be hired from Manali agencies or at Solang Nullah from ₹500 per day. The piste offers limited options for experienced skiers, but there is off-piste powder and backcountry skiing for the experienced from the top of the cable car. In April and May there's snowshoe ski touring in areas like the Hamta valley, upper Solang valley and around Gulaba, with snowshoe-trekking up peaks. Agencies such as Himalayan Caravan (p309), **Himalayan Adventurers** (Map p314; ☎01902-252750; www.himalayanadventurers.com; 44 The Mall; ⏰9am-9pm) and Himalayan Extreme Centre (p309) offer ski touring packages. Heli-skiing packages to high-altitude powder in February and March can be arranged through **Himalayan Heli Adventures** (☎9816025899; www.himachal.com).

Walking & Trekking

Manali is a popular jumping-off point for organised mountain treks. Most agencies offer multiday treks for ₹1600 to ₹3000 per person per day including guides, transport, porters or pack animals, food and camping equipment. Generally the larger the group, the lower the price per person. June, September and October are overall the best months. Popular shorter options include Beas Kund (three days, with the option of extra days hiking up surrounding mountains), the 4250m-high Bhrigu Lake (three days), the Hamta Pass (p318) to Lahaul (four days) and the Chandrakani Pass (p308) from Naggar to Malana (two or three days). More demanding and usually more expensive routes include the six- to nine-day Pin-Parvati Trek (p304) and routes west to the isolated village of Bara Bhangal and on to the Chamba or Kangra Valleys (11 days or more).

Plenty of shorter walks are possible from Manali. The usual rules on safe trekking apply – tell someone where you are going and don't walk alone. Guides for day hikes typically cost ₹1500. One good day hike (about five hours up, four hours down) is up to **Lama Dugh meadow** at 3380m: the way starts along the uphill path from a **water tank** (Map p310) above Hotel Delfryn in the Log Huts Area of town. A good short walk (about an hour each way) goes north from Vashisht to **Jogini waterfalls** and back.

Manali Yes Please HOTEL $
(Map p310; ☎9418523125; www.manaliyesplease.com; Manu Temple Rd; r ₹1000) A relatively large place by Old Manali standards with three floors of rooms along broad verandahs. Rooms are a bit worn but clean enough, and outside June and July they are usually available for ₹500, which makes them popular.

Dragon Guest House HOTEL $$
(Map p310; ☎01902-252290; www.dragoninn-manali.com; r ₹1760-2860, ste ₹4950; 📶) Dragon has comfortable, wood-panelled rooms opening on to long verandahs on four floors – the higher the better, and best of all are the Swiss-chalet-style rooms on the top floors.

Drifters' Inn HOTEL $$
(Map p310; ☎9805033127; http://driftersinn.in; Manu Temple Rd; r ₹1100-2000, f ₹1900-2500; 📶) The hipness of the ground-floor restaurant (p315) doesn't quite extend into the rooms, but it's a spotless and comfy place with outdoor terraces on all three floors, and the wi-fi reaches all rooms.

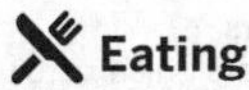

Eating

Manali

Chopsticks ASIAN $$
(Map p314; The Mall; mains ₹120-300; ⏰9am-11pm; 📶) The most popular traveller choice in central Manali, tightly packed Chopsticks serves a big range of Tibetan, Chinese and Japanese dishes with professional efficiency. Amid Tibetan lutes and Chinese lanterns, it does good *momos* (Tibetan dumplings), *gyoza* (their Japanese equivalent), *thenthuk* (a Tibetan soup with short, flat noodles) and Sichuan chicken and lamb.

Cold beers, wine and local fruit wines too.

Central Manali

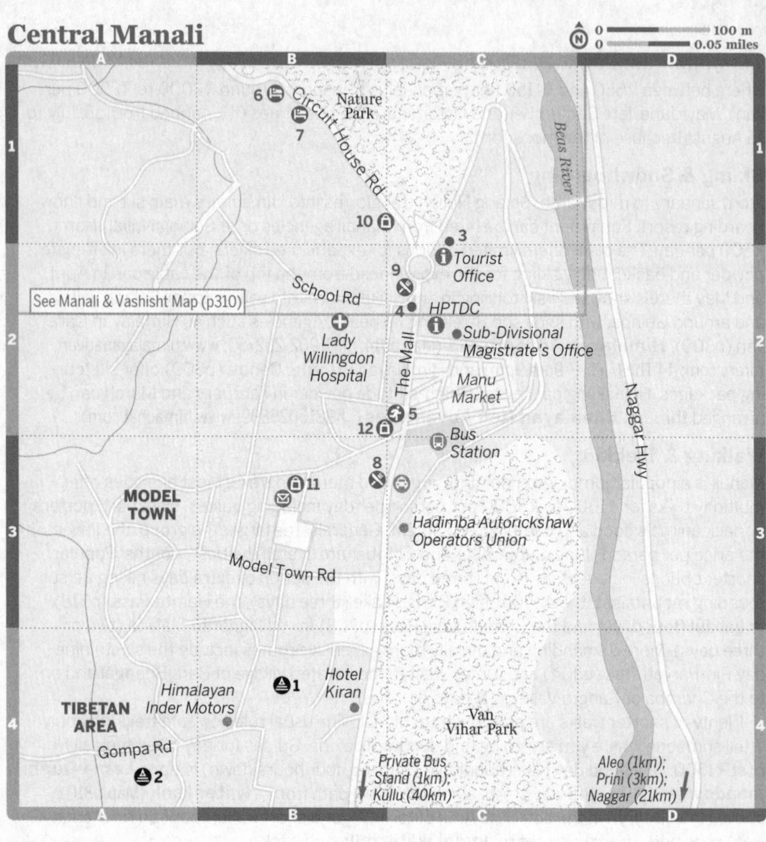

Central Manali

Sights

1 Himalayan Nyinmapa Buddhist Temple B4
2 Von Ngari Monastery A4

Activities, Courses & Tours

3 Him-aanchal Taxi Operators Union C1
4 Himalayan Adventurers C2
5 Himalayan Bike Bar C2

Sleeping

6 Johnson Hotel B1
7 Johnson Lodge B1

Eating

8 Chopsticks B3
Johnson's Cafe .... (see 6)
9 Khyber C2

Shopping

10 Bhuttico B1
11 Bookworm B3
12 Shashni Communications B2

Transport

Railway Reservation Office .... (see 3)

Johnson's Cafe INTERNATIONAL $$$
(Map p314; Circuit House Rd; mains ₹300-550; ⏲8am-11pm; 📶) The restaurant at Johnson Hotel is tops for European food, with specialities such as lamb and mint gravy, wood-oven-baked trout, and apple crumble with ice cream. The restaurant-bar is cosy, but the garden terrace is the place to be, especially during happy hour (4pm to 8pm).

Il Forno ITALIAN $$$
(Map p310; Hadimba Rd; mains ₹180-500; ⏲10.30am-10.30pm; 📶) The pretty flower garden of this 150-year-old traditional stone-

and-timber house makes a lovely stop on the way to or from Hadimba Temple – and the pizzas are pretty good too!

Old Manali

Numerous inexpensive, half-open-air restaurants serve all the usual backpacker-town suspects – *momos* (Tibetan dumplings), omelettes, banana pancakes, apple pie and the three Is (Italian/Israeli/Indian dishes). A lot of these places close by November. The best include friendly and efficient **Shiva Garden Cafe** (Map p310; Manu Temple Rd; mains ₹100-250; ⏲8am-11pm; 📶) and riverside **Kathmandu Cafe** (Map p310; Manu Temple Rd; mains ₹100-350; ⏲10am-11pm; 📶).

Dylan's Toasted & Roasted CAFE $
(Map p310; www.dylanscoffee.com; Manu Temple Rd; coffees & breakfasts ₹50-170; ⏲9am-10pm Mon-Sat; 📶) This ever popular hole-in-the-wall cafe serves the best coffee in town, plus cinnamon tea, hearty breakfasts, pancakes and wicked desserts including 'Hello to the Queen' – ice cream, melted chocolate and fried banana chunks on a bed of broken biscuits.

★**La Plage** FRENCH $$$
(Map p310; ☎9805340977; www.facebook.com/la.plage.manali; mains ₹400-700; ⏲noon-11pm late May–late Aug, closed Mon Aug) Dinner at this outpost of a chic Goan eatery is like being invited to the hip Paris apartment of your much, much cooler friend. French standards such as onion soup or mushroom quiche are joined by specialities such as overnight-cooked lamb, smoked trout, broccoli-and-courgette lasagne and a decadent chocolate thali dessert. Decent Indian and international wines too.

Food flavours are perhaps not quite so sensational as you'd hope for the prices, but it's still well worth the trip – 1km from Old Manali bridge in an apple orchard. It will provide free transport from and back to the bridge if you call.

Drifters' Inn MULTICUISINE $$$
(Map p310; Manu Temple Rd; mains ₹230-380; ⏲9.30am-11pm; 📶) A loungey restaurant-cafe that's good for hearty breakfasts, strong coffee, international dishes from eggs Florentine to Thai curries, and imaginative beverages such as seabuckthorn fizz, as well as plenty of alcoholic options.

Lazy Dog Lounge MULTICUISINE $$$
(Map p310; Manu Temple Rd; mains ₹180-600; ⏲11am-1am; 📶) This slick restaurant-bar features big plates of fresh, flavourful international food – from pumpkin-and-coconut soup to oven-baked trout and Thai rice bowls, as well as good Indian dishes – that's well above typical backpacker fare. Sit on chairs, benches or cushions in a space that's classy yet earthy, or relax in the riverside garden.

Casa Bella Vista CONTINENTAL $$$
(Map p310; Log Huts Rd; mains ₹350-500; ⏲10am-10.30pm May-Sep; 🖉) Not the cheapest, but the best pizzas in the Old Manali area – thin-crust, log-oven pizzas with tasty topping combinations. The salads and pasta are good too.

Drinking & Entertainment

Restaurants doubling as bars provide the bulk of Manali's nightlife, and their live-music nights (mostly in Old Manali, of diverse musical genre and equally diverse quality) are often the liveliest. All-night trance parties happen in Old Manali with place and time circulated by word of mouth and the occasional poster.

A particularly popular spot is the **Hangout** (Map p310; Manu Temple Rd; mains ₹150-500; ⏲noon-midnight, from 5pm Thu), with its outdoor firepits and jam sessions (and also good food). Other places to check out for music evenings include Lazy Dog Lounge, **Rendez-Vous** (Map p310; Manu Temple Rd; mains ₹120-590; ⏲8am-11pm; 📶), Drifters' Inn, Kathmandu Cafe and, down towards central Manali, the bar at Johnson Lodge (p311).

Johnson's Cafe and Banon Resorts (p311) also have good, relatively upmarket bars. In Manali town, the best places for a drink are **Khyber** (Map p314; The Mall; mains ₹180-500; ⏲10am-11pm) and Chopsticks (p313).

Shopping

Manali is crammed with shops selling souvenirs from Himachal, Tibet and Ladakh, including turquoise jewellery and lots of brass Buddhas. The local speciality is Kullu shawls (p307), for which a good place to start is **Bhuttico** (Map p314; ☎01902-252196; The Mall; ⏲9am-7pm Mon-Sat), which charges fair, fixed prices and has several shops around town.

Bookworm BOOKS
(Map p314; ☎01902-252920; Shop No 5, near Post Office; ⏲10am-7pm Mon-Sat) Excellent selection of books including many on the Himalaya, and maps including Leomann trekking maps.

Information

MEDICAL SERVICES

Lady Willingdon Hospital (Map p314; ☎01902-252379; www.manalihospital.com; School Rd) Considered the best hospital in the Kullu Valley; has 24-hour emergency service.

TELEPHONE

You can buy SIM cards for foreign phones at several phone shops on and around the Mall.

Shashni Communications (Map p314; off The Mall; ⏰10am-9pm) charges ₹500 for a SIM with 2GB of data and around ₹40 of call credit.

TOURIST INFORMATION

HPTDC (Map p314; ☎01902-252116; The Mall; ⏰8am-8pm mid-April–mid-Jul & mid-Sep–mid-Nov, 9am-7pm rest of year) Can book HPTDC buses and hotels.

Tourist Office (Map p314; ☎01902-252175; The Mall; ⏰10am-5pm Mon-Sat, closed 2nd Sat of the month) Readily answers questions and has a few give-away leaflets.

Getting There & Away

Manali's closest airport is 50km south at Bhuntar.

There's a **Railway Reservation Office** (Map p314; The Mall; ⏰8am-1.30pm Mon-Fri, 8am-12.30pm Sat) at the top of the Mall.

BUS

Government-run Himachal Road Transport Corporation (HRTC) buses go from the **bus station** (Map p314; The Mall). Himachal Tourism (HPTDC) runs a few services to Delhi, Leh and Shimla and these are generally the most comfortable on their routes. They leave from the bus station but tickets are sold at the **HPTDC office**. Private buses to a few destinations start from the **private bus stand** (Hwy 3), 1.2km south of the bus station; tickets are sold at travel agencies along the Mall.

For the Parvati Valley, take a bus to Bhuntar and change there.

Delhi The HPTDC's comfortable AC Volvo coaches (₹1300, 14 hours) go at 5.30pm and, in busy seasons, 5pm and/or 6pm. Private bus companies run similar overnight services for ₹900 to ₹1800 depending on season. The HRTC runs five AC Volvos (₹1412) each afternoon, plus an AC deluxe (₹1122) at 5.50pm, and seven ordinary or 'semi-deluxe' services daily.

Lahaul & Spiti The Rohtang La, between Manali and Lahaul, is normally open from mid-May to early November, and the Kunzum La, between Lahaul and Spiti, from early June to some time in November (exact dates depend on snow conditions). A tunnel bypassing the Rohtang La may open by 2018, which hopefully will open up Lahaul to year-round visits. In season, the HRTC runs up to seven daily buses to Keylong (Lahaul) and one to Kaza (Spiti).

Ladakh The bone-shaking, exhausting and spectacular road to Leh is normally open from early June to some time in October (exact dates depend on road conditions). On all journeys to Leh, bring snacks and warm clothing and be alert to the symptoms of Acute Mountain Sickness. Fare-wise the cheapest option is to take a bus to Keylong and then the early morning HRTC bus the next day from there to Leh, though you do need a night in Keylong in between.

HRTC BUSES FROM MANALI

DESTINATION	FARE (₹)	DURATION (HR)	DEPARTURES
Amritsar	542-594	11-14	1.45pm & 3.30pm
Bhuntar	15	30	every 15-30min, 5am-9pm
Chandigarh	451-854	9	18 daily
Dehra Dun	665-1187	15	3 daily
Delhi	684-1412	14-16	13 daily
Dharamsala	360-820	10	Volvo AC 8pm, ordinary 8.20am & 7pm
Haridwar	662-1311	15	4 daily
Jammu	562-1363	12	ordinary 4pm, Volvo AC 8pm
Kaza	300	11	6.30am, approximately mid-Jun–mid-Oct
Keylong	175	7	7 daily, approximately mid-May–early Nov
Kullu	60	1½	every few minutes, 4am-10pm
Mandi	170	4	half-hourly, 5am-9pm
Naggar	30	1	hourly, 8am-6pm
Shimla	390-544	9	6 daily

From early July to mid-September, an HPTDC bus (₹3000, 34 hours) departs Manali at 9am every second day, with an overnight stop at Keylong, where dormitory accommodation, dinner and breakfast are included in the fare. Throughout the season the **Him-aanchal Taxi Operators Union** (Map p314; ☎01902-252120; The Mall) runs minibuses to Leh departing at 2.30am without an overnight halt (₹1800 to ₹3000 depending on demand, about 18 hours), or departing at 6am with an overnight halt en route (₹2000 to ₹3500, accommodation and meals not included); book a day in advance. Some travel agencies offer similar services.

MOTORCYCLE

Many people tackle the mountain passes to Ladakh or Spiti on bought or rented bikes. You can book into a group tour with accommodation, food and backup vehicles included at around ₹5000 per day, or just rent a bike and head off on your own.

For rentals, expect to pay ₹1200 or ₹1300 per day for a 350cc Enfield, ₹1400 to ₹1500 for a 500cc Enfield, and around ₹800 for 220cc bikes. Make sure the deal includes spares, tools, at least third-party insurance, and the registration and pollution certificates needed for your Rohtang La permit.

Anu Auto Works (Royal Moto Touring; Map p310; ☎9816163378; www.royalmototouring.com; Vashisht Rd; ⊙office 9am-9pm or later, approx Jun-Sep) Established, highly regarded and professional outfit that offers Enfield motorbike tours, and rents and repairs Enfields too.

Bike Rentals Manali (Map p310; ☎9816044140; www.bikerentalsmanali.com; Vashisht; ⊙9.30am-11pm Apr-Oct) Enfield rentals and tours.

Enfield Club (Map p310; ☎9805146389; Vashisht Rd; ⊙9am-9.30pm mid-Apr–Jan) Tiny enthusiasts' workshop doing Enfield rentals and repairs.

Himalayan Inder Motors (Map p314; ☎9816113973; Gompa Rd) Rents Enfields and other makes; owner Kaku has been in business 25 years.

TAXI & JEEP

The **Him-aanchal Taxi Operators Union** (Map p314; ☎01902-252205; The Mall) charges between ₹14,000 and ₹24,000 for an MUV (multi-utility vehicle, often called jeeps), carrying six people in reasonable comfort, to Leh. Prices are highest from about mid-June to late July. Private travel agencies offer similar deals and may also sell individual seats for ₹2000 to ₹3000.

For Kaza (Spiti), a jeep is around ₹9000 one way. For 6am share jeeps to Kaza (₹1000 per seat), ask the day before at **Hotel Kiran** (Map p314; ☎01902-253066) in the south of Manali, where drivers from Spiti hang out. These run as long as the Rohtang La and Kunzum La are open.

Multiday rentals of a jeep with a driver normally cost ₹3000 to ₹3500 per day. This is a relatively economical way of touring areas such as Spiti or Ladakh, especially if shared between five or six people. Vehicle types vary from the fairly basic high-clearance Sumo or Spacio to the comfier, less rugged Innova, Xylo or Tavera. You can organise them through almost any travel agency. Some of the best prices are available from **Shalom Travels** (Map p310; ☎9816746264; Manu Temple Rd) and **Nirvana Travels** (Map p310; ☎9816023222; off Manu Temple Rd) in Old Manali.

Other typical one-way taxi fares:

DESTINATION	FARE (₹)
Bhuntar airport	1500
Dharamsala	5000
Keylong	5000
Kullu	1100
Manikaran	2000
Naggar	800
Solang Nullah	800

ℹ Getting Around

Hadimba Autorickshaw Operators Union (Map p314; ☎01902-253366; The Mall) has an office at the south end of the Mall, but drivers waiting at the top of the Mall tend to be a little more reasonable about fares and with luck will go to Old Manali bridge for ₹50, Hadimba Temple for ₹60 or Vashisht for ₹70. But they'll get more out of you if they can, especially after dark (if you can get one at all).

Around Manali

Vashisht

☎01902 / POP 1600 / ELEV 1970M

About 2km north of Manali on the hillside above the Beas River, Vashisht village is a slightly quieter and more compact version of Old Manali and a popular travellers' hangout. Indian tourists mostly come to bathe in the hot springs and tour the temples, while foreign travellers largely come for the cheap accommodation, chilled atmosphere and charas. Many guesthouses and restaurants close down from about November to April.

Vashisht Mandir HINDU TEMPLE

(Map p310; ⊙9am-9pm) Vashisht's sulphur-laden hot springs are channelled into small

public baths (Map p310; ⏲9am-9pm) FREE inside the ancient stone Vashisht Mandir, which is dedicated to the sage Vashisht. There's another open-air **public pool** (Map p310; ⏲6am-9pm) FREE, for men only, just uphill, past a set of hot-water spouts where locals wash clothes and dishes. Nearby are a *sikhara*-type **Rama temple** (Map p310), with old stone carvings and a wooden canopy, and a relatively plain **Shiva temple** (Map p310).

Sleeping & Eating

Many small, inexpensive guesthouses and homestays are tucked away along the village lanes and up paths towards the hills.

Hotel Dharma HOTEL $
(Map p310; ☎01902-252354; www.hoteldharmamanali.com; r ₹300-1200; ⏲closed Jan & Feb; @ 📶) A short, steep walk above the Vashisht Mandir is rewarded with some of the best views from any hotel on either side of the Beas River. The older wing, with a big terrace out front, has basic but clean rooms from ₹300 to ₹600 that are pretty good value, while the pricier new section has nicer, carpeted rooms with balconies.

Hotel Surabhi HOTEL $$
(Map p310; ☎9816042796; www.surabhihotel.in; r incl breakfast ₹1660-2760; 📶) One of a few big, modernish places on the main street, Surabhi's spacious, carpeted, decently maintained rooms have balconies with great views. This is one place where you don't really need to spring for the most expensive rooms.

Hotel Valley of Gods HOTEL $$
(Map p310; ☎01902-251111; www.hotelvalleyofgods.com; r ₹3000-3500, ste ₹4000; @ 📶) This impressive stone-and-wood building, owned and run by a local family, has bright, spacious, pine-floored rooms with good, big bathrooms and fine balconies overlooking the valley.

Rasta Cafe MULTICUISINE $$
(Map p310; mains ₹100-240; ⏲8am-11pm; 📶) Rasta is the top traveller hang-out for its well-prepared breakfasts, soups, salads, *momos*, Indian dishes, falafel, hummus, pasta, pizza, desserts, juices, smoothies (and we could go on...). Friendly service in a bright, airy space with pine tables and cane chairs or low-table cushion seating. And plenty of reggae too!

World Peace Cafe MULTICUISINE $$
(Map p310; Hotel Surabhi; mains ₹120-300; ⏲7am-10pm; 📶) This rooftop restaurant has great valley views from its expansive patio, plus an inside room with low tables and floor cushions. The kitchen does a decent job on a wide-ranging international menu, and it sometimes holds music jams in summer.

Getting There & Away

The regular autorickshaw fare to or from Manali is ₹70; don't rely on being able to get one in either direction after 7pm. On foot it's about 30 minutes; a footpath down beside Bike Rentals Manali comes out on the main road 300m north of the Vashisht turn-off.

Solang Nullah

☎01902

From January to March, skiers and snowboarders can enjoy 1.5km of alpine-style runs here at Himachal's main winter-sports resort, 13km north of Manali in the lower part of the Solang valley. A **cable car** (ropeway, gondola; one-way or return ₹600; ⏲10am-

HAMTA PASS TREK

Easily accessible from Manali, this camping trek crosses from the Kullu Valley to Lahaul's Chandra Valley via the 4270m Hamta Pass. Most people drive up the Hamta valley from Prini village to the spot known as Jobri, where the Hamta Nullah and Jobri Nullah streams meet. Two easy days to start off, with a combined ascent of around 800m, are good for acclimatisation. The climb to the pass from the campsite at Balu Ka Gera is steep and tiring, but there are sublime snow-peak views from the top. Best times for this trek are the second half of September and October, after the monsoon. Chatru is on the road between the Rohtang La and Spiti.

STAGE	ROUTE	DURATION (HR)	DISTANCE (KM)
1	Jobri to Chikka	2	5
2	Chikka to Balu Ka Gera	4	9
3	Balu Ka Gera to Shiagouru via Hamta Pass	8	15
4	Shiagouru to Chatru	4	10

6.30pm) climbs up to 3200m, and there's also off-piste powder and backcountry skiing from the top of it.

Solang is also a year-round 'beauty spot', with paragliding (p312), quad bikes and a general carnival-like atmosphere in the pre-monsoon tourist season. The cable car operates year-round. The surrounding hills are good for walking and climbing – Patalsu peak (4472m) to the north is an excellent if quite strenuous one- or two-day hike.

WESTERN HIMACHAL PRADESH

Western Himachal Pradesh is most famous as the home of the Tibetan government-in-exile and residence of the Dalai Lama at McLeod Ganj, which is a major traveller hub with many opportunities to volunteer or take yoga, meditation or other courses. The Dhauladhar and Pir Panjal ranges make for some excellent trekking and the Chamba Valley lying between them is beautiful and culturally intriguing. Elsewhere, the Bir-Billing area is attracting growing numbers of adventurers and spiritual seekers with its world-class paragliding and numerous Tibetan monasteries.

Dharamsala

01892 / POP 20,000 / ELEV 1380M

Dharamsala (also spelled Dharamshala) is known as the home of the Dalai Lama, but the untidy market town where the buses pull in is actually Lower Dharamsala. The Tibetan spiritual leader is based 3km up the hill in Upper Dharamsala, also known as McLeod Ganj, and that's where most visitors are heading. When people locally talk about Dharamsala, they usually mean Lower Dharamsala.

Museum of Kangra Art MUSEUM

(Map p320; Indian/foreigner ₹20/100; 10am-1.30pm & 2-5pm Tue-Sun) This museum, just off the main street, displays some fine miniature paintings from the Kangra school, and Chamba *rumal* embroideries, along with traditional costumes from the area and photos from the devastating 1905 Kangra earthquake.

Hotel Dhauladhar HOTEL $$

(Map p320; 01892-224926; www.hptdc.gov.in; s ₹1720-2050, d ₹2290-2730, ste from ₹3270;) This centrally located HPTDC hotel has clean, spacious rooms and a broad restaurant terrace enjoying good valley views, plus a bar.

Getting There & Away

Dharamsala airport is at Gaggal, 13km southwest. Air India and SpiceJet both fly daily to/from Delhi, though flights are sometimes cancelled in bad weather.

Buses run from **Dharamsala bus station** (Map p320) to McLeod Ganj (₹15, 35 minutes) about every half-hour from 6am to 9pm. Services to Delhi include Volvo AC buses (₹1240) at 5.15am, 6.30pm, 8pm and 9.30pm, and an AC deluxe bus (₹950) at 8.30pm.

BUSES FROM DHARAMSALA

DESTINATION	FARE (₹)	DURATION (HR)	DEPARTURES
Amritsar	255	7	5am
Chamba	364	8	3 daily
Dalhousie	171	5	7am
Dehra Dun	535-1045	12	3 daily
Delhi	542-1240	12	10 daily
Gaggal	15	40min	every 15min
Jawalamukhi	60	1½	frequent
Kangra	25	1	every 15-30min
Manali	360-815	10	Volvo AC 9.30pm, ordinary 7am & 6pm
Mandi	195-400	6	4 HRTC daily, also private buses
Palampur	50	2	about half-hourly to 8.45pm
Pathankot	136	3½	about hourly, 5am-5.30pm
Shimla	363-522	10	7 daily (morning & evening)

Dharamsala

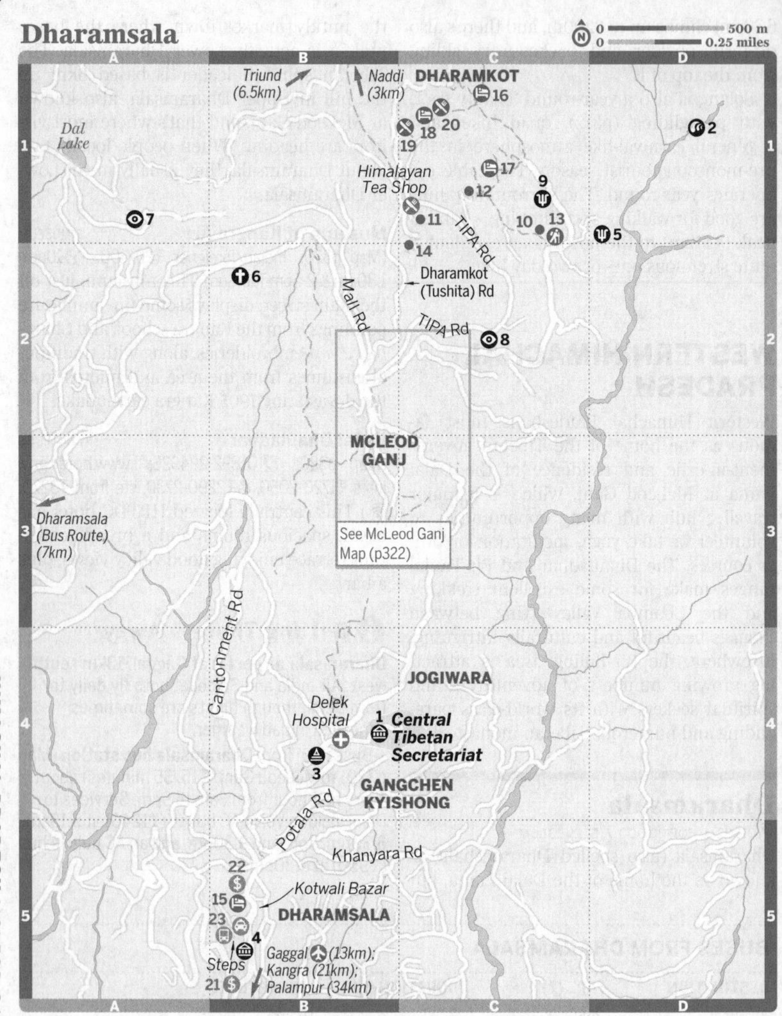

Dharamsala Taxi Union (Map p320; ☎01892-222105) is up a flight of 185 steps from the bus station. Cabs to McLeod Ganj cost ₹200.

McLeod Ganj

☎01892 / POP 10,000 / ELEV 1740M

When travellers talk of heading up to Dharamsala (to see the Dalai Lama...), this is where they mean. Three kilometres north of Dharamsala town (or 10km via the looping bus route), McLeod Ganj is the residence of His Holiness the 14th Dalai Lama and home to a large Tibetan population, including many monks and nuns. The Tibetan government-in-exile is based just downhill at Gangchen Kyishong. McLeod attracts thousands of international visitors each year to volunteer with the Tibetan community, take courses in Buddhism, meditation or yoga, trek in the Dhauladhar mountains, shop for Tibetan crafts, or just hang out and enjoy the low-budget spiritual/alternative vibe and the many good cafes and restaurants dishing up Indo-Italo-Israeli-Tibetan food.

With an interesting mix of travellers, volunteers, maroon-robed monks and nuns, the international dharma crowd and an increas-

Dharamsala

Top Sights
1 Central Tibetan Secretariat....B4

Sights
2 Bhagsu Waterfall....D1
Cultural Museum....(see 1)
Library of Tibetan Works & Archives....(see 1)
3 Men-Tsee-Khang....B4
Men-Tsee-Khang Museum....(see 3)
4 Museum of Kangra Art....B5
Nechung Gompa....(see 1)
5 Shiva Temple....D1
6 St John in the Wilderness....B2
7 Tibetan Children's Village....A1
8 Tibetan Institute of Performing Arts....C2
9 Vashnu Mata Temple....C1

Activities, Courses & Tours
10 Ayuskama Ayurvedic Clinic....C1
Buddhist Philosophy Courses....(see 1)
11 Himachal Vipassana Centre....C1
12 Himalayan Iyengar Yoga Centre....C1
13 Terrestrial Adventures....C1
Tibetan Language Courses....(see 1)
14 Tushita Meditation Centre....C2

Sleeping
15 Hotel Dhauladhar....B5
16 Raj Residency....C1
17 Trimurti Garden Cafe....C1
18 Valley View....C1

Eating
19 Cool Talk Cafe....C1
20 Space Out....C1

Information
21 SBI....B5
22 SBI ATM....B5

Transport
23 Dharamsala Bus Station....B5

ing flow of Indian tourists, you're never far from an interesting conversation here.

Named after Donald McLeod, Lieutenant-Governor of Punjab, McLeod began life in the 1850s as a civilian settlement outside the British garrison of Dharamsala. It was devastated by the 1905 Kangra earthquake and sank into obscurity after Independence – until the Dalai Lama arrived to establish his base here in 1960. Since then, McLeod has become a vibrant centre of Tibetan culture and Buddhism.

The monsoon (late June to early September) is particularly wet here, and warm clothes are useful between November and March. Many shops and businesses close on Monday.

Sights & Activities

★Tsuglagkhang Complex BUDDHIST TEMPLE
(Map p322; Temple Rd; ⏲5am-8pm Apr-Oct, 6am-6pm Nov-Mar) The main focus of visiting pilgrims, monks and many tourists, the Tsuglagkhang complex includes the Tsuglagkhang itself (the main Tibetan temple), the Namgyal Gompa and the excellent Tibet Museum.

➡ Tsuglagkhang
(Map p322) The revered Tsuglagkhang is the exiles' concrete equivalent of the Jokhang temple in Lhasa and was built in 1969. The central image is a gilded statue of the Sakyamuni Buddha. To its left are gilded statues of Avalokitesvara (the bodhisattva of compassion, Tibet's patron deity) and Padmasambhava, the Indian sage believed to have helped spread Buddhism in 8th-century Tibet, and a wooden 'starving Buddha' representing the Buddha near the end of his six years of ascetic meditation at Bodhgaya.

➡ Namgyal Gompa
(Map p322) Namgyal Gompa is the monastery in the Tsuglagkhang Complex. You can watch the monks in lively debate in the courtyard from 2pm to 3pm daily except Sunday, sealing points of argument with a foot stamp and theatrical clap of the hands. The entrance to the Dalai Lama's residence, not open to the public, is on the south side of the courtyard.

➡ Kalachakra Temple
(Map p322) Before visiting the Tsuglagkhang itself, pilgrims first visit the Kalachakra Temple on its west side, which contains mesmerising murals of the Kalachakra (Wheel of Time) mandala, specifically linked to Avalokitesvara, of whom the Dalai Lama is a manifestation.

➡ Tibet Museum
(Map p322; http://tibetmuseum.org; ⏲9am-1pm & 2-6pm Sun & Tue-Fri & 1st Sat of the month, to 5pm Oct-Mar) FREE The museum tells the story of Tibetan history, the Chinese occupation and the continuing Tibetan resistance and exodus, through photographs, video and clear English-language display panels. It also covers the Dalai Lama and his life's work. A visit here is a must.

McLeod Ganj

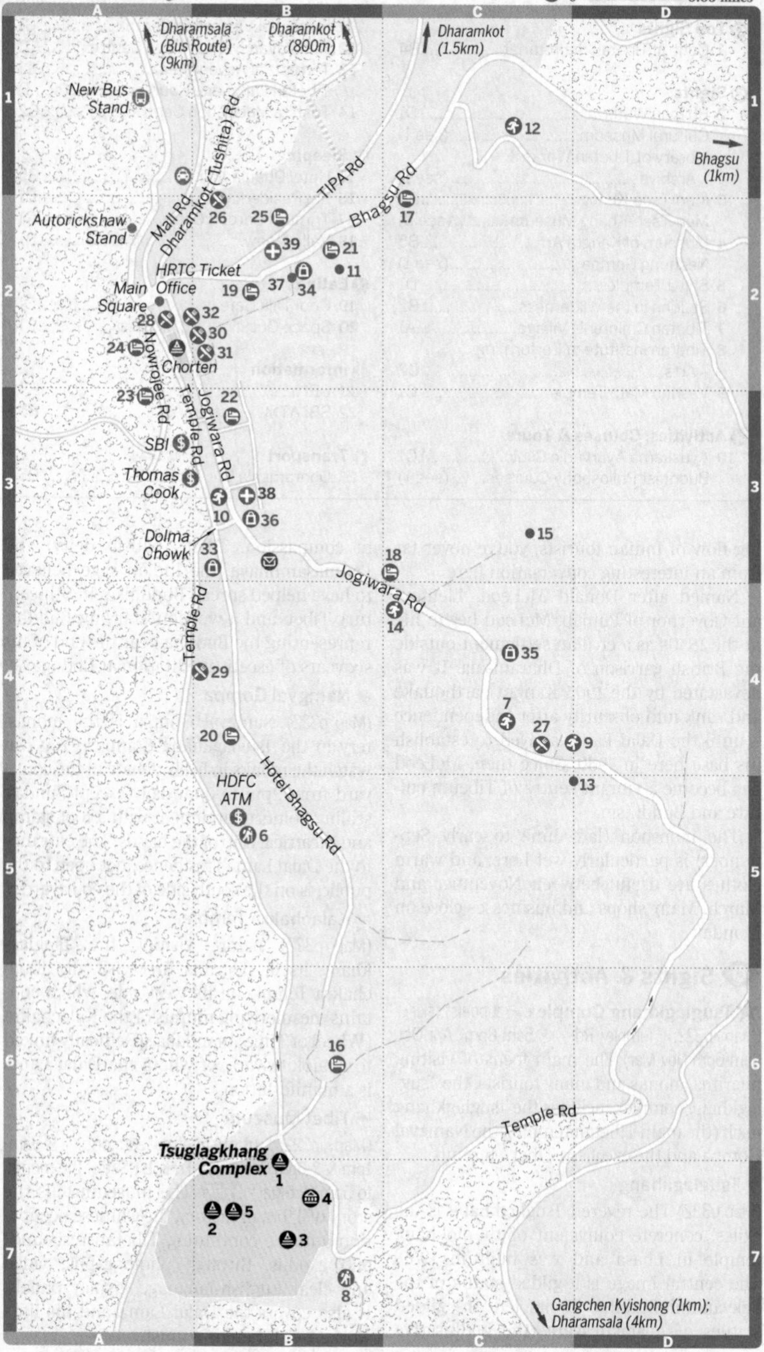

0 100 m
0 0.05 miles
Dharamsala (Bus Route) (9km)
Dharamkot (800m)
Dharamkot (1.5km)
New Bus Stand
Dharamkot (Tushita) Rd
TIPA Rd
Bhagsu Rd
Bhagsu (1km)
Mall Rd
Autorickshaw Stand
HRTC Ticket Office
Main Square
Nowrojee Rd
Chorten
Temple Rd
Jogiwara Rd
SBI
Thomas Cook
Dolma Chowk
Jogiwara Rd
Temple Rd
Hotel Bhagsu Rd
HDFC ATM
Temple Rd
Tsuglagkhang Complex
Gangchen Kyishong (1km); Dharamsala (4km)
1 2 3 4 5 6 7 8 9 10 11 12 13 14 15 16 17 18 19 20 21 22 23 24 25 26 27 28 29 30 31 32 33 34 35 36 37 38 39

McLeod Ganj

Top Sights
1 Tsuglagkhang Complex B7

Sights
Gu-Chu-Sum Movement Gallery .... (see 27)
2 Kalachakra Temple B7
3 Namgyal Gompa B7
4 Tibet Museum B7
5 Tsuglagkhang B7

Activities, Courses & Tours
6 High Point Adventure B5
High Point Adventure .... (see 20)
7 Holistic Centre of Ayurveda C4
8 Kora Circuit B7
9 Learning & Ideas for Tibet D4
10 Lha B3
11 Lhamo's Kitchen B2
12 Rogpa C1
13 Sangye's Kitchen D5
14 Tibet World C4
15 Universal Yoga Centre C3

Sleeping
16 Chonor House B6
17 Green Hotel C2
18 Hotel Mount View C3
19 Hotel Tibet B2
20 Kareri Lodge B4
21 Kunga Guesthouse B2
22 Loseling Guest House B3
23 Om Hotel A3
24 Serkong House A2
25 Seven Hills Guest House B2

Eating
26 Common Ground Cafe B2
Green Hotel Restaurant .... (see 17)
27 Lung Ta C4
28 McLlo Restaurant A2
29 Moonpeak B4
Namgyal Cafe .... (see 23)
Nick's Italian Kitchen .... (see 21)
30 Shangrila Vegetarian Restaurant B2
31 Snow Lion Restaurant B2
32 Tibet Kitchen A2

Shopping
33 Bookworm B3
34 Green Shop B2
35 Pick & Speak Mobile Shop C4
36 Tibetan Handicraft Center B3

Information
37 Branch Security Office B2
38 Dr Yeshi Dhonden B3
39 Men-Tsee-Khang Therapy Centre B2

➡ Kora Circuit
(Map p322) Most Tibetan pilgrims make a clockwise *kora* (ritual circuit) around the outside of the Tsuglagkhang Complex. To join them, take the downhill road to the left at the complex's entrance then follow the prayer-flag-draped path off to the right after 150m.

St John in the Wilderness CHURCH
(Map p320; 9am-5pm) Amid tall cedars 1.5km west of McLeod on the road to Forsyth Ganj, this brooding Gothic church (dating from 1852) is one of the few remaining traces of McLeod's days as a British hill station. The cemetery contains the graves of many victims of the 1905 earthquake, as well as the rocket-like tomb of the Earl of Elgin, the second Viceroy of India.

Tibetan Children's Village SCHOOL
(Map p320; 01892-221348; www.tcv.org.in; office 9am-12.30pm & 1.30-5pm Mon-Fri) Just a short hop from the underwhelming Dal Lake, 3km northwest of McLeod, the Tibetan Children's Village provides free education for nearly 2000 refugee children and lodging for most of them. Founded in the 1960s, it's now one of 12 such schools around India. Visitors are welcome.

★ Central Tibetan Secretariat MUSEUM
(Map p320; Gangchen Kyishong) Inside the government-in-exile compound, nearly 2km downhill from the Tsuglagkhang Complex, the **Library of Tibetan Works & Archives** (Map p320; 9218422467; www.ltwa.net; 9am-1pm & 2-5pm Mon-Sat, closed 2nd & 4th Sat of the month) began life as a collection of sacred manuscripts saved from the Cultural Revolution. Today it has more than 120,000 manuscripts and books in Tibetan, and more than 15,000 books on Tibet, Buddhism and the Himalayan region in English and other languages.

Upstairs is a fascinating **cultural museum** (Map p320; ₹20) with statues, old Tibetan artefacts and books, and some astonishing three-dimensional mandalas in wood and sand.

➡ Nechung Gompa
(Map p320) Worth a look if you're in the Central Tibetan Secretariat complex, the colourful Nechung Gompa is seat of the Tibetan state oracle. If you should want to consult the oracle, a monk named Thupten Ngodup,

MEETING THE DALAI LAMA

Meeting the Dalai Lama is a lifelong dream for many travellers and certainly for Buddhists, but private audiences are rarely granted. Put simply, the Dalai Lama is too busy with spiritual duties to meet everyone who comes to Dharamsala. Tibetan refugees are automatically guaranteed an audience, but travellers must make do with the occasional public teachings held at the Tsuglagkhang (p321), normally in September or October and after Losar (Tibetan New Year) in February or March, and on other occasions depending on his schedule. For schedules and just about everything you need to know about His Holiness, visit www.dalailama.com. To attend a teaching, register with your passport at the **Branch Security Office** (Map p322; ☎221560; Bhagsu Rd, McLeod Ganj; ⏲9am-1pm & 2-5pm Mon-Fri & 1st Sat of the month) in the days leading up to the teaching (if you don't manage this, registration is usually also possible in the early morning at the temple before the teaching starts). To get the most out of the teachings bring a cushion and an FM radio with headset (around ₹450 in local shops) for simultaneous translation.

ask in the office here for an appointment with the oracle's secretary.

★Men-Tsee-Khang BUDDHIST SITE

(Tibetan Medical & Astrological Institute; Map p320; ☎01892-223113; www.men-tsee-khang.org; Gangchen Kyishong; ⏲9am-1pm & 2-5pm Mon-Sat, closed 2nd & 4th Sat of the month) Established to preserve the traditional arts of Tibetan medicine and astrology, Men-Tsee-Khang is a college, clinic, museum, research centre and astrological institute rolled into one. The astrological folk can do a 45-minute oral consultation (₹2000; register in person half a day ahead with your birth date, time and place), or a detailed life-horoscope online, which you'll receive by email and a hard copy within four months (US$85 plus US$20 taxes).

The **Men-Tsee-Khang Museum** (Map p320; ₹20; ⏲9am-1pm & 2-5pm Mon-Sat, closed 2nd & 4th Sat) has three floors of fascinating displays on the sophisticated sciences of Tibetan astrology and medicine, told via illustrative *thangkas* as well as samples of medicines, their plant and mineral sources, and instruments that have been used for some treatments – such as a brass hammer for treating tumours, insanity and body ache. Learn useful facts: cinnamon wards against flatulence; cumin and coriander combat anorexia; gold helps longevity.

Men-Tsee-Khang also runs occasional short courses on the basics of Tibetan medicine.

Yoga, Ayurveda & Massage

McLeod Ganj and neighbouring Dharamkot and Bhagsu (p331) have dozens of practitioners of holistic and alternative therapies, some reputable and some making a fast buck at the expense of gullible travellers. Talking to friends and other travellers is the best way to find good practitioners.

Holistic Centre of Ayurveda MASSAGE

(Map p322; ☎9418493871; holisticmassage16@gmail.com; Ladies Venture Hotel, Jogiwara Rd; 1hr ₹800-1000; ⏲10.30am-7pm) Resident masseur Shami is very popular, so book a day or two ahead. He offers relaxation, ayurvedic and deep-tissue massages, and can attend to your head, back, face, feet or whole body.

Universal Yoga Centre YOGA

(Map p322; ☎9882222011; www.vijaypoweryoga.com; Youngling School, Jogiwara Rd; 1½hr class ₹200-400; ⏲Apr-Sep) Gets good reports for daily drop-in classes in a variety of techniques at all levels; also does teacher-training courses.

Trekking

It's possible to trek to the Chamba or Kullu Valleys and even Lahaul, and several agencies in McLeod and in Dharamkot or Bhagsu (p329) can make the necessary arrangements for camping, guides and porters or pack animals. Apart from the demanding Indrahar La trek (p330) to the Chamba Valley, the most popular option is the easy three- to five-day loop to Kareri Lake. Guided treks with food, camping and porter(s) can cost anywhere from ₹1500 to ₹3000 per person per day: be sure to check exactly what's being provided for your money – items such as food and any necessary return transport for the workers may not be included in the initial price.

High Point Adventure TREKKING (Map p322; ☎9816120145; highpointadventure@gmail.com; Kareri Lodge, Hotel Bhagsu Rd) This place has an experienced, knowledgeable team offering some of the best prices in town. It also has an **office** (Map p322; ⏲9am-6pm) on Temple Rd.

Volunteering

McLeod Ganj has more volunteering opportunities than almost anywhere else in India, mostly geared to supporting the Tibetan community in one way or another. Some language conversation classes welcome drop-in participants. For other opportunities it's ideal to make contact a couple of weeks in advance. Many volunteer opportunities are publicised in the free magazine, *Contact* (www.contactmagazine.net). Travellers should always investigate any volunteer opportunity themselves to assess the standards and suitability of the project. Experts recommend that volunteering should be at least a three-month commitment. Lonely Planet cannot vouch for any organisation that we do not work with directly.

Volunteers generally arrange their own accommodation and meals, though Lha offers homestays with Tibetan families (US$20 per day including breakfast and dinner, minimum one week).

The following organisations are among those that offer, or can provide information on, volunteer opportunities.

Lha (Map p322; ☎9882323453; www.lhasocialwork.org; Temple Rd; ⏲office 9am-1pm & 2-5pm Mon-Fri, 9-11am 1st & 3rd Sat) This NGO arranges placements at a host of community projects, including for teachers of English and other languages, fundraisers, and healthcare or IT professionals. Minimum periods range from one week to two months. Anyone can participate in English conversation classes with refugees at the office from 4pm to 5pm Monday to Friday.

Learning & Ideas for Tibet (Map p322; ☎9882439815; http://learningandideasfortibet.blogspot.com; Jogiwara Rd; ⏲9am-5pm Mon-Fri) Gives free classes for Tibetan refugees and has a variety of volunteer positions teaching English, French, German, Mandarin or Japanese, and computing skills for beginners. Volunteers can drop in to the 2pm English conversation classes (1½ hours). The office is down the steps leading to Seed Cafe and Pawan Guest House.

Tibet World (Map p322; ☎9816999928; http://tibetworld.org; Jogiwara Rd; ⏲office 9am-5pm Mon-Fri) Has some 600 refugee students each year and uses volunteers for a variety of jobs including teaching English, German, French and Mandarin, preferably for one month minimum. Its yoga classes are also taught by volunteers. It runs drop-in conversation classes in English at 11am and 4pm, and in French and Mandarin at 4pm.

TIBETAN EXILES

In October 1950, about a year after Mao Zedong declared the founding of the People's Republic of China, Chinese troops invaded Tibet. At the time, Tibet was a de facto independent state led by the Dalai Lama, with a hazy, complicated relationship with China. A year later, in October 1951, Lhasa, the Tibetan capital, fell. Resistance simmered for years in the countryside, and protests against the Chinese occupation broke out in Lhasa in 1959. As the Chinese army moved against the uprising, it fired upon the Norbulingka, the Dalai Lama's summer palace. Believing his life or his freedom was at risk, the Dalai Lama fled across the Himalayas to India, where he received asylum.

China says its army was sent to Tibet as liberators, to free Tibetans from feudal serfdom and improve life on the vast high plateau. It hasn't worked out that way. While the sometimes-quoted figure of 1.2 million Tibetans killed since 1950 is seriously disputed, no independent observers question the suffering and human-rights abuses, as well as huge losses to Tibet's cultural legacy, that have occurred under Chinese occupation. Many Tibetans still risk the dangerous crossing into India. Today there are 100,000 or more Tibetans in India, including those born here. Many new arrivals come first to the Dharamsala area, where they find support from their community (more than 10,000 strong), their government-in-exile and a legion of NGOs. There are also large Tibetan communities in Karnataka state, where several settlements have been set up since the 1960s.

Courses

The most established and best reputed schools of yoga and meditation are mainly found in Dharamkot and Bhagsu (p331). The Library of Tibetan Works & Archives conducts serious **Buddhist philosophy courses** (Map p320; ☎9218422467; www.ltwa.net; Library of Tibetan Works & Archives, Central Tibetan Secretariat; per month ₹300, registration ₹50; ⏰classes 9am & 10.30am Mon-Sat) in English lasting from 1½ to four months (1¼ hours daily), plus monthly five-day evening courses (one hour per day), sometimes in Tibetan, sometimes in English.

The Library also runs 4½-month **Tibetan language and speaking courses** (Map p320; per month ₹500, registration ₹50) for beginner, intermediate and experienced students, starting around 1 March and 1 August (five hours a week). Students can join the basic course at any time.

Lhamo's Kitchen COOKING
(Map p322; ☎9816468719; lhamoskitchen@gmail.com; Bhagsu Rd; 2hr class ₹300; ⏰10am-noon & 5-7pm) Recommended courses in vegetarian Tibetan cooking. Each day focuses on *momos*, soups or breads, with two or three types of each.

A minimum of two people is required, and you should register at least five hours in advance.

Sangye's Kitchen COOKING
(Map p322; ☎9816164540; Jogiwara Rd; classes ₹250; ⏰10am-noon & 4-6pm Thu-Tue) Tibetan treats, focusing on *momos* (including chocolate *momos!*) every Sunday and Thursday, and noodles on Tuesday and Saturday.

Festivals & Events

In late January, February or early March, McLeod celebrates **Losar** (Tibetan New Year) with processions and masked dances at local monasteries. The Dalai Lama often gives public teachings at this time.

The **Tibetan Opera Festival** (⏰Mar/Apr), held most years at the Tibetan Institute of Performing Arts (p328), sees 12 performances on successive days by different groups from India and Nepal, each lasting seven or eight hours.

Several film festivals liven up McLeod's autumn. The **Free Spirit Film Festival** (www.freespiritfilmfestival.com; ⏰late Oct) and **Dharamsala International Film Festival** (http://diff.co.in; ⏰late Oct/early Nov) screen eclectic selections of independent features, documentaries and shorts, while the **Tibet Film Festival** (http://tibetfilmfestival.org; ⏰Sep or Oct) spotlights films made by Tibetans.

Sleeping

Popular places fill up quickly; advance bookings are advisable, especially from April to June and in October.

Kunga Guesthouse GUESTHOUSE $
(Map p322; ☎9857421180; www.kungaguesthouse.com; Bhagsu Rd; r ₹400-1500; 📶) Above (and below) Nick's Italian Kitchen (p327), which is its greatest asset, Kunga offers a huge range of dull but clean rooms in sever-

TIBETAN MEDICINE

Traditional Tibetan medicine is a centuries-old holistic healing practice and a popular treatment for all kinds of minor and persistent ailments. Its methods include massages, compresses, bath and steam therapies, pills made from plants and minerals, and diet and lifestyle advice. There are several clinics around town, including the **Men-Tsee-Khang Therapy Centre** (Map p322; ☎01892-221484; www.men-tsee-khang.org; TIPA Rd; ⏰9am-1pm & 2-5pm Mon-Sat, closed 2nd & 4th Sat of the month), run by the Tibetan Medical & Astrological Institute.

The most popular *amchi* (Tibetan doctor) in town is the former physician to the Dalai Lama, **Dr Yeshi Dhonden** (Map p322; ☎01892-221461; Ashoka Niwas; ⏰9am-1pm Sun-Fri), whose tiny clinic is squirrelled away in a passage off Jogiwara Rd. The fantastic reputation of his holistic treatments brings him many cancer patients, among others. On an appointed day every month or two, from 8am, tokens for consultations are given out to all who queue up outside the nearby Ashoka Guest House. Dr Yeshi sees 45 patients a day, six days a week, but he's in such demand that two months' supply of tokens may be given out on a single day. At the actual consultation, patients must bring a sample of urine, which, along with a quick examination, is all the doctor needs to prescribe the appropriate herbal pills.

al buildings, and has a helpful travel-booking service. The cheapest rooms share bathrooms.

Om Hotel HOTEL $
(Map p322; ☎9816329985; Nowrojee Rd; r ₹550-650, without bathroom ₹300-350; 📶) Friendly, family-run Om, down a lane from the main square, has simple but pleasing rooms with good views, and its terrace catches the sunset over the valley. No reservations are taken so try to go in the morning for a room.

The popular **Namgyal Cafe** (Map p322; mains ₹90-350; ⏰9.30am-10pm) here serves well-laden if chewy pizzas, plus decently prepared tofu and potato dishes, soups and more

Loseling Guest House GUESTHOUSE $
(Map p322; ☎9218923305; off Jogiwara Rd; d ₹350-500; 📶) In an alley off Jogiwara Rd, Loseling is run by a Tibetan monastery in Karnataka. It's a good cheapie and all rooms have a hot shower; the three rooftop rooms are easily the best.

Hotel Mount View HOTEL $
(Map p322; ☎9816261717; mountmagic786@yahoo.co.in; Jogiwara Rd; r ₹500-1200; 📶) A no-frills but well-run budget hotel down busy Jogiwara Rd, Mount View has a travel desk and rooftop cafe as well as a range of rooms, all with attached bath. Look at a few as they vary in view, size, light and airiness.

Seven Hills Guest House GUESTHOUSE $
(Map p322; ☎9736597593; TIPA Rd; d ₹450-600, s without bathroom ₹250; @📶) A smallish guesthouse with a big sunny terrace, Seven Hills offers clean rooms and a cafe in a convenient location on TIPA Rd.

Green Hotel HOTEL $$
(Map p322; ☎01892-221479; www.greenhotel.in; Bhagsu Rd; r ₹800-2500; ❄📶) A favourite with midrange travellers and small groups, the Green has a diverse range of sunny, super-clean rooms in three buildings, most with balconies and valley and mountain views. It's very well run by the ever-cheerful Choekyi and has an excellent cafe.

Hotel Tibet HOTEL $$
(Map p322; ☎01892-221587; hoteltibetdasa@yahoo.com; Bhagsu Rd; r ₹1190-2380; 📶) Bang in the centre of town, this well-run place has a faintly upmarket feel, but reasonable prices. Rooms have parquet floors and there's a cosy multicuisine licensed restaurant and a useful in-house travel office.

Kareri Lodge HOTEL $$
(Map p322; ☎01892-221132; karerilodge@gmail.com; Hotel Bhagsu Rd; r ₹770-2120; 📶) Kareri, squeezed in among a string of mostly more upmarket hotels, has five spotless and comfy rooms with soft beds, four of them enjoying great long-distance views from huge windows. There's a good vibe here, helped by the friendly manager who offers a reliable trekking service.

★**Chonor House** BOUTIQUE HOTEL $$$
(Map p322; ☎9882976879; www.norbulingka.org; off Temple Rd; r ₹5360-7860; ❄@📶) Up a lane near the Tsuglagkhang, Chonor House is a real gem. It's run by the Norbulingka Institute (p333), and is decked out with wonderful handmade Norbulingka furnishings and fabrics. Each of the 18 bright and sunny rooms has a Tibetan theme that runs from the carpets to the bedspreads to the murals. Even the cheapest rooms are spacious.

★**Serkong House** HOTEL $$$
(Map p322; ☎9857957131; www.norbulingka.org; Nowrojee Rd; s ₹2740-4110, d ₹3430-4790, ste s/d ₹5480/6160; 📶) Belonging to the Norbulingka Institute, the Serkong is tasteful, comfortable and well run. Spacious rooms boast Tibetan rugs and Norbulingka-made tables, and the more expensive ones have fine views. Staff are polite and efficient, and the good Tibetan-Indian-Continental restaurant (mains ₹150 to ₹240) eschews white flour and MSG.

Eating & Drinking

McLeod Ganj is crammed with traveller restaurants serving pretty similar menus – omelettes, pancakes, Indian, Tibetan and Chinese staples, pizzas, pasta and assorted other European food. Happily, many of them do a pretty good job. McLeod also has some of North India's best cafes, with good coffee and English-style tea. For a quick snack, Tibetans sell veg *momos* on the upper part of Jogiwara Rd and outside the entrance to the Tsuglagkhang.

Nick's Italian Kitchen ITALIAN $
(Map p322; Bhagsu Rd; mains ₹80-190; ⏰7am-9pm; 📶) Unpretentious, well-run Nick's has been serving up tasty vegetarian pizzas, lasagne, ravioli, gnocchi and quiches for years. Follow up a ground coffee with one of their desserts – apple pie or a heavenly slice of lemon cheesecake.

Shangrila Vegetarian Restaurant TIBETAN, INDIAN $
(Map p322; Jogiwara Rd; mains ₹70-90; ⌚7.30am-8.30pm; 📶) Shangrila is run by monks of the Gyudmed monastery, some of whom wait on tables and help to engender a notably friendly atmosphere. It serves up tasty, well-priced Tibetan staples including *momos* in soup and *baglebs* (large fried *momos*).

Snow Lion Restaurant MULTICUISINE $
(Map p322; Jogiwara Rd; mains ₹80-150, breakfasts ₹160-195; ⌚7am-9pm; 📶) Especially popular for its good-value set breakfasts and decent coffee, the Snow Lion does good *momos* and *thukpa* too, and has comfy seating and shelves of books.

★**Moonpeak** MULTICUISINE $$
(Map p322; www.moonpeak.org; Temple Rd; mains ₹150-300; ⌚7am-9pm; 📶) A little chunk of Seattle, transported to India. Come for excellent coffee, breakfasts, cakes, imaginative brown-bread open sandwiches (try the poached chicken with mango, lime and coriander sauce), soups, salads and plenty of well-prepared veg and nonveg main dishes.

It's also a gallery and has a great laid-back bluesy taste in music.

Green Hotel Restaurant MULTICUISINE $$
(Map p322; Bhagsu Rd; mains ₹110-180; ⌚6.30am-9.30pm; 📶) This traveller-oriented hotel restaurant, with a sunny terrace and comfy couches inside, serves very good vegetarian food and the earliest breakfasts in town.

Common Ground Cafe ASIAN $$
(Map p322; www.facebook.com/commongroundcafe09; Dharamkot Rd; mains ₹80-230; ⌚9am-9pm; 📶) The menu is a sizzling variety of Chinese and Tibetan speciality dishes, from Taiwan-style tofu to *sha tag* (a rich meat-and-veg stir-fry), available without MSG if you like, plus all-day Western-type breakfasts. The coffee's good, too. The atmosphere is pleasingly laid-back and sociable, with shared tables and floor cushions.

Tibet Kitchen TIBETAN $$
(Map p322; Jogiwara Rd; mains ₹120-300; ⌚noon-9.30pm) It's worth queueing here to try the spicy Bhutanese food including *kewa datse* (potatoes, beans and chilli in cheese sauce) and unusual Tibetan dishes including *shapta* (roasted lamb slices with capsicum and onion). The *momos* are good too, and there are also Thai and Chinese flavours. Its three floors of tables are often full of travellers, monks and locals.

Lung Ta JAPANESE $$
(Map p322; Jogiwara Rd; set meals ₹200; ⌚noon-8.30pm Mon-Sat) The daily set menus are the best choice at this popular, vegetarian Japanese restaurant, especially on Tuesdays and Fridays when they include sushi rolls and miso soup. The food and ambience are authentic enough to attract Japanese travellers looking for a taste of home. Profits go to the NGO Gu-Chu-Sum.

McLlo Restaurant MULTICUISINE $$
(Map p322; Main Sq; mains ₹200-400; ⌚9.30am-11.30pm) Crowded nightly and justifiably popular, this large, four-floor place serves a mind-boggling menu of Indian, Chinese and international fare, including pizzas and pasta. The semi-open-air top floor is one of McLeod's best places to enjoy a cold beer (₹220-plus).

☆ Entertainment

Irregular live-music nights or jam sessions are advertised around town. The **Tibetan Institute of Performing Arts** (TIPA; Map p320; ☎9418087998; http://tipa.asia; TIPA Rd; ⌚9am-5pm Mon-Sat, closed 2nd & 4th Sat of the month) stages irregular cultural performances, including a 1½-hour show of folk and ritual dance and song, Dances from the Roof of the World, and concerts by the electric folk fusion group Aa Ka Ma. Check its Facebook page or website for upcoming events. Tibet World (p325) puts on a Tibetan folk show at 6.30pm on Thursdays (₹200) and shows documentary films (free) at 4pm on Saturdays.

Shopping

Dozens of shops and stalls sell Tibetan artefacts, including *thangkas*, bronze statues, metal prayer wheels, turquoise necklaces, yak-wool shawls and 'singing' bowls. Some are Tibetan-run, but others are run by Kashmiri traders who apply a degree of sales pressure. Several local cooperatives offer the same goods without the hassle. And – book lovers rejoice! – McLeod undoubtedly has the highest bookshop-to-population ratio in India.

Tibetan Handicraft Center ARTS & CRAFTS
(Map p322; ☎01892-221415; www.tibetanhandicrafts.com; Jogiwara Rd; ⌚9am-5pm Mon-Sat) This cooperative employs refugees

for the weaving of Tibetan carpets. You'll pay around ₹13,500 for a 0.9m by 1.8m traditional wool carpet, and they'll ship it if you like (₹2500 to ₹3500 to Europe, ₹4500 to the USA). Visitors are welcome to watch the weavers in action. There's also a shop with other attractive goods, including quality *thangkas* (₹20,000-plus).

Bookworm BOOKS
(Map p322; ☎01892-221465; Hotel Bhagsu Rd; ⏰9am-7pm Tue-Sun) McLeod's best all-round bookshop.

Green Shop ARTS & CRAFTS
(Map p322; Bhagsu Rd; ⏰9.30am-7pm Mon-Sat) Sells appealing handmade, recycled paper products, organic peanut butter, tahini and more.

Information

Contact (www.contactmagazine.net) is an informative, free local magazine with useful information about courses and volunteer work. Available online and in paper form at several cafes, restaurants and hotels in McLeod Ganj.

Delek Hospital (Map p320; ☎01892-222053; www.delekhospital.org/delek; Gangchen Kyishong; consultations before/after noon ₹10/50; ⏰outpatient clinic 9am-1pm & 2-5pm Mon-Fri & 1st Sat of the month, 9am-1pm 3rd, 4th & 5th Sat of the month) A small, Tibetan-run hospital practising allopathic medicine, with a 24-hour emergency service.

Pick & Speak Mobile Shop (Map p322; Jogiwara Rd; ⏰8.30am-8.30pm) Sells SIM cards for ₹200 (not including data or calls). Bring your phone and passport.

Thomas Cook (Map p322; Temple Rd; ⏰9.30am-6.30pm Mon-Sat) Changes cash and travellers cheques with 0.15% tax (minimum ₹35) and a ₹50 transaction fee, and gives advances on credit cards for a 3% charge.

Getting There & Around

Many travel agencies in McLeod will book train tickets for a commission of ₹100.

AIR

Dharamsala airport (p319) has flights to/from Delhi.

AUTORICKSHAW

The **autorickshaw stand** (Map p322) is just north of the main square. Fares are around ₹60 to Bhagsu and ₹70 to Dharamkot.

BUS

Buses start from and arrive at the **New Bus Stand** (Map p322), 150m north of the main square. Buses and overcrowded jeeps to Dharamsala (both ₹15, 35 minutes) run about every 15 to 30 minutes from 4am to 8pm.

Some long-distance buses start from McLeod, but there are more frequent departures from Dharamsala bus station. You can book government (HRTC) buses from both places at McLeod's **HRTC ticket office** (Map p322; Main Sq; ⏰9am-7pm). In addition, travel agencies sell seats on private buses to Delhi (₹900 to ₹1100, 12 hours, 6pm to 7pm), Manali (₹400 to ₹600, 11 hours, 8.30pm and 9.30pm), Amritsar (₹600, seven hours, morning and evening) and elsewhere.

TAXI

McLeod's **taxi stand** (Map p322; ☎01892-221034; Mall Rd) is just north of the main square. A taxi for the day, travelling less than 80km, should cost ₹1600. One-way fares include ₹100 to Gangchen Kyishong, Dharamkot or Bhagsu, ₹200 to Dharamsala bus station, ₹800 to Dharamsala airport, ₹4000 to Chamba and ₹4500 to Manali.

Around McLeod Ganj

Bhagsu & Dharamkot

☎01892

Through pine trees north and east of McLeod lie the villages of Bhagsu (officially Bhagsunag) and Dharamkot, more rural and laid-back and alternative than McLeod itself. These are the abodes of choice for many budget travellers and long-stayers, and especially popular among Israelis. Here

HRTC BUSES FROM MCLEOD GANJ

DESTINATION	FARE (₹)	DURATION (HR)	DEPARTURES
Dehra Dun	550-1080	12	3 daily
Delhi	580-1275	12-13	4am, 6pm & 7.30pm (ordinary); 5pm (semi-deluxe); 6.30pm & 7.45pm (deluxe); 5.30pm & 7pm (Volvo AC)
Manali	400	11	4.30pm
Pathankot	150	4	5 daily

you can take classes in tarot, Reiki, numerology, crystal healing and varieties of yoga you've never heard of, do sitar, tabla or flute lessons, get or learn to give a dozen types of massage, have your hair dreadlocked, dyed or extended, or just lounge in cafes and practise your juggling. Some of the area's best and most serious yoga and meditation schools are here too.

Sights

Dharamkot retains a quiet village vibe, with the scattered houses of upper Dharamkot stretching almost to the little Gallu Devi Temple on the ridge above. Lower Bhagsu, in contrast, is busy with concrete hotels, shops and discos aimed squarely at domestic visitors. But two minutes up from the main road in Bhagsu you're back in backpackerland: upper Bhagsu is very similar to upper Dharamkot, with which it effectively merges. Lower Bhagsu's small, 16th-century **Shiva temple** (Map p320) has a cold, clean, spring-fed swimming pool in front of it, and from there it's a 1km walk to **Bhagsu waterfall** (Map p320), most impressive during the monsoon. En route to upper Bhagsu, 200m up from the main road, drop into the awesomely kitsch **Vashnu Mata Temple** (Map p320), where you access the inner grotto through a concrete lion's mouth and emerge via the jaws of a crocodile.

Activities

Terrestrial Adventures TREKKING
(Map p320; 9418656758, 9882858628; kcnehria@yahoo.com; Main Sq, Bhagsu; 8am-7pm) An experienced and well-reputed firm offering a range of serious treks including the Indrahar and Minkiani Pass routes to the Chamba Valley, routes to the Kullu Valley, and a 10-day trek to the Pattan Valley over both the Dhauladhar and Pir Panjal ranges. Indrahar treks cost around ₹3000 per person per day.

Gallu Devi & Triund Hikes

To reach the little Gallu Devi temple, on the ridge above Dharamkot, head along the left side of the water tank opposite Dharamkot's **Himalayan Tea Shop** (Map p320; items ₹30-80; 6am-8.30pm), and after 50m turn up a path to the right. This lovely trail winds up through the forest to emerge on a jeep track after 1km: go 500m to the right to reach Gallu Devi.

Alternatively you can walk straight up from the top of Dharamkot in 20 or 30 minutes. A couple of cafes and guesthouses are set on the panoramic ridge where the little temple stands. From here, one track leads gently west downhill to Naddi village (2.5km) and Dal Lake (3km), with the Tibetan Children's Village (p323) nearby; another heads about 2km north down to a waterfall; and the main track climbs east through rho-

INDRAHAR LA TREK

This popular four- or five-day route crosses the Indrahar La (4420m) to the Chamba Valley, and can be done in either direction. The pass is normally open from June to early November, but the best months are September and October.

The first day climbs three or four hours to the mountain meadow of Triund, where you can camp and which also has a couple of basic guesthouses, plus *dhabas* that will rent you a sleeping bag and/or tent. The next stage climbs to the alpine meadow of Laka Got (3350m) and then the rocky shelter known as Lahesh Cave (3600m). With an early start the next day, you can cross the Indrahar La – and be rewarded for the tough climb with astounding views – before descending steeply to the meadow campground at Chata Parao.

The track on down to Kuarsi, crossing summer meadows, can be tricky to find in places. On the final day you reach a road at Hilling, about 5km before Lamu. It's 3km to 5km (depending on short cuts) down from Lamu to Holi-Kharamukh-Chamba road, plied by several buses a day (a couple of these come up to Lamu or Hilling). To reach Bharmour, take a bus as far as Kharamukh and change there.

STAGE	ROUTE	DURATION (HR)	DISTANCE (KM)
1	McLeod Ganj to Triund	3-4	9
2	Triund to Lahesh Cave	3-4	8
3	Lahesh Cave to Chata Parao over Indrahar La	6	10
4	Chata Parao to Kuarsi	5-6	15
5	Kuarsi to Lamu	4	10

dodendron woods towards the panoramic mountain meadow of Triund (2900m) – a beautiful walk that gains 800m altitude in a fairly strenuous 2½ to three hours. You pass a couple of tea shops, and Triund has a few *dhabas* offering simple meals, tents, sleeping bags and beds. An overnight stop gives you the best chance of clear weather, and time to hike one hour up to the teashop and viewpoint at Laka Got meadow (3350m), sometimes called 'Snowline', before heading back down – or continuing upward if you're on the Indrahar La trek.

Courses

Dharamkot and Bhagsu have many of the area's best options for learning yoga, meditation, Buddhist philosophy and ayurveda. Some places have strict rules on silence, alcohol and smoking.

Tushita Meditation Centre MEDITATION, PHILOSOPHY
(Map p320; http://tushita.info; Dharamkot; 10-day course incl accommodation & meals from ₹6000; Feb-Nov) Tushita conducts 10-day 'Introduction to Buddhism' silent retreat courses and drop-in meditation sessions at 9.30am daily, except Sunday.

Himalayan Iyengar Yoga Centre YOGA
(Map p320; www.hiyogacentre.com; TIPA Rd, Dharamkot; 5-day course SAARC citizens/others ₹3200/4000, advance booking fee ₹1000; Mar-Oct) Five-day courses introducing the Iyengar method start every Monday in the large purpose-built hall here amid green surroundings.

Intensive and teacher-training courses and therapy take place at the ashram west of McLeod.

Ayuskama Ayurvedic Clinic AYURVEDA
(Map p320; 9736211210; www.ayuskama.com; Hotel Anand Palace Bldg, Bhagsu; 9am-5pm) Dr Arun Sharma's ayurvedic treatments and courses get rave reviews. Courses range from a week on massage or nutrition (₹6500 to ₹7500) to three-month diploma courses (₹65,000) and practitioner courses of up to two years.

Sleeping & Eating

Both villages have plenty of inexpensive guesthouses (many unsigned). Long-stayers can get rooms in small family-run places for around ₹6000 a month, often with kitchen use too.

Trimurti Garden Cafe GUESTHOUSE $
(Map p320; 9816869144; www.trimurtigarden.in; Lower Dharamkot; r ₹600, s/d without bathroom ₹300/400;) Friendly, secluded Trimurti has eight neat, spotless rooms centred on a lovely green garden. The cafe, open to all (8am to 9pm), serves excellent homemade food from muesli to salads to cakes to vegetarian thali. You can learn tabla, flute, sitar or vocals from Ashoka, the father of the family, and two friendly dogs enhance the homey atmosphere.

The rooms are booked out from April to June and mid-September to mid-October for popular yoga teacher-training courses (www.trimurtiyoga.com).

Raj Residency GUESTHOUSE $
(Map p320; 9736129703, 9418607040; Upper Dharamkot; r ₹700-1000;) There are fine views from this two-storey stone house and its wide front lawn towards the top of Dharamkot, and the eight rooms are spacious and clean, with some arty bathroom tiling. Breakfast is available. It's popular for stays of two to three weeks or more.

Valley View GUESTHOUSE $
(Map p320; 9418054693; Dharamkot; s/d ₹500/600;) There's no sign but it's easy to find this four-storey building behind Himachal Trekkers as you walk up through Dharamkot. It has plenty of no-frills but adequately clean rooms and a sociable atmosphere.

Cool Talk Cafe MULTICUISINE $
(Map p320; 9736365156; Dharamkot; dishes ₹90-200; 9am-9pm) A neat, clean little place up a quiet lane above Dharamkot's main street, with cushion or chair seating and well-done dishes ranging from Indian staples to *momos*, hummus, baba ganoush or toasted sandwiches, and teas, coffees, juices or lassi to drink. It also has two bright rooms (₹800) with sunny balconies.

Space Out MULTICUISINE $$
(Map p320; Dharamkot; mains ₹160-190; 8.30am-11pm) Polish-run Space Out is a space to relax on floor cushions beneath mural-daubed walls and enjoy good couscous, Thai curries, pasta, vegie burgers or whatever else is chalked up on the board.

Kangra

01892 / POP 9500 / ELEV 734M

Once capital of the princely state of Kangra, this bustling town 18km from Dharamsala is a good day trip from McLeod Ganj, with a dramatic fort and important Hindu temple. You can combine Kangra with the impressive 10th-century temples at Masrur, 40km west.

Sights

Kangra Fort FORT

(www.royalkangra.com; Indian/foreigner ₹15/200, audio guide ₹100/200; ⌚ dawn-dusk) The impregnable-looking Kangra Fort, at least 1000 years old, soars on a high promontory of land between the Manjhi and Banganga Rivers. Head up through a series of gates and passages to the palace area at the top for views north to the mountains and south to the plains.

The fort is at the south end of town, a ₹100 autorickshaw ride from the bus stand. It was occupied by Hindu rajas, Mughal and Sikh conquerors and even the British (from 1846), before it was finally toppled by the 1905 Kangra earthquake.

Maharaja Sansar Chand Museum MUSEUM

(☎01892-265866; Indian/foreigner ₹30/100, audio guide ₹150/200; ⌚9am-5.30pm) About 200m up the road from Kangra Fort is the well-displayed Maharaja Sansar Chand Museum, whose ornate palanquins, peacock-feather fans and pashmina fly-whisks give fine insights into the lifestyle of the erstwhile Kangra royal family, the Katochs – a dynasty so ancient that early members fought against the Pandavas of the Mahabharata (or so a history panel tells us).

Brajeshwari Devi Temple HINDU TEMPLE

Hindus visit Kangra to pay homage at the Brajeshwari Devi Temple, one of the 51 *Shakti peeths*, famous temples marking the sites where body parts from Shiva's first wife, Sati, fell after the goddess was consumed by flames (the temple marks the final resting place of Sati's left breast).

KANGRA VALLEY TOY TRAIN

Lumbering narrow-gauge trains run east from Pathankot, providing a scenic if slow route to Kangra (five hours), Palampur (six hours), Baijnath (seven hours) and Jogindernagar (nine hours). Two trains go all the way to Jogindernagar; the other four only go as far as Baijnath. Fares are ₹35 or less to any destination, but carriages are generally packed and seats cannot be booked in advance. Board early to grab a window seat and enjoy the views.

It's reached through an atmospheric bazaar lined with shops selling *prasad* (religious food offerings) and religious trinkets, winding 10 minutes uphill from the main road 1km south of the bus stand.

Sleeping & Eating

Kangra hotels are mostly dreary. Easily best is **Hotel Grand Raj** (☎01892-260901; www.hotelgrandraj.com; Dharamshala Rd; d ₹2250-5820; ❄📶), opposite the bus station, though the cheapest rooms are small and can be stuffy and noisy. The **Royal Hotel** (☎01892-265013; royalhotel@rediffmail.com; opposite Civil Hospital; r without/with AC ₹900/1500; ❄), 800m further south along the main road, is a reasonable budget option offering neat, good-sized, tiled rooms with hot showers. Both these hotels have decent restaurants.

Getting There & Away

Buses run about every 30 minutes to Dharamsala (₹25, one hour), Palampur (₹55, 1½ hours) and Pathankot (₹130, three hours).

A return taxi from McLeod Ganj to Kangra Fort costs ₹1300, including waiting time.

Masrur

Winding roads through pleasant green hills lead 40km west from Kangra (or 31km southwest from Gaggal) to the impressive 10th-century **Masrur temples** (Indian/foreigner ₹15/200; ⌚dawn-dusk). Though badly damaged by the 1905 earthquake, the elaborately carved sandstone *sikharas* – very rare examples of rock-cut temples in northern India – bear a passing resemblance to the Hindu temples at Angkor Wat in Cambodia and to Ellora in Maharashtra. You can climb to the upper level for mountain views and the tank in front provides photogenic reflections.

The easiest way to get here is a taxi day trip (around ₹2500 from McLeod Ganj if combined with Kangra, or ₹2000 without Kangra). Alternatively you can reach Lunj (₹50, 1½ hours) from Dharamsala by bus, then take a Nagrota Surian–bound bus 4km southwest to the junction at Pir Bindli, then either walk the last 2.5km or wait for one of the hourly buses to the temples.

Dharamsala to Mandi

The scenery along the wide valley stretching southeast from Dharamsala is dramatic, with the Dhauladhar Range rising to the

NORBULINGKA INSTITUTE

The wonderful **Norbulingka Institute** (☎9418436410; www.norbulingka.org; local & Tibetan ₹20, tourist ₹50; ⏲9am-5.30pm), 6km southeast of Dharamsala, was established in 1988 to teach and preserve traditional Tibetan art forms and is a fascinating place to visit.You can watch artisans at work on woodcarving, metal statue–making, *thangka* painting and embroidery on free tours. Also set among the institute's delightful Japanese-influenced gardens are the **Deden Tsuglakhang temple**, with a 4m-high gilded Sakyamuni statue, and the **Losel Doll Museum** (local & Tibetan ₹5, tourist ₹20), which uses charming dioramas with dolls dressed in traditional costumes to illustrate aspects of traditional Tibetan culture. On Sundays and the second Saturday of each month, the workshops are closed but the rest of the complex is open.

The institute's shop sells some of the expensive but beautiful craftworks made here, including jewellery, painted boxes and embroidered clothes and cushions. Visitors can join one of the craft studios to do customised workshops, for any period, at ₹1500/2000 per half-day/day. Book at least two days ahead.

Peaceful and stylish **Norling House** (☎9816646423; www.norbulingka.org; r/ste ₹3690/5430; ❄📶), in the institute's gardens, offers comfortable rooms decked out with Buddhist murals and Norbulingka handicrafts, arranged around a sunny atrium. Vegetarian food, and good coffee, are available at **Hummingbird Cafe** (mains ₹150-200; ⏲7am-9pm; 📶).

To get here, catch a Palampur-bound bus from Dharamsala and get off at Sacred Heart School, Sidhpur (₹7, 15 minutes), from where it's a 1km gentle uphill walk (or ₹80 taxi ride). A taxi to/from McLeod Ganj costs ₹350.

north, and the valley sweeping away down towards the plains.

Palampur

☎01894 / POP 10,000 / ELEV 1260M

About 35km southeast of Dharamsala, Palampur is a bustling little market town surrounded by tea plantations and rice fields at the foot of the Dhauladhar range. You can visit tea factories and temples and hike in the hills just above the town.

Sights & Activities

There are good walks in and above the lush, green Bundla valley that reaches back into the hills north of town. **Vindhyavasini temple**, high on the east side of the valley, is a scenic walk of some 9km, gaining 500m altitude, about three hours from the 'Water Tank Point', 4km north of the centre (around ₹350 by taxi). A good hiking and sightseeing guide who knows the Palampur area and its hills well is **Atul Sharma** (☎9816272105; atulsharma2k@yahoo.co.in).

Vaidyanath Temple HINDU TEMPLE

(Baijnath) High above the Binwa River at Baijnath, 17km southeast of Palampur, this exquisitely carved 13th-century temple is sacred to Shiva in his incarnation as Vaidyanath, Lord of the Physicians. Buses between Palampur and Mandi stop at Baijnath bus station, almost opposite the temple.

Wah Tea Estate TEA ESTATE

(☎9418026354; www.wahtea.com; Deogran; ⏲9am-5pm Tue-Sun) FREE On the hour-long visits you walk through tea and herb gardens, tour the drying, rolling, heating and grading operations, and get the chance to taste the green and black teas. It's 7km south of Palampur, around ₹600 round trip by taxi.

Sleeping

The pick in town is **Norwood Green** (☎9736031300; www.norwoodgreen.in; Bundla Tea Estate, Lohna village; incl half-board r ₹8000-9000, cottage ₹32,000-36,000; 📶), with bright, sparkling clean four-room cottages (but individual rooms are usually only available Monday to Thursday nights). The area's most atmospheric and luxurious stay is **Taragarh Palace** (☎01894-242034, in Delhi 011-24692317; http://taragarh.com; r ₹7000-10,000; ❄📶🏊), 12km southeast along the Mandi road, formerly a palace of the royal family of Jammu and Kashmir. The **Tea Bud** (☎01894-231298; www.hptdc.gov.in; s ₹1520-2150, d ₹2030-2860; 📶) is an acceptable midranger.

Getting There & Away

From Palampur's bus station, 1km south of the centre, buses leave all day for Dharamsala (₹60, two hours) and Mandi (₹175, 3½ hours). Palampur is also a stop on the Pathankot–Jogindernagar railway.

Bir & Billing

The village of Bir (elevation: 1400m), 2km north of Hwy 154 between Palampur and Jogindernagar, is internationally famous as the base for some of the best paragliding in the world. The take-off point is at Billing, 14km up a winding road from Bir and 1000m higher. Bir-Billing hosts major competitive flying events most years in October or November. Experienced paragliders fly as far as Dharamsala, Mandi and Manali from here.

Bir is also a centre of the Tibetan exile community and home to several gompas (Tibetan Buddhist monasteries) founded since the 1960s, some of which attract foreigners for courses and retreats. There are at least three gompas in the village itself, and two of the biggest and most impressive gompas in India, **Sherabling Monastery** (www.palpung.org; Bhattu village) and the **Dzongsar Khyentse Chökyi Lodrö Institute** (http://khyentsefoundation.org/dzongsar-khyentse-chokyi-lodro-college; Chauntra), lie a few kilometres outside Bir. As a rule, the gompas welcome visitors and normally no special permission is needed to visit their main temples and open-air areas.

Bir Portal (http://birhp.com) has useful info.

Activities

Several agencies offer tandem **paragliding** flights of around 30 minutes for ₹1600 to ₹2500 (including transport), depending on the experience and quality of the pilot. A GoPro camera is ₹500 extra. October and November have the best flying conditions. The monsoon prevents flying from mid-July to mid-September.

Paragliding regulation in India is minimal: the best recommendation of who to fly with is word of mouth from others who have done it. One reputable operator is **Golden Eagle Paragliding** (☎9816577607; www.geparagliding.org). For training courses of three to six days, **PG-Gurukul** (www.paragliding.guru; Blue Umbrella Bldg) comes recommended. **Himalayan Sky Safaris** (www.himalayanskysafaris.com), run by top paragliders from the UK, provides guided paragliding tours for solo and tandem flyers.

As well as paragliding, the Bir-Billing area is good for walking, trekking and mountain biking.

Courses

Deer Park Institute ARTS, PHILOSOPHY

(☎01894-268508; www.deerpark.in; Tibetan Colony, Bir; course payment by donation, r without/with bathroom ₹400/600, dm ₹100; ⏲office 9am-noon & 2-6pm Mon-Sat) Deer Park attracts around 5000 students from dozens of countries each year to its courses and workshops ranging over Buddhist and Indian philosophy, arts including photography, writing and film-making, the Sanskrit, Pali, Tibetan and Chinese languages, and meditation retreats led by Buddhist masters. Courses are non-academic and experiential, lasting from two days to one month, and are open to all.

Sleeping & Eating

Several places to stay have restaurants. There is also a number of small restaurants, serving Tibetan or other food.

Chhokling Guest House GUESTHOUSE $

(☎8894112325; chodak_tenzin@yahoo.com; Tibetan Colony; r ₹600-1500; 📶) Well-kept, well-managed Chhokling Guesthouse is run by Chhokling Gompa across the street, the largest of the Tibetan monasteries in Bir itself. The guesthouse is open to all, with 16 clean rooms ranging from no-frills cheapies with hard beds to bright abodes with softer beds and big bathrooms.

★**Colonel's Resort** HOTEL $$

(Colonel's Retreat; ☎9882377469; www.colonelsresort.com; Chougan, Bir; incl breakfast standard s/d ₹2200/3300, deluxe r ₹4400, tent s/d ₹700/1200; 📶) The pick of the crop, Colonel's is set in spacious gardens and has options for several budgets, the spacious deluxe rooms being very comfortable by any standards, with big soft beds, large bathrooms with good toiletries, Tibetan rugs and well-made wooden furniture. Excellent, mainly Indian buffet dinners (₹450) are served and management is helpful with arrangements and activities.

Getting There & Away

Most buses between Palampur and Mandi will drop you at the Bir Road stop on Hwy 154, about 2.5km west of Chauntra. From there local buses (₹10) or taxis (₹100) will take you up to Bir. Taxis cost around ₹1500 to Mandi and ₹800 to Palampur.

Dalhousie

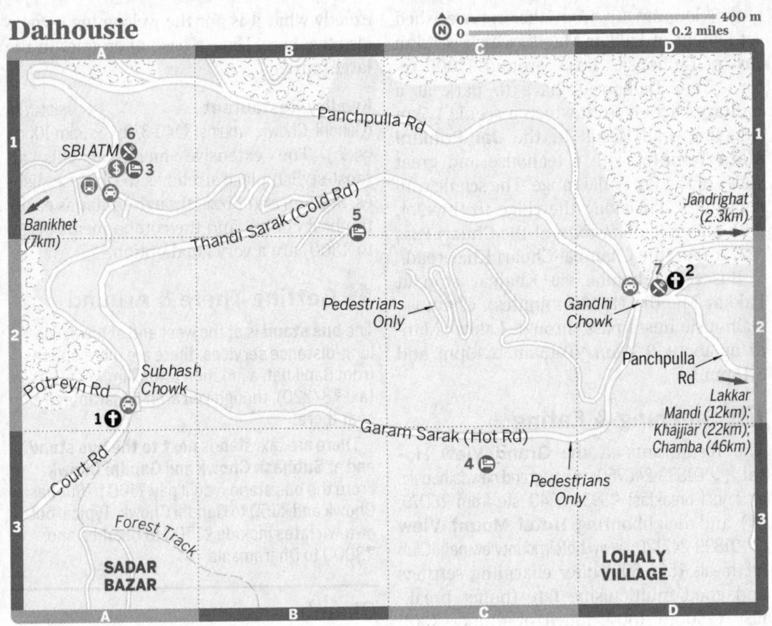

Dalhousie

Sights

1 St Francis Church A2
2 St John Church D2

Sleeping

3 Grand View Hotel A1
4 Hotel Monal C3
5 Silverton Estate Guest House B1

Eating

6 Hotel Mount View A1
7 Kwality Restaurant D2

Chamba Valley

The scenic Chamba Valley is a splendidly isolated valley system, separated from the Kangra Valley by the Dhauladhar Range and from Lahaul and Kashmir by the Pir Panjal. This area was ruled for centuries as the princely state of Chamba, one of the most ancient states in North India. It's great for temple buffs, trekkers and scenery addicts but well off most tourists' radars.

Dalhousie

☎01899 / POP 10,500 / ELEV 2050M

With its plunging pine-clad valleys and distant mountain views, Dalhousie is another of those cool hill retreats left behind by the British. Founded in the 1850s by the viceroy whose name it bears, its heyday came in the 1920s, '30s and '40s when Lahore society flocked here for its hols. Come Partition, Lahore found itself in Pakistan and Dalhousie has never been quite the same again. Today it survives as a relatively staid escape for honeymooners and families from the plains.

Sights

There's not a lot to see or do except stroll the tree-shaded lanes. Unusually for a hill station, there are few truly steep roads. The market areas at Subhash Chowk and Gandhi Chowk are linked by the lanes Thandi Sarak (Cold Rd) and Garam Sarak (Hot Rd). The latter receives more sunshine. There's a nice 2.5km road walk northeast from Gandhi Chowk to **Jandrighat**, a summer home of the former Chamba rulers (not open to visitors). The British-era churches of **St John** (1863) and **St Francis** (1894) are set among the pines at opposite ends of the ridge.

DHAINKUND

The most uplifting spot around Dalhousie is the upland area Dhainkund (2745m), reached by a 4km side road (with short-cut paths) looping up from the impoverished settlement of Lakkar Mandi, which is 12km east of Dalhousie. Taxis (around ₹1000 return from Dalhousie) have to park at a military barrier, from which a scenic 1.5km ridgeline walk leads to the **Jai Pohlani Mata Temple**, with a teahouse and great views of the Pir Pinjal range. The scenic trail continues 5km along the ridge to tiny Jot, with a couple of *dhabas*, at the Chuari Pass (2772m) on the Chamba–Chuari Khas road.

Buses to Chamba via Khajjiar stop at Lakkar Mandi (₹15, 30 minutes). Chamba–Dalhousie buses pass through Lakkar Mandi at about 8.30am, 10.45am, 2.45pm and 3.45pm.

Sleeping & Eating

The restaurants at the **Grand View Hotel** (01899-240760; www.grandviewdalhousie.in; r incl breakfast ₹3930-5240, ste from ₹6070;) and neighbouring **Hotel Mount View** (01899-242120; www.hotelmountview.net; Club Rd; meals ₹500-600) offer charming settings and good multicuisine fare (buffet breakfast ₹250 to ₹300, lunch or dinner ₹500 to ₹600). For cheap eats, there are Punjabi *dhabas* around Subhash Chowk.

Hotel Monal HOTEL $$
(9418106230; www.hotelmonal.com; Garam Sarak; r ₹2000-2500) A 10-year-old hotel with bright, clean, decently maintained rooms and superb valley views. Best are the top-floor quarters with private balconies. Vegetarian meals are available and the hotel is good value from about mid-August to mid-April, when rates are slashed by more than half.

Silverton Estate Guest House GUESTHOUSE $$$
(9418010674; www.heritagehotels.com/silverton; above Circuit House, Moti Tibba; r ₹5000-8000; Apr-Nov;) Silverton is secluded among trees above Thandi Sarak and is the choice pick for colonial character and an old-fashioned kind of comfort. If it feels like staying in a cosy and beloved family home, that's exactly what it is, for the welcoming owners also live here. Have a bash at croquet in the large gardens.

Kwality Restaurant INDIAN $$
(Gandhi Chowk; mains ₹140-370; 9am-10pm;) The extensive menu at this almost-stylish place stretches to Chinese dishes, burgers and pizza, though Indian is easily the best choice, and the combo meals (₹250 to ₹300) are a very good option.

Getting There & Around

The **bus stand** is at the west end of town. For long-distance services, there are more options from Banikhet, a junction town 7km west (bus/taxi ₹8/220), though you aren't guaranteed a seat there.

There are taxi stands **next to the bus stand** and at **Subhash Chowk** and **Gandhi Chowk**. From the bus stand, you'll pay ₹100 to Subhash Chowk and ₹150 to Gandhi Chowk. Typical out-of-town fares include ₹1500 to Chamba and ₹3000 to Dharamsala.

Chamba

01899 / POP 20,000 / ELEV 930M

Ensconced in the valley of the fast-flowing Ravi River, the capital of Chamba district is a beguiling old town with some beautiful temples, a good museum and bustling markets. Chamba was founded in AD 920 when Raja Sahil Varman moved his capital here from Bharmour, and it remained capital of the Chamba kingdom until the merger with India in 1947, though under British control from 1846.

Chamba's de facto centre is the large grassy field known as the Chowgan, a focus for festivals, cricket games, picnics and general hanging out.

Sights

★Lakshmi Narayan Temple Complex HINDU TEMPLE
(dawn-dusk) Standing in a compound at the top of the Dogra Bazar, this superb line

BUSES FROM DALHOUSIE

DESTINATION	FARE (₹)	DURATION (HR)	DEPARTURES
Chamba via Banikhet	80	2½	7am, 9.15am, 10.30am, 11.15am
Chamba via Lakkar Mandi & Khajjiar	80	2½	9am, 9.30am, 2.30pm, 4.30pm
Delhi	610-1380	14	3 daily
Dharamsala	170	5	7.15am, 11.50am, 1.15pm, 2pm
Pathankot	100	3	7 daily

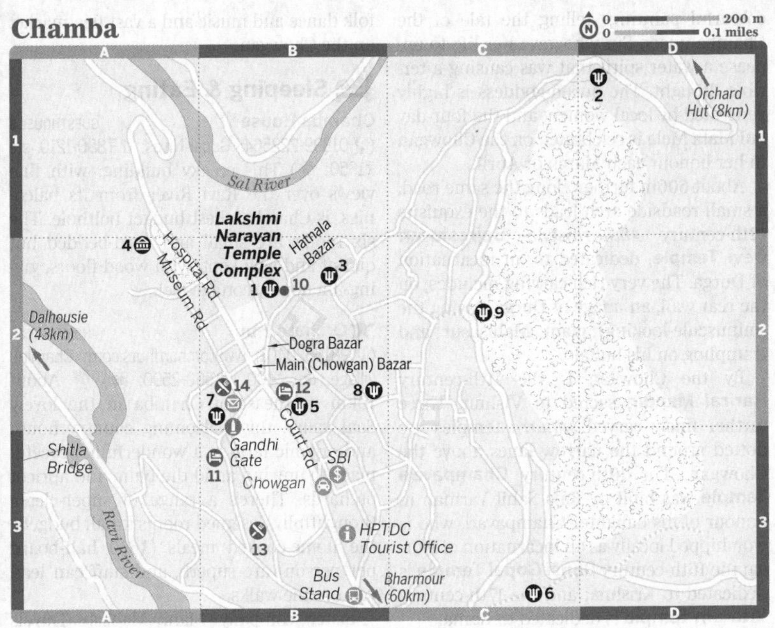

Chamba

Top Sights

1 Lakshmi Narayan Temple Complex..... B2

Sights

2 Bajreshwari Devi Temple..... D1
3 Bansi Gopal Temple..... B2
4 Bhuri Singh Museum..... A2
5 Champavati Temple..... B2
6 Chamunda Devi Temple..... C3
7 Harirai Mandir..... B2
8 Sitaram Temple..... B2
9 Sui Mata Shrine..... C2

Activities, Courses & Tours

10 Mani Mahesh Travels..... B2

Sleeping

11 Chamba House..... B3
12 Hotel City Heart..... B2

Eating

13 Cafe Ravi View..... B3
14 Jagan Restaurant..... B2

of six beautiful stone *sikharas,* covered in carvings, dates from the 10th to the 19th centuries. The largest (and oldest) is dedicated to Lakshmi Narayan (Vishnu). Of the others, three are dedicated to versions of Shiva (recognisable by the statues of the bull Nandi, Shiva's vehicle, outside them) and two to Vishnu.

Bhuri Singh Museum MUSEUM

(☎01899-222590; Museum Rd; Indian/foreigner ₹20/100, camera ₹50/100; ⊙10am-5pm Tue-Sun) This well-displayed museum, one of Himachal's best, includes a wonderful collection of Pahari (Hill Country) miniature paintings from the Chamba and other schools. Also here are intriguing copper-plate inscriptions (formerly a way of preserving important documents) and ornately carved, centuries-old fountain slabs – a unique Chamba Valley tradition.

Other Temples

A steep 378 steps up from near the bus stand (or take a taxi), the **Chamunda Devi Temple**, dating from 1762, affords wonderful views over the town and valley. It's dedicated to a wrathful aspect of the mother goddess Devi, and its front *mandapa* (pavilion) features a forest of bells and rich ceiling carving. Just above the road about 500m north is the small, modern **Sui Mata Shrine**, with colourful paintings telling the tale of the Chamba queen Sui who gave her life to appease a water spirit that was causing a terrible drought. The queen-goddess is highly venerated by local women, and the four-day Sui Mata Mela is celebrated on the Chowgan in her honour each March or April.

About 600m further along the same road, a small roadside arch leads to the exquisite 12th-century *sikhara*-style **Bajreshwari Devi Temple**, dedicated to an incarnation of Durga. The very rich carving includes, on the rear wall, an image of Durga slaying the (minuscule-looking) giant Mahisasur and trampling on his buffalo.

By the Chowgan is the 11th-century **Harirai Mandir**, sacred to Vishnu. Three further finely carved *sikhara* temples are dotted around the narrow lanes above the Chowgan. The 10th-century **Champavati Temple** was built by Raja Sahil Varman in honour of his daughter Champavati, who is worshipped locally as an incarnation of Durga; the 16th-century **Bansi Gopal Temple** is dedicated to Krishna; and the 17th-century **Sitaram Temple** is dedicated to Rama.

Activities

Mani Mahesh Travels TREKKING
(9816620401, 9418020401; www.orchardhuts.com; outside Lakshmi Narayan Temple Complex; 9am-9pm Mon-Sat) Professional and experienced Mani Mahesh can arrange treks with guides and porters in and across the surrounding Pir Panjal and Dhauladhar ranges, as well as informative tours of Chamba's temples (from ₹550). Treks cost ₹2000 to ₹2800 per person per day within the Chamba Valley, or ₹3500 to ₹4500 across the Pir Panjal or Dhauladhar passes, plus any transport costs.

It's run by the same family who run the excellent Orchard Hut. Ask about stays in their deliciously isolated Ridgemoor Cottage, three or four hours' walk (1000m higher) above Orchard Hut. Mani Mahesh also organises far-ranging jeep safaris and motorbike tours.

Festivals & Events

Minjar Festival CULTURAL
(last Sun Jul-1st Sun Aug) Every year since 935, Chamba has celebrated the annual harvest with the Minjar Festival in honour of the deity Raghuvir (an incarnation of Rama) – nowadays a week of processions, sports, folk dance and music and a vast flea market on the Chowgan.

Sleeping & Eating

Chamba House GUESTHOUSE $
(01899-222564; Gopal Nivas; d ₹880-1210, ste ₹1650;) This creaky building, with fine views over the Ravi River from its balconies, is Chamba's best budget bolthole. The six rooms are small and hard-bedded but quaint and well kept, with wood floors, giving it a homey cottage feel.

★ **Orchard Hut** HOMESTAY $$
(9816620401; www.orchardhuts.com; Chaminu village; dm ₹400, r ₹560-2590;) About 10km northeast of Chamba in the lovely Saal valley, this welcoming country house and organic farm is a wonderfully peaceful place to unwind amid the plum and apricot orchards. There's a range of super-clean, thoughtfully designed rooms for all budgets, the home-cooked meals (₹650 half-board per person) are superb, and staff can lead you on fine walks.

Sister company Mani Mahesh Travels (p338) in Chamba will arrange transfers, either by taxi (₹450) or public bus (₹25), to Chaminu village, from where it's a 20-minute uphill walk to the house. You'll thank yourself if you schedule an extra day or two here. Kitchen use is available for ₹100 per day.

Jamwal Villa HOMESTAY $$
(8894555246; www.jamwalvilla.com; Kuranh village; r ₹1500-1800; @) In a beautiful spot beside the Ravi River, 10km southeast of Chamba, this is a charming little hideaway with ducks and rabbits in its pretty garden. The three appealing rooms feature tasteful modern art and individual touches including walls of river stones, and everything is very comfy and spotless. Excellent breakfast and dinner thalis of local dishes cost from ₹150.

Hotel City Heart HOTEL $$
(01899-222032; www.hotelcityheartchamba.com; r ₹2600-3430, ste ₹3790-5450;) Rooms here are spacious, clean and well decorated. The suites and some 'super deluxe' rooms have expansive Chowgan views, and the good restaurant does Continental and Chinese as well as Indian fare (mains ₹180 to ₹300).

Cafe Ravi View INDIAN $$
(Chowgan; mains ₹95-225; 9am-10pm;) This HPTDC-run snack house is worth a visit for

its icy-cold beers (₹150) and excellent river views as well as for its Indian and Chinese veg food – including dosas and bargain thalis (₹125 to ₹175).

It has a sunny terrace as well as indoor air-con.

Jagan Restaurant INDIAN $$
(Museum Rd; mains ₹90-200; ⊙11.30am-10.30pm) It's nothing flash but the uniformed waiters at this upstairs restaurant serve up the tasty *chamba madhra* (kidney beans with curd and ghee) for ₹110, plus a good selection of veg curries and chicken dishes.

Getting There & Away

BUS

A mix of government-run HRTC and private buses runs to many destinations from the often crowded and chaotic **bus stand**. For the spectacular trip to Bharmour, sit on the left for the best views. For Dharamsala, if there's no direct bus soon, you can get one to Gaggal (₹230, five to seven hours) where buses leave every few minutes to Dharamsala (₹15, 40 minutes); for the best scenery try to get one going via Jot, over the 2772m Chuari Pass. The best Delhi service is the Volvo AC bus at 6pm.

TAXI & JEEP

Taxis at the Court Rd **stand** ask around ₹1500 to Bharmour, ₹1800 to Dalhousie and ₹3500 to Dharamsala.

Most days from July to September there are shared jeeps (₹500) crossing the Sach Pass to Killar in the Pangi Valley – ask at **Mani Mahesh Travels** (p338).

Bharmour

01895 / POP 2000 / ELEV 2195M

Hovering on the edge of the seemingly bottomless Budil Valley, Bharmour is reached by a mountain road as scenic as it is perilous, winding 60km east of Chamba (it gets really interesting once you leave the Ravi Valley at Kharamukh). This ancient settlement was the area capital until replaced by Chamba in AD 920, and there are some beautiful old temples, though the main reason to come here is for treks to the surrounding valleys and passes. The villages around Bharmour are home to communities of seminomadic Gaddis, pastoralists who move their flocks to alpine pastures during the summer, and return here (or to the Kullu or Kangra Valleys) in winter.

Sights & Activities

Chaurasi Temples HINDU TEMPLE
(⊙6am-8.30pm) The Chaurasi temples, 500m up the street from the bus stand, occupy a wide flagstone courtyard that doubles as an outdoor classroom and cricket practice ground. There are three main Shaivite temples, plus a couple of dozen smaller shrines (*chaurasi* means 84, seemingly an exaggeration). The central **Manimahesh Temple** is a classic stone *sikhara,* built in the 7th century AD. The squat **Lakshna Devi Temple** is of a similar date, with a weathered but wildly carved wooden doorway.

For the best valley views, hike 3km up from the Chaurasi entrance to the **Brahmani Mata Temple** above town. The route passes through the upper village, still full of traditional slate-roofed, wooden houses.

Trekking

The trekking season lasts from May to late October, though July and August see some monsoon rain. The many treks starting in the district include from Kugti to Jhalma in Lahaul over the 5040m Kugti Pass (five days); from Lamu in the Ravi Valley to McLeod Ganj over the 4420m Indrahar La (five days); and demanding longer treks via the isolated village of Bara Bhangal to Manali or Bir.

BUSES FROM CHAMBA

DESTINATION	FARE (₹)	DURATION (HR)	DEPARTURES
Amritsar	277	7	11.15pm
Bharmour	95	3½	hourly 5am-5pm
Dalhousie via Banikhet	80	2½	4 daily
Dalhousie via Khajjiar	80	2½	4 daily
Delhi	675-1516	15	3 daily
Dharamsala	260-330	6-8	5 daily
Killar	260	12	6am Jul-Sep

A popular shorter trek is to the sacred Manimahesh Lake, a two- or three-day return hike (about 13km each way, with an altitude difference of 2100m) starting at Hadsar, 13km east of Bharmour. It can be done without a tent thanks to the many *dhabas* en route. In the two weeks following Janmastami (Krishna's birthday; late August or early September), up to 300,000 pilgrims take this route in the **Manimahesh Yatra** pilgrimage in honour of Lord Shiva, climaxing with a freezing dip in the lake. The whole Chamba Valley throngs with people travelling to or from the lake at this time.

Anna Adventures & Tours (☎8894687758, 9805659622; www.bharmourtreks.com; Main Bazar) arranges a full range of treks in the Bharmour region and across the surrounding ranges. Ask for Gopal Chauhan.

Sleeping & Eating

Hotel Mahadev HOTEL $
(☎9816544000; Main Bazar; r ₹400-1000;) Occupying three upstairs floors on the right of the street leading up to the Chaurasi Temples, Mahadev has rooms ranging from the dingy and windowless to large and bright (front rooms on the top floor).

Chaurasi Hotel HOTEL $$
(☎9418025004; http://hotelchourasi.in; Main Bazar; r ₹800-2000;) You can't miss this red multistorey building up the street towards the Chaurasi Temples. Rooms are generous in size and many have soaring views; those in the new block at the side are generally in better condition. The restaurant (mains ₹70 to ₹190) is Bharmour's best, but it doesn't have much competition.

Getting There & Away

Buses leave about hourly from 5.30am to 5.30pm for the rugged trip to Chamba (₹95, 3½ hours). Taxis charge ₹1500 to ₹2000; some go on a shared basis for ₹200 per person.

A bus to Dharamsala (₹450, 12 hours) departs at 5.30pm. A few daily buses head to Hadsar (₹35, one hour); there are also shared jeep-taxis for ₹30 per person. For buses up the Ravi Valley as far as Holi, take a Chamba-bound bus to Kharamukh and change there.

LAHAUL & SPITI

The desolate northern and eastern tracts of Himachal Pradesh are among the most spectacular and sparsely populated regions on Earth. Crossing the Rohtang La from Manali, you arrive first in Lahaul's relatively green Chandra Valley. Head west down the Chandra then up the Bhaga Valley through Keylong (Lahaul's capital) and you're on the road to Ladakh. If you travel east up the Chandra Valley and over the Kunzum La into Spiti, you pass into the rain shadow of the Great Himalayan Range. Spiti is 7000 sq km of snow-topped mountains and high-altitude desert, punctuated by tiny patches of greenery and villages of whitewashed houses clinging to the sides of rivers and meltwater streams. As in Zanskar and Ladakh, Tibetan Buddhism is the dominant religion in both Spiti and Lahaul, though Hinduism is prominent in lower Lahaul. Some Lahauli temples encompass both religions.

History

Buddhism is believed to have arrived in Spiti and Lahaul during the 8th century AD with the legendary Indian sorcerer-sage-missionary Padmasambhava (Guru Rinpoche in Tibetan) who helped to spread Buddhism in Tibet. In the 10th century, upper Lahaul, Spiti, Zanskar and Ladakh were incorporated into the vast Guge kingdom of western Tibet, with Lahaul and Spiti eventually being ruled from Ladakh. The Great Translator, Ringchen Zangpo, founded a series of centres of Buddhist learning in Spiti in the late 10th and early 11th centuries, including Tabo, one of the most remarkable Buddhist monasteries in the Indian Himalaya.

The Kullu rajas took control of Lahaul in the 16th century and established a loose hold over Spiti in the 17th. The region came under British control following the 1846 Anglo-Sikh War, yet it maintained strong links with Tibet right up until the Chinese invasion there in 1950.

Recent decades have seen a resurgence in the region's cultural and religious life, aided by the work of the Tibetan government-in-exile in Dharamsala. Many gompas in Lahaul and Spiti have been restored, and money from tourism and hydroelectricity is improving living conditions for the farming communities who get snowed in here each winter.

Climate

Rainfall is minimal, especially in Spiti, and the high altitude ensures low temperatures. Winter temperatures can plummet below -30°C, but on the plus side, summer daytime temperatures often rise into the 20s, and when monsoons are soaking the rest of the state (mid-July to mid-September), it's usually dry and sunny here. Whenever you travel, bring some clothing for cold weather.

Getting There & Away

The road north from Manali over the Rohtang La (3978m) is normally open from about mid-May to early November. From the north side of the Rohtang you can head west to Keylong or east to Spiti.

From Keylong, the road to Ladakh continues over the mighty Baralacha La (4950m) and Taglang La (5328m) and is normally open from about early June to some time in October. The road to Spiti over the Kunzum La (4551m) is open from about mid-June to some time in November.

You can cross these passes by minibus, jeep, motorbike or bus, all of which can be arranged in Manali.

When the passes are closed, Lahaul is virtually cut off from the outside world, and Spiti is connected only by the rugged road from the south looping through Kinnaur. Check the status of the passes before visiting late in the season – once the snows arrive, you might be stuck for the winter! The websites www.bcmtouring.com and http://devilonwheels.com have updates.

Lahaul (but not Spiti or Ladakh) should be opened to year-round traffic from Manali when the tunnel bypassing the Rohtang La opens (possibly in 2018). The tunnel will run for 8.85km underneath the mountains from the Solang Valley, north of Manali, to Lahaul's Chandra Valley.

Lahaul

Manali to Keylong

From Manali, Hwy 3 strikes north along the Beas River and climbs slowly through pine forests and endless switchbacks to the bare rocky slopes below the **Rohtang La**. The pass's name literally translates as 'pile of dead bodies' – hundreds of travellers have frozen to death here over the centuries. In the domestic tourist season, it's busy with day trippers from Manali enjoying the novelty of a snowball fight. Near the top, look out for the small, dome-shaped temple that marks the source of the Beas River.

Once over the pass, the road soon deteriorates as it makes the steep descent into the Chandra Valley, where the Chandra River rages along between towering rocky peaks ribboned with waterfalls plunging from high-level glaciers. After a zig-zagging 14km, **Gramphu** (four stone buildings) marks the turn-off to Spiti. **Khoksar**, in the valley bottom, has several *dhabas* and a checkpoint where police note down foreigners' passport details. The new tunnel bypassing the Rohtang La will join this road 7km west of Khoksar.

Tandi, 8km before Keylong, marks the confluence of the Chandra River with

ROHTANG RULES

Anyone planning to drive or ride a motorcycle north over the Rohtang La from Manali must obtain a permit beforehand from the town's **Sub-Divisional Magistrate's Office** (SDM Office; Map p314; ☎01902-254100; behind HPTDC, The Mall; ⏰10am-4.30pm Mon-Sat, 10am-1pm Sun & 2nd Sat of the month). The process normally takes about one hour and the permit is free (though some applicants have been asked for donations). Take your passport and driving licence and the vehicle's registration and pollution-under-check documents, and complete a form. You have to show your permit at a checkpoint at Gulaba on the way up to the pass.

The pass is closed on Tuesdays from 6am to all private northbound traffic, including taxis, to facilitate maintenance work. If you're through Gulaba before 6am, you can continue.

Southbound vehicles need no permit and can cross the pass any day of the week.

A different permit (₹550), issued online (www.hpkullu.nic.in), is required for vehicles just making a day trip from Manali to the pass and back. In practice it's usually very difficult for individual tourists to obtain these, and almost everyone making a Rohtang day trip does so by taxi.

Details of the Rohtang regulations change frequently. With any luck the opening of the Rohtang tunnel, possibly in 2018, will eliminate the permit requirement for those travelling to Lahaul or beyond.

the Bhaga (together they become the Chandra-Bhaga). From the south end of the Bhaga bridge here you can walk 100m up to Tupchiling Gompa and ask there for the keys to **Guru Ghantal Gompa**, a further hour's walk uphill, which is the oldest monastery in Lahaul, allegedly founded by Padmasambhava. Although crumbling, the gompa contains ancient *thangkas*, a painted ceiling mandala, unusual wooden statues of Padmasambhava, other bodhisattvas and the Hindu deity Brajeshwari, and a black stone image of Kali.

Keylong

☎01900 / POP 1150 / ELEV 3100M

Keylong stretches along the north side of the green Bhaga Valley just below the Manali–Leh road, and it's an overnight stop for many travellers on that route. Many people only see Keylong briefly and in the dark, but a longer stay reveals grand mountain views, a laid-back, small-town lifestyle, some scenic walks and historic Buddhist monasteries.

The main street, optimistically named the Mall, winds for 1km below and roughly parallel to the highway, with the bus station (New Bus Stand) just above its east end.

Sights & Activities

Lahaul-Spiti Tribal Museum MUSEUM

(The Mall; 10am-1.30pm & 2-5pm Tue-Sun) FREE At the west end of town, this semi-interesting museum displays traditional artefacts including *chaam* dance masks and a *thod-pa* (part of a skull formerly used by *amchis* or lamas to store healing or sacred liquids), plus historical photos and prints, and contemporary photos of local monasteries and villages.

Kardang Gompa BUDDHIST MONASTERY

On concrete stilts facing Keylong across the valley, Kardang Gompa has existed for 900 years, but the current building dates from 1912. Maintained by an order of Drukpa Kagyu (Red Hat) monks and nuns, the monastery enshrines a mighty prayer wheel said to contain a million paper strips bearing the mantra *Om mani padme hum* ('Hail to the jewel in the lotus'). There are excellent frescos, but you may have to find a monk or nun to open the doors.

The monastery also has a large library of sacred texts and collections of *thangkas*, old weapons and musical instruments. To get here, head for the hospital at the bottom of the west end of Keylong and take a path down to the left 30m before the hospital. This crosses the River Bhaga on a footbridge, then climbs 1km to a road. Turn right into Kardang village and ask directions to the gompa, 800m further uphill. For a different route back, return to Kardang village then head to the right along the road for 3km to Lapchang village, where a path descends 1km to another footbridge, then climbs 1.25km to the main road. Keylong is 1.5km to the left.

Shashur Gompa BUDDHIST MONASTERY

About 2km of uphill walking (or a 7km drive) above Keylong, Shashur Gompa was founded in the 17th century by the Zanskari lama Deva Gyatsho. The original gompa, featuring 5m-high *thangkas*, is now enshrined inside a modern concrete one, with fine views over the valley.

Brokpa Adventure Tours TREKKING

(☎9418165176; brokpatrek@yahoo.com; Hotel Dupchen, The Mall; internet & wi-fi per hr ₹60; 9am-8pm May, Jun & Sep, 7am-10pm Jul & Aug) For tips on day hikes or to arrange longer treks in the local area or over to Zanskar, talk to Amar here. The office also has public internet service.

Sleeping & Eating

Most guesthouses and hotels are open only from about May to October. A couple of places up the street from the bus station have basic dorms for minimum-cost sleeping before early-morning bus departures.

Nordaling Guest House HOTEL $

(☎01900-222294; www.nordalingkeylong.in; r ₹800-1500; May-Oct; wi-fi) Just 100m above the bus station is this pleasant place with large, spotless rooms, and a relaxing restaurant (mains ₹80 to ₹180) in the apple orchard outside. It's an excellent choice and rates can drop steeply when things are quiet.

Hotel Tashi Deleg HOTEL $$

(☎01900-222450; hotel_tashideleg@yahoo.in; The Mall; r ₹1250-3050; May-Oct; wi-fi) This big white hotel, towards the western end of the Mall, is Keylong's nicest. Rooms in the new wing are large, with soft chairs, good showers and (mostly) balconies. The old wing is also fine, and cheaper (rates rise as you climb the floors).

The wi-fi is in the restaurant, which is Keylong's best, serving Indian, Chinese and

Continental food (mains ₹100 to ₹220), plus cold beers.

Hotel New Gyespa HOTEL $$

(☎9418136055; r ₹1200-1800; ⊙May-Oct) Only 20m up from the bus station, most of the clean, carpeted rooms here have views across the valley. Best are the spacious top-floor rooms, new in 2016. The hotel also possesses an attractive pine-panelled restaurant (mains ₹100 to ₹300). The affiliated, cheaper **Hotel Gyespa** (☎9418133522; The Mall; r ₹800-1200; ⊙May-Oct) is another worthy option and also has a restaurant. Both places offer discounts early and late in the season.

Information

The **State Bank of Patiala ATM** (The Mall), opposite Hotel Dupchen, accepts international cards.

Getting There & Away

From mid-June to mid-September, an HRTC bus departs for Leh (₹540, about 14 hours) at 5am – get tickets at the bus station between 4am and 4.30am. Privately operated minibuses and shared jeeps run until October, depending on snow conditions: one place you can book seats is **Brokpa Adventure Tours**. Seats cost between ₹1500 and ₹3000 (most expensive from June to August).

The HRTC also runs six or seven daily buses to Manali (₹173, seven hours, 4.30am to 1.30pm), one to Shimla (₹565, 16 hours, 1.30pm) and two to Delhi (₹850, 23 hours) from about mid-May to early November.

From about May to mid-November there are buses at 6.30am and 1pm to Chika (₹60, two hours) in the Darcha Valley, on the way up to the Shingo La pass into Zanskar. Services depend on road conditions in all cases.

For Kaza, take the 4.30am or 6.30am Manali-bound bus and change at Gramphu (₹75, 2½ hours), where the Manali–Kaza pulls in around 9am.

Pattan & Pangi Valleys

At Tandi, 8km southwest of Keylong, a road branches northwest along the beautiful, fertile, little-visited Pattan Valley, carved by the Chandra-Bhaga (Chenab) River. The river and road then curve northward into the Pangi Valley, even more beautiful and more remote (and often completely cut off from December to March). Snowy peaks rise above the many beautiful, steep-sided side valleys, climbing into the Pir Panjal range on the west and the Great Himalayan Range on the east, with demanding trekking routes crossing to the Chamba Valley and Zanskar respectively.

Probably the scariest of all Himachal's mountain roads continues along the Chenab valley from Pangi's only town, Killar, enabling intrepid travellers to make an epic 'K3' journey from Keylong to Killar to Kishtwar (p280) in Jammu & Kashmir.

Sights & Activities

If you have time, explore some of the scenic side valleys, especially on the east side of the river – such as the Miyar Valley running up from Udaipur in the Pattan Valley, or the Saichu, Parmar, Hudan and Sural Valleys heading up from Pangi. The Hindu population lower down gives way higher up to Tibetan Buddhists known as Bots. There is daily bus service up most of these valleys from Udaipur or Killar.

Triloknath Temple TEMPLE

Some 36km down the Pattan Valley from Tandi, a side road leads 5km to the hilltop village of Triloknath, whose squat stone temple is a remarkable example of Hindu-Buddhist syncretism. The white-marble main idol is revered by Buddhists as Avalokitesvara, the bodhisattva of compassion, while Hindus worship it as Shiva. It's a pilgrimage site for both religions, especially during the three-day **Pauri Festival** (⊙3rd week of Aug) honouring the temple deity.

Markula Devi Temple HINDU TEMPLE

(Udaipur) In Udaipur, the Pattan Valley's largest village, the Markula Devi Temple looks plain on the outside but the inside is covered with fabulous, detailed wood carvings from the 11th to 16th centuries, including scenes from the Mahabharata and Ramayana around the top of the walls.

Sleeping

Udaipur and Killar have a few small hotels, guesthouses and government rest houses that take tourists when space is available. Killar's **Raj Hotel** (☎9418890045; Killar; r ₹1000-1500, ste ₹4500; ⊙Apr-Nov), two minutes' walk from the bus stand, is an unexpectedly clean and comfortable option with good views, and its restaurant (mains ₹70 to ₹200) is the only one in town with much choice. Two hairpins up from the bus stand (past the Raj Hotel), **Killar Rest House** (Killar; r from ₹500) has six well-kept rooms. It's unsigned but directly after the well-marked Senior Secondary School.

Information

Udaipur and Killar have ATMs on their main streets.

Getting There & Away

Udaipur has year-round bus connections with Keylong (₹85, three hours, seven buses daily). From about mid-April to mid-November two buses daily from Keylong continue to Killar (₹210 from Keylong, taking about 10 hours to cover the 125km). These stop at Udaipur at about 9.15am and 1.45pm. The route is dusty, bumpy and often as narrow as a ribbon but stunningly beautiful, with the road teetering along a series of precarious ledges high above the fast-flowing river for much of the last 50km into Killar. Buses back to Keylong leave Killar at 5am and 10am.

From Killar there's a road to Chamba over the Sach Pass (4390m), open from about late June to early October. In season a bus (₹260, about 12 hours) leaves Killar at 6.30am daily, and there are shared jeeps (₹500) between 7am and 9am.

For Kishtwar in Jammu & Kashmir, you'll usually need to head first from Killar to Gulabgarh (53km) along one of India's most perilous but scenic roads. For the intrepid only! The Luj–Tayari section bumps over bare rocks then along terrifyingly narrow ledges after Ishtiyari, sometimes overhung by daggers of unstable rock. Most days there's likely to be a J&K jeep leaving Killar around mid-morning for Gulabgarh (₹300, four hours). Look around for vehicles with JK number plates. Chartering a jeep should cost ₹3000.

Spiti

Separated from fertile Lahaul by the soaring 4551m Kunzum La, the trans-Himalayan region of Spiti is another chunk of Tibet marooned in India. The scattered villages in this serrated moonscape arrive like mirages, clusters of whitewashed mud-brick homes huddled amid green barley fields below monasteries perched on crags a thousand feet above. The turquoise-grey ribbon of the Spiti River is your near-constant companion, running along a fairly broad valley before turning south at Sumdo into the precipitous gorges of the Hangrang Valley.

Spiti attracts many travellers, including streams of Indian motorcyclists, as a kind of 'mini-Ladakh without tourist crowds', which is fair enough, since its pristine nature (high-altitude desert) and culture (Tibetan Buddhist) are still intact. The approaches to Spiti remain among the most rugged and scenically spectacular roads in India, and the Spiti–Kinnaur loop is one of Asia's great road trips.

Gramphu to Kaza

From Gramphu, on the northern side of the Rohtang La, the road to Spiti runs up the awe-inspiring, glacier-carved Chandra Valley. One kilometre past tiny Batal, a rough but driveable track runs north up towards **Chandratal** (Moon Lake), a 2km-long glacial lake among snow peaks at 4270m, whose blue hue changes constantly following the moods of the sky. The track ends after 12km; a footpath runs the final 1km to the lake. You can break the journey in this inspiringly beautiful area at nearby tent camps. From Chandratal, trekkers can reach the Baralacha La on the Manali–Leh road in three strenuous but heavenly days.

The main road switchbacks precipitously up to the **Kunzum La**, where vehicles perform a respectful circuit of prayer-flag-strewn stupas before continuing down into Spiti. There's also a 10.5km walking trail down to Chandratal starting from the stupas.

The first Spitian village of any size is **Losar**, where there's a passport check. From here the road follows the Spiti River downstream along its spectacular valley to Kaza.

Sleeping

Tashi Gatsel Hotel HOTEL $

(☎9418931909; Losar; r ₹800-1000; ⏲late May-late Oct) Tashi Gatsel, almost beside the Losar checkpoint, offers good clean rooms with big comfy beds and hot-water bathrooms, expansive views from its terrace, and Indian/Continental/Chinese food (mains ₹100 to ₹200).

Nomad's Cottage GUESTHOUSE $$

(☎9650824268; www.nomadscottage.in; Losar; s/d ₹1300/1900, without bathroom ₹1300/1500; ⏲May-Oct) Has excellent rooms with wood-beam ceilings and big comfy beds, plus a cosy sitting area with a wood-burning stove and low tables where good breakfasts and Indian or Tibetan-Spitian dinners (₹300 to ₹400) are served.

Parasol Camps TENTED CAMP $$

(☎9418845817; parasolcamps@gmail.com; Chandratal Camps; d tent with beds & full board ₹3000, with mattress & half-board ₹1600; ⏲mid-Jun–mid-

Oct) One of the best Chandratal camps, Parasol provides cosy tents, good Indian meals (including garlic soup, good for altitude), sit-down toilets and buckets of hot water for washing.

Kaza

01906 / POP 1700 / ELEV 3640M

The capital of Spiti, Kaza sits on the eroded flood plain of the Spiti River, with jagged mountains rising on either side, and is the biggest settlement you'll encounter in this empty corner of the planet. It feels a bit like a small frontier town with an easygoing pace. The often-dry Kaza Nullah stream divides New Kaza (west of the nullah) from the bazaar area, Old Kaza, to the east. The bus and taxi stands are at the bottom of the bazaar.

Most people stay at least one night to arrange an inner line permit for travel beyond Tabo. Kaza is also the starting point for trips to Ki Gompa and the villages of Kibber, Langza, Hikkim, Komic and Demul, high on the east side of the valley, and a good place to organise treks and tours in or beyond Spiti.

Activities

A few agencies run by highly experienced locals can set you up with treks, jeep safaris, day tours and other travel arrangements.

Incredible Spiti ADVENTURE SPORTS
(www.incrediblespiti.com) Incredible Spiti specialises in treks and motorbike and jeep tours. It's closely associated with Sakya Abode hotel, (p346) which also has wide-ranging travel and activities services, so can assist in organising almost anything you fancy.

Spiti Holiday Adventure TREKKING
(9418638071; www.spitiholidayadventure.com; Main Bazar; office 8.30am-9.30pm Mar-Nov) Organises all-inclusive treks from two days upwards, as well as jeep tours and mountain-bike and motorbike rentals. It runs a number of fixed-departure trips, which individuals can join. It's a good place for travel information generally.

Spiti Valley Tours TREKKING
(9418537689; www.spitivalleytours.com; Main Bazar; office 8am-7pm Jun-Oct) Treks, jeep tours, wildlife trips, mountaineering and more, with an emphasis on local homestay accommodation.

INNER LINE PERMITS IN KAZA

To travel between Sumdo in eastern Spiti and Rekong Peo (Kinnaur), foreign travellers need an inner line permit. These are issued free in around 20 minutes at the **Assistant Deputy Commissioner's Office** (8988384472; New Kaza; 10am-1.30pm & 2-5pm Mon-Sat, closed 2nd Sat of the month) in New Kaza – a large white building diagonally opposite the Community Health Centre (hospital). Bring two passport photos and photocopies of your passport's identity and visa pages, plus application and permit forms (sold for ₹20 from the government canteen outside). Solo travellers have no problems getting permits here.

Sleeping

Kunzaum Guest House GUESTHOUSE $
(9418521541; New Kaza; r ₹500, without bathroom ₹250; Apr-Oct) A clean, friendly, family-run guesthouse whose best rooms are the three upstairs facing Kaza Nullah. It's just above the footbridge.

Butith Gangri Home Stay HOMESTAY $
(9459228510; tnguisem@gmail.com; New Kaza; r without bathroom ₹400; May-Oct) The three rooms at this friendly family home are neat and spotless though beds are hard. The kitchen and dining room, shared bathrooms (hot water by bucket) and the courtyard, with pretty flowers, are equally pristine. It's close to Kaza Nullah, 90m down from the footbridge.

Ösel Rooms GUESTHOUSE $
(off Main Bazar, Old Kaza; s ₹800, d & tr ₹1000-1200; Apr-Nov) Seven large, clean rooms with solar hot water above Taste of Spiti restaurant. It's run by Ecosphere (p348): contact them for bookings.

★**Hotel Deyzor** HOTEL $$
(9418402660; www.hoteldeyzor.com; behind BSNL office, New Kaza; r ₹900-1750; mid-Apr–mid-Nov;) The bright, well-kept rooms have comfy beds and a cosy charm with ethnic fabrics and Spiti-theme photos. The owners are real Spiti enthusiasts, full of info, and can help arrange hikes, wildlife-spotting or fossil-hunting trips and more. And the restaurant is our favourite in Kaza. Not

surprisingly the dozen rooms can fill up so it's advisable to book.

Sakya Abode HOTEL $$
(☎9418208987; www.sakyaabode.com; New Kaza; s ₹900-1300, d ₹1100-1500; ⏲late Apr-Nov; @📶) On the main road near the Sakya Gompa, this is Kaza's longest-running (since 1992) and one of its best-value hotels. Comfy rooms line shared terraces overlooking a grassy courtyard, and the Indian-Tibetan-Chinese restaurant (mains ₹100 to ₹250) is good – try the addictive 'copper Eliza' dessert! The hotel also offers full travel and activities services.

Eating

Sol Cafe CAFE $
(Main Bazar; hot drinks & snacks ₹50-110; ⏲9am-8pm Mon-Sat May-Nov) This cool little cafe, operated by Ecosphere (p348), offers super-strong coffee, herbal and other teas, and light dishes such as French toast, pancakes and wholewheat baked goods, as well as items showcasing sea-buckthorn, a berry with an amazing list of health-giving properties.

★Hotel Deyzor Restaurant MULTICUISINE $$
(New Kaza; mains ₹100-350; ⏲8am-10pm mid-Apr–mid-Nov) The Deyzor restaurant does a great job on an eclectic range of dishes, doubtless partly inspired by the owner's own world travels. The menu ranges over Indian, Spitian (similar to Tibetan), Continental and beyond, with good, freshly prepared daily specials and an emphasis on seasonal local produce.

Himalayan Café MULTICUISINE $$
(www.facebook.com/thehimalayancafe; off Main Bazar, Old Kaza; mains ₹100-350; ⏲8am-10.30pm May-Oct; 📶) The Himalayan, run by an escaped lawyer from Mumbai, takes the concept of bright, clean and cheerful to new levels for these parts and it's a big hit. The satisfying food runs from muesli with fresh fruit to *momos*, salads, pancakes and a full Indian range from aloo gobi to mutton rogan josh.

Information

There's an **internet cafe** (per hr ₹80; ⏲9am-7pm) opposite Shambhala Homestay in the bazaar, and an SBI ATM nearby.

Getting There & Away

The bus to Manali (₹350, 11 hours) leaves at 6.30am, mid-June to mid-October; be there 30 to 60 minutes before to buy tickets. For Keylong, change at Gramphu (₹230, nine hours). A bus leaves for Rekong Peo (₹357, 11 hours) at 7.30am, going via Tabo (₹73, 2½ hours) and Nako (₹177, 5½ hours). There's a second Tabo bus at 3pm.

Lhungta Traveller Union (☎9418190083; opposite bus stand, Old Kaza) has fixed-rate taxis everywhere including to Dhankar (₹1550, 1½ hours), Tabo (₹2000, 1½ hours), Ki (₹700, 45 minutes), Keylong (₹10,000, eight hours) and Manali (₹10,000, eight hours). Most vehicles can take 10 or 11 passengers. For return trips with a one-hour wait, add 20%; for each extra hour, add ₹100 more. It also runs a shared jeep to Manali (₹1000) at 6am, approximately mid-June to October (when the passes are passable).

Around Kaza

The small, high-altitude villages on the east side of the Spiti valley (all well above 4000m) have a pristine, desolate beauty all their own – clusters of whitewashed, flat-roofed houses against a stark mountain backdrop with minimal vegetation except their carefully tended fields of barley and other crops. Several villages have seasonal guesthouses or homestays and interesting old temples or monasteries. You can visit them in day trips from Kaza but you can also stay over and take local walks – or trek between several of the villages along the homestay trek route (p348), which links Langza, Komic and Demul with Lhalung and Dhankar – a great way to get a sense of the lifestyle of Spiti's amazingly resilient people.

A daily bus leaves Kaza for Ki (₹25, 30 minutes) and Kibber (₹34, 50 minutes), starting back from Kibber at 8.30am. But for the villages on the homestay trek route it's foot or taxi (unless you have your own wheels). The circuit from Kaza to Langza, Hikkim, Komic, Demul and back to Kaza is 70km and can be done in a one-day trip drive.

KI

POP 370 / ELEV 3800M

About 12km northwest of Kaza, on the road to Kibber, tiny Ki is dominated by the whitewashed buildings of the photogenic **Ki Gompa** (⏲6am-7pm). Set atop a conical hillock, this is the largest gompa in Spiti, with around 350 senior and student monks. An atmospheric *puja* is held in the new prayer hall every morning around 8am. On request, the monks will open up the medieval prayer rooms, including the Zimshung Lhakhang, which houses a bed slept in by the Dalai Lama in 1960 and 2000. Dance masks and highly colourful costumes are brought out for **Losar** and the **Ki Chaam Festival** (Guitor Festival; ⏲ Jul/Aug), a week long series of rituals seeking good fortune for the coming year, which culminates in a day of lively dancing by lamas to the sound of horns, percussion and deep-throated chanting – and free lunch for all present.

KIBBER

☎ 01906 / POP 370 / ELEV 4200M

Eight kilometres beyond Ki, this relatively large but still traditional village is the trailhead for the demanding eight- to 10-day trek over the 5578m Parang La to Tso Moriri lake in Ladakh (mid-July to mid-September), and also a good base to just stay in guesthouses and do local hikes.

The Kibber area is a good one for sighting Spiti wildlife including blue sheep, ibex, red fox and Himalayan griffon vulture. In winter it offers better-than-average prospects of sighting the ever-elusive snow leopard (best in March).

You can walk to the higher hamlets of **Gete** (about two hours, with small lakes nearby) or **Tashigang** (about three hours), where you can ask about the meditation cave with rock-carved Buddhist deities about 45 minutes further on. The peak **Khanamo** (5964m) is a fine two- or three-day round-trip trek (non-technical), best in August or the first half of September.

Several guesthouses and homestays offer rooms and meals. Most close from some time in October to March or April. Solar-powered **Norling Home Stay** (☎ 9418556107; r ₹500-700, mains ₹90-140) 🍃, overlooking most of the village, has some of the best rooms, dishes up excellent organic food and stays open all year. **Norling Guest House** (☎ 9459662148; r ₹600-700, without bathroom ₹300; ⏲ Apr–mid-Sep) at the village entrance provides decent clean rooms and has a public restaurant with open terrace serving good Israeli, Continental and Indian food (mains ₹100 to ₹200).

LANGZA

Tiny Langza, a switchback 14km drive north of Kaza, sits at 4325m below the pointed 6300m peak of Chau Chau. A large modern **medicine-Buddha statue** stares across the valley from the top of the village; the temple behind it is around 500 years old. About a 2km walk away is an area rich in **ammonite fossils** around 100 million years old. Village men participate in a drunken **horse race** to Komic and back (or Komic to Langza and back, depending on the year) on a variable date in the first half of August, imbibing large amounts of local homebrews before, during and after the race.

Several of the village's 20 or so houses are homestays, typically charging ₹500 per person including three meals. Most have squat toilets (flushing or dry) and some have floor mattresses rather than beds. Have a look around to see which ones appeal.

There's no bus service. Taxis from Kaza cost ₹950/1140 one way/return.

HIKKIM

Six kilometres south of Langza, a slight detour down from the road to Komic, little Hikkim is home to what's claimed to be the **world's highest post office** (⏲ 9am-5pm Mon-Sat), 4440m above sea level. Some spoilsports say the post office at Everest Base Camp in Tibet is higher (5200m) but this is almost certainly the highest in India! It's also a house, and customers are often offered a cup of tea. They may have postcards to sell, but it's an idea to bring some anyway.

It's possible to hike direct from Kaza to Hikkim up the Kaza Nullah in two or three hours – steeper and harder, but shorter, than the 15km road route.

KOMIC

A sign outside the monastery here proclaims Komic to be the highest motorable village in the world at 4587m. Santa Bárbara in Bolivia (4754m) would disagree, but Komic may well claim the Asian crown! The village comprises about 10 houses and, above them, the **Tangyud Gompa**, with about 50 lamas. The monastery's history goes back many centuries, but its fort-like main building was seemingly constructed after it relocated from near Hikkim following a 1975 earthquake. *Pujas* are offered at 8am to Mahakala, a wrathful emanation of Avalokitesvara. A smaller, older building nearby has a stuffed leopard (believed to impart strength to those who touch it) hanging inside the entrance: women are not permitted in its inner prayer room.

At research time most families in Komic were participating in a community homestay

THE HOMESTAY TRAIL

In one of India's most successful ecotourism programs, five mostly remote, high-altitude villages on the east side of the Spiti Valley (Langza, Komic, Demul, Lhalung and Dhankar) offer homestays in real village homes, giving a taste of authentic Spitian life. For ₹500 to ₹600 per night per person (including meals), visitors sleep in simple but clean traditional houses, eat home-cooked food and get the chance to experience village life. Hot water is normally by bucket and squat toilets are prevalent.

The villages are accessible by road but are also linked in a popular 'Homestay Trail' trekking route. Trained guides (per day ₹1000 to ₹2000) – not required but recommended – can accompany you between villages or on day hikes and explain about the culture and the unique natural environment. Wildlife-watching hikes offer the chance of spotting ibex, blue sheep *(bharal)* and possibly the Himalayan wolf *(shanku)*, the world's oldest wolf species.

It's a good example of how an area's tourism potential can be harnessed for the benefit of the local community. Some of the villages (at research time, Demul and Komic) operate a cooperative system with the families taking turns to host tourists; in the others the homestays operate individually. Either way, the program brings invaluable extra income into communities subsisting in extremely harsh natural conditions.

It's possible just to roll up in a village and ask for a homestay, or you can organise visits or treks through agencies including the Spiti conservation and development NGO **Ecosphere** (☎9418860099; www.spitiecosphere.com; Main Bazar, Kaza; ⊙office & shop 10am-7pm Mon-Sat Apr–mid-Dec), which was closely involved in setting up the homestay program. If you want a guide, it's definitely best to arrange this in advance.

Ecosphere also offers travellers numerous other activities including mountain-bike, culture or wildlife tours, yak safaris, cooking/pottery/yak-rope-twining classes, other multiday treks, and 'nun for a day' in Spiti's Buddhist convents. If you can get here in deep winter (February is best) and stay in high-altitude villages for seven to 10 days, Ecosphere offers a 90% chance of seeing snow leopards (₹2500 to ₹4000 per person per day).

scheme, taking turns to host tourists for ₹600 per person including three meals, though one or two families were going it alone and asking ₹500. Ask for the homestay coordinator or find the Kunga Homestay (on the left as you go down), where he lives. Most houses have ecological dry pit toilets and hot water by bucket. Homestays operate from May to October.

Taxis from Kaza cost ₹1500/1800 one way/return. From Komic it's about a 16km walk south to Demul, the next village on the 'Homestay Trail', or 26km by road. Whether you walk or drive, you'll reach an altitude of nearly 4700m a couple of kilometres south of Komic; this is the best leg of the homestay trek for long-distance panoramas. It's also good for sightings of blue sheep.

DEMUL

One of the larger villages on the homestay route, with 280 inhabitants, Demul sits in a high valley surrounded by its vegetable fields and awesome mountain vistas. Its weavers make many of the colourful, patterned shawls worn by women throughout Spiti. Villagers lead a semi-nomadic existence, taking their cows and yaks off to summer pastures for four or five months each year.

Demul operates a fully cooperative homestay scheme, with families taking turns to host tourists for ₹600 per person including meals. Ask for the coordinator who will organise you a house to stay in.

The next leg of the homestay trek is a sharp descent to Lhalung, 600m lower to the east (trail only; not possible for vehicles). To the west, a dramatic road zig-zags down to the main Spiti Valley road at Lidang, 800m lower than Demul. Taxis from Kaza cost around ₹2000.

Pin Valley

Southeast of Kaza, the Spiti River is joined by the Pin River, flowing out of a wind-scoured but beautiful valley from the heights of the Great Himalayan Range. Geological strata tilted at all conceivable angles, including vertical, bear witness to the immense tectonic forces that created the world's mightiest mountains.

Mudh (3770m), 33km up the valley road from the highway, is the trailhead for the spectacular and demanding Pin-Parvati trek (p304), and also for the easier but beautiful four-day trek over the 4850m **Bhaba (Bawa) Pass** to Kaphnu in Kinnaur, normally passable June to September. Mudh is a fine spot to ramble around for a couple of days, even if you're not trekking.

A short distance into either trek, you enter the 675-sq-km Pin Valley National Park, reputed as the 'land of ibex and snow leopards'. You may well see ibex (and blue sheep).

Ugyen Sangnak Choling Gompa BUDDHIST MONASTERY
At Kungri, 3km above Gulling, which is 16km up the valley, this 680-year-old monastery has a huge new building and three much more interesting medieval shrines, featuring blackened murals, festival masks and carved wooden snow lions. Women are not allowed past the threshold of two of them.

★Tara Homestay GUESTHOUSE $
(☎8988062293; www.facebook.com/taraguesthousespiti; Mudh; r ₹800, without bathroom ₹300-600, mains ₹60-110; ⌚May-Oct) The excellent Tara Homestay is the pick of several guesthouses in Mudh, and its little restaurant serves up thalis, *momos*, omelettes and fried rice to all comers. Owner Sonam Gialson can arrange full treks with porters, and other tours including jeep safaris.

Getting There & Away

The road into the Pin Valley branches off the Tabo road 15km southeast of Kaza. Mudslides at **Kirgarang Nullah**, 8km along, can block the road, sometimes for weeks, from some time in June, so take soundings before heading into the valley.

Buses to Mudh (₹82, two hours) leave Kaza daily at 4pm, starting back at 6am. Some days there's a shared jeep (₹100 per person) from Mudh to Kaza at about 6am, returning around 3pm. Kaza taxis charge ₹2100 to Mudh.

Dhankar

POP 300 / ELEV 3880M

High above the confluence of the Spiti and Pin Rivers, an 8km walk or drive up from Sichling on the Kaza–Tabo road, Dhankar village is the former capital of the Nono kings who ruled Spiti. Its old gompa is one of the most spectacular sights in Spiti.

Sights

The spectacular 1200-year-old **Dhankar Gompa** (₹25; ⌚usually 7am-6pm) perches precariously between eroded pinnacles on the edge of a cliff. Its top-floor courtyard has a stuffed goat hanging above the stairwell, a room where the Dalai Lama slept, a meditation cave, and a shrine containing ceremonial masks. Another prayer hall, with murals of the Buddha of healing, stands on top of the rock above, accessed by separate concrete steps. The views from these buildings are phenomenal. Dhankar's lamas no longer inhabit the old gompa, having moved to the large, gleaming **New Monastery**, 800m away, in 2009.

On the hilltop above the gompa are the ruins of the abandoned mud-brick **fort-palace** that sheltered the valley's population during times of war and gave the village its name (*khar* means 'citadel' and *dhak* means 'cliff'). An hour's steep walk up from the village, the small lake **Dhankar Tso** offers views over the valley and southeast to the twin peaks of Manirang (6593m).

Sleeping & Eating

Dhankar Monastery Guesthouse GUESTHOUSE $
(☎9418646578; dm ₹200, r ₹500-1200; ⌚Apr-mid-Oct, restaurant 7am-9.30pm) Beside the New Monastery, this place belongs to the monastery but is geared to tourists. The rooms and terrace have picture-postcard views, and the restaurant prepares a wide choice of good food (mains ₹120 to ₹280).

Manirang Home Stay & Cafe HOMESTAY $
(☎8988053409; dm ₹150-200, r without bathroom per person incl half-board ₹500, incl full board ₹600; ⌚cafe 7am-8pm) Below the road between the old and new monasteries, Manirang has five pleasant, clean rooms and a dorm with floor mattresses, plus a cafe with an international menu (mains ₹60 to ₹120). Owner Anil Kumar is a trekking guide and has a jeep for transport.

Getting There & Away

Buses between Kaza and Tabo pass through Sichling (₹40, one hour from Kaza); you might find a ride from Sichling. A taxi from Kaza to Dhankar is ₹1550/1860 one way/return.

Lhalung

Hidden up the Lingti Valley, 12km northeast of Dhankar along a fairly level dirt road, the charming traditional village of Lhalung is worth a detour for its fantastic medieval **monastery** (₹25). The atmospheric main chapel contains superb old murals and an incredibly ornate, carved, wooden back frieze. The separate Langkharpo chapel holds a unique four-sided statue of the white deity atop a plinth of snow lions. Don't miss the skin prayer wheel in a side chapel.

The village has several homestays charging around ₹600 per person including meals, which you can arrange on the spot or through agencies including Ecosphere (p348).

A bus to Lhalung (₹43, two hours; not via Dhankar) leaves Kaza at 5.30pm, coming back at 8am the next day.

Tabo

☎01906 / POP 600 / ELEV 3280M

Little Tabo, in a dramatic valley setting hemmed in by scree slopes, 48km southeast of Kaza, is the only other town in Spiti. The mud-brick walls of Tabo Gompa enclose some of the finest of all Indo-Tibetan art, and Tabo makes a fine place to kick back for a couple of days.

Sights

★Tabo Gompa BUDDHIST MONASTERY

(www.tabomonastery.com; donations accepted; ⏲shrines 9am-1pm & 2-5pm) The gompa was founded in AD 996, possibly by Ringchen Zangpo, the Great Translator, as Tibet's Guge kingdom expanded into these outlying territories, and is reckoned to be the oldest continuously functioning Buddhist monastery in India. Five of the nine shrines inside its mud-walled buildings date from the 10th and 11th centuries, when they were painted by some of the best Buddhist muralists of their era, blending Tibetan, Indian and Kashmiri styles. Bring a torch as lighting is dim.

The other shrines mostly date from the 15th to 17th centuries. While the old gompa is still used for some monastic activities, most of the monastery's life today goes on in the modern gompa beside the ancient compound.

The old gompa's spectacular main assembly hall, the **Tsuglkang**, is entered through the Zal-ma antechamber. Large sculptures of four blue protector deities (one for each compass point) flank the Tsuglkang's doorway (two inside, two outside), and its walls are lined with stunning, near life-size clay sculptures of 28 bodhisattvas. The hall's focus is a statue of a four-bodied Vairochana Buddha turning the wheel of law – the whole room being a 3D representation of the Vajradhatu mandala, which has the Vairochana at its centre. Murals below the bodhisattvas depict 10th-century life. Behind the Vairochana, the inner sanctuary holds a stucco Amitabha Buddha and two smaller bodhisattvas. The ambulatory behind that is adorned with hundreds of small and large lotus-position figures.

You may have to ask a lama to open up other temples in the compound. The other worthwhile early temples are the **Ser-Khang** (Golden Temple), second to the left from the Tsuglkang, with outstanding murals on its north wall of the green Tara and the goddess Usnishavijaya; the **Kyil-Khang** (Mystic Mandala Temple) behind the Ser-Khang, with a Vairochana mural facing the entrance and mandalas depicting deities surrounded by eight other deities on the north and south walls; and the **Byams-Pa Chen-po Lha-Khang** (Bodhisattva Maitreya Temple), immediately right of the Tsuglkang, with a 3m-high statue of the Maitreya (future Buddha).

The modern gompa outside the ancient compound has a sparkling gilded chorten and a brand-new temple, and holds a well-attended *puja* at 6am (guests welcome).

Caves CAVE

A number of caves on the hillside above the main road were part of the old monastery complex – a 200m walk starting up the steps opposite the Vijay Kumar shop.

Sleeping & Eating

★Tashi Khangsar Hotel GUESTHOUSE $

(☎9418817761; vaneetrana23@gmail.com; r ₹600-800, camping per tent ₹200; ⏲Apr-Oct) The four bright, clean, inviting rooms here are set beside an expansive, grassy garden where table and chairs sit beneath a large parachute canopy. There's good international food at decent prices, and plenty of camping space, and the relaxed, friendly vibe makes it a great spot to chill out for a night or a few.

From the new monastery's gate, head towards the river and turn right at the helipad.

Tiger Den GUESTHOUSE $
(☎9459349711; naveen.chauhan82@gmail.com; r ₹900-1200; ⏲Apr-Oct) Almost next to the new monastery's entrance, this is a fine choice with clean, pink, medium-sized rooms with hot showers.

It has one of Tabo's best **restaurants** (mains ₹120-300; ⏲7am-10pm Apr-Oct), with indoor and outdoor seating, and a great range of Indian, Tibetan and traveller food, plus delectable chilled apple juice.

Sonam Homestay GUESTHOUSE $
(☎9418503966; www.prospiti.ch; s/d ₹800/1000, r without bathroom ₹400-500; ⏲May-Oct) Rooms here are some of the best value in Tabo: neat and clean, with solar-heated water. The locally born owner also runs his own travel and trekking firm.

Also here is the good **Cafe Kunzum Top** (Sonam Homestay; mains ₹100-150; ⏲7am-9.30pm), serving up tasty Tibetan, Spitian, Indian and Continental dishes, and good coffee, in its sunny garden and cosy interior.

Dewachen Retreat HOTEL $$$
(☎9459566689; www.dewachenretreats.com; s/d ₹4320/4800, incl half-board ₹5490/6100; ⏲mid-Apr–mid-Nov) The impressiveness of the carved wooden doorway doesn't quite extend inside, but the pine-panelled rooms, with good tiled bathrooms and temple and mountain views, are Tabo's nearest thing to luxury. It's on the main road at the back of town, and is sometimes full with groups. The good restaurant is open to all.

ℹ Information

There's an SBI ATM near the new monastery's gate.

ℹ Getting There & Away

Buses to Kaza (₹73, 2½ hours) pass through Tabo around 9am (coming from Chango) and 3pm (coming from Rekong Peo, so its time is pretty variable). There's a daily bus to Rekong Peo (₹270, nine hours) at 9am or 10am, via Nako (₹105, three hours), but since this originates in Kaza, it can be packed, especially in May and October when seasonal workers are on the move.

Taxis charge around ₹1900 to Kaza, ₹1600 to Dhankar, ₹1900 to Nako and ₹6000 to Rekong Peo.

Agra & the Taj Mahal

Includes ➡

Best Places to Eat

- ➡ Pinch of Spice (p366)
- ➡ Mama Chicken (p366)
- ➡ Esphahan (p366)
- ➡ Vedic (p366)

Best Places to Sleep

- ➡ Tourists Rest House (p364)
- ➡ N Homestay (p363)
- ➡ Oberoi Amarvilas (p363)
- ➡ The Retreat (p363)

Why Go?

The magical allure of the Taj Mahal draws tourists to Agra like moths to a wondrous flame. And despite the hype, it's every bit as good as you've heard. But the Taj is not a standalone attraction. The legacy of the Mughal empire has left a magnificent fort and a liberal sprinkling of fascinating tombs and mausoleums; and there's also fun to be had in the bustling *chowks* (marketplaces). The downside comes in the form of hordes of rickshaw-wallahs, touts, unofficial guides and souvenir vendors, whose persistence can be infuriating at times.

Agra straddles a large bend along the holy Yamuna River. The fort and the Taj, 2km apart, both overlook the river on different parts of the bend. The main train and bus stations are a few kilometres southwest.

When to Go

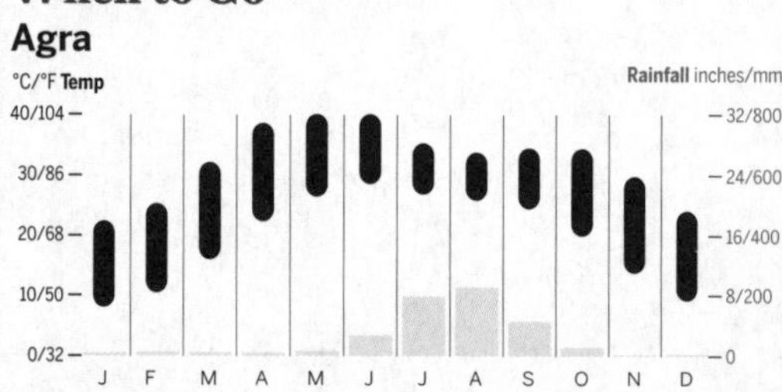

Sep–Oct The best time to visit. Most of the monsoon rains are over and summer temperatures have cooled.

Nov–Feb Daytime temperatures are comfortable but big sights are overcrowded. Evenings are nippy.

Mar Evening chill is gone but raging-hot midsummer temperatures haven't yet materialised.

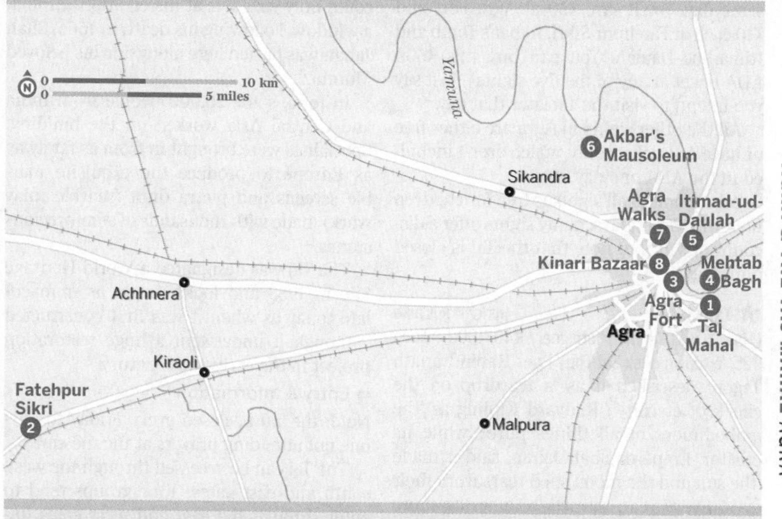

Agra & the Taj Mahal Highlights

1. **Taj Mahal** (p354) Basking in the beauty of one of the most famous buildings in the world – a must-see!
2. **Fatehpur Sikri** (p371) Roaming a sprawling palace complex from Mughal times, with an immense and fascinating 450-year-old mosque next door.
3. **Agra Fort** (p358) Wandering the many rooms of one of India's most impressive ancient forts.
4. **Mehtab Bagh** (p358) Relaxing in gardens with perfect sunset views of the Taj.
5. **Itimad-ud-Daulah** (p360) Marveling at the marble-work of an exquisite tomb nicknamed the Baby Taj.
6. **Akbar's Mausoleum** (p360) Visiting the impressive resting place of the greatest Mughal emperor.
7. **Agra Walks** (p361) Strolling deeper into ancient Agra with local guides.
8. **Kinari Bazaar** (p367) Boggling your senses in one of India's most mesmerising – and hectic – markets.

History

In 1501 Sultan Sikander Lodi established his capital here, but the city fell into Mughal hands in 1526, when Emperor Babur defeated the last Lodi sultan at Panipat. Agra reached the peak of its magnificence between the mid-16th and mid-17th centuries during the reigns of Akbar, Jehangir and Shah Jahan. During this period the fort, the Taj Mahal and other major mausoleums were built. In 1638 Shah Jahan built a new city in Delhi, and his son Aurangzeb moved the capital there 10 years later.

In 1761 Agra fell to the Jats, a warrior class who looted its monuments, including the Taj Mahal. The Marathas took over in 1770, but were replaced by the British in 1803. Following the First War of Independence of 1857, the British shifted the administration of the province to Allahabad. Deprived of its administrative role, Agra developed as a centre for heavy industry, quickly becoming famous for its chemicals industry and air pollution, before the Taj and tourism became a major source of income.

Agra

0562 / POP 1.7 MILLION

Sights

The entrance fee for Agra's five main sights – the Taj, Agra Fort, Fatehpur Sikri, Akbar's Tomb and Itimad-ud-Daulah – comprises charges from two different bodies: the Archaeological Survey of India (ASI) and the Agra Development Association (ADA). Of the ₹1000 ticket for the Taj Mahal, ₹500 is a special ADA ticket, which gives you small savings on the other four sights if visited in the same day. You'll save ₹50 at Agra Fort and ₹10 each at Fatehpur Sikri, Akbar's Tomb and Itimad-ud-Daulah. You can buy this ₹500 ADA ticket at any of the five sights – just say you intend to visit the Taj later that day.

All the other sights in Agra are either free or have ASI tickets only, which aren't included in the ADA one-day offer.

Admission to all sights is free for children under 15. On Fridays, many sights offer a discount of ₹10 (but note that the Taj is closed on Friday).

★**Taj Mahal** HISTORIC BUILDING

(Map p362; Indian/foreigner ₹40/1000, video ₹25; ⏲dawn-dusk Sat-Thu) Poet Rabindranath Tagore described it as 'a teardrop on the cheek of eternity'; Rudyard Kipling as 'the embodiment of all things pure'; while its creator, Emperor Shah Jahan, said it made 'the sun and the moon shed tears from their eyes'. Every year, tourists numbering more than twice the population of Agra pass through its gates to catch a once-in-a-lifetime glimpse of what is widely considered the most beautiful building in the world. Few leave disappointed.

The Taj was built by Shah Jahan as a memorial for his third wife, Mumtaz Mahal, who died giving birth to their 14th child in 1631. The death of Mumtaz left the emperor so heartbroken that his hair is said to have turned grey virtually overnight. Construction of the Taj began the following year; although the main building is thought to have been built in eight years, the whole complex was not completed until 1653. Not long after it was finished, Shah Jahan was overthrown by his son Aurangzeb and imprisoned in Agra Fort, where for the rest of his days he could only gaze out at his creation through a window. Following his death in 1666, Shah Jahan was buried here alongside his beloved Mumtaz.

In total, some 20,000 people from India and Central Asia worked on the building. Specialists were brought in from as far away as Europe to produce the exquisite marble screens and pietra dura (marble inlay work) made with thousands of semiprecious stones.

The Taj was designated a World Heritage Site in 1983 and looks nearly as immaculate today as when it was first constructed – though it underwent a huge restoration project in the early 20th century.

➡ **Entry & Information**

Note: the Taj is closed every Friday to anyone not attending prayers at the mosque.

The Taj can be accessed through the west, south and east gates. Tour groups tend to enter through the east and west gates. Independent travellers tend to use the south gate, which is nearest to Taj Ganj, the main area for budget accommodation, and generally has shorter queues than the west gate. The east gate has the shortest queues of the lot, but this is because the ticket office is inconveniently located a 1km walk away at Shilpgram, a dire, government-run tourist centre. There are separate queues for men and women at all three gates. Once you get your ticket, you can skip ahead of the lines of Indians waiting to get in – one perk of your pricey entry fee.

Cameras and videos are permitted but you can't take photographs inside the mausoleum itself, and the areas in which you can take videos are quite limited. Tripods are banned.

Remember to retrieve your free 500ml bottle of water and shoe covers (included in Taj ticket price). If you keep your ticket you get small entry-fee discounts when visiting Agra Fort, Fatehpur Sikri, Akbar's Tomb or the Itimad-ud-Daulah on the same day. You can also pick up an **audio guide** (₹120). Bags much bigger than a money pouch are not allowed inside; free bag storage is available at the west gate. Any food or tobacco will be confiscated when you go through security.

From the south gate, entry to the inner compound is through a very impressive 30m red-sandstone **gateway** on the south side of the forecourt, which is inscribed with verses from the Quran.

BEST TIMES TO SEE THE TAJ

The Taj is arguably at its most atmospheric at sunrise. This is certainly the most comfortable time to visit, with far fewer crowds. Sunset is another magical viewing time.

You can also view the Taj for five nights around the full moon. Entry numbers are limited, though, and tickets must be bought a day in advance from the **Archaeological Survey of India office** (p368); see its website for details. (Note: this office is known as the Taj Mahal Office by some rickshaw riders.)

TAJ MAHAL MYTHS

The Taj is a Hindu Temple

The well-publicised theory that the Taj was originally a Shiva temple built in the 12th century, and only later converted into Mumtaz Mahal's famous mausoleum, was developed by Purushottam Nagesh Oak in 1989. (Oak also claims that the Kaaba, Stonehenge and Vatican City all have Hindu origins.) He petitioned parliament to open the Taj's sealed basement rooms to prove his theory (request denied) and in 2000 India's Supreme Court dismissed his plea to officially name a Hindu king as the builder of the Taj. But the matter is still alive, with a similar court case filed as recently as 2015, this one naming a form of Shiva as one of the plaintiffs. Archaeologists and the Indian government remain unconvinced.

The Black Taj Mahal

The story goes that Shah Jahan planned to build a negative image of the Taj Mahal in black marble on the opposite side of the river as his own mausoleum, and that work began before he was imprisoned by his son Aurangzeb in Agra Fort. Extensive excavations at Mehtab Bagh have found no trace of any such construction.

Craftsmen Mutilations

Legend has it that on completion of the Taj, Shah Jahan ordered the hands of the project's craftsmen to be chopped off, preventing them from ever building anything as beautiful again. Some even say he went so far as to have their eyes gouged out. Thankfully, no historical evidence supports either story.

Sinking Taj

Some experts believe there is evidence to show that the Taj is slowly tilting towards and sinking into the riverbed due to the changing nature of the soil beside an increasingly dry Yamuna River. The Archaeological Survey of India has dismissed any marginal change in the elevation of the building as statistically insignificant, adding that it has not detected any structural damage at its base in the seven decades since its first scientific study of the Taj was carried out, in 1941.

➡ Inside the Grounds

The **ornamental gardens** are set out along classical Mughal *charbagh* (formal Persian garden) lines – a square quartered by watercourses, with an ornamental marble plinth at its centre. When the fountains are not flowing, the Taj is beautifully reflected in the water.

The Taj Mahal itself stands on a raised marble platform at the northern end of the ornamental gardens, with its back to the Yamuna River. Its raised position means that the backdrop is only sky – a masterstroke of design. Purely decorative 40m-high white **minarets** grace each corner of the platform. After more than three centuries they are not quite perpendicular, but they may have been designed to lean slightly outwards so that in the event of an earthquake they would fall away from the precious Taj. The red-sandstone **mosque** (Map p362) to the west is an important gathering place for Agra's Muslims. The identical building to the east, the **jawab** (Map p362), was built for symmetry.

The central Taj structure is made of semitranslucent white marble, carved with flowers and inlaid with thousands of semiprecious stones in beautiful patterns. A perfect exercise in symmetry, the four identical faces of the Taj feature impressive vaulted arches embellished with pietra dura scrollwork and quotations from the Quran in a style of calligraphy using inlaid jasper. The whole structure is topped off by four small domes surrounding the famous bulbous central dome.

Directly below the main dome is the **Cenotaph of Mumtaz Mahal**, an elaborate false tomb surrounded by an exquisite perforated marble screen inlaid with dozens of different types of semiprecious stones. Beside it, offsetting the symmetry of the Taj, is the **Cenotaph of Shah Jahan**, who was interred here with little ceremony by his usurping son Aurangzeb in 1666. Light is admitted into the central chamber by finely cut marble screens. The real tombs of Mumtaz

Taj Mahal

TIMELINE

1631 Emperor Shah Jahan's beloved third wife, Mumtaz Mahal, dies in Buhanpur while giving birth to their 14th child. Her body is initially interred in Buhanpur itself, where Shah Jahan is fighting a military campaign, but is later moved, in a golden casket, to a small building on the banks of the Yamuna River in Agra.

1632 Construction of a permanent mausoleum for Mumtaz Mahal begins.

1633 Mumtaz Mahal is interred in her final resting place, an underground tomb beneath a marble plinth, on top of which the Taj Mahal will be built.

1640 The white-marble mausoleum is completed.

1653 The rest of the Taj Mahal complex is completed.

1658 Emperor Shah Jahan is overthrown by his son Aurangzeb and imprisoned in Agra Fort.

1666 Shah Jahan dies. His body is transported along the Yamuna River and buried underneath the Taj, alongside the tomb of his wife.

1908 Repeatedly damaged and looted after the fall of the Mughal empire, the Taj receives some long-overdue attention as part of a major restoration project ordered by British viceroy Lord Curzon.

1983 The Taj is awarded Unesco World Heritage Site status.

2002 Having been discoloured by pollution in more recent years, the Taj is spruced up with an ancient recipe known as multani mitti – a blend of soil, cereal, milk and lime once used by Indian women to beautify their skin.

Today More than three million tourists visit the Taj Mahal each year. That's more than twice the current population of Agra.

ARIS ABDULLAH/SHUTTERSTOCK ©

Pishtaqs

These huge arched recesses are set into each side of the Taj. They provide depth to the building while their central, latticed marble screens allow patterned light to illuminate the inside of the mausoleum.

Minaret

Plinth

Entra

Marble Relief Work

Flowering plants, thought to be representations of paradise, are a common theme among the beautifully decorative panels carved onto the white marble.

FABIOIM/SHUTTERSTOCK ©

GO BAREFOOT

Help the environment by entering the mausoleum barefoot instead of using the free disposable shoe covers.

LIGHT THE WAY

Bring a small torch into the mausoleum to fully appreciate the translucenc of the white marble and semiprecious stones.

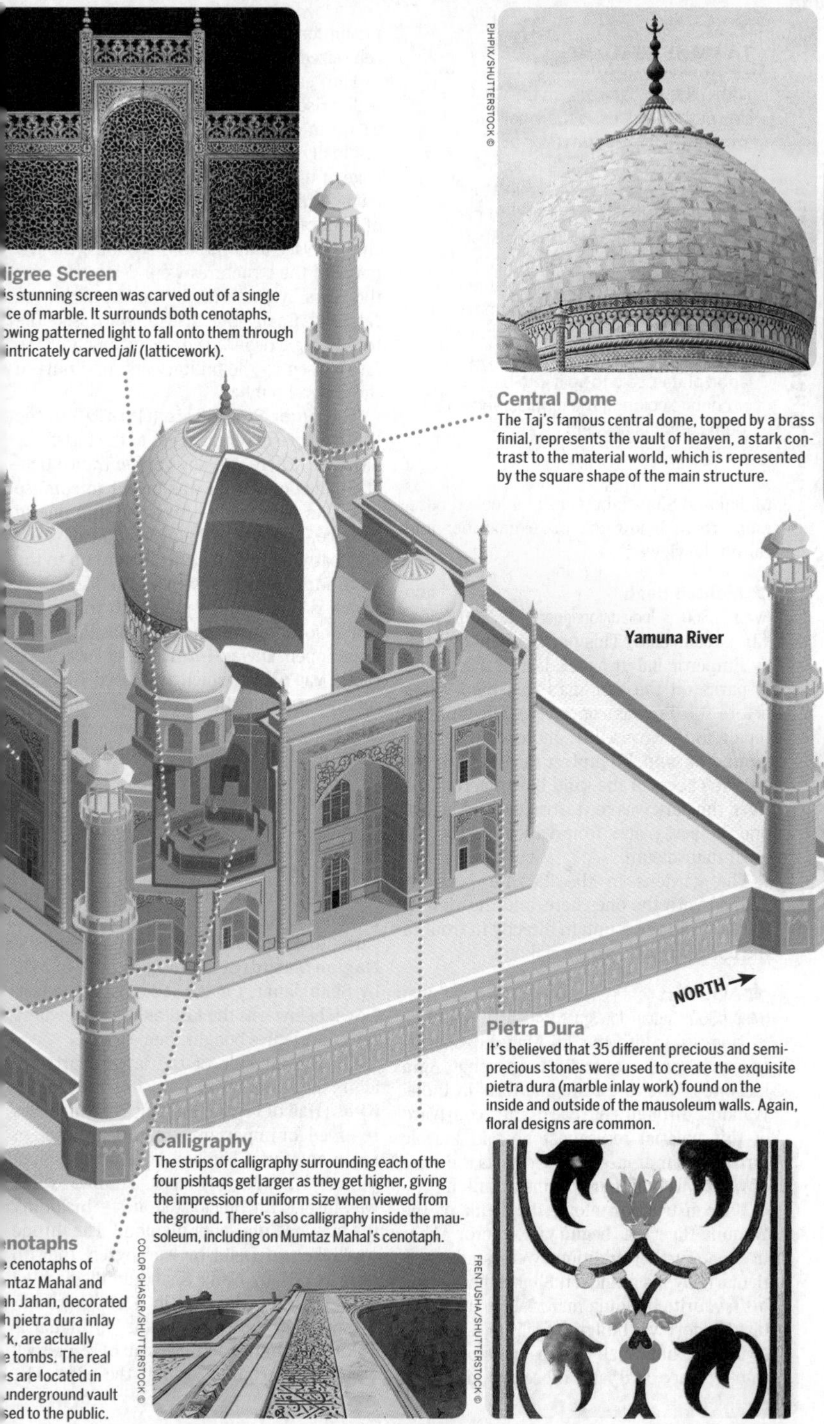

ligree Screen

's stunning screen was carved out of a single ce of marble. It surrounds both cenotaphs, owing patterned light to fall onto them through intricately carved *jali* (latticework).

Central Dome

The Taj's famous central dome, topped by a brass finial, represents the vault of heaven, a stark contrast to the material world, which is represented by the square shape of the main structure.

Pietra Dura

It's believed that 35 different precious and semi-precious stones were used to create the exquisite pietra dura (marble inlay work) found on the inside and outside of the mausoleum walls. Again, floral designs are common.

Calligraphy

The strips of calligraphy surrounding each of the four pishtaqs get larger as they get higher, giving the impression of uniform size when viewed from the ground. There's also calligraphy inside the mausoleum, including on Mumtaz Mahal's cenotaph.

enotaphs

e cenotaphs of mtaz Mahal and ah Jahan, decorated h pietra dura inlay k, are actually e tombs. The real s are located in underground vault sed to the public.

TAJ MUSEUM

Within the Taj complex, on the western side of the gardens, is the small but excellent **Taj Museum** (Map p362; 9am-5pm Sat-Thu) FREE, housing a number of original Mughal miniature paintings, including a pair of 17th-century ivory portraits of Emperor Shah Jahan and his beloved wife Mumtaz Mahal. It also has some very well-preserved gold and silver coins dating from the same period, plus architectural drawings of the Taj and some nifty celadon plates, said to split into pieces or change colour if the food served on them contains poison.

Mahal and Shah Jahan are in a locked basement room below the main chamber and cannot be viewed.

★Mehtab Bagh PARK

(Map p360; Indian/foreigner ₹15/200, video ₹25; dawn-dusk) This park, originally built by Emperor Babur as the last in a series of 11 parks on the Yamuna's east bank (long before the Taj was conceived), fell into disrepair until it was little more than a huge mound of sand. To protect the Taj from the erosive effects of the sand blown across the river, the park was reconstructed and is now one the best places from which to view the great mausoleum.

The gardens in the Taj are perfectly aligned with the ones here, and the view of the Taj from the fountain directly in front of the entrance gate is a special one.

★Agra Fort FORT

(Map p360; Indian/foreigner ₹40/550, video ₹25; dawn-dusk) With the Taj Mahal overshadowing it, one can easily forget that Agra has one of the finest Mughal forts in India. Walking through courtyard after courtyard of this palatial red-sandstone and marble fortress, your amazement grows as the scale of what was built here begins to sink in.

Its construction along the bank of the Yamuna River was begun by Emperor Akbar in 1565. Further additions were made, particularly by his grandson Shah Jahan, using his favourite building material – white marble. The fort was built primarily as a military structure, but Shah Jahan transformed it into a palace, and later it became his gilded prison for eight years after his son Aurangzeb seized power in 1658.

The ear-shaped fort's colossal double walls rise more than 20m and measure 2.5km in circumference. The Yamuna River originally flowed along the straight eastern edge of the fort, and the emperors had their own bathing ghats here. It contains a maze of buildings, forming a city within a city, including vast underground sections, though many of the structures were destroyed over the years by Nadir Shah, the Marathas, the Jats and finally the British, who used the fort as a garrison. Even today, much of the fort is used by the military and off-limits to the general public.

The **Amar Singh Gate** (Map p360) to the south is the sole entry point to the fort these days and where you buy your entrance ticket. Its dogleg design was meant to confuse attackers who made it past the first line of defence – the crocodile-infested moat.

A path leads straight from here up to the large **Moti Masjid** (Pearl Mosque; Map p360), which is closed to the public. To your right, just before you reach Moti Masjid, is the large, open **Diwan-i-Am** (Hall of Public Audiences; Map p360), which was used by Shah Jahan for domestic government business, and features a throne room where the emperor listened to petitioners. In front of it is the small and rather incongruous **grave of John Colvin**, a lieutenant-governor of the northwest provinces who died of an illness in the fort during the 1857 First War of Independence.

A tiny staircase just to the left of the Diwan-i-Am throne leads up to a large courtyard. To your left is the tiny but exquisite **Nagina Masjid** (Gem Mosque), built in 1635 by Shah Jahan for the ladies of the court. Down below was the **Ladies' Bazaar**, where the court ladies bought their goods.

On the far side of the large courtyard, along the eastern wall of the fort, is **Diwan-i-Khas** (Hall of Private Audiences), which was reserved for important dignitaries or foreign representatives. The hall once housed Shah Jahan's legendary Peacock Throne, which was inset with precious stones – including the famous Koh-i-noor diamond. The throne was taken to Delhi by Aurangzeb, then to Iran in 1739 by Nadir Shah and dismantled after his assassination in 1747. Overlooking the river and the distant Taj Mahal is **Takhti-i-Jehangir**, a huge slab of black rock with an inscription around the edge. The throne that stood here was made for Jehangir when he was Prince Salim.

Off to your right from here (as you face the river) is **Shish Mahal** (Mirror Palace), with walls inlaid with tiny mirrors. At the time of research it had been closed for some time due to restoration, although you can peek through cracks in the doors at the sparkling mirrors inside.

Further along the eastern edge of the fort you'll find **Musamman Burj** and **Khas Mahal**, (Map p360) the wonderful white-marble octagonal tower and palace where Shah Jahan was imprisoned for eight years until his death in 1666, and from where he could gaze out at the Taj Mahal, the tomb of his wife. When he died, Shah Jahan's body was taken from here by boat to the Taj. The now closed **Mina Masjid**, set back slightly from the eastern edge, was his private mosque.

The large courtyard here is **Anguri Bagh**, a garden that has been brought back to life in recent years. In the courtyard is an innocuous-looking entrance – now locked – that leads down a flight of stairs into a two-storey labyrinth of underground rooms and passageways where Akbar used to keep his 500-strong harem.

Continuing south, the huge red-sandstone **Jehangir's Palace** (Map p360) was probably built by Akbar for his son Jehangir. It blends Indian and Central Asian architectural styles, a reminder of the Mughals' Afghani cultural roots. In front of the palace is **Hauz-i-Jehangir**, a huge bowl carved out of a single block of stone, which was used for

TOP TAJ VIEWS

Inside the Taj Grounds

You may have to pay ₹1000 for the privilege, but it's only when you're inside the grounds themselves that you can really get up close and personal with the world's most beautiful building. Don't miss inspecting the marble inlay work (pietra dura) inside the *pishtaqs* (large arched recesses) on the four outer walls. And don't forget to bring a small torch with you so that you can shine it on similar pietra dura work inside the dark central chamber of the mausoleum. Note the translucency of both the white marble and the semiprecious stones inlaid into it.

From Mehtab Bagh

Tourists are no longer allowed to wander freely along the riverbank on the opposite side of the Yamuna River, but you can still enjoy a view of the back of the Taj from the 16th-century Mughal park Mehtab Bagh, with the river flowing between you and the mausoleum. A path leading down to the river beside the park offers the same view for free, albeit from a more restricted angle.

Looking up from the South Bank of the River

This is a great place to be for sunset. Take the path that hugs the outside of the Taj's eastern wall and walk all the way down to the small temple beside the river. You should be able to find boat-hands down here willing to row you out onto the water for an even more romantic view. Expect to pay around ₹100 per boat. For safety reasons, it's best not to wander down here on your own for sunset.

From a Rooftop Cafe in Taj Ganj

Perfect for sunrise shots: there are some wonderful photos to be had from the numerous rooftop cafes in Taj Ganj. We think the cafe on Saniya Palace Hotel (p362) is the pick of the bunch, with its plant-filled design and great position, but many of them are good. And all offer the bonus of being able to view the Taj with the added comfort of an early-morning cup of coffee.

From Agra Fort

With a decent zoom lens you can capture some fabulous images of the Taj from Agra Fort, especially if you're willing to get up at the crack of dawn to see the sun rising up from behind it. The best places to snap from are probably Musamman Burj and Khas Mahal, the octagonal tower and palace where Shah Jahan was imprisoned for eight years until his death.

Agra

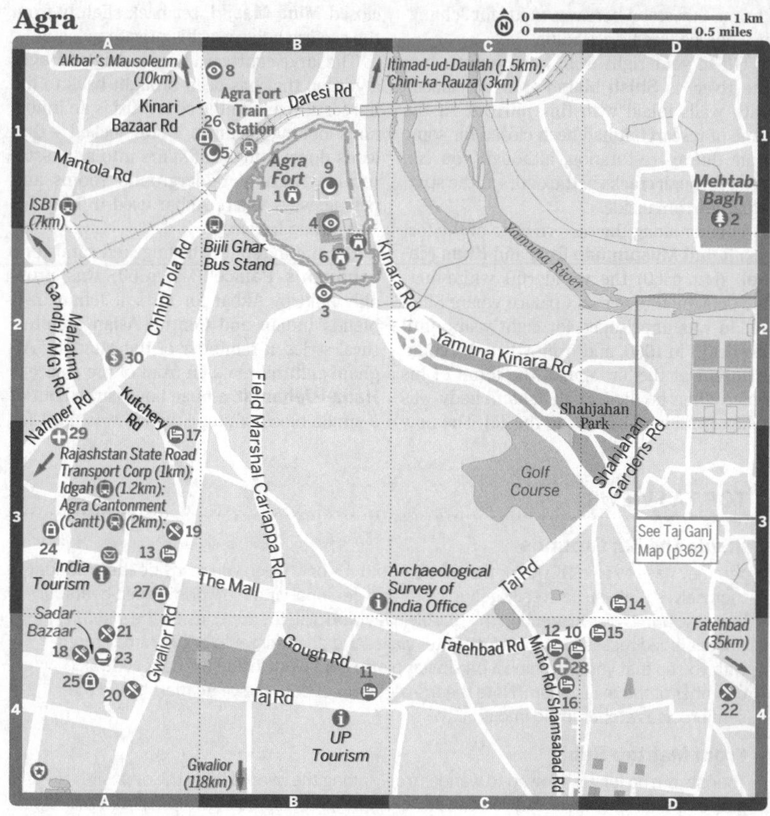

bathing. Walking past this brings you back to the main path to Amar Singh Gate.

You can walk here from Taj Ganj, or else take a cycle-rickshaw for ₹40.

Akbar's Mausoleum HISTORIC BUILDING

(Indian/foreigner ₹15/300, video ₹25; ⏲ dawn-dusk) This outstanding sandstone and marble tomb commemorates the greatest of the Mughal emperors. The huge courtyard is entered through a stunning gateway. It has three-storey minarets at each corner and is built of red sandstone strikingly inlaid with white-marble geometric patterns.

The mausoleum is at Sikandra, 10km northwest of Agra Fort. Catch a bus (₹25, 45 minutes) headed to Mathura from Bijli Ghar bus stand (p370); they go past the mausoleum. Or else take a taxi (return trip about ₹800).

Itimad-ud-Daulah HISTORIC BUILDING

(Indian/foreigner ₹20/210, video ₹25; ⏲ dawn-dusk) Nicknamed the Baby Taj, the exquisite tomb of Mizra Ghiyas Beg should not be missed. This Persian nobleman was Mumtaz Mahal's grandfather and Emperor Jehangir's *wazir* (chief minister). His daughter, Nur Jahan, who married Jehangir, built the tomb between 1622 and 1628, in a style similar to the tomb she built for Jehangir near Lahore in Pakistan.

It doesn't have the same awesome beauty as the Taj, but it's arguably more delicate in appearance thanks to its particularly finely carved *jalis* (marble lattice screens). This was the first Mughal structure built completely from marble, the first to make extensive use of pietra dura and the first tomb to be built on the banks of the Yamuna, which until then had been a sequence of beautiful pleasure gardens.

You can combine a trip here with Chini-ka-Rauza and Mehtab Bagh, all on the east bank. A cycle-rickshaw covering all four should cost about ₹300 return from the Taj,

Agra

Top Sights
1 Agra Fort ... B1
2 Mehtab Bagh ... D1

Sights
3 Amar Singh Gate ... B2
4 Diwan-i-Am ... B1
5 Jama Masjid ... B1
6 Jehangir's Palace ... B2
7 Khas Mahal ... B2
8 Kinari Bazaar ... B1
9 Moti Masjid ... B1

Sleeping
10 Bansi Homestay ... C4
11 Clarks Shiraz Hotel ... B4
Dasaprakash ... (see 28)
12 Hotel Amar ... C4
13 Hotel Yamuna View ... A3
14 Howard Plaza ... D3
15 Mansingh Palace ... D4
16 N Homestay ... C4
17 Tourists Rest House ... A3

Eating
18 Brijwasi ... A4
19 Dasaprakash ... A3
Dasaprakash ... (see 28)
20 Lakshmi Vilas ... A4
21 Mama Chicken ... A4
22 Pinch of Spice ... D4
Vedic ... (see 19)

Drinking & Nightlife
23 Café Coffee Day ... A4
Costa Coffee ... (see 10)

Shopping
24 Khadi Gramodyog ... A3
25 Modern Book Depot ... A4
26 Subhash Bazaar ... B1
27 Subhash Emporium ... A3

Information
28 Amit Jaggi Memorial Hospital ... C4
Bagpacker Travel ... (see 17)
29 SR Hospital ... A3
30 State Bank of India ... A2

including waiting time. An autorickshaw should be ₹450.

Chini-ka-Rauza HISTORIC BUILDING
(dawn-dusk) FREE This Persian-style riverside tomb of Afzal Khan, a poet who served as Shah Jahan's chief minister, was built between 1628 and 1639. Rarely visited, it is hidden away down a shady avenue of trees on the east bank of the Yamuna.

Jama Masjid MOSQUE
(Map p360; Jama Masjid Rd) This fine mosque, built in the Kinari Bazaar (p367) by Shah Jahan's daughter in 1648, and once connected to Agra Fort, features striking marble patterning on its domes.

Activities

Hotels allowing nonguests to use their swimming pools include Howard Plaza (p364), per hour ₹500, and Amar (p364), all day ₹575 – with slide.

Tours

Agra Walks WALKING
(9027711144; www.agrawalks.com; ₹2200) Many folks spend but a day in Agra, taking in the Taj and Agra Fort and sailing off into the sunset. If you're interested in digging a little deeper, this excellent walking/cycle-rickshaw combo tour will show you sides of the city most tourists don't see.

The guides are darling and Old Agra highlights include going deeper into Kinari Bazaar and a few off-the-beaten-path temples such as Mankameshwar Mandir and Radha Krishna Mandir. A delectable **food tour** is also offered (₹2000, includes tastings).

Amin Tours CULTURAL
(9837411144; www.daytourtajmahal.com) If you can't be bothered handling the logistics, look no further than this recommended agency for all-inclusive private Agra day trips from Delhi by car (from ₹9900, depending on number in group) or train (from ₹10,200). Caveat: if they try to take you shopping and you're not interested, politely decline.

UP Tourism BUS
(0562-2421204; www.uptourism.gov.in; incl entry fees Indian/foreigner ₹650/3000) UP Tourism runs coach tours that leave Agra Cantonment train station at 10.30am Saturday to Thursday, after picking up passengers arriving from Delhi on the Taj Express. The tour includes the Taj Mahal, Agra Fort and Fatehpur Sikri, with a 1¼-hour stop in each place.

Tours return to the station so that day trippers can catch the Taj Express back to Delhi at 6.55pm. Contact either of the UP Tourism offices – at the train station (p369) or on Taj Rd (p369) – to book a seat, or just turn up at the train station tourist office at 9.45am to sign up for that day. Tours only

Taj Ganj

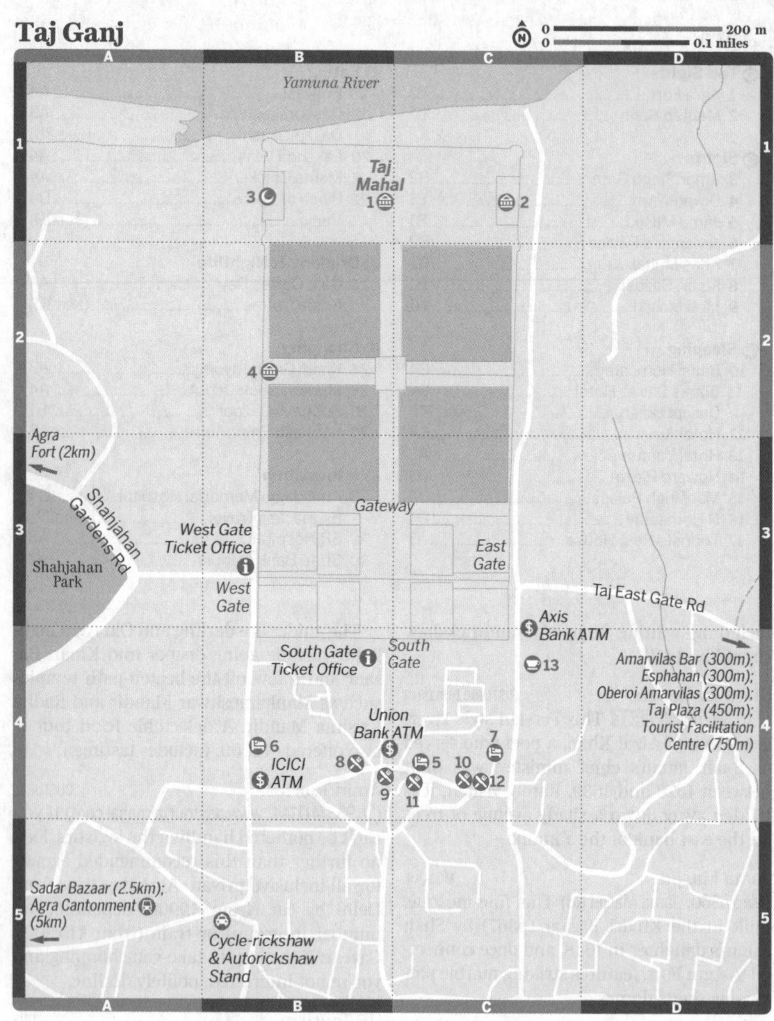

depart with five people or more, unless you book via the UP Tourism website – in that case, we've been told, your tour will go no matter how many sign up. (The website is a bit difficult to navigate: From the home page, click Online Booking Portal > Package Tours at a Glance > Agra Package Tour (under Package Tours, *not* One Day Tour) and take it from there...)

Sleeping

The main place for budget accommodation is the bustling area of Taj Ganj, immediately south of the Taj, while there's a high concentration of midrange hotels further south, along Fatehabad Rd. Sadar Bazaar, an area boasting good-quality restaurants, offers another option.

Be forewarned: free wi-fi hasn't really caught on in Agra's nicer hotels; expect to pay upwards of ₹500 for 24 hours.

Taj Ganj Area

Saniya Palace Hotel HOTEL $
(Map p362; ☎0562-3270199; www.saniyapalace.in; Chowk Kagziyan, Taj South Gate; r without/with AC from ₹600/1300; ❄@🛜) Set back from

Taj Ganj

Top Sights

1 Taj Mahal B1

Sights

2 Jawab C1
3 Mosque B1
4 Taj Museum B2

Sleeping

5 Hotel Kamal C4
6 Hotel Sidhartha B4
7 Saniya Palace Hotel C4

Eating

8 Joney's Place B4
Saniya Palace Hotel .... (see 7)
9 Shankara Vegis B4
10 Shanti Lodge Restaurant C4
11 Taj Cafe C4
12 Yash Cafe C4

Drinking & Nightlife

13 Café Coffee Day C4

the main strip down an undesirable alleyway, this isn't the sleekest Taj Ganj option, but it tries to imbue character with marble floors and Mughal-style framed carpet wall hangings. The rooms are clean and large enough, although the bathrooms in the non-AC rooms are minuscule.

The real coup is the very pleasant, plant-filled (and recently expanded) rooftop, which trumps its rivals for optimum Taj views.

Hotel Kamal HOTEL $

(Map p362; ☎0562-2330126; hotelkamal@hotmail.com; Taj South Gate; r ₹700-1400, with AC ₹2000; ❄📶) The smartest hotel in Taj Ganj proper, Kamal has clean, comfortable rooms with nice touches, such as framed photos of the Taj on the walls and rugs on the tiled floors. Five rooms in the newer annexe are a definite step up, with welcoming woodwork, extra space and stone-walled showers.

There's a cosy, bamboo-enclosed ground-floor restaurant and an underused rooftop restaurant with a somewhat obscured Taj view.

Hotel Sidhartha HOTEL $

(Map p362; ☎0562-2230901; www.hotelsidhartha.com; Taj West Gate; r incl breakfast from ₹950, with AC from ₹1200; ❄@📶) Of the 21 rooms in this West Gate staple, those on the ground floor are stylish for the price, with marble walls, cable TV and clean bathrooms with hot water (room 111A is the standard to which all future ground-floor rooms will eventually be renovated). Upper-floor rooms are smaller and not as exciting.

Either way, all rooms surround or overlook a small, leafy courtyard over-run by a shade-providing *tameshwari* plant.

Taj Plaza HOTEL $$

(☎0562-2232515; www.hoteltajplazaagra.com; Shilpgram VIP Rd; d ₹1500, with AC ₹2500, Taj-facing ₹3200; ❄@📶) Depending on demand, this well-positioned hotel fluctuates between budget and midrange; when slow, prices can drop 50%. You won't be disappointed if you stay here. It has professional reception and clean rooms with TV – six of which look out at the Taj. There's also a pleasant rooftop with decent Taj and sunset views.

It's a whole lot closer to the Taj than most hotels in the same price range.

★Oberoi Amarvilas HOTEL $$$

(☎0562-2231515; www.oberoihotels.com; Taj East Gate Rd; d with/without balcony ₹97,750/80,500; ❄@📶🏊) Following Oberoi's iron-clad MO of maharaja-level service, exquisite dining and properties that pack some serious wow, Agra's best hotel by far oozes style and luxury. Elegant interior design is suffused with Mughal themes, a composition carried over into the exterior fountain courtyard and swimming pool, both of which are set in a delightful water garden.

All rooms (and even some bath-tubs) have wonderful Taj views.

The Retreat BOUTIQUE HOTEL $$$

(☎8810022200; www.theretreat.co.in; Shilpgram Rd; s/d incl breakfast from ₹5750/6900; ❄@📶🏊) Everything in this sleek, 52-room hotel is done up boutique-style with Indian sensibilities (lots of soothing mauve, mocha and turquoise throughout) and modern fixtures abound. There's a small pool and multicuisine restaurant offering countrywide specialities such as Goan fish curries and Lahori kebabs. Free wi-fi.

Fatehabad Road Area

★N Homestay HOMESTAY $$

(Map p360; ☎9690107860; www.nhomestay.com; 15 Ajanta Colony, Vibhav Nagar; s/d incl breakfast ₹1800/2000; ❄@📶) Matriarch Naghma and her helpful sons are a riot at this wonderful homestay. Their beautiful home, tucked away in a residential neighbourhood 15 minutes' walk from the Taj's Western

SLEEPING PRICE RANGES

Accommodation price ranges for this region:

$ below ₹1500

$$ ₹1500–4000

$$$ above ₹4000

Gate, is nothing short of a fabulous place to stay.

The three-storey house features marble floors throughout, and some of the six large and authentically appointed rooms have pleasant balconies (first-come, first-served). Naghma will even cook you dinner (₹400) – and what a cook she is! You'll rarely break through the cultural surface with such ease.

Bansi Homestay HOMESTAY **$$**
(Map p360; ☎0562-2333033; www.bansihomestayagra.com; 18 Handicraft Nagar, Fatehabad Rd; s/d incl breakfast ₹3000/3500; ❄📶) 🍃 A retired director of Uttar Pradesh Tourism is your host at this wonderful upscale homestay tucked away in a quiet residential neighbourhood near Fatahabad Rd. The five large rooms boast huge bathrooms with pressurised solar-powered rain-style showers and flank extremely pleasant common areas with bespoke furniture and Krishna paintings. It feels more like a boutique hotel than a homestay.

The immensely pleasurable 2nd-floor garden is a fabulous retreat for watching the world go by, and the food – notably the homemade pickles and *aloo paratha* (potato-stuffed flatbread) – excels, along with the hospitality in general. Bansi is Krishna's flute, a symbol of peace and tranquillity, which is exactly what you'll find here.

Dasaprakash HOTEL **$$**
(Map p360; ☎0562-4016123; www.dasaprakashgroup.com; 18/163A/6 Shamshabad Rd; s/d incl breakfast ₹3100/3450; ❄📶) This friendly and clean retreat offers 28 modern and functional rooms with small desks, flat-screen TVs and nice bathrooms, all of which haven't been around long enough to show signs of deterioration. It all works well as a good-value escape from the diesel and dust, and is located far enough from Fatahabad Rd to offer relative R&R. Free wi-fi.

Walk-ins can easily get discounts of more than 50% if rooms are available.

Howard Plaza HOTEL **$$$**
(Map p360; ☎0562-4048600; www.howardplazaagra.com; Fatehabad Rd; s/d incl breakfast from ₹8050/9200; ❄@📶🏊) Standard rooms in this very welcoming hotel are decked out in elegant dark-wood furniture and stylish decorative tiling. Deluxe rooms boast soothing aqua colour schemes. You won't find much to fault in either category.

The pool is starting to show its age, but there's a small, well-equipped gym and a very pleasant spa offering a whole range of ayurvedic and massage treatments, including the so-called 'erotic bath'. The breezy, open-air rooftop restaurant doubles as one of the few atmospheric bars in town at night (beer from ₹175, cocktails ₹400), and distant Taj views are on offer from the 4th-floor terrace. Wi-fi is enabled throughout.

Hotel Amar HOTEL **$$$**
(Map p360; ☎0562-4027000; www.hotelamar.com; Fatehabad Rd; s/d incl breakfast from ₹4000/4600; ❄@📶🏊) Though a little worn, the 66 rooms at the friendly Amar come with wi-fi, big TVs and clean bathrooms. The marble-inlay entrance halls and funky, mirrored-ceiling hallways drive home a palpable sense of place. There's a great pool area, complete with a lush green lawn and a 3.5m-tall water slide. Rooms are usually discounted by at least 15%.

Mansingh Palace HOTEL **$$$**
(Map p360; ☎0562-2331771; www.mansinghhotels.com; Fatehabad Rd; r from ₹5200; ❄@🏊) The service isn't up to scratch for the quality of this hotel, but if you can put up with the grumpy staff on reception you'll find plush rooms inside a complex crammed with Mughal design themes and exotic furnishings. The garden has an interestingly shaped pool and outdoor barbecue area. There's a gym and the quality **Sheesh Mahal** restaurant has live *ghazal* (Urdu songs) nightly.

Sadar Bazaar Area

★**Tourists Rest House** HOTEL **$**
(Map p360; ☎0562-2463961; www.dontworrychickencurry.com; 4/62 Kutchery Rd; s/d from ₹500/600, with AC from ₹950/1100; ❄@📶) If you aren't set on sleeping under the nose of the Taj, this centrally located travellers' hub offers better value than most Agra spots. It's been under the watchful eye of the same family since 1965 (though you can't tell it's going on 50 years old).

If you can forgo AC, the newly renovated cheapies are great value – and things only get better from there. All rooms come with free wi-fi, TV, hot water and large windows, and are set around a peaceful plant-filled, palm-shaded courtyard (a real highlight) and a North Indian pure veg restaurant. The bend-over-backwards owners speak English and French. They couldn't be more helpful, right down to occasionally carting you off somewhere in their hotel rickshaw. Phone ahead for a free pick-up; otherwise, it's ₹40 in a cycle-rickshaw from the train station. Damn fine masala chai, too.

Clarks Shiraz Hotel HOTEL **$$$**
(Map p360; 0562-2226121; www.hotelclarksshiraz.com; 54 Taj Rd; r incl breakfast from ₹9200;) Agra's original five-star hotel, opened in 1961, has done well to keep up with the hotel Joneses. The standard doubles are nothing special for this price range, but the marble-floored deluxe versions are a pleasant step up and all bathrooms have been re-tiled and are spotless.

There are three very good restaurants, two bars (three in season), a gym, a shaded garden and pool area (one of Agra's best) and ayurvedic massages. Some rooms have distant Taj views.

Hotel Yamuna View HOTEL **$$$**
(Map p360; 0562-3293777; www.hotelyamunaviewagra.com; 6B The Mall; s/d from ₹7500/8500;) This reliably excellent hotel was getting a full makeover when we visited – when completed we expect it to be even more modern and more comfortable than before. Prices listed here are estimates of what they might be when the hotel reopens.

There's a great garden pool, a sleek cocktail bar and a plush Chinese restaurant (with a real Chinese chef – good for a sabbatical from Indian food).

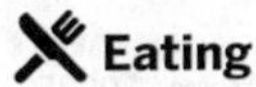

Eating

Dalmoth is Agra's famous version of *namkin* (spicy nibbles). *Peitha* is a square-shaped sweet made from pumpkin and glucose that is flavoured with rosewater, coconut or saffron. You can buy it all over Agra. From October to March look out for *gajak*, a slightly spicy sesame-seed biscuit strip.

Taj Ganj Area

Saniya Palace Hotel MULTICUISINE **$**
(Map p362; mains ₹100-200; 6am-10pm;) With cute tablecloths, dozens of potted plants and a bamboo pergola for shade, this is the most pleasant rooftop restaurant in Taj Ganj. It also has the best rooftop view of the Taj, bar none. The kitchen is a bit rough and ready, but its mix of Western dishes and Western-friendly Indian dishes usually go down without complaints.

Taj Cafe MULTICUISINE **$**
(Map p362; mains ₹50-200; 7am-11pm;) Up a flight of steps and overlooking Taj Ganj's busy street scene, this friendly, family-run restaurant is a nice choice if you're not fussed about Taj views. There's a good choice of breakfasts, thalis (₹90 to ₹140) and pizza (₹160 to ₹200), and the lassis here won't disappoint.

Shanti Lodge Restaurant MULTICUISINE **$**
(Map p362; mains ₹90-250; 6.30am-10pm) The rooftop Taj view here is superb so this is a great place for breakfast or a sunset beer. There's some shade for hot afternoons, although it's not as comfortable as nearby Saniya Palace (p365). The only let-down is

TOP AGRA FESTIVALS

Taj Mahotsav (www.tajmahotsav.org; Feb) This 10-day carnival of culture, cuisine and crafts is Agra's biggest and best party. Held at Shilpgram, the festival features more than 400 artisans from all over India, a pot-pourri of folk and classical music, dances from various regions and enough regional food to induce a curry coma.

Kailash Fair (Aug/Sep) Held at the Kailash temple, 12km from Agra, this cultural and religious fair honours Lord Shiva, who legendarily appeared here in the form of a stone lingam. It attracts devotees from all over North India.

Ram Barat (Sep) Celebrated before the Hindu festival of Dussehra, Ram Barat is a dramatic recreation of the royal/divine wedding procession of Rama and Sita. Expect three days of colourful lights and pounding Hindu rhythms, highlighted by the 12-hour parade itself, featuring caparisoned elephants, horses, more than 125 mobile floats depicting mythological events and 30 marching bands.

the menu which, although not bad, lacks invention. Banana pancakes, anyone?

Shankara Vegis VEGETARIAN $
(Map p362; Chowk Kaghzi; mains ₹90-150; ⏲8am-10.30pm;) Most restaurants in Taj Ganj ooze a distinctly average air of mediocrity – Shankara Vegis is different. This cosy old-timer, with its red tablecloths and straw-lined walls, stands out not only for its decor, but for great vegetarian thalis (₹120 to ₹160) and, most pleasantly, the genuinely friendly, non-pushy ethos of its hands-on owners.

Joney's Place MULTICUISINE $
(Map p362; Kutta Park, Taj Ganj; mains ₹70-120; ⏲5am-10.30pm) This pocket-sized institution whipped up its first creamy lassi in 1978 and continues to please despite cooking its meals in what must be Agra's smallest kitchen. The cheese and tomato 'jayfelles' (toasted sandwich), the banana lassi (with money-back guarantee) and the *malai* kofta all come recommended, but it's more about crack-of-dawn sustenance than culinary dazzle.

Yash Cafe MULTICUISINE $$
(Map p362; 3/137 Chowk Kagziyan; mains ₹100-260; ⏲7am-10.30pm;) This chilled-out, 1st-floor cafe has wicker chairs, sports channels on TV, DVDs shown in the evening and a good range of meals, from good-value set breakfasts to thalis (₹90), pizza (₹90 to ₹300) and Indian-style French toast (with coconut – we think they made that up). It also offers a shower and storage space (₹50 for both) to day visitors.

★**Esphahan** NORTH INDIAN $$$
(☎2231515; Taj East Gate Rd, Oberoi Amarvilas Hotel; mains ₹1550-3500; ⏲dinner 6.30pm & 9pm; ❄) There are only two sittings each evening at Agra's finest restaurant (6.30pm and 9.30pm), so booking a table is essential. The exquisite menu is chock-full of unique delicacies and rarely seen regional heritage dishes.

Anything that comes out of the succulent North Indian tandoor is a showstopper (especially the *bharwan aloo,* a potato kebab stuffed with nuts, spices, mint and coriander). Melt-in-your-mouth dishes such as *aloobukhara maaz* (a Mughlai lamb kebab stuffed with prunes) and *safri gosht* (braised lamb with pickled onions, dried tomatoes and spiced pickle) redefine lamb as most know it. It's all set to a romantic background soundtrack of a live *santoor* (a stringed instrument) player.

Fatehabad Road Area

Dasaprakash SOUTH INDIAN $$
(Map p360; www.dasaprakashgroup.com; 18/163A/6 Shamshabad Rd; thalis ₹230-330, mains ₹230-330; ⏲7am-11pm) The Vibhav Nagar branch of this perennial South Indian upscale staple ups the ante with a North Indian tandoor. You get the pure veg love of other Dasaprakash branches, plus North Indian options such as veg tandoori kebabs, available from noon (that tandoor needs a few hours to heat up). It's inside the hotel of the same name.

Vedic NORTH INDIAN $$
(Map p360; www.vedicrestaurant.com; 1 Gwalior Rd; mains ₹150-275; ⏲11am-10.45pm; ❄) Modern decor meets traditional ambience at this North Indian veg hot spot, with paneer (unfermented cheese) dishes featuring highly. The paneer tikka masala and Navaratan korma are particularly good. There's also a range of delicious vegetarian kebabs.

★**Pinch of Spice** MODERN INDIAN $$$
(Map p360; www.pinchofspice.in; Fatehabad Rd; mains ₹280-410; ⏲noon-11.30pm) This modern North Indian superstar is the best spot outside five-star hotels to indulge yourself in rich curries and succulent tandoori kebabs. The *murg boti masala* (chicken tikka swimming in a rich and spicy country gravy) and the paneer *lababdar* (unfermented cheese cubes in a spicy red gravy with sauteed onions) are outstanding. Located opposite the ITC Mughal Hotel.

Portions are huge.

Sadar Bazaar Area

★**Mama Chicken** DHABA $
(Map p360; Stall No 2, Sadar Bazaar; items ₹40-440; ⏲noon-midnight) This superstar *dhaba* is a must: duelling veg and nonveg glorified street stalls employing 24 cooks during the rush, each of whom is handling outdoor tandoors or other traditional cookware. They whip up outrageously good *kathi* (flatbread wrap) rolls (try chicken tikka or paneer tikka), whole chickens numerous ways, curries and chow meins for a standing-room-only crowd hell-bent on sustenance.

Bright lights, obnoxious signage and funky Indian tunes round out the festive atmosphere – a surefire Agra must.

Lakshmi Vilas SOUTH INDIAN $
(Map p360; 50A Taj Rd; mains ₹110-130; ⏲11am-10.30pm; ❄) This no-nonsense, plainly

THE SPA MAHAL

If India's most glorious monument looks particularly glowing on your visit, it could come down to a day at the spa. After years of research, Indian and American scientists have identified the culprits behind the ongoing discolouration of the mausoleum, which was originally gleaming white. The dust and air pollution that's a feature of daily life in Agra have tarnished the surface of the Taj over the years, giving it a brownish hue. More recently, a greenish tint has begun to appear, due to the excrement of millions of insects that breed in the polluted Yamuna River and are drawn to the Taj's white-ish walls.

In an effort to restore the marble to some of its earlier glory, a mud-pack cleanse has been developed – based on a traditional recipe used by Indian women to restore their own facial radiance. The next full treatment is scheduled to last from April 2017 to March 2018, using a newly improved formula that experts say won't mar the Taj's surface, as previous applications may have done. Though it should look brilliant when finished, note that if you plan to visit during cleaning time, you'll find this wonder of the world covered by scaffolding! And of course, things may not go according to schedule... So if seeing the Taj is a top priority, check to confirm that the work is complete before you book your flights.

decorated, nonsmoking restaurant is *the* place in Agra to come for affordable South Indian fare. The thali meal (₹145), served from noon to 3.30pm and 7pm to 10.30pm, is good though comes across as relatively expensive.

Brijwasi SWEETS $

(Map p360; Sadar Bazaar; sweets from ₹320 per kg, mains ₹95-170; ⌚7am-11pm; ❄) Sugar-coma–inducing selection of traditional Indian sweets, nuts and biscuits on the ground floor, with a decent-value Indian restaurant upstairs. It's most famous for its *peda* (milk-based sweets).

Dasaprakash SOUTH INDIAN $$

(Map p360; www.dasaprakashgroup.com; Meher Theater Complex, Gwailor Rd; mains ₹210-325; ⌚noon-10.45pm; ❄🖉) Fabulously tasty and religiously clean, Dasaprakash whips up consistently great South Indian vegetarian food, including spectacular thalis (₹230 to ₹330), dosas and a few token Continental dishes. The ice-cream desserts (₹100 to ₹220) are another speciality. Comfortable booth seating and wood-lattice screens make for intimate dining.

Drinking & Nightlife

A night out in Agra tends to revolve around sitting at a rooftop restaurant with a couple of bottles of beer. None of the restaurants in Taj Ganj are licensed, but they can find alcohol for you if you ask nicely, and don't mind if you bring your own drinks, as long as you're discreet.

Amarvilas Bar BAR

(Taj East Gate Rd, Oberoi Amar Vilas Hotel; ⌚noon-midnight) For a beer or cocktail in sheer opulence, look no further than the bar at Agra's best hotel. A terrace opens out to views of the Taj. Nonguests can wander onto the terrace, but staff can be funny about it.

Costa Coffee CAFE

(Map p360; www.costacoffee.com; 8 Handicraft Nagar, Fatehabad Rd; ⌚8am-11pm; 📶) Agra's only outlet of this UK coffee chain offers a cool and clean caffeine fix (coffee ₹90 to ₹240) off Fatahabad Rd – and wi-fi.

Café Coffee Day CAFE

(Map p362; www.cafecoffeeday.com; 21/101 Taj East Gate; ⌚6am-8pm) This AC-cooled branch of the popular cafe chain is the closest place to the Taj selling proper coffee (₹90 to ₹140). Another branch is located at **Sadar Bazaar** (Map p360; ⌚9am-11pm).

Shopping

Agra is well known for its marble items inlaid with coloured stones, similar to the pietra dura work on the Taj. Sadar Bazaar, the old town and the area around the Taj are full of emporiums.

Other popular buys include rugs, leather and gemstones, though the latter are imported from Rajasthan and are cheaper in Jaipur.

Be sure to wander narrow streets behind Jama Masjid, where the crazy maze of overcrowded lanes bursting with colourful markets is known collectively as **Kinari Bazaar** (Map p360; ⌚11am-9pm Wed-Mon).

STAYING AHEAD OF THE SCAMS

As well as the usual commission rackets and ever-present gem-import scam, some specific methods to relieve Agra tourists of their hard-earned cash include the following.

Rickshaws

When taking an auto- or cycle-rickshaw to the Taj, make sure you are clear which gate you want to go to when negotiating the price. Otherwise, almost without fail, riders will take you to the roundabout at the south end of Shahjahan Gardens Rd – where expensive tongas (horse-drawn carriage) or camels wait to take tour groups to the west gate – and claim that's where they thought you meant. Only nonpolluting autos can go within a 500m radius of the Taj because of pollution rules, but they can get a lot closer than this.

Fake Marble

Lots of 'marble' souvenirs are actually alabaster, or even just soapstone. So you may be paying marble prices for lower quality stones. The mini Taj Mahals are always alabaster because they are too intricate to carve quickly in marble.

★ **Subhash Emporium** ARTS & CRAFTS
(Map p360; ☎9410613616; www.subhashemporium.com; 18/1 Gwalior Rd; ⏰9.30am-7pm) Some of the pieces on display at this renowned marble shop are simply stunning. While more expensive than many other shops, you definitely get what you pay for: high-quality stone and master craftsmanship. Some of the work is decorative, but some is functional, such as tabletops, trays, lamp bases, and candle holders that glow from the flame inside.

Subhash Bazaar MARKET
(Map p360; ⏰8am-8pm Apr-Sep, 9am-8pm Oct-Mar) Skirts the northern edge of Agra's Jama Masjid and is particularly good for silks and saris.

Modern Book Depot BOOKS
(Map p360; Sadar Bazaar; ⏰10.30am-9.30pm Wed-Mon) Great selection of novels (plus Lonely Planet guides) at this friendly, 60-year-old establishment.

Khadi Gramodyog CLOTHING
(Map p360; MG Rd; ⏰11am-7pm Wed-Mon) Stocks simple, good-quality men's Indian clothing made from the homespun *khadi* fabric famously recommended by Mahatma Gandhi. There's no English sign – on Mahatma Gandhi (MG) Rd, look for the *khadi* logo of hands clasped around a mud hut.

ℹ Information

Agra is more wired than most, even in restaurants. Taj Ganj is riddled with internet cafes, most charging from ₹40 per hour.

Archaeological Survey of India Office
(ASI; Map p360; ☎0562-2227261; www.asiagracircle.in; 22 The Mall; Indian/foreigner ₹540/1000; ⏰9.30am-5pm Mon-Fri) The place to buy your full-moon Taj tickets. See its website for more info.

EMERGENCY

Tourist Police (☎0562-2421204; Agra Cantonment Train Station; ⏰6.30am-9.30pm) The helpful crew in sky-blue uniforms are based on Fatahabad Rd, but have an office here in the Tourist Facilitation Centre. Officers also hang around the East Gate ticket office and the UP Tourism office on Taj Rd, as well as at major sites.

MEDICAL SERVICES

Amit Jaggi Memorial Hospital (Map p360; ☎0562-2230515, 9690107860; www.ajmh.in; off Minto Rd, Vibhav Nagar) If you're sick, Dr Jaggi, who runs this private clinic, is the man to see. He accepts most health-insurance plans from abroad; otherwise a visit runs ₹1000 (day) or ₹2000 (night). He'll even do house calls.

SR Hospital (Map p360; ☎0562-4025200; Laurie's Complex, Namner Rd) Agra's best private hospital.

MONEY

ATMs are everywhere. There are four close to the Taj, one near each gate (though the East Gate Axis Bank ATM is often on the fritz) and another next to the East Gate ticket office complex. If you need to change money and are worried about being swindled in Taj Ganj, there is a government-sanctioned money changer at the East Gate ticket office complex as well.

POST

India Post (Map p360; www.indiapost.gov.in; The Mall; ⏰10am-5pm Mon-Fri, to 4pm Sat)

Agra's historic GPO (General Post Office) dates to 1913 and includes a handy 'facilitation office' for foreigners.

TOURIST INFORMATION

India Tourism (Map p360; ☎0562-2226378; www.incredibleindia.org; 191 The Mall; ⊙9am-5.30pm Mon-Fri) Very helpful branch; has brochures on local and India-wide attractions.

Tourist Facilitation Centre (Taj East Gate; ⊙9.30am-5pm Sat-Thu) This helpful tourist office is part of the East Gate ticket office complex at Shilpgram.

UP Tourism (☎0562-2421204; www.up-tourism.com; Agra Cantonment Train Station; ⊙6.30am-9.30pm) The friendly train-station branch inside the Tourist Facilitation Centre on Platform 1 offers helpful advice and is where you can book day-long bus tours of Agra. This branch doubles as the Tourist Police. There's another UP Tourism (Map p360; ☎0562-2226431; www.uptourism.gov.in; 64 Taj Rd; ⊙10am-5pm Mon-Sat) office on Taj Rd.

TRAVEL AGENCIES

Bagpacker Travel (Map p360; ☎9997113228; www.bagpackertravels.com; 4/62 Kutchery Rd; ⊙9am-9pm) An honest agency for all your travel and transport needs, run by the friendly Anil at Tourists Rest House. English and French spoken.

Getting There & Away

AIR

There are currently no commercial flights departing from Agra's Kheria Airport, but Agra will probably see better air service in the near future, as a long-planned Taj International Airport finally received approval to be built in 2016. Officials say they plan to have it operational sometime in 2017, but it's too early to tell whether or not they'll meet that goal.

BUS

The opening of the 165km Yamuna Expressway toll highway in 2012 cut drive time from Delhi to Noida, a southeastern suburb, by 30%. Some luxury coaches now use this route and reach central Delhi faster.

Some services from **Idgah Bus Stand** (off National Hwy 2, near Sikandra):

Bharatpur (₹65, 1½ hours, every 30 minutes, 6am to 6.30pm)

Delhi Non-AC (₹180, 4½ hours, every 30 minutes, 5am to 11pm)

Fatehpur Sikri (₹40, one hour, every 30 minutes, 6am to 6.30pm)

Gwalior (₹115, three hours, hourly, 6am to 6.30pm)

Jaipur (₹262, six hours, every 30 minutes, 5am to 11pm)

Jhansi (₹215, six hours, 8.30pm and 10.30pm)

A block east of Idgah, just in front of Hotel Sakura, the **Rajasthan State Road Transport Corporation** (RSRTC; ☎0562-2420228; www.rsrtc.rajasthan.gov.in) runs more comfortable coaches to Jaipur throughout the day. Services include non-AC (₹256, 5½ hours, 7.30am, 10am, 1pm and 11.59pm), AC (₹440, five hours, 6.30am and 8.30am) and luxury Volvo (₹530, 4½ hours, 11.30am and 2.30pm).

From **ISBT Bus Stand** (☎0562-2603536), luxury Volvo coaches leave for Delhi (₹595, four hours, 7am, 1pm, 3.30pm and 6.30pm) and Lucknow (₹930, 7½ hours, 10am and 10pm); there are also standard non-AC services to Gorakhpur (₹625, 16 hours, 3.30pm and 9.30pm) and Allahabad (₹450, nine hours, 4.30am, 5.30am and 4pm) which continue on to Varanasi (₹600, 13 hours). Several classes of buses to Dehra Dun

DELHI–AGRA TRAINS FOR DAY TRIPPERS

TRIP	TRAIN NO & NAME	FARE (₹)	DURATION (HR)	DEPARTURES
New Delhi–Agra	12002 Shatabdi Exp	550/1010 (A)	2	6am
Agra–New Delhi	12001 Shatabdi Exp	690/1050 (A)	2	9.15pm
Hazrat Nizamuddin–Agra	12280 Taj Exp	100/370 (B)	2¾	7am
Agra–Hazrat Nizamuddin	12279 Taj Exp	100/370 (B)	3	6.55pm
Hazrat Nizamuddin–Agra*	12050 Gatimaan Exp	755/1505 (A)	1¾	8.10am
Agra–Hazrat Nizamuddin*	12049 Gatimaan Exp	755/1505 (A)	1¾	5.50pm

Fares: (A) AC chair/ECC, (B) 2nd-class/AC chair; * departs Saturday to Monday

also depart from here: Volvo (₹1190, 9.30pm); AC (₹700, 4.30pm); non-AC (₹425, 7pm, 8pm, 9pm and 9.30pm). A few evening buses also run to Haridwar (AC/non-AC ₹1050/400, 10 hours), from where you can transfer to a bus for Rishikesh.

Bijli Ghar Bus Stand (Agra Fort Bus Stand; Map p360) serves Mathura (₹65, 90 minutes, every 30 minutes, 6am to 6.30pm), and also Tundla (₹35, one hour, every 30 minutes, 8am to 7pm), from where you can catch the 12382 Poorva Express train to Varanasi at 8.15pm if the trains from Agra are sold out.

Shared autos (₹10) run between Idgah and Bijli Ghar bus stands. To get to ISBT, catch an autorickshaw (₹200 to ₹250, depending on where your trip starts).

TRAIN

Most trains leave from **Agra Cantonment (Cantt) train station**, although some go from Agra Fort station. A few trains, such as Kota PNBE Express, run as slightly different numbers on different days than those listed, but timings remain the same.

Express trains are well set up for day trippers to/from Delhi but trains run to Delhi all day. If you can't reserve a seat, just buy a 'general ticket' for the next train (about ₹90), find a seat in sleeper class then upgrade when the ticket collector comes along (most of the time, he won't even make you pay any more). A new semi-express train between Delhi and Agra, the Gatimaan Express, is now up and running. It travels 160km per hour (India's fastest), a full 30km per hour faster than the Shatabdi Express.

For Orchha, catch one of the many daily trains to Jhansi (sleeper from ₹165, three hours), then take a shared auto to the bus stand (₹10), from where shared autos run all day to Orchha (₹20). An autorickshaw runs ₹200 for the same route.

If you are heading to Jaipur on Thursday, the best option is 12403/12404 ALD JP Express, departing Agra at 7.15am.

Getting Around

AUTORICKSHAW

Just outside Agra Cantt station is the **prepaid autorickshaw booth** (24hr), which gives you a good guide for haggling elsewhere. Usually, trips shorter than 3km should not cost more than ₹50. Always agree on the fare before entering the rickshaw.

Sample prices from Agra Cantt station: Fatahabad Rd ₹150; ISBT bus stand ₹200; Sadar Bazaar ₹70; Sikandra ₹400; Taj Mahal (Taj West Gate) ₹100, Taj South Gate ₹130, Shilpgram (Taj East Gate) ₹150; half-day (four-hour) Agra tour ₹400; full-day (eight-hour) Agra tour ₹600. If you just want to shoot to the Taj and back with waiting time, they will charge ₹250. Note: autorickshaws aren't allowed to go to Fatehpur Sikri.

CYCLE-RICKSHAW

Prices from the Taj Mahal's South Gate: Agra Cantt train station ₹80; Agra Fort ₹40; Biili Ghar bus stand ₹50; Fatahabad Rd ₹30; Kinari Bazaar ₹100; Sadar Bazaar ₹50; half-day tour ₹400. Tack on another ₹10 to ₹20 if two people are riding.

TAXI

Outside Agra Cantt the **prepaid taxi booth** (24hr) gives a good idea of what taxis should cost. Non-AC prices: Delhi ₹3500; Fatahabad Rd ₹200; Sadar Bazaar ₹100; Taj Mahal ₹200; half-day (four-hour) tour ₹750; full-day (eight-

MORE HANDY TRAINS FROM AGRA

DESTINATION	TRAIN NO & NAME	FARE (₹)	DURATION (HR)	DEPARTURES
Gorakhpur*	19037/9 Avadh Exp	335/910/1305 (A)	15¾	10pm
Jaipur*	12036 Shatabdi Exp	660/1225 (C)	3½	5.40pm (except Thu)
Khajuraho	12448 UP Sampark Kranti	280/720/1010 (A)	7½	11.10pm
Kolkata (Howrah)	13008 UA Toofan Exp	555/1500 (B)	31	12.15pm
Lucknow	12180 LJN Intercity	145/515 (D)	6	5.50am
Mumbai (CST)	12138/7 Punjab Mail	580/1530/2215 (A)	23	8.35am
Varanasi*	14854/64/66 Marudhar Exp	340/930/1335 (A)	14	8.30pm

Fares: (A) sleeper/3AC/2AC, (B) sleeper/3AC only, (C) AC chair/ECC, (D) 2nd-class/AC chair; * leaves from Agra Fort station

DANCING BEAR RETIREMENT HOME

For hundreds of years, sloth bear cubs were stolen from their mothers (who were often killed) and forced through painful persuasion to become 'dancing bears', entertaining kings and crowds with their fancy footwork. In 1996, Wildlife SOS (www.wildlifesos.org) – an animal rescue organisation that is often called around Agra to humanely remove pythons and cobras from local homes – began efforts to emancipate all of India's 1200 or so dancing bears. By 2009, nearly all were freed, and more than 200 of them live at the **Agra Bear Rescue Facility** (9756205080; www.wildlifesos.org; Sur Sarovar Bird Sanctuary; 2hr/full day ₹2000/₹4000; 9am-4pm), inside Sur Sarovar Bird Sanctuary, 30km outside of Agra on the road to Delhi.

Visitors are welcome to tour the park-like grounds and watch the bears enjoying their new, better lives. Wildlife SOS also runs a **refuge for rescued circus elephants** (two-hour/full day ₹1500/₹3000), closer to Mathura, which is more hands-on, as you can feed and walk with the elephants. Email or phone in advance to arrange visits.

hour) tour ₹1000. Prices here do not include the ₹10 booking fee and tolls or parking charges (if applicable).

Around Agra

Fatehpur Sikri

05613 / POP 30,000

This magnificent fortified ancient city, 40km west of Agra, was the short-lived capital of the Mughal empire between 1572 and 1585, during the reign of Emperor Akbar. Earlier, Akbar had visited the village of Sikri to consult the Sufi saint Shaikh Salim Chishti, who predicted the birth of an heir to the Mughal throne. When the prophecy came true, Akbar built his new capital here, including a stunning mosque, still in use today, and three palaces, one for each of his favourite wives – one a Hindu, one a Muslim and one a Christian (though Hindu villagers in Sikri dispute these claims). The city was an Indo-Islamic masterpiece, but erected in an area that supposedly suffered from water shortages and so was abandoned shortly after Akbar's death.

It's easy to visit this World Heritage Site as a day trip from Agra, but there are a couple of decent places to stay. In addition to the main attractions, the colourful bazaar in the village of **Fatehpur**, just below the ruins, as well as the small village of **Sikri**, a few kilometres north, are worth exploring.

The palace buildings lie beside the Jama Masjid mosque. Both sit on top of a ridge that runs between Fatehpur and Sikri. The red-sandstone palace walls are at their most atmospheric and photogenic near sunset.

Sights

Jama Masjid MOSQUE

This beautiful, immense mosque was completed in 1571 and contains elements of Persian and Indian design. The main entrance, at the top of a flight of stone steps, is through the spectacular 54m-high **Buland Darwaza** (Victory Gate), built to commemorate Akbar's military victory in Gujarat. Inside is the stunning white marble **tomb of Sufi saint Shaikh Salim Chishti**, where women hoping to have children come to tie a thread to the *jalis* (carved lattice screens).

The saint's tomb was completed in 1581 and is entered through an original door made of ebony. Inside it are brightly coloured flower murals, while the sandlewood canopy is decorated with mother-of-pearl shell, and the marble *jalis* are among the finest in India. To the right of the tomb lie the gravestones of family members of Shaikh Salim Chishti and nearby is the entrance to an underground tunnel (barred by a locked gate) that reputedly goes all the way to Agra Fort. Behind the entrance to the tunnel, on the far wall, are three holes, part of the ancient ventilation system; you can still feel the rush of cool air forcing its way through them. Just east of Shaikh Salim Chishti's tomb is the red-sandstone **tomb of Islam Khan**, the final resting place of Shaikh Salim Chishti's grandson and one-time governor of Bengal.

On the east wall of the courtyard is a smaller entrance to the mosque – the **Shahi Darwaza** (King's Gate), which leads to the palace complex.

Palaces & Pavilions PALACE

(Indian/foreigner ₹40/510, video ₹25; dawn-dusk) The main sight at Fatehpur Sikri is the

Fatehpur Sikri

A WALKING TOUR OF FATEHPUR SIKRI

You can enter this fortified ancient city from two entrances, but the northeast entrance at Diwan-i-Am (Hall of Public Audiences) offers the most logical approach to this remarkable Unesco World Heritage site. This large courtyard (now a garden) is where Emperor Akbar presided over the trials of accused criminals. Once through the ticket gate, you are in the northern end of the 1 **Pachisi Courtyard**. The first building you see is 2 **Diwan-i-Khas** (Hall of Private Audiences), the interior of which is dominated by a magnificently carved central stone column. Pitch south and enter 3 **Rumi Sultana**, a small but elegant palace built for Akbar's Turkish Muslim wife. It's hard to miss the 4 **Ornamental Pool** nearby – its southwest corner provides Fatehpur Sikri's most photogenic angle, perfectly framing its most striking building, the five-storey Panch Mahal, one of the gateways to the Imperial Harem Complex, where the 5 **Lower Haramsara** once housed more than 200 female servants. Wander around the Palace of Jodh Bai and take notice of the towering ode to an elephant, the 21m-high 6 **Hiran Minar**, in the distance to the northwest. Leave the palaces and pavilions area via Shahi Darwaza (King's Gate), which spills into India's second-largest mosque courtyard at 7 **Jama Masjid**. Inside this immense and gorgeous mosque is the sacred 8 **Tomb of Shaikh Salim Chishti**. Exit through the spectacular 9 **Buland Darwaza** (Victory Gate), one of the world's most magnificent gateways.

JAN S/SHUTTERSTOCK ©

Buland Darwaza

Most tours end with an exit through Jama Masjid's Victory Gate. Walk out and take a look behind you: Behold! The magnificent 15-storey sandstone gate, 54m high, is a menacing monolith to Akbar's reign.

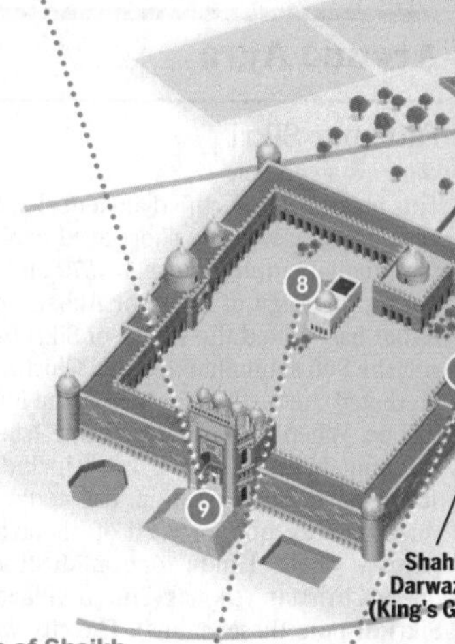

Tomb of Shaikh Salim Chishti

Each knot in the strings tied to the 56 carved white marble designs of the interior walls of Shaikh Salim Chishti's tomb represents one wish of a maximum three.

Jama Masjid

The elaborate marbl inlay work at the Badshahi Gate and throughout the Jama Masjid complex is sa to have inspired simi work 82 years later a the Taj Mahal in Agra

IGOR PLOTNIKOV/SHUTTERSTOCK ©

DUSHI82/SHUTTERSTOCK ©

iran Minar

is bizarre, seldom-visited tower off the north-st corner of Fatehpur Sikri is decorated with ndreds of stone representations of elephant sks. It is said to be the place where Minar, bar's favourite execution elephant, died.

CECOLUSSI/GETTY IMAGES ©

Pachisi Courtyard

Under your feet just past Rumi Sultana is the Pachisi Courtyard where Akbar is said to have played the game *pachisi* (an ancient version of ludo) using slave girls in colourful dress as pieces.

ROOP_DEY/SHUTTERSTOCK ©

Diwan-i-Khas

Emperor Akbar modified the central stone column inside Diwan-i-Khas to call attention to a new religion he called Din-i-Ilahi (God is One). The intricately carved column features a fusion of Hindu, Muslim, Christian and Buddhist imagery.

Panch Mahal

Diwan-i-Am (Hall of Public Audiences)

Rumi Sultana

Don't miss the headless creatures carved into Rumi Sultana's palace interiors: a lion, deer, an eagle and a few peacocks were beheaded by jewel thieves who swiped the precious jewels that originally formed their heads.

Ornamental Pool

Tansen, said to be the most gifted Indian vocalist of all time and one of Akbar's treasured nine *Navaratnas* (Gems), would be showered with coins during performances from the central platform of the Ornamental Pool.

wer aramsara

bar reportedly t more than 5000 ncubines, but the) or so female vants housed in Lower Haramsara re strictly business. ots were tied to se sandstone rings support partitions ween their individual arters.

CANAN KAYA/SHUTTERSTOCK ©

stunning imperial complex of pavilions and palaces spread among a large, abandoned 'city' peppered with Mughal masterpieces: courtyards, intricate carvings, servants quarters, vast gateways and ornamental pools.

A large courtyard dominates the northeast entrance at **Diwan-i-Am** (Hall of Public Audiences). Now a pristinely manicured garden, this is where Akbar presided over the courts – from the middle seat of the five equal seatings along the western wall, flanked by his advisors. It was built to utilise an echo sound system, so Akbar could hear anything at any time from anywhere in the open space. Justice was dealt with swiftly if legends are to be believed, with public executions said to have been carried out here by elephants trampling convicted criminals to death.

The **Diwan-i-Khas** (Hall of Private Audiences), found at the northern end of the Pachisi Courtyard, looks nothing special from the outside, but the interior is dominated by a magnificently carved stone central column. This pillar flares to create a flat-topped plinth linked to the four corners of the room by narrow stone bridges. From this plinth Akbar is believed to have debated with scholars and ministers who stood at the ends of the four bridges.

Next to Diwan-i-Khas is the **Treasury**, which houses secret stone safes in some corners (one has been left with its stone lid open for visitors to see). Sea monsters carved on the ceiling struts were there to protect the fabulous wealth once stored here. The so-called **Astrologer's Kiosk** in front has roof supports carved in a serpentine Jain style.

Just south of the Astrologer's Kiosk is **Pachisi Courtyard**, named after the ancient game known in India today as ludo. The large, plus-shaped game board is visible surrounding the block in the middle of the courtyard. In the southeast corner is the most intricately carved structure in the whole complex, the tiny but elegant **Rumi Sultana**, which was said to be the palace built for Akbar's Turkish Muslim wife. Other theories say it was used by Akbar himself as a palace powder room or for a rest break during court sessions. On one corner of the **Ladies Garden** just west of Pachisi is the impressive **Panch Mahal**, a pavilion with five storeys that decrease in size until the top consists of only a tiny kiosk. The lower floor has 84 different columns; in total there are 176 columns.

Continuing anticlockwise will bring you to the **Ornamental Pool**. Here, singers and musicians would perform on the platform above the water while Akbar watched from the pavilion in his private quarters, known as **Daulat Khana** (Abode of Fortune). Behind the pavilion is the **Khwabgah** (Dream House), a sleeping area with a huge stone bunk bed. Nowadays the only ones sleeping here are bats, hanging from the ceiling; the small room in the far corner is full of them.

Heading west from the Ornamental Pool reveals the **Palace of Jodh Bai**, and the one-time home of Akbar's Hindu wife, said to be his favourite. Set around an enormous courtyard, it blends traditional Indian columns, Islamic cupolas and turquoise-blue Persian roof tiles. Just outside, to the left of Jodh Bai's former kitchen, is the **Palace of the Christian Wife**. This was used by Akbar's Goan wife Mariam, who gave birth to Jehangir here in 1569. (Some believe Akbar never had a Christian wife and that Mariam was short for Mariam-Ut-Zamani, a title he gave to Jodh Bai meaning 'Beautiful like a Rose', or 'Most Beautiful Woman on Earth'.) Like many of the buildings in the palace complex, it contains elements of different religions, as befitted Akbar's tolerant religious beliefs. The domed ceiling is Islamic in style, while remnants of a wall painting of the Hindu god Shiva can also be found.

Walking past the Palace of the Christian Wife once more will take you west to **Birbal Bhavan**, ornately carved inside and out, and thought to have been the living quarters of one of Akbar's most senior ministers. The **Lower Haramsara**, just to the south, housed Akbar's large number of live-in female servants.

Plenty of ruins are scattered behind the whole complex, including the **Caravanserai**, a vast courtyard surrounded by rooms where visiting merchants stayed. Badly defaced carvings of elephants still guard **Hathi Pol** (Elephant Gate), while the remains of the small **Stonecutters' Mosque** and a **hammam** (bath) are also a short stroll away. Other unnamed ruins can be explored north of what is known as the **Mint** but is thought to have in fact been stables, including some in the interesting village of **Sikri** to the north.

Archaeological Museum MUSEUM
(near Diwan-i-Am; ⏰9am-5pm Sat-Thu) **FREE**
Inaugurated in 2014 inside Akbar's former

Treasury house, this museum about 100m from Diwan-i-Am showcases pre-Mughal artefacts excavated over many years at Fatehpur Sikri. Small but well presented, highlights include a few remarkably preserved sandstone Jain *tirthankars* (the 24 holy Jain supreme beings) dating between AD 982 and 1034.

Tours

Official Archaeological Society of India guides can be hired from the ticket office for ₹450 (English), but they aren't always the most knowledgeable (some are guides thanks to birthright rather than qualifications). The best guides are available in Agra, and charge ₹750. Our favourite is **Pankaj Bhatnagar** (☎8126995552; ₹750); he prefers to be messaged on WhatsApp.

Sleeping & Eating

Fatehpur Sikri's culinary specialty is *khataie,* the biscuits you can see piled high in the bazaar. For restaurants, head to one of the hotels.

Hotel Goverdhan HOTEL $
(☎05613-282643; www.hotelfatehpursikriviews.com; Agra Rd; r ₹750-950, with AC ₹1300; ❄@☜) There are a variety of rooms at this old-time favourite, all of which surround a very well-kept garden. There's a communal balcony and terrace seating, free wi-fi, new beds in every room, air-coolers in the non-ACs and CCTV. The restaurant does decent work as well (meals ₹70 to ₹180).

Hotel Ajay Palace GUESTHOUSE $
(☎9548801213; Agra Rd; r ₹500) This friendly family-run guesthouse isn't pretty but offers a few very simple and cheap double rooms with marble floors and sit-down flush toilets. It's also a very popular lunch stop (mains ₹50 to ₹150). Sit on the rooftop at the large, elongated marble table and enjoy a view of the village streets with the Jama Masjid towering above.

Note that it's not 'Ajay Restaurant By Near Palace' at the bus stand – it's 50m further along the road.

Information

DANGERS & ANNOYANCES

Take no notice of anyone who gets on the Fatehpur Sikri–Agra bus before the final stop at Idgah Bus Stand, telling you that you have arrived at the city centre or the Taj Mahal. You haven't. You're still a long autorickshaw ride away, and the man trying to tease you off the bus is – surprise surprise – an autorickshaw driver.

Getting There & Around

From the Fatehpur bus stand, buses run to Agra's **Idgah Bus Stand** (p369) every half-hour (₹40) from 5.30am to 6.30pm. If you miss those, walk 1km to Agra Gate and another 350m to Bypass Crossing Stop on the main road and wave down an Agra-bound bus. They pass every 30 minutes or so, day and night.

For Bharatpur (₹25, 40 minutes) or Jaipur (₹190, 4½ hours), wave down a westbound bus from Bypass Crossing Stop.

Regular trains for Agra Fort Station leave Fatehpur Sikri at 4.43am (59811 Haldighati Pass) and 8.16pm (19037/9 Avadh Express), but there are simpler passenger trains at 10.14am and 3.54pm, as well as four other trains that fly through at various times. Just buy a 'general' ticket at the station and pile in (₹20, one to two hours).

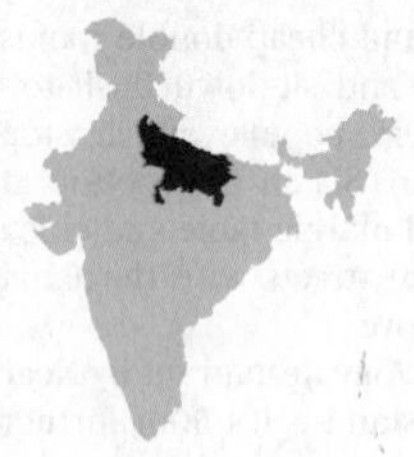

Uttar Pradesh

Includes ➡

Best Places to Eat

- ➡ Oudhyana (p400)
- ➡ Darbangha (p388)
- ➡ Tunday Kababi (p399)
- ➡ Eat On (p407)

Best Places to Sleep

- ➡ Brijrama Palace (p387)
- ➡ Kanchan Villa (p407)
- ➡ Hotel Ganges View (p387)
- ➡ Ganpati Guesthouse (p386)

Why Go?

There are few states more quintessentially Indian than Uttar Pradesh. The subcontinent's historic and religious roots – Hindu, Buddhist, Islamic and secular – intertwine in this land of sacred rivers and vast plains, manifesting in sights of profound importance.

Aside from iconic Agra, UP is home to Varanasi, India's holiest city, famed for its cremation ghats and vibrant ceremonies along the Ganges River. Stories tell us that Krishna was born in Mathura, while Rama was born in Ayodhya – a place of tragic conflict in modern times that reveals much about the shadow side of the collective Indian psyche. Buddha gave his first sermon in Sarnath and died in Kushinagar, now tranquil pilgrimage destinations. And the Mughals and the Nawabs made their marks as well, leaving behind architectural and gastronomic masterpieces – particularly in Lucknow (and of course Agra). UP offers more than enough to satisfy the senses – and curiosities – of any traveller.

When to Go

Varanasi

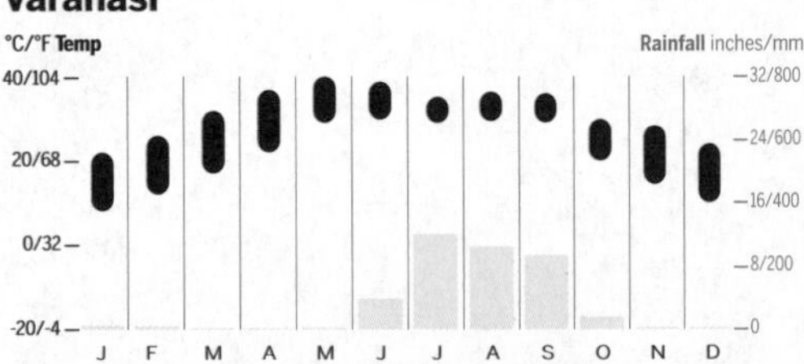

mid-Sep–Oct Monsoon rains are mostly over and temperatures have cooled...just enough.

Nov–Feb Comfortable winter days and nippy nights means it's cool but overcrowded.

Mar With evening chills subsided and raging midsummer heat still at bay, some say it's perfect.

History

More than 2000 years ago this region was part of Ashoka's great Buddhist empire, remnants of which can be found in the ruins at the pilgrimage centre of Sarnath near Varanasi. Muslim raids from the northwest began in the 11th century, and by the 16th century the region was part of the Mughal empire, with its capital in Agra, then Delhi and, for a brief time, Fatehpur Sikri.

Following the decline of the Mughal empire, Persians stepped in briefly before the Nawabs of Avadh rose to prominence in the central part of the region, notably around the current capital of Lucknow. The Nawabs were responsible for turning Lucknow into a flourishing centre for the arts, culture and culinary delights, which continues to this day. But their empire came to a dramatic end when the British East India Company deposed the last nawab, triggering the First War of Independence (Indian Uprising) in 1857. During the 147-day Siege of Lucknow, British Chief Commissioner Sir Henry Lawrence was killed defending the British Residency, which remains in remarkable preservation in Lucknow.

Agra was later merged with Avadh and the state became known as United Province. It was renamed Uttar Pradesh after Independence and has since been the most dominant state in Indian politics, producing half of the country's prime ministers, most of them from Allahabad (locus of the Nehru/Gandhi dynasty). The people of UP don't seem to have benefited much from this, though, as poor governance, a high birth rate, a low literacy rate and an erratic electricity supply have held back the state's economic progress over the past 70 years.

In 2000, the mountainous northwestern part of the state was carved off to create the new state of Uttaranchal, now called Uttarakhand.

VARANASI

0542 / POP 1.4 MILLION

Varanasi is the India of your imagination. One of the most colourful and fascinating places on earth, surprises abound around every corner.

This is one of the world's oldest continually inhabited cities, and one of the holiest in Hinduism. Pilgrims come to the ghats lining the Ganges to wash away sins in the sacred waters or to cremate their loved ones. It's a particularly auspicious place to die, since expiring here offers moksha (liberation from the cycle of rebirth).

Most visitors agree Varanasi is magical – but not for the faint-hearted. Intimate rituals of life and death take place in public, and the sights, sounds and smells on the ghats – not to mention almost constant attention from touts – can be intense. Still, the so-called City of Light may turn out to be your favourite stop of all. Walking the ghats and alleyways or watching sunrise from a boat can be unforgettable.

History

Thought to date back to around 1200 BC, Varanasi really rose to prominence in the 8th century AD, when Shankaracharya, a reformer of Hinduism, established Shiva worship as the principal sect. The Afghans destroyed Varanasi around AD 1300, after laying waste to nearby Sarnath, but the fanatical Mughal emperor Aurangzeb was the most destructive, looting and destroying almost all of the temples.

The old city of Varanasi may look antique, but few buildings are more than a couple of hundred years old. Rajas and other wealthy families from around India built palaces and mansions along the ghats to be close to the sacred river; most of these are now in states of serious disrepair, though a few have been bought by hotel companies and renovated into something resembling their previous glory.

TOP STATE FESTIVALS

Magh Mela (Allahabad; Jan/Feb) A huge annual religious fair that transforms into the world's largest human gathering, the Kumbh Mela, every 12th year (next in 2025).

Holi (p410) Perhaps the world's most colorful festival. Prepare to be powdered!

Purnima (Apr or May) Buddha's birthday party.

Janmastami (p410) Krishna's birthday party.

Dev Diwali (Ganga Diwali; Varanasi; Nov) A festival of light in the 'City of Light'.

Ram Lila (Varanasi; Sep/Oct) The dramatic retelling of Lord Rama's quest to reclaim his wife, Sita, from the demon Ravana.

Uttar Pradesh Highlights

❶ **Varanasi** (p377) Having your mind blown in India as you've always imagined it, with sacred ghats along the Ganges and a maze of alleyways with surprises around every corner.

❷ **Lucknow** (p397) Eating in the kebab capital of India, then strolling among impressively ornamented Mughal architecture.

❸ **Sarnath** (p392) Roaming the peaceful park where Buddha delivered his first sermon.

❹ **Allahabad** (p404) Joining 100 million devotees who converge at the confluence of two (or three) sacred rivers during the Kumbh Mela.

❺ **Chitrakut** (p404) Experiencing Hindu devotions on a less overwhelming scale at this laid-back riverside town.

❻ **Vrindavan** (p410) Temple-hopping at this spiritual centre and international home of the Hare Krishnas.

❼ **Ayodhya** (p402) Veering off the beaten path to Lord Rama's mythic birthplace.

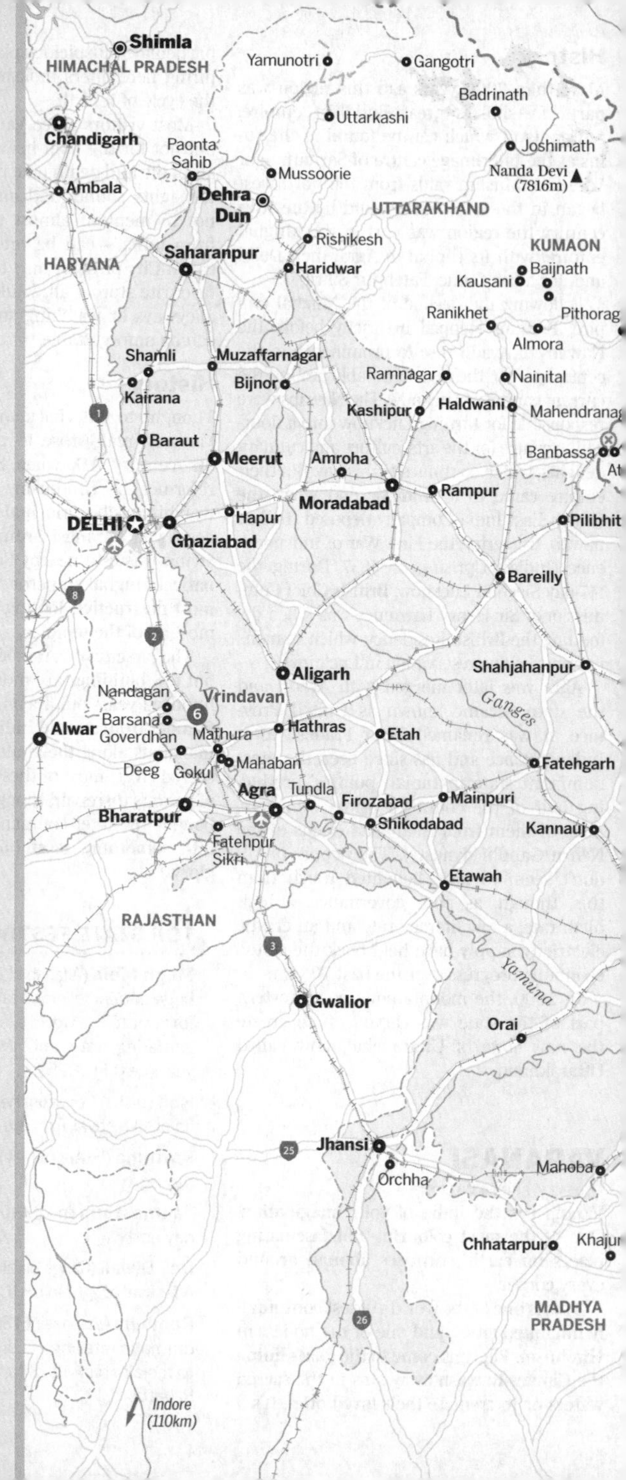

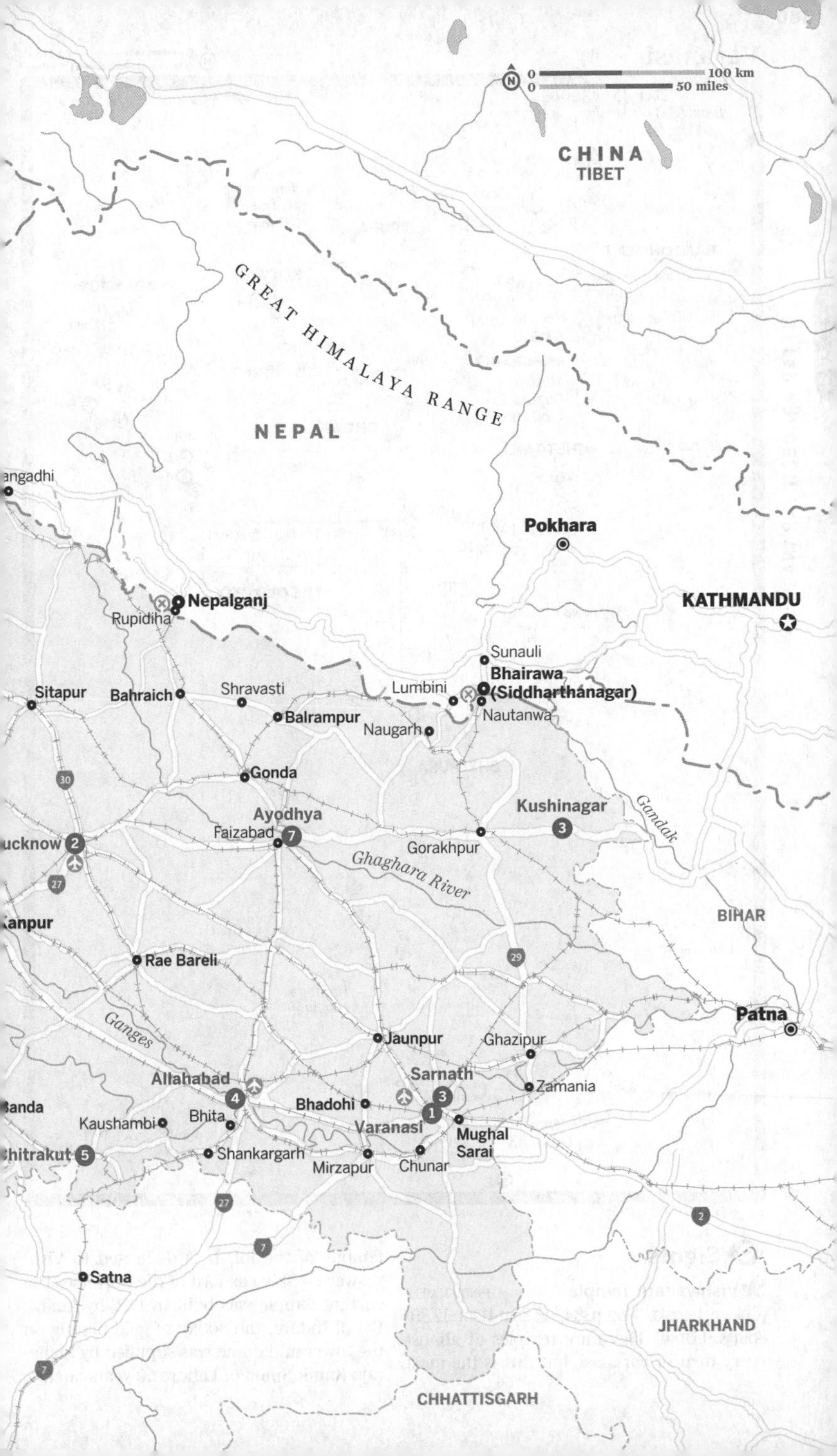

0
100 km
0
50 miles
CHINA
TIBET
GREAT HIMALAYA RANGE
NEPAL
angadhi
Pokhara
Nepalganj
Rupidiha
KATHMANDU
Sunauli
Bhairawa
(Siddharthanagar)
Lumbini
Nautanwa
Sitapur
Bahraich
Shravasti
Balrampur
Naugarh
Gonda
Kushinagar
3
Gandak
Ayodhya
Faizabad
7
ucknow
2
Gorakhpur
Ghaghara River
30
27
BIHAR
anpur
29
Rae Bareli
Patna
Ganges
Jaunpur
Ghazipur
Sarnath
Allahabad
4
Zamania
Banda
Bhadohi
1
Kaushambi
Bhita
Varanasi
Mughal
Sarai
hitrakut
5
Shankargarh
Mirzapur
Chunar
27
2
7
Satna
JHARKHAND
7
CHHATTISGARH

Varanasi

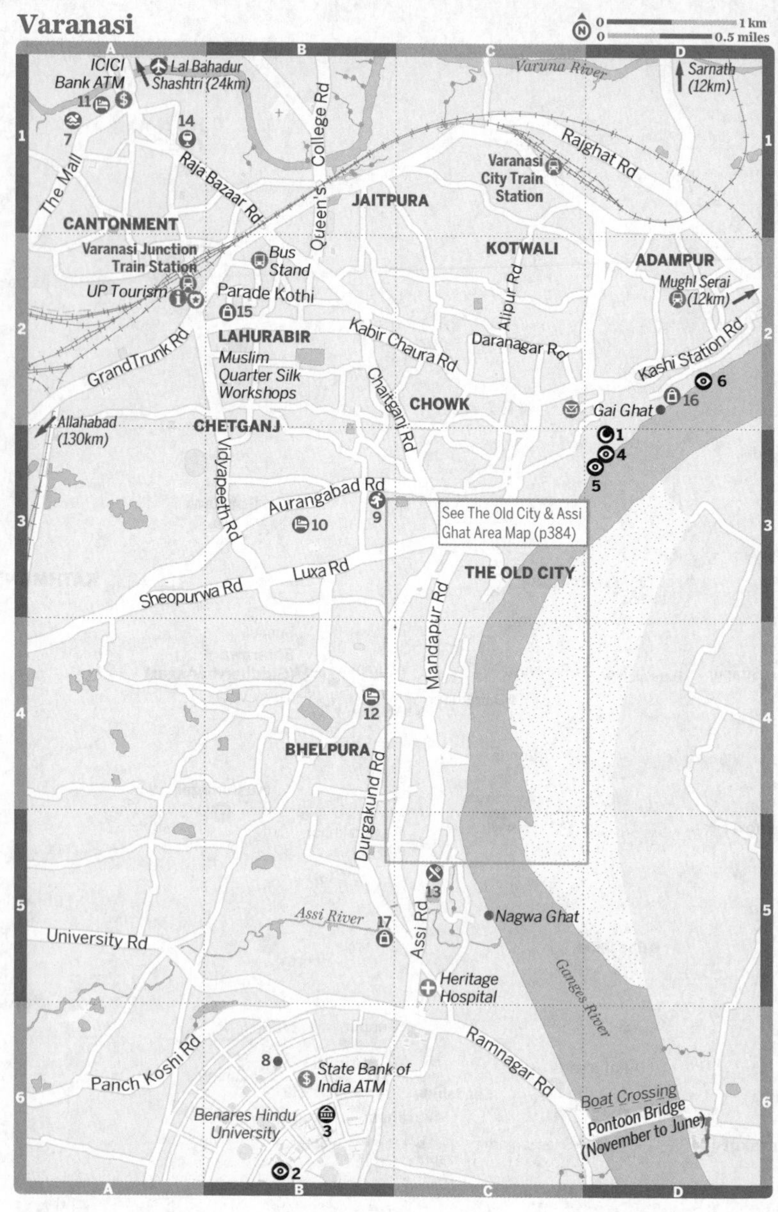

Sights

★Vishwanath Temple HINDU TEMPLE

(Golden Temple; Map p384; 3am-11am, 12.30-8pm & 9-11pm) There are temples at almost every turn in Varanasi, but this is the most famous of the lot. It is dedicated to Vishveswara – Shiva as lord of the universe. The current temple was built in 1776 by Ahalya Bai of Indore; the 800kg of gold plating on the tower and dome was supplied by Maharaja Ranjit Singh of Lahore 50 years later.

Varanasi

Sights

1 Alamgir Mosque ... D3
2 Benares Hindu University ... B6
3 Bharat Kala Bhavan ... B6
4 Panchganga Ghat ... D3
5 Ram Ghat ... D3
6 Trilochan Ghat ... D2

Activities, Courses & Tours

Aarna Spa ... (see 11)
7 Hotel Clarks Varanasi ... A1
8 International Centre ... B6
9 Learn for Life Society ... B3

Sleeping

10 Homestay ... B3
11 Hotel Surya ... A1
12 Stops Hostel ... B4

Eating

Canton Royale ... (see 11)
13 Open Hand ... C5

Drinking & Nightlife

Mangi Ferra ... (see 11)
14 Prinsep Bar ... A1

Shopping

15 Mehrotra Silk Factory ... B2
16 Mehrotra Silk Factory ... D2
17 Shri Gandhi Ashram Khadi ... B5

The area is full of soldiers because of security issues and communal tensions. Bags, cameras, mobile phones, pens and any electronic device must be deposited in lockers (₹20) before you enter the alleyway it's in – or just leave your stuff at your hotel. Though accounts vary as to whether or not foreigners can go in the temple itself, we found it to be fairly straightforward: Head to **Gate 2** (Map p384), where security will instruct you to walk past the long lines of Indians waiting in the queue, then go through a metal detector and security check. Walk past another line of Indians until you are pointed to a desk, where you must show your passport (not a copy) and leave your shoes. Then enter the temple through a door across the alley.

Once inside, things can be quite intense, with people pushing and tripping over each other for a chance to give an offering and touch the lingam (phallic symbol of Shiva), which resolves one of all sins. At other times, it's much more peaceful. Hindus routinely wait in lines for 48 hours to enter on particularly holy days.

On the northern side of Vishwanath Temple is the **Gyan Kupor Well** (Well of Knowledge; Map p384). The faithful believe drinking its water leads to a higher spiritual plane, though they are prevented from doing so by a strong security screen. Non-Hindus are not allowed to enter here, and the rule is strictly enforced.

Benares Hindu University UNIVERSITY, HISTORIC SITE

(BHU; Map p380; www.bhu.ac.in) Long regarded as a centre of learning, Varanasi's tradition of top-quality education continues today at Benares Hindu University, established in 1916. The wide, tree-lined streets and parkland of the 5-sq-km campus offer a peaceful atmosphere a world away from the city outside. On campus is **Bharat Kala Bhavan** (Map p380; Indian/foreigner ₹10/150; 10am-5.30pm Mon-Fri), a roomy museum with a wonderful collection of miniature paintings, as well as 12th-century palm-leaf manuscripts, sculptures and local history displays.

Ghats

Spiritually enlightening and fantastically photogenic, Varanasi is at its brilliant best by the ghats, the long stretch of steps leading down to the water on the western bank of the Ganges. Most are used for bathing but there are also several 'burning ghats' where bodies are cremated in public. The main one is Manikarnika (p382): you'll often see funeral processions threading their way through the backstreets to this ghat.

The best time to visit the ghats is at dawn, when the river is bathed in a mellow light as pilgrims come to perform *puja* (prayers) to the rising sun, and at sunset when the main *ganga aarti* (river worship ceremony) takes place at Dashashwamedh Ghat (p382).

About 80 ghats border the river, but the main group extends from Assi Ghat (p382), near the university, northwards to **Raj Ghat**, near the road and rail bridge.

A boat trip along the river provides the perfect introduction, although for most of the year the water level is low enough for you to walk freely along the whole length of the ghats. It's a world-class 'people-watching' stroll as you mingle with the fascinating mixture of people who come to the Ganges not only for a ritual bath but also to wash clothes, do yoga, offer blessings, sell flowers, get a massage, play cricket, wash their buffaloes, improve their karma by giving to beggars or simply hang around.

Southern Stretch

★Assi Ghat
GHAT

(Map p384) The furthest south of the main ghats and one of the biggest, Assi Ghat is particularly important as the River Assi meets the Ganges near here and pilgrims come to worship a Shiva lingam (phallic image of Shiva) beneath a peepul tree. Evenings are particularly lively, as the ghat's vast concreted area fills up with hawkers and entertainers. There's also music and yoga at sunrise. It's a popular starting point for boat trips and there are some excellent hotels here.

Tulsi Ghat
GHAT

(Map p384) Named after a 16th-century Hindu poet, Tulsi Ghat has fallen down towards the river, but in the month of Kartika (October/November) a festival devoted to Krishna is celebrated here.

Bachraj Ghat
GHAT

(Map p384) This small ghat is marked by three Jain temples.

Shivala Ghat
GHAT

(Map p384) A small Shiva temple and a 19th-century mansion built by Nepali royalty sit back from Shivala Ghat, built by the local maharaja of Benares.

Hanuman Ghat
GHAT

(Map p384) Popular with Rama devotees (Hanuman was Rama's stalwart ally in his quest to rescue Sita from the demon Ravana).

★Harishchandra Ghat
GHAT

(Map p384) Harishchandra Ghat is a cremation ghat – smaller and secondary in importance to Manikarnika, but one of the oldest ghats in Varanasi.

Kedar Ghat
GHAT

(Map p384) A colourful ghat with many steps and a small pool, where a fire *aarti* is held every evening at 6.30pm.

Old City Stretch

★Dashashwamedh Ghat
GHAT

(Map p384) Varanasi's liveliest and most colourful ghat. The name indicates that Brahma sacrificed *(medh)* 10 *(das)* horses *(aswa)* here. In spite of the oppressive boat owners, flower sellers, massage practitioners and touts trying to drag you off to a silk shop, it's a wonderful place to linger and people-watch while soaking up the atmosphere. Every evening at 7pm an elaborate *ganga aarti* (river worship) ceremony with *puja* (prayers), fire and dance is staged here.

It's easily reached at the end of the main road from Godaulia Crossing.

Man Mandir Ghat
GHAT

(Map p384) Just north of Dashashwamedh Ghat, Man Mandir Ghat was built in 1600 by Raja Man Singh, but was poorly restored in the 19th century. The northern corner of the ghat has a fine stone balcony.

★Manikarnika Ghat
GHAT

(Map p384) Manikarnika Ghat, the main burning ghat, is the most auspicious place for a Hindu to be cremated. Dead bodies are handled by outcasts known as *doms*, and are carried through the alleyways of the Old City to the holy Ganges on a bamboo stretcher, swathed in cloth. The corpse is doused in the Ganges prior to cremation.

Huge piles of firewood are stacked along the top of the ghat; every log is carefully weighed on giant scales so that the price of cremation can be calculated. Each type of wood has its own price, sandalwood being the most expensive. There is an art to using just enough wood to completely incinerate a corpse. You can watch cremations but always show reverence by behaving respectfully. Photography is strictly prohibited. You're almost guaranteed to be led by a priest, or more likely a guide, to the upper floor of a nearby building from where you can watch cremations taking place, and then asked for a donation (in dollars) towards the cost of wood. If you don't want to make a donation, don't follow them.

Above the steps here is a tank known as the **Manikarnika Well**. Parvati is said to have dropped her earring here and Shiva dug the tank to recover it, filling the depression with his sweat. The **Charanpaduka**, a slab of stone between the well and the ghat, bears footprints made by Vishnu. Privileged VIPs are cremated at the Charanpaduka, which also has a temple dedicated to Ganesh.

Dattatreya Ghat
GHAT

(Map p384) Dattatreya takes its name from a Brahmin saint, whose footprint is preserved in a small temple nearby.

Scindhia Ghat
GHAT

(Map p384) Scindhia Ghat was originally built in 1830, but was so huge and magnificent that it collapsed into the river and had to be rebuilt.

Northern Stretch

Ram Ghat GHAT

(Map p380) North from Scindhia Ghat, Ram Ghat was built by a maharaja of Jaipur.

Panchganga Ghat GHAT

(Map p380) Just beyond Ram Ghat, this ghat marks where five holy rivers are supposed to meet.

Alamgir Mosque MOSQUE

(Map p380) Dominating Panchganga Ghat, this small mosque was built by Aurangzeb on the site of a large Vishnu temple.

Trilochan Ghat GHAT

(Map p380) At Trilochan, two turrets emerge from the river, and the water between them is especially holy.

Activities

It's worth an early rise for two of your mornings in Varanasi, one to take in the action on a river-boat trip and another to experience the hubbub of activity on the ghats themselves. Nonguests can use the outdoor **swimming pools** at Hotel Surya (p387) for ₹300 and **Hotel Clarks Varanasi** (Map p380; The Mall; nonguests ₹500; 9am-6pm).

DarkLotus YOGA

(www.banarasyoga.com) Taking yoga out of the studio and around the sacred sites of Varanasi, these highly recommended classes are set along the river and at temples around the city. Contact through the website for courses and prices.

Aarna Spa MASSAGE

(Map p380; 0542-2508465; www.hotelsuryavns.com; Hotel Surya, S-20/51A-5 The Mall Rd; massage from ₹1400; 8am-8pm) Hotel Surya's spa is a nice choice for soothing ayurvedic massages.

Swasthya Vardhak AYURVEDA

(Map p384; 0542-2312504; www.swasthyavardhak.in; Assi Crossing; 8am-7.30pm) Varanasi is full of ayurvedic imposters. Serious seekers should come here, the city's real-deal ayurvedic pharmacy. Consultations with a doctor are free (from 9am to noon and 5pm to 7.30pm); prescriptions run from ₹20 to ₹2000. Additionally, it works with a government initiative that encourages struggling local farmers to turn over a new leaf planting ayurvedic herbs.

Volunteering

Learn for Life Society VOLUNTEERING

(Map p380; 0542-2390040; www.learn-for-life.net; D55/147 Aurangabad) This small charity, run by two foreigners and contacted through Brown Bread Bakery (p388), supports a unique school for disadvantaged children

THE VARANASI SHAKEDOWN

- Don't take photos at the 'burning' ghats and resist offers to 'follow me for a better view', where you'll be pressured for money and possibly be placed in an uncomfortable situation.
- Do not go to any shop with a guide or autorickshaw driver. Be firm and don't do it. Ever. You will pay 40% to 60% more for your item due to insane commissions, and you'll also be passively encouraging this practice. Do yourself a favour and walk there, or have your ride drop you a block away.
- Imposter stores are rampant in Varanasi, usually spelled one letter off or sometimes exactly the same. The shops we have recommended are the real deal. Ask for a visiting card (ie business card) – if the info doesn't match, you have been had.
- When negotiating with boatmen, confirm the price and currency before setting out. Many just love to say '100!' and then at the end claim they meant dollars or euros.
- Do not book unofficial guides, which are whom most guesthouses hire. If you want a guide, go through UP Tourism (p390) to avoid most of the hassles above. If not, have fun shopping!
- Be wary of bhang lassis – these are made with hash (degraded cannabis) and can be very strong if that's not what you're looking for (we've heard reports of robberies of intoxicated people).
- Beware of fake 'yoga teachers' who are mainly interested in hands-on lessons with young women.

The Old City & Assi Ghat Area

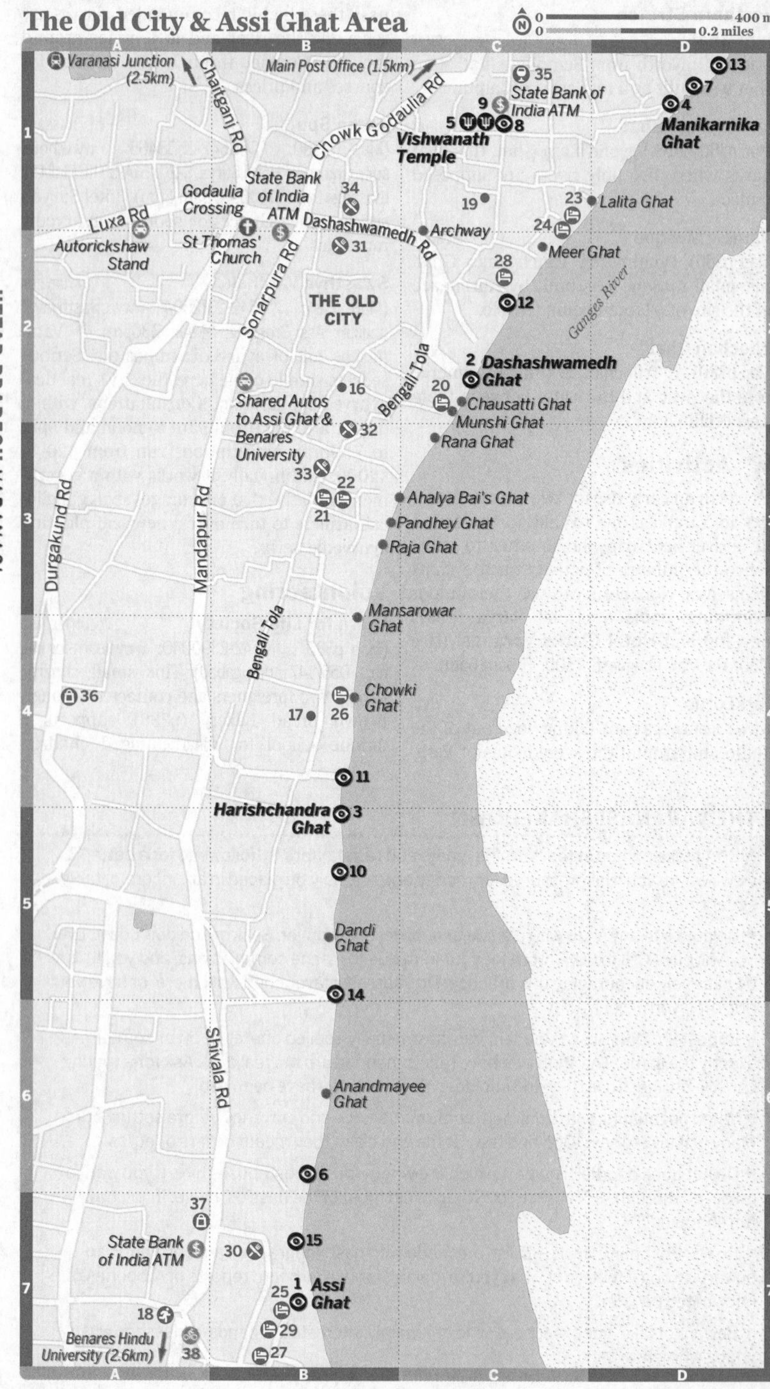

The Old City & Assi Ghat Area

Top Sights
1 Assi Ghat B7
2 Dashashwamedh Ghat C2
3 Harishchandra Ghat B5
4 Manikarnika Ghat D1
5 Vishwanath Temple C1

Sights
6 Bachraj Ghat B6
7 Dattatreya Ghat D1
8 Gate 2 .... C1
9 Gyan Kupor Well C1
10 Hanuman Ghat B5
11 Kedar Ghat B4
12 Man Mandir Ghat C2
13 Scindhia Ghat D1
14 Shivala Ghat B5
15 Tulsi Ghat B7

Activities, Courses & Tours
16 International Music Centre Ashram B2
17 Pragati Hindi B4
18 Swasthya Vardhak A7
19 Yoga Training Centre C1

Sleeping
20 Brijrama Palace C2
21 Brown Bread Bakery Guesthouse B3
22 BunkedUp Hostel B3
23 Ganpati Guesthouse C1
24 Hotel Alka C1
25 Hotel Ganges View B7
26 Kedareswar B4
27 Palace on Ganges B7
28 Rashmi Guest House C2
29 Sahi River View Guesthouse B7

Eating
30 Aum Cafe B7
31 Ayyar's Cafe B2
32 Bhumi French Bakers B3
33 Bona Cafe B3
Brown Bread Bakery .... (see 21)
Darbangha .... (see 20)
Dolphin Restaurant .... (see 28)
34 Keshari Restaurant B1
Vegan & Raw .... (see 37)

Drinking & Nightlife
35 Blue Lassi C1

Shopping
36 Baba Blacksheep A4
37 Organic by Brown Bread Bakery A7

Transport
38 Cycle Repair Shop A7

and a women's empowerment group, offering fairly paid work to local women. While there are some opportunities for short-term volunteers, volunteering in a classroom requires a commitment of at least a few months.

Courses

Pragati Hindi LANGUAGE
(Map p384; ☎9335376488; www.pragatihindi.com; B-7/176 Harar Bagh) Readers recommend the flexibility of the one-to-one classes taught here by the amiable Rajeswar Mukherjee (Raju). Private classes start from ₹300 per hour. Call ahead, or just drop in to meet Raju and arrange a schedule. Walk up the stairs opposite Chowki Ghat and take the first left, following the 'Hindi' signs.

International Music Centre Ashram MUSIC
(Map p384; ☎9415987283; tablateeteteete@gmail.com; D33/81 Khalishpura; per class ₹400) This family-run centre is hidden in the tangle of backstreets off Bengali Tola. It offers sitar, tabla, flute and classical-dance tuition, and performances are held every Saturday and Wednesday evening at 8pm (₹150). There's a small, easy-to-miss sign on Bengali Tola directing you here.

International Centre LANGUAGE
(Map p380; ☎0542-2368130; www.bhu.ac.in; C/3/3 Tagore House; ⏰10am-5pm Mon-Sat) If you're interested in studying at Benares Hindu University, contact this centre. Courses on offer include Hindi, Sanskrit and yoga, among others.

Yoga Training Centre YOGA
(Map p384; ☎9919857895; www.yogatrainingcentrevaranasi.in; 5/15 Sakarkand Gali; 2hr class group/private ₹300/800, reiki from ₹800; ⏰8am, 10am & 4pm) Former army clerk and yoga master Sunil Kumar and partners run set classes four times a day on the 2nd and 3rd floors of this small backstreet building near Meer Ghat (but you can drop in anytime for a session).

He teaches an integrated blend of hatha, shivananda, satyananda, pranayama and Iyengar, and serious students can continue on certificate and diploma courses in both yoga and reiki.

Tours

If time is short, UP Tourism (p390) can arrange guided tours by taxi of the major sites, including a 5.30am boat ride and an afternoon trip to Sarnath (p392).

★**Varanasi Walks** WALKING
(☎9793714111; www.varanasiwalks.com; tours ₹1000-1600) The cultural walks on offer from this agency specialising in themed walks explore beyond the most popular ghats and temples, giving eye-opening insight into this holy city. The American founder, Jai, has lived in Varanasi for years, and most of the guides were born and raised here. Walks are available by reservation, booking online or by phone.

Sleeping

Most of Varanasi's budget hotels – and some midrange gems – are tucked among the narrow streets off the ghats. There's a concentration around Assi Ghat; others are in the bustling alleys of the Old City, between Scindhia and Meer Ghat. To experience local life, stay in a guesthouse.

For five-star luxury, there are some great choices in the neighborhoods west of the river, such as Bhelpura, Aurangabad Rd and Cantonment.

Old City Area

Brown Bread Bakery Guesthouse GUESTHOUSE $
(Map p384; ☎0542-2450472, 9838888823; www.brownbreadbakery.com; Bengali Tola, Pandey Ghat; s without bathroom ₹250, with AC or heater ₹750, d with/without AC or heater from ₹1200/750;) With the cleanest budget rooms in Varanasi, this well-run guesthouse is one of the best deals in town. Bonus: it shares space with the excellent restaurant (p388) of the same name and offers the best deals around on reliable sunrise boat tours – you can even arrange for breakfast on your boat! A two-minute walk from Pandey Ghat.

Hotel Alka GUESTHOUSE $
(Map p384; ☎0542-2401681; www.hotelalkavns.com; 3/23 Meer Ghat; r ₹1200, with AC ₹1800-6300, without bathroom ₹700; @) This excellent ghat-side option could use an attentive eye on its exteriors, but the pretty much spotless rooms – either opening onto, or overlooking, a large, plant-filled courtyard over the Ganges – draw the lion's share of care here. In the far corner, a terrace juts out over Meer Ghat for one of the best views in all of Varanasi, a view shared from the balconies of eight of the pricier rooms.

BunkedUp Hostel HOSTEL $
(Map p384; ☎0542-2450508; www.bunkeduphostels.com; off Bengali Tola; dm with/without AC ₹460/360, r with/without AC ₹1500/1000;) This brand-new hostel aims to please, with a couple of mixed-gender dorm rooms and a women-only dorm, plus some private rooms. The rooftop cafe has great views of the river, and there's a movie theatre in the basement. Currently, it's the only hostel in the Old City.

★**Ganpati Guesthouse** GUESTHOUSE $$
(Map p384; ☎0542-2390057; www.ganpatiguesthouse.com; 3/24 Meer Ghat; r ₹1300-5630; @) This old red-brick favourite has a pleasant, shaded courtyard as well as plenty of balcony space dotted around offering fine river views. Rooms are clean, brightly painted from the ceilings down and feature tasteful framed wall hangings and modern bathrooms. The best have private river-view balconies.

The least expensive rooms – very much budget offerings – are in an annexed building down the alley, which lacks the ambience of the main guesthouse. Be *very* wary of the aggressive monkeys!

Homestay HOMESTAY $$
(Map p380; ☎9415449348; www.homestayvaranasi.in; 61/16 Sidhgiri Bagh; s ₹2300-2800, d ₹2500-3000; @) This homestay in a 1936 colonial home in a residential neighborhood 1.5km from the Old City back alleys is a true catch. Good-hearted host Harish, a 30-year veteran of the textile industry (well-regarded, fixed-price shop on premises) has six exquisitely maintained deluxe and enormous super-deluxe rooms that are shielded from light, noise and mosquitoes. You'll truly appreciate the rest.

His wife, Malika, whips up exquisite home-cooked meals and has been known to give impromptu cooking classes. If you don't mind being a bit away from the heart of the action, it's a delightful choice.

Kedareswar HOTEL $$
(Map p384; ☎0542-2455568; www.kedareswarguesthouse.com; B14/1 Chowki Ghat; r ₹1840, with river view ₹3680, all incl breakfast;) Housed in a brightly painted aquamarine-green building, this friendly six-room place has cramped but immaculate rooms with sparkling bathrooms. Breakfast is served on the rooftop when it's not too hot or rainy. It's popular, so you'll want to book ahead.

Rashmi Guest House HOTEL $$$
(Map p384; ☎0542-2402778; www.rashmiguesthouse.com; 16/28A Man Mandir Ghat; r incl breakfast ₹3200-6900; @) Incense-scented,

white-tile corridors and marble staircases lead to a variety of cramped but smart rooms boasting high marks for cleanliness and style. Many have artistically patterned walls and views of Man Mandir Ghat. Dolphin (p388), the hotel's rooftop restaurant, is a fine place for a beer-chased evening meal and one of the Old City's few nonveg options.

★ **Brijrama Palace** HERITAGE HOTEL $$$
(Map p384; ☎9129414141; www.brijrama.in; Munshi/Darbhanga Ghat; r ₹21,850-42,550; ❄📶) This meticulously renovated riverfront palace, built in 1812 and known as the Darbangha Mahal, is simply exquisite. From the period chandeliers to the oriental rugs to the carved stone columns and artwork on the walls, this is the most authentic and luxurious heritage hotel along the ghats. Its Darbangha restaurant (p388) may well be the best in Varanasi.

Enter from the ghats by elevator – the original was one of India's first, hoisted by horse and pulley!

Assi Ghat Area

Stops Hostel HOSTEL $
(Map p380; ☎9506118023; www.gostops.com; B20/47A2, Vijaya Nagaram Colony; tent Nov-Feb ₹250, dm from ₹500, d with AC ₹2000, all incl breakfast; ❄@📶) Varanasi's original hostel is in a four-story residential mansion 2km or so from Assi Ghat. Dorms in six-, eight- and 14-bed variations are livened up by colourful lockers, and there are ample hang-out spaces on various floors that cultivate the right vibe – a rare find in UP.

The few privates are basic and a bit overpriced; the real draws are the dorms, common areas and the rooftop showers, each uniquely painted by various artistic volunteers. The hostel offers all sorts of tours and activities, from cooking classes to sunrise river trips, making it easy to get the most out of your stay. It's a solid choice for the socially inclined – the only downside is its distance from the ghats.

Sahi River View Guesthouse GUESTHOUSE $
(Map p384; ☎0542-2366730; www.sahiriverview.co.in; B1/158 Assi Ghat; s/d ₹400/800, r with AC from ₹1450, all incl breakfast; ❄@📶) You'll find a huge variety of rooms at this friendly place, which is better than it looks from its entrance down a side alley. Most rooms are good quality and clean, and some have interesting private balconies. Each floor has a pleasant communal seating area with river view, creating a great feeling of space throughout.

> **SLEEPING PRICE RANGES**
>
> Accommodation price ranges for this region are:
>
> **$** below ₹1500
>
> **$$** ₹1500–4000
>
> **$$$** above ₹4000

★ **Hotel Ganges View** HOTEL $$$
(Map p384; ☎0542-2313218; www.hotelgangesview.co.in; Assi Ghat; r with AC ₹5100-8000; ❄@📶) Simply gorgeous, this beautifully restored and maintained colonial-style house overlooking Assi Ghat is crammed with books, artwork and antiques. Rooms are spacious and immaculate and there are some charming communal areas in which to sit and relax, including a lovely 1st-floor garden terrace. Book ahead.

Palace on Ganges HOTEL $$$
(Map p384; ☎0542-2315050; www.palaceonganges.com; B1/158 Assi Ghat; r ₹6900-9200; ❄@📶) Each room is individually themed on a regional Indian style, using antique furnishings and colourful design themes. The colonial, Rajasthan and Jodhpur rooms are among the best, but look at a few if you can, as the more expensive rooms aren't necessarily better than the less expensive ones.

Cantonment Area

Hotel Surya HOTEL $$
(Map p380; ☎0542-2508465; www.hotelsuryavns.com; S-20/51 A-5 The Mall Rd; s/d incl breakfast from ₹3450/4025; ❄@📶🏊) Varanasi's cheapest hotel with a swimming pool, Surya has standard three-star Indian rooms, but a modern makeover in the superior and premium rooms means everything has been tightened up a bit, with stylish new furnishings, upholstery and the like – yours for ₹1500 or so more above standard rates.

Value here is palpable, as all is built around a huge lawn area that includes a colourful lounge-style bar and cafe flanked by a gorgeous, nearly 200-year-old heritage building (the former stomping grounds of a Nepali king), where the excellent-value **Canton Royale** (Map p380; mains ₹200-390; ⏰11am-11pm) is housed. There's also the good (but smoky) Sol Bar and the recommended Aarna Spa (p383).

Eating

Look for locally grown *langda aam* (mangoes) in summer or *sitafal* (custard apples) in autumn. *Singharas* are water chestnuts that are sold raw (green) or cooked (black) – there's a risk of intestinal parasites with the raw ones.

Many eateries in the Old City shut in summer due to unbearable humidity and water levels that often flood the ghats and around.

Old City Area

Bhumi French Bakers BAKERY $

(Map p384; Bengali Tola; pastries ₹50; ⏰6am-6pm; 📶) This casual cafe creates some of the best pastries in Varanasi, and what might be the best chocolate croissants in all of India.

Keshari Restaurant INDIAN $

(Map p384; 14/8 Godaulia; mains ₹130-200; ⏰9.30am-10.30pm; 📝) Known as much for excellent cuisine as for surly service, this atmospheric spot (carved-wood panelling dons the walls and ceilings) has been famously at it for nearly a half-century. Indians pack in here for high-quality veg cuisine from all over India – a dizzying array of dishes are on offer (more than 40 paneer curries alone).

Those who like to dance with the devil should spring for the paneer Kadahi (spicy tomato-based gravy), sure to make your nose run. Note: this restaurant is about 20 metres down a side street off Dashashwamedh Rd. Do not confuse it with the less-desirable Keshari Ruchiker Byanjan around the corner on Dashashwamedh Rd.

Ayyar's Cafe SOUTH INDIAN $

(Map p384; Dashashwamedh Rd; mains ₹35-120; ⏰9.30am-8.30pm) Excellent, no-nonsense choice off the tourist-beaten path for South Indian *masala dosa*, and its spicier cousin, the Mysore dosa; and one of the few cheapies to serve filtered coffee. It's tucked away at the end of a very short alley signed 'New Keshari Readymade' off Dashashwamedh Rd.

★ **Brown Bread Bakery** MULTICUISINE $$

(Map p384; ☎9792420450; www.brownbreadbakery.com; Bengali Tola, near Pandey Ghat; mains ₹125-400; ⏰7am-10pm; ❄📶) 🍃 This restaurant's fabulous menu includes more than 40 varieties of European-quality cheese and more than 30 types of bread, cookies and cakes – along with excellent pastas, sandwiches, pizzas and more. Sit downstairs at street level (AC in summer) or upstairs at the casual rooftop cafe, with seating on cushions around low tables and glimpses of the Ganges.

Pop in for the shockingly European breakfast buffet (7am to noon; ₹300) or the free, nightly live classical-music performances (7.30pm). Part of the profits go to the Learn for Life (p383) school. Warning: don't be fooled by imposters who pretend to be the BBB. Note this new location (on Bengali Tola, near Pandey Ghat), and remember: the real BBB will never accept cash donations for Learn for Life.

Bona Cafe KOREAN $$

(Map p384; Bengali Tola; mains ₹100-500; ⏰9am-10pm) This cosy restaurant does everything well, but you really want to come here for the quality Korean food. Tasty full meals, such as *jabchaebab* (glass-noodle stir-fry), include soup and kimchi. Sit on floor cushions, at tables or on the patio overlooking Bengali Tola. The owner, Bona, is as kind as they come.

Dolphin Restaurant INDIAN $$

(Rashmi Guest House; Map p384; 16/28A Man Mandir Ghat; mains ₹130-340; ⏰7am-10pm) The atmosphere trumps the food at Dolphin – the rooftop restaurant at Rashmi Guest House (p386) – which is perched high above Man Mandir Ghat, but it's still a fine place for an evening meal. The breezy balcony is the most refined table in the Old City and one of the few that serves nonveg as well.

★ **Darbangha** INDIAN, MULTICUISINE $$$

(Map p384; ☎9129414141; Brijrama Palace Hotel, Munshi/Darbhanga Ghat; mains ₹750-1100, thalis ₹1750; ⏰noon-3pm & 7.30-10.30pm) Seriously some of the best Indian food we've ever had. The *palak chaman* (paneer in spinach and spices) is heaven in your mouth and the *aloo chaat* is a gourmet-street-food revelation. There's also a good list of continental and Thai options. For nonguests there's a minimum charge of ₹1000 per person. It's worth it.

Assi Ghat Area

Aum Cafe CAFE $

(Map p384; www.touchoflight.us; B1/201 Assi Ghat; mains ₹70-180; ⏰8am-4.30pm Tue-Sun; 📶📝) 🍃 Run by an American woman who has been coming to India for more than 20 years, this colourful cafe has breakfast all day (good lemon pancakes!), astounding lemon-

DON'T MISS

NO 1 LASSI IN ALL VARANASI

Your long, thirsty search for the best lassi in India is over. Look no further than **Blue Lassi** (Map p384; lassi ₹40-90; ⌚9am-10pm; 📶), a tiny, hole-in-the-wall yoghurt shop that has been churning out the freshest, creamiest, fruit-filled lassis since 1925. The grandson of the original owner still works here, sitting by his lassi-mixing cauldron in front of a small room with wooden benches for customers to sit on and walls plastered with messages from happy drinkers.

There are more than 80 delicious flavour combos, divided by section – plain, banana, apple, pomegranate, mango, papaya, strawberry, blueberry, coconut and saffron. We think banana and apple, the latter flecked with fresh apple shreds, just about top the long list. (What the hell, make it banana-apple!)

The whole scene here is surreal: the lassi takes ages to arrive while a UN-rivalling group of thirsty nationalities chats away; when it does, it's handed off to you with the care of a priceless work of art as the deceased are carried by the front of the shop on the way to Burning Ghat (Manikarnika). *Namaste!*

and-organic-green-tea lassis and a handful of light sandwiches and mains that offer a respite from all the curry. There's also massage therapy and body piercing available.

★Open Hand CAFE $$

(Map p380; www.openhand.in; 1/128-3 Dumraub Bagh; mains ₹160-280; ⌚8am-8pm; 📶) 🌿 This shoes-off cafe-cum–gift shop serves real espresso and French-press coffee alongside breakfast platters featuring pancakes, omelettes and muesli. There's also a range of salads, sandwiches, pastas and baked goods, which are excellent. Sit on the narrow balcony or lounge around the former home all day on the free wi-fi.

There's also a large selection of gorgeous handicrafts (jewellery, toys, clothing) made in the local community. Couldn't be more pleasant.

Vegan & Raw VEGAN $$

(Map p384; Shivala Rd, near Tulsi Ghat; mains ₹170-220; ⌚9am-9.30pm; 📶) This casual courtyard restaurant is an offshoot of Brown Bread Bakery (p388), featuring excellent vegan dishes, including a full page of salads from spinach-radish-walnut to papaya-pomegranate-linseed. Entrées lean toward pastas, but there's also tofu, *momo* (Tibetan dumplings) and couscous. Eclectic live music is performed Tuesday, Thursday and Saturday at around 7pm. It's behind the Organic by Brown Bread Bakery (p390) shop.

🍷 Drinking & Nightlife

Wine and beer shops are dotted discreetly around the city, usually away from the river. (Note that it is frowned upon to drink alcohol on or near the holy Ganges.) Liquor laws regarding proximity of temples ensure nobody is licensed, but rooftops here can usually discreetly fashion up a beer. For bars, head to midrange and top-end hotels away from the ghats.

Mangi Ferra CAFE

(Map p380; www.hotelsuryavns.com; S-20/51A-5 The Mall Rd; ⌚11am-11pm) This colourful, laid-back lounge in the garden at Hotel Surya (p387) is a relaxing place where you can sip on espresso (₹70), a cold one or a cocktail (₹120 to ₹480) in the garden, or on waves of couches and armchairs.

Prinsep Bar BAR

(Map p380; www.tajhotels.com; Gateway Hotel Ganges, Raja Bazaar Rd; ⌚noon-11pm Mon-Sat, to midnight Sun) For a quiet drink with a dash of history, try this tiny bar named after James Prinsep, who drew wonderful illustrations of Varanasi's ghats and temples (but stick to beer as the 25ml cocktail pour is weak).

☆ Entertainment

There's nightly live Indian classical music at Brown Bread Bakery.

The International Music Centre Ashram (p385) has small performances (₹150) on Wednesday and Saturday evenings.

🔒 Shopping

Varanasi is justifiably famous for silk brocades and beautiful Benares saris, but don't believe much of what the silk salesmen tell you about the relative quality of products, even in government emporiums. Instead, shop around and judge for yourself.

There are loads of musical instrument shops on Bengali Tola (near Rana Ghat), many of which offer lessons.

★**Baba Blacksheep** FASHION & ACCESSORIES
(Map p384; B12/120 A-9, Bhelpura; ⏲9am-8pm) If the deluge of traveller enthusiasm is anything to go by, this is the most trustworthy, non-pushy shop in India. Indeed it is one of the best places you'll find for silks (scarves/saris from ₹500/4000) and *pashmina* (shawls from ₹1700).

Prices are fixed (though unmarked) and the friendly owner refuses to play the commission game, so autorickshaws and taxis don't like to come here (ignore anyone who says you cannot drive here, and make sure you're in the right place, not an imposter). It's located at Bhelpura crossing under the mosque. It's not the cheapest, but it's a pleasant experience.

Mehrotra Silk Factory FASHION & ACCESSORIES
(Map p380; www.mehrotrasilk.in; 4/8A Lal Ghat; ⏲10am-8pm) In a labyrinth of alleys behind Lal Ghat, this fixed-price shop, its floor cushioned for seating, offers fine silks for fair prices. Grab something as small as a scarf or as big as a bedcover. There's another **branch** (Map p380; www.mehrotrasilk.in; 21/72 Englishia Line; ⏲10am-8pm) near the railway station.

Organic by Brown Bread Bakery COSMETICS, FOOD
(Map p384; www.brownbreadbakery.com; 2/225 Shivali; ⏲7am-8pm; 📶) 🍃 This small shop sells natural cosmetics from the government-sponsored Khadi program, as well as baked goods, muesli and cheese from Brown Bread Bakery (p388).

Shri Gandhi Ashram Khadi CLOTHING
(Map p380; Sankat Mochan Rd; ⏲10am-7.30pm) Stocks shirts, kurta shirts, saris and headscarves, all made from the famous homespun *khadi* fabric.

BUYER BEWARE: 'THROUGH' BUS TICKETS

Be wary of buying 'through' tickets from Kathmandu or Pokhara to Varanasi. Some travellers report being intimidated into buying another ticket once over the border. Travelling in either direction, it's better to take a local bus to the border, walk across and take another onward bus (pay the conductor onboard) – though there is one legit, direct Varanasi–Kathmandu bus each day (you can buy tickets from its booth at the bus stand).

Travellers have also complained about being pressured into paying extra luggage charges for buses out of Sunauli. You shouldn't have to, so politely decline.

ℹ Information

There are several ATMs scattered around town, including State Bank of India in the lobby as you exit the train station.

Heritage Hospital (Map p380; ☎0542-2368888; www.heritagehospitals.in; Lanka) English-speaking staff and doctors; 24-hour pharmacy.

Main Post Office (GPO; Map p380; www.indiapost.gov.in; off Rabindranath Tagore Rd, Visheshwarganj; ⏲10am-6pm Mon-Sat) Best PO for sending parcels abroad.

Tourist Police (Map p380; UP Tourism office, Varanasi Junction train station; ⏲5am-9pm) Tourist police wear sky-blue uniforms.

UP Tourism (Map p380; ☎0542-2506670; www.uptourism.gov.in; Varanasi Junction Train Station; ⏲10am-6pm) The patient Mr Umashankar at the office inside the train station has been dishing out reasonably impartial information to arriving travellers for years; he's a mine of knowledge, so this is a requisite first stop if you arrive here by train.

ℹ Getting There & Away

AIR

Lal Bahadur Shashtri Airport, 24km north of town in Babatpur, is served by several airlines with nonstop flights to select cities in India, including Delhi, Mumbai, Benguluru (Bangalore), and Hyderabad. Thai Airways flies directly to Bangkok on Monday, Tuesday and Thursday.

BUS

The main **bus stand** (Map p380) is opposite Varanasi Junction train station. Lucknow Volvo AC buses can be reserved in advance at a dedicated ticket window at the station.

Allahabad ₹120, three hours, every 30 minutes, 4am to 10pm; also eight daily AC buses for ₹193

Delhi AC buses ₹1227, 16 hours, 10am and 2.30pm

Faizabad ₹195, seven hours, frequent service from 5am to 9pm

Gorakhpur ₹185, seven hours, every 30 minutes, 4am to 10pm; also siz daily AC buses for ₹317

Lucknow Non-AC ₹275, 7½ hours, every 30 minutes, 4am to 11pm; also AC buses

₹480-900, 7½ hours, 8am, 10.30am, 9pm, 9.30pm and 10.30pm

TRAIN

Varanasi Junction train station, also known as Varanasi Cantonment (Cantt), is the main station.

There are several daily trains to Allahabad, Gorakhpur and Lucknow. A few daily trains leave for New Delhi and Kolkata/Howrah, but none go to Agra. (But there are daily trains from Mughal Sarai Junction, 18km from Varanasi, to Tundla, 24km from Agra). The direct train to Khajuraho only runs on Monday, Wednesday and Saturday. On other days, go via Satna, a much larger rail transit hub from where you can catch buses to Khajuraho.

Luggage theft has been reported on trains to and from Varanasi so you should take extra care. Reports of drugged food and drink aren't unheard of, so it's probably best to politely decline any offers from strangers.

Getting Around

TO/FROM THE AIRPORT

An autorickshaw to the airport in Babatpur, 24km northwest of the city, costs ₹350. A taxi is about ₹800.

BICYCLE

You can hire bikes from a small **cycle repair shop** (Map p384; ☎7860154166; 1/105 Assi-Dham; bike hire per day ₹30; ⌚8am-7pm) near Assi Ghat.

CYCLE-RICKSHAW

A small ride – up to 2km – costs ₹50. Rough prices from Godaulia Crossing include Assi Ghat (₹50), Benares Hindu University (₹60) and Varanasi Junction train station (₹60). Be prepared for hard bargaining.

TAXI & AUTORICKSHAW

Prepaid booths for autorickshaws and taxis are directly outside Varanasi Junction train station and give you a good benchmark for prices around town – though it doesn't work as well as some other cities as there are usually no officials policing it, so you'll have to haggle here, too.

If the drivers are playing by the system, you'll pay an administration charge (₹5 for autorickshaws, ₹10 for taxis) at the booth then take a ticket which you give to your driver, along with the fare, once you've reached your destination. Note that taxis and autorickshaws cannot access the Dashashwamedh Ghat area between the hours of 9am and 9pm due to high pedestrian traffic. You'll be dropped at Godaulia Crossing and will need to walk the remaining 400m or so to the entrance to the Old City, or 700m or so all the way to Dashashwamedh Ghat. During banned hours, autorickshaws line up near Godaulia Crossing at a **stand** (Map p384; Luxa Rd) on Luxa Rd.

Sample fares:

Airport auto/taxi ₹225/650

Assi Ghat auto/taxi ₹90/300

Godaulia Crossing auto/taxi ₹95/250

Sarnath auto/taxi ₹120/400

Half-day tour (four hours) taxi ₹500

Full-day tour (eight hours) taxi ₹900

Autorickshaws do not offer half-/full-day tours. **Shared autos** (Map p384; Mandapur Rd; ₹15) to Assi Ghat and Benares University leave from Mandapur Rd.

GETTING TO NEPAL

From Varanasi's bus stand there are regular services to Sunauli (p395) (₹293, 10 hours, every 30 minutes, 4am to 11pm), plus one nightly AC bus that goes all the way to Kathmandu (₹1370, 16 hours, 10pm). By train, go to Gorakhpur then transfer to a Sunauli bus. By air, you'll be connecting through Delhi. Nepali visas are available on arrival.

HANDY TRAINS FROM VARANASI

DESTINATION	TRAIN NO & NAME	FARE (₹)	DURATION (HR)	DEPARTURE
Agra Fort	14853 Marudhar Exp	350/950/1365 (A)	13	5.25pm
Allahabad	15159 Sarnath Exp	140/490/695 (A)	3	12.25pm
Gorakhpur	15003 Chaurichaura Exp	170/490/695 (A)	6½	12.35am
Jabalpur	12168 BSB-LTT Sup Exp	315/810/1140 (A)	8½	10.25am
Khajuraho	21108 BSB-Kurj Link E	265/720 (B)	11½	5.45pm*
Kolkata (Howrah)	12334 Vibhuti Exp	415/1100/1565 (A)	13½	6.08pm
Lucknow	14235 BSB-BE Exp	210/570/810 (A)	7¼	11.40pm
New Delhi	12561 Swatantra S Exp	415/1100/1565 (A)	12	12.40am

Fares: (A) sleeper/3AC/2AC, (B) sleeper/3AC; * Monday, Wednesday, Saturday only

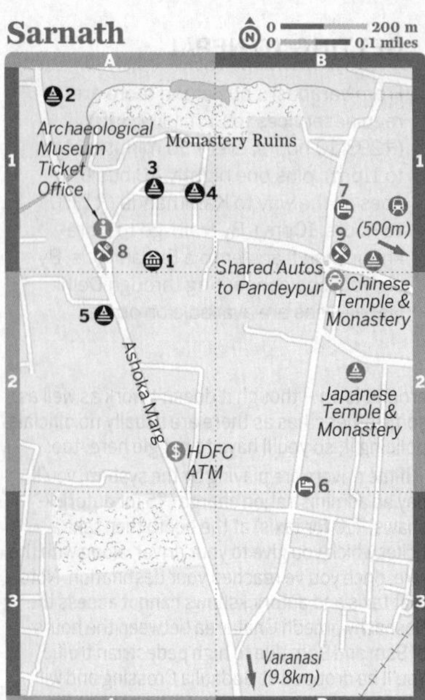

Sarnath

Sights

1 Archaeological Museum A1
2 Burmese Temple & Monastery A1
3 Dhamekh Stupa & Monastery Ruins A1
4 Mulgandha Kuti Vihar A1
5 Thai Temple & Monastery.................. A2

Sleeping

6 Agrawal Paying Guest House B2
7 Jain Paying Guest House B1

Eating

8 Green Hut... A1
9 Vaishali Restaurant B1

SARNATH

0542

Buddha came to Sarnath to preach his message of the middle way to nirvana after he achieved enlightenment at Bodhgaya, and gave his famous first sermon here. In the 3rd century BC, Emperor Ashoka had magnificent stupas and monasteries erected here, as well as an engraved pillar. When Chinese traveller Xuan Zang dropped by in AD 640, Sarnath boasted a 100m-high stupa and 1500 monks living in large monasteries. However, soon after, Buddhism went into decline and, when Muslim invaders sacked the city in the late 12th century, Sarnath disappeared altogether. It was 'rediscovered' by British archaeologists in 1835.

Today it's one of the four key sites on the Buddhist circuit (along with Bodhgaya, Kushinagar and Lumbini in Nepal) and attracts followers from around the world, especially on Purnima (or, informally, Buddha's birthday), when Buddha's life, death and enlightenment are celebrated, usually in April or May.

Sights

Purchase tickets for Sarnath's sights at the **ticket office** opposite the Archaeological Museum gardens. In addition to the main sights, check out some of the temples and gardens created by various Buddhist nations.

Dhamekh Stupa & Monastery Ruins BUDDHIST SITE

(Indian/foreigner ₹15/200, video ₹25; dawn-dusk) Set in a peaceful park of monastery ruins is this impressive 34m stupa, marking the spot where the Buddha preached his first sermon. The floral and geometric carvings are 5th century AD, but some of the brickwork dates back as far as 200 BC.

Nearby is the 3rd-century-BC **Ashoka Pillar**, engraved with an edict. It once stood 15m tall and had the famous four-lion capital, now in the museum, perched atop; all that remains are five fragments of its base.

Thai Temple & Monastery BUDDHIST TEMPLE

(6.30am-6pm Apr-Sep, 7.15am-5pm Oct-Mar) With its unique, red-walled, white-roofed design, the temple is worth a look, but the real reason to visit are the peaceful **gardens** that surround it.

Burmese Temple & Monastery BUDDHIST TEMPLE

(7.30am-6pm) The Burmese Temple features a triple-pagoda roof and several statues of the Buddha, set in lush gardens.

Archaeological Museum MUSEUM

(₹5; 9am-5pm) This fully modernised, 100-year-old sandstone museum houses wonderfully displayed ancient treasures, such as the very well-preserved, 3rd-century-BC lion capital from the Ashoka Pillar, which has been adopted as India's national emblem, and a huge 2000-year-old **stone umbrella**, ornately carved with Buddhist symbols.

Mulgandha Kuti Vihar BUDDHIST TEMPLE
(video ₹25; ⏲6am-6pm) This turreted temple was completed in 1931 by the Mahabodhi Society, and is noted for its unique **wall frescoes**, which look almost like animation stills. Buddha's first sermon is chanted daily, starting between 6pm and 7pm, depending on the season. A **bodhi tree** growing outside was transplanted in 1931 from the tree in Anuradhapura, Sri Lanka, which in turn is said to be the offspring of the original tree in Bodhgaya.

Entry is through the Dhamekh Stupa grounds.

Sleeping & Eating

Agrawal Paying Guest House GUESTHOUSE $
(☎0542-2595316; agrawalpg@gmail.com; 14/94 Ashok Marg; r ₹700-800, with AC ₹1400; ❄📶) A peaceful place with a refined owner, and spotless marble-floored rooms overlooking a large garden.

Jain Paying Guest House GUESTHOUSE $
(☎0542-2595621; www.visitsarnath.com; Sa 14/37; s/d ₹500/750, r without bathroom ₹400; 📶) This simple guesthouse is run by a friendly doctor of geography, whose wife whips up home-cooked pure veg thalis (₹180). The five rooms are rustic and well worn, but have mosquito window screens. Prices drop to ₹300 between April and September.

Vaishali Restaurant INDIAN, CHINESE $
(mains ₹80-230; ⏲8am-9pm) Large and modern 1st-floor restaurant serving mostly Indian dishes, but some Chinese too. It's the best in town.

Green Hut INDIAN, CHINESE $
(mains ₹60-230; ⏲9am-7.30pm) A breezy, open-sided cafe-restaurant offering snacks, thalis (₹90 to ₹140) and Chinese dishes.

Information

HDFC has an ATM.

Getting There & Away

Local buses to Sarnath (₹20, 40 minutes) pass in front of Varanasi Junction train station, but you may wait a long time for one.

An autorickshaw costs ₹150 from Varanasi Junction train station (use that as your bargaining base if you catch one from the Old City); pay the same to get back. Or if you prefer, you can return to Varanasi in a shared auto or *vikram* (₹15) to Pandeypur, where you'll need to switch to another shared auto to Benia Bagh (₹15), which is just a ₹40 cycle-rickshaw ride from Godaulia.

There are unreserved trains from Varanasi to Sarnath at 6.55am (daily), 9.40am (Monday to Saturday) and 9.50pm (Sunday to Friday); hop on and pay ₹20. From Sarnath to Varanasi, catch train 15159 at 11.35am (Sarnath Express; sleeper/3AC ₹140/490, 45 minutes), or take an unreserved train at 5.43am (Sunday to Friday) or 3.38pm (Monday to Friday).

GORAKHPUR

☎0551 / POP 675,000

There's little to see in Gorakhpur itself, but this well-connected transport hub is a short hop from the pilgrimage centre of Kushinagar – the place where Buddha died – making it a possible stopover on the road between Varanasi and Nepal.

Sleeping & Eating

Grand Kaushal Inn HOTEL $
(☎0551-2200690; Railway Station Rd; r from ₹600, with AC from ₹990; ❄📶) Definitely the best choice of the hotels in front of the railway station. Rooms are on the smallish side but are modern and well kept. They offer 24-hour checkout.

Chowdhry Sweet House MULTICUISINE, DESSERTS $
(Cinema Rd; mains ₹70-200; ⏲7am-11pm; 🌶) This bi-level madhouse is packed with locals taking in an extensive array of delicious Indian and Chinese veg dishes in a diner atmosphere, including ginormous *dosas* and excellent thalis (₹160 to ₹210). It specialises in sundaes, too, with a tasty boatload from which to choose. You can get a cycle-rickshaw ride (₹30) here from the railway station.

Shahanshah INDIAN $$
(Royal Residency Hotel, Golghar Rd; mains ₹170-375; ⏲11am-10.30pm) At the Royal Residency Hotel, this restaurant is an homage to Bollywood icon Amitabh Bachhaan, featuring a wall full of headshots and a mural of the star. The atmosphere is modern and pleasant, with tasteful lighting and e-tablet menus. The food is good, too – definitely worth a visit.

Information

There are State Bank of India ATMs in the train station parking lot and across from Hotel Adarsh Palace.

UP Tourism Office (☎0551-2335450; ⏲10am-5pm Mon-Sat) Inside Gorakhpur's train station.

Getting There & Away

Frequent bus services run from the main bus stand to Faizabad (₹155, 3½ hours, every 30 minutes), Kushinagar (₹56, 1½ hours, every 30 minutes) and Sunauli (₹90, three hours, every 30 minutes). Private AC buses to Faizabad (₹245, 3½ hours) and Lucknow (₹500, six hours) also depart from here throughout the day. Faster collective cars and jeeps leave for Sunauli (per person ₹150 to ₹300, two hours) when full between 5am and 6pm, directly across from the train station.

Buses to Varanasi (₹200, seven hours, express at 7.30am then hourly 10am to 10pm) leave from the Katchari bus stand, as do buses to Allahabad (₹250, 10 hours, express at 7am, then hourly 10am to 10pm).

For the main bus stand, exit the train station and keep walking straight for about 400m. For Varanasi buses you need the Katchari bus stand, about 3km further south.

There are three daily trains (four on Tuesday and Thursday, five on Friday and Saturday) from big and bustling Gorakhpur Junction to Varanasi (sleeper/3AC/2AC ₹170/490/695, 5½ hours). A number of daily trains also leave for Lucknow (sleeper/3AC/2AC ₹190/490/695, five hours) and Delhi (sleeper/3AC/2AC ₹395/1080/1555, 14 to 17 hours) and one for Agra Fort (19038/40 Avadh Express, sleeper/3AC/2AC ₹335/910/1305, 14½ hours, 1.20pm).

The train ticket reservation office is 500m to the right as you exit the station.

KUSHINAGAR

05564 / POP 23,000

One of the four main pilgrimage sites marking Buddha's life – the others being Lumbini (Nepal), Bodhgaya and Sarnath – Kushinagar is where Buddha died. There are several peaceful, modern temples where you can stay, chat with monks or simply contemplate your place in the world, and there are three main historical sights, including the simple but wonderfully serene stupa where Buddha is said to have been cremated.

Sights

In addition to the main ruins, Kushinagar's one road is lined with elaborate temples run by various Buddhist nations.

★ Mahaparinirvana Temple BUDDHIST TEMPLE
(Buddha Marg; 6am-dusk) The highlight of this modest temple, rebuilt in 1927 and set among extensive lawns and ancient excavated ruins with a circumambulatory path, is its serene 5th-century reclining Buddha, unearthed in 1876. Six metres long, it depicts Buddha on his ancient death-bed and is one of the world's most moving Buddhist icons. At sunset, monks cover the statue to the shoulders with a long saffron-coloured silk sheet, as though putting Buddha to bed for the night.

Behind the temple is an ancient 19m-tall **stupa**, and in the surrounding park is a large **bell** erected by the Dalai Lama.

Wat Thai Complex BUDDHIST TEMPLE
(www.watthaikusinara-th.org; Buddha Marg; 9-11.30am & 1.30-4pm) Features an elaborate temple, beautifully maintained **gardens** with bonsai-style trees, a monastery and a **temple** containing a gilded Buddha. There's also a Sunday school and health clinic across the street, both of which welcome visitors. Unfortunately for the rest of us, accommodation is reserved for Thai citizens only.

Ramabhar Stupa BUDDHIST SITE
Architecturally, this half-ruined 15m-high stupa is little more than a large, dome-shaped clump of red bricks, but there's an unmistakable aura about this place that is hard to ignore. This is where Buddha's body is said to have been cremated and monks and pilgrims can often be seen meditating by the palm-lined path that leads around the structure.

Mathakuar Temple BUDDHIST TEMPLE
(Buddha Marg; dawn-dusk) This small shrine, set among monastery ruins, marks the spot where Buddha is said to have made his final sermon. It now houses a 3m-tall blue-stone Buddha statue, thought to date from the 10th century AD.

Sleeping & Eating

Some of the temples, which have basic accommodation for pilgrims, also welcome tourists.

Tibetan Temple GUESTHOUSE $
(8795569357; Buddha Marg; d/tr ₹600/800) By far the nicest of Kushinagar's pilgrim accommodation offerings, this a great temple choice – rooms are even nicer than in the more expensive neighbouring hotels. There's also a dormitory offering rooms by donation. Tibetan monks from Dharamsala do a one- to two-year managerial stint here and usually speak decent English.

Linh Son Vietnam Chinese Temple GUESTHOUSE $
(9936837270; www.linhsonnepalindiatemple.org; Buddha Marg; s/d/tr ₹400/550/800;)

Kushinagar

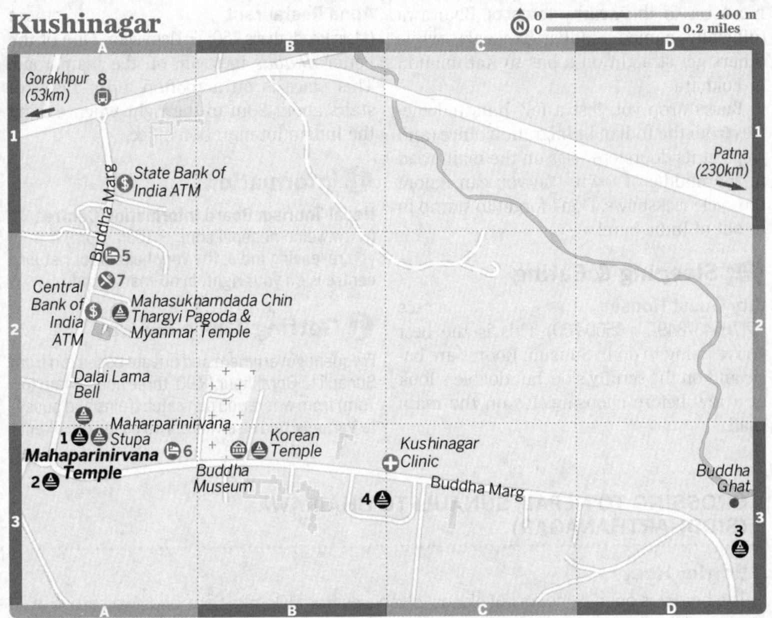

Simple, clean triples with private bathroom, hot water and a rare wi-fi signal.

Yama Cafe MULTICUISINE $

(☎9956112749; Buddha Marg; mains ₹60-100; ⏰8am-7.30pm) Run by the welcoming Mr and Mrs Roy, this Kushinagar institution has a traveller-friendly menu that includes toast, omelettes, fried rice and *thukpa* (Tibetan noodle soup). It's also the best place to come for information about the area, including about the so-called **Holy Hike**, a 13km walk in the surrounding farmland.

Information

There are two ATMs in town and a couple of private money changers.

Central Bank of India (Buddha Marg)

State Bank of India (Buddha Marg)

Kushinagar Clinic Medical services operated by nearby Wat Thai.

Getting There & Away

A new international airport has been approved nearby, but there's no firm date for its completion.

Frequent buses to Gorakhpur (₹56, 1½ hours) can be flagged down along the main road, in the middle lane across from the yellow archway entrance to town.

Kushinagar

Top Sights
1 Mahaparinirvana Temple A3

Sights
2 Mathakuar Temple A3
3 Ramabhar Stupa D3
4 Wat Thai Complex B3

Sleeping
5 Linh Son Vietnam Chinese Temple A2
6 Tibetan Temple A3

Eating
7 Yama Cafe A2

Transport
8 Buses to Gorakhpur A1

SUNAULI & THE NEPAL BORDER

☎05522 / POP 700

Sunauli is a dusty town that offers little more than a bus stop, a couple of hotels, a few shops and a border post. The border is open 24 hours and the crossing is straightforward, so most travellers carry on into Nepal without stopping here, pausing just long enough to get their passport stamped. Some move on to the nearby town of Bhairawa (officially named Siddharthanagar), while others get straight on a bus to Kathmandu or Pokhara.

Buses drop you just a few hundred metres from the Indian immigration office (and jeeps at its doorstep) – it's on the main road in the middle of town – so you can ignore the cycle-rickshaws. Don't forget to stamp in or out of India here!

Sleeping & Eating

City Guest House HOTEL $
(☎7054378491; r ₹500-700) This is the best you're going to do in Sunauli. Rooms are basic and on the scruffy side, but doable – look at a few before choosing. It's on the main road.

Apna Restaurant DHABA $
(Main Road; thalis ₹50; ⊙11am-9pm) One of the better *dhabas* in town, on the main road. This place is on a rooftop, up a flight of stairs about 30m to the right when exiting the Indian immigration office.

Information

Nepal Tourism Board Information Centre (www.welcomenepal.com; ⊙10am-5pm) If you're leaving India, the very helpful tourist info centre is on your right, in no-man's land.

Getting There & Away

Frequent government and private buses run from Sunauli to Gorakhpur (₹90, three hours, 4am to 7pm) from where you can catch trains and buses to Varanasi and elsewhere. Two buses run direct

CROSSING TO NEPAL: SUNAULI TO BHAIRAWA (SIDDHARTHANAGAR)

Border Hours

The border is open 24 hours but closes to vehicles from 10pm to 6am, and if you arrive in the middle of the night you may have to wake someone to get stamped out of India.

For further information, head to shop.lonelyplanet.com to purchase a downloadable PDF of the Kathmandu chapter from Lonely Planet's *Nepal* guide.

Foreign Exchange

There are a couple of money changers in Sunauli. On the Nepal side, there are a few ATMs on the Nepali side, including a State Bank of India adjacent to Hotel Akash – all accept international cards.

Small denominations of Indian currency are accepted for bus fares on the Nepal side.

Onward Transport

The most comfortable option to Kathmandu is the **Golden Travels** (☎071-520194) AC bus (US$15, six to seven hours); it leaves from 100m beyond Nepali immigration at 7am. AC micros (minivans) depart from the same spot every 30 minutes from 6am to 10am (₹800, six hours).

Local buses (₹20) and autorickshaws (₹100) can take you from the border to Siddharthanagar, 4km away, where you can also catch non-AC buses to Kathmandu (₹550, eight hours) via Narayangarh (₹350, three hours) and Pokhara (₹550, nine hours) via Tansen (₹250, five hours) along the Siddhartha Hwy or via the Mugling Hwy (₹650, eight hours). Local buses for Buddha's birthplace at Lumbini (₹80, one hour) leave from the junction of the Siddhartha Hwy and the road to Lumbini, about 1km north of Bank Rd.

Buddha Air (www.buddahair.com) and **Yeti Airlines** (www.yetiairlines.com) offer flights to Kathmandu from Siddharthanagar (from US$135).

Visas

Multiple-entry visas (15-/30-/90-day US$25/40/100) are available at the Nepal immigration post (note: you must pay with US cash, not rupees). You can now save time by applying online at http://online.nepalimmigration.gov.np/tourist-visa. Your receipt, which you must produce at the border within 15 days of your application, outlines the border procedures.

Always check with the **Nepal Department of Immigration** (☎+977-1-4429659; www.nepalimmigration.gov.np; Kalikasthan, Kathmandu) for the latest information on visas.

to Varanasi (11 hours) – AC at 5pm (₹466), non-AC at 6pm (₹292) – but it's a long, bumpy ride.

Faster collective cars and jeeps to Gorakhpur hang out alongside the road beyond Indian immigration and leave when full (₹150 to ₹300, two hours).

LUCKNOW

0522 / POP 3.3 MILLION

Sprinkled with exceptional British Raj–era buildings, boasting two superb mausoleums and famed throughout India for its food, the capital of Uttar Pradesh is something of a sleeper: plenty worth seeing, but often overlooked by travellers. Central Lucknow features wide boulevards, outsized monuments and several parks and gardens, but feels a bit worn out, creating an atmosphere of tired grandiosity. Locals tend to be welcoming, and you'll experience little of the hassle of more touristy towns.

The city rose to prominence as the home of the Nawabs of Avadh (Oudh) who were great patrons of the culinary and other arts, particularly dance and music. Lucknow's reputation as a city of culture, gracious living and rich cuisine has continued to this day – the phrase for which conveniently rhymes in Hindi: *Nawab, aadaab* ('respect'), *kebab* and *shabab* ('beauty').

Sights

★Residency — HISTORIC SITE

(Indian/foreigner ₹10/105, video ₹25; dawn-dusk) The large collection of gardens and ruins that makes up the Residency offers a fascinating historical glimpse of the beginning of the end for the British Raj. Built in 1800, the Residency became the stage for the most dramatic events of the 1857 First War of Independence (Indian Uprising): the Siege of Lucknow, a 147-day siege that claimed the lives of thousands.

The compound has been left as it was at the time of the final relief and the walls are still pockmarked from bullets and cannon balls.

The focus is the well-designed **museum** (8am to 4.30pm) in the main Residency building, which includes a scale model of the original buildings. Downstairs are the huge basement rooms where many of the British women and children lived throughout the siege.

The **cemetery** around the ruined St Mary's church is where 2000 of the defenders were buried, including their leader, Sir Henry Lawrence, who – according to the famous inscription on his weathered gravestone – 'tried to do his duty'.

★Bara Imambara — ISLAMIC TOMB

(Hussainabad Trust Rd; Indian/foreigner ₹50/500; 6am-6pm) This colossal *imambara* (tomb dedicated to a Shiite holy man) is worth seeing in its own right, but the highly unusual labyrinth of corridors inside its upper floors make a visit here particularly special. The ticket price includes entrance to Chota Imambara (p397), the clock tower (p398) and the Hussainabad Picture Gallery (p398), all walking distance from here.

The complex is accessed through two enormous gateways that lead into a huge courtyard. On one side is an attractive **mosque**, on the other a large **baori** (step-well), which can be explored – bring a torch (flashlight). At the far end of the courtyard is the huge **central hall**, one of the world's largest vaulted galleries. *Tazia* (small replicas of Imam Hussain's tomb in Karbala, Iraq) are stored inside and are paraded around during the Shiite mourning ceremony of Muharram.

But it's what is beyond the small entrance – intriguingly marked 'labyrinth' – to the left of the central hall that steals the show. It leads to the **Bhulbhulaiya**, an enticing network of narrow passageways that winds its way inside the upper floors of the tomb's structure, eventually leading out to rooftop balconies. As with the step-well, it's handy to have a torch.

Just beyond the Bara Imambara is the unusual but imposing gateway **Rumi Darwaza** (Hussainabad Trust Rd), said to be a copy of an entrance gate in Istanbul; 'Rumi' (relating to Rome) is the term Muslims applied to Istanbul when it was still Byzantium, the capital of the Eastern Roman empire. Across the road is the beautiful white mosque **Tila Wali Masjid**, a deceptively shallow building built in 1680. The interior is repainted periodically over the original designs.

If you are visiting as part of an opposite-sex couple, you will be required to pay for a guide (₹100) to prevent any hanky-panky in the labyrinth (yes, we're serious).

Chota Imambara — ISLAMIC TOMB

(Hussainabad Imambara; Hussainabad Trust Rd; Indian/foreigner ₹20/200, incl with Bara Imambara ticket; 6am-6pm) This elaborate tomb was constructed by Mohammed Ali Shah (who is buried here, alongside his mother) in 1832. Adorned with calligraphy, it has a serene

Lucknow

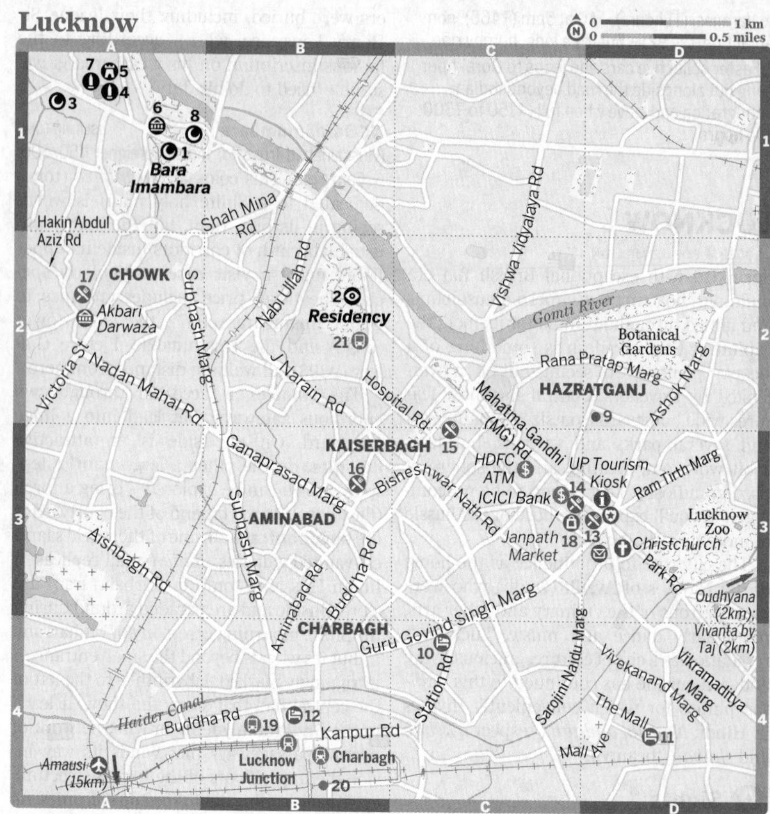

and intimate atmosphere. Mohammed's silver throne and red crown can be seen here, as well as countless chandeliers and some brightly decorated *tazia*.

In the garden is a water tank and two replicas of the Taj Mahal that are the tombs of Mohammed Ali Shah's daughter and her husband. A traditional **hammam** is off to one side.

Outside the complex, the decaying watchtower on the other side of the road is known as **Satkhanda** (Seven Storey Tower; Hussainabad Trust Rd). It has only four storeys because construction was abandoned in 1840 when Mohammed Ali Shah died.

The 67m red-brick **clock tower** (free with Bara Imambara ticket; ⏲dawn-dusk), the tallest in India, was built in the 1880s. Nearby is the **Hussainabad Picture Gallery** (Baradari; Indian/foreigner ₹20/200, free with Bara Imambara ticket; ⏲7am-6pm), a striking red-brick *baradari* (pavilion) built in 1842 that was once a royal summer house. It overlooks an artificial lake and houses portraits of the nawabs.

Tours

★UP Tourism Heritage Walking Tour

WALKING

(☎9415013047; 3hr tour ₹300; ⏲tours 7am Apr-Sep, 8am Oct-Mar) This fabulous tour run by UP Tourism could well turn out to be the best ₹300 you ever spend. Meet your English-speaking guide outside Tila Wali Masjid, then follow them first around the mosque and the Bara Imambara before delving in to the architectural delights of the crazy maze of alleyways in the fascinating Chowk district.

You'll sample interesting nibbles such as refreshing *thandai* (made from milk, cardamom, almonds, fennel, saffron etc and – in this case – with or without marijuana!) and get an insider glimpse into various traditions, from indigo block printing to traditional *unani* medicine or *vark* making

Lucknow

Top Sights
1 Bara Imambara....A1
2 Residency....B2

Sights
3 Chota Imambara....A1
4 Clock Tower....A1
5 Hussainabad Picture Gallery....A1
6 Rumi Darwaza....A1
7 Satkhanda....A1
8 Tila Wali Masjid....A1

Activities, Courses & Tours
9 UP Tourism Heritage Walking Tour....D2

Sleeping
10 Hotel Ganga Maiya....C4
11 Lucknow Homestay....D4
12 SSJ International....B4

Eating
13 Moti Mahal Restaurant....D3
14 Royal Cafe....C3
15 Sakhawat....C3
16 Tunday Kababi....B3
17 Tunday Kebabi....A2

Drinking & Nightlife
EOS....(see 13)

Shopping
18 Sugandhco....C3

Information
UP Tourism....(see 9)

Transport
19 Charbagh Bus Stand....B4
20 Foreign Tourist Help Desk....B4
21 Kaiserbagh Bus Stand....B2

(edible silver foil). This is an eye-popping way to get your bearings among Lucknow's oldest neighbourhoods. Note: tours are best booked directly by phone and last between 2½ and three hours.

Sleeping

Lucknow Homestay HOMESTAY $
(☎9838003590; lucknowhomestay@gmail.com; 110D Mall Ave; s/d ₹1000/1100, without bathroom ₹600/700, with AC ₹1500/1600;) Lucknow's most accommodating budget option is in the leafy neighbourhood home of Naheed and her family, who keep their distance but offer six rustic rooms – four with private bathrooms. Breakfast is included with your stay. There's a sign in front – enter and go up one flight of stairs. Book ahead – it's popular for long stays.

Rickshaw drivers know Mall Ave, which is actually a neighbourhood (not merely an avenue), but you'll need to orient yourself upon arrival if you want to find your way back home, as the address is amid the maze if you enter the neighbourhood from anywhere other than the Mahatma Gandhi (MG) Rd side. Better yet, get to know Naheed's favourite rickshaw driver: the honest, reliable and English-speaking Guatam.

SSJ International HOTEL $$
(☎0522-406609; www.ssjinternational.com; 46 Chandran Gupt Nagar, Charbagh; s/d ₹1725/2200) If you want to be close to the railway station or bus stand but don't want to slum it, this is your place. New and modern, with excellent management and rooms that offer many business-quality comforts. It's on a small cross street just east of Subash Marg, about a block north of Kanpur Rd.

Hotel Ganga Maiya HOTEL $$
(☎9335282783; www.hotelgangamaiya.com; 62/9 Station Rd; s/d from ₹1400/1600) Clean and well run, and even the cheapest rooms have wi-fi, flat-screen TVs and good beds; the higher-priced rooms offer more space and a bit of extra glitz. What sets this place apart is the incredibly helpful staff. Overall one of Lucknow's best-value hotels. Conveniently located between the railway station and MG Road. Discounts usually available.

Eating

Lucknow is the undisputed king of UP cuisine. The refined palates of the Nawabs left the city with a reputation for rich, meaty and impossibly tasty Mughlai cuisine. Restaurants here are famous for mouth-watering kebabs and delicious biryanis.

In addition to its renowned kebabs, Lucknow is also famous for *dum pukht* – the art of steam-pressure cooking, in which meat and vegetables are cooked in a sealed clay pot. In winter, look out for *namash,* a surprisingly light and tasty concoction made from milk, cream and morning dew.

★**Tunday Kababi** NORTH INDIAN $
(Naaz Cinema Rd, off Aminabad Rd; dishes ₹95-200; ⏲11am-11.30pm) This is the cleaner, more hospitable outlet of Lucknow's renowned,

100-year-old, impossible-to-find kebab shop in **Chowk** (near Akbari Gate; kebabs ₹5; ⏲10am-11pm), where buffalo-beef kebabs go for ₹5! Here the prices are higher, but the boys put on quite a show streetside for to-go orders, while the proper restaurant behind dishes up scrumptious plates of mutton biryani, kebabs and tandoori chicken for throngs of carnivores.

The minced-mutton kebab (₹95 for four, eat them with *paratha*) here is impossibly delicious and a spicy punch in the gut. Rickshaw riders know how to find this place. It's tucked away down a narrow street in the bustling Aminabad district. You'll find other Tunday kebab restaurants around the city – some of which are franchises, most of which are copies.

Sakhawat NORTH INDIAN **$**
(www.sakhawatrestaurant.com; 2 Kaiserbagh Ave, behind Awadh Gymkhana Club; kebabs ₹110-140; ⏲4.30-10.30pm Wed-Mon) This highly recommended hole-in-the-wall doesn't look like much, but the daily-changing kebabs (*galawat* etc) at this locals' haunt are fabulous – the smoky, perfectly crispy char makes the difference – and, despite appearances, it has won international accolades and doubles as an Awadh cooking institute. Also serves biryanis and several curries.

Royal Cafe MULTICUISINE **$$**
(51 MG Rd; chaat ₹50-180, mains ₹190-470; ⏲noon-11pm) Even if you don't step inside this excellent restaurant, don't miss its exceedingly popular *chaat* (spicy snack) stand at the front, where mixed *chaats* are served in an *aloo* (potato) basket or in mini *puris*.

Inside, you'll find it does a mouth-watering job of Mughlai cuisine and everything else, including Chinese, Continental, pizza and shakes and sundaes, which are whipped out along with classy service to a wildly mixed crowd that runs the gamut: Sikhs and Muslims over there, Hindus and hipsters over here. Our boneless *murg mirch masala* (chicken cooked with chilli peppers and ground spices with onion and tomatoes) was perfect.

Moti Mahal Restaurant INDIAN **$$**
(75 MG Rd; mains ₹125-210; ⏲7am-11pm; ❄📝) If Mughlai meat country has got you down, seek refuge in this popular veg hideaway on MG Rd. It's perfect for breakfast (with great *poori sabji* – deep-fried bread rounds served with potato curry) or lunch. Come evening, head upstairs for more refined dining in the good-quality, low-lit, AC restaurant.

You could do worse here than try the Lucknow *dum aloo* (potatoes stuffed with nuts and paneer in a tomato-based sauce) and the *kadhai paneer* (paneer in a gravy made of capsicum, tomato, onion and traditional Indian spices) makes a stunning case for vegetarianism. It's all excellent.

★**Oudhyana** MUGHLAI, NORTH INDIAN **$$$**
(www.vivantabytaj.com; Vivanta by Taj Hotel, Vipin Khand, Gomti Nagar; mains ₹780-1350) If you want to savor the flavours of the Nawabs

LUCKNOW'S KEBABS DECONTRUCTED

Kakori Kebab

Originates from Kakori, a small town outside Lucknow. Legend has it that the old and toothless Nawab of Kakori asked his royal *bawarchi* (chef) to make kebabs that would simply melt in the mouth. So these kebabs are made adding papaya (as a tenderiser) to raw mincemeat and a mix of spices. They are then applied to skewers and barbecued over charcoals.

Galawat

This is the mouth-watering creation that is served up in Lucknow's most famous kebab restaurant, **Tunday Kababi** (p399). There it is simply referred to as a mutton kebab, and in other restaurants it is often called Tunday. Essentially, they're the same as Kakori kebabs, except that rather than being barbecued they are made into patties and shallow-fried in oil or ghee.

Shami

Raw mincemeat is boiled with spices and black gram lentil. It is then ground on stone before being mixed with finely chopped onions, coriander leaves and green chillies, then shaped into patties and shallow-fried.

performing at their culinary best, look no further than Oudhyana, where Chef Nagendra Singh gives Lucknow's famous Awadh cuisine its royal due at this signature restaurant inside the city's **top hotel** (☎0522-6771000; s/d from ₹13,110/14,375; ❄@📶🏊).

The flavours of everything Singh does, from the famous *galawat* and *kakori* kebabs to an entire menu of long-lost heritage dishes, unravel like an intricate gastronomic spy novel in your mouth. The intimate room is impossibly striking as well, dressed up in soothing baby-blues with chandelier accoutrements. A special night out.

Drinking & Nightlife

EOS BAR

(72 MG Rd; ⏲noon-11:45pm Mon-Fri, to 1am Sat) This chic bar on the rooftop of the Best Western Levana is Lucknow's attempt at a genuinely trendy bar. It draws the young and restless, especially for Saturday night DJ sets. Otherwise, the breezy, plant- and bamboo-filled spot is pleasant enough for a cocktail (₹350 to ₹450), either in the open air or within the smart AC lounge.

Shopping

Lucknow is famous for *chikan,* an embroidered cloth worn by men and women. It is sold in a number of shops in the labyrinthine bazaars of Chowk (near the Tunday Kebabi there), and in the small, traffic-free **Janpath Market**, just south of MG Rd in Hazratganj.

Sugandhco PERFUME

(www.sugandhco.com; D-4 Janpath Market; ⏲noon-7.30pm Mon-Sat) A family business since 1850, the sweet-scented Sugandhco sells *attar* (pure essence oil extracted from flowers by a traditional method) in the form of women's perfume, men's cologne, household fragrances and incense sticks. Sweet-smelling stuff.

Information

ICICI Bank (Shalimar Tower, 31/54 MG Rd, Hazratganj; ⏲8am-8pm Mon-Fri, 9am-2pm Sat) Changes travellers cheques (Monday to Friday only, 10am to 5pm) and cash, and has an ATM.

Main Post Office (www.indiapost.gov.in; MG Rd; ⏲10am-4pm Mon-Sat) In a building of Grand Raj–era architecture.

Sahara Hospital (☎0522-6780001; www.saharahospitals.com; Gomti Nagar) The best private hospital in Lucknow.

Tourist Police (MG Road, Hazratganj; ⏲8am-9pm Mon-Sat) Located at the UP Tourism kiosk on MG Road.

UP Tourism (☎0522-2615005; www.up-tourism.com; 6 Sapru Marg; ⏲9am-7pm Mon-Sat) Not a particularly helpful or well-informed government tourist office, but it happens to run Lucknow's excellent Heritage Walking Tour (though they couldn't tell us one single detail about it!). It operates a smaller kiosk (MG Rd, Hazratganj; ⏲8am-9pm Mon-Sat) on MG Rd's main drag as well as a Tourist Helpline (☎0522-3303030).

Getting There & Away

AIR

The modern Chaudhary Charan Singh International Airport is 15km southwest of Lucknow in Amausi, with a number of different airlines offering direct daily service to many domestic cities, including Delhi, Mumbai, Ahmedabad, Kolkata and Benguluru (Bangalore). Nonstop international flights head to Gulf destinations including Abu Dhabi, Dubai, and Muscat (Oman).

BUS

Most long-distance buses leave from **Charbagh Bus Stand** (Kanpor Rd, at Subhash Marg), opposite the railway station. Services include the following:

Agra Non-AC (₹395, seven hours, 4.30pm and 8.30pm), regular AC (₹530, six hours, 8.45pm and 9.45pm), Scania AC (₹905, six hours, 10am and 10.30pm)

Allahabad Non-AC (₹175, five hours, every 30 minutes), regular AC (₹280, five hours, departs throughout day), Volvo AC (₹480, 4½ hours, 10 daily)

Delhi Non-AC (₹510, 11 hours), AC Volvo/Scania (₹835/1510, nine hours). Departs throughout the day.

Faizabad Non-AC (₹145, four hours, every 30 minutes), Volvo AC (₹345, three hours, 10am and 10pm)

Gorakhpur Non-AC (₹285, 7½ hours, every 30 minutes), Volvo AC (₹718, six hours, 10am, 10pm and 11pm)

Jhansi Non-AC (₹350, eight hours, 6pm, 7pm and 9.30pm)

Varanasi Non-AC (₹290, eight hours, every 30 minutes), regular AC (₹405, six hours, 9am and 10.30pm), Volvo AC (₹710, six hours, 3pm and 10pm)

Kaiserbagh Bus Stand (☎0522-2622503; J Narain Rd) also has services to Faizabad (₹145, four hours) and Gorakphur (₹285, eight hours, every 30 minutes, 6am to 10pm), as well as buses to Rupaidha (₹210, seven hours, 9.30am, 11am, 7.30pm, 8.30pm, 9.30pm and 11pm), where there is a rarely used Nepal border crossing.

TRAIN

The two main stations, Lucknow NR (usually called Charbagh) and Lucknow Junction, are side by side about 4.5km or so south of the main sites. Services for most major destinations leave from Charbagh, including several daily to Agra, Varanasi, Faizabad, Gorakhpur and New Delhi. Lucknow Junction handles the one daily train to Mumbai and trains to Haldwani. Check your ticket and make sure you go to the right station!

The **Foreign Tourist Help Desk** (Rail Reservation & Booking Centre, Charbagh Station; 8am-1.50pm & 2-8pm) for booking train tickets is at window 601 inside the Rail Reservation and Booking Centre complex, 150m to your right as you exit Charbagh.

Getting Around

TO/FROM THE AIRPORT

An autorickshaw to the airport from the prepaid taxi stand outside the train station costs ₹125 (plus ₹20 airport entry) and takes about 30 minutes.

LOCAL TRANSPORT

A short cycle-rickshaw ride is ₹30. Dealing with autorickshaws demands some serious haggling. From the train station/Charbagh bus stand, pay about ₹80 to reach Hazratganj, or ₹120 to Bara Imambara.

The best way to get around is by shared autorickshaw – flag one down and tell them the neighbourhood you're headed for (like Hazratganj, for MG Road, or Charbagh, for the railway station) and they'll wave you in if they're going that way. Pay ₹5 to ₹15 depending on the length of the trip.

A metro system is under construction – we were told that the first phase was supposed to be completed in early 2017, but from what we saw, that seemed highly optimistic.

AYODHYA & AROUND

05278 / POP 58,000

With monkeys galore, the usual smattering of cows and even the odd working elephant, the relatively traffic-free streets of Ayodhya would be an intriguing place to spend some time even if not for the religious significance of the place.

Ayodhya is revered as the birthplace of Rama – and as such one of Hinduism's seven holy cities – as well as the birthplace of four of Jainism's 24 *tirthankars* (religious teachers). It was also the site of one of modern India's most controversial religious disputes (p1136), but the only evidence you'll see of that today is a more robust police presence than a town of this size would usually warrant, and intense security precautions around the site where Rama is said to have been born.

The slightly larger town of **Faizabad**, 7km away, is the jumping-off point for Ayodhya and where you'll find more accommodation.

Sights

Bahu Begum Ka Maqbara HISTORIC BUILDING
(dawn-dusk) FREE In Faizabad, the so-called 'Taj Mahal of the East' (OK, an overstatement) is a unique mausoleum built for the queen of Nawab Shuja-ud-Daula. It has three domes built above each other, with wonderfully ornate decoration on the walls and ceilings, and is considered to be a prime example of Awadhi architecture.

Hanumangarhi HINDU TEMPLE
(dawn-dusk) This is one of the town's most popular temples, and the closest of Ayodhya's major temples to the main road. Walk up the 76 steps to the ornate carved gateway and the

HANDY TRAINS FROM LUCKNOW

DESTINATION	TRAIN NO & NAME	FARE (₹)	DURATION (HR)	DEPARTURE
Agra	12179 LJN AGC INTRCT	145/515 (C)	6	3.55pm
Allahabad	14216 Ganga Gomti Exp	340 (B)	4¼	6pm
Faizabad	13010 Doon Exp	140/490/695 (A)	2½	8.45am
Gorakhpur	13020 Bagh Exp	190/490/695 (A)	6	6.20am
Jhansi	11016 Kushinagar Exp	195/490/695 (A)	6½	12.40am
Kolkata (Howrah)	13006 ASR-HWH Mail	480/1300/1890 (A)	20½	10.50am
Mumbai (CST)*	12533 Pushpak Exp	626/1627/2337 (A)	24	7.45pm
New Delhi	12553 Vaishali Exp	335/865/1220 (A)	8	10.25pm
Varanasi	14236 BE-BSB Exp	210/570/810 (A)	7½	11.25pm

Fares: (A) sleeper/3AC/2AC, (B) AC chair only, (C) 2S/AC chair; * leaves from Lucknow Junction

TRANSIT HUB: JHANSI

This nondescript town near the Madhya Pradesh border is famous for its link to Rani Lakshmibai of Jhansi, a key player in the 1857 First War of Independence (Indian Uprising). It's commonly used as a transit hub and gateway to Orchha, Khajuraho and Gwalior.

Buses leave from the bus stand for Chhatarpur (₹130, three hours, hourly, 5am to 10pm), where you can switch for Khajuraho (₹50, 1½ hours); Chitrakut (₹250, six hours, 8.30am); and Gwalior (₹100, three hours, hourly). Tempos (₹20) go between Jhansi bus stand and Orchha all day; private autorickshaws charge ₹200. Handy trains include:

TRAIN & DESTINATION	TRAIN NO.	CLASSES	DURATION (HR)	DEPARTURE
Punjab Mail to Gwailior	12137	sleeper/3AC/2AC ₹170/535/735	1½	2.30pm
Punjab Mail to Agra	12137	sleeper/3AC/2AC ₹195/540/740	3½	2.30pm
Punjab Mail to Mumbai	12138	sleeper/3AC/2AC ₹530/1395/2010	19	12.35pm
Grand Trunk Express to Delhi	12615	sleeper/3AC/2AC ₹280/830/1010	7½	11.40pm
Bundelkhand Express to Varanasi	11107	sleeper/3AC/2AC ₹305/720/1190	12½	10.25pm
Udz Kurj Express to Khajuraho	19666	sleeper/3AC/2AC ₹160/490/695	3	3.30pm

fortress-like outer walls, and join the throng inside offering *prasad* (temple-blessed food).

Kanak Bhavan HINDU TEMPLE
(Palace of Gold; ⏲8.30-11.30am & 4.30-9.30pm Apr-Sep, 9am-noon & 4-9pm Oct-Mar) This palace rebuilt into a temple is one of the most impressive in Ayodhya, It was supposedly given to Lord Rama and his wife Sita as a wedding present, and the interior features three shrines dedicated to the holy couple.

Ramkatha Museum MUSEUM
(☎9415328511; ⏲10.30am-5pm Tue-Sat) FREE Beyond the northern end of the main road, this museum houses paintings and ancient sculptures. Every evening but Monday, the museum hosts free performances of the Ram Lila – a dramatic re-enactment of the battle between Lord Ram and Ravan, as described in the Hindu epic the Ramayana – at **Tulsi Smarg Bhawan**, a nearby park, from 6pm to 9pm.

Walk about 500m or so along the main road deeper into Ayodhya, turn right at the police station across from Akash Cycle Company, and the museum is another 500m or so on your right.

Ram Janam Bhumi HINDU TEMPLE
(⏲7-11.30am & 12.30-5pm) This is the highly contentious spot said to be the site of Lord Rama's birth. Security here is staggering (think crossing from West Bank into Israel!). You must first show your passport, then leave all belongings apart from your passport and money (even your belt!) in nearby lockers. You are then searched several times before being accompanied through a long, caged corridor that leads to a spot 20m away from a makeshift tent shrine, which marks Rama's birthplace.

You get about 10 seconds to look at it before being hustled away. Go for the surreal experience, not the unremarkable tent shrine (and if lines are very long, skip it). To get there, turn left at Dashrath Bhavan, when coming from Hanumanghari.

Sleeping & Eating

Hotel Shane Avadh HOTEL $
(☎05278-222075; www.hotelshaveavadh.com; Civil Lines, Faizabad; s/d from ₹450/550, with AC from ₹1300/1600; ❄) There's a huge range of rooms at this well-run establishment in Faizabad (though only a few recently renovated ones are as smart as their website would have you believe). The cheapest ones are a bit gritty, but they improve rapidly if you pay a little more. Beds are rock-hard. Book ahead.

WORTH A TRIP

CHITRAKUT: VARANASI IN MINIATURE

Known as a mini Varanasi because of its many temples and ghats, this small, peaceful town on the banks of the River Mandakini is the stuff of Hindu legends. It is here that Hinduism's principal trinity – Brahma, Vishnu and Shiva – took on their incarnations. It is also the place where Lord Rama is believed to have spent 11½ years of his 14-year exile after being banished from his birthplace in Ayodhya at the behest of a jealous stepmother. Today Chitrakut attracts throngs of pilgrims, giving the area a strong religious quality, particularly by Ram Ghat, the town's centre of activity, and at the holy hill of Kamadgiri, 2km away.

Dozens, sometimes hundreds, of devotees descend onto **Ram Ghat** to take holy dips at dawn before returning at the end of the day for the evening *aarti* (an auspicious lighting of lamps/candles). Colourful rowboats (with rabbits!) wait here to take you across to the opposite bank, which is actually in Madhya Pradesh, or to scenic spots along the river.

The 2km trip to the **Glass Temple**, a building covered in religious mosaics made with thousands of pieces of coloured glass, is popular. During the day, many people make their way to Kamadgiri, a hill revered as the holy embodiment of Lord Rama. A 5km circuit (90 minutes) around the base of the hill takes you past prostrating pilgrims, innumerable monkeys and temples galore.

Awantika MULTICUISINE $$
(Civil Lines, Faizabad; mains ₹95-235; ⌚11am-10.30pm; ☑) Clean and hip, this out-of-place restaurant does a seriously good all-veg menu that runs the gamut from Chinese to Italian to Indian. The special thali (₹200) is a real treat, and it's all set to trendy tunes in a funky lounge atmosphere. It's across the street from Bharat Petroleum. (Don't mistake it for the nearby New Awantika snack house.)

Information

There are a number of ATMs in Faizabad around **Hotel Shane Avadh**.

Cyber Zone (Civil Lines, Faizabad; per hr ₹20; ⌚10am-8.30pm) A rudimentary internet cafe at the first intersection 50m on the right after Hotel Shane Avadh, on the road heading towards Ayodhya.

Getting There & Away

From the Faizabad bus stand turn left onto the main road, where you'll find shared rickshaws (₹10 to ₹20, 20 minutes) to Ayodhya.

From Faizabad bus stand, frequent buses run to Lucknow (₹140, three hours), Gorakhpur (₹150, 3½ hours, 5am to 8pm) and Allahabad (₹150, five hours, 7am to 10pm). AC coaches head to Lucknow (₹190) every hour or so.

There are several handy trains from Faizabad:

Lucknow 13307 Gangasutlej Express, sleeper/3AC/2AC ₹140/485/690, 3½ hours, 11.08am
Varanasi 13010 Doon Express, sleeper/3AC/2AC ₹140/490/695, five hours, 11.10am
Delhi 12225 Kaifiyat Express, sleeper/3AC/2AC ₹380/995/1410, 11¼ hours, 7.52pm

A cycle-rickshaw from the bus stand to the train station is ₹30.

ALLAHABAD

☎0532 / POP 1.2 MILLION

Brahma, the Hindu god of creation, is believed to have landed on earth in Allahabad (or Prayag, as it was originally known), and to have named it the king of all pilgrimage centres. Indeed, Sangam, a river confluence on the outskirts of the city, is the most celebrated of India's four Kumbh Mela locations. Allahabad was also home to the Nehru family, whose house served as a headquarters for the independence movement against the British Raj.

Yet for all its importance in Hindu mythology, Indian history and modern politics, Allahabad today is a much humbler place. Though there are a few surprisingly good places to stay and eat, the main sights are of modest appeal – and the mix of dust, exhaust fumes and burning trash makes for eye-stinging air by late afternoon.

Sights

★Sangam RELIGIOUS SITE
This is the particularly auspicious point where two of India's holiest rivers, the Ganges and the Yamuna, meet one of Hinduism's mythical rivers, the Saraswati. All year round, pilgrims row boats out to this holy spot, but their numbers increase dramatically during the annual Magh Mela, a six-week festival held between January and March, which culminates in six communal 'holy dips'.

Every 12 years the massive **Maha (Great) Kumbh Mela** takes place here, attracting millions of people, while an **Ardh Mela** (Half Mela) is held here every six years.

In the early 1950s, 350 pilgrims were killed in a stampede trying to get to the soul-cleansing water, an incident recreated vividly in Vikram Seth's essential novel *A Suitable Boy*. The last Ardh Mela, in 2007, attracted more than 70 million people – considered to be the largest-ever human gathering until the 2013 Kumbh Mela, which attracted about 32 million on Mauni Amavasya, the main bathing day, and 100 million across the 55-day festival; expect equally astonishing numbers at the next Allahabad Kumbh Mela in 2025.

Old hands will row you out to the sacred confluence for around ₹50 per person (hard-bargaining Indian) or ₹100 (hard-bargaining foreigner), or ₹600 to ₹800 per boat.

Around the corner from Sangam (skirt the riverbank around the front of Akbar's Fort) is **Saraswati Ghat**; further along the shore is **Nehru Ghat**. Both host a nightly *aarti* (an auspicious lighting of lamps/candles), but neither is as impressive as what you'd see in Varanasi or Mathura.

Khusru Bagh PARK

(dawn-dusk) **FREE** This intriguing park, surrounded by huge walls, contains four highly impressive **Mughal tombs**. One is that of **Prince Khusru**, the eldest son of Emperor Jehangir, who tried to overthrow his father in 1606, but was instead apprehended, imprisoned and blinded. He was finally murdered in 1622 on the orders of his half-brother, who later took the throne under the name Shah Jahan. If Khusru's coup had succeeded, Shah Jahan would not have become emperor – and the Taj Mahal would not exist.

A second tomb belongs to **Shah Begum**, Khusru's mother (Jehangir's first wife), who committed suicide in 1603 with an opium overdose, distraught over the ongoing feud between her son and his father. Between these two, a third, particularly attractive tomb was constructed by **Nesa Begum**, Khusru's sister, although was never actually used as a tomb. A smaller structure, called **Tamolon's Tomb**, stands to the west of the others, but its origin is unknown.

If you linger around the tombs of Prince Khusru and Shah Begum, someone will appear with keys to let you inside, where you can see a beautiful array of nature paintings and unique, tree-shaped window *jalis* (carved lattices). You'll have to negotiate a price – but don't pay more than ₹100 for all four tombs.

Anand Bhavan MUSEUM

(Indian/foreigner ₹10/100; 9.30am-1pm & 1.30-5pm Tue-Sun) This picturesque two-storey house is a shrine to the Nehru family, which has produced five generations of leading politicians, from Motilal Nehru to the latest political figure, Rahul Gandhi. This stately home is where Mahatma Gandhi, Jawaharlal Nehru and others successfully planned the overthrow of the British Raj. It is full of books, personal effects and photos from those stirring times.

Akbar's Fort & Patalpuri Temple FORT, HINDU TEMPLE

(by donation; 6am-5.30pm) Built by the Mughal Emperor Akbar, this 16th-century **fort** on the northern bank of the Yamuna has massive walls with three gateways flanked by towers. Most of it is occupied by the Indian army and cannot be visited, but a small door in the eastern wall by Sangam leads to one part you can enter: the underground **Patalpuri Temple**.

This unique temple is crowded with all sorts of idols; pick up some coins from the change dealers outside so you can leave small offerings as you go. (You may be pressured

DIP DATES

The vast riverbanks at Sangam attract tens of millions of pilgrims every six years for either the Kumbh Mela (p1129) or the Ardh (Half) Mela, but every year there is a smaller **Magh Mela**. The next **Ardh Mela** is in 2019; the next full Kumbh Mela is in 2025.

The following are auspicious bathing dates during upcoming Magh Melas:

BATHING DAY	2018	2019	2020	2021
Makar Sankranti	14 Jan	15 Jan	15 Jan	14 Jan
Mauni Amavasya	16 Jan	4 Feb	20 Jan	11 Feb
Vasant Panchami	22 Jan	10 Feb	29 Jan	16 Feb
Magh Purnima	31 Jan	19 Feb	9 Feb	27 Feb
Mahashivatri	14 Feb	5 Mar	21 Feb	11 Mar

Allahabad

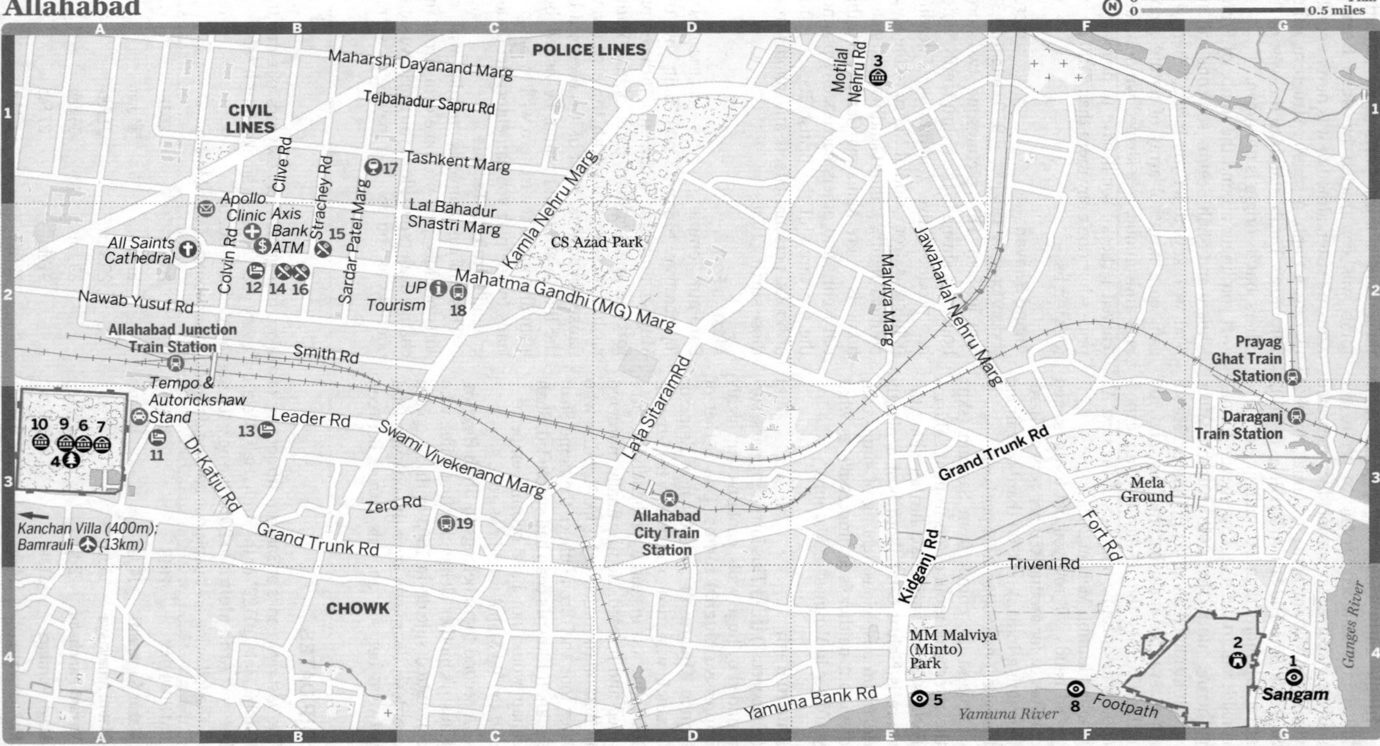
0 1 km
0 0.5 miles
POLICE LINES
CIVIL LINES
CHOWK
Maharshi Dayanand Marg
Tejbahadur Sapru Rd
Tashkent Marg
Lal Bahadur Shastri Marg
Clive Rd
Strachey Rd
Sardar Patel Marg
Colvin Rd
Nawab Yusuf Rd
Kamla Nehru Marg
CS Azad Park
Mahatma Gandhi (MG) Marg
Motilal Nehru Rd
Malviya Marg
Jawaharlal Nehru Marg
Apollo Clinic
Axis Bank ATM
All Saints Cathedral
UP Tourism
Allahabad Junction Train Station
Smith Rd
Tempo & Autorickshaw Stand
Leader Rd
Swami Vivekenand Marg
Lala SitaramRd
Dr Katju Rd
Zero Rd
Grand Trunk Rd
Allahabad City Train Station
Kanchan Villa (400m); Bamrauli (13km)
Prayag Ghat Train Station
Daraganj Train Station
Mela Ground
Fort Rd
Triveni Rd
Kidganj Rd
MM Malviya (Minto) Park
Yamuna Bank Rd
Yamuna River
Footpath
Sangam
Ganges River
1
2
3
4
5
6
7
8
9
10
11
12
13
14
15
16
17
18
19

Allahabad

Top Sights
1 Sangam G4

Sights
2 Akbar's Fort & Patalpuri Temple G4
3 Anand Bhavan E1
4 Khusru Bagh A3
5 Nehru Ghat E4
6 Nesa Begum's Tomb A3
7 Prince Khusru's Tomb A3
8 Saraswati Ghat F4
9 Shah Begum's Tomb A3
10 Tamolon's Tomb A3

Sleeping
11 Hotel Prayag A3
12 Hotel U.R. B2
13 Milan Hotel B3

Eating
14 Eat On B2
15 El Chico B2
El Chico Cafe .... (see 15)
16 Kamdhenu Sweets B2

Drinking & Nightlife
17 Patiyala Peg Bar B1

Transport
18 Civil Lines Bus Stand C2
19 Zero Road Bus Stand C3

into giving ₹10 to ₹100 at some shrines, but a few coins are perfectly acceptable.)

Outside the temple – though its roots can be seen beneath ground – is the **Undying Banyan Tree**. Pilgrims used to leap to their deaths from it, believing this would liberate them from the cycle of rebirth.

Sleeping

Hotel Prayag HOTEL $
(0532-2656416; www.prayaggroupofhotels.com; 73 Noorullah Rd; s/d from ₹500/700, without bathroom ₹300/350, s/d with AC ₹1200/1350;) A stone's throw south of the train station, this sprawling, well-run place is helpful and boasts an internet cafe (₹30 per hour) with free wi-fi, a State Bank of India ATM and a funky restaurant. There's a wide variety of old-fashioned, basic rooms in various states of dilapidation, but staff are friendly and will even help negotiate autorickshaws.

Milan Hotel HOTEL $$
(0532-2403776; www.hotelmilan.in; 46 Leader Rd; s ₹2300-4000, d ₹3000-4900;) One of the best values in Allahabad in this price range: rooms are modern and clean, with mellow colour schemes and good beds. You can pay more for more space, but even the cheapest rooms are of good quality.

Hotel U.R. HOTEL $$
(0532-2427334; mj1874@gmail.com; 7/3, A/1 MG Marg, Civil Lines; r ₹1600-2200;) This professionally run 20-room midrange hotel is in a good location along MG Marg and offers a slight step up from similarly priced competition. A glass elevator leads to somewhat cramped (due to big beds) but clean rooms, the best of which open onto a plant-lined terrace. Staff is better trained than elsewhere in this price range. Discounts often available.

★ **Kanchan Villa** HOMESTAY $$$
(9838631111; www.kanchanvilla.com; 64 Lukerganj; s/d from ₹3000/3850, ste from ₹4950;) Ivan – a guitar-wielding Indian rum enthusiast – and his wife, Purnima, are your South Indian/Bengali hosts at this fabulous homestay offering a window into a rarely seen side of Christian Indian culture. In a historic home nearing its centennial milestone, six rooms are decked out with period furnishings (our fave: Bengali); breakfast (included) can be taken on the lush, 2nd-floor patio.

The lovely staff will cook for you as well, serving up fresh kebabs from the outdoor tandoor, for example. You'll feel right at home in the living room–bar. Pick-up and drops-offs included; otherwise it's a short cycle-rickshaw ride (₹20) from the train station.

Eating

★ **Eat On** MUGHLAI $
(MG Marg; mains ₹50-200; 11.30am-10pm Wed-Mon) This standing-room-only food shack does four things, and does them astonishingly cheap and well: mouth-watering *shami* kebabs (minced mutton with black lentils and spices), perfectly spiced chicken biryani, roasted chicken (evenings only) and a lovely, thin *paratha* to accompany it all. Prepare to wait – this is one of Allahabad's best.

Kamdhenu Sweets SWEETS $
(37, Palace Cinema Compound, MG Marg; snacks ₹20-80; 8.30am-10.30pm) Very popular snack shop selling absolutely delicious house-made sweets, as well as cakes, samosas, sandwiches and ice cream.

El Chico Cafe MULTICUISINE $$

(24/28 MG Marg; mains ₹200-400; ⏲noon-10.30pm) Cure your homesick hungries in a heartbeat among a forward-thinking Indian crowd. Big breakfasts all day – cinnamon pancakes, waffles, espresso – sandwiches, wood-fired pizzas and more sophisticated fusion fare fill out the menu. Try the Sizzlin' Brownie! The cafe is attached to El Chico.

El Chico MULTICUISINE $$

(26/28 MG Marg; mains ₹200-500; ⏲10am-10.30pm; ❄) This refined restaurant serves up absolutely wonderful Indian (the chicken-chilli-garlic kebab is every bit as delicious as it sounds), tasty-looking Chinese, popular sizzlers and Continental cuisine, along with coffee in pewter carafes. It's below the modern El Chico Cafe.

Drinking & Nightlife

Patiyala Peg Bar BAR

(Grand Continental Hotel, Sardar Patel Marg; ⏲7-11pm) Allahabad's most interesting bar for tourists has live *ghazal* (Urdu love songs) performed nightly from 7.30pm to 10.30pm. Serves mostly beers (from ₹300) and whisky.

Information

ATMs dot the Civil Lines area.

Axis Bank

Apollo Clinic (☎0532-2421132; www.apolloclinic.com; 28B MG Marg; ⏲24hr) A modern private medical facility with a 24-hour pharmacy.

Post Office (www.indiapost.gov.in; Sarojini Naidu Marg; ⏲10am-1.30pm & 2-5pm Mon-Fri, 10am-4pm Sat)

UP Tourism (☎0532-2408873; www.up-tourism.com; 35 MG Marg; ⏲10am-5pm Mon-Sat, closed 2nd Sat each month) At the Rahi Ilawart Tourist Bungalow, next to Civil Lines Bus Stand. Of marginal use.

Getting There & Away

AIR

Allahabad Airport is 15km west of Allahabad. **Air India** (☎0532-258360; www.airindia.com) has one daily flight to Delhi (from ₹3800, 3pm). An autorickshaw to the airport costs ₹450 and a taxi ₹600.

BUS

From the **Civil Lines Bus Stand** (MG Marg) regular non-AC buses run to Varanasi (₹120, three hours, every 10 minutes), Faizabad (₹170, five hours, every 30 minutes, 4.30am to 1am), Gorakhpur (₹250, 10 hours, every 30 minutes, 4am to midnight) and Lucknow (₹176, five hours, hourly, noon to 8pm). AC buses run to Varanasi (₹195, three hours) and Lucknow (₹510, five hours) throughout the day, and to Delhi (₹1680, 14 hours) at 7pm. To go to Delhi or Agra, you can change in Lucknow, or take a train.

To reach Chitrakut go to the **Zero Road Bus Stand** (Zero Rd) and hop a bus for Karwi (₹125, three hours, every 30 minutes, 4am to 8.30pm), from where you can travel the final 10km by shared autorickshaw (₹10).

TRAIN

Allahabad Junction is the main station. A few daily trains run to Lucknow, Varanasi, Delhi, Agra and Kolkata. Frequent trains also run to Satna, from where you can catch buses to Khajuraho.

Getting Around

Cycle-rickshaws are plentiful; pay ₹20 for a short trip of 1km to 2km but be prepared to haggle for it.

The stand at the train station or MG Marg are your best bet for autorickshaws. Consider hiring one for a half-day (₹500, four hours) to take in more of the sights.

Vikrams (large shared autos) hang about on the south side of the train station. Destinations include Zero Road Bus Stand (₹10), Civil Lines Bus Stand (₹10) and Sangam (₹15).

HANDY TRAINS FROM ALLAHABAD

DESTINATION	TRAIN NO & NAME	FARE (₹)	DURATION (HR)	DEPARTURE
Agra	12403 ALD JP Exp	295/765/1075 (A)	7½	11.30pm
Kolkata (Howrah)	12312 Kalka Mail	435/1150/1640 (A)	14½	5.20pm
Lucknow	14209 PRG-LKO Intercity	330 (B)	4	3.40pm
New Delhi	12559 Shiv Ganga Exp	375/985/1395 (A)	9¾	10.30pm
Satna	12428 ANVT REWA Exp	170/540/740 (A)	3	6.55am
Varanasi	15017 Gorakhpur Exp	140/490/695 (A)	4	8.45am

Fares: (A) sleeper/3AC/2AC, (B) AC chair only

WESTERN UTTAR PRADESH

Side by side in the west of Uttar Pradesh, on the road from Delhi to Agra, Mathura and Vrindavan are a pair of sacred towns that have played a pivotal role in India's religious history.

Mathura

☎0565 / POP 540,000

Famed for being the birthplace of the much-loved Hindu god Krishna, Mathura is one of Hinduism's seven sacred cities and attracts floods of pilgrims, particularly during Janmastami (Krishna's birthday) in August/September and Holi in February/March. The town is dotted with temples from various ages and the stretch of the sacred Yamuna River which flows past here is lined with 25 ghats. They're best seen at dawn, when many people take their holy dip, and just after sunset, when hundreds of candles are sent floating out onto the river during the evening *aarti* ceremony.

Mathura was once a Buddhist centre with 20 monasteries that housed 3000 monks, but after the rise of Hinduism, and later sackings by Afghan and Mughal rulers, all that's left of the oldest sights are the beautiful sculptures recovered from ruins, now on display in the Archaeological Museum.

Sights

★Kesava Deo Temple HINDU TEMPLE
(Shri Krishna Janambhoomi; 5am-9.30pm summer, 5.30am-8.30pm winter) In the most important temple complex in Mathura, the small, bare room known as **Shri Krishna Janambhoomi** marks the spot where Krishna is said to have been born in prison more than 5000 years ago. The much larger main temple is decked with murals depicting scenes from Krishna's life, and houses several statues of the god and his consort, Radha. Destroyed and rebuilt a number of times over the past thousand years, the current temple was erected in the 1950s.

Vishram Ghat GHAT
A string of ghats and temples lines the Yamuna River north of the main road bridge. The most central and most popular is Vishram Ghat, where Krishna is said to have rested after killing the tyrannical King Kansa. Boats gather along the banks here

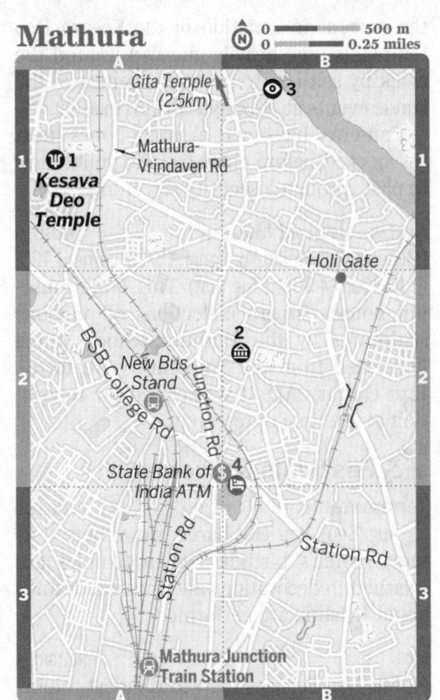

Mathura

Top Sights
1 Kesava Deo Temple........................A1

Sights
2 Archaeological Museum B2
Katra Masjid..............................(see 1)
3 Vishram Ghat B1

Sleeping
4 Hotel Brijwasi Royal..........................B2

Eating
Status Restaurant ....(see 4)

to take tourists along the Yamuna (₹150 per hour for two people, ₹300 for a full boat).

Gita Temple HINDU TEMPLE
(dawn-dusk) This serene marble temple on the road to Vrindavan has the entire Bhagavad Gita (Hindu Song of the Divine One) written on a red pillar in the garden.

Katra Masjid MOSQUE
This fine sandstone mosque was built by the Mughal ruler Aurangzeb in 1661. To clear the site, he ordered the destruction of the then-standing incarnation of the Kesava Deo temple, which marked the spot of Krishna's birth. The mosque, which sits directly beside

the current incarnation of the Kesava Deo temple, is now heavily guarded around the clock by soldiers to prevent a repeat of the tragic events at Ayodhya (p1136) in 1992.

Cameras, bags, and mobile phones must be checked before entering, and you'll have to pass through a security screening.

Archaeological Museum MUSEUM
(Museum Rd; Indian/foreigner ₹5/25, camera ₹20; ⏲10.30am-4.30pm Tue-Sun) This large museum houses superb collections of religious sculptures by the Mathura school, which flourished from the 3rd century BC to the 12th century AD. It was closed for renovation at the time of research.

Festivals & Events

Janmastami RELIGIOUS
(⏲Aug/Sep) You can barely move here during Krishna's birthday, when temples are swathed in decorations and musical dramas about Krishna are performed.

Holi RELIGIOUS
(⏲Feb/Mar) Perhaps the world's most colourful festival – you've probably seen pictures of people covered in all shades of fluorescent powder – this nationwide party celebrates the arrival of spring and the triumph of good over evil. The action is particularly intense around Mathura and Vrindavan, the birthplace and spiritual home of Krishna.

Sleeping & Eating

Hotel Brijwasi Royal HOTEL $$$
(☎8191818818; www.brijwasihotels.com; SBI Crossing, Station Rd; r incl breakfast ₹3500-4900; ❄📶) A clean and contemporary hotel, with 40 business-like rooms that come with either marble floors or carpets and bath-tubs; some overlook a buffalo pond behind the building. Substantial discounts are available if business is slow.

Status Restaurant INDIAN $$
(SBI Crossing, Station Rd; mains ₹195-275; ⏲7am-11pm) At the Hotel Brijwasi Royal (p410), this well-staffed place serves up some tasty Indian veg plates, and is deservedly popular. Go for the tandoori platter.

Information

There is a **State Bank of India ATM** (Station Rd) at SBI Crossing, next door to Brijwasi Royal and not far from the New Bus Stand. There is a second one at Shri Krishna Janmbhoomi.

Getting There & Around

BUS

The so-called **New Bus Stand** (Vrindavan Rd) has buses to Delhi (₹135, four hours, every 30 minutes, 5am to 10pm) and Agra (₹65, 90 minutes, every 15 minutes, 4am to 9pm).

Shared autos and tempos that ply Station and Mathura-Vrindaven Rds charge ₹15 for the 13km Mathura–Vrindavan run.

TRAIN

Frequent trains go to Delhi (sleeper/AC chair ₹170/260, two to three hours), Agra (sleeper/AC chair ₹170/330, one hour), and Bharatpur (sleeper/AC chair ₹100/270, 45 minutes). The Bharatpur trains continue to Sawai Madhopur (for Ranthambore National Park; two hours) and Kota (5½ hours).

Vrindavan

☎0565 / POP 65,000

The village of Vrindavan is where the young Krishna is said to have grown up. Pilgrims flock here from all over India – and in the case of the Hare Krishna community, from all over the world. Dozens of temples, old and modern, dot the area. They come in all shapes and sizes and many have their own unique peculiarities, making a visit here more than just your average temple hop.

Sights

Most temples are open from dawn to dusk and admission is free. Among those worth a stop are **Rangaji Temple** (⏲5.30-10.30am & 4-9pm summer, 6-11am & 3.30-8.30pm winter), Vrindavan's largest; **Madan Mohan Temple**, Vrindavan's oldest; **Radha Ballabh Temple**, dedicated to Krishna's consort, Radha; and **Nidhivan Temple** (⏲dawn-dusk), which Krishna is said to visit every night.

★**Krishna Balaram Temple Complex** HINDU TEMPLE
(Iskcon; ⏲7.30am-12.45pm & 4-9pm winter, 4.30-9pm summer) The **International Society for Krishna Consciousness** (Iskcon; ☎0565-2540343; www.iskcon.org), also known as the Hare Krishnas, is based at the Krishna Balaram temple complex (Iskcon Temple). Accessed through a beautiful, white marble gate, the temple houses the tomb of Swami Prabhupada (1896–1977), the founder of the Hare Krishna organisation.

Inside the temple is a whirl of activity, filled with chanting and singing, and devotees prostrating in prayer, playing drums, and consulting with monks. Several hundred foreigners attend courses and seminars here annually.

The temple is closed to the public at various times of the day, most significantly from 12.45pm to 4pm (4.30pm in summer). If you're carrying a bag, you must use the side entrance.

Pagal Baba Temple HINDU TEMPLE
(⏲6am-noon & 3.30-8.30pm winter, 5-11.30am & 3-9pm summer) This 10-storey temple, a fairy-tale-castle lookalike, has an amusing succession of animated puppets and dioramas behind glass cases on the ground floor, which depict scenes from the lives of Rama and Krishna. Puppet shows telling the story are performed year-round.

Govind Dev Temple HINDU TEMPLE
(⏲8am-12.30pm & 4.30-8pm) This cavernous, red-sandstone temple, built in 1590 by Raja Man Singh of Amber, has cute bells carved on its pillars. The resident monkeys here are as cheeky as any in India, so stay alert!

Sleeping & Eating

It's possible to stay at the **guesthouse** (☎0565-2540021; www.iskconvrindavan.com; r with AC ₹950; ❄) at the back of the Hare Krishna temple complex (though devotees are prioritised). Otherwise, there are several hotels, ranging from modest to fancy, on the main road west of the complex.

Sri Govinda Restaurant INDIAN $
(mains ₹100-200; ⏲8am-2.30pm & 6-9.30pm) Does Indian veg dishes, pasta, cakes, shakes, salads and soups. Located inside Krishna Balaram Temple Complex.

Information

The closest ATM is **Andhra Bank**, 250m down from the main entrance of the temple complex (near the Bhaktivedanta Swami gate).

Krishna Balaram Welcome Office
(☎9557849475; ⏲10am-1pm & 5-8pm) Has lists of places to stay in Vrindavan and can help with booking Gita (studies in the Bhagavad Gita, an ancient Hindu scripture) classes as well as all travel agency services.

Vrindavan

Top Sights
1 Krishna Balaram Temple Complex A2

Sights
2 Govind Dev Temple B1
3 Madan Mohan Temple A1
4 Nidhivan Temple B1
5 Pagal Baba Temple A2
6 Radha Ballabh Temple B1
7 Rangaji Temple B1

Sleeping
ISKCON Guest House .... (see 1)

Eating
Sri Govinda Restaurant .... (see 1)

Information
International Society for Krishna Consciousness .... (see 1)
Krishna Balaram Welcome Office .... (see 1)

Getting There & Around

Tempos, shared autos and buses all charge ₹15 between Vrindavan and Mathura.

The temples here are spread out, so a cycle-rickshaw tour is a good way to see them. Expect to pay ₹200 to ₹250 for a half-day tour (₹350 to ₹400 in an autorickshaw).

Uttarakhand

Includes ➡

Best Places to Eat

➡ Prakash Lok (p423)

➡ Chetan Puriwallah (p428)

➡ Little Buddha Cafe (p419)

Best Places to Sleep

➡ Mohan's Binsar Retreat (p449)

➡ Gateway Resort (p442)

➡ Haveli Hari Ganga (p423)

➡ Kasmanda Palace Hotel (p431)

Why Go?

Uttarakhand is a place of myth and mountains. Hindus think of it as Dev Bhoomi – the Land of Gods – and the dramatic terrain is covered with holy peaks, lakes and rivers. Twisting roads and high-altitude hiking trails lead to spectacular pilgrimage sites where tales from Hindu epics are set. Though the presence of Shiva and Parvati (in a few of her forms) tower over the state, the imprint of the British is equally apparent: the legend of Jim Corbett lives on in the famed tiger reserve that bears his name; popular holiday towns were once Raj-era hill stations; and the Beatles turned Rishikesh into a magnet for spiritual seekers and yoga practitioners worldwide.

Uttarakhand may seem like a silver medallist: it's the state with the second-highest tiger population (after Karnataka) and boasts India's second-highest peak (Nanda Devi); but its diversity of activities and sheer natural beauty are pure travellers' gold.

When to Go

Rishikesh

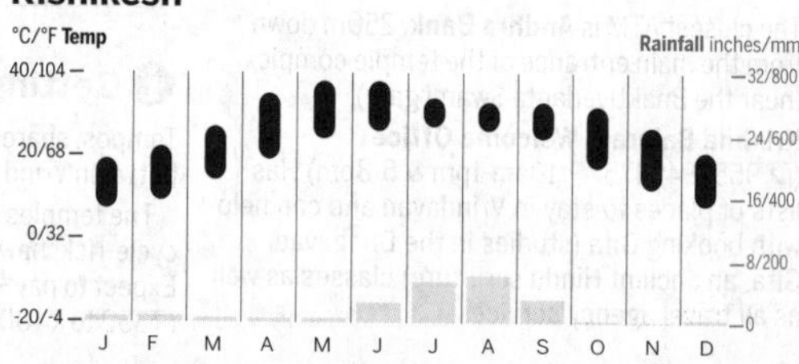

Apr–mid-Jun The best season for tiger spotting at Corbett Tiger Reserve.

Jul–mid-Sep Monsoons may make travel difficult; Valley of Flowers blooms July and August.

Mid-Sep–Nov The perfect time to trek the Himalaya.

Uttarakhand Highlights

1. **Gaumukh** (p433) Hiking below stunning peaks to the source of the holy Ganges.
2. **Har-ki-Pairi Ghat** (p421) Floating a candle down the Ganges at the gorgeous nightly ceremony in Haridwar.
3. **Corbett Tiger Reserve** (p440) Spotting some stripes at India's first national park.
4. **Rishikesh** (p414) Pursuing inner peace at the yoga and meditation capital of the universe.
5. **Nainital** (p443) Cooling off from the heat at this scenic Raj-era hill station.
6. **Valley of Flowers National Park** (p439) Strolling among a dazzling display of wildflowers, framed by snowy summits.
7. **Kuari Pass** (p434) Trekking amid a mind-blowing Himalayan landscape.

History

Over the centuries various dynasties have dominated the region, including the Guptas, Kuturyi and Chand rajas. In the 18th century the Nepalese Gurkhas attacked first the kingdom of Kumaon, then Garhwal, prompting the British to step in and take most of the region as part of the Sugauli Treaty in 1816.

After Independence, the region was merged with Uttar Pradesh, but a vocal separatist movement followed, and the present-day state of Uttaranchal was formed in 2000. In 2007 it was officially renamed Uttarakhand, a traditional name meaning 'northern country'.

Climate

Temperatures are determined by altitude in this state of elevation extremes. Trekking the Himalaya is possible from May to October, but can be dangerous between July and mid-September, during the monsoon, when violent cloudbursts cause landslides. Hill stations offer a welcome escape from summertime heat, while low-lying Rishikesh is most comfortable from October to March.

Information

Most towns in the region have an Uttarakhand Tourism office, however, the main responsibility for the region's tourism rests with the **Garhwal Mandal Vikas Nigam** (GMVN; www.gmvnl.in), in the Garhwal district and **Kumaon Mandal Vikas Nigam** (KMVN; http://kmvn.gov.in), in the Kumaon district.

Getting Around

Tough old government buses are the main means of travelling around Uttarakhand. In addition, crowded shared jeeps criss-cross the state, linking remote towns and villages to important road junctions. Pay 10 times the share-taxi rate to hire the whole vehicle and travel in comfort. Roads that snake through the hills can be nerve-racking and stomach-churning, and are sometimes blocked by monsoon-season landslides.

TOP STATE FESTIVALS

Kumbh Mela, Haridwar (p421)

International Yoga Festival, Rishikesh (p418)

Shivaratri, Dehra Dun (p426)

Nanda Devi Fair, Almora (p447)

RISHIKESH

☎0135 / POP 102,200 / ELEV 356M

Ever since the Beatles rocked up at the ashram of the Maharishi Mahesh Yogi in the late '60s, Rishikesh has been a magnet for spiritual seekers. Today it styles itself as the 'Yoga Capital of the World', with masses of ashrams and all kinds of yoga and meditation classes. Most of this action is north of the main town, where the exquisite setting on the fast-flowing Ganges, surrounded by forested hills, is conducive to meditation and mind expansion. In the evening, an almost supernatural breeze blows down the valley, setting temple bells ringing as sadhus ('holy' men), pilgrims and tourists prepare for the nightly *ganga aarti* (river worship ceremony). You can learn to play the sitar or tabla; try Hasya yoga (laughter therapy), practise meditation or take a punt on crystal healing.

But Rishikesh is not all spirituality and contorted limbs; it's now a popular white-water rafting centre, backpacker hang-out and Himalayan-trekking gateway.

Rishikesh is divided into two main areas: the crowded, unattractive downtown area (Rishikesh town), where you'll find the bus and train stations as well as the Triveni Ghat (a popular and auspicious bathing ghat and place of prayer on the Ganges); and the riverside communities a few kilometres upstream around Ram Jhula and Lakshman Jhula, where most of the accommodation, ashrams, restaurants and travellers are ensconced. The two *jhula* (suspension bridges) that cross the river are pedestrian-only – though scooters and motorcycles freely use them. Swarg Ashram, located on the eastern bank, is the traffic-free 'spiritual centre' of Rishikesh, while High Bank, west of Lakshman Jhula, is a small enclave popular with backpackers.

Sights

Lakshman Jhula

The defining image of Rishikesh is the view across the Lakshman Jhula hanging bridge to the huge, 13-storey wedding-cake temple of **Swarg Niwas and Shri Trayanbakshwar**. Built by the organisation of the guru Kailashanand, it resembles a fairy-land castle and has dozens of shrines to Hindu deities on each level, interspersed with jewellery and textile shops. Sunset is an especially good time to photograph the temple from the bridge itself, and you'll hear the bell-clanging and chanting of devotees in the morning and evening. Shops selling devotional CDs add to the cacophony of noise on this side of the river. Markets, restaurants, ashrams and guesthouses sprawl on both sides of the river; in recent years the area has grown into the busiest and liveliest part of upper Rishikesh.

Swarg Ashram

A pleasant 2km walk south of Lakshman Jhula, along the path skirting the east bank of the Ganges, leads to the spiritual community of Swarg Ashram, made up of temples, ashrams, a crowded bazaar, sadhus and the bathing ghats (steps or landing on a river) where religious ceremonies are performed at sunrise and sunset. The colourful, though rather touristy, *ganga aarti* is held at the riverside temple of the Parmarth Niketan Ashram every evening around sunset, with singing, chanting, musicians and the lighting of candles.

Maharishi Mahesh Yogi Ashram HISTORIC BUILDING
(Indian/foreigner ₹100/600; 9am-4pm) Just south of Swarg Ashram is what's left of the original Maharishi Mahesh Yogi Ashram, where the Beatles stayed and apparently wrote much of the *White Album*. After decades of neglect, the Forest Department has decided to reclaim it from the jungle growth that had nearly consumed it, turning it into a pilgrimage site for Beatles fans, as well as an evolving graffiti-art museum. Don't miss the meditation hall, with bizarre warrens of rock-lined hallways, plus striking new paintings.

Activities

Yoga & Meditation

Yoga and meditation are ubiquitous in India's yoga capital. Teaching and yoga styles vary tremendously, so check out a few classes and ask others about their experiences before committing yourself to a course. Many places also offer ayurvedic massage, and some residential ashrams have strict rules forbidding students from consuming drugs, alcohol, tobacco and meat during their stay.

Omkarananda Ganga Sadan YOGA
(0135-2430763; www.iyengaryoga.in; Lakshman Jhula Rd; r with/without AC ₹2000/600, minimum 3-day stay) On the river at Ram Jhula, this ashram has comfortable rooms and specialises in highly recommended Iyengar yoga classes. There are intensive seven- to 10-day courses (₹1200) from October to May; advance reservations recommended. In the gaps between the intensives, day classes are offered (₹300, beginners 4pm to 5.30pm, general 6pm to 7.30pm, Monday to Saturday, prices go down if you do more than one class).

Anand Prakash Yoga Ashram YOGA
(0135-2442344; www.anandprakashashram.com; Badrinath Rd, Tapovan; private/share r incl full board ₹1200/900) About 1km north of Lakshman Jhula, you can stay at this ashram for as long or as little as you like, taking part in morning and afternoon Akhanda yoga classes (included in the price). The food is excellent and rooms are simple but comfortable and clean. Silence is the rule from 9pm to 9am. If you're not staying, drop in for classes for ₹200.

Parmarth Niketan Ashram YOGA
(0135-2434301; www.parmarth.com; Swarg Ashram; r with/without AC ₹1600/600) Dominating the centre of Swarg Ashram and drawing visitors to its evening *ganga aarti* on the riverbank, Parmarth has a wonderfully ornate and serene garden courtyard. The price includes a room with a private bathroom and basic hatha yoga sessions.

Rishikesh Yog Peeth YOGA
(0135-2440193; www.rishikeshyogpeeth.com; Swarg Ashram; 40-day course US$1400) With its excellent reputation, this popular yoga-teacher-training school has become something of a local industry.

GARHWAL & KUMAON

Uttarkhand is split into two administrative districts: Garhwal and Kumaon. Locals consider the region of Garhwal, covering the western part of Uttarkhand, to be the masculine half of the state due to its exceptionally burly topography. The character of the landscape – and, some say, the people – is largely defined by the four major rivers that flow from Himalayan glaciers and have carved the terrain into a rugged network of ridges and canyons.

Blessed by a landscape that's gentler and sweeter than that of Garhwal, Kumaon is said to be the feminine half of Uttarakhand. With its rolling, terraced hills and graceful Himalayan summits, as well as the strength of its goddess-worshipping culture, there's something incredibly special here that's easy to experience but impossible to define.

Rishikesh

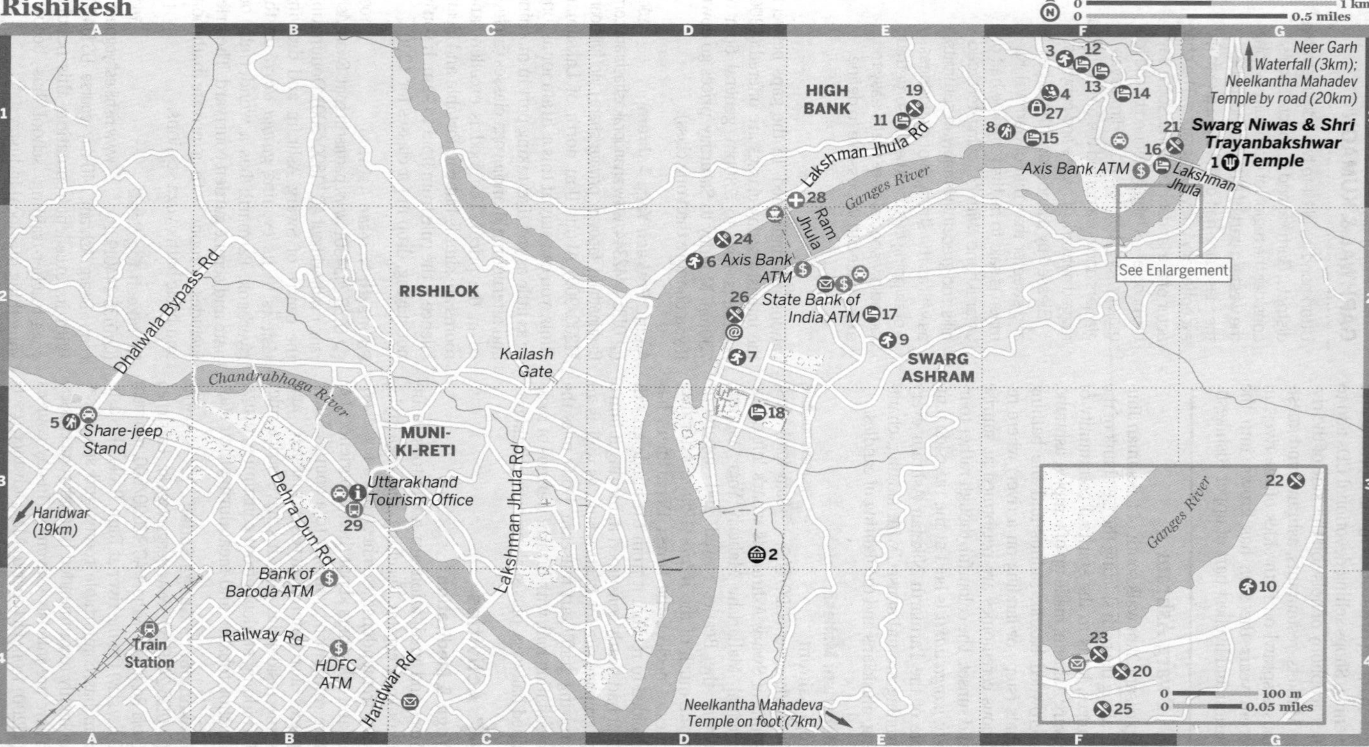
0 1 km
0 0.5 miles
A
B
C
D
E
F
G
1
2
3
4
Neer Garh Waterfall (3km); Neelkantha Mahadev Temple by road (20km)
Swarg Niwas & Shri Trayanbakshwar Temple
HIGH BANK
Lakshman Jhula Rd
Ganges River
Axis Bank ATM
Lakshman Jhula
Ram Jhula
Axis Bank ATM
State Bank of India ATM
See Enlargement
RISHILOK
Dhalwala Bypass Rd
Kailash Gate
SWARG ASHRAM
Chandrabhaga River
Share-jeep Stand
MUNI-KI-RETI
Uttarakhand Tourism Office
Lakshman Jhula Rd
Dehra Dun Rd
Haridwar (19km)
Bank of Baroda ATM
Railway Rd
Train Station
HDFC ATM
Haridwar Rd
Neelkantha Mahadeva Temple on foot (7km)
Ganges River
0 100 m
0 0.05 miles
1
2
3
4
5
6
7
8
9
10
11
12
13
14
15
16
17
18
19
20
21
22
23
24
25
26
27
28
29

Rishikesh

Top Sights
1 Swarg Niwas & Shri Trayanbakshwar Temple G1

Sights
2 Maharishi Mahesh Yogi Ashram D3

Activities, Courses & Tours
3 Anand Prakash Yoga Ashram F1
4 De-N-Ascent Expeditions F1
5 GMVN Trekking & Mountaineering Division A3
6 Omkarananda Ganga Sadan D2
7 Parmarth Niketan Ashram D2
8 Red Chilli Adventure F1
9 Rishikesh Yog Peeth E2
10 Shiva Yoga Peeth G4
Sri Sant Seva Ashram .... (see 10)

Sleeping
11 Bhandari Swiss Cottage E1
12 Dewa Retreat F1
13 Dhiraj Guest House F1
14 Divine Ganga Cottage F1
15 Divine Resort F1
16 Hotel Ishan F1
New Bhandari Swiss Cottage .... (see 11)
17 Sudesh Guest House E2
18 Vashishth Guest House D3

Eating
19 Bistro Nirvana E1
20 Chatsang Cafe F4
21 Devraj Coffee Corner F1
22 Ganga Beach Restaurant G3
23 Little Buddha Cafe F4
24 Madras Cafe D2
Oasis Restaurant .... (see 11)
25 Pyramid Cafe F4
26 Tip Top Restaurant D2

Shopping
27 Adventure Axis F1

Information
28 Shivananda Ashram E1

Transport
Jeep Stand .... (see 22)
29 Main Bus Stand B3
Taxi & Autorickshaw Stand .... (see 24)
Yatra/GMOU Bus Stand .... (see 29)

Sri Sant Seva Ashram YOGA
(☎0135-2430465; www.santsewaashram.org.in; r without/with AC ₹600/1500) Sri Sant Seva Ashram overlooks the Ganges in Lakshman Jhula, and its large rooms are popular, so book ahead. The more expensive rooms have balconies with superb river views. The yoga classes are mixed styles and open to all. Beginner (₹100), and intermediate and advanced (₹200) sessions run daily. It is also home to the well-regarded **Shiva Yoga Peeth** (☎9622724204; www.shivayogapeeth.org; 200/300/500hr $210/315/420) yoga-teacher-training program.

Rafting, Kayaking & Trekking

More than 100 operators offer full- and half-day rafting trips, launching upstream and paddling down to Rishikesh. Some also offer multiday rafting trips, with camping along the river. The official rafting season runs from 15 September to 30 June. A half-day trip starts at about ₹1000 per person, while a full day costs from ₹1800. Most companies also offer all-inclusive Himalayan treks to places such as Kuari Pass, Har-ki Dun and Gangotri/Tapovan from around ₹3500 per day.

Red Chilli Adventure TREKKING, RAFTING
(☎0135-2434021; www.redchilliadventure.com; Lakshman Jhula Rd; ⌚9am-8pm) Reliable outfit offering Himalayan trekking and rafting trips throughout Uttarakhand and to Himachal Pradesh and Ladakh.

De-N-Ascent Expeditions KAYAKING, TREKKING
(☎0135-2442354; www.kayakhimalaya.com; Badrinath Rd, Tapovan) De-N-Ascent Expeditions are specialists in kayaking lessons and expeditions. Learn to paddle and Eskimo roll with an experienced instructor, or go on multiday kayaking or rafting adventures. Also organises trekking trips.

GMVN Trekking & Mountaineering Division TREKKING
(☎0135-2431793; www.gmvnl.in; Lakshman Jhula Rd, Muni-ki-Reti; ⌚10am-5pm) Can arrange high-altitude treks in the Garhwal Himalaya, and hires out trekking equipment, guides and porters.

Walks & Beaches

An easy, 15-minute walk to two small **waterfalls** starts 3km north of Lakshman Jhula bridge on the south side of the river. The start is marked by drink stalls and a roadside shrine, and the path is easy to find. 4WD taxis cost ₹100 from Lakshman Jhula.

On the other side of the river, a 20-minute uphill walk (signposted) to lovely **Neer Garh Waterfall** (₹30) starts about 2km north of Lakshman Jhula.

For a longer hike, follow the dedicated pilgrims who take water from the Ganges to offer at **Neelkantha Mahadev Temple**, a 7km three-hour walk along a forest path from Swarg Ashram. You can also reach the temple by road (about 20km) from Lakshman Jhula.

Festivals & Events

International Yoga Festival YOGA

(www.internationalyogafestival.com; ⏲ Mar) In the first week of March, swamis and yoga masters from around the world flock to Rishikesh for lectures and training. Most of the action is centred on the Parmarth Niketan Ashram (p415) in Swarg Ashram.

Sleeping

Most of the accommodation is spread on both sides of the river around Lakshman Jhula; there are a handful of hotels among the ashrams at Swarg Ashram and directly across the river around Ram Jhula, and some good budget places at High Bank.

Though many hotels have backpackers in mind, more and more decent midrange options are appearing each year, and the few top-end hotels are good.

Lakshman Jhula

There are several good budget options on both sides of the river here, the liveliest part of Rishikesh. Some of the best-value places are at the guesthouses in the Tapovan area, along the lane that leads to Divine Ganga Cottage.

Dhiraj Guest House GUESTHOUSE $

(☎ 9719357411; s/d ₹450/550) Clean, friendly and cheap – this family-run place hits the trifecta. Rooms are simple and pleasant, and each has use of its own little kitchen (gas is extra). It's about a seven-minute walk from the bridge at Lakshman Jhula.

Divine Ganga Cottage HOTEL $$

(☎ 0135-2442175; www.divinegangacottage.com; r ₹2400, with AC ₹3200-3800; ❄@📶) This neat hotel is surrounded by small rice paddies and local homes with gardens. The huge upstairs terrace has supreme river views. Non-AC rooms downstairs are small and overpriced but the larger stylish AC rooms upstairs are some of the best in town, with writing tables and modern bathrooms.

Hotel Ishan HOTEL $$

(☎ 0135-2431534; r ₹2000-4000; ❄@📶) This long-running riverfront place near Lakshman Jhula recently went upscale. Rooms are comfortable and tastefully furnished, with shared or private terraces overlooking the Ganges.

Divine Resort HOTEL $$$

(☎ 0135-2442128; www.divineresort.com; r ₹3500-7000, ste ₹10,000-15,000; ❄📶🏊) Some rooms in this top-end hotel have stunning river views – but few rival that of the Ganges-facing glass elevator, which could be a tourist attraction all its own. Then there's the infinity pool, perched above the river bank... We'd say it's the top hotel around Lakshman Jhula. About half of the rooms are being freshly renovated.

Dewa Retreat HOTEL $$$

(☎ 0135-2442382; www.dewaretreat.com; r without/with river view ₹4500/5000; ❄📶🏊) Lakshman Jhula's newest top-end hotel features immaculate rooms that blend simplicity with luxury. The best rooms have balconies with Ganges valley views, and the outdoor swimming pool takes the edge off a sultry day.

High Bank

Bhandari Swiss Cottage HOTEL $

(☎ 0135-2432939; www.bhandariswisscottagerishikesh.com; r from ₹300, with AC from ₹800; ❄@📶) This backpacker favourite has rooms in several budgets – the higher up you stay, the higher the price. Rooms are varying degrees of worn and could use a bit of love, but the big balconies are winners, with expansive views of the green mountains. It has an excellent little courtyard restaurant, internet cafe and yoga classes.

New Bhandari Swiss Cottage HOTEL $

(☎ 0135-2435322; www.newbhandariswisscottage.com; r ₹400-800, with AC ₹1000-1500; ❄@📶) One of the last places on the High Bank lane, this is a large, popular place with rooms ranging from clean and simple to simply impressive. Many have been renovated recently. There's a massage centre and a good restaurant, **Oasis Restaurant** (mains ₹90-170; ⏲ 8am-10pm), with a menu that covers oodles of world cuisines.

Swarg Ashram

If you're serious about yoga and introspection, stay at one of Swarg's numerous ashrams. Otherwise, there's a knot of hotels a block back from the river towards the southern end of Swarg.

Sudesh Guest House GUESTHOUSE $

(☎ 9760313572; sudeshguesthouse771@gmail.com; r without/with AC ₹300/800; ❄) A good budget choice in Swarg Ashram, here you'll find some of the best-value rooms in the neighbourhood. There's a yoga hall, rooftop terrace, shared kitchen, and filtered water available.

★**Vashishth Guest House** BOUTIQUE HOTEL $$
(☎0135-2440029; www.vashishthgroup.com; r without AC ₹950, with ₹1500-1800; ❄📶) This sweet little boutique hotel has colourfully painted walls, comfortable mattresses and a small lending library. A couple of the rooms boast good-sized kitchens with cooking utensils, table and chairs. For what you get, this is one of the best deals in Rishikesh.

Eating

Virtually every restaurant in Rishikesh serves only vegetarian food, but there are lots of travellers' restaurants whipping up various interpretations of Continental and Israeli food, as well as Indian and Chinese. High Bank is the only area where you'll find meat on the menu.

Lakshman Jhula

★**Devraj Coffee Corner** CAFE $
(snacks & mains ₹50-230; ⏲8am-9pm) Perched above the bridge and looking across the river to Shri Trayanbakshwar temple, this German bakery is a sublime spot for a break at any time of the day. The coffee is the best in town and the menu ranges from specialities such as brown bread with yak cheese to soups and sizzlers, along with croissants, apple strudel and more.

There's a good bookshop next door.

Pyramid Cafe MULTICUISINE $
(mains ₹110-180; ⏲8am-10pm; 📶) Sit on cushions under open-sided, pyramid-shaped roofs and choose from a menu of home-cooked Indian food, plus a few Tibetan and Western dishes including pancakes. The family that runs it is superfriendly and they also rent out a couple of peaceful, well-kept pyramid tents with double beds and attached baths (₹600).

Chatsang Cafe FUSION $$
(mains ₹150-250; ⏲8am-10pm) The clatter of chopping knives and sizzling pans coming from the open kitchen raises expectations that something delicious will soon be placed on your table – and you won't be disappointed. With innovative twists on Indian and international dishes, including several varieties of *khichdi* (spiced rice and lentils), the food here seems fresher than anywhere else in town.

★**Little Buddha Cafe** MULTICUISINE $$
(mains ₹110-250; ⏲8am-11pm; 📶) This funky treehouse-style restaurant has an ultralounge top floor, tables overlooking the Ganges River and really good international food. Pizzas are big and the mixed vegetable platter is a serious feast. It's one of the busiest places in Lakshman Jhula, for good reason.

SLEEPING PRICE RANGES

The following price ranges refer to a double room with bathroom and are inclusive of tax:

$ less than ₹1000

$$ ₹1000–3000

$$$ more than ₹3000

Ganga Beach Restaurant MULTICUISINE $$
(mains ₹100-200; ⏲7.30am-10.30pm; 📶) Ganga Beach Restaurant has a great riverside location, with a spacious terrace and a big menu including crêpes and ice-cold lassis.

High Bank

Bistro Nirvana INTERNATIONAL $$
(mains ₹80-250; ⏲9am-10pm) This new joint hits the right groove, with a shaded patio and elevated tables with cushioned bench seating. The theme is bamboo and the multi-regional food is tasty.

Swarg Ashram & Ram Jhula

Madras Cafe INDIAN $
(Ram Jhula; mains ₹100-180; ⏲8am-9pm; 📶) This local institution recently underwent a modern facelift but still dishes up tasty South and North Indian vegetarian food, thalis, a mean mushroom curry, wholewheat pancakes and the intriguing Himalayan 'health pilau', as well as superthick lassis.

Tip Top Restaurant MULTICUISINE $
(Swarg Ashram; mains ₹90-200; ⏲9am-9.30pm) This friendly little joint is perched up high, catching river views and breezes. Customise your own sandwich, or dig into Indian, Italian or Israeli dishes.

Shopping

Swarg Ashram is the place to go for bookshops, ayurvedic herbal medicines, clothing, handicrafts and tourist trinkets such as jewellery and Tibetan singing bowls, though there are also plenty of stalls around Lakshman Jhula. If you need outdoor gear, your best bet is well-stocked **Adventure Axis** (Badrinath Rd, Lakshman Jhula; ⏲10am-8pm).

Information

DANGERS & ANNOYANCES

Be cautious of befriending sadhus – while some are on genuine spiritual journeys, the orange robes have been used as a disguise by fugitives from the law since medieval times, and people have been robbed and worse.

The current in some parts of the Ganges is very strong and people occasionally drown here. Don't swim beyond your depth.

INTERNET ACCESS

Internet access is available all over town, including **The Great Himalaya** (per hour ₹30; ⏲8am-9.30pm; 📶), usually for ₹30 per hour.

MEDICAL SERVICES

Himalayan Institute Hospital (☎0135-2471200, emergency 0135-2471225; ⏲24hr) The nearest large hospital, 17km along the road to Dehra Dun and 1km beyond Jolly Grant Airport.

Shivananda Ashram (☎0135-2430040; www.sivanandaonline.org; Lakshman Jhula Rd) Provides free medical services and has a pharmacy.

MONEY

Some travel agents around Lakshman Jhula and Swarg Ashram will exchange travellers cheques and cash.

TOURIST INFORMATION

Uttarakhand Tourism Office (☎0135-2430209; Main Bus Stand; ⏲10am-5pm Mon-Sat) In a building behind the main bus stand, with eager staff.

Getting There & Away

BUS

There are frequent buses to Haridwar and Dehra Dun; for Mussoorie change at Dehra Dun. Buses run north to Char Dham sites during the *yatra* season (May to October), though direct buses to Gangotri were infrequent at the time of research – to get there, connect in Uttarkashi; likewise, there are no buses to Yamunotri – you'll have to change in Dehra Dun and Barkot.

Private AC and Volvo buses run to Delhi (₹600 to ₹900, seven hours) several times a day.

Private night buses to Jaipur (seat/sleeper/AC sleeper ₹600/700/1200, 13 hours) and Pushkar (seat/sleeper ₹650/700, 16 hours) can be booked at travel agents in Lakshman Jhula, Swarg Ashram and High Bank, but they leave from Haridwar. You can also book a bus to Agra (AC sleeper/Volvo ₹750/1300, 12 hours) that departs from Dehra Dun.

SHARE JEEPS & TAXI

Share jeeps to Uttarkashi (₹280, five hours) and Joshimath (₹380, eight hours) leave when full from Natraj Chowk, near the corner of Dehra Dun Rd and Dhalwala Bypass Rd. It's best to get here between 5am and 7am.

To hire cars for out-of-town destinations, go to the **taxi stand** at Lakshman Jhula; the **taxi stand** between the main and *yatra* (pilgrimage) bus stands; or the **taxi and autorickshaw stand** at Ram Jhula. Rates include Haridwar (₹920, one hour), Dehra Dun (₹1250, 1½ hours), Jolly Grant Airport (₹820, one hour), Uttarkashi (for Gangotri; ₹4080, seven hours), Joshimath (₹5610, nine hours) and Almora (₹7000, 10 hours). For long-distance trips you may find a cheaper rate by asking around at travel agents and guesthouses.

Vikrams (large autorickshaws) charge ₹400 to make the trip to Haridwar.

TRAIN

Very few trains run from Rishikesh itself, so your best bet is to take a bus or taxi to the train station in Haridwar and hop on-board there. Bookings for trains from Haridwar can be made at the train station in Rishikesh, or at travel agents around Lakshman Jhula and Swarg Ashram (for a fee).

Getting Around

Shared *vikrams* run from the downtown Ghat Rd junction up past Ram Jhula (₹10 per person) and the High Bank turn-off to Lakshman Jhula. To hire

BUSES FROM RISHIKESH

The following buses depart from the **main bus stand (A)** or the **Yatra/GMOU bus stand (B)**.

DESTINATION	FARE (₹)	DURATION (HR)	DEPARTURES
Badrinath (B)	425	14	5am
Dehra Dun (A)	51	1½	half-hourly
Delhi (A)	255/500 (ordinary/AC)	7	half-hourly
Gangotri (B)	380	12	5.30am
Haridwar (A)	35	1	half-hourly
Joshimath (B)	360	12	half-hourly 3.30-6am, 9am
Kedarnath (B)	400	12	6am
Uttarkashi (B)	240	7	8 buses 4.15am-noon

a private *vikram* or autorickshaw from downtown to Lakshman Jhula should cost ₹100 to 'upside' – the top of the hill on which the Lakshman Jhula area sits – and ₹120 to 'downside' – closer to the bridge. Be prepared to haggle, hard. From Ram Jhula to High Bank or Lakshman Jhula is ₹50.

To get to the eastern bank of the Ganges you either need to walk across one of the suspension bridges or take the **ferry** (one way/return ₹10/15; 7.30am-6.15pm) from Ram Jhula.

On the eastern bank of the Ganges, taxis and share jeeps wait to take passengers to waterfalls and Neelkantha Mahadev Temple (shared/private ₹120/1000), but it's a 16km trip by road to get from one side of the river to the other. Lakshman Jhula to Swarg Ashram costs ₹10 in a shared jeep, or ₹80 for the whole vehicle. Find rides at the **taxi stand** in Swarg Ashram, or the **jeep stand** in Lakshman Jhula.

Bicycles (per day ₹100), scooters (per day ₹300) and motorcycles (per day ₹400 to ₹700) can be hired around the Lakshman Jhula area. There are no actual shops – rent from guys on the street or ask at guesthouses.

HARIDWAR

01334 / POP 311,000 / ELEV 249M

Propitiously located at the point where the Ganges emerges from the Himalaya, Haridwar (also called Hardwar) is Uttarakhand's holiest Hindu city, and pilgrims arrive here in droves to bathe in the fast-flowing Ganges. The sheer number of people gathering around Har-ki-Pairi Ghat give Haridwar a chaotic but reverent feel. Within the religious hierarchy of India, Haridwar is much more significant than Rishikesh, an hour further north, and every evening the river comes alive with flickering flames as floating offerings are released onto the Ganges. It's especially busy during the *yatra* (pilgrimage) season from May to October, in particular during July, when hundreds of thousands of Shiva devotees, known as Kanwarias, descend upon the city.

Haridwar's main street is Railway Rd, becoming Upper Rd, which runs parallel to the Ganges canal (the river proper runs further to the east). Generally only cycle-rickshaws are allowed between Laltarao Bridge and Bhimgoda Jhula (Bhimgoda Bridge), so vehicles travel around the opposite riverbank. The alleyways of Bara Bazaar run south of Har-ki-Pairi Ghat.

Sights

★Har-ki-Pairi Ghat — GHAT

Har-ki-Pairi (The Footstep of God) is where Vishnu is said to have dropped some divine nectar and left behind a footprint. Every evening, hundreds of worshippers gather for the *ganga aarti* (river worship ceremony). Officials in blue uniforms collect donations and, as the sun sets, bells ring out a rhythm, torches are lit, and leaf baskets with flower petals inside and a candle on top (₹10) are lit and placed on the river to drift away downstream.

Tourists can mingle with the crowd to experience the rituals of an ancient religion that still retains its power in the modern age. Someone may claim to be a priest and help you with your *puja* before asking for ₹200 or more. If you want to make a donation, it's best to give to a uniformed collector.

The best times to visit the ghat are early morning or just before dusk.

Mansa Devi & Chanda Devi Temples

To get to the crowded hilltop temple of **Mansa Devi**, a wish-fulfilling goddess, take the **cable car** (return ₹95; 7am-7pm Apr-Oct, 8am-6.30pm Nov-Mar). The path to the cable car is lined with stalls selling packages of *prasad* (a food offering used in religious ceremonies) to bring to the goddess on the hill. You can walk up (a steep 1.5km) but beware of *prasad*-stealing monkeys.

Many visitors and pilgrims combine this with another **cable car** (return ₹163; 8am-6pm) up Neel Hill, 4km southeast of Haridwar, to **Chandi Devi Temple**, built by Raja Suchet Singh of Kashmir in 1929.

Pay ₹312 at Mansa Devi to ride both cable cars and take an AC coach between the two temples. Photography is forbidden inside the shrines.

Tours

Mohan's Adventure Tours — ADVENTURE

(9837100215, 9412022966; www.mohansadventure.in; Railway Rd; 8am-10.30pm) Sanjeev Mehta of Mohan's Adventure Tours can organise any kind of tour, including trekking, fishing, birdwatching, cycling, motorcycling and rafting. An accomplished wildlife photographer, he specialises in five-hour safaris (₹2250 per person with two or more, singles pay ₹3500) within Rajaji Tiger Reserve. Sanjeev also runs overnight trips to Corbett Tiger Reserve (from ₹9950). Tours operate year-round.

Festivals & Events

Kumbh Mela — RELIGIOUS

The largest religious gathering on earth, drawing millions of worshippers, the Kumbh Mela

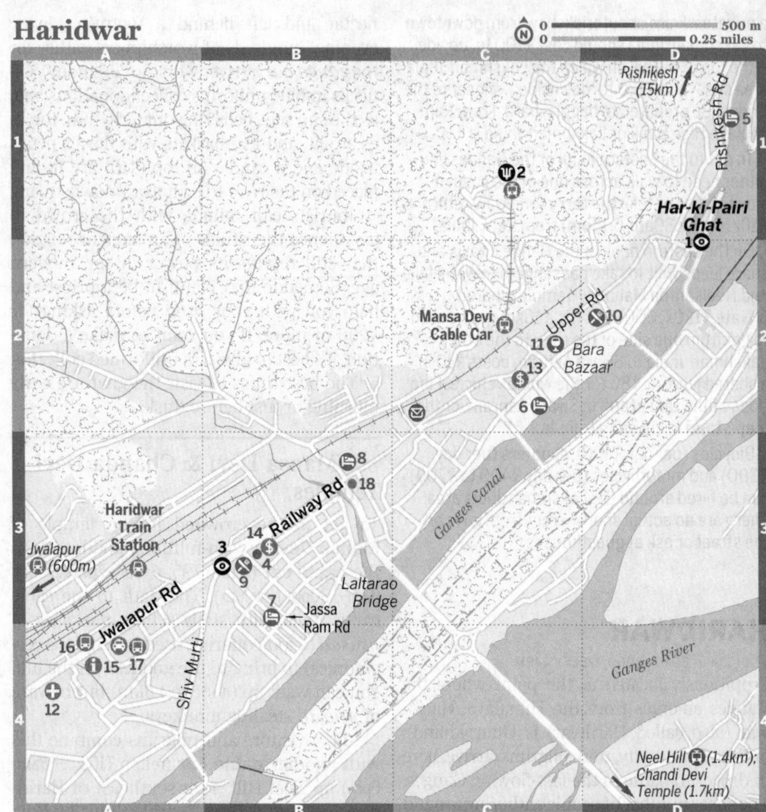

Haridwar

Top Sights
1 Har-ki-Pairi Ghat D2

Sights
2 Mansa Devi Temple C1
3 Shiva Statue B3

Activities, Courses & Tours
4 Mohan's Adventure Tours B3

Sleeping
5 Bhaj-Govindam D1
6 Haveli Hari Ganga C2
7 Hotel Arjun B3
8 Hotel La Casa B3

Eating
9 Big Ben Restaurant B3
Haveli Hari Ganga Restaurant .... (see 6)
10 Hoshiyar Puri D2

Drinking & Nightlife
11 Prakash Lok C2

Information
12 Rishikul Ayurvedic Hospital A4
13 Sai Forex C2
14 State Bank of India B3
15 Uttarakhand Tourism Office A4

Transport
16 GMOU Bus Stand A4
17 UK Roadways Bus Stand A4
18 Vikrams to Rishikesh B3

is an auspicious time to wash away sins in a sacred river. It's celebrated in Haridwar every 12 years (rotating between Allahabad, Ujjain and Nasik for the years between). Every sixth year, the Ardh (half) Kumbh Mela is held, also bringing huge crowds to Haridwar.

Sleeping

Haridwar has loads of hotels catering to Hindu pilgrims. The busiest time of year is the May–October *yatra* season – outside this you'll find rooms discounted by 20% to 50%.

Jassa Ram Rd and other alleys running off Railway Rd have budget hotels, although most are grim. Rishikesh has far superior budget accommodation.

Down by the ghats are a number of high-rise hotels that have good views but worse-than-average rooms.

Hotel Arjun HOTEL **$**
(☎01334-220409; www.hotelarjun.com; Jassa Ram Rd; r with/without AC from ₹950/750; ❄📶) The best of the budget choices, the Arjun beats its neighbours for cleanliness and comfort. Some rooms have balconies. Most have their quirks, though – one a broken TV, another a dead overhead light – so take a look at a few if you can. It's walking distance from the train and bus stations.

Hotel La Casa HOTEL **$$**
(☎01334-221197; www.lacasahotels.in; Bilkeshwar Rd, opposite Gurdwara; r from ₹2200; ❄📶) One of Haridwar's few solid midrange choices, La Casa boasts some of the least scuffed rooms in town. They strive for character, with splashes of colour, tasteful furnishings and modern bathrooms. In all, good value (though not quite as nice as it looks on the hotel website).

Bhaj-Govindam HOTEL **$$**
(☎8881007007; http://hotelbhajgovindam.com; Upper Rd; r from ₹1500; ❄📶) About 100m north of Bhimgoda Jhula, Bhaj-Govindam is the most peaceful hotel in town, set around a grassy garden, with river frontage on the banks of the Ganges (easily accessed behind a metal wall). Rooms are comfortable, suites are huge, while cleanliness can be inconsistent. Fortunately, prices are negotiable.

★ **Haveli Hari Ganga** HERITAGE HOTEL **$$$**
(☎01334-226443; www.havelihariganga.com; 21 Ram Ghat; r incl breakfast ₹8000-10,000; ❄📶) Hidden away in Bara Bazaar, but right on the Ganges, this superb 1918 *haveli* (traditional, ornately decorated residence) is Haridwar's finest hotel. Interior courtyards and marble floors give it a regal charm. It's worth shelling out extra for a Ganges View room, with an airy balcony overlooking the river.

The hotel's **restaurant** (lunch thali ₹450, dinner buffet ₹650; ⏲12.30-2.30pm & 7.30-10pm) is the classiest in Haridwar. Come for the thali lunch or buffet dinner.

Eating

Being a holy city, only vegetarian food and nonalcoholic drinks are available.

Hoshiyar Puri INDIAN **$**
(Upper Rd; mains ₹90-175; ⏲11am-4.30pm & 7-10pm) Established in 1937, this place still has a loyal (and well-deserved) local following. The *dhal makhani* (black lentils and red kidney beans with cream and butter), *lacha paratha* (layered fried bread), *aloo gobi* (potato and cauliflower curry) and *kheer* (creamy rice pudding) are lip-smackingly good.

Big Ben Restaurant MULTICUISINE **$$**
(Railway Rd, Hotel Ganga Azure; mains ₹110-200; ⏲8am-10.30pm) Watch the passing parade through the big windows and enjoy some of Haridwar's best food in this restaurant of mirrors, soft music and polite staff. It's a solid choice for breakfast, with good coffee. There's wi-fi in the adjoining lobby.

Drinking & Nightlife

★ **Prakash Lok** LASSI
(Bara Bazaar; ⏲10am-midnight) Don't miss a creamy lassi at this Haridwar institution, famed for its ice-cold, best-you'll-ever-have lassis served in tin cups (₹50). Just about anyone in the Bara Bazaar can point you to it.

Information

Rishikul Ayurvedic Hospital (☎01334-221003; Railway Rd) A long-established medical college and hospital with a good reputation.

Sai Forex (Upper Rd; ⏲10am-2pm & 4-9pm) Changes cash and travellers cheques for a commission of 1%. Also has internet for ₹50 per hour.

Uttarakhand Tourism Office (☎01334-265304; Railway Rd, Rahi Motel; ⏲10am-5pm Mon-Sat) You can get a Char Dham biometric card here.

Getting There & Away

Haridwar is well connected by bus and train, but book ahead for trains during the pilgrimage season (May to October).

BUS

Government buses run from the **UK Roadways bus stand** (Railway Rd) on the main road through town. Private deluxe buses buses run to Delhi (₹400), Agra (seat/sleeper ₹500/600), Jaipur (₹580/680) and Pushkar (₹500/600). Ask the travel agent who makes your booking where to find your bus.

TAXI

The main **taxi stand** (Railway Rd) is outside the train station. Destinations include Chilla (for Rajaji Tiger Reserve, ₹570), Rishikesh (₹820, one hour), Dehra Dun (₹1320), and Jolly Grant Airport (₹1120), but it's usually possible to arrange a taxi for less than these official rates. You can also hire taxis to go to one or all of the pilgrimage sites on the Char Dham between April and October. One-way rates to single temples range from ₹6550 to ₹7550; a nine-day tour of all four is ₹22,600. Hiring a jeep for the Char Dham costs marginally more, and can be well worth it in monsoon season, or for groups of four or more.

TRAIN

Haridwar Junction is well connected by train to Delhi, Haldwani and beyond. There are many more trains to/from Haridwar than to/from nearby Rishikesh.

Getting Around

Cycle-rickshaws cost ₹10 for a short distance and ₹30 for longer hauls, such as from the Haridwar train station to Har-ki-Pairi. Shared **vikrams** run up and down Railway Rd (₹10) and all the way to Rishikesh (₹40, one hour) from Upper Rd at Laltarao Bridge, but for that trip buses are more comfortable. Hiring a taxi for three hours to tour the local temples and ashrams costs around ₹800; an autorickshaw costs ₹350.

RAJAJI TIGER RESERVE

Unspoilt **Rajaji Tiger Reserve** (Rajaji National Park; ☎0135-2621669; www.rajajitigerreserve.co.in; Indian/foreigner per day ₹150/600, vehicle fee ₹250/500; ⏲15 Nov-15 Jun), covering over 1000 sq km in the forested foothills near Haridwar, was declared an official tiger park in 2015, despite having only about 13 of the striped cats within its boundaries. It's best known for wild elephants – around 600 at last count – and leopards (about 250). The village of Chilla, 13km northeast of Haridwar, is the base for visiting the park.

The thick deciduous forests are also home to chital, sambars, rarely seen sloth bears and some 300 species of birds. Though your chances of spotting a tiger are slim, you're

BUSES FROM HARIDWAR

The following buses depart from the UK Roadways bus stand. Information about buses to Dharamsala and Shimla is available at counter 6.

DESTINATION	FARE (₹)	DURATION (HR)	DEPARTURES
Agra	350	12	early morning
Chandigarh	211	10	hourly
Dehra Dun	68	2	half-hourly
Delhi (AC Volvo)	665	6	5 daily
Delhi (standard)	230	6	half-hourly
Dharamsala (ordinary/AC Volvo)	555/1190	15	2pm, 4pm/5pm
Haldwani	265	8	hourly
Jaipur (ordinary/AC)	484/930	12	4.30pm, 6.40pm, midnight/5.30pm
Rishikesh	35	1	half-hourly
Shimla	430	14	10am, 11am, noon
Uttarkashi	315	8	5am

In the *yatra* (pilgrimage) season from May to October, the following buses run from the **GMOU bus stand** (Railway Rd). During monsoon season (July to mid-September), service is occasionally suspended. For info call 01334-265008. For Yamunotri, go to Dehra Dun, then take a bus to Barkot.

DESTINATION	FARE (₹)	DURATION (HR)	DEPARTURES
Badrinath (via Joshimath)	480	15	3.15am, 5am, 8am, 11am
Gangotri	450	13	5.30am
Joshimath	395	10	7.45am
Kedarnath	345	10	5.15am
Uttarkashi	280	8	7am, 10am

TRAINS FROM HARIDWAR

DESTINATION	TRAIN NAME & NUMBER	FARE (₹)	DURATION (HR)	DEPARTURE/ ARRIVAL
Amritsar	12053 Jan Shatabdi	2nd class/chair car 185/615	7½	2.45pm/10.05pm (Fri-Wed)
	14631 Dehra Dun-Amritsar Exp	sleeper/3AC 250/670	10	9.25pm/7.30am
Delhi (New Delhi Station)	12018 Shatabdi Exp	chair car/executive 805/1275	4½	6.15pm/10.45pm
	12056 Jan Shatabdi Exp	2nd class/chair car 140/470	4½	6.22am/11.15am
Delhi (Old Delhi Station)	14042 Mussoorie Exp	sleeper/3AC/2AC/1AC 195/490/695/1160	8½	11.15pm/8.30am
Haldwani (for Nainital & Almora)	14120 Dehra Dun-Kathgodam Exp	sleeper/2AC/1AC 190/695/1160	6½	12.25am/6.48am
Kolkata/Howrah	13010 Doon Exp	sleeper/3AC/2AC 595/1600/2340	32¾	10.15pm/6.55am (2 nights later)
Lucknow	13010 Doon Exp	sleeper/3AC/2AC 285/765/1095	10¼	10.15pm/8.35am
Varanasi	13010 Doon Exp	sleeper/3AC/2AC 405/1105/1595	17¾	10.15pm/4pm

likely to see some wildlife, and will get a feel for the wilderness.

Rajaji's forests include the traditional winter territory of more than 1000 families of nomadic Van Gujjar buffalo herders – most of whom have been evicted from the park against their will. Visit www.himalayanmigration.com for more on this and other issues affecting this unique tribe.

Tours

At the Forest Ranger's office, close to the tourist guesthouse at Chilla, you can organise a jeep tour (taking up to six people and starting at ₹885 per person for a standard safari, plus a ₹500 entry fee for the vehicle) – the price includes a guide.

For a more personalised experience of Rajaji Tiger Reserve with expert guides, go with Mohan's Adventure Tours (p421), out of Haridwar, who offer abridged safaris even when the park is officially closed. These five-hour trips include a safari, a jungle walk and a visit to a Van Gujjar forest camp.

Sleeping

The **Chilla Guesthouse** (☎0138-266678; www.gmvnl.com; r from ₹2200; ❄) is the GMVN rest house and the most comfortable place to stay in Chilla.

You can stay inside the park at one of the rest houses run by the Forest Department. For information and reservations, contact the director at the **Rajaji National Park Office** (☎0135-2621669; 5/1 Ansari Rd, Dehra Dun; ⏰10am-5pm Mon-Fri). Mohan's Adventure Tours (p421) can also make bookings. Also within the park, **Camp King Elephant** (☎9871604712; cottage incl full board Indian/foreigner from ₹8500/US$240) has solar power, private bathrooms, full meal service and jeep tours.

Getting There & Away

Buses to Chilla (₹35, one hour) leave the GMOU bus stand in Haridwar every hour from 7am to 2pm. The last return trip leaves Chilla at 5.30pm. Taxis charge ₹700 one way for the 13km journey.

DEHRA DUN

☎0135 / POP 600,000 / ELEV 640M

Perhaps best known for the institutions the British left behind – the huge Forest Research Institute Museum, the Indian Military Academy, the Wildlife Institute of India and the Survey of India – the capital of Uttarakhand is a hectic, congested city sprawling in the Doon Valley between the Himalayan foothills and the Siwalik Range. Most travellers merely pass through on their way to nearby Rishikesh, Haridwar, Mussoorie or Himachal Pradesh, but if you have time, there's enough to do here to make Dehra Dun worth a stop.

Sights

Mindrolling Monastery BUDDHIST MONASTERY
(0135-2640556; www.mindrolling.org) The region around Dehra Dun is home to a thriving Tibetan Buddhist community, mainly focused on this monastery, about 10km south of the centre in Clement Town. Everything here is on a grand scale: at more than 60m tall its **Great Stupa** is believed to be the world's tallest and contains a series of shrine rooms displaying relics, murals and Tibetan art. Presiding over the monastery is the impressive 35m-high gold **Sakyamuni Buddha Statue**, dedicated to the Dalai Lama.

The streets around the monastery are lined with Tibetan cafes. Unfortunately, due to new government regulations, foreigners are no longer allowed to stay overnight in Clement Town – but the manager of the Devaloka House hotel on the monastery grounds may be willing to bend the rules. Simple rooms cost ₹350; the bed sheets have seen better days. Take *vikram* 5 from the city centre (₹10). An autorickshaw costs about ₹200.

Survey of India Museum MUSEUM
(Survey Chowk; 10.30am-5pm Mon-Fri) FREE Instruments used to accomplish the monumental task of mapping India in the 19th century are displayed here, including some designed especially for the mission by its leader, George Everest. See beautiful brass transits and scopes, plus a part-iron part-brass bar, which allowed surveyors to compensate for inaccuracies in measurements caused by the expansion and contraction of their instruments in heat and cold. The museum is not officially open to the public – you'll need permission to visit.

To get permission, go to the Surveyor General's office at the Survey of India Compound in Harthibarkala. There, you'll have to write a brief letter explaining why you want to view the collection. Permits are given only to those with an academic or professional interest in the subject – like a geography student or a historian – but proof of your vocation or college major isn't demanded.

Forest Research Institute Museum NOTABLE BUILDING
(http://fri.icfre.gov.in; ₹25; 9pm-5pm) The prime attraction of this museum is the building itself. Set in a 5-sq-km park, this grand remnant of the Raj era – where most of India's forest officers are trained – is larger than Buckingham Palace. Built between 1924 and 1929, this red-brick colossus has Mughal towers, perfectly formed arches and Roman columns in a series of quadrangles edged by elegant cloisters. Six huge halls have displays on Indian forestry that look like leftovers from a middle-school science fair.

Highlights include beautiful animal, bird and plant paintings by Afshan Zaidi, exhibits on the medicinal uses of trees, and a cross-section of a 700-year-old deodar tree. A return autorickshaw from the city centre, including one-hour wait time, costs around ₹300. Or take *vikram* 6 from Connaught Place and get out at the institute's entry gate.

Tapkeshwar Temple HINDU TEMPLE
(dawn-dusk) In a scenic setting on the banks of the Tons Nadi River, you'll find an unusual and popular Shiva shrine inside a small, dripping cave, which is the site of the annual **Shivaratri festival** (usually Mar). Turn left at the bottom of the steps for the main shrine. Cross the bridge over the river to visit another shrine, where you have to squeeze through a narrow cave to see an image of Mata Vaishno Devi.

The temple is about 5km north of the centre. Take a rickshaw for ₹300 (round trip).

Ram Rai Darbar MAUSOLEUM
(Paltan Bazaar; dawn-dusk) FREE The unique mausoleum of Ram Rai, the errant son of the seventh Sikh guru, Har Rai, is made of white marble, with paintings covering the walls, archways and ceilings. Four smaller tombs in the garden courtyard are those of Ram Rai's four wives. A communal lunch of dhal, rice and chapatis is offered to anyone who wants it, for a donation.

Activities

Har Ki Dun Protection & Mountaineering Association TREKKING
(9412918140, 9410134589; www.harkidun.org) Highly regarded company that offers guided treks in Har-ki-Dun, around the Garhwal Himalaya and beyond.

Sleeping

There are plenty of grungy cheapies along the Haridwar road outside the train station, some charging as little as ₹350 a double, but the better places can be found along Rajpur Rd.

Samar Niwas Guest House GUESTHOUSE $$
(0135-2740299; www.samarniwas.com; M-16 Chanderlok Colony; d ₹1600-1800;) This charming four-room guesthouse, in a peaceful residential area just off Rajpur Rd, is as welcoming as it gets. The owners are de-

Dehra Dun

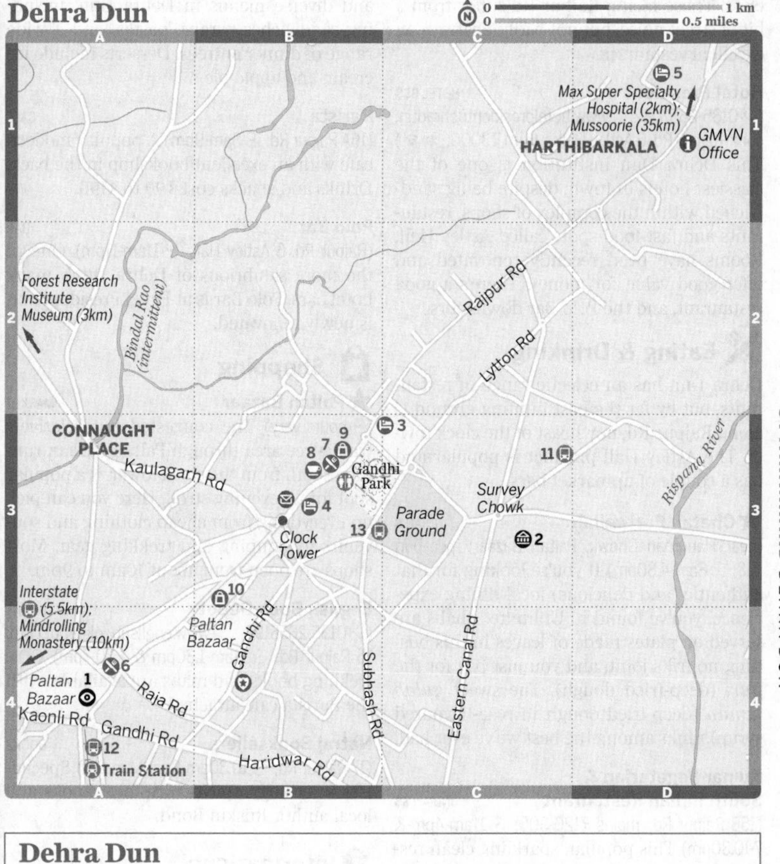

Dehra Dun

Sights
1 Ram Rai Darbar A4
2 Survey of India Museum C3

Sleeping
3 Hotel President C3
4 Moti Mahal Hotel B3
5 Samar Niwas Guest House D1

Eating
6 Chetan Puriwallah A4
7 Kumar Vegetarian & South Indian Restaurant B3
Moti Mahal .... (see 4)
Salt & Cravings .... (see 3)

Drinking & Nightlife
8 Barista B3
Polo Bar .... (see 3)

Shopping
English Book Depot .... (see 8)
9 Natraj Booksellers B3
10 Paltan Bazaar B3

Transport
11 Chunabata Bus Stand C3
12 Mussoorie Bus Stand A4
13 Parade Ground Bus Stand B3
Taxi Stand .... (see 12)

scendants of the Tehri royal family, but the rulers of the house seem to be the friendly pugs that roam the comfortable lounge-cum-lobby. Rooms are well appointed, but cleanliness can be hit or miss.

Moti Mahal Hotel HOTEL $$
(☎0135-2651277; www.motimahal.net; 7 Rajpur Rd; s/d from ₹1600/1900; ❄📶) Centrally located, Moti Mahal offers well-kept rooms, with upholstered furnishings adding a touch of

class. Those facing Rajpur Rd suffer from a bit of street noise, but not badly. Features an excellent restaurant.

Hotel President HOTEL **$$$**
(☎0135-2657082; www.hotelpresidentdehradun.com; Rajpur Rd, 6 Astley Hall; r from ₹3000; ❄📶) This Dehra Dun institution is one of the classiest hotels in town, despite being sandwiched within the complex of shops, restaurants and fast-food spots called Astley Hall. Rooms have been recently renovated and offer good value for money. There's a good restaurant, and the Polo Bar downstairs.

Eating & Drinking

Dehra Dun has an eclectic range of restaurants, but by far the best hunting ground is along Rajpur Rd, northeast of the clock tower. The Astley Hall precinct is popular and has a couple of upmarket bars.

★**Chetan Puriwallah** INDIAN **$**
(near Hanuman Chowk, Paltan Bazaar; per puri ₹18; ⊙8am-4.30pm) If you're looking for that authentic (and delicious) local dining experience, you've found it. Unlimited thalis are served on plates made of leaves in this bustling no-frills joint, and you just pay for the *puri* (deep-fried dough). The sweet *gulab jamun* (deep-fried dough in rose-flavoured syrup) ranks among the best we've ever had.

Kumar Vegetarian & South Indian Restaurant INDIAN **$$**
(15B Rajpur Rd; mains ₹120-300; ⊙11am-4pm & 7-10.30pm) This popular, sparkling clean restaurant serves what surely comes close to the Platonic Form of a *masala dosa* (curried vegetables inside a crisp pancake), which is the main reason locals flock here. Other Indian dishes are also cooked to near perfection and even the Chinese food is quite good. The waitstaff are very attentive.

Moti Mahal SOUTH INDIAN **$$**
(7 Rajpur Rd; mains ₹160-450; ⊙8am-10.45pm; 📶) Locals consistently rate Moti Mahal as one of the best midrange diners along Rajpur Rd. An interesting range of vegetarian and non-vegetarian options include Goan fish curry and Afghani *murg* (chicken), along with traditional South Indian fare and Chinese food.

Salt & Cravings INTERNATIONAL **$$$**
(Astley Hall; mains ₹300-500; ⊙11am-10.45pm) This international bistro connected to Hotel President features one of the more modern and diverse menus in Dehra Dun, including sandwiches, wraps, pastas, and a wide range of dinner entrées. Desserts include ice cream and apple pie.

Barista CAFE
(15A Rajpur Rd; ⊙8am-9pm) A popular modern cafe with an excellent bookshop in the back. Drinks and snacks cost ₹90 to ₹190.

Polo Bar BAR
(Rajpur Rd, 6 Astley Hall; ⊙11am-11pm) One of the more salubrious of Dehra Dun's many hotel bars, Polo Bar is at Hotel President and is newly renovated.

Shopping

★**Paltan Bazaar** MARKET
(⊙hours vary) The congested but relatively traffic-free area through Paltan Bazaar, running south from the clock tower, is a popular spot for an evening stroll. Here you can pick up everything from cheap clothing and souvenirs to camping and trekking gear. Most shops are open from about 10am to 9pm.

English Book Depot BOOKS
(☎0135-2655192; www.englishbookdepot.com; 15 Rajpur Rd; ⊙11am-1.30pm & 2.30-7pm) CDs, trekking books and maps are available, with the Barista cafe attached.

Natraj Booksellers BOOKS
(17 Rajpur Rd; ⊙10.30am-8pm Mon-Sat) Specialises in ecology, spirituality, local books and local author Ruskin Bond.

Information

The banks located on Rajpur Rd exchange travellers cheques and currency, and there are numerous ATMs that accept foreign credit cards.

GMVN Office (74/1 Rajpur Rd; ⊙10am-5pm Mon-Sat) For information on trekking in Garhwal, whether booking a GMVN trip or going independently, talk to BS Gusain on the ground floor of the tourism office, or call him on 9568006695.

Max Super Specialty Hospital (☎0135-6673000; Mussoorie Diversion Rd) The best hospital in Dehra Dun; it's north of the centre.

Getting There & Away

AIR

A few airlines (Jet Airways, SpiceJet and Air India) fly daily between Delhi and Dehra Dun's Jolly Grant Airport – about 20km east of the city on the Haridwar road – with fares starting at around ₹3200 each way. A taxi to/from the airport costs ₹600, or take the AC coach for ₹100.

BUS

Nearly all long-distance buses arrive and depart from the huge Inter State Bus Terminal (ISBT), 5km south of the city centre. To get there take a local bus (₹5), *vikram* 5 (₹10) or an autorickshaw (₹150). A few buses to Mussoorie leave from here but most depart from the **Mussoorie bus stand** (₹56, 1½ hours, half-hourly between 6am and 8pm) next to the train station. Some head to Mussoorie's Picture Palace bus stand while others go to Mussoorie's Library bus stand, across town. There are also buses from the Mussoorie bus stand to Barkot – for Yamnotri – (₹220, five hours, 5.30am and noon); Purola – for Har-ki-Dun – (₹230, seven hours, 6.30am, 9am and 1.30pm); Uttarkashi (₹255, seven hours, 5.30am) and Joshimath (₹480, 12 hours, 5.30am).

Private buses to Joshimath (₹400, 12 hours, 7am) and Uttarkashi (₹280, eight hours, 7am, 9am and 1.30pm) leave from the **Parade Ground bus stand**, where you can show up and get your ticket on the bus. If you want to secure seats in advance, go to the ticket office at the **Chunabata Bus Stand**, on Raipur Rd, a day early.

TAXI

A full taxi to Mussoorie costs ₹1060, while a share taxi should cost ₹180 per person; both can be found in front of the train station at the **taxi stand**. Taxis charge ₹1410 to Haridwar or Lakshman Jhula in Rishikesh, and ₹910 to Jolly Grant Airport.

TRAIN

Dehra Dun is well connected by train to Delhi, and there are a handful of services to Lucknow, Varanasi, Chennai (Madras) and Kolkata (Calcutta). Of the multiple daily trains from Dehra Dun to Delhi, the best are the expresses: Shatabdi (train 12018; chair/executive ₹885/1405; six hours; 5pm); Janshatabdi (train 12056; 2nd class/chair ₹160/520; six hours; 5.10am); and Nanda Devi Express (train 12206; 3AC/2AC/1st class ₹590/825/1375; six hours; 11.30pm).

The overnight Dehradun–Amritsar Express (train 14631; sleeper/3A class ₹270/730; 13 hours) to Amritsar departs nightly at 7pm.

Getting Around

Hundreds of eight-seater *vikrams* (₹5 to ₹10 per trip) race along five fixed routes (look at the front for the number). Most useful is *vikram* 5, which runs between the ISBT stand, the train station and Rajpur Rd, and as far south as the Tibetan colony at Clement Town. *Vikram* 1 runs up and down Rajpur Rd above Gandhi Park, and also to Harthibarkala (check with the driver to see which route he's on). Autorickshaws cost ₹30 for a short distance, ₹150 from ISBT to the city centre or ₹180 per hour for touring around the city.

MUSSOORIE

☎0135 / POP 30,200 / ELEV 2000M

Perched on a ridge 2km high, the 'Queen of Hill Stations' vies with Nainital as Uttarakhand's favourite holiday destination. When the mist clears, views of the green Doon Valley and the distant white-capped Himalayan peaks are superb, and in the hot months the cooler temperatures and fresh mountain air make a welcome break from the plains below.

Established by the British in 1823, Mussoorie became hugely popular with the Raj set. The ghosts of that era linger on in the architecture of the churches, libraries, hotels and summer palaces. The town is swamped with visitors between May and July, when it can seem like a tacky holiday camp for families and honeymooners, but at other times

BUSES FROM DEHRA DUN

The following buses depart from the Inter State Bus Terminal (ISBT).

DESTINATION	FARE (₹)	DURATION (HR)	DEPARTURES
Chandigarh	230	6	hourly 4am-10pm
Delhi (AC/Volvo)	538/750 ordinary/AC	7	frequent
Delhi (ordinary)	270	7	hourly 4am-10pm
Dharamsala	576	14	5pm
Haldwani (for Nainital & Almora)	320	10	hourly
Haridwar	68	2	half-hourly
Manali	500	14	6.45am, 3pm, 10.15pm
Ramnagar	300	7	7 daily
Rishikesh	51	1½	half-hourly
Shimla	440	10	5 daily

Mussoorie

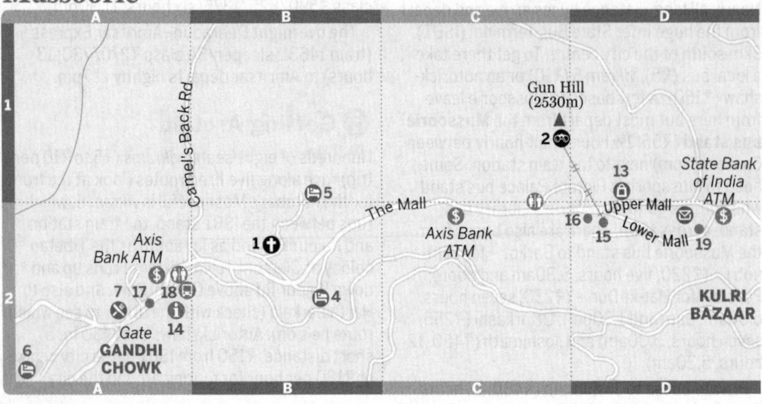

Mussoorie

Sights
1 Christ Church B2
2 Gun Hill C1

Activities, Courses & Tours
Trek Himalaya .... (see 13)

Sleeping
3 Hotel Broadway E1
4 Hotel Padmini Nivas B2
5 Kasmanda Palace Hotel B1
6 Savoy A2

Eating
7 Imperial Square A2
8 Lovely Omelette Centre E1
9 Neelam E1
10 Urban Turban E1

Shopping
11 Star Walking Stick Mfg F1
12 Vinod Kumar F1
13 Wildcraft D1

Information
14 GMVN Booth A2
Trek Himalaya .... (see 13)

Transport
15 Cable Car D2
16 Cycle-Rickshaw Stand D2
17 Cycle-Rickshaw Stand A2
18 Library Bus Stand A2
19 Northern Railway Booking Agency D2
20 Picture Palace Bus Stand F2
Taxi Stand .... (see 18)
Taxi Stand .... (see 20)

many of the 300 hotels have vacancies and their prices drop dramatically. During monsoon, the town is often shrouded in clouds.

Central Mussoorie consists of two developed areas: Gandhi Chowk (also called Library Bazaar) at the western end, and the livelier Kulri Bazaar and Picture Palace at the eastern end, linked by the 2km Mall, which is still dominated by pedestrians but has sadly seen a notable increase in vehicle traffic and noise. Beyond Kulri Bazaar a narrow road leads 1.5km to the atmospheric Landour Bazaar.

Sights & Activities

Gun Hill VIEWPOINT

From midway along the Mall, a **cable car** (return ₹100; ⊙10am-7pm) runs up to Gun Hill (2530m), which, on a clear day, has views of several big peaks. A steep path also winds up to the viewpoint. The most popular time to go up is an hour or so before sunset. There's a minicarnival atmosphere in high season, with kids' rides, food stalls, magic shops and honeymooners having their photos taken in Garhwali costumes.

Christ Church CHURCH

(off the Mall) Built in 1836 and featuring stained-glass windows, this is purported to be the oldest church in the Himalaya.

Trek Himalaya TREKKING

(☎9837258589; www.trekhimalaya.com; Upper Mall; ⊙11am-9pm) Trek Himalaya can organise one- to three-day treks in the Mussoorie area, as well as longer customised treks to Har-ki-Dun, Darwa Top and beyond. If weather or road conditions are bad, they don't go. Based out of the Wildcraft outdoor-gear store.

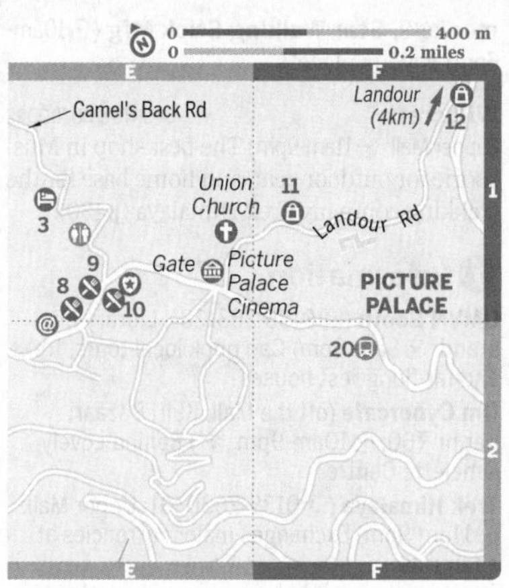

Walks

When the clouds don't get in the way, the walks around Mussoorie offer great views. **Camel's Back Rd** is a popular 3km promenade from Kulri Bazaar to Gandhi Chowk, and passes a rock formation that looks like a camel. There are a couple of good mountain viewpoints along the way, and you can ride a rickshaw (one way/return ₹200/350) along the trail if you start from the Gandhi Chowk end. An enjoyable, longer walk (5km one way) starts at the **Picture Palace Cinema** and goes past **Union Church** to Landour and the Sisters' Bazaar area.

West of Gandhi Chowk, a more demanding walk is to the **Jwalaji Temple** on Benog Hill (about 20km return) via Cloud's End Hotel. The route passes through thick forest and offers some fine views. Taking a taxi to Cloud's End (one way/return ₹600/1100) cuts the walk by more than half. A slightly shorter walk is to the abandoned **Everest House** (16km return), former residence of Sir George Everest, first surveyor-general of India and namesake of the world's highest mountain. You can also take a cycle-rickshaw (₹130) to Park Toll, cutting 5km off the distance.

Courses

Landour Language School LANGUAGE
(☎0135-2631487; www.landourlanguageschool.com; Landour; per hr group/private ₹350/575; ⊙Feb-Dec) One of India's leading schools for teaching conversational Hindi at beginner, intermediate and advanced levels. There's an enrolment fee of ₹750, and course books are an extra ₹2200.

Sleeping

Peak season is summer (May to July) when hotel prices shoot up to ridiculous heights. There's a midseason during the honeymoon period around October and November, and over Christmas and New Year. At other times you should be able to get a bargain.

Budget places are scarce – you'll find some dives near Picture Palace. But many hotels offer budget rates out of season.

Hotel Broadway HOTEL $
(☎0135-2632243; Camel's Back Rd, Kulri Bazaar; midseason d ₹650-1500) The best of the budget places by a country mile, this historic 1880s wooden hotel with colourful flowerboxes in the windows oozes character. It's in a quiet location but close to the Mall. Cheaper downstairs rooms could use a refresh, but upstairs rooms are nice; the best has lovely sunlit bay windows.

★**Kasmanda Palace Hotel** HERITAGE HOTEL $$$
(☎0135-2632424; www.welcomheritagehotels.in; midseason s/d from ₹7400/8500) Located off the Mall, this is Mussoorie's most romantic hotel. The white Romanesque castle was built in 1836 for a British officer and was bought by the Maharaja of Kasmanda in 1915. The red-carpeted hall has a superb staircase flanked by moth-eaten hunting trophies. All the rooms have charm but the wood-panelled and antique-filled Maharaja Room is the royal best.

Hotel Padmini Nivas HERITAGE HOTEL $$$
(☎0135-2631093; www.hotel-padmininivas.com; The Mall; midseason d ₹3900-5550, ste ₹6670-7520; @) Built in 1840 by a British colonel, this heritage hotel has real old-fashioned charm. Large rooms with quaint sunrooms are beautifully furnished; those in the main house are significantly nicer than those in the side building. The dining room, with its antique furniture, is an outstanding feature. The whole place is set on 2 hectares of landscaped gardens.

Savoy HERITAGE HOTEL $$$
(☎0135-2637000; www.fortunehotels/savoy.in; behind Gandhi Chowk; midseason r from ₹13,680) This famous Mussoorie hotel, built in 1902, has reopened after undergoing a seven-year renovation. Inside and out, the public spaces are magnificent, imparting a regal aesthetic with none of the rundown air that often infuses historic properties. The restaurant is as much an aesthetic as a culinary experience. Bedrooms, however, feel strangely generic.

Eating & Drinking

Most of Mussoorie's best spots to eat are at the Kulri Bazaar and Picture Palace end of town. True to the holiday feel there are lots of fast-food places, and most hotels have their own restaurants.

★Lovely Omelette Centre FAST FOOD $
(The Mall, Kulri Bazaar; mains ₹60-90; ⏰8am-10pm) Mussoorie's most famous eatery is also its smallest – a cubbyhole along the Mall that serves what many say are the best omelettes in India. The speciality is the cheese omelette, with chillies, onions and spices, served over toast, but the maestro at the frying pan will whip up a chocolate omelette on request. On weekends you might have to wait.

Urban Turban PUNJABI $$
(mains ₹190-400; ⏰11am-11pm) This new Punjabi bistro packs in the flavour, with perfectly spiced veg and nonveg options: the Turban Tikka Masala rocked our taste buds to a very happy place. Staff are exceptionally eager to please. If the music on the 1st floor is too loud for you, head up to the quieter 2nd floor. Windows overlook the street.

Neelam PUNJABI $$
(Kulri Bazaar; mains ₹160-570; ⏰9am-11pm) Around in one form or another since 1949, Neelam specialises in paneer dishes, and boasts a long list of chicken and lamb. In high season they break out the *tawa* – a heated metal plate, which slow-cooks meat to perfection. The affable manager, Sam, is exceptionally welcoming.

Imperial Square INTERNATIONAL $$$
(☎0135-2632632; Gandhi Chowk; mains ₹300-700; ⏰7.30am-11pm; 📶) With huge windows overlooking Gandhi Chowk, Imperial Square satisfies, but for a price. The menu emphasises Continental dishes, with long lists of platters and sizzlers, plus big toasted sandwiches. For breakfast you can even have waffles. The attached hotel has excellent rooms (from ₹5700) with valley views.

Shopping

Mussoorie has plenty of souvenir shops selling generic mementos. The most interesting store is the antiques and miscellany shop run by **Vinod Kumar** (Clock Tower, Landour Bazaar; ⏰10am-6pm), near the clock tower at the bottom of Landour Bazaar – a 10- to 15-minute walk from Picture Palace. And if you want something to protect yourself from monkeys, **Star Walking Stick Mfg** (⏰10am-6pm) is your place!

Wildcraft SPORTS & OUTDOORS
(Upper Mall; ⏰11am-9pm) The best shop in Mussoorie for outdoor gear, and home base for the trekking company Trek Himalaya (p430).

Information

GMVN Booth (☎0135-2631281; Library bus stand; ⏰8am-5pm) Can book local tours, treks and far-flung rest houses.

Om Cybercafe (off the Mall, Kulri Bazaar; per hr ₹60; ⏰10am-9pm; 📶) Behind Lovely Omelette Centre.

Trek Himalaya (☎0135-2630491; Upper Mall; ⏰11am-9pm) Exchanges major currencies at a fair rate.

Getting There & Away

BUS

Frequent buses head to Mussoorie (₹56, 1½ hours) from Dehra Dun's Mussoorie bus stand. Some go to the **Picture Palace bus stand** (☎0135-2632259) while others go to the **Library bus stand** (☎0135-2632258) at the other end of town – if you know where you're staying, it helps to be on the right bus. There's no direct transport from Mussoorie to Rishikesh or Haridwar – change at Dehra Dun.

To reach the mountain villages of western Garhwal, grab one of the buses passing through Gandhi Chowk. For Yamunotri, hop on a bus to Barkot (₹147, 3½ hours, 6.30am, 7.30am and 1.30pm), then transfer to another to Janki Chatti (₹65, three hours). A couple of buses go to Purola (₹158, five hours, 7.30am and 2.30pm). For Uttarkashi, take a bus to Barkot and transfer there, or head to the Tehri bus stand at Landour, hop a bus to Chamba, and transfer there.

TAXI

From taxi stands at both the **Picture Palace bus stand** and the **Library bus stand** you can hire taxis to Dehra Dun (₹1050) and Rishikesh (₹2250), or Uttarkashi (₹4550). A shared taxi to Dehra Dun should cost ₹180 per person.

TRAIN

The **Northern Railway Booking Agency** (☎0135-2632846; Lower Mall, Kulri Bazaar; ⏰8am-2pm Mon-Sat) books tickets for trains from Dehra Dun and Haridwar.

Getting Around

Central Mussoorie is very walkable – for a hill station, the Mall and Camel's Back Rd are surprisingly flat. Cycle-rickshaws along the Mall cost ₹50, but can only go between **Gandhi Chowk** and the **cable-car station**.

THE CHAR DHAM

High in the Garhwali Himalaya sit some of the holiest sites in the Hindu religion – Yamunotri, Gangotri, Kedarnath, and Badrinath – where temples mark the spiritual sources of four sacred rivers: the Yamuna, the Ganges, the Mandakini and the Alaknanda. Together, they make up one of the most important *yatra* (pilgrimage) circuits in all of India, known as the *char dham* (four seats). Every year between April and November, hundreds of thousands of worshippers brave hair-raising mountain roads and high-altitude trails to reach them.

Travelling to one or more of the *char dam* temples is a great way to get a feel for the religious pulse of the subcontinent, amid incredible alpine scenery. Numerous buses, share jeeps, porters, ponies – and now helicopters – are on hand for transport, and there's a well-established network of guesthouses, ashrams and government rest houses. As a result, getting to these temples is easy enough without hiring guides or carrying supplies, and Gangotri and Badrinath temples can be visited without even having to hike. Monsoons in summer, however, can produce dangerous conditions, triggering landslides that block roads and trails for days or weeks.

In June 2013, a torrential cloudburst produced an epic flood that swept away entire villages – and thousands of local people and pilgrims. The official death toll is around 6000, but locals insist the real number was closer to 50,000. Since then the people and government of Uttarakhand have worked to rebuild confidence in the area's safety, in an effort to revive the region's main economic engine. After a few years of decline, the *char dham* has surged back to life. Note that before visiting *char dham* sites, you are supposed to obtain a free photometric ID card (the government's way of tracking people in the event of another natural disaster), which are easily available in many cities and towns around the state. You may never be asked to show yours, but you should get one anyway.

Vegetarian food is available around all *char dham* sites.

Yamunotri

Yamunotri Temple (⌚late Apr-late Oct) is tucked in a tight gorge close to the source of the Yamuna, Hinduism's second-most sacred river after the Ganges. Yamunotri is the least visited and therefore least developed of the *char dham* sites, but once you get to the trailhead it's an easy trek in.

The 5km, 1½-hour hike begins at the tiny village of **Janki Chatti**. At Yamunotri Temple there are several **hot-spring pools** where you can take a dip, and others where pilgrims cook potatoes and rice as *prasad*. You'll find plenty of priests to help you make *puja* for a price. One kilometre beyond the temple, the Yamuna River spills from a frozen lake of ice and glaciers on the **Kalinda Parvat mountain** at an altitude of 4421m, but this is a very tough climb that requires mountaineering skills.

Across the river from Janki Chatti is the friendly village of **Kharsali**, which is worth a stroll if you have the time.

Accommodation is available at basic guesthouses or at the GMVN tourist lodges in Janki Chatti and Hanuman Chatti.

During peak *yatra* season (May to June), buses run from Dehra Dun, Mussoorie and Rishikesh to Janki Chatti, but the most frequent transport services originate in Barkot. Buses (₹65, three hours) depart Barkot for Janki Chatti at 9am, 1pm and 3pm; they make return runs to Barkot at 6am, 8.30am and 2pm. You can find sporadic share jeeps making the same runs (₹80, 2½ hours). A full taxi costs about ₹2000 each way.

Gangotri & Gaumukh Glacier Trek

In a remote setting at an altitude of 3042m, **Gangotri Temple** (⌚late Apr-late Oct) is one of the holiest places in India. Near the source of the Ganges (known as the Bhagirathi until it reaches Devprayag), the shrine is dedicated to the origin of Hinduism's most sacred river. Nearby is the rock on which Shiva is said to have cushioned the impact of the water in his matted locks as it poured from the heavens, saving the earth from the destructive force of this great gift.

Erected by Gorkha commander Amar Singh Thapa in the 18th century, the temple – for a site of such significance – is surprisingly underwhelming. Unless you're a devout Hindu, to get a real sense of awe you'll probably have to trek from Gangotri to the true source of the river, at **Gaumukh**, 18km upstream. There, the water flows out of **Gangotri Glacier** beneath the soaring west face of **Bhagirathi Parvat** (6856m),

TREKKING THE HIMALAYA

There are many sublime trekking routes in Uttarakhand. For more information, contact GMVN (p428) in Dehra Dun or local trekking outfitters.

Har-ki-Dun Valley Trek

The wonderfully remote Har-ki-Dun Valley (3510m), within **Govind Wildlife Sanctuary & National Park** (Indian/foreigner up to 3 days ₹150/600, subsequent days ₹50/250), is a botanical paradise criss-crossed by glacial streams, surrounded by pristine forests and snowy peaks. You might be lucky enough to glimpse the elusive snow leopard above 3500m.

The three-day, 38km trail to Har-ki-Dun begins at Sankri (also called Saur), where the best place to stay is the new **Wild Orchid Inn** (☎9411500044; www.wildorchidin@gmail.com; Sankri; s/d ₹600/800). There are very basic GMVN tourist bungalows at Sankri and along the way in the villages of Taluka and Osla, but at the valley itself you have to stay in the Forest Department rest house or bring a tent. You can cut a day off the hike by taking a share jeep to Taluka and starting from there. A side trip to Jamdar Glacier takes another day. The trek can be busy during June and October.

A couple of reputable guides work out of Sankri – Chain Singh and Bhagat Singh – who run the Har Ki Dun Protection & Mountaineering Association (p426). In addition to outfitting trips to Har-ki-dun, they can take you to the unique villages of the Rupin and Supin Valleys. They also lead treks from Sankri to the Sangla (Baspa) Valley in Himachal Pradesh and along other beautiful routes. Make arrangements in advance by email if possible – these guys are busy!

To get to Sankri, take a direct bus from Gandhi Chowk in Mussoorie or from Dehra Dun's Mussoorie Bus Stand – or hop a series of buses and shared or private jeeps until you get there.

Kuari Pass Trek

Also known as the Curzon Trail (though Lord Curzon's party abandoned its attempt on the pass following an attack of wild bees), the trek over the Kuari Pass (3640m) was popular in the Raj era. It's still one of Uttarakhand's finest and most accessible treks, affording breathtaking views of the snow-clad peaks around Nanda Devi – India's second-highest mountain, at 7816m – while passing through the outer sanctuary of Nanda Devi Sanctuary. The trailhead is at Auli (p438) and the 75km trek to Ghat past lakes, waterfalls, forests, meadows and small villages takes five days, though it's possible to do a shorter version that finishes

with the peak of **Shivling** (the 6543m 'Indian Matterhorn') towering to the south.

Don't be daunted by the trek – the trail rises gradually and is completely solid. Four to six hours (14km) up the trail, at Bhojbasa (3790m), there's a **GMVN Tourist Bungalow** (Bhojbasa; dm ₹320) and other basic lodging; Gaumukh is 4km (1½ hours) past that. On clear days, the best time to visit the source is early to mid-afternoon, when it's out of the shadows. Porters (₹1000 each way) and horses (one way/return ₹1700/2500) can be hired in Gangotri. More ambitious hikers with camping gear often continue to the gorgeous meadow at **Tapovan**, 6km beyond Gaumukh.

Before trekking to Gaumukh, you must first get a permit, since access is limited to 150 people per day. This can be obtained from the **District Forest Office** (☎01377-225693; ⏲10am-5pm Mon-Sat, closed 2nd Sat of month), 3km north of the Uttarkashi bus stand, or from the satellite office above the bus stand at Gangotri, which is open every day from 6am to 2pm. At both places, you'll need to bring a copy of your passport ID page and visa. The permit is valid for two days and costs ₹150/600 per Indian/foreigner (then ₹50/250 for each extra day).

Gangotri village has plenty of guesthouses, ashrams and *dharamsalas* charging ₹300 or less per room. When hungry, follow the Indian families to the **Hotel Gangaputra Restaurant** (mains ₹70-150; ⏲7am-11pm), which is busy for a good reason.

Bus service to Gangotri is sporadic. The best way to get there is to take a shared jeep (₹200) or full taxi (one way/return ₹3000/4000) from Uttarkashi, though taxis can also be hired from Rishikesh or Haridwar.

in Tapovan in three days. A tent, guide, permit and your own food supplies are necessary, all of which can be organised easily in Joshimath.

Milam Glacier Trek

This challenging eight-day, 118km trek to the massive Milam Glacier (3450m) is reached along an ancient trade route to Tibet that was closed in 1962 following the war between India and China. It passes through magnificent rugged country to the east of Nanda Devi (7816m) and along the sometimes spectacular gorges of the river, Gori Ganga. You can also take a popular but tough side trip to Nanda Devi East base camp, adding another 32km or three days.

Free permits (passport required) are available from the District Magistrate in Munsyari (p451). You will also need a tent and your own food supplies, as villages on the route may be deserted. KMVN organises all-inclusive eight-day treks (from ₹10,500). These are best arranged at KMVN Parvat Tours (p444) in Nainital but the KMVN Rest House in Munsyari should be able to set you up too.

The base for this excursion is the spectacularly located village of Munsyari, where a guide, cook and porters can be hired and package treks can be arranged through **Nanda Devi Tour N Trek** (☎05961-222015, 9411130330; beerubugyal@yahoo.co.in).

Less travelled but equally (or more) stunning treks include the Begini/Dunagiri route north of Joshimath and the Panchachuli East/Chota Kailash route, north of Dharchula.

Pindari Glacier Trek

This six-day, 94km trek passes through truly virgin country that's inhabited by only a few shepherds. It offers wonderful views of Nanda Kot (6860m) and Nanda Khat (6611m) on the southern rim of Nanda Devi Sanctuary. The 3km-long, 365m-wide Pindari Glacier is at 3353m, so take it easy to avoid altitude sickness. Permits aren't needed but bring your passport.

The trek begins and finishes at Loharket (1700m), a village 36km north of Bageshwar. Guides and porters can be organised easily there, or in the preceding village of Song (1400m), or you can organise package treks through companies in Almora. KMVN operates all-inclusive eight-day treks starting from Song for ₹7000 per person, staying at government rest houses. KMVN dorms (mattresses on the floor for ₹200), basic guesthouses or *dhaba* huts (₹100 to ₹300) are dotted along the route, and food is available. KMVN tours are best arranged through KVMN Parvat Tours (p444) in Nainital.

Buses (₹50, two hours) or share jeeps (₹60, 1½ hours) run between Song and Bageshwar. Private taxis between Bageshwar and Song/Loharket cost ₹3500/4000.

Kedarnath

In the epic Mahabharata, after the Pandavas defeated the Dhartarashtras, they sought forgiveness for killing their own family members, as their enemies also happened to be their cousins. Shiva refused them, but the Pandavas were so relentless in their quest for absolution that Shiva, in the form of a bull, dove into the ground to elude them. He left his hump behind at Kedarnath, below the source of the sacred Mandakini River, where a magnificent stone temple – built in the 8th century by Guru Shankara – marks the spot. (Other portions of Shiva's bull-form body are worshipped at the other four *panch kedar* shrines, which take some effort to reach but can be visited: the arms at Tungnath, the face at Rudranath, the navel at Madmaheshwar and the hair at Kalpeshwar.)

Tucked at the base of 6970m peaks, 18km from the nearest road, Kedarnath is in the most dramatic location of any of the *char dham* temples. The *puja* offered inside, especially around the stone 'hump', is fervent and can be quite intense. The site is so auspicious that pilgrims used to throw themselves from one of the cliffs behind the temple in the hope of instantly attaining moksha (liberation).

Kedarnath was at the epicentre of the devastating flood of 2013. Thousands of people – pilgrims and locals, porters and horse guides, among others – perished here. Much of the village around the temple was destroyed by the raging waters and the huge rocks that washed down from the surrounding slopes. Today, nearly as much reverence is paid to a massive boulder that sits behind the temple – which, incredibly, shielded it from the worst of the onslaught and saved it from collapse – as to the temple itself.

Kedarnath is slowly recovering, and the experience of visiting evolves year by year. Getting there involves an 18km uphill trek from the village of Gaurikund, which was an uninhabitable mess after the flood but has been revived into a scaled-down version of its formerly bustling self. Prior to hitting the trail, however, you must get a free photometric ID card in Sonprayag, a village 5km before Gaurikund, where all buses and taxis end their runs. From Sonprayag, shared jeeps (₹20) make the trip to the trailhead.

You'll walk alongside pilgrims on a stone-paved pathway etched into the steep slopes of canyon cut by the Mandakini, following the river upstream. On a clear day, you'll see the skyscraping, snow-covered summits that tower over the temple long before you reach it. In Kedarnath village, life is springing up around the wreckage from the flood, with a few shops, restaurants and hotels beginning to emerge between giant rocks and pulverised buildings. Currently, the best place to stay in Kedarnath is the Himachal House, which is a one-minute walk from the temple.

Basic accommodation is also available in Sonprayag and Gaurikund (rooms from ₹200 to ₹400) – Gaurikund is much quieter and more atmospheric, making it a better place to stay before or after trekking. A handful of better hotels can be found about 2km before Sonprayag, at Sitapur.

The main transit hub for the area is Guptkashi, from where you can take a shared/private jeep (₹80/1000) to Sonprayag. Alternatively, take a GMOU bus to Sonprayag from Rishikesh or Haridwar. From Sonprayag, morning buses run to Rishikesh (₹310, seven hours), Haridwar (₹340, eight hours), and Dehra Dun (₹350, nine hours). If you get stuck in Guptkashi, the **New Viswanath Hotel** (9720895992; Guptkashi Bus Stand; r from ₹500), at the bus stand, is a good choice.

Going to or from Kedarnath by helicopter is becoming an increasingly popular option for Indians, and a handful of operators have begun flying the route. It costs ₹3000 to ₹3500 to fly up, ₹2500 to ₹3000 to fly down, and ₹6000 to ₹6500 round trip. Several companies fly out of – and have offices in – Phata, between Guptkashi and Sonprayag, while **Himalayan Heli Services** (7895479452; www.himalayanheli.com; Guptkashi-Sonprayag Rd) is based in nearby Sersi. All companies have offices at the Kedarnath helipad. Flights typically end by early afternoon. Note that scientists are concerned about the impact of frequent helicopter flights on wildlife in the Kedarnath Wildlife Sanctuary, which surrounds the area.

Badrinath & Mana Village

01381 / POP 850 / ELEV 3133M

Basking in a superb setting in the shadow of snow-topped Nilkantha, **Badrinath Temple** (late Apr-Nov) appears almost lost in the tatty village that surrounds it. Sacred to Lord Vishnu, this vividly painted temple is the most easily accessible and popular of the *char dham* temples. It was founded by Guru Shankara in the 8th century, but the current structure is much more recent.

A scenic 3km walk beyond Badrinath along the Alaknanda River (cross over to the temple side to pick up the path), past fields divided by dry-stone walls, leads to tiny but charismatic **Mana Village**; you can also take a taxi there for ₹250. The village is crammed with stone laneways and traditional houses, some with slate walls and roofs while others are wooden with cute balconies. You can wander around and watch the villagers at work and play. They migrate to somewhere warmer and less remote – usually Joshimath – between November and April.

Just outside Mana village in a small cave is the tiny, 5000-year-old **Vyas Temple**. Nearby is **Bhima's Rock**, a natural rock arch over a river that is said to have been made by Bhima, strongest of the Pandava brothers, whose tale is told in the Mahabharata. The 5km hike along the Alaknanda to the 145m **Vasudhara Waterfall** has a great reward-to-effort ratio, with views up the valley of the Badrinath massif jutting skywards like a giant fang.

Sleeping & Eating

Badrinath can easily be visited in a day from Joshimath if you get an early start, but it's worth staying if you also want to see Mana Village and do any hiking. There is a slew of grim budget guesthouses lining the main road into town (₹400 to ₹600 per room); they can be loud with pilgrims.

Hotel Urvashi HOTEL $

(9411565459; r ₹800) One of the few decent budget accommodations in Badrinath, with friendly staff.

Badriville Resort BUNGALOW $$$

(9412418725; www.badrivilleresort.in; r from ₹3000) Our favourite hotel in Badrinath,

Badriville Resort has clean and comfortable individual bungalow rooms, with the best beds in town. Most have patios with full valley views. The staff are helpful and friendly, and the restaurant serves up delicious fresh food. It's set back about 100m from the main road, just as you enter Badrinath. Major discounts available when slow.

Hotel Snow Crest HOTEL $$$

(☎9412082465; www.snowcrest.co.in; r ₹2500-4000) The best standard hotel in Badrinath. While overpriced, it's modern and passably clean, and rooms have heaters, TVs and geysers. Prices rise in May and June.

Getting There & Away

From the large bus station at the entrance to Badrinath, GMOU buses run to Haridwar (₹455) via Rishikesh (₹420) at 5.30am, 7am, and 8am, but double-check departure times, as these may change. For Joshimath or Govindghat (for Valley of Flowers), try to grab a shared jeep at around 7am or earlier.

UTTARKASHI

☎01374 / POP 17,500 / ELEV 1158M

Uttarkashi, 155km from Rishikesh and the largest town in northern Garhwal, is a major stop on the road to Gangotri Temple and the Gaumukh Glacier trek. The main bazaar is worth a wander and has all the supplies you might need. A number of outfitters can arrange treks in the region, including to Tapovan (beyond Gangotri/Gaumukh).

The town is probably best known for the Nehru Institute of Mountaineering (p437), which trains many of the guides running trekking and mountaineering outfits in India. The centre is across the river from the main market and has a museum and outdoor climbing wall. Basic and advanced mountaineering and adventure courses are open to all – check the website for details and admission information.

Uttarkashi also hosts the **Makar Sankranti festival** (Jan).

Nehru Institute of Mountaineering OUTDOORS

(☎01374-222123; www.nimindia.net; 10am-5pm) Offers highly regarded mountaineering courses, guide training and trekking-guide services throughout the Garhwal Himalaya and beyond.

Sleeping & Eating

Monal Guest House HOTEL $

(☎01374-222270; www.monaluttarkashi.com; Kot Bungalow Rd; r ₹700-2300; @) This hillside hotel feels like a large, comfortable house, and has clean, airy rooms, a big-windowed restaurant and peaceful garden setting. Wing A has a more homely feel than Wing B. It's off the Gangotri road 3km north of town, about 100m from the office that issues permits to Gamukh.

Hotel Govind Palace HOTEL $

(☎01374-223815, 9411522058; near bus stand; r from ₹500) One of the best-value choices if you have to catch an early morning bus. It has good beds, hot showers and TVs, and the manager GS Bhandari is superhelpful. It also has one of the better restaurants in town.

Getting There & Away

To get to Gangotri, take a shared jeep/full taxi (₹200/3000, five hours). Buses leave for Rishikesh (₹230, seven hours) at least every hour between 5am and 2pm. Buses go to Haridwar (₹280, eight hours) at 6.45am and 12.30pm, and to Dehra Dun (₹200, nine hours) at 6am, 7.30am and noon. Buses to Srinagar (₹210, eight hours) leave at 5.30am, 8am and 8.30am, and those to Barkot (₹120, five hours) run frequently until 3pm. In summer, a 7.45am bus runs directly to Janki Chatti (₹190, nine hours) for Yamunotri temple. Seats may sell out on some routes, so it's a good idea to buy tickets a day in advance.

Full taxis to Rishikesh cost ₹4500.

JOSHIMATH

☎01389 / POP 13,860 / ELEV 1875M

As the gateway to Badrinath Temple and Hem Kund, Joshimath sees a steady stream of Hindu and Sikh pilgrims from May to October. And as the base for the Valley of Flowers and Kuari Pass treks, and Auli ski resort, it attracts adventure travellers year-round.

Reached from Rishikesh by a serpentine mountain road, Joshimath is a thoroughly utilitarian two-street town with erratic power supply and limited places to eat. Although the big mountain views are lost from the town itself, it's only a short cable-car ride (p439) from here to Auli, which has magnificent vistas of Nanda Devi.

Activities

To trek the Kuari Pass and other routes in Nanda Devi Sanctuary, you need a permit and a registered guide. There are excellent operators in town who can organise everything, including further-flung and intensely adventurous multiday expeditions.

★ **Himalayan Snow Runner** OUTDOORS
(☎9756813236, 9412082247; www.himalayansnowrunner.com) Highly recommended outfit for trekking (from around ₹3000 per person per day), skiing and adventure activities, with camping gear provided. The owner, Ajay, can customise unique trekking routes, takes cultural tours to Bhotia and Garhwali villages, and runs a guesthouse in his home in Mawari village, 5km from Joshimath (rooms ₹1550 to ₹4550).

Adventure Trekking OUTDOORS
(☎9837937948; www.adventuretrekking.org; opposite Hotel Mount View Joshimath) Treks of anything from two to 10 days can be arranged here for around US$50 per person per day (with more than one person), as well as white-water rafting, skiing and peak ascents. The helpful owner, Santosh, runs a guesthouse on the way up to Auli (rooms ₹1000 to ₹2000).

Eskimo Adventures OUTDOORS
(☎9756835647; www.eskimoadventure.com) Offers treks and rock-climbing expeditions from about ₹3000 per day, equipment rental (for trekking and skiing), and white-water rafting trips on the Ganges.

Sleeping & Eating

Hotel New Kamal HOTEL $
(☎9411577880; Main Market; r ₹500) Small and clean with TVs and bucket hot water; though the beds are hard, this is one of the better cheapies in Joshimath.

Malari Inn HOTEL $$
(☎01389-222257; www.hotel-malari-inn.weebly.com; Main Market; r ₹1800-3500) This is the best place in Joshimath. Standard rooms are basic but spacious and clean; you pay more for more amenities, a fatter mattress and a balcony with valley views. All rooms have geysers. Discounts are offered outside peak season (May through to September).

Hotel Mount View Annexy HOTEL $$
(☎9634255572; r ₹1000) Mount View Annexy is a short walk down the main road from where the buses stop. The rooms at this standard hotel deliver what many others in Joshimath lack: reliable cleanliness, soft mattresses, flat-screen TVs, 24-hour hot water, and a sense of being well maintained.

Auli D's Food Plaza MULTICUISINE $$
(Main Market; mains ₹90-450; ⏲7am-10pm) Featuring a full menu of Indian, Chinese and Continental food, including veg and nonveg choices, this 1st-floor restaurant has plastic tablecloths and covered seats, and feels like a banquet hall.

Information

GMVN Tourist Office (☎01389-222181; ⏲10am-5pm Mon-Sat) Located just north of the town (follow the Tourist Rest House sign off Upper Bazaar Rd).

Getting There & Away

Although the main road up to Joshimath is maintained by the Indian army, and a hydroelectric plant on the way to Badrinath has improved that road, the area around Joshimath is inevitably prone to landslides, particularly in the rainy season from mid-June to mid-September.

The best way to get to Badrinath/Govindghat (for Valley of Flowers and Hem Kund) is by shared jeep (₹100/50), leaving from the Badrinath taxi stand at the far end of Upper Bazaar Rd. Hiring the whole jeep costs ₹1000. A few buses (₹65) leave throughout the day from the same place.

Buses run from Joshimath to Rishikesh (₹360, 10 hours) and Haridwar (₹400, 11½ hours), at 4am, 4.30am, 6am and 7am, departing from the tiny **GMOU booth** (Upper Bazaar Rd; ⏲3am-7pm), where you can also book tickets. From the main jeep stand, private buses leave occasionally for Chamoli (₹80, two hours) and Karanprayag (₹130, four hours), with some continuing to Rishikesh.

To get to the eastern Kumaon region, take any bus or shared taxi to Chamoli then transfer onward to Karanprayag, from where a series of local buses and share jeeps can take you along the beautiful road towards Kausani, Bageshwar and Almora. You may have to change several times along the way. Transport winds down in the late afternoon, so get an early start.

Full taxis are best hired through a travel agency or hotel, as there is no taxi stand for these. Taking one to Rishikesh would cost about ₹6000.

AROUND JOSHIMATH

Auli

☎01389 / POP 300 / ELEV 3048M

Rising above Joshimath, 14km by road – and only 4km by the gondola-style cable car – Auli is India's premier ski resort. But you don't have to visit in winter to enjoy the awesome views of Nanda Devi (India's second-highest peak) from the top of the cable-car station.

As a ski resort, Auli is hardly spectacular, with gentle 5km-long slopes, one 500m rope tow (₹100 per trip) that runs beside the main slope, and an 800m chairlift (₹200) that connects the upper and lower slopes. The snow is consistently good, though, and the setting is superb. The season runs from January to March, and equipment hire and instruction can be arranged here or in Joshimath.

The state-of-the-art **cable car** (return ₹750; ⏲ every 20min 8am-5pm), India's longest, links Joshimath to the upper slopes above Auli. There's a cafe, of sorts, at the top, serving hot chai and tomato soup.

A handful of hotels are spread around the ski resort. The **Clifftop Club** (☎ 7417936606; www.clifftopclubauli.com; studio ₹8500, ste ₹16,000) wouldn't look out of place in the Swiss Alps. Meals and all-inclusive ski packages, including equipment, are available.

If on a tighter budget, stay at the surprisingly good **GMVN Tourist Rest House** (☎ 01389-223208; www.gmvnl.in; incl breakfast dm ₹280, r ₹1650-4500) at the start of the chairlift. **Devi Darshan** (☎ 9719316777; www.mountainshepherds.com; r incl meals from ₹4000) has a restaurant and common room with full-on Nanda Devi views, with dark bedrooms.

VALLEY OF FLOWERS & HEM KUND

British mountaineer Frank Smythe stumbled upon the Valley of Flowers in 1931. The *bugyals* (high-altitude meadows) of tall wildflowers are a glorious sight on a sunny day, rippling in the breeze, and framed by mighty 6000m mountains that have glaciers and snow decorating their peaks all year.

The 300 species of flowers make this World Heritage Site a unique and valuable pharmaceutical resource. Unfortunately, most flowers bloom during the monsoon season in July and August, when the rains make access difficult and hazardous. There's a widespread misconception that the valley isn't worth visiting outside peak flower season, but even without its technicolour carpet it's still ridiculously beautiful. And it's more likely to be sunny.

Overnight stays aren't permitted in the Valley of Flowers or at the sacred lake of Hem Kund so you must stay in Ghangaria. This one-street village shuts down outside the pilgrimage season (1 June to 1 October or thereabouts).

To reach the 87-sq-km **Valley of Flowers National Park** (Indian/foreigner up to 3 days ₹150/600, subsequent days ₹50/250; ⏲ 7am-5pm Jun-Oct, last entry 2pm) first requires a full-day hike from **Govindghat** to the village of **Ghangaria** (also called Govinddham), which is just outside the park. The fabled valley begins 2km uphill from Ghangaria's ticket office and continues for another 5km. Tracks are easy to follow.

A tougher hike from Ghangaria involves joining hundreds of Sikh pilgrims toiling up to the 4300m **Hem Kund** (⏲ May-Oct), the sacred lake surrounded by seven peaks where Sikh Guru Gobind Singh is believed to have meditated in a previous life. Ponies (₹500) are available if you prefer to ride up

TUNGNATH & CHANDRISILLA

One of the best day hikes in Uttarakhand, the trail to **Tungnath Mandir** (3680m) and **Chandrisilla Peak** (4000m) features a sacred Panch Kedar temple and a stunning Himalayan panorama.

The trail starts at Chopta, a small village with no electricity, which is found on the winding road between Chamoli (south of Joshimath) and Kund (south of Gaurikund). A well-paved path switchbacks 3.5km uphill, gaining 750m in elevation, to Tungnath, the highest Shiva temple in the world. A dirt trail continues 1.5km further to the top of Chandrisilla. From the summit, the Garhwali and Kumaoni Himalaya stretch out before you, with awesome vistas of major mountains including Nanda Devi, Trishul and the Kedarnath group. Start early before the clouds move in, or head up in the afternoon, stay at one of the spartan guesthouses around Tungnath and hit Chandrisilla for sunrise. There's basic accommodation in Chopta: **Hotel Neelkanth** (☎ 7500139051; www.neelkanthcampchopta.in; r from ₹600) has the best rooms, but **Hotel Rajkamal** (r ₹400) is the friendliest.

The drive from Chamoli to Chopta is a worthwhile diversion in itself, as it traverses steeply terraced hillsides dotted with rural villages before entering a lushly forested musk-deer sanctuary pierced by dramatic cliffs.

the 6km zigzag trail. Remarkably, the climb is often undertaken by small children and people with weak legs or lungs – they ride up in a wicker chair hauled on the back of a *kandi* man or reclining in a *dandi* (litter), carried on the shoulders of four men like the royalty of old.

The trek to Ghangaria is a scenic but strenuous 14km uphill from Govindghat, which takes five to seven hours – though recent 'improvements' to the route have seen the paving of the first 3km into a driveable road, which many people choose to cover in a shared jeep (₹30). You can also ease the hike and help the local economy by hiring a pony (₹800) or a porter (₹800) at the bridge over the Alaknanda River, or at the end of the paved road. Top tip: if you have the time, sleep at Badrinath the night before you trek to Ghangaria to acclimatise your body to the altitude; it'll make the hike easier.

Sleeping & Eating

In Ghangaria, water and electricity supplies are erratic. It can get cold, so bring warm layers. All the accommodation here is relatively spartan, and none has heat, but they do have heaps of blankets.

At Govindghat, there are several hotels with rooms for around ₹300, but the **Hotel Bhagat** (☎9412936360; www.hotelbhagat.com; Badrinath Rd; r ₹2100-3000), up on the main road between Joshimath and Badrinath, has very clean rooms with river views, geysers and meals.

You don't need to carry food, as *dhabas* and drink stalls serve the army of pilgrims heading to Hem Kund, and there are plenty of restaurants in Ghangaria.

Hotel Kuber Annex HOTEL **$**
(Ghangaria; r ₹400-800) The super-deluxe rooms here are marginally better than any other options in Ghangaria.

Getting There & Away

All buses and share jeeps between Joshimath and Badrinath pass by Govindghat, so you can easily find transport travelling in either direction, though this trickles off later in the day and stops dead at night.

If you want to see the Valley of Flowers but are daunted by the trek, it's possible to get a helicopter from Govindghat to Ghangaria with **Deccan Air** (☎9412051036; www.deccanair.com; one way/return ₹3500/7000); the booking office is along the Joshimath–Badrinath road, just above Govindghat.

CORBETT TIGER RESERVE

☎05947 / ELEV 400-1210M

World-renowned **Corbett Tiger Reserve** (www.corbetttigerreserve.in; ⏲15 Nov-15 Jun, Jhirna & Dhela zones open year-round) was established in 1936 as India's first national park, and covers 1318 sq km of wild forests. It's named for legendary British hunter Jim Corbett (1875–1955), who brought this region international fame with his book *The Man-Eaters of Kumaon*. Greatly revered by local people for killing tigers that preyed on people, Corbett eventually shot more wildlife with his camera than with his gun and became a prominent voice for conservation.

Though tiger attacks are on the rise in villages around Corbett Tiger Reserve, tiger sightings on safaris take some luck, as the 230 or so striped cats that roam the reserve are neither baited nor tracked. Your best chance of spotting one is late in the season (April to mid-June), when the forest cover is low and animals come out in search of water.

Notwithstanding tiger sightings, few serious wildlife enthusiasts will leave disappointed, as the park has a variety of wildlife and birdlife in grassland, sal forest and river habitats, and a beautiful location in the foothills of the Himalaya on the Ramganga River. Commonly seen wildlife include wild elephants (200 to 300 live in the reserve), sloth bears, langur monkeys, rhesus macaques, peacocks, romps of otters and several types of deer including chital (spotted deer), sambars, hog deer and barking deer. You might also see leopards, mugger crocodiles, gharials, monitor lizards, wild boars and jackals. The Ramganga Reservoir attracts large numbers of migrating birds, especially from mid-December to the end of March, and more than 600 species have been spotted here.

Of Corbett's six zones – Bijrani, Dhikala, Dhela, Durga Devi, Jhirna and Sonanadi – Dhikala is the highlight of the park, 49km northwest of Ramnagar and deep inside the reserve. This is the designated core area, where the highest concentration of the animals you probably hope to see are found. It's open from 15 November to 15 June and only to overnight guests, or as part of a one-day tour available through the park's **reception centre** (☎05947-251489; Ranikhet Rd; ⏲6am-4pm), almost opposite Ramnagar's bus stand.

Jhirna and Dhela, in the southern part of the reserve, are the only zones that remain open all year, but your chances of seeing serious megafauna in those areas are iffy – at least for now. Dhela, which opened to the public in December 2014, may eventually include a large fenced section meant to house rescued tigers, which should be fairly easy to spot. There are also plans to create two nature trails in Dhela; we're told that these will mainly be for birdwatching, and that the trails will be protected by fences, so you don't have to worry about becoming tiger prey. Note that in some years, depending on conditions, the other four zones may open in October, but the only way to find out is to check online.

Be sure to bring binoculars (you can hire them at park gates) and plenty of mosquito repellent and mineral water.

Visiting the Reserve

The reception centre in Ramnagar runs daily **bus tours** (☎05947-251489; Ranikhet Rd; Indian/foreigner ₹1125/2250; ⊙6am & noon) to Dhikala – called Canter Safaris – at 6am and noon.

Jeeps can be hired at the reception centre in Ramnagar, or through your accommodation or a tour agency. Jeep owners have formed a union, so in theory rates are fixed (on a per-jeep basis, carrying up to six people). Half-day safaris (leaving in the morning and afternoon) should cost ₹1600 to Bijrani, ₹1750 to Jhirna, ₹1750 to Dhela and ₹2350 to Durga Devi – not including the entry fees for you and your guide. Full-day safaris cost double. Overnight excursions to Dhikala cost ₹5200, while those to Sonanadi run ₹7000. Check current prices at the reception centre and at your hotel before hiring a jeep. Safaris offered by Karan Singh, who runs Karan's Corbett Motel (p442), are highly recommended.

Two-hour **elephant rides** (Indian/foreigner ₹300/1000; ⊙6am & 4pm) are available only at Dhikala and Bijrani on a first-come, first-served basis. However, animal welfare groups warn that carrying passengers can cause spinal damage to elephants.

Sleeping & Eating

For serious wildlife-viewing, Dhikala – deep inside the reserve – is the prime place to stay, though prices for foreigners are exorbitant. Book through the park's website (www.corbettonline.uk.gov.in) at least one month in advance. The town of Ramnagar has budget accommodation, while upmarket resorts are strung out along the road skirting the eastern side of the park between Dhikuli and Dhangarhi Gate.

Dhikala

Easily the cheapest lodgings in the park are at **Log Huts** (☎05947-251489, 9759363344; www.corbettonline.uk.gov.in; dm Indian/foreigner

CORBETT PERMITS

Corbett Tiger Reserve controls tourist impact by limiting the number of vehicles into each zone each day. You must book your entry permit in advance, via the park's website (www.corbettonline.uk.gov.in) or by signing up for a trip with a safari outfit. If you book online (fee ₹50), give your reservation confirmation to your driver, whether you hire one from the reservation centre or use a tour operator. Day trips can be booked 45 days in advance; if you can't plan ahead, you can probably still visit the park; safari operators will ask each other if anyone is running a jeep with open seats that you can fill. Overnight trips to Dhikala are best booked by a safari company.

For a day trip, the vehicle entry fee (not including passengers) costs ₹250/500 for Indians/foreigners; for an overnight jaunt, it's ₹500/1500. Then there's the visitor entry fee, which is about the craziest system we've seen in a while. Officially, the single-day fee (valid for four hours, available for every zone except Dhikala) is ₹100/450 per Indian/foreigner; three-day permits cost ₹200/900. But the park makes you pay visitor fees for every seat in the jeep, *even if they are empty*. Kindly, they imagine that unoccupied seats are filled by Indians, so jeep passengers will pay their own entry fees, plus ₹100 for the driver's entry, plus an extra ₹100 per seat for their invisible companions! On top of all of that, there's a ₹450 road tax.

How much does this all cost? Add up your jeep hire fee, vehicle entry fee, visitor entry fees, driver's entry fee and empty seat fees, road tax, and online booking fee...and that's your total. Taking a safari or hotel tour costs marginally more than arranging everything yourself, but since they provide expert guides fluent in English, they can be well worth the few extra rupees.

₹200/400), with 24 basic beds. **Tourist Hutments** (☎05947-251489, 9759363344; www.corbettonline.uk.gov.in; Indian/foreigner ₹1250/2500) offer the best-value accommodation in Dhikala and sleeps up to six people. Book via www.dhikalaforestlodge.in or www.corbettonline.uk.gov.in. Dhikala has a couple of restaurants serving vegetarian food. No alcohol is allowed in the park.

Accommodation at the **New Forest Rest House** (☎05947-251489, 9759363344; www.corbettonline.uk.gov.in; r Indian/foreigner ₹1250/2500), **Annexe** (☎05947-251489, 9759363344; r Indian/foreigner from ₹1000/2000) and the VIP **Old Forest Rest House** (☎9759363344, 05947-251489; www.corbettonline.uk.gov.in; r Indian ₹1500-2500, foreigner ₹3000-5000) can all be booked at the reception centre in Ramnagar.

Elsewhere in the Reserve

Most rest houses outside of Dhikala offer kitchen facilities but not restaurants, so check with your guide to see if you should bring your own food.

Bijrani Rest House LODGE $$
(☎05947-251489, 9759363344; www.corbettonline.uk.gov.in; s/d Indian ₹500/1250, foreigner ₹1000/2500) The first place in from Amdanda Gate at the Corbett Tiger Reserve; meals are available.

Khinnanauli Rest House BUNGALOW $$$
(☎9759363344, 05947-251489; /www.corbettonline.uk.gov.in; r Indian/foreigner ₹5000/12,000) VIP lodging near Dhikala, deep in the reserve.

Sarapduli Rest House HOTEL $$$
(☎05947-251489, 9759363344; www.corbettonline.uk.gov.in; r Indian/foreigner ₹2000/4000) Clean and simple rooms, set in an area with lots of wildlife, especially birds and crocodiles, but tigers and elephants too.

Gairal Rest House BUNGALOW $$$
(☎9759363344, 05947-251489; www.corbettonline.uk.gov.in; r Indian/foreigner from ₹1250/2500) On the Ramnagar River, accessed from Dhangarhi Gate; meals are available.

Ramnagar

A busy, unappealing town, Ramnagar has plenty of facilities, including internet cafes (₹30 per hour), ATMs (State Bank of India ATM at the train station and a Bank of Baroda ATM on Ranikhet Rd) and transport connections – mostly along Ranikhet Rd.

★**Karan's Corbett Motel** HOTEL $$
(☎9837468933; www.karanscorbettmotel.com; Manglar Rd; r ₹1000-1200; ❄) On the fringes of town, surrounded by gardens and mango trees, here the rooms are spacious and have terraces with tables and chairs. The owner, Karan Singh, is as knowledgable and helpful as you could ask for. Hands-down the best place to stay in Ramnagar (not to be confused with the Corbett Motel). Karan runs highly recommended jeep safaris in Corbett.

Hotel Corbett Kingdom HOTEL $$
(☎7500668883; www.corbettkingdom.com; Bhaghat Singh St; r from ₹2500; ❄📶) This straightforward hotel is a comfortable, well-kept option right in Ramnagar. Marble floors add a touch of class.

Delhi Darbar Restaurant INDIAN $
(Ranikhet Rd; mains ₹80-160; ⏲9am-11pm) The cleanest and quietest place to eat near the bus stand, with a typical Indian menu, plus pizza.

North of Ramnagar

A growing number of upmarket African-style safari resorts are strung along the Ramnagar–Ranikhet road that runs along the reserve's eastern boundary. Most are around a settlement called Dhikuli – not to be confused with Dhikala. When most of the reserve is closed (15 June to 15 November), discounts of up to 50% are offered. Most rates are for a room only, but most have packages that include meals and safaris. All places have resident naturalists, recreational facilities, restaurants and bars. Note that a substantial number of resorts in this area were put on notice for polluting the Kosi River.

★**Gateway Resort** RESORT $$$
(☎05947-284133; www.thegatewayhotels.com; r/cottage ₹15,000-16,500; ❄📶🏊) At the Taj Group's luxury offering, modern rooms and cottages are spread around a verdant garden. There's an outdoor pool and a full-service spa, but the real gem is the restaurant, whose outdoor terrace has picture-perfect views of the Kosi River. It's the best place on the resort strip.

Namah RESORT $$$
(☎05947-266666; www.namah.in; r ₹12,000-13,000, ste ₹20,000; 📶🏊) On the outside, this new resort looks and feels like a condo complex. Rooms, however, have personality, with two-toned walls and jungle-themed

artwork. The playground, open spaces, pool and rec room make this a good choice for families. Prices fluctuate greatly depending on demand.

Tiger Camp RESORT $$$

(☎05947-284101; www.habitathotels.com; Dhikuli; r/cottage ₹10,700/11,700; ❄📶) This mellow, good-value resort is nestled in a shady jungle-style garden by the Kosi River, 8km from Ramnagar. Cosy cottages are much better than the 'superior' rooms, with modern facilities. Nature walks and village tours are offered.

Getting There & Away

Buses run almost hourly from Ramnagar to Delhi (₹260, seven hours), Haridwar (₹200, six hours) and Dehra Dun (₹275, seven hours). Frequent buses run to Haldwani (₹64, two hours), from where you can connect to just about anywhere. For Nainital, take a UK Roadways bus to Haldwani and change there, or hop on a private bus that runs direct to Nainital (₹80) – several depart throughout the morning from outside the main bus stand.

Ramnagar train station is 1.5km south of the main reception centre. The nightly Ranikhet Express-Slip 15013 (sleeper/3AC/2AC ₹175/490/695) leaves Old Delhi at 10.30pm, arriving in Ramnagar at 4.50am. The return trip on train 25014 leaves Ramnagar at 10pm, arriving in Old Delhi at 3.55am. A daytime run from Old Delhi on train 15035-Slip (2nd class/chair ₹100/375) departs at 4pm, reaching Ramnagar at 8.40pm; the return on train 25036 departs Ramnagar at 9.50am, hitting Delhi at 3.25pm.

NAINITAL

☎05942 / POP 42,000 / ELEV 2084M

Crowded around a deep, green volcanic lake, Nainital is Kumaon's largest town and favourite hill resort. It occupies a steep forested valley around the namesake lake Naini and was founded by homesick Brits reminded of the Cumbrian Lake District.

Plenty of hotels are set on the hillside around the lake. There's a busy bazaar, and a spider's web of walking tracks covers the forested slopes to viewpoints overlooking distant Himalayan peaks. For travellers it's an easy place to kick back and relax, eat well, and ride horses or paddle on the lake. In peak seasons – roughly May to mid-July and October – Nainital is packed to the gills with holidaying families and honeymooners, and hotel prices skyrocket.

Tallital (Lake's Foot) is at the southeastern end of the lake, where you'll find the bus stand and the main road heading east towards Bhowali. The 1.5km promenade known as the Mall leads to Mallital (Lake's Head) at the northwestern end of the lake. Most hotels, guesthouses and restaurants are strung out along the Mall between Mallital and Tallital. You'll find most shops, including pharmacies, in Bara Bazaar.

Sights & Activities

★Naini Lake LAKE

This pretty lake is Nainital's centrepiece and is said to be one of the emerald green eyes of Shiva's wife, Sati (*naina* is Sanskrit for eye) that fell to earth after her act of self-immolation. Boatmen will row you around the lake for ₹210 in the brightly painted gondola-like **boats**, or the **Nainital Boat Club** (www.boathouseclub.in; Mallital; ⏰10am-4pm) will sail you around for ₹500. **Pedal boats** can also be hired for ₹150 per hour.

Naina Devi Temple is on the precise spot where the eye is believed to have fallen. Nearby is the **Jama Masjid** and a **gurdwara**. You can walk around the lake in about an hour – the southern side is more peaceful and has good views of the town.

Raj Bhavan HISTORIC BUILDING

(₹50; ⏰8am-5pm Mon-Sat Jan-Mar, Sep & Oct, to 6pm Apr-Aug, to 4pm Nov & Dec) About 3km south of Tallital, this is the official residence of the Governor of Uttarakhand. Styled on Buckingham Palace, it's a prime example of British Raj architecture, set among gardens, lawns and forests. Tours of the grounds are available but the residence itself is only open when the governor is away.

On the grounds is a lovely 18-hole golf course (green fee men/women ₹800/100); club hire and caddies are available. A taxi to Raj Bhavan from Tallital should cost about ₹200 round trip, or you can hike 1km by trail.

Snow View VIEWPOINT

A **cable car** (return adult/child ₹290/130; ⏰8am-8pm May & Jun, 10.30am-4.30pm Jul-Apr) runs up to the popular Snow View at 2270m, which (on clear days) has panoramic Himalayan views, including of Nanda Devi. The ticket office is at the bottom. At the top you'll find the usual food, souvenir and carnival stalls, as well as **Mountain Magic**, an amusement park with kids' entertainment including bumper cars, trampolines and a flying fox.

Nainital

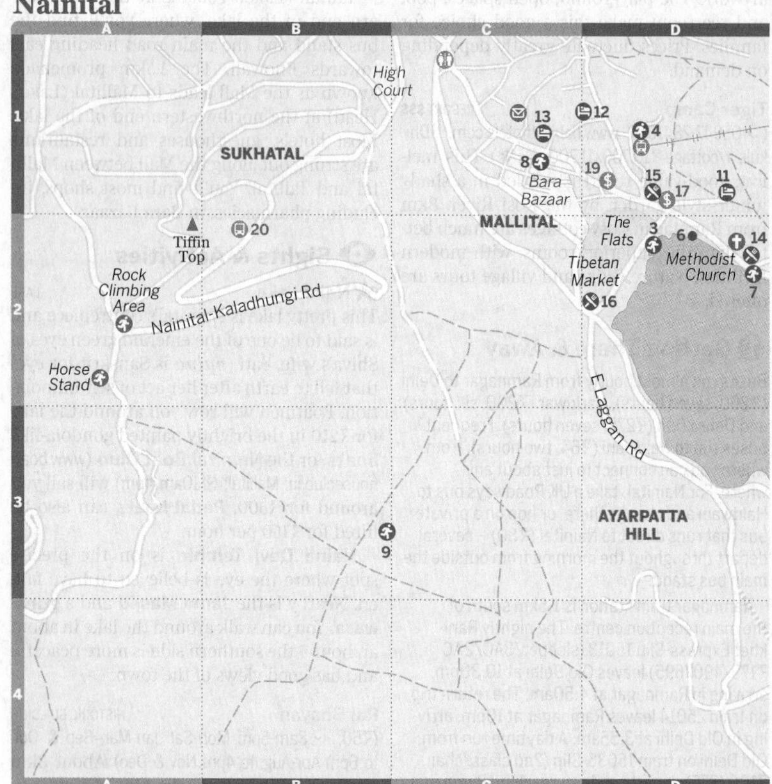

A highlight of the trip to Snow View is hiking to viewpoints such as Cheena/Naina Peak, 4km away. Local guides may offer to lead you there. If you want to get up to Snow View for sunrise, taxis charge ₹200.

Tiffin Top & Land's End HORSE RIDING, WALKING

A 4km walk west of the lake brings you to Tiffin Top (2292m), also called Dorothy's Seat. From here it's a lovely 30-minute walk to Land's End (2118m) through a forest of oak, deodar and pine. Mangy horses gather 3km west of town on the road to Ramnagar to take you on rides to these spots.

★Tranquility Treks TREKKING

(☎9411196837; www.tranquilitytreks.in) Experienced guide Sunil Kumar leads hikes and focuses on bird- and wildlife-watching. He can take you on day walks (₹1500), overnight hikes where you stay in local villages (₹2000), and two-week all-inclusive nature trips (from ₹75,000).

Snout Adventures OUTDOORS

(☎9412306615; www.snoutadventure.com; Bara Bazaar) A recommended outfit offering treks in the Nainital area (from ₹2200 per day, all inclusive, depending on group size). It also conducts rock-climbing courses (₹700 per day) and organises adventure camps.

KMVN Parvat Tours TREKKING

(☎05942-231436; www.kmvn.org; Tallital; ⊙8am-7pm) A helpful office for information and booking KMVN's rest houses and trekking packages.

Sleeping

Traveller's Paradise HOTEL $$

(☎7417743236; www.travellersparadise.in; Mallital; r ₹2000-4500; wi-fi) A bit north of the Mall, this exceptionally friendly hotel features spacious rooms with flat-screen TVs, couches, faux-wood panelling, wi-fi and quality beds. It's run by the amiable Anu Consul, who spent

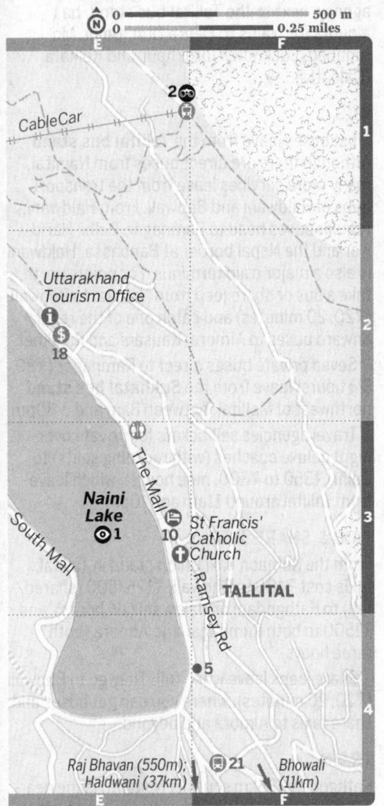

Nainital

Top Sights
1 Naini Lake........E3

Sights
2 Snow View........E1

Activities, Courses & Tours
3 Boat Hire........D2
4 Cable Car........D1
5 KMVN Parvat Tours........F4
6 Nainital Boat Club........D2
7 Pedal-boat Hire........D2
8 Snout Adventures........C1
9 Tiffin Top & Land's End........B3

Sleeping
10 Evelyn Hotel........E3
11 Hotel City Heart........D1
12 Palace Belvedere........D1
13 Traveller's Paradise........C1

Eating
14 Embassy........D2
15 Sakley's Restaurant........D1
16 Sonam Chowmein Corner........D2

Drinking & Nightlife
Nainital Boat Club........(see 6)

Information
17 Bank of Baroda ATM........D1
Cyberden........(see 8)
18 HDFC Bank........E2
19 State Bank of India........D1

Transport
20 Sukhatal Bus Stand........B2
21 Tallital Bus Stand........F4
Train Booking Agency........(see 21)

10 years living in Mexico, and his wonderful father. Off-season prices start at ₹1800.

Hotel City Heart HOTEL $$
(☎05942-235228; www.cityhearthotelnainital.com; Mallital; d ₹2000-5500) Located off the Mall, with rooms ranging from small but cute to fabulous deluxe ones with a view. This place discounts more than most and is one of Nainital's best off-season bargains, with prices from ₹800. The rooftop terrace restaurant has fine lake views.

Evelyn Hotel HOTEL $$
(☎05942-235457; www.hotelevelynnainital.com; The Mall, Tallital; d ₹2000-3500, ste ₹5000-6500) This Victorian-looking hotel overlooking the lake is quintessential Nainital – charming and slightly eccentric. It's big, with stairways and terraces cascading down the hillside, and is a bit old-fashioned, but the well-tended rooms with retro furniture have a nice, cosy feel. Look at a few.

Palace Belvedere HERITAGE HOTEL $$$
(☎05942-237434; www.palacebelvedere.com; Mallital; s/d/ste from ₹6700/7900/10,200; 📶) Built in 1897, this was the summer palace of the rajas of Awagarh. Animal skins and old prints adorn the walls and lend a faded Raj-era charm. Rooms are spacious, high-ceilinged, and have an aged, if worn, soul. Upstairs gets much more light. Downstairs has an elegant dining room, lounge and verandah. It can be cold in winter.

Eating & Drinking

Sonam Chowmein Corner FAST FOOD $
(The Flats, Mallital; mains ₹30-60; ⏲11am-7.30pm) In the covered alley of the Tibetan Market, this authentic Tibetan *dhaba* whips up fabulous chow mein and *momos* (dumplings) for the best cheap eats in town.

Embassy INDIAN **$$**

(The Mall, Mallital; meals ₹150-450; ⌚9am-10.30pm) With a wood-lined chalet interior and snappily dressed staff, Embassy has been serving up five pages of menu items for more than 40 years. For drinks try 'dancing coffee' or a rosewater lassi. There's a good terrace for people-watching.

Sakley's Restaurant MULTICUISINE **$$$**

(Mallital; snacks from ₹125, mains ₹250-650; ⌚9.30am-9.30pm) A spotless restaurant found off the Mall, serving up a range of unusual global items such as Thai curries, honey chicken, roast lamb, pepper steaks, and plenty of Chinese dishes, pizzas and sizzlers. The cakes and pastries are great; even if you don't dine here, swing by and pick up some dessert to take back to your room.

Nainital Boat Club BAR

(The Mall, Mallital; ⌚10am-10pm) This club is a classic remnant of the Raj era. Temporary membership is ridiculously steep (men/women/couples ₹870/440/870), but the atmospheric bar – with timber beams, buttoned-up barmen with handlebar moustaches and an outdoor deck overlooking the lake – is perfect for an afternoon drink. The dress code specifies no shorts or slippers, and signs warn that 'decorum should be maintained'.

ℹ Information

Cyberden (per hr ₹40; ⌚9am-9pm) Upstairs in a quaint old building in Bara Bazaar.

State Bank of India (The Mall, Mallital; ⌚10am-4pm Mon-Fri, to 1pm Sat) Exchanges foreign currencies and travellers cheques.

Uttarakhand Tourism Office (☎05942-235337; The Mall; ⌚10am-5pm Mon-Sat) Doesn't always follow official hours.

ℹ Getting There & Away

Train Booking Agency (⌚9am-noon & 2-5pm Mon-Fri, 9am-2pm Sat) The train booking agency, next to the Tallital bus stand, has a quota for trains to Dehra Dun, Delhi, Moradabad, Lucknow, Gorakhpur and Kolkata (Calcutta).

BUS

Most buses leave from the **Tallital bus stand**. Although there are direct buses from Nainital, many more services leave from the transport hubs of Haldwani and Bhowali. From Haldwani, regular buses head to Ramnagar, Delhi, Haridwar and the Nepal border at Banbassa. Haldwani is also a major train terminus. For points north, take a bus or share jeep from Nainital to Bhowali (₹20, 20 minutes) and catch one of the regular onward buses to Almora, Kausani and Ranikhet.

Seven private buses direct to Ramnagar (₹80, 3½ hours) leave from the **Sukhatal bus stand**, northwest of Mallital, between 8am and 3.30pm.

Travel agencies sell tickets for private overnight deluxe coaches (with reclining seats) to Delhi (₹350 to ₹800, nine hours), which leave from Tallital around 11am and 10pm.

TAXI & SHARE JEEP

From the Kumaon Taxi Union stand in Tallital, taxis cost ₹400 to Bhowali, ₹125/500 (shared/full) to Kathgodam or Haldwani (1½ hours), and ₹1500 to both Ramnagar and Almora (both three hours).

Share jeeps leave when full. They go to Bhowali (₹20, 20 minutes), where you can get buses and share taxis to Almora and beyond.

TRAIN

Kathgodam (35km south of Nainital) is the nearest train station, but Haldwani, one stop further south, is the regional transport hub. The **train booking agency** (p446), next to the Tallital bus stand, can book trains to Dehra Dun, Delhi, Moradabad, Lucknow, Gorakhpur and Kolkata (Calcutta). The daily 12039 Kathgodam–New Delhi Shatabdhi (AC chair/Exec ₹745/1320) departs Kathgodam at 3.35pm, stops at Haldwani at 3.50pm, and reaches New Delhi station at 9.05pm. In the other direction, train 12040 departs New Delhi station at 6am, arriving at Haldwani at 11.18am and Kathgodam at 11.40am.

BUSES FROM NAINITAL

The following buses leave from the Tallital bus stand. For Kathgodam, take the Haldwani bus.

DESTINATION	FARE (₹)	DURATION (HRS)	DEPARTURES
Almora	110	3	2pm
Dehra Dun	480	10	4 early morning, 3 evening
Delhi (AC/non-AC)	660/410	9	9am, 9.30am, 8.30pm, 9pm (AC)
Haldwani	60	2	half-hourly
Haridwar	350	8	6.30pm
Rishikesh	330	9	5am

CROSSING TO NEPAL: BANBASSA TO MAHENDRANAGAR (BHIMDATTA)

Banbassa is the closest Indian village to the Nepal border post of Mahendranagar (Bhimdatta), 5km away. Check the current situation in western Nepal before crossing here, as roads during monsoon or immediate postmonsoon season may be impassable due to landslides and washed-out bridges.

Banbassa is easily reached by bus from Haldwani and Pithoragarh. The nearby town of Tanakpur has even more connections.

The border is open 24 hours, but before 6am and after 6pm you're unlikely to find anyone to stamp you out of India and into Nepal. While the border is officially open to vehicles only from 6am to 8am, 10am to noon, 2pm to 4pm and 6pm to 7pm, rickshaws and motorcycles are usually allowed to make the 1km trip across the bridge between the border posts at any time. Otherwise you have to walk it.

Single-entry Nepali visas valid for 15/30/90 days cost US$25/40/100 and are available at the Nepali side of the border between 9am and 5pm. Bring US dollars.

Hotels in Banbassa exchange Indian and Nepali rupees, as will a small office near the Nepal border post. Nabil Bank in Mahendranagar has an ATM and foreign-currency exchange. ATMs can be found in Banbassa.

Onward Transport

From the Nepali border, take an autorickshaw (₹100) or shared taxi to Mahendranagar. The bus station is about 1km from the centre on the Mahendra Hwy, from where eight daily buses depart for Kathmandu between 5.30am and 4.30pm. There's also a single Pokhara service at 2.20pm (16 hours).

ALMORA

05962 / POP 35,500 / ELEV 1650M

Set along a steep-sided ridge, Almora is the regional capital of Kumaon, first established as a summer capital by the Chand rajas of Kumaon in 1560. These days you'll find colonial-era buildings, reliable trekking outfits and a couple of community-based weaving enterprises. Don't be put off by the utilitarian main street when you're first deposited at the bus stand – head one block south to the pedestrian-only cobbled Lalal Bazaar, lined with intricately carved and painted traditional wooden shop facades. It's a fascinating place to stroll, people-watch and shop. On clear days, you can see Himalayan snow peaks from various spots around town.

Sights & Activities

Nanda Devi Temple HINDU TEMPLE

(Lalal Bazaar) The stone Nanda Devi Temple dates back to the Chand raja era, and is covered in folk-art carvings, some erotic. Every September the temple hosts the five-day Nanda Devi Fair (p447).

Panchachuli Weavers Factory FACTORY

(05962-232310; www.panchachuli.com; off Bageshwar Rd; 10am-5pm Mon-Sat) FREE The Panchachuli Weavers Factory employs some 700 women to weave, market and sell woollen shawls. The shop here has a wider range of products than the small shop in the Mall. Taxis charge ₹150 return to the factory, or you can walk the 3km – follow the continuation of Mall Rd to the northeast and ask for directions.

High Adventure TREKKING, MOUNTAIN BIKING

(9412044610; www.trekkinghimalayas.in) Organises treks around Uttarakhand, and mountain-bike trips near Almora and Nainital. Prices vary depending on route and group size, so call for details.

Festivals & Events

Nanda Devi Fair CULTURAL

(Sep) During this five-day fair, thousands of devotees parade the image of the goddess around and watch dancing and other cultural shows. The ritual slaughtering of a male buffalo at the fair's culmination was suspended in recent years due to controversy over the practice, though it still goes on in more remote Kumaoni villages.

Sleeping

Bansal Hotel HOTEL $

(05962-230864; Lalal Bazaar; r ₹400) Above Bansal Cafe in the bustling bazaar, but easily reached from the Mall, this is a fine budget choice with small, tidy rooms (some with TV) and a rooftop terrace.

Hotel Shikhar HOTEL $$
(05962-230253; www.hotelshikhar.in; The Mall; r ₹600-3500, ste ₹5000;) Dominating the centre of town and built to take in the views, this large, boxlike hotel offers a maze of rooms covering all budgets. The cheaper rooms are soulless and worn, but not too awful. The top-tier rooms are Almora's nicest.

Savoy Hotel HOTEL $$
(05962-230329; www.ashoknainital.com; The Mall; r ₹1000-1800) At the southern end of the Mall, just past the tourist office, the Savoy is in a quiet location. Some cheaper downstairs rooms are simple, musty affairs, but the pricier upstairs rooms strive for comfort and style; best of all, they have tables and chairs on a shared terrace that overlooks the valley below Almora.

Eating

Saraswati Sweet & Restaurant TIBETAN $
(Pithoragarh Rd; dishes ₹30-60; 7.30am-7.30pm) This busy place with upstairs tables quickly dishes up veg and nonveg *momos* and other Tibetan food, along with Chinese. The *thukpa* (Tibetan noodle soup) is spicy enough to clear your sinuses. It also has mutton burgers and a full list of cold drinks.

Glory Restaurant INDIAN $
(LR Sah Rd; mains ₹65-190; 9am-10pm) This long-running family eatery features popular South and North Indian veg and nonveg dishes, including biryanis and lemon chicken. Pizzas are extra cheesy.

Information

Joshi's Cybercafe (per hr ₹30; 9am-8pm Mon-Sat, 9am-1pm Sun;) One of several places with internet. It's opposite the main post office.

Uttarakhand Tourism Office (05962-230180; Upper Mall; 10am-5pm Mon-Sat)

Getting There & Away

The vomit-splattered sides of the buses and jeeps pulling into Almora tell you all you need to know about what the roads are like around here.

KMOU buses operate from the Mall – starting early morning until 2.30pm or 3pm – to Kausani (₹85, 2½ hours), Bageshwar (₹120, two hours) and Haldwani (₹125, three hours) via Bhowali (₹80, two hours) near Nainital. Buses to those places – except Ranikhet – also leave from the adjacent Roadways stand, where you'll find buses to Delhi (₹448, 12 hours) at 5.30pm and 6.30pm – it's best to book Delhi tickets in the morning. For Pithoragarh, head to the Dharanaula bus stand east of the bazaar on Bypass Rd, where several buses (₹165, five hours) depart between about 8.30am and 11am. For Banbassa on the Nepal border, take a bus to Haldwani and change there.

You can get a taxi or jeep to Kausani (shared/full ₹120/1200, 2½ hours), Bageshwar (₹250/1800, two hours), Bhowali (₹200/1000, three hours), Kasar Devi (₹30/300), Pithoragarh (₹350/2000, five hours) and Munsyari (full taxi only, ₹5000, 10 hours). All leave from the Mall, except the shared taxis to Pithoragarh, which leave from Dharanaula bus stand. We can recommend Kishan Bisht (9410915048) as a remarkably sane driver.

The nearest railway stations are at Kathgodam and Haldwani. There's a **Railway Reservation Centre** (05962-230250; KMVN Holiday Home, Mall; 9am-noon & 2-5pm Mon-Sat) at the southern end of town.

AROUND ALMORA

Kasar Devi

ELEV 2100M

This peaceful spot about 8km north of Almora has been luring alternative types for close to 100 years – as a result, it's also known as Crank's Ridge. The list of luminaries who've visited, some for extended stays, includes Bob Dylan, Cat Stevens, Timothy Leary, Allen Ginsberg and Swami Vivekananda, who meditated at the hilltop **Kasar Devi Temple**. Today, the village is a low-key backpacker destination, with a mellow vibe and clear-day Himalayan views. There's not a lot to do here, but it's a great place to chill. And Mohan's Binsar Retreat (p449) can arrange multiday fishing, rafting or trekking trips.

Sleeping & Eating

Manu Guest House GUESTHOUSE $
(9410920696; below Binsar Rd; r ₹400-600) Set amid an orchard with a couple of cows, this place feels like a rural homestay. The largest stone or brick cottages include kitchenettes, making it a great choice for long stays.

Kripal House HOTEL $
(9690452939; off Binsar Rd; r from ₹800, without bathroom from ₹600) This basic guesthouse,

down a dirt lane off the main road, boasts mind-blowing views of the Himalaya from its unfurnished rooftop terrace. The more expensive rooms have private kitchens, others share a kitchen with another room.

★Freedom Guest House GUESTHOUSE **$$**
(☎7830355686; www.freedomguesthouse.in; Binsar Rd; r from ₹1500) Big, immaculately clean rooms open onto shared terraces with sublime valley views, catching the afternoon and sunset light. The newer rooms on the upper floors have a touch more luxury, but each one is a winner. The owners, Sunder and Gita, go out of their way to please.

★Mohan's Binsar Retreat GUESTHOUSE **$$$**
(☎9412977968, 05962-251215; www.mohans-binsarretreat.com; Binsar Rd; r incl breakfast from ₹5250; wifi) Arguably the nicest place in Kasar Devi, Mohan's has huge, beautiful rooms with luxurious beds and wooden ceilings and floors. The real draw is the indoor-outdoor terrace restaurant, with great views of the valley below and a shot of distant Himalayan peaks. It's said that Bob Dylan hung out here when it was a humble tea shop in the 1960s.

Rainbow Restaurant INTERNATIONAL **$$**
(☎9720320664; mehra.harsh145@gmail.com; Binsar Rd; mains ₹100-250; ⏲9am-9pm; wifi) Sit at tables or cushions on the floor while ordering Indian, Asian, Western or Middle Eastern food, and choose from a long list of fresh juices. Everything we tried was delicious – especially dessert! The owners also run a brand new, top-notch guesthouse and yoga retreat with rooms from ₹3500 (discounts often available).

Binsar

ELEV 2420M

Beyond Kasar Devi, picturesque Binsar, 26km from Almora, was once the hilltop summer capital of the Chand rajas. Now it's a sanctuary protecting 45 sq km. You may spot a leopard or some barking deer, but many people come here for the 200-plus species of birds. On clear days, the Himalayan panorama is breathtaking – from the tower at 'Zero Point,' Binsar's summit (2420m), you can see Kedarnath, Trishul, Nanda Devi, Panchachuli and more. Hiking trails wend throughout the lush forest; their main nexus is the KMVN Rest House. There is one good map of Binsar put out by the Forest Department, with trails and topo lines, but this is very hard to find; it's not offered at the entry gate.

The fee to enter the sanctuary is ₹150/600 per Indian/foreigner, plus a ₹250 to ₹500 vehicle fee depending on what you're driving. Guides, who can be hired at the sanctuary gate or the Rest House, charge ₹250 for a 1½-hour hike.

A return taxi from Almora costs about ₹1100.

Two highly recommended outfits run single- and multiday trekking tours between the villages in and around the sanctuary, offering a deeper experience of the natural environment and rural culture of the area. **Village Ways** (☎9759749283; www.villageways.com) has its own private guesthouses in several villages. The **Grand Oak Manor** (☎9412094277; shikhatripathi.travel@gmail.com) is run by adventure travel writer Shikha Tripathi and her husband Sindhu Shah, whose family has been in Binsar for over 100 years, and customises treks with overnight stays in the homes of villagers.

Jageshwar

ELEV 1870M

An impressive and active **temple complex** is set along a creek in a forest of deodars at the village of Jageshwar, 38km northeast of Almora. The 124 temples and shrines date to the 7th century AD and vary from linga shrines to large *sikhara* (Hindu temples) dedicated to different gods and goddesses. Down the street is the **Jageshwar Archaeological Museum** (www.asi.nic.in; ⏲10am-5pm Sat-Thu) FREE, which houses a small collection of exquisite religious carvings taken from the temples for preservation purposes and is well worth a look. An October instalment of the International Yoga Festival (p418) was first held here in 2016.

A 3km trail that starts below the centre of the village leads to the top of the ridge behind it. The ridge has dizzying views of the sculpted valley on the other side and the big peaks in the distance.

There are a handful of hotels. The best of the bunch is **Tara Guest House** (☎9411544736; www.jageshwar.co.uk; r from ₹400; wifi).

The easiest way to get from Almora to Jageshwar is by taxi (₹1200 return) or shared taxi (₹75). There's one direct bus daily at around noon. It returns to Almora at 8am the following day. You can also take any bus going through Artola, get off there, and either walk 4km to Jageshwar or take a taxi for ₹80.

KAUSANI

05962 / POP 4100 / ELEV 1890M

Perched high on a forest-covered ridge, this tiny village has lovely panoramic views of distant snowcapped peaks, fresh air and a relaxed atmosphere. Mahatma Gandhi found Kausani an inspirational place to write his Bhagavad Gita treatise *Anasakti Yoga* in 1929, and there is still an ashram devoted to him here. Baijnath village, 19km north, has an intriguing complex of 12th-century *sikhara*-style temples in a lovely location shaded by trees, with other shrines in the nearby old village.

Sights

Kausani Tea Estate PLANTATION
(9am-6pm mid-Mar–mid-Nov) FREE At Kausani Tea Estate – a tea plantation that involves private enterprise, the government and local farmers – you can look around and sample and buy products that are exported around the world. It's 3.5km north of the village on the road to Baijnath, an easy and scenic walk.

Anasakti Ashram HISTORIC SITE
(05962-258028; Anasakti Ashram Rd) FREE About 1km uphill from the bus stand, Anasakti Ashram is where Mahatma Gandhi spent two weeks pondering and writing *Anasakti Yoga*. It has a small **museum** (Anasakti Ashram Rd; 6am-noon & 4-7pm) FREE that tells the story of Gandhi's life through photographs and words. Visit at 6pm to attend nightly prayers in his memory.

Sleeping & Eating

Outside the two short peak seasons (May to June and October to November), accommodation is often discounted by 50%.

Hotel Uttarakhand HOTEL $$
(05962-258012; www.uttarakhandkausani.com; d ₹1250-2550; @) Just north of the bus stand, but in a quiet location with a panoramic view of the Himalaya from your verandah, this is Kausani's best-value accommodation. The cheaper rooms are small, with bucket hot water, but upper-floor rooms are spacious and have hot showers and TVs. The manager is helpful and friendly.

Krishna Mountview HOTEL $$$
(9927944473; www.krishnamountview.com; Anasakti Ashram Rd; d ₹3650-6250, ste ₹8550-10,250;) Just past Anasakti Ashram, this is one of Kausani's smartest hotels, with clipped formal gardens (perfect for mountain views). Try to get a spacious upstairs room; they have balconies, bay windows and rocking chairs.

Garden Restaurant MULTICUISINE $$
(mains ₹80-250; 7am-10pm) In front of Hotel Uttarkhand and enjoying fine Himalayan views, this bamboo and thatch-roofed restaurant is Kausani's coolest. The food comprises first-class dishes from Swiss rösti to chicken tikka and imported pasta, as well as some Kumaon specialities, using fresh ingredients.

Getting There & Away

Buses and share jeeps stop in the village centre. Several buses run to Almora (₹125, 2½ hours), but in the afternoon they generally stop at Karbala on the bypass road, from where you need to take a share jeep (₹10). Heading north, buses run every hour or so to Bageshwar via Baijnath (₹55, 1½ hours). Share jeeps (₹30, 30 minutes) run to Garur, 16km north of Kausani, which is a much more active transport hub, and where you can find share jeeps to Gwaldam for onward buses and jeeps to Garhwal (via Karanprayag).

A taxi to Almora costs around ₹1500; to Nainital or Karanprayag about ₹3200.

BAGESHWAR

05963 / POP 9100 / ELEV 975M

Hindu pilgrims visit Bageshwar, at the confluence of the Gomti and Saryu Rivers, for its ancient stone **Bagnath Temple**. For travellers, it's more important as a transit town connecting Munsyari and other points east with Kausani and Almora. There are a couple of internet cafes around, and there's a State Bank of India ATM in the main bazaar. The valley around the town, with fields sculpted above the riverbanks, is strikingly beautiful, and the main market is worth a wander.

The bare-bones **Hotel Annapurna** (05963-220109; r ₹300-400, s/d without bathroom ₹100/200) is conveniently next to the bus stand, but for something much better, head for **Hotel Narendra Palace** (05963-220166; Pindari Rd; r ₹500-1500;), about 1km from the bus stand on Pindari Rd.

Getting There & Away

Several daily buses go to Almora (₹120, three hours) and Kausani (₹50, 1½ hours). Frequent buses run to Bhowali (₹185, six hours) and Haldwani (₹230, 7½ hours). For connections to Garhwal, take a bus to Gwaldam (₹60, two hours) and change there. There are several morning buses to Pithoragarh (₹170, seven hours) and one at 9am to Munsyari (₹160, six hours).

There's a jeep stand near the bus stand, along with a few other spots around town. Share jeeps go to Garur (₹35, 45 minutes), Kausani (₹55, 1½ hours) and Gwaldam (₹85, two hours). A shared/private jeep costs ₹200/2000 to Song (two hours), ₹300/3000 to Loharket (2½ hours), ₹400/4000 to Munsyari (five hours), ₹350/4000 to Pithoragarh (six hours) and ₹200/2000 to Almora (two hours).

PITHORAGARH

☎05964 / POP 56,050 / ELEV 1514M

Spread across the hillsides above a scenic valley that's been dubbed 'Little Kashmir', Pithoragarh is the main town of a little-visited region that borders Tibet and Nepal. Its sights include several Chand-era temples and an old fort, but the real reason to come here is to get off the tourist trail. The busy main bazaar is good for a stroll, and townspeople are exceptionally friendly. Picturesque hikes in the area include the rewarding climb up to **Chandak** (7km) for views of the gorgeous **Panchachuli (Five Chimneys)** massif.

For a good meal at a good price, locals swear by **Jyonar Restaurant** (Gandhi Chowk; mains ₹90-250; ⏲10am-9.30pm) in the bazaar.

Hotel Yash Yatharth HOTEL $$
(☎05964-225005; www.punethahotels.com; Naya Bazaar; dm ₹200, r ₹1200-3500) The best value accommodation in Pithoragarh, rooms here range from simple with shared bath to large and ornately furnished. In the main bazaar, it's close to the bus stand, and rates are negotiable.

ℹ Information

A State Bank of India ATM is in the bazaar.

Tourist Office (☎05964-225527; ⏲10am-5pm Mon-Fri, to 2pm Sat) Located 50m uphill from the jeep stand; can help with trekking guides and information.

ℹ Getting There & Away

Buses leave at 5.30am and 9am for Almora (₹280, five hours) and Haldwani (₹336, 10 hours). Frequent buses go to Delhi until 4pm (₹600, 18 hours); there are hourly services from 5am to 2pm to Banbassa (₹260, six hours), the border crossing into Nepal. To get to Munsyari, take a share jeep (₹300, seven hours).

MUNSYARI

Perched on a mountainside surrounded by plunging terraced fields, where the 6000m Panchachuli peaks scrape the sky across the Johar Valley, Munsyari (2290m) is one of the most scenic villages in Uttarakhand. Visited mostly by trekkers heading to the Milam Glacier, the surrounding landscape makes this a worthwhile destination even if you don't plan on lacing up your boots and hitting the trail.

There are some nice day hikes in the area – ask how to get to Kalya Top (it's a couple of miles off the road that heads uphill, toward Bageshwar) with views of Nanda Devi and Nanda Kot, as well as the Panchachulis. The small **Tribal Heritage Museum** (☎9411337094; ₹10; ⏲10am-5pm most days), 2km downhill from the bazaar, is run by the charming scholar SS Pangtey and has artefacts from the days when Munsyari was an important nexus of trade with Tibet. Munsyari is also a unique place to experience the Nanda Devi Festival in September.

Several new, modern hotels have popped up in Munsyari, but we still like **Hotel Pandey Lodge** (☎9411130316; www.munsyarihotel.com; r ₹550-1500), by the bus stand, with its range of good-value rooms, some with amazing views. Across the street, **Snow View Hotel** (☎7534881686; r ₹500-1200; 📶) is exceptionally friendly.

Buses run to Bageshwar (₹150, six hours) at 7.30am. Another bus at 6.30am goes all the way to Dehra Dun. Share jeeps run to Pithoragarh (₹180, eight hours), Almora (₹180, eight hours) and Thal (₹120, three hours), where you can change for onward transport. If travelling to Munsyari via Thal, get a right-side window seat for the best views along the road. If you came from Thal and are heading to Pithoragarh, consider taking the longer route via Jauljibi for a change of scenery, including some amazing vistas of the Kumaon and Nepali Himalaya.

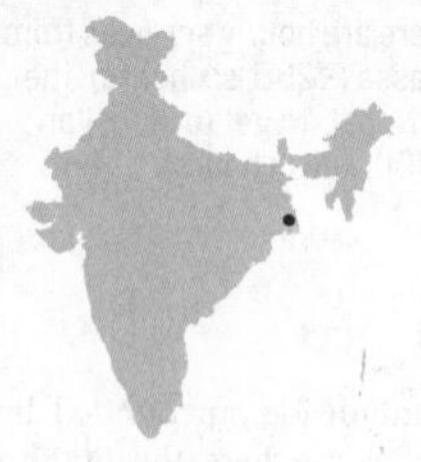

Kolkata (Calcutta)

033 / POP 14.5 MILLION

Includes ➡

Best Places to Eat

- 6 Ballygunge Place (p475)
- Arsalan (p473)
- Kewpies (p474)
- Fire and Ice (p474)
- Tamarind (p475)

Best Places to Sleep

- Astor (p470)
- Corner Courtyard (p472)
- Oberoi Grand (p469)
- Park Hotel (p470)
- Sunflower Guest House (p470)

Why Go?

India's second-biggest city is a daily festival of human existence, simultaneously noble and squalid, cultured and desperate, decidedly futuristic while splendid in decay. By its old spelling, Calcutta readily conjures images of human suffering to most Westerners – although that's not a complete picture of this 350-year-old metropolis. Locally, Kolkata is regarded as India's intellectual, artistic and cultural capital. Although poverty is certainly apparent, the self-made middle class drives the city's core machinery, a nascent hipster culture thrives among its millennial residents and its dapper Bengali gentry frequent grand, old colonial-era clubs.

As the former capital of British India, Kolkata retains a feast of colonial-era architecture contrasting starkly with urban slums and dynamic new-town suburbs. Kolkata is the ideal place to experience the mild yet complex tang of Bengali cuisine. Friendlier than India's other metropolises, this is a city you 'feel' more than simply visit.

When to Go

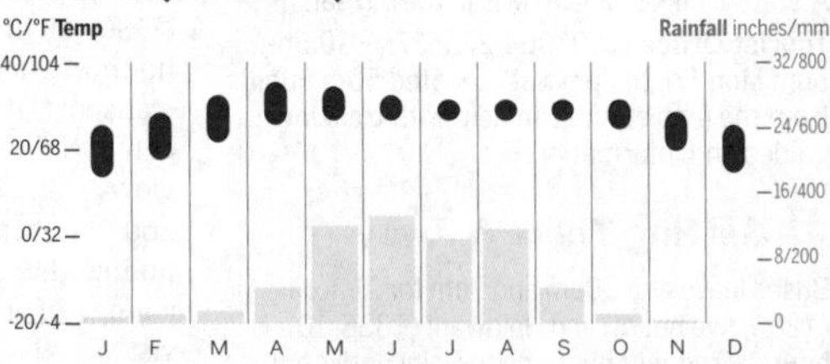

May–Sep Best avoided due to heavy rains that leave the city drenched.

Sep & Oct The city dresses up magnificently for the colourful mayhem of Durga Puja.

Nov–Jan Cool and dry, the winter months are a time for film and music festivals.

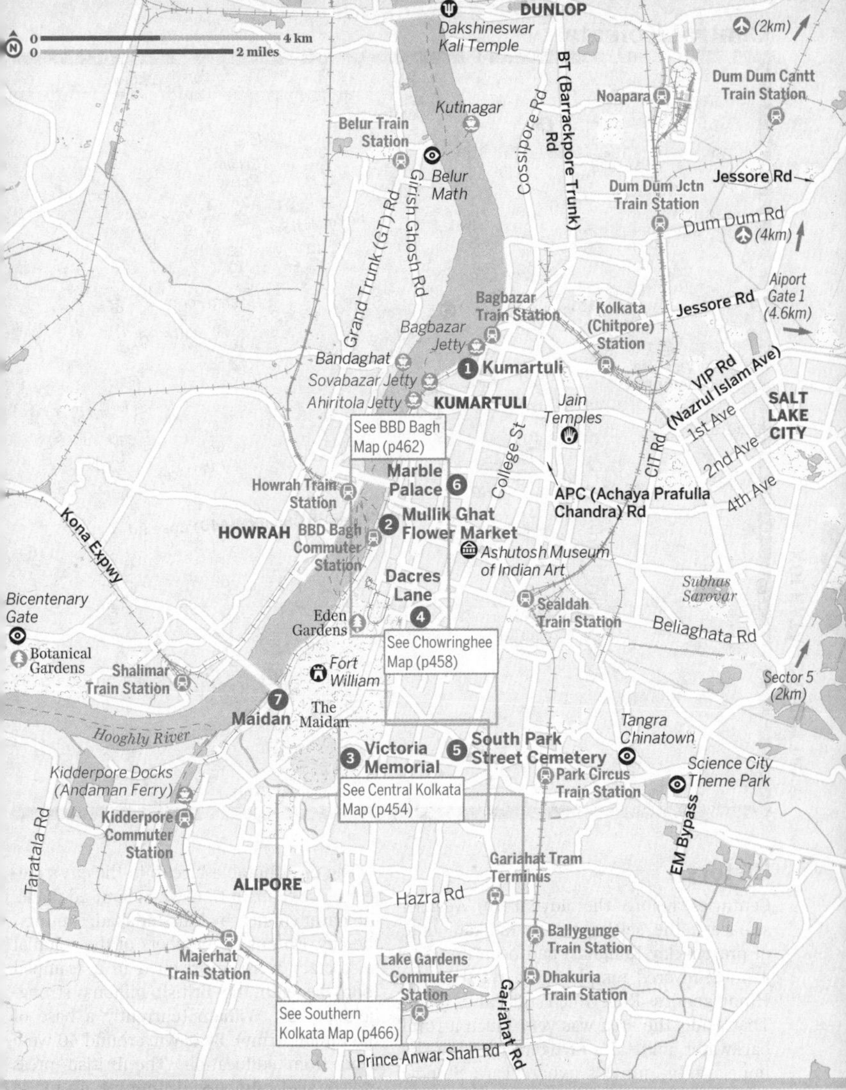

Kolkata Highlights

❶ **Kumartuli** (p464) Watching clay goddesses come to life in this atmospheric neighbourhood.

❷ **Mullik Ghat Flower Market** (p461) Visiting colourful stalls selling tropical blossoms.

❸ **Victoria Memorial** (p456) Pondering the architectural brilliance of the British Raj's tribute to Queen Victoria.

❹ **Dacres Lane** (p475) Sampling lip-smacking creole cuisine at street-food stalls in this serpentine lane.

❺ **South Park Street Cemetery** (p456) Discovering stories from the city's past etched on tombstones.

❻ **Marble Palace** (p463) Being intrigued by the idiosyncratic exuberance of zamindars in arguably the city's most curious museum.

❼ **Maidan** (p457) Enjoying a fun ride through this lush green colonial-era park.

Central Kolkata

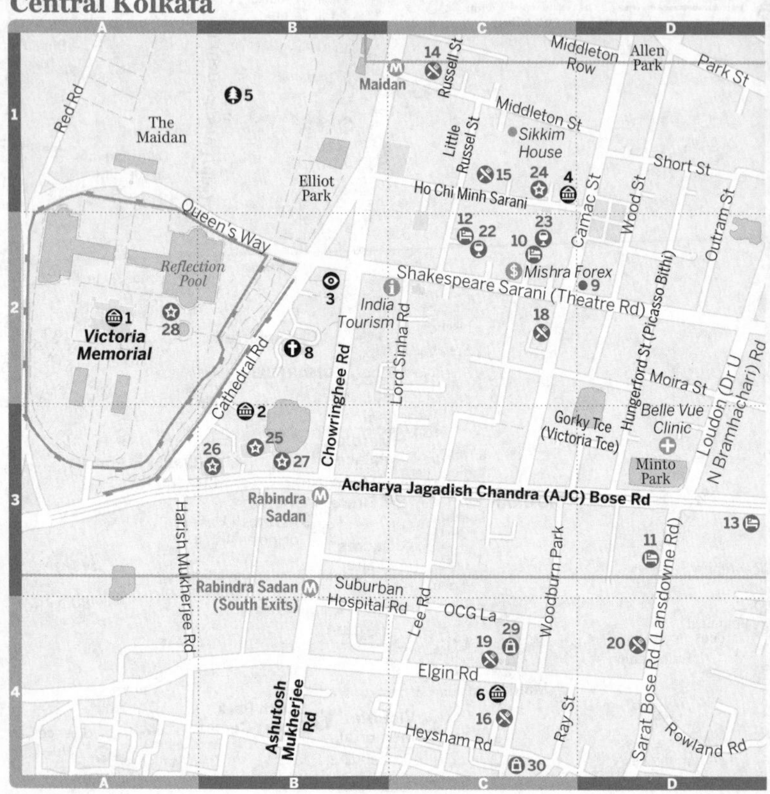

History

Centuries before the advent of Western seafarers, the settlement of Kalikata (site of present-day Kalighat) had been home to a much-revered temple consecrated to the Hindu goddess Kali, which still stands today. That aside, the area was very much a rural backwater, and tales of tigers roaming the impenetrable jungles (where Park St now runs!) are rife in the city's lores. When British merchant Job Charnock showed up in 1690, he considered the site appropriate for a new, defendable colonial settlement, and within a few decades a miniature version of London – christened Calcutta – was sprouting stately buildings and English churches amid wide boulevards and grand formal gardens. The grand European illusion, however, vanished abruptly at the new city's frayed edges, where Indians servicing the Raj mostly lived in cramped, overcrowded slums.

The most notable hiccup in the city's meteoric rise came in 1756, when Siraj-ud-daula, the nawab of nearby Murshidabad, captured the city. Dozens of members of the colonial aristocracy were imprisoned in a cramped room beneath the British military stronghold of Fort William (currently a base of the Indian Army). By dawn, around 40 were dead from suffocation. The British press exaggerated numbers, drumming up moral outrage back home: the legend of the 'Black Hole of Calcutta' was born.

The following year, Lord Robert Clive – then Viceroy of India – retook Calcutta for Britain. The nawab sought aid from the French but was defeated at the Battle of Plassey (now Palashi), thanks to the treachery of former allies. A stronger moated 'second' Fort William was constructed in 1758, and Calcutta became British India's official capital, though well into the 18th century

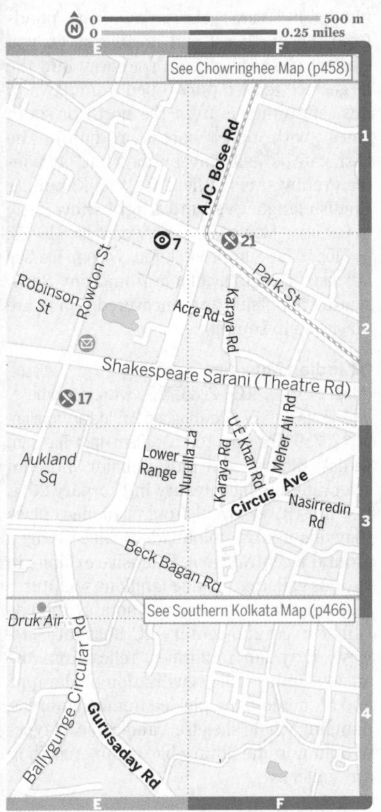

Central Kolkata

Top Sights
1 Victoria Memorial A2

Sights
2 Academy of Fine Arts B3
3 Birla Planetarium B2
4 Harrington Street Arts Centre C1
5 Maidan B1
6 Netaji Bhawan C4
7 South Park Street Cemetery E2
8 St Paul's Cathedral B2

Activities, Courses & Tours
9 Mystic Yoga Studio D2

Sleeping
10 Astor C2
11 Central B&B D3
12 Kenilworth C2
13 Park Prime D3

Eating
14 Fire and Ice C1
15 Gabbar's Bar & Kitchen C1
16 Kewpies C4
17 Kookie Jar E2
18 Monkey Bar C2
19 Oh! Calcutta C4
20 Picadilly Square D4
21 Shiraz F2

Drinking & Nightlife
22 Big Ben C2
23 Plush C2

Entertainment
24 ICCR C1
Nandan Cinema .... (see 25)
25 Nandan Complex B3
26 Rabindra Sadan B3
27 Sisir Mancha B3
28 VM Sound & Light Show A2

Shopping
29 Anokhi C4
30 FabIndia C4

one could still hunt leopards in the bamboo forests around where Sudder St lies today.

The late-19th-century Bengali Renaissance movement saw a great cultural reawakening among middle-class Calcuttans. This was further galvanised by the massively unpopular 1905 division of Bengal, which sowed the seeds of the Indian Independence movement. Bengal was reunited in 1911, but the British promptly transferred their colonial capital to less troublesome New Delhi.

Initially, loss of political power had little effect on Calcutta's economic status. However, the impact of 1947's partition was devastating. While West Pakistan and Punjab saw a fairly equal (and bloody) exchange of populations, migration in Bengal was largely one way. Around four million Hindu refugees from East Bengal arrived, choking Calcutta's already overpopulated *bastis* (slums). For a period, people were literally dying of hunger in the streets, creating Calcutta's abiding image of abject poverty. No sooner had these refugees been absorbed than a second wave arrived during the 1971 India-Pakistan War.

After India's partition, the port of Calcutta was hit very hard by the loss of its main natural hinterland, which lay behind the closed East Pakistan (later Bangladesh) border. Labour unrest spiralled out of control while the city's dominant party (Communist Party of India) spent most of its efforts attacking the feudal system of land ownership and representing proletarian demands and interests. Despite being well intentioned, many of these moves backfired. *Bandhs* (strikes) were called by labour unions almost fortnightly, severely affecting the commercial productivity of the region. Strict rent controls to protect tenants' interests were abused to the extent that even today some tenants pay only a few hundred rupees occupying quarters in the grandest heritage buildings, which are sadly crumbling away because landlords have no interest in maintaining these loss-making properties.

In 2001 Calcutta officially adopted the more phonetic spelling, Kolkata. Around the same time the city administration implemented a new, relatively business-friendly attitude that has encouraged a noticeable economic resurgence. The most visible results are numerous suburban shopping malls and apartment towers, plus the rapid emergence of Salt Lake City's Sector 5 as Kolkata's alternative corporate and entertainment centre (albeit well off tourists' radars). In 2011 the Trinamool Congress Party swept the state elections to end the Communist Party's 34-year reign in West Bengal, and promised to usher in large-scale *paribartan* (change). It's a work in progress that continues to the present day.

Sights

Chowringhee

★Victoria Memorial HISTORIC BUILDING
(VM; Map p454; ☎033-22235142; www.victoriamemorial-cal.org; Indian/foreigner incl park ₹20/200; ⏲10am-4.30pm Tue-Sun) The incredible Victoria Memorial is a vast, beautifully proportioned festival of white marble: think US Capitol meets Taj Mahal. Had it been built for a beautiful Indian princess rather than a colonial queen, this domed beauty flanking the southern end of the Maidan would surely be considered one of India's greatest buildings. Commissioned by Lord Curzon, then Viceroy of India, it was designed to commemorate Queen Victoria's demise in 1901, but construction wasn't completed until 20 years after her death.

Inside, highlights are the soaring central chamber and the **Calcutta Gallery**, an excellent, even-handed exhibition tracing the city's colonial-era history. Even if you don't want to go in, the building is still worth admiring from afar: there are magnificently photogenic views across reflecting ponds from the northeast and northwest. Or you can get closer by paying your way into the large, well-tended **park**, open from dawn to dusk. Entrance is from the north or south gates (with ticket booths at both). The east gate is exit-only by day, but on winter evenings, enter here for the 45-minute English-language **sound & light show** (Story of Calcutta; Map p454; Indian/foreigner ₹10/20; ⏲7.15pm Tue-Sun mid-Oct–Feb, 7.45pm Tue-Sun Mar-Jun). Tickets available from 5pm. Show seating is outside and uncovered. There are no shows in summer.

★Indian Museum MUSEUM
(Map p458; ☎033-22861702; www.indianmuseumkolkata.org; 27 Chowringhee Rd; Indian/foreigner ₹20/500, camera ₹50; ⏲10am-4pm Tue-Sun) India's biggest and oldest major museum celebrated its bicentenary in February 2014. It's mostly a lovably old-fashioned place that fills a large colonnaded palace ranged around a central lawn. Extensive exhibits in various galleries include fabulous sculptures dating back two millennia (notably the lavishly carved 2nd-century-BC Bharhut Gateway), Egyptian mummies, relics from the ancient Indus Valley civilisation of Harappa and Mohenjo-daro, pickled human embryos, dangling whale skeletons and some 37 types of opium in the library-like commercial botany gallery.

St Paul's Cathedral CHURCH
(Map p454; Cathedral Rd; ⏲9am-noon & 3-6pm) Arguably Kolkata's most iconic Gothic superstructure, decorated with a central crenellated tower, St Paul's would look quite at home in Cambridgeshire but cuts an equally impressive profile against Kolkata's skyline. Built between 1839 and 1847, it has a remarkably wide nave and features a stained-glass west window by pre-Raphaelite maestro, Sir Edward Burne-Jones. Reputedly the first cathedral built outside of the UK, St Paul's takes centre stage on Christmas Eve, when hundreds of people flock in to attend midnight Mass.

South Park Street Cemetery CEMETERY
(Map p454; Park St; donation ₹20, guide booklet ₹100; ⏲8am-4pm) Active from 1767 to about 1840, this historic cemetery remains a wonderful oasis of calm, featuring surreal mossy Raj-era graves from rotundas to soaring pyramids, all jostling for space in a lightly manicured jungle. Apart from their sculp-

tural beauty, some of the crumbling graves here house mortal remains of eminent citizens from Kolkata's colonial era, including academic Henry Derozio, scholar William Jones and eminent botanist Robert Kyd. Entry is from the north gate on Park St, and photography is allowed.

New Market MARKET

(Hogg Market; Map p458; Lindsay St) Marked by a distinctive red-brick **clocktower** (Map p458), this enormous warren of market halls dates to 1874, but was substantially rebuilt after a 1980s fire. By day, handicraft touts can be a minor annoyance, and the crowds can swell in the evenings, especially on weekends. It's more engrossing just after dawn, when there's a harrowing (and a wee morbid) fascination in watching the arrival of animals at the meat market, with its grizzly chopping blocks, blood-splattered floors and pillared high ceilings.

Within the main market, **Chamba Lama** (Map p458; ⌚11am-8pm Mon-Sat) is one of the best-known shops to pick up silver and semiprecious jewellery. Another curiosity is **Nahoum Bakery** (Map p458; Stall F-20; snacks/brownies ₹30/50; ⌚9.30am-8pm Mon-Sat, to 1pm Sun), with plum cakes and lemon tarts displayed in its showcases. Little has changed here since 1902, when its original Jewish owners arrived from Baghdad. The little teak cash desk is more than 80 years old.

Mother Teresa's Motherhouse HISTORIC BUILDING

(Map p458; ☎033-22497115; www.motherteresa.org; 54A AJC Bose Rd; ⌚8am-noon & 3-6pm Fri-Wed) FREE A regular flow of mostly Christian pilgrims visits the Missionaries of Charity's 'Motherhouse' to pay homage at Mother (and now Saint) Teresa's large, sober tomb. A small adjacent museum room displays Teresa's worn sandals and battered enamel dinner bowl. Located upstairs is the room where she worked and slept from 1953 to 1997, preserved in all its simplicity. From Sudder St, walk for about 15 minutes along Alimuddin St, then two minutes' south. It's in the second alley to the right.

Maidan PARK

(Map p454) A vast expanse of green in the heart of the city's brick-and-mortar matrix, the Maidan is where Kolkata's residents congregate for walks, spirited cricket and football matches, family outings, dates, tonga rides and general idling. The grounds are flanked by the Victoria Memorial (p456) and St Paul's Cathedral to the south and the **Hooghly riverbanks** to the west. A tram line cuts through the greens, and hopping onto of the carriages for a slow ride is great fun.

Historically, the Maidan was created in in 1758, in the aftermath of the 'Black Hole' fiasco. A moated 'second' Fort William, it was shaped in octagonal, Vaubanesque

KOLKATA IN...

Three Days

On the first day, admire the Victoria Memorial (p456) and surrounding attractions, then visit India Tourism to grab a Marble Palace permit (to be used two days hence). Steal an evening boat ride from a pier on the Hooghly Riverbanks and then drink and dine at a Park St institution, such as OlyPub (p476) or Peter Cat (p473).

On day two, wander through the colonial-era wonderland of BBD Bagh (p460), experience the fascinating (albeit wistful) alley life of Old Chinatown (p461) and Barabazar (p460), and observe Howrah Bridge (p461) from the colourful Mullik Ghat Flower Market (p461).

Day three is best spent visiting Marble Palace (p463) and its surrounding attractions, continuing to Kumartuli (p464) directly or by a vastly longer detour via the spiritual stops of **Dakshineswar** (www.dakshineswarkalitemple.org; ⌚6am-12.30pm & 3.30-8pm) FREE and Belur Math (p464).

One Week

In addition to the three-day itinerary, experience the contrasts of **Southern Kolkata**, with its art galleries, textile boutiques, buzzing cafes, green areas, fancy shopping malls, delicious Bengali food and the ritualistic splendour of Kalighat Temple (p464). Then take a short tour to the **Sunderbans** (p486) in the lower Ganges Delta, and explore the charming former European outposts located up the Hooghly.

Chowringhee

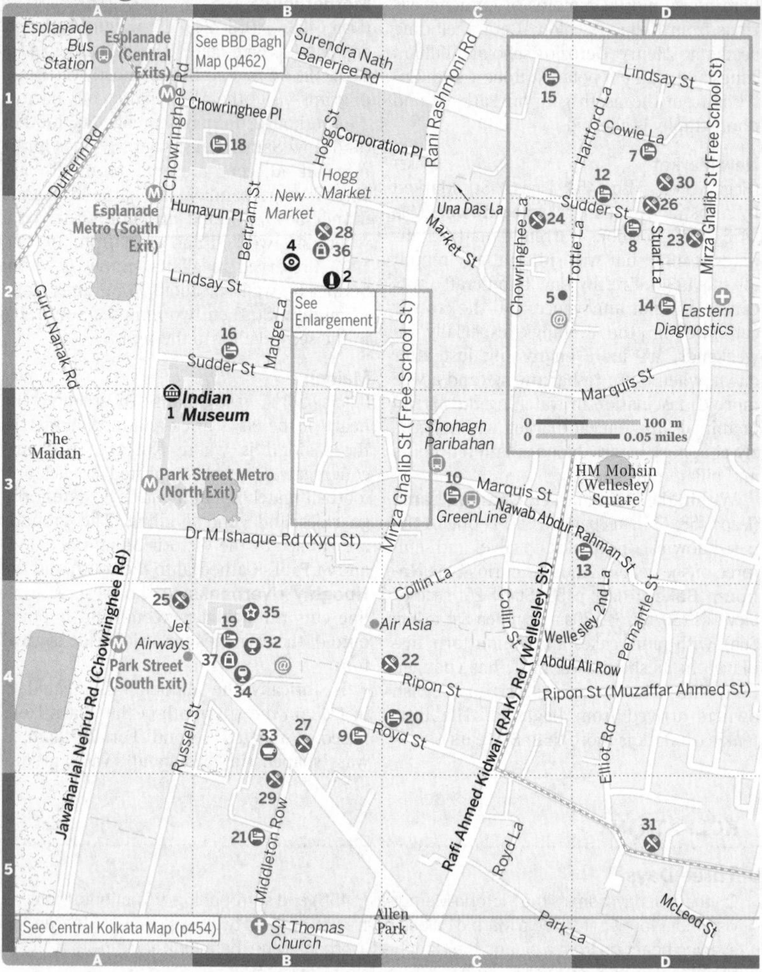

A B C D
1 2 3 4 5
Esplanade Bus Station
Esplanade (Central Exits)
See BBD Bagh Map (p462)
Surendra Nath Banerjee Rd
Rani Rashmoni Rd
Chowringhee Rd
Chowringhee Pl
Corporation Pl
Hogg St
Hogg Market
New Market
Dufferin Rd
Esplanade Metro (South Exit)
Humayun Pl
Bertram St
Una Das La
Market St
Lindsay St
See Enlargement
Madge La
Guru Nanak Rd
Sudder St
Mirza Ghalib St (Free School St)
Indian Museum
The Maidan
Shohagh Paribahan
Park Street Metro (North Exit)
Marquis St
GreenLine
Nawab Abdur Rahman St
HM Mohsin (Wellesley) Square
Dr M Ishaque Rd (Kyd St)
Collin La
Collin St
Jawaharlal Nehru Rd (Chowringhee Rd)
Jet Airways
Air Asia
Park Street (South Exit)
Russell St
Ripon St
Wellesley 2nd La
Pemantle St
Abdul Ali Row
Ripon St (Muzaffar Ahmed St)
Royd St
Rafi Ahmed Kidwai (RAK) Rd (Wellesley St)
Elliot Rd
Middleton Row
Royd La
See Central Kolkata Map (p454)
St Thomas Church
Allen Park
Park La
McLeod St
Lindsay St
Hartford La
Cowie La
Free School St
Sudder St
Chowringhee La
Tottle La
Stuart La
Mirza Ghalib St
Eastern Diagnostics
Marquis St
0 100 m
0 0.05 miles

form, and the whole village of Gobindapur was flattened to give the new fort's cannons a clear line of fire. Though sad for then-residents, this created a 3km-long park that is today as fundamental to Kolkata as Central Park is to New York City. Fort William itself remains hidden within a walled military zone.

Birla Planetarium PLANETARIUM

(Map p454; Chowringhee Rd; ₹30; ⏲in English 1.30pm & 6.30pm) Loosely styled on Sanchi's iconic Buddhist stupa, this 1962 planetarium presents slow-moving, half-hour audio-visual programs on the wonders of the universe and mysteries of deep space. It's quite convenient as a rest stop in between your day's explorations of nearby sights, and the shows aren't half bad in their execution (the baritone voice-over is particularly dramatic!).

Netaji Bhawan MUSEUM

(Map p454; ☎033-24868139; www.netaji.org; 38/2 Elgin Rd; adult/child ₹5/2; ⏲11am-4pm Tue-Sun) Celebrating the life and vision of controversial Bengali leader and pro-Independence radical Subhas Chandra Bose is this house-turned-museum, which also houses an academic research bureau.

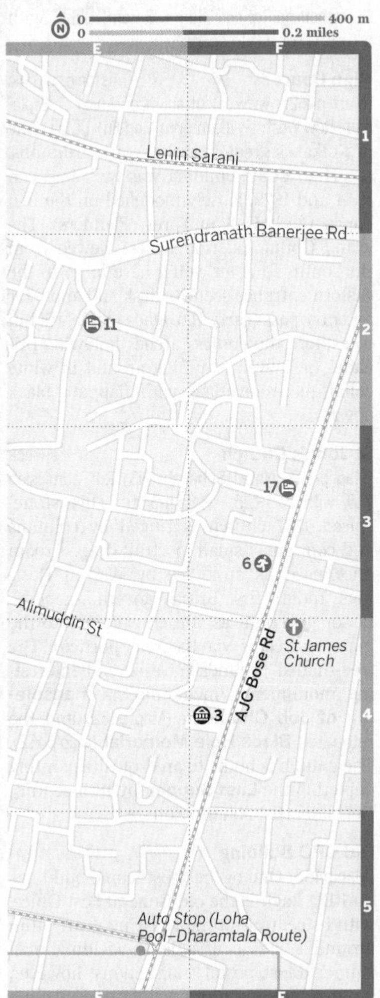

Chowringhee

The yellow limewashed building was Bose's brother's residence, from where he made his famous 'Great Escape' from British-imposed house arrest in January 1941, before eventually joining hands with the Japanese to wage war against British forces. Some rooms retain a 1940s feel, and the original Wanderer getaway car is parked in the drive.

Academy of Fine Arts GALLERY
(Map p454; 2 Cathedral Rd; 2-8pm) FREE Several bright, ground-floor gallery rooms in this 1933 building feature changing exhibitions by local artists. It's a good place to check out young-and-upcoming city talents, as well as some senior artists from the academic circuit. There's also a theatre on-site, where local groups often stage their plays that are mostly written and performed in regional languages. Information regarding

ongoing and upcoming productions can be found at the main entrance.

Harrington Street Arts Centre GALLERY
(Map p454; ☎033-22829220; www.hstreetartscentre.com; 2nd fl, 8 Ho Chi Minh Sarani; ⏲2-8pm) FREE Imaginative exhibitions of contemporary artworks, by Indian and international artists in diverse media, are spread through four spacious rooms of this classic Kolkata colonial building, restored painstakingly by the gallery proprietors. The verandah with chequered floor tiles leads to a cosy cafe. Interestingly, the gallery has two charming guest rooms (double including breakfast ₹5000) adjoining the exhibition space, which are normally reserved for visiting artists but opened up for tourists when they're vacant. Call the gallery for details.

BBD Bagh

One of Raj-era Calcutta's foremost squares, BBD Bagh (formerly Dalhousie Sq) is centred on a palm-lined central reservoir-lake called **Lal Dighi**, which once supplied the young city's water. Although concrete intrusions detract from the overall spectacle, many a splendid colonial-era edifice remains. Some of them still serve as office buildings and wandering in is prohibited, but you are free to admire the structures from outside.

Foremost is the 1780 **Writers' Buildings** (Map p462), a twin-block office complex whose glorious south facade looks something like a French provincial city hall. It was originally built as a workplace for clerks ('writers') of the East India Company, and has been under restoration since 2013. Behind, past the joyously repainted **Eastern Railways Building** (Map p462; NS Rd), the former **Chartered Bank Building** (Map p462; India Exchange Pl) has a vaguely Moorish feel with shrubs sprouting from the untended upper turrets. The 1860s GPO (p460) has a soaring rotunda, and the **Standard Life Building** (Map p462; 32 BBD Bagh) sports cherubic details that have been given a fresh lease of life by a new restoration project. Although dilapidated, the ruins of the once-grand **Currency Building** (Map p462; BBD Bagh East; ⏲10am-5pm Mon-Fri) FREE have been stabilised, making an interesting venue for an exhibition-bookshop of the Archaeological Survey of India. Standing proud to the north is **St Andrews Church** (Map p462; 15 Brabourne Rd; ⏲7-11am & 3-6pm) FREE with a fine Wren-style spire.

High Court HISTORIC BUILDING
(Map p462; www.calcuttahighcourt.nic.in; Esplanade Row West; ⏲10am-5pm Mon-Fri) FREE One of Kolkata's greatest architectural triumphs, the High Court building was built between 1864 and 1872, loosely modelled on the medieval Cloth Hall in Ypres (Flanders). The grand Gothic exterior is best viewed from the south. To enter, you'll have to go to the eastern entrance security desk and apply for an entry pass (carry ID). Once inside, it's fun to explore the endless arches following brigades of lawyers shuffling around in white collar pieces overlaid with flapping black gowns.

St John's Church CHURCH
(Map p462; Netaji Subhash (NS) Rd; admission ₹10, with car ₹25; ⏲8am-5pm) This stone-spired 1787 church is ringed by columns and contains a small, portrait-draped room once used as an office by Warren Hastings, India's first British governor-general. It's on the right as you enter (entry to the main church is via the rear portico). The tree-shaded grounds have several interesting monuments, including the **mausoleum of Job Charnock** (Map p462) and the relocated **Black Hole Memorial** (Map p462). The church is home to an exquisite painting depicting the **Last Supper**, by 18th-century German artist Johann Zoffany.

Old GPO Building ARCHITECTURE
(Map p462) One of the most iconic buildings on BBD Bagh is the old General Post Office, with its central rotunda soaring nearly 40m around a statue of a lance-wielding mail runner. Most postal transactions, however, are in a building 100m further up Koilaghat St. Outside that is a philatelic bureau where you can get commemorative issues or design yourself a sheet of ₹5 stamps incorporating your own photo (₹300). However, these can take up to seven days to be delivered.

Barabazar & Howrah

The following walk links several minor religious sights, but much of the fun comes from exploring the vibrantly chaotic alleys en route that teem with traders, rickshaw couriers and baggage-wallahs hauling impossibly huge packages balanced on their heads. Hidden away amid the paper merchants of **Old China Bazaar St**, the Armenian Church of Nazareth (Map p462; Armenian St; ⊙9am-4pm Mon-Sat) was founded in 1707 and is claimed to be Kolkata's oldest place of Christian worship. The larger 1797 Portuguese-Catholic **Holy Rosary Cathedral** (Map p462; Brabourne Rd; ⊙6am-11am & 5-6pm) has eye-catching crown-topped side towers and an interior whose font is festively kitsch.

Kolkata's Jewish community once numbered around 30,000 but these days barely 30 ageing co-religionists turn up at **Maghen David Synagogue** (Map p462; Canning St). Around the corner, the **Neveh Shalome Synagogue** (Map p462; Brabourne Rd) is almost invisible behind shop stalls. Once you've fought your way across Brabourne St, go down **Pollock St** between very colourful stalls selling balloons, tinsel and plastic plants to the decrepit **Pollock St Post Office** (Map p462; Pollock St), once a grand Jewish school building. Opposite, **BethEl Synagogue** (Map p462; Pollock St) FREE has a facade that looks passingly similar to a 1930s cinema. The synagogue has a fine colonnaded interior, but to get into this or the other synagogues you'll generally need to have contacted the **Jewish Community Affairs Office** (☎9831054669; 63 Park St).

Parallel to Pollock St, wider **Ezra St** has a brilliant old **perfumerie** (Map p462; 55 Ezra St; ⊙10am-7pm Mon-Fri), just before the **Shree Cutchi Jain Temple** (Map p462; Ezra St). From there, follow Parsee Church St east to reach Old Chinatown or swing back up the ever-fascinating **Rabindra Sarani** to find the shop-clad 1926 Nakhoda Mosque (p461) that was loosely modelled on Akbar's Mausoleum at Sikandra.

Howrah Bridge LANDMARK

(Rabindra Setu; Map p462) Howrah Bridge is a 705m-long abstraction of shiny steel cantilevers and rivets, which serves as a carriageway of nonstop human and motorised traffic across the Hooghly River. Built during WWII, it's one of the world's busiest bridges and a Kolkatan architectural icon. Photography of the bridge is prohibited, but you might sneak a discreet shot from one of the various ferries that ply across the river to the vast 1906 Howrah train station.

To lessen traffic load on the bridge and provide easy access to the city's southern districts from Howrah, a newer **Vidyasagar Setu** bridge was inaugurated in 1992. It can be seen about 3km downstream, cutting a Golden Gate Bridge–like profile across the river, if you look south from Howrah Bridge.

Mullik Ghat Flower Market MARKET

(Map p462; off Strand Rd) Near the southeast end of Howrah Bridge, this flower market is fascinatingly colourful virtually 24 hours a day. However, if you visit at daybreak, you'll see wholesellers arrive with huge consignments of flowers that are then auctioned to retailers. Many workers live in makeshift shacks, bathing in the river behind from a ghat with sunset views of Howrah Bridge. At around 7am, local wrestlers practise their art on a small caged area of sand set slightly back from the river.

Nakhoda Mosque MOSQUE

(Map p462; Zakaria St) FREE Located amid the din and chaos of Rabindra Sarani, the 1926 red-sandstone Nakhoda Mosque rises impressively above the bustling shopfronts of its neighbouring commercial establishments. Its roof, which is adorned with emerald green domes and minarets, was loosely modelled on Akbar's Mausoleum at Sikandra, while the main entrance gate was inspired by the Buland Darwaza at Fatehpur Sikri. The mosque is Kolkata's largest, and is at the centre of festive action every evening during the holy month of Ramadan.

Old Chinatown

For nearly two centuries, the area around Bentinck St and Phears Lane was Kolkata's Chinatown, populated by Chinese merchants who settled here during Kolkata's maritime heydays. However, dwindling business prospects, relocation to newer suburban colonies and the migration of later generations to the USA and Australia have taken their toll, and today 'old' Chinatown is predominantly Muslim. However, just after dawn, there's a lively market scene in the tiny square of **Tiretta Bazaar**. It's closed by 10am, as is the archetypal old shop, **Hap Hing** (Map p462; 10 Sun Yat Sen St; ⊙6am-10am), whose owner Stella Chen can tell you lots more about the Chinese community.

Other historic shops nearby include musical instrument makers Mondal & Sons (p479) and the fascinating 1948 gun shop **ML Bhunja** (Map p462; ☎9831134146; 301 BB Ganguli St, Lal Bazar; ⊙11am-6.30pm Mon-Fri), with its musty old cases of rifles, sabres, a flintlock and many an old bayonet laced with snake venom.

BBD Bagh

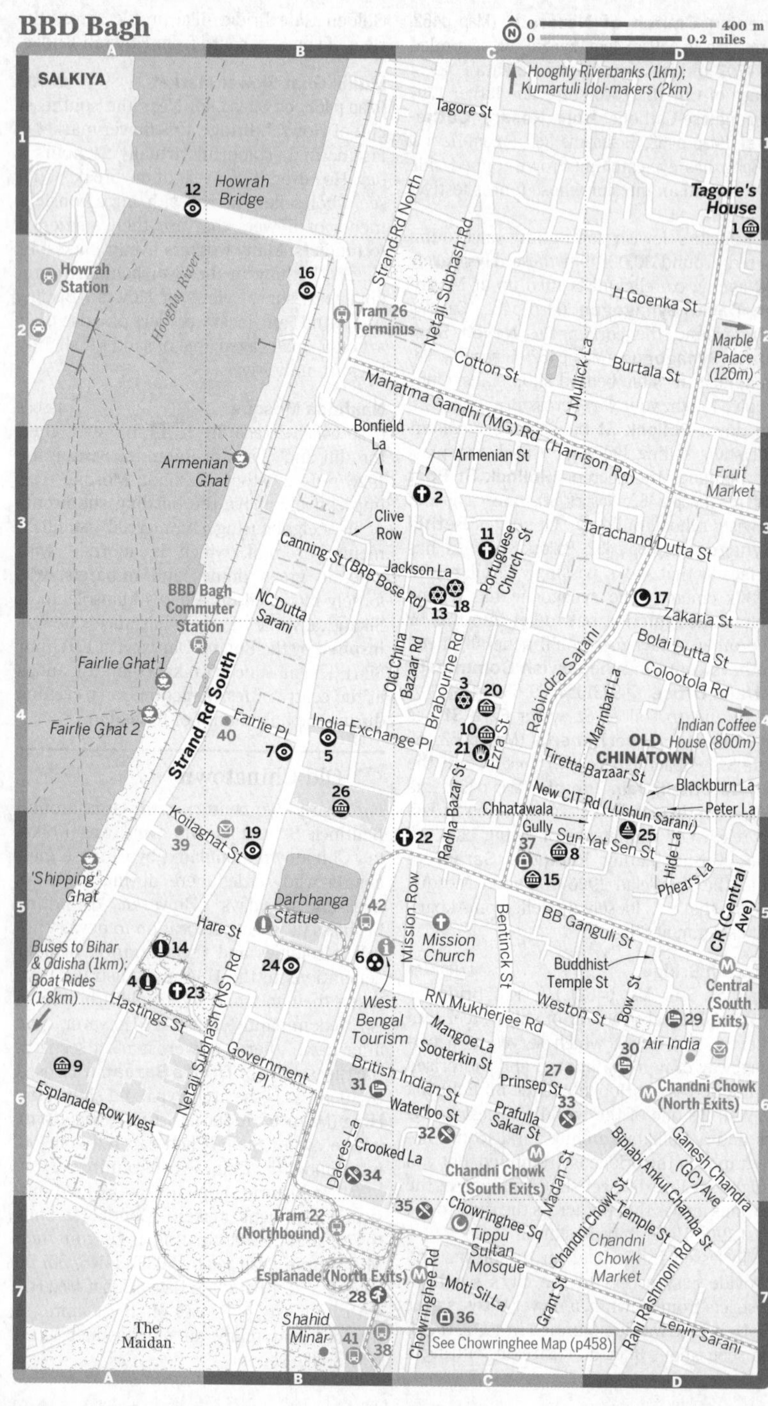

0 400 m
0 0.2 miles
SALKIYA
Hooghly Riverbanks (1km); Kumartuli Idol-makers (2km)
Tagore St
Howrah Bridge
Tagore's House
Howrah Station
Hooghly River
Tram 26 Terminus
Strand Rd North
Netaji Subhash Rd
H Goenka St
Marble Palace (120m)
Cotton St
Burtala St
J Mullick La
Mahatma Gandhi (MG) Rd (Harrison Rd)
Bonfield La
Armenian St
Armenian Ghat
Fruit Market
Clive Row
Tarachand Dutta St
Canning St (BRB Bose Rd)
Jackson La
Portuguese Church St
NC Dutta Sarani
Zakaria St
BBD Bagh Commuter Station
Bolai Dutta St
Colootola Rd
Fairlie Ghat 1
Strand Rd South
Old China Bazaar Rd
Brabourne Rd
Rabindra Sarani
Marinbari La
Fairlie Ghat 2
Fairlie Pl
India Exchange Pl
Ezra St
Indian Coffee House (800m)
OLD CHINATOWN
Tiretta Bazaar St
Radha Bazar St
Blackburn La
New CIT Rd (Lushun Sarani)
Peter La
Chhatawala Gully
Koilaghat St
Sun Yat Sen St
Hide La
Phears La
'Shipping' Ghat
Darbhanga Statue
Mission Row
Bentinck St
BB Ganguli St
CR (Central Ave)
Hare St
Mission Church
Buddhist Temple St
Bow St
Buses to Bihar & Odisha (1km); Boat Rides (1.8km)
Netaji Subhash (NS) Rd
West Bengal Tourism
RN Mukherjee Rd
Weston St
Central (South Exits)
Hastings St
Mangoe La
Air India
Government Pl
Sooterkin St
British Indian St
Princep St
Chandni Chowk (North Exits)
Esplanade Row West
Waterloo St
Prafulla Sakar St
Crooked La
Dacres La
Madan St
Biplabi Ankul Chamba St
Ganesh Chandra (GC) Ave
Chandni Chowk (South Exits)
Chowringhee Sq
Tippu Sultan Mosque
Tram 22 (Northbound)
Chandni Chowk St
Temple St
Chandni Chowk Market
Rani Rashmoni Rd
Esplanade (North Exits)
Chowringhee Rd
Moti Sil La
Grant St
The Maidan
Shahid Minar
See Chowringhee Map (p458)
Lenin Sarani

BBD Bagh

Around the once-grand 1924 **Toong On Temple** (Map p462; Blackburn Lane) FREE, destitute scavengers sift through rubbish heaps, sleeping in tent-and-box shacks on neighbouring pavements. It's a very humbling experience; take care to respect the dignity of others while walking around the area.

Rabindra Sarani & Around

The ever-fascinating **Rabindra Sarani**, a street of densely packed shops and workshops, is threaded through by trams running north from Esplanade via the clay idolmakers' workshops of **Kumartuli**, before terminating at **Galiff St**, the site of Kolkata's curious Sunday-morning pet and bird market. There are a few interesting sights around the **Kolkata University** building on College St, east of Rabindra Sarani, including the impressive facade of the 1817 **Presidency University**.

★ Marble Palace — MUSEUM

(46 Muktaram Babu St; 10am-3pm, closed Mon & Thu) FREE Built in 1835 by a raja from the prosperous Mallick family, this resplendent mansion is as grand as it is curious. Arguably one of India's best-preserved royal homes, its marble-draped halls are overstuffed with dusty statues of thinkers and dancing girls, much Victoriana, ample Belgian glassware, game trophies of moose heads and fine paintings, including supposedly original works by Murillo, Joshua Reynolds and Rubens. Admission is free, but you need prior written permission from West Bengal Tourism (p480).

Of particular note within the building is the music room, lavishly floored with marble inlay, where Napoleons beat Wellingtons three to one. The ballroom retains its vast array of candle chandeliers with globes of silvered glass to spread illumination (original 19th-century disco balls!). There's also a private menagerie on the mansion's grounds, dating back to the early years, which is home to a few monkey and bird species.

To find Marble Palace from MG Rd metro, walk north and turn left at the first traffic light – 171 Chittaranjan (CR) Ave. From the east, it's on the lane that leaves Rabindra Sarani between Nos 198 and 200.

★Tagore's House MUSEUM

(Jorasanko Thakurbari; Map p462; www.rbu.ac.in/museum; Dwarkanath Tagore Lane, off Rabindra Sarani; Indian/foreigner adult ₹10/50, student ₹5/25; ⏲10.30am-4.30pm Tue-Sun) The stately 1784 family mansion of Rabindranath Tagore has become a shrine-like museum to India's greatest modern poet. Even if his personal effects don't inspire you, some of the well-chosen quotations might spark an interest in Tagore's deeply universalist and modernist philosophy. There's a decent gallery of paintings by his family and contemporaries, and an exhibition on his literary, artistic and philosophical links with Japan. There's also a 1930 photo of Tagore with Einstein shot during a well-publicised meeting.

Northern Kolkata

★Kumartuli Idol-makers AREA

(Banamali Sarkar St) Countless clay effigies of deities and demons immersed in the Hooghly during Kolkata's colourful *pujas* (offering or prayers) are created in specialist *kumar* (sculptor) workshops in this enthralling district, notably along Banamali Sarkar St, the lane running west from Rabindra Sarani. Craftsmen are busiest from August to October, creating straw frames, adding clay coatings, and painting divine features on idols for Durga and Kali festivals. In November, old frameworks wash up on riverbanks and are often repurposed the following year.

★Belur Math RELIGIOUS SITE

(☎033-26541144; www.belurmath.org; Grand Trunk Rd; ⏲6.30am-noon & 3.30-6pm; 🚌54, 56) FREE Set very attractively amid palms and manicured lawns, this large religious centre is the headquarters of the Ramakrishna Mission, inspired by 19th-century Indian sage Ramakrishna Paramahamsa, who preached the unity of all religions. Its centrepiece is the 1938 **Ramakrishna Mandir** (⏲6.30am-noon & 3.30-6pm), which somehow manages to look like a cathedral, Indian palace and Istanbul's Aya Sofya all at the same time. Several smaller shrines near the Hooghly riverbank include the **Sri Sarada Devi Temple** (⏲6.30am-noon & 3.30-6pm) FREE, entombing the spiritual leader's wife, Sarada.

Accessed from the car park, a beautifully presented dual-level **museum** (⏲8.30-11.30am & 3.30-5.30pm Tue-Sun) FREE charts Ramakrishna's life and the travels of his great disciple Swami Vivekananda. During Durga Puja, the institution comes to life with absorbing spells of ritual and festive splendour, and the immersion of the goddess on the ultimate day in the Hooghly River is a spectacular draw.

From the main road outside, six daily suburban trains run between Belur Math and Howrah (25 minutes), most usefully at 10.45am and 4.45pm. Picking up next door to Belur Math train station, minibuses as well as buses 54 and 56 run to Esplanade/Howrah in stop-start traffic. Southbound, they pass almost beside Bandaghat from where you can take the thrice-hourly ferry to Ahiritola, then switch to the Bagbazar boat for Kumartuli. From **Belur Jetty**, ferries (hourly) and open boats (when full) operate to Dakshineswar. Southbound ferries to Howrah via Bagbazar depart at 6.30pm and 8pm (plus 9.15am/1.30pm weekdays/Sunday).

Kalighat

Surrounding Kalighat Temple is a fascinating maze of alleys jammed with market stalls selling votive flowers, brassware and religious artefacts. The ritualistic splendour is worth a few hours of your exploration, preferably camera in hand.

Kalighat Temple HINDU TEMPLE

(Map p466; Kali Temple Rd; ⏲5am-10pm, central shrine closed 2-4pm) This ancient Kali temple is Kolkata's holiest spot for Hindus, and possibly the source of the city's name. Today's version is the 1809 rebuild, with floral- and peacock-motif tiles that look more Victorian than Indian. More interesting than the architecture are the jostling pilgrim queues that snake into the main hall to fling hibiscus flowers at a crowned, three-eyed Kali image with a gold-plated tongue. Behind the bell pavilion, goats are ritually beheaded (generally mornings) to honour the Tantric goddess.

Ballygunge, Gariahat & Lansdowne

East of Kalighat, these modern and cosmopolitan residential and commercial areas are a fascinating mixture of new and old, with a generous scattering of fancy restaurants, glitzy shopping malls, sophisticated galleries, urban-chic boutiques and espresso-punching cafes.

Rabindra Sarovar PARK

(Map p466; off Southern Ave) FREE The lakes here prettily reflect hazy sunrises, while middle-class Kolkatans jog, row and meditate around the tree-shaded parkland that was once the site of an Allied Forces medical camp during WWII. Some form circles to do group yoga routines culminating in forced, raucous laugh-ins, engagingly described by Tony Hawks as Laughing Clubs in *The Weekenders: Adventures in Calcutta.* Young love birds match the park's avian residents in numbers, and street musicians enthral listeners with soulful tunes, mostly on weekends.

Birla Mandir HINDU TEMPLE

(Map p466; Gariahat Rd; ⏲6-11am & 5-9pm) FREE A graceful 20th-century structure built in cream-coloured sandstone, this temple is consecrated to the Hindu gods Narayan (Vishnu) and his wife Lakshmi. The three corn-cob shaped towers are more impressive for their size than their carvings, and the courtyards are a nice place to sit and spend a few moments in quiet contemplation. There's a state-of-the-art auditorium adjacent to the temple complex called **GD Birla Sabaghar** (Map p466; www.gdbirlasabhaghar.com; Queens Park Rd) that often hosts musical programs and other performances; see website for upcoming schedules.

CIMA GALLERY

(Map p466; ☎033-24858717; www.cimaartindia.com; Sunny Towers, 43 Ashutosh Chowdhury Ave; ⏲noon-7pm Tue-Sat, 3-7pm Mon) FREE A cutting-edge contemporary art gallery located on the 2nd floor of an upmarket South Kolkata building complex, CIMA is a great place to check out works by some of India's top-line contemporary artists as well as old masters. Exhibitions change on a biweekly or monthly basis, and there are occasionally specially curated shows. There's also a design shop and gift store within the premises, selling an eclectic and highly desirable collection of souvenirs, handicrafts and urban-chic designware.

Alipore & Around

★**Botanical Gardens** PARK

(Indian/foreigner ₹10/100; ⏲6am-5pm Tue-Sun; 🚌55, 213) Despite being an awkward journey by public transport, Kolkata's lovely 109-hectare Botanical Gardens makes for a great place to escape from the city's frazzling sounds and smells. Founded in 1786, the gardens – home to more than 12,000 plant species – played an important role in cultivating tea bushes smuggled in from China by the British, long before the drink became a household commodity. Today, there's a cactus house, palm collection, river-overlook and a boating lake with splendid Giant Amazon Lily pads.

The most touted attraction in the park is the 250-year-old **'world's largest banyan tree'**. That's a little misleading – the central trunk rotted away in the 1920s, leaving an array of cross-branches and linked aerial roots that collectively look more like a copse than a single tree. The banyan is five minutes' walk from the park's Bicentenary Gate on buses 55 and 213, or a 30-minute walk from the main gate where minibuses as well as bus 55 terminate after a painfully slow journey from Esplanade via Howrah. Taxis from Shakespeare Sarani charge around ₹200 via the elegant Vidyasagar Setu.

MOTHER TERESA

For many people, Mother Teresa (1910–97) was the living image of human compassion and sacrifice. Born Agnes Gonxha Bojaxhiu to Albanian parents in then-Ottoman Üsküp (now Skopje in Macedonia), she joined the Irish Order of Loreto nuns and worked for more than a decade teaching in Calcutta's St Mary's High School. Horrified by the city's spiralling poverty, she established a new order, the Missionaries of Charity (p467) and founded refuges for the destitute and dying. The first of these, **Nirmal Hriday** (Map p466; 251 Kalighat Rd), opened in 1952. Although the order swiftly expanded into an international charity, Mother Teresa herself continued to live in absolute simplicity. She was awarded the Nobel Peace Prize in 1979, beatified by the Vatican in 2003 and eventually made a saint in 2016.

However, there are some who detract and question the social worker's call of duty. Feminist author Germaine Greer has accused Mother Teresa of religious imperialism, while journalist Christopher Hitchens' book, *The Missionary Position,* decried donations from dictators and corrupt tycoons. Many have also questioned the order's minimal medical background as well as Teresa's staunch views against contraception. Regardless, her defenders continue to look up to her for her noble lifelong mission to offer love, care and dignity to the dying and the destitute, while inspiring several others to follow in her charitable steps.

Southern Kolkata

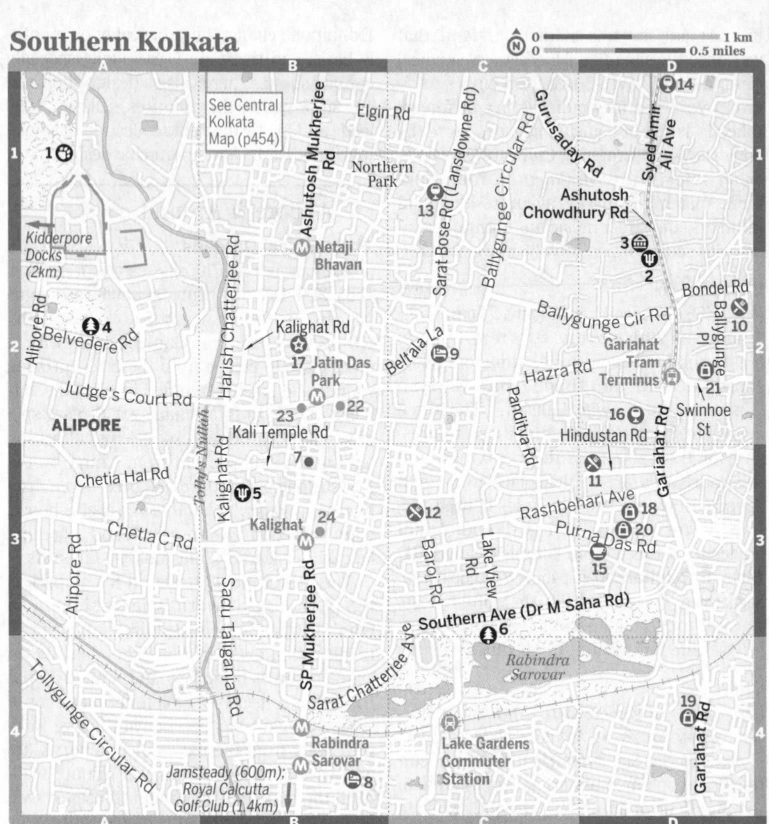

Horticultural Gardens PARK

(Map p466; Belvedere Rd; ₹10; ⏲6-10am & 2-7pm) A hidden island of tranquillity in the heart of Kolkata, this delightful garden complex offers visitors an opportunity to acquaint themselves with tropical plant species, even while feasting their eyes on its placid green surroundings. Hundreds of tropical shrubs and flowering plants blossom around the central lawn, as well as in the themed Japanese Garden and around a cute stony waterfall. There's also an orchard with fruit trees (no plucking), and separate gardens for cacti and orchids.

Alipore Zoo ZOO

(Map p466; www.kolkatazoo.in; Alipore Rd; admission ₹20, video ₹250; ⏲9am-5pm Fri-Wed) Kolkata's 16-hectare zoo opened its doors in 1875 as one of British India's showpiece zoological gardens, but has gradually dropped in stature and standards over the years. The spacious lawns and lakeside promenades are very popular with weekend picnickers (hence all the rubbish). Avoid visiting between Christmas and New Year as the place is swamped by locals. You'll find toilets and stalls selling snacks and bottled water within the premises.

Activities

Boat Rides BOATING

(Outram Ghat) A fantastic way to watch the sun go down over the Hooghly River is by riding a skiff into the waters at dusk. Oarsmen line up their boats along the pier at **Outram Ghat**, and offer rides that take you under the **Vidyasagar Setu** bridge on a round trip from the jetty. Prices range around ₹500 for an hour's ride.

Heritage Tram TRAM RIDE

(Map p462; tickets incl snacks ₹260; ⏲7am & 2pm Sat & Sun) The state-owned Calcutta Tramways Company operates a few trams in Kolkata only on select routes. For a special experience of Kolkata's tramways, however, you

Southern Kolkata

could hop onto a renovated air-conditioned heritage tram from the Esplanade tram depot, and embark on a pleasure ride across the Maidan or the charming northern districts extending along Rabindra Sarani.

Royal Calcutta Golf Club GOLF
(☎033-24731352; www.rcgc.in; 18 Golf Club Rd; nonmember green fees ₹6500, 9-/18-hole caddy fee ₹225/450) The magnificent Royal Calcutta Golf Club was established in 1829, making it the oldest golf club in the world outside Britain. It's also one of India's few colonial golf clubs where you can tee off as a walk-in nonmember, although for a steep fee. For other facilities (such as swimming or tennis), you'll have to come as a member's guest.

Responsible Charity VOLUNTEERING
(www.responsiblecharity.org) This US-based humanist charity works with destitute families in the Jadavpur area of Kolkata. Volunteers should ideally be trained in medicine or have educational exerience. Alternatively just donate (decent) old clothes to its collection bank at JoJo's Cafe (p473).

Missionaries of Charity VOLUNTEERING
(☎033-22497115; www.motherteresa.org) This charitable religious order, founded by Mother (St) Teresa, helps large numbers of the city's destitute sick and dying. Volunteers are universally welcome, with no minimum service period, experience or specific skills required other than a warm heart and patience to listen to and empathise with those whose language they may not understand.

Volunteers need to attend an orientation briefing, held three times weekly at **Sishu Bhavan** (Map p458; 78 AJC Bose Rd; ⏲3pm Mon, Wed & Fri), two blocks north of Mother Teresa's Motherhouse (p457). A volunteering 'day' starts at 7am with a bread-and-banana breakfast at the Motherhouse, and is generally over by early afternoon.

Courses

Mystic Yoga Studio YOGA
(Map p454; www.mysticyoga.in; 2nd fl, 20A Camac St; drop-in sessions ₹600; ⏲8am-8pm) This mirror-walled commercial studio offers one-hour guided yoga sessions (mostly basic) for drop-in guests. If you're on a long stay, try one of its monthly courses, which are more structured. There's an attached juice bar and organic cafe that plays recorded mantras. Hours vary on weekends, when they remain open till 5pm.

Kali Travel Home COOKING
(☎033-25550581; www.traveleastindia.com; courses per person from ₹1200) Enthusiastic expats at Kali Travel Home offer personalised Bengali cooking courses with local families. Courses range from basic dishes to special fare (both vegetarian and non-vegetarian), including

tossing up a full Bengali lunch platter. Kali also offers guided tours of Kolkata and neighbouring areas. Call for more information.

Tours

★Calcutta Walks WALKING
(Map p462; ☎033-40052573, 9830184030, 9830604197; www.calcuttawalks.com; 9A Khairu Pl; per person from ₹2000) A super-professional outfit run by the knowledgeable conservationist Iftekhar, this organisation offers a wide range of walking, cycling and motorbike tours, plus homestays with local families. It produces what is arguably the best printed map of Kolkata. Apart from fixed departure shared walks, you can also customise a private walk for a higher price.

Backpackers MOTORBIKE TOURS
(Map p458; ☎9836177140; www.tourdesundarbans.com; Tottee Lane; per person per bike incl lunch ₹2200) Best known for their Sundarban mangrove trips, the inspiring 'brothers' at Backpackers also offer innovative pillion-ride city tours on the back of an iconic Royal Enfield motorbike. Classic tours (from 8.30am to 3pm) drive past several well-known sites, such as Old Chinatown, Victoria Memorial, South Park Street Cemetery, Howrah Bridge and Kumartuli, and might also throw in a few curiosities.

Bomti TOURS
(Surajit Iyengar; ☎9831314990; bomtiyengar@yahoo.com; per group per day ₹8000-10000, plus per person for meals ₹2500-3000) More than merely a tour guide, Bomti is an art collector and a veritable well of information on the city's heritage. Residing in a fascinating heritage apartment stuffed with art and artisana that was once featured in *Elle Decor*, tailor-made personalised tours for up to four people typically end with a lavish and traditional Bengali meal in Bomti's home.

Calcutta Photo Tours PHOTOGRAPHY
(☎9831163482; www.calcuttaphototours.com; per person from ₹1750) A range of photography tours on foot, themed on Kolkata's culture, colonial heritage and markets, is offered by this professional outfit. Tours start at 6am or 2pm, and are offered throughout the year.

Sleeping

Decent accommodation is expensive in Kolkata, and budget places are often dismal. Top-end hotels have significant discounts online. Midrange hotels are usually better value as walk-ins, while budget places rarely take bookings. The Salt Lake area has many business hotels, but it's badly connected so travellers might regret staying there. Accommodation fills to bursting before and during Durga Puja (p471), and demand is high from mid-November to February.

Around Sudder Street

The nearest Kolkata gets to a traveller ghetto is around helpfully located Sudder St. There's a range of backpacker-oriented ser-

TOP FESTIVALS

Dover Lane Music (www.doverlanemusicconference.org; Nazrul Mancha, Rabindra Sarovar; ⏲late Jan) Conference Indian classical music and dance at Rabindra Sarovar.

Saraswati Puja (⏲late Jan/early Feb) Prayers for educational success, all dress in yellow.

Kolkata Book Fair (www.kolkatabookfair.net; Milan Mela, EM Bypass; ⏲late Jan/early Feb) Asia's biggest book fair.

Eid-ul-fitr Celebrated after the Islamic holy month of Ramadan.

Rath Yatra (⏲late Jul/early Aug) Major Krishna chariot festival similar to the Puri equivalent.

Durga Puja (⏲late Sep/early Oct) Kolkata's biggest festival (p471).

Kolkata Film Festival (www.kff.in; ⏲mid-Nov) Weeklong festival of Indian and international movies.

Kolkata Jazzfest (www.jazzfest.in; Dalhousie Institute; ⏲late Nov) Three days of jazz, blues and world music.

Boro Din Kolkata's version of Christmas.

There is also a wide range of village craft festivals in the area outside the city. Bangla Natak (www.banglanatak.com) is an NGO that helps raise awareness and encourage visitors.

vices, and virtually every second building is a guesthouse or hotel, from charming heritage palaces to ultra-budget dives that represent a whole new league of nastiness. When we list Sudder St area accommodation under ₹1000, we're usually identifying the least objectionable options rather than making a recommendation.

Hotel Lindsay HOTEL **$$**

(Map p458; ☎033-30218866; www.thelindsay.in; 8 Lindsay St; s/d incl breakfast from ₹4150/4750;) A thorough redecoration gives an attractive old-Kolkata 'heritage' ambience to the Lindsay's guest rooms and corridors, belying the 1970s architecture of the tower in which they lie. Some of the rooms overlook the atmospheric New Market area. Walk-in rates can be lower, but thanks to its unbeatable location and great in-house terrace bar-restaurant, rooms are hard to find without prior bookings.

Afridi International HOTEL **$**

(Map p458; ☎033-66077525; goldenapplegroup hotels@gmail.com; 3 Cowie Lane; d incl breakfast ₹1450;) Possibly the most professionally managed budget hotel in Sudder St, the furniture and fittings are top-notch, while the entrance is floored in crystalline marble. Some rooms are small and suffer from a trace of damp, but maintenance is regular and the smart upholstery and comfy beds ensure a pleasant stay.

Golden Apple Hotel GUESTHOUSE **$$**

(Map p458; ☎033-66077500; www.goldenapple hotel.in; 9 Sudder St; dm cubicles ₹700, d incl breakfast from ₹3550) The Golden Apple has accommodation that's mostly fresh and tastefully appointed for the price. Even the cramped cheapest rooms somehow jam in a small desk. A handy and stylish backpacker feature is the set of 15 top-floor deluxe dorm cubicles, each a lockable bedspace partitioned off by smoked-glass walls and equipped with a storage area beneath the mattress.

Bawa Walson Spa'O'Tel BOUTIQUE HOTEL **$$**

(Map p458; ☎033-22521512; 5A Sudder St; s/d incl breakfast ₹3600/4230;) Plenty of brass mudra-hands, Buddha heads and pretty metal leaf sculptures along with multicoloured fabrics give the Walson visual hints of a Thai boutique hotel. However, while pretty, the less pricey rooms are undersized, lack enough natural light and are prone to damp. The lounge bar has film posters of Hollywood classics doubling as decor.

SLEEPING PRICE RANGES

The following price ranges refer to a double room including tax (5% on rooms over ₹1000, 17.42% on those over ₹3000). When bargaining, double-check whether the quote is 'plus plus'.

$ less than ₹2000

$$ ₹2000–6000

$$$ more than ₹6000

★**Oberoi Grand** HERITAGE HOTEL **$$$**

(Map p458; ☎033-22492323; www.oberoihotels.com; 15 Chowringhee Rd; s/d incl breakfast from ₹12,100/14,200;) Saluting guards usher you out of the chaos of Chowringhee Rd and into a regal oasis of genteel calm that deserves every point of its five stars. Immaculate accommodation exudes timeless class, the swimming pool is ringed with five-storey palms and proactive staff anticipate your every need. Remarkably comfortable rooms come with a five-choice pillow menu and soothing pool views.

Online bargains available from ₹8454.

Hotel Aafreen HOTEL **$**

(Map p458; ☎033-22654146, 033-32261780; www.goldenapplehotel.in; Nawab Abdur Rahman St; d with/without AC ₹1400/1250;) Offering midrange quality at budget prices, the Aafreen has patterned pink-marble floors and ample-sized rooms that are regularly repainted and boast smart furniture and clean linen. The fan-cooled rooms make the deal a notch more attractive for those travelling on a budget.

Hotel Galaxy GUESTHOUSE **$**

(Map p458; ☎033-22524565; hotelgalaxy.kol@gmail.com; 3 Stuart Lane; d/tr ₹900/1200;) This quiet, ever-popular guesthouse looks dowdy from outside but the tiny rooms are unexpectedly comfortable and well appointed. Hot water flows freely in the en-suite bathrooms and there's free wi-fi (add ₹200 for air-con). There's a small front-porch sitting area, with a mini library, where you can leave your hand imprint on a wall that serves as a guestbook.

DK International HOTEL **$$**

(Map p458; ☎033-22522540, 033-40019283; www.dkinthotel.com; 11/1A Marquis St; d from ₹2400;) This five-storey glass tower has a certain neo–art deco feel in its corridors, soap-stone 'jade' ornamentation and rooms with golden curtains. Despite its affordability, it tries to emulate a business hotel, throwing in complimentary newspapers and fruit baskets, and offers prompt and efficient service.

Lytton Hotel BOUTIQUE HOTEL **$$$**
(Map p458; 033-22491872, 033-39841900; www.lyttonhotelindia.com; 14 Sudder St; s/d incl breakfast ₹5800/7100;) Sudder St's only 'real' top-end hotel is slightly old-fashioned, but well maintained with polite service and little Tiffany-style panels in the stairwells. There are sitting areas in the attractively appointed bedrooms along with kettle, safe, fridge and wi-fi, but mattresses could be thicker and the bathrooms more modern. Room sizes vary significantly.

Around Park Street

Sunflower Guest House GUESTHOUSE **$**
(Map p458; 033-22299401; www.sunflowerguesthouse.com; 5th fl, 7 Royd St; d with/without AC from ₹1650/1450;) The Sunflower is what all budget hotels in Kolkata should strive to be. It's housed in a grand 1865 residential building – take the vintage lift to the top then climb one floor to check in. Rooms can be slightly spartan but they're assiduously cleaned, with high ceilings. Pleasant communal spaces are available, and the rooftop garden at dusk is delightful.

YWCA HOSTEL **$**
(Map p458; 033-22292494; www.ywcacalcutta.org; 1 Middleton Row; s/d ₹700/1000, without bathroom ₹450/750, with AC ₹1000/1300;) You don't have to be a woman to get a room in this well-kept, imposing but basic 1925 building. Old high-ceilinged rooms have slatted green doors opening onto a wide arched corridor whose other open side faces a central tennis court. Large, sparse sitting rooms have a sense of times gone by, without the slightest hint of luxury.

★**Park Hotel** HOTEL **$$$**
(Map p458; 033-22499000; www.theparkhotels.com; 17 Park St; s/d incl breakfast from ₹6250/7250;) A top central choice for hip, upmarket accommodation. Modern rooms are snug and feature snazzy decor, while hidden to the rear of the 1st floor is a trio of classy restaurants and a passage past waterfall foliage to Aqua, one of India's coolest poolside bars. Curiously, the hotel's main entrance is through the Street, a cafe-deli.

Corporate HOTEL **$$**
(Map p458; 033-22267551, 8981011686; www.thecorporatekolkata.com; 4 Royd St; d incl breakfast ₹4650;) In the suave designer lobby of this slick hotel, the receptionist seems to float in luminous marble. Compact well-maintained rooms in beige and brown tones have comfy thick mattresses with satin sashes and pale polished stone bathrooms. Suites have small balconies and there's a four-table 'garden' behind the kitchen windows. Creature comforts such as kettle, fridge and hairdryer are provided.

Southern Chowringhee

Central B&B B&B **$$**
(Map p454; 9836465400; www.centralbnb.com; Flat 28, 7th fl, Lansdowne Crt, 5B Sarat Bose Rd; d incl breakfast ₹3550;) Probably the best Kolkata apartment-guesthouse to have made its name on the B&B circuit, Central lives up to all its promises. The four rooms are huge and comfortable, with a large shared lounge and communal kitchen. There's fast wi-fi, a basic but sumptuous breakfast, a basket of complimentary snacks and ever-obliging (if usually invisible) hosts.

Astor HERITAGE HOTEL **$$$**
(Map p454; 033-22829950; www.astorkolkata.com; 15 Shakespeare Sarani; s/d ₹8300/8900;) Artful evening floodlighting brings out the best of the Astor's solid 1905 architecture, while inside walls are lavished with B&W photos of old Kolkata. A creative palette of chocolate, beige and iridescent butterfly blue brings to life beautifully furnished rooms, fully refurbished in 2012. Some suites include a four-poster bed. Sizes and shapes vary. There's no lift, however.

Kenilworth HOTEL **$$$**
(Map p454; 033-22823939; www.kenilworthhotels.com; 1 Little Russell St; d incl breakfast from ₹7150;) The pleasingly bright, fully equipped rooms in this classy Kolkata address have some of the city's most comfortable beds. The deep lobby of marble, dark wood and chandeliers contrasts successfully with a more contemporary cafe that spills out onto an attractive quadrangle of lawn. The Irish-style in-house pub attracts the city's beautiful people in the evenings.

Park Prime BUSINESS HOTEL **$$$**
(Map p454; 033-30963096; www.chocolatehotels.in; 226 AJC Bose Rd; s/d incl breakfast from ₹6800/7600;) Sleep in an artistic

statement with an exterior that looks like a seven-storey computer punch card and rooms that have optical-illusion decor. Bedboards carry up across the ceiling and sweep down the wall to emerge as a dagger of desk. It's all done without compromising comfort, the foyer is spaciously inviting and the rooftop swimming pool nestles beside hip Henry's Lounge Bar.

Motherhouse Area

The Motherhouse and Park St areas feature a few prosaic hotels and guesthouses that are handy for those wishing to visit points of interest in the area. However, they are rather scattered, and lack backpacker facilities or any sense of 'traveller community'.

Monovilla Inn GUESTHOUSE **$**
(Map p458; ☎033-40076752; www.monovillainn.com; 79/26/D AJC Bose Rd; s/d ₹1200/1500, with AC ₹1800/2100; ❄@) Fresh and modern rooms here back a 1940s three-storey building with just two guest rooms per floor. Those located upstairs have better light. There's minimal communal space so you'll be confined to your room most of the time. The toilets are very good for the price.

Georgian Inn GUESTHOUSE **$**
(Map p458; ☎9830156625, 9830068355; www.georgianin.com; 1 Doctor Lane; s/d ₹1150/1350, with AC ₹1500/1750; ❄) Very functional but friendly and cheap, this hotel gains in atmosphere thanks to the fascinating melee of Taltala Market that surrounds it. Streetscapes of Doctor Lane to the direct east have architectural hints of old Penang. It's within walking distance of the New Market and Sudder St areas.

BBD Bagh

Bengal Buddhist Association GUESTHOUSE **$**
(Bauddha Dharmankur Sabha; Map p462; ☎033-22117138; bds1892@yahoo.com; 1 Buddhist Temple St; d/tr without bathroom ₹300/400; ❄) Although meant for visiting Buddhist students, the guesthouse opens its doors to all travellers, as long as they maintain house decorum (the gates are locked from 10pm to 6am – and you can't hobble in drunk). The simple rooms share basic common bathrooms with geysers, although there are a few en-suite rooms with air-con (₹750).

Broadway Hotel HOTEL **$**
(Map p462; ☎033-22363930; www.broadwayhotel.in; 27A Ganesh Chandra (GC) Ave; s/d/tr/ste ₹980/1150/1610/1980; ❄📶) The Broadway is a simple colonial-era hotel that has kept its character without going upmarket. An antiquated lift accesses plain but well-maintained rooms with high ceilings and reupholstered 1950s-style furniture. There's good service and a free newspaper under the door, but hot water is by the bucket in cheaper rooms. The in-house bar is delightfully atmospheric.

Lalit Great Eastern HOTEL **$$$**
(Map p462; ☎033-44447777; www.thelalit.com; 1 Old Court House St; d incl breakfast from ₹8400; ❄📶🏊) The 1840 Great Eastern Hotel was once one of India's finest hotels. It lay derelict for years, and the original west-facing facade still remains a work in progress. Behind that, however, is an entirely new, sleek business hotel. Rooms are spacious and modernist, with very comfortable super-king beds and stylish black-pebble surround showers. Enter via Waterloo St.

DURGA PUJA

Much as Carnival transforms cities such as Rio or New Orleans, **Durga Puja** brings Kolkata to a fever pitch of colourfully chaotic mayhem, as the city's biggest festival celebrates the maternal essence of the divine. For five days in late September or early October, people venerate ornate idols of the 10-armed goddess Durga and her entourage, displayed in *pandals* (temporary shrines) that dominate yards and little parks and block roads.

Over the past 30 years, design competitions and increasing corporate sponsorship have seen *pandals* growing ever more ornate and complex, some with topical or political messages. **West Bengal Tourism** (p480) tours try to take tourists around a selection of the best *pandals*, but getting anywhere within the city can take hours given the general festive pandemonium. At the festival's climax, myriad Durga idols are thrown into the sacred Hooghly River amid singing, water throwing, fireworks and indescribable traffic congestion. If you just want *pandal* photos and not the festival aspect, consider visiting just after Durga Puja when the idols have gone but *pandals* have yet to be deconstructed. Note that the city is virtually on shutdown mode during these five days. Do not schedule any important work during the festival.

Southern Kolkata

★Corner Courtyard BOUTIQUE HOTEL $$
(Map p466; ☎033-40610145; www.thecornercourtyard.com; 92B Sarat Bose Rd; d incl breakfast ₹5000; ❄📶) Seven perfectly pitched rooms at this stylish address are named after colours, but they also take photographic subthemes – such as Bengali cinema in 'Charcoal', Kumartuli goddesses in 'Vermilion' and Kolkata's architectural heritage in 'Ivory'. Rooms are on two storeys above a superb little restaurant in a recently restored 1904 townhouse, which includes a charming roof garden drooping with bougainvillea.

Bodhi Tree GUESTHOUSE $$
(Map p466; ☎033-24246534, 8017133921; www.bodhitreekolkata.com; 48/44 Swiss Park; d incl breakfast from ₹2500; ❄📶) Atmospheric and characterful, a bunch of stone-walled, rustic Buddha-themed guest rooms are attached to this intriguing little 'monastery of art' gallery cafe, which positions itself as a hippie-chic address for flashpackers. Access is from behind Rabrindra Sarovar metro's southeast exit, walking east for around 10 minutes.

Airport Area

Celesta BOUTIQUE HOTEL $$
(☎033-71000131; www.celesta.in; VIP Rd, Ragunathpur; d incl breakfast from ₹3600; ❄📶) Celesta is the suavest of over a dozen hotels in the Raghunathpur area that target travellers in transit (the airport is 15 minutes away by taxi). It makes a style statement with big plate-glass lobby walls and an upper exterior looking like a Mondrian painting. Luxurious beds are piled with pillows in retro art-deco rooms with rain showerheads.

It's beside the well-signed KFC on the east side of VIP Rd, 4km south of the airport.

Hotels Balaji & Tirupati HOTEL $$
(☎033-25120065, 033-25132005; www.hotelbalajiinternational.in; 32 Jessore Rd; d Balaji/Tirupati from ₹1550/1850; ❄📶) Off Jessore Rd between Airport Gates 1 and 2, this smart twin-hotel (named after South Indian divinities) has heavy timber doors, plants on the stairs and good rooms with decent bathrooms, though the mattresses are thin and there's a Donald Duck painted incongruously on some mirrors. Prices include a ride to the airport.

Eating

Bengali cuisine is a wonderful discovery once you've mastered a new culinary vocabulary. Cheaper eateries often serve tapas-sized portions, so order two or three dishes per person along with rice or *luchi* (deep-fried Bengali *puris*). Most restaurants add 19.4% tax to food bills (included in prices quoted). Posher places add service fees. Tips are welcome at cheaper places and expected at most expensive restaurants. Check **Times Food Guide** (book ₹239) and **Zomato** (www.zomato.com/kolkata).

Around Sudder Street

Bhoj Company BENGALI $
(Map p458; Sudder St; mains veg ₹60-90, nonveg ₹100-200; ⏲8.30am-11.30pm; ❄) Excellent, inexpensive Bengali food comes to your table in this tiny restaurant, where colourful naive art sets off white walls inset with little terracotta-statuette niches. A deliciously safe bet here is the *rui kalia* (ginger- and garlic-based fish curry) or giant prawn *malaikari* (in coconut milk gravy), and dhal and rice with *jhuri alu bhaja* – crispy potato whisps to add crunch.

Suruchi BENGALI $$
(Map p458; ☎033-22290011; 89 Elliot Rd; mains ₹150-200; ⏲10am-5pm; ❄) This canteen-style eatery run by an NGO committed to women's empowerment serves fabulous fish, meat and vegetarian dishes redolent with homemade flavours and aromas. The decor is spartan yet ethnic, featuring reed blinds on windows, and food is served in an elaborate arrangement of stainless-steel tableware. It's behind an easy-to-spot vermilion-coloured door on Elliot Rd.

Raj Spanish Cafe CAFE $
(Map p458; off Sudder St; mains ₹90-150, pizzas ₹240-390; ⏲8.30am-10pm; 📶) Popular as a hang-out for medium-term charity volunteers, this unpretentious place serves good coffee, lassis, pancakes, and a range of Italian, Mexican and Spanish dishes. The pizzas come out of a wood-fired oven, which is a rarity in town. There's a small outdoor area with some cursory foliage. It's hidden in a lane behind the Roop Shringar fabric shop.

Blue Sky Cafe CAFE $
(Map p458; Chowringhee Lane; mains ₹70-250, juices ₹100; ⏲8am-11pm; ❄) Wise-cracking staff at this travellers' cafe serve up a vast selection of reliable standbys (including great old-style banana pancakes and milkshakes)

BENGALI FOOD

Bengali food is an exceptionally evolved cuisine that is characterised by the astringent aroma of mustard oil, its principal cooking medium. A typical Bengali meal starts with a few preparations of leafy greens and a selection of fried vegetables such as eggplant, bitter gourd or potatoes. The next course comprises a few curries, many of which are accented with the generous use of *posto* (poppy seeds). Other excellent vegetarian choices include *mochar ghonto* (mashed banana flower with potato and coconut), *doi begun* (eggplant in curd) and *shukto,* a favourite starter combining at least five different vegetables in a coconut-milk-based sauce, topped with fried bitter gourd and *bori* (crunchy savouries made from mashed dhal paste).

Next comes fish, for which Bengal has earned a legendary reputation. Typical Bengali fish curry types include the light, cumin- or nigella-scented *jhol,* the drier and spicier *jhal* or the richer, ginger- and garlic-based *kalia.* Strong mustard notes feature in *shorshe* curries and *paturi* dishes that come steamed in a banana leaf. Popular fish species include *chingri* (river prawns), meaty *rohu* (white rui), fatty *chital* and the snapper-like *bhetki*. If you can handle the bones, *ilish* (hilsa) is considered the tastiest fish. While it's not *de rigueur,* meat or *murgi* (chicken) dishes also often feature towards the end of a meal. All of this is polished off with *gobindobhog bhaat* (steamed aromatic rice) or *luchi* (small puris).

Mishti (desserts), the final items on the menu, form an important part of Bengali meals. Subtly flavoured *mishti doi* (sweetened yoghurt), *roshogolla* (deep-fried spongy cottage cheese balls soaked in sugar syrup) and *cham-cham* (double-textured curd-based desserts) are the more iconic sweetmeats.

In between meals, Bengal's trademark fast food is the *kati* roll, an oily *paratha* fried with a coating of egg and filled with sliced onions, chilli and your choice of stuffing (curried chicken, grilled meat or paneer). It is generally eaten as a takeaway from hole-in-the-wall serveries. You could also try the spicy *phuchka,* hollow semolina balls stuffed with spicy potato masala dipped in tamarind sauce, or *jhal muri,* a spicy mixture with a base of puffed rice and peanuts.

For a colourful and very affectionate portrait of Kolkata's cuisine, along with a historical record of myriad colonial-era influences and adaptations over centuries, buy a copy of *The Calcutta Cookbook* (₹399), written by Minakshie Dasgupta, Bunny Gupta and Jaya Chaliha, available at leading bookstores.

at long glass tables set close enough to make conversation between strangers a little more likely. The place fills up quickly during meals. The salads are safe to consume as they're washed in bottled water only.

JoJo's Restaurant CAFE **$**

(Map p458; Sudder St; snacks ₹50-70, mains ₹80-120; ⏲8am-11pm; ❄📶) This pleasant, well-run backpacker cafe flaunts some original fresh juices and smoothies with evocative names (Liquid Breakfast, Kung Flu Fighter etc). There's free wi-fi, flags and frescoes for wall decor and an overall cheerful ambience.

Blue & Beyond MULTICUISINE **$$**

(Map p458; 9th fl, Lindsay Hotel, Lindsay St; mains ₹250-350, beer/cocktails from ₹220/300; ⏲noon-10.45pm; ❄) The drawcard here is an open-air rooftop terrace with wide views over New Market, plus a small glass-walled cocktail bar that falls somewhere between 1970s retro and a space-station acid trip. The globetrotting menu swerves from *khawsuey* (Burmese-style curried noodles) and Roquefort prawn sizzler to Greek chicken and Mexican 'veg-steak'.

Around Park Street

Peter Cat MULTICUISINE **$$**

(Map p458; ☎033-22298841; Middleton Row; mains ₹200-430; ⏲11am-11pm; ❄) This phenomenally popular Kolkata institution is best known for its Iranian-style *chelo* kebabs (barbequed fingers of spiced, minced meat on buttered rice). Other dishes such as the tandoori mixed grill and the chicken sizzler also fly thick and fast. Beer (₹190) comes in pewter tankards and waiters wear Rajasthani costumes. No reservations – just join the queue!

★**Arsalan** MUGHLAI **$$**

(Map p458; 119 Ripon St; mains ₹120-280; ⏲11.30am-11.30pm; ❄) Consistently popular with locals, this central branch of Kolkata's best biriyani house is high ceilinged and attractively modern without being fashion-conscious. The main attractions are the celebrated biryanis – aromatic basmati rice, steamed potato and huge chunks of juicy mutton or chicken – that are best paired with melt-in-mouth chicken tikka, skewer-grilled mutton *seekh* kebab and the creamy mutton *galawati* kebab.

Hot Kati Rolls BENGALI **$**
(Map p458; Park St; rolls from ₹40; ⏲11am-10.30pm) This is one of Kolkata's best known hole-in-the-wall places for a *kati roll*. For first-timers, this hit snack is essentially a *paratha*, fried one-sided with a coating of egg and then filled with sliced onions, chilli and your choice of stuffing (curried chicken, grilled meat or paneer). Eat it rolled up in a twist of paper as a takeaway.

Mocambo MULTICUISINE **$$**
(Map p458; Mirza Ghalib St; mains ₹300-450; ⏲11am-11pm; ❄) Mocambo dates back to 1956, but with old-fashioned seats in scalloped red leather, it feels more like a mood-lit 1970s steakhouse. A very loyal following comes regularly for its mixed grills, devilled crabs, fish Wellington, chicken Kiev and *bhetki* meunière (barramundi fillets in lemon butter sauce). An unwritten admission code applies.

Southern Chowringhee

★Kewpies BENGALI **$$**
(Map p454; ☎033-24861600; 2 Elgin Lane; thalis ₹450-1050, mains ₹150-500; ⏲12.30-3pm & 7.30-10.30pm Tue-Sun; ❄) Kewpie's is a Kolkata gastronomic institution, and dining here feels like a lavish dinner party in a gently old-fashioned home. Reared to perfection by a speciality Bengali chef, this place serves impeccably traditional and authentic Bengali dishes made from the best local ingredients, and though on the pricy side, the food (as well as the experience) is worth every rupee.

Kookie Jar CAFE **$**
(Map p454; Rawdon St; pastries/savouries from ₹60/80; ⏲8.30am-9pm; ❄) This confectionery is a long-time favourite with Kolkata's pastry lovers. Try the myriad forms of chocolate cakes and brownies, or bite into a freshly baked slice of pizza, a meaty puff or a subtly flavoured sandwich. For vegans, there are a few eggless preparations available.

★Fire and Ice ITALIAN **$$$**
(Map p454; ☎033-22884073; www.fireandicepizzeria.com; Kanak Bldg, Middleton St; mains ₹500-700, beer/cocktails from ₹200/450; ⏲11.30am-11.30pm; ❄) Founded and directed by an Italian lady from Naples, Fire and Ice's waiters bring forth real Italian-style pastas and Kolkata's best thin-crust pizzas. Old film posters give character to the spacious dining room set behind foliage in a huge heritage building. Few other Kolkata restaurants keep serving as late, or as consistently.

It has a well-stocked cellar, so you can pair a good glass of wine with your food. The proprietor is often around to offer her suggestions.

Picadilly Square CAFE **$$**
(Map p454; ☎033-30990354; 15B Sarat Bose Rd; mains ₹150-300, beverages from ₹120; ⏲11am-10pm; ❄✍) This cute six-table cafe with two Victorian-style lampposts and a serving counter is fashioned like a street cart, with flooring designed to feel like a Parisian sidewalk. It serves imaginative savoury crepes (try the Rakakat Jibneh), pitas, pastas, ice creams, waffles and very good espressos to a seemingly endless Bruno Mars soundtrack.

Gabbar's Bar & Kitchen MULTICUISINE **$$$**
(Map p454; ☎033-40602507; 11/1 Ho Chi Minh Sarani; mains ₹350-650, beers ₹200; ⏲12.30-11pm; ❄) This excellent eatery has evolved from what used to be Kolkata's coolest Tex-Mex restaurant. It's now a Bollywood-themed resto-bar, the name being a take on a famous Hindi movie villain. The setting is easy and relaxed, the menu is a mix of hearty Indian, Chinese, Italian and Mexican fare, and there's chilled beer to go with the spicy grub.

Shiraz MUGHLAI **$$**
(Map p454; 135 Park St; mains ₹180-300; ⏲5am-11.30pm) Synonymous with Kolkata's signature biryani (basmati rice with juicy mutton chunks and steaked potatoes), Shiraz also offers a range of curries, including a superb ₹100 mutton *keema* (spiced minced meat) breakfast until noon.

Monkey Bar GASTRONOMY **$$$**
(Map p454; ☎033-30990381; Fort Knox Bldg, Camac St; mains ₹350-600; ⏲4pm-midnight; ❄) A fancy new entrant in Kolkata's fine dining scene, this upscale eatery tosses up an imaginative range of fusion and experimental delicacies within its grunge-modern environs. Take your pick from items such as five-spice duck confit in pita pockets, peppered calamari with garlic and curry leaves, or baked brie with caramelised onion and marmalade. The only downer – there's no alcohol.

Oh! Calcutta BENGALI **$$$**
(Map p454; ☎033-22837161; 4th fl, Forum Mall, Elgin Rd; mains ₹250-600, cocktails from ₹290; ⏲12.30-3pm & 7.30-11pm; ❄) Situated within a shopping mall, the shutter-edged mirror 'windows', bookshelves, paintings and B&W photographs create a casually upmarket feel for enjoying some of the city's best Bengali-fusion food. The mild, subtle and creamy *Daab Chingri* (₹790) is served in a green coconut, its subtleties brought out particularly well by a side dish of fragrant lime salad (₹90).

BBD Bagh

Amber INDIAN **$$**
(Map p462; ☎033-22486520; 11 Waterloo St; mains ₹200-450, beer ₹250; ⏲noon-11pm; ❄) This two-hall middle-class restaurant serves reliable Indian food, though the signature brain curry isn't to everyone's taste. Of the two dining areas, Amber (1st floor) is more family oriented, while Essence (2nd floor) is more dimly lit and predominantly for businesspeople. Menus are essentially the same at both places.

Dacres Lane STREET FOOD **$**
(Map p462; James Hickey Sarani; mains from ₹20; ⏲8am-9pm) A series of food stalls selling a unique combination of creole cuisine is interspersed by a few somewhat dodgy bar-restaurants, whose fairy lights add some warmth to the narrow and dingy lane. Choose from quick-and-easy bites, including *paratha* (Indian-style flaky bread) and curry, toasted bread with mutton, papaya and carrot stew, vegetable fritters, wok-fried noodles and chicken curry with rice.

KC Das SWEETS **$**
(Map p462; Lenin Sarani; sweets from ₹20; ⏲7.30am-9.30pm; ❄) This bustling Bengali sweet shop claims to have invented the iconic *roshogolla* (rosewater-scented, deep-fried cheese balls dipped in sugar syrup) way back in 1868. Try the *mishti doi* – Bengali sweet; curd sweetened with jaggery – as well. Seating is available in the form of simple wrought-iron tables and chairs.

Anand SOUTH INDIAN **$**
(Map p462; 19 CR Ave; dosas ₹80-130, fresh juice ₹70; ⏲9am-9.30pm, closed Wed; ❄🖉) Unbelievably tasty pure-veg dosas are served in this well-kept if stylistically dated family restaurant with octagonal mirror panels and timber strips on the somewhat low upper ceiling. It also serves a delicious milky South Indian coffee (₹50) through the day to go with your food of choice.

Southern Kolkata

★6 Ballygunge Place BENGALI **$$**
(Map p466; ☎033-24603922; 6 Ballygunge Pl; mains ₹200-300; ⏲noon-3.30pm & 7-10.30pm; ❄) Housed in a superbly renovated mid-20th-century mansion, this top-notch restaurant serves some of the best Bengali fare in town. If you're confused about the ingredients, spices and gravies, skip the menu and hit the lunch buffet (vegetarian/non-vegetarian ₹600/700), and you'll be treated to a fantastic sampling of classic and contemporary Bengali cuisine.

Flavours here are less intense and more subtle than several other speciality Bengali restaurants, and are suited to a wide range of palates.

★Tamarind SOUTH INDIAN **$$**
(Map p466; ☎033-30990434; 177 Sarat Bose Rd; mains ₹250-400; ⏲noon-3.30pm & 7-11pm; ❄) This unpretentious restaurant on one of South Kolkata's main thoroughfares serves a melange of traditional and improvised dishes curated from Kerala, Karnataka and Tamil Nadu. Dishes such as Coorgi mutton fry, Chettinad chicken, *kottu* paratha (a fluffy crumble featuring a *paratha*, eggs and spices) and *appams* (South Indian rice pancake) with mutton stew are simply unbeatable, probably even by restaurants in South India.

Bhojohori Manna BENGALI **$$**
(Map p466; www.bhojohorimanna.com; 18/1 Hindustan Rd; mains ₹50-270, small/large veg thali ₹210/280; ⏲12.30-10.30pm; ❄) Each Bhojohori Manna branch in town feels very different, but all feature good-quality Bengali food at sensible prices. The branch on Hindustan Rd is comparatively spacious, decorated with tribal implements, and the menu allows you to pair a wide selection of fish types with the sauce of your choice. Don't miss the *echorer dalna* (green jackfruit curry) in summer.

★Corner Courtyard FUSION **$$$**
(Map p466; ☎9903990597; 92B Sarat Bose Rd; mains ₹350-650, beers/cocktails ₹180/300; ⏲8am-11pm, reduced menu 3-7pm; ❄) This reincarnated 1904 mansion has had its walls artistically splattered with doorknobs, locks and old books, complementing its stylish distressed-look decor. The menu is creative, imaginative and designed to please discerning foodies, from Thai curry-spiced risotto and Brazilian salmon to Finnish fondue and Uruguayan calamari, with many a daring flavour combination.

Drinking & Nightlife

Central Kolkata & Chowringhee

OlyPub BAR
(Map p458; 21 Park St; beers ₹190; ⏲11am-11pm) This grungy yet oddly convivial central watering hole is a low-key Kolkata classic. The upper-floor bar has comfortable sofa seating, although the ground-floor lounge with rickety chairs and boisterous drinkers is far more atmospheric. Special promotional offers on select booze brands are often available. Chateaubriand-style steaks (₹250 a platter) are served by the dozens every evening.

Big Ben PUB
(Map p454; Kenilworth Hotel, Little Russel St; beers ₹300; ⏲noon-midnight) An upscale pub with a 'Britain' theme, this cosy watering hole features a good selection of beers and has live sports on TV. It's a fairly casual setting, but avoid wearing shorts or flip-flops.

Flury's CAFE
(Map p458; Park St; coffee/tea from ₹130/140; ⏲7.30am-10pm) Dating back to 1927, Flury's is an enticing art-deco palace that's a real Kolkata institution. The best time to drop by is during breakfast, or in the evenings when you can just drink coffee and eat slices of gooey Sacher-Torte (cake from ₹70). It's surely the only major iconic world cafe to cite beans on toast as a heritage speciality.

Plush LOUNGE
(Map p454; Astor Hotel, 15 Shakespeare Sarani; beers ₹200; ⏲4pm-2am) This stylish yet unthreateningly casual bar is most appealing on Thursday evenings when young local musicians perform jazz, blues and progressive sets (from 9pm). It's also one of the city's few nightlife spots to remain open well past midnight. A 'smart casual' dress code applies to all guests.

Aqua LOUNGE
(Map p458; ☎033-22499000; Park Hotel, Park St; cocktails ₹400; ⏲7pm-midnight) This luxurious yet laid-back open-air lounge allows you to nurse your booze while soothing your eyes on the dreamy waters of the neon-lit pool around which it is located. Dress for the evening to be allowed entry (no shorts or flip-flops).

Irish House PUB
(Map p466; Quest Mall, Syed Amir Ali Ave; beers ₹200; ⏲noon-11.30pm) While not really Irish at all, this is the nearest Kolkata gets to a fully fledged non-hotel pub-sports bar. There's lots of weekend ambience and a showman holding fort at the well-stocked bar.

REVOLUTIONARY CAFE

If you're walking down College St to the Ashutosh Museum of Indian Art from MG Rd, after one block turn left, take the fourth doorway on the left and climb the stairs to the mythic **Indian Coffee House** (1st fl, 15 Bankim Chatterjee St; ⏲9am-9pm Mon-Sat, 9am-12.30pm & 5-9pm Sun). The cheap, dishwater coffee can't be recommended, but it's incredibly fascinating to look inside this unpretentious high-ceilinged place that was once a meeting place of freedom fighters, bohemians and revolutionaries.

BBD Bagh

Broadway Bar BAR
(Map p462; Broadway Hotel, 27A GC Ave; beers ₹150, shots ₹50-150; ⏲noon-10.30pm) Backstreet Paris? Chicago in the 1930s? Prague circa 1980s? This cavernous, unpretentious old-men's pub defies easy parallels, but has a compulsive left-bank fascination with cheap booze, heavy ceiling fans, bare walls, marble floors and, thankfully, no music.

Southern Kolkata

Smoke Shack ROOFTOP BAR
(Map p466; Hotel Park Plaza, Dover Pl; cocktails/beers ₹450/300; ⏲4-11.30pm) Fancy to the hilt, this open-air terrace bar attracts stylish people and serves a good selection of mojitos and cocktails through the evening. There's tasty kebabs and other assorted finger food to go with your drinks.

Dolly's Tea Shop TEAHOUSE
(Map p466; G62 Dakshinapan; teas/mocktails ₹100/150; ⏲11am-7pm) For sampling authentic Darjeeling teas as well as refreshing mocktails featuring the brew, visit this popular teahouse run by a veteran tea taster. Try the orange mint julep tea or the lemon barley tea, with a grilled bacon sandwich on the side if you like.

Mrs Magpie CAFE
(Map p466; 570 Lake Tce; coffee from ₹50; ⏲9am-10.30pm) Cosy, cheerfully lit and adorned with pretty wallpapers, this popular cafe serves cheap and tasty cupcakes (from ₹40)

in a wide range of flavours, best paired with a cup of fresh espresso. It also serves breakfast platters and afternoon-tea sets.

Basement CLUB

(Map p466; Samilton Hotel, Sarat Bose Rd; beers ₹200; ⌚7pm-midnight) A relaxed and inexpensive mini-club with live music from 9pm on Thursday evenings, this is a good place to unwind after a long day of sightseeing. The piped music can get a bit loud at times, though.

☆ Entertainment

Seagull Arts & Media Resource Centre ARTS CENTRE

(Map p466; www.seagullindia.com; Rupchand Mukherjee Lane; ⌚11am-8pm) Owned by the same management that operates Seagull Bookstore, this acclaimed institution regularly organises art and media exhibitions, film screenings, workshops, panel discussions and a host of other activities, with themes ranging from sociology and philosophy to religion and politics. Most events are free; check the website for details.

Someplace Else LIVE MUSIC

(Map p458; www.theparkhotels.com/kolkata/someplace-else.html; Park Hotel, Park St) This nightclub has been steadily promoting live music in Kolkata since the mid-1990s. Acts perform nightly, although you'll have to be lucky to catch some original music. Most are cover bands who belt out regulation rock and blues hits. The ambience is laid-back, and the crowd gets rather raucous on weekends.

Jamsteady LIVE MUSIC

(www.jamsteady.in; Princeton Club, Prince Anwar Shah Rd) The most happening place in Kolkata's underground and indie-music circuit, Jamsteady has packed gigs every Friday evening featuring a diverse array of musicians playing jazz, blues, electronica, folk and world music. There's a minimum cover charge that secures entry, and cheap booze is available against prepurchased coupons.

ICCR CULTURAL PROGRAM

(Rabindranath Tagore Centre; Map p454; ☎033-22822895; www.tagorecentreiccr.org; 9A Ho Chi Minh Sarani) This state-run cultural melting pot is a large, multilevel operation that regularly hosts exhibitions, dance shows, recitals and lectures in its many galleries and auditoriums. The programs are often free, and snacks (also free!) are usually offered to guests on inauguration days.

Inox (Quest Mall) CINEMA

(Map p466; www.inoxmovies.com; Syed Amir Ali Ave) This is one of Kolkata's top-tier multiplexes, screening brand-new Hollywood, Bollywood and local Bengali flicks. It's located on the top floor of the Quest Mall.

Nandan Complex CULTURAL PROGRAM

(Map p454; ☎033-22235317; 1/1 AJC Bose Rd) This complex is made up of the auditoriums and theatre halls at **Rabindra Sadan** (Map p454), **Sisir Mancha** (Map p454) and the central **Nandan Cinema** (Map p454). Apart from sundry cultural programs through the year, the complex also hosts the popular Kolkata Film Festival (p468). Tourist information offices and pamphlets give extensive listings of events here and at many other venues.

Shopping

Sienna Store & Cafe GIFTS & SOUVENIRS

(Map p466; ☎033-40002828; 49/1 Hindustan Park; ⌚11.30am-10pm) Very hipster, very chic, yet unbelievably affordable. Housed in a tastefully renovated mansion, this boutique specialises in a delightful collection of wearables, souvenirs, lifestyle products and tiny bits and bobs that double as great gifts for people back home. There's a cosy, buzzy cafe to the rear, which makes light and delicious organic sandwiches, juices, pasta and salads (dishes ₹250).

Byloom CLOTHING

(Map p466; www.byloom.co.in; 58B Hindusthan Park; ⌚11am-8pm) Some of Kolkata's most exquisite handmade saris are sold at this speciality boutique. There's also a fair smattering of semiprecious jewellery, and an impressive collection of shawls and scarves. Look for pieces that feature the intricate *kantha* embroidery style, or the *khesh* method of weaving employing strips of cloth. A cafe on-site dishes up tasty bites (snacks ₹100).

Weaver's Studio CLOTHING

(Map p466; www.weaversstudio.in; 5/1 Ballygunge Pl; ⌚10am-6pm Mon-Sat) Gorgeous handmade textiles and traditional fabrics vie for your attention at this upmarket boutique, run by an organisation that works with artisanal communities. Choose from a plethora of styles, such as exquisite hand-block prints, appliques, tribal designs, batik and embroidery, and expect to pay a premium price for your unique and indulgent purchase.

Aranya GIFTS & SOUVENIRS

(Map p466; F56 Dakshinapan Shopping Centre, Gariahat Rd; ⌚11am-7.30pm) Thoughtfully designed toys, stationery and souvenirs, made mostly from recycled materials, feature at this boutique run by a city-based designer duo. There's also a range of dresses to choose from, mostly in the smart-casual category.

Anokhi CLOTHING

(Map p454; Shop 209, Forum Mall; ⏲11am-8pm) This boutique sells tasteful ethno-chic garments made from hand-dyed and hand-printed fabrics. Creations featuring Gujarati block prints seem to be the most popular, although tie-dye and batik have a strong presence as well. Most of the collection caters to women, while men have a limited choice of shirts to browse through.

Central Cottage Industries ARTS & CRAFTS

(Map p462; Metropolitan Bldg, Chowringhee Rd; ⏲10am-7pm Mon-Sat) An impressive array of traditional arts and tribal crafts are on sale at this well-stocked government emporium. Service is a bit impersonal and prices can be steeper than some street establishments, but you can rest assured that you're only buying genuine and well-curated merchandise here. There are separate sections for textiles, artefacts, metalwork, woodwork and handmade paper, among others.

FabIndia FABRICS, HANDICRAFTS

(Map p454; www.fabindia.com; 11A Allenby Rd; ⏲11am-8.30pm) India's top consumer line of ethno-chic dresses and Indo-Western apparel has one of its city stores in this central location. Apart from garments, there's a wide selection of upholstery, jewellery, ceramics, woodwork, home decor and organic food products. Look for items bearing the 'Craftmark' seal, imply-

STREET NAMES

Since Independence, street names with Raj-era connotations have been officially changed, but while street signs and business cards use the new variant, citizens and taxis often still refer to the British-era names. The following *italicised* street names are what we have found, quite unscientifically, to be the most commonly employed variant and these have been used in our listings.

OLD NAME	NEW NAME
Allenby Rd	Dr Sisir Kumar Bose Sarani
Ballygunge Rd	Ashutosh Chowdhury Ave *(AC Rd)*
Brabourne Rd	Biplabi Trailokya Maharaja Rd
Camac St	Abinindranath Tagore St
Central Ave	*Chittaranjan (CR) Ave*
Chitpore Rd	*Rabindra Sarani*
Chowringhee Rd	Jawaharlal Nehru Rd
Dalhousie Sq	*BBD Bagh*
Free School St	*Mirza Ghalib St*
Harrington St	*Ho Chi Minh Sarani*
Harrison Rd	*Mahatma Gandhi (MG) Rd*
Hungerford St	Picasso Bithi
Kyd St	Dr M Ishaque Rd
Lansdowne Rd	*Sarat Bose Rd*
Loudon St	Dr UN Brahmachari St
Lower Circular Rd	*AJC Bose Rd*
Old Courthouse St	Hemant Basu Sarani
Park St	Mother Teresa Sarani
Rawdon St	Sarojini Naidu Sarani
Theatre Rd	*Shakespeare Sarani*
Victoria Terrace	*Gorky Terrace*
Waterloo St	Nawab Siraj-ud-Daula Sarani
Wellesley St	*RAK (Rafi Ahmed Kidwai) Rd*
Wood St	Dr Martin Luther King Sarani

ing they are of a premium quality and made in association with traditional artisans.

Dakshinapan Shopping Centre SHOPPING CENTRE
(Map p466; Gariahat Rd; ⌚11am-7pm Mon-Sat) It's worth facing the soul-crushing 1970s architecture for Dakshinapan's wide range of government emporia, which brings together a mind-boggling artisanal diversity from across India under one roof. There's plenty of tack, but many shops offer excellent-value souvenirs, crafts and fabrics. Prices are usually fixed, but buying at an emporium means that authenticity and quality are never called into question.

Oxford Bookstore BOOKS
(Map p458; ☎033-22297662; www.oxfordbookstore.com; 17 Park St; ⌚11am-8pm) This is an excellent full-range bookshop that sells a variety of titles, including an impressive catalogue of coffee-table books on India. It stocks Lonely Planet guides and the indispensable *Calcutta Walks Tourist Map* (₹100). Value additions come in the form of a stationery section, a DVD section, and a cafe where you can sit and browse titles.

Mondal & Sons MUSICAL INSTRUMENTS
(Map p462; ☎9804854213; 8 Rabindra Sarani; ⌚10am-6pm Mon-Fri, to 2pm Sat) For sitars (from ₹5000) or violins (from ₹3000), visit Mondal & Sons, a family-run musical establishment dating back to the 1850s. Do not be misled by the modest appearance of the store: the Mondals count Yehudi Menuhin among their satisfied customers.

ℹ Information

DANGERS & ANNOYANCES

Kolkata feels remarkably unthreatening, and is usually safe (though stray incidents involving tourists can and do occur).

- Predictable beggar-hassle is a minor irritant around Sudder St.
- *Bandhs* (strikes) occasionally stop all land transport, including suburban trains and taxis to the airport.
- Monsoon-season waterlogging can be severe.

INTERNET ACCESS

Inexpensive and widespread 4G/LTE cellular services have slowly begun to phase out internet cafes. A central survivor is **Cyber Zoom** (Map p458; 27B Park St; per hr ₹20; ⌚10am-9pm), which also does passport photos. Around Sudder St, some back-alley cubby-hole places charge ₹20 per hour for internet access, but it's worth paying a little more for fast connections and more comfortable seating at the travel agency with internet cafe **R-Internet Travels** (Map p458; ntrncf@gmail.com; Tottee Lane; per hour ₹20; ⌚9am-10pm).

MEDICAL SERVICES

Medical contacts (including chemists, doctors, hospitals and clinics) are widely listed on the popular web portal www.justdial.com/kolkata.

Apollo Gleneagles (☎033-23202122, emergency 033-60601066; www.apollogleneagles.in; off EM Bypass; ⌚24hr)

Belle Vue Clinic (Map p454; ☎9163058000; www.bellevueclinic.com; Loudon (Dr UN Brahmachari) St, Minto Park; ⌚24hr)

Eastern Diagnostics (Map p458; ☎033-22178080; www.easterndiagnostics.com; 13C Mirza Ghalib St; ⌚9am-2pm Mon-Sat)

MONEY

You won't have to walk far to find ATMs that accept Visa, MasterCard, Cirrus and Maestro cards. International credit cards are widely accepted at stores.

Money Changers

Many private money changers around Sudder St offer commission-free exchange rates that are significantly better than banks. Some will exchange travellers cheques. Shop around and double-check the maths. In the city centre, **Mishra Forex** (Map p454; 11 Shakespeare Sarani; ⌚10am-8pm Mon-Sat, to 4pm Sun) gives reasonable rates and opens daily.

Airport money changers give predictably poor rates and charge up to 5% in commission. There's an ATM in the arrival lounge (booth 22) between exit gates 3B and 4A.

POST

The new **General Post Office** (Map p462; 7 Koilaghat St; ⌚7.30am-8.30pm Mon-Sat, 10am-4pm Sun, parcel service 10am-2.30pm, philatelic office 10am-6pm Mon-Fri) is located along Koilaghat St. The philatelic bureau sells commemorative issues, or can turn your own photos into a sheet of ₹5 stamps (₹300), which can take up to seven days to be ready.

CR Ave Post Office (Map p462; CR Ave; ⌚10am-7pm Mon-Sat) is handy for the Chandni Chowk area, and has snail mail, speed post and parcel facilities.

Shakespeare Sarani Post Office (Map p454; Shakespeare Sarani; ⌚10am-4pm Mon-Fri, to 2pm Sat) is a minor but helpful and conveniently located central post office, with general and speed post services.

TELEPHONE

Sudder St agency-shops will sell you a SIM card (₹200), given a copy of your ID, a passport photo and details of your address/hotel. SIMs are available in micro and nano versions for use with smartphones, but make sure your handset is unlocked. Local/national calls can be made and text messages sent for only a few rupees, while 4G data packs start from ₹250 per GB.

TOURIST INFORMATION

India Tourism (Map p454; ☎033-22821475; www.incredibleindia.org; 4 Shakespeare Sarani; ⏰10am-6pm Mon-Fri, to 1pm Sat) This office hands out free maps of greater Kolkata, with major sights and stops marked, and also has useful information about travelling to other parts of India.

West Bengal Tourism (Map p462; ☎033-22488271; www.wbtdc.gov.in; 3/2 BBD Bagh; ⏰10.30am-1.30pm & 2-5.30pm Mon-Fri, 10.30am-1pm Sat) The office primarily sells its own tours (last sales 4.30pm), and has good free city maps. Its website is useful for local travel information, as well as booking state-operated hotels and lodges across the state.

ℹ Getting There & Away

AIR

Rebuilt in 2013, the glassy **Netaji Subhash Chandra Bose International Airport** (NSCBIA (CCU); ☎033-25118036) has an impressive terminal building, although services can get strangely bottlenecked at times, especially in the departures area. If you're flying out, arrive with ample time and expect long queues at passport control and security check.

Kolkata has a vast selection of domestic connections from early morning to late night. It's also a useful hub for regional flights linking Bangladesh (Air India, Biman, Jet Airways and Regent Airways), Bhutan (Bhutan Airlines and Druk Air), Myanmar (Air India) and Nepal (Air India). East Asian destinations include Bangkok (Air Asia, IndiGo, Jet Airways, SpiceJet and Thai), Hong Kong (Dragonair), Kuala Lumpur (Air Asia), Kunming (China Eastern Airlines) and Singapore (SilkAir). For long-haul connections to Europe and the USA, there are daily flights via Abu Dhabi (Etihad), Doha (Qatar Airways) and Dubai (Emirates).

Several airlines have offices with booking counters in the city.

Air Asia (Map p458; ☎033-33008000; www.airasia.com; 55A Mirza Ghalib St; ⏰10am-8pm Mon-Sat)

Air India (Map p462; ☎033-22110730; www.airindia.in; 39 CR Ave; ⏰10am-4pm Mon-Sat)

Druk Air (Map p454; ☎033-22900050; www.drukair.com; 51 Tivoli Crt; ⏰10am-5pm Mon-Sat)

Emirates (☎033-40099555; www.emirates.com; Trinity Tower, 83 Topsia Rd; ⏰10am-6pm Mon-Sat)

Jet Airways (Map p458; ☎033-39893333; www.jetairways.com; Park St; ⏰10am-7pm Mon-Sat)

BOAT

Shipping Corporation of India has five ships that depart on scheduled monthly dates to Port Blair. The vessels sail from **Kidderpore Docks**, accessed via Gate 3 opposite Kidderpore commuter train station. Tickets (bunk/cabin/deluxe ₹2500/6420/9750) go on sale from the 1st floor of the corporation's office around 10 days prior to the voyage.

BUS

Domestic

For Darjeeling or Sikkim, start by taking a bus to Siliguri (12 to 14 hours). All drive overnight departing **Esplanade bus station** (Map p458; Esplanade) between 5pm and 8pm (seat/sleeper from ₹550/650, with AC ₹1200/1400). An NBSTC bus for Cooch Behar leaves at 8pm (₹520, 18 hours).

Buses to Bihar and Odisha (Strand Rd) line up along the road running parallel to the riverbank south of Eden Gardens commuter train station. Most run overnight, departing between 5pm and 8.30pm. Arrive very early if you have baggage. Destinations:

Bhubaneswar (fan/AC ₹380/430, 10 hours)

Gaya (seat/sleeper ₹300/450, 13 hours)

Puri (seat/sleeper ₹410/460, 12 hours)

Ranchi (seat/sleeper from ₹250/290, 10 hours)

International

Bangladesh Buses advertised to Bangladesh actually run to Benapol (international checkpost), where you walk across and board another vehicle operated by the same company on to Dhaka. **Shohagh Paribahan** (Map p458; ☎033-22520696; shohagh12@sify.com; 23 Marquis St; ⏰5am-10.30pm) has five morning 'Dhaka' services (fan/AC ₹900/1550, 14 hours). **GreenLine** (Map p458; ☎033-22520571; 12 Marquis St; ⏰5am-10.30pm) has three AC buses to Benapol (₹400), all leaving by 7am. Connecting tickets to Dhaka cost Tk1200 (about ₹1000).

Bhutan A Bhutan government-operated bus to Phuentsholing (₹600, 15 hours) leaves at 7pm daily, except Sunday, from the walled northeast yard of Esplanade bus station where there are two special **ticket booths** (Map p462; ☎033-22627735; Esplanade bus station; ⏰9.30am-1pm & 2-6pm Mon-Sat). It's faster and more comfortable to take the 13149 Kanchankanya Express (sleeper/3AC/2AC ₹370/1000/1450, 8.30pm, 14 hours) from Sealdah train station to Hasimara, and then travel the last 18km by bus or taxi to Phuentsholing. Note that you may have to camp a night at this border town for your visa to be processed.

TRAIN

Stations

Long-distance trains depart Kolkata from three major stations. Gigantic Howrah (pronounced 'hao-rah'; HWH) has the most connections and is across the river, often best reached by ferry. Sealdah (pronounced 'shey-al-dah'; SDAH) is at the eastern end of MG Road; and the eponymous Kolkata (or Chitpore; KOAA) is around 5km further north (near Belgachia metro station).

Tickets

To buy long-distance train tickets with 'tourist quota', foreigners should use the **Eastern Railways' International Tourist Bureau** (Map p462; ☎033-22224206; 6 Fairlie Pl; ⏰10am-4pm Mon-Sat, to 2pm Sun). Bring your passport, as well as a book to read as waits can be very long, but there are usually seats. On arrival, take and fill in a booking form (forms are numbered and double as queuing chits). Lines form well before opening. If you're travelling as a group, just one of you can be present, as long as you have everyone else's passports. Note that it's sometimes quicker to use the nearby standard **computerised train booking office** (Map p462; Koilaghat St; ⏰8am-8pm Mon-Sat, to 2pm Sun), although that has no tourist quota.

Getting Around

Tickets for buses, trams and the metro on most city transport routes cost ₹5 to ₹20. Men shouldn't sit in clearly assigned 'Ladies' seats.

Note that between 1pm and 9pm, much of the city's one-way road system reverses direction, so bus routes invert and taxis hailed on one-way thoroughfares may be reluctant to make journeys in the other direction.

TO/FROM THE AIRPORT

NSCBIA Airport is around 16km northeast of central Kolkata. A dedicated feeder road accesses the new combined terminal from the south (VIP Rd) via Airport Gate 1. Integrated within the arrival lounge of the terminal are several public-transport options into the city, including a computerised train ticket booking counter (booth 25) for trains out of the city.

MAJOR TRAINS FROM KOLKATA

DESTINATION	TRAIN NO & NAME	FARE (₹; SLEEPER/ 3AC/2AC UNLESS OTHERWISE STATED)	DURATION (HR)	DEPARTURE
Bhubaneswar	12839 Chennai Mail	290/745/1045	6½	11.45pm (HWH)
Chennai	12841 Coromandal	665/1745/2540	26½	2.50pm (HWH)
	12839 Chennai Mail	665/1745/2540	28	11.45pm (HWH)
Delhi	Poorva (Nos 12303/81)	630/1665/2415	23½	8.05am (HWH)
	12313 SDAH Rajdhani	3AC/1AC 2105/4875	17½	4.50pm (SDAH)
Gorakhpur	Purvanchal/KOAA-GKP (Nos 15047/49/51)	420/1140/1650	17¼-19	2.30pm (KOAA)
Guwahati	12345 Saraighat	500/1315/1890	17¾	3.50pm (HWH)
	15657 Kanchanjunga	455/1235/1795	21¾	6.35am (SDAH)
Hooghly	Bandel Local	unreserved ₹10	50min	several hourly (HWH)
Lucknow	13151 Jammu Tawi	470/1270/1845	22¾	11.45am (KOAA)
	Upasana/Kumbha (Nos 12327/69)	510/1350/1980	18¼	1pm (HWH)
Mumbai CST	12810 Mumbai Mail	740/1945/2840	33	8.15pm (HWH)
New Jalpaiguri	12343 Darjeeling Mail	350/920/1295	10	10.05pm (SDAH)
	12377 Padatik	350/920/1295	10¼	11.15pm (SDAH)
Patna	13005 Amritsar mail	315/840/1205	9	7.10pm (HWH)
	12351 Danapur	340/890/1250	9½	8.35pm (HWH)
Puri	18409 Sri Jagannath	300/815/1160	9¾	7pm (HWH)
	12837 Howrah-Puri	330/860/1210	8¾	10.35pm (HWH)
Varanasi	13005 Amritsar Mail	385/1055/1530	14	7.10pm (HWH)

HWH = ex-Howrah, SDAH = ex-Sealdah, KOAA = ex-Chitpur

AC Bus

Airport buses start from a stand that's a minute's walk south of Arrivals Gate 1A. Pay onboard. The punctual **AC-39** (⌚ 8am-8pm) departs hourly, stopping en route at the Esplanade bus station (₹80, one hour) before terminating at Howrah train station (₹100, 1½ hours).

City Bus

Cheap ordinary buses and minibuses are available if you walk about 500m south of the airport terminal building to reach the VIP Rd crossing. Look out for carriages to BBD Bagh (₹20) and Howrah (₹25). Bus 237 will take you to the ferry pier at Babughat (₹20), while bus L238 connects to Howrah train station (₹25). The ride will be crowded and sweaty, and there may not be room for large bags or suitcases.

Taxi

Fixed-price yellow taxis cost ₹320/380 to Sudder St/Howrah train station, taking around one hour when traffic is kind. Prepay at booth 12 in the new arrivals area between exits 3B and 4A. Radio taxis offer an air-con ride into town, charging around ₹20 per kilometre, and are available at booth 11.

AUTORICKSHAW

Tuk-tuk-style autorickshaws ('autos') operate as fixed-route hop-on share taxis with three passengers in the back and one beside the driver. Fares are typically ₹6 to ₹10, depending on distance.

Key routes:

Loha Pool–Dharamtala (Map p458; Elliot Rd) Starts from Park Circus using Park St (or after 1pm looping via Nasreddin and Karaya roads), goes up AJC Bose Rd (near Mother Teresa's Motherhouse), then along Elliot Rd/Royd St and finally up Mirza Ghalib St/RAK Rd (mornings/afternoons) near Sudder St. Loop reverses after 1pm.

Hazra–Bondel (Map p466; Hazra Rd) Runs along Hazra Rd, starting a block east of Jatin Das Park metro station, and goes to Ballygunge.

Hazra–Kiddepore (Map p466; Hazra Rd) Goes west from Jatin Das Park metro station, past the Kalighat idol-makers and on through Alipore.

Rashbehari–Gariahat (Map p466; Rashbehari Ave) This is the mid-segment of a longer route, and connects the Kalighat metro station to the shopping district of Gariahat along Rashbehari Ave.

BUS & TRAM

Buses in Kolkata come in different forms. The best are a limited fleet of shiny new air-con buses, but the standard tumbles quickly down to crowded blue-and-yellow rattletraps and red-and-yellow minibuses, mostly run by manic drivers and motormouth conductors. A large selection of minbuses start from the **Minibus Station** (Map p462) on the eastern side of BBD Bagh, including a service to Airport Gate 1 via Dum Dum.

Dinky but photogenic trams follow more predictable routes along select city tracks, and are immune to one-way traffic.

FERRY

Crossing the Hooghly River is generally faster and more agreeable by boat than by using the clogged road bridges, especially during rush hour. **River ferries** (tickets ₹5-10; ⌚ 8am-8pm) depart every 15 to 20 minutes from Howrah to jetties in central Kolkata. Convenient drop-off points include Chandpal (for Babughat), Bagbazar (for Kumartuli), Belur and Dakshineswar.

METRO

Kolkata's busy and crowded **metro** (www.kmrc.in; tickets ₹5-20; ⌚ 6.45am-9.55pm Mon-Sat, 9.45am-9.55pm Sun) has trains every five to 15 minutes (fewer on Sundays). For Sudder St, use Esplanade or Park St. Some trains are air-con, although you pay the same fare for fan-cooled carriages.

Only one line (running in a north–south direction) is operational so far, but several extensions are planned. Line 2 linking Howrah, Sealdah and Salt Lake is due by late 2017.

Theoretically you may not carry bags over 10kg. If you're staying in the city for a while, consider buying a multiride ticket to save yourself the hassle of queuing every time you ride the service.

RICKSHAW

Human-powered '*tana* rickshaws' work within limited areas, notably around New Market and some southern zones. Although rickshaw pullers sometimes charge foreigners disproportionate fares, many are virtually destitute, sleeping on the pavements beneath their rented vehicles at night, so tips are heartily appreciated.

TAXI

Kolkata's yellow Ambassador cabs charge ₹25 for up to 2km, and ₹12 per kilometre thereafter. Meters are digital and show the exact fare due. A few air-con taxis (white with blue stripe) also use the same fare structure, with a 25% air-con surcharge on the metered fare. Taxis are generally easy to flag down, except during the 5pm to 6pm rush hour and after 10pm when some cabs refuse to use the meter. There are prepaid taxi booths at **Howrah train station** (Map p462; Howrah train station), Sealdah train station and at the airport.

Clean and cool Uber cabs currently abound in Kolkata, and can be accessed by updated versions of the app on your smartphone. The minimum fare is ₹60. Surge fares during peak demand can be many times the fare of a regular yellow taxi.

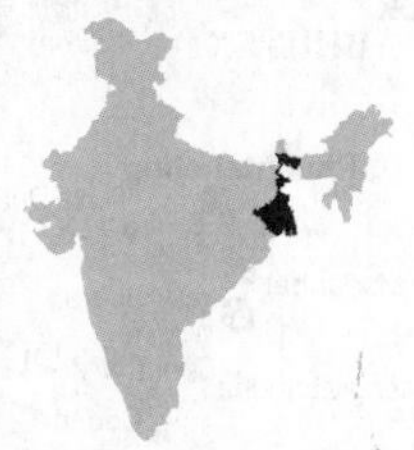

West Bengal & Darjeeling

Includes ➡

Best Places to Eat

- ➡ Glenary's (p503)
- ➡ Cochrane Place (p496)
- ➡ Amber (p493)

Best Places to Sleep

- ➡ Dekeling Hotel (p502)
- ➡ Holumba Haven (p512)
- ➡ Vedic Village (p489)

Why Go?

A sliver of fertile land running from the tea-draped Himalayan foothills to the sultry mangroves of the Bay of Bengal, West Bengal offers a remarkable range of destinations and experiences within a single state. In the tropical southern areas, the sea-washed hamlet of Mandarmani vies for attention with Bishnupur's ornate terracotta-tiled Hindu temples and palaces. The striped Bengal tiger stealthily swims through muddy rivulets in the Sunderbans, while a bunch of European ghost towns line the banks of the Hooghly (a branch of the Ganges) further upstream as reminders of the state's maritime heyday. In the cool northern hills, the 'toy train' chugs its way up the charming British-era hill station of Darjeeling, revered for its ringside views of massive Khangchendzonga. West Bengal also boasts a vibrant art scene, delectable cuisine and a genuinely hospitable population.

When to Go

Darjeeling

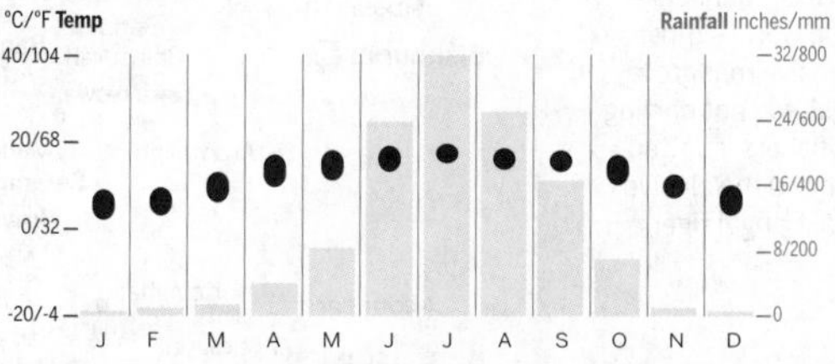

Jan Ideal for navigating the dense mangrove forests of the Sunderbans Tiger Reserve.

Mar–May & Oct–Dec Best for hill views, trekking and spring blooms up north, but high season in October.

Oct–Mar Best time for avoiding the heat on the lower southern plains.

West Bengal & Darjeeling Highlights

1 Singalila Ridge Trek (p508) Enjoying 360-degree mountain views over breakfast at hilltop lodges on this ridgeline walk.

2 Toy train (p507) Riding the tiny colonial-era steam-driven train as it puffs and pants its way between the tea towns of Kurseong and Darjeeling.

3 Shantiniketan (p488) Exploring rural wonders and getting arty on a visit to this university town.

4 Darjeeling (p497) Visiting a tea estate, sipping a delicate local brew and enjoying fantastic mountain views from this historic hill station.

5 Bishnupur (p488) Admiring intricate scenes from the Hindu epics carved on the many medieval terracotta temples.

6 Sunderbans (p486) Cruising the river channels of the world's most extensive mangrove forest, to spot darting kingfishers, spotted deer and the elusive Royal Bengal tiger.

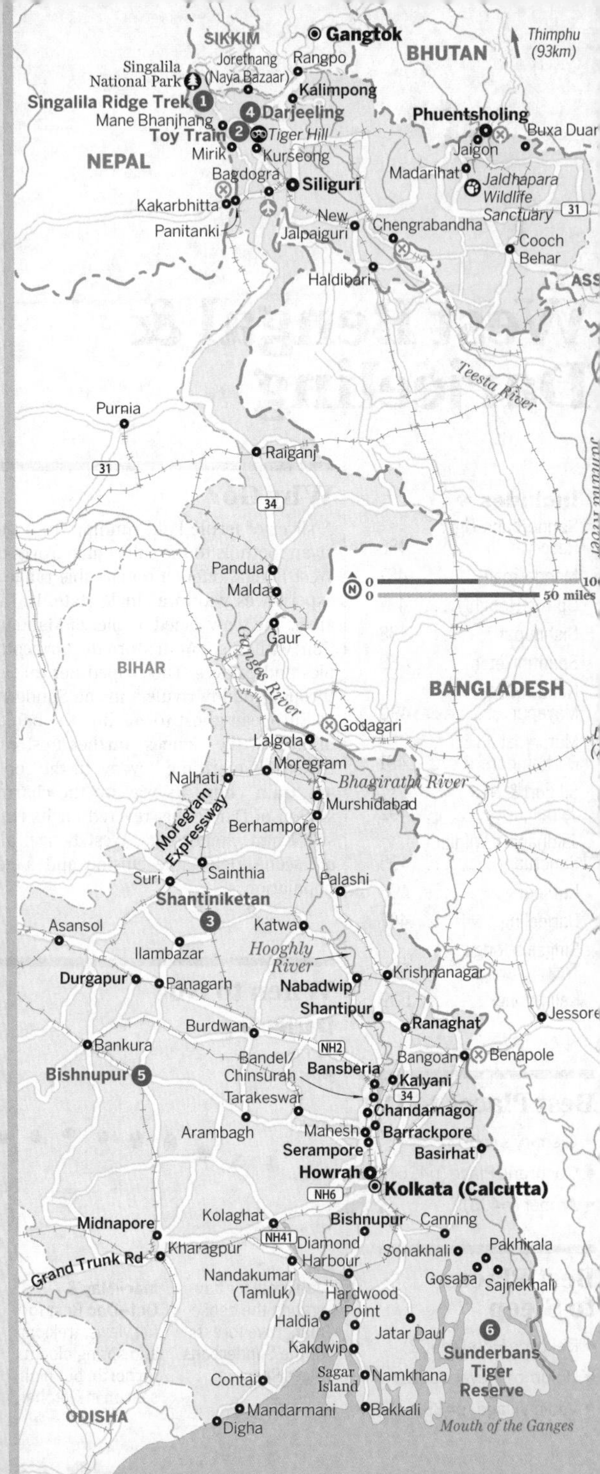

History

Referred to as Bongo in the Mahabharata, Bengal was part of the Mauryan empire in the 3rd century BC, and was successively controlled by the Guptas, the Buddhist Palas and the Islamic sultans of Delhi. Following the death of Aurangzeb in 1707, Bengal became an independent Islamic state.

The British East India Company established a trading post in Kolkata (Calcutta) in 1698, which quickly prospered and outshone other European outposts along the Hooghly River belonging to Portuguese, Dutch and Danish merchants. Annoyed by rapid British expansion, Siraj-ud-daula, the nawab of Bengal, marched out of his capital at Murshidabad and easily took Kolkata in 1756. Robert Clive defeated him the following year at the Battle of Plassey, helped by the treachery of Siraj-ud-daula's uncle, Mir Jafar, a commander in the nawab's army. Jafar succeeded his nephew as nawab, but after the Battle of Buxar in 1764 the British took full control of Bengal.

West Bengal was the cradle of the Indian Renaissance and national freedom movement, and has long been considered the country's cultural and intellectual heartland – Calcutta was the political capital of India until the British shifted office to Delhi in 1931. In 1947 Indian independence from Britain – and the subsequent partition of the country – saw the state of Bengal (which had already been split for administrative purposes in 1905) divided into Hindu-predominant West Bengal and Muslim-oriented Bangladesh, causing the upheaval and migration of millions of Bengalis.

Since the late 1980s, Darjeeling's demand for political autonomy saw phases of unrest in the state's northern mountains. This eventually led to the establishment of the Gorkhaland Territorial Administration in 2012, which has stabilised the situation for the time being.

Activities

Trekking

There are enjoyable walks along pine-scented trails in all of West Bengal's hill stations, but the most popular place for a multiday trek is Singalila Ridge, near Darjeeling, where teahouse-style trekking is possible. Kalimpong boasts some fantastic walks, both in the town's backstreets and along the surrounding ridges for Himalayan views.

Wildlife-Watching

The Sunderbans remains the state's prime forest area for spotting such species as crocodiles, Gangetic dolphins, deer, water monitors, myriad birds and the Royal Bengal tiger. In the jungles of Jaldhapara, you can get up close with elephants and grumpy rhinos.

Getting There & Away

Kolkata is the natural gateway to the southern half of the state, with flights and trains from across India, as well as a sprinkling of international flights. Bagdogra airport and New Jalpaiguri train station at Siliguri are the main gateways to the northern hills, whether via India's northeastern states or overland from neighbouring

TOP STATE FESTIVALS

Ganga Sagar Mela (Sagar Island; mid-Jan) Hundreds of thousands of Hindu pilgrims converge where the Ganges meets the sea, to bathe en masse in a riotous festival.

Bengali New Year (Naba Barsha; Statewide; mid-Apr) A holiday celebrating the first day of the Bengali calendar, also called Nabo Barsho.

Rath Yatra (Chariot Festival; Mahesh, Serampore; Jul/Aug) Attendees celebrate by dragging the juggernaut chariot of Lord Jagannath between temples.

Durga Puja (statewide; Sep/Oct) Across the state, especially in Kolkata, temporary *pandals* (pavilions) are raised and celebrations take place to worship the Hindu goddess Durga. After four colourful days, beautiful clay idols of the 10-armed deity are immersed in the rivers. Celebrated as Dussehra or Dashain in the Himalayan foothills. Banks and offices can be closed for a week.

Jagaddhatri Puja (Chandarnagar; Nov) Honours the Hindu goddess Jagaddhatri, an incarnation of Durga.

Poush Mela (p489) Folk music, dance, theatre and Baul songs radiate across the university town of Shantiniketan.

northern Bangladesh. Bagdogra Airport has international flights to Paro and Bangkok, and helicopter passenger flights to Gangtok. Frequent sleeper trains and air-conditioned day and night buses shuttle between Kolkata and Siliguri (12 hours).

SOUTH OF KOLKATA

Sunderbans Tiger Reserve

Home to one of the largest concentrations of Royal Bengal tigers on the planet, the 2585-sq-km Sunderbans Tiger Reserve (admission/video ₹60/200) is a network of channels and semi-submerged mangroves that forms the world's largest river delta. The ecosystem here is contiguous with the Sunderbans delta in Bangladesh, which lies eastward across the international border along the same shoreline. Tigers (officially estimated to number a few more than 100) lurk in the impenetrable depths of the mangrove forests, and also swim the delta's innumerable channels. Although they do sometimes attack villagers and prey on livestock, tigers are typically shy and sightings are rare. Nevertheless, cruising the broad waterways through the world's biggest mangrove sanctuary (now a Unesco World Heritage Site) and watching wildlife, whether it be gangetic dolphins, water monitors, 5m-long saltwater crocodiles or luminescent kingfishers, is a world away from Kolkata's chaos. The best time to visit is between November and February – the warmer months of March and April are better for tiger-spotting.

SAGAR ISLAND

According to Hindu legend, Sagar Island – at the confluence of the Ganges – was where King Sagar's 60,000 sons were brought back to life by the flowing river after they had been reduced to ashes by a sage named Kapil Muni. Each year in January, the Ganga Sagar Mela (p485) is held here near the **Kapil Muni Temple**, honouring the legend. The best way to see the festival is the two-day, one-night boat tour operated from Kolkata by West Bengal Tourism, with accommodation on-board (per person all-inclusive from ₹8800). The island hibernates for the rest of the year.

Buses (₹60, two hours) run frequently from Kolkata's Esplanade bus station to Namkhana pier, from where ferries head to the island. Buses and share taxis shuttle around the island between points of tourist interest.

Sights

Mangrove Interpretation Centre MUSEUM
(Sajnekhali; 8.30am-5pm) FREE This tree-shaded complex located at the entrance of the reserve is looked after by the forest department, and has some useful information on the local ecosystem, a small turtle and crocodile hatchery, a museum of wildlife and a blackboard where the date of the last tiger-spotting is routinely updated.

Activities

India Beacons BOATING
(9903295920; www.indiabeacons.com) Motorboats and guides are available for hire in Godkhali, en route to Sajnekhali. Expect to pay about ₹8000 for groups of up to four people. India Beacons has a good selection of boats for cruising the waterways deep in the Sunderbans.

Tours

Organised tours are the best way to navigate this tricky and harsh landscape, not least because all your permits, paperwork, guiding duties and logistical problems are taken care of. In fact, travelling alone is not recommended.

Tour prices vary widely. They typically include return transport from Kolkata, accommodation, food, park entry fees, as well as guide- and boat-hire charges. Do check what is and isn't included. Motorboats and guides are available for hire at Godkhali port, en route to Sajnekhali. Expect to pay about ₹8000 for groups of up to four people. India Beacons has a good selection of boats.

Backpackers WILDLIFE
(9836177140; www.tourdesundarbans.com; 11 Tottee Lane, Kolkata; 1/2 nights per person all-inclusive ₹4000/4500; 10am-7pm) Reliable yet laid-back, fun yet spiritual, this very knowledgeable 'three brothers' outfit conducts highly recommended tours of the jungle, including birdwatching and local music. Accommodation is either on a cruise boat converted from a fishing trawler, or in a traditional village-style guesthouse, with

folk music in the evenings. Rates depend on group size and number of days.

Sunderban Tiger Camp WILDLIFE
(☎033-32935749; www.waxpolhotels.com; 71 Ganesh Chandra Ave, Kolkata; 1/2 nights per person all-inclusive from ₹4940/9880) This well-managed outfit provides expert guides and quality accommodation (on dry land) in huts and lovely red-brick cottages with forest-themed wall murals. The huts are the cheapest, but come with a sense of adventure. The staff can arrange cultural shows and birdwatching tours on prior request.

Help Tourism WILDLIFE
(Map p466; ☎033-24550917; www.helptourism.com; 67A Kali Temple Rd, Kalighat, Kolkata; 2 nights per person all-inclusive ₹16,400) Actively associated with local communities, this tour operator takes you up close to rural life in the delta, and provides wonderful access into the forest. Accommodation is in a luxury eco-themed camp. Prices drop dramatically as group size increases; enquire directly.

West Bengal Tourism CRUISE
(☎033-22488271; www.wbtdc.gov.in; 2 nights per person all-inclusive from ₹6600) West Bengal's state tourism board organises weekly boat cruises from September to April, including food and on-board accommodation in dedicated vessels. It's mostly booked out by local tourists through the high season between December and February. Reserve online and well in advance.

ℹ Getting There & Away

Guided tours include pick-up and drop-off facilities in Kolkata, so you'll never have to worry about transport. If you intend to go it alone, the best option is to take a local train from Kolkata's Sealdah train station to Canning (₹15, 1½ hours), from where you'll find shuttle minibuses (₹50) to Godkhali. The last stretch to Sajnekhali is by local boat (₹20).

Mandarmani

☎03220

About 180km south of Kolkata, the sleepy fishing village of Mandarmani sports a heavenly beach stretching nearly 15km. It remains one of the more unpolluted beaches in the country, and supports countless colonies of sand bubbler crabs. The beaches see some additional action at dawn, when fishing boats drop anchor and disgorge their catches of marine goodies.

Adventure Zone (☎9830033896) conducts parasailing (₹800) on the beaches, and offers an adventure-sports package (₹1500) that includes kayaking, zip-lining, rock climbing and rappelling.

Most of Mandarmani's accommodation is thrown along the beach, and can vary widely in quality. **Sana Beach** (☎9330633111; www.mandarmanihotels.com; d incl breakfast from ₹3750; ❄🏊), at the far end of the sands, is by far the best among all the resorts lining the sea. It has a mix of comfy rooms done up in cheerful hues, ethno-chic cottages and tents, a lovely swimming pool and a good bar restaurant.

To get to Mandarmani, take the 6.40am 12857 Tamralipta Express (2nd class/chair ₹100/370, 3½ hours) from Kolkata's Howrah train station to Digha. A taxi drop from Digha train station to Mandarmani costs about ₹500.

NORTH OF KOLKATA

Up the Hooghly

Located on the Hooghly River about 25km north of Kolkata, **Serampore** was a Danish trading centre until Denmark's holdings in India were transferred to the British East India Company in 1845. **Serampore College** was founded in 1818 by the first Baptist missionary to India, William Carey, and houses a library that was once one of the largest in the country.

Further upstream is the former French outpost of **Chandarnagar**. Here you can visit the **Eglise du Sacre Coeur** (Sacred Heart Church) and the nearby 18th-century mansion now housing the **Cultural Institut de Chandarnagar** (⏰11am-5.30pm, closed Thu & Sat) FREE, which has several collections documenting the glorious era of this colonial trading outpost. In November, there are gorgeous public lighting displays for **Jagaddhatri Puja**, a festival devoted to the worship of an incarnation of the Hindu mother goddess. Enthusiastic locals throng festive arenas to pay their respects to gigantic clay idols of the four-armed deity, housed in temporary pavilions called *pandals*.

In 1571, the Portuguese set up a factory in **Bandel**, 41km north of Kolkata and close to Saptagram, which was an important Portuguese trading port long before Kolkata rose to prominence. Here, In Bandel, you can climb the lofty clock tower of the romantically crumbling **Imambara** (admission ₹10; ⏲10am-6pm Apr-Jul, to 5.30pm Aug-Nov, to 5pm Dec-Mar), which has breathtaking views of the Hooghly River and houses a giant mechanical clock. The building was inaugurated in 1861 as a centre for learning and worship, and its grand Indo-Saracenic profile offers some very interesting photo ops.

Only 1km south of Bandel, **Chinsurah** was ceded by the Dutch to the British in exchange for Sumatra in 1825. There are dilapidated ruins of a fort and a cemetery, about 1km to the west.

About 6km north of Bandel, **Bansberia** has two interesting temples. The imposing **Hanseswari Temple** is devoted to an avatar of the goddess Kali. Its tower, comprising 13 sikharas (Hindu temple-spires), looks like something you'd expect to see in Moscow. Within the temple premises is the small but elegant terracotta-tiled **Vasudev Temple**, which resembles terracotta temples seen in Bishnupur.

To visit these settlements on a day tour from Kolkata, take any Bandel-bound local train (₹15, one hour, hourly) from Howrah train station. From Bandel train station, you'll find autorickshaws going to all places of interest – you can reserve one for a day's sightseeing for about ₹500. Alternately, hire a taxi for the day from Kolkata (₹3000).

RIVER CRUISES

For those with a Piscean bent of mind (and pockets deep enough to match), the Hooghly River doubles as a corridor for luxury boat cruises, which slosh their guests with a host of fine on-board comforts while allowing them to visit the Ganges Delta in a most memorable manner. Cruises usually range from four days to about two weeks, and stop in places such as Chandarnagar, Bandel, Mayapur, Murshidabad and Farakka (for Gaur and Pandua), along with side excursions to some little-known places along the way. **Bengal Ganga** (☎011-41085922; www.bengalganga.com; per person per day all-inclusive from ₹46,800) and **Assam Bengal Navigation** (☎9207042330; www.assambengalnavigation.com; per person per day all-inclusive from US$210) come highly recommended.

Bishnupur

☎03244

Known for its beautiful terracotta temples, Bishnupur flourished as the capital of the Malla kings from the 16th to the early 19th centuries. The architecture of these intriguing **temples** (Indian/foreigner ₹30/750; ⏲dawn-dusk) is a bold mix of Bengali, Islamic and Oriya (Odishan) styles. Intricately detailed facades of numerous temples play out scenes of the Hindu epics, the Ramayana and Mahabharata.

Bishnupur is in Bankura district, famous for its **Baluchari silk saris** and its pottery, particularly the stylised and iconic **terracotta Bankura horse**. Reproductions of detailed terracotta tiles from the temples are sold everywhere.

The most striking structures include **Jor Bangla**, **Madan Mohan Temple**, the multi-arched **Ras Mancha** and the elaborate **Shyam Rai Temple**. You need to pay for your ticket at Ras Mancha and show it at the other temples. Cycle-rickshaw-wallahs offer tours (the best way to negotiate the labyrinth of lanes) for ₹300. There's a small **museum** (admission ₹15; ⏲11am-7pm Tue-Sun) that's worth a look for its collection of painted manuscript covers, stone friezes, musical instruments and folk art.

Bishnupur Tourist Lodge (☎03244-252013; www.wbtdc.gov.in; College Rd; d from ₹880; ❄), flaunting a red-and-white exterior, is perhaps the best place to sleep in town, with clean pastel-shaded rooms and a good bar restaurant. It's close to the museum and a ₹80 rickshaw ride from the train station. It's often full, so book ahead.

ℹ Getting There & Away

Regular buses run between Bishnupur and Kolkata (₹160, five hours). For Shantiniketan (₹120, four hours) you have to change in Durgapur. Two fast trains run daily from Howrah (2nd class/chair ₹110/395, four hours): the 6.25am 12883 Rupashi Bangla Express and the 4.50pm 12827 Howrah Purulia Express.

Shantiniketan

☎03463

In addition to epitomising its Bengali name – meaning 'abode of peace' – the university town of Shantiniketan is a veritable nerve centre of Bengal's art and culture. Nobel laureate, poet and artist Rabindranath Tagore (1861–1941) founded a school here amid pas-

DON'T MISS

SPA TREATS

Looking to experience the best of rural Bengal while treating yourself to a spot of wellness and luxury? Head to one of these two recommended spa resorts, set amid scenic landscapes, and indulge in some of the best comforts and therapies, while soaking up the bucolic charms of the region.

Hemmed by blooming vegetable gardens and centred around a tree-lined lake only an hour's drive north of Kolkata is **Vedic Village** (☎033-66229900; www.thevedicvillage.com; Shikharpur village, Rajarhat; spa package from ₹8500; ❄@≋), a luxury resort known as much for its fine hospitality as its showcase facility – a speciality spa-cum-naturopathy clinic that's touted to be the first (and best) medical spa in the country. Long-stay treatment packages, built around several sessions of consultation with in-house doctors, can be customised upon prior notice. Casual holidaymakers can simply kick back in one of the luxury villas, de-stress to the chirping of myriad bird species, tuck into mouth-watering cuisine, or float in the ultramarine waters of the swimming pool.

En route to Diamond Harbour, about two hours south of Kolkata, stands **Ganga Kutir** (☎033-40404040; www.raichakonganges.com; Sarisa village, Raichak; r incl breakfast from ₹8550; ❄@≋), another popular destination for those wanting some solitude. Located on the banks of the Hooghly, this swish resort offers a range of wellness packages that – paired with yoga and meditation – are a great nourisher for tired sinews. Accommodation is in chic suites appointed with snazzy mural-covered walls and great river views.

toral settings in 1901. It later developed into the famous university called **Visva Bharati**, with an emphasis on the study of liberal arts as well as humanity's relationship with nature. A relaxed place, it attracts students from all over India and overseas.

Sights

Spread throughout the leafy university grounds of Visva Bharati are a rush of eclectic **statues**, the celebrated **Shantiniketan murals** and the Belgian glass-panelled **university prayer hall**.

Uttarayan Complex MUSEUM
(Visva Bharati Campus; adult/student ₹10/5; ⏲10am-1pm & 2-4pm Thu-Mon, to 1pm Tue) This beautiful complex thrown around tree-lined avenues, gravelled courtyards and exotic gardens boasts several buildings built in architectural styles varying from art deco to rural Bengal. Once the residence of Rabindranath Tagore, the complex now houses a few offices of the university, as well as a **museum** and an **art gallery** that are both worth a peek if you are a Tagore aficionado. Reproductions of his sketches and paintings are sold here from a publications sales counter by the main entrance.

Festivals & Events

Poush Mela CULTURAL
(Shantiniketan; ⏲23-26 Dec) The highpoint of Shantiniketan's festive calendar, the Poush Mela fair brings together artists, musicians, artisans and poets from nearby villages and far-flung continents. You can spend time with the *bauls* – the wandering minstrels of Bengal – and listen to their songs about life and love, or roam stalls selling tribal artefacts, clothing and jewellery. There's some lip-smacking regional food available at the food stalls.

Magh Mela CULTURAL
(Shantiniketan; ⏲6-8 Feb) At the three-day Magh Mela held in the village of Sriniketan (contiguous to Shantiniketan), crafts and rural arts take centre stage. On the second evening, a spectacular fireworks show attracts a huge audience.

Sleeping

Shantiniketan Tourist Lodge HOTEL $
(☎03463-252699; www.wbtdc.gov.in; Bhubandanga; d from ₹1180; ❄) Industrial but friendly, this large-scale government operation is worth considering only if you go for one of its deluxe air-conditioned rooms (₹2950), located in cottages standing around a pretty lawn. There's a decent restaurant (mains ₹80 to ₹140) that works up delicious local Bengali fare.

Mitali Homestay HOMESTAY $$
(☎9433075853; krishno.dey@gmail.com; Phool Danga; d incl breakfast ₹3500; ❄) Located about 2km north of the university in verdant Phool Danga village, this charming home of a retired diplomat and his designer

PALACES GALORE

Thrown around the vicinity of Kolkata's city limits are a handful of *rajbaris* (palaces) belonging to families of erstwhile zamindars (landowners). While most of them stand dilapidated and forlorn, a few have recently made a promising turnaround and joined the top-end tourism bandwagon. Among the palaces offering a luxury experience woven around the bygone regal life is the palace of **Itachuna** (☎9830142389; www.itachunarajbari.com; Halusai village; d from ₹2100; ❄), 110km from Kolkata. It packs a punch with its renovated stately interiors, fine Bengali food and an overall bucolic ambience. The palace of **Bawali** (☎9830383008; www.therajbari.com; Bawali village; d incl breakfast from ₹8000; ❄), a one-hour drive south of Kolkata, also makes for a lovely getaway, with a striking doric-pillared facade, carefully preserved distressed decor and excellent overall hospitality.

wife promises a languid and bucolic experience featuring great company, snug air-con rooms (both within the family home and in an annexe) and some delicious home-style food (lunch or dinner per person ₹400). An autorickshaw from the campus costs ₹50.

Discounts are often thrown in for stays longer than three nights.

Chhuti Holiday Resort RESORT **$$**
(☎03463-252692; www.chhutiresort.co.in; Charu Palli; d from ₹1800; ❄) This tree-shaded property offers cottage-style rooms with ethnic trimmings, good food in its multicuisine restaurant and an overall sense of peace and quiet. There's no wireless connectivity comped in, but the reception can arrange for cultural programs upon prior request. It's located close to the Jambuni bus stand in Bolpur, and an autorickshaw to the university will cost you ₹50.

Park Guest House GUESTHOUSE **$$**
(☎9434012420; www.parkguesthouse.in; Deer Park; d incl breakfast from ₹1730; ❄📶) Bordering a quaint tribal village, this modest place appeals to those who like a dash of rustic essence and solitude on their holidays. The basic but comfortable rooms sport some tribal decor, and the elaborate thali meals (prepared upon advance notice) are simply awesome. There's a lovely lawn where you can nurse a quiet beer in the evening.

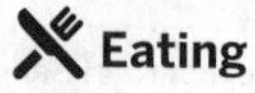

Eating

Alcha Foods BENGALI **$$**
(Tourist Lodge Rd; thalis vegetarian/fish ₹100/190; noon-3pm & 4-8pm Mon-Sat) This tiny restaurant is known for its yummy lunch platters that feature a fabulous spread of traditional Bengali dishes. Unique seasonal menus are followed for each day of the week. In the evenings, you can order yourself a range of crispy fried snacks to go with a cup of aromatic filter coffee.

Ghare Baire BENGALI **$$**
(Geetanjali Cinema complex; meals ₹190; 11.30am-9.30pm) A restaurant specialising in traditional Bengali fare, this cafeteria-style eatery churns out sumptuous and delectable platters for lunch and dinner. There are a few generic snacks and Chinese preparations on offer as well. There's a souvenir store on-site, selling a line of exquisite pottery and textiles that you might want to check out in between morsels.

Information

Post Office (Shantiniketan Rd; 10am-4pm Mon-Sat) Located on the main road, this post office has speed post and parcel facilities.

State Bank of India (Shantiniketan Rd; 10am-4pm Mon-Fri, to 2pm Sat) This bank has an ATM that accepts foreign cards.

Getting There & Away

The town of Bolpur, contiguous to Shantiniketan, serves as its transport hub. Several daily trains ply the route between Kolkata and Bolpur train station, 2km south of the university. The best is 12337 Shantiniketan Express (2nd class/chair ₹95/305, 2½ hours) departing at 10.10am from Howrah train station. For New Jalpaiguri, take the 9.20am 15657 Kanchenjunga Express (sleeper/3AC ₹250/670, nine hours). There's a **train booking office** (Shantiniketan Rd; 8am-noon & 12.30-2pm Thu-Tue) within the university campus for information and ticketing.

Bolpur's Jambuni bus stand has connections to Berhampore/Murshidabad (₹110, four hours) and Bishnupur (₹100, four hours). Change in Suri and Durgapur respectively.

Nabadwip & Mayapur

☎03472

About 115km north of Kolkata, Nabadwip is an important Krishna pilgrimage centre, attracting throngs of devotees, and is also an ancient centre of Sanskrit culture. The last Hindu king of Bengal, Lakshman Sen, moved his capital here from Gaur.

Across the river from Nabadwip, Mayapur is the headquarters of the Iskcon (Hare Krishna) movement. There's a large, colourful temple and the basic but clean **Iskcon Guest House** (☎03472-245620; mghb@pamho.net; Main Complex; d/tr/q from ₹600/800/900; ❄), which has a variety of rooms for guests wishing to spend a night. Iskcon also runs a package bus tour from Kolkata, leaving early on Friday, Saturday and Sunday mornings, returning the subsequent evening. For details or to make a booking, call Iskcon Kolkata.

Besides the Iskcon Guest House, there are no hotels catering to foreign tourists. It's quite easy, however, to visit Mayapur on a day trip from Kolkata.

A simple cafeteria within the Iskcon premises has vegetarian snacks (₹40 to ₹70) on offer. You can also sit in for the communal vegetarian lunch (₹70), served daily at 1pm at Gada Bhavan.

ℹ Getting There & Away

Local suburban trains (₹20, two hours, hourly) connect Kolkata's Sealdah train station to the town of Krishnagar, from where shared autorickshaws (₹20) can shuttle you to Mayapur. Alternately, join the bus tour operated by **Iskcon Kolkata** (☎033-64588777; 22 Gurusaday Rd).

Murshidabad & Berhampore

☎03482 / POP 195,200

In Murshidabad, rural Bengali life and 18th-century architecture meld on the verdant shores of the Hooghly River, locally also known as the Bhagirathi River. When Siraj-ud-daula was nawab of Bengal, Murshidabad was his capital, and he was assassinated here after his defeat by Robert Clive at Plassey (now Palashi) in 1757.

The main draw here is the palace of **Hazarduari** (Indian/foreigner ₹30/750; ⏲10am-4.30pm Sat-Thu), a royal mansion famous for its 1000 doors (real and false), built for the

OFF THE BEATEN TRACK

GAUR & PANDUA

Rising from the flooded paddy fields of Gaur (355km from Kolkata) are mosques and other crumbling ruins of the 13th- to 16th-century capital of the Muslim nawabs of Bengal. Little remains from the 7th- to 12th-century pre-Islamic period, when Gaur was the capital of the successive Buddhist Pala and Hindu Sena dynasties.

Malda, 340km north of Kolkata, is a convenient base for exploring both Gaur and Pandua. Malda is also famed for its mangoes ripening in summer. Even if it's not mango season when you visit, you can buy delicious mango pickle and candied mango from the local market.

Hiding behind lush mango orchards, the most graceful monuments in Gaur are the impressive **Baradwari Mosque** (1526) – the arcaded aisle of its corridor still intact – and the fortress-like gateway of **Dakhil Darwaza** (1425). The **Qadam Rasul Mosque** enshrines the flat footprint of the Prophet Mohammed. Remnants of colourful enamel cling to the **Chamkan Mosque** and the **Gumti Gate** nearby.

In Pandua (about 25km from Gaur) are the vast ruins of the 14th-century **Adina Masjid**, once India's largest mosque. About 2km away is the **Eklakhi Mausoleum**, so called because it cost ₹1 lakh (₹100,000) to build back in 1431.

Malda has a few very basic hotels catering to local travellers. The best of the lot is **Hotel Kalinga** (☎03512-283567; www.hotelkalingamalda.com; NH34, Ram Krishna Pally; d ₹1050; ❄), with OK-ish rooms and a multicuisine restaurant. The reception arranges taxis for touring the ruins.

Several express trains run daily from Kolkata's Howrah train station to Malda, including the 12041 Shatabdi Express (chair ₹750, five hours, 2.15pm) and the 13011 Howrah-Malda Intercity Express (2nd class/chair ₹130/470, 7½ hours, 3.25pm). The former continues to New Jalpaiguri (chair ₹600, three hours, 7.10pm), which is the access point for Darjeeling.

Buses depart regularly for Siliguri (₹150, six hours), Berhampore/Murshidabad (₹90, four hours) and Kolkata (₹200, 10 hours).

For touring the monuments in Gaur and Pandua, you have to hire a taxi for the day (₹2500) in Malda. There's no public transport to the ruins.

nawabs in 1837. It houses an astonishing collection of antiquities from the 18th and 19th centuries. Other beautiful structures within the complex include the **Nizamat Imambara** with a **clock tower**, the **Wasef Manzil** (a former regal residence) and the elegant **Madina Mosque**.

Murshid Quli Khan, who moved the capital here in 1700, is buried beneath the stairs at the impressive ruins of the **Katra Mosque**. Siraj-ud-daula was assassinated at the **Nimak Haram Deori** (Traitor's Gate). Within the **Kathgola Gardens** (admission ₹10; ⏲6.30am-5.30pm) is an interesting family mansion of a Jain trading family, dating back to 1873.

Sleeping & Eating

Hotel Sagnik HOTEL $

(☎09434021911; Omrahaganj; d from ₹950; ❄) Conveniently located between Murshidabad and Berhampore, this friendly place has good-value rooms and a decent restaurant, but scores mostly on service, which is prompt and personalised. It's a 10-minute cycle-rickshaw ride from Murshidabad train station.

Hotel Samrat HOTEL $

(☎03482-251147; NH34 Panchanantala; d incl breakfast from ₹1150; ❄) This is one of Berhampore's longest-running operations. It offers spacious and clean rooms opening along corridors painted in orange and cream. The Mahal restaurant (mains ₹80 to ₹150) downstairs is a good place for meals. It's located on the main highway, though, so expect some vehicle noise at night.

Getting There & Around

The 13113 Hazarduari Express (2nd class/chair ₹85/320, 3½ hours) departs Kolkata train station at 6.50am. Regular buses leave for Kolkata (₹150, six hours) and Malda (₹90, four hours). For Shantiniketan/Bolpur (₹110, four hours) you'll have to change in Suri.

SLEEPING PRICE RANGES

The following price ranges refer to a double room with bathroom in high season. Unless otherwise stated tax is included in room rates.

$ less than ₹1300

$$ ₹1300–3000

$$$ more than ₹3000

Shared autorickshaws (₹50) whiz between Murshidabad and Berhampore through the day. Cycle-rickshaws/autorickshaws offer guided half-day tours to see the spread-out sites for ₹500/800.

WEST BENGAL HILLS

Siliguri & New Jalpaiguri

☎0353 / POP 701,000 / ELEV 120M

The crowded and noisy transport hub encompassing the twin towns of Siliguri and New Jalpaiguri (NJP) is the jumping-off point for Darjeeling, Kalimpong, Sikkim, the Northeast States, eastern Nepal and Bhutan. However, despite this being one of the largest cities in the state, there's little to see or do here, apart from staying the night in transit, if you have to.

Most of Siliguri's hotels, restaurants and services are spread along riotously noisy Tenzing Norgay Rd, better known as Hill Cart Rd. NJP Station Rd leads southward 6km to NJP train station. Branching northeastward off Hill Cart Rd are Siliguri's other main streets, Sevoke and Bidhan Rds.

If you have time to kill, visit the colourful Tibetan-style **Salugara Monastery** (Sed-Gyued Gompa; www.sed-gyued.org; Sevoke Rd), 5km north of town, adorned with an imposing 30m tall chorten (Tibetan-style stupa).

Sleeping

Hotel Rajdarbar HOTEL $$

(☎0353-2511189; rajdarbarhotel@yahoo.com; Hill Cart Rd; s/d incl breakfast ₹2050/2280; ❄📶) A fresh and tidy option in a group of similar hotels, this place has well-maintained rooms, a good restaurant and lobby wi-fi. Rooms come with free breakfast. Best by far are the spacious and quiet top-floor premium suites (single/double ₹3930/4170).

Evergreen Inn HOTEL $

(☎0353-2510426; innevergreen@yahoo.in; Pradhan Nagar, Ashana Purna Sarani; d with/without AC from ₹1440/990; ❄📶) Located just 100m from the central bus terminal, this hotel down a side street is surprisingly peaceful. Each of the 11 rooms is different, but they all are clean and fresh with flat-screen TVs and stylish bathrooms. You'll find it down a lane on the opposite side of the bus terminal.

Hotel Conclave HOTEL $

(☎0353-2516155; hotelconclave@rediffmail.com; Hill Cart Rd; s/d with AC from ₹1865/2035, without

AC ₹850/990; ❄📶) Located conveniently close to town's bus stands, Hotel Conclave has quality beds and prim cedar-themed decor. The cheaper rooms are quieter and the pricier rooms come with complimentary breakfast. All have a small balcony.

Hotel Himalayan Regency HOTEL $
(☎0353-2516624; himalayanhatchery@gmail.com; Hill Cart Rd, Pradhan Nagar; d with/without AC ₹1500/800; ❄📶) Despite some eyebrow-raising decor choices, rooms here are clean and comfortable, with circular beds in the air-con rooms. You'll find it near Pradhan Nagar police station.

Hotel Sinclairs HOTEL $$$
(☎0353-2512675; www.sinclairshotels.com; off NH31; s/d incl breakfast from ₹5800/6200; ❄📶🏊) This comfortable three-star hotel, 1km north of the central bus terminal, offers an escape from the noise of Hill Cart Rd. It's one of Siliguri's longest-standing luxury addresses, and offers fresh, modern and comfortable rooms with good bathrooms. There's an excellent patio restaurant-bar and a cool clean pool, perfect for escaping the heat of the plains.

Eating

★**Khana Khazana** MULTICUISINE $$
(Hill Cart Rd; mains ₹120-200; ⏲9am-10pm) On a side alley off the busy main highway, the secluded outdoor garden here offers merciful relief from the thunderous chaos outside. The extensive menu ranges from fine curries and naan (tandoor-cooked flat bread) to Mumbai street snacks, with plenty of hearty vegetarian options and *kulfi,* flavoured (often with pistachio) firm-textured ice cream.

Amber INDIAN $$
(☎0353-2431682; Hill Cart Rd; mains ₹190-330; ⏲10am-11pm; ❄) This trusted and air-conditioned restaurant attached to Hotel Saluja Residency serves mouth-watering dishes, including fluffy naans, lip-smacking curries, tender meat dishes and subtly flavoured biryanis that go down extremely well with the city's food lovers. Evenings are an especially buzzy time to be here.

Sartaj INDIAN $$
(☎0353-2431758; Hill Cart Rd; mains ₹120-220; ⏲9am-11pm; ❄) In a cluster of similar bar restaurant operations, this sophisticated eatery boasts a huge range of first-rate North Indian tandooris and curries, some decent Continental sizzlers and top-notch service, including a fantastic uniformed doorman. It's also a good place for a cold beer.

Information

INTERNET ACCESS

Krishna Travels (Hill Cart Rd; per hr ₹80; ⏲9am-9pm Mon-Sat) Internet access (but no wi-fi) down a side street across from Hotel Conclave.

MEDICAL SERVICES

Sadar Hospital (☎0353-2436526; Hospital Rd) Siliguri's main state-run hospital with emergency and outpatient services.

MONEY

Delhi Hotel (Hill Cart Rd; ⏲9am-2pm) Cash foreign currency exchanged, opposite the Tenzing Norgay central bus terminal. Flexible hours often extend into the evening.

TOURIST INFORMATION

Sikkim Tourist Office (☎0353-2512646; SNT terminal, Hill Cart Rd; ⏲10am-4pm Mon-Sat) Issues permits for Sikkim on the spot. Bring copies of your passport and visa, and one passport-sized photo.

West Bengal Tourism (WBTDC; ☎bookings 9832492417, information 0353-2511974; www.wbtdc.gov.in; Hill Cart Rd; ⏲10.30am-5.30pm Mon-Fri, to 1.30pm Sat) Can book accommodation online for Jaldhapara Wildlife Sanctuary, including forestry lodges.

TRAVEL AGENCIES

Private transport booking agencies line Hill Cart Rd.

Help Tourism (☎0353-2535896; www.help-tourism.com; 143 Hill Cart Rd) A recommended agency with a strong environmental and community-development focus, including voluntourism. It has links to dozens of homestays and lodges around the hills, including a historic tea estate at Damdin and the stylish Neora Valley Jungle Camp outside Lava.

Getting There & Away

AIR

Bagdogra Airport is 12km west of Siliguri. There are daily flights to Delhi, Kolkata and Guwahati, plus seasonal international connections on Druk Air to Bangkok and Paro.

Five-seater helicopters (₹3500, 30 minutes, 10kg luggage limit) travel daily from Bagdogra to Gangtok at 2.30pm in good weather. You need to book in advance through **Sikkim Tourism Development Corporation** (☎03592-203960, 03592-209031; www.sikkimstdc.com/HeliServiceGeneral/HeliGeneralReservation.aspx) in Gangtok; or book at the airport.

A prepaid taxi stand at Bagdogra Airport offers fixed fares to Darjeeling (₹1800), Kalimpong (₹1410), Gangtok (₹2200) and Kakarbhitta (₹500) on the Nepal border, allowing you to bypass Siliguri completely. It's not difficult to hook up with other airline passengers to share the cost. Prices indicated are to the local jeep stand; a hotel drop will cost a little more.

BUS

Most North Bengal State Transport Corporation (NBSTC) buses leave from **Tenzing Norgay central bus terminal** (Hill Cart Rd), as do many private buses plying the same routes. Private long-distance bus companies line the entrance.

NBSTC buses include frequent buses to Malda (₹175, 6½ hours), plus six daily services to Kolkata (₹390 to ₹420). Assam State Transportation Corporation runs a daily 4pm bus to Guwahati (₹550, 15 hours). The Hill Region Minibus Owners Association booth has minibuses to Kalimpong (₹200, 2½ hours) every 30 minutes.

For a 6pm Patna departure (seat/sleeper ₹350/400, 12 hours) try **Gupta Travels** (☎0353-2513451; Hill Cart Rd), just outside the bus station. Deluxe air-con Volvo buses for Kolkata (₹1200, 11 hours) leave around 7pm from this company and many other agencies. Non-air-con coaches cost around ₹400.

Sikkim Nationalised Transport (SNT) buses to Gangtok (₹150, 4½ hours) leave every 40 minutes between 6am and 3pm from the **SNT terminal** (Hill Cart Rd), 250m southeast of the bus terminal. Arrange your permit in advance at the Sikkim Tourist Office next door.

JEEP

An efficient if somewhat cramped way of getting around the hills is by shared jeep. There are a number of jeep stands lining Hill Cart Rd: for Darjeeling (₹130, three hours) and Kurseong (₹70, 1½ hours) look around opposite the bus terminal or outside the Conclave Hotel until late afternoon; for Kalimpong (₹130, 2½ hours) head to the Panitanki Mall stand on Sevoke Rd (take an autorickshaw for ₹20); and for Gangtok (₹200, four hours) jeeps leave from next to the SNT terminal until around 4pm. Shared and chartered jeeps for all these destinations also leave from NJP train station. Mirik-bound jeeps (₹100, 2½ hours) leave most frequently from Siliguri train station, 200m southwest of Tenzing Norgay central bus terminal.

Chartering a jeep privately costs roughly 15 times that of a shared ticket. A recommended

BORDER CROSSING: BANGLADESH, BHUTAN & NEPAL

To/From Bangladesh

A number of private agencies in Siliguri, including **Shyamoli** (☎9932628243; Hotel Central Plaza complex, Mallagauri More, Hill Cart Rd, 1km northwest of central bus terminal), run daily air-con buses direct to Dhaka (₹1200, 18 hours), departing at 1.30pm. You'll need to complete border formalities at Chengrabandha. Book a day or two in advance.

Buses also run every 45 minutes from the Tenzing Norgay central bus terminal to Chengrabandha (₹60, 2½ hours) between 7am and 5pm. The border post is open from 8am to 6pm daily. From near the border post you can catch buses on to Rangpur, Bogra and Dhaka. Visas for Bangladesh can be obtained in Kolkata and New Delhi.

To/From Bhutan

Bhutan Transport Services runs two daily buses from Sevoke Rd to Phuentsholing inside Bhutan (₹100, departs 7.15am and noon), but it makes more sense to take one of the more frequent local buses to Jaigaon (₹106, four hours) on the Indian side of the border, where you clear Indian immigration. The gate between Phuentsholing and Jaigaon opens at 6am and closes at 9pm for vehicles, but people can cross on foot until 10pm.

A chartered jeep from Bagdogra Airport to Jaigaon costs ₹2510. Non-Indian nationals need visa clearance from a Bhutanese tour operator to enter Bhutan.

To/From Nepal

For Nepal, local buses pass the Tenzing Norgay central bus terminal on Hill Cart Rd every 30 minutes for the border town of Panitanki (₹25, one hour). Nearby shared jeeps to Kakarbhitta (₹125) are faster but only leave when full. The Indian border post in Panitanki is officially open 24 hours but the Nepali post in Kakarbhitta is open from 7am to 7pm.

Onward from Kakarbhitta there are numerous buses to Kathmandu (17 hours) and other destinations. Bhadrapur Airport, 23km southwest of Kakarbhitta, has regular flights to Kathmandu (US$185) on Buddha Air (www.buddhaair.com). Visas for Nepal can be obtained at the border (bring two passport photos).

option for XL-sized travellers is to pay for and occupy the front two or three seats next to the driver.

TRAIN

When booking tickets to/from Siligrui be sure to confirm whether your ticket is from central Siliguri Junction or New Jalpaiguri (NJP) train stations, 6km to the southeast.

Buy tickets at Siliguri junction train station or at the **train booking office** (☎0353-2537333; cnr Hospital & Bidhan Rds; ⏲8am-noon, 12.30-2pm & 2.15-8pm Mon-Sat, to 2pm Sun), 1.5km southeast of the Hotel Conclave.

The 8pm 12344 Darjeeling Mail is the fastest of the many daily services to Kolkata (sleeper/3AC ₹350/915, 10 hours), via Malda.

For Delhi, the 1.15pm 12423 Rajdhani Express is your best and quickest bet (3AC/2AC ₹2200/3020, 21 hours). Alternatively, board the 5.15pm 12505 North East Express (sleeper/3AC ₹625/1630, 26 hours).

The easiest train to get tickets for to head to Patna (sleeper/3AC/2AC ₹280/750/1490, 13 hours) is the Capital Express, though it arrives at an unsociable 3.20am. For Guwahati, board the 8.35am 12506 North East Express going in the other direction (sleeper/3AC ₹275/710, eight hours).

ℹ Getting Around

From Tenzing Norgay central bus terminal to NJP train station, a taxi/autorickshaw costs ₹230/100. Taxis/autorickshaws between Bagdogra Airport and Siliguri cost ₹460/250.

Shared autorickshaws (₹7) run continuously along the length of Tenzing Norgay Rd.

Jaldhapara Wildlife Sanctuary

☎03563 / ELEV 60M

The little-visited **Jaldhapara Wildlife Sanctuary** (☎03563-262239; www.jaldapara.in; Indian/foreigner ₹60/200, camera/video ₹50/500; ⏲mid-Sep–mid-Jun) protects 114 sq km of lush forests and grasslands along the Torsa River and is a refuge for 150 Indian one-horned rhinoceros *(Rhinoceros unicornis)*. It's not the easiest place to visit independently and booking accommodation inside the park needs to be done months in advance, so plan ahead. The best time to visit is mid-November to April, with March and April being the best months for wildlife-spotting. Bring mosquito repellent.

Your best chance of spotting a rhino is on an **elephant ride** (☎03563-262230; Indian/foreigner per person ₹600/1000; ⏲5-8am), though these limited lumbering safaris are often booked out by the tourist lodges, and are discouraged by animal welfare groups because of the potential harm that this can cause to the elephants. Even if you are staying at Jaldhapara Tourist Lodge (p496) for a night, you are not guaranteed a ride, as full occupancy is double that of their daily elephant quota. An hour-long elephant ride will cost at least US$50 per person, after all costs are added in. Bear in mind that tourists ride in a *howdah* (wooden seat) on the elephant's back, a practice that animal welfare groups discourage.

Jeep safaris (☎03563-262230; 4-/6-person jeep foreigners ₹1840/2240, Indians ₹1520/1640) operate in the early morning and afternoon and stop at viewing platforms, but these can also be hard to arrange unless you are on a tour or staying at one of the two tourist lodges.

Mithun of **Wild Planet Travel Desk** (☎9735028733; easthimalayan3@yahoo.com) and Hotel Relax can often book accommodation and safaris when no one else can and are probably your best option for a DIY trip, including cycling and birdwatching options.

Sleeping & Eating

Hollong Tourist Lodge LODGE $$
(☎03563-262228; www.wbtourism.gov.in; d ₹2850) This green-coloured wooden lodge right in the heart of the park is perhaps the best place to stay, though booking one of the six non-air-con rooms can be a real challenge. You can spot animals right from the verandah and the package includes a morning elephant ride, but you may want to avoid this because of the animal welfare issues. Book up to six months in advance.

The lodge doesn't take direct bookings, bookings are made online at www.wbtdc.gov.in or via West Bengal Tourism (p480).

TOY TRAIN WOES

The toy train to Darjeeling continues to remain suspended from Siliguri, due to damaged tracks near Tindharia. Until it's repaired, the only option will be to drive to Kurseong and then catch the toy train on to Darjeeling. Even when it's open, the daily 9.30am departure for Darjeeling (seat ₹350) is for die-hards only, since it takes seven hours to cover 88km, well over twice as long as by road!

Jaldhapara Tourist Lodge HOTEL $$
(☎9733008795, 03563-262230; www.wbtourism.gov.in; Madarihat; d with AC ₹2200-3200, without AC ₹1600; ❄) This functional but comfortable West Bengal Tourism Development Corporation (WBTDC) hotel is just outside the park in Madarihat town. It has rooms in wooden and concrete blocks or in new cottages. Weekends can be swamped with noisy local families and youth groups.

The lodge doesn't take direct bookings; bookings are made online at www.wbtdc.gov.in or via West Bengal Tourism (p480).

Getting There & Away

Jaldhapara is 124km east of Siliguri. Local buses run every 30 minutes from Siliguri bus terminal to Madarihat (₹87, four hours) until 3.30pm. Book at the 'Inter District Minibus Owners Association' booth.

There are also slow but scenic mail trains (unreserved seat ₹40 to ₹65, three to four hours), leaving Siliguri Junction train station at 6am, 7.15am, 5pm and 6pm, returning from Madarihat at 6.05am, 7.50am and 1.30pm.

From Madarihat, it's a 7km trip to the park headquarters. A return taxi costs ₹700, including waiting time, plus you'll also have to pay the ₹275 vehicle entry fee.

Kurseong

☎0354 / POP 40,100 / ELEV 1460M

Kurseong, 32km south of Darjeeling, is a tiny but bustling hill town best known for its tea estates and Raj-era boarding schools. Its name derives from the Lepcha word *khorsang*, a reference to the small white orchid prolific in this area. Flanked by hilly slopes draped with manicured tea estates, it is also currently the southern terminus for the charming toy trains of the Darjeeling Himalayan Railway.

Hill Cart Rd (Tenzing Norgay Rd) – the noisy, traffic-choked main thoroughfare from Siliguri to Darjeeling – and its remarkably close shadow, the railway line, wind through town.

Sights

Makaibari TEA ESTATE
(☎0353-2510071; www.makaibari.com; Pankhabari Rd; ⏲Tue-Sat mid-Mar–mid-Nov) FREE If you like tea, you should visit this organic and biodynamic tea estate; the factory is open to visitors. In-between the huge sorting and drying machines, and the fields of green bushes, you may run into the owner, tea guru and local character, Rajah Banerjee. Short visits are free, or you can opt for a plantation walk with tea plucking and tasting (per person ₹200 to ₹300, with lunch in a local homestay an additional ₹200 or so).

Mornings before 10am between mid-March and mid-November are the best time to see the production process. There's no picking on Sunday or processing on Monday. Horse riding and even canopy climbing are planned, and a spa resort is under construction.

The estate is 3km below Kurseong along Pankhabari Rd, and 1km below Cochrane Place. A taxi here costs ₹200, or it's a pleasant downhill walk (it's much steeper coming back so take a ₹20 shared taxi from Cochrane Place). En route, the lush, overgrown old graveyard at St Andrew's has poignant reminders of the tea-planter era.

Makaibari runs a homestay and volunteer program from a separate office 50m below the main entrance. Volunteers can find placements in teaching, health and community projects; for details, see www.volmakaibari.org. Ask for Nayan Lama. This is also the place to book a plantation walk.

Ambootia Tea Estate TEA ESTATE
(☎9434045602; www.ambootia.com) FREE The organic Ambootia Tea Estate welcomes visitors to its aromatic factory and is a good walking destination from nearby Cochrane Place.

Sleeping

Makaibari Homestays HOMESTAY $$
(☎9832447774; www.volmakaibari.org; Makaibari tea estate; per person incl full board ₹800) This pioneering program aims to harness tourism to empower local women tea pickers. There are 16 family houses currently involved in the project, and more are planned in a new environmentally sustainable and midrange bamboo village nearby. Houses are simple but comfortable and families speak basic English. Activities on offer include tea picking and birdwatching trips (guide ₹100).

Cochrane Place BOUTIQUE HOTEL $$$
(☎9932035660; www.cochraneplacehotel.com; 132 Pankhabari Rd; s/d from ₹3050/3820; @📶) With 360-degree plantation views and the twinkling lights of Siliguri below, this charming getaway offers oodles of quaintness in the form of period furniture and quirky artefacts in its bright and airy pas-

tel-shaded rooms. There's a delicious mix of Anglo-Indian, Continental and Indian food on offer, and a fine selection of Darjeeling teas at Chai Country, the in-house cafe.

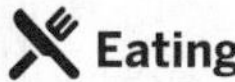

Eating

Kurseong Tourist Lodge NORTH INDIAN $

(☎0354-2345608; Hill Cart Rd; mains ₹80-140; ⏰7am-8.30pm) This old-fashioned, government-run lodge has a popular cafe where you can snack on excellent chicken or vegetarian *momos* as the toy train whistles past just outside. The restaurant serves a wider range of Indian treats for lunch and dinner. It's a 10-minute walk out of town along the main road towards Darjeeling.

There are also some rooms with balcony (single/double ₹1850/2050).

Getting There & Away

Numerous shared jeeps run to Darjeeling (₹70, 1½ hours) and Siliguri (₹70, 1½ hours) until around 4pm, with 8am and 1pm departures for Kalimpong (₹150, 3½ to four hours) and Mirik (₹80, 2½ hours).

The Darjeeling Himalayan Railway's toy train to Darjeeling (1st/2nd class ₹210/60, three hours) is scheduled to leave at 7am and 3pm but takes twice as long as a shared jeep. The 3pm service was not running at the time of research.

Darjeeling

☎0354 / POP 120,400 / ELEV 2135M

Spread in ribbons over a steep mountain ridge, surrounded by emerald-green tea plantations and towered over by majestic Khangchendzonga (8598m), Darjeeling is the definitive Indian hill station and is arguably West Bengal's premier attraction. When you aren't gazing open-mouthed at Khangchendzonga, you can explore colonial-era architecture, visit Buddhist monasteries, and spot snow leopards and red pandas at the nearby zoo. The adventurous can arrange a trek to Singalila Ridge or hire a mountain bike for a guided ride around the hilltops. Meanwhile the steep and winding bazaars below the town bustle with an array of Himalayan products and faces from across Sikkim, Bhutan, Nepal and Tibet. And finally, when energies start to flag, a good, steaming Darjeeling brew is never far away.

History

Darjeeling originally belonged to the Buddhist chogyals (kings) of Sikkim until 1780, when it was annexed by invading Gurkhas from Nepal. The East India Company gained control of the region in 1816, but soon returned most of the lands to Sikkim in exchange for British control over any future border disputes.

During one such dispute in 1828, two British officers stumbled across the Dorje Ling monastery, on a tranquil forested ridge, and passed word to Kolkata (Calcutta) that it would be a perfect site for a sanatorium (they were sure to have also mentioned its strategic military importance in the region). The chogyal of Sikkim (still grateful for the return of his kingdom) agreed to lease the uninhabited land to the East India Company for the annual fee of £3000. In 1835 the hill station of Darjeeling was born and the first tea bushes were planted. By 1857 the population of Darjeeling had reached 10,000, mainly because of a massive influx of Gurkha tea labourers from Nepal.

Since Independence, the Gurkhas have become the main political force in Darjeeling. Friction with the state government led to calls for a separate state of Gorkhaland in the 1980s. In 1986 violence and riots orchestrated by the Gorkha National Liberation Front (GNLF) brought Darjeeling to a standstill. As a result, the Darjeeling Gorkha Hill Council (DGHC) was given a large measure of autonomy from the state government, later replaced by the Gorkhaland Territorial Administration (GTA). The political situation is now calm but political agitation and strikes could reappear any time.

Sights

Tiger Hill VIEWPOINT

To watch the dawn light break over a spectacular 250km stretch of Himalayan horizon, including Everest (8848m), Lhotse (8501m) and Makalu (8475m) to the far west, rise early and take a jeep out to Tiger Hill (2590m), 11km south of Darjeeling, above Ghum. The skyline is dominated by Khangchendzonga ('great five-peaked snow fortress'), India's highest peak and the world's third-highest. On either side of the main massif are Kabru (7338m), Jannu (7710m) and Pandim (6691m), all serious peaks in their own right.

This daily morning spectacle (views are best in autumn and spring) is a major tourist attraction, and you'll find hundreds of jeeps leaving Darjeeling for Tiger Hill every morning at 4am – traffic snarls en route are quite common. At the summit you can pay

Darjeeling

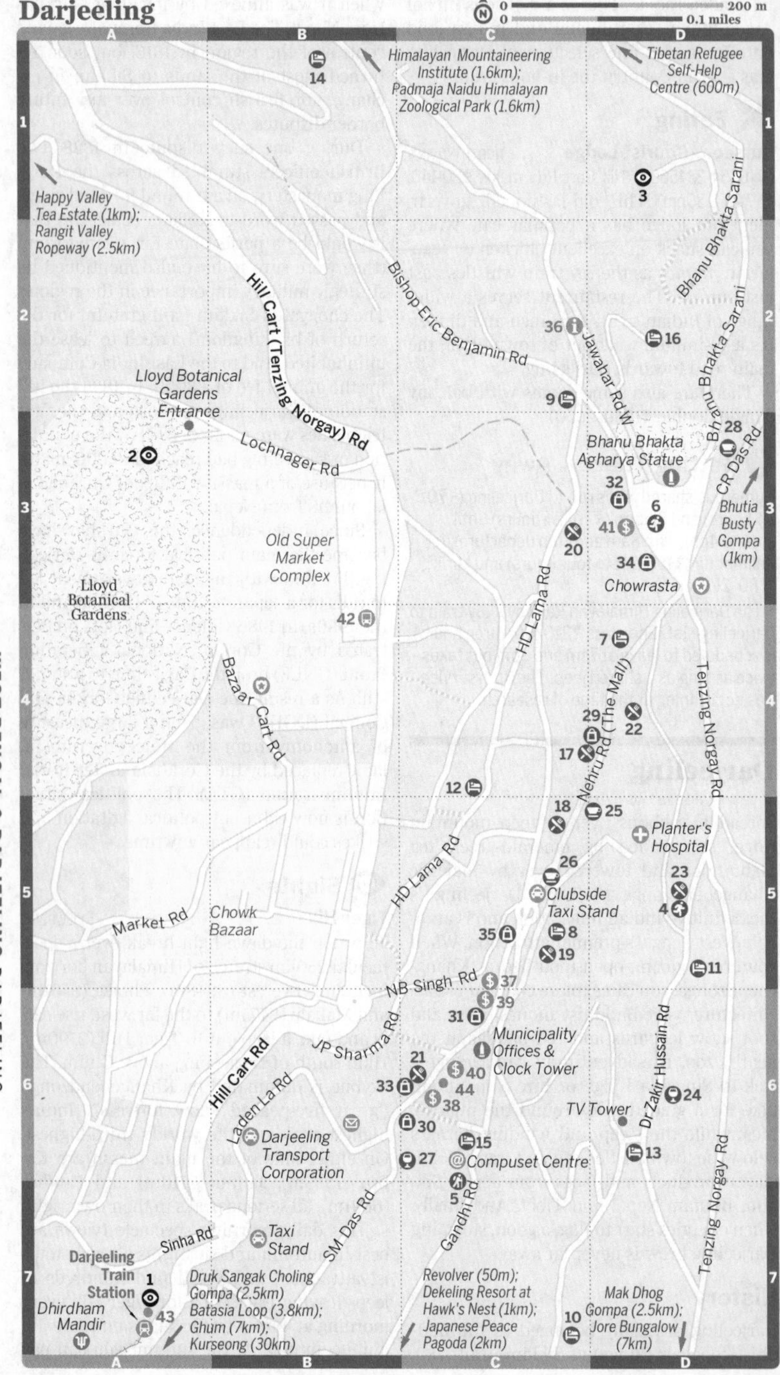
0 200 m
0 0.1 miles
Himalayan Mountaineering Institute (1.6km); Padmaja Naidu Himalayan Zoological Park (1.6km)
Tibetan Refugee Self-Help Centre (600m)
Happy Valley Tea Estate (1km); Rangit Valley Ropeway (2.5km)
Hill Cart (Tenzing Norgay) Rd
Bishop Eric Benjamin Rd
Jawahar Rd W
Bhanu Bhakta Sarani
Lloyd Botanical Gardens Entrance
Lochnager Rd
Bhanu Bhakta Agharya Statue
CR Das Rd
Bhutia Busty Gompa (1km)
Old Super Market Complex
HD Lama Rd
Chowrasta
Lloyd Botanical Gardens
Bazaar Cart Rd
Nehru Rd (The Mall)
Tenzing Norgay Rd
Planter's Hospital
Clubside Taxi Stand
Market Rd
Chowk Bazaar
NB Singh Rd
JP Sharma Rd
Hill Cart Rd
Laden La Rd
Municipality Offices & Clock Tower
Dr Zakir Hussain Rd
TV Tower
Darjeeling Transport Corporation
Compuset Centre
Gandhi Rd
SM Das Rd
Sinha Rd
Taxi Stand
Darjeeling Train Station
Dhirdham Mandir
Druk Sangak Choling Gompa (2.5km) Batasia Loop (3.8km); Ghum (7km); Kurseong (30km)
Revolver (50m); Dekeling Resort at Hawk's Nest (1km); Japanese Peace Pagoda (2km)
Mak Dhog Gompa (2.5km); Jore Bungalow (7km)

Darjeeling

Top Sights
1 Darjeeling Himalayan Railway A7

Sights
2 Lloyd Botanical Gardens A3
3 Observatory Hill D1

Activities, Courses & Tours
4 Adventures Unlimited D5
5 Himalayan Travels C6
Manjushree Centre of Tibetan Culture .... (see 15)
6 Pony Rides D3

Sleeping
7 Bellevue Hotel D4
8 Dekeling Hotel C5
9 Elgin Darjeeling C2
10 Hotel Aliment C7
11 Hotel New Galaxy D5
12 Hotel Seven Seventeen C4
13 Hotel Tranquillity D6
14 Mayfair Darjeeling B1
15 Tibet Home C6
16 Windamere Hotel D2

Eating
Dekeva's .... (see 19)
17 Glenary's C4
18 Hasty Tasty C5
19 Kunga C5
Lunar Restaurant .... (see 8)
20 Mamta Pizza C3
21 Park Restaurant C6
22 Shangri-La D4
23 Sonam's Kitchen D5

Drinking & Nightlife
24 Gatty's Cafe D6
Glenary's .... (see 17)
25 Himalayan Java D5
26 House of Tea C5
27 Joey's Pub C6
28 Sunset Lounge D3
Windamere Hotel .... (see 16)

Shopping
29 Das Studios D4
30 Dorjee Himalayan Artefacts C6
31 Hayden Hall C6
32 Life & Leaf Fair Trade Shop D3
33 Nathmull's Tea Room C6
34 Oxford Book & Stationery Company D3
35 Rope C5

Information
36 GTA Tourist Reception Centre C2
37 ICICI Bank ATM C6
38 Poddar's C6
39 Ridhi Siddhi C5
40 State Bank of India C6
41 State Bank of India ATM D3

Transport
42 Chowk Bazaar Bus & Jeep Station B4
43 Darjeeling Train Station A7
44 Samsara Tours, Travels & Treks C6

to stand in the pavilion grounds or warm up in one of the heated lounges (₹30 to ₹100 with tea). It can be a real bunfight here, so if you prefer your Himalayan views in solitude you might want to try somewhere else.

Organised sunrise trips (usually with a detour to Batasia Loop and the monasteries in Ghum on the way back) can be booked through a travel agency or directly with jeep drivers at the Clubside taxi stand. Return trips cost ₹1300 per vehicle, or ₹250 per seat.

Observatory Hill RELIGIOUS SITE

Sacred to both Buddhists and Hindus, this hill was the site of the original Dorje Ling monastery that lent Darjeeling its name. Today, devotees come to a temple in a small cave to honour Mahakala, a Buddhist protector deity also worshipped in Hinduism as a wrathful avatar of Shiva the destroyer. The summit is marked by several shrines, a flurry of colourful prayer flags and the ringing notes from numerous devotional bells, but sadly no mountain views.

Bhutia Busty Gompa BUDDHIST MONASTERY

This temple originally stood on Observatory Hill, but was rebuilt in its present location by the chogyals of Sikkim in the 19th century. It houses fine murals depicting the life of Buddha, with Khangchendzonga providing a spectacular backdrop. Come for prayers at 4pm; it's often locked during the day. To get here, follow CR Das Rd downhill for five minutes from Chowrasta Sq, past a trinity of Buddhist rock carvings.

Japanese Peace Pagoda BUDDHIST TEMPLE

(4.30am-7pm, prayers 4.30-6am & 4.30-6.30pm)

Perched on a hillside at the end of AJC Bose Rd, this gleaming white pagoda is one of more than 70 pagodas built around the world by the Japanese Buddhist Nipponzan Myohoji organisation. During the drumming *puja* (prayers) sessions, visitors are offered a hand drum and encouraged to join in the rituals. Getting here involves a pleasant, gentle 30-minute walk from Clubside junction along Gandhi and AJC Bose Rds, past the curiously named Institute of Astroparticle Physics and Space Science.

Padmaja Naidu Himalayan Zoological Park ZOO

(☎0354-2254250; www.pnhzp.gov.in; Indian/foreigner incl Himalayan Mountaineering Institute ₹50/100; camera/video ₹10/25; ⏰8.30am-4pm Fri-Wed, ticket counter closes 3.30pm) This zoo, one of India's best, was established in 1958 to study, conserve and preserve Himalayan fauna. Housed within its rocky and forested environment are species such as Asiatic black bears, cloud leopards, red pandas and Tibetan wolves. The zoo, and its attached snow leopard–breeding centre (closed to the public), are home to the world's largest single captive population of snow leopards (currently 11). The zoo is a pleasant 20-minute downhill walk from Chowrasta along Jawahar Rd West.

Himalayan Mountaineering Institute MUSEUM

(HMI; ☎0354-2254087; www.hmi-darjeeling.com; Indian/foreigner incl zoo ₹50/100; ⏰8.30am-4.30pm Fri-Wed) Tucked away within the grounds of the zoo, this prestigious mountaineering institute was founded in 1954 and has provided training for some of India's leading mountaineers. Within the complex is the fascinating **Mountaineering Museum**. It houses sundry details and memorabilia from the 1922 and 1924 Everest expeditions, which set off from Darjeeling, as well as more recent summit attempts. Look for the Carl Zeiss telescope presented by Adolf Hitler to the head of the Nepali Army.

Rangit Valley Ropeway CABLE CAR

(return adult/child ₹175/90; ⏰10am-4pm, ticket office closes 2pm, closed 19th of every month) This scenic ropeway reopened in 2012, after a fatal accident halted operations in 2003. The 20-minute ride takes you from North Point down to the Takvar Valley tea estate, gliding over manicured tea bushes that look like giant broccoli growing on mountain slopes. Get here early if you want to explore the village and tea plantation. The last lift back is 5pm.

Tibetan Refugee Self-Help Centre FACTORY

(☎2255938; www.tibetancentredarjeeling.com; Lebong Cart Rd; ⏰9am-4.30pm Mon-Sat) Established in 1959, this refugee centre comprises a home for the aged, a school, an orphanage, a clinic, a gompa (Tibetan Buddhist monastery) and craft workshops that produce carpets, woodcarvings and woollen items. There's also an interesting, politically charged **photographic exhibition** portraying Tibetan history through B&W photos. Visitors are welcome to wander through the workshops. The handicrafts are for sale in the showroom (p505) and proceeds go straight back into the Tibetan community.

SEEING THE SIGHTS IN DARJEELING

Darjeeling's sights are quite spread out and road transport is a bit of a hassle. You'll make things easier by visiting certain sights together as clusters.

One popular idea is to jump out of bed at 4am and take a jeep up to Tiger Hill (p497) in time for the spectacular sunrise over **Khangchendzonga**. After a regulation photo op with the mountain in the backdrop, continue down to Ghum and spend the morning/day visiting Batasia Loop (p501) and the monasteries there. An alternative 90-minute walking route back to Darjeeling is along quiet Tenzing Norgay Rd from the junction at Jore Bungalow, via the charming **Mak Dhog Gompa** (Alu Bari). Despite the lack of mountain views, this also makes a nice cycling route.

If you can't face a dawn trip to Tiger Hill, take an early-morning stroll around **Bhanu Bhakta Sarani**, which runs from Chowrasta around the north side of Observatory Hill and offers several stunning viewpoints. Combine the stroll with a visit down to Bhutia Busty Gompa (p499) or up to Observatory Hill (p499).

A good half-day itinerary is to walk 20 minutes from Chowrasta Sq to the zoo and Himalayan Mountaineering Institute, then continue around the hill on the road above busy Hill Cart Rd for 15 minutes to the Rangit Valley Ropeway. From here take a shared minivan from North Point back to Darjeeling, getting off at Happy Valley Tea Estate (p501). Then walk the short-cut footpath to Chowk Bazaar jeep stand via Lloyd Botanical Gardens (p501). Alternatively, walk 20 minutes from the ropeway along Lebong Cart Rd to the Tibetan Refugee Self-Help Centre and hike back steeply uphill to Chowrasta via Bhutia Busty Gompa.

GHUM

The junction of Ghum, 7km southwest from Darjeeling, is home to three colourful Buddhist monasteries, all 10 minutes' walk from each other. You can get to Ghum from Darjeeling by toy train (2nd/1st class ₹30/145), shared taxi (₹30), chartered taxi (one way ₹300) or on the way back from Tiger Hill.

Yiga Choling Gompa (dawn-dusk), the region's most famous monastery, has wonderful old murals and is home to some 30 monks of the Gelugpa school. Built in 1850, it enshrines a 5m-high statue of Jampa (Maitreya or 'Future Buddha') and 300 beautifully bound Tibetan texts. It's just west of Ghum, about a 10-minute walk off Hill Cart Rd.

Other gompas of interest nearby include the fortress-style **Guru Sakya Gompa** (dawn-dusk), which conducts prayer sessions between 5.30am and 7.30am (useful if returning from a dawn visit to Tiger Hill). The active **Samten Choling Gompa** (New Monastery; dawn-dusk), just downhill, has the largest Buddha statue in West Bengal, a memorial chorten dedicated to German mystic Lama Govinda and a small cafe.

Happy Valley Tea Estate PLANTATION
(8017700700; www.ambootia.com; Lebong Cart Rd; tour ₹100; 8am-4pm Tue-Sun) This 1854 tea estate below Hill Cart Rd is worth visiting, especially when the plucking and processing are in progress (March to November). An employee will guide you through the aromatic factory and its withering, rolling, fermenting and drying processes, explaining how green, black and white teas all come from the same leaf. Take the marked turn-off about 1km northwest of town on Hill Cart Rd.

Lloyd Botanical Gardens GARDENS
(0354-2252358; 8am-4.30pm) FREE These pleasant gardens contain an impressive collection of Himalayan plants, most famously orchids and rhododendrons. Follow the signs along Lochnager Rd from the Chowk Bazaar bus and jeep station, until the hum of cicadas replaces the honking of jeeps at the main entrance. A map is posted at the office at the top of the park.

Batasia Loop MONUMENT
(₹10) If you're travelling on the toy train, or walking back from Tiger Hill, look out for this famous railway loop that goes around the open-air Gorkha War Memorial, erected in honour of the brave soldiers from the region who laid down their lives in WWI and WWII. Some tours stop here after the sunrise trip to Tiger Hill. The views are almost as good and the atmosphere much more serene.

Druk Sangak Choling Gompa BUDDHIST MONASTERY
(Dali Gompa; dawn-dusk) About halfway between Ghum and Darjeeling is the huge Druk Sangak Choling Gompa, inaugurated by the Dalai Lama in 1993. Known for its vibrant frescoes, it is home to 300 Himalayan monks who study philosophy, literature, astronomy, meditation, dance and music. Come for prayers between 4pm and 6pm.

Activities

Adventures Unlimited OUTDOORS
(9933070013; www.adventuresunlimited.in; Dr Zakir Hussain Rd; 10am-6pm Mon-Sat) Offers treks to Singalila Ridge (US$50 per person per day) and Sikkim (US$60 to US$75 per person per day), plus Enfield motorbike hire (₹1500 to ₹1850) and mountain-bike hire and trips. Ask for Gautam.

Himalayan Travels TREKKING
(0354-2252254; kkguring@cal.vsnl.net.in; 18 Gandhi Rd, Darjeeling) Experienced company that's been arranging treks (US$60 to US$70 per person per day) and mountaineering expeditions in Darjeeling and Sikkim since 1975.

Pony Rides HORSE RIDING
From Chowrasta, children can take a ride around Observatory Hill for ₹200, or through tea estates to visit a monastery for ₹400 per hour (two-hour minimum). A horseman accompanies the horse at all times, and the activity is fairly safe. No riding helmets are provided though.

Courses

Himalayan Mountaineering Institute CLIMBING
(HMI; 0354-2254087; www.hmi-darjeeling.com; Indian/foreigner ₹7500/US$800) The HMI runs 28-day basic and advanced mountaineering

courses from March to May and September to December. These courses are oriented to teach candidates a broad range of skills required for high-altitude climbing. Foreigners should apply at least three months in advance.

The first week is spent in Darjeeling, learning theory, knots and basic mores, before moving to Sikkim for two weeks. The price includes food and dormitory/tent accommodation. Figure on up to 60 people in a class.

Manjushree Centre of Tibetan Culture LANGUAGE
(☎0354-2252977; www.manjushreetibcentre.org; 12 Gandhi Rd; tuition per hr ₹200; ⏰mid-Mar–mid-Dec) Private lessons in written and spoken Tibetan can be organised through this cultural centre, which has a good library and can arrange for students to stay in local Tibetan homes. The office is above the Himalayan Tibet Museum.

Sleeping

Darjeeling has a large selection of hotels. The main backpacker enclave is Dr Zakir Hussain Rd, which follows the highest ridge in Darjeeling, so be prepared for a hike to the best budget places.

Prices given are for the high season (October to early December and mid-March to mid-May), when it's wise to book ahead. In the low season prices can drop by 50%.

Hotel New Galaxy HOTEL $
(☎9775914939; Dr Zakir Hussain Rd; d from ₹700) A simple budget option, with small but neat rooms and hot-water buckets in the cheaper rooms. Rooms vary considerably; corner rooms with a mountain view are easily the best (try for room 104). Unexpected pluses include a sun terrace and an authentic Thai restaurant.

Hotel Tranquillity HOTEL $
(☎0354-2257678; hoteltranquillity@yahoo.com; 13A Dr Zakir Hussain Rd; d/tr ₹700/900; 📶) This good-value place is sparkling clean, with 24-hour hot water, nice lobby seating, views from the rooftop and small but neat baby-blue rooms. The helpful owner is a local schoolteacher, and can provide all kinds of info about the area.

★Dekeling Hotel GUESTHOUSE $$
(☎0354-2254159; www.dekeling.com; Gandhi Rd; d ₹2380-3810, without bathoom ₹998; @📶) Spotless Dekeling is full of charming touches such as coloured diamond-pane windows, a traditional *bukhari* (wood-fired oven) in the cosy and sociable lounge-library, wood panelling and sloping-attic ceilings, plus superb views. Tibetan owners Sangay and Norbu play perfect hosts and the service is excellent. The central location is also a plus, even if some rooms suffer from traffic noise.

★Revolver BOUTIQUE HOTEL $$
(☎8371919527; www.revolver.in; 110 Gandhi Rd; d ₹1310-1760; 📶) This Beatles-themed hotel is a must for fans. Five small but stylish rooms are each named after one of the Fab Four (plus Brian Epstein), so you can choose your favourite Moptop (John fills up first; Ringo brings up the rear). It's chock-a-block with Beatles memorabilia, and well thought out (free filtered water), but there's a certain coolness to the hospitality.

The downstairs restaurant serves good fresh-ground coffee and interesting local and Naga set meals (₹150). The entrance is easily missed behind the Union Church.

Hotel Seven Seventeen HOTEL $$
(☎0354-2255099; www.hotel717.com; 26 HD Lama Rd; s/d from ₹2620/2975; 📶) This friendly Tibetan-run place on the edge of the bazaar has pleasant wood-skirted rooms with clean toilets. Upper-floor rooms are best; back rooms have great views overlooking the valley. The excellent-value ground-floor restaurant (mains ₹150) is spacious and civilised, and if you get chatting to the owners you might get invited upstairs for tea and biscuits.

Hotel Aliment HOTEL $
(☎0354-2255068; alimentweb98@gmail.com; 40 Dr Zakir Hussain Rd; r ₹870-1950; @📶) A budget travellers' favourite, with a good top-floor restaurant (and cold beer), lending library, helpful owners and wood-lined rooms. There's a wide range of rooms, from the cheapest small singles to upstairs doubles (₹1950) with a TV and valley views. All the double rooms have geysers, but these only operate in the mornings and evenings.

Bellevue Hotel HOTEL $$
(☎0354-2254075; www.bellevuehotel-darjeeling.com; d from ₹2420; @📶) This atmospheric but somewhat faded old-school building has a variety of renovated wood-panelled rooms, most of which come with grass-mat floors and a *bukhari*. The communal breakfast-lounge area and location by Chowrasta com-

pensate for the idiosyncratic management. Head to the rooftop terrace for fine views. Don't confuse it with the rival Olde (Main) Bellevue Hotel up the road.

Tibet Home GUESTHOUSE $$
(☎0354-2252977; tibethome2006@gmail.com; 12 Gandhi Rd; r ₹1900) Clean, bright and modern rooms make this a solid, central option, with profits going to the attached Manjushree Centre of Tibetan Culture. There are great views from the rooftop.

★**Windamere Hotel** HERITAGE HOTEL $$$
(☎0354-2254041; www.windamerehotel.com; Jawahar Rd West; s/d incl full board from ₹12,630/15,750; @📶) This quaint, rambling relic of the Raj on Observatory Hill offers one of Darjeeling's most atmospheric digs. The charming colonial-era Ada Villa was once a boarding house for British tea planters, and the well-tended grounds are spacious with lots of pleasant seating areas. The comfortable rooms, fireplaces and hot-water bottles offer just the right measures of comfort and mothballed charm.

Nonguests can book afternoon tea, Sunday lunch or a set dinner (₹1400) and sample the vintage charm of the place. Keep your eyes peeled for the Jan Morris poem in the tearoom. It's a particularly great place to spend Christmas.

Elgin Darjeeling HERITAGE HOTEL $$$
(☎0354-2257226; www.elginhotels.com; HD Lama Rd; s/d incl half-board ₹10,970/11,350; @📶) Grand yet friendly and full of classy ambience, the Elgin was once the summer residence of the maharaja of Cooch Bihar. The restaurant is elegant and the garden terrace is the perfect place to nurse a beer (₹250). For historic charm, ask for the 'attic room' underneath the dripping eaves; for the biggest rooms, try the new, modern wing.

Dekeling Resort at Hawk's Nest HERITAGE HOTEL $$$
(☎0354-2253298; www.dekeling.com; 2 AJC Bose Rd; d from ₹4760; 📶) Run by the good people at Dekeling Hotel, this is a quiet, exclusive place, 1km outside of Darjeeling en route to the Japanese Pagoda. The four 140-year-old, colonial-style, two-room suites have antique touches and fireplaces, and there's a nice sunny terrace. Seven fresh and modern mountain-facing super-deluxe rooms were recently added. It's a great escape from Darjeeling's increasingly noisy centre.

Mayfair Darjeeling HOTEL $$$
(☎0354-2256376; www.mayfairhotels.com; Jawahar Rd West; s/d incl half-board from ₹10,533/13,220; 📶) Originally a maharaja's summer palace but renovated within an inch of its life, this plush choice sits among manicured gardens and a bizarre collection of kitschy sculptures. The communal areas don't have quite the charm of some of Darjeeling's other historic hotels, but the plush rooms are well decorated and many have balconies.

Eating

Most restaurants close by 9pm. Tax will add on 14.5% to most bills, with service on top of that.

Dekeva's TIBETAN $
(51 Gandhi Rd; mains ₹100-180; ⏰9am-9pm) Next door to Kunga, this cosy place offers generous servings of Tibetan staples and tasty Chinese dishes, and a range of noodles for connoisseurs who can tell their *thenthuk* (Tibetan noodles) from their *sogthuk* (also Tibetan noodles). Prices include tax, so are particularly good value.

★**Glenary's** MULTICUISINE $$
(Nehru Rd; mains ₹235-300; ⏰noon-9pm; 📶) This elegant restaurant sits atop the famous bakery and cafe of the same name and is a Darjeeling staple. Of note are the Continental and Chinese dishes and the tandoori specials; try the beef steak and potato or the delicious-smelling baked-cheese macaroni. The wooden floors, linen tablecloths and recently expanded window seating add to the classy atmosphere.

Kunga TIBETAN $
(51 Gandhi Rd; mains ₹120-190; ⏰7.30am-8.30pm) Kunga is a cosy wood-panelled place run by a friendly Tibetan family, strong on noodles and *momos,* and with excellent juice, fruit muesli curd and *shabhaley* (Tibetan pies). The clientèle includes locals, which is a mark of its culinary authenticity. You'll find it at street level below Dekeling Hotel.

Sonam's Kitchen INTERNATIONAL $
(142 Dr Zakir Hussain Rd; mains ₹90-180; ⏰8am-2.30pm & 5.30-9pm Mon-Sat, 8am-2pm Sun; 📶) Sonam's serves up strong brewed coffee, authentic French toast, fluffy pancakes (breakfasts until 2.30pm), fresh soups (nettle in season) and yummy pasta, from two dining rooms across the road from each

TEA TOURISM

Darjeeling's most famous export is its aromatic muscatel tea, known for its amber colour, tannic astringence and a musky and spicy flavour. These days, however, other teas including green, oolong and premium white varieties are produced alongside the traditional black tea. Most of the produce is now organic, and the best grades fetch several hundred dollars per kilogram at auctions. Purists will tell you that Darjeeling teas are best taken alone or with a slice of lemon (and/or a pinch of sugar), but never with milk.

While in Darjeeling, a pot of this fine brew is best enjoyed at Sunset Lounge or House of Tea. The true-blue afternoon-tea experience at **Windamere Hotel** (afternoon tea ₹800; ⏲4-6pm) is a joy for aficionados of all things colonial, with shortcake, scones, cheese and pickle sandwiches, and brews from the reputed Castleton Tea Estate; book in advance

For a more absorbing and enlightening experience, we recommend a day visit to one of the tea estates that currently welcomes visitors. The easiest places to learn about tea production are Makaibari (p496) in Kurseong and Happy Valley (p501) outside Darjeeling. Spring, monsoon and autumn are the busiest times, when the three respective 'flushes' are harvested. There's no plucking on Sunday, which means most of the machinery isn't working on Monday.

If you wish to spend a night amid the plantations, try a tea pickers' family at a homestay (p496) at Makaibari, where you'll get to join your hosts for a morning's work in the tea bushes. If you have three days to spare, you can pick your own leaves, watch them being processed and then return home with a batch of your very own hand-plucked Darjeeling tea.

If you're in the mood for splurging, accommodation doesn't get any more exclusive than top-end **Glenburn** (☎9830070213; www.glenburnteaestate.com; Darjeeling; s/d incl full board ₹19,900/31,500), between Darjeeling and Kalimpong, a working tea estate and resort that boasts five members of staff for every guest. A stay at Glenburn is rumoured to have given director Wes Anderson inspiration for his film *The Darjeeling Limited*.

To learn more about the past and present of Darjeeling's tea history, read Jeff Koehler's 2016 book *Darjeeling: A History of the World's Greatest Tea*.

other. The chunky wholemeal sandwiches can be packed to go for picnics. Book the Nepali-style dinners three hours in advance.

Hasty Tasty INDIAN $

(Nehru Rd; mains ₹90-140, set meals ₹160-190; ⏲8.30am-8.30pm) There's nothing fancy at this vegetarian self-service canteen, but the bustling open kitchen churns out great paneer *masala dosas* (curried vegetables inside a crisp pancake) and several types of set meals. It's a hit with domestic tourists, so expect some rush during mealtimes. Prices include tax.

Shangri-La CHINESE $$

(Nehru Rd; mains ₹200-300; ⏲noon-9.30pm) This classy and modern bar-restaurant near the top of the Mall specialises in local Chinese and Indian offerings in stylish surrounds, with sleek wooden floors, clean tablecloths and roaring fires in winter. There are also a couple of stylish hotel rooms upstairs (doubles ₹4640).

Mamta Pizza ITALIAN $$

(☎8967203905; HD Lama Rd; pizza ₹150-220; ⏲10am-7pm) An unlikely address (or name) for a pizzeria, this cramped but sociable one-table place tosses up excellent European-accented pizza, pasta, panini and salads, alongside delicatessen rarities such as bacon, beef merguez sausage and Nepali cheese (₹500 per kg). Expect to wait about 20 minutes for a pizza.

Lunar Restaurant INDIAN $$

(51 Gandhi Rd; mains ₹160-200; ⏲7.30am-9pm) This bright and clean space just below Dekeling Hotel is perhaps the best vegetarian Indian restaurant in town, with good service and great views from the large windows. The *masala dosas* come with delicious dried fruit, nuts and cheese. Access to this 1st-floor joint is via the same staircase as Hotel Dekeling.

Park Restaurant INDIAN, THAI $$

(☎0354-2255270; 41 Laden La Rd; mains ₹200-350; ⏲noon-9pm) The intimate Park is deservedly very popular for its tasty North Indian curries (great chicken tikka masala) and surprisingly authentic Thai dishes, including the tasty *tom kha gai* (coconut chicken soup) and spicy green papaya salad. Renovations plan to move the Thai dishes to a separate pan-Asian dining area; look for the ornate Thai-style entrance.

Drinking & Nightlife

The top-end hotels all have classy bars; the Windamere (p503) is the most atmospheric place to kick back with an early-evening gin and tonic if you are having dinner there.

Gatty's Cafe BAR
(Dr Zakir Hussain Rd; beer ₹170; 6-11pm;) Backpacker-friendly Gatty's is the only place in town that has a pulse after 9pm, with live music on the weekend and open mic and movie nights during the week. The food (mains ₹170 to ₹200) includes housemade lasagne, and pita with hummus and felafel, plus good espresso and cold Kingfisher and Tuborg.

Joey's Pub PUB
(SM Das Rd; beer ₹180-250; 1-10pm) Joey's has suffered from the eponymous owner's passing but if your preferred beverage comes in a pint not a pot, this long-standing pub near the post office is a decent place to meet other travellers. It has sports on TV, cold beer and hot toddys in winter.

Himalayan Java CAFE
(Nehru Rd; coffee ₹100; 7am-8.30pm;) Branch of the Nepal cafe chain, serving up good coffee and cakes, plus breakfast pancakes, waffles and sandwiches (snacks ₹150 to ₹250), in a stylish industrial interior.

Sunset Lounge TEAHOUSE
(Chowrastra Sq; cup of tea ₹25-400; 9.30am-9pm;) This tearoom run by Nathmull's Tea offers aficionados a range of white, green and black teas by the cup, with inhouse baked treats, fine valley views and free wi-fi. Ask for its six-cup tasting sample for two people (it's not on the menu).

Glenary's TEAHOUSE
(Nehru Rd; pot ₹80; 7.30am-7.30pm;) This teahouse and bakery (pastries ₹30 to ₹60) has massive windows and good views from the new outdoor balcony. Order your tea, select a cake, grab your book and sink into a cosy wicker chair. It's a good place to grab breakfast, from oatmeal to eggs and bacon.

House of Tea TEAHOUSE
(Nehru Rd; cup of tea ₹30-80; 10am-8pm;) Sit and sip a range of brewed teas from several local Goodricke estates before purchasing a package of your favourite leaves.

Shopping

Nathmull's Tea Room TEA
(www.nathmulltea.com; Laden La Rd; 9am-8pm Mon-Sat, daily Mar-May, Oct & Nov) Darjeeling produces some of the world's finest teas and Nathmull's is the best place to pick up some, with more than 50 varieties. Expect to pay ₹200 to ₹400 per 100g for a decent tea, and up to ₹5000 per 100g for the finest flushes. There are also attractive teapots, strainers and cosies as souvenirs. To taste the teas for sale here head to Sunset Lounge.

Hayden Hall ARTS & CRAFTS
(www.haydenhalldarjeeling.org; Laden La Rd; 10am-5pm) Sells Tibetan-style yak wool carpets as part of its charitable work (₹10,800 for a 0.9m by 1.8m carpet) and offers shipping. You can see the carpets being made out the back. There are also good jumpers, caps, gloves, shrugs and bags made by local women.

Oxford Book & Stationery Company BOOKS
(Chowrasta Sq; 10am-7.30pm Mon-Sat, daily Mar-May, Oct & Nov) The best bookshop east of Kathmandu, selling a good selection of novels and Himalayan titles.

Dorjee Himalayan Artefacts ARTS & CRAFTS
(Laden La Rd; 11am-7pm Mon-Sat) This tiny Aladdin's cave is crammed full of Himalayan knick-knacks, some antique, some made yesterday, from Tibetan *gau* (amulets) to cast Buddhas and silver prayer wheels. A good collection of masks and *thangkas* is also on offer.

Tibetan Refugee Self-Help Centre CARPETS
(0354-2252552; www.tibetancentredarjeeling.com; Lebong Cart Rd; carpet incl shipping from US$380) This centre makes gorgeous Tibetan carpets to order, if you don't mind waiting six months for one to be made. Choose from the catalogue and staff will ship the finished carpet to your home address.

Das Studios PHOTOGRAPHY
(Nehru Rd; 10am-7pm Mon-Sat) Digital photo accessories, printing and instant passport photos (six for ₹75). The reprinted early-20th-century photographs depicting old Darjeeling and Himalayan scenes make for

great souvenirs (₹500); ask to look at the catalogue.

Rope SPORTS & OUTDOORS
(NB Singh Rd; ⌚10am-7pm Mon-Sat) This shop stocks quality imported gear alongside decent Chinese knock-offs, including backpacks, stoves and trek boots. The fakes come at nearly half-price; you get what you pay for.

Life & Leaf Fair Trade Shop ARTS & CRAFTS
(www.lifeandleaf.org; Chowrasta Sq; ⌚10am-7pm Mon-Sat) Supports local artisans and environmental projects through the sale of organic honey and tea sourced from local small farmers, plus jute bags and Assamese silk scarves. The selection is small.

Information

EMERGENCY

Police Assistance Booth (Chowrasta Sq)

Sadar Police Station (☎0354-2254422; Market Rd)

INTERNET ACCESS

Compuset Centre (Gandhi Rd; per hr ₹30; ⌚9am-7pm Mon-Sat; wi-fi) Offers printing and passport photos (₹40) but no Skype.

MEDICAL SERVICES

Planter's Hospital (D&DMA Nursing Home; ☎0354-2254327; Nehru Rd) The best private hospital in town.

MONEY

A number of shops and hotels around Darjeeling can change cash and travellers cheques at fairly good rates; shop around.

ICICI Bank Atm (49 Laden La Rd)

Poddar's (☎0354-2252841; Laden La Rd; ⌚10am-9pm) Better rates, longer hours and shorter queues than the State Bank of India next door. Changes most currencies and travellers cheques at no commission. It's inside a clothing store.

Ridhi Siddhi (Laden La Rd; ⌚9.30am-8pm) Changes cash at good rates with no commission.

State Bank of India (Laden La Rd; ⌚10am-2pm & 2.30-4pm Mon-Fri, to noon every other Sat) Changes major foreign currencies plus US-dollar Amex travellers cheques, with a commission of ₹100 per transaction. It has an adjacent ATM, and another in **Chowrasta** (Chowrasta Sq; ⌚24hr).

POST

Main Post Office (Laden La Rd; ⌚10am-6pm Mon-Sat, to 4pm Sun)

TOURIST INFORMATION

GTA Tourist Reception Centre (☎9434247927; Silver Fir Bldg, Jawahar Rd West; ⌚9am-6pm Mon-Sat, to 1pm every other Sat) The staff are friendly, well organised and the best source of information on Darjeeling.

TRAVEL AGENCIES

Most travel agencies in town can arrange local tours.

Samsara Tours, Travels & Treks (☎0354-2252874; www.samsaratourstravelsandtreks.com; Laden La Rd)

Getting There & Away

AIR

The nearest airport is 90km away at Bagdogra, about 12km from Siliguri. A chartered taxi from Darjeeling costs ₹2200. Allow four hours for the drive, to be safe.

BUS

Samsara Tours, Travels & Treks can book 'luxury' air-con buses from Siliguri to Kolkata (₹1300 to ₹1700, 12 hours), and ordinary night buses to Guwahati (₹600, 10 hours, 4pm), Patna (₹550 to ₹700, 10 hours, 6pm) and Gaya (₹750, 4pm). These tickets don't include transfers to Siliguri.

Foreigners can only cross the border (p494) into Nepal at Kakarbhitta/Panitanki (not at Pasupatinagar, en route to Mirik).

Samsara Tours, Travels & Treks can book day and night buses from Kakarbhitta to Kathmandu (₹1000 to ₹1500, departure 4am and 4pm), leaving you to hire a jeep to Kakarbhitta or catch a shared jeep to Siliguri and then Karkabhittha. Samsara can also book Nepali domestic flights from Bhadrapur to Kathmandu (US$182), or book online directly with Buddha Air (www.buddhaair.com).

Any tickets you see advertised from Darjeeling to Kathmandu are not direct buses and involve transfers in Siliguri and at the border – leaving plenty of room for problems – it's just as easy to do it yourself.

JEEP & TAXI

Numerous shared jeeps leave the crowded **Chowk Bazaar Bus & Jeep Station** (Old Super Market Complex) for Siliguri (₹130, three hours) and Kurseong (₹70, 1½ hours). Jeeps for Mirik (₹100, 2½ hours) leave from the northern end about every 30 minutes. A ticket office inside the ground floor of the Old Super Market Complex sells advance tickets for the frequent jeeps to Kalimpong (₹130, 2½ hours), while two roadside stands sell advance tickets for Gangtok (₹200, four hours). All jeeps depart between 7am and 3.30pm.

THE TOY TRAIN

The **Darjeeling Himalayan Railway** (steam/diesel joy ride ₹1100/630), known affectionately as the toy train, is one of the few hill railways still operating in India. The panting train made its first journey along its precipice-topping, 2ft-wide tracks in September 1881. These days, it passes within feet of local shopfronts as it weaves in and out of the main road, bringing traffic to a standstill and tooting its whistle incessantly for almost the entire trip. The train has been a Unesco World Heritage Site since 1999.

Services on the section of line south of Kurseong are constantly in flux and monsoon rains seem to block sections of track as fast as engineers can repair them. At the time of research it was suggested that services to and from New Jalpaiguri (NJP) train station should resume soon.

At the time of research there was only one daily passenger service between Darjeeling and Kurseong. Train No 52588 departs Darjeeling at 4pm, stopping in Ghum at 4.30pm and arriving in Kurseong at 6.50pm. Fares (1st/2nd class) are ₹145/30 to Ghum and ₹210/60 to Kurseong. The 10.15am departure from Darjeeling was not running at the time of research but might resume in the future.

Steam-powered joy rides (₹1100) leave Darjeeling at 10.40am, 1.20pm and 4.05pm for a two-hour return trip. The same trips on a diesel service leave at 8am, 11am and 1.30pm and are cheaper at ₹630. During high season (March to May and October to November) there are often an additional three steam departures. All joy rides pause for 10 minutes at the scenic Batasia Loop and then stop for 20 minutes in Ghum, India's highest train station, to visit the small **railway museum** (Ghum; ₹20; ⊙10am-1pm & 2-4pm). Enthusiasts can see the locomotives up close in the shed across the road from Darjeeling train station.

Book joy rides at least a day or two ahead at the Darjeeling train station (p507) or online at www.irctc.co.in.

To New Jalpaiguri or Bagdogra, get a connection in Siliguri, or charter a jeep or taxi from Darjeeling for ₹2200.

Darjeeling Transport Corporation (Laden La Rd) offers chartered jeeps to Gangtok (₹3000), Kalimpong (₹2500), Kurseong (₹1500), Kakarbhitta (₹3500) and Mirik (₹2000).

TRAIN

The nearest major train station is at New Jalpaiguri (NJP), near Siliguri. Tickets can be bought for major services out of NJP at the **Darjeeling train station** (☎0354-2252555; www.irctc.co.in; Hill Cart Rd; ⊙8am-5pm Mon-Sat, to 2pm Sun). Fares from Darjeeling include Ghum (2nd/1st class ₹140/20, 30 minutes) and Kurseong (2nd/1st class ₹30/210, three hours).

Getting Around

There are several taxi stands around town, including at **Clubside** (Clubside) and on **Hill Cart Road** (Hill Cart Rd) near the train station, but rates are absurdly high for short hops. Darjeeling's streets can be steep and hard to navigate. You can hire a porter to carry your bags up to Chowrasta Sq from Chowk Bazaar for around ₹100.

Shared minivans to anywhere north of the town centre (eg to North Point) leave from the northern end of the **Chowk Bazaar Bus & Jeep Station** (p506). For Ghum, get a shared jeep (₹20) from along Hill Cart Rd.

Singalila Ridge Trek

The most popular multiday walk from Darjeeling is the five-day Singalila Ridge Trek from Mane Bhanjhang to Phalut, through the scenic **Singalila National Park** (Indian/foreigner ₹100/200, camera/video ₹100/500). The highlights are the great views of the Himalayan chain stretching from Nepal to Sikkim and Bhutan. Sandakhphu in particular offers a superb panorama that includes Lhotse, Everest and Khangchendzonga peaks. October and November's clear skies and warm daytime temperatures make it an ideal time to trek, as do the long days and incredible rhododendron blooms of late April and May.

Local guides (₹1200 per day, including food and accommodation) are mandatory within the park and must be arranged at the office of the **Highlander Trekking Guides Association** (☎9734056944; www.highlanderguidesandporters.com; Mane Bhanjang), if you don't already have one, along with porters (₹700) if required.

Mane Bhanjhang is 26km from Darjeeling and is served by frequent shared jeeps (₹70, 1½ hours), as well as a 7am bus from Darjeeling's Chowk Bazaar bus & jeep station (p506). A chartered jeep costs ₹1200. From Rimbik, there are shared jeeps back to Darjeeling (₹150, five hours) at 7am and noon, and a bus at 6.30am (₹90). Book seats in advance. Roads now reach Sri Khola, so you could arrange private transport to pick you up there.

If you have to stay overnight in Rimbik, the best lodges are **Hotel Sherpa** (Rimbik; d ₹900), with pleasant lawns and Alpine-style huts, and **Green Hill** (☎9593720817; Rimbik; r ₹500-700), with quieter wooden rooms out the back.

The usual trekking itinerary is 83km over five days. A shorter four-day option is possible by descending from Sandakhphu to Sri Khola on day three. A rough jeep road follows the trek from Mane Bhanjhang to Phalut but traffic is light and the walking trail partly avoids the road. Some organised groups start in Dhodrey and agencies offer a day hike from here to Tumling. Fit die-hards cycle the route on mountain bikes in three days, though the section from Kalipokhari to Sandakphu is generally too steep to ride.

Private lodges, some with attached bathrooms, are available along the route for around ₹200 for a dorm bed or ₹700 to ₹1400 per room. All offer food, normally a filling combo of rice, dhal and vegetables (₹200). Rooms have clean bedding and blankets so sleeping bags are not strictly necessary, though they are nice to have. At a minimum, bring a sleeping bag liner and warm clothes for dawn peak viewing. The only place where finding a bed can be a problem is at Phalut where there is only one reliable place to stay. Bottled and boiled water is available along the route, though it's better and cheaper to purify your own water. Trekkers' huts can be booked at the GTA Tourist Reception Centre (p506) in Darjeeling but even they will tell you that you are better off at one of the private lodges.

The main lodges for each overnight stop are listed below in ascending order of price and quality:

Day 1: Trekkers' Hut, Mountain Lodge, Siddharta Lodge and Shikhar Lodge in Tumling; Trekkers' Hut in Tonglu

Day 2: Chewang Lodge in Kalipokhari; Trekkers' Hut, Namobuddha, Sunrise and Sherpa Chalet Lodge in Sandakphu

Day 3: Trekkers' Hut and Forest Rest House in Phalut

Day 4: Eden Lodge in Gorkhey; Trekkers' Hut, Namobuddha Lodge and Sherpa Lodge in Rammam

All-inclusive guided treks on this route are offered by Darjeeling agencies for about ₹3000 per person per day, though it's easy enough to arrange a DIY trek for less. Lodges can get booked out in the busy month of October and early November, so consider a mid- to late November itinerary if you're planning the trek in autumn.

Remember to bring your passport, as you'll have to register at half a dozen army checkpoints. The ridge forms the India–Nepal border and the trail actually enters Nepal in several places.

For a relaxing end to a trek, consider a stay at **Karmi Farm** (www.karmifarm.com; per person incl full board ₹2000), a two-hour drive from Rimbik near Bijanbari. It's managed by Andrew Pulger-Frame, whose Sikkimese grandparents once ran an estate from the main house here. The simple but comfortable rooms are attractively decorated with colourful local fabrics, and bathrooms have 24-hour hot water. A small clinic for villagers is run from the farm, providing a volunteer opportunity for medical students and doctors. Singalila treks and other activities

SINGALILA RIDGE TREK

DAY	ROUTE	DISTANCE (KM)
1	Mane Bhanjhang (2130m) to Tonglu (3070m)/Tumling (2980m) via Meghma Gompa	14
2	Tonglu to Sandakphu (3636m) via Kalipokhari & Garibas	17
3	Sandakphu to Phalut (3600m) via Sabarkum	17
4	Phalut to Rammam (2530m) via Gorkhey	16
5	Rammam to Sri Khola or Rimbik (2290m)	19

Around Darjeeling

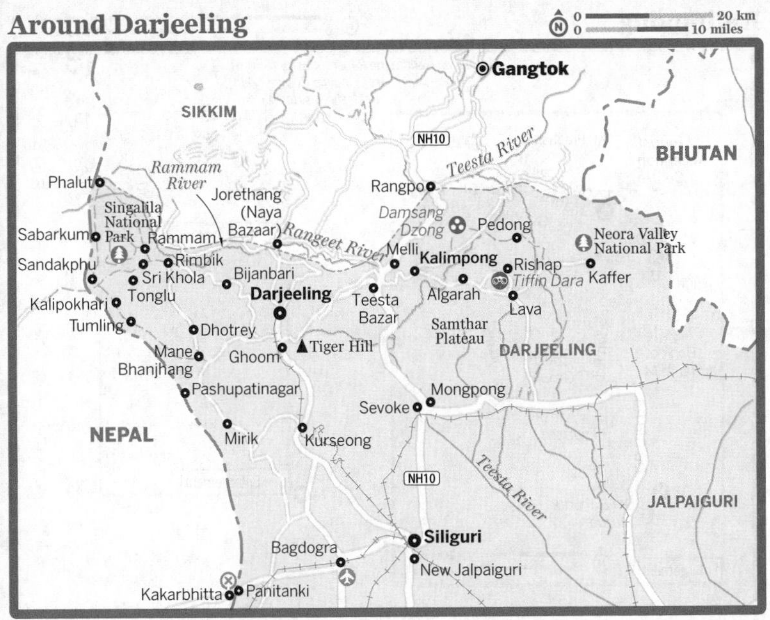

can be organised, but it is just as easy to sit here for a week with a book and a pot of tea, overlooking the bird- and flower-filled gardens in the foreground and towering peaks in the distance. Staff can arrange transport given advanced notice.

Kalimpong

03552 / POP 43,000 / ELEV 1250M

This bustling bazaar town sprawls along a saddle-shaped mountain ridge overlooking the roaring Teesta River and lorded over by the summit of Khangchendzonga. It's not a must-see, but it does boast Himalayan views, Buddhist monasteries, colonial-era architecture and a fascinating nursery industry, all linked by some fine hikes. You could easily fill three days here.

History

Kalimpong's early development as a major Himalayan trading centre focused on the tea and wool trade with Tibet, across the Jelep La Pass, as well as a staging base for Victorian travellers headed into Tibet. Like Darjeeling, Kalimpong once belonged to the chogyals of Sikkim, but it fell into the hands of the Bhutanese in the 18th century and later passed to the British, before becoming part of India at Independence. Scottish missionaries, particularly the Jesuits, made great efforts to win over the local Buddhists in the late 19th century and the town remains an important educational centre for the entire eastern Himalaya.

Sights

Durpin Gompa BUDDHIST MONASTERY

FREE Kalimpong's largest monastery, formally known as Zangtok Pelri Phodang, sits atop panoramic Durpin Hill (1372m) and was consecrated by the Dalai Lama in 1976. There are impressive religious murals in the main prayer room downstairs (photography is permitted), interesting 3D mandalas (visual meditational aids) on the 2nd floor, and stunning Khangchendzonga views from the terrace. Prayers are at 6am and 3pm.

MacFarlane Church CHURCH

One of Kalimpong's most imposing churches, this 1870 church was severely damaged by a 2011 earthquake, when one of its steeples came crashing to the ground. After renovations, the church is now open to visitors and believers alike, and its wood-buttressed Gothic interiors are a wonderful place to spend a few moments in quiet contemplation.

Kalimpong

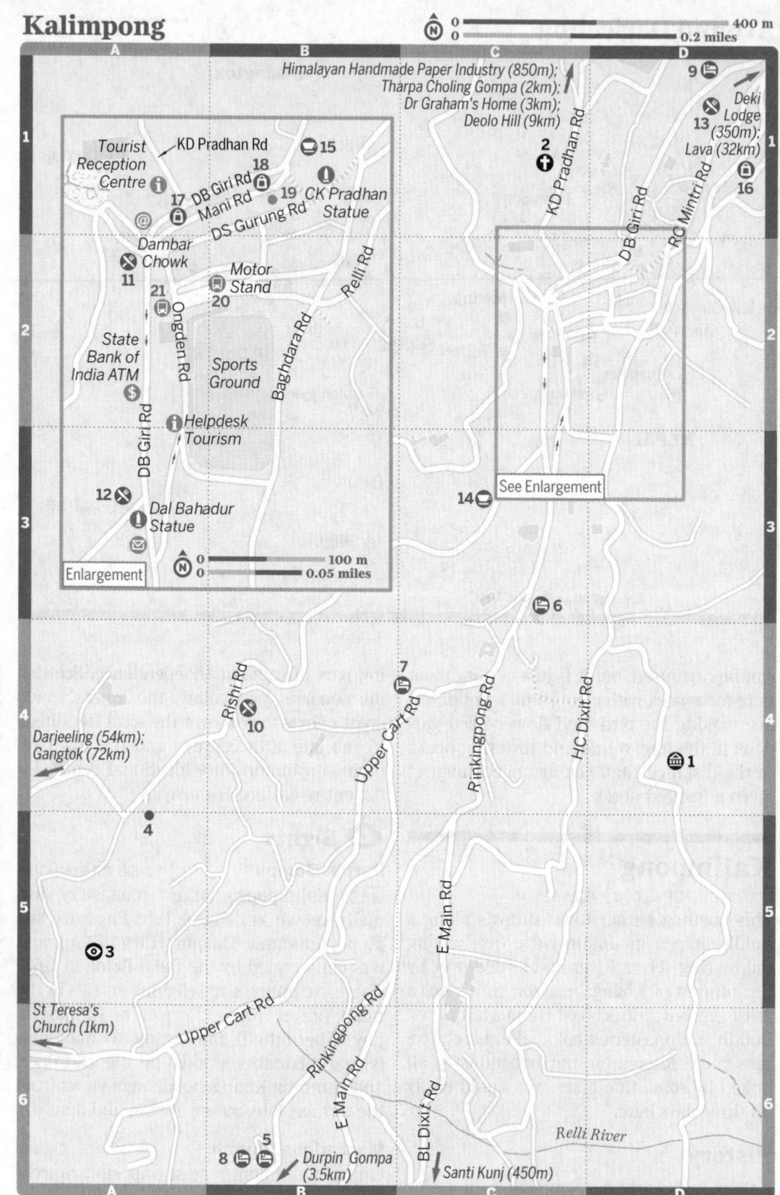

Tharpa Choling Gompa BUDDHIST MONASTERY
(off KD Pradhan Rd; ⊙5.30am-5pm) FREE Built in 1922, this Gelugpa-school Tibetan monastery of 50 monks contains statues of the past, present and future Buddhas. Don't miss the fascinating **museum**, next to an unusual Chinese temple, just above the main monastery. It's a 30-minute walk (uphill) from town along KD Pradhan Rd, 50m past Tripai Rd.

Deolo Hill VIEWPOINT
(9km from Kalimpong; ₹50; ⊙dawn-dusk) On a clear day the morning views of Khangchendzonga from this hilltop park are sim-

Kalimpong

ply superb. After savouring the views you can have breakfast (₹100 to ₹150) at the attached **Tourist Lodge** (from 8am) and then walk down to Kalimpong via Dr Graham's Home. A taxi here costs around ₹300.

Dr Graham's Home HISTORIC BUILDING
(museum 9am-noon & 1.15-3.30pm Mon-Fri) FREE This orphanage and school was built in 1900 by Dr JA Graham, a Scottish missionary, to educate children of tea-estate workers, and now has 1300-odd students. There's a **museum** that commemorates Graham and his wife, Katherine. The 1925 chapel above the school seems lifted straight out of a Scotland parish, with its grey slate, spire and fine stained-glass windows.

The gate is 4km up the steep KD Pradhan Rd. Many people charter a taxi to get here (₹150) and then do the downhill walk back to town via Tharpa Choling Gompa and the Himalayan Handmade Paper Industry workshop. Shared minivans (₹30) run sporadically from below One Cup cafe.

Himalayan Handmade Paper Industry WORKSHOP
(9932388321; Panlook Compound, KD Pradhan Rd; 9am-noon & 1-3pm Mon-Sat) FREE Visitors are welcome to drop into this small unsigned workshop to see traditional paper-making processes, from boiling and pulping of the local *argayli* (daphne) bush to sifting, pressing and drying. The resulting insect-resistant paper is used to block-print monastic scriptures, but it is also sold as notebooks and cards. Morning is the best time to see production. It's a 15-minute walk from town, on the right side of the road.

Lepcha Heritage Museum MUSEUM
(9933780295; 10.30am-4.30pm Mon-Fri) FREE This offbeat collection of Lepcha treasures could be likened to rummaging through the attic of your grandfather's house (if he were a Lepcha elder). A guide explains Lepcha creation myths, while pointing out religious texts, sacred porcupine quill hats and old pangolin skins. It's a 10-minute walk downhill below the Sports Ground. Times vary so call ahead.

St Teresa's Church CHURCH
A fascinating missionary church built in 1929 by Swiss Jesuits, St Teresa was constructed to incorporate designs from a Bhutanese gompa. The wooden apostles resemble Buddhist monks, and carvings on the doors resemble the *tashi tagye,* eight auspicious symbols of Himalayan Buddhism. The church is off 9th Mile, about 2km downhill from town. If it's locked, ask the next-door neighbours.

Activities

Himalayan Eagle PARAGLIDING
(9635156911; www.himalayaneagle.in) Manali-based pilots offers paragliding flights from

Deolo Hill. Tandem flights cost ₹3000/5000 for a 5/15km flight from Deolo Hill. Weather conditions have to be perfect for flights.

Courses

Anandavan Yog Peeth YOGA
(☎3552-256936; www.anandavanyogpeeth.com) This Yoga Alliance–registered organisation runs 17-day yoga teacher-training courses for US$1400, based at Holumba Haven.

Tours

Gurudongma Tours & Travels TREKKING
(☎03552-255204; www.astonishingindiatours.com; Rinkingpong Rd, Hilltop) This local operator run by 'General Jimmy' organises interesting trekking, mountain-biking and birdwatching tours, based out of its luxury farmhouse on the Samthar Plateau.

Sleeping

Manokamana Lodge GUESTHOUSE $
(☎03552-257047; manokamanalodge@gmail.com; DB Giri Rd; s/d ₹500/700; @ 📶) This simple, family-run place is somewhere between a local hotel and a backpackers' dive. Its central location, combined with an internet cafe and an excellent-value restaurant add to its shoestring appeal, even though accommodation is fairly basic, characterised by linoleum-floored rooms and bucket hot water in clean attached bathrooms. Ask for one of the quieter rear rooms.

Deki Lodge GUESTHOUSE $
(☎03552-255095; www.dekilodge.yolasite.com; Tripai Rd; s/d from ₹990/1100; 📶) This friendly Tibetan-owned place is set around a peaceful flower-hemmed family house, and boasts an airy terrace cafe. The rooms are plain and a tad overpriced for what's on offer, but the pricier upper-floor rooms (₹1330/1760) are comfortable, with shared balconies. It's a 10-minute walk northeast of the town centre, just up a side road.

★ **Holumba Haven** BOUTIQUE HOTEL $$
(☎03552-256936; www.holumba.com; 9th Mile; r ₹1800-3000; 📶) A unique and utterly charming property combining a nursery and a family-run guesthouse, Holumba is located amid sylvan settings a walkable 1km below town. The spotless, comfy rooms are arranged in cosy cottages spread around the lush orchid gardens, and good homestyle meals (preorders only) are available in the sociable dining room.

The owner Norden is a great source of information on local hikes and trips.

Kalimpong Park Hotel HERITAGE HOTEL $$
(☎03552-255304; www.kalimpongparkhotel.com; Rinkingpong Rd; s/d ₹2530/3200; @ 📶) This former summer home of the maharajas of Dinajpur is perched on a mountain shelf overlooking the Relli Valley, and packs in oodles of Raj-era charm. Wicker chairs and scarlet blossoms line the verandah and there's a charming lounge bar, along with a restaurant offering British boarding-school staples, such as jelly custard (order in advance).

Cloud 9 HOTEL $$
(☎03552-255410; cloudnine.kpg@gmail.com; Rinkingpong Rd; s/d from ₹1000/1400; 📶) The five wood-panelled rooms on the 1st floor of this cheerful property are irreverently homey, and the restaurant below serves interesting Bhutanese dishes and chilled beer. Binod the owner is a Beatles junkie and loves to bond over music in the late evenings – he might even buy you a beer if you're good with the guitar! Front-facing rooms are brighter but slightly more expensive.

Himalayan Hotel HERITAGE HOTEL $$$
(☎03552-255248; www.himalayanhotel.com; Upper Cart Rd; s/d ₹2400/3600; 📶) This historic hotel was opened by David MacDonald, an interpreter from Francis Younghusband's 1904 Lhasa mission, and over the years has housed such Himalayan legends as Alexandra David-Neel, Heinrich Harrer and Charles Bell. The brash Mayfair chain recently bought the property and renovations are underway, so it remains to be seen how much ambience will survive.

DON'T MISS

NURSERIES

Kalimpong is a major flower exporter and produces about 80% of India's gladioli and sundry orchid varieties. Visit **Nurseryman's Haven** (☎03552-256936; Holumba Haven, 9th Mile) at Holumba Haven to see some 200-odd species of orchids; **Santi Kunj** (BL Dixit Rd; ⊙8.30am-noon & 1.30-4pm Sun-Fri) to see anthuriums and the bird of paradise; and **Pineview Nursery** (☎03552-255843; Atisha Rd; admission ₹10; ⊙9am-5pm Mon-Sat) to gaze at its eminently photographable cactus collection.

OFF THE BEATEN TRACK

KALIMPONG WALKS

There's plenty of scope for some great walking around Kalimpong, so allow an extra day or two to stretch your legs. **Helpdesk Tourism** (p515) at Sherpa Lodge and **Holumba Haven** offer information on all these walks and can arrange guides (per day ₹800 to ₹1500) and transport if needed.

In Kalimpong itself, Helpdesk can arrange a half-day guided crafts walk (guide ₹600 to ₹800), taking in a traditional incense workshop, working silversmiths, noodle makers and a *thangka* (Tibetan cloth painting) studio, all hidden in the backstreet bazaars near Haat Bazaar.

One easy half-day walk close to town leads from near Holumba Haven to the villages of **Challisey** and **Chibo Busty** to a grand viewpoint over the Teesta River. En route, you can drop by the **LK Pradhan Cactus Nursery** and a small **curd production centre** at Tharker Farm, with the option of descending to see two fascinating traditional **Lepcha houses** at Ngassey village.

Heading further afield, one potential DIY hike starts at a wide track at 20th Mile, 2km past Algarah on the road to Pedong. The track climbs gently along a forested ridge to the faint 17th-century ruins of **Damsang Dzong**, site of the last stand of the Lepcha kings against the Bhutanese. Continue along the ridge and then descend to views of Khangchendzonga at Tinchuli Hill, before following the dirt road back from Sillery to the main Algarah–Pedong road. From here you can walk back 4km to Algarah to catch a shared jeep to Kalimpong (last jeep 3pm), or continue 3km to Pedong via the Bhutanese-influenced **Sangchen Dorje Gompa** in Sakyong Busty, just below Pedong. Buses and jeeps leave Kalimpong for Pedong (₹30 to ₹50) and Algarah (₹30) at 8.15am, or charter a return taxi for the day (₹1000 to ₹1500). If you want to stay overnight, the five cottages at the laid-back **Silk Route Retreat** (p514), 1.5km before Pedong, offer a fine hiking base.

For the ultimate dawn and dusk views of Khangchendzonga, head to the **Tiffin Dara viewpoint**, just above the village of Rishap, about 30km from Kalimpong. A rough road branches off the main Kalimpong–Lava road and climbs for 3km to a signed footpath 1km before Rishap. The path detours left after 20 minutes to the viewpoint and, once back at the junction, it continues through forest for 45 minutes to rejoin the main Kalimpong–Lava road. Just before this junction, by some prayer flags, a shortcut footpath drops down to Lava village via the Forest Lodge. For transport take the 7am shared jeep to Lava (₹80) or the slower 8am bus (₹60). The last bus back to Kalimpong is at 1.30pm. A chartered one-way jeep costs ₹1600 to Rishap or ₹2000 for a day's return hire, taking in Lava.

Lava (2353m), 34km from Kalimpong, is a worthy destination in itself, especially if you time your walk with the bustling Tuesday market, or the 10am debating or 3.30pm prayers at the modern **Kagyupa Thekchenling Gompa**. Adjoining Lava is **Neora Valley National Park** (Indian/foreigner ₹60/200, vehicle hire ₹1500, guide ₹200; ⏲15 Sep-15 Jun), whose lush forests are home to red pandas, clouded leopards and myriad bird species. Jeep tours are available (₹1300 to ₹1600) and travel agents can arrange a four-day camping trek to Roche La (3155m), at the high junction of West Bengal, Sikkim and Bhutan. The cottages of the **Lava Forest Lodge** (☎033-23350064; www.wbfdc.com; Lava; d ₹800-1500) just above town offer the nicest accommodation but can be hard to book; try through **West Bengal Tourism** (p493) in Siliguri or Holumba Haven in Kalimpong. The private **Hotel Orchid** (p514) is another decent choice. Avoid October, when Bengali tourists flood the town. Shared jeeps (₹80) run back to Kalimpong when full, until around 3.30pm and there is one bus at 1.30pm.

Elgin Silver Oaks HERITAGE HOTEL **$$$**
(☎03552-255296; www.elginhotels.com; Rinkingpong Rd; s/d incl full board ₹8100/8400; @📶) This Raj-era homestead-turned-heritage-hotel is centrally located and packs plenty of atmosphere but isn't brilliantly run. The rooms are plushly furnished and offer grand views down the valley towards the Relli River (ask for a garden-view room). The tariff includes all meals in the classy restaurant.

Hotel Orchid HOTEL $$

(☎03552-282213; www.hotelorchid.com; Lava; d ₹1200-2200) A middle-of-town inn featuring 12 bright pine-skirted rooms, fresh linen and clean bathrooms with hot water, the Orchid is one of Lava's few overnight options. There's some decent Chinese food available in the in-house restaurant on the ground floor.

Silk Route Retreat RESORT $$

(☎9932828753; www.thesilkrouteretreat.com; 21st Mile, Pedong; s/d cottage ₹1600/2500; 📶) The five clean and modern cottages make a good base for hiking or biking the region (hiking guides are available) and the food is good (mains ₹180 to ₹250), with a sociable verandah hang-out.

Eating

Gompu's Bar & Restaurant TIBETAN $$

(Gompu's Hotel, off DB Giri Rd; mains ₹120-200; ⏱7am-9pm) Gompu's is known for its signature oversized pork *momos* (₹130), which have been drawing locals and travellers alike for as long as anyone can remember. Lunchtime is the best time to find them. It's also a good place for a cold beer (₹210) chased by a plate of garlic chilli potatoes or crispy pork.

Lee's CHINESE $$

(☎9593305812; DB Giri Rd; mains ₹80-150, set meal ₹250; ⏱11am-7.30pm Mon-Sat) Mr Lee and his daughter serve up fantastic and unique Chinese-style dishes at this eatery with a red interior. Stand-out dishes include the *mun* wontons (dumplings fried in egg), *mun chu nyuk* (red pork), homemade *mefun* (rice noodles), a delectable golden chicken in garlic gravy and a refreshing pot of good-quality green tea. It's on the top floor above One Cup cafe.

Paris Kalimpong Bakery BAKERY $

(DB Giri Rd; pastries ₹30-50; ⏱9am-6pm Mon-Sat) Surprising French-owned bakery that serves up excellent baguettes, eclairs, cheese brioches, quiches and cakes, plus coffee. Opening hours can be erratic but it's worth persevering.

King Thai CHINESE $$

(3rd fl supermarket, DB Giri Rd; mains ₹160-200; ⏱11am-9pm) A multicultural hang-out with a Thai name, Chinese food and Bob Marley posters on the walls, this place draws in monks, businessmen and Tibetan cool kids. The generously portioned food is mainly Chinese with some Indian accents, and there's a bar with comfy chairs.

Cafe Refuel INTERNATIONAL

(www.caferefuel.com; Rishi Rd, 9th Mile; ⏱10.30am-8pm) Cool place with a motorbike-themed decor that uses classic old Vespas for counter seats. The food has a Mexican twist, with homemade nachos and burritos, hamburgers, pizza and pita sandwiches, plus espresso coffee and a foosball table to keep things lively.

Drinking & Nightlife

★**Art Cafe** CAFE

(Rishi Rd; coffee ₹40; ⏱10am-7pm) Cool cafe with a breezy terrace offering fine views over the Teesta Valley towards Darjeeling. There is good coffee, shakes, lemonade coolers (served in Mason jars) and great thin-crust pizzas (₹160 to ₹180), plus magazines to read. It's a good place to meet Kalimpong's hip set, especially as there's no wi-fi.

One Cup CAFE

(DB Giri Rd; coffee ₹50-90; ⏱11am-6pm Mon-Sat) Kalimpong's first coffee house serves a decent espresso hit, alongside some quality cakes, brownies and ice-cream specials. No wi-fi.

Shopping

Lark's Provisions FOOD & DRINKS

(DB Giri Rd; ⏱9.30am-6.30pm) This is the best place to pick up local cheese (per kg ₹600), produced in Kalimpong since the Jesuits established a dairy here in the 19th century. It also sells locally made milky lollipops (₹30) and yummy homemade pickles.

Haat Bazaar MARKET

(btwn Relli & RC Mintri Rds) On Wednesdays and especially Saturdays, this normally quiet bazaar roars to life with a plethora of merchandise ranging from food and textiles, to objects of daily life and sundry other knick-knacks.

Kashi Nath & Sons BOOKS

(DB Giri Rd; ⏱10am-6.30pm Mon-Sat) This, and the attached stationary shop next door, has a modest collection of Himalayan titles, plus some international bestselling novels and nonfiction titles.

Information

Cyber Infotech (per hr ₹30; 10am-7pm Mon-Sat;) Tiny internet cafe opposite Gompu's that offers computers and wi-fi.

Helpdesk Tourism (7363818059, 8967938378; helpdesktourism@gmail.com; Sherpa Lodge; 9am-5pm) This private information centre on the ground floor of Sherpa Lodge offers guides, a useful map and information on trips around Kalimpong, including hikes and regional homestays. Ask for Jigme or Norden.

Post Office (Rinkingpong Rd; 9am-5pm Mon-Fri, to 4pm Sat)

State Bank of India ATM (DB Giri Rd) One of several ATMs located together.

Tourist Reception Centre (DGHC; 03552-257992; DB Giri Rd; 10am-4.30pm Mon-Sat, closed 2nd & 4th Sat of the month) Sleepy staff can organise local tours and accommodation.

Getting There & Away

All the bus and jeep options and their offices are found next to each other at the chaotic **Motor Stand**.

BUS & JEEP

Bengal government NBSTC buses run hourly to Siliguri (₹80, 2½ hours).

Himalayan Travellers (9434166498; Motor Stand) This helpful transport company runs shared jeeps to Lava (₹80, 1½ hours, five daily from 7am).

Kalimpong Mainline Taxi Driver's Welfare Association (KMTDWA; Motor Stand) Frequent shared jeeps to Siliguri (₹130, 2½ hours) and two daily to Jorethang (₹100, two hours, 7.30am and noon).

Kalimpong Motor Transport (Motor Stand) Frequent shared jeeps (₹130, three hours) to Darjeeling until midafternoon, plus charters (₹1800).

Kalimpong, Sikkim All Highway Taxi Driver's Owner's Association (259544; Motor Stand) Shared jeeps to Gangtok (₹140, three hours, hourly until 11.30am), Ravangla (₹150, 3½ hours, 2pm) and Namchi (₹110, 8am and 1pm) in Sikkim.

Sikkim Nationalised Transport (SNT; Ongden Rd) Operates a single bus to Gangtok (₹105, three hours) departing at 1pm from opposite the Motor Stand.

TRAIN

Kalimpong Railway Out Agency (Mani Rd; 10am-5pm Mon-Sat, to 1pm Sun) Sells train tickets from New Jalpaiguri (NJP) train station but has no tourist quota.

Getting Around

Taxis (mostly unmarked minivans) can be chartered for local trips from along DB Giri Rd. A half-day rental to see most of the sights should cost ₹1000.

Bihar & Jharkhand

Includes ➡

Best Places to Eat

- ➡ Mohammad Restaurant (p528)
- ➡ Be Happy Cafe (p528)
- ➡ Pind Balluchi (p520)
- ➡ Nook (p533)

Best Places to Sleep

- ➡ Rahul Guest House (p527)
- ➡ Hotel Nalanda Regency (p530)
- ➡ Chanakya BNR Hotel (p533)
- ➡ Hotel President (p519)

Why Go?

Remote and rural, Bihar is the birthplace of Buddhism – indeed its very name derives from *vihara,* the Sanskrit word for Buddhist monastery. Thousands of pilgrims from around the world throng its many places of religious significance, most extraordinary of which is Bodhgaya, the site of Buddha's enlightenment, where getting caught up in the spiritual atmosphere is a major draw for travellers. In tribal Jharkhand, holy Parasnath Hill is a revered Jain pilgrimage site, and joining devotees on the hike to the top is a surreal highlight for those who like to get off the beaten track.

Truth be told, the whole of this region is off the beaten track. Outside Bodhgaya, foreign tourists are almost nonexistent, so if you're looking to sidestep mainstream travel, and especially if you have an interest in Buddhism, this unfashionable pocket of India could be an unexpected highlight.

When to Go

Patna

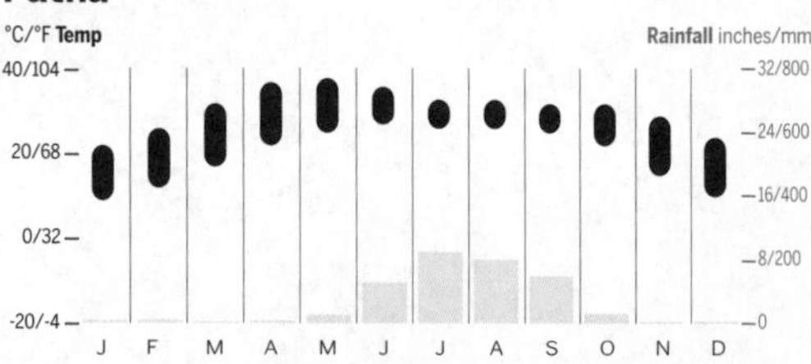

Jan & Feb Temperatures hover between a chilly-to-pleasant 12°C and 25°C.

Jun–Sep Monsoon season. Steer clear – Bihar is India's most flood-prone state.

Oct & Nov Warm days in October and comfortably cool in November.

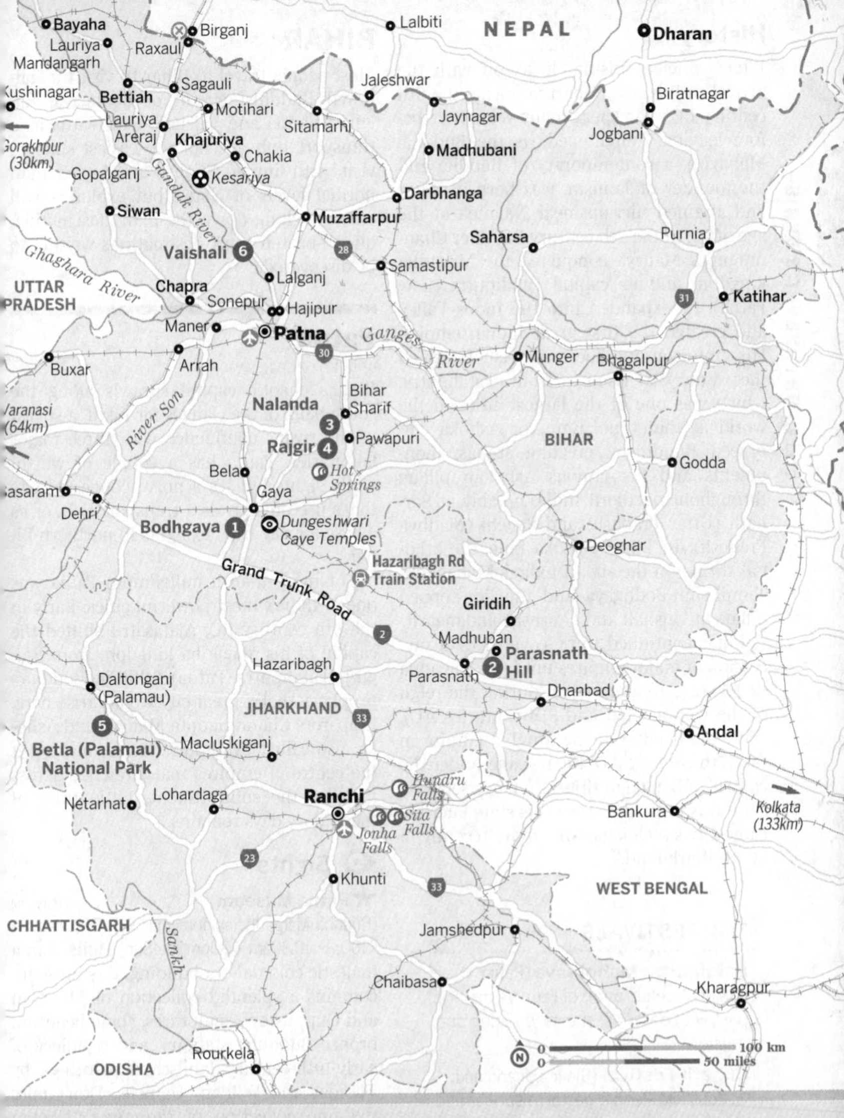

Bihar & Jharkhand Highlights

❶ **Bodhgaya** (p525) Witnessing Buddhists from around the world praying, prostrating and meditating at the powerfully serene site of Buddha's enlightenment.

❷ **Parasnath Hill** (p532) Getting up at 4am for the surreal day-long Jain pilgrimage to the top of Jharkhand's tallest peak.

❸ **Nalanda** (p531) Visiting the peaceful ruins of this once-huge ancient university.

❹ **Rajgir** (p529) Hiring a tonga (two-wheeled horse-drawn carriage) for the day to explore the Buddhist sites and stupas of this laid-back village.

❺ **Betla (Palamau) National Park** (p533) Touring the deliciously peaceful forests of this protected area to spot wild elephants and spotted deer.

❻ **Vaishali** (p522) Walking through villages to the ancient stupas and ruins of this Buddhist pilgrimage spot.

History

Bihar's ancient history kicks off with the arrival of Prince Siddhartha during the 6th century BC, who spent many years here before leaving, enlightened, as the Buddha. Mahavira, a contemporary of Buddha and the founder of Jainism, was born in Bihar and attained nirvana near Nalanda at the age of 72. In the 4th century BC, after Chandragupta Maurya conquered the Magadha kingdom and its capital Pataliputra (now Patna), he expanded into the Indus Valley and created the first great Indian empire. His grandson and successor, Ashoka, ruled the Mauryan empire from Pataliputra, which was one of the largest cities in the world at that time. Emperor Ashoka embraced Buddhism, erecting stupas, monuments and his famous Ashokan pillars throughout northern India, notably at Sarnath (Uttar Pradesh) and Sanchi (Madhya Pradesh). In Bihar, Ashoka built the original shrine on the site of today's Mahabodhi Temple in Bodhgaya and the lion-topped pillars at Vaishali and Lauriya Nandangarh.

Bihar continued to be coveted by a succession of major empires until the Magadha region rose to glory again during the reign of the Guptas (7th and 8th centuries AD). With the decline of the Mughal empire in the 17th century AD, Bihar came under the control of Bengal until 1912, when a separate state was formed. Part of this state later became Orissa (Odisha) and, more recently in 2000, Jharkhand.

TOP FESTIVALS

Pataliputra Mahotsava (Patna; Mar) A celebration of Patna's historic past with parades, sports, dancing and music.

Chhath Festival (Bihar & Jharkhand; Oct/Nov) People perform sunset and sunrise rituals on the banks of rivers and ponds to honour Surya, the Sun God.

Rajgir Mahotsava (p529) A performing-arts gala with dances, devotional songs and instrumental music.

Sonepur Mela (Sonepur; Nov/Dec) With 700,000 attendees and countless thousands of animals taking part, this three-week festival is four times the size of Pushkar's **Camel Fair** (p138).

BIHAR

Most people travel to Bihar to visit the hallowed Buddhist circuit of Bodhgaya, Rajgir, Nalanda and Vaishali, with Patna as a transport hub. It's not the easiest state to visit, with limited English and higher than normal levels of chaos, but explorers will enjoy tracking down the many fascinating, off-the-beaten track destinations waiting to be discovered.

Patna

0612 / POP 1,697,900

Bihar's chaotic capital sprawls along the south bank of the Ganges for 15km, just east of the river's confluence with three major tributaries. Patna has a couple of worthwhile sights but it's a noisy, congested city that's used mostly as a transport hub, or as a base for day trips to sights in northern Bihar.

For more than a millennium Patna was one of India's most powerful cities. Early in the 5th century BC, Ajatasatru shifted the capital of his Magadha kingdom from Rajgir to Pataliputra (Patna), fulfilling Buddha's prophecy that a great city would arise here. Emperors Chandragupta Maurya and Ashoka also called Pataliputra home, making it the centre of empires that stretched across most of the subcontinent. Little trace of these glory days remains.

Sights

★Patna Museum MUSEUM

(Buddha Marg; Indian/foreigner ₹15/250, camera ₹100; 10.30am-4.30pm Tue-Sun) Housed in a majestic colonial-era building, this museum contains a splendid collection of Mauryan and Gupta stone sculptures, some beautiful bronze Buddhist statuary, and a gallery of early-19th-century landscape paintings by Thomas and William Daniells. Don't miss the fine collection of *thangkas* (Tibetan cloth paintings) brought to India by the Benagli Tibetologist and traveller Rahul Sankrityayan in the early 20th century.

★Golghar HISTORIC BUILDING

(Danapure Rd; ₹5; 10am-6pm) For a dome with a view, climb this massive, bulbous granary, built by the British army in 1786 and renovated in 2016. The idea behind its construction was to avoid a repeat of the terrible 1770 famine – look for the old carved sign on one side, reading: 'For the perpetual prevention of famine in these provinces' – although fortunately it was never required.

Bihar Museum MUSEUM
(☎0612-2235732; www.biharmuseum.org; Bailey Rd (Jawaharlal Nehru Marg)) This impressive new museum, one of the largest in south Asia, was only partially opened at time of research but when finished it will boast three impressive history galleries, plus displays on contemporary art and ethnic groups of Bihar. It may well poach some of the finer pieces of the Patna Museum, including the famous Mauryan-era *Didarganj Yakshi* statue, dating from the 3rd century BC.

Buddha Smriti Park PARK
(Muzharal Haque Path (Fraser Rd); park ₹20, museum ₹40; ⏲9am-7pm Tue-Sun) This peaceful 9-hectare park, inaugurated by the Dalai Lama in 2010, is notable for its massive sandblasted charcoal stupa (₹50), which houses a unique, bulletproof relic chamber, and sapling plantings from both the Bodhi Tree in Bodhgaya and Anuradhapura in Sri Lanka. The strikingly modern Buddhist museum is worthwhile, and there is a library (₹50) and a meditation centre (free).

Sleeping

Most budget hotels in Patna do not accept foreigners.

Hotel Clark Inn HOTEL $
(☎9939726620; Jamal Rd; r from ₹660) The cheapest hotel we could find that welcomed foreigners, Clark Inn has simple budget rooms with TVs and squat toilets, or bigger and cleaner rooms with air coolers (₹1100). Some have small balconies.

★**Hotel President** HOTEL $$
(☎0612-2209203; www.hotelpresidentpatna.com; off Fraser Rd; s/d ₹2020/2620; ❄@🛜) This recently remodelled, family-run hotel is in a useful and relatively quiet location off Fraser Rd and close to Patna Museum. Rooms – all with air-con – are spacious, stylish and fresh, with TV, seating areas and hot-water bathrooms. Some have small balconies. It's an excellent lower midrange choice, especially if you can get a discount.

Hotel City Centre HOTEL $$
(☎0612-2208687; www.hotelcitycentre.in; Station Rd; d incl breakfast with/without AC ₹2000/1000; ❄🛜) This modern glass tower to your right just as you exit the train station is temptingly convenient for a transit overnighter. Rooms are simple but decent value (non-air-con rooms have squat toilets), staff are helpful and there are several restaurants on the ground floor. The upper floors are a bit of a rabbit warren.

SLEEPING PRICE RANGES

Accommodation price ranges for this chapter (referring to double rooms with bathroom in high season, and including taxes):

$ less than ₹1000

$$ ₹1000–2500

$$$ more than ₹2500

Hotel Maurya Patna HOTEL $$$
(☎0612-2203040; www.maurya.com; Gandhi Maidan; s/d incl breakfast ₹15,780/17,000; ❄@🛜🏊) Patna's top business hotel has tastefully furnished rooms, a rather barren pool, a couple of nice restaurants and a gym. It all adds up to comfort rather than luxury. Booking online can bring discounts of 50%.

Eating

Baba Hotel INDIAN $
(Dak Bungalow Rd; mains ₹70-110; ⏲9am-10pm) Clean, good-value, pocket-sized restaurant serving Indian and Chinese dishes (including some good vegetarian options), as well as ₹85 to ₹95 thalis.

Litti Chokha Stall STREET FOOD $
(opposite Gandhi Maidan; per plate ₹15) One of numerous streetside stalls dotted around the city cooking up Patna's signature snack: *litti chokha* (grilled chickpea-powder dough balls served with a side sauce of mashed tomatoes, aubergine and potatoes).

Bollywood Treats FAST FOOD $
(Gandhi Maidan; mains ₹80-150; ⏲noon-9pm) This somewhat anaemic fast-food place dishes out South Indian snacks, Chinese stir-fries, decent pizza and tempting brownies to Patna's blossoming middle class. There is a Baskin-Robbins ice-cream kiosk, and it serves instant coffee (₹115). Opens at noon, but doesn't start serving food until 1pm.

★**Bellpepper Restaurant** INDIAN $$
(Hotel Windsor, Braj Kishore Path (Exhibition Rd); mains ₹120-320; ⏲11am-3pm & 7-10.30pm; ❄) Intimate and contemporary, this small restaurant inside Hotel Windsor is popular for

Patna

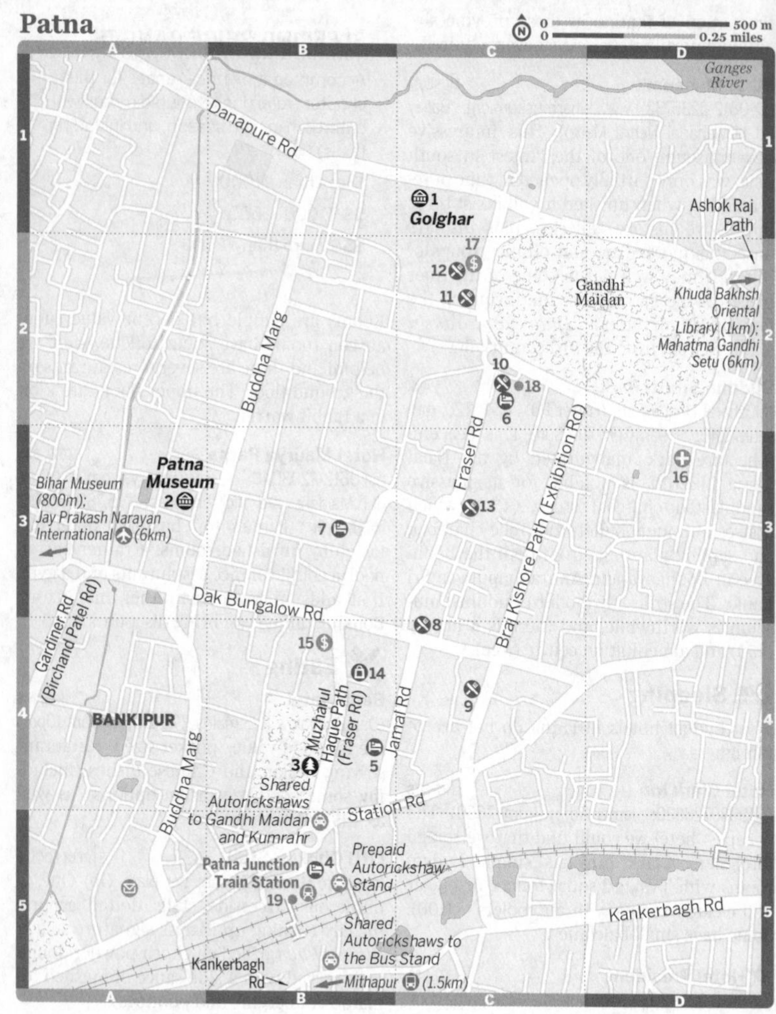

its tandoori dishes. The *murg tikka lababdar* (boneless tandoori chicken basted with garlic, ginger, green chillies, and a pistachio- and cashew-nut paste) is melt-in-your-mouth sinful. The biryanis are good here too.

Pind Balluchi NORTH INDIAN $$
(☎0612-2219101; www.pindballuchi.com; 16-18 fl, Biscomaun Tower, Gandhi Maidan; ⊙noon-10pm; ❄) For Patna's best food and views, head to this revolving restaurant with ever-shifting vistas over Gandhi Maidan, Golghar and the Ganges beyond. The kebabs are excellent (try the *murgh malai* kebab), and there is a full range of vegetarian dishes such as *kadai paneer,* and fine *kheer* for dessert. Enter on the north side of the building.

Tandoor Hut INDIAN $$
(☎delivery 9386851333; Fraser Rd; kebabs ₹150-180; ⊙11am-11pm) Streetside grill that serves delicious kebabs and other tandoor offerings, as well as huge biryanis and curries. Eat on-site or take them back to your hotel. The chicken *malai* and *reshmi kebabs* are both superb.

Shopping

Ajanta ARTS & CRAFTS
(Fraser Rd; ⊙10.30am-9pm Mon-Sat, 1-8pm Sun) This unassuming little shop has a delightful

Patna

Top Sights
1 Golghar....C1
2 Patna Museum....A3

Sights
3 Buddha Smriti Park....B4

Sleeping
4 Hotel City Centre....B5
5 Hotel Clark Inn....B4
6 Hotel Maurya Patna....C2
7 Hotel President....B3

Eating
8 Baba Hotel....C4
9 Bellpepper Restaurant....C4
10 Bollywood Treats....C2
11 Litti Chokha Stall....C2
12 Pind Balluchi....C2
13 Tandoor Hut....C3

Shopping
14 Ajanta....B4

Information
15 Axis Bank....B4
16 Dr Ruban Memorial Hospital....D3
17 State Bank of India....C2
18 Thomas Cook....C2

Transport
19 Foreign-Tourist Ticket Counter....B5

selection of colourful Mithila (Madhubani) paintings secreted away in drawers and cupboards. Prices range from ₹300 (handmade paper) to ₹950 (silk). It's next to Harrison's Hotel.

Information

MEDICAL SERVICES

Dr Ruban Memorial Hospital (0612-2320446, 0612-2320404; www.rubanpatliputrahospital.com; Gandhi Maidan; 24hr) Emergency room, clinic and pharmacy.

MONEY

Axis Bank (Fraser Rd; 9.30am-3.30pm Mon-Fri & 1st & 3rd Sat of month) Exchanges currency and has ATMs.

State Bank of India (Gandhi Maidan; 10am-4pm Mon-Fri & 1st & 3rd Sat of month) Exchanges currency and travellers cheques. Has ATMs.

TRAVEL AGENCIES

Thomas Cook (0612-2221699, 9334942188; www.thomascook.in; Hotel Maurya, Patna Arcade; 10am-6pm Mon-Sat) Helpful for booking airline tickets and car rental. Also exchanges currency with a ₹150 commission. Contact Sami.

Getting There & Away

AIR

Patna's Jay Prakash Narayan International Airport is 8km southwest of the city centre. Between them, **Air India** (0612-2223199; www.airindia.in; Patna airport), **IndiGo** (1800 1803838; www.goindigo.in; Patna airport), **Go Air** (0612-2227148; Patna airport) and **Jet Airways** (0612-2223045; www.jetairways.com; Patna airport) fly direct daily to Delhi and Kolkata, with onward connections to other cities.

BUS

The main bus stand occupies a large, dusty space about 1.5km southwest of the train station (₹10 shared autos run here from the back of the train station). It's a noisy, anarchic place, with little English and no booking offices, but if you walk into the chaos telling people where you want to go, you'll eventually get directed to the right bus; buy tickets on-board.

There are frequent services throughout the day to the following destinations:

Gaya ₹100, three hours; there are also a couple of direct buses a day to Bodhgaya (₹120)

Kesariya ₹80, three hours

Motihari ₹145 to ₹170, 4½ hours

Ranchi AC/non-AC ₹350/280, eight hours

Raxaul AC/non-AC ₹230/180, six hours

Vaishali ₹50, two hours

There are also 9pm sleeper buses to Ranchi and Raxaul.

CAR

Hiring a car and driver can be done through **Thomas Cook** (p521), starting from ₹12 per kilometre (minimum 200km) plus a driver allowance of ₹300 per overnight stay. A taxi from Patna to Bodhgaya costs around ₹3000.

TRAIN

Patna Junction has a **foreign-tourist ticket counter** (Window 3, Patna Junction train station; 8am-8pm Mon-Sat, to 2pm Sun) at the 1st-floor reservation office, in the right-hand wing of the train station.

NO ALCOHOL

Since 2016 Bihar has been a dry state, so there's no alcohol of any kind for sale.

Trains leave roughly hourly for Gaya (2nd class/AC chair ₹25/260, two to three hours), with the 11.40am Patna-Hatiya Express offering air-con chair seats. For other trains just buy a 2nd-class 'general' ticket and hop on the next available service.

More than a dozen daily trains leave for New Delhi (sleeper/3AC/2AC ₹490/1300/1860, 12 to 18 hours); the quickest and most convenient time-wise is the RJPB Rajdhani (3AC/2AC/1AC ₹2180/2660/3765), which leaves at 7.25pm and arrives in Delhi at 7.40am.

Ten daily trains go to Kolkata (sleeper/3AC/2AC ₹340/890/1250, eight to 14 hours). The best time-wise is probably the Vibhuti Express (10.35pm, nine hours).

At least 20 daily trains go to Varanasi (sleeper/3AC/2AC ₹200/540/740, four to six hours) between 5am and 9pm.

Three fast trains go to Ranchi (sleeper/3AC/2AC ₹250/670/960, eight to 10 hours), leaving at 6am, 11.40am and 9.45pm. The first two trains offer chair-car class (₹540 to ₹630)

The most comfortable option to Rajgir is air-con chair car (₹260, three hours) on the 9.15am 13234 Rajgriha Express.

Note that you may also find trains arriving at Patna's minor stations, such as Rajendra Nagar, 3km east of Patna Junction, or inconvenient Patna Sahib, 11km east.

Getting Around

Autorickshaws/taxis to Patna airport cost ₹160/350 from the **prepaid autorickshaw stand** (Patna Junction train station) by the train station.

Cramped **shared autorickshaws** depart from in front of the train station for Gandhi Maidan (₹7). Head to the rear of the train station for **autorickshaws** to the bus stand (₹10).

A metro system is currently under construction, allegedly due for completion in 2021.

PRECAUTIONS

Bihar and Jharkhand have a reputation for lawlessness. Conditions have improved in recent years, and bandit activity – such as holding up cars, buses and trains – is only a remote possibility.

➡ Locals will advise you to avoid travelling after dark or hiking in the hills alone, and this is a sensible precaution.

➡ Although tourists are not specific targets, it's a good idea to keep up to date with the latest info; check the newspapers *Bihar Times* (www.bihartimes.in) or *Patna Daily* (www.patnadaily.com) before arrival.

Vaishali

☎06225

A quiet, yet significant Buddhist pilgrimage site, Vaishali, 55km northwest of Patna, makes a lovely rural escape from hectic Patna. The small museum is engaging, while the ruins of Kolhua are wonderfully serene. Simply walking around the surrounding villages and farmland is a treat in itself.

The bus from Patna will drop you at a junction, from where it's a 1km walk west past monasteries built by Thai, Cambodian and Vietnamese Buddhists to the large ancient coronation water tank known as Abhishek Pushkarini. On the left side of the tank is the modern, whitewashed, Japanese-built **World Peace Pagoda** (dawn-dusk) FREE.

On the opposite side of the tank, and of more historical interest, is the **Buddha Relic Stupa** (dawn-dusk) FREE. The 5th-century stupa, originally 12m tall, is now in ruins, but it was once one of the eight locations in which Buddha's ashes were interred. The soapstone relic casket housing the ashes now resides in Patna Museum. The small **Archaeological Museum** (admission ₹10; 9am-5pm Sat-Thu) here contains some fine 1000-year-old Buddhist statuary and an intriguing 1st- to 2nd-century-AD toilet pan. It also has an interesting scale model of the nearby site of Kolhua.

Between the Buddha Relic Stupa and the Archaeological Museum, a single-lane countryside road winds its way north through farming villages to the **Kolhua Complex** (Indian/foreigner ₹15/200; dawn-dusk), 5km away. It's worth making time for this very pleasant walk, although shared autos also make the trip. Set in a landscaped park, Kolhua comprises a large, hemispherical brick stupa guarded by a lion crouching atop a 2300-year-old Ashoka pillar. The pillar is plain and contains none of the Ashokan edicts usually carved onto these pillars. Nearby are the ruins of smaller stupas, monastic buildings where Buddha spent several monsoons, and also one of the first ever Buddhist nunneries. According to legend, Buddha was given a bowl of honey here by monkeys, who also dug out the rainwater tank for his water supply.

Eating options are limited in Vaishali. The best place to grab lunch is the **Buddha Fun & Food Village** (☎997316874; mains ₹80-200), located at the southeastern corner of the ceremonial tank. The outdoor seating of thatched huts is pleasant and cottage accommodation is available.

OFF THE BEATEN TRACK

LAURIYA NANDANGARH

Fans of Buddhist history will enjoy the off-beat trip to the huge stupa at Lauriya Nandangarh, 25km northwest of Bettiah. The 2000-year-old, 25m-tall brick stupa consists of five circular and zig-zag terraces. The upper section remains covered in foliage and you can climb up for views of the pancake-flat countryside. To get here from the west end of town head 2km south and take a left just past the sugar/ethanol factory, following the factory wall for 1km. An autorickshaw costs around ₹150 return.

Also at the west end of town, 500m north of the main junction, is an 18.5m tall Ashoka pillar, one of only a handful remaining that feature all six of Ashoka's edicts, along with a seated lion carving on top, and the only such pillar still in its original location. Look for the colonial-era graffiti dating from 1873.

To get here from Motihari take one of the frequent buses to Bettiah (₹40, 90 minutes) and then take a Ramnagar-bound bus to Lauriya Nandangarh (₹30, 45 minutes). On the return you might find a Patna-bound bus direct to Motihari. For Raxaul take a cramped share jeep to Sagauli (₹30) and change there, or hire an entire jeep to the border for ₹1200.

If you are travelling in a hired vehicle from Patna and Kesariya, you can stop to visit another Ashoka pillar en route, just west of the village of Lauriya Areraj, 37km southeast of Bettiah.

Buses run every hour or so from Patna to Vaishali, and on to Kesariya. The last bus back to Patna swings by the main road at around 4pm.

Kesariya

Rising high out of the earth from where the dying Buddha donated his begging bowl, the enormous **Kesariya Stupa** (dawn-dusk) FREE is an enthralling example of how nature can reclaim a deserted monument. Excavated from under a grassy and wooded veil is one of the world's tallest (38m) Buddhist stupas dating from the Pala period (200–750 AD). Five uniquely shaped terraces above the 425m-circumference pedestal form a gargantuan Buddhist tantric mandala. Each terrace has a number of niches containing disfigured Buddha statues, which were destroyed during attacks by foreign invaders in the Middle Ages. The rural setting is a joy, but there is nothing else to see here apart from the stupa and you are not allowed to climb it.

Buses from Patna (via Vaishali) can drop you by the stupa, which is visible from the main road. The last bus back swings by at around 3.30pm. Buses from Motihari will drop you at the main crossroads in the village of Kesariya, where there are roadside *dhabas* (casual eateries, serving snacks and basic meals) that you could have lunch in, leaving you with a 2km walk or rickshaw ride south. If you can't find a direct onward bus to Motihari from Kesariya village, take one to the junction of Khajuriya and change there.

Motihari

06252 / POP 100,000

Bustling Motihari is not a particularly pleasant town but you may need to change buses here en route to Kesariya, Raxaul or Lauriya Nandangarh. If you need to stay, the modern and friendly **Hotel Rajeshwari Palace** (06252-222222; Main (Bank) Rd; r with/without AC from ₹2000/1000;) has fresh, clean rooms 10 minutes' walk west of the bus stand.

Frequent buses head to Patna (₹145 to ₹170, 4½ hours), Raxaul (₹50, 2½ hours) and Kesariya (₹40, two hours), from where you can catch passing buses to Vaishali.

Raxaul

06255 / POP 41,600

Raxaul is a dusty, congested border town that provides passage into Nepal via a hassle-free border post. It's no place to linger, but if you must spend the night, **Hotel Kaveri** (06255-221148; Main Rd; r with/without AC ₹1200/500;), on the main road leading to the border (about 1km from the border), has decent air-con rooms with modern bathrooms, and very basic non-AC rooms with tap-and-bucket showers, but shared toilets. Restaurants are scarce and none have English menus; the *dhaba* opposite Hotel Kaveri is probably your best bet.

CROSSING TO NEPAL: RAXAUL TO BIRGANJ

The busy border crossing between Raxual and Birganj, open from 6am to 10pm, is the most direct route to Kathmandu and eastern Nepal.

Nepali 15-, 30- and 90-day visas (US$25/40/100 and one passport photo) are only available from 6am to 6pm on the Nepal side of the border.

No banks change money in Raxaul but there are many private money changers on both sides of the border. The **State Bank of India** (⏲10.30am-4.30pm Mon-Fri, to 1.30pm Sat), on the main road in Raxaul, has an ATM. Note that Nepali rupees trade at a different rate to Indian rupees.

Onward Transport

On the Nepal side, the town of Birganj is about 3km from the border. You are free to walk across the border to Birganj, or shared autorickshaws and tongas (two-wheeled horse carriages) charge NRs25 per person from the border to Birganj. A cycle-rickshaw costs about NRs300.

From Birganj, there are frequent buses to Kathmandu (ordinary/deluxe/AC NRs550/600/800, six to seven hours, 5am to 8pm). However, the most comfortable and quickest option is to get a Tata Sumo '4WD' (NRs550 to NRs800, four to five hours, every 20 minutes until 5pm). There are also morning buses to Pokhara (NRs600, eight hours) via Narayangarh (NRs250, four hours) at 5am, 6.30am and 7.30am.

Buddha Air (www.buddhaair.com) has up to five daily flights between Simara (the airport for Birganj) and Kathmandu (US$105, 20 minutes). The airport is 22km from Birganj and a taxi costs around NRs1000.

The bus stand is 200m down a lane off the main road, about 2km from the border on the right. There are frequent buses, day and night, to Patna (AC/non-AC ₹230/180, seven to eight hours) via Motihari (₹50, 2½ hours). The road to Motihari is dreadfully bumpy so sit near the front of the bus if you can.

The train station is off the main road, 750m from the border, but isn't well connected. The Mithila Express runs daily to Kolkata (sleeper/3AC/2AC ₹365/990/1425, 18 hours, 10am). The Satyagrah Express runs daily to New Delhi (sleeper/3AC/2AC ₹455/1215/1765, 24 hours, 9.05am).

Gaya

☎0631 / POP 395,000

The hectic town of Gaya is a religious centre for Hindu pilgrims, who believe that offerings at the town's riverside Vishnupad Temple relieve the recently departed from the cycle of birth and rebirth. For foreign tourists, it merely serves as a transit point for Bodhgaya, 13km away.

Sleeping & Eating

Ajatsatru Hotel HOTEL $

(☎0631-2222961; Station Rd; r with/without AC ₹1430/840; ❄📶) If you get stuck for the night in Gaya, this hotel is the best value of a cluster of hotels directly opposite the train station. It has decent-sized but noisy rooms and an OK vegetarian restaurant. There are a few cheaper (and smaller) single rooms.

Getting There & Around

AUTORICKSHAW

Shared autos leave when full from Gaya Junction train station for Bodhgaya (₹20 per person), Manpur bus stand (₹10) and Gandhi Maidan bus stand (₹5).

A private auto from Gaya to Bodhgaya should cost ₹150, although they usually start at ₹200 or more.

BUS

Patna (₹100, three hours, hourly) Buses leave from the train station.

Rajgir (₹55, 2½ hours, hourly) Buses leave from Manpur bus stand, across the river to the east.

Ranchi (₹180, seven hours, twice hourly) Buses leave from the Gandhi Maidan bus stand.

TRAIN

Passenger trains leave every couple of hours for Patna (2nd class/AC chair ₹25/260, two to three hours). Buy a 2nd-class 'general' ticket and hop on. Express trains (two hours) run at 1.15pm and 8.25pm and offer comfortable chair-car seats.

The fastest overnight trains to New Delhi (sleeper/3AC/2AC from ₹490/1560/2585, 11 hours) leave at 10.38pm, 10.55pm and 11.11pm.

At least eight trains run daily to Kolkata (sleeper/3AC/2AC ₹270/730/1045, eight to 10 hours), the most convenient being the Doon Express (9½ hours, 9.27pm).

Almost a dozen daily trains go to Varanasi (sleeper/3AC/2AC ₹195/540/740, three to six hours). The quickest are the Purushottam Express (to Mughal Serai; 2.05pm) and Poorva Express (2.55pm).

Bodhgaya

☎0631 / POP 30,900

The crucible of Buddhism, Bodhgaya was where Prince Siddhartha attained enlightenment beneath a bodhi tree 2600 years ago and became Buddha (the 'Awakened One'). In terms of blessedness, this tiny temple town is to Buddhists what Mecca is to Muslims. Unsurprisingly, it attracts thousands of pilgrims from around the world every year, who come for prayer, study and meditation.

The most hallowed spot in town is the bodhi tree that flourishes inside the Mahabodhi Temple complex, amid a beautiful garden setting, its roots embedded in the same soil as its celebrated ancestor. Additionally, many monasteries and temples dot the town, built in their national style by foreign Buddhist communities. The ambience is a mix of monastic tranquillity, backpacker comforts and small-town hustle, underpinned by an intensity of devotion that makes it endlessly interesting.

The best time to visit is November to March when the weather is cool and Tibetan pilgrims come down from McLeod Ganj in Dharamsala. The high season is from December to January, which is also when the Dalai Lama often visits to teach in the large central Kalachakra Maidan.

Sights & Activities

★Mahabodhi Temple BUDDHIST TEMPLE

(camera ₹100; ⏲5am-9pm) FREE The magnificent Unesco World Heritage–listed Mahabodhi Temple, marking the hallowed ground where Buddha attained enlightenment and formulated his philosophy of life, forms the spiritual heart of Bodhgaya. Built in the 6th century AD atop the site of a temple erected by Emperor Ashoka almost 800 years earlier, it was razed by foreign invaders in the 11th century, and subsequently underwent several major restorations.

Topped by a 50m pyramidal spire, the inner sanctum of the ornate structure houses a 10th-century, 2m-high gilded image of a seated Buddha. Amazingly, four of the original sculpted stone railings surrounding the temple, dating from the Sunga period (184–72 BC), have survived amid the replicas. Others are now housed inside the archaeological museum.

Pilgrims and visitors from all walks of life and religions come to worship or just soak up the atmosphere of this sacred place. An enthralling way to start or finish the day is to stroll around the inside of the perimeter of the temple compound (in an auspicious clockwise pattern) and watch a sea of maroon and yellow dip and rise, while Tibetan monks perform endless prostrations on their prayer boards. There's a less atmospheric **Meditation Park** (Mahabodhi Temple; visitors/meditators ₹20/25; ⏲visitors 10am-5pm, meditators 5-10am & 5-9pm) for those seeking extra solitude within the temple grounds.

Leave your bags and MP3 players in the lockers 50m to the west of the entrance. Security has been fairly tight since bombs exploded in the complex in 2013.

Bodhi Tree BUDDHIST SITE

Undoubtedly, the most sacred fig tree ever to grace the Earth was the Bodhi Tree at Bodhgaya, under which Prince Siddhartha, the founder of Buddhism, achieved enlightenment. Buddha was said to have stared unblinkingly at the tree in an awed gesture of gratitude and wonder after his enlightenment. Today, pilgrims and tourists alike flock here to pray and meditate at the most important of Buddhism's four holiest sites.

Known as Sri Maha Bodhi, the original tree was paid special attention by Ashoka, a mighty Indian emperor who ruled most of the subcontinent from 269 to 232 BC, a century or two after Buddha's believed death. His wife, Tissarakkhā, wasn't such a fan of the tree and in a fit of jealousy and rage, caused the original Bodhi Tree's death by poisonous thorns shortly after becoming queen.

Thankfully, before its death, one of the tree's saplings was carried off to Anuradhapura in Sri Lanka by Sanghamitta (Ashoka's daughter), where it continues to flourish. A cutting was later carried back to Bodhgaya and planted where the original once stood. The red sandstone slab between the tree and the adjacent Mahabodhi Temple was placed by Ashoka to mark the spot of Buddha's enlightenment – it's referred to as the Vajrasan (Diamond Throne).

Great Buddha Statue BUDDHIST, MONUMENT

(off Temple St; ⏲7am-5.30pm) FREE This 25m-high Japanese-style statue towers above

Bodhgaya

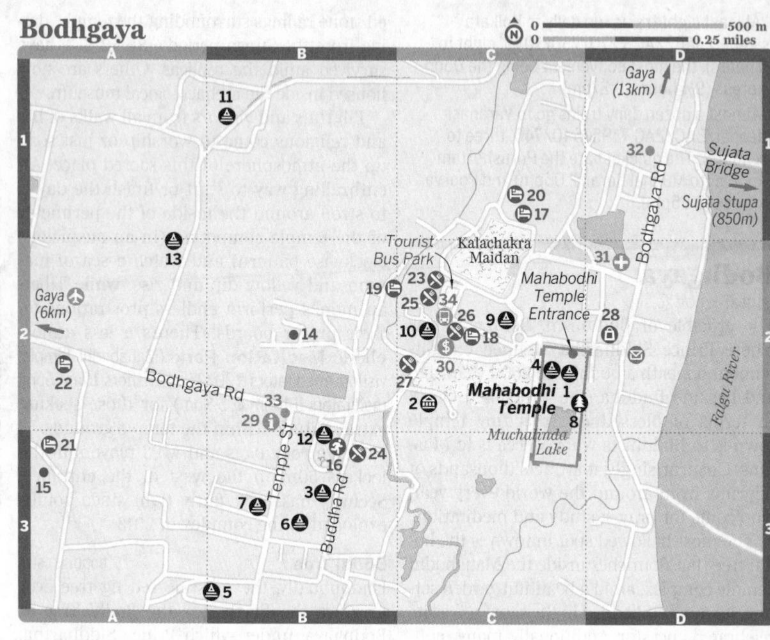

Bodhgaya

Top Sights
1 Mahabodhi Temple C2

Sights
2 Archaeological Museum C2
3 Bhutanese Monastery B3
4 Bodhi Tree C2
5 Great Buddha Statue B3
6 Indosan Nipponji Temple B3
7 Karma Temple B3
8 Meditation Park C2
9 Namgyal Monastery C2
10 Shechen Monastery C2
11 Tergar Monastery B1
12 Thai Temple B3
13 Vietnamese Monastery A2

Activities, Courses & Tours
14 International Meditation Centre B2
15 Root Institute for Wisdom Culture A3
Tergar Monastery .... (see 11)
16 Thai Massage B3

Sleeping
17 Gupta House C1
18 Kirti Guest House C2
19 Mohammad House B2
20 Rahul Guest House C1
21 Shantidevi Ashram's Guesthouse A3
22 Taj Darbar A2

Eating
23 Be Happy Cafe C2
24 Bodhgaya City Cafe Restaurant B3
Hari Om International Cafe .... (see 17)
25 Mohammad Restaurant C2
26 Ram Sewak Tea Corner C2
27 Siam Thai C2

Shopping
28 Middle Way Bookshop D2

Information
29 BSTDC Tourist Complex B2
30 State Bank of India C2
31 Verma Health Care Centre D2

Transport
32 Autorickshaws to Gaya D1
33 Indian Railways Reservation Counter B2
34 Jayjagdamba Travels C2

a pleasant garden at the end of Temple St. The impressive monument was unveiled by the Dalai Lama in 1989 and is surrounded by 10 smaller sculptures of Buddha's disciples. The statue is partially hollow and is said to contain some 20,000 bronze Buddhas.

Archaeological Museum MUSEUM
(off Bodhgaya Rd; ₹10; ⏲9am-5pm, closed Fri) This museum contains a number of (mostly headless) stone Buddhist sculptures dating from the 8th to 12th centuries, but the highlight is the collection of 2000-year-old granite and sandstone railings and pillars rescued from the Mahabodhi Temple. No photos.

Dungeshwari Cave BUDDHIST SITE
(Mahakala Cave; ⏲dawn-dusk) FREE This fairly nondescript cave in the Pragbodhi Hills northeast of Bodhgaya is where Buddha is said to have spent seven years living as an ascetic, almost dying from starvation in the process. There's not much to see but getting here is fun; either on a motorbike tour or on foot.

Sujata Stupa BUDDHIST STUPA
The huge Sujata Kuti stupa, across the Fagu River from Bodhgaya, was built to commemorate the residence of Sujata, the cow-herder who fed the starving Buddha rice pudding, thus ending his seven years of asceticism and spurring him to follow the Middle Way. The ancient brick stupa was originally covered with lime plaster and painted white. It's a 20-minute walk from Bodhgaya.

Thai Massage MASSAGE
(☎8294782534; Thai Temple; 1/2hr massage ₹800/1500; ⏲8am-noon & 1-6pm) Authentic Thai massage in a clinic at the Thai Hospital, located within the grounds of the Thai Temple; take the entrance to the left of the main temple entrance. Book a day or two in advance.

Other Temples & Monasteries

One of Bodhgaya's great joys is its collection of monasteries and temples, each offering visitors a unique opportunity to peek into different Buddhist cultures and compare architectural styles.

The **Indosan Nipponji Temple** (Japanese Temple; Buddha Rd; ⏲6am-noon & 2-6pm) is an exercise in quiet Japanese understatement and has meditation at 5pm. In contrast is the nearby ornate **Bhutanese Monastery** (Buddha Rd), which has images of the kings of Bhutan and the bearded Zhabdrung, Bhutan's religious leader, as well as some unusual 3D frescoes. The most impressive of all the modern monasteries is the **Tergar Monastery** (Sujata Bypass Rd) of the Karmapa school of Tibetan Buddhism, where the 17th Karmapa is often in residence. It has a small cafe. Nearby is the calming **Vietnamese Monastery** with lush gardens and an eight-storey pagoda. Another stunner is the sublime **Thai Temple** (Bodhgaya Rd), a brightly coloured *wat* with gold leaf shimmering from its arched rooftop and manicured gardens. Meditation is held here mornings and evenings.

The Tibetan **Karma Temple** (Temple St) (note the double-dragon brass door knockers) and **Namgyal Monastery** (Tibetan Temple; Kalachakra Maidan Rd) each contain large prayer wheels. The Nyingmapa-school **Shechen Monastery** has a large stupa that contains bone fragments of the Buddha.

Monasteries are open sunrise to sunset, closed noon to 2pm. Between 4pm and 6pm is a good time to visit, as there is often chanting and meditation.

Courses

Root Institute for Wisdom Culture MEDITATION
(☎0631-2200714; www.rootinstitute.ngo; ⏲office 9am-noon & 1.15-5pm) Located in a tranquil, tree-shaded corner of town, this foreign-run institute holds various meditation courses (from two to 21 days) between October and March. Courses cost around ₹1000 per day, including meals and accommodation. The 6.45am meditation session is open to all.

Tergar Monastery MEDITATION
(☎0631-2201256) Offers courses on Tibetan Buddhism and welcomes long-term qualified volunteer English teachers.

Sleeping

Budget guesthouses are concentrated on the northern side of the Kalachakra Maidan.

If there's space, you can stay at the peaceful Root Institute for Wisdom Culture (p527) even if you're not attending any of its courses. Dorm beds cost ₹250, while double rooms go for ₹900, or ₹1500 with a private bathroom.

★**Rahul Guest House** GUESTHOUSE $
(☎0631-2200709; rahul_bodhgaya@yahoo.co.in; near Kalachakra Maidan; s/d ₹500/700, with AC ₹800-1000; 📶) Clean and serene, with sociable balcony seating, this family home makes for an excellent stay away from the din, even if the welcome is slightly cool. The rooms upstairs, with whitewashed walls, nice breezes and simple furnishings, are better than those on the ground floor, but all

are good value, particularly the four air-con rooms. Laundry service is available.

Mohammad House GUESTHOUSE $
(9934022691, 9431085251; yasmd_2002@gmail.com; r ₹300-600;) There's an authentic village atmosphere at this hard-to-find, no-frills guesthouse, which is hidden away from the more touristy parts of town. Ducks and chickens scuttle around the narrow lanes that link villagers' colourfully painted homes to the Kalachakra Maidan area.

The guesthouse has two buildings, almost side by side; the older one has very basic rooms with shared squat bathrooms (₹300). The newer one has cleaner, nicer modern twin rooms with clean attached bathrooms and powerful, hot-water showers (₹600). Both have rooms on upper floors with lovely views of the surrounding paddy fields. To find this guesthouse, either take the lane beside Mohammad Restaurant (same owners), and walk through the village, turning left then right, or take the lane diagonally opposite the Thai Temple (signposted towards the International Meditation Centre) and keep walking straight.

Gupta House GUESTHOUSE $
(0631-2200933; jyoti_gupta2000in@yahoo.com; beside Kalachakra Maidan; d ₹500-600;) Rooms are spartan but comfortable enough at this newly renovated guesthouse, with back rooms looking out onto a huge new Tibetan monastery. The alfresco Hari Om International Cafe out the front is an advantage.

★ Shantidevi Ashram's Guesthouse GUESTHOUSE $$
(9852053186; www.shantideviashramguesthouse.com; r ₹2000;) This unassuming but tastefully decorated boutique-like guesthouse makes a simple Zen-like retreat from the hustle and bustle of the main drags. Fan-cooled rooms come with pieces of artwork, colourful rugs on concrete floors and super-hard beds. Bathrooms are small but spotless. There's no restaurant, but guests can use the kitchen and washing machine.

Kirti Guest House HOTEL $$
(0631-2200744; kirtihouse744@yahoo.com; off Bodhgaya Rd; s/d incl breakfast ₹2500/2750;) Run by the Kiirti Monastery in Dharamsala, this central hotel offers a quiet atmosphere despite its central location. It's set back from the road slightly and has 60 comfortable modern rooms.

Taj Darbar HOTEL $$$
(7739320524, 0631-2200053; www.hoteltajdarbar.com; Bodhgaya Rd; s/d incl breakfast from ₹5490/6570;) A somewhat old-fashioned, upper midrange choice, this smart hotel comes with polished marble hallways and spacious rooms with ivory-white bed sheets, small seating areas, desks and sporadic bath-tubs. It's comfortable but not luxurious. Discounts of 20% are standard.

Eating

★ Mohammad Restaurant MULTICUISINE $
(mains ₹80-220; 7.30am-9.30pm;) Tucked away behind the market stalls at the Tourist Bus Park (take the lane beside Fujiya Green restaurant), Mohammad's whips up a fine array of food from across the Buddhist world – Tibetan, Chinese, Thai, Indian – as well as doing a strong line in Western favourites, including breakfasts and espresso coffee. The fresh fruit juices are superb and there's pleasant outdoor seating.

Hari Om International Cafe MULTICUISINE $
(Kalachakra Maidan; mains ₹80-120; 7am-10pm;) This informal, shanty-like, alfresco restaurant on the north side of the Kalachakra maidan has a backpacker-friendly menu, with lots of vegetarian options. Among the banana pancakes you'll find local specialities such as *litti chokha* and *khichdi* (a rice thali with chutneys and mashed potato).

Bodhgaya City Cafe Restaurant INDIAN $
(Buddha Rd; mains ₹60-200; 8am-9.30pm) Good-value local food with pleasant outdoor seating in a newly built restaurant-and-cafe complex. It's conveniently close to many of the monasteries.

Ram Sewak Tea Corner FAST FOOD $
(dishes ₹50-100; 6am-10pm) If you're seeking sustenance at rock-bottom prices, look no further than this *dhaba*-style eatery, little more than a glorified roadside stand, for excellent snacks (including samosa, dosa and *idli* – a South Indian spongy, round, fermented rice cake), sweets, lassis and basic thalis. The outdoor bench seating is a great spot to lounge with a cup of masala chai and watch Bodhgaya go by.

★ Be Happy Cafe ITALIAN $$
(beside Kalachakra Maidan; mains ₹150-420; 8am-8.30pm;) Quaint, cosy, cafe serving fresh coffee (₹100), herbal teas and healthy Italian cuisine: salads, pastas and

freshly baked pizza. This is one place where you can trust the salads and fresh vegetables, and the desserts are the best in town. Reservations are a good idea for lunch.

Siam Thai THAI
(Bodhgaya Rd; curries ₹200; ⏲8.30am-10pm) Authentically delicious curries made from ingredients flown in from Thailand, plus interesting starters such as fish cakes and *larb kai* (minced chicken with lemon, lemongrass and mint). The chicken *paenang* is addictive; for something sweeter try the *massaman* curry. The yellow-robed monks who fill the place know a good curry when they see it.

Shopping

Middle Way Bookshop BOOKS
(⏲10am-9pm) A good selection of new and used novels and books on Buddhism and spirituality.

Information

BSTDC Tourist Complex (☎0631-2200672; cnr Bodhgaya Rd & Temple St; ⏲10.30am-5pm Tue-Sat) Basic information available.

Main Post Office (cnr Bodhgaya & Godam Rds; ⏲10am-3pm Mon-Fri, to 2pm Sat)

State Bank of India (Bodhgaya Rd; ⏲10.30am-4.30pm Mon-Fri, to 1.30pm Sat) Best rates for cash and travellers cheques; has an ATM.

Verma Health Care Centre (☎0631-2201101, 9934290324; ⏲24hr) Emergency room and clinic. Staffed round the clock, but a doctor is only on location from 11.30am to 8pm.

Getting There & Away

Gaya airport is 8km west of Bodhgaya, on the back route to Gaya. **Air India** (☎0631-2201155; www.airindia.com; Airport) flies daily to Delhi and Varanasi, and twice weekly to Kolkata. Between October and March there are direct international flights from Bangkok (Thailand), Colombo (Sri Lanka), Paro (Bhutan) and Yangon (Myanmar).

Shared **autorickshaws** (₹25) leave from north of the Mahabodhi Temple for the 13km trip to Gaya, though not all go as far as the train station. A private autorickshaw to Gaya costs ₹150.

Note, autos occasionally take the back route from Gaya to Bodhgaya, via Sikadia More, and then drop passengers on the approach to Mahabodhi Temple on Bodhgaya Rd.

A few noiseless electric autorickshaws run in Bodhgaya; you can encourage this trend by taking these whenever possible.

Jayjagdamba Travels (☎9472964873; Tourist Bus Park) operates non-air-con buses to Varanasi (₹350, seven hours) at 7am, 9am and 5pm, as well as a 2pm bus to Siliguri (₹700 to ₹750, 16 hours), and can arrange a private car to Varanasi for ₹4500.

You can buy train tickets from the **Indian Railways Reservation Counter** (Bodhgaya Rd; ⏲8am-noon & 12.30-2pm Mon-Sat), next to the BSTDC Tourist Complex.

Rajgir

☎06112 / POP 33,700

The fascinating surrounds of Rajgir are bounded by five semiarid rocky hills, each lined with ancient stone walls – vestiges of the ancient capital of Magadha. As both Buddha and the Mahavira spent some serious time here, Rajgir is an important pilgrimage site for Buddhists and Jains. And a mention in the Mahabharata also means that Rajgir sees a large number of Hindu pilgrims, who come to bathe in the hot springs at the Lakshmi Narayan Temple.

Rajgir is littered with historic sites, so bank on spending a couple of days here, including a side trip to Nalanda. It's a lovely part of Bihar; greener and more rural than other places in the region, and relatively hassle-free.

Rajgir Mahotsava (Rajgir; ⏲end Nov) is the town's major cultural festival, featuring three days of classical Indian music, folk music and dance at the end of November, or sometimes December.

Sights & Activities

The most pleasant way to see Rajgir's scattered sites is to rent a tonga (two-wheeled horse-drawn carriage). A half-day tour including the ropeway (chairlift) to Vishwa Shanti Stupa and surrounding sights is around ₹500. You can also pay for one-way journeys to single sites (eg ₹100 to Vulture Hill).

★ **Vishwa Shanti Stupa** BUDDHIST STUPA
(Shanti Stupa Rd; chairlift return ticket ₹60; ⏲ropeway 8.15am-1pm & 2-5pm) Constructed in 1965, this blazing-white, 40m stupa stands atop Ratnagiri Hill about 5km south of town. Recesses in the stupa feature golden statues of Buddha in four stages of his life – birth, enlightenment, preaching and death. A fun, but wobbly, single-person chairlift runs to the summit, which affords expansive views of hills and a few Jain shrines dotting the landscape.

Vulture Hill BUDDHIST SITE

(Griddhakuta) Buddha is thought to have preached the Lotus sutra on this rock outcrop. There are some faint remains of a 1500-year-old stupa, some prayer flags and a small shrine where Buddhist pilgrims come to pray. Get here by walking down from the Vishwa Shanti Stupa and detouring for a 10-minute walk uphill along a processional way built by King Bimbisara 2500 years ago.

Saptaparni Cave BUDDHIST SITE

(dawn-4pm) A 40-minute uphill hike from the back of the Lakshmi Narayan Temple takes you past Jain and Hindu temples to this atmospheric cave and natural rock platform, where Buddha is said to have meditated. It's the likely location for the First Buddhist Council, held six months after Buddha's death to define the direction of the new faith.

Lakshmi Narayan Temple HINDU TEMPLE

(dawn-dusk) FREE Hindu pilgrims visit the Lakshmi Narayan Temple, about 2km south of town (turn right out of the bus stand and keep walking), to enjoy the health benefits of the hot springs here. The murky grey Brahmakund, the hottest spring, is a scalding 45°C. Temple priests will show you around, pour hot water on your head as a blessing and ask for generous donations (there's no obligation to give).

Buddha Jal Vihar SWIMMING

(swimming ₹25; men 5-10am & noon-9pm, women 10am-noon) Next to the Lakshmi Narayan Temple complex (on your left as you approach the temple), the Jaipur-pink Buddha Jal Vihar is an inviting, crystal-clear swimming pool set in well-manicured gardens and perfect to beat the heat.

Sleeping

Hotel Vijay Niketan GUESTHOUSE $

(06112-255555, 9334647881; www.hotelvijayniketan.com; Police Station Rd; r ₹750-900;) The budget rooms here are a bit rough at the edges but are decent for the price (which is often negotiable). It's run by two helpful English-speaking brothers, who can fix any issues with hot water or wi-fi. Upper-floor rooms are best but can be hot, and there are a couple of overpriced air-con rooms (₹1650).

Hotel Nalanda Regency HOTEL $$

(7766969099; www.hotelnalandaregency.com; r incl breakfast ₹4500;) Perhaps the best-run hotel in town, rooms here are fresh and modern with hot-water bathrooms and an excellent restaurant (mains ₹125 to ₹225), just two minutes' walk north of the bus stand. Walk-in discounts of 40% can make it excellent value.

Indo Hokke Hotel BOUTIQUE HOTEL $$$

(06612-255245; www.theroyalresidency.co; Veerayatan Rd; s/d incl breakfast ₹6000/6500;) Surrounded by 3 hectares of lovely gardens, this modern, red-brick building features clean, modern rooms and good service. It's a quiet place with a Buddhist chapel and hot bath for groups. The rooms with tiled floors are biggest. It's 500m beyond Veerayatan museum, 3km south and then west of the bus stand.

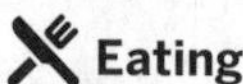

Eating

Hotel Anand PUNJABI $

(Dharmshala Rd; mains ₹50-100; 8am-10pm;) This small, fan-cooled, vegetarian restaurant serves good-value Punjabi and South Indian dishes, including good thalis (₹90 to ₹150). It's 100m beyond the Hotel Raj.

Green Hotel INDIAN $

(mains ₹60-150, thali ₹125-250; 7.30am-9.30pm) Diagonally opposite the Lakshmi Narayan Temple complex, this simple restaurant is one of several in a row that offers very pleasant alfresco seating. The food is good and it's a great place to relax at the end of the day.

Lotus Restaurant INDIAN, JAPANESE $$$

(Veerayatan Rd; mains ₹150-375, Japanese dishes ₹300-600; 11am-3pm & 7-10pm;) The air-conditioned restaurant at the Indo Hokke Hotel has superb Indian food and a pricier Japanese menu featuring soba noodles, teriyaki and tempura, with authentic flavours and fresh ingredients (including pepper, pickles and green tea).

Information

Tourist Information Centre (8292984850; 10am-5pm) The tourist information centre near the bus stand has a few leaflets and a map of Rajgir.

Getting There & Away

Buses run every 30 minutes to Gaya (₹50 to ₹55, 2½ hours) and Nalanda (₹10, 20 minutes) from the bus stand. For Nalanda take a bus bound for Bihar Sharif.

Two fast trains runs daily to Patna (2nd class/sleeper/AC chair ₹50/140/260, 2½ hours) at 8.10am (sleeper) and 2.40pm (chair car).

The bus stand is in the centre of town, with the train station 1km to the north; turn left out of the bus stand and take the third left to reach the train station. Turn right out of the train station road to reach the bus stand and the town centre.

Nalanda

☎06112

Founded in the 5th century AD, Nalanda – 15km north of Rajgir – was one of the ancient world's great universities and an important Buddhist centre of academic excellence. When Chinese scholar and traveller Xuan Zang visited sometime between 685 and 762 AD, about 10,000 monks and students lived here, studying theology, astronomy, metaphysics, medicine and philosophy. It's said that Nalanda's three libraries were so extensive they burnt for six months when foreign invaders sacked the university in 1193.

Buses from Rajgir (₹10) drop you at Nalanda village. From there you can take a shared tonga (per person/cart ₹5/50) for the final 2km to the ruins.

Allow at least an hour or two for wandering the extensive monastery **ruins** (Indian/foreigner ₹15/200, video camera ₹25; ⌚9am-5.30pm). They're peaceful and well maintained with a parklike atmosphere of clipped lawns and shrubs. The red-brick ruins consist of 11 monasteries and six temples. Most impressive is the Great Stupa (Number Three), with steps, terraces, monks' residences and a few intact Gupta-era stupas. It is thought that a huge statue of Buddha once crowned the building. Climbing the structures is not allowed. Unofficial guides (₹100) will approach you, but each of the ruins has signboards beside them including explanatory text in English.

Across from the entrance to the ruins is the **archaeological museum** (admission ₹5; ⌚9am-5pm, closed Fri), a small but fascinating museum housing the Nalanda University seal and a host of beautiful stone sculptures and bronzes unearthed from Nalanda and Rajgir. Among the many Buddha figures and *kirtimukha* (gargoyle) is a bizarre multiple-spouted pot (probably once used to contain perfumed water).

About 2km further on from the museum and the ruins (take the first right) is the huge, modern **Xuan Zang Memorial Hall** (Indian/foreigner ₹5/50; ⌚8am-5pm), built by the Chinese in honour of the famous Chinese pilgrim who walked to India from China before studying and teaching for several years at Nalanda, and eventually returning home with Buddhist scriptures he would later translate into Chinese. His epic trip was immortalised in *Journey to the West,* one of China's classic pieces of literature. The story was then turned into the cult 1970s TV show, *Monkey.* Modern-day backpackers will appreciate the statue of Xuan Zang at the front of the memorial hall. A return tonga ride here costs ₹100.

About 1.5km beyond the Nalanda ruins (bear left, then right, then take the first right turn after Surya Kund pond), you'll find the striking **Nandyavarta Mahal** (⌚5am-9pm) at Kundalpur, a temple complex believed by the Digambar Jain sect to be the birthplace of Lord Mahavira, the final *tirthankar* and founder of Jainism. You can also walk here from the Xuan Zang Memorial Hall.

On the pathway leading to the archaeological museum, **Cafeteria Nalanda** (mains ₹150-250; ⌚8am-7pm) makes a pleasant spot for lunch. Otherwise a few simple roadside stalls sell snacks.

JHARKHAND

Hewn out of neighbouring Bihar in 2000 to meet the autonomy demands of the Adivasi (tribal) population, Jharkhand is a land of immense natural and anthropological wealth. However, despite boasting an incredible 40% of the country's mineral wealth (mostly coal, copper and iron ore), rich forests and cash-rich industrial hubs, it is plagued by poverty, social injustice, corruption, and sporadic outbursts of Maoist and Naxalite violence. For travellers, Jharkhand's prime attractions are the Jain pilgrimage centre at Parasnath Hill, its national parks, and the chance to explore a relatively tourist-free and unspoilt part of India.

Ranchi

☎0651 / POP 1.1 MILLION

Set on a plateau at 700m and marginally cooler than the plains, Jharkhand's capital, Ranchi, was the summer capital of Bihar under the British. There's little of interest here for travellers, but the city acts as a gateway to Betla (Palamau) National Park, and there are numerous waterfalls you can visit in the surrounding countryside.

Sights

State Museum MUSEUM
(☎0651-2270011; www.statemuseumranchi.in; Hotwar, Khelgaon; Indian/foreigner ₹5/100,

OFF THE BEATEN TRACK

HIKING HOLY PARASNATH

For a fabulously off-beat experience with a spiritual leaning, consider joining the hundreds of Jain pilgrims who hike each morning to the top of holy Parasnath Hill.

Also known as Shikarji (Venerated Peak), Parasnath is the highest mountain in Jharkhand at 1336m, and is a major Jain pilgrimage centre. The ridge top is studded with 31 *tonk* (shrines), including the striking white Parasnath Temple, where 20 of the 24 Jain *tirthankars* (including Parasnath, at the age of 100) are believed to have reached salvation.

The approach to the hill is from the small temple town of Madhuban, 13km northeast of Parasnath train station. The daily pilgrimage begins from the town at around 4am; it's a 9km hike to the top, gaining 1000m elevation, followed by a 9km clockwise loop around a ridgeline, before reaching the highest peak at Parasnath Temple. For the correct clockwise circuit, take the left branch about halfway up the hill, rather than the right-hand trail straight up to Parasnath Temple. The entire 27km circuit – up, round and back down – takes about eight hours; three hours up, three hours circuiting the peaks, and two hours back down. You could start later in the day and still get back before dark, but hiking while you're half asleep with hundreds of pilgrims as dawn breaks across the mountain is a big part of the experience, and it means you avoid the worst of the midday heat. Water, chai and snacks are available along the way. During holidays and major festivals, you could end up walking with as many as 15,000 people, many of whom pay to be carried up in a *dholi* (litter).

You're likely to spend at least one night in Madhuban. There are three or four hotels in town (plus numerous *dharamsalas* – pilgrims' rest houses). Best value is the ageing government-run **Yatri Nivas** (☎9470184432, 8102761253; Madhuban; r ₹400-500) with simple but huge rooms. It's at the bottom end of the main road leading up to the mountain, next to a creek, and just before you reach the museum; there's no English sign. Just before Yatri Nivas, turn left down a lane off the main road, and keep walking for 500m to reach the **Shikarji Continental** (☎9323360708, 9334294965; Madhuban; r ₹1500; ❄📶). This is Madhuban's best-quality hotel, with modern but grubby air-con rooms; the massage room (per hour ₹400) is perfect after your hike. **Hotel Sapna & Veg Restaurant** (☎06558-232234; Main Rd, Madhuban; mains ₹50-130; ⏰11am-10pm; 🌱), towards the top end of the main road at a bend, has a 1st-floor restaurant serving simple South Indian and Punjabi dishes.

Parasnath is most easily reached from Gaya, from where there are frequent trains (two hours). For maximum comfort book an air-con chair-car class (₹285 to ₹355) on the 8.20am Janshatabdi Express or the 2.08pm Patna-Hatia Express. Returning to Gaya these trains leave at 10.10am and 5.45pm. Alternatively, just buy a 'general' 2nd-class ticket (₹65 to ₹80) and hop on the next train; you'll usually get a seat, and if not, it's only two hours.

Cramped shared vehicles (jeeps, autos and even the odd bus) carry passengers from Parasnath train station to Madhuban (per person ₹30). A chartered minivan costs ₹300.

From Parasnath there are also trains to Ranchi (2nd class ₹110, AC chair ₹300 to ₹375, four hours, 10.20am and 4.25pm) and Varanasi (2nd class/sleeper ₹130/255, six hours, 11.21am), and a handful of trains to Kolkata, the most convenient being the Doon Express (sleeper/3AC/2AC ₹210/555/790, seven hours, 11.55pm).

camera/video ₹25/100; ⏰10.30am-4.30pm Tue-Sun) This surprisingly large state museum has some ethnographic displays, featuring ornate bows and jewellery, but the main draw is the sculpture gallery, with its fine carvings and intriguing photos of remote architectural sites across Jharkhand. It's 8km northeast of the train station; figure on a one-way autorickshaw ride of around ₹200.

Sleeping

Station Rd, running between the train and bus stations, is lined with hotels and a convenient place to stay, but most budget places don't have permits for hosting foreigners.

Hotel AVN Plaza HOTEL $$

(☎0651-2462231; www.hotelavnplaza.com; off Station Rd; s/d incl breakfast from ₹1700/2190; ❄📶)

This neat, modern hotel has small but spotlessly clean rooms with TV, wi-fi and modern hot-water showers. Some rooms have no windows. There are only six standard non-air-con rooms (double ₹1070), but these are small and stuffy, with no natural light. It's down a lane, off Station Rd, so is pretty quiet. It has 24-hour checkout. Ask for a 15% discount.

★**Chanakya BNR Hotel** HERITAGE HOTEL **$$$**
(☎0651-2461211; www.chanakyabnrranchi.com; Station Rd; s/d incl breakfast ₹6350/7880; ❄@🛜🏊) This charming hotel could be your sole reason for visiting Ranchi. A part-historic railways property located outside the train station, it's a superbly renovated terracotta-roofed Raj relic that oozes vintage and boutique appeal. The property's trees are home to parrots, and it has a small outdoor pool, two excellent restaurants and a modern bar.

✕ Eating

Hotel AVN Plaza (p532) and Chanakya BNR Hotel (p533) both have restaurants that are open to nonguests; Chanakya BNR's two restaurants are particularly good (mains ₹400).

Nook INDIAN **$$**
(Station Rd; mains ₹100-200; ⌚7.30am-11pm) Arguably the best midrange hotel restaurant in the train-station area, this in-house dining facility at Hotel Kwality Inns is comfortable and the service attentive without being obsequious. The tandoori dishes are excellent, especially the creamy *murgh tikka lababdar*.

ℹ Orientation

Turn left out of the train station to reach Chanakya BNR Hotel (100m), Nook, Suhana Tour & Travels (200m), Hotel AVN Plaza (300m) and the government bus stand (500m), just beyond the junction where shared autorickshaws pick up passengers.

ℹ Getting There & Around

AIR

Ranchi's Birsa Munda Airport is 6km south of the city centre. Between them **Air India** (☎2503255; www.airindia.com), Indigo and **GoAir** (☎1800 222111; www.goair.in) fly daily to Kolkata, Delhi, Patna and Mumbai.

A prepaid taxi to Station Rd from the airport is ₹250. An autorickshaw in the opposite direction is ₹150.

BUS

From the government bus stand on Station Rd, there are hourly buses to Gaya throughout the day (₹160, six hours) and numerous overnight services to Patna (standard/AC ₹250/450, nine hours), which leave from around 9pm onwards.

Private sleeper and air-con buses to cities such as Kolkata (seat/sleeper ₹250/300, AC bus ₹360 to ₹850, 10 hours, from 8pm onwards) and Bhubaneswar (sleeper ₹500, 13 hours, 7pm) leave from Khartatoli bus stand, 2km northeast of Station Rd (shared/private autorickshaw ₹10/100).

Buses to Daltonganj leave from ITI bus stand, 8km northwest of Station Rd (shared/private autorickshaw ₹20/200).

TRAIN

The handy 12366 Janshatabdi Express departs daily at 2.25pm to Patna (2nd class/chair ₹185/630, seven hours), via Parasnath (₹110/375, three hours) and Gaya (₹160/530, 5½ hours). Alternatively, try the 18626 Hatia-Patna Express, departing at 6.35am.

For Kolkata (chair car/3AC/2AC ₹980/670/960, nine hours) the handiest trains are the daytime Shatabdi Express (1.45pm), or the overnight Kriya Yoga Express (9.40pm).

The once-daily Tapaswini Express goes to Bhubaneswar (sleeper/3AC/2AC ₹340/930/1335, 13 hours, 3.55pm).

Betla (Palamau) National Park

☎06562

Wild elephants freely roam the virgin forests of this lovely, rarely visited **national park** (☎06562-222650, 9939341211; ⌚6-10am & 2-5pm), spread over the hilly landscape of picturesque Palamau district, 140km west of Ranchi. Tiger sightings are extremely rare, but a trip to this primeval region of Jharkhand offers a glimpse into the rich tribal heritage of the state. The park covers around 1026 sq km, much of which comprises the Palamau Tiger Reserve. Hiding behind stands of sal forest, rich evergreens, teak trees and bamboo thickets are some 17 tigers, 52 leopards, 216 elephants and four lonely nilgai (antelope). You'll also see plenty of monkeys, spotted deer and possibly some gaur (Indian bison).

The park is open year-round, but the best time to visit is November to April. If you can stand the heat, May is prime for tiger spotting as forest cover is reduced and animals venture out in search of waterholes.

JEEP SAFARI COSTS

Jeep safaris can be arranged at the Betla (Palamau) National Park gate. The breakdown of the costs for jeep safaris is as follows:

Park entry (per vehicle, per hour) ₹150

Compulsory guide (per vehicle, per hour) ₹100

Jeep hire (per vehicle, per hour) ₹500

Camera fee (per person, per safari) ₹100

So, for example; a two-hour jeep safari for two people, both with cameras, would cost a total of ₹1700. For a single person, it would cost ₹1600. Jeep safaris can last from one hour to up to three or four hours, depending on how long you wish to spend in the park.

Activities

The two main ways to visit Betla are on a jeep safari or on elephant-back, and both can be arranged at the park gate. However, elephant rides involve the use of a *howdah* – a common practice in India but one which is discouraged by animal-welfare groups because of the injuries that this can cause to elephants.

Jeep safaris can be taken either during the park's morning session (between 6am and 10am) or afternoon session (between 2pm and 5pm), but elephant safaris can only be taken in the morning and cost a flat-rate ₹400 per elephant (for up to four people). The elephant takes you off-piste, into thick forest cover, although not as deep into the park as the jeeps do.

It's a good idea to book a morning safari the night before. If you take a morning safari, wrap up warm; it's freezing in the forest before the sun comes up properly. If you don't have any warm clothes, borrow a blanket from your guesthouse to wrap yourself up in.

If you have time on your hands, consider the hour-long jeep excursion to the ruined Palamau Fort, a 16th-century citadel of the local tribal Chero dynasty sited spectacularly within the forest. Alternatively, plan a picnic on the sandy banks of the scenic Kechki River. A jeep tour to the fort or Kechki River costs the same as a jeep safari, minus the ₹150 park entry fee.

Sleeping & Eating

The majority of visitors stay overnight at the government-run **Van Vihar** (☎9102403882; d ₹1580; ❄), 100m before the park entrance. Rooms are comfortable, spacious and clean, with hot-water bathrooms and a balcony, though the exuberant groups can be noisy.

The other sleeping options are just inside the park gate and can only be booked through the Forestry Department in Daltonganj, which can be a hassle. The most atmospheric accommodation is **Tourist Lodge** (☎bookings 06562-222650; d from ₹1180; ❄). It's not luxurious, but boasts large clean rooms with TV, spacious bathrooms and private balconies with views of the deer-filled meadow in front of the forest.

About 50 paces from the lodge, and also just inside the park entrance, is the **Tree House** (☎bookings 06562-222650; r ₹690), with two elevated sets of rooms, a bathroom and an observation deck with the same views as Tourist Lodge. It's more basic, but great value.

Food options can be limited in Betla, so bring some snacks. The well-priced canteen beside the Tourist Lodge does post-safari breakfasts and arranges a hearty vegetarian thali (₹100) for lunch and dinner with advance notice.

Getting There & Away

The nearest town to the park entrance is Daltonganj, about 20km away, which has frequent bus services to Ranchi throughout the day (₹150, 4½ hours). From Daltonganj take a local bus (₹20, roughly hourly until around 4pm) or shared autorickshaw (₹30) to Betla. A private auto from Daltonganj will cost around ₹300. You can save some time by getting off the Ranchi bus at Dubiamar, the turn-off for Betla, about 10km before Daltonganj. From here you can wave down a passing bus (₹10) or hire a private auto (₹200) to the park. Buses run from Betla back to Daltonganj and on to Ranchi until around 4pm.

If you don't fancy going it alone, **Suhana Tour & Travels** (☎9431171394; suhana_jharkhandtour@yahoo.co.in; Gurunanak Market, Station Rd; ⊙8am-8pm Mon-Sat, to 2pm Sun), based in Ranchi, does two-day trips to Betla for ₹4600 per person (minimum two people).

Sikkim

Includes ➡

Best Places to Sleep

- Chumbi Mountain Retreat (p553)
- Bamboo Retreat (p546)
- Lake View Nest (p554)
- Mayallyang Homestay (p547)
- Hotel Garuda (p552)

Best Monasteries

- Resum Gompa (p558)
- Tashiding Gompa (p557)
- Lingdum Gompa (p545)
- Palchen Choeling Monastery (p550)
- Ngadak Gompa (p549)

Why Go?

Sikkim was its own mountain kingdom till 1975 and still retains a very distinctive personality. The meditative, mural-filled traditional monasteries of Tibetan Buddhism coexist with Hindu shrines of the ever-growing Nepali community, both religions creating some astonishing latter-day mega-sculptures to adorn the skyline.

Hassle-free and warm-hearted, it's a state that's all too easy to fall in love with, explaining perhaps why permit regulations prevent foreigners staying too long or going too far. Clean, green and 'all organic' since 2016, Sikkim is mostly a maze of plunging, super-steep valleys thick with lush subtropical woodlands and rhododendron groves, rising in the north to the spectacular white-top peaks of the eastern Himalaya. When clouds clear, an ever-thrilling experience from many a ridgetop perch is spotting the world's third-highest mountain, Khangchendzonga (8598m), on the northwestern dawn horizon.

When to Go

Gangtok

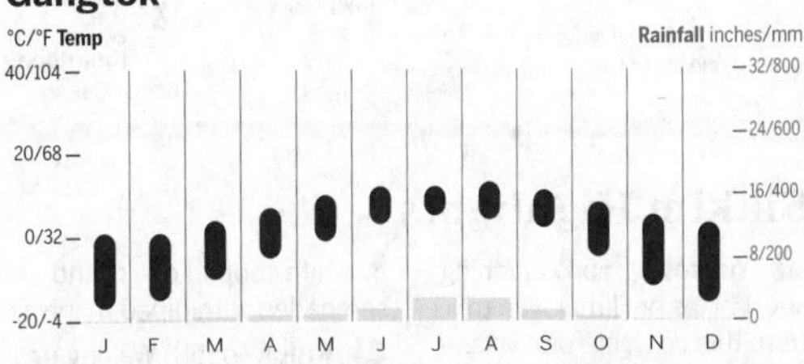

Apr & May Beautiful spring blossoms, partly clear skies, high-season crowds.

Mid-Jun–Sep Monsoon plays spoilsport, but there are great discounts on offer.

Mid-Oct–mid-Nov Clearest weather for fabulous views but gets cold at altitude.

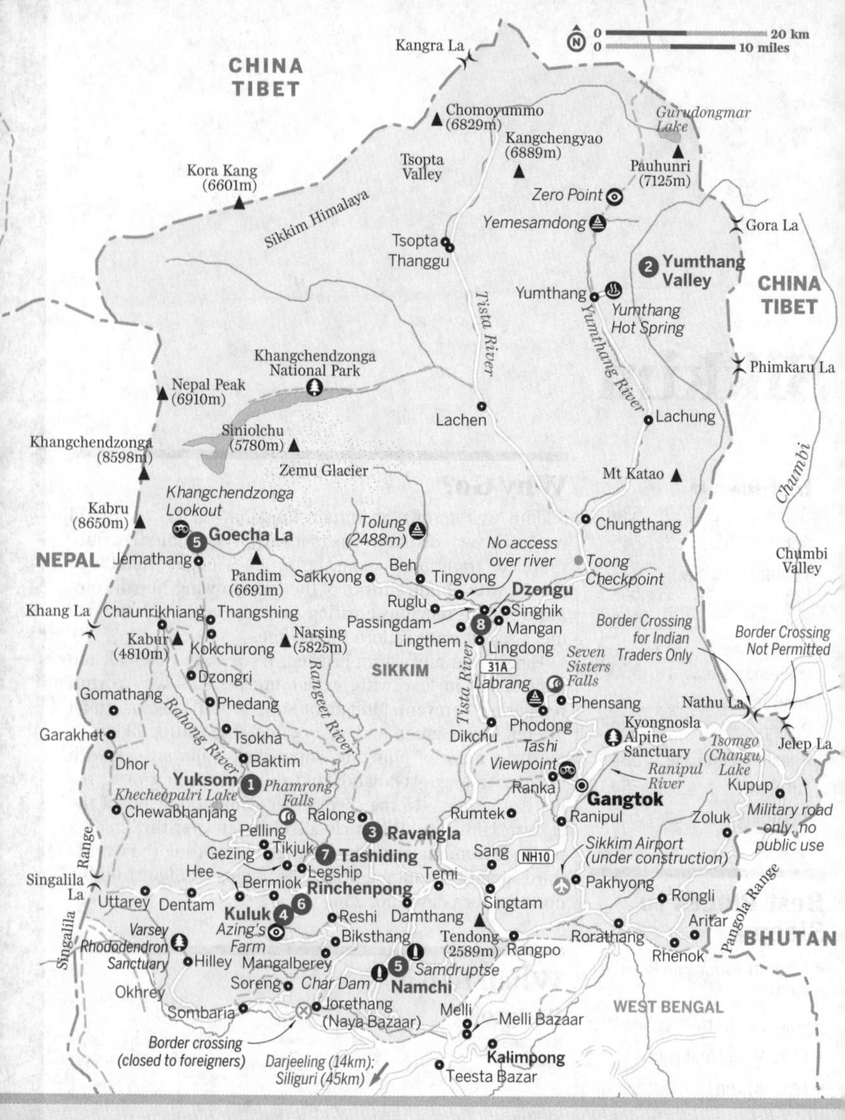

Sikkim Highlights

1. **Yuksom** (p554) Planning short hikes or Himalayan treks from this cosy, historic village.
2. **Yumthang Valley** (p548) Driving through a kaleidoscope of sceneries to and through this picture-perfect valley.
3. **Buddha Park** (p550) Gazing at Ravangla's giant, serene Buddha statue, backed by white-topped peaks and serenaded with piped mantras.
4. **Kuluk** (p558) Waking up to dazzling Khangchendzonga views.
5. **Namchi** (p549) Finding a gigantic Shiva statue overshadowing a selection of India's greatest Hindu temples all recreated on a ridge.
6. **Rinchenpong** (p558) Exploring half-forgotten monasteries with stunning views.
7. **Tashiding Gompa** (p557) Wandering among prayer flags, flower hedges and ancient chortens (stupas).
8. **Dzongu** (p547) Learning about Lepcha culture in an authentic Dzongu homestay.

History

The etymology of Sikkim's traditional place names indicates that the Lepcha people were Sikkim's earliest long-term inhabitants, arriving by the 13th century from Assam or Myanmar/Burma. They were followed by Bhutias who struck south from Tibet in the 15th century, having secured a much-celebrated bond of friendship with the Lepchas at Kabi Lunchok (p547). However, the ascendency of the Bhutias and their Nyingmapa form of Vajrayana (Tibetan) Buddhism was underlined when three Tibetan lamas met in Yuksom in 1641 to crown Phuntsog Namgyal (a Bhutia) as first chogyal (king) of Sikkim. The capital later moved to Rabdentse (near Pelling), then to Tumlong in North Sikkim, before finally settling in Gangtok.

In their heydays, the chogyals ruled parts of what is now eastern Nepal, upper Bengal and Darjeeling. However, much territory was lost during wars with Bhutan and Nepal. In 1835, the British bamboozled the chogyal into ceding Darjeeling to the East India Company for a nominal rent, a move that was strongly opposed by Tibet, which had regarded Sikkim as a vassal state. In 1849, the British annexed the entire area between the present Sikkim border and the Ganges plains, and subsequently repulsed a counter-invasion by Tibet in 1886. The later 19th century saw large numbers of Hindu migrants, encouraged by the British, arriving from Nepal; these migrants would ultimately form a majority of Sikkim's population.

When India gained independence in 1947, Sikkim's status was nebulous, as there had never been a formal agreement with Britain and the chogyal hoped to follow the Nepali and Bhutanese examples of independence. This worked for a couple of decades, with the Sikkimese kingdom retaining formal autonomy but allowing India to direct all foreign policy. However, in 1975 the last chogyal and his American-born queen were deposed when Sikkim became incorporated as an Indian state.

Activities

Trekking is a high point of any Sikkim sojourn. Mountaineers considering the state's numerous 6000-plus-metre peaks should plan carefully with Namgyal Treks & Tours (p539) in Gangtok. Paragliding is possible in Gangtok and Pelling. BB Line (p539) arranges motorbike tours and is developing rafting, kayaking and bungee-jumping plans. It and **Hub Outdoor** (9443203848; www.huboutdoor.in; NH31A, Bojoghari; bike rental per day ₹1000; call ahead) have mountain-biking trips for the super-fit.

Permits

STANDARD PERMITS

Foreigners require an **Inner Line Permit (ILP)** to enter Sikkim (Indians don't). These are free and getting one is a formality, although to apply you'll need a passport-sized photo and photocopies of your passport and visa (show the original too). You can usually apply on the spot at the entry checkpoints at Melli (24 hours) and Rangpo (permits issued 8am to 7.30pm), though a few unlucky travellers report having found offices temporarily unstaffed. If you are arriving towards Gangtok outside the Rangpo hours you'll need the permit in advance. If you fly into Bagdogra, there's a small Sikkim Tourism booth (open 10am to 4pm or 5pm) at the airport that will usually issue the permit for you. You can also apply at **Sikkim House** (Map p454; 4/1 Middleton St; 10am-5pm Mon-Sat) in Kolkata, at the **Sikkim Tourist Office** (p493) in Siliguri, at **Sikkim House** (Map p72) in Delhi or by a more complicated two-stage process in Darjeeling (p497) involving first visiting the FRO (Foreigners' Registration Office) then crossing town to the DCO (District Commissioner's Office). You could also ask for a 15-day Sikkim permit at Indian embassies abroad when applying for your Indian visa.

A new checkpoint at Jorethang is planned.

The standard ILP is valid for 15 days, though longer validity is sometimes provided on request.

The permit allows you to travel to:

- Gangtok, Rumtek and Lingdum
- the southern parts of East Sikkim as far east as Rhenock and Aritar

TOP STATE FESTIVALS

Losar (Feb/Mar) Sikkim's biggest *chaam* (masked dance) rings in the Tibetan New Year.

Bumchu (Feb/Mar) Lamas open a *bum* (pot) containing *chu* (holy water) to foretell the year's fortunes.

Saga Dawa (May/Jun) Religious ceremonies and parades commemorate Buddha's birth, enlightenment and death.

Pang Lhabsol (Aug) Prayers and religious dances are performed in honour of Sikkim's guardian deity.

Losoong (Namsoong; Dec/Jan) The Sikkimese harvest festival is preceded by flamboyant *chaam* dances.

- all of South Sikkim
- North Sikkim as far as Singhik (just beyond Mangan)
- most of West Sikkim where paved roads extend.

SPECIAL PERMITS

High-altitude treks require **trekking permits**, organised by trekking agents, but you must be accompanied by a guide. Application is made in Gangtok, so if you join a tour in Yuksom or Utterey, allow at least a day (and pay suitable expenses) for your documents to be delivered to the capital and back.

For travel beyond Singhik up the Lachung and Lachen valleys in North Sikkim, foreigners need **restricted area permits**. These allow travel up to the Tsopta and Yumthang valleys. Indian citizens need a **police permit** to travel north of Singhik but can venture further up the Thanggu valley to Gurudongmar Lake, or to Yume Samdong (Zero-Point) past Yumthang. Permits can be procured in Gangtok on the morning of departure, or in Mangan in advance, but always through a registered agency and (for foreigners) requiring a minimum of two travellers.

For Dzongu (the Lepcha area north of Dikchu) you'll also need a special permit, usually organised through your pre-booked homestay. While the permit is free, homestay owners incur significant costs copying documents and taking taxis to Mangan to make arrangements on your behalf so will normally charge around ₹500 for the service.

A restricted area permit is required to visit Tsomgo (Changu) Lake, with only Indian citizens permitted to travel onward to the Tibetan border post at Nathu La. Again, tours are required and a minimum group of two foreigners.

Getting There & Away

AIR

Sikkim's new **airport** at Pakyong might have been completed a year or two back had it not been for a catastrophic collapse of the runway's high-tech mud-banking. Even when it does open, most travellers will probably still arrive at busy Bagdogra airport near Siliguri in West Bengal. There's a daily helicopter shuttle from there to Gangtok, but only five passengers are carried and it gets cancelled in inclement weather.

LAND

The nearest train station is at New Jaipalguri near Siliguri. The transfer to Siliguri from most tourist centres in Sikkim should take four to six hours by jeep, but potentially huge delays due to landslides and chaotic traffic mean that locals allow at least nine hours. Consider staying a night in Darjeeling or Kurseong the night before a flight or train journey to make the NJP–Bagdogra a lot dash less stressful.

BORDER CROSSING: TIBET

None of Sikkim's international border crossings are open to non-locals, though longer term there are discussions about opening the Nathu La. It is currently open only to select traders and groups of pilgrims. Indeed non-Indians aren't even allowed to visit the border zone.

Border Crossings

Sikkim's internal border with West Bengal has several crossing points, but due to permit-check procedures, foreigners are only supposed to use the Melli and Rangpo ones (both open 24 hours, but Rangpo issues permits between 8am and 7.30pm only). For now there's significant inconvenience if you want to link Pelling to Darjeeling via Jorethang, where the crossing has been only for Indians since 2016, though a new checkpoint there is planned.

Permit rules also blur the issue of legally trekking near Aritar, as some major trails cross into West Bengal.

EAST SIKKIM

Gangtok

03592 / POP 106,300 / ELEV 1620M

Irreverent, cheerful and pleasantly boisterous, Sikkim's modern capital is layered along a precipitous mountain ridge, descending the hillside in steep tiers. It's a confusing spaghetti of winding lanes flanked by tall, mostly concrete-block buildings that might appear to be two storeys high from one side but often have several more floors descending behind. As well as a handful of minor sights, there are countless viewpoints with panoramas that encompass plunging green valleys and, if you're lucky weather-wise, glimpses of Khangchendzonga on the distant skyline.

More than anything, Gangtok's a good place for post-trek R&R, for organising tours and permits, and for meeting fellow travellers to make up a necessary group.

The NH31A (Rangpo–Mangan road) is Gangtok's crooked north–south spine. Mostly pedestrianised Mahatma Ghandi (MG) Marg, the social-commercial hub, is packed with restaurants, shops, travel agents and a bustling early-evening *passeggiata* of relaxed wanderers.

Sights

★Namgyal Institute of Tibetology MUSEUM

(NIT; www.tibetology.net; Deorali; ₹10; ⏲10am-4pm) The NIT's 1958 core building feels like a Tibetan fantasy palace, with corner towers, colourful mural frontage and a forest-glade setting. The main hall houses a priceless and well-explained collection of culturally Tibetan/Buddhist iconography and artefacts, ranging from *thangkas* (cloth paintings), coins and amulets to tantric skull-cap bowls and trumpets made from human thigh bones. Beautiful Buddhist statuary includes an eight-armed bronze image of victory goddess Namgyalama, who appears to be texting on an invisible phone.

Few tourists venture upstairs to the shrine-like library, whose teak-and-glass cases house mostly wrapped religious scriptures along with the 135-volume *Encyclopaedia Tibetica*. The rooftop has pleasant views.

The institute is six minutes' walk from **Deorali Bazaar Ropeway Station** (Deorali Chowk) and Deorali taxi stand.

★Tsuklakhang BUDDHIST TEMPLE

(Bhanu Path; ⏲dawn-dusk, prayers 6am & 4pm) Gangtok's 'royal' monastery has a very impressive centrepiece temple whose superb interior incorporates a pair of carved dragon columns flanking the main images. The whole compound is an oasis of calm and, though surrounding monastic quarters are contrastingly neutral, you can get a decent glimpse of the private Chogyal Palace while wandering across the monks' football pitch.

Tashi Viewpoint VIEWPOINT

(Gangtok-Mangan Rd Km1.4; observation tower ₹5) FREE When clouds lift, Gangtok's best glimpses of Khangchendzonga are from this roadside knoll at the junction of routes to Mangan and Nathu La, around 7km northwest of the centre.

Ganesh Tok VIEWPOINT

Named for the tiny associated Hindu temple, this viewpoint tower is an eagle's perch surveying a vast sweep of cityscape. Notice the Royal Palace visible amid trees way beyond Enchey Gompa.

The Ridge AREA

With gorgeous views to east and west through the trees, the city's green heart consists of manicured gardens at the northern end along with a handful of park cafes. Further south, you enter what almost feels like jungle as you skirt the Chogyal Palace (former royal residence).

Himalayan Zoological Park ZOO

(Gangtok Zoo; Indian/foreigner ₹25/50, motorbike/car/jeep ₹10/40/100, video ₹500; ⏲9.30am-4pm Fri-Wed) Among India's better-maintained zoos, the Himalayan Zoological Park occupies an entire hillside. The star attraction is a pair of red pandas, Sikkim's animal emblem, looking a little like small foxes. There are also Himalayan bears, clouded leopards and snow leopards roaming extensive forested enclosures. These are very widely separated, such that without a vehicle you'll need around three hours to see the main sites. With a car, an hour should suffice. The **ticket booth** is opposite the Ganesh Tok viewpoint but is a long way from the main enclosures.

Enchey Gompa MONASTERY

(⏲prayer hall 5am-11am & noon-4pm Mon-Sat, to 1pm Sun) FREE On the city's northern outskirts, approached through rustling conifers, Enchey is a small but appealing Buddhist monastery that is, in a sense, Gangtok's raison d'être: it was the site's perceived sanctity that attracted people to this once-obscure area. A small, vibrant prayer hall sports tantric statues and a three-dimensional scene that plays out behind the central Buddha figure.

Flower Exhibition Centre GARDENS

(₹10; ⏲9am-6pm) Especially during late March and April, when alpine flowers are in bloom, it's worth peeping inside this modestly sized covered garden, which has changing displays of potted flowers around a central pond. It's often blasted with Bollywood hits – perhaps orchids thrive on rhythm?

Activities

Namgyal Treks & Tours OUTDOORS

(☎03592-203701, 9434033122; www.namgyaltreks.com; Enchey Compound, Tibet Rd; ⏲10am-5pm Mon-Sat) One of Sikkim's best established agencies for treks and especially mountaineering expeditions, founded in 1991 by Namgyal Sherpa, a highly experienced climber and now president of the local Rotary club.

BB Line ADVENTURE SPORTS

(☎03592-206110; www.bbline.co.in; 2nd fl, Yama House, MG Marg; ⏲9.30am-6.30pm) BB Line is

Gangtok

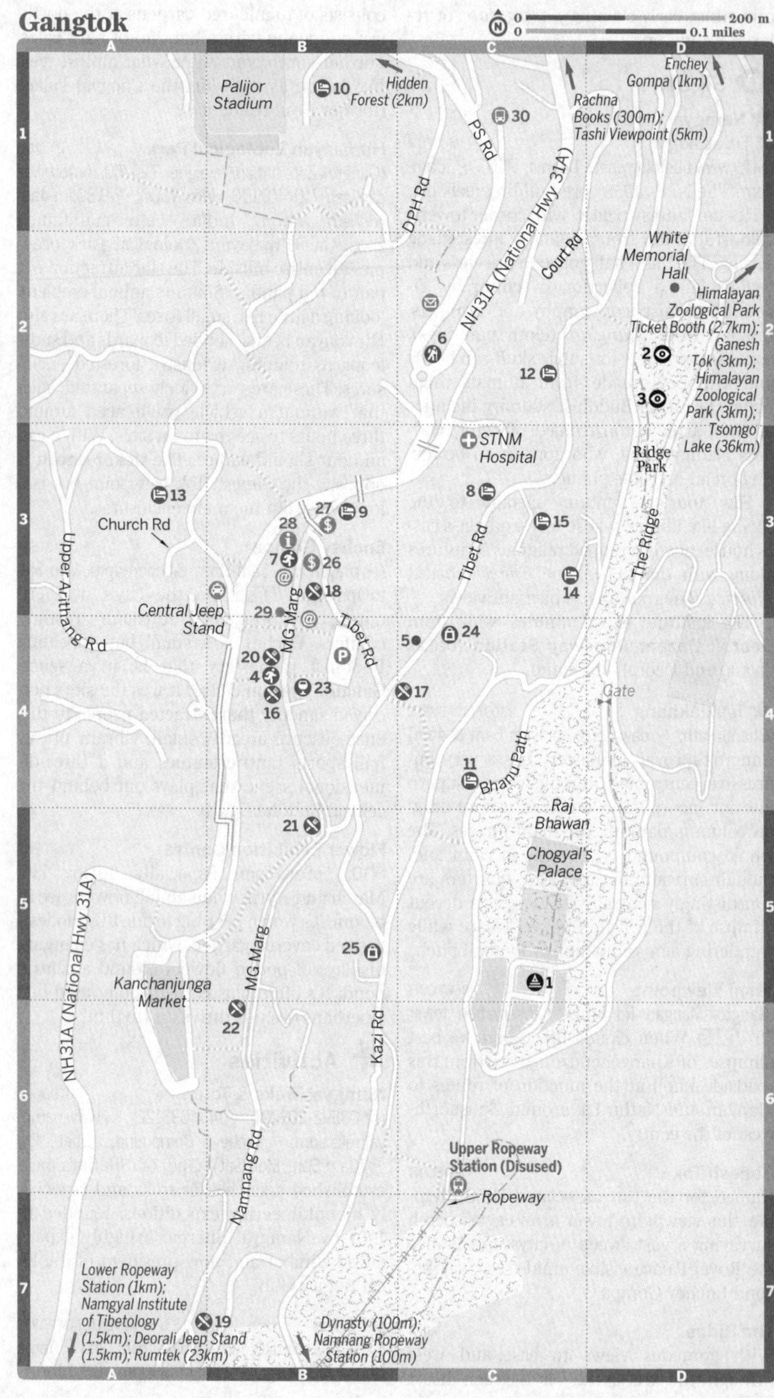
0 200 m
0 0.1 miles
Palijor Stadium
10
Hidden Forest (2km)
30
Rachna Books (300m); Tashi Viewpoint (5km)
Enchey Gompa (1km)
PS Rd
DPH Rd
NH31A (National Hwy 31A)
Court Rd
White Memorial Hall
Himalayan Zoological Park Ticket Booth (2.7km); Ganesh Tok (3km); Himalayan Zoological Park (3km); Tsomgo Lake (36km)
6
2
3
12
STNM Hospital
Ridge Park
8
15
14
The Ridge
Tibet Rd
13
Church Rd
27
9
28
7
26
18
Upper Arithang Rd
Central Jeep Stand
29
MG Marg
Tibet Rd
5
24
20
4
23
16
17
Gate
11
Bhanu Path
Raj Bhawan
21
Chogyal's Palace
NH31A (National Hwy 31A)
MG Marg
25
1
Kanchanjunga Market
22
Kazi Rd
Namnang Rd
Upper Ropeway Station (Disused)
Ropeway
Lower Ropeway Station (1km); Namgyal Institute of Tibetology (1.5km); Deorali Jeep Stand (1.5km); Rumtek (23km)
19
Dynasty (100m); Namnang Ropeway Station (100m)

Gangtok

Top Sights
1 Tsuklakhang ... C5

Sights
2 Flower Exhibition Centre ... D2
3 The Ridge ... D2

Activities, Courses & Tours
4 BB Line ... B4
Blue Sky Treks & Travels ... (see 7)
5 Namgyal Treks & Tours ... C4
6 Potala Tours & Treks ... C2
7 STDC ... B3

Sleeping
8 Chumbi Residency ... C3
9 Gangtok Lodge ... B3
10 Hotel Nor-Khill ... B1
11 Hotel Pandim ... C4
12 Hotel Sonam Delek ... C2
13 Hotel Yavachi ... A3
14 Mintokling Guest House ... C3
15 Netuk House ... C3

Eating
16 Bakers Cafe ... B4
17 Dekid ... C4
18 Golden Dragon ... B3
19 Mu Kimchi ... A7
20 Parivar Restaurant ... B4
21 Taste of Tibet ... B5
22 The Coffee Shop ... B6

Drinking & Nightlife
Clique ... (see 19)
23 Downtown ... B4
The Square ... (see 22)

Entertainment
Cafe Live & Loud ... (see 5)

Shopping
24 Climate Zone ... C4
Golden Tips ... (see 4)
25 Golden Tips II ... B5

Information
Pankhuri Enterprises ... (see 29)
26 RS Enterprises ... B3
27 SBI ... B3
28 Tourist Office ... B3

Transport
29 DJ Mandap Tours ... B3
Railway Booking Counter ... (see 30)
30 SNT Bus Station ... C1

one of Sikkim's most forward-thinking adventure-tourism agencies. The first major outfit to offer motorbike rental and tours, it's also developing mountain-bike tours, kayaking and rafting, and it has plans for a bungee-jumping experience in Dzongu.

STDC SCENIC FLIGHTS
(Sikkim Tourism Development Corporation; ☎03592-203960; www.sikkimtourism.gov.in; MG Marg; ⏲9am-7pm) This well-organised office offers a pre-booked taxi service (cars collect you at your hotel) and sells helicopter tickets both for transfers to Bagdogra and for pleasure flights, most affordably a 15-minute buzz over Gangtok (₹9500 for up to five people). Longer variants can take you as far as the Khangchendzonga ridge (₹90,000 for four people, 75 minutes). Book early.

Potala Tours & Treks TREKKING
(☎9434257036; www.potalatreks.in; PS Rd) Treks, tours, mountain biking and trips for school groups that can be linked up with routes in Darjeeling and Bhutan.

Fly Sikkim Adventure PARAGLIDING
(☎9197207767; www.paraglidingsikkim.com; Banjhankri Rd) One of Gangtok's main paragliding operators.

Blue Sky Treks & Travels TREKKING
(☎03592-205113; www.blueskysikkim.com; Tourism Bldg, MG Marg; ⏲10.30am-7pm) This is a go-to agent for foreigners looking to share relatively inexpensive but decent-quality budget tours to Lachung. It also arranges treks.

Sleeping

★Hotel Pandim HOTEL $
(☎03592-207540, 9832080172; www.hotelpandim.com; Bhanu Path; dm/d from ₹500/1500; 📶) Almost too good to be true, this family hotel has jaw-dropping mountain panoramas from its top-floor deluxe rooms (₹2000 to ₹2300), from super-clean four-bed dorms, and especially from the delightful Tibetan-styled top-floor cafe-restaurant where you check in. Even the cheaper basement rooms are eminently liveable, with ample space and *thangkas* (cloth paintings) as decoration.

Gangtok Lodge GUESTHOUSE $
(☎03592-206562; NH31A; d ₹1500) Formerly the Modern Central Lodge, this neat little eight-room guesthouse has simple rooms with small double beds. Nepali curtains and hand-painted Sikkimese cabinets add a little colour. Curfew 10pm.

★Hidden Forest GUESTHOUSE **$$**
(☎03592-205197; www.hiddenforestretreat.org; NH10, Middle Sichey; s/d ₹2750/3300,; @📶) 🍃 This collection of high-quality, lovingly maintained cottage rooms and houselets is interspersed with countless blooming shrubs and orchids. Though partly masked by new building work below, valley vistas remain gorgeous, and there's a well-stocked library downstairs and a nursery full of flowers. By advance arrangement you can enjoy delicious home-cooked meals (₹220/330 for breakfast/dinner).

It's around 2km from central Gangtok, ₹150 by taxi. Enter via the garden path behind Hotel Vajrakila.

Hotel Yavachi DESIGN HOTEL **$$**
(☎03592-204666; www.hotelyavachi.com; Church Rd; r from ₹3300, walk-in from ₹2400; 📶) Despite the modest rates, Yavachi is a well-executed festival of comfortable modernism, with ceiling-panel lighting and abstract art thoughtfully designed to coordinate with the fabrics in each room. Views are limited – those from the very inviting rooftop Rockefeller Bar (beer ₹100) are better than the mere glimpses you get from some guest rooms.

Hotel Tashi Tagey HOTEL **$$**
(☎03592-231631; www.tashitagey.com; NH10, Tadong; d ₹1500-3500; @) For quality at affordable prices, it's worth venturing to this hotel in Tadong, 3km below Gangtok. Corridors with botanical prints lead to spotless rooms, wi-fi is available in a lounge adorned with the hostess's needlepoint, and unbeatable rooftop views are framed by a priceless collection of bonsai trees, some more than 50 years old. A shared taxi from town costs ₹20.

Hotel Sonam Delek HOTEL **$$**
(☎03592-202566; www.hotelsonamdelek.com; Tibet Rd; r without/with view from ₹1870/3960, ste ₹5610; 📶) The view, the view! Most of the 20 highly comfortable if slightly dated rooms have it, and even the other three have access to a communal vista-gazing terrace. Upper rooms and suites have private balconies for that top-of-the-world feeling.

SLEEPING PRICE RANGES

Accommodation price ranges for Sikkim:

$ below ₹1500

$$ ₹1500–5000

$$$ above ₹5000

Service is obliging and efficient. Parking is a squeeze.

Mintokling Guest House GUESTHOUSE **$$**
(☎03592-208553; www.mintokling.com; Bhanu Path; s/d/ste ₹2530/2750/3300; @📶) Nestled amid exotic greenery and set around pretty lawns, this oasis of peace and quiet has a dozen large, well-kept if slightly austere rooms that are partly wood-panelled. There's a family-style warmth in the welcome, yet the dining room offers a restaurant-worthy range of guest meals, including several genuine Sikkimese options.

★Netuk House HERITAGE HOTEL **$$$**
(☎03592-206778; www.netukhouse.com; r/ste ₹5500/7500) Netuk House is a luxurious 'heritage' B&B with a dozen rooms in three very different buildings. The most visually exciting is the two-storey temple-esque 'Annex', a festival of colourful Sikkimery with superb panoramas from upper rooms set back from a gorgeous crazy-paved view patio. The octagonal 'Heritage' building has three huge rooms with lashings of old wood. It's off Tibet Rd.

Chumbi Residency BOUTIQUE HOTEL **$$$**
(☎03592-206618; www.thechumbiresidency.com; Tibet Rd; s/tw/d ₹4740/5920/7100; 📶) In a building whose half-timbered exterior has an almost Japanese vibe, rooms are tastefully understated, and on upper floors you'll easily forgive the lacklustre old bathrooms as you sit in your window gazing towards Khangchendzonga. Most lower floors have views too, albeit partly tree-obstructed. Four floors down (no lift) is the appealing bar-restaurant Tangerine and a delightful shady garden area.

Hotel Nor-Khill HERITAGE HOTEL **$$$**
(☎03592-205637; www.elginhotels.com; s/d/ste incl half-board ₹11,565/11,945/13,335; P📶) Checking into the Nor-Khill is like time travelling back to the pre-Independence era, when this stately property served as the royal guesthouse. Countless historical photos, splendid period furniture and crystal chandeliers lend a vintage feel to the hallways and the indulgent lobby-lounge. Rooms are spaciously classy, too, though some can smell a little musty. The hotel is off PS Rd.

✕ Eating

Taste of Tibet TIBETAN **$$**
(MG Marg; mains ₹160-230, momos ₹90-140; ⊙11am-8.30pm) With a perfect central loca-

tion and a reputation for Gangtok's best Tibetan food, this place always draws throngs of diners chomping *shyabhale* (fried meat pasties) and slurping *thentuk* (*thukpa*; noodle soup), but the decor (or lack thereof) offers little romance. Try for a people-watching window seat.

Dekid BHUTANESE **$$**
(1st fl, Tibet Rd; mains ₹90-150, half/full portion rice ₹60/120; ⌚8.30am-8.30pm) Fancy trying Bhutanese food? This pleasantly unsophisticated three-table place makes it straightforward by offering just two main styles to choose from: red-orange *shakam* curry using dried meat, and deliciously creamy, mid-spiced *datshi* cheese-based dishes with *kawa* (potato), pepper, beef or short strips of fatty pork. The complimentary bowl of soup is a nice touch.

The Coffee Shop INTERNATIONAL **$$**
(www.facebook.com/thecoffeeshopgangtok; pizza ₹290-380, snacks ₹130-220, mains ₹280-320; ⌚9.30am-9.30pm; 📶) Upstairs above The Square, this ever-popular cafe-diner is known not just for excellent coffee and smoothies but also for familiar international meals from nachos and falafels to grilled chops, rosemary tenderloin and various thin-crust pizzas. Behind a tempting cake display, the Dalai Lama raises his mug in approval.

Bakers Cafe BAKERY **$$**
(MG Marg; pastries/snacks from ₹20/65, mains ₹80-220, mixed grill ₹380; ⌚8am-8pm) Lilting twangs of country music often serenade this timber-panelled cafe that's especially popular with families and local women. Robust espressos (₹70), organic ginger tea (₹60) and other exotic infusions wash down a range of paninis and Western-style pastries from the bakery counter. The menu also offers fast food and traveller favourites including banana pancakes, hummus and all-day breakfasts.

★Mu Kimchi KOREAN **$$$**
(☎9593340401; https://www.facebook.com/MuKimchi/; 5th fl, Clique Bldg, Namnang Rd; snacks ₹190-310, meals ₹300-700; ⌚10am-10.30pm) Longing for perfectly prepared, authentic Korean cuisine? Then it's well worth climbing the 80 steps to Mu Kimchi, with an interior that cleverly cultivates a special ambience, balancing original bamboo ceilings and woven lamps with a pared-down contemporary minimalism matching the sound system's insistent, bass-heavy mash-ups.

SIKKIMESE FOOD

The most common dishes are Tibetan/pan-Himalayan favourites, including *momos* (dumplings) and rich noodle soups including *thentuk/thukpa*, *gyathuk* and *bhathuk*. More archetypally Sikkimese soups use local organic vegetables, whether fermented (*gundruk* spinach, *sinki* radishes) or fresh (*karela* bitter gourds, *sisnoo* nettles). Curries might incorporate fried *ningro* (fiddlehead ferns), *bareh* (ground-orchid bud heads) or *fing* (rice-noodle strands). Unusually for India, beef is popular. If ordering pork, beware: locals like it indulgently fatty, often with rind.

Beer/cocktails/soju cost from ₹150/350/250.

Parivar Restaurant SOUTH INDIAN **$**
(MG Marg; curries ₹100-180, dosas ₹110-150, rice ₹70, small/large thalis ₹180/280; ⌚9.30am-9pm; 🌿) Ever popular for pure-veg South Indian food, the reliable Parivar plays a stylistically straight bat with red-leatherette bench booths and almost no decor beyond a token ornate dragon column.

Dynasty CHINESE **$$$**
(☎03592-206444; 1st fl, Namnang Ropeway Bldg, Kazi Rd; mains ₹180-440, half/whole Peking duck ₹800/1400, rice ₹80; ⌚11.30am-9.30pm; 📶) Enjoy some of Gangtok's most authentic Chinese cuisine while settled into black-patterned sofas upstairs in the **Namnang Ropeway Station building** (Kazi Rd). Dynasty does a passable approximation of Thai food too.

Drinking & Nightlife

There's no beating the regal setting of the Hotel Nor-Khill for an indulgent, very British Empire–style afternoon tea (₹495) with engraved pewter teapots and scones on doilied stands. If you just want to taste Sikkimese Temi tea (₹40), head for Golden Tips (p544) or Cafe Fiction within Rachna Books (p544), which also has good French press coffee. For espresso, hit The Coffee Shop or Bakers Cafe.

Clique BAR
(Namnang Rd; beer/juice from ₹120/110; ⌚10am-11pm) Decorated with old 33rpm records, this cube of a bar often offers live music (pop

to Nepali traditional) on weekend nights. It supplements its range of alcoholic drinks with a series of healthy fresh-juice alternatives saddled with brutal names such as Liver Cleanser and Go Nuts Shake.

★Downtown BAR

(MG Marg; beer/wine/shots from ₹130/60/40; ⊙noon-9pm) Central Gangtok's most alternative little bar has seats like midget sofas with stuffing coming out, and guests seem to flout the no-smoking rules. Yet somehow the low-lit atmosphere works, with its curtained balconies, little performance space, informal jam sessions and murals of Marley, Lennon and Hendrix.

The Square BAR

(MG Marg; beer/shots/cocktails/wine from ₹149/33/193/83; ⊙10am-9.30pm) Moodily lit, with booth seating, pacey music, and walls chock-a-block with black-and-white portrait photos, The Square pulls off a clever balance between 'family friendly' and 'comfortably contemporary'. The drink list includes a selection of cocktails and various wines by the glass. Food ranges from spicy barbeque ribs to bacon-wrapped shrimps to an array of curries (mains ₹190 to ₹440).

☆ Entertainment

★Cafe Live & Loud LIVE MUSIC

(www.facebook.com/CafeLiveAndLoud; Tibet Rd; beer/cocktails/tea/coffee from ₹160/350/54/95, hookah ₹250; ⊙11am-11pm Sun-Fri, to 1am Sat; wi-fi) Gangtok's most happening music bar bathes its drinkers in a tsunami of sound Wednesday to Friday evenings, when live bands typically crank out rock or alternative-pop sets. On Saturday, pay ₹300 after 6pm to join the DJ party. By day there's a relaxed, jazzy vibe, especially on the plush, partly curtained balcony terrace. Full food menu (mains ₹200 to ₹600).

Service, tax and food VAT add a whopping 25.5% to meal bills.

Shopping

★Golden Tips TEA

(www.goldentipstea.in; MG Marg; ⊙9.30am-8.30pm) This boutique tea store stocks a fine selection of beautifully packaged teas, mostly premium Darjeeling and Temi (Sikkimese) variants. A cafe-style tasting area allows you to sip from a choice of 48 types. A cup/pot costs from ₹40/160, but drinking delicate white tea made from hand-selected buds picked before sunrise can set you back ₹160/800.

There's a **second shop** (Kazi Rd; ⊙9am-7.30pm).

★Rachna Books BOOKS

(☎03592-204336; www.rachnabooks.com; Jeewan Theeng Marg, Development Area; tea/coffee from ₹40/90; ⊙9.30am-7pm Mon-Sat, closed during Dasain) Gangtok's 'alternative cultural hub' as well as the city's best-stocked and most convivial bookshop, Rachna also has a three-room B&B (rooms ₹1500 to ₹1900) and a jazzy little cafe serving French-press and filter coffees, Temi teas and snacks. Occasional events include possible film shows.

Climate Zone SPORTS & OUTDOORS

(Tibet Rd; ⊙9.30am-9pm) Reasonably well-stocked outdoors shop for hiking and camping equipment, including trekking sticks, umbrellas and various sizes of backpack.

ℹ Information

INTERNET ACCESS

Some hotels offer wi-fi, as do a handful of restaurants and cafes. Speeds can be far from impressive. **Internet Cafe** (MG Marg; per hr ₹30, minimum charge ₹20; ⊙8.30am-7.30pm) allows customers to use wi-fi on their own computers; **Cyber Cafe** (MG Marg; per hr ₹30; ⊙9am-9pm) doesn't. For ₹198 you can get 1GB of data valid for a month on a BSNL sim. That works OK in the city but barely functions in rural Sikkim.

MEDICAL SERVICES

STNM Hospital (☎03592-222059; NH31A) Government hospital with emergency and outpatient facilities. Take a copy of your travel insurance for major treatments.

MONEY

ATMs are widespread. Gangtok is essentially the only place in Sikkim with currency-exchange facilities.

Money changers aren't particularly common. A good place to look is MG Marg, where you can compare rates at a trio of of tiny booths in the building opposite **Golden Dragon** (MG Marg; mains ₹200-440; ⊙11am-9pm). **Pankhuri Enterprises** (www.pankhurienterprises.com; MG Marg; ⊙9.30am-6.30pm) offers OK deals, but the best rates are from **RS Enterprises** (MG Marg; ⊙9.15am-7.15pm) opposite the Gandhi statue. Other than **SBI** (State Bank of India; NH31A; ⊙10am-4pm Mon-Fri, every 2nd Sat), banks that claim to offer forex services usually require you to have an account before changing money, and rates are usually poor.

POST

Main Post Office (PS Rd; ⏲ for stamps 10am-4pm Mon-Sat, to 2pm Sun) This is one of relatively few GPOs in India to offer the 'My Stamp' service, where you can get your own photograph turned into a postage stamp (sheet of 12 stamps for ₹300).

TOURIST INFORMATION

STDC (p541) Makes practical arrangements including helicopter and taxi bookings.

Tourist Office (☎03592-209090; www.sikkimtourism.gov.in; MG Marg; ⏲9am-7pm) Relatively helpful at answering questions; offers a comprehensive info pamphlet that includes useful schematic maps.

Getting There & Away

AIR

Until the much-delayed Pakyong airport opens, the nearest airport to Sikkim is at Bagdogra, near Siliguri in West Bengal. It has plentiful flights to Kolkata, Delhi and Guwahati.

Foreigners without pre-arranged Sikkim permits can get one quickly at the airport's Sikkim Tourism counter, important if you've arrived after around 3pm and are thus unlikely to reach the Rangpo border before 7.30pm, when it stops issuing permits.

BUS & JEEP

Government buses from the **SNT bus station** (PS Rd; ⏲ tickets 6am-6pm) run approximately hourly to Siliguri (₹190) between 6am and 1.30pm, and there are daily services to Pakyong (₹45, 4.15pm) and Rhenock via Rangpo (₹80, 2pm).

Most jeeps running to destinations within Sikkim start from the three-layered **Central Jeep Stand** (Church Rd).

Vehicles to Rumtek and Ranka start from the top, jeeps to West and South Sikkim use the midlevel, and to Singtam, Pakyong and Rhenock they start from the bottom. The booking offices will only sell same-day tickets, but locals call the driver to reserve seats, especially for early departures. Some main-road hotels, including **Tashi Tagey** (p542), are happy to do this for you so that you're picked up from your door and don't need to go to the jeep stand at all.

Useful departures:

Dentam ₹250, six hours, 6.15am

Geyzing ₹250, 4½ hours, 6.30am, 7am, 7.30am, 7.45am

Jorethang ₹150, three hours, every half-hour 6.45am to 4.30pm via West Bengal

Namchi ₹150, four hours, every half-hour 7am to 3pm

Pelling ₹300, five hours, 1pm, or use Geyzing vehicles

Ravangla ₹140, four hours, 7am, 7.45am, noon, 12.30pm, 1.30pm, 2pm

Rhenock ₹120, 2½ hours, 7am, 9.30am, 10.30am, 12.30pm, 3.30pm

Singtam ₹60, one hour, three or more hourly 7am to 5pm. Can take two hours in heavy traffic

Tashiding ₹250, five to 6½ hours, 7am

Yuksom ₹300, 6½ to eight hours, 7am

Note that journey times can vary enormously according to road conditions and traffic. Estimates above might sound pessimistic but are in fact realistic.

TRAIN

The nearest major train station is about 125km away at New Jalpaiguri (NJP). Tickets can be purchased through the computerised **railway booking counter** (SNT bus stand; ⏲8am-2pm Mon-Sat, to 11am Sun & public holidays) at the SNT bus station or more centrally at **DJ Mandap Tours** (☎9832373337; MG Marg; commission ₹100; ⏲10am-6pm).

Rumtek

ELEV 1660M

Facing Gangtok distantly across a plunging green valley, Rumtek's extensive gompa complex (p545) is one of Tibetan Buddhism's most venerable institutions as the home-in-exile of the Kagyu (Black Hat) sect. The main route up starts near Ranipul and passes some lovely city views as it climbs. You can also make Rumtek part of a day-trip loop that includes more peaceful and arguably lovelier **Lingdum Gompa** (www.zurmangkagyud.org; Ranka; butter-lamp donation small/medium/large ₹10/20/100; ⏲dawn-dusk) FREE. Though stretches of the road are in dire need of repair, the route winds through mossy forests, bamboo groves and terraced paddy fields, presenting many more super viewpoints. Nearer to Gangtok you'll pass minor attractions, including the try-hard **Kanchendzonga Tourist Centre** (www.ktcranka.com/; Ranka; adult/child/parking ₹100/50/25, simulator/panorama show/mini train ₹80/90/40; ⏲11am-8pm, rides till 6pm) and the modest **Banjhakri Waterfalls** (Lower Sichey; ₹50, parking ₹20; ⏲7.30am-6.30pm) in a park of garish figures portraying pre-Buddhist animist myths.

Sights

Rumtek Gompa MONASTERY
(Rumtek Dharma Chakra Centre; ☎03592-252329; www.rumtek.org; monastery ₹10; ⏲6am-6pm)

Rumtek is Sikkim's most spiritually significant monastery complex. It's essentially a self-contained village with a colourful main prayer hall that was built (1961–66) to replace Tibet's Tsurphu Monastery, destroyed during the Chinese Cultural Revolution (though since rebuilt). The interior's centrepiece is a giant yellow throne awaiting the long-overdue coronation of the Kagyu spiritual leader, the (disputed) 17th Karmapa. He currently resides in Dharamsala due to the Karmapa controversy (p546), sensitivity over which explains all the armed soldiers and why foreigners must show their passport and Sikkim permit on entry.

Behind the monastery, stairs rise beside the distinctively painted Karma Shri Nalanda Institute of Buddhist Studies, leading quickly to a smallish room containing an ornate **Golden Stupa** (6-11.45am & noon-5pm) FREE studded with turquoise and amber gemstones. That's the reliquary of the 16th Karmapa, founder of the current complex and considered almost a saint hereabouts.

The gompa hosts some of Sikkim's finest *chaam* masked dances, notably at Saga Dawa (p537) and especially at the Gutor Chaam directly before Losar (p537), Tibetan New Year.

Old Rumtek Gompa MONASTERY
(dawn-dusk) FREE Old Rumtek Gompa, around 1.5km beyond the Rumtek main gate, is an oasis of peace away from the tourist crowds. Originally founded in 1734 but thoroughly rebuilt, the prayer hall has an intensely colourful interior. Valley views can be glimpsed through the trees from foreground lawns, on which three rotundas are provided for people to picnic.

Festivals & Events

Rumtek holds impressive masked *chaam* dances during the annual drupchen (group meditation) in May/June, and at Old Rumtek Gompa two days before Losar (p537). The much-fancied **Mahakala Dance** takes place in February, when giant figurines of fierce protector deities come to life in the central courtyard.

Sleeping & Eating

★**Bamboo Retreat** BOUTIQUE HOTEL $$$
(9434382036, 3592252516, 9647851055; www.bambooretreat.in; Sajong; incl breakfast s without/with view ₹4700/6700, d ₹6000/7000, apt ₹15,000; P) Climb stone steps through terraced organic gardens to reach this fabulous pseudo-temple resort, set gloriously alone in partly cleared forest. Comfy rooms are named for their coordinating colours, and all but three have balconies offering superb views. Communal spaces ooze atmosphere and include a library, a museum-like dining room with fireplace, a TV lounge (no TVs in rooms) and a meditation room.

THE KARMAPA CONTROVERSY

The 'Black Hat' sect takes its name from the priceless ruby-topped black headgear traditionally worn by the Karmapas (reincarnated spiritual leaders). Said to be woven from the hair of *dakinis* (female spirits who carry the souls of the dead), the hat must be kept locked in a box to prevent it from flying back to the heavens. Nobody, however, has actually seen the hat since 1993, when a bitter controversy arose within the Kagyu sect over the legitimacy of two candidates, with both claiming their right to the throne following the death of the 16th Karmapa in 1981.

The main candidate, recognised by the Dalai Lama, is Ogyen Trinley Dorje (http://kagyuoffice.org), who fled Tibet in 2000. He holds 'temporary' office at the Gyuto Tantric Monastery near Dharamsala, but Indian authorities are believed to have prevented him from officially taking up his Rumtek seat for fear of upsetting Chinese-government sensibilities. His rival, Thaye Dorje (www.karmapa.org), operates from the Karmapa International Buddhist Institute in Delhi. Supporters of the two lamas have now been locked in a legal dispute over who can control Rumtek for more than two decades. During 2016 supporters of Ogyen Trinley Dorje launched a renewed series of demonstrations and hunger strikes aimed at persuading the Indian government to allow their candidate to finally take up his Rumtek seat.

Only when the dispute is resolved and the 17th Karmapa is finally crowned will anyone dare to unlock the box and reveal the sacred black hat. To learn more about the controversy, read *The Dance of 17 Lives* by Mick Brown.

Tsomgo (Changu) Lake

ELEV 3750M

Mysterious for its lack of feeder river, **Tsomgo** (pronounced Changu) is not the prettiest mountain lake in the world, but excursions here are the quickest way to get above the tree line, making it a wildly popular destination for those in-a-hurry Indian tourists who have never before experienced alpine scenery. Short yak rides (₹200) potter along the shore, completing the tourist experience. The altitude might make you short of breath, but don't believe scare stories that suggest you'll need to carry oxygen or take diamox for a day trip.

Permits are required for foreigners and Indians alike, but these can generally be arranged for a next-day departure by virtually any Gangtok agent (photos and document copies required).

Only Indians can continue to **Nathu La**, the Chinese border post, and only then to snap a few photos, not to cross into Tibet – at least for now.

At the lakeside, food stalls sell hot chai, chow mein and *momos* (dumplings).

The lake is 38km from Gangtok. A budget day tour typically costs around ₹4500 per vehicle. Joining a group tour is easy for Indians (around ₹800 per person including Nathu La) but pretty much impossible for foreigners, since they can't do the Nathu La section, leading to the logistical problem of who stays with them while the rest of the group continues to the Chinese border.

NORTH SIKKIM

Gangtok to Mangan

The frail, narrow and sometimes infuriatingly muddy NH31A winds tortuously through thickly wooded slopes high above the Teesta River. Streams cascade between mossy boulders half-hidden by curtains of foliage and bamboo thickets. Larger white-water rivers are glimpsed from bridges fluttering with prayer flags. But Yumthang-bound tour jeeps generally zoom right by, stopping only at Tashi Viewpoint (p539) and the impressive **Seven Sisters Waterfall** (Gangtok-Mangan Rd Km30). To see **Kabi Lunchok** (Gangtok-Mangan Rd, Km17.6) FREE and **Tumlong** (Gangtok-Mangan Rd Km36), which are only vaguely worthwhile, you'll need to ask, as the reluctant driver will be rushing to reach Lachung before dark.

GUIDED TOURS

There are essentially two valleys to explore: Lachen and Lachung. But since foreigners aren't permitted to visit Gurudongmar Lake (the Lachen area's main attraction), most visitors choose Lachung-Yumthang. From Gangtok you'll need three days to do justice to Yumthang and Zero Point. Starting from Mangan makes things far more relaxed – two days would suffice.

All-inclusive two-night, three-day tours from Gangtok to Yumthang start from around ₹6000 per person (including bed and board) if you're in a group of four. Vehicle-only 'tours' from Mangan cost around ₹3500 per day for the jeep, accommodation extra. Double-check what accommodation is offered, and whether the second day includes a trip to Zero Point or only to Yumthang (the official fare for Yumthang and Zero Point is ₹2500).

Mangan, North Sikkim's regional capital, is a good place to organise DIY Lachung tours. Its commercial centre is a dreary, Y-shaped concrete scar high on a steep, jungle-covered hillside, but attractive outskirts hide two appealing accommodation choices. Across the Teesta, the Lepcha protected area of **Dzongu** is delightful for low-key village homestay experiences.

Sleeping & Eating

★**Mayallyang Homestay** HOMESTAY
(☎9647872434, 8348332721; www.mayallyang.com; Passingdang, Dzongu; per person incl full board ₹1800) One of Sikkim's most magical getaways. Youthful host Gyatshe is an energetic anti-dam campaigner who sees homestays as an important part of sharing his message about ecological and cultural sustainability. Watch interesting videos in the inviting lounge, or relax on the half-timbered homestead's enchanting porch. Rooms are simple, with shared bathrooms. It's down nearly 100 steps from Passingdang's main street.

Far North Sikkim

Lachung

☎03592 / ELEVATION 2680M

Soaring, rock-pinnacled valley walls embroidered with long ribbons of waterfalls

OFF THE BEATEN TRACK

THANGGU & TSOPTA

Beyond a sprawling army camp 32km north of Lachen, Thanggu (3850m) is essentially a summer herders' settlement with an end-of-the-world feel. A few hardy travellers spend the night here, but most groups just stop for breakfast en route to **Gurudongmar Lake** (5150m), a memorable sight reflecting its backdrop of snowy peaks in mirror-calm water, at least when it isn't frozen. **Chomalu**, around 10km further, is India's highest lake. Unfortunately, foreigners are not permitted to visit either lake.

Foreigners usually can wander in the **Tsopta Valley** though, reached by a boulder-strewn stream some 2km from Thanggu. Just above the tree line, the scenery takes on the added drama of a glacier-toothed mountain wall framing the western horizon. A two-hour hike leads up to a pair of **meditation caves**, one of which was reputedly used for two years by the famous French traveller and mystic Alexandra David-Neel.

A few houses in Thanggu offer homestay-style accommodation but most visitors stay in Lachen.

surround the scattered village of Lachung. To appreciate the full drama of its setting, take the metal cantilever bridge across the wild Yumthang River and wander up through the older part of town to the colourful **Lachung Gompa** (Sarchok Gompa; Katao Rd, Km1.8), established 1880, or along to a viewpoint field in which stands the distinctive **Shakathang Stupa**.

Much more of this wonderful scenery is to be found along the majestic Yumthang Valley – excursions here are the main reason visitors stay in Lachung in the first place.

Sleeping & Eating

★**Kalden Residency** GUESTHOUSE $

(☎8900085244; Yumthang Rd; r ₹1000-2000, full board extra ₹500) Our favourite budget digs in Lachung, the Kalden Residency is based around a local-style timber house, with a couple of newer, house-like buildings around a yard blooming with pot plants. Rooms are simple but far better than average for the price, and the family owners are charming.

Yarlam Resort RESORT $$$

(☎9434330033; www.yarlamresort.com; Yumthang Rd Km1.3; d without/with view ₹10,000/11,000, ste ₹15,000; ⏲Mar–mid-Jun & Aug-Dec; @) Remarkably luxurious for remote Lachung, Yarlam greets new arrivals with tea in the part-Tibetanised lobby lounge or serene library. Indulgent rooms have comfy beds overloaded with pillows and DVD-TVs; suites have spacious balcony seating (notably room 301). Their wonderful mountain views are shared by the communal games room (snooker, table tennis, Carrom, chess). No wi-fi.

Yumthang Valley

One of North Sikkim's greatest highlights is driving the 52km route between Lachung and Zero Point through the ever-changing scenic kaleidoscope of the Yumthang Valley. Though you'll no doubt hope for clear skies to see the mountains' full magnificence, swirling clouds can actually help emphasise their contours and let you focus on their natural botanical beauty. Ascending over 2000m, you'll pass through lush mixed forest, rhododendon groves, sturdy old pines draped with garlands of moss, and wild, tundra-like uplands above the tree line.

Around halfway, don't miss **Yumthang Hot Springs** (Yumthang Rd Km21.9) FREE: not for the tiny, unappealing bathing pool but for the approach across prayer-flag-draped suspension footbridges, with picture-postcard views of the towering valley wall. Beyond Yumthang's basic gaggle of shop and cafes, stop again to stroll **Yumthang Meadow** (Yumthang Rd Km23). Some tours end here; others continue another 30km up a seemingly endless series of hairpins to **Zero Point** (at a breathless 4825m).

Transport is by tour jeep with pre-approved permits. It takes around an hour to reach Yumthang Meadow from Lachung, and as long again to Zero Point. Start early – there are plenty of photo stops en route and you'll need to be back in Lachung by around 2pm as per army rules.

Lachen

ELEV 2700M

Lachen was once a quaint village of old wooden homes on sturdy stone bases with ornate Tibetan-style window frames. These days, however, it's largely a mass of concrete box hotels serving streams of Indian tourists heading for Gurudongmar Lake. The scene is more attractive up by the **Lachen (Nyudrup Choeling) Gompa**, a 15-minute walk above the town.

Lachen can also be used as the trailhead for eight-day expeditionary treks to **Green Lake** (5050m) towards Khangchendzonga's northeast face. The trek is partly along the **Zemu Glacier**, considered the legendary home of the yeti (aka 'the abominable snowman'). Until 2015, permits had to be applied for in Delhi and could take months. But that's changed – at least for a trial period – and the paperwork can now be sorted in a week or so. Contact Namgyal Treks & Tours (p539) in Gangtok for information and assistance.

As you'll almost certainly arrive on a tour, it's likely that your hotel will be pre-selected. If you get to choose, and you're seeking luxury a little away from the main centre, hospitable **Apple Orchard Resort** (☎9474837640; www.theappleorchardresort.com; s/d incl full board ₹7479/9619; P) next to the *ani gompa* (nunnery) is worth considering. In smart buildings set around a leafy, tiered complex, its cosy, inviting rooms have graceful wooden flooring and panelling.

SOUTH SIKKIM

Namchi

☎03595 / POP 12,920 / ELEV 1470M

Two hulking religious superstructures on the the jagged horizon around Namchi are the town's great 'sights', but it's pleasant enough as a staging post, with a convivial pedestrianised centre formed from twin plazas, each with an ancient tree.

Sights

★Samdruptse BUDDHIST MONUMENT

(Padmasambhava Statue; ₹30, parking ₹30; ⏲dawn-dusk) Visible for miles, this 45m-high **statue of Padmasambhava** (Guru Rimpoche) is painted in shimmering copper and gilt and sits on a lotus plinth high above Namchi on the forested Samdruptse ridge. Completed in 2004 on a foundation stone laid in 1997 by the Dalai Lama, the statue turns his back on a superlative view of the **Khangchendzonga Massif**, which is best seen from beside his right haunch.

Around the base are some fading historical photos of old Sikkim and within is a prayer room. From the car park, a 15-minute **cable car** (return ₹173; ⏲9.30am-5pm) excursion takes you down to a **rock garden** (⏲9.30am-5.30pm) FREE and back.

Samdruptse is 7km from Namchi, 2km off the Damthang/Ravangla road. Taxis from town charge ₹330 return. Or pay ₹930 to charter a one-way to Ravangla with a Samdruptse side trip en route.

★Char Dham HINDU MONUMENT

(Siddesvara Dham; adult/student/parking ₹50/25/30; ⏲6am-7pm) This unmissable feast of colour is a remarkable Hindu religious theme park crowning Solophuk hilltop, 5km southwest of Namchi. It brings together replicas of great Indian pilgrimage sites, including Rameshwarm, Dwarka and Jagarnath, beneath a towering 33m **Shiva statue**. Whether you find it moving or kitschy, the views and photo opportunities are spectacular.

Be prepared to walk a fair distance barefooted. A taxi here from Namchi, with a one-hour wait, costs ₹330 return.

Ngadak Gompa BUDDHIST MONASTERY

The Ngadak gompa complex is dominated by a gigantic 2014 prayer hall containing some of the richest new paintings in Sikkim; beside it is the ruinous, unpainted shell of a far older monastery building. Exuding a sense of antique Sikkim and reputedly haunted, it was previously the palace of Pedi Wangmu, the Sikkimese queen who temporarily overthrew her half-brother in 1700 and finally had him killed years later (only to be murdered by his followers).

Sleeping & Eating

Dungmali Heritage Resort GUESTHOUSE $

(☎9734126039; minurai81@yahoo.com; Solophuk Rd; s ₹600, d rear/front ₹1200/1500, cottage ₹2500; 📶) Some 4km from Namchi, overlooking town from the first hairpin as you climb to Char Dham, this family-run guesthouse has great-value rooms in an organic cardamon grove, with valley views from the front doubles. Upon prior request, the proprietors can organise **forest walks** and **birdwatching tours** nearby.

Summit Sobralia Resort HOTEL $$$

(☎9083246084, central reservations 0359-520113; www.summithotels.in; Chardham Rd; s/d

₹7000/8000, walk-in ₹4000/5000;) Namchi's swankiest option so far has framed views of Khangchendzonga from its little outdoor pool and from several of the smart (if somewhat formulaic) top-end rooms. It's 1.8km southwest of Namchi on the road towards Char Dham.

Hotel Sangay TIBETAN, INDIAN $
(mains ₹70-160; 8am-8pm) Overlooking the central fountain and an ancient bodhi tree, this gently stylish restaurant is cleaner and more inviting than most of the competition – but other than *momo* (Tibetan dumplings) and a basic veg thali, the majority of the extensive menu requires you to order an hour or two before you dine.

Getting There & Away

The multi-storey **jeep-stand** building is directly east of the pedestrianised town centre. Buses and shared jeeps start from the base; private taxis with fixed rates queue on the 1st floor.

Pre-purchase tickets for shared jeeps to Gangtok (₹150, four hours) and Siliguri (₹150, three to six hours depending on traffic), which leave once or twice an hour from 6.30am to 3pm. For Jorethang (₹40, two hours) and Ravangla (₹60, 1¼ hours) vehicles depart when full, with few services after noon.

There are daily morning buses for Siliguri (₹90) and Gangtok (₹90), plus two to Ravangla at 11.30am and 2pm (₹35).

Ravangla (Rabongla)

03595 / ELEVATION 2050M

The small, ridge-top settlement of Ravangla (aka Rabongla or Rabong) is one of Sikkim's must-see destinations thanks to the remarkable new Buddha Park, whose gigantic golden statue sits serenely with a stunning dawn backdrop of white-topped Himalayan peaks.

Views aren't nearly as dramatic from the two main streets where the majority of Ravangla's central hotels are clustered, but a central taxi stand is handily placed to explore nearby sights, most notably the monasteries at Ralang and Yungdrung Kundrakling.

Sights

★Buddha Park BUDDHIST MONUMENT
(Tathagata Tsal; www.tathagatatsal.com; Ralang Rd Km2; Indian/foreigner ₹50/200; 9am-5.30pm) With a breathtaking backdrop of Himalayan peaks, this gigantic, 41m-tall **Buddha statue** contains holy relics from 11 countries. A spiral interior gallery showcases scenes from Buddha's life in two very different but colourfully intricate styles. Blessed by the Dalai Lama in 2013, the statue is set in manicured lawns behind a central fountain; piped-in mantras add a meditative atmosphere.

Palchen Choeling Monastery BUDDHIST MONASTERY
(New Ralang Gompa; Ralang; P) Near Ralang, 10.5km northwest of Ravangla, this monastery complex built in 1995 is home to more than 300 monks. It's highly significant in Kagyu Buddhism as residence of Gyaltsap Rinpoche, one of the order's five top figures. The main prayer hall is a spectacular feast of coloured walls and gilded roofs set around a wide courtyard with swastika-patterned tiling. The superb, two-storey-high golden Buddha inside sports an iridescent-blue haircut.

Yungdrung Kundrakling MONASTERY
(Ravangla-Kewzing Rd; dawn-dusk) One of only two Bon monasteries in India, this small, double-prayer-hall complex enjoys superb mountain views but has only around 25 monks and three teachers, plus a school full of (mostly orphaned) youngsters. It's beside the main Legship road, 5.5km from central Ravangla, just beyond an area of beautiful deep forest. If you visit, a donation to the monastery will be greatly appreciated.

Old Ralang Gompa BUDDHIST MONASTERY
(Ralang) About 1.5km downhill from Palchen Choeling (p550), Old Ralang monastery was established in 1768. The main temple has been totally rebuilt since 2012 but the complex does retain a handful of old stone-and-timber monks' dwellings preserved as examples of historic Bhutia architecture – and there are unforgettable mountain panoramas to your right as you pass through the outer gate. The **Mahakala Puja** (Dec) festival is held here.

Mane Choekhorling Gompa BUDDHIST MONASTERY
(dawn-dusk) Built between 1984 and 2008 according to classic traditional designs, this flamboyant gompa has an impressive central temple with an octagon stone base. The annual Pang Lhabsol (p537) festival honours Kanchendzonga here. It makes an attractive quick stop if you're walking back from the Buddha Park to Ravangla's Main Bazaar.

Activities

Maenem Hill Hike HIKING

For a fairly strenuous day hike ask at **Kanchan Himalayas** (☎8768442600; khtoursntravels@gmail.com; Kewzing Rd; ⊙9.30am-6pm) or find yourself a guide (from ₹500) and trek through the woodlands, springtime-blooming rhododendrons and magnolias of the **Maenam Wildlife Sanctuary**, continuing up Maenem Hill and on to **Bhaledunga Rock** for sweeping views. There's just a chance that you'll encounter **red pandas** and **monal pheasants** (Sikkim's state animal and bird, respectively).

Sleeping & Eating

Red Panda GUESTHOUSE $$

(☎9733193884, 9735264819; Buddha Park Rd; without/with view ₹1500/2000) Above a snack cafe (great chicken *momo)* that looks far from promising are nine new guest rooms, almost all of which have views of the Buddha with a full Himalayan peak backdrop that is unbeatable. Conditions are comfortable without particular luxury.

Mt Narsing Village Resort RESORT $$

(☎8145841614, 8145294900; www.mtnarsingresorts.com; off Kewzing Rd; d from ₹3025) Set 1km off the Ravanla–Legship road, this gaggle of rustic bungalows is arrayed on pretty garden lawns with Himalayan views that would be perfect were it not for an annoying electricity pylon. Room conditions are a tad scraggy for the price but the central restaurant is a complete delight, overflowing with character and packed with local artefacts.

Blue Spring Residency HOTEL $$

(☎8927479246, 9733121105; raju1881975@gmail.com; Main Bazaar; d/tr ₹2200/2500, off-season ₹1600/1800) Slightly smarter than Ravangla's average boxy hotels, Blue Spring's smallish rooms have two-colour pastel walls and decent bathrooms. Fifteen of the 19 rooms have balconies with lovely mountain views (albeit not encompassing the full range of peaks). The pleasantly airy multicuisine restaurant (mains ₹60 to ₹180) has similarly fine panoramas, thought not necessarily every dish listed on the menu.

Taste of Sikkim MULTICUISINE $$

(Main Bazaar; mains ₹80-180; ⊙8.30am-9pm) The name is misleading as the only Sikkimese dishes served are Tibetan standards *momo* (dumplings) and *thukpa* (noodle soup), but it's the cutest of the Main Bazaar's restaurants, with B&W travel prints and small framed weapons. The food is tasty and imaginatively presented: the fried rice is a star streaked with decorative lines of carrot.

Kookay Restaurant TIBETAN, INDIAN $

(Main Bazaar; mains ₹80-120; ⊙8.30am-8pm) Right at the jeep stand, this long-standing favourite offers Tibetan soups, *shaya phalays* (deep-fried meat turnovers), Chinese sizzlers (₹250 to ₹300) and six delicious thali variants (₹100 to ₹200).

Getting There & Away

Buses leave for Siliguri (₹170, five hours, 7am) and Namchi (₹35, one hour, 9am and 2.30pm); the 9am service continues to Jorethang (₹70). The **SNT bus office** (Main Bazaar) is beneath Hotel 10Zing at the main junction and taxis wait near the same point. Shared jeeps use a **multi-storey garage** (Yangang Rd) 500m down the Yangyang Rd from there. Departures include the following:

Gangtok (₹140, 7am, 7.30am, 8am, 11am and noon) Or take the (sometimes cancelled) 2.30pm Singtam service and change.

Geyzing For Pelling (₹100, two hours, 9am only). Or change at Legship.

Legship (₹60) Leaves when full; no set timetable, but fairly regular till around 2pm.

Siliguri (₹220, 7am and 7.30am)

Jeeps to Namchi (₹60) fill slowly, as most locals take the bus.

Temi Tea Garden

As you wind up, up and up again on the beautiful (if seriously potholed) Singtam-Damthang lane, much of the upper route passes through the very extensive jade-green Temi Tea Garden. The meticulous steep terracing is impressive in itself, but if the weather is clear, it's the stupendous views that you'll remember – across a vast green valley with the Khangchendzonga Massif towering above.

Accommodation with superb views is available in the midst of the tea fields at the slightly institutional **Cherry Resort** (☎8016488737; www.cherryresort.com; Temi Tea Estate; s/d from ₹3040/3490).

The Cherry Resort has a passable restaurant and there are two additional roadside cafes in the tea gardens for a cuppa and a few very basic snacks; **Organic Tea Point** (⊙7am-9pm) is the nicer one.

If you've rented your own vehicle it's easy to stop off at the tea factory, the resort and one of the roadside cafes. Each is a few kilometres from the next over bumpy switchback roads, though far closer on foot using paths through the tea bushes.

A return taxi from Namchi or Ravangla costs ₹800. Namchi to Ravangla one way with a Temi side trip en route costs ₹1100, including waiting time while you visit the factory.

Gangtok–Temi shared jeeps do exist but these only go to **Temi village** (1400m), which is far below the tea estate.

WEST SIKKIM

Pelling

☎03595 / ELEV 1930M

Pelling's raison d'être is to provide hordes of visitors with stride-stopping dawn views of white-robed Khangchendzonga. At first glance the small town is an architecturally uninteresting cascade of concrete hotels tumbling down an otherwise gorgeous woodland ridge – but walk a little and you'll quickly find yourself wandering through beautiful natural forest.

Helpful agencies make excursions easy to organise. Within 3km of Pelling along the same ridge-top are two historic monasteries: busy Pemayangtse Gompa (p552) and peaceful Sanghak Choeling (p552), plus the ruins of the 18th-century royal palace of Rabdentse (p552). Directly below the latter is Tikjuk, West Sikkim's administrative complex (for permit extensions), from where it's another 3km to the commercial and transport centre at Geyzing (Gyalshing).

Sights

Pemayangtse Gompa BUDDHIST MONASTERY
(☎03595-250656; www.sangchenpemyangtse.org; ₹20; ⊙7am-5pm) One of Sikkim's oldest and most significant Nyingmapa monasteries, Pemayangtse is atmospherically backed by traditional wood-and-stone monastic cottages descending from a 2080m hilltop towards the Rabdentse ruins (p552). The oft-remodelled central temple's most memorable attraction is the top floor's seven-tiered model representing Zangtok Palri (Padmasambhava's heavenly abode), handmade over five laborious years by a single dedicated lama. Unheralded in a surrounding attic passage is an underlit, museum-like collection of costumes, implements and remnants from previous incarnations of the monastic buildings.

There has been a Buddhist shrine on the site since 1647. Literally translated, Pemayangtse means 'Perfect Sublime Lotus'. The monastery is 500m off the Geyzing Road – turn north 1.5km east of Upper Pelling.

Rabdentse HISTORIC SITE, RUINS
(parking ₹20; ⊙8am-5pm, last entry 4pm) FREE A few partially rebuilt wall-stubs are all that remains of the palace complex at Rabdentse, which was Sikkim's royal capital from 1670 until it was sacked by Nepali forces in the 18th century. Its main selling point today is the fabulous **viewpoint** on which the ruins are located, best photographed between a trio of small, bare-stone stupas.

The site's **entrance gateway** is 2.3km along the Geyzing road from Upper Pelling, 800m further east than the Pemayangtse turn-off. From the gate the ruins are 1km through woodland, passing a large new aviary area, and only accessible on foot.

Sanghak Choeling Gompa BUDDHIST MONASTERY
(⊙dawn-dusk) At least until the vast new **Chenrezig Statue** (Sanghak Choeling Rd) is completed, this monastery complex is a calm, meditative place with fabulous views, set photogenically behind a collection of seven stone stupas, attractively unpainted other than their golden spires.

Sleeping

★**Hotel Garuda** HOTEL $
(☎9647880728, 9733076484; www.hotelgaruda-pelling.com; Main Rd, Upper Pelling; dm/s/d from ₹250/600/700, online s/d from ₹850/1100; wi-fi) Great for meeting fellow travellers, Pelling's backpacker classic offers specially low walk-in rates for foreigners. Even the more basic rooms are remarkably clean, spacious and equipped with geyser, towels and soap. Smarter, brighter upstairs rooms can still cost less than ₹1500, even with Khangchendzonga views. With free wi-fi, bookswap library, travel assistance and authentic Sikkimese food, the Garuda is very hard to beat.

Rabdentse Residency HOTEL $
(☎9681292163, 03592-92163; www.saikripa.in; Main Rd, Lower Pelling; d without/with balcony ₹1200/1500, ste without/with view ₹3000/3500) A good notch up from most budget hotels, with rooms with bright white linens, *thangka* and

wood-panelling and small but functional bathrooms; north-facing rooms have brilliant views. The restaurant has a lounge area and opens onto a large, concrete terrace with more unimpeded views. It's hidden down a stepped path opposite Hotel Sand & Snow.

Hotel Phamrong HOTEL **$$**
(☎9733085318, 9733240742; www.hotelphamrong.com; Main Rd, Upper Pelling; s/d/ste incl breakfast ₹2450/3135/4290) This pleasant mid-range choice throws in curiosities such as a Tibetan-styled reception booth, four-storey atrium with dangling streamers and ethnographic corner on the 2nd-floor landing, along with a hodgepodge of artefacts, maps and faded mountain photos. Rooms are well-enough appointed minus the odd dusty surface and faded mirror. Some upper versions have superb views.

★Chumbi Mountain Retreat HERITAGE HOTEL **$$$**
(☎9933126619; www.thechumbimountainretreat.com; Chumbong Rd; d incl half-board walk-in/rack-rate ₹9800/17,250; P 📶) This truly exceptional resort blows visitors away with its artful blend of traditional Sikkimese architecture and 21st-century luxury. Just a kilometre from Pelling yet with a secluded forest setting, it has fabulous mountain views, curious public spaces with Bhutanese antique fireplaces and a museum-like thatched farm building, all genteelly directed by ever-helpful staff.

★Elgin Mount Pandim HERITAGE HOTEL **$$$**
(☎03595-250756; www.elginhotels.com; Pemayangtse; s/d/ste incl half-board ₹9295/9625/10,725; P @ 📶) This erstwhile royal getaway is perched on a hilltop with stupendous views in all directions. Highlights are the manicured lawns and the welcoming lobby; it's everything you'd want in a heritage hotel, busy with uniformed staff and packed with interest but welcomingly unstuffy. Cosily luxurious rooms come with very fresh but unflashy bathrooms.

It's a 10-minute stroll from Pemayangtse Gompa, less than 2km from Upper Pelling.

Norbu Ghang RESORT **$$$**
(☎03595-258272; www.norbughanghotels.com; Main Rd, Upper Pelling; d resort/retreat from ₹6630/11,664; 📶) Sharing oblique views of Khangchendzonga, Norbu Ghang has two entrances and two personas. The 'Resort' places Sikkimese-style half-timbered duplex cottages amid exuberant gardens (very pretty but masking views). The upper 'Retreat' welcomes guests with inviting lounges and the huge rooms come with fireplaces and corner-tub baths in what look like semi-detatched English houses dressed for a Tibetan fancy-dress party.

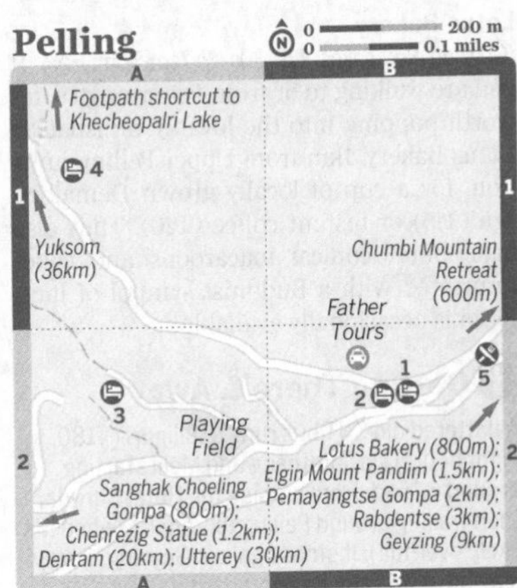

Pelling

Sleeping

1	Hotel Garuda	B2
2	Hotel Phamrong	B2
3	Norbu Ghang	A2
4	Rabdentse Residency	A1

Eating

	Hotel Garuda	(see 1)
5	Kabur Resto-Bar	B2

Eating

Kabur Resto-Bar TIBETAN, CHINESE **$$**
(Geyzing Rd; mains ₹90-250; ⏰9am-9pm) This Pelling traveller classic creates a wonderfully cosy atmosphere at night with candles and colourful, half-lit globe lamps; by day the balcony has great views. The menu favours Tibetan soups, *momo* and *taipoo* – a delicious, fist-sized, filled steamed bun. But there's also plenty of Chinese options.

Hotel Garuda MULTICUISINE
(Upper Pelling; 📶) It doesn't advertise its dining room as a restaurant and will only serve nonguests when the kitchen is quiet, but if you're staying at the Garuda don't miss their home-cooked Sikkimese food, including excellent *churpi* (tomato-cheese soup), fried cheese *momo* and nicely balanced *ema datshi* (chilli-cheese curry).

Lotus Bakery CAFE

(Geyzing Rd; cakes ₹10-30; ⏰7am-5pm; P) If you are walking to or from Pemayangtse, it's worth popping into the lovably ramshackle Lotus Bakery, 1km from Upper Pelling junction, for a cup of locally grown Demajong Tea (₹15) or instant coffee (₹20). They also bake buns, conical macaroons and cakes imprinted with a Buddhist symbol of luck. Pizza is occasionally available.

Getting There & Away

A battered old SNT bus runs to Siliguri (₹180, eight hours) via Jorethang and Melli starting around 6.15am from outside the Hotel Garuda, then trailing around Pelling till 7am (by when it's likely over-full). It stops again in Geyzing, finally leaving at 7.45am. Pay on-board.

Shared jeeps from Pelling depart at 7am to Gangtok (₹300, six hours) and Siliguri (₹350, six hours); book ahead through **Father Tours** (☎7797283512; Upper Pelling). There's also a Pelling–Kalimpong jeep but oddly you can only book that in Geyzing. Almost all other transport starts from Geyzing's packed **jeep stand** (Mani Rd), which is West Sikkim's de facto transport hub.

For Yuksom, Utterey, Khecheopalri and Dentam, ask your hotel to phone possible shared-jeep drivers to try to arrange a pick-up at Upper Pelling, since they all pass through on their way back from Geyzing, mid-afternoon – but that doesn't always work as most will be full of locals. Many tourists simply book a private vehicle through one of the numerous Pelling agencies.

Khecheopalri Lake

ELEV 1800M

Pronounced like 'ketchup-perry', **Khecheopalri Lake** (Kechuperi Lake; ₹10; ⏰tickets sold 5am-5.30pm) is a placid 'holy' reservoir precipitously ringed with thickly forested hills. Its attraction is its serenity, rather than any great visual drama: you'll do best to avoid arriving mid-morning in high season, when streams of day trippers disturb the peace. Late afternoon is a fine time to arrive – most tourists have left and the low light glows beautifully through the trees and endlessly flapping multicoloured prayer flags.

Better still, hike around a half-hour up from the car park through dense forest to idyllic **Khacheopalri Village** on the ridgetop above (south). The place has a wonderful timeless quality, a 400-year-old stupa, 360-degree views and two particularly wonderful, if simple, homestays. Ask your hosts about day hikes, or practise meditation with Pala, an octogenarian monk who was once a cook for the Dalai Lama.

Sleeping & Eating

Flanking the lake's car park are a series of small, simple restaurants and shops serving instant noodles and *momo*. In the village, homestays provide guests with meals; **Sonam's Homestay** (☎9735589678; zamyang22@gmail.com; Khecheopalri village; per person incl meals ₹600) 🍃 can provide day-hiking nonguests with lunch for ₹100 (with around an hour's notice).

★**Lake View Nest** HOMESTAY $$

(☎9735945598, 9593976635; lakeviewnest@gmail.com; Khecheopalri village; per person incl meals ₹850-1250) 🍃 All alone at the western end of Khecheopalri village, around 10 minutes' walk from the gompa, this delightful homestay has four guesthouse-standard rooms with wicker lamps, *thangka* (Tibetan cloth painting) and comfy beds, sharing one remarkably clean bathroom downstairs, with sit-down flush toilet and giant geyser.

Getting There & Away

Two or three shared jeeps to Geyzing via Pelling (₹60, 1½ hours) leave the car park around 6am, returning early afternoon via Pelling. A private taxi from Yuksom or Pelling typically costs around ₹1500/2200 one way/return with all-day waiting. Hitching a ride back to Pelling with other tourist vehicles is often possible in the mid-morning if you ask nicely.

Yuksom

☎03595 / ELEV 1750M

Charming and still relatively unspoilt, Yuksom is the historical starting point of the Sikkimese nation, its first capital and the coronation place of its first chogyal (king). For adventurers the village is also a starting point – as the main trailhead for treks towards **Mt Khangchendzonga**. If you don't have that kind of energy, though, it's just the ticket as a relaxed, friendly place to kick back quietly for a few nights.

Sights

Norbugang Park HISTORIC SITE

(₹20; ⏰5am-6pm) Yuksom means 'meeting place of the three lamas', referring to the trio of Tibetan holy men who crowned the first chogyal of Sikkim at this historic site in 1641. Aflutter with prayer flags, the charming woodland garden contains a small temple,

OFF THE BEATEN TRACK

YUKSOM TO TASHIDING HIKE

This wonderful one-day hike requires no permits and can be done quite easily if you start in Yuksom. Figure on at least six hours of walking (19km), excluding stops. Porter-guides are available in Yuksom for around ₹600 if you're not confident with way-finding.

Start by ascending to **Dubdi Gompa**, descending behind the monastery and contouring around on the road to **Tsong** (around 4km total). There are some rough steps up to the left of the road around 100m before you reach Tsong's three-jeep parking stand and shop; if you miss them there's a second chance with clearer steps rising up to the volleyball court. The stone-reinforced trail runs behind, heading up, then down, finally steeply up again in around 45 minutes to reach lonely **Hongri Gompa** (keep left when the path splits). At the toilet block directly behind the gompa the path splits, offering three directions – take the grassy central option, then five minutes beyond take the lower path. Allow around an hour to reach upper **Nessa** hamlet, staying high at any major junction. Some 10 minutes further is the village of **Pokhari Dara**, locally famed for its little pea-green pond. After another 3km by road (slightly less using a rather overgrown parallel footpath) you reach the access path for **Silnon Gompa**. From here it's an hour or so down steps and steep trails to Tashiding (p557), starting behind the yellow school building – but check with monks that you're on the right path, because if you miss the key shortcuts, it's a 12km plod by road.

If you arrive at Tashiding by 2pm it's usually possible to find a shared jeep back to Yuksom the same afternoon.

a huge prayer wheel, a chorten containing earth from each corner of Sikkim and the supposedly original four-seat **Coronation Throne** (Norbugang).

Dubdi Gompa BUDDHIST MONASTERY
(₹20; ⏲9am-3pm) High on the ridge above Yuksom, this compact, peaceful gompa is beautifully set in tended gardens, with dawn views of white peaks between high green folds of forested foothills. Established in 1647 in honour of Lhatsun Chenpo, Dubdi is said to be Sikkim's oldest still-functioning monastery, though many signs oddly misdate it to 1701.

Tashi Tenka VIEWPOINT
When Yuksom was Sikkim's capital, a royal palace complex known as Tashi Tenka sat on a ridge to the south of town. Today, barely a stone remains but the views are superb. To get here, walk around five minutes towards Pelling and take the long stairway up through a 'heritage garden' near the school football pitch for anothern 10 minutes. The best viewpoint is beyond the four-house hamlet on the top.

Activities

Heavenly Traveller TREKKING
(☎9733084983; www.goechalatrek.org) Responsive and good-value, DS Limboo offers a well-oiled service for standard Dzongri and Goecha La treks. There's also a guesthouse.

Red Panda Tours & Travels TREKKING
(☎9733196470, 9002322885; www.redpandatreks.weebly.com; Main Rd; ⏲8am-6pm) Beside Gupta Restaurant, 'Panda' is a former-porter-turned-guide with considerable expertise and experience. As well as standard trekking packages, he offers guide-only Goecha La treks and permits for those with all their own equipment.

Sleeping & Eating

★**Limboo Homestay** GUESTHOUSE $
(☎09733084983; www.limboohomestay.com; s/d/cottage ₹800/1000/1200) Above a shop and highly reputable trekking agency (p555), rooms here are sparkling clean. There's little decor but the forest is close enough for dawn birdsong choruses, there are fine views from the roof and the glorious vegetable garden behind produces most of the food for delicious home-cooked food (by pre-order).

Hotel Tashi Gang HOTEL $$
(☎9933007720, 9733077249; hoteltashigang@gmail.com; Main Rd; s/d from ₹1650/2200) Half-timbered inside and out, the Tashi Gang has an old-fashioned heritage feel set in spacious lawns hemmed with flowers and subtle lighting. Beyond the fireplace lounge, grey-marble corridors with B&W photo portraits lead to pleasant rooms with Sikkimese floral headboards and colourful *thangka* (cloth paintings), but somewhat dated bathrooms.

Hotel Yangrigang HOTEL $

(☎03595-241217, 9434164408; Main Rd; s/d from ₹600/800) At first glance there's not much to this fairly functional hotel near the start of Yuksom's main street. But the family are helpful, the food is good and the rooms are large and very fair value, with geysers that heat up well (given a half-hour).

Hotel Red Palace HERITAGE HOTEL $$

(☎9593668773; www.hotelredpalace.com; Nghadak Monastery Rd; s ₹1830-2830, d ₹1980-3190, ste ₹3790) Looking from the outside like a Darjeeling mansion but with Sikkimese lintels, this hotel has a lobby that feels more like a sofa-strewn temple, and a dining hall with token Tibetan motifs. Basic rooms are simpler but comfy and clean.

Mama's Kitchen SIKKIMESE, BAKERY $

(Mangsabung Path; mains ₹30-200; ⌚6am-10pm) Charming hostess Pema serves delicious, very genuine Sikkimese home cuisine, along with fresh muffins, sponge cake and even bowls of creamy pasta in this tiny one-room cafe. Preparation takes a while so it's worth pre-ordering and fixing a dining time.

Gupta Restaurant MULTICUISINE $

(Main Rd; mains ₹50-120; ⌚5.30am-8pm) Yuksom's foremost traveller meeting point is little more than a shack with a one-table thatched rotunda, but it's an old-school classic serving thali, *thukpa* (noodle soup), pizzas and paneer curries, as well as curious quesadillas that take your taste buds south of the border (even if it's only the Tibetan one).

ℹ Getting There & Away

At around 6.30am, several shared jeeps leave for Jorethang (₹250, three to four hours) via Tashiding (₹60, 1½ hours); Geyzing via Pelling (₹100, 2½ hours); and Gangtok (₹300, six hours) – book the day before at the shop next to Gupta Restaurant. There's also a Gangtok service around 2pm, as well as a Geyzing via Tashiding jeep at around 12.30pm (call the driver on ☎8763952216 to book, but be aware that as many as 15 people have been known to squeeze into the seven seats).

Dzongri & Goecha La – The Khangchendzonga Trek

For guided groups (no lone hikers) Sikkim's classic trek is a five- to nine-day epic from Yuksom to the 4940m **Goecha La** and back. The route showcases more than a dozen massive peaks; a gruelling, pre-dawn slog gets you unforgettable views of the awesome **Khangchendzonga Massif** (weather permitting). With less time, a five-day return to **Dzongri** still gives superb panoramas of **Mt Pandim**; even a two-day return to **Tsokha** is a memorable experience, with waterfalls, hanging bridges and lovely valley views. While the trek is not a technical climb, the high altitude, long days and pre-dawn summit-day start make it comparatively challenging, especially when the trail is foggy or slippery after rain.

The trek is only feasible several months a year. Late March to mid-May offers the best temperatures but rain is common in the afternoons and trails get muddy. October to November have the highest chance of clear skies, but snow and subzero temperatures are possible; upper camps will see frost in November.

You must have a permit and guide organised through a registered agency. The permits are only available in Gangtok, but (miraculously) if you book in the evening, most Yuksom fixers can send copies of your documents by the next morning's jeep and

KHANGCHENDZONGA TREK SCHEDULE

STAGE	ROUTE	DURATION (HR)
1	Yuksom to Baktim/Tsokha	7-8
2	Optional acclimatisation day at Tsokha	
3	Tsokha to Dzongri	4-5
4	Acclimatisation day at Dzongri, or continue to Kokchurong	
5	Dzongri (or Kokchurong) to Lamuni	6-7
6	Lamuni to Goecha La and back (most groups descend further to Thangsing)	9-12 (11-14)
7	Lamuni (Thangsing) to Tsokha	8 (7)
8	Tsokha to Yuksom	5-7

have everything arranged for departure the day after.

Technically, foreigners are required to be at least in pairs or bigger groups. However, we twice encountered exceptions – one foreigner alone with guide; one Indian/non-Indian couple (also with guide) – so the rule may be bendable in certain circumstances.

If you carry your own gear and pay for your own food and lodging along the way, the cost for the guide of a return trek will be about ₹20,000 total, split among the group.

With tents, cook, porter yaks and all food, you're looking at around ₹30,000 per person for a couple, or as little as ₹20,000 per person in a large group of a dozen or more.

Tashiding

ELEV 1240M

Little Tashiding is essentially a low-rise one-street market village sloping up from its jeep stand and briefly bypassed by the Yuksom–Legship road. It's notable as the access point for the Tashiding Gompa and its enchanting stupas, set on an isolated ridge 3.5km away. While you don't see many white-top mountains from here, views over plunging green valleys, forested slopes and occasional stripes of rice terracing more than compensate.

Tashiding is also the destination of a popular one-day hike from Yuksom (p555) via isolated monasteries Hongri and Silnon.

If you arrive by 2pm you can generally nip back to Yuksom by shared jeep. If you pay for a whole taxi you can admire several waterfalls en route, the most impressive of which is Phamrong.

Sights

Tashiding Gompa MONASTERY

(dawn-dusk, main hall closes around 3pm) FREE The ridge between Ralang and Yuksom ends with an upturned promontory (1450m) on which sits the multi-building complex of Tashiding Gompa, an important Nyingmapa monastery. At its heart, a beautifully proportioned **prayer hall** has a delicate topknot that contrasts with the two lower stone floors. The murals inside are somewhat time-darkened and the main images fronted with numerous colourful butter sculptures. Behind the Guru Lakhang building is a unique **'forest' of chorten stupas**, mantra stones and a dharma bell, overlooked by two ancient Kashmir cypress trees.

Dzongri & Goech La

Phamrong Falls WATERFALL

(Yuksom-Tashiding Rd, Km6) FREE The most dramatic of four waterfalls between Yuksom and Tashiding, the Phamrong's powerful flow fires itself through a high, green notch then crashes down a steep cliff. Viewed from the road, it's fronted by several sub-cascades; climbing an overgrown path for around five minutes gets you to a vandalised octagonal viewing pavilion, beyond which are a couple of natural pools just before the main spray. Locals bathe here but access can be rather dicey.

Sleeping & Eating

Sanu Homestay HOMESTAY $

(Sanoo Homestay; 9635060062; www.facebook.com/sanu.bhutia.94; Tashiding Gompa Path; per person incl meals ₹600) With a minor cult following among foreign backpackers, Sanu and her mother offer great food and very simple lodging in a wild garden reached after about 15 minutes' walk off the road to Tashiding Gompa.

Getting There & Away

The **jeep stand** (Tashiding Bazaar) is at the south end of the short bazaar street. Departures for Gangtok (₹200, six hours), Jorethang (₹150, three hours) and Siliguri (₹250, seven hours) all leave by around 7am. Several Geyzing jeeps (₹100, two hours) leave between 6.30am and 8.30am, with one more around 2pm. For Yuksom (₹70, 2½ hours) there's one jeep at around 9am (usually very full on arrival) and several more between 2pm and 3pm.

Chartering a vehicle to Yuksom (₹600, 1½ hours) costs a lot more but you'll save an hour in travel time.

Kuluk & Rinchenpong

ELEV 1600M

The small ridge-top settlements of **Martam**, **Bermiok**, **Kaluk** and **Rinchenpong** stare north across a gaping valley, towards a magnificent mountain panorama taking in a series of white Himalayan peaks and a saw-toothed range of lower crags to the east of the main massif. The scene is arguably even more memorable than from much more developed Pelling, especially viewed from Rinchenpong, which also has a pair of historic monasteries, and from Kuluk, 3km east, where there's a handy junction bazaar and taxi stand.

Sights

★Resum Gompa BUDDHIST MONASTERY

(Rinchenpong) If you love forgotten, naively painted temples, little Resum Gompa is likely to be one of the highlights of your monastic wanderings in Sikkim. Adding to the fun is the lack of any access road, forcing you to walk around 20 minutes through the forest, encountering occasional collapsing stupas and *mani* walls with sacred inscriptions. With 360-degree views, this wobbly old place is a peaceful delight with an incredible mountain panorama.

Sleeping & Eating

★Ghonday Village Resort HOTEL $$

(☎9593979695, 03595-210339; www.ghondayresort.com; Kuluk; r ₹3500-4500, walk-in from ₹1500; wifi) A complimentary coffee and traditional silk-scarf welcome underline the high-quality service and upmarket feel to this lovely resort, which has jaw-dropping panoramic views. Sturdy fittings work remarkably well in large, well-appointed rooms. Some units are airy cottages set in lush, sloped gardens, where there's a playground-sized chess set.

★Biksthang FARMSTAY $$$

(☎9593779077; www.biksthang.com; Mangalbarey Rd; s incl half-board ₹6000-13,000, d ₹6450-22,050; P) If you'd like to escape from techno-modernity, yet unwind with highly educated, thoughtful hosts, it's hard to imagine anywhere better than this isolated but very classy farmstay. Eight artistically appointed cottages are tucked between turmeric, mandarin and cardamon groves; the unique dining room is within a photogenic 19th-century farmhouse and Khangchendzonga reflects grandly in the infinity pool.

Getting There & Away

Shared jeeps operate on two main routes, Rinchenpong–Dentam–Pelling–Geyzing and Dentam–Bermiok–Kuluk–Soreng–Jorethang, heading outbound early morning and returning from Jorethang or Geyzing in the early afternoon.

Kuluk's tiny bazaar, where the Rinchenpong road turns off the main Dentam–Soreng road, is a good place to find a private taxi; Dentam–Jorethang shared jeeps drop passengers off here fairly regularly. Central Rinchenpong has a small, slightly less busy **taxi rank**, 2.6km from Kuluk.

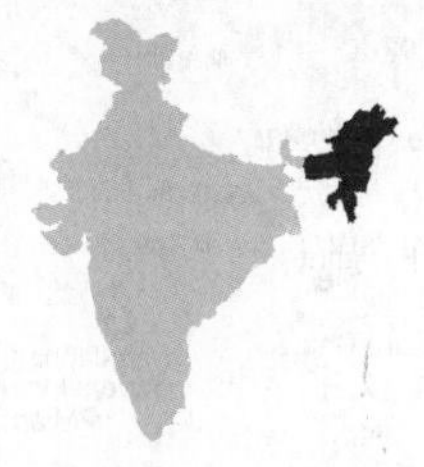

Northeast States

Includes ➡

Best Places to Eat

- Paradise (p563)
- Luxmi Kitchen (p584)
- Moti Mahal (p571)
- Maihang (p568)
- Trattoria (p591)

Best Places to Sleep

- Diphlu River Lodge (p568)
- Puroni Bheti (p569)
- Ri Kynjai (p591)
- Prabhakar Homestay (p563)

Why Go?

Thrown across the farthest reaches of India, obscured from the greater world by ageless forests and formidable mountain ranges, the Northeast States are one of Asia's last great natural and anthropological sanctuaries. Sharing borders with Bhutan, Tibet, Myanmar (Burma) and Bangladesh, these remote frontiers are a region of rugged beauty, and a collision zone of tribal cultures, climates, landscapes and peoples. In this wonderland for adventurers, glacial Himalayan rivers spill onto Assam's vast floodplains, faith moves mountains on the perilous pilgrimage to Tawang, rhinos graze in Kaziranga's swampy grasslands and former headhunters slowly embrace modernity in their ancestral longhouses in Nagaland.

Of course, it's not all smooth sailing in these faraway states, and there's a horde of obstacles to battle along the way (bad roads, poor infrastructure and rebel armies, to name a few). Only those with a taste for raw adventure need apply.

When to Go

Assam (Guwahati)

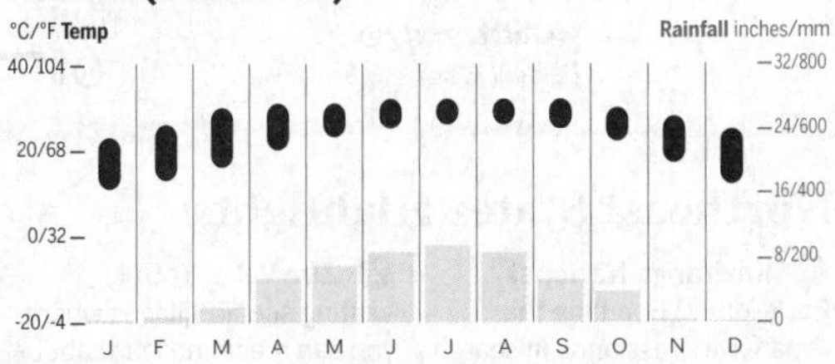

Mar The best season for rhino-spotting in Kaziranga.

Oct A time for dazzling Himalayan vistas and trips to remote outposts.

Dec Fierce Naga warriors in ethnic regalia assemble for Kohima's spectacular Hornbill Festival.

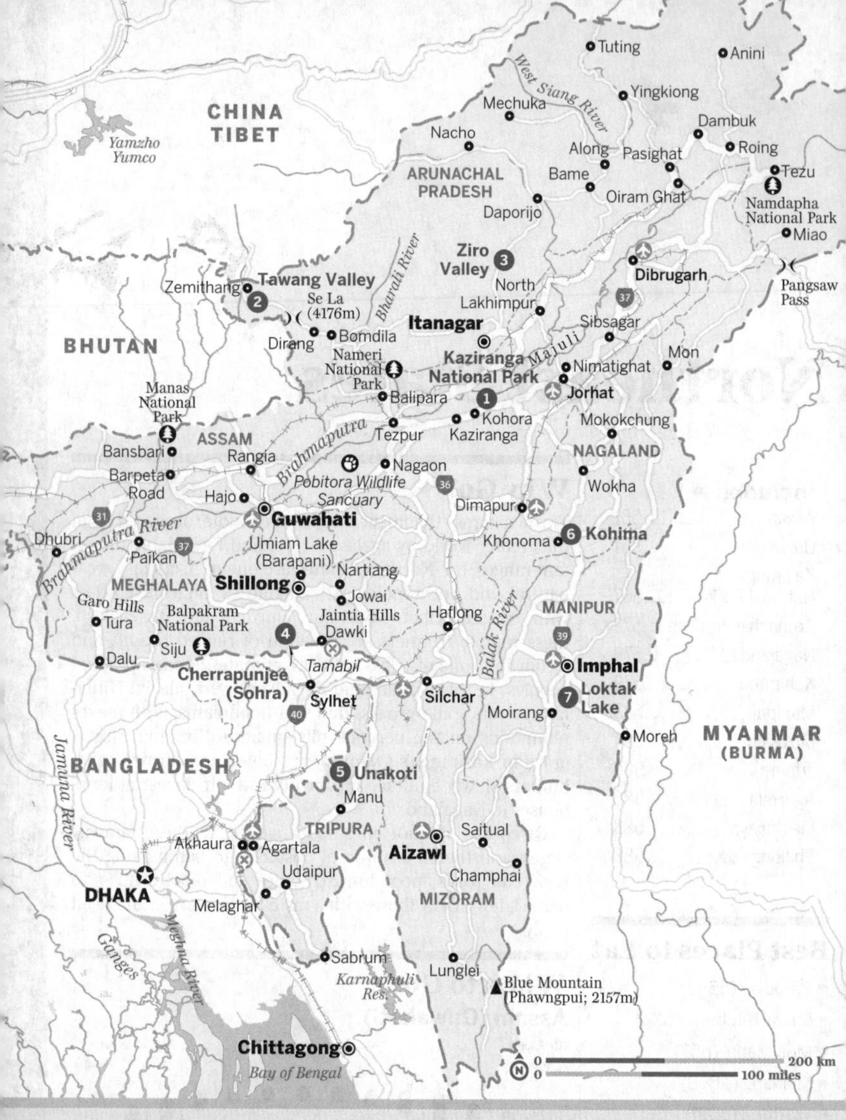

Northeast States Highlights

1. **Kaziranga National Park** (p567) Roaming the expansive grasslands in search of rhinos.
2. **Tawang Valley** (p578) Touching the clouds at the 4176m Se La pass before descending to the Tawang Valley, a Tibetan Buddhist hot spot.
3. **Ziro Valley** (p574) Visiting scenic villages where you can meet and learn about the intriguing Apatani tribe.
4. **Cherrapunjee** (p592) Gazing down on the plains of Bangladesh from a lofty escarpment.
5. **Unakoti** (p588) Staring in awe at massive rock-cut sculptures of gods amid the wilderness.
6. **Kohima** (p579) Visiting a quaint WWII cemetery and sampling traditional Naga hospitality.
7. **Loktak Lake** (p584) Exploring the lake's unique ecosystem and floating islands.

ASSAM

Sprawled like a prehistoric leviathan along the length of the Brahmaputra valley, Assam (also known as Ahom) is the biggest and most accessible of the Northeast States. A hospitable population, a cuisine with its own distinctive aromas and flavours, a vibrant artistic heritage marked by exotic dance forms, and a string of elegant Hindu temples top its list of innumerable attractions. The archetypal Assamese landscape is a picturesque golden-green vista of rice fields and manicured tea estates, framed by the blue mountains of Arunachal in the north and the highlands of Meghalaya and Nagaland to the south.

Assam's culture is proudly sovereign. The *gamosa* (a red-and-white scarf worn around the neck by men) and the *mekhola sador* (the traditional dress for women) are visible proclamations of regional costume and identity, while the subtly flavoured fish *tenga* (sour curry) is distinctly different from its regional culinary cousins.

Guwahati

0361 / POP 810,000

History

Guwahati is considered the site of Pragjyotishpura, a semi-mythical town founded by Asura king Naraka (son of an avatar of Vishnu who later transformed into a demon), later killed by Krishna for a pair of magical earrings. The city was a vibrant cultural centre well before the Ahoms arrived from Southeast Asia around the 13th century, and it was subsequently the theatre of intense Ahom–Mughal strife, changing hands eight times in 50 years before 1681. In 1897, a huge earthquake – followed by a series of devastating floods – wiped out most of the old city.

Dormant through much of India's colonial history, Guwahati gained metropolitan prominence after the formation of Assam state in the post-Independence era. Though technically not the state capital (the title goes to contiguous Dispur), Guwahati is Assam's number-one city.

Sights

Kamakhya Mandir HINDU TEMPLE

(no queue/short queue/queue ₹500/100/free; 8am-1pm & 3pm-dusk) According to Hindu legend, when an enraged Shiva divided his deceased wife Sati's body into 108 pieces and scattered them across the land, her *yoni* (vagina) fell on Kamakhya Hill. This makes Kamakhya Mandir one of the most hallowed shrines for practitioners of *shakti* (tantric worship of female spiritual power). It is here that the Ambubachi Mela festival takes place. Kamakhya is 7km west of central Guwahati and 3km up a spiralling side road.

Assam State Museum MUSEUM

(GNB Rd; ₹5, camera/video ₹10/100; 10am-5pm Wed-Mon Mar-Oct, to 4pm Nov-Feb) Housed in an imposing colonial-era building, this museum has a large sculpture collection and upper floors devoted to informative tribal-culture displays. In the anthropological galleries, you can walk through reconstructed tribal homes that give a glimpse of everyday rural life. Time permitting, it's worth a visit.

Old Guwahati AREA

This quaint area of Guwahati, bordering the Brahmaputra River, is best explored on foot. Walk past the beehive dome of the **Courthouse** (MG Rd), which rises above attractive **Dighulipukhuri Park** (HB Rd; ₹10;

TOP REGIONAL FESTIVALS

Losar (Feb) Masked Tibetan Buddhist dances in Tawang.

Rongali Bihu (Apr) Assamese New Year festivities.

Ambubachi Mela (Jun/Jul) A melange of tantric fertility rituals at Kamakhya Mandir in Guwahati.

Ziro Music Festival (www.zirofestival.com; Sep) The region's very own Glastonbury takes place in Ziro Valley.

Wangala (Oct/Nov) Garo harvest festival with dancing and drumming.

Ras Mahotsav (Nov) Much song and dance in praise of Lord Krishna on Majuli Island.

Hornbill Festival (www.hornbillfestival.com; 1-10 Dec) Naga tribes take the stage in full warrior gear just outside Kohima in Nagaland.

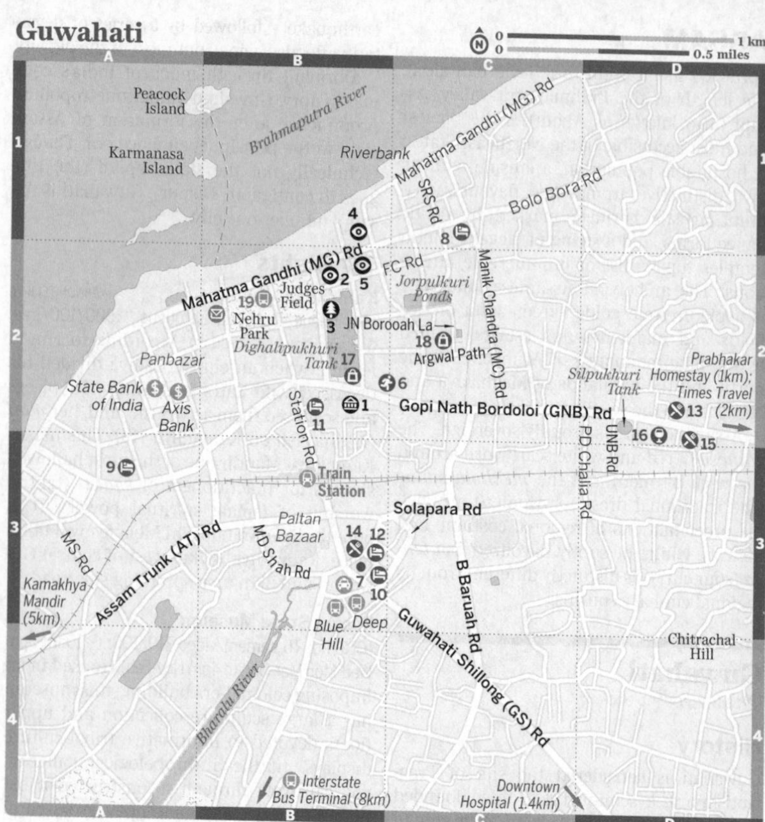

Guwahati

Sights
1 Assam State Museum B2
2 Courthouse B2
3 Dighulipukhuri Park B2
4 Guwahati Planetarium B1
5 Old Guwahati B2

Activities, Courses & Tours
6 Assam Bengal Navigation B2
Jungle Travels India .... (see 6)
7 Network Travels B3

Sleeping
8 Baruah Bhavan C1
9 Dynasty A3
10 Hotel Siroy Lily B3
11 Prashanti Tourist Lodge B2
12 Sundarban Guest House B3

Eating
13 Khorikaa D2
14 New Maa Kali B3
15 Paradise D2

Drinking & Nightlife
16 Trafik D2

Shopping
17 Artfed B2
18 Northeast Network C2

Information
Assam Tourism .... (see 11)

Transport
19 Kachari Bus Stand B2
Network Travels .... (see 7)

⏲9.30am-8pm). The nearby **Guwahati Planetarium** (MG Rd; shows ₹20; ⏲noon & 4pm, closed 1 & 15 of month) looks somewhere between a mosque and a landed UFO and and offers entertainment in the form of space shows projected on a dome-like screen. A short walk due northwest takes you to the **riverbank**, where you can take in sweeping views of the Brahmaputra along a well-maintained promenade.

Sleeping

Prashanti Tourist Lodge HOTEL $

(☎0361-2544475; Station Rd; s/d from ₹1000/1550; ❄) This central hotel is convenient for the train station. A fancy elevator takes you up to your room, which will be clean and tidy and might overlook an inviting (but out-of-bounds) swimming pool to the rear. There are drinking-water dispensers at the end of each corridor, some train noise to put up with, and no room service after 9pm.

Sundarban Guest House HOTEL $

(☎0361-2730722; Paltan Bazaar; s/d/tr from ₹800/900/1000; ❄) Reminiscent of a classic backpacker hang-out, this cheery, busy hotel sits in Guwahati's central market area and offers great value for those travelling on a budget. Rooms are typically featureless but clean and tidy, with fresh sheets, and the management is helpful. The in-house restaurant offers a decent range of basic dishes.

★**Baruah Bhavan** GUESTHOUSE $$

(☎0361-2541182; www.baruahbhavan.com; MC Rd, Uzanbazar; d incl breakfast from ₹2750; ❄@) Owned and managed by the affable and hospitable Baruah family, this charming 1970s bungalow on Manik Chandra (MC) Rd oozes nostalgia in the form of innumerable antiques and memorabilia strewn across its living areas. The six plush rooms are appointed with elegant period furniture and brocaded upholstery. The home-cooked food is matchless in terms of local flavour and character.

The manicured front lawns go extremely well with chilled beer in the evenings (just remember to carry mosquito repellent).

Hotel Siroy Lily HOTEL $$

(☎0361-2608492; www.hotelsiroygroup.com; Solapara Rd; s/d incl breakfast from ₹1550/1950; ❄☰) This trusted oldie is professionally run and offers superb value for money, and is thus a favourite with midrange travellers transiting through Guwahati. Rooms are well serviced; those with AC offer a significantly better deal for a few hundred extra rupees. Book in advance, as it's packed most of the time.

★**Prabhakar Homestay** HOMESTAY $$$

(☎9435033222; www.prabhakarhomestay.com; House 2, Bylane 2, KP Barua Rd, Chandmari; s/d incl breakfast ₹4180/4640; ❄☰) In a quiet residential area, this utterly delightful place run by ex-professor Sheila and her husband, Mahesh, is probably one of the best homestays in all India. The property is hemmed by lush gardens outside and adorned with ecochic decor within. The Assamese meals (₹650) prepared by in-house chef Pankaj give serious competition to restaurants in town.

Dynasty HOTEL $$$

(☎0361-2516021; www.dynastyhotel.in; SS Rd; d incl breakfast from ₹5500; ❄@☰) Once the best among Guwahati's hotels, the Dynasty on Sir Shahdullah (SS) Rd retains a sense of nostalgia and offers magnificent rooms with a colonial flavour. It has all the facilities you'd expect from a top-end hotel, including a couple of superb restaurants, a sauna and a spa.

> DON'T MISS
>
> **RIVER CRUISES**
>
> To experience the beauty of Assam from a unique perspective (and all of it in style), consider a plush river cruise. Departing Guwahati between September and April, these multiday luxury rides take you upstream along the Brahmaputra River to Dibrugarh, dropping anchor at essential stops such as Kaziranga National Park, Majuli Island and Sivasagar. Activities en route include wildlife tours, cultural excursions and simply lazing on the sun deck with a drink in hand. Guwahati-based **Assam Bengal Navigation** (☎9207042330; www.assambengalnavigation.com; Dirang Arcade, GNB Rd; per person per day all-inclusive from US$195) has all the information.

Eating

New Maa Kali ASSAMESE $

(Paltan Bazaar, ME Rd; mains ₹70-120; ⏲9am-11pm) This straightforward, no-frills restaurant serves a rustic but delicious version of local Assamese dishes, with an accent on fish. The menu is in Assamese, but waiters are happy to help you choose your food.

★**Paradise** INDIAN $$

(☎9435548812; GNB Rd; mains ₹100-200; ⏲10.30am-10.30pm; ❄) The lunch thali at Paradise is considered by many to be the archetypal Assamese spread, bringing together a wide range of local culinary flavours on one platter. Try the subtly flavoured fish

GUIDED TOURS

While joining a tour might seem restrictive, remember that independent travel in the Northeast can be a very tricky affair on the ground. Licensed tour agents in the region are highly experienced in dealing with permit-related red tape and negotiating with local officials, and will also help you bridge linguistic and cultural barriers in a way that would be almost impossible if you were travelling independently. Indeed, it would be very difficult to have any meaningful encounters with tribal people without a local go-between to explain the proper etiquette. A tour agent will also help you steer clear of insurgent hot spots and situations.

A few reputable tour companies in the region:

Abor Country Travels & Expeditions (☎9436053870, 0360-2292969; www.aborcountrytravels.com; B Sector)

Alder Tours & Travels (☎9402905046; www.aldertoursntravels.com; Imphal Rd; ⊙9am-5pm Mon-Sat)

Jungle Travels India (☎0361-2667871; www.jungletravelsindia.com; Dirang Arcade, GNB Rd)

Network Travels (☎0361-2605335; GS Rd; ⊙10am-7pm Mon-Sat)

Purvi Discovery (☎0373-2301120; www.purviweb.com; Medical College Rd, Jalan Nagar)

tenga (sour curry) and you're bound to become a fan for life. A vegetarian version of the thali is also available, featuring a few additional no-meat delights.

Khorikaa ADIVASI **$$**
(☎9864157454; GNB Rd; mains ₹100-180; ⊙11am-4pm & 7-10.30pm; ❄) Named after Assamese *khorikaa* (barbecued dishes), this restaurant serves a superb selection of regional fare in upscale air-conditioned comfort. Try the barbecued small fish and fried pigeon meat, or go for the delicious pork seasoned with sesame seeds.

Drinking & Nightlife

Trafik BAR
(GNB Rd; beer ₹140; ⊙11am-10pm) Dim and buzzy, this popular bar is a hit with the city's office workers and, true to its name, attracts heavy traffic after sundown. There's a vast TV screen for cricket matches and Bollywood music, and a tiny platform where live bands play local hits at weekends.

Shopping

Northeast Network CLOTHING
(☎9435017824; www.northeastnetwork.org; JN Borooah Lane; ⊙11am-4pm Mon-Fri) This NGO seeds self-help projects in villages to empower rural women and works as an umbrella organisation for several handloom-weaving cooperatives. Buying beautiful (and good-value) woven products here supports this social mission.

Artfed GIFTS & SOUVENIRS
(☎0361-2548987; GNB Rd; ⊙10am-8pm) Fine bamboo crafts, textiles, wickerwork, bell-metal and terracotta handicrafts, and many a carved rhino, are on offer at this state-operated emporium.

Information

MEDICAL SERVICES

Downtown Hospital (☎0361-2331003, 9864101111; www.downtownhospitals.in; GS Rd, Dispur) Among the best hospitals in town for emergencies. Dispur, Assam's state administrative district, is contiguous to Guwahati along GS Rd in an easterly direction.

MONEY

ATMs and banks abound all around town. It's a good idea to stock up on some local currency here if you're planning long excursions into remote parts of Northeast India.

Axis Bank (M Nehru Rd; ⊙10am-4pm Mon-Sat) Has an ATM and handles foreign exchange.

State Bank of India (Pan Bazaar; ⊙10am-4pm Mon-Fri, to 2pm Sat) Has an ATM and changes major currencies. Off Hem Barua Rd.

POST

Main Post Office (Ananda Ram Barua Rd; ⊙10am-4pm Mon-Sat)

TOURIST INFORMATION

Arunachal House (☎0361-2840215; GS Rd, Rukmini Gaon; ⊙10am-5pm Mon-Sat) Has info on travel in Arunachal Pradesh and processes permits. Also sells helicopter tickets for flights to Naharlagun helipad near Itanagar.

Assam Tourism (☎0361-2544475; www.assamtourism.gov.in; Prashaanti Tourist Lodge, Station Rd; ⊙10am-5pm Mon-Sat) Little more than an informal help desk in the Prashaanti Tourist Lodge and a tour booth just outside the building.

Getting There & Away

AIR

Air India (☎011-24624075; www.airindia.in), **IndiGo** (☎9212783838; www.goindigo.in), **GoAir** (☎9223222111; www.goair.in), **Jet Airways** (☎1800225522; www.jetairways.com) and **SpiceJet** (☎9654003333; www.spicejet.com) connect Guwahati to most major Indian cities (often with a stopover in Kolkata).

Arunachal Helicopter Service (☎0361-2842175; www.pawanhans.nic.in; Guwahati Airport; ⊙9am-2pm Mon-Sat) For those with permits, Arunachal Helicopter Service has flights to Naharlagun helipad near Itanagar (₹4000, 1½ hours, 1.30pm Monday, Wednesday and Friday, 2pm Tuesday, Thursday and Saturday).

Meghalaya Helicopter Service (☎9859021473; Guwahati Airport; ⊙flights 9am-2.50pm) Shuttles to Shillong (₹1500, 30 minutes, 9am and 12.30pm) and Tura (₹1900, 45 minutes, 10.30am and 2pm). Note that helicopters won't fly in bad weather.

BUS & SUMO

Long-distance buses leave from the Interstate Bus Terminal (ISBT), 8km from the town centre along NH37. Private bus operators run shuttle services from their offices to the ISBT. **Blue Hill** (☎0361-2609440; HPB Rd; ⊙6am-8pm), **Deep** (☎9435118527; HPB Rd; ⊙6am-9pm) and **Network Travels** (☎0361-2605335; www.networkbus.in; Paltan Bazaar, GS Rd; ⊙5am-9pm) have extensive networks. All companies hire out Sumos and other sturdy 4WD vehicles for travel in the region, and charge the same regulated fares of ₹4000 per day, including fuel and driver.

Times Travel (☎9435110947; timestravel24@gmail.com; GM Path, New Guwahati) has a good fleet of cabs and 4WD vehicles for multiday hire.

TRAIN

Four daily trains connect Guwahati to Delhi, among which the 12423 Dibrugarh–Rajdhani Express (3AC/2AC ₹2560/3565, 28 hours, 7am) is the fastest and most comfortable. The best daily train to Kolkata (Howrah) is the 12346 Saraighat Express (sleeper/3AC/2AC ₹500/1315/1885, 17 hours, 12.30pm). If travelling to Darjeeling and Sikkim, get off at New Jalpaiguri (sleeper/3AC/2AC ₹295/765/1075, seven hours).

Several trains also serve Dimapur (2nd seating/sleeper/3AC ₹105/180/460, four to six hours), Jorhat (2nd seating/sleeper/3AC ₹175/235/585, seven to 11 hours) and Dibrugarh (sleeper/3AC/2AC ₹180/315/860, 10 to 14 hours).

Getting Around

Getting into town from Guwahati's orderly Lokpriya Gopinath Bordoloi International Airport (23km away) costs ₹500/150/100 for a taxi/shared taxi/airport bus. **Shared taxis** (per person/car ₹150/500) travel to the airport from outside Hotel Mahalaxmi on GS Rd. Autorickshaws charge ₹50 to ₹100 for short hops within the city. You could also call an Uber through your mobile-based app and enjoy a comfortable aircon ride for less than ₹10 per kilometre within town or to the airport.

Buses leave for several local destinations from **Kachari bus stand** (MG Rd).

Around Guwahati

Hajo & Poa Mecca

Some 30km northwest of Guwahati, the pleasant little town of Hajo attracts Hindu and Buddhist pilgrims to its five ancient

BUSES FROM GUWAHATI

DESTINATION	FARE (₹)	DURATION (HR)
Agartala (Tripura)	950	24-26
Aizawl (Mizoram)	760	28
Dibrugarh	510	10
Imphal (Manipur)	750	17
Jorhat	320	7
Kaziranga	260-350	6
Kohima (Nagaland)	410	13
Shillong (Meghalaya)	120	2½
Sivasagar	410	8
Tezpur	190	5

temples topping assorted hillocks. **Hayagriva Madhav Temple** is the main shrine, which is accessed by a long flight of steps through an ornate quasi-Mughal gateway. The images inside of Madhav, an avatar of Krishna, are believed to be 6000 years old. To get here, take local bus 25 from the Adabari bus stand in Guwahati (₹60, one hour).

Two kilometres east of Hajo is **Poa Mecca mosque**, sheltering the tomb of Hazarat Shah Sultan Giasuddin Aulia Rahmatullah Alike, an emperor-saint from Iraq who came here to preach Islam and died some 800 years ago. Muslims need to walk (the less pious may drive) 4km up a spiral road to reach the mosque, which is architecturally unremarkable.

Pobitora National Park

Located about 40km east of Guwahati, **Pobitora** (Indian/foreigner ₹50/500, camera ₹50/500, video ₹500/1000; ⌚4WD access 7.30am-noon & 2.30pm-dusk Nov-Apr) is known for its thriving population of one-horned rhinoceros: nearly 100 of these hulking creatures call this 17-sq-km park their home. Besides, Pobitora is also popular among wildlife enthusiasts for other species such as leopard, wild buffalo, wild boar and almost 2000 resident and migratory bird types. Getting into the park involves a boat ride over the river boundary to the elephant-mounting station, from where you could embark on a one-hour trip atop an elephant, lumbering through boggy grasslands and stirring up petulant rhinos. Note, however, that elephant rides here incorporate the use of *howdahs*, which have been known to cause spinal injuries to the jumbos; many prefer to avoid these rides in the interests of elephant welfare. To get here, hire a half-day cab (₹1500) from Guwahati.

Tezpur

☎03712 / POP 105,500

Little more than a utilitarian stopover for travellers journeying into Arunachal Pradesh or Upper Assam, Tezpur is a charming town with some beautifully kept parks, attractive lakes and enchanting views of the mighty Brahmaputra River as it laps the town's edge.

Sights

Chitralekha Udyan PARK

(Cole Park; Jenkins Rd; ₹20, camera/video ₹20/100; ⌚9am-7pm) Chitralekha Udyan has a U-shaped pond (paddle-boat hire ₹20 per person) wrapped around pretty manicured lawns dotted with fine ancient sculptures. From April to September, the park also contains bumper cars and water slides. A block east, then south, stands **Ganeshgarh Temple**, which backs onto a ghat overlooking the surging Brahmaputra. It's a good place to take in river sunsets.

Sleeping & Eating

Prashaanti Tourist Lodge HOTEL $

(☎03712-221016; touristlodgetezpur@gmail.com; Jenkins Rd; s/d/tr ₹850/950/1300) Facing Chitralekha Udyan south of the bus station, this government-run hotel has been spruced up to cater to international budget travellers. The spacious, good-value rooms have clean attached bathrooms, fresh sheets and mosquito nets. The staff is extremely efficient and obliging by government standards.

Hotel KRC Palace HOTEL $$

(krc.tezpur@rediffmail.com; JN Rd; s/d from ₹2530/2970; ❄📶) Touting itself as 'one of the finest hotels in Assam', this smart midrange address offers great value for money. The spacious rooms have comfy beds, large windows, clean and airy loos, and mod cons such as flat-screen TVs and wi-fi. It's a five-minute walk along JN Rd from Mission Chariali.

KF HOTEL $$$

(☎03712-255203; kfhotel@gmail.com; Mission Charali; s/d from ₹2420/2970; ❄📶) With slick, contemporary rooms, good customer service and plenty of attention to detail, this hotel – located about 3km north of the town centre – has lots going for it. There's an in-house restaurant, a coffeeshop and, most importantly, a well-stocked department store downstairs where you can buy essentials before venturing into remote areas.

Chat House FAST FOOD $

(Baliram Bldg, cnr NB & NC/SC Rds; snacks from ₹50; ⌚8am-9.30pm; 🌶) On the rooftop terrace, Chat House has an open-sided, but roofed, dining area boasting cooling breezes, good views, Indian snacks, noodles, pizzas and *momos* (Tibetan dumplings).

Spring Valley CAFETERIA $

(NC Rd; snacks/mini meals ₹40/60; ⌚7.30am-9pm; 🌶) This incredibly busy and popular cafeteria serves hot, tasty all-day snacks and mini meals – the *puris* (deep-fried flatbreads) are simply scrumptious – through the day. The bakery section has a decent range of puffs, pastries and bread, while the upstairs vegetarian restaurant comes alive during lunch and dinner.

Getting There & Away

Jeep-booking counters are located on Jenkins Rd and run to Bomdila (₹400, eight hours), Dirang (₹400, six hours) and Tawang (₹750, 12 hours) in Arunachal Pradesh. Bargain for a private taxi on the same street for Nameri National Park (₹800) and Kaziranga National Park (₹1500). A little further on is the **bus station** (Jenkins Rd) with frequent services to Guwahati (₹190, five hours), Jorhat (₹200, four hours) and Kohora village (₹100, two hours) for Kaziranga.

Nameri National Park

Scenic Nameri National Park specialises in low-key, walk-in birdwatching treks.

Sights

Nameri National Park NATURE RESERVE
(Indian/foreigner ₹70/520, camera/video ₹50/500; dawn-dusk) Around 374 bird species have been recorded in Nameri, including such rarities as the greater spotted eagle and the white-winged duck. Birdwatching treks are a park speciality; make arrangements through Eco-Camp (p567) and **Jia Bhorelli Wild Resort** (03715-247109; d ₹2200). Mammals include wild elephants, a few rarely seen tigers and the critically endangered dwarf hog. Park fees include the compulsory armed guard. Access is from Potasali, 2km off the Tezpur–Bhalukpong road.

Sleeping & Eating

Eco-Camp TENTED CAMP $$
(9854019932, 8472800344; ecocampnameri@gmail.com; Nameri National Park; dm/d ₹400/1900) Eco-Camp organises park visits, including two-hour birdwatching rafting trips (₹1650/2200 in a two/four seater). Accommodation is in 'tents', but colourful fabrics, private bathrooms, sturdy beds and thatched-roof shelters make the experience relatively luxurious. The camp is set within lush gardens full of tweeting birds and butterflies drunk on tropical nectar, while the exotic plants are all labelled for easy identification.

Eastern Himalayan Botanic Gardens RESORT $$$
(Wild Mahseer; 03714-234354; wildmahseer@gmail.com; d incl full board from ₹12,000;) Set amid rolling tea gardens about 5km from Balipara and 30km northeast of Tezpur, this resort offers luxury accommodation in four superbly renovated planter's bungalows on a picturesque 9-hectare campus canopied with evergreen trees. The showcase Heritage Bungalow (₹29,500 per double including full board) is a stately 100-year-old building that preserves a slice of the high life from its past.

Getting There & Away

You can hire a taxi from Tezpur to Nameri National Park for ₹800.

Kaziranga National Park

03776

The famed one-horned rhinoceros, one of India's best-known tourism wildlife mascots, calls the expansive grasslands of the Kaziranga National Park home.

The park consists of western, central and eastern ranges, with the central range doubling as the venue for early-morning elephant safaris.

Sights

Kaziranga National Park NATURE RESERVE
(Indian/foreigner ₹50/500, camera ₹50/500, video ₹500/1000; 4WD access 7.30am-noon & 2.30pm-dusk Nov-Apr) The park's population of 1800-odd rhinos represents more than two-thirds of the world's total (in 1904, there were just 200). Kaziranga offers popular 4WD (p568) and elephant safaris (p567) that allow you to get close to the rhinos. Pay park fees at the range office (p568), in the Kaziranga Tourist Complex (marked by an obvious rhino gate) about 800m south of Kohora village.

Tours

Elephant Safaris TOURS
(03776-262428; Kaziranga Tourist Complex; incl park Indian/foreigner ₹875/1875; safaris 5.30-8.30am, book the previous night) These popular safaris can be arranged at the Kaziranga Tourist Complex (located about 800m south of Kohora village and marked by an obvious rhino gate) or directly with your accommodation. Note that, while the safari elephants are well cared for by forest authorities, the rides incorporate the use of howdahs, which have the potential to cause spinal injuries to jumbos.

While no control or restrictions on elephant rides are currently in place, you may prefer to avoid them.

An armed guard accompanies some elephants as they enter the park. A ₹100 tip for mahouts and guards is customary.

4WD Safaris TOUR
(☎03776-262428; Kaziranga Tourist Complex; per vehicle incl toll fee western/central/eastern ranges ₹1600/1500/2000) These popular safaris can be arranged at the Kaziranga Tourist Complex (located about 800m south of Kohora village and marked by an obvious rhino gate) or directly with your accommodation. An armed guard accompanies all vehicles entering the park. A ₹100 tip for drivers and guards is customary.

Sleeping & Eating

Tourist Complex

Jupuri Ghar RESORT $$$
(☎9435196377, 0361-2605335; www.jupurigharkaziranga.com; d incl breakfast ₹4200; ❄) A holiday atmosphere adds to the appeal of this pretty property, comprising traditional-style cabins set around pleasant, mature gardens in a tranquil setting. It's well managed and has an open-air restaurant where you can compare your safari notes with other guests over the complimentary breakfast.

Aranya Tourist Lodge HOTEL $$
(☎03776-262429; d from ₹1250; ❄) A somewhat characterless and boxy government operation masquerading as a forest getaway, this garden-fronted hotel features clean rooms, prompt service, decent food and a well-stocked bar. It's popular with large groups, so expect some noisy company. At the time of research, renovations were due to be completed that might work a few wonders on the place.

★Maihang INDIAN $$
(☎9435600879; Kohora Village; mains ₹200-250; ⏲noon-3.30pm & 7-10pm) Fried duck, fish in sesame-paste gravy, fried pork with dried bamboo shoots or spicy mutton chunks – local cuisine can't get more varied than at this tiny roadside restaurant. A defunct vintage car repurposed into a reception desk leads to a cane-furnished dining area, where you can sample some of Assam's best ethnic delights in their most authentic form.

Beyond The Complex

Wild Grass Resort RESORT $$
(☎8876747357, 03776-262085; wildgrasskaziranga@gmail.com; d incl breakfast ₹2450) This slightly ramshackle yet cheerful resort, about 10km east of Kohora, is so popular that it doesn't bother with a sign – it carefully labels all the trees instead! Its colonial-era decor makes you feel the clock has slowed. Tasty Indian food is served in the dining room. Bookings essential in peak season.

★Diphlu River Lodge RESORT $$$
(☎0361-2667871, 9954205360; www.diphluriverlodge.com; jungle plan per person Indian/foreigner ₹10,000/18,000; ❄📶) Easily the classiest place to stay in the Kaziranga region, this fantastic resort combines fine luxuries with a rustic look and an ethno-chic theme. The bamboo cottages lining the Diphlu River boast soft beds, rain showers in stylish bathrooms, and pleasant sit-outs from where lucky guests might spot rhinos grazing the grasslands. Oh, and the food is delicious.

Bonhabi Resort RESORT $$
(☎03776-262675; www.bonhabiresort.com; d from ₹2010; ❄) This quiet, friendly place consists of an old villa with a colonial-era look and feel, plus a series of comfortable cottages set amid gorgeous gardens. The food is well cooked but somewhat unimaginative. It's well signposted on the way to the eastern range.

Iora RESORT $$$
(The Retreat; ☎9957193350; info@kazirangasafari.com; s/d incl breakfast from ₹6150/7380; ❄@📶🏊) Somewhat formal and oversized for a place like Kaziranga, this sprawling property has excellently maintained rooms (42 in all) featuring tasteful decor, modern amenities and efficient service. The swimming pool is a big draw for kids, while adults can spend a lazy afternoon indulging in a range of therapies at the in-house spa.

ℹ Information

Range Office (☎03776-262428; Kaziranga Tourist Complex; per person forest tax/road tax/wildlife-society tax ₹100/300/100; ⏲24hr) Pay park fees at this office, located at the Kaziranga Tourist Complex (marked by an obvious rhino gate) about 800m south of Kohora village. Note that the approachway to the park entrance is via a dirt track diverting to the right 1km west of the tourist complex.

ℹ Getting There & Away

Buses travel from Kohora village to Guwahati (₹350, four hours, hourly 7.30am to 4.30pm), Dibrugarh (₹300, four hours) and Tezpur (₹100, two hours).

A private taxi from Tezpur should cost ₹1500.

Jorhat

0376 / POP 140,000

Apart from being the access point for Majuli Island, bustling Jorhat has little on offer for travellers. Gar Ali, the town's commercial street, meets the main AT Rd (NH37) in front of a lively **central market**.

Sleeping & Eating

Conveniently tucked behind the Assam State Transport Corporation (ASTC) bus station, Solicitor Rd has a bunch of reasonable hotels.

Hotel Paradise HOTEL $

(0376-2321521; paradisejorhat@gmail.com; Solicitor Rd; s/d incl breakfast from ₹770/1050;) Hotel Paradise has well-kept interiors, chequered blankets, friendly service, deep-fried snacks and free wi-fi in the lobby.

New Park HOTEL $

(0376-2300721; hotelnewparkjorhat@gmail.com; Solicitor Rd; s/d from ₹1050/1150;) At the end of Solicitor Rd is New Park, a smart establishment with tidy, breezy rooms, hot showers and lots of daylight.

★**Puroni Bheti** GUESTHOUSE $$$

(9954150976; rajibbarooah@yahoo.co.in; Haroocharai Tea Estate; d incl breakfast from ₹5000;) The highlight of Jorhat is the delightful Puroni Bheti, standing amid lush tea gardens on the western edge of town and run by a super-hospitable planter and his family. Personalised attention, premium accommodation, lip-smacking homemade food and song- and laughter-filled evenings with the hosts guarantee a memorable and luxurious stay. House dogs Elsa and Bamby are great company.

Getting There & Away

The **ASTC bus station** (AT Rd) has frequent services to Sivasagar (₹80, one hour), Tezpur (₹160, four hours), and Guwahati (₹320, seven hours, eight buses 6am to noon), passing Kaziranga en route.

Jorhat's train station is in the heart of town, about 500m south of AT Rd along Gar Ali. The 12068 Jan Shatabdi Express (AC chair ₹585, seven hours, 2.30pm Monday to Saturday) is the most convenient of the three trains to Guwahati.

The windswept sandbank of **Nimati Ghat**, pockmarked with chai shacks, is the departure point for overcrowded ferries to Majuli Island (adult/4WD ₹20/600, 1½ hours, 8.30am, 10.30am, 1.30pm and 3pm). Nimati Ghat is a 12km ride from Jorhat by bus (₹30, 40 minutes).

Majuli Island

03775 / POP 168,000

Beached amid the mighty Brahmaputra River's ever-shifting puzzle of ochre sandbanks is Majuli, which at around 450 sq km is India's largest river island. For a place continually ravaged by the primal forces of nature (much of the island disappears under water every monsoon), Majuli flaunts unparalleled scenic beauty. The island is a relaxed, shimmering mat of glowing rice fields and water meadows bursting with hyacinth blossoms.

The two main villages are **Kamalabari**, 3km from the ferry port, and **Garamur**, 5km further north. Highlights of a visit here include birdwatching (nearly 100 species live here) and learning about neo-Vaishnavite philosophy at Majuli's 22 ancient *satras* (Hindu Vaishnavite monasteries and centres for art).

Surveys indicate that, at current levels of erosion, the island will cease to exist within the next two decades.

Tours

Majuli Tourism BIRDWATCHING

(9435657282; jyoti24365@gmail.com; Garamur Village; full-day tour ₹1000, bicycle hire per day ₹200) Run by the friendly and knowledgeable Jyoti Narayan Sarma, Majuli Tourism conducts birdwatching tours and rents bicycles.

Sleeping & Eating

Some of the *satras* on Majuli Island have very basic guesthouses (per person ₹200). Remember to dress conservatively on the premises.

La Maison de Ananda GUESTHOUSE $

(9957186356; monjitrisong@yahoo.in; Garamur Village; r ₹600-900) In Garamur, this thatched guesthouse on bamboo stilts has rooms decked out in locally made fabrics, giving it a hippie-chic atmosphere. There's also a new concrete block that sticks out like a sore thumb. It's run by a friendly tribal family, and the kitchen serves a delicious range of local Mishing dishes (meals ₹250).

Ygdrasill Bamboo Cottage GUESTHOUSE $

(8876707326; bedamajuli@gmail.com; Garamur Village; d/q ₹600/1200) En route from Kamalabari to Garamur, this stilted guesthouse perches on a marshy, bird-spotted lake. Listen to the chorus of a thousand cicadas before dropping off to sleep in a comfy bamboo bed in one of the spartan, traditionally furnished cottages (bring that insect repellent along!). Dinner (₹250) can be organised by prior request.

Mepo Okum GUESTHOUSE $$
(☎9435203165; Garamur Village; d ₹1800) A pretty complex of eight cottages ranged around a grassy lawn trimmed by seasonal blossoms, this place is often booked out by top-end international tour groups and is clearly the best of Majuli's overnight options. A very tasty local meal (₹500) can be enjoyed with advance arrangement.

Getting There & Around

Ferries (adult/4WD ₹20/600, 1½ hours) leave Nimati Ghat in Jorhat for Majuli Island at 8.30am, 10.30am, 1.30pm and 3pm; return trips are at 7.30am, 8.30am, 1.30pm and 3pm. Departures depend on tidal conditions and season.

Jam-packed buses/vans (₹20/30) meet arriving ferries at the pier and then drive to Garamur via Kamalabari. For long stays, consider arranging a bicycle (per day ₹200) through **Majuli Tourism** (p569).

Sivasagar

☎03772 / POP 53,800

Once the capital of the Ahom dynasty, sleepy Sivasagar (literally 'the ocean of Shiva') takes its name from the expansive and graceful reservoir complex in the heart of town. It's otherwise a chaotic suburban settlement, important to tourists as a base for exploring some beautiful outlying Ahom ruins, as well as a transit point into Nagaland.

Sights

Ahom Temples HINDU TEMPLE
(Shiva Dol; dawn-dusk) FREE Three typical Ahom temple towers rise proudly above the partly wooded southern banks of Sivasagar tank. To the west stands **Devi Dol**, to the east **Vishnu Dol** and, in the centre, the 33m-high **Shiva Dol**, consecrated to the mother goddess, Lord Vishnu and Lord Shiva respectively. It's a good place to spend some time, quietly watching pilgrims go about their rituals within the atmospheric complex shaded by tropical trees. Ask before taking photographs.

Rang Ghar MONUMENT
(Indian/foreigner ₹15/300; dawn-dusk) About 4km south along AT Rd from central Sivasagar, approximately 2km past a WWII-era metal lift-bridge, look right to see the rather beautiful Rang Ghar, a two-storey, oval-shaped pavilion that has now been impeccably restored and stands amid pretty lawns. Its gleaming sienna exterior sports some subtle stucco work in the form of floral motifs. The interiors are mostly unadorned, but you can walk up to the top floor, from where the Ahom monarchs once watched buffalo and elephant fights.

Talatal Ghar RUINS
(Indian/foreigner ₹15/300; dawn-dusk) The ruins of Talatal Ghar are located about 4km south of central Sivasagar on AT Rd. Designed as a subterranean palace complex for the Ahom kings, this sprawling structure is now mostly in ruins, although it's possible to walk

SATRAS

A *satra* is a monastery for Vishnu worship, Assam's distinctive form of everyman Hinduism. Formulated by 15th-century Assamese philosopher Sankardev, the faith eschews the caste system and idol worship, focusing on Vishnu as God, especially in his Krishna incarnation. Much of the worship is based on dance and melodramatic play-acting of scenes from the holy Bhagavad Gita. The heart of any *satra* is its *namghar* (a large, simple prayer hall), housing an eternal flame, the Gita and possibly a horde of instructive (but not divine) images. Traditionally, *satras* have also patronised the elegantly choreographed Satriya dance form and the folk-performing-arts tradition of Ankiya Bhawna, in which masked dancers play out tales from Hindu mythology. To purchase traditional dance masks (₹300 to ₹2000) as souvenirs, visit **Samaguri Satra**, a 15-minute drive from Garamur village.

The most interesting and accessible *satras* in Majuli are the large, beautifully peaceful **Uttar Kamalabari** (1km north, then 600m east of Kamalabari) and **Auni Ati** (5km west of Kamalabari), where monks are keen to show you their little **museum** (Auni Ati Satra; Indian/foreigner ₹10/50, camera/video ₹50/200; 9.30-11am & noon-4pm) of Ahom royal artefacts. The best chances of observing chanting, dances or drama recitations are around dawn and dusk or during the big **Ras Mahotsav Festival** (p561), in celebration of the birth, life and feats of Krishna.

along its ramparts and explore some of the arched portals that now stand above ground level. Adjacent to the palace is **Gola Ghar**, an elegant structure with a vaulted roof that is believed to have been the royal armoury.

Gauri Sagar HINDU TEMPLE

(Indian/foreigner ₹15/300; ⏲dawn-dusk) The somewhat grandiose complex of Gauri Sagar has an attractive central tank and a trio of distinctive 1720s temples – **Vishnudol**, **Shivadol** and **Devidol** – built by the Ahom queen Phuleswari. The most impressive of the three stuctures is Vishnudol, not as tall as Sivasagar's Shivadol but with much finer (though eroded) carvings. Gauri Sagar is on the main AT Rd about 16km south of Sivasagar en route to Kaziranga.

Sleeping & Eating

Hotel Shiva Palace HOTEL $

(☎03772-222629; hotelshivapalace.1811@rediffmail.com; AT Rd; s/d ₹990/1320, with AC from ₹1650/1980; ❄📶) Around 500m south of Shiva Dol along AT Rd is this surprisingly appealing hotel, where you'll find a line of super-smart rooms with comfy beds, clean sheets, tasteful laminate furniture and good bathrooms. It's clearly the best of Sivasagar's meagre budget options, and the pricier rooms easily conjure a faithful illusion of a business hotel. There's a good in-house restaurant.

Hotel Brahmaputra HOTEL $$$

(☎03772-222200; www.hotelbrahmaputra.com; BG Rd; s/d incl breakfast from ₹1800/2970; ❄📶) Now in its 25th year of operation, this trusted address features 34 rooms that – despite offering varying standards of comfort – all guarantee excellent value for money. Service is professional and prompt, and in-house restaurant Kaveri does a good job of Indian and Chinese staples.

Sky Chef MULTICUISINE $$

(Hotel Shiva Palace, AT Rd; mains ₹160; ⏲noon-10.30pm; ❄) Smartly appointed and featuring a good range of North Indian, Chinese and local Assamese fare, this restaurant is a great place to grab dinner after a long day's sightseeing around town. The staff will happily explain the nuances of local cuisine and help you order your preferred dishes.

Getting There & Away

The **ASTC Bus Station** (cnr AT & Temple Rds) has frequent services to Jorhat (₹80, one hour), Dibrugarh (₹100, two hours), Tezpur (₹250, five hours) and Guwahati (₹410, eight hours, hourly from 7am).

For local sightseeing trips to Rang Ghar, Talatal Ghar, Gauri Sagar and Kareng Ghar, use a tempo (half/full day ₹300/600). You'll find them at an unmarked stop about 300m up BG Rd from AT Rd.

Dibrugarh

☎0373 / POP 137,500

Cheerful and clement Dibrugarh, Assam's original tea city, usefully closes a loop between Kaziranga National Park and the Ziro–Along–Pasighat route in Arunachal Pradesh. It's also the terminus (or starting point) for the fascinating ferry ride along the Brahmaputra River to Pasighat.

Sleeping & Eating

Hotel Rajawas HOTEL $

(☎0373-2323307; www.hotelrajawas.com; AT Rd; s/d incl breakfast from ₹1000/1400; ❄@📶) Hotel Rajawas has 30 delightful rooms with modern amenities. Management does an excellent job of maintaining the property.

Hotel Little Palace HOTEL $$

(☎0373-2328700; www.hotellp.com; AT Rd; s/d from ₹1320/1920; ❄📶) Anything but little, Hotel Little Palace has 48 well-appointed rooms with clean linen. The views of the Brahmaputra from the verandah at the end of the corridor are free.

Mancotta Heritage Chang Bungalow RESORT $$$

(☎0373-2301120; purvi@sancharnet.in; Mancotta Rd; d incl meals ₹8500; ❄📶) The best place to enjoy a planter-style cuppa, Mancotta offers accommodation in a charming planter's bungalow fronted by lawns. It also arranges tea tours and river cruises on request.

Moti Mahal NORTH INDIAN $$

(AT Rd; mains ₹180-250; ⏲11am-3pm & 7-11pm; ❄) Hotel Rajawas boasts the highly recommended Moti Mahal restaurant, an upmarket eatery popular with the town's gastronomes that serves superb North Indian food, including staples such as naan, butter chicken, *palak paneer* (unfermented cheese chunks in pureed-spinach gravy) and *tarka dhal* (lentils seasoned and tempered with spices).

Getting There & Away

From Mohanbari Airport, 16km northeast of Dibrugarh and 4km off the Tinsukia road, Air India and Jet Airways fly to Guwahati, Kolkata and Delhi, and IndiGo flies to Guwahati and Kolkata.

From the main **bus station** (Mancotta Rd), both ASTC and private buses depart for Sivasagar (₹100, two hours, frequent 6am to 9am), Jorhat (₹200, three hours, frequent 6am to 9am), Tezpur (₹400, six hours, hourly 6am to 6pm) and Guwahati (₹550, nine hours, hourly 6am to 8am and 8pm to 10pm). There's also an AC Volvo service to Guwahati (₹790, seven hours, 8.30pm).

From the train station in the town centre, the overnight 12423 Dibrugarh–Rajdhani Express leaves for Guwahati (3AC/2AC ₹1150/1560, 8.35pm, 10 hours).

Rattletrap **ferries** (person/vehicle ₹60/1000; ⏲ hourly 9am-3pm) cruise daily to Bogibil Ghat (1½ hours) on the Arunachal side of the Brahmaputra River, where they're met by a bus to Pasighat in Arunachal Pradesh. Challenging the basic laws of flotation, the rickety steamboats carry up to four cars, a few dozen motorcycles and an army of humans. There's little shelter, so bring hat, sunglasses, water and sunscreen. Exact departure times depend on the Brahmaputra's water level. During the dry season, ferries cruise further upstream to Oiram Ghat, which can take up to five hours. Many hotels in Dibrugarh sell 4WD-ferry-4WD combination tickets (per person ₹300) for travel to Pasighat.

Manas National Park

☎ 03666

About 180km from Guwahati, along the Assam–Bhutan border, lies Bodoland's **Manas National Park** (☎ 03666-261413; incl elephant safari Indian/foreigner ₹1100/2100, camera/video ₹50/500; ⏲ Nov-Apr). The park has three forest ranges, of which the central **Bansbari Range** is the most accessible, reached from the town of Barpeta Road, northwest of Guwahati. The forests here are contiguous with the wilderness zone on the Bhutanese side of the international border, which bears the same name.

Sleeping & Eating

Bansbari Lodge LODGE **$$$**
(☎ 0361-2667871; www.assambengalnavigation.com/bansarilodge.html; per person incl full board ₹4500; ❄) The Bansbari Range can be appreciated in delightful comfort at Bansbari Lodge. Jungle packages (per person ₹9000) cover full board, an early-morning elephant safari, a jeep safari, a guide and the park entry fee. However, you may prefer to avoid the elephant ride because of the animal welfare issues. Ask about river rafting, village tours and tribal cultural programs. Access is from Barpeta Road. Book through the Guwahati-based Assam Bengal Navigation (p563).

Bear in mind that the elephant safaris here incorporate the use of *howdahs*, which can be harmful to the animals.

Getting There & Away

Guwahati–Kokrajhar buses (₹120) serve Pathsala junction and pass within 3km of Barpeta Road.

The 15960 Kamrup Express (sleeper/3AC ₹140/490, 2½ hours, 7.45am) and 14055 Brahmaputra Mail (sleeper/3AC ₹100/490, 2½ hours, 12.50pm) connect Guwahati and Barpeta Road.

Jeep rental is available at Barpeta Road and at Bansbari Lodge (for guests only).

ARUNACHAL PRADESH

Virginal Arunachal Pradesh appears as a giant patch of green on the country's map. India's wildest and least explored state, Arunachal (literally the 'land of dawn-lit mountains') rises abruptly from the Assam plains as a mass of densely forested and impossibly steep hills, culminating in snowcapped peaks along the Tibetan border. Home to 26 indigenous tribes, Arunachal is perhaps the last sanctuary for India's natural and anthropological heritage. Much of the state remains beyond tourism's reach, but new areas are slowly being opened to visitors.

China has never formally recognised Indian sovereignty here, and it took the surprise Chinese invasion of 1962 for Delhi to begin funding significant infrastructure (the Chinese voluntarily withdrew after a few days). Border passes are heavily guarded by the Indian military, but the atmosphere is generally calm. Arunachal has been relatively untouched by political violence, though Naga rebels are active in the state's far-eastern corner.

Permits

Foreigners can access Arunachal Pradesh only if they have a Protected Area Permit (PAP) from the Indian government, which is usually only granted if you are travelling in a group. Permits are issued through registered travel agents, meaning that even if you plan to travel independently, you will have to approach a tour operator to process the PAP for you. In practice, almost everyone joins a tour because of the difficulties of dealing with local officials and avoiding

ARUNACHAL'S TRIBAL GROUPS

An astonishing patchwork quilt of ethnic populations, Arunachal is home to 26 tribal groups, including the Adi (Abor), Nishi, Tagin, Galo, Apatani and Monpa people. Many tribes are related to each other, while some consider themselves unique.

Modernity is slowly making inroads into the local society, but most tribes straddle the boundary between old and new – it's not uncommon to see a modern concrete building outfitted with a traditional open-hearth kitchen over stilted bamboo flooring.

The traditional animistic religion of Donyi-Polo (sun and moon worship) is still prevalent in the region, although Christian missionaries have had a significant impact on the religious beliefs and way of life in this area. For ceremonial occasions, village chiefs typically wear scarlet shawls and a bamboo wicker hat spiked with porcupine quills or hornbill beaks. Women favour hand-woven wraparounds like Southeast Asian sarongs, while some of the older men still wear their hair long, with a topknot above their foreheads. The artistic traditions of weaving and wickerwork are very much alive in these hills.

Architecture varies from tribe to tribe – traditional Adi villages are generally the most photogenic, with luxuriant palmyra-leaf thatching and wobbly bamboo suspension bridges strung across river gorges.

political unrest and insurgent groups without a guide who speaks the local language.

The rules in the other states change regularly. Manipur, Mizoram and Nagaland (all under permit clauses at different times) enjoyed 'permit free' status as of 2016, but the scene could well be different by 2018. Check ahead before you travel.

Itanagar

☎0360 / POP 35,000 / ELEV 770M

Arunachal's capital takes its name from the mysterious **Ita Fort**, the brick ruins of which crown a hill above the burgeoning mercantile town. Awash in concrete, this somewhat characterless urban hub serves as the state's power centre (travel permits for Arunachal Pradesh are issued here).

Sights

Jawaharlal Nehru State Museum MUSEUM
(Museum Rd; Indian/foreigner ₹10/75, camera/video ₹20/100; ⏲9.30am-4pm Sun-Thu) The spruced-up and well-maintained Jawaharlal Nehru State Museum has a decent representation of Arunachal Pradesh's tribal and natural heritage. The brightly coloured gompa of the **Centre for Buddhist Culture** is set in the gardens nearby.

Sleeping & Eating

Hotel SC Continental HOTEL $$
(☎9436075875; www.hotelsccontinental.com; Vivek Vihar; s/d from ₹2200/2640; ❄@) This upscale, well-maintained hotel offers Itanagar's equivalent of business-class luxury in a quiet neighbourhood southwest of the bustling Ganga Market. The in-house Fire & Ice restaurant (p573) serves good Indian and Chinese fare. To get here, walk about 1km downhill along the main road from the town centre, then take the slip road hairpinning to the right.

Hotel Arun Subansiri HOTEL $$
(☎0360-2212806; Zero Point Tinali; s/d from ₹1540/1760; ❄📶) With an oversized foyer better suited to a car showroom, Hotel Arun Subansiri has comfortably large rooms with clean bathrooms, soft beds and in-room wireless connectivity. It's within walking distance of the museum (p573).

Fire & Ice MULTICUISINE $$
(Hotel SC Continental, Vivek Vihar; mains ₹120-180; ⏲11am-10pm; ❄) Sporting tasteful woodwork and smart maroon-and-white table linen, this eatery serves a good range of Indian and Chinese fare and vies for the moniker of Itanagar's prime fine-dining spot. It doubles as a lounge bar in the evenings (beers ₹100).

Getting There & Away

The **APST bus station** (Ganga Market) has services to Guwahati (₹550, 11 hours, 6am), Bomdila (₹380, eight hours, 6am), Pashighat (₹320, 10 hours, 5.30am and 6am) and Shillong (₹450, 12 hours, 4.30pm). Most buses depart in the morning, and there may not be connections available every day.

Across the road from the bus station, shared jeeps depart for Ziro (₹350, four hours, 5.30am and 2.50pm), Along (₹700, 15 hours, 5.30am) and Pasighat (₹400, eight hours, 5.30am).

OFF THE BEATEN TRACK

NAMDAPHA NATIONAL PARK

The staggering **Namdapha National Park** (☎03807-222249; www.changlang.nic.in/namdapha.html; Indian/foreigner ₹500/1000), spread over 1985 sq km of dense forest in far-eastern Arunachal Pradesh, is an ecological hot spot with a mind-boggling array of animal and plant species, and habitats ranging from warm tropical plains to icy Himalayan highlands. Namdapha is famous for being the only park in India to have four big-cat species (leopard, tiger, clouded leopard and snow leopard). It's also a birdwatcher's delight, with around 500 recorded species.

The park is a long haul from anywhere, and visiting can be a pain unless you're travelling with a tour operator.

The gateway to Namdapha is Dibrugarh in Assam, from where you need to travel about 150km to get to the small town of **Miao**. From here it's a 26km drive to **Deban**, where the park headquarters are located. Simple accommodation is available in Miao at the **Eco-Tourist Guest House** (☎03807-222296; Miao; per person Indian/foreigner ₹400/600), or in Deban at the **Forest Rest House** (☎03807-222249; Deban; d Indian/foreigner ₹300/500).

The 22411 Naharlagun–New Delhi Express (3AC/2AC ₹2005/2940, 38 hours, 9.35pm) departs Tuesday from a new railway station in Naharlagun, about 12km east of Itanagar. There's also the daily 15168 Intercity Express (sleeper/3AC ₹215/580, nine hours, 10pm), connecting Naharlagun to Guwahati.

Itanagar is serviced by the Naharlagun helipad, which has daily flights (except Sunday) to Guwahati (₹4000). Ask your hotel reception or tour operator about tickets.

Central Arunachal Pradesh

For intrepid travellers, Central Arunachal Pradesh promises some great adventures, from tribal encounters in the picturesque Ziro Valley to rafting on the Siang River and thrilling excursions to remote settlements such as Mechuka.

Ziro Valley

☎03788 / POP 32,000 / ELEV 1750M

One of the prettiest landscapes in all of India, the fertile Ziro Valley nestles within Arunachal's formidable mountains like a mythical kingdom. A layered landscape of rice fields, rivers and picture-postcard villages of the Apatani tribe, it is an undisputed high point of any trip to Arunachal.

Scenery and village architecture apart, the main attraction here is meeting the older Apatani people, who have the traditional ornamentation of facial tattoos and nose plugs. The most authentic Apatani villages are **Hong** (the biggest and best known), **Hija** (more atmospheric), **Hari**, **Bamin** and **Duta**, none of which are more than 10km apart. It's vital to have a local guide to take you to these villages, otherwise you won't see much and might even be made to feel quite unwelcome.

Sprawling **Hapoli** (New Ziro), about 6km south of the Ziro Valley, has basic urban infrastructure and road transport.

Sleeping & Eating

Homestays are the best way to experience traditional Apatani hospitality. At present, there are more than 30 registered homestays in all the villages combined, although standards vary widely. The best of the homestays are clustered in Siiro village, about 3km southeast of Hapoli. There are also a couple of hotels in the region.

Hibu Tatu's Homestay HOMESTAY $$
(☎9436224834; hibuatotatu@gmail.com; Siiro village; per person incl half-board ₹1500) Hibu Tatu's Homestay offers superb access into the lives of local villagers, and also provides guides (₹1000) and bicycles (₹500) for village tours. The homestay is located at the far end of Siiro village.

Abasa Homestay HOMESTAY $$
(☎9402709164; abasahomestay@gmail.com; Siiro village; per person incl half-board ₹1500) For a memorable homestay experience (and a sampling of superb home-cooked food), consider a night or two at the lovely Abasa Homestay. It's run by the friendly and hospitable Kago Kampu, who is known for her expertise in making fine fruit wine.

Siiro Homestay HOMESTAY $$
(☎9856209494; punyochada@gmail.com; Siiro village; per person incl half-board ₹1500) Siiro is one of the most popular homestays in the Ziro Valley, its operator, Punyo Chada, easily qualifying as India's most jovial host. The rooms here – featuring soft beds and large windows – are unmatched in the region in terms of quality.

Getting There & Away

Sumos depart from MG Rd in Hapoli, near the SBI ATM, for Itanagar (₹350, four hours, 5am and 11am), Lakhimpur (₹350, four hours, hourly 7am to 9am) and Daporijo (₹450, six hours, around 9.30am).

Ziro to Pasighat

DAPORIJO

☎03792 / POP 15,700 / ELEV 250M

A necessary stopover midway along the long drive from Ziro to Pasighat, Daporijo is dirty, characterless and unsophisticated. However, its location on the banks of the Subansiri River gives you the option of a few walks and hikes. Start early from Ziro, and you'll be here by lunch.

Sleeping & Eating

Hotel Singhik HOTEL $$
(☎03792-223103; singhikhotel@gmail.com; d from ₹1900; ❄📶) The surprisingly comfortable Hotel Singhik, with colourful interiors, an excellent restaurant and free wi-fi, is the best place to stop for the night on the Ziro–Pasighat route.

Ligu Tourist Resort RESORT $
(☎03792-223114; Ligu village; d ₹1350) This comfortable resort is located in the thatched village of Ligu (coming from Ziro, take the left turn just before the bridge at the entrance to Daporijo). The proprietor's family cooks up fantastic traditional meals, and you can spend the evening wandering in the shadows of trees, exploring the village and meeting the friendly locals.

Getting There & Away

Sumos leave New Market in Daporijo's town centre at 6am for Itanagar (₹600, 10 hours) and Ziro (₹450, six hours).

ALONG

☎03783 / POP 20,500 / ELEV 600M

A nondescript highway town en route to Pasighat from Daporijo, Along (aa-low) is a dusty, scruffy settlement with little for travellers apart from a small, informative **district museum** (Main Rd; ⏰10am-4pm Mon-Fri) FREE.

Sleeping & Eating

Hotel West HOTEL $$
(☎03783-222566; hotelwest@rediffmail.com; Medical Rd; d from ₹1650; ❄) The saving grace of Along is the well-kept Hotel West, which has spacious and comfortable rooms, good service and a central location, making it the

MEET THE APATANI

Numbering around 25,000 and native to the Ziro Valley, the Apatani are one of Northeast India's most intriguing tribes. Believed to have migrated to the valley from the less hospitable northern highlands, the Apatani are strongly rooted in their ancient culture. Most people are adherents of the animistic Donyi-Polo (sun-and-moon worship) religion, and continue to live in traditional houses fabricated out of bamboo and wood (the interiors are very modern, though). Apatani villages are immensely photogenic, with T-shaped totem poles called *babohs* towering over rows of huts that line every thoroughfare. Farmers by occupation, the Apatani practise a unique system of agriculture in which terraced rice fields are flooded with water to double as shallow fish farms. The Apatani also excel in arts such as weaving and wickerwork.

Historically famous for their beauty, Apatani women have elaborate facial tattoos as well as extraordinary cane plugs known as *dat*, fitted into holes cut in their upper nostrils. Elders say the practice derived from a tribal legend that pronounced the adornments to be the ultimate complement to the innate beauty of Apatani women. However, some others believe it was an act of defacement to prevent the women from being kidnapped by warriors of the neighbouring Nishi tribe. Peace with the Nishis in the 1960s ended the practice, and only a few locals from older generations can now be seen wearing *dat*. Photography is a sensitive issue, so always ask first.

perfect place to retire to after your day-long road journey.

Hotel Toshi Palace HOTEL $
(☎9436638196; Main Rd; d from ₹900; ❄) Hotel Toshi Palace, opposite the APST bus station, has clean rooms and a pleasant terrace restaurant where beers flow freely after sundown.

Getting There & Away

Sumos from the town centre head to Itanagar (₹700, 15 hours, 5.30am) and Pasighat (₹250, five hours, 5.30am and 11.30am).

Pasighat

☎0368 / POP 25,000

Laid out along forested plains by the banks of the Siang River, Pasighat feels more like Assam than Arunachal Pradesh. In September the town hosts the Adi festival of **Solung** (⏲1-5 Sep), but through the rest of the year the most interesting sight is the sunrise over the gorgeous Siang.

Sleeping & Eating

Hotel Serene Abode HOTEL $$
(☎0368-2222382; theserenεabode@gmail.com; NH52; d incl breakfast without/with AC ₹1650/2650; ❄📶) The new and smart Hotel Serene Abode ups the hospitality ante in Pasighat, with modern rooms, stylish loos, flat-screen TVs and efficient service.

Hotel Aane HOTEL $$
(☎0368-2222777; MG Rd; d from ₹1650; ❄) Most tourists passing through Pasighat sleep at Hotel Aane, which has pastel shades adorning its walls, clean sheets, and a good in-house restaurant.

Siang Tea Garden Lodge RESORT $$$
(☎9436675824; Oyan village; per person incl full board ₹3000; 📶) Lounge amid lush tea gardens at the Siang Tea Garden Lodge, which has simple but comfy rooms with ethnic decor, garden-fresh tea and awesome food prepared by Babul, the in-house chef. Rates here are flexible; those willing to participate in community-development and welfare programs often get a rebate. Oyan is about 25km south of Pasighat.

Getting There & Away

Sumos run to Along (₹250, five hours, 6am and noon) and Itanagar (₹400, eight hours, 6am). **Ferries** (per person/vehicle ₹60/1000) drift lazily down the Brahmaputra to Dibrugarh in Assam from Bogibil Ghat (and from Oiram Ghat during the dry season). Sumos take two hours to reach Bogibil Ghat from Pasighat, departing at 6am. Combined Sumo-and-ferry tickets (₹200) are sold by agents at the Sumo stand in town.

Western Arunachal Pradesh

Bomdila

☎03782 / ELEV 2680M

Halfway between Tezpur and Tawang, Bomdila is a tiny settlement incorporating administrative offices, hotels, markets and wayside eateries. If you're overnighting here, there isn't much to do apart from exploring the local market or visiting the large **monastery** in the town's higher reaches.

Sleeping & Eating

Doe-Gu-Khil Guest House GUESTHOUSE $
(☎9402292774; yipe_bg@yahoo.com; Monastery Hill; d ₹900; 📶) The traditionally decorated Doe-Gu-Khil Guest House, located just below the large monastery, provides fabulous views of Bomdila town spread out below. Rooms are simply appointed but well kept, the food in the canteen is fresh and tasty, and there's free wireless connectivity in rooms.

Hotel Tsepal Yangjom HOTEL $$
(☎03782-223473; www.hoteltsepalyangjom.in; Main Bazaar; d from ₹2450; 📶) With wood-panelled rooms and a busy restaurant screening cricket matches on a cricket-field-sized TV, this is the town's most popular inn. It's centrally located, and offers free wi-fi in its cosy lobby.

Getting There & Away

Shared jeeps plying the long route from Tezpur to Tawang break at Bomdila for the night. You'll find connections departing from the town centre for Tawang (₹400, eight hours, 7am).

Dirang

☎03780 / ELEV 1620M

Dirang is the gateway to the Tawang Valley and serves as a useful overnight stop, especially for those travelling in their own vehicles. Tiny **Old Dirang**, located 5km south of New Dirang, is a picture-perfect Monpa stone village. The main road separates its rocky mini **citadel** from a huddle of pretty streamside houses, above which rises a steep

OFF THE BEATEN TRACK

FRONTIER ADVENTURES

Mechuka

The drive from Along to Mechuka – a remote outpost very close to the Tibetan border – is one of the most enthralling road trips in Arunachal Pradesh. Mechuka often goes by the moniker of 'forbidden valley' – indeed, until recently, the only way to reach the village was on foot. Populated by the Buddhist Memba tribe, this tiny settlement on the banks of the Siang River is notable for the 400-year-old **Samten Yongcha Monastery** and its stunning landscapes, which culminate in a massive hulk of snow-draped mountains running along the border.

Sumos ply the 180km road from Along (₹550, seven hours, 5.30am), but connections are contingent on the weather and vehicle availability, and rides may not be possible every day. Unless you're able to find accommodation with a local family, the only place to stay is the government **Circuit House**, which rents out rooms on an ad hoc basis (and tariff). Remember that bookings can be overridden by visiting government officials. Owing to security issues, most places here won't accommodate independent travellers without a reference, so it is strongly recommended that your Mechuka trip be arranged through a local tour operator.

Tuting & Pemako

In the far north of Arunachal Pradesh lies the isolated town of **Tuting**, visited yearly by a handful of pilgrims and hard-core adventure seekers. Accessible from Pasighat by a long, rough road, it sits near the Tibetan border, where the Tsang Po River, having left the Tibetan Plateau and burrowed through the Himalayas via a series of spectacular gorges, enters the Indian subcontinent and becomes the Siang (which in turn becomes the Brahmaputra in Assam). Steadily gaining a reputation as a thrilling whitewater-rafting destination, the perilous 180km route from Tuting to Pasighat is littered with grade IV to V rapids, strong eddies and inaccessible gorges. This is for pros only.

Tuting also serves as the launch pad for the fabulous land of **Pemako**, known in Buddhist legend as a hidden paradise and the earthly representation of Dorje Phangmo (a Tibetan goddess). This isolated mountain valley is populated by Memba Buddhists and most visitors here are Buddhist pilgrims travelling on foot. However, a sealed road due to be completed by 2018 will result in a surge in tourist numbers.

If you do manage to get here, consider kicking back for a few nights at **Yamne Abor** (☎9436053870; Damroh Village; per person incl full board ₹2500), a lovely resort comprising a mix of luxury tents and eco-cottages in the remote Yamne Valley amid pretty Adi villages, rice fields and verdant forests. On your way down, stay a night or two at the **Aborcountry River Camp** (☎9436053870; Rane Ghat; per person incl full board ₹3000), situated amid a bamboo grove on the banks of the Siang and offering eco-chic rooms in traditional thatched cottages. Book both properties through Abor Country Travels & Expeditions (p564).

ridge topped by a timeless **gompa**. Heading the other way, just north of New Dirang, the valley opens out and its floor becomes a patchwork of rice and crop fields, through which gushes the icy-blue Dirang River.

Sleeping & Eating

Hotel Pemaling HOTEL $$

(☎9402783255; www.hotelpemaling.com; d from ₹1500; 🛜) Hotel Pemaling, 2km south of New Dirang, is a wonderful family-run hotel with smart rooms, great service and a very pleasant garden where you can enjoy views of the river below and the mountains above.

Norphel Retreat HOTEL $$

(☎7085499595; www.norphelretreat.in; d ₹2500) On the left bank of the Dirang River, about 1km north of New Dirang, stands the gargantuan Norphel Retreat, boasting luxurious rooms, tasty finger food and river views.

Getting There & Away

Shared jeeps leave for Tawang (₹350, six hours, 5.30am) and Tezpur (₹400, six hours, 6am) every morning from the central market area of New Dirang.

Dirang to Tawang Valley

Climbing from Dirang, Arunachal's most perilous road is a seemingly endless series of bombed-out zigzags, which cross several army camps and landslide zones to finally top off at **Se La**, an icy 4176m pass that breaches the mountains and provides access to Tawang. The pass is likely to be snowed under during winter and high monsoon months, so enquire in advance if the road is open.

From the pass, the road plummets down the mountainside into the Tawang Valley. En route, you will cross the beautiful **Nuranang Falls**, cascading down the steep cliffs and continuing as a streak of silvery rivulet down the gorge.

There are no sleeping options along the way, so complete the 140km stretch from Dirang to Tawang well before sundown. Indian Army cafeterias at Se La and Jaswantgarh War Memorial – 20km down the road – serve piping-hot samosas (₹10), veg *momos* (dumplings; ₹20) and noodles (₹40), along with cups of free tea.

Tawang Valley

☎03794 / ELEV 3050M

A mighty gash in the earth fringed by hulking mountains, Tawang Valley works a special magic on the minds of travellers. The valley is a gorgeous patchwork of mountain ridges, vast fields and clusters of Buddhist monasteries and Monpa villages. Autumn is a particularly beautiful season for travelling this route, when waterfalls are in spate and cosmos shrubs lining the tarmac come alive in riotous reds and pinks. The setting is more beautiful than the town itself, but murals of auspicious Buddhist emblems and colourful prayer wheels add interest to the central Old Market area. The prayer wheels are turned by a stream of Monpa pilgrims, many of whom wear traditional black yak-wool *gurdam* (skullcaps that look like giant Rastafarian spiders).

Sights

★Tawang Gompa MONASTERY
(camera/video ₹20/100; dawn-dusk) Tawang's biggest attraction is the magical Tawang Gompa, founded in 1681. Reputedly the world's second-largest Buddhist-monastery complex after Drepung Monastery (in Lhasa, Tibet), Tawang is famed in Buddhist circles for its priceless library. Within its fortified walls, narrow alleys lead to the magnificently decorated prayer hall, containing an 8m-high Buddha statue. Come at dawn (4am to 5am) to see monks performing early-morning prayers. Spectacular masked *chaam* dances are held in the courtyard during the Torgya, Losar and Buddha Mahotsava festivals.

Urgeyling Gompa MONASTERY
(dawn-dusk) FREE The ancient if modest Urgeyling Gompa is where the sixth Dalai Lama was born. Before he left for Lhasa, it's said that he stuck his walking stick into the ground and it eventually grew into a giant oak tree that flanks the entrance to the monastery. Within the main hall are hand-painted portraits of all the Dalai Lamas, and imprints of the forehead and feet of the sixth Dalai Lama.

Sleeping & Eating

Hotel Gakyi Khang Zhang HOTEL $$
(☎03794-224647; www.gkztawang.com; Monastery Rd; d from ₹1650;) A kilometre out of town on the road to Tawang Gompa, this hotel offers by far the best rooms in Tawang: colourful pastel affairs with polished wood floors. There's power back-up, good wi-fi and a 1st-floor bar, and the distant views of the monastery (from most rooms) clinch the deal.

Hotel Tashi Ga-Tsel HOTEL $$
(☎03794-222351; www.hoteltashigatsel.com; d incl breakfast from ₹2500;) Pleasantly removed from the din of town, yet within walking distance of the main drag (near the General Parade Ground), this large operation offers a range of comfortable rooms with tasteful furniture, large bathrooms, clean linen, large windows and prompt service. Some of the pricier rooms also have private sit-outs.

Hotel Nefa HOTEL $
(☎03794-222419; Nehru Market; d from ₹800) Hotel Nefa has tidy, wood-panelled rooms and hot showers but lackadaisical service. It fills up very quickly with domestic tourists, especially over weekends and local holidays.

Dragon Restaurant CHINESE $$
(Old Market; mains ₹100-180; 8am-8pm) The cosy Dragon Restaurant is Tawang's best eatery, serving freshly made local dishes such as *churpa* (delicious fermented-cheese broth with fungi and vegetables), *momos*

(Tibetan dumplings), fiery chilli chicken and salted Tibetan yak-butter tea.

Getting There & Away

Shared jeeps with kamikaze drivers ply the route from Tawang to Tezpur (₹750, 12 hours, 5.30am), calling at Dirang (₹400, six hours), Bomdila (₹550, eight hours) and Bhalukpong (₹700, 10 hours). **Himalayan Holidays** (9436291868; Old Market), a reliable tour agency at the old market, sells tickets and arranges local tours and hikes.

NAGALAND

The uncontested 'wild east' of India, Nagaland is probably one of the reasons you came to the Northeast in the first place. Rich in primeval beauty, Nagaland's dazzling hills and valleys – right on the edge of the India–Myanmar border – are an other-worldly place where, until very recently, some 16-odd headhunting Naga tribes valiantly fought off intruders. Of course, Nagaland today is a shadow of its once fierce self, and much of the south of the state is fairly developed. In the north, however, you still stand a good chance of meeting tribespeople in exotic attire who continue to live a traditional lifestyle. Note that a number of insurgent groups are active in the state and you should check the political situation before you travel.

Dimapur

03862 / POP 122,800 / ELEV 260M

Dimapur, the flat, uninspiring commercial centre of Nagaland, has very little up its sleeve to draw international (or even domestic) tourists. However, thanks to its airport (4km from town), it serves as an important access point, especially during the ultra-busy Hornbill Festival (p561) in Kohima in December.

Sleeping & Eating

★Longchen Homestay GUESTHOUSE $$
(9436160888; ajmynsong@yahoo.com; Airport Rd, Ao Yimti Village; d from ₹2000;) A charming quasi-traditional home adorned with bamboo trimmings and hemmed by lush paddies and vegetable fields, Longchen is reason enough to visit Dimapur. Hosts Anne and Toshi (a colonel in the Indian Army) and their house dogs provide great company, and the deliciously spicy Naga food is to die for (meals ₹350). Ao Yimti village is 3.5km from Dimapur.

Hotel Acacia HOTEL $$
(8415935254; www.hotelacacia.co.in; d incl breakfast from ₹2530;) The impeccably maintained Hotel Acacia has clean, spacious rooms, comfy beds, spotless linen, speedy wi-fi, prompt service and good in-house food. You'll find it opposite East Police Station along the main drag. A couple of on-site travel kiosks can arrange bus and flight bookings at short notice.

Getting There & Away

From Dimapur's tiny airport, located 400m off the Kohima road, 3km out of town, **Air India** (011-24624074; www.airindia.in) and **Indigo** (9910383838; www.goindigo.in) fly daily to Kolkata. The **NST bus station** (Kohima Rd) runs services to Kohima (₹100, three hours, hourly) and Imphal (₹450, seven hours, 6am).

Kohima

0370 / POP 268,000 / ELEV 1450M

If not for its crazy traffic and rampant urbanisation, Nagaland's agreeable capital – scattered across a series of forested ridges and hilltops – could easily rub shoulders with the best hill stations of India. That said, it's still a nice place to stop by on your tour of the Northeast, and the festive Christmas week is a particularly beautiful time to be in town. Avoid Kohima on a Sunday if you can: apart from hotels, virtually everything is shut.

Sights

★War Cemetery HISTORIC SITE
(9am-5pm Mar-Oct, to 4pm Nov-Feb) FREE This immaculately maintained cemetery contains the graves of 1400 British, Commonwealth and Indian soldiers – killed in action during WWII – laid out across stepped and manicured lawns. It stands at the strategic junction of the Dimapur and Imphal roads, a site that saw intense fighting against the Japanese during the 64-day Battle of Kohima, now widely considered the bloodiest of all WWII battles.

Central Market MARKET
(Stadium Approach; 6am-4pm) In this fascinating market that supplies the bulk of Kohima's kitchen supplies, tribal people buy and sell local delicacies such as *borol* (wriggling hornet grubs), tadpoles, bullfrogs, silkworms, exotic condiments such as dried

WORTH A TRIP

VILLAGES AROUND KOHIMA

Cultural tours are slowly catching on in Nagaland, and it's now possible to take a day trip to remote villages, interact with villagers, and even stay with local families thanks to the establishment of homestays in places such as Khonoma and Kisama. Contact **Explore Nagaland** (9856343037; www.explorenagaland.com; per person per night incl full board from ₹1500).

Khonoma

This historic Angami-Naga village was the site of two major British–Angami siege battles in 1847 and 1879. Built on an easily defended ridge, Khonoma looks beautifully traditional, with emerald paddy patchworks carpeting valley floors between towering ridges. There are a few simple homestay options in the village, and tour guides can work out overnight arrangements with local proprietors if informed in advance.

Kisama Heritage Village

Kisama Heritage Village has a representative selection of traditional Naga houses and *morungs* (clubhouse-dormitories) with full-size log drums and architectural ornamentation specific to each of Nagaland's tribes. Nagaland's biggest annual jamboree, the Hornbill Festival (p561), is celebrated here. Within the village is the **WWII Museum** (Kisama Heritage Village; ₹10; 10am-4pm), which has a collection of memorabilia from WWII battles fought around Kohima. Kisama is 10km from central Kohima along the Imphal road.

Kigwema

A 10-minute drive past Kisama along Imphal Rd brings you to Kigwema, an Angami village of historic importance where Japanese forces arrived and set up camp before the final showdown with Allied forces in 1944. The modest valley-view home of General Saito, commanding officer of the Japanese troops, still stands within the village and bears bullet marks from the battle that raged here. Several households in the village welcome tourists (preferably accompanied by local guides), and you can get a peek into the daily lives of resident tribespeople if you stay a night.

and fermented bamboo shoots, fiery Raja chili peppers, *jabrang* (hill peppercorns), fermented soybeans and a mind-boggling range of meat and vegetables. Ask for permission before taking photos, although if you buy something, vendors will usually let you snap pictures of their stalls.

State Museum MUSEUM
(₹5, camera/video ₹20/100; 9.30am-3.30pm Mon-Sat) This well-presented government museum, 3km north of Kohima's centre, has galleries on two floors featuring tribal artefacts, jewellery mannequin tableaux, and a display of headhunted skulls, curated from old village collections. It's a good place to acquaint yourself with the genealogy of different Naga tribes and their diverse customs, cultures and crafts.

Sleeping

Accommodation becomes many times pricier and extremely scarce during the Hornbill Festival (early December). Some hotels open reservations a year ahead, so book well in advance.

★Heritage GUESTHOUSE $$
(9436215259; theheritagekohima@gmail.com; Old DC Bungalow, Raj Bhavan Rd; s/d ₹2000/2500;) This stately guesthouse was once the official residence of Kohima's serving deputy commissioners, and overlooks the town from the summit of Officer's Hill. With nostalgia reigning supreme in each of its four charming and luxurious rooms, the place preserves a slice of the high administrative life from a bygone era. Delicious meals (mains ₹120 to ₹180) are available with notice.

Razhu Pru HERITAGE HOTEL $$
(0370-2290291; razhupru@yahoo.co.in; Mission Compound; d incl breakfast from ₹2500;) A family home thoughtfully converted into a heritage hotel, Razhu Pru packs a diverse array of heirlooms and artefacts into its wood-panelled living areas. Elegant cane furniture and potted ferns add to the appeal.

Rooms sport comfy beds, ethnic upholstery and fireplaces for cold winter nights. The kitchen does a superb Naga meal (thalis ₹500) if you order in advance.

Blue Bayou HOTEL $$

(☎0370-2292008; thebluebayoukohima@gmail.com; s/d incl breakfast from ₹1600/2680; ❄📶) Across the road from the War Cemetery, this central hotel has spacious, well-kept rooms, many of which have gorgeous valley views to the rear. Its competitive tariff makes it one of the first hotels to be booked out during December's Hornbill Festival, so book well in advance if you're planning to come during the bash.

Hotel Vivor HOTEL $$$

(☎0370-2806243; contact@hotelvivor.in; NH61; s/d incl breakfast from ₹3600/4150; ❄📶) The upscale Vivor, 3km south of town, has rooms lavishly fitted with spongy beds, snow-white linen, ultra-clean bathrooms and large windows. Service is prompt, a cafe below squeezes out fresh espressos, and there's a souvenir shop by the main entrance that boasts a decent collection of reasonably priced handicrafts.

Eating

Dream Café CAFE $

(cnr Dimapur & Imphal Rds; mains ₹80-120; ⏲10am-6pm Mon-Sat) The place to be for most of Kohima's youth, this busy, cheerful place offers daily lunch specials such as fried noodles or pizza, as well as fresh coffee and snacks. Great hill views can be taken in from the bay windows, and displays by local artists and lots of friendly diners make this a good place to linger.

Ozone Cafe CAFE $

(Imphal Rd; mains ₹80-120; ⏲noon-8pm; 📶) Hip and happening, this central cafe opposite ICICI Bank has a sprawling gymnasium-style dining area, where Kohima's young guns spend hours catching up over a variety of dishes including *momos* (Tibetan dumplings), pizza, noodles and ginger ale. Free wi-fi.

Arudupa Spur Cafe MULTICUISINE $$

(Arudupa Hotel; mains ₹120-160; ⏲11am-9pm Mon-Sat) Part of the Arudupa Hotel, this is one of Kohima's busiest restaurants, with youngsters relaxing on sofas and tucking into a pan-Asian menu. There's good music through the day, and lots of heaters for cold winter nights.

ℹ Getting There & Away

The **NST bus station** (Main Rd) has services to Dimapur (₹100, three hours, hourly), Mokokchung (₹200, six hours, 6am) and Imphal (₹220, seven hours, 7am). The taxi stand opposite has shared taxis to Dimapur (₹200, 2½ hours). A reserved car and driver for a day out to Kisama and Khonoma costs about ₹1500.

Northern Nagaland

Kohima to Mon

The scenic but insufferably bumpy road from Kohima to Mon passes through beautiful forested hills, at one point briefly entering Assam. Along the way, you will pass several tribal settlements inhabited by the dominant **Ao**, who once excelled in warfare and continue to weave spectacular clan shawls with elaborate animal motifs. Laid-back **Mokokchung**, with a spectacular hill setting, is the

HEADHUNTING

Long feared for their ferocity in war and their sense of independence, Naga tribes considered headhunting a sign of strength and machismo. Every inter-village war saw the victors lopping off the heads of the vanquished and instantly rising in social stature (as well as in the eyes of women). Among certain tribes such as the Konyaks of Mon, men who claimed heads were adorned with face tattoos and V-shaped marks on their torsos, in addition to being allowed to wear brass pendants called *yanra* denoting the number of heads they had taken.

Headhunting was outlawed in 1953 (the last recorded occurrence was in 1963). Much of the credit for the change, however, goes to Christian missionaries in the region who preached non-violence and peaceful coexistence over decades. Almost 90% of the Nagas now consider themselves Christian, their unshakeable faith marked by behemoth-like churches that are a prominent landmark in any settlement. Most hamlets have got rid of their grisly human trophies, which are now seen as immoral possessions.

biggest town en route and is a great place to acquaint yourself with Nagaland life.

Sights

Rendikala Subong Museum MUSEUM
(Town Hall Rd, Mokokchung; ₹10) This tiny, privately run museum houses a number of tribal artefacts relating to the local Ao culture, along with what is touted to be the world's smallest Bible. It's usually shut, but the onsite caretaker will open the doors if you turn up at a reasonable time.

Sleeping & Eating

Hotel Metsuben HOTEL $
(☎8014587442; metsuben@yahoo.com; Mokokchung; d from ₹990; ❄@☎) The spiffy Hotel Metsuben is the best place in Mokokchung to look for a bed and a range of hearty and fiery Naga dishes. Its hilltop location – off Kohima Rd, near Town Park – also means that you're comfortably distanced from the din of the town centre.

Tuophema Tourist Village HOMESTAY $$
(☎9436005002; Tuophema; d ₹2750) Sleep in Naga thatched huts and eat traditional food in a glass-paned cafeteria (meals ₹250) at this tourist village 45km north of Kohima. Notify it of your arrival in advance or it will probably be closed.

A tiny museum (with erratic hours) within the tourist village has a small collection of tribal artefacts and animal parts.

Getting There & Away

Shared jeeps leave Kohima's **NST bus station** (p581) early in the morning and inch along the 150km stretch to reach Mokokchung (₹200, six hours, 6am). From there, you'll find a few connections the following morning to Sonari (₹100, four hours, 7am), which in turn has jeeps going to Mon (₹150, three hours, 9am and noon).

Mon & Around

The haggard hill town of Mon serves as an access point for the many Konyak villages in the area. Note that local day-tripping taxis are difficult to book in Mon and many of the outlying villages are not served by regular public transport. Having a reserved car with guide certainly helps in getting around these remote parts.

Sights

Konyak Villages
The most popular among tourist-friendly hamlets is **Longwa**, about 35km from Mon, where the headman's longhouse spectacularly straddles the India–Myanmar border and contains a fascinating range of weapons, dinosaur-like totems and a WWII metal aircraft seat salvaged from debris scattered in nearby jungles. You can spend some time at a local house here and several tattooed former headhunters can be photographed for a fairly standard ₹100 fee. Tribal jewellery, carved masks and other collectibles (₹200 to ₹1000) can also be bought from many households. In high season, the village charges a per-person entry fee of ₹200.

Other villages that can be visited from Mon include **Old Mon** (5km), with countless animal skulls adorning the outer walls of the headman's house; **Singha Chingnyu** (20km), which has a huge longhouse decorated with animal skulls and three stuffed tigers; and **Shangnyu** (25km), with a friend-

TRAVELLING SAFELY IN THE NORTHEAST STATES

In recent decades, many ethno-linguistic groups in the Northeast have jostled – often violently – to assert themselves in the face of illegal immigration from neighbouring countries, governmental apathy and a heavy-handed defence policy. Some want independence from India, others autonomy, but most are fighting what are effectively clan or turf wars. While peace mostly prevails, trouble in these regions can flare up suddenly and unpredictably. In 2010, bombings hit parts of Assam and the Garo Hills area of Meghalaya. Ethnic violence erupted in Assam, while a bomb blast and curfews shattered the veneer of peace in Manipur in late 2012. In December 2014, strikes by Bodo groups killed more than 70 people across Assam. In June 2015, guerrillas ambushed an army convoy and killed 18 soldiers in Manipur, while in late 2016, the state was ravaged by nearly two months of arson, violence and curfews. To make things worse, Assam and Manipur are often paralysed by strikes and shutdowns. It pays to keep abreast of the headlines on TV and in local papers. If you're with a tour company, talk to the operators to make sure your field guide is up to date with the situation.

ly headman and a wooden shrine full of fertility references.

Sleeping & Eating

Helsa Resort HUT $

(9436000028; Mon; d from ₹1200) This place is located on the edge of town en route to Longwa village, and has six traditional thatched Konyak huts with springy bamboo floors, sparse furnishings and hot water by the bucket. Meals can be arranged by prior request.

Konyak Tea Retreat FARMSTAY $$

(www.konyaktearetreat.com; Shiyong village; per person incl full board ₹2500) Located 20km short of Mon along the main road in Shiyong village, this fantastic homestay is run by the friendly Phejin, descendant of a legendary Konyak headhunter, and she does an excellent job familiarising guests with her tribal roots. Accommodation is in charming eco-chic rooms overlooking a tea garden, and the traditional Naga meals are delicious to the last morsel.

Getting There & Away

Shared jeeps from Mon bounce painfully to Dimapur (₹450, 13 hours, 3pm) and Sonari in Assam (₹100, three hours, 6am and 9am), where you can change for Jorhat (₹100, two hours) and Mokokchung (₹150, four hours). No public transport leaves Mon on the weekend, so schedule your trip accordingly.

MANIPUR

A breeding ground for graceful classical dance traditions, intricate art forms, sumptuous cuisine and (it's said) the sport of polo, Manipur sits pretty amid rolling hills along India's border with Myanmar. This 'Jewelled Land' is home to Thadou, Tangkhul, Paite, Kuki Naga, Mao Naga and many other tribal peoples, but the predominant community is the Hindu Meitei tribe, who adhere to a neo-Vaishnavite order. Much of the state is carpeted with dense forests, which provide cover for rare birds, drug traffickers and guerrilla armies, making it by far the Northeast's most dangerous state.

Foreign travellers are currently restricted to Imphal and its outskirts, an area that is deemed 'safe'. Most foreigners fly into Imphal; it is also possible to drive in from Kohima (Nagaland) or Silchar (Assam) if you have a dedicated vehicle and guide.

Imphal

0385 / POP 268,500

Located close to the India–Myanmar border, Imphal is a vibrant mix of cultures and customs. Members of several local tribes live and work here, in what is Manipur's only major city. Due to a long history of insurgency, however, heavy militarisation, random shutdowns and curfews have become a way of life, which means there's little to do, especially after dark.

Sights

★Khwairamband Bazaar MARKET

(Ima Market; 7am-5pm) Housed in colonnaded buildings, this vast all-women's market – the largest in the world – is run by some 4000 *ima* (mothers), who have traditionally dominated the socio-economic matrix of Manipuri society. One section of the market sells vegetables, fruit, fish and groceries, while the other deals in household items, fabrics and pottery. It's a spectacular place for photographs (of course, ask first before photographing people). A 2015 earthquake caused severe damage to the buildings, but repairs have begun and it's business as usual.

Kangla Fort FORT

(Myanmar Rd; indian/foreigner ₹10/50; 9am-4pm Thu-Tue) This expansive, low-walled fort was the on-again, off-again regal capital of Manipur until the Anglo-Manipuri War of 1891 saw the defeat of the Manipuri maharaja and a subsequent British takeover. Entrance is by way of an exceedingly tall gate on Myanmar Rd, past a wide moat. While the entire complex contains several minor sights, the more interesting older buildings are at the rear, guarded by three restored large white *kangla sha* (dragons).

Imphal War Cemetery CEMETERY

(Imphal Rd; 8am-4.30pm) FREE This peaceful, well-kept memorial contains the graves of more than 1600 British and Commonwealth soldiers killed in the Battle of Imphal, which took place here in 1944 and is acknowledged as one of the most intense battles of WWII. You'll find the cemetery across a shaded public park at the end of a lane off Imphal Rd.

Sleeping & Eating

★Classic Hotel HOTEL $$

(0385-2443967; www.theclassichotel.in; North AOC Rd; s/d incl breakfast from ₹2000/2540;) Featuring large, spotless rooms

WORTH A TRIP

LOKTAK LAKE

An intriguing, picturesque ecosystem, Loktak Lake is one of the few places in Manipur that a foreigner is allowed to visit apart from Imphal. Its shimmering blue waters are broken into small lakelets by (rapidly vanishing) clumps of matted weeds called *phumdis,* and the lake is inhabited by villagers who build thatched huts on the floating 'islands' and make their way about in dugout canoes. Large, perfectly circular fishing ponds are created out of floating rings of weeds. The best view is atop **Sendra Island** (₹15). You can also embark on a **boat ride** (per boat ₹200) in order to get a closer look at lake life.

On the southern edge of the lake is the sleepy hamlet of **Moirang**, where on 14 April 1944 the anti-colonial Indian National Army first asserted Indian sovereignty against the British Raj.

You'll find a few shacks offering bottled water, snacks and tea by the lake near Sendra Island. For a lakeside picnic, bring along a packed lunch and beverages from Imphal.

Loktak Lake is 45km by road from Imphal. A return taxi costs about ₹2500, including waiting time.

stuffed with the requisite creature comforts, this long-standing property is one of Northeast India's best-value business hotels. The English-speaking staff love to please, and the restaurant serves a range of delicious dishes (place advance orders for regional delicacies). The clean and smartly plumbed bathrooms are a plus, and the wi-fi is speedy enough for video calling.

Hotel Imphal HOTEL $$
(0385-2421373; www.hotelimphal.com; North AOC Rd; s/d incl breakfast from ₹2280/2800;) This hulking operation attracts guests with its pearl-white exteriors, manicured lawns, decent cafe dispensing fresh coffee, bright pine-skirted rooms with snug beds and fresh white linen, tiled bathrooms with giant tubs, and super-friendly, prompt service. Public receptions are big here, though, so it could get a bit noisy during one of these galas.

Anand Continental HOTEL $$
(0385-2449422; hotel_anand@rediffmail.com; Khoyathong Rd; s/d from ₹1350/1550;) A trusted oldie with cheerful lime-coloured interiors, this tidy hotel has smallish rooms with more furniture than legroom. The management, however, is exceptionally friendly and you have the advantage of power backup. The in-house food is unexciting. Reception is on the 1st floor, up a narrow flight of stairs.

★ **Luxmi Kitchen** INDIAN $$
(Jiribam Rd, Wahengbam Leikai; thalis ₹140; 11am-2pm) The last word in Manipuri lunch platters, this ultra-popular restaurant does a fabulous thali comprising more than a dozen local delicacies such as tangy fish stew, fried fish, leafy greens, fried vegetables, local varieties of dhal, *iromba* (fermented fish chutney) and *ngapi* (fermented shrimp paste). A sumptuous meal here could well be one of the highlights of your Manipur trip.

Getting There & Away

The airport is 9km southwest of Imphal. From here, Air India, IndiGo and Jet Airways fly to Guwahati and Kolkata. Air India also flies to Aizawl and Dimapur.

Private buses head to Guwahati (₹750, 17 hours, hourly 6am to 10am) and Dimapur (₹450, seven hours, 10am) via Kohima (₹390, five hours). If you're heading to Aizawl, you must change in Dimapur first. **Manipur Golden Travels** (MG Ave; 5.30am-7pm) – among several other agents – sells tickets on North AOC crossing, a T-junction midway between Classic Hotel and Hotel Imphal.

To get to the **Moreh international checkpost** (Moreh-Tamu; 8am-4pm), it's best to hire a private taxi for about ₹3000.

MIZORAM

Seated precariously along rows of north-south-running mountain ridges, pristine Mizoram is more of an experiential journey than a tourist destination. Ethnically, the majority of the local population shares similarities with communities in neighbouring Southeast Asian countries such as Myanmar, and the predominant religion is Christianity. Mizo culture is liberated from caste or gender distinctions: in Aizawl girls smoke openly, wear modern clothes and hang out in unchaperoned posses meeting up with their beaus at music concerts.

Mizoram runs to its own rhythm. Most businesses open early and shut by 6pm; virtually everything closes tight on Sunday. Upon arrival, you should theoretically register at the **Office of the Superintendent of Police** (☎0389-2335339; CID Office, Bungkawn; ⏲10am-4pm Mon-Sat) in Aizawl.

Aizawl

☎0389 / POP 293,500

Clinging to a near-vertical ridge by its fingernails, Aizawl (eye-zole) is easily the most languid and unhurried of all Indian state capitals. There's very little to do here, apart from soaking up its relaxed feel and peaceful way of life. The area around Chanmari, the heart of Aizawl's residential and shopping district, is the most interesting, and most tourist establishments are located in or near it.

Sights

Saturday Street Market MARKET

(Mission Veng St) This interesting Saturday street market – Aizawl's buzziest occasion through its otherwise quiet weekends – sees village women selling fruit, vegetables, fish, poultry and maybe even live pigs in individual wickerwork carry-away baskets. Gastronomes could swing by to pick up a few sundried kitchen rations and local spices to enhance food back home.

Salvation Army Temple CHURCH

(Zodin Sq) FREE The Salvation Army Temple has bell chimes that are endearingly complex and can be heard throughout the city, especially on a quiet Sunday morning. Its hulking white Gothic-inspired exteriors are worth a photo. To get here, you could take a taxi from the town's central Chanmari area (₹50) or walk for about 30 minutes.

Sleeping & Eating

Hotel Regency HOTEL $$

(☎0389-2349334; www.regencyaizawl.com; Zarkawt Main St; s/d incl breakfast from ₹2120/2490; ❄📶) Posh by Aizawl's standards, this stylish hotel has inviting rooms off marbled corridors, each with cosy beds, clean bathrooms and LCD TVs. The staff is smart and cooperative, and there's a great in-house restaurant overlooking the main street that serves tasty Indian, Chinese and Continental fare. Some lower-floor rooms out the front suffer from street noise.

David's Hotel Clover HOTEL $$

(☎0389-2305736; www.davidshotelclover.com; G16, Chanmari; s/d incl breakfast from ₹950/1500; @📶) It may not be the plushest address in town, but it's definitely the friendliest. The well-kept rooms here have colourful accent lighting and fancy bathroom fittings, the wi-fi works all the time and the in-house restaurant serves the best Chinese and Mizo food in town. It's a flight of steps down from street level.

Aizawl Masala CHINESE $

(Zarkawt Main St; mains ₹80-120; ⏲noon-8pm Mon-Sat) One flight of stairs below street level, this trendy place serves a host of the usual quasi-Chinese suspects (noodles, fried rice, meat in chilli/garlic/pepper sauce etc). There's good music to go with your food.

Getting There & Away

Lengpui airport is 35km west of Aizawl; a reserved taxi/shared jeep will charge ₹1500/150 to get here. **Air India** (☎011-24624074; www.airindia.in), **Indigo** (☎9910383838;

OFF THE BEATEN TRACK

RURAL MIZORAM

Mizoram's pretty, green hills get higher as you head east towards the Myanmar border. **Champhai** is widely considered the most attractive district, where you'll find **Murlen National Park**, known for its resident population of hoolock gibbons. The small town of **Saitual** is a good stopover on the road to Champhai. Very close to Champhai is pretty **Tamdil Lake**, ringed by lush mountains. Further afield is the stunning **Blue Mountain** (Phawngpui), Mizoram's highest peak at 2147m. It's considered by Mizos to be the abode of gods, but its slopes are said to be haunted by ghosts. Hiking options are also available in the region, but it's advisable to enter the wilderness only with an experienced local tour guide.

Limited homestay options are available in the countryside, but come with a local guide or you may not know where to look for them or even communicate with host families. There are no hotels.

www.goindigo.in) and **Jet Airways** (☎1800225522; www.jetairways.com) operate daily flights to Guwahati and Kolkata.

Counters for long-distance Sumos are conveniently clustered around the Zarkawt area's Sumkuma Point. Destinations include Guwahati (₹1200, 20 hours, 6pm Monday to Saturday), Shillong (₹1000, 16 hours, 6pm Monday to Saturday) and Silchar (₹500, six hours, four daily).

TRIPURA

Far from India's popular tourist circuits, Tripura is a culturally charming place that thrives on the hope that its handful of royal palaces and temples will draw the world's attention someday. For the moment, though, foreign travellers remain very rare, despite the fact that no permit is currently required to visit the state. Southern Tripura's best-known sights can be combined into a long day trip from Agartala.

Agartala

☎0381 / POP 400,000

Tripura's only 'city', low-key Agartala with its semi-rural atmosphere feels like an India of yore. It's a congested but relaxed place, and in many ways feels more like a small town than a state capital. The pace of life is unhurried, and the people are extremely friendly.

Sights

Apart from the town's main sights, there are several royal mausoleums decaying quietly on the riverbank behind Battala market (walk west down HGB Rd, turn left at Ronaldsay Rd and right along the riverbank).

Ujjayanta Palace PALACE
(museum ₹10; ⏲11am-5pm Tue-Sun) Agartala's centrepiece is this striking, dome-capped palace, fronted by two large reflecting ponds. Within the superstructure is the wonderfully preserved **Tripura Government Museum**, which is the only section of the main palace building open to visitors. It contains an imposing collection of regal and cultural memorabilia and artefacts, along with relics from Northeast India's centuries-old artistic heritage. The tree-lined lakeside promenades flanking the building are open to the public throughout the day.

State Academy of Tribal Culture MUSEUM
(Chowmuhani; ⏲10am-5pm Mon-Sat) FREE The well-maintained State Academy of Tribal Culture, off Central Rd in Chowmuhani, has an impressive display of tribal costumes, handicrafts, instruments, utensils and objects of daily life sourced from across 19 tribal cultures in the state. It gives visitors a comprehensive insight into Tripura's ethnic matrix, and is definitely worth a visit if you have some time to spare.

Sleeping & Eating

Ginger HOTEL $$$
(☎0381-2411333; www.gingerhotels.com; Airport Rd; s/d from ₹3290/3650; ❄@📶) Part of the Tata-owned Ginger chain of hotels, this superbly managed, low-cost business hotel has smart rooms done up in orange and blue pastel shades. There's free wi-fi, real coffee, a restaurant with delicious buffets, a small gym and an in-house SBI ATM. Coming from the airport, you'll find the hotel on your right about 2km short of town.

Hotel Rajdhani HOTEL $$
(☎0381-2323387; BK Rd; d from ₹1980; ❄@) Located close to the Ujjayanta Palace, this trusted address has an assortment of clean and tidy rooms, some of which have direct views of the palace's lofty ramparts. The staff is helpful and easygoing, and there's a popular eatery serving decent multicuisine fare and local meals.

Restaurant Kurry Klub INDIAN, CHINESE $$
(Hotel Welcome Palace, HGB Rd; mains ₹120-180; ⏲11am-10pm; ❄) The restaurant at Hotel Welcome Palace serves generous helpings of tasty Indian food, including some fantastic local fish dishes. It's particularly busy dur-

BORDER CROSSING: AKHAURA TO BANGLADESH

From central Agartala, the border is just 3km along Akhaura Rd (₹60 by rickshaw). On the Bangladesh side the nearest town is Akhaura, 5km beyond the border, reached by 'CNG' (autorickshaw). From Akhaura, trains head to Dhaka, Comilla and Sylhet. From the **International Bus Terminal**, off Hospital Rd opposite the TRTC, there's a 1.30pm bus connection to Dhaka (₹480, six hours). The border at Agartala is open from 8am to 6pm. There's no currency-exchange booth, so ask local traders or border officials.

Agartala

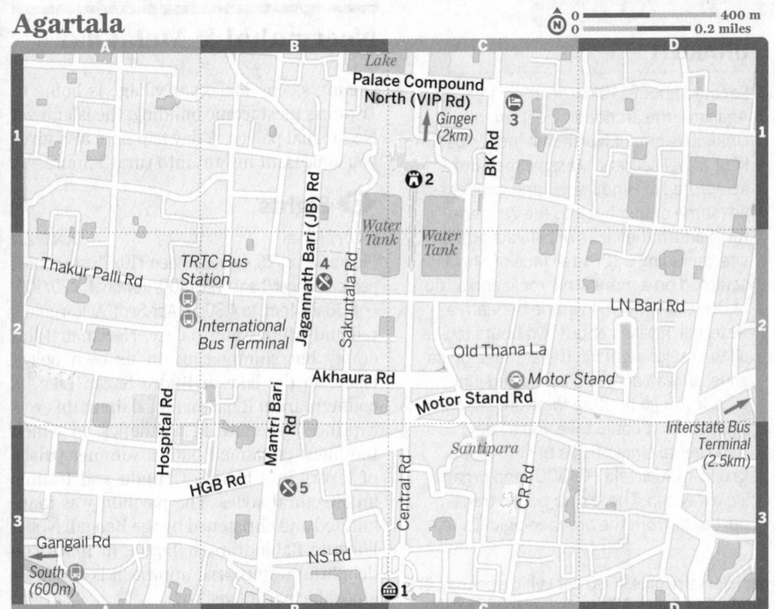

ing dinner, when walk-in diners turn up in chatty groups.

Abhishek Restaurant INDIAN $

(LN Bari Rd; mains ₹80-130; noon-10pm;) Choose between a marine-themed AC dining room and an outdoor seating area with tables set amid bushes and sculptures, and then put away a hearty meal comprising some eminently enjoyable North Indian and local fare. The lighting could be less tacky, but the atmosphere is cheerful.

Agartala

Sights

1 State Academy of Tribal Culture C3
2 Ujjayanta Palace C1

Sleeping

3 Hotel Rajdhani C1

Eating

4 Abhishek Restaurant B2
5 Restaurant Kurry Klub B3

Information

BANGLADESH VISAS

Northeast India's only **Bangladesh visa office** (0381-2324807; Airport Rd, Kunjaban; application 9am-1pm Mon-Thu, to noon Fri, collection 4pm) hides down a small lane in Agartala, about 2km north of the Ujjayanta Palace. On paper, tourist visas for Bangladesh are supposed to be issued free of charge. However, speedy service often comes with a 'processing fee' of ₹400, in which case visas are generally granted within one working day.

Getting There & Away

Agartala's airport is 12km north; a taxi costs ₹250. **Air India** (011-24624075; www.airindia.in), **Jet Airways** (1800225522; www.jetairways.com), **Indigo** (9910383838; www.goindigo.in) and **SpiceJet** (9654003333; www.spicejet.com) fly from here to Kolkata and Guwahati daily.

Private bus operators are clustered on LN Bari Rd. From the **Interstate Bus Terminal** (Chandrapur), 3km east of Agartala's town centre in Chandrapur (rickshaw ₹50), buses head to Guwahati (₹950, 24 hours, 6am and noon), Shillong (₹800, 20 hours, 6am and noon) and Silchar (₹350, 12 hours, 6am). Sumos use the **Motor Stand** (Motor Stand Rd) and **South Bus Station** (SBS).

Government-operated buses connecting Agartala with smaller towns in Tripura leave from the **TRTC bus station** (Thakur Palli Rd).

Taxis can be hired on a day-long basis for sightseeing in and around Agartala, for about ₹8

OFF THE BEATEN TRACK

UNAKOTI

Located about 140km northeast of Agartala, the archaeological site of Unakoti is one of Northeast India's best-kept travel secrets. Massive rock-cut sculptures of Hindu gods and goddesses (some dating back to the 7th century) adorn the faces of hillocks at the site, including a 10m-tall face of Shiva sculpted on a monolithic rock, and a trio of Ganeshas hewn in stone beneath a waterfall. It takes about two hours to see all the major sights in the archaeological zone, spread across hillocks and jungles. If you go hunting for more obscure sculptures, it could take you all day.

To get to Unakoti, it's best to hire a taxi from Agartala (₹3000) and organise a day trip. There's no public transport to or from the archaeological site.

per kilometre plus ₹600 per vehicle per day. Try **Hindustan Tours & Travels** (☎9206348911; Ginger Hotel, Airport Rd).

Udaipur

☎03821

Udaipur was Tripura's historic capital and remains dotted with ancient temples and tanks. According to Hindu legend, when Shiva – blinded by sorrow and rage – divided the corpse of his beloved wife Sati into 108 pieces, her right leg dropped onto Matabari, the site of Udaipur's main drawcard: the vivid Tripura Sundari Mandir (p588).

Sights

Tripura Sundari Mandir HINDU TEMPLE

(Matabari; ⏲4.30am-1.30pm & 3.30-9.30pm) The red-spired Tripura Sundari Mandir is a 1501 Kali temple where pilgrims come to be showered with the blessings of the Hindu mother goddess. Even more people come here during Kali Puja (October/November) to bathe in the fish-filled tank by the temple. The temple is 4km south of Udaipur; an autorickshaw costs ₹50.

Getting There & Away

Udaipur's bus station has daily connections to Agartala (₹60, two hours) and Melaghar (₹40, 45 minutes).

Neermahal & Melaghar

☎0381

Quaint, sleepy Melaghar village is home to Tripura's most iconic building, the island-set Neermahal palace. A day trip here also gives you a pleasant insight into rural Tripura.

Sights

Neermahal MONUMENT

(Rudra Sagar; ₹5, camera/video ₹10/25, speedboat per passenger/boat ₹20/400, rowboat ₹20/100; ⏲8.30am-4pm, to 4.30pm Apr-Sep) A gorgeous red-and-white water palace, Neermahal lies empty but shimmering on its own boggy island in the lake of Rudra Sagar. Like its counterpart in Rajasthan's Udaipur, this was a princely exercise in aesthetics, in which the finest craftsmen built a summer palace of luxury in a blend of Hindu and Islamic architectural styles. The pavilion was inaugurated and christened by the Bengali Nobel laureate Rabindranath Tagore in 1930. The delightful waterborne approach is the most enjoyable part of visiting.

Getting There & Away

Melaghar has hourly bus connections to Agartala (₹60, two hours) through the morning and afternoon. The last bus leaves around 4pm.

MEGHALAYA

Separating the Assam valley from the plains of Bangladesh, hilly Meghalaya – the 'abode of clouds' – is a cool, pine-fresh mountain state set on dramatic horseshoes of rocky cliffs. Cherrapunjee and Mawsynram are statistically among the wettest places on Earth; most of the rain falls between June and September, creating very impressive waterfalls and carving out some of Asia's longest caves.

The state's population predominantly comprises the Jaintia, Khasi and Garo tribes, who live in the eastern, central and western parts respectively. A good time to be in Meghalaya is during the Wangala (p561) drum festival in the Garo Hills in autumn.

Shillong

☎0364 / POP 145,000

Irreverent Shillong was the capital of British-created Assam until 1972. Since becoming the state capital of Meghalaya, it

Shillong

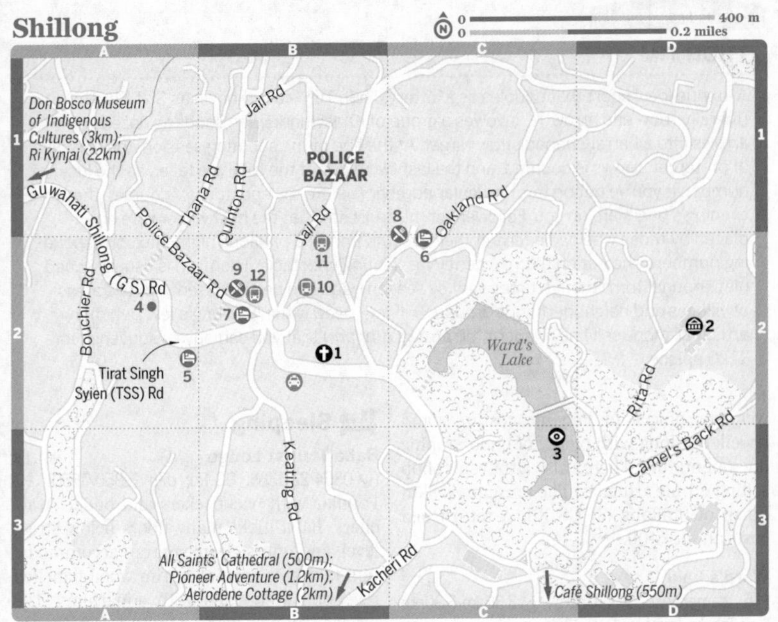

Shillong

Sights
1 Anglican Church B2
2 Pinewood Hotel D2
3 Ward's Lake C3

Activities, Courses & Tours
4 Campfire Trails A2

Sleeping
5 Baba Tourist Lodge A2
6 Earle Holiday Home C2
7 Hotel Centre Point B2

Eating
8 City Hut Dhaba C1
9 Trattoria B2

Transport
10 Deep B2
11 MTC Bus Station B2
12 Network Travels B2

has rapidly developed into a typical modern Indian town, but it retains some of its colonial-era charm in certain pockets. Overhauled cars are all the rage here – take a ride in one of Shillong's many taxis and you'll see.

Sights

The city's half-timbered architecture has been swamped by lots of drab modern concrete, but areas such as Oakland and Lumsohphoh retain many older houses. More centrally located is the **Pinewood Hotel** (Rita Rd), a 1920s tea-growers' retreat that is particularly representative of colonial-era architecture and looks great at night. The 1902 **All Saints' Cathedral** (Kacheri Rd) would look perfect pictured on a biscuit tin. The **Anglican Church**, perched above Police Bazaar, is a graceful structure fronted by pretty lawns.

★ **Don Bosco Museum of Indigenous Cultures** MUSEUM
(☎0364-2550260; www.dbcic.org; Mawlai; Indian/foreigner ₹100/200; ⏲9am-5.30pm Mon-Sat, to 4.30pm Dec & Jan) This well-maintained museum is a fabulous repository of innumerable tribal artefacts interspersed with galleries on Christian missionary work. Compulsory tours depart on the half-hour and last over an hour. Sights in the seven-storey museum include tribal basketry, musical instruments,

DON'T MISS

THOH TIM

A unique local sport that doubles as a lottery, Thoh Tim – also known as Siat Khnam (literally, 'bow and arrow') – involves a group of Khasi marksmen shooting dozens of arrows into a barrel-shaped straw target. At the end of the shooting session, the number of on-target arrows is counted, and the last two digits of the total are taken as the lucky number. If you've bet on this particular number (before the shootout, of course), the evening's beers are on you. Followers of the sport say that the best wagers are often placed by those who can interpret their dreams from the previous night into corresponding numbers and bet on them! A gently fascinating spectacle, Thoh Tim is usually scheduled around 4pm (though times vary by season), and can be witnessed in public areas of villages and neighbourhoods around Shillong. Deep within Shillong's Iew Duh market, artisanal shops sell fine handcrafted arrows *(khnam)* that you can buy as souvenirs for ₹120 apiece.

weapons, objects of daily life, costumes and jewellery, along with plenty of photographic documentation. There's also a souvenir shop selling ethnic artefacts. The museum is 3km north of Shillong off GS Rd. A return taxi costs about ₹400.

Ward's Lake LAKE
(₹5, camera/video ₹10/20; ⏲8.30am-5.30pm Nov-Feb, to 7pm Mar-Oct) The central landscaping element of colonial-era Shillong, this attractive lake has a pretty ornamental bridge, flower beds, manicured lawns, courting couples, boating facilities and gaggles of geese.

Activities

Campfire Trails OUTDOORS
(☎9856001871; www.campfiretrails.com; DD Laloo & Co, GS Rd; per person per night incl full board ₹1700-2000) Campfire Trails specialises in authentic village tourism experiences in rustic settings across central Meghalaya. Four previously unexplored villages are run as self-sustaining units in cooperation with local tribal stakeholders. Activities to accompany your village experience (complete with utterly delicious local food) include kayaking, mountain biking, zip lining and trekking.

Pioneer Adventure OUTDOORS
(☎9049442647; www.pioneeradventuretour.com; Jarman Villa, Hopkinson Rd) This agency has introduced diving in the hills! Open-water facilities (per person ₹2500) are available at its camp near Dawki, where the Umngot River offers up to 10m visibility. PADI-recognised courses are also available. Other activities include snorkelling, rock climbing, rafting, caving and camping. All-inclusive overnight packages (per person ₹7000) allow you to sample a bit of everything.

Sleeping

Baba Tourist Lodge HOTEL $
(☎0364-2211285; GS Rd; d/tr ₹1350/1550; wi-fi) Popular with backpackers and budget travellers, Baba hides many floors below street level, and offers clean, spartan accommodation in rooms beyond a prim wood-panelled reception area lined with aquariums. The pricier rooms have running hot water. There's basic in-house food, and free wi-fi in the lobby.

Earle Holiday Home HOTEL $
(☎9089184830; Oakland Rd; d from ₹800; ❄) This hotel has character but is amusingly disorganised. The cheaper rooms are original half-timbered affairs within a classic 1920 Shillong hill house adorned with sweet little turrets. Pricier rooms in the concrete annexe are less atmospheric but more comfortable.

Hotel Centre Point HOTEL $$$
(☎0364-2220480; www.shillongcentrepoint.com; Police Bazaar Rd; d incl breakfast from ₹4160; ❄ wi-fi) Located bang on Police Bazaar, this is arguably the best business hotel in Shillong. Run by professional and helpful staff, it has smart rooms with wood panelling and large windows overlooking the town centre. All creature comforts are at your disposal, and the Cloud 9 rooftop lounge bar is a good place for evening beers and (occasionally) live music.

Royal Heritage Tripura Castle HERITAGE HOTEL $$$
(☎0364-2501149; www.tripuracastle.com; Cleve Colony; d incl breakfast from ₹5850; ❄@ wi-fi) Behind the distinctively turreted summer villa of the former Tripura maharajas, this private 'castle' offers luxurious rooms in a new (pseudo-heritage) building. Pine-framed

rooms have a gently stylish vibe, with period furniture and excellent service. For the full royal experience, opt for a suite. The hotel is 2.5km southeast of Shillong.

Aerodene Cottage GUESTHOUSE **$$$**
(☎9774065366; www.aerodene.in; Lower Cleve Colony; d incl breakfast from ₹3500;) An appealing garden-fronted Assam-style bungalow converted into a guesthouse, Aerodene has atmospheric rooms with soft beds, wooden floors, period decor and lots of light and fresh air. The newer annexe to the right has rooms that are less charming but equally comfortable. The food is simply delicious; dinner costs an additional ₹250 per person.

★**Ri Kynjai** RESORT **$$$**
(☎9862420300; www.rikynjai.com; Umiam Lake; d incl breakfast from ₹10,300;) This divine resort on the banks of pristine Umiam Lake, 22km from Shillong, is a gem of a getaway. Spacious wood-pillared cottages with fabulous lake views lie scattered about its lush, green gardens, and each is impeccably presented, with elegant furnishings and lavish bathrooms. There's a traditionally decorated spa and a multicuisine restaurant-bar with lake views.

Eating

★**Trattoria** ADIVASI **$**
(Police Bazaar Rd; mains ₹100-120; noon-4pm) No visit to Shillong is complete without a midday meal at this busy eatery patronised by locals. Some of the best Khasi dishes, including *ja doh* and curried pig innards, are (literally) hot favourites here. For a sampling, try the immensely popular lunch platter (₹150). A contiguous stall sells packs of exotic pickles, squashes and condiments.

City Hut Dhaba MULTICUISINE **$**
(Oakland Rd; mains ₹100-150; 10am-9pm) Guarded by signage gnomes, City Hut serves a variety of Indian, Chinese and barbecue dishes in four rooms, including a family-only room and an attractive, flower-decked straw pavilion. The quality of food is fairly commendable, and the place sees plenty of locals.

Drinking & Nightlife

Café Shillong CAFE
(☎0364-2505759; Laitumkhrah; coffee ₹60; 11am-9pm;) This cool hang-out in bustling Laitumkhrah (lai-muk-rah) has the best coffee in town, yummy steaks (mains ₹140 to ₹200), and rock, jazz and blues on tap. Its fashionable decor features a Les Paul guitar signed by performing musicians. Weekends, when there are live acts, are the busiest.

Getting There & Away

The **MTC bus station** (Jail Rd) has a computerised train-reservation counter (the nearest train station is in Guwahati). Private buses depart from Dhankheti Point; book tickets from counters around Police Bazaar, including **Deep** (Ward's Lake Rd) and **Network Travels** (☎0364-2210981; Shop 44, MUDA Complex, Police Bazaar Rd).

Departing from the MTC bus station, frequent buses and Sumos go to Aizawl (Sumo ₹1000, 16 hours), Cherrapunjee (bus/Sumo ₹120/200, three hours), Dimapur (bus ₹450, 10 hours), Guwahati (bus/Sumo ₹120/200, 2½ hours), Silchar (bus ₹400, six hours), Siliguri (bus ₹550, 12 hours) and Tura (bus/Sumo ₹350/450, nine hours via Guwahati).

Khasi Hills Tourist Taxi Cooperative
(☎0364-2223895; Kacheri Rd) charges ₹2200 to ₹2500 for a day trip to Cherrapunjee; for a ride to the Bangladesh border near Dawki it's ₹2000. For Guwahati airport, a full taxi costs ₹2000, or you can share with other passengers for ₹500.

Garo & Jaintia Hills

Far off the beaten track, the lush Garo Hills in the far west of Meghalaya are worth exploring if you have a few days to spare (and a sense of adventure). Easier to reach from Guwahati than Shillong, the region's urban hub is the tiny settlement of **Tura**, where the friendly **tourist office** (10am-4pm Mon-Fri) can arrange local guides. In autumn, the Garo Hills come alive with the four-day Wangala (p561) drum festival. In the Jaintia Hills, located in the east of the state, **Nartiang** is a lonesome town specked with pine trees and pretty tribal villages, where you can sample the region's rich and undiluted heritage.

Sights

Nokrek Biosphere Reserve NATURE RESERVE
(dawn-dusk) FREE About 17km from Tura, the forested Nokrek Biosphere Reserve is home to the endangered Hoolock gibbon, as well as red pandas, elephants and a few species of macaque. The reserve can be visited if you hire a vehicle (₹1000) in Tura for the day.

Nartiang Monoliths MONUMENT
(Nartiang; dawn-dusk) FREE The Jaintia Hills is home to the village of Nartiang,

BORDER CROSSING: DAWKI TO BANGLADESH

The India–Bangladesh border post is at Tamabil, a Bangladeshi settlement 1.5km from Dawki market (a taxi costs ₹100). There are frequent Tamabil–Sylhet minibuses on the other side. The border is open from 9am to 6pm. There's no foreign-exchange booth here, but you will find helpful non-official personnel on the Bangladesh side willing to change cash for a steep rate.

where you can visit an intriguing complex of stone monoliths erected by different clans between the 16th and 19th centuries. It's unattended and overgrown – beware of snakes in the undergrowth.

Sleeping & Eating

Rikman Continental HOTEL $$

(☎03651-220744; www.hotelrikman.com; Circular Rd; s/d incl breakfast from ₹1200/1500; ❄📶) Just seconds from Tura's central market and transport booths is this ultra-friendly place. The upper floors have a string of more expensive rooms, with AC, huge windows and tiled bathrooms with hot water. Rikman's restaurant is probably the best place to taste Garo cuisine; try the lunch buffet (₹250). The attached bar has a decent stock of booze.

Getting There & Away

Quick, comfortable minivans (₹300, six hours, 6am) ply the 200km stretch from Tura to Guwahati every day. To visit Nartiang, you'll have to hire a taxi (₹1800) for the day from Shillong, 62km away.

Cherrapunjee (Sohra)

☎03637 / POP 14,500

Laid out along razor-like ridges of a high mountain wall, Cherrapunjee (known locally as Sohra) sits at the edge of the Himalayas, overlooking the pancake-flat plains of Bangladesh. The village was once feted as the wettest place on Earth because of its prodigious monsoon rainfall. The road from state capital Shillong passes through pretty scenery that becomes dramatic at the **Dympep viewpoint**, where a photogenic V-shape valley cuts deeply into the plateau.

Sights

★ **Root Bridges** BRIDGE

The most fascinating sights around Cherrapunjee are the incredible root bridges – living rubber fig-tree roots that ingenious Khasi villagers have, over decades, trained across streams to form natural pathways. Three of these root bridges (including an amazing 'double-decker') are near **Nongriat**. Access is via the pretty village of **Tyrna**, 2km from Mawshamok. The round trip into the canyon where these root bridges stand is an eight-hour slog from Tyrna, involving a 2000-step ascent and descent through very steep terrain.

Nohkalikai Falls WATERFALL

(viewpoint ₹10, camera/video ₹20/50; ⏲8am-5pm) Nohkalikai Falls are particularly dramatic during the monsoon, when their capacity increases 20-fold. You can see them from the **viewpoint** located on a plateau at the end of a mountain ridge 4.4km from Cherrapunjee's market. Local taxis (₹50) shuttle passengers to the viewpoint.

Sleeping & Eating

Cherrapunjee Holiday Resort RESORT $$$

(☎09436115925; www.cherrapunjee.com; Laitkynsew Village; d incl half-board from ₹3700; 📶) Run by an affable Khasi woman and her South Indian husband, this delightful resort comprises an older building (with cheaper rooms set around a spacious refectory) and a new multistorey block (with modern deluxe rooms). The home-cooked meals are simply fantastic. The resort provides guides for local hikes and organises tented accommodation in the dry season.

Polo Orchid RESORT $$$

(☎0364-2222341; www.hotelpolotowers.com; Seven Sisters Falls; d incl breakfast ₹7600; ❄📶) A stylish place with a spectacular setting, this resort has clusters of rooms located along a ridge overlooking the vast sweep of the Bangladeshi plains. Rooms feature eco-chic furnishings and bright upholstery, but it all appears somewhat lavish for the otherwise sylvan location.

Getting There & Away

Although straggling for several kilometres, Cherrapunjee has a compact centre. Huddled beside the marketplace is the Sumo stand, with connections to Shillong (₹200, three hours).

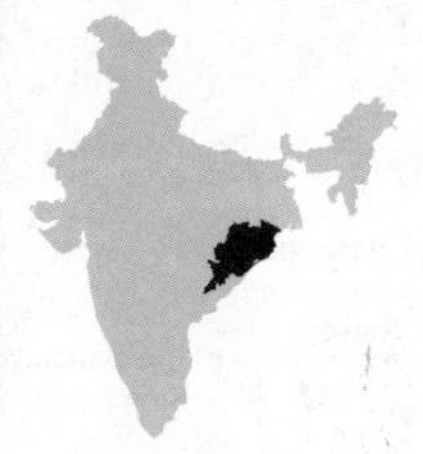

Odisha

Includes ➡

Best Places to Eat

- Wildgrass Restaurant (p607)
- Kila Dalijoda (p616)
- Kanika (p600)
- Odisha Hotel (p600)

Best Places to Sleep

- Kila Dalijoda (p616)
- Chandoori Sai (p614)
- Desia (p615)
- Gajlaxmi Palace (p616)
- Nature Camp Bhitarkanika (p619)
- Garh Dhenkanal Palace (p616)

Why Go?

An off-the-beaten-track favourite for more adventurous types, Odisha (Orissa) rewards those who make the effort with an intricate patchwork of history, fascinating tribal culture and natural beauty, along with an old-fashioned sprinkling of sun and sand.

The forested hills of the southwest keep Adivasi (tribal) groups largely hidden from mainstream tourism, but it is still possible to visit their fascinating weekly markets and interact with villagers leading traditional lives. Forests elsewhere – both inland and along the coast – are home to some of Odisha's wonderful nature reserves, where you can spy on 6m-long crocs, rare dolphins, endangered sea turtles and thousands of nesting birds.

Foodies will relish a whole new set of regional flavours cooked up in Odishan kitchens, while history buffs will be left salivating over long-lost Buddhist universities, ancient Jain rock carvings and centuries-old Hindu relics, including Konark's unparalleled Sun Temple.

When to Go

Bhubaneswar

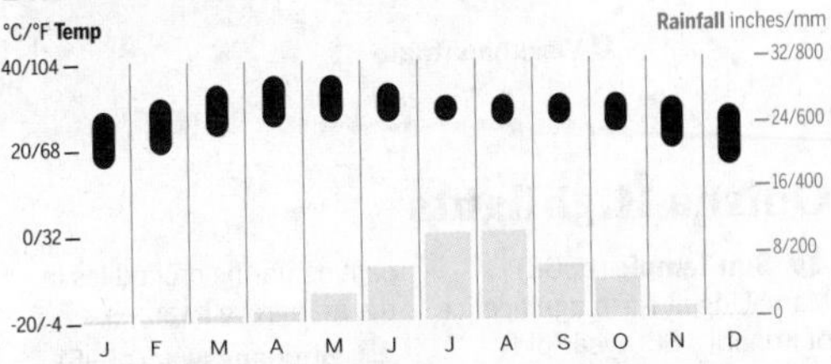

Nov–Mar Warm and dry; best for wildlife-spotting in the nature reserves.

Jun & Jul It's baking, but Puri's Rath Yatra festival is Odisha's biggest celebration.

Dec The Unesco-protected Sun Temple is the magnificent backdrop for the seductive Konark Festival.

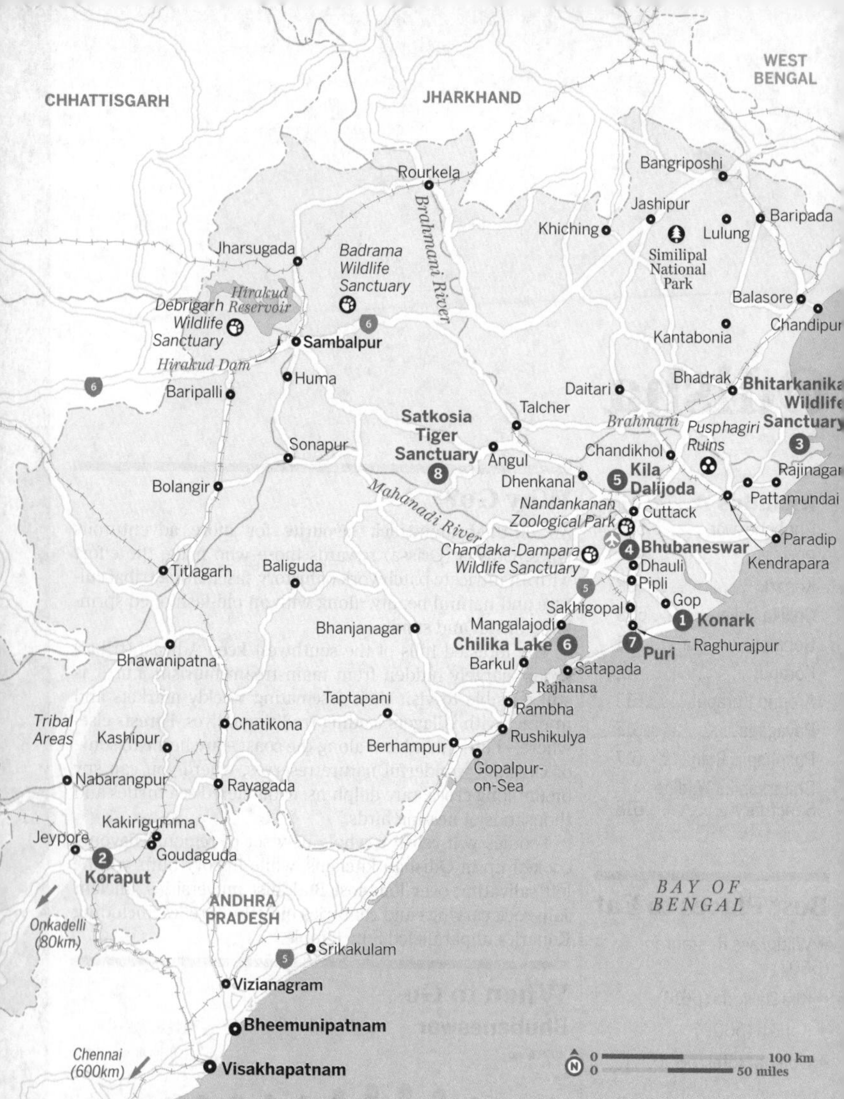

Odisha Highlights

1. **Sun Temple** (p608) Marvelling at the magnificence of Konark's 800-year-old Unesco-protected edifice.
2. **Koraput** (p612) Venturing deep into the hills of Odisha's tribal country to visit tribal markets and villages.
3. **Bhitarkanika Wildlife Sanctuary** (p618) Cruising past estuarine crocodiles in the mangrove swamps.
4. **Bhubaneswar** (p595) Touring some of the 50-odd ancient temples that still remain in Odisha's capital city.
5. **Kila Dalijoda** (p616) Cycling through pristine villages while staying at this heritage home.
6. **Chilika Lake** (p609) Spotting rare Irrawaddy dolphins and a wealth of birdlife.
7. **Puri** (p604) Tapping into the traveller vibe in Odisha's most appealing town.
8. **Satkosia Tiger Sanctuary** (p603) Gazing across the sands of the Mahanadi River from your tent.

History

Formerly known as Kalinga, Utkala and more recently Orissa, Odisha (per a long-standing name-change campaign that finally received government approval in 2010) was once a formidable maritime empire that had trading routes leading down into Indonesia, but its history is somewhat hazy until the demise of the Kalinga dynasty in 260 BC at the hands of the great emperor Ashoka. Appalled at the carnage he had caused, Ashoka forswore violence and converted to Buddhism.

Around the 1st century BC, Buddhism declined and Jainism was restored as the faith of the people. During this period the monastery caves of Udayagiri and Khandagiri (in Bhubaneswar) were excavated as important Jain centres.

By the 7th century AD, Hinduism had supplanted Jainism. Under the Kesari and Ganga kings, trade and commerce increased and Odishan culture flourished – countless temples from that classical period still stand. The Odishans defied the Muslim rulers in Delhi until finally falling to the Mughals during the 16th century, when many of Bhubaneswar's temples were destroyed.

Until Independence, Odisha was ruled by Afghans, Marathas and the British.

Since the 1990s a Hindu fundamentalist group, Bajrang Dal, has undertaken a violent campaign against Christians in Odisha in response to missionary activity. The often illiterate and dispossessed tribal people have suffered the most from the resulting communal violence, which has been as much about power, politics and land as religious belief.

Violence flared up again in 2008 after the killing of a Hindu leader in Kandhamal district, and thousands of Christians were moved to government relief camps outside the district after their homes were torched. There has been little Bajrang Dal activity in Odisha since, but the group has been implicated in violent acts in recent years in Uttar Pradesh.

The creation of the neighbouring states of Jharkhand and Chhattisgarh has prompted calls for the formation of a separate, tribal-oriented state, Koshal, in the northwest of Odisha, with Sambalpur as the capital. A separatist political party, the Kosal Kranti Dal (KKD), fielded candidates in the 2009 state election and took to disruptive transport protests in 2010. Maoist activity flares up occasionally in Odisha's tribal country.

ℹ Dangers & Annoyances

Mosquitoes in some parts here have a record of being dengue and malaria carriers. Arm yourself with repellent and cover up.

ℹ Tourist Information

Odisha Tourism (www.orissatourism.gov.in) has a presence in most towns, with offices for information and tour/hotel bookings. **Odisha Tourism Development Corporation** (www.otdc.in), the commercial arm of Odisha Tourism, runs tours and hotels throughout the state.

ℹ Getting There & Away

Air routes connect Bhubaneswar with Bengaluru (Bangalore), Delhi, Hyderabad, Mumbai (Bombay), Kolkata (Calcutta) and Chennai (Madras). Major road and rail routes between Kolkata and Chennai pass through coastal Odisha and Bhubaneswar with spur connections to Puri. Road and rail connect Sambalpur with Kolkata, Chhattisgarh and Madhya Pradesh.

BHUBANESWAR

☎0674 / POP 885,363

Once dubbed the 'Temple City', chaotic Bhubaneswar is a worthwhile pit stop for a day or two as you take in the old city's holy centre around the ceremonial tank called Bindu Sagar. Here once stood thousands of medieval stone temples; now around 50 remain. Temples aside, there are a couple of highly worthwhile museums, an ancient cave complex and

TOP STATE FESTIVALS

Adivasi Mela (p599) Features art, dance and handicrafts of Odisha's tribal groups in Bhubaneswar.

Rath Yatra (p605) Immense chariots containing Lord Jagannath, brother Balbhadra and sister Subhadra are hauled from Jagannath Mandir to Gundicha Mandir.

Puri Beach Festival (p605) Song, dance, food and cultural activities on the beach in Puri.

Bali Yatra (⏲Nov/Dec) Immense state fair in Cuttack, with fine silver filigree, *ikat* weaving and other crafts for sale.

Konark Festival (p609) Features traditional music and dance and a seductive temple ritual.

Bhubaneswar

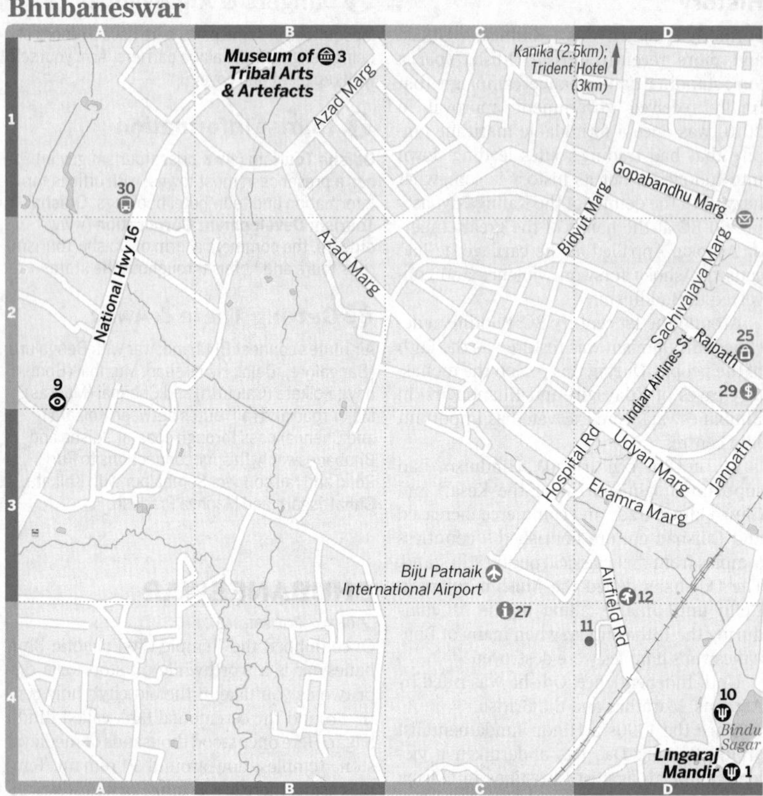

the most varied dining scene in Odisha, along with a smattering of decent hotels.

Sights

★Lingaraj Mandir HINDU TEMPLE

(Lingaraj Temple Rd; dawn-dusk) The 54m-high Lingaraj Mandir, dedicated to Tribhuvaneswar (Lord of Three Worlds), dates from 1090 to 1104 (though parts are more than 1400 years old) and is surrounded by dozens of smaller temples and shrines. The granite block, representing Tribhuvaneswar, is bathed daily with water, milk and bhang (marijuana). The main gate, guarded by two mustachioed yellow lions, is a spectacle in itself as lines of pilgrims approach, *prasad* (temple-blessed food offering) in hand. Take bus 333 here from Master Canteen bus stand.

Because the temple is surrounded by a wall and closed to non-Hindus, foreigners can see it only from a viewing platform (this can also include foreign Hindus). Face the main entrance, walk right, then follow the wall around to the left and find the viewing platform on your left, just before you reach Chitrakarini Temple. There is occasional aggressive hassling for 'donations' at the viewing platform. The money will not go to the temple; stand your ground and do not pay.

★Mukteswar Mandir HINDU TEMPLE

(Kedar Gouri Ln; dawn-dusk) This small but beautiful 10th-century temple is one of the most ornate temples in Bhubaneswar; you'll see reproductions of it on posters across Odisha. Intricate carvings show a mixture of Buddhist, Jain and Hindu styles – look for Nagarani (Snake Queen), easily mistaken by Westerners for a mermaid, whom you'll also see at the nearby Rajarani Mandir. The ceiling carvings and stone arch are particularly striking, as is the arched *torana* (architrave) at the front, clearly showing Buddhist influence.

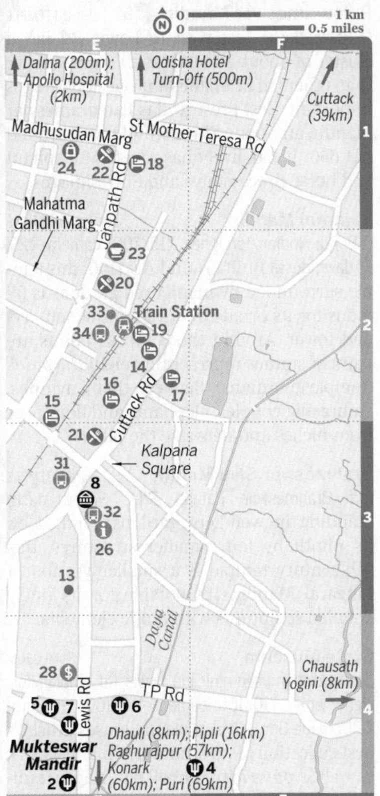

Bhubaneswar

Top Sights
1 Lingaraj Mandir D4
2 Mukteswar Mandir E4
3 Museum of Tribal Arts & Artefacts B1

Sights
4 Brahmeswar Siva Mandir F4
5 Parsurameswar Mandir E4
6 Rajarani Mandir E4
7 Siddheswara Mandir E4
8 State Museum E3
9 Udayagiri & Khandagiri Caves A2
10 Vaital Mandir D4

Activities, Courses & Tours
11 Alternative Tours D4
12 Kerala Panchakarma D3
13 Odisha Tourism Development Corporation E3

Sleeping
14 Hotel Grand Central E2
15 Hotel Nirmal Inn E2
16 Hotel Upasana E2
17 Mango Hotel E2
18 New Marrion E1
19 Railway Retiring Rooms E2

Eating
20 Hare Krishna Restaurant E2
21 Khana Khazana E3
22 Sri Ram Mandir Tiffin Centre E1
Truptee .... (see 21)

Drinking & Nightlife
23 BNC E2

Shopping
24 Ekamra Haat E1
25 Utkalika D2

Information
India Tourism .... (see 26)
26 Odisha Tourism E3
Odisha Tourism .... (see 19)
27 Odisha Tourism C4
28 SBI E4
29 State Bank of India D2

Transport
30 Baramunda Bus Stand A1
31 Buses to Cuttack E3
32 Buses to Puri E3
33 Computerised Reservation Office E2
34 Master Canteen Bus Stand E2

★Museum of Tribal Arts & Artefacts MUSEUM
(off National Hwy 16; ⏲10am-5pm Tue-Sun) FREE This superb musum is a must for anthropologically inclined visitors interested in Odisha's 62 tribes or considering a visit to Odisha's tribal areas. Complete with interactive elements, its galleries display traditional dress, bead ornaments, heavy silver collars, coin necklaces, elaborate headdresses, ornate wine pipes and musical instruments. One gallery is dedicated entirely to weaponry, fishing, hunting and agricultural equipment. You can buy colourful cloth paintings by the Saora people here. Bus 801 goes to nearby Azad Marg.

Behind the museum are replicas of traditional houses of the Gadaba, Kandha, Santal, Saora and other tribes.

Udayagiri & Khandagiri Caves HISTORIC SITE
(entry both sites Indian/foreigner ₹15/200, video ₹25; ⏲dawn-dusk) Six kilometres west of the city centre are two hills riddled with rock-cut shelters. Khandagiri is topped with a fine temple. Many of the caves are ornately

carved and thought to have been chiselled out for Jain ascetics in the 1st century BC. Buses don't go to the caves, but bus 801 runs to the nearby Baramunda bus stand. A shared/private autorickshaw shouldn't cost much more than ₹30/250.

Ascending the ramp at Udayagiri (Sunrise Hill), note **Swargapuri** (Cave 9) to the right with its devotional figures. **Hathi Gumpha** (Cave 14) at the top has a 117-line inscription relating the exploits of its builder, King Kharavela of Kalinga, who ruled from 168 to 153 BC.

Around to the left you'll see **Bagh Gumpha** (Tiger Cave; Cave 12), with its entrance carved as a tiger mouth. Nearby are **Pavana Gumpha** (Cave of Purification) and small **Sarpa Gumpha** (Serpent Cave), where the tiny door is surmounted by a three-headed cobra. On the summit are the remains of a defensive position. Around to the southeast is the single-storey elephant-guarded **Ganesh Gumpha** (Cave 10), almost directly above the two-storey **Rani ka Naur** (Queen's Palace Cave; Cave 1), carved with Jain symbols and battle scenes.

Continue back to the entrance via **Chota Hathi Gumpha** (Cave 3), with its carvings of elephants, and the double-storey **Jaya Vijaya Cave** (Cave 5), with a bodhi tree carved in the central area.

Across the road, Khandagiri offers fine views over Bhubaneswar from its summit. The steep path splits about one-third of the way up the hill. The right path goes to **Ananta Cave** (Cave 3), with its carved figures of athletes, women, elephants and geese carrying flowers. Further along is a series of **Jain temples**; at the top is another (18th-century) Jain temple.

Siddheswara Mandir HINDU TEMPLE
(Kedar Gouri Ln; dawn-dusk) In the same compound as Mukteswar Mandir, Siddheswara Mandir is a later but plainer temple with a fine red-painted Ganesha.

Vaital Mandir HINDU TEMPLE
(Rath Rd; dawn-dusk) This 8th-century temple, with a double-storey 'wagon roof' influenced by Buddhist cave architecture, was a centre of tantric worship, eroticism and bloody sacrifice. Look closely and you'll see some very early erotic carvings on the walls. Chamunda (a fearsome incarnation of Devi), representing old age and death, can be seen in the dingy interior, although her necklace of skulls and her bed of corpses are usually hidden beneath her temple robes.

Parsurameswar Mandir HINDU TEMPLE
(dawn-dusk) Just west of Lewis Rd lies a cluster of about 20 temples that are smaller than others in Bhubaneswar but nonetheless important. Best preserved is Parsurameswar Mandir, an ornate Shiva temple built around AD 650. It has lively bas-reliefs of elephant and horse processions, and Shiva images.

Rajarani Mandir HINDU TEMPLE
(TP Rd; Indian/foreigner ₹15/200, camera ₹25; dawn-dusk) Built around AD 1100, this temple surrounded by manicured gardens is famous for its ornate *deul* (temple sanctuary) and tower. Around the compass points are pairs of statues representing eight *dikpalas* (temple guardians). Between them, nymphs, embracing couples, elephants and lions peer from niches and decorate the pillars.

Brahmeswar Siva Mandir HINDU TEMPLE
(off Brahmeswar Patana Rd; dawn-dusk) Standing in well-kept gardens, flanked on its plinth by four smaller structures, this 9th-century temple is a smaller version of Lingaraj Mandir. It's notable for its finely detailed sculptures with erotic elements.

State Museum MUSEUM
(www.odishamuseum.nic.in; Lewis Rd; Indian/foreigner entry ₹10/100, camera ₹10/100; 10am-4.30pm Tue-Sun) This museum houses Odisha's best collection of rare palm-leaf manuscripts, as well as *patachitra* (scroll paintings), traditional and folk musical instruments, Bronze Age tools, an armoury, and an impressive collection of Buddhist, Jain and Brahmanical sculptures (look for the haunting 8th-century sculpture of Chamunda).

Activities

Kerala Panchakarma AYURVEDA, MASSAGE
(0674-2590053; 240/90 Airfield Rd, Airport Sq; treatments from ₹600; 6am-9pm) A small ayurvedic clinic offering stress-busting full-body massages.

Tours

Odisha Tourism Development Corporation CULTURAL
(OTDC; 0674-2431515; www.otdc.in; Lewis Rd; 7am-8pm) Daily bus tours by OTDC include city tours (₹300, 9am) to Nandankanan Zoo, Dhauli, the Lingaraj and Mukteswar temples, the State Museum, and Udayagiri and Khandagiri Caves. Another tour goes to Pipli, Konark and Puri (₹380, 9am), while a third takes in Puri and Satapada on Chilika

Lake (₹400, 8am). Book the day before from this OTDC office behind Panthanivas Hotel.

Tour prices do not include entry fees.

Alternative Tours TOURS
(☎0674-2590830; www.alternativetoursindia.com; Room 5, BDA Market Complex, off Airfield Rd; ⏲10am-6.45pm Mon-Sat) A veteran for tribal tours in Odisha, Nagaland and Arunachal Pradesh, its prices start at around ₹9000 per person per day, all inclusive. It also runs multiday wildlife and heritage tours of Odisha and organises private day tours to Puri and Konark.

Festivals & Events

Adivasi Mela CULTURAL
(⏲26-31 Jan) Bhubaneswar goes tribal for the annual Adivasi Mela festival, celebrating the art, dance and handicrafts of Odisha's tribal groups.

Sleeping

Many hotels have 24-hour checkout. The cheapest and less salubrious hotels are clustered around the train station. There are several midrange places along Janpath and Cuttack Rds, while the city's plushest offerings are found just north of Route 16 that circles the city, in BDA Colony.

Mango Hotel HOTEL $$
(☎0674-7119000; www.staymango.com; Cuttack Rd; r ₹2616-3815;) With friendly front-desk staff, a decent restaurant serving a mix of North Indian and Odishan dishes, and spotless rooms with comfy beds and decent wi-fi, this is the best midrange choice along Cuttack Rd. The train station is a five-minute walk.

Hotel Upasana HOTEL $$
(☎9439865225, 9439865227; www.hotelupasana.com; 2282 Laxmisagar, off Cuttack Rd; r ₹990, with AC from ₹1300; @) This family-run place, located behind Bhubaneswar Hotel, has rather rundown rooms that could be cleaner, with hot showers and small balconies. There are computer terminals in the lobby and wi-fi extends to some rooms. No restaurant.

Hotel Nirmal Inn HOTEL $$
(☎0674-2534411; Rajpath; r ₹1000, with AC ₹1400;) This no-frills place has good-value rooms, which are of the can't-swing-a-cat variety but are relatively clean and modern. Has a restaurant, but wi-fi is in the lobby only.

Railway Retiring Rooms GUESTHOUSE $
(Platform 1, Bhubaneswar train station; dm ₹90-300, r ₹260-520, r with AC ₹480-940;) These large but simple rooms are a place for ultra-shoestringers to rest for a few hours before catching a train. Rooms are in a quiet corner of the station, but it's still a train station so it's pretty noisy. Secure your room at the booking window beside 'Enquiries', which is just inside the station's main entrance.

> **SLEEPING PRICE RANGES**
>
> The following price ranges refer to a double room with bathroom and are inclusive of tax:
>
> **$** less than ₹800
>
> **$$** ₹800–₹2500
>
> **$$$** more than ₹2500

★**Trident Hotel** RESORT $$$
(☎0674-3010000; ww.tridenthotels.com; CB-1 Nayapalli; r/ste from ₹12,000/22,000;) The spacious, stylish rooms at the Trident, decorated with fine examples of Odishan stonework, textiles and metalwork, look out onto the peaceful gardens. There's a private jogging track, luxurious pool and one of the best restaurants in town. It's located 6km north of the train station.

Hotel Grand Central HOTEL $$$
(☎9437001152, 9937439074; www.hotelgrandcentral.com; Old Station Bazaar; s/d incl breakfast from ₹2800/3200;) Whitewashed corridors and marble floors lead to smart, well-fitted rooms at this business-class hotel, located just behind the train station. There's a restaurant, bar and car rental.

New Marrion HOTEL $$$
(☎0674-2380850; www.hotelnewmarrion.com; 6 Janpath Rd; s/d from ₹6100/6500; @) A central top-end hotel, Marrion has rooms with a contemporary, classy design – LCD TVs, dark-wood panelling and a small sofa space. Restaurants include South Indian, Italian-Mexican combo and Chinese, a great kebab house, a Café Coffee Day in the building out front and a contemporary Scottish bar. There's a Thai spa to round off the allure, and service is top-notch.

Eating

Dalma ODISHAN $
(www.dalmahotels.com; 157 Madhusudan Nagar; mains ₹70-180, thali ₹150-240; ⏲11am-4pm & 7-10.30pm) This outlet of the small Bhubaneswar chain is widely regarded by locals as

ODIA CUISINE

Mustard is the staple in Odishan kitchens, used ubiquitously in seed, paste and oil forms, giving many Odia dishes a distinct pungent flavour. A typical meal consists of *bhata* (rice) served alongside a variety of tasty side dishes such as *kaharu phula bhaja* (fried pumpkin flower); *dalma* (dhal cooked with pumpkin, potato, plantains and eggplant, then fried in a five-spice oil of fenugreek, cumin, black cumin, anise and mustard, topped with grated coconut); and *besara* (vegetables or river fish with mustard-paste gravy). *Saga bhaja* (leafy greens lightly fried with garlic paste and a five-seed mixture called *pancha phutan* (cumin, mustard, anis, black cumin and chilli) is also a treat here. On the coast, fish and prawns are omnipresent: *sarison macha* is a superb favourite fish dish cooked in a mustard-based curry.

the best place in town to sample authentic Odia cuisine, including *aloo bharta* (a delicious mashed potato and aubergine combination), *dalma* (the restaurant's speciality dhal dish, cooked with coconut), *chenna poda* (Orissa's cottage-cheese dessert from heaven) and numerous Odishan thalis.

It's nothing flash – there's a canteen feel to the place, with dishes served on metal trays – but the food is nothing short of sensational, especially when you consider the prices. First-time visitors to the region will welcome the well-translated menu with clear, English descriptions of every dish.

Khana Khazana INDIAN **$**
(Kalpana Sq; mains ₹50-170; ⏲5.30-10.30pm) This long-standing evening-only street stall – with plastic chairs and tables spread across the pavement – does a bang-up job with tandoori chicken, delicious chow mein and tasty biryanis. The *chicken dum biryani* (₹100) is particularly popular with the locals, as are the great-value rolls (roti wraps that come with various fillings and are a speciality of Kolkata; ₹40 to ₹60).

★Kanika ODISHAN **$$$**
(www.mayfairhotels.com; Jaydev Vihar, Mayfair Lagoon; mains ₹429-995; ⏲noon-3pm & 7-11pm) Located at the Mayfair Lagoon hotel, tiny Kanika does a don't-miss job with regional Odishan recipes, excelling with local seafood. Specialities include *kankada yarkari* (crab curry); slow-cooked, spiced pomfret; mustard-based dishes; and Odisha's most traditional dessert, the seriously addictive *chhena poda* (literally 'burnt cheese', cooked with sugar, cashew nuts and raisins). There are also excellent veg and nonveg thalis (from ₹399).

Odisha Hotel ODISHAN **$$**
(Market Bldg, Sahid Nagar; thali ₹140-340; ⏲12.30-10.30pm) This dead-simple restaurant is one of the best spots to try authentic Odia cuisine, served in huge proportions thali-style. The menu board is entirely in Odia, so just order veg or nonveg and sit back and await this Hindu last supper! It's on the second street on the left if heading east along Maharishi College Rd, past Bhawani Mall.

Make sure you ask for a small spread, and double-check the price of it before you tuck in. Otherwise you'll be given the enormous ₹400 thali, which one person could never finish.

Truptee SOUTH INDIAN **$**
(Cuttack Rd; mains ₹70-160; ⏲7am-10.30pm) A great choice for South Indian breakfasts, this clean, family-friendly restaurant does a fine line in dosas (large savoury crêpes), *vada* (doughnut-shaped deep-fried lentil savoury) and *idlis* (spongy, fermented rice cakes) before bringing out the curries and tandoor flat breads later in the day. Also does thalis (₹100 to ₹150).

Sri Ram Mandir Tiffin Centre STREET FOOD **$**
(Janpath Rd; dishes ₹10-40; ⏲6.30am-9pm) *Dahi vada* (*vada* in a slightly spicy yoghurt sauce) is the classic Odishan breakfast dish, and locals flock to this streetside stall beside Sri Ram Mandir to have their fill of it, along with other tasty offerings such as samosas, *alu chops* (deep-fried potato snacks) and small portions of veg curry. Point at what you want and tuck in.

Hare Krishna Restaurant INDIAN **$$**
(Lalchand Shopping Complex, Janpath Rd; mains ₹120-260; ⏲11.30am-3.30pm & 7-10.45pm) The beautifully lacquered Gujarati *sankheda* furniture stands out at this stylish but unpretentious veg restaurant where you can enjoy delicious curries, biryanis and tandoor flat breads in a soothing atmosphere. Enter through Lalchand Shopping Complex.

Drinking & Nightlife

BNC CAFE
(Brown n Cream; Janpath Rd; ⏲8am-10.30pm) An AC-cooled coffeeshop with good-value fresh

coffee (₹80), plus sandwiches, muffins and ice cream.

Shopping

Utkalika ARTS & CRAFTS

(Odisha State Handloom Cooperative; ☎0674-2530187; http://utkalika.co.in/contactus.php; Eastern Tower, Market Bldg; ⊙10am-8.30pm) Located in the busy all-day market streets known as Market Building, Utkalika features Odishan textiles, including appliqué and *ikat* (a technique involving tie-dyeing the thread before it's woven), as well as traditional palm-leaf paintings, fine stone carvings, silver filigree from Cuttack, brasswork and tribal jewellery.

Ekamra Haat MARKET

(www.ekamrahaat.in; Madhusudan Marg; ⊙9am-9pm) A wide-ranging exposition of Odishan handicrafts (and snack stalls) can be found at the 50 or so stalls at this permanent market, located within pleasant, well-tended gardens.

Information

MEDICAL SERVICES

Apollo Hospital (☎0674-7150382, 0674-6661016; www.apollohospitals.com; Plot No 251, Old Sainik School Rd; ⊙24hr) Private medical facility with a 24-hour trauma centre and pharmacy.

MONEY

ATMs including **SBI** (Lewis Rd) are plentiful along Janpath Rd, Cuttack Rd and Lewis Rd. There are also a couple at the train station.

State Bank of India (Rajpath; ⊙10am-4pm Mon-Fri, to 1pm Sat) Exchanges foreign currencies and has ATMs.

POST

Post Office (www.indiapost.gov.in; cnr Mahatma Gandhi & Sachivajaya Margs; ⊙9am-7pm Mon-Sat, 3-7pm Sun) Main post office.

TOURIST INFORMATION

Odisha Tourism (☎0674-2432177; www.orissatourism.gov.in; Paryatan Bhavan, 2nd fl, Museum Campus, Lewis Rd; ⊙10am-5pm Mon-Sat) The main branch of the tourist office, with maps and lists of recommended guides. Other branches are at the **airport** (⊙by flight schedule) and **train station** (⊙6am-10pm).

India Tourism (www.incredibleindia.org; Paryatan Bhavan, 2nd fl, Lewis Rd; ⊙9am-6pm Mon-Fri, to 1pm Sat) Info on nationwide attractions; in the same building as the main Odisha Tourism office.

Getting There & Away

AIR

Bhubaneswar's modern **Biju Patnaik International Airport** (http://airport-departures-arrivals.com) is 2km from the centre.

Destinations served by Air India, IndiGo and GoAir:

Bengaluru ₹5585, two hours, three daily
Delhi ₹5720, 2½ hours, 10 daily
Hyderabad ₹2790, 1½ hours, five daily
Kolkata ₹3130, one hour, five daily
Mumbai ₹5360, 2½ hours, four daily

BUS

For destinations northeast of Bhubaneswar, it's quicker catching a bus to Cuttack's Badambari bus stand and then catching an onwards service from there; jump on any of these **buses** heading east along Cuttack Rd. Puri-bound buses from Baramunda bus stand spend ages going around the city and picking up passengers; catch them **outside the State Museum** to save time, though they'll be pretty full by then.

Baramunda bus stand is reachable by bus 801 from Master Canteen bus stand (₹10, 20 minutes) or autorickshaw/Uber (around ₹100 from the centre).

Services from **Baramunda bus stand** (National Hwy 16) are listed below:

DESTINATION	FARE (₹)	DURATION (HR)	DEPARTURES
Baripada	300	6	hourly 9am-11pm
Berhampur	150	4	every 2 hours
Cuttack	25	40min	frequent
Jeypore	433-540	13-16	5 daily
Kolkata	non-AC seat/sleeper 340/700, AC seat/sleeper 475/800	9	frequent 7.30-9pm
Konark	55	2	hourly
Koraput	non-AC seat 420	14	five daily
Puri	40	2	hourly

TRAIN

Foreigners queue at window 3 at the **computerised reservation office** (⏲8am-10pm Mon-Sat, to 2pm Sun), in a separate building in front of the train station. Destinations:

Berhampur (Brahmapur) 2nd class/sleeper ₹35/170, two to four hours, more than a dozen, 7am to 9.25pm

Kolkata 2nd class/3AC ₹160/745, seven to eight hours, at least 10 daily, 4.55am to 11.55pm

Puri 2nd class/general ₹55/70, two hours, more than a dozen, 7am to midnight

Getting Around

AUTORICKSHAW

An autorickshaw to the airport, if hailed on the street, costs around ₹200; an autorickshaw summoned with the Uber/Ola app costs around ₹60. The Uber/Ola apps also give you the option of hiring an autorickshaw by the hour if you want a tour of the city. Shared rickshaws ply main routes around the city and charge locals ₹5; they tend to demand considerably more from foreigners unless you just pay your fare and hop out.

BUS

Bhubaneswar has a relatively foreign-friendly numbered city-bus system that runs between 7am and 9pm from the bus stand known as **Master Canteen**, by the train station. Double-check your bus is going where you want it to, as some bus numbers run along more than one route.

City buses leaving from Master Canteen bus stand:

Airport Bus 207A, ₹10, 15 minutes

Baramunda Bus Stand Bus 801, ₹10, 20 minutes

Dhauli Bus 225, ₹10, 30 minutes

Lingaraj Mandir Bus 333, ₹10, 20 minutes

Mayfair Hotel Bus 207N, ₹10, 20 minutes

Mukteswar Mandir Bus 225, ₹10, 15 minutes

Pipli Bus 701, ₹50, 50 minutes

Puri Bus 701, ₹100, two hours

Udayagiri Caves Bus 801 or 405, ₹10, 30 minutes

CAR & TAXI

Uber and Ola trips all the way across the city cost around ₹100 or less. Ola also gives you the option of hiring a car on a per-hour basis (around ₹80) and organising a one-way drop-off (to, say, Puri or Konark).

Odisha Tourism Development Corporation (p598) offers car-and-driver services for tours around the area. For destinations within 200km, the charges are ₹110 per hour and ₹11 per kilometre for an AC Indigo, or ₹72 per hour and ₹7 per kilometre for a non-AC Ambassador. Book in person at least a day in advance.

There's a prepaid taxi stand at the airport; taxis to the centre cost ₹300.

AROUND BHUBANESWAR

Scattered around the countryside, south, east and west of the capital, several worthwhile sites make easy half-day trips from Bhubaneswar. These include a zoo, wildlife sanctuary, craft village, tantric temple and centuries-old rock edicts.

Sights

★Chausath Yogini HINDU MONUMENT

(⏲dusk-dawn) Rediscovered in the 1950s among rice fields 15km south of Bhubaneswar, this small but serene 9th-century open-roofed temple (pronounced 'chorsat jorgini') is dedicated to *yoginis* (female tantric mystics) and is one of only four of its kind in India. The temple – no larger than a village hut – contains 64 *(chausath)* carved *yoginis,* each shown standing on top of her *vaharna* (vehicle; often in animal form). No buses go here; a return trip by rickshaw/Uber costs around ₹450/540.

TRAINS FROM BHUBANESWAR

DESTINATION	TRAIN NO & NAME	FARE (₹)	DURATION (HR)	DEPARTURE
Chennai	12841 Coromandal Exp	560/1470/2110	19½	9.25pm
Kolkata (Howrah)	18410 Sri Jagannath Exp	270/715/1015	8¼	11.55pm
Koraput	18447 Hirakhand Exp	370/995/1425	14	8.25pm
Mumbai	12880 Bbs Ltt S Exp	705/1845/2685	30½	7.10am
New Delhi	12801 Purushottam Exp	705/1845/2685	29¼	11.15pm
Ranchi	18452 Tapaswini Exp	350/950/1355	13¾	9.20pm
Rayagada	18447 Hirakhand Exp	310/830/1180	8¾	8.25pm

Fares: sleeper/3AC/2AC

SATKOSIA TIGER SANCTUARY

Comprising the Satkosia Gorge Sanctuary and the Baisipalli Wildlife Sanctuary, 964-sq-km forested **Satkosia Tiger Sanctuary** (☎8763102681; www.satkosia.org; per day Indian/foreigner ₹40/2000; ⏰6am-6pm), 125km northwest of Bhubaneswar, is straddled by a breathtaking gorge, cut by the mighty Mahanadi River, and is one of the most beautiful natural spots in Odisha. However, tourists are not allowed inside the park's core zone, where most of the wildlife is found, and 4WD safaris are not on offer. The main appeal of coming here is to spend some time amid the stunning natural scenery.

The sanctuary as a whole is home to significant populations of gharial and mugger crocodiles, plus 38 species of mammals, including elephants, leopards, sambar deer, wild dogs, jackals, giant squirrels and around a dozen tigers. As of 2016, boat trips on the river have been discontinued but you may still spot crocodiles and birds from the river bank.

The main entry gate of the reserve is at Pampasar, 30km southwest of Angul.

You'll need to stop by **Satkosia Wildlife Division** (☎8763102681, 06764-236218; www.satkosia.org; Hakimpada, Angul) for permissions and reservations – a mere formality, but bring a copy of your passport and visa. From the train station it costs around ₹100 to get here in an autorickshaw.

Few tourists make it out here, which adds to the tranquillity of the location. For unique Odishan crafts, check out **Soumya Handicraft** (⏰hours vary) nearby.

Dhauli BUDDHIST MONUMENT

(Ashoka Rock Edicts) In about 260 BC, 11 of of Ashoka's 14 famous edicts were carved onto a rock at Dhauli, 8km south of Bhubaneswar. Above the edicts, the earliest Buddhist sculpture in Odisha – a carved elephant, representing Buddha – emerges from a rock.

From the Dhauli turn-off, accessed by Bhubaneswar–Puri buses (₹14, 30 minutes), it's a tree-shaded 3km walk or shared/private autorickshaw ride (₹10/70 one way) to the rock edicts and then a short, steep walk to the stupa. Uber drop off costs around ₹120.

Just beyond the rock edicts, each translated into English, is the huge, white Shanti Stupa (Peace Pagoda), built by Japanese monks in 1972 on a hill to the right. Older Buddhist reliefs are set into the modern structure, and there are great views of the surrounding countryside from the top.

Pipli VILLAGE

This colourful village, 16km southeast of Bhubaneswar, is notable for its locally made brilliant appliqué craft, which incorporates small mirrors and is used for door and wall hangings and the more traditional canopies hung over Jagannath and family during festival time. Inexpensive lampshades and parasols hanging outside the shops turn the main road into an avenue of rainbow colours. During Diwali the place is particularly vibrant. Take any Bhubaneswar–Puri bus and hop off en route.

Nandankanan Zoological Park ZOO

(www.nandankanan.org; Indian/foreigner ₹25/100, digital camera/video ₹10/500; ⏰7.30am-5.30pm Tue-Sun Apr-Sep, 8am-5pm Tue-Sun Oct-Mar) Famous for its blue-eyed white tigers, the zoo – one of India's better ones – also boasts rare Asiatic lions, rhinoceros, copious reptiles, monkeys and deer. Don't get food out of your bag in front of any of the monkeys that roam free around the zoo; trust us. Forty-five-minute safaris to see the lions and tigers cost ₹30 per person. Uber autorickshaw/car drop-off costs around ₹200/250.

ℹ Getting There & Away

Pipli and Dhauli are easily accessible by frequent bus from Bhubaneswar. To visit the other attractions, you have to go as part of an organised tour or commandeer an autorickshaw or car with driver for a day or half-day.

SOUTHEASTERN ODISHA

Southeastern Odisha hugs the coast of the Bay of Bengal and is home to the state's most visited spots, including the backpacker outpost of Puri and the Unesco-protected Sun Temple at Konark. Tiny Raghurajpur is craft central, Chilika Lake offers ample birding and dolphin-watching opportunities, and you can hit the beach at Golpalpur-on-Sea.

Puri

☎06752 / POP 200,564

Hindu pilgrims, Bengali holidaymakers and foreign travellers all make their way to Puri. For Hindus, Puri is one of the holiest pilgrimage places in India, with religious life revolving around the great Jagannath Mandir and its famous Rath Yatra (Car Festival). The town's other attraction is its long, sandy beach – better for strolling than swimming.

In the 1970s, travellers on the hippie trail through Asia were attracted here by the sea and bhang (marijuana), which is legal in Shiva's Puri. There's little trace of that scene today (though the bhang hasn't departed); travellers come to chill out and visit the Sun Temple in nearby Konark.

The action is along a few kilometres of coast. The backpacker part of town is bunched up towards the eastern end of Chakra Tirtha (CT) Rd, while Bengali holidaymakers flock to busy New Marine Rd, where there is lots of hang-out action on the long esplanade.

Sights

★Jagannath Mandir HINDU TEMPLE

This mighty temple belongs to Jagannath (Lord of the Universe), an incarnation of Vishnu. Built in its present form in 1198, the temple (closed to non-Hindus) is surrounded by two walls, but you can spot its 58m-high *sikhara* (spire) topped by the flag and wheel of Vishnu.

Non-Hindus can spy from the Raghunandan Library roof opposite for a 'donation' (₹50 is fine; don't believe the numbers in the ledger). On Sundays, touts who help you to nearby rooftops demand ₹100.

Jannagath, the jet-black deity with large, round, white eyes, is hugely popular across Odisha; his images are tended and regularly dressed in new clothes at shrines across the state.

Guarded by two stone lions and a pillar crowned by the Garuda that once stood at the Sun Temple at Konark, the eastern entrance (Lion Gate) to the temple is the passageway for the chariot procession of Rath Yatra.

Jagannath, brother Balbhadra and sister Subhadra reside supreme in the central *jagamohan* (assembly hall). Priests continually garland and dress the three throughout the day for different ceremonies. Incredibly, the temple employs about 6000 men to perform the complicated rituals involved in caring for the gods. An estimated 20,000 people – divided into 36 orders and 97 classes – are dependent on Jagannath for their livelihood.

Model Beach BEACH

(www.puribeach.net) Puri is no palm-fringed paradise – the beach is wide, shelves quickly with a nasty shore break and is shadeless – but Model Beach, part of a sustainable, community-run beach tourism initiative, offers a 700m stretch of sand that's easily Puri's finest and cleanest. Palm umbrellas provide shade and cabana boys/lifeguards, known as Sea Riders, hawk fixed-price beach chairs (₹20) and massages (₹50 to ₹200) and are responsible for keeping the beach clean. They'll expect money for rescuing you, though.

WORTH A TRIP

RAGHURAJPUR

The fascinating artists' village of Raghurajpur, 14km north of Puri, consists of a single street lined with thatched brick houses, adorned with murals of geometric patterns and mythological scenes – a traditional art form that has almost died out in Odisha.

Most houses double as artists' workshops, selling a mix of crafts, from palm-leaf etchings to colourful silk prints. The designs are copied from Odisha's Saora people, but Raghurajpur is particularly famous for its *patachitra* (Odishan cloth paintings). With eye-aching attention and a very fine brush, artists mark out animals, flowers, deities and demons, illuminated with bright colours.Some are traditional designs, of the kind that decorate temple walls; others are more contemporary, but both make unique souvenirs.

There is considerable competition for your business. Particularly fine *patachitra* examples are found at the far end of the street, in a house with red and white patterns. His neighbour does fine palm-leaf etchings.

To get here, take the Bhubaneswar bus from Puri and look for the 'Raghurajpur The Craft Village' signpost 11km north of Puri, then walk the last 1km.

Swargdwar RELIGIOUS SITE

(off New Marine Rd; ⏲24hr) These hallowed cremation grounds are the end stop of choice for eastern India's Hindu population and beyond – some 40 bodies are cremated here daily. You can watch or walk among the open-air ceremonies as long as you behave in a respectful manner and avoid taking photos. It's an obviously solemn affair, but a fascinating glimpse into Puri's role as one of India's holiest cities.

Activities

Barefoot VOLUNTEERING

(www.heritagetoursodisha.com) This small local NGO, started by Heritage Tours, works to improve community lifestyles through sustainable tourism development. Volunteers must commit to a two-week minimum, which can involve teaching English, beach maintenance supervision and training in tourism. From ₹1500 per week including lodging and meals.

Tours

Grass Routes CULTURAL

(☎9437029698; www.grassroutesjourneys.com; CT Rd) Grass Routes' Indian-Australian husband-and-wife team has a stellar reputation for sensitive, all-inclusive, multiday tours of tribal Odisha as well as historical and nature tours. Pulak and Claire also organise excellent overnight island stays at a private tented camp at Chilika Lake and day trips by bicycle into the picturesque countryside around Puri. Contact them in advance.

Heritage Tours CULTURAL

(☎06752-223656; www.heritagetoursorissa.com; Mayfair Heritage Hotel, CT Rd; ⏲8am-8pm) Bubu is a tribal and cultural tourism veteran whose tour company focuses on rural and special-interest ethnic tourism. In addition to multiday tribal tours with stays at Desia, and Puri walking tours, Heritage also offers cycle-rickshaw tours (two hours ₹300) around old Puri, and Odishan-cuisine cookery classes (half-day ₹500) at Bubu's home, lunch included (₹1500/2500 for one/two people).

OTDC CULTURAL

(☎06752-223524; www.otdc.in; CT Rd; ⏲6am-10pm) Runs three day trips from Puri: Tour 1 (₹430, 6.30am Tuesday to Sunday) skips through Konark, Dhauli, Bhubaneswar's temples, the Udayagiri and Khandagiri Caves plus Nandankanan zoo; Tour 2 (₹300, 6.30am daily) goes for a boat jaunt on Chilika Lake; while Tour 3 (₹80, 8am) is a two-hour trip to Raghurajpur village. Admission fees are not included.

Festivals & Events

Rath Yatra RELIGIOUS

(Car Festival; ⏲Jun/Jul) Immense chariots containing Lord Jagannath, brother Balbhadra and sister Subhadra are hauled from Jagannath Mandir to Gundicha Mandir, beside Puri's main bus stand.

Puri Beach Festival CULTURAL

(www.puribeachfestival.com; ⏲late Nov) Song, dance, food and cultural activities, including sand artists, on the beach.

Sleeping

Lodgings accommodating foreigners are found east of VIP Rd, along CT Rd, while hotels catering to domestic tourists front Marine Dr. Book well in advance for Rath Yatra, Durga Puja (Dussehra) and Diwali. Many hotels have early-morning checkout times.

Hotel Lotus HOTEL $

(☎06752-227033; www.hotellotuspuri.com; CT Rd; r ₹750, with AC ₹1650; ❄📶) Friendly and humbly run, Lotus is probably the most popular budget choice among foreign backpackers, offering a range of inexpensive rooms that are clean and comfortable. The non-AC rooms, with small balconies, are great value. Long-term visitors fight over the one non-AC rooftop room (₹950).

Backpackers' Inn HOSTEL $$

(☎06752-223656; www.heritagetoursorissa.com; off VIP Rd; r ₹1000; ❄📶) This welcome newcomer on the backpacker scene, hidden on a quiet street off VIP Rd, is run by Heritage Tours. There are common areas for mingling, including the fantastic roof terrace – ideal for sunset-gazing – and you can choose between cosy en suites and a dorm.

Hotel Gandhara HERITAGE HOTEL $$

(☎06752-224117; www.hotelgandhara.com; CT Rd; heritage r ₹850-1250, new-block s/d incl breakfast ₹1500/1570, with AC ₹2290/2700; ❄📶🏊) Gandhara continues to steamroll the competition in this price bracket for its friendliness and value. The 200-year-old pillared heritage building – the former holiday home of a rich Bengali family – has three wonderfully atmospheric fan-cooled rooms. More expensive but unmemorable, modern AC rooms are in a new block at the back of the

Puri

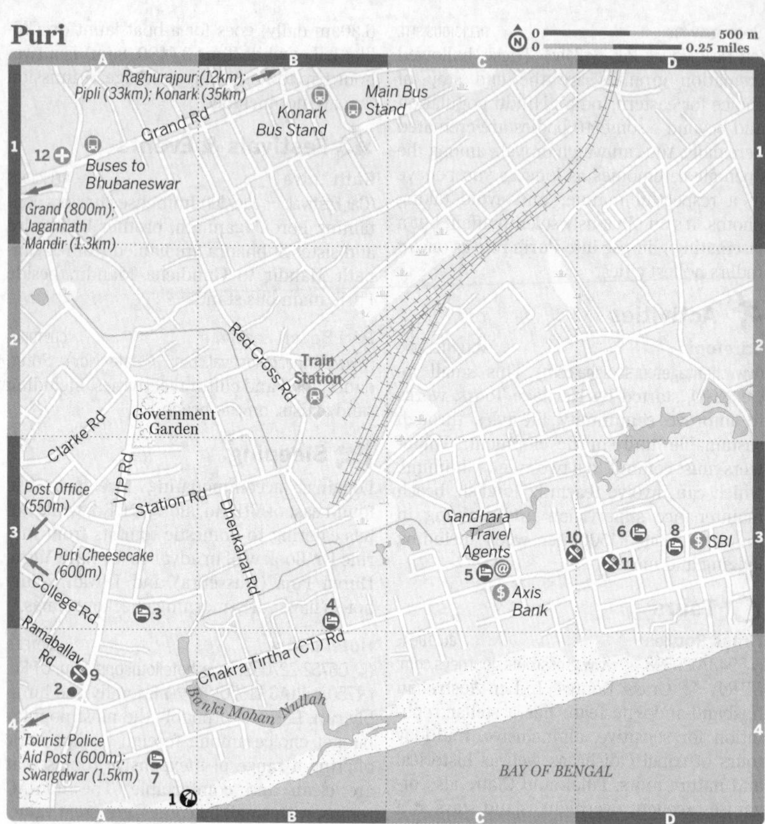

lawned garden, overlooking the swimming pool.

The wi-fi is super quick (for India), you get newspapers slipped under your door and there are beers (₹120) waiting for you in a fridge.

Z Hotel HERITAGE HOTEL $$
(06752-222554; www.zhotelindia.com; CT Rd; r from ₹2100;) This charming yet understated heritage hotel (pronounced 'jed') – the former raja's home – remains one of Puri's most atmospheric choices. Rooms are large and airy, and come with high ceilings, chunky wooden furniture and spotless bathrooms. There's a restaurant, evening films shown in the TV room, and wi-fi in common areas.

Chanakya BNR Hotel HERITAGE HOTEL $$$
(06752-223006; www.therailhotel.com; CT Rd; r incl breakfast ₹4400;) Conjuring up images of the Raj, this splendid 150-year-old railway hotel features beautiful bygone touches throughout, including 90-year-old Lac mural art in the lobby stairwell and restaurant. Inside the enormous rooms, entered through 2.7m-tall wooden doors, there's period furniture and old framed Indian Railways photographs. The 1st-floor rooms open out onto a large shared verandah with sea views.

Mayfair RESORT $$$
(06752-227800; www.mayfairhotels.com; off CT Rd; d incl breakfast & dinner from ₹11,000, cottage/ste from ₹13,000;) The benchmark for Puri luxury, this modern hotel is split between two buildings side by side. The 12-year-old Mayfair Heritage has spacious, stylish rooms and cottages, all with sea views, dotted around freshly clipped gardens, while the contemporary Mayfair Waves has luxury rooms and suites as well as a gym and spa. Both buildings have garden pools and top-notch restaurants.

Puri

Sights

1 Model Beach...A4

Activities, Courses & Tours

Grass Routes...(see 11)
Heritage Tours...(see 7)
2 OTDC...A4

Sleeping

3 Backpackers' Inn...A3
4 Chanakya BNR Hotel...B3
5 Hotel Gandhara...C3
6 Hotel Lotus...D3
7 Mayfair...A4
8 Z Hotel...D3

Eating

9 Chung Wah...A4
10 Honey Bee Bakery & Pizzeria...C3
11 Peace Restaurant...D3
Two States...(see 7)
Wildgrass Restaurant...(see 9)

Information

12 District Headquarters Hospital...A1
Odisha Tourism Office...(see 2)

Eating

Puri has a decent dining scene that ranges from excellent Odishan specialities to Indo-Chinese and Western food. Many restaurants are clustered along CT Rd and VIP Rd; there are plenty of cheap eateries in the labyrinthine Old Town.

Peace Restaurant MULTICUISINE $
(CT Rd; mains ₹50-260; ⏲7am-4pm & 6-11pm) This Puri stalwart, with seating in a shaded front courtyard, is still the most pleasant budget option, doing nice work with Western breakfasts and pasta, but excelling at simple thalis. Save room for house desserts, a fried empanada-like banana or apple turnover laced with sugar, cinnamon and honey.

★**Wildgrass Restaurant** ODISHAN $$
(☎9437023656; VIP Rd; mains ₹100-240, thali ₹120-240; ⏲11am-11pm) At delightful, tranquil Wildgrass, grab a table at one of the thatched pavilions dotted around the lush garden and tuck into excellent local and regional specialities categorised by their origins (Odishan, Chilikan and Puriwala). The tandoori pomfret is one of the best things we've ever had, anywhere, and the seasonal vegetable specialities are not to be missed either.

Ask about their Odishan-cuisine cookery classes (₹500), which include a morning trip to the local food market to buy the ingredients you'll cook for lunch.

Grand NORTH INDIAN $$
(Grand Centre, Grand Rd; mains ₹100-150; ⏲11.30am-3.30pm & 7.30-10.30pm) This large, pure-veg locals' favourite offers plenty of off-menu dishes, so even if you don't see the *bhindi chatpati* (okra), *gobi Hyderabadi* (cauliflower), or *kadhai* veg (creamy curried vegies) on the menu, ask for them anyway. Also has a healthy list of dosas (₹40 to ₹80). From the open-air terrace there are striking views of Jagannath Mandir.

Chung Wah CHINESE $$
(VIP Rd; mains ₹220-360; ⏲11.30am-3pm & 6.30-11.30pm) Inside the Lee Garden Hotel, this place certainly has the look of a classic Chinese restaurant: dark-wood booths, lattice screens, lots of red and gold and dragon imagery. The food, courtesy of Chinese transplants from Kolkata, is excellent Indo-Chinese: we particularly like the hot garlic prawns.

Honey Bee Bakery & Pizzeria CAFE $$
(CT Rd; pizza ₹220-340, mains ₹100-350; ⏲8.30am-2pm & 6-10pm) Decent pizzas and pancakes, espresso-machine coffee (₹80), toasted sandwiches and breakfast fry-ups (including bacon!) – are here at this cute cafe-restaurant with rooftop seating. Popular for breakfast but otherwise fairly forlorn.

Two States INDIAN $$$
(Mayfair Heritage; mains ₹275-600; ⏲12.30-3pm & 7.30-10.30pm) This excellent new restaurant inside the Mayfair Heritage hotel specialises in two cuisines: Odishan and Bengali. Seafood is the star here and all items on the succinct menu are well executed. Try the prawn cutlet or the prawn *malai* curry.

Puri Cheesecake SWEETS $
(Temple Rd, Dolamandap Sahi; per piece ₹20; ⏲7am-11pm) Bikram Sahoo and his six brothers have been churning out this unique Odishan delight, known as *chhena poda* ('burnt cheese') – a cross between a cheesecake and a flan – for more than 45 years from their sweetshop in Puri's holy quarter. It's cottage cheese, sugar and cardamom cooked in an iron pan over an open flame – a real treat.

To find it, walk down Temple Rd from Jagganath Mandir, pass a small public square about 300m on the right, and it's another 100m on your right next door to Jagganath Pump House.

Information

Axis Bank and **SBI** (CT Rd) are two of several ATMs along CT Rd.

District Headquarters Hospital (☎06752-224097; Grand Rd; ⏲24hr). Has 24-hour emergency treatment.

Gandhara Travel Agents (www.gandharatravels.com; Hotel Gandhara, CT Rd; internet per hr ₹40; ⏲8am-7pm Mon-Sat, to 1pm Sun) All-in-one internet cafe and money changer.

Odisha Tourism Office (☎06752-222664; www.odishatourism.gov.in; cnr VIP Rd & CT Rd; ⏲10am-5pm Mon-Sat, closed 2nd Sat of the month) Some info on local attractions.

Post Office (www.indiapost.gov.in; cnr Kutchery & Temple Rd; ⏲10am-6pm Mon-Sat) Main post office.

Getting There & Away

BUS

Frequent buses to Konark (₹30, 45 minutes) leave from the **Konark bus stand** (off Grand Rd). The last bus back is at 6.30pm. Next to the Konark bus stand is the sprawling **main bus stand** (off Grand Rd), where frequent buses head to Bhubaneswar (₹40, two hours) and Satapada (₹40, two to three hours), as well as AC buses (seat ₹950, 11 hours, 6pm to 6.30pm, two daily) and non-AC buses (seat ₹400, 13 hours, from 3pm) to Kolkata. Buses to Bhubaneswar can also be taken from **Grand Rd**.

For Pipli and also the Raghurajpur turn-off, take a Bhubaneswar-bound bus.

CAR

Heritage Tours (p605) and the **tourist office** (p608) can arrange cars and drivers for round trips to Konark (around ₹1500) and Satapada (around ₹2000).

TRAIN

At least a dozen daily trains run to Bhubaneswar (2nd-class unreserved seat ₹15 to ₹55, two hours, from 5.45am to 1.50pm).

Konark

☎06758 / POP 16,779

The iconic Sun Temple at Konark – a Unesco World Heritage Site – is one of India's signature buildings and Odisha's raison d'être. Most visitors are day trippers from Bhubaneswar or Puri, which makes sense, as the temple is Konark's sole attraction.

Originally nearer the coast (the sea has receded 3km), Konark was visible from far out at sea and known as the 'Black Pagoda' by sailors, in contrast to Puri's whitewashed Jagannath. The inland lighthouse near Chandrabhaga Beach is an odd testament to that fact.

Sights

★Sun Temple — HINDU TEMPLE

(Indian/foreigner ₹20/500, video ₹25, guide per hr ₹150; ⏲dawn-8pm) Conceived as the cosmic chariot of the sun god Surya, this massive, breathtakingly splendid temple was constructed in the mid-13th century, probably by Odishan king Narashimhadev I to celebrate his military victory over the Muslims. Seven rearing horses (representing the days of the week) move this stone leviathan on 24 stone cartwheels (representing the hours of the day) around the base. The temple was positioned so that dawn light would illuminate the *deul* (temple sanctuary) interior and the presiding deity.

The temple was in use for maybe only three centuries. In the late 16th century the 40m-high *sikhara* (spire) partially collapsed: speculation about causes ranges from marauding Mughals removing the copper over the cupola to a ransacking Kalapahad displacing the Dadhinauti (arch stone), to simple wear and tear from recurring cyclones – the truth was apparently lost with Konark's receding shoreline. The presiding deity may have been moved to Jagannath Mandir in Puri in the 17th century – the interior of the temple was filled in with stone in 1903 on the orders of Sir James Austin Bourdillon, the Lieutenant Governor of Bengal.

The *gajasimha* (main entrance) is guarded by two stone lions crushing elephants and leads to the intricately carved *nritya mandapa* (dancing hall). Steps, flanked by straining horses, rise to the still-standing *jagamohan* (assembly hall). Behind is the spireless *deul*, with its three impressive chlorite images of Surya aligned to catch the sun at dawn, noon and sunset.

The base and walls present a chronicle in stone of Kalinga life; you'll see women cooking and men hunting. Many are in the erotic style for which Konark is famous and include entwined couples as well as solitary exhibitionists.

Persistent guides will approach you at the entrance. Guides can be useful here as the temple's history is a complicated amalgam of fact and legend, and religious and secular imagery, and the guides' explanations can be thought provoking. But make sure you get a government-approved one; the tourist office at Yatrinivas hotel, beside the Archaeological Museum, can help.

Archaeological Museum MUSEUM

(₹20; ⏲10am-5pm Sat-Thu) This museum contains many impressive sculptures and carvings found during excavations of the Sun Temple.

Festivals & Events

Konark Festival DANCE

(⏲1-5 Dec) Steeped in traditional music and dance, the Konark Festival takes place in an open-air auditorium with the gorgeous Sun Temple as a backdrop.

Information

There's an ATM in the dusty lane leading to the Sun Temple.

Odisha Tourism Development Corporation (☎06758-236821; www.odishatourism.gov.in; Yatrinivas hotel; ⏲10am-5pm Mon-Sat) This tourist office can line up a registered guide to meet you at the Sun Temple. The temple can be visited as part of an OTDC day tour from Bhubaneswar or Puri.

Getting There & Away

The bus stand is set back from the main road, 200m further away from the temple. Hourly buses ply the 33km road between Konark and Puri (₹30, one hour); a return trip from Puri by autorickshaw/car costs around ₹800/1500. There are also frequent buses to Bhubaneswar (₹50, two hours).

Chilika Lake

Chilika Lake is Asia's largest brackish lagoon. Swelling from 600 sq km in April and May to 1100 sq km in the monsoon, the shallow lake is separated from the Bay of Bengal by a 60km-long sand bar called Rajhansa.

The lake is noted for the million-plus migratory birds – including grey-legged geese, herons, cranes and pink flamingos – that flock here in winter (from November to mid-January) from as far away as Siberia and Iran and concentrate in a 3-sq-km area within the bird sanctuary on Nalabana Island.

Other attractions are rare Irrawaddy dolphins near Satapada, the pristine beach along Rajhansa, and Kalijai Island temple, where Hindu pilgrims flock for the Makar Mela festival in January.

Satapada

Little more than a bus stand, a hotel, and a cluster of road-shack restaurants beside a jetty, the tiny village of Satapada, on a headland jutting southwestwards into Chilika Lake, is the starting point for boat trips. These range from short dolphin-spotting excursions to all-day boat outings that take in several islands and a spot of birdwatching. The boats are noisy, so serious birdwatching is out; also, they tend to get too close to the dolphins, so make it clear this isn't what you want. In spite of this, it's a tranquil experience being out on this great watery expanse, watching fishermen pull in their catch, as their boats move through the labyrinthine reeds.

DON'T MISS

COASTAL RETREATS

For an idyllic getaway that's still within shouting distance of both Puri and Konark, consider one of these coastal retreats.

Nature Camp, Konark Retreat (☎9337505022, 8908621654; www.naturecampindia.com; tent incl breakfast ₹3000) This friendly, laid-back camp has fan-cooled, comfortable rather than luxurious tented rooms dotted around a slightly unkempt forest clearing. Tents come with cute attached shower rooms with sit-down flush toilets. Sumptuous Odia thalis are served. The camp is 500m off the main Puri–Konark road, on the banks of the Ramchandi River; jump off the bus when you see the sign. Book ahead.

Lotus Resorts (☎9090093464; www.lotusresorthotels.com; Puri-Konark Marine Dr; cottage incl breakfast from ₹4199; ❄) This collection of weathered Canadian pine cottages is a beautiful getaway across a calm and swimmable islet. Amenities include a small ayurvedic spa (high-season only) and a nice sandside restaurant. It's about 6km from Konark, on pretty Ramchandi Beach. Take any bus between Puri (₹25) and Konark (₹8) and look for the sign.

In the village, you can see a 12m-long baleen whale skeleton at the small **Chilika Ecopark** (Satapada Jetty).

OTDC (06752-262077; Yatrinivas Hotel; per person ₹220-300, depending on the number of people) runs a three-hour tour of the lake, which leaves between 9.30am and 10am each morning.

Dolphin Motor Boat Association (7377653372; Satapada Jetty; 1/3/7hr trips per boat ₹700/1300/2500), a cooperative of local boat owners, runs seven set-price trips, including dolphin-watching (₹700, one hour); dolphin-watching plus the river mouth and Kalijai Island Temple (₹1300, three hours); and dolphin-watching, Kalijai Island Temple and Nalabana Island bird sanctuary (₹2500, seven hours).

There is only one place to stay in Satapada – the mediocre, government-run hotel **Yatrinivas** (06752-262077; d ₹630, with AC ₹1650; ❄). Those coming with a Grass Routes trip (p605) from Puri can stay in a private tented camp on one of the islands.

Chilika Visitor Centre (entry ₹10; 10am-5pm) has exhibitions on the lake, its wildlife and human inhabitants. The centre has an upstairs observatory with a telescope and bird-identification charts.

Getting There & Away

Frequent ferries (pedestrians/bicycles/motorbikes/cars ₹10/10/20/350, 30 minutes) ply between Satapada and the Janhikuda jetty just to the west, where vehicles can then head west, and around to the north side of the lake. It's a wonderfully scenic route. Daily departures are at 7.30am, 10am, 1pm and 4pm, returning at 8am, 10.30am, 1.30pm and 4.30pm.

A bus to Berhampur (₹150, 3½ hours), near Gopalpur-on-Sea, starts off from Puri's main bus stand at 6am and travels on the 7.30am ferry before following the beautiful countryside road for two hours until it meets up with the main highway. Wait for the bus on the ferry, then jump on as it drives off. It will already be full of villagers by the time it reaches Satapada so don't expect a seat. The bus will drop you at the turn-off for Gopalpur-on-Sea, if you ask, from where you can wave down any passing bus (₹15, 20 minutes). The return bus leaves Berhampur at 12.40pm and crosses Chilika Lake on the 4.30pm ferry to Satapada.

Pretty much every hotel and travel agent in Puri does day trips to Chilika Lake (around ₹1500 return by car), but it's easy to come here independently by bus (₹38, two to three hours). The last bus back to Puri leaves Satapada at around 6pm.

Mangalajodi

On Chilika's north shore, 60km southwest of Bhubaneswar, this small fishing village is the jumping-off point for the resident and migratory bird haven of Chilika Lake, an ecotourism success story virtually unknown to the outside world until 2006. Six years prior, NK Bhujabal started Wild Orissa (www.wildorissa.org), a waterfowl safeguard committee that converted bird poachers into protectors...and now ecotourism guides. In just a decade, the waterfowl population has climbed from 5000 to an estimated 300,000, spread among some 160 species.

A packed-earth levee leads out into the lake for around 1.5km, with fishing boats sheltering to one side and animal herders taking their buffalo to pasture across shallow waters, and a forest of reeds sheltering birds on the other side. Towards the end of the levee is a birdwatching tower and the dock from which birding trips depart, with guides slowly propelling their narrow boats through reed tunnels using poles, Venetian-gondola-style.

There are only two sleeping options in the village: a mediocre guesthouse and guest cottages run by Mangalajodi Eco Tourism.

Getting There & Away

Mangalajodi is 10km south of the main highway between Bhubaneswar and Berhampur. Buses run from Bubaneswar to Tangi, the nearest village to Mangalajodi; you'll have to catch an autorickshaw the rest of the way. **Grass Routes** (p605) in Puri runs birdwatching trips to Mangalajodi.

Barkul

On the northern shore of Chilika Lake, Barkul is just a scattering of houses, small guesthouses and food stalls on a lane that runs from the main highway down to the government-run hotel property Panthanivas Barkul. From here boats make trips to Nalabana Island (full of nesting birds in December and January) and Kalijai Island (which has a temple on it), though you could charter you own boat to anywhere; deal directly with the boat hands.

Panthanivas Barkul hotel runs two-hour round trips to Kalijai Island Temple for ₹1500 per speedboat (up to seven passengers), including some time on the island. The four-hour trip to Kalijai and Nalabana costs ₹4000 per boat, but tends only to be done in December and January when the birds are on Nalabana. Barkul is also trying to reinvent itself as a water-sports centre; unfortunately, this involves seriously eco-unfriendly jet-ski rental.

The only decent place to stay is the government-run **Panthanivas Barkul** (☎06756-227488; pns.barkul@gmail.com; d ₹1100, with AC ₹2400, AC cottage ₹2780, all incl breakfast; ❄). There's also a handful of cheaper guesthouses on the lane leading to Panthanivas Barkul.

Getting There & Away

Frequent buses dash along National Hwy 5 between Bhubaneswar (₹90, 1½ hours) and Berhampur (₹68, 1½ hours). You can get off anywhere en route.

Panthanivas Barkul is around 2km from the main highway. If you don't have much luggage it's a lovely, signposted walk past village homes. Alternatively, hop in a passing autorickshaw (shared/private ₹20/60).

Rambha

The village of Rambha, on the northwestern shore of Chilika Lake, is the nearest place to stay for turtle-watching on Rushikulya beach, but many tourists come for boat trips on the lake in general. Tours of the lake by seven-person speedboats (per hour ₹2300) or 10-person motorboats (per hour ₹750) are bookable at the government-run Panthanivas Rambha hotel.

There is only one place to stay here – the government-run, waterfront **Panthanivas Rambha** (☎06810-278346; rabi.dash09@gmail.com; dm ₹330, d ₹900, d with AC ₹1610, AC cottage ₹3300, all incl breakfast; ❄).

Getting There & Away

The hotel is a 2km walk from the main highway if you're entering the village from the west end, and around 3km from the east end. Alternatively, hop in a passing autorickshaw (₹20).

From the highway you can easily wave down buses to Barkul (₹35, 30 minutes), Berhampur (₹35, one hour) and Bhubaneswar (₹140, two hours).

Gopalpur-on-Sea

☎0680 / POP 7221

If you dig nosing about seaside resorts past their prime, Gopalpur-on-Sea, a seaside town the British left to slide into history until Bengali holidaymakers rediscovered its attractions in the 1980s, could be just your thing. Prior to this, it had a noble history as a seaport with connections to Southeast Asia, the evidence of which is still scattered through the town in the form of romantically deteriorating old buildings.

The waves are too rough for swimming, but the relatively clean beach is great for a stroll or a paddle, and it's oddly charismatic in its own strange, antiquated way.

The main village is a couple of hundred metres back from the beach, along the road to Berhampur.

Sleeping & Eating

Hotel Seaside Breeze HOTEL $$
(☎0680-2343075; s/d ₹600/950, with AC ₹1100/1350; ❄) Right on the beach, this friendly lime-green hotel has clean, brightly painted rooms with sea-facing terraces. Cute corner room No 15 has a private balcony with sweeping views of the beach – it's the smallest and cheapest, but we think the best. The balconies have tables and chairs, and the great-value menu (mains ₹50 to ₹140) includes fresh fish.

Hotel Sea Pearl HOTEL $$
(☎0680-2343557; www.hotelseapearlgopalpur.com; d ₹900, with AC ₹1330-1780; ❄) Right on the beach, Sea Pearl is a decent midrange option. Rooms are of the can't-swing-a-cat variety, but all have a sea view of some description (except the cheapest non-AC ones). Has a restaurant.

Mayfair Palm Beach HOTEL $$$
(☎0680-6660101; www.mayfairhotels.com; r incl breakfast & dinner from ₹12,100; ❄📶🏊) This renovated 1914 historic property is Golpalpur-on-Sea's most luxurious, though the service doesn't live up to expectations. The grounds contain winding walkways, a beautiful pool, spa and immaculate terraced gardens leading down to the beach. It's worth paying the extra ₹2000 for the deluxe-category rooms, which have fabulous beach-facing balconies. There's also an excellent restaurant and a striking teak-wood bar.

Sea Shell Fast Food INDIAN, CHINESE $
(mains ₹50-120; ⏰8am-10.30pm) Cheap and cheerful alfresco dining on the esplanade overlooking the beach; noodles dishes and biriyanis are both served.

Getting There & Away

Between 7am and 7.45pm, comfortable half-hourly buses shuttle between the beachfront and Berhampur (₹24, 30 minutes), from where you can catch onward transport by rail or bus.

From Berhampur's new bus stand there are frequent buses throughout the day to Bhubaneswar (₹170, three hours, frequent), via Rambha (₹35, one hour) and Barkul (₹70, 1½ hours). There are two buses to Rayagada (₹180, eight hours, 9.45am and 1.45pm), and one daily bus to Satapada (₹85, three hours, 12.40pm) via the scenic route along the southeast shore of Chilika Lake and then on the ferry.

SOUTHWESTERN ODISHA

Southwestern Odisha is one of the richest regions in India when it comes to traditional tribal culture. Of the 62 tribes that inhabit Odisha as a whole, the majority, including the Bonda, Koya, Paraja, Kondh, Mali and Didayi, reside in the villages around Koraput, Jeypore and Rayagada, leading lives that have remained largely unchanged for centuries, revolving largely around subsistence farming. For most visitors, the highlight of travel in this part of Odisha involves using the main towns of Koraput and Rayagada as springboards for visiting the colourful tribal markets and witnessing traditional village life – a vanishing world.

Koraput

06852 / POP 47,468

Up in the cool, forested hills, the small market town of Koraput is by far the nicest of places from which to launch yourself into this region's tribal country. There's a hill-station feel to it, a weekly tribal market, and the main temple here is fascinating, especially for non-Hindus, who can't enter the Jagannath Mandir in Puri.

Sights

Jagannath Temple HINDU TEMPLE

(dawn-dusk) Jagannath Temple, whose whitewashed *sikhara* (temple spire) overlooks the town, is worth visiting. The courtyard around the *sikhara* contains numerous colourfully decorated statues of the wide-eyed Jagannath, the deity of Odisha, which you'll see painted on homes across the state. Below the *sikhara,* in a side hall, you'll walk past more than two dozen linga (an auspicious symbol of Shiva), before reaching some attractive displays of local *ossa* (traditional patterns made with white and coloured powders on doorsteps).

The temple is 200m behind the bus stand. At the bus stand, facing the police station, turn left up Post Office Rd then take the first left and look for the temple steps up to your right at the small staggered crossroads.

Koraput Market MARKET

(8am-5pm) There's a market here every day, but it's Koraput's big all-day Sunday Market that's worth exploring. Tribespeople and local traders alike buy and sell food produce and handmade goods in the lanes around the bus stand and behind the police station, and buying stuff from them is a rare opportunity for you to interact with tribespeople on your own.

Sleeping & Eating

Maa Mangala Residency HOTEL $

(06852-251228; Jeypore Rd; r ₹599, with AC ₹799, ste ₹1199;) The pick of Koraput's rather lacklustre offerings, this new hotel on the outskirts of town actually has wi-fi in its spotless rooms, and there's a travel desk and a good restaurant. It's a bit of a trek down into town, though, if you're hoofing it.

Atithi Bhavan HOTEL $

(06852-250610; atithibhaban@gmail.com; d with fan ₹300, with AC ₹600;) A decent budget hotel run by the Jagannath Temple. Rooms are relatively clean and attached bathrooms have bucket showers.

Raj Residency HOTEL $$

(06852-251591; www.hotelrajresidency.com; Post Office Rd; s/d ₹750/950, with AC from ₹1250/1500;) Raj Residency has some of the best digs in town, offering clean, modern rooms with plasma TVs, friendly service and free wi-fi (in the lobby only). The Indian/Chinese **restaurant** (mains ₹80-200; 7.30am-11am, noon-3pm & 7.30-10.30pm;) is also one of the best places for food in Koraput. To get here, turn left up Post Office Rd, walk past the post office and keep going straight (for 400m).

Information

There are ATMs along Koraput's main street.

A few internet cafes are dotted around town.

Getting There & Away

BUS

From the Koraput bus stand, there are half-hourly buses to Jeypore (₹25, 40 minutes) between 6am and 8.30pm. Seven buses

LOCAL KNOWLEDGE

WEEKLY MARKETS

There are weekly *haats* (markets) held every day at different villages in Koraput district, sometimes two or three at different places on the same day. Tribespeople from surrounding villages will descend on the market of the day to buy clothes, jewellery and foodstuffs. They are fabulously colourful places to visit, and the best chance foreign tourists have to interact with Odishan tribespeople.

Onkadelli Market (busiest at lunchtime) is the best known and, as a result, more touristy than the others: expect to be approached by enterprising Bonda women wishing to sell you bead necklaces and metal collars. Koraput itself has a Sunday *haat*, which, because of its location in the town centre, is open to foreigners even without special permission. At many markets you'll see tribeswomen selling alcohol brewed from sago palm and imbibed from a wine pipe (₹10 a shot).

Selected *haats*:

Monday Subai (5am-4pm Mon) Small produce market, 34km from Koraput.

Tuesday Ramgiri (5am-5pm Tue) Produce market, 64km from Koraput; **Kotapad** (5am-5pm Tue) Textile market, 63km from Koraput.

Wednesday Podagada (p614) Produce market attended by Paraja and Mali people, 18km from Koraput; **Chatikona** (p615) Dongria Kondh and Desia Kondh produce market, 39km from Rayagada.

Thursday Onkadelli (p614) Produce market, 65km from Jeypore, with numerous tribes represented, including Bonda.

Thursday/Friday Kundli (p614) The region's largest produce market, with a cattle section. Also numerous tribes represented; 20km from Koraput.

Saturday Laxmipur (p614) Kondh and Paraja produce market, 56km from Koraput.

Sunday Koraput (p612) In the Koraput town centre; also one of the bigger produce markets.

make the scenic trip to Rayagada (₹110, four hours) between 6am and 7pm. And at least four evening buses leave for Bhubaneswar (₹420, 12 hours) between 5pm and 7pm.

To get a bus to Onkadelli Market, you'll have to first catch a bus to the scruffy town of Jeypore and then the 7.30am or 9.30am bus to Onkadelli (₹45, three hours). The Onkadelli buses leave from Jeypore's private bus stand, which is located in front of Jeypore's government bus stand. From Jeypore's government bus stand, there are frequent buses to Visakhapatnam (₹270, six hours, 5am to 11pm) in Andhra Pradesh.

TRAIN

The train station is 3km from the centre; it costs around ₹10/60 in a shared/private autorickshaw to get here from the bus stand. Destinations:

Bhubaneswar 18448 Hirakhand Express (sleeper/3AC/2AC ₹370/995/1425, 14½ hours, 5.25pm)

Jagdalpur (Chhattisgarh) 18447 Hirakhand Express (sleeper/3AC/2AC ₹150/510/715, three hours, 1pm)

Kolkata 18006 Koraput Howrah Express (sleeper/3AC/2AC/1AC ₹490/1320/1910/3245, 23¼ hours, 7.10am)

Visakhapatnam (Andhra Pradesh) 58502 (general/2nd class/sleeper ₹45/60/110, seven hours, 1.45pm)

The journey to Jagdalpur is particularly scenic.

Around Koraput

Koraput is not a destination in its own right, but the countryside around the town is. This unique, remote part of India is particularly rich in tribal culture that has survived largely intact. Most of the tribespeople are subsistence farmers and you'll see the villagers planting and harvesting in a traditional fashion and carrying heavy loads on their heads to sell at the region's many markets, often walking long distances as transport is scarce here. The gentle rhythm of rural life entices visitors to linger longer and explore, on foot and by bicycle.

Sights

The biggest attractions around Koraput are the colourful tribal markets and villages. Until recently, foreigners technically had to be accompanied by a government-approved guide to visit any of the tribal areas where the markets are held, with an itinerary lodged with the local police station, though this wasn't strictly enforced. The guides themselves processed the 'prior permission' required for foreigners to visit these markets. All you needed to do was give them a copy of your passport and visa, and tell them where you wished to visit. This may still be the case, though since there is no longer a tourist office in Koraput, the information available to travellers is incomplete and conflicting.

Furthermore, there were plenty of complaints about these government-approved guides: that they would take their customers' money and abandon them at the market, for instance. In practical terms, there is nothing to stop travellers from getting on a public bus or chartering a car and driver in Koraput or Rayagada, and getting to their market of choice under their own steam.

★Onkadelli Market MARKET
(10am-6pm Thu) A particularly popular tribal produce market, with Bonda, Mali, Kondh and Paraja people attending.

Kundli Market MARKET
(6pm Thu-5pm Fri) The region's largest produce market, taking place from Thursday afternoon until Friday afternoon. Homemade alcohol is sold near the cattle section.

Laxmipur Market MARKET
(5am-5pm Sat) A produce market attended by Kondh and Paraja people, 56km from Koraput. Reachable on any Rayagada-bound bus.

Podagada Market MARKET
(5am-5pm Wed) Paraja and Mali people attend this produce market, 18km from Koraput.

Sleeping & Eating

★Chandoori Sai LODGE $$$
(9443342241; www.chandoorisai.com; Goudaguda Village; per person incl meals ₹4000;)
Run by Aussie Leon, this is an earthen-walled refuge with beautiful terracotta flooring, a colourful sari ceiling and five contemporary rooms. The Western food is fabulous, but the real coup is the guest interaction with tribal women on the property, and sensitive trips to nearby villages and markets. Trains between Bhubaneswar and Koraput stop at nearby Kakirigumma, as do Koraput–Rayagada buses.

Guests are free to do as little or as much as they like; some come as part of tribal tour packages arranged through Puri-based Grass Routes (p605), but independent guests are most welcome. Leon is passionate about local culture and about protecting it from unscrupulous tour operators. He has books for guests to peruse on India's tribes. Sometimes he'll drive the guests around himself; other times he'll get a local guide to take guests to nearby markets and for walks around nearby villages, including the potters' village of Goudaguda that's right outside the front door.

ODISHA'S INDIGENOUS TRIBES

Sixty-two Adivasi (tribal) groups live in an area that encompasses Odisha, Chhattisgarh and Andhra Pradesh. In Odisha they account for one-quarter of the state's population and mostly inhabit the jungles and hilly regions of the centre and southwest. Their distinctive cultures are expressed in music, dance and arts.

Of the more populous tribes, the **Kondh** number about one million and are based around Koraput in the southwest, Rayagada and the Kandhamel district in the central west. The 500,000-plus **Santal** live around Baripada and Khiching in the far north. The 300,000 **Saura** live near Gunupur near the border with Andhra Pradesh. The **Bonda**, known as the 'Naked People' for wearing minimal clothing but incredibly colourful and intricate accessories, such as beadwork, have a population of about 5000 and live in the hills near Koraput.

In 2012, permission from the District Collector was required to visit specific areas designated as home to Particularly Vulnerable Tribal Groups (PVTGs) and bans on overnight lodging and private home visits were put in place. This has recently changed. It is possible to visit tribal regions independently, but most travellers choose a customised tour, best organised through reputable private tour agencies in Puri or through Chandoori Sai (p614) and Desia (p614) in Odisha's tribal country.

The 18447 Hirakhand Express from Bhubaneswar to Koraput gets in to Kakirigumma at around 8.20am every morning. From Koraput the reverse journey stops there at 7pm. Three trains daily stop at Laxmipur Rd, 25km from Chandoori Sai, en route from Koraput to Kolkata. Call ahead for pick-up.

★Desia LODGE $$$

(☎9437023656, 9437677188; www.desiakoraput.com; Bantalabiri Village, Lamptaput; s/d incl meals Apr-Sep ₹3000/4000, Oct-Mar ₹3500/5500) This gorgeous rural four-room lodge, made of local materials and decorated by tribal artists, is run by Heritage Tours (p605). Activities on offer include half- and full-day walks to nearby villages, cooking, cycling through the countryside, craftwork, cooking and local market trips. Desia is 70km southwest of Koraput, near the village of Machkund. It's best to call for a pick-up from Koraput.

This place is seriously remote: no wi-fi, little phone signal, total silence after dark and the most beautiful starry sky on a clear night. You can come here independently or with an all-inclusive 'tribal tour' package, starting at ₹19,000 for a four-day trip for two people. Since the lodge is along the rural road to Onkadelli Market, visitors to the market are welcome to drop by for a delicious lunch (book in advance). If you're seriously interested in cultural immersion, an overnight stay in a nearby village can be arranged; evening visits are also possible and you might get sucked into a local full-moon dance. Desia also runs a nursery and primary school for children from surrounding villages, teaching them English.

Getting There & Around

Some of the markets, including Laxmipur, Onkadelli, Koraput and Chatikona, can be reached by public transport; for the rest you have to hire a car. Consider the tribal people, many of whom walk for hours to get to the markets!

Rayagada

☎06856 / POP 71,208

The only reason for staying in the industrial town of Rayagada is to use it as the base for visiting the weekly Wednesday Chatikona market. The market is considered tourist-friendly.

Rayagada's own daily market, between the train station and the bus stand, is where colourfully dressed tribespeople weave bamboo baskets alongside local traders selling fruit and veg, spices, dried fish and the like.

Sights

★Chatikona Market MARKET

(⏰5am-4pm Wed) The weekly Chatikona market takes place at Bissamcuttack (about 40km north) and is mostly attended by the Dongria Kondh and Desia Kondh villagers from the surrounding Niayamgiri Hills. It's largely a produce market, but also for sale are bronze animal sculptures made locally using the lost-wax method.

Rayagada Market MARKET

(off R 326; ⏰7am-5pm) Rayagada's daily market is between the train station and the bus stand; turn right out of the bus stand, take the second right and it's on your left. Here you'll see colourfully dressed tribespeople weaving bamboo baskets alongside local traders selling fruit and veg, spices, dried fish and more.

Sleeping & Eating

Hotel Rajbhavan HOTEL $

(☎06856-223777; Main Rd; d/tr ₹700/990, with AC from ₹1360/1670; ❄) Friendly Hotel Rajbhavan is a decent option and has a good multicuisine restaurant (mains ₹60 to ₹200). It's located across the main road from the train station – don't confuse it with nearby Hotel Raj, which isn't as good.

Tejasvi International BUSINESS HOTEL $$

(☎06856-224925; www.hoteltejasvi.in; Collector Residence Rd, Gandhi Nagar; s/d incl breakfast from ₹1500/1800, ste ₹4000; ❄📶) Tejasvi International is an architectually odd business hotel with good service, comfortable rooms and wi-fi throughout. To get here, take a right out of the train station, then take the first left and keep walking to the end (500m).

Getting There & Away

The bus stand is a 1km-walk from the train station; turn right out of the train station, walk over the railway line and it's on your left; both are on main Rte 326.

From Rayagada bus stand, there are three early-morning local buses to Chatikona (₹38, two hours, 4.45am, 6.30am and 9.30am). Buses to Jeypore (₹120, five hours, five daily) all go via Koraput (₹100, four hours); the route over the forested hills is fabulously scenic. There are frequent evening buses to Bhubaneswar (non-AC ₹390, 12 hours) between 4pm and 7pm.

Of the three trains between Bhubaneswar and Rayagada, the 18447 Hirakhand Express (sleeper/3AC/2AC ₹310/830/1180) departs Bhubaneswar daily at 8.25pm, reaching Rayagada at 5.10am – good timing for catching the market bus. The return (18448) leaves Rayagada at 10.30pm.

NORTHERN & NORTHEASTERN ODISHA

Northeastern Odisha is best known for its nature sanctuaries, notably Bhitarkanika Wildlife Sanctuary and Similipal National Park, and the excellent Buddhist ruins at Ratnagiri, Udayagiri and Lalitgiri. To the north of Bhubaneswar you can stay in heritage palaces and explore the peaceful countryside by foot and by bicycle. While Cuttack is not a particularly attractive city, it's worth stopping here to check out the new Odisha State Maritime Museum (p616), which puts Odisha's history into context.

Sights

Odisha State Maritime Museum MUSEUM
(www.odishastatemaritimemuseum.org; Jobra, Cuttack; ₹300; 10am-4.30pm Tue-Sun) This excellent new museum, sitting on the bank of the Mahanadi River, focuses on Odisha's centuries-old maritime history of trade and boat-building. The partially interactive displays walk you through the Kalingas' maritime activities, rituals and tools. The boat display shed features river-boat models from different parts of India, while the Jobra workshop gallery introduces you to the world of sluice gates and boat repair. An aquarium entertains visitors with displays of Odisha's marine life, while the temporary gallery showcases contemporary art.

Ushakothi Wildlife Sanctuary WILDLIFE RESERVE
(per day Indian/foreigner ₹20/1000; Oct-May) The Ushakothi Wildlife Sanctuary, 45km east of Sambalpur, shelters elephants, tigers, panthers and bears. It can be closed with no notice in the event of bad weather. Transport (4WDs) can be arranged through your hotel in Sambalpur if you don't have your own wheels.

Sleeping & Eating

★**Kila Dalijoda** HERITAGE HOTEL $$$
(9438667086; www.kiladalijoda.com; s/d ₹4500/5500;) In the village of Mangarajpur, an hour's drive from Bhubaneswar, Debjit and his family welcome visitors into his ancestral home, a rambling mansion surrounded by peaceful countryside. The home-cooked food is among the best we've had in Odisha, and Debjit takes his guests on walks and bicycle rides through tribal villages. Visits to tribal markets and nearby temples are also arranged.

The former hunting lodge of a local raj, this castle-like stone home was built in 1931 and features three well-appointed guest rooms with antique furniture and enormous bathrooms. Instead of AC, the rooms use traditional root curtains, dampened with water during the summer to cool the rooms down. The family are a delight and Debjit likes to introduce his guests to the quirks of rural life – by visiting an old cows' home, or walking through jungle to a tribal village of subsistence farmers who get raided nightly by wild elephants. The roads around the property are empty and ideal for two-wheeled exploration. Food-wise, duck and quail is served instead of chicken due to a rule regarding the family deity.

Kila Dalijoda can be used as a base for trips further afield; Debjit arranges day trips to Bhitarkanika Wildlife Sanctuary and to the craft villages and temples north of Cuttack. Pick-up can be arranged from Bhubaneswar or Cuttack.

★**Garh Dhenkanal Palace** HERITAGE HOTEL $$$
(9437292448; www.dhenkanalpalace.com; r ₹6000) This mighty fort-cum-palace full of rooms, courts and gardens nestles against the foothills of the Eastern Ghats in the village of Dhenkanal. The 19th-century home of the Raja of Dhenkanal, it now accepts guests; sumptuous rooms have en-suite bathrooms and guests have access to the present Raja's library. Trips to surrounding crafts and tribal villages can be arranged.

★**Gajlaxmi Palace** HERITAGE HOTEL $$$
(9861011221, 9337411020; www.gajlaxmipalace.com; Borapada, Dhenkanal; s/d incl meals & nature walk ₹3500/6000;) Located 10km from Dhenkanal, this heritage palace, tucked away amid stunning scenery in the untapped forests of the Dhenkanal district, dates back to 1935. The palace belonged to a member of the Dhenkanal royal family. Today, his grandson, JP Singh Deo, and Navneeta, his lovely wife, have opened up two rooms inside their tranquil slice of royal history to guests.

Sleeping here is like overnighting in a museum – the whole place is chock-full of Singh Deo's antiques collected from around the world and the palace lives and breathes of decadent days gone by. The surrounding forest hides at least 22 wild elephants, a common sight on JP's morning and evening nature walks. Wild boar, jungle fowl and barking deer also roam freely outside the palace doors. JP grew up here and is ever too pleased to take you to rarely visited Sabara tribal villages or nearby Joranda temples, or tell tales of elephant and tiger kills in crazier days over wonderful meals sourced from their own organic gardens. Paradise found.

Dhenkanal is an easy train ride from Bhubaneswar.

Getting There & Away

The village of Dhenkanal, with its palaces, is easily reachable by train from Bhubaneswar, while Kila Dalijoda arranges pick-up from Bhubaneswar or Cuttack. It's easy to combine a visit to both. From Kila Dalijoda, Bhitarkanika Wildlife Sanctuary is a viable day trip, while Dhenkanal is within easy reach of Angul and the Satkosia Tiger Reserve.

Pusphagiri Ruins

These fascinating Buddhist ruins, the oldest of which date back to around 200 BC, are the remnants of one of India's earliest *mahaviharas* (Buddhist monasteries, which were, effectively, the universities of their day). Pusphagiri Mahavihara had three campuses – Ratnagiri, Udayagiri and Lalitgiri – each built upon a small hilltop in the low-lying Langudi Hills. The Kelua River provided a scenic backdrop, and these days supports small farming communities and their mud-and-thatch villages, which dot the rural landscape.

If you start early, it's possible to visit the area in a day trip by bus from Bhubaneswar, but having your own wheels or staying overnight in one of the villages gives you the chance to explore each of the three sites properly. Stop by the excellent museum at Ratnagiri first, as it puts the three sites into context.

Sights

★Udayagiri ARCHAEOLOGICAL SITE
(dawn-dusk) FREE These two monastery complexes date back to the 10th to 12th centuries AD. At the first one, there's a large pyramidal brick stupa with a seated Buddha image on each of the four sides. Beyond, a large Buddha statue is locked away behind some fine doorjamb carvings. The second site, marred by graffiti, features an exquisite deity carving, a seated Buddha statue and monastic cells. Unhelpful 'guides' fish for donations (not compulsory). The ruins are a 2km walk from the main road.

★Ratnagiri ARCHAEOLOGICAL SITE
(Indian/foreigner ₹15/200, video ₹25; dawn-dusk) Ratnagiri has the most interesting and extensive of the Pusphagiri ruins. Two large monasteries flourished here from the 5th to 13th centuries. Noteworthy are an exquisitely carved doorway inside the first monastary complex and an intact Buddha statue beyond. Up on the small hillock are the remains of a 10m-high stupa, surrounded by smaller votive stupas; all are covered in graffiti in spite of a security guard presence.

Lalitgiri ARCHAEOLOGICAL SITE
(Indian/foreigner ₹15/200, video ₹25; dawn-dusk) Several monastery ruins, some dating back to 200 BC, consisting largely of brick foundations, are scattered along a gentle incline; one is surrounded by several dozen small votive stupas. Next to a small museum housing some fine carvings from the site, steps lead up a hillock crowned with a shallow stupa. During excavations in the 1970s, a casket containing gold and silver relics was found. A museum was being built near the site entrance at the time of research.

Ratnagiri Museum MUSEUM
(₹5; 9am-5pm) The four galleries at this fine museum tell the story of the Pusphagiri ruins. Two of them display beautifully preserved sculpture from all three Pusphagiri sites, while the other two galleries are devoted to terracotta plaques, copper plates engraved with Sanskrit, sacred bronzes and other objects found on-site.

Sleeping & Eating

Toshali Ratnagiri Resort HOTEL $$$
(9937023791, 06725-281044; www.toshaliratnagiri.com; r from ₹6000;) The Toshali Ratnagiri Resort, opposite the Ratnagiri Museum at the far end of Ratnagiri village, is surrounded by rice fields and a peaceful village pond. Tastefully decorated rooms flank an interior courtyard and there's a restaurant (mains ₹100 to ₹250) and a bar. It's overpriced, but you're a captive audience.

Toshali Udayagiri Resort HOTEL $$$
(☎ 9937212110; www.toshaliudayagiri.com; r ₹4000; ❄) This hotel is in the Udayagiri village, around 2km from the Udayagiri ruins. Facilities include an ayurvedic spa and decent multicuisine restaurant.

Toshali Lalitgiri Resort HOTEL $$$
(☎ 9937003223; www.toshalilalitgiri.com; r ₹4000; ❄) Comfortable hotel near Lalitgiri with a small ayurvedic spa on-site.

Getting There & Away

Udayagiri is 23km from Chandikhol. Ratnagiri is 9km past Udayagiri. Lalatgiri is 22km from Chandikhol, but down a different lane, 8km beyond the Ratnagiri/Udayagiri turn-off.

If coming by public transport from Bhubaneswar, catch a bus to Cuttack (₹25, one hour, frequent) then change for a bus to Chandikhol (₹31, one hour, frequent) where, from the road leading off to the right, you can catch shared minivans to Ratnagiri (₹30, 45 minutes) via Udayagiri (₹24, 30 minutes), or to Lalitgiri (₹24, 30 minutes) via Hotel Toshali Pusphagiri. Minivans start drying up at around 3.30pm.

A day trip to the three sites with a car and driver from Bhubaneswar costs around ₹3500.

Bhitarkanika Wildlife Sanctuary

Spanning mangrove forests, vast wetlands, and three rivers flowing into the Bay of Bengal, Bhitarkanika Wildlife Sanctuary is an immensely wildlife-rich ecosystem, home to crocodiles, diverse birdlife and endangered turtles.

Sights

★Bhitarkanika Wildlife Sanctuary NATURE RESERVE
(www.bhitarkanika.org; per day ₹40, camera/video ₹200/10,000; ⏲7am-4pm Aug–mid-May) Three rivers flow out to sea at Bhitarkanika, forming a tidal maze of muddy creeks and mangroves. This is India's second-largest mangrove region, and most of the 672-sq-km delta forms this wonderful sanctuary, a significant biodiversity hot spot. The only way to get around most of the sanctuary is

ODISHA'S OLIVE RIDLEY MARINE TURTLES

One of the smallest sea turtles and a threatened species, the olive ridley marine turtle swims up from deeper waters beyond Sri Lanka to mate and lay eggs on Odisha's beaches. The main nesting sites are Gahirmatha (in Bhitarkanika Wildlife Sanctuary), Devi river mouth near Konark, and Rushikulya River mouth by Chilika Lake.

Turtle deaths due to fishing practices are unfortunately common. Although there are regulations, such as requiring the use of turtle exclusion devices (TEDs) on trawl nets and banning fishing from certain prohibited congregation and breeding areas, these laws are routinely flouted in Odisha.

Casuarina trees have been planted to help preserve Devi beach but they occupy areas of soft sand that are necessary for a turtle hatchery. Other potential threats include the upcoming Astaranga Seaport and Thermal Power Plant and the proposed Palur port, which is planned right next to the Rushikulya River mouth nesting site (which it would destroy if allowed to continue as planned).

In January and February the turtles congregate near nesting beaches and, if conditions are right, come ashore. If conditions aren't right, they reabsorb their eggs and leave without nesting.

Hatchlings emerge 50 to 55 days later and are guided to the sea by the luminescence of the ocean and stars. They can be easily distracted by bright lights; unfortunately NH5 runs within 2km of Rushikulya beach. Members of local turtle clubs in Gokharkuda, Podampeta and Purunabandha village gather up disoriented turtles and take them to the sea. It's best to visit the nesting beach at dawn when lights are not necessary.

The best place to see nesting and hatching is on the northern side of Rushikulya River, near the villages of Purunabandha and Gokharkuda, 20km from the nearest accommodation in Rambha. During nesting and hatching, activity takes place throughout the night: don't use lights.

Ask staff at Panthanivas Rambha (p611) what conditions are like, or contact the Wildlife Society of Odisha (p620). Rickshaws between Rambha and Rushikulya cost around ₹500 return for a half-day and ₹1000 for the full day.

WORTH A TRIP

SIMLIPAL NATIONAL PARK

The 2750-sq-km **Similipal National Park** (06792-259126; www.similipal.org; per day Indian/foreigner ₹40/1000, camera per 3 days ₹50/100; Oct–mid-Jun) has long been Odisha's prime wildlife sanctuary. However, due to on-off Maoist activity in the region, the park has been off-limits to foreign tourists in recent years. At the time of research it was open again to visitors, but check ahead with the **Similipal National Park office** (06792-259126; rccfbaripada@gmail.com; 9am-5pm Mon-Fri) or Odisha Tourism (p601) in Bhubaneswar before visiting, as the security situation is volatile and subject to change. There are waterfalls to see and wild elephants are relatively common, tigers less so. Most visitors tend to be Bengali tourists who come with their own vehicles; if you don't have your own wheels, the easiest way to visit the park is by organised tour. Odisha Tourism can arrange a car and driver, otherwise some of the lodgings in Baripada can arrange transport to the park, 25km away.

There are several basic hotels in Baripada.

Most accommodation options either have basic restaurants or offer meals.

Regular buses go from Baripada to Kolkata (₹200, five hours), Bhubaneswar (₹210 to ₹240, five hours) and Balasore (₹45 to ₹60, 1½ hours). The 12892 Bhubaneswar–Baripada Express (2nd class/AC chair ₹135/475, five hours, 5.10pm) runs from Bhubaneswar every day except Saturday, and returns as the 12891 at 5.10am every day except Sunday. A car and driver to the park from Baripada should cost around ₹2500.

by boat, and the main reason to come is to spot crocodiles and birds (particularly at the Bagagahana heronry).

There are long-snouted gharials, short squat muggers, and enormous estuarine crocodiles, or 'salties', which bask on mud flats before diving into the water for cover as your boat chugs past. One particular 23-foot beast that you're likely to see has made the Guinness Book of World Records.

The best time to visit is from December to February, but you'll see crocs all year round, and may also see monitor lizards, spotted deer, wild boar and all sorts of birds, including eight species of brilliantly coloured kingfishers. Herons arrive in early June and nest until early December, when they move on to Chilika Lake, while raucous open-billed storks have set up a permanent rookery here. A short walk through the mangroves from one of the docks inside the sanctuary leads to a birding tower. There is also a 5km nature walk along one of the islands, though that's best done on weekdays when there are fewer visitors.

It's also worth knowing that this area has the highest concentration of king cobras found anywhere in India, as well as half a dozen other potentially deadly viper species.

The park entrance is at the beautiful, but very poor, mud-hut village of Dangmal (Dang-ger-mal), and all tour boats depart from the same dock at 7.30am. You can learn more about the crocodile conservation program at Dangmar Island; the sanctuary is off-limits to visitors during the May–August crocodile breeding season.

Sleeping & Eating

★Aul Palace HERITAGE HOTEL **$$$**

(Rajbati; 9437690565; www.kilaaulpalace.com; r incl breakfast ₹4000;) In the village of Aul, this centuries-old former royal palace has been converted into an intimate retreat. The rooms are splendidly furnished with antique furniture, the tranquil grounds and the riverfront location add charm, and meals may include giant river prawns. Half-/full-day boat trips (₹4000/6000) into Bhitarkanika are arranged. Several direct buses serve Aul from Cuttack (₹70, three hours).

The raja splits his time between Cuttack and Aul, and it's particularly interesting to stay here when he's around to host you.

★Nature Camp Bhitarkanika CAMPGROUND **$$$**

(9437029989, 9437016054; www.bhitarkanikatour.com; per person incl meals & transfer from Bhubaneswar s/d/tr/q ₹12,000/6675/4821/3894; Oct-Apr) A special experience awaits at this small, sustainable, privately run tented camp at the heart of Dangmal village, built with the help of villagers and just 200m before the sanctuary gate. The stylish Swiss Cottage tents are a tad musty but fully equipped with electricity, fans, sit-down flush toilets and pleasant terraces, and the rustic Odisha cuisine is excellent.

Nature Camp does accept walk-ins, though you'd be wise to contact them in advance. The majority of their customers come as part of overnight or multinight packages that include transfers from Bhubaneswar, visits to the Pusphagiri ruins en route, park entry, boat trips and nature hikes in the reserve and all meals. A two-night all-inclusive trip for one/two/three people costs ₹22,000/25,000/29,000.

Dangmal Forest Rest House GUESTHOUSE **$$**
(www.bhitarkanika.org; d ₹1500-2500) The Forestry Department–run Forest Rest House is located just inside the sanctuary's main gate. Annoyingly, rooms have to be pre-booked through the Wildlife Warden at Rajnagar village, about an hour's drive back up the road. Cheaper rooms are available for Indian tourists.

Information

PERMITS

The powers that be at the Bhitarkanika Wildlife Sanctuary are prone to changing the rules regarding permits. At research time, advance registration of foreign visitors was required, so get in touch with **Nature Camp Bhitarkanika** (p619) or **Aul Palace** (p619) in advance if you're interested in going on a boat tour.

TOURIST INFORMATION

Wildlife Society of Odisha (☎9437024265; www.facebook.com/wildlifesocietyoforissa; Shantikunj, Link Rd, Cuttack) Has information on the plight of Odisha's olive ridley marine turtles.

Wildlife Warden (☎9437037370, 06729-242460; Rajnagar) Book the Dangmal Forest Rest House accommodation through this guy.

Getting There & Away

The easiest way to visit the Bhitarkanika Wildlife Sanctuary is by an organised trip with **Nature Camp Bhitarkanika** (p619), which includes pick-up from Bhubaneswar and visits to the Pusphagiri ruins en route.

Getting here by public transport is a bit of a mission. Two or three direct buses to Dangmal leave from Cuttack between noon and 1pm. Otherwise, frequent buses go from Cuttack to Pattamundai (₹70, three hours), from where you can catch onward buses to Dangmal (₹45, 2½ hours, last bus 5pm), passing Rajnagar en route.

There are three early-morning buses from Dangmal. The 5am and 7am both go as far as Kendrapara (a small town just past Pattamundai), from where you can catch onward transport to Cuttack or Chandikhol (for the Pusphagiri ruins). The 6am bus goes all the way to Cuttack. After that, you'll have to catch an autorickshaw from Dangmal to Rajnagar (around ₹600) from where the last bus to Cuttack leaves at 2pm. You can also take one of the 10 or so trains (2¼ to three hours) to Bhadrak (the nearest railhead, 60km away from Bhitarkanika) from Bhubaneswar and request to be picked up from there by Nature Camp Bhitarkanika.

Getting Around

The only way to get around the sanctuary is by boat.

Madhya Pradesh & Chhattisgarh

Includes ➡

Best Places to Eat

- Under the Mango Tree (p649)
- Ahilya Fort (p671)
- Sarafa Bazar (p661)
- Mediterra (p661)
- Baghvan (p681)
- Silver Saloon (p627)

Best Places to Sleep

- Kipling Camp (p677)
- Orchha Home-Stay (p634)
- Sarai at Toria (p645)
- Baghvan (p681)
- Salban (p677)

Why Go?

The spotlight doesn't hit Madhya Pradesh (MP) with quite the same brilliance as it shines on more celebrated neighbouring states, so you can experience travel riches ranking with the best without that feeling of just following a tourist trail.

Khajuraho's temples bristle with some of the finest stone carving in India, their exquisite erotic sculptures a mere slice of the architectural wonders of a region exceedingly well endowed with palaces, forts, temples, mosques and stupas, most gloriously in the villages of Orchha and Mandu. Tigers are the other big news here, and your chances of spotting a wild Royal Bengal in MP are as good as anywhere in India.

Pilgrimage-cum-traveller havens such as Maheshwar and Omkareshwar on the Narmada River are infused with the spiritual and chill-out vibes for which India is renowned, while the adventurous can foray into the tribal zones of Chhattisgarh, fascinatingly far removed from mainstream Indian culture.

When to Go

Bhopal

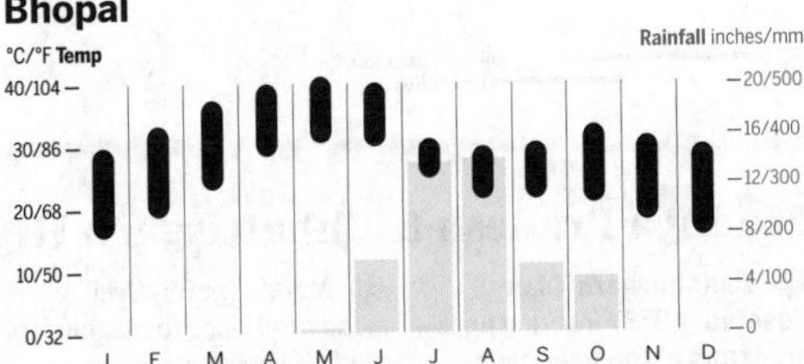

Nov–Feb The most pleasant time to visit central India, despite chilly mornings.

Apr–Jun Hot, but best chance of spotting tigers; thin vegetation and few water sources.

Jul–Sep Monsoon time, but places such as Chhattisgarh are at their most beautiful.

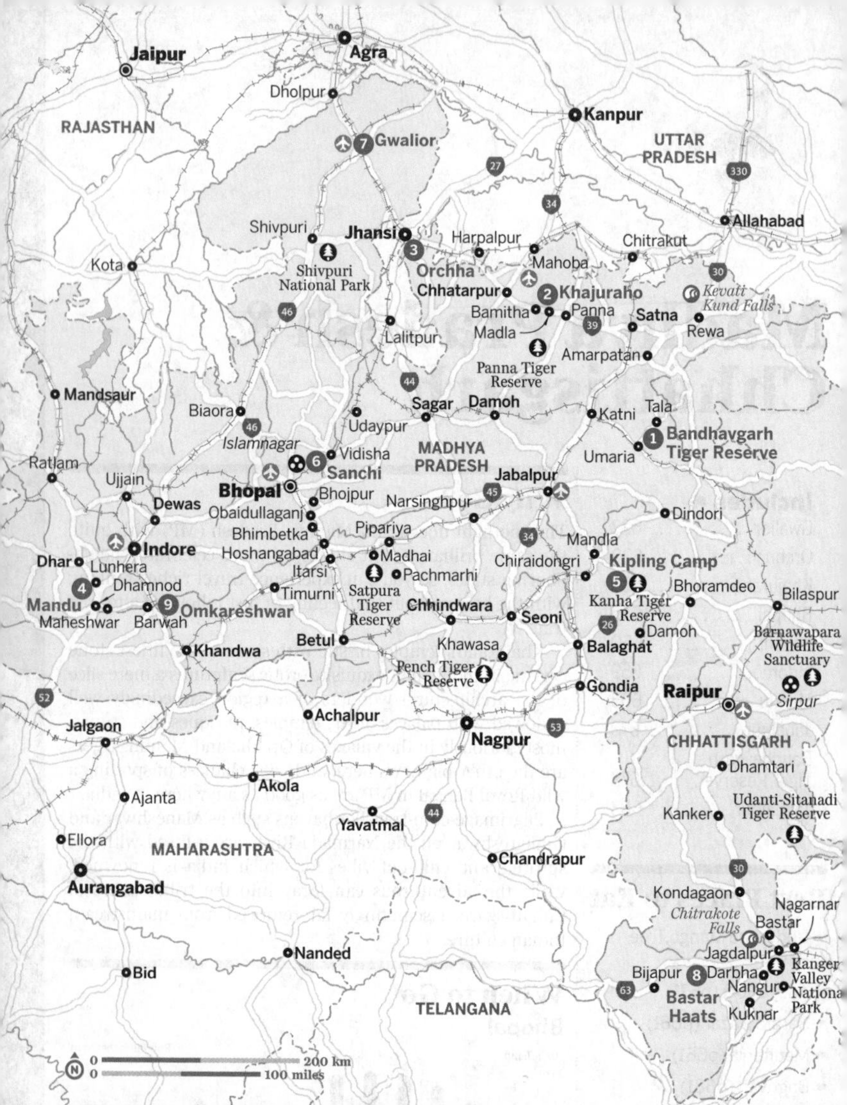

Madhya Pradesh & Chhattisgarh Highlights

1. **Bandhavgarh Tiger Reserve** (p678) Tracking apex predators at top tiger parks.
2. **Khajuraho** (p635) Blushing at the erotic carvings on the Chandela dynasty's exquisite temples.
3. **Orchha** (p630) Bedding down in a village homestay at this beautiful, laid-back town.
4. **Mandu** (p665) Cycling along rural lanes to magnificent medieval buildings.
5. **Jungle Lodges** (p677) Obeying the call of the wild in comfort and style at top-class lodges such as Kipling Camp.
6. **Sanchi** (p650) Travelling back two millennia to the golden age of Indian Buddhism.
7. **Gwalior** (p625) Exploring the city's historic cliff-girt fort.
8. **Bastar Haats** (p684) Experiencing tribal culture at fascinating markets.
9. **Omkareshwar** (p672) Absorbing the spiritual atmosphere at the riverside pilgrimage centre.

History

Plum in the centre of India, Madhya Pradesh and Chhattisgarh have been subject to a mind-boggling array of empires, kingdoms, sultanates and competing local dynasties. The great Mauryan Buddhist emperor Ashoka chose Sanchi for the site of his Great Stupa. Gupta emperor Chandragupta II had a series of remarkable Hindu cave shrines cut from the rock at nearby Udaigiri six centuries later.

By the 11th century the Paramaras, a Rajput dynasty, established a powerful kingdom in Malwa (western MP and southeastern Rajasthan), with capitals variously at Ujjain, Mandu and Dhar. Around the same time another Rajput dynasty, the Chandelas, established themselves in Bundelkhand (northern MP and southern Uttar Pradesh) and their nimble-fingered sculptors enlivened some 85 temples at Khajuraho with now-famous erotic scenes.

Between the 12th and 16th centuries, the region experienced continuing struggles between local Hindu rulers and Muslim rivals from the north. Much of Madhya's monumental architecture was erected during these centuries by rulers such as the Muslim Ghuris and Khiljis of Mandu, and the Hindu Bundelas of Orchha and Tomars of Gwalior.

The Delhi-based Mughals took control of the region in the 16th century until they were expelled by the Marathas, the rising Hindu power in central India, after a 27-year war (1681–1707). Powerful Maratha clans like the Holkars of Maheshwar and Indore and the Scindias of Gwalior held sway until the Marathas' 1818 defeat by the British, for whom the Scindias became powerful allies.

Madhya Pradesh took on its modern identity in 1956, when several smaller states were combined into one. Chhattisgarh was separated as an independent state in 2000.

NORTHERN MADHYA PRADESH

Gwalior

☎0751 / POP 1.05 MILLION

Famous for its dramatic and dominant hilltop fort, which Mughal emperor Babur reputedly described as the pearl of Indian fortresses, Gwalior makes an interesting stop en route to some of the better-known destinations in this part of India. The city also houses the elaborate Jai Vilas Palace, the historic seat of the Scindia family, who have been playing important roles in Indian history for more than two centuries.

History

The legend of Gwalior's beginning goes that a 6th- or 8th-century hermit named Gwalipa cured a Rajput chieftain, Suraj Sen, of leprosy using water from Suraj Kund tank (which remains in Gwalior Fort). Renaming the chieftain Suhan Pal, Gwalipa foretold

TOP STATE FESTIVALS

Festival of Dance (p642) The cream of Indian classical dancers perform amid the floodlit temples of Khajuraho.

Shivaratri Mela (p658) Up to 100,000 Shaivite pilgrims, sadhus (holy men) and Adivasis (tribal people) attend celebrations at Pachmarhi's Mahadeo Cave then make a pilgrimage up Chauragarh hill to plant tridents by the Shiva shrine.

Kumbh Mela (p663) Ujjain is one of the four cities where India's biggest religious festival happens once every 12 years, attracting tens of millions of pilgrims. Next in 2028.

Ahilyabai Holkar Jayanti Mahotsav (p671) The birthday of the revered Holkar queen, Ahilyabai, is celebrated with particular fervour in Maheshwar.

Navratri (p663) Celebrated with particular fervour in Ujjain, where lamps are lit at Harsiddhi Mandir.

Tansen Music Festival (Tansen Samaroh; ⏲1st week Dec) Gwalior music festival featuring classical musicians and singers from all over India.

Bastar Dussehra (p683) Dedicated to local goddess Danteshwari, this 75-day festival culminates in a week and a half of (immense) chariot-pulling through the streets of Jagdalpur.

Gwalior

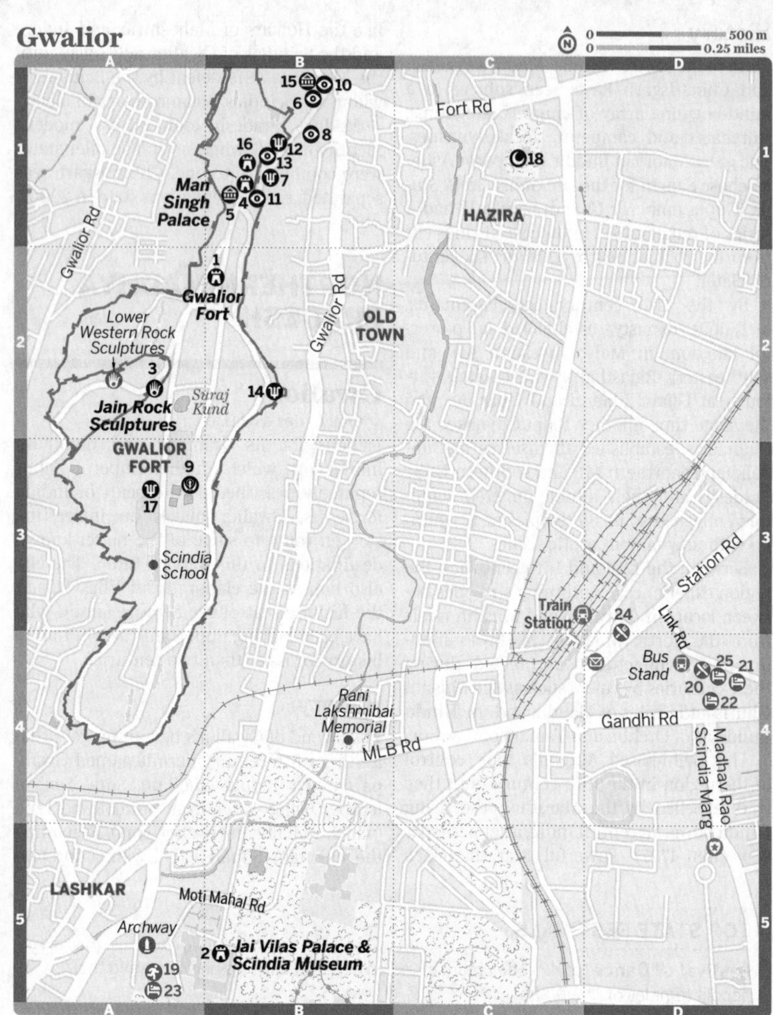

that Suhan's descendants would remain in power as long as they retained the name Pal. Suhan's first 83 descendants did just that, but number 84 changed his name to Tej Karan and, naturally, lost his kingdom.

Gwalior owes its importance to its much coveted hilltop fort, in existence since at least the 9th century, which commands important north–south trade routes and changed hands many times before the Tomar dynasty was founded here by Bir Singh Deo in 1398. The dynasty reached its ascendancy under Raja Man Singh (r 1486–1516) but ended in 1526 to be followed by two centuries of Mughal rule. The Scindia clan of Marathas took over in 1765 and made Gwalior their capital in 1810, though it became a British tributary after the Third Anglo-Maratha War of 1818.

During the First War of Independence (Indian Uprising) in 1857, Maharaja Jayajirao remained loyal to the British but his troops rebelled. The British reconquest of Gwalior Fort a year later marked the effective end of the uprising, and it was in the final British assault that the famous rebel leader, the Rani (Queen) of Jhansi, was killed.

Gwalior

Sights

★Gwalior Fort FORT

(dawn-dusk) Stretched majestically along the top of a 3km-long plateau overlooking Gwalior, the fort is a dominant, unmissable sight, and full of fascinating palaces, temples, museums and other buildings. Much of the fort is now occupied by the prestigious private Scindia School, established by Maharaja Madho Rao Scindia in 1897 for the education of Indian nobility.

➡ **Eastern Approach**

From the east a series of five gates punctuates the worn path up to Gwalior Fort (two of the former seven gates have disappeared). You enter by the **Gwalior Gate** (Alamgiri Gate), dating from 1660, which is followed quickly by the **Badalgarh Gate** (Hindola Gate), named after Badal Singh, Man Singh's uncle. The State Archaeological Museum (p625) is on the right immediately after this.

Further up is the 15th-century **Ganesh Gate**, and then a small four-pillared **Hindu temple** to the hermit Gwalipa, after whom both fort and city are supposedly named. You pass a 9th-century rock-cut Vishnu shrine, the **Chaturbhuj Mandir** (Temple of the Four-Armed God), before the **Lakshman Gate**, probably dating from the 14th century. Finally you enter the palace area through the two-towered **Hathi Gate** (Elephant Gate), built in 1516.

➡ **State Archaeological Museum**

(Gujari Mahal; Indian/foreigner ₹10/100, camera/video ₹50/200; 10am-5pm Tue-Sun) This museum is housed in the 15th-century Gujari Mahal palace, built by Man Singh for his favourite rani (queen), next to the Badalgarh Gate. The entrance is flanked by two extraordinary 14th-century *sardulas* (mythological man-lion creatures) from the town of Sihoniya. Inside is a large collection of Hindu, Jain and Buddhist sculptures, including the famed Shal Bhanjika, a small but exceptionally well-carved 10th-century female figure from Gyaraspur (ask in the curator's office for its room to be unlocked).

➡ **Man Singh Palace**

(Indian/foreigner ₹15/200, video ₹25; 6am-6pm) This imperial-style palace, built by Tomar ruler Man Singh between 1486 and 1516, is definitely one of India's more quirkily decorated monuments: its colourful exterior tilework includes a frieze of yellow ducks and mosaics of elephants, crocodiles and tigers in blue, yellow and green! Hence its alternative identity of Chit Mandir (Painted Palace). Man Singh, a connoisseur of the arts, would surely be delighted to know that his creation is now considered the only intact pre-Mughal palace in India.

It's a labyrinth of a building on four levels. Two circular, columned halls on the lower levels were designed for hot weather and connected by 'speaking tubes' built into the walls – and later used by the Mughals as cells for high-ranking prisoners.

The ticket counter is opposite the palace. You can also hire official guides here for ₹470 for up to four hours. To the north are

WORTH A TRIP

SHIVPURI & MADHAV NATIONAL PARK

A possible day trip from Gwalior is to the old Scindia summer capital of Shivpuri, 117km southwest.

The **Scindia chhatris** (Shivpuri; ₹40, camera/video ₹10/40; ⌚8am-6pm), 2.5km east of the bus stand (autorickshaw ₹30 to ₹40), are the magnificent cenotaphs of maharajas and maharanis gone by – walk-in marble structures the size of large houses, with Mughal-style pavilions and *sikharas* (Hindu temple-spires) facing each other across a pool with a criss-cross of walkways. The *chhatri* to Madhorao Scindia, built between 1926 and 1932, is exquisitely decorated with intricate pietra dura (precious- and semi-precious-stone inlay work).

Two kilometres past the *chhatris* is the entrance to **Madhav National Park** (☎07492-223379; per vehicle incl guide ₹1110, 6-passenger jeep rental ₹1600; ⌚dawn-dusk), 355 sq km of forest, lakes and grassland that's home to antelopes, deer, sloth bears, langurs and a few leopards, and is scattered with relics from the Scindias' hunting days – a shooting box, hunting lodge and sailing club. A 20km jeep tour takes two to 2½ hours.

Buses leave frequently from the Shivpuri bus stand for Gwalior (₹110, 2½ hours), and also for Jhansi (₹95, three hours), where you can make connections for Orchha and Khajuraho.

the ruins of the Vikram Mahal, Karan Mahal and other dilapidated palaces in the north of the fort, grouped under the name **State Protected Monuments** (Indian/foreigner ₹10/250, photography ₹25; ⌚9am-5pm). Just south is the small **Archaeological Survey of India museum** (ASI; ₹5; ⌚9am-5pm Sat-Thu), housing a ho-hum collection of Gwalior-area antiquities.

Ticket also covers admission to Sasbahu Temples and Teli ka Mandir.

➡ Sasbahu Temples

(Mother-in-Law & Daughter-in-Law Temples; Indian/foreigner ₹15/200, video ₹25; ⌚6am-6pm) The Sasbahu, dating from the 9th to 11th centuries, are reminiscent of Central American Maya temples, with their dome- and pillar-covered roofs looking like miniature cities. Mother-in-Law, dedicated to Vishnu, has four gigantic and many smaller pillars supporting its heavy roof, layered with carvings.

➡ Teli ka Mandir

(Indian/foreigner ₹15/200, video ₹25; ⌚6am-6pm) Used as a drinks factory and coffee shop by the British after the First War of Independence (Indian Uprising) of 1857, this 30m-high, 9th-century temple is the oldest monument in the compound.

The modern, gold-topped **gurdwara** nearby is dedicated to Sikh Guru Hargobind Singh, who was imprisoned in Man Singh Palace from 1617 to 1619. (You have to walk around past Suraj Kund to reach it.)

➡ Jain Rock Sculptures

While there are sculptures carved into the rock at a few points around the fort, including on the way up from the Gwalior Gate, the most impressive is the upper set on the western approach, between Urvai Gate and the inner fort walls. Mostly carved from the cliff-face in the mid-15th century, they represent nude figures of *tirthankars* (the 24 great Jain teachers). They were defaced by Babur's Muslim army in 1527 but have been more recently repaired.

★ Jai Vilas Palace & Scindia Museum

PALACE, MUSEUM

(http://jaivilasmuseum.org; Indian/foreigner ₹100/600, camera ₹100; ⌚10am-6pm Tue-Sun, to 5.30pm Nov-Feb) The museum occupies some 35 rooms of the Scindias' opulent Jai Vilas Palace, built by Maharaja Jayajirao in 1874 using prisoners from the fort. The convicts were rewarded with the 12-year job of weaving the hall carpet, one of the largest in Asia.

Supposedly, eight elephants were suspended from the ceiling of the durbar (royal court) hall to check it could cope with two 12.5m-high, 3.5-tonne chandeliers, said to be the largest pair in the world.

Bizarre items fill the rooms: cut-glass furniture, stuffed tigers and a ladies-only swimming pool with its own boat. The cavernous dining room displays the pièce de résistance, a model railway with a silver train that carried after-dinner brandy and cigars around the table.

Note: only the northern entrance to the palace grounds was open for visitors at research time, and it had to be approached from the west (no entry from Moti Mahal Rd).

Tomb of Tansen ISLAMIC TOMB
(⏲dawn-dusk) Tucked away in a lawned compound in the Hazira neighbourhood, just off the southwest corner of the resplendent tomb of the Sufi saint Mohammed Ghaus, is the smaller, simpler tomb of Tansen, a singer much admired by the Mughal emperor Akbar and held to be the father of Hindustani classical music. Chewing the leaves from the tamarind tree here supposedly enriches your voice. Both men lived in the 16th century.

Sleeping

Hotel DM HOTEL $
(☎0751-2341049; Link Rd; s ₹500-1200, d ₹600-1500; ❄📶) Rooms are a bit cramped but they're slightly better than other budget options, and the chirping birds at the end of the corridor are, well, chirpy. Best rooms have air-con and sit-down toilets; the cheapest have coolers and squat toilets. All have an old TV locked inside a cabinet. (When did you last steal a hotel TV?)

Tansen Residency HOTEL $$
(☎0751-2340370; www.mptourism.com; 6A Gandhi Rd; s/d incl breakfast from ₹2830/3260; ❄📶🏊) Not bad at all for a government-run hotel, this MP Tourism offering has large-ish rooms with comfy beds, updated bathrooms, a 1st-floor bar (with a mostly male clientele), a satisfactory buffet breakfast and even a good rooftop pool.

★**Usha Kiran Palace** HERITAGE HOTEL $$$
(☎0751-2444000; www.tajhotels.com; Jayendraganj; s/d incl breakfast from ₹10,280/11,450; ❄@🏊) Live like royalty in this grand, nearly 140-year-old building with expansive gardens that was built as a guesthouse for the Prince of Wales (later King George V). Every room has its unique touches, including different hand-made tiles, but all feature understated heritage luxury, though the cheapest rooms ('superior' category) can be smaller than you'd hope.

Room prices veer around: you may strike a better offer than the mid-January rates given here. The hotel boasts a gorgeous outdoor pool with separate kids' pool, the soothing **Jiva Spa** (☎0751-2444000; Usha Kiran Palace; massage treatments from ₹1875; ⏲8am-8pm) with massage treatments from ₹1875, and the excellent Silver Saloon restaurant (p627). The spiffing **Bada Bar** with its century-old, 4-tonne, Italian-slate snooker table was closed at research time for what was hopefully just a temporary licensing hiccup.

Hotel Gwalior Regency BUSINESS HOTEL $$$
(☎0751-2340670; www.hotelregencygroup.com; Link Rd; s/d incl breakfast from ₹3930/5000; ❄@📶) A superior Indian business hotel. Rooms are spacious, with tile floors, good toiletries, tea/coffee equipment and wi-fi. Some have glass-walled shower rooms. There's a good, licensed, multicuisine restaurant, and a legitimate bar with DJs each night too.

Eating

Indian Coffee House SOUTH INDIAN $
(Station Rd; mains ₹70-300; ⏲7am-10.30pm) Hugely popular branch that does all the breakfast favourites – real coffee, dosas, scrambled eggs – but also has a main-course menu, including excellent thalis (₹140 to ₹250).

Moti Mahal Delux NORTH INDIAN $$
(Link Rd; mains ₹225-395; ⏲11am-11pm) Flavours pop on anything coming out of the tandoor at this stylish nonveg Delhi transplant. They work magic with northwest frontier cuisine, especially the chicken tikka biryani and the green-coloured *murg hariyali tikka* (tandoor-baked chicken marinated in spices, yoghurt and herbs such as coriander and mint). It's next to the bus stand.

★**Silver Saloon** INDIAN $$$
(Usha Kiran Palace, Jayendraganj; mains ₹520-1390; ⏲7am-11pm; ❄) Mouth-watering Indian and Continental dishes, as well as some Thai, Nepali and Marathi specialities, are served in the air-con restaurant or on the palm-shaded verandah of this exquisite heritage hotel.

SLEEPING PRICE RANGES

Price ranges are for two people, including taxes, excluding meals:

$ less than ₹1500

$$ ₹1500–₹4000

$$$ more than ₹4000

Sacred Centre

With its melting pot of religious denominations, India is blessed with a formidable array of sacred sites, from ancient cave temples and solemn contemporary shrines to more frisky architectural creations, such as the sensuous temples of Khajuraho.

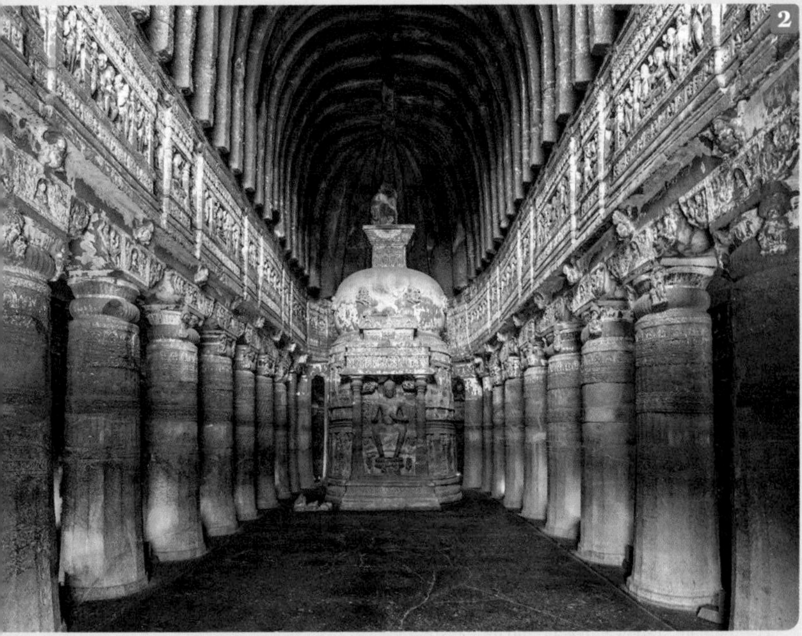

2

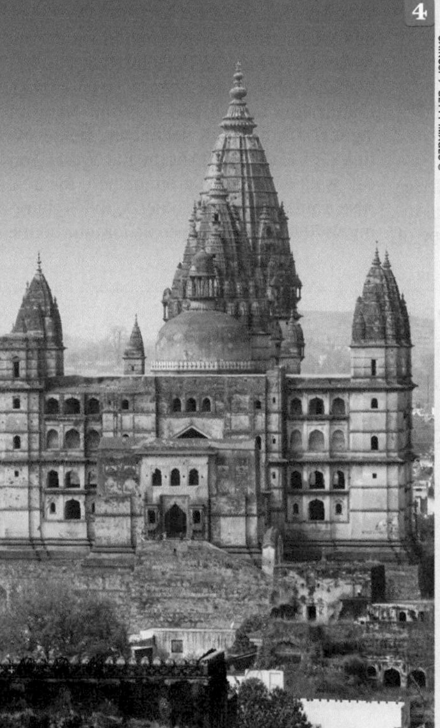

4

1. Khajuraho (p635), Madhya Pradesh
The erotic and other carvings on the World Heritage–listed temples are what's made Khajuraho famous.

2. Ajanta Caves (p787), Maharashtra
These caves date from around the 2nd century BC to the 6th century AD.

3. Jama Masjid (p371), Fatehpur Sikri
Completed in 1571, the mosque contains elements of Indian and Persian design.

4. Chaturbhuj Temple (p631), Orchha
This Hindu temple's spectacular soaring spires are visible from all over Orchha.

3

Information

MP Tourism (☎0751-2234557; Tansen Residency, 6A Gandhi Rd; ⏲10.30am-5.30pm Mon-Sat) The helpful tourist office is outside Tansen Residency hotel.

Getting There & Away

AIR

The airport is 10km northeast of the centre. Air India (www.airindia.in) flies three times weekly to/from Mumbai.

BUS

Services from the **bus stand** (Link Rd):

Agra ₹120, three hours, half-hourly 4.30am to 10pm

Delhi ₹300, eight hours, seven daily

Jhansi ₹110, three hours, half-hourly 5.30am to 11pm

Shivpuri ₹110, 2½ hours, half-hourly 5am to 10pm

TRAIN

The main station, Gwalior Junction, is centrally located, 2.5km southeast of the fort's eastern entrance. More than 30 daily trains go to Agra's Cantonment station and Delhi, and to Jhansi (for Orchha). More than 20 go to Bhopal, but for Khajuraho and Jaipur there's just one each. For Khajuraho you can also go to Jhansi and get a bus from there.

Orchha

☎07680 / POP 11,500

This historic small town on the Betwa River showcases a supreme display of Mughal-influenced Rajput architecture in the shape of spectacular palaces, temples and royal *chhatris* (cenotaphs). The atmosphere in Orchha is far more laid-back and hassle-free than in northern Madhya Pradesh's other famed monument village, Khajuraho, making for a relaxed stay. There are great homestay options as well as opportunities to enjoy the surrounding pastoral countryside, with walking, cycling and rafting all on the agenda.

History

Orchha owes its glories to the Bundela clan of Rajputs, who set up their HQ here in 1531 and ruled over the Bundelkhand region (from Jhansi in the west to Panna in the east and Narsinghpur in the south) from Orchha till 1783. Orchha reached its zenith under Bir Singh Deo (r 1605–27), who was on good terms with the Mughal emperor Jehangir. In the 1630s Bir Singh Deo's son Jhujar Singh unwisely rebelled against Jehangir's son Shah Jahan, whose armies trashed the Orchha kingdom and damaged some of the town's fine buildings.

Sights

The combined ticket (Indian/foreigner ₹10/250, camera/video ₹25/200) for Orchha's sights covers seven monuments – the Jehangir Mahal, Raj Mahal, Rai Praveen Mahal, camel stables, *chhatris* (cenotaphs), Chaturbhuj Temple and Lakshmi Narayan Temple – and is only sold at the **ticket office** (⏲7.30am-5.30pm) at the Raj Mahal. You can walk around the grounds here for free. Also available here are official guides charging ₹470 for up to five people for four hours.

HANDY TRAINS FROM GWALIOR

DESTINATION	TRAIN NO & NAME	FARE (₹)	DURATION (HR)	DEPARTURE
Agra	12617 Mangala Lakshadweep	170/540/740 (A)	2	8.10am
Bhopal	12002 Bhopal Shatabdi	770/1525 (B)	4¼	9.33am
Delhi	12625 Kerala Exp	240/605/840 (A)	5½	8.25am
Indore	12920 Malwa Exp	385/1005/1425 (A)	12	12.35am
Jaipur	19665 Udaipur-Khajuraho Exp	225/605/860 (A)	7	3.45pm
Jhansi	12002 Bhopal Shatabdi	310/650 (B)	1¼	9.33am
Khajuraho	19666 Udaipur-Khajuraho Exp	120/490/695 (A)	5	1.40pm

Fares: (A) sleeper/3AC/2AC, (B) chair/1AC

Palace Area

Crossing the granite bridge from the village centre over the often dry water channel brings you to a fortified complex created by the Bundelas and dominated by two wonderful palaces – the Raj Mahal and Jehangir Mahal.

In several rooms of the 16th-century **Raj Mahal** (dawn-dusk), deities such as Brahma, Vishnu, Rama, Krishna and Sita, plus Orchha royalty, wrestle, hunt, fight and dance their way across walls and ceilings in vivid, colourful murals. The upper floors give great views across the town through their pretty *jali* (stone lattice) windows. A **sound-and-light show** (Indian/Foreigner ₹100/250; English 7.30pm Mar-Nov, 6.30pm Dec-Feb, Hindi 8.45pm Mar-Nov, 7.45pm Dec-Feb) that's more sound than light, and is only likely to enthuse those interested in Orchha's history, takes place outside the Raj Mahal each evening.

The massive **Jehangir Mahal** (dawn-dusk), an assault course of steep staircases and precipitous walkways, represents a zenith of Indo-Islamic architecture. More decorative than the Raj Mahal, it was built, or at least completed, in the early 17th century by Bir Singh Deo, possibly for a visit by emperor Jehangir. Its walls are crowned by eight domed turrets and eight slender domed pavilions, and superbly devised sightlines carry your gaze through successive arches and doorways to *jali* screens with views over the countryside or town around.

Behind the palace, the **'camel stables'** (Ount Khana; dawn-dusk) (maybe actually a royal pleasure pavilion), overlook a green landscape dotted with monuments. Downhill from here are the **Khana Hammam** (Royal Bathhouse; dawn-dusk), with fine vaulted ceilings, and the **Rai Praveen Mahal** (9am-5pm), a pavilion built for a famous 16th-century courtesan, with a semi-well-kept formal Mughal garden. Murals inside the building immortalise Praveen, dancing, and her lover, Raja Indrajit, on horseback.

Town Centre

★Ram Raja Temple HINDU TEMPLE

(9am-12.30pm & 7-10.30pm Oct-Mar, 8am-12.30pm & 8-10.30pm Apr-Sep) At the west end of a lively square is the pink- and tangerine-domed Ram Raja Temple, the only temple where Rama is worshipped as a king and busy with crowds of devotees every day. Built as a palace for Madhukar Shah's wife in the 16th century, it became a temple when an image of Rama, temporarily installed by the rani, proved impossible to move.

★Chaturbhuj Temple HINDU TEMPLE

(9am-5pm) The spectacular soaring spires of the 16th-century Chaturbhuj Temple are visible from all over town. The Chaturbhuj has never been used for its intended purpose of housing the Rama idol that remains in the Ram Raja Temple next door. You can climb a steep, dark staircase, from the door at the northwest corner of its central interior space, to emerge among the mossy roof pinnacles for the best views in town.

Phool Bagh GARDENS

(8am-8pm) Prince Dinman Hardol is venerated as a hero in Bundelkhand for committing suicide to 'prove his innocence' over a supposed affair with his brother's wife. His memorial is in the Phool Bagh, a traditional *charbagh* (formal Persian garden, divided into quarters) adjacent to his palace, the Palaki Mahal. It's an animated scene here with women singing songs about him, tying threads onto the memorial's *jali* (carved lattice screen) and walking around it five times, making wishes they hope he'll grant.

Other Areas

★Chhatris ISLAMIC TOMB

(9am-5pm) Funerary monuments to Orchha royalty, the huge and serene *chhatris* rise beside the Betwa River at the south end of town. They're best seen at dusk, when birds reel above the children splashing at the river ghats and cinematic sunsets drop across the river. Bir Singh Deo's *chhatri* is set slightly apart, right on the riverbank.

Lakshmi Narayan Temple HINDU TEMPLE

(9am-5pm) This soaring temple-cum-fort, on the road out to Ganj village, has fine rooftop views and well-preserved murals on the ceilings of its domed towers.

Activities

If your hotel lacks a pool, you could just cool off in the Betwa – it's one of India's cleanest rivers.

Orchha Wildlife Sanctuary CYCLING, WALKING

(Indian/foreigner ₹15/150; dawn-dusk) This 44-sq-km sliver of wooded island between the Betwa and the rock-strewn Jamni River makes an enjoyable few hours' cycling or

Orchha

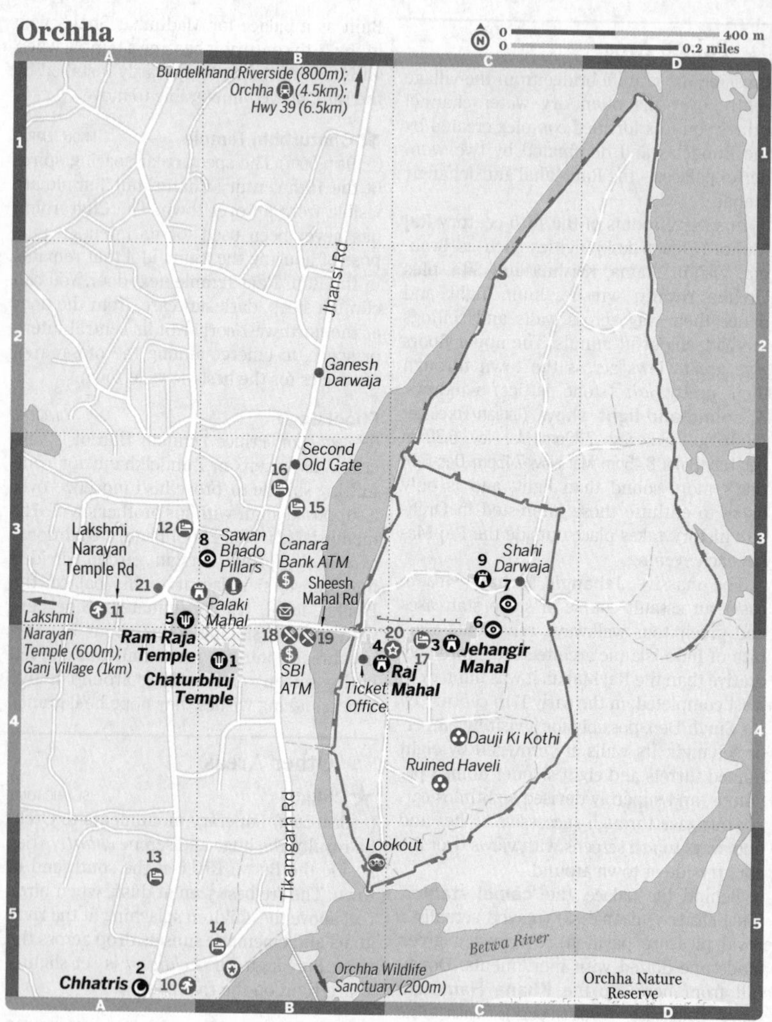

(in temperate weather) walking. The ticket office is 250m after the causeway at the south end of Orchha. Most people follow a route of about 8km starting from the entry gate 1km past the ticket office, visiting the riverside spot Pachmariya and two lookout towers, before emerging on the road again 2km south of where you entered.

River-Rafting RAFTING

(per raft per 1½hr ₹1500) There are some minor rapids upstream from the *chhatris* (cenotaphs) and below the causeway, but this is really just an enjoyable scenic float. Buy tickets at the Betwa Retreat (p633): trips start from the boat club just in front. Rafts take up to six people. There's no minimum number.

Raju Bike CYCLING

(Lakshmi Narayan Temple Rd; per hr/day ₹10/50; ⏲6am-9pm) Hires out rickety bicycles at unbeatable prices.

Kairali Spa AYURVEDA

(☎07680-252222; www.orchharesort.com; treatments ₹900-2500; ⏲8.30am-8.30pm) Orchha Resort offers good-quality ayurvedic massage treatments.

Orchha

Sleeping

Aditya Hotel HOTEL $

(07680-252027; adityahotelorchha@gmail.com; r ₹700-1500;) Just behind Phool Bagh, Aditya provides clean, medium-sized, all-white rooms with prices depending on whether they're upstairs or down and are or aren't air-conditioned. Some upstairs rooms have temple and palace views, and you can have breakfast on a nice little roof terrace up there.

Hotel Monarch Rama HOTEL $

(07680-252015; hotelmonarchrama@gmail.com; Jhansi Rd; r ₹800, with AC ₹1200;) Rooms here are cleaner and more appealing than at most of the budget competition, and staff are friendly too. Sheets are clean, the bathrooms don't smell, and there are even Indian miniature prints on the walls. No natural light, however, except a little in the two air-con rooms, upstairs, where there's also a small restaurant.

Hotel Fort View HOTEL $

(07680-252701; fortvieworchha@rediffmail.com; Jhansi Rd; r ₹400-600, with AC ₹1000;) Rooms at this recently repainted budget hotel are set beside a long courtyard and have clean sheets on hardish beds. Best are rooms 108, 111 and 112, with good views to the river and the Jehangir Mahal and Raja Mahal beyond.

★**Hotel Sheesh Mahal** HERITAGE HOTEL $$

(07680-252624; www.mptourism.com; incl breakfast s/d ₹1950/2830, ste ₹5390-6570;) Literally palatial and like sleeping with history, this hotel occupies an 18th-century former royal guesthouse adjoining the Jehangir Mahal. The eight different rooms are all gorgeous, with colourful traditional-style paintings, thick, pelmeted curtains, cute alcoves and bathrooms that could give you agoraphobia. (The only single, however, is disappointingly claustrophobic.)

Betwa Retreat HOTEL $$

(07680-252618; www.mptourism.com; cottage/r/ste ₹2830/3260/5040;) MP Tourism's main Orchha property makes a pretty good choice, with the accommodation and a good pool set amid well-kept gardens with views to the river and the *chhatris* (cenotaphs). The 'cottages' are large safari-style tents with solid floors and half-walls, plus bathrooms, good beds, air-con and minibars. Rooms, in vaguely traditional style, are similarly comfy and have tea/coffee equipment.

★**Amar Mahal** HOTEL $$$

(07680-252102; www.amarmahal.com; s/d from ₹5460/6650, ste ₹11,760;) Kick your feet up like a maharaja in rooms featuring lovely wood-carved four-poster beds, set around gorgeous courtyards with white-pillar verandahs or a large pristine pool. The architecture is in traditional Orchha style but the building is modern (opened in 2003) and has all mod cons – including the good **Kerala Ayurvedic Centre** (07680-252102 ext 167; treatments ₹500-2000; 8am-9pm). This is probably Orchha's most luxurious stay.

Bundelkhand Riverside HOTEL $$$
(9009749630; www.bundelkhandriverside.com; s/d incl breakfast ₹4300/4600;) Owned by the grandson of Orchha's last king, this hotel feels authentically heritage, although the main building is less than 20 years old. Antique-style furniture abounds and some of the maharaja's personal art collection is displayed in the corridors. Exquisite rooms overlook either the river or the graceful gardens, which contain four 16th-century temples as well as a small swimming pool.

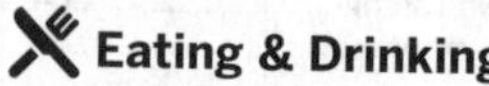

Eating & Drinking

Laxmi Betwa Tarang INDIAN, CONTINENTAL $
(Sheesh Mahal Rd; mains ₹80-180; 7am-10pm;) This place does the best veg food of any of Orchha's budget restaurants – the thalis (₹130 to ₹350) are particularly good. It also has the attraction of a rooftop terrace where you can sit with stupendous views of the Raj Mahal. Beers are off menu but available.

RamRaja Restaurant INDIAN, CONTINENTAL $
(Sheesh Mahal Rd; mains ₹75-395; 7am-10.30pm;) No hygiene awards here, but this friendly, family-run streetside restaurant offers eggy breakfasts, muesli, pancakes, tasty vegetarian fare and pretty decent espresso under the shade of a large tree. Can also scare up a beer.

Bundela Restaurant INDIAN $$
(Betwa Retreat; mains ₹140-350; 8am-10.30pm) Continental and Chinese dishes are on offer as well as the reliably good Indian fare at this licensed hotel restaurant – and the live traditional Bundelkhandi music by a trio and singer on the terrace makes evenings a bit special.

Jharokha Restaurant INDIAN $$
(Hotel Sheesh Mahal; mains ₹140-350; 8am-10.30pm;) Good food and friendly waiters, in the elegant pillared hall of a former royal guesthouse, are a cut above what you'd normally expect from a government-run hotel. Indian, Chinese and Continental dishes are on offer, but as usual the Indian (especially tandoori items) are recommended. They can usually supply beer or whisky, too.

Information

Orchha Tourist Service (OTS; 9981749660; www.otstoursindia.com; behind Ram Raja Temple; 8.30am-9.30pm) This agency, run by Romi Samele, is the representative in town for

VILLAGE IMMERSION HOMESTAYS IN GANJ

Thanks to **Orchha Home-Stay** (9993385405, 9410762072; www.orchha.org; s ₹700-800, d ₹1000-1200, meals ₹50-250;), a successful and popular homestay program started by the non-profit organisation Friends of Orchha in 2009, travellers have a wonderful opportunity to stay with local people and experience village life in Ganj, 1km west of central Orchha. You'll be staying in simple village homes and eating simple village meals, but you may be amazed at how spotlessly clean the houses are, and you can rent bikes (₹50 per day) to explore Orchha and the surrounding area.

Don't expect luxury – you'll be sleeping on charpoys (rope beds) in most cases – but the eight rooms, in six homes in the small village, are better and more charming than a lot of budget hotels. Rooms have insulated walls and tiled roofs and are equipped with fans and mosquito nets. Most houses have sit-down toilets, while others have dry-composting squat toilets or a squat toilet linked to a bio-gas digester.

The interaction with villagers and immersion into village life is priceless (so you probably won't want the wi-fi; ₹100 per day) and guests are provided with a helpful information folder, which includes ideas about what to do and where to go around Ganj and Orchha.

If you want to stay one night only, you can, but room rates will be slightly higher than for longer stays. In any case, the slow pace of life in Ganj is something to be savoured and most guests stay several nights.

Friends of Orchha has an office, open from 3pm, on the right-hand side of the road as you enter Ganj, but it's easy to book directly online through their website, or make arrangements through the program's manager, Romi Samele, at **Orchha Tourist Service** (p634) in Orchha.

Friends of Orchha also runs an after-school youth club for village children. Options to volunteer (eg for teachers and doctors) and donate are available.

Orchha Home-Stay at Ganj, and is also good for all kinds of travel bookings.

Getting There & Away

Getting to or from Orchha by public transport almost always involves getting to the larger town of Jhansi, 18km northwest, first. Jhansi is on the Delhi–Agra–Gwalior–Bhopal rail route, with more than 30 daily trains in each direction. From Jhansi train station an autorickshaw to Orchha (45 minutes) costs ₹200 to ₹250; a taxi (30 minutes) is ₹500 to ₹600. Or get a tempo (₹10) from the train station to the bus station, 4km east, then another tempo to Orchha (₹20, 45 minutes).

TO/FROM KHAJURAHO

Buses from Jhansi go to Chhatarpur (₹130, three hours, hourly 5am to 10pm), where you can switch for Khajuraho (₹50, 1½ hours). Coming from Khajuraho, you can ask the bus driver to drop you at the Orchha turn-off on Hwy 39, where you should be able to wave down a vehicle to take you to Orchha.

Train 19666, the Udaipur-Khajuraho Express, theoretically departs Jhansi at 3.30pm, reaching Khajuraho (sleeper/3AC/2AC ₹160/490/695) at 6.30pm, but it averages two hours late out of Jhansi. Even less reliable is train 54159, which leaves Orchha's tiny train station, 5km north of town on the Jhansi road, at 7.25am for Mahoba (₹30, 2¾ hours). From Mahoba train 51821 departs at 10.40am, reaching Khajuraho (₹15) at noon. These trains are slow, with unreserved 2nd-class seating only, and are often very crowded. If you miss the connection at Mahoba (quite likely) the next train to Khajuraho isn't due till 6.05pm.

Or take a taxi (₹2500 from Orchha to Khajuraho, four hours).

Khajuraho

07686 / POP 24,500

The erotic and other carvings that swathe Khajuraho's three groups of World Heritage–listed temples are among the finest temple art in the world. The Western Group of temples, in particular, contains some stunning sculptures.

Khajuraho is fully on the tour bus map, and the touts infesting the town can be a pain in the neck. But they're not so bad that you should contemplate missing out on these beautiful temples.

The temples are superb examples of north Indian architecture, but it's their liberally embellished carvings that have made Khajuraho famous. Around the outsides of the temples are bands of exceedingly artistic stonework showing a storyboard of life a millennium ago – gods, goddesses, warriors, musicians, dancers and real and mythological animals.

Two elements appear repeatedly – women and sex. Sensuous, posturing *surasundaris* and *apsaras* (heavenly nymphs) and *nayikas* (heroines) have been carved with a half-twist and slight sideways lean that make the playful figures dance and swirl out from the temple. The *mithunas* (pairs, threesomes etc of men and women depicted in erotic poses) display the great skill of the sculptors and the dexterity of the Chandelas.

History

Legend has it that Khajuraho was founded by Chandravarman, son of the moon god Chandra, who descended and saw a beautiful maiden, Hemavati, as she bathed in a stream. Historians tell us that most of the 85 original temples (of which 25 remain) were built between AD 930 and 1050 during the zenith of the Chandela dynasty, a Rajput clan who ruled varying amounts of Bundelkhand (straddling northern Madhya Pradesh and southern Uttar Pradesh) between the 9th and 16th centuries. It's not clear whether Khajuraho was the Chandelas' capital or more of a sacred ceremonial centre. Mahoba, 50km north, was certainly their capital from some time in the 11th century, though the Khajuraho temples remained active long after this.

Khajuraho's isolation may well have helped preserve it from the desecration Muslim invaders inflicted on 'idolatrous' temples elsewhere. Perhaps for the same reason the area was slowly abandoned and overtaken by jungle, with many buildings falling into ruin. The wider world remained largely ignorant until British officer TS Burt was apparently guided to the ruins by his palanquin bearers in 1838.

Sights

Western Group – Inside the Fenced Enclosure

Khajuraho's most striking and best-preserved temples are those within the fenced-off section of the **Western Group** (Indian/foreigner ₹30/500, video ₹25; dawn-dusk) and these are the only temples here that you have to pay to see. An Archaeological Survey of India (ASI) guidebook to Khajuraho

Khajuraho

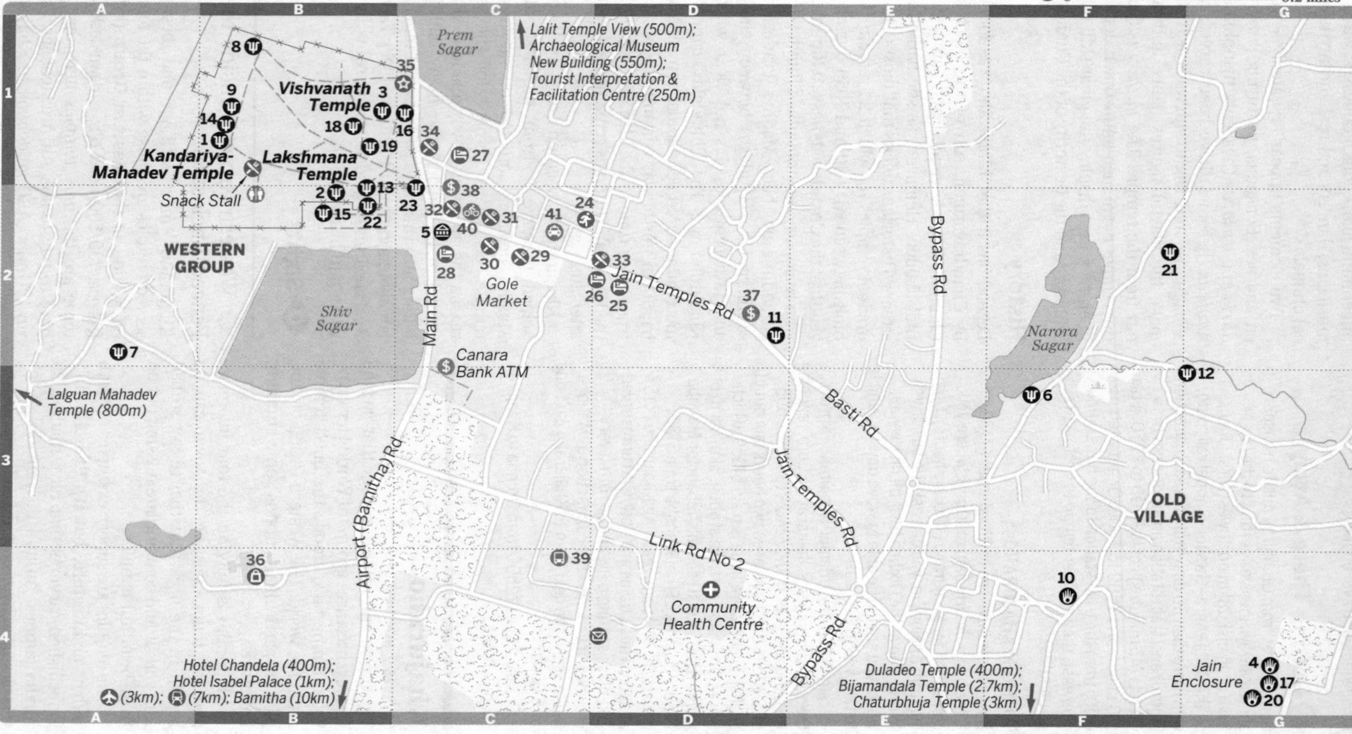
0 400 m
0 0.2 miles
Lalit Temple View (500m); Archaeological Museum New Building (550m); Tourist Interpretation & Facilitation Centre (250m)
Prem Sagar
Vishvanath Temple
Kandariya-Mahadev Temple
Lakshmana Temple
Snack Stall
WESTERN GROUP
Shiv Sagar
Main Rd
Gole Market
Canara Bank ATM
Jain Temples Rd
Bypass Rd
Basti Rd
Narora Sagar
OLD VILLAGE
Link Rd No 2
Airport (Bamitha) Rd
Community Health Centre
Lalguan Mahadev Temple (800m)
Hotel Chandela (400m); Hotel Isabel Palace (1km); (3km); (7km); Bamitha (10km)
Duladeo Temple (400m); Bijamandala Temple (2.7km); Chaturbhuja Temple (3km)
Jain Enclosure
1
2
3
4
5
6
7
8
9
10
11
12
13
14
15
16
17
18
19
20
21
22
23
24
25
26
27
28
29
30
31
32
33
34
35
36
37
38
39
40
41
A
B
C
D
E
F
G

Khajuraho

Top Sights
1 Kandariya-Mahadev Temple.................B1
2 Lakshmana Temple.................B2
3 Vishvanath Temple.................B1

Sights
4 Adinath Temple.................G4
5 Archaeological Museum.................C2
6 Brahma Temple.................F3
7 Chausath Yogini Temple.................A2
8 Chitragupta Temple.................B1
9 Devi Jagadamba Temple.................B1
10 Ghantai Temple.................F4
11 Hanuman Temple.................D2
12 Javari Temple.................G3
13 Lakshmi Shrine.................B2
14 Mahadeva Temple.................B1
15 Matangesvara Temple.................B2
16 Nandi Shrine.................C1
17 Parsvanath Temple.................G4
18 Parvati Temple.................B1
19 Pratapeswar Temple.................B1
20 Shantinath Temple.................G4
21 Vamana Temple.................F2
22 Varaha Shrine.................B2
23 Western Group.................C2

Activities, Courses & Tours
24 Ayur Arogyam.................C2

Sleeping
25 Hotel Harmony.................D2
26 Hotel Surya.................D2
27 Hotel Yogi Lodge.................C1
28 Zostel.................C2

Eating
29 Evening Food Stalls.................C2
30 La Bella Italia.................C2
31 Lassi Corner.................C2
32 Madras Coffee House.................C2
33 Mediterraneo.................D2
34 Raja Cafe.................C1

Entertainment
35 Sound-&-Light Show.................C1

Shopping
36 Kandariya.................B4

Information
37 SBI ATM.................D2
38 State Bank of India.................C2
Union Bank ATM.................(see 34)

Transport
Bus Reservation Office.................(see 39)
39 Bus Stand.................C4
40 Mohammed Bilal.................C2
41 Yashowarman Taxi Driver Union.................C2

(₹60) may be available at the ticket office. Officially licensed guides cost ₹1190/1508 for a half-/full day, plus ₹476/635 for languages other than English or Hindi.

A nightly **sound-and-light show** (Indian/foreigner ₹200/500, child ₹100/250; English 6.30pm Oct-Feb, 7.30pm Mar-Sep, Hindi 7.40pm Oct-Feb, 8.40pm Mar-Sep) sees technicolour floodlights sweep across the temples of the Western Group as Indian classical music accompanies a potted history of Khajuraho narrated by the 'master sculptor'. Photography is prohibited.

★Lakshmana Temple — HINDU TEMPLE

The large Lakshmana Temple took 20 years to build and was completed in about AD 954 during the reign of Dhanga, according to an inscription in its *mandapa* (pillared front pavilion). It's arguably the best preserved of all the Khajuraho temples. On the southern side of its base are some of Khajuraho's most orgiastic carvings, including one gentleman proving that a horse can be a man's best friend while a shocked figure peeps out from behind her hands.

You'll see carvings of battalions of soldiers on the frieze around the base – the Chandelas were generally at war when they weren't inventing new sexual positions – as well as musicians, hunters and plenty of elephants, horses and camels. Some superb carvings can also be found around the *garbhagriha* (inner sanctum). The temple is dedicated to Vishnu, although it's similar in design to the Shiva temples Vishvanath and Kandariya-Mahadev.

The two small shrines facing Lakshmana's east end are the **Lakshmi Temple** (usually locked) and the **Varaha Temple**, containing a wonderful, 1.5m-high sandstone carving of Vishnu as his boar avatar, dating from AD 900 and meticulously carved with a pantheon of gods.

★Kandariya-Mahadev Temple — HINDU TEMPLE

The 30.5m-long Kandariya-Mahadev, built between 1025 and 1050, is the largest Western Group temple and represents the highpoint of Chandela architecture. It also has the most representations of female beauty and sexual acrobatics of any Khajuraho

Khajuraho Temples

WESTERN-GROUP TOUR

The sheer volume of artwork at Khajuraho's best-preserved temples can be overwhelming. Initiate yourself with this introductory tour, which highlights some of those easy-to-miss details.

First, admire the ❶ **sandstone boar** in the Varaha shrine before heading to the ❷ **Lakshmana Temple** to study the south side of the temple's base, which has some of the raunchiest artwork in Khajuraho: first up, a nine-person orgy; further along, a guy getting very friendly with a horse. Up on the temple platform see a superb dancing Ganesh carved into a niche (south side), before walking to the west end for graceful *surasundaris* (nymphs): removing a thorn from a foot or draped in a wet sari (northwest corner) or looking into a mirror (southwest corner).

Next is Khajuraho's largest temple, ❸ **Kandariya-Mahadev**. Carvings to look for here include the famous headstand position (south side), but the most impressive thing about this temple is the scale of it, particularly its soaring rooftops.

❹ **Mahadeva** and ❺ **Devi Jagadamba** share the same stone plinth as Kandariya-Mahadev, as do four beautifully carved *sardulas* (part-lion, part-human mythical beasts), each caressing a nymph – one is at the entrance to Mahadeva; the other three stand alone on the plinth.

Walk north from here to the ❻ **Chitragupta Temple**, with miniature elephants and hunting scenes among its lowest band of reliefs. Inside, spot the tiny sculpture of the seven horses pulling sun god Surya's chariot.

Continue east to the ❼ **Vishvanath Temple** for more fabulous carvings before admiring the impressive statue of Shiva's bull in the ❽ **Nandi shrine** opposite.

BODOM/SHUTTERSTOCK ©

Headstand Position
Perhaps Khajurah most famous carv ing, this flexible flirtation is above you as you stand c the south side of t awesome Kandari Mahadev.

Sikharas
Despite its many fine statues, perhaps the most impressive thing about Kandariya-Mahadev is its soaring *sikharas* (temple rooftops), said to represent the Himalayan abode of the gods.

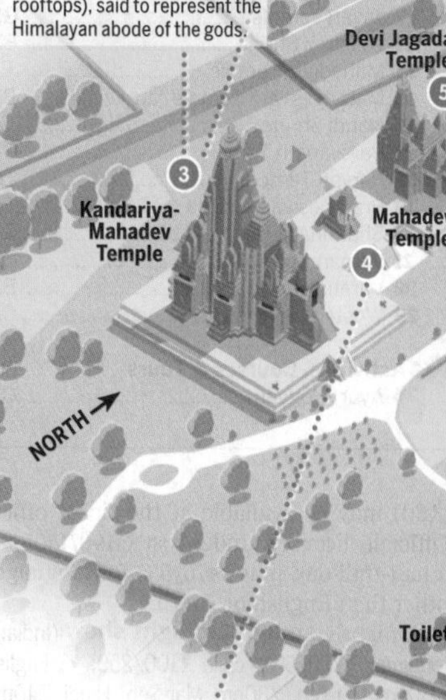

Sardula Statue
There are four nymph-caressing *sardulas* on this huge stone plinth, but this one, guarding the entrance to Mahadeva, is our favourite.

ELENA MIRAGE/SHUTTERSTOCK ©

Kama Sutra Carvings
Although commor referred to as Kam Sutra carvings, Khajuraho's erotic artwork does not properly illustrate Vatsyayana's famous sutra. Debate continues to its significance: fertility symbolism or to imply rulers here were virile, th powerful? Interest ingly, the erotic carvings are never located close to th temple deity.

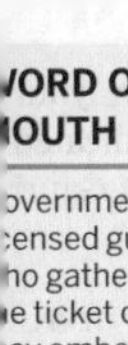

ᴉORD OF ᴉOUTH

ᴐvernment-
ᴄensed guides,
ᴉno gather near
ᴉe ticket office,
ᴉay embellish
ᴉe history a bit
ᴉt they do help
ᴉring the old
ᴉones to life.

JEREMYRICHARDS/GETTY IMAGES

JEREMYRICHARDS/SHUTTERSTOCK ©

6 Chitragupta Temple

Toilets

7 Vishvanath Temple

JUST THE TICKET

For an extra-close look at Khajuraho artwork, use your ticket for entrance to the town's Archaeological Museum.

Parvati Temple

8 Nandi Shrine

ᴉakshmana Temple

2

Pratapeswar Temple

Lakshmi Shrine

1 Varaha Shrine

Entrance

Matangesvara Temple

Nandi Statue

This massive 2.2m-long statue of Nandi, the bull-vehicle of Shiva, is enshrined in a pavilion facing Vishvanath Temple.

ᴉurasundaris

ᴉautifully graceful depictions of nymphs are ᴉnd on a number of Khajuraho temples. And ᴉspite all the depictions of gymnastic orgies, ᴉe seductive *surasundari* draped in a wet sari is ᴉuably the most erotic of all.

Vishnu's Boar

This 9th-/10th-century statue of Varaha, the boar incarnation of Vishnu, is carved all over with figures of Brahmanical gods and goddesses. At Varaha's feet notice the serpent Seshanaga in a devotional posture, and the feet of a goddess, now missing.

FOTOEMBER/GETTY IMAGES ©

temple. There are 872 statues, most nearly 1m high – taller than those at the other temples. One frequently photographed sculpture on the south side illustrates the feasibility of the headstand position.

The 31m-high *sikhara* (temple spire) here is, like a lingam, a phallic Shiva symbol, worshipped by Hindus hoping to seek deliverance from the cycle of reincarnation. It and the *mandapa* (pillared pavilion) are decorated with 84 subsidiary spires, which make up a mountain-like rooftop scene reminiscent of the Himalayan abode of the gods.

Mahadeva Temple HINDU TEMPLE

Mahadeva, a small, partly ruined temple on the same platform as Kandariya-Mahadev and Devi Jagadamba, is dedicated to Shiva, who is carved on the lintel of its doorway. It houses one of Khajuraho's finest sculptures – a *sardula* (mythical beast that's part lion, part other animal – possibly human) engaged in a mutual caress with a kneeling woman.

Devi Jagadamba Temple HINDU TEMPLE

Devi Jagadamba was originally dedicated to Vishnu, but later to Parvati and then Kali. The carvings include *sardulas* accompanied by Vishnu, *surasundaris* (heavenly nymphs), and *mithunas* (pairs of men and women) frolicking in the third band up. Its three-part design is simpler than that of the Kandariya-Mahadev and Chitragupta Temples. It has more in common with Chitragupta, but is less embellished with carvings so is thought to be a little older.

Chitragupta Temple HINDU TEMPLE

The Chitragupta Temple (1000–25) is unique in Khajuraho – and rare among North Indian temples – in being dedicated to the sun god Surya. While its condition is not as good as the other Western Group temples, it has some fine carvings of *apsaras* and *surasundaris*, elephant fights and hunting scenes, *mithunas* and a procession of stone-carriers.

In the dark inner sanctum, at the base of the statue, you can make out the seven horses that pull Surya's chariot, while in the lower of the two main niches beneath the *sikhara* on the south side is an 11-headed carving of Vishnu, representing the god and 10 of his 22 incarnations.

Parvati Temple HINDU TEMPLE

Walking around the Western Group enclosure from the Chitragupta Temple you come to the closed-up Parvati Temple on your right, a small temple originally dedicated to Vishnu and now with an image of Gauri (Parvati) riding an iguana.

★Vishvanath Temple HINDU TEMPLE

Believed to have been built in 1002, the Vishvanath Temple anticipates the plan and style of the Kandariya-Mahadev Temple. Dedicated to Shiva, it's a superlative example of Chandela architecture, with a riot of carved figures continuing up to the highest levels of the *sikharas*. Sculptures include a female doing a headstand in the north-side recess; sensuous *surasundaris* writing letters, cuddling babies, looking in mirrors and scratching their backs; and miniature camels, horses, musicians, elephants, warriors and dancers in the lowest frieze.

At the east end of the platform, a 2.2m-long statue of **Nandi**, Shiva's bull vehicle, faces the temple. The basement of this 12-pillared shrine is decorated with an elephant frieze that recalls similar work on the Lakshmana Temple's facade.

Pratapeswar Temple HINDU TEMPLE

Near the Vishvanath Temple, the white Pratapeswar is a much more recent bricks-and-mortar structure built around 200 years ago.

Western Group – Outside the Fenced Enclosure

Matangesvara Temple HINDU TEMPLE

(dawn-dusk) Right next to the Lakshmana Temple but separated from it by the enclosure fence, Matangesvara is the only temple in the Western Group still in everyday use. It may be the plainest temple here (suggesting an early construction), but inside it sports a polished 2.5m-high lingam (phallic symbol of Shiva).

Chausath Yogini Temple HINDU TEMPLE

The ruins of Chausath Yogini, beyond Shiv Sagar lake, date from the late 9th century and are probably the oldest at Khajuraho. You may find it locked up. Constructed entirely of granite, this is the only temple not aligned east–west. *Chausath* means 64 – the temple once had 64 cells for statues of the *yoginis* (female attendants) of Kali, while the 65th sheltered the goddess herself. It's reputedly India's oldest *yogini* temple.

Lalguan Mahadev Temple TEMPLE

About 800m west from the Chausath Yogini Temple (p640), down a track and across a couple of fields (just ask the locals), is the sandstone-and-granite Lalguan Mahadev Temple (AD 900), a small ruined shrine to Shiva.

Archaeological Museum MUSEUM

(www.museumkhajurahoasi.nic.in; Main Rd; 9am-5pm Sat-Thu) The Archaeological Museum has a good collection of sculptures from around Khajuraho, starting in the entrance hall with a wonderful 11th-century statue of Ganesh dancing remarkably sensuously for an elephant-headed deity, with a tiny mouse (his vehicle) at his feet. Admission is only with a same-day ticket for the Western Group (p635). A brighter, purpose-built, new museum building, north of the Western Group, opened in 2016, containing more Khajuraho sculptures plus information panels on Chandela history and art.

The new building's displays were still works in progress at research time, and it's not clear whether the old museum will eventually close or whether both buildings will remain open.

Eastern Group

The eastern group includes several Hindu temples scattered around the old village and four Jain temples further south, three of which are in a walled enclosure.

Hanuman Temple HINDU TEMPLE

(Basti Rd) The small, white Hanuman Temple contains a 2.5m-tall orange-painted statue of the Hindu monkey god. Its interest is in the pedestal inscription from AD 922, the oldest dateable inscription in Khajuraho.

Brahma Temple HINDU TEMPLE

The granite Brahma Temple, with its sandstone *sikhara* (temple spire) overlooking Narora Sagar, is one of the oldest in Khajuraho, dating from about AD 900. Inside is an unusual Shiva lingam with four faces (which led to the temple being incorrectly named after the four-faced Brahma) – but the image of Vishnu above the sanctum doorway reveals its original dedication to Vishnu.

Javari Temple HINDU TEMPLE

(dawn-dusk) Resembling the Chaturbhuja Temple in the southern group, the Javari Temple (1075–1100) stands just north of the old village. It's dedicated to Vishnu and is a good example of small-scale Khajuraho architecture for its crocodile-covered entrance arch and slender *sikhara*.

Vamana Temple HINDU TEMPLE

(dawn-dusk) The Vamana Temple (1050–75), 300m north of the old village, is dedicated to the dwarf incarnation of Vishnu. It has quirky touches such as elephants protruding from the walls, but its *sikhara* is devoid of subsidiary spires and there are few erotic scenes.

Ghantai Temple JAIN TEMPLE

Located between the old village and the Jain Enclosure, the small Ghantai Temple, also Jain, is named after the *ghanta* (chain and bell) decorations on its pillars. It was once similar to the nearby Parsvanath Temple, but only the pillared shell of its porch and *mandapa* (pillared pavilion) remain, and it's normally locked.

Shantinath Temple JAIN TEMPLE

Shantinath, a mixture of old and modern construction, is the main place of worship in the Jain group. It has a collection of components from older temples, including a 4.5m-high Adinath statue with a plastered-over inscription on the pedestal dating to about 1028.

Parsvanath Temple JAIN TEMPLE

(dawn-dusk) While not competing in size or erotica with the Western Group temples, this largest of the Jain temples in the walled enclosure is notable for the exceptional precision of its construction as well as for its sculptural beauty. Some of the best preserved examples of Khajuraho's most famous images can be seen here, including the woman removing a thorn from her foot and another applying eye makeup, both on the southern side.

Adinath Temple JAIN TEMPLE

The late-11th-century Adinath has been partially restored over the centuries. With fine carvings on its three bands of sculptures, it's similar to Khajuraho's Hindu temples, particularly Vamana. Only the striking black image in the inner sanctum triggers a Jain reminder.

Southern Group

A paved road running south from near the Jain enclosure leads to three temples that are not Khajuraho's most spectacular but make for a pleasant cycle into the countryside.

Duladeo Temple HINDU TEMPLE

(⏲dawn-dusk) The Duladeo Temple, dedicated to Shiva and set among well-tended gardens just above a small river, is Khajuraho's youngest temple, dating to 1100–50. Its relatively wooden, repetitive carvings suggest that Khajuraho's sculptors had passed their artistic peak by this point, although they had certainly lost none of their zeal for eroticism.

Chaturbhuja Temple HINDU TEMPLE

(⏲dawn-dusk) The small Chaturbhuja Temple (c 1100) anticipates Duladeo and its flaws, but has a fine 2.7m-high, four-armed statue of Vishnu in the sanctum. It is Khajuraho's only developed temple without erotic sculptures.

It's 1.7km past Duladeo: go through Jatkara village and turn left at the T-junction 350m later.

Bijamandala Temple HINDU TEMPLE

(⏲dawn-dusk) The 700m track to Bijamandala veers left (signposted) 200m before you reach Chaturbhuja Temple. This is the excavated mound of an 11th-century temple, dedicated to Shiva (judging by the white marble lingam at the apex of the mound).

There are remnants of a small-scale frieze with elephants and dancers, but unfinished carvings were also excavated, suggesting that what would have been Khajuraho's largest temple was abandoned as resources flagged.

Activities

Many budget hotels offer cheap ayurvedic massage treatments of varying levels of authenticity. Top-end hotels offer more luxurious versions.

Ayur Arogyam MASSAGE

(☎07686-272572; www.ayurarogyam.in; Jain Temples Rd; treatments ₹1000-1900) For the real deal, head to Ayur Arogyam, run by a lovely, professionally qualified and experienced Keralan couple.

Treatments range from half-hour head or back/neck massages to a supremely soothing one-hour *abhyangam* (full-body massage with medicated oils).

Festivals & Events

Festival of Dance DANCE, CRAFTS

(⏲late Feb) Free nightly Indian dance performances amid the Western Group temples are the focus of this weeklong festival, which packs Khajuraho with visitors.

Sleeping

Hefty discounts (20% to 50%) are available out of season (approximately April to September). Hotel staff are more than happy to organise tours and travel.

Zostel HOSTEL $

(☎07686-297009; www.zostel.com; Main Rd; dm/r ₹400/2000, with AC ₹500/2200; 📶) This bright new hostel painted in red, yellow and orange is perfectly positioned overlooking Shiv Sagar lake and offers well-kept accommodation in five six-bunk dorms and five spacious doubles. There's a great rooftop cafe doing inexpensive breakfasts and thalis, and everything is good and clean, including the guest kitchen.

Hotel Surya HOTEL $

(☎9425146203; www.hotelsuryakhajuraho.com; Jain Temples Rd; r ₹800-1000, with AC ₹1000-1500; ❄@📶) There's quite a range of rooms in this sprawling, well-run, decently kept hotel with whitewashed corridors, marble staircases and a lovely courtyard and garden out the back. Some rooms have balconies. Yoga and massage are available; wi-fi costs ₹50 per day.

Hotel Harmony HOTEL $

(☎07686-274135; www.hotelharmonyonline.com; Jain Temples Rd; r ₹1000, with AC ₹1500; ❄📶) Cosy, well-equipped rooms off marble corridors are tastefully decorated and come with mostly effective mosquito screens and cable TV. Good food is available at Zorba the Buddha restaurant and you can eat under the stars on the rooftop. Wi-fi is ₹50 per day.

Hotel Yogi Lodge HOTEL $

(☎9993687416; yogi_sharm@yahoo.com; off Main Rd; s ₹200-300, d ₹300-400; ❄@📶) Rooms at this backpacker-favourite cheapie are simple, but they're reasonably neat and well kept, and the sheets do seem to have been laundered. The small courtyards, free morning rooftop yoga, free wi-fi, and the upstairs patio restaurant with cute stone tables and an eclectic menu (mains ₹100 to ₹260), all give this place character and value.

★**Hotel Isabel Palace** HOTEL $$

(☎07686-274770; www.hotelisabelpalace.com; off Airport Rd; dm ₹450, r incl breakfast ₹1500-3500; ❄📶) This newish hotel along a quiet dirt road 1.5km south of town, in a far more pastoral setting than Khajuraho's main drag, is a star. The sparkling-clean rooms vary according to view (garden or sunrise), decor and furnishings, but all are spacious, very comfortable and with sizeable bathrooms and terrace or balcony. For budget travellers there's also a small dorm.

Surendra, the manager, is delightful and takes his family's hospitality business very seriously. You could eat off the floor in the stylish restaurant, which offers sunset views, as does the rooftop terrace, which is the best by far in town and candlelit for romantic dinners for guests at night.

★Lalit Temple View HOTEL **$$$**
(☎07686-272111; www.thelalit.com; Main Rd; d incl breakfast ₹13,510-14,120; ❄@📶≋) Sweeps aside all other five-star pretenders with supreme luxury, impeccable service and high prices. Rooms are immaculate with marble bathrooms, wood-carved furniture and tasteful artwork. If you're not fussed about temple views, there's a block of 'budget' rooms hidden away from the main grounds – all the same amenities for less than half the price, bookable only by phone or email.

Hotel Chandela HOTEL **$$$**
(☎07686-272366; www.tajhotels.com; Airport Rd; s ₹5950-7920, d ₹6500-8500; ❄📶≋) This Taj Group property, while not in the first flush of youth, is a good choice for solidly comfortable rooms, two good restaurants, a bar, a big pool, free bicycles and professional service, at less than stratospheric prices.

Eating & Drinking

For cheap eats, **evening food stalls** (dishes ₹20-60; ⏲approximately 7-11pm) selling omelettes, *momos* (Tibetan dumplings), South Indian items and paneer patties open up after sunset towards the west end of Jain Temple Rd.

You can get a beer at several of the rooftop restaurants in town, and the more expensive hotels all have bars or licensed restaurants.

Madras Coffee House SOUTH INDIAN **$**
(cnr Main & Jain Temples Rds; mains ₹60-200; ⏲8.30am-8.30pm) They've been serving great, honest South Indian fare for three generations in this narrow, friendly cafe – dosas, *idlis* (spongy round fermented rice cakes), *uttapams* (thick savoury rice pancakes), thalis – as well as coffee (Madras-style with chicory) and chai. The unique house speciality is the tasty egg, cheese and veg dosa (₹200).

Lassi Corner INDIAN **$**
(Jain Temples Rd; dishes ₹15-60, lassis ₹15-80; ⏲7.30am-10pm) This tin-and-brick shack is a great place for a quick chai break, lazy lassi (including 'special'), breakfast or simple Indian fare.

★Raja Cafe MULTICUISINE **$$**
(www.rajacafe.com; Main Rd; mains ₹170-370; ⏲8am-10pm; 📶) Raja's has been on top of its game for nearly 40 years, with espresso coffee, English breakfasts, wood-fired pizzas, superb Indian (including tandoori), Italian and Chinese dishes, and an otherwise eclectic menu full of things you might miss, depending on your passport (rosti, fish and chips, Belgian waffles...).

The temple-view terrace is great, as is the courtyard shaded by a 170-year-old neem tree. But it's the food that steals the show.

La Bella Italia ITALIAN **$$**
(Jain Temples Rd; mains ₹150-350; ⏲7.30am-10.30pm) The roof-terrace setting is prettily lit at night and the homemade pasta and sauces are among the most authentically Italian-tasting you'll find in India.

Mediterraneo ITALIAN **$$**
(Jain Temples Rd; mains ₹215-475, pizzas ₹375-525; ⏲7.30am-10pm; 📶) Mediterraneo manages acceptable Italian fare served on a lovely terrace overlooking the street. Dishes includes crêpes, salads, organic wholewheat pasta and surprisingly good wood-fired pizzas. Beer and Indian Sula wine are also available.

Shopping

Kandariya ARTS & CRAFTS
(☎07686-274031; Airport Rd; ⏲9am-8pm) Huge emporium where full-size replicas of some of Khajuraho's temple carvings can be bought – if you have a spare ₹10,000 to ₹1,000,000! Smaller, more affordable versions, along with textiles, brassware, wood carvings and marble inlay, can be found indoors.

Information

Community Health Centre (☎07686-272498, emergency 108; Link Rd No 2; ⏲24hr, consultations 8am-1pm & 5-6pm Mon-Fri) Helpful staff but with limited English.

State Bank of India (Main Rd; ⏲10.30am-2.30pm & 3-4.30pm Mon-Sat, closed 2nd & 4th Sat of the month) Exchanges foreign cash.

Tourist Interpretation & Facilitation Centre (☎07686-274051; khajuraho@mptourism.com; Main Rd; ⏲10am-6pm Mon-Sat, closed 2nd & 3rd Sat of the month) Has guidebooks and free leaflets on statewide tourist destinations. Also has stands at the airport and train station.

Tourist Police (☎07686-274690; Main Rd; ⏰24hr) Handy booth near the western temples.

Getting There & Away

AIR

Khajuraho airport, with a brand new terminal opened in 2016, is 5km south of town. **Jet Airways** (www.jetairways.com) flies from Delhi to Khajuraho and back, via Varanasi in both directions, daily from October to April. **Air India** (☎07686-274035; www.airindia.in; Temple Hotel, Airport) flies three times weekly from Delhi to Khajuraho via Varanasi and Agra, then back to Delhi via Varanasi, year-round.

BUS

If the **reservation office** (⏰7.30am-6pm) at the **bus stand** is closed, the owner of the Madhur coffee stand, across the yard, is very helpful and trustworthy with schedule information.

For Orchha, Jhansi and Gwalior, you have to catch a bus to Chhatarpur (₹50, 1½ hours, every 30 or 60 minutes, 7.30am to 7.30pm) and switch there. Jhansi-bound buses from Chhatarpur can drop you at the Orchha turn-off on Hwy 39, where you can wave down a tempo (₹10) to Orchha.

Buses also run to Madla (for Panna Tiger Reserve; ₹40, one hour, 8.30am, 10am, 12.30pm, 1pm, 3pm and 7.30pm), and there's a bus to Jabalpur (seat/sleeper ₹300/350, eight hours) at 7.30pm.

Much more frequent buses can be caught at Bamitha, 11km south on Hwy 39, where buses between Gwalior, Jhansi and Satna shuttle through all day. You can reach Bamitha by tempo or shared jeep (both ₹10) or autorickshaw (₹100) from the bus stand or as they drive down Airport Rd.

TAXI

Yashowarman Taxi Driver Union (Jain Temples Rd) is just off Jain Temples Rd, under a neem tree. Fares in non-AC cabs including all taxes and tolls: Satna ₹2500, Orchha ₹3200, Bandhavgarh ₹6000, Varanasi ₹8000, Agra ₹8000. Air-con cabs cost 15% to 25% more.

TRAIN

Three useful long-distance trains leave from Khajuraho station, 8km south of town:

Delhi 22447 Uttar Pradesh Sampark Kranti Express (sleeper/3AC/2AC ₹365/955/1350, 11 hours, 6.20pm daily), via Jhansi (₹190/540/740, five hours) and Agra (₹280/720/1010, eight hours)

Udaipur 19665 Khajuraho Udaipur Express (sleeper/3AC/2AC ₹485/1320/1915, 21 hours, 9.25am daily), via Jhansi (₹160/490/695, four hours), Gwalior, Jaipur and Ajmer

Varanasi 21107 Bundelkhand Link Express (sleeper/3AC ₹265/720, 11 hours, 11.50pm Tuesday, Friday and Sunday)

For Orchha you can take train 19665 to Jhansi and then local transport (p635) for the final 18km (total travel time about five hours).

The station's **reservation office** (⏰8am-noon & 1-4pm Mon-Sat, 8am-2pm Sun) makes bookings for all reservable trains in India.

Coming to Khajuraho, train 21108 leaves Varanasi Junction on Monday, Wednesday and Saturday at 5.45pm, reaching Khajuraho at 5.15am. The 12448 U P Sampark Kranti leaves Delhi's Hazrat Nizamuddin station daily at 8.10pm and passes Agra (11.05pm) before reaching Mahoba (5.08am) where part of the train continues to Khajuraho (6.35am). If you book a seat through from Nizamuddin to Khajuraho, you'll automatically be seated in the right carriages. From Jhansi, the 19666 Udaipur Khajuraho Express theoretically departs at 3.30pm and arrives in Khajuraho at 6.30pm, but is often an hour or two late.

Getting Around

Taxis to or from the airport cost ₹300; autorickshaws are ₹80. If you don't have too much luggage, it's easy enough to wave down a bus, tempo or shared jeep (₹10) as they head along Airport Rd into or out of town.

CONNECTIONS AT SATNA

The town of Satna, 120km east of Khajuraho on Hwy 39, is a hub for transport between Khajuraho, eastern Madhya Pradesh and Varanasi.

From Khajuraho there's one daily bus to Satna (₹150, 4½ hours, 3pm). In the other direction, the Satna–Khajuraho bus leaves at 2.30pm. Much more frequent buses travelling between Chhatarpur and Satna along Hwy 39 pass through Bamitha, 11km south of Khajuraho, and Madla (for Panna Tiger Reserve). You may have to change at Panna town, 19km east of Madla.

Satna's bus and train stations are 2.5km apart (autorickshaw ₹50). There are about 20 daily trains to Jabalpur (sleeper/3AC/2AC ₹170/540/740, three hours), 12 to Varanasi (₹240/605/840, six to eight hours), and trains to Umaria (for Bandhavgarh Tiger Reserve) at 4.40am and 7.10pm (₹140/490/695, 3½ hours) and at 7.25pm and 10.25pm (sleeper-class only, ₹100, 4½ hours).

An autorickshaw to or from the train station costs ₹100. Taxis charge ₹350/450 non-AC/AC.

Mohammed Bilal (☎9893240074; Jain Temples Rd; per day ₹100-150; ⏰8am-7pm) Bicycle is a great way to get around. Mohammad has been in the bike business since 1982. He rents bikes and mountain bikes in varying conditions.

Panna Tiger Reserve

Tigers are making a comeback after being reintroduced in 2009 to **Panna Tiger Reserve** (☎07732-252135; www.pannatigerreserve.in; reserve entry per 6-passenger jeep/s seat ₹1500/250, obligatory guide ₹360, jeep rental ₹2000; ⏰2½–5hr safaris morning & afternoon, except Wed afternoon, Oct-Jun) from other Madhya Pradesh reserves. By 2016 there were thought to be more than 35 tigers in the reserve, plus a lot of other wildlife. On safaris here there's a better than even chance of seeing at least one of leopards, sloth bears or tigers. You can visit on an excursion from Khajuraho, or stay in one of the lodges near the reserve's main gate at Madla, 26km southeast of Khajuraho.

Panna is much less visited than Bandhavgarh, Kanha or Pench, and safaris here are rarely booked out. The reserve's core zone is the Panna National Park, 543 sq km of beautiful forests and grasslands, with the crocodile-inhabited Ken (Karnavati) River flowing through it.

Eighteen seats in six-passenger jeeps are available on a walk-up basis for morning safaris at Madla (12 for afternoon safaris). Tickets are sold at **Karnavati Interpretation Centre** (☎07732-252135; Madla; Indian/foreigner ₹5/50; ⏰6am-6pm), 1km from Madla gate, where you can also hire a park-registered safari jeep (₹2000). Tickets for up to a further 24 jeeps are sold online (http://forest.mponline.gov.in), but the website doesn't accept foreign cards for payment. Most people get their hotel or a travel agency to organise everything, typically for a total ₹4500 to ₹6000 for up to six people.

Sleeping & Eating

Jungle Camp TENT RESORT **$$**
(☎07732-275275; www.mptourism.com; Madla; r incl breakfast ₹3260; ❄📶) Right by Madla gate, MP Tourism's Jungle Camp offers nine comfortable air-conditioned tents with proper bathrooms and tiger-paw-print sheets, plus a restaurant (mains ₹120 to ₹280) and a nicely kept garden dotted with children's play areas.

★ **Sarai at Toria** LODGE, RESORT **$$$**
(☎9891796671, 9685293130; www.saraiattoria.com; s/d incl full board ₹15,500/19,800; ⏰Oct-mid-Apr; 📶) 🍃 This riverside lodge 2km from Madla gate is a superb base. Eight large, very comfortable cottages are spread around the grounds, with thick, cooling, mud walls and a wonderful rustic-chic aesthetic. Everything including the attractive wooden furniture is created from local materials, and the excellent meals include homemade bread and vegetables from the Sarai's organic garden.

Run by a pair of passionate wildlife enthusiasts and conservationists, this is a perfect base not just for Panna but also for visiting Khajuraho (a half-hour drive away) and the little known but spectacular Chandela forts of Ajaigarh and Kalinjar to the northeast. Boating on the Ken River and a walk to nearby Toria village are included in rates. Most guests stay three or four days and if you feel like just unwinding, pick a book from the library and relax by the riverside or in the open-air dining and lounge area.

Getting There & Away

Six daily buses run between Madla and Khajuraho (₹40, one hour) and there are many more between Madla and Bamitha, 11km of Khajuraho. There's also frequent service between Madla and Satna (₹120, three hours), although for Satna you sometimes have to change at the nearby town of Panna.

Khajuraho's **Yashowarman Taxi Driver Union** (p644) offers ₹4000 round-trips to Panna Tiger Reserve in 4WDs which can be used for safaris.

CENTRAL MADHYA PRADESH

Bhopal

☎0755 / POP 1.80 MILLION

Split by a pair of lakes, the capital of Madhya Pradesh offers two starkly contrasting cityscapes. North of the lakes is Bhopal's Muslim-dominated old city, a fascinating, labyrinthine area of mosques and crowded bazaars. About a quarter of Bhopal's population is Muslim, and the women in black

Bhopal

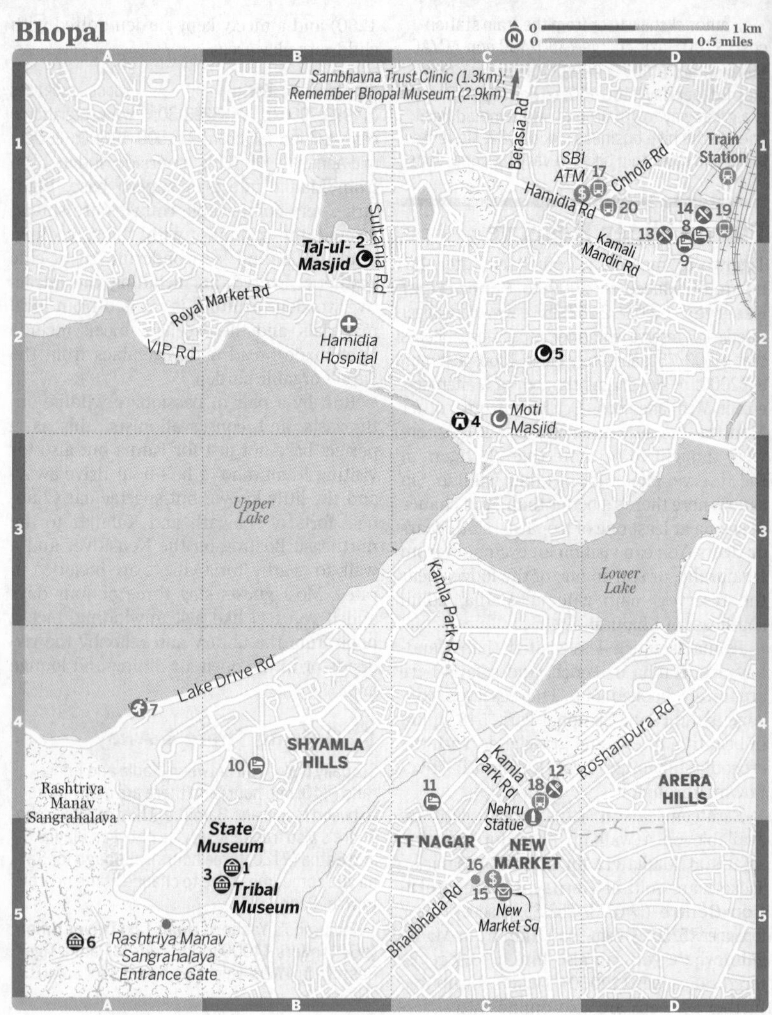

niqabs (veils) are reminders of the four female Islamic rulers, known as the Begums of Bhopal, who developed the city in the 19th and early 20th centuries. North of the old city is a reminder of a more recent, tragic history – the Union Carbide chemical plant, site of the world's worst industrial disaster.

South of the lakes, Bhopal is more modern, with wide roads, some excellent museums, and upmarket hotels and restaurants nestled comfortably in the Arera and Shyamla Hills. The central district here is known as New Market.

Bhopal was founded by Raja Bhoj, a king of Malwa (western Madhya Pradesh and southeast Rajasthan) in the 11th century. Conquests and plunder by the Delhi Sultanate, Mandu and the Mughals sank it into oblivion after the 13th century. It was reborn in the 1720s when Dost Mohammed Khan of nearby Islamnagar built a fort here and then made Bhopal his capital.

Sights

★Tribal Museum MUSEUM

(http://mptribalmuseum.com; Shyamla Hills; Indian/foreigner ₹10/100, camera ₹50; noon-8pm

Bhopal

Tue-Sun Feb-Oct, to 7pm Nov-Jan) Step through the looking glass into what feels like an enchanted forest at this extremely well-done museum dedicated to the tribal peoples who make up more than 10 million of Madhya's population. Opened in 2013, the exhibits were created by 1500 tribespeople using no materials from outside their villages. The results are divided into five large, surreal galleries featuring replica tribal houses, ritual sites and stunning artisan pieces including trees carved into elaborate wedding pillars.

If you have another couple of hours, visit the nearby **Rashtriya Manav Sangrahalaya** (National Museum of Man; http://igrms.gov.in; Indian/foreigner ₹30/500, video ₹50; ⏲10am-5.30pm Tue-Sun Sep-Feb, 11am-6.30pm Tue-Sun Mar-Aug), which does a similar job to the Tribal Museum, but for the whole of India, on a large, mostly open-air site.

★State Museum — MUSEUM

(Shyamla Hills; Indian/foreigner ₹10/100, camera/video ₹50/200; ⏲10.30am-5.30pm Tue-Sun) This first-class archaeological museum spread over 17 galleries includes some wonderful temple sculptures as well as 87 10th- and 11th-century Jain bronzes unearthed by a surprised farmer in western Madhya Pradesh.

★Taj-ul-Masjid — MOSQUE

(⏲closed to non-Muslims noon-3pm Fri) Bhopal's third female ruler, Shah Jahan Begum, wanted to create the largest mosque in the world, so in 1877 she set about building the Taj-ul-Masjid. Still incomplete at her death in 1901, it was not finally finished until the 1980s. Fortress-like pink walls surround a 99-sq-metre courtyard and a prayer hall with 27 scalloped ceiling domes and three gleaming eggshell-like domes on top, all overlooked by two towering minarets.

Gauhar Mahal — PALACE

(VIP Rd; ⏲10am-6pm Mon-Sat) FREE This early-19th-century royal palace, chiefly associated with Qudsia Begum (r 1819–37), now stands empty, but its pretty courtyards, balconies and hallways, in a confection of Mughal, Rajput and other styles, are worth a wander.

Jama Masjid — MOSQUE

The gold spikes crowning the squat minarets of the Jama Masjid Mosque, built in the 1830s by Qudsia Begum, glint serenely above the skull caps and veils swirling through the bazaar below.

Activities

MP Tourism Boat Club — BOATING

(☎0775-3295043; Lake Drive Rd; ⏲10am-7pm) Offers motorboat ('speedboat') rides (₹210, five minutes, three passengers), pedal boats (per boat ₹60, 30 minutes), jet-skiing (per person ₹400, five minutes) and even parasailing (₹500, 20 minutes).

Children might enjoy feeding the gaggle of geese here. An autorickshaw from New Market costs ₹80.

Sleeping

Hotel Sonali Regency — HOTEL $

(☎0755-2740880; www.hotelsonaliregency.com; Plot 3, Hamidia Rd, near Radha Talkies; s/d from

THE BHOPAL DISASTER – A CONTINUING TRAGEDY

Shortly after midnight on 3 December 1984, 27 tonnes of deadly methyl isocyanate (MIC) leaked out over Bhopal from the US-owned Union Carbide chemical plant. Blown by the wind, a 40ft wall of toxic cloud coursed through the city. In the ensuing panic, people were trampled trying to escape, while others were so disorientated that they ran into the gas.

Estimates of initial fatalities range from 3800 to 16,000. The total death toll, including those who have died since, stands at around 25,000 according to people working with victims. More than 400,000 people have suffered a catalogue of illnesses ranging from diabetes, cancer and paralysis to premature menopause and skin disorders, while their children have suffered problems such as birth malformations and reduced stature. Separately, dumping of toxic waste since well before the gas leak is thought to have contaminated groundwater around the Union Carbide factory with chemicals that cause cancer, birth defects and organ damage. In 2014, 22 communities around the factory finally received a new, piped water supply, but activists say there is also high toxicity beyond these communities.

The gas leak is generally thought to have resulted from a saga of negligent maintenance and cost-cutting measures (though Union Carbide blames sabotage). Damages of US$3 billion were demanded, and in 1989 Union Carbide paid the Indian government US$470 million, but compensation reaching the victims has generally been meagre and distribution has been dogged by disputes over who is entitled to it. Union Carbide was bought by Dow Chemical in 2001. Dow denies ongoing liability.

A multimillion-dollar hospital was funded from the sale of Union Carbide's Indian subsidiary, while charity **Sambhavna Trust Clinic** (☎0755-2923195; www.bhopal.org; Bafna Colony, off Berasia Rd; ⏲8.30am-3pm Mon-Sat), opened in 1996, gives free treatment to 150 to 200 Union Carbide victims a day using yoga, ayurveda, conventional medicine and herbal remedies. Visitors and donations are welcome. Volunteers (minimum 15 days) can work in a range of areas from water testing and medical research to the clinic's library, pharmacy or medicinal herb garden; they are hugely appreciated and offered board and lodgings in the medical centre.

To find Sambhavna, head 1km north up Berasia Rd from Hamidia Rd, turn right at the Reliance petrol station, and you'll soon see Sambhavna signs. The derelict Carbide factory (not open to casual visitors) is 1km north of here.

The very moving **Remember Bhopal Museum** (☎9589345134; http://rememberbhopal.net; Sr HIG 22, Housing Board Colony, Berasia Road, Karond; ⏲10am-5pm Tue-Sun) FREE was opened in 2014 in Karond, 3km north up Berasia Rd from Hamidia Rd (turn left at its small sign, then left again after 250m). Run by a dedicated activist team, the museum preserves belongings and pictures of victims as well as audio recordings from survivors, doctors and forensic experts, and relates the continuing efforts to win justice for the victims.

₹700/850, with AC incl breakfast from ₹1450/1650; ❄📶) Excellent service, right down to the errand boys, makes Sonali a great option near Hamidia Rd. Air-con rooms have tile floors, funky-shaped beds and working hot showers. The 'executive' non-AC rooms (doubles from ₹995) are almost as good as 'business' air-con rooms.

Hotel Ranjeet HOTEL $$
(☎0755-2740500; www.ranjeethotels.com; 3 Hamidia Rd; s/d incl breakfast from ₹1550/2070; ❄📶) Recently renovated, the Ranjeet has air-con rooms with *moderne* rectangular washbasins and toilets, kettles and a slight attempt at artful decor. Beds are soft though the laundering is less than immaculate.

★ **Jehan Numa Palace Hotel** HERITAGE HOTEL $$$
(☎0755-2661100; www.jehannuma.com; 157 Shyamla Hills; incl breakfast s ₹5490-10,360, d ₹6700-11,570, ste from ₹19,490; ❄@📶🏊) This former 19th-century palace lost none of its colonial-era charm through conversion into a top-class hotel. Pillared walkways and immaculate lawns lead you to beautifully decorated rooms. The fact that you can sleep in

a patio room – perfectly great – for US$100 in a five-star hotel is ridiculous. Worth a splurge.

The hotel has a palm-lined pool and excellent spa plus three restaurants, two bars and a coffeeshop that are all among the very best in town.

Palash Residency HOTEL $$$
(☎0755-2553066; www.mptourism.com; TT Nagar; s/d incl breakfast ₹4280/4750; ❄ 📶) This large-ish MP Tourism hotel is walking distance from New Market. Long corridors lead to large rooms that are mostly in good condition (except for the odd wall stain due to 'seepage'). They're equipped with heavy wood furniture, wall-mounted flat-screen TVs, tea/coffee facilities and toiletries.

There's a bar and a reasonable restaurant.

Eating & Drinking

Zam Zam INDIAN $
(Hamidia Rd; mains ₹80-250; ⏰9am-midnight) Crowds pack this fast-food hot spot day and night for some of Bhopal's best biryani, but it's the finger-lickin' chicken tikka, grilled over hot coals outside the door and dipped in green-chilli yoghurt sauce, that's the true showstopper.

For vegetarians, the paneer tikka ain't bad either.

Manohar INDIAN $
(6 Hamidia Rd; mains ₹90-160, thali ₹140-190; ⏰8am-11pm) Bright, clean, canteen-style Manohar does a brisk business in South Indian breakfasts, thalis, snacks, shakes and a load of presumably more hygienic versions of many Indian street-food favourites. In truth, it's a bit of a madhouse and rightfully so.

Bapu Ki Kutia INDIAN $
(Roshanpura Rd, TT Nagar; mains ₹60-165, thali ₹140-160; ⏰10am-11pm; 📝) Papa's Shack has been serving up delicious Indian veg dishes since 1964. Prepare to get cosy with the locals – it's so popular you'll often share a table. There's an English menu, but no English sign. Look for the picture of a beach hut and palm tree above the door.

★Under the Mango Tree MUGHLAI $$$
(Jehan Numa Palace Hotel, 157 Shyamla Hills; mains ₹400-750; ⏰7-11pm) Jehan Numa Palace's best restaurant specialises in barbecue kebabs and tandoor dishes (including vegetarian options). Most things on the menu are top-class, but the sampler platter of varied kebabs (from ₹825) may well be the best meal you have anywhere in Madhya Pradesh.

Great food, wine, draft beer (Woodpecker, a local swill) and cocktails all combine under a romantic white pavilion and the heavy boughs of a venerable centenarian mango tree.

Information

State Bank of India (TT Nagar Sq; ⏰10.30am-4pm Mon-Sat) The International Division, upstairs, changes foreign cash. Has an ATM too.

Transport

AIR

Air India (☎0755-2770480; www.airindia.in; Bhadbhada Rd; ⏰10am-1pm & 2-5pm Mon-Sat) and **Jet Airways** (☎0755-2645676; www.jetairways.com; ⏰9.30am-6pm Mon-Sat) fly daily to Delhi and Mumbai. Air India flies three or four times weekly to Jabalpur, Hyderabad, Raipur and Pune.

BUS

Bhopal has two main bus stations: **Nadra Bus Stand** (Old Bus Stand; ☎9755102080; Chhola Rd), just off Hamidia Rd, and the **ISBT** (Inter State Bus Terminus; Habibganj) in Habibganj, 5km east of New Market. For superior comfort to Indore, several companies run Volvo AC buses including **Chartered Bus** (☎9993288888; www.charteredbus.in; ISBT) from the ISBT (₹330, 4½ hours, two or three hourly, 5am to 9.30pm), which can be booked at its **city ticket office** (☎7389921709; Shop No 3, Shalimar Trade Centre, Hamidia Rd; ⏰7am-10pm).

Services from Nadra Bus Stand:

Gwalior seat/sleeper ₹300/350, 10 hours, 9pm (Bhopal Travels)

Indore ₹200, five hours, every 15 minutes, 4am to 11pm

Pachmarhi AC seat/sleeper ₹360/460, seven hours, 11.55pm (Verma Travels)

Sanchi ₹40, 1½ hours, half-hourly, 5am to 10pm

Services from the ISBT:

Jabalpur ₹320, nine hours, 4.55am, 5.45am, 9.25am, 7.15pm, sleeper 9.25pm (seat/sleeper ₹350/450, by Verma Travels)

Khajuraho seat/sleeper ₹450/550, 11 hours, 7.20pm and 10.20pm (both Om Sai Ram company)

Pachmarhi ₹250, seven hours, 6.15am, 8am, 10.15am, AC sleeper 12.45am (seat/sleeper ₹360/460), non-AC sleeper 2.30am (₹300/400); sleeper buses are by Verma Travels.

The **Bhopal Travels** (☎0755-4083544; 35 JK Bldg, Chhola Rd) office is across the road from Nadra Bus Stand.

TRAIN

There are around 30 daily trains to Gwalior, Agra and Delhi, and at least nine to Ujjain and eight to Jabalpur and Mumbai.

Getting Around

The airport is 11km northwest of central Bhopal – at least ₹200 by autorickshaw or around ₹500 by taxi.

Minibuses and buses (both ₹10) shuttle between New Market and Hamidia Rd all day and all evening. Catch ones to New Market at the **eastern end of Hamidia Rd**. Returning from New Market, they leave from **near the Nehru Statue**. Autorickshaws cost about ₹60 for the same journey. **My Cab** (☎0755-6666666; www.mycabindia.com) operates metered taxis (₹23 per kilometre) and fixed-price transfers and day trips (eg ₹1500 for a day trip to Sanchi).

Sanchi

☎07482 / POP 7305

Rising from the plains, 46km northeast of Bhopal, is a rounded hill topped with some of India's oldest Buddhist structures.

In 262 BC, repentant of the horrors he had inflicted on Kalinga (Odisha), the Mauryan emperor Ashoka embraced Buddhism. As a penance he built the Great Stupa at Sanchi, a domed edifice to house religious relics, near the home town (Vidisha) of his wife Devi. Sanchi became an important Buddhist monastic centre and over the following centuries further stupas and other monuments were added. After about the 13th century it was abandoned and forgotten, until rediscovered in 1818 by a British army officer.

Today, the remarkably preserved Great Stupa is the centrepiece of Sanchi's World Heritage–listed Buddhist monuments.

Although you can visit Sanchi in a day trip from Bhopal, this crossroads village is a relaxing spot to spend the night, and a number of side trips can be taken from here.

Sights

The hilltop **Buddhist monuments** (Indian, SAARC or BIMSTEC citizen ₹30, others ₹500, video ₹25; dawn-dusk) stand at the top of Monuments Rd, a continuation of the road that leaves the train station. The **ticket office** (dawn-dusk) is near the beginning of Monuments Rd, in front of the Archaeological Museum. If you don't want to walk up the hill, autorickshaws will deposit you at the top for ₹30. The **Publication Sales Counter** (dawn-dusk) beside the monuments entrance sells the Archaeological Survey of India's good *Sanchi* guide for ₹60 (assuming stocks haven't run out). If you are interested in a human guide, licensed government guides mill about here and charge ₹475/750 for four/eight people for three or four hours.

Remember, it's auspicious to walk clockwise around Buddhist monuments.

Great Stupa BUDDHIST STUPA

(Stupa 1) Beautifully proportioned, the Great Stupa is the centrepiece of the monumental area, directly ahead as you enter the complex from the north. Originally constructed by Ashoka, it was enlarged a century later and the original brick stupa enclosed within a stone one. Today it stands 16m high and 37m in diameter. Encircling the stupa is a wall with four magnificently carved *toranas* (gateways) that have few rivals as the finest Buddhist works of art in India.

HANDY TRAINS FROM BHOPAL

DESTINATION	TRAIN NO & NAME	FARE (₹)	DURATION (HR)	DEPARTURE
Agra	12627 Karnataka Exp	330/855/1205	7	11.30pm
Delhi	12621 Tamil Nadu Exp	400/1055/1495	11	8.20pm
Gwalior	11077 Jhelum Exp	235/635/910	6	9.10am
Indore	12920 Malwa Exp	215/540/740	5	7.40am
Jabalpur	18233 Narmada Exp	215/580/830	7	11.25pm
Mumbai (CST)	12138 Punjab Mail	445/1175/1675	15	4.55pm
Raipur	18238 Chhattisgarh Exp	365/985/1420	15	6.45pm
Ujjain	12920 Malwa Exp	170/540/740	3½	7.40am

Fares: sleeper/3AC/2AC

WORTH A TRIP

BEYOND BHOPAL

Several sites in villages and countryside outside Bhopal make good day trips. Public transport is not very convenient, but a taxi for a day should cost between ₹1400 (eight hours, 80km) and ₹2000 (12 hours, 120km).

Islamnagar

This now-ruined fortified town 13km north of central Bhopal was the first capital of the Bhopal princely state, established by Dost Mohammed Khan in the early 18th century. The still-standing walls enclose two small villages as well as two palaces with gardens: the **Chaman Mahal** (Indian/foreigner ₹5/100; ⏲8am-6pm) and **Rani Mahal** (Indian/foreigner ₹5/100; ⏲8am-6pm).

Bhojpur

Built by Bhopal's 11th-century founder, Raja Bhoj, Bhojpur originally stood beside a 400-sq-km artificial lake, which was emptied in the 15th century by the dam-busting Mandu ruler Hoshang Shah. Thankfully, the magnificent **Bhojeshwar Temple** survived the attack. It's 23km southeast of the city. Remains of one of the lake's **dams** can be seen down in the river valley about 400m northwest of the temple.

Bhimbetka

In forests on craggy hills 45km south of Bhopal are the World Heritage–listed **Bhimbetka rock shelters** (Indian/foreigner ₹50/100; ⏲7am-7pm), containing thousands of paintings of animals, people and other subjects from the Stone Age to medieval times. Fifteen of the best shelters are linked by an easy 1.4km round-trip walking trail.

Toranas

The Great Stupa's four *toranas* (gateways) were erected around 35 BC, more than two centuries after the stupa itself. They had all fallen down by the time the site was rediscovered, but have since been put back up. The wonderful carving on their pillars and triple architraves mainly depicts scenes from the Buddha's life, the history of Buddhism and the Jatakas, episodes from the Buddha's earlier lives.

At this stage in Buddhist art, the Buddha himself was never represented directly – only his presence was alluded to through symbols. The lotus stands for his birth, the bodhi tree for his enlightenment, the wheel for his teachings, and the footprint and throne for his presence. The stupa itself also symbolises the Buddha.

Northern Gateway — BUDDHIST MONUMENT

The Northern Gateway, topped by a broken wheel of law, is the best preserved of the *toranas*. Elephants support the architraves above the columns, while delicately carved *yakshis* (mythical fairy-like beings) hang nonchalantly on each side. Scenes include a monkey offering a bowl of honey to the Buddha, who is represented by a bodhi tree (western pillar, east face, second panel down).

Eastern Gateway — BUDDHIST MONUMENT

The breathtakingly carved figure of a *yakshi*, hanging from an architrave on the Eastern Gateway, is one of Sanchi's best-known images. The middle architrave depicts the Great Departure, when the Buddha (shown four times as a riderless horse) renounced the sensual life and set out to find enlightenment. On the bottom architrave is Ashoka's visit to the bodhi tree: the emperor is seen dismounting from an elephant then approaching the tree with clasped hands.

The rear of the middle architrave shows the Buddha being worshipped by lions, buffalo and other animals. On the south face of the northern pilllar (second panel down) is shown the dream of an elephant standing on the moon, dreamt by the Buddha's mother Maya when he was conceived.

Southern Gateway — BUDDHIST MONUMENT

The back-to-back lions on the pillars of the monuments compound's Southern Gateway (the oldest) were a favourite Ashokan motif and now form the state emblem of India, which can be seen on every banknote. The gateway narrates Ashoka's life as a Buddhist, with another representation of the Great Departure (rear of top architrave, east end).

Sanchi

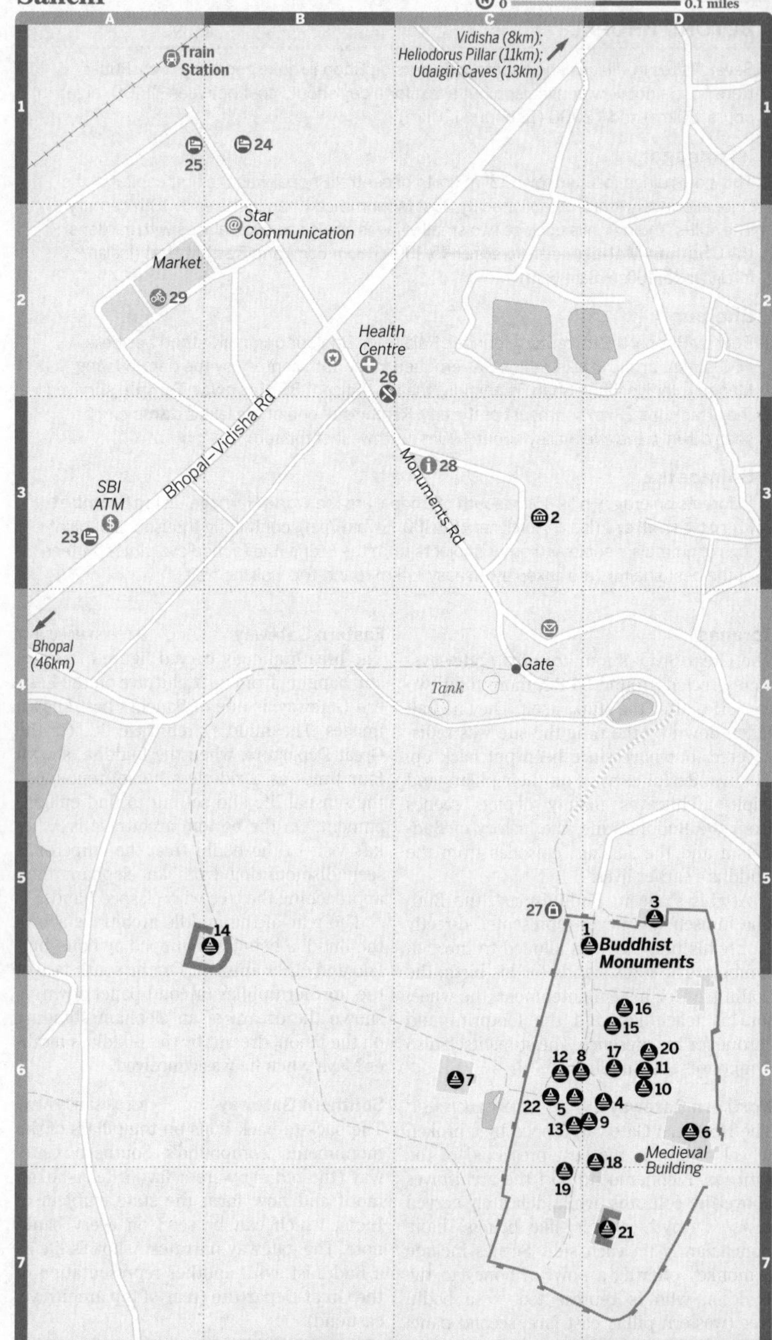

0 200 m
0 0.1 miles
Vidisha (8km); Heliodorus Pillar (11km); Udaigiri Caves (13km)
Train Station
25
24
Star Communication
Market
29
Health Centre
26
Bhopal–Vidisha Rd
Monuments Rd
28
SBI ATM
23
2
Bhopal (46km)
Gate
Tank
27
3
1
Buddhist Monuments
14
16
15
12
8
17
20
11
10
7
22
5
4
13
9
6
Medieval Building
18
19
21

Sanchi

Top Sights

1 Buddhist Monuments D5

Sights

2 Archaeological Museum C3
3 Chetiyagiri Vihara D5
4 Eastern Gateway D6
Great Bowl .... (see 7)
5 Great Stupa C6
6 Monasteries 45 & 47 .... D6
7 Monastery 51 .... C6
8 Northern Gateway C6
9 Pillar 10 .... D6
10 Pillar 25 .... D6
11 Pillar 26 .... D6
12 Pillar 35 .... C6
13 Southern Gateway C6
14 Stupa 2 .... B5
15 Stupa 3 .... D6
16 Stupa 4 .... D6
17 Stupa 5 .... D6
18 Temple 17 .... D6
19 Temple 18 .... C7
20 Temple 31 .... D6
21 Temple 40 .... D7
22 Western Gateway C6

Sleeping

23 Gateway Retreat A3
24 Mahabodhi Society of Sri Lanka B1
25 New Jaiswal Lodge A1

Eating

26 Gateway Cafeteria B2
Gateway Retreat Restaurant .... (see 23)

Shopping

27 Publication Sales Counter C5

Information

28 Ticket Office C3

Transport

29 Usman A2

Western Gateway

BUDDHIST MONUMENT

Pot-bellied dwarves support the architraves of the Western Gateway, which has some of the site's most interesting scenes. The back of the bottom architrave and the south pillar's north-face top panel both show the Buddha resisting the temptation and assault by Mara (the Buddhist personification of evil), while demons flee and angels cheer.

The front of the top architrave shows the Buddha along with six Manushi-Buddhas (Buddhas who preceded him), all represented as stupas or trees. On the back of the middle architrave we see the siege of Kushinagar by seven cities that wanted a portion of the Buddha's bone relics after his death, and above that the transport of the relics after the agreement to divide them into eight shares.

Other Stupas

You pass **Stupa 3** on your left as you approach the Great Stupa from the main entrance. It's similar in design to the Great Stupa, but smaller, with a single, rather fine gateway. One of Sanchi's earliest monuments after the Great Stupa, it dates from the 2nd century BC and once contained relics of two important disciples of the Buddha: Sariputta and Moggallana. These were moved to London in the 19th century but relics thought to be the same ones were returned in 1952 to the modern *vihara* (resting place) outside the monuments compound.

Only the base is left of the 2nd-century-BC **Stupa 4**, behind Stupa 3. Between Stupa 3 and the Great Stupa is the small **Stupa 5**, unusual in that it once contained a statue of Buddha, now displayed in the museum.

Stupa 2 is halfway down the hill to the west from the Great Stupa. You can walk back down to the village via Stupa 2 (but be prepared for some fence-hopping at the bottom). Instead of gateways, 'medallions' decorate its surrounding wall – naive in design, but full of energy and imagination. Flowers, animals and people – some mythological – ring the stupa.

Temples

The rectangular **Temple 31**, beside Stupa 5, was built in the 6th or 7th century but reconstructed during the 10th or 11th century. It contains a well-executed image of the Buddha.

Temple 18, behind the Great Stupa, is a *chaitya* (prayer room or assembly hall) remarkably similar in appearance to classical-Greek columned buildings. It dates from around the 7th century AD, but traces of earlier wooden buildings have been discovered beneath it. To its left is the small, also Greek-like **Temple 17**. Beyond both of them, the large **Temple 40** dates back in part to the Ashokan period.

Monasteries

The earliest of Sanchi's monasteries were made of wood and are long gone. The usual plan was of a central courtyard surrounded by monastic cells. These days only the courtyards and stone foundations remain. **Monasteries 45 and 47**, standing on the ridge east of the Great Stupa, date from the 7th to 10th centuries, and have strong Hindu elements in their design. The former has two sitting Buddhas. The one housed inside is exceptional.

The remains of **Monastery 51** sit a short distance downhill west of the Great Stupa. Outside its west gate is the **Great Bowl**, carved from a boulder, into which food and offerings were placed for distribution to the monks.

Pillars

Of the scattered pillar remains, the most important is **Pillar 10**, erected by Ashoka but later broken. Two upper sections of this beautifully proportioned and executed shaft lie side by side behind the Great Stupa; its superb lions-on-lotus capital is in the museum. **Pillars 25** and **26**, east of the Great Stupa, and **Pillar 35**, to its northwest, are less impressive but their capitals (lions from 25 and 26, a figure of the Bodhisattva Vajrapani from 35) can also be seen in the museum.

Other Sights

Archaeological Museum MUSEUM

(⌚9am-5pm Sat-Thu) This fine museum has a small collection of sculptures from the site. The centrepiece is the 3rd-century-BC lions-on-lotus capital from the Ashoka-era Pillar 10. Other highlights include a *yakshi* (mythical fairy-like being) hanging from a mango tree, and beautifully serene Buddha figures in red sandstone. There are also some interesting photos showing the site pre-restoration. Admission is with a ticket for the monuments compound (p650).

Chetiyagiri Vihara BUDDHIST TEMPLE

(⌚9am-5pm) The *vihara* (literally 'resting place'), just outside the monuments compound, was built to house relics of the Buddha's disciples Sariputta and Moggallana on their return from Britain in 1952.

The relics are brought out for public viewing for the Chetiyagiri Vihara festival on the last Sunday of November, an event that attracts tens of thousands of Buddhist monks and pilgrims.

Sleeping & Eating

Mahabodhi Society of Sri Lanka GUESTHOUSE, HOSTEL $

(☎07482-266699; wimalatissasanchi@yahoo.co.in; Monuments Rd; dm ₹100, r ₹1000, with AC ₹1500; 📶) This friendly, well-run place is primarily geared to Sri Lankan Buddhist pilgrims but also welcomes international travellers except when full (most likely around the late-November Chetiyagiri Vihara festival). The rear building has good, clean, carpeted air-con rooms with big bathrooms, and wearier but still clean non-AC rooms. Dorms around the shady front courtyard share clean squat toilets and unheated showers.

New Jaiswal Lodge GUESTHOUSE $

(☎9713758366; pranjaljaiswal@gmail.com; Monuments Rd; s/d/tr ₹400/500/600) This friendly place has four basic but colourful rooms with ceiling fans, mosquito screens and small private bathrooms with sit-down toilets. Does basic meals and air-coolers can be provided.

★**Gateway Retreat** HOTEL $$

(☎07482-266723; www.mptourism.com; Bhopal-Vidisha Rd; incl breakfast s ₹1740-3920, d ₹2170-4280; ❄📶🏊) This MP Tourism hotel is Sanchi's most comfortable lodging, with smart, air-con rooms and bungalows set among well-kept gardens. The **restaurant** (Gateway Retreat; mains ₹170-360; ⌚8am-10.30pm; 📶) is Sanchi's best, and there's a small bar tucked into its corner. Note: the two cheapest rooms are 400m away at Gateway Cafeteria but are also fine, and recently modernised.

The hotel has a small children's play area and a rather big slide leading to a rather small kiddie pool!

Gateway Cafeteria INDIAN $

(Monuments Rd; mains ₹120-175; ⌚8am-10.30pm) This simple but clean MP Tourism place has a very basic Indian menu and coffee in addition to housing the two cheapest rooms of Gateway Retreat.

Information

Health Centre (☎07482-266724; Monuments Rd; ⌚8am-1pm & 5-6pm Mon-Sat) Small clinic near the central crossroads.

Star Communication (internet per hr ₹40; ⌚9am-10pm) Offers internet access and books train and bus tickets.

Getting There & Around

You can rent bicycles from **Usman** (per hr/day ₹10/50; 8.30am-7pm Mon-Sat) in the market.

BUS

Every half-hour buses connect Sanchi with Bhopal (₹40, 1½ hours, 5am to 10pm) and Vidisha (₹10, 20 minutes, 6am to 11pm). Catch them at the village crossroads.

TRAIN

Train is a decent option for getting to Sanchi from Bhopal. It takes less than an hour so you can just turn up in time to queue for a 'general' ticket (₹10 to ₹30) and then squeeze on. There are at least six trains a day – 8am, 10.35am, 3.05pm, 4.10pm, 6.15pm and 10.55pm from Bhopal to Sanchi, and 4.15am, 8am, 10.30am, 4.30pm, 6.15pm and 7.35pm from Sanchi to Bhopal.

For longer trips, there are far more trains from Vidisha, 8km northeast of Sanchi.

Around Sanchi

Several historic sites are accessible from Sanchi by bicycle or autorickshaw, with the Udaigiri Caves especially worth the trip. En route, the busy market town of Vidisha is an interesting place for a wander or a chai break, and its **District Museum** (Block Colony, Durga Nagar, Vidisha; Indian/foreigner ₹5/50, camera ₹50; 10am-5pm Tue-Sun), on Hwy 146, 800m past the central railway bridge, houses some beautiful sculptures from local sites.

Getting There & Around

For Udaigiri Caves, fork left following a sign for Udaigiri as you enter Vidisha, continue across the Betwa River, then take the first road to the left and follow it for 3km. For the Heliodorus Pillar, continue straight on after crossing the Betwa and after 1km you'll see a sign pointing to the pillar, along a small road on your right.

An autorickshaw from Sanchi to Udaigiri Caves costs ₹350 return, or ₹450 with the Heliodorus Pillar and Vidisha included. Or take a bus to Vidisha then a rickshaw (₹150 return).

Udaigiri Caves

Cut into a sandstone hill 5km northwest of Vidisha are some 20 Gupta-period **cave shrines** (dawn-dusk) FREE from the time of Chandragupta II (AD 382–401). All are Hindu except two Jain shrines – interesting evidence of how both these religions, as well as Buddhism at Sanchi, all coexisted in the same area at the same time. You need at least an hour to explore the caves fully.

You first reach **Cave 19**, dedicated to Shiva, with a finely carved portal and the remains of a multi-columned portico outside. The main group of caves is 400m past here. Especially remarkable is **Cave 5** with its superb, large-scale image of Vishnu as Varaha, his boar incarnation, rescuing the earth goddess Bhudevi (or Prithvi) from the ocean of chaos with his tusk, while ranks of divine beings look on. **Cave 4** contains an unusual Shiva lingam with Shiva's face (complete with third eye) carved on it and the River Ganges flowing from the top of his head. **Cave 13** shows Vishnu sleeping on a bed of cobras: past here you can walk up on the hilltop where there are ruins of a 6th-century **Gupta temple** dedicated to the sun god. **Cave 1**, on the hillside 350m south of the main group, is one of the two Jain shrines: it contains an image of the *tirthankar* Parasnath, but you can only look through the fence as it's closed for safety reasons.

Heliodorus Pillar

The Heliodorus Pillar (Kham Baba) was erected by a Greek, Heliodorus, who came to this region as an ambassador from Taxila (now in Pakistan), in about 140 BC. Dedicated to Vasudeva (Vishnu), the 6m-tall pillar records Heliodorus' conversion to Vaishnavism, which makes him one of the very first Westerners to adopt an Indian religion.

Pachmarhi

07578 / POP 13,700 / ELEV 1067M

Madhya Pradesh's only hill station is surrounded by waterfalls, canyons, natural pools, cave temples and the forested ranges of the Satpura Tiger Reserve, and offers a refreshing escape from steamy central India. It's popular with Indians but few foreign travellers get here.

The most popular tourist activity is touring a selection of places of interest, beauty spots and natural pools by jeep (with a few shortish walks from parking places). It's also possible to reach some places by foot, bicycle or normal car.

British army Captain James Forsyth came across Pachmarhi in 1857 and set up India's first Forestry Department at Bison Lodge in

Pachmarhi

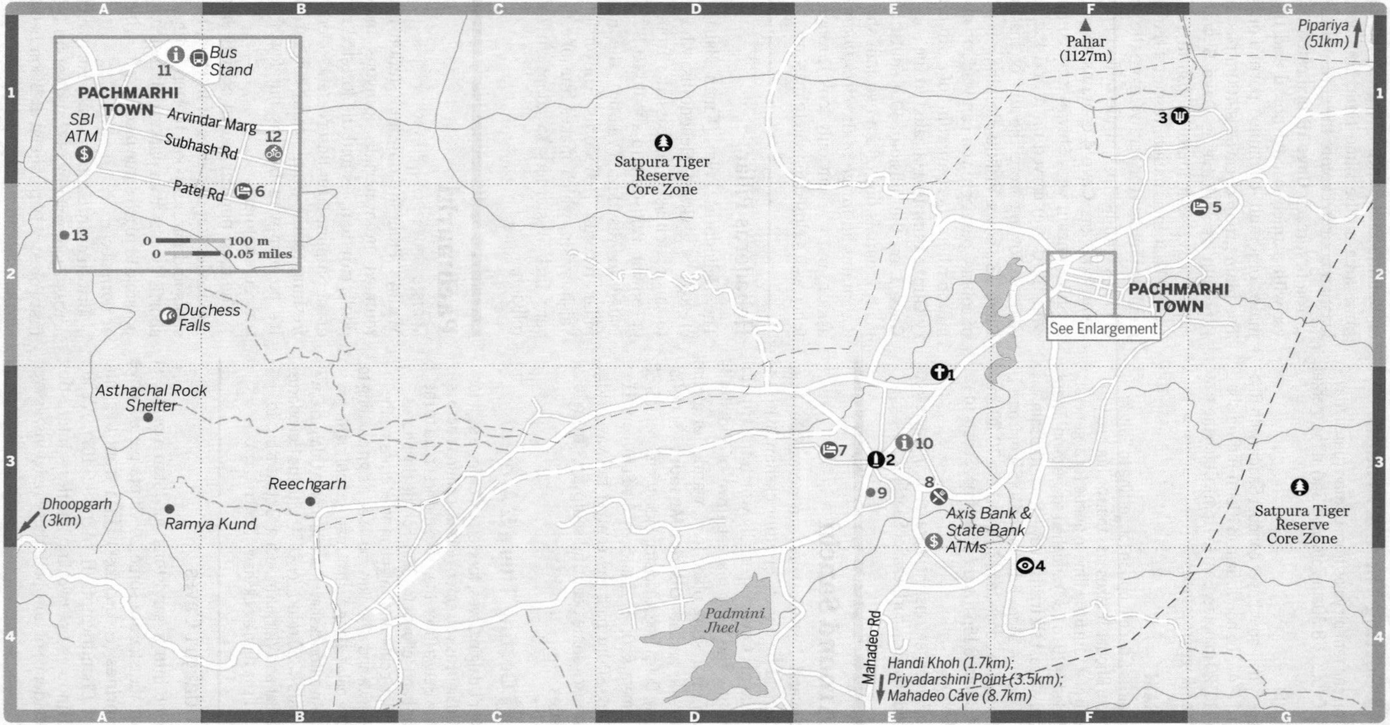

0 1 km
0 0.5 miles

Pahar (1127m)
Pipariya (51km)
3
Satpura Tiger Reserve Core Zone
5
PACHMARHI TOWN
See Enlargement
1
10
7
2
8
9
Axis Bank & State Bank ATMs
4
Satpura Tiger Reserve Core Zone
Padmini Jheel
Mahadeo Rd
Handi Khoh (1.7km); Priyadarshini Point (3.5km); Mahadeo Cave (8.7km)
Duchess Falls
Asthachal Rock Shelter
Reechgarh
Ramya Kund
Dhoopgarh (3km)

Bus Stand
11
PACHMARHI TOWN
SBI ATM
Arvindar Marg
Subhash Rd
12
Patel Rd
6
13
0 100 m
0 0.05 miles

Pachmarhi

Sights

Sleeping

Eating

Information

Transport

1862. Soon after, the British army set up regional headquarters here, starting an association with the military that remains today.

Pachmarhi has moderate temperatures year-round. During the monsoon (July to September) there are no jungle safaris from Madhai, and some of the sights around Pachmarhi may be closed too.

Budget hotels and the bus station are in the main, northeastern part of town. To the southwest across a small valley are the broad streets, churches and colonial bungalows of the Jai Stambh area, named after a **pillar** at a seven-way junction, commemorating Indian independence.

Sights & Activities

Pachmarhi sits inside the Satpura Tiger Reserve: the town and some surrounding countryside constitute an island of buffer zone, surrounded by the reserve's core zone.

Buffer Zone Sights

Sights in the buffer zone can be visited freely: these include the **Pandav Caves**, five ancient rock dwellings believed to have been carved by Buddhists as early as the 4th century; **Mahadeo Cave**, 10km south of the Jai Stambh by paved road, where a path leading 30m into the damp gloom reveals a lingam with attendant priest; the **Handi Khoh** and **Priyadarshini Point** (Forsyth Point) lookouts along the road to Mahadeo Cave; and **Jata Shankar**, a Shiva cave temple in a beautiful gorge 1km along a road that's signed just north of the town limits. You can rent bicycles or jeeps in the town's market area to visit these places.

In town, the handsome Gothic-revival **Christchurch** was built back in 1875, entirely of sandstone.

Core Zone Sights near Pachmarhi

Apart from Chauragarh hill (which can be accessed freely by a five-hour return hike from Mahadeo Cave) entry to the core zone requires a permit, available at Bison Lodge (p659), and in most cases a guide is obligatory too. Most people rent a jeep with driver (₹1425 per day for up to six passengers, plus ₹730 for the core-zone entry permit and ₹300 for a guide) at Bison Lodge for tours. Core-zone entry on foot or bicycle costs ₹70, and by motorcycle ₹190. Bison Lodge can also provide guides for day hikes (₹310 for the entry permit and ₹700 for the guide, for up to six people).

Apsara Vihar Underneath a small waterfall, this is the best of Pachmarhi's natural pools for swimming. It's a drive of about 1.5km past Pandav Caves, followed by a walk of about 700m.

Rajat Prapat Viewpoint Steps up from Apsara Vihar lead to a point with magnificent views of Rajat Prapat, central India's highest single-drop waterfall (107m), and the gorge below it.

Dhoopgarh An almost mandatory final stop on jeep tours, Dhoopgarh lookout faces west over endless valleys, hills and forests and has a broad stepped terrace for everyone to do their sunset selfies on.

Bee Falls This pretty waterfall and pools can almost be reached by bike (you have to walk the last 250m or so).

Chauragarh Madhya Pradesh's third-highest peak (1308m) is topped by a panoramic Shiva temple that attracts tens of thousands of pilgrims during the Shivaratri Mela (p658). It's a return hike of about five hours from Mahadeo Cave – 3.5km each way, with 1365 steps to climb and descend.

Jungle Safaris

Jungle Safaris SAFARI
(reserve entry per 6-passenger jeep/seat ₹1500/250, obligatory guide ₹300, jeep rental approximately ₹2000; Oct-Jun) Jeep safaris (2½ to five hours) from Madhai, on the

northern edge of Satpura Tiger Reserve, are an entirely different experience from the beauty-spot-focused jeep tours starting from Pachmarhi. You travel through dense, pristine forests in search of wildlife. Don't expect to see any of the tiger reserve's 20-odd tigers, but there are decent prospects of spotting sloth bears (especially in winter) and leopards.

Up to 12 six-passenger jeeps are allowed in each session, but only one of these is available for walk-up customers. The rest are sold online (http://forest.mponline.gov.in) – but the website doesn't accept foreign credit or debit cards for payment, so it's best to organise things through a travel agency or one of the hotels or lodges near Madhai (they typically charge around ₹1000 for doing this). Boat safaris can also be organised at Madhai.

Taxis to Madhai from Pachmarhi cost ₹2000 (2½ to three hours), or you can get a bus to Sohagpur (₹80, 2½ hours, 12 daily), then a shared jeep (₹25, one hour) 20km south to Madhai.

Festivals & Events

Shivaratri Mela RELIGIOUS
(Feb/Mar) Up to 100,000 Shaivite pilgrims, sadhus (holy men) and Adivasis attend celebrations at Mahadeo Cave then make a pilgrimage up Chauragarh hill to plant tridents by the Shiva shrine.

Sleeping & Eating

Pachmarhi

A number of colonial-era bungalows and houses in the Jai Stambh area have been converted into delightful guesthouses and hotels, no less than 14 of them run by MP Tourism. Places fill up and room rates may rise during high season (May to July, national holidays and major festivals).

Hotel Saket HOTEL $$
(07578-252165; www.sakethotel.in; Patel Rd; r ₹1900, with AC ₹3100-3570;) The wide range of warmly decorated rooms, comfy beds, bright new lobby and dining area and friendly welcome make this one of the best of many similar-looking hotels in town. Prices drop by half outside high season, meaning excellent value.

The **restaurant** (Hotel Saket, Patel Rd; mains ₹80-180; 8am-11pm) does good and cheap Gujarati, North and South Indian and Chinese dishes. Wi-fi costs ₹100 for your stay.

Hotel Highlands HOTEL $$
(07578-252099; www.mptourism.com; Pipariya Rd; r incl breakfast ₹3090;) This MP Tourism property at the north end of town has great-value rooms with high ceilings, dressing rooms, modern bathrooms and verandahs, dotted around well-tended gardens. There's a children's play area and a bar-restaurant.

Rock-End Manor HERITAGE HOTEL $$$
(07578-252079; www.mptourism.com; s/d incl full board ₹5470/6420;) A gorgeous colonial-era building, whitewashed Rock-End overlooks the fairways of the army golf course. It's well and helpfully managed and the six spacious rooms have wonderfully high ceilings, luxurious furnishings with quality upholstery, framed paintings and full-body massage showers.

★ **Rasoi** DHABA $
(Company Garden; mains ₹80-200; 9am-11.30pm) Not your average roadside *dhaba* (casual eatery)! A scrumptious, long-winded, South Indian, nonveg and Chinese menu is served here in several open or partially open-air seating areas. Our waiter's recommendation – veg tawa (₹150) – was downright delicious.

Madhai

Options in the Madhai area include a few midrange hotels, a forest rest house and a few luxurious top-end jungle lodges.

Madhai Forest Rest House REST HOUSE $
(07574-254838, bookings 07574-254394; dirsatpuranp@mpforest.org; Madhai; r ₹1000) On the south bank of the Denwa River, where jungle safaris start, this Forest Department–run rest house has six bare but quite comfortable rooms with sit-down toilets. The canteen serves simple Indian meals. Access is by boat from the north bank. It's best to reserve ahead by phone or email.

There's no air-con and no coolers, something to bear in mind in the pre-monsoon months when temperatures can get into the 40s.

Madhai Resort HOTEL $$
(9424437150; www.themadhairesort.com; Bija Kheri village; r ₹1500, with AC ₹2000-2500;) Not far from the north bank of the Den-

wa River, this is a good midrange option if you're planning a safari from Madhai. Rooms are sizeable and pastel-hued, and it's run by the same people as Hotel Saket in Pachmarhi.

Information

Bison Lodge (07574-254394; near Jai Stambh; 9am-5pm Thu-Tue, 9-11.30am Wed) The lodge was built by Captain Forsyth for his own use in 1862, and also housed the region's Forest Department for more than half a century. This is where you must come for permits and jeeps to visit sites in the Pachmarhi area that fall within the Satpura Tiger Reserve's core zone – it's usually pretty busy around opening time in the morning.

The lodge building houses a bright, colourful **Wildlife & Cultural Interpretation Centre** (admission ₹10), with displays on the tiger reserve and its flora, fauna and people.

MP Tourism (07578-252100; Amaltas Complex; 10am-5pm) Main office near the Jai Stambh. Also has a kiosk at the bus stand (07578-252029; 10am-5pm).

Getting There & Away

From the **bus stand** in Pachmarhi town, six daily buses go to Bhopal (₹200, six hours). The 6.30pm and 9pm buses are sleepers and continue to Indore (seat/sleeper to Bhopal ₹270/300, to Indore ₹500/550, 12 hours). Buses to Nagpur (₹280 to ₹300, seven hours) leave at 3.30am and 5pm.

Buses run at least hourly to Pipariya (₹60, 1½ hours), where you can catch trains to destinations such as Jabalpur and Varanasi without having to go all the way to Bhopal. Train tickets are sold at the **railway booking office** (Army Area Main Gate; 8.30am-2pm & 4.30-7.30pm, closed Sun & Thu afternoons) and by agencies in the town.

If you're coming from Pipariya, shared jeeps to Pachmarhi (₹60 to ₹100 per person) leave from the bus stand far more often than buses.

Getting Around

The standard rate for a jeep and driver for a day, from Bison Lodge or from the bus stand/market area, is ₹1450.

Most Pachmarhi sights can be reached by bicycle, although in many cases you have to walk the last part. The roads are mostly fairly flat except for the last stretches to Dhoopgarh and Mahadeo Cave. You can rent bikes from **Baba Cycles** (Subhash Rd; per hr/day ₹20/100; 10am-9pm) and other shops in the market area.

WESTERN MADHYA PRADESH

Indore

0731 / POP 1.96 MILLION

Madhya Pradesh's biggest city and commerical powerhouse has much more of a cosmopolitan buzz than anywhere else in the state. Apart from some splendid buildings created by the Holkar dynasty, there's a shortage of outstanding sights, and Indore's traffic and crowds are as hectic as in any Indian city of this size, so for most tourists this is little more than a gateway to Mandu, Maheshwar or Omkareshwar. But with its bustling bazaars, good eating scene and a better-than-average crop of hotels, Indore is a place you may well grow to like if you spend a couple of nights here.

Sights

Lal Bagh Palace PALACE
(Lal Bagh Rd; Indian/foreigner ₹10/250; 10am-5pm Tue-Sun) Built between 1886 and 1921, Lal Bagh is the finest building left by the Holkar dynasty. As was the fashion among many late-Raj-era Indian nobility, the lavish interior is dominated by European styles, with striated Italian marble pillars reminiscent of a stracciatella-and-chocolate gelato, lots of chandeliers and classical columns, murals of Greek deities, a baroque-cum-rococo dining room, an English-library-style office with leather armchairs, a Renaissance sitting room and a Palladian queen's bedroom (with sadly ripped furnishings in some rooms).

An autorickshaw from the city centre costs about ₹50. Imitations of the Buckingham Palace gates creak at the entrance to the 28-hectare grounds, where, close to the palace, there's a statue of Queen Victoria.

Rajwada PALACE, TEMPLE
(Rajwada Chowk; Indian/foreigner ₹10/250, camera/video ₹25/100, temple free; 10am-5pm Tue-Sun, temple 7am-9pm) The Holkars' original Indore palace, begun in 1749, was almost annihilated by fire in 1984 and is still being rebuilt. Its seven-storey Mughal-influenced facade is striking but work on the interior still has a way to go. The temple in its rear, however, has already been restored and is a lovely little refuge from the hectic city, with a charming wood-pillared courtyard (enter from the north side of the building).

Indore

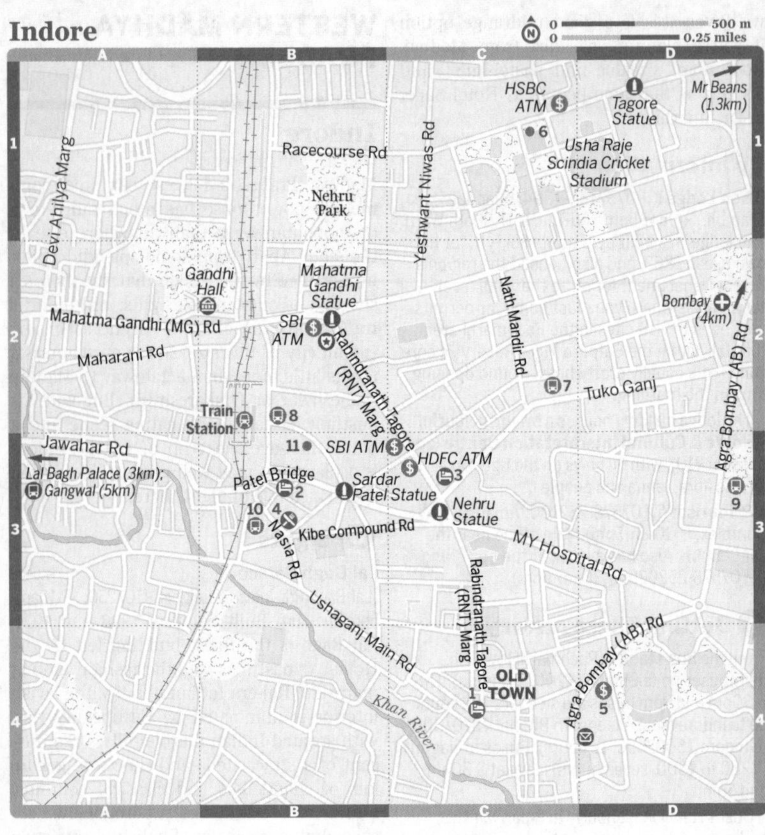

Indore

Sleeping
1 Hotel Chanakya C4
2 Hotel Neelam B3
3 Hotel Shreemaya C3

Eating
4 Hotel Apna B3

Information
5 State Bank of India D4

Transport
6 Air India C1
Chartered Bus .... (see 9)
7 Hans Travels C2
Metro Taxi .... (see 9)
8 Minivans to Gangwal Bus Stand B2
9 Royal Bus D3
10 Sarwate Bus Stand B3
11 Train Reservation Office B3

Central Museum MUSEUM
(AB Rd; Indian/foreigner ₹10/100, camera/video ₹50/200; ⏰10am-5pm Tue-Sun) Housed in a fine Holkar building on the Agra Bombay (AB) Rd, this museum has a good, if uninspiringly presented, collection of medieval (and earlier) Hindu sculptures, along with tools, weaponry and copper-engraved land titles. Skirmishes took place here during the First War of Independence (Indian Uprising) – the well in the garden was poisoned during the struggle.

Sleeping

Hotel Chanakya HOTEL $
(☎0731-4075191; 57-58 RNT Marg, Chhawni Chowk; s/d ₹880/1100, with AC from ₹1210/1540; ❄📶) Rooms here aren't as flashy as the disco-lit

Krishna mini-waterfall in the entrance hallway but they are functional nonetheless. The non-AC rooms have coolers and some of them are brighter than some of the ACs so it's worth comparing. Staff are friendly and it's in an interesting section of the old town.

Autorickshaws know it best by the sweet shop on the ground floor, Mathurawala.

Hotel Neelam HOTEL $
(☎0731-2466001; 33/2 Patel Bridge Corner; s/d from ₹525/725, with AC ₹850/1050; ❄📶) One of the few budget places near the train and bus stations that happily accepts foreigners. Neelam is well run and has simple but clean rooms with upgraded bathrooms around a central atrium.

★**Hotel Shreemaya** BUSINESS HOTEL $$
(☎0731-2515555; www.shreemaya.com; 12 RNT Marg; incl breakfast s ₹2840-4170, d ₹3600-5000; ❄@📶) Faults are hard to come by in this professionally run and extremely friendly business hotel. Modern rooms, in immaculate condition, feature good wi-fi, tea/coffee makers and balconies peppered with potted plants, and rates include airport pick-up and drop-off. The multicuisine restaurant is one of the best in town (mains ₹170 to ₹370).

Eating & Drinking

Hotel Apna INDIAN $
(Nasia Rd; mains ₹90-200; ⏲6am-11.30pm) This licensed restaurant right opposite Sarwate bus stand has been around more than 50 years and serves up delicious veg and meat dishes from an all-Indian menu, as well as the usual selection of beers and cheap whiskies. It's a popular spot to stow away in dark booths for some hard afternoon drinking as well. The upstairs has a brighter ambience than downstairs.

Mr Beans CAFE, CONTINENTAL $$
(www.mrbeans.in; 100 Saket Nagar; dishes ₹175-460; ⏲10am-11pm; 📶) With sophisticated European-style interiors throughout its seven open-plan rooms, this is one of India's nicest cafes. Beyond the Indorean in-crowd and excellent coffee (₹50 to ₹150) and tea, the menu specialises in homesickness-remedy overload: shepherd's pie, herbed chicken, three flavours of hummus, quesadillas, pastas, outstanding thin-crust pizzas and fantastic desserts.

★**Mediterra** MEDITERRANEAN $$$
(☎0731-4006666; Hotel Sayaji, Vijay Nagar; mains ₹580-1150; ⏲7.30-11.30pm) Cure the curry blues at this romantic rooftop restaurant on Indore's main avenue of upscale shopping and hotels north of the centre. Main dishes run from paella and rack of lamb to ratatouille and risotto, but many of the excellent mezze and starters – the likes of paneer satay or coconut prawns – are big enough to be mains themselves.

Information

Bombay Hospital (☎emergency 0731-4077000; www.bombayhospitalindore.com; Eastern Ring Rd) Indore's best general hospital.

State Bank of India (AB Rd; ⏲10.30am-4.30pm Mon-Sat) Changes foreign cash and has an ATM.

Getting There & Around

AIR

The airport is 9km west of the city.

SARAFA BAZAR

Many Indoreans consider this **street-food market** (snacks ₹20-70; ⏲9pm-midnight) to be the most exciting thing about their city. It's a great experience not just for the taste sensations of the local snacks but also for the friendly atmosphere among the nightly crowds. The street is lined with jewellers' shops and after they close, the snack stalls set up in front. The most famous spot is **Joshi Dahi Vada** which doles out hundreds of serves of *dahi vada* (lentil dumplings in yoghurt with chutney) nightly. It's about halfway along the strip on the south side – easily identified by the crowds in front. Mr Joshi likes to toss dishes of yoghurt into the air to show off its consistency.

The best plan is simply to come hungry and wander along and try what takes your fancy, but two top local favourites definitely worth asking for are *bhutte ka kees* (grated maize sautéed with spices and herbs) and *sabudana khichdi* (soaked sago tossed with spices, herbs and crushed peanuts).

Follow the street along the south side of the Rajwada palace and you'll hit the food stalls within 200m.

IndiGo (www.goindigo.in) operates the most flights out of Indore: Delhi four times daily, Mumbai three times, Hyderabad, Kolkata and Raipur twice, and Ahmedabad, Bengaluru (Bangalore), Goa, Nagpur and Pune all six or seven days a week. **Jet Airways** (www.jetairways.com) flies to Mumbai four times daily, Delhi three times, and Ahmedabad, Bengaluru, Chennai, Pune six or seven days a week. **Air India** (☎0731-2431595; www.airindia.in; Racecourse Rd; ⏲10am-1pm & 2-5pm Mon-Sat) flies once daily to Mumbai and Delhi.

Allow 45 minutes to get to/from the airport. Autorickshaws charge around ₹150, taxis ₹250 to ₹300. Prepaid taxi stands at the airport offer out-of-town rides (Ujjain ₹900, Omkareshwar ₹1800) as well as trips into the city.

City bus 11 runs from the road outside the airport into the centre (Sardar Patel Circle, Madhumilan Chauraha) about every 20 minutes, and returns by the same route.

BUS

For Mandu, catch a bus from the **Gangwal bus stand** (☎0731-2380688; Dhar Rd) to Dhar (₹70, three hours, frequent 6am to 11.30pm) from where you can change for Mandu (₹40, one hour, last bus 9pm). **Minivans** go between the centre (opposite the train station) and Gangwal bus stand for ₹20. Autorickshaws charge around ₹60.

Buses from the **Sarwate bus stand** (☎0731-2364444; Chhoti Gwaltoli) include those listed below. For Maheshwar, change at Dhamnod.

Bhopal ₹180, five hours, frequent 6am to 8pm

Dhamnod ₹77, 2½ hours, frequent 5am to 10.30pm

Omkareshwar ₹70, three hours, about hourly 6am to 6.30pm

Pachmarhi (Verma Travels, 12 hours) AC bus 8pm seat/sleeper ₹500/600, non-AC 9.40pm ₹450/500

Ujjain ₹60, two hours, frequent 24 hours

For more comfort, **Chartered Bus** (☎0731-4288888; http://charteredbus.in; AICTSL Campus, AB Rd) runs AC Volvo coaches to Bhopal (₹330, four hours) two or three times hourly from 5am to 9.30pm, and every hour or two through the night. It also has one or two daily air-con services to Ahmedabad, Jabalpur, Jaipur, Pune and Udaipur. From the same terminal, **Royal Bus** (☎0731-4027999; www.royalbus.info; AICTSL Campus, AB Rd) has air-con buses to Ujjain (₹70, two hours) every 45 minutes, 7.30am to 8.15pm.

Hans Travels (☎0731-2510007; www.hanstravel.in; Dhakkanwala Kua, South Tukoganj) runs nine daily Volvo AC buses to Bhopal (₹330, four hours), and a host of sleeper buses departing between 5pm and 10pm, including these:

Agra non-AC/AC ₹500/800, 16 hours, two daily

Ahmedabad non-AC/AC ₹400/600, 11 hours, two daily

Gwalior non-AC/AC ₹400/600, 12 hours, four daily

Jaipur non-AC/AC ₹400/700, 13 to 15 hours, three daily

Jalgaon (for Ajanta) non-AC ₹350 to ₹400, eight hours, 9pm and 10pm

Mumbai non-AC/AC/Volvo AC ₹600/900/1250, 12 to 15 hours, five daily

Nagpur non-AC/AC/Volvo AC ₹500/660/1200, 10 to 13 hours, four daily

Pune non-AC/AC/Volvo AC ₹600/900/1200, 12 to 15 hours, eight daily

TAXI

Metro Taxi (☎0731-4288888; AICTSL Campus, AB Rd) has new cars and professional drivers and charges ₹2000 one way to Mandu or Omkareshwar, and ₹2200 to Maheshwar. Day hire up to 12 hours and 250km is ₹2500.

TRAIN

There are seven daily trains to Bhopal and 12 to Ujjain. The **train reservation office** (⏲8am-10pm Mon-Sat, to 2pm Sun) is 200m east of the station.

HANDY TRAINS FROM INDORE

DESTINATION	TRAIN NO & NAME	FARE (₹)	DURATION (HR)	DEPARTURE
Bhopal	12919 Malwa Exp	215/535/735	5	12.25pm
Delhi	12415 Indore-Delhi Sarai Rohilla Intercity Exp	440/1160/1655	14½	4pm
Mumbai (Central station)	12962 Avantika Exp	440/1160/1655	14	4.25pm
Ujjain	12919 Malwa Exp	170/540/740	1½	12.25pm

Fares: sleeper/3AC/2AC

Ujjain

0734 / POP 515,215

First impressions don't always impress. And that's the case with Ujjain. But wander away from the chaotic station area towards the river ghats and some of Ujjain's famous temples, via the city's maze of alleyways, and you'll discover an older, more spiritual side to Ujjain that has been attracting traders and pilgrims for hundreds of years. An undeniable energy pulses through the sacred sites here – not surprising given this is one of Hinduism's seven sacred cities and also one of the four cities that hosts, every 12 years, the gigantic Kumbh Mela pilgrimage festival. An estimated 75 million people crowded into Ujjain during the month of its most recent Kumbh Mela in 2016.

Sights

★Mahakaleshwar Mandir HINDU TEMPLE

(4am-11pm) While this is not visually the most stunning temple, tagging along behind a conga-line through the underground chambers can be magical. At nonfestival times, the marble walkways are a peaceful preamble to the subterranean chamber containing one of India's 12 *jyoti linga* – naturally occurring, especially sacred Shiva linga believed to derive currents of *shakti* (creative energies perceived as female deities) from within themselves rather than being ritually invested with *mantra-shakti* by priests.

The temple was destroyed by the Delhi sultan Iltutmish in 1235 and restored by the Scindias in the 19th century. You can jump the queues by paying ₹150 for a 'VIP' entry ticket.

★Ram Ghat GHAT

The most central and popular of Ujjain's river ghats, strung with orange- and pink-roofed shrines, is busy all day with people bathing and presenting gifts of milk or flowers to the Shipra. It's most atmospheric at dawn or dusk when the devout chime cymbals and light candles at the water's edge.

Harsiddhi Mandir HINDU TEMPLE

Built during the Maratha period, this temple enshrines a famous vermilion-painted image of goddess Annapurna. At the entrance, two tall blackened stone towers bristling with lamps are a special feature of Maratha art. They add to the spectacle of **Navratri** (Festival of Nine Nights; Sep/Oct) when filled with oil and ignited.

Sinhasan Battisi MONUMENT

Vikram Teela, a small island in Rudra Sagar lake, is covered with statuary (installed in 2016) that recreates the magical throne and court of the legendary Ujjain king Vikramaditya. The enthroned king sits surrounded by his legendary circle of nine scholars, the *nava-ratna*, which includes the great (historical) Sanskrit poet Kalidas.

Gopal Mandir HINDU TEMPLE

(7am-noon & 4-10pm) The Scindias built this marble-spired temple, a fine example of Maratha architecture, in the 19th century. The sanctum's silver-plated doors originated at the Somnath Temple in Gujarat but were taken from there to Ghazni, Afghanistan, by Muslim raiders. Ahmad Shah Durani later took them to Lahore (in present-day Pakistan), before Mahadji Scindia brought them here.

The bazaar alleyways in this part of town are wonderful places to explore.

Vedh Shala HISTORIC BUILDING

(Observatory, Jantar Mantar; Indian/foreigner ₹10/100; 8am-6pm) Ujjain has been India's Greenwich since the 4th century BC, and this simple-looking but surprisingly complicated observatory was built by Maharaja Jai Singh between 1725 and 1730. Each of its five structures (for tracking celestial bodies and recording time) has quite detailed explanations in English, but you'd need to be an astronomer to understand them!

Festivals & Events

Kumbh Mela RELIGIOUS

(Simhastha; Apr/May) Ujjain is one of four sites in India that hosts the incredible Kumbh Mela, during which millions bathe in the Shipra River. It takes place here every 12 years, normally during April and May. The next one is due in 2028.

Sleeping & Eating

Hotel Naman Palace HOTEL $

(0734-2564086; 8 Choubis Khamba Marg; r ₹1000, with AC ₹1300;) One of several new hotels in the Mahakaleshwar Mandir area, the Naman provides (for now at least) modern rooms in brown, copper and white, with soft beds, sofas, wi-fi and big square shower heads. Only a few have natural light, though.

Ujjain

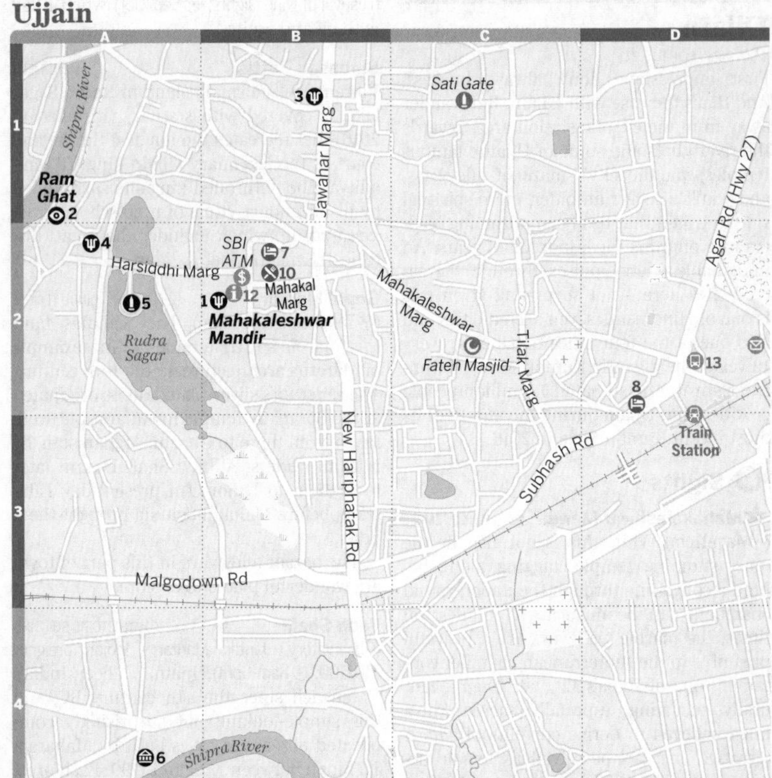

Hotel Ramakrishna HOTEL **$**
(☎0734-2557012; www.hotelramakrishna.co.in; Subhash Rd; s/d/tr ₹500/1000/1300, with AC ₹900/1300/1700; ❄📶) This cleaner-than-average Subhash Rd hotel has the best air-con rooms of those considered, with tiled floors, semi-stylish trimmings and tight bathrooms. The non-ACs are well-worn versions of the same, some with squat toilets. Rooms vary in light and size.

The adjoining New Sudama restaurant does inexpensive vegetarian food (mains ₹75 to ₹150).

★**Hotel Shipra Residency** HOTEL **$$**
(☎0734-2551495; www.mptourism.com; Dewas Rd; incl breakfast r ₹3560-4280, ste ₹5470; ❄📶) Easily the best option anywhere near the centre, this MP Tourism hotel added a new block of 30 bright, contemporary deluxe rooms and suites in 2015. The original rooms, on three floors around a courtyard, are smaller, with older bathrooms, but are still fine, with comfy beds, tea/coffee equipment and toiletry kits.

There's also a stylish restaurant, the **Meghdoot** (mains ₹150-400; ⏲11am-3pm & 7-10.30pm).

Damaru Wala INDIAN **$**
(138 Mahakal Marg; thali ₹100-140; ⏲9.30am-midnight) It just does thalis (all-you-can-eat meals) but they're tasty, home-style ones, and served up in a bright, clean, purpose-designed space with white-top tables and black chairs.

The restaurant is up a flight of stairs, with a big black, red and white sign in Hindi only.

Shree Ganga SWEETS, SOUTH INDIAN **$**
(50 Amarsingh Marg; sweets per kg from ₹360, mains ₹70-120; ⏲7am-11pm) Since 1949 this epic sweet shop has been satiating Ujjaini sugar cravings. There's no English sign or menu, but staff can steer you in the right

Ujjain

Top Sights

1 Mahakaleshwar Mandir........B2
2 Ram Ghat........A1

Sights

3 Gopal Mandir........B1
4 Harsiddhi Mandir........A2
5 Sinhasan Battisi........A2
6 Vedh Shala........A4

Sleeping

7 Hotel Naman Palace........B2
8 Hotel Ramakrishna........D2
9 Hotel Shipra Residency........E3

Eating

10 Damaru Wala........B2
Meghdoot........(see 9)
11 Shree Ganga........F3

Information

12 MP Tourism........B2

Transport

13 Dewas Gate Bus Stand........D2

direction. One speciality is their milk cake, another the *caju barfi* (a fudge-like cashew sweet). They also do thirst-quenching freshly squeezed juices such as pomegranate and pineapple.

Upstairs, there's a great savoury menu from 11am that includes creative South Indian (green chutney *masala dosa*) and Chinese. It's just to the right of Baker's Lounge.

Information

MP Tourism (0734-2552263; www.mptourism.com; 10am-6pm Mon-Sat) In the grounds of the Mahakaleshwar Mandir.

Transport

BUS

Services from the **Dewas Gate Bus Stand** (State Hwy 27):

Dhar ₹160, 3½ hours, 8am and 2pm
Indore ₹55, two hours, frequent 5am to 11pm
Omkareshwar ₹140, 3½ hours, 6am, 8am, 9am, 2pm, 4pm

For Maheshwar or Mandu, change at Dhar.

Buses to Bhopal, including six daily air-con services by Chartered Bus (www.charteredbus.in; ₹280, 4½ hours), go from the **Nanakheda Bus Stand** (Sanwer Rd), a 4km autorickshaw ride (₹30) south of the train station.

TRAIN

There are about 10 daily trains to Bhopal and 15 to Indore, both of which have many more trains than Ujjain. The only train going every day to Gwalior and Agra is the Delhi-bound 12919 Malwa Express at 2.10pm; otherwise you can take any train to Bhopal and change there.

Getting Around

Prepaid autorickshaws from the booth outside the train station charge ₹50 to Ram Ghat and₹400 for a four-hour tour around Ujjain.

Mandu

07292 / POP 10,300 / ELEV 590M

Perched on a pleasantly green, thinly forested 25-sq-km plateau, picturesque Mandu is home to some of India's finest examples of Afghan architecture as well as impressive baobab trees, originally from Africa. The plateau is littered with World Heritage–listed

HANDY TRAINS FROM UJJAIN

DESTINATION	TRAIN NO & NAME	FARE (₹)	DURATION (HR)	DEPARTURE
Bhopal	12919 Malwa Exp	170/535/740 (A)	3½	2.10pm
Delhi	12415 Nizamuddin Exp	415/1090/1555 (A)	12½	5.35pm
Indore	18234 Narmada Exp Passenger	100/490/695 (A)	2½	8.30am
Jaipur	12465 Ranthambore Exp	185/335/700/865 (B)	9	7.45am
Mumbai (Central)	12962 Avantika Exp	415/1095/1555 (A)	12½	5.55pm

Fares: (A) sleeper/3AC/2AC, (B) 2nd class/sleeper/chair car/3AC

palaces, tombs, monuments and mosques. Some cling to the edge of ravines, others stand beside lakes, while Rupmati's Pavilion, the most romantic of them all, sits serenely on the edge of the plateau, overlooking the vast plains below. Mandu is a great place to spend a couple of days exploring grand and beautiful architecture in a relaxed rural setting, easily toured by bicycle – and pondering the mutation of the capital of a once powerful kingdom into just another Indian village.

History

Mandu came to prominence in the 10th century as a fort-capital of the Hindu Paramara dynasty that ruled Malwa (western Madhya Pradesh and southeastern Rajasthan) at the time. Malwa was conquered by the Muslim Delhi sultanate in 1305. After Timur sacked Delhi in 1401, the sultanate's governor in Malwa, the Afghan Dilawar Khan, set up his own kingdom and Mandu's golden age began. His son Hoshang Shah shifted the capital from Dhar to Mandu and raised the place to its greatest splendour. Their Ghuri dynasty was short-lived, however. Hoshang's son was poisoned by a rival, Mahmud Khilji (or Khalji), whose Khilji dynasty ruled Malwa from 1436 until Bahadur Shah of Gujarat conquered it in 1526.

Mandu and Malwa then fell in quick succession to the Mughal emperor Humayun (1534), Mallu Khan, an officer from the Khilji dynasty (1536), and Humayun's north Indian rival Sher Shah (1542). In 1555 Baz Bahadur, a son of Sher Shah's local governor, crowned himself sultan. Baz however fled Mandu in 1561 as the Mughal emperor Akbar's troops invaded.

Akbar's successors Jehangir and Shah Jahan enjoyed visiting Mandu but its importance had waned. When the Holkar clan of Marathas defeated the Mughals near Dhar in 1732, Mandu came under Maratha control from Dhar and the slide in its fortunes that had begun with the absconding of Baz Bahadur became a plummet.

Sights

There are three main groups of ruins: the Royal Enclave, the Village Group and the Rewa Kund Group. Each requires its own separate ticket. All other sights are free.

★Royal Enclave HISTORIC BUILDING
(Indian/foreigner ₹15/200, video ₹25; dawn-dusk) The Royal Enclave is the largest group of monuments, with several beautiful buildings from the 15th- and 16th-century Ghuri and Khilji dynasties set near two picturesque tanks. This is the only group that's fenced off into a single compound. There's a **Publication Sales Counter** (9am-5pm) selling guidebooks beside the ticket office.

➡ Jahaz Mahal
(Ship Palace) Dating from the 15th century, this is the most famous building in Mandu. Built on a narrow strip of land between Munja and Kapoor tanks, with an upper terrace like a ship's bridge (use your imagination), it's far longer (120m) than it is wide (15m). The pleasure-loving sultan Ghiyas-ud-din Khilji, who is said to have had a harem of 15,000 maidens, constructed its lookouts, scalloped arches, airy rooms and beautiful pleasure pools.

➡ Hindola Mahal
(Swing Palace) Just north of Ghiyas' stately pleasure dome is the Hindola Mahal, so-

called because the slope of its walls sort of resembles that of the ropes of a swing. Thought to have been a royal reception hall, it's often ascribed to Hoshang Shah though some writers attribute it to Ghiyas-ud-Din. Either way it's an impressive and eye-catching design.

➡ Dilawar Khan's Mosque

Built by Dilawar Khan in 1405, this is Mandu's earliest Islamic building. It was built mainly with material from earlier Hindu temples – particularly obvious in the pillars and ceilings of the roofed western end.

➡ Champa Baodi

So-called because its water supposedly smelled as sweet as the champak flower, the Champa Baodi is a circular step-well with vaulted side-niches. It was accessed by a series of vaulted passages and chambers, called the Tahkhana, some of which you can explore from nearby entrances, though you can't actually reach the well. You can, however, look down into it from above.

➡ Turkish Bath

Stars and octagons perforate the domed roofs of this tiny bathhouse, which had hot and cold water and a hypocaust (underfloor-heated) sauna.

➡ Jal Mahal

(Water Palace) This palace on an island-like spit of land at the corner of Munja Tank is thought to have been a private retreat for noble couples. It has several step-wells and pools in which they could disport.

Village Group

This group, straddling the main road in the centre of the village, comprises three grand edifices constructed in the 15th-century by the Ghuri and Khilji dynasties – a mosque, a tomb and a madrasa (Islamic college). One **ticket** (Indian/foreigner ₹15/200, video; ⏲ dawn/dusk), sold at the entrance to the Jama Masjid, covers all three.

Jama Masjid MOSQUE

Entered by a flight of steps leading to a 17m-high domed porch, this disused redstone mosque dominates Mandu village centre. Hoshang Shah begun its construction around 1406, basing it on the great Omayyad Mosque in Damascus in Syria, and Mahmud Khilji completed it in 1454. It's a relatively austere but harmonious building, and reckoned to be the finest and largest example of Afghan architecture in India.

Hoshang Shah's Tomb ISLAMIC TOMB

Reputed to be India's oldest marble mausoleum, this imposing tomb is crowned with a tiny crescent thought to have been imported from Persia or Mesopotamia. Light filters into the echoing, domed interior through stone *jalis* (carved lattice screens), intended to cast an appropriately subdued light on the tombs. An inscription records Shah Jahan sending his architects – including Ustad Hamid, who worked on the Taj Mahal – here in 1659 to pay their respects to the tomb's builders of two centuries before.

Ashrafi Mahal ISLAMIC SITE

The Ashrafi Mahal was built as a madrasa (Islamic college) by Hoshang Shah between 1405 and 1422. It was a quadrangle with rows of cells and arcaded corridors on the outside, and four corner towers. Mahmud Khilji of the following dynasty converted the northwest tower into a seven-storey victory tower, and roofed the courtyard as a platform for his own grand marble tomb. Tomb and tower have vanished but you can climb a grand staircase and walk around the roof.

Rewa Kund Group

A pleasant 4km cycle south of Mandu village brings you to the Rewa Kund tank and the two monuments of the Rewa Kund Group, Baz Bahadur's Palace and Rupmati's Pavilion – all infused with the legends of sultan Baz Bahadur and his shepherdess beloved, Rupmati. The **ticket office** (Indian/foreigner ₹15/200, video ₹25; ⏲ dawn/dusk) is opposite the tank, just before Baz Bahadur's Palace.

Baz Bahadur's Palace PALACE

Baz Bahadur (r 1555–61) was the last independent ruler of Mandu. His palace, a curious mix of Rajasthani and Mughal styles, was built in 1508–09 by the Khilji sultan Nasir-ud-Din. Baz Bahadur supposedly took a liking to it because of his infatuation with the singing shepherdess Rupmati who, according to legend, used to frequent the nearby Rewa Kund.

Rupmati's Pavilion NOTABLE BUILDING

Standing at the top of an escarpment falling 366m to the plains, Rupmati's Pavilion has a delicacy of design and beauty of location unmatched by Mandu's other monuments. According to Malwa legends, the music-loving Baz Bahadur built it to persuade his golden-voiced shepherdess beloved, Rupmati, to move here from her home on the plains.

Mandu

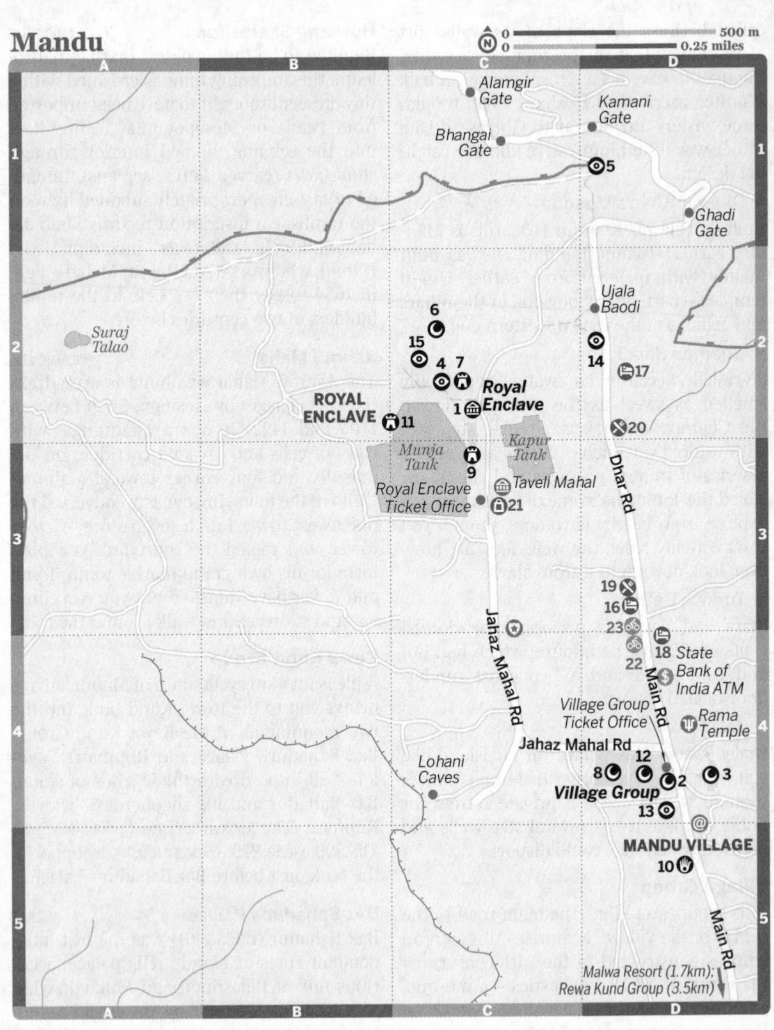

From its terrace and domed pavilions, Rupmati could gaze at the distant glint of the sacred Narmada River.

In fact, the pavilion probably began life as a watchtower a century or more before Rupmati's time. Nonetheless, the love story is a subject of Malwa folk songs – not least because of its tragic ending. Lured by tales of Rupmati's beauty, Akbar's general Adham Khan marched on Mandu and Baz Bahadur fled, leaving his lover to poison herself rather than fall into the invader's hands.

This place is simply gorgeous at sunset.

Other Sights

Shop of Gada Shah NOTABLE BUILDING

Almost resembling a Gothic cathedral, this looks more like an emporium than a mere shop. It was a warehouse for saffron and musk, imported and sold at a handsome profit when there were enough wealthy people to buy. Its owner's name, meaning 'beggar master', is thought to identify him as Rajput chief Medini Ray, a powerful subject of the early-16th-century Khilji sultan Mahmud II.

Delhi Gate GATE

It's worth wandering up to the north end of town to the Delhi Gate, which was the main

Mandu

Top Sights
1 Royal Enclave C2
2 Village Group D4

Sights
3 Ashrafi Mahal D4
4 Champa Baodi C2
5 Delhi Gate D1
6 Dilawar Khan's Mosque C2
7 Hindola Mahal C2
8 Hoshang Shah's Tomb D4
9 Jahaz Mahal C3
10 Jain Temple D5
11 Jal Mahal C2
12 Jama Masjid D4
13 Saturday Haat D4
14 Shop of Gada Shah D2
15 Turkish Bath C2

Sleeping
16 Hotel Gurukripa Villa D3
17 Hotel Rupmati D2
18 Shivani Resort D4

Eating
19 Shivani Restaurant D3
20 Yatrika D2

Shopping
21 Publication Sales Counter C3

Information
Tourist Interpretation Centre .... (see 20)

Transport
22 Ritik Cycles D4
23 Sonu Bicycles D3

entrance to Mandu. You can walk up on top of it and along a short stretch of the walls for fine views over the country beyond.

Saturday Haat MARKET
(10am-dusk Sat) This colourful weekly *haat* (market), behind the Jama Masjid, is similar to ones held in many central Indian areas with a tribal population. Adivasis (tribal people) walk kilometres to buy and sell goods ranging from mountains of red chillies to dried *mahua* (a flower used to make a potent liquor of the same name).

Jain Temple JAIN TEMPLE
Entered through a kaleidoscopic pot-pourri of a gate, this complex is a splash of kitsch among the Islamic monuments. The temples feature marble, silver and gold *tirthankars* (the 24 great Jain teachers) with jade eyes, and at the far right-hand end is a theme-park–like museum with a walk-on model of the Shatrunjaya hilltop temple complex in Gujarat. In its colourful murals, bears devour sinners' arms, demons poke out their eyes, and men and women are tied together and burnt.

You'll probably have to ask around for someone to open the museum.

Nil Kanth Palace HINDU TEMPLE
If you're looking for a great reason to cycle out into the countryside, consider visiting this unusual former palace turned temple. It stands at the head of a ravine, on the site of an earlier Shiva shrine – its name means God with Blue Throat – and is now again used as a place of worship. A stream built by one of Akbar's governors trickles through a delightful spiral channel and is usually filled with sweet-scented water.

To get here cycle south from the Jama Masjid for 850m and turn right at a large water tower. Follow the road as it twists and turns past outlying houses all the way to Nil Kanth (2.2km). You can continue from here, past more remote settlements, for just over 1km to reach the still-standing gateway of the now ruined, Maratha-built **Songarh Fort**, from where there are more great views.

Sagar Talao Group ISLAMIC SITE
If you have time, this group of handsome buildings is worth a detour between Mandu village and Rewa Kund. The main ones are **Malik Mughith's Mosque**, built by Mahmud Khilji's father in 1432 using carvings from earlier Hindu buildings; a large, courtyarded **caravanserai** (1437); the **Dai-ki-Chhoti Bahen-ka-Mahal** (Wetnurse's Younger Sister's Palace), actually a striking octagonal domed tomb on a raised platform; and the **Dai-ka-Mahal** (Wetnurse's Palace), another domed tomb, on an arcaded platform that also supports a mosque.

If coming from the village, turn left 200m after the Malwa Resort hotel and the buildings soon appear on the right.

Sleeping & Eating

Hotel Gurukripa Villa HOTEL $
(07292-263243; Dhar Rd; r ₹700, with AC ₹1500) Has reasonably clean but stuffy rooms with the occasional blue, yellow or pink wall but no natural light.

Malwa Resort HOTEL $$

(☎07292-263235; www.mptourism.com; Main Rd; r incl breakfast ₹3920-5110;) The best thing about this MP Tourism property, 2km south of the village, is morning chai in the lakeside gazebo, watching local fishermen cast their nets over Sagar Talao. The large gardens contain comfortable rooms in cottages, children's play areas and a pool, and the hotel has a restaurant, a bar and bicycles to rent.

Hotel Rupmati HOTEL $$

(☎07292-263270; www.hotelrupmati.com; Dhar Rd; r ₹2000, with AC ₹2500;) A row of clean rooms with large bathrooms (though smelling of bug spray) is perched on the edge of a cliff with good views of the valley below. There's an adequate restaurant and you can eat out on the delightful lawn.

Shivani Resort HOTEL $$

(☎9425334777; Dhar Rd; r with fan/cooler/AC ₹1000/1500/1850) New in 2016, Shivani offers big, bare, mostly bright rooms with efforts at contemporary style in the shape of pictorial bathroom tiles, rectangular toilets and square washbasins. We hope they'll be kept in the condition they deserve.

Shivani Restaurant INDIAN $

(Dhar Rd; mains ₹100-180, thali ₹80-180; 9am-10pm;) The plain, clean, canteen-style interior of this no-nonsense diner is in welcome contrast to the hectically gaudy exterior, but it's the good, honest and cheap food that overshadows both. The pure-veg menu is extensive and includes solid thalis plus local specialities such as *Mandu malai kofta* (dumplings in a mild sauce).

Yatrika INDIAN $

(Malwa Retreat, Dhar Rd; mains ₹130-320; 8-10am, noon-3pm & 7-10pm;) The cafe-restaurant at Malwa Retreat dishes out veg and nonveg Indian meals in relatively flash contemporary premises with an open kitchen. It has wi-fi but unfortunately if you want a cold beer you'll need to head to the sister property, the Malwa Resort (p670).

Shopping

Roopayan TEXTILES

(Main Rd; 8am-9pm) Next to Malwa Resort, this small shop sells good-quality scarves, shawls, bedspreads and clothing made from material (mostly cotton) that has been block-printed, usually with natural dyes, in the nearby village of Bagh.

Information

Internet (Main Rd; per hr ₹30; 7am-10pm) You can get online at Gayan Dut Sucnalay's fabric shop (no English sign), about 100m south of the Jama Masjid.

Tourist Interpretation Centre (☎07292-263221; Malwa Retreat, Dhar Rd; 9am-6pm) They can answer questions and arrange government-certified guides (per half-day/day ₹470/660).

Getting There & Away

Buses stop at various spots around the central intersection by the Jama Masjid. There are four buses to Indore (₹100, 3½ hours, 7.15am, 9am, 1.30pm and 3.30pm) and one to Ujjain (₹150, six hours, 6am). Buses leave every half-hour for Dhar (₹40, one hour, 6am to 7pm), where you can change for Dhamnod (₹50, two hours), then, in turn, for Maheshwar (₹15, 30 minutes) or for Barwah (₹70, two hours) where you can catch another bus or a tempo on to Omkareshwar (₹20, 30 minutes). In fact it's quicker to get off 22km before Dhar at the junction at Lunhera (₹15, 30 minutes), where you can flag down Dhamnod-bound buses (₹50, 1½ hours). You should leave Mandu not later than 3pm if heading to Maheshwar and by 1pm for Omkareshwar.

Taxis cost about ₹700 to Maheshwar and ₹1500 to Indore. Ask around the market area in front of the Jama Masjid.

Getting Around

Cycling is the best way to get around, as the terrain is flat, the air clear and the countryside beautiful. Mandu doesn't appear to have any autorickshaws. Neighbours **Ritik Cycles** (☎9000157920; Dhar Rd; per day ₹100) and **Sonu Bicycles** (Dhar Rd; per day ₹100) both rent reasonable bikes near the village centre.

Maheshwar

☎07283 / POP 24,400

The peaceful riverside town of Maheshwar has long held spiritual significance – it's mentioned in the Mahabharata and Ramayana under its old name, Mahishmati, and still draws sadhus and *yatris* (pilgrims) to its ancient ghats and temples on the holy Narmada River. The town enjoyed a golden age in the 18th century under the Holkar queen Ahilyabai (r 1767–95), who moved the Holkar capital here from Indore and built the palace within Maheshwar's fort, and is still much revered for her wisdom, benevolence and temple-building. Away from the ghats and historic buildings, Maheshwar's colourful streets display some brightly painted wooden houses with overhanging balconies.

It's a captivating place that packs a lot of punch in a very small area around the ghats, palace and temples – a sort of refined, spitshone Varanasi in miniature.

Sights

Maheshwar Palace PALACE

Maheshwar is dominated by its fort, whose huge, imposing ramparts, towering above the river ghats, were built by Emperor Akbar. The Maheshwar Palace and several temples within the fort were added by Queen Ahilyabai in the 18th century. The palace is part public courtyards, part posh hotel. Entering the fort complex from the town side, a 'Maheshwar Palace' sign indicates a **museum** (9am-6pm) FREE about the queen in part of her living quarters.

Rehwa Society WORKSHOP

(8120001381; www.rehwasociety.org; 10am-6pm Wed-Mon, shop daily) On the way down from the palace to the ghats, a small doorway announces the NGO Rehwa Society, a craft cooperative where profits are ploughed back into the education, housing and welfare of the weavers and their families. A local school, run entirely by Rehwa, is behind the workshop. Maheshwar saris are famous for their unique weave and simple, geometric patterns.

You can watch the weavers at work and buy shawls (from ₹1800), saris (₹4000 to ₹13,000), scarves (₹1100 to ₹2500) and fabrics made from silk, cotton and wool. There are also volunteer possibilities here.

★ **Chhatris** HINDU SHRINE

(Cenotaphs) Down to the right of the ramp descending towards the ghats are the *chhatris* (cenotaphs) of Ahilyabai and Vithoji Rao, a Holkar prince who was trampled to death by elephants in 1801 on orders of his enemies during an inter-Maratha conflict. Ahilyabai's *chhatri,* the larger and more elaborate of the two, with fine stone carving, is known as the Ahilyeshwar Temple. It contains a small statue of the queen, wearing a sari, with a Shiva lingam in front of her.

Festivals & Events

Ahilyabai Holkar Jayanti Mahotsav PARADE

(May/Jun) The birthday of the revered Holkar queen, Ahilyabai, is celebrated with particular fervour in Maheshwar on or close to her birth date, 31 May, with percussion-heavy processions of palanquins (enclosed seats carried on poles on four men's shoulders) throughout the town.

Sleeping & Eating

Hansa Heritage HOTEL $

(07283-273296; http://hansaheritage.in; Fort Rd; r ₹800, with AC ₹1150-1550;) This place 150m from the fort gate has been built with style and quality throughout. Smart, modern rooms have a rustic feel with mud-and-grass-daubed walls, antique-looking wooden furniture and attractive coloured-glass window panes.

Aakash Deep GUESTHOUSE $

(9827809455; aakashdeeplodge@gmail.com; Fort Rd; s/d/q ₹350/400/600, q with AC ₹1200;) Friendly Aakash has a variety of clean, medium-sized or large rooms. Those on the two upper floors have balconies and softer mattresses than the dark ground-floor quarters. Breakfast is available; hot water is by bucket. It's 150m from the fort gate, behind Hansa Heritage.

★ **Laboo's Café & Lodge** GUESTHOUSE $$

(7771004818; info@ahilyafort.com; Fort Gate; s/d incl breakfast ₹1450/1650, snacks ₹15-40; cafe 7am-8pm;) Laboo's is not only a delightful cafe in a tree-shaded courtyard, but also has five wonderful air-conditioned rooms. Each is different, being part of the fort gate and walls, but is decorated with care and attention. The biggest and brightest, upstairs (single/double ₹2300/2750), features its own fort-wall verandah. For guests, staff will whip up a delicious, unlimited thali (₹250).

★ **Ahilya Fort** HERITAGE HOTEL $$$

(011-41551575; www.ahilyafort.com; per person incl full board Indian ₹7900-9020, foreigner ₹11,500-13,650;) Mick Jagger, Demi Moore and Sting have all indulged in this heritage hotel in Maheshwar Palace owned by Prince Shivaji Rao (Richard) Holkar, an Indian-American directly descended from the palace's founder Queen Ahilyabai. The best rooms are indeed palatial and some come with fabulous river views, while lush gardens house exotic fruit trees, organic vegetable patches and history at every turn.

Rates include all meals as well as sunset boat trips. Booking ahead is essential. Nonguests who fancy a night to remember should not miss dining here. The sumptuous menu is set, as is the ₹3675 per person price (including alcohol). You'll need to book 24 hours in advance. Dinner begins at 7.30pm with candlelit cocktails courtesy (when he's here) of the Prince himself, who divides his time between here and Paris.

Information

There's an SBI ATM on the main road 400m before the fort entrance gate.

Getting There & Away

There are buses to Indore (₹90, 2½ hours) about every 1½ hours, 6am to 5pm. For Mandu, first head west to Dhamnod (₹15, 30 minutes, buses about every 15 minutes, 6am to 9pm) then take a Dhar-bound bus as far as the junction at Lunhera (₹50, 1½ hours, about half-hourly). From there flag down a bus or tempo (both ₹15, 30 minutes) for the final 14km to Mandu.

For Omkareshwar take a bus to Barwah (₹50, 1½ hours, about half-hourly) and then another bus or a tempo to Omkareshwar (₹20, 30 minutes).

Omkareshwar

☎07280 / POP 10,062

This Om-shaped island in the holy Narmada River attracts pilgrims in large numbers and has become a spiritual chill-out destination for some travellers. A controversial dam just upstream has changed the look of Omkareshwar considerably, but the island has retained its spiritual vibe and remains a pleasant and authentic – if typically commercialised – pilgrimage point.

Much activity takes place off the island, in the town on the south side of the river. Two footbridges 400m apart link town and island: the western old bridge crosses from the market square called Getti Chowk, and the eastern new bridge crosses from a large parking area. Halfway between the bridges you'll find the ghats (landings), where you can cross the river on boats for ₹10 per person.

The new bus stand is 1.5km southwest from Getti Chowk along Mamaleshwar Rd, and the old bus stand is 1km nearer town along the same road. Arriving buses may drop you at either.

The hub of activity on the island is the street leading from the old bridge to Shri Omkar Mandhata temple.

Sights

Tourists can rub shoulders with sadhus in the island's narrow lanes, browse the colourful stalls selling souvenir linga, piles of orange and yellow powder for tikka marks and flower offerings for the temples, or join pilgrims attending the thrice daily *puja* (prayer) at the **Shri Omkar Mandhata**. This salmon-pink, cave-like temple, towering above the island ghats just east of the old bridge, houses the only shapeless *jyoti lingam* (the *jyoti linga* are 12 especially important Shiva linga dotted around India). It's one of many Hindu and Jain monuments on the island.

Most Hindu pilgrims make a 7km *parikrama* (ritual circumnavigation) along a clearly marked path around the island. From the old bridge, the route heads to **Sangam Ghat** at the western tip of the island, where sadhus bathe in the holy Narmada. It then climbs back east to the 11th-century **Gaudi Somnath Temple** on the highest point, with a mighty 2m-high Shiva lingam inside. (You can go directly to the Gaudi Somnath by turning right 150m from the old bridge and climbing 287 steps.)

From the Gaudi Somnath the path continues east, passing in front of a modern, 30m-high, golden Shiva statue, then loops round, down and up hills and passing a number of temple ruins, to the Shri Omkar Mandata. Don't miss the beautifully sculpted **Siddhanath Temple** with marvellous elephant carvings around its base.

Sleeping & Eating

★ **Manu Guest House** GUESTHOUSE $

(☎9826749004; r without bathroom ₹350) A special experience awaits at this welcoming island guesthouse with inspiring views, where Manu and family treat you like one of their own. The six rooms are simple yet well looked after, and the shared bathrooms (cold showers) are kept clean. If asked in advance, your hosts can whip up a delicious thali (₹150), served village-style on the open-air patio floor.

This is pretty much the only place to stay on the island that isn't a *dharamsala* (pilgrims' rest house). It's a bit hard to find: cross the old bridge from Getti Chowk, come around and down the stairs and turn left. After 15m, turn left into a narrow alley with a painted blue wall saying 'Kalyan Bhattacharya', and head up a steep set of steps. Continue to the left at the top and ask for Manu's.

Ganesh Guest House GUESTHOUSE $

(☎9993735449; sumitbhoi1137@gmail.com; r ₹150-200, tr ₹300-400) Follow the signs zig-zagging off the path down to the ghats from Mamaleshwar Rd to reach Ganesh, with its decidedly budget rooms and thin mattresses. Upstairs rooms are airier and brighter, while the shaded garden restaurant (mains ₹60 to ₹160), overlooking the ghats, has a multicuisine menu including Western breakfasts and a peaceful ambience.

Brahmin Bhojanalaya INDIAN, DHABA **$**
(Mamaleshwar Rd; dishes ₹50-130, thali ₹50-150; ⌚9.30am-10pm) There's no English sign, but this casual eatery does have a friendly English-speaking chapati-wallah. The cheapest thalis tend towards soupy, so it's worth spending more. It's on your left as you walk in from the bus stand, 40m before the road bears left towards Getti Chowk.

Information

Sarita Photo Studio (Mamaleshwar Rd; internet per hr ₹60; ⌚8am-9pm; wi-fi) The very friendly, English-speaking Mamta has laptops and wi-fi at this magnet for tourist information. The tiny shop is on the right just as the main road bears left to Getti Chowk. Also exchanges money and is a Western Union rep.

SBI ATM (Mamaleshwar Rd) Two hundred metres towards town from the bus stand.

Getting There & Away

Buses may start from the old bus stand or new bus stand or both. Departures:

Indore ₹85, 2½ hours, half-hourly 5.30am to 10am, every one to two hours 10am to 7pm

Maheshwar ₹70, two hours, 6am and 10am; or take a bus or tempo to Barwah (₹20, 30 minutes, every 30 to 60 minutes), where Maheshwar buses (₹50, 1½ hours) leave about half-hourly till 5pm

Ujjain ₹140, four hours, 5.45am, 9.30am, 2pm, 3.30pm

For Mandu, first take a bus or tempo to Barwah (₹20, 30 minutes, every 30 to 60 minutes). At Barwah you might just find a bus all the way to Mandu (₹100, four hours) but more likely you'll have to change at Dhamnod and Lunhera en route.

If you're heading for Ajanta (Maharashtra), take a bus to Khandwa (₹70, two hours, about half-hourly) from the new bus stand. From Khandwa there are about 15 daily trains to Jalgaon (2½ hours), which has frequent buses to Ajanta.

EASTERN MADHYA PRADESH

Jabalpur

☎0761 / POP 1.27 MILLION

Domestic tourists mostly come here to visit Marble Rocks, an attractive river gorge nearby, but for foreigners this industrial city of *chowks* (market areas) and working men's taverns is mainly useful as a launchpad for Madhya Pradesh's famous tiger parks – Kanha, Bandhavgarh and Pench.

WORTH A TRIP

MARBLE ROCKS

Known locally as Bhedaghat, the magnesium-limestone cliffs at this gorge on the holy Narmada River, 20km west of Jabalpur, change colours in different lights, from pink to black. They're particularly impressive by moonlight, and parts are floodlit at night.

More pleasant than awe-inspiring (during the day, anyway), the trip up the 2km-long gorge is made in a shared **motorboat** (per person 30-50min ₹50; ⌚dawn-dusk, closed during monsoon approximately mid-Jun–mid-Oct) from the jetty at Panchvati Ghat (private boats cost around ₹1000 for up to 20 people). Sticking around? The **Dhuandhar (Smoke Cascade) waterfall** is a worthwhile 1.5km walk uphill from the ghat. Along the way is the much-revered **Chausath Yogini**, a circular 10th-century temple dedicated to the Hindu goddess Durga, accessed via a steep flight of steps on the right-hand side of the road. Once at the falls, you can take a short cable-car ride (₹75 return) across the gorge.

Local city bus 7 or 9 leaves about every 15 minutes, 6.15am to 9pm, for Bhedaghat (₹20, 45 minutes to one hour) from **Model Rd**. They drop you at a junction 100m from Panchvati Ghat. To return, you can also squeeze into Jabalpur-bound shared autorickshaws (₹20).

Jabalpur

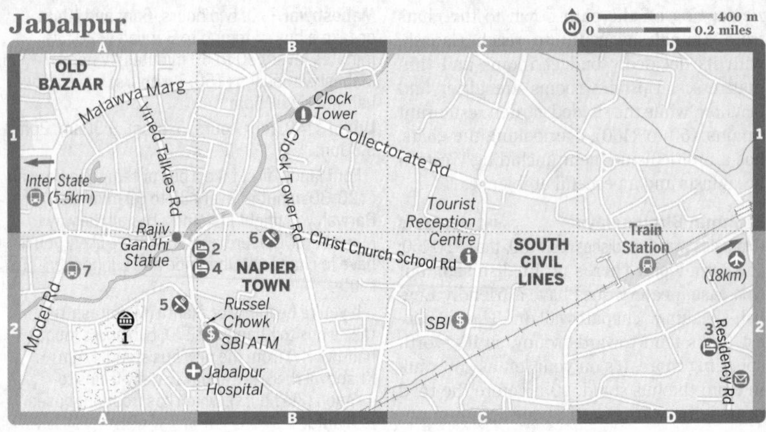

Jabalpur

Sights
1 Rani Durgawati Museum A2

Sleeping
2 Hotel Rahul B2
3 Kalchuri Residency D2
4 Lodge Shivalaya B2

Eating
Olives Restaurant ....(see 2)
5 Saheb's Food Junction A2
6 Yellow Chili B2

Transport
7 Buses to Bhedaghat A2

Sights

Rani Durgawati Museum MUSEUM
(Napier Town; Indian/foreigner ₹10/100, camera/video ₹50/200; 10am-5pm Tue-Sun) Displays a collection of 10th- and 11th-century sculpture from local sites, while upstairs are galleries for stone and copper inscriptions, ancient coins and a photograph exhibition of Bhedaghat's Chausath Yogini Temple.

Tours

Tiger Safari WILDLIFE
(8120445454; www.thetigersafari.com) This very well organised and efficient agency, inherently involved in tiger conservation, can customise safari tours throughout eastern MP and other major Indian tiger reserves. Photography wildlife tours are a speciality, but it handles birding and cultural itineraries as well.

Expect to pay ₹13,500 (budget) to ₹66,000 (top end) per day for all-inclusive custom safari tours for two people, depending on a variety of factors (type of vehicle, accommodation, number of safaris, number of days etc). Prices come down for groups of more than two people.

Sleeping & Eating

Lodge Shivalaya HOTEL $
(0761-2625188; Napier Town; s ₹550-600, d ₹650-750, r with AC ₹1200-1400;) Rooms are basic, but are clean enough for one night and come with TVs and small bathrooms. Non-AC rooms open onto shared terraces overlooking the bustling (and noisy) street below; air-con rooms are interior, without natural light. Checkout is 24 hours.

Hotel Rahul HOTEL $$
(hotelrahul768@gmail.com; Naudra Bridge; incl breakfast s ₹1430-1930, d ₹1780-2130;) Everything is good and clean at this 20-room hotel, especially the sparkling, recently renovated 'superior' rooms with tea/coffee equipment and mini-fridges. One of Jabalpur's better eateries, **Olives Restaurant** (mains ₹170-370; 7am-10pm), is in the basement.

★**Kalchuri Residency** HOTEL $$$
(0761-2678492; www.mptourism.com; South Civil Lines; s/d incl breakfast ₹5110/5500;) One of MP Tourism's nicest properties, the Kalchuri is located in the quieter Civil Lines area just south of the train station. Rooms are large and modern in soothing earth tones with TVs, kettles and spacious bathrooms.

There's a decent restaurant (mains ₹240 to ₹420) and a spacious pub (beer from ₹250). Anecdote: your absent-minded author left his phone charging in the hotel's lobby, and they came and found him on the train station platform to return it to him!

Saheb's Food Junction MUGHLAI $$
(Russel Chowk; meals ₹150-290; ⏲11am-11pm) The best nonveg in Russel Chowk is better than it looks from outside (the dining room is upstairs and air-conditioned), and isn't afraid to spice things up in its fiery gravies (mutton curry, *kadhai* chicken).

Yellow Chilli MODERN INDIAN $$$
(www.theyellowchilli.com; Dixit Pride, Napier Town; mains ₹330-770; ⏲noon-11.30pm) This higher-end Indian chain, the domain of celeb chef Sanjeev Kapoor, might not be top choice in Delhi, but it's a gastro-godsend in Jabalpur. Creative takes on gourmet Indian fare rule here and everything is a flavour bomb. The coconut saffron *shorba* soup is a fine way to start and you're spoilt for choice among the chicken and lamb dishes and veg and nonveg curries to follow.

Information

SBI (South Civil Lines; ⏲10.30am-4.30pm Mon-Sat, closed 2nd & 4th Sat of the month) Changes cash and has an ATM.
Tourist Reception Centre (☎0761-2677690; www.mptourism.com; Christ Church School Rd; ⏲10.30am-7.30pm) Has tourist information and makes bookings for MP Tourism hotels.

Getting There & Away

AIR

The airport is 15km east of the centre.

Air India (☎0761-6459333; www.airindia.com) flies to Delhi daily and Bhopal and Hyderabad four times weekly. **SpiceJet** (☎9871803333; www.spicejet.com) flies to Delhi, Mumbai and Hyderabad daily.

BUS

The **ISBT** (Inter State Bus Terminus; ☎8359998002; Damoh Rd) is 6km northwest of the centre. Departures (sleeper places available on night buses only):
Bamitha (for Khajuraho) seat/sleeper ₹250/350, six hours, half-hourly 7.30am to 11.30am and 7.30pm to 11.30pm
Bhopal seat/sleeper ₹300/400, eight hours, nine daily
Nagpur seat/sleeper ₹270/350, eight hours, half-hourly 5.30am to 12.30am (Volvo AC ₹450, 9.30am, 11am, 2.30pm, 11pm)
Pachmarhi ₹180, seven hours, 8.30am, 3.30pm, 4.30pm
Raipur seat/sleeper ₹400/450, 10 hours, 9.30am, 3pm, 6.30pm, 7.30pm, 9.30pm

To the Tiger Reserves

Pench Tiger Reserve Take a Nagpur bus as far as Khawasa (₹200, six hours, half-hourly 5.30am to 12.30am), then take a shared 4WD (₹20) for the final 12km to Turia.

HANDY TRAINS FROM JABALPUR

DESTINATION	TRAIN NO & NAME	FARE (₹)	DURATION (HR)	DEPARTURE
Agra	12189 Mahakaushal Exp	425/1115/1590	14	6.10pm
Bhopal	11472 Jabalpur-Indore Exp	215/575/820	6½	11.30pm
Delhi	12192 Shridham SF Exp	505/1330/1910	19	5.30pm
Kolkata (Howrah)	12322 Kolkata Mail	535/1415/2040	23	1.20pm
Mumbai (CST)	12321 Howrah–Mumbai Mail	490/1300/1860	17½	5.55pm
Raipur	12854 Amarkantak Exp	335/865/1220	9½	9.25pm
Satna	Different trains each day	140/490/695	3	8.50am
Umaria	18233 Narmada Exp	100/490/695	4	6.35am
Varanasi	12165 Lokmanya Tilak Exp	330/855/1205	10	8.50pm (Mon, Thu & Fri)
Varanasi	12669 Ganga Kaveri Exp	330/855/1205	10	8.50pm (Tue & Sun)

Fares: sleeper/3AC/2AC

AMERICAN/JUNGLE PLAN

Many of the resorts at the tiger reserves have part- and all-inclusive packages rather than straight accommodation prices. The so-called American Plan includes accommodation and all meals, while the Jungle Plan includes accommodation and meals plus safaris (often two a day).

Kanha Tiger Reserve There are buses to Khatia (₹160, 5½ hours) at 6.25am, 10.30am and 11.30am – or take a bus to Mandla (₹110, 3½ hours, every 15 to 20 minutes 5.30am to 7pm), from where there are eight buses daily to Khatia (₹60, 2½ hours).

Bandhavgarh Tiger Reserve It's best to take a train direct to Umaria, but you can also take a bus to Katni (₹110, three hours, half-hourly 7am to 8.30pm), from where there are trains and buses to Umaria.

TRAIN

About 20 daily trains (sleeper/3AC/2AC ₹170/540/740, three hours) leave for Satna (p644), where you can take buses to Khajuraho (usually with a change at Panna and/or Bamitha). For Bandhavgarh Tiger Reserve, take a train to Umaria, then a 1½-hour bus ride.

Getting Around

Autorickshaws charge around ₹50 from the train station to Russel Chowk, or ₹100 from the ISBT.

Kanha Tiger Reserve

Madhya Pradesh is one of the kings of the Indian jungle when it comes to tiger parks, and **Kanha** (www.kanhatigerreserve.com; core zone entry per 6-passenger jeep/s seat ₹1500/250, obligatory guide ₹360, jeep rental ₹2000; 2½–5hr safaris morning & afternoon, except Wed afternoon, Oct-Jun) is its most famous. The forests are vast, and while your chances of seeing a tiger are a bit slimmer than at nearby Bandhavgarh, this is still one of India's best parks for sightings. And here you can really go deep into the forest for a perhaps more complete safari experience than the rush-and-grab outings that some complain of at Bandhavgarh.

Kanha's sal forests and vast meadows contain somewhere around 90 tigers and 100 leopards and support huge populations of deer and antelopes, including some 400 southern swamp deer *(barasingha)* which exist nowhere else in the world. You'll see plenty of langurs, the odd gaur (Indian bison), maybe a family or two of wild boar and the odd lonesome jackal or two. Over 260 bird species have been recorded here too.

Activities

Jeep Safaris

The tiger reserve covers 2059 sq km including the 940-sq-km Kanha National Park which is the reserve's core zone. Jeep safaris venture into four zones within the core zone, of which Kisli and Mukki zones have the best reputations for tiger sightings, followed by Kanha zone then Sarhi zone. Kisli and Kanha zones are best accessed from Khatia gate in Khatia village on the western edge of the core zone. Mukki zone is best accessed from Mukki gate on the south side, a 54km, 1½-hour drive from Khatia.

Up to 140 six-passenger safari jeeps (known as Gypsies because most of them are the Suzuki Gypsy model) are allowed into the core zone per day, but most of these can only be booked online (http://forest.mponline.gov.in, up to 120 days in advance) and the website does not accept foreign cards for payment. Save yourself immense hassle by having hotels/agencies make your safari bookings (for a typical extra price of around ₹1000) – and make arrangements as far ahead as possible, because popular zones sell out months ahead for popular dates. There are two safari slots each day: morning (roughly 6am to 11am) and afternoon (roughly 3pm to 6pm). Morning safaris are longer and tend to produce more tiger sightings.

Tickets for the 15 jeeps per day (90 seats) that can be booked in person are sold at the park gates in the early evening for safaris the next morning, and in late morning for safaris the same afternoon (exact times may vary). But queues can form many hours ahead.

Other Options

If you just can't get seats in regular jeep safaris, you can book a ride in a **canter** (₹510), lumbering 18-seat open 'minibuses' operating from Khatia and Mukki gates. Or you can opt for a **buffer zone safari** (per jeep ₹3110; dawn-11am & 3pm or 4pm-dusk) from Khatia gate. Tickets for both are sold early the previous evening for morning rides, and in late morning for afternoon sessions.

Nature Trail WALKING
(guide ₹500; ⏲ dawn-11am & 3pm or 4pm-dusk) A 4km trail starts from Khatia gate and skirts the edge of the reserve's core zone before looping back to the village. Mostly you'll see monkeys and birds, but tigers do venture into this area on occasions and an accompanying guide is essential.

Sleeping & Eating

Plenty of midrange and top-end lodges and resorts are dotted around the countryside within about 10km of the Khatia and Mukki gates. Nearly all these places can organise safaris for you, often in their own park-registered jeeps. Budget accommodation is very limited.

Near Khatia Gate

Motel Chandan HOTEL **$$**
(☎9009345333, 9424989289; www.motelchandan.com; Khatia; incl full board dm ₹1240, s ₹1800-2870, d ₹2820-3660; ❄@📶) Only 200m from Khatia gate, Chandan represents excellent value for Kanha. Modernish rooms are set around a courtyard garden, and the new eight-bed dorm will be the area's best budget bet. The friendly owner is a smooth guy with two of his own 4WDs and two resident naturalists for safaris, and he can put travellers together to share safari costs.

European Plan (without meals) and Jungle Plan (room, meals and safari) rates are good-value too.

Baghira Jungle Resort HOTEL **$$**
(☎07642-216027; www.mptourism.com; Mocha; incl full board s ₹4140-4900, d ₹5000-5440; ❄) This new MP Tourism hotel on the bank of the Banjar River, 5km west of Khatia, is a solid choice. Accommodation comprises seven villas each with three large rooms on two floors. All rooms have air-con and river views of varying scope, and are comfy and reasonably tasteful in tigerish golds and browns, with tiger-stripe rugs and tiger-pug pillowcases.

Pugmark Resort LODGE **$$**
(☎07649-277291; www.pugmarkresort.com; Khatia; incl full board s/d ₹2400/3600, AC ₹3000/4800; ❄📶) These spacious village-like cottages, 700m off the main road in Khatia, are just a step above basic but bright and airy and set around a pleasant, albeit slightly overgrown, garden. It's a well-oiled, family-run operation, and Rahul, the owner/manager, is very knowledgeable and nails five-star service for three-star prices (in addition to being resident naturalist and artist).

From breakfast on up, the food is outstanding – they even use milk from their own two Holsteins. Wi-fi throughout.

★**Kipling Camp** LODGE **$$$**
(☎07649-277218, 011-65196377; www.kiplingcamp.com; Mocha; incl full board Indian s ₹12,390-13,630, d ₹18,700-21,180, foreigner s ₹17,350-19,830, d ₹24,780-29,740; ⏲mid-Oct–early May; ❄📶) 🍃 A wonderful, laid-back wildlife lodge hosted by one of India's most dedicated tiger campaigners, filmmaker, photographer and writer Belinda Wright. It's as informative as it is relaxing to stay in this jungle setting just 3km from Khatia gate, where wildlife discussions follow excellent communal meals and guests retire to delightful rustic-chic cottages slightly scented with essence of British colonialism.

Nature abounds in the fenceless grounds where langurs and chitals make regular appearances, only to be outshone by an occasional tiger or leopard flyby. Expert, professional and charming staff can guide you on varied walks and excursions, and you can also swim in the river with Tara, the camp's memorable sexagenarian elephant, a truly extraordinary experience. Founded back in 1982, this was India's first-ever wildlife lodge and is run on an ecosensitive, not-for-profit basis, with profits channelled to numerous local community causes.

Near Mukki Gate

Kanha Safari Lodge HOTEL **$$**
(☎07636-290715; www.mptourism.com; Mukki; incl full board s ₹3920-4900, d ₹5000-5440; @) Decent but unimaginative rooms with firm beds are set in one- and two-storey villas around a central garden equipped with a rope bridge and several climbing devices for children. With a bar and reliable restaurant, this MP Tourism hotel is a dependable choice, well positioned just 1km from Mukki gate.

★**Salban** HOMESTAY **$$$**
(☎9818403038, 7692835206; www.facebook.com/salbankanhahomestay; Baherakhar village; s/d incl full board ₹4500/6000; @) 🍃 This beautiful, spacious home of a wildlife-and-travel-expert couple makes a great base. Between safaris you can sip a G&T and

spot birds from the gorgeous wide verandah, enjoy great home-cooking, dip into their fabulous library or wander around their acres of forest and organic garden. It's 7km southeast of Mukki gate, right on the edge of the core zone.

Information

A Central Bank of India ATM next to Motel Chandan at Khatia accepts foreign cards.

Getting There & Away

BUS

There are six daily buses from Khatia to Mandla (₹60, 2½ hours, 6.30am, 8am, 8.30am, 12.45pm, 2.15pm, 5.30pm). The 6.30am, 8.30am and 12.45pm continue to Jabalpur (₹160, 5½ hours). There's also an 8am bus from Khatia to Nagpur (₹250, eight hours). For Raipur, there's one daily bus from Mocha (₹220, six hours, 8am).

Services from Mandla bus stand:

Jabalpur ₹100, 3½ hours, every 20 or 30 minutes 5am to 6pm, hourly 6pm to 11pm

Khatia ₹60, 2½ hours, 9.30am, 10am, 11.30am, 12.15pm, 1.50pm, 2.30pm, 4.15pm, 5.20pm

Nagpur (buses go via Khawasa for transfer to Pench Tiger Reserve) ₹250, eight hours, 8am, 2pm, 7pm, 9pm, 11pm

Raipur seat/sleeper ₹400/450, eight hours, 9.30pm and 10.30pm

Travelling by bus from Kanha to the Bandhavgarh Tiger Reserve involves changes at Mandla, Shahpura and Umaria.

TAXI

Taxis from Khatia should cost ₹2500 to Jabalpur station, ₹2800 to its airport, and ₹4500 to Nagpur or Raipur.

TRAIN

The nearest train stations, at Chiraidongri and Mandla, 32km and 51km northwest of Khatia, were closed at research time for conversion of the Seoni-Mandla line from narrow gauge to broad gauge. When work is completed (due late 2018) it should be possible to reach these stations by train from Jabalpur and elsewhere.

Bandhavgarh Tiger Reserve

☎07627

If your sole reason for visiting an Indian tiger reserve is to see a tiger, look no further. Two or three days at **Bandhavgarh** (☎9424794315; www.facebook.com/pg/Bandhavgarh-National-Park-Tiger-Reserve-789482291185683; core zone entry per 6-passenger jeep/s seat ₹1500/250, obligatory guide ₹360, jeep rental ₹2200; ⌚2½–5hr safaris morning & afternoon, except Wed afternoon, Oct-Jun) should net you a tiger sighting, except perhaps in October. India's 2014 tiger census counted 68 tigers here, the great majority of them in the relatively small (453 sq km) territory of Bandhavgarh National Park, which forms part of the reserve's core zone. Neck and neck with Rajasthan's Ranthambhore for sightings, this is one of India's top tiger playgrounds. There are also more than 40 rarely seen leopards and more commonly sighted animals such as deer, wild boar and langurs.

The main base for visits is the small, laidback village of Tala, 32km northeast of Umaria, the nearest train station. February to June are generally the best months for tiger sightings, but April to June is very hot with temperatures often climbing above 40°C.

Sights

Interpretation Centre MUSEUM

(Tala; ⌚11am-2pm & 6-8pm, closed Wed evening) FREE Interesting exhibits detailing the history and legends of Bandhavgarh, plus some superb tiger photos on the 1st floor. It's behind the safari ticket office by the main road in Tala.

Note: the ticket office is due to move to a new building 1km away. It's unclear whether the interpretation centre will move with it.

Activities

Safaris

All safaris start from Tala and head into three zones of Bandhavgarh National Park. Tala zone is entered from the village itself; the entrances to Khitauli and Maghdi (or Magadhi) zones are about 5.5km and 6km southwest of Tala along the Umaria road.

Up to 111 six-passenger safari jeeps (known as Gypsies) are allowed into the park per day, but most of these can only be booked online (http://forest.mponline.gov.in, up to 120 days in advance) and the website does not accept foreign cards for payment. Save yourself immense hassle by having hotels/agencies make your safari bookings (for a typical extra price of around ₹1000) – and make arrangements as far ahead as possible, because safaris can sell out months ahead, especially for Tala zone which has the general reputation of being best for tiger sightings. Morning safaris, starting between 5.30am and 6.45am (depending on season) are longer than afternoon safaris (starting at 3pm) and tend to produce more tiger sightings.

Tickets for the 12 jeeps per day (72 seats) that can be booked in person go on sale at the ticket office in Tala village half an hour before safari starting times, but queues for these can start forming as early as the night before.

You can usually arrange for pick up and drop-off at your hotel for around ₹300 extra on top of the basic ₹2200 for jeep-and-driver rental.

Canter Tours

If all else fails, you can book a ride in a **canter** (per person ₹510), lumbering 18-seat open 'minibuses' traversing the Maghdi and Khitauli zones. Tickets go on sale at the Tala ticket office half an hour before regular safari start times.

Sleeping & Eating

Kum Kum Lodge HOTEL $

(9424330200; Main Rd, Tala; r ₹500-1000;) Rooms are very basic and bare but decently clean, with verandahs, and set around a patch of shady ground (with swings!). They have fans or coolers but no heaters for winter.

★Tigergarh LODGE $$$

(7489826868; www.tigergarh.com; Ranchha Rd; s/d incl half-board ₹4500/6000, incl full board ₹5000/7500; Oct-Jun;) This stylish 11-room lodge sits under the nose of the surrounding hills in a peaceful spot 3.5km northwest of downtown Tala. The rustic-chic cottages (earthy tones with splashes of brighter colours and bits of folk art) provide considerable comfort, including four-poster beds and rain-style showers. A sustainability mantra permeates the property and the well-kept gardens still have a natural feel.

★Treehouse Hideaway LODGE $$$

(9810253436; www.treehousehideaway.com; s/d incl full board ₹18,000/20,000, Jungle Plan ₹32,000/34,000; Oct-Jun;) Undoubtedly the most special beds in Bandhavgarh, these five massive tree houses clock in at 625 sq metres each and are dismantled and reassembled each season 5m off the ground in all their luxurious glory. Beautiful four-poster beds and spacious porches frame the jungle surrounds with poetic aplomb and privacy is paramount.

Nature Heritage Resort HOTEL $$$

(07627-265351; www.natureheritageresort.com; Tala; incl full board s ₹5500-6500, d ₹6500-7500;) An excellent choice with a lively atmosphere and slick safari operation (₹5500 per jeep door-to-door with guide from hotel and tea service on return). The adobe-toned rooms verge on jungle kitsch but are pleasant and comfortable, and set in cottages around a shady bamboo grove.

The buffet meals (mainly Indian) are satisfying and staff are friendly and helpful.

★Malaya Cafe CAFE $$

(Main Rd, Tala; dishes ₹80-150, breakfast ₹375; 9am-8pm Oct-Jun;) This welcoming cafe run by an extroverted escapee from the marketing business in Ahmedabad does fabulous pure-veg breakfast/brunches (bookings the previous day advisable) that are the perfect finish to a morning safari. Real filter coffee or homemade lemonade, fresh and dried fruit, porridge and lentil pancakes with salad or mashed potatoes typically find their way to your plate.

Indian and Western snacks and light dishes are available all day – and Malaya is also an excellent crafts and souvenir shop: owner Neelam spends two months every year driving around India picking up some rare and individual artisan products.

Kolkata Restaurant DHABA $$

(Main Rd, Tala; mains ₹120-250, thalis ₹80-250; 8am-10pm) Friendly chef and owner Amal Jana is a one-man show at this glorified *dhaba* (eatery serving snacks and basic meals), where he whips up honest, down-home, extremely tasty thalis – he reckons it's due to the mustard oil – that can be kicked up a notch with a side of his spicy tomato chutney. Also omelettes, Chinese and limited Continental.

Information

All Tala's services are along a 100m stretch of the single main street, including the post office, internet cafes (per hour ₹50), restaurants and a State Bank of India ATM.

Getting There & Away

A cycle-rickshaw between Umaria's bus stand and train station is ₹10 (10 minutes). Buses to Tala (₹35, one hour) go about half-hourly, 8am to 7pm. Outside those hours, you'll have to take an autorickshaw from the train station (before/after 7pm ₹400/600) or arrange a taxi in advance (from ₹900).

The last bus from Tala back to Umaria bus stand is 7.30pm. There are no autorickshaws in Tala.

TRAIN

Trains from Umaria include the 18477 Utkal Express at 8.55pm to Delhi (Nizamuddin station; sleeper/3AC/2AC ₹425/1150/1665, 18 hours) via Gwalior (₹320/865/1245, 11 hours), Agra (₹365/985/1420, 14 hours) and Mathura (₹380/1035/1490, 15 hours), and the 18234 Narmada Express at 4.36pm to Jabalpur (₹100/490/695, 4½ hours), Bhopal (₹280/750/1080, 12 hours), Ujjain (₹360/975/1405, 16 hours) and Indore (₹385/1055/1520, 18½ hours).

There are two daily trains to Varanasi: the 15160 Sarnath Express (₹275/740/1065, 12 hours, 4.19am) and the 15232 Gondia Barauni Express (₹280/750/1080, 12½ hours, 7.17am). Both call at Satna, where you can catch buses to Khajuraho.

For Raipur (Chhattisgarh) there are three daily trains including the 15159 Sarnath Express (₹230/615/880, eight hours, 10.16pm)

An alternative to Umaria is Katni, a busier railway junction with direct trains to places like Jabalpur, Satna and Varanasi. You can get to Katni by bus from Umaria (₹60, 2½ hours, 7.30am and half-hourly 9am to 6pm).

Pench Tiger Reserve

☎07695

The third of Madhya Pradesh's trio of well-known tiger reserves, **Pench** (☎07692-223794; www.penchtiger.co.in; core zone entry per 6-passenger jeep/s seat ₹1500/250, obligatory guide ₹360, jeep rental ₹2500; ⏲2½–5hr safaris morning & afternoon, except Wed afternoon, Oct-Jun) is made up mostly of teak-tree forest rather than sal and so it has a different flavour from nearby Kanha or Bandhavgarh. It also sees fewer tourists (and fewer tigers); you'll often feel like you have the whole forest to yourself. Even if no tigers appear, there'll be a variety of other wildlife, and the forests are beautiful in their own right.

Pench Tiger Reserve has a total area of 1921 sq km – 60% in Madhya Pradesh, the rest in Maharashtra. The majority of its tigers are on the MP side and specifically in Pench National Park (part of the tiger reserve's core area), which has around 50 of the big stripeys. By far the easiest reached and most used of the park's three entry points is Turia gate, 12km west of Khawasa on the Jabalpur-Nagpur Hwy 44.

Activities

Jeep Safaris from Turia Gate

Up to 34 six-passenger safari jeeps ('Gypsies') per day are allowed into the national park at the Turia gate for each morning or evening safari slot. But most of these are sold online (http://forest.mponline.gov.in, up to 120 days in advance) and the website doesn't accept foreign cards for payment. Tickets for the three jeeps (18 seats) per safari that can be booked in person are sold at the Turia gate from one hour before the safaris start. At busiest times queues for these may start to form the night before. On the other hand, at quiet times unsold seats from the online quota may also go on sale at Turia gate the evening or morning before safaris or even in the hour before they start. But you certainly can't count on this, so overall it's safest to get hotels or agencies to make your safari bookings (for a typical extra price of around ₹1000 per safari). Do this as far ahead as possible, as safaris often sell out two or three weeks ahead, and months ahead for popular dates including holidays and some weekends.

Morning safaris tend to produce more tiger sightings.

You can usually arrange for pick up and drop-off at your hotel for an extra few hundred rupees on top of the basic ₹2500 for jeep-and-driver rental.

Other Safaris

If you get shut out of a regular national-park safari, you can try a **buffer-zone safari** (per 6-passenger jeep incl guide ₹3510), starting at the same times as regular safaris from three points: one near Turia village; one at Teliya, about 5km south of Turia; and one at Rukhad, about 24km north of Khawasa. There are also two-hour night safaris from the forest office in Khawasa starting about 6pm. Another option is a safari in Pench Maharashtra, from Khursapar gate about 17km south of Turia.

Sleeping & Eating

Tiger 'N' Woods LODGE $$

(☎8888399166; http://tigernwoods.com; r incl full board ₹5000; ❄📶🏊) Friendly young staff help give this place a relaxed, informal atmosphere and the rooms, in wooden stilt houses, are plain but pleasing, with forest-view bathrooms and verandahs. The in-house naturalist leads nature walks (₹100) and you can have a *desi* (ghee) massage while you're here too.

Kipling's Court HOTEL **$$**
(07695-232830; www.mptourism.com; incl full board dm ₹1300, r ₹5460-5940;) This government-run property, 2km from Turia gate, wins in both the budget category (considering prices include all meals, the two well-kept, six-bed dorms are fine value) and family category (it boasts the best playground in Turia plus indoor games). The rooms, in cottages around dutifully manicured gardens, aren't bad either and all have air-con.

★ **Baghvan** RESORT **$$$**
(07695-232847; www.tajsafaris.com; incl full board s ₹22,000-50,000, d ₹29,000-67,000;) Taj Hotels has luxury properties at all of MP's major tiger parks, but this discerning choice is the most jungly and worth the splurge. Twelve massive bamboo, sal and concrete cottages are hidden away amid the forest and feature exquisite artwork and furniture, indoor/outdoor showers and massive elevated *machans* (open-air patios).

The common areas follow suit, pleasantly offset by some whimsical art and artefacts. Food is expectedly divine. It's 1km from Turia gate and reservations are required. Rates vary wildly with season and demand; B&B and jungle plan (full board plus safaris) are also available.

Mowgli's Den LODGE **$$$**
(07695-232832; www.mowglisdenpench.com; r full-board ₹6500;) Mowgli's, 2.5km from Turia gate, has 10 large, comfortable, circular cottages in verdant gardens, all with bamboo furnishings and big bathrooms. The welcoming owners are real wildlife enthusiasts, with plenty of Pench information, and sometimes accompany guests on safaris.

Good meals too, in a bamboo-lined dining room.

Information

A Bank of Maharashtra ATM in Khawasa accepts foreign cards.

Getting There & Away

Frequent buses link Khawasa with Nagpur (₹90, two hours, every half-hour) and Jabalpur (₹180, six hours, every half-hour). Shared jeeps (₹20) run between Khawasa and Turia when full. The national park gate is 3km beyond Turia village. The nearest airport and major train station are at Nagpur (₹2000 to ₹2500 by taxi).

You can go to Kanha Tiger Reserve from Khawasa without going all the way to Jabalpur or Mandla. Flag down any northbound bus to Seoni (₹50, one hour, every half-hour) then take a Mandla-bound bus to Chiraidongri (₹95, three hours, about hourly, 6.40am to 10.40pm) where there are nine daily buses to Khatia gate (₹35, one hour, 11am to 6pm).

CHHATTISGARH

Chhattisgarh is remote, short on major 'sights' and limited in tourist infrastructure, but for the adventurous traveller, time spent here may well prove to be a highlight of your trip to this part of India. The country's most densely (44%) forested state is blessed with considerable natural beauty – waterfalls and unspoilt nature reserves abound. More interestingly, it's home to 42 different tribes whose pointillist paintings and spindly sculptures are as vivid as the colourful *haats* (markets) that take place across the region, particularly around Jagdalpur in the southern Bastar region.

Chhattisgarh is one of the eastern states where ultra-leftist Naxalite guerrillas are active. They carry out occasional attacks on police, government officials and politicians, including on roads, mainly in the southern half of the state, but there have been no reported incidents involving foreigners in recent years, if ever.

Raipur

0771 / POP 1.01 MILLION

Chhattisgarh's ugly, busy capital is a centre for the state's steel and other industries and, apart from the ruins at Sirpur, a day trip away, has little to detain you. The **Chhattisgarh Tourism Board office** (0771-6453336, 9926781331; www.tourism.cg.gov.in; Raipur Junction Station; 7am-10pm) is worth visiting, though: it can help organise tribal visits, transport, accommodation and guides. The state government, as well as new educational institutions, hospitals, offices, a technology park and an international cricket stadium, is located in the new city of Naya Raipur, 20km southeast.

There are many budget and midrange hotels outside the main train station (Raipur Junction) and east along Station Rd, and a few in the centre around Jaistambh Chowk and on LIC Rd outside Pandri Bus Stand. Top-end hotels are mostly 4km to 12km east of the centre along the Hwy 53 or VIP Rd leading to the airport.

Hotel Jyoti HOTEL $
(☎0771-2428777; hoteljyoti@gmail.com; LIC Rd, Pandri; s/d from ₹750/1000, with AC from ₹1200/1450; ❄📶) The Jyoti is a decent retreat after a long bus journey, on the main road outside Pandri Bus Stand. The basic rooms have flourishes of colour (though some bathrooms are on the nose), and the manager is helpful.

In the rear of the building, **Hotel Saatvik** (☎0771-2420420; www.hotelsaatvik.org; LIC Rd, Pandri; s/d from ₹1400/1600; ❄📶) is a step up in quality.

★**Hotel LeRoi** HOTEL $$
(☎0771-2971354; www.leroihotels.com; MFC Bldg, beside Raipur Junction station; incl breakfast s ₹3190-3640, d ₹3640-4100; ❄📶) If you're in this price bracket, don't waste time looking any further than the bright, friendly, efficient LeRoi, right beside the station. Spotless, good-sized, pine-accented rooms have good wi-fi, good air-con, tea/coffee facilities and up-to-date bathrooms where it's a delight to step into the shower.

There's a 24-hour restaurant and coffeeshop too. Airport transfers ₹500.

ℹ Getting There & Away

AIR

Raipur's busy airport (www.aai.aero/allairports/raipur_generalinfo.jsp), 14km southeast of the centre, has at least two daily flights to Delhi, Mumbai, Bhopal, Bengaluru, Indore, Kolkata and Hyderabad, plus flights to six other Indian cities. It's served by **Air India** (☎0771-2972321, airport 0771-2418201; www.airindia.in; CII/1 Aiswarya Chamber, GE Rd, Telebhanda; ⏲9.30am-5pm Mon-Sat), **IndiGo** (☎9212783838; www.goindigo.in; Airport) and **Jet Airways** (☎0771-2107613; www.jetairways.com).

BUS

The main terminal is the somewhat chaotic **Pandri Bus Stand** (LIC Rd), 2.5km southeast of the train station (₹50 by autorickshaw from the prepaid stand outside the train station). **Mahendra Travels** (☎0771-4054444; www.mahendrabus.in) is a reliable company with buses to Jagdalpur (seat ₹330 to ₹380, sleeper ₹400 to ₹430, eight hours, every 15 minutes, 5.15am to midnight), Jabalpur (seat/sleeper ₹300/400, 11 hours, 4.30am, 6pm, 9pm) and Nagpur (seat/sleeper non-AC ₹300/350, AC ₹400/500, eight hours, seven buses daily).

TRAIN

Useful trains include the 18237 Chhattisgarh Express to Delhi (Nizamuddin station; sleeper/3AC/2AC ₹565/1515/2215, 28 hours, 4.20pm) via Nagpur (5½ hours), Bhopal (14 hours), Jhansi (21 hours), Gwalior (22 hours) and Agra (24 hours), and the 12859 Gitanjali Express to Kolkata (Howrah station; ₹445/1165/1665, 13 hours, 11.35pm). Other daily trains head to Bhubaneswar, Visakhapatnam, Jabalpur and Varanasi.

ℹ Getting Around

From the 24-hour prepaid booth outside the train station (the one with the hard-hat-shaped roof), autorickshaws run to Paldri Bus Stand (₹50), Jaistambh Chowk (₹55) and the airport (₹240 including parking fee). Shared autos (₹10) also head to the bus station.

Sirpur & Around

A possible day or overnight trip from Raipur, the village of Sirpur, 80km east, is dotted with the remains of dozens of Buddhist and Jain monasteries and Hindu temples from the 6th and 7th centuries AD. Many of the excavations are works in progress. The 7th-century **Laxman Temple** (Indian/foreigner ₹15/200; ⏲dawn-dusk) is mostly intact and is one of the oldest brick temples in India. The other main highlights (free to enter, normally open 8am to 6pm) are **Teevardwo Buddhist Monastery**, with very fine sculptures; the **Surang Tila**, a highly unusual, pyramid-like Shiva temple faced in white stone; the **Anand Prabhu Kuti Vihara** (another Buddhist monastery); and the 18th-century **Gandeshwar Temple** on the bank of the Mahanadi River, still very much a living shrine to Shiva.

To delve deeper into the Chhattisgarh countryside, take a safari in the forests of **Barnawapara Wildlife Sanctuary** (⏲Nov-Jun), east of Sirpur. It's home to a few dozen sometimes-seen leopards, many deer and antelopes, around 300 sloth bears and a few wild elephants.

Jeeps and guides for safaris of three to five hours (starting around 6am and 2.30pm) are available at Barbaspur, 15km northeast of Sirpur, and at Rawan, 32km southeast of Sirpur, for a total cost of ₹3000 to ₹4000 including guide and park fees.

Hiuen Tsiang Tourist Resort (☎0771-4066415; s/d ₹1500/2200; ❄) provides big, spotlessly white, air-con rooms with comfy beds and large bathrooms, plus good Indian meals (mains ₹90 to ₹170). They can do meals for nonguests with a couple of hours' notice.

Buses from Raipur's Pandri Bus Stand go to Mahasamund (₹45, 1½ hours, half-hourly), from where there are buses to Sirpur (₹30, one hour) every hour. A taxi day trip from Raipur should cost around ₹1600.

Jagdalpur

07782 / POP 125,000

The capital of the southern Bastar region is an ideal base for exploring tribal Chhattisgarh. The town itself hosts a *haat* (market) every Sunday where you'll see Adivasis (tribal people) buying, selling and bartering alongside town traders, but it's in the surrounding villages where Adivasi life can be fully appreciated. Some villages are extremely remote, and only really accessible with a guide. Others, though, are just a bus ride away and, particularly on market days, can be explored independently.

Sanjay Market, which hosts the Sunday *haat*, is the heartbeat of Jagdalpur. The gaily painted maharaja's palace, 500m north at the end of Palace Rd, is the town's main landmark.

Sights

Anthropological Museum MUSEUM

(Chitrakote Rd; 10.30am-5.30pm Mon-Fri) FREE Jagdalpur's old-fashioned-looking museum, 3km west of the centre, has illuminating exhibits on tribal customs and culture as well as many artefacts collected from tribal villages in the 1970s and 1980s.

Festivals & Events

Bastar Dussehra CULTURAL

(Sep/Oct) In Bastar the Dussehra date (usually in early October) is just the last of 75 days of rituals and preparations that give Bastar Dussehra claim to be one of the world's longest festivals. Things climax in the final 10 days, and especially the last two nights, with a gigantic wooden chariot *(rath)* being tugged around Jagdalpur by teams of rope-pullers.

Sleeping & Eating

There are some cheap and mostly grungy hotels near the bus stand and a handful of better places around the centre. The top place in the area, though not actually luxurious, is **Dandami Luxury Resort** (18001026415, 0771-4224999; www.tourism.cg.gov.in; Chitrakote; s/d ₹2000/2500;) out at Chitrakote Falls.

Hotel Rainbow HOTEL $

(07782-221684; hotelrainbow@rediffmail.com; d/tr ₹760/945, with AC ₹1050/2190;) Even the cheap, squat-toilet, non-AC rooms are big and decently furnished at this well-worn, good-value hotel (wi-fi throughout) while the in-house Indian restaurant (mains ₹120 to ₹270) is one of the best in town and there's a very blue bar to boot. Management can be extra helpful and there's 24-hour checkout. It's opposite Sanjay Market.

Devansh Residency HOTEL $$

(07782-221199; devanshresidency@gmail.com; Collectorate Rd; incl breakfast s/d ₹1700/2160, ste ₹4780;) The best place in town: large, clean, white-and-lime-green rooms are equipped with wi-fi and good toiletry kits, and the in-house pure-veg **Vaishnavi** (mains ₹140-250; 7.30am-10.30pm;) restaurant is also the best in town.

Shopping

Shabari ARTS & CRAFTS

(Chandni Chowk; 10.30am-8pm Mon-Sat) A fixed-price government emporium selling a good range of Adivasi handicrafts, from small, spindly iron figures to more expensive, heavy bell-metal statues.

WORTH A TRIP

KONDAGAON CRAFTS

Some 77km north of Jagdalpur, the admirable NGO **Saathi** (9993861686; tiwaribhupesh@gmail.com; Kondagaon; 8am-6pm Mon-Sat), run by the affable Bhupesh Tiwari and his team, works with more than 300 villages, providing crafts training and marketing, and assistance with health, education and hygiene. It has workshops and a sales showroom on-site, and can provide guides to visit area artisans (₹500 to ₹1000 per day) and tuition for one week or longer in bell metal, wrought iron, terracotta or woodcarving. Head west off the Raipur road along Hwy 130D about 3km north of Kondagaon, and within 1km you'll see the Saathi sign.

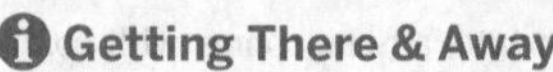

Information

Tourism Information Centre (☎07782-2008001; ctbbastar@rediffmail.com; beside Shahid Park; ⏰10am-7pm Mon-Sat) Can help with arrangements for visiting tribal villages, and also sells Bastar handicrafts. It's just off Main Rd, 1km east of the centre.

Getting There & Away

BUS

The bus stand is about 1.5km south of the centre (₹20 by autorickshaw). **Mahendra Travels** (p682) and **Kanker Roadways** (☎9826185795; www.kankerroadways.in) run buses to Raipur (non-AC ₹330 to ₹400, AC seat/sleeper

BASTAR HAATS & ADIVASI VILLAGES

There are eight main tribes in Bastar spread among more than 3500 villages, ranging from the Ghadwa (specialists in bell metal) to the Doria in the far southern forests, the only tribe to make their homes from tree branches and leaves (instead of mud thatch). One of the most fascinating ways to get a taste of Bastar's vibrant Adivasi culture is the colourful *haats* (markets). These are the lifeblood of tribal Chhattisgarh. Tribal people walk up to 20km to trade (often barter) everything from their distinctive, almost fluorescent, saris to live red ants.

You'll find all kinds of fascination here, including bell-metal craftwork (a mix of bronze and brass), a skill passed down through generations for some 300 years in some cases. The large piles of what look like squashed dates are in fact dried *mahuwa* flowers, either eaten fresh, or dried then boiled to create steam, which is fermented to produce a potent liquor, the favourite tipple of many Bastar Adivasis.

You can get to many local Adivasi villages by bus from Jagdalpur (most start from Sanjay Market) and this is certainly an option on market days – but some are pretty inaccessible, and if you want to actually meet tribespeople, rather than just look at them, a guide is essential as a translator if nothing else. They can also help you arrange homestays. A day with **Awesh Ali** (☎9425244925; aweshali@gmail.com; per day ₹1500) is a truly enlightening experience. He's a highly experienced guide who speaks nine languages (four of which are tribal). Contact him directly, or through Jagdalpur's Tourism Information Centre (p684). A car and driver (which the tourist office can organise) will cost from ₹1200 to ₹1600 per day including fuel.

Most *haats* run from around noon to 5pm. There are many of them – the following are just some of the more popular ones. Ask at Jagdalpur's Tourism Information Centre for details. Shared jeeps normally hang around markets to take people back to Jagdalpur.

WHEN	WHERE	DISTANCE FROM JAGDALPUR	BUS FROM JAGDALPUR (FARE, DURATION)	FEATURES
Mon	Tokapal	16km	₹25, 30min	bell-metal craftwork from Ghadwa Adivasis
Wed	Darbha	35km	₹40, 1hr	attended by Dhurwa Adivasis
Thu	Bastar	20km	₹30, 30min	easy to reach from Jagdalpur
Fri	Lohandiguda	36km	₹40, 1¼hr	halva, Muria and Maria tribes; 1km off Chitrakote road
Fri	Nangur	22km	no direct bus	attended by distant forest Adivasis
Fri	Nagarnar	24km	no direct bus	colourful Bhatra Adivasis
Sat	Kuknar	70km	₹60, 2hr	bison-Horn Maria stronghold
Sun	Jagdalpur	-	-	city location, open late into the evening
Sun	Pamela	12km	₹10, 20min	animated crowds bet on cockfighting

₹380/430, eight hours) every 15 or 30 minutes, 5am to midnight.

TRAIN

India's highest broad-gauge line heads over the Eastern Ghats to Vizianagram near the Andhra Pradesh coast. The 18448 Hirakhand Express leaves at 3pm for Bhubaneswar (sleeper/3AC/2AC ₹395/1080/1555, 18 hours). The 58502 Kirandul-Visakhapatnam Passenger leaves at 10.38am for Visakhapatnam (sleeper/AC ₹140/810, 10½ hours). Both trains stop at Koraput, Odisha (Orissa), about three hours from Jagdalpur.

Around Jagdalpur

Chitrakote Falls

The 'Indian Niagara', 300m wide and 32m high, is India's widest waterfall and is at its roaring best after rains, but beautiful all year round, particularly at sunset.

When the water isn't too strong (about December to June) it's possible to paddle in pools at the top (take extreme care). You can also swim in the river downstream from the falls, or get a local fisherman to row you up to the spray (₹50 per person): take the steps down beside the government-only hotel next to the falls.

The falls are on the Indravati River, 40km northwest of Jagdalpur. Buses (₹45, 1½ hours, 9am, 11pm, 2pm and 7pm) leave from Anupama Chowk, on Chitrakote Rd 500m from Sanjay Market. The last one back to Jagdalpur is at 4pm. A taxi round trip costs about ₺1500.

Kanger Valley National Park

An enjoyable and locally very popular day or half-day outing from Jagdalpur, this **park** (Indian/foreigner ₹25/150, car ₹50; ⏲9am-5pm) covers 200 sq km of a thickly forested valley south of Jagdalpur. Visitors head to two main sites. One is **Tirathgarh Falls**, tumbling 35m in several sections down a canyon formed by the Mugabahar River, a Kanger tributary. The other is **Kutumsar Cave** (guide ₹75; ⏲8am-3pm Nov-Jun), where guides lead you through up to 300m of narrow passages, concrete steps and large chambers with many stalactites and stalagmites. A taxi round trip from Jagdalpur is ₹1200 to either the falls or the caves, or ₹1500 for both.

Gujarat

Includes ➡

Best Places to Eat

- Vishalla (p696)
- Nilambag Palace Restaurant (p706)
- Peshawri (p703)
- Gopi Dining Hall (p696)
- Bhatiyar Gali (p695)

Best Places to Sleep

- House of MG (p695)
- Deewanji Ni Haveli (p695)
- Bhuj House (p727)
- São Tome Retiro (p710)
- Rann Riders (p733)

Why Go?

Unfairly overlooked by many travellers scurrying between Mumbai (Bombay) and Rajasthan, Gujarat is an easy side-step off the well-beaten tourist trail. While the capital, Ahmedabad, can draw you in with its remarkable architecture and excellent dining scene, the countryside holds most of this state's many treasures. Traditional artisans in tribal villages weave, embroider, dye and print some of India's finest textiles, and pristine parks harbour unique wildlife, including wild asses and the last remaining prides of Asiatic lions. For the spiritually inclined, sacred Jain and Hindu pilgrimage sites sit atop mountains that rise dramatically from vast flatlands. And colourful festivals burst with a cornucopia of culture.

Gujarat also claims a special relationship to the life and work of Mahatma Gandhi: he was born here, he ignited the satyagraha movement from here, he made his Salt March here – and his legacy remains a vibrant part of public discourse and private lives.

When to Go

Ahmedabad

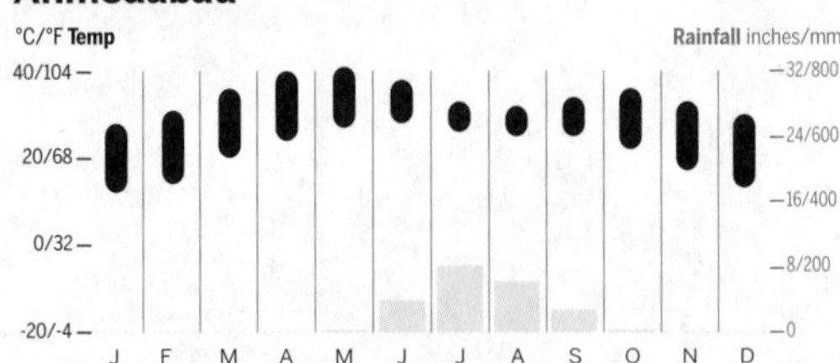

Sep & Oct Navratri festival brings music and dancing to every town and village.

Nov–Dec Mango milkshake time in Junagadh.

Nov–Mar Best for Gujarat's national parks and wildlife sanctuaries.

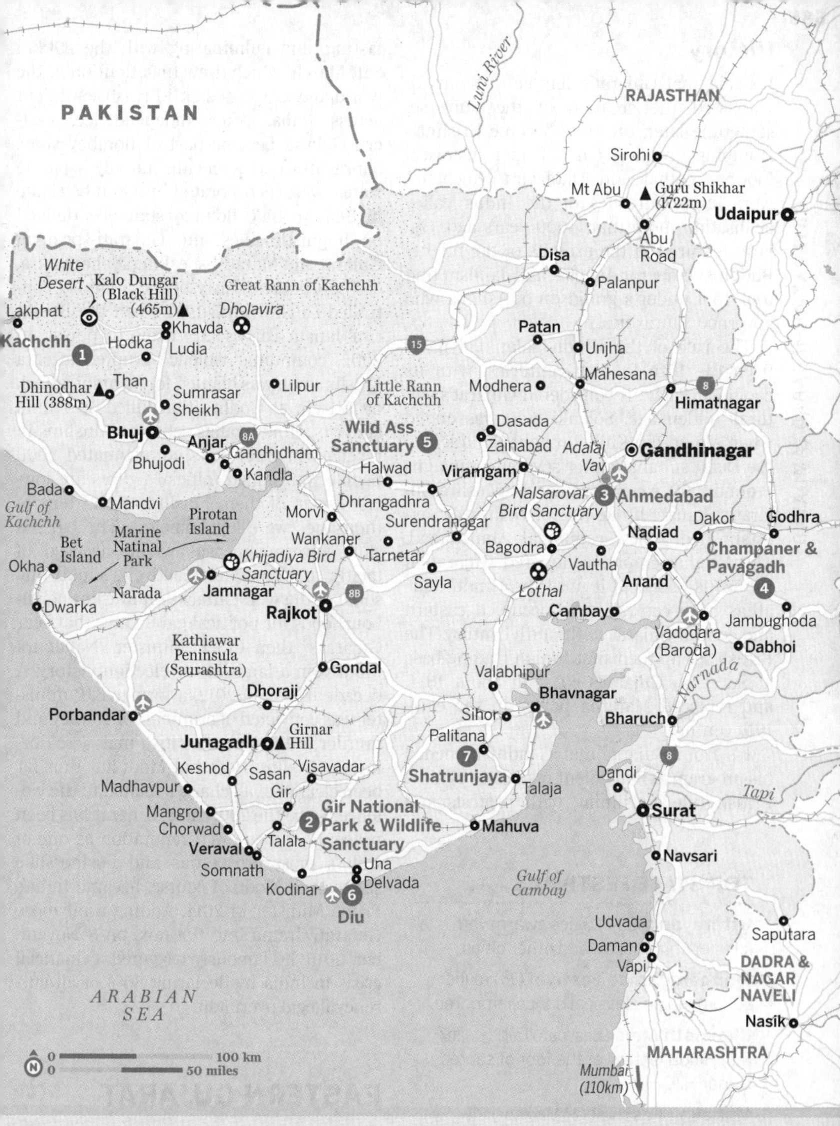

Gujarat Highlights

1 **Kachchh** (p724) Exploring tribal villages to admire and acquire some of India's best textiles.

2 **Gir National Park & Wildlife Sanctuary** (p713) Taking a forest safari in search of Asia's only wild lions.

3 **Ahmedabad** (p688) Tackling a thali, exploring the old-city mosques, and paying homage to Mahatma Gandhi.

4 **Champaner & Pavagadh** (p703) Exploring an abandoned capital city and following pilgrims at two adjacent World Heritage Sites.

5 **Wild Ass Sanctuary** (p732) Looking for Indian wild ass, wolves, hyenas and nilgai antelope amid the flat salt plains of the Little Rann.

6 **Diu** (p708) Letting loose in this former Portuguese enclave and scootering around its near-empty roads.

7 **Shatrunjaya** (p707) Undertaking a challenging dawn pilgrimage to the hilltop Jain temple near Palitana.

History

It's said that Gujarat's Temple of Somnath witnessed the creation of the universe; sometime later, the state became Krishna's stomping grounds. On a firmer historical footing, Lothal and Dholavira (Kachchh) were important sites of the Indus Valley civilisation more than 4000 years ago. Gujarat featured in the exploits of the mighty Buddhist emperor Ashoka, and Jainism first took root under a grandson of Ashoka who governed Saurashtra.

The rule of the Hindu Solanki dynasty from the 10th to 13th centuries, with its capital at Patan, is considered Gujarat's cultural golden age. Solanki rule was ended when Ala-ud-din Khilji brought Gujarat into the Delhi sultanate after several campaigns around 1300. A century later the Muslim Gujarat sultanate broke free of Delhi rule and established a new capital at Ahmedabad. The Mughal empire conquered Gujarat in the 1570s and held it until the Hindu Marathas from central India occupied eastern and central Gujarat in the 18th century. The British set up their first Indian trading base at Surat on Gujarat's coast in about 1614, and replaced Maratha power in the early 19th century.

It's from Gujarat that Gandhi launched his program of nonviolent resistance against British rule, beginning with protests and fasting, and culminating with the 390km Salt March, which drew the attention of the world and galvanised anti-British sentiment across India. After Independence, eastern Gujarat became part of Bombay state. Saurashtra and Kachchh, initially separate states, were incorporated into Bombay state in 1956. In 1960 Bombay state was divided on linguistic lines into Gujarati-speaking Gujarat and Marathi-speaking Maharashtra.

The Congress Party of India largely controlled Gujarat until 1991 when the Bharatiya Janata Party (BJP) came to power. In 2002, communal violence erupted after a Muslim mob was blamed for an arson attack on a train at Godhra that killed 59 Hindu activists. Hindu gangs set upon Muslims in revenge. In three days, an estimated 2000 people were killed (official figures are lower) – most of them Muslims – and tens of thousands were left homeless. The BJP-led state government was widely accused of tacitly, and sometimes actively, supporting some of the worst attacks on Muslim neighbourhoods for political gain. Later that year Gujarat's then–Chief Minister Nahendra Modi won a landslide re-election victory. A decade hence, in 2012, a former BJP minister was convicted of criminal conspiracy and murder in the Naroda Patiya massacre during the Godhra riots, but Modi has thus far been cleared of all charges related to the violence. Since the 2002 riots, Gujarat has been peaceful, and enjoys a reputation as one of India's most prosperous and businesslike states. And Modi, of course, became India's Prime Minister in 2014. Adding a bit more Gujarati drama into the mix, on 8 November, 2016, he famously triggered a financial crisis in India by declaring 86% of all currency illegal overnight.

TOP STATE FESTIVALS

Uttarayan (p694) Skies swarm with kites in Ahmedabad and other cities.

Modhera Dance Festival (around 20 Jan) Indian classical dance jamboree.

Bhavnath Mela (Bhavnath Fair; Jan/Feb) Hindu festival at the foot of sacred Girnar Hill.

Mahakali Festival (Mar/Apr) Pilgrims pay tribute to Kali at Pavagadh hill.

Navratri (p694) Nine nights of dancing all around Gujarat.

Kartik Purnima (Somnath & Shatrunjaya; Nov/Dec) A multifaceted holy day for Hindus, Jains, and Sikhs (who celebrate it as Guru Nanak Jayanti). There's a large fair at Somnath (p713) and Jain pilgrims flock to Shatrunjaya hill (p707).

EASTERN GUJARAT

Ahmedabad (Amdavad)

079 / POP 6.36 MILLION

Ahmedabad (also called Amdavad, Ahmadabad or Ahemdavad), Gujarat's major city, grows on you. Yes, during peak hours with traffic, noise, and air so thick you can chew it, the place can be a little overwhelming, but it's well worth taking the time to get to know this remarkable city. It wins you over with its wealth of architecture – from centuries-old mosques and mausoleums to cutting-edge contemporary design. Then there's the fascinating maze of an old quarter, excellent museums, fine restaurants, a bustling street-food scene and the tranquility of the Sabarmati Ashram (Gandhi's former headquarters).

The old city, on the east side of the Sabarmati River, used to be surrounded by a 10km-long wall, of which little now remains except 15 formidable gates standing as forlorn islands amid swirling, cacophonous traffic. The new city on the west side of the river has wider streets, several major universities, and many middle-class neighbourhoods.

History

Ahmedabad was founded in 1411 by Gujarati sultan Ahmed Shah at the spot where, legend tells, he saw a hare chasing a dog and was impressed by its bravery. The city quickly spread beyond his citadel on the east bank of the Sabarmati, and by the 17th century it was considered one of the finest cities in India, a prospering trade nexus adorned with an array of fine Islamic architecture. Its influence waned, but from the second half of the 19th century Ahmedabad rose again as a huge textile centre (the 'Manchester of the East'). By the late 20th century many of the mills had closed and the subsequent economic hardship may have been a contributing factor to the communal violence that split the city in 2002, when about 2000 people, mostly Muslims, were killed. Today Ahmedabad is booming again as a centre for IT, education and chemical production on top of its traditional textiles and commerce, and has been officially dubbed a 'megacity'.

ALCOHOL PERMITS

Gujarat is, officially, a dry state, because Gandhi disapproved of the evils of alcohol, but alcohol permits for foreign visitors are easy to get. They're free upon arrival at the airport, or can be picked up – usually for a small charge – at the 'wine shops' found in many large hotels. Just show your passport to receive a one-month permit. There are plans to issue permits over the internet in the near future. The permit allows you two units over the month, which equates to 20 bottles of standard beer or two 750ml bottles of liquor, which you must drink in private. Cheers!

Sights

The most interesting part of Ahmedabad is the old city, east of the Sabarmati River – particularly the areas of Lal Darwaja, Bhadra Fort and Teen Darwaja, and the market streets that radiate from them.

★Calico Museum of Textiles MUSEUM
(☎079-22868172; www.calicomuseum.org; Sarabhai Foundation; ⏲tour 10.30am-1pm Thu-Tue) FREE This museum contains one of the world's finest collections of antique and modern Indian textiles, all handmade and up to 500 years old. There are some astoundingly beautiful pieces, displaying incredible virtuosity and extravagance. You'll see Kashmiri shawls that took three years to make, and double-*ikat* cloths whose 100,000 threads were each individually dyed before weaving. A single tour is offered each day the museum is open; advance booking is absolutely essential as spaces are limited (20); call well ahead.

The tour takes in the main textile galleries, where you get to see remarkable examples of tapestries, royal garments, exquisite saris, tribal costumes, Patola and Mashru weaves and Bandhani tie-dye. A separate gallery showcases different examples of needlework from around the world, and you can also see sacred bronzes, *pichwais* (devotional cloth hangings) and miniature paintings.

Kids under 10 are not welcome. Photography is not permitted and bags are not allowed inside. The museum is in the Shahibag area, 3.5km north of the old centre, opposite the Shahibag Underbridge. An autorickshaw from Lal Darwaja should cost about ₹50.

★Hutheesingh Temple JAIN TEMPLE
(Balvantrai Mehta Rd; ⏲6am-8pm) Outside Delhi Gate, this Jain temple is one of 300 *derasars* in Ahmedabad. Even if you've already seen some, this one will make your jaw drop in wonder at its delicate carvings of deities, flowers, and celestial damsels in white marble. Built in 1848, it's dedicated to Dharamanath, the 15th Jain *tirthankar* (great teacher), and each of the 52 sub-shrines in the courtyard is home to his likeness with bejewelled eyes. The caretaker may let you go on the roof.

Ahmedabad (Amdavad)

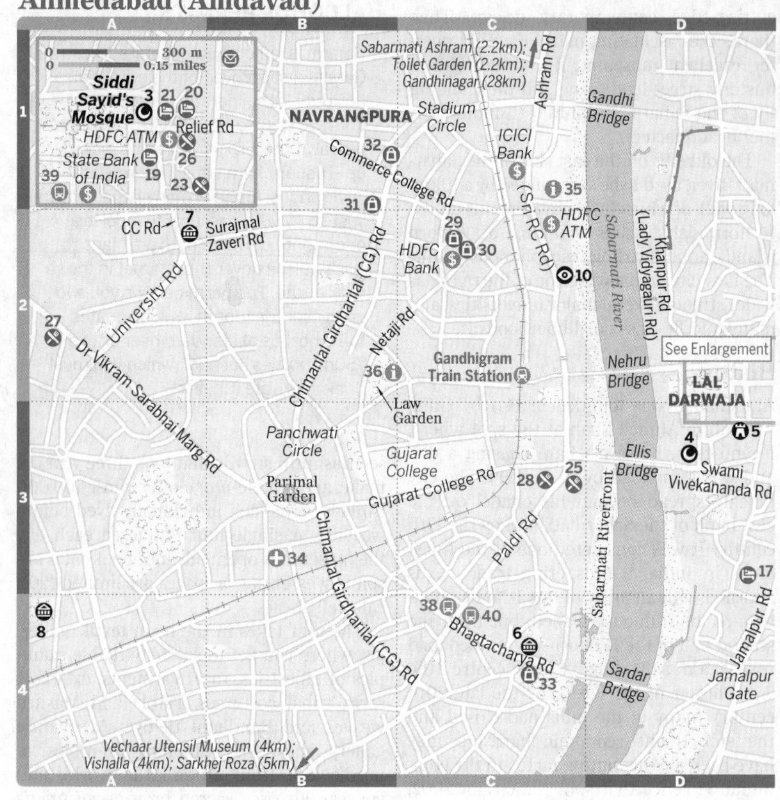

★Sabarmati Ashram HISTORIC SITE

(www.gandhiashramsabarmati.org; Ashram Rd; 8.30am-6.30pm) FREE In peaceful, shady grounds on the Sabarmati River's west bank, this ashram was Gandhi's headquarters from 1917 to 1930 during the long struggle for Indian independence. It's said he chose this site because it lay between a jail and a cemetery, and any *satyagrahi* (nonviolent resister) was bound to end up in one or the other. Gandhi's poignant, spartan living quarters are preserved, and there's a museum that presents a moving and informative record of his life and teachings.

It was from here, on 12 March 1930, that Gandhi and 78 companions set out on the famous Salt March to Dandi, on the Gulf of Cambay, in a symbolic protest, with Gandhi vowing not to return to the ashram until India had gained independence. The ashram was disbanded in 1933, later becoming a centre for Dalit welfare activities and cottage industries. After Gandhi's death some of his ashes were immersed in the river in front of the ashram.

It's about 5km north of Lal Darwaja. An autorickshaw from the city centre is about ₹50.

Lokayatan Folk Museum MUSEUM

(www.shreyasfoundation.in; Indian/foreigner ₹25/100; 3-5.30pm Tue-Sat, 10.30am-1.30pm & 3-5.30pm Sun) This museum, 3km west of the river in Bhudarpura, displays a fascinating range of Gujarati folk arts – particularly from Kachchh – including wood carvings, metalwork and some wonderful embroidered textiles and amazing tie-dyed quilts. Look out for elaborate headdresses, beadwork, dowry boxes, household utensils, camel and horse ornaments made by the Rabari people and more. The curator can give you a free tour. An autorickshaw from the centre costs around ₹50; say you want to go to the Shreyas Foundation.

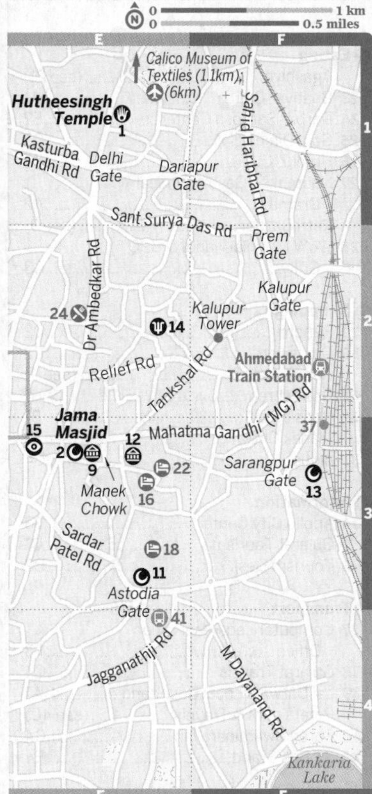

Sarkhej Roza HISTORIC BUILDING
(⏲9am-dusk) This mosque, tomb and palace complex is dedicated to the memory of Ahmed Shah I's spiritual adviser, Ahmed Khattu Ganj Baksh. The elegant, dilapidated buildings cluster around a great (often dry) tank, constructed by Sultan Mahmud Begada in the mid-15th century. It's an atmospheric place once used as a retreat by Ahmedabad's rulers. It's located in the Sarkhej area, 8km southwest of the old centre; a return autorickshaw from the city centre will cost around ₹150. Combine with dinner at Vishalla (p696).

The mausoleums of Mahmud Begada (by the entrance, with geometric *jalis* casting patterns of light on the floor) and Ganj Baksh (the largest in Gujarat) are both here.

Bhadra Fort FORT
(Lal Darwaja; ⏲dawn-dusk) Built immediately after the founding of Ahmedabad in 1411, Bhadra Fort houses government offices and a Kali temple. Its mighty gate formed the eastern entrance of the Ahmedabad citadel, which stretched west to the river. From the roof (take left doorway), you can see the formidable structure and views of surrounding streets. Between the fort and the **Teen Darwaja** (Triple Gateway) to its east was the Maidan Shahi (Royal Square), now a seething marketplace, where royal processions and polo games took place.

Mill Owners' Association Building ARCHITECTURE
(www.atmaahd.com; Ashram Rd; ⏲10am-4.30pm Mon-Fri, to 12.30pm Sat) FREE One of four buildings in Ahmedabad designed by legendary Swiss-French architect Le Corbusier, this one is the most striking. A dramatic ramp rises up the building, with slanted concrete brise-soleil (sun breakers) that make up the east and west facades allowing for air to circulate while blocking out the harsh sunlight. The mezzanine hosts temporary art exhibitions. If you wish to photograph the building, you need to seek permission first.

Kalpana Mangaldas Museum MUSEUM
(⏲3-5.30pm Tue-Sat, 10am-1.30pm & 3-5.30pm Sun) FREE Part of the Shreyas Museum complex, this one features festival masks from around India, toys, crafts, musical instruments and, just to round things off, an elephant skeleton. Admission is free with entry to Lokayatan Folk Museum.

NC Mehta Gallery MUSEUM
(University Rd; ⏲10.30am-5.30pm Tue-Sun) FREE In the same building as the Lalbhai Dalpatbhai Museum (p691), this gallery has an important collection of jewel-like illustrated manuscripts and miniature paintings. Best known is *Chaurapanchasika* (Fifty Love Lyrics of a Thief), written by Vilhana, an 11th-century Kashmiri poet sentenced to be hanged for loving the king's daughter. Before his execution he was granted one final wish: he chose to recite these 50 poems, which so impressed the king that he gave Vilhana his daughter in marriage.

Lalbhai Dalpatbhai Museum MUSEUM
(LD Museum; www.ldmuseum.co.in; University Rd; ⏲10.30am-5.30pm Tue-Sun) FREE Part of the LD Institute of Indology, this museum houses a gorgeous collection of ancient and medieval Indian art treasures, including Buddhist, Hindu and Jain deities in stone, marble and bronze, 75,000 Jain manuscripts

Ahmedabad (Amdavad)

Top Sights
1 Hutheesingh Temple E1
2 Jama Masjid E3
3 Siddi Sayid's Mosque A1

Sights
4 Ahmed Shah's Mosque D3
5 Bhadra Fort D3
6 City Museum C4
Kalpana Mangaldas Museum .... (see 8)
7 Lalbhai Dalpatbhai Museum A2
8 Lokayatan Folk Museum A4
9 Mausoleum of Ahmed Shah E3
10 Mill Owners' Association Building C2
NC Mehta Gallery .... (see 7)
11 Rani Sipri's Mosque E3
12 Rani-na-Hazira E3
13 Sidi Bashir Mosque F3
14 Swaminarayan Temple E2
15 Teen Darwaja E3

Activities, Courses & Tours
Heritage Walk .... (see 14)
House of MG Walks .... (see 21)

Sleeping
16 Deewanji Ni Haveli E3
17 Diwan's Bungalow D3
18 French Haveli E3
19 Hotel Cadillac A1
Hotel Good Night .... (see 21)
20 Hotel Volga A1
21 House of MG A1
22 Mangaldas Ni Haveli E3

Eating
Agashiye .... (see 21)
23 Bhatiyar Gali A1
24 Darbar Samosa Center E2
25 Gopi Dining Hall C3
26 Hotel ZK A1
27 Nautanki – Gastronomical Drama A2
Ratri Bazaar .... (see 9)
28 WoW Mughlai Handi & BBQ Grill C3

Shopping
29 Bandhej C2
30 Crossword C2
Gamthiwala .... (see 9)
31 Gramshree B1
32 Hansiba B1
Manek Chowk .... (see 9)
33 nidus C4

Information
34 Apollo City Center B3
35 Gujarat Tourism C1
36 Tourism Desk B2

Transport
37 Computerised Reservation Office F3
38 Gujarat Travels C4
39 Lal Darwaja Local Bus Stand A1
Patel Tours & Travels .... (see 40)
40 Shree Swaminarayan C4
41 ST Bus Stand E4

and miniature paintings. A 6th-century-AD sandstone carving from Madhya Pradesh is the oldest-known carved image of the god Rama.

Swaminarayan Temple HINDU TEMPLE
(Kalupur; dawn-dusk) The glorious, multicoloured, wood-carved Swaminarayan Temple, in the old city, was built in 1822 as the first temple of the Swaminarayan Hindu sect. Followers believe the sect's founder, Swaminarayan (1781–1830), was the supreme being. The daily Heritage Walk (p694) starts here at 8am and usually coincides with worship at the temple, with chanting and music on full display.

Vechaar Utensil Museum MUSEUM
(www.vishalla.com; Bye-Pass Rd; Indian/foreigner ₹15/50; 2-4pm & 5-10.30pm Tue-Sun) At Vishalla restaurant (p696), this excellent museum displays the graceful practicality of pots and utensils, with more than 4500 items from all over India, some 1000 years old. Look out for enormous oil containers, nutcrackers shaped like buxom women and a prototype samovar. It's around 7km southwest of the centre.

City Museum MUSEUM
(Sanskar Kendra, Bhagtacharya Rd; 10am-6pm Tue-Sun) FREE Inside one of four buildings designed by Le Corbusier, this museum covers Ahmedabad's history, craft, art, architecture and literature. It includes sections on the city's religious communities, Gandhi and the Independence struggle, as well as an excellent photography gallery and works by Gujarat's notable artists. On the ground floor there's a collection of 100 colourful kites, along with the history of kite-flying (the Chinese were the first to do so, in 200 BC).

Toilet Garden MUSEUM
(Safai Vidyalaya, Ashram Rd; ⏲10am-6pm Mon-Sat) Located next door to Sabarmati Ashram (p690), it's well worth popping in here to see the ecofriendly toilet models and diagrams displayed in the garden. Ishwardada Patel (also known as Mr Toilet) made it his life's work to promote sanitation across India, where around 40% of the population still don't have access to clean latrines. His other aim was to free the human scavengers, belonging to the untouchables caste, from their degrading and dangerous job of cleaning dry latrines by hand.

Tours

★Nirav Panchal TOURS
(☎9825626387; nirupanchal@yahoo.co.in) One of Gujarat's most knowledgeable guides, the charming Nirav Panchal leads customised tours, from single-day experiences in Ahmedabad to multiday trips across all parts of

MOSQUES & MAUSOLEUMS

Under the Gujarat sultanate in the 15th and 16th centuries, and especially under Ahmed Shah I (1411–42) and Mahmud Begada (1459–1511), Ahmedabad was endowed with a remarkable collection of stone mosques in a unique style incorporating elements of Hindu and Jain design. Note that women are not allowed into the actual prayer halls, and at some mosques are restricted to the periphery.

Jama Masjid (Friday Mosque; MG Rd; ⏲6am-6pm) Built by Ahmed Shah in 1423, the Jama Masjid ranks as one of India's most beautiful mosques. Demolished Hindu and Jain temples provided the building materials, and the mosque displays some architectural fusion with these religions, notably in the lotus-like carving of some domes, which are supported by the prayer hall's 260 columns. The two 'shaking' minarets lost half their height in the great earthquake of 1819; their lower portions still flank the prayer hall's central portico.

Mausoleum of Ahmed Shah (Badshah-na-Hazira; MG Rd; ⏲dawn-dusk) This atmospheric mausoleum, outside the Jama Masjid's east gate, may have been constructed by Ahmed Shah himself before his death in 1442. His cenotaph is the central one under the main dome. An 11pm drumming session in the mausoleum's eastern gateway used to signal the closing of the city gates and still happens nightly, carrying on a nearly 600-year-old tradition. No women allowed inside.

Rani-na-Hazira (Manek Chowk Rd) The tomb of Ahmed Shah's queen sits on a raised platform that's engulfed by market stalls. Though it's not in great shape, the *jali* screens are worth a look.

Siddi Sayid's Mosque (Lal Darwaja; ⏲dawn-dusk) One of Ahmedabad's most stunning buildings, this mosque is famed for its exquisite *jali* windows, spiderweb fine, two of them depicting the intricate intertwining branches of the 'tree of life'. Built in the year the Mughals conquered Gujarat (1573), by an Abyssinian in the Gujarati army, it was once part of the old citadel wall.

Ahmed Shah's Mosque (Swami Vivekananda Rd; ⏲dawn-dusk) Southwest of Bhadra Fort and dating from 1414, this is one of the city's earliest mosques, built for the sultan and nobles within Ahmedabad's original citadel. The prayer hall is a forest of beautifully carved stone pillars and *jali* (carved lattice) screens, and the elaborately carved insides of its cupolas have a circular symmetry reminiscent of Hindu and Jain temples.

Rani Sipri's Mosque (Astodia Gate Circle; ⏲dawn-dusk) This small mosque near the ST bus stand is also known as the Masjid-e-Nagira (Jewel of a Mosque) because of its graceful construction, with delicately carved minarets and domed tomb with fine *jali* screens. It was commissioned in 1514 by Rani Sipri, the Hindu wife of Sultan Mahmud Begada; after her death, she was buried here.

Sidi Bashir Mosque (⏲dawn-dusk) Between Ahmedabad train station and Sarangpur Gate, the Sidi Bashir Mosque, built in 1452, is famed for its 21.3m-high shaking minarets *(jhulta minara)*, built to shake to protect against earthquake damage. The delicate stonework around the base is particularly fine.

the state. He speaks perfect English, and his French isn't bad either. Call or email him for details and prices, based on your interests.

★ **Saiyed Badrudin** CULTURAL

(☎7622884557, 9510225587; easywaysaiyed@gmail.com) Saiyed is a very knowledgeable local guide, a native of Ahmedabad who's a fluent English speaker and who is happy to arrange tailor-made sightseeing city excursions, depending on your interest.

Heritage Walk WALKING

(☎9824032866; Swaminarayan Temple; Indian/foreigner ₹30/50; ⊙8am daily) Ahmedabad's Municipal Corporation runs a fascinating daily walking tour through the old city. It starts at 8am (show up at 7.45am) at the Swaminarayan Temple (p692) in Kalupur and finishes at the Jama Masjid (p693) around 10.30am. Meandering through the narrow, confusing streets and past dilapidated, carved wooden houses, it is an excellent way to get a feel for old Ahmedabad with its 600 *pols* – nook-like neighbourhoods with common courtyards, wells and *chabutaras* (bird-feeding towers).

The tours are in English and there's a brief slideshow beforehand. Wear slip-on footwear as you'll be visiting plenty of temples.

House of MG Walks WALKING

(☎079-25506946; House of MG, Lal Darwaja; breakfast walk ₹350, night walk ₹250; ⊙breakfast walk 7.30-9.30am, night walk 9.30-11pm) The House of MG heritage hotel offers two excellent guided walking tours. The Breakfast Walk, offered October to March, covers the old city's highlights and ends at the hotel where breakfast is served. The hour-long Heritage Night Walk, offered year-round, gives a glimpse of some of Ahmedabad's historic neighbourhoods at night, including the markets of Manek Chowk.

NAVRATRI & DUSSEHRA

Navratri (Festival of Nine Nights; ⊙Sep/Oct) is celebrated India-wide, but Gujarathas made it its own. This nine-night festival celebrates the feminine divinity in the forms of the goddesses Durga, Lakshmi and Saraswati – particularly Durga's slaying of the demon Mahishasura. Celebrations centre on special shrines at junctions, marketplaces and, increasingly, large venues that can accommodate thousands. People dress up in sparkling finery to whirl the night away in entrancing garba or dandiya rasa circle dance still the early hours. The night after Navratri is **Dussehra** (⊙Oct), which celebrates the victory of Rama over Ravana, with more nocturnal dancing and fireworks, plus the burning of giant effigies of the defeated demon king.

Festivals & Events

Uttarayan CULTURAL

(Makar Sakranti; ⊙14-15 Jan) From 14 to 15 January, Ahmedabad hosts Uttarayan, a traditional kite festival that attracts international participants and is well worth the stiff neck, as visitors flood the city and kites fill the sky.

Sleeping

Budget hotels are mostly clustered in the noisy, traffic-infested Lal Darwaja area, close to the old city, while the majority of midrange and top-end places are found on Khanpur Rd (paralleling the eastern bank of the Sabarmati), a more congenial environment but further from most of the interesting sights. There are also several beautiful heritage properties right in the heart of the old city.

Hotel Cadillac HOTEL $

(☎079-25507558; Advance Cinema Rd, Lal Darwaja; s/d from ₹500/600) If you're counting every last rupee, you could do worse than this friendly option – an old-timer from 1934, which has kept its wooden balustrade. Mattresses are lumpy and smaller rooms are cell-like; larger rooms are OK, just grungy. Try to get a room on the balcony.

Hotel Volga HOTEL $$

(☎079-25509497; www.hotelvolga.in; Hanuman Ln, off Relief Rd, Lal Darwaja; s/d ₹950/1100, with AC ₹1200/1400; ❄📶) This surprisingly good option tucked down a narrow street behind the House of MG is worth searching out. Rooms are smart and respectably clean, with many recently upgraded and decorated with curved or padded headboards and accent lighting. The front desk is efficient and you can order decent multicuisine food to your room. Avoid rooms below the 3rd-floor kitchen.

Hotel Good Night HOTEL $$

(☎079-25507181; www.hotelgoodnight.co.in; Lal Darwaja; s/d from ₹1700/1900; ❄📶) This tidy hotel has a few categories of rooms, all of which have been renovated in sparkling whites. The top-grade 'executive' rooms are surprisingly arty; the ground-floor 'economy' ones can be a bit stuffy. Great central location, but the air-con and fan sounds like a helicopter taking off.

★**Deewanji Ni Haveli** HERITAGE HOTEL **$$$**
(079-22140830; www.cityhc.org; opposite Ganga Dhiya ni Pol, Sankadi Sheri, Manek Chowk; r ₹2970-5515;) Part of the movement to regenerate heritage buildings in Ahmedabad, this striking 250-year-old *haveli* has been painstakingly restored to its former glory. Surrounding a tranquil courtyard, its luxurious rooms – with stuccoed walls, heavy wooden beams and antique furnishings – are one of the most atmospheric places to stay in the old town. Excellent breakfast included.

★**House of MG** HERITAGE HOTEL **$$$**
(079-25506946; www.houseofmg.com; Lal Darwaja; s/d from ₹4400/4600, ste from ₹9900, all incl breakfast;) This 1920s building – once the home of textile magnate Sheth Mangaldas Girdhardas – was converted into a beautiful heritage hotel by his great-grandson. All the rooms are vast, verandah-edged and masterfully decorated, with homey yet luxurious ambience. Service is first-rate, there are two excellent restaurants, and the indoor swimming pool and gym are divine. Discounts available for advance online bookings.

Don't miss the antique textiles gallery on the first floor. You can also buy artisanal gifts of excellent quality at the on-site shop, as well as coffee-table books on India's textiles, heritage and culture. The hotel runs three excellent walking tours (p694), for guests and nonguests alike.

French Haveli HOMESTAY **$$$**
(9978910730, 9016430430; www.frenchhaveli.com; opposite Jain Temple, Khida Sheri, Dhal-ni-pol, Astodia Chakra; r ₹2500-4300, ste ₹5700;) In the heart of one of the old city's *pols* (micro-neighbourhoods), this is a beautifully restored 150-year-old Gujarati heritage home with five individually decorated rooms. Agaashi on the 2nd floor has its own open-air terrace, whereas the Mahajan Suite is the most spacious. Terrific breakfast included. Not suitable for those with mobility difficulties due to steep stairs.

SLEEPING PRICE RANGES

The following price ranges refer to a double room with private bathroom and are inclusive of tax:

$ less than ₹800

$$ ₹800–₹2500

$$$ more than ₹2500

Mangaldas Ni Haveli BOUTIQUE HOTEL **$$$**
(www.houseofmg.com; Sankadi Sheri, Manek Chowk; r ₹6000;) Owned by the House of MG, the six rooms at this intimate boutique hotel face a tranquil courtyard and a mezzanine patio with traditional Gujarati swings. The animal-themed rooms are uniquely decorated using local stencil art; cow rooms are the most spacious. There are enviable views of the *pol* from the upstairs terrace and the restaurant serves Gujarati fast food.

Diwan's Bungalow HERITAGE HOTEL **$$$**
(079-25355428; www.neemranahotels.com; MB Kadri Rd; r ₹5900-8800;) Tucked away in a lively neighborhood a 10-minute walk from Badra Fort, this restored 19th-century mansion has an air of casual elegance. The lobby and dining room are hung with period chandeliers and an interior terrace opens onto a garden courtyard. Every room is different, but each is large and tastefully appointed, blending modern amenities with historic touches.

Eating

Ahmedabad has the best range of restaurants in Gujarat, serving anything from Gujarati thalis and Mughlai curries to molecular cuisine. There are excellent food stalls and no-frills eateries in the old city, night markets at Manek Chowk and Law Garden, and more upmarket restaurants found largely in the west half of the city and inside hotels.

★**Bhatiyar Gali** INDIAN **$**
(Khaas Bazaar, Lal Darwaja; dishes from ₹30; noon-1am) The narrow 'Cook's Lane' and adjoining alleyways really come into their own in the evenings, with no-frills eateries and stalls preparing meaty delights. Bera Samosa serves tiny, delicious, spicy meat samosas and deep-fried meatballs, while Bari Handa is the place for stews simmered in clay ovens overnight. Spicy skewers char-

GUJARATI CUISINE

Gujarat is strong on vegetarian cuisine, partly thanks to the Jain influence here, and the quintessential Gujarati meal is the all-veg thali. It's sweeter, lighter and less spicy and oily than Punjabi thali and locals – who are famously particular about food – have no doubt it's the best thali in the world. It begins with a large stainless-steel dish, onto which teams of waiters will serve most or all of the following: curries, chutneys, pickles, dhal, kadhi (a yoghurt and gram-flour preparation), raita, rotis, rice, *khichdi* (a blend of lightly spiced rice and lentils), *farsan* (savoury nibbles), salad and one or two sweet items – to be eaten concurrently with the rest. Buttermilk is the traditional accompanying drink. Normally the rice and/or *khichdi* don't come till you've finished with the rotis. In most thali restaurants, the waiters will keep coming back until you can only say, 'No more'.

coal-grilled are good, too. It's just east of Teen Darwaza.

★Ratri Bazaar MARKET $
(Manek Chowk; dishes from ₹40; ⏲7.30pm-1.30am) This is by far the most popular night market in the city, and it heaves nightly with hungry locals. Favourites include the dosa stall that dishes out the South Indian crispy pancake with a myriad of fillings, the biriyani stalls, kulfi from Asharfi Kulfi and Cadbury pizza (crisp base with melted chocolate and cheese).

Darbar Samosa Center GUJARATI $
(Gheekanta Rd, opposite Navtad Ni Pol, Vishwa Karma Bhuwan; 12 samosas ₹45; ⏲9am-8.30pm) This standout samosa joint is one of several along this lane that specialises in *navtad ni samosa* – small vegetable samosas stuffed with pulses, potato or peas and served either with a sweet-and-sour wood-apple sauce with chilli and jaggery or a spicy chickpea gravy.

Gopi Dining Hall GUJARATI $$
(off Paldi Rd; thali ₹210-300; ⏲10.30am-3.30pm & 6.30-10.30pm; ❄) Just off the western end of Ellis Bridge, this little restaurant is a much-loved thali institution, with a small garden and an air-conditioned dining room. You can choose from 'fix', 'full' (unlimited) and 'with one sweet' options depending on how hungry you are.

WoW Mughlai Handi & BBQ Grill NORTH INDIAN $$
(☎079-30257202; www.wowrestaurant.co.in; Rangoli Complex, Ashram Rd, Ellis Bridge; mains from ₹140; ⏲noon-3pm & 7-11pm; ❄) The cheesy Seven Wonders of the World decor aside, this place specialises in rich, flavourful Mughlai curries and tasty kebabs. In the evenings, grill your own over the charcoal burners on its 2nd-floor open-air terrace.

Hotel ZK INDIAN, CHINESE $$
(Relief Rd, Lal Darwaja; mains ₹190-300; ⏲11am-11.30pm; ❄) This popular nonveg restaurant has air-con, tinted windows, low lighting and impeccable service. The boneless mutton *kadhai* is fantastic and (like a number of dishes here) comes served over a flame. The kebabs and the Afghani chicken curry are also recommended.

★Nautanki – Gastronomical Drama MODERN INDIAN $$$
(☎079-65555560; www.nautankiamd.com; Dr Vikram Sarabhai Marg, opposite ATIRA near IIM-Ahmedabad; mains ₹450-850, tasting menu ₹1350; ⏲noon-3pm & 7-11pm; ❄) This daring establishment pushes Ahmedabad's gastronomic boundaries by experimenting with molecular gastronomy and reinventing traditional dishes by using non-traditional techniques. The tasting menu is a great introduction for first-time diners, with its deconstructed *panipuri* sphere, flavourful mutton biriyani and excellent desserts. A worthy splurge.

★Vishalla INDIAN $$$
(☎079-26602422; www.vishalla.com; Bye-Pass Rd; lunch ₹340, dinner ₹670; ⏲11am-3pm & 7.30-11pm) On the southwestern outskirts of town, Vishalla is a magical eating experience in an open-air, lantern-lit, rural village fantasy setting. An endless thali of Gujarati dishes you won't find elsewhere is served on leaf plates, at low wood tables under open-air awnings. Dinner includes excellent folk music, dance and puppet shows. An autorickshaw from central Ahmedabad costs about ₹150 return.

★Agashiye GUJARATI $$$
(☎079-25506946; www.houseofmg.com; House of MG, Lal Darwaja; set meal regular/deluxe ₹770/1050; ⏲noon-3.30pm & 7-10.30pm) On the rooftop terrace of the city's finest herit-

age hotel, Agashiye's daily-changing, all-veg menu begins with a welcoming drink and is a cultural journey around the traditional thali, with a multitude of diverse dishes delivered to your plate. It finishes with hand-churned ice cream. For dinner, book ahead.

Shopping

★Hansiba ARTS & CRAFTS
(8 Chandan Complex, CG Rd; ⏲11am-9pm Mon-Sat, 11.30am-7.30pm Sun) The retail outlet of the Self-Employed Women's Association (SEWA), Hansiba sells colourful woven and embroidered shawls, saris, beautifully embroidered ladies' tunics and wall hangings.

Manek Chowk HANDICRAFTS
(Manek Chowk; ⏲dawn-dusk) This busy space and surrounding narrow streets are the commercial heart of the old city. Weave your way through the crowds to soak up the atmosphere and browse the vegetable and sweet stalls and silver and textile shops.

Gamthiwala TEXTILES
(Manek Chowk; ⏲11am-7pm Mon-Sat) Gamthiwala, by the entrance to the Mausoleum of Ahmed Shah in the old city, sells quality block-printed and tie-dyed textiles.

Bandhej FASHION & ACCESSORIES
(www.bandhej.com; Shree Krishna Centre, Netaji Rd) Traditional and contemporary saris, embroidered tunics, accessories and gifts – all are handcrafted by expert craftspeople from around the country using ecofriendly materials. There's beautiful glassware made in Ahmedabad, too.

nidus GIFTS & SOUVENIRS
(☎079-26623692; National Insititute of Design Campus, Paldi; ⏲11am-7pm Mon-Sat) This gift shop on the NID (National Institute of Design) campus stocks an excellent range of independent designs by the Institute's alumni and students. Choose between funky jewellery, unconventional crockery, beautiful stainless-steel dining implements, toys, clothing, leather bags and funky stationery.

Gramshree ARTS & CRAFTS
(☎079-22146530; www.gramshree.org; 4th fl, Shopper's Plaza, CG Rd; ⏲8am-8pm) Beautiful handcrafted gifts – from embroidered pillowcases and traditional leather sandals to clothing, accessories, stationery and more. Gramshree is a grassroots organisation that supports and empowers more than 500 slum and rural women and invests in various community programs.

Crossword BOOKS
(Shree Krishna Centre, Netaji Rd; ⏲10.30am-9pm) A large, bustling bookshop, with a good selection of Lonely Planet guides, as well as regional maps and guidebooks (get your *101 Things to Do in Ahmedabad* here).

Information

Apollo City Center (☎079-66305800; www.apolloahd.com; 1 Tulsibaug Society) Small but recommended private hospital opposite Doctor House, near Parimal Garden.

Gujarat Tourism (☎079-26578044; www.gujarattourism.com; HK House, off Ashram Rd; ⏲10.30am-6pm Mon-Sat, closed 2nd & 4th Sat of the month) The very helpful HK House office has all sorts of information at its fingertips and you can also hire cars with drivers here. There is also an office at the Ahmedabad train station.

ICICI Bank (Ashram Rd, 2/1 Popular House; ⏲9am-6pm Mon-Fri) Foreign currency and changes travellers cheques.

Main Post Office (Ramanial Sheth Rd; ⏲10am-7.30pm Mon-Sat, to 1pm Sun) Postal services.

State Bank of India (Lal Darwaja; ⏲11am-4pm Mon-Fri, to 1pm Sat) Changes travellers cheques and currency.

Tourism Desk (☎079-32520878; Law Garden; ⏲10.30am-6pm Mon-Sat, closed 2nd & 4th Sat

ADVANCED BUS RESERVATIONS

These days, it's becoming much more common for passengers using public intercity buses run by Gujarat State Road Transport Corporation (GSRTC, ST) to reserve seats in advance. Theoretically, you should be able to do this online by registering at www.gsrtc.in. None of our attempts to book tickets by computer were successful, but we had no problem connecting to their internet system via smartphone – using an Indian SIM card with a data plan. (The system is also very useful for checking most bus route timings.) Alternatively, if you don't have the technology, many bus stands have online reservation windows, where you can make advance bookings in person. Doing so is not absolutely necessary, but depending on the route, you just might get stuck standing for a few hours.

of the month) Ahmedabad Municipal Corporation's office has city maps and puts effort into answering questions.

Getting There & Away

AIR

Ahmedabad's **international airport** (www.ahmedabadairport.com) is 9km north of central Ahmedabad. Air India, IndiGo, Jet Airways, SpiceJet and GoAir serve the following national destinations:

DESTINATION	COST (₹)	FREQUENCY
Bengaluru	3380	7 daily
Chennai	3095	7 daily
Delhi	2300	22 daily
Goa	2460	3 daily
Hyderabad	1829	5 daily
Jaipur	2778	daily
Kolkata	2942	2 daily
Mumbai	1050	30 daily

Etihad Airways and Jet Airways also fly to Abu Dhabi.

BUS

Private buses coming from the north may drop you on Naroda Rd, about 7km northeast of the city centre – an autorickshaw will complete the journey for around ₹70 to ₹80.

From the main **ST bus stand** (Gita Mandir Rd), also known as Gita Mandir or Astodia, around 1km southeast of Lal Darwaja, destinations served by state buses include the following:

DESTINATION	COST (₹)	TIME (HR)	FREQUENCY
Bhavnagar	123	3¾	17 daily
Bhuj	188	6¾	28 daily, mostly evening
Diu	207	9	daily at 8am
Jaipur	502	12	3 daily
Jamnagar	171	7	16 daily, morning and evening
Jodhpur	362	8½	5 daily
Junagadh	176	7½	26 daily
Rajkot	136	5½	half-hourly
Udaipur	220	5½	10 daily
Vadodara	89	2½	half-hourly

For long distances, private buses are more comfortable and quicker; most offices are close to Paldi Char Rasta bus station. **Patel Tours & Travels** (079-26576807; www.pateltoursandtravels.com; Paldi Char Rasta Bus Stand,

MAJOR TRAINS FROM AHMEDABAD

DESTINATION	TRAIN NO & NAME	COST (₹)	TIME (HR)	DEPARTURE
Bhavnagar	12971 Bandra-Bhavnagar Exp	240/560/760 (A)	5½	5.15am
Bhuj	19115 Sayaji Nagari Exp	235/625/880 (A)	7¼	11.59pm
Delhi (NDLS)	12957 Rajdhani	N/A/2049/1445 (B)	14	5.40pm
Delhi (DLI)	12915 Ashram Exp	485/1270/1810/3060 (C)	15¾	6.30pm
Jaipur	14312 Ala Hazrat Exp	350/950/1355 (A)	12¼	8.20pm
Jamnagar	22945 Saurashtra Mail	225/600/850/1405 (C)	6½	5.55am
Junagadh	22957 Somnath Exp	230/615/865 (A)	6¼	10.10pm
Mumbai	12010 Shatabdi	780/1655 (D)	6¾	2.40pm (Mon-Sat)
Mumbai	12902 Gujarat Mail	325/830/1160/1950 (C)	8½	10pm
Vadodara (Baroda)	12010 Shatabdi	330/670 (D)	1¾	2.40pm (Mon-Sat)

Fares: (A) sleeper/3AC/2AC, (B) 3AC/2AC/1AC, (C) sleeper/3AC/2AC/1AC, (D) AC chair/exec

Paldi Rd) has Volvo AC buses to Rajkot (₹450, four hours, hourly), Jamnagar (₹600, six hours, hourly) and Mumbai (sleeper ₹1000, 11 hours), plus non-AC buses to Mumbai (seat/sleeper ₹800/1000, 3pm to 10pm) and six daily buses to Bhuj (non-AC seat/sleeper ₹300/450, AC seat/sleeper ₹400/550). **Shree Swaminarayan** (☎079-26576544; www.sstbus.in; 22 Anilkunj Complex) runs to Diu in non-AC buses (seat/sleeper ₹300/400, 10 hours, 10.15pm), while **Gujarat Travels** (☎079-26575951; www.gujarattravels.co.in; Paldi Char Rasta Bus Stand, Paldi Rd) has departures to Mt Abu (seat/sleeper ₹460/510, seven hours, 7am, 11pm and 11.25pm).

Lal Darwaja Local Bus Stand has buses running to various destinations around the city and beyond; the most useful for visitors are the buses to Gandhinagar.

TRAIN

There's a **computerised reservation office** (⏲8am-8pm Mon-Sat, to 2pm Sun) just outside main Ahmedabad train station, which is the most convenient for departures. Window 6 handles the foreign-tourist quota. There are numerous daily services to the destinations below (especially Mumbai); we have picked some of the most convenient departures.

Getting Around

The airport is 9km north of the centre; a prepaid taxi should cost around ₹600, depending on your destination. An autorickshaw costs about ₹250 to the old city.

Autorickshaw drivers are supposed to turn their meter to zero at the start of a trip then calculate the fare using a conversion chart at the end, but few are willing to use them at all for foreigners, so negotiate before setting off. Short hops around the city should be around ₹30 to ₹40, and from the train station to Lal Darwaja no more than ₹50.

Around Ahmedabad

Nalsarovar Bird Sanctuary

This 121-sq-km **sanctuary** (www.nalsarovar.com; Indian/foreigner ₹40/600, car ₹20, camera/video ₹100/2500; ⏲6am-6pm), 60km southwest of Ahmedabad, protects Nalsarovar Lake, a flood of island-dotted blue dissolving into the sky and iron-flat plains, and its surrounding wetlands. Between November and February, the sanctuary sees flocks of indigenous and migratory birds, with as many as 250 species passing through. To see the birds, it's best to hire a boat (around ₹200, negotiable, per hour). A taxi from Ahmedabad costs around ₹4500 for a day trip; combine with visiting Lothal (40km south). Ducks, geese, eagles, spoonbills, cranes, pelicans and flamingos are best seen at daybreak and dusk, so it's worth staying overnight in the **luxury tent** (☎9427725090; s/d ₹1300/1800; ❄) accommodations run by Gujarat Tourism, 1.5km from the lake. The sanctuary is busiest at weekends and on holidays, and best avoided then. The only way to get here is under your own steam. A taxi from Ahmedabad costs around ₹4500 for a day trip, and gives you the option of combining Nalsarovar with Lothal (40km south).

WORTH A TRIP

ADALAJ VAV STEP-WELL

The **Adalaj Vav** (Adalaj Vav; ⏲dawn-dusk), 19km north of Ahmedabad, is among the finest of the Gujarati step-wells. Built by Queen Rudabai in 1499, it has three entrances leading to a huge platform that rests on 16 pillars, with corners marked by shrines. The octagonal well is five storeys deep and is decorated with exquisite stone carvings; subjects range from eroticism to buttermilk. From Ahmedabad, an autorickshaw costs around ₹550 return.

Lothal

About 80km southwest of Ahmedabad, the city that stood at this **archaeological site** (⏲dawn-dusk) 4500 years ago was one of the most important of the Indus Valley civilisation, which extended into what is now Pakistan. Excavations have revealed the world's oldest known artificial dock, which was connected to an old course of the Sabarmati River. Artefacts suggest that trade may have been conducted with Mesopotamia, Egypt and Persia. Access to the site is difficult if you don't have your own wheels and you'll need a strong imagination to make the ruins come to life.

Palace Utelia (☎9825012611; www.thepalaceutelia.com; Utelia; r from ₹6000; ❄), 7km from the archaeological site, by the Bhugavo River – complete with aged retainers – dwarfs the village it oversees. The dark, large rooms with antique furniture are overpriced, but it's an unusual place with charm if not comfort.

WORTH A TRIP

VAUTHA FAIR

Each November, Gujarat's largest **livestock fair** is held at Vautha, at the confluence of the Sabarmati and Vatrak Rivers, 50km south of Ahmedabad. Thousands of donkeys, camels and cows change hands, and some 25,000 people – including many maldhari pastoralists – camp for several days of buying, selling, eating, dancing, and making sunset *puja* (prayers) in the river. Contact Gujarat Tourism for exact dates.

Lothal is a long day trip from Ahmedabad, and a taxi (around ₹4600 return) is the easiest bet. Five daily trains run from Ahmedabad's Gandhigram station to Lothal-Bhurkhi station (2nd-class ₹20, 1½ to 2½ hours), 6km from the site, from where you can catch one of the infrequent buses. Take water and food.

Modhera

Built in 1027 by King Bhimdev I, Modhere's **Sun Temple** (Indian/foreigner ₹15/200; ⏲9am-5pm) is one of the greatest monuments of the Solanki dynasty, whose rulers were believed to be descended from the sun. Like the better-known Sun Temple at Konark in Odisha, which it predates by 200 years, the Modhera temple was designed so that the dawn sun shone on the image of Surya during the equinox. Surya Kund, an extraordinary rectangular step-well inside the complex, contains more than 100 shrines, resembling a sunken art gallery. Each year, around 20 January, the temple is the scene for a three-day classical dance festival (p688) with dancers from all over India.

Modhera is 100km northwest of Ahmedabad. You can take a bus (₹76, two hours, half-hourly) from Ahmedabad's ST bus stand to Mahesana (Mehsana), and then another bus 26km west to Modhera (₹34, one hour). There are also trains from Ahmedabad to Mahesana. A taxi from Ahmedabad is much easier, and will cost about ₹3800 round trip, including a visit to nearby Patan.

Patan

About 130km northwest of Ahmedabad, Patan was Gujarat's capital for six centuries before Ahmedabad was founded in 1411. It was ruined by the armies of Ala-ud-Din Khilji around 1300, and today is a dusty, little town with narrow streets lined by elaborate wooden houses.

Patan is famed, far and wide, for its beautiful Patola silk textiles, produced by the torturously laborious double-*ikat* method. Both the warp (lengthways) and weft (transverse) threads are painstakingly tie-dyed to create the pattern before the weaving process begins. It takes about six months to make one sari, which might cost ₹180,000.

Sights

★Rani-ki-Vav HISTORIC SITE
(Indian/foreigner ₹15/200; ⏲9am-5pm) The only real sign of Patan's former glory is this astoundingly beautiful step-well. Built in 1063 by Rani Udayamati to commemorate her husband, Bhimdev I, the step-well is the oldest and finest in Gujarat and is remarkably preserved. Steps lead down through multiple levels with lines of carved pillars and more than 800 sculptures, mostly on Vishnu-avatar themes, as well as striking geometric patterns. It's signposted in the northwest corner of the city.

★Patan Patola Heritage Museum WORKSHOP
(☎02766-232274; www.patanpatola.com; Patola House, Kalika Rd; Indian/foreigner ₹10/100; ⏲10am-6pm) Run by the multiple-award-winning Salvi family, this purpose-built museum is an excellent place to see Patola silk weaving in action. The family has specialised in double-*ikat* weaving (a process that their ancestors brought from Southeast Asia) since the 11th century – yes, you've read this correctly! – and inside you can get a demonstration on the loom and compare the family's craft with beautifully displayed single-*ikat* textiles from around the world, from Uzbekistan and northern Thailand to Holland.

The Salvi family mostly uses natural dyes such as indigo and turmeric and their hand-woven silk saris start from around ₹180,000 (US$2500) and can cost triple that amount, depending on the design. There's a three-year waiting list. They can also execute single-*ikat* weavings, which are considerably more affordable and quicker to make.

Upstairs you can see a demonstration of a less ancient yet fascinating and elaborate craft of paper carving.

Panchasara Parshvanath JAIN TEMPLE
(Hemchandracharya Rd) Among more than 100 Jain temples around Patan, this is the largest, with all the domes and sacred carvings your eyes can absorb.

Sleeping & Eating

Apple Residency HOTEL $$
(02766-297033; www.appleresidency.co.in; Panchvati Complex; s/d from ₹1045/1375;) Finally, a recommendable hotel in Patan! Not far from the railway station and under the same management as Food Zone (p701), this neat place lures travellers with its spick-and-span rooms decked out in neutral creams and browns, all with modern bathrooms and plasma-screen TVs.

Food Zone INDIAN $
(mains ₹90-170; 11am-3pm & 7-11pm;) This place near the railway tracks has modern booth seating, great thalis and a mix of Gujarati and Indo-Chinese dishes.

Getting There & Away

Patan is 40km northwest of Mahesana. Buses leave Ahmedabad's ST bus stand about every hour (₹99, three to 3½ hours). There are also buses to/from Zainabad (₹74, 2½ hours, four daily), via Modhera. A day trip in a private taxi from Ahmedabad costs about ₹3800; combine with a visit to the Sun Temple in Modhera.

Vadodara (Baroda)

0265 / POP 1.72 MILLION

Vadodara (or Baroda as it's often known) lies 106km southeast of Ahmedabad, little over an hour's drive along National Expressway 1. Vadodara has some interesting city sights, but the main reason for coming here is the stunning Unesco World Heritage Site of Champaner and Pavagadh nearby. The city is way less hectic than Ahmedabad, and parts of the Sayajigunj area near the university have a college-town feel.

After the Marathas expelled the Mughals from Gujarat in the 18th century, their local lieutenants, the Gaekwad clan, made Vadodara their capital. Vadodara retained a high degree of autonomy even under the British, right up to Independence in 1947. Maharaja Sayajirao III (1875–1939) was a great moderniser and laid the foundations of Vadodara's modern reputation as Gujarat's cultural capital, and the city's main attraction – the palace – is part of his legacy.

Sights

★**Laxmi Vilas Palace** PALACE
(Nehru Rd; Indian/foreigner ₹225/400; 10am-5pm Tue-Sun) Still the residence of Vadodara's royal family, Laxmi Vilas was built in full-throttle 19th-century Indo-Saracenic flourish at a cost of ₹6 million. The most impressive Raj-era palace in Gujarat, its elaborate interiors boast well-maintained mosaics, chandeliers and artworks, as well as a highly impressive collection of weaponry. It's set in expansive park-like grounds, which include a golf course. A one-hour audio guide is included with admission.

There are plans to turn some of the rooms into a heritage hotel.

Baroda Museum & Picture Gallery MUSEUM
(Sayaji Bagh; Indian/foreigner ₹10/200; 10.30am-5pm) Within Sayaji Bagh park, this museum houses a diverse collection, much of it gathered by Maharaja Sayajirao III, including statues and carvings from several Asian regions, fine ivory carvings from India, Japan and China, a modest Egyptian room with a mummy and an entire floor of stuffed and pickled wildlife specimens. The gallery has lovely Mughal miniatures and a motley crew of unsympathetically lit European masters; check out the small contemporary art gallery instead.

Sleeping

Most accommodation is in the conveniently central Sayajigunj area; there are a number of very cheap hotels (₹250 to ₹400) there, as well as decent, if cookie-cutter, midrange places.

Hotel Valiant HOTEL $$
(0265-2363480; www.hotelvaliant.com; 7th fl, BBC Tower, Sayajigunj; s/d ₹890/1270, with AC from ₹1300/1620;) The Valiant offers surprisingly fresh digs on the upper floors of a high-rise building. Take the lift up from the street entrance to find reception in a spacious lobby on the 7th floor. The clean if bland rooms are some of the best value in town.

Hotel Ambassador HOTEL $$
(0265-2362727; www.hotelambassadorindia.com; Sayajigunj; s/d from ₹1460/1780;) With stylish rooms and comfortable beds, the Ambassador offers very good value. The cheapest 'deluxe' rooms have a vaguely Japanese air, while the 'executive' quarters have

Vadodara (Baroda)

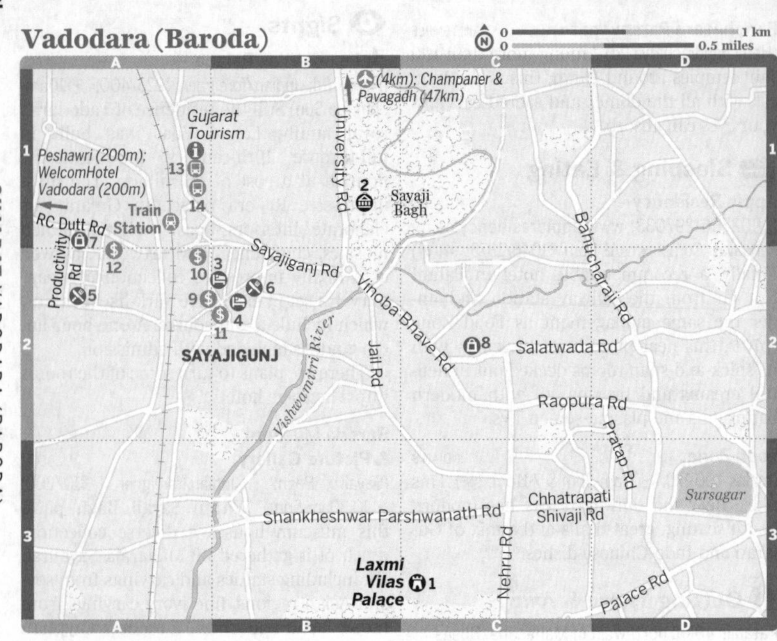

Vadodara (Baroda)

Top Sights
1 Laxmi Vilas Palace ... C3

Sights
2 Baroda Museum & Picture Gallery ... B1

Sleeping
3 Hotel Ambassador ... B2
4 Hotel Valiant ... B2

Eating
5 Aamantran ... A2
6 Kalyan ... B2

Shopping
7 Baroda Prints ... A1
8 Baroda Prints & Workshop ... C2

Information
9 Bank of Baroda ATM ... A2
10 HDFC ATM ... A2
11 ICICI Bank ... B2
12 State Bank of India ATM ... A2

Transport
13 ST Bus Stand ... A1
14 Sweta Travels ... A1

a slick contemporary feel, all pinks, oranges, squares and rectangles. There's civilised 24-hour checkout and a very helpful front desk.

★ **WelcomHotel Vadodara** HOTEL **$$$**
(☎0265-2330033; www.itchotels.in; RC Dutt Rd; r incl breakfast from ₹9550-13,150, ste ₹21,500; ❄📶🏊) A swish five-star complex with well-appointed rooms, an unusual outdoor pool, plenty of cool lounge areas, a good but expensive 24-hour multicuisine restaurant, a wine shop, and the best restaurant in Vadodara.

Eating

Kalyan SOUTH INDIAN **$**
(Sayajigunj; dishes ₹80-210; ⏰7am-11pm; 🥬) Kalyan is a breezy student hang-out serving healthy portions of South Indian food and less healthy attempts at Western fast food (though all dishes are vegetarian).

Aamantran INDIAN **$$**
(Sampatrao Colony; mains ₹150-330, thali ₹300; ⏰11am-3pm & 7-10.30pm; ❄) Hailed by many as the best thali in Vadodara, it's an all-you-can-eat taste of Gujarat. À la carte dishes

include a variety of veg tandoor selections, along with North Indian and Jain specialities. Look for the sign in Gujarati.

★ **Peshawri** NORTH INDIAN $$$
(☎0265-2330033; WelcomHotel Vadodara, RC Dutt Road; mains ₹1675-2900; ⏲7.30-11.30pm; ❄) Rough stone walls, heavy wooden beams and hanging copper vessels conjure a northwest frontier feel at Vadodara's best restaurant, with loyal customers coming all the way over from Ahmedabad and beyond. North Indian and clay oven dishes are the speciality here; standouts include tandoori *jhinga* (prawns) and *murgh malai* (marinated chicken) kebab, as well as imaginative stuffed naans. Book ahead.

Shopping

Baroda Prints ARTS & CRAFTS
(3 Aires Complex, Productivity Rd; ⏲9am-9pm Mon-Sat, 8am-6pm Sun) Hand-printed dress materials in original, colourful and attractive designs.

Baroda Prints & Workshop ARTS & CRAFTS
(Salatwada Rd; ⏲10am-8pm Mon-Sat, 11am-5pm Sun) At this Baroda Prints branch you can see printers at work upstairs, then buy the finished product downstairs.

Information

There are ATMs at the **train station**, on **RC Dutt Rd**, and in **Sayajigunj**.

ICICI Bank (p703) has an ATM and changes travellers cheques and cash.

Gujarat Tourism (www.gujarattourism.com; ⏲10am-6pm Mon-Sat, closed 2nd & 4th Sat of the month) Located inside the new VED Transcube Mall next to the ST bus stand. Friendly, but don't expect much.

ICICI Bank (Sayajigunj; ⏲10am-4pm Mon-Fri, to 1pm Sat) Has an ATM and changes travellers cheques and cash.

Getting There & Away

AIR

Vadodara International Airport (☎0265-2485356) is 4km northeast of the centre and has numerous daily departures to Delhi and Mumbai with Jet Airways, IndiGo and Air India.

BUS

The **ST bus stand** (Old Chhani Rd), integrated with a shopping mall, is just north of the train station. Frequent buses run to numerous destinations.

DESTINATION	COST (₹)	TIME (HR)	FREQUENCY
Ahmedabad	ordinary/AC 89/180	2	at least hourly
Bhavnagar	137	5½	12 daily
Diu	229	10	1.30am & 6am
Mumbai	368	9	7.30pm
Udaipur	260	8½	3.15am & 6am

Across from the train station, **Sweta Travels** (☎0265-2786917) sends AC Volvo buses to Mumbai (seat/sleeper ₹1500/1800, eight hours, three nightly). Many other companies have private buses to other destinations in Gujarat and Rajasthan from the plethora of offices at Pandya Bridge, 2km north of the train station.

TRAIN

Around 40 trains a day run to Ahmedabad, including the 12009 Shatabdi (AC chair/exec ₹330/670, two hours, 11.07am Monday to Saturday). The 44 daily trains to Mumbai include the 12010 Shatabdi (AC chair/exec ₹670/1415, 5¼ hours, 4.19pm Monday to Saturday).

Around Vadodara

Champaner & Pavagadh

This spectacular Unesco World Heritage Site, 47km northeast of Vadodara, combines a sacred 762m volcanic hill (Pavagadh) that rises dramatically from the plains and a ruined Gujarati capital with beautiful mosque architecture (Champaner). The whole area is referred to as Pavagadh.

Sights

★ **Pavagadh** HISTORIC SITE
This scenic hilltop may have been fortified as early as the 8th century. Today, throngs of pilgrims ascend Pavagadh to worship at the important **Kalikamata Temple**, dedicated to the evil-destroying goddess Kali, who sits atop the summit. You can either walk up the pilgrim trail (two to three hours), or take a shuttle (₹24) halfway up the hill from along the Champaner Citadel south wall, from where a **ropeway** (return ₹113; ⏲6am-6.45pm) glides you up to within a 700m walk of the temple.

Pavagadh became the capital of the Chauhan Rajputs around 1300, but in 1484 was taken by the Gujarat Sultan Mahmud

Begada, after a 20-month siege; the Rajputs committed *jauhar* (ritual mass suicide) in the face of defeat.

Near the top of the hill are also Pavagadh's oldest surviving monument, the 10th- to 11th-century Hindu **Lakulisha Temple** and several Jain temples. The views are fantastic and so are, if you're lucky, the cooling breezes. During the nine days of Navratri (p694) and the Mahakali festival (p688), the usual flow of pilgrims becomes a flood.

★ **Champaner** HISTORIC SITE

(Indian/foreigner ₹20/500; ⏲8am-6pm) Following his capture of Pavagadh, Sultan Mahmud Begada turned Champaner, at the base of the hill, into a splendid new capital. But its glory was brief: when it was captured by Mughal emperor Humayun in 1535, the Gujarati capital reverted to Ahmedabad, and Champaner fell into ruin. The heart of this historic site is the Citadel, whose most impressive features are its 16th-century monumental mosques (no longer used for worship), with their beautiful blending of Islamic and Hindu architecture.

The huge **Jami Masjid**, just outside the Citadel's east gate, boasts a wonderful carved entrance porch that leads into a lovely courtyard surrounded by a pillared corridor. The prayer hall has two tall central minarets, further superb stone carving, multiple domes, finely latticed windows and seven mihrabs (prayer niches) along the back wall.

Other beautiful mosques include the **Saher ki Masjid**, behind the ticket office inside the Citadel, which was probably the private royal mosque, and the **Kevda Masjid**, 300m north of the Citadel and about 600m west of the Jami Masjid. Here you can climb narrow stairs to the roof, and higher up the minarets, to spot other mosques even further out into the countryside – **Nagina Masjid**, 500m north, with no minarets but exquisite geometric carving, particularly on the tomb next to it, and **Lila Gumbaj ki Masjid**, 800m east, on a high platform and with a fluted central dome. The twin minarets resembling factory chimneys, about 1km west, adorn the **Brick Minar ki Masjid**, a rare brick tomb.

Sleeping & Eating

★ **Kathiwada Raaj Mahal** HERITAGE HOTEL $$$

(☎022-69995505; www.kathiwada.com; Kathiwada, Madhya Pradesh; r ₹5500; ❄☒) Nestling next to the village of Kathiwada in Madhya Pradesh, this lovingly restored 1895 family home of the Kathiwada royal family is draped in flowering bougainvillea and overlooks the beautiful Ratanman Hill Plateau. The rooms are airy, spacious and decked out with 1960s art-deco furniture; meals are vegetarian and delicious and the place is 1½ hours' drive from Champaner.

Apart from drinking in the tranquillity of the surroundings, guests can visit tribal villages, trek to the nearby RatanMal wildlife sanctuary via a waterfall, or just go wandering through the property's mango orchards.

Getting There & Away

Buses to Pavagadh run at least once hourly from Vadodara (₹50, 1¼ hours); a return taxi costs around ₹1200. Most buses from Pavagadh to Vadodara carry on to Ahmedabad (₹112, four hours).

SAURASHTRA

Before Independence, Saurashtra, also known as the Kathiawar Peninsula, was a jumble of more than 200 princely states. Today it has a number of hectic industrial cities, but most of them retain a core of narrow old streets crowded with small-scale commerce. Outside the cities it's still villages, fields, forests and a timeless, almost feudal feel, with farmers and *maldhari* herders dressed head to toe in white, and rural women as colourful as their neighbours in Rajasthan.

Saurashtra is mainly flat and its rare hills are often sacred, including the spectacular, temple-topped Shatrunjaya and Girnar. The peninsula is liberally endowed with wildlife sanctuaries, notably Sasan Gir, where Asia's last wild lions roam. On the south coast lies the quaint, laid-back, ex-Portuguese island enclave of Diu. Saurashtra is also where Mahatma Gandhi was born and raised: you can visit several sites associated with his life.

Bhavnagar

☎0278 / POP 605,880

Bhavnagar is a hectic, sprawling industrial centre with a colourful old core that makes a base for journeys to nearby Shatrunjaya and Blackbuck National Park.

Sights

Old City AREA

North of Ganga Jalia Tank, Bhavnagar's old city is well worth a wander, especially in the

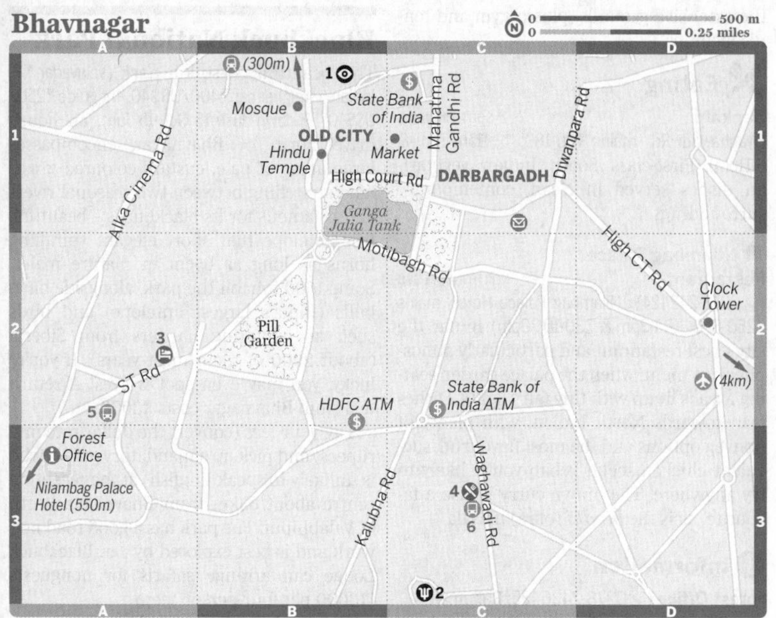

early evening – it's busy with small shops and cluttered with dilapidated elaborate wooden buildings leaning over the colourful crowded bazaars. Don't miss the vegetable market!

Takhteshwar Temple HINDU TEMPLE

(Takhteshwar Tarheti Rd; ⏰dawn-dusk) Perched atop a small hillock, this temple is up high enough to provide splendid views over the city and out onto the Gulf of Cambay.

Sleeping

The budget hotels, mostly in the old city and near the train station, are fairly grim, but midrange hotels are reasonable, and there's a beautiful, museum-like heritage palace.

Hotel Sun 'n' Shine HOTEL **$$**

(☎0278-2516131; www.hotelsunnshine.in; Panwadi Chowk, ST Rd; r incl breakfast from ₹2300, ste from ₹4200; ❄📶) This well-run, three-star hotel is decent value. It has a Mediterranean-inspired and vertigo-inducing atrium, a welcoming front desk, and a reliable vegetarian restaurant. The rooms are fresh and clean with comfortable beds and soft pillows: the more you pay, the more windows you get. Breakfast is substantial, and free airport transfers are offered.

Bhavnagar

Sights
1 Old City ... B1
2 Takhteshwar Temple ... C3

Sleeping
3 Hotel Sun 'n' Shine ... A2

Eating
4 Sankalp ... C3

Transport
5 ST Bus Stand ... A2
6 Tanna Travels ... C3

Nilambag Palace Hotel HERITAGE HOTEL **$$$**

(☎0278-2424241; cottage room ₹3400, palace r ₹3950-10,400; ❄📶🏊) In large gardens beside the Ahmedabad road, 600m southwest of the bus station, this former maharaja's palace was built in 1859. The lobby looks like an understated regal living room, with a beautiful mosaic floor. The sizeable palace rooms retain a stately early-20th-century feel; the 'cottage' rooms are mediocre and could be cleaner. The restaurant (p706) is the best in town.

Guests have use of a circular swimming pool (nonguests ₹100) in the Vijay Mahal in the extensive grounds, plus a gym and tennis facilities.

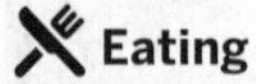

Eating

Sankalp SOUTH INDIAN $

(Waghawadi Rd; mains ₹90-180; 11am-3pm & 6-11pm) First-class South Indian vegetarian dishes served in clean, contemporary surroundings.

★ **Nilambag Palace Restaurant** NORTH INDIAN $$$

(0278-2424241; Nilambag Palace Hotel; mains ₹250-650; 1-3pm & 7.30-10.30pm) By far the city's best restaurant and particularly atmospheric at night, when the palace garden seating area is lit up with tiny fairy lights. Dishes lean towards North Indian, with plenty of nonveg options and the most flavourful, succulent chicken seekh kebab you're likely to try anywhere. The prawn curry is also a favourite, as is the *bindhi* (okra) masala.

Information

Forest Office (0278-2426425; Bahumali Bhavan, Annexe, ST Rd; 10.30am-6.30pm Mon-Sat, closed 2nd & 4th Sat of the month) Book accommodation for Blackbuck National Park here. It's near the STC bus stand.

State Bank of India (Darbargadh; 10.30am-4.30pm Mon-Fri) The State Bank of India changes cash and travellers cheques and has a 24-hour ATM.

Getting There & Around

AIR

Bhavnagar Airport (0278-2203113) is about 3.5km from town and has four weekly flights to Mumbai with Air India. A taxi/rickshaw to/from the airport costs around ₹170/110.

BUS

From the **ST bus stand** (ST Rd) there are frequent services to Rajkot (₹124/225 seat/sleeper, four hours, 11 daily), Ahmedabad (₹123, 4½ hours, at least once hourly), Vadodara (seat/sleeper ₹147/247, 5½ hours), Palitana (₹47, 1½ hours, three daily) and Diu (₹125, 7½ hours, five daily).

Private bus companies include **Tanna Travels** (0278-2425218; Waghawadi Rd), with AC buses to Ahmedabad (₹270, four hours, 15 daily).

TRAIN

The 12972 Bhavnagar-Bandra Express departs at 6.35pm and arrives in Ahmedabad (sleeper/3AC/2AC ₹240/560/760) at 11.40pm on its way to Mumbai (sleeper/3AC/2AC ₹435/1135/1610).

Blackbuck National Park

This beautiful, 34-sq-km **park** (Velavadar NP; Indian/foreigner car ₹400/US$40, 4hr guide ₹250/US$10; dawn-dusk 16 Oct–15 Jun), an hour's drive north of Bhavnagar, encompasses large areas of pale, custard-coloured grassland stretching between two seasonal rivers and is famous for its blackbucks – beautiful, fast antelope that sport elegant spiralling horns as long as 65cm in mature males. Some 1600 inhabit the park, alongside bluebulls (India's largest antelope) and birds such as wintering harriers from Siberia (about 2000 of them most years). If you're lucky, you may even spot wolves! A return taxi from Bhavnagar costs ₹3000.

Pay your fees (convert the dollar rate into rupees) and pick up a mandatory guide (who is unlikely to speak English) at the reception centre about 65km from Bhavnagar, north of Valabhipur. The park has a good road network and is best explored by car. Blackbuck Lodge can arrange safaris for nonguests (₹3000 per four-person jeep).

A taxi day trip from Bhavnagar costs about ₹3000.

Sleeping

★ **Blackbuck Lodge** HOTEL $$$

(9978979728; www.theblackbucklodge.com; s/d incl breakfast Oct-Mar ₹14,400/15,000, Apr-Sep ₹9600/9000) This cluster of tastefully decorated, comfortable stone villas is just outside the park's western entrance. Packages with dinner included are also offered, as are safaris, and blackbucks are easily spotted on the property grounds.

Kaliyar Bhavan Forest Lodge HOTEL $$$

(Indian/foreigner dm ₹200/US$20, d ₹600/US$55, with AC ₹1700/US$80) Near the park's reception centre, this basic lodge is run by the Forest Office (p706) in Bhavnagar. Choose between two 13-bed dorms, an air-con room and a non-AC room. Good vegetarian meals served; hideously overpriced for foreigners, but the location within the park is amazing for animal-spotters.

Palitana

02848 / POP 64,500

The hustling, dusty town of Palitana, 51km southwest of Bhavnagar, has grown rapidly to serve the pilgrim trade around Shatrunjaya. During the Kartik Purnima (p688) festival, accommodation around town floods with pilgrims and is best booked in advance.

Sights & Activities

★Shatrunjaya RELIGIOUS SITE

(temples 6.30am-6pm) One of Jainism's holiest pilgrimage sites, Shatrunjaya is an incredible hill studded with temples, built over 900 years. It is said that Adinath (also known as Rishabha), the founder of Jainism, meditated beneath the rayan tree at the summit. The temples are grouped into *tunks* (enclosures), each with a central temple flanked by minor ones. The 500m climb up 3300 steps (1½ hours) to the temples adds to the extraordinary experience. It costs ₹30 by autorickshaw to the steps.

Most days, hundreds of pilgrims make the climb; crowds swell into the thousands around Kartik Purnima (p688), which marks the end of Chaturmas, a four-month period of spiritual retreat and material self-denial that coincides with the monsoon season.

As you near the top of the hill, the track forks. The main entrance, **Ram Pole**, is reached by bearing left, though the best views are to the right, where on a clear day you can see the Gulf of Cambay. Inside the Nav Tonk Gate, one path leads left to the Muslim shrine of **Angar Pir** – a Muslim saint who protected the temples from a Mughal attack; women who want children come here and make offerings of miniature cradles. To the right, the second *tunk* you reach is the Chaumukhji Tunk, containing the **Chaumukh** (Four-Faced Shrine), built in 1618 by a wealthy Jain merchant. Images of Adinath, the first Jain *tirthankar* (believed to have attained enlightenment here), face the four cardinal directions.

You can easily spend a couple of hours wandering among the hundreds of temples up here. The biggest and one of the most splendid and important, with a fantastic wealth of detailed carving, is the **Adinath Temple**, on the highest point on the far (south) side.

Shri Vishal Jain Museum MUSEUM

(₹20; 8.30am-12.30pm & 3.30-8.30pm) This dusty museum features some remarkable exhibits of Jain artwork and artefacts up to 500 years old and beautiful ivory carvings. In the basement is a surprising circular temple with mirror walls and centuries-old images of four *tirthankars* (great Jain teachers). It's 500m down the street from the foot of the Shatrunjaya steps.

SHATRUNJAYA PRACTACALITIES

It's best to start the ascent around dawn, before it gets too hot. Dress respectfully (no shorts etc), leave behind leather items (including belts and bags), and don't eat or drink inside the temples. If you wish, you can be carried up and down the hill in a *dholi* (portable chair with two bearers), for about ₹1000 round trip. Photos may be taken on the trail and outside the temples, but not inside them.

Sleeping & Eating

Takhatgadh Mangal Bhuvan GUESTHOUSE $

(02848-252167; opposite Shri Vishal Jain Museum; r ₹300) Palitana being a place of pilgrimage, it's little wonder that there are so many pilgrims' rest houses. This is the pick of the lot – no-frills and no AC, but clean, tidy, and just a short walk from the steps up the mountain.

★Vijay Vilas Palace HERITAGE HOTEL $$$

(9427182809, 02848-282371; vishwa_adpur@yahoo.co.in; Adpur; r incl breakfast ₹3750;) This small former palace built in 1906 sits in the countryside beneath the western end of Shatrunjaya, 4km west of Palitana. There are four courtyard rooms and six large rooms in the main building with original furniture. Three have terraces/balconies looking towards Shatrunjaya – which can be climbed from here by a slightly shorter, steeper path than the one from Palitana.

Vijay Vilas is family-run, with delicious home-cooked food (a mix of Gujarati and Rajasthani, veg and nonveg). You can also just pop in for lunch (₹300) – it's best to call first.

Jagruti Restaurant INDIAN $

(thali ₹45-80; 24hr) Opposite the bus stand, Jagruti is a wildly busy thali house.

Getting There & Away

ST buses run to/from Bhavnagar (₹47, 1½ hours, three daily) and Ahmedabad (₹137, five hours, seven daily). Take a bus to Talaja (₹37, one hour, hourly), where you can change for Diu (₹125, 5¾ hours, five daily).

Four passenger trains run daily to/from Bhavnagar (2nd class ₹15, 1½ hours).

Diu

☎02875 / POP 23,990

Tiny Diu island, linked by a bridge to Gujarat's southern coast, is infused with Portuguese history. The streets of the main town are clean and quiet once you get off the tourist-packed waterfront strip; and alcohol is legal here. If you've been spending time immersed in the intensity of Gujarati cities, or just really need a beer, Diu offers a refreshing break.

Diu town sits at the east end of the island. The northern side of the island, facing Gujarat, is tidal marsh and salt pans, while the southern coast alternates between limestone cliffs, rocky coves and sandy beaches, better for people-watching than sun-worshipping. Diu is one of the safest places in India to ride a scooter, with minimum traffic and excellent roads, and zipping along the coast with the wind in your hair is a joy.

The siesta is very much observed here, with very little open in mid-afternoon.

History

Diu was the first landing point for the Parsis when they fled from Persia in the 7th century AD, and it became a major port between the 14th and 16th centuries, when it was the trading post and naval base from which the Ottomans controlled the northern Arabian Sea shipping routes.

The Portuguese secured control of Diu in 1535 and kept it until India launched Operation Vijay in 1961. After the Indian Air Force unnecessarily bombed the airstrip and terminal near Nagoa, it remained derelict until the late 1980s. Diu, Daman and Goa were administered as one union territory of India until 1987, when Goa became a state.

Like Daman and Goa, Diu was a Portuguese colony until taken over by India in 1961. With Daman, it is still governed from Delhi as part of the Union Territory of Daman and Diu and is not part of Gujarat. It includes Diu Island, about 11km by 3km, separated from the mainland by a narrow channel, and two tiny mainland enclaves. One of these, housing the village of Ghoghla, is the entry point to Diu from Una.

Sights & Activities

Diu Town

The town is sandwiched between the massive fort at its east end and a huge city wall on the west. The main **Zampa Gateway**, painted bright red, has carvings of lions, angels and a priest, while just inside it is a chapel with an image of the Virgin and Child dating from 1702.

Cavernous **St Paul's Church** (8am-6pm) is a wedding cake of a church, founded by Jesuits in 1600 and then rebuilt in 1807. Its neoclassical facade is the most elaborate of any Portuguese church in India. Inside, it's a great barn, with a small cloister next door, above which is a school. Daily Mass is heard here. Nearby is white-walled **St Thomas' Church**, a lovely, simple building that is now the **Diu Museum** (9am-9pm) FREE, with a spooky, evocative collection of wooden Catholic saints going back to the 16th century and particularly creepy armless angels. Once a year, on All Saints Day (1 November), this is used for a packed-out Mass. The Portuguese-descended population mostly live in the church-studded, southern part of Diu town, still called Farangiwada (Foreigners' Quarter). The **Church of St Francis of Assisi**, founded in 1593, had previously been used as a hospital and for occasional religious services, but when we visited it was locked up and possibly due to be renovated.

Many other Diu buildings show a lingering Portuguese influence. The western part of town is a maze of narrow, winding streets and many houses are brightly painted, with the most impressive being in the Panchwatiarea, notably **Nagar Sheth Haveli**, an old merchant's house laden with stucco scrolls and fulsome fruit.

Around the Island

★Diu Fort FORT

(Fort Rd; 8am-6pm) Built in 1535, with additions made in 1541, this massive, well-preserved Portuguese fort with its double moat (one tidal) must once have been impregnable, but sea erosion and neglect are leading to a slow collapse. Cannonballs litter the place, and the ramparts have a superb array of cannons. The lighthouse, which you can climb, is Diu's highest point, with a beam that reaches 32km. There are several

Diu Town

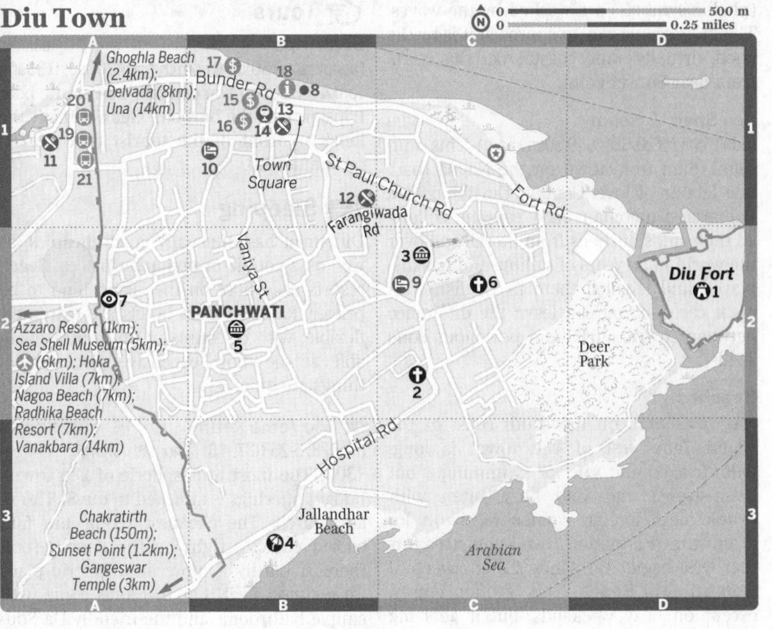

Diu Town

Top Sights
1 Diu Fort ... D2

Sights
2 Church of St Francis of Assisi ... C2
3 Diu Museum ... C2
4 Jallandhar Beach ... B3
5 Nagar Sheth Haveli ... B2
6 St Paul's Church ... C2
7 Zampa Gateway ... A2

Activities, Courses & Tours
8 Boat Trips ... B1

Sleeping
9 Casa Lourdes ... C2
Herança Goesa ... (see 9)
10 Hotel The Grand Highness ... B1
São Tome Retiro ... (see 3)

Eating
11 Fish Market ... A1
12 O'Coqueiro ... B1
13 Ram Vijay ... B1

Drinking & Nightlife
14 Casaluxo Bar ... B1

Information
15 ICICI Bank ATM ... B1
Post Office ... (see 14)
16 State Bank of India ... B1
17 State Bank of India ATM ... B1
18 Tourist Office ... B1

Transport
19 Ekta Travels ... A1
20 Jethibai Bus Stand ... A1
21 JK Travels ... A1

small chapels, one holding engraved tombstone fragments.

Part of the fort also serves as the island's jail.

★Vanakbara VILLAGE
At the extreme west of the island, Vanakbara is a fascinating little fishing village and one of the highlights of the island. It's great to wander around the port, packed with colourful fishing boats and bustling activity – best around 7am to 8am when the fishing fleet returns and sells off its catch.

Gangeswar Temple HINDU TEMPLE
Gangeswar Temple, on the south coast 3km west of town, just past Fudam village, is a small coastal cave where five Shiva linga

(phallic symbols) are washed by the waves. The most scenic way to approach it is by the good, virtually empty coastal road that starts from near Sunset Point.

Sea Shell Museum MUSEUM
(adult/child ₹20/10; 9.30am-5pm) This museum, 6km from town on the Nagoa road, is a labour of love. Captain Devjibhai Vira Fulbaria, a merchant navy captain, collected thousands of shells from literally all over the world in 50 years of sailing, and has displayed and labelled them in English with great care, so you can learn the difference between cowrie shells and poisonous cone shells.

Beaches

Nagoa Beach, on the south coast of the island 7km west of Diu town, is long, palm-fringed and safe for swimming – but trash-strewn and very busy, often with drunk men: foreign women receive a lot of unwanted attention. Two kilometres further west begins the sandy, 2.5km sweep of **Gomptimata Beach**. This is often empty, except on busy weekends, but it gets big waves – you need to be a strong swimmer here. Within walking distance of Diu town are the rocky **Jallandhar Beach**, on the town's southern shore; the longer, sandier **Chakratirth Beach**, west of Jallandhar; and pretty **Sunset Point Beach**, a small, gentle curve beyond Chakratirth that's popular for swimming and relatively hassle-free. **Sunset Point** itself is a small headland at the south end of the beach, topped by the INS Khukhri Memorial, commemorating an Indian Navy frigate sunk off Diu during the 1971 India–Pakistan War. Unfortunately the region around Sunset Point is also a dumping ground, and any early-morning excursion will reveal that the tidal zone here is a popular toilet venue.

The best beach is **Ghoghla Beach**, north of Diu. A long stretch of sand, it's got less trash and fewer people than the others, along with gentle waves and some decent restaurants behind it.

DANGERS & ANNOYANCES

More an annoyance than a danger, drunk males can be tiresome, particularly for women, and particularly around Nagoa Beach. Also, beware of broken glass in the sand.

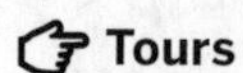

Tours

Boat Trips BOATING
(per person ₹50, minimum charge ₹300; 9.30am-1pm & 3-6.30pm) You can take 20-minute boat trips around the harbour. Get tickets at the kiosk in front of the tourist office (p711) on Bunder Rd.

Sleeping

Diu town has unusually good cheapies, as well as a couple of upmarket places. Beach resorts elsewhere on the island tend to be pricier. Rates at most hotels are extremely flexible, with discounts of up to 60% available at the more expensive places when things are quiet.

★ **São Tome Retiro** GUESTHOUSE $
(02875-253137; St Thomas Church; r from ₹300) The most atmospheric of Diu town's budget offerings is attached to the St Thomas' church. The cheapest rooms are fan-cooled cubicles right on the church roof; there is hardly a more atmospheric place for a sunset beer! Larger rooms come with simple bathrooms and the friendly Da Souza family throws barbecues every other evening; nonguests welcome with advance notification.

Herança Goesa GUESTHOUSE $
(02875-253851; heranca_goesa@yahoo.com; Farangiwada; r ₹500-1000) Behind Diu Museum, this friendly home of a Portuguese-descended family has eight absolutely spotless rooms that represent good value. Take one of the upstairs rooms that captures the sea breeze and just relax. Good breakfasts are served and delicious fish/seafood dinners may be available if several guests ask in advance.

Casa Lourdes GUESTHOUSE $$
(9426230335; gibu1102@gmail.com; Farangiwada; s/d from ₹800/1000;) Run by a cheerful local musician, Gilbert Almeida, this bright yellow guesthouse is a newcomer on the budget scene, with compact, colourful ensuites and kitchen use for guests. Your host family can also prepare Portuguese dishes on request.

★ **Hotel The Grand Highness** BUSINESS HOTEL $$$
(02875-254000; www.thegrandhighness.com; Main Bazaar; r from ₹4500;) By far the grandest place in Diu town, this brand new

hotel comes with spotless rooms, rain showers, comfortable beds, and plasma-screen TVs. The stunning atrium is decorated with contemporary sculptures and the hotel shares a restaurant with Hotel Prince next door.

★ Azzaro Resort HOTEL $$$
(☎02875-255421; www.azzarodiu.com; Fudam Rd; r ₹6529, ste ₹10,845;) A kilometre outside the city gate, this is hands down Diu's most luxurious hotel. It features tastefully luxurious rooms with high-tech lighting controls and stylish glass walls between the bedroom and bath. All look out onto the garden surrounding the sapphire-blue pool, many with balconies. There's a spa, a gym, two decent restaurants and a 24-hour cafe. Worth the money.

Nagoa Beach

Hoka Island Villa HOTEL $$$
(☎02875-253036; www.resorthoka.com; r ₹5395-5750;) Hoka is a great place to stay, with colourful, clean and cool rooms in a small, palm-shaded complex with a swimming pool. Some rooms have terraces over the palm trees. Management is helpful, you can hire mopeds, and the food is excellent. On the main road, pass the turn into Nagoa Beach, and it's on the left after 150m.

Radhika Beach Resort HOTEL $$$
(☎02875-275551; www.radhikaresort.com; d ₹5505-7685;) An immaculate, smart, modern place and Diu's best-located upmarket option, with comfortable, condo-like villas in grassy grounds, just steps from Nagoa Beach. Rooms are spacious and clean, and there's a very good multicuisine restaurant. The classic and VIP rooms are set around a large kidney-shaped pool.

Eating

Diu's delicious fresh fish and seafood features heavily on restaurant menus, and most guesthouses will cook anything you buy; there's a daily **fish market** (⏲7am-5pm) opposite Jethibai bus stand. A couple of places serve Portuguese dishes.

Ram Vijay ICE CREAM $
(scoop ₹40; ⏲8.30am-1.30pm & 3.30-9.30pm) For a rare treat head to this small, squeaky-clean, old-fashioned ice-cream parlour near the town square for delicious handmade ice cream and milkshakes. Going since 1933, this family enterprise started with soft drinks, and still makes its own brand (Dew) in Fudam village – try a ginger lemon soda and then all the ice creams!

★ O'Coqueiro MULTICUISINE $$
(Farangiwada Rd; breakfast ₹80-140, lunch & dinner ₹170-380; ⏲8am-9pm;) Here, the dedicated Kailash Pandey has developed a soul-infused garden restaurant celebrating freshness and quality. The menu offers uncomplicated but very tasty pasta, chicken and seafood, plus a handful of Portuguese dishes, such as prawns in a coconut gravy, learnt from a local Diu matriarch. There's also good coffee, cold beer and friendly service.

Cat's Eye View MULTICUISINE $$
(Hoka Island Villa, Nagoa Beach; breakfast ₹70-170, lunch & dinner ₹165-395; ⏲8-10am, noon-2.30pm & 7-9.30pm;) The open-air restaurant at Hoka Island Villa has excellent food, with inviting breakfasts and delicious choices such as penne with tuna and tomato, fish and chips, prawn coconut curry and grilled aubergine with yoghurt. It's relaxed, pleasant and brightened up by contemporary art pieces.

Sea View Restaurant SEAFOOD $$
(Ghoghla Beach; meals ₹110-250; ⏲8am-11pm) Fronting Ghoghla Beach, next to the eponymous hotel, the open-air Sea View has a full menu of Indian and seafood, with the sand a stone's throw away. The Goan prawn curry (₹170) is big and spicy. Except at holiday time, the clientele is mostly men.

Drinking & Nightlife

Casaluxo Bar BAR
(⏲9am-1pm & 4-9pm Tue-Sun) The almost pub-like Casaluxo Bar, facing the town square, has a salubrious air. It opened in 1963 and, except for some sexy swimsuit posters in the back room, might not have updated its decor since.

Information

Post Office (⏲9am-5pm Mon-Sat) Upstairs, facing the town square.

State Bank of India (Main Bazaar; ⏲10am-4pm Mon-Fri) Changes cash and travellers cheques and has an ATM.

Tourist Office (☎02875-252653; www.visitdiu.in; Bunder Rd; ⏲9.30am-1.30pm & 2.30-6pm Mon-Sat) Has maps, bus schedules and hotel prices.

Getting There & Away

AIR

Alliance Air, a budget subsidiary of Air India, flies to/from Mumbai four times weekly from **Diu Airport** (☎02875-254743; North Beach Rd). The airport is 6km west of town, just before Nagoa Beach.

BUS & CAR

Visitors arriving in Diu by road may be charged a border tax of ₹50 per person, though the practice seems to be erratic.

From **Jethibai bus stand** there are buses to numerous destinations.

DESTINATION	COST (₹)	TIME (HR)	FREQUENCY
Bhavnagar	144	5½	4 daily
Junagadh	142	4½	3 daily
Rajkot	182	5½	3 daily
Veraval	102	2½	3 daily

More frequent departures go from Una, 14km north of Diu. Buses run between Una bus stand and Diu (₹19, 40 minutes, half-hourly) between 6.30am to 8pm. Outside these hours, shared autorickshaws go to Ghoghla or Diu from Tower Chowk in Una (1km from the bus stand), for about the same fare. An autorickshaw costs ₹300. Una rickshaw-wallahs are unable to proceed further than the bus station in Diu, so cannot take you all the way to Nagoa Beach (an additional ₹100).

JK Travels (☎02775-252515; http://jkbus.in) runs private buses from the Diu bus stand to Ahmedabad at 7.30pm (non-AC sleeper ₹350, 10 hours) and to Mumbai at 11.30am (non-AC sleeper ₹700, 19 hours). **Ekta Travels** (☎9898618424) is another decent option for both routes.

TRAIN

Delvada is the nearest railhead, 8km from Diu on the Una road. The 52951 MG Passenger at 2.25pm runs to Sasan Gir (2nd class ₹25, 3½ hours) and Junagadh (₹35, 6¼ hours), while 52950 Passenger at 8.05am heads to Veraval (₹25, 3¼ hours). Half-hourly Diu–Una buses stop at Delvada (₹23, 20 minutes).

GETTING AROUND

Travelling by autorickshaw anywhere in Diu town should cost no more than ₹40. From the bus stand into town is ₹50. To Nagoa Beach and beyond pay ₹120 and to Sunset Point ₹60.

Scooters are a perfect option for exploring the island – the roads are deserted and in good condition. The going rate is ₹350 per day (not including fuel), and motorcycles can be had for ₹400. Most hotels can arrange rentals, although quality varies. You will normally have to show your driving licence and leave a deposit of ₹1500.

Local buses from Diu town to Nagoa and Vanakbara (both ₹12) leave Jethibai bus stand at 7am, 11am and 4pm. From Nagoa, they depart for Diu town from near the police post at 1pm, 5.30pm and 7pm.

TRANSIT HUB: VERAVAL

Cluttered and chaotic, Veraval is one of India's major fishing ports; its busy harbour is full of bustle and boat building. It was also the major seaport for Mecca pilgrims before the rise of Surat. The main reason to come here now is to visit the Temple of Somnath, 6km southeast; while the town of Somnath is a nicer place to stay, Veraval is more convenient to public transport.

From the centrally located bus stand on Bus Stand Rd, buses go to Ahmedabad (₹207, 9½ hours, eight daily), Junagadh (₹79, two hours, half-hourly), Rajkot (₹124, five hours) and Una (for Diu, ₹74, 2¼ hours), Diu (₹90, 2¾ hours) and Sasan Gir (₹41, one hour, daily at 3pm).

Patel Tours & Travels (☎02876-222863; www.pateltoursandtravels.com), opposite the ST bus stand, offers a nightly non-AC jaunt to Ahmedabad (seat/sleeper ₹320/420) at 9.30pm and 10pm.

Four trains daily run to Junagadh, including the 11463 Jabalpur Express departing at 9.50am (sleeper/3AC/2AC ₹150/510/750, 1¾ hours). The 11463, the 59460 at 1.20pm and the 22958 at 9.35pm continue to Rajkot (₹150/510/715, 4¼ hours) and Ahmedabad (₹270/715/1015, 8¾ hours). Second-class-only trains with unreserved seating head to Sasan Gir (₹10) at 9.45am (two hours) and 1.55pm (1¼ hours). There's a **computerised reservation office** (⏲8am-10pm Mon-Sat, to 2pm Sun) at the station.

The quickest way to get to Somnath is by autorickshaw, which costs around ₹15/150 for shared/private.

Somnath

☎ 02876

Somnath's famous, phoenix-like temple stands in neat gardens above the beach, 6km southeast of Veraval. The sea below gives it a wistful charm. The small town of Somnath is an agglomeration of narrow, interesting market streets with no car traffic, so it's easy to walk around and enjoy. Somnath celebrates Kartik Purnima (p688), marking Shiva's killing of the demon Tripurasura, with a large colourful fair.

Sights

Temple of Somnath HINDU TEMPLE

(⏲6am-9pm) It's said that Somraj (the moon god) first built a temple in Somnath, made of gold; this was rebuilt by Ravana in silver, by Krishna in wood and by Bhimdev in stone. The current serene, symmetrical structure was built to traditional designs on the original coastal site: it's painted a creamy colour and boasts a little fine sculpture. The large, black Shiva lingam at its heart is one of the 12 most sacred Shiva shrines, known as *jyoti linga*.

A description of the temple by Al-Biruni, an Arab traveller, was so glowing that it prompted a visit in 1024 by a most unwelcome tourist – the legendary looter Mahmud of Ghazni from Afghanistan. At that time, the temple was so wealthy that it had 300 musicians, 500 dancing girls and even 300 barbers. Mahmud of Ghazni took the town and temple after a two-day battle in which it's said 70,000 Hindu defenders died. Having stripped the temple of its fabulous wealth, Mahmud destroyed it. So began a pattern of Muslim destruction and Hindu rebuilding that continued for centuries. The temple was again razed in 1297, 1394 and finally in 1706 by Aurangzeb, the notorious Mughal ruler. After that, the temple wasn't rebuilt until 1950.

Cameras, mobile phones and bags must be left at the cloakroom before entering. Colourful dioramas of the Shiva story line the north side of the temple garden, though it's hard to see them through the hazy glass. A one-hour **sound-and-light show** highlights the temple nightly at 7.45pm.

Prabhas Patan Museum MUSEUM

(Indian/foreigner ₹5/50; ⏲10.30am-5.30pm Thu-Tue, closed 2nd & 4th Sat of the month) This museum, 300m north of the Somnath temple along the market street, has intricately carved stone fragments from previous temples exposed to the elements in the courtyard. The highlight is the reconstructed 12th-century shrine from the main temple, complete with delicately carved ceilings.

Sleeping & Eating

Hotel Swagat HOTEL $

(☎02876-233839; www.hotelswagatsomnath.elisting.in; r from ₹600, with AC from ₹1000; ❄) This hotel, diagonally across from Somnath Temple on the market street, is the best option close to the temple and the markets. Rooms are in good shape, and have modern air-con units and flat-screen TVs.

New Bhabha Restaurant INDIAN, CHINESE $

(mains ₹100-140; ⏲11.30am-2pm & 7-10pm; ❄) The pick of a poor bunch of eateries, vegetarian New Bhabha sits 50m north of the ST bus stand, which is one block east of Somnath Temple. You can eat in a small air-con room or outside open to the street.

Getting There & Away

From the ST bus stand one block east of the temple, buses run to Diu (₹87, 2½ hours, daily at 5.50pm), Junagadh (₹83, 2½ hours, half-hourly) and Ahmedabad (₹236, 10 hours, six daily).

Mahasagar Travels (www.mahasagartravels.com), near the ST bus stand, is one of a few companies running several evening buses to Ahmedabad (seat/sleeper ₹320/410, 10 hours), with one AC departure (₹519) at 9.30pm.

Ashapura Travels (☎9879048590; Tanna Complex, next to Somnath Temple car park) runs a nightly non-AC sleeper to Bhuj (₹550, 11¼ hours).

Gir National Park & Wildlife Sanctuary

☎ 02877

The last refuge of the Asiatic lion *(Panthera leo persica)* is this forested, hilly, 1412-sq-km sanctuary about halfway between Veraval and Junagadh, where visitors may go lion-spotting between mid-October and mid-June (December to April is best). Taking a safari through the thick, undisturbed forests is a joy – even without the added excitement of spotting lions, other wildlife and myriad bird species.

Access to the sanctuary is by safari permit only, bookable in advance online. If you miss out on a permit, your other option for lion encounters is at the Devalia Safari Park, a fenced-off part of the sanctuary where sightings are guaranteed but more stage-managed.

The gateway to the Gir National Park is **Sasan Gir** village, on a minor road and railway between Veraval and Junagadh (about 40km from each).

Sights

★Gir National Park NATIONAL PARK

(9971231439; www.girnationalpark.in; per 6-person jeep Indian/foreigner Mon-Fri ₹800/4800, Sat & Sun ₹1000/6000; 6am-9am, 9am-noon, 3-6pm mid-Oct–mid-Jun) The last refuge of the Asiatic lion *(Panthera leo persica)* is this forested, hilly, 1412-sq-km sanctuary about halfway between Veraval and Junagadh. Taking a safari through the thick, undisturbed forests would be a joy even if there wasn't the excitement of lions and other wildlife to spot. The sanctuary access point is Sasan Gir village, on a minor road and railway between Veraval and Junagadh (about 40km from each). The best time to visit is from December to April.

The sanctuary was set up in 1965, and a 259-sq-km core area was declared a national park in 1975. Since the late 1960s, lion numbers have increased from under 200 to over 400. The sanctuary's 37 other mammal species, most of which have also increased in numbers, include dainty chital (spotted deer), sambar (large deer), nilgais (large antelopes), chousinghas (four-horned antelopes), chinkaras (gazelles), crocodiles and rarely seen leopards. The park is a great destination for birders too, with more than 300 bird species, most of them resident.

While the wildlife has been lucky, more than half the sanctuary's human community of distinctively dressed *maldhari* (herders) have been resettled elsewhere, ostensibly because their cattle and buffalo were competing for food resources with the antelopes, deer and gazelles, while also being preyed upon by the lions and leopards. About 1000 people still live in the park, however, and their livestock accounts for about a quarter of the lions' diet.

Gir is no longer big enough for the number of lions that currently live here; some have already been moved to other patches of wilderness around the country and there is talk of introducing some to tiger country in Madhya Pradesh, but the Gujarat government opposes this plan, vying to remain the sole home of India's lions.

Devalia Safari Park NATURE RESERVE

(Indian/foreigner ₹190/3000; 8-11am & 3-5pm) Twelve kilometres west of Sasan Gir village at Devalia, within the sanctuary precincts, is the Gir Interpretation Zone, better known as simply Devalia. The 4.12-sq-km fenced-off compound is home to a cross-section of Gir wildlife. Chances of seeing lions and leopards here are guaranteed, with 45-minute bus tours departing along the trails hourly. You may also see foxes, mongoose and blackbuck – the latter being lion fodder. An autorickshaw/taxi round trip to Devalia from Sasan Gir village costs around ₹150/350.

Activities

★Safaris WILDLIFE-WATCHING

(www.girlion.in; permit vehicle with up to 6 passengers Indian/foreigner Mon-Fri ₹400/US$40, Sat &

THE LAST WILD ASIATIC LIONS

The Asiatic lion *(Panthera leo persica)* once roared as far west as Syria and as far east as India's Bihar. Widespread hunting decimated the population, with the last sightings recorded near Delhi in 1834, in Bihar in 1840 and in Rajasthan in 1870. In Gujarat, too, they were almost hunted to extinction, with as few as 12 remaining in the 1870s. It was not until one of their erstwhile pursuers, the enlightened Nawab of Junagadh, decided to set up a protection zone at the beginning of the 20th century that the lions began slowly to recover. This zone now survives as the Gir Wildlife Sanctuary (p713) and the population is thriving to such an extent that some of the lions have had to be repopulated elsewhere in Gujarat.

Separated from their African counterpart *(Panthera leo leo)* for centuries, Asiatic lions have developed unique characteristics. Their mane is less luxuriant and doesn't cover the top of the head or ears, while a prominent fold of skin runs the length of the abdomen. They are also purely predatory, unlike African lions, which sometimes feed off carrion.

Sun ₹500/US$50, guide 3hr ₹250, camera Indian/foreigner ₹100/600) Lion safaris are done in 4WDs (Gypsys) and visiting hours are split into three, three-hour time slots – 6am to 9am, 9am to noon, and 3pm to 6pm. Only 30 Gypsys are allowed in the park at any one time. Your best bet for seeing wildlife is early morning or a bit before sunset. Permits must be booked online in advance.

Most hotels and guesthouses in and around Sasan Gir have Gypsys and drivers or will arrange them for you, charging ₹3000 or more per vehicle for up to six passengers. Alternatively, you can hire an open 4WD and driver for around ₹2700 outside the sanctuary reception centre, in Sasan Gir village. Once you have a vehicle sorted, you must queue up at the reception centre to collect your permit and a guide, and pay photography fees. Your driver will usually help with this.

As a general rule, about one in every two safaris has a lion sighting. So if you're determined to see lions, allow for a couple of trips. You'll certainly see a variety of other wildlife, such as blackbuck and foxes, and the guides are adept spotters.

Sleeping & Eating

★Nitin Ratanghayara Family Rooms GUESTHOUSE $$
(☎9979024670, 02877-285686; www.nitinbhaihomestay.in; SBI Bank St; r ₹800, with AC ₹1400; ❄@📶) At his family's courtyard-style home in Sasan, friendly, golden-toothed Nitin Ratanghayara has several very good rooms for travellers. They're well kept, and much better value than any of the budget joints on the main street. Plus, you get to eat his sister-in-law's home cooking, and can help her in the kitchen if you like. Look for his sign over his shop along Sasan's main drag.

Hotel Umang HOTEL $$
(☎02877-285728; www.sasangirhotels.in; Rameshwar Society, SBS Rd; r without/with AC ₹850/1450; ❄📶) This is a quiet option with perfectly good rooms, helpful management and decent meals. Discounts are available when business is slow. It's 200m south off the main road near the town centre; follow the signs.

★Asiatic Lion Lodge LODGE $$$
(☎9099079965, 02877-281101; www.asiaticlionlodge.com; Sasan Gir-Bhalchhel-Haripur Rd; r ₹4700; ❄📶) Around 5km west of Sasan Gir village, this peaceful lodge consists of bungalow-style, tastefully decorated, spacious rooms with thatched roofs. Food is excellent vegetarian and in the evenings they do open-air screenings of an interesting documentary on the lion sanctuary.

Gir Birding Lodge HOTEL $$$
(☎9266519519, 9723971842; www.girbirdinglodge.com; Rte 100A; r or cottage incl meals s/d ₹5600/6800; ❄) This peaceful place, situated in a mango grove that borders a forest, has six simple and sweet cottages, with a few nice touches such as handmade wooden beds. The 16 hotel rooms are new and modern, if a bit plain. Particularly good for birders, plus there's also yoga and meditation sessions. It's 2.5km from the village off the Junagadh road.

Bird and river walks are available; naturalist guides cost ₹2000 per day.

Gateway Hotel HOTEL $$$
(☎02877-285551; www.thegatewayhotels.com; r incl breakfast from ₹9900, ste from ₹13,200; ❄📶🏊) 🍃 The remodelling of an old government property by the Taj Group is easily the finest – and greenest – choice near Gir National Park. The rooms and huge suites are lush with comforts – they even come with yoga mats! All overlook a river where buffaloes wade and lions have been spotted.

Booking online in advance gets serious discounts, and promotional packages that include all meals and safaris are offered.

Gir Rajwadi Hotel GUJARATI $
(mains ₹110-170; ⏱11am-4pm & 7-11pm) This vegetarian joint is the best of several simple restaurants along the village's main street and serves up tasty Gujarati thalis.

Information

Gir Orientation Centre (⏱8am-6pm) Next to the reception centre at Devalia, this has an informative exhibition on the sanctuary and its wildlife and a small shop.

Getting There & Away

Buses run from Sasan Gir village to both Veraval (₹41, one hour) and Junagadh (₹62, two hours) throughout the day.

Second-class, unreserved-seating trains run to Junagadh (₹20, 2¾ hours, 5.58pm), to Delvada (for Diu; ₹25, 3½ hours, 9.58am), and to Veraval (₹10, 1½ hours, 11.58am and 4.27pm).

Junagadh

☎0285 / POP 319,460

Reached by few tourists, Junagadh is nestled against some of the most impressive topography in Gujarat. It's an ancient, fortified city (its name means 'old fort') with 2300 years of history, at the base of holy Girnar Hill. The Nawab of Junagadh opted to take his tiny state into Pakistan at the time of Partition – a wildly unpopular decision as the inhabitants were predominantly Hindu, so the nawab departed on his own. Junagadh makes a good jumping-off point for seeing the lions at Gir National Park.

Sights & Activities

While parts of the centre are as traffic-infested, crowded and hot as any other city, the area up towards Uparkot Fort and around Circle and Diwan Chowks is highly atmospheric, dotted with markets and half-abandoned palaces in Euro-Mughal style with grass growing out of their upper storeys.

★Girnar Hill RELIGIOUS SITE

This sacred mountain, rising dramatically from the plains, is covered with Jain and Hindu temples. Pilgrims from far and wide come to tackle the long climb up 10,000 stone steps to the summit, which is best begun at dawn. Be prepared to spend a full day if you want to reach the uppermost temples. Ascending in the early morning light is a magical experience, as pilgrims and porters trudge up the steps. An autorickshaw to Girnar Taleti costs about ₹100.

The Jain temples, a cluster of mosaic-decorated domes interspersed with elaborate stupas, are about two-thirds of the way up. The largest and oldest is the 12th-century **Temple of Neminath**, dedicated to the 22nd *tirthankar:* go through the first left-hand doorway after the first gate. Many temples are locked from around 11am to 3pm, but this one is open all day. The nearby triple **Temple of Mallinath**, dedicated to the ninth *tirthankar,* was erected in 1177 by two brothers. During festivals this temple is a sadhu magnet.

Further up are various Hindu temples. The first peak is topped by the **Temple of Amba Mata**, where newlyweds worship to ensure a happy marriage. Beyond here there is quite a lot of down as well as up to reach the other four peaks and further temples. The **Temple of Gorakhnath** is perched on Gujarat's highest peak at 1117m. The steep peak Dattatraya is topped by a shrine to a three-faced incarnation of Vishnu. Atop the final outcrop, Kalika, is a shrine to the goddess Kali.

The trail begins 4km east of the city at **Girnar Taleti**. A motorable road, which may or may not be open, leads to about the 3000th step, which leaves you only 7000 to go! Refreshment stalls on the ascent sell chalk, so you can graffiti your name on the rocks. If you can't face the walk, *dholis* carried by porters cost ₹4000 (round trip) if you weigh between 50kg and 70kg, and ₹4500 for heavier passengers. If your weight range isn't obvious, you suffer the indignity of being weighed on a huge beam scale before setting off. Note that while photography is permitted on the trail, it's not allowed inside the temples.

The Bhavnath Mela (p688), over five days in the month of Magha, brings folk music and dancing and throngs of *nagas* (naked sadhus or spiritual men) to Bhavnath Mahadev Temple at Girnar Taleti. It marks the time when Shiva is believed to have danced his cosmic dance of destruction.

★Uparkot Fort FORT

(⌚dawn-dusk) This ancient fort is believed to have been built in 319 BC by the Mauryan emperor Chandragupta, though it has been extended many times. In places the ramparts reach 20m high. It's been besieged 16 times, and legend has it that the fort once withstood a 12-year siege. The views over the city and east to Girnar Hill are superb, and within its walls there is a magnificent former mosque, a set of millenia-old Buddhist caves and two fine step-wells.

Jama Masjid, the disused mosque inside the fort, was converted from a palace in the 15th century by Gujarat Sultan Mahmud Begada and has a rare roofed courtyard with three octagonal openings, which may once have been covered by domes. It's a shame about the graffiti, but the delicate mihrab stonework and the forest of columns are still stunning. From the roof, the city views are excellent.

Close to the mosque, the **Buddhist caves** (Indian/foreigner ₹15/200; ⌚8am-6pm) are not actually caves, rather monastic quarters carved out of rock, 2nd century AD. Descend into the eerie three-storey carved complex to

Junagadh

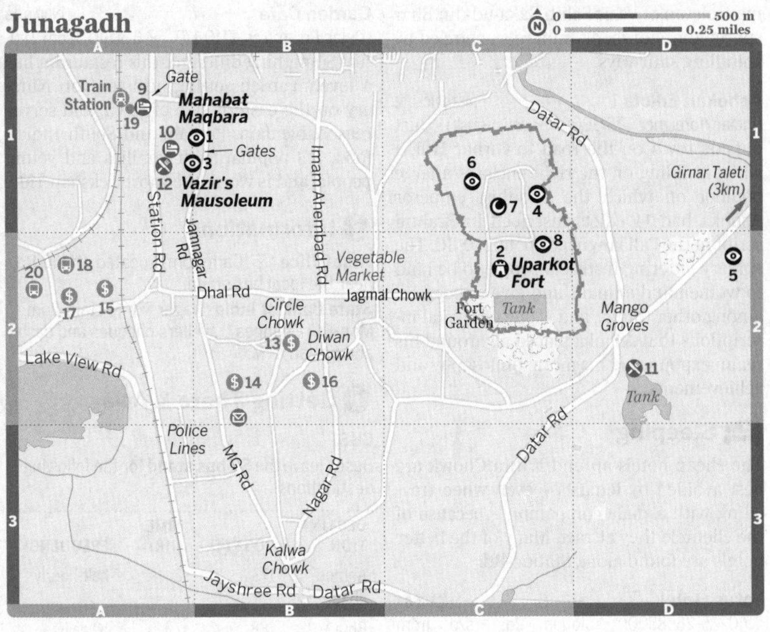

Junagadh

Top Sights

1 Mahabat Maqbara B1
2 Uparkot Fort C2
3 Vazir's Mausoleum A1

Sights

4 Adi Kadi Vav C1
5 Ashokan Edicts D2
6 Buddhist Caves C1
7 Jama Masjid C1
8 Navghan Kuvo C2

Sleeping

9 Click Hotel A1
10 Lotus Hotel A1

Eating

11 Garden Cafe D2
12 Geeta Lodge A1

Information

13 Axis Bank ATM B2
14 Bank of Baroda B2
15 State Bank of India A2
16 State Bank of India B2
17 State Bank of India ATM A2

Transport

18 Mahasagar Travels A2
19 Railway Station Reservation Office A1
20 ST Bus Stand A2

see the main hall and its pillars with weathered carvings.

The fort has two fine step-wells both cut from solid rock. The circular, 41m-deep **Adi Kadi Vav** was cut in the 15th century and named after two slave girls who used to fetch water from it. **Navghan Kuvo**, 52m deep and designed to help withstand sieges, is almost 1000 years old and its magnificent staircase spirals around the well shaft. Look for the centuries-old dovecotes.

★Mahabat Maqbara MAUSOLEUM
(MG Rd) This stunning mausoleum of Nawab Mahabat Khan II of Junagadh (1851–82) seems to bubble up into the sky. One of Gujarat's most glorious examples of Euro-Indo-Islamic architecture, with French windows and Gothic columns, its lavish appeal is topped off by its silver inner doors.

★Vazir's Mausoleum MAUSOLEUM
(MG Rd) Boasting even more flourish than neighbouring Mahabat Maqbara, the 1896

mausoleum of Vazir Sahib Baka-ud-din Bhar sports four storybook minarets encircled by spiralling stairways.

Ashokan Edicts HISTORIC SITE

(Indian/foreigner ₹5/100; ⊙dawn-dusk) Just outside town on the road to Girnar Hill, a white building on the right encloses a large boulder on which the Buddhist emperor Ashoka had 14 edicts inscribed in Brahmi script in the Pali language about 250 BC. The spidery lettering instructs people to be kind to women and animals and give to beggars, among other things, and is one of several inscriptions that Ashoka placed all around his realm expounding his moral philosophy and achievements.

Sleeping

The cheap hotels around Kalwa Chowk are best avoided by females – even when travelling with a male companion – because of the clientele they attract. Many of the better hotels are found along Station Rd.

Lotus Hotel HOTEL $$

(☎0285-2658500; Station Rd; s/d from ₹2000/2500; ❄📶) This luxurious and comfortable option occupies the totally renovated top floor of a former *dharamsala* (pilgrim rest house). Pilgrims never had it so good, with split-system air-con and LCD TVs. Rooms are beautifully bright, spacious and pristine, the beds are great, and everything works – incredible value for such quality. There isn't a restaurant, but there is room service.

★Click Hotel HOTEL $$$

(☎02832-244 077; www.theclickhotels.com; Station Rd; r ₹2800; 🚭❄📶) Conveniently located next to the train station, this excellent new hotel is the most comfortable place to stay in town. Rooms are absolutely spotless and come with comfy beds and plasma-screen TVs, the wi-fi is reliable and though the food choices at the on-site vegetarian restaurant are limited, the staff are eager to please.

Eating

★Geeta Lodge GUJARATI $

(Station Rd; thali ₹100; ⊙10am-3.30pm & 6.30-10pm; 🌿) Geeta's army of waiters are constantly on the move serving up top-class, all-you-can-eat veg Gujarati thalis at a bargain price. Finish off with sweets, such as fruit salad or puréed mango, for an extra ₹20.

Garden Cafe INDIAN $$

(Datar Rd; mains ₹110-170; ⊙6.30-10.30pm Thu-Tue) Something different: this restaurant has a lovely garden setting next to Jyoti Nursery on the eastern side of town, and serves reasonable Jain, Punjabi and South Indian food. It's popular with families and young people, and is worth the short rickshaw ride.

Information

Post Office (⊙10am-3pm) Located off MG Rd, near the local bus stand.

State Bank of India (Nagar Rd; ⊙11am-2pm Mon-Fri) Changes travellers cheques and cash and has an ATM.

Getting There & Away

BUS

Buses leave the **ST bus stand** for the following destinations:

DESTINATION	COST (₹)	TIME (HR)	FREQUENCY
Ahmedabad	173	8	half-hourly
Bhuj	188	7	10 daily
Diu	127	5	4 daily
Jamnagar	102	4	10 daily
Rajkot	86	2¾	half-hourly
Sasan Gir	62	2	hourly
Una (for Diu)	113	4	10 daily
Veraval	79	2½	half-hourly

Various private bus offices, including **Mahasagar Travels** (☎0285-2629199; Dhal Rd), are on Dhal Rd, near the railway tracks. Services:

DESTINATION	COST (₹)	TIME (HR)	FREQUENCY
Ahmedabad	non-AC/AC/Volvo 270/320/425	8	half-hourly
Mumbai	sleeper 943	17	5 daily

TRAIN

There's a computerised **reservation office** (⊙8am-10pm Mon-Sat, to 2pm Sun) at the railway station.

The Jabalpur Express (train 11463/5) departs at 11.10am for Gondal (sleeper/3AC/2AC ₹173/556/761, one hour), Rajkot (₹173/556/761, 2¾ hours) and Ahmedabad (₹240/661/911, 7¼ hours). The Somnath Express (train 22958) overnighter to Ahmedabad (same prices, 6½ hours) departs at 11.02pm.

WORTH A TRIP

WANKANER'S PALACES

Wankaner, an appealing small town 60km northeast of Rajkot, is famous for its two palaces and its scenic setting on the banks of the River Machchhu (*wanka* means 'bend' and *ner* means 'river'). The grand 1907 **Ranjit Villas Palace** (☎02828-220000; ₹200/free for Royal Oasis guests) – an architectural melange of Victorian Gothic arches, splendid stained-glass windows and chandeliers, Mughal domes and Doric columns – was the official residence of the Maharajah of Wankaner until 2012, when the family decamped to a smaller place. A tour takes in the main hall, decorated with the Maharajah's hunting trophies, the games room and the grand bedrooms upstairs. There are plans to put the Maharajah's 1921 Rolls Royce Silver Ghost on display. Call ahead to visit – you might even get to meet the friendly family of the Maharajah. Bed down at **Royal Oasis** (☎02828-222000; www.wankanerheritagehotels.com; r ₹5000; ❄ 🏊), another gorgeous 1937 palace that used to be the summer residence of the Maharajah of Wankaner and has now been converted into an intimate hotel.

Buses run from Rajkot (₹24, one hour, half-hourly) to Wankaner's bus stand in the southeast of town. Wankaner is on the main train line between Rajkot and Ahmedabad and 11 trains pass through daily in each direction.

Second-class train 52952 heads to Sasan Gir (₹20, 2¾ hours) and Delvada (for Diu; ₹35, 5¾ hours) at 7.15am.

Gondal

☎02825 / POP 112,195

Gondal is a small, leafy town, 38km south of Rajkot, that sports a string of palaces and a gentle river. It was once capital of a 1000-sq-km princely state ruled by Jadeja Rajputs who believe they are descendants of Krishna.

Sights & Activities

★Naulakha Museum MUSEUM

(www.heritagepalacesgondal.com; Naulakha Palace, DCR Pandeya Marg; ₹50; ⏱9am-noon & 3-6pm) This eclectic museum in the old part of town is housed in a beautiful, 260-year-old riverside royal palace that was built in a mixture of styles, with striking gargoyles and delicate stone carvings. It shows royal artefacts, including scales used to weigh Maharaja Bhagwat Sinhji in 1934 against gold, with proceeds going to charity, a nine-volume Gujarati dictionary compiled by the same revered maharaja, and Dinky Toy collections. See two stables full of mint-condition horse carriages for an extra ₹20.

Shri Bhuvaneshwari Aushadhashram HISTORIC BUILDING

(www.bhuvaneshwaripith.com; Ghanshyam Bhuvan; ⏱9am-noon & 3-5pm Tue-Sat) Founded in 1910 by Gondal's royal physician, this ayurvedic pharmacy manufactures ayurvedic medicines and it's possible to see all the weird machinery involved, as well as buy medicines for treating hair loss, vertigo, insomnia etc. The founding physician, Brahmaleen Acharyashree, is said to have coined the title 'Mahatma' (Great Soul) for Gandhi. Also here is a temple to the goddess Bhuvaneshwari.

Udhyog Bharti Khadi Gramodyog WORKSHOP

(Udhyog Bharti Chowk; ⏱9am-noon & 3-5pm Mon-Sat) A large *khadi* (homespun cloth) workshop where women work spinning cotton upstairs, while downstairs embroidered *salwar kameez* (traditional dresslike tunic and trouser combination for women) and saris are on sale.

Vintage & Classic Car Collection MUSEUM

(Orchard Palace Hotel, Palace Rd; Indian/foreigner ₹120/250; ⏱9am-noon & 3-6pm) This is the royal collection of cars – 32 impressive vehicles, from a 1907 car made by the New Engine Company Acton and a 1935 vintage Mercedes saloon to racing cars raced by the present maharaja. Most are still in working condition.

Sleeping & Eating

Orchard Palace HERITAGE HOTEL $$$

(☎02825-220002; www.heritagepalacesgondal.com; Palace Rd; s/d ₹5200/6600; ❄) This small palace, once the royal guesthouse, has seven well-kept, rather luxurious, high-ceilinged rooms of different sizes, filled with 1930s and '40s furniture. The parlors and patios, with more of the same, have an inviting, relaxed kind of charm. The royal kitchens provide meals that use vegetables from the on-site organic garden; book in advance.

Riverside Palace HERITAGE HOTEL **$$$**
(☎02825-220002; www.heritagepalacesgondal.com; Ashapura Rd; s/d ₹5200/6600; ❄) This is the erstwhile ruling family's main palace-hotel, built in the 1880s and formerly the crown prince's abode. Well worn, adorned with hunting trophies and four-poster beds, its 11 rooms are kind of like a royal time machine you can sleep in, with river views. Meals for the guests come from the royal kitchens; reserve in advance.

Getting There & Around

Buses run frequently from the ST stand on Gundana Rd, 500m south of Orchard Palace, to/from Rajkot (₹30, one hour) and Junagadh (₹65, two hours). Slow passenger trains between Rajkot (₹10, one hour, 14 daily) and Junagadh (₹25, 1¾ to three hours, 11 daily) also stop at Gondal. Hiring an autorickshaw to take you to all the sights and wait while you see them costs about ₹150 per hour.

Jamnagar

☎0288 / POP 600,945

Jamnagar is a little-touristed but interesting city, brimming with ornate, decaying buildings and colourful bazaars displaying the town's famous, brilliant-coloured *bandhani* (tie-dye) – produced through a laborious 500-year-old process involving thousands of tiny knots in a piece of folded fabric. The city is also a good jumping-off point for visiting a nearby bird sanctuary and marine national park.

Before Independence, Jamnagar was capital of the Nawanagar princely state. Today, Jamnagar is quite a boom town, with the world's biggest oil refinery, belonging to Reliance Petroleum, not far west of the city. The whole central area is one big commercial zone, with more brightly lit shops and stalls at night than you'll find in many a larger city.

Sights

With its beautiful Jain temples, crumbling city gates and towers, busy produce markets and tranquil lake promenade, wandering

RAJKOT: GANDHI'S CHILDHOOD HOME

In otherwise hectic and industrial Rajkot, 40km north of Gondal, Gandhi enthusiasts will find **Kaba Gandhi No Delo** (Ghee Kanta Rd; ⏱9am-6pm) FREE, the house where Gandhi lived from the age of six (while his father was diwan of Rajkot). It features many photos of the family and lots of interesting information on his life. The Mahatma's passion for the handloom is preserved in the form of a small weaving school. If you come this way and are into weaving, Rajkot has quickly developed a Patola-weaving industry. This skill comes from Patan, and is a torturous process that involves dyeing each thread before it is woven. However, in Patan both the warp and weft threads are dyed (double *ikat*), whereas in Rajkot only the weft is dyed (single *ikat*), so the product is more affordable. You can visit workshops that are located in people's houses in the Sarvoday Society area about 1km southwest of Shastri Maidan, including **Mayur Patola Art** (☎0281-2464519; www.facebook.com/Mayur-patola-art-1563670977185321; Sarvoday Society; ⏱10am-6pm), behind Virani High School.

Around 18km southwest of Rajkot, the splendid 16th-century **Heritage Khirasara Palace** (☎02827-234444; www.khirasarapalace.in; Kalawad Rd, Khirasara; r from ₹4000, ste ₹8000-25,000; ❄📶🏊), painstakingly rebuilt at its lofty hillock location, is the sleep of choice in Rajkot. Inside, there are manicured lawns, a mosaic-tiled pool and spacious, luxurious rooms. The Maharajah Suite comes with antique furniture, though we prefer the Maharani Suite for the ambience.

Rajkot is reached by air via Air India, Jet Airways, JetKonnect and Alliance Air flights from Mumbai and Delhi. Buses departing from the **ST bus stand** (Dhebar Rd) connect Rajkot with Jamnagar (₹86, two hours, half-hourly), Junagadh (₹89, 2¾ hours, half-hourly), Bhuj (₹161, seven hours, about hourly) and Ahmedabad (from ₹137, 4½ hours, half-hourly). There are numerous train connections as well, including Ahmedabad and Mumbai.

Jamnagar

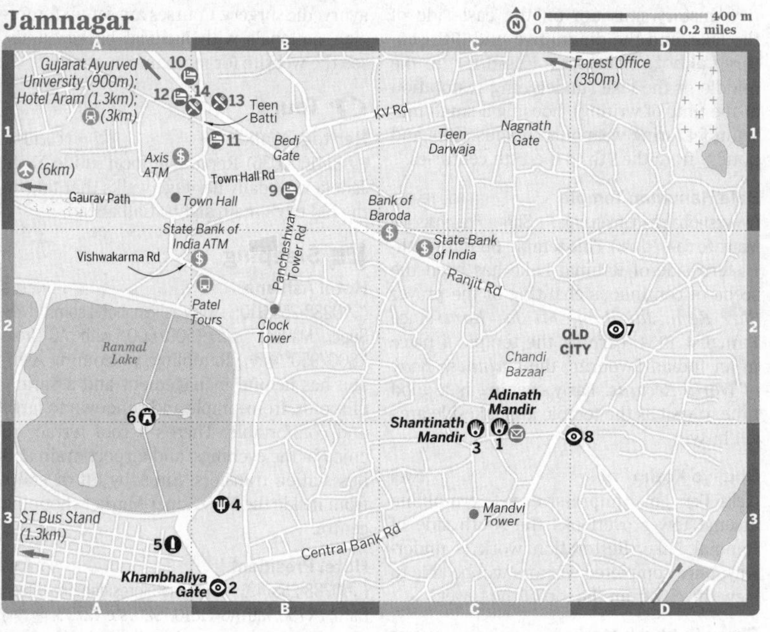

Jamnagar

Top Sights
1 Adinath Mandir ... C3
2 Khambhaliya Gate ... B3
3 Shantinath Mandir ... C3

Sights
4 Bala Hanuman Temple ... B3
5 Bhujiyo Kotho ... A3
6 Lakhota Palace ... A2
7 Shree Subhash Market ... D2
8 Willingdon Crescent ... D3

Sleeping
9 Hotel Ashiana ... B1
10 Hotel Kalatit ... A1
11 Hotel President ... B1
12 Hotel Punit ... A1

Eating
7 Seas Restaurant ... (see 11)
13 Brahmaniya Dining Hall ... B1
14 Hotel Kalpana ... B1

aimlessly is perhaps the best way to experience the old city.

★Khambhaliya Gate GATE
(Central Bank Rd) Built in the 17th century by Wazir Meraman Khawa, and one of two remaining city gates from that period, this genteelly decaying landmark has been recently restored to former glory. Upstairs is a gallery due to open with displays on the city's history.

★Shantinath Mandir JAIN TEMPLE
(Chandi Bazaar Rd; ⏲dawn-dusk) One of the largest Jain temples in old town, the Shantinath Mandir is particularly beautiful, with coloured columns and a gilt-edged dome of concentric circles.

★Adinath Mandir JAIN TEMPLE
(Chandi Bazaar Rd; ⏲dawn-dusk) Adinath Mandir, one of the two largest and most elaborate Jain temples in the old town, is dedicated to the 16th and first *tirthankars* (great Jain teachers) and explodes with fine murals, mirrored domes and elaborate chandeliers.

★Ranmal Lake LAKE
(₹10; ⏲dawn-10.30pm) The attractive, tree-lined promenades around Ranmal Lake have been seriously upgraded and surrounded by a fence with several gateways. There's a bona fide astroturf running track, a brand

new history museum on the east side of the lake, and the diminutive mid-19th-century **Lakhota Palace**, an island fort in the middle of the lake (undergoing restoration at the time of writing), housing a small museum featuring weaponry, manuscripts and pottery from the 9th to the 18th centuries.

Bala Hanuman Temple HINDU TEMPLE
(www.shribalahanuman.org; Shri Premhikshuji Marg; ⏲ dawn-dusk) This temple on the southeastern side of Ranmal Lake has been the scene of continuous chanting of the prayer *Shri Ram, Jai Ram, Jai Jai Ram* since 1 August 1964, earning the temple a place in an Indian favourite, the *Guinness Book of World Records*. Early evening is a good time to visit as the temple and lakeside area get busy.

Bhujiyo Kotho TOWER
(Lake Dr) This impressive yet crumbling arsenal tower overlooks the south side of Ranmal Lake. Restoration work is underway; once completed, visitors will be able to view the city from the top of the tower.

Shree Subhash Market MARKET
(Ranjit Rd, Kadiawad; ⏲ 5am-8pm) Jamnagar's colourful vegetable market dates back to the 18th century and resembles a crumbling coliseum.

Willingdon Crescent LANDMARK
(Central Bank Rd) This European-style arcaded crescent was built by Jam Ranjitsinhji to replace Jamnagar's worst slum. It now houses an assortment of shops, and is commonly known as Darbargadh, after the now-empty royal residence across the street.

Courses

Gujarat Ayurved University HEALTH & WELLBEING
(☎ 0288-2664866; www.ayurveduniversity.com; Chanakya Bhavan, Hospital Rd) The world's first ayurvedic university, founded in 1967, is 1.5km northwest of the centre. It has played a big part in the revival of ayurvedic medicine since Independence and also has a public hospital treating 800 to 1000 inpatients and outpatients daily. Its International Center for Ayurvedic Studies runs a full-time, three-month introductory course (registration US$25, tuition per month US$475).

There are also longer certificate and degree courses in several subjects, including ayurvedic surgery. Courses are set up for foreign nationals with medical backgrounds; see the website for more information.

Tours

Heritage Walk CULTURAL
(☎ 8141600036) Reputable local guide Yashi Jadela runs daily heritage walks that take in the old city's main sights. Call ahead.

Sleeping

Hotel Ashiana HOTEL $
(☎ 0288-2559110; www.ashianahotel.com; New Super Market; s/d ₹500/600, with AC from ₹800/950; ❄ 📶) Rambling, welcoming Ashiana has helpful management and a variety of rooms, from simple and rundown to large and comfortable. There's a roof terrace to enjoy in the evenings, and airport, train and bus station transfers. Enter by lift or stairs from inside the New Super Market shopping centre.

Hotel President HOTEL $$
(☎ 0288-2557491; www.hotelpresident.in; Teen Batti; r ₹780, with AC ₹1810-1920, ste ₹2795; ❄ 📶) This hotel has exceptionally helpful management and a range of reasonable rooms, many with balconies. The air-con rooms have street views and are bigger and generally better than the non-AC, which are at the rear.

Hotel Punit HOTEL $$
(☎ 0288-2670966; www.hotelpunit.com; Teen Batti; s/d from ₹850/950, ste ₹1700; ❄ 📶) Currently one of the best budget spots in town, rooms are simple but in decent shape, with modern air-con units and LCD TVs. Suites are roomy but not terribly worth the splurge. Just a quick walk from a number of restaurants and convenient to the old city.

Hotel Kalatit HOTEL $$
(☎ 0288-2660105; www.hotelkalatit.com; Teen Batti; s/d from ₹1520/1820, ste ₹5500; ❄ 📶) This modern hotel feels new and stylish, with creative lighting and artfully patterned walls. With a gym and a good restaurant, this is one of the best options in town.

Hotel Aram HERITAGE HOTEL $$$
(☎ 0288-2551701; www.hotelaram.com; Pandit Nehru Marg; r ₹2230-3960, ste ₹4320-6500; ❄ 📶) This former royal property has had an upgrade, creating an interesting mix of historic and contemporary. Rooms vary widely, from simple standards up to luxuri-

ous superdeluxe rooms and suites, some of which can't decide on a style. Still, it's the nicest place around. There's a good multicuisine veg restaurant with garden seating. It's 1.5km northwest of city centre.

Eating

Brahmaniya Dining Hall GUJARATI $
(1st fl, Badri Complex, Teen Batti Chowk; thali ₹199; 11.30am-2.30pm & 7.30-10.30pm) Bottomless vegetarian thalis is what this local place specialises in. The dishes are a little oily but tasty. Find it on the 1st floor of the Badri Complex.

Hotel Kalpana MULTICUISINE $$
(Teen Batti; mains ₹90-170; 9am-11pm Tue-Sun) Clean and modern, with cushy booths, there's a full list of Punjabi, Gujarati and Chinese food, along with pizza. If you want chicken or mutton, you'll get it here!

7 Seas Restaurant MULTICUISINE $$
(Hotel President, Teen Batti; mains ₹140-320; 6-10am & 11am-11pm;) This cool, clean, efficient hotel restaurant has a nautical theme and a touch of class, offering a good range of veg and nonveg dishes, including seafood, Indianised Chinese and tandoori options, and real breakfasts. The tandoori *bhindi* (okra) is a triumph.

Information

The city's website (www.jamnagar.org) is full of useful information for visitors.

State Bank of India changes foreign currency at its central **branch** and has a handy **ATM** just south of the town hall. There's also an **Axis ATM** north of the town hall, and a **Bank of Baroda** branch and ATM on Ranjit Rd.

Forest Office (0288-2679357; Indira Gandhi Marg, Forest Colony; 10.30am-6pm Mon-Sat, closed 2nd & 4th Sat of the month) The Forest Office provides permits for exploring the Gulf of Kachchh, with its marine park, as well as the nearby Khijadiya Bird Sanctuary, however, not much English is spoken and there is very little useful information. Your best bet is to contact **Hotel President** (p722) for assistance in visiting these two parks.

Post Office (Central Bank Rd; 9am-5pm) Main post office.

Getting There & Away

AIR

Jamnagar Airport (0288-2712187) is located 6km west of the city. Air India has daily flights to Mumbai.

BUS

ST buses run to/from the **ST bus stand** (Government Colony) to Rajkot (₹81, two hours, half-hourly), Junagadh (₹102, four hours, about hourly) and Ahmedabad (₹176, 7¼ hours, about hourly). There are also three morning and evening buses to Bhuj (₹162, 6½ hours).

Private companies based along Vishwakarma Rd include the reliable **Patel Tours** (0288-2660243), which has 22 daily Volvo AC buses to Ahmedabad (₹600, seven hours), 34 buses to Rajkot (₹150, two hours), and five non-AC buses to Bhuj (seat/sleeper ₹300/400, six hours), mostly overnighters.

TRAIN

One of the most useful trains is the 22946 Saurashtra Mail, which departs at 4.05pm for Rajkot (sleeper/3AC/2AC/1AC ₹150/510/715/1180, 1¾ hours) via Wankaner, continuing on to Ahmedabad (₹225/600/850/1405, 6¾ hours) and Mumbai (₹420/1135/1625/2745, 16 hours).

Getting Around

An autorickshaw from the airport, 6km west, should be around ₹150, and a taxi ₹300. An autorickshaw from the ST bus stand to Bedi Gate costs around ₹30; autorickshaws to the railway station from the centre cost the same.

Around Jamnagar

Khijadiya Bird Sanctuary WILDLIFE RESERVE
(entry US$10, vehicle with up to 6 people US$40, motorcycle US$10; 7am-noon & 3-6pm) This small, 6-sq-km sanctuary, about 12km northeast of Jamnagar, encompasses both salt- and fresh-water marshlands and hosts more than 200 bird species, including rarities such as the Dalmatian pelican, painted stork and crab plover. It's best visited between October and March and in the early morning or at sunset. The evening arrival of cranes for roosting can be spectacular and there are six towers for birdwatching. Hiring a car from Jamnagar to drive you around the sanctuary costs around ₹1500.

You'll have to show your passport at the new interpretation centre before going in.

Marine National Park NATIONAL PARK
(up to 6 people ₹900, camera ₹450) Consisting of three parts, this national park and the adjoining marine sanctuary encompass the intertidal zone and 42 small islands along some 120km of coast east and west of Jamnagar – an area rich in wildlife that faces growing challenges from industrialisation. Coral, octopus, anemones, puffer fish, sea

OFF THE BEATEN TRACK

WESTERN SAURASHTRA

Mahatma Gandhi was born in 1869 in the port town of **Porbandar**, 130km southwest of Jamnagar. You can visit **Gandhi's birthplace** (9am-noon & 3-6pm) FREE – a 22-room, 220-year-old house with photographic exhibitions of his family's life – and a memorial next door, **Kirti Mandir** (7.30am-7pm) FREE. En route to Porbandar, the **Barda Wildlife Sanctuary** (Rte 27; 8am-5pm) is a hilly, forested area with stone-built villages, old temples and good hiking.

Dwarka, 104km northwest of Porbanar at the western tip of the Kathiawar Peninsula, is one of the four holiest Hindu pilgrimage sites in India. Its **Dwarkadhish Temple** (7-8am, 9am-12.30pm & 5-9.30pm) is believed to have been founded more than 2500 years ago, and has a fantastically carved, 78m-high spire. Dwarka's **lighthouse** (₹10; 5-6.30pm) affords a beautiful panoramic view, though photography is not allowed (neither are mobile phones). The town swells to breaking point for Janmastami in celebration of Krishna's birthday in August/September. There are some good beaches, including the beautiful, long, clean **Okhamadhi**, 22km south of Dwarka.

A good contact for arranging visits to western Saurashtra is **Mustak Mepani** (p724) at Jamnagar's Hotel President.

horses, lobsters and crabs are among the marine life you may see in shallow water at low tide. **Mustak Mepani** (9824227786) at Jamnagar's Hotel President arranges tours, cars, drivers and permits.

There are three sections of the park: Narada, Poshitra and Pirotan Island. Narada is more interesting – from the entry gate, you park and hike 2.3km over rock and reef to the Gulf of Kachchh, where you can spot a variety of sea life. (You'll want to wear footwear with decent soles, as the terrain is sharp.) Narada is best reached from Jamnagar, which is 65km away; hiring a car to get you there and back costs about ₹2200. Poshitra's main draw is the coral; you won't see many animate creatures there; Poshitra is closed to visitors until 2018 to allow for coral recovery. Pirotan Island is 7 nautical miles from Rozi dock, a 25-minute drive from Jamnagar. The boat ride is good for dolphin- and bird-spotting. Hiring a vehicle from Jamnagar costs ₹4500 whether you go one way or round trip.

The best time to visit is December to March, when wintering birds are plentiful.

Narada and Poshitra are only open during low tide, so the entry schedule shifts daily. Before you enter, you'll have to show your passport and fill out some paperwork.

KACHCHH (KUTCH)

Kachchh, India's wild west, is a geographic phenomenon. The flat, tortoise-shaped land, edged by the Gulf of Kachchh and Great and Little Ranns, is a seasonal island. During the dry season, the Ranns are vast expanses of dried mud and blinding-white salt. Come the monsoon, they're flooded first by seawater, then by fresh river water. The salt in the soil makes the low-lying marsh area almost completely barren. Only on scattered 'islands' above the salt level is there coarse grass, which provides fodder for the region's wildlife.

The villages dotted across Kachchh's arid landscape are home to a jigsaw of tribal groups and subcastes who produce some of India's finest handicrafts, above all, textiles that glitter with exquisite embroidery and mirrorwork. In spite of the mammoth earthquake in 2001 that completely destroyed several villages, the residents of this harsh land have determinedly rebuilt their lives and are welcoming to visitors.

Bhuj

02832 / POP 188,240

The capital of Kachchh is an interesting city, largely resurrected following the massive 2001 earthquake that destroyed most of the place. It sells amazing Kachchh handicrafts, and historic buildings such as the Aina Mahal and Prag Mahal possess an eerie beauty. Bhuj is an ideal springboard for visits to the surrounding villages and to places of great natural beauty in the Great Rann, and textile tourism is attracting visitors from around the world.

The Jadeja Rajputs who took control of Kachchh in 1510 made Bhuj their capital 29 years later, and it has remained Kachchh's most important town ever since.

Bhuj

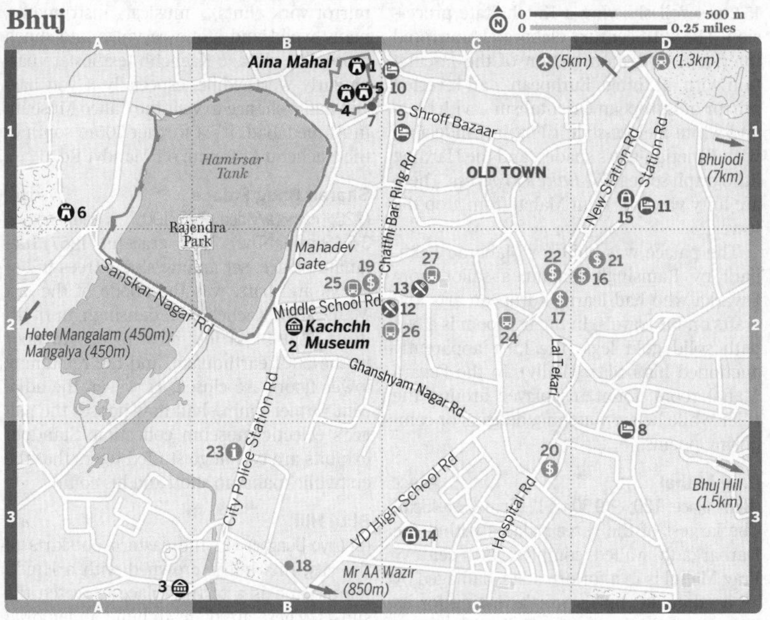

Bhuj

Top Sights
1 Aina Mahal....B1
2 Kachchh Museum....B2

Sights
3 Folk Art Museum....A3
4 Prag Mahal....B1
5 Rani Mahal....B1
6 Sharad Baug Palace....A1

Activities, Courses & Tours
7 Pramod Jethi....B1

Sleeping
8 Bhuj House....D3
9 City Guest House....C1
10 Hotel Gangaram....C1
11 Hotel Ilark....D1

Eating
12 Green Rock....C2
Jesal....(see 15)
13 Shankar Vadapav....C2
Toral....(see 15)

Shopping
14 Kutch Mahila Vikas Sangathan (Qasab)....C3
15 Qasab....D1

Information
16 Ashapura Money Changer....D2
17 Bank of Baroda ATM....C2
18 District Superintendent of Police....B3
19 HDFC ATM....B2
20 State Bank of India....C3
21 State Bank of India ATM....D2
22 State Bank of India ATM....C2
23 Tourist Information Bureau....B3

Transport
24 4WD for Mandvi....C2
Jay Somnath Travels....(see 25)
25 Patel Tours & Travels....B2
26 Shree Sahjanand Travels....C2
27 ST Bus Stand....C2

Sights

At the heart of the old town is the Darbargadh palace complex; Prag Mahal, Aina Mahal and Rani Mahal are located inside its walls.

★Aina Mahal PALACE

(Old Palace; ₹20, camera ₹30; ⌚9-11.45am & 3-5.45pm Fri-Wed) This beautiful palace, built in 1752, lost its top storey in an earthquake, but the lower floor is open, with a fantastic

15.2m scroll showing a Kutch state procession. The 18th-century elaborately mirrored interior is a demonstration of the fascination with all things European – an inverted mirror of European Orientalism – with blue-and-white Delphi-style tiling, a candelabra with Venetian-glass shades, and the Harding lithograph series *The Rake's Progress*. There are lofty views of Rani Mahal from atop the tower.

The palace was built for Maharao Lakhpatji by Ramsingh Malam, a sailor from Dwarka who had learnt European arts and crafts on his travels. In the bedroom is a bed with solid gold legs (the king apparently auctioned his bed annually). In the Fuvara Mahal room, fountains played around the ruler while he sat watching dancers or composing poems.

Prag Mahal PALACE

(New Palace; ₹20; ⏲9.30am-12.15pm & 3-5.45pm) The largest of the three palaces within the Darbargadh walled complex, 19th-century Prag Mahal is in a forlorn state, damaged by an earthquake, but is worth visiting for its ghostly, exuberant Durbar Hall, with its vast chandeliers, the Maharajah's taxidermied contribution to the demise of India's wildlife, and gold-skirted classical statues that wouldn't look out of place decorating a gay nightclub. Several scenes from *Lagaan*, the much-acclaimed Bollywood cricket blockbuster, were filmed here.

Rani Mahal PALACE

The 17th-century Rani Mahal, the former main royal residence, is completely closed up, though you can still admire the latticed windows of its *zenana* (women's quarters). It's particularly beautiful around sunset.

★Kachchh Museum MUSEUM

(City Police Station Rd; Indian/foreigner ₹5/100; ⏲10am-1pm & 2.30-5.30pm Thu-Tue, closed 2nd & 4th Sat of the month) Opposite Hamirsar Tank, Gujarat's oldest museum has eclectic and worthwhile displays spanning textiles, weapons, silverware, sculpture, wildlife, geography and dioramas of Kachchh tribal costumes and artefacts, with labelling in English and Gujarati.

Folk Art Museum MUSEUM

(Bhartiya Sanskriti Darshan; near City Police Station Rd; ₹100, camera ₹200; ⏲11am-1.15pm & 3-6pm Tue-Sun) This museum has excellent displays on traditional Kachchh culture, including reconstructed Rabari *bhungas* (mud-and-mirrorwork huts), musical instruments, many wood and stone carvings and much more. The vintage Kachchh textiles are particularly worthwhile, especially if you haven't had a chance to visit the Calico Museum in Ahmedabad. It's a further 700m south of the Kachchh Museum, off Mandvi Rd.

Sharad Baug Palace PALACE

(₹20, camera/video ₹20/100; ⏲9am-noon & 3-5.45pm Sat-Thu) This graceful 1867 Italianate palace, set among shade trees full of crows and bats, was the abode of the last Maharao of Kachchh, Madansingh, until his death in 1991. It lost most of its 3rd floor in the 2001 earthquake, and the remaining lower floors are closed. However, the adjacent former dining hall now houses the palace's eclectic museum collection. Standout exhibits are two huge stuffed tigers that the erstwhile maharao shot, and his coffin.

Bhuj Hill HILL

(Bhujiyo Dungar) On the eastern outskirts of the city, this hill is crowned with a Hindu temple and is a terrific place to watch the sunset. There are plans to build a memorial to the 2001 earthquake victims atop the hill. Autorickshaws to the bottom of the steps from central Bhuj should cost around ₹80.

Sleeping

City Guest House GUESTHOUSE $

(☎9913922669; www.cityguesthousebhuj.com; Langa St; d ₹500, s/d without bathroom from ₹300/400; ❄) Just off Shroff Bazaar, this place is unusually bright and cheery for a budget guesthouse, and has clean, basic rooms with colourful bedspreads. Avoid the windowless ones. Bathrooms have either squat toilets or the hybrid variety. Breakfast is available, there are two airy rooftop terraces, and manager Latif rents motorbikes for ₹500 per day.

Hotel Mangalam HOTEL $$

(☎9227593130; www.mangalamhotels.com; Mangalam Cross Rd; r ₹1500, s/d with AC from ₹2000/2500; ❄📶) Towards the southern edge of town, the new Mangalam has big, bright rooms with comfy furnishings. Some have good views. Free airport transfers are offered, and there's an excellent restaurant on the ground floor.

Hotel Gangaram HOTEL $$

(☎9429377131; www.hotelgangaram.com; off Shroff Bazaar; s/d ₹1000/1200, with AC ₹1200/1400; ❄📶) In the old city, near the

Darbargadh, this is a good, if weary-looking, place run by a kindly manager and well away from the din of Bhuj's main thoroughfares. The rooms vary, so look at a few. Meals here are pretty decent.

★Bhuj House HOMESTAY $$$
(9098187346; www.thebhujhouse.com; Camp Area, opposite Camp Police Chowki; r ₹4600-5600;) Run by the delightful Indian-British couple, Jehan and Katie, this lovingly restored 19th-century heritage house – Jehan's ancestral home – surrounds a tranquil courtyard. The four fan-cooled, en-suite rooms feature Khachch embroidery and antique furnishings, delicious meals are available on request and your hosts can help you arrange your travels around the villages of Khachch.

Hotel Ilark HOTEL $$$
(02832-258999; www.hotelilark.com; Station Rd; s/d from ₹3250/3550, ste from ₹5240;) One of Bhuj's top hotels, the stylish wood-panelled, wood-furnished rooms live up to the promise of the modern glass-and-red-paint exterior. Service is very professional and there's a good restaurant on-site.

Eating

★Shankar Vadapav STREET FOOD $
(Middle School Rd; snacks from ₹20) This food stall is a local legend. Try a *vadapav* (basically a spiced fried potato with chutney in a sandwich) or go big and get the *mirchvada* (fluffy fried dough covering a whole chilli pepper that's stuffed with a paste of spices and served on bread). The sign is in Gujarati; it's right next to the Gopi Gola Ghar ice-cream shop.

★Toral VEGETARIAN $$
(Hotel Prince, Station Rd; thali ₹299; 11.30am-3pm & 7.30-11pm;) This stylish restaurant inside Hotel Prince gets packed at lunchtime as locals and visitors alike pile in for the excellent bottomless Gujarati thali.

★Mangalya MUGHLAI $$
(Hotel Mangalam, Mangalam Cross Rd; mains from ₹160, buffet lunch ₹230;) Creative twists on all-veg Mughlai cuisine are sure to please your palate. The tandoor options and paneer varieties are outstanding – try the delicious Mix Grill Platter if you can't decide. There are also dosas and other South Indian dishes. And if you feel like a taste of home – they've got pizza!

Jesal NORTH INDIAN $$
(Hotel Prince, Station Rd; mains from ₹190; 7am-3pm & 7-11pm;) Jesal serves up a good mix of North Indian dishes (particularly all things tandoori), along with an extensive menu of Indo-Chinese dishes and a few Western ones for homesick or spiced-out guests.

Green Rock MULTICUISINE $$
(Middle School Rd; mains ₹100-210, thali ₹220; 11am-3pm & 7-10.30pm;) This 1st-floor, air-conditioned place serves up tasty lunchtime thalis as well as an extensive all-veg menu.

Information

Ashapura Money Changer (Station Rd; 9.30am-7pm Mon-Sat) Changes currency and travellers cheques.

District Superintendent of Police (DSP Rd; 10am-6pm Mon-Sat, closed 2nd & 4th Sat)

EXPLORING KACHCHH

It is possible to get out to some of Kachchh's villages by public transport – for example, there are three buses a day to Khavda (₹55, two hours). You can also take autorickshaws to villages not too far from the city. But you'll have many more options and more flexibility if you hire a car and driver; most Bhuj hotels can organise this for you.

Thoughtfully themed and customised autorickshaw tours (half-/full day ₹800/1400) to villages outside Bhuj are organised by **Pramod Jethi** (p728), former curator at the Aina Mahal and expert on everything Kachchhi. However, there has been some negative traveller feedback regarding some of the rickshaw drivers he uses. **Salim Wazir** (p728) is a textiles expert and an excellent local guide who can arrange tailor-made tours of Kachchh villages, depending on what you want to see; his 4WD can reach interesting villages where autorickshaws may not go. **Kuldip Gadhvi** (p728) also has an excellent reputation as a Kachchh guide. All three can arrange single and multiday tours around the region; guide services per day tend to be around ₹2000, with another ₹3000 for a car/4WD.

KACHCHH CREATIVITY

Kachchh is one of India's richest areas for handicrafts, particularly famed for its beautiful, colourful embroidery work (of which there are 16 distinct styles), but it also has many artisans specialising in weaving, tie-dying, block printing, wood carving, pottery, bell-making and other crafts. The diversity of Kachchh crafts reflects the differing traditions of its many communities. Numerous local cooperatives invest in social projects and help artisans produce work that is marketable yet still preserves their artistic heritage. For those interested in embroidery, a visit to the new Living & Learning Design Centre (LLDC) Crafts Museum (p730) in Ajrakhpur is an absolute must. Try to get hold of the Kutch Craft Map, printed by the **Somaiya Kala Vidya** (www.somaiya-kalavidya.org) organisation that works with individual artisans across Kachchh in a bid to preserve and enhance traditional craft.

The tourist office may suggest autorickshaw guides to take you around most of the local cooperatives (half-/full day ₹800/1400) and can include visits to Ajir and Rabari villages, but not all are reliable and there's a language barrier. Ex–tourism director **Pramod Jethi** (9374235379; near Darbargadh; 9am-noon & 3.30-6pm Mon-Sat) can accompany you on tours of the surrounding cooperatives, as can the excellent local guides **Salim Wazir** (9825715504, 02832-224187; salimwazir@gmail.com) and **Kuldip Gadhvi** (9327054172; www.kutchadventuresindia.com); with them, you can specify exactly what you want to see and they can explain the creative processes. You can purchase items of superb quality at the locations below; the cooperatives take cards, but individual craftspeople generally don't, so bring plenty of cash.

Local Handicrafts Cooperatives

Kutch Mahila Vikas Sangathan (02832-256281; www.kmvs.org.in; 21 Nootan Colony, Dr Urmila Mehta Hospital Lane; 10am-6pm) This grassroots organisation comprises 12,000 rural women (1200 artisans) and pays members a dividend of the profits and invests money to meet social needs. The embroidery and patchwork are exquisite, employing the distinctive styles of several communities. Products go under the brand name Qasab and range from bags and bedspreads to cushion covers and wall hangings. Visit the Qasab outlet at **Hotel Prince** (Hotel Prince, Station Rd; 1-3pm & 7-10pm), or Khavda, a village about 80km north of Bhuj.

Kala Raksha (02832-277237; www.kala-raksha.org; 10am-2pm & 3-6pm Mon-Sat) Based at Sumrasar Sheikh, 25km north of Bhuj, Kala Raksha is a nonprofit trust working to preserve and promote Kachchh arts. It works with about 1000 embroiderers and patchwork and appliqué artisans from six communities in some 26 villages. The trust has a small museum and shop, and can help arrange visits to villages to meet artisans. Up to 80% of the sale price goes to the artisans, who also help design and price the goods.

Get your permits here for visiting some of the outlying villages.

State Bank of India (Hospital Rd; 10am-4pm Mon-Fri, to 1pm Sat) Changes travellers cheques and currency.

Tourist Information Bureau (02832-224910; www.gujarattourism.com; Bahumali Bhavan Rd; 9am-6pm Mon-Sat) Helpful tourist office opposite the Bahumali Bhavan building.

Getting There & Away

AIR

Bhuj Airport, 4km north of the centre, has daily flights to Delhi and Mumbai with Air India.

BUS

Numerous buses run from the **ST bus stand** to Ahmedabad (₹188, eight hours, hourly), Rajkot (₹153, seven hours), Jamnagar (₹151, six hours, hourly) and Mandvi (₹67, 1½ hours). Book private buses with **Patel Tours & Travels** (02832-220556; www.pateltoursandtravels.com; Middle School Rd), just outside the bus station, for Ahmedabad (non-AC/AC sleeper ₹350/500, nine hours) or the Volvo AC sleeper (₹588, 9pm) with **Shree Sahjanand Travels** (02832-222236; www.shreesahjanandtravels.com; opposite ST bus stand). Patel Tours & Travel also run non-AC sleepers to Jamnagar (seat/sleeper ₹300/400, seven hours, 3.30pm, 8.30pm, 9pm, 10.30pm), while **Jay Somnath Travels** (9979869670; Middle School Rd; 8am-9pm) has departures

Vankar Vishram Valji (☎02832-240723; Bhujodi; ⏲8am-8pm) A family operation and one of the leading weavers in Bhujodi; it sells beautiful blankets, shawls, stoles and rugs.

Shrujan (☎02832-240272; www.shrujan.org; Bhujodi; ⏲10am-7.30pm) Just past the Bhujodi turn-off, behind the GEB Substation, Shrujan is a nonprofit trust working with more than 3000 women embroiderers of nine communities in 114 villages. Its showroom sells top-class shawls, saris, cushion covers and more. Their other wares are on display at the LCDC Crafts Museum.

Dr Ismail Mohammad Khatri (☎02832-299786, 9427719313; dr.ismail2005@gmail.com; Ajrakhpur; ⏲9am-5pm) In Ajrakhpur, 6km east of Bhujodi along the Bhachau road, Dr Khatri heads a 10-generation-old block-printing business of real quality, using all natural dyes in bold geometric designs. Go in the morning if you want to see a demonstration of the fascinating, highly skilled process. You can buy tablecloths, shawls, skirts, saris and other attractive products.

Parmarth (☎9909643903, 9712411959; 106 Ramkrushn Nagar, New Dhaneti; ⏲8.30am-9pm) Run by a delightful family whose work has won national awards, Parmarth specialises in Ahir embroidery. New Dhaneti is 17km east of Bhujodi, on the Bhachau road.

Khamir (☎02832-271272; www.khamir.org; Kukma Rd, Lakhond Crossroad, Kukma; ⏲10am-5.30pm) This umbrella organisation is dedicated to preserving and encouraging Kachchh crafts in all their diversity. At the Kukma centre you can see demonstrations and buy some of the artisans' products. It's about 4km beyond Bhujodi, in the Anjar direction.

Traditional Rogan Art (☎02835-277788; www.traditionalroganart.com; Nirona) The village of Nirona, 40km northwest of Bhuj, features several distinctive crafts (laquerwork, bell-making), but none more so than the award-winning ancient art of rogan painting, brought over from Iran 300 years ago and practised by just one extended family in India in this village. These delicate, detailed cloth paintings take months of work and Narendra Modi famously presented one fine piece to Barack Obama during the American president's visit.

Textile Dealers

In Bhuj, textile dealers line Shroff Bazaar just east of the Darbargadh. However, plenty of so-called block-printed fabric is in fact screen-printed.

Mr AA Wazir (☎02832-224187; awazir1@rediffmail.com; Plot 107B, Lotus Colony, Bhuj) If you're interested in antique embroidery, contact Mr AA Wazir, opposite the General Hospital. He has a stunning collection of more than 3000 pieces, about half of which are for sale.

to Rajkot (₹200). The quickest way to get to Mandvi is by shared **jeep**.

TRAIN

Bhuj station is 1.5km north of the centre and has a **reservations office** (⏲8am-8pm Mon-Sat, to 2pm Sun). Of the four to five Ahmedabad-bound trains, the 14312 Ala Hazrat Express leaves at 12.40pm (Tuesday, Thursday, Sunday) and arrives at Ahmedabad (sleeper/3AC/2AC ₹235/625/880) at 7.45pm, continuing to Abu Road, Jaipur and Delhi. The 19116 Bhuj BDTS Express leaves at 12.15pm daily and hits Ahmedabad (sleeper/3AC/2AC/1AC ₹235/625/880/1465) at 5.05am and Mumbai/Bandra Station (₹425/1140/1640/2765) at 2.05pm.

Getting Around

The airport is 5km north of town – a taxi will cost around ₹300, an autorickshaw ₹150. Autorickshaws from the centre to the train station cost around ₹50.

Around Bhuj

Bhuj is an excellent jumping-off point for visiting the local Jat, Ahir, Meghwal, Harijan, nomadic Rabari and other communities that have distinct, colourful craft traditions that make their villages fascinating to visit. The best of the crafts are found in the villages on the road north to Khavda, as well as southeast of Bhuj. Other attractions include an important, remote archaeological site and the stark landscape of the Great Rann of Kachchh. Permits are required to visit certain parts of the Rann; if travelling with a guide, they can easily obtain them for you.

Sights

★Living & Learning Design Centre (LLDC) Crafts Museum MUSEUM
(www.shrujan.org; Bhuj-Bhachau Rd, Ajrakhpur; ₹50; ⊙10am-6pm Tue-Sun) Fifteen kilometres east of Bhuj, this superb NGO-run museum is an absolute must for anyone interested in the centuries-old crafts practised by Kachchh artisans. One of three planned galleries is now open, showcasing the 42 different embroidery styles of the Ahir, Maghwal, Rabari and others. The pieces on display are breathtaking and the multimedia features let you learn about individual exhibits in greater depth. The gift shop sells embroidered items and books on Kachchh embroidery.

There are plans to eventually document the full range of Kachchh creativity, from metalwork and leatherwork to silverwork and rogan printing.

★White Desert NATURE RESERVE
(₹100) West of Khavda and north of Hodka, the white desert is the one accessible corner of the Great Rann of Kachchh – the 30,000-sq-km desert between the Gulf of Kutch and the mouth of the Indus River in southern Pakistan. A 1.3km trail leads from the parking area to the viewing tower overlooking the great salt expanse. During the winter months, when the water dries up, the place is mesmerising. The fee is payable en route.

Bhujodi VILLAGE
Bhujodi, about 7km southeast of Bhuj, is a village of weavers, mostly using pit looms, operated by both feet and hands. You can look into many workshops, which produce attractive shawls, blankets and other products. The village is 1km off Hwy 42. You can take a bus towards Ahmedabad and ask the driver to drop you at the turn-off for Bhujodi (₹14). A return rickshaw from Bhuj costs around ₹350.

Than MONASTERY
In the hills about 60km northwest of Bhuj is the eerie 12th-century monastery at Than. This is a laid-back place, with architecture ranging from crumbling mud brick to Portuguese-style stucco, blue and whitewashed bell towers. There's one bus daily to Than from Bhuj (₹55, two hours) at 5pm, returning early next morning. The monastery has very basic guest rooms (not recommended for female travellers) with mattresses on the floor and simple food (pay by donation) but no drinking water.

The holy man Dhoramnath, as penance for a curse he had made, stood on his head on top of Dhinodhar hill for 12 years. The gods pleaded with him to stop, and he agreed, provided the first place he looked at became barren – hence the Great Rann. He then established the monastic order of Kanphata (Split Ears, because of large piercings through the ear's concha), whose monastery stands at the foot of the hill.

Tejsibhai Dhanabhai Marwada HANDICRAFTS WORKSHOP
(☎9913491374; Sanjot Nagar; ⊙8am-6pm) In a small village near Bhujodi, several kilometres east of Bhuj, this master craftsman is the only one in the area who specialises in hand-weaving carpets, rugs and wall hangings of superb quality made out of camel wool.

Dholavira ARCHAEOLOGICAL SITE
A long drive northeast from Bhuj is the fascinating and remote archaeological site of Dholavira, on a seasonal island in the Great Rann. Excavations have revealed a complex town of stone buildings 1 sq km in area, inhabited by the Harappan civilisation from around 2900 to 1500 BC. It's best to organise your own transport (₹5000 one way or return): the only bus to Dholavira leaves Bhuj at 2pm (₹86, six hours) and starts back at 5am.

It will become cheaper and considerably faster to reach Dholavira once the road from Khavda to Dholavira is completed.

Tana Bana HANDICRAFTS WORKSHOP
(☎9998082332; ramji.vankar@gmail.com; Sumrasar Shekh) One of the graduates of the Somaiya Kala Vidya design school for artisans, weaver Ramji Maheshwari demonstrates his craft on a traditional pit loom. Scarves, shawls and other quality items for sale.

Hodka VILLAGE
Inhabited by the Meghwal and Halepotra people, this village specialises in leatherwork and embroidery. It's around 55km north of Bhuj, off Rte 341.

Bhirandiyara VILLAGE

You can find some excellent embroidery and leatherwork at this Meghwal village. It's an hour's drive north of Bhuj, off Rte 341.

Khavda VILLAGE

The Kumbhar village of Khavda, 70km north of Bhuj, is known for its pottery and textiles.

Kalo Dungar HILL

(Black Hill) North of the village of Khavda, the Black Hill marks Kutch's highest point (462m), with remarkable views over the Great Rann salt flat (or inland sea if you're visiting during the monsoon). You'll need your own transport to visit.

Activities

Centre for Desert & Ocean BIRDWATCHING

(CEDO; ☎8511981245, 9825248135, 02835-221284; www.cedobirding.com; Moti Virani; s/d incl meals ₹2500/5000) Around 53km northwest of Bhuj, this wildlife conservation organisation, run by passionate environmentalist Jugal Tiwari and his son Shivam, does birding trips focusing on the wildlife-rich Banni grasslands. Accommodation is in well-kept rooms with 24-hour solar-heated hot water; meals are Gujarati vegetarian. Safaris cost ₹3500 per half-day for a car and driver; an expert naturalist and birder guide costs an extra ₹2000 per day.

Sleeping

Toran Tourist Complex HOTEL $

(☎9825026813; s/d ₹400/600, with AC ₹800/1000; ❄) The only place to stay at Dholavira consists of circular *bhunga* huts with attached bathrooms, some with AC. Gujarati thalis are served in the adjoining cafeteria.

★**Devpur Homestay** HOMESTAY $$$

(☎9825711852, 02835-283065; www.devpurhomestay.in; Devpur; incl breakfast s ₹2000-4500, d ₹2500-5000, tent s/d ₹1500/1800; ❄) In the village of Devpur, 40km northwest of Bhuj, this 1905 sandstone manor is the ancestral home of the friendly host Krutarthsinh, who is related to the Bhuj royal family. Guests stay either in the uniquely decorated air-con rooms or fan-cooled annex rooms overlooking the tranquil courtyard, or in luxury tents on the farm. Excellent home-cooked meals arranged on request.

Shaam-e-Sarhad Village Resort HOTEL $$$

(☎02803-296222; www.hodka.in; Hodka; all incl meals tent s/d ₹2800/3400, bhunga s/d ₹3800/5700; ⊙Oct-Mar) Set in the beautiful Banni grasslands just outside Hodka, 70km north of Bhuj, this safari camp consists of three *bhungas* (traditional mud huts) and six luxurious tents with private bathrooms. Owned and operated by the Halepotra people, it's a fascinating opportunity to witness the daily life of an indigenous community and the positive impact of thoughtful tourism. Superb thali meals available.

Local (non-English-speaking) guides cost ₹350 per day for birdwatching or visits to villages in the area, but you need to provide your own transport.

Getting There & Away

Buses that serve the villages of Khavda and Dholavira are few and sporadic. Most visitors organise multiday tours of the region with a car and knowledgeable guide; there are several excellent guides (p727) in Bhuj that you can contact in advance. A day's driving in a 4WD with a guide costs around ₹5000.

Mandvi

☎02834 / POP 51,375

Mandvi is an hour down the road from Bhuj and is a busy little place with an amazing shipbuilding yard. Hundreds of men construct, by hand, these wooden beauties for faraway Arab merchants. The massive timbers apparently come from Malaysian rainforests. Mandvi suffered far less destruction than Bhuj in the 2001 earthquake, so the heart of town (around Mochi Bazar) is lined with beautiful old buildings in faded pastel hues and temples with wildly sculpted, cartoonlike facades. There are also some sweeping beaches, including the glorious, long, clean private beach near Vijay Vilas Palace, and public Kashivishvanath Beach, with food stalls and camel rides, 2km from the centre just east of the Rukmavati River.

Sights

Vijay Vilas Palace PALACE

(Mon-Sat ₹30, Sun ₹40, vehicle ₹50, camera/video ₹50/200; ⊙7am-7pm) This crumbling 1920s palace, 7km west of town amid extensive orchards, is set by a trash-strewn private beach. Originally a summer abode for the Kachchh rulers, its 1st floor is now the main residence of the elderly Maharajah of Bhuj. The view from the roof is worth the climb, and the rooms, with their stuffed wildlife and faded grand furniture, are worth a peek.

Autorickshaws charge about ₹200/300 one way/return from Mandvi.

Sleeping & Eating

Hotel Sea View HOTEL $
(☎9825376063; www.hotelseaviewmandvi.com; cnr ST & Jain Dharamsala Rds; r ₹850, with AC ₹1250-2300; ❄) This small hotel on the main road facing the river has brightly decorated rooms with big windows that make the most of the views of the shipbuilding.

★**Beach at Mandvi Palace** RESORT $$$
(☎9879013118, 02834-277597; www.mandvibeach.com; s/d incl meals ₹7000/9000; ❄) This small tent resort is set in a peaceful location on a superb swath of clean beach that stretches down from Vijay Vilas Palace. The luxurious air-cooled tents have big beds, white-tiled bathrooms and solid wooden furniture. Nonguests may come for excellent lunch (₹550, 10am to 3pm) or dinner (₹650, 7pm to 9pm) – all-day access to the private beach is included.

Osho Restaurant GUJARATI $
(1st fl, Osho Hotel, Bhid Gate; thali ₹120; ⏲11.45am-3pm & 7-9pm) In the heart of the town, Osho is a massively popular place that dishes out an excellent vegetarian thali. All you can eat! Look for the big 'Osho Hotel' sign.

Getting There & Away

Regular buses to/from Bhuj (₹35) take 1½ to two hours. Or you can take faster shared 4WD taxis (₹45), which depart from the street south of Bhuj's main vegetable market. **Patel Tours & Travels** (☎9925244272) and **Royal Express** (☎02834-232135) offer comfortable long-distance services to Amehdabad, the latter with AC.

Little Rann of Kachchh

The barren, salt-tinted land of the Little Rann is nature at its harshest and most compelling. The Wild Ass Sanctuary, covering a large part of the Rann, is the home of the last remaining population of the chestnut-coloured Indian wild ass (khur). Wildlife and birding safaris are the big attraction here.

The Little Rann is punctuated by desolate, illegal salt farms, where people eke out a meagre living by pumping up groundwater and extracting the salt; the excellent Swedish documentary by Farida Pacha, *My Name Is Salt*, captures their plight. Heat mirages disturb the vast horizon – bushes and trees seem to hover above the surface. Rain turns the desert into a sea of mud, and even during the dry season the solid-looking crust is often deceptive, so it's essential you take a local guide when exploring the area.

Sights

★**Wild Ass Sanctuary** NATURE RESERVE
(4WD safari with up to 6 passengers Indian/foreigner Mon-Fri ₹400/2000, Sat & Sun ₹500/2200, camera ₹200/1000) This 4953-sq-km sanctuary covers a chunk of the parched land of the Little Rann and is the home of the only remaining population of the chestnut-coloured Indian wild ass (khur), as well as bluebulls, blackbuck and chinkara. There's also a huge bird population from October to March (this is one of the few areas in India where flamingos breed in the wild). Guides will arrange your permits for the reserve; the cost of these is normally additional to safari prices.

About 2500 khurs live in the sanctuary, surviving off the flat, grass-covered expanses or islands, known as *bets*, which rise up to around 3m. These remarkable, notoriously untamable creatures are capable of running at an average speed of 50km/h for long distances.

Easily accessible from Ahmedabad, the Wild Ass Sanctuary can be visited in a combined trip with Nalsarovar Bird Sanctuary, Modhera and Patan.

Activities

★**Desert Coursers** WILDLIFE-WATCHING
(☎9998305501, 9426372113; www.desertcoursers.net) Excellent safari outfit with expert guides, based out of Camp Zainabad.

Sleeping

★**Camp Zainabad** HOTEL $$
(☎02757-241333, 9426372113; www.desertcoursers.net; Zainabad; per person incl full board ₹2500-3000; ⏲Oct-Mar; ❄📶) Camp Zainabad is 10km from the eastern edge of the Little Rann, just outside Zainabad, 105km northwest of Ahmedabad. The lodge has air-conditioned *koobas* (thatch-roofed huts) and excellent meals, in a peaceful setting. Desert Coursers (p732), run by infectiously enthusiastic naturalist Dhanraj Malik, organises excellent Little Rann safaris and village tours from here. Prices include a 4WD safari. Advance booking advised.

Eco Tour Camp HOTEL $$
(☎9825548090; www.littlerann.com; near Kidi Village; s/d incl full board from ₹1500/2000; ⊙Oct-Apr) This simple camp, situated right on the Wild Ass Sanctuary's edge, is run by the personable Devjibhai Dhamecha; his son Ajay runs 4WD safaris (₹2000/3000 per 4WD). Accommodation is in basic cement huts, plusher rooms and atmospheric *koobas*. Pick-ups (autorickshaw/taxi ₹700/1200) can be arranged from Dhrangadhra, 45km away, en route between Ahmedabhad (three hours) and Bhuj (5½ hours).

★**Rann Riders** COTTAGE $$$
(☎9925236014; www.rannriders.com; Dasada; s/d incl all meals & safari ₹7000/8000; ❄📶🏊) Luxurious Rann Riders, near Dasada, offers accommodation in either mirror-pattern-studded *bhungas* (circular Rabari huts) or *kubas* (square huts) with rain showers and mosaic-tiled outdoor bathrooms, surrounded by lush gardens. Price includes excellent 4WD and camel safaris. Horseback safaris cost ₹3000/7000 per half-day/full day; visits to nearby tribal villages also arranged. Dining options consist of an Indian buffet and Japanese restaurant.

Bell Guest House HERITAGE HOTEL $$$
(☎9724678145; www.bellguesthouse.com; Sayla; s/d incl breakfast ₹3750/5000; ❄) Presided over by the erstwhile ruling family of Sayla (and their yellow labs), Bell Guest House is an ageing heritage hotel retreat down a lane off the Sayla roundabout on Hwy 8A. Rooms have modern en-suite bathrooms. Look for bluebulls in the surrounding countryside or take trips further afield to see wild asses, blackbuck, or artisans in nearby villages.

If you wish to learn more about Rajput culture, dinner with the owners can be booked by prior appointment.

ℹ Getting There & Away

To get to Zainabad from Ahmedabad, hiring a private car is easiest but you can also take a bus from Ahmedabad's ST bus stand to Dasada, 10km away (₹85, 2½ hours, about hourly), from where **Desert Coursers** (p732) and **Rann Rider** (p733)s offer free pick-ups. There are direct buses between Zainabad and Patan (₹80, 2½ hours, four daily) via Modhera.

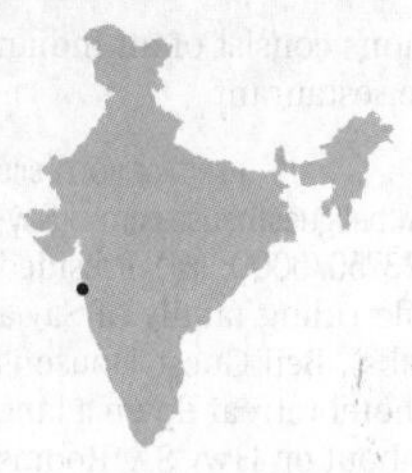

Mumbai (Bombay)

☎022 / POP 21.1 MILLION

Includes ➡

Best Places to Eat

- Peshawri (p760)
- Bastian (p761)
- Bademiya Seekh Kebab Stall (p756)
- Bombay Canteen (p761)
- Masala Library (p761)

Best Places to Sleep

- Taj Mahal Palace, Mumbai (p754)
- Abode Bombay (p754)
- Residency Hotel (p754)
- Sea Shore Hotel (p752)
- Juhu Residency (p755)

Why Go?

Mumbai, formerly Bombay, is big. It's full of dreamers and hard-labourers, starlets and gangsters, stray dogs and exotic birds, artists and servants, fisherfolk and *crorepatis* (millionaires), and lots and lots of people. It has India's most prolific film industry, some of Asia's biggest slums (as well as the world's most expensive home) and the largest tropical forest in an urban zone. Mumbai is India's financial powerhouse, fashion epicentre and a pulse point of religious tension.

If Mumbai is your introduction to India, prepare yourself. The city isn't a threatening place but its furious energy, limited public transport and punishing pollution make it challenging for visitors. The heart of the city contains some of the grandest colonial-era architecture on the planet but explore a little more and you'll uncover unique bazaars, hidden temples, hipster enclaves and India's premier restaurants and nightlife.

When to Go

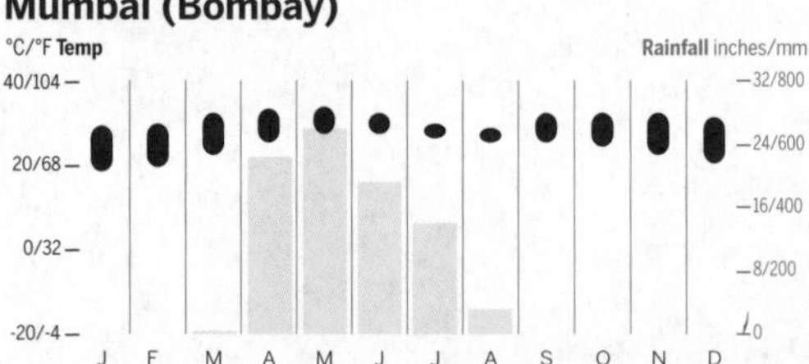

Dec & Jan The very best, least sticky weather.

Aug & Sep Mumbai goes Ganesh-crazy during its most exciting festival, Ganesh Chaturthi.

Oct–Apr There's very little rain, post-monsoon; the best time of year for festivals.

Mumbai (Bombay) Highlights

1. **Chhatrapati Shivaji Terminus** (p739) Marvelling at Mumbai's colonial-era architecture, including this monumental train station.

2. **Bazaars** (p766) Investigating the labyrinthine lanes and stalls in the ancient bazaar district.

3. **Restaurants** (p760) Dining like a maharaja at one of India's best restaurants, such as Peshawri.

4. **Iskcon Temple** (p748) Feeling the love with the Krishna crowd at this unique temple.

5. **Dharavi Slum** (p744) Taking a tour through of Asia's largest shantytown.

6. **Taj Mahal Palace, Mumbai** (p754) Sleeping at one of the world's most iconic hotels, or having a drink at its bar, Mumbai's first.

7. **Dr Bhau Daji Lad Mumbai City Museum** (p744) Ogling this museum's gorgeous Renaissance revival interiors.

8. **Elephanta Island** (p749) Beholding the commanding triple-headed Shiva on this island.

9. **Girgaum Chowpatty** (p745) Catching the sea breeze among playing kids, big balloons and a hot-pink sunset.

History

Koli fisherfolk have inhabited the seven islands that form Mumbai from as far back as the 2nd century BC. Remnants of this culture remain huddled along the city shoreline today. A succession of Hindu dynasties held sway over the islands from the 6th century AD until the Muslim Sultans of Gujarat annexed the area in the 14th century, eventually ceding it to Portugal in 1534. The only memorable contribution the Portuguese made to the area was christening it Bom Bahai. They handed control to the English government in 1665, which leased the islands to the East India Company.

Bombay flourished as a trading port. The city's fort was completed in the 1720s, and a century later ambitious land reclamation projects joined the islands into today's single landmass. The city continued to grow, and in the 19th century the fort walls were dismantled and massive building works transformed the city in grand colonial style. When Bombay became the principal supplier of cotton to Britain during the American Civil War, the population soared and trade boomed as money flooded into the city.

Bombay was a major player in the Independence movement, and the Quit India campaign was launched here in 1942 by Mahatma Gandhi. The city became capital of the Bombay presidency after Independence, but in 1960 Maharashtra and Gujarat were divided along linguistic lines – and Bombay became the capital of Maharashtra.

The rise of the pro-Marathi, pro-Hindu regionalist movement in the 1980s, spearheaded by the Shiv Sena (literally 'Shivaji's Army'), shattered the city's multicultural mould when it was accused of actively discriminating against Muslims and non-Maharashtrians. Communalist tensions increased, and the city's cosmopolitan self-image took a battering when 900 people were killed in riots in late 1992 and 1993. The riots were followed by a dozen retaliatory bombings which killed 257 people and damaged the Bombay Stock Exchange.

Shiv Sena's influence saw the names of many streets and public buildings – as well as the city itself – changed from their colonial monikers. In 1996 the city officially became Mumbai (derived from the Hindu goddess Mumba). The airport, Victoria Terminus and Prince of Wales Museum were all renamed after Chhatrapati Shivaji, the great Maratha leader.

Religious tensions deepened and became intertwined with national religious conflicts and India's relations with Pakistan. A series of bomb attacks on trains killed over 200 in July

MUMBAI IN ...

Two Days

Begin at one of Mumbai's architectural masterpieces, the **Chhatrapati Shivaji Maharaj Vastu Sangrahalaya museum** (p742), before grabbing lunch Gujarati-style at **Samrat** (p758).

In the afternoon head to Colaba and tour the city's iconic sights, the **Gateway of India** (p738) and **Taj Mahal Palace hotel** (p754). That evening, fine dine at **Indigo** (p757) or chow down at **Bademiya Seekh Kebab Stall** (p756), followed by cocktails at hip **Colaba Social** (p761).

The next day, take in the grandaddy of Mumbai's colonial-era giants, **Chhatrapati Shivaji Terminus** (p739); and **Crawford Market** (p766) and its maze of bazaars, hidden temples and unique street life. Kill the afternoon wandering the tiny lanes of **Khotachiwadi** (p749), followed by beach *bhelpuri* at **Girgaum Chowpatty** (p745). Need a drink? Hip nightlife hub Lower Parel beckons for dinner and craft beers at **White Owl** (p762) or **Woodside Inn** (p762).

Four Days

Sail to Unesco-listed **Elephanta Island** (p749), returning for lunch in artsy Kala Ghoda at **Burma Burma** (p759). In the evening, head north for exquisite seafood at **Bastian** (p761), followed by seriously happening bar action in Bandra.

Spend your last day visiting the **Mahalaxmi Dhobi Ghat** (p745), **Mahalaxmi Temple** (p745) and **Haji Ali Dargah** (p745); or **Sanjay Gandhi National Park** (p743) for a peaceful walk in the woods. Call it a night after exploring modern Indian fare at **Bombay Canteen** (p761) or **Masala Library** (p761).

TOP FESTIVALS IN MUMBAI

Mumbai Sanskruti (www.asiaticsociety.org.in; ⏲ Jan) This free, two-day celebration of Hindustani classical music is held on the steps of the gorgeous Asiatic Society Library in the Fort area.

Kala Ghoda Festival (www.kalaghodaassociation.com; ⏲ Feb) Getting bigger and more sophisticated each year, this two-week-long art fest held in Kala Ghoda and the Fort area sees tons of performances and exhibitions.

Elephanta Festival (www.maharashtratourism.gov.in; ⏲ Feb/Mar) This classical music and dance festival takes place on the waterfront Apollo Bunder at the Gateway of India.

Nariyal Poornima (⏲ Aug) This Koli celebration in Colaba marks the start of the fishing season and the retreat of monsoon winds.

Ganesh Chaturthi (www.ganeshchaturthi.com; ⏲ Aug/Sep) Mumbai gets totally swept up by this 10- to 12-day celebration of the Hindu god Ganesh. On the festival's first, third, fifth, seventh and 11th days, families and communities take their Ganesh statues to the seashore at Chowpatty and Juhu beaches and auspiciously submerge them.

Mumbai Film Festival (MFF; www.mumbaifilmfestival.com; ⏲ Oct) New films from the subcontinent and beyond are screened at the weeklong MFF at cinemas across Mumbai.

2006. Then, in November 2008, a coordinated series of devastating attacks (by Pakistani gunmen) targeted landmark buildings across the city, as the Taj Mahal Palace hotel burned, passengers were gunned down inside the Chhatrapati Shivaji railway station and 10 killed inside the Leopold Cafe backpacker haunt.

In late 2012, when the Sena's charismatic founder Bal Thackeray died (500,000 attended his funeral), the Shiv Sena mission begin to falter, and in the 2014 assembly elections, President Modi's BJP became the largest party in Mumbai.

Mumbaikars are a resilient bunch. Increased security is very much part of everyday life today and the city's status as the engine room of the Indian economy remains unchallenged. However, Mumbai politicians certainly have their work cut out, with the megacity's feeble public transport, gridlocked streets, pollution and housing crisis all in desperate need of attention.

Sights

Mumbai is an island connected by bridges to the mainland. The city's commercial and cultural centre is at the southern, claw-shaped end of the island known as South Mumbai. The southernmost peninsula is Colaba, traditionally the travellers' nerve centre, with many of the major attractions.

Directly north of Colaba is the busy commercial area known as Fort, where the British fort once stood. This part of the city is bordered on the west by a series of interconnected grassy areas known as maidans (pronounced may-*dahns*).

Continuing north you enter 'the suburbs', which contain the airport and many of Mumbai's best restaurants, shops and nightspots. The upmarket districts of Bandra, Juhu and Lower Parel are key areas (the bohemians and hippies that used to claim Bandra have now moved further north to Andheri West and Vesova).

Colaba

Along the city's southernmost peninsula, Colaba is a bustling district packed with elegant art deco and colonial-era mansions, budget-to-midrange lodgings, bars and restaurants, street stalls and a fisherman's quarter. Colaba Causeway (Shahid Bhagat Singh Marg) dissects the district.

If you're here in August, look out for the Koli festival Nariyal Poornima, which is big in Colaba.

★**Taj Mahal Palace, Mumbai** LANDMARK
(Map p738; https://taj.tajhotels.com; Apollo Bunder) Mumbai's most famous landmark, this stunning hotel is a fairy-tale blend of Islamic and Renaissance styles, and India's second-most photographed monument. It was built in 1903 by the Parsi industrialist JN Tata, supposedly after he was refused entry to nearby European hotels on account of being 'a native'. Dozens were killed inside the hotel when it was targeted during the 2008 terrorist attacks, and images of its burning facade were

Colaba

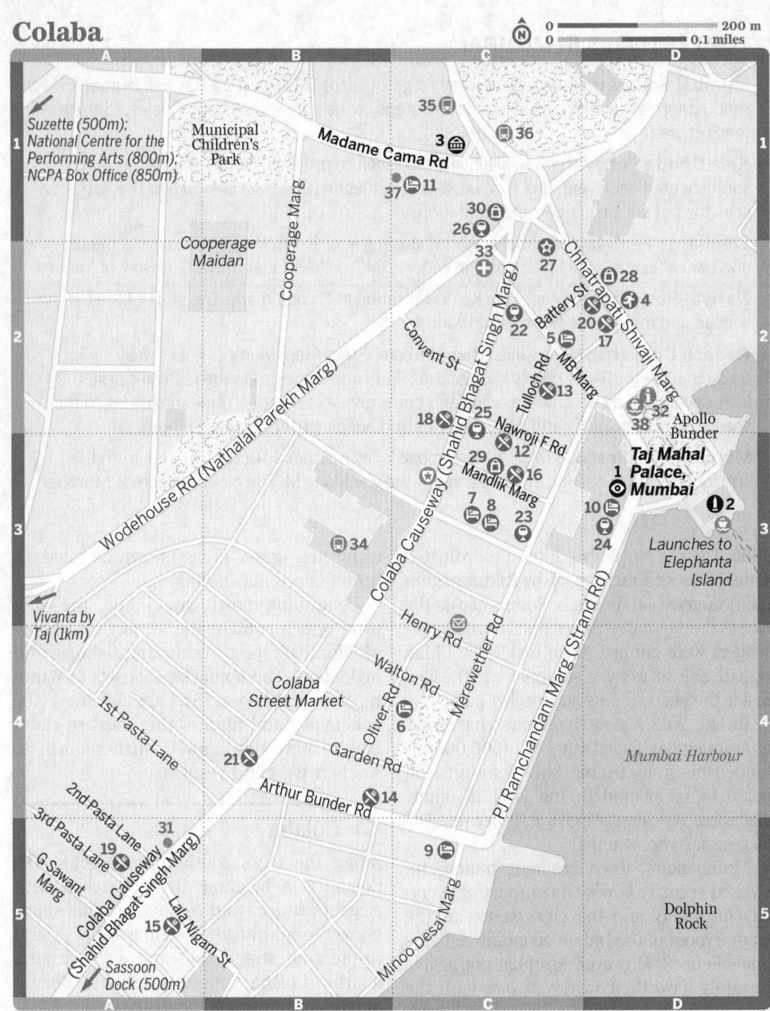

beamed worldwide. The fully restored hotel reopened on Independence Day 2010.

Much more than an iconic building, the Taj's history is intrinsically linked with the nation: it was the first hotel in India to employ women, the first to have electricity (and fans), and it also housed freedom-fighters (for no charge) during the struggle for independence.

Today the Taj fronts the harbour and Gateway of India, but it was originally designed to face the city (the entrance has been changed).

Gateway of India MONUMENT

(Map p738) This bold basalt arch of colonial triumph faces out to Mumbai Harbour from the tip of Apollo Bunder. Incorporating Islamic styles of 16th-century Gujarat, it was built to commemorate the 1911 royal visit of King George V, but wasn't completed until 1924. Ironically, the British builders of the gateway used it just 24 years later to parade the last British regiment as India marched towards independence.

These days, the gateway is a favourite gathering spot for locals and a top place for people-watching. Giant-balloon sellers, photographers, vendors making *bhelpuri* (puffed rice tossed with fried rounds of dough, lentils, onions, herbs and chutneys) and touts rub shoulders with locals and

Colaba

Top Sights
1 Taj Mahal Palace, Mumbai D3

Sights
2 Gateway of India D3
3 National Gallery of Modern Art C1

Activities, Courses & Tours
4 Palms Spa D2

Sleeping
5 Abode Bombay C2
6 Bentley's Hotel C4
7 Hotel Moti C3
8 Regent Hotel C3
9 Sea Shore Hotel C5
10 Taj Mahal Palace, Mumbai D3
11 YWCA C1

Eating
12 Bademiya Restaurant C3
13 Bademiya Seekh Kebab Stall C2
14 Basilico B4
15 Colaba Market A5
16 Indigo C3
17 Indigo Delicatessen D2
18 Olympia C2
19 Star Daily A5
20 The Table D2
21 Theobroma B4

Drinking & Nightlife
22 Cafe Mondegar C2
23 Colaba Social C3
24 Harbour Bar D3
25 Leopold Cafe C2
26 Woodside Inn C1

Entertainment
27 Regal Cinema C2

Shopping
28 Central Cottage Industries Emporium D2
29 Cottonworld Corp C3
30 Phillips C1

Information
31 Akbar Travels A5
32 Maharashtra Tourism Development Corporation Booth D2
33 Sahakari Bhandar Chemist C2

Transport
34 BEST Bus Depot B3
35 BEST Bus Stand C1
36 BEST Bus Stand C1
37 Jet Airways C1
38 Maldar Catamarans D2
PNP ..... (see 38)

tourists, creating all the hubbub of a bazaar. In February/March they are joined by classical dancers and musicians who perform during the Elephanta Festival (p737).

Boats depart from the gateway's wharves for Elephanta Island.

Sassoon Dock WATERFRONT

Sassoon Dock is a scene of intense and pungent activity at dawn (around 5am) when colourfully clad Koli fisherfolk sort the catch unloaded from fishing boats at the quay. The fish drying in the sun are *bombil,* used in the dish Bombay duck. Photography at the dock is prohibited.

Fort Area & Churchgate

Lined up in a row and vying for your attention with aristocratic pomp, many of Mumbai's majestic Victorian buildings pose on the edge of **Oval Maidan**. This land, and the **Cross** and **Azad Maidans** immediately to the north, was on the oceanfront in those days, and this series of grandiose structures faced west directly to the Arabian Sea.

Kala Ghoda, or 'Black Horse', is a hip, atmospheric sub-neighbourhood of Fort just north of Colaba. It contains many of Mumbai's museums, galleries and design boutiques alongside a wealth of colonial-era buildings and some of the city's best restaurants and cafes.

★Chhatrapati Shivaji Terminus HISTORIC BUILDING

(Victoria Terminus; Map p740) Imposing, exuberant and overflowing with people, this monumental train station is the city's most extravagant Gothic building and an aphorism for colonial-era India. It's a meringue of Victorian, Hindu and Islamic styles whipped into an imposing Daliesque structure of buttresses, domes, turrets, spires and stained glass.

Some of the architectural detail is incredible, with dog-faced gargoyles adorning the magnificent central tower and peacock-filled windows above the central courtyard. Designed by Frederick Stevens, it was completed in 1887, 34 years after the first train in India left this site.

Officially renamed Chhatrapati Shivaji Terminus (CST) in 1998, it's still better known locally as VT. Sadly, its interior is far less impressive, with ugly modern additions

Fort Area & Churchgate

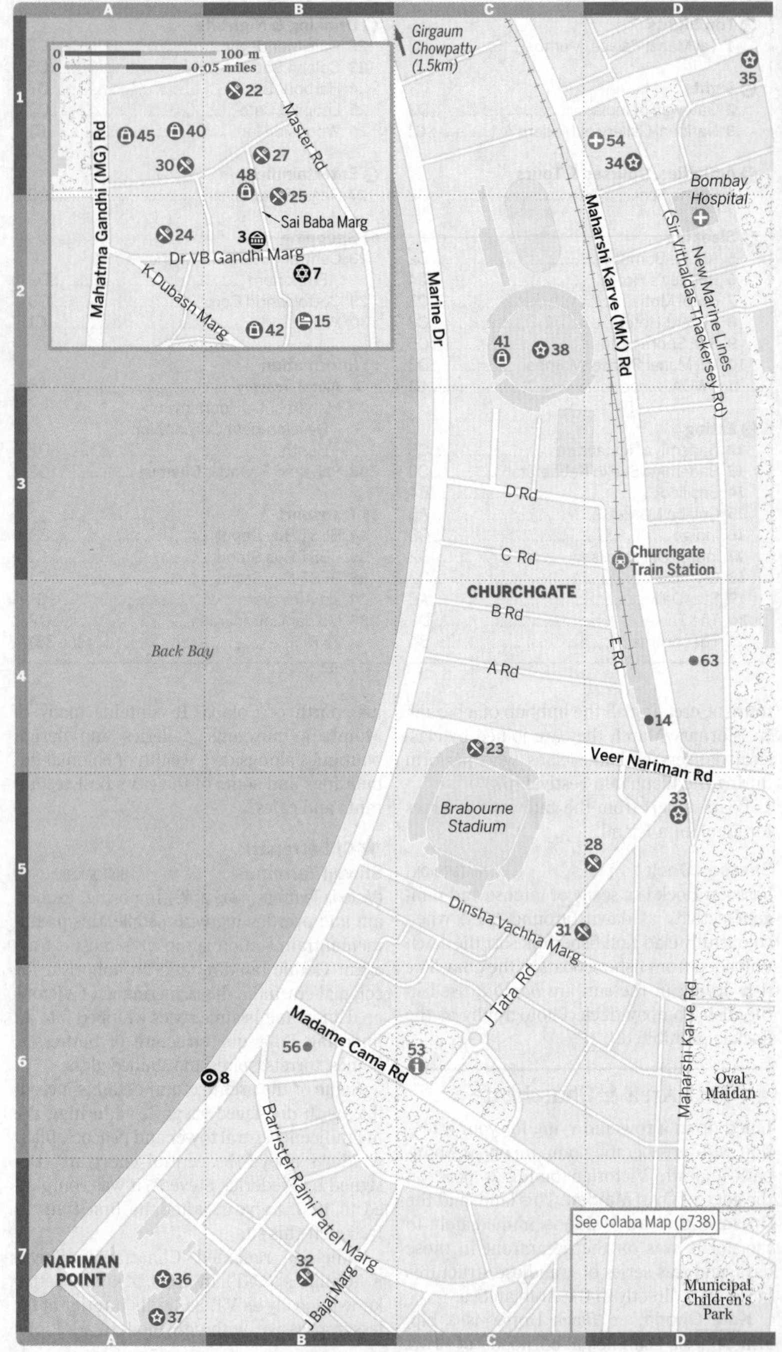

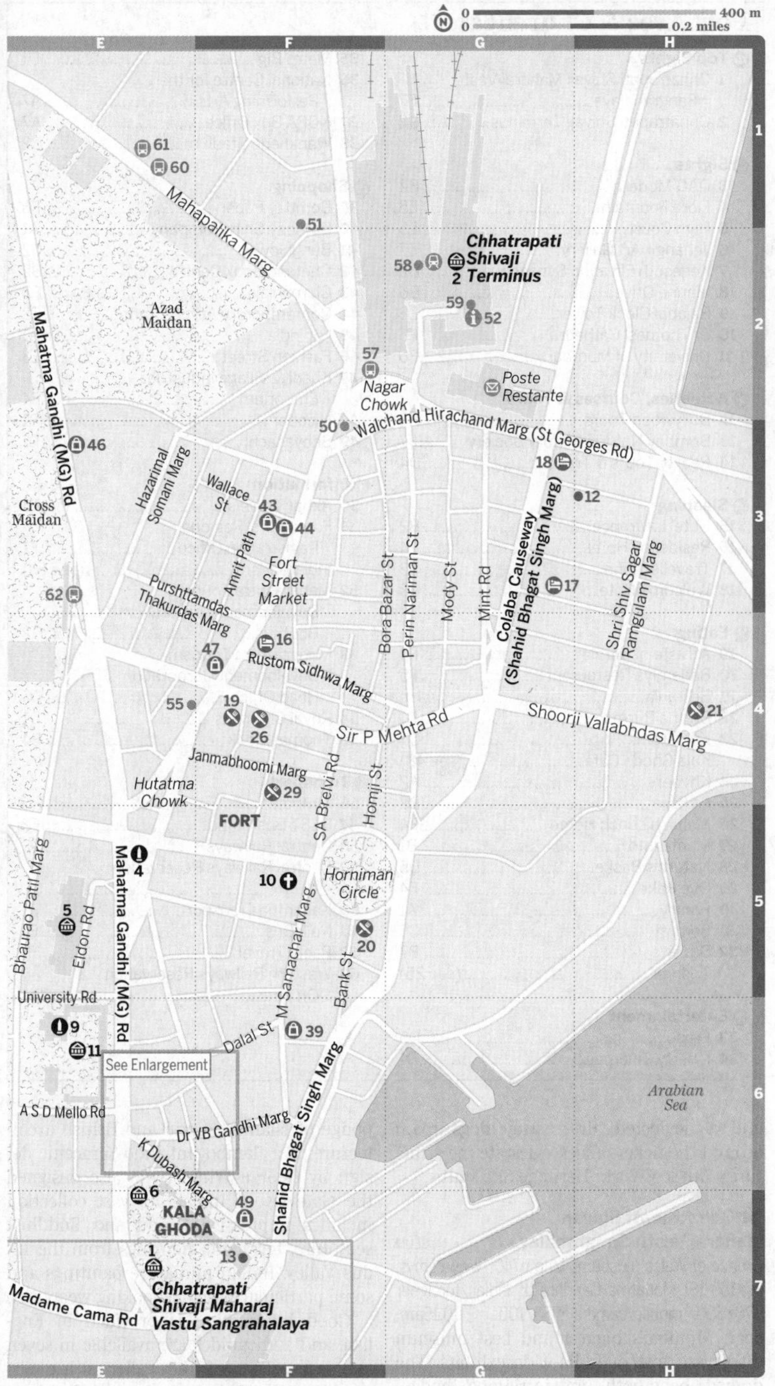

0 400 m
0 0.2 miles
Mahapalika Marg
Azad Maidan
Chhatrapati Shivaji Terminus
Nagar Chowk
Poste Restante
Walchand Hirachand Marg (St Georges Rd)
Mahatma Gandhi (MG) Rd
Hazarimal Somani Marg
Wallace St
Cross Maidan
Amrit Path
Fort Street Market
Purshttamdas Thakurdas Marg
Rustom Sidhwa Marg
Bora Bazar St
Perin Nariman St
Mody St
Mint Rd
Colaba Causeway (Shahid Bhagat Singh Marg)
Shri Shiv Sagar Ramgulam Marg
Shoorji Vallabhdas Marg
Sir P Mehta Rd
Janmabhoomi Marg
Hutatma Chowk
FORT
SA Brelvi Rd
Homji St
Horniman Circle
Bhaurao Patil Marg
Eldon Rd
M Samachar Marg
Bank St
University Rd
Dalal St
See Enlargement
A S D Mello Rd
Dr VB Gandhi Marg
Shahid Bhagat Singh Marg
K Dubash Marg
KALA GHODA
Arabian Sea
Madame Cama Rd
Chhatrapati Shivaji Maharaj Vastu Sangrahalaya

Fort Area & Churchgate

Top Sights
1 Chhatrapati Shivaji Maharaj Vastu Sangrahalaya ... E7
2 Chhatrapati Shivaji Terminus ... G2

Sights
3 DAG Modern ... B2
4 Flora Fountain ... E5
5 High Court ... E5
6 Jehangir Art Gallery ... E7
7 Keneseth Eliyahoo Synagogue ... B2
8 Marine Drive ... B6
9 Rajabai Clock Tower ... E6
10 St Thomas' Cathedral ... F5
11 University of Mumbai ... E6

Activities, Courses & Tours
12 Bollywood Tours ... H3
13 Bombay Natural History Society ... F7
14 Reality Tours & Travel ... D4

Sleeping
15 Hotel Lawrence ... B2
16 Residency Hotel ... F4
17 Traveller's Inn ... G3
18 Welcome Hotel ... G3

Eating
19 A Taste of Kerala ... F4
20 Bademiya Restaurant ... F5
21 Brittania ... H4
22 Burma Burma ... B1
23 K Rustom ... C4
Kala Ghoda Café ... (see 48)
24 Khyber ... A2
25 La Folie ... B2
26 Mahesh Lunch Home ... F4
27 Mamagoto ... B1
28 Nature's Basket ... D5
29 Oye Kake ... F4
30 Pantry ... A1
31 Samrat ... C5
32 Suzette ... B7
Trishna ... (see 25)

Entertainment
33 Eros ... D5
34 Liberty Cinema ... D1
35 Metro Big ... D1
36 National Centre for the Performing Arts ... A7
37 NCPA Box Office ... A7
38 Wankhede Stadium ... C2

Shopping
39 Bombay Paperie ... F6
40 Bombay Shirt Company ... A1
41 Bungalow 8 ... C2
42 Chetana Book Centre ... B2
43 Chimanlals ... F3
44 Contemporary Arts & Crafts ... F3
45 Fabindia ... A1
46 Fashion Street ... E3
47 Khadi & Village Industries Emporium ... F4
48 Nicobar ... B1
49 Sabyasachi ... F7

Information
50 Akbar Travels ... F3
51 Foreigners' Regional Registration Office ... F1
Indiatourism ... (see 63)
52 Maharashtra Tourism Development Corporation Booth ... G2
53 Maharashtra Tourism Development Corporation Head Office ... C6
54 Royal Chemists ... D1
55 Thomas Cook ... E4

Transport
56 Air India ... B6
57 BEST Bus Stand ... F2
58 Central Railways ... G2
59 Central Railways Reservation Centre ... G2
60 Kadamba Transport ... E1
61 Naik Bus ... E1
62 Paolo Travel ... E3
63 Western Railways Reservation Office ... D4

and a neglected air – stray dogs roam around the ticket offices – despite the structure's Unesco World Heritage Site status.

★Chhatrapati Shivaji Maharaj Vastu Sangrahalaya MUSEUM

(Prince of Wales Museum; Map p740; www.csmvs.in; 159-161 Mahatma Gandhi Rd; Indian/foreigner ₹70/500, mobile/camera ₹50/100; ⏲10.15am-6pm) Mumbai's biggest and best museum displays a mix of India-wide exhibits. The domed behemoth, an intriguing hodgepodge of Islamic, Hindu and British architecture, is a flamboyant Indo-Saracenic design by George Wittet (who also designed the Gateway of India). Its vast collection includes impressive Hindu and Buddhist sculpture, terracotta figurines from the Indus Valley, Indian miniature paintings and some particularly vicious-looking weaponry.

Good information is provided in English, and audioguides are available in seven languages. Five of the galleries are air-conditioned, offering a welcome relief from

WORTH A TRIP

SANJAY GHANDI NATIONAL PARK

Within 1½ hours of Mumbai's teeming metropolis is 104 sq km of protected tropical forest at **Sanjay Gandhi National Park** (022-28868686; https://sgnp.maharashtra.gov.in; Borivali; adult/child ₹44/23, vehicle ₹105, safari admission ₹50; 7.30am-6pm Tue-Sun, last entry 4pm). Bright flora, birds, butterflies and leopards replace pollution and concrete, surrounded by forested hills on the city's northern edge. Urban development exists on the park's fringes, but the heart of the park is very peaceful.

The easiest way to take a walk in the woods is by going with Bombay Natural History Society (p749) – many of the park's highlights require advanced permission, which BNHS takes care of for you. You might see Shilonda waterfall, Vihar and Tulsi lakes or even the park's highest point, Jambol Mal. **Kanheri Caves** (Indian/foreigner ₹15/200; 9am-5pm), a set of 109 dwellings and monastic structures for Buddhist monks 6km inside the park, is the most intriguing option. From the 1st century BC, the caves were developed over 1000 years as part of a sprawling monastic university complex. Avoid the zoo-like lion and tiger 'safari' as the animals are in cages and enclosures. October to April is the best time to see birds, and August to November to see butterflies. At time of research a huge restoration project – a new lakeside promenade, tourist huts, mangrove walkway, taxidermy gallery, nature trails and nature interpretation centres – had been approved.

An information centre with a small exhibition on the park's wildlife is inside the park's main northern entrance. The nearest station is Borivali, served by trains on the Western Railway line from Churchgate station (₹15 to ₹140, 30 minutes, frequent).

the summer heat. For a quick historical overview of Mumbai, the new 20-minute Mumbai Experience (Indian/foreigner ₹40/50) is shown in English five times per day. There's a fine cafeteria at the entrance and the museum shop is also excellent.

High Court HISTORIC BUILDING

(Map p740; Eldon Rd; 10.45am-2pm & 2.45-5pm Mon-Fri) A hive of daily activity, packed with judges, barristers and other cogs in the Indian justice system, the High Court is an elegant 1848 neo-Gothic building. The design was inspired by a German castle and was obviously intended to dispel any doubts about the authority of the justice dispensed inside.

Keneseth Eliyahoo Synagogue SYNAGOGUE

(Map p740; Dr VB Gandhi Marg, Kala Ghoda; camera/video ₹100/500; 11am-5pm Sun-Thu) Built in 1884, this unmistakable sky-blue synagogue still functions and is tenderly maintained by the city's dwindling Jewish community. It's protected by very heavy security, but the caretaker is welcoming (and will point out a photo of Madonna, who dropped by in 2008). Bring a copy of your passport.

Marine Drive WATERFRONT

(Map p740; Netaji Subhashchandra Bose Rd) Built on reclaimed land in 1920, Marine Dr arcs along the shore of the Arabian Sea from Nariman Point past Girgaum Chowpatty and continues to the foot of Malabar Hill. Lined with flaking art deco apartments, it's one of Mumbai's most popular promenades and sunset-watching spots. Its twinkling nighttime lights have earned it the nickname 'the Queen's Necklace'.

University of Mumbai HISTORIC BUILDING

(Bombay University; Map p740; Bhaurao Patil Marg) Looking like a 15th-century French-Gothic mansion plopped incongruously among Mumbai's palm trees, this structure was designed by Gilbert Scott of London's St Pancras train station fame. There's an exquisite **University Library** and **Convocation Hall**, as well as the 84m-high **Rajabai Clock Tower** (Map p740), decorated with detailed carvings. Since the 2008 terror attacks there's no public access to the grounds, but it's still well worth admiring from the street.

Jehangir Art Gallery GALLERY

(Map p740; www.jehangirartgallery.com; 161B Mahatma Gandhi Rd, Kala Ghoda; 11am-7pm) FREE Renovated in recent years, this excellent gallery hosts exhibitions of all types of visual arts by Mumbaikar, national and international artists.

National Gallery of Modern Art MUSEUM

(NGMA; Map p738; www.ngmaindia.gov.in; Mahatma Gandhi Rd; Indian/foreigner ₹20/500; 11am-6pm Tue-Sun) Well-curated shows of Indian and international artists in a bright and spacious five-floor exhibition space.

DAG Modern GALLERY

(Map p740; www.dagmodern.com; 58 Dr VB Gandhi Marg, Kala Ghoda; 11am-7pm Mon-Sat) FREE This gallery is spread over four floors of a beautifully restored cream-coloured colonial-era structure. With well-curated exhibitions it showcases important modern Indian art from its extensive collection.

St Thomas' Cathedral CHURCH

(Map p740; Veer Nariman Rd; 7am-6pm) This charming cathedral, begun in 1672 and finished in 1718, is the oldest British-era building standing in Mumbai and the city's first Anglican church: it was once the eastern gateway of the East India Company's fort (the 'Churchgate'). The cathedral is a marriage of Byzantine and colonial-era architecture, and its airy interior is full of grandiose colonial memorials.

Kalbadevi to Mahalaxmi

★ Dr Bhau Daji Lad Mumbai City Museum MUSEUM

(Map p746; www.bdlmuseum.org; Dr Babasaheb Ambedkar Rd; Indian/foreigner ₹10/100; 10am-6pm Thu-Tue) This gorgeous museum, built in Renaissance revival style in 1872 as the Victoria & Albert Museum, contains 3500-plus objects centring on Mumbai's history – photography, maps, textiles, books, manuscripts,

DHARAVI SLUM

Mumbaikars were ambivalent about the stereotypes in 2008's *Slumdog Millionaire*, but slums are very much a part of – some would say the foundation of – Mumbai city life. An astonishing 60% of Mumbai's population lives in slums, and one of the city's largest slums is Dharavi, originally inhabited by fisherfolk when the area was still creeks, swamps and islands. It became attractive to migrant workers from South Mumbai and beyond when the swamp began to fill in due to natural and artificial causes. It now incorporates 2.2 sq km of land sandwiched between Mumbai's two major railway lines, and is home to perhaps as many as a million people.

While it may look a bit shambolic from the outside, the maze of dusty alleys and sewer-lined streets of this city-within-a-city is actually a collection of abutting settlements. Some parts of Dharavi have mixed populations, but in other parts inhabitants from different regions of India, and with different trades, have set up homes and tiny factories. Potters from Saurashtra (Gujarat) live in one area, Muslim tanners in another; embroidery workers from Uttar Pradesh work alongside metalsmiths; while other workers recycle plastics as women dry pappadams in the searing sun. Some of these thriving industries, as many as 20,000 in all, export their wares, and the annual turnover of business from Dharavi is thought to exceed US$700 million.

Up close, life in the slums is fascinating to witness. Residents pay rent, most houses have kitchens and electricity, and building materials range from flimsy corrugated-iron shacks to permanent multistorey concrete structures. Perhaps the biggest issue facing Dharavi residents is sanitation, as water supply is irregular – every household has a 200L drum for water storage. Very few dwellings have a private toilet or bathroom, so some neighbourhoods have constructed their own (to which every resident must contribute financially) while other residents are forced to use run-down public facilities.

Many families have been here for generations, and education achievements are higher than in many rural areas: around 15% of children complete a higher education and find white-collar jobs. Many choose to stay, though, in the neighbourhood they grew up in.

Slum tourism is a polarising subject, so you'll have to decide for yourself. If you opt to visit, the award-winning Reality Tours & Travel (p752) has an illuminating tour (from ₹850), and puts 80% of profits back into Dharavi social programs. They can also now arrange a meal with a local family for further insight.

Some tourists opt to visit on their own, which is OK as well – just don't take photos. Take the train from Churchgate station to Mahim, exit on the west side and cross the bridge into Dharavi.

To learn more about Mumbai's slums, check out Katherine Boo's 2012 book *Behind the Beautiful Forevers*, about life in Annawadi, a slum near the airport, and *Rediscovering Dharavi*, Kalpana Sharma's sensitive and engrossing history of Dharavi's people, culture and industry.

MUMBAI FOR CHILDREN

Kidzania (www.kidzania.in; 3rd fl, R City, LBS Marg, Ghatkopar West; child/adult Tue-Fri ₹950/500, Sat & Sun ₹1200/550; ⏲10am-9pm Tue-Sun) is Mumbai's latest attraction, an educational activity centre where kids can learn all about flying, fire-fighting and policing, and get stuck into lots of arts and crafts. It's on the outskirts on the city, 10km northeast of the Bandra Kurla Complex.

Little tykes with energy to burn will love the Gorai Island amusement parks, **Esselworld** (www.esselworld.in; adult/child ₹949/699; ⏲10.30am-6.30pm) and **Water Kingdom** (www.waterkingdom.in; adult/child ₹999/699; ⏲10am-7pm). Both have lots of rides, slides and shade. Combined tickets are adult/child ₹1299/899.

The free **Hanging Gardens**, in Malabar Hill, have animal topiaries, swings and coconut-wallahs. **Kamala Nehru Park**, across the street, has a two-storey 'boot house'.

Bombay Natural History Society (p749) conducts nature trips for kids.

Bidriware, lacquerware, weaponry and exquisite pottery. The landmark building was renovated in 2008, with its Minton tile floors, gilded ceiling mouldings, ornate columns, chandeliers and staircases all gloriously restored.

Haji Ali Dargah MOSQUE
(Map p746; www.hajialidargah.in; off V Desai Chowk) Floating like a sacred mirage off the coast, this Indo-Islamic shrine located on an offshore inlet is a striking sight. Built in the 19th century, it contains the tomb of the Muslim saint Pir Haji Ali Shah Bukhari. Legend has it that Haji Ali died while on a pilgrimage to Mecca and his casket miraculously floated back to this spot.

It's only possible to visit the shrine at low tide, via a long causeway (check tide times locally). Thousands of pilgrims, especially on Thursday and Friday (when there may be *qawwali;* devotional singing), cross it daily, many donating to beggars who line the way. Sadly, parts of the shrine are in a poor state, damaged by storms and the saline air, though a renovation plan exists. It's visited by people of all faiths.

Mahalaxmi Dhobi Ghat GHAT
(Map p746; Dr E Moses Rd; ⏲4.30am-dusk) This 140-year-old dhobi ghat (place where clothes are washed) is Mumbai's biggest human-powered washing machine: every day hundreds of people beat the dirt out of thousands of kilograms of soiled Mumbai clothes and linen in 1026 open-air troughs. The best view is from the bridge across the railway tracks near Mahalaxmi train station.

Babu Amichand Panalal Adishwarji Jain Temple JAIN TEMPLE
(Walkeshwar Marg, Malabar Hill; ⏲5am-9pm) This temple is renowned among Jains for its beauty – given how beautiful Jain temples are, that's saying a lot. Check out the paintings and especially the ecstatically colourful zodiac dome ceiling. It's a small, actively used temple; visitors should be sensitive and dress modestly.

Girgaum Chowpatty BEACH
(Map p746) This city beach is a favourite evening spot for courting couples, families, political rallies and anyone out to enjoy what passes for fresh air. Evening *bhelpuri* at the throng of stalls at the beach's southern end is an essential part of the Mumbai experience. Forget about taking a dip: the water's toxic.

Mahalaxmi Temple HINDU TEMPLE
(Map p746; off V Desai Chowk) It's only fitting that in money-mad Mumbai one of the busiest and most colourful temples is dedicated to Mahalaxmi, the goddess of wealth. Perched on a headland, it is the focus for Mumbai's Navratri (Festival of Nine Nights) celebrations in September/October.

Malabar Hill AREA
(around BG Kher Marg) Mumbai's most exclusive neighbourhood, at the northern end of Back Bay, surprisingly contains one of Mumbai's most sacred oases. Concealed between apartment blocks is **Banganga Tank**, an enclave of serene temples, bathing pilgrims, meandering, traffic-free streets and picturesque old *dharamsalas* (pilgrims' rest houses). According to Hindu legend, Lord Ram created this tank by piercing the earth with his arrow.

For some of the best views of Chowpatty, about 600m east, and the graceful arc of Marine Dr, visit **Kamala Nehru Park**.

Mani Bhavan MUSEUM
(Map p746; www.gandhi-manibhavan.org; 19 Laburnum Rd, Gamdevi; donations appreciated; ⏲9.30am-5.30pm) As poignant as it is tiny, this museum is in the building where

Kalbadevi to Mahalaxmi

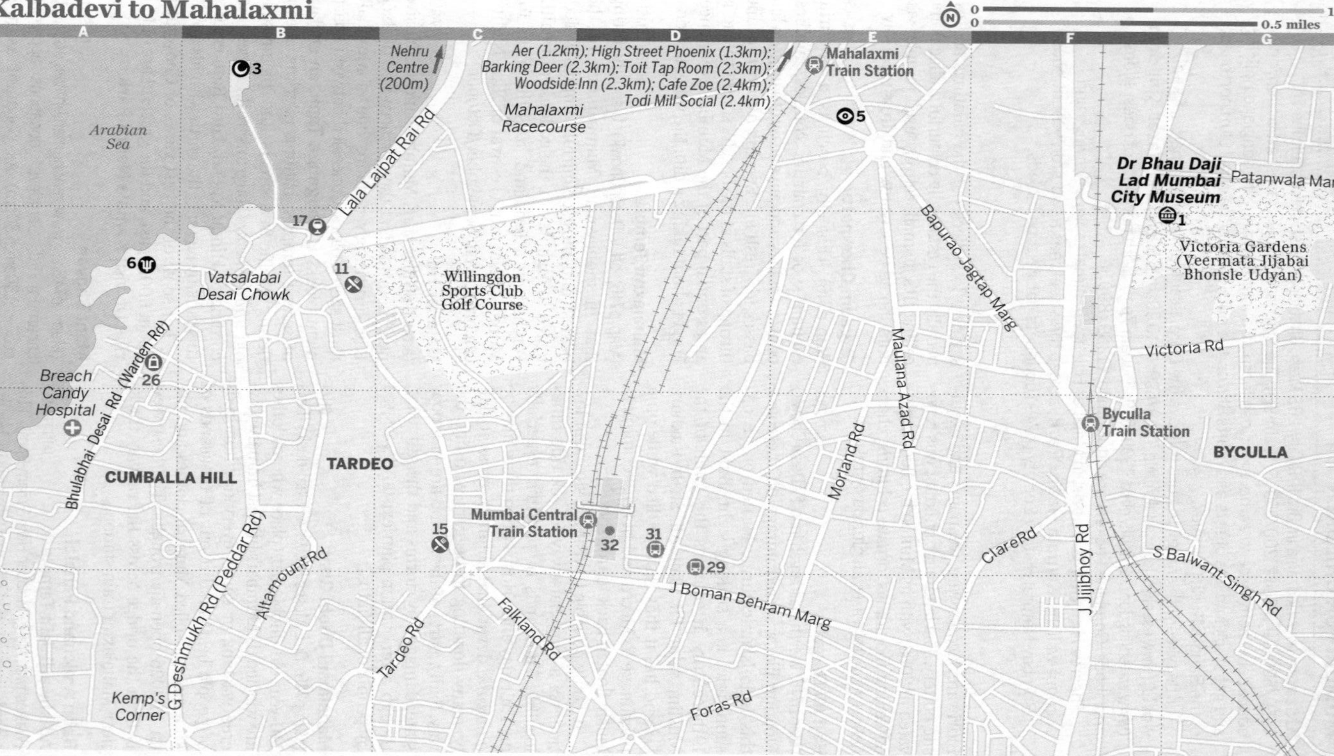

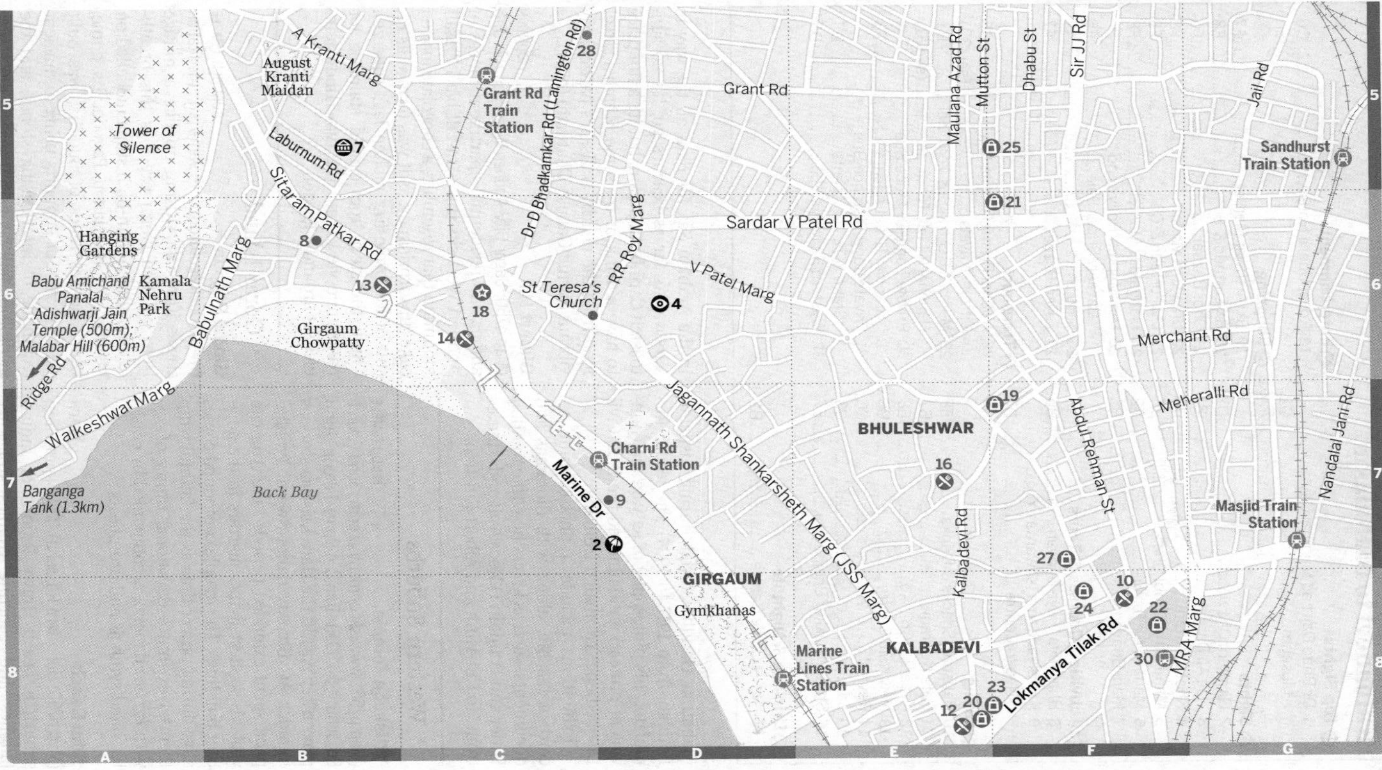
A Kranti Marg
August Kranti Maidan
Tower of Silence
Laburnum Rd
Grant Rd Train Station
Dr D Bhadkamkar Rd (Lamington Rd)
Grant Rd
Maulana Azad Rd
Mutton St
Dhabu St
Sir JJ Rd
Jail Rd
Sandhurst Train Station
Sitaram Patkar Rd
Sardar V Patel Rd
Hanging Gardens
Babulnath Marg
RR Roy Marg
V Patel Marg
Babu Amichand Panalal Adishwarji Jain Temple (500m); Malabar Hill (600m)
Kamala Nehru Park
St Teresa's Church
Girgaum Chowpatty
Merchant Rd
Ridge Rd
Walkeshwar Marg
Jagannath Shankarsheth Marg (JSS Marg)
Meheralli Rd
BHULESHWAR
Abdul Rehman St
Nandalal Jani Rd
Charni Rd Train Station
Banganga Tank (1.3km)
Back Bay
Marine Dr
Masjid Train Station
Kalbadevi Rd
GIRGAUM
Gymkhanas
KALBADEVI
Marine Lines Train Station
Lokmanya Tilak Rd
MRA Marg
A
B
C
D
E
F
G
5
6
7
8
28
7
25
21
8
13
18
4
14
19
16
9
2
27
10
24
22
30
23
20
12

Kalbadevi to Mahalaxmi

Mahatma Gandhi stayed during visits to Bombay from 1917 to 1934. The leader formulated his philosophy of satyagraha (nonviolent protest) and launched the 1932 Civil Disobedience campaign from here.

Exhibitions include a photographic record of his life, along with dioramas and documents, such as letters he wrote to Adolf Hitler and Franklin D Roosevelt and tributes from Ho Chi Minh and Albert Einstein.

Western Suburbs

★ Iskcon Temple — HINDU TEMPLE

(Map p750; www.iskconmumbai.com; Juhu Church Rd, Juhu; 4.30am-1pm & 4-9pm) Iskcon Juhu plays a key part in the Hare Krishna story, as founder AC Bhaktivedanta Swami Prabhupada spent extended periods here (you can visit his modest living quarters in the adjacent building). The temple compound comes alive during prayer time as the faithful whip themselves into a devotional frenzy of joy, with *kirtan* dancing accompanied by crashing hand symbols and drumbeats.

Juhu Beach — BEACH

(Map p750; Juhu Tara Rd, Juhu) This sprawling suburban beach draws legions of Indian families and courting couples frolicking in the Arabian Sea for 6km all the way to Versova. As far as beaches go, it's no sun-toasted Caribbean dream, but it's a fun place to have a drink or try some Mumbai street food from the nearby stalls. It's particularly vibrant during Ganesh Chaturthi (p737).

Gilbert Hill — MOUNTAIN

(Map p750; Sagar City, Andheri West) Smack dab among the residential apartment blocks of Andheri West sits this 61m-tall black basalt mountain that resembles a chocolate molten cake (unsurprisingly, as it was formed as result of Mesozoic Era molten lava squeeze). Climb the steep rock-carved staircase for panoramic views and the two Hindu temples set around a garden.

Gorai Island

Global Pagoda — BUDDHIST TEMPLE

(www.globalpagoda.org; 9am-7pm, meditation classes 10am-6pm) Rising up like a mirage from polluted Gorai Creek is this breathtaking, golden 96m-high stupa modelled on Myanmar's Shwedagon Pagoda. Its dome, which houses relics of Buddha, was built entirely without supports using an ancient technique of interlocking stones, and the meditation hall beneath it seats 8000.

OFF THE BEATEN TRACK

KHOTACHIWADI

The storied *wadi* (hamlet) of **Khotachiwadi** (Map p746), a heritage village nearly 180 years old, is clinging onto Mumbai life as it was before high-rises. A Christian enclave of elegant two-storey Portuguese-style wooden mansions, it's 500m northeast of Girgaum Chowpatty, lying amid Mumbai's predominantly Hindu and Muslim neighbourhoods. The winding lanes allow a wonderful glimpse into a quiet(ish) life away from noisier Mumbai.

It's not large, but you can spend a while wandering the alleyways and admiring the old homes and, around Christmas, their decorations. You can also plan an East Indian feast in advance at the home of celebrated fashion designer, Khotachiwadi activist and amateur chef James Ferreira (www.jamesferreira.co.in).

To find Khotachiwadi, head for St Teresa's Church, on the corner of Jagannath Shankarsheth Marg (JSS Marg) and Rajarammohan Roy Marg (RR Rd/Charni Rd), then head directly opposite the church on JSS Marg and duck down the third lane on your left (look for the Khotachiwadi wall stencil map that says 'Khotachiwadi Imaginaries').

There's a museum dedicated to the life of the Buddha and his teaching. Twenty-minute meditation classes are held daily; an on-site meditation centre also offers 10-day courses. To get here, take a train from Churchgate to Borivali (exit the station at the 'West' side), then take bus 294 (₹5) or an autorickshaw (₹40) to the ferry landing, where Esselworld ferries (return ₹50) depart every 30 minutes. The last ferry to the pagoda is at 5.30pm.

Elephant Island

★Elephanta Island HINDU TEMPLE
(Gharapuri; Indian/foreigner ₹30/500; ⏲caves 9am-5pm Tue-Sun) Northeast of the Gateway of India in Mumbai Harbour, the rock-cut temples on Gharapuri, better known as Elephanta Island, are a Unesco World Heritage Site. Created between AD 450 and 750, the labyrinth of cave temples represent some of India's most impressive temple carving.

The main Shiva-dedicated temple is an intriguing latticework of courtyards, halls, pillars and shrines; its magnum opus is a 6m-tall statue of Sadhashiva, depicting a three-faced Shiva as the destroyer, creator and preserver of the universe, his eyes closed in eternal contemplation.

It was the Portuguese who dubbed the island Elephanta because of a large stone elephant near the shore (this collapsed in 1814 and was moved by the British to Mumbai's Jijamata Udyan). There's a small museum on-site, with informative pictorial panels on the origin of the caves.

Pushy, expensive guides are available – but you don't really need one as Pramod Chandra's *A Guide to the Elephanta Caves,* widely for sale, is more than sufficient.

Launches (Map p738; economy/deluxe ₹145/180) head to Gharapuri from the Gateway of India every half-hour from 9am to 3.30pm. Buy tickets at the booths lining Apollo Bunder. The voyage takes about an hour.

The ferries dock at the end of a concrete pier, from where you can walk or take the miniature train (₹10) to the stairway (admission ₹10) leading up to the caves. It's lined with souvenir stalls and patrolled by pesky monkeys. Wear good shoes.

Activities

Mumbai has surprisingly good butterfly- and birdwatching opportunities. Sanjay Gandhi National Park (p743) is popular for woodland birds, while the mangroves of Godrej (13km east of Bandra) are rich in waders. The **Bombay Natural History Society** (BNHS; Map p740; ☎022-22821811; www.bnhs.org; Hornbill House, Shahid Bhagat Singh Marg; ⏲9am-5.30pm Mon-Fri) runs excellent trips every weekend. The mudflats viewable from the Sewri Jetty (p751) also receive thousands of migratory pink flamingos from November to March.

Outbound Adventure OUTDOORS
(☎9820195115; www.outboundadventure.com) Runs one-day rafting trips on the Ulhas River from July to early September (₹2300 per person). After a good rain, rapids can get up to Grade III+, though the rafting is calmer. Also organises guided nature walks, birdwatching, camping (from ₹2000 per person per day) and canoeing trips in the Western Ghats.

Yogacara YOGA, MASSAGE
(Map p750; ☎022-26511464; www.yogacara.in; 1st fl, SBI Bldg, 18A New Kant Wadi Rd, Bandra West; ⏲yoga per class/week ₹650/1600) Classic ha-

Western Suburbs

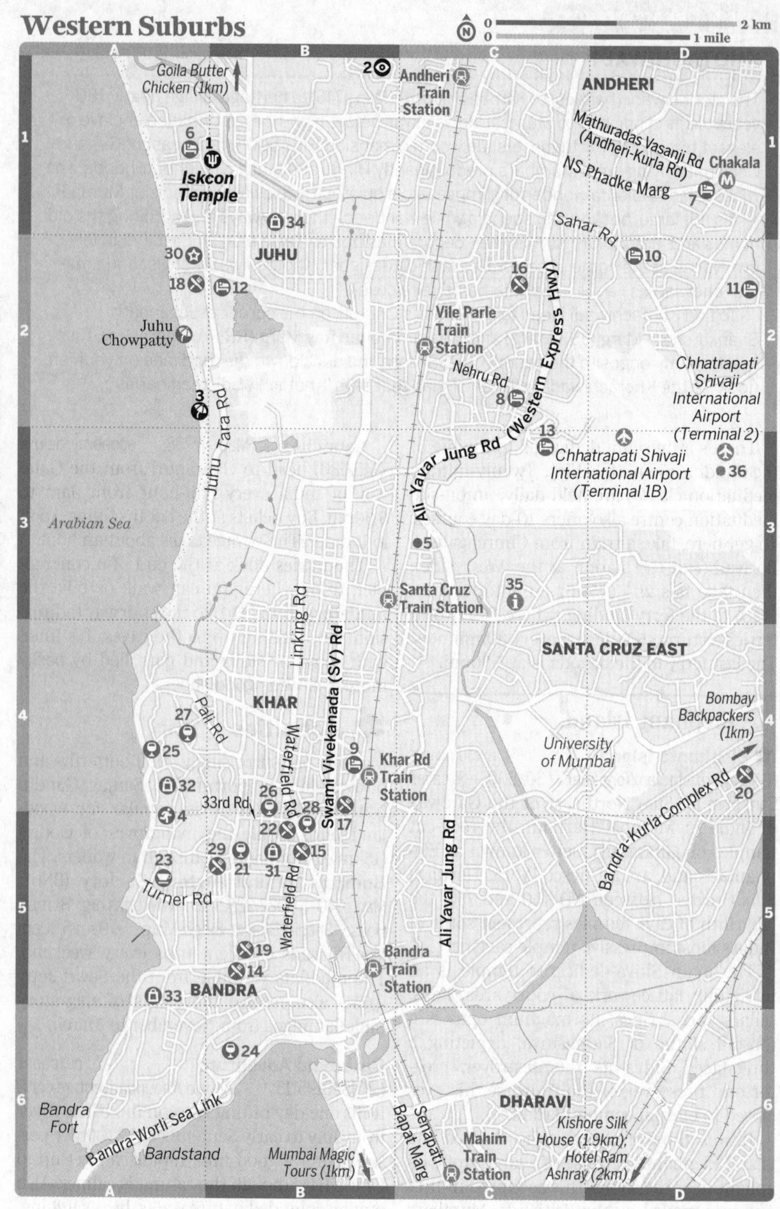

tha and iyengar yoga institute, with excellent massages (from ₹1850 per hour) and treatments; the Abhyangam rejuvenating massage is recommended. Ayurvedic cooking, meditation and Chakra healing classes are also offered sporadically.

Yoga House YOGA

(Map p750; ☎022-65545001; www.yogahouse.in; Nargis Villa/Water Bungalow Sherly Rajan Rd, Bandra West; class ₹700; ⊙8am-9.30pm Tue-Sun) A variety of yoga traditions are taught at this homey, traditional-style yoga centre. There's

Western Suburbs

Top Sights
1 Iskcon Temple B1

Sights
2 Gilbert Hill B1
3 Juhu Beach A2

Activities, Courses & Tours
4 Yoga House A5
5 Yoga Institute C3
Yogacara .... (see 23)

Sleeping
6 Anand Hotel A1
7 Backpacker Panda D1
8 Hotel Columbus C2
9 Hotel Regal Enclave B4
10 Hotel Suba International D2
Iskcon .... (see 1)
11 ITC Maratha D2
12 Juhu Residency B2
13 Taj Santacruz C3

Eating
14 Basilico B5
15 Bastian B5
Dakshinayan .... (see 6)
16 Gajelee C2
17 Khar Social B4
Kitchen Garden by Suzette .... (see 21)
18 Mahesh Lunch Home A2
19 Mamagoto B5
20 Masala Library D4
Peshawri .... (see 11)
Prithvi Cafe .... (see 30)
Raaj Bhog .... (see 9)
21 Suzette B5
22 Theobroma B5
Yoga House .... (see 4)

Drinking & Nightlife
23 Bad Cafe A5
24 Doolally Taproom B6
25 Masala Bar A4
26 Monkey Bar B4
27 Olive Bar & Kitchen A4
28 One Street Over B5
29 Toto's Garage B5

Entertainment
30 Prithvi Theatre A2

Shopping
31 Bombay Shirt Company B5
32 Indian Hippy A4
33 Kulture Shop A5
34 Shrujan B1

Information
35 Humsafar Trust C3

Transport
36 GoAir D3
IndiGo .... (see 36)
SpiceJet .... (see 36)
Vistara .... (see 36)

also a charming cafe (p760) on the 3rd floor of the bright-green colonial-style bungalow.

Sewri Jetty BIRDWATCHING
(Sewri) This jetty about 5km east of Lower Parel is an ideal place for gawking at thousands of migratory pink flamingos that come from as far away as Siberia between November and March. The birds descend on the surrounding mudflats to forage for sustenance. The best time to visit is between 6am and 10am.

Enquire at Bombay Natural History Society (p749) for trips here. Or come on your own by taking a taxi from Sewri station on the Harbour Railway line from CST.

Palms Spa SPA
(Map p738; 022-66349898; www.thepalmsspaindia.com; Dhanraj Mahal, Chhatrapati Shivaji Marg, Colaba; 1hr massage from ₹3200; 10am-10pm) Indulge in a rub, scrub or tub at this renowned Colaba spa. The exfoliating lemongrass and green-tea scrub is ₹2500.

Courses

★Yoga Institute YOGA, HEALTH & WELLBEING
(Map p750; 022-26122185; www.theyogainstitute.org; Shri Yogendra Marg, Prabhat Colony, Santa Cruz East; per 1st/2nd month ₹700/500) At its peaceful leafy campus, the respected Yoga Institute has daily classes as well as weekend and weeklong programs, and longer residential courses including teacher training (with the seven-day course a prerequisite).

★Bharatiya Vidya Bhavan LANGUAGE, MUSIC
(Map p746; 022-23631261; www.bhavans.info; 2nd fl, cnr KM Munshi Marg & Ramabai Rd, Girgaum; language per hr ₹500, music per month ₹900; 4-8pm) Excellent private Hindi, Marathi, Gujarati and Sanskrit language classes. Contact Professor Ghosh (a Grammy Award–winning composer and musician) for lessons in tabla, vocals, sitar or classical dance.

Kaivalyadhama Ishwardas Yogic Health Centre HEALTH & WELLBEING
(Map p746; 022-22818417; www.yogcenter.com; 43 Netaji Subhash Rd, Marine Dr; 6am-7pm

Mon-Sat) Several daily yoga classes as well as workshops; fees include a ₹1000 monthly membership fee and a ₹700 admission fee. A four-month teaching certification course is ₹20,000.

Tours

Fiona Fernandez' *Ten Heritage Walks of Mumbai* (₹395) has walking tours of the city, with fascinating historical background. The Government of India tourist office can provide a list of approved multilingual guides; official prices are ₹1368/1734 per half/full day for up to five people.

★Reality Tours & Travel TOURS
(Map p740; ☎9820822253; www.realitytoursandtravel.com; 1/26 Unique Business Service Centre, Akber House, Nowroji Fardonji Rd; most tours ₹750-1700; ⏲8am-9pm) Compelling tours of the Dharavi slum, with 80% of post-tax profits going to the agency's own NGO, Reality Gives (www.realitygives.org). Street food, market, bicycle and Night Mumbai tours are also excellent.

New offerings further afield include socially responsible multiday tours of South India, the Golden Triangle and Rajasthan, including community visits.

Bombay Heritage Walks WALKING
(☎9821887321; www.bombayheritagewalks.com; per 2hr tour (up to 5 people) from ₹3750) Started by two enthusiastic architects and operating with a slew of colleagues and art historians, BHW has terrific tours of heritage neighbourhoods.

Mumbai Magic Tours TOURS
(☎9867707414; www.mumbaimagic.com; 5 Bhaskar Mansion, Sitladevi Temple Rd; 2hr tour per 2/4 people from ₹1750/1500; ⏲10am-5pm Mon-Fri, to 2pm Sat) Designed by the authors of the fabulous blog Mumbai Magic (www.mumbai-magic.blogspot.com), these city tours focus on Mumbai's quirks, culture, community, food, bazaars, festivals, Jewish heritage and more.

MTDC/Nilambari Bus Tours BUS
(MTDC; ☎020-22845678; www.maharashtratourism.gov.in; 1hr tour lower/upper deck ₹60/180; ⏲7pm & 8.15pm Sat & Sun) Nilambari in partnership with Maharashtra Tourism runs open-deck bus tours of illuminated heritage buildings on weekends. Buses depart from and can be booked at both the MTDC booth (p768) and the MTDC office (p768). Cash only.

Sleeping

Mumbai has the most expensive accommodation in India and you'll never quite feel like you're getting your money's worth.

Colaba is compact, has the liveliest tourist scene and many budget and midrange options. The neighbouring Fort area is convenient for the main train stations and is a dining and shopping epicentre. Most top-end places are along Marine Dr and in the western suburbs.

No matter where you stay, always book ahead.

Colaba

★Sea Shore Hotel GUESTHOUSE $
(Map p738; ☎022-22874237; 4th fl, 1-49 Kamal Mansion, Arthur Bunder Rd; s/d without bathroom ₹700/1100; wi-fi) This place is really making an effort, with small but immaculately clean and inviting rooms, all with flat-screen TVs, set off a railway-carriage-style corridor. Half the rooms even have harbour views (the others don't have a window). The modish communal bathrooms are well scrubbed and have a little gleam and sparkle. Wi-fi in the reception and *some* rooms.

Bentley's Hotel HOTEL $
(Map p738; ☎022-22841474; www.bentleyshotel.com; 17 Oliver Rd; r incl breakfast ₹2350-3150; air-con wi-fi) A welcoming Parsi-owned place in the heart of Colaba that travellers either love or hate depending on which of the five apartment buildings they end up in. First choice are the spacious, colonial-style rooms in the main building (snag 31 or 39 for generous balconies); avoid Henry Rd and JA Allana Marg. Air-conditioning is ₹350 extra. Cash only.

★YWCA GUESTHOUSE $$
(Map p738; ☎022-22025053; www.ywcaic.info; 18 Madame Cama Rd; s/d/tr with AC incl breakfast & dinner ₹2450/3720/5560; air-con @ wi-fi) Efficiently managed, and within walking distance of all the sights in Colaba and Fort, the YMCA is a good deal and justifiably popular. The spacious, well-maintained rooms boast desks and wardrobes and multi-chanelled TVs (wi-fi is best from the lobby). Tariffs include a buffet breakfast, dinner and a daily newspaper. In addition to the room rates there's a one-time ₹50 membership fee.

Hotel Moti GUESTHOUSE $$
(Map p738; ☎9920518228; hotelmotiinternational@yahoo.co.in; 10 Best Marg; d/tr with fan

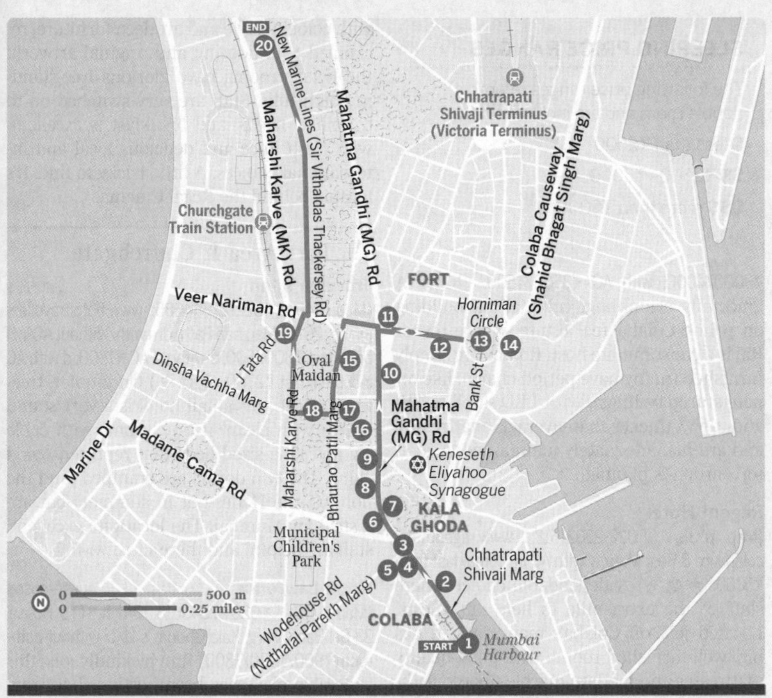

City Walk
Architectural Mumbai

START GATEWAY OF INDIA
END LIBERTY CINEMA
LENGTH 3.5KM; 1¾ HOURS

Mumbai's defining feature is its distinctive mix of colonial-era and art deco architecture. Starting from the 1 **Gateway of India** (p738), walk up Chhatrapati Shivaji Marg past the art deco residential-commercial complex 2 **Dhunraj Mahal**, towards 3 **Regal Circle**. Walk the circle for views of the surrounding buildings – including the art deco 4 **Regal Cinema** (p764) and the 5 **Majestic Hotel**, now the Sahakari Bhandar cooperative store. Continue up Mahatma Gandhi (MG) Rd, past the beautifully restored facade of the 6 **National Gallery of Modern Art** (p743). Opposite is the landmark 7 **Chhatrapati Shivaji Maharaj Vastu Sangrahalaya** (p742), built in glorious Indo-Saracenic style. Back across the road is the 'Romanesque Transitional' 8 **Elphinstone College** and the 9 **David Sassoon Library & Reading Room**, where members escape the afternoon heat lazing on planters' chairs on the upper balcony.

Continue north to admire the vertical art deco stylings of the 10 **New India Assurance Company Building**. On an island ahead lies 11 **Flora Fountain**, depicting the Roman goddess of flowers. Turn east down Veer Nariman Rd, walking towards 12 **St Thomas' Cathedral** (p744). Ahead lies the stately 13 **Horniman Circle**, an arcaded ring of buildings laid out in the 1860s around a beautifully kept botanical garden. It's overlooked from the east by the neoclassical 14 **Town Hall**, home to the Asiatic Society library. Backtrack to Flora Fountain, turning south onto Bhaurao Patil Marg to see the august 15 **High Court** (p743) and the ornate 16 **University of Mumbai** (p743). Unfortunately, the university's 84m-high 17 **Rajabai Clock Tower** (p743) is off-limits for visitors, but is best observed from within the 18 **Oval Maidan**. Turn around to compare the colonial edifices with the row of art deco beauties lining Maharshi Karve (MK) Rd – most notably the wedding cake tower of the 19 **Eros cinema** (p764).

Wrap things up by heading 1km north to the 20 **Liberty Cinema** (p764), a dazzling, 1200-capacity single-screen art deco gem.

SLEEPING PRICE RANGES

The following price ranges refer to a double room and are inclusive of tax.

$ less than ₹2500

$$ ₹2500–₹6000

$$$ more than ₹6000

₹3000/4000, with AC ₹3500/4500;) A gracefully crumbling, colonial-era building on prime Colaba real estate, where owner Raj is a consummate host. Rooms are simply furnished (many have period charm, like ornate stucco ceilings), with LED satellite TVs and new, thicker-than-average mattresses, and are *just* adequately maintained. A rooftop garden is planned.

Regent Hotel HOTEL **$$**
(Map p738; 022-22021518; www.regenthotelcolaba.in; 8 Best Marg; r with AC incl breakfast from ₹5360;) A dependable choice where staff go the extra mile to help out guests. Located just off Colaba's main drag, it has big, well-furnished rooms with good-quality mattresses and modern marble-floored bathrooms. Falconry art and Gulf state flags hint at its most popular clientele.

★**Taj Mahal Palace, Mumbai** HERITAGE HOTEL **$$$**
(Map p738; 022-66653366; https://taj.tajhotels.com; Apollo Bunder; s/d tower from ₹16,000/17,500, palace from ₹21,000/22,500;) The grande dame of Mumbai is one of the world's most iconic hotels and has hosted a roster of presidents and royalty. Sweeping arches, staircases and domes, and a glorious garden and pool ensure an unforgettable stay. Rooms in the adjacent tower lack the period details of the palace itself, but many have spectacular, full-frontal Gateway of India views.

With a myriad of excellent in-house eating and drinking options, plus spa and leisure facilities, it can be a wrench to leave the hotel premises. There's even a new (small but discernibly curated) art gallery. Heritage walks for guests at 5pm daily provide illuminating context about the hotel's role in the city's history.

★**Abode Bombay** BOUTIQUE HOTEL **$$$**
(Map p738; 8080234066; www.abodeboutiquehotels.com; 1st fl, Lansdowne House, MB Marg; r with AC incl breakfast ₹4760-16,000;) A terrific 20-room boutique hotel, stylishly designed with colonial-style and art deco furniture, reclaimed teak flooring and original artwork; the luxury rooms have glorious free-standing bath tubs. Staff are very switched on to travellers' needs, and breakfast is excellent, with fresh juice and delicious local and international choices. A little tricky to find, it's located behind the Regal Cinema.

Fort Area & Churchgate

Traveller's Inn HOTEL **$**
(Map p740; 022-22644685; www.hoteltravellersinn.co; 26 Adi Marzban Path; dm with/without AC incl breakfast ₹800/600, d without AC ₹1800, d with AC incl breakfast ₹2300;) On a quiet, tree-lined street, this small hotel is a very sound choice with clean, if tiny, rooms with cable TV and king-sized beds that represent good value. The two dorms are cramped (and the non-AC one Hades-hot in summer) but are a steal for Mumbai. The location's excellent, staff are helpful and there's free wi-fi.

Hotel Lawrence GUESTHOUSE **$**
(Map p740; 022-22843618; 3rd fl, ITTS House, 33 Sai Baba Marg, Kala Ghoda; s/d/tr without bathroom ₹900/1000/1800) Run by kindly folk, this venerable place has been hosting shoestring travellers for years. Rooms are certainly basic but kept pretty tidy, as are the communal bathrooms. It boasts an excellent Kala Ghoda location, on a quiet little lane accessed by a ramshackle old lift. No breakfast or wi-fi.

★**Residency Hotel** HOTEL **$$**
(Map p740; 022-22625525; www.residencyhotel.com; 26 Rustom Sidhwa Marg; s/d with AC incl breakfast from ₹4640/5120;) The Residency is the kind of dependable place where you can breathe a sigh of relief after a long journey and be certain you'll be looked after well. It's fine value too, with contemporary rooms, some boasting mood lighting, mini-bars, flat-screens and hip en suite bathrooms. Best of all, staff are friendly, polite and understand the nuance of unforced hospitality.

Its Fort location is also excellent. The best-run midranger in Mumbai.

Welcome Hotel HOTEL **$$**
(Map p740; 022-66314488; www.welcomehotel.co.in; 257 Shahid Bhagat Singh Marg; s/d incl breakfast from ₹3330/3870, without bathroom from ₹1900/2080;) Service is a little hit and miss and the hallways are dark but the simple rooms here are spacious and comfortable, and shared bathrooms are well

kept. Top-floor executive rooms are more boutique than midrange.

Western & Northern Suburbs

Backpacker Panda HOSTEL $

(Map p750; 022-28367141; www.backpackerpanda.com; Shaheed Bhagat Singh Society, Andheri East; dm with AC ₹900-950;) Mumbai's first vaguely hostel-like backpackers features a rather makeshift lobby (improvised palette-supported lounges, for example) but the six- and eight-bed dorms are cool, clean and climate-controlled (though cramped). There's a tiny kitchen and outdoor patio and it sits next to Chakala Metro (which connects with the main train line at Andheri), 10 minutes by taxi from both of Mumbai's airports.

Bombay Backpackers HOSTEL $

(9096162246; 1 Uttam Jeevan, LBS Rd, Kurla West; dm ₹1000;) In an oddly east (but lively) location at Mumbai's BKC business district, this artsy backpackers is another welcome newcomer to a previously nonexistent scene. Sturdy six- and eight-bed teak-like dorm beds in some cases come triple-stacked, and there's a colourful kitchen. It's just a few minutes' walk from Kurla Junction and a five-minute rickshaw ride to Bandra.

★ **Juhu Residency** BOUTIQUE HOTEL $$

(Map p750; 022-67834949; www.juhuresidency.com; 148B Juhu Tara Rd, Juhu; s/d with AC incl breakfast from ₹6250;) The aroma of sweet lemongrass greets you in the lobby at this excellent boutique hotel with an inviting atmosphere (and a fine location, five minutes' walk from Juhu beach). The chocolate-and-coffee colour scheme in the modish rooms works well, each room boasting marble floors, dark woods, artful bedspreads and flat-screen TVs. There are three restaurants – good ones – for just 18 rooms.

To top it all off, free airport pick-ups are included.

Iskcon GUESTHOUSE $$

(Map p750; 022-26206860; www.iskconmumbai.com/guest-house; Juhu Church Rd, Juhu; r from ₹3000, with AC ₹4000;) An intriguing place to stay inside Juhu's lively Iskcon complex. Though the hotel building is a slightly soulless concrete block, some rooms enjoy vistas over the Hare Krishna temple compound. Spartan decor is offset by the odd decorative flourish such as Gujarati *sankheda* (lacquered country wood) furniture, and staff are very welcoming.

Anand Hotel HOTEL $$

(Map p750; 022-26203372; anandhote@yahoo.co.in; Gandhigram Rd, Juhu; s/d with AC from ₹2620/4170;) Yes, the decor's in 50 shades of beige but the Anand's rooms are comfortable, spacious and represent decent value, considering the prime location on a quiet street next to Juhu beach. The excellent in-house Dakshinayan restaurant (p760) scores highly for authentic, inexpensive meals too. It's a particularly good deal for solo travellers.

Hotel Columbus HOTEL $$

(Map p750; 022-42144343; www.hotelcolumbus.in; 344 Nanda Patkar Rd, Vile Parle East; s/d with AC incl breakfast from ₹4170/4700;) Rooms at the best midrange option in the domestic airport area aren't new – they're a little scuffed up – but are very homey. Staff are helpful and willing to solve issues. Just 900m away is the local's secret seafooder **Gajelee** (Map p750; 022-26166470; www.gajalee.com; Kadamgiri Complex, Hanuman Rd, Vile Parle East; mains ₹275-875; 11.30am-3.30pm & 7-11.30pm).

★ **ITC Maratha** HOTEL $$$

(Map p750; 022-28303030; www.itchotels.in; Sahar Rd, Andheri East; s/d incl breakfast from ₹21,450/23,240;) The five-star hotel with the most luxurious local character – from the Muhammed Ali Rd–inspired *jharokas* (lattice windows) around the atrium to the Maratha-influenced Resident's Bar (a guest-only level overlooking public areas), the details are extraordinary. The rooms, awash in lush colour schemes, exude Indian opulence. Peshawri (p760), Mumbai's most memorable Northwest Frontier restaurant, is located here.

★ **Taj Santacruz** BOUTIQUE HOTEL $$$

(Map p750; 022-62115211; https://taj.tajhotels.com/en-in/taj-santacruz-mumbai; Chhatrapati Shivaji International Airport (Domestic Terminal); s/d from ₹14,500/16,500;) Forget the 3500 hand-blown chandelier bulbs or the 75-species aquarium in the lobby of this recently opened hotel connected to the domestic airport terminal – at the lap-of-luxury Taj Santacruz it's all about the gorgeous Tree of Life art installation forged from 4000 pieces of broken glass (a Rajasthani technique) in the Tiqri bar and restaurant.

The standard rooms, decked out in soothing yellow, fuchsia and orange, are the city's largest at nearly 54 sq metres (some have direct runway views). If you cannot stay here, visit on a layover for a massage at Jiva Spa (from ₹4600) or a cocktail.

THE PARSIS

Mumbai is home to the world's largest surviving community of Parsis, people of the ancient Zoroastrian faith, who fled Iran in the 10th century to escape religious persecution by the new Muslim rulers of Persia. 'Parsi' literally means Perisan. Zoroastrians believe in a single deity, Ahura Mazda, who is worshipped at *agiaries* (fire temples) across Mumbai, which non-Parsis are forbidden to enter. Parsi funeral rites are unique: the dead are laid out on open-air platforms to be picked over by vultures. The most renowned of these, the **Tower of Silence**, is located below the Hanging Gardens in Malabar Hill, yet screened by trees and hidden from public view.

The Mumbai Parsi community is extremely influential and successful, with a 98.6% literacy rate (the highest in the city). Famous Parsis include the Tata family (India's foremost industrialists), author Rohinton Mistry and Freddie Mercury. The best way for travellers to dig into the culture is by visiting one of the city's Parsi cafes. These atmospheric time capsules of a bygone era are a dying breed, but several sail on, including the excellent Brittania restaurant, **Kyaani and Co** (Map p746; Ratan Heights, Dr DB Rd; snacks ₹15-120; ⏲7am-8.30pm Mon-Sat, to 6pm Sun) and tourist hotbed Cafe Mondegar.

Hotel Regal Enclave HOTEL **$$$**
(Map p750; ☎022-67261111; www.regalenclave.com; 4th Rd, Khar West; r with AC incl breakfast from ₹7740; ❄📶) Hotel Regal Enclave enjoys a stellar location in an exceedingly leafy part of Khar, right near the station (some rooms have railway views) and close to all of Bandra's best eating, drinking and shopping. Rooms are spacious and comfortable – save the tight bathrooms – with pleasant if unoriginal decor. Rates include airport pick-up.

Hotel Suba International BOUTIQUE HOTEL **$$$**
(Map p750; ☎022-67076707; www.hotelsubainternational.com; Sahar Rd, Andheri East; s/d with AC incl breakfast from ₹7600/8700; ❄📶) A 72-room 'boutique business' hotel that's very close to the international airport (free transfers included) and boasts rooms with stylish touches, iPads and a wee bit of chipped paint.

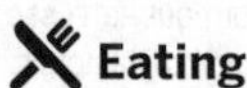

Eating

Flavours from all over India collide with international trends and taste buds in Mumbai. Colaba has most of the cheap tourist haunts, while Fort and Churchgate are more upscale, a trend that continues in Mahalaxmi and the western suburbs, where you'll find Mumbai's most international and expensive restaurants.

Subscribe to **Brown Paper Bag** (http://brownpaperbag.in/mumbai) for daily news on the latest and hottest dining destinations.

Colaba

★Bademiya Seekh Kebab Stall MUGHLAI, FAST FOOD **$**
(Map p738; www.bademiya.com; Tulloch Rd; light meals ₹110-220; ⏲5pm-4am) These side-by-side, outrageously popular late-night street stalls (split between veg and nonveg) are in Bademiya's original location, where they remain a key Colaba hang-out for their trademark buzz and bustle and delicious meat-heavy menu. Expect spicy, fresh-grilled kebabs and tikka rolls hot off the grill. They also have sit-down restaurants in **Colaba** (Map p738; 19A Ram Mention, Nawroji Furdunji St; meals ₹150-290; ⏲1pm-2am) and **Fort** (Map p740; ☎022-22655657; Botawala Bldg, Horniman Circle; mains ₹190-410; ⏲11.30am-1.30am).

Olympia MUGHLAI **$**
(Map p738; Rahim Mansion, 1 Shahid Bhagat Singh Marg; meals ₹80-140; ⏲7am-11.45pm) This old-school Mughlai cheapie does a recommended *masala kheema* (spicy minced meat; ₹50) for breakfast – scoop it up with some roti. A simple place renowned for its pocket-friendly meat dishes; the *seekh* kebab (₹160) and chicken butter fry masala (₹90) are also great.

Theobroma CAFE **$$**
(Map p738; www.theobroma.in; 24 Cusrow Baug, Shahid Bhagat Singh Marg; confections ₹60-190, light meals ₹180-200; ⏲7am-11pm) Perfectly executed cakes, tarts and brownies go well with the coffee at this staple Mumbai patisserie. The pastries change regularly; if you're lucky, you'll find popular decadence like the chocolate opium pastry, but it's all great. For brunch have the *akoori* – Parsi-style scrambled eggs – with green mango. The **Bandra branch** (Map p750; 33rd Rd, near Linking Rd, Bandra West; confections ₹60-190; ⏲8am-midnight) is big and airy, though with a smaller menu.

★Indigo FUSION, CONTINENTAL $$$
(Map p738; ☎022-66368980; www.foodindigo.com; 4 Mandlik Marg; mains ₹885-2185; ⊙noon-3pm & 7-11.45pm;) This incredibly classy Colaba institution is a colonial-era property converted into a temple of fine dining. It serves inventive, expensive European and Asian cuisine and offers a long wine list, sleek ambience and a gorgeous rooftop deck. Favourites include creamed pumpkin and sage ravioli and maple orange-glazed duck breast – if you can pass on mac and cheese lasagne, that is!

Reserve ahead.

Indigo Delicatessen CAFE $$$
(Map p738; www.indigodeli.com; Pheroze Bldg, Chhatrapati Shivaji Marg; sandwiches/mains from ₹625/645; ⊙8.30am-midnight;) A bustling and fashionable cafe-restaurant with cool tunes and massive wooden tables. The menu includes all-day breakfasts (₹399 to ₹725) and straightforward international classics like pork ribs, thin-crust pizza and inventive sandwiches. It's always busy so service can get stretched.

Table FUSION $$$
(Map p738; ☎022-22825000; www.thetable.in; Kalapesi Trust Bldg, Apollo Bunder Marg; small plates ₹405-1075, mains ₹825-1375; ⊙noon-4pm & 7pm-1am, tea 4.30-6.30pm;) San Francisco chef Alex Sanchez is all the rage in Colaba, where his market-fresh, globally inspired fusion menu changes daily and does everything in its power to satisfy your cravings for a curry-free evening out. There's a lot to love: a crunchy kale salad with Iranian dates and toasted pistachios, zucchini spaghetti with almonds and Parmesan and house-made black truffle taglierini.

Basilico MEDITERRANEAN $$$
(Map p738; ☎022-66345670; www.cafebasilico.com; Sentinel House, Arthur Bunder Rd; mains ₹320-950; ⊙9am-12.30am;) Euro-style Basilico does decadent sweets and especially creative fare when it comes to vegans and vegetarians. There are exquisite salads (from ₹320) like quinoa, organic avocado and papaya, and numerous other interesting options like veg Moroccan tagines. It draws a top-end Indian crowd. If you can walk past that crunchy chocolate cake without biting, you're better than us.

The Bandra **branch** (Map p750; St John Rd, Pali Naka, Bandra West; mains ₹320-950; ⊙9am-midnight;) has outdoor seating.

Self-Catering

Colaba Market MARKET $
(Map p738; Lala Nigam St; ⊙7am-11pm) A colourful and atmospheric fresh fruit and vegetables street market.

Star Daily SUPERMARKET $
(Map p738; www.starbazaarindia.com; Sanghvi House, 3rd Pasta Lane, Colaba; ⊙10am-9.30pm) This new Tata/Tesco initiative is easily Colaba's best supermarket for self-caterers. It's an air-con, Western-style affair with all your daily needs, including fresh produce.

Fort Area & Churchgate

K Rustom SWEETS $
(Map p740; 87 Stadium House, Veer Nariman Rd, Churchgate; desserts ₹30-80; ⊙9.30am-11pm Mon-Sat, 3-11pm Sun) K Rustom has nothing but a few metal freezers, but the ice-cream sandwiches (pick from 48 flavours) here have been pleasing Mumbaikar palettes since 1953.

STREET EATS

Mumbai's street cuisine is vaster than many Western culinary traditions. Stalls tend to get started in late afternoon, when chai complements much of the fried deliciousness; items are ₹10 to ₹80.

Most street food is vegetarian. Chowpatty Beach is a great place to try Mumbai's famous *bhelpuri* (puffed rice tossed with fried rounds of dough, lentils, onions, herbs and chutneys). Stalls offering samosas, *pav bhaji* (spiced vegetables and bread), *vada pav* (deep-fried spiced lentil-ball sandwich), *bhurji pav* (scrambled eggs and bread) and *dabeli* (a mixture of potatoes, spices, peanuts and pomegranate, also on bread) are spread through the city.

For a meaty meal, Mohammed Ali and Merchant Rds in Kalbadevi are famous for kebabs. In Colaba, Bademiya Seekh Kebab Stall is a late-night Mumbai rite of passage, renowned for its chicken tikka rolls.

The office workers' district on the north side of Kala Ghoda is another good hunting ground for street snacks.

Badshah Snacks & Drinks INDIAN $

(Map p746; 52/156 Umrigar Bldg, Lokmanya Tilak Marg; snacks & drinks ₹55-240; ⏲7am-12.30am) Opposite Crawford Market, Badshah has been serving snacks, fruit juices and its famous *falooda* (rose-flavoured drink made with milk, cream, nuts and vermicelli), *kulfi falooda* (with ice cream) and *kesar pista falooda* (with saffron and pistachios) to hungry bargain-hunters for more than 100 years.

★ **La Folie** CAFE $$

(Map p740; www.lafolie.in; 16 Commerce House, Kala Ghoda; cakes ₹260; ⏲noon-11pm) Chocoholics and cake fetishistas look no further – this minuscule Kala Ghoda place will seduce and hook you. Owner Sanjana Patel spent seven years in France studying the art (addiction?) of pastry- and chocolate-making, which was obviously time well spent. Try the delectable Madagascar cake (chocolate with raspberry mousse) or the Infinite Caramel (salted caramel and hazelnut) with a latte (₹150).

★ **Samrat** GUJARATI $$

(Map p740; www.prashantcaterers.com; Prem Ct, J Tata Rd; thali lunch/dinner ₹330/415; ⏲noon-11pm; ❄) Samrat has an à la carte menu but most rightly opt for the famous Gujarati thali – a cavalcade of taste and texture, sweetness and spice that includes four curries, three chutneys, curd, rotis and other bits and pieces. Samrat is air-conditioned and beer is available.

A Taste of Kerala KERALAN $$

(Map p740; Prospect Chambers Annex, Pitha St, Fort; mains ₹96-250, thali from ₹170; ⏲9am-midnight) An inexpensive Keralan eatery with lots of coconut and southern goodness on the menu; try one of the epic thalis (served on a banana leaf) or the seafood specials like prawn pepper masala. Don't skip the *payasam* (rice pudding with jaggery and coconut milk) for dessert. Staff are very welcoming, and there's an air-conditioned dining room.

Brittania PARSI $$

(Map p740; Wakefield House, Ballard Estate; mains ₹250-900; ⏲noon-4pm Mon-Sat) This Parsi institution is the domain of 95-year-old Boman Kohinoor, who will warm your heart with his stories (and he still takes the orders!). The signature dishes are the *dhansak* (meat with curried lentils and rice) and the berry *pulao* – spiced and boneless mutton or chicken, veg or egg, buried in basmati rice and tart barberries imported from Iran.

Cash only.

Oye Kake NORTH INDIAN $$

(Map p740; 13C Cawasji Patel Rd; mains ₹209-289; ⏲11am-4pm & 7-11pm) An intimate all-veg Punjabi place where the daily thali (₹219) is wildly popular with local office workers and renowned for its authenticity. Signature dishes include the paneer tikka masala, *sarson da saag* (mustard leaf curry; seasonal from December to February) and *parathas* (flaky flatbread); lassis are excellent too. Prepare to wait for a table.

Pantry CAFE $$

(Map p740; www.thepantry.in; ground fl, Yashwanth Chambers, Military Square Lane, B Bharucha Marg, Kala Ghoda; breakfast/meals from ₹195/275; ⏲8.30am-11pm; 📶) 🌿 Pantry is a bakery-cafe that offers a choice of fine pies and organic breads, soups and sandwiches (the gourmet cheese toastie is exceptional) plus delicious mains. Cold-brew coffee, too. Breakfasts are legendary: try the scrambled eggs with tomato, gruyère and local ham, or some organic-flour waffles with fruit. The elegantly restored historic building channels a Martha Stewart vibe.

Shree Thakkar Bhojnalaya INDIAN $$

(Map p746; 31 Dadisheth Agyari Lane, Marine Lines; thali ₹500; ⏲11.30am-3pm & 7-10.30pm Mon-Sat, 11.30am-3.30pm Sun) With a cult following and festive lavender tables to boot, this thali mainstay, one of the oldest in the city, puts on the full-court flavour press with their never-ending Gujarati/Rajasthani set meals, full of *farsans* (bite-size snacks) and scrumptious veg curries. The air-con environs are a welcome retreat from the busy congestion below. They've been at it since 1945.

Suzette FRENCH $$

(Map p740; www.suzette.in; Atlanta Bldg, Vinayak K Shah Marg, Nariman Point; meals ₹300-450; ⏲9am-11pm Mon-Sat; 📶) 🌿 Relaxed Parisian-style place steeped where possible in organically sourced ingredients. Delectable crêpes, croques, salads, juices and soothing lounge music attract flocks of foreigners in need of a curry recess. On the crêpe front, sweet tooths should try the organic jaggery; for a savoury flavour, order a croque feta (with tomato, mozzarella, creamed spinach and feta).

The **Bandra branch** (Map p750; St John St, Pali Naka, Bandra West; mains ₹220-560; ⏲9am-11pm) 🌿 has outdoor seating and is open daily.

Kala Ghoda Café CAFE $$

(Map p740; www.kgcafe.in; 10 Ropewalk Lane, Kala Ghoda; mains ₹170-530; ⏲8.30am-11.45pm Mon-Fri, from 8am Sat & Sun; 📶) 🌿 Once tiny, this

DABBA-WALLAHS

A small miracle of logistics, Mumbai's 5000 *dabba-wallahs* (literally 'food container person'; also called tiffin-wallahs) work tirelessly to deliver hot lunches to office workers throughout the city (and to the poor later on in the evenings, a 2015 initiative).

Lunch boxes are picked up each day from restaurants and homes and carried on heads, bicycles and trains to a centralised sorting station. A sophisticated system of numbers and colours (many wallahs don't read) identifies the destination of each lunch. More than 200,000 meals are delivered – always on time, come (monsoon) rain or (searing) shine.

This system has been used for over a century and there's only about one mistake per six million deliveries. (In a 2002 analysis, *Forbes Magazine* found that the *dabba-wallahs* had a six-sigma, or 99.999999%, reliability rating.) The system was also the subject of a Harvard Business School study in 2010.

Look for these master messengers mid-morning at Churchgate and CST stations.

boho cafe was expanded in 2016 with the addition of a vintage Mumbai backroom, and now turns away fewer of its artsy and creative fanbase. It serves organic coffee and tea, sandwiches, salads and breakfasts, and there's usually some interesting art or photography on the walls.

★Burma Burma BURMESE **$$$**

(Map p740; ☎022-40036600; www.burmaburma.in; Oak Lane, off Mahatma Gandhi Rd; meals ₹330-500; ⏰noon-2.45pm & 7-11pm; 📶) A sleek, stylish restaurant that marries contemporary design with a few traditional artefacts (prayer wheels line one wall), providing a beautiful setting for the cuisine of Myanmar (Burma). The menu is well priced, intricate and ambitious, with inventive salads (the pickled tea leaf is extraordinary), curries and soups: *Oh No Khow Suey* is a glorious coconut-enriched noodle broth. No alcohol.

★Khyber MUGHLAI, INDIAN **$$$**

(Map p740; ☎022-40396666; www.khyberrestaurant.com; 145 Mahatma Gandhi Rd; mains ₹510-1100; ⏰12.30-4pm & 7.30-11.30pm) The much-acclaimed Khyber has a Northwest Frontier–themed design that incorporates murals depicting turbaned Mughal royalty, lots of exposed brickwork and oil lanterns – just the sort of place an Afghan warlord might feel at home. The meat-centric menu features gloriously tender kebabs, rich curries and lots of tandoori favourites roasted in the Khyber's famous red masala sauce.

Mahesh Lunch Home SEAFOOD **$$$**

(Map p740; ☎022-22023965; www.maheshlunchhome.com; 8B Cowasji Patel St, Fort; mains ₹230-640; ⏰11.30am-4pm & 6-11pm) A great place to try Mangalorean or Chinese-style seafood in Mumbai. It's renowned for its ladyfish, pomfret, lobster, crab (try it with butter garlic pepper sauce) and anything else out of the sea.

There's also a bigger Juhu **branch** (Map p750; ☎022-66955554; Juhu Tara Rd; mains ₹350-975; ⏰12-3.30pm & 7pm-12.30am; 📶) with an extended menu.

Trishna SEAFOOD **$$$**

(Map p740; ☎022-22703214; www.trishna.co.in; Ropewalk Lane, Kala Ghoda; mains ₹400-1800; ⏰noon-3.30pm & 6.15pm-midnight Mon-Sat, noon-3.30pm & 7pm-midnight Sun) Behind a modest entrance on a quiet Kala Ghoda lane is this often-lauded, intimate South Indian seafood restaurant. It's not a trendy place – the decor is old school, the seating a little cramped and the menu perhaps too long – but the cooking is superb. Witness the Hyderabadi fish tikka, jumbo prawns with green pepper sauce and the outstanding crab dishes.

Mamagoto ASIAN **$$$**

(Map p740; ☎022-61054586; www.mamagoto.in; 5 Surya Mahal, B Bharucha Marg, Kala Ghoda; mains ₹529-799; ⏰noon-11.30pm; 📶) Mamagoto means 'play with food' in Japanese and this zany hot spot is certainly fun, with a relaxed vibe, cool tunes and kooky decor (think pop and propaganda art). The menu really delivers, with punchy Pan-Asian flavours: the authentic Malay-style Penang curry is terrific and the fiery Bangkok bowl packs a wallop of spice.

There's also a branch in **Bandra** (Map p750; ☎022-61054585; Gazebo House, 133 Hill Rd, Bandra West; mains ₹529-799; ⏰noon-11.30pm; 📶).

Self-Catering

Nature's Basket SUPERMARKET **$**

(Map p740; www.naturesbasket.co.in; 27 Khetan Bhavan, 198 Jamshedi Tata Rd, Churchgate; ⏰8am-10pm) An eco-leaning well-to-do supermarket chain with fresh produce, a deli counter, loads of international items as well as a sizeable organic section.

Kalbadevi to Mahalaxmi

Sardar STREET FOOD $
(Map p746; 166A Tardeo Rd Junction, Tulsiwadi; pav bhaji from ₹125; ⏲11am-2am) If you're spooked about Indian street food, try one of the city's most beloved street staples, *pav bhaji*, at this Mumbai institution. The curried veg mish-mash is cooked to death on a series of scalding *tawas* (hotplates) and served with a butter floater the size of a Bollywood ego. Get in line; the entire restaurant turns over at once.

New Kulfi Centre ICE CREAM $
(Map p746; 556 Marina Mansion, Sukh Sagar, Sardar V Patel Rd, Girgaon; kulfi per 100g ₹40-90; ⏲9.30am-1am) Serves 36 flavours of the best *kulfi* (Indian firm-textured ice cream) you'll have anywhere. Killer flavours include pistachio, *malai* (cream) and mango.

Cafe Noorani NORTH INDIAN $$
(Map p746; www.cafenoorani.com; Tardeo Rd, Haji Ali Circle; mains ₹140-450; ⏲8am-11.30pm) Inexpensive, old-school eatery that's a requisite stop before or after visiting Haji Ali Dargah (p745). Mughlai and Punjabi staples dominate, with kebabs chargrilled to perfection and great biryanis; try the chicken tikka biryani (₹300).

Western Suburbs

North Mumbai is home to the city's trendiest dining, centred on Bandra West and Juhu.

Hotel Ram Ashraya SOUTH INDIAN $
(Bhandarkar Rd, King's Circle, Matunga East; light meals ₹40-75; ⏲5am-9.30pm) In the Tamil enclave of King's Circle, 80-year-old Ram Ashraya is beloved by southern families for its spectacular dosas, *idli* (spongy, round, fermented rice cake) and *uttapa* (pancake with toppings). Filter coffee is strong and flavoursome. The menu (no English) changes daily. It's just outside Matunga Rd train station's east exit.

★Dakshinayan SOUTH INDIAN $$
(Map p750; Anand Hotel, Gandhigram Rd, Juhu; mains ₹130-250; ⏲11am-11pm Mon-Sat, from 8am Sun) With *rangoli* on the walls, servers in lungis and sari-clad women lunching (*chappals* – sandals – off under the table), Dakshinayan channels Tamil Nadu. There are delicately textured dosas, *idli* and *uttapam*, village-fresh chutneys and perhaps the best *rasam* (tomato soup with spices and tamarind) in Mumbai. Finish off with a South Indian filter coffee, served in a stainless-steel set.

Kitchen Garden by Suzette CAFE $$
(Map p750; www.suzette.in; 9 Gasper Enclave, St John St, Bandra West; light meals ₹190-550; ⏲9am-11pm; 📶) 🍃 From the same French trio that brought us Suzette comes this new, superb organic cafe, a haven of health and homesick-remedying salads, sandwiches, cold-press juices and coffee sourced from local cooperatives and organic farms around Maharashtra and worldwide. The burrata, made by an American-Indian Hare Krishna in Gujarat, is outstanding, but then again so is everything.

★Yoga House CAFE $$
(Map p750; www.yogahouse.in; Nargis Villa/Water Bungalow Sherly Rajan Rd, Bandra West; light meals ₹140-390; ⏲8am-9.30pm; 📶) This haven of pastel shades, scatter cushions and greenery in the bungalow of Yoga House (p750) is the perfect little retreat from Mumbai's mean streets. The menu is very creative and healthy – much of it vegan, raw and all of it wholesome. Signature items include its famous salads (₹215 to ₹370), 10-grain toasts (₹130), soups and gussied-up hash browns (with spinach, mozzarella and peppers).

Goila Butter Chicken INDIAN $$
(☎8080809102; www.goilabutterchicken.com; 26 Sai Kanwal Complex, JP Rd, Andheri West; mains ₹275-335; ⏲noon-3pm & 6pm-midnight) Don't miss this takeaway/delivery-only gourmet stand dedicated to celebrity chef Saransh Goila's take on one of India's most iconic dishes: butter chicken. Goila, who won India n TV's *Food Food Maha Challenge*, gets the gravy just right – a perfect marriage of tang and spice – and whips it up various ways (traditional, with paneer, in biryani or rolls). Delivers to airport-area hotels.

Raaj Bhog GUJARATI $$
(Map p750; 3rd Rd, Cosmos Commercial Center, Khar West; meals ₹180-300; ⏲11am-3.30pm & 7-11pm) Modestly priced restaurants are not easy to find in this part of town, so this friendly Gujarati place by Khar train station is a welcome addition. The (unlimited) deluxe thali costs ₹330 and is filling and varied; hilarious staff will talk your ears off.

★Peshawri NORTH INDIAN $$$
(Map p750; ☎022-28303030; www.itchotels.in; ITC Maratha, Sahar Rd, Andheri East; mains ₹1600-3000; ⏲12.45-2.45pm & 7-11.45pm) Make this Northwest Frontier restaurant, outside the

international airport, your first or last stop in Mumbai. It's a carbon-copy of Delhi's famous Bukhara (p89), with the same menu and decor. Folks flock here for the buttery *dhal bukhara* (a 24-hour simmered black dhal; ₹800), but its kebabs are sublime: try the *Murgh Malai* (tandoor-grilled chicken marinated in cream cheese, malt vinegar, green chilli and coriander).

Despite the five-star surrounds (and prices) you're encouraged to eat with your hands and the seating is low.

★Bastian SEAFOOD **$$$**

(Map p750; www.facebook.com/BastianSeafood; B/1, New Kamal Bldg, Linking Rd, Bandra West; mains for 2 ₹700-2600; 7pm-12.45am Tue-Sun; wi-fi) All the praise bestowed upon this trendy seafooder is indisputably warranted. Chinese-Canadian chef Boo Kwang Kim and his culinary sidekick, American-Korean Kelvin Cheung, have forged an East-meets-West gastronomic dream. Go with the market-fresh side menu: choose your catch (prawns, fish, mud crab or lobster) then pick from an insanely difficult list of impossibly tasty Pan-Asian sauces.

Don't miss the stir-fried lotus root, either.

★Bombay Canteen INDIAN **$$$**

(022-49666666; www.thebombaycanteen.com; Process House, Kamala Mills, SB Rd, Lower Parel; small plates ₹175-450, mains ₹300-975; noon-1am; wi-fi) Bombay Canteen is Mumbai's hottest restaurant, courtesy of former New York chef and Top Chef Masters winner Floyd Cardoz and executive chef Thomas Zacharias, who spent time at New York's three-Michelin-star Le Bernardin. India-wide regional dishes and traditional flavours dominate – Kejriwa toast, Goan pulled-pork vindaloo tacos, smoked mutton guijiya curry – each dish an explosion of texture and flavour.

Excellent cocktails (₹350 to ₹900) like Incredible India (vodka, basil, ginger, pineapple juice and orange juice) are perfect for jump-starting a night out in Lower Parel. Reservations are essential (7.30pm/8pm and 10pm/10.30pm seatings only). Don't miss the comment card – it's a riot.

★Masala Library MODERN INDIAN **$$$**

(Map p750; 022-66424142; www.masalalibrary.co.in; ground fl, First International Financial Centre, G Block, Bandra East; mains ₹500-900, tasting menu ₹2300-2500, with wine ₹3800-4000; noon-2.15pm & 7-11pm) Daring and imaginative Masala Library dangles the contemporary Indian carrot to foodies and gastronauts, challenging them to rethink their notions of subcontinent cuisine. The tasting menus are an exotic culinary journey – think pan-tossed mushrooms with black pepper, dill crust and truffle haze; kashmiri chilli duck, *jalebi* caviar and a betel-leaf candy floss to finish.

Drinking & Nightlife

Colaba

★Colaba Social BAR

(Map p738; www.socialoffline.in; ground fl, Glen Rose Bldg, BK Boman Behram Marg, Apollo Bunder; 9am-1.30am; wi-fi) Colaba is the best of the locations of the hip Social chain, which combines a restaurant/bar with a collaborative work space. The happening bar nails the cocktails (₹295 to ₹450) – the Acharroska is the perfect East-meets-West marriage of Indian pungency and Brazilian sweet. The food (mains ₹160 to ₹360) spans everything from fish and chips and *poutine* (French fries and cheese curds topped with gravy) to Punjabi and Mangalorean (with great Parsi dishes for breakfast).

There are also Social locations in Lower Parel – **Todi Mill** (242 Mathuradas Mill Compound; 9am-1am; wi-fi) – and **Khar** (Map p750; Rohan Plaza, 5th Rd, Ram Krishna Nagar; mains ₹160-360; 9am-1am; wi-fi).

★Harbour Bar BAR

(Map p738; Taj Mahal Palace, Apollo Bunder; 11am-11.45pm) With unmatched views of the Gateway of India and harbour, this timeless bar inside the Taj Mahal Palace is an essential visit. Drinks aren't uberexpensive (from ₹450/670/900 for a beer/wine/cocktail) given the surrounds and the fact that they come with very generous portions of nibbles (including jumbo cashews).

Woodside Inn PUB

(Map p738; www.facebook.com/WoodsideInn; Indian Mercantile Mansion, Wodehouse Rd; 11am-1am Mon-Fri, from 10am Sat & Sun; wi-fi) As close as you'll get to a London pub in Mumbai, this cosy place has a gregarious vibe and serves Gateway and Independence craft beers on draught (pints from ₹295). There's comfort food (mains ₹425 to ₹895) and a great two-for-one happy hour (4pm to 8pm daily).

Cafe Mondegar PUB

(Map p738; Metro House, 5A Shahid Bhagat Singh Marg; 7.30am-12.30am Sun-Wed, to 1am Thu-Sat) Iranian-founded 'Mondy's' has been drawing a heady mix of foreigners and locals since

DON'T MISS

CRAFT BREW BOMBAY

Few visitors to India would argue that an ice-cold Kingfisher in a dingy, smoke-filled bar isn't a quintessential Indian experience, but craft-beer connoisseurs might also add that India's ubiquitous native lager gets old pretty quick. And then there's those distinctly disgusting YouTube videos of oily, urine-coloured *something* being drained out from beer bottles before drinking (it's usually glycerine, widely used in Indian beers as a preservative). Cheers? Not really.

While certainly late to the craft-brew boozefest, Mumbai has finally embraced hop-heavy IPAs, roasty, chocolatey porters and refreshing saisons, thanks to the city's very own craft-beer wallah, American expat Greg Kroitzsh. Kroitzsh opened Mumbai's first microbrewery, **Barking Deer** (www.barkingdeer.in; Mathuradas Mill Compound, Senapati Bapat Marg, Lower Parel; 🕒 noon-1.30am; 📶), in 2013, and the taps began flowing in Mumbai as they already had been for some time in craftier Indian cities like Pune, Bangalore and Gurgaon.

Fancy a pint? In Andheri West, **Independence Brewing Company** (www.independencebrewco.com; Boolani Estate Owners Premises Co-Op, New Link Rd, Andheri West; 🕒 1pm-1.15am; 📶) and **Brewbot** (www.brewbot.in; Morya Landmark 1, off New Link Rd, Andheri West; 🕒 4pm-1am Mon-Fri, noon-1am Sat; 📶) are worth the journey north, as is the excellent **Doolally Taproom** (Map p750; www.facebook.com/godoolallybandra; Shop 5/6, Geleki, ONGC Colony, Bandra West; 🕒 7am-1am; 📶) in Bandra. In Lower Parel are Barking Deer, **White Owl** (www.whiteowl.in; One Indiabulls Center, Tower 2 Lobby, Senapati Bapat Marg, Lower Parel; 🕒 noon-1am), **Toit Tap Room** (www.toit.in; Zeba Centre, Mathuradas Mill Compound, Senapati Bapat Marg, Lower Parel; 🕒 noon-1.30am) and, to get a sampling of nearly all of them, the new, 25-tap **Woodside Inn** (www.facebook.com/WoodsideInn; Mathuradas Mills Compound, NM Joshi Marg, Lower Parel; 🕒 11am-1am Mon-Fri, from 10am Sat & Sun) – all are within walking distance of each other. It's only a matter of time before taps start flowing in Fort and Colaba as well. Ubiquitous draught-only craft beer includes Gateway Brewing Company and Bira 91 ('Bira' meaning 'Bro' in Punjabi, '91' for the country code!).

The city's signature brew has quickly become Belgian Wit – citrusy and refreshing, it's a perfect accompaniment for hot and humid Mumbai. *Jai ho!*

1871. It's first and foremost a rowdy bar serving ice-cold mugs of Kingfisher (₹220), but don't discount it for its wide range of American, English and Parsi breakfast choices (₹130 to ₹350).

Leopold Cafe BAR

(Map p738; www.leopoldcafe.com; cnr Colaba Causeway & Nawroji F Rd; 🕒 7.30am-midnight) Love it or hate it, most tourists end up at this clichéd Mumbai travellers' institution at one time or another. Around since 1871, Leopold's has wobbly ceiling fans, crap service and a rambunctious atmosphere conducive to swapping tales with strangers. There's also food and a cheesy DJ upstairs on weekend nights.

Kalbadevi to Mahalaxmi

Haji Ali Juice Centre JUICE BAR

(Map p746; Lala Lajpat Rai Rd, Haji Ali Circle; 🕒 5am-1.30am) Serves fresh juices and milkshakes (₹80 to ₹380), mighty fine *falooda* and fruit salads. Strategically placed at the entrance to Haji Ali mosque, it's a great place to cool off after a visit. Try the Triveni, a gorgeous trifecta of mango, strawberry and kiwi (₹280).

Western Suburbs

★ **One Street Over** COCKTAIL BAR

(Map p750; Navarang Bldg, 35th Rd, off Linking Rd, Khar West; 🕒 7pm-1am Tue-Sun; 📶) With an emphasis on Prohibition-era craft mixology, this shotgun-style cocktail bar (cocktails ₹500 to ₹850), housed where high-class orgies once went down, is currently Khar's drinkery of desire. DJs spin hip-hop to a beautiful and trendy crowd, who are content to gaggle away at the long and sociable central share table over drinks and internationally inspired tapas.

★ **Aer** LOUNGE

(www.fourseasons.com/mumbai; Four Seasons Hotel, 34th fl, 114 Dr E Moses Rd, Worli; 🕒 5.30pm-midnight; 📶) Boasting astounding sea, sunset and city views, Aer is Mumbai's premier sky bar. Drink prices are steep (cocktails ₹1000 to ₹1500), but that's kind of the point. DJs spin house and lounge tunes nightly, including over groovy happy hour sundowner specials, concocted by some of Mumbai's best mixologists.

Monkey Bar BAR

(Map p750; Summerville, cnr 14th & 33rd Rd, Linking Rd, Bandra West; ⏲6pm-1am Mon-Fri, from noon Sat & Sun; 📶) Successful ventures in Delhi and Bangalore led this chill gastropub to Bandra, where scenesters gather on the excellent patio – particularly great when it's pouring rain a metre or so away. Cheekily named cocktails (ask a local to get in on the joke; ₹320 to ₹650) and Gateway Brewing craft beer on tap ensure a fun and festive mood over DJ-spun hip-hop/Latin hits.

Masala Bar COCKTAIL BAR

(Map p750; www.masalabar.co.in; 1st fl, Gagangiri Apt, Carter Rd, Bandra West; ⏲12.30-4pm & 5pm-1am) Take unorthodox ingredients like thyme foam, mudfig purée, orange-skin oil and sattu fizz, then shake, stir, cook or otherwise manipulate them along with alcohol using things like vacuum-sealing machines, rotovaps, siphons, centrifuges and sous-vide machines, and you have an idea of what to expect from the innovative molecular cocktails at this new Bandra hot spot overlooking the beach on Carter Rd. Signature cocktails are ₹550.

Toto's Garage BAR

(Map p750; ☎022-26005494; 30th Rd, Bandra West; ⏲6pm-1am) A highly sociable, down-to-earth local dive done up in a car-mechanic theme, where you can go in your dirty clothes, drink draught beer (₹200 a glass) and listen to classic rock. Check out the upended VW Beetle above the bar. It's always busy and has a good mix of guys and gals.

Olive Bar & Kitchen BAR

(Map p750; ☎022-26058228; www.olivebarandkitchen.com; 14 Union Park, Khar West; ⏲8pm-1am daily, plus 12.30-3.30pm Sat & Sun; 📶) A perennial watering hole of choice for Bandra's filmi elite and aspiring starlets, Olive is a Mediterranean-style bar-restaurant whose white-washed walls, candle-lit terraces and rooms

QUEER MUMBAI

Homosexuality remains illegal in India, so Mumbai's LGBTQ scene is still quite underground, especially for women, but it's gaining momentum. No dedicated LGBTQ bars/clubs have opened yet, but gay-friendly 'safe house' venues often host private gay parties (announced on Gay Bombay).

Humsafar Trust (Map p750; ☎022-26673800; www.humsafar.org; 3rd fl, Manthan Plaza Nehru Rd, Vakola, Santa Cruz East) Runs tons of programs and workshops; one of its support groups organises the weekly gathering 'Friday Workshop' and another, Umang, organises monthly events (called 'Chill Outs'), workshops and runs a helpline (☎99300-95856). It's also closely connected to the erratically published but pioneering magazine Bombay Dost (www.bombaydost.co.in).

Gaylaxy (www.gaylaxymag.com) India's best gay e-zine; well worth consulting and has lots of Mumbai content.

Gay Bombay (www.gaybombay.org) A great place to start, with event listings including meet-ups in Bandra, GB-hosted bar and film nights (including somewhat regular gay Saturday nights at Liquid Lounge in Girgaum Chowpatty), plus hiking trips, picnics and other queer-community info.

Kashish Mumbai International Queer Film Festival (www.mumbaiqueerfest.com) Excellent annual event in May, with a mix of Indian and foreign films; in 2016 182 films from 54 countries were featured.

LABIA (Lesbian & Bisexuals in Action; www.labiacollective.org) Lesbian and bi support group based in Mumbai; provides a counselling service for women.

Queer Azaadi Mumbai (www.queerazaadi.wordpress.com) Organises Mumbai's Pride Parade (www.mumbaipride.in), which is usually held in early February.

Queer Ink (www.queer-ink.com) Online publisher with excellent books, DVDs and merchandise. Also hosts a monthly arts event with speakers, workshops, poetry, comedy, music and a marketplace.

Salvation Star A Facebook community organising and promoting gay events and parties.

evoke Ibiza and Mykonos. It's the perfect setting for inspired Greek and Italian food (mains ₹600 to ₹1500) and vibing DJ sounds. Thursdays and weekends are packed.

Bad Cafe CAFE

(Map p750; www.thebadcafe.com; 22G Kapadia House, New Kantwadi Rd, Bandra West; 9am-11pm;) Thoroughly hidden down a quiet lane off Perry Cross Rd, this is the caffeinated stomping grounds of the Bandra cool and creative set. Co-owner and coffee fiend Amit Dhanani sources organic, 80% Arabica beans from South India, which are turned into espressos, ristretto, cortados, flat whites and the like by old-school trained baristas. Porch-swing seating and globally inspired tapas (₹250 to ₹520) encourage lingering.

Cafe Zoe BAR

(www.cafezoe.in; Mathurdas Mills Compound, NM Joshi Marg, Lower Parel; 7.30am-1.30am) This cafe/bar is not merely another unassuming hipster enclave hidden away in the redeveloped cotton mill at Mathurdas Mills Compound. Exposed brick and railing dominate the bi-level space that's long on atmosphere and serves strong, fruit-forward cocktails (₹470 to ₹600) like black grape caipiroskas and watermelon martinis. Old black-and-white photos of its former life dot the walls.

☆ Entertainment

Mumbai has an exciting live-music scene, some terrific theatres, an emerging network of comedy clubs and, of course, cinemas and sporting action.

Consult **Time Out Mumbai** (www.timeout.com/mumbai) and **Insider** (https://insider.in) for events and/or live-music listings. Unfortunately, Hindi films aren't shown with English subtitles. You can book movies, theatre and sporting events online with **Book My Show** (https://in.bookmyshow.com).

Royal Opera House OPERA

(Map p746; 022-23690511; Mama Parmanand Rd; box office 11am-6pm) India's only surviving opera house reopened to suitably dramatic fanfare with a 2016 performance by Mumbai-born British soprano Rozario, after a meticulous six-year restoration project that saw the regal address returned to full British-rule glory. Architect Abha Narain Lambah combed through old photographs of gilded ceilings, stained-glass windows and a baroque Indo-European foyer to restore the three-level auditorium.

Liberty Cinema CINEMA, LIVE MUSIC

(Map p740; 022-22084521; www.thelibertycinema.com; 41/42 New Marine Lines, Fort) The stunning art deco Liberty was once the queen of Hindi film – think red-carpet openings with Dev Anand. It fell on hard times in recent years, but is on the rebound and now hosts private events and more. It's near the Bombay Hospital.

National Centre for the Performing Arts THEATRE, LIVE MUSIC

(NCPA; Map p740; www.ncpamumbai.com; Marine Dr & Sri V Saha Rd, Nariman Point; tickets ₹150-7500) This vast cultural centre is the hub of Mumbai's highbrow music, theatre and dance scene. In any given week, it might host experimental plays, poetry readings, photography exhibitions, a jazz band from Chicago or Indian classical music. Many performances are free. The **box office** (Map p740; 022-66223724; www.ncpamumbai.com; Marine Dr & Sri V Saha Rd, Nariman Point; 9am-7pm) is at the end of NCPA Marg.

Regal Cinema CINEMA

(Map p738; 022-22021017; www.regalcinema.in; Shahid Bhagat Singh Marg, Regal Circle, Apollo Bunder; tickets ₹100-200) A faded art deco masterpiece that's good for Hollywood blockbusters.

Wankhede Stadium SPECTATOR SPORT

(Mumbai Cricket Association; Map p740; 022-22795500; www.mumbaicricket.com; D Rd, Churchgate; ticket office 9am-6pm) Test matches and one-day internationals are played a few times a year here in season (October to April). Contact the Cricket Association for ticket information; for a test match you'll probably have to pay for the full five days.

Prithvi Theatre THEATRE

(Map p750; 022-26149546; www.prithvitheatre.org; Juhu Church Rd, Juhu; tickets ₹175-500) A Juhu institution that's a great place to see both Hindi- and English-language theatre or an arthouse film, with the **Prithvi Cafe** (Map p750; light meals ₹35-150; 10am-10.45pm) for drinks. Its excellent theatre festival in November showcases contemporary Indian theatre and includes international productions.

Eros CINEMA

(Map p740; www.eroscinema.co.in; Maharshi Karve Rd, Churchgate; tickets ₹130-180) To experience Bollywood blockbusters in situ, the Eros cinema is the place.

BOLLYWOOD DREAMS

Mumbai is the glittering epicentre of India's gargantuan Hindi-language film industry. The Lumière brothers screened the first film ever shown in India at the Watson Hotel in Mumbai in 1896, and beginning with the 1913 silent epic *Raja Harishchandra* (with an all-male cast, some in drag) and the first talkie, *Lama Ara* (1931), Bollywood now churns out more than 1000 films a year – doubling Hollywood's output, and not surprising considering it has a captive audience of one-sixth of the world's population.

Every part of India has its regional film industry, but Bollywood continues to entrance the nation with its escapist formula in which all-singing, all-dancing lovers fight and conquer the forces keeping them apart. These days, Hollywood-inspired thrillers and action extravaganzas vie for moviegoers' attention alongside the more family-oriented saccharine formulas.

Bollywood stars can attain near godlike status in India and star-spotting is a favourite pastime in Mumbai's posher establishments. You can also see the stars' homes as well as a film/TV studio with **Bollywood Tours** (Map p740; ☎9820255202; www.bollywood-tours.in; 8 Lucky House, Goa St, Fort; per person 4/8hr tour ₹8000/10,000), but you're not guaranteed to see a dance number and you may spend much of it in traffic.

Extra! Extra!

Studios sometimes want Westerners as extras to add a whiff of international flair (or provocative dress, which locals often won't wear) to a film. If you're game, just hang around Colaba (especially the Salvation Army hostel) where studio scouts, recruiting for the following day's shooting, will find you.

A day's work, which can be up to 16 hours, pays around ₹500 (more for speaking roles). You'll get lunch, snacks and (usually) transport. The day can be long and hot with loads of standing around the set; not everyone has a positive experience.

Complaints range from lack of food and water to dangerous situations and intimidation when extras don't comply with the director's orders. Others describe the behind-the-scenes peek as a fascinating experience. Before agreeing to anything, always ask for the scout's identification and go with your gut feeling.

Metro Big CINEMA
(Map p740; ☎022-39894040; www.bigcinemas.com; Mahatma Gandhi Rd, New Marine Lines, Fort; tickets ₹150-800) This grande dame of Bombay talkies has been renovated into a multiplex cinema.

Shopping

Mumbai is India's great marketplace, with some of the best shopping in the country. Spend a day at the markets north of CST for the classic Mumbai shopping experience. Booksellers set up daily on the sidewalks along the main thoroughfare between Colaba and Fort. Snap up a bargain backpacking wardrobe at **Fashion Street** (Map p740; Mahatma Gandhi Rd). Kemp's Corner and Kala Ghoda have good shops for designer threads.

Colaba

Cottonworld Corp CLOTHING
(Map p738; www.cottonworld.net; Mandlik Marg, Colaba; ⏲10.30am-8pm Mon-Sat, noon-8pm Sun) A great shop for stylish Indian-Western-hybrid goods made from cotton, linen and natural materials. Think Indian Gap, but cooler.

Phillips ANTIQUES
(Map p738; www.phillipsantiques.com; Wodehouse Rd, Colaba; ⏲10am-7pm Mon-Sat) Art deco and colonial-era furniture, wooden ceremonial masks, silver, Victorian glass, plus high-quality reproductions of old photos, maps and paintings.

Bungalow 8 FASHION & ACCESSORIES
(Map p740; www.bungaloweight.com; North Stand, E & F Block, Wankhede Stadium, D Rd, Churchgate; ⏲10.30am-7.30pm) Original, high-end, artisanal clothing, jewellery, home decor and other objects of beauty under the bleachers of the cricket stadium. Enter via Gate 2 from Vinoo Mankad Rd.

Central Cottage Industries Emporium ARTS & CRAFTS
(Map p738; www.cottageemporium.in; Chhatrapati Shivaji Marg, Apollo Bunder; ⏲10am-7pm Mon-Sat, to 6pm Sun) Fair-trade-like souvenirs including pashminas.

WORTH A TRIP

BAZAAR DISTRICT

Mumbai's main market district is one of Asia's most fascinating, an incredibly dense combination of humanity and commerce that's a total assault on the senses. If you've just got off a plane from the West, or a taxi from Bandra – hold on tight. This working-class district stretches north of Crawford Market up as far as Chor Bazaar, a 2.5km walk away. Such are the crowds (and narrowness of the lanes), you'll need to allow yourself two to three hours to explore it thoroughly.

You can buy just about anything here, but as the stores and stalls are very much geared to local tastes, most of the fun is simply taking in the street life and investigating the souk-like lanes rather than buying souvenirs. The markets merge into each other in an amoeba-like mass, but there are some key landmarks so you can orientate yourself.

Crawford Market (Mahatma Phule Market; Map p746; cnr DN & Lokmanya Tilak Rds; ⌚10.30am-9pm) Crawford Market is the largest in Mumbai, and contains the last whiff of British Bombay before the tumult of the central bazaars begins. Bas-reliefs by Rudyard Kipling's father, Lockwood Kipling, adorn the Norman Gothic exterior. Fruit and vegetables, meat and fish are mainly traded, but it's also an excellent place to stock up on spices.

If you're here during alphonso mango season (May to June) be sure to indulge.

Mangaldas Market (Map p746) Mangaldas Market, traditionally home to traders from Gujarat, is a mini-town, complete with lanes of fabrics. Even if you're not the type to have your clothes tailored, drop by DD Dupattawala (Map p746; ☎022-22019719; Shop 217, 4th Lane; ⌚11am-8pm Mon-Sat) for pretty scarves and dupattas at fixed prices. Zaveri Bazaar (Map p746) for jewellery and Bhuleshwar Market (Map p746; cnr Sheikh Memon St & M Devi Marg; ⌚10am-9pm) for fruit and veg are just north of here.

Just a few metres further along Sheikh Memon St from Bhuleshwar are a Jain pigeon feeding station, a flower market and a religious market.

Chor Bazaar (Map p746; Mutton St, Kumbharwada) Chor Bazaar is known for antiques, though nowadays much of them are reproductions. The main area of activity is Mutton St, where shops specialise in these 'antiques' and miscellaneous junk. Dhabu St, to the east, is lined with fine leather goods.

Fort Area & Churchgate

★Contemporary Arts & Crafts HOMEWARES
(Map p740; www.cac.co.in; 210 Dr Dadabhai Naoroji Rd, Fort; ⌚10.30am-7.30pm) Modish, high-quality takes on traditional crafts: these are not your usual handmade souvenirs.

★Sabyasachi CLOTHING
(Map p740; www.sabyasachi.com; Ador House, 6 K Dubash Marg, Fort; ⌚11am-7pm Mon-Sat) It's worth popping in to this high-end wedding shop to see the space itself, a gorgeous, cavernous, rose-oil-scented stunner chock-full of owner and designer Sabyasachi Mukherjee's collection of chandeliers, antiques, ceramics, paintings and carpets. As far as retail goes it's unlike anything you have ever seen.

Chimanlals ARTS & CRAFTS
(Map p740; www.chimanlals.com; Wallace St, Fort; ⌚9.30am-6pm Mon-Fri, to 5pm Sat) The beautiful traditional printed papers here will make you start writing letters.

Fabindia CLOTHING, HOMEWARES
(Map p740; www.fabindia.com; Jeroo Bldg, 137 Mahatma Gandhi Rd, Kala Ghoda; ⌚10am-9pm) Ethically sourced cotton and silk fashions and homewares in everybody's favourite modern-meets-traditional Indian shop.

Nicobar HOMEWARES, CLOTHING
(Map p740; www.nicobar.com; 10 Ropewalk Lane, Kala Ghoda; ⌚11am-8pm) This new and excellent high-end boutique from the same folks who brought us Good Earth is a great spot to pick up carefully curated homewares, travel totes and select Indian hipsterware.

Bombay Shirt Company CLOTHING
(Map p740; ☎022-40043455; www.bombayshirts.com; ground fl, 3 Sassoon Bldg, Kala Ghoda; ⌚10.30am-9pm) A trendy, bespoke shirt tailor for men and women. You can customise everything (collars, buttons, cuffs and twill tapes), the results are stunning and the prices a fraction of those back home (unless home is Vietnam). Shirts (from ₹2000) take two weeks, and they will deliver or ship in-

ternationally. They're also in **Bandra** (Map p750; ☎022-26056125; ground fl, Kamal Vishrantee Kutir, 24th Rd; ⊙10.30am-9pm).

Bombay Paperie ARTS & CRAFTS
(Map p740; ☎022-66358171; www.bombaypaperie.com; 63 Bombay Samachar Marg, Fort; ⊙10.30am-6pm Mon-Sat) Championing a dying art, this fascinating shop sells handmade, cotton-based paper crafted into charming cards, sculptures and lampshades.

Chetana Book Centre BOOKS
(Map p740; www.chetana.com; K Dubash Marg, Kala Ghoda; ⊙10.30am-7.30pm Mon-Sat) This great spirituality bookstore has lots of books on Hinduism, and the attached restaurant does excellent Gujarati and Rajasthani thalis (₹459 to ₹595).

Khadi & Village Industries Emporium CLOTHING
(Khadi Bhavan; Map p740; 286 Dr Dadabhai Naoroji Rd, Fort; ⊙10.30am-6.30pm Mon-Sat) A dusty, 1940s time warp full of traditional Indian clothing, silk, *khadi* (homespun cloth) and shoes, plus very popular Khadi natural soaps and shampoos.

Kalbadevi to Mahalaxmi

LM Furtado & Co MUSIC
(Map p746; ☎022-22013163; www.furtadosonline.com; 540-544 Kalbadevi Rd, Kalbadevi; ⊙10.30am-8pm Mon-Sat) The best place in Mumbai for musical instruments – sitars, tablas, accordions and local and imported guitars. Another branch under the same Furtados umbrella (but with a slightly different name) is **BX Furtado & Sons** (Map p746; ⊙10.30am-8pm Mon-Sat), located on Lokmanya Tilak Rd.

Shrujan ARTS & CRAFTS
(Map p750; ☎022-26183104; www.shrujan.org; Hatkesh Society, 6th North South Rd, JVPD Scheme; ⊙10am-7.30pm Mon-Sat) Nonprofit Shrujan aims to help women from 114 villages in Kutch, Gujarat, earn a livelihood while preserving their spectacular embroidery traditions – the intricate embroidery work sold here makes great gifts. Shrujan also has a branch in **Breach Candy** (Map p746; ☎022-23521693; ground fl, Krishnabad Bldg, 43 Bhulabhai Desai Marg; ⊙10am-7.30pm Mon-Sat).

Mini Market/Bollywood Bazaar/Super Sale ANTIQUES, SOUVENIRS
(Map p746; ☎9820032923; 33/31 Mutton St; ⊙11am-8pm Sat-Thu) Sells vintage Bollywood posters and other movie ephemera.

Western Suburbs

★**Kulture Shop** DESIGN
(Map p750; www.kultureshop.in; 241 Hill Rd, Bandra West; ⊙11am-8pm) Behold Bandra's – and Mumbai's – coolest shop, featuring exclusive graphic art and illustrations sourced from a global army of Indian artists. You'll find thought-provoking and conceptually daring T-shirts, art prints, coffee mugs, notebooks, stationery and other cutting-edge objets d'art.

It's co-owned by well-known American-Indian street artist Jas Charanjiva, her urban culture and design enthusiast husband, and their curator friend.

Indian Hippy ART
(Map p750; ☎8080822022; www.hippy.in; 17C Sherly Rajan Rd, Bandra West, off Carter Rd; ⊙by appointment) Indian Hippy will put your name in lights, with custom-designed vintage Bollywood posters hand-painted on canvas by the original studio artists (a dying breed since the advent of digital illustrating). Bring (or email) a photo and your imagination (or let them guide you). Also sells LP clocks, vintage film posters and all manner of (frankly bizarre) Bollywood-themed products. Portraits cost ₹7500 to ₹15,000. Ships worldwide.

Kishore Silk House CLOTHING, HANDICRAFTS
(Dedhia Estate 5/353, Bhandarkar Rd, Matunga East; ⊙10am-8.30pm Tue-Sun) Handwoven saris (from ₹300) and dhotis (from ₹250) from Tamil Nadu and Kerala.

High Street Phoenix MALL
(www.highstreetphoenix.com; 462 Senapati Bapat Marg, Lower Parel; ⊙11am-11pm) High Street Phoenix, one of India's first and largest shopping malls, and its mall-within-a-mall, the luxury-oriented Palladium, is an indoor/outdoor retail orgy that hosts top shops, great restaurants, fun bars and clubs, a 20-lane bowling alley and an IMAX cineplex. It's also where you go when you want a horn-free few hours.

Information

EMERGENCY

As of 2017, a single number for emergencies (112) will be in operation across India, though the following will continue to work until 2018.

AMBULANCE	☎102 (public) or 1298 (private)
POLICE	☎100
FIRE	☎101

INTERNET ACCESS

While cyber cafes are increasingly scarce, all but the simplest hotels, restaurants, cafes and bars now have wi-fi. Commercial establishments generally require a connection via social media accounts or via a mobile phone number, to which a unique one-time password is sent.

MEDIA

Newspapers The *Hindustan Times* is the best paper; its *Ht Café* insert has a good what's-on guide.

Websites *Time Out Mumbai* (www.timeout.com/mumbai) no longer publishes a Mumbai magazine but its website is worth consulting.

MEDICAL SERVICES

Bombay Hospital (Map p740; ☎022-22067676; www.bombayhospital.com; 12 New Marine Lines) A private hospital with the latest medical technology and equipment.

Breach Candy Hospital (Map p746; ☎022-23672888, emergency 022-23667890; www.breachcandyhospital.org; 60 Bhulabhai Desai Marg, Breach Candy) The best hospital in Mumbai, if not India. It's 2km northwest of Girgaum Chowpatty.

Royal Chemists (Map p740; www.royalchemists.com; 89A Queen's Chambers, Maharshi Karve Rd, Marine Lines; ⏲8.30am-8.30pm Mon-Sat) Delivers also.

Sahakari Bhandar Chemist (Map p738; cnr Colaba Causeway & Wodehouse Rd, Colaba; ⏲10am-8.30pm) Handy Colaba pharmacy.

MONEY

ATMs are everywhere, and foreign-exchange offices are also plentiful.

Thomas Cook has a branch in the Fort area with foreign exchange.

POST

Main Post Office (Map p740; www.indiapost.gov.in; Walchand Hirachand Marg; ⏲9am-8pm Mon-Sat, to 4pm Sun) The main post office is an imposing building beside CST. Poste restante (Map p740; Walchand Hirachand Marg; ⏲10am-3pm Mon-Sat) is at the 'Delivery Department'. Opposite the post office are parcel-wallahs who will stitch up your parcel for between ₹50 and ₹200 (find them under the banyan tree).

TELEPHONE

Call ☎197 for directory assistance.

TOURIST INFORMATION

Indiatourism (Government of India Tourist Office; Map p740; ☎022-22074333; www.incredibleindia.com; Western Railways Reservation Complex, 123 Maharshi Karve Rd; ⏲8.30am-6pm Mon-Fri, to 2pm Sat) Provides information for the entire country, as well as contacts for Mumbai guides and homestays. Oddly, branches at the airports had been shut at the time of research.

Maharashtra Tourism Development Corporation Head Office (MTDC; Map p740; ☎022-22845678; www.maharashtratourism.gov.in; Madame Cama Rd, Nariman Point; ⏲10am-5.30pm) The MTDC's head office has helpful staff and lots of pamphlets and information on Maharashtra and bookings for MTDC hotels. This is also the only MTDC office of note that accepts credit cards. There are additional booths at Apollo Bunder (MTDC; Map p738; ☎022-22841877; ⏲9am-4pm Tue-Sun) and Chhatrapati Shivaji Terminus (MTDC; Map p740; ☎022-22622859; ⏲10am-5pm Mon-Sat), but airport booths were closed at the time of research.

TRAVEL AGENCIES

Akbar Travels (Map p738; ☎022-22823434; www.akbartravels.com; 30 Alipur Trust Bldg, Shahid Bhagat Singh Marg, Colaba; ⏲10am-7pm Mon-Fri, to 6pm Sat) Extremely helpful and can book long-distance car/drivers and buses with advance notice. Also has good exchange rates. There's another branch in Fort (Map p740; ☎022-22633434; www.akbartravels.com; 167/169 Dr Dadabhai Naoroji Rd, Fort; ⏲10am-7pm Mon-Fri, to 6pm Sat).

Thomas Cook (Map p740; ☎022-61603333; www.thomascook.in; 324 Dr Dadabhai Naoroji Rd, Fort; ⏲9.30am-6pm Mon-Sat) Flight and hotel bookings, plus foreign exchange.

VISAS

Foreigners' Regional Registration Office (FRRO; Map p740; ☎022-22621169; www.boi.gov.in; Annexe Bldg No 2, CID, Badaruddin Tyabji Marg, near Special Branch; ⏲9.30am-1pm Mon-Fri) Tourist and transit visas can no longer be extended except in emergency situations; check the latest online.

Getting There & Away

AIR

Mumbai's **Chhatrapati Shivaji International Airport** (Map p750; ☎022-66851010; www.csia.in), about 30km from the city centre, was recently modernised to the tune of US$2 billion. Now handling all international arrivals is the impressive, remodelled international Terminal 2 (T2), which includes India's largest public art program (a skylighted, 3.2km multistorey Art Wall along moving walkways, boasting over 5000 pieces of art from every corner of India).

Domestic flights operate out of both the new T2 and the older Terminal 1B (T1B), also known locally as Santa Cruz Airport, 5km away. An inter-terminal fixed-rate taxi service (₹230 from T1B to T2, ₹245 from T2 to T1B) operates between the terminals. Both terminals have ATMs and foreign-exchange counters, and T2 also houses a luxurious transit hotel.

Air India (Map p740; ☎022-27580777, airport 022-28318666; www.airindia.com; Air India Bldg, cnr Marine Dr & Madame Cama Rd, Nariman Point; ⌚9.15am-6pm Mon-Fri, 9.15am-1pm & 2-6pm Sat), **Jet Airways** (Map p738; ☎022-39893333; www.jetairways.com; B1, Amarchand Mansion, Madam Cama Rd, Colaba; ⌚9.30am-6pm Mon-Sat) and **Vistara** (Map p750; ☎0186-1089999; www.airvistara.com) operate out of T2, while **GoAir** (Map p750; ☎022-26156113; www.goair.in), **IndiGo** (Map p750; ☎call centre 099-10383838; www.goindigo.in) and **SpiceJet** (Map p750; ☎airport 0987-1803333; www.spicejet.com) operate out of T1B – be sure to check ahead for any changes on the ground. Travel agencies and the airlines' websites are usually best for booking flights.

There are also normally MTDC tourist information booths at both terminals but these had been removed at the time of research due to the airport renovations, with no planned time frame for their return.

BUS

Numerous private operators and state governments run long-distance buses to and from Mumbai.

Long-distance government-run buses depart from the **Mumbai Central bus terminal** (Map p746; ☎enquiries 022-23024075; Jehangir Boman Behram Marg, RBI Staff Colony) right by Mumbai Central train station. They're cheaper and more frequent than private services, but standards are usually lower. The website of the **Maharashtra State Road Transport Corporation** (MSRTC; ☎022-23023900; www.msrtc.gov.in) theoretically has schedules and is supposed to permit online booking, though in practice it's next to useless.

Private buses are usually more comfortable and simpler to book (if a bit more costly). Most depart from Dr Anadrao Nair Rd near Mumbai Central train station, but some buses to southern destinations depart from Carnac Bunder near Crawford Market or Dadar TT Circle (free transport is usually provided to both by ticketing agents). Check departure times and prices with **Citizen Travels** (Map p746; ☎022-23459695; www.citizenbus.com; G Block, Sitaram Bldg, Palton Rd) or **National NTT/CTC** (Map p746; ☎022-23074854, 022-23015652; Dr Anadrao Nair Rd; ⌚6.20am-11.30pm). Fares to popular destinations (like Goa) are up to 75% higher during holiday periods.

Private buses to Goa are more convenient; these vary in price from as little as ₹450 (a bad choice) to ₹1000. Many leave from way out in the suburbs, but **Naik Bus** (Map p740; ☎022-23676840; www.naibus.com; ⌚6pm, 7pm, 8.30pm & 9pm), **Paolo Travel** (Map p740; ☎022-26433023; www.paulotravels.com; ⌚5.30pm & 8pm) and government-run **Kadamba Transport** (Map p740; ☎9969561146; www.goakadamba.com; ⌚6pm) are convenient for the centre, leaving from in front of Azad Maidan. The trip takes 14 hours.

Private long-distance bus stands and ticket agents are on **Palton Road** (Map p746; Palton Rd) and **Dr Anadrao Nair Road** (Map p746; Dr Anadrao Nair Rd, RBI Colony).

TRAIN

Three train systems operate out of Mumbai, but the most important services for travellers are Central Railways and Western Railways. Tickets for either system can be bought from any station that has computerised ticketing.

Central Railways (Map p740; ☎139; www.cr.indianrailways.gov.in), handling services to the east, south, plus a few trains to the north, operates from CST (also known as 'VT'). Foreign-tourist-quota tickets and Indrail passes

MAJOR LONG-DISTANCE BUS ROUTES

DESTINATION	PRIVATE NON-AC/AC SLEEPER (₹)	GOVERNMENT NON-AC (₹)	DURATION (HR)
Ahmedabad	300-1500/700-1500	N/A	7-12
Aurangabad	500-700/500-1300	600 (two daily)	9-11
Hyderabad	800-5000 (all AC)	N/A	16
Mahabaleshwar*	500-900 (all AC)	400 (five daily)	7-8
Murud	N/A	200 (10 daily)	8-10
Nasik	200-300/500-600	290 (half-hourly, 6am-11.15pm)	13-16
Panaji (Panjim)	600-750/700-3000	N/A	14-16
Pune*	508-730/425-2800	250 (half-hourly, 6.45am-12.30am)	3-5
Udaipur	200-812/1000-2500	N/A	14-17

* Leaves from Dadar TT Circle.

can be bought at Counter 52 on the 1st floor of the **reservation centre** (Map p740; ⊙8am-8pm Mon-Sat, to 2pm Sun). There is a prepaid taxi scheme near the MTDC tourist information booth (₹160 to Colaba, ₹360 to Bandra, ₹430 to the domestic terminal and ₹500 to the international terminal).

Some Central Railways trains depart from Dadar (D), a few stations north of CST, or Lokmanya Tilak (LTT), 16km north of CST.

Western Railways (Map p746; ☎139; www.wr.indianrailways.gov.in) has services to the north from Mumbai Central train station, usually called Bombay Central (BCT). The **reservation office** (Map p740; ⊙8am-8pm Mon-Sat, to 2pm Sun), opposite Churchgate station, has foreign-tourist-quota tickets.

Getting Around

M-Indicator (http://m-indicator.soft112.com) is an invaluable app for Mumbai public transit – from train schedules to rickshaw fares it covers the whole shebang.

TO/FROM THE AIRPORTS

Terminal 2

Prepaid Taxi Set-fare taxis cost ₹680/820 (non-AC/AC; including one piece of luggage) to Colaba and Fort and ₹400/480 to Bandra. The journey to Colaba takes about an hour at night (via the Sea Link) and 1½ to two hours during the day.

Autorickshaw Although available, they only go as far south as Bandra – walk out of the terminal and follow the signs. Prices are ₹18 per kilometre (a traffic warden *should* keep them honest).

Train If you arrive during the day (but not during 'rush hour' – 6am to 11am) and are not weighed down with luggage, consider the train: take an autorickshaw to Andheri train station and then the Churchgate or CST train (₹10, 45 minutes).

Taxi The trip from South Mumbai to the international airport in an AC taxi should cost from ₹650 to ₹800, plus the ₹60 toll if you take the time-saving Sea Link Bridge. Allow two hours for the trip if you travel between 4pm and 8pm. From Colaba, an UberGo is around ₹385 off-peak.

Terminal 1B

Taxi There's a prepaid taxi counter in the arrivals hall. A non-AC/AC taxi costs ₹560/683 to Colaba or Fort and ₹283/340 to Bandra (a bit more at night).

Autorickshaw Alternatively, if it's not rush hour, catch an autorickshaw (between ₹22 and ₹27) to Vile Parle station, where you can get a train to Churchgate (₹10, 45 minutes).

MAJOR TRAINS FROM MUMBAI

DESTINATION	TRAIN NO & NAME	SAMPLE FARE (₹)	DURATION (HR)	DEPARTURE
Agra	12137 Punjab Mail	613/1596/2281/3856 (A)	22	7.40pm CST
Ahmedabad	12901 Gujarat Mail	348/876/1206/1996 (A)	9	10pm BCT
	12009 Shatabdi Exp	860/1701 (E)	7	6.25am BCT
Aurangabad	11401 Nandigram Exp	268/691/961/1571 (A)	7	4.35pm CST
	17617 Tapovan Exp	173/571 (C)	7	6.15am CST
Bengaluru	11301 Udyan Exp	533/1416/2031/3421 (A)	24	8.05am CST
Chennai	12163 Chennai Exp	603/1561/2226/3766 (A)	23½	8.30pm CST
Delhi	12951 Mumbai Rajdhani	1856/2641/4481 (D)	16	5pm BCT
Hyderabad	12701 Hussainsagar Exp	458/1191/1671/2781 (A)	14½	9.50pm CST
Indore	12961 Avantika Exp	473/1226/1721/2866 (A)	14	7.10pm BCT
Jaipur	12955 Bct Jp Sf Exp	568/1481/2106/3546 (A)	18	6.50pm BCT
Kochi	16345 Netravati Exp	648/1711/2481 (B)	25½	11.40am LTT
Madgaon (Goa)	10103 Mandovi Exp	423/1131/1601/2661 (A)	12	7.10am CST
	12133 Mangalore Exp	453/1176/1646 (B)	9	10pm CST
	11085 Mao Doubledecker	906 (F)	12	5.33am Wed, Fri & Sun LTT
Pune	11301 Udyan Exp	173/556/761/1226 (A)	3½	8.05am CST

Station abbreviations: CST (Chhatrapati Shivaji Terminus); BCT (Mumbai Central); LTT (Lokmanya Tilak)

Fares: (A) sleeper/3AC/2AC/1AC; (B) sleeper/3AC/2AC; (C) second class/CC; (D) 3AC/2AC/1AC; (E) CC/Exec CC; (F) CC

BOAT

PNP (Map p738; ☎ 022-22885220) and **Maldar Catamarans** (Map p738; ☎ 022-22829695) run regular ferries to Mandwa (one way ₹125 to ₹165), useful for access to Murud-Janjira and other parts of the Konkan Coast, avoiding the long bus trip out of Mumbai. Buy tickets at their Taj Gateway Plaza offices.

BUS

Few travellers bother with city buses but **BEST** (Map p738; www.bestundertaking.com) has a useful search facility for hardcore shoestringers and masochists – you'll also need to read the buses' Devanagari numerals and beware of pickpockets. Fares start at ₹8.

BEST bus stands are on the **east** (Map p738) and **west** (Map p738) sides of Mahatma Gandhi Rd and at CST.

CAR & MOTORCYCLE

Cars with drivers can be hired for moderate rates. Air-conditioned cars start at ₹1550/1800 for half-/full-day rental with an 80km limit. For long-distance treks out of Mumbai, prices vary by type of car and service but expect to pay between ₹13 (non-AC) to ₹15 (AC) per kilometre. **Clear Car Rental** (☎ 8888855220; www.clearcarrental.com) is a handy online car-booking service.

Allibhai Premji Tyrewalla (Map p746; ☎ 022-23099417, 022-23099313; www.premjis.com; 205/20 Dr D Bhadkamkar (Lamington) Rd; ⏲ 10am-7pm Mon-Sat) sells new and used motorcycles with a guaranteed buy-back option. Long-term rental schemes (two months or more) start at around ₹35,000, with a buy-back price of around 60% after three months.

METRO

Line 1 of Mumbai's **metro** (www.mumbaimetroone.com) opened in 2014, the first of a long-phase project expected to finish by 2020. It connects 12 stations in the far northern suburbs to Ghatkopar Station in the east, mostly well away from anywhere of interest to visitors save the growing nightlife hubs of Andheri West and Versova, accessed by DN Nagar and Versova stations, respectively. However, Line 1 of the monorail was scheduled to be extended south as far as Jacob Circle (5km north of Chhatrapati Shivaji Terminus) by early 2017 (after missing deadlines in 2010, 2011 and 2016), bringing it past nightlife hub Lower Parel.

Single fares are based on distance and cost between ₹10 and ₹45, with monthly Trip Passes (₹725 to ₹950) also available. Access to stations is by escalator, carriages are air-conditioned, and there are seats reserved for women and the disabled.

Line 3 (a 33.5km, 27-station underground line connecting Cuffe Pde south of Colaba, all the main railway terminals, Bandra and the airport) is the next line to be constructed. It's been approved and contracted but won't open until at least 2020.

TAXI & AUTORICKSHAW

Mumbai's black-and-yellow taxis are very inexpensive and the most convenient way to get around southern Mumbai; drivers *almost* always use the meter without prompting. The minimum fare is ₹22 (for up to 1.5km); a 5km trip costs about ₹80. **Meru Cabs** (☎ 022-44224422; www.merucabs.com) is a reliable call-ahead taxi service.

Game-changing taxi apps in play include **Uber** (www.ubercom) and **Ola** (www.olacabs.com); the latter is good for booking autorickshaws as well – no more rickshaw-wallah price gouging!

Autorickshaws are the name of the game north of Bandra. The minimum fare is ₹18, up to 1.5km; a 3km trip is about ₹36 during daylight hours.

Both taxis and autorickshaws tack 50% onto the fare between midnight and 5am.

Tip: Mumbaikars tend to navigate by landmarks, not street names (especially new names), so have some details before heading out.

TRAIN

Mumbai's suburban train network is one of the world's busiest; forget travelling during rush hours. Trains run from 4am to 1am and there are two main lines of most interest to travellers:

Western Line The most useful; operates out of Churchgate north to Charni Rd (for Girgaum Chowpatty), Mumbai Central, Mahalaxmi (for the Dhobi Ghat), Bandra, Vile Parle (for the domestic airport), Andheri (for the international airport) and Borivali (for Sanjay Gandhi National Park), among others. Make sure you don't catch an express train when you need a slow train – the screens dictate this by an 'S' (Slow) or 'F' (Fast) under 'Mode'.

Central Line Runs from CST to Byculla (for Veermata Jijabai Bhonsle Udyan, formerly Victoria Gardens), Dadar and as far as Neral (for Matheran).

From Churchgate, 2nd-/1st-class fares are ₹5/50 to Mumbai Central, ₹10/55 to Vile Parle, and ₹15/75 to Borivali. 'Tourist tickets' permit unlimited travel in 2nd/1st class for one (₹75/275), three (₹115/440) or five (₹135/515) days.

To avoid the queues, buy a rechargeable **SmartCard** (₹100, ₹52 of which is retained in credit), good for use on either train line, then print out your tickets at the numerous automatic ticket vending machines (ATVMs) before boarding (place your card on the reader, touch the zone of your station, pick the specific station, choose the amount of tickets, choose 'Buy Ticket' and then 'Print').

Watch your valuables, and gals, stick to the ladies-only carriages except late at night, when it's more important to avoid empty cars.

Maharashtra

Includes ➡

Best Places to Eat

- Malaka Spice (p804)
- Sadhana (p777)
- Bhoj (p782)
- Green Leaf (p782)
- Kinara Dhaba Village (p799)

Best Places to Sleep

- Beyond by Sula (p776)
- Verandah in the Forest (p797)
- Tiger Trails Jungle Lodge (p792)
- Hotel Sunderban (p803)
- Hotel Plaza (p790)

Why Go?

India's third-largest and second-most populous state, Maharashtra is an expansive canvas showcasing many of India's iconic attractions. There are palm-fringed beaches; lofty, cool-green mountains; Unesco World Heritage Sites; and bustling cosmopolitan cities. In the far east of the state are some of the nation's most impressive national parks, including Tadoba-Andhari Tiger Reserve.

Inland lie the extraordinary cave temples of Ellora and Ajanta, undoubtedly Maharashtra's greatest monuments, hewn by hand from solid rock. Matheran, a colonial-era hill station served by a toy train, has a certain allure, while pilgrims and inquisitive souls are drawn to cosmopolitan Pune, a city famous for its 'sex guru' and alternative spiritualism. Westwards, the romantic Konkan Coast, fringing the Arabian Sea, is lined with spectacular, crumbling forts and sandy beaches; some of the best are around pretty Malvan resort, which is fast becoming one of India's premier diving centres.

When to Go

Nasik

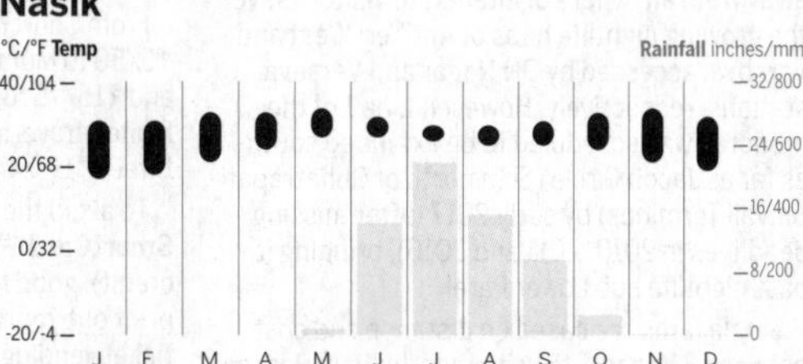

Jan It's party time at Nasik's wineries, marked by grape harvesting and crushing galas.

Sep The frenzied, energetic Ganesh Chaturthi celebrations reach fever pitch.

Dec Clear skies, mild temperatures; the secluded beaches of Murud, Ganpatipule and Tarkali are lovely.

Maharashtra Highlights

1 **Kailasa Temple** (p784) Being amazed by the beauty in the Ellora temple complex.

2 **Ajanta** (p787) Wandering through ancient cave galleries and admiring Buddhist art.

3 **Tadoba-Andhari Tiger Reserve** (p792) Searching for big cats inside the reserve.

4 **Nasik** (p774) Sipping on a Chenin Blanc or Cab-Shiraz in this gorgeous wine country.

5 **Malvan** (p795) Diving or snorkelling in the big blue off this picturesque seaside town.

6 **Janjira** (p793) Pondering the might of a lost civilisation at a colossal fort.

7 **Pune** (p799) Delving into spiritualism and Indian cuisine in this progressive centre.

8 **Bhandardara** (p777) Riding out a monsoon tucked away amid mountain scenery.

9 **Matheran** (p797) Exploring the spectacular hill station viewpoints.

10 **Lonar Meteorite Crater** (p783) Contemplating Mother Nature at a primordial crater.

History

Maharashtra was given its political and ethnic identity by Maratha leader Chhatrapati Shivaji (1627–80), who lorded over the Deccan plateau and much of western India from his stronghold at Raigad. Still highly respected today, Shivaji is credited for instilling a strong, independent spirit among the region's people, as well as establishing Maharashtra as a dominant player in the power relations of medieval India.

From the early 18th century, the state was under the administration of a succession of ministers called the Peshwas, who ruled until 1819, ceding thereafter to the British. After Independence in 1947, western Maharashtra and Gujarat were joined to form Bombay state. But it was back to the future in 1960, when modern Maharashtra was formed with the exclusion of Gujarati-speaking areas and with Mumbai (Bombay) as its capital.

Since then the state has forged ahead to become one of the nation's most prosperous, with India's largest industrial sector, mainly thanks to agriculture, coal-based thermal energy, nuclear electricity and technology parks and software exports.

ℹ Getting There

Mumbai is Maharashtra's main transport hub, though Pune, Aurangabad and Nagpur also have busy airports. Jalgaon station is an important gateway for Ajanta.

Goa airport is handily placed for the far southern resort of Malvan.

ℹ Getting Around

Because the state is so large, internal flights (eg Pune to Nagpur) will really speed up your explorations.

The **Maharashtra State Road Transport Corporation** (MSRTC; www.msrtc.gov.in) runs a comprehensive bus network spanning all major towns and many remote places. Private operators also have comfortable Volvo and Mercedes Benz services between major cities.

Renting a car and driver to explore the Konkan coastline is a good option as public transport is poor on this stretch: allow four or five days to travel between Mumbai and Goa.

NORTHERN MAHARASHTRA

Nasik

0253 / POP 1.57 MILLION / ELEV 565M

Located on the banks of the holy Godavari River, Nasik (or Nashik) gets its name from the episode in the Ramayana where Lakshmana, Rama's brother, hacked off the *nasika* (nose) of Ravana's sister. Today this large provincial city's old quarter has some intriguing wooden architecture, interesting temples that reference the Hindu epic and some huge bathing ghats. The city is notice-

TOP STATE FESTIVALS

Naag Panchami (Jul/Aug) A traditional snake-worshipping festival held in Pune and Kolhapur.

Ganesh Chaturthi (Aug/Sep) Celebrated with fervour all across Maharashtra; Pune goes particularly hysterical in honour of the elephant-headed deity.

Dussehra (Sep & Oct) A Hindu festival, but it also marks the Buddhist celebration of the anniversary of the famous humanist and Dalit leader BR Ambedkar's conversion to Buddhism.

Ellora Ajanta Aurangabad Festival (Oct/Nov) Aurangabad's cultural festival brings together the best classical and folk performers from across the region while promoting a number of artistic traditions and handicrafts on the side.

Kalidas Festival (Nov) Commemorates the literary genius of legendary poet Kalidas through spirited music, dance and theatre in Nagpur.

Sawai Gandharva Sangeet Mahotsav (Dec) An extravaganza of unforgettable performances in Pune by some of the heftiest names in Indian classical music.

SulaFest (www.sulafest.com; Sula Vineyards, Gat 36/2, Govardhan Village, off Gangapur-Savargaon Rd; tickets ₹1700-4700; Feb) Nasik's biggest party and one of India's best boutique music festivals.

Nasik

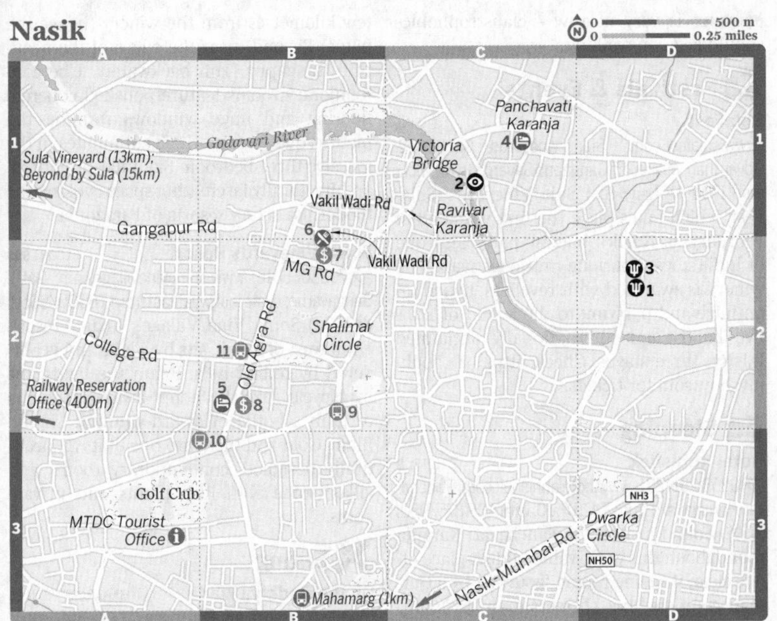

ably cleaner, better maintained and greener than many Indian cities of its size.

As Indian wine continues its coming of age, Nasik's growth potential as a wine tourism destination is wide open. India's best wines are produced locally and an afternoon touring the gorgeous vineyards (p778) in the countryside surrounding the city is a great reason to point your nose in Nasik's direction.

Every 12 years Nasik plays host to the grand **Kumbh Mela**, the largest religious gathering on Earth (the last one was in 2015, the next one in 2027).

Sights

Ramkund GHAT

This bathing ghat in the heart of Nasik's old quarter sees hundreds of Hindu pilgrims arriving daily to bathe, pray and – because the waters provide *moksha* (liberation of the soul) – to immerse the ashes of departed friends and family. There's an adjacent market that adds to the alluring and fascinating scene.

Kala Rama Temple HINDU TEMPLE

(6am-10pm) The city's holiest shrine dates back to 1794 and contains unusual black-stone representations of Rama, Sita and Lakshmana. Legend has it that it occupies the site where Lakshmana sliced off Surpanakha's nose.

Sita Gumpha HINDU TEMPLE

(6am-9.30pm) Sita is said to have hidden in this cave-like temple while being assailed by the evil Ravana. You'll have to stoop and shuffle your way into the cave as the

Nasik

Sights
1 Kala Rama Temple D2
2 Ramkund C1
3 Sita Gumpha D2

Sleeping
4 Hotel Abhishek C1
5 Hotel Samrat B2

Eating
6 Dhaba B1

Information
7 HDFC ATM B2
8 State Bank of India ATM B2

Transport
9 Dwarka Circle B2
10 New Central Bus Stand B3
11 Old Central Bus Stand B2

entrance is very narrow – claustrophobics should keep on walking.

Festivals & Events

SulaFest WINE

(www.sulafest.com; Sula Vineyards, Gat 36/2, Govardhan Village, off Gangapur-Savargaon Rd; tickets ₹1700-4700; Feb) Sula Vineyard's SulaFest, which takes place the first weekend of February, is Nasik's biggest party and one of India's best boutique music festivals. The winery is swarmed with revellers, hyped up on juice and partying to the sound of 120+ live bands and internationally acclaimed DJs on three stages. Check https://in.bookmyshow.com for tickets.

Sleeping

Hotel Abhishek HOTEL $

(0253-2514201; www.hotelabhishek.com; Panchavati Karanja; s/d from ₹425/560, with AC ₹875/980;) Found just off the Panchavati Karanja roundabout, this great-value budget place offers clean if ageing rooms, 'gourmet by a German company' hot showers (6am to 10am) and appetising vegetarian food. The economy rooms are in way too good a shape to be going this cheap. The hands-on owner is tuned into foreign-traveller needs and is around most days.

Hotel Samrat HOTEL $

(0253-2306100; www.hotelsamratnasik.com; Old Agra Rd; s/d from ₹950/1330, with AC ₹1640/1960;) Its veg restaurant has fallen out of favour as a local hot spot, but Samrat's hotel still offers superb value, with comfortable rooms, some of which have large windows and pine furniture. Located right next to the bus stand, with a private bus agent at its doorstep, it's a sensible choice. Wi-fi is speedy but their system is maddening.

★**Beyond by Sula** RESORT $$$

(7875555725; www.sulawines.com; Gangavarhe; r week/weekend incl breakfast ₹7870/9680, Sky Villa from ₹32,670;) Sula Vineyard's brand-new seven-room flagship resort sits a few kilometres from the winery (hence the name: Beyond) near the edges of the beautiful Gangapur Dam backwaters. Ubercontemporary rooms feature polished concrete flooring and huge windows framing the picturesque setting, which culminates in the massive three-bedroom Sky Villa, a modern, architecturally fascinating space evoking the modernist luxury resorts of Patagonia.

Soma Vineyards Resort RESORT $$$

(7028066016; www.somavinevillage.com; Gat 1, Gangavarhe; d/ste incl breakfast from ₹6000/9650;) Soma Vine Village's luxury resort, 17km west of Nasik, sits by a lake and is bordered by rolling hills. Roam the landscape by bicycle, laze the hours away at the spa or grab a bottle of award-winning Chenin Blanc Gold and tuck into one of its 32 beautifully designed, contemporary rooms and villas, some with lush plants and private pools.

EATING PRICE RANGES

The following price ranges refer to the price of a main course.

$ below ₹150

$$ ₹150 to ₹300

$$$ above ₹300

Eating

Divtya Budhlya Wada MAHARASHTRIAN $$

(Anadwali, Gangapur Rd; mains ₹130-340, thalis ₹210-350; 11am-3.30pm & 7-11pm) If you're looking for a spicy kick in the gut, this local hot spot is the place to come for authentic Maharashtrian food that'll make your nose run. Under an atmospheric, lantern-lit bamboo canopy, locals devour the special mutton thali (which could be more generous) and rustic à la carte countryside dishes bone-in, grease, fat and all. Tasty stuff.

It's located 5km northwest of the centre – order an Uber for ₹85 or so. Signed in Marati only.

Dhaba INDIAN $$

(Hotel Panchavati, 430 Vakil Wadi Rd; thali ₹260; 11.30am-3pm & 7-10.30pm) This wildly popular restaurant known as Panchavati around town (but actually called Dhaba) will take your tastebuds on a roller coaster of flavour via its Gujarati thalis spruced up with local touches like mini *bakri* (bread made with sorghum) and served with bullet-train efficiency. Great *dhal tadka* (dhal flavoured with tempered ghee and spices), too. It's inside Hotel Panchavati.

Information

MTDC Tourist Office (0253-2570059; www.maharashtratourism.gov.in; T/I, Golf Club, Old Agra Rd, Matoshree Nagar; 10am-6pm) About 1km south of the Old Central bus stand; helpful staff.

DON'T MISS

MISAL PAV!

Nasik's undeniable breakfast of champions is *misal pav*, an unusual Maharashtrian dish prepared locally with bean sprouts and pulses, topped with a *potato-chiwda* (flattened puffed rice) mixture, *gathiya sev* (crunchy chickpea flour noodles), onions, lemon and coriander and served with a buttered bun – a cornucopia of flavour and texture born in Kolhapur but religiously adopted by Nashikkars.

Opinions are heated, but **Sadhana** (www.facebook.com/sadhanarestaurant.misal; Hardev Bagh, Motiwala College Rd, Barden Phata; meals ₹80; ⌚8am-3pm), 8km west of the city centre (a ₹110 or so Uber ride), is consistently awarded the best in town. Chefs at this rustic institution light up a 560L wood-fired cauldron at 5am every morning, three hours ahead of a breakfast rush that will see bow-tied waiters dance among the jam-packed, straw-topped tables and cot seating within minutes of opening.

So how do you eat it? Fill your bowl with small torn bits of bread, throw a wallop of onions and coriander in the mix and a squeeze of fresh lemon, drizzle a bit of *tari* (a heavily spiced oil mix) to taste (careful now!) and pour a healthy portion of *rassa*, a soupy red masala-laced liquid, over the whole thing until it's all floating in favourful goodness. Dig in with a spoon. Finish things off with *gulachi jalebi* (*jalebi* are orange-coloured coils of deep-fried batter made with jaggery rather than refined sugar) and its absolutely excellent chai. You're welcome!

Getting There

BUS

The **New Central Bus Stand** (☎0253-2309308) has services to Aurangabad (from ₹237, 4½ hours, hourly 6am to 3am), Mumbai (₹275, four hours, hourly) and Pune (non-AC/AC ₹350/650, 4½ hours, hourly). Nasik's **Old Central Bus Stand** (CBS; ☎0253-2309310) has buses to Trimbak (₹33, 45 minutes, hourly 5am to 11pm) and Igatpuri (₹57, one hour, hourly 10.30am to 11pm). South of town, the Mahamarg Bus Stand has services to Mumbai (non-AC ₹250, 4½ hours, hourly), Shirdi (non-AC ₹108, 2½ hours, hourly 6am to 10.30pm) and Ghoti (non-AC ₹45, 1¾ hours, hourly).

Private buses head to Ahmedabad (non-AC/AC sleeper from ₹600/1000, 12 hours), Mumbai (from ₹250/450, four hours), Pune (from ₹300/450, six hours) and Nagpur (AC sleeper f₹1000, 12 hours). There is a handy private bus agent outside Hotel Samrat.

Most private buses depart from Dwarka Circle and most Mumbai-bound buses terminate at Dadar TT Circle in Mumbai.

TRAIN

The Nasik Rd train station is 8km southeast of the town centre, but a useful **railway reservation office** (1st fl, Palika Bazaar, Sharanpur Rd; ⌚8am-8pm Mon-Sat, to 2pm Sun) is 500m west of the Old Central Bus Stand. There are around 15 daily trains to Mumbai so you won't have to wait long; these include the daily Pushpak Express (1st/2AC/sleeper ₹1301/806/203, 4½ hours, 3.15pm). Connections to Aurangabad are not good, with only four daily departures; try the Tapovan Express (2nd class/chair ₹118/391, 3½ hours, 9.50am). An autorickshaw to the station costs about ₹150.

Around Nasik

Bhandardara

The picturesque village of Bhandardara is nestled deep in the folds of the Sahyadris, about 70km from Nasik. A little-visited place surrounded by craggy mountains, it is one of Maharashtra's best escapes from the bustle of urban India. The lush mountain scenery, especially during the monsoon, is extraordinary.

Most of Bhandardara's habitation is thrown around **Arthur Lake**, a horseshoe-shaped reservoir fed by the waters of the Pravara River, which counts as one of India's largest. The lake is barraged on one side by the imposing Wilson Dam, a colonial-era structure dating back to 1910. Hikers should consider a hike to the summit of **Mt Kalsubai**, which at 1646m was once used as an observation point by the Marathas. Alternatively, you could hike to the ruins of the **Ratangad Fort**, another of Shivaji's erstwhile strongholds; or to several Bollywood-preferred waterfalls like **Randha Falls** or **Umbrella Falls**. Guided highlight tours run ₹600.

The charming **Anandvan Resort** (☎02424-257320; www.anandvanresorts.com; Ghatghar Rd,

WORTH A TRIP

GRAPES OF NASIK

From wimpy raisins to full-bodied wines, the grapes of Nasik have come a long way. The surrounding region had been producing table grapes since ancient times; however, it was only in the early 1990s that a couple of entrepreneurs realised that Nasik, with its fertile soils and temperate climate, boasted good conditions for wine cultivation. In 1997 industry pioneer **Sula Vineyards** fearlessly invested in a crop of Sauvignon Blanc and Chenin Blanc and the first batch of domestic wines hit the shelves in 2000. Nasik hasn't looked back.

'Over the last 10 years, quality and wine consistency have been ramped up, as has investment (both by mergers/takeovers and via foreign investment and know-how)', says international wine consultant, writer and sommelier Harshal Danger-Shah. 'The results are in the glass: Indian wine is tasting fresher and more enjoyable than ever before.'

These days the wine list in most of Nasik's wineries has stretched to include Shiraz, Merlot, Cabernet, Semillon and Zinfandel as well as a few sparkling wines; and bars and restaurants in India's bigger cities have finally got hip to domestic wines. Even the pairings have evolved: ever tried a nice Indian Chenin Blanc alongside Keralan seafood? Or an Indian Chardonnay with butter chicken?

It's well-worth sampling these drops firsthand by visiting one of the region's beautiful estates. Oenophiles should enlist **Wine Friend** (9822439051; www.winefriend.in), the only experienced guide doing wine speciality tours around Nasik's vineyards (₹6000 plus tasting fees). If you're just looking for a designated driver, cars can be hired from ₹2400. Try the friendly and English-speaking Sanil at **SCK Rent-A-Car** (8888080525; scktravels2015@gmail.com) for a horn-free ride.

Sula Vineyards (9970090010; www.sulawines.com; Gat 36/2, Govardhan Village, off Gangapur-Savargaon Rd; 11am-11pm), located 15km west of Nasik, offers a professional tour (around 45 minutes) of its impressive estate and high-tech facilities. This is rounded off with a wine-tasting session (four/six wines ₹150/250) that features its best drops, including at least one from its top-end Rasa line. The cafe here has commanding views of the countryside.

York Winery (0253-2230701; www.yorkwinery.com; Gat 15/2, Gangavarhe Village, Gangapur-Savargaon Rd; noon-10pm, tours 12.30-6pm) A further kilometre from Sula Vineyards, family-owned York Winery offers tours and wine-tasting sessions (five/seven wines ₹150/250) in a top-floor room that has scenic views of the lake and surrounding hills. Four reds, including its flagship barrel-aged Cab Shiraz, three whites, a Rosé and a sparkling are produced. There's a large garden where Western snacks (olives, cheeses) are offered.

Soma Vine Village (7028066016; www.somavinevillage.com; Gat 1, Gangavarhe; 11.30am-6.30pm) One of Nasik's newest wineries, Soma Vine Village, 17km west of the city centre on the same road as Sula and York, offers 45-minute tours that end in a sampling plucked from its 11-wine portfolio (five/seven wines ₹250/350), including its award-winning Chenin Blanc Gold and its new Rosé dessert wine, both excellent.

Chandon (9561065030; www.chandon.co.in; Gat 652/653, Taluka-Dindori Village; 9am-6pm) Nasik's newest winery is a world-class facility on meticulously manicured grounds that easily rank as Nasik's most peaceful and beautiful. Tastings (₹500), by appointment only, feature India's leading sparkling wines, Chandon Brut (Chenin Blanc/Chardonnay/Pinot Noir) and Brut Rosé (Shiraz/Pinot Noir). Sip your bubbly in the upscale contemporary lounge, wine gallery or on the tremendously picturesque terrace. It's 26km north of Nasik.

Grover Zampa (02553-204379; www.groverzampa.in; Gat 967/1026, Village Sanjegaon, Tallgatpuri; 10am-5.30pm, tours 10.30am, 2.30pm & 4pm) It first produced juice with imported French vines at its Karnataka estate in 1992. Today, it's India's oldest surviving winery and easily its most most lauded (74 international awards between 2014 and 2016 alone). Tours and tastings at its Nasik estate, 53km southwest of the city, take place in its cinematic cave (five/seven wines ₹500/650). The Soireé Brut Rosé and the top-end Chêne Grand Réserve Tempranillo-Shiraz are fantastic. If you come out this way, do dine at nearby **Malaka Spice** (www.malakaspice.com; Vallonné Vineyard, Gat 504, Kavnai Shiver; mains ₹285-535; 11.30am-11.30pm), Nasik's best and most scenic wine country restaurant.

Village Shendi; s/d from ₹5450/5950; ❄📶), a hilltop hotel with a choice of comfy cottages and villas overlooking Arthur Lake, allows you to sleep in style.

Bhandardara can be accessed by taking a local bus from Nasik's **Mahamarg bus stand** to Ghoti (₹64, one hour), from where shared jeeps carry on the remaining kilometres to Bhandardara (₹40, 45 minutes). A taxi from Nasik can also drop you at your resort for about ₹2000.

Igatpuri

Vipassana International Academy MEDITATION

(☎02553-244076; www.giri.dhamma.org; Dhamma Giri, Igatpuri; donations accepted; ⏱visitors centre 9.30am-5.30pm) Located about 44km south of Nasik, Igatpuri is home to the headquarters of the world's largest *vipassana* meditation institution, the Vipassana International Academy. Ten-day residential courses (advance bookings compulsory) are held throughout the year, though teachers warn that it requires rigorous discipline. Basic accommodation, food and meditation instruction are provided free of charge, but donations upon completion are accepted. Visitors can watch a 20-minute intro video or take part in a 10-minute mini Anapana meditation session.

This strict form of meditation was first taught by Gautama Buddha in the 6th century BC and was reintroduced to India by teacher SN Goenka in the 1960s.

Buses (₹57, one hour, hourly 10.30am to 11pm) and shared taxis (per person ₹500) for Igatpuri depart from Nasik's Old Bus Stand. Numerous daily trains call at Igatpuri from Nasik Rd station and Mumbai's CST.

Trimbak

Trimbakeshwar Temple HINDU TEMPLE

(entrance ₹200, to avoid queue ₹200; ⏱6am-10pm) The moody Trimbakeshwar Temple stands in the centre of Trimbak, 33km west of Nasik. It's one of India's most sacred temples, containing a highly venerated *jyoti linga,* one of the 12 most important shrines to Shiva. Although the sign says only Hindus are allowed in, it's outdated and non-Hindus are welcome to enter (expect mere seconds in the inner sanctum as security corrals the crowd through). Mobile phones are prohibited.

Nearby, the waters of the Godavari River flow into the Gangadwar bathing tank, where all are welcome to wash away their sins.

Trimbak is a quick day trip from Nasik so most folks don't spend the night. But there are loads of guesthouses and resorts, many of which have panoramic views of the striking Bhahmagiri mountain range. The road leading to the temple is chock-full of snack stalls and restaurants if you fancy a bite.

Buses for Trimbak depart Nasik's Old Bus Stand hourly 5am to 11pm (₹33, 45 minutes). The last bus back to Nasik departs at 10.30pm

Aurangabad

☎0240 / POP 1.28 MILLION / ELEV 515M

Aurangabad laid low through most of the tumultuous history of medieval India and only hit the spotlight when the last Mughal emperor, Aurangzeb, made the city his capital from 1653 to 1707. With the emperor's death came the city's rapid decline, but the brief period of glory saw the building of some fascinating monuments, including Bibi-qa-Maqbara, a Taj Mahal replica, and these continue to draw a steady trickle of visitors. Alongside other historic relics, such as a group of ancient Buddhist caves, these Mughal relics make Aurangabad a good choice for a weekend excursion from Mumbai. But the real reason for traipsing here is because the town is an excellent base for exploring the World Heritage Sites of Ellora and Ajanta.

Silk fabrics were once Aurangabad's chief revenue generator and the town is still known across the world for its hand-woven Himroo and Paithani saris.

Sights

★Bibi-qa-Maqbara MONUMENT

(Indian/foreigner ₹15/200; ⏱6am-8pm) Built by Aurangzeb's son Azam Khan in 1679 as a mausoleum for his mother Rabia-ud-Daurani, Bibi-qa-Maqbara is widely known as the poor man's Taj. With its four minarets flanking a central onion-domed mausoleum, the white structure certainly does bear a striking resemblance to Agra's Taj Mahal.

Aurangabad Caves CAVE

(Indian/foreigner ₹15/200; ⏱6am-6pm) Architecturally speaking, the Aurangabad Caves aren't a patch on Ellora or Ajanta, but they do shed light on early Buddhist architecture and make for a quiet and peaceful outing. Carved out of the hillside in the 6th or 7th century AD, the 10 caves, comprising two

Aurangabad

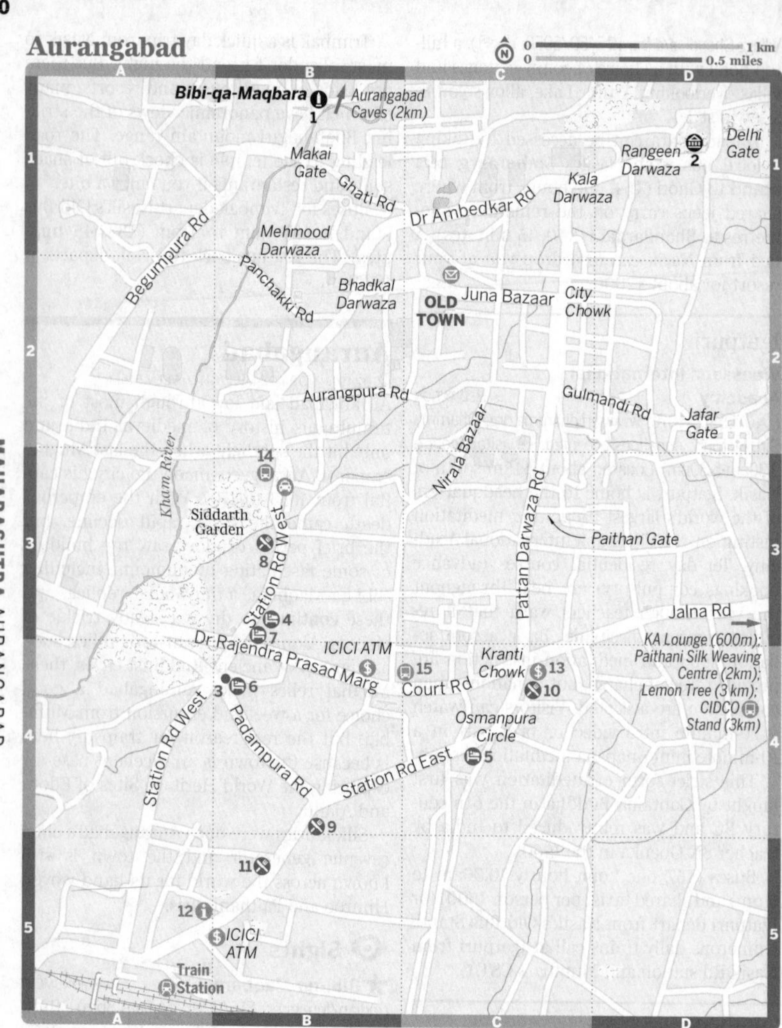

groups 1km apart (retain your ticket for entry into both sets), are all Buddhist.

Shrimat Chatrapati Shivaji Museum MUSEUM
(Dr Ambedkar Rd; ₹5; ⊙10.30am-6.30pm Fri-Wed)
This simple museum is dedicated to the life of the Maratha hero Shivaji. Its collection includes a 500-year-old chain-mail suit and a copy of the Quran, handwritten by Aurangzeb.

Tours

MSRTC (☎0240-2242164; www.msrtc.gov.in; Central Bus Stand, Station Rd West) operates daily Volvo AC bus tours to the Ajanta (₹682) and Ellora (₹265) Caves. Be aware that these are mass-market tours popular with domestic tourists and designed to cover as much ground as possible in a short period of time. Prices are transport only – they do not cover a guide or admission fees. The Ellora tour also includes all the other major Aurangabad sites along with Daulatabad Fort, which is a lot to swallow in a day. Though tours technically start at the Central Bus Stand (p783), you can hop on at the second stop at MTDC Holiday Resort (Station Rd East) at 7.30am (Ajanta) and

Aurangabad

8.30am (Ellora), which is also the best spot for information.

Ashoka Tours & Travels SIGHTSEEING
(☎9890340816, 0240-2359102; www.touristaurangabad.com; Hotel Panchavati, Station Rd West; ⏰7am-8pm) The stand-out Aurangabad agency, with excellent city and regional tours and decent car hire at fair rates. Prices for an air-con car with up to four people are ₹1450 for Ellora and ₹2450 for Ajanta. Run by Ashok T Kadam, a knowledgeable former autorickshaw driver.

Sleeping

★Hotel Panchavati HOTEL $
(☎0240-2328755; www.hotelpanchavati.com; Station Rd West; s/d ₹1000/1130, r with AC ₹1250; ❄@📶) A traveller-oriented budget hotel in town, the Panchavati is run by ever-helpful, switched-on management who understand travellers' needs. Rooms are compact but thoughtfully appointed, with crown moulding, comfortable beds (with paisley-style bedspreads) and thick bath towels. There are two decent restaurants and a 'bar' (read: drinking room) and it's a great place to hook up with fellow intrepid nomads.

Hotel Raviraj HOTEL $
(☎0240-2352124; www.hotelraviraj.in; Rajendra Prasad Marg; r with AC from ₹1690; ❄📶) The standard rooms at this pleasant midrange option masquerading as a budget hotel are easily Aurangabad's best deal. Spacious, comfy linens, flat-screen TVs, good bathrooms (with motion-sensor lighting) and (weak) wi-fi. The pricier executives are basically the same, with more polished furniture. Tack on a friendly staff, a leafy foyer, restaurant/bar and beer-friendly 1st-floor terrace and it's tough to beat.

Hotel Gurjas HOTEL $
(☎0240-2323841; www.hotelgurjas.com; Osmanpura Circle, Station Rd East; s/d ₹1026/1139, with AC ₹1250/1370; ❄📶) The former Hotel Oberoi was manhandled by the well-known, five-star luxury chain into changing its name. Voila! Hotel Gurjas was born. Owned by the same people behind Hotel Panchavati, this means good service and helpful staff. The spacious rooms are modern with flat-screen TVs, comfy beds, desks and attractive, newly renovated bathrooms.

Call for a free pick-up from the train or bus stations.

Hotel Green Olive HOTEL $$
(☎0240-2329490; www.hotelgreenolive.com; 13/3 Bhagya Nagar, CBS Rd; s/d from ₹3570/4760; ❄📶) Cramped bathrooms aside, this boutique-ish business hotel offers stylish, well-equipped and -maintained rooms. The friendly staff here looks after guests commendably and can organise transport and tours; there's a good bar and restaurant on the premises.

★Lemon Tree HOTEL $$$
(☎0240-6603030; www.lemontreehotels.com; R7/2 Chikalthana, Airport Rd; s/d incl breakfast from ₹7790/9350; ❄@📶🏊) The Lemon Tree offers elegance and class, looking more like a billionaire's luxury whitewashed Mediterranean villa than an Indian hotel. It's well designed too: all rooms face inwards, overlooking perhaps the best pool in the Decca plateau – all 50m of it. The artsy standard rooms, though not large, are brightened by vivid tropical tones offset against snow-white walls.

Eating

Kailash INDIAN $
(Station Rd East; mains ₹50-150; ⏰8am-11pm; ❄) This bustling pure-veg restaurant looks and

feels vaguely like an half-hearted Indian take on an American diner, with big portions of food in familial surrounds. There's lots of Punjabi and South Indian food, as well as rice and noodle dishes, and an extensive list of *pav bhaji* options, a Mumbai street-food staple. It's rightfully popular.

★Bhoj INDIAN $$
(Station Rd West; thali ₹210; ⌚11am-3pm & 7-11pm) Rightly famous for its delicious, unlimited Rajasthani and Gujarati thalis, Bhoj is a wonderful place to refuel and relax after a hard day on the road (or rail). It's on the 1st floor of a somewhat scruffy little shopping arcade, but the decor, ambience, service and presentation are all first rate. Best thali in Maharashtra!

Green Leaf INDIAN $$
(www.greenleafpureveg.com; Shop 6-9, Fame Tapadiya Multiplex, Town Centre; mains ₹140-280; ⌚noon-11pm; 📶) Aurangabad's favourite modern vegetarian is loved for delectable pure-veg dishes that really pop with flavour (try the veg handi or paneer Hyderabadi) and come with spice level indicators (one chilli pepper equals medium!). Teal-panted servers gracefully navigate the clean, contemporary surrounds. So clean, in fact, the kitchen is open for all to see. It's 400m from CIDCO Bus Stand.

Swad Restaurant INDIAN $$
(Station Rd East, Kanchan Chamber; thali ₹200) Though prices are similar, always-packed Swad is the simpler, more local and slightly greasier counterpart to some of our other favourite spots in town. Waiters clad in bright Rajasthani-style turbans sling spicy *sabzi* (vegetables), dhal and other Gujarati-Rajasthani thali delights – an endless flavour train under the benevolent gaze of patron saint swami Yogiraj Hanstirth.

Tandoor NORTH INDIAN $$
(Station Rd East, Shyam Chambers; mains ₹150-380; ⌚11am-11pm) Offers fine tandoori dishes, flavoursome North Indian veg and nonveg options and an extensive beer list (for Aurangabad) in a weirdly Pharaonic atmosphere. Try the wonderful sizzler kebabs. A few Chinese dishes are also on offer, but patrons clearly prefer the dishes coming out of... well... the tandoor.

Drinking & Nightlife

KA Lounge BAR
(Satya Dharam Complex, Akashwari Cir, Jalna Rd; cocktails from ₹320; ⌚noon-11pm Mon-Fri, to 1am Sat & Sun; 📶) Aurangabad's one and only trendy cocktail bar is brand-spanking new and caters to the city's upwardly hip who plop down on cosy lounge seating amid exposed brick walls and groove to DJ-spun hip-hop, jazz and house on Saturday and Sunday. Try the basil and green chilli mojito for a cool burn.

Shopping

Himroo material is a traditional Aurangabad speciality made from cotton, silk and metallic threads. Most of today's Himroo shawls and saris are produced using power looms, but some showrooms still stock hand-loomed cloth.

Himroo saris start at around ₹2000 for a cotton and silk blend. Paithani saris, which are of superior quality, range from ₹8000 to ₹150,000 – but some of them take more than a year to make. If you're buying, make sure you get authentic Himroo, not 'Aurangabad silk'.

Paithani Silk Weaving Centre TEXTILES
(www.paithanisilk.com; 54, P-1, Town Center, Lokmat Nagar; ⌚9.30am-9pm) One of the best places to come and watch weavers at work is the Paithani Silk Weaving Centre where you'll find good-quality products for sale. It's about 6km east of Kranti Chowk (behind the Air India office), so take a taxi.

Information

Indiatourism (Government of India Tourism; ☎0240-2364999; www.incredibleindia.org; MTDC Holiday Resort, Station Rd East; ⌚9.30am-6pm Mon-Fri) India-wide information is available at India's national tourist board office in Aurangabad.

MTDC Office (☎0240-2343169; www.maharashtratourism.gov.in; MTDC Holiday Resort, Station Rd East; ⌚10am-1pm & 1.30-5.30pm Mon-Sat) Quite helpful and has a stock of brochures.

Post Office (www.indiapost.gov.in; Juna Bazaar; ⌚10am-6pm Mon-Sat)

Getting There & Away

AIR

Aurangabad Airport (Chikkalthana Airport) is 10km east of town. Daily direct flights go to Delhi and Mumbai with both **Air India** (☎0240-2483392; www.airindia.in; Airliens House, Town Centre, Jalna Rd; ⌚10am-1pm & 2-5pm Mon-Sat) and **Jet Airways** (☎0240-2441392; www.jetairways.com; 4, Santsheel, Vidyanagar 7 Hills, Jalna Rd) and to Hyderabad with **Trujet**

(☎0240-2471818; www.trujet.com; Aurangabad Airport).

BUS

Buses leave about every half-hour from the **MSRTC/Central Bus Stand** (☎0240-2242164; Station Rd West) to Pune (non-AC/AC ₹341/661, 5½ hours, 5am to 11.30pm) and Nasik (non-AC ₹214, 4½ hours, 6am to 12.15pm). Private bus agents are clustered on Dr Rajendra Prasad Marg and Court Rd; a few sit closer to the bus stand. Deluxe overnight bus destinations include Mumbai (AC sleeper ₹774 to ₹1400, 7½ to 9½ hours), Ahmedabad (AC/non-AC sleeper from ₹800/500, 13 to 15 hours) and Nagpur (AC sleeper ₹660 to ₹1100, non-AC ₹800, 8½ to 10 hours).

Ordinary buses head to Ellora from the MSRTC bus stand every half-hour (AC/non-AC ₹251/32, 30 minutes, 5am to 12.30am) and Jalgaon (non-AC ₹177, four hours, 5am to 8pm) via Fardapur (₹120, three hours), which is the drop-off point for Ajanta.

From the **CIDCO Bus Stand** (☎0240-2240149; Airport Rd), by the Lemon Tree hotel junction, six ordinary buses leave direct for the Lonar meteorite crater (₹180, 4½ hours, 5am, 6am, 8am, 10am, 12.30pm and 1pm).

TRAIN

Aurangabad's **train station** (Station Rd East) is not on a main line, but it has four daily direct trains to/from Mumbai. The Tapovan Express (2nd class/chair ₹173/571, 7½ hours) departs Aurangabad at 2.35pm. The Janshatabdi Express (2nd class/chair ₹223/686, 6½ hours) departs Aurangabad at 6am. For Hyderabad, trains include the Ajanta Express (sleeper/2AC ₹233/1226, 10 hours, 10.45pm). To reach northern or eastern India, take a bus to Jalgaon and board a train there.

ℹ Getting Around

Autorickshaws are common here and are bookable (along with taxis) with Ola Cabs (www.olacabs.com). The taxi stand is next to the MSRTC/Central Bus Stand; shared 4WDs also depart from here for Ellora and Daulatabad but are usually very packed. Renting a car and driver is a much better option.

You can hire a car and driver through **Ashoka Tours & Travels** (p781): a return trip to Ellora is ₹1250/1450 in a car/AC car, to Ajanta it's ₹2250/2450.

WORTH A TRIP

LONAR METEORITE CRATER

If you like offbeat adventures, travel to Lonar to explore a prehistoric natural wonder. About 50,000 years ago, a meteorite slammed into the earth here, leaving behind a massive crater 2km across and 170m deep (it's said to be the world's third largest). In scientific jargon, it's the only hypervelocity natural-impact crater in basaltic rock in the world. In lay terms, it's as tranquil and relaxing a spot as you could hope to find, with a shallow green lake at its base and wilderness all around, including aquatic birds. The lake water is supposedly alkaline and excellent for the skin. Scientists think the meteorite is still embedded about 600m below the southeastern rim of the crater.

The crater's edge is home to several Hindu temples as well as wildlife, including langurs, peacocks, deer and numerous birds.

There are regular buses between Lonar and the CIDCO bus stand in Aurangabad (₹180, 4½ hours, 5am, 6am, 8am, 10am, 12.30pm and 1pm).

Around Aurangabad

Daulatabad

This one's straight out of a Tolkien fantasy. A most beguiling structure, the 12th-century hilltop fortress of **Daulatabad** (Indian/foreigner ₹15/200; ⏰6am-6pm) is located about 15km north of Aurangabad, en route to Ellora. Now in ruins, the citadel was originally conceived as an impregnable fort by the Yadava kings. Its most infamous high point came in 1328, when it was named Daulatabad (City of Fortune) by eccentric Delhi sultan Mohammed Tughlaq and made the capital – he even marched the entire population of Delhi 1100km south to populate it. Ironically, Daulatabad – despite being better positioned strategically than Delhi – soon proved untenable as a capital due to an acute water crisis, and Tughlaq forced the weary inhabitants all the way back to Delhi, which had by then been reduced to a ghost town.

Daulatabad's central bastion sits atop a 200m-high craggy outcrop known as Devagiri (Hill of the Gods), surrounded by a 5km **fort** (Indian/foreigner ₹15/200; ⏰6am-6pm). The climb to the summit takes about an hour, and leads past an ingenious series of defences, including multiple doorways designed with odd angles and spike-studded doors to prevent elephant charges. A tower of victory, known as the Chand Minar (Tower of the Moon), built in 1435, soars 60m above the ground to the right; it's closed to visitors. Higher up, you can walk into the Chini Mahal, where Abul Hasan Tana Shah, king of Golconda, was held captive for 12 years before his death in 1699. Nearby, there's a 6m cannon, cast from five different metals and engraved with Aurangzeb's name.

Part of the ascent goes through a pitch-black, bat-infested, water-seeping, spiralling tunnel. Guides (₹500) are available near the ticket counter to show you around, and their torch-bearing assistants will lead you through the dark passageway for a small tip. On the way down you'll be left to your own devices, so carry a torch.

As the fort is in ruins (with crumbling staircases and sheer drops) and involves a steep ascent, the elderly, children and those suffering from vertigo or claustrophobia will find it a tough challenge. Allow 2½ hours to explore the structure, and bring water.

Ellora

02437

Give a man a hammer and chisel and he'll create art for posterity. Come to the Unesco World Heritage Site **Ellora cave temples** (Indian/foreigner ₹30/500; 6am-6pm Wed-Mon), located 30km from Aurangabad, and you'll know exactly what we mean. The epitome of ancient Indian rock-cut architecture, these caves were chipped out laboriously over five centuries by generations of Buddhist, Hindu and Jain monks. Monasteries, chapels, temples – the caves served every purpose and they were stylishly embellished with a profusion of remarkably detailed sculptures.

Undoubtedly Ellora's shining moment is the awesome Kailasa Temple (Cave 16), the world's largest monolithic sculpture, hewn top to bottom against a rocky slope by 7000 labourers over a period of 150 years. Dedicated to Lord Shiva, it is clearly among the best that ancient Indian architecture has to offer.

Sights

Ellora has 34 caves in all: 12 Buddhist (AD 600–800), 17 Hindu (AD 600–900) and five Jain (AD 800–1000) – though the exact time scales of these caves' construction is the subject of academic debate.

Unlike the caves at Ajanta, which are carved into a sheer rock face, the Ellora caves line a 2km-long escarpment, the gentle slope of which allowed architects to build elaborate courtyards in front of the shrines and render them with sculptures of a surreal quality.

The established academic theory is that Ellora represents the renaissance of Hinduism under the Chalukya and Rashtrakuta dynasties, the subsequent decline of Indian Buddhism and a brief resurgence of Jainism under official patronage. However, due to the absence of inscriptional evidence, it's been impossible to accurately date most of Ellora's monuments – some scholars argue that some Hindu temples predate those in the Buddhist group. What is certain is that their coexistence at one site indicates a lengthy period of religious tolerance.

Official guides can be hired at the ticket office in front of the Kailasa Temple for ₹1370 (up to five people). Guides have an extensive knowledge of cave architecture so are worth the investment. If your tight itinerary forces you to choose between Ellora or Ajanta, Ellora wins hands down in terms of architecture (though Ajanta's setting is more beautiful and more of a pleasure to explore).

Ellora is very popular with domestic tourists; if you can visit on a weekday, it's far less crowded.

★Kailasa Temple — HINDU TEMPLE

One of India's greatest monuments, this astonishing temple, carved from solid rock, was built by King Krishna I in AD 760 to represent Mt Kailasa (Kailash), Shiva's Himalayan abode. To say that the assignment was daring would be an understatement. Three huge trenches were bored into the sheer cliff face, a process that entailed removing 200,000 tonnes of rock by hammer and chisel, before the temple could begin to take shape and its remarkable sculptural decoration could be added.

Covering twice the area of the Parthenon in Athens and being half as high again, Kailasa is an engineering marvel that was executed straight from the head with zero margin for error. Modern draughtsmen might have a lesson or two to learn here.

The temple houses several intricately carved panels, depicting scenes from the Ramayana, the Mahabharata and the adventures of Krishna. Also worth admiring are the immense monolithic pillars that stand in the courtyard, flanking the entrance on both sides, and the southeastern gallery that has 10 giant and fabulous panels depicting the different avatars (incarnations of a deity) of Lord Vishnu.

After you're done with the main enclosure, bypass the hordes of snack-munching day trippers to explore the temple's many dank, bat urine-soaked corners with their numerous forgotten carvings. Afterwards, hike up an overgrown foot trail (or bypass the scaffolding to walk up sturdier rock) to the south of the complex that takes you to the top perimeter of the 'cave', from where you can get a bird's-eye view of the entire temple complex.

Buddhist Caves CAVE

Calm and contemplation infuse the 12 Buddhist caves, which stretch to the south of Kailasa. All are Buddhist *viharas* (monasteries) used for study and worship, but these multistoreyed structures also included cooking, living and sleeping areas. The one exception is Cave 10, which is a *chaitya* (assembly hall). While the earliest caves are simple, Caves 11 and 12 are more ambitious; both comprise three storeys and are on par with the more impressive Hindu temples.

Cave 1, the simplest *vihara,* may have been a granary. **Cave 2** is notable for its ornate pillars and the imposing seated Buddha that faces the setting sun. **Cave 3** and **Cave 4** are unfinished and not well preserved.

Cave 5 is the largest *vihara* in this group at 18m wide and 36m long; the rows of stone benches hint that it may once have been an assembly hall.

Cave 6 is an ornate *vihara* with wonderful images of Tara, consort of the Bodhisattva Avalokitesvara, and of the Buddhist goddess of learning, Mahamayuri, looking remarkably similar to Saraswati, her Hindu equivalent. **Cave 7** is an unadorned hall. **Cave 8** is the first cave in which the sanctum is detached from the rear wall. **Cave 9**, located above Cave 8, is notable for its wonderfully carved fascia.

Cave 10 is the only *chaitya* in the Buddhist group and one of the finest in India. Its ceiling features ribs carved into the stonework; the grooves were once fitted with wooden panels. The balcony and upper gallery offer a closer view of the ceiling and a frieze depicting amorous couples. A decorative window gently illuminates an enormous figure of the teaching Buddha.

Cave 11, the Do Thal (Two Storey) Cave, is entered through its third basement level, not discovered until 1876. Like Cave 12, it

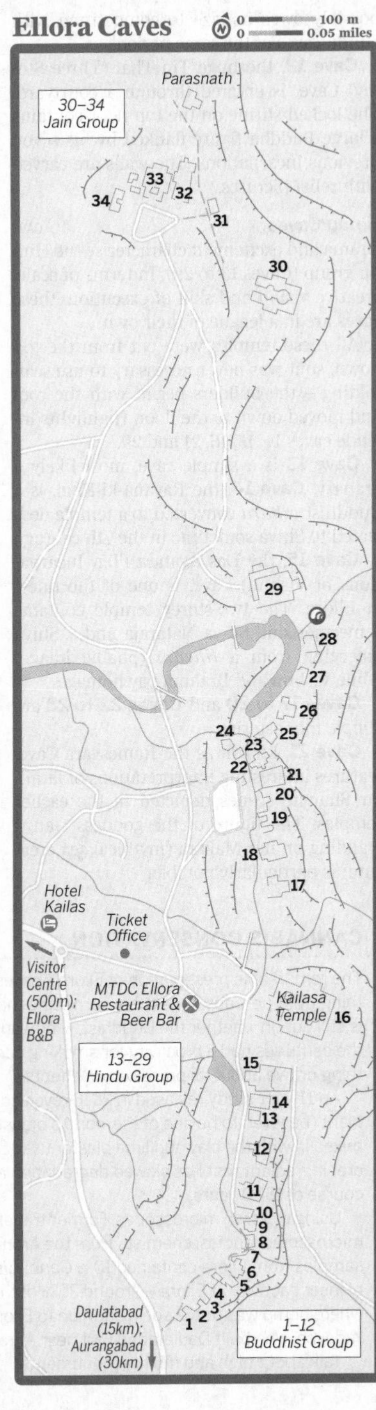

possibly owes its size to competition with Hindu caves of the same period.

Cave 12, the huge Tin Thal (Three Storey) Cave, is entered through a courtyard. The locked shrine on the top floor contains a large Buddha figure flanked by his seven previous incarnations. The walls are carved with relief pictures.

Hindu Caves
CAVE

Drama and excitement characterise the Hindu group (Caves 13 to 29). In terms of scale, creative vision and skill of execution, these caves are in a league of their own.

All these temples were cut from the top down, so it was never necessary to use scaffolding – the builders began with the roof and moved down to the floor. Highlights include caves 14, 15, 16, 21 and 29.

Cave 13 is a simple cave, most likely a granary. **Cave 14**, the Ravana-ki-Khai, is a Buddhist *vihara* converted to a temple dedicated to Shiva sometime in the 7th century.

Cave 15, the Das Avatara (Ten Incarnations of Vishnu) Cave, is one of the finest at Ellora. The two-storey temple contains a mesmerising Shiva Nataraja and a Shiva emerging from a *lingam* (phallic image) while Vishnu and Brahma pay homage.

Caves 17 to 20 and **Caves 22 to 28** are simple monasteries.

Cave 21, known as the Ramesvara Cave, features interesting interpretations of familiar Shaivite scenes depicted in the earlier temples. The figure of the goddess Ganga standing on her Makara (mythical sea creature) is particularly notable.

The large **Cave 29**, the Dumar Lena, is thought to be a transitional model between the simpler hollowed-out caves and the fully developed temples exemplified by the Kailasa. It has views over a nearby waterfall, though the path was inaccessible at time of writing. It's best reached via the MSRTC bus.

Jain Caves
CAVE

The five Jain caves, the last created at Ellora, may lack the ambitious size of the best Hindu temples, but they are exceptionally detailed, with some remarkable paintings and carvings.

The caves are 1km north of the last Hindu temple (Cave 29) at the end of the bitumen road; there is a MSRTC bus departing from in front of Kailasa Temple that runs back and forth (₹21 return).

Cave 30, the Chhota Kailasa (Little Kailasa), is a poor imitation of the great Kailasa Temple and stands by itself some distance from the other Jain temples. It's reached via the unmarked stairway between Caves 31 and 32.

In contrast, **Cave 32**, the Indra Sabha (Assembly Hall of Indra), is the finest of the Jain temples. Its ground-floor plan is similar to that of the Kailasa, but the upstairs area is as ornate and richly decorated as the downstairs is plain. There are images of the Jain *tirthankars* (great teachers) Parasnath and Gomateshvara, the latter surrounded by wildlife. Inside the shrine is a seated figure of Mahavira, the last *tirthankar* and founder of the Jain religion.

CANNABIS CONSERVATION

The remarkable preservation of Ellora's caves and paintings could be attributed to many things, but perhaps none more surprising than a healthy dose of hemp. While the jury is still out on whether the Buddhist, Hindu and Jain monks that called Ellora home over the centuries had a proclivity for smoking cannabis, archaeologists are sure they knew a thing or two about its preservation effects.

An 11-year study released in 2016 revealed that hemp, a variety of the *Cannabis sativa* plant (believed to be one of the world's oldest domesticated crops), has been discovered mixed in with the clay and lime plaster used at Ellora and is credited with being the secret ingredient that has slowed degradation at the Unesco World Heritage Site over the course of 1500 years.

Using electron microscopes, Fourier transforms, infra-red spectroscopy and stereomicroscopic studies, chemists from the Archaeological Survey of India found that samples from Ellora contained 10% *Cannabis sativa*, which resulted in reduced levels of insect activity at Ellora – around 25% of the paintings at Ajanta have been destroyed, where hemp was not used. In addition to Ellora, hemp was also implemented by the Yadavas, who built Daulatabad Fort near Aurangabad in the 12th century.

Talk about high and mighty monuments!

Cave 31 is really an extension of Cave 32. **Cave 33**, the Jagannath Sabha, is similar in plan to Cave 32 and has some well-preserved sculptures. The final temple, the small **Cave 34**, also has interesting sculptures. On the hilltop over the Jain temples, a 5m-high image of Parasnath looks down on Ellora.

Sleeping & Eating

Ellora B&B GUESTHOUSE **$**
(☎9960589867; ellorabedandbreakfast@gmail.com; Ellora Village; s/d incl breakfast from ₹500/800) For a bit of rustic cultural immersion, good-hearted man about town Sadeek and his uncle Rafiq have four simple rooms in their village home, 2km from the caves (and the crowds). The three best rooms open out onto a breezy terrace with farmland and mountain views and feature renovated en suite bathrooms with sit-down flush toilets and 24-hour hot water.

Grandma cooks up *poha* (flattened rice with spices), *upma* (semolina cooked with onions, spices, chilli peppers and coconut) and *aloo paratha* (potato-filled flatbread) for breakfast. Fancy it ain't, but the hospitality makes up for it.

Hotel Kailas HOTEL **$$**
(☎02437-244446; www.hotelkailas.com; r with/without AC ₹3570/2500; ❄📶) The sole decent hotel near the site, with attractive air-con stone cottages set in leafy grounds. The restaurant (mains ₹90 to ₹280) is excellent, with a menu chalked up on a blackboard that includes sandwiches, breakfasts, curries and tandoori favourites. Sold in increments of three hours for ₹100, wi-fi, however, is ridiculous.

Information

Ellora Visitor Centre (⏲9am-5pm Wed-Mon) Ellora's impressive visitor centre, 750m west of the site, is worth dropping by to put the caves in historical context. It features modern displays and information panels, a 15-minute video presentation and two galleries: one on the Kailasa Temple (with a diorama of the temple) and the other dedicated to the site itself.

Getting There & Away

Note that the temples are closed on Tuesday. Buses depart Aurangabad every half-hour (AC/non-AC ₹251/32, 30 minutes, 5am to 12.30am); the last bus departs from Ellora at 9pm. Share 4WDs are also an option, but get packed; they leave when full and stop outside the bus stand in Aurangabad (₹30). A full-day tour to Ellora, with stops en route, costs ₹1450 in an air-con car; try **Ashoka Tours & Travels** (p781). Autorickshaws ask for ₹800.

Ajanta

☎02438

Superbly set in a remote river valley 105km northeast of Aurangabad, the remarkable cave temples of Ajanta are this region's second World Heritage Site. Much older than Ellora, these secluded caves date from around the 2nd century BC to the 6th century AD and were among the earliest monastic institutions to be constructed in the country. Ironically, it was Ellora's rise that brought about Ajanta's downfall and historians believe the site was abandoned once the focus shifted to Ellora.

As the Deccan forest claimed and shielded the caves, with roots and shoots choking the sculptures, Ajanta remained deserted for about a millennium, until 1819 when a British hunting party led by officer John Smith stumbled upon it purely by chance.

Sights

One of the primary reasons to visit Ajanta is to admire its renowned 'frescoes', actually temperas, which adorn many of the caves' interiors. With few other examples from ancient times matching their artistic excellence and fine execution, these paintings are of unfathomable heritage value.

Despite their age, the paintings in most caves remain finely preserved and many attribute this to their relative isolation from humanity for centuries. However, it would be a tad optimistic to say that decay hasn't set in.

It's believed that the natural pigments for these paintings were mixed with animal glue and vegetable gum to bind them to the dry surface. Many caves have small, crater-like holes in their floors, which acted as palettes during paint jobs.

Most buses ferrying tour groups don't arrive until noon. To avoid the crowds stay locally in Fardapur or make an early start from Aurangabad.

★Ajanta Caves CAVE
(Indian/foreigner ₹30/500, video ₹25, authorised guide ₹1370; ⏲9am-5.30pm Tue-Sun) Ajanta's caves line a steep face of a horseshoe-shaped gorge bordering the Waghore River. Five of the caves are *chaityas* while others are *viharas*. Caves 8, 9, 10, 12, 13 and part of 15 are

Ajanta Caves

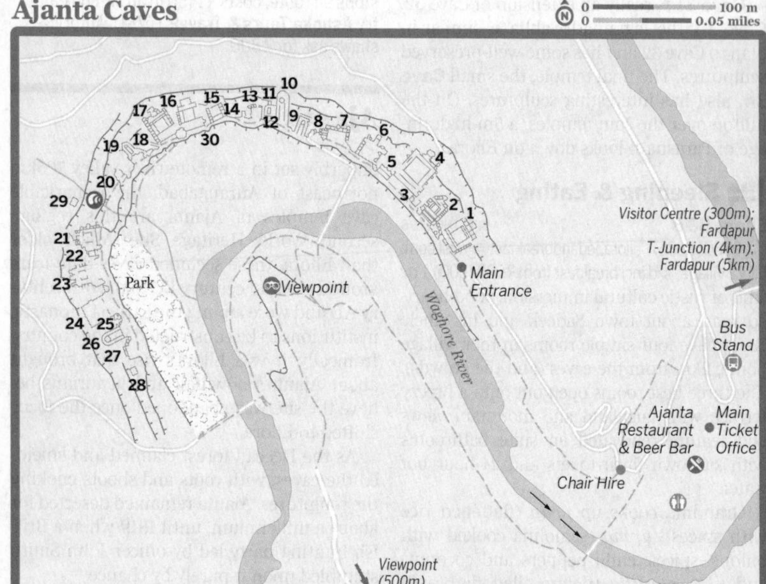

early Buddhist caves, while the others date from around the 5th century AD (Mahayana period). In the austere early Buddhist school, the Buddha was never represented directly but always alluded to by a symbol such as the footprint or wheel of law.

During busy periods, viewers are allotted 15 minutes within the caves, which have to be entered barefoot (socks/shoe covers allowed; flip-flops will make your life a lot easier). Caves 3, 5, 8, 22, 28, 29 and 30 remain either closed or inaccessible.

Cave 1 CAVE

Cave 1, a Mahayana *vihara,* was one of the last to be excavated and is the most beautifully decorated. This is where you'll find a rendition of the *Bodhisattva Padmapani,* the most famous and iconic of the Ajanta artworks. A verandah in front leads to a large congregation hall housing sculptures and narrative murals known for their splendid perspective and elaborate detailing of dress, daily life and facial expressions.

The colours in the paintings were created from local minerals, with the exception of the vibrant blue made from Central Asian lapis lazuli. Look up to the ceiling to see the carving of four deer sharing a common head.

Cave 2 CAVE

Cave 2 is a late Mahayana *vihara* with deliriously ornamented columns and capitals and some fine paintings. The ceiling is decorated with geometric and floral patterns. The murals depict scenes from the Jataka tales, including Buddha's mother's dream of a six-tusked elephant, which heralded his conception.

Cave 4 CAVE

Cave 4 is the largest *vihara* at Ajanta and is supported by 28 pillars. Although never completed, the cave has some impressive sculptures, such as the four statues surrounding a huge central Buddha. There are also scenes of people fleeing from the 'eight great dangers' to the protection of Avalokitesvara.

Cave 6 CAVE

Cave 6 is the only two-storey *vihara* at Ajanta, but parts of the lower storey have collapsed. Inside is a seated Buddha figure and an intricately carved door to the shrine. Upstairs the hall is surrounded by cells with fine paintings on the doorways.

Cave 7 CAVE

Cave 7 has an atypical design, with porches before the verandah leading directly to the four cells and the elaborately sculptured shrine.

Cave 9 CAVE

Cave 9 is one of the earliest *chaityas* at Ajanta. Although it dates from the early Buddhist period, the two figures flanking the entrance door were probably later Mahayana additions. Columns run down both sides of the cave and around the 3m-high dagoba (pagoda) at the far end.

Cave 10 CAVE

Cave 10 is thought to be the oldest cave (200 BC) and was the first one to be spotted by the British hunting party. Similar in design to Cave 9, it is the largest *chaitya*. The facade has collapsed and the paintings inside have been damaged, in some cases by graffiti dating from soon after their rediscovery. One of the pillars to the right bears the engraved name of Smith, who left his mark here for posterity.

Cave 16 CAVE

Cave 16, a *vihara,* contains some of Ajanta's finest paintings and is thought to have been the original entrance to the entire complex. The best known of these paintings is of the 'dying princess', Sundari, wife of the Buddha's half-brother Nanda, who is said to have fainted at the news her husband was renouncing the material life (and her) in order to become a monk.

Carved figures appear to support the ceiling and there's a statue of the Buddha seated on a lion throne teaching the Noble Eightfold Path.

Cave 17 CAVE

With carved dwarfs supporting the pillars, cave 17 has Ajanta's best-preserved and most varied paintings. Famous images include a princess applying make-up, a seductive prince using the old trick of plying his lover with wine and the Buddha returning home from his enlightenment to beg from his wife and astonished son.

A detailed panel tells of Prince Simhala's expedition to Sri Lanka: with 500 companions he is shipwrecked on an island where ogresses appear as enchanting women, only to seize and devour their victims. Simhala escapes on a flying horse and returns to conquer the island.

Cave 19 CAVE

Cave 19, a magnificent *chaitya,* has a remarkably detailed facade; its dominant feature is an impressive horseshoe-shaped window. Two fine, standing Buddha figures flank the entrance. Inside is a three-tiered dagoba with a figure of the Buddha on the front. Outside the cave, to the west, sits a striking image of the Naga king with seven cobra hoods around his head. His wife, hooded by a single cobra, sits by his side.

Cave 26 CAVE

A largely ruined *chaitya,* cave 26 is now dramatically lit and contains some fine sculptures that shouldn't be missed. On the left wall is a huge figure of the reclining Buddha, lying back in preparation for nirvana. Other scenes include a lengthy depiction of the Buddha's temptation by Maya.

Viewpoints

Two lookouts offer picture-perfect views of the whole horseshoe-shaped gorge. The first is a short walk beyond the river, crossed via a bridge below Cave 8. A further 40-minute uphill walk (not to be attempted during the monsoons) leads to the lookout from where the British party first spotted the caves.

AJANTA PHOTOGRAPHY ETIQUETTE

Flash photography is strictly prohibited within the caves, due to its adverse effect on the natural dyes used in the paintings. Authorities have installed rows of tiny pigment-friendly lights, which cast a faint glow within the caves, as additional lighting is required for glimpsing minute details, but you'll have to rely on long exposures for photographs.

Sleeping

Padmapani Park HOTEL $

(☎0240-244280; www.hotelpadmapaniparkajanta.com; Jalgaon-Aurangabad Hwy, Fardapur; s/d ₹800/1000, with AC ₹1500; ❄📶) It's definitely not going to thrill you, but this is one of the better run-down options in Fardapur, mainly due to the friendly, English-speaking manager, wi-fi in the reception/restaurant and the free rides they will give you to the Ajanta Visitor Centre.

MTDC Ajanta Tourist Resort HOTEL $$

(☎02438-244230; www.maharashtratourism.gov.in; Aurangabad-Jalgaon Rd, Fardapur; d with/without AC ₹1900/2260; ❄) This government hotel is pricey but the best option at Ajanta, set amid lawns in a peaceful location off the main road in Fardapur, 5km from the caves. Air-con rooms, in apple green structures, are spacious; non-AC rooms are less interesting but fine. There's a bar, garden and restaurant with veg thalis (₹160 to ₹225) and cold beer (₹175).

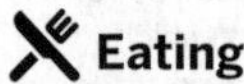

Eating

Hotel Radhe Krishna DHABA $

(Aurangabad-Jalgaon Hwy, Fardapur; mains ₹90-160, thalis from ₹180; ⏲24hr) The best of Fardapur's streetside dhabas (casual eatery serving basic meals), this excellent spot is fresh, cheap and satisfying. The famous cook, Babu, and his team (Sunil on the chapati!) get a big kick out of foreigners dropping in, and just watching these guys whip up various curries, fries and thalis is pure entertainment.

Information

Ajanta Visitor Centre (⏲9am-5.30pm Tue-Sun) This new, state-of-the-art facility is one of India's very best, with highly impressive replicas of four caves (Nos 1, 2, 16 and 17) in real scale, audioguides available in many languages, excellent painting and sculpture galleries detailing the story of Buddhism in India, an audiovisual arena and a large cafe.

Getting There & Away

Buses from Aurangabad or Jalgaon will drop you at the Fardapur T-junction (where the highway meets the road to the caves), 4km from the site. From here, after paying an 'amenities' fee (₹10), walk to the departure point for the buses (with/without AC ₹22/16), which zoom up to the caves. Buses return half-hourly to the T-junction; the last bus is at 5pm. Note that the caves are closed on Monday.

All MSRTC (www.msrtc.gov.in) buses passing through Fardapur stop at the T-junction. After the caves close you can board buses to either Aurangabad or Jalgaon outside the MTDC Holiday Resort in Fardapur, 1km down the main road towards Jalgaon. Taxis are available in Fardapur; ₹1500/2500 should get you to Jalgaon/Aurangabad.

Jalgaon

☎0257 / POP 468,300 / ELEV 208M

Apart from being a handy base for exploring Ajanta 60km away, the industrial city of Jalgaon is really nothing more than a convenient transit town. It has rail connections to all major cities across India.

Sleeping & Eating

★**Hotel Plaza** HOTEL $

(☎9370027354, 0257-2227354; hotelplaza_jal@yahoo.com; Station Rd; dm ₹300, s/d from ₹650/950, r with AC incl breakfast ₹1300-1650; ❄@📶) This extremely well-managed and well-presented hotel is only a short hop from the station. Rooms vary in size and layout, but with whitewashed walls, a minimalist feel and bathrooms cleaner than a Jain temple, it's modestly boutique and brilliant value. Everything from the hospitality to the bed linens exceeds expectations.

Hotel Arya INDIAN $

(Navi Peth; mains ₹50-110; ⏲11am-10.30pm) Delicious vegetarian food, particularly Punjabi cuisine, though a few Chinese and South Indian dishes are also offered. It's a short walk south along Station Rd, left at MG Rd and left at the clock tower. You may have to queue for a table at lunchtime.

Information

There is a State Bank of India ATM at the station and an Axis Bank ATM just off to the left when exiting; otherwise, you'll find ATMs spread out along Nehru Rd, which runs along the top of Station Rd.

Internet cafes can be found along Nehru Rd.

Getting There & Around

Jalgaon's train station and bus stand are about 2km apart (₹30 by autorickshaw).

Several express trains connecting Mumbai (sleeper/2AC ₹313/1076, eight hours), Delhi (₹558/2051, 18 hours), Ahmedabad (₹373/1316, 14 hours) and Varanasi (₹518/1981, 20 hours) stop at Jalgaon train station. Nine daily trains head for Nagpur (₹313/1076, seven to nine hours).

Buses to Fardapur T-junction (₹71, 1½ hours), for access to Ajanta, depart hourly from the bus stand between 6am and 9pm, continuing to Aurangabad (₹177, four hours).

Private bus companies on Station Rd offer services to Mumbai (₹500 to ₹1400, 9½ hours) and Nagpur (₹750, nine hours).

Nagpur

☎0712 / POP 2.43 MILLION / ELEV 305M

Way off the main tourist routes, the isolated city of Nagpur holds the distinction of being the dead geographical centre of India. It lacks must-see sights but is an important gateway to several reserves and parks including Tadoba-Andhari Tiger Reserve and

Pench National Park. It's also close to the temples of Ramtek and the ashrams of Sevagram. Summer is the best time to taste the city's famous oranges.

Sleeping

Hotel Blue Moon HOTEL $

(☎0712-2726061; www.hotelbluemoon.org; Central Ave; s/d from ₹720/960, with AC ₹1350/1600; ❄📶) Large, plain rooms that don't win any awards for imagination but are among the better budget options in this pricey city. It's one of the closest hotels to the train station. Management is helpful and friendly, which eases the blow of those sickly marble bathtubs and poor man's stained glass.

Legend Inn HOTEL $$

(☎0712-6658666; www.thelegendinn.com; 15 Modern Society, Wardha Rd; s/d from ₹4180/4840; ❄@📶) On the main highway for the Tadoba-Andhari Tiger Reserve, this is an efficiently run hotel, owned by an Indian mountaineering legend, with well-appointed rooms, a good restaurant, smoky bar and smiley staff (which might make up for the low water pressure). Free pick-ups from the airport, 1km away, are included.

Peanut Hotel HOTEL $$

(☎0712-3250320; www.peanuthotels.com; Bharti House, 43 Kachipura Garden, New Ramdaspeth; s/d incl breakfast from ₹2500/3200; ❄📶) Located on a leafy residential street, this hotel's modern, whitewashed rooms are spruced up with orange throws and are kept spick and span. It's 2km southeast of the train station and the best overall value in town.

Eating

Krishnum SOUTH INDIAN $

(www.krishnum.com; Central Ave; mains ₹60-160; ⏲8am-10pm) This popular place dishes out South Indian snacks and generous Punjabi thalis, as well as freshly squeezed fruit juices. There are branches in other parts of town.

★**Breakfast Story** CAFE $$

(www.facebook.com/thebreakfastorynagpur; Sai Sagar Apt, Hingna Rd; mains ₹100-300; ⏲8am-2.30pm & 3.30-7pm Mon-Tue & Thu-Sat, 8am-3pm Sun; 📶) This stylish all-day breakfast-only hot spot in a residential building 7km southwest of the centre is worth a diversion. English, American and Belgian breakfast combos, sandwiches, pancakes and waffles, along with daily chalkboard specials, are served up on artsy wooden tables covered in comics. Cassette tapes, newspapers and other pop art line the walls, completing the cosy, hipster atmosphere.

Information

Numerous ATMs line Central Ave.

MTDC (☎0712-2533325; www.maharashtratourism.gov.in; West High Court Rd, Civil Lines; ⏲10am-6pm) Staff here can help with getting to national parks near Nagpur. There is also an airport counter (☎9405143376; www.maharashtratourism.gov.in; Arrivals Hall, Dr Babasaheb Ambedkar International Airport; ⏲7am-7pm Mon-Sat).

Getting There & Around

AIR

Dr Babasaheb Ambedkar International Airport (☎0712-2807501) is 8km southwest of the centre. Domestic airlines, including Air India, IndiGo, Jet Airways and GoAir, fly direct to Delhi, Mumbai, Kolkata, Ahmedabad, Bengaluru, Chennai and Pune. Internationally, Qatar and Air Arabia fly to Doha and Sharjah, respectively.

BUS

The main **MSRTC/Ganesh Peth Bus Stand** (☎0712-2726221) is 2km south of the train station. Ordinary buses head for Aurangabad (₹750 to ₹1200, six daily), Pune (₹1100, 1pm, 4pm, 5pm and 6.30pm), Ramtek (₹50, 1½ hours, every 30 minutes 6.15am to 9.30pm) and Wardha (₹45, three hours, every 10 minutes 6am to 10pm).

Government buses to Madhya Pradesh leave from the **MP Bus Stand** (☎0712-2533695), 350m south of the train station. Destinations include Khawasa (for access to Pench Tiger Reserve; ₹90, every 30 minutes, 6am to 1.30am) and Jabalpur (from ₹270, 2.30pm and 11pm).

Private buses leave from the Bhole Petrol Pump, 3km southwest of the train station. **Sanjay Travels** (☎0712-2550701; www.sanjaytravels.com; near Bhole Petrol Pump) books air-con seaters and sleepers with the best companies, such as Purple (www.prasannapurple.com), to Mumbai (₹1400, 4.45pm), Pune (₹900 to ₹1100, 3pm and 10pm), Aurangabad (₹750, hourly, 3pm to 10pm), Jalgaon (₹700, 5pm, 7pm, 9pm and 10pm) and Hyderabad (₹750 to ₹1000, 9pm and 10.30pm). For Jabalpur, **Nandan Bus** (☎7620941415; www.nandanbus.com; Gitanjali Cinema Sq) goes daily at 2.30pm and 11pm (₹450 to ₹500) from Central Ave.

TRAIN

From Mumbai's CST, the Duronto Express runs daily to Nagpur (sleeper/2AC ₹523/1946,

WORTH A TRIP

TADOBA-ANDHARI TIGER RESERVE

The seldom-visited **Tadoba-Andhari Tiger Reserve** (⌚6am-10am & 3-6pm with seasonal variations), 150km south of Nagpur, is one of the best places to see tigers in India. Seeing fewer visitors than most other Indian forest reserves – it gets around 60% less visitors than neighbouring parks in Madhya Pradesh – this is a place where you can get up close to wildlife without having to jostle past truckloads of shutter-happy tourists. Rather than restrict access to certain zones of the park like other tiger parks in India, Tadoba-Andhari opted to limit the number of gypsy safaris per day instead (48) but give them free rein throughout the park. The results are excellent for wildlife-sighting opportunities. The park also remains open throughout the year, unlike many in India.

You'll find comfortable, well-furnished rooms and cottage at the **MTDC Resort** (☎9579314261; Moharli Gate; r with/without AC from ₹2380/1900; ❄), but the true treat in these parts is **Tiger Trails Jungle Lodge** (☎0712-6541327; www.tigertrails.in; Khutwanda Gate; s/d incl all meals ₹9500/19,500; ❄📶✖) 🍃, where Passionate enthusiasts have run this conservation-minded lodge deeply entrenched in studying Tadoba tigers for two decades. It's located in the wildlife-rich buffer zone and has its own private park gate. Accommodation is spacious and divided between rooms nearer to forest or watering holes – there's also the option of overnighting under the stars in a 6m-high observation tower. Save room for the absolutely excellent tribal-style Maharashtra thalis!

Most folks reach the park by private vehicle. That said, to reach Khutwanda Gate on public transport, catch a Chandrapur-bound bus from Nagpur to Warora (₹120, three hours), where you can catch a second bus for the last 42km to Khutwanda Gate (₹57, 1½ hours). For Moharli, stay on the bus to Chandrapur (₹175, four hours) and catch a second bus on to Moharli (₹29, one hour).

10 hours, 8.15pm). From Nagpur it departs at 8.40pm and arrives at 7.55am the following morning. Heading north to Kolkata is the Gitanjali Express (sleeper/2AC ₹563/2076, 17½ hours, 7.05pm). Several expresses bound for Delhi and Mumbai stop at Jalgaon (sleeper/2AC ₹313/1076, eight hours) for Ajanta caves.

Around Nagpur

Ramtek

About 40km northeast of Nagpur, Ramtek is believed to be the place where Lord Rama, of the epic Ramayana, spent some time during his exile with his wife, Sita, and brother Lakshmana. The place is marked by a cluster of 10 or so ancient **temples** (⌚6am-9pm), which sit atop the Hill of Rama and have their own population of resident langur monkeys.

Ramtek is beginning to fancy itself as a burgeoning adventure sports destination. MTDC was building an adventure sports training centre and hotel at the time of research and Khindsi Lake is indeed a beautiful spot for kayaking, paragliding or hot-air ballooning.

Mansar, 7km west of Ramtek, is an important archaeological site believed to be the 5th-century remains of Pravarapura, the capital ruled by the Vakataka King Pravarasena II.

Buses run half-hourly between Ramtek and the MSRTC bus stand in Nagpur (₹50, 1½ hours). The last bus to Nagpur is at 9.30pm.

Sevagram

☎07152

About 85km from Nagpur, Sevagram (Village of Service) was chosen by Mahatma Gandhi as his base during the Indian Independence Movement. Throughout the freedom struggle, the village played host to several nationalist leaders, who would regularly come to visit the Mahatma at his **Sevagram Ashram** (☎07152-284754; www.gandhiashramsevagram.org; ⌚6am-5.30pm). The overseers of this peaceful ashram, which is built on 40 hectares of farmland, have carefully restored the original huts where Gandhi lived and worked and which now house some of his personal effects. There is a **small museum** (Sevagram Ashram; ⌚10am-6pm) as well.

Very basic lodging is available at **Rustam Bhavan** (☎07152-284754; nayeetaleem.75@gmail.com; r per person ₹150) and **Yatri Nivas**

(☎7276160260; sevagram_ashram@yahoo.in; r without AC ₹200-300), across the road from the entry gate; advance booking is recommended. Simple organic meals are available at the atmospheric **Prakrutik Ahar Kendra** (Sevagram Ashram; meals ₹120-150; ⊙11.30am-6pm).

Sevagram can be reached by taking a bus from Nagpur to Wardha (₹85, three hours), where you'll need to switch to a Sevagram-bound bus (₹12, 10 minutes), which drops you at Medical Sq, 1km from the ashram; or catch a shared autorickshaw (₹20).

SOUTHERN MAHARASHTRA

Konkan Coast

A little-developed shoreline running south from Mumbai all the way to Goa, this picturesque strip of coast is peppered with picture-postcard beaches, fishing villages and magnificent ruined forts. Travelling through this tropical backwater can be sheer bliss, whether you're off to dabble in the sands with Mumbaikars in Ganpatipule, visit the stunning Janjira Fort at Murud-Janjira or head into the blue at Malvan, the last beach town of significance before the sands give way to Goa.

Murud-Janjira

☎02144 / POP 13,100

The sleepy fishing hamlet of Murud-Janjira – 165km from Mumbai – should be on any itinerary of the Konkan Coast. The relaxed pace of life, fresh seafood, stupendous offshore Janjira fort (and the chance to feel the warm surf rush past your feet) make the trip here well worthwhile.

Murud-Janjira's beach is fun for a run or game of cricket with locals and it comes alive with street stalls and beach tomfoolery nightly. Alternatively, you could peer through the gates of the off-limits Ahmedganj Palace, estate of the Siddi Nawab of Murud, or scramble around the decaying mosque and tombs on the south side of town.

Sights

★Janjira FORT

(⊙7am-dusk) FREE The commanding, brooding fortress of Janjira, built on an island 500m offshore, is the most magnificent of the string of forts that line the Konkan coastline. This citadel was completed in 1571 by the Siddis, descendants of slaves from the Horn of Africa, and was the capital of a princely state.

Over the centuries Siddi alignment with Mughals provoked conflict with local kings, including Shivaji and his son Sambhaji, who attempted to scale the walls and tunnel to it, respectively. However, no outsider (including British, French and Portuguese colonists) ever made it past the fort's 12m-high granite walls which, when seen during high tide, seem to rise straight from the sea. Unconquered through history, the fort is finally falling to forces of nature as its mighty walls slowly crumble and wilderness reclaims its innards.

Still, there's a lot to see today, including the remarkable close-fitting stonework that's protected the citadel against centuries of attack by storms, colonists and gunpowder. You approach the fort via a brooding grey-stone gateway and can then explore its ramparts (complete with giant cannons) and 19 bastions, large parts of which are intact. Its inner keep, palaces and mosque are in ruins, though the fort's huge twin reservoirs remain. As many of the surviving walls and structures are in poor shape, tread carefully while you explore the site, which is unfortunately littered with trash.

The only way to reach Janjira is by boat (₹61 return, 20 minutes) from Rajpuri port. Boats depart with a minimum 20 people from 7am to noon and 2pm to 5.30pm on weekdays and 7am to 5.30pm on weekends, and allow you 45 minutes to explore the fort. To get to Rajpuri from Murud-Janjira, take an autorickshaw (₹150) or hire a bicycle.

Sleeping & Eating

Sea Shore Resort GUESTHOUSE $

(☎9209240603; www.seashoreresortmurud.com; Darbar Rd; r with/without AC ₹2000/1500; ❄📶) The advantage at this dead-simple guesthouse is a palm-fringed sea-view room with a small balcony and wi-fi for ₹2000 or less. The beach-facing garden is a bit ramshackle, but there are a few hammocks. Faisal, the friendly man about the place, speaks some English.

Devakinandan Lodge GUESTHOUSE $

(☎9273457057; Darbar Rd; r with/without AC ₹2000/1500; ❄) This sparkling little green-and-red guesthouse has clean, basic rooms with TV and attached bathrooms with hot water. The family owners are friendly but speak very little English.

Sea Shell Resort HOTEL **$$**
(☎02144-274306; www.seashellmurud.com; Darbar Rd; r with/without AC from ₹2500/2000; ❄☒) Set back from the beachside road, this cheery place has glistening, spacious and breezy sea-facing rooms with hot-water bathrooms (rain-style showers, thick bath towels) that look far better than the facade would indicate. There's a tiny pool as well.

Hotel Vinayak INDIAN **$$**
(Darbar Rd; mains ₹120-400; ⏲7am-10pm) Its sea-facing terrace is the perfect place to tuck into a delicious and fiery Konkani thali (₹120 to ₹300), with fish curry, *tawa* (hotplate) fish fry, *sol kadhi* (pink-coloured, slightly sour digestive made from coconut milk and kokum fruit) and more. Fresh fish, prawn dishes and good breakfasts are also available.

Getting There & Around

Ferries and catamarans (₹125 to ₹165) from the Gateway of India in Mumbai cruise to Mandva pier between 6am and 7pm. The ticket includes a free shuttle bus to Alibag (30 minutes). Rickety local buses from Alibag head down the coast to Murud-Janjira (₹70, two hours, every 30 minutes). Alternatively, 10 buses depart Mumbai Central bus stand between 6am and 1am and take almost six hours to reach Murud-Janjira (non-AC ₹200). Four buses a day continue on to Pune (₹215, seven hours, 7.30am, 2pm, 3pm and 4pm).

The nearest railhead is at Roha, two hours away and poorly connected.

Bicycles (per hour/day ₹150/250) and cars (₹15 per kilometre) can be hired at the **Golden Swan Beach Resort** (☎9225591131; www.goldenswan.com; Darbar Rd).

Around Murud-Janjira

RAIGAD FORT

Alone on a high and remote hilltop, 24km off Hwy 66, the enthralling **Raigad Fort** (Indian/foreigner ₹15/200; ⏲8am-5.30pm) served as Shivaji's capital from 1648 until his death in 1680. The fort was later sacked by the British and some colonial structures added, but monuments such as the royal court, plinths of royal chambers, the main marketplace and Shivaji's tomb still remain – it's worth an excursion.

You can hike a crazy 1475 steps to the top, but for a more 'levitating' experience, take the vertigo-inducing **ropeway** (www.raigadropeway.com; return ₹250; ⏲8am-7pm) – actually a cable car – which climbs up the cliff and offers a bird's-eye view of the deep gorges below. Be warned this is a very popular attraction with domestic tourists and you may have to wait up to an hour for a ride during holiday times. Guides (₹500) are available within the fort complex. **Sarja Restaurant** (snacks ₹35-80; ⏲8am-7pm), adjoining the ropeway's base terminal, is a basic place for lunch or snacks.

Autorickshaws shuttle up to the ropeway from the town of Mahad on Hwy 66 (look out for the 'Raigad Ropeway' sign) for ₹700 return including wait time. Mahad is 158km south of Mumbai and 88km from Murud-Janjira. The Mahad–Raigad road is paved and in good condition. Car and drivers charge ₹15 per kilometre for a day trip here from Murud-Janjira. There are buses every two to three hours from Mahad to Mahabaleshwar (₹70, two hours).

Ganpatipule

☎02357

The tiny beach resort of Ganpatipule has been luring a steady stream of beach lovers over the years with its warm waters and wonderful stretches of sand. Located about 375km from Mumbai, it's a village that snoozes through much of the year, except during holidays such as Diwali or Ganesh Chaturthi. These are times when hordes of boisterous tourists turn up to visit the seaside **Swayambhu Temple** (⏲6am-9pm), which houses a monolithic Ganesh (painted a bright orange). For more solitude, the beaches just south of the main beach (such as Neware Beach) are both more spectacular than Ganpatipule and less crowded – have an autorickshaw take you there.

To reach Ganpatipule, you'll pass through the transport hub of Ratnagiri, home to the crumbling **Thibaw Palace** (Thibaw Palace Rd; ⏲10am-5.30pm Tue-Sun) FREE, where the last Burmese king, Thibaw, was interned by the British.

Sleeping & Eating

Grand Konkan Resort GUESTHOUSE **$**
(☎02357-235291; www.atithilodgeganpatipule.com; r with/without AC ₹1800/1500) A tad ambitiously named, but this family-run guesthouse behind the simple and cheaper Atithi Lodge (same owners) offers quite nice rooms with a wee bit of character (curtains, wood-

WORTH A TRIP

ALL ABOARD THE KONKAN RAILWAY

One in a long list of storied Indian train rides, the Konkan Railway hugs the southwest Indian coast along a 738km journey between Maharashtra, Goa and Karnataka. The line, which has hosted passenger trains since 1998, is considered the biggest and most expansive infrastructure project the country has undertaken (and completed) since independence. So much so, the very idea was dismissed outright in the early 20th century by the British, who deemed the whole adventure an impossible task of construction and engineering, leaving it to the locals to finish the job over the course of several decades (10 of whom lost their lives in the disaster-plagued process).

Today, the ridiculously scenic route, chock-full of picturesque paddy fields, rolling green hills, craggy mountaintops, storybook sea views and numerous tunnels, waterfalls, viaducts and jungly landscapes, is made possible by 92 tunnels and 2000 bridges, including Panval Viaduct, India's highest (and Asia's third) viaduct at 64m tall.

Most travellers enjoy the Konkan ride on the Mandovi Express from Mumbai to Goa, but train enthusiasts can take in the whole shebang on the Mangalore Express, a 14-hour journey from Mumbai to Mangalore.

framed art) just five minutes' walk from the beach. Hardwood flooring and shelving give off a rustic forest lodge feel. Brothers Jayesh and Rajesh speak English and are more than helpful.

MTDC Resort HOTEL **$$**
(☎02357-235248; www.mararashtratourism.gov.in; d with/without AC from ₹2740/2380; ❄📶) Spread over prime beachfront, this huge operation is something of a holiday camp for Mumbaikar families. Its concrete rooms and cottages would benefit from a little updating, but all boast magnificent full-frontal ocean views. It also packs in a decent restaurant that serves cold beer.

Bhau Joshi Bhojnalay INDIAN **$**
(mains ₹55-125; ⏲11.30am-3pm & 7.30-10.30pm) It's not the easiest place to eat (no English sign, nearly no English spoken and no napkins, so bring some baby wipes!), but the delicious Maharashtrian food in this clean, orderly restaurant inland from the beach makes up for the struggles. Try the fantastic *baingan masala* (eggplant curry; ₹90). Jain and Punjabi dishes also on offer.

Hotel Naivedya INDIAN **$**
(mains ₹80-170, thali ₹85; ⏲10am-7pm) A simple local's joint in the village serving up a wonderful daily veg thali with a kick (₹85) and the most refreshing *sol kadhi* we had on the coast.

ℹ Information

There are several ATMs in Ganpatipule, including one about 400m inland from the MTDC Resort.

ℹ Getting There & Around

Ganpatipule has limited transport links. Ratnagiri, 40km to the south, is the nearest major town. Hourly buses (₹33, 1½ hours) connect the two places; autorickshaws cost ₹400.

Two government buses per day leave Ganpatipule for Pune (₹350, five hours, 6.45am and 7.30pm). For Mumbai and Kolhapur (or more timely government departures in general), head back to Ratnagiri (₹33, 1¼ hours, every 30 minutes 7am to 8pm).

There are private buses to Mumbai (Volvo non-AC seater/AC sleeper ₹700/1000, 10 hours, 7pm) and Pune (Volvo AC sleeper ₹800, nine hours, 7pm).

Ratnagiri train station is on the Konkan Railway line. From Ratnagiri, the Mandovi Express goes daily to Mumbai (2nd class/sleeper/2AC ₹188/293/1061, 7½ hours, 2.05pm). The return train heading for Goa (₹163/248/896, 5½ hours) is at 1.15pm. From Ratnagiri's old bus stand, buses leave for Goa (semideluxe ₹270, six hours) and Kolhapur (₹160, four hours).

Malvan

☎02365

A government tourism promo promotes the emerging Malvan region as comparable to Tahiti, which is a tad ambitious, but it does boast near-white sands, sparkling seas and jungle-fringed backwaters. Offshore there are coral reefs, sea caves and vibrant marine life – diving is becoming a huge draw with the opening of a new world-class diving school.

Malvan town is one of the prettiest on the Konkan Coast. It's a mellow, bike-friendly place with a good stock of old wooden buildings, a busy little harbour and bazaar and a slow, tropical pace of life. Stretching directly south of the centre is lovely Tarkali beach, home to many hotels and guesthouses.

Sights & Activities

There are several dive shops operating in Malvan that allow unqualified diving; if you want to dive, stick with a registered operator. The Malvan Marine Sanctuary is the region's top scuba draw with its 67-nautical-mile reef often hailed as India's Great Barrier Reef.

The southern end of Tarkali beach is bordered by the broad, beautiful Karli River. Several boat operators (you'll find them moored on the northern bank) offer multistop boat trips along this backwater to Seagull Island, Golden Rock, Dolphin Point and cove beaches and/or Vengurla Rock lighthouse. Trips range from ₹1200 to ₹3500 per boat for up to 10 people.

Sindhudurg Fort FORT

Built by Shivaji and dating from 1664, this monstrous fort lies on an offshore island and can be reached by frequent ferries (adult/child ₹70/40, 8am to 5.30pm) from Malvan's harbour. It's not as impressive as Janjira up the coast, and today lies mostly in ruins, but it remains a powerful presence. You can explore its ramparts and the coastal views are impressive. Boat operators allow you one hour on the island.

Tarkali Beach BEACH

A golden arc south of Malvan, this crescent-shaped sandy beach is a vision of tropical India, fringed by coconut palms and casuarina trees, plus the odd cow. At dusk (between October and February) fishermen work together to haul in huge, kilometre-long nets that are packed with sardines. A rickshaw here from Malvan town is ₹150.

★**IISDA** DIVING

(Indian Institute of Scuba Diving & Aquasports; ☎02365-248790; www.maharashtratourism.gov.in; Tarkali Beach; per dive ₹3700, PADI Open Water course ₹22,000; ⏲7am-7pm) This state-of-the-art PADI diving centre, an initiative of Maharashtra Tourism, is India's finest, run by marine biologist and all-round diving pro Dr Sarang Kulkarni. It offers professional instruction, a 20m-long and 8m-deep pool for training, air-conditioned classrooms and comfortable sleeping quarters for students. IISDA is also a marine conservation centre and there's even a restaurant, bar and tennis court.

Located 7km south of Malvan.

Sleeping & Eating

Vicky's Guest House GUESTHOUSE $

(☎9823423046; www.malvanvickysguesthouse.com; near Heravi Batti, Dandi Beach; r with/without AC from ₹1500/1000; ❄📶) Down a quiet residential lane surrounded by lush palms 400m from Dandi Beach and steps form Malvan town, cool and mellow Vicky has five purpose-built rooms that don't look like much on arrival but are actually spacious, well-equipped and extremely comfortable for the price. Vicky himself is super helpful

MALVAN MARINE SANCTUARY

The shoreline around Malvan is incredibly diverse, with rich wetlands, sandy and rocky beaches, mangroves and backwaters. But underwater it's arguably even more compelling, with coral patches and caves that shelter abundant marine life and extensive forests of *sargassum* seaweed that acts as a nursery for juvenile fish. Rocky offshore islands attract schools of snapper and large grouper, butterfly fish, yellow-striped fusilers, manta and sting rays and lobster. Pods of dolphins are regularly seen between October to May and the world's largest fish, the whale shark, even puts in an appearance every now and then.

Presently only a small section is protected as the **Malvan Marine Sanctuary**, which encompasses the Sindhudurg Fort; yet such is its rich diversity that marine biologists, including the director of the Indian Institute of Scuba Diving & Aquasports (IISDA), Dr Sarang Kulkarni, feel it's essential that the boundaries are extended. The reef extends for 67 nautical miles offshore and has been described as India's Great Barrier Reef. A submerged plateau, the **Angria Bank**, is 40km long and 20km wide, with healthy coral and an abundance of sealife: nurse sharks are seen on almost every dive. IISDA has big plans in the works to operate day trips and live-aboard excursions to Angria.

and hospitable as is the downright gracious family.

★Chaitanya MALVANI $$

(502 Dr Vallabh Marg; mains ₹150-325; ⊙11am-11pm) On Malvan's main drag, this great, family-run place specialises in Konkan cuisine including *bangda tikhale* (fish in thick coconut sauce), prawns *malvani* and very flavoursome crab *masala;* portions won't thrill you, but it's first-rate seafood. Its vegetarian dishes are also excellent. It's always packed with locals and has an air-con section.

Athithi Bamboo MALVANI $$

(Church St, Chival; thalis ₹80-325; ⊙noon-4pm & 8-10.30pm) On the north side of the harbour, this large casual place offers excellent Malvani thalis and lots of fresh fish. There's no sign or menu in English and you sit under a tin roof (so it gets very hot during the day), but the seafood is surf-fresh and the cooking Konkan-authentic.

Getting There & Away

The closest train station is Kudal, 38km away. Frequent buses (₹38, one hour) cover the route from **Malvan Bus Stand** (☎02365-252034; Shri Babi Hadkar Marg) or an autorickshaw is about ₹500. Malvan has ordinary buses to Kolhapur (non-AC from ₹189, five hours), Mumbai (₹562, 12 hours, 8am), Panaji (non-AC from ₹102, four hours, 6.45am, 7.45am, 2.30pm and 3.15pm) and Ratnagiri (non-AC from ₹190, five hours, 6am, 7.45am and 11.15am). Slightly quicker to Goa are the blue-and-white Kadamba Goan government buses (₹135, 3½ hours, 7.45am, 2.30pm and 3pm) to Mapusa and Panaji.

There are private bus agents on Dr Vallabh Marg selling more comfortable seats on Volvo buses to Mumbai and Pune, but these depart 33km inland from Malvan in Kasal and transport is not provided.

Malvan is only 80km from northern Goa; private drivers charge ₹2000 (non-AC) to ₹2500 (AC) for the two-hour trip.

Matheran

☎02148 / POP 5750 / ELEV 803M

Matheran, literally 'Jungle Above', is a tiny patch of peace and quiet capping a craggy Sahyadri summit within spitting distance of Mumbai's heat and grime. Endowed with shady forests criss-crossed with foot trails and breathtaking lookouts, it still retains an elegance and colonial-era ambience, though creeping commercialism and illegal construction are marring its appeal (it could do without the Ferris wheel and wax museum, for example).

In the past, getting to Matheran was really half the fun. While speedier options were available by road, nothing beat arriving in town on the narrow-gauge toy train that chugged up to the heart of the settlement, but derailment woes caused the suspension of the train in 2016, with no planned timetable for getting it moving again.

Motor vehicles are banned within Matheran, making it an ideal place to give your ears and lungs a rest and your feet some exercise.

Sights & Activities

You can walk along shady forest paths to most of Matheran's viewpoints in a matter of hours; it's a place well suited to stress-free ambling. To catch the sunrise, head to **Panorama Point**, while **Porcupine Point** (also known as Sunset Point) is the most popular (read: packed) as the sun drops. **Louisa Point** and **Little Chouk Point** also have stunning views of the Sahyadris.

If you're here on a weekend or public holiday you might want to avoid the most crowded section around **Echo Point**, **Charlotte Lake** and **Honeymoon Point**, which get rammed with day trippers.

You can reach the valley below One Tree Hill down the path known as **Shivaji's Ladder**, supposedly trod upon by the Maratha leader himself.

Sleeping & Eating

Hope Hall Hotel HOTEL $

(☎8149621803; www.hopehallmatheran.com; MG Rd; d Mon-Fri ₹1200, Sat & Sun ₹1500) Run by a very hospitable family, this long-running place has been hosting happy travellers for years; the house dates back to 1875. Spacious rooms with high ceilings and arty touches are in two blocks at the rear of the leafy garden. Good breakfasts and drinks are available.

★Verandah in the Forest HERITAGE HOTEL $$$

(☎02148-230296; www.neemranahotels.com; Barr House; d incl breakfast Sun-Thu from ₹4760, Sat & Sun from ₹5950; 📶) This deliciously preserved 150-year-old bungalow exudes undiluted nostalgia, with quaintly luxurious rooms. Reminisce about bygone times in the company of ornate candelabras, oriental rugs, antique teak furniture, Victorian canvases and grandfather clocks. The verandah has a lovely aspect over Matheran's wooded hillsides.

The in-house restaurant offers a terrific four-course Continental dinner (₹700; guests only for dinner, lunch is open to the public).

Shabbir Bhai INDIAN $
(Merry Rd; mains ₹100-210; ⏲9am-10.30pm) Known locally as the 'Byrianiwala', this funky joint has a full North Indian menu, but it's all about the spicy biryanis: spiced steamed rice with chicken, mutton and veg. To find it, take the footpath uphill beside the Jama Masjid on MG Rd and follow your nose.

ℹ Information

Entry to Matheran costs ₹50 (₹25 for children), which you pay at the Dasturi car park.

ℹ Getting There & Away

TAXI

Shared taxis (₹70) run from just outside Neral train station to Matheran's Dasturi car park (30 minutes). Horses (₹350 to all hotels except Verandah in the Forest, which is ₹550) and hand-pulled rickshaws (₹700) wait here to whisk you (relatively speaking) to Matheran's main bazaar. The horse-wallahs are unionised and their prices are officially posted, but do not agree on a price until you have seen the board, which is located 50m *after* the Matheran ticket counter (hotel fares bottom-right in smaller font than the rest of the board). You can also walk this stretch in a little under an hour (around 3.5km uphill) and your luggage can be hauled for around ₹250.

TRAIN

Matheran's toy train was suspended in 2016 after two derailments. It normally chugs between Matheran and Neral Junction six times daily.

From Mumbai's CST station there are two daily express trains to Neral Junction at 7am and 8.40am (2nd class/chair car ₹93/326, 1½ hours), but they cannot be booked online as Neral and Mumbai are considered the same metropolitan area by IRCTC. You must book a further destination (Lonavla, for example) and then hop down at Neral. Alternatively, numerous local trains ply the route from Mumbai CST and Dadar.

Other expresses from Mumbai stop at Karjat, down the line from Neral, from where you can backtrack on a local train or catch a bus to Matheran (₹31, 30 minutes, four times daily 5.45am, 11am, 1.30pm and 4.15pm). From Pune there are numerous daily departures to Karjat. Note: trains from Pune don't stop at Neral Junction.

ℹ Getting Around

Apart from hand-pulled rickshaws and horses, walking is the only other transport option in Matheran. Horse-wallahs will hustle you constantly for rides (about ₹400 per hour).

Lonavla

☎02114 / POP 57,400 / ELEV 625M

Lonavla is a raucous resort town about 106km southeast of Mumbai. Its main drag consists almost exclusively of garishly lit shops flogging *chikki*, the rock-hard, brittle sweet made in the area, and you get fun-for-the-whole-family kind of stuff like wax museums, go-carts and India's largest water park. But there are some pleasant side streets, serene residential areas and destination yoga places along with the pastoral surrounding countryside that means you can choose your own path here.

The main reason you'd want to come here is to visit the nearby Karla and Bhaja Caves which, after those at Ellora and Ajanta, are the best in Maharashtra.

Hotels, restaurants and the main road to the caves lie north of the train station. Most of the Lonavla township and its markets are located south of the station.

Activities

Kaivalyadhama Yoga Hospital YOGA
(☎8551092986, 02114-273039; www.kdham.com; 40-day course incl full board US$1000) This progressive yoga centre is located in neatly kept grounds about 2km from Lonavla, en route to the Karla and Bhaja Caves. Founded in 1924 by Swami Kuvalayananda, it combines yoga courses with naturopathic therapies. Courses cover full board, yoga classes, programs and lectures.

Nirvana Adventures PARAGLIDING
(☎022-26053724; www.flynirvana.com) Mumbai-based Nirvana Adventures offers paragliding courses (two-day learner course ₹12,000 per person including full board) and short tandem flights (from ₹2500) in a charming rural setting near the town of Kamshet, 25km from Lonavla.

Sleeping & Eating

★**Ferreira Resort** HOTEL $
(☎02114-272689; http://ferreiraresortlonavala.blogspot.co.uk; DT Shahani Rd; r Mon-Thu ₹1300, Fri-Sun ₹1800-2100, with AC Mon-Thu ₹1500, Fri-Sun ₹2000-2500; ❄📶) It's certainly not

a resort, but it is something of a rarity in Lonavla: a well-priced, family-run place in a quiet residential location that's close to the train station. Ten of the 15 clean but worn air-con rooms have a balcony and there's a little garden as well as room service.

Hotel Rama Krishna SOUTH INDIAN, PUNJABI **$$**
(Mumbai Pune Rd; mains ₹40-420; ⏲7am-11.45pm) It seems everyone in town – along with passing motorcycle road warriors – gathers on this restaurant's pleasant terrace at breakfast, where great South Indian staples (generously portioned dosas etc) are the way to go. As the day wears on, diners pack in for spicy Punjabi dishes and there's plenty of cold beer to go around.

★**Kinara Dhaba Village** NORTH INDIAN, CHINESE **$$$**
(www.thekinaravillage.com; Vaksai Naka, Old Mumbai Pune Hwy; mains ₹280-560; ⏲11am-11.30pm; 👪) A bit of a *dhaba* Disneyland, but therein lies the fun. About 5km east of Lonavla nearer Karla and Bhaja Caves is this fun-for-all restaurant/entertainment venue. Dine under traditional *shamiana* huts amid obnoxious festival lighting, camel and donkey rides, *jalebi* (deep-fried batter dunked in sugar syrup) carts, fish pedicure pools and live *ghazal* (Urdu love songs) music nightly (7pm).

ℹ Getting There & Away

Lonavla is serviced by MSRTC buses departing from the bus stand to Dadar in Mumbai (from ₹150, two hours) and Pune (from ₹100, two hours). From Lonavla, **Neeta Bus** (☎8652222640; www.neetabus.in; 57/2/2/A Valvan Dam, Old Mumbai Pune Hwy) offers luxury air-con buses to Pune (₹250, hourly 8am to 11pm) and Mumbai (₹400, hourly 7am to 11pm) from its fancy station 3km northeast of the train station. It stops at Sion Station (for access to Churchgate) then heads north through the suburbs, stopping in Vila Parle for the domestic airport and on to Borivali.

All express trains from Mumbai's CST to Pune stop at Lonavla (2nd class ₹98 to ₹123, chair ₹326 to ₹371, 2½ to three hours).

Karla & Bhaja Caves

While they pale in comparison to Ajanta or Ellora, the Karla and Bhaja rock-cut caves, which date from around the 2nd century BC, are among the better examples of Buddhist cave architecture in India. They are also low on commercial tourism, making them ideal places for a quiet excursion. Karla has the most impressive single cave, but Bhaja is a quieter site to explore.

⊙ Sights

Karla Caves CAVE
(Indian/foreigner ₹15/200, video ₹25; ⏲9am-5pm) Karla Cave, the largest early *chaitya* in India, is reached by a 20-minute climb from a minibazaar at the base of a hill. Completed in 80 BC, the *chaitya* is around 40m long and 15m high and sports a vaulted interior and intricately executed sculptures of Buddha, human and animal figures.

Excluding Ellora's Kailasa Temple, this is probably the most impressive cave temple in the state. A semicircular 'sun window' filters light in towards a dagoba or stupa (the cave's representation of the Buddha), protected by a carved wooden umbrella, the only remaining example of its kind. The cave's roof also retains ancient teak buttresses. The 37 pillars forming the aisles are topped by kneeling elephants. The carved elephant heads on the sides of the vestibule once had ivory tusks.

There's a **Hindu temple** in front of the cave, thronged by pilgrims whose presence adds colour to the scene.

Bhaja Caves CAVE
(Indian/foreigner ₹15/200, video ₹25; ⏲8.30am-5.30pm) On the other side of the expressway from Karla Caves in a lush setting 3km off the main road, Bhaja Caves is the greener and quieter of the region's caves. Thought to date from around 200 BC, 10 of the 18 caves here are *viharas,* while Cave 12 is an open *chaitya* containing a simple dagoba.

ℹ Getting There & Around

Karla is 11km east of Lonavla, and Bhaja 9km. Both can be visited on a local bus to the access point, from where it's about a 6km return walk on each side to the two sites – but that would be exhausting and hot. Autorickshaws charge between ₹800 and ₹1000 (depending on the day of the week) from Lonavla for the tour, including waiting time.

Pune

☎020 / POP 5.14 MILLION / ELEV 535M

A thriving, vibrant metropolis, Pune is a centre of academia and business that epitomises 'New India' with its baffling mix of capitalism and spiritualism (ancient and modern). It's also globally famous, or notorious, for an ashram, the Osho International

Pune

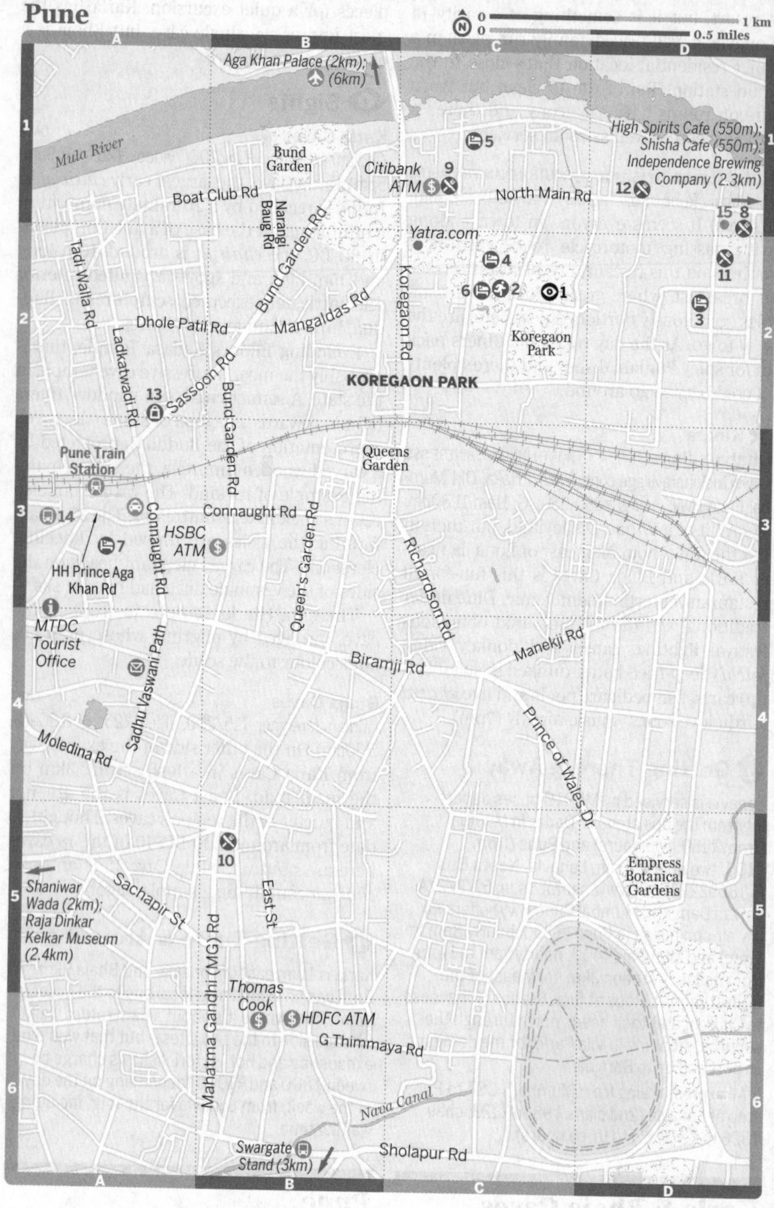

Meditation Resort (p802), founded by the late guru Bhagwan Shree Rajneesh.

Pune was initially given pride of place by Shivaji and the ruling Peshwas, who made it their capital. The British took the city in 1817 and, thanks to its cool and dry climate, soon made it the Bombay Presidency's monsoon capital. Globalisation knocked on Pune's doors in the 1990s, following which it went in for an image overhaul. However, some colonial-era charm was retained in a few old buildings and residential areas, bringing

Pune

Sights

1 Osho Teerth Gardens ... C2

Activities, Courses & Tours

2 Osho International Meditation Resort ... C2

Sleeping

3 Hotel Lotus ... D2
4 Hotel Sunderban ... C2
5 Hotel Surya Villa ... C1
6 Osho Meditation Resort Guesthouse ... C2
7 Samrat Hotel ... A3

Eating

8 Arthur's Theme ... D1
Dario's ... (see 4)
9 German Bakery ... C1
10 Juice World ... B5
11 Malaka Spice ... D2
12 Prem's ... D1

Shopping

13 Fabindia ... A2

Transport

14 Pune Train Station Stand ... A3
15 Simran Travels ... D1

about a pleasant coexistence of the old and new, which (despite the pollution and hectic traffic) makes Pune a worthwhile place to explore.

Sights

★Raja Dinkar Kelkar Museum MUSEUM

(www.rajakelkarmuseum.com; Kamal Kunj, Natu Baug, 1377-78, Shukrawar Peth; Indian/foreigner ₹50/200, mobile/camera ₹100/500; ⏲10am-5.30pm) An oddball of a museum that's one of Pune's true delights, housing only a fraction of the 20,000-odd objects of Indian daily life painstakingly collected by Dinkar Kelkar (who died in 1990). The quirky pan-Indian collection includes hundreds of hookah pipes, writing instruments, lamps, textiles, toys, entire doors and windows, kitchen utensils, furniture, puppets, ivory playing cards and betel-nut cutters.

And there's an amazing gallery of musical instruments, including peacock sitars!

Joshi's Museum of Miniature Railway MUSEUM

(www.minirailways.com; 17/1 B/2 GA Kulkarni Rd, Kothrud; ₹90; ⏲9.30am-5.30pm Mon-Fri, 9.30am-4pm & 5-8pm Sat, 5-8pm Sun) Inside the small Soudamini Instruments factory in eastern Pune is what is claimed to be India's only miniature city, the lifelong obsession of model train enthusiast Bhau Joshi. In short, it's one of the world's great model train layouts, a detailed, fully functional and passionate display of mechanical and engineering wow.

It's the stuff of boyhood dreams (and many adults, frankly). It features 65 signals, 26 points, fences, lamp posts and flyovers, a swimming pool, circus fairground (with roller coaster), drive-in theatre and dual-carriageway with moving vehicles among other bells and whistles, all controlled by a panel boasting 5km of wiring.

Aga Khan Palace PALACE

(Pune Nagar Rd, Kalyani Nagar; Indian/foreigner ₹15/200, video ₹25; ⏲9am-5.30pm) The grand Aga Khan Palace is set in a peaceful wooded 6.5-hectare plot northeast of the centre. Built in 1892 by Sultan Aga Khan III, this graceful building was where Mahatma Gandhi and other prominent nationalist leaders were interned by the British following Gandhi's Quit India campaign in 1942.

The main palace now houses the **Gandhi National Memorial** where you can peek into the room where the Mahatma used to stay. Photos and paintings exhibit moments in his extraordinary life. Both Kasturba Gandhi, the Mahatma's wife, and Mahadeobhai Desai, his secretary for 35 years, died here in confinement. You'll find their shrines (containing their ashes) in a quiet garden to the rear.

Osho Teerth Gardens GARDENS

(www.osho.com; DH Dhunjibhoy Rd, Koregaon Park; ⏲6-9am & 3-6pm) The 5-hectare Osho Teerth Gardens are a verdant escape from urban living with giant bamboo, jogging trails, a gurgling brook and smooching couples. You don't have to be an Osho member, they're accessible to all.

Shaniwar Wada FORT

(Shivaji Rd; Indian/foreigner ₹15/200, sound-and-light show ₹50/100; ⏲9am-5.30pm) The remains of this fortressed palace of the Peshwa rulers are located in the old part of the city. Built in 1732, Shaniwar Wada was destroyed by a fire in 1828, but the massive walls and ramparts remain, as does a mighty fortified gateway.

Activities

Osho International Meditation Resort MEDITATION
(☎020-66019999; www.osho.com; 17 Koregaon Park) Indelibly linked with Pune's identity, this iconic ashram-resort, located in a leafy, upscale northern suburb, has been drawing thousands of *sanyasins* (seekers) since the death of Osho in 1990. With its swimming pool, sauna and spa, 'zennis' and boutique guesthouse, it is, to some, the ultimate place to indulge in some luxe meditation.

Alternatively, detractors point fingers at the blatant commercialisation and high cost and accuse it of marketing a warped version of the mystic East to rich, gullible Westerners.

To make up your own mind you'll have to cough up the (steep) registration and daily meditation fees. Tours of the facilities are no longer permitted – the only way to access Osho is to pay an initial ₹1560, which covers registration (passport required) and a mandatory on-the-spot HIV test (sterile needles used). You'll also need two robes (one maroon and one white, ₹1000 per robe) and will have to attend a welcome session (daily at 9.30am). Note that the rules and regulations are very strict, even pedantic: swimmers are only allowed to wear, and have to pay for, Osho maroon swimwear (₹400 to ₹700) and there are mandatory (Osho maroon) clothes for the gym. Indian nationals are also lectured about behaviour (eg not hassling Western women) in special etiquette classes – female security is taken extremely seriously.

Once you've got all this out of the way, you can then pay for a meditation pass (₹870/1790 per day Indian/foreigner, with discounts for longer stays). Oh, that's apart from the fee to enter the Basho Spa (where the pool, Jacuzzi, gym, saunas and tennis courts are all located), which will be a further ₹290. Cash only for day trippers.

The main centre for meditation and the nightly white-robed spiritual dance is in the Osho Auditorium (no coughing or sneezing, please). The Osho Chuang Tzu, where the guru's ashes are kept, is also open for meditation. The commune's 'Multiversity' runs a plethora of courses in meditation and other esoteric techniques.

In the evenings, as well as meditation sessions, there's a 'nightlife' program, with parties, cinema, theatre and 'creativity nights'.

Photography is not permitted anywhere in the resort. The Welcome Center is open daily from 9am to 12.30pm and 2pm to 3.30pm.

OSHO GURU OF SEX

Ever tried mixing spirituality with primal instincts and garnishing with oodles of expensive trinkets? Well, Bhagwan Shree Rajneesh (1931–90) certainly did. Osho, as he preferred to be called, was one of India's most flamboyant 'export gurus' to market the mystic East to the world and undoubtedly the most controversial.

Initially based in Pune, he followed no particular religion or philosophy and outraged many across the world with his advocacy of sex as a path to enlightenment. A darling of the international media, he quickly earned himself the epithet 'sex guru'. In 1981, Rajneesh took his curious blend of Californian pop psychology and Indian mysticism to the USA, where he set up an agricultural commune in Oregon. There, his ashram's notoriety, as well as its fleet of (material and thus valueless!) Rolls Royces grew, until raging local opposition following a bizarre, infamous food poisoning incident (designed to manipulate local elections) moved the authorities to charge Osho with immigration fraud. He was fined US$400,000 and deported.

An epic journey then began, during which Osho and his followers, in their search for a new base, were either deported from or denied entry into 21 countries. By 1987, he was back at his Pune ashram, where thousands of foreigners soon flocked for his nightly discourses and meditation sessions.

They still come from across the globe. Such is the demand for the resort's facilities that prices are continually on the rise, with luxury being redefined every day. Interestingly, despite Osho's discourse on how nobody should be poor, no money generated by the resort goes into helping the disadvantaged.

In recent years the Osho institute has embraced the digital age, with its online iOsho portal offering iMeditate programs, Osho radio and Osho library; subscriptions are required.

Ramamani Iyengar Memorial Yoga Institute YOGA
(☎020-25656134; www.bksiyengar.com; 1107 B/1 Hare Krishna Mandir Rd, Model Colony) To attend classes at this famous institute, 7km northwest of the train station, you need to have been practising yoga for at least eight years.

Sleeping

Pune's main accommodation hubs are around the train station (where budget places proliferate) and leafy Koregaon Park, where you'll find good midrange options. Many upmarket places are on the road to the airport, 6km or so from the centre.

Hotel Surya Villa HOTEL $
(☎020-26124501; www.hotelsuryavilla.com; 294/2 German Bakery Lane, Koregaon Park; r with/without AC from ₹2380/1690; ❄📶) The Surya's functional, tiled rooms are well-kept and generously proportioned and, though a little spartan, they do have bathrooms with hot water, wi-fi and cable TV. It enjoys a good location on a quiet street in Koregaon Park, close to popular cafes.

Samrat Hotel HOTEL $$
(☎020-26137964; www.thesamrathotel.com; 17 Wilson Garden; s/d from ₹1700/2100, with AC from ₹2100/2600; ❄📶) It's not quite as grand as its fancy reception area would indicate, but with a central location just a few steps from the train station and spacious, well-maintained rooms, the 49-room Samrat represents good value. The staff is courteous and eager to please. Complimentary airport pick-up (not drop-off!) and breakfast.

Hotel Lotus HOTEL $$
(☎020-26139701; www.hotelsuryavilla.com; Lane 5, Koregaon Park; s/d ₹1930/2260, with AC ₹2260/2860; ❄📶) Hotel Lotus is good value for the quiet, Koregaon Park location and though the rooms are not that spacious, they are light and airy, and all but four have balconies. There's no restaurant, but they offer room service and there are plenty of good eating options close by.

★ **Hotel Sunderban** HOTEL $$$
(☎020-26124949; www.tghotels.com; 19 Koregaon Park; s/d without bathroom ₹1100/1430, incl breakfast from ₹4760/5950; ❄📶) Set around a manicured lawn right next to the Osho resort, this renovated art deco bungalow effortlessly combines colonial-era class with boutique appeal. Deluxe rooms in the main building sport antique furniture, while even the cheapest options are beautifully presented and spacious (though lack a private bathroom). The best-value rooms are the lawn-facing studios.

There is a yoga centre, spa and two restaurants on the premises, including highly regarded Dario's (p804).

Osho Meditation Resort Guesthouse GUESTHOUSE $$$
(☎020-66019900; www.osho.com; Koregaon Park; s/d ₹6020/6620; ❄📶) This uberchic, 60-room place will only allow you in if you come to meditate at the Osho International Meditation Resort. The rooms and common spaces are an elegant exercise in modern minimalist aesthetics with several ultraluxe features – including Biotique amenities and purified fresh air supplied in all rooms!

Eating

Juice World CAFE $
(2436/B East St, Camp; snacks ₹40-200, juices ₹65-300; ⏰11am-11.30pm) Delicious fresh fruit juices and shakes. This casual cafe with outdoor seating serves wholesome snacks such as *pav bhaji* (spiced vegetables and bread). On a hot day it's impossible to walk past its fruit displays and not drop in for a drink. Try the seasonal *kabuli amar* (pomegranate).

Arthur's Theme EUROPEAN $$
(☎020-26152710; www.arthurstheme.com; 2, Vrindavan Apts, Lane No 6, Koregaon Park; mains ₹280-990; ⏰11.30am-11.30pm; 📶) This eclectic European bistro has rave reviews seeping from its pores. Indeed the food, a lengthy list that includes rarely seen proteins like turkey and duck in addition to extensive choices of veg, fish, chicken and buffalo, presents a tantalising opportunity for a sophisticated curry-free evening. Most dishes fall in the ₹300 to ₹400 range, so the price is right.

German Bakery BAKERY $$
(North Main Rd, Koregaon Park; cakes ₹100-140, mains ₹90-380; ⏰7am-11pm; 📶) A Pune institution famous for its traveller-geared grub, including omelettes, cooked breakfasts, Greek salads, cappuccinos and lots of sweet treats (try the mango cheesecake). Located on a very busy traffic-plagued corner. A fatal terrorist attack took place here in 2010 – a painful memory in this peace-loving city.

Prem's MULTICUISINE $$
(www.facebook.com/PremsResto.Pune; North Main Rd, Koregaon Park; mains ₹60-550; ⏰8am-12.15am; 📶) In a quiet, tree-canopied courtyard, Prem's is perfect for a lazy, beery daytime

TRANSIT HUB: MAHABALESHWAR

Once a summer capital under the British, today the best thing about the hill station of Mahabaleshwar (1327m) is the jaw-dropping mountain scenery on the road to get here. It's an overdeveloped mess, tainted by an ugly building boom and traffic chaos as tourists attempt a mad dash to tick off its viewpoints and falls. There's no compelling reason to visit – it's basically one big bustling bazaar surrounded by resorts and views – though the town can be used as a base to visit the impressive **Pratapgad Fort** (p807) or Kass Plateau of Flowers, both nearby.

Forget about coming during the monsoon when the whole town virtually shuts down (and an unbelievable 6m of rain falls). If you have an hour or so to kill between buses, budget-friendly **Nature Care Spa** (☎7066327423; Hotel Shreyas, opposite ST Bus Stand; massages from ₹1899; ⏲8am-8pm), across the street from the bus stand at Hotel Shreyas, hits the spot in a place like Mahabaleshwar. And don't miss **Grapevine** (☎02168-261100; Masjid Rd; mains ₹160-700; ⏲9.30am-3pm & 5-10pm) – its gourmet Parsi cuisine and Maharashtran wine are a godsend in Mahabaleshwar.

From Mahabaleshwar bus stand, state buses leave regularly for Pune (non-AC ₹180, four hours, hourly 7.30am to 6.30pm), Kohlapur (non-AC ₹265, 5½ hours, hourly from 8am) and Satara (non-AC ₹57, two hours, hourly 6am to 7pm). Seven daily buses head to Mumbai Central between 9am and 9.30pm (non-AC ₹400, seven hours) and one ordinary bus to Goa (non-AC ₹423, 12 hours, 8am).

RB Travels, located on a corner between an alley shortcut to Masjid Rd and the bazaar (across from Meghdoot restaurant), books luxury coaches to Goa (non-AC seater/Volvo AC sleeper ₹850/1800, 12 hours). You will depart from the bazaar in a car at 7.30pm to Surur Phata junction, 42km away, to wait for the bus on the way from Pune. Transport to Mumbai (Volvo AC seater/sleeper ₹500/600, six hours, noon and 9pm) and Pune (Volvo AC seater ₹375, 3½ hours, 11.30am) is available as well.

For the Pratapgad Fort, a state bus (₹130 return, one hour, 9.15am) does a daily round-trip, with a waiting time of around one hour; taxi drivers charge a fixed ₹1000 return.

drinking session on the breezy patio, with some decent local craft beers to try, perhaps with one of its famous sizzlers. The morning after? Well, Prem's is the logical choice again, with the city's best breakfast selection: eggs Benedict with smoked salmon (₹160), pancakes and detox shots.

Its sister bar next door, Swig, is its wilder counterpart, quite a happy hour hot spot.

★Malaka Spice ASIAN **$$$**
(www.malakaspice.com; Lane 5, North Main Rd, Koregaon Park; mains ₹305-780; ⏲11.30am-midnight; ❄📶) Maharashtra's shining culinary moment is a fury of Southeast Asian fantasticness; trying to choose one dish among the delectable stir-fries, noodles and curries – all strong on seafood, vegetarian options, chicken, duck and mutton – is futile. Dine alfresco under colourful tree lights and relish the spicy and intricate flavour cavalcade from star chefs reared on a Slow Food, stay-local philosophy.

Many of their ingredients come from their own farm as well. Reserve ahead and starve yourself all day in preparation!

Dario's ITALIAN **$$$**
(www.darios.in; Hotel Sunderban, 19 Koregaon Park; mains ₹480-610, pizza ₹260-680; ⏲8am-11.30pm) At the rear of Hotel Sunderban, this Italian-run veg paradise is one of Pune's most elegant dining experiences, providing you plant yourself on the gorgeous and intimate courtyard for an alfresco meal. Homemade pastas, very good pizzas and fine salads (try the Bosco; ₹480), including wholewheat, vegan and gluten-free options, fill the extensive menu of delectable homesick remedies.

Drinking & Nightlife

★Independence Brewing Company CRAFT BEER
(☎020-66448308; www.independencebrewco.com; Zero One, 79/1, Pingle Vasti, Mundhwa Rd, Mundhwa; pints from ₹300) Reserve a table in the outstanding beer garden at this industrially hip craft brewery – Pune's finest – and you'll swear you're in California. The seven taps change often – Four Grain saison, Method to Madness IPA and the chocolate-bomb Ixcacao porter are standouts – and the funky-flavoured, Indian-Asian bar

grub means it's very easy to settle in for the night.

High Spirits Cafe BAR
(www.dahigh.com; 35A/1, North Main Rd, Mundhwa; cocktails ₹300-575; ⌚8-11.45pm) Pune's most happening evenings take place in this artistically inclined bar with a ramshackle, good-time outdoor patio. Every night something cool is on, such as comedy Wednesdays, disco Saturdays and an unskippable Sunday barbecue (1.30pm to 4.30pm). The crowd, stretching from starving artists to wayward soul-searchers to 40-something trendsetters, goes bananas. No cover!

☆ Entertainment

★Shisha Cafe JAZZ
(☎020-26880050; www.facebook.com/shishajazzcafe; ABC Farms, Mundhwa; Thu ₹250) It's a magical atmosphere anytime, but live jazz Thursday nights at alfresco Shisha are a Pune institution. Snuggle up on Iranian-style lounges downstairs or reserve a seat at a marble table under hanging Arabian carpets in the elevated main stage area. It's inside a nightlife enclave in Mundhwa called ABC Farms.

Shopping

Fabindia CLOTHING
(www.fabindia.com; Sakar 10, Sassoon Rd; ⌚10.30am-8.30pm) Sells Indian saris, silks and cottons, as well as linen shirts for men, and diverse accessories including bags and jewellery.

ℹ Information

For exchange services, there is a Thomas Cook branch on General Thimmaya Rd. There are dozens of ATMs spread through the city and at the train station.

Citibank ATM (Tulsidas Apartment, N Main Rd)
HDFC ATM (East St)
HSBC ATM (Bund Garden Rd)

You'll find several internet cafes along Pune's main thoroughfares. Wi-fi is common in trendier bars and restaurants and most hotels.

Main Post Office (www.indiapost.gov.in; Sadhu Vaswani Path; ⌚10am-6pm Mon-Sat)

MTDC Tourist Office (☎020-26128169; www.maharashtratourism.gov.in; I Block, Central Bldg, Dr Annie Besant Rd; ⌚10am-6pm Mon-Sat, to 5pm Sun, closed 2nd & 4th Sat) Buried in a government complex south of the train station.

Thomas Cook (☎020-66007903; www.thomascook.in; Thackers House, 2418 General Thimmaya Rd; ⌚9.30am-6pm Mon-Sat) Cashes travellers cheques and exchanges foreign currency.

Yatra.com (☎020-65007605; www.yatra.com; Koregaon Park Rd; ⌚10am-7pm Mon-Sat) The city office of the reputed internet ticketing company.

ℹ Getting There & Away

AIR

A flashy new international airport is planned but infighting over the exact location was stalling the project at time of writing. Until then, airlines fly daily from **Pune International Airport** (PNQ; New Airport Rd, Mhada Colony, Lohgaon) to Mumbai, Delhi, Jaipur, Bengaluru (Bangalore), Nagpur, Goa, and Chennai, among others.

BUS

Pune has three bus stands. Buses leave the **Pune train station stand** (☎020-26126218) for Belgaum (₹700, seven hours, 11pm), Goa (₹600 to ₹1000, 10 hours, 6.30pm and 7.30pm), Kolhapur (₹400, six hours, hourly 5.30am to 11.30pm), Lonavla (₹62, hourly), Mahabaleshwar (₹230, four hours, hourly 5.30am to 5.30pm) and Mumbai's Dadar TT Circle station (₹266 to ₹531, four hours, every 15 minutes).

From the **Shivaji Nagar bus stand** (☎020-24431240; Shivajinagar Railway Station Rd), air-con buses go to Aurangabad (from ₹661, five to six hours, hourly 6am to 11.30pm), Nasik (from ₹611, every 20 minutes, 6am to 12.30am) and Mumbai (₹650, frequent). Non-AC buses also go

MAJOR TRAINS FROM PUNE

DESTINATION	TRAIN NO & NAME	FARE (₹)	DURATION (HR)	DEPARTURE
Bengaluru	11301 Udyan Express	460/1785	21	11.45am
Chennai	12163 Chennai Express	525/1980	19½	12.10am
Delhi	11077 Jhelum Express	625/2435	27½	5.20pm
Hyderabad	17031 Hyderabad Express	340/1310	13½	4.35pm
Mumbai CST	12124 Deccan Queen	115/395	3½	7.15am

Express fares are sleeper/2AC; Deccan Queen fares are 2nd class/AC chair.

to Mahabaleshwar (₹230, four hours, 6.15am, 8.30am and 9.30am).

Ticket agents selling private long-distance bus tickets are across the street from Shivaji Nagar station – try **Sana Travels** (☎8888808984; 2, Sita Park, Shivajinagar). Destinations (all AC sleepers) include Bengaluru (₹1050, 14 hours, hourly 1pm to 10pm), Hyderabad (₹500, 10 hours, hourly 7pm to 1am), Goa (₹1000, 10 hours, 7pm and 10pm), Mangalore (₹1500, 14 hours, 6pm and 10pm) and Nagpur (₹800, 14 hours, hourly 4am to 10pm). Buses for Bengaluru and Mangalore as well as Sinhagad leave from the **Swargate bus stand** (☎020-24441591; Satara Rd).

TAXI

Shared taxis (up to four passengers) link Pune with Mumbai airport around the clock. They leave from the **taxi stand** (☎020-26121090) in front of Pune train station (per seat ₹400 to ₹475, 2½ hours). To rent a car and driver try **Simran Travels** (☎020-26153222; www.mumbaiairportcab.com; 1st fl, Madhuban Bldg, Lane No 5, Koregaon Park; ⏲24hr).

TRAIN

Pune train station (sometimes called Pune Junction) is in the heart of the city on HH Prince Aga Khan Rd. There are very regular, roughly hourly services to Mumbai and good links to cities including Delhi, Chennai and Hyderabad.

ℹ Getting Around

The modern airport is 8km northeast of the city. From Koregaon Park an autorickshaw costs about ₹150 and a taxi around ₹200, but an UberGo at nonsurge pricing is only around ₹115. Autorickshaws can be found everywhere; a trip from the train station to Koregaon Park costs about ₹50 (more at night).

Around Pune

Sinhagad

The ruined **Sinhagad** (Lion Fort; ⏲dawn-dusk) FREE, about 24km southwest of Pune, was wrested by Maratha leader Shivaji from the Bijapur kings in 1670. In the epic battle (where he lost his son Sambhaji), Shivaji is said to have used monitor lizards yoked with ropes to scale the fort's craggy walls. Today, it's in a poor state, but worth visiting for the sweeping views and opportunity to hike in the hills. Bus 50 runs frequently to Donje (Golewadi) village from Swargate (₹30, 45 minutes), from where it's a 4km hike if you want to walk or catch a shared 4WD (₹50) that can cart you 10km to the base of the summit.

Shivneri

Situated 90km northwest of Pune, above the village of Junnar, **Shivneri Fort** (⏲dawn-dusk) FREE holds the distinction of being the birthplace of Shivaji. Within the ramparts of this ruined fort are the old royal stables, a mosque dating back to the Mughal era and several rock-cut reservoirs. The most important structure is Shivkunj, the pavilion in which Shivaji was born.

About 8km from Shivneri, on the other side of Junnar, is an interesting group of Hinayana Buddhist caves called **Lenyadri** (Indian/foreigner ₹15/200; ⏲8am-6pm). Of the 27 caves, cave 7 is the most impressive and, interestingly, houses an image of the Hindu god Ganesh.

Views from both monuments are spectacular.

There are seven or so buses per day (₹88, two hours) connecting Pune's Shivaji Nagar terminus with Junnar (a day cab from Pune will cost about ₹2625). From Junnar's bus stand, a return rickshaw including one hour's wait time runs ₹200 to Shivneri and ₹300 to Lenyadri.

Kolhapur

☎0231 / POP 561,300 / ELEV 550M

A little-visited city, Kolhapur is the perfect place to get intimate with the flamboyant side of India. Only a few hours from Goa, this historic settlement boasts an intensely fascinating temple complex. In August Kolhapur is at its vibrant best when Naag Panchami (p774), a snake-worshipping festival, is held in tandem with one at Pune. Gastronomes take note: the town is also the birthplace of the famed, spicy Kolhapuri cuisine, especially chicken and mutton dishes.

Sights

The atmospheric old town quarter around the Mahalaxmi Temple and Old Palace has a huge (traffic-free) plaza and is accessed by a monumental gateway.

★Shree Chhatrapati Shahu Museum MUSEUM

(Indian/foreigner ₹25/80; ⏲9.15am-5.30pm) 'Bizarre' takes on a whole new meaning at this 'new' palace, an Indo-Saracenic behemoth designed by British architect 'Mad' Charles

Mant for the Kolhapur kings in 1884. The madcap museum is a maze of countless trophies from the kings' trigger-happy jungle safaris, including walking sticks made from leopard vertebrae and ashtrays fashioned out of tiger skulls and rhino feet. The armoury houses enough weapons to stage a minicoup. The horror-house effect is brought full circle by the taxidermy section.

Don't miss the highly ornate Durbar Hall, where the rulers held court sessions, and dotted around the palace you'll find dozens of portraits of the portly maharajas to admire. Photography is prohibited inside.

It's located about 2.5km north of the train station. A rickshaw from the train station/bus stand will cost ₹35/50.

★Mahalaxmi Temple HINDU TEMPLE

(⌚3am-11pm) One of Maharastra's most important and vibrant places of worship, the Mahalaxmi Temple is dedicated to Amba Bai (Mother Goddess). The temple's origins date back to AD 10, but much of the present structure is from the 18th century. It draws an unceasing tide of humanity, as pilgrims press to enter the holy inner sanctuary and bands of musicians and worshippers chant devotions. Non-Hindus are welcome and it's a fantastic place for people-watching.

Motibag Thalim TRAINING CENTRE

(⌚4am-4pm) Kolhapur is famed for the calibre of its Kushti wrestlers and at the Motibag Thalim you can watch young athletes train in an earthen pit. The *akhara* (training ground) is reached through a low doorway and passage to the left of the entrance to Bhavani Mandap (ask for directions). You are free to walk in and watch, as long as you don't mind the sight of sweaty, seminaked men and the stench of urine emanating from the loos.

Sleeping & Eating

Hotel K Tree HOTEL $$

(☎0231-2526990; www.hotelktree.com; 517E, Plot 65, Shivaji Park; s/d incl breakfast from ₹3330/3700; ❄📶) With high service standards and 26 very inviting modish rooms, this newer hotel is fine value and wildy popular with Indians for its 15-item buffet breakfast. It's a toss up between the clandestine bathrooms in deluxe rooms or elevated Asian-style beds in executive rooms.

Hotel Pavillion HOTEL $$

(☎0231-2652751; www.hotelpavillion.co.in; 392E Assembly Rd, Shaupuri; s/d incl breakfast ₹1850/2080, with AC from ₹2260/2500; ❄@) Located at the far end of a leafy park-cum-office-area, this hotel guarantees a peaceful stay, occasionally uninspired bathrooms aside. Its large, well-equipped rooms are perhaps a little dated, but many have windows that open out to delightful views of seasonal blossoms. Book room 101 to catch the lobby-only wi-fi signal in-room.

Chorage Misal INDIAN $

(Mahadwar Rd, near Gujri Corners; mains ₹40; ⌚8.30am-8pm) Near Mahalaxmi Temple, this hole-in-the-wall *misal* (spicy curry made from moth bean sprouts) joint has been at it since 1963 and is the spiciest of the city's classic joints. Rajesh is the third generation behind the recipe and acts as a one-man show. There's no English sign. It's directly to the right of the beautiful Jain temple with the Coca-Cola signage.

★Dehaati INDIAN $$

(Ayodha Park, Old Pune-Bangalore Hwy, Nimbalkar Colony; thalis ₹230-320; ⌚12.30-3.30pm & 7.30-10.30pm) The city's Kolhapuri thali specialist. Meals come in a variety of mutton variations as well as chicken and veg. The vibrant curries, the spiced-up dhal, the rich *aakkha masoor* (Kolhapuri-style whole lentil curry), the intricate *tambda rassa* (spicy red mutton curry), the perfectly flaky chapatis – it's all delicious.

DON'T MISS

PRATAPGAD FORT

Pratapgad Fort (⌚9am-dusk) FREE, built by Shivaji in 1656 (and still owned by his descendants), straddles a high mountain ridge 24km northwest of the town of Mahabaleshwar. In 1659, Shivaji agreed to meet Bijapuri General Afzal Khan here in an attempt to end a stalemate. Despite a no-arms agreement, Shivaji, upon greeting Khan, disembowelled his enemy with a set of iron *baghnakh* (tiger's claws). Khan's tomb (out of bounds) marks the site of this painful encounter at the base of the fort. Pratapgad is reached by a 500-step climb that affords brilliant views.

From the bus stand in Mahabaleshwar, a state bus tour (₹165 return, one hour, 9.30am) does a daily shuttle to the fort, with a waiting time of around one hour. Taxi drivers in Mahabaleshwar charge a fixed ₹1000 for the return trip, including one hour's waiting time.

Little Italy ITALIAN $$

(☎0231-2537133; www.littleitaly.in; 517 A2 Shivaji Park; pizza ₹225-445, pasta ₹215-365; ⊙11.30am-10pm) If you've been clocking up some hard yards on India's roads, this authentic, professionally run restaurant is just the place to sustain you for the next trip. All the flavours are to savour, with a delicious, veg-only menu of antipasti, thin-crust pizzas (from a wood-fired oven), al dente pasta and a great Indian-heavy wine list (by the glass available).

Don't pass on the desserts, particularly the panna cotta.

Information

ICICI Bank ATM Located next to Mahalaxmi Temple.

MTDC Tourist Office (☎0231-2652935; www.maharashtratourism.gov.in; 254B Udyog Bhavan, Assembly Rd; ⊙10am-5.30pm Mon-Sat) Located behind the Collector's Office near Hotel Pavillion. At the time of research, it had opened a far more convenient booth (☎0231-2652935; www.maharashtratourism.gov.in) near Mahalaxmi Mandir on a trial basis.

State Bank of India ATM Handy ATM across the street from Hotel Pavillion.

Getting There & Around

BUS

From the **Kolhapur bus stand** (☎0231-2650620; Benadikar Path, Shahupur), services head regularly to Pune (non-AC from ₹396, five hours, hourly 5am to 11pm), Ratnagiri (ordinary/semideluxe ₹177/199, 4½ hours, every 30 minutes 5am to 1am), five ordinary-only buses to Malvan (₹201, five hours, 5.15am, 6.5am, noon, 1.30pm and 5pm) and 12 daily buses to Mumbai (ordinary/semideluxe ₹480/600, 10 hours). There is a reservation counter for all buses.

The best private bus agents gather at the Royal Plaza building at Dabholkar Corner, 300m north of the bus stand. **Paulo Travels** (☎0231-6681812; www.paulotravels.com; B/22, Royal Plaza, Dhabolkar Corner) heads to Goa (Volvo AC seater/sleeper from ₹500/600, eight hours, 9am, noon, 2am, 3am, 4am, 5am and 6am). **Neeta Travels** (☎0231-3290061; www.neeta-bus.in; B/16, Royal Plaza, Dabholkar Corner) is a good bet for overnight air-con services heading to Mumbai (Volvo AC sleeper from ₹850, nine hours, 5pm, 9.45pm and 10.45pm) and Pune (Volvo AC seater from ₹350, five hours, 7am, 9am, 4pm, 5pm, 8pm and 11.30pm).

TRAIN

The train station, known as Chattrapati Shahu Maharaj Terminus, is 10 minutes' walk west of the bus stand. Three daily expresses, including the 10.50pm Sahyadri Express, go to Mumbai (sleeper/2AC ₹338/1241, 13 hours, 10.50pm) via Pune (₹243/876, eight hours). The Rani Chennama Express makes the long voyage to Bengaluru (₹433/1636, 17½ hours, 2.05pm). There are no direct trains to Goa.

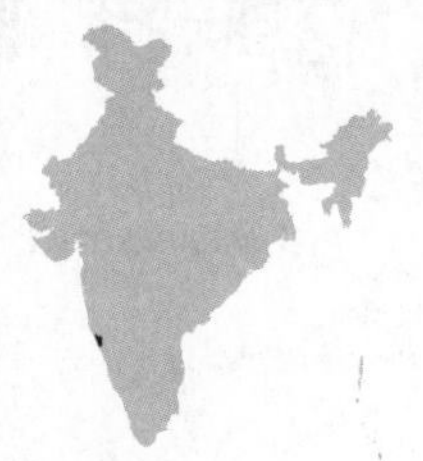

Goa

Includes ➡

Best Beaches

- ➡ Palolem (p846)
- ➡ Mandrem (p837)
- ➡ Cola & Khancola (p844)
- ➡ Anjuna (p829)
- ➡ Arambol (p838)

Best Places to Sleep

- ➡ Panjim Inn (p816)
- ➡ Red Door Hostel (p829)
- ➡ Mandala (p838)
- ➡ Indian Kitchen (p827)
- ➡ Ciaran's (p846)

Why Go?

Pint-sized Goa is much more than beaches and trance parties. A kaleidoscopic blend of Indian and Portuguese cultures, sweetened with sun, sea, sand, seafood and spirituality, there's nowhere in India quite like it.

The central region (practically beach-free) is Goa's historic and cultural heart, home to capital Panaji, Old Goa's glorious churches, inland islands, bird sanctuaries, spice plantations and the wild Western Ghats.

North Goa is the Goa you've heard all about: busy beaches, upbeat nightlife, Goan trance, great food, hippie markets and yoga retreats. Calangute and Baga are the epicentre. Anjuna (with its famous Wednesday market) and Vagator still exude some hippie cool and party vibe. Laid-back Morjim, Aswem and Mandrem are burgeoning family-friendly beach resorts. Northern, budget-loving Arambol hosts paragliding.

South Goa is the state's more serene half, with cleaner, whiter, quieter beaches ranging from village-feel Benaulim to beach-hut bliss at Palolem, Patnem and Agonda.

When to Go

Panaji

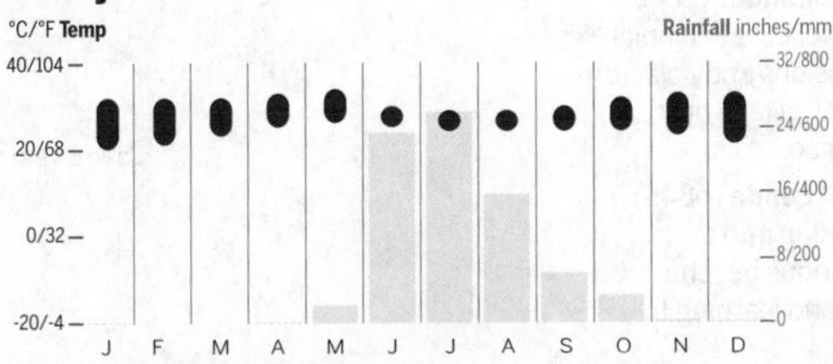

Sep–Nov Some shacks up, but prices are lower and crowds fewer; humid weather post-monsoon.

Nov–Mar Wonderful weather; yoga, festivals in full swing; peak prices and crowds mid-Dec to early Jan.

Mar–Apr Carnival and Easter celebrations as the season winds down.

Goa Highlights

❶ **Panaji** (p813) Exploring the historic Latin Quarter, shopping and eating well in India's most laid-back state capital.

❷ **Assagao** (p832) Dropping in to a yoga class at Assagao, Anjuna, Arambol or Mandrem.

❸ **Anjuna Flea Market** (p832) Haggling for a bargain at this touristy but fun Wednesday market.

❹ **Old Goa** (p819) Standing in silence in the extraordinary churches and cathedrals of Old Goa.

❺ **Cola Beach** (p844) Trekking down to secluded Cola, one of Goa's prettiest beaches.

❻ **Mandrem** (p837) Sleeping in style and stretching out with a good book at this peaceful beach.

❼ **Palolem** (p846) Checking into a beach hut on beautiful Palolem Beach, where you can kayak, learn to cook and relax.

❽ **Chandor** (p842) Marvelling at colonial mansions and *palácio* in this village near Margao.

❾ **Agonda** (p845) Booking into a luxurious beachfront hut and learning to surf.

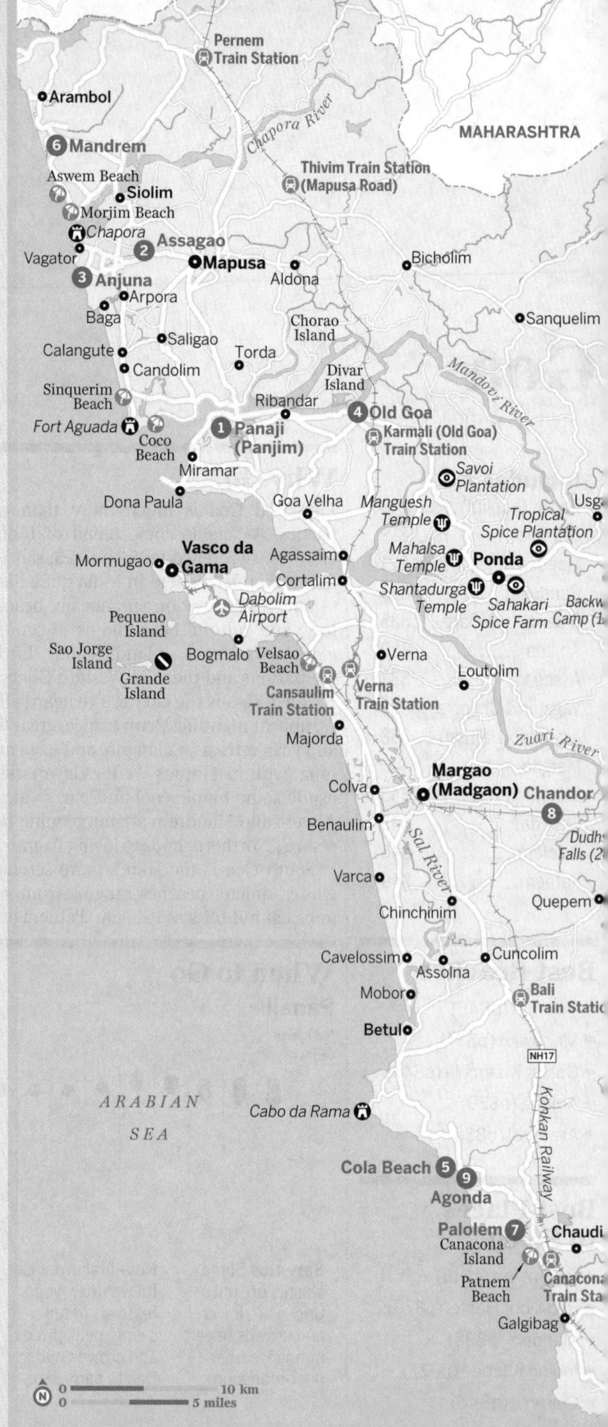

History

A 100,000-year look back through the history of Goa offers a keen insight into some of the region's most mysterious and alluring archaeological and historic remains, and into the Goan psyche itself.

Goa went through a dizzying array of rulers from Ashoka's Mauryan empire in the 3rd century BC to the long-ruling Kadambas from the 3rd century AD. Subsequent conflict saw rival sultanates fighting the Hindu Vijayanagar empire for control, before the Adil Shahs of Bijapur created the capital we now call Old Goa in the 15th century.

The Portuguese arrived in 1510 and steadily extended their power from their grand capital at Old Goa out into the provinces, zealously converting the locals to Christianity. Their 400-year reign came to an end in 1961, after a three-day siege by the Indian Army, but the Portuguese legacy lives on in the state's colonial-era mansions, its cuisine, churches and even in its language.

Activities

Yoga & Alternative Therapies

Every imaginable form of yoga, meditation, reiki, ayurvedic massage and other spiritually orientated health regime is practised, taught and relished in Goa. The best time is mid-November to early April, when all outfits or retreats are open and courses are in full swing. A handful of classes operate year-round.

Palolem, Agonda and Patnem in the south, and Arambol, Mandrem, Anjuna and Assagao in the north, are particularly great places for yoga classes and courses.

Ayurvedic treatments can be found at most beach villages. Ask around for personal recommendations and ensure that massages are conducted by a female if you're a woman and a male if you're a man. The spas at Goa's five-star hotels offer a superluxurious alternative.

Wildlife-Watching

Goa's hinterland is great for spotting wildlife, from the blazing kingfishers that fleck the coastal strip's luminescent paddy fields, to the water buffalo that wander home come sunset. Goa's wildlife sanctuaries host hard-to-spot wonders such as gaurs (Indian bison), porcupines, wild boar and the occasional pangolin (scaly anteater) or leopard. A loud rustle in the leaves overhead often signals the arrival of mischievous langur monkeys. Taking a riverine trip inland, you might spot crocodiles, otters, and yet more birdlife.

John's Boat Tours (p823) in Candolim runs dolphin- and crocodile-spotting trips.

Water Sports

Most water-sports outfits run on a seasonal, itinerant basis; it's enough to turn up at a beach and look around for a shack offering your chosen activity. Calangute and Colva are the busiest water-sports beaches. Activities include jet skiing, parasailing, wake-boarding, kayaking, surfing and kitesurfing. Paragliding (p838) is popular at Arambol. The best places for kayaking are Palolem's calm bay or Goa's numerous rivers and estuaries. Surfing outfits include Vaayu Waterman's Village (p837) in Aswem, Surf Wala (p839) in Arambol and Aloha Surf School (p845) in Agonda.

TOP STATE FESTIVALS

Feast of the Three Kings (Chandor & Reis Magos; 6 Jan) Boys re-enact the story of the three kings bearing gifts for Christ.

Shigmotsav of Holi (Shigmo; statewide; Feb/Mar) Goa's version of the Hindu festival Holi sees coloured powders thrown about and parades in most towns.

Sabado Gordo (Panaji; Feb/Mar) A procession of floats and street parties on the Saturday before Lent.

Carnival (statewide; Mar) A four-day festival kicking off Lent; the party's particularly jubilant in Panaji.

Fama de Menino Jesus (Colva; 2nd Mon in Oct) Statue of the baby Jesus is paraded through the streets of Colva.

Feast of St Francis Xavier (Panaji, Old Goa; 3 Dec) A 10-day celebration of Goa's patron saint.

Feast of Our Lady of the Immaculate Conception (Margao, Panaji; 8 Dec) Fairs and concerts around Panaji's famous church.

Although Goa is not an internationally renowned diving destination, its waters are India's third-best diving spot (after the Andaman and Lakshadweep Islands). Dive season runs from late October to April. Recommended Professional Association of Dive Instructors (PADI) accredited operations in Goa include Barracuda Diving (p825) in Baga, Dive Goa (p823) in Candolim, Goa Aquatics (p825) in Calangute and **Goa Diving** (☎9049442647; www.goadiving.com; courses from ₹11,000, 1-/2-tank dive ₹3000/5000) in Bogmalo.

Information

The **Goa Tourism Development Corporation** (www.goa-tourism.com) provides maps and information, operates hotels throughout the state and runs a host of tours.

Getting There & Away

AIR

Goa's airport, **Dabolim** (Goa International Airport; ☎0832-2540806), is served directly by domestic flights, a handful of international flights from the Middle East, and seasonal package-holiday charters (mostly from Russia, Europe and the UK).

> **SLEEPING PRICE RANGES**
>
> The following price ranges refer to a double room with bathroom:
>
> **$** below ₹1200
>
> **$$** ₹1200–₹5000
>
> **$$$** above ₹5000
>
> Accommodation prices in Goa can vary considerably depending on the season and demand. The high season runs from November to late February, but prices climb even higher during the crowded Christmas and New Year period (around 22 December to 3 January). Mid-season is October and March to April, and low season is the monsoon (May to September). These dates can vary a little depending on the monsoon and the granting of shack licences, which are renewed every couple of years.
>
> All accommodation rates listed are for the high season – but not for the peak Christmas period, when you'll almost certainly have to book in advance. Always call ahead for rates and ask about discounts.

Unless you're on a charter, you'll generally have to fly into a major city such as Mumbai or Delhi and change to a domestic flight with Jet Airways, Air India, SpiceJet or IndiGo.

BUS

Private and state-run long-distance buses run to/from Goa daily; in many cases you simply turn up at the bus station and jump on the next available bus. State-run and private companies offer 'ordinary', 'deluxe' 'superfast' and VIP services. Most comfortable are Volvo buses, with reclining seating and air-conditioning. Note that travel into and out of Mumbai by road is interminably slow; the train is faster and more comfortable.

Buses for Mumbai and other cities depart from Panaji, Margao and Mapusa between 5.30pm and 8.30pm daily; there are dozens of operators and departures, but fares are standard to/from anywhere in Goa. **Kadamba** (www.goakadamba.com), the state government bus company, serves the state and neighbouring regions. For booking private buses, try www.redbus.in.

TRAIN

The 760km-long **Konkan Railway** (www.konkanrailway.com), completed in 1998, is the main train line running through the state, connecting Goa with Mumbai to the north and Mangalore to the south.

The biggest station in Goa is Margao's Madgaon station (p841), and many trains also pass through Karmali station near Old Goa, 12km from Panaji. Smaller stations on the line include Pernem for Arambol, Thivim for Mapusa and the northern beaches, and Canacona for Palolem.

Getting Around

TO/FROM THE AIRPORT

From Dabolim Airport, prepaid taxis to central Panaji or Margao charge ₹870 (₹920 for AC). Alternatively, if you don't have much luggage, catch a bus from the main road to Vasco da Gama, then a bus direct from Vasco to Panaji (₹30, 45 minutes).

BUS

Goa's extensive network of buses shuttle to and from almost every tiny town and village; the main hubs are Panaji, Margao and Mapusa. Travelling between north and south Goa you'll generally need to change at Margao, Panaji or both. Fares range from ₹5 to ₹40.

CAR & MOTORCYCLE

It's easy in Goa to organise a private car with driver (or simply a taxi) for long-distance day trips. Expect to pay from ₹2000 for a full day (usually eight hours and 80km). Self-drive hire cars start from ₹900 to ₹1200 per day for a small Maruti to upwards of ₹2000 for a large

4WD, excluding fuel and usually with a per kilometre limit. Your best bet for rentals is online at sites such as www.goa2u.com.

You'll rarely go far on a Goan road without seeing a local or tourist whizzing by on a scooter or motorbike, and renting one is a breeze. You'll likely pay from ₹200 to ₹400 per day for a scooter, ₹400 to ₹500 for a smaller Yamaha motorbike, and ₹450 to ₹600 for a Royal Enfield Bullet. Prices can drop considerably if you're renting for more than a few days or if it's an off-peak period – bargain if there are lots of machines around.

Goan roads can be treacherous, filled with human, bovine, canine, feline, mechanical and avian obstacles, as well as potholes and hairpin bends. Take it slowly, be on the lookout for 'speed breakers', try not to drive at night (country lanes are poorly lit), and don't attempt a north–south day trip on a 50cc bike.

TAXI & AUTORICKSHAW

Taxis are widely available for town-hopping, but the local union cartel means prices are high, especially at night and more so around expensive hotels. A full day's sightseeing, depending on the distance, is likely to be around ₹1500 to ₹2000. Agree on a price beforehand.

A new initiative by Goa Tourism is the **Women's Taxi Service** (☎0832-2437437), with female drivers, phone-only bookings and only women, couples or families accepted as passengers. The vehicles are fitted with accurate meters and GPS monitoring, and the drivers are trained in first aid and self-defence. Fares can even be paid with a credit card.

Autorickshaws are about a third cheaper than taxis and generally better for short trips; count on ₹50 minimum for a short journey and ₹100 for a slightly longer one. Negotiate the fare before you jump in.

Motorcycle taxis, known as 'pilots', are also a licensed form of taxi in Goa, identified by a yellow front mudguard. They're only really common around major taxi stands and beach resorts, and cost half the price of a taxi.

PANAJI & CENTRAL GOA

Panaji (Panjim)

☎0832 / POP 115,000

One of India's most relaxed state capitals, Panaji (Panjim) crowds around the peninsula overlooking the broad Mandovi River, where cruise boats and floating casinos ply the waters, and advertising signs cast neon reflections in the night.

A glorious whitewashed church lords over the animated city centre, a broad leafy boulevard skirts around the river, and grand colonial-era buildings rub shoulders with arty boutiques, old-school bookshops, state-of-the-art malls and backstreet bars.

But it's the tangle of narrow streets in the old Latin Quarter that really steal the show. Nowhere is the Portuguese influence felt more strongly than here, where the late afternoon sun lights up yellow houses with purple doors, and around each corner you'll find restored ochre-coloured mansions with terracotta-tiled roofs, wrought-iron balconies and arched oyster-shell windows.

A day or two in Panaji really is an essential part of the Goan experience.

OFF THE BEATEN TRACK

DUDHSAGAR FALLS

Goa's most impressive **waterfall** splashes 603m down on the eastern border with Karnataka, in the far southeastern corner of the Bhagwan Mahavir Wildlife Sanctuary. The falls are best visited as soon after monsoon as possible (October is perfect), when water levels are highest.

Get here via Colem village, 7km south of Molem, by car or by the scenic 8.15am local train from Margao (return train times vary seasonally). From Colem, pick up a shared jeep (₹500 per person for six people) for the bumpy remaining 45-minute journey. An easier option is a taxi or a full-day Goa Tourism 'Dudhsagar Special' tour (₹1200), starting at 9am from Calangute, Mapusa, Panaji or Miramar on Wednesday and Sunday, and returning at 6pm. Private travel agents also offer tours.

Sights & Activities

Some of Panaji's great pleasures are leisurely strolls through the sleepy Portuguese-era districts of **Fontainhas and Sao Tomé** and **Altinho**. Riverside **Campal Gardens**, west of the centre, and **Miramar Beach**, 4km southwest of the city, are also popular spots.

★Church of Our Lady of the Immaculate Conception CHURCH

(cnr Emilio Gracia & Jose Falcao Rds; ⏲10am-12.30pm & 3-5.30pm Mon-Sat, 11am-12.30pm & 3.30-5pm Sun, English Mass 8am daily) Panaji's spiritual, as well as geographical, centre is this elevated, pearly white church, built in

Panaji (Panjim)

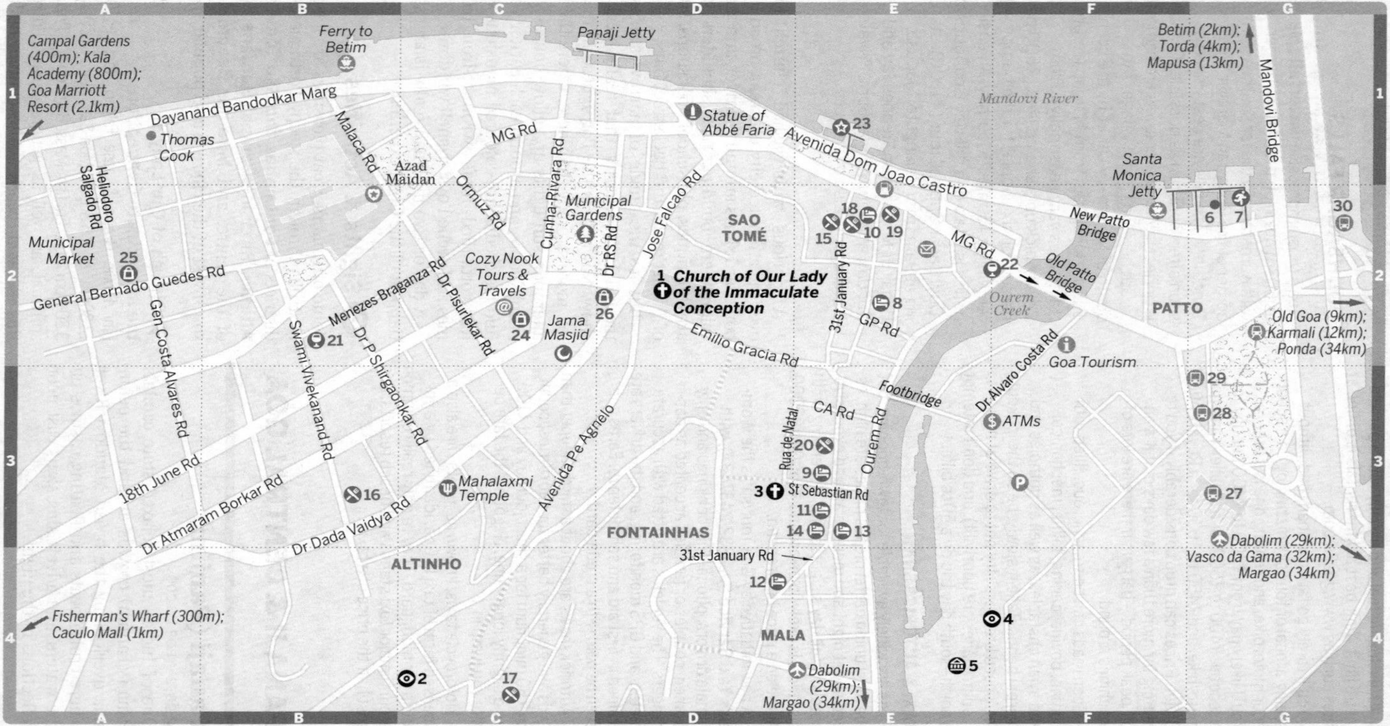

0 — 400 m
0 — 0.2 miles

A B C D E F G
1 2 3 4

Campal Gardens (400m); Kala Academy (800m); Goa Marriott Resort (2.1km)
Ferry to Betim
Panaji Jetty
Betim (2km); Torda (4km); Mapusa (13km)
Mandovi River
Mandovi Bridge
Dayanand Bandodkar Marg
Thomas Cook
Malaca Rd
Azad Maidan
MG Rd
Statue of Abbé Faria
23
Avenida Dom Joao Castro
Santa Monica Jetty
6
7
30
Heliodoro Salgado Rd
Ormuz Rd
Cunha-Rivara Rd
Municipal Gardens
Dr RS Rd
Jose Falcao Rd
SAO TOMÉ
18
10
19
15
New Patto Bridge
Municipal Market
25
Cozy Nook Tours & Travels
24
Menezes Braganza Rd
Dr Pisurlekar Rd
26
1 Church of Our Lady of the Immaculate Conception
31st January Rd
8
GP Rd
MG Rd
22
Old Patto Bridge
Ourem Creek
PATTO
General Bernado Guedes Rd
Gen Costa Alvares Rd
21
Swami Vivekanand Rd
Dr P Shirgaonkar Rd
Jama Masjid
Emilio Gracia Rd
Old Goa (9km); Karmali (12km); Ponda (34km)
Dr Alvaro Costa Rd
Goa Tourism
29
Footbridge
CA Rd
ATMs
28
Rua de Natal
20
9
Ourem Rd
18th June Rd
Avenida Pe Agnelo
Mahalaxmi Temple
16
3 St Sebastian Rd
27
Dr Atmaram Borkar Rd
Dr Dada Vaidya Rd
FONTAINHAS
11
14
13
Dabolim (29km); Vasco da Gama (32km); Margao (34km)
ALTINHO
31st January Rd
12
Fisherman's Wharf (300m); Caculo Mall (1km)
4
MALA
5
2
17
Dabolim (29km); Margao (34km)

Panaji (Panjim)

1619 over an older, smaller 1540 chapel, and stacked like a fancy white wedding cake. When Panaji was little more than a sleepy fishing village, this church was the first port of call for sailors from Lisbon, who would give thanks for a safe crossing, before continuing to Ela (Old Goa) further east up the river. The church is beautifully illuminated at night.

Goa State Museum MUSEUM
(☎0832-2438006; www.goamuseum.gov.in; EDC Complex, Patto; ⏱9.30am-5.30pm Mon-Sat) FREE This spacious museum east of town houses an eclectic, if not extensive, collection of items tracing aspects of Goan history. As well as some beautiful Hindu and Jain sculptures and bronzes, there are nice examples of Portuguese-era furniture, coins, an intricately carved chariot and a pair of quirky antique rotary lottery machines.

Goa State Central Library LIBRARY
(Sanskruti Bhavan, Patto; ⏱9am-7.30pm Mon-Fri, 9.30am-5.45pm Sat & Sun) FREE Panaji's ultra-modern new state library, near the state museum, has six floors of reading material, a bookshop and gallery. The 2nd floor features a children's book section and internet browsing (free, but technically only for academic research). The 4th floor has Goan history books and the 6th a large collection of Portuguese books.

Tours

Organised boat cruises are a popular way to see the Mandovi River.

Paradise Cruises CRUISE
(☎0832-2437960; http://paradisecruises.in; Tourist Boat Jetty; per person ₹300; ⏱cruises 5.30pm & 7pm) This private operator runs two evening 'party' cruises on the Mandovi River aboard its triple-decker boat. There's a bar on board and usually a cultural or dance show on the upper deck.

Mandovi River Cruises CRUISE
(sunset cruise ₹300, dinner cruise ₹650, backwater cruise ₹900; ⏱sunset cruise 6pm, sundown cruise 7.15pm, dinner cruise 8.45pm Wed & Sat, backwater cruise 9.30am-4pm Tue & Fri) Goa Tourism operates a range of entertaining hour-long cruises along the Mandovi River aboard the *Santa Monica* or *Shantadurga*. All include a live band and usually performances of Goan folk songs and dances. There are also twice-weekly, two-hour dinner cruises and backwater cruises, which takes you down the Mandovi to Old Goa, a spice plantation and then heads back past Divar and Chorao

WARNING: DRUGS

Acid, ecstasy, cocaine, charas (hashish), marijuana and most other forms of drugs are illegal in India (though still readily available in Goa), and purchasing or carrying drugs is fraught with danger. Goa's Fort Aguada jail houses a number of prisoners, including some foreigners, serving drug-related sentences. Being caught in possession of even a small quantity of illegal substances can mean a 10-year stretch.

Islands. All cruises depart from the Santa Monica Jetty next to the Mandovi Bridge.

Festivals & Events

Carnival RELIGIOUS
(statewide; Mar) A four-day festival kicking off Lent; Panaji's party is particularly jubilant.

Feast of Our Lady of the Immaculate Conception RELIGIOUS
(Margao, Panaji; 8 Dec) Fairs and concerts are held, as is a beautiful church service at Panaji's Church of Our Lady of the Immaculate Conception.

Sleeping

Panaji has its fair share of accommodation for all budgets. In the middle range are some of Goa's better boutique heritage hotels and guesthouses, mostly in the Fontainhas area.

★**Old Quarter Hostel** HOSTEL $
(0832-6517606; www.thehostelcrowd.com; 31st Jan Rd, Fontainhas; dm ₹550-600, d with AC ₹1600-2000;) In an old Portuguese house in historic Fontainhas, this flamboyant hostel offers slick four-bed dorms with lockers as well as private doubles in a separate building, along with the Urban Cafe, arty murals, good wi-fi and bikes for hire. Noon checkout.

A Pousada Guest House GUESTHOUSE $
(9850998213, 0832-2422618; sabrinateles@yahoo.com; Luis de Menezes Rd; s/d from ₹800/1050, d with AC ₹1575;) The five rooms in this bright-yellow place are simple but clean and come with comfy spring-mattress beds and TV. Owner Sabrina is friendly and no-nonsense, and it's one of Panaji's better budget guesthouses.

Afonso Guesthouse GUESTHOUSE $$
(9764300165, 0832-2222359; www.afonsoguesthouse.com; St Sebastian Rd; d ₹2900-3250;) Run by the friendly Jeanette, this pretty Portuguese townhouse offers spacious, well-kept rooms with timber ceilings. The little rooftop terrace makes for sunny breakfasting (not included) with Fontainhas views. It's a simple, serene stay in the heart of the most atmospheric part of town. Checkout is 9am and bookings are accepted online but not by phone.

La Maison BOUTIQUE HOTEL $$
(0832-2235555; www.lamaisongoa.com; 31st January Rd; r incl breakfast ₹4700-5300;) Another boutique heritage hotel in Fontainhas, La Maison is historic on the outside but thoroughly modern and swanky within. The eight rooms are deceptively simple and homely but five-star comfortable with soft beds, cloud-like pillows, writing desks and flat-screen TVs. Breakfast is included and attached is the European fusion **Desbue** restaurant.

Caravela Homestay BOUTIQUE HOTEL $$
(0832-2237448; www.caravela.in; 27 31st January Rd; s/d incl breakfast from ₹2000/2500, ste ₹4000;) In a beautiful Sao Tome heritage building, Caravela has 10 minimalist but comfortable rooms with extra touches such as minibar and toiletries. Across the lane is the cafe where breakfast is served.

★**Panjim Inn** HERITAGE HOTEL $$$
(9823025748, 0832-2226523; www.panjiminn.com; 31st January Rd; s ₹5100-8000, d ₹5750-9200;) One of the original heritage hotels in Fontainhas, the Panjim Inn has been a long-standing favourite for its character and charm, friendly owners and helpful staff. This beautiful 19th-century mansion has 12 charismatic rooms in the original house, along with newer rooms with modern touches to complement four-poster beds, colonial furniture and artworks. There's also a day spa and rooftop jacuzzi.

Goa Marriott Resort HOTEL $$$
(0832-2463333; www.marriott.com; Miramar Beach; d ₹11,700-17,000;) Miramar's plush Goa Marriott Resort is the best in the area. It's expertly choreographed, with the five-star treatment beginning in the lobby and extending right up to the rooms-with-a-view. The 24-hour Waterfront Terrace & Bar is a great place for a sundowner overlooking the pool, while its Simply Grills restaurant is a favourite with well-heeled Panjimites.

Panjim Pousada GUESTHOUSE $$$
(0832-2226523; www.panjiminn.com; 31st January Rd; s ₹5100-8000, d ₹5750-9200;) In an

old Hindu mansion, the nine divine, colonial fantasy rooms at Panjim Pousada are set off by a stunning central courtyard, with antique furnishings and lovely art on the walls. Various doorways and spiral staircases lead to the rooms; those on the upper level are the best.

Eating

A stroll down 18th June or 31st January Rds will turn up a number of cheap but tasty canteen-style options, as will a quick circuit of the Municipal Gardens. The Latin Quarter has a developing foodie scene, where you can dine on traditional Goan specialities or Western comfort food.

Anandashram INDIAN, GOAN **$**
(31st January Rd; thalis ₹90-140, mains ₹100-350; noon-3.30pm & 7.30-10.30pm Mon-Sat, noon-3pm Sun) This little place is renowned locally for seafood, serving up simple but tasty fish curries, as well as veg and nonveg thalis for lunch and dinner.

Vihar Restaurant INDIAN **$**
(MG Rd; veg thali ₹100-150; 7-9am, 11am-3pm & 7.30-10.30pm) A vast menu of 'pure veg' food, great big thalis, South Indian dosas and a plethora of fresh juices make this clean, simple canteen a popular place for locals and visitors. One of the few places in this area that's still busy late into the evening.

★Viva Panjim GOAN **$$**
(0832-2422405; 31st January Rd; mains ₹130-220; 11.30am-3.30pm & 7-11pm Mon-Sat, 7-11pm Sun) Well known to tourists, this little side-street eatery, in an old Portuguese house and with a few tables out on the laneway, still delivers tasty Goan classics at reasonable prices. There's a whole page devoted to pork dishes, along with tasty *xacuti* (a spicy chicken or meat dish cooked in red coconut sauce) and *cafreal* (a marinated chicken dish) style meals, seafood such as kingfish vindaloo and crab *xec xec,* and desserts such as *bebinca* (richly layered Goan dessert made from egg yolk and coconut).

★Cafe Bodega CAFE **$$**
(0832-2421315; Altinho; mains ₹140-340; 10am-7pm Mon-Sat, 10am-4pm Sun;) It's well worth a trip up to Altinho Hill to visit this serene cafe-gallery in a lavender-and-white Portuguese mansion in the grounds of Sunaparanta Centre for the Arts. Enjoy good coffee, juices and fresh-baked cakes around the inner courtyard or lunch on super pizzas and sandwiches.

Verandah GOAN **$$**
(0832-2226523; 31st January Rd; mains ₹180-420; 11am-11pm) The breezy 1st-floor restaurant at Panjim Inn is indeed on the balcony, with just a handful of finely carved tables, Fontainhas street views and snappy service. Goan cuisine is the speciality, but there's also a range of Indian and continental dishes and local wines.

Fisherman's Wharf SEAFOOD **$$**
(8888493333; http://thefishermanswharf.in; Dr Braganza Pereira Rd; mains ₹220-450; noon-11pm) The successful formula from its long-running restaurant down in Mobor has been transplanted in the capital with fresh seafood, North Indian tandoor, kebabs and Goan specialities. The atmosphere on the open-side restaurant is relaxed but upmarket.

★Black Sheep Bistro EUROPEAN **$$$**
(0832-2222901; www.blacksheepbistro.in; Swami Vivekanand Rd; tapas ₹190-280, mains ₹320-650; noon-4pm & 7-10.45pm) Among the best of Panaji's burgeoning boutique restaurants, Black Sheep's impressive pale-yellow facade gives way to a sexy dark-wood bar and loungy dining room. The tapas dishes are light, fresh and expertly prepared in keeping with their farm-to-table philosophy. Salads, pasta, seafood and dishes like lamb osso bucco grace the menu, while an internationally trained sommelier matches food to wine.

★Hotel Venite GOAN **$$$**
(31st January Rd; mains ₹340-460; 9am-10.30pm) With its cute rickety balcony tables overhanging the cobbled street, Venite has long been among the most atmospheric of Panaji's Goan restaurants. The menu is traditional, with spicy sausages, fish curry

GOAN CUISINE

Goan cuisine is a tantalising fusion of Portuguese and South Indian flavours. Goans tend to be hearty meat and fish eaters, and fresh seafood is a staple: the quintessential Goan lunch of 'fish-curry-rice' is fried mackerel steeped in coconut, tamarind and chilli sauce. Traditional dishes include vindaloo (a fiery dish in a marinade of vinegar and garlic), *xacuti* (a spicy chicken or meat dish cooked in red coconut sauce) and *cafreal* (dry-fried chicken marinated in a green masala paste and sprinkled with toddy vinegar). For dessert try the layered *bebinca* cake.

WORTH A TRIP

BACKWOODS CAMP

In a forest near Bhagwan Mahavir Wildlife Sanctuary, in far east Goa, rustic **Backwoods Camp** (9822139859; www.backwoodsgoa.com; Matkan, Tambdi Surla; 2-/3-day stay per person ₹8500/12,000;) is a magical, serene spot. The area is one of Goa's richest birding spots, with everything from Ceylon frogmouths and Asian fairy bluebirds to puff-throated babblers and Indian pittas putting in regular appearances. Accommodation is in tents on raised forest platforms, bungalows or farmhouse rooms; rates include meals and birdwatching guides.

rice, pepper steak and *bebinca,* but Venite is popular with tourists and prices are consequently inflated. Drop in for a beer or shot of *feni* (Goan spirit) before deciding.

Drinking & Nightlife

Panaji's local drinking scene is in the town's tiny, tucked-away bars, mostly equipped with rudimentary plastic tables, a fridge, a few stools and an almost-exclusively male clientele. More upscale bars can be found in high-end hotels, along with a few English-style pubs.

Cafe Mojo BAR
(www.cafemojo.in; Menezes Braganza Rd; 10am-4am Mon-Thu, to 6am Fri-Sun) The decor is cosy English pub, the clientele young and up for a party, and the novelty is the e-beer system. Each table has its own beer tap and LCD screen: you buy a card (₹500), swipe it at your table and start pouring – it automatically deducts what you drink (you can use the card for spirits, cocktails or food too).

Riverfront & Down the Road BAR
(cnr MG & Ourem Rds; 11am-1am) The balcony of this restaurant-bar overlooking the creek and Old Patto Bridge makes for a cosy beer or cocktail spot with carved barrels for furniture. The ground-floor bar (from 6pm) is the only real nightspot on the Old Quarter side of town, with occasional live music.

Entertainment

Panaji's most visible form of entertainment are the casino boats anchored out in the Mandovi River, but the city is also home to India's biggest **international film festival** (www.iffi.nic.in; Nov) and the cultural offerings of the excellent Kala Academy.

Kala Academy CULTURAL CENTRE
(0832-2420452; http://kalaacademygoa.org; Dayanand Bandodkar Marg) On the west side of the city, in Campal, is Goa's premier cultural centre, which features a program of dance, theatre, music and art exhibitions throughout the year. Many shows are in Konkani, but there are occasional English-language productions. The website has an up-to-date calendar of events.

Deltin Royale CASINO
(8698599999; www.deltingroup.com/deltin-royale; Noah's Ark, RND Jetty, Dayanand Bandodkar Marg; weekday/weekend ₹3000/4000, premium package ₹4500/5500; 24hr, entertainment 9pm-1am) Goa's biggest and best luxury floating casino, Deltin Royal has 123 tables, the Vegas Restaurant, a Whisky Bar and a creche. Entry includes gaming chips worth ₹2000/3000 weekday/weekend and to the full value of your ticket with the premium package. Unlimited food and drinks included.

Shopping

Caculo Mall MALL
(0832-2222068; http://caculomall.in; 16 Shanta, St Inez; 10am-9pm) Goa's biggest mall is four levels of air-conditioned family shopping heaven with brand-name stores, food court, kids' toys and arcade games.

Municipal Market MARKET
(Heljogordo Salgado Rd; from 7.30am) This atmospheric place, where narrow streets have been converted into covered markets, makes for a nice wander, offering fresh produce, clothing stalls and some tiny, enticing eateries. The fish market is a particularly interesting strip of activity.

Singbal's Book House BOOKS
(Church Sq; 9.30am-1pm & 3.30-7.30pm Mon-Sat) On the corner opposite Panaji's main church, Singbal's has an excellent selection of international magazines and newspapers, and lots of books on Goa and travel.

Khadi India ARTS & CRAFTS
(Dr Atmaram Borkar Rd; 9am-1pm & 3-7pm) Goa's only outpost of the government's Khadi & Village Industries Commission has a fine range of hand-woven cottons, oils, soaps, spices and other handmade products

that come straight from (and directly benefit) regional villages.

Marcou Artifacts ARTS & CRAFTS
(☎0832-2220204; www.marcouartifacts.com; 31st January Rd; ⊙9am-8pm) This small Fontainhas shop showcases one-off painted tiles, fish figurines and hand-crafted Portuguese and Goan ceramics at reasonable prices. Also has showrooms at Caculo Mall, Hotel Delmon and Margao's market.

Information

Goa Medical College Hospital (☎0832-2458700; www.gmc.goa.gov.in; Bambolim; ⊙24hr) This 1000-bed hospital is 9km south of Panaji on NH17 in Bambolim.

Goa Tourism (GTDC; ☎0832-2437132; www.goa-tourism.com; Paryatan Bhavan, Dr Alvaro Costa Rd; ⊙9.30am-5.45pm Mon-Fri) Better known as Goa Tourism, the GTDC office is in the large Paryatan Bhavan building across the Ourem Creek and near the bus stand. However, it's more marketing office than tourist office and is of little use to casual visitors, unless you want to book one of GTDC's host of tours.

Government of India Tourist Office (☎0832-2223412; www.incredibleindia.com; Communidade Bldg, Church Sq; ⊙9.30am-1.30pm & 2.30-6pm Mon-Fri, 10am-1pm Sat) The staff at this central tourist office can be helpful, especially for information outside Goa. This office is planning a move to the same building as Goa Tourism in Patto.

Main Post Office (MG Rd; ⊙9.30am-5.30pm Mon-Sat) Offers swift parcel services and Western Union money transfers.

Getting There & Away

BUS

All local buses depart from Panaji's **Kadamba bus stand** (☎interstate 0832-2438035, local 0832-2438034; www.goakadamba.com; ⊙reservations 8am-8pm), with frequent local services every few minutes (to no apparent timetable); major destinations are Mapusa (₹30, 30 minutes) in the north, Margao (₹30, 45 minutes) to the south and Ponda (₹20, one hour) to the east. Most bus services run from 6am to 10pm.

For South Goa's beaches, take an express bus to Margao and change there; to get to beaches north of Baga, head to Mapusa and change there. There are direct buses to Candolim (₹20, 20 minutes), Calangute (₹25, 25 minutes) and Baga (₹30, 30 minutes).

State-run long distance services also depart from the Kadamba bus stand, but private operators offer similar prices and greater choice in type of bus and departure times. Many private operators have booths outside the entrance to the bus stand, but most private interstate services depart from the interstate bus stand across the highway next to the New Patto Bridge.

Paulo Travels (☎0832-2438531; www.paulobus.com; G1, Kardozo Bldg)

TRAIN

The closest train station to Panaji is Karmali (Old Goa), 12km east near Old Goa. A number of long-distance services stop here, including services to and from Mumbai. Many trains coming from Margao also stop here (but check in advance). Panaji's **Konkan Railway Reservation Office** (☎0832-2712940; www.konkanrailway.com; ⊙8am-8pm Mon-Sat) is on the 1st floor of the Kadamba bus stand (*not* at the train station).

Getting Around

A taxi from Panaji to Dabolim Airport costs ₹900 and takes 45 minutes, but allow an hour for traffic. From the airport, prepaid taxis charge ₹870 (₹920 for AC).

It's easy enough to get around central Panaji and Fontainhas on foot. Taxis and autorickshaws charge extortionately for short trips. A return taxi to Old Goa costs ₹400; an autorickshaw should charge ₹300. Lots of taxis hang around at the Municipal Gardens. Autorickshaws and motorcycle taxis can be found in front of the post office, on 18th June Rd, and just south of the church.

Local buses run to Miramar (₹4, 10 minutes), Dona Paula (₹6, 15 minutes) and Old Goa (₹10, 20 minutes).

Taking the rusty but free passenger/vehicle **ferry** (⊙every 20min 6am-10pm) across the Mandovi River to the fishing village of Betim makes a fun shortcut en route to the northern beaches. It departs the jetty on Dayanand Bandodkar Marg.

Old Goa

☎0832

From the 16th to the 18th centuries, when Old Goa's population exceeded that of Lisbon or London, Goa's former capital was considered the 'Rome of the East'. You can still sense that grandeur as you wander what's left of the city, with its towering churches and cathedrals and majestic convents. Its rise under the Portuguese, from 1510, was meteoric, but cholera and malaria outbreaks

EMERGENCIES

Dialling ☎112 will connect you to the police, fire brigade or medical services.

forced the abandonment of the city in the 1600s. In 1843 the capital was officially shifted to Panaji. Some of the most imposing churches and cathedrals are still in use and are remarkably well preserved, while other historical buildings have become museums or simply ruins. It's a fascinating day trip, but it can get crowded: consider visiting on a weekday morning.

Sights

Remember to cover your shoulders and legs when entering the churches and cathedral.

★Basilica of Bom Jesus CHURCH
(7.30am-6.30pm) Famous throughout the Roman Catholic world, the imposing Basilica of Bom Jesus contains the tomb and mortal remains of St Francis Xavier, the so-called Apostle of the Indies. St Francis Xavier's missionary voyages throughout the East became legendary. His 'incorrupt' body is in the mausoleum to the right, in a glass-sided coffin amid a shower of gilt stars. Freelance guides at the entrance will show you around for ₹100.

★Sé Cathedral CATHEDRAL
(9am-6pm; Mass 7am & 6pm Mon-Sat, 7.15am, 10am & 4pm Sun) At over 76m long and 55m wide, the cavernous Sé Cathedral is the largest church in Asia. Building commenced in 1562, on the orders of King Dom Sebastiao of Portugal, and the finishing touches were finally made some 90 years later. The exterior is notable for its plain style, in the Tuscan tradition. Also of note is its rather lopsided look resulting from the loss of one of its bell towers, which collapsed in 1776 after being struck by lightning.

Church of St Francis of Assisi CHURCH
(9am-5pm) West of the Sé Cathedral, the Church of St Francis of Assisi is no longer in use for worship, and consequently exudes a more mournful air than its neighbours.

Archaeological Museum MUSEUM
(adult/child ₹10/free; 9am-5pm) The archaeological museum houses some lovely fragments of sculpture from Hindu temple sites in Goa, and some Sati stones, which once marked the spot where a Hindu widow com-

Old Goa

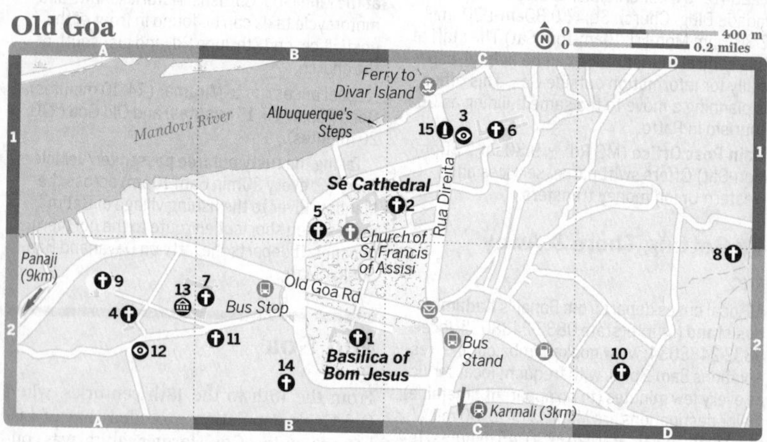

Old Goa

Top Sights
1 Basilica of Bom Jesus B2
2 Sé Cathedral C1

Sights
3 Adil Shah Palace Gateway C1
Archaeological Museum .... (see 5)
4 Chapel of St Anthony A2
5 Chapel of St Catherine B1
6 Church & Convent of St Cajetan C1
7 Church & Convent of St Monica B2
8 Church of Our Lady of the Mount D2
9 Church of Our Lady of the Rosary A2
10 Church of St Francis Xavier D2
11 Convent & Church of St John B2
12 Monastery of St Augustine A2
13 Museum of Christian Art A2
14 Sisters' Convent B2
15 Viceroy's Arch C1

WORTH A TRIP

SPICE UP YOUR LIFE

The Ponda region, southeast of Panaji, is the centre of commercial spice farms in Goa and several have opened their doors as tourist operations, offering guided plantation tours, buffet thali-style lunches and, in some cases, cultural shows.

These farms typically produce spices such as vanilla, pepper, cardamom, nutmeg, chilli and turmeric, along with crops such as cashew, betel nut, coconut, pineapple and papaya. To reach them you'll need your own transport or a taxi.

Savoi Plantation (0832-2340272, 9423888899; http://savoiplantations.com; adult/child ₹700/350; 9am-4.30pm) This 200-year-old plantation, 12km north of Ponda, is the least touristy in the region (and elephant-free). Knowledgeable guides will walk you through the 40-hectare plantation. Local crafts are also for sale and there are a couple of cottages for overnight stays.

Pascoal Spice Farm (0832-2344268; farm tour & lunch ₹400; 9am-4.30pm) About 7km east of Ponda, Pascoal offers bamboo river-rafting and cultural shows, along with farm tours and lunch.

Tropical Spice Plantation (0832-2340329; www.tropicalspiceplantation.com; Keri; tour incl lunch ₹400; 9am-4pm) Accessed via a bamboo bridge, around 5km north of Ponda, this is one of the most popular farms with tour groups, so is often busy. An entertaining 45-minute tour of the spice plantation is followed by a banana-leaf buffet lunch.

mitted suicide by flinging herself onto her husband's funeral pyre.

Church & Convent of St Cajetan CHURCH
(8am-6pm) Modelled on the original design of St Peter's in Rome, this impressive church was built by Italian friars of the Order of Theatines, sent here by Pope Urban VIII to preach Christianity in the kingdom of Golconda (near Hyderabad). The friars, however, were refused entry to Golconda, so settled instead at Old Goa in 1640. The construction of the church began in 1655, and although it's perhaps less interesting than the other churches, it's still a beautiful building and the only domed church remaining in Goa.

Museum of Christian Art MUSEUM
(www.museumofchristianart.com; ₹50, camera ₹100; 9.30am-4.30pm Mon-Sat) This museum, in a beautifully restored space within the 1627 Convent of St Monica, contains a collection of statues, paintings and sculptures. Interestingly, many of the works of Goan Christian art made during the Portuguese era, including some of those on display here, were produced by local Hindu artists.

Other Sights

There are plenty of other monuments in Old Goa to explore, including the Viceroy's Arch, Adil Shah Palace Gateway, the Chapel of St Anthony, the Chapel of St Catherine, the **Church & Convent of St Monica** (8am-5pm), the Convent & Church of St John, the Sisters' Convent, the **Church of Our Lady of the Rosary** (8am-5pm), the Monastery of St Augustine and, 2km east of the centre, the Church of Our Lady of the Mount.

Getting There & Away

There are frequent buses to Old Goa (₹10, 25 minutes) from the Kadamba bus stand in Panaji to Old Goa's bus stand. Buses to Panaji or Ponda from Old Goa leave when full (around every 10 minutes) from either the main roundabout or the bus stop/ATM just beside the Tourist Inn restaurant.

NORTH GOA

Mapusa

0832 / POP 40,500

Mapusa (pronounced 'Mapsa') is the largest town in northern Goa, and is most often visited for its busy Friday **market** (8am-6.30pm Mon-Sat), which attracts scores of buyers and sellers from neighbouring towns and villages. It's a good place to pick up the usual range of embroidered bed sheets and the like, at prices far lower than in the beach resorts.

Many travellers pass through Mapusa anyway as it's the major transport hub for northern Goa buses. Most amenities are arranged around the Municipal Gardens, just north of the Kadamba bus station and main market site.

Activities

Mango Tree Goa VOLUNTEERING
(☎9881261886; www.mangotreegoa.org; The Mango House, near Vrundavan Hospital, Karaswada) Offers one- to three-month placements for volunteers providing teaching support for disadvantaged children around Mapusa.

Sleeping

With the northern beaches so close and most long-distance buses departing in the late afternoon or early evening, it's hard to think of a good reason to stay in Mapusa, but there are a few options if you do.

Hotel Satyaheera HOTEL $$
(☎0832-2262949; www.hotelsatyaheeragoa.com; d without/with AC from ₹1950/2300; ❄) Next to the little Maruti temple in the town centre, this is Mapusa's best central hotel, which isn't saying much. Rooms are comfortable enough and **Ruchira** (mains ₹90-190; ⏲11am-11pm), the roof garden restaurant, is a decent place to eat.

Eating & Drinking

Hotel Vrundavan INDIAN $
(thalis from ₹80; ⏲7am-10pm Wed-Mon) This all-veg place bordering the Municipal Gardens is a great place for a hot chai, *pav bhaji* (bread with curried vegetables) or a quick breakfast.

Pub PUB
(mains from ₹100; ⏲11am-4pm & 6.30-11pm Mon-Sat) Don't be put off by the dingy entrance or stairwell: once you're upstairs, this breezy place opposite the market is great for watching the milling crowds over a cold beer or *feni*. Eclectic daily specials make it a good spot for lunch.

Shopping

Other India Bookstore BOOKS
(☎0832-2263306; www.otherindiabookstore.com; Mapusa Clinic Rd; ⏲9am-5pm Mon-Fri, to 1pm Sat) This friendly and rewarding little bookshop, at the end of an improbable, dingy corridor, specialises in books about Goa and India with a focus on spirituality, environment, politics and travel. It's signposted near the Mapusa Clinic, a few hundred metres up the hill from the Municipal Gardens.

Getting There & Away

BUS

If you're coming to Goa by bus from Mumbai, Mapusa's **Kadamba bus stand** (☎0832-2232161) is the jumping-off point for the northern beaches. Local bus services run every few minutes. For buses to the southern beaches, take one of the frequent buses to Panaji, then Margao, and change there.

Local services include:

Anjuna ₹15, 20 minutes
Arambol ₹30, one hour

GREEN GOA

Goa's environment has suffered from an onslaught of tourism over the last 40 years, but also from the effects of logging, mining and local customs (rare turtle eggs have traditionally been considered a delicacy). Construction proceeds regardless of what the local infrastructure or ecosystem can sustain, while plastic bottles pile up in vast mountains. There are, however, a few easy ways to minimise your impact on Goa's environment.

Take your own bag when shopping and refill water bottles with filtered water wherever possible. Rent a bicycle instead of a scooter, for short trips at least; bicycle rentals are declining as a result of our scooter infatuation and the bikes are poor quality, but they'll bounce back if the demand is there. Goa Tourism now employs cleaners to comb the beaches each morning picking up litter, but all travellers should do their part by disposing of cigarette butts and any litter in bins.

Turtles are protected by the **Forest Department** (www.forest.goa.gov.in), which operates information huts on beaches such as Agonda, Galgibag and Morjim, where turtles arrive to lay eggs. Also doing good work over many years is the **Goa Foundation** (☎0832-2256479; www.goafoundation.org; St Britto's Apartments, G-8 Feira Alta), the state's main environmental pressure group based in Mapusa. It has spearheaded a number of conservation projects since its inauguration in 1986, including pressure to stop illegal mining, and its website is a great place to learn more about Goan environmental issues. The group's excellent *Fish Curry & Rice*, a sourcebook on Goa's environment and lifestyle, is sold at Mapusa's Other India Bookstore. The Foundation occasionally runs volunteer projects.

Calangute ₹12, 20 minutes
Candolim ₹15, 35 minutes
Panaji ₹30, 30 minutes
Thivim ₹15, 20 minutes

Long-distance services are run by both government and private bus companies. Private operators have booking offices outside the bus stand (opposite the Municipal Gardens). Most long-distance buses depart in the late afternoon or evening. Sample fares include:

Bengaluru ₹900, with AC ₹1200; 13-14 hours
Hampi sleeper ₹1000; 9½ hours
Mumbai ₹850, with AC ₹900; 12-15 hours
Pune ₹700, with AC ₹900, 11-13 hours

TAXI

There's a prepaid taxi stand in the town square with a signboard of fixed prices. Cabs to Anjuna or Calangute cost ₹280; Candolim ₹350; Panaji ₹350; Arambol ₹600; and Margao ₹1100. An autorickshaw to Anjuna or Calangute should cost ₹200.

TRAIN

Thivim, about 12km northeast of town, is the nearest train station on the Konkan Railway. Local buses to Mapusa meet trains (₹15); an autorickshaw to or from Thivim station costs around ₹200.

Candolim

0832 / POP 8600

Candolim's long and languid beach, which curves to join smaller Sinquerim Beach to the south, is largely the preserve of charter tourists from the UK, Russia and, increasingly, elsewhere in India. It's fringed with an unabating line of beach shacks, all offering sunbeds and shade in exchange for your custom.

In all it's an upmarket, happy holiday strip, but independent travellers may find it a little soulless. The post office, supermarkets, travel agents, pharmacies and plenty of banks with ATMs are all located on the main Fort Aguada Rd, running parallel to the beach.

Sights & Activities

Fort Aguada FORT

(8.30am-5.30pm) FREE Standing on the headland overlooking the mouth of the Mandovi River, Fort Aguada occupies a magnificent and successful position, confirmed by the fact it was never taken by force. A highly popular spot to watch the sunset, with uninterrupted views both north and south, the fort was built in 1612, following the increasing threat to Goa's Portuguese overlords by the Dutch, among others.

John's Boat Tours TOURS

(0832-6520190, 9822182814; www.johnboattours.com; Fort Aguada Rd; 9am-9pm) A respected and well-organised Candolim-based operator offering a wide variety of boat and jeep excursions, as well as overnight houseboat cruises (₹6000 per person including meals). Choose from dolphin-watching cruises (₹1000) or the renowned 'Crocodile Dundee' river trip (₹1200), to catch a glimpse of the Mandovi's mugger crocodile.

Sinquerim Dolphin Trips BOATING

(per person ₹300; 8.30am-5.30pm) The boatmen on the Nerul River below Fort Aguada have banded together, so trips are fixed price. A one-hour dolphin-spotting and sightseeing trip costs ₹300 per person with a minimum of 10 passengers. Trips pass Nerul (Coco) Beach, Fort Aguada Jail, the fort and 'Jimmy Millionaire's House'.

Dive Goa DIVING

(9325030110; www.divegoa.com; Fort Aguada Rd) Based next to SinQ Beach Club, this established scuba-diving outfit offers PADI and SSI courses, and boat dives to Netrani Island, Grande Island and more.

Sleeping

★ Bougainvillea Guest House GUESTHOUSE $$

(0832-2479842, 9822151969; www.bougainvilleagoa.com; Sinquerim; r incl breakfast ₹3000-4000, penthouse ₹6000;) A lush, plant-filled garden leads the way to this gorgeous family-run guesthouse, located off Fort Aguada Rd. The eight light-filled suite rooms are spacious and spotless, with fridge, flat-screen TV and either balcony or private sit-out; the top-floor penthouse has its own rooftop terrace. This is the kind of place guests come back to year after year. Book ahead.

D'Hibiscus BOUTIQUE HOTEL $$

(www.dehibiscus.com; 83 Sinquerim; d ₹3300, penthouse ₹4950;) Huge modern rooms with balconies are the draw at this newly renovated Portuguese home off Sinquerim beach. The top-floor penthouse rooms, with jacuzzi, big-screen TV and balcony sunbeds, are worth a splurge.

D'Mello's Sea View Home HOTEL $$

(0832-2489650; www.dmellos.com; Monteiro's Rd, Escrivao Vaddo; d ₹1200-1800; @)

D'Mello's has grown up from small beginnings, but is still family-run and occupies four buildings around a lovely garden. The front building has the sea-view rooms so check out a few, but all are clean and well-maintained. Add ₹500 if you want aircon. Wi-fi is available in the central area.

★Marbella Guest House BOUTIQUE HOTEL **$$$**
(☎0832-2479551, 9822100811; www.marbellagoa.com; Sinquerim; r ₹3600-6000, ste ₹5400-7000; ❄📶) This beautiful Portuguese villa, filled with antiques and enveloped in a peaceful courtyard garden, is a romantic and sophisticated old-world remnant. Rooms are individually themed, including Moghul, Rajasthani and Bouganvillea. The penthouse suite is a dream of polished tiles, four-poster bed with separate living room, dining room and terrace. The kitchen serves up some imaginative dishes. No kids under 12.

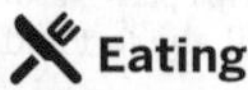

Eating

Candolim has a high concentration of international restaurants and seafront beach shacks serving world cuisine and fresh seafood. Much of the best on offer is along Fort Aguada Rd, though if you take the side streets towards the beach you'll find a few gems, along with local joints serving a cheap, tasty breakfast *pav bhaji* or lunchtime thali.

Viva Goa! GOAN **$**
(Fort Aguada Rd; mains ₹90-200; ⏲11am-midnight) This inexpensive, locals-oriented little place, also popular with in-the-know tourists, serves fresh fish and Goan seafood specialities such as a spicy mussel fry. Check the market price of seafood before ordering.

★Café Chocolatti CAFE **$$**
(409A Fort Aguada Rd; sweets ₹50-200, mains ₹250-420; ⏲9am-7pm Mon-Sat; 📶) The lovely garden tearoom at Café Chocolatti may be on the main Fort Aguada Rd, but it's a divine and peaceful retreat where chocolate brownies, waffles and banoffee pie with a strong cup of coffee or organic green tea taste like heaven. Also has a great range of salads, paninis, crepes and quiches for lunch. Take away a bag of chocolate truffles, homemade by the in-house chocolatier.

Moroccan Shisha & Grill MOROCCAN **$$**
(☎8600544442; Calangute-Candolim Rd; mains ₹200-500, sheesha ₹600; ⏲11am-2am) Relax on cushions amid wafts of fragrant sheesha smoke at this Arabian-style cafe. Naturally there's strong coffee, mint tea and North African dishes such as shish kebab and chicken tagine.

Stone House STEAKHOUSE **$$**
(Fort Aguada Rd; mains ₹200-800; ⏲11am-3pm & 7pm-midnight) Surf 'n' turf's the thing at this venerable old Candolim venue, inhabiting a stone house and its leafy front courtyard, with the improbable-sounding 'Swedish Lobster' topping the list, along with some Goan dishes. It's also a popular blues bar with live music most nights of the week in season.

★Bomra's BURMESE **$$$**
(☎9767591056; www.bomras.com; 247 Fort Aguada Rd; mains ₹470-580; ⏲noon-2pm & 7-11pm) Wonderfully unusual food is on offer at this sleek little place serving interesting modern Burmese cuisine with a fusion twist. Aromatic curries include straw mushroom, lychee, water-chestnut, spinach and coconut curry, and duck curry with sweet tamarind and groundnut shoot. Decor is palm-thatch style huts in a lovely courtyard garden.

Tuscany Gardens ITALIAN **$$$**
(☎0832-6454026; www.tuscanygardens.in; Fort Aguada Rd; mains ₹300-465; ⏲1-11pm) You can easily be transported to Tuscany at Candolim's cosy, romantic Italian restaurant with check tablecloths and imported wine. Perfect antipasti, pasta, pizza and risotto are the order of the day; try the seafood pizza or buffalo mozzarella salad.

Drinking & Nightlife

LPK Waterfront CLUB
(couples ₹1500; ⏲9.30pm-4am) The initials stand for Love, Peace and Karma: the whimsical, sculpted waterfront LPK across the Nerul River from Candolim is the biggest club in the area, attracting party-goers from all over with huge indoor and outdoor dance areas.

Bob's Inn BAR
(Fort Aguada Rd; ⏲noon-4pm & 7pm-midnight) The African wall hangings, palm-thatch, communal tables and terracotta sculptures are a nice backdrop to the *rava* (semolina) fried mussels, but this Candolim institution is really just a great place to drop in for a drink.

Shopping

Broadway Book Centre BOOKS
(☎0832-6519777; www.booksingoa.com; Fort Aguada Rd; ⏲10am-8pm) With four stores in Goa, Broadway is the state's biggest book-

store chain, and a publisher, so you should be able to find what you're looking for here. Staff here are friendly and helpful.

Getting There & Away

Buses run about every 10 minutes to and from Panaji (₹15, 35 minutes), and stop at the central bus stop near John's Boat Tours. Some continue south to the Fort Aguada bus stop at the bottom of Fort Aguada Rd, then head back to Panaji along the Mandovi River road, via the villages of Verem and Betim.

Frequent buses also run from Candolim to Calangute (₹8, 15 minutes) and can be flagged down on Fort Aguada Rd.

Calangute & Baga

0832 / POP 16,000

For many visitors, particularly cashed-up young Indian tourists from Bangalore and Mumbai plus Europeans on package holidays, this is Goa's party strip, where the raves and hippies have made way for modern thumping nightclubs and wall-to-wall drinking. The Calangute market area and the main Baga road can get very busy but everything you could ask for – from a Thai massage to a tattoo – is in close proximity and the beach is lined with an excellent selection of restaurant shacks with sunbeds, wi-fi and attentive service.

Stretching between the blurred lines of Candolim and Baga, Calangute is centred on the busy market road leading to the beachfront. To the north, Baga beach consists of jostling shacks, peppered with water sports, and late-night clubs along infamous Tito's Lane.

Sights

Museum of Goa ARTS CENTRE
(07722089666; www.museumofgoa.com; 79, Pilerne Industrial Estate, Calangute; Indian/foreigner ₹100/300; 10am-6pm) Not so much a museum as a repository for art, MOG features artworks, exhibitions, workshops, courses, sitar concerts and an excellent cafe. It's the brainchild of well-known local artist and sculptor Subodh Kerkar, with the philosophy of making art accessible to all.

Activities

Yoga classes pop up around Calangute and Baga each season. You don't have to go far to find beach water sports along the Calangute–Baga strip.

Two local scuba-diving operators are recommended: **Goa Aquatics** (9822685025; www.goaaquatics.com; 136/1 Gaura Vaddo, Calangute; dive trip from ₹5000, dive course ₹22,000) and **Barracuda Diving** (9822182402, 0832-2279409; www.barracudadiving.com; Sun Village Resort, Baga; dive trip/course from ₹5000/17,000).

Baga Snow Park SNOW SPORTS
(9595420781; http://snowparkgoa.com; Tito's Lane 2; ₹495; 11am-8pm;) This giant fridge is a mini wonderland of snowmen, igloos, slides and ice sculptures. You get kitted out with parka, pants and gloves (included) – it's very cold! Good for kids.

GTDC Tours TOURS
(Goa Tourism Development Corporation; 0832-2276024; www.goa-tourism.com) Goa Tourism's tours can be booked online or at the GTDC Calangute Residency hotel beside the beach. The full-day North Goa tour (₹300, 9.30am to 6pm daily) departs from Calangute or Mapusa and takes in the Mandovi estuary, Candolim, Calangute, Anjuna and inland to Mayem Lake.

Sleeping

Quite a few places remain open year-round, though it's not a particularly budget-friendly destination, except in the off-season.

Calangute

★**Ospy's Shelter** GUESTHOUSE $
(7798100981, 0832-2279505; ospeys.shelter@gmail.com; d ₹800-1000) Tucked away between the beach and St Anthony's Chapel, in a quiet, lush little area full of palms and sandy paths, Ospey's is a traveller favourite and only a two-minute walk from the beach. Spotless upstairs rooms have fridges and balconies and the whole place has a cosy family feel. Take the road directly west of the chapel – but it's tough to find, so call ahead.

Johnny's Hotel HOTEL $
(0832-2277458; www.johnnyshotel.com; s ₹500-600, d ₹800-900, with AC ₹1200-1400;) The 15 simple rooms at this backpacker-popular place make for a sociable stay, with a downstairs restaurant-bar and regular yoga and reiki classes. A range of apartments and houses are available for longer stays. It's down a lane lined with unremarkable midrange hotels and is just a short walk to the beach.

Zostel HOSTEL $
(917726864942; www.zostel.com; Calangute; dm ₹450-550, d ₹1800;) Zostel brings budget dorm beds to package-tour central

Calangute & Baga

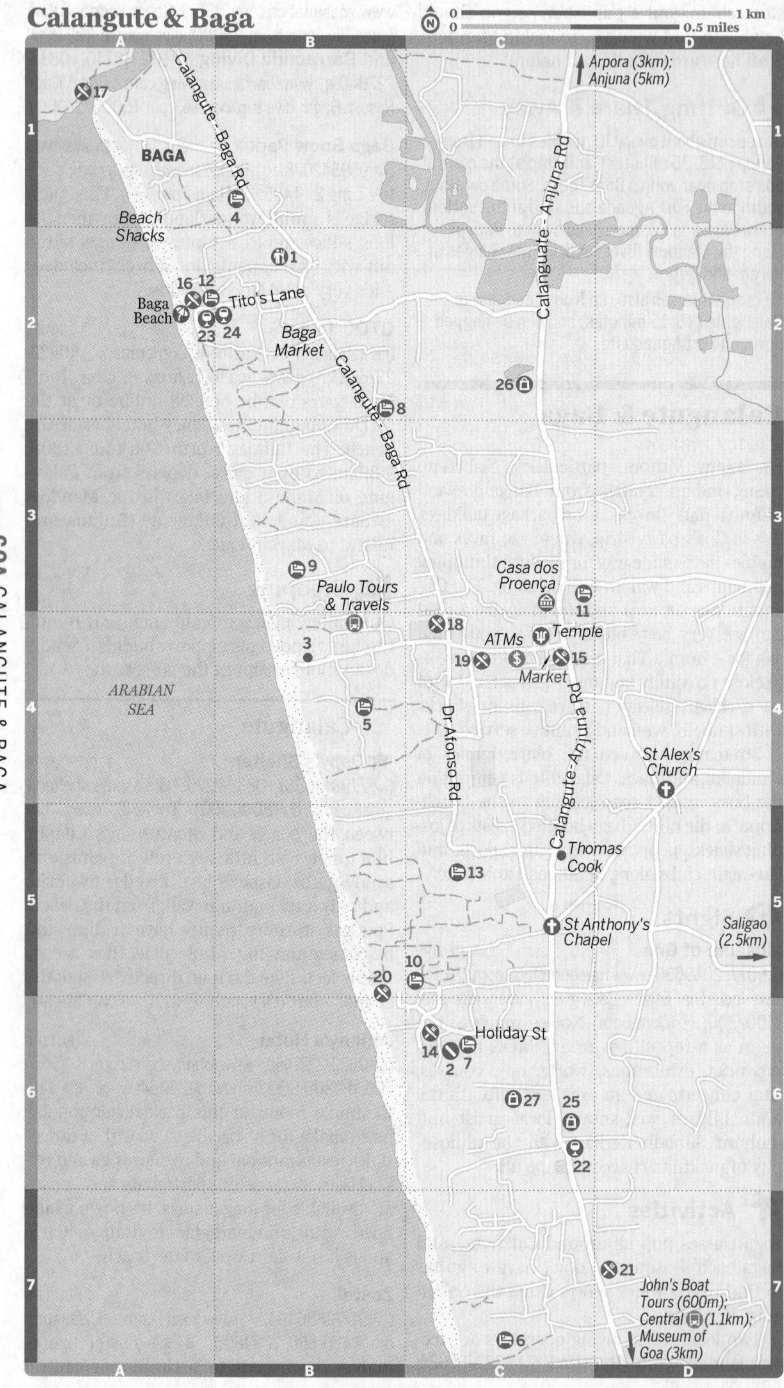

Calangute & Baga

Activities, Courses & Tours
1 Baga Snow Park ... B2
2 Goa Aquatics ... C6
3 GTDC Tours ... B4

Sleeping
4 Alidia Beach Cottages ... B1
5 Coco Banana ... B4
6 D'Mello's Sea View Home ... C7
7 Hotel Seagull ... C6
8 Indian Kitchen ... B2
9 Johnny's Hotel ... B3
10 Ospy's Shelter ... C5
11 Pousada Tauma ... C3
12 Resort Fiesta ... A2
13 Zostel ... C5

Eating
14 A Reverie ... C6
15 Cafe Sussegado Souza ... C4
16 Fiesta ... A2
17 Go With the Flow ... A1
18 Infantaria ... C4
19 Plantain Leaf ... C4
20 Pousada by the Beach ... B5
21 Viva Goa! ... D7

Drinking & Nightlife
22 Bob's Inn ... C6
23 Café Mambo ... A2
24 Tito's ... B2

Shopping
25 Broadway Book Centre ... C6
26 Karma Collection ... C2
27 Literati Bookshop & Cafe ... C6

with four- to 12-bed dorms, some with air-con, all in a whitewashed two-storey house set back from the main road. Facilities include a kitchen, free wi-fi, common room and lockers. There's just one double room.

Coco Banana GUESTHOUSE $
(☎9960803790; d ₹1200, with AC ₹1500; ❄📶) Among the palms south of the main entrance to Calangute Beach, colourful Coco Banana has been providing a soothing retreat for travellers for many years. Run by the friendly Walter, rooms are spacious and spotless and the vibe mellow. For families or groups, ask about the self-contained apartments at nearby Casa Leyla.

Hotel Seagull HOTEL $$
(☎0832-2179969; http://seagullgoa.com; Holiday St; d from ₹2800; ❄📶🏊) Bright, friendly and welcoming, the Seagull's rooms, set in a cheerful blue-and-white house in south Calangute, are light and airy with air-con, and a small pool out back. Downstairs is the fine Blue Mariposa bar-restaurant, serving Goan, Indian and continental dishes.

★ **Pousada Tauma** BOUTIQUE HOTEL $$$
(☎0832-2279061; www.pousada-tauma.com; ste incl meals US$360-530; ❄📶🏊) If you're looking for luxury with your ayurvedic regime, this gorgeous little boutique hotel in busy Calangute is appropriately shielded from the outside world. Spacious, nicely furnished suites are set around a super fountain-fed pool. Rates include all meals at the romantic little open-air Copper Bowl restaurant, though ayurvedic treatments in the private centre are extra.

Baga

★ **Indian Kitchen** GUESTHOUSE $
(☎0832-2277555, 9822149615; www.indiankitchen-goa.com; s/d/chalet ₹770/880/1500; ❄@📶🏊) If a colourful budget stay is what you're after, look no further than this family-run guesthouse, which offers a range of rooms from basic to more spacious, comfy apartments and wooden chalets by the pool. There's a neat central courtyard and a sparkling-clean pool. Each room has its own terrace or sit-out. Add ₹600 for air-con.

★ **Alidia Beach Cottages** GUESTHOUSE $$
(☎9822876867, 0832-2279014; Calangute-Baga Rd, Saunta Waddo; d ₹2000, with AC from ₹3300; ❄📶🏊) Set back behind a whitewashed chapel off busy Baga Rd, this convivial but quiet place has beautifully kept Mediterranean-style rooms orbiting a gorgeous pool. The cheaper non-AC rooms at the back are not as good, but all are in good condition, staff are eager to please, and there's a path leading directly to Baga Beach.

Resort Fiesta BOUTIQUE HOTEL $$$
(☎9822104512; http://fiestagoa.com; Tito's Lane, Baga; d & ste incl breakfast ₹5000-8000; ❄@📶🏊) Large, light-filled rooms are the signature at this beautifully designed boutique resort behind the beachfront restaurant of the same name. The labour of love by owner Yellow Mehta is stylishly appointed with a lovely garden and pool, large verandahs and modern touches like TV, minibar and dual wash basins.

Eating

The beach shacks are an obvious go-to, but there are some interesting gems along the 'Strip' and excellent upmarket offerings on the north side of the Baga River.

Calangute

Plantain Leaf INDIAN $

(☎0832-2279860; veg thali ₹120, mains ₹110-250; ⊙11am-5pm & 7-11.45pm) In the heart of Calangute's busy market area, 1st-floor Plantain Leaf has consistently been the area's best pure veg restaurant for many years, with classic South Indian banana leaf thalis and dosas, along with more North Indian flavours. Most dishes sneak in to the budget category.

Cafe Sussegado Souza GOAN $$

(☎09850141007; Calangute-Anjuna Rd; mains ₹160-300; ⊙noon-11pm) In a little yellow Portuguese house just south of the Calangute market area, Cafe Sussegado is the place to come for Goan food such as fish curry rice, chicken *xacuti* and pork *sorpotel* (a vinegary stew made from liver, heart and kidneys), with a shot of *feni* to follow. Authentic, busy and good atmosphere.

Infantaria ITALIAN $$

(Calangute-Baga Rd; pastries ₹50-200, mains ₹140-580; ⊙7.30am-midnight) Once Calangute's best bakery, Infantaria is now a popular Italian-cum-Indian fondue-meets-curry restaurant. The bakery roots are still there, though, with homemade cakes, croissants, little flaky pastries and real coffee. Get in early for breakfast before the good stuff runs out. Regular live music in season.

★A Reverie INTERNATIONAL $$$

(☎8380095732; www.areverie.com; Holiday St; mains ₹475-700; ⊙7pm-late) A gorgeous lounge bar, all armchairs, cool jazz and whimsical outdoor space, this is the place to spoil yourself, with the likes of Serrano ham, grilled asparagus, French wines and Italian cheeses. A Reverie likes to style itself as 'fun dining' and doesn't take itself too seriously.

Pousada by the Beach SEAFOOD, GOAN $$$

(Holiday St; mains ₹550-710; ⊙11am-7pm) This permanent beachfront restaurant is simple in appearance but the lunch-only menu is bona fide fine dining – the chef also oversees Pousada Tauma's upmarket Copper Bowl. The menu is kept uncluttered with just a handful of expertly prepared Goan and seafood specialities.

SATURDAY NIGHT MARKETS

There are two well-established evening markets, **Saturday Night Market** (www.snmgoa.com; ⊙from 6pm Sat late Nov-Mar) in Arpora and **Mackie's** (⊙from 6pm Sat Dec-Apr) in Baga, that make an interesting evening alternative to the Anjuna flea market.

The attractions here are as much about food stalls and entertainment as shopping, but there's a big range of so-so stalls, flashing jewellery, laser pointers and other novelties that would be difficult to sell during daylight hours.

Both start up in late November and are occasionally known to be cancelled at short notice, so check locally or with taxi drivers.

Baga

★Go With the Flow INTERNATIONAL $$$

(☎7507771556; www.gowiththeflowgoa.com; Baga River Rd; mains ₹200-650; ⊙noon-10.30pm) Stepping into the fantasy neon-lit garden of illuminated white-wicker furniture is wow factor enough, but the food is equally out of this world. With a global menu leaning towards European and Asian flavours, this remains one of Baga's best dining experiences. Try some of the small bites (ask about a tasting plate) or go straight for the signature pork belly or prawn laksa.

★Fiesta ITALIAN $$$

(☎0832-2279894; www.fiestagoa.in; Tito's Lane; mains ₹350-950; ⊙7pm-late) Long-running Fiesta has undergone a classy makeover: a rustic beachfront bar with all-day dining, and fine dining by candlelight around the pool in the evening. Overseen by style queen Yellow Mehta, it's an intimate and sophisticated Mediterranean-style dining experience that starts with homemade pizza and pasta and extends to French-influenced seafood dishes and tiramisu.

Drinking & Nightlife

Baga's boisterous club scene, centred on Tito's Lane, has long been well known among the tourist crowd looking for a good time. Some find the scene here a little sleazy and the bar staff indifferent. Solo women are welcomed into clubs (usually free) but should exercise care and take taxis to and from venues.

Café Mambo CLUB

(☎7507333003; www.cafemambogoa.com; Tito's Lane, Baga; cover charge couples ₹800; ⊙6pm-3am) Part of the Tito's empire, Mambo is one of Baga's most happening clubs with an indoor/outdoor beachfront location and nightly DJs pumping out house, hip hop and Latino tunes. Couples or women only.

Tito's CLUB

(☎9822765002; www.titosgroup.com; Tito's Lane, Baga; cover charge couples/women/stags from ₹8000/free/2000; ⏰8pm-3am) The long-running titan of Goa's clubbing scene, Tito's has done its best to clean up the locals-leering-at-Western-women image of yesteryear. It's generally couples or ladies only – solo men (stags) might get in at an inflated rate, depending on the mood of door staff.

Shopping

Literati Bookshop & Cafe BOOKS

(☎0832-2277740; www.literati-goa.com; Calangute; ⏰10am-6.30pm Mon-Sat) A refreshingly different bookstore, in the owners' South Calangute home, and a very pleasant Italian-style garden cafe. Come for a fine espresso or pizza and browse the range of books by Goan and Indian authors as well as antiquarian literature. Check the website for readings and other events.

Karma Collection GIFTS & SOUVENIRS

(www.karmacollectiongoa.com; Calangute-Arpora Rd, Calangute; ⏰9.30am-10.30pm) Beautiful home furnishings, textiles, ornaments, bags and other enticing stuff – some of it antique – has been sourced from across India, Pakistan and Afghanistan and gathered at Karma Collection, which makes for a mouth-watering browse. Fixed prices mean there's no need to bargain, though it's not cheap.

Getting There & Around

Frequent buses go to Panaji (₹15, 45 minutes) and Mapusa (₹12, 30 minutes) from both the Calangute and Baga bus stands.

A taxi from Calangute or Baga to Panaji costs around ₹450 and takes about half an hour. A prepaid taxi from the airport to Calangute costs ₹1150.

A local bus runs between the Calangute and Baga stands every few minutes (₹5); catch it anywhere along the way, though when traffic is bad it might be quicker to walk.

Taxis between Calangute and northern Baga Beach charge an extortionate ₹100.

Anjuna

☎0832 / POP 9640

Good old Anjuna has been a stalwart of the hippie scene since the 1960s and still drags out the sarongs and sandalwood each Wednesday (in season) for its famous flea market. Though it continues to pull in droves of backpackers, midrange and domestic tourists are increasingly making their way here for a dose of hippie-chic. Anjuna is continuing to evolve, with a heady beach party scene and a flowering of new restaurants and bars.

The village itself is a bit ragged around the edges and is spread out over a wide area. Do as most do: hire a scooter or motorbike and explore the back lanes and southern beach area and you'll find a place that suits. Anjuna will grow on you.

Sights & Activities

Anjuna's charismatic, narrow **beach** runs for almost 2km from the rocky, low-slung cliffs at the northern village area right down beyond the flea market in the south. In season there are water sports here, including jet skis (₹400), banana boats (₹1000 for four people) and parasailing (₹700).

Lots of yoga, ayurveda and other alternative therapies and regimes are on offer in season (p833); look out for noticeboards at popular cafes such as Artjuna (p831).

Courses

Mukti Kitchen COOKING

(☎0800-7359170; www.muktikitchen.com; Anjuna-Baga Rd, Arpora; veg/nonveg/Goan class ₹1500/2000/2500; ⏰11am-2pm & 5-8pm) Mukti shares her cooking skills twice daily at these recommended classes on the Anjuna Rd in Arpora. Courses include around five dishes which can be tailored – veg or nonveg, Goan, Indian or ayurvedic. Minimum four people, maximum six; book one day ahead.

Sleeping

Dozens of basic rooms are strung along Anjuna's northern clifftop, while pricier places front the main beach. Plenty of small, family-run guesthouses are also tucked back from the main beach strip, offering nicer double rooms for a similar price; look out for signs announcing 'rooms to let' or 'house to let'.

Red Door Hostel HOSTEL $

(☎0832-2274423; reddoorhostels@gmail.com; dm without/with AC ₹550/660, d without/with AC ₹1900/2200; ❄📶) Red Door is a welcoming backpacker place close to Anjuna's central crossroads with clean four- and six-bed

Anjuna

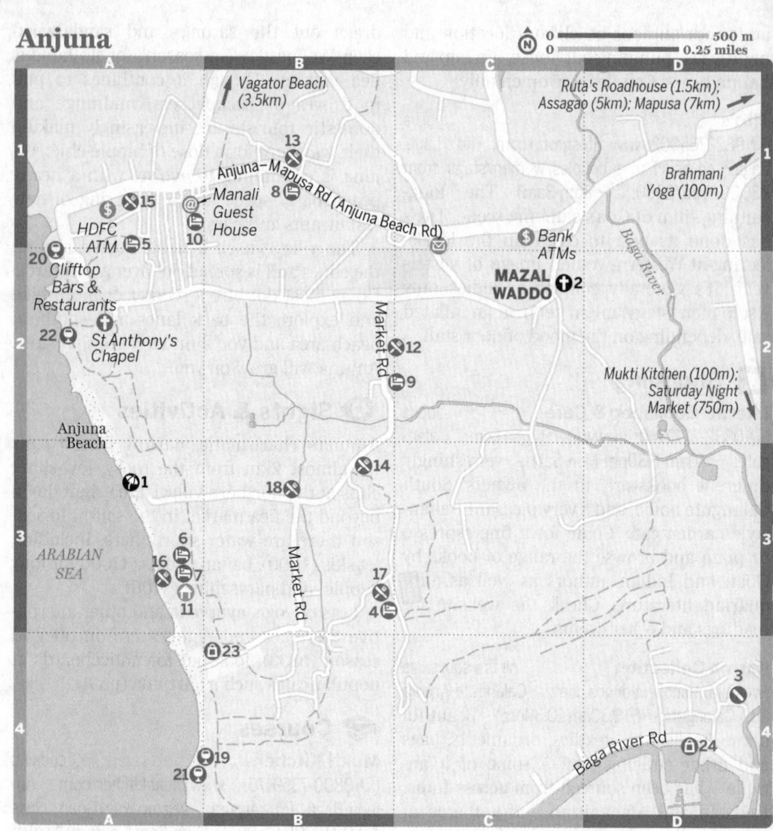

dorms plus a few private rooms. Facilities include lockers, free wi-fi, a garden, good communal areas – including a well-equipped kitchen – and a sociable cafe-bar. There's a laid-back vibe and resident pet dogs.

Prison Hostel HOSTEL $
(☎0832-2273745; www.thehostelcrowd.com; 940 Market Rd; dm ₹400, with AC ₹500, d ₹1500; ❄📶) This quirky backpacker hostel on Anjuna's Market Rd is themed like a jail with bars on the windows, B&W decor and, strangely, an old bus for a cafe. Clean four- to 10-bed dorms have individual lockers and bed-lights, there's a good kitchen, and breakfast and wi-fi are included.

Florinda's GUESTHOUSE $
(☎9890216520; s/d ₹500/800, with AC ₹1500; ❄📶) One of the better budget places near the beach, Florinda's has clean rooms, with 24-hour hot water, window screens and mosquito nets, set around a pretty garden. The few air-con rooms fill up fast.

Paradise GUESTHOUSE $
(☎9922541714; janet_965@hotmail.com; Anjuna-Mapusa Rd; d ₹1000, with AC ₹1500-2000; ❄@📶) This friendly place is fronted by an old Portuguese home and offers neat, clean rooms with well-decorated options in the newer annexe. The better rooms have TVs, fridges and hammocks on the balcony. Friendly owner Janet and family also run the pharmacy, general store, restaurant, internet cafe, Connexions travel agency and money exchange!

Palms N Tides COTTAGE $$
(☎9988882021; www.palmsntides.com; d ₹3800-4300) The dome-shaped cottages here are some of the roomiest and best-designed on the beachfront. Set in a garden they feature huge beds and bathrooms, and air-con to justify the price. It's behind Elephant Art Cafe.

Anjuna

Sights

1 Anjuna Beach ... A3
2 Our Lady of Good Health ... C2

Activities, Courses & Tours

3 Barracuda Diving ... D4

Sleeping

4 Banyan Soul ... B3
5 Casa Anjuna ... A1
6 Florinda's ... A3
7 Palms N Tides ... A3
8 Paradise ... B1
9 Prison Hostel ... C2
10 Red Door Hostel ... A1
11 Sea Horse ... A3

Eating

12 Artjuna Cafe ... C2
13 Burger Factory ... B1
14 Café Diogo ... B3
15 Dhum Biryani & Kebabs ... A1
16 Elephant Art Cafe ... A3
17 German Bakery ... B3
18 Goa's Ark ... B3

Drinking & Nightlife

19 Curlies ... B4
20 Purple Martini ... A2
21 Shiva Valley ... A4
22 UV Bar ... A2

Shopping

23 Anjuna Flea Market ... B4
24 Mackie's Saturday Nite Bazaar ... D4

Sea Horse HUT $$
(9764465078; www.vistapraiaanjuna.com; hut without/with AC ₹2000/3000;) A line-up of timber cabins behind the beach restaurant of the same name, Sea Horse has a good location. The huts are small and get a little hot – go for the air-con rooms if it's humid. Staff are friendly and accommodating. The same owners have a pricier beachfront set-up called Vista Praia Anjuna.

Banyan Soul BOUTIQUE HOTEL $$
(9820707283; www.thebanyansoul.com; d ₹2500;) A slinky 12-room option, tucked down the lane off Market Rd, and lovingly conceived and run by Sumit, a young Mumbai escapee. Rooms are chic and well equipped with AC and TV, and there's a lovely library and shady seating area beneath a banyan tree.

Casa Anjuna HERITAGE HOTEL $$$
(0832-2274123; www.casaboutiquehotels.com; D'Mello Vaddo 66; d incl breakfast from ₹9850;) This heritage hotel is enclosed in lovely plant-filled gardens around an inviting pool, managing to shield itself from the hype of central Anjuna. All rooms have antique furnishings and period touches; like many upmarket places it's better value out of season, when rates halve.

Eating

Café Diogo CAFE $
(Market Rd; snacks ₹80-160; 8.30am-3pm) Excellent fruit salads are sliced and diced at Café Diogo, a small family-run cafe on the way down to the market. The generous avocado, cheese and mushroom toasted sandwiches and the range of lassis are also worth a try.

★**Artjuna Cafe** CAFE $$
(0832-2274794; www.artjuna.com; Market Rd; mains ₹130-350; 8am-10.30pm;) Artjuna is right up there with our favourite cafes in Anjuna. Along with all-day breakfast, outstanding espresso coffee, salads, sandwiches and Middle Eastern surprises like baba ganoush, tahini and falafel, this sweet garden cafe has an excellent craft and lifestyle shop, yoga classes and a useful noticeboard. Great meeting place.

★**Burger Factory** BURGERS $$
(Anjuna-Mapusa Rd; burgers ₹300-450; 11.30am-3.30pm & 6.30-10.30pm Thu-Tue) There's no mistaking what's on offer at this little alfresco diner/kitchen. The straightforward menu of burgers isn't cheap, but they are interesting and expertly crafted. Choose between beef or chicken burgers and toppings such as cheddar or beetroot and aioli.

Goa's Ark MIDDLE EASTERN $$
(Market Rd; mains ₹150-670, meze from ₹50; 10am-11pm;) Set in a lovely garden, Goa's Ark is a Middle Eastern–style restaurant with meze, barbecued meat and falafel. It's also a petting zoo with farmyard animals, birds and a kids' playground.

Elephant Art Cafe BEACH CAFE $$
(mains ₹190-370; 8am-10pm;) A standout among the restaurants lining the beach, Elephant Art Cafe does a great range of tapas, sandwiches, fish and chips and speciality breakfasts.

DON'T MISS

ANJUNA FLEA MARKET

Anjuna's weekly Wednesday **flea market** (8am-late Wed, Nov-Apr) is as much part of the Goan experience as a day on the beach. More than three decades ago, it was conceived and created by hippies smoking jumbo joints, convening to compare experiences on the heady Indian circuit. Nowadays things are far more mainstream and the merchandise comes from all over India: sculptures and jewellery courtesy of the Tibetan and Kashmiri traders; colourful Gujarati tribal women selling T-shirts; richly colourful saris, bags and bedspreads from Rajasthan; sacks of spices from Kerala; and the hard-to-miss tribal girls from Karnataka pleading passers-by to 'come look in my shop'.

For a rest from the shopping there are chai stalls and a couple of restaurant-bars with live music. **Cafe Looda** has a fabulous sunset beachfront location and live music from 5pm. The best time to visit is early (from 8am) or late afternoon (around 4pm till close just after sunset).

German Bakery MULTICUISINE **$$**
(www.german-bakery.in; bread & pastries ₹20-160, mains ₹160-470; 8.30am-11pm;) Leafy and adorned with prayer flags, occasional live music and garden lights, German Bakery is a long-standing favourite for hearty and healthy breakfasts, fresh-baked bread and organic food, but the menu also runs to pasta, burgers and pricey seafood. Has healthy juices (think wheatgrass) and espresso coffee.

Dhum Biryani & Kebabs INDIAN **$$**
(Anjuna-Mapusa Rd; mains ₹180-350; 9am-1am) Loved by visitors and locals alike, Dhum Biryani serves up consistently good kebabs as well as plates of biryani (steamed rice with meat or vegetables) and other usual suspects.

Drinking & Nightlife

Anjuna vies with Vagator as the trance party capital of Goa and the southern end of the beach has several nightclubs that are the most happening places in North Goa when the night is right. Market day is always fun, with live music at one or both of the two bars there.

Curlies BAR
(www.curliesgoa.com; 9am-3am) Holding sway at South Anjuna Beach, Curlies mixes laid-back beach-bar vibe with sophisticated nightspot – the party nights here are notorious and loud. There's a rooftop lounge bar and an enclosed late-night dance club. Thursday and Saturday are big nights, as are full moon nights.

Purple Martini COCKTAIL BAR
(9823772890; Sunset Point; 9pm-midnight) The clifftop sunset views, blue-and-white colour scheme and swanky bar at this beautifully situated restaurant-bar could easily transport you to Santorini. Come for a sundowner cocktail and check out the menu of Greek kebabs and Mediterranean salads.

Getting There & Away

Buses to Mapusa (₹15, 30 minutes) depart every half-hour or so from the main bus stand at the end of the Anjuna–Mapusa Rd near the beach; some buses coming from Mapusa continue on to Vagator and Chapora.

A couple of direct daily buses head south to Calangute; otherwise, take a bus to Mapusa and change there.

Plenty of motorcycle taxis and autorickshaws gather at the main crossroads and you can also easily hire scooters and motorcycles here from ₹250 to ₹400 – most Anjuna-based travellers get around on two wheels.

Assagao

On the road between Mapusa and Anjuna or Vagator, Assagao is one of North Goa's prettiest villages, with almost traffic-free country roads passing old Portuguese mansions and whitewashed churches. The area is inspiring enough to be home to several of North Goa's best yoga retreats.

Activities

International Animal Rescue VOLUNTEERING
(Animal Tracks; 0832-2268272; www.internationalanimalrescuegoa.org.in; Madungo Vaddo; 9am-4pm) The well-established International Animal Rescue collects and cares for stray dogs, cats and other four-legged animals in distress, carrying out sterilisations and vaccinations. Volunteers are welcome to help with dog walking and playing with puppies

and kittens, but must have evidence of rabies vaccination.

El Shaddai VOLUNTEERING
(☎0832-6513286, 0832-2461068; www.childrescue.net; El Shaddai House, Socol Vaddo) El Shaddai is a British-founded charity that aids impoverished and homeless children throughout Goa. Volunteers able to commit to more than four weeks' work with El Shaddai can apply through the website. There's a rigorous vetting process, so start well in advance.

Courses

Spicy Mama's COOKING
(☎9623348958; www.spicymamasgoa.com; 138/3 Bairo Alto; 1-day course veg/nonveg ₹2000/3000, 3-day ₹5000/7000, 5-day ₹10,000/12,000) For cooking enthusiasts, Spicy Mama's specialises in spicy North Indian cuisine, from butter chicken to *aloo gobi* (cauliflower and potato curry) and *palak paneer* (cheese in a puréed spinach gravy), prepared at the country home of Suchi. The standard one-day course is four hours; book online for in-depth multiday masterclasses.

Sleeping

Hopping Frog HOSTEL $
(☎8007669996; www.hoppingfrog.in; dm/d ₹400/1500;) This new hostel in leafy Assagao is a fun backpacker alternative to the beach. The four dorms are clean, and open out to a very cool garden space. The loungy cafe-bar is very sociable and there are bikes available for cruising Assagao's back lanes.

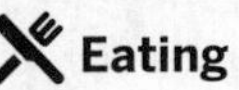

Eating

★ **Villa Blanche Bistro** CAFE $$
(www.villablanche-goa.com; 283 Badem Church Rd; breakfast ₹90-200, mains ₹320-480; 9am-11pm Mon-Sat, 10am-4pm Sun, Oct-Apr) This lovely, chilled garden cafe in the back lanes of Assagao is run by a German-Swiss couple. Salads, sandwiches, filled bagels and cakes are specialities, but you'll also find Thai curry and German sausages. For an indulgent breakfast or brunch try the waffles and pancakes.

Ruta's Roadhouse INTERNATIONAL $$
(☎8380025757; www.rutas.in; Mapusa Rd; breakfast ₹300, small/big plates ₹200/300; 8.30am-6.30pm) Ruta's has found a new home in an old Portuguese house in Assagao, serving up excellent set breakfasts and global culinary offerings from jambalaya to spicy laksa.

Getting There & Away

Local buses between Mapusa and Anjuna (about 15 minutes from each) or Siolim pass through Assagao, but the village is best explored on a rented scooter or by taxi from your beach resort.

Vagator & Chapora

☎0832

Dramatic red stone cliffs, thick palm groves and a crumbling 17th-century Portuguese fort give Vagator and its diminutive village neighbour Chapora one of the prettiest settings on the North Goan coast. Once known for their wild trance parties and heady, hippie lifestyles, things have slowed down

NORTH GOA YOGA RETREATS

The Anjuna/Vagator/Assagao area has a number of yoga retreats where you can immerse yourself in courses, classes and a Zen vibe during the October-March season.

Purple Valley Yoga Retreat (☎0832-2268363; www.yogagoa.com; 142 Bairo Alto; dm/s 1 week from £690/820, 2 weeks £1100/1350) Popular yoga resort in Assagao offering one- and two-week residential and nonresidential courses in Ashtanga yoga.

Swan Yoga Retreat (☎8007360677, 0832-2268024; www.swan-yoga-goa.com; drop-in classes ₹350, 1 week from ₹23,300) In a peaceful jungle corner of Assagao, Swan Retreat is a very Zen yoga experience. Daily drop-in classes are available, or minimum week-long yoga retreats start every Saturday.

Yoga Magic (☎0832-6523796; www.yogamagic.net; Mapusa-Chapora Rd, Anjuna; lodge s/d ₹6750/9000, ste ₹9000/12,000) Solar lighting, vegetable farming and compost toilets are just some of the worthy initiatives practised in this luxurious yoga resort. The lodge features dramatic Rajasthani tents under a thatched shelter.

Brahmani Yoga (☎9545620578; www.brahmaniyoga.com; Tito's White House, Aguada-Siolim Rd; class ₹700, 10-class pass ₹5000; classes 9.30am) Drop-in classes at Tito's White House.

Vagator & Chapora

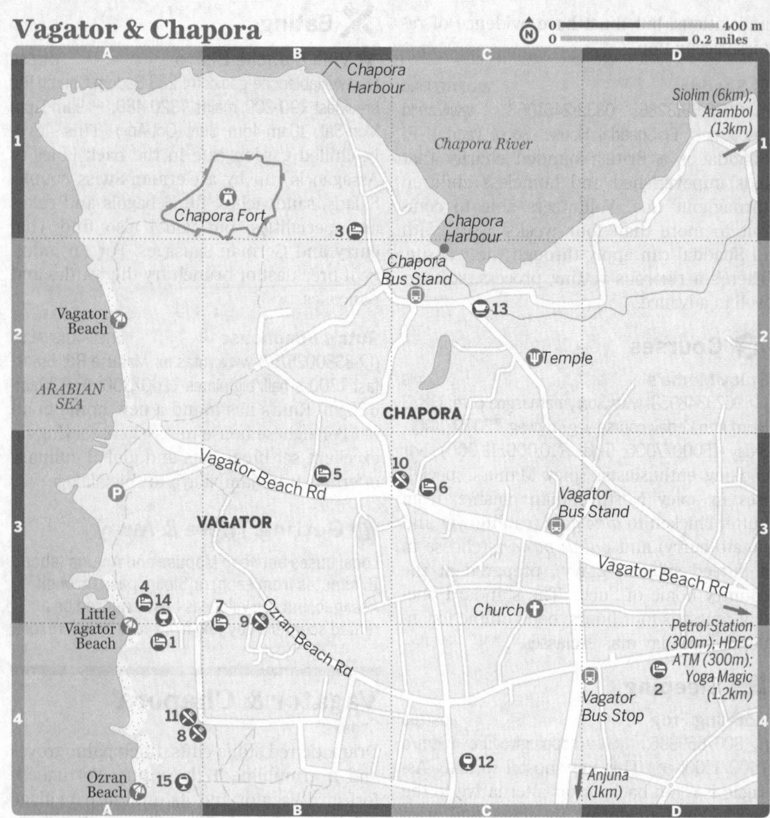

Vagator & Chapora

Sleeping

1 Alcove Resort ... A4
2 Bean Me Up ... D4
3 Casa de Olga ... B1
4 Casa Vagator ... A3
5 Dreams Hostel ... B3
6 Jungle Hostel ... C3
7 Pappi Chulo ... B3

Eating

8 Antares ... A4
Bean Me Up ... (see 2)
9 Bluebird ... B3
10 Mango Tree Bar & Cafe ... C3
11 Thalassa ... A4

Drinking & Nightlife

12 Hilltop ... C4
13 Jai Ganesh Fruit Juice Centre ... C2
14 Nine Bar ... A3
15 Waters Beach Lounge ... A4

considerably these days and upmarket restaurants are more the style, though Vagator has some of Goa's best clubs. Chapora – reminiscent of the Mos Eisley Cantina from *Star Wars* – remains a favourite for hippies and long-staying smokers, with the smell of charas (resin of the marijuana plant) clinging heavily to the light sea breeze.

Sleeping

Budget accommodation, much of it in private rooms, ranges along Ozran Beach Rd and Vagator Beach Rd; you'll see lots of signs for 'rooms to let' on the side roads in simple private homes and guest houses, from ₹400 to ₹600 per double.

Head down the road to the harbour at Chapora and you'll find lots of rooms – and whole homes – for rent.

Vagator

★Jungle Hostel HOSTEL $
(☎0832-2273006; www.thehostelcrowd.com; Vagator Beach Rd; dm without/with AC ₹500/600, s/d ₹1000/1500; ❄@📶) One of the original backpacker hotels in North Goa, Jungle brought the dorm experience and an international vibe to Vagator and has expanded to three properties. The six-bed dorms are clean and bright and things like lockers, wifi, breakfast, a communal kitchen and travel advice are free.

Enterprise Guest House GUESTHOUSE $
(☎7769095356; www.beanmeup.in; 1639/2 Deulvaddo; d incl breakfast without/with bathroom ₹1100/1400; 📶) Set around a leafy, parachute-silky courtyard that's home to Vagator's best vegan restaurant Bean Me Up, rooms at the Enterprise Guest House look simple but are themed with individual exotic decor, earthy shades, mosquito nets and shared verandahs. The mellow yoga-friendly vibe matches the clientele and the included breakfast is decadent.

Pappi Chulo HOSTEL $
(☎9075135343; pappichulohostel@gmail.com; Ozran Beach Rd; dm without/with AC ₹400/500) Unashamedly Vagator's party hostel, Pappi's has a bar in the garden, movie nights and an international vibe of travellers just hanging out. Themed dorms have lockers and bunk beds.

Dreams Hostel HOSTEL $
(☎9920651760; dreamshostel.com; off Vagator Beach Rd; dm ₹500) With a philosophy of 'art, music, wellness', former backpacker and DJ Ravi has established a great little creative space for like-minded travellers with a spacious garden, three clean dorms and chilled common areas.

Alcove Resort HOTEL $$
(☎0832-2274491; www.alcovegoa.com; Little Vagator Beach; d ₹4500-8500; ❄@📶🏊) The location overlooking Little Vagator Beach is hard to beat at this price. Attractively furnished rooms, slightly larger cottages, and four suites surrounding a decent central pool, restaurant and bar, make this a good place for those who want a touch of affordable luxury.

Casa Vagator HOTEL $$$
(☎0832-2416738; www.casaboutiquehotels.com; d incl breakfast from ₹11,200; ❄@📶🏊) A successfully rendered outfit in the deluxe Casa boutique mould, this is one of Vagator's most stylish accommodation options, with gorgeous rooms offering equally gorgeous views out to the wide blue horizon. A bit close to techno-heavy Nine Bar.

Chapora

Casa de Olga GUESTHOUSE $
(☎0832-2274355, 9822157145; eadsouza@yahoo.co.in; r ₹700-1200, without bathroom from ₹400) This welcoming family-run homestay, set around a nice garden on the way to Chapora harbour, offers spotless rooms of varying sizes in a three-storey building. The best are the brand-new top-floor rooms with swanky bathrooms, TV and balcony.

Eating

Vagator has a handful of outstanding dining spots along its clifftop, along with the usual range of much-of-a-muchness shacks down on the beach.

The dining scene at tiny Chapora isn't as evolved as Vagator, but that's what the people who hang out there like about it. With a couple of popular juice joints and a handful of nondescript restaurants, Chapora stays cool while the fine dining is elsewhere.

★Bean Me Up VEGAN $$
(www.beanmeup.in; 1639/2 Deulvaddo; mains ₹180-380; ⏰8am-11pm; 📶) Bean Me Up is vegan, but even nonveg travellers will be blown away by the taste, variety and filling plates on offer in this relaxed garden restaurant. The extensive menu includes vegan pizzas, ice creams, housemade tofu curry and innovative salads. Ingredients are as diverse as coconut, cashew milk and cashew cheese, quinoa, tempeh and lentil dhal.

Bluebird GOAN $$
(www.bluebirdgoa.com; Ozran Beach Rd; mains ₹250-480; ⏰8.30am-11pm) Bluebird specialises in Goan cuisine, with genuine vindaloos, chicken *cafreal* (marinated in a sauce of chillies, garlic and ginger), fish curry rice and Goan sausages among the temptations, as well as some delicately spiced seafood dishes. Dine in the lovely open garden cafe.

Mango Tree Bar & Cafe MULTICUISINE $$
(Vagator Beach Rd; mains ₹130-430; ⏰24hr) With loud reggae, crappy service, dark-wood

furniture, a sometimes rambunctious bar scene, ancient expats leaning over the bar, draught beer and an overall great vibe, the Mango Tree is a classic Vagator meeting place. It's open late (24 hours if it's busy enough) with a menu from Goan to European, pizza and Mexican.

★Thalassa GREEK $$$
(☎9850033537; www.thalassagoa.com; mains ₹300-750; ⏲4pm-midnight) Authentic and awesomely good Greek food is served alfresco on a breezy clifftop terrace. Kebabs, souvlaki and thoughtful seafood dishes are the speciality, but this is also a great bar and fills up late in the evening when you might see some Greek dancing and plate smashing. Come early, order a jug of sangria and enjoy the sunset.

Antares MODERN AUSTRALIAN $$$
(☎7350011528; www.antaresgoa.com; Ozran Beach Rd; mains ₹200-1400; ⏲11.30am-midnight) The latest addition to Vagator's clifftop dining scene, Antares is known as the project of Australian Masterchef contestant Sarah Todd. The atmosphere is beachfront chic and the food Modern Australian meets Indian, with some Goan dishes such as crab *xacuti*.

Drinking & Nightlife

Waters Beach Lounge CLUB
(☎9767200012; ⏲from 6pm Thu-Sun) Terracing down the hillside on the Vagator cliffs, this deluxe restaurant, bar and club is best known for its party nights, with open-air dance floors overlooking the Arabian Sea and a soundproof room for late at night. Top DJs come to play.

Nine Bar BAR
(⏲5pm-4am) Once the hallowed epicentre of Goa's trance scene, the open-air Nine Bar terrace, on the clifftop overlooking Little Vagator Beach, has now moved into a soundproof indoor space so the parties can still go all night. Look out for flyers and local advice to see when the big party nights are on.

Jai Ganesh Fruit Juice Centre CAFE
(juices ₹50-80; ⏲8.30am-midnight) Thanks to its corner location, with views up and down Chapora's main street, this may be the most popular juice bar in Goa. It's a prime meeting spot and, once parked, most people are reluctant to give up their seat.

Hilltop CLUB
(⏲sunset-late) Hilltop is a long-serving Vagator trance and party venue that's deserted by day but comes alive from sunset. Its edge-of-town neon-lit coconut grove location allows it, on occasion, to bypass noise regulations to host concerts, parties and international DJs. Sunday sessions (5pm to 10pm) are legendary.

Getting There & Away

Fairly frequent buses run to both Chapora and Vagator from Mapusa (₹15, 30 minutes) throughout the day, many via Anjuna. Practically anyone with legs will rent you a scooter/motorcycle from ₹250/400 per day.

Vagator has North Goa's most popular petrol station.

Morjim

☎0832

Morjim Beach was once very low-key (almost deserted) and its southern end is still protected due to the presence of rare olive ridley marine turtles, which lay their annual clutches of eggs between November and February. These days Morjim is popular with Russian tourists and there's a bit of an in-season clubbing

WHERE'S THE PARTY?

Though Goa was long legendary among Western visitors for its all-night, open-air hippie trance parties, a central government 'noise pollution' ban on loud music in open spaces between 10pm and 6am largely curtailed its often notorious, drug-laden party scene. Of course, the parties quickly moved inside and the big trance and dance clubs still go all night in season.

The trance party scene is going strong in Anjuna at Curlies (p832); in Vagator at Hilltop, Nine Bar and Waters; in Aswem/Morjim at Club M; and in Palolem at Leopard Valley (p849), which runs silent discos (p848). In Baga, the clubs on Tito's Lane are as wild as ever.

Over the busy Christmas–New Year period the authorities tend to turn a blind eye to parties so you might find some of the old-school variety happening. Taxi drivers will know. Online check out www.goa-freaks.com or www.whatsupgoa.com.

scene, but the southern beach is more black sand than golden due to river run-off.

Sleeping

★Wanderers Hostel HOSTEL $
(9619235302; www.wanderershostel.com; dm ₹500, shared tent ₹300, luxury tent d ₹1700-2000;) About five minutes' walk back from Morjim Beach, Wanderers is a real find for budget travellers. The main building, decorated with original travellers murals, has spotless air-con dorms with lockers, bed lights and wi-fi, full kitchen, cosy communal areas and a pool table. In the garden next door is a tent village with swimming pool and yoga retreat centre and outdoor cinema.

Goan Café & Resort RESORT $$
(0832-2244394; www.goancafe.com; apt & cottage from ₹1800, with AC ₹2200, treehouse without/with bathroom from ₹1200/1700;) Fronting Morjim Beach, this excellent family-run resort has a fine array of beachfront stilted 'treehouse' huts and more solid rooms (some with AC) at the back. The Friends Corner restaurant is good.

Getting There & Away

Occasional local buses run between Siolim and Morjim village (₹8, 15 minutes), but most travellers taxi to their chosen accommodation, then either hire a scooter/motorbike or use taxis from there.

Aswem

0832

Aswem Beach is growing busier each year, but it's still overshadowed by Mandrem to the north. Beach-hut accommodation and beach-shack restaurants spring up each season on its very broad stretch of clean, white sand (with few hawkers). The main Morjim-Mandrem road is set some way back from the sands.

Activities

★Vaayu Waterman's Village SURFING
(9850050403; http://vaayuoceanadventures.in; surfboard hire per hr ₹500, lessons ₹2500) Goa's premier surf shop is also an activity and art centre where you can arrange lessons and hire equipment for surfing, kiteboarding, stand up paddleboarding, kayaking and wakeboarding. A highlight is the full-day SUP tour to Paradise Lagoon in Maharashtra. The enthusiastic young owners also run an art gallery, cafe and **funky accommodation** (9850050403; http://vaayuoceanadventures.in; hut ₹2250-4000, d without/with AC ₹3500;) across the road from Aswem Beach.

Sleeping & Eating

You can still find basic beach huts and rooms back from the beach for ₹1000 (less out of high season).

Yab Yum HUT $$$
(0832-6510392; www.yabyumresorts.com; hut/cottage from ₹8500/9700;) This top-notch choice has unusual, stylish, dome-shaped huts – some look like giant hairy coconuts – made of a combination of all-natural local materials, including mud, stone and mango wood, as well as more traditional AC cottages. A host of yoga and massage options are available, and it's set in one of the most secluded beachfront jungle gardens you'll find in Goa.

Marbela Beach Resort TENTED CAMP $$$
(0832-6450599, 9158881180; www.marbelabeach.com; tent/villa/ste ₹8000/9000/20,000;) The luxury tents and 'Spanish-style' villas at this slick resort are pricey but fitted out like five-star hotel rooms. Even if you don't stay here, the beachfront cabanas are a divine spot for a drink and for the resort's thumping **Club M** (0832-6450599; www.marbelabeach.com; Marbela Beach Resort; Fri-Sun) parties, till late from Friday to Sunday.

La Plage MEDITERRANEAN $$
(9822121712; Aswem Beach; mains ₹200-450; 9am-10pm Nov-Apr) Renowned in these parts, La Plage takes beach shack to the next level with its inspired gourmet French-Mediterranean food. Along with excellent salads, seafood and fabulous desserts (try the chocolate thali), La Plage stocks great wines. It's usually open from late November to April.

Getting There & Away

Buses run between Siolim and Aswem, but it's easier to get a taxi to your accommodation, then use a scooter/motorbike or taxis.

Mandrem

Mellow Mandrem has developed in recent years from an in-the-know bolt-hole for those seeking respite from the relentless traveller scene of Arambol and Anjuna to a fairly mainstream but still very lovely beach hangout. There's plenty of yoga, meditation and ayurveda on offer here, plus good dining and space to lay down with a good book. Many believe there's no better place in North Goa.

Sights & Activities

Shanti Ayurvedic Massage Centre AYURVEDA
(☎8806205264; 1/1½hr massage from ₹1000/1500; ⏰9am-8pm) Ayurvedic massage is provided here by the delightful Shanti. Try the rejuvenating 75-minute massage and facial package, or go for an unusual 'Poulti' massage, using a poultice-like cloth bundle containing 12 herbal powders. You'll find her place on the right-hand side as you head down the beach road.

Himalaya Yoga Valley YOGA
(☎9960657852; www.yogagoaindia.com; Mandrem Beach) The winter home of a popular Dharamsala outfit, HYV specialises in hatha and ashtanga residential teacher-training courses, but also has daily drop-in classes (₹2000 for five).

Sleeping & Eating

★**Dunes Holiday Village** HUT $
(☎0832-2247219; www.dunesgoa.com; r & hut ₹1000-1200; @📶) The pretty huts here are peppered around a palm-filled lane leading to the beach; at night, lamps light up the place like a palm-tree dreamland. Huts range from basic to more sturdy 'treehouses' (huts on stilts). It's a friendly, good-value place with a decent beach restaurant, massage, yoga classes and a marked absence of trance.

★**Mandala** RESORT $$
(☎9158266093; www.themandalagoa.com; r & hut ₹1600-5500; ❄📶) Mandala is a very peaceful and beautifully designed eco-village with a range of huts and a couple of quirky air-con rooms in the 'Art House'. Pride of place goes to the barn-sized two-storey villas inspired by the design of a Keralan houseboat. The location, overlooking the tidal lagoon, is serene, with a large garden, daily yoga sessions and an organic restaurant.

Elsewhere COTTAGE $$$
(www.aseascape.com; tent ₹9000, beachhouse ₹14,400-29,000; @📶) The exact location of this heavenly place, on some 500m of beachfront, is a closely guarded secret. Choose from four beautiful beachfront houses, intriguingly named the Piggery, Bakery, Priest's House and Captain's House, or from three luxury tents, and revel in the solitude that comes with a hefty price tag and a 60m walk across a bamboo bridge.

Bed Rock MULTICUISINE $$
(mains ₹130-370; ⏰8am-11pm; 📶) Bed Rock is a welcome change from the beach shacks with a reliable menu of Indian and continental faves (pizza, pasta etc) and a cosy chill-out lounge upstairs.

Getting There & Away

Buses run between Siolim and Mandrem village (₹10, 20 minutes) hourly, but it's hard work trying to get anywhere in a hurry on public transport. Most travellers taxi to their chosen accommodation, then either hire a scooter/motorbike or use taxis from there.

Arambol (Harmal)

☎0832 / POP 5320

Arambol (also known as Harmal) is the most northerly of Goa's developed beach resorts and is still considered the beach of choice for many long-staying budget-minded travellers in the north.

Arambol first emerged in the 1960s as a mellow paradise for long-haired long-stayers escaping the scene at Calangute. Today things are still cheap and cheerful, with budget accommodation in little huts clinging to the cliffsides, though the main beach is now an uninterrupted string of beach shacks, many with beach-hut operations stacked behind.

The main beach is gently curved and safe for swimming but often crowded – head south towards Mandrem for a quieter beach scene. A short walk around the northern headland brings you to little Kalacha Beach, another popular place thanks to the 'Sweetwater Lake' back from the beach. The headland above here is the best place in Goa for paragliding.

Activities

Arambol Paragliding PARAGLIDING
(10min flight ₹2000; ⏰noon-6pm) The headland above Kalacha Beach (Sweetwater Lake) is an ideal launching point for paragliding. There are a number of independent operators: ask around at the shack restaurants on the beach, arrange a pilot, then make the short hike to the top of the headland. Most flights are around 10 minutes, but if conditions are right you can stay up longer.

Himalayan Iyengar Yoga Centre YOGA
(www.hiyogacentre.com; Madhlo Vaddo; 5-day yoga course ₹4000; ⏰9am-6pm Tue-Sun Nov-Mar) Arambol's reputable Himalayan Iyengar

Yoga Centre, which runs five-day courses in hatha yoga from mid-November to mid-March, is the winter centre of the Iyengar yoga school in Dharamkot, near Dharamsala in north India. First-time students must take the introductory five-day course, and can then continue with more advanced five-day courses at a reduced rate.

Surf Wala SURFING
(☎9011993147; www.surfwala.com; Surf Club, Arambol Beach; 1½hr lesson from ₹2500, 3-/5-day course ₹6500/11,000) If you're a beginner looking to get up on a board, join the international team of surfers based on the beach just north of Arambol's Surf Club. Prices include board hire, wax and rashie. Check the website for instructor contact details – between them they speak English, Russian, Hindi, Konkani and Japanese! Board-only rental is ₹500.

Sleeping

Accommodation in Arambol has expanded from the basic huts along the clifftop walk and the guesthouses back in the village to a mini-Palolem of beach huts behind the shacks along the main beach. Enter at the 'Glastonbury St' entrance and walk north to find plenty of places clinging to the headland between here and Kalacha Beach, or enter at the south end and ask at any of the beach shacks.

★Happy Panda HOSTEL $
(☎9619741681; www.happypanda.in; dm ₹300; 📶) Traveller-painted murals cover the walls in this very chilled backpacker place near the main village. Young owners have worked hard making the three dorms, neon common area, bar and garden into a well-equipped and welcoming budget place to crash. Bikes for hire.

Chilli's HOTEL $
(☎9921882424; d ₹600, apt with AC ₹1200; ❄📶) Near the beach entrance on Glastonbury St, this friendly canary-yellow place is one of Arambol's better nonbeachfront bargains. There are 10 decent, no-frills rooms, all with attached bathroom, fan and a hot-water shower. The top-floor apartment with AC and TV is good value. Owner Derek hires out motorbikes and scooters.

Pitruchaya Cottages COTTAGES $
(☎9404454596; r ₹800) The sea-facing timber cottages here are among the best on the cliffs, with attached bathrooms, fans and verandahs.

Lotus Sutra RESORT $$
(☎9146096940; www.lotussutragoa.com; s ₹1420, d with AC ₹2130-3320, cottages ₹6500-7100; ❄📶) The fanciest place on Arambol's beachfront has a series of bright rooms in a quirky two-storey building and cute individual timber cottages facing a garden-lawn setting. The restaurant-bar features live music.

Surf Club GUESTHOUSE $$
(www.facebook.com/surfclubgoa; d ₹1650-2300; 📶) In a quiet space at the end of a lane, on the southern end of Arambol Beach, the Surf Club is one of those cool little hang-outs that offer a bit of everything: simple but clean rooms, yoga and a fun bar with live music.

Eating & Drinking

Arambol certainly hasn't escaped the beach shack invasion, and you'll find about two dozen of them wall to wall along the main beach in season, complete with sunbeds and beach umbrellas.The northern cliff walk has a string of budget restaurants with good views, and the road down to the beach also has some interesting dining options. In the upper village, chai shops and small local joints will whip up a chai for ₹5 and a thali for ₹80.

★Shimon MIDDLE EASTERN $
(☎9011113576; Glastonbury St; meals ₹120-200; ⏲9am-11pm; 📶) Just back from the beach, and understandably popular with Israeli backpackers, Shimon is the place to fill up on exceptional falafel or *sabich* (crisp slices of eggplant stuffed into pita bread along with boiled egg, boiled potato and salad). The East-meets-Middle-East thali (₹450) comprises a little bit of almost everything on the menu.

Dylan's Toasted & Roasted CAFE $
(☎9604780316; www.dylanscoffee.com; coffee & desserts from ₹70; ⏲9am-11pm Nov-Apr; 📶) The Goa (winter) incarnation of a Manali institution, Dylan's is a fine place for an espresso, chocolate chip cookies and old-school dessert. It's a nice hang-out, just back from the southern beach entrance, with occasional live music and open-mic nights.

Fellini ITALIAN $$
(☎9881461224; Glastonbury St; mains ₹200-380; ⏲from 6.30pm) On the left-hand side just before the beach, this unsignposted but long-standing Italian joint is perfect if you're craving a carbonara or calzone. More than 40 wood-fired, thin-crust pizza varieties are

on the menu, but save space for a very decent rendition of tiramisu.

Double Dutch MULTICUISINE **$$**
(mains ₹120-400, steaks ₹420-470; ⏲7am-10pm) In a peaceful garden set back from the main road to the Glastonbury St beach entrance, Double Dutch has long been popular for its steaks, salads, Thai and Indonesian dishes, and famous apple pies. It's a relaxed meeting place with secondhand books, newspapers and a useful noticeboard for current Arambolic affairs.

Information

The closest ATM is on the main highway in Arambol's village, about 1.5km back from the beach. If it's not working there's another about 3km north in Paliyem or about the same distance south in Mandrem.

Getting There & Away

Frequent buses to/from Mapusa (₹30, one hour) stop on the main road at the 'backside' (as locals say) of Arambol village. From here, it's a 1.5km trek down through the village to the main beach drag; an autorickshaw or taxi charges at least ₹50.

Plenty of places in the village hire scooters and motorbikes (per day scooter/motorbike ₹250/350).

A taxi to Mapusa or Anjuna should cost ₹600. If you're heading north to Mumbai, travel agents can book bus tickets and you can board at a stop on the highway in the main village.

SOUTH GOA

Margao

☎0832 / POP 94,400

Margao (also known as Madgaon) is the capital of South Goa, a busy – at times traffic-clogged – market town of a manageable size for getting things done. As the major transport hub of the south, lots of travellers pass through Margao's train station or Kadamba bus stand; fewer choose to stay here, but it's a useful place for shopping, catching a local sporting event or simply enjoying the busy energy of big-city India in small-town form.

Margao's compact town centre ranges around the oblong Municipal Gardens, with shops, restaurants, ATMs and the covered market all within easy reach. To the north of town is the old Portuguese-influenced Largo de Igreja district; about 1km north further is the main (Kadamba) bus station, and 1.5km southeast of the Municipal Garden is Margao's train station.

Sights

The city's **Largo de Igreja** district features a number of traditional old Portuguese mansions; the most famous is the grand 1790 **Sat Burnzam Ghor** (Seven Gabled House). It's also home to the whitewashed **Church of the Holy Spirit**, built in 1565 on the site of an important Hindu temple.

At the southern end of the Municipal Gardens, on the west side of the canary-yellow **Secretariat Building**, the prim **Municipal Library** (Abade Faria Rd; ⏲8am-8pm Mon-Fri, 9am-noon & 4-7pm Sat & Sun) houses good books about Goa.

Sleeping

Nanutel Margao HOTEL **$$**
(☎0832-6722222; www.nanuhotels.in; Padre Miranda Rd; s/d incl breakfast ₹3800/4500, ste ₹5000-5500; ❄📶🏊) Margao's best business-class hotel by some margin, Nanutel is modern and slick with a lovely pool, good restaurant, bar and coffee shop, and clean air-con rooms. The location, between the Municipal Gardens and Largo de Igreja district, is convenient for everything.

Om Shiv Hotel HOTEL **$$**
(☎0832-2710294; www.omshivhotel.com; Cine Lata Rd; d ₹3000-4250, ste ₹5400; ❄@📶) In a bright-yellow building tucked away behind the Bank of India, Om Shiv does a decent line in fading 'executive' rooms, all of which have air-con and balcony. The suites have good views, there's a gym and the 7th-floor **Rockon Pub**.

Eating

Café Tato INDIAN **$**
(Valaulikar Rd; thalis ₹90; ⏲7am-10pm Mon-Sat) A favourite local lunch spot: tasty vegetarian fare in a bustling backstreet canteen, and delicious all-you-can-eat thalis.

Swad INDIAN **$**
(New Market; ₹60-110; ⏲7.30am-8pm; ❄) Some of Margao's best veg food is dished up at the family-friendly, lunch-break favourite Swad, across from Lotus Inn. The thalis, South Indian tiffins and other mains are all reliably tasty.

★Longhuino's GOAN, MULTICUISINE $$
(Luis Miranda Rd; mains ₹110-250; ⊙8.30am-10pm) A local institution since 1950, quaint old Longhuino's serves up tasty Indian, Goan and Chinese dishes, popular with locals and tourists alike. Go for a Goan dish like *ambot tik* (a slightly sour but fiery curry dish), and leave room for the retro desserts like rum balls and tiramisu. Service is as languid as the whirring ceiling fans but it's a great place to watch the world go by over a coffee or beer.

Martin's INTERNATIONAL $$
(mains ₹290-500; ⊙11am-3.30pm & 7-11pm) It's a welcome feeling to step off Margao's hot and busy street into the cool and classy interior of Martin's. There's just 10 tables, attentive service and an eclectic menu of tapas starters, pan-Indian dishes and stone-cooked steaks. Just off the north end of the Municipal Gardens.

Shopping

Golden Heart Emporium BOOKS
(Confidant House, Abade Faria Rd; ⊙10am-1.30pm & 4-7pm Mon-Sat) One of Goa's best bookshops, Golden Heart is crammed from floor to ceiling with fiction, nonfiction, children's books, and illustrated volumes on the state's food, architecture and history. It also stocks otherwise hard-to-get titles by local Goan authors. It's down a little lane off Abade Faria Rd.

MMC New Market MARKET
(⊙8.30am-9pm Mon-Sat) Margao's crowded, covered canopy of colourful stalls is a fun but busy place to wander around, sniffing spices, sampling soaps and browsing the household merchandise.

Information

There are plenty of banks offering currency exchange and 24-hour ATMs ranged around the Municipal Gardens.

Getting There & Around

BUS

Local and long-distance buses use the Kadamba bus stand, 2km north of the Municipal Gardens. Buses to Palolem (₹30, one hour), Colva (₹15, 20 minutes), Benaulim (₹15, 20 minutes) and Betul (₹20, 40 minutes) stop both at the Kadamba bus stand and at informal bus stops on the east and west sides of the Municipal Gardens. For Panaji (₹30), take any local bus to the Kadamba bus stand and change to a frequent express bus.

Daily AC state-run buses go to Mumbai (₹700, 16 hours), Pune (₹660, 13 hours) and Bengaluru (₹650, 13 hours). Non-AC buses are about one-third cheaper. Private long-distance buses depart from the stand opposite Kadamba. You'll find booking offices all over town; **Paulo Travels** (☎0832-2702405; www.paulobus.com; Padre Miranda Rd) is among the best.

TAXI & AUTORICKSHAW

Taxis are plentiful around the Municipal Gardens and Kadamba bus stand, and are a quick and comfortable way to reach any of Goa's beaches, including Palolem (₹1150), Calangute (₹1355), Anjuna (₹1500) and Arambol (₹1900). Prepaid taxi stands are at the train station and main bus stand.

For Colva and Benaulim, autorickshaws will happily do the trip for around ₹120.

TRAIN

Margao's well-organised train station (Madgaon on train timetables), 2km south of town, serves the Konkan Railway and local South Central Railways routes, and is the main hub for trains

MAJOR TRAINS FROM MARGAO (MAGDAON)

DESTINATION	TRAIN NO & NAME	FARE (₹)	DURATION (HR)	DEPARTURES
Bengaluru	02779 Vasco da Gama-SBC Link (D)	390/1025	15	3.50pm
Chennai (Madras); via Yesvantpur	17312 Vasco da Gama-Chennai Express (C)	475/1285/1865	21	3.20pm Thu
Delhi	12431 Rajdhani Express (A)	2765/3800	14½	10.10am
Ernakulam (Kochi)	12618 Lakshadweep Express (C)	445/1175/1665	14½	7.20pm
Mangalore	12133 Mangalore Express (C)	290/745/1035	5½	7.10am
Mumbai (Bombay)	10112 Konkan Kanya Express (C)	390/1065/1535	12	6pm
Pune	12779 Goa Express (C)	335/935/1325	12	3.50pm

Fares: (A) 3AC/2AC, (B) 2S/CC, (C) sleeper/3AC/2AC, (D) sleeper/3AC

WORTH A TRIP

HAMPI

The surreal ruins of the Vijayanagar empire at Hampi (p896), in Karnataka, are a popular detour or overnight trip from Goa. Hampi can be reached by train from Margao to Hospet on the VSG Howrah Express which departs at 7.10am Tuesday, Thursday, Friday and Saturday (sleeper/3AC/2AC ₹235/620/885, eight hours). More convenient are the overnight sleeper buses direct to Hampi from Margao and Panaji operated by Paulo Travels (₹800 to ₹1500, 10 to 11 hours, two to three daily).

from Mumbai to Goa and south to Kochi and beyond. Its **reservation hall** (☎0832-2712790; Train Station; ⏰8am-2pm & 2.15-8pm Mon-Sat, 8am-2pm Sun) is on the 1st floor; there's a foreign-tourist quota counter upstairs.

Outside the station you'll find a prepaid taxi stand. Taxis or autorickshaws to/from the town centre cost around ₹80.

Chandor

The small village Chandor, about 15km east of Margao, is an important stop for its collection of once-grand Portuguese mansions, exemplified by the wonderful Braganza House. It's a photogenic place, with fading but still grand facades and gables – many topped with typically Portuguese carved wooden roosters – and the looming white Nossa Senhora de Belem church.

Between the late 6th and mid-11th centuries Chandor was better known as Chandrapur, the most spectacular city on the Konkan coast. This was the grand seat of the ill-fated Kadamba dynasty until 1054, when the rulers moved to a new, broad-harboured site at Govepuri, at modern-day Goa Velha. When Govepuri was levelled by the Muslims in 1312, the Kadambas briefly moved their seat of power back to Chandrapur, though it was not long before Chandrapur itself was sacked in 1327, and then its glory days were finally, definitively, over.

Sights

Braganza House HISTORIC BUILDING

Braganza House, built in the 17th century and stretching along one whole side of Chandor's village square, is the biggest Portuguese mansion of its kind in Goa and the best example of what Goa's scores of once-grand and glorious mansions have today become. Granted the land by the King of Portugal, the Braganza family built this oversized house, which was later divided into the east and west wings when it was inherited by two sisters from the family.

Fernandes House HISTORIC BUILDING

(☎0832-2784245; donation ₹200; ⏰9am-6pm) A kilometre east past the church, and open to the public, is the Fernandes House, whose original building dates back more than 500 years, while the Portuguese section was tacked on by the Fernandes family in 1821. The secret basement hideaway, full of gun holes and with an escape tunnel to the river, was used by the family to flee attackers. Admission includes a guided tour.

Getting There & Away

Local buses run infrequently from Margao to Chandor (₹10, 30 minutes) but the best way to get here is with your own transport. A taxi from Margao should cost ₹400 round trip, including waiting time.

Colva

☎0832 / POP 10,200

Once a sleepy fishing village, and in the '60s a hang-out for hippies escaping the scene up at Anjuna, Colva is still the main town-resort along this stretch of coast, but these days it has lost any semblance of beach paradise. Travel a little way north or south, though, and you'll find some of the peace missing in central Colva.

Activities

Colva's beach entrance throngs with water-sports operators keen to sell you **parasailing** (₹1000), **jet skiing** (15 minutes single/double ₹400/600) and **dolphin-watching trips** (per person around ₹330). Rates are fixed, but ensure that life jackets are supplied.

Sleeping

Sam's Guesthouse HOTEL $

(☎0832-2788753; r ₹650; wi-fi) Away from the fray, north of Colva's main drag on the road running parallel to the beach, Sam's is a big, cheerful place with friendly owners and spacious rooms that are a steal at this price. Rooms are around a pleasant garden courtyard and there's a good restaurant and whacky 'cosy cave'. Wi-fi in the restaurant only.

La Ben HOTEL $
(☎0832-2788040; www.laben.net; Colva Beach Rd; r without/with AC ₹1100/1400; ❄📶) Neat, clean and not entirely devoid of atmosphere. If you're not desperately seeking anything with character, La Ben has decent, good-value rooms and has been around for ages. A great addition is the adjacent **Garden Restaurant** (mains ₹100-320; ⊙7-10am & 6-11pm; 📶).

★**Skylark Resort** HOTEL $$
(☎0832-2788052; www.skylarkresortgoa.com; d with AC ₹3350-4500, f ₹5000; ❄📶🏊) A serious step up from the budget places, Skylark's clean, fresh rooms are graced with bits and pieces of locally made teak furniture and block-print bedspreads, while the lovely pool makes a pleasant place to lounge. The best (and more expensive) rooms are those facing the pool.

Eating & Drinking

Sagar Kinara INDIAN $
(Colva Beach Rd; mains ₹70-190; ⊙7am-10.30pm) A pure-veg restaurant upstairs (nonveg is separate, downstairs) with tastes to please even committed carnivores, this place is clean, efficient and offers cheap and delicious North and South Indian cuisine all day.

★**Leda Lounge & Restaurant** BAR
(⊙7.30am-midnight) Part sports bar, part music venue, part cocktail bar, Leda is Colva's best nightspot by a long shot. There's live music from Thursday to Sunday, fancy drinks (Mojitos, Long Island iced teas) and good food at lunch and dinner.

Information

Colva has plenty of banks and ATMs, as well as the odd internet cafe and travel agent, strung along Colva Beach Rd.

Getting There & Away

Buses from Colva to Margao run roughly every 15 minutes (₹15, 20 minutes) from 7.30am to about 7pm, departing from the parking area at the end of the beach road. A taxi to Margao is ₹300.

Benaulim

☎0832

A long stretch of largely empty sand peppered with a few beach shacks and water-sports enthusiasts, the beaches of Benaulim and nearby Sernabatim are much quieter than Colva, partly because the village is a good kilometre back from the beach and linked by several laneways. Out of season there's a somewhat desolate feel, but the lack of traffic or serious beachfront development is an obvious attraction.

Most accommodation, eating options, grocery shops and pharmacies are concentrated along the Vasvaddo Beach Rd near the Maria Hall intersection.

Sights

★**Goa Chitra** MUSEUM
(☎0832-6570877; www.goachitra.com; St John the Baptist Rd, Mondo Vaddo; ₹300; ⊙9am-6pm Tue-Sun) Artist and restorer Victor Hugo Gomes first noticed the slow extinction of traditional objects – from farming tools to kitchen

IT'S A DOG'S LIFE

South Goa has two animal welfare shelters that welcome volunteers or visitors to help walk or play with rescued stray dogs.

The **Goa Animal Welfare Trust** (☎9763681525, 0832-2653677; www.gawt.org; Curchorem; ⊙9am-5.30pm Mon-Sat, 10am-1pm & 2.30-5pm), in the small inland town of Curchorem, works hard at providing veterinary help for sick animals, shelter for puppies and kittens, sterilisation programs for street dogs and low-cost veterinary care (including anti-rabies injections) for Goan pets. Volunteers are welcome, even just for a few hours on a single visit, to walk or play with the dogs. Items such as your old newspapers can be used for lining kennel floors, as can old sheets, towels and anything else you might not be taking home.

You can make contact with the shelter at the **Goa Animal Welfare Trust Shop** (☎0832-2653677; ⊙9.30am-1pm & 4-7pm Mon-Sat) in Colva, a charity shop selling souvenirs and secondhand books.

At Chapolim, a few kilometres northeast of Palolem Beach, the small **Animal Rescue Centre** (☎0832-2644171; Chapolim; ⊙10am-1pm & 2.30-5pm Mon-Sat) also takes in sick, injured or stray animals. Volunteers welcome. Look out for the sign on the road to Chaudi; it's about 2km north near the Chapolim dam.

DON'T MISS

COLA BEACH

Cola Beach is one of those hidden gems of the south coast – a relatively hard-to-reach crescent of sand enclosed by forested cliffs and with a gorgeous emerald lagoon stretching back from the beach.

It has been discovered of course and in November and April several hut and tent villages set up here, but it's still a beautiful place and popular with day trippers from Agonda and Palolem.

Further north around the headland is an even more remote beach known as **Khancola Beach**, or Kakolem, with one small resort reached via a steep set of jungly steps from the clifftop above.

utensils to altarpieces – as a child in Benaulim. He created this ethnographic museum from the more than 4000 cast-off objects that he collected from across the state over 20 years. Admission is via a one-hour guided tour, held on the hour. Goa Chitra is 3km east of Maria Hall – ask locally for directions.

San Thome Museum MUSEUM
(☎9822363917; www.goamuseum.com; Colva Rd; ₹200; ⊙9am-6pm) This quirky new museum, dubbed 'Back in Time', has three floors of carefully presented technology through the ages, from old cameras and typewriters to gramophones, clocks and projectors. Highlights include a Scheidmier grand piano, Raleigh bicycle and an anchor cast from the same pattern as the *Titanic*.

Sleeping

Lots of budget rooms for rent can be found along the roads towards Benaulim and Sernabatim Beach; the big five-stars are further south. The best of the budget beachfront accommodation is at Sernabatim Beach, a few hundred metres north of Benaulim.

D'Souza Guest House GUESTHOUSE $
(☎0832-2770583; d ₹600) With just three rooms, this traditional blue-painted house in the back lanes is run by a local Goan family and comes with bundles of homely atmosphere and a lovely garden. It's often full so book ahead.

Anthy's Guesthouse GUESTHOUSE $
(☎0832-2771680; anthysguesthouse@rediffmail.com; Sernabatim Beach; d ₹1500, with AC ₹1800; ❄📶) One of a handful of places lining Sernabatim Beach, Anthy's is a favourite with travellers for its good restaurant, book exchange and well-kept chalet-style rooms, which stretch back from the beach, surrounded by a garden. Ayurvedic massage is available.

★ **Blue Corner** HUT $$
(☎9850455770; www.bluecornergoa.com; huts ₹1200; 📶) Behind the beach shack restaurant a short walk north of the main beach entrance, this group of sturdy palm-thatch cocohuts – not so common around here – are the best in Benaulim, with fan and verandah. The restaurant gets good reviews from guests.

Taj Exotica HOTEL $$$
(☎0832-6683333; www.tajhotels.com; d ₹17,000-28,000; ❄@🏊) Bollywood stars and sheiks are known to stay at the Taj Exotica, one of Goa's plushest resorts. Set in 23 hectares of tropical gardens 2km south of Benaulim, it has all the spas, restaurants and pools that you would expect. Most travellers will be content to visit its swish restaurants, including the Goan cuisine of Allegria and the beachfront Lobster Shack.

Eating & Drinking

Cafe Malibu INDIAN $
(mains ₹110-200; ⊙8am-11pm) This unpretentious little family-run cafe offers a nice dining experience in its roadside garden setting on a back lane a short walk back from the beach. It does a good job of Goan specialities as well as Indian and continental dishes.

Pedro's Bar & Restaurant MULTICUISINE $$
(Vasvaddo Beach Rd; mains ₹120-360; ⊙7am-midnight; 📶) Set amid a large, shady garden on the beachfront and popular with local and international travellers, Pedro's offers standard Indian, Chinese and Italian dishes, as well as Goan choices and 'sizzlers'.

Club Zoya CLUB
(☎9822661388; www.clubzoya.com; ⊙from 8pm) The party scene has hit sleepy little Benaulim in the form of barn-sized Club Zoya, with international DJs, big light shows and a cocktail bar featuring speciality flavoured and infused vodka drinks. Something is on most nights here in season but check the website for upcoming events and DJs.

Transport

Buses from Margao to Benaulim are frequent (₹15, 15 minutes). Buses stop at the Maria Hall crossroads, or at the junctions to Sernabatim or Taj Exotica (ask to be let off). From Maria Hall, autorickshaws cost ₹60 for the five-minute ride to the sea.

Agonda

0832 / POP 3800

Travellers have been drifting to Agonda for years and seasonal hut villages – some very luxurious – now occupy almost all available beachfront space, but it's still more low-key than Palolem and a good choice if you're after some beachy relaxation. The coast road between Betul and Palolem passes through Agonda village, while the main traveller centre is a single lane running parallel behind the beach.

Sights & Activities

Agonda Beach is a fine 2km stretch of white sand framed between two forested headlands. The surf can be fierce and swimming is not as safe as at Palolem, but lifeguards are on patrol. Olive ridley marine turtles nest (and are protected) at the northern end in winter.

South of Agonda are pretty **Honeymoon Beach** and then **Butterfly Beach** (from ₹1700), both accessible on foot or by boat (but there are no facilities).

Lots of local and foreigner-run yoga, meditation and ayurveda courses and classes set up in season. Local boats can take you on dolphin-spotting trips.

Aloha Surf School SURFING

(7507582933; 1hr/2hr/full day board rental ₹300/500/1500, lesson from ₹1500; 8am-6pm) The first surf school in Goa's deep south, Aloha is run by a passionate local crew. Learn to surf on Agonda's gentle waves or hire a board.

Sleeping

Agonda has gone seriously upmarket in its beach-hut operations in recent years, with the best beachfront resorts offering air-con, TV and giant open-sky bathrooms and all with a restaurant and bar, usually beach-facing. As with any seasonal accommodation, standards and ownership can change.

Back from the beach on the parallel road are a few cheaper guesthouses and rooms to let.

Fatima Guesthouse GUESTHOUSE $

(0832-2647477; www.fatimasguesthouse.com; d ₹1000-1500, with AC ₹1500-2500;) An ever-popular budget guesthouse set back from the beach, with clean rooms, a good restaurant and obliging staff. Rooftop yoga classes in season.

★ **Agonda White Sand** HUT $$

(9823548277; www.agondawhitesand.com; Agonda Beach; hut from ₹4200-5200;) Beautifully designed and constructed cottages with open-air bathrooms and spring mattresses surround a central bar and restaurant at this stylish beachfront place.

Chattai HUT $$

(9423812287; www.chattai.co.in; hut ₹2100) Overlooking the north end of the beach, Chattai offers lovely, airy huts on the sands, and popular yoga classes under its secluded Yoga Dome.

H2O Agonda HUT $$$

(9423836994; www.h2oagonda.com; d incl breakfast ₹4500-6500;) With its purple and mauve muslin curtains and Arabian nights ambience, H2O is among the most impressive of Agonda's luxury cottage setups. From the hotel-style reception, walk through a leafy garden to the spacious cottages with air-con and enormous open-air bathrooms. The more expensive sea-facing cottages with king-size beds may be worth paying extra for.

Eating

★ **Blue Planet Cafe** VEGAN $$

(0832-2647448; mains ₹110-250; 9.30am-3pm & 6.30-9pm) With a soul-food and healthy vibe and a small, mostly vegan menu, Blue Planet is a welcoming detox from the beach scene. The menu offers salads, smoothies and innovative veg dishes. It's in an off-track jungle location about 2km from Agonda village (follow the signs off the main Agonda–Palolem road).

Kopi Desa EUROPEAN $$

(7767831487; mains ₹120-450; 8am-11pm) The name translates from Indonesian as 'coffee village' but this new expat restaurant and cocktail bar is making waves with its imaginative Euro-centric menu and live music.

Getting There & Away

Scooters and motorbikes can be rented from places on the beach road for around ₹300/400. Autorickshaws depart from the main T-junction near Agonda's church to Palolem (₹250) and Patnem (₹300). Taxis are around ₹50 more.

Local buses run from Chaudi sporadically throughout the day (₹12), but ask for Agonda Beach, otherwise you'll be let off in the village about 1km away.

Palolem

☎0832 / POP 12,440

Palolem is undoubtedly one of Goa's most postcard-perfect beaches: a gentle curve of palm-fringed sand facing a calm bay. But in season the beachfront is transformed into a toytown of colourful and increasingly sophisticated timber and bamboo huts fronted by palm-thatch restaurants. It's still a great place to be and is popular with backpackers, long-stayers and families. The protected bay is one of the safest swimming spots in Goa and you can comfortably kayak and paddleboard for hours here.

Away from the beach you can learn to cook, drop in to yoga classes or hire a motorbike and cruise to surrounding beaches, waterfalls and wildlife parks.

Activities

Palolem offers no shortage of yoga, reiki and meditation classes in season. Locations and teachers tend to change seasonally – ask around locally to see whose hands-on healing powers are hot this season.

Palolem's calm waters are perfect for **kayaking** and **stand-up paddleboarding**. Kayaks are available for hire for around ₹150 per hour, paddleboards for ₹500. **Mountain bikes** (₹100 per day) can be hired from **Seema Bike Hire** (Ourem Rd).

Local fishermen will take you on dolphin-spotting and fishing expeditions on their outrigger boats. They charge a minimum of ₹1200, or ₹1600 for four or more people, for a one-hour trip. They also do trips to nearby Butterfly and Honeymoon Beaches, or Agonda and Cola Beaches.

★Goa Jungle Adventure OUTDOORS

(☎9850485641; www.goajungle.com; trekking & canyoning trips ₹2090-3990; ⊙Oct-May) This adventure company, run by experienced French guide Manu, will take you out for thrilling trekking and canyoning trips in the Netravali area at the base of the Western Ghats, where you can climb, jump and abseil into remote waterfilled plunges. Trips run from a half-day to several days, and extended rafting trips into Karnataka are also sometimes offered.

Courses

Rahul's Cooking Class COOKING

(☎07875990647; www.rahulcookingclass.com; Palolem Beach Rd; per person ₹1500; ⊙11am-2pm & 6-9pm) Rahul's is one of the original cooking schools, with three-hour morning and afternoon classes each day. Prepare five dishes including chapati and coconut curry. Minimum two people; book at least one day in advance.

Masala Kitchen COOKING

(per person ₹1000) Well-established cooking classes; enquire at the Butterfly Book Shop (p849) and book a day in advance.

Sleeping

Most of Palolem's accommodation is of the seasonal beach-hut variety, though there are plenty of old-fashioned guesthouses or family homes with rooms to rent back from the beach. It's still possible to find a basic palm-thatch hut or plywood cottage somewhere near the beach for as little as ₹800, but many of the huts these days are more thoughtfully designed – the very best have air-con, flat-screen TV and sea-facing balcony.

Travellers Blues Bus HOSTEL $

(☎9665510281; Ourem Rd; dm ₹300-500, d ₹2000-2500; ❄📶) There's a blue-and-white Kombi parked in the open-air bar and travellers handing around a guitar. The atmosphere is chilled at TBB, an excellent new hostel just off the beach. Spotless four- to 10-bed dorms (no bunks), private rooms and seasonal huts are all good value.

Sevas HUT $

(☎9422065437; www.sevaspalolemgoa.com; d hut ₹800, family cottage ₹1800; @📶) Hidden in the jungle on the Colomb Bay side of Palolem, Sevas has a range of simple palm-thatch huts with open-air bathrooms and larger family huts and rooms set in a lovely shaded garden area.

★Ciaran's HUT $$

(☎0832-2643477; www.ciarans.com; hut incl breakfast ₹3000-3500, r with AC ₹4500; ❄📶) Ciaran's has some of the most impressive huts on the beachfront. Affable owner John has worked hard over the years to maintain a high standard and his beautifully designed cottages around a plant-filled garden and pond are top-notch. There's a popular multi-cuisine restaurant, tapas restaurant and quality **massage and spa centre** (1hr massage from ₹1900).

Palolem

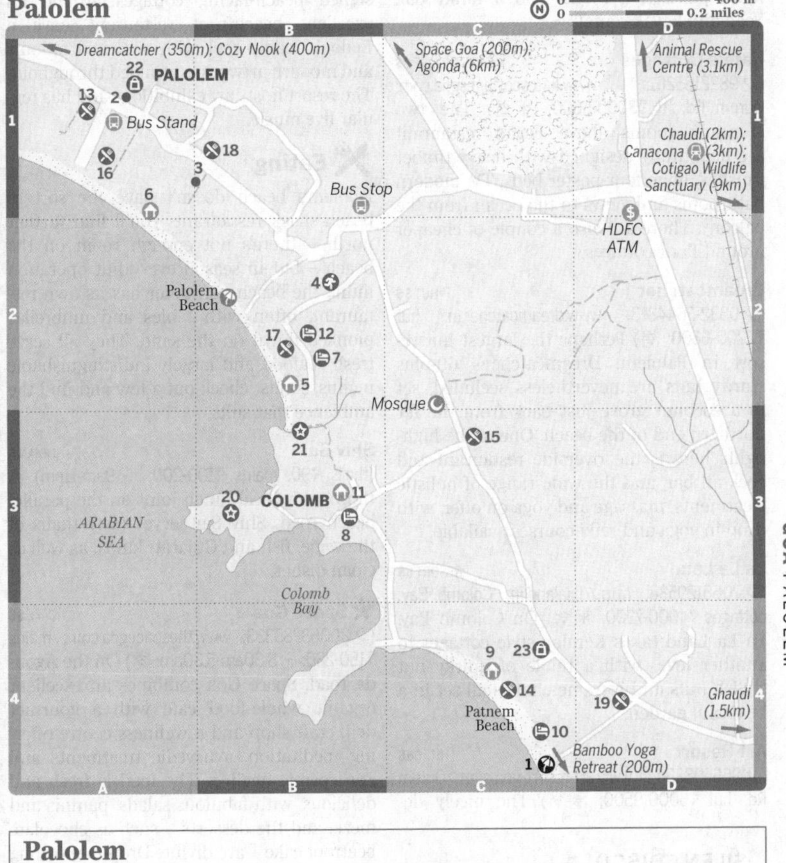

Palolem

Sights
1 Patnem Beach C4

Activities, Courses & Tours
Humming Bird Spa .... (see 6)
2 Masala Kitchen A1
3 Rahul's Cooking Class B1
4 Seema Bike Hire B2

Sleeping
5 Art Resort B2
6 Ciaran's A1
7 Kate's Cottages B2
8 La La Land B3
9 Micky's C4
10 Papaya's C4
11 Sevas B3
12 Travellers Blues Bus B2

Eating
13 Café Inn A1
14 Home C4
Jaali Cafe .... (see 23)
15 Karma Cafe & Bakery C3
16 Magic Italy A1
17 Ourem 88 .... B2
18 Shiv Sai B1
19 Zest Patnem D4

Entertainment
20 Neptune Point Headphone Disco B3
21 Silent Noise B3

Shopping
22 Butterfly Book Shop A1
23 Jaali C4

★ **Cozy Nook** HUT $$
(9822584760, 0832-2643550; www.cozynookgoa.com; hut ₹2500-3500) Long-running Cozy Nook, at the northern end of the beach, has some well-designed cottages including two-storey pads, upstairs chill-out deck,

more pedestrian rooms and a funky bar. Yoga and kayak rental.

Kate's Cottages GUESTHOUSE **$$**
(9822165261; www.katescottagesgoa.com; Ourem Rd; d ₹3000-5000;) The two stunning rooms above Fern's restaurant are beautifully designed with heavy timber finishes, huge four-poster beds, TV, modern bathrooms and views to the ocean from the balcony. There are also a couple of cheaper ground-floor cottages.

Dreamcatcher HUT **$$**
(0832-2644873; www.dreamcatcher.in; hut ₹2200-6600;) Perhaps the largest hut resort in Palolem, Dreamcatcher's 60-plus sturdy huts are nevertheless secluded, set in a coconut grove just back from the far northern end of the beach. One of the highlights here is the riverside restaurant and cocktail bar, and the wide range of holistic treatments, massage and yoga on offer, with drop-in yoga and reiki courses available.

La La Land RESORT **$$**
(7066129588; http://lalaland.in; Colomb Bay; cottages ₹4000-7200;) On Colomb Bay, La La Land takes Keralan-style cottages to another level with a range of quirky but stylish huts and A-frame chalets all set in a beautiful garden.

Art Resort HUT **$$$**
(9665982344; www.art-resort-goa.com; Ourem Rd; hut ₹6000-9500;) The nicely designed beach-facing cottages around an excellent beachfront restaurant have a Bedouin camp feel with screened sit-outs and modern artworks sprinkled throughout. The resort hosts art exhibitions and has regular live music.

SILENT DISCO

Neatly sidestepping Goa's statewide ban on loud music in open spaces after 10pm, Palolem's 'silent parties' are the way to dance the night away without upsetting the neighbours.

Turn up around 10pm, don your headphones with a choice of two or three channels featuring Goan and international DJs playing trance, house, hip hop, electro and funk, and then party the night away in inner bliss but outer silence. At the time of research there were two headphone parties in Palolem:

Silent Noise (www.silentnoise.in; On the Rocks; cover charge ₹600; 9pm-4am Sat Nov-Apr)

Neptune Point (www.neptunepoint.com; Neptune's Point, Colomb Bay; cover charge ₹600; 9.30am-4am Sat Nov-Apr)

Eating

Palolem's beach doesn't have the sort of beach shack restaurants you'll find further north – there's not enough room on the beach – but in season every hut operation lining the beach perimeter has its own restaurant, often with tables and umbrellas plonked down on the sand. They all serve fresh seafood and largely indistinguishable menus, so just check out a few and find the ambience that suits.

Shiv Sai INDIAN **$**
(thalis ₹90, mains ₹100-200; 9am-11pm) A thoroughly local lunch joint on the parallel beach road, Shiv Sai serves tasty thalis of the vegie, fish and Gujarati kinds, as well as Goan dishes.

★ **Space Goa** CAFE **$$**
(80063283333; www.thespacegoa.com; mains ₹150-280; 8.30am-5.30pm;) On the Agonda road, Space Goa combines an excellent organic whole-food cafe with a gourmet deli, craft shop and a wellness centre offering meditation, ayurvedic treatments and Zen cosmic healing. The food is fresh and delicious, with fabulous salads, paninis and meze, and the desserts – such as chocolate beetroot cake – are divine. Drop-in morning yoga classes are ₹500.

★ **Magic Italy** ITALIAN **$$**
(8805767705; Palolem Beach Rd; mains ₹260-480; 5pm-midnight) On the main beach road, Magic Italy has been around for a while and the quality of its pizza and pasta remains high, with imported Italian ingredients like ham, salami, cheese and olive oil, imaginative wood-fired pizzas and homemade pasta. Sit at tables, or Arabian-style on floor cushions. The atmosphere is busy but chilled.

Café Inn CAFE **$$**
(7507322799; Palolem Beach Rd; mains ₹100-450; 8am-11pm;) If you're craving a cappuccino or a rum-infused slushie, semi-open-air Café Inn, which grinds its own blend of beans to perfection, is one of Palolem's favourite hang-outs – and it's not even on the beach. Breakfasts are filling, and

WORTH A TRIP

DAY-TRIPPING DOWN SOUTH

Goa's far south is tailor-made for day-tripping. Hire a motorbike or charter a taxi and try these road trips from Palolem, Patnem or Agonda.

Tanshikar Spice Farm (☎0832-2608358, 9421184114; www.tanshikarspicefarm.com; Netravali; tour incl lunch ₹500; ⏲10am-4pm) About 35km inland from Palolem via forest and farms is this excellent spice plantation, along with jungle treks to waterfalls and the enigmatic 'bubble lake'.

Talpona & Galgibag These two near-deserted beach gems are scenically framed (naturally) by the Talpona and Galgibag Rivers. Olive ridley turtles nest on Galgibag and there are a couple of excellent shack restaurants and huts. The winding country drive here is half the fun.

Polem Beach Goa's most southerly beach, 25km south of Palolem, has just one set of beach huts and a real castaway feel. A trip here should be combined with the detour to Talpona and Galgibag.

comfort-food burgers and panini sandwiches hit the spot.

★**Ourem 88** FUSION $$$
(☎8698827679; mains ₹540-750; ⏲6-10pm Tue-Sun) British-run Ourem 88 is a gastro sensation with just a handful of tables and a small but masterful menu. Try baked brie, tender calamari stuffed with Goan sausage, braised lamb shank or fluffy souffle. Worth a splurge.

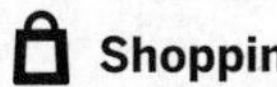

Drinking & Nightlife

Leopard Valley CLUB
(www.leopardvalley.com; Palolem-Agonda Rd; entry from ₹600; ⏲9pm-4am Fri) South Goa's biggest outdoor dance club is a sight (and sound) to behold, with 3D laser light shows, pyrotechnics and state-of-the-art sound systems blasting local and international DJs on Friday nights. It's in an isolated but easily reached location between Palolem and Agonda.

Shopping

Butterfly Book Shop BOOKS
(☎9341738801; ⏲10am-1pm & 3-8pm) The best of several good bookshops in town, this cosy place stocks best sellers, classics, and a good range of books on yoga, meditation and spirituality. This is also the contact for yoga classes and cooking courses (p846).

Getting There & Around

Frequent buses run to nearby Chaudi (₹7) from the **bus stop** on the corner of the road down to the beach. Hourly buses to Margao (₹40, one hour) depart from the same place, though these usually go via Chaudi anyway. From Chaudi you can pick up regular buses to Margao, from where you can change for Panaji, or south to Polem Beach and Karwar in Karnataka.

The closest train station is Canacona, 2km from Palolem's beach entrance.

An autorickshaw from Palolem to Patnem should cost ₹100, or ₹150 to Chaudi. A taxi to Dabolim Airport is around ₹1500.

Scooters and motorbikes can be hired on the main road leading to the beach from around ₹300.

Patnem

☎0832

Smaller and less crowded than neighbouring Palolem, pretty Patnem makes a much quieter and more family-friendly alternative. The waters aren't as calm and protected as Palolem's, but relaxed **Patnem Beach** is patrolled by lifeguards and safe for paddling. It's easy enough to walk around the northern headland to Colomb Bay and on to Palolem.

Sleeping

Long-stayers will revel in Patnem's choice of village homes and apartments available for rent from ₹10,000 to ₹40,000 per month. There are a dozen or so beach-hut operations lining the sands; many change annually, so walk along to find your perfect spot.

Micky's HUT $
(☎9850484884; www.mickyhuts.com; Patnem Beach; d ₹800-1000; 📶) Micky's is an old-timer at the north end of Patnem Beach with a range of simple budget huts (some without

attached bath) and rooms. It's run by a friendly family and open for most of the year. There's a cruisy beachfront bar and cafe.

Papaya's COTTAGE $$
(☎9923079447; www.papayasgoa.com; hut ₹2000-3000, with AC ₹5000; ❄📶) Solid huts constructed with natural materials head back into the palm grove from Papaya's popular restaurant, which does great versions of all the beachfront classics. Each hut is lovingly built, with lots of wood, four-poster beds and floating muslin.

Bamboo Yoga Retreat HUT $$$
(☎9637567730; www.bamboo-yoga-retreat.com; s/d from ₹6500/10,000; 📶) This laid-back yoga retreat, exclusive to guests, has a wonderful open-sided *shala* facing the ocean at the southern end of Patnem Beach, and three more *shalas* among the village of comfortable timber and thatched huts. Yoga holiday rates include brunch, meditation and two daily yoga classes, but there are also training courses and ayurvedic treatments.

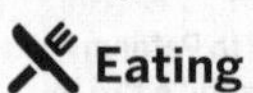

Eating

Karma Cafe & Bakery CAFE $
(☎9764504253; Patnem Rd, Colomb; baked goods from ₹60; ⏲7.30am-6pm; 📶) Pull up a cushion at this chilled cafe and bakery opposite the Colomb road and delve into a superb range of fresh baked breads, yak cheese croissants and pastries as well as coffee and smoothies.

★ **Jaali Cafe** CAFE $$
(☎8007712248; small plates ₹150-250; ⏲9am-6pm Tue-Sun, dinner Thu-Sat) The menu at this lovely garden cafe is something special with a delicious range of tapas-style Middle Eastern and Mediterranean plates – choose two or three dishes each and share. Sunday brunch is a popular event with local expats. There's also an excellent **boutique** (⏲9.30am-6.30pm) and a highly regarded massage therapist on-hand.

Home INTERNATIONAL $$
(☎0832-2643916; www.homeispatnem.com; Patnem Beach; mains ₹120-300; ⏲8am-10pm; 📶) Standing out from the beach shacks like a beacon, this bright white, relaxed vegetarian restaurant serves up good breakfasts, pastas, risotto and salads. A highlight here is the dessert menu – awesome chocolate brownies, apple tart and cheesecake. Home also rents out eight nicely decorated, light rooms (from ₹1800).

Zest Patnem CAFE $$
(☎8806607919; mains ₹190-320; ⏲8am-8pm; 📶🌿) Bowls of pad Thai, plates of meze or sushi and Mexican dishes, all freshly prepared, make Zest a popular hang-out. With similar cafes in Palolem and Agonda, they're certainly doing something right among the beach-loving, health-conscious crowd.

ℹ Getting There & Away

The main entrance to Patnem Beach is reached from the country lane running south from Palolem, then turning right at the Hotel Sea View. Alternatively, walk about 20 minutes along the path from Palolem via Colomb Bay, or catch a bus heading south (₹5). An autorickshaw charges around ₹100 from Palolem.

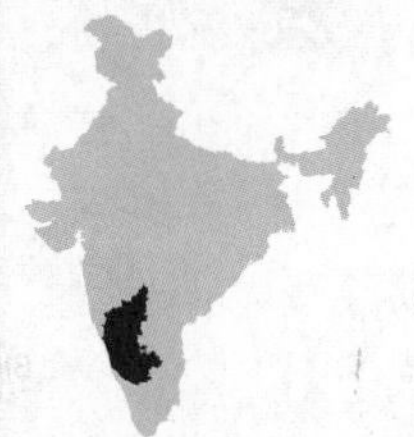

Karnataka & Bengaluru

Includes ➡

Best Places to Eat

- Karavalli (p861)
- Mavalli Tiffin Rooms (p861)
- Vinayaka Mylari (p875)
- Lalith Bar & Restaurant (p887)
- Fatty Bao (p861)

Best Places to Sleep

- Uramma Cottage (p903)
- Electric Cats B&B (p859)
- Dhole's Den (p879)
- Honey Valley Estate (p883)

Why Go?

A stunning introduction to southern India, Karnataka is a prosperous, compelling state loaded with a winning blend of urban cool, glittering palaces, national parks, ancient ruins, beaches, yoga centres and legendary hang-outs.

At its nerve centre is the capital Bengaluru (Bangalore), a progressive city famous for its craft beer and restaurant scene. Heading out of town you'll encounter the evergreen rolling hills of Kodagu, dotted with spice and coffee plantations, the regal splendour of Mysuru (Mysore), and jungles teeming with monkeys, tigers and Asia's biggest population of elephants.

If that all sounds too mainstream, head to the countercultural enclave of tranquil Hampi with hammocks, psychedelic sunsets and boulder-strewn ruins. Or the blissful, virtually untouched coastline around Gokarna, blessed with beautiful coves and empty sands. Or leave the tourist trail behind entirely, and take a journey to the evocative Islamic ruins of northern Karnataka.

When to Go

Bengaluru

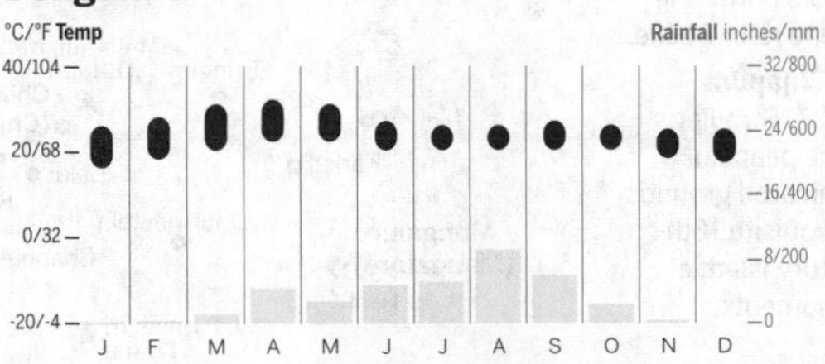

Mar–May The best season to watch tigers and elephants in Karnataka's pristine national parks.

Oct Mysuru's Dussehra (Dasara) carnival brings night-long celebrations and a jumbo parade.

Dec & Jan The coolest time to explore Hampi and the northern forts, palaces, caves and temples.

Karnataka & Bengaluru Highlights

1 **Hampi** (p896) Soaking up the surreal landscapes, sociable travellers' scene and epic ruins in this magical, evocative destination.

2 **Gokarna** (p893) Searching for the perfect cove beach in this low-key coastal hideaway, then touring its atmospheric temples.

3 **Bengaluru** (p853) Sampling craft beers, dining out in style and enjoying the museums and sights of this cosmopolitan city.

4 **Kodagu** (p881) Savouring aromatic coffee and hiking trails in these temperate, evergreen highlands.

5 **Mysuru Palace** (p868) Getting bowled over by one of India's most grandiose structures and touring its glittering halls.

6 **Nagarhole National Park** (p880) Spying on lazy tuskers in the forests bordering serene Kabini Lake.

7 **Vijapura** (p907) Strolling in the peaceful manicured grounds of exquisite 16th-century Islamic monuments.

History

A rambling playing field of religions, cultures and kingdoms, the Karnataka region has been ruled by a string of charismatic rulers through history. India's first great emperor, Chandragupta Maurya, made the Karnataka area his retreat when he embraced Jainism at Sravanabelagola in the 3rd century BC. From the 6th to the 14th centuries, the land was under a series of dynasties such as the Chalukyas, Cholas, Gangas and Hoysalas, who left a lasting mark in the form of stunning cave shrines and temples across the state.

In 1327 Mohammed Tughlaq's army sacked Halebid. In 1347 Hasan Gangu, a Persian general in Tughlaq's army, led a rebellion to establish the Bahmani kingdom, which was later subdivided into five Deccan sultanates. Meanwhile, the Hindu kingdom of Vijayanagar, with its capital in Hampi, rose to prominence. Having peaked in the early 1550s, it fell in 1565 to a combined effort of the sultanates.

In subsequent years the Hindu Wodeyars of Mysuru grew in stature and extended their rule over a large part of southern India. They remained largely unchallenged until 1761, when Hyder Ali (one of their generals) deposed them. Backed by the French, Hyder Ali and his son Tipu Sultan set up capital in Srirangapatna and consolidated their rule. However, in 1799 the British defeated Tipu Sultan and reinstated the Wodeyars. Historically, this battle consolidated British territorial expansion in southern India.

Mysuru remained under the Wodeyars until Independence – post-1947, the reigning maharaja became the first governor. The state boundaries were redrawn along linguistic lines in 1956 and the extended Kannada-speaking state of Mysore was born. It was renamed Karnataka in 1972, with Bangalore (now Bengaluru) as the capital.

SOUTHERN KARNATAKA

Bengaluru (Bangalore)

080 / POP 11.5 MILLION / ELEV 920M

Cosmopolitan Bengaluru (formerly Bangalore) is one of India's most progressive and developed cities, blessed with a benevolent climate and a burgeoning drinking, dining and shopping scene. Yes, its creature comforts are a godsend to the weary traveller who has done the hard yards and it's a great city for mixing with locals in craft beer joints or quirky independent cafes. Though there are no world-class sights, you'll find lovely parks and striking Victorian-era architecture.

The past decade has seen a mad surge of development, coupled with traffic congestion

TOP STATE FESTIVALS

Udupi Paryaya (Jan/Feb) Held even-numbered years, with a procession and ritual marking the handover of swamis at Udupi's Krishna Temple in January.

Classical Dance Festival (Jan/Feb) Some of India's best classical dance performances take place in Pattadakal.

Vijaya Utsav (p896) A three-day extravaganza of culture, heritage and the arts in Hampi.

Tibetan New Year (Jan/Feb) Lamas in Tibetan refugee settlements in Bylakuppe take shifts leading nonstop prayers that span the weeklong celebrations.

Vairamudi Festival (Mar/Apr) Lord Vishnu is adorned with jewels at Cheluvanarayana Temple in Melkote, including a diamond-studded crown belonging to Mysore's former maharajas, attracting 400,000 pilgrims.

Ganesh Chaturthi (Sep) Families march their Ganesh idols to the sea in Gokarna at sunset in September.

Dussehra (p869) Mysuru Palace is lit up in the evenings and a vibrant procession hits town to the delight of thousands.

Lakshadeepotsava (p888) Thousands and thousands of lamps light up the Jain pilgrimage town of Dharmasthala in November, offering spectacular photo ops.

Huthri (Nov/Dec) The Kodava community in Madikeri celebrates the start of the harvesting season with ceremony, music, traditional dances and much feasting for a week.

Bengaluru (Bangalore)

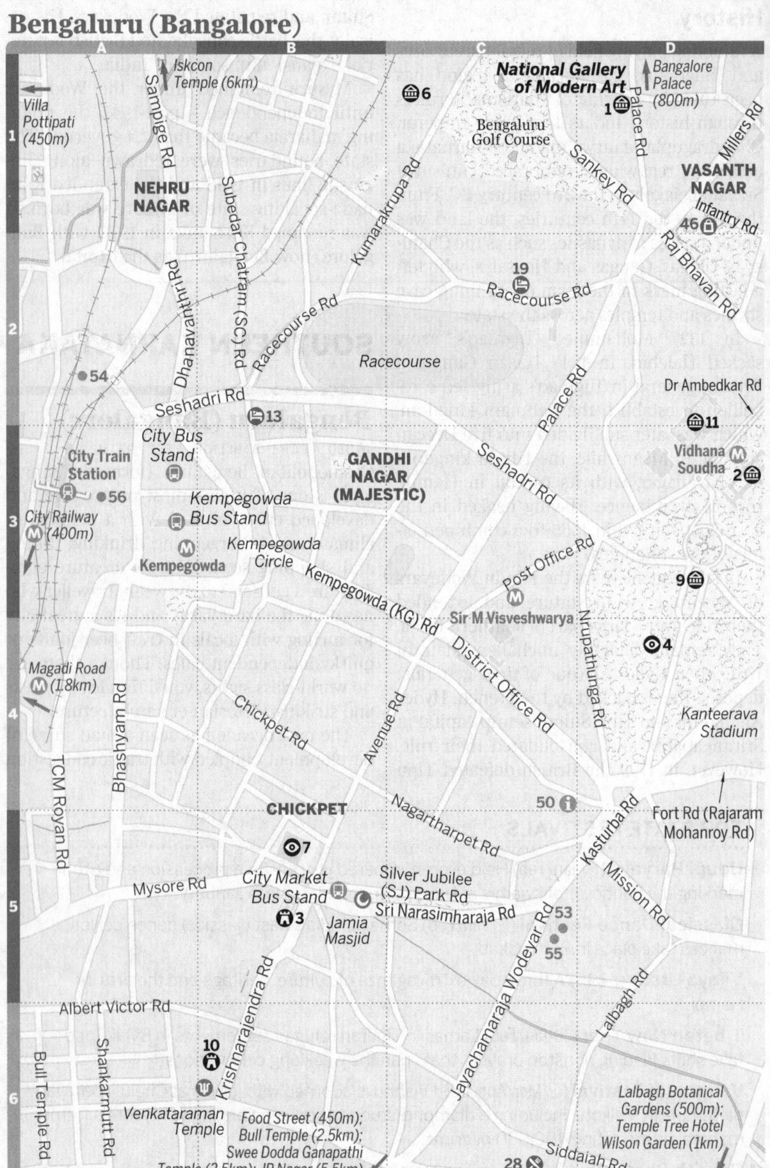

and rising pollution levels. But the central district (dating back to the British Raj years) remains little changed, and the landmark corporate HQs and business parks of the city's booming IT industry are mostly in the outer suburbs.

History

Literally meaning 'Town of Boiled Beans', Bengaluru supposedly derived its name from an ancient incident involving an old village woman who served cooked pulses to a lost and hungry Hoysala king. Kempegowda, a

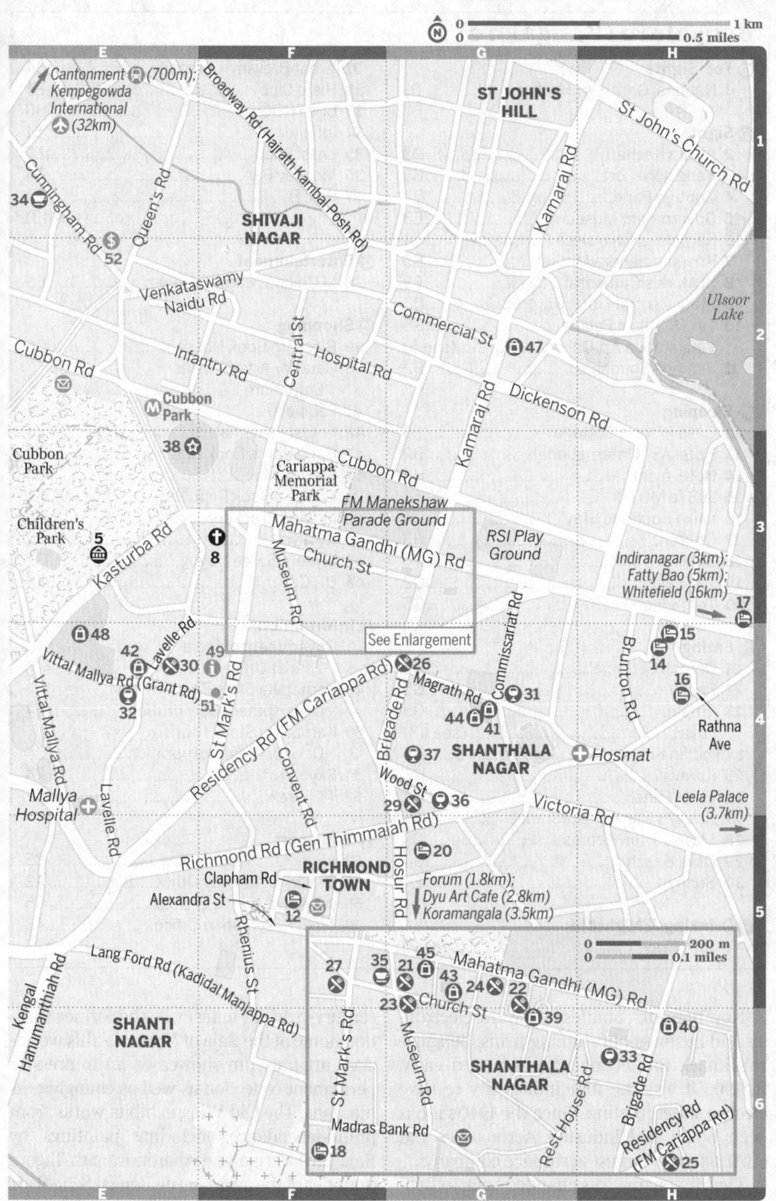

feudal lord, was the first person to mark out Bengaluru's extents by building a mud fort in 1537. The town remained obscure until 1759, when it was gifted to Hyder Ali.

The British arrived in 1809 and made it their regional administrative base in 1831, renaming it Bangalore. During the Raj era the city played host to many a British officer, including Winston Churchill, who enjoyed life here during his greener years and famously left a debt (still on the books) of ₹13 at the Bangalore Club.

Bengaluru (Bangalore)

Top Sights
1 National Gallery of Modern Art D1

Sights
2 Attara Kacheri D3
3 Bangalore Fort B5
4 Cubbon Park D4
5 Government Museum E3
6 Karnataka Chitrakala Parishath C1
7 Krishnarajendra Market B5
8 St Mark's Cathedral F3
9 State Central Library D3
10 Tipu Sultan's Palace B6
Venkatappa Art Gallery .... (see 5)
11 Vidhana Soudha D2

Sleeping
12 Casa Piccola Cottage F5
13 Hotel ABM International B2
14 Hotel Ajantha H4
15 JüSTa MG Rd H4
16 Laika Boutique Stay H4
17 Oberoi H3
18 St Mark's Inn F6
19 Taj West End C2
20 Tom's Hotel G5

Eating
21 Church St Social G5
22 Ebony G5
23 Empire G5
Fava .... (see 48)
24 Indian Kitchen G5
25 Karavalli H6
26 Khan Saheb G4
27 Koshy's Bar & Restaurant F5
28 Mavalli Tiffin Rooms C6
29 Olive Beach G4
30 Sunny's E4

Drinking & Nightlife
13th Floor .... (see 22)
31 Arbor Brewing Company G4
32 Biere Club E4
33 blueFROG H6
34 Infinitea E1
35 Lassi Shop F5
36 Monkey Bar G4
37 Plan B G4
Shiro .... (see 48)

Entertainment
38 M Chinnaswamy Stadium E3

Shopping
39 Blossom Book House G6
40 Cauvery Arts & Crafts Emporium H6
41 Fabindia G4
42 Forest Essentials E4
43 Gangarams Book Bureau G5
44 Garuda Mall G4
Goobe's Book Republic .... (see 35)
45 Indiana Crockery G5
46 Kynkyny Art Gallery D1
47 Mysore Saree Udyog G2
48 UB City E4

Information
Government of India Tourist Office .... (see 43)
49 Karnataka State Tourism Development Corporation F4
50 Karnataka State Tourism Development Corporation C4
51 Skyway F4
52 TT Forex E2

Transport
53 Air India C5
54 Divisional Railway Office A2
55 Jet Airways C5
56 Train Reservation Office A3

Now home to countless software, electronics and business-outsourcing firms, Bengaluru's knack for technology developed early. In 1905 it was the first Indian city to have electric street lighting. Since the 1940s it has been home to Hindustan Aeronautics Ltd (HAL), India's largest aerospace company.

The city's name was changed back to Bengaluru in November 2006, though few care to use it in practice.

Sights

★National Gallery of Modern Art GALLERY
(NGMA; ☎080-22342338; www.ngmaindia.gov.in/ngma_bangaluru.asp; 49 Palace Rd; Indian/foreigner ₹20/500; ⊙10am-5pm Tue-Sun) Housed in a century-year-old mansion – the former vacation home of the Raja of Mysuru – this world-class art museum showcases an impressive permanent collection as well as changing exhibitions. The Old Wing exhibits works from pre-Independence, including paintings by Raja Ravi Varma and Abanindranath Tagore (founder of the avant-garde Bengal School art movement). Interconnected by a walk bridge, the sleek New Wing focuses on contemporary post-Independence works by artists including Sudhir Patwardhan and Vivan Sundaram.

Karnataka Chitrakala Parishath GALLERY
(www.karnatakachitrakalaparishath.com; Kumarakrupa Rd; ₹50; ⊙10am-7.30pm Mon-Sat) A superb gallery with a wide range of Indian and

international contemporary art, as well as permanent displays of Mysuru-style paintings and folk and tribal art from across Asia. A section is devoted to the works of Russian master Nicholas Roerich, known for his vivid paintings of the Himalaya, and the Pan Indian Panorama collection, which includes progressive art from SG Vasudev and Yusuf Arakkal.

★ Cubbon Park GARDENS

(www.horticulture.kar.nic.in/cubbon.htm; Kasturba Rd; Ⓜ Cubbon Park) In the heart of Bengaluru's business district is Cubbon Park, a well-maintained 120-hectare garden where Bengaluru's residents converge to steal a moment from the rat race that rages outside. The gardens encompass the red-painted Gothic-style **State Central Library**. Unfortunately, Cubbon is not completely closed to traffic, except on Sundays when there are concerts, fun runs, yoga and even a small farmers market.

Other wonderful colonial architecture around the park includes the colossal neo-Dravidian-style **Vidhana Soudha** (Dr Ambedkar Rd; Ⓜ Vidhana Soudha), built in 1954 and which serves as the legislative chambers of the state government, and neoclassical **Attara Kacheri** (High Court) built in 1864 and housing the High Court. The latter two are closed to the public.

Government Museum MUSEUM

(Kasturba Rd; ₹4; ⏲10am-5pm Tue-Sun, closed every 2nd Sat; Ⓜ Cubbon Park) In a beautiful red colonial-era building dating from 1877, you'll find a dusty, neglected collection of ancient stone carvings and artefacts excavated from Halebid, Hampi and Attriampakham. Your ticket also gets you into the **Venkatappa Art Gallery** (Kasturba Rd; ⏲10am-5pm Tue-Sun; Ⓜ Cubbon Park) FREE next door, where you can see works and personal memorabilia of K Venkatappa (1887–1962), court painter to the Wodeyars (the former maharajas of the state).

St Mark's Cathedral CHURCH

(www.saintmarks.in; MG Rd; Ⓜ MG Rd) Atmospheric cathedral built in 1812 with a distinct domed roof based on St Paul's Cathedral. Check out the entrance's ornate carvings. There are four services on Sundays.

Lalbagh Botanical Gardens GARDENS

(www.horticulture.kar.nic.in/lalbagh.htm; Lalbagh Rd; ₹10; ⏲6am-7pm) Spread over 96 hectares of landscaped terrain, the expansive Lalbagh Botanical Gardens were laid out in 1760 by the famous ruler Hyder Ali. As well as amazing centuries-old trees it claims to have the world's most diverse species of plants. Try to visit in the early morning for the bird chorus. You can take a guided tour with Bangalore Walks (p858).

Krishnarajendra Market MARKET

(City Market; Silver Jubilee Park Rd; ⏲6am-10pm) For a taste of traditional urban India, dive into the bustling Krishnarajendra Market and the dense grid of commercial streets that surround it. Weave your way around this lively colourful market past fresh produce, piles of vibrant dyes, spices and copperware. The colourful **flower market** in the centre is the highlight.

Bangalore Fort FORT

(KR Rd) This ruined 1761 fort is a peaceful escape from the chaotic city surrounds, with its manicured lawn and stone pink walls. The fort remained in use until its destruction by the British in 1791, and today the gate and bastions are the only structures remaining. There's a small dungeon here, and Ganesh temple with its Mooshak (ratlike creature) statue.

Bangalore Palace PALACE

(Palace Rd; Indian/foreigner ₹230/460, mobile/camera/video ₹285/685/1485; ⏲10.30am-5.30pm) The private residence of the Wodeyars, erstwhile maharajas of the state, Bangalore Palace preserves a slice of bygone royal splendour. Still the residence of the current maharaja, an audio guide provides a detailed explanation of the building, and you can marvel at the lavish interiors and galleries featuring hunting memorabilia, family photos and a collection of nude portraits.

Tipu Sultan's Palace PALACE

(Albert Victor Rd; Indian/foreigner ₹15/200, video ₹25; ⏲8.30am-5.30pm) The elegant Indo-Islamic summer residence of the ruler Tipu Sultan is notable for its teak pillars and ornamental frescoes.

Bull Temple HINDU TEMPLE

(Basavanagudi; Bull Temple Rd, Basavanagudi; ⏲7am-8.30pm; 🐾) FREE Built by Kempegowda in the 16th-century Dravidian style, the Bull Temple contains a huge stone monolith of Nandi (Shiva's bull), which is always embellished with lavish flower garlands. This is one of Bengaluru's most atmospheric temples and is located about 1km south of Tipu Sultan's Palace.

Iskcon Temple HINDU TEMPLE

(www.iskconbangalore.org; Chord Rd, Hare Krishna Hill; ⏲7.15am-1pm & 4.15-8.20pm Mon-Fri,

7.15am-8.30pm Sat & Sun; Ⓜ Mahalakshmi) Built by the International Society of Krishna Consciousness (Iskcon), also referred to as the Hare Krishnas, this impressive hilltop temple, inaugurated in 1997, is lavishly decorated in a mix of ultra-contemporary and traditional styles. There are many food stalls here so bring an appetite, and concerts and lectures are regularly held. It's around 8km northwest from the centre of town.

HAL Aerospace Museum & Heritage Centre MUSEUM
(www.hal-india.com; Airport-Varthur Rd; ₹50, camera/video ₹50/75; ⏲9am-5pm Tue-Sun) For a peek into India's aeronautical history, visit this wonderful museum past the old airport, where you can see some of the indigenous aircraft models designed by HAL. Interesting exhibits include a MIG-21, home-grown models such as the Marut and Kiran, and a vintage Canberra bomber.

Activities

Equilibrium CLIMBING
(☎8861684444; www.equilibrium.co.in; 3rd fl, 546 CMH Rd, Indiranagar; from ₹150; ⏲6am-11pm) India's first climbing centre is more indoor bouldering, which will suit those en route to Hampi, a world-renowned climbing destination. It also arranges weekend climbing excursions.

Soukya YOGA
(☎080-28017000; www.soukya.com; Soukya Rd, Samethanahalli, Whitefield; per day incl treatments, meals & accommodation from US$1400; ⏲6am-8.30pm) Very upmarket, internationally renowned retreat on a picture-perfect 12-hectare organic farm running programs in ayurvedic therapy and yoga, as well as medical and therapeutic skin treatments.

Ayurvedagram AYURVEDA, YOGA
(☎080-65651090; www.ayurvedagram.com; Hemmandanhalli, Whitefield; day package from ₹4000) Set over 3 hectares of tranquil gardens with heritage homes transplanted from Kerala, this centre has specifically tailored ayurvedic treatments, yoga and rejuvenation programs. It's in the outer suburb of Whitefield, around 25km from central Bengaluru.

Tours

★Bangalore Walks WALKING
(☎9845523660; www.bangalorewalks.com; adult/child from ₹500/300; ⏲7-10am Sat & Sun) Highly recommended tours including guided walks through Lalbagh Botanical Gardens and Cubbon Park, a medieval Old City history walk or 19th-century Victorian walk. Most walks include a delicious breakfast. Customised tours are also possible.

★Unhurried Tours WALKING
(☎919880565446; www.unhurried.in; half-day tours ₹2500) Led by Poornima Dasharathi, an author and history enthusiast, these excellent walking tours explore backstreets, temples, streetlife and local cuisine in Bengaluru. Out-of-town trips are also offered.

Bus Tours TOURS
(www.karnatakaholidays.net; half day ₹255, full day ₹485, without AC ₹230/385) The government tourism department runs city bus tours which are worth considering (though they do cover a lot of places in a short space of time). Basic half-day city tours run twice daily at 7.30am and 2pm, while the full-day tour departs at 7.15am Wednesday to Sunday.

Day trips around Bengaluru are also offered, including a daily departure to Srirangapatna and Mysuru that takes in several temples, palaces and gardens.

Sleeping

Choosing a place to stay near a metro station is a wise idea for those who want to really explore the city. Decent budget rooms are in short supply but you'll find a stack of dive lodges on Subedar Chatram (SC) Rd, east of the bus stands and around the train station.

MG Road Area

JüSTa MG Road BOUTIQUE HOTEL $$
(☎080-41135555; www.justahotels.com/mg-road-bangalore; 21/14 Craig Park Layout, MG Rd; r/ste incl breakfast ₹3520/4840; ❄📶; Ⓜ Trinity) A stylish alternative to Bengaluru's plethora of generic business hotels, this intimate arty hotel has slick and spacious rooms with Japanese-inspired motifs throughout. It's well located with a metro station and shopping malls close by.

Hotel Ajantha HOTEL $$
(☎080-25584321; www.hotelajantha.in; 22A MG Rd; s/d incl breakfast with fan ₹1500/2000, with AC from ₹2300; ❄📶; Ⓜ Trinity) Dependable, affordable budget favourite Ajantha is very close to Trinity metro station and has decent, well-maintained rooms with cable TV. There's a well-regarded restaurant in the compound and the complimentary breakfast is generous.

Tom's Hotel HOTEL $$
(☎080-25575875; www.hoteltoms.com; 1/5 Hosur Rd; s/d incl breakfast with fan ₹2200/2400, with AC ₹2310/2560;) An excellent place with high cleanliness standards, and bright cheerful rooms, Tom's allows you to stay in a central location (it's a 15-minute walk from MG Rd) and has friendly staff and free wi-fi. There's a restaurant which serves well-priced Indian dishes.

★ **Casa Piccola Cottage** HERITAGE HOTEL $$$
(☎080-22990337; www.casacottage.com; 2 Clapham Rd; r incl breakfast from ₹4400;) A tastefully renovated heritage hotel, Casa Piccola's atmospheric rooms offer a tranquil sanctuary. Its personalised brand of hospitality has garnered it a solid reputation and rooms come with tiled floors and traditional bedspreads while the garden boasts papaya and avocado trees.

★ **Oberoi** HOTEL $$$
(☎080-41358222; www.oberoihotels.com; 39 MG Rd; s/d from ₹13,400/14,600; ; M Trinity) Top dog (and top dollar) in Bengaluru, the opulent Oberoi is set in lush gardens around an enchanting 120-year-old tree, yet its central location could not be more convenient. It mixes colonial-era ambience with modern touches like tablet-controlled in-room devices and TVs in the bathrooms. Rooms all have balconies with garden views and the spa and restaurants are superb.

Laika Boutique Stay B&B $$$
(☎9482806630; www.laikabangalore.in; Rathna Rd; r from ₹4235; ; M Trinity) Hidden down a leafy side street, this welcoming guesthouse is a wonderful choice for those seeking a more local experience combined with style and comfort. Extra touches, including thoughtful service and home-cooked breakfasts, make it a great choice.

St Mark's Inn HOTEL $$$
(☎080-41122783; www.stmarkshotel.com; St Mark's Rd; s/d incl breakfast ₹4870/5880; ; M MG Rd) Designer hotel with immaculate rooms decked out with modern decor, big comfy beds and sparkling stainless-steel bathroom fittings. The buffet breakfast is quite a spread. Rates vary considerably day to day according to demand.

Other Areas

★ **Electric Cats B&B** HOSTEL $
(☎9845290679; www.facebook.com/ElectricCatsHostel; 1794 6th Cross Rd; dm ₹500-600; ; M Indiranagar) A really well-organised, sociable hostel close to the buzzing Indiranagar area with good dorms (one female-only with a shared bathroom), all beds have good linen, private reading lamps and charging facilities. Drinking water and wi-fi are free, there's no curfew and staff are very switched on to travellers' needs, even organising pub crawls and barbecues.

Cuckoo Hostel HOSTEL $
(☎9535034683; www.facebook.com/cuckoohostel; 561 17 A Main Rd, Koramangala; dm/s ₹650/850;) A lot of thought has gone into this new hostel which is run by and attracts a creative crowd, with regular craft, art, music sessions and occasional debates about the environment and global issues. There are cycles for hire, laundry facilities and clean, well-presented dorms. It's about 6km south-west of the centre.

Meditating Monkeys HOSTEL $
(☎918861459156; http://themeditatingmonkeys.com; 9/24 Lloyd Rd, Cooke Town; dm incl breakfast ₹500;) Founded by a local musician/traveller this excellent new hostel offers a comfy, social base in a business city. There's a free veg breakfast, wi-fi, tea and coffee, kitchen and washing machine. Dorms are well-presented and communal bathrooms are clean. It's a smoke- and alcohol-free zone. Located 4km north of MG Rd.

Temple Tree Hotel Wilson Garden HOTEL $$
(☎080-46622000; http://templetreehotel.com; 9th Cross Rd, Mavalli; r ₹3765-4499;) Ticking the right contemporary boxes, including hip bathrooms and modish design touches, this sleek hotel won't fail to impress. Garden view rooms have great balconies, and there's a rooftop restaurant and a small gym. It's not far from the Lalbagh Botanical Gardens.

Mass Residency GUESTHOUSE $$
(☎9945091735; massresidency@yahoo.com; 18, 2nd Main Rd, 11th Cross, JP Nagar; r incl breakfast with fan/AC ₹1600/2000;) Welcoming guesthouse,

SLEEPING PRICE RANGES

The following price ranges are for a double room with bathroom and are inclusive of tax:

$ less than ₹1500

$$ ₹1500–₹4000

$$$ more than ₹4000

run by two brothers who are world travellers themselves. It has comfortable enough rooms, but wins rave reviews for its warm hospitality and free neighbourhood walking tours. Located 8km south of the centre.

Hotel ABM International HOTEL $$
(☎080-41742030; 232 Subedar Chatram Rd, near Anand Rao Circle; r ₹1400-1700, with AC ₹1600-2200; ❄📶; Ⓜ Kempegowda) Offering good value for money, this budget hotel has neat, simple, well-presented rooms. There is a popular juice bar and restaurant downstairs and it's walking distance from the Kempegowda Bus Stand and metro.

★**Taj West End** HERITAGE HOTEL $$$
(☎080-66605660; www.tajhotels.com; Racecourse Rd; s/d incl breakfast from ₹12,600/13,700; ❄📶🏊) Spread over 8 hectares of stunning tropical gardens the West End saga flashbacks to 1887, when it was first established as a base for British officers, and it still oozes colonial class. Some of the city's best dining options include the Blue Ginger for Vietnamese cuisine and the Masala Klub for superb Indian food.

Leela Palace HOTEL $$$
(☎080-25211234; www.theleela.com; 23 HAL Airport Rd; s/d from ₹18,800/19,300; ❄@📶🏊) Modelled on Mysuru Palace, the astonishing Leela isn't actually a palace (it was built in 2003), but it's fit for royalty. Gleaming marble, luxuriant carpets, regal balconies and period features are done superbly, as are its beautiful gardens, classy restaurants, bars and boutique galleries. It's within the Leela Galleria complex, 5km east of MG Rd next to a golf course.

Villa Pottipati GUESTHOUSE $$$
(☎080-41144725; www.villa-pottipati.neemranahotels.com; 142 8th Cross, 4th Main, Malleswaram; s/d incl breakfast from ₹4800/7600; ❄@📶🏊) This heritage building makes an atmospheric base, with antique furniture and kindly staff. Indeed it was once the home of the wealthy expat Andhra family. Its garden is full of ancient trees and has a dunk-sized pool. However, the property is close to a busy intersection and there's some traffic noise.

Eating

Bengaluru's adventurous dining scene keeps pace with the whims and rising standards of its hungry, moneyed locals and IT expats. You'll find high-end dining, gastropubs and cheap local favourites.

MG Road Area

Khan Saheb INDIAN $
(www.khansaheb.co; 9A Block, Brigade Rd; rolls from ₹60; ⏰noon-11.30pm; Ⓜ MG Rd) Famous for its terrific rolls (wholewheat chapatis), filled with anything from charcoal-grilled meats and tandoori prawns to paneer and sweetcorn tikka.

Koshy's Bar & Restaurant INDIAN $$
(39 St Mark's Rd; mains ₹160-350; ⏰9am-11pm; Ⓜ MG Rd) Serving the city's intelligentsia for decades, this buzzy, decidedly old-school resto-pub is where you can put away tasty North Indian dishes in between fervent discussions and mugs of beer. The decor is all creaky ceiling fans and dusty wooden shuttered windows and lashings of nostalgia. Between lunch and dinner it's 'short eats' only (colonial-era snacks like chicken liver on toast).

Church Street Social GASTROPUB $$
(http://socialoffline.in; 46/1 Church St; mains ₹170-350; ⏰9am-11pm Mon-Thu, to 1am Fri & Sat; 📶; Ⓜ MG Rd) Bringing hipsterism to Bengaluru, this industrial warehouse-style space serves cocktails in beakers and its napkins are toilet paper–style (on a roll). The menu takes in fine breakfasts, meze platters, southern fried chicken burgers and 'gunpowder' calamari.

Empire NORTH INDIAN $$
(www.facebook.com/hotelempire; 36 Church St; mains ₹120-240; ⏰11am-11pm; Ⓜ MG Rd) Famous in the city, Empire is all about authentic, inexpensive tandoori and meat dishes in unpretentious surrounds (plastic banquette seating and fake wood); try their butter chicken, kebabs or a mutton biryani. It's busy day and night and its streetside kitchen dishes out tasty shawarma (spit-roasted kebab) to time-pushed peeps on the go. There are numerous other branches around the city.

★**Olive Beach** MEDITERRANEAN $$$
(☎080-41128400; www.olivebarandkitchen.com; 16 Wood St, Ashoknagar; mains ₹525-795; ⏰noon-3.30pm & 7-11pm; 📶) A whitewashed villa straight from the coast of Santorini, Olive Beach does a menu that evokes wistful memories of sunny Mediterranean getaways. Things change seasonally, but expect Moroccan lamb tagines, prawns *pil pil* (with garlic and hot peppers) and plenty of veg choices. The addition of a new alfresco lounge bar here has only added to Olive Beach's allure.

★Karavalli SEAFOOD $$$

(☎080-66604545; Gateway Hotel, 66 Residency Rd; mains ₹500-1575; ⏰12.30-3pm & 6.30-11.30pm; Ⓜ MG Rd) For the finest Indian seafood, look no further. The wonderfully atmospheric interior is perfect for a special meal, with subtle lighting, traditional thatched roof, vintage woodwork and beaten brassware – though the garden seating is equally appealing. Choose from fiery Mangalorean fish dishes, spicy Kerala-style prawns, crab Milagu in a pepper masala and superb lobster *balchao* (cooked in a spicy sauce; ₹1495).

Ebony MULTICUISINE $$$

(☎080-41783333; www.ebonywithaview.com; 13th fl, Barton Centre, 84 MG Rd; mains ₹300-560; ⏰12.30-3pm & 7-11pm; 📶; Ⓜ MG Rd) While there's a delectable menu of Indian, Thai and European dishes, here it's all about the romantic views from the 13th-floor rooftop. On weekday lunchtimes two courses are just ₹445. There's a cool lounge zone, too, buzzing with Bengaluru's cocktail-sipping classes on weekends.

Indian Kitchen MODERN INDIAN $$$

(☎080-25598995; 86 Oak Shot Pl, MG Rd; 250-825; ⏰noon-3pm & 7pm-1am; Ⓜ MG Rd) Destination restaurant that's a big hit with the city's bright young things. The menu raids the nation for inspiration; standouts include the Chingri Malai (Bengali-style curry with prawns and coconut) and chicken gassi (with spicy tamarind sauce). Doubles as a bar, with a good selection of beers, wines and cocktails.

Fava MEDITERRANEAN $$$

(www.fava.in; UB City, 24 Vittal Mallya Rd; mains ₹350-850; ⏰11am-11pm; 📶; Ⓜ Cubbon Park) Dine alfresco on Fava's canopy-covered decking, feasting on large plates of delectable dishes like duck leg confit, fish kebabs or something from the organic menu. The fixed-price Med lunch is great value at ₹475/570 for two/three courses.

Sunny's ITALIAN $$$

(☎080-41329366; www.sunnysbangalore.in; 50 Lavelle Rd; mains ₹350-730; ⏰12.30-11.30pm; 📶) A well-established fixture on Bengaluru's restaurant scene, classy Sunny's has a lovely terrace for alfresco dining. On the menu you'll find authentic thin-crust pizzas, homemade pastas, imported cheese and some of the best desserts in the city.

DON'T MISS

FOOD STREET

For a local eating experience, head to VV Puram, aka **Food Street** (Sajjan Rao Circle, VV Puram; meals from ₹100; ⏰from 5.30pm), with its strip of hole-in-the-wall eateries cooking up classic street-food dishes from across India. It's quite a spectacle, with rotis being handmade and spun in the air and *bhajia* (vegetable fritters) dunked into hot oil before packed crowds.

It's an all-vegetarian affair with a range of dosas, *idli* (fermented rice cake), Punjabi-style snacks and curries.

Other Areas

★Mavalli Tiffin Rooms SOUTH INDIAN $

(MTR; ☎080-22220022; www.mavallitiffinrooms.com; 14 Lalbagh Rd; snacks from ₹50, meals from ₹130; ⏰6.30-11am & 12.30-9.30pm, closed Mon) A legendary name in South Indian comfort food, this super-popular eatery has had Bengaluru eating out of its hands since 1924. Head to the dining room upstairs, queue for a table, and then admire the images of southern beauties etched on smoky glass as waiters bring you delicious *idlis* (fermented rice cakes) and dosas (savoury crêpes), capped by frothing filter coffee served in silverware.

Gramin INDIAN $

(☎080-41104104; 20, 7th Block, Raheja Arcade, Koramangala; mains ₹136-180; ⏰12.30-11pm) Translating to 'from the village', Gramin offers a wide choice of flavourful rural North Indian fare at this cosy, eclectic all-veg place. Try the excellent range of lentils and curries with oven-fresh rotis, accompanied by sweet rose-flavoured lassi served in a copper vessel. The lunchtime thali (₹136) is always a good bet. Between 3.30pm and 7pm there's a limited snack menu.

★Fatty Bao ASIAN $$$

(☎080-44114499; www.facebook.com/thefattybao; 610 12th Main Rd, Indiranagar; mains ₹380-650; ⏰noon-3pm & 7-10.30pm; 📶; Ⓜ Indiranagar) This hip rooftop restaurant serves up Asian hawker food to a crowd of fashionable, young foodies in a vibrant setting with colourful chairs and wooden bench tables. There's ramen, Thai curries and Malaysian street food, as well as Asian-inspired cocktails such as lemongrass mojitos.

Drinking & Nightlife

Bengaluru's rock-steady reputation and wide choice of chic watering holes makes it the place to indulge in a spirited session of pub-hopping in what's the original beer town of India. Many microbreweries have sprung up in the past few years, producing quality ales. All serve food too.

The trendiest nightclubs will typically charge a cover of around ₹1000 per couple, but it's often redeemable against drinks or food.

Lassi Shop CAFE

(41 Church St; drinks ₹30-90; ⏲noon-midnight; 📶) Kitsch-kool cafe on two levels run by a couple of enthusiasts that's perfect for lassis, mocktails and cold-pressed juices: try the ABC (apple, beetroot and carrot). There's ample lounge seating so you can spread out, plus a few streetside tables too.

blueFROG CLUB, BAR

(www.bluefrog.co.in; 3 Church St; ⏲noon-11pm Sun-Thu, to 12.30am Fri & Sat; Ⓜ MG Rd) Upmarket club that draws a hip, lively crowd with its fine roster of house, techno and trance DJs and live bands. Entrance is free to ₹500 depending on the night.

13th Floor BAR

(13th fl, Barton Centre, 84 MG Rd; ⏲5-11pm Sun-Thu, to 1am Fri & Sat; 📶) Forget your superstitions and head up to 13th Floor's terrace, with all of Bengaluru glittering at your feet. There's an excellent selection of martini, sangria and mojito combinations. Happy hour is 5pm to 7pm.

Dyu Art Cafe CAFE

(www.dyuartcafe.yolasite.com; 23 MIG, KHB Colony, Koramangala; ⏲10am-10.30pm; 📶) An atmospheric cafe-gallery in a leafy neighbourhood with a peaceful courtyard reminiscent of a Zen temple. It has coffee beans from Kerala and does good French press, espresso and iced coffee, to go with homemade cakes, sandwiches and mains.

Monkey Bar PUB

(14/1 Wood St, Ashoknagar; ⏲noon-11pm; 📶) Gastropub that draws a mixed, jovial crowd knocking back drinks around the bar or at wooden booth seating. Otherwise head

BENGALURU'S MICROBREWERIES

Arbor Brewing Company (www.arborbrewing.com/locations/india; 8 Magrath Rd; ⏲noon-12.30am Sun-Thu, to 1am Fri & Sat; 📶) This classic brewpub was one of the first microbreweries to get the craft beer barrel rolling in Bengaluru. Choose from stout, porter, IPA, Belgian beers, spiced, sour and fruit beers.

Toit Brewpub (www.toit.in; 298 100 Feet Rd, Indiranagar; ⏲noon-11.30pm Mon-Tue, to 12.30am Wed, Thu & Sun, to 1am Fri & Sat; 📶) A brick-walled gastropub split over three levels where lively punters sample its quality beers brewed on-site, including two seasonals and a wheat beer on tap. Sample six beers for ₹220.

Vapour (www.vapour.in; 773 100 Feet Rd, Indiranagar; ⏲noon-11.30pm; 📶) Multilevel complex divided into several bars and restaurants, though its highlight is the rooftop with big screen to enjoy its six microbrews, including a rice beer and guest ale.

Prost (www.prost.in; 811 5th Cross Rd, Koramangala; ⏲noon-11.30pm Sun-Thu, to 1am Fri & Sat; 📶) Prost has eclectic industrial decor, a rooftop with several quality craft beers on tap and a tempting food menu. Things kick off on weekend evenings with DJs and dancing.

Brewsky (www.brewsky.in; 4th & 5th Fl Goenka Chambers, 19th Main Rd, JP Nagar; ⏲noon-12.30am; 📶) A very cool spot, with city views from its fine roof terrace, a mezzanine terrace and a funky restaurant with vintage decor. It brews six beers on-site including a golden ale, wheat beer and stout. Tasty 'small bites' and substantial sharing platters are good value.

Biere Club (www.thebiereclub.com; 20/2 Vittal Mallya Rd; ⏲11am-11pm Sun-Thu, to midnight Fri & Sat; 📶) Beer lovers rejoice as South India's first microbrewery serves up handcrafted beers on tap, some of which are brewed on-site. There's plenty on the menu (platters, burgers) to nibble on while you sup.

Barleyz (www.barleyz.com; 100 Feet Rd, Koramangala; ⏲11am-11.30pm Sun-Thu, to 1am Fri & Sat; 📶) A suave rooftop beer garden with potted plants, artificial grass and tables with built-in BBQ grills. Offers free tastings of its six beers, as well as rotating seasonal brews. There's also excellent wood-fired pizza, Indian snacks and Western food.

down to the basement to join the 'party' crew shooting pool, playing foosball and rocking out to bangin' tunes.

Another branch is in **Indiranagar** (925 12th Main Rd; noon-11pm, till midnight weekends;).

Infinitea CAFE

(www.infinitea.in; 2 Shah Sultan Complex, Cunningham Rd; pot of tea from ₹100; 11am-11pm;) This smart yet homely place has an impressive menu including orthodox teas from the best estates, and a few fancy selections. Their food (soups, salads, smoked chicken wings) also scores highly and they sell loose tea by the gram.

Atta Galatta CAFE

(080-41600677; www.attagalatta.com; 134, KHB Colony, 5th Block, Koramangala; 11am-8.30pm;) This fine cafe and bakery offers good sandwiches on nutritious bread, cookies and snacks and also doubles as a bookshop and art venue, hosting readings and performances.

Plan B PUB

(20 Castle St, Ashoknagar; 11am-11.30pm Sun-Thu, to 1am Fri & Sat;) This popular student hang-out has 3.5L beer towers, a long cocktail list and is famous for its chicken wings (six for ₹215) which are half-price on Tuesdays.

Also runs industrial-chic gastropub **Plan B Loaded** (https://holycowhospitality.com; 13 Rhenius St, Richmond Town; mains ₹295-475; noon-1am;).

Shiro BAR

(www.shiro.co.in; UB City, 24 Vittal Mallya Rd; 12.30-11.30pm Sun-Thu, to 1am Fri & Sat;) A sophisticated lounge to get sloshed in style, Shiro has elegant interiors complemented by the monumental Buddha busts and *apsara* (celestial nymph) figurines. There's also outdoor deck seating. Has good Japanese food and its 'Special Shiro' cocktails are the bomb.

☆ Entertainment

Humming Tree LIVE MUSIC

(9945532828; www.facebook.com/thehummingtree; 12th Main Rd, Indiranagar; 11am-11.30pm Sun-Thu, to 1am Fri & Sat; M Indiranagar) This popular warehouse-style venue has bands (starting around 9pm), DJs and a rooftop terrace. Cover charge is anything from free to ₹300. There's a good finger food menu and happy hour until 7pm.

Ranga Shankara THEATRE

(080-26592777; www.rangashankara.org; 36/2 8th Cross, JP Nagar) All kinds of interesting theatre (in a variety of languages and spanning various genres) and dance are held at this cultural centre. Hosts an annual mini-festival in late October/early November.

M Chinnaswamy Stadium SPECTATOR SPORT

(www.ksca.cricket; MG Rd; M Cubbon Park) A mecca for cricket lovers, hosting many matches per year. Check online for upcoming schedule of tests, one-dayers and Twenty20s.

B Flat LIVE MUSIC

(080-41739250; www.facebook.com/thebflatbar; 776 100 Feet Rd, Indiranagar; cover charge ₹300; 11am-3pm & 7pm-1am; M Indiranagar) A pub and live music venue that features some of India's best blues and jazz bands.

Indigo Live Music Bar LIVE MUSIC

(080-25535330; www.facebook.com/IndigoLiveMusicBar; 5/6th fl, Elite Bldg, Jyoti Nivas College Rd, Koramangala; 5-11pm Sun-Thu, to 1am Fri & Sat) Hosting bands, DJs, acoustic musicians and even stand-up comedy this popular spot is always lively. On the upper (6th floor) there's a large terrace for dining and lounging.

Shopping

Bengaluru's shopping options are abundant, ranging from teeming bazaars to glitzy malls. Some good shopping areas include Commercial St, Vittal Mallya Rd and the MG Rd area.

★Mysore Saree Udyog CLOTHING

(www.mysoresareeudyog.com; 1st fl, 316 Kamaraj Rd; 10.30am-8.30pm) A great choice for top-quality silk saris, blouses, fabrics and men's shirts, this fine store has been in business for over 70 years and has something to suit all budgets. Most garments are made with Mysuru silk. Also stocks 100% *pashmina* (wool shawls).

Cauvery Arts & Crafts Emporium GIFTS & SOUVENIRS

(45 MG Rd; 10am-8pm; M MG Rd) Government-run store famous for its expansive collection of quality sandalwood and rosewood products as well as handmade weavings, silks and bidriware (metallic handicrafts). Fixed prices.

Forest Essentials COSMETICS

(www.forestessentialsindia.com; 4/1 Lavelle Junction Bldg, Vittal Mallya Rd; 10am-9pm) High-end natural beauty products including

WHAT'S ON, BENGALURU?

The following cover all the latest restaurant openings, cultural events, nightlife and shopping in the city:

➡ Time Out Bengaluru (www.timeout.com/bangalore)

➡ What's Up Bangalore (www.whatsupguides.com)

➡ Explocity (https://bangalore.explocity.com)

potions and lotions for hair, face and body as well as all-organic ayurvedic essential oils.

Fabindia CLOTHING, HOMEWARES
(Garuda Mall, Magrath Rd; ⊙10am-8pm) Hugely successful chain with a range of stylish traditional clothing, homewares and accessories in traditional cotton prints and silks. Quality skincare products too.

Branches at **Commercial Street** (152 Commercial St; ⊙10am-8.30pm), **MG Road** (www.fabindia.com; 1 MG Rd, Lido Mall, Kensington Rd; ⊙10.30am-9pm; Ⓜ Trinity) and **Koramangala** (www.fabindia.com; 54 17th Main Rd; ⊙10am-8pm).

★ **Kynkyny Art Gallery** ART
(www.kynkyny.com; Embassy Sq, 148 Infantry Rd; ⊙10am-7pm Mon-Sat; Ⓜ Cubbon Park) A sophisticated commercial gallery inside a stunning colonial-era building with works by contemporary Indian artists, priced suitably for all budgets. Also sells outstanding designer furniture.

Goobe's Book Republic BOOKS
(www.goobes.wordpress.com; 11 Church St; ⊙10.30am-9pm Mon-Sat, noon-9pm Sun) Great little bookshop selling new and secondhand, cult and mainstream books and comics. Run by informed, helpful staff.

Garuda Mall MALL
(www.garudamall.in; McGrath Rd; ⊙10am-10pm, to 10.30pm Fri & Sat) A modern mall in central Bengaluru with a wide selection of clothing chains and a multiplex Inox cinema.

UB City MALL
(www.ubcitybangalore.in; 24 Vittal Mallya Rd; ⊙10.30am-10pm) Global haute couture (Louis Vuitton, Jimmy Choo, Burberry) and Indian high fashion come to roost at this towering mall in the central district. Also boasts good restaurants and a spa.

Forum MALL
(www.theforumexperience.com/forumbangalore.htm; Hosur Rd, Koramangala; ⊙10am-11pm) Shiny mall complex in the happening district of Koramangala with lots of fashion stores and a cinema.

Gangarams Book Bureau BOOKS
(www.facebook.com/Gangaramsbookbureau; 3rd fl, 48 Church St; ⊙10am-8pm Mon-Sat) Excellent selection of Indian titles, guidebooks and Penguin classics. Has knowledgeable staff and author-signing sessions.

Indiana Crockery HOMEWARES
(97/1 MG Rd; ⊙10.30am-9pm) Good spot to buy thali trays, brass utensils and chai cups for that dinner party back home.

Blossom Book House BOOKS
(www.blossombookhouse.com; 84/6 Church St; ⊙10.30am-9.30pm; Ⓜ MG Rd) Great deals on new and secondhand books.

Orientation

Finding your way around Bengaluru can be difficult at times. In certain areas, roads are named after their widths (eg 80 Feet Rd). The city also follows a system of mains and crosses: 3rd Cross, 5th Main, Residency Rd, for example, refers to the third lane on the fifth street branching off Residency Rd. New affluent pockets are springing up across the city, including the ritzy suburbs of Indirangar, JP Nagar, Koramangala and Whitefield – all with Western-style malls, nightlife and restaurants.

Information

LEFT LUGGAGE

The City train station and Kempegowda bus stand have 24-hour cloakrooms (per day ₹15). You need a valid journey ticket and proof of ID. Your bag must be locked.

MEDICAL SERVICES

Hosmat (☎080-25593796; www.hosmatnet.com; 45 Magrath Rd) Hospital for critical injuries and general illnesses.

Mallya Hospital (☎080-22277979; www.mallyahospital.net; 2 Vittal Mallya Rd) Emergency services and 24-hour pharmacy.

MONEY

ATMs are everywhere, as are moneychangers around MG Rd.

TT Forex (☎080-22254337; 33/1 Cunningham Rd; ⊙9.30am-6.30pm Mon-Fri, 9.30am-1.30pm Sat) Changes travellers cheques and foreign currency.

TOURIST INFORMATION

Government of India Tourist Office (GITO; ☎080-25585417; indtourblr@dataone.in; 2nd level, 48 Church St; ⏲9.30am-6pm Mon-Fri, 9.30am-1pm Sat; Ⓜ MG Rd) Very helpful for Bengaluru and beyond.

Karnataka State Tourism Development Corporation (KSTDC; ☎080-41329211; www.kstdc.co; Karnataka Tourism House, 8 Papanna Lane, St Mark's Rd; ⏲10am-7pm Mon-Sat; Ⓜ MG Rd) Bookings can be made for KSTDC city and state tours.

Karnataka State Tourism Development Corporation (KSTDC; ☎080-43344334; www.kstdc.co; Badami House, Kasturba Rd; ⏲10am-7pm Mon-Sat) Useful office just south of Cubbon Park.

TRAVEL AGENCIES

Skyway (☎080-22111401; www.skywaytour.com; 8 Papanna Lane, St Mark's Rd; ⏲9am-6pm Mon-Sat) Thoroughly professional and reliable outfit for booking long-distance taxis and air tickets.

Getting There & Away

AIR

International and domestic flights arrive at Bengaluru's **Kempegowda International Airport** (☎1800 4254425; www.bengaluruairport.com), about 40km north from the MG Rd area. Domestic flights also leave here with daily connections to major cities including Chennai (Madras), Mumbai (Bombay), Hyderabad, Delhi and Goa. Carriers include:

Air India (☎080-22978427; www.airindia.com; Unity Bldg, JC Rd; ⏲10am-5pm Mon-Sat)

GoAir (☎080-47406091; www.goair.in; Bengaluru Airport)

IndiGo (☎9910383838; www.goindigo.in)

Jet Airways (☎080-39893333; www.jetairways.com; Unity Bldg, JC Rd; ⏲9.30am-6pm Mon-Sat)

BUS

Bengaluru's huge, well-organised **Kempegowda bus stand** (Majestic; Gubbi Thotadappa Rd), also commonly known as both the Majestic and Central, is directly in front of the City train station. Karnataka State Road Transport Corporation (KSRTC; www.ksrtc.in) buses run to destinations in Karnataka and neighbouring states. **Mysuru Road Satellite Bus Stand** (Mysuru Rd) 8km southwest of the centre is another important terminal: most KSRTC buses to Mysuru, Mangaluru (Mangalore) and other destinations southwest of Bengaluru leave from here as does the Flybus to Bengaluru airport.

The KSRTC website lists current schedules and fares. Booking online isn't always possible using international credit cards, but travel agents can. Book long-distance journeys in advance.

Private bus operators line the street facing Kempegowda bus stand.

TRAIN

Bengaluru's **City train station** (www.bangalorecityrailwaystation.in; Gubbi Thotadappa Rd) is the main train hub. There's also **Cantonment train station** (Station Rd), a sensible spot to disembark if you're arriving and headed for the MG Rd area, while **Yeshvantpur train station** (Rahman Khan Rd), 8km northwest of downtown, is the starting point for trains to Goa.

The computerised **reservation office** (☎139; ⏲8am-8pm Mon-Sat, to 2pm Sun) has separate counters for credit card purchase, women and foreigners. Head to the **Divisional Railway Office** (Gubbi Thotadappa Rd) for last-minute reservations. Luggage can be left at the 24-hour cloakroom on Platform 1 at the City train station.

MAJOR BUSES FROM BENGALURU (BANGALORE)

DESTINATION	FARE (₹)	DURATION (HR)	DEPARTURES
Chennai	398 (R)/491 (V)/693 (S)	6-7	25 daily, 5.35am-11.30pm
Ernakulam	619 (R)/1139 (V)	10-12	7 daily, 4pm-9.45pm
Hampi	629 (R)	7½	1 daily, 11pm
Hosapete	334 (R)/599 (V)/696 (S)	8	17 daily, 4.30pm-11.30pm
Hyderabad	713 (R)/989 (V)/1190 (S)	9-11	27 daily, 7.30am-11.30pm
Mumbai	1383 (V)	18	3 daily, 3pm-8pm
Mysuru*	123 (R)/299 (V)	2-3	51 daily, 24hr
Ooty*	639-839 (V)	7-9½	9 daily, 6.15am-11.15pm
Panaji	919 (V)1800 (S)	11-13	5 daily, 6.30pm-8.30pm
Gokana	549 (R) 789 (V) 882 (S)	9-11½	4 daily, from 8.30pm-10.15pm

Fares: (R) Rajahamsa Semideluxe, (V) Airavath AC Volvo, (S) AC Sleeper
*leave from Mysuru Rd Satellite Bus Stand.

Getting Around

TO/FROM THE AIRPORT

Metered AC taxis from the airport to the centre cost between ₹750 and ₹1000, while Uber/Ola cab rates are around ₹500 to ₹600; these rates include the ₹120 airport toll charge.

Flybus (www.ksrtc.in) KSRTC runs the Flybus to/from Mysuru (₹739, four hours) departing the airport 10 times daily, it travels via the Mysuru Rd Satellite Bus Stand.

Vayu Vajra (1800 4251663; www.mybmtc.com) Vayu Vajra's airport shuttle service has regular AC buses to destinations including Kempegowda (Majestic) bus stand, MG Rd and Indiranagar departing 24 hours.

AUTORICKSHAW

Very few autorickshaw drivers use meters but if yours does 50% is added to the metered rate after 10pm.

BUS

Bengaluru has a comprehensive local bus network, operated by the Bangalore Metropolitan Transport Corporation (BMTC; www.mybmtc.com), with a useful website for timetables and fares. Red AC Vajra buses criss-cross the city, while green Big10 deluxe buses connect the suburbs. Ordinary buses run from the **City bus stand** (Sayyali Rao Rd), next to Kempegowda bus stand; a few operate from the City Market bus stand further south.

To get from the City train station to the MG Rd area, catch any bus from Platform 17 or 18 at the City bus stand. For the City Market, take bus 31, 31E, 35 or 49 from Platform 8.

METRO

Bengaluru's shiny new AC metro service, known as Namma Metro, is still a work in progress, but it does have two lines up and running. There was *no* interchange between the two, despite what the official maps indicate, at the time of research. The most relevant route to tourists is the Purple Line, which runs east–west: useful stops include Kempegowda (for the bus terminal), MG Rd (for shopping and bars) and Indiranagar (for restaurants and nightlife). Trains run about every 15 minutes, 6am to 10pm, and tickets are priced at ₹10 to ₹22 for most journeys. For the latest updates on the service, log on to www.bmrc.co.in.

TAXI

There are thousands of Uber and Ola drivers in Bengaluru. To hire a conventional cab for a day allow around ₹2000 for eight hours.

Meru Cabs (080-44224422; www.merucabs.com) Available at the airport.

Olacabs (080-33553355; www.olacabs.com) Professional, efficient company with modern air-con cars. Online and phone bookings.

Around Bengaluru

Hesaraghatta

080 / POP 9200

Located 30km northwest of Bengaluru, the small town of Hesaraghatta is home to Nrityagram, a leading dance academy.

Sights

Nrityagram ARTS CENTRE
(080-28466313; www.nrityagram.org; self-guided tour ₹50, children under 12 free; 10am-2pm Tue-Sun) This leading dance academy was established in 1990 to revive and popularise Indian classical dance. The brainchild and living legacy of celebrated dancer Protima Gauri Bedi (1948–98), the complex was designed like a village by Goa-based architect Gerard da

MAJOR TRAINS FROM BENGALURU (BANGALORE)

DESTINATION	TRAIN NO & NAME	FARE (₹)	DURATION (HR)	DEPARTURES
Chennai	12658 Chennai Mail	255/910	6	10.40pm
Chennai	12028 Shatabdi	785/1060	5	6am & 4.25pm Wed-Mon
Hosapete	16592 Hampi Exp	255/970	9½	10pm
Hubballi	16589 Rani Chennamma Exp	270/1045	8½	9.15pm
Madgaon, Goa	17311 Mas Vasco Exp	360/1405	15	8.10pm Fri
Mysuru	12007 Shatabdi	300/835	2	11am Thu-Tue
Mysuru	12614 Tippu Exp	90/310	2½	3pm
Trivandrum	16526 Kanyakumari Exp	410/1605	16½	8pm

Fares: Shatabdi fares are AC chair/AC executive; Express (Exp/Mail) fares are 2nd-class/AC chair for day trains and sleeper/2AC for night trains.

WORTH A TRIP

WHISKY & WINE

In a country not known for being a big exponent of fine wines and liquors (anyone who has stepped foot into one of India's ubiquitous 'wine shops' can attest to this), Bengaluru is very much an exception to the rule. It's a city that's not only gained a thirst for craft beer, but has on its doorstep one of India's premier wine-growing regions in **Nandi Hills** (per person ₹10, car ₹150; 6am-6pm). While an emerging industry, it's fast gaining a reputation internationally with some 18 wineries in the area. Also a few clicks out of town is India's first single-malt whisky distillery, which allows tastings.

Grover Wineries (080-27622826; www.groverzampa.in; 1½hr tour Mon-Fri ₹850, Sat & Sun ₹1000) At an altitude of at 920m this winery produces quality white and red varietals. Tours include tastings of five wines in the cellar rooms accompanied by cheese and crackers, followed by lunch. From February to May you'll also see grape crushing and can visit its vineyards. It's located on the approach to Nandi Hills, around 40km north of Bengaluru.

Amrut (080-23100402; www.amrutdistilleries.com; Mysuru Rd) FREE Established in 1948, Amrut, India's first producer of single malt whisky, offers free distillery tours run by knowledgeable guides. You get taken through the entire process before tasting its world-class single malts and blends. It's 20km outside Bengaluru on the road to Mysuru; prebookings essential.

Cunha. Long-term courses in classical dance are offered here to deserving students, while local children are taught for free on Sundays. Check their website for upcoming performances (₹1000 per person).

You can also book a tour package that includes a guided tour, lecture, dance demonstration and vegetarian meal (per person ₹1500 to ₹2000, minimum 10 people, advance booking required).

Sleeping

Taj Kuteeram HOTEL $$$
(080-28466326; www.tajhotels.com; d from ₹4660;) Opposite Nrityagram dance village, Kuteeram isn't as luxurious as other Taj Group hotel offerings, but it's still atmospheric with a balance of comfort and rustic charm, and designs by Gerard da Cunha. It also offers ayurveda and yoga sessions.

Getting There & Away

From Bengaluru's City Market, buses 266, 253 and 253E run to Hesaraghatta (₹26, one hour), with bus 266 continuing on to Nrityagram. From Hesaraghatta an autorickshaw will cost ₹75 to Nrityagram.

Janapada Loka Folk Arts Museum

Janapada Loka Folk Arts Museum MUSEUM
(www.jaanapadaloka.org; Bengaluru-Mysuru Rd; Indian/foreigner ₹20/100; 9am-5.30pm Wed-Mon) A worthwhile stopover between Bengaluru and Mysuru, this museum is dedicated to the preservation of rural local culture. It has a wonderful collection of folk-art objects, including 500-year-old shadow puppets, festival costumes, musical instruments, a superb temple chariot and a replica of a traditional village. There's also a children's playground. It's situated 53km south of Bengaluru, 3km from Ramnagar; any Mysuru–Bengaluru bus can drop you here.

Mysuru (Mysore)

0821 / POP 912,000 / ELEV 707M

The historic settlement of Mysuru (which changed its name from Mysore in 2014) is one of South India's most enchanting cities, famed for its glittering royal heritage and magnificent monuments and buildings. Its World Heritage–listed palace brings most travellers here, but Mysuru is also rich in tradition with a deeply atmospheric bazaar district littered with spice stores and incense stalls. Ashtanga yoga (p874) is another drawcard and there are several acclaimed schools which attract visitors from across the globe.

History

Mysuru owes its name to the mythical Mahisuru, a place where the demon Mahisasura was slain by the goddess Chamundi. Its regal history began in 1399, when the

Wodeyar dynasty of Mysuru was founded, though they remained in service of the Vijayanagar empire until the mid-16th century. With the fall of Vijayanagar in 1565, the Wodeyars declared their sovereignty, which – save for a brief period of Hyder Ali and Tipu Sultan's supremacy in the late 18th century – remained unscathed until Independence in 1947.

Sights

Mysuru isn't known as the City of Palaces for nothing, being home to a total of seven and an abundance of majestic heritage architecture dating from the Wodeyar dynasty and British rule. The majority of grand buildings are owned by the state, and used as anything from hospitals, colleges and government buildings to heritage hotels. Visit www.karnatakatourism.org/Mysore/en for a list of notable buildings.

★Mysuru Palace PALACE

(Maharaja's Palace; www.mysorepalace.gov.in; Purandara Dasa Rd; Indian/foreigner/child under 10 incl audio guide ₹40/200/free; ⏲10am-5.30pm) Among the grandest of India's royal buildings, this was the seat of the Wodeyar maharajas. The original palace was gutted by fire in 1897; the one you see today was completed in 1912 by English architect Henry Irwin for ₹4.5 million. The lavish Indo-Saracenic interior – a kaleidoscope of stained glass, mirrors and gaudy colours – is undoubtedly over the top. It's further embellished by carved wooden doors, mosaic floors and a series of paintings depicting life here during the Edwardian Raj era.

The way into the palace takes you past a fine collection of sculptures and artefacts. Don't forget to check out the armoury, with an intriguing collection of 700-plus weapons.

Every Sunday and national holiday, from 7pm to 7.30pm, the palace is illuminated by nearly 100,000 light bulbs that accent its majestic profile against the night.

Entrance to the palace grounds is at the **South Gate** (Purandara Dasa Rd). While you are allowed to snap the palace's exterior, photography within is strictly prohibited.

Devaraja Market MARKET

(Sayyaji Rao Rd; ⏲6am-8.30pm) Dating from Tipu Sultan's reign, this lively bazaar has local traders selling traditional items such as flower garlands, spices and conical piles of *kumkum* (coloured powder used for bindi dots), all of which makes for some great photo ops. Refresh your bargaining skills before shopping.

Jaganmohan Palace PALACE

(Jaganmohan Palace Rd; adult/child ₹120/30; ⏲8.30am-5pm) Built in 1861 as the royal auditorium, this stunning palace just west of the Mysuru Palace now houses the **Jayachamarajendra Art Gallery**. Set over three floors it has a huge collection of Indian paintings, including works by noted artist Raja Ravi Varma, traditional Japanese art and some rare musical instruments. However, presentation is poor and the building is sadly neglected.

Rail Museum MUSEUM

(KRS Rd; adult/child ₹15/10, camera/video ₹20/30; ⏲9.30am-6pm) This open-air museum's main exhibit is the Mysuru maharani's saloon, a wood-panelled beauty dating from 1899 that provides an insight into the stylish way in which the royals once rode the railways. There are also steam engines, locomotives and carriages to investigate. A toy train (₹10) rides the track around the museum.

Jayalakshmi Vilas Mansion Museum Complex MUSEUM

(Mysore University Campus; ⏲10am-1pm & 3-5pm Tue-Sun) FREE On the university campus west

MYSURU (MYSORE) COLONIAL-ERA ARCHITECTURE

Mysuru's colonial heritage is considerable, with numerous grand edifices and quirky reminders to investigate. Dating from 1805, **Government House** (Irwin Rd), formerly the British Residency, is a Tuscan Doric building set in 20 hectares of gardens. Facing the north gate of Mysuru Palace is the 1927 **Silver Jubilee Clock Tower** (Dodda Gadiara; Ashoka Rd). The beauty of towering **St Philomena's Cathedral** (St Philomena St; ⏲8am-5pm), built between 1933 and 1941 in neo-Gothic style, is emphasised by wonderful stained-glass windows. **Wellington Lodge** is an unassuming early colonial landmark which today houses a museum: **Indira Gandhi Rashtriya Manav Sangrahalaya** (National Museum of Mankind; www.igrms.com; Wellington Lodge, Irwin Rd; ⏲10am-5.30pm Tue-Sun) FREE.

DUSSEHRA

Mysuru is at its carnivalesque best during the 10-day **Dussehra** (Dasara; ⌚ Sep/Oct) festival held in September or October. During this time the Mysuru Palace is dramatically lit up every evening, while the town is transformed into a gigantic fairground, with concerts, dance performances, sporting demonstrations and cultural events running to packed houses.

On the last day the celebrations are capped off in grand style. A dazzling procession of richly costumed elephants, garlanded idols, liveried retainers and cavalry march through the streets to the rhythms of clanging brass bands.

Mysuru is chock-a-block with tourists during the festival, especially on the final day. To bypass suffocating crowds, consider buying a Dasara VIP Gold Card (₹7500 for two adults). Only 1000 are available, and though expensive, it assures you good seats at the final day gala and helps you beat the entry queues at other events, while providing discounts on accommodation, dining and shopping. It's also possible to buy tickets (₹250 to ₹1000) just for entering the palace and Bannimantap for the final day's parades.

of town, this museum specialises in folklore, with artefacts, stone tablets and sculptures, including rural costumes and a wooden puppet of the 10-headed demon king Ravana. The building itself (restored in 2006) was originally built as a mansion for Princess Jayalakshmi Ammani, the eldest daughter of the Maharaja Chamaraja Wodeyar.

Chamundi Hill VIEWPOINT

This 1062m hill is crowned with the **Sri Chamundeswari Temple** (http://chamundeshwaritemple.kar.nic.in; ⌚ 7am-2pm, 3.30-6pm & 7.30-9pm). It's a fine half-day excursion, offering spectacular views of the city below. Queues are long at weekends, so visit during the week. From Central bus stand take bus 201 (₹28; AC); a return autorickshaw/Uber trip is around ₹450/700.

Alternatively, you can take the foot trail comprising 1000-plus steps that Hindu pilgrims use to visit the temple. One-third of the way down is a 5m-high statue of **Nandi** (Shiva's bull) that was carved out of solid rock in 1659.

Mysuru Zoo ZOO

(http://mysorezoo.info; Indiranagar; adult/child Mon-Fri ₹50/20, Sat & Sun ₹60/30, camera ₹20; ⌚ 8.30am-5.30pm Wed-Mon) A well-managed zoo set in pretty gardens. Highlights include white tigers, lowland gorillas, giraffes and rhinos. It's situated around 2km southeast of Mysuru Palace.

Activities

Emerge Spa AYURVEDA, MASSAGE

(☎ 0821-2522500; www.thewindflower.com; Windflower Spa & Resort, Maharanapratap Rd, Nazarbad; massages from ₹2275; ⌚ 7am-9pm) Wonderful resort spa offering over 30 ayurvedic treatments including hot-stone massages and pampering rituals. Day packages include access to the hotel pool. It's located 3km southeast of Mysuru Palace; rates include pick-up and drop-off.

Indus Valley Ayurvedic Centre AYURVEDA

(☎ 0821-2473263; www.ayurindus.com; Lalithadripura) Set on 10 hectares of gardens, this classy centre derives its therapies from ancient scriptures and prescriptions. The overnight package (single/double including full board from US$180/310) includes one session each of ayurveda, yoga and beauty therapy.

Courses

Shruthi Musical Works MUSIC

(☎ 9845249518; 1189 3rd Cross, Irwin Rd; per hr ₹400; ⌚ 10.30am-9pm Mon-Sat, to 2pm Sun) Music teacher Jayashankar gets good reviews for his tabla (drum) instruction.

Tours

★ **Royal Mysore Walks** WALKING, TOURS

(☎ 9632044188; www.royalmysorewalks.com; from ₹500) An excellent way to familiarise yourself with Mysuru's epic history and heritage. Offers a range of weekend walks (themes include royal history and food) as well as cycle and jeep tours.

KSTDC Transport Office BUS

(☎ 080-43344334; www.kstdc.co; city tour ₹210) KSTDC runs a daily Mysuru city tour, taking in city sights (excluding the palace), Chamundi Hill, Srirangapatna and Brindavan

Mysuru Palace

A HALF-DAY TOUR

The interior of Mysuru Palace houses opulent halls, royal paintings, intricate decorative details, as well as sculptures and ceremonial objects. There is a lot of hidden detail and much to take in, so be sure to allow yourself at least a few hours for the experience. A guide can also be invaluable.

After entering the palace the first exhibit is the ❶ **Doll's Pavilion**, which showcases the maharaja's fine collection of traditional dolls and sculptures acquired from around the world. Opposite the ❷ **Elephant Gate** you'll see the seven cannons that were used for special occasions, such as the birthdays of the maharajas. Today the cannons are still fired as part of Dasara festivities.

At the end of the Doll's Pavilion you'll find the ❸ **Golden Howdah**. Note the fly whisks on either side; the bristles are made from fine ivory.

Make sure you check out the paintings depicting the Dasara procession in the halls on your way to the ❹ **Marriage Pavilion** and look into the courtyard to see what was once the wrestling arena. It's now used during Dasara only. In the Marriage Pavilion, take a few minutes to scan the entire space. You can see the influence of three religions in the design of the hall: the glass ceiling represents Christianity, stone carvings along the hallway ceilings are Hindu design and the top-floor balcony roof (the traditional ladies' gallery) has Islamic-style arches.

When you move through to the ❺ **Private Durbar Hall**, take note of the intricate ivory inlay motifs depicting Krishna in the rosewood doors. The ❻ **Public Durbar Hall** is usually the last stop where you can admire the panoramic views of the gardens through the Islamic arches.

Private Durbar Hall
Rosewood doors lead into this hall, which is richly decorate with stained-glass ceilings, steel grill work and chandeliers. houses the Golden Throne, only on display to the public dur Dasara.

Doll's Pavilion
The first exhibit, the Doll's Pavilion, displays the gift collecti of 19th- and early-20th-century dolls, statues and Hindu ido that were given to the maharaja by dignitaries from around the world.

blic Durbar Hall

open-air hall contains a priceless collection of paintings aja Ravi Varma and opens into an expansive balcony ported by massive pillars with an ornate painted ceiling of carnations of Vishnu.

Marriage Pavilion

This lavish hall used for royal weddings features themes of Christianity, Hindu and Islam in its design. The highlight is the octagonal painted glass ceiling featuring peacock motifs, the bronze chandelier and the colonnaded turquoise pillars.

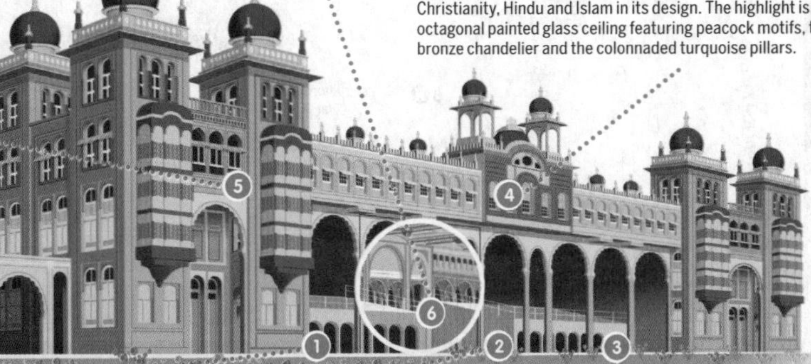

ephant Gate

t to the Doll's Pavilion, this brass gate has four bronze hants inlaid at the bottom, an intricate double-headed e up the top and a hybrid lion-elephant creature (the state blem of Karnataka) in the centre.

Golden Howdah

At the far end of the Doll's Pavilion, a wooden elephant howdah decorated with 80kg of gold was used to carry the maharaja in the Dasara festival. It now carries the idol of goddess Chamundeswari.

Mysuru (Mysore)

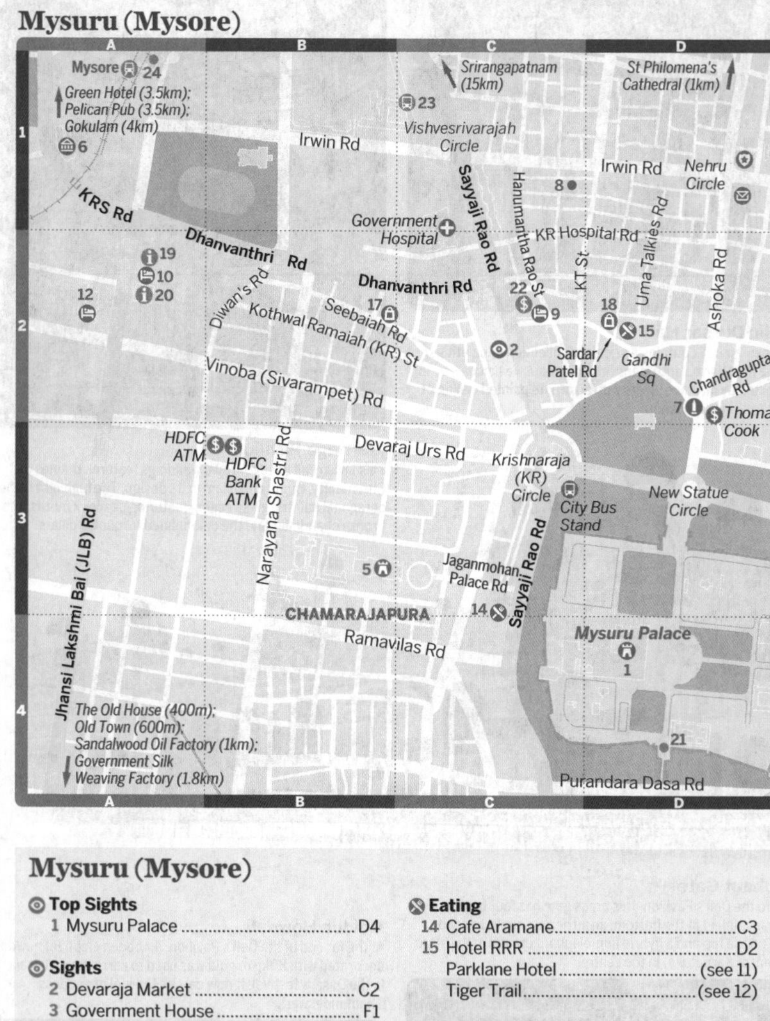

Mysuru (Mysore)

Top Sights

1 Mysuru Palace D4

Sights

2 Devaraja Market C2
3 Government House F1
4 Indira Gandhi Rashtriya Manav Sangrahalaya E1
5 Jaganmohan Palace B3
6 Rail Museum A1
7 Silver Jubilee Clock Tower D2

Activities, Courses & Tours

8 Shruthi Musical Works C1

Sleeping

9 Hotel Maurya C2
10 Hotel Mayura Hoysala A2
11 Parklane Hotel E3
12 Royal Orchid Metropole A2
13 The Mansion 1907 .... F2

Eating

14 Cafe Aramane C3
15 Hotel RRR D2
Parklane Hotel .... (see 11)
Tiger Trail .... (see 12)

Drinking & Nightlife

16 Infinit Doora E3

Shopping

17 Sri Sharada Grand Musical Works B2
18 Sumangali Silks D2

Information

19 Karnataka Tourism A2
20 KSTDC Transport Office A2
21 South Gate Ticket Office D4
22 State Bank of Mysore C2

Transport

23 Private Bus Stand C1
24 Railway Reservation Office A1

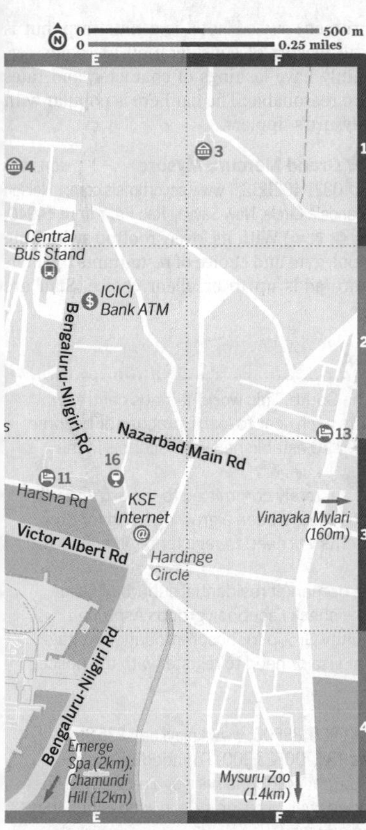

Gardens. It starts daily at 8.30am, ends at 8.30pm and is likely to leave you breathless! Other tours go to Belur, Halebid and Sravanabelagola (₹550) on Tuesday and Thursday from 7.30am to 9pm.

All tours leave from the KSTDC transport office (p876) next to Hotel Mayura Hoysala, from where bookings are made, or at travel agencies around town.

Sleeping

Mysuru attracts tourists throughout the year and can fill up very quickly during Dussehra (p869). Booking early is recommended.

★Mansion 1907 HOSTEL $

(☎9886523472; www.facebook.com/themansion1907; 36 Shalivahana Rd; dm with fan/AC ₹500/600, r from ₹1400; ❄📶) Deservedly popular hostel in a historic house that shows Indian and British architectural influences. It's very well set up, with spacious dorms and private rooms, cool communal areas, good bathrooms, a kitchen and speedy wi-fi. And it's a great place to meet other travellers and plan your next journey.

Sonder HOSTEL $

(www.sonderhostel.com; 66, 3rd Block, Jayalaxmipuram; dm incl breakfast ₹500; ❄📶) Backpackers hostel located about 3km from the centre in a tranquil, leafy suburb not far from many yoga schools. It's a well-designed space with comfy dorms, lockers, board games and books, a kitchen and a friendly vibe. There are regular events like movie nights and cooking classes.

Hotel Maurya HOTEL $

(☎0821-2426677; 9/5 Hanumantha Rao St; s/d from ₹195/350; ❄📶) Very centrally located, the Maurya is a good budget choice with a wide range of large, unremarkable but very cheap rooms. It offers more upmarket choices with TV and AC too. The manager and his staff are extremely helpful and welcoming.

Anokhi Garden Guest House GUESTHOUSE $$

(☎0821-4288923; www.anokhigarden.com; 408 Contour Rd, 3rd Stage, Gokulam; s/d from ₹2200/3200; 📶) Very popular with yoga students and young travellers, this homely French-run guesthouse offers neat, tidy rooms in a property which also boasts a lovely garden cafe.

Parklane Hotel HOTEL $$

(☎0821-4003500; www.parklanemysore.com; 2720 Harsha Rd; r ₹1755-3267; ❄@📶🏊) The Parklane is very well located for the palace and city and represents fine value. Decor is over-the-top kitsch but it's hard to dislike with its massive and immaculate rooms, ultracomfortable and thoughtfully outfitted with mobile-chargers and considerate toiletry kits. Its lively open-air restaurant is always buzzing, and there's a small rooftop pool too.

Mystic School Studios HOTEL $$

(☎0821-4288490; www.mysoreyoga.in; 100 3rd Main Rd, Gokulam; r with/without kitchen per month ₹25,000/15,000; ❄📶🏊) This yoga school offers squeaky-clean rooms with private bathrooms and studios with kitchenettes and balconies. There's a great cafe, Finnish sauna, plunge pool and rooftop chill-out zone.

Urban Oasis HOTEL $$

(☎0821-4006332; www.urbanoasis.co.in; 7 Contour Rd, 3rd Stage, Gokulam; r ₹1200-2000, monthly from ₹30,000; ❄📶) More of a business hotel, but popular with yoga students for its clean, functional and modern rooms with cable TV. There are four price categories from compact single to spacious rooms with balconies and AC.

Hotel Mayura Hoysala HOTEL $$
(☎0821-2426160; www.karnatakaholidays.net; 2 Jhansi Lakshmi Bai Rd; r incl breakfast with fan/AC from ₹1550/2900; ❄📶) Near the train station, the potential of this beautiful historic building remains unrealised. Yes, this government-owned hotel is a timewarp, but is still worthy of consideration as rooms certainly have lashings of character, and rates are reasonable. The bar here is popular with Mysuru's tipplers.

★**Grand Mercure Mysore** HOTEL $$$
(☎0821-4021212; www.accorhotels.com; Nelson Mandela Circle, New Sayyaji Rao Rd; r from ₹4940; ❄@📶🏊) With its lovely rooftop swimming pool, gym and choice of restaurants the Mercure adds up to excellent choice. Staff are

MYSURU (MYSORE) ASHTANGA YOGA

What Rishikesh is to North India, Mysuru is to the South. This world-famous centre for yoga attracts thousands of international students each year to learn, practise or become certified in teaching Ashtanga. There are now over 20 established yoga schools in the city.

For the most part students are required to be austerely committed to the art, and will need at least a month. While in more recent times there's been a growing trend for drop-in classes or week-long courses, long-term students will need to register far in advance, as courses are often booked out.

Most foreign yoga students congregate in the upmarket residential suburb of Gokulam. Several schools now offer accommodation – check Facebook groups Ashtanga Community in Mysore and Mysore Yoga Community Group for accommodation rentals.

Yogis in India no longer need a special student visa or need to register with the police.

Yoga Centres

Ashtanga Yoga Research Institute (AYRI; ☎9880185500; www.kpjayi.org; 235 8th Cross, 3rd Stage, Gokulam; 1st/2nd month plus taxes ₹34,700/23,300) Founded by the renowned ashtanga teacher K Pattabhi Jois, who taught Madonna her yoga moves. He has since passed away and the reins have been handed over to his grandson, who is proving very popular. You need to register two months in advance.

IndeaYoga (Ānanda Yoga India; ☎0821-2416779; www.indeayoga.com; 144E 7th Main Rd, Gokulam; incl food and lodging US$1999) Offering hatha and ashtanga yoga with guru Bharath Shetty (who practised under the late BKS Iyengar) and his wife Archana. Courses include anatomy and yoga philosophy. Drop-in classes and student accommodation are also offered.

Mystic School (☎0821-4288490; www.mysoreyoga.in; 100 3rd A Main Rd, Gokulam; drop-in/1-month yoga classes ₹500/17,000) Well-established school with a diverse program covering hatha and ashtanga, meditation and lectures. Suitable for short- and long-term students at all levels, and has drop-in classes. Reiki and massage courses are also offered. There's accommodation (studios with kitchenettes), sauna, plunge pool and cafe.

Atmavikasa Centre (☎0821-2341978; www.atmavikasayoga.com; 18 Rd, 6th Cross, Ramakrishnanagar) Classical hatha yoga school set up by Acharya Venkatesh and Acharye Hema offering training, therapy and workshops. Enjoys a garden setting in a peaceful suburb 5km southwest of the palace.

Yogadarshanam (☎0821-2412143; http://yogadarshanam.org; 77/A, 4th Main Rd, 3rd Stage; courses ₹6000-29,600) Classical Indian yoga centre offering classes, teacher training, workshops and retreats. Their one-month foundation course covers the yoga fundamentals and is perfect for beginners.

Yoga Bharata (☎0821-4242342; www.yogabharata.com; 1st fl, 810 Contour Rd; 20-class pass ₹4500) Professional centre offering ashtanga, vinyasa, hatha and yoga therapy with experienced teachers. Linked to IndeaYoga. Drop-in classes (₹300) are available.

super attentive and rooms are sleek, well-equipped and have a wide selection of international TV channels. Located 4km north of the city centre.

Royal Orchid Metropole HERITAGE HOTEL $$$
(☎0821-4255566; www.royalorchidhotels.com; 5 Jhansi Lakshmi Bai Rd; s/d incl breakfast from ₹6880/7250;) Originally built by the Wodeyars to serve as the residence of the maharaja's British guests, this is undoubtedly one of Mysuru's leading heritage hotels. The charming colonial-era structure has 30 rooms oozing historical character, just with all mod cons. There's a fitness centre and lovely outdoor pool area.

Green Hotel GUESTHOUSE $$$
(☎0821-4255000; www.greenhotelindia.com; 2270 Vinoba Rd, Jayalakshmipuram; s/d incl breakfast from ₹3880/4480;) The historic Green Hotel was originally built as a palace in the 1920s by the maharajah for his daughters. Today it's a heritage hotel set among charming gardens. Commendably, all 31 rooms run on solar power and have plenty of character, though maintenance could be a little better and some fixtures are looking a tad tired. There's a good **cafe** (cakes from ₹40, snacks from ₹70; 10am-7pm;), restaurant and travel agent here.

Profits are distributed to charity and environmental projects across India.

Eating

★Vinayaka Mylari SOUTH INDIAN $
(769 Nazarbad Main Rd; dosas ₹30-50; 6.30-1.30pm & 3-8.30pm) This no-nonsense place is one of the best eateries in town to try South Indian classics of *masala dosa* (large South Indian savoury crêpe stuffed with spiced potatoes), which are beautifully light and fluffy and *idlis*. Locals eat them with coconut chutney and a coffee.

Depth 'n' Green VEGETARIAN $
(www.facebook.com/depthngreen; 228/3, 1st Main Rd, Gokulam; dishes ₹80-170; 10.30am-10.30pm;) Wildly popular with local yogis, this buzzing healthy cafe offers a menu of satisfying Indian and Western dishes, including great salads, served up on tree trunk tables. Their green smoothies and lassis and other drink concoctions (beet and ginger lemonade) are also superb.

Hotel RRR SOUTH INDIAN $
(Gandhi Sq; mains ₹90-135; noon-4pm & 6-11pm) Classic Andhra-style food is ladled out at this ever-busy eatery, and you may have to queue for a table during lunch. Try their famous chicken or mutton biryanis (served on a banana leaf).

Cafe Aramane SOUTH INDIAN $
(Sayyaji Rao Rd; mains ₹90-110; 8am-10pm) In a character-filled heritage building, this typically busy South Indian eatery rolls out steaming breakfast platters for Mysuru's office-goers, thalis for lunch (from ₹80) and welcomes them back in the evenings with aromatic filter coffee and a convoy of delicious snacks. There are speciality dosas each day of the week.

Parklane Hotel MULTICUISINE $$
(Parklane Hotel, 2720 Harsha Rd; mains ₹100-160;) Mysuru's most social restaurant with outdoor tables, lit up moodily by countless lanterns, and there's often live traditional music. The menu does delicious regional dishes from across India as well as Chinese and continental options and cold beers.

Anu's Bamboo Hut HEALTH FOOD $$
(☎9900909428; www.facebook.com/CafeinGokulam; 367, 2nd Main, 3rd Stage, Gokulam; lunch buffet ₹250; 1-3pm & 5-7pm Mon-Sat;) Rooftop shack cafe catering mainly to yoga students with healthy vegetarian lunch buffets (from 1pm) and evening smoothies. Chef-owner Anu is a great source of info and offers cooking classes (₹700, lunch included).

Tiger Trail INDIAN $$$
(☎0821-4255566; Royal Orchid Metropole, 5 Jhansi Lakshmi Bai Rd; mains ₹200-650; 7.30-10am, 12.30-3.30pm & 7.30-11pm;) This sophisticated hotel restaurant works up delectable Indian cuisine in a courtyard that twinkles with fairy lights at night. The North Indian dishes are particularly good; try a Lucknow chicken korma (₹300). Also has a fine lunch buffet.

Old House ITALIAN $$$
(☎0821-2333255; 451 Jhansi Rani Lakshmi Bai Rd; mains ₹175-399; 7.30am-9.45pm;) Classy Italian with delightful terrace for tasty salads, pasta and risotto and pizzas (baked in a wood-fired oven). They serve a full range of mocktails and coffees but no alcohol.

Drinking & Nightlife

Pelican Pub PUB
(Hunsur Rd; mains ₹100-190; 11am-11pm) A venerable, still-popular watering hole located on the fringes of upmarket Gokulam.

Serves draught beer and food (try the chilli pork) at bargain basement rates in the indoor classic pub or alfresco-style garden setting out back. There's live music some nights.

Infinit Doora BAR

(Hotel Roopa, 2724/C, Bangalore Nilgiris Rd; noon-11pm;) The nearest thing to a lounge in Mysuru, this rooftop bar has a classy ambience and comprehensive drinks selection, smoking and nonsmoking zones and fine city views.

Shopping

Mysuru is a great place to shop for sandalwood products, silk saris and wooden toys. It is also one of India's major incense-manufacturing centres. Look for the butterfly-esque 'Silk Mark' on your purchase; it's an endorsement for quality silk.

The bazaar area around the Devaraja Market is a real highlight for those in search of spices (and photographs).

Government Silk Weaving Factory CLOTHING

(8025586550; www.ksicsilk.com; Mananthody Rd, Ashokapuram; 8.30am-4pm Mon-Sat, outlet 10.30am-7pm daily) Given that Mysuru's prized silk is made under its very sheds, this government-run outlet, set up in 1912, is the best and cheapest place to shop for the exclusive textile. Behind the showroom is the factory, where you can drop by to see how the fabric is made. It's around 2km south of town.

Sumangali Silks CLOTHING

(off Gandhi Sq; 10.30am-8.30pm) Exceptionally popular with Indian ladies, this multilevel store is another option to pick up a silk sari, with quality of varying degrees depending on how much you want to spend.

Sandalwood Oil Factory GIFTS & SOUVENIRS

(Mananthody Rd, Ashokapuram; outlet 9.30am-6.30pm, factory closed Sun) A quality-assured place for sandalwood products including incense, soap, cosmetics and the prohibitively expensive pure sandalwood oil (if in stock). Guided tours are available to show you around the factory.

Sri Sharada Grand Musical Works MUSIC

(2006 Seebaiah Rd) Sells a variety of traditional musical instruments including tabla (drum) sets and assorted percussion instruments.

Information

MEDICAL SERVICES

Government Hospital (0821-4269806; Dhanvanthri Rd) Centrally located and has a 24-hour pharmacy.

Left Luggage

The city bus stand's left-luggage cloakroom is open from 6am to 11pm and costs ₹15 per bag for 12 hours.

TOURIST INFORMATION

Karnataka Tourism (0821-2422096; www.karnatakatourism.org; 1st fl, Hotel Mayura Hoysala, 2 Jhansi Lakshmi Bai Rd; 10am-5pm Mon-Sat) Helpful and has plenty of brochures.

KSTDC Transport Office (0821-2423652; www.karnatakaholidays.net; Yatri Navas Bldg, 2 Jhansi Lakshmi Bai Rd; 8.30am-8.30pm) Main office which offers general tourist information and provides a useful map.

BUSES FROM MYSURU (MYSORE)

DESTINATION	FARE (₹)	DURATION (HR)	DEPARTURES
Bandipur	77 (O)	2	11 daily via Ooty
Bengaluru	123 (O)/209 (R)/299 (V)	2-3	every 30min
Bengaluru Airport	739 (V)	3½-4	12 daily
Channarayapatna	83 (O)/160 (V)	2	hourly
Chennai	632 (R)/1026 (V)	9-11	6 daily from 4.30pm
Ernakulam	739 (V)	8-9	3 daily from 6pm
Gokarna	478 (O)	12	1 daily
Hassan	112 (O)	3	hourly
Hosapete (Hospet)	381 (O)/608 (R)	9-12	7 daily
Mangaluru	245 (O)/390 (R)/502 (V)	6-7	hourly
Ooty	131 (O)/193 (R)/529 (V)	4-5	12 daily

Fares: (O) Ordinary, (R) Rajahamsa Semideluxe, (V) Airavath AC Volvo

TRAINS FROM MYSURU (MYSORE)

DESTINATION	TRAIN NO & NAME	FARE (₹)	DURATION (HR)	DEPARTURES
Bengaluru	16518 Bengaluru Exp	2AC/3AC 695/490	3	5.30am
Bengaluru	12613 Tippu Exp	2nd class/AC chair 90/305	2½	11.15am
Bengaluru	12008 Shatabdi Exp	AC chair/AC executive chair 305/770	2	2.15pm daily except Wed
Chennai	12008 Shatabdi Exp	AC chair/AC executive chair 1280/1845	7	2.15pm daily Thu-Tue
Hosapete (for Hampi)	16592 Hampi Exp	3AC/2AC sleeper 840/1205	12	7pm
Hubballi	17301 Mysore Dharwad Exp	sleeper/2AC 275/1065	9½	10.30pm

Getting There & Away

AIR

Mysuru's airport was not operating at research time, but flights may resume.

BUS

The **central bus stand** (Bengaluru-Nilgiri Rd) handles all KSRTC long-distance buses.

The **city bus stand** (Sayyaji Rao Rd) is for city, Srirangapatna and Chamundi Hill buses.

The **private bus stand** (Sayyaji Rao Rd) serves Hubballi (Hubli), Vijapura (Bijapur), Mangaluru, Ooty (Udhagamandalam) and Ernakulam. You'll find several ticketing agents around the stand.

TRAIN

Train tickets can be bought from Mysuru's **railway reservation office** (☎131; ⏰8am-8pm Mon-Sat, to 2pm Sun).

Getting Around

Uber and Ola cabs are everywhere in Mysuru. Agencies at hotels can organise drivers for around ₹1800 per day in town, or from ₹2500 per day for out of town trips.

Count on around ₹1000 for a day's sightseeing in an autorickshaw.

Around Mysuru

Consider one of KSTDC's (p869) tours for visiting sights around Mysuru.

Srirangapatna (Srirangapatnam)

☎08236 / POP 26,300

Steeped in bloody history, the fort town of Srirangapatna, 16km from Mysuru, is built on an island straddling the Cauvery River. The seat of Hyder Ali and Tipu Sultan's power, this town was the de facto capital of much of southern India during the 18th century. The ramparts, battlements and some of the gates of the fort still stand, as do a clutch of monuments.

Sights

Daria Daulat Bagh PALACE

(Summer Palace; Indian/foreigner ₹20/100; ⏰9am-5pm) Set within lovely manicured grounds, Srirangapatna's star attraction is Tipu's summer palace, 1km east of the fort. Built from teak and rosewood, the lavish decoration that covers every inch of its interiors is impressive. The ceilings are embellished with floral designs, while the walls bear murals depicting courtly life and Tipu's campaigns against the British. There's a small museum within displaying artefacts and interesting paintings.

Gumbaz MAUSOLEUM

(⏰8am-6.30pm) FREE In a serene garden, the historically significant Persian-style Gumbaz is the resting place of the legendary Tipu Sultan, his equally famed father, Hyder Ali, and his wife. Most inscriptions are in Farsi. The interior of the onion-dome mausoleum is impressive and painted in a tiger-like motif as a tribute to the sultan.

Sri Ranganathaswamy Temple HINDU TEMPLE

(⏰7.30am-1pm & 4-8pm) Constructed in AD 894, this attractive Vaishnavite temple has a mix of Hoysala and Vijayanagar design. Within are cavernous walkways, pillars and the centrepiece 4.5m-long reclining statue of Ranganatha, a manifestation of Vishnu.

Jamia Masjid MOSQUE

This cream-coloured mosque with two minarets was built by the sultan in 1787 and features an interesting blend of Islamic and Hindu architecture. Climb the stairs at the back for panoramic views of the site.

Colonel Bailey's Dungeon HISTORIC SITE

FREE North of the island, on the banks of the Cauvery, is this well-preserved 18th-century white-walled dungeon used to hold British prisoners of war, including Colonel Bailey who died here in 1780. Jutting out from the walls are stone fixtures used to chain the naked prisoners, who were immersed in water up to their necks.

Ranganathittu Bird Sanctuary NATURE RESERVE

(Indian/foreigner incl 15min boat ride ₹60/120, long lens camera/video ₹500; 8.30am-5.45pm) The Ranganathittu Bird Sanctuary includes six islets and the banks of the Cauvery River. Storks, ibises, egrets, spoonbills and cormorants are best seen in the early morning or late afternoon on an extended **boat ride** (₹1000 per hour). There are also plenty of crocodiles around, which are quite easy to spot. You'll find a restaurant on-site.

Sleeping & Eating

Mayura River View HOTEL $$

(0823-6252114; www.kstdc.co/hotels; d with fan/AC from ₹2300/3300;) These government rooms and cottages are in pretty decent shape and have a fine location on a quiet patch of riverbank. Day trippers can pop in for lunch (mains ₹150 to ₹180) to gaze at the river while guzzling beer.

Getting There & Away

Hourly buses (₹22 to ₹30, 45 minutes) depart from Mysuru's City bus stand. Passenger trains travelling from Mysuru to Bengaluru also stop here. Bus 307 (₹18, 30 minutes) heading to Brindavan Gardens is just across from Srirangapatna's main bus stand. A return autorickshaw from Mysuru is about ₹600, and a taxi around ₹1000.

Getting Around

The sights are spread out, so hiring an autorickshaw (around ₹300 for three hours) is the best option for getting around.

Melukote (Melkote)

Life in the devout Hindu town of Melukote (also called Melkote), about 50km north of Mysuru, revolves around the atmospheric 12th-century **Cheluvanarayana Temple** (Raja St; 8am-1pm & 5-8pm), with its rose-coloured *gopuram* (gateway tower) and ornately carved pillars. Get a workout on the hike up to the hilltop Yoganarasimha Temple, which offers fine views of the surrounding hills.

Three KSRTC buses shuttle daily between Mysuru and Melukote (₹100, 1½ hours).

Somnathpur

The astonishingly beautiful **Keshava Temple** (Indian/foreigner ₹5/100; 8.30am-5.30pm) is one of the finest examples of Hoysala architecture, on par with the masterpieces of Belur and Halebid. Built in 1268 AD, this star-shaped temple, 33km from Mysuru, is adorned with superb stone sculptures depicting various scenes from the Ramayana, Mahabharata and Bhagavad Gita, and the life and times of the Hoysala kings.

Somnathpur is 12km south of Bannur and 10km north of Tirumakudal Narsipur. Take one of the half-hourly buses from Mysuru to either village (₹35, 30 minutes) and change there.

Bandipur National Park

08229

Part of the Nilgiri Biosphere Reserve, **Bandipur National Park** (http://bandipurtigerreserve.in; Indian/foreigner ₹75/1000, video ₹1000; 6am-9.30am & 4-6pm) is one of South India's most famous wilderness areas. Covering 880 sq km, it was once the Mysuru maharajas' private wildlife reserve, and is now a protected zone for over 100 species of mammals, including tiger, elephant, leopard, gaur (Indian bison), chital (spotted deer), sambar, sloth bear, dhole (wild dog), mongoose and langur. It's also home to an impressive 350 species of bird. It's only 80km south of Mysuru on the Ooty road.

Activities

Only government-approved vehicles are permitted to run safaris within the park.

Bandipur Safari Lodge JEEP SAFARI

(08229-233001; www.junglelodges.com; 2hr safari per person ₹2700; 6am & 4pm) Bandipur Safari Lodge has open-air 4WDs and minibuses, accompanied by knowledgeable guides.

Forest Department Safari SAFARI

(08229-236043; directorbandipur@gmail.com; 1hr safari per person incl permit in bus/jeep/Gypsy

WORTH A TRIP

BILIGIRI RANGANNA TEMPLE WILDLIFE SANCTUARY

Much less known than Bandipur or Nagarhole, the **Biligiri Ranganna Temple Wildlife Sanctuary** in the BR Hills makes a great alternative to live out your *Jungle Book* fantasies. Set over 570 sq km, it was declared a tiger reserve in 2011 – but as with most parks, you'd be extremely lucky to spot one. Elephants, leopards, sloth bears and dholes (wild dogs) also roam the hills here.

The **Kyathdevaraya Gudi Wilderness Camp** (☎080-40554055; www.junglelodges.com/kyathadevara-gudi-wilderness-camp; Yelandur; per person incl full board Indian/foreigner from ₹8036/9804) has a fantastic site among the peaceful forest, with grazing warthog and spotted deer. Accommodation (in tented cottages or delightful stilted log cabins) is pricey, but rates include all meals, a safari, guided walk and all taxes.

The wildlife sanctuary is a 4½-hour drive from Bengaluru. It's best to hire a vehicle, although it is theoretically possible to get there by public transport. You can catch a direct 7.45am bus from Mysuru to K Gudi, or a bus to Chamarajanagar and connect to a 1.30pm bus to K Gudi. From Chamarajanagar you can arrange a jeep for ₹700.

₹1200/2000/3000; ⏲departures 6.30-8.30am & 3.30-5.30pm) The forest department has rushed drives on buses (capacity 20) arranged at the park headquarters. It's worth paying extra for a jeep or 4WD. Avoid weekends when it gets very crowded.

Sleeping & Eating

Hotel Bandipur Plaza HOTEL $
(☎08229-233200; Ooty-Mysuru Hwy; r ₹1500; 📶) Its highway location is a drawback, but this basic hotel's rooms are affordable and adequate in an otherwise pricey destination. It's nearby to Bandipur Safari Lodge, so convenient for safaris into the park, and has a decent restaurant.

Forest Department Bungalows GUESTHOUSE $
(☎08229-236051; www.bandipurtigerreserve.in; 9-/20-bed dm ₹720/1000, bungalow foreigner from ₹3000; 📶) Basic lodging at the park HQ is convenient for location and atmosphere, but the downside is foreigners have to pay an additional ₹1000 per night for park entry fees. Dorms are rented out in the entirety, so you won't need to share with strangers. You can book online.

Tiger Ranch LODGE $$
(☎8095408505; www.tigerranch.net; Mangala Village; per person incl full board ₹1510) Offering a genuine wilderness experience, the very rustic Tiger Ranch has basic but attractive cottages, an atmospheric thatched-roof dining hall and fine home-cooked food. There's good walking in the surrounding forest, and a you're sure to encounter wildlife. Evenings can be enjoyed around a bonfire. It's located 10km from the park; call ahead to arrange a pick-up (₹300).

★**Dhole's Den** LODGE $$$
(☎9444468376; www.dholesden.com; Kaniyanapura Village; camping/s/d incl full board from ₹3000/11,000/12,000; 📶) Flawlessly presented, Dhole's Den offers contemporary design in lovely pastoral surrounds. Stylish, modernist rooms and bungalows are decked out with art and colourful fabrics, plus couches and deckchairs. It's environmentally conscious with solar power, tank water and organic vegies. Camping is available for those on a budget. It's a 20-minute drive from the park headquarters; rates include a guided nature walk.

Serai RESORT, LODGE $$$
(☎08229-236075; www.theserai.in; Kaniyanapura Village; r incl full board from ₹21,000; ❄📶🏊) Set in a coffee plantation that backs onto the national park, this luxurious resort has gorgeous Mediterranean-inspired villas (some with private pool) that are in harmony with the natural surrounds. Thatched-roof rooms feature elegant touches such as copper bathroom fixtures, stone-wall showers and wildlife photography on the walls. Its glassed-in restaurant and infinity pool both maximise outlooks to Nilgiri Hills.

MC Resort HOTEL $$$
(☎9019954162; www.mcresort.in; Bengaluru-Ooty Rd, Melukamanahally; s/d incl full board from ₹4000/5000; 📶🏊) Decent resort-style place with spacious, well-equipped rooms, a large swimming pool, kids' pool, a multicuisine restaurant and a convenient location near the park. Rates are inclusive of meals.

Getting There & Away

Buses between Mysuru and Ooty can drop you at Bandipur (₹78, 2½ hours), an 88km journey. Taxis from Mysuru are about ₹2000.

Nagarhole National Park

Rich in wildlife, jungle and boasting a scenic lake, the 643-sq-km **Nagarhole National Park** (Rajiv Gandhi National Park; Indian/foreigner ₹200/1000, video ₹1000; 6am-6pm) (pronounced *nag*-ar-hole-eh) is one of Karnataka's best wildlife getaways, containing good numbers of animals including tigers and elephants. Flanking the **Kabini River**, it forms an important protected region that includes neighbouring Bandipur National Park (p878) and several other reserves. The lush forests here are home to tigers, leopards, elephants, gaurs, muntjacs (barking deer), wild dogs, bonnet macaques and common langurs, and 270 species of birds. The park can remain closed for long stretches between July and October, when the rains transform the forests into a giant slush-pit.

The Kabini River empties into the Kabini Reservoir, creating a vast watering hole for Nagarhole's wildlife. Herds of wild elephants and other animals gather on the banks, and the high concentration of wildlife has made this one of Karnataka's top wildlife-spotting locations.

The traditional inhabitants of the land, the hunter-gatherer Jenu Kuruba people, still live in the park, despite government efforts to relocate them.

Activities

Government-Run Safaris SAFARI
(Kabini River Lodge; 2½hr 4WD safari ₹3000) Leave at 6am and 3pm when conditions permit in the dry season.

20-Seater Motorboat Rides BOATING, WILDLIFE
(Kabini River Lodge; per person ₹2000) Organised by the Kabini River Lodge for relaxed wildlife viewing, and excellent for birders.

Sleeping & Eating

Kabini Lake (home to most lodges) makes a wonderful base, but has no real budget hotels. For inexpensive places head to the park HQ.

Karapur Hotel GUESTHOUSE $$
(9945904840; Karapura roundabout; r ₹1200) The only budget option close to Kabini is this simple lodge with a few rooms above a shop in the township of Karapura, 3km from the park.

★ **Waterwoods Lodge** GUESTHOUSE $$$
(082-28264421; www.waterwoods.in; d incl full board from ₹13,200;) On a grassy embankment overlooking scenic Kabini Lake, Waterwoods is a stunning lodge. Most rooms have balconies with wonderful lake views, swing chairs, hardwood floors and designer flair. It's kid-friendly with trampoline, infinity pool, free canoe hire and wood-fired pizzas. Pamper yourself in the spa which has massage rooms, Jacuzzi and a steam bath.

Serai Kabini LODGE $$$
(080-40012200; http://theserai.in/kabini; r incl full board from ₹16,450;) Perfectly set up for wildlife spotting, this luxury lodge has wonderful lake-facing bungalows, and organises tip-top jungle safaris, boat trips and nature walks. The restaurant is beautifully designed and the cuisine excellent. There's a beautiful spa too. Located on the north shore of Kabini Reservoir.

Bison Resort LODGE $$$
(080-41278708; www.thebisonresort.com; Gundathur Village; camping per person from ₹2500, s/d incl full board from US$320/370;) Inspired by luxury safari lodges in Africa, Bison succeeds in replicating the classic wilderness experience with a stunning waterfront location and choice between canvas-walled cottages, stilted bungalows or bush camping. They offer a wide selection of activities including treks to local tribal villages and sunset boat rides. Service standards are top-notch and there are expert naturalists at hand.

KAAV Safari Lodge LODGE $$$
(08228-264492; www.kaav.com; Mallali Cross, Kabini; incl full board s/d from ₹10,400/13,200, tent from ₹12,000;) A kind of designer safari lodge, KAAV has open-plan rooms with polished concrete floors, hip bathrooms and spacious balconies that open directly to the national park. Yes, the attention to detail is superb. Head up to the viewing tower to lounge on plush day beds, or take a dip in the infinity pool. No children under 10.

Getting There & Away

The park's main entrance is 93km southwest of Mysuru. Two buses depart daily from Mysuru to Karapuram (₹68, 2½ hours), around 3km from Kabini Lake. A taxi from Mysuru is around ₹2000.

Kodagu (Coorg) Region

Nestled amid evergreen hills that line the southernmost edge of Karnataka is the luscious Kodagu (Coorg) region, gifted with emerald landscapes and hectares of plantations. A major centre for coffee and spice production, this rural expanse is also home to the Kodava people, who are divided into 1000 clans. The uneven terrain and cool climate make it a fantastic area for trekking, birdwatching or lazily ambling down little-trodden paths winding around carpeted hills. All in all, Kodagu is rejuvenation guaranteed.

Kodagu was a state in its own right until 1956, when it merged with Karnataka. The region's chief town and transport hub is Madikeri, but for an authentic Kodagu experience, you have to venture into the countryside. Avoid weekends if you can, when places can quickly get filled up by weekenders from Bengaluru.

Activities

Exploring the region by foot is a highlight for many visitors. Treks are part cultural experience, part nature encounter, involving hill climbs, plantation visits, forest walks and homestays.

The best season for trekking is October to March; there are no treks during monsoon. The most popular peaks are the seven-day trek to Tadiyendamol (1745m), and to Pushpagiri (1712m) and Kotebetta (1620m). Plenty of day hikes are possible too; Rainforest Retreat (p882) organises several. A trekking guide is essential for navigating the labyrinth of forest tracks.

Madikeri (Mercara)

☎08272 / POP 34,200 / ELEV 1525M

Madikeri (also known as Mercara) is a congested market town spread out along a series of ridges. The only reason for coming here is to organise treks or sort out the practicalities of travel.

Sights

Madikeri Fort HISTORIC SITE

There are good views from this hilltop fort, built by Tipu Sultan in the 16th century, though today it's the less glamorous site of the municipal headquarters. You can walk a short section of ramparts and within the fort's walls are the hexagonal palace (now the dusty district commissioner's office) and colonial-era church, which houses a quirky museum (⏲10am-5.30pm Sun-Fri) FREE.

Raja's Seat VIEWPOINT

(MG Rd; ₹5; ⏲5.30am-7pm) A very popular spot to enjoy sunset, as the raja himself did, with fantastic outlooks to rolling hills and endless valleys.

Raja's Tombs HISTORIC BUILDING

(Gaddige) FREE These domed tombs are built in Indo-Sarcenic style and serve as the resting place for Kodava royalty and dignitaries. Located 7km from Madikeri, so take an autorickshaw (₹200).

Abbi Falls WATERFALL

A spectacular sight after the rainy season, these 21.3m-high falls can pack a punch.

Activities

Coorg Sky Adventures SCENIC FLIGHTS

(☎9448954384; www.coorgskyadventures.com; short/long flight ₹2500/8000) Soar over plantation and paddy valleys on a microlight flight for tremendous views of Coorg's lush scenery. An experienced, professional operator.

Ayurjeevan AYURVEDA

(☎944974779; www.ayurjeevancoorg.com; Kohinoor Rd; 1hr from ₹1400; ⏲7am-7pm) An ayurvedic 'hospital' that offers a whole range of intriguing and rejuvenating techniques including rice ball massages and oil baths. It's a short walk from the State Bank India.

Sleeping

With fantastic guesthouses in the surrounding plantations, there's no real reason to stay in Madikeri, unless you arrive very late.

Hotel Chitra HOTEL $

(☎08272-225372; www.hotelchitra.co.in; School Rd; dm ₹270, d from ₹780, with AC ₹1760; ❄) Concrete hotel close to Madikeri's main intersection, so expect some background traffic noise. Provides low-cost, no-frills rooms and friendly service.

Hotel Mayura Valley View HOTEL $$

(☎08272-228387; www.kstdc.co/hotels/hotel-mayura-valley-view-madikeri; Stuart Hill; d/ste incl breakfast from ₹3250/4950; ❄📶) On the hilltop past Raja's Seat, this government hotel is one of Madikeri's best, with large bright rooms, a peaceful ambience and fantastic valley views. Its restaurant-bar with terrace overlooking the valley is a great spot for a beer.

Eating

Coorg Cuisine INDIAN $

(Main Rd; mains ₹100-130; noon-4pm & 7-10pm) Championing unique Kodava specialities such as *pandhi barthadh* (pork dry fry) and *kadambuttu* (rice dumplings), this restaurant is well worth trying. It's not exactly atmospheric, located above a shop on the main road, but there are a few portraits on the walls and the seating is comfy.

★**Raintree** MULTICUISINE $$

(www.raintree.in; 13-14 Pension Lane; meals ₹170-260; 11.30am-10pm) A welcome surprise in a humdrum town, this cute converted bungalow makes a homely place for a delicious meal, with solid wooden furniture and some tribal art. The food does not disappoint either, with local specialities and dishes from the coast. They also sell wine and great Kodagu coffee. Located just behind Madikeri Town Hall.

Information

Travel Coorg (08272-223333; www.travel-coorg.in; outside KSRTC bus stand; 24hr) Provides a good overview of things to do, as well as arranging homestays, trekking guides and other activities. Also offers transport.

Getting There & Away

Very regular buses depart from the KSRTC bus stand for Bengaluru (fan/AC ₹350/539, 5½ to seven hours), stopping in Mysuru (₹162/250, 2½ to four hours) en route. Buses go roughly every two hours in the daytime to Mangaluru (₹135/283, three to four hours), while infrequent ordinary buses head to Hassan (₹117, four hours).

Around Madikeri

The beguiling highlands around Madikeri offer some of the Kodagu's most enchanting countryside. Dotted around its lush hills are numerous spice and coffee plantations, and some tea is grown too.

Activities

★**Jiva Spa** AYURVEDA, MASSAGE

(08272-2665800; www.tajhotels.com/jivaspas/index.html; Vivanta, Galibeedu; treatments from ₹2700; 9am-9pm) Surrounded by rainforest, Jiva Spa at the stunning Vivanta hotel (p882) is *the* place to treat yourself with a range of rejuvenating treatments. With soak tubs, a relaxation lounge, beauty salon and a yoga and meditation zone, it's one of the best in South India. Appointments essential.

Swaasthya Ayurveda Retreat Village AYURVEDA

(www.swaasthya.com; Bekkesodlur Village; per person per day incl full board & yoga class ₹7000) For an exceptionally peaceful and refreshing ayurvedic vacation, head to south Coorg to soothe your soul among the lush greenery on 1.6 hectares of coffee and spice plantations. Prices include up to six treatments a day.

Sleeping & Eating

Rainforest Retreat GUESTHOUSE $$

(08272-265638, 08272-265639; www.rainforestours.com; Galibeedu; s/d tent ₹1500/2000, cottage from ₹2500/3000;) A great place to socialise with eco-minded Indians, this nature-soaked refuge is immersed within forest and plantations and an organic, sustainable set-up. Accommodation is lazy camping (prepitched tents with beds) or cottages with solar power. Rates include plantation tours and treks. Check the website for volunteering opportunities. An autorickshaw from Madikeri is ₹240.

Victorian Verandaz B&B $$

(08272-200234; http://victorianverandaz.com; Modur Estate, Kadagadal Village; d self-catering ₹2000-5500, B&B ₹2950;) Fine family-owned lodgings on a huge estate that grows coffee, pepper, cardamom and rice. There's a choice of accommodation, with two rental cottages that have kitchens which are available on a self-catering basis and two rooms in a cottage which operate on a B&B basis. There's good birding and trail walking on the estate.

Golden Mist HOMESTAY $$

(9448903670, 08272-265629; www.golden-mist.net; Galibeedu; s/d incl full board ₹2500/4000) An incredibly peaceful, very rustic Indian-German-managed tea, coffee and rice-growing farm. The cottages have character though they are basic and best suited for outdoor types rather than those who prize their creature comforts. Meals are tasty local dishes made from the farm's organic produce and staff are very hospitable. It's tricky to find and not signposted, an autorickshaw costs ₹250 from Madikeri.

★**Vivanta** HOTEL $$$

(08272-665800; www.vivantabytaj.com; Galibeedu; r from ₹15,800;) Built across 72 hectares of misty rainforest this effortlessly stylish hotel incorporates principles of space

DON'T MISS

BYLAKUPPE

The small, beautifully kept village of Bylakuppe, just south of the Mysuru–Mangaluru highway, forms South India's largest Tibetan community. Established in 1961, it was among the first refugee camps set up in South India to house thousands of Tibetans who fled from Tibet following the 1959 Chinese invasion. Over 10,000 Tibetans live here (including 3300 monks).

Foreigners are not allowed to stay overnight without a Protected Area Permit (PAP) from the Ministry of Home Affairs in Delhi, which can take months to process. Contact the **Tibet Bureau Office** (11-26479737; www.tibetbureau.in; New Delhi) for details. Day trippers are welcome to visit, however.

The area's highlight is the atmospheric **Namdroling Monastery** (www.namdroling.org; 7am-6pm), home to the spectacular **Golden Temple** (Padmasambhava Buddhist Vihara; 7am-6pm), presided over by three 18m-high gold-plated Buddha statues. The temple is at its dramatic best when prayers are in session and it rings out with gongs, drums and the drone of hundreds of young monks chanting. You're welcome to meditate. The **Zangdogpalri Temple** (7am-6pm), a similarly ornate affair, is next door.

If you have a permit, the simple **Paljor Dhargey Ling Guest House** (08223-258686; pdguesthouse@yahoo.com; r ₹275-375) is opposite the Golden Temple. For delicious *momos* (Tibetan dumplings) or *thukpa* (noodle soup), pop into the Tibetan-run **Malaya Restaurant** (momos ₹60-90; 7am-9pm). **Thirsty Crow** (south of Namdroling Monastery) offers fine fresh juices, milkshakes, lime sodas, teas and coffees. Otherwise there are many hotels in nearby Kushalnagar – including modern, well-presented **Hotel White Wings** (9741155900; http://whitewingscoorg.com; 1-86, BM Rd, Kushalnagar; r with AC ₹2100;) – and the surrounding countryside.

Autorickshaws (shared/solo ₹15/30) run to Bylakuppe from Kushalnagar, 5km away. Buses frequently do the 34km run to Kushalnagar from Madikeri (₹45, 45 minutes) and Hassan (₹80, 2½ hours). Most buses on the Mysuru–Madikeri route stop at Kushalnagar.

and minimalism, and effectively blends into its environment. Old cattle tracks lead to rooms, with pricier ones featuring private indoor pools, fireplaces and butlers. There are astonishing highland views from the lobby and infinity pool, and a top-class ayurvedic spa (p882).

Kakkabe

08272 / POP 580

Surrounded by forested hills, this tranquil village and hiking hot spot is an ideal base to plan an assault on Kodagu's highest peak, Tadiyendamol, or just enjoy a wander along scenic highland trails.

Sleeping & Eating

★Honey Valley Estate GUESTHOUSE $

(08272-238339; www.honeyvalleyindia.in; r from ₹800, without bathroom from ₹550;) A homestay on a hilltop, this wonderful trekking guesthouse, at 1250m above sea level, transports you into a lovely cool, fresh, natural environment. The owners' friendliness, eco-mindedness and local knowledge of wildlife is excellent. There are 18 local trekking routes and six different accommodation options. It's accessible by 4WD only (₹200, book via hotel) from Kakkabe.

Chingaara GUESTHOUSE $$

(08272-238633; www.chingaara.com; Kabbinakad; r incl half board ₹2300-3200;) This delightful farmhouse is surrounded by verdant coffee plantations, with good birding in the vicinity. Rooms are spacious, and most have good views – especially room 9. Good home-style cooking is served and staff will light a bonfire at night. It's 2.5km up a rocky steep hill (4WD only); call ahead and Chingaara's jeep will pick you up from Kabbinakad junction.

Tamara Resort RESORT $$$

(080-71077700; www.thetamara.com; Yavakapadi Village; r incl meals & activities from ₹23,800;) Set in a coffee estate, this romantic nature resort has stilted cottages that soar above the lush green surrounds. Luxurious rooms all have teak floorboards, balconies and king-sized beds. Its memorable restaurant is raised above the plantations with a glass-bottom floor to look down upon. There are three good local treks, yoga classes and a spa. No children under 12.

Hassan

☎08172 / POP 138,000

This sprawling, congested transport hub (with decent accommodation) has minimal appeal other than as a base to visit nearby Belur, Halebid or Sravanabelagola. The helpful **tourist office** (☎08172-268862; AVK College Rd; ⏰10am-5.30pm, Mon-Fri) advises on transport options.

Sleeping

SS Residency HOTEL $$
(☎08172-233466; www.ssresidency.co.in; BM Rd; r from ₹1960; ❄📶) Modern, centrally located hotel with a wide choice of rooms, all attractively styled with cream furnishings, cable TV and minibars. There's no restaurant, however.

Getting There & Away

From the **New Bus Stand** (Hwy 71), 500m south of the town centre, buses depart to Mysuru (₹112, three hours), Bengaluru (₹192 to ₹469, 3½ to 4½ hours) and Mangaluru (₹163 to ₹355, 3½ to 4½ hours). A day tour of Belur and Halebid or Sravanabelagola will cost you about ₹1400.

From Hassan's well-organised train station, three to four trains head to Mysuru daily (sleeper/2AC ₹140/695, two to three hours), all in the dead of night. For Bengaluru, there's the red-eye 3am 16518 Bangalore Express (sleeper/2AC ₹180/695, 5½ hours).

Belur (Beluru)

☎08177 / POP 9320 / ELEV 968M

The Hoysala temples at Belur (also Beluru) and nearby Halebid are the apex of one of the most artistically exuberant periods of ancient Hindu cultural development. Architecturally, they are South India's answer to Khajuraho in Madhya Pradesh and Konark near Puri in Odisha (Orissa).

Sights

Channakeshava Temple HINDU TEMPLE
(Temple Rd; guide ₹250; ⏰7.30am-7.30pm) Commissioned in AD 1116 to commemorate the Hoysalas' victory over the neighbouring Cholas, this temple took more than a century to build, and is currently the only one among the three major Hoysala sites still in daily use – try to be there for the *puja* (offerings or prayer) ceremonies at 9am, 3pm and 7.30pm.

Some parts of the temple, such as the exterior lower friezes, were not sculpted to completion and are thus less elaborate. However, the work higher up is unsurpassed in detail and artistry, and is a glowing tribute to human skill.

Particularly intriguing are the angled bracket figures depicting women in ritual dancing poses. While the front of the temple is reserved for images depicting erotic sections from the Kama Sutra, the back is strictly for gods. The roof of the inner sanctum is held up by rows of exquisitely sculpted pillars, no two of which are identical in design.

Sleeping & Eating

Hotel Mayura Velapuri HOTEL $$
(☎0817-7222209; www.kstdc.co/hotels; Kempegowda Rd; d with fan/AC from ₹1200/1550; ❄) A renovated state-run hotel located on the way to Channakeshava Temple with pretty comfortable, spacious rooms. Its restaurant-bar serves a variety of Indian dishes (from ₹80) to go with beer.

Getting There & Away

There are frequent buses to/from Hassan (₹44 to ₹96, 45 minutes), 38km away, and Halebid (₹25, 30 minutes). It's also possible to visit on day-trip KSTDC tour from Bengaluru or Mysuru.

Halebid

☎08177 / POP 9348

Halebid (also called Halibidu, or Halebeedu) is a small town that's home to a stunning Hoysala temple and some other minor Jain sites. Most travellers visit on a day trip from Belur, 15km west.

Sights

Hoysaleswara Temple HINDU TEMPLE
(⏰dawn-dusk) Construction of the Hoysaleswara Temple, Halebid's claim to fame, began around AD 1121 and went on for more than 80 years. It was never completed, but nonetheless stands today as a masterpiece of Hoysala architecture. The interior of its inner sanctum, chiselled out of black stone, is marvellous. On the outside, the temple's richly sculpted walls are covered with a flurry of Hindu deities, sages, stylised animals and friezes depicting the life of the Hoysala rulers.

Museum MUSEUM
(₹5; ⏰9am-5pm Sat-Thu) Adjacent to Hoysaleswara Temple is this small museum with a collection of beautiful sculptures from around Halebid.

Sleeping

Hotel Mayura Shanthala HOTEL $$
(08177-273224; www.kstdc.co/hotels/; d incl breakfast from ₹1600;) Set in a leafy garden right opposite the temple complex, Hotel Mayura Shanthala is the best sleeping option.

Getting There & Away

Regular buses depart for Hassan (₹35, one hour), 33km away; buses to Belur are ₹25. KSTDC tours from Bengaluru and Mysuru also visit Halebid.

Sravanabelagola

08176 / POP 5660

Atop the bare rocky summit of Vindhyagiri Hill, the 17.5m-high statue of the Jain deity Gomateshvara (Bahubali) is visible long before you reach the pilgrimage town of Sravanabelagola (also spelt Shravanabelagola). Viewing the statue close up is the main reason for heading to this sedate town, whose name means 'Monk of the White Pond'.

Sights

Gomateshvara Statue JAIN SITE
(Bahubali; 6.30am-6.30pm) A steep climb up 614 steps takes you to the top of Vindhyagiri Hill, the summit of which is lorded over by the towering naked statue of the Jain deity Gomateshvara (Bahubali). Commissioned by a military commander in the service of the Ganga king Rachamalla and carved out of a single piece of granite by the sculptor Aristenemi in AD 98, it is said to be the world's tallest monolithic statue. Leave your shoes at the foot of the hill.

Bahubali was the son of emperor Vrishabhadeva, who later became the first Jain *tirthankar* (revered teacher), Adinath. Embroiled in fierce competition with his brother Bharatha to succeed his father, Bahubali realised the futility of material gains and renounced his kingdom. As a recluse, he meditated in complete stillness in the forest until he attained enlightenment. His lengthy meditative spell is denoted by vines curling around his legs and an ant hill at his feet.

Every 12 years, millions flock here to attend the **Mastakabhisheka** (Feb) ceremony, when the statue is dowsed in holy waters, pastes, powders, precious metals and stones. The next ceremony is slated for 2018.

Sleeping & Eating

The local Jain organisation **SDJMI** (08176-257258) handles bookings for its 15 guesthouses (double/triple ₹250/310). The office is behind the Vidyananda Nilaya Dharamsala, past the post office.

Hotel Raghu HOTEL $
(08176-257238; s/d from ₹400/500, d with AC ₹900;) Very basic rooms that are something of a last resort should you be stranded in town. However, the vegetarian restaurant downstairs works up an awesome veg thali (₹90).

Getting There & Away

There are no direct buses from Sravanabelagola to Hassan or Belur – you must go to Channarayapatna (₹40, 20 minutes) and catch an onward connection there. One daily bus runs direct to Mysuru (₹149, 1½ hours).

SRAVANABELAGOLA (SHRAVANABELAGOLA) JAIN TEMPLES

Apart from the Gomateshvara statue, there are several interesting Jain temples in town. The **Chandragupta Basti** (Chandragupta Community; 6am-6pm), on Chandragiri Hill opposite Vindhyagiri, is believed to have been built by Emperor Ashoka. The **Bhandari Basti** (Bhandari Community; 6am-6pm), in the southeast corner of town, is Sravanabelagola's largest temple. Nearby, **Chandranatha Basti** (Chandranatha Community; 6am-6pm) has well-preserved paintings depicting Jain tales.

KARNATAKA COAST

Mangaluru (Mangalore)

0824 / POP 492,500

Alternating between relaxed coastal town and hectic nightmare, Mangaluru (more commonly known as Mangalore) has a Jekyll and Hyde thing going, but it's a useful gateway for the Konkan coast and inland Kodagu region. While there's not a lot to do here, it has an appealing off-the-beaten-path feel, and the spicy seafood dishes are sensational.

Mangaluru sits at the estuaries of the picturesque Netravathi and Gurupur Rivers on the Arabian Sea and has been a major port on international trade routes since the 6th century.

Mangaluru (Mangalore)

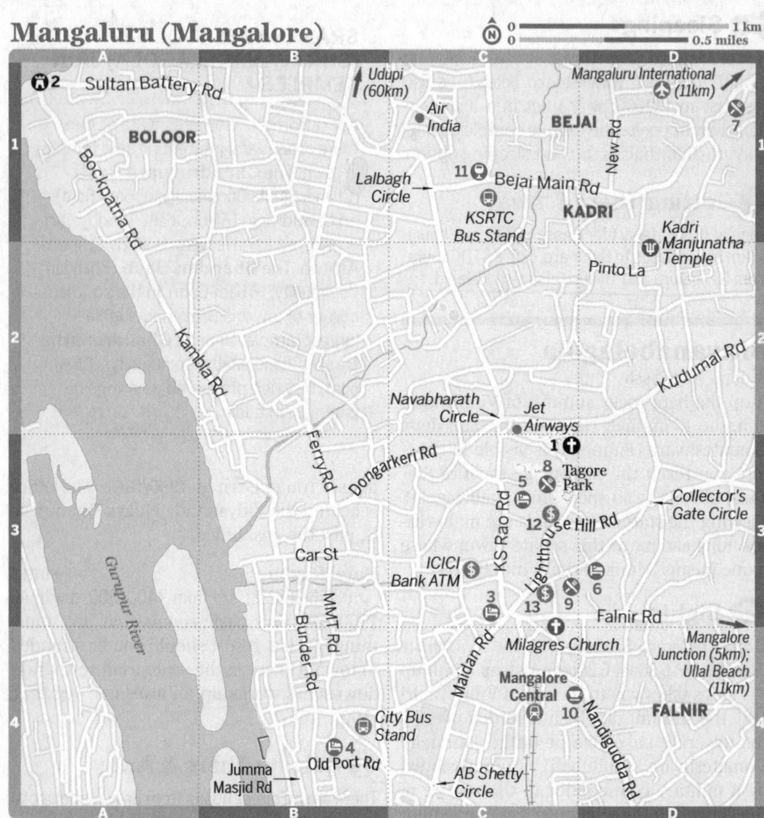

Mangaluru (Mangalore)

Sights
1 St Aloysius College Chapel C3
2 Sultan's Battery A1

Sleeping
3 Adarsh Hotel C3
4 Gateway Hotel B4
5 Hotel Manorama C3
6 Hotel Roopa D3

Eating
7 Gajalee D1
8 Kadal C3
9 Lalith Bar & Restaurant C3

Drinking & Nightlife
10 #45 .... C4
11 Spindrift C1

Information
12 HDFC C3
13 State Bank of Mysore ATM C3

Sights

St Aloysius College Chapel CHURCH
(Lighthouse Hill; 9am-6pm) Catholicism's roots in Mangaluru date back to the arrival of the Portuguese in the early 1500s. One impressive legacy is the 1880 Sistine Chapel-like St Aloysius chapel, with its walls and ceilings painted with brilliant frescoes. No photography is permitted.

Sultan's Battery FORT
(Sultan Battery Rd; 6am-6pm) The only remnant of Tipu Sultan's fort is this small lookout with views over scenic backwaters. It's 4km from the city centre on the headland of the old port.

Ullal Beach BEACH

This stretch of golden sand is a good destination to escape the city heat. It's 12km south of Mangaluru, across the Netravathi estuary. An Uber/autorickshaw is ₹200 one way, or take bus 44A or 44C (₹10) from the City bus stand.

Sleeping

Hotel Roopa HOTEL $

(☎0824-2421272; www.roopahotel.com; Balmatta Rd; r with fan/AC from ₹450/1300; ❄📶) One of the city's best-value hotels, close to the KSRTC bus stand, and combines good prices with professional management and decent, very affordable rooms. It has an excellent basement restaurant and bar.

Hotel Manorama HOTEL $

(☎0824-2440306; KS Rao Rd; s/d from ₹620/640, with AC from ₹1120; ❄) Offering fine value with clean, good-value rooms and a lobby that provides a memorable first impression with its display of Hindu statues and artefacts. It's close to the City Center mall for shopping and a food court.

Adarsh Hotel HOTEL $

(☎0824-2440878; Market Rd; s/d ₹340/500) Enjoying a good location in the thick of things, this old-school cheapie has very low rates and fairly well-maintained rooms.

Gateway Hotel HOTEL $$$

(☎0824-6660420; www.tajhotels.com; Old Port Rd; s/d incl breakfast from ₹5840/6260; ❄@📶🏊) Owned by the Taj group, this is a well-run hotel where the spacious rooms have plasma TVs and large beds laden with pillows, though bathrooms are somewhat dated. The lovely 20m swimming pool is surrounded by lawn and loungers, and there's a small spa and a fine restaurant.

Eating

Lalith Bar & Restaurant SEAFOOD $$

(Balmatta Rd; mains ₹150-400; ⏰11.30am-3.30pm & 6.30-11.30pm; ❄) Specialising in authentic Mangalorean seafood delights such as spicy masala fish fry smothered in saucy red coconut curry, or scrumptious deep-fried prawn rava fry, this scruffy restaurant is always popular. It all goes beautifully with a cold beer from its fully stocked bar.

Kadal SOUTH INDIAN $$

(www.kadalrestaurant.in; Nalapad Residency, Lighthouse Hill Rd; mains ₹150-230; ⏰11am-3.30pm & 6.30-11pm; 📶) This high-rise restaurant affords wonderful city views and elegant and warmly lit interiors. Try the spicy chicken *uruval* (a coconut coastal curry) or the yummy prawn ghee roast. Prices are moderate for the quality and experience.

Gajalee SEAFOOD $$$

(☎0824-2221900; www.gajalee.com; Circuit House, Kadri Hills; mains ₹160-1280; ⏰10am-11pm) In a town famous for seafood, locals often cite this as the best. Their fish curries are superb, prepared in a spicy coconut sauce, while the clam *koshimbir* is cooked in a rich green masala.

WORTH A TRIP

SURFING SWAMIS

While there has always been a spiritual bond between surfer and Mother ocean, the **Surfing Ashram** (Mantra Surf Club; ☎9663141146; www.surfingindia.net; 6-64 Kolachikambla, Mulki; board hire/lessons per day ₹700/2200) at Mulki, 30km north of Mangaluru, takes things to a whole new plane. At this Hare Krishna ashram, which was established by its American guru who's been surfing since 1963, devotees follow a daily ritual of *puja* (prayers), chanting, meditation and vegetarian diet in between catching barrels.

There's surf year-round, but the best waves are May to June and September to October. The swamis can also assist with information on surfing across India. Board hire is ₹700 per day and lessons are ₹2200 per day.

If there are no waves they have SUP boards for the river or ocean, sea kayaks and a jet ski for wakeboarding. Snorkelling trips to offshore islands are also possible.

The centre has a homely beachhouse feel, and rates (per person/couple including full board ₹2800/3900).

All are welcome to visit, but it's important to be aware that it's strictly a place of worship and there are guidelines to abide by, including abstinence from meat, alcohol, tobacco and sex during your stay.

Drinking & Nightlife

★Spindrift MICROBREWERY

(www.facebook.com/SpindriftMangalore; 5th Fl, Bharath Mall, Lalbagh; ⏲11am-11pm; 📶) The first microbrewery in town is a big space with indoor and outdoor seating and the acoustic artists, indie bands and DJs create quite a vibe on weekend nights. Beers on tap (from ₹230) include a wheat beer, pilsner and IPA and there's good finger food too.

#45 CAFE

(Trinity Commercial Complex, Attavara Rd; ⏲10.30am-10.30pm; 📶) Very popular with students, this hip little cafe does a wide range of huge milkshakes (including Ferrero Rocher and Nutella flavours), fresh juices, good coffees, wraps, burgers and breakfasts.

Getting There & Away

AIR

Mangaluru International Airport (☎0824-2254252; www.mangaloreairport.com) is about 15km northeast of town. There are daily flights to Mumbai, Delhi, Bengaluru, Hyderabad and Chennai and international connections to Abu Dhabi, Doha and Dubai.

Airlines include:

Air India (☎0824-2451046; Hathill Rd; ⏲9am-5.30pm Mon-Sat)

Jet Airways (☎0824-2441181; Ram Bhavan Complex, KS Rao Rd; ⏲9am-5.30pm Mon-Sat)

BUS

The **KSRTC bus stand** (☎0824-2211243; Bejai Main Rd) is 3km from the city centre. Deluxe buses depart half-hourly to Bengaluru (₹406 to ₹815, seven to nine hours) via Mysuru (₹245 to ₹505, five to six hours).

Dharmasthala ₹49-82, one to two hours, 8.05am and 2.20pm daily

Ernakulam ₹845, nine hours, 9pm

Gokarna ₹234, 5½ hours, 12.45pm daily

Hassan ₹163 to ₹355, three to five hours, 12 daily

Madikeri ₹135 to ₹305, 3½ to four hours, 11 daily

Panaji ₹359 to ₹698, 8-9½ hours, one to three daily

For Udupi (₹58, 1½ hours) head to the **City bus stand** (State Bank stand).

TRAIN

The main train station, Mangaluru Central, is south of the city centre.

Getting Around

To get to the airport, take buses 47B or 47C from the City bus stand. An Uber is around ₹350.

Dharmasthala

☎08256 / POP 10,340

Inland from Mangaluru are a string of Jain temple towns, such as Venur, Mudabidri and Karkal. The most interesting among them is Dharmasthala village, 75km east of Mangaluru by the Netravathi River. Tens of thousands of pilgrims pass through this tiny settlement every day. During holidays and major festivals, such as the five-day pilgrim festival of **Lakshadeepotsava** (⏲Nov), the footfall can go up tenfold.

Sights

Manjunatha Temple HINDU TEMPLE

(⏲6.30am-2.30pm & 5-8.45pm) This striking Kerala-style temple has a pyramidal roof of gold-plated copper plates and its wood carvings have recently been meticulously renovated. Three elephants trunk out blessings to pilgrims outside the Manjunatha Temple; men have to enter bare-chested, with legs covered. You can fast-track the queue if you pay ₹200.

Car Museum MUSEUM

(₹5; ⏲8.30am-1pm & 2-7pm) Don't forget to visit the fantastic Car Museum, home to 48 vintage autos, including a 1903 Renault and 1920s Studebaker President used by Mahatma Gandhi, plus classic Mercedes Benz, Chevrolet and Rolls-Royce models. No photos are allowed.

TRAINS FROM MANGALURU (MANGALORE)

DESTINATION	TRAIN NO & NAME	FARE (₹)	DURATION (HR)	DEPARTURES
Bengaluru	16524 Bangalore Exp	sleeper/2AC 280/1080	11½	8.55pm
Chennai	12686 Chennai Exp	sleeper/2AC 460/1725	15½	4.20pm
Gokarna	16523 Karwar Exp	sleeper/2AC 190/6900	5½	7.55am
Gokarna	12620 Matsyaganda Exp	sleeper/2AC 235/825	4	2.35pm
Thiruvananthapuram	16630 Malabar Exp	sleeper/2AC 340/1320	15	6.15pm

RANI ABBAKKA: THE WARRIOR QUEEN

The legendary exploits of Rani Abbakka, one of India's first freedom fighters – who happened to be a female – is one that gets surprisingly little attention outside the Mangaluru region. An Indian Joan of Arc, her inspiring story is just waiting to be picked up by a Bollywood/Hollywood screenwriter.

As the Portuguese consolidated power along India's western coastline in the 16th century, seizing towns across Goa and down to Mangalore, their attempts to take Ullal proved more of a challenge. This was thanks to its 'fearless queen', who proved to be a major thorn in their grand plans to control the lucrative spice trade. Her efforts to continually repel their advances is the stuff of local legend.

Well trained in the art of war, both in strategy and combat, Rani Abbakka knew how to brandish a sword. And while she was eventually defeated, this wasn't from a loss on the battlefield, but by her treacherous ex-husband, who conspired against her in leaking intelligence to the enemy.

Her efforts to rally her people to defeat the powerful Portuguese is not forgotten by locals: Rani Abbakka is immortalised in a bronze statue on horseback at the roundabout on the road to Ullal beach, and has an annual festival dedicated to her.

The shore temple that looks over the beautiful Someshwara beach a few kilometres south from Ullal was the former site of her fort, but only sections of its wall remains intact.

Sleeping

There are only very simple sleeping options. Contact the **temple office** (☎08256-277121; www.shridharmasthala.org) for help with lodging.

Rajathadri Guest House LODGE $
(www.shridharmasthala.org/online-accommodation; r with fan/AC ₹500/1000) About 700m north of the main temple, this clean guesthouse is used by pilgrims and can be booked online. Rooms sleep up to three.

Eating

Manjunatha Temple Kitchen INDIAN
(⏲11.30am-2.15pm & 7.30-10pm) FREE Offers simple free meals, attached to a hall that can seat up to 3000. Very efficiently managed.

Getting There & Away

There are frequent buses to Dharmasthala from Mangaluru (₹75, 2½ hours).

Udupi

☎0820 / POP 177,800

Just inland from the coast, Udupi is a holy town home to an ancient Hindu temple and several monasteries.

Sights

Krishna Temple HINDU TEMPLE
(www.udupisrikrishnamatha.org; Car St; ⏲3.30am-10pm) Udupi is home to the atmospheric, 13th-century Krishna Temple, which draws thousands of Hindu pilgrims through the year. Surrounded by eight *maths* (monasteries), it's a hive of activity, with musicians playing at the entrance, elephants on hand for *puja* (prayer rituals) and pilgrims constantly coming and going. Non-Hindus are welcome inside the temple; men must enter bare-chested. Elaborate rituals are also performed in the temple during the Udupi Paryaya festival.

Sleeping

Shri Vidyasamuda Choultry HOTEL $
(☎0820-2520820; Car St; r ₹150-350) There are several pilgrim hotels near the temple, but this simple offering is the best with views looking over the ghat.

Hotel Sriram Residency HOTEL $$
(☎0820-2530761; www.hotelsriramresidency.in; Head Post Office Rd; r with fan/AC from ₹1035/1868; ❄📶) A well-run place with good choice of rooms, some on the upper floors overlooking the Krishna temple. There are two bars and a good seafood restaurant here.

Eating

Udupi is famed for its vegetarian food, and recognised across India for its sumptuous thali and as the birthplace of the humble dosa.

Woodlands INDIAN $
(Dr UR Rao Complex; dosas from ₹60, meals from ₹100; ⏲8am-3.15pm & 5.30-10.30pm)

The Southern Shores

Pretty palm-fringed stretches of sun-warmed sand peering over shimmering waters. Welcome to India's southern peninsula, which is particularly famed for its bounty of beautiful beaches that make ideal spots to swap the hustle and bustle of India's dusty roads for the revivifying bliss of cool ocean waters.

ELENA MIRAGE / SHUTTERSTOCK ©

TIM MAKINS / GETTY IMAGES ©

1. Palolem beach (p846), Goa
With its colourful huts, Palolem is one of Goa's most postcard-perfect beaches.

2. Varkala (p953), Kerala
A small strand of beach nuzzles Varkala's cliff edge.

3. Gokarna Beach (p893), Karnataka
The chilled-out beach holiday town of Gokarna is among travellers' favourite Indian beaches.

4. Lighthouse Beach, Kovalam (p949), Kerala
Candy-striped Vizhinjam Lighthouse stands out at the southern end of Lighthouse Beach.

FRANCKY38 / SHUTTERSTOCK ©

Woodlands is regarded as the best vegetarian place in town and has an AC dining room where you can escape the heat. It's a short walk south of Krishna Temple.

Mitra Samaja INDIAN $
(Car St; meals from ₹80; ⊙8am-9pm) A famous old establishment that serves delicious snacks, dosas and coffee. Can get crowded. It's just south of the Krishna Temple.

Getting There & Away

Udupi is 58km north of Mangaluru along the coast; very regular buses ply the route (₹40 to ₹62, 1½ hours). There's a daily bus to Gokarna (₹180, four hours) at 2pm and many services (mostly at night) to Bengaluru (₹434 to ₹880, eight to 10 hours). Regular buses head to Malpe (₹9, 30 minutes).

Malpe

☎0820 / POP 1980

A laid-back fishing harbour on the west coast 4km from Udupi, Malpe has nice beaches ideal for flopping about in the surf (though on weekends and holidays jet skis, banana boats and quad bikes taint the scene).

Sights & Activities

St Mary's Island ISLAND
This tiny island off Malpe is where Portuguese explorer Vasco da Gama supposedly landed in 1498, and has curious hexagonal basalt formations that jut out of the sand. No boats run here between June and mid-October. From Malpe pier you can take a ferry (₹100 return, 45 minutes, departing at 11am or when demand is sufficient) or charter a private boat from Malpe Beach here.

Sleeping & Eating

Paradise Isle Beach Resort HOTEL $$
(☎0820-2538777; www.theparadiseisle.com; r ₹3000-5500; ❄@☎≋) This large concrete hotel is right on the sands and has comfortable rooms, many with sea views. They offer a lot of ayurvedic packages, which include massages and specialised diet programs, water sports such as banana boat rides and jet skiing, and can organise **boats** (per couple ₹4000; ⊙Oct-Mar) in the backwaters of Hoode nearby.

Getting There & Away

Buses to Udupi are ₹9, and an autorickshaw ₹60.

Jog Falls

☎08186

The second-highest waterfalls in India, **Jog Falls** (₹5) only come to life during the monsoon. The tallest of the four falls is the Raja, which drops 293m. For a good view of the falls, bypass the area close to the bus stand and hike to the foot of the falls down a 1200-plus step path. Watch out for leeches during the wet season.

Sleeping

Hotel Mayura Gerusoppa Jogfalls HOTEL $$
(☎08186-244732; www.kstdc.co/hotels/hotel-mayura-gerusoppa-jogfalls; dm ₹300, d with fan/AC incl breakfast from ₹1950/2400; ❄☎) Located near Jog Falls' car park, this government-run hotel has enormous rooms that are in decent shape, all with spectacular views, though they can be a tad musty off-season. The dorm has 10 beds and is more geared to local school groups. Note prices rise weekends and wi-fi is confined to the lobby area only.

Getting There & Away

Most people hire a taxi; a return trip from Gokarna costs ₹2200. Otherwise, you can get a string of buses which head via Kumta and turn off at Honavar (₹68), or Shivamogga (Shimoga) if coming via Bengaluru (₹470, nine hours).

FORMULA BUFFALO

Call it an indigenous take on the Grand Prix, Kambla, or traditional buffalo racing, is a hugely popular pastime among villagers along the southern Karnataka coast. Popularised in the early 20th century and born out of local farmers habitually racing their buffaloes home after a day in the fields, the races have now hit the big time. Thousands of spectators attend each edition, and racing buffaloes are pampered and prepared like thoroughbreds.

Kambla events are held between November and March, usually on weekends. Parallel tracks are laid out in a paddy field, along which buffaloes hurtle towards the finish line. In most cases the man rides on a board fixed to a ploughshare, literally surfing his way down the track behind the beasts. The faster creatures can cover the 120m-odd distance through water and mud in around 14 seconds!

Gokarna

08386 / POP 28,880

A regular nominee among travellers' favourite beaches in India, Gokarna attracts a crowd for a low-key, chilled-out beach holiday and not for full-scale parties. Most accommodation is in thatched bamboo huts along its several stretches of blissful coast.

In fact there are two Gokarnas; adjacent to the beaches is the sacred Hindu pilgrim town of Gokarna, full of ancient temples that come to life during important festivals such as Shivaratri and Ganesh Chaturthi (p853). While its lively bazaar is an interesting place to visit, most foreign tourists don't hang around overnight, instead making a beeline straight to the adjoining beaches.

Sights

The best beaches are south of Gokarna town: first Kudle Beach (5km by road from Gokarna), then Om Beach (6.5km by road). Well hidden south of Om Beach lie the small sandy coves of Half Moon Bay and Paradise Beach, without road access. A lovely coastal trail links all the beaches, but, as there have been (very occasional) reports of muggings, it's best not to walk it alone.

★Om Beach BEACH

One of Karnataka's best beaches, Gokarna's most famous stretch of sand twists and turns over several kilometres in a form that resembles the outline of an Om symbol. It comprises several gorgeous coves, with wide stretches interspersed with smaller patches of sand, perfect for sunbathing and swimming. There's fine swimming most of the season when the sea is not choppy, though signs officially ban swimming (local tourists have drowned here in rough seas).

Kudle Beach BEACH

This lovely wide cove, backed by wooded headlands, offers plenty of room to stretch out on along its attractive sands. Restaurants, guesthouses and yoga camps are dotted around the rear of the beach, but they're well spaced and development remains peaceful and attractive.

Half Moon Bay BEACH

Small, attractive cove with a lovely sweep of powdery sand and basic hut accommodation. There's no road, only a path to this beach. It's about a 30-minute hike from Om Beach (itself 5km from Gokarna town), or boats run here on demand from Gokarna town.

GOKARNA'S TEMPLES

This is a deeply holy town and foreigners should be respectful in and around its many temples: do not try to enter their inner sanctums, which are reserved for Hindus only. It's customary for pilgrims to bathe in the sea and fast, and many shave their heads, before entering Gokarna's holy places.

Paradise Beach BEACH

Paradise Beach is a mix of sand and rocks, and a haven for the long-term 'turn-on-tune-in-drop-out' crowd. Unfortunately, the government routinely destroys all the huts out this way, leaving it in a ramshackle state – hence it's BYO everything here. If you've a hammock or tent it's a great choice for total isolation.

★Mahaganapati Temple HINDU TEMPLE

(Car St; 6am-8.30pm) FREE Deeply atmospheric temple complex, encircled by lanes, but peaceful inside. Here there's a (rare) stone statue of an upright, standing Ganesh, said to be over 1500 years old, who is depicted with a flat head – said to mark the spot where the demon Ravana struck him. This is the second-most holy site in Gokarna and it's customary for pilgrims to visit here first before heading to the neighbouring Mahabaleshwara Temple. Foreigners are not allowed inside the inner sanctum.

★Mahabaleshwara Temple HINDU TEMPLE

(Car St; 6am-8.30pm) FREE Dedicated to Lord Shiva, this is a profoundly spiritual temple, built of granite by Mayurasharma of the Kadamba dynasty and said to date back to the 4th century. Hindus believe it brings blessings to pilgrims who even glimpse it, and rituals are performed for the deceased. A *gopura* (gateway tower) dominates the complex, while inside a stone nandi faces the inner chamber, home to Shiva's lingam. Foreigners may enter the complex but not the inner sanctum.

Koorti Teertha HINDU SITE

A large temple tank where locals, pilgrims and immaculately dressed Brahmins perform their ablutions.

Gokarna Beach BEACH

Gokarna's main town beach isn't clean and is not good for casual bathing. The main section is popular with domestic tourists but if you walk away from here to the north you'll

OFF THE BEATEN TRACK

MURUDESHWAR

A worthwhile stopover for those taking the coastal route from Gokarna to Mangaluru, Murudeshwar is a beachside pilgrimage town. It's most notable for its colossal seashore **statue of Lord Shiva**, which sits directly on the shore overlooking the Arabian Sea. For the best views, take the lift 18 storeys to the top of the skyscraper-like **Shri Murudeshwar Temple** (lift ₹10; lift 7.45am-12.30pm & 3.15-6.45pm).

Murudeshwar is 3km off the main highway, accessed by train or bus passing up and down the coast. If you'd like to stay overnight, beachfront homestay **Mavalli Beach Heritage Home** (9901767993; http://mavallibeachheritage.com; r ₹4200;) has four stylish rooms, a warm ambience and great home-cooked food, though the approach road is in poor shape.

find a long stretch of sand that seems to go forever. There's some surf here in season.

Activities

Cocopelli Surf School SURFING
(8105764969; www.cocopelli.org; Gokarna Beach; lesson per person ₹2000, board rental per 2hr ₹750; Oct-May) Offers lessons by internationally certified instructors and rents boards.

Festivals & Events

★ **Shivaratri** RELIGIOUS
(Feb/Mar) A chariot bearing a statue of Lord Shiva and his lingam is pulled through the streets by hundreds of pilgrims to conclude this nine-day festival.

Sleeping & Eating

For most foreigners Gokarna means sleeping right on the beach in a simple shack. However, there are a growing number of more upmarket lodges and hotels, so if you don't want to rough it you don't have to. Note that most places close from November to March.

Om Beach

★ **Nirvana Café** GUESTHOUSE $
(9742466481; cottage ₹700-900;) These attractive cottages, towards the eastern end of the beach, are some of Om's best, all with front porches that face a slim central garden. On the premises you'll find a good beachfront restaurant, laundry and travel agency.

Namaste Café GUESTHOUSE $
(08386-257141; www.namastegokarna.com; r with fan/AC from ₹1080/1720;) At the beginning of Om, this long-standing guesthouse is the most upmarket place on the beach, with well-constructed accommodation in leafy gardens and the comforts of AC and wi-fi and hot water.

Dolphin Shanti GUESTHOUSE $
(9740930133; r from ₹300) Rooms are basic yet appealing at this simple guesthouse at the far eastern end of Om Beach. It's perched upon the rocks with fantastic ocean views, and lives up to its name with dolphins often spotted.

Sangham BUNGALOW $
(9448101099; Om Beach; r ₹650, without bathroom ₹400) The no-frills concrete bungalows at the back of this beachfront restaurant are set in a garden area. Rooms are basic and a bit soulless, with OK mattresses and mossie nets.

★ **SwaSwara** HOTEL $$$
(08386-257132; www.swaswara.com; s/d 5 nights from €1820/2450;) 'Journeying into the self' is the mantra at SwaSwara and you certainly have the infrastructure in place to achieve that here, as this is one of South India's finest retreats. Yoga, ayurveda, treatments, a meditation dome and elegant private villas with open-air showers and lovely sitting areas await. No short stays are possible.

Sunset Point INDIAN $
(mains ₹120-200; 7.30am-10pm) Family-run place at the eastern end of Om Beach with a great perch overlooking the waves. There's a long menu that takes in breakfasts, sandwiches, Indian and Chinese dishes; grilled kingfish is around ₹180.

Om Shree Ganesh MULTICUISINE, INDIAN $
(meals ₹80-170; 8am-3pm & 6-10.30pm) Across a stream on Om Beach, this atmospheric double-storey restaurant does tasty dishes such as tandoori prawns, mushroom tikka and *momos* (Tibetan dumplings).

Namaste Cafe MULTICUISINE $$
(mains ₹120-230; 8.30am-4pm & 6-11pm) The only 'proper' restaurant on Om Beach, this

attractive double-deck affair has dreamy, romantic sea views, cold beer and good seafood, pasta and Indian dishes.

Kudle Beach

Strawberry Farmhouse GUESTHOUSE $

(☎7829367584; r ₹700-1000; ❄) A good guesthouse at the northern section of Kudle with spacious cottages (some with AC), all with verandahs and a prime position looking out to the water.

Uma Garden GUESTHOUSE $

(☎9916720728; www.facebook.com/uma.garden kudlebeach; r without bathroom ₹350) Tucked around the corner at the beginning of Kudle, this bucolic guesthouse has a laid-back owner and sea-facing vegetarian restaurant.

Ganga Cafe GUESTHOUSE $

(☎8095766058; r from ₹350; 📶) At the north end of Kudle, these concrete rooms are above a popular restaurant and have partial sea views from a shared balcony. Bathrooms are shared.

★**Arya Ayurvedic Panchakarma Centre** SPA HOTEL $$

(☎9611062468; www.ayurvedainindien.com; r from ₹1800; ❄📶) Some of the best rooms in Gokarna, the simple yet elegant, accommodation on Kudle Beach has been carefully planned and designed using quality furnishings. Priority is given to those booking ayurvedic packages and there's a fine in-house **cafe** (mains ₹130-200; ⏰8am-10pm; 📶).

Namaste Yoga Farm BUNGALOW $$$

(☎08386-257454; www.spiritualland.com; incl breakfast & yoga r €50-94, cottage €80-104; 📶) On the hillside above the northern end of Kudle this popular place is owned by an excellent, patient German yoga instructor. The accommodation, in a patch of jungle, is pretty functional and does not have a 'wow' factor but the yoga (two daily classes are included) and breakfast (cooked to order) are exceptional and there's a very welcoming vibe.

Half Moon Beach

Half Moon Garden Cafe BUNGALOW $

(☎9743615820; hut from ₹300) 🍃 A throwback to the hippie days, this hideaway has a blissful beach and pretty decent huts in a coconut grove. It runs on solar power.

Gokarna Town

Shree Shakti Hotel HOTEL $

(☎9036043088; chidushakti@gmail.com; Gokarna Beach Rd; s/d ₹400/600) On Gokarna's main strip, this friendly hotel is excellent value with immaculate lime-green rooms. There's a popular restaurant downstairs.

Greenland Guesthouse GUESTHOUSE $

(☎9019651420; r from ₹300; 📶) Hidden down a jungle path on the edge of town, this mellow family-run guesthouse has clean rooms in vibrant colours and a lovely verdant garden to enjoy. There's a daily charge (₹200) for wi-fi.

★**Prema** INDIAN, MULTICUISINE $

(Gokarna Beach Rd; meals ₹80-150; ⏰8am-10pm) Always packed, this humble-looking place has a prime location just before the beach. Offers Western food but it's best to stick to the South Indian classics. They accept cards for payments.

Shree Shakti ICE CREAM, INDIAN $

(Gokarna Beach Rd; meals from ₹110; ⏰8am-10pm; 📶) Attractive, casual cafe-restaurant in Gokarna town that's rightly renowned for its ice cream, juices and flavoursome local food.

Shopping

Shree Radhakrishna Bookstore BOOKS

(Car St, Gokarna Town; ⏰10am-6pm) Secondhand novels, postcards and maps.

Information

Post Office (Main St; ⏰10am-4.30pm Mon-Sat)

SBI ATM (Main St)

Getting There & Away

Trains from Mumbai or Goa and private buses from Hampi/Hospet may get you into Gokarna at ungodly hours: it's worth notifying your guesthouse.

BUS

Local and private buses depart daily to Bengaluru (₹505 to ₹714, 12 hours) and Mysuru (from ₹570, 12 hours), as well as Mangaluru (from ₹255, 6½ hours) and Hubballi (₹195, four hours).

For Hampi, **Paulo Travels** (☎08394-225867; www.paulobus.com) is a popular choice which heads via Hosapete (Hospet; fan/AC ₹1500/1550, seven hours). Note if you're coming from Hampi, you'll be dropped at Ankola from where there's a free transfer for the 26km journey to Gokarna.

There's also regular buses to Panaji (₹120, three hours) and Mumbai (₹754 to ₹980, 12 hours).

TRAIN

Many express trains stop at Gokarna Rd station, 9km from town. There are other options from Ankola, 26km away. Hotels and travel agencies in Gokarna can book tickets.

The 3am 12619 Matsyagandha Express goes to Mangaluru (sleeper/2AC ₹220/740, 4½ hours); the return train leaves Gokarna Rd at 6.40pm for Madgaon in Goa (sleeper/2AC ₹170/740, two hours) and Mumbai (sleeper/2AC, ₹455/1700, 12 hours).

Autorickshaws charge ₹220 to go to Gokarna Rd station (or ₹450 to Ankola); a bus from Gokarna town charges ₹30 and leaves every 30 minutes.

CENTRAL KARNATAKA

Hampi

☎08394 / POP 3500

The magnificent ruins of Hampi dot an unearthly landscape that has captivated travellers for centuries. Heaps of giant boulders perch precariously over kilometres of undulating terrain, their rusty hues offset by jade-green palm groves, banana plantations and paddy fields. While it's possible to see this World Heritage Site in a day or two, plan on lingering for a while.

The main travellers' ghetto has traditionally been Hampi Bazaar, a village crammed with budget lodges, shops and restaurants, and towered over by the majestic Virupaksha Temple. Tranquil Virupapur Gaddi across the river has become a new popular hang-out. However, recent demolitions (p901) in both areas have seen businesses closed, with the future of Hampi bitterly contested between locals and authorities.

History

Hampi and its neighbouring areas find mention in the Hindu epic Ramayana as Kishkinda, the realm of the monkey gods. In 1336 Telugu prince Harihararaya chose Hampi as the site for his new capital Vijayanagar, which – over the next couple of centuries – grew into one of the largest Hindu empires in Indian history. By the 16th century it was a thriving metropolis of about 500,000 people, its busy bazaars dabbling in international commerce, brimming with precious stones and merchants from faraway lands. All this, however, ended in a stroke in 1565, when a confederacy of Deccan sultanates razed Vijayanagar to the ground, striking it a death blow from which it never recovered.

Sights

Set over 36 sq km, there are some 3700 monuments to explore in Hampi, and it would take months if you were to do it justice. The ruins are divided into two main areas: the **Sacred Centre**, around Hampi Bazaar with its temples, and the **Royal Centre**, towards Kamalapuram, where the Vijayanagara royalty lived and governed.

Sacred Centre

★Virupaksha Temple HINDU TEMPLE

(Map p900; ₹2, camera/video ₹50/500; ⏲dawn-dusk) The focal point of Hampi Bazaar is the Virupaksha Temple, one of the city's oldest structures, and Hampi's only remaining working temple. The main *gopuram*, almost 50m high, was built in 1442, with a smaller one added in 1510. The main shrine is dedicated to Virupaksha, an incarnation of Shiva.

An elephant called Lakshmi blesses devotees as they enter in exchange for donations; it doesn't seem hugely rewarding for the pachyderm, but she gets time off for a morning bath down by the river ghats

Hemakuta Hill HISTORIC SITE

(Map p898) To the south, overlooking Virupaksha Temple, Hemakuta Hill has a scattering of early ruins, including monolithic sculptures of Narasimha (Vishnu in his man-lion incarnation) and Ganesh. It's worth the short walk up for the view.

Nandi Statue STATUE

(Map p898) At the east end of Hampi Bazaar is a Nandi statue, around which stand some of the colonnaded blocks of the ancient marketplace. This is the main location for **Vijaya Utsav** (Hampi Festival; ⏲Jan), the Hampi arts festival.

★Vittala Temple HINDU TEMPLE

(Map p898; Indian/foreigner/child under 15 ₹30/500/free; ⏲8.30am-5.30pm) The undisputed highlight of the Hampi ruins, the 16th-century Vittala Temple stands amid the boulders 2km from Hampi Bazaar. Work possibly started on the temple during the reign of Krishnadevaraya (r 1509–29). It was never finished or consecrated, yet the temple's incredible sculptural work remains the pinnacle of Vijayanagar art.

The ornate **stone chariot** that stands in the courtyard is the temple's showpiece and represents Vishnu's vehicle with an image of Garuda within. Its wheels were once capable of turning.

The outer 'musical' pillars reverberate when tapped. They were supposedly designed to replicate 81 different Indian instruments, but authorities have placed them out of tourists' bounds for fear of further damage, so no more do-re-mi.

As well as the main temple, whose sanctum was illuminated using a design of reflective waters, you'll find the marriage hall and prayer hall, the structures to the left and right upon entry, respectively.

Lakshimi Narasmiha HINDU TEMPLE
(Map p898) An interesting stop-off along the road to the Virupaksha Temple is the 6.7m monolithic statue of the bulging-eyed Lakshimi Narasmiha in a cross-legged lotus position and topped by a hood of seven snakes.

Krishna Temple HINDU TEMPLE
(Map p898) Built in 1513, the Krishna Temple is fronted by an *apsara* and 10 incarnations of Vishnu. It's on the road to the Virupaksha Temple near Lakshimi Narasmiha.

Sule Bazaar HISTORIC SITE
(Map p898) Halfway along the path from Hampi Bazaar to Vittala Temple, a track to the right leads over the rocks to deserted Sule Bazaar, one of ancient Hampi's principal centres of commerce and reputedly its red-light district. At the southern end of this area is the beautiful 16th-century **Achyutaraya Temple** (Map p898).

Royal Centre & Around

While it can be accessed by a 2km foot trail from the Achyutaraya Temple, the Royal Centre is best reached via the Hampi–Kamalapuram road. A number of Hampi's major sites stand here.

Mahanavami-diiba RUINS
(Map p898) The Mahanavami-diiba is a 12m-high three-tiered platform with intricate carvings and panoramic vistas of the walled complex of ruined temples, stepped tanks and the King's audience hall. The platform was used as a royal viewing area for the Dasara festivities, religious ceremonies and processions.

Zenana Enclosure RUINS
(Map p898; Indian/foreigner ₹30/500; 8.30am-5.30pm) Northeast of the Royal Centre within the walled ladies' quarters is the Zenana Enclosure. Its peaceful grounds and manicured lawns feel like an oasis amid the arid surrounds. Here are the **Lotus Mahal** (Map p898) and **Elephant Stables** (Map p898; 8.30am-5.30pm).

Hazarama Temple HINDU TEMPLE
(Map p898) Features exquisite carvings that depict scenes from the Ramayana, and polished black granite pillars.

Queen's Bath RUINS
(Map p898; 8.30am-5.30pm) South of the Royal Centre you'll find various temples and elaborate waterworks, including the Queen's Bath, deceptively plain on the outside but amazing within, with its Indo-Islamic architecture.

Archaeological Museum MUSEUM
(Map p898; Kamalapuram; 10am-5pm Sat-Thu) Boasts a fine collection of sculptures from local ruins, plus neolithic tools, 16th-century weaponry and a large floor model of the Vijayanagar ruins. There's a fine photographic record of the site dating back to 1856.

Activities

Hampi Waterfalls WATERFALL
About a 2km walk west of Hampi Bazaar, past shady banana plantations, you can scramble over the boulders to reach the attractive Hampi 'waterfalls', a series of small whirlpools among the rocks amid superb scenery.

Bouldering

Hampi is the undisputed bouldering capital of India. The entire landscape is a climber's adventure playground made of granite crags and boulders, some bearing the marks

HAMPI RUINS TICKET

The ₹500 ticket for Vittala Temple entitles you to same-day admission into most of the paid sites across the ruins (including around the Royal Centre and the Archaeological Museum), so don't lose your ticket.

Hampi & Anegundi

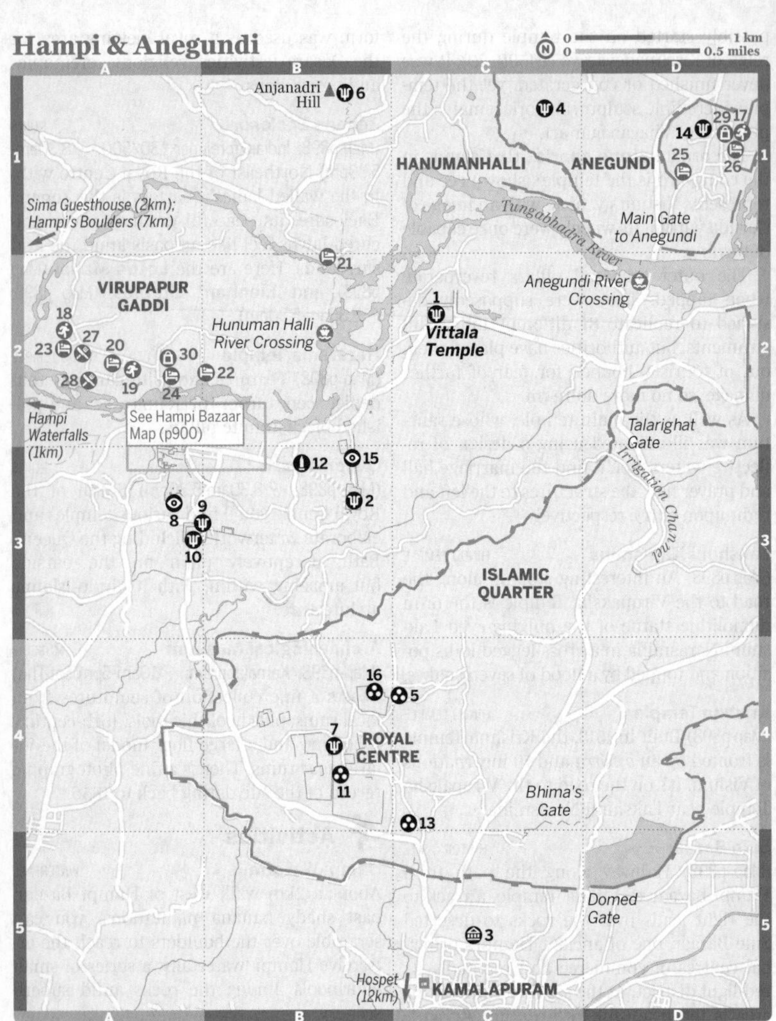

of ancient stonemasons. *Golden Boulders* (2013) by Gerald Krug and Christiane Hupe has a tonne of info on bouldering in Hampi.

Tom & Jerry CLIMBING
(Map p898; ☎9482746697, 8277792588; www.facebook.com/TomJerry-Climbing-Shop; Virupapur Gaddi; 2½hr class ₹500) Two local lads who are doing great work in catering to climbers' needs, providing quality mats, shoes and local knowledge and running climbing classes.

Thimmaclimb CLIMBING
(Map p898; ☎8762776498; www.thimmaclimb.wix.com/hampi-bouldering; Shiva Guesthouse, Virupapur Gaddi; class from ₹400) A small professional operation run by local pro Thimma, who guides, runs lessons and stocks professional equipment for hire and sale. He also runs three-day trips (₹5000) to Badami for sandstone climbing.

Birdwatching

Get in touch with **Kishkinda Trust** (TKT; ☎08533-267777; http://tktkishkinda.org) in Anegundi for info on birdwatching in the area, which has over 230 species, including the greater flamingo. *The Birds of Hampi* (2014) by Samad Kottur is the definitive guide.

Hampi & Anegundi

Festivals & Events

Virupaksha Car Festival RELIGIOUS

(Mar/Apr) The Virupaksha Car Festival is a big event, with a colourful procession characterised by a giant wooden chariot (the temple car from Virupaksha Temple) being pulled along the main strip of Hampi Bazaar.

Sleeping

Most guesthouses are cosy family-run digs, perfect for the budget traveller. More upmarket places are located further from the centre.

Hampi Bazaar

This little enclave is a classic travellers' ghetto. However, its existence is under threat as there are plans to demolish it.

★Manash Guesthouse GUESTHOUSE $

(Map p900; 9448877420; manashhampi@gmail.com; r with fan/AC ₹1200/1500;) Owned by the legendary Mango Tree people, this place has only two rooms set off a little yard, but they are the best in Hampi Bazaar, each with quality mattresses, attractive decorative touches and free fast wi-fi.

Thilak Homestay GUESTHOUSE $

(Map p900; 9449900964; www.facebook.com/thilak.homestay; r with fan/AC ₹1000/1500;) A commendably clean, orderly place with eight well-presented rooms (and more in another block) that have spring mattresses and hot water. The owner is helpful and can arrange transport from Hosapete or around Hampi.

Pushpa Guest House GUESTHOUSE $

(Map p900; 9448795120; pushpaguesthouse99@yahoo.in; d from ₹900, with AC from ₹1300;) Pushpa is a good all-rounder with comfortable, attractive and spotless rooms that have mossie nets. It has a lovely sit-out on the 1st floor, and reliable travel agency.

Ganesh Guesthouse GUESTHOUSE $

(Map p900; vishnuhampi@gmail.com; r ₹500-800, with AC from ₹1500;) A welcoming place, the small family-run Ganesh has been around for over 20 years, and has four tidy, neat rooms. Also has a nice rooftop restaurant.

Archana Guest House GUESTHOUSE $

(Map p900; 08394-241547; addihampi@yahoo.com; d from ₹800;) On the riverfront, quiet and cheerful Archana has two plain rooms with river views above a restaurant. The others are in a separate block over the street.

Vicky's GUESTHOUSE $

(Map p900; 9480561010; vikkyhampi@yahoo.co.in; r from ₹350;) Dependable cheapie with decent, basic rooms with mossie nets done up in pop purple and green and a friendly owner. There's a good travel agent here too.

Hampi Bazaar

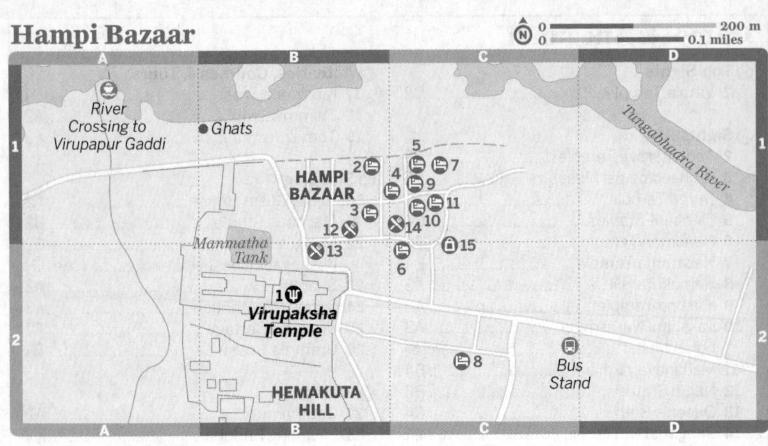

Hampi Bazaar

Top Sights
1 Virupaksha Temple B2

Sleeping
2 Archana Guest House B1
3 Ganesh Guesthouse B1
4 Gopi Guest House C1
5 Kiran Guest House C1
6 Manash Guesthouse C2
7 Netra Guesthouse C1
8 Padma Guest House C2
9 Pushpa Guest House C1
10 Thilak Homestay C1
11 Vicky's C1

Eating
12 Mango Tree B1
13 Moonlight B2
14 Ravi's Rose C1

Shopping
15 Akash Art Gallery & Bookstore C2

Information
Tourist Office .... (see 1)

Padma Guest House GUESTHOUSE $
(Map p900; 08394-241331; padmaguesthouse@gmail.com; d ₹900-1600;) Away from the main bazaar area, this guesthouse has a choice of basic, decent rooms, many with views of Virupaksha Temple, though bathrooms could do with an upgrade. The owners can arrange bus and train tickets.

Kiran Guest House GUESTHOUSE $
(Map p900; 9448143906; kiranhampi2012@gmail.com; r ₹600-800;) No-frills guesthouse close to the riverfront and banana groves. Rooms are basic but clean, the showers are warmish and the family owners are helpful.

Netra Guesthouse GUESTHOUSE $
(Map p900; 9480569326; r from ₹500, without bathroom from ₹300) Basic, clean rooms for shoestringers, with an ambient open-air restaurant.

Gopi Guest House GUESTHOUSE $$
(Map p900; 08394-241695; www.gopi-guesthouse.com; r with fan/AC ₹2000/2500; @) Split over two properties on the same street, long-standing Gopi offers friendly service and has good-quality rooms that are almost upscale for Hampi's standards. There are temple views from its rooftop cafe. Walk-in rates are usually lower than online bookings.

Virupapur Gaddi & Around

The rural tranquillity of Virupapur Gaddi, across the river from Hampi Bazaar, has real appeal, particularly with Israelis – locals nickname the place 'Little Jerusalem'. However, authorities demolished buildings here in 2016, and its long-term status is unclear.

Sunny Guesthouse GUESTHOUSE $
(Map p898; 9448566368; www.sunnyguesthouse.com; r ₹450-1200; @) Sunny both in name and disposition, this popular guesthouse is a hit among backpackers for its characterful huts, very well-maintained tropical garden, hammocks and chilled-out restaurant.

Shanthi GUESTHOUSE $
(Map p898; ☎8533287038; http://shanthihampi.com/; cottages ₹1000-1800; @) Enjoys a stunning, peaceful setting next to rice fields and primed for sunset. Shanthi's attractive earth-themed, thatched cottages have couch swings dangling in their front porches and the restaurant serves good grub.

Hema Guest House GUESTHOUSE $
(Map p898; ☎8762395470; rockyhampi@gmail.com; Virupapur Gaddi; d from ₹600; 📶) Worth considering, with rows of cute and comfy colourful cottages in a shady grove, all with a table or chair for company and a hammock; though mattresses could be better. Its restaurant is perpetually full with lazing tourists.

Manju's Place GUESTHOUSE $
(Map p898; ☎9449247712; r ₹500, without bathroom from ₹250) The place for those who like things quiet, with attractive mud-brick huts in a bucolic setting among rice fields.

★ **Hampi's Boulders** LODGE $$$
(☎9448034202; www.hampisboulders.com; Narayanpet; r incl full board from ₹5600; ❄📶🏊) Beautifully designed, Hampi Boulders is the only luxury option in these parts, an 'eco-wilderness' resort in leafy gardens 7km west of Virupapur Gaddi. There's a choice of themed rooms and chic cottages with elegant furnishings, river views and outdoor showers. There's a stunning natural pool for chlorine-free swims. Rates include guided walks, and the restaurant's food is from their organic farm.

Eating

Due to Hampi's religious significance, meat is strictly off the menu in all restaurants, and alcohol is banned (though some restaurants can order it for you).

Laughing Buddha MULTICUISINE $
(Map p898; mains from ₹80; ⏰8am-10pm; 📶) Laughing Buddha is perhaps Hampi's most atmospheric place to eat, with serene river views that span beyond to the temples and ruins and a loyal crowd of diners. Its menu includes curries, burgers and pizzas but service can be slow.

Gouthami MULTICUISINE $
(Map p898; mains ₹90-180; ⏰8am-11pm) A well-run place with the usual cushioned seating (or dining tables) and an excess of

HAMPI BAZAAR DEMOLITION

While in 1865 it was the Deccan sultanates who levelled Vijayanagar, today a different battle rages in Hampi, between conservationists bent on protecting Hampi's architectural heritage and the locals who have settled there.

In 1999, Unesco placed Hampi on its list of World Heritage Sites in danger because of 'haphazard informal urbanisation' around the temples, particularly the ancient bazaar area near Virupaksha Temple.

The government consequently produced a masterplan which aimed to classify all of Hampi's ruins as protected monuments. After years of inaction this plan was dramatically and forcefully put into action in July 2011. Shops, hotels and homes in Hampi Bazaar were bulldozed overnight, reducing the atmospheric main strip to rubble in hours, as 1500 villagers who'd made the site a living monument were evicted.

Villagers were compensated with a small plot of land in the village of Kaddirampur, 18km from the bazaar. There's talk of new guesthouses eventually opening up here but such is its distance from Hampi few villagers are keen to start building guesthouses. Meanwhile the displaced await their payout.

Then in May 2016 history repeated itself as homes, guesthouses and shops in the old village of Virupapur Gaddi were demolished. Larger establishments avoided the clearance by contesting eviction orders in court. Angry locals blame HWHAMA (Hampi World Heritage Area Management Authority) and the ASI (Archaeological Survey of India) for the demolitions and argue that the masterplan is causing a lifeless 'museumification' of what was a vibrant cultural monument.

The main temple road today is devoid of buildings and bustle, and legendary hangouts like the (original) Mango Tree have been knocked down. By early 2017 Hampi Bazaar consisted of an enclave of guesthouses and restaurants north of Virupaksha Temple, but its future is in doubt as there are more clearance plans in place.

psychedelic wall hangings. Serves tasty Indian, Israeli and Western food; they've an espresso machine and the bakery at the front has good cakes.

Moonlight MULTICUISINE $
(Map p900; mains ₹80-150; ⌚7.30am-10pm) Simple, family-owned place that has a good set breakfast, espresso coffee and tasty pancakes and egg dishes and, of course, curries.

Ravi's Rose MULTICUISINE $
(Map p900; mains from ₹100; ⌚8am-10.30pm; 📶) This is the bazaar's most social hang-out, with a good selection of dosas and thalis, but most are here for the, erm, special lassis (cough, cough, nudge, nudge).

★ **Mango Tree** MULTICUISINE $$
(Map p900; mains ₹140-310; ⌚7.30am-9.30pm) Hampi's most famous restaurant has relocated to the bazaar inside an ambient tented restaurant but is still run by three generations of the same local family. It's an efficiently run place with good service and delicious Indian cuisines including thalis and spinach paneer with chapati (₹160).

Shopping

Akash Art Gallery & Bookstore BOOKS
(Map p900; Hampi Bazaar; ⌚6am-9pm) Excellent selection of books on Hampi and India, plus secondhand fiction. It has a free Hampi map.

Gali Djembe Music Shop MUSIC
(Map p898; ☎9449982586; www.facebook.com/pg/Galidurugappa; Virupapur Gaddi; ⌚10am-7pm) Run by an amiable musician who teaches djembe (drums) and didgeridoo this store sells Indian and Western musical instruments at fair prices.

DAROJI SLOTH BEAR SANCTUARY

About 30km south of Hampi, amid scrubby undulated terrain, lies the **Daroji Sloth Bear Sanctuary** (₹25, vechicle ₹500; ⌚2-6pm), which nurses a large population of free-ranging sloth bears in an area of 83 sq km. You have a good chance of spotting them (but only from afar at the viewing platform), as honey is slathered on the rocks to coincide with the arrival of visitors. Bring binoculars, or there's no point showing up. Late afternoon is the best time to visit.

Information

DANGERS & ANNOYANCES

Hampi is generally a safe, peaceful place. However, exercise normal precautions and don't wander around the ruins after dark; female travellers should avoid being alone in the site's more remote parts. Alcohol and narcotics are illegal in Hampi.

MONEY

There's no ATM in Hampi; the closest is 3km away in Kamalapuram – an autorickshaw costs ₹80 for a return trip.

TOURIST INFORMATION

Tourist Office (Map p900; ☎08394-241339; ⌚10am-5.30pm Sat-Thu) Has brochures but is more useful for arranging cycling tours (per person ₹400 including bike and guide), walking guides (from ₹600) and bus tours (₹350, seven hours), all of which head to the ruins.

Getting There & Away

Hosapete (Hospet) is the gateway to Hampi. There's only one daily direct (very slow) bus from Hampi Bazaar to Goa (₹663, 11 hours, 7pm). Travel agents in Hampi Bazaar can book bus tickets to Bengaluru, Hyderabad, Goa and other destinations; many of these include a minibus transfer from Hampi to Hosapete.

Local buses connect Hampi with Hosapete (₹22, 30 minutes, half-hourly) between 5.45am and 7.30pm. An autorickshaw costs around ₹180.

Hosapete is Hampi's nearest train station.

Getting Around

Bicycles cost ₹30 to ₹50 per day in Hampi Bazaar, while mopeds can be hired for ₹150 to ₹400. Traffic is very light around Hampi, except on the road to Hosapete.

A small boat shuttles frequently across the **river crossing** (Map p900; person/bicycle/motorbike ₹10/10/20; ⌚6am-6pm) to Virupapur Gaddi. After dark it costs ₹50 to ₹100 per person depending on how late you cross. There are also boats to **Anegundi** (Map p898; person/bicycle/motorbike ₹10/10/20; ⌚6am-5.45pm) and **Hunuman Halli** (Map p898; person/bicycle ₹10/10; ⌚6am-5.45pm).

Walking the ruins is possible, but expect to cover at least 7km just to see the major sites. The beautiful river section between Hampi Bazaar and Vittala Temple is a delight to stroll. Autorickshaws and taxis are available for sightseeing, and an autorickshaw for the day costs around ₹750.

Organised tours depart from Hosapete and Hampi.

Around Hampi

Anegundi

08394 / POP 5600

Anegundi is an ancient fortified village that's part of the Hampi World Heritage Site, but predates Hampi by way of human habitation. The settlement has been spared the blight of commercialisation, and retains a delightfully rustic feel where the seasons dictate the cycle of change and craft traditions endure.

It's accessed by a river crossing or via a long loop from Virupapur Gaddi.

Sights & Activities

Mythically referred to as Kishkinda, the kingdom of the monkey gods, Anegundi retains many of its historic monuments, such as sections of its defensive wall and gates, and the **Ranganatha Temple** (Map p898; dawn-dusk) devoted to Rama. Also worth visiting is the **Durga Temple** (Map p898; dawn-dusk), an ancient shrine closer to the village and the hilltop Hanuman Temple. A new museum is scheduled to open here in 2017 in a meticulously restored old structure and other royal residences are also being renovated.

Hanuman Temple HINDU TEMPLE
(Map p898; dawn-dusk) The whitewashed Hanuman Temple, accessible by a 570-step climb up the Anjanadri Hill, has fine views of the rugged terrain around. Many believe this is the birthplace of Hanuman, the Hindu monkey god who was Rama's devotee and helped him in his mission against Ravana. The hike up is pleasant, though you'll be courted by impish monkeys. At the temple you may encounter chillum-puffing sadhus. It's a very popular sunset spot, with panoramic views over the Hampi region.

Kishkinda Trust CULTURAL PROGRAMS, OUTDOOR ADVENTURE
(TKT; Map p898; 08533-267777; www.tktkishkinda.org; Main Rd) For cultural events, activities and volunteering opportunities, get in touch with Kishkinda Trust, an NGO based in Anegundi that works with local people.

Sleeping & Eating

Anegundi has fantastic homestays in restored heritage buildings. It's ideal for experiencing Indian village life.

Peshegaar Guest House GUESTHOUSE $
(Map p898; 9449972230; www.urammaheritagehomes.com; Hanumanahalli; s/d ₹500/1000) In the middle of the village this homely, heritage place has five simple yet stylish rooms decorated with tribal textiles around a pleasant common area with courtyard garden. Bathrooms are shared, but there are four.

Uramma House GUESTHOUSE $$
(Map p898; 9449972230; www.urammaheritagehomes.com; s/d per r ₹2100/4200;) This 4th-century heritage house is a gem, with traditional-style rooms with exposed beams featuring boutique touches. It has two bedrooms and is ideal for a family or small group, with a dining room.

★ **Uramma Cottage** COTTAGE $$$
(Map p898; 08533-267792; www.urammaheritagehomes.com; s/d incl breakfast from ₹2100/4200;) Close to the river crossing, this wonderfully atmospheric village lodge has thatched-roof cottages with farmhouse charm scattered around a large grassy plot. The attention to detail is all-evident with rustic chic furniture, lovely bed linen and handmade textiles adding a splash of colour. Staff could not be more helpful and the restaurant serves very fine food (and beer).

Machaan Studio APARTMENT $$$
(Map p898; 9448284658; www.urammaheritagehomes.com; apt incl breakfast ₹5000;) A gorgeous fully equipped loft-style place with a huge living space, sunken bathtub and terrace. It's been imaginatively designed with a mix of rustic and contemporary touches and has views of the Vittala Temple and river. It's in the neighbouring village of Hunuman Halli.

Shopping

Banana Fibre Craft Workshop ARTS & CRAFTS
(Map p898; 10am-1pm & 2-5pm Mon-Sat) Watch on at this small workshop as workers ply their trade making a range of handicrafts and accessories using the bark of a banana tree, and recycled materials. Of course they sell it all too.

Getting There & Away

Anegundi is 7km from Hampi, and reached by crossing the river on a boat (₹10) from the pier east of the Vittala Temple. From Hampi get here by moped or bicycle (if you're feeling energetic). An autorickshaw to the Anegundi crossing costs ₹120 from Hampi.

OFF THE BEATEN TRACK

DANDELI

Located in the jungles of the Western Ghats about 100km from Goa, emerging **Dandeli** is a wildlife getaway that promises close encounters with wildlife such as elephants, leopards, sloth bears, gaur, wild dogs and flying squirrels. It's a chosen birding destination too, with resident hornbills, golden-backed woodpeckers, serpent eagles and white-breasted kingfishers. Also on offer are a slew of adventure activities, from kayaking to bowel-churning white-water rafting on the swirling waters of the Kali River.

Kali Adventure Camp (08284-230266; www.junglelodges.com/kali-adventure-camp; Dandeli; incl full board Indian/foreigner tent from ₹4168/5052, r from ₹4948/5832;) is a well-managed government lodge adhering to ecofriendly principles, with rooms, tented cottages and accommodating staff. It organises white-water rafting on the Kali (possible most of the year), guided canoe adventures, canyoning and mountain-biking trips.

Frequent buses connect Dandeli to both Hubballi (₹58, two hours) and Dharwad (₹46, 1½ hours), with onward connections to Goa, Gokarna, Hosapete and Bengaluru.

Hosapete (Hospet)

08394 / POP 168,600

A hectic, dusty regional city, Hosapete (still called Hospet by many) is notable only as a transport hub for Hampi.

Sleeping & Eating

Hotel Malligi HOTEL **$$**

(08394-228101; www.malligihotels.com; Jabunatha Rd; r ₹2200-4000, ste from ₹5000;) Boasts a choice of modern, well-serviced rooms, an aquamarine swimming pool, spa, a good multicuisine restaurant and lounge bar for TV sports events.

Udupi Sri Krishna Bhavan SOUTH INDIAN **$**

(Bus Stand; thali ₹45, mains ₹70-90; 6am-11pm) This bustling place dishes out Indian vegie fare, including thalis and dosas, plus some North Indian dishes. It's opposite the bus stand.

Getting There & Away

BUS

Hosapete's bus stand has services to Hampi every half-hour (₹22, 30 minutes). Overnight private sleeper buses ply to/from Goa (₹1200 to 1600, seven to 10 hours), Gokarna (₹700, 6½ hours), Bengaluru (₹510 to ₹660, seven hours), Mysuru (₹380 to ₹605, 8½ hours) and Hyderabad (₹890 to ₹1120, seven to eight hours).

Paulo Travels (p895) runs overnight buses to Gokarna and Goa.

TRAIN

Hosapete's train station is a ₹20 autorickshaw ride from the town centre. The 18047 Amaravathi Express heads to Magdaon, Goa (sleeper/2AC ₹225/860, 7½ hours) daily at 6.20am. The 16591 Hampi Express departs nightly at 9pm for Bengaluru (3AC/2AC/1AC ₹625/895/1505, nine hours) and Mysuru (₹840/1205/2015, 12 hours). For Hyderabad there's a daily train at 7pm (sleeper/2AC ₹305/1175, 12 hours).

Hubballi (Hubli)

0836 / POP 958,600

Industrial Hubballi (still called by its old name Hubli by many) is a hub for rail routes for Mumbai, Bengaluru, Goa and northern Karnataka. There's no other reason to visit.

Sleeping & Eating

Hotel Ajanta HOTEL **$**

(0836-2362216; Koppikar Rd; s/d from ₹455/565) A simple crash pad near the train station with a popular ground-floor restaurant that serves delicious regional-style thalis.

Hotel Metropolis HOTEL **$$**

(0836-4266666; www.hotelmetropolishubli.com; Koppikar Rd; s/d with fan ₹1134/1242, with AC ₹1755/1989;) In the city centre and convenient for the train station, with a choice of clean, attractive, spacious and good-value rooms. Staff are eager to help travellers and there are two restaurants, including a multicuisine rooftop option.

Getting There & Away

The train station is 1.5km from the centrally located KSRTC Old Bus Stand, ₹50 in an autorickshaw. There's also a KSRTC New Bus Stand 4km west of the centre where many services originate, but nearly all also stop at the Old Bus Stand too.

AIR

The airport is 6km west of the centre. Currently only Air India Regional operates a daily flight to Bengaluru. Buses (₹6, 20 minutes) run between Gokul Rd, 400m south of the terminal, and the centre; taxis cost ₹180.

BUS

There are very regular services to Bengaluru, most being overnight (₹420 to ₹650, seven to 8½ hours), and plenty daily to Vijapura (₹197 to ₹241, five to six hours) and mainly night-time buses to Hosapete (₹144 to ₹189, four hours). There's an 8am bus to Gokarna (₹158, four hours) and regular connections to Mumbai (₹715 to ₹1300, 11 to 14 hours), Mysuru (₹452 to ₹808, nine hours) and Panaji (₹171 to ₹347, five to six hours).

TRAIN

From the train station, plenty of expresses head to Hosapete (sleeper/2AC ₹140/695, 2½ hours, six daily), Bengaluru (sleeper/2AC ₹270/1045, eight hours, three daily), Mumbai (sleeper/2AC ₹380/1435, 15½ hours) and Goa (sleeper/3AC ₹190/540, 6½ hours, two daily).

NORTHERN KARNATAKA

Badami

08357 / POP 26,600

Once the capital of the mighty Chalukya empire, today Badami is famous for its magnificent rock-cut cave temples, and red sandstone cliffs that resemble the Wild West. While the dusty main road is an eyesore that will have you wanting to get the hell out of there, its backstreets are a lovely area to explore with old houses, carved wooden doorways and the occasional Chalukyan ruin.

History

From about AD 540 to 757, Badami was the capital of an enormous kingdom stretching from Kanchipuram in Tamil Nadu to the Narmada River in Gujarat. It eventually fell to the Rashtrakutas, and changed hands several times thereafter, with each dynasty sculpturally embellishing Badami in their own way.

The sculptural legacy left by the Chalukyan artisans in Badami includes some of the earliest and finest examples of Dravidian temples and rock-cut caves.

Sights & Activities

The bluffs and horseshoe-shaped red sandstone cliff of Badami offer some great low-altitude climbing. For more information, visit www.indiaclimb.com.

Badami's caves overlook the 5th-century **Agastyatirtha Tank** and the waterside **Bhutanatha temples**. The stairway behind the Archaeological Museum climbs to the **North Fort**.

Cave Temples CAVE

(Indian/foreigner ₹15/200, children under 15 free, tour guide ₹300; 9am-5.30pm) Badami's highlights are its beautiful cave temples, three Hindu and one Jain, which display exquisite sculptures and intricate carvings. They're a magnificent example of Chalukya architecture and date back to the 6th century. All have a columned verandah, interior hall and a shrine at their rear.

Cave One, just above the entrance to the complex, is dedicated to Shiva. It's the oldest of the four caves, probably carved in the latter half of the 6th century. On the wall to the right of the porch is a captivating image of Nataraja striking 81 dance moves in the one pose. On the right of the porch area is a huge figure of Ardhanarishvara. On the opposite wall is a large image of Harihara, half Shiva and half Vishnu.

Dedicated to Vishnu, **Cave Two** is simpler in design. As with caves one and three, the front edge of the platform is decorated with images of pot-bellied dwarfs in various poses. Four pillars support the verandah, their tops carved with a bracket in the shape of a *yali* (mythical lion creature). On the left wall of the porch is the bull-headed figure of Varaha, the emblem of the Chalukya empire. To his left is Naga, a snake with a human face. On the right wall is a large sculpture of Trivikrama, another incarnation of Vishnu.

Between the second and third caves are two sets of steps to the right. The first leads to a natural cave with a small image of Padmapani (an incarnation of the Buddha). The second set of steps – sadly, barred by a gate – leads to the hilltop South Fort.

Cave Three, carved in AD 578, is the largest and most impressive. On the left wall is a carving of Vishnu, to whom the cave is dedicated, sitting on a snake. Nearby is an image of Varaha with four hands. The pillars have carved brackets in the shape of *yalis*. The ceiling panels contain images, including Indra riding an elephant, Shiva on a bull and Brahma on a swan. Keep an eye out for the image of drunken revellers, in particular one lady being propped up by her husband. There's also original colour on the ceiling;

the divots on the floor at the cave's entrance were used as paint palettes.

Dedicated to Jainism, **Cave Four** is the smallest of the set and dates to between the 7th and 8th centuries. The right wall has an image of Suparshvanatha (the seventh Jain *tirthankar*) surrounded by 24 Jain *tirthankars*. The inner sanctum contains an image of Adinath, the first Jain *tirthankar*.

Archaeological Museum MUSEUM
(₹5; ⏲9am-5pm Sat-Thu) The archaeological museum houses superb examples of local sculpture, including a remarkably explicit Lajja-Gauri image of a fertility cult that once flourished in the area. There are many sculptures of Shiva in different forms and there's a diorama of the Shidlaphadi cave.

Sleeping & Eating

Mookambika Deluxe HOTEL $
(☎08357-220067; hotelmookambika@yahoo.com; Station Rd; d with fan/AC from ₹1200/1800; ❄📶) For 'deluxe' read 'decent' – this hotel offers fair value with rooms done up in matt orange and green. Staff are a good source of travel info. It's opposite the bus stand.

Hotel Mayura Chalukya HOTEL $
(☎08357-220046; www.kstdc.co/hotels; Ramdurg Rd; d with fan/AC from ₹962/1282; ❄📶) Away from the bustle, this government hotel has large, clean rooms with an OK restaurant serving Indian staples.

Krishna Heritage HOTEL $$$
(☎08357-221300; www.krishnaheritagebadami.com; Ramdurg Rd; s/d incl breakfast ₹4000/6000; ❄📶) Located 2km west of the centre this attractive hotel is set in landscaped grounds. Rooms are massive with open-air showers and balconies and the large restaurant has delightful views over gardens and fields.

Bridge Restaurant MULTICUISINE $$
(Clarks Hotel, Veerpulakeshi Circle; mains ₹130-320; ⏲7am-10.30pm; 📶) Just the place when you need some AC relief, this business hotel's restaurant makes a good stab at Western dishes like pasta and pizza as well as Chinese and North Indian fare.

Getting There & Away

Badami is not served by many direct services. From Badami's bus stand on Station Rd there's one direct bus to both Vijapura (₹157, four hours, 5pm) and Hubballi (₹100, five hours, 3.15pm) but otherwise head on one of the regular buses to Kerur (₹26, 45 minutes), which has many more connections.

Getting Around

Theoretically, you can visit Aihole and Pattadakal in a day from Badami by bus if you get moving early. Start with Aihole (₹38, one hour), then move to Pattadakal (₹22, 30 minutes), and finally return to Badami (₹40, one hour). The last bus from Pattadakal to Badami is at 4pm.

However, it's much easier and less stressful to arrange an autorickshaw (₹1000) or taxi (₹2000) for a day trip to Pattadakal, Aihole and nearby Mahakuta.

Around Badami

Pattadakal

☎08357 / POP 1630

A secondary capital of the Badami Chalukyas, Pattadakal is known for its finely carved Hindu and Jain temples, which are collectively a World Heritage Site. The surrounding village of Pattadakal is tiny; most travellers visit the site from nearby Badami.

Sights

Barring a few that date back to the 3rd century AD, most of Pattadakal's World Heritage Site–listed temples were built during the 7th and 8th centuries AD. The main **Virupaksha Temple** (⏲6am-6pm) is a massive structure, its columns covered with intricate carvings depicting episodes from the Ramayana and Mahabharata. A giant stone sculpture of Nandi sits to the temple's east. The **Mallikarjuna Temple**, next to the Virupaksha Temple, is almost identical in design.

About 500m south of the main enclosure is the Jain **Papanatha Temple**, its entrance flanked by elephant sculptures.

Getting There & Away

Pattadakal is 20km from Badami, with buses (₹28) departing every 30 minutes until about 5pm. There's a morning and afternoon bus to Aihole (₹20), 13km away.

Aihole

☎08351 / POP 3200

Some 100 temples, built between the 4th and 6th centuries AD, speck the ancient Chalukyan regional capital of Aihole (*ay*-holeh). Most, however, are either in ruins or engulfed by the modern village. Aihole documents the embryonic stage of South Indian Hindu architecture, from the earliest simple shrines, such as the most ancient Ladkhan Temple, to the later and more complex buildings, such as the Meguti Temple.

Aihole is about 40km from Badami and 13km from Pattadakal.

Sights

The most impressive of all the temples in Aihole is the 7th-century **Durga Temple** (Indian/foreigner ₹5/200, camera ₹25; 6am-6pm), notable for its semicircular apse (inspired by Buddhist architecture) and the remains of the curvilinear *sikhara* (temple spire). The interiors house intricate stone carvings. The small **museum** (₹5; 9am-5pm Sat-Thu) behind the temple contains further examples of Chalukyan sculpture.

To the south of the Durga Temple are several other temple clusters, including early examples. About 600m to the southeast, on a low hillock, is the Jain **Meguti Temple**. Watch out for snakes if you're venturing up.

Getting There & Away

Regular buses run from Badami to Aihole (₹38, one hour).

Vijapura (Bijapur)

08352 / POP 337,200

A historic city epitomising the Deccan's Islamic era, dusty Vijapura (renamed in 2014 but still widely called Bijapur) tells a glorious tale dating back some 600 years. Blessed with a heap of mosques, mausoleums, palaces and fortifications, it was the capital of the Adil Shahi kings from 1489 to 1686, and one of the five splinter states formed after the Islamic Bahmani kingdom broke up in 1482. Despite its strong Islamic character, Vijapura is also a centre for the Lingayat brand of Shaivism, which emphasises a single personalised god. The **Lingayat Siddeshwara Festival** (Jan or Feb) runs for eight days.

Sights

★Golgumbaz MONUMENT
(Indian/foreigner ₹15/200; 10am-5pm) Set in tranquil gardens, the magnificent Golgumbaz mausoleum houses the tombs of emperor Mohammed Adil Shah (r 1627–56), his two wives, his mistress (Rambha), one of his daughters and a grandson. Octagonal seven-storey towers stand at each corner of the monument, which is capped by an enormous dome. Climb the steep, narrow stairs up one of the towers to reach the 'whispering gallery' within the dome, which has terrific acoustics (which excitable schoolchildren love to prove to loud effect).

Archaeological Museum MUSEUM
(₹5; 10am-5pm Sat-Thu) A well-presented archaeological museum set in the Golgumbaz lawns. Skip the ground floor and head upstairs; there you'll find an excellent collection of artefacts, such as oriental carpets, china crockery, weapons, armoury and scrolls.

Jama Masjid MOSQUE
(Jama Masjid Rd; 9am-5.30pm) Constructed by Ali Adil Shah I (r 1557–80), the finely proportioned Jama Masjid has graceful arches, a fine dome and a vast inner courtyard with room for more than 2200 worshippers. Women should make sure to cover their heads and not wear revealing clothing.

Asar Mahal HISTORIC BUILDING
(6am–8.30pm) FREE Built by Mohammed Adil Shah in about 1646 to serve as a Hall of Justice, the graceful Asar Mahal once housed two hairs from Prophet Mohammed's beard. The rooms on the upper storey are decorated with frescoes and a square tank graces the front. It's out of bounds for women.

Citadel FORT
FREE Surrounded by fortified walls and a wide moat, the citadel once contained the palaces, pleasure gardens and durbar (royal court) of the Adil Shahi kings. Now mainly in ruins, the most impressive of the remaining fragments are the colossal arches of the **Gagan Mahal** FREE, built by Ali Adil Shah I around 1561. The gates here are locked, but someone will be on hand to let you in.

The ruins of Mohammed Adil Shah's seven-storey palace, the **Sat Manzil** FREE, are nearby. Across the road stands the delicate **Jala Manzil**, once a water pavilion surrounded by secluded courts and gardens. On the other side of Station Rd (MG Rd) are the graceful arches of **Bara Kaman** FREE, the ruined mausoleum of Ali Roza.

Central Market MARKET
(Station Rd; 9am-9pm) This lively market is an explosion of colour and scents with flowers, spices and fresh produce on sale.

Vijapura (Bijapur)

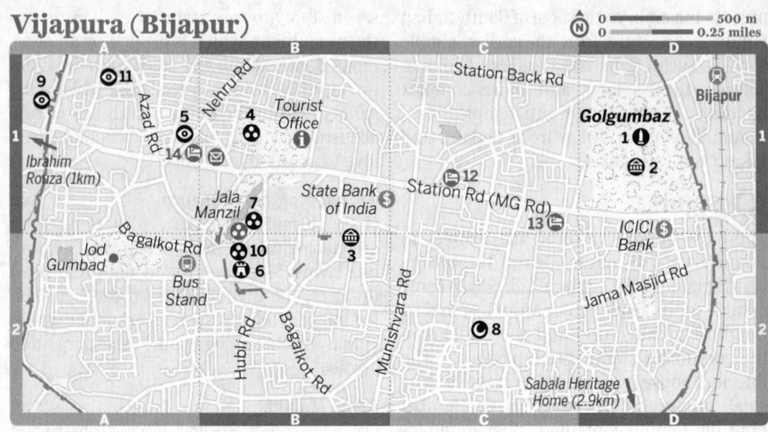

Vijapura (Bijapur)

Top Sights
1 Golgumbaz D1

Sights
2 Archaeological Museum D1
3 Asar Mahal B2
4 Bara Kaman B1
5 Central Market A1
6 Citadel B2
7 Gagan Mahal B1
8 Jama Masjid C2
9 Malik-e-Maidan A1
10 Sat Manzil B2
11 Upli Buruj A1

Sleeping
12 Hotel Madhuvan International C1
13 Hotel Pearl C1
14 Hotel Tourist A1

Upli Buruj HISTORIC SITE
FREE Upli Buruj is a 16th-century, 24m-high watchtower near the western walls of the city. An external flight of stairs leads to the top, where you'll find two hefty cannons and good views of other monuments around town.

Malik-e-Maidan HISTORIC SITE
(Monarch of the Plains) Perched upon a platform is this beast of a cannon – over 4m long, almost 1.5m in diameter and estimated to weigh 55 tonnes. Cast in 1549, it was supposedly brought to Vijapura as a war trophy thanks to the efforts of 10 elephants, 400 oxen and hundreds of men!

★Ibrahim Rouza MONUMENT
(Indian/foreigner ₹15/200; 6am-6pm) The beautiful Ibrahim Rouza is among the most elegant and finely proportioned Islamic monuments in India. Its 24m-high minarets are said to have inspired those of the Taj Mahal, and its tale is similarly poignant: built by emperor Ibrahim Adil Shah II (r 1580–1627) as a future mausoleum for his queen, Taj Sultana. Ironically, he died before her, and was thus the first person to be rested there. Also interred here with Ibrahim Adil Shah are his queen, children and mother.

For a tip (₹150 is fine), caretakers can show you around the monument, including the dark labyrinth around the catacomb where the actual graves are located.

Sleeping & Eating

Hotel Tourist HOTEL $
(08352-250655; Station Rd; s/d from ₹220/360) A dive bang in the middle of the bazaar, with no-frills rooms; their 'deluxe' options cost slightly more but are worth it.

★Sabala Heritage Home HERITAGE HOTEL $$
(9448118204; www.sabalaheritagehome.org; Bijapur Bypass, NH-13, near Ganesh Nagar; r incl breakfast & dinner ₹3000;) On the edge of the city this heritage hotel has attractive, artistically decorated rooms overlooking farmland. Food is home-cooked, flavoursome and inventive. The hotel is linked to an NGO that empowers women and trades

fine handicrafts (there's a store here too). It's 4km south of the centre.

Hotel Pearl HOTEL **$$**
(☎08352-256002; www.hotelpearlbijapur.com; 633 Station Rd; d with fan/AC from ₹1600/2200; ❄📶) Offering good value, this midrange hotel has clean motel-style rooms around a central atrium, and is conveniently located to Golgumbaz. Wi-fi is a bit spotty but its in-house **Qaswa Hills restaurant** (Pearl Hotel, Station Rd; meals ₹120-280; ⏰7am-4pm & 7-10pm) is very popular.

Hotel Madhuvan International HOTEL **$$**
(☎08352-255571; Station Rd; d with fan/AC ₹1600/2100; ❄📶) An ongoing renovation program means most rooms are in good shape at this pleasant hotel which has a courtyard garden. It's hidden down a lane off Station Rd and has a great in-house **restaurant** (mains ₹60-100; ⏰9-11am, noon-4pm & 7-11pm). There's no lift, however.

Shopping

Sabala Handicrafts ARTS & CRAFTS
(http://sabalahandicrafts.com; NH13, Bijapur Bypass; from ₹800; ⏰8am-5.30pm) Beautiful handmade textiles, bags, saris, kurtas and accessories. Profits benefit an NGO that empowers village women. It's 4km south of the centre.

Information

Tourist Office (☎08352-250359; Hotel Mayura Adil Shahi Annexe, Station Rd; ⏰10am-5.30pm Mon-Sat) Has good Vijapura brochures with map.

Getting There & Away

BUS

The following services leave from the **bus stand** (☎08352-0251344; Meenakshi Chowk Rd; ⏰24hr):

Bengaluru ordinary/sleeper ₹576/757, 12 hours, four daily

Bidar ₹265, 6½ hours, four evening buses

Kalaburgi (Gubarga) ₹164, four hours, three day buses

Hosapete ₹241, five hours, five daily

Hubballi ₹193 to ₹241, five hours, two daily

Hyderabad ₹373 to ₹729, eight to 10 hours, six daily

Mumbai ₹660, 12 hours, four daily, via Pune (₹428, eight hours)

Panaji (Goa) ₹335 to ₹415, 10 hours, two daily

TRAIN

Trains from Vijapura station go to:

Badami 17320 Hubli-Secunderabad Express, sleeper/2AC ₹140/695, 2½ hours, 1am and two other daily trains

Bengaluru 16536 Golgumbaz Express, sleeper/2AC ₹355/1395, 15½ hours, 5pm

Hyderabad 17319 Secunderabad Express, sleeper/2AC ₹250/960, 11 hours, 1am

Getting Around

Given the amount to see and distance to cover, ₹700 is a fair price to hire an autorickshaw for a day of sightseeing. Short hops around town cost ₹50.

Bidar

☎08482 / POP 218,500

Despite being home to amazing ruins and monuments, Bidar, hidden away in Karnataka's far northeastern corner, gets very little tourist traffic – which of course makes it all the more appealing. It's a city drenched in Islamic Indian history, with this old-walled town being first the capital of the Bahmani kingdom (1428–87) and later the capital of the Barid Shahi dynasty. This is one of the least Westernised parts of Karnataka, with many niqab-wearing women and turbaned Sikh pilgrims, and though locals are welcoming to visitors, conservative values predominate.

Sights

★**Bidar Fort** FORT
(⏰6am-6pm) FREE Keep aside a few hours for peacefully wandering around the remnants of this magnificent 15th-century fort, the largest in South India – and once the administrative capital of much of the region. Surrounded by a triple moat hewn out of solid red rock and many kilometres of defensive walls, the fort has a fairy-tale entrance that twists in an elaborate chicane through three gateways.

Information at the site is minimal so consider hiring a guide from the archaeological office (who can unlock the most interesting ruins within the fort). These include the **Rangin Mahal** (Painted Palace), with elaborate tilework, teak pillars and panels with mother-of-pearl inlay, **Solah Khamba Mosque** (Sixteen-Pillared Mosque), and **Tarkash Mahal** with exquisite Islamic inscriptions and wonderful rooftop views.

There's a small **museum** in the former royal bath with local artefacts.

Khwaja Mahmud Gawan Madrasa RUIN, HISTORIC SITE
(dawn-dusk) FREE Dominating the heart of the old town are the ruins of Khwaja Mahmud Gawan Madrasa, a college for advanced learning built in 1472. To get an idea of its former grandeur, check out the remnants of coloured tiles on the front gate and one of the minarets which still stands intact.

Guru Nanak Jhira Sahib SIKH TEMPLE
(Shiva Nagar; 24hr) FREE This large Sikh temple on the northwestern side of town is dedicated to the guru Guru Nanak and was built in 1948. It's centred around the Amrit Kund (a water tank) where pilgrims cleanse their souls.

Bahmani Tombs HISTORIC SITE
(dawn-dusk) FREE The huge domed tombs of the Bahmani kings in Ashtur, 3km east of Bidar, were built to house the remains of the sultans, of which the painted interior of Ahmad Shah Bahman's tomb is the most impressive.

Sleeping & Eating

Hotel Mayura HOTEL $
(08482-228142; Udgir Rd; d with fan/AC from ₹1100/2200;) Its concrete exterior is unappealing but rooms are cheerful and well-appointed. There's a bar and restaurant and it's opposite the central bus stand. Look out for its NBC-peacock symbol.

Hotel Mayura Barid Shahi HOTEL $
(08482-221740; Udgir Rd; s/d ₹500/600, r with AC ₹900;) Maintenance could be better at this old-timer which has simple, institutional rooms, a central location and a popular garden bar-restaurant.

Jyothi Fort INDIAN $
(Bidar Fort; mains ₹70-120; 9am-5pm) A peaceful setting at the fort's entry with tables set up on the grass under sprawling tamarind trees has delicious vegetarian meals.

Kamat Hotel SOUTH INDIAN $
(Udgir Rd; meals ₹80-150; 7.30am-10pm) Scores highly for South Indian classics at very affordable rates. It's busy through the day and there's an AC room.

Getting There & Away

From the bus stand, frequent buses run to Kalaburagi (₹124, three hours) and there are two evening buses to Vijapura (₹280, seven hours). There are also buses to Hyderabad (₹142, four hours, 6.30pm) and Bengaluru (semideluxe/AC ₹750/900, 13 hours, five daily).

Trains head to Hyderabad (sleeper ₹100, five hours, 2am) and Bengaluru (sleeper/2AC ₹370/1435, 13 hours, 6.05pm).

Getting Around

You can arrange a day tour in an autorickshaw for around ₹600.

Telangana & Andhra Pradesh

Includes ➡

Best Places to Eat

- ➡ Sea Inn (p936)
- ➡ Shah Ghouse Cafe (p923)
- ➡ SO – The Sky Kitchen (p924)
- ➡ Hotel Mayura (p939)
- ➡ Dhaba By Claridges (p925)
- ➡ TFL (p933)

Best Off the Beaten Track

- ➡ Ramappa Temple (p930)
- ➡ Sankaram (p937)
- ➡ Moula Ali Dargah (p919)
- ➡ Guntupalli (p933)

Why Go?

Hyderabad, one of Islamic India's greatest cities, is reason enough on its own to visit this region. Its skyline is a sight to behold, defined by the great domes and minarets of ancient mosques, mausoleums and palaces of once-mighty dynasties. Delve inside the city's fabled old quarter for fascinating street markets, teahouses and biryani restaurants, then journey to the city's fringes to the majestic Golconda fort. Meanwhile, Hyderabad's newer districts are awash with the classy restaurants and boutiques of IT-fuelled economic advancement.

The other attractions of these two states (which were one state until they split in 2014) are less brazen, but dig around and you will unearth gems – like the wonderful medieval temple sculptures of Ramappa, the beauty of ancient Buddhist sites such as Sankaram and Guntupalli hidden in deep countryside, the cheery coastal holiday vibe of Visakhapatnam, and the positive vibrations emanating from the vast pilgrim crowds at Tirumala's temple.

When to Go

Hyderabad

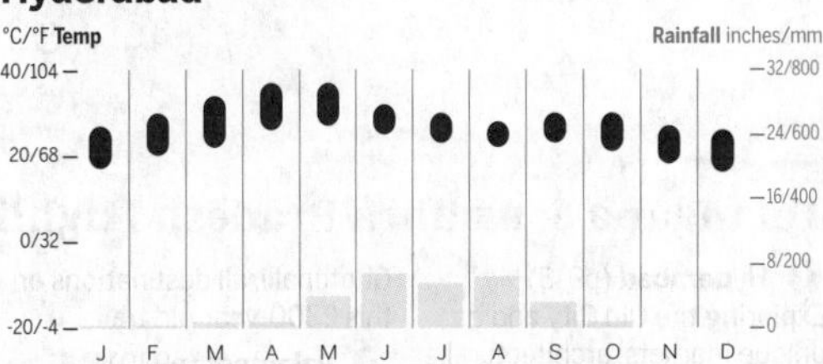

May–Jun Join locals digging into *haleem*, a Ramadan (Ramzan) favourite.

Nov–Feb Explore Hyderabad's sights in balmy 22–28°C weather.

Dec–Apr The best time to enjoy Vizag's coastal attractions – there's little rain and it's not *too* hot.

Telangana & Andhra Pradesh Highlights

1. **Hyderabad** (p913) Exploring the Old City and its unique markets, architectural marvels and restaurants.

2. **Monastic trail** (p937) Absorbing the meditative ambience at beautiful Sankaram, as well as Bavikonda, Thotlakonda and Guntupalli, all destinations on this 2300-year-old trail.

3. **Palampet** (p930) Revelling in the genius of Kakatiya sculptors at the temple near this village.

4. **Tirumala** (p938) Going with the crowd and finding a spiritual calling with Hindu pilgrims.

5. **Araku** (p938) Enjoying the delightful train ride here through the lush forests and wide green valleys of the Eastern Ghats.

History

From the 3rd century BC to 3rd century AD the Satavahana empire, also known as the Andhras, ruled over much of the Deccan plateau from a base in this region. The Satavahanas helped Buddhism to flourish after it arrived with emperor Ashoka's missionary monks, and today Andhra Pradesh has more ancient Buddhist sites than almost any other Indian state.

The Hindu Kakatiyas, based at Warangal, ruled most of Telangana and Andhra Pradesh from the 12th to 14th centuries, a period that saw the rise of Telugu culture and language. Warangal eventually fell to the Muslim Delhi Sultanate and then passed to the Deccan-based Bahmani Sultanate. Then, in 1518, the Bahmanis' governor at Golconda, Sultan Quli Qutb Shah, claimed independence. His Qutb Shahi dynasty developed Golconda into the massive fortress we see today. But a water shortage there caused Sultan Mohammed Quli Qutb Shah to relocate a few kilometres east to the south bank of the Musi River, where he founded the new city of Hyderabad in 1591.

The Qutb Shahis were ousted by the Mughal emperor Aurangzeb in 1687. When the Mughal empire in turn started fraying at the edges, its local viceroy Nizam ul-Mulk Asaf Jah took control of much of the Deccan, launching Hyderabad's second great Muslim dynasty, the Asaf Jahis – the famously fabulously wealthy nizams of Hyderabad – in 1724. His capital was Aurangabad, but his son Asaf Jah II moved to Hyderabad in 1763. Hyderabad rose to become the centre of Islamic India and a focus for the arts, culture and learning. Its abundance of rare gems and minerals – the world-famous Kohinoor diamond is from here – furnished the nizams with enormous wealth.

The whole region was effectively under British control from around 1800, but while Andhra Pradesh was governed from Madras (now Chennai), the princely state of Hyderabad – which included large territories outside the city populated by Telugu-speaking Hindus – remained nominally independent. Come Indian Independence in 1947, nizam Osman Ali Khan wanted to retain sovereignty, but Indian military intervention saw Hyderabad state join the Indian union in 1948.

When Indian states were reorganised along linguistic lines in 1956, Hyderabad was split three ways. What's now Telangana joined other Telugu-speaking areas to form Andhra Pradesh state; other districts became parts of Karnataka and Maharashtra. Telangana was never completely happy with this arrangement, and after prolonged campaigning, it was split off from Andhra Pradesh as a separate state in 2014. Hyderabad remains capital of both states until Andhra Pradesh gets its new capital at Amaravati (next to Vijayawada) up and running. Amaravati, designed by Singapore city planners, should be smart, green and ultramodern – though completion will doubtless take many decades.

HYDERABAD

☎040 / POP 7.68 MILLION / ELEV 600M

Steeped in history, thronged with people and buzzing with commerce, the Old City of Hyderabad is one of India's most evocative ancient quarters. Exploring the lanes of this district, with its chai shops and spice merchants, you'll encounter a teeming urban masala of colour and commerce. Looming over the Old City is some of Islamic India's most impressive architecture, in varying states of repair. Most visitors concentrate their time in this area, though the magnificent Golconda Fort should not be missed either.

Hyderabad's other pole is far younger and west of the centre – its Hi-Tech City, or 'Cyberabad', and other districts like Banjara Hills and Jubilee Hills are replete with glittery malls, multiplexes, clubs, pubs and sleek restaurants.

TOP STATE FESTIVALS

Sankranti (⌚Jan) This important regionwide Telugu festival marks the end of harvest season. Kite-flying abounds, doorsteps are decorated with colourful *kolams* (rice-flour designs) and men adorn cattle with bells and fresh horn paint.

Brahmotsavam (⌚Sep/Oct) This nine-day festival sees the Venkateshwara temple at Tirumala awash in vast crowds of worshippers. Special *pujas* (offerings) and chariot processions are held, and it's an auspicious time for *darshan* (deity-viewing).

Muharram (⌚Sep/Oct) Commemorates the martyrdom of Mohammed's grandson Hussain. A huge procession throngs the Old City in Hyderabad.

One thing you have to accept wherever you are in Hyderabad: the traffic is appalling. A (long-delayed) Metro Rail rapid-transit system should ease things somewhat in the coming years.

Sights

Old City

★Charminar MONUMENT

(Map p916; Indian/foreigner ₹5/100; ⏲9am-5.30pm) Hyderabad's principal landmark and city symbol was built by Mohammed Quli Qutb Shah in 1591 to commemorate the founding of Hyderabad and the end of epidemics caused by Golconda's water shortage. The gargantuan four-column, 56m-high structure has four arches facing the cardinal points, with minarets atop each column (hence the name Charminar, 'four minarets'). It's certainly an impressive sight, though the relentless traffic that swirls around the structure, crowds and queues make it somewhat less rewarding to visit.

The Charminar stands at the heart of Hyderabad's main bazaar area (also known as Charminar), a labyrinth of lanes crowded with shops, stalls, markets and shoppers. You can climb to the 1st floor for a view of the district. The 2nd floor, home to Hyderabad's oldest mosque, and the upper columns, are not open to the public. The structure is illuminated from 7pm to 9pm.

★Chowmahalla Palace PALACE

(Map p916; http://chowmahalla.co.in; Indian/foreigner ₹50/200, camera ₹50; ⏲10am-5pm Sat-Thu) This opulent 18th- and 19th-century palace compound, the main residence of several nizams, comprises several grandiose buildings and four garden courtyards. Most dazzling is the Khilwat Mubarak, a magnificent durbar hall where nizams held ceremonies under 19 enormous chandeliers of Belgian crystal. Its side rooms today house historical exhibits, arts and crafts and exhibits of nizams' personal possessions. In the southernmost courtyard is a priceless collection of carriages and vintage cars including a 1911 yellow Rolls-Royce and 1937 Buick convertible.

Salar Jung Museum MUSEUM

(Map p916; www.salarjungmuseum.in; Salar Jung Rd; Indian/foreigner ₹20/500, camera ₹50; ⏲10am-5pm Sat-Thu) This vast collection was amassed by Mir Yousuf Ali Khan (Salar Jung III), who was briefly grand vizier to the seventh nizam. The 39 galleries include early South Indian bronzes and wood and stone sculptures, Indian miniature paintings, European fine art, historic manuscripts, a room of jade and the remarkable *Veiled Rebecca* by 19th-century Italian sculptor Benzoni. Note the entrance ticket for foreigners is very steep and the museum is very popular (near bedlam on Sundays).

HEH The Nizam's Museum MUSEUM

(Purani Haveli; Map p916; www.hehnmh.com; off Dur-e-Sharwah Hospital Rd; adult/child ₹80/15, camera ₹150; ⏲10am-5pm Sat-Thu) The Purani Haveli was a home of the sixth nizam, Mahbub Ali Khan (r 1869–1911). He was rumoured to have never worn the same thing twice: hence the 54m-long, two-storey Burmese teak wardrobe. Much of the museum is devoted to personal effects of the seventh nizam, Osman Ali Khan, including his silver cradle, gold-burnished throne and lavish Silver Jubilee gifts. The displays, lighting and information could be improved, but it's still a worthwhile visit.

Mecca Masjid MOSQUE

(Map p916; Shah Ali Banda Rd; ⏲4.30am-9pm) This mosque is one of the world's largest, with 10,000 men praying here at major Muslim festivals, and also one of Hyderabad's oldest buildings, begun in 1617 by the city's founder Mohammed Quli Qutb Shah. Women are not allowed inside the main prayer hall, and male tourists are unlikely to be let in either (they can look through the railings). Female tourists, even with headscarves, may not even be allowed into the vast courtyard if their clothing is judged too skimpy or tight.

Several bricks embedded above the prayer hall's central arch are made with soil from Mecca, hence the mosque's name. An enclosure alongside the courtyard contains the tombs of several Hyderabad nizams.

Badshahi Ashurkhana ISLAMIC SITE

(Map p916; High Court Rd) The 1594 Badshahi Ashurkhana (literally 'royal house of mourning') was one of the first structures built by the Qutb Shahs in their new city of Hyderabad. In a courtyard set back from the road, its walls are practically glowing with intricate, brightly coloured tile mosaics. The Ashurkhana is packed during Muharram, as well as on Thursdays, when local Shiites gather to commemorate the martyrdom of Hussain Ibn Ali. Visitors should remove shoes and dress modestly (including a headscarf for women).

Hyderabad

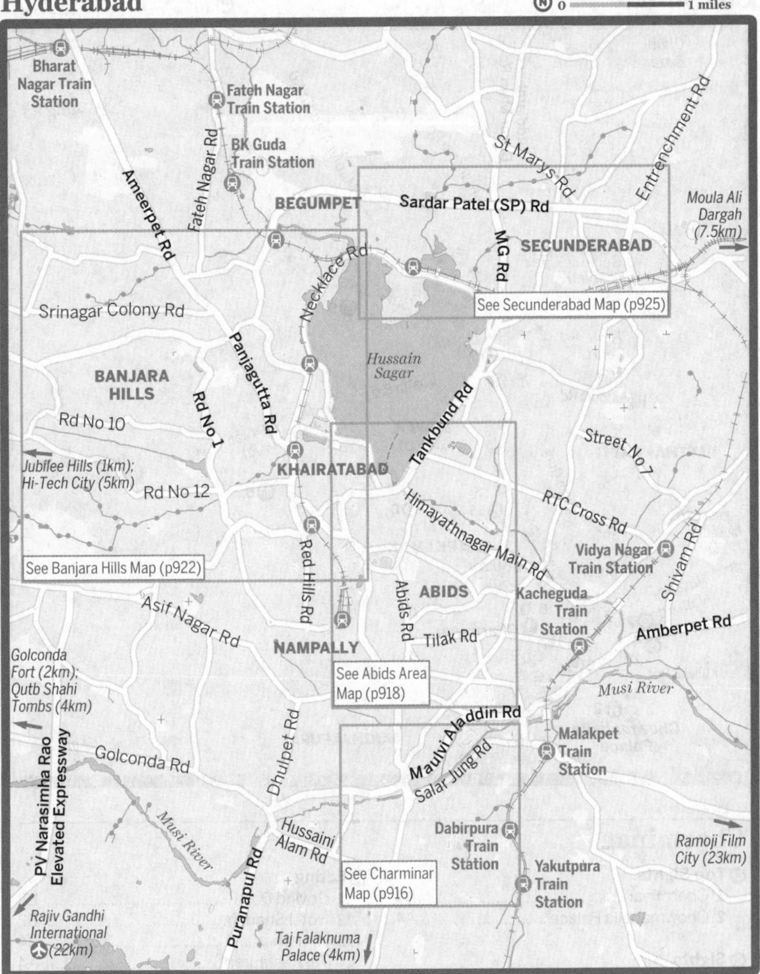

Abids Area

State Museum MUSEUM

(Map p918; Public Gardens Rd, Nampally; ₹10, camera/video ₹100/500; ⏲10.30am-4.30pm Sat-Thu, closed 2nd Sat of month) This sprawling museum is in a fanciful Indo-Saracenic building constructed by the seventh nizam as a playhouse for one of his daughters. It hosts a collection of important archaeological finds as well as an exhibit on the region's Buddhist history. There's an interesting decorative-arts gallery, where you can learn about Bidriware inlaid metalwork and *kalamkari* textile painting, plus a bronze-sculpture gallery and a 4500-year-old Egyptian mummy.

British Residency HISTORIC BUILDING

(Koti Women's College; Map p918; Koti Main Rd) This palatial Palladian residence, built in 1803–06 by James Achilles Kirkpatrick, the British Resident (official East India Company representative) in Hyderabad, features in William Dalrymple's brilliant historical love story *White Mughals*. Work is ongoing to restore the building to its former glory, a project which will take many years to accomplish. There's no official access but Detours (p920)

Charminar

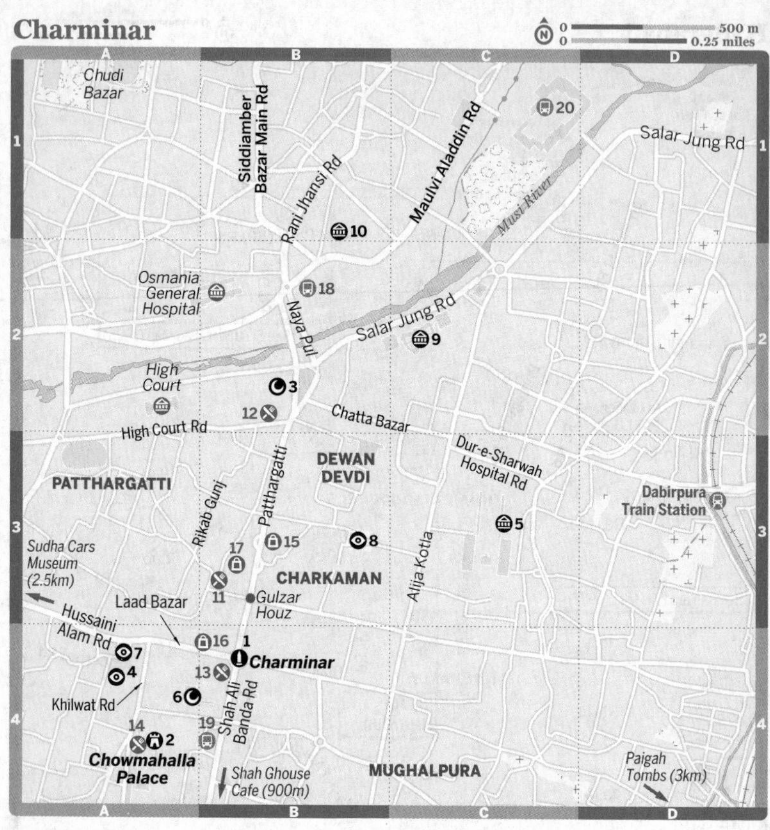

Charminar

Top Sights
- 1 Charminar B4
- 2 Chowmahalla Palace A4

Sights
- 3 Badshahi Ashurkhana B2
- 4 Chiddi Bazar A4
- 5 HEH The Nizam's Museum C3
- 6 Mecca Masjid A4
- 7 Mehboob Chowk A4
- 8 Mir Alam Mandi B3
- 9 Salar Jung Museum C2
- 10 State Library B1

Activities, Courses & Tours
- Heritage Walks .... (see 1)

Eating
- 11 Govind Dosa B3
- 12 Hotel Shadab B2
- 13 Nimrah B4
- 14 Taj Restaurant A4

Shopping
- 15 Hyderabad Perfumers B3
- 16 Laad Bazar B4
- 17 Patel Market B3

Transport
- 18 Afzalgunj Bus Stop B2
- 19 Charminar Bus Stop B4
- 20 Mahatma Gandhi Bus Station C1

can usually gain entry for those booking one of its fascinating White Mughal tours.

Kirkpatrick became enchanted by Hyderabad courtly culture, converted to Islam and married Khair-un-Nissa, a teenage relative of the Hyderabad prime minister. The Residency and its extensive gardens became the Osmania University College for Women, known as Koti Women's College, in 1949. Beyond the grand classical portico is the (newly renovated) Durbar Hall, with Islamic geometric designs on its high ceiling above the chandeliers and classical columns and an elaborate curving staircase behind. In the overgrown gardens to the southwest you'll find a British cemetery, the surviving entrance to the Residency's zenana (women's quarters) and a model of the Residency building made by Kirkpatrick for Khair-un-Nissa.

Birla Mandir HINDU TEMPLE

(Map p922; ⏲7am-noon & 3-9pm) The ethereal Birla Mandir, constructed of white Rajasthani marble in 1976, graces Kalapahad (Black Mountain), one of two rocky hills overlooking the lake of Hussain Sagar. Dedicated to Venkateshwara, it's a popular Hindu worship centre, with a relaxed atmosphere, and affords magnificent views over the city, especially at sunset. There are several imposing statues including a huge granite image of Venkateshwara. Disabled access is good: there's a lift in the curious clock tower.

Birla Modern Art Gallery MUSEUM

(Map p918; www.birlasciencecentre.org; Naubat Pahad Lane, Adarsh Nagar; ₹50; ⏲10.30am-8pm) This skilfully curated collection of modern and contemporary art includes paintings by superstars Jogen Chowdhury, Tyeb Mehta and Arpita Singh.

Banjara Hills

★Lamakaan CULTURAL CENTRE

(Map p922; ☎9642731329; www.lamakaan.com; next to JVR Park, Banjara Hills; ⏲10am-10.30pm Tue-Sun) This noncommercial 'inclusive cultural space' is an open centre that hosts plays, films, musical events, exhibitions, organic markets and lectures. It also has a great Irani cafe, with cheap tea and snacks and free wi-fi. On a lane off Rd No 1.

Kalakriti Art Gallery GALLERY

(Map p922; www.kalakritiartgallery.com; Rd No 10, Banjara Hills; ⏲11am-7pm) FREE One of the city's best contemporary galleries, Kalakriti hosts excellent exhibitions by some of India's leading artists, and collaborative programs with the Alliance Française and Goethe Zentrum.

Other Areas

★Golconda Fort FORT

(Indian/foreigner ₹20/200, 1hr sound-and-light show ₹140; ⏲9am-5.30pm, English-language sound-and-light show 6.30pm Nov-Feb, 7pm Mar-Oct) Hyderabad's most impressive sight, this monumental fort lies on the western edge of town. In the 16th century the Qutb Shahs made Golconda a fortified citadel, built atop a 120m-high granite hill surrounded by mighty ramparts, all ringed by further necklaces of crenellated fortifications, 11km in perimeter. From the summit there are stunning vistas across dusty Deccan foothills and the crumbling outer ramparts, over the domed tombs of Qutb Shahs, past distant shanty towns to the horizon haze of the inner city.

By the time of the Qutb Shahs, Golconda Fort had already existed for at least three centuries under the Kakatiyas and Bahmani sultanate, and was already famed for its diamonds, which were mostly mined in the Krishna River valley, but cut and traded here. The Qutb Shahs moved to their new city of Hyderabad in 1591, but maintained Golconda as a citadel until the Mughal emperor Aurangzeb took it in 1687 after a year-long siege, ending Qutb Shahi rule.

KITSCHABAD

Mixed in with Hyderabad's world-class sights are some attractions that err on the quirkier side.

Ramoji Film City (www.ramojifilmcity.com; adult/child from ₹1000/900; ⏲9am-8pm) The Telangana/Andhra Pradesh film industry, 'Tollywood', is massive, and so is the 6.7-sq-km Film City, where films and TV shows in Telugu, Tamil and Hindi, among others, are made. The day-visit ticket includes a bus tour, funfair rides and shows. **Telangana Tourism** (p920) runs tours here.

Sudha Cars Museum (www.sudhacars.com; 19-5-15/1/D, Bahadurpura; Indian/foreigner ₹50/200, camera ₹50; ⏲9.30am-6.30pm) The eccentric creations of auto-enthusiast K Sudhakar include cars and bikes in the shape of a cricket bat, computer and lipstick, among other wacky designs. And they all work. The museum is 3km west of Charminar.

Abids Area

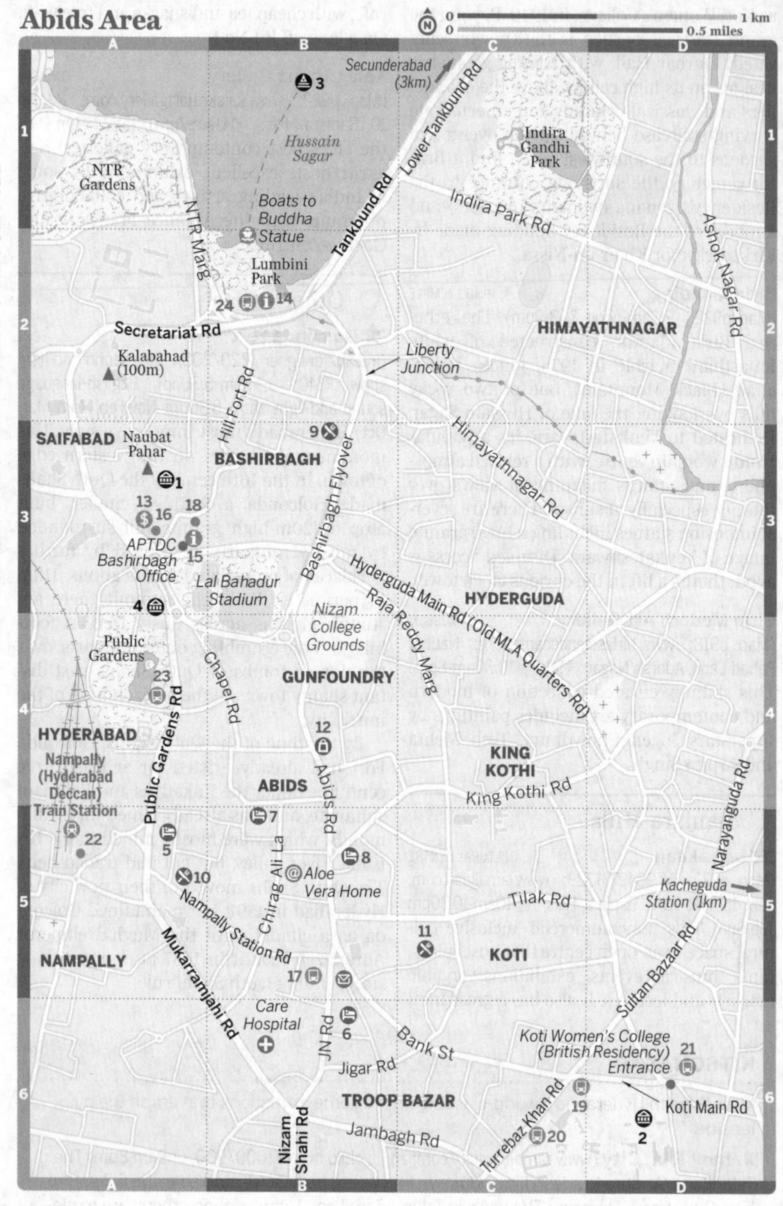

Golconda's massive gates were studded with iron spikes to obstruct war elephants. Within the fort, a series of concealed glazed earthenware pipes ensured a reliable water supply, while the ingenious acoustics guaranteed that even the smallest sound from the entrance would echo across the fort complex.

Allow at least a couple of hours to explore the site. Guides charge at least ₹600 per 90-minute tour. Small ₹20 guide booklets are also available. Inside the citadel gate, an

Abids Area

Sights
1 Birla Modern Art Gallery A3
2 British Residency D6
3 Buddha Statue & Hussain Sagar B1
4 State Museum A3

Sleeping
5 Hotel Rajmata A5
6 Hotel Suhail B6
7 Royalton Hotel B5
8 Taj Mahal Hotel B5

Eating
Dakshina Mandapa .... (see 8)
9 Gufaa B3
10 Kamat Hotel A5
11 Santosh Dhaba C5

Shopping
12 Bidri Crafts B4

Information
13 State Bank of India A3
14 Telangana Tourism B2
15 Telangana Tourism A3

Transport
16 Air India A3
17 GPO Abids Bus Stop B5
18 Jet Airways A3
19 Koti Bus Stand C6
20 Koti Bus Stop C6
21 Koti Women's College Bus Stand D6
22 Nampally Reservation Complex A5
23 Public Gardens Bus Stop A4
24 Secretariat Bus Stop (Pushpak) B2

anticlockwise circuit leads through gardens and up past mostly minor buildings to the top of the hill, where you'll find the functioning Hindu Jagadamba Mahakali Temple and the three-storey durbar hall, with fine panoramas. You then descend to the old palace buildings in the southeastern part of the fort and return to the entrance passing the elegant three-arched Taramati Mosque.

Golconda is about 10km west from Abids or Charminar: an Uber cab or auto is around ₹250 one way. Buses 65G and 66G run from Charminar to Golconda via GPO Abids hourly; the journey takes about an hour.

★ Qutb Shahi Tombs — HISTORIC SITE

(Tolichowki; Indian/foreigner ₹15/100, camera/video ₹50/100; ⏲9.30am-5.30pm Sat-Thu) These 21 magnificent domed granite tombs, with almost as many mosques, sit serenely in landscaped gardens about 2km northwest of Golconda Fort, where many of their occupants spent large parts of their lives. Seven of the eight Qutb Shahi rulers were buried here, as well as family members and a few physicians, courtesans and other favourites. An exhibition near the entrance provides helpful explanatory information (including the ambitious plans to renovate the structures and create a Heritage Park).

The tombs' great domes are mounted on cubical bases, many of which have beautiful colonnades and delicate lime stucco ornamentation. Among the finest is that of Mohammed Quli, the founder of Hyderabad, standing 42m tall on a platform near the edge of the complex, with views back towards Golconda.

The tombs are about 2km from Golconda Fort, ₹30 by autorickshaw or Uber cab.

Paigah Tombs — HISTORIC SITE

(Santoshnagar; ⏲9.30am-5pm) FREE The aristocratic Paigah family, purportedly descendants of the second Caliph of Islam, were fierce loyalists of the nizams, serving as statespeople, philanthropists and generals. The Paigahs' necropolis, in a quiet neighbourhood 4km southeast of Charminar, is a small compound of exquisite mausoleums made of marble and lime stucco. It's signposted down a small lane opposite Owaisi Hospital on the Inner Ring Rd.

The complex contains 27 carved-marble tombs in enclosures with delicately carved walls and pillars, stunning geometrically patterned filigree screens and, overhead, tall, graceful turrets. At the western end a handsome mosque is reflected in its large ablutions pool.

Moula Ali Dargah — ISLAMIC SITE

Out on the city's northeastern fringes, the dramatic rock mound of Moula Ali hill has long-distance views, cool breezes and at the top, up 500 steps, a dargah (shrine to a Sufi saint) containing what's believed to be a handprint of Ali, the son-in-law of the Prophet Mohammed. The dargah's reputed healing properties make it a pilgrimage site for the sick.

Visitors are normally allowed inside the dargah, which is covered in thousands of tiny mirrors, only during the three-day Moula Ali *urs* festival during Muharram, but you can admire them outside at other times.

Moula Ali hill is 9km northeast of Secunderabad – around ₹250 in an Uber cab, or take bus 16A or 16C from Rathifile bus stand to ECIL bus stand, and an autorickshaw 2km from there.

Buddha Statue & Hussain Sagar BUDDHIST MONUMENT
(Map p918; boats adult/child ₹55/35) Set magnificently on a plinth in the Hussain Sagar, a lake created by the Qutb Shahs, is a colossal stone statue of the Buddha (18m tall). The Dalai Lama consecrated the monument in 2006, which is evocatively illuminated at night.

Frequent boats make the 30-minute return trip to the statue from both Eat Street (⊙launches 3-8pm) and popular Lumbini Park (admission ₹10; ⊙9am-9pm). The Tankbund Rd promenade, on the eastern shore of Hussain Sagar, has great views of the statue.

Activities

Blue Cross of Hyderabad VOLUNTEERING
(☎9642229858; www.bluecrosshyd.in; Rd No 35, Jubilee Hills; ⊙9am-5pm) This large shelter rescues animals, and vaccinates and sterilises stray dogs. Volunteers can help in the shelter (grooming and feeding animals), in the adoption centre (walking and socialising dogs) or in the office. A minimum 20 hours is requested.

Tours

★Detours TOURS
(☎9000850505; www.detoursindia.com; per person 3hr walk ₹2500) Outstanding cultural tours led by the enthusiastic, knowledgable Jonty Rajagopalan and her small team. Options cover off-the-beaten-track corners of Hyderabad, Warangal, plus markets, food (including cooking lessons and eating), religion and crafts.

★Heritage Walks WALKING
(Map p916; ☎9849728841; www.telanganatourism.gov.in/heritagewalks; per person ₹50; ⊙7.30-9am Sun & every 2nd Sat) Starting at Charminar and ending at the Chowmahalla Palace, these highly informative (and incredibly inexpensive) walks were designed and are sometimes led by architect and historian Madhu Vottery. The price includes breakfast.

SIA Photo Walks WALKING
(☎8008633354; http://siaphotography.in/tours; group walks from ₹300) Excellent street-photography tours of the city curated by Saurabh Chatterjee, who is a knowledgable guide and experienced photographer. Smartphone users will also benefit from his expertise.

Telangana Tourism TOURS
(☎1800 42546464; www.telanganatourism.gov.in) Offers fine weekend tours, such as a 'Nizam Palace' trip that includes the Chowmahalla Palace, Falaknuma Palace and the Golconda Fort (for the sound-and-light show) for ₹3100/2000 with/without high tea at Falaknuma. Also has daily bus tours of city sights (from ₹350 plus admission tickets) and evening Golconda sound-and-light trips. Book at any Telangana Tourism office (p927).

Courses

Vipassana International Meditation Centre HEALTH & WELLBEING
(Dhamma Khetta; ☎040-24240290; www.khetta.dhamma.org; Nagarjuna Sagar Rd, Km12.6) Intensive 10-day silent meditation courses (10 hours a day) in peaceful grounds 20km outside the city. Apply online. There's no official charge; you donate according to your means.

Festivals & Events

Pandit Motiram–Maniram Sangeet Samaroh MUSIC
(⊙Nov) This four-day music festival, named for two renowned classical musicians, celebrates Hindustani music. It's held in the Chowmahalla Palace.

Sleeping

The inner-city Abids area is convenient for Nampally station and the Old City. For more space and greenery head to middle-class Banjara Hills, about 4km northwest of Abids.

In addition to the uberluxurious Taj Falaknuma Palace (p921), the swish Taj Group also runs three of Hyderabad's top high-end hotels, in Banjara Hills: the opulent **Taj Krishna** (Map p922; ☎040-66662323; www.tajhotels.com; Rd No 1; s/d from ₹8700/9300; ❄@🛜🏊), stylish **Taj Deccan** (Map p922; ☎040-66669999; www.tajhotels.com; Rd No 1; s/d from ₹7540/7980; ❄@🛜🏊) and lakeside **Taj Banjara** (Map p922; ☎040-66669999; www.tajhotels.com; Rd No 1; s/d from ₹8970/10,280; ❄@🛜🏊).

Golden Glory Guesthouse GUESTHOUSE $
(Map p922; ☎040-23554765; www.goldengloryguesthouse.com; off Rd No 3, Banjara Hills; s/d incl breakfast ₹1100/1300, with AC ₹1300/1700; ❄🛜) Boasting an enviable location in upmarket Banjara Hills, with ample cafes and eateries close by, this modestly priced place has clean

simple rooms, some with balconies. There's free wi-fi throughout and staff are eager to please.

Hotel Rajmata HOTEL $
(Map p918; ☎040-66665555; www.hotelrajmata.chobs.in; Public Gardens Rd; s/d ₹850/1200, with AC ₹2250/2400; ❄📶🏊) This popular long-running hotel is only 250m from Nampally station, but set back from the busy main road, which keeps things relatively quiet. Standard quarters are aged but roomy; AC rooms are overpriced but fresh. There's 24-hour room service.

Hotel Suhail HOTEL $
(Map p918; ☎040-24610299; www.hotelsuhail.in; Troop Bazar; s/d/tr from ₹700/850/1200, with AC ₹1200/1400/1700; ❄@📶) Reasonable value if you want to be in the thick of things, though standards of cleanliness could be better. Has friendly staff and large, quiet rooms with balconies and hot water. It's tucked away on a lane off Bank St.

Fresh Living APARTMENT $$
(Map p922; ☎9849563056; www.freshlivingrooms.in; 61 Banjara Green Colony, Rd No 12; 🕐d ₹2166, apt from ₹5130; ❄@📶) This modern place enjoys a good location off Rd No 12 and has well-presented, comfortable rooms and also spacious apartments (sleeping up to nine) that are ideal for families. Breakfast is included.

Raj Classic Inn HOTEL $$
(Map p925; ☎040-27815291; rajclassicinn@gmail.com; 50 MG Rd, Secunderabad; s/d incl breakfast from ₹1630/2050; ❄📶) A very good-value hotel, with clean, well-maintained and spacious rooms and friendly, courteous staff. Expect some traffic noise due to its busy location (a short rickshaw ride from Secunderabad station). In-house Chilly's restaurant is recommended for veg food.

Treebo GN International HOTEL $$
(Map p925; ☎9322800100; www.treebo.com; Padmarao Nagar; r ₹2660; ❄📶) Rooms here give more than a nod to contemporary style, and reliable wi-fi. There's no in-house restaurant facility but lots close by as the location is near Secunderabad station. The Treebo budget chain operates around a dozen other places around town.

Taj Mahal Hotel HOTEL $$
(Map p918; ☎040-24758250; www.hoteltajmahalindia.com; Abids Rd; incl breakfast s ₹1840-3010, d ₹2620-3250; ❄📶) The original 1924 building oozes class and houses the reception and a few bedrooms ('heritage' rooms have some character, the others are plain); the majority of rooms are in a functional modern block to the side. Staff are ever-helpful but facilities like (spotty) wi-fi are poor and the decor needs an upgrade. Still, it's very convenient for sightseeing.

SLEEPING PRICE RANGES

The following price ranges refer to a double room with bathroom:

$ less than ₹1500

$$ ₹1500–₹4000

$$$ more than ₹4000

★Taj Falaknuma Palace HERITAGE HOTEL $$$
(☎040-66298585; www.tajhotels.com; Engine Bowli, Falaknuma; s/d from ₹37,800/40,780; ❄@📶) One of the nation's most impressive hotels, the former residence of the sixth nizam, this 1884 neoclassical palace now run by the Taj group has nizam-esque embossed-leather wallpaper and 24-karat-gold ceiling trim. The rooms are stunning, and the whole place is astoundingly opulent.

Nonguests can come for lunch/dinner or 'high tea' (₹2340) on the Jade Room terrace. Guests (including those just there to eat) get a free palace tour. Book meals two days ahead, or you won't get past the outer gate of the 1.2km driveway.

Marigold HOTEL $$$
(Map p922; ☎040-67363636; www.marigoldhotels.com; Ameerpet Rd, Greenlands; s/d incl breakfast from ₹6920/7970; ❄@📶🏊) The Marigold is as practical as it is stylish. Rooms are smart but not try-hard, with golds, neutrals and fresh flowers, while the in-house Mekong restaurant offers good Thai food. The rooftop pool is also a great feature.

Fortune Park Vallabha HOTEL $$$
(Map p922; ☎040-39884444; www.fortunehotels.in; Rd No 12, Banjara Hills; s/d incl breakfast from ₹5180/6300; ❄@📶🏊) Enjoys a good location and has large contemporary rooms with stained-glass panels, many with balconies. Room service is available at reasonable prices and the South Indian food and breakfast buffet are excellent.

Royalton Hotel HOTEL $$$
(Map p918; ☎040-67122000; www.royaltonhotel.in; Fateh Sultan Lane, Abids; s/d incl breakfast from ₹4460/4750; ❄📶) In a relatively quiet part

Banjara Hills

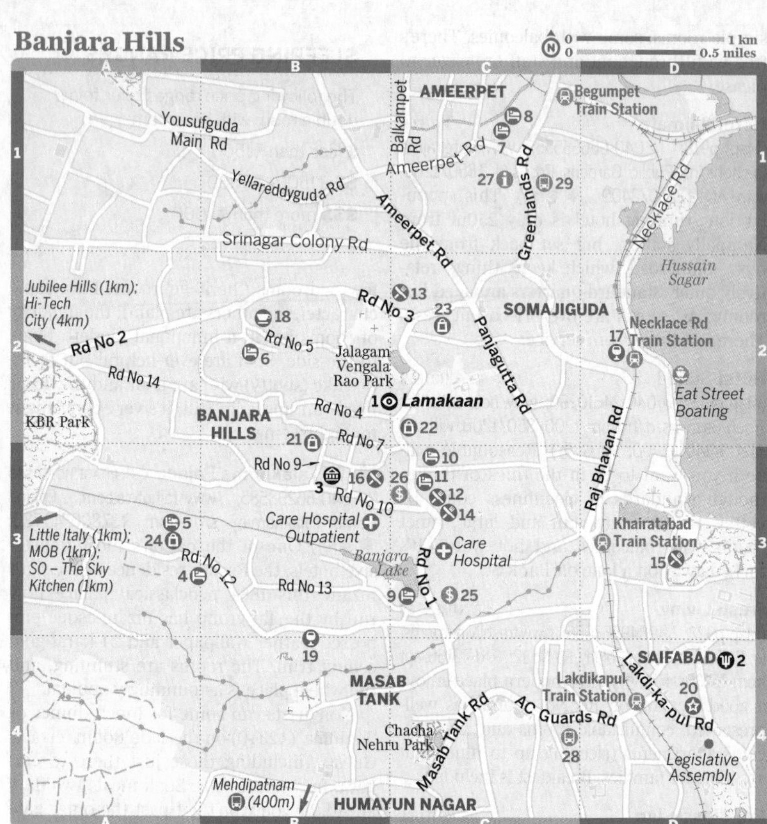

of Abids, Royalton's gargantuan black lobby chandelier and mirrored lifts give off a slight Manhattan vibe. Rooms have tasteful textiles, glass showers and tea/coffee makers. The hotel is vegetarian, and alcohol-free.

GreenPark HOTEL **$$$**

(Map p922; ☎040-66515151; www.hotelgreenpark.com; Ameerpet Rd, Greenlands; s/d incl breakfast from ₹5320/6550; ❄@🛜) The GreenPark has decent standard rooms that have sleek desks, wood flooring and a dash of art; the posher options aren't quite as good value. Staff are attentive and you'll dine well in the in-house Once Upon a Time restaurant.

Eating

In the early evenings, look out for *mirchi bhajji* (chilli fritters), served at street stalls with tea. The Hyderabadi style is famous: chillis are stripped of their seeds, stuffed with tamarind, sesame and spices, dipped in chickpea batter and fried.

Local usage refers to 'thalis' as 'meals'.

Old City & Abids Area

Govind Dosa STREET FOOD **$**

(Map p916; Charkaman; snacks ₹40-100; ⏱6am-noon) A famous breakfast spot, cheery Govind's street-corner stand is permanently surrounded by happy Hyderabadis savouring his delicious dosas (try the butter cheese) and *idlis* (spongy, round, fermented rice cake; the *tawa idlis* topped with chilli powder and spices is a great way to kickstart the day). Always very busy, so be prepared to wait.

Nimrah CAFE **$**

(Map p916; Charminar; baked goods ₹3-12; ⏱5.30am-11pm) This classic Irani cafe, always packed to the rafters, is located almost underneath the Charminar's arches. It offers a particularly tasty range of Irani baked goods to accompany your chai pick-me-up. The classic dunk is Osmania biscuits (melt-in-

Banjara Hills

Top Sights
1 Lamakaan ... B2

Sights
2 Birla Mandir ... D4
3 Kalakriti Art Gallery ... B3

Sleeping
4 Fortune Park Vallabha ... A3
5 Fresh Living ... A3
6 Golden Glory Guesthouse ... B2
7 GreenPark ... C1
8 Marigold ... C1
9 Taj Banjara ... C3
10 Taj Deccan ... C3
11 Taj Krishna ... C3

Eating
12 Barbeque Nation ... C3
13 Chutneys ... C2
Deli 9 ... (see 14)
Firdaus ... (see 11)
14 Fusion 9 ... C3
Gallery Cafe ... (see 3)
15 Paradise ... D3
16 Utupura ... B3

Drinking & Nightlife
17 Kismet ... D2
18 OCD ... B2
19 Vertigo ... B4

Entertainment
20 Ravindra Bharathi Theatre ... D4

Shopping
21 Fabindia ... B2
22 GVK One ... C2
23 Himalaya Book World ... C2
24 Suvasa ... A3

Information
25 Citibank ATM ... C3
Citibank ATM ... (see 22)
26 Citibank ATM ... C3
Indiatourism ... (see 27)
27 Telangana Tourism ... C1

Transport
28 AC Guards Bus Stop (Pushpak) ... C4
29 Paryatak Bhavan Bus Stop (Pushpak) ... C1

the-mouth shortbreads) but there are many other options including sponge breads and plum slices.

Santosh Dhaba NORTH INDIAN $
(Map p918; Hanuman Tekdi Rd, off Bank St, Abids Circle; mains ₹140-170; ⏲11am-1am) A pure-veg place that serves up tasty North Indian classics (try the paneer butter masala), great roti and naan, plus some Chinese dishes. Prices are easy on the pocket, service is prompt and there's an air-con section upstairs.

Kamat Hotel SOUTH INDIAN $
(Map p918; Nampally Station Rd; mains ₹110-185; ⏲7am-10pm) Cheap and reliably good for tasty South Indian fare. It's a good option for breakfast or a speedy lunch – try their *idli* or *masala vada* (spicy, deep-fried lentil savoury). There's also a larger AC branch in Saifabad, and two in Secunderabad.

★ **Shah Ghouse Cafe** HYDERABADI $$
(Shah Ali Banda Rd; mains ₹120-240; ⏲5am-1am) During Ramadan, Hyderabadis line up for Shah Ghouse's famous *haleem* (a thick soup of pounded spiced wheat, with goat, chicken or beef, and lentils) and at any time of year the biryani is near-perfect. Don't expect ambience: just good, hard-working, traditional food, in a no-frills upstairs dining hall. Wash it down with a delicious lassi (₹60).

Hotel Shadab HYDERABADI $$
(Map p916; High Court Rd, Charminar; mains ₹170-350; ⏲noon-11.30pm) The timewarp decor looks like it's been based on a 1970s disco but the cuisine is great at this hopping Hyderabadi restaurant. Great for biryani, kebabs and mutton in all configurations and, during Ramadan, *haleem*. Downstairs it's very solo-male; head upstairs to the AC room for more of a family vibe.

Dakshina Mandapa SOUTH INDIAN $$
(Map p918; Taj Mahal Hotel, Abids Rd; mains & meals ₹170-240; ⏲7am-10.30pm) Highly regarded spot for South Indian vegetarian food. You may have to wait for a lunch table, but order the South Indian thali and you'll be brought heap after heap of rice and refills of authentic dishes. The AC room upstairs does a superb ₹320 lunch buffet (noon to 3.30pm).

Taj Restaurant HYDERABADI $$
(Map p916; Khilwat Rd; mains ₹100-200; ⏲10am-9pm) Specialising in biryani and delicious chicken and mutton curries, this bustling place is just around the corner from the Chowmahalla Palace. There's an AC room on the upper floor.

Gufaa NORTH INDIAN $$$
(Map p918; Ohri's Cuisine Court, Bashirbagh Rd; mains ₹210-660; ⏲noon-3.30pm & 7-11pm) For

an authentic taste of the north, the great veg and nonveg kebabs and curries at Gufaa will satisfy all. Try a Lahori *mahi* (fish curry) or *dal bukhara* (dhal prepared with cream and tomatoes). The premises are gloriously kitsch, with fake cave walls, goblets and lots of zebra and leopard prints in evidence.

Banjara Hills & Jubilee Hills

Gallery Cafe CAFE $$
(Map p922; http://gallerycafe.in; Rd No 10, Banjara Hills; meals ₹160-210; 11.30am-10.30pm;) A tranquil cafe, well set off busy Rd No 10, with a tempting array of coffees, sandwiches and pasta dishes at moderate prices. It hosts art, musical and stand-up comedy events most Wednesdays and adjoins the excellent Kalakriti Art Gallery.

Chutneys SOUTH INDIAN $$
(Map p922; Shilpa Arcade, Rd No 3; mains & meals ₹178-272; 7am-11pm;) Chutneys is famous for its South Indian meals and all-day dosas, *idlis* and *uttapams* (thick, savoury rice pancake with finely chopped onions, green chillies, coriander and coconut). Its dishes are low on chilli, so you can get the full 'Andhra meals' experience without the pain. It's a bustling place with teams of neatly purple-shirted waiters.

Deli 9 CAFE $$
(Map p922; www.deli9.in; 1st Ave, Rd No 1, Banjara Hills; snacks ₹140-275; 9am-10pm;) Renowned for its desserts and cakes, this cafe also offers good breakfasts, wraps, soups, pies, sandwiches and crêpes in a tranquil ambience.

Utupura KERALAN $$
(Map p922; Rd No 10, Banjara Hills; mains ₹110-200; 11.30am-4pm & 6-10pm Mon-Fri, noon-10pm Sat & Sun) Hidden down a lane west of the GVK One mall, this low-key, unpretentious place serves tasty South Indian classics, a mean lunchtime thali (from ₹180), fish curries and *appam* (rice pancake).

★ **SO – The Sky Kitchen** ASIAN, MEDITERRANEAN $$$
(040-23558004; www.notjustso.com; Rd No 92, near Apollo Hospital, Jubilee Hills; mains ₹375-520; noon-midnight;) On a quiet Jubilee Hills rooftop, with candles and loungy playlists, this is one of the most atmospheric eating spots in town. The superb menu has been crafted carefully, mixing pan-Asian and Mediterranean dishes and with a nod to healthy eating: most dishes are grilled, baked or stir-fried. It's 4km west of Banjara Hills' Rd No 1.

Fusion 9 MULTICUISINE $$$
(Map p922; 040-65577722; www.fusion9.in; Rd No 1; mains ₹425-975; 12.30-3.30pm & 7-11.30pm;) With a warm ambience and cosy decor, Fusion 9 offers one of the best international menus in town. Food is creatively presented; try a shot of gazpacho blanco and then perhaps the Moroccan veg tagine with lemon couscous. Very popular for Sunday brunch (₹1188).

Southern Spice SOUTH INDIAN $$$
(Rd No 10, Jubilee Hills; mains ₹215-485; noon-3.30pm & 7-11pm) Now in new (less intimate) premises in the wealthy western district of Jubilee Hills, Southern Spice offers specialities from across the south. Try *natu kodi iguru* ('country chicken') or a special veg thali (₹325).

Firdaus INDIAN $$$
(Map p922; 040-66662323; Taj Krishna hotel, Rd No 1; mains ₹520-1180; 12.30-3pm & 7.30-

HYDERABAD CUISINE

Hyderabad has a food culture all its own and Hyderabadis take great pride and pleasure in it. It was the Mughals who brought the tasty biryanis, skewer kebabs and *haleem* (a thick Ramadan soup of pounded, spiced wheat with goat, chicken or beef, and lentils). Mutton (goat or lamb) is the classic biryani base, though chicken, egg and vegetable biryanis are plentiful too. Biryanis come in vast quantities and one serve may satisfy two people.

If you're in Hyderabad during Ramadan (known locally as Ramzan), look out for the clay ovens called *bhattis*. You'll probably hear them before you see them. Men gather around, taking turns to vigorously pound *haleem* inside purpose-built structures. Come nightfall, the serious business of eating begins. The taste is worth the wait.

Andhra cuisine, found in Telangana as well as Andhra Pradesh, is more curry- and pilau-based, often with coconut and/or cashew flavours, and famous across India for its delicious spicy hotness. Vegetarians are well catered for, but you'll find plenty of fish, seafood and meat dishes too.

Secunderabad

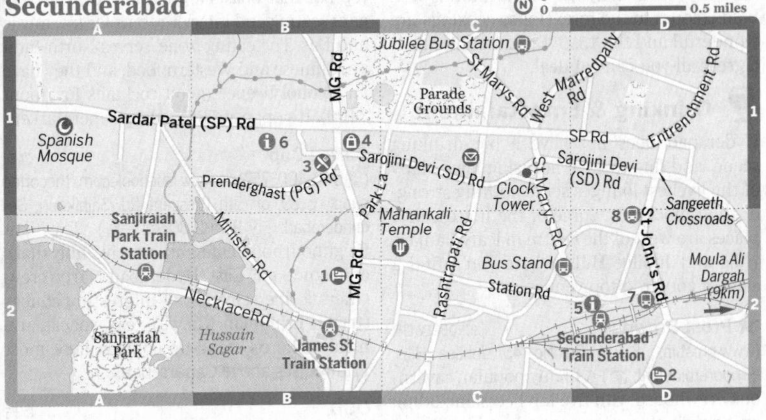

Secunderabad

Activities, Courses & Tours

Sleeping

Eating

Shopping

Information

Transport

11.30pm;) A classy hotel restaurant, Firdaus offers great Hyderabadi (and other) dishes to the strains of live *ghazals* (classical Urdu love songs, accompanied by harmonium and tabla). They even serve *haleem* outside Ramadan and have good vegetarian choices too.

Barbeque Nation INDIAN $$$
(Map p922; 040-64566692; www.barbequenation.com; ANR Centre, Rd No 1; veg/nonveg lunch ₹627/752, dinner ₹946/1071; noon-3.30pm & 6.30-10.30pm;) All-you-can-eat kebabs, curries, salads and desserts, with many veg and nonveg options. A great-value place to come when you're hungry! Prices fluctuate a little depending on the day and time. Slurp on one of their excellent Indian wines while you dine.

Secunderabad

Paradise HYDERABADI $$
(Persis; Map p925; www.paradisefoodcourt.com; cnr SD & MG Rds; biryani ₹200-254; 11.30am-11pm) Paradise is synonymous with biryani in these parts. The main Secunderabad location has five different dining areas: head to the attractive 'roof garden', complete with whirring fans, or pay an AC surcharge to eat inside. Also serves lots of (less pleasing) Chinese dishes.

There's a large, modern **branch** (Map p922; 040-67408400; NTR Gardens; mains ₹200-378; 11am-11pm) closer to Abids and Banjara Hills, though we found the biryani there a bit less flavoursome.

Other Areas

★ **Dhaba By Claridges** MODERN INDIAN $$$
(040-29706704; www.dhababyclaridges.com; Western Pearl Bldg, Survey 13, Kondapur; mains ₹265-445; noon-11.30pm;) A good reason to head out west to Hi-Tech City, this hip hang-out offers a contemporary take on North Indian street food (minus the fumes and traffic of course). Dhaba's decor

is kooky, with Bollywood-style murals and bold colours to the fore. House cocktails are wonderful and the ₹599 'Da Lunch Bomb' is a great all-you-can-eat deal.

 Drinking & Entertainment

Hyderabad does not have a big drinking scene, and due to local licensing laws many of the liveliest lounges serve nothing stronger than mocktails. Some of the hottest new places are west of the centre in leafy Banjara Hills and Jubilee Hills, where you'll find a slew of good rooftop venues.

★Prost Brewpub MICROBREWERY
(www.prost.in; 882/A Rd No 45, Jubilee Hills; ⏲noon-midnight; 📶) A highly popular, cavernous brewhouse with five tap beers, including an English ale and a stout, plus cider. There are several zones, all stylishly lit, including ample outdoor space and an extensive East-meets-West pub-grub menu. Rammed on weekend nights. Also hosts comedy and DJs.

★MOB BAR
(www.facebook.com/itismob; Aryan's, Rd No 92, near Apollo Hospital, Jubilee Hills; ⏲noon-11.30pm; 📶) A stylish, sociable Belgium beer house that draws a refreshingly mixed-gender, mixed-age crowd. Order a 'beer platter' for a sample of four choice brews or try the set lunch (₹799), which includes a draught beer. There's live music on Saturday nights. It's on a side road off the south side of KBR National Park, 4km west of Banjara Hills' Rd No 1.

Vertigo BAR
(Map p922; www.vertigothehighlife.in; 5th fl, Shiv Shakti Tower, Rd No 12; ⏲11am-midnight) A rooftop bar that boasts a great terrace, with elegant seating and interior rooms for live music and DJs. The eating 'zone' serves North Indian, Chinese and Western food, and they have an alcohol licence (good cocktails for about ₹400). It's opposite Ratnadeep supermarket.

Coffee Cup CAFE
(☎040-40037571; www.facebook.com/thecoffeecupp; E 89, off 5th Crescent Rd, Sainikpuri, Secunderabad; ⏲9am-11.30pm; 📶) Excellent neighbourhood cafe and creative hub that's a magnet for East Hyderabad's arty crew. Offers a fine selection of interesting coffees (try an Ethiopian Khawa), teas, snacks and meals. There's stand-up comedy here most Fridays. It's above Canara Bank.

OCD CAFE
(Map p922; Rd No 5, Banjara Hills; ⏲10am-10pm) Located on a quiet leafy street in Banjara Hills, OCD (Obsessive Coffee Disorder) attracts a fashionable crowd with its zany decor, pool table and terrace for hookah puffing. There's decent grub (Chinese and Western snacks), great mocktails and, of course, superb coffee.

Kismet CLUB
(Map p922; ☎040-23456789; www.theparkhotels.com; The Park, Raj Bhavan Rd, Somajiguda; admission per couple ₹700-2000; ⏲9pm-midnight or later Wed-Sun) A sleek, upmarket nightclub, with loungy booth seating, a big dance floor and a pumping bass-driven sound system. Men won't get past the ranks of bouncers without female companions. Drinks are pricey (cocktails around ₹600), not that the wealthy crowd are too bothered. Musically things range from EDM to Bollywood.

CHARMINAR MARKETS

Hyderabadis and visitors of every stripe flock to the Charminar area's labyrinthine lanes to browse, buy and wander. Patthargatti, the broad avenue leading in from the Musi River, is lined with shops selling clothes (especially wedding outfits), perfumes and Hyderabad's famous pearls. **Laad Bazar** (Map p916; ⏲10am-8.30pm), running west from the Charminar, is famed for its sparkling bangle shops: lac bangles, made from a resinous insect secretion and encrusted with colourful beads or stones, are a Hyderabad speciality. In Laad Bazar you'll also find perfumers, wedding goods and fabrics.

Laad Bazar opens into **Mehboob Chowk** (Map p916), a square with shops selling antiquarian books and antiques, a livestock market on its south side, and a market in exotic birds, **Chiddi Bazar** (Map p916; ⏲7am-7pm), just southwest.

A short distance north, the **Patel Market** (Map p916; ⏲approximately 11am-8pm) sells cloth fabrics and cranks into action from around 11am in the back lanes between Patthargatti and Rikab Gunj. Further north again and on the other side of Patthargatti, the wholesale vegetable market **Mir Alam Mandi** (Map p916; Patthargatti Rd; ⏲6.30am-6.30pm) trades in all kinds of fresh stuff from 6.30am to 6.30pm daily.

Ravindra Bharathi Theatre THEATRE
(Map p922; ☎040-23233672; www.ravindrabharathi.org; Ladki-ka-pul Rd, Saifabad) Well-curated music, dance and drama performances, and cinema.

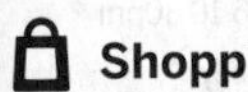

Shopping

Charminar is the most exciting place to shop: you'll find exquisite pearls, slippers, gold and fabrics alongside billions of bangles. Upmarket boutiques and malls are scattered around Banjara Hills and the western suburbs.

Bidri Crafts ARTS & CRAFTS
(Map p918; http://bidrihandicraft.com; Gunfoundry, Basheer Bagh; ⏰11am-9pm) *Bidri* is a metal craft (originating in Iran) that involves intricate inlay work. The famous family-run business sells top-quality plates, vases, bowls, jewellery (earrings from ₹180) and accessories at moderate prices.

Malkha CLOTHING
(Map p925; www.malkha.in; 229, 2nd fl, B Wing, Chandralok Complex; ⏰10am-9pm Mon-Sat) Malkha cloth is made near the cotton fields, by hand and with natural dyes, reducing strain on the environment and putting primary producers in control. The result is gorgeous; here you can pick up fabric (from ₹320 per yard), shawls and saris (from ₹2200) at reasonable prices. It's opposite Paradise Hotel.

Fabindia CLOTHING
(Map p922; www.fabindia.com; Rd No 9, Banjara Hills; ⏰11am-9.30pm) Lovely women's (and some men's) clothes in artisanal fabrics with contemporary prints and colours. They also sell homeware including bed linen, cushions and *dhurries* (rugs). Prices are fair.

There's another **branch** (Fateh Maidan; ⏰10.30am-8.30pm) in Bashirbagh.

Suvasa CLOTHING
(Map p922; www.suvasa.in; Rd No 12, Banjara Hills; ⏰11am-7.30pm) Suvasa's block-printed kurtas (long shirts with a short or no collar), baggy *salwar* pants and dupattas (scarves) are all high quality. They also sell homeware including gorgeous bed and table linen.

Hyderabad Perfumers PERFUME
(Map p916; Patthargatti; ⏰10am-8.30pm Mon-Sat) This fourth-generation family business can conjure something aromatic up for you on the spot. They specialise in *ittar*, natural perfume oils from flowers and herbs; prices start as low as ₹200 and rise to over ₹7000 per bottle.

GVK One MALL
(Map p922; www.gvkone.com; Rd No 1, Banjara Hills; ⏰11am-11pm) An upmarket mall with a good selection of clothes shops, ATMs, a small food court, cafes and a cinema.

Himalaya Book World BOOKS
(Map p922; Panjagutta Circle, Banjara Hills; ⏰10.30am-10.30pm) A fine selection of English-language fiction and nonfiction by Indian and international authors. They have several other branches in town.

Information

MEDICAL SERVICES

Reputable Care Hospitals are on **Mukarramjahi Road** (Map p918; ☎040-30417777; www.carehospitals.com) and **Road No 1** (Map p922; ☎040-30418888; www.carehospitals.com). There's also an outpatient hospital on **Road No 10** (Map p922; ☎040-39310444; 4th Lane).

POST

General Post Office (Map p918; Abids Circle; ⏰8am-7pm Mon-Sat, 10am-1pm Sun)

TOURIST INFORMATION

Indiatourism (Map p922; ☎040-23409199; www.incredibleindia.org; Tourism Plaza, Greenlands Rd; ⏰9.30am-6pm Mon-Fri, 9.30am-1pm Sat) A useful office, with good information on Hyderabad, Telangana and beyond.

Telangana Tourism (☎1800 42546464; www.telanganatourism.gov.in; ⏰7am-8.30pm) Tourist information and bookings for state-government-run tours, heritage walks and hotels in Telangana. Branches at **Bashirbagh** (Map p918; ☎040-66745986; Shakar Bhavan; ⏰6.30am-8pm), **Tankbund Road** (Map p918; ☎040-65581555; ⏰6.30am-8pm), **Greenlands Road** (Map p922; ☎040-23414334; Tourism Plaza; ⏰7am-8pm), **Hyderabad airport** (☎040-24253215), **Secunderabad** (Map p925; ☎040-27893100; Yatri Nivas Hotel, SP Rd; ⏰6.30am-8.30pm) and **Secunderabad train station** (Map p925; ☎040-27801614; ⏰10am-8pm).

Getting There & Away

AIR

Hyderabad's massive, modern, efficient **Rajiv Gandhi International Airport** (☎040-66546370; http://hyderabad.aero; Shamshabad) is 25km southwest of the city centre. It has direct daily flights, including with **Air India** (Map p918; ☎040-23389711; www.airindia.com; HACA Bhavan, Saifabad; ⏰9.30am-6pm

BUSES FROM HYDERABAD

DESTINATION	FARE (₹)	DURATION (HR)	FREQUENCY
Bengaluru	687-1040	8-11	22 buses 9am-10.30pm
Chennai	694-1191	11-14	18 buses 6-10.30pm
Hospet	522-850	8-11	3 buses daily
Mumbai	1070-2550	12-14	27 buses 2-11.55pm
Mysore	1050-1733	11-13	9 buses 6.30-9.30pm
Tirupati	652-1485	16	half-hourly 1.30-10pm
Vijayawada	340-480	4-5	half-hourly 5am-11.55pm
Visakhapatnam	660-1650	11-13	hourly 4-11pm
Warangal	180-240	4	half-hourly

Mon-Sat) and **Jet Airways** (Map p918; ☎020-39893333; www.jetairways.com; Summit Apartments, Hill Fort Rd; ⊙10am-6pm Mon-Sat), to over 20 Indian cities plus international destinations including Chicago, London and several Southeast Asian and Gulf destinations.

BUS

The main terminal is the vast **Mahatma Gandhi bus station** (MGBS; Imlibun Bus Station; Map p916; ☎040-24614406; ⊙advance booking offices 8am-10.30pm) near Abids. Air-con services by the **TSRTC** (Telangana State Road Transport Corporation; ☎1800 2004599; http://tsrtcbus.in) are quite good; for Karnataka, go with KSRTC near platform 30. Nearly all long-distance services depart in the evening. When booking ahead, women should request seats up front as these are reserved for female passengers.

Secunderabad's **Jubilee bus station** (Map p925; ☎040-27802203; Gandhi Nagar, Secunderabad) is smaller; frequent city buses run here from St Mary's Rd near Secunderabad station. From Jubilee there are buses to cities including Chennai (Madras), Mumbai and these routes:

Bengaluru (Bangalore) ordinary/Volvo AC/sleeper ₹687/from 827/1370, eight to 11 hours, 19 daily

Vijayawada non-AC/AC ₹317/437, four to six hours, 17 daily

Other useful bus stops include the **bus stand** (Map p925) on St Mary's Rd, the **Charminar bus stop** (Map p916; Shah Ali Banda Rd) for the Old City, **Koti bus stand** (Map p918; Turrebaz Khan Rd), **Koti Women's College bus stand** (Map p918) and **Rathifile bus stand** (Map p925; Station Rd) for Secunderabad.

TRAIN

Secunderabad, Nampally (officially called Hyderabad Deccan) and Kacheguda are Hyderabad's three major train stations. Most through trains stop at Kacheguda.

The reservation complexes at **Nampally** (Map p918; ☎040-27829999; Public Gardens Rd; ⊙8am-8pm Mon-Sat, 8am-2pm Sun) and **Secunderabad** (Rathifile; Map p925; St John's Rd; ⊙8am-8pm Mon-Sat, 8am-2pm Sun), both in separate buildings away from the stations, have foreign-tourist-quota counters (bring your passport and visa photocopies, along with originals). For enquiries and PNR status, phone ☎139.

There are 12 daily trains to both Warangal (sleeper/3AC/2AC ₹170/540/735, 2½ hours) and Vijayawada (₹220/650/910, six hours), mostly from Secunderabad.

Getting Around

TO/FROM THE AIRPORT

Bus

The TSRTC's Pushpak air-conditioned bus service runs between about 4am or 5am and 11pm to/from various stops in the city including:

AC Guards (Map p922; AC Guards Rd) (₹212, two or three buses hourly) About 1.5km from Abids.

Paryatak Bhavan (Map p922) (₹265, about hourly) On Greenlands Rd.

Secretariat (Map p918; NTR Marg) (₹265, about hourly) About 1.5km from Abids.

Secunderabad (Map p925; Rail Nilayam Rd) (₹265, twice hourly)

The trip takes around one hour. Contact **TSRTC** or check http://hyderabad.aero for exact timings.

Taxi

The prepaid taxi booth is on the lowest level of the terminal. Fares to Abids or Banjara Hills are ₹600 to ₹750. **Meru Cabs** (☎040-44224422) and **Sky Cabs** (☎040-49494949) charge similar rates. Uber is cheaper: around ₹350 to ₹500.

AUTORICKSHAW

Expect to pay ₹30 to ₹50 for a short ride, and around ₹120 for 4km. Few drivers use meters.

BUS

Few travellers bother with local buses (₹6 to ₹12 for most rides) but there are some useful routes. Try www.hyderabadbusroutes.com (although it can be inaccurate).

City stops include **Afzalgunj** (Map p916), **GPO Abids** (Map p918; JN Rd), **Koti** (Map p918), **Mehdipatnam**, **Public Gardens** (Map p918) and **Secunderabad Junction** (Map p925).

Hyderabad City Bus Routes

BUS NO	ROUTE
65G, 66G	Charminar–Golconda Fort, via Afzalgunj, GPO Abids; both about hourly
49M	Secunderabad Junction–Mehdipatnam via Rd No 1 (Banjara Hills); frequent
8A	Charminar–Secunderabad Junction via Afzalgunj, GPO Abids; frequent
40, 86	Secunderabad Junction–Koti Bus Stop; both frequent
127K	Koti Bus Stop–Jubilee Hills via GPO Abids, Public Gardens, Rd Nos 1 & 12 (Banjara Hills); frequent

CAR

Arrange car hire through your hotel. The going rate for a small AC car with a driver is ₹1200 to ₹1500 per day for city sightseeing (eight hours/80km maximum), and ₹2800 to ₹3500 per day for out-of-town trips (up to 300km).

METRO RAIL

Hyderabad Metro Rail, a (long-delayed) 72km rapid-transit network is scheduled to start (perhaps) in late 2017 or 2018. Trains will run on elevated tracks above Hyderabad's streets, with 66 stations on three lines.

TAXI

There are thousands of Uber and Ola drivers in Hyderabad and fares are very fair indeed (often cheaper than those quoted by autorickshaw drivers). A 3km ride will be around ₹80 to ₹100.

TRAIN

The suburban **MMTS trains** (www.mmtstraintimings.in; fares ₹5-10) are not very useful for travellers, but infrequent trains (every 30 to 45 minutes) run between Hyderabad (Nampally) and Lingampalli via Necklace Rd, Begumpet and Hi-Tech City. There's also a route between Falaknuma (south of Old City) and Lingampalli via Kacheguda and Secunderabad stations.

TELANGANA

Bhongir

Most Hyderabad–Warangal buses and trains stop at the town of Bhongir, 60km from Hyderabad. It's worth stopping to climb the fantastical-looking 12th-century Chalukyan **hill fort** (off DVK Rd; ₹5, camera ₹10; ⏲10am-5pm), sitting on what resembles a gargantuan

MAJOR TRAINS FROM HYDERABAD & SECUNDERABAD

DESTINATION	TRAIN NO & NAME	FARE (₹)	DURATION (HR)	DEPARTURE TIME & STATION
Bengaluru	22692 or 22694 Rajdhani	1690/2460 (B)	12	6.50pm Secunderabad
	12785 Bangalore Exp	360/945/1335 (A)	11½	7.05pm Kacheguda
Chennai	12604 Hyderabad-Chennai Exp	400/1055/1495 (A)	13	4.50pm Nampally
	12760 Charminar Exp	425/1115/1590 (A)	14	6.30pm Nampally
Delhi	12723 Telangana Exp	665/1745/2450 (A)	27	6.25am Nampally
	22691 or 22693 Rajdhani	3145/4675 (B)	18	7.50am Secunderabad
Hosapete (Hospet; for Hampi)	17603 Exp	275/740/1065 (A)	11½	9pm Kacheguda
Kolkata	18646 East Coast Exp	615/1645/2415 (A)	31	9.50am Nampally
Mumbai (Bombay)	12702 Hussainsagar Exp	410/1085/1540 (A)	14½	2.45pm Nampally
Tirupati	12734 Narayanadri Exp	385/1005/1425 (A)	12	6.05pm Secunderabad
Visakhapatnam	12728 Godavari Exp	395/1035/1465 (A)	12½	5.15pm Nampally

Fares: (A) – sleeper/3AC/2AC; (B) – 3AC/2AC

stone egg on the eastern side of town. You can leave backpacks at the ticket office.

Warangal

0870 / POP 633,000

Warangal was the capital of the Kakatiya kingdom, which ruled most of present-day Telangana and Andhra Pradesh from the 12th to early 14th centuries. The city merges with the town of Hanumakonda.

Sights

Ancient temples in Hanumakonda include the lakeside **Bhadrakali Temple** (Bhadrakali Temple Rd), 2km southeast of the 1000-Pillared Temple, whose idol of the mother goddess Kali sits with a weapon in each of her eight hands, and the small **Siddeshwara Temple** on the south side of Hanumakonda Hill.

Fort FORT

(Fort Rd) Warangal's fort, on the southern edge of town, was a massive construction with three circles of walls (the outermost 7km in circumference). Most of it is now either fields or buildings, but at the centre is a huge, partly reassembled Shaivite **Svayambhu Temple** (Indian/foreigner ₹15/100, camera ₹25; 9am-6pm), with handsome, large *torana* (architrave) gateways at its cardinal points. An autorickshaw from Warangal station costs around ₹300 return.

The Svayambhu Temple ticket also covers the Kush Mahal (Shitab Khan Mahal), a 16th-century royal hall 400m west. Almost opposite the Svayambhu entrance is a **park** (₹10; 7am-7pm) containing the high rock Ekashila Gutta, which is topped by another Kakatiya temple overlooking a small lake.

1000-Pillared Temple HINDU TEMPLE

(south of NH163, Hanumakonda; 6am-6pm) FREE The 1000-Pillared Temple, constructed in the 12th century, is in a leafy setting and is a fine example of Kakatiya architecture and sculpture. Unusually, the cross-shaped building has shrines to the sun god Surya (to the right as you enter), Vishnu (centre) and Shiva (left). Despite the name, it certainly does not have 1000 pillars. Behind rises Hanumakonda Hill, site of the original Kakatiya capital.

Sleeping & Eating

Vijaya Lodge HOTEL $

(0870-2501222; Station Rd; s ₹290, d ₹550-800) Conveniently close (around 350m) to Warangal's bus and train stations, the Vijaya is certainly basic but has helpful enough staff. Rooms are borderline dreary, with showers by bucket. The upper floors are best.

Hotel Ashoka HOTEL $$

(0870-2578491; www.hotelashoka.in; Main Rd, Hanumakonda; r ₹1760-2650;) This large hotel, dating from the 1980s, has a selection of AC rooms in several price categories. It's near the Hanumakonda bus stand and 1000-Pillared Temple. Also here is the good veg restaurant **Kanishka** (mains ₹140-260; 6.30am-10.30pm), plus a nonveg restaurant and a bar.

Hotel Landmark HOTEL $$

(0870-2546333, 0870-2546111; landmarkhotel3@yahoo.co.in; Nakkalagutta; r ₹1920;) Behind the mirrored facade you'll find clean if smallish rooms that have a dash of contemporary style. The in-house restaurant serves a wide variety of South Indian dishes.

Sri Geetha Bhavan ANDHRA $

(Market Rd, Hanumakonda; mains ₹90-130; 6am-11pm) Good South Indian meals in pleasant AC surroundings. Follow the Supreme Hotels sign.

Seasons MULTICUISINE $$

(www.facebook.com/seasonsrestauranthnk; NH 163, Hanumakonda, near National Institute of Technology; mains ₹160-240; 1-10.30pm) With subtle lighting, attractive seating and a varied menu that includes popular Chinese, Middle Eastern and Indian dishes, Seasons is a good choice for an atmospheric meal.

Getting There & Around

Buses to Hyderabad (₹135 to ₹215, four hours) leave about three times hourly from **Hanumakonda bus stand** (New Bus Stand Rd), and seven times daily (express/deluxe ₹115/150, seven hours) from **Warangal bus stand** (0870-2565595; Station Rd) opposite the train station.

From Warangal several trains daily run to Hyderabad (sleeper/3AC/2AC ₹170/540/740, three hours), Vijayawada (₹190/535/740, three hours) and Chennai (₹375/985/1395, 10½ to 12 hours).

Shared autorickshaws (₹15) ply fixed routes around Warangal and Hanumakonda.

Palampet

About 70km northeast of Warangal, the stunning **Ramappa Temple** (camera ₹25; 6am-6pm) is near the village of Palampet. Built in the early 13th century, it's the outstanding gem of Kakatiya architecture, covered in wonderfully detailed carvings of animals, lovers, wrestlers, musicians, dancers, deities and Hindu legends. Brackets on its external pillars support superb black-basalt carvings of mythical creatures and sinuous women twined with snakes. The large temple tank, **Ramappa Cheruvu**, 1km south, is popular with migrating birds.

Getting There & Away

The easiest way to get here is by chartered taxi (around ₹2000 return from Warangal), but buses also run half-hourly from Hanumakonda to Mulugu (₹58, one hour), then a further 13km to Palampet (₹20).

ANDHRA PRADESH

The state of Andhra Pradesh stretches 972km along the Bay of Bengal between Tamil Nadu and Odisha, and inland up into the picturesque Eastern Ghats. Its the epicentre of Telugu language and culture, and one of the nation's wealthier states. Explorers will discover one of India's most visited temples (at Tirumala), some fascinating and remote ancient sites from the earliest days of Buddhism and one of the nicest stretches of India's east coast, north of Visakhapatnam – plus you'll be able to enjoy the spicily delicious Andhra cuisine everywhere.

Andhra's tourism websites are www.aptourism.gov.in and www.aptdc.gov.in.

Vijayawada

☎0866 / POP 1.12 MILLION

The commercial and industrial city of Vijayawada, on the north bank of the Krishna River, will become Andhra's new state capital. Construction has started on a showpiece capital complex called Amaravati (named after a nearby Buddhist site), encompassing 30 existing villages on the southwest side of the river. It's projected Vijayawada-Amaravati will have 2.5 million inhabitants by 2025.

Right now there's not much of interest for travellers in the city itself, but Vijayawada is a good base for visiting some fascinating old Buddhist sites in the lush and green surrounding area.

Sights

★Undavalli Cave Temples HINDU TEMPLE
(Indian/foreigner ₹5/100; ⏲9am-5.30pm) This stunning four-storey cave temple was probably originally carved out of the hillside for Buddhist monks in the 2nd century AD, then converted to Hindu use in the 7th century. The shrines are now empty except those on the third level, one of which houses a huge reclining Vishnu. Three gnome-like stone Vaishnavaite gurus/preachers gaze out over the rice paddies from the terrace. It's 6km southwest of downtown Vijayawada: autorickshaws or Ola/Uber cabs here cost ₹125 one way.

Kanaka Durga Temple HINDU TEMPLE
(www.kanakadurgatemple.org; Durga Temple Ghat Rd, Indrakeeladri Hill; ⏲4am-9pm) Dating back to the 12th century, this important temple is located on Indrakeeladri Hill, close to the Krishna River, and draws many pilgrims.

Sleeping & Eating

Hotel Sripada HOTEL $
(☎0866-2579641; hotelsripada@rediffmail.com; Gandhi Nagar; s ₹900-1460, d ₹1010-1690; ❄📶) A short walk from the train station, this is

AMARAVATI

On 21 October 2015, the Chief Minister of Andhra Pradesh chartered a helicopter bearing soil and holy water from Mecca, Jerusalem and Hindu holy sites and sprinkled a holy blessing over nondescript flatlands west of the city of Vijayawada. Three days later President Modi laid a founding stone during a grandiose event said to have been witnessed by 500,000 people.

These ceremonies were to mark the founding of Andhra Pradesh's new capital city, Amaravati (named after an important Buddhist site close by). City planners from Singapore and experts from Japan will help in its construction. The main capital area will cover 16.7 sq km and include a vast civic centre, a new business hub dotted with skyscrapers, canals, an island park and a waterfront promenade along the Krishna River. A rapid transit bus system is proposed, plus expressways linking the town to its sister city of Vijayawada.

All this is going to take some time – decades – to achieve. For now Hyderabad remains the joint capital of both Telangana and Andhra Pradesh, but the transfer of power has to occur before 2024.

one of the few budget hotels in Vijayawada authorised to accept foreign guests. Offers small but decent AC rooms in reasonable condition, and helpful staff. However, there's no in-house restaurant.

Hotel Southern Grand HOTEL **$$**
(☎0866-6677777; www.hotelsoutherngrand.com; Papaiah St, Gandhi Nagar; incl breakfast s ₹2400-2800, d ₹2800-3200; ❄📶) A good deal for the tariffs charged, with inviting, spotless and contemporary rooms. Just 600m from the train station, the hotel also has an excellent veg restaurant, **Arya Bhavan** (Hotel Southern Grand, Papaiah St, Gandhi Nagar; mains ₹130-165, thalis ₹110-170; ⏰7am-11pm), a useful travel desk, **Southern Travels** (☎0866-6677777; Hotel Southern Grand, Papaiah St, Gandhi Nagar), and offers free airport and station transfers.

★**Minerva Hotel** HOTEL **$$$**
(☎0866-6678888; www.minervahotels.in; MG Rd; ⏰s/d ₹3500/4000; ❄📶) Offering excellent value, this renovated hotel has rooms with a pleasing contemporary touch, large flat-screen TVs, wooden floors, safe and minibar. The Blue Fox restaurant here is good, there's a coffee shop and you'll find a cinema and good shopping close by.

Gateway Hotel HOTEL **$$$**
(☎0866-6644444; www.thegatewayhotels.com; MG Rd; s/d from ₹5220/6160; ❄📶🏊) Part of the Taj Group, this classy hotel has six floors of well-equipped, contemporary rooms around its high atrium lobby, plus two stylish restaurants, a bar, gym and a lovely rooftop pool. Staff are very welcoming and management is helpful. It's 3km southeast of the train station near two malls.

★**Minerva Coffee Shop** INDIAN **$$**
(Museum Rd; mains ₹170-270; ⏰7am-11pm) This outpost of the excellent Minerva chain does great North and South Indian veg cuisine in bright, spotless AC premises. Meals (thalis) are only available from 11.30am to 3.30pm but top-notch dosas, *idlis* and *uttapams* (₹35 to ₹75) are served all day and the biryanis are also good. There's another **branch** (Minerva Hotel, MG Rd; mains ₹180-270; ⏰7am-11pm) in airy, sophisticated surrounds on MG Rd.

STATE OF GOOD KARMA

Lying at a nexus of major Indian land routes and sea routes across the Bay of Bengal, Andhra Pradesh played an important role in the early history of Buddhism. Andhra and Telangana have about 150 known Buddhist stupas, monasteries, caves and other sites. They speak of a time when Andhra Pradesh, or 'Andhradesa', was a hotbed of Buddhist activity, when Indian monks set off for Sri Lanka and Southeast Asia to spread the Buddha's teachings, and monks came from far and wide to learn from renowned Buddhist teachers.

Andhradesa's Buddhist culture lasted around 1500 years from the Buddha's own lifetime in the 6th century BC. The dharma really took off in the 3rd century BC under the Mauryan emperor Ashoka, who dispatched monks across his empire to teach and construct stupas enshrining relics of the Buddha. (Being near these was thought to help progress on the path to enlightenment.)

After Ashoka's death in 232 BC, succeeding rulers of central Andhra Pradesh, the Satavahanas and then the Ikshvakus, continued to support Buddhism. At their capital Amaravathi, the Satavahanas adorned Ashoka's stupa with elegant decoration. They built monasteries across the Krishna Valley and exported the dharma through their sophisticated maritime network. It was under Satavahana rule that Nagarjuna, considered the progenitor of Mahayana Buddhism, is believed to have lived, in the 2nd or 3rd centuries AD. The monk, equal parts logician, philosopher and meditator, wrote several ground-breaking works that shaped Buddhist thought.

Today, even in ruins, you can get a sense of how large some of the stupas were, how expansive the monastic complexes, and of how the monks lived, sleeping in caves and fetching rainwater from stone-cut cisterns. Many of the sites have stunning views across seascapes or countryside. The complexes at **Nagarjunakonda** (p934) and **Amaravathi** (p933) have good infrastructure and helpful museums on-site. For a bit more adventure, head out from Vijayawada to **Guntupalli** (p933) or Bhattiprolu, or from Visakhapatnam to **Thotlakonda** (p937), **Bavikonda** (p937) and **Sankaram** (p937).

OFF THE BEATEN TRACK

GUNTUPALLI

Well off the beaten path, the Buddhist site of **Guntupalli** (Indian/foreigner ₹5/100; ⏲10am-5pm) makes a very scenic adventure. This former monastic compound, high on a hilltop overlooking a vast expanse of forest and paddy fields, is specially noteworthy for its circular rock-cut *chaitya-griha* shrine. The cave's domed ceiling is carved with 'wooden beams' designed to look like those in a hut. The *chaitya-griha* has a well-preserved stupa and, like the monks' dwellings lining the same cliff, a gorgeous arched facade also designed to look like wood. Check out the stone 'beds' in the monks' cells, and the compound's 60-plus votive stupas. The monastery was active from the 2nd century BC to the 3rd century AD.

From Eluru, on the Vijayawada–Visakhapatnam road and railway, take a bus 35km north to Kamavarapukota (₹42, 1½ hours, half-hourly), then an autorickshaw 10km west to Guntupalli. A taxi from Eluru costs around ₹1800 return.

★**TFL** MULTICUISINE, ITALIAN **$$$**
(http://thefoodlounge.in; Santhi Nagar First Lane; mains ₹175-345; ⏲10am-11.30pm; 📶) This new place is in a stylishly converted suburban bungalow with a great (covered) terrace. Offers great Italian, Mexican, American, European (and East Asian) dishes including risotto, good pizza and excellent Western breakfasts (from ₹110). Don't skip on their desserts.

ℹ Information

Department of Tourism (☎0866-2578880; Train Station; ⏲10am-5pm) Has helpful staff and can assist with travel planning.

ℹ Getting There & Around

The train and bus stations have prepaid autorickshaw stands.

BUS

Services from the large **Pandit Nehru bus station** (Arjuna St; ⏲24hr) include:

Chennai non-AC/AC/semi-sleeper ₹450/760/1050, seven to nine hours, 14 daily

Eluru non-AC/AC ₹70/90, 1½ hours, half-hourly

Hyderabad non-AC/AC ₹335/574, four to six hours, half-hourly

Tirupati non-AC/AC ₹474/698, nine hours, half-hourly

Visakhapatnam non-AC/AC ₹430/674, eight hours, half-hourly

Many private bus companies depart from stops around Benz Circle, 4km east of the centre.

CAR

Southern Travels (p932) Good rates for car-and-driver hire.

TRAIN

Vijayawada Junction station is on the main Chennai–Kolkata (Calcutta) and Chennai–Delhi railway lines. The 12841/12842 Coromandel Express between Chennai and Kolkata is quick for journeys up and down the coast. Typical journey times and frequencies, for sleeper/3AC/2AC fares:

Chennai ₹290/735/1045, seven hours, 12 daily

Hyderabad ₹240/605/880, six hours, 12 daily

Kolkata ₹555/1465/2115, 18 hours, five daily

Tirupati ₹235/670/890, nine hours, seven daily

Warangal ₹190/535/740, three hours, 14 daily

Visit the **Advance-Booking Office** (☎enquiries 0866-139; ⏲8am-8pm Mon-Sat, 8am-2pm Sun) at the train station for reservations.

Around Vijayawada

Amaravathi

The historic Buddhist site of Amaravathi (not to be confused with the new state capital, Amaravati) is 43km west of Vijayawada. This was the earliest centre of Buddhism in the southern half of India, with the nation's biggest **stupa** (Indian/foreigner ₹5/100; ⏲7am-7pm), 27m high and 49m across, constructed here in the 3rd century BC. Amaravathi flourished as a capital of the Satavahana kingdom, which ruled from Andhra across the Deccan for four or five centuries, becoming a fountainhead of Buddhist art. All that remains of the stupa now are its circular base and a few parts of the surrounding stone railing. The great hemispherical dome is gone – but the neighbouring **museum** (Amaravathi village; ₹5; ⏲9am-5pm Sat-Thu) has a model of the stupa and some of the intricate marble carvings, depicting the Buddha's life, with which the Satavahanas covered and surrounded it. The giant modern **Dhyana Buddha statue** (Amaravathi) of a seated Buddha overlooks the Krishna River nearby.

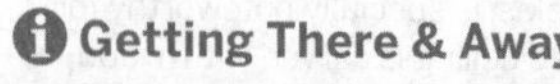

Getting There & Away

Bus 301 from Vijayawada bus station runs to Amaravathi (₹64, two hours) every 20 minutes, via Unduvalli. Drivers charge around ₹1800 for a half-day excursion from Vijayawada.

Eluru

08812 / POP 201,050

The city of Eluru, 60km east of Vijayawada on the road and railway to Visakhapatnam, is the jumping-off point for the remote old Buddhist site of Guntupalli (p933) and the Dhamma Vijaya meditation centre at Vijayarai.

Courses

Dhamma Vijaya HEALTH & WELLBEING

(9441449044, 08812-225522; www.vijaya.dhamma.org; Eluru-Chintalapudi Rd, Vijayarai) Monthly intensive 10-day *vipassana* silent meditation courses are offered in lush palm- and cocoa-forested grounds; apply in advance. Payment is by donation.

Getting There & Away

Buses depart Eluru for Vijayarai every 30 minutes (₹16, 20 minutes).

Nagarjunakonda

08680

The unique island of Nagarjunakonda is peppered with ancient Buddhist structures. The Ikshvaku dynasty had its capital here in the 3rd and 4th centuries AD, when the area was probably the most important Buddhist centre in South India.

Sights

Nagarjunakonda Museum MUSEUM

(incl monuments Indian/foreigner ₹20/120; 9am-4pm Sat-Thu) The thoughtfully laid-out Nagarjunakonda Museum has Buddha statues and some superbly detailed carvings depicting local contemporary life and the Buddha's lives. The reassembled remains of several buildings, including stupa bases, walls of monastery complexes and pits for horse sacrifice, are arranged on a 1km path running along the island. The largest stupa, in the Chamtasri Chaitya Griha group, contained a bone fragment thought to be from the Buddha himself.

Sri Parvata Arama BUDDHIST SITE

(Buddhavanam; 9.30am-6pm) FREE This Buddhism Heritage park, featuring a recreation of the huge Amaravathi stupa, is 8km north of the dam. It's been under construction by the state tourism authorities for several years. The 9m replica of the Avukana Buddha statue was donated by Sri Lanka. There's also an attractive meditation area, Dhyanavanam, with fine lake views. Alight at Buddha Park when coming by bus from Hyderabad.

Courses

Dhamma Nagajjuna HEALTH & WELLBEING

(9440139329, 9348456780; www.nagajjuna.dhamma.org; Hill Colony) Keeping the Buddha's teachings alive in the region, this centre offers 10-day silent meditation courses in charming flower-filled grounds overlooking Nagarjuna Sagar. Apply in advance; payment is by donation. Alight at Buddha Park when coming by bus from Hyderabad.

Sleeping & Eating

Nagarjuna Resort HOTEL $

(08642-242471; Vijayapuri South; r without/with AC ₹800/1500;) Nagarjuna Resort has spacious, though drab, rooms, while the balconies enjoy good views. It's conveniently located across the road from the boat launch.

Haritha Vijaya Vihar HOTEL $$

(08680-277362; r with AC incl breakfast Mon-Thu ₹1400-1700, Fri-Sun ₹2400-2700;) Telangana Tourism's Haritha Vijaya Vihar is 6km north of the dam, with decent rooms, nice gardens, a good pool (guest admission ₹50) and lovely lake views. It's a little overpriced, but the location is exceptional, the restaurant is quite decent and there's a bar.

Hotel Siddhartha INDIAN $$

(Buddhavanam, Hill Colony; mains ₹130-240; 6am-11pm) Beside Sri Parvata Arama, with tasty curries, biryanis, fish dishes and lots of snacks served in a pleasant, airy pavilion.

Getting There & Away

The easiest way to visit Nagarjunakonda, other than with a private vehicle, is on a bus tour (₹550) from Hyderabad with **Telangana Tourism** (p920), running on weekends only. It's a very long (15 hours!) day trip, however.

Public buses from Hyderabad's Mahatma Gandhi Bus Station run hourly to Hill Colony/

Nagarjuna Sagar (₹220, four hours): alight at Pylon and catch an autorickshaw (shared/private ₹20/120) 8km to Vijayapuri South.

Boats (₹120 return) depart for the island from Vijayapuri South, 7km south of the dam, theoretically at 9.30am, 11.30am and 1.30pm (but they invariably leave late), and stay for one to two hours. The first two boats may not go if not enough people turn up, but the 1.30pm boat goes every day (barring high winds) and starts back from the island around 4.30pm.

Visakhapatnam

0891 / POP 1.76 MILLION

Visakhapatnam – also called Vizag (*vie*-zag) – is Andhra Pradesh's largest city, famous for steel and its big port but also doubling as a beach resort for sea-breeze-seeking domestic tourists. During the main December–February holiday season there's a distinctly kitschy vibe, with camel rides and thousands of bathers (though no swimmers).

The pedestrian promenade along Ramakrishna Beach is pleasant for a stroll, and nearby Rushikonda Beach is Andhra's best. The surrounding area contains one of Andhra's most important Hindu temples, several ancient Buddhist sites and the rural Araku Valley.

Every mid-January the city hosts **Visakha Utsav** (mid-Jan), a festival with food stalls on Ramakrishna Beach, exhibitions and cultural events.

Sights & Activities

Ramakrishna Beach BEACH

(Beach Rd) Ramakrishna (RK) Beach stretches 4km up the coast from the large port area in the south of town, overlooking the Bay of Bengal with its mammoth ships and brightly painted fishing boats. Its pedestrian promenade is great for strolling. Swimming is officially prohibited (and the sea polluted). On Sunday mornings the adjacent Beach Rd is closed to traffic (from 6am to 9am) in an initiative called 'Happy Streets', as cricket, football and basketball games replace the cars and buses.

★ **Submarine Museum** MUSEUM

(Beach Rd; adult/child ₹40/20, camera ₹50; 2-8.30pm Tue-Sat, 10am-12.30pm & 2-8.30pm Sun) A fantastic attraction located towards the north end of Ramakrishna Beach, the 91m-long, Soviet-built, Indian navy submarine *Kursura* is now a fascinating museum. You're given about 15 minutes to explore the incredibly confined quarters and check out the torpedoes, kitchens and sleeping areas. Some staff speak a little English.

Rushikonda BEACH

Rushikonda, 10km north of town, has a wild beauty and is one of the nicest beaches on India's east coast. Swimming is officially prohibited (there have been drownings), but it's the best beach for a knee-high dip. Women should opt for modest beachwear. Weekends are busy and festive. Surfers and kayakers can rent decent boards and kayaks from local surf pioneer **Melville Smythe** (9848561052; per hr surfboard ₹400-600, 2-person kayak ₹300, surf tuition ₹250), by the jet-ski hut.

You can reach Rushikonda by bus 900K from the train station or RTC Complex, or shared autorickshaws from Beach Rd.

Simhachalam Temple HINDU TEMPLE

(7-11.30am, 12.30-2.30pm & 3.30-7pm) Andhra's second-most visited temple (after Tirumala) is a 16km drive northwest of town. It's dedicated to Varahalakshmi Narasimha, a combination of Vishnu's boar and lion-man avatars, and can get crowded. A ₹100 ticket will get you to the deity (and a sip of holy water) much quicker than a ₹20 one. Buses 6A and 28 go here from the RTC Complex and train station.

The temple's architecture bears much Odishan influence, including the 13th-century main shrine with its carved stone panels (the lion-man can be seen disembowelling a demon on the rear wall).

Sleeping

Beach Rd is the best place to stay, but it's low on inexpensive hotels.

SKML Beach Guest House GUESTHOUSE $

(9848355131; ramkisg.1074@gmail.com; Beach Rd, Varun Beach; r ₹1100-1250, with AC ₹1700-2200;) SKML is towards the less select southern end of Ramakrishna Beach but its 12 rooms are clean and decent. Best are the two top-floor 'suites' with sea views, a terrace and a bit of art.

Hotel Morya HOTEL $

(0891-2731112; www.hotelmorya.com; Bowdara Rd; s/d from ₹490/690, r with AC ₹1390;) A good choice, and just 600m south of the train station. Standard rooms here are small and lack ventilation, but their better AC options are quite spacious, bright and relatively smart. There's a lift, but no restaurant.

Dolphin Hotel HOTEL $$
(☎0891-2567000; http://dolphinhotelsvizag.com; Dabagardens; r incl breakfast ₹2700-4800;) A dependable hotel with quite spacious, well-equipped rooms and an attractive restaurant. Its trump card is the 20m pool and excellent gym, one of the best in the city.

★**Novotel Visakhapatnam Varun Beach** HOTEL $$$
(☎0891-2822222; www.accorhotels.com; Beach Rd; r/ste incl breakfast ₹8230/15,076;) Novotel Visakhapatnam Varun Beach boasts a commanding position on Beach Rd and its rooms are very well-appointed and immaculately presented, all with direct sea views. Dining options are first class, the bar is great for a tipple, the spa is excellent and the pool area and gym overlook the Bay of Bengal. Both the Indian and English cricket teams stayed here in 2016.

Park HOTEL $$$
(☎0891-3045678; www.theparkhotels.com; Beach Rd; s/d incl breakfast from ₹8450/10,880;) Tasteful seafront property, with lovely beachfront gardens that contain a fine pool and three of the hotel's four restaurants. Guests also have access to a private beach. Rooms are cosy and generally well-maintained, though some furnishings are looking a tad dated.

Eating & Drinking

★**Sea Inn** ANDHRA $$
(Raju Ka Dhaba; ☎9989012102; http://seainn.info; Beach Rd, Rushikonda; meals ₹220-300; noon-4pm Tue-Sun) This delightful place is owned by chef Devi, who cooks Andhra-style curries the way her mum did. Fish, seafood, chicken and veg are served up in a simple, semi-open-air dining room with bench seating, about 300m north of the Haritha Beach Resort turn-off. Cash only.

★**Dharani** INDIAN $$
(Daspalla Hotel, off Town Main Rd, Suryabagh; thalis & mains ₹175-240; noon-3.30pm & 7-10.30pm) Bustling family veg place that's one of the town's best-regarded restaurants, with simply superb South Indian thalis. The hotel has several other restaurants too, including Andhra nonveg and North Indian veg options. Be sure to round off your meal with a Daspalla special filter coffee.

Little Italy ITALIAN $$
(http://littleitaly.in; 1st fl, South Wing, ATR Towers, Vutagedda Rd, Paandurangapuram; mains ₹240-440; 11.30am-11pm;) Behind Ramakrishna Beach, this renowned restaurant does fine thin-crust pizza, pasta and reasonable salads in stylish surrounds. No alcohol, but good fruit mocktails.

Vista MULTICUISINE $$$
(The Park, Beach Rd; mains ₹360-960; dinner 7.30-11pm;) A wonderful setting for a meal, the Vista overlooks the stunning pool in the grand Park hotel. It's a fine choice for its long, truly global menu and excellent all-you-can-eat dinner buffet.

Moksha Restocafé CAFE
(www.facebook.com/moksha.restocafe; Ootagadda Rd, Daspalla Hills; noon-11pm;) A great independent cafe popular with a hip young Vizag crowd, it has distant sea views. There's fine coffee, including espresso options, and good juices (try the minty lemon). On the menu you'll find Western, Thai, Tibetan and Indian dishes.

Information

APTDC (☎0891-2788820; www.aptdc.gov.in; RTC Complex; 7am-9pm Mon-Sat) Useful office for tours, hotel bookings and tourist information.

Getting There & Away

AIR

Vizag airport has direct daily flights to cities including Bengaluru, Bhubaneswar, Chennai, Delhi, Hyderabad, Kolkata, Mumbai and Vijayawada. There are also international connections to Dubai, Kuala Lumpur and Singapore.

BOAT

Boats depart roughly once a month for Port Blair in the Andaman Islands. Call or email for schedules or check www.andamanbeacon.com. Book for the 56-hour journey (bunk ₹2410, cabin berth from ₹4640) at **AV Bhanojirow, Garuda Pattabhiramayya & Co** (☎0891-2565597; ops@avbgpr.com; Harbour Approach Rd, next to NMDC, port area; 9am-5pm). Tickets go on sale two or three days before departure. Bring your passport, two photocopies of its data page, and two passport photos.

BUS

Services from Vizag's well-organised **RTC Complex** (☎0891-2746400; RTC Complex Inner Rd) include the following:

Hyderabad non-AC/AC ₹745/1290, 13 hours, almost hourly 2.30pm to 10pm

Jagdalpur non-AC ₹236, eight hours, two daily

Vijayawada general/superluxury/AC ₹375/448/640, eight hours, hourly 5am to midnight

CAR

English-speaking **Srinivasa 'Srinu' Rao** (7382468137) is a reliable, friendly driver for out-of-town trips. He charges around ₹3000 for an Araku Valley day trip and ₹1600 to Sankaram and back.

Reliable **Guide Tours & Travels** (9848265559, 0891-2754477; Shop 15, Sudarshan Plaza; 7am-10pm) charges around ₹3200 plus tolls for a day trip up to 300km.

TRAIN

Visakhapatnam station (Station Rd), on the western edge of town, is on the main Kolkata–Chennai line. Typical journey times, frequencies and sleeper/3AC/2AC fares:

Bhubaneswar ₹260/705/1055, six hours, 10 daily

Chennai ₹425/1125/1605, 13 hours, two to three daily

Hyderabad ₹370/1025/1450, 11 hours, five to six daily

Kolkata ₹460/1210/1725, 14 hours, five to six daily

Tirupati ₹410/1070/1520, 10 hours, three to four daily

Vijayawada ₹255/650/910, six hours, 16 to 19 daily

The **railway reservation centre** (Station Approach Rd; 8am-10pm Mon-Sat, 8am-2pm Sun) is 300m south of the main station building.

Getting Around

There are over 2000 Uber (and a similar number of Ola) drivers in Visakhapatnam, so you won't have to wait long for a ride.

For the airport, 12km west of downtown, app-cabs or autorickshaws charge about ₹240. Or take bus 38 from the RTC Complex (₹18, 30 minutes). The airport's arrivals hall has a prepaid taxi booth.

The train station has a prepaid autorickshaw booth. Shared autorickshaws run along Beach Rd from the port at the south end of town to Rushikonda, 10km north of Vizag, and Bheemunipatnam, 25km north, charging between ₹5 (for a 1km hop) and ₹40 (Vizag to Bheemunipatnam).

Around Visakhapatnam

Sankaram

Located 40km southwest of Vizag, the stunning Buddhist complex of **Sankaram** (near Anakapalle; 8am-5pm) FREE, also known by the names of its two parts, Bojjannakonda and Lingalakonda, occupies a rocky outcrop about 300m long. Used by monks from the 2nd to 9th centuries AD, the outcrop is covered with rock-cut caves, stupas, ruins of monastery structures and reliefs of the Buddha. Bojjannakonda, the eastern part, has a pair of rock-cut shrines with several gorgeous carvings of the Buddha inside and outside. Above sit the ruins of a huge stupa and a monastery. Lingalakonda, at the western end, is piled with tiers of rock-cut stupas, some of them enormous. Both parts afford fabulous views over the surrounding rice paddies.

Getting There & Away

A private car from Vizag costs around ₹1600. Or take a frequent train (₹38, one hour), or bus (₹48, 1½ hours) from Vizag's **RTC Complex** (p936), to Anakapalle, 3km away, and then an autorickshaw (₹120 return including waiting).

Bavikonda & Thotlakonda

Bavikonda (9am-5pm) FREE and **Thotlakonda** (pedestrian/car ₹5/30; 8am-5.30pm) were Buddhist monasteries on scenic hilltop sites north of Vizag that each hosted up to 150 monks, with the help of massive rainwater tanks. Their remains were unearthed in the 1980s and 1990s.

The monasteries flourished from around the 3rd century BC to the 3rd century AD, and had votive stupas, congregation halls, *chaitya-grihas, viharas* and refectories. Thotlakonda has sea views, and Bavikonda has special importance because a relic vessel found in its Mahachaitya stupa contained a piece of bone believed to be from the Buddha himself.

Getting There & Away

Bavikonda and Thotlakonda are reached from turn-offs 14km and 15km, respectively, from Vizag on the Bheemunipatnam road: Bavikonda is 3km off the main road and Thotlakonda 1.25km. Vizag autorickshaw or Uber drivers charge around ₹650 return to see both.

Bheemunipatnam

This former Dutch settlement, 25km north of Vizag, is the oldest municipality in mainland India, with bizarre sculptures on the beach, an 1861 lighthouse, an interesting Dutch cemetery, and Bheemli Beach, where local grommets surf not-very-clean waters on crude homemade boards.

Araku Valley

📞08936 / ELEV 975M

Andhra's best train ride is through the beautiful, lushly forested Eastern Ghats to the Araku Valley, centred on Araku town, 115km north of Visakhapatnam. The area is home to isolated tribal communities and known for its tasty organic coffee and lovely green countryside. En route you can visit the impressive Borra Caves.

Sights

Borra Caves CAVE

(adult/child ₹60/45, camera/mobile camera ₹100/25; ⏰10am-1pm & 2-5pm) Illuminated with fancy lighting, the huge million-year-old limestone Borra Caves are 38km before Araku town and can be combined with a visit to the Araku Valley. Watch out for monkeys. There are snack stands close to the entrance.

Museum of Habitat MUSEUM

(₹40; ⏰8am-1.30pm & 2.30-8pm) This museum has extensive exhibits on the tribal peoples of eastern Andhra Pradesh, including full-scale mock-ups of hunting, ceremonial and other scenes, and a few craft stalls. Worthwhile, but displays and information could be better. Located next to the bus station and 2km east of the train station.

Sleeping & Eating

Hotel Rajadhani HOTEL $

(📞08936-249580; www.hotelrajadhani.com; r without/with AC ₹880/1350; ❄📶) Budget hotel with over 30 rooms, seven of which have AC, and all have attached bathrooms with hot water. They could all be better presented, but those on the upper floor enjoy valley views from their balconies. There's an **in-house restaurant** (meals ₹130-220; ⏰7am-10pm).

Haritha Valley Resort HOTEL $$

(📞08936-249202; incl breakfast r ₹1200-2150, with AC ₹2350; ❄📶🏊) The best place to stay in Araku, with a pool and landscaped grounds. It's a government-run hotel and rooms are maintained quite well, though service is very leisurely. Favoured by Tollywood film crews.

Haritha Hill Resort HOTEL $$

(Mayuri; 📞08936-249204; incl breakfast cottage ₹945, r ₹1468-2522; ❄📶) Not bad for a government hotel, this decent APTDC place is just behind the Museum of Habitat and its cottages offer adequate comfort for the reasonable prices asked.

Star Annapurna INDIAN $

(meals ₹125-240; ⏰7.30am-10pm) Perhaps the best restaurant in the Araka area, offering a wide choice of flavoursome dishes including a good chicken biryani, fish dishes and lots of well-spiced vegetable curries.

Araku Valley Coffee House CAFE $

(coffee ₹25-100; ⏰8.30am-9pm) You can sample and buy local coffee and all kinds of chocolatey goods (brownies, chocolate-covered coffee beans) at Araku Valley Coffee House, which also has a tiny **coffee museum** (₹25; ⏰8.30am-9pm).

Shopping

Araku Aadiwasi Arts & Crafts ARTS & CRAFTS

(⏰8am-8pm) Located between the Coffee House and bus station, it has a good selection of tribal jewellery, jute bags and ornaments.

Getting There & Away

From Visakhapatnam a train (₹100, four hours) leaves daily at 7.05am, returning from Araku at 4.10pm. Get to Visakhapatnam early to secure a seat and be aware that the return train often leaves late. Buses (roughly hourly) from Visakhapatnam (from ₹128) take 4½ hours. A taxi day trip costs ₹3000 to ₹4000. The APTDC runs tours that all include the Borra Caves, 38km before Araku; however, its day trips are very rushed.

Tirumala & Tirupati

📞0877 / POP 292,000 (TIRUPATI) / 7900 (TIRUMALA)

One of the globe's largest pilgrimage destinations, the holy hill of Tirumala is, on any given day, thronged with thousands of devotees who've journeyed to see Lord Venkateshwara here, at his home. Around 60,000 pilgrims come each day, and *darshan* runs 24/7. The **Tirumala Tirupathi Devasthanams** (TTD; 📞0877-2233333, 0877-2277777; www.tirumala.org; KT Rd; ⏰9am-5.30pm Mon-Fri, 9am-1pm Sat) efficiently administers the multitudes, employing 20,000 people to do so. Despite the crowds, a sense of order, serenity and ease mostly prevails, and a trip to the Holy Hill can be fulfilling even if you're not a pilgrim. Queues during the annual nine-day **Brahmotsavam festival** (⏰Sep/Oct) can stretch for kilometres.

Tirupati, the humdrum town at the bottom of the hill, is the gateway to Tirumala.

Sights

Venkateshwara Temple HINDU TEMPLE

(www.tirumala.org) Devotees flock to Tirumala to see Venkateshwara, an avatar of Vishnu. Among the many powers attributed to Venkateshwara is the granting of any wish made at this holy site. 'Ordinary *darshan*' requires a wait of anywhere from two to eight hours in claustrophobic metal cages ringing the temple. Special-entry *darshan* (deity-viewing) tickets (₹300, bookable online) will get you through the queue faster though you'll still have to brave the cages, which is part of the fun, kind of...

There are different hours for special-entry *darshan* each day: check the website. Upon entry, you'll have to sign a form declaring your faith in Lord Venkateshwara.

Legends about the hill itself and the surrounding area appear in the Puranas, and the temple's history may date back 2000 years. The main temple is an atmospheric place, though you'll be pressed between hundreds of devotees when you see it. Venkateshwara inspires bliss and love among his visitors from the back of the dark and magical inner sanctum; it smells of incense and resonates with chanting. You'll have a moment to say a prayer and then you'll be shoved out again. Don't forget to collect your delicious *ladoo* from the counter: Tirumala *ladoos* (sweet balls made with chickpea flour, cardamom and dried fruits) are famous across India.

Many pilgrims donate their hair to the deity – in gratitude for a wish fulfilled, or to renounce ego – so hundreds of barbers attend to devotees. Tirumala and Tirupati are filled with tonsured men, women and children.

Sleeping

Avoid weekends, when Tirupati is uber-rammed. The Tirumala Tirupathi Devasthanams (TTD) runs vast **dormitories** (beds free) and **guesthouses** (r ₹50-3000; ❄) near the temple in Tirumala, intended for pilgrims. To stay here, check in at the Central Reception Office.

★ Athidhi Residency — HOTEL $

(☎ 0877-2281222; www.facebook.com/Athidhi-Residency; Peddakapu Layout; r ₹900-1400; ❄📶) Keenly priced, this is a deservedly popular place with well-presented rooms that have flat-screen TVs, ceiling fans and attractive en suites. It's a short drive from the train station or walkable from the bus stand.

Hotel Annapurna — HOTEL $

(☎ 0877-2250666; www.hotelannapurna.in; 349 G Car St, Tirupati; r without/with AC ₹1180/1980; ❄📶) Rooms at this long-running place are simply furnished and painted pink. Front rooms can be noisy. Its **veg restaurant** (mains ₹125-220; ⏰5.30am-11pm; 📶) has fresh juices and tasty food. There's a lift.

Minerva Grand — HOTEL $$

(☎ 0877-6688888; http://minervahotels.in; Renigunta Rd, Tirupati; s/d with AC from ₹2300/2700; ❄📶) A well-run establishment with some of the best rooms in town – comfy business-style abodes with desks, plump pillows and good mattresses. Its two restaurants, both with icy AC, are great too and there's a small gym.

Hotel Regalia — HOTEL $$

(☎ 0877-2238699; www.regaliahotels.com; Ramanuja Circle, Tirupati; r/ste incl breakfast ₹2999/4999; ❄📶) On the east side of town, 1.5km from the train station, the Regalia provides attractive, inviting, contemporary rooms with sleek en suites. The inclusive breakfast is a generous buffet. Excellent value.

Eating & Drinking

Tirupati is well-endowed with restaurants. Huge **dining halls** (meals free; ⏰hours vary) on the hill feed thousands of pilgrims daily; veg restaurants also serve meals for ₹25.

★ Hotel Mayura — INDIAN $$

(209 TP Area; meals ₹150-280; ⏰7am-10pm) Opposite the bus station, this comfortable hotel restaurant is one of the best places in town for South Indian thalis (₹220), with delicious dishes and lots of chutneys neatly arranged on a banana leaf. North Indian dishes are also offered.

★ Minerva Coffee Shop — INDIAN $$

(Minerva Grand, Renigunta Rd; thalis ₹190-230; ⏰7am-11.30pm; 📶) The veg-only Minerva Coffee Shop does superb Andhra thalis (with free refills) and dynamite filter coffee. Staff are efficient and the ambience is family orientated. It's a good choice for a local breakfast.

Blue Fox — INDIAN, CHINESE $$

(Minerva Grand, Renigunta Rd; mains ₹220-380; ⏰7am-11.30pm; 📶) The Blue Fox 'fine dining bar', with besuited waiters, serves Indian and Chinese veg and nonveg dishes, as well as alcoholic drinks.

Aroma Coffee House — CAFE

(Tirumala Bypass; ⏰9am–11pm) Hits the spot when you need that espresso or latte. In modern, AC surrounds; they also sell sandwiches and snacks.

Getting There & Away

It's possible to visit Tirumala on a long day trip from Chennai. The Andhra Pradesh State Road Transport Corporation (APSRTC) runs half-hourly buses direct to Tirumala (₹112 to ₹303, three to four hours) from **Chennai's CMBT bus station** (p1021).

AIR

Tirupati Airport (www.tirupatiairport.com; Renigunta Airport Rd) is at Renigunta, 14km east of town. There are daily flights to Delhi, Hyderabad and other cities with **Air India** (☎0877-2283981, airport 0877-2283992; www.airindia.in; Srinivasam Pilgrim Amenities Complex, Tirumala Bypass Rd; ⊙9.30am-5.30pm Mon-Sat), SpiceJet, Air Costa and TruJet.

BUS

Tirupati's **bus station** (☎0877-2289900; Tirupati Rd; ⊙24hr) has services, all once or twice hourly, including the following:

Chennai express/Volvo ₹112/293, three to four hours

Bengaluru express/Volvo/semi-sleeper ₹229/323/377, four to six hours

Hyderabad superluxury/Volvo ₹652/1023, nine to 13 hours

Vijayawada express/semi-sleeper ₹474/698, seven to nine hours

TRAIN

There are numerous daily departures; the **reservation office** (Netaji Rd; ⊙8am-8pm Mon-Sat, 8am-2pm Sun) is opposite Tirupati station's east end. Typical journey times and fares for sleeper/3AC/2AC:

Bengaluru ₹210/615/860, seven hours

Chennai ₹140/490/695, three to four hours

Hyderabad ₹380/1035/1495, 12 hours

Vijayawada ₹235/625/935, seven hours

Visakhapatnam ₹380/1035/1490, 15 hours

Getting Around

BUS

There's a stand for buses to Tirumala opposite the train station, with departures every few minutes. The scenic one-hour trip costs ₹48/85 one-way/return; going up, sit on the left side for views.

TAXI

There's a prepaid taxi booth outside the east end of the train station. Ola and Uber cabs are in Tirupati.

WALKING

The Tirumala Tirupathi Devasthanams has constructed probably the best footpath in India, for pilgrims to walk up to Tirumala. It's about 12km from the start of the path at Alipiri on the north side of Tirupati (₹50 by autorickshaw), and takes three to six hours. You can leave your luggage at Alipiri and it will be transported free to the reception centre. There are shady rest points along the way, and a few canteens.

Around Tirumala & Tirupati

Chandragiri Fort

This fort complex, 15km west of Tirupati, dates back 1000 years but its heyday came in the late 16th century when the rulers of the declining Vijayanagar empire, having fled from Hampi, made it their capital. At the heart of a 1.5km-long stout-walled enclosure beneath a rocky hill, the **palace area** (Indian/foreigner ₹10/100; ⊙9am-5pm Sat-Thu) contains nice gardens and the Raja Mahal, a heavily restored Vijayanagar palace reminiscent of Hampi buildings, with a reasonably interesting **museum** (⊙9am-5pm Sat-Thu) of bronze and stone sculptures. The upper fort on the hillside is (frustratingly) out of bounds.

Getting There & Away

Buses for Chandragiri (₹10) leave Tirupati hourly. Cabs charge around ₹600 return.

Sri Kalahasti

☎08578 / POP 82,521

The holy town of Sri Kalahasti, 37km east of Tirupati, is known for its important **Sri Kalahasteeswara Temple** (www.srikalahasthitemple.com; ⊙6am-9.30pm) and for being, along with Machilipatnam near Vijayawada, a centre for the ancient textile-painting art of *kalamkari*. Cotton cloth is primed with *myrabalam* (resin) and cow's milk; figures are drawn with a pointed bamboo stick dipped in fermented jaggery and water; and the dyes are made from cow dung, ground seeds, plants and flowers. You can see artists at work, and buy some of their products, in the Agraharam neighbourhood, 2.5km from the bus stand. **Sri Vijayalakshmi Fine Kalamkari Arts** (☎9441138380; Door No 15-890; ⊙by appointment) is a 40-year-old family business employing over 60 artists. Dupatta scarves start at around ₹1500.

Getting There & Away

Buses leave Tirupati for Sri Kalahasti every 15 minutes (₹32, one hour). Taxis charge around ₹1400 return including waiting time.

Kerala

Includes ➡

Best Places to Eat

- Villa Maya (p947)
- Dal Roti (p985)
- Bait (p952)
- Malabar Junction (p985)
- Paragon Restaurant (p993)

Best Places to Sleep

- Green Woods Bethlehem (p981)
- Varnam Homestay (p997)
- Kaiya House (p955)
- Ashtamudi Villas (p959)
- Reds Residency (p981)

Why Go?

For many travellers, Kerala is South India's most serenely beautiful state. A slender coastal strip is shaped by its layered landscape: almost 600km of glorious Arabian Sea coast and beaches; a languid network of glistening backwaters; and the spice- and tea-covered hills of the Western Ghats. Just setting foot on this swath of soul-quenching, palm-shaded green will slow your subcontinental stride to a blissed-out amble. Kerala is a world away from the frenzy of elsewhere, as if India had passed through the Looking Glass and become an altogether more laid-back place.

Besides its famous backwaters, elegant houseboats, ayurvedic treatments and delicately spiced, taste-bud-tingling cuisine, Kerala is home to wild elephants, exotic birds and the odd tiger, while vibrant traditions such as Kathakali plays, temple festivals and snake-boat races frequently bring even the smallest villages to life. It's hard to deny Kerala's liberal use of the slogan 'God's Own Country'.

When to Go

Thiruvananthapuram

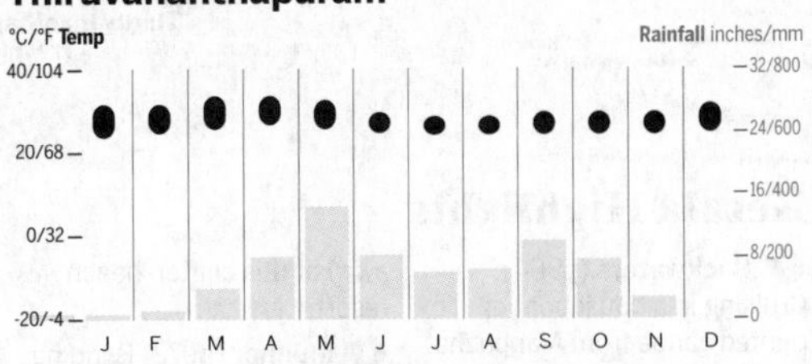

Dec–Feb Perfect beach and backwater weather. Festival season throughout the state.

Apr Kathakali at Kottayam and Kollam festivals, and the elephant procession in Thrissur.

Aug–Oct End of the monsoon period: Onam festival, snake-boat races.

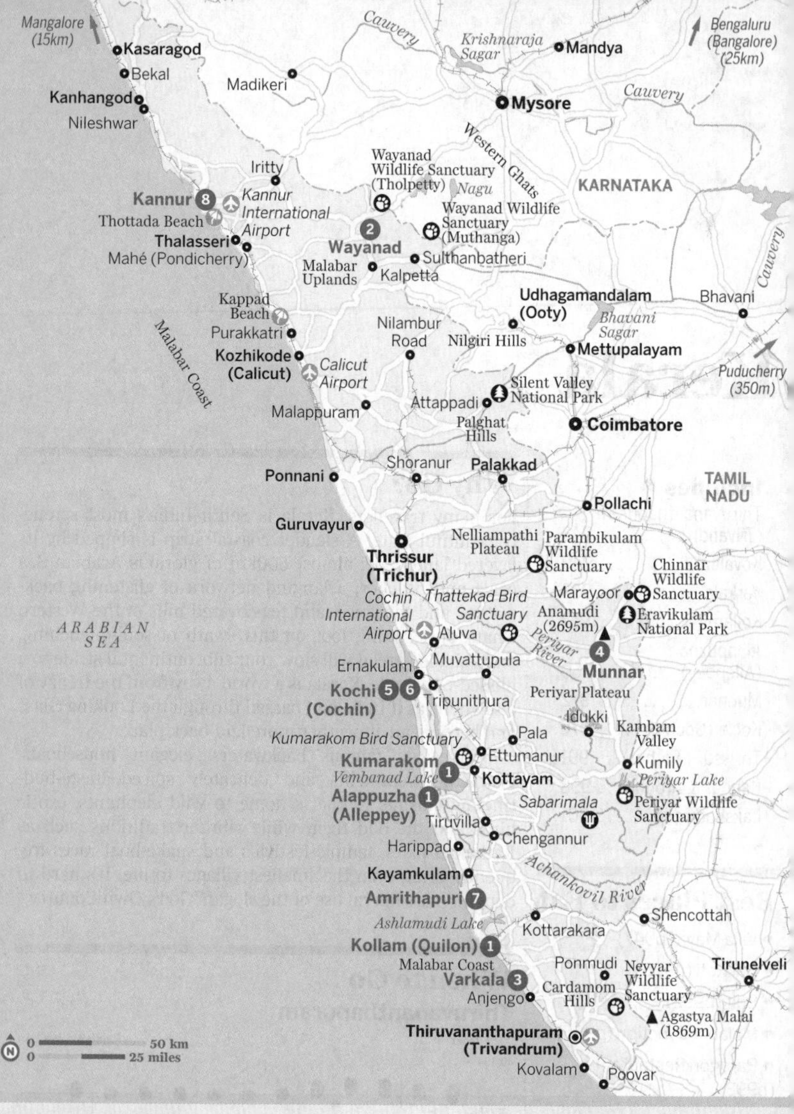

Kerala Highlights

1. **Backwaters** (p964) Cruising in a houseboat or punted canoe from Alappuzha, Kollam or Kumarakom.

2. **Wayanad** (p995) Spotting wild elephants, trekking and relaxing in remote forest accommodation.

3. **Varkala** (p953) Watching the days slip-slide away at this clifftop beach resort.

4. **Munnar** (p972) Bedding down in a beautifully remote resort and trekking through emerald tea plantations.

5. **Fort Cochin** (p977) Feeling the history and dining with a local family in a homestay.

6. **Kathakali** (p990) Experiencing a performance in Kochi.

7. **Matha Amrithanandamayi Mission** (p960) Calling in for a cuddle at the ashram of Amma, in Amrithapuri.

8. **Kannur** (p998) Exploring unspoilt beaches and *theyyam* rituals in the north.

History

Traders have been drawn to the scent of Kerala's spices for more than 3000 years. The coast was known to the Phoenicians, the Romans, the Arabs and the Chinese, and was a transit point for spices from the Moluccas (eastern Indonesia).

The kingdom of Cheras ruled much of Kerala until the early Middle Ages, competing with kingdoms and small fiefdoms for territory and trade. Vasco da Gama's arrival in 1498 opened the floodgates to European colonialism as Portuguese, Dutch and English interests fought Arab traders, and then each other, for control of the lucrative spice trade.

The present-day state of Kerala was created in 1956 from the former states of Travancore, Kochi and Malabar. A tradition of valuing the arts and education resulted in a post-Independence state that is one of the most progressive in India, with the nation's highest literacy rate.

In 1957 Kerala had the first freely elected communist government in the world, which has gone on to hold power regularly since – though the Congress-led United Democratic Front (UDF) has been in power since 2011. Many Malayalis (speakers of Malayalam, the state's official language) work in the Middle East and their remittances play a significant part in the economy. A big hope for the state's future is the relatively recent boom in tourism, with Kerala emerging in the past decade as one of India's most popular new tourist hot spots. According to Kerala Tourism almost 13.5 million visitors arrived in 2015 – more than double the number of a decade ago – though fewer than a million of these were foreign tourists.

SOUTHERN KERALA

Thiruvananthapuram (Trivandrum)

0471 / POP 958,000

Thiruvananthapuram, Kerala's capital – still usually referred to by its colonial name, Trivandrum – is a relatively compact but energetic city and an easygoing introduction to urban life down south. Most travellers merely springboard from here to the nearby beach resorts of Kovalam and Varkala, but Trivandrum has enough sights – including a zoo and cluster of Victorian museums in glorious neo-Keralan buildings – to justify a stay.

Sights

Zoological Gardens ZOO

(0471-2115122; adult/child ₹20/5, camera/video ₹50/75; 9am-5.15pm Tue-Sun) Yann Martel famously based the animals in his novel *Life of Pi* on those he observed here in Trivandrum's zoological gardens. Shaded paths meander through woodland, lakes and native forest, where tigers, macaques and hippos gather in reasonably large open enclosures.

★Napier Museum MUSEUM

(adult/child ₹10/5; 10am-5pm Tue & Thu-Sun, 1-5pm Wed) Housed in an 1880 wooden building designed by Robert Chisholm, a British architect whose Fair Isle–style version of the Keralan vernacular shows his enthusiasm for local craft, this museum has an eclectic display of bronzes, Buddhist sculptures, temple carts and ivory carvings. The carnivalesque interior is stunning and worth a look in its own right.

★Museum of History & Heritage MUSEUM

(9567019037; www.museumkeralam.org; Park View; adult/child Indian ₹20/10, foreigner ₹200/50, camera ₹25; 10am-5.30pm Tue-Sun) In a lovely heritage building within the Kerala Tourism complex, this beautifully presented museum traces Keralan history and culture through superb static displays and interactive

TOP STATE FESTIVALS

As well as the major state festivals, Kerala has hundreds of annual temple festivals, *theyyam* rituals, boat-race regattas and street parades. *A Hundred Festivals for You*, a free publication produced by Kochi's Tourist Desk, lists many of them.

Ernakulathappan Utsavam (p981) Eight days of festivities culminating in a parade of elephants, music and fireworks.

Thrissur Pooram (p991) The elephant procession to end all elephant processions.

Nehru Trophy Boat Race (p961) The most popular of Kerala's boat races.

Onam (Aug/Sep) The entire state celebrates the golden age of mythical King Mahabali for 10 days.

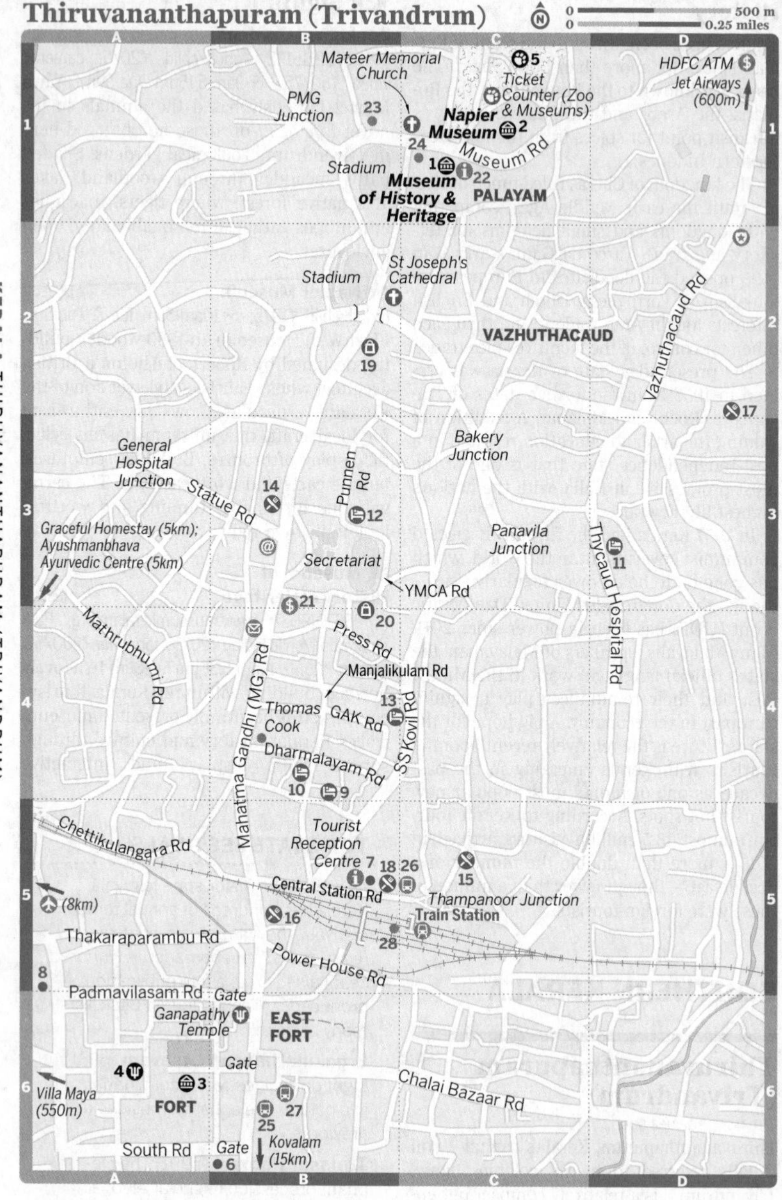

audiovisual presentations. Exhibits range from Iron Age implements to bronze and terracotta sculptures, murals, *dhulichitra* (floor paintings) and recreations of traditional Keralan homes.

Puthe Maliga Palace Museum MUSEUM
(Fort; Indian/foreigner ₹30/100, camera/video ₹50/250; ⏲9.30am-12.30pm & 2-4.45pm Tue-Sun) The 200-year-old palace of the Travancore maharajas has carved wooden ceilings, marble sculptures and imported Belgian

Thiruvananthapuram (Trivandrum)

Top Sights
1 Museum of History & Heritage....C1
2 Napier Museum....C1

Sights
3 Puthe Maliga Palace Museum....A6
4 Shri Padmanabhaswamy Temple....A6
5 Zoological Gardens....C1

Activities, Courses & Tours
6 CVN Kalari Sangham....B6
7 KTDC Tours....B5
8 Margi Kathakali School....A5

Sleeping
9 Hotel Regency....B4
10 Princess Inn....B4
11 Taj Vivanta....D3
12 Varikatt Heritage....B3
13 Vedanta Wake Up Trivandrum....B4

Eating
14 Ananda Bhavan....B3
15 Ariya Nivaas....C5
16 Azad Restaurant....B5
17 Cherries & Berries....D2
18 Indian Coffee House....B5

Shopping
19 Connemara Market....B2
20 SMSM Institute....B4

Information
21 State Bank of India ATM....B3
22 Tourist Facilitation Centre....C1

Transport
23 Air India....B1
24 Airtravel Enterprises....C1
25 East Fort Bus Stand....B6
26 KSRTC Central Bus Stand....C5
27 Municipal Bus Stand....B6
28 Train Station Reservation Office....B5

glass. Inside you'll find Kathakali images, an armoury, portraits of maharajas, ornate thrones and other artefacts. Admission includes an informative one-hour guided tour, though you can just visit the outside of the palace grounds (free), where you'll also find the **Chitrali Museum** (₹50), containing loads of historical memorabilia, photographs and portraits from the Travancore dynasty.

Shri Padmanabhaswamy Temple HINDU TEMPLE

(Hindu-only inner sanctum 3.30am-7.30pm) Trivandrum's spiritual heart is this 260-year-old temple in the Fort area. The main entrance is the 30m-tall, seven-tier eastern *gopuram* (gateway tower). In the inner sanctum (Hindus only), the deity Padmanabha reclines on the sacred serpent and is made from over 10,000 *salagramam* (sacred stones) that were purportedly transported from Nepal by elephant.

The path around to the right of the gate offers good views of the *gopuram*.

Courses

Ayushmanbhava Ayurvedic Centre AYURVEDA, YOGA

(0471-2556060; www.ayushmanbhava.com; Pothujanam; massage from ₹900; yoga classes 6.30am) This centre, 5km west of MG Rd, offers massage, daily therapeutic-yoga classes, as well as longer ayurvedic treatments and a herbal garden.

Margi Kathakali School CULTURAL PROGRAM

(0471-2478806; www.margitheatre.org; Fort) Conducts courses in Kathakali and Kootiattam (traditional Sanskrit drama) for beginner and advanced students. Fees average ₹300 per two-hour class. Visitors can peek at uncostumed practice sessions held from 10am to noon Monday to Friday. It's in an unmarked building behind the Fort School, 200m west of the fort.

CVN Kalari Sangham MARTIAL ARTS

(0471-2474182; www.cvnkalari.in; South Rd; 15-day/1-month course ₹1000/2000) Offers long-term courses in *kalarippayat* for serious students (aged under 30) with some experience in martial arts. Visitors are welcome to watch training sessions from 7am to 8.30am Monday to Saturday.

Tours

KTDC Tours BUS

(0471-2330031; www.ktdc.com) KTDC runs several tours, all leaving from the Tourist

SLEEPING PRICE RANGES

The following price ranges refer to a double room with bathroom:

$ less than ₹1200

$$ ₹1200–₹5000

$$$ more than ₹5000

Reception Centre at the Hotel Chaithram on Central Station Rd. The City Tour (₹300) includes the zoo, museums and other local sights; the Kanyakumari Day Tour (₹700) visits Padmanabhapuram Palace, Kanyakumari in Tamil Nadu and the nearby Suchindram Temple. Other trips include Neyyar Dam (₹400) and Kovalam (₹200).

Sleeping

There are several decent budget and midrange hotels along Manjalikulam Rd, north of Central Station Rd.

Vedanta Wake Up Trivandrum HOSTEL **$**
(☎0471-2334351; www.vedantawakeup.com; SS Kovil Rd; dm/d ₹650/1450; ❄📶) A good central bet for backpackers and solo travellers, with spotless air-con dorms and a private double.

Princess Inn HOTEL **$**
(☎0471-2339150; princess_inn@yahoo.com; Manjalikulam Rd; s/d from ₹600/800, with AC from ₹1000/1200; ❄📶) In a glass-fronted building, the Princess Inn promises a relatively quiet budget sleep in a central side street location. It's comfortable, with satellite TV and immaculate bathrooms; it's worth paying a little more for the spacious 'deluxe' rooms.

Hotel Regency HOTEL **$**
(☎0471-2330377; www.hotelregency.com; Manjalikulam Cross Rd; s/d ₹650/800, with AC ₹1000/1600; ❄📶) This tidy, welcoming place offers small but spotless rooms with satellite TV; the deluxe rooms are larger and there's wi-fi in the lobby, as well as a rooftop garden.

THE INDIAN COFFEE HOUSE STORY

The Indian Coffee House is a place stuck in time. Its India-wide branches feature old-India prices and waiters dressed in starched white with peacock-style head-dresses. It was started by the Coffee Board in the early 1940s, during British rule. In the 1950s the Board began to close down cafes across India, making employees redundant. At this point, the Keralan-born communist leader Ayillyath Kuttiari Gopalan Nambiar began to support the workers and founded with them the India Coffee Board Workers' Co-operative Society. The Coffee House has remained ever since, always atmospheric, and always offering bargain snacks and drinks such as Indian filter coffee, rose milk and *idlis* (fermented rice cakes). It's still run by its employees, all of whom share ownership.

★Graceful Homestay HOMESTAY **$$**
(☎9847249556, 0471-2444358; www.gracefulhomestay.com; Pothujanam Rd, Philip's Hill; incl breakfast downstairs s/d ₹1550/1800, upstairs & ste s/d ₹2450/3000; @📶) In Trivandrum's leafy western suburbs, this lovely, serene family house set in a couple of hectares of garden has four rooms, neatly furnished with individual character and access to kitchen, living areas and balconies. The pick of the rooms has an amazing covered terrace overlooking a sea of palms. Call ahead for directions.

Varikatt Heritage HOMESTAY **$$$**
(☎0471-2336057, 9895239055; www.varikattheritage.com; Punnen Rd; r/ste incl breakfast ₹5000/6000; 📶) Trivandrum's most charismatic place to stay is the 250-year-old home of Colonel Roy Kuncheria. It's a wonderful Indo-Saracenic bungalow with four rooms flanked by verandahs facing a pretty garden. Every antique – and the home itself – has a family story attached. Lunch and dinner are available (₹500).

Taj Vivanta HOTEL **$$$**
(☎0471-6612345; vivanta.tajhotels.com; Thycaud Hospital Rd; s/d incl breakfast from ₹8500/11,000; ❄@📶🏊) The lobby here is bigger than most hotels in town, so the Taj doesn't disappoint with the wow factor. Rooms are sufficiently plush, the lawn and pool area is well maintained, and there's a spa, 24-hour gym and several good restaurants, including the Smoke on the Water poolside grill.

Eating

★Ariya Nivaas SOUTH INDIAN **$**
(Manorama Rd; mains ₹40-150, thalis ₹100; ⏲6.45am-10pm, lunch 11.30am-3pm) Trivandrum's best all-you-can-eat South Indian veg thalis mean Ariya Nivaas is always busy at lunchtime, but service is snappy and the food fresh.

Indian Coffee House INDIAN **$**
(Maveli Cafe; Central Station Rd; snacks ₹10-60; ⏲7am-10.30pm) This branch of Indian Coffee House serves its strong coffee and snacks in a crazy red-brick tower that looks like a cross between a lighthouse and a pigeon coop, and has a spiralling interior lined with

concrete benches and tables. You have to admire the hard-working waiters.

Azad Restaurant INDIAN $

(MG Rd; dishes ₹60-200; ⏰11am-11.30pm) A busy family favourite serving up authentic Keralan seafood dishes such as *molee* (fish pieces in coconut sauce), and excellent biryanis and tandoori. There's a takeaway barbecue on street level and the restaurant is downstairs.

Ananda Bhavan SOUTH INDIAN $

(☎0471-2477646; MG Rd; dishes ₹20-80; ⏰noon-3pm & 6-10pm) Classic cheap veg place specialising in tiffin snacks and dosas.

Cherries & Berries CAFE $$

(☎0471-2735433; www.cherriesandberries.in; Carmel Towers, Cotton Hill; items ₹130-220; ⏰10am-10pm; 📶) For serious comfort food, icy air-con and free wi-fi that really works, take a trip east of the centre to Cherries & Berries. The menu includes waffles, mini-pizzas, hot dogs, toasties, good coffee and indulgent chocolate-bar milkshakes – try the KitKat shake (₹165).

★Villa Maya KERALAN $$$

(☎0471-2578901; www.villamaya.in; 120 Airport Rd, Injakkal; starters ₹200-600, mains ₹400-1500; ⏰11am-11pm) Villa Maya is more an experience than a restaurant. Dining is either in the magnificent 18th-century Dutch mansion or in private curtained niches in the tranquil courtyard garden. The Keralan cuisine is expertly crafted, delicately spiced and beautifully presented. Seafood is a speciality, with dishes like stuffed crab with lobster butter, but there are some tantalising veg dishes too.

Between lunch and dinner (3pm to 7pm) you can order snacks like sandwiches, pizzas and calzones. Ask the friendly staff for a free tour of the historic manor.

Shopping

Connemara Market MARKET

(MG Rd; ⏰6am-9pm) At the busy Connemara Market vendors sell vegetables, fish, goats, fabric, clothes, spices and more.

SMSM Institute ARTS & CRAFTS

(www.keralahandicrafts.in; YMCA Rd; ⏰9am-8pm Mon-Sat) A Kerala Government–run handicraft emporium with an Aladdin's cave of fix-priced crafts, souvenirs and antiques.

Information

KIMS (Kerala Institute of Medical Sciences; ☎0471-3041400, emergency 0471-3041144; www.kimskerala.com; Kumarapuram; ⏰24hr) The best choice for treating medical problems; about 7km northwest of Trivandrum railway station.

Tourist Facilitation Centre (☎0471-2321132; Museum Rd; ⏰24hr) Near the zoo; supplies maps and brochures.

Tourist Reception Centre (KTDC Hotel Chaithram; ☎0471-2330031; Central Station Rd; ⏰7am-9pm) Arranges KTDC-run tours.

Getting There & Away

AIR

Trivandrum International Airport (www.trivandrumairport.com), around 5km west of the city, serves international destinations with direct flights to/from Colombo in Sri Lanka, Malé in the Maldives and major Gulf destinations such as Dubai, Sharjah, Muscat, Bahrain and Kuwait.

BUSES FROM THIRUVANANTHAPURAM (TRIVANDRUM)

DESTINATION	FARE (₹)	DURATION (HRS)	DEPARTURES
Alleppey	132, AC 221	3½	every 15min
Chennai	AC from 850	12	15 daily (overnight)
Ernakulam (Kochi)	177, AC 291	5½	every 15-30min
Kanyakumari	70	2	4 daily
Kollam	63, AC 111	1½	every 15min
Kumily (for Periyar)	226	8	7.30am
Munnar	245	8	3 daily
Neyyar Dam	35	1½	every 40min
Thrissur	224, AC 391	7½	hourly
Varkala	65	1¼	hourly

Within India, **Air India** (☎0471-2317341; www.airindia.com; Mascot Sq; ⏰9am-5pm Mon-Sat), **Jet Airways** (☎0471-2728864; www.jetairways.com; Sasthamangalam Junction; ⏰9am-6pm) and **IndiGo** (☎9212783838; www.indigo.in) fly between Trivandrum and Mumbai (Bombay), Kochi (Cochin), Bengaluru (Bangalore), Chennai (Madras) and Delhi. **SpiceJet** (☎9871803333; www.spicejet.com; Trivandrum Airport) flies to Chennai once a week.

All airline bookings can be made at the efficient travel agency **Airtravel Enterprises** (☎0471-3011300; www.ate.travel; MG Rd, New Corporation Bldg; ⏰9am-7pm).

BUS

State-run and private buses use Trivandrum's giant new concave **KSRTC central bus stand** (☎0471-2462290; www.keralartc.com; Central Station Rd, Thampanoor), opposite the train station.

Buses leave for Kovalam beach (₹17, 30 minutes, every 20 minutes) between 6am and 9pm from the southern end of the **East Fort bus stand** on MG Rd.

TRAIN

Trains are often heavily booked, so it's worth visiting the **reservation office** (☎139; ⏰8am-8pm Mon-Sat, to 2pm Sun) at the main train station or booking online. There's a foreign tourist counter on the 1st floor. While most major trains arrive at Trivandrum Central Station close to the city centre, some express services terminate at Vikram Sarabhai Station (Kochuveli), about 7km north of the city – check in advance.

Within Kerala there are frequent express trains to Varkala (2nd class/sleeper/3AC ₹45/140/490, one hour), Kollam (₹55/140/490, 1¼ hours) and Ernakulam (₹90/165/490, 4½ hours), with trains passing through either Alappuzha (Alleppey; ₹80/140/490, three hours) or Kottayam (₹80/140/490, 3½ hours). There are also numerous daily services to Kanyakumari (2nd class/sleeper/3AC ₹60/140/490, three hours).

Getting Around

For the airport, take local bus 14 from the **East Fort** and **Municipal** bus stands (₹10). Prepaid taxi vouchers from the airport cost ₹350 to the city and ₹500 to Kovalam (13km away).

Autorickshaws are the easiest way to get around, with short hops costing ₹30 to ₹50.

Around Trivandrum

Sights

Neyyar Wildlife Sanctuary NATURE RESERVE
(☎0471-2272182; Indian/foreigner ₹10/100; ⏰9am-4pm Tue-Sun) Surrounding an idyllic lake created by the 1964 Neyyar Dam 35km north of Trivandrum, this sanctuary features a **Lion Safari Park** (☎9744347582, 0471-2272182; Indian/foreigner ₹200/300; ⏰9am-4pm Tue-Sun), deer park and Crocodile Production Centre (named for Australian legend Steve Irwin). The fertile forest lining the shore is home to gaurs, sambar deer, sloth, elephants, lion-tailed macaques and the occasional tiger.

Get here from Trivandrum's KSRTC bus stand by frequent bus (₹35, 1½ hours). A taxi is about ₹1000 return (with two hours' waiting time) from Trivandrum, or ₹1400 from Kovalam. The KTDC office in Trivandrum also runs tours to Neyyar Dam (₹400).

Sivananda Yoga Vedanta Dhanwantari Ashram YOGA
(☎0471-2273093; www.sivananda.org.in/neyyardam; dm/tent ₹800, tw ₹1000-1250, with AC ₹1850) Just before Neyyar Dam, this superbly located ashram established in 1978 is renowned for its hatha yoga courses. Courses start on the 1st and 16th of each month, run for a minimum of two weeks and include various levels of accommodation and vegetarian meals. Low season (May to September) rates are ₹100 less.

MAJOR TRAINS FROM THIRUVANANTHAPURAM (TRIVANDRUM)

DESTINATION	TRAIN NAME & NO	FARE (₹; SLEEPER/3AC/2AC)	DURATION (HRS)	DEPARTURES (DAILY)
Bengaluru	16525 Bangalore Exp	415/1120/1620	18	12.45pm
Chennai	12696 Chennai Exp	470/1240/1775	16½	5.15pm
Coimbatore	17229 Sabari Exp	255/685/980	9¼	7.15am
Mangalura	16604 Maveli Exp	340/915/1320	12½	7.25pm
Mumbai	16346 Netravathi Exp	670/1795/2645	31	9.50am

Kovalam

0471 / POP 25,700

Once a calm fishing village clustered around its crescent beaches, Kovalam competes with Varkala as Kerala's most developed resort. The touristy main stretch, **Lighthouse Beach**, has hotels and restaurants built up along the shore, while **Hawa Beach** to the north is usually crowded with day trippers heading straight from the taxi stand to the sand. Neither beach could be described as pristine, but at less than 15km from the capital it's a convenient place to have some fun by the sea, there are some promising waves (and a surf club), and it makes a good base for ayurvedic treatments and yoga courses.

About 2km further north, **Samudra Beach** has several upmarket resorts, restaurants and a peaceful but steep beach.

Sights & Activities

Vizhinjam Lighthouse LIGHTHOUSE

(Indian/foreigner ₹10/25, camera/video ₹20/25; 10am-5pm) Kovalam's most distinguishing feature is the working candy-striped lighthouse at the southern end of Lighthouse Beach. Climb the spiral staircase – or the brand-new elevator – for vertigo-inducing views up and down the coast.

Cool Divers & Bond Safari DIVING

(9946550073; www.bondsafarikovalam.com; introductory dive ₹6000, 3hr ocean safari ₹6000; 9am-7pm) This new dive outfit offers state-of-the-art equipment, PADI courses and guided trips to local dive sites. It also has nifty Bond submarine scooters, where your head is enclosed in a helmet with an airhose to the surface – no diving experience required!

Kovalam Surf Club SURFING

(9847347367; www.kovalamsurfclub.com; 1½hr lesson ₹1000, rental from ₹400) This surf shop and club just back from Lighthouse Beach offers introductory lessons and 'guided surfing' with a community focus.

Ayur Kerala Ayurvedic Health Care AYURVEDA

(9947027226; www.ayurkerala.org; Lighthouse Beach Rd; massage from ₹1200; 9am-8pm) Recommended massages and ayurvedic treatments.

Sleeping

Kovalam is tightly packed with hotels and guesthouses, though true budget places are in the minority in high season. Beachfront properties are the most expensive and sought after, but look out for smaller places in the labyrinth of sandy paths behind Lighthouse Beach among palm groves and rice paddies; they're usually much better value. Samudra Beach has upmarket resorts. All places offer discounts outside the December–January high season; book ahead in peak times.

Vedanta Wake Up Kovalam HOSTEL $

(0471-2484211; www.vedantawakeup.com; behind Lighthouse Beach; dm/d ₹600/1800;) Kovalam's first backpacker hostel is a five-storey joint a short walk back from Lighthouse Beach. The two air-con dorms are very clean, while the private rooms come with TV and bathroom. It has helpful staff, but lacks common areas and personality.

Green Valley Cottages GUESTHOUSE $

(0471-2480636; indira_ravi@hotmail.com; r ₹800-1000) Back among the palm trees and overlooking a lily pond, this serene complex feels a little faded but it's quiet and decent value. The 22 rooms are simple, but the upper rooms have good views from the front terraces.

Hotel Greenland GUESTHOUSE $

(0471-2486442; hotelgreenlandin@yahoo.com; r ₹700-1400) This friendly family-run place has refurbished rooms in a multilevel complex just back from Lighthouse Beach. It's not flash but rooms have lots of natural light and the larger upstairs rooms have balconies.

Paradesh Inn GUESTHOUSE $$

(9995362952; inn.paradesh@yahoo.com; Avaduthura; s/d incl breakfast ₹2300/2700, superior ₹3000/3400; Oct-Mar; @) Set back from Lighthouse Beach high above the palms, tranquil Italian-run Paradesh Inn resembles a whitewashed Greek island hideaway. Each of the six fan-cooled rooms has a hanging chair outside, there are views from the rooftop, nice breakfasts and *satya* cooking ('yoga food') for guests.

WARNING: LIGHTHOUSE BEACH CURRENTS

There are strong rips at both ends of Lighthouse Beach that carry away several swimmers every year. Swim only between the flags in the area patrolled by lifeguards and avoid swimming during the monsoon.

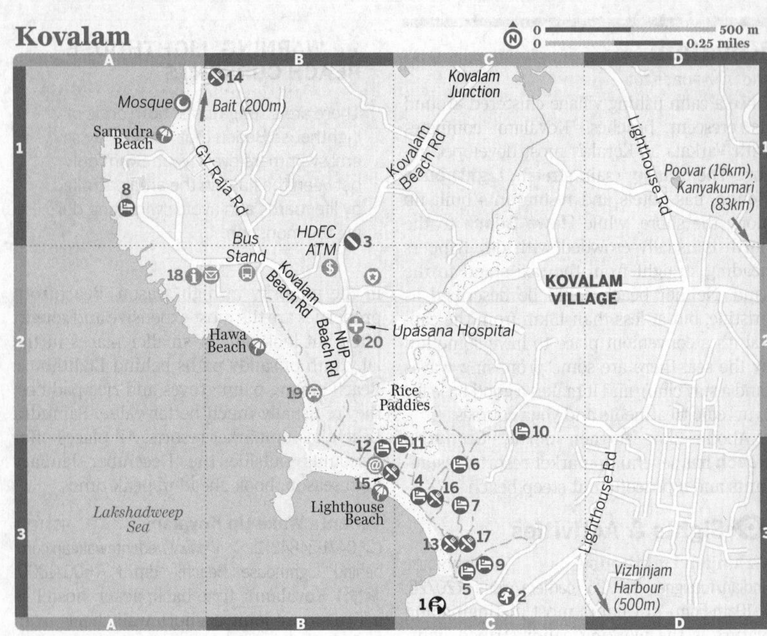

Kovalam

Sights

1 Vizhinjam Lighthouse C3

Activities, Courses & Tours

2 Ayur Kerala Ayurvedic Health Care C3
3 Cool Divers & Bond Safari B1
Kovalam Surf Club .... (see 12)

Sleeping

4 Beach Hotel C3
5 Beach Hotel II C3
6 Green Valley Cottages C3
7 Hotel Greenland C3
8 Leela A1
9 Maharaju Palace C3
10 Paradesh Inn C2
Treetops .... (see 10)
11 Vedanta Wake Up Kovalam C3
12 Wilson Ayurvedic Resort B3

Eating

13 Beatles Cafe C3
14 Curry Leaf B1
Fusion .... (see 5)
15 Malabar Cafe B3
16 Suprabhatham C3
17 Varsha Restaurant C3
Waves Restaurant & German Bakery .... (see 4)

Information

18 Tourist Facilitation Centre A2

Transport

19 Autorickshaw & Taxi Stand B2
20 K Tours & Travel B2

Beach Hotel II HOTEL $$

(☎9400031243, 0471-2481937; www.thebeachhotel-kovalam.com; d ₹4400, with AC ₹5500; ❄📶) Tucked into the southern end of Lighthouse Beach, this stylish pad has 10 sea-facing rooms all with balcony and large sliding French windows. Decor is simple chic. It's also home to the excellent terrace restaurant Fusion.

Treetops GUESTHOUSE $$

(☎9847912398; treetopsofkovalam@yahoo.in; d ₹1500; @📶) Indeed in the treetops high above Lighthouse Beach, this friendly expat-owned place is a peaceful retreat from the action below. The three bright, clean rooms have hanging chairs on the terraces and TVs, and there are rooftop views and a guest kitchen; yoga classes are available. Call ahead to book and get directions.

Beach Hotel GUESTHOUSE $$
(☎0471-2481937; www.thebeachhotel-kovalam.com; d ₹3300; 📶) Location alert! Below Waves Restaurant and German Bakery, the eight beach-facing rooms here are designed with minimalist flair, ochre tones and finished with smart, arty touches.

Maharaju Palace GUESTHOUSE $$
(☎9946854270; www.maharajupalace.com; s/d incl breakfast from ₹1650/1980, cottage ₹3300/3600, summer house ₹7150; ❄📶) More of a peaceful retreat than a palace, this quirky Dutch-owned place in a lane just back from Lighthouse Beach has more character than most, with timber furnishings, including the odd four-poster bed, and a separate cottage in the garden. The lovely breakfast terrace is hung with chintzy chandeliers.

Wilson Ayurvedic Resort HOTEL $$
(☎9847363831; Lighthouse Beach; d ₹1500, with AC ₹2500; ❄📶🏊) Wilson has simple but reasonably well-maintained rooms orbiting a shady pool just back from Lighthouse Beach. There's a leafy holiday-resort vibe and it offers ayurvedic treatments.

Leela HOTEL $$$
(☎0471-2480101; www.theleela.com; d from ₹18,000, ste from ₹66,000; ❄@📶🏊) The sumptuous Leela is set in extensive grounds on the headland north of Hawa Beach. You'll find three swimming pools, an ayurvedic centre, a gym, two 'private beaches', several restaurants and more. Spacious rooms have period touches, colourful textiles and Keralan artwork.

Vivanta By Taj Green Cove HOTEL $$$
(☎0471-6613000; vivanta.tajhotels.com; Samudra Beach; d from ₹17,500, ste from ₹28,000; ❄@📶🏊) The Kovalam branch of this swanky Indian hotel chain is set among sprawling green grounds and has direct access to a secluded stretch of Samudra Beach. The individual thatched cottages here are simply but tastefully adorned, some with private gardens and others with primo sea views. There are several restaurants and the usual top-end amenities.

Eating & Drinking

Lighthouse Beach is the main restaurant hub, with lots of seafood places. Samudra Beach, to the north, is quieter but also has some restaurants worth seeking out. For a romantic dining splurge, the restaurants at Leela and Vivanta By Taj Green Cove are pricey but top class.

Each evening a dozen or so restaurants lining the Lighthouse Beach promenade display the catch of the day – just pick a fish or lobster, settle on a price and decide how you want it prepared. Market prices vary enormously depending on the day's catch, but at the time of research it was around ₹400 per fish fillet, tiger prawns were ₹900 per half kilo, and lobster was ₹3500 per kilo.

★Varsha Restaurant SOUTH INDIAN $
(dishes ₹100-200; ⌚8am-10pm; 📶) This little restaurant just back from Lighthouse Beach serves some of Kovalam's best vegetarian food at budget prices. Dishes are fresh and carefully prepared. It's a great spot for breakfast and lunch in particular.

Suprabhatham KERALAN $
(meals ₹90-250; ⌚7am-11pm; 📶) This little veg place hidden back from Lighthouse Beach doesn't look like much, but it dishes up excellent, inexpensive Keralan cooking, vegetarian thalis and fresh fruit juices in a rustic setting.

Waves Restaurant & German Bakery MULTICUISINE $$
(Beach Hotel; mains ₹220-550; ⌚7.30am-11pm; 📶) With its broad, burnt-orange balcony, ambient soundtrack and wide-roaming menu, Waves is usually busy with foreigners. It morphs into the German Bakery, a great spot for breakfast with fresh bread, croissants, pastries and decent coffee, while dinner turns up Thai curries, German sausages, pizza and seafood. There's a small bookshop attached. Wi-fi (unusually) costs ₹30 per half hour.

Fusion MULTICUISINE $$
(mains ₹200-450; ⌚7.30am-10.30pm; 📶) This terrace restaurant at Beach Hotel II is one of the better dining experiences on Lighthouse

WORTH A TRIP

PADMANABHAPURAM PALACE

About 60km southeast of Kovalam, just over the border in Tamil Nadu, **Padmanabhapuram Palace** (p1069) is considered the finest surviving example of traditional Keralan architecture. It's accessible by bus or taxi from Kovalam or Kanyakumari, via Thuckalay. A return taxi from Kovalam including waiting time costs ₹2000.

Beach, with an inventive East-meets-West menu, a range of Continental dishes, Asian fusion and interesting seafood numbers like lobster steamed in vodka. It also serves French press coffee and herbal teas.

Malabar Cafe INDIAN $$

(mains ₹110-450; 8am-11pm;) The busy tables tell a story: with candlelight at night and views through pot plants to the crashing waves, Malabar offers tasty food, including the nightly fresh seafood display, and good service.

Beatles Cafe MULTICUISINE $$

(Lighthouse Beach; mains ₹100-400; 8am-11pm;) This sweet little cafe on the promenade has been around for a long time and is a good little spot for breakfast or a burger, but the menu ranges from pizza to *momos* (Tibetan dumplings) and South Indian curries.

Curry Leaf MULTICUISINE $$

(Samudra Beach; mains ₹100-380; 8am-8.30pm) On a small hilltop overlooking Samudra Beach, this two-storey restaurant boasts enviable ocean and sunset views, eager staff and a menu ranging from fresh seafood and tandoori to Continental dishes. It requires a bit of a walk along paths or uphill from the beach, but the uncrowded location is part of the charm.

★Bait SEAFOOD $$$

(Vivanta by Taj Green Cove; mains ₹300-800; 12.30-3pm & 6-10.30pm) The seafood restaurant at the Vivanta (p951) fronts Samudra Beach, a golf-buggy ride from the hotel itself. It's designed as an upmarket alfresco beach shack, where you can watch the waves on one side and the chefs at work in the open kitchen on the other; the seafood and spicy preparations are top-notch.

Information

About 500m uphill from Lighthouse Beach are HDFC and Axis ATMs, and there are Federal Bank and ICICI ATMs at Kovalam Junction.

Tourist Facilitation Centre (0471-2480085; Kovalam Beach Rd; 9.30am-5pm Mon-Sat) This helpful office is in the main entrance to Leela hotel near the bus stand.

Upasana Hospital (0471-2480632) Has English-speaking doctors who can take care of minor injuries.

Getting There & Around

BUS

Buses start and finish at an unofficial bus stand on the main road outside the entrance to Leela hotel, and all buses pass through Kovalam Junction, about 1.5km north of Lighthouse Beach. Buses connect Kovalam and Trivandrum every

AYURVEDIC RESORTS

Between Kovalam and Poovar (16km southeast), amid seemingly endless swaying palms, laid-back village life and empty golden-sand beaches, are a string of upmarket ayurvedic resorts that are worth a look if you're serious about immersing yourself in ayurvedic treatments. They're all between 6km and 10km southeast of Kovalam. A taxi from Kovalam costs between ₹250 and ₹450.

Dr Franklin's Panchakarma Institute (0471-2480870; www.dr-franklin.com; Chowara; s/d hut €25/33, r from €30/40, with AC €45/66;) For those serious about ayurvedic treatment, this is a reputable and less expensive alternative to the flashier resorts. Daily treatment with full meal plan costs €75. Accommodation is tidy and comfortable but not resort-style.

Niraamaya Surya Samudra (8589982204, 0471-2229400; www.niraamaya.in; Pulinkudi; r incl breakfast ₹16,800-30,000;) Surya Samudra offers A-list-style seclusion. The 22 transplanted traditional Keralan homes come with four-poster beds and open-air bathrooms, set in a palm grove above sparkling seas. There's an infinity pool carved out of a single block of granite, renowned Niraamaya Spa, ayurvedic treatments, a gym and spectacular outdoor yoga platforms.

Bethsaida Hermitage (0471-2267554; www.bethsaidahermitage.com; Pulinkudi; s/d incl meals ₹1760/5500, with AC ₹4000/6050;) This charitable organisation helps support two nearby orphanages and several other worthy causes. As a bonus, it's also a luxurious and remote beachside escape, with sculpted gardens, seductively slung hammocks, putting-green-perfect lawns, palms galore and professional ayurvedic treatments and yoga classes.

WORTH A TRIP

POOVAR & KERALA'S DEEP SOUTH BACKWATERS

About 16km southeast of Kovalam, almost at the Tamil Nadu border, Poovar is the gateway to a region of beaches, estuaries, villages and upmarket resorts that comprise the 'mini backwaters' of Kerala's far south.

Numerous 'boat clubs' and operators along the Neyyar River or backwater canals will take you on 1½- to two-hour cruises through the waterways visiting the beach, bird-filled mangrove swamps and forested Poovar Island for ₹1500 to ₹2500 per boat (you can bargain down outside high season). Kovalam travel agents also arrange trips.

Poovar Island Resort (☎0471-2212068, 9895799044; www.poovarislandresorts.com; d cottage from ₹11,400, floating cottage from ₹16,800; ❄📶🏊), accessible only by boat, is popular for its romantic 'floating' cottages, though most rooms are on land, in Keralan architectural style.

Local buses head south from Kovalam Junction to Poovar, from where you'll need to take an autorickshaw to the backwaters. A taxi/autorickshaw from Kovalam to Poovar costs ₹1000/800, or hire a scooter.

20 minutes between 7am and 8pm (₹17, 30 minutes).

For northbound onward travel it's easiest to take any bus to Trivandrum and change there, although there is one bus to Varkala at 3.30pm (₹120, 2½ hours).

There are two buses at 9.30am and 5.30pm for Kanyakumari (₹100, 2½ hours).

MOTORCYCLE

K Tours & Travel (☎9847259507; per day scooters/Enfields from ₹400/600; ⏱9am-5pm), next door to Devi Garden Restaurant just above Hawa Beach, rents out scooters and Enfields.

TAXI & AUTORICKSHAW

A taxi between Trivandrum and Kovalam Beach is around ₹500; an autorickshaw should cost ₹350. From the bus stand to the north end of Lighthouse Beach costs around ₹50.

The main autorickshaw and taxi stand is at Hawa Beach.

Varkala

☎0470 / POP 42,300

Perched almost perilously along the edge of 15m-high red laterite cliffs, the North Cliff part of Varkala has a naturally beautiful setting that has steadily grown into Kerala's most popular backpacker hang-out. A small strand of beach nuzzles Varkala's cliff edge, where restaurants play innocuous world music and stalls sell T-shirts, baggy trousers and silver jewellery. It's touristy and the sales pitch can be tiring, but Varkala is still a great place to watch the days slowly turn into weeks, and it's not hard to escape the crowds further north or south where the beaches are cleaner and quieter.

Despite its backpacker vibe, Varkala is essentially a temple town, and the main Papanasham Beach is a holy place where Hindus come to make offerings for passed loved ones, assisted by priests who set up shop beneath the Hindustan Hotel. About 2km east of here is busy Varkala town.

Sights

The gently undulating path from the northern clifftop continues for a photogenic 7km to Kappil Beach, passing a subtly changing beach landscape, including Odayam Beach and the fishing village of Edava. The walk is best done early in the morning.

Janardhana Temple HINDU TEMPLE
Varkala is a temple town and Janardhana Temple is the main event – its technicolour Hindu spectacle hovers above Beach Rd. It's closed to non-Hindus, but you may be invited into the temple grounds where there is a huge banyan tree and shrines to Ayyappan, Hanuman and other Hindu deities.

Sivagiri Mutt ASHRAM
(☎0470-2602807; www.sivagirimutt.org) Sivagiri Mutt is the headquarters of the Shri Narayana Dharma Sanghom Trust, the ashram devoted to Shri Narayana Guru (1855–1928), Kerala's most prominent guru. This is a popular pilgrimage site and the resident swami is happy to talk to visitors.

Varkala Aquarium AQUARIUM
(adult/child ₹30/15, camera ₹10; ⏱10am-7pm) Varkala's new aquarium, between Black

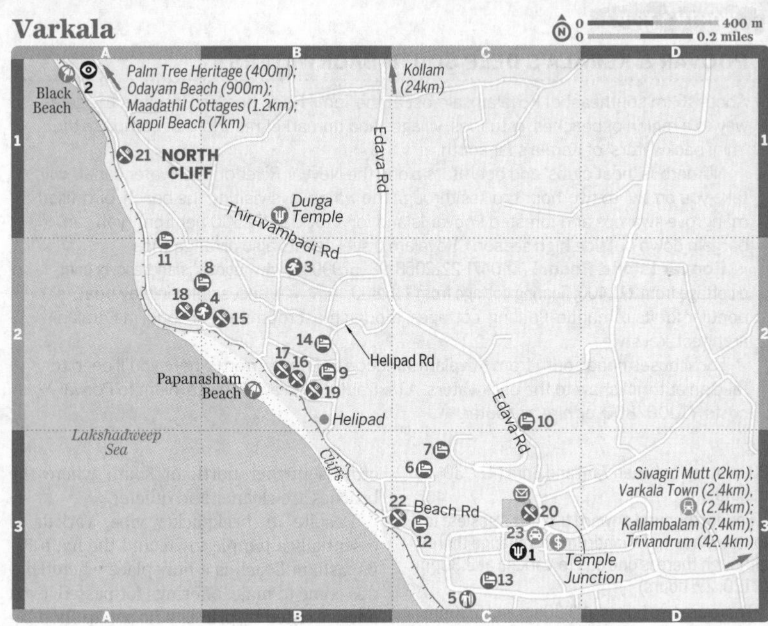

Varkala

Sights

1 Janardhana Temple C3
2 Varkala Aquarium A1

Activities, Courses & Tours

3 Can Fly B2
Cooking Class .... (see 11)
Eden Garden .... (see 6)
4 Haridas Yoga B2
5 Soul & Surf C3

Sleeping

6 Eden Garden C3
7 Gateway Hotel Janardhanapuram C3
8 InDa Hotel B2
9 Jicky's B2
10 Kaiya House C2
11 Kerala Bamboo House A2
12 Omsam Guesthouse C3
13 Villa Jacaranda C3
14 Wake Up Vedanta Varkala B2

Eating

15 Café del Mar B2
16 Coffee Temple B2
17 God's Own Country Kitchen B2
18 Juice Shack A2
19 Oottupura Vegetarian Restaurant B2
20 Sreepadman C3
21 Trattorias A1
22 Wait n Watch C3

Transport

23 Autorickshaw Stand C3

Beach and Odayam Beach, has large tanks, viewed from a spiralling walkway, that are full of exotic species including piranha, sea snakes, scorpion fish and the local karimeen. A worthwhile diversion from the beach.

Kappil Beach BEACH

About 9km north of Varkala by road, Kappil Beach is a pretty and, as yet, undeveloped stretch of sand. It's also the start of a mini network of backwaters.

Ponnumthuruthu (Golden) Island ISLAND

(boat ride 2/3/4 people ₹500/600/700, island admission per person ₹50) About 10km south of Varkala, this island in the middle of a backwater lake is home to the Shiva-Parvati Hindu temple, also known as the Golden Temple. It's closed to non-Hindus but the main reason to venture down here is the scenic punt-powered boat ride to and around the island. An autorickshaw from Varkala should cost ₹500 with waiting time.

Activities

Yoga (₹300 to ₹400 per session) is offered at several guesthouses, and boogie boards (₹100) can be hired from places along the beach; be wary of strong currents. Many of the resorts and hotels along the north cliff offer ayurvedic treatments and massage.

Eden Garden MASSAGE
(☎0470-2603910; www.edengarden.in; massages ₹1000-3000) Eden Garden offers an upmarket ayurvedic experience, including single treatments and packages.

Soul & Surf SURFING, YOGA
(☎9895580106; www.soulandsurf.com; South Cliff; surf lessons ₹2300, surf guide ₹1150, board rental half-/full day ₹850/1600; ⏰Oct-May) This UK outfit organises surfing trips and yoga retreats in season, with accommodation and a garden restaurant at its South Cliff pad. It also offers 1½-hour lessons and board rental. If you already surf and there's space, join one of the regular surf tours (₹1150).

Can Fly PARAGLIDING
(☎9048795781; canflyindia@gmail.com; 20min flight ₹3500) Tandem paragliding from the North Cliff car park, depending on the wind. The French owner also runs stand-up paddleboarding tours and a budget guesthouse, Pooja House.

Haridas Yoga YOGA
(☎9846374231; www.pranayogavidya.com; Hotel Green Palace; classes ₹300; ⏰8am & 4.30pm Aug-May) Recommended drop-in 1½-hour hatha yoga classes with experienced teachers.

Sleeping

Most places to stay are crammed along and behind the north cliff where backpackers tend to congregate, but there are some nice places down by the southern cliffs. Less-developed Odayam Beach is a tranquil alternative.

Practically all accommodation places can be reached by taxi or autorickshaw via the network of lanes leading to the cliffs, but the commission racket is alive and well – be sure your driver takes you to the place you've asked for.

★Jicky's GUESTHOUSE $
(☎9846179325, 0470-2606994; www.jickys.com; s ₹600, d ₹800-1500, AC cottage ₹2500-3000; ❄📶) In the palm groves just back from the cliffs and taxi stand, family-run Jicky's is as friendly as they come and has blossomed into several buildings offering plenty of choice for travellers. The rooms in the main whitewashed building are fresh, and nearby are two charming octagonal double cottages, and some larger air-con rooms. Good off-season discounts.

Wake Up Vedanta Varkala HOSTEL $
(☎0470-2051341; www.vedantawakeup.com; North Cliff; dm/d ₹600/1500, huts ₹1500; ❄📶) This large house on the road to the helipad has spotless six-bed air-con dorms, good-value private rooms and neat bamboo huts. It's a good deal for backpackers.

★Kaiya House GUESTHOUSE $$
(☎9746126909, 9995187913; www.kaiyahouse.com; d incl breakfast ₹2750, d with AC ₹3300; ❄📶) Not your typical Varkala address, Kaiya House has bags of charm, a warm welcome and sheer relaxation. Each of the five rooms is thoughtfully furnished and themed (African, Indian, Chinese, Japanese and English), with four-poster beds and artworks. There's a lovely rooftop terrace and expat owner Debra welcomes you with tea, advice and free walking tours. The clifftop is a 10-minute walk away.

Eden Garden RESORT $$
(☎0470-2603910; www.edengarden.in; cottages ₹1200-2000, deluxe cottages ₹5500; 📶) Stylish rooms come with high wooden ceilings and attractive furniture, set around a lush lily pond. There are also bamboo cottages and deluxe cottages organically shaped like white space mushrooms, with intricate paintwork, round beds and mosaic circular baths. All-inclusive ayurvedic packages range from three to 30 days.

InDa Hotel GUESTHOUSE $$
(☎7025029861; North Cliff; s/d incl breakfast ₹1900/2400; 📶) Tucked away behind the North Cliff restaurants, InDa Hotel is a friendly and highly regarded hotel with ruthlessly clean rooms and individual cottages in a leafy garden. A big plus is the serene cafe serving healthy snacks such as wraps and the Buddha bowl.

Kerala Bamboo House RESORT $$
(☎9895270993; www.keralabamboohouse.com; huts d ₹2000, r with AC ₹3000; ❄📶) For that simple bamboo-hut experience, this popular place squishes together dozens of pretty Balinese-style huts and a neatly maintained garden about halfway along the North Cliff walk. Ayurvedic treatments, yoga and **cooking classes** (☎9895270993; www.keralabamboohouse.com; Kerala Bamboo House; per person ₹1500; ⏰8am-8pm Nov-Mar) are on offer.

Palm Tree Heritage RESORT $$
(☎9946055036; www.palmtreeheritage.com; Odayam Beach; d from ₹3350, with AC ₹4500-8000, ste from ₹9000; ❄📶) Set in a lovely garden just steps from quiet Odayam Beach, Palm Tree Heritage is an antidote to Varkala's backpacker scene. A wide variety of rooms are neatly furnished and tables and chairs from the restaurant spill out onto the sand.

Omsam Guesthouse GUESTHOUSE $$
(☎0470-2604455; www.omsamguesthome.com; South Cliff; d ₹2500-2900, d with AC ₹4200; ❄📶) The seven rooms in this beautiful Keralan-style guesthouse are a delight, with heavy timber stylings and furniture. Good location south of the main beach.

Maadathil Cottages GUESTHOUSE $$
(☎9746113495; www.maadathilcottages.com; Odayam Beach; d incl breakfast without/with AC ₹4000/5000; ❄📶) The 10 beachfront cottages here are designed in traditional Keralan style with heritage furniture and big beds. All have sea views from the spacious balconies and some overlook a large lotus pond. Excellent location on quiet Odayam Beach.

Villa Jacaranda GUESTHOUSE $$$
(☎0470-2610296; www.villa-jacaranda.biz; Temple Rd West; d incl breakfast ₹6850-9600; ❄📶) This understated but romantic retreat back from the southern beach has just four spacious, bright rooms in a large two-storey house, each with a balcony and decorated with a chic blend of minimalist modern and period touches. The divine top-floor room has its own rooftop garden with sea views.

Gateway Hotel Janardhanapuram HOTEL $$$
(☎0470-6673300; www.thegatewayhotels.com; d incl breakfast from ₹9600; ❄@📶🏊) Varkala's flashiest hotel and part of the Taj group, the Gateway is all gleaming linen and mocha cushions in capacious rooms overlooking the garden, while the more expensive rooms have sea views and private balconies. There's a fantastic pool with bar, a tennis court and the highly regarded GAD restaurant.

✗ Eating

Most restaurants in Varkala offer a similar traveller menu of Indian, Asian and Western fare but these days some of the cliffside 'shacks' are impressive multilevel hang-outs and most offer free wi-fi and espresso coffee. Join in the nightly Varkala saunter till you find a place that suits.

Coffee Temple CAFE $
(coffee ₹80-110, mains ₹80-350; ⏰6am-8pm; 📶) For your early morning coffee fix it's hard to beat this place at the start of the North Cliff trail, where the beans are freshly ground, there's fresh bread and a daily paper. The menu also features crêpes, baguettes and Mexican burritos, fajitas and tacos.

Sreepadman SOUTH INDIAN $
(thalis ₹80; ⏰5am-10pm) For cheap and authentic Keralan fare – think dosas and thalis – in a spot where you can rub shoulders with rickshaw drivers and pilgrims rather than tourists, pull up a seat at Sreepadman, opposite the Janardhana Temple and overlooking the large bathing tank.

Juice Shack MULTICUISINE $
(juices from ₹80, mains ₹80-300; ⏰7am-11.30pm; 📶) The Juice Shack has moved into less shack-like premises (after the old one burnt down) but still turns out great health juices, smoothies and now has a full menu including good breakfast choices.

Oottupura Vegetarian Restaurant SOUTH INDIAN $
(mains ₹40-180; ⏰7am-10pm) Near the taxi stand, this budget eatery has a respectable range of cheap veg dishes, including breakfast *puttu* (flour with milk, bananas and honey) and a good thali (₹100).

God's Own Country Kitchen MULTICUISINE $$
(North Cliff; mains ₹100-500; ⏰7am-11pm; 📶) This fun place doesn't really need to play on Kerala Tourism's tagline in its name – the food is good, there's a great little upper-floor deck and there's live music some nights in season.

Trattorias MULTICUISINE $$
(meals ₹100-400; ⏰8.30am-11pm) Trattorias sounds Italian and has a decent range of pasta and pizza, but the menu is equally pan-Asian and Indian and the food consistently good. This was one of the original places here with an Italian coffee machine, and the wicker chairs and sea-facing terrace are cosy.

Café del Mar MULTICUISINE $$
(mains ₹100-420; ⏰7am-11pm; 📶) It doesn't have the big balcony of some of its neighbours, but Café del Mar is usually busy thanks to efficient service, decent coffee and consistently good food.

Wait n Watch INDIAN $$
(Hindustan Beach Retreat; mains ₹120-280; ⏰11am-10.30pm; 📶) The top-floor restaurant

AYURVEDA

With its roots in Sanskrit, the word ayurveda comes from *ayu* (life) and *veda* (knowledge); the knowledge or science of life. Principles of ayurvedic medicine were first documented in the Vedas some 2000 years ago, but may have been practised centuries earlier.

Ayurveda sees the world as having an intrinsic order and balance. It argues that we possess three *doshas* (humours): *vata* (wind or air); *pitta* (fire); and *kapha* (water/earth), known together as the *tridoshas*. Deficiency or excess in any of them can result in disease: an excess of *vata* may result in dizziness and debility; an increase in *pitta* may lead to fever, inflammation and infection. *Kapha* is essential for hydration.

Ayurvedic treatment aims to restore the balance, and hence good health, principally through two methods: panchakarma (internal purification) and herbal massage. Panchakarma is used to treat serious ailments, and is an intense detox regime, a combination of five types of different therapies to rid the body of built-up endotoxins. These include: *vaman* – therapeutic vomiting; *virechan* – purgation; *vasti* – enemas; *nasya* – elimination of toxins through the nose; and *raktamoksha* – detoxification of the blood. Before panchakarma begins, the body is first prepared over several days with a special diet, oil massages *(snehana)* and herbal steam-baths *(swedana)*. Although it may sound pretty grim, panchakarma purification might only use a few of these treatments at a time, with therapies like bloodletting and leeches only used in rare cases. Still, this is no spa holiday. The herbs used in ayurveda grow in abundance in Kerala's humid climate – the monsoon is thought to be the best time of year for treatment, when there is less dust in the air, the pores are open and the body is most receptive to treatment – and every village has its own ayurvedic pharmacy.

and bar at this ugly beachfront hotel block offers tasty-enough Indian fare and seafood, but the main reason to take the elevator is for the view from the balcony (with just a few tables) over the action of the beach. There's another alfresco restaurant by the pool.

Information

An **ATM** (24hr) at Temple Junction takes Visa cards; more ATMs and banks in Varkala town.

DANGERS & ANNOYANCES

The beaches at Varkala have strong currents; even experienced swimmers have been swept away. During the monsoon the beach all but disappears, and the cliffs themselves are slowly being eroded. Take care walking on the cliff path, especially at night – some of it is unfenced and it can be slippery in parts.

If women wear bikinis or even swimsuits on the main beach at Varkala, they are likely to feel uncomfortably exposed to stares. Wearing a sarong when out of the water will help avoid offending local sensibilities. Dress conservatively if going into Varkala town.

Getting There & Away

There are frequent local and express trains to Trivandrum (2nd class/sleeper/3AC ₹45/140/490, one hour) and Kollam (₹45/140/490, 40 minutes), as well as seven daily services to Alleppey (₹95/140/490, two hours).

Varkala is off the main highway and the main bus stand is buried in Varkala town; there are frequent buses to Trivandrum and seven daily to Kollam. If you can time it right, three daily buses pass by Temple Junction on their way to Trivandrum (₹65, 1½ to two hours), with one heading to Kollam (₹45, one hour).

If you're opting for a taxi or autorickshaw to Kollam (₹600), Trivandrum or Kovalam (both ₹1300), ask for the scenic coast road rather than the highway.

Getting Around

It's about 3km from the train station to Varkala beach, with autorickshaws going to Temple Junction for ₹80 and North Cliff for ₹100. Taxis and autorickshaws gather at the helipad at the North Cliff and at a stand near the Janardhana Temple. Local buses also travel regularly between the train station and Temple Junction (₹8).

A few places along the cliff hire out scooters/motorbikes for ₹350/450 per day.

Kollam (Quilon)

0474 / POP 349,000

Kollam (Quilon) is the southern approach to Kerala's backwaters and one end of the popular backwater ferry trip to Alleppey. One of the oldest ports in the Arabian Sea, it was once a major commercial hub that saw Roman, Arab, Chinese and later Portuguese,

Kollam (Quilon)

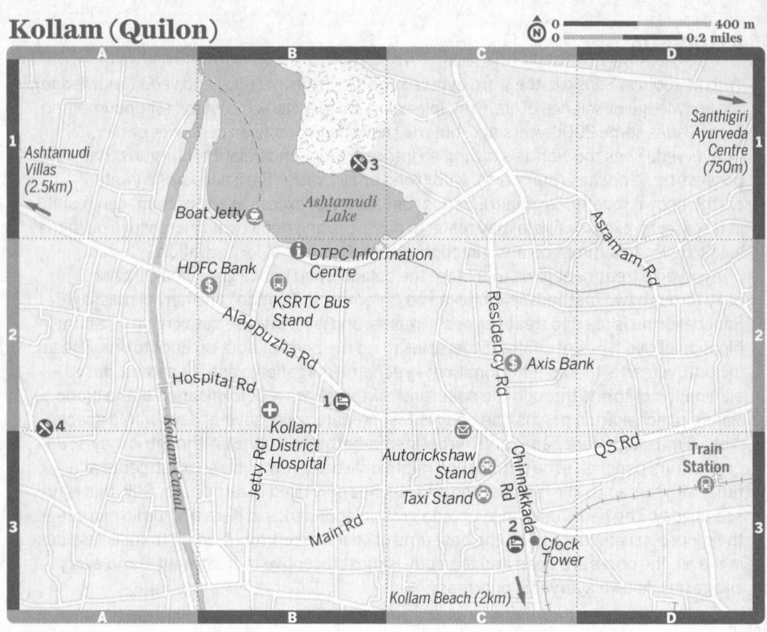

Kollam (Quilon)

Sleeping

1 Hotel Sudarsan B2
2 Nani Hotel C3

Eating

3 8 Point Art Cafe B1
Prasadam .... (see 2)
4 Wok & Grill A2

Dutch and British traders jostle into port – eager to get their hands on spices and the region's cashew crops. The centre of town is reasonably hectic, but surrounding it are the calm waterways of Ashtamudi Lake, fringed with coconut palms, cashew plantations and traditional villages – a great place to get a feel for the backwaters without the crowds.

Sights

There's a rowdy fish market and harbour north of **Kollam Beach** where customers and fisherfolk alike pontificate on the value of the day's catch. Kollam's beach is 2km south of town but there are better stretches of sand further south at Eravipuram and Mayyanad. The northern end of the harbour is marked by the **Thangassery Lighthouse** (₹10, lift Indian/foreigner ₹20/50; ⏲10am-1pm & 2-6pm Tue-Sun).

Activities

★ **Munroe Island Cruise** BOATING

(www.dtpckollam.com; tours per person ₹500; ⏲9am-1.30pm & 2-6.30pm) Excellent tours through the canals of Munroe Island are organised by the DTPC (p959) and a number of private operators, including Ashtamudi Villas and Munroe Island Backwaters Homestay. The trip begins about 15km north of Kollam, where you take a leisurely three-hour punted canoe ride through a network of canals.

On the canals you can observe daily village life, see *kettuvallam* (rice barge) construction, toddy (palm beer) tapping, coir-making, prawn and fish farming, and do some birdwatching on spice-garden visits.

Houseboat Cruises BOATING

(www.dtpckollam.com; overnight cruise ₹9200, Kollam-Alleppey cruise ₹20,000-28,000) Kollam has far fewer houseboats than Alleppey, which can mean a less touristy experience. The DTPC organises various houseboat cruise packages, along with two private operators with offices at the jetty who also offers trips from Kollam to Alleppey.

Santhigiri Ayurveda Centre AYURVEDA

(☎9287242407, 0474-2763014; www.santhigiriashram.com; Asramam Rd, Kadappakada; massage from ₹1200) An ayurvedic centre with more of an institutional than a spa vibe, popular for its seven- to 21-day treatment packages.

Festivals & Events

The Kollam region hosts many festivals and boat regattas – from November to March there are temple festivals somewhere in the region virtually every day.

Kottamkulangara Chamaya Vilakku RELIGIOUS
(Mar/Apr) An unusual festival event in Chavara, 15km north of Kollam, where local men dress as women and carry lamps to the temple.

Kollam Pooram CULTURAL
(Asraman Shri Krishna Swami Temple, Kollam; Apr) A 10-day festival with full-night Kathakali performances and a procession of 40 ornamented elephants.

President's Trophy Boat Race SPORTS
(1 Nov) Held on Ashtamudi Lake, this is the most prestigious boat regatta in the Kollam region.

Sleeping

Munroe Island Backwaters Homestay HOMESTAY $
(9048176186; Chittamula Rd, Munroe Island; d incl breakfast ₹1200;) The three colourful cottages built in Keralan style and hidden away in the backwaters of Munroe Island north of Kollam are popular with travellers wanting to immerse themselves in the village experience. Vijeesh and his friendly family also run backwater canoe tours (₹450 per person).

Hotel Sudarsan BUSINESS HOTEL $
(0474-2744322; www.hotelsudarsan.com; Hospital Rd; d ₹950, with AC from ₹1900, ste ₹3500;) Sudarsan is well located near the boat jetty and surprisingly good value. Rooms are arranged around a central courtyard with the Kedar Restaurant and Golden Tavern beer parlour on-site. The suite rooms are particularly spacious.

★ Ashtamudi Villas GUESTHOUSE $$
(9847132449, 0474-2706090; www.ashtamudivillas.com; near Kadavoor Church, Mathilil; d/f ₹1500/2500;) These charming lakeside cottages are easily the best choice for a relaxing, affordable stay in Kollam. Host Prabhath Joseph offers a warm welcome, with thoughtful architectural design, colourful decor, gleaming bathrooms, hammocks swinging between palm trees by the lake and a library of books on Kerala. Free kayaks are available, and canoe tours of Munroe Island can be organised from here.

Access is by road or boat – call ahead for directions.

Nani Hotel HOTEL $$
(0474-2751141; www.hotelnani.com; Chinnakkada Rd; d incl breakfast ₹1460, with AC ₹2250-3650, ste ₹7800; @) This boutique business hotel is a good-value surprise in Kollam's chaotic centre. Built by a cashew magnate, its beautifully designed architecture mixes traditional Keralan elements and modern lines for a sleek look. Even the cheaper rooms have flat-screen TVs, feathery pillows and sumptuous bathrooms.

Eating

★ 8 Point Art Cafe CAFE $
(0474-2970256; mains ₹70-190; 11.30am-9pm) On the fun side of Ashtamudi Lake, this excellent cafe in a restored heritage building is part local art gallery, part trendy hang-out, with changing free exhibitions, good coffee, soups, pasta and a small library.

Wok & Grill ASIAN $$
(0474-2753400; High School Junction Rd; mains ₹185-290; noon-10.30pm) The combination of Indian, Chinese, Thai, Arabic and Chettinad cuisines offers some tasty, meaty dishes at this modern, clean restaurant. Choose from *kung pao* chicken, green curry, ginger garlic prawns and shawarma rolls.

Prasadam MULTICUISINE $$
(0474-2751141; Chinnakkada Rd, Nani Hotel; mains ₹160-280, lunch thali ₹160; noon-2.30pm & 7-10pm) The restaurant at the Nani Hotel has a slightly formal feel with high-backed chairs amid intricate copper-relief artwork depicting Kollam history. Meals, including Keralan dishes, tandoori and Chinese, are well prepared, and the tasty thalis are good value at lunchtime.

Information

DTPC Information Centre (0474-2745625; www.dtpckollam.com; 8am-7pm) Helpful and can organise backwater trips and yoga classes; opposite the KSRTC bus stand near the boat jetty.

Getting There & Away

BOAT

Many travellers take the government canal boat to or from Alleppey (₹400, eight hours,

10.30am); it's not necessary to book, but be at the ferry dock by 9.30am. From the main boat jetty there are frequent public ferry services across Ashtamudi Lake to Guhanandapuram (one hour). Fares are around ₹10 return, or ₹3 for a short hop.

BUS

Kollam is on the Trivandrum–Kollam–Alleppey–Ernakulam bus route, with buses departing every 10 or 20 minutes to Trivandrum (₹84, two hours), Alleppey (₹80, 2½ hours) and Ernakulam (Kochi, standard/AC ₹122/225, 3½ hours). There's a 5am bus to Kumily (₹125, five hours) and a handful of local buses to Varkala (₹40, 30 minutes), though the train is a better option for Varkala.

Buses depart from the **KSRTC bus stand** (☎0474-2752008), conveniently near the boat jetty.

TRAIN

There are frequent express trains to Ernakulam (sleeper/3AC ₹140/490, three hours, 20 daily) via Alleppey (₹140/490, 1½ hours) and Trivandrum (₹140/490, 1½ hours, 21 daily) via Varkala (₹140/490, 30 minutes).

Around Kollam

Krishnapuram Palace Museum MUSEUM
(☎0479-2441133; ₹10, camera/video ₹25/250; ⏲9.30am-4.30pm Tue-Sun) Two kilometres south of Kayamkulam (between Kollam and Alleppey), this restored palace is a fine example of grand Keralan architecture. Inside are paintings, antique furniture, sculptures and a renowned 3m-high mural depicting the Gajendra Moksha (the liberation of Gajendra, chief of the elephants) as told in the Mahabharata.

Buses (₹27, one hour) leave Kollam every few minutes for Kayamkulam. Get off at the bus stand near the temple gate, 2km before the palace.

Alappuzha (Alleppey)

☎0477 / POP 74,200

Alappuzha – most still call it Alleppey – is the hub of Kerala's backwaters, home to a vast network of waterways and more than a thousand houseboats. Wandering around the small but chaotic city centre and bus-stand area, with its modest grid of canals, you'd be hard-pressed to agree with the 'Venice of the East' tag. But head west to the beach or in practically any other direction towards the backwaters and Alleppey becomes graceful and greenery-fringed, disappearing into a watery world of villages, punted canoes, toddy shops and, of course, houseboats. Float along and gaze over paddy fields of succulent green, curvaceous rice barges and village life along

MATHA AMRITHANANDAMAYI MISSION

The incongruously pink **Matha Amrithanandamayi Mission** (☎0476-2897578; www.amritapuri.org; Amrithapuri) is the famous ashram of one of India's few female gurus, Amrithanandamayi, also known as Amma (Mother) or 'The Hugging Mother' because of the *darshan* (audience) she offers, often hugging thousands of people in marathon all-night sessions. The ashram runs official tours at 4pm and 5pm daily – check the website or download the Amma app for details.

It's a huge complex, with about 3500 people living here permanently – monks, nuns, students and families, both Indian and foreign. It offers food, ayurvedic treatments, and a daily schedule of yoga, meditation and *darshan*. Amma travels around for much of the year, so you might be out of luck if in need of a cuddle (check her schedule online). A busy time of year at the ashram is around Amma's birthday on 27 September.

Visitors should dress conservatively and there is a strict code of behaviour. With prior arrangement – register online – you can stay at the ashram in a triple room for ₹250 per person, ₹500 for a single (including simple vegetarian meals).

Since the ashram is on the main canal between Kollam and Alleppey, many travellers break the ferry ride by getting off here, staying a day or two, then picking up another cruise. Alternatively, cross to the other side of the canal and grab a rickshaw 10km south to Karunagappally or 12km north to Kayankulam (around ₹200), from where you can catch onward buses or trains.

If you're not taking the cruise, catch a train to either Karunagappally or Kayankulam and take an autorickshaw (around ₹200) to Vallickavu and cross the pedestrian bridge from there. If you intend to stay a while, you can book online for an ashram taxi – they pick up from as far away as Kochi or Trivandrum.

the banks. This is one of Kerala's most mesmerisingly beautiful and relaxing experiences.

Sights

Alleppey Beach BEACH

Alleppey's main beach is about 2km west of the city centre; there's no shelter at the beach itself and swimming is fraught due to strong currents, but the sunsets are good and there are a few places to stop for a drink or snack, including a good coffeeshop. The beach stretches up and down the coast.

Alleppey Lighthouse LIGHTHOUSE

(Indian/foreigner ₹10/25, camera/video ₹20/25; ⏲9-11.45am & 2-5.30pm Tue-Sun) The candy-striped lighthouse is a few blocks back from the beach. There's a small museum containing an original oil lamp and you can climb to the top via the spiralling staircase for 360-degree views of a surprisingly green Alleppey.

RKK Memorial Museum MUSEUM

(☎0477-2242923; www.rkkmuseum.com; NH47, near Powerhouse Bridge; Indian/foreigner ₹150/350; ⏲9am-5pm Tue-Sun) The Revi Karuna Karan (RKK) Memorial Museum, in a grand building fronted by Greco-Roman columns, contains a lavish collection of crystal, porcelain, Keralan antiques, furniture, artworks and (sadly) ivory from the personal collection of wealthy businessman Revi Karuna Karan. The museum was created as a memorial after he passed away in 2003.

Activities

Kerala Kayaking KAYAKING

(☎9846585674, 8547487701; www.keralakayaking.com; per person 4/7/10hr ₹1500/3000/4500) The original and best kayaking outfit in Alleppey. The young crew here offer excellent guided kayaking trips through narrow backwater canals. Paddles in single or double kayaks include a support boat and motorboat transport to your starting point. There are four-hour morning and afternoon trips, seven- or 10-hour day trips, and multiday village tours can also be arranged.

Houseboat Dock BOATING

(dtpcaly@yahoo.com; ⏲prepaid counter 10am-5pm) Where dozens of houseboats gather; this is a good place to wander down and compare a few. There's a government-run prepaid counter where you can see the 'official' posted prices, starting at ₹7000 for two people, up to ₹24,000 for a five-berth boat. Even these prices fluctuate depending on demand.

Shree Krishna Ayurveda Panchkarma Centre AYURVEDA

(☎9847119060; www.krishnayurveda.com; 3-/5-/7-day treatments from €275/420/590) For ayurvedic treatments; one-hour rejuvenation massages are ₹1200, but it specialises in three-, five- and seven-night packages with accommodation and yoga classes. Rates are cheaper with two people sharing accommodation. It's near the Nehru boat race finishing point.

Tours

Any guesthouse, hotel, travel agent or the DTPC can and will arrange canoe or houseboat tours of the backwaters.

Kashmiri-style *shikaras* (covered boats) gather along the North Canal on the road to the houseboat dock. They charge ₹300 to ₹400 per hour for motorised canal and backwater trips. Punt-powered dugout canoes are slower but more ecofriendly. They charge from ₹250 per hour and most tours require four to five hours, with village visits, walks and a visit to a toddy bar.

It can be hard to get a good seat for the Nehru Trophy Boat Race, but for the best seat in the house check out Johnson's Houseboat at www.alleppeysnakeboatrace.com.

Festivals & Events

Nehru Trophy Boat Race SPORTS

(www.nehrutrophy.nic.in; tickets ₹50-2000; ⏲Aug) This is the most renowned and fiercely contested of Kerala's boat-race regattas. Thousands of people, many aboard houseboats, gather around the starting and finishing points on Alleppey's Punnamada Lake to watch snake boats with up to 100 rowers battle it out.

Sleeping

Even if you're not planning on boarding a houseboat, Alleppey has some of Kerala's most charming and best-value accommodation, from heritage homes and resorts to family-run homestays with backwater views.

The rickshaw-commission racketeers are at work here, particularly at the train and bus stations; ask to be dropped off at a landmark close to your destination, or if you're booked in, call ahead to say you're on the way – some places will pick you up.

Matthews Residency GUESTHOUSE $

(☎9447667888, 0477-2235938; www.palmyresidency.com; off Finishing Point Rd; r ₹450-800; @🛜) One of the better budget deals in

Alappuzha (Alleppey)

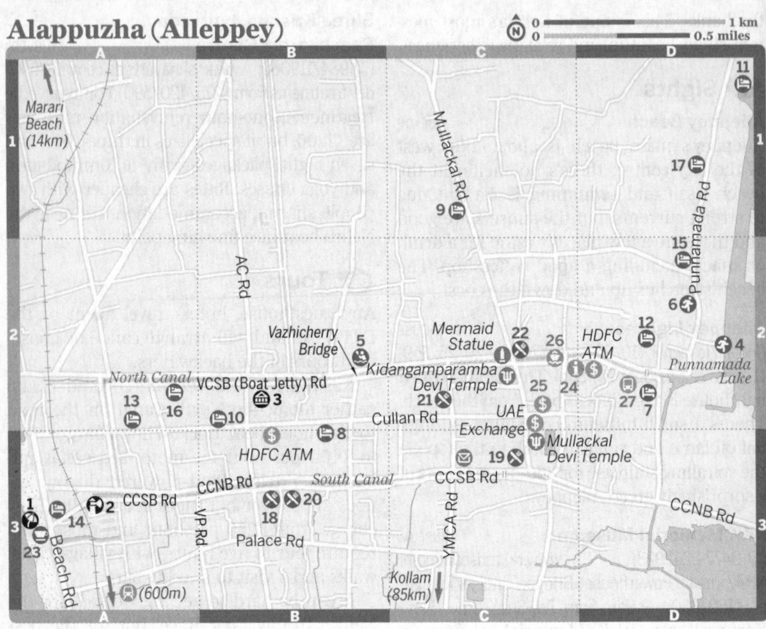

Alappuzha (Alleppey)

Sights
1 Alleppey Beach ... A3
2 Alleppey Lighthouse ... A3
3 RKK Memorial Museum ... B2

Activities, Courses & Tours
4 Houseboat Dock ... D2
5 Kerala Kayaking ... B2
6 Shree Krishna Ayurveda Panchkarma Centre ... D2

Sleeping
7 Cherukara Nest ... D2
8 Dream Nest ... B3
9 Gowri Residence ... C1
10 Johnson's ... B2
11 Malayalam ... D1
12 Matthews Residency ... D2
13 Nanni Backpackers Hostel ... A2
14 Raheem Residency ... A3
15 Sona Heritage Home ... D2
16 Tharavad ... A2
17 Vedanta Wake Up! ... D1

Eating
Chakara Restaurant ... (see 14)
18 Halais ... B3
Harbour Restaurant ... (see 14)
19 Kream Korner Art Cafe ... C3
20 Mushroom ... B3
21 Royale Park Hotel ... C2
22 Thaff ... C2

Drinking & Nightlife
23 Le Coffee Time ... A3

Information
24 DTPC Tourist Reception Centre ... C2
Federal Bank ATM ... (see 21)
25 SBI Bank ... C2
Tourist Police ... (see 24)

Transport
26 Boat Jetty ... C2
27 KSRTC Bus Stand ... D2
Nanni Tours & Travel ... (see 13)

Alleppey, this place has six spotless rooms with Italian marble floors, three with garden-facing verandahs. It's north of the canal, five minutes' walk from the bus stand but set well back from the road amid lush greenery.

Johnson's GUESTHOUSE $
(9846466399, 0477-2245825; www.johnsonskerala.com; d ₹800-1200, with AC ₹1850;) This longtime backpacker favourite in a quirky two-storey home is run by the gregarious Johnson Gilbert. It's a rambling res

idence with themed rooms filled with funky furniture, hanging chairs, outdoor bathtubs and a garden with open-air barbecue and pet horse. Johnson also has an excellent 'eco-houseboat' (www.ecohouseboat.com; ₹8000 to ₹13,000) – book ahead for a spot at the Nehru boat race.

Nanni Backpackers Hostel HOSTEL $
(☎9895039767; www.nannitours.com; Cullan Rd; dm/d ₹250/700) A very good deal, this easy-going backpacker place is a short walk from the beach and 1.5km north of the train station. There are two six-bed dorms and some spacious private rooms upstairs, along with a street cafe and a rooftop lounge. Young owner Shibu is a good source of local information and scooter hire, and works hard at making the place homely.

Vedanta Wake Up! HOSTEL $
(☎0477-2231132; www.vedantawakeup.com; Punnamada Rd; dm ₹400, d with AC from ₹1400; ❄📶) In a quiet location just north of the houseboat dock, this hostel has clean air-con dorms, cosy common areas, a cafe and the usual extras like lockers and wi-fi. It's a good place to meet other travellers, especially if you're looking to get a houseboat group together.

Dream Nest GUESTHOUSE $
(☎9895860716; www.thedreamnest.com; Cullan Rd; d ₹500-900, with AC ₹1200; ❄📶) The colourful rooms set back from the road are a good deal at this budget guesthouse. There's a social communal lounge and a youthful traveller vibe.

Cherukara Nest HOMESTAY $$
(☎0477-2251509, 9947059628; www.cherukaranest.com; d/tr incl breakfast ₹900/1200, with AC ₹1500, AC cottage ₹1500; ❄@📶) Set in well-tended gardens, this lovely heritage home has the sort of welcoming family atmosphere that makes you want to stay. In the main house there are four large characterful rooms, with high ceilings, lots of polished wood touches and antediluvian doors with ornate locks. Owner Tony also has a good-value houseboat (two/four people ₹6000/8500) and organises village tours (₹900).

Tharavad HOMESTAY $$
(☎0477-242044; www.tharavadheritageresort.com; west of North Police Station; d ₹2500-3500; ❄📶) In a quiet canalside location between the town centre and beach, this charming ancestral home has lots of glossy teak and antiques, shuttered windows, five characterful rooms and well-maintained gardens.

Malayalam RESORT $$
(☎9496829424, 0477-2234591; malayalamresorts@yahoo.com; Punnamada; r ₹1500-2500; 📶) This little family-run pad has bamboo cottages and a pair of spacious two-storey four-room houses facing the lake near the Nehru Trophy Boat Race starting point. Views from the upstairs rooms with balcony are sweet. It's a bit hard to find: walk past the Keraleeyam resort reception and along the canal bank.

Canoe Ville COTTAGE $$
(☎9895213162; http://canoeville.com; d cottage incl meals ₹3500) This quirky lakefront place 5km north of Alleppey has created artificial canals and floating mini houseboat cottages for a 'houseboat on land' experience. The comfortable double cottages have attached bath, large verandah and come with meals, free hammocks and activities such as bamboo rafting. There are plans to add budget safari tents (per person ₹500).

Punnamada Homestay HOMESTAY $$
(☎0484-2371761, 9847044688; d incl breakfast & dinner ₹3000; 📶) This attractive heritage-style family home is north of Alleppey in a peaceful location close to Punnamada Lake. The two rooms are neat, well-furnished, and have private balconies, and the home cooking is first-rate.

Sona Heritage Home GUESTHOUSE $$
(☎0477-2235211; www.sonahome.com; Lakeside, Finishing Point; r ₹900, with AC ₹1400; ❄📶) Run by the affable Joseph, this beautiful old heritage home has high-ceilinged rooms with faded flowered curtains, Christian motifs and four-poster beds overlooking a well-kept garden.

Gowri Residence GUESTHOUSE $$
(☎0477-2236371, 9847055371; www.gowriresidence.com; Mullackall Rd; d ₹600-1200, AC cottages ₹1500-2000; ❄📶) This rambling complex about 800m north of the North Canal has an array of rooms and cottages in a large garden: traditional wood-panelled rooms in the main house, and several types of bungalows made from stone, wood, bamboo or thatch – the best have cathedral ceilings, air-con and flat-screen TVs. Overall the place is looking a little faded.

★Raheem Residency HOTEL $$$
(☎0477-2239767; www.raheemresidency.com; Beach Rd; d ₹9600-12,500; ❄📶🏊) This thoughtfully renovated beachside 1860s heritage home is a

BOATING KERALA'S BACKWATERS

The undisputed highlight of a trip to Kerala is travelling through the 900km network of waterways that fringe the coast and trickle inland. Long before the advent of roads, these waters were the slippery highways of Kerala, and many villagers still use paddle-power as their main form of transport. Trips through the backwaters traverse palm-fringed lakes studded with cantilevered Chinese fishing nets, and wind their way along narrow, shady canals where coir (coconut fibre), copra (dried coconut kernels) and cashews are loaded onto boats. Along the way are isolated villages where farming life continues as it has for eons.

Tourist Cruises

The popular tourist cruise between Kollam and Alleppey (₹400) departs from either end at 10.30am, arriving at 6.30pm, daily from July to March and every second day at other times, though it may start running later in the season. Generally, there's a 1pm lunch stop and a brief afternoon chai stop. Bring drinks, snacks, sunscreen, a hat and a good book.

It's a scenic and leisurely way – the journey takes eight hours – to get between the two towns, but the boat travels along only the major canals – you won't have many close-up views of the village life that makes the backwaters so magical. Another option is to take the trip halfway (₹200) and get off at the Matha Amrithanandamayi Mission (p960).

Houseboats

If the stars align, renting a houseboat designed like a *kettuvallam* (rice barge) could well be one of the highlights of your trip to India. It can be an expensive experience (depending on your budget) but for a couple on a romantic overnight jaunt or split between a group of travellers, it's usually worth every rupee. Drifting through quiet canals lined with coconut palms, eating delicious Keralan food, meeting local villagers and sleeping on the water – it's a world away from the usual clamour of India.

Houseboats cater for couples (one or two double bedrooms) and groups (up to seven bedrooms!). Food (and an onboard chef to cook it) is generally included in the quoted cost, as is a driver/captain. Houseboats can be chartered through a multitude of private operators in Alleppey, Kollam and Kottayam. This is the biggest business in Kerala and the quality of boats varies widely, from ageing boats to floating palaces – try to inspect the boat before agreeing on a price. Travel-agency reps will be pushing you to book a boat as soon as you set foot in Kerala, but it's better to wait till you reach a backwater hub: choice is greater in Alleppey (an extraordinary 1000-plus boats), and you're much more likely to be able to bargain down a price if you turn up and see what's on offer. Most guesthouses and homestays can also book you on a houseboat.

joy. The 10 rooms have been restored to their former glory by owner and Irish personality Bibi Baskin and have bathtubs, antique furniture and period fixtures. The common areas include pretty indoor courtyards, a great pool and an excellent restaurant.

Eating & Drinking

★Mushroom ARABIAN, INDIAN $
(CCSB Rd; mains ₹70-150; noon-midnight) A breezy open-air restaurant with wrought-iron chairs, specialising in cheap, tasty and spicy halal meals like chicken *kali mirch*, fish tandoori and chilli mushrooms. Lots of locals and travellers give it a good vibe.

Kream Korner Art Cafe MULTICUISINE $
(0477-2260005; www.kreamkornerartcafe.com; Mullackal Rd; dishes ₹40-160; 9am-10pm) The most colourful dining space in town, this food-meets-art restaurant greets you with brightly painted tables and contemporary local art on the walls. It's a relaxed, airy place popular with Indian and foreign families for its inexpensive and tasty menu of Indian and Chinese dishes.

Thaff INDIAN $
(VCNB Rd; meals ₹45-120; 9am-9pm Sun-Thu, 9am-10pm Sat & Sun) This popular restaurant serves tasty South Indian bites, with some North Indian and Chinese flavours mixed in. It does succulent roast spit-chicken, biryanis and brain-freezing ice-cream shakes.

Halais INDIAN, ARABIAN $$
(9447053338; www.halaisrestaurant.com; mains ₹70-400, biryani from ₹170; 24hr) Famous for its chicken and mutton biryanis, Halais

In the busy high season or during domestic holidays (such as Pooja, Onam or Diwali) when prices peak, you're likely to get caught in backwater-gridlock – some travellers are disappointed by the number of boats on the water. It's possible to travel by houseboat between Alleppey and Kollam and part way to Kochi – though these trips spend more time on open lakes and large canals than true backwaters and take longer than most travellers expect. Expect a boat for two people for 24 hours to cost about ₹6000 to ₹8000 at the budget level; for four people ₹10,000 to ₹12,000; for larger boats or for air-conditioning expect to pay ₹15,000 to ₹30,000. Shop around to negotiate a bargain – though this will be harder in the peak season. Prices triple from around 20 December to 5 January.

Village Tours & Canoe Boats

Village tours are an excellent way to see the backwaters at a slow pace by day. Village tours usually involve small groups of five to six people, a knowledgable guide and an open canoe or covered *kettuvallam*. The tours (from Kochi, Kollam or Alleppey) last 2½ to six hours and cost around ₹400 to ₹1000 per person. They include visits to villages to watch coir-making, boat building, toddy (palm beer) tapping and fish farming. The Munroe Island trip from Kollam is an excellent tour of this type; the Tourist Desk (p981) in Kochi also organises recommended tours.

Public Ferries

If you want the local backwater transport experience for just a few rupees, there are State Water Transport (www.swtd.gov.in) boats between Alleppey and Kottayam (₹15, 2½ hours) five times daily starting from Alleppey at 7.30am. The trip crosses Vembanad Lake and has a more varied landscape than the Kollam–Alleppey cruise. Other ageing boats operate from the boat jetty at Alleppey, ferrying locals around to backwater villages.

Environmental Issues

Pollution from houseboat motors is becoming a major problem as boat numbers increase. The Keralan authorities have introduced an ecofriendly and safety accreditation system for houseboat operators. Among the criteria an operator must meet before being issued with the Gold Star, Silver Star or Green Palm certificate are the installation of solar panels and sanitary tanks for the disposal of waste – ask operators whether they have the requisite certification. Consider choosing one of the few remaining punting, rather than motorised, boats if possible, though these can only operate in shallow water.

packs them in at this clean restaurant behind the street-front sweet shop. It's also popular for Arabian and Yemeni dishes.

Harbour Restaurant MULTICUISINE **$$**
(☎0484-2230767; Beach Rd; meals ₹110-300; ⏰10am-10pm) This enjoyable beachside place is run by the nearby Raheem Residency. It's more casual and budget-conscious than the hotel's restaurant, but promises a range of well-prepared Indian, Chinese and Continental dishes, and the coldest beer in town.

Royale Park Hotel INDIAN **$$**
(YMCA Rd; meals ₹130-310; ⏰7am-10.30pm, bar from 10am; 📶) There's an extensive menu at this air-con hotel restaurant, and the food, including veg and fish thalis, is consistently good. You can order from the same menu in the surprisingly nice upstairs beer parlour and wash down your meal with a cold Kingfisher.

★Chakara Restaurant MULTICUISINE **$$$**
(☎0477-2230767; Beach Rd; mini Kerala meal ₹500, mains from ₹450; ⏰12.30-3pm & 7-10pm) The restaurant at Raheem Residency is Alleppey's finest, with seating on a bijou open rooftop, reached via a spiral staircase, with views over to the beach. The menu creatively combines traditional Keralan and European cuisine, specialising in locally caught fish.

Le Coffee Time CAFE
(Alleppey Beach; coffee & snacks ₹70-150; ⏰8am-9pm; 📶) A friendly beachfront place with a genuine Italian espresso machine, some shady tables, good breakfasts and free wi-fi.

WORTH A TRIP

GREEN PALM HOMES

Around 12km from Alleppey on a backwater island, **Green Palm Homes** (9495557675, 0477-2724497; www.greenpalmhomes.com; Chennamkary; r incl full board ₹3500-5000;) is a series of homestays in a picturesque village, where you sleep in simple rooms in villagers' homes among rice paddies (though 'premium' rooms with attached bathroom and air-con are available). There are no roads but you can take a guided walk, hire bicycles or canoes and take cooking classes.

To get here, call ahead and catch one of the hourly ferries from Alleppey to Chennamkary (₹10, 1¼ hours).

Information

DTPC Tourist Reception Centre (0477-2253308; www.dtpcalappuzha.com; Boat Jetty Rd; 9am-5pm) Close to the bus stand and boat jetty. Staff can advise on local tours.

Tourist Police (0477-2251161; 24hr) Next door to the DTPC Tourist Reception Centre.

Getting There & Away

BOAT

Ferries run to Kottayam (₹15) and daily at 10am to Kollam (₹400) from the boat jetty on VCSB (Boat Jetty) Rd.

BUS

From the KSRTC bus stand, frequent buses head to Trivandrum (₹132, 3½ hours, every 20 minutes), Kollam (₹73, 2½ hours) and Ernakulam (Kochi; ₹55, 1½ hours). Buses to Kottayam (₹40, 1¼ hours, every 30 minutes) are much faster than the ferry. Three buses leave for Kumily at 6.40am, 1.10pm and 2.50pm (₹126, 5½ hours) and Munnar at 4.30am, 7am and 2pm (₹132, five hours). The Varkala bus (₹90, 3½ hours) leaves daily at 8.15am, 8.45am and 10.40am.

TRAIN

There are numerous daily trains to Ernakulam (2nd class/sleeper/3AC ₹50/140/490, 1½ hours) and Trivandrum (₹80/140/490, three hours) via Kollam (₹60/140/490, 1½ hours). Six trains a day stop at Varkala (2nd class/AC chair ₹65/260, two hours). The train station is 4km southwest of town.

Getting Around

An autorickshaw from the train station to the boat jetty and KSRTC bus stand is around ₹60.

Several guesthouses around town hire out scooters for ₹300 per day, or try the reliable **Nanni Tours & Travel** (9895039767; Cullan Rd).

Around Alleppey

Kattoor & Marari Beaches

The beaches at Kattoor and Marari, 10km and 14km north of Alleppey respectively, are popular beachside alternatives to the backwaters.

Marari is the flashier of the two, with some exclusive five-star beachfront accommodation, while Kattoor, sometimes known as 'Secret Beach', is more of a fishing village, where development is at a minimum and sandy back lanes lead down to near-deserted sands.

Sleeping

★ **Secret Beach Yoga Homestay** HOMESTAY $
(9447786931; www.secretbeach.in; Kattoor Beach; d ₹1000-1500;) The location is sublime at this three-room homestay, with a small lagoon separating the property from a near-deserted piece of Kattoor Beach; get here by floating mat or walking through the village. Home-cooked meals are available and the talented and welcoming young owner Vimal is an accredited yoga and *kalari* instructor; yoga lessons and free bikes available.

A Beach Symphony COTTAGE $$$
(9744297123; www.abeachsymphony.com; cottages ₹14,000-17,900; Sep-May;) With just four individually designed cottages at the main beach entrance, this is one of Marari's most exclusive beachfront resorts. The Keralan-style cottages are plush and private – Violin Cottage even has its own plunge pool in a private garden.

Kottayam

0481 / POP 335,000

Between the backwaters and the Western Ghats, Kottayam is renowned for being the centre of Kerala's spice and rubber trade, rather than for its aesthetic appeal. For most travellers it's a hub town, well connected to both the mountains and the backwaters, with many travellers taking the public canal cruise to or from Alleppey before heading east to Kumily or north to Kochi. The city itself has an unappealing, crazy, traffic-clogged centre.

Sleeping

There's enough accommodation in Kottayam to justify a stay if you're coming off the Alleppey ferry, but there are better lakeside stays (at a price) at Kumarakom.

Ambassador Hotel HOTEL $
(0481-2563293; ambassadorhotelktm@yahoo.in; KK Rd; s/d from ₹550/950, d with AC from ₹1100;) This old-school place is one of the better budget hotels in the town centre. Rooms with TV are spartan but fairly clean, spacious and quiet for this price. It has a bar, an adequate restaurant and a boat-shaped fish tank in the lobby.

Windsor Castle & Lake Village Resort HOTEL $$
(0481-2363637; www.thewindsorcastle.net; MC Rd; s/d from ₹3300/3850, Lake Village cottages ₹6600;) This grandiose white box has some of Kottayam's best hotel rooms, but the more impressive accommodation is in the Lake Village behind the hotel. Deluxe cottages, strewn around the private backwaters and manicured gardens, are top-notch. There's a pleasant restaurant overlooking landscaped waterways.

Eating

Thali SOUTH INDIAN $
(KK Rd; meals ₹40-175; 8am-8pm) A lovely, spotlessly kept 1st-floor dining room with slatted blinds, Thali is a swankier version of the typical Keralan set-meal place. The food here is great, including Malabar fish curry and thalis.

Meenachil MULTICUISINE $
(KK Rd; dishes ₹60-180; noon-3pm & 6-9.30pm) A favourite place in Kottayam to fill up on Indian and Chinese fare. There's a friendly, family atmosphere, the dining room is modern and tidy, and the menu expansive.

★ **Nalekattu** SOUTH INDIAN $$$
(MC Rd, Windsor Hotel; dishes ₹200-550; noon-3pm & 7-10pm) This traditional Keralan restaurant at the Windsor Castle overlooks some picturesque backwaters and serves tasty Keralan specialities like *chemeen* (prawn curry). Buffet deals are offered on weekends.

Information

DTPC office (0481-2560479; www.dtpckottayam.com; 10am-5pm Mon-Sat) At the boat jetty; has local information and can arrange pricey backwater cruises. Private operators nearby charge around ₹4000 for a full-day cruise to Alleppey.

Getting There & Away

BOAT

Daily ferries run to Alleppey from the boat jetty (₹15) five times a day.

BUS

The KSRTC bus stand has buses to Trivandrum (₹127, four hours, every 20 minutes), Alleppey (₹37, 1¼ hours, hourly), Ernakulam (Kochi; ₹60, two hours, every 20 minutes), Kumily for Periyar Wildlife Sanctuary (₹97, four hours, every 30 minutes) and Munnar (₹130, five hours, five daily). There are also frequent buses to nearby Kumarakom (₹9, 30 minutes, every 15 minutes) and to Kollam (₹85, three hours, four daily), where you can change for Varkala.

TRAIN

Kottayam is well served by frequent trains running between Trivandrum (2nd class/sleeper/3AC ₹80/140/490, 3½ hours) and Ernakulam (₹50/140/490, 1½ hours).

Getting Around

The KSRTC bus stand is 1km south of the centre, with the boat jetty a further 2km (at Kodimatha). An autorickshaw from the jetty to the KSRTC bus stand is around ₹50, and from the bus stand to the train station about ₹40.

Around Kottayam

Kumarakom

0481

Kumarakom, 16km west of Kottayam and on the shore of vast Vembanad Lake – Kerala's largest lake – is an unhurried backwater village with a smattering of dazzling top-end sleeping options and a renowned bird sanctuary. You can arrange houseboats through Kumarakom's less-crowded canals, but expect to pay considerably more than in Alleppey.

Arundhati Roy, author of the 1997 Booker Prize–winning *The God of Small Things*, was raised in the nearby Aymanam village.

Sights

Kumarakom Bird Sanctuary NATURE RESERVE
(0481-2525864; Indian/foreigner ₹50/150; 6am-5pm) This reserve on the 5-hectare site of a former rubber plantation on Lake Vembanad is the haunt of a variety of domestic and migratory birds. October to February is the time for travelling birds like the garganey

teal, osprey, marsh harrier and steppey eagle; May to July is the breeding season for local species such as the Indian shag, pond herons, egrets and darters. A guide costs ₹300 for a two-hour tour (₹400 from 6am to 8am).

Sleeping

Cruise 'N Lake RESORT $$
(☎9846036375, 0481-2525804; www.homestaykumarakom.com; Puthenpura Tourist Enclave, Cheerpunkal; d ₹1500, with AC ₹2000;) Location, location. Surrounded by backwaters on one side and a lawn of rice paddies on the other, this is the affordable Kumarakom getaway. The rooms in two separate buildings are plain but all have verandahs facing the water. Go a couple of kilometres past the sanctuary to Cheerpunkal and take a left; it's then 2km down a rugged dirt road.

Tharavadu Heritage Home GUESTHOUSE $$
(☎0481-2525230; www.tharavaduheritage.com; d from ₹1200, with AC ₹2000-2200, bamboo cottage ₹1100; @) Rooms here are either in the superbly restored 1870s teak family mansion or in equally comfortable individual creekside bamboo cottages. All are excellently crafted and come with arty touches. It's 4km before Kumarakom Bird Sanctuary.

Getting There & Away

Kumarakom is an easy bus ride from Kottayam (₹15, 30 minutes, every 15 minutes).

Sree Vallabha Temple

Devotees make offerings at **Sree Vallabha Temple**, 2km from Tiruvilla, in the form of regular, traditional all-night Kathakali performances that are open to all. Around 10km east of here, the **Aranmula Boat Race** (near Shri Parthasarathy Temple; Aug/Sep), one of Kerala's biggest snake-boat races, is held during Onam in August/September.

OFF THE BEATEN TRACK

SABARIMALA

Deep in the Western Ghats, about 20km west of Gavi and some 50km from the town of Erumeli, is a place called Sabarimala, home to the Ayyappan temple. It's said to be one of the world's most visited pilgrimage centres, with anywhere between 40 and 60 million Hindu devotees trekking here each year. Followers believe the god Ayyappan meditated at this spot. Non-Hindus can join the pilgrimage but strict rules apply, and women aged 12 to 50 are only allowed as far as the Pampa checkpoint. For information see www.sabarimala.kerala.gov.in or www.sabarimala.org.

THE WESTERN GHATS

Periyar Wildlife Sanctuary

☎04869 / POP KUMILY 30,300

South India's most popular wildlife sanctuary, **Periyar** (☎04869-224571; www.periyartigerreserve.org; Indian/foreigner adult ₹33/450, child ₹5/150, camera/video ₹38/300; 6am-6pm, last entry 5pm), also called Thekkady, encompasses 777 sq km and a 26-sq-km artificial lake created by the British in 1895. The vast region is home to bison, sambar, wild boar, langur, 900 to 1000 elephants and 35 to 40 hard-to-spot tigers. It's firmly established on both the Indian and foreigner tourist trails and has a typical boat cruise that doesn't scream 'wildlife experience', but if you dig deeper and do a trek led by a tribal villager, the hills and jungle scenery make for a rewarding visit. Bring warm and waterproof clothing.

Kumily is the closest town and home to a growing strip of hotels, homestays, spice shops, chocolate shops and Kashmiri emporiums. Thekkady, 4km from Kumily, is the sanctuary centre with the KTDC hotels and boat jetty. Confusingly, when people refer to the sanctuary they tend to use Thekkady, Kumily and Periyar interchangeably.

Sights & Activities

Various tours and trips access Periyar Wildlife Sanctuary, all arranged through the Ecotourism Centre. Most hotels and homestays around town can arrange three-hour jeep **jungle safaris** (per jeep ₹1800), which cover around 40km of trails and viewpoints in jungle bordering the park, though many travellers complain that at least 30km of the trip is on sealed roads.

Connemara Tea Factory FACTORY
(☎04869-252233; Vandiperiyar; tours ₹150; tours hourly 9am-4pm) About 13km from Kumily, this 77-year-old working tea factory and plantation offers guided tours of the tea-making process and tea garden, and ends with some tea tastings. Regular buses

from Kumily pass by the entrance; ask to be let off at the tea factory or Vandiperiyar.

Ecotourism Centre OUTDOORS
(☎8547603066, 04869-224571; www.periyartiger reserve.org; Thekkady Rd; ⊙9am-1pm & 2-5pm) The Forest Department's Ecotourism Centre runs all tours within the park. These include border hikes (₹1000 per person), 2½-hour nature walks (from ₹800), bamboo rafting (₹1500) and night 'jungle scouts' (₹750), accompanied by trained tribal guides. Rates are per person and trips usually require a minimum of four.

There are also overnight 'tiger trail' treks (per person ₹4000), covering 20km to 30km, which are run by former poachers retrained as guides.

Periyar Lake Cruise BOATING
(₹225; ⊙departures 7.30am, 9.30am, 11.15am, 1.45pm & 3.30pm) These 1½-hour boat trips around the lake are the main way to tour the sanctuary without taking a guided walk. You might see deer, boar, otters and birdlife but it's generally more of a cruise than a wildlife-spotting experience. Boats are operated by the KTDC – you need to buy a ticket from the main building above the boat jetty before boarding the boat.

In high season get to the ticket office 1½ hours before each trip to buy tickets. The first and last departures offer the best prospects for wildlife spotting, and October to March is generally the best time to see animals.

Santhigiri Ayurveda AYURVEDA
(☎8113018007, 04869-223979; www.santhigiri ashram.org; Munnar Rd, Vandanmedu Junction; ⊙9am-8pm) An authentic place for an ayurvedic experience, offering top-notch massage (₹900 to ₹1800) and long-term treatments lasting seven to 14 days.

Cooking Classes

Cooking classes are offered by many local homestays for around ₹400 to ₹600. There are recommended two-hour classes at **Bar-B-Que** (☎9895613036; KK Rd; ₹500; ⊙6.30pm), about 1km from the bazaar on the road to Kottayam.

Spice Plantations

Several spice plantations are open to visitors and most hotels can arrange tours (₹450/750 by autorickshaw/taxi for two to three hours).

Abraham's Spice Garden FARM
(☎04869-222919; www.abrahamspice.com; Spring Valley; tours ₹100; ⊙7.30am-5.30pm) Abraham's Spice Garden, 3km from Kumily, is a family-run farm that's been operating for more than 50 years. Informative one-hour tours here take you through the spice gardens.

Spice Walk TOURS
(☎04869-222449; www.spicewalk.com; Churakulam Coffee Estate; 1hr tour ₹150; ⊙9am-5pm) Part of Churakulam Coffee Estate, Spice Walk is a 44-hectare plantation surrounding a small lake. Informative walks take around one hour and include explanations of coffee and cardamom processing, but there's also fishing and boating and a small cafe at the front. It's 2km from Kumily.

Sleeping

Inside the Park

The KTDC runs three steeply priced hotels in the park: Periyar House, Aranya Nivas and the grand Lake Palace. Note that there's effectively a curfew at these places – guests are not permitted to roam the sanctuary after 6pm.

The Ecotourism Centre can arrange tented accommodation inside the park at the **Jungle Camp** (d incl meals ₹6000). Another option is **Bamboo Grove** (d incl breakfast ₹1500), a group of basic cottages and tree houses not far from Kumily town.

Lake Palace HOTEL $$$
(☎04869-223887; www.lakepalacethekkady.com; r incl all meals ₹24,000-30,000) There's a faint whiff of royalty at this restored old summer palace, located on Periyar Lake and accessible only by boat. The six charismatic rooms are decorated with flair and antique furnishings. Staying in the sanctuary gives you a good chance of seeing wildlife from your private terrace, and rates include meals, boat trip and trekking.

Kumily

Mickey Homestay GUESTHOUSE $
(☎9447284160, 04869-223196; www.mickey homestay.com; Bypass Rd; r & cottages ₹750-1000; 📶) Mickey is a genuine homestay with just a handful of intimate rooms in a family house and a rear cottage, all with homely touches that make them some of the cosiest in town. Balconies have rattan furniture and hanging bamboo seats and the whole place is surrounded by greenery.

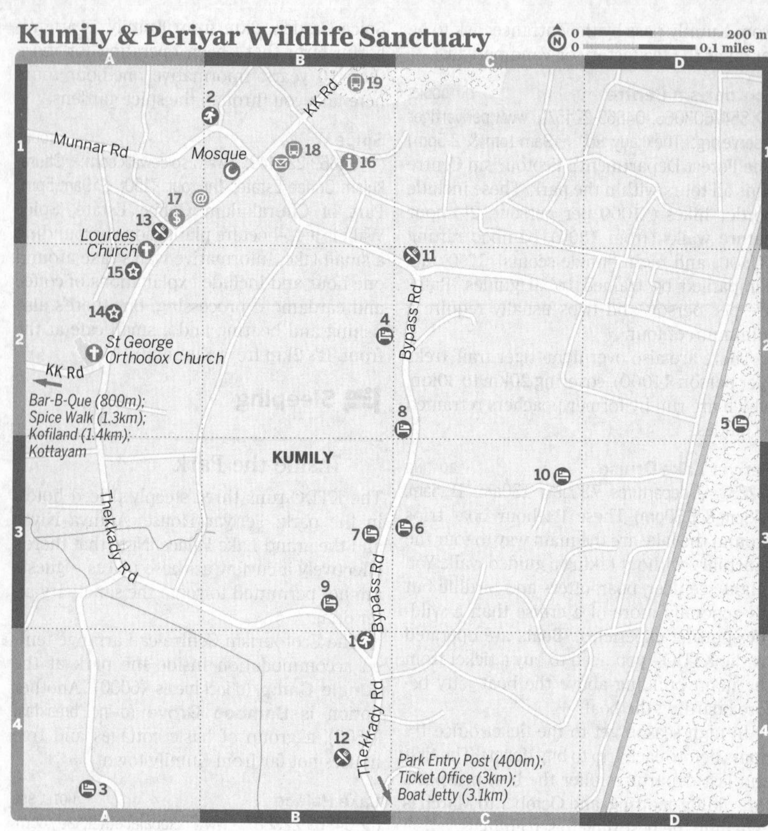

Kumily & Periyar Wildlife Sanctuary

Activities, Courses & Tours
1 Ecotourism Centre B4
Jungle Safaris .... (see 18)
2 Santhigiri Ayurveda B1

Sleeping
3 Bamboo Grove A4
4 Chrissie's Hotel B2
5 Claus Garden D2
6 El-Paradiso C3
7 Green View Homestay B3
8 Mickey Homestay C2
9 Spice Village B3
10 Tranquilou C3

Eating
Chrissie's Cafe .... (see 4)
11 Ebony's Cafe C2
12 French Restaurant & Bakery B4
13 Shri Krishna A1

Entertainment
14 Kadathanadan Kalari & Navarasa Kathakali Centre A2
15 Mudra Cultural Centre A2

Information
16 DTPC Office B1
Ecotourism Centre .... (see 1)
17 Federal Bank ATM A1

Transport
18 Kumily Bus Stand B1
19 Tamil Nadu Bus Stand B1

Tranquilou HOMESTAY $
(☎04869-223269; off Bypass Rd; r incl breakfast ₹600-1200; 📶) One of Kumily's friendly, family homestays, Tranquilou is in a peaceful location with seven neatly furnished rooms surrounding a pleasant garden; the two dou-

bles that adjoin a shared sitting room are a good family option.

★Green View Homestay HOMESTAY $$
(☎9447432008, 04869-224617; www.sureshgreenview.com; Bypass Rd; r incl breakfast ₹500-1750;) It's grown from its humble homestay origins but Greenview is a lovely place that manages to retain its personal and friendly family welcome from owners Suresh and Sulekha. The two buildings house several classes of well-maintained rooms with private balconies – the best are the upper-floor rooms overlooking a lovely rear spice garden. They also have excellent vegetarian meals and cooking lessons (veg/nonveg ₹450/600).

Claus Garden HOMESTAY $$
(☎04869-222320, 9567862421; www.homestay.in; Thekkumkadu; d/tr/f ₹1600/1800/2000;) Set well away from the hustle and bustle and up a steep hill with good views, this German-run place has gently curving balconies, spotless rooms and a rooftop overlooking a lush green garden. The 'family room' comprises two adjoining rooms sharing a bathroom. Organic breakfast with fresh-baked bread is available for ₹300.

El-Paradiso HOMESTAY $$
(☎04869-222350, 9447431950; www.goelparadiso.com; Bypass Rd; d ₹1500-2500; @) This immaculate family homestay has fresh rooms that have balconies and hanging chairs, or open onto a terrace overlooking greenery at the back. Cooking classes (₹500) are a speciality here.

Chrissie's Hotel GUESTHOUSE $$
(☎9447601304, 04869-224155; www.chrissies.in; Bypass Rd; s/d/f from ₹2200/2400/3900;) This four-storey building behind the popular restaurant of the same name somehow manages to blend in with the forest-green surrounds. The chic rooms are spacious and bright, with cheery furnishings, lamps and colourful pillows. Yoga classes are offered and a rooftop pool was being installed when we visited. Wi-fi in the lobby only.

Spice Village HOTEL $$$
(☎0484-3011711; www.cghearth.com; Thekkady Rd; villas ₹18,400-30,900;) This CGH Earth place takes its green credentials very seriously and has captivating, spacious cottages that are smart yet cosily rustic, in pristinely kept grounds. Its restaurant does lavish lunch and dinner buffets, there's a colonial-style bar and the Wildlife Interpretation Centre has a resident naturalist. Better value out of high season when rates halve.

Eating

There are a few good cheap veg restaurants in Kumily's busy bazaar area, and some decent traveller-oriented restaurants on the road to the wildlife sanctuary. Most homestays offer home-cooked meals on request.

Shri Krishna INDIAN $
(KK Rd; meals ₹70-140; noon-2pm & 6-10pm) A local favourite in the bazaar, serving up spicy pure-veg meals including several takes on the lunchtime thali.

Chrissie's Cafe MULTICUISINE $$
(www.chrissies.in; Bypass Rd; meals ₹120-350; 8am-9pm) A perennially popular traveller haunt, this 1st-floor rooftop cafe is clean and airy and satisfies with cakes and snacks, excellent coffee, well-prepared Western faves like pizza and pasta, and even a Middle Eastern meze platter or falafel.

Ebony's Cafe MULTICUISINE $$
(Bypass Rd; meals ₹120-275; 8am-10.30pm) This long-standing breezy rooftop joint has lots of pot plants and traveller-friendly tunes, while the menu serves up a simple assortment of Indian and Western food from mashed potato to basic pasta dishes and cold beer.

French Restaurant & Bakery CAFE, BAKERY $$
(☎9961213107; meals ₹100-300; 8am-9pm) This family-run shack set back from the main road is a good spot for breakfast or lunch, mainly for the fluffy tuna or cheese baguettes baked on-site, but also for pasta, pizza and noodle dishes.

Kofiland MULTICUISINE $$$
(www.kofiland.in; mains ₹210-650; 8am-9pm) For a dining splurge, head to the cavernous *palapa*-style restaurant at the new Kofiland Resort on the outskirts of town. Overlooking the pool and lagoon through floor-to-ceiling glass windows, it has a vast menu of North and South Indian dishes with an emphasis on Keralan cuisine.

☆ Entertainment

Mudra Cultural Centre LIVE PERFORMANCE
(☎9061263381; www.mudraculturalcentre.com; Lake Rd; entry ₹200, video ₹200; Kathakali 5pm & 7pm, kalarippayat 6pm & 7.15pm) Kathakali shows at this cultural centre are highly entertaining.

OFF THE BEATEN TRACK

PARAMBIKULAM TIGER RESERVE

Possibly the most protected environment in South India – nestled behind three dams in a valley surrounded by Keralan and Tamil Nadu sanctuaries – **Parambikulam** (9442201690; www.parambikulam.org; Indian/foreigner ₹10/150, camera/video ₹25/150; 7am-6pm, last entry 4pm) constitutes 285 sq km of Kipling-storybook scenery and wildlife-spotting goodness. Far less touristed than Periyar, it's home to elephants, bison, gaur, sloths, sambar, crocodiles, tigers, panthers and some of Asia's largest teak trees. The sanctuary is best avoided during monsoon (June to August) and sometimes closes in March and April.

Contact the sanctuary office in Anappady to arrange tours of the park's buffer zones, including treks from ₹500 per person, bamboo rafting (₹8800 for 10 people) and jungle safaris (₹8000 for 10 people). Park accommodation includes treetop huts (₹2750 to ₹3300) or niche tents (from ₹5500), inclusive of some activities. Entry to the reserve is via Pollachi (40km from Coimbatore and 49km from Palakkad) in Tamil Nadu. There are two buses in either direction between Pollachi and Parambikulam via Annamalai daily (₹20, 1½ hours). A taxi costs around ₹2400.

Make-up and costume starts 30 minutes before each show; use of still cameras is free and welcome. Arrive early for a good seat. There also two *kalarippayat* performances nightly.

Kadathanadan Kalari & Navarasa Kathakali Centre LIVE PERFORMANCE
(9961740868; www.kalaripayattu.co.in; Thekkady Rd; ₹200; kalarippayat 6-7pm, Kathakali 7-8pm) Hour-long demonstrations of the exciting Keralan martial art of *kalarippayat,* as well as Kathakali, are staged here every evening. Tickets are available from the box office throughout the day.

Information

DTPC Office (04869-222620; 10am-5pm Mon-Sat) Uphill behind the main bus stand; you can pick up a map and have a chat but that's about it.

Ecotourism Centre (8547603066, 04869-224571; www.periyartigerreserve.org; 6.30am-1pm & 2-8.30pm) For park tours, information and guided walks.

Getting There & Away

Kumily's **bus stand** is at the northeastern edge of town. Eleven buses daily operate between Ernakulam (Kochi) and Kumily (₹150, five hours). Buses leave every 30 minutes for Kottayam (₹87, four hours), with three direct buses to Trivandrum (₹190, eight hours) and two to Alleppey (₹130, 5½ hours). Private buses to Munnar (₹100, four to five hours) also leave from this bus stand.

Tamil Nadu buses leave every 30 minutes to Madurai (₹100, four hours) from the **Tamil Nadu bus stand** just over the border.

Getting Around

It's only about 1.5km from **Kumily bus stand** (p972) to the main park entrance, but it's another 3km from there to Periyar Lake; an autorickshaw from the entry post is around ₹70, or set off on foot – but bear in mind there's no path so you'll have to walk on the road. Autorickshaws will take you on short hops around town for ₹30.

Kumily town is small enough to explore on foot but some guesthouses rent out bicycles (₹200) and most can arrange scooter hire (₹500) if you want to explore further afield.

Munnar

04865 / POP 68,200 / ELEV 1524M

The rolling hills around Munnar, South India's largest tea-growing region, are carpeted in emerald-green tea plantations, contoured, clipped and sculpted like ornamental hedges. The low mountain scenery is magnificent – you're often up above the clouds watching veils of mist clinging to the mountaintops. Munnar town itself is a scruffy, traffic-clogged administration centre, not unlike a North Indian hill station, but wander just a few kilometres out of town and you'll be engulfed in a sea of a thousand shades of green.

Once known as the High Range of Travancore, today Munnar is the commercial centre of some of the world's highest tea-growing estates. The majority of the plantations are operated by corporate giant Tata, with some in the hands of local cooperative Kannan Devan Hills Plantation Company (KDHP).

Sights & Activities

The main reason most travellers visit Munnar is to explore the lush, tea-filled hillocks that surround it. Hotels, homestays, travel agencies, autorickshaw drivers and practically every passerby will want to organise a day of sightseeing for you: shop around, though rates are fairly standard.

Tea Museum MUSEUM
(04865-230561; adult/child ₹125/40, camera ₹20; 9am-7pm Tue-Sun) About 1.5km northwest of town, this museum is a demo model of a working tea factory, but it still shows the basic process. A collection of old bits and pieces from the colonial era, including photographs and a 1905 tea-roller, are also kept here. The walk to or from town follows the busy road with views of tea plantations; an autorickshaw charges ₹25 from the bazaar.

★ **Nimi's Lip Smacking Classes** COOKING
(9745513373, 9447330773; www.nimisrecipes.com; ₹2000; 3pm Mon-Fri, 2pm Sat & Sun) Nimi Sunilkumar has earned a solid reputation for Keralan cooking, publishing her own cookbooks, website and blog, and offers popular daily hands-on cooking classes in her home (next to Munnar's DTPC). You'll learn traditional Keralan recipes and the class includes a copy of her book *Lip Smacking Dishes of Kerala*.

Trekking

The best way to experience the hills is on a guided trek, which can range from a half-day 'soft trekking' around tea plantations (from ₹600 per person) to more arduous full-day mountain treks (from ₹800), which open up some stupendous views when the mist clears. Trekking guides can easily be organised through your accommodation, or ask at the DTPC Tourist Information Office (p976).

Bear in mind that the tea plantations are private property and trekking around without a licensed guide is trespassing.

Tours

The DTPC (p976) runs three fairly rushed but inexpensive full-day tours to points around Munnar. The **Sandal Valley Tour** (per person ₹400; tour 9am-6pm) visits Chinnar Wildlife Sanctuary, several viewpoints, waterfalls, plantations, a sandalwood forest and villages. The **Tea Valley tour** (per person ₹400; tour 10am-6pm) visits Echo Point, Top Station and Rajamalai (for Eravikulam National Park), among other places. The **Village Sightseeing Tour** (₹400; 9.30am-6pm) covers Devikulam, Anayirankal Dam, Ponmudy and a farm tour, among others. You can hire a taxi to visit the main local sights for around ₹1100 to ₹1500.

Sleeping

Munnar has plenty of accommodation but it seems a shame to stay in Munnar town when the views and peace are out in the hills and valleys. There are some good budget options just south of the town centre; if you really want to feel the serenity and are willing to pay a bit more, head for the hills.

Around Town

JJ Cottage HOMESTAY $
(9447228599, 04865-230104; jjcottagemnr@gmail.com; d ₹350-800;) The sweet family at this little purple place 2km south of town

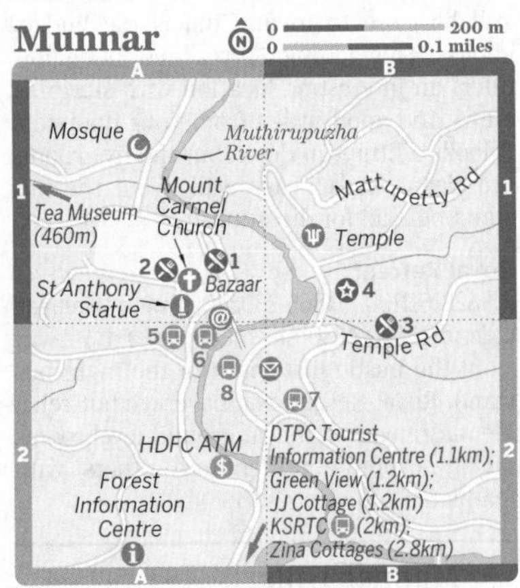

Munnar

Eating
1 Rapsy Restaurant A1
2 Saravana Bhavan A1
3 Sree Mahaveer Bhojanalaya B2

Entertainment
4 Thirumeny Cultural Centre B1

Transport
Autorickshaw Stand .... (see 8)
5 Buses to Coimbatore A2
6 Buses to Ernakulam & Trivandrum A2
7 Buses to Kumily & Madurai B2
8 Buses to Top Station A2

(easy walking distance from the main bus stand) offers a varied and uncomplicated set of clean, bright, great-value rooms with TV and hot water. The one deluxe room on the top floor has a separate sitting room and sweeping views.

Green View GUESTHOUSE $
(☎9447825447, 04865-230940; www.greenviewmunnar.com; d ₹600-850; @☎) This tidy guesthouse has 10 fresh budget rooms, a friendly welcome and reliable tours and treks. The best rooms are on the upper floor and there's a super rooftop garden where you can sample 15 kinds of tea. Young owner Deepak organises trekking trips (www.munnartrekking.com) and also runs **Green Woods Anachal** (☎04865-230189; Anachal; d incl breakfast ₹900; ☎).

Zina Cottages GUESTHOUSE $
(☎04865-230349; r ₹900-1200; ☎) If you want to be immersed in lush tea plantations but still be close to town, Zina is the budget choice. This fading 50-year-old bungalow offers an interesting location with stunning views and good walks from your doorstep; it looks a little run down but the five rooms are clean. It's an easy walk from the bus stand but call for directions.

Royal Retreat HOTEL $$
(☎8281611100, 04865-230240; www.royalretreat.co.in; d ₹3030-4230, ste ₹4830; ❄@☎) Away from the bustle just south of the main bus stand, Royal Retreat is an average but reliable midranger with neat ground-level rooms facing a pretty garden and others with tea-plantation views.

Munnar Hills

★Green Valley Vista GUESTHOUSE $$
(☎9447432008, 04865-263261; www.greenvalleyvista.com; Chithirapuram; d incl breakfast ₹2200-3850; ☎) The valley views are superb, accommodation top-notch and the welcome warm. Rooms on three levels all face the valley and have private balconies with dreamy greenery views, as well as flat-screen TVs and modern bathrooms. Staff can organise trekking, jeep safaris and tours to the wild elephant village. It's 11km south of Munnar on the back road to Kochi.

★Rose Gardens HOMESTAY $$
(☎9447378524, 04864-278243; www.munnarhomestays.com; NH49 Rd, Karadipara; r incl breakfast ₹5000; @☎) This is a true family homestay in a peaceful spot overlooking owner Tomy's idyllic plant nursery and organic mini spice and fruit plantation. The five rooms are large and immaculate with balconies overlooking the valley, and the family is charming. Cooking lessons are free, and include fresh coconut pancakes for breakfast and delicately spiced Keralan dishes for dinner.

Its handy location is on the main road to Kochi, around 10km south of Munnar and with good bus connections.

Aranyaka RESORT $$
(☎9443133722, 04865-230023; www.aranyakaresorts.com; Pallivasal Tea Estate; cottages ₹4800-6000; ☎) These neat modern cottages set in a landscaped garden have fine views over the Pallivasal Tea Estate, one of Tata's largest tea holdings. The valley setting, with views of waterfalls and the Muthirappuzhayar River, feels remote but is only 8km from Munnar town.

Anna Homestay HOMESTAY $$
(☎8156980088; www.annahomestay.com; d incl breakfast ₹2800, with AC ₹5000; ❄☎) Near Anachal village, Anna Homestay is a welcoming family home with nine very tidy rooms and spacious rooftop common areas. The best are the corner rooms with balconies and there are a couple of large air-con rooms.

British County GUESTHOUSE $$
(☎0484-2371761; http://touristdesk.in/britishcounty.htm; d incl meals ₹3500) Around 11km southeast of Munnar, this appealing little guesthouse has four fresh rooms with balconies facing a stunning valley panorama. Steps lead down to the valley for treks. Rates include meals and the owners offer packages from Kochi.

Windermere Estate RESORT $$$
(☎04865-230512; www.windermeremunnar.com; Pothamedu; d incl breakfast ₹10,100-12,200; ❄@☎) Windermere is a charming boutique-meets-country-retreat and cardamom plantation 4km southeast of Munnar. There are supremely spacious garden- and valley-view rooms, but the best are the suite-like 'Plantation Villas', surrounded by 26 hectares of cardamom and coffee plantations, with spectacular views. There's a cosy library above the country-style restaurant.

Bracknell Forest GUESTHOUSE $$$
(☎9446951963; www.bracknell.in; Bison Valley Rd, Ottamaram; r incl breakfast ₹5000-6000; @☎)

WORTH A TRIP

THATTEKKAD BIRD SANCTUARY

Thattekkad Bird Sanctuary (9048355288; Indian/foreigner ₹35/175, camera/video ₹38/225; 6.30am-5.30pm) is a serene 25-sq-km park in the foothills of the Western Ghats and home to over 320 fluttering species, which are unusually mostly forest, rather than water birds, and include Malabar grey hornbills, Ripley owls, jungle nightjars, grey drongos, darters and rarer species like the Sri Lankan frogmouth. Also here are kingfishers, flycatchers, warblers, sunbirds and tiny 4g flowerpeckers. Boating on the river (₹250 per person) can be organised at the park office; accommodation places offer guided birdwatching trips.

Park accommodation includes the **Frogmouth Watchtower** (Thattekkad Bird Sanctuary; d ₹2500) and **Hornbill View Tower** (Thattekkad Bird Sanctuary; per person ₹1000). Better budget options are **Jungle Bird Homestay** (0485-2588143, 9947506188; www.junglebirdhomestay.blogspot.com.au; per person incl meals ₹1300;) or **Bird Song Homestay** (d incl meals ₹2500, with AC ₹3250;), both inside the main park boundary.

For more luxury, visit the lovely **Soma Birds Lagoon** (0471-2268101, 8113876665; www.somabirdslagoon.com; Palamatton; s/d incl breakfast €60/70, with AC from €75/90;). Set deep in the villages near Thattekkad, this low-key ecoresort lies on a seasonal lake among spacious and manicured grounds. The basic rooms here are roomy and the whole place feels refreshingly remote although it's just 16km from Kothamangalam.

The tented **Hornbill Camp** (0484-2092280; www.thehornbillcamp.com; d incl full board US$100) has accommodation in large permanent tents and a sublimely peaceful location facing the Periyar River. Kayaking, cycling, a spice-garden tour and all meals are included. It's about 8km from Thattekkad by road.

Thattekkad is on the Ernakulam–Munnar road. Take a bus from Ernakulam (₹35, two hours) or Munnar (₹60, three hours) to Kothamangalam, from where a Thattekkad bus travels the final 12km (₹12, 25 minutes), or catch an autorickshaw (₹300).

The 11 neat rooms here have balconies and views of a lush valley and cardamom plantation. It's surrounded by deep forest on all sides. The small restaurant has wraparound views. A transfer from Munnar costs around ₹400 but call ahead for directions. It's 9.5km southeast of Munnar.

Eating

Early morning food stalls in the bazaar serve breakfast snacks and cheap meals, but some of the best food is served up at the homestays and resorts.

★ Rapsy Restaurant INDIAN $
(Bazaar; dishes ₹50-150; 7am-10pm) This spotless glass-fronted sanctuary from the bazaar is packed at lunchtime, with locals lining up for Rapsy's famous *paratha* (Indian-style flaky bread) or biryani. It also makes a decent stab at fancy international dishes like Spanish omelette and Israeli *shakshuka* (eggs with tomatoes and spices).

Saravana Bhavan SOUTH INDIAN $
(mains ₹25-110; 7am-9.30pm) Branch of the popular South Indian pure-veg chain serving all the *idlis* and dosas you could want.

Taste the Brews CAFE $
(drinks ₹30-50; 8am-noon & 3-8pm) A cool cafe near the bus stand for Continental-style breakfasts and tastings of local tea and coffee.

Sree Mahaveer Bhojanalaya NORTH INDIAN $$
(Mattupetty Rd; thalis ₹130-220; 7.30am-9.30pm) This pure-veg restaurant in SN Annex Hotel is madly popular with families for its great range of thalis: take your pick from Rajasthani, Gujarati, Punjabi and more, plus a dazzling array of veg dishes.

Entertainment

Punarjani Traditional Village LIVE PERFORMANCE
(04865-216161; www.punarjanimunnar.org; 2nd Mile, Pallivasal; ₹200-300; shows 5pm & 6pm) Touristy but entertaining daily performances of Kathakali (5pm) and *kalarippayat* (6pm). Arrive at 4pm if you want to see the ritual Kathakali make-up session. Tickets are available on the day but for the best seats consider bookings a day in advance. It's about 8km south of Munnar town.

Thirumeny Cultural Centre LIVE PERFORMANCE
(9447827696; Temple Rd; shows ₹300; Kathakali shows 5-6pm & 7-8pm, kalarippayat 6-7pm &

WORTH A TRIP

CHINNAR WILDLIFE SANCTUARY

About 60km northeast of Munnar, **Chinnar Wildlife Sanctuary** (www.chinnar.org; entry with 3hr trek Indian/foreigner ₹230/600; ⌚8am-5pm) protects deer, leopards, elephants and the endangered grizzled giant squirrel. Trekking and **tree house** (d ₹2600) or **hut** (d ₹2600-3100) accommodation within the sanctuary are available, as well as ecotour programs like river-trekking, cultural visits (two tribal groups inhabit the sanctuary) and waterfall treks (around ₹600 per person). For details contact the Forest Information Centre (p976) in Munnar. Buses from Munnar can drop you off at Chinnar (₹40, 1½ hours), or a taxi costs around ₹1500.

8-9pm) On the road behind the Eastend hotel, this small theatre stages one-hour Kathakali shows and *kalarippayat* martial arts demonstrations twice nightly.

Information

DTPC Tourist Information Office (☎04865-231516; www.dtpcidukki.com; Munnar Rd; ⌚8.30am-7pm) Marginally helpful; operates a number of tours and can arrange trekking guides.

Forest Information Centre (☎8301024187; ⌚9am-3pm) Advance bookings for Chinnar Wildlife Sanctuary and information on Chinnar and Eravikulam National Park.

Getting There & Away

Roads around Munnar are winding and often in poor condition following monsoon rains, so bus times may vary. The main **KSRTC bus station** (AM Rd) is south of town, but it's easier to catch buses from stands in Munnar town (where more frequent private buses also depart). The main stand is in the bazaar.

There are around 18 daily **buses** to Ernakulam (Kochi; ₹124, 5½ hours), six buses to Trivandrum (ordinary/deluxe ₹251/371, nine hours) and two to Alleppey (₹168/226, five hours). **Private buses** go to Kumily (₹80, four hours) at 11.25am, 12.20pm and 2.25pm. There are separate stands for buses to **Top Station** and **Coimbatore**.

A taxi to Ernakulam costs around ₹2800; to Alleppey is ₹3800 and to Kumily ₹2400.

Getting Around

Gokulam Bike Hire (☎9447237165; per day ₹400-500; ⌚9am-6pm), in the former bus stand south of town, has motorbikes and scooters for hire. Call ahead.

Autorickshaws ply the hills around Munnar with bone-shuddering efficiency; they charge up to ₹850 for a day's sightseeing.

Around Munnar

Top Station

High above Kerala's border with Tamil Nadu, Top Station (elevation 1880m) is popular for its spectacular views over the Western Ghats. From Munnar, four daily buses (₹40, 1½ hours, from 7.30am) make the steep 32km climb in around an hour, or you could book a return taxi (₹1200). You may see wild elephants on the way up.

Eravikulam National Park

Eravikulam National Park NATIONAL PARK
(☎04865-208255; www.eravikulam.org; Indian/foreigner ₹95/360, camera/video ₹38/300; ⌚7.30am-4pm Apr-Jan) This park, 13km from Munnar, is home to the endangered, but almost tame, Nilgiri tahr (a type of mountain goat). A safari bus will take you into the Rajamala tourist zone where the likelihood of a sighting is high. Guided treks cost ₹300. The park is also home to Anamudi, Kerala's highest peak (2695m), though it was closed to climbers at the time of research.

From Munnar, an autorickshaw/taxi costs around ₹300/400 return; a government bus will take you the final 4km from the checkpoint (₹40).

CENTRAL KERALA

Kochi (Cochin)

☎0484 / POP 601,600

Serene Kochi has been drawing traders, explorers and travellers to its shores for over 600 years. Nowhere else in India could you find such an intriguing mix: giant fishing nets from China, a 400-year-old synagogue, ancient mosques, Portuguese houses and the crumbling remains of the British Raj. The result is an unlikely blend of medieval Portugal, Holland and an English village grafted onto the tropical Malabar Coast. It's a delightful place to spend some time and nap in some of India's finest homestays and heritage accommodation. Kochi is also a

Kochi (Cochin)

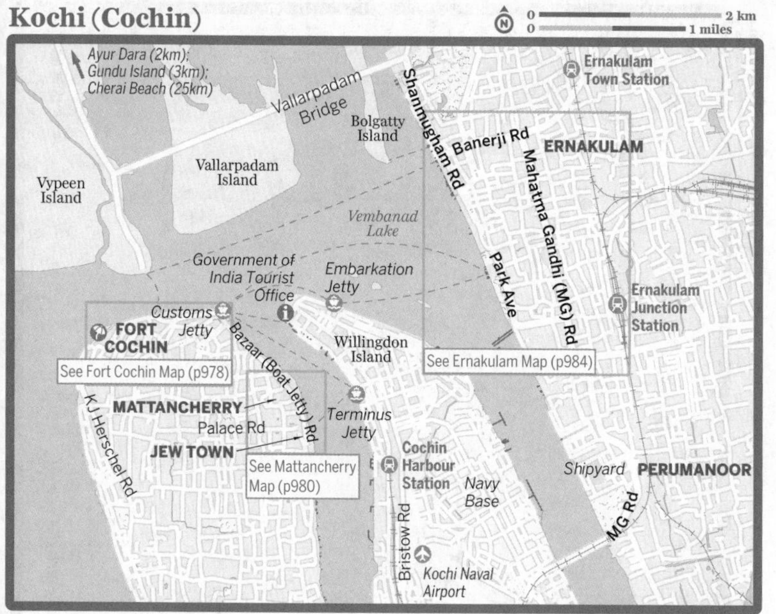

centre for Keralan arts and one of the best places to see Kathakali and *kalarippayat*.

Mainland Ernakulam is the hectic transport and cosmopolitan hub of Kochi, while the historical towns of Fort Cochin and Mattancherry, though well-touristed, remain wonderfully atmospheric – thick with the smell of the past. Other islands, including Willingdon and Vypeen, are linked by a network of ferries and bridges.

Sights

Fort Cochin

Fort Cochin has a couple of small, sandy beaches, which are only really good for people-watching in the evening and gazing out at the incoming tankers. A popular promenade winds around from Mahatma Gandhi Beach to the Chinese fishing nets and fish market.

Look out along the shore for the scant remains of Fort Immanuel, the 16th-century Portuguese fort from which the area takes its name.

Chinese Fishing Nets LANDMARK
(Map p978) The unofficial emblems of Kerala's backwaters, and perhaps the most photographed, are the half dozen or so giant cantilevered Chinese fishing nets on Fort Cochin's northeastern shore. A legacy of traders from the AD 1400 court of Kublai Khan, these enormous, spider-like contraptions require at least four people to operate their counterweights at high tide.

Modern fishing techniques are making these labour-intensive methods less and less profitable, but they supply much of the fresh lake fish you'll see on display for sale. Smaller fishing nets are dotted around the shores of Lake Vembanad – some of the best are north of Cherai Beach on Vypeen Island.

Indo-Portuguese Museum MUSEUM
(Map p978; 0484-2215400; Indian/foreigner ₹10/25; 9am-1pm & 2-6pm Tue-Sun) This museum in the garden of the Bishop's House preserves the heritage of one of India's earliest Catholic communities, including vestments, silver processional crosses and altarpieces from the Cochin diocese. The basement contains remnants of Fort Immanuel.

Maritime Museum MUSEUM
(Beach Rd; adult/child ₹40/20, camera/video ₹100/150; 10am-3.30pm & 4.30-5.30pm Tue-Sun) In a pair of former bomb shelters, this museum traces the history of the Indian navy, as well as maritime trade dating back to the Portuguese and Dutch, through

Fort Cochin

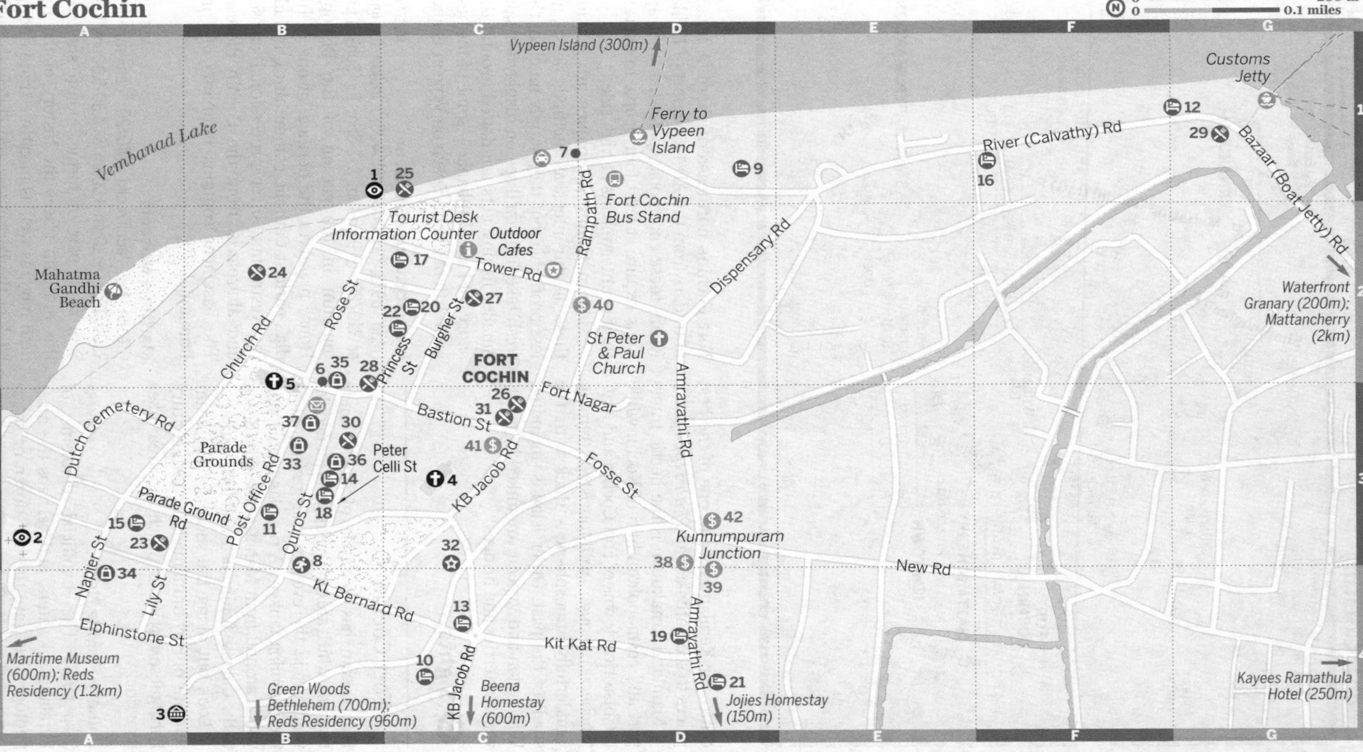
Fort Cochin
200 m
0.1 miles
Vypeen Island (300m)
Customs Jetty
Vembanad Lake
Ferry to Vypeen Island
River (Calvathy) Rd
Bazaar (Boat Jetty) Rd
Fort Cochin Bus Stand
Rampath Rd
Tourist Desk Information Counter
Outdoor Cafes
Tower Rd
Dispensary Rd
Mahatma Gandhi Beach
Waterfront Granary (200m); Mattancherry (2km)
Rose St
Church Rd
Princess St
Burgher St
FORT COCHIN
St Peter & Paul Church
Amravathi Rd
Fort Nagar
Bastion St
Dutch Cemetery Rd
Parade Grounds
Post Office Rd
Quiros St
Peter Celli St
KB Jacob Rd
Fosse St
Parade Ground Rd
Napier St
Lily St
Kunnumpuram Junction
New Rd
KL Bernard Rd
Elphinstone St
Kit Kat Rd
Maritime Museum (600m); Reds Residency (1.2km)
Green Woods Bethlehem (700m); Reds Residency (960m)
Beena Homestay (600m)
Jojies Homestay (150m)
Kayees Ramathula Hotel (250m)

Fort Cochin

Sights
1 Chinese Fishing Nets........B1
2 Dutch Cemetery........A3
3 Indo-Portuguese Museum........A4
4 Santa Cruz Basilica........C3
5 St Francis Church........B2

Activities, Courses & Tours
6 Art of Bicycle Trips........B2
Cook & Eat........(see 14)
7 KTDC........C1
8 SVM Ayurveda Centre........B3

Sleeping
9 Brunton Boatyard........D1
10 Daffodil........C4
11 Delight Home Stay........B3
12 Fort House Hotel........G1
13 Happy Camper........C4
14 Leelu Homestay........B3
15 Malabar House........A3
16 Maritime........F1
17 Old Harbour Hotel........C2
18 Raintree Lodge........B3
19 Saj Homestay........D4
20 Spice Fort........C2
21 Tea Bungalow........D4
22 Walton's Homestay........C2

Eating
23 Dal Roti........A3
24 Drawing Room........B2
25 Fishmongers........C1
26 Fusion Bay........C3
27 Kashi Art Cafe........C2
28 Loafers Corner........B2
Malabar Junction........(see 15)
29 Solar Cafe........G1
30 Teapot........B3
31 Upstairs Italian........C3

Entertainment
32 Kerala Kathakali Centre........C3

Shopping
33 Cinnamon........B3
34 Fabindia........A4
35 Idiom Bookshop........B2
36 Niraamaya........B3
37 Tribes India........B3

Information
38 Federal Bank ATM........D3
39 ICICI ATM........D4
40 SBI ATM........D2
41 South India Bank ATM........C3
42 UAE Exchange........D3

a series of rather dry relief murals and information panels. There's plenty of naval memorabilia, including a couple of model battleships outside in the garden.

St Francis Church CHURCH
(Map p978; Church Rd; 8.30am-5pm) Constructed in 1503 by Portuguese Franciscan friars, this is believed to be India's oldest European-built church. The edifice that stands here today was built in the mid-16th century to replace the original wooden structure. Explorer Vasco da Gama, who died in Cochin in 1524, was buried in this spot for 14 years before his remains were taken to Lisbon – you can still visit his tombstone in the church.

Santa Cruz Basilica CHURCH
(Map p978; cnr Bastion St & KB Jacob Rd; 9am-1pm & 2.30-5.30pm Mon-Sat, 10.30am-1pm Sun) The imposing Catholic basilica was originally built on this site in 1506, though the current building dates to 1902. Inside you'll find artefacts from the different eras in Kochi and a striking pastel-coloured interior.

Dutch Cemetery CEMETERY
(Map p978; Beach Rd) Consecrated in 1724, this cemetery near Kochi beach contains the worn and dilapidated graves of Dutch traders and soldiers. Its gates are normally locked but a caretaker might let you in, or ask at St Francis Church.

Mattancherry & Jew Town

About 3km southeast of Fort Cochin, Mattancherry is the old bazaar district and centre of the spice trade. These days it's packed with spice shops and pricey Kashmiri-run emporiums that autorickshaw drivers will fall over backwards to take you to for a healthy commission – any offer of a cheap tour of the district will inevitably lead to a few shops. In the midst of this, Jew Town is a bustling port area with a fine synagogue. Scores of small firms huddle together in dilapidated old buildings and the air is filled with the biting aromas of ginger, cardamom, cumin, turmeric and cloves, though the lanes around the Dutch Palace and synagogue are packed with antique and tourist-curio shops rather than spices.

★ **Mattancherry Palace** MUSEUM
(Dutch Palace; Map p980; 0484-2226085; Palace Rd; adult/child ₹5/free; 9am-5pm Sat-Thu) Mattancherry Palace was a generous gift presented to the Raja of Kochi, Veera Kerala

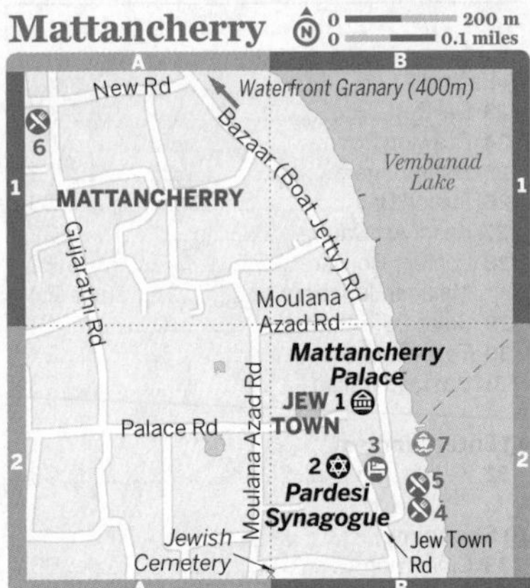

Mattancherry

Top Sights

Sleeping

Eating

Transport

Varma (1537–61), as a gesture of goodwill by the Portuguese in 1555. The Dutch renovated the palace in 1663, hence its alternative name, the Dutch Palace. The star attractions here are the astonishingly preserved Hindu murals, depicting scenes from the Ramayana, Mahabharata and Puranic legends in intricate detail.

★**Pardesi Synagogue** SYNAGOGUE
(Map p980; ₹5; ⏲10am-1pm & 3-5pm Sun-Thu, closed Jewish holidays) Originally built in 1568, this synagogue was partially destroyed by the Portuguese in 1662, and rebuilt two years later when the Dutch took Kochi. It features an ornate gold pulpit and elaborate hand-painted, willow-pattern floor tiles from Canton, China, which were added in 1762. It's magnificently illuminated by Belgian chandeliers and coloured-glass lamps. The graceful clock tower was built in 1760. There's an upstairs balcony for women, who worshipped separately according to Orthodox rites.

Note that shorts, sleeveless tops, bags and cameras are not allowed inside.

Ernakulam

Kerala Folklore Museum MUSEUM
(☎0484-2665452; www.keralafolkloremuseum.org; Folklore Junction, Thevara; Indian/foreigner ₹100/200, camera ₹100; ⏲9am-6pm) Created in Keralan style from ancient temples and beautiful old houses collected by its owner, an antique dealer, this museum includes over 4000 artefacts and covers three architectural styles: Malabar on the ground floor, Kochi on the 1st and Travancore on the 2nd. There's a beautiful wood-lined theatre, with a 17th-century wooden ceiling. It's about 6km south of Ernakulam Junction train station.

A rickshaw from Ernakulam should cost ₹90, or you can take any bus to Thevara from where it's a ₹25 rickshaw ride. An autorickshaw from Fort Cochin should cost ₹200.

Activities

Ayur Dara AYURVEDA
(☎0484-2502362, 9447721041; www.ayurdara.com; Murikkumpadam, Vypeen Island; ⏲9am-5.30pm) Run by third-generation ayurvedic practitioner Dr Subhash, this delightful waterside treatment centre specialises in treatments of one to three weeks (₹1650 per day). By appointment only. It's 3km from the Vypeen Island ferry.

SVM Ayurveda Centre AYURVEDA
(Kerala Ayurveda Pharmacy Ltd; Map p978; ☎9847371667; www.svmayurveda.com; Quiros St; massage from ₹900, rejuvenation from ₹1200; ⏲9.30am-7pm) This small Fort Cochin centre offers daily therapeutic massages and Hatha yoga classes (₹500). Longer rejuvenation packages are also available.

Courses

The Kerala Kathakali Centre (p986) has lessons in classical Kathakali dance, music and make-up (short and long-term courses from ₹350 per hour).

For a crash course in the martial art of *kalarippayat*, head out to Ens Kalari (p986), a famed training centre, which offers short intensive courses from one week to one month.

Cook & Eat COOKING
(Map p978; ☎0484-2215377; www.leeluhomestay.com; Quiros St; classes veg/nonveg ₹700/750; ⏲4-6pm) Mrs Leelu Roy runs popular two-hour cooking classes in her big family kitch-

en at Leelu Homestay (p982), teaching five dishes and her homemade garam masala to classes of five to 10 people.

Tours

Tourist Desk TOURS
(Map p984; ☎0484-2371761, 9847044688; www.touristdesk.in; Ernakulam Boat Jetty; ⊙8am-6pm) This high-profile private tour agency runs the popular full-day Water Valley Tour (₹1250, departs 8am) by houseboat through local backwater canals and lagoons. A canoe trip through smaller canals and villages is included. It also offers a sunset dinner cruise (₹850 per person) by canoe from Narakkal Village on Vypeen Island, with the option of an overnight stay at a beach bungalow.

Art of Bicycle Trips CYCLING
(Map p978; ☎08129945707; www.artofbicycletrips.com; Bastion St; 3hr/half-day tours ₹1450/2500; ⊙9am-6pm) Guided bicycle tours on quality mountain bikes include a morning tour of the historic Fort area and a half-day ride around the backwaters. A great way to see the area at a slow pace.

Kerala Bike Tours MOTORCYCLING
(☎0484-2356652, 9388476817; www.keralabiketours.com; Kirushupaly Rd, Ravipuram) Organises motorcycle tours around Kerala and the Western Ghats, and hires out touring-quality Enfield Bullets (from US$155 per week) for serious riders with unlimited mileage, full insurance and free recovery/maintenance options.

KTDC BOATING
(Map p978; ☎0484-2353234; Marine Dr, Kochi; backwater tours half-/full day ₹750/1250; ⊙10am-5pm Mon-Sat) The KTDC has half-day backwater tours at 8.30am and 2pm, and full-day trips visiting village weaving factories, spice gardens and toddy tappers, as well as local cruises and city tours.

Festivals & Events

Ernakulathappan Utsavam RELIGIOUS
(⊙Jan/Feb) At the Shiva Temple, Ernakulam; eight days of festivities culminating in a parade of 15 splendidly decorated elephants, plus music and fireworks.

Cochin Carnival CARNIVAL
(www.cochincarnival.org; ⊙21 Dec) The Cochin Carnival is Fort Cochin's biggest bash, a 10-day festival culminating on New Year's Eve. Street parades, colourful costumes, embellished elephants (which won't appeal to all), music, folk dancing and lots of fun.

Sleeping

Fort Cochin is the homestay capital of India with some 200 to choose from, but it also has some of Kerala's best heritage accommodation. It can feel a bit touristy and crowded in season, but it's a great place to escape the noise and chaos of the mainland. Ernakulam is cheaper and more convenient for onward travel, but the ambience and accommodation choices are less inspiring.

Book ahead during December and January. At other times you may snag a discount.

Fort Cochin

Happy Camper HOSTEL $
(Map p978; ☎9742725668; KB Jacob Rd; dm incl breakfast ₹550; ❄📶) Billing itself as a boutique hostel, Happy Camper is a relaxed place with just three air-con dorms (one female-only), a small kitchen, an excellent little cafe and rooftop area and friendly staff. Good location just south of the main tourist hub.

Maritime HOSTEL $
(Map p978; ☎0484-6567875; www.thehostelcrowd.com; 2/227 Calvathy Rd; dm ₹500, d ₹1200-1600; ❄📶) This Goan hostel chain has now opened in Kochi with a great location not far from Customs jetty. The nautical theme is a nice touch, the air-con dorms and double rooms are clean and well-kept, and there's a small kitchen, laundry and library.

Jojies Homestay HOMESTAY $
(☎9995396543; 1/1276 Chirattapallam Rd, off KB Jacob Rd; d/tr ₹800/1200; 📶) Clean, friendly and welcoming homestay popular with travellers thanks to helpful owners and big breakfasts served on the rooftop garden.

★ **Reds Residency** HOMESTAY $$
(☎0484-3204060, 9388643747; www.redsresidency.in; 11/372 A KJ Herschel Rd; d incl breakfast ₹900-1200, with AC from ₹1200, AC rooftop cottage ₹1500; ❄📶) Reds is a lovely homestay with hotel-quality rooms but a true family welcome from knowledgable hosts Philip and Maryann. The five rooms – including a triple and four-bed family room – are modern and immaculate, and there's a brilliant self-contained 'penthouse' cottage with kitchen on the rooftop. It's in a peaceful location south of the centre.

★ **Green Woods Bethlehem** HOMESTAY $$
(☎9846014924, 0484-3247791; greenwoodsbethlehem1@vsnl.net; opposite ESI Hospital; d incl breakfast ₹1200-1400, with AC ₹1500-1800; ❄📶)

With a smile that brightens weary travellers, welcoming owner Sheeba looks ready to sign your adoption papers the minute you walk through her front door. Down a quiet laneway and with a walled garden thick with plants and palms, this is one of Kochi's most serene homestays. The rooms are humble but cosy; breakfast is served in the fantastic, leafy rooftop cafe.

Raintree Lodge BOUTIQUE HOTEL **$$**
(Map p978; ☎9847029000, 0484-3251489; http://raintree-lodge.viewhotel.co; 1/618 Peter Celli St; r ₹3100; ❄📶) The intimate and elegant rooms at this historic place flirt with boutique-hotel status. Each of the five rooms has a great blend of contemporary style and heritage carved-wood furniture, and the front upstairs rooms have gorgeous vine-covered Romeo-and-Juliet balconies. Good value.

Delight Home Stay GUESTHOUSE **$$**
(Map p978; ☎98461121421, 0484-2217658; www.delightfulhomestay.com; Post Office Rd; r incl breakfast ₹2500-4500; ❄📶) One of Fort Cochin's original homestays, this grand house's exterior is adorned with frilly white woodwork, and the six rooms are spacious and polished. There's a charming little garden, elegant breakfast room and an imposing sitting room covered in wall-to-wall teak. Good food is served and cooking classes are offered in the open kitchen.

Beena Homestay HOMESTAY **$$**
(homestaykochi.com; XI/359B KB Jacob Rd; d incl breakfast & dinner ₹3000; ❄📶) Beena has been feeding and sheltering travellers in the family homestay for quite a few years and maintains a high standard with six spotless air-con rooms and home-cooked meals taken in the dining room.

Walton's Homestay GUESTHOUSE **$$**
(Map p978; ☎9249721935, 0484-2215309; www.waltonshomestay.com; Princess St; r incl breakfast ₹1600-3500; ❄📶) The fastidious Mr Walton offers big wood-furnished rooms in his lovely old house that's painted a nautical white with blue trim and buried behind a bookstore. Downstairs rooms open onto a lush garden while upstairs rooms have a balcony, and there's a nice communal breakfast room.

Saj Homestay HOMESTAY **$$**
(Map p978; ☎8086565811, 9847002182; www.sajhome.com; Amravathi Rd, near Kunnumpuram Junction; d incl breakfast from ₹2500; ❄📶) There are six upstairs rooms at this welcoming and spotless homestay run by helpful Saj. It can be a bit street-noisy at the front but the air-con rooms are well soundproofed and travellers rave about the balcony breakfasts.

Leelu Homestay HOMESTAY **$$**
(Map p978; ☎0484-2215377; www.leeluhomestay.com; 1/629 Quiros St; s/d incl breakfast ₹1500/2500; ❄📶) Central and very homely, Leelu has four air-con rooms upstairs, a rooftop terrace (yoga can be arranged) and sociable lounge areas with nanna furniture. The kitchen is a popular venue for Leelu's Cook & Eat cooking classes (p980).

Daffodil GUESTHOUSE **$$**
(Map p978; ☎9895262296, 0484-2218686; www.daffodilhomestay.com; Njaliparambu Junction; d incl breakfast without/with AC ₹1800/2500; ❄@📶) Run by a welcoming local couple, Daffodil has eight big and brightly painted modern rooms with a sense of privacy, but the best feature is the carved-wood Keralan balcony upstairs.

★Malabar House HOTEL **$$$**
(Map p978; ☎0484-2216666; www.malabarhouse.com; Parade Ground Rd; r €275, ste incl breakfast €300-400; ❄@🏊) What may just be one of the fanciest boutique hotels in Kerala, Malabar flaunts its uberhip blend of modern colours and period fittings like it's not even trying. While the suites are huge and lavishly appointed, the standard rooms are more snug. The award-winning restaurant and wine bar are top-notch.

★Brunton Boatyard HOTEL **$$$**
(Map p978; ☎0484-2215461; www.cghearth.com/brunton-boatyard; River Rd; d from ₹22,000; ❄@📶🏊) This imposing hotel faithfully reproduces grand 16th- and 17th-century Dutch and Portuguese architecture. All of the rooms look out over the harbour, and have bathtubs and balconies with a refreshing sea breeze that beats air-con. The hotel is also home to the excellent History Restaurant and Armoury Bar, along with a couple of open-air cafes.

Spice Fort BOUTIQUE HOTEL **$$$**
(Map p978; ☎9364455440; www.duneecogroup.com; Princess St; r ₹10,500-12,600; ❄📶🏊) The chic red-and-white spice-themed rooms here have TVs built into the bed heads, cool tones and immaculate bathrooms. They all orbit an inviting pool in a heritage courtyard shielded from busy Princess St. Great location, excellent restaurant, friendly staff.

Tea Bungalow HOTEL $$$
(Map p978; ☎0484-2216337; www.teabungalow.in; 1/1901 Kunumpuram; r incl breakfast from ₹10,500;) This mustard-coloured colonial building was built in 1912 as headquarters of a UK spice trading company before being taken over by Brooke Bond tea. The 10 graceful boutique rooms – all named after sea ports – are decorated with flashes of strong colour and carved colonial wooden furniture, and have Bassetta-tiled bathrooms. Off-season rates drop by 60%.

Old Harbour Hotel HOTEL $$$
(Map p978; ☎0484-2218006; www.oldharbourhotel.com; 1/328 Tower Rd; r ₹12,700-15,700, ste ₹16,500;) Set around an idyllic garden with lily ponds and a small pool, the dignified Old Harbour is housed in a 300-year-old Dutch/Portuguese heritage building. The elegant mix of period and modern styles lends it a more intimate feel than some of the more grandiose competition. There are 13 rooms and suites, some facing directly onto the garden, and some with plant-filled, open-air bathrooms.

Fort House Hotel HOTEL $$$
(Map p978; ☎0484-2217103; www.hotelforthouse.com; 2/6A Calvathy Rd; r incl breakfast ₹6500;) Close to the ferry point, this is one of Fort Cochin's few truly waterfront hotels, though the 16 smart air-con rooms are set back in a lush garden, with the restaurant taking prime waterside position.

Mattancherry & Jew Town

Caza Maria HERITAGE HOTEL $$
(Map p980; ☎9846050901; cazamaria@rediffmail.com; Jew Town Rd, Mattancherry; r incl breakfast ₹5000;) Right in the heart of Jew Town, this unique unsigned place has just two large heritage rooms above shops overlooking the bazaar. Fit for a maharaja, the rooms feature an idiosyncratic style, with each high-ceilinged room painted in bright colours, filled to the brim with antiques.

Waterfront Granary BOUTIQUE HOTEL $$$
(☎98952847000, 0484-2211177; www.thewaterfrontgranary.com; 6/641 Bazaar Rd, Mattancherry; d ₹10,200-14,400, ste ₹21,600;) The first thing you'll notice when entering the Waterfront Granary is the 1928 Ford vintage car in the lounge. This is a museum hotel, where many relics from the owner's personal collection are on show. The main building itself, a former granary, dates to 1877, while the 16 spacious room have a heritage feel with modern touches.

The location on the lakefront is superb, with a large terrace and small pool looking out to Willingdon Island.

Ernakulam

John's Residency HOTEL $
(Map p984; ☎8281321395, 0484-2355395; TG Rd; s/d from ₹550/750, with AC ₹1550;) John's is a genuine backpacker place and the best budget bet in Ernakulam, especially if John is in residence. Quiet location but a short walk from the boat jetty. Rooms are small (deluxe rooms are bigger) but decorated with flashes of colour that give them a welcoming funky feel in this price bracket.

Boat Jetty Bungalow HOTEL $$
(Map p984; ☎0484-2373211; www.boatjettybungalow.com; Cannon Shed Rd, Ernakulam; s/d ₹650/950, with AC ₹1400/1900;) This 140-year-old former jetty manager's house has been refurbished with 22 compact and very clean rooms with TV. It's a short walk from here to the boat jetty for Fort Cochin.

Grand Hotel HOTEL $$
(Map p984; ☎9895721014, 0484-2382061; www.grandhotelkerala.com; MG Rd; s/d incl breakfast from ₹3500/4300, ste ₹6500;) This 1960s hotel, with its polished original art deco fittings, exudes the sort of retro cool that modern hotels would love to recreate. The spacious rooms have gleaming parquet floors and large modern bathrooms, and there's a good restaurant and Ernakulam's most sophisticated bar.

Around Kochi

Kallanchery Retreat HOMESTAY $$
(☎9847446683, 0484-2240564; www.kallancheryretreat.com; Kumbalanghi Village; r & cottage without/with AC ₹2000/2500;) Escape the Kochi tourist crowds at this serene budget waterfront homestay and expansive garden in the village of Kumbalanghi about 15km south of Fort Cochin. Rooms are either in the family home or in a sublime lakefront cottage. Chinese fishing nets are on your doorstep, and boat trips, village tours and home-cooked meals are available.

The Bungalow HOMESTAY $$
(☎9846302347; www.thebungalow.in; Vypeen Island; d incl breakfast ₹4500-5500;) A short walk from the ferry dock on Vypeen Island, this beautiful old Keralan heritage home

Ernakulam

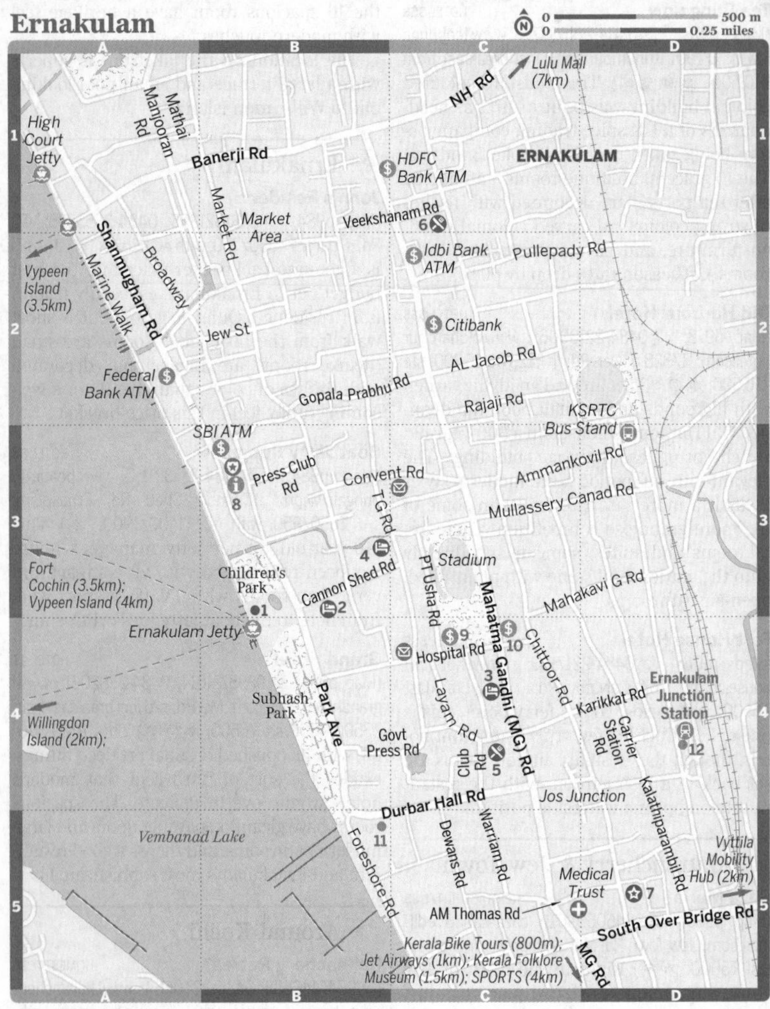

Ernakulam

Activities, Courses & Tours
1 Tourist Desk ... B3

Sleeping
2 Boat Jetty Bungalow ... B3
3 Grand Hotel ... C4
4 John's Residency ... B3

Eating
5 Chillies ... C4
6 Frys Village Restaurant ... C1
Grand Pavilion ... (see 3)

Entertainment
7 See India Foundation ... D5

Information
8 KTDC Tourist Reception Centre ... B3
Tourist Desk Information Counter ... (see 1)
9 UAE Exchange ... C4
10 UAE Exchange ... C4

Transport
11 Air India ... B5
12 Reservations Office ... D4

has just two large connecting rooms with four-poster beds and quaint furnishings. Owner Neema is a great cook and offers cooking lessons (₹500).

Olavipe HOMESTAY $$$
(☎0478-2522255; www.olavipe.com; Olavipe; s/d incl meals ₹6000/10,000; 📶) This gorgeous 1890s traditional Syrian-Christian home is on a 16-hectare farm surrounded by backwaters, 28km south of Kochi. A restored mansion of rosewood and glistening teak, it has several large and breezy rooms beautifully decorated in original period decor.

Eating & Drinking

Some of Fort Cochin's best cooking can be found in the homestays, but there are lots of good restaurants and cafes.

Fort Cochin

Behind the Chinese fishing nets are **fishmongers** (Map p978; Fort Cochin; seafood ₹400-1000; ⏲restaurants 8am-9pm), from whom you can buy the day's catch – fresh fish, prawns, crab and lobster – then take your selection to one of the simple but popular restaurants on nearby Tower Rd where they will cook it and serve it to you for an additional charge. Market prices vary but you'll easily get a feel for prices if you wander along and bargain.

Loafers Corner CAFE $
(Map p978; ☎0484-2215351; Princess St; snacks from ₹60; ⏲9am-9pm) If you get a window seat there are few better people-watching spots on Princess St than this. It's a good spot for a coffee, lassi, breakfast or light snack.

Solar Cafe CAFE $
(Map p978; Calvathy Rd; meals ₹60-240; ⏲8am-6pm) This arty upstairs cafe serves organic breakfasts and lunches, cinnamon coffee and fresh juice in a lime-bright, book-lined setting opposite the Customs Jetty.

★**Dal Roti** INDIAN $$
(Map p978; ☎9746459244; 1/293 Lily St; meals ₹150-250; ⏲noon-3pm & 6.30-10pm Wed-Mon) There's a lot to like about busy Dal Roti. Friendly and knowledgable owner Ramesh will hold your hand through his expansive North Indian menu, which even sports its own glossary, and help you dive into his delicious range of vegetarian, eggetarian and non-vegetarian options. From *kati* rolls (kebabs wrapped in a hot *paratha*) to seven types of thali, you won't go hungry. No alcohol.

★**Kashi Art Cafe** CAFE $$
(Map p978; Burgher St; breakfast & snacks ₹160-280; ⏲8.30am-10pm) An institution in Fort Cochin, this natural-light-filled place has a Zen, casual vibe and solid wood tables that spread out into a semi-courtyard space. The coffee is strong and the daily Western breakfast and lunch specials are excellent. A small gallery shows off local artists.

Teapot CAFE $$
(Map p978; Peter Celli St; tea ₹50-120, mains ₹200-300; ⏲8.30am-8.30pm) This atmospheric cafe is the perfect venue for 'high tea', with 16 types of tea, sandwiches, cakes and a few meals served in chic, airy rooms. Witty tea-themed accents include loads of antique teapots, tea chests for tables and a gnarled, tea-tree-based glass table.

Drawing Room CAFE $$
(Map p978; Church Rd; mains ₹150-450; ⏲noon-10.30pm) In the Grand Cochin Club, this slick new restaurant enjoys a wonderful location with large windows facing out to the water. The light menu features platters, salads and pasta dishes. Occasional live music in the evenings.

Fusion Bay SEAFOOD $$
(Map p978; ☎9995105110; KB Jacob Rd; mains ₹250-400; ⏲noon-10.30pm) This unassuming little family restaurant in central Fort Cochin is renowned locally for its Kerala Syrian fish delicacies cooked in the *pollichathu* style (masala spiced and grilled in a banana leaf), and assorted seafood dishes such as spicy fish pappas and fish in mango curry.

★**Malabar Junction** INTERNATIONAL $$$
(Map p978; ☎0484-2216666; Parade Ground Rd; mains ₹420-750, 5-course degustation ₹2000; ⏲12.30-3pm & 7-11pm) Set in an open-sided pavilion, the restaurant at Malabar House (p982) is movie-star cool, with white-tableclothed tables in a courtyard close to the small pool. There's a seafood-based, European-style menu – the signature dish is the impressive seafood platter with grilled vegetables. Upstairs, the wine bar serves upmarket tapas-style snacks and fine wine by the glass.

Upstairs Italian ITALIAN $$$
(Map p978; ☎9745682608; Bastion St; mains ₹250-600; ⏲10am-11pm) For authentic Italian – imported gorgonzola, prosciutto, olive oil, parmesan – head upstairs to this cosy little place serving Kochi's best pizza, pasta and antipasto. Pricey but worth the effort.

Mattancherry & Jew Town

Kayees Ramathula Hotel INDIAN $
(Map p980; Kayees Junction, Mattancherry; biryani ₹60-145; ⏲noon-2.30pm) This place is legendary among locals for its lunchtime chicken and mutton biryanis – get here early or miss out. Don't be confused by the lime-green biryani place on the corner – Kayees is next door.

Cafe Crafters CAFE $$
(Map p980; ☎0484-2223345; www.crafters.in; Jew Town Rd, Mattancherry; mains ₹100-350; ⏲9.30am-6.30pm) In the heart of Mattancherry's Jewish Quarter and above a large antique store, this charming little 1st-floor restaurant cooks up Keralan seafood and Western efforts like sandwiches and burgers. Prime position is the small balcony overlooking the street.

★ **Ginger House** INDIAN $$$
(Map p980; ☎8943493648; www.gingerhousecochin.com; Jew Town Rd, Jew Town; mains ₹200-720; ⏲9am-6.30pm, to 10pm Dec-May) Hidden behind a massive antique-filled godown (warehouse) is this weird and wonderful waterfront restaurant, where you can feast on Indian dishes and snacks – ginger prawns, ginger ice cream, ginger lassi…you get the picture. To get to the restaurant, walk through the astonishing Heritage Arts showroom with amazing sculptures and antiques – check out the giant snake-boat canoe.

Caza Maria MULTICUISINE $$$
(Map p980; Bazaar Rd; mains ₹200-700; ⏲9am-8pm) This enchanting 1st-floor place is a bright-blue, antique-filled heritage space with soft music and a changing daily menu of North Indian, South Indian and French dishes.

Ernakulam

Ernakulam's mega shopping malls provide food-court dining. Another interesting development is the leafy Panampilly Ave, in a residential area south of the main train station, which is lined with modern fine-dining and fast-food restaurants.

Frys Village Restaurant KERALAN $
(Map p984; Chittoor Rd; mains ₹90-180; ⏲noon-3.30pm & 7-10.30pm) This brightly decorated and breezy place with an arched ceiling is a great family restaurant with authentic Keralan food, especially seafood like *pollichathu* or crab roast. Fish/veg thalis are available for lunch.

Chillies INDIAN $$
(Map p984; Layam Rd; meals ₹140-280, thali ₹150; ⏲11.30am-3.30pm & 7.30-11pm) A dark, buzzing 1st-floor place, serving Kochi's best spicy Andhra cuisine on banana leaves. Try a thali, for all-you-can-eat joy.

Grand Pavilion INDIAN $$$
(Map p984; MG Rd; meals ₹260-390; ⏲noon-3pm & 6-9pm) The restaurant at the Grand Hotel (p983) is as elegant and retro-stylish as the hotel itself, with cream-coloured furniture and stiff tablecloths. It serves a tome of a menu that covers dishes from the West, North India, South India and most of the rest of the Asian continent.

☆ Entertainment

There are several places where you can view Kathakali. Performances are designed for tourists, but they're a good introduction. Standard programs start with the intricate make-up application and costume-fitting, followed by a demonstration and commentary on the dance and then the performance – usually two hours in all. The fast-paced traditional martial art of *kalarippayat* can also be easily seen, often at the same theatres.

Kerala Kathakali Centre LIVE PERFORMANCE
(Map p978; ☎0484-2217552; www.kathakalicentre.com; KB Jacob Rd, Fort Cochin; shows ₹250-300; ⏲make-up from 5pm, show 6-7.30pm) In an intimate, wood-lined theatre, this recommended place provides a useful introduction to Kathakali, complete with handy translations of the night's story. The centre also hosts performances of classical music from 8pm to 9pm Sunday to Friday and traditional dance on Saturday.

See India Foundation LIVE PERFORMANCE
(Map p984; ☎0484-2376471; devankathakali@yahoo.com; Kalathiparambil Lane, Ernakulam; entry ₹300; ⏲make-up 6pm, show 7-8pm) One of the oldest Kathakali theatres in Kerala, this intimate venue has small-scale shows with an emphasis on the religious and philosophical roots of Kathakali.

Ens Kalari LIVE PERFORMANCE
(☎0484-2700810; www.enskalari.org.in; Nettoor; entry by donation; ⏲demonstrations 7.15-8.15pm, training from 5.30pm) If you want to see real professionals practising *kalarippayat*, travel

out to this renowned *kalarippayat* training centre, 8km southeast of Ernakulam. There are daily one-hour demonstrations (one day's notice required) or you can watch training sessions from 5.30pm daily except Sunday.

Shopping

Broadway in Ernakulam is good for local shopping, spice shops and clothing. On Jew Town Rd in Mattancherry you'll find Gujarati-run shops selling genuine antiques mingled with knock-offs. Most shops in Fort Cochin are identikit Kashmiri-run stores selling North Indian crafts. Many shops around Fort Cochin and Mattancherry operate lucrative commission rackets, with autorickshaw drivers getting kickbacks (added to your price) for dropping tourists at their door.

Lulu Mall MALL
(0484-2727777; www.lulumall.in; NH47, Edapally; 9am-11pm;) India's largest shopping mall, Lulu is an attraction in its own right with people coming from all over to shop here, hang out in the food courts or cinema, go ice-skating or tenpin bowling. Sprawling over 7 hectares, this state-of-the-art air-con, wi-fi-connected mall has more than 215 brand outlets from Calvin Klein to KFC. It's in Edapally, about 9km from the Ernakulam boat jetty.

Niraamaya CLOTHING
(Map p978; 0484-3263465; www.ayurvastraonline.com; Quiros St, Fort Cochin; 10am-5.30pm Mon-Sat) Popular throughout Kerala, Niraamaya sells 'ayurvedic' clothing and fabrics – all made of organic cotton, coloured with natural herb dyes, or infused with ayurvedic oils. There's another branch in Mattancherry.

Idiom Bookshop BOOKS
(Map p978; Bastion St; 9am-8pm) Huge range of quality new and used books in Fort Cochin.

Cinnamon CLOTHING
(Map p978; 0484-2217124; www.cinnamonthestore.com; 1/658 Ridsdale Rd, Parade Grounds; 10am-7pm Mon-Sat) Cinnamon sells gorgeous Indian-designed clothing, jewellery and homewares in an ultrachic white retail space.

Fabindia CLOTHING, HOMEWARES
(Map p978; 0484-2217077; www.fabindia.com; Napier St, Fort Cochin; 9.30am-9pm) This renowned brand has fine Indian textiles, fabrics, clothes and household linen.

Tribes India ARTS & CRAFTS
(Map p978; 0484-2215077; Ridsdale Rd; 10am-6.30pm Mon-Sat) Tucked behind the post office, this Trifed (Tribal Cooperative Marketing Development Federation of India) enterprise sells tribal artefacts, paintings, shawls, figurines and more at reasonable fixed prices, with the profits going towards supporting the artisans.

Information

DANGERS & ANNOYANCES

Tourist police are at **Ernakulam** (Map p984; 0484-2353234; Shanmugham Rd, Ernakulam; 8am-6pm) and **Fort Cochin** (Map p978; 0484-2215055; Tower Rd, Fort Cochin; 24hr).

MEDICAL SERVICES

Lakeshore Hospital (0484-2701032; www.lakeshorehospital.com; NH Bypass, Marudu) Modern hospital 8km southeast of central Ernakulam.

Medical Trust (Map p984; 0484-2358001; www.medicaltrusthospital.com; MG Rd) Central hospital in Ernakulam.

MONEY

UAE Exchange Foreign exchange and travellers cheques. Has branches on **MG Road** (Map p984; 0484-2383317; MG Rd, Perumpillil Bldg, Ernakulam; 9.30am-6pm Mon-Fri, to 2pm Sat) and **PT Usha Road** (Map p984; 0484-3067008; Chettupuzha Towers, PT Usha Rd Junction, Ernakulam; 9.30am-6pm Mon-Fri, to 2pm Sat) in Ernakulam and in **Fort Cochin** (Map p978; 0484-2216231; Amravathi Rd, Fort Cochin; 9.30am-6pm Mon-Fri, to 2pm Sat).

TOURIST INFORMATION

There's a tourist information counter at the airport. Many places distribute a free brochure that includes a map and walking tour entitled *Historical Places in Fort Cochin*.

Government of India Tourist Office (0484-2669125; indtourismkochi@sify.com; Willingdon Island; 9am-5.30pm Mon-Fri, to 1pm Sat) On Willingdon Island.

KTDC Tourist Reception Centre (Map p984; 0484-2353234; Shanmugham Rd, Ernakulam; 8am-7pm) Near Ernakulam's main jetty.

Tourist Desk Information Counter At this private tour agency, with offices at **Ernakulam's ferry terminal** (Map p984; 0484-2371761, 9847044688; www.touristdesk.in; Boat Jetty, Ernakulam; 8am-6pm) and in **Fort Cochin** (Map p978; 0484-2216129; Fort Cochin; 8am-7pm), the staff are extremely knowledgable and helpful about Kochi and beyond. They run several popular and recommended tours, including a festival tour, and publish information on festivals and cultural events.

Getting There & Away

AIR

Cochin International Airport (0484-2610115; http://cial.aero) is at Nedumbassery, 30km northeast of Ernakulam. It's a popular hub, with international flights to/from the Gulf states, Sri Lanka, the Maldives, Malaysia, Bangkok and Singapore.

On domestic routes, **Jet Airways** (0484-2359633; www.jetairways.com; MG Rd; 9am-6pm Mon-Sat), **Air India** (Map p984; 0484-2371141; www.airindia.com; Durbar Hall Rd; 9am-5pm Mon-Sat), Indigo, SpiceJet and GoAir fly direct daily to Chennai (Madras), Mumbai (Bombay), Bengaluru (Bangalore), Hyderabad, Delhi and Trivandrum (but not Goa). Air India flies to Delhi daily and to Agatti in the Lakshadweep islands six times a week.

BUS

All long-distance services operate from Ernakulam. The **KSRTC bus stand** (Map p984; 0484-2372033; reservations 6am-10pm) still has a few services but most state-run and private buses pull into the massive **Vyttila Mobility Hub** (0484-2306611; www.vyttila mobilityhub.com; 24hr), a state-of-the-art transport terminal about 2km east of Ernakulam Junction train station. Numerous private bus companies have super-deluxe, air-con, video and Volvo buses to long-distance destinations such as Bengaluru, Chennai, Mangaluru (Mangalore), Trivandrum and Coimbatore; prices vary depending on the standard. Agents in Ernakulam and Fort Cochin sell tickets. Private buses also use the Kaloor bus stand, 1km north of the city.

A prepaid autorickshaw from Vyttila costs ₹86 to the boat jetty, ₹215 to Fort Cochin and ₹400 to the airport.

TRAIN

Ernakulam has two train stations, Ernakulam Town and Ernakulam Junction. Reservations for both are made at the **reservations office** (Map p984; 132; 8am-8pm Mon-Sat, 8am-2pm Sun) at Ernakulam Junction.

There are local and express trains to Trivandrum (2nd class/sleeper/3AC ₹95/165/490, 4½ hours), via either Alleppey (₹50/140/490, 1½ hours) or Kottayam (₹50/140/490, 1½ hours). Trains also run to Thrissur (2nd class/AC chair ₹60/260, 1½ hours), Kozhikode (sleeper/3AC/2AC ₹170/540/740, 4½ hours) and Kannur (₹220/490/695, 6½ hours).

Getting Around

TO/FROM THE AIRPORT

AC Volvo buses run between the airport and Fort Cochin (₹80, one hour, eight daily) via Ernakulam. Taxis to/from Ernakulam cost around ₹850, and to/from Fort Cochin around ₹1200, depending on the time of night.

BOAT

Ferries are the fastest and most enjoyable form of transport between Fort Cochin and the mainland. The main stop at Fort Cochin is called **Customs** (Map p978), with another stop at the Mattancherry Jetty near the synagogue. **Ferries**

MAJOR BUSES FROM ERNAKULAM (KOCHI)

The following bus services operate from the KSRTC bus stand and Vyttila Mobility Hub. In addition, private buses operate on long-haul routes.

DESTINATION	FARE (₹)	DURATION (HR)	DEPARTURES
Alleppey	55	1½	every 10min
Bengaluru	530-890	14	8 daily
Calicut	170	5	hourly
Chennai	600	16	1 daily, 2pm
Coimbatore	162	4½	10 daily
Kannur	260	8	5 daily
Kanyakumari	237	8	1 daily, 7pm
Kollam	124	3½	every 30min
Kottayam	60	2	every 30min
Kumily (for Periyar)	135	5	8 daily
Mangaluru	400	12	3 daily
Munnar	124	4½	every 30min
Thrissur	68	2	every 15min
Trivandrum	177-290	5	every 30min

MAJOR TRAINS FROM ERNAKULAM (KOCHI)

DESTINATION	TRAIN NO & NAME	FARES (₹)	DURATION (HR)	DEPARTURES (DAILY)
Bengaluru	16525 Bangalore Exp (A)	345/940/1345	13	6pm
Chennai	12624 Chennai Mail (A)	395/1045/1480	12	7.25pm
Delhi	12625 Kerala Exp (B)	885/2290/3400	46	3.45pm
Goa (Madgaon)	16346 Netravathi Exp (B)	445/1175/1630	15	2.10pm
Mumbai	16346 Netravathi Exp (B)	615/1645/2465	27	2.10pm

Trains: (A) departs from Ernakulam Junction; (B) departs from Ernakulam Town
Fares: Sleeper/3AC/2AC

(Map p980) also run from Mattancherry to Willingdon Island. The jetty on the eastern side of Willingdon Island is called Embarkation; the west one, opposite Mattancherry, is Terminus. One-way fares are ₹4 (₹6 between **Ernakulam** (Map p984) and Mattancherry). Ferries run to Vypeen Island from **Ernakulam** (Map p984) and **Fort Cochin** (Map p978). Ferries to Bolgatty Island depart from **High Court Jetty** (Map p984).

Ernakulam

There are services to both Fort Cochin jetties (Customs and Mattancherry) every 25 to 50 minutes from Ernakulam's main jetty between 4.40am and 9.10pm. Ferries run every 20 minutes or so to Willingdon and Vypeen Islands.

Fort Cochin

Ferries run from Customs Jetty to Ernakulam regularly between 5am and 9.50pm. Ferries also hop between Customs Jetty and Willingdon Island 18 times a day. Car and passenger ferries cross to Vypeen Island from Fort Cochin virtually nonstop.

LOCAL TRANSPORT

There are no regular bus services between Fort Cochin and Mattancherry Palace, but it's an enjoyable 30-minute walk through the busy warehouse area along Bazaar Rd. Autorickshaws should cost around ₹80, much less if you promise to look in a shop. Most short autorickshaw trips around Ernakulam shouldn't cost more than ₹50.

To get to Fort Cochin after ferries (and buses) stop running you'll need to catch a taxi or autorickshaw – Ernakulam Town train station to Fort Cochin should cost around ₹400; prepaid autorickshaws during the day cost ₹250.

Local buses from Ernakulam and airport buses use the **Fort Cochin bus stand** (Map p978).

Uber drivers are becoming a popular alternative to **taxis** (Map p978) for trips around Kochi.

Scooters (₹300 per day) or Enfields (₹400 to ₹600 per day) can be hired from a number of agents in Fort Cochin.

METRO

An elevated metro (www.kochimetro.org) is under construction in Ernakulam, with the first phase expected to be completed mid-2017. It will connect bus and train stations and suburbs including Edappally, and will eventually connect the airport with the city.

Around Kochi

Cherai Beach

On Vypeen Island and 25km from Fort Cochin, Cherai Beach makes a fun day trip or getaway from Kochi, especially if you hire a scooter or motorbike in Fort Cochin. The main beach entrance can get busy at times but with kilometres of lazy backwaters just a few hundred metres from the seafront, it's a pleasant place to explore.

Sleeping & Eating

Brighton Beach House GUESTHOUSE **$$**
(9946565555; www.brightonbeachhouse.org; d ₹2400-3300;) Brighton Beach House has a handful of basic rooms in a small building right near the shore. The beach is rocky here, but the garden is filled with hammocks to loll in, and has a neat, elevated stilt-restaurant that serves perfect sunset views with dinner.

★ **Les 3 Elephants** RESORT **$$$**
(9349174341, 0484-2480005; www.3elephants.in; Convent St; cottages incl breakfast ₹6000-10,000, with AC ₹12,500;) Hidden back from the beach but with the backwaters on your doorstep, Les 3 Elephants is a superb French-run ecoresort. The 11 beautifully designed boutique cottages are all different but have private sit-outs, thoughtful personal touches and lovely backwater views out to Chinese fishing nets. The restaurant serves home-cooked French-Indian fare. Worth the trip.

Chilliout Cafe CAFE **$$**
(mains ₹180-450; 9.30am-11pm Thu-Tue Oct-May) For European-style comfort food by

TRADITIONAL KERALAN ARTS

Kathakali

The art form of Kathakali crystallised at around the same time as Shakespeare was scribbling his plays. The Kathakali performance is the dramatised presentation of a play, usually based on the Hindu epics the Ramayana, the Mahabharata and the Puranas. All the great themes are covered – righteousness and evil, frailty and courage, poverty and prosperity, war and peace.

Drummers and singers accompany the actors, who tell the story through their precise movements, particularly *mudras* (hand gestures) and facial expressions.

Preparation for the performance is lengthy and disciplined. Paint, fantastic costumes, ornamental headpieces and meditation transform the actors both physically and mentally into the gods, heroes and demons they are about to play. Dancers even stain their eyes red with seeds from the *chundanga* plant to maximise the drama.

Traditional performances can last for many hours, but you can see cut-down performances in tourist destinations such as Kochi, Munnar and Kumily, and there are Kathakali schools in Thiruvananthapuram (Trivandrum; p945) and near Thrissur (p990) that encourage visitors.

Kalarippayat

Kalarippayat (or *kalari*) is an ancient tradition of martial arts training and discipline, still taught throughout Kerala. Some believe it is the forerunner of all martial arts, with roots tracing back to the 12th-century skirmishes among Kerala's feudal principalities.

Masters of *kalarippayat*, called Gurukkal, teach their craft inside a special arena called a *kalari*. You often can see *kalarippayat* performances at the same venues as Kathakali.

The three main schools of *kalarippayat* can be divided into northern and central, both practised in northern Kerala and the Malabar region, and southern *kalarippayat*. As well as open hand combat and grappling, demonstrations of the martial art are often associated with the use of weapons, including sword and shield *(valum parichayum)*, short stick *(kurunthadi)* and long stick *(neduvadi)*.

the beach – think burgers, pizzas, crêpes and barbecue – Chilliout Cafe is a breezy open-sided hang-out with sea views and a relaxed vibe. No alcohol.

Getting There & Away

From Fort Cochin, catch the vehicle-ferry to Vypeen Island (per person ₹3, two-wheeler ₹9) and hire an autorickshaw from the jetty (around ₹400) or catch one of the frequent buses (₹15, one hour) and get off at Cherai village, 1km from the beach. Buses also go here direct from Ernakulam via the Vallarpadam bridge.

North Paravur & Chennamangalam

Nowhere is the tightly woven religious cloth that is India more apparent than in North Paravur, 35km north of Kochi. Here, one of the oldest **synagogues** (₹5; 9am-5pm Tue-Sun) in Kerala, at Chennamangalam, 8km from Paravur, has been fastidiously renovated. Inside you can see door and ceiling wood-reliefs in dazzling colours, while just outside lies one of the oldest tombstones in India – inscribed with the Hebrew date corresponding to 1269. The Jesuits first arrived in Chennamangalam in 1577 and there's a Jesuit church and the ruins of a Jesuit college nearby. Nearby are a Hindu temple on a hill overlooking the Periyar River, a 16th-century mosque, and Muslim and Jewish burial grounds.

In Paravur town, you'll find the *agraharam* (place of Brahmins) – a small street of closely packed and brightly coloured houses originally settled by Tamil Brahmins.

Travel agencies in Fort Cochin can organise tours to both places.

Thrissur (Trichur)

0487 / POP 315,600

While the rest of Kerala has its fair share of celebrations, untouristy, slightly chaotic Thrissur is the cultural cherry on the festival cake with a list of energetic festivals as long as a temple-elephant's trunk. Centred around a large park (known as the 'Round') and Hindu temple complex, Thrissur is also home to a Nestorian Christian community whose denomination dates to the 3rd century AD.

Sights

Thrissur is renowned for its central temple, as well as for its numerous impressive churches, including the massive **Our Lady of Lourdes Cathedral**, towering, whitewashed **Puttanpalli (New) Church** and the **Chaldean (Nestorian) Church**.

Vadakkunathan Kshetram Temple HINDU TEMPLE
Finished in classic Keralan architecture and one of the oldest Hindu temples in the state, Vadakkunathan Kshetram Temple crowns the hill at Thrissur. Only Hindus are allowed inside, though the mound surrounding the temple has sweeping views and the surrounding park is a popular spot to linger.

Archaeology Museum MUSEUM
(adult/child ₹20/5, camera/video ₹50/250; 9.30am-1pm & 2-4.30pm Tue-Sun) The refurbished Archaeology Museum is housed in the wonderful 200-year-old Sakthan Thampuran Palace. Its mix of artefacts includes 12th-century Keralan bronze sculptures and giant earthenware pots, weaponry, coins and a lovely carved chessboard. To the side is a shady heritage garden.

Festivals & Events

Thypooya Maholsavam RELIGIOUS
(Jan/Feb) This festival stars a procession of *kavadiyattam* (a form of ritualistic dance), in which dancers carry tall, ornate structures called *kavadis*.

Uthralikavu Pooram RELIGIOUS
(Mar/Apr) The climactic day of this event sees 20 elephants circling the Uthralikavu Temple shrine.

Thrissur Pooram RELIGIOUS
(Apr/May) The most colourful and largest of Kerala's temple festivals, with huge processions of caparisoned elephants. Held at the Vadakkunathan Kshetram Temple.

Sleeping

Gurukripa Heritage HERITAGE HOTEL $
(0487-2421895; http://gurukripaheritage.in; Chembottil Lane; d without/with AC ₹930/1470, AC cottage ₹2800;) Almost a century old but recently refurbished, Gurukripa is a fine budget heritage hotel in an excellent location just off the Round. Simple rooms and family cottages are unpretentious but clean.

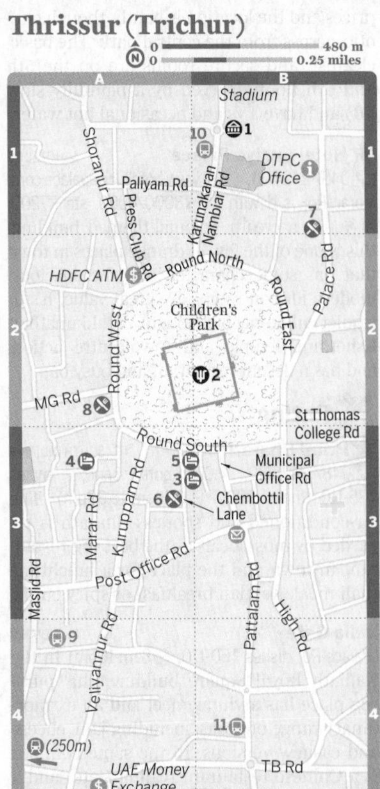

Thrissur (Trichur)

Sights
1 Archaeology Museum ... B1
2 Vadakkunathan Kshetram Temple ... B2

Sleeping
3 Gurukripa Heritage ... A3
4 Hotel Luciya Palace ... A3
5 Pathans Hotel ... A3

Eating
6 Hotel Bharath ... A3
7 India Gate ... B1
8 Navaratna Restaurant ... A2

Transport
9 KSRTC Bus Stand ... A4
10 Priyadarshini (North) Bus Stand ... B1
11 Sakthan Thampuran Bus Stand ... B4

Pathans Hotel HOTEL $
(0487-2425620; www.pathansresidentialhotel.in; Round South; s/d from ₹600/800, with AC ₹1100/1500;) No-frills rooms at no-frills

prices and the location is handy, though chaotic, across from the central park. The basic, cleanish and secure rooms are on the 5th and 6th floors (served by a painfully slow lift) and have TVs and occasional hot water.

★Hotel Luciya Palace HOTEL **$$**
(☎0487-2424731; www.hotelluciyapalace.com; Marar Rd; s/d with AC ₹3000/4000, ste ₹7200;) In a cream, colonial-themed building, this is one of the few midrange places in town that has some character, and the spacious, modern air-con rooms are great value. It's in a quiet cul-de-sac but close to Vadakkunathan Kshetram Temple and town-centre action, and has a decent restaurant and busy bar.

Eating

★Hotel Bharath SOUTH INDIAN **$**
(☎0487-2421720; Chembotil Lane; mains ₹85-110, thalis ₹90; ⊙6.30am-10.30pm) The air-conditioned and spotless Bharath is regarded by most locals as the best veg restaurant in town and the place for a lunchtime thali meal, Keralan breakfast or spicy curry.

India Gate INDIAN **$**
(Palace Rd; dishes ₹60-170; ⊙8am-10pm) In the Kalliath Royal Square building, this pure-veg place has a vintage feel and an extraordinary range of dosas, including jam, cheese and cashew versions. In the same complex is a Chinese restaurant (China Gate) and a fast-food joint (Celebrations).

Navaratna Restaurant MULTICUISINE **$$**
(Round West; dishes ₹100-200; ⊙noon-9.30pm) Cool, dark and intimate, this is one of the classier dining experiences in the town centre, with seating on raised platforms. Downstairs is veg and upstairs is nonveg, with lots of North Indian specialities, Chinese and a few Keralan dishes.

Information

DTPC Office (☎0487-2320800; Palace Rd; ⊙10am-5pm Mon-Sat) You might be able to pick up some local brochures from this tourist office.

Getting There & Away

BUS

State buses leave around every 30 minutes from the **KSRTC bus stand** bound for Trivandrum (₹235, 7½ hours), Ernakulam (Kochi; ₹68, two hours), Calicut (₹112, 3½ hours), Palakkad (₹60, 1½ hours) and Kottayam (₹115, four hours). Hourly buses go to Coimbatore (₹98, three hours).

Local services also chug along to Guruvayur (₹27, one hour), Irinjalakuda (₹27, one hour) and Cheruthuruthy (₹30, 1½ hours). Two private bus stands – **Sakthan Thampuran** and **Priyadarshini (North)** – have more frequent buses to these destinations, though the chaos involved in navigating each station hardly makes using them worthwhile.

TRAIN

Services run regularly to Ernakulam (2nd class/AC chair ₹60/260, 1½ hours), Calicut (₹70/260, three hours) and Coimbatore (₹90/305, three hours).

Getting Around

Hundreds of autorickshaws gather at the Round and are usually happy to use the meter. Short trips are ₹20.

Around Thrissur

The Thrissur region supports several institutions that are nursing the dying classical Keralan performing arts back to health.

Courses

Kerala Kalamandalam CULTURAL PROGRAMS
(☎0488-4262418; www.kalamandalam.org; courses per month ₹600; ⊙Jun-Mar) Using an ancient Gurukula system of learning, students undergo intensive study in Kathakali, *mohiniyattam* (dance of the enchantress), Kootiattam, percussion, voice and violin. A Day with the Masters (₹1400, including lunch) is a morning program allowing visitors to tour the theatre and classes and see various art and cultural presentations. Email to book in advance. It's 26km north of Thrissur.

Natana Kairali Research & Performing Centre for Traditional Arts CULTURAL PROGRAMS
(☎0480-2825559; www.natanakairali.org) This school, 20km south of Thrissur near Irinjalakuda, offers training in traditional arts, including rare forms of dance and puppetry. Short appreciation courses lasting up to a month are sometimes available to interested foreigners.

Sleeping

River Retreat GUESTHOUSE **$$**
(☎0488-4262244; www.riverretreat.in; Palace Rd, Cheruthuruthy; s/d from ₹3600/4900, ste ₹7200-9200;) River Retreat is an excellent heritage hotel and ayurvedic resort in the

former summer palace of the Maharajas of Cochin. Along with ayurvedic treatments, it includes a pool, gym and business centre. It's about 30km north of Thrissur.

NORTHERN KERALA

Kozhikode (Calicut)

☎0495 / POP 432,100

Northern Kerala's largest city, Kozhikode (still widely known as Calicut), was always a prosperous trading town and was once the capital of the formidable Zamorin dynasty. Vasco da Gama first landed near here in 1498, on his way to snatch a share of the subcontinent for king and country (Portugal that is). These days, trade depends mostly on exporting Indian labour to the Middle East, while agriculture and the timber industry are economic mainstays. For travellers it's mainly a jumping-off point for Wayanad or for the long trip over the ghats to Mysuru (Mysore) or Bengaluru.

Sights

Mananchira Square, a large central park, was the former courtyard of the Zamorins and preserves the original spring-fed tank. South of the centre, the 650-year-old Kuttichira Mosque is in an attractive wooden four-storey building that is supported by impressive wooden pillars and painted brilliant aquamarine, blue and white. The central **Church of South India** was established in 1842 by Swiss missionaries and has unique Euro-Keralan architecture.

About 1km west of Mananchira Sq, Kozhikode Beach is good enough for a sunset promenade.

Sleeping

Beach Hotel HOTEL **$$**
(☎0495-2762055, 9745062055; www.beachheritage.com; Beach Rd; r incl breakfast ₹3550-3850;) Built in 1890 to house the Malabar British Club, this is a slightly worn but charming 10-room hotel. Some rooms have bathtubs and secluded sea-facing verandahs; others have original polished wooden floors and private balconies. Restaurant and bar on-site.

Hyson Heritage HOTEL **$$**
(☎0495-4081000; www.hysonheritage.com; Bank Rd; s/d incl breakfast from ₹3600/4200;) You get a bit of swank for your rupee at this central business hotel. Rooms are spick and span and shielded from the main road. There's a good restaurant and a gym.

Alakapuri HOTEL **$$**
(☎0495-2723451; www.hotelalakapuri.com; MM Ali Rd; s/d from ₹750/1800, with AC from ₹1350/1900;) Built motel-style around a green lawn (complete with fountain!), this place is set back from a busy market area. Various rooms are a little scuffed, but reasonable value, and there's a restaurant and modern bar.

★**Harivihar** HOMESTAY **$$$**
(☎9388676054, 0495-2765865; www.harivihar.com; Bilathikulam; s/d incl meals & yoga €150/230;) In northern Calicut, the ancestral home of the Kadathanadu royal family is as serene as it gets – a traditional Keralan family compound with pristine lawns. The seven rooms are large and beautifully furnished with dark-wood antiques, but this is primarily an ayurvedic and yoga centre, with packages available.

Eating

Famous for its Malabar cuisine, Calicut is regarded as the foodie capital of northern Kerala.

Zains SOUTH INDIAN **$**
(☎0495-2366311; dishes ₹40-180; 6am-10pm) A local favourite for its Malabar dishes, biryanis and snacks, Zains is usually busy in the afternoons and evenings.

★**Paragon Restaurant** INDIAN **$$**
(Kannur Rd; dishes ₹120-350; 8am-midnight, lunch from noon) You might struggle to find a seat at this always-packed restaurant, founded in 1939. The overwhelming menu is famous for fish dishes such as fish in tamarind sauce, and its legendary chicken biryani.

Salkaram & Hut INDIAN **$$**
(Beach Rd; mains ₹110-300; 7am-10.30pm) At the back of the Beach Hotel are two restaurants with the same menu: the air-con Salkaram, and the cool open-sided bamboo 'hut' restaurant-bar serving a big range of fish and chicken dishes, and Malabari cuisine. It's a breezy place for an informal lunch or cold beer. Snacks are also served out on the front lawn.

Getting There & Away

AIR

Kozhikode Airport (www.kozhikodeairport.com) is about 25km southeast of the city in Karipur. It serves major domestic routes as well as international flights to the Gulf.

Kozhikode (Calicut)

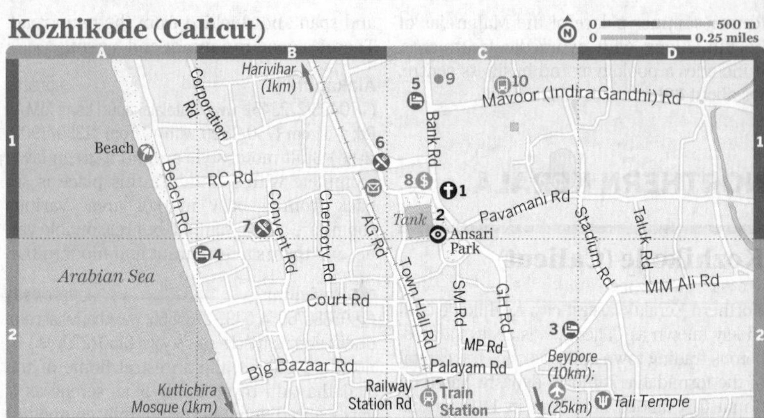

Kozhikode (Calicut)

Sights
1 Church of South India C1
2 Mananchira Square C1

Sleeping
3 Alakapuri C2
4 Beach Hotel B2
5 Hyson Heritage C1

Eating
6 Paragon Restaurant B1
Salkaram & Hut .... (see 4)
7 Zains B1

Information
8 State Bank of India C1

Transport
9 Air India C1
10 KSRTC Bus Stand C1

SpiceJet (www.spicejet.com; Kozhikode Airport) has the best domestic connections, with direct flights to Mumbai, Bengaluru and Chennai. **Air India** (☎0495-2771974; 5/2521 Bank Rd, Eroth Centre; ⊙9am-5pm) flies to Kochi and Coimbatore. **Jet Airways** (☎0495-2712375; Kozhikode Airport) has one daily flight to Mumbai. Flights to Goa go via Bengaluru or Mumbai.

BUS

The new **KSRTC bus stand** (Mavoor Rd) has government buses to Bengaluru (₹326 to ₹700, eight hours, 14 daily) via Mysuru (₹195 to ₹400, five hours), Mangaluru (₹240 to ₹340, seven hours, three daily) and to Ooty (Udhagamandalam; ₹130, 5½ hours, 5am and 6.45am). There are frequent buses to Thrissur (₹112, 3½ hours) and Kochi (₹170 to ₹280, four hours, 14 daily).

For Wayanad district, buses leave every 15 minutes heading to Sultanbatheri (₹80, three hours) via Kalpetta (₹55, two hours). Private buses for various long-distance locations also use this bus stand.

TRAIN

The train station is 1km south of Mananchira Sq. There are frequent trains to Kannur (2nd class/sleeper/3AC ₹75/140/490, two hours), Mangaluru (sleeper/3AC/2AC ₹165/490/695, five hours), Ernakulam (₹170/490/695, 4½ hours), and all the way to Trivandrum (₹240/650/930, 11 hours).

Heading southeast, trains go to Coimbatore (sleeper/3AC/2AC ₹140/490/695, 4½ hours), via Palakkad.

Getting Around

Calicut has a glut of autorickshaws and most are happy to use the meter. It costs about ₹40 from the station to the KSRTC bus stand or most hotels. An autorickshaw/taxi to the airport costs around ₹450/650.

Wayanad Region

☎04935 & 04936 / POP 816,600

Many Keralans rate the elevated Wayanad region as the most beautiful part of their state. Encompassing part of a remote forest reserve that spills into Tamil Nadu and Karnataka, Wayanad's landscape combines mountain scenery, rice paddies of ludicrous green, skinny betel nut trees, bamboo, red earth, spiky ginger fields, and rubber, cardamom and coffee plantations. Foreign travellers stop here on the bus route between Mysuru, Bengaluru or Ooty and Kerala, but it's still fantastically unspoilt and satisfyingly remote. It's also an excellent place to spot wild elephants.

The 345-sq-km sanctuary has two separate pockets – **Muthanga** in the east bordering Tamil Nadu, and **Tholpetty** in the north bordering Karnataka. Three main towns in Wayanad district make good bases and transport hubs for exploring the sanctuary – **Kalpetta** in the south, **Sultanbatheri** (Sultan Battery) in the east and **Mananthavadi** in the northwest – though the best of the accommodation is scattered throughout the region.

Sights & Activities

★Wayanad Wildlife Sanctuary NATURE RESERVE
(www.wayanadsanctuary.org; entry to each part Indian/foreigner ₹115/300, camera/video ₹40/225; 7-10am & 3-5pm) Entry to both parts of the sanctuary is only permitted as part of a two-hour jeep safari (₹650), which can be arranged at the sanctuary entrances. At the time of research the government was planning to introduce minibuses to supplement the jeeps. Trekking is no longer permitted in the sanctuary. Both Tholpetty and Muthanga close during April, but remain open during the monsoon.

Whether you go to Tholpetty or Muthanga essentially depends on whether you're staying in the north or south of Wayanad, as there's no difference in the chances of spotting wildlife. At both locations arrive at least an hour before the morning or afternoon openings to register and secure a vehicle, as there are a limited number of guides and jeeps permitted in the park at one time.

Thirunelly Temple HINDU TEMPLE
(dawn-dusk) Thought to be one of the oldest temples on the subcontinent, Thirunelly Temple is 10km from Tholpetty. Non-Hindus cannot enter, but it's worth visiting for the otherworldly cocktail of ancient and intricate pillars. Follow the path behind the temple to the stream known as Papanasini, where Hindus believe you can wash away all your sins.

Edakkal Caves CAVE
(adult/child ₹20/10, camera ₹30; 9am-4pm Tue-Sun) The highlight of these remote hilltop 'caves' – more accurately a small series of caverns – is the ancient collection of petroglyphs in the top cave, thought to date back over 3000 years. From the car park near Ambalavayal it's a steep 20-minute walk up a winding road to the ticket window, then another steep climb up to the light-filled top chamber. On a clear day there are exceptional views out over the Wayanad district. The caves get crowded on weekends.

Wayanad Heritage Museum MUSEUM
(Ambalavayal; adult/child ₹20/10, camera/video ₹20/150; 9am-5.30pm) In the small village of Ambalavayal, about 5km from Edakkal Caves, this museum exhibits tools, weapons, pottery, carved stone and other artefacts dating back to the 14th century, shedding light on Wayanad's significant Adivasi population.

Uravu HANDICRAFTS WORKSHOP
(04936-231400; www.uravu.net; Thrikkaippetta; 8.30am-5pm Mon-Sat) Around 6km from Kalpetta a collective of workers creates all sorts of artefacts from bamboo. You can visit the artists' workshops, where they work on looms, painting and carving, and support their work by buying vases, lampshades, bangles and baskets.

Kannur Ayurvedic Centre AYURVEDA
(9497872562, 9495260535; www.ayurvedawayanad.com; Kalpetta; massage from ₹1200, yoga & meditation ₹1200) For rejuvenation and curative ayurvedic treatments, visit this excellent small, government-certified and family-run clinic in the leafy backstreets of Kalpetta. Accommodation and yoga classes are available.

Trekking

There are some good opportunities for trekking around the district (though not in

MAHÉ

Mahé is an anomaly in Kerala. On the Malabar Coast about 10km south of Thalassery, Mahé is surrounded by, but not actually part of, Kerala – it's part of the Union Territory of Puducherry (Pondicherry), formerly under French India. Apart from the riverfront promenade with its Parisian-style street lamps, the province is similar to other towns along the Keralan coast, and Malayalam and English are the main languages. The other obvious difference is that there is no restriction on the sale of alcohol here (unlike in Kerala) and sales tax is low. Unsurprisingly, every third shop is an open-fronted liquor store with giant brandname signs!

the wildlife sanctuary itself), but it's tightly controlled by the Forest Department and various trekking areas open and close depending on current environmental concerns. At the time of research three treks were open: Chembra Peak (but only to the midway point) and Banasura Hills in the south, and Brahmagiri Hills in the north. Permits and guides are mandatory and can be arranged at forest offices in south or north Wayanad or through your accommodation. The standard cost for a permit and guide is ₹2500 for up to five people – try to arrange a group in advance.

Sleeping & Eating

There's plenty of accommodation in Wayanad's three main towns of Kalpetta, Sultanbatheri and Mananthavadi, but the isolated homestays and resort accommodation scattered throughout the region are much better choices.

Kalpetta

PPS Residency HOTEL $

(☎04936-203431; www.ppsresidency.com; Kalpetta; s/d ₹400/500, with AC ₹1320/1540; ❄) This friendly budget place in the middle of Kalpetta has a variety of reasonably clean rooms in a motel-like compound, which includes the reasonably popular multicuisine Pankaj restaurant and a beer parlour. Helpful management can arrange trips around Wayanad.

Haritagiri HOTEL $$

(☎04936-203145; www.hotelharitagiri.com; Kalpetta; s/d incl breakfast from ₹1650/2100, with AC from ₹2100/2750; ❄📶🏊) Set back from Kalpetta's busy main streets, this is a comfortable midrange option, with balconied rooms and more private garden cottages. There are two good restaurants, a pool, gym and an ayurvedic 'village' on-site.

Sultanbatheri

Mint Flower Residency HOTEL $$

(☎04936-222206, 9745222206; www.mintflowerresidency.com; Sultanbatheri; s/d ₹830/1375, with AC ₹1075/1670) The budget annexe of Mint Flower Hotel is in great condition. It's no frills but rooms are spotless and come with hot water and TV.

Issac's Hotel Regency HOTEL $$

(☎04936-220512; www.issacsregency.com; Sultanbatheri; dm ₹250, s/d/tr from ₹1150/1600/1800, with AC from ₹1550/2000/2250; ❄@📶🏊) This remarkably well-equipped complex near the private bus stand in the town centre has everything from a cinema to a swim-

Wayanad District

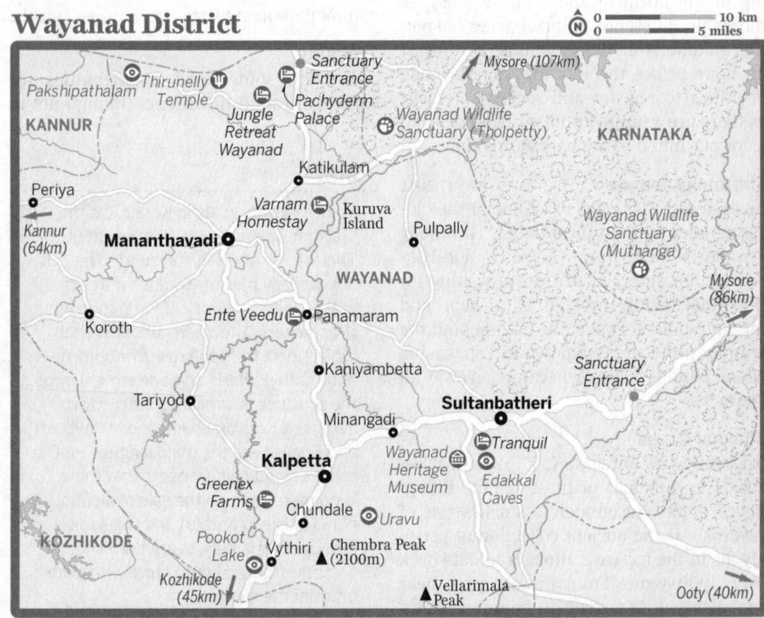

ming pool at a reasonable price. The air-con 'dorm' has only mattresses on the floor.

Wilton Restaurant MULTICUISINE **$$**
(☎04936-226444; Kalpetta Rd; mains ₹120-440; ⊙7am-10pm) Wilton's is a stand-out restaurant in Sultanbatheri with an eclectic menu of Indian, Arabian, Asian and burgers served in the air-con upstairs dining room. Downstairs is a snack and sweet shop with pastries, dried fruits and coffee. Snappy service.

Around Wayanad

★Varnam Homestay HOMESTAY **$$**
(☎9745745860, 04935-215666; www.varnamhomestay.com; Kurukanmoola, Kadungamalayil House; s/d r incl meals ₹1500/2600, villa ₹1800/3000; ❄📶) This oasis of peace and calm is a lovely place to stay a few kilometres from Katikulam in northern Wayanad. Varghese and Beena will look after you with Wayanad stories, local information and delicious home cooking with organic farm-fresh ingredients. Rooms are in a traditional family home or a newer elevated 'tree-house' villa, and the property is surrounded by jungle and spice plantations.

Ente Veedu HOMESTAY **$$**
(☎9446834834, 04935-5220008; www.enteveedu.co.in; Panamaram; r incl breakfast ₹2500-5500, with AC ₹3500-4000; ❄@📶) Secluded and set in a lovely location overlooking sprawling banana plantations and rice paddies, this homestay halfway between Kalpetta and Mananthavadi is definitely worth seeking out. There are several large rooms, two bamboo-lined ones with private balconies, hammocks and wicker lounges to enjoy the sensational views. Lunch and dinner are available. Call to arrange a pick-up.

Greenex Farms RESORT **$$**
(☎9645091512; www.greenexfarms.com; Chundale Estate Rd, Moovatty; r ₹2250-7800; 📶🏊) Greenex Farms is a wonderfully remote-feeling place surrounded by spice, coffee and tea plantations about 8km southwest of Kalpetta. Each of the private cottages is individually designed with separate lounge, bathroom, balcony and superb views. Restaurants, campfire, walks and activities.

Jungle Retreat Wayanad GUESTHOUSE **$$**
(☎9742565333; www.jungleretreatwayanad.com; d incl breakfast ₹2500; 📶) The location on the boundary of Tholpetty Wildlife Sanctuary is exceptional and the rooms and cottages comfortable at this jungle guesthouse. The best rooms are the rustic cottages with terraces facing the reserve. Meals are ₹500 extra and a host of activities can be arranged.

★Tranquil HOMESTAY **$$$**
(☎04936-220244; www.tranquilresort.com; Kuppamudi Estate, Kolagapara; d incl breakfast ₹11,900-16,500, tree house ₹18,800, tree villa ₹19,350; 📶🏊) This wonderfully serene and exclusive homestay is in the middle of an incredibly lush 160 hectares of pepper, coffee, vanilla and cardamom plantations. The elegant house has sweeping verandahs filled with plants and handsome furniture, and there are two tree houses that may be the finest in the state. A network of marked walking trails meanders around the plantation.

ℹ Information

International ATMs can be found in each of Wayanad's three main towns.

DTPC Office (☎9446072134; www.wayanadtourism.org; Kalpetta; ⊙9.30am-5.30pm Mon-Sat) The DTPC has two useful offices in Kalpetta: one in town and the other upstairs at the new bus stand. They have a map and can advise on trekking.

ℹ Getting There & Away

Although remote, Wayanad is easily accessible by bus from Calicut and Kannur in Kerala, and from Mysuru (Karnataka) and Ooty (Tamil Nadu). Buses brave the winding roads – including a series of nine spectacular hairpin bends – between Calicut and Kalpetta (₹65 to ₹95, two hours) every 15 minutes, with some continuing on to Sultanbatheri (₹80 to ₹150, three hours) and others to Mananthavadi (₹87, three hours). Hourly buses run between Kannur and Mananthavadi (₹55, 2½ hours).

From Sultanbatheri, an 8am bus heads out for Ooty (₹100, four hours), with a second one passing through town at around 12.45pm. The Ooty bus leaves Mananthavadi at 11.15am. Buses run from Kalpetta to Mysuru (₹143, four hours, hourly) via Sultanbatheri, but note that the border gate is closed between 7pm and 6am. There are six daily buses to Mysuru (₹167, three hours) on the alternative northern route from Mananthavadi, where the border is open 24 hours.

ℹ Getting Around

The Wayanad district is quite spread out but plenty of private buses connect the main towns of Mananthavadi, Kalpetta and Sultanbatheri every 10 to 20 minutes during daylight hours (₹15 to ₹25, 45 minutes to one hour). From Mananthavadi, regular buses also head to

Tholpetty (₹15, one hour). You can hire jeeps or taxis to get between towns for ₹600 to ₹800 each way, or hire a vehicle to tour the region for around ₹2000 per day.

There are plenty of autorickshaws and taxis for short hops within the towns.

Kannur & Around

0497 / POP 1.2 MILLION

Kerala's northern coast is far less touristed than the south, which for many is an attraction in its own right. The main draws in this part of coastal Kerala are the beautiful, undeveloped beaches and the enthralling theyyam possession rituals (p999).

Under the Kolathiri rajas, Kannur (formerly Cannanore) was a major port bristling with international trade – explorer Marco Polo christened it a 'great emporium of spice trade'. Since then, the usual colonial suspects, including the Portuguese, Dutch and British, have had a go at exerting their influence on the region, leaving behind the odd fort. Today it is an unexciting, though agreeable, town known mostly for its weaving industry and cashew trade.

This is a predominantly Muslim area, so local sensibilities should be kept in mind: wear a sarong over your bikini on the beach.

Sights

Kannur's main town beach is the 4km-long **Payyambalam Beach** (beach park ₹10, camera/video ₹25/150; 8am-8pm), which starts about 1.5km east of the train station, just past the military cantonment. The beach park gets busy in the evening when families and couples come down to watch the sunset and picnic.

Arakkal Museum MUSEUM
(Indian/foreigner ₹20/100, camera ₹25; 9.30am-5.15pm Mon-Sat) Housed in part of the royal palace of the Arakkal family, a 16th-century Kannur dynasty, this harbourfront museum features antiques, furniture, weapons, silver and portraits. It's a fascinating look into the life of Kerala's only Muslim royal family.

Kerala Dinesh Beedi Co-Operative WORKSHOP
(0497-2701699; www.keraladinesh.com; 8am-6pm Mon-Sat) FREE The Kannur region is known for the manufacture of *beedis,* those tiny Indian cigarettes deftly rolled inside green leaves. This is one of the largest and purportedly best manufacturers, with a factory at Thottada, 7km south of Kannur and about 4km from Thottada beach. A skilled individual can roll up to 1000 a day! Visitors are welcome to look around; an autorickshaw should cost around ₹120 return from Kannur town.

Sleeping & Eating

Although there are plenty of hotels in Kannur town, the best places to stay are homestays near the beach at Thottada (8km south) and towards Thalassery.

Kannur Town

Hotel Meridian Palace HOTEL $
(9995999547, 0497-2701676; www.hotelmeridianpalace.com; Bellard Rd; s/d from ₹550/700, deluxe ₹935/1100, with AC ₹1425-1650;) In the market area opposite the main train station, this place is hardly palatial but it's friendly enough and offers a cornucopia of clean budget rooms and a Punjabi restaurant.

Hotel Odhen's INDIAN $
(Onden Rd; mains ₹30-100; 8.30am-5pm) This popular local restaurant in Kannur's market area is usually packed at lunchtime. The speciality is Malabar cuisine, including tasty seafood curries and banana-leaf thalis.

Thottada Beach & Around

Blue Mermaid Homestay HOMESTAY $$
(9497300234; www.bluemermaid.in; Thottada Beach; s/d incl breakfast & dinner ₹2500/3500, cottage ₹4000;) With a prime location among the palms facing Thottada Beach, Blue Mermaid is a charming and immaculate guesthouse with rooms in a traditional home, bright air-con rooms in a newer building and a whimsical stilted 'honeymoon cottage'. Friendly young owners cook up fine Keralan meals.

Waves Beach Resort HOMESTAY $$
(9495050850, 9447173889; www.wavesbeachresort.co.in; Adikadalayi, Thottada Beach; s/d incl meals ₹2000/3500;) Crashing waves will lull you to sleep at these very cute hexagonal laterite huts overlooking a semi-private little crescent beach. The welcoming owners, Seema and Arun, also have rooms in two other nearby properties, including cheaper rooms in an old Keralan house.

Costa Malabari GUESTHOUSE $$
(0944-7775691, reservations 0484-2371761; www.touristdesk.in; Thottada Beach; d incl meals

THEYYAM

Kerala's most popular ritualistic art form, *theyyam* is believed to predate Hinduism, originating from folk dances performed during harvest celebrations. An intensely local ritual, it's often performed in *kavus* (sacred groves) throughout northern Kerala.

Theyyam refers both to the shape of the deity/hero portrayed, and to the actual ritual. There are around 450 different *theyyams*, each with a distinct costume, made up of face paint, bracelets, breastplates, skirts, garlands and exuberant, intricately crafted headdresses that can be up to 6m or 7m tall. During performances, each protagonist loses his physical identity and speaks, moves and blesses the devotees as if he were that deity. Frenzied dancing and wild drumming create an atmosphere in which a deity indeed might, if it so desired, manifest itself in human form.

From November to April there are annual rituals at each of the hundreds of *kavus*. *Theyyams* are often held to bring good fortune to important events such as marriages and housewarmings.The best place for visitors to see *theyyam* is in village temples in the Kannur region of northern Kerala. In peak times (December to February) there should be a *theyyam* ritual happening somewhere almost every night.

Although tourists are welcome to attend, this is not a dance performance but a religious ritual, and the usual rules of temple behaviour apply: dress appropriately, avoid disturbing participants and villagers; refrain from displays of public affection. Photography is permitted, but avoid using a flash. For details on where and when, ask at your guesthouse or contact Kurien at Costa Malabari.

₹3000-4000; ❄📶) Costa Malabari pioneered tourism in this area and there are three lovely homestay properties just back from Thottada Beach. Costa Malabari 1 has spacious rooms in an old hand-loom factory, while rooms are offered in two other nearby bungalows. The home-cooked Keralan food is included. Manager Kurien is an expert on the *theyyam* ritual and can help arrange a visit.

Kannur Beach House HOMESTAY **$$**
(☎0497-2708360, 9847184535; www.kannurbeachhouse.com; Thottada Beach; s/d ₹2600/3600) This original beachfront homestay is a traditional Keralan building with handsome wooden shutters. Rooms are looking a little worn but you can enjoy sensational ocean sunset views from your porch or balcony. A small lagoon separates the house from the beach. Breakfast and dinner included.

Ezhara Beach House HOMESTAY **$$**
(☎0497-2835022; www.ezharabeachhouse.com; 7/347 Ezhara Kadappuram; s/d incl meals from ₹1500/3000; 📶) Fronting the unspoilt Kizhunna Ezhara beach, midway between Kannur and Thalassery railway stations (11km from each), Ezhara Beach House is run by welcoming and no-nonsense Hyacinth. Rooms are simple but the house has character and guests rave about the meals.

Thalassery

Ayisha Manzil HOMESTAY **$$$**
(☎9496189296; www.ayishamanzil.com; Thalassery; d incl meals ₹15,500; ❄📶🏊) The four rooms in this 150-year-old heritage homestay are enormous and filled with antique furniture, but most guests come for the Mappila (Muslim) cuisine and the famous cooking classes (₹2500) overseen by Mrs Faiza Moosa. A visit to the local market is part of the culinary experience. Book well ahead.

Getting There & Away

AIR

Kannur International Airport, 25km east of Kannur, is due to open in 2017 and will be the largest in Kerala.

BUS

Kannur has several bus stands: the enormous central bus stand – one of the largest in Kerala – is the place to catch private and some government buses, but most long-distance state buses still also use the KSRTC bus stand near the Caltex junction, 1km northeast of the train station.

There are daily buses to Mysuru (₹203 to ₹298, eight hours, five daily), Madikeri (₹85, 2½ hours, 11am) and Ooty (via Wayanad; ₹221, nine hours, 7.30am and 10pm).

For the Wayanad region, buses leave every hour from the central bus stand to Mananthavadi (₹80, 2½ hours).

For Thottada Beach, take bus 22 or 29 (₹9) from Plaza Junction opposite the train station and get off at Adikadalayi village.

TRAIN

There are frequent daily trains to Calicut (2nd class/AC chair ₹60/295, 1½ hours), Ernakulam (sleeper/3AC/2AC ₹220/540/740, 6½ hours) and Alleppey (₹215/580/830). Heading north there are express trains to Mangaluru (sleeper/3AC/2AC ₹170/540/740, three hours) and up to Goa (sleeper/3AC/2AC ₹350/915/1295, eight hours).

Bekal & Around

0467

Bekal and nearby Palakunnu and Udma, in Kerala's far north, have long, white-sand beaches begging for DIY exploration. The area is gradually being colonised by glitzy five-star resorts catering to fresh-from-the-Gulf millionaires, but it's still worth the trip for off-the-beaten-track adventurers.

Sights & Activities

The laterite-brick **Bekal Fort** (Indian/foreigner ₹15/200; 8am-5pm), built between 1645 and 1660, sits on Bekal's rocky headland. Next door, **Bekal Beach** (₹5) encompasses a grassy park and a long, beautiful stretch of sand that turns into a circus on weekends and holidays when local families descend for rambunctious leisure time. Isolated **Kappil Beach**, 6km north of Bekal, is a lonely stretch of fine sand and calm water, but beware of shifting sandbars.

Sleeping & Eating

Apart from the five-star Vivanta Taj and Lalit hotels, there are lots of cheap, average-quality hotels scattered between Kanhangad (12km south) and Kasaragod (10km north), with a few notable exceptions.

Nirvana@Bekal COTTAGE $$
(0467-2272900, 9446463088; www.nirvanabekal.com; Bekal Fort Rd; d incl breakfast ₹1800-4700;) Right below the walls of Bekal Fort, these laterite-brick cottages in a beachfront palm-filled garden are the best value in town. Rooms come with air-con and TV, there's a good restaurant, ayurvedic treatments and even a cricket bowling machine!

★**Neeleshwar Hermitage** RESORT $$$
(0467-2287510; www.neeleshwarhermitage.com; Ozhinhavalappu, Neeleshwar; s/d cottages from ₹13,900/16,600;) This spectacular beachfront ecoresort consists of 18 beautifully designed thatch-roof cottages modelled on Keralan fisherman's huts but with modern touches like iPod docks and a five-star price tag. Built according to the principles of Kerala Vastu, the resort has an infinity pool, nearly 5 hectares of lush gardens fragrant with frangipani, superb organic food and ayurvedic massage, meditation and yoga programs.

Getting There & Away

A couple of local trains stop at Fort Bekal station, right on Bekal beach. Kanhangad, 12km south, and Kasaragod, 10km to the north, are major train stops. Frequent buses run from

OFF THE BEATEN TRACK

VALIYAPARAMBA BACKWATERS

Kerala's 'northern backwaters' offer an intriguing alternative to better-known waterways down south. This large body of water is fed by five rivers and fringed by ludicrously green groves of nodding palms. One of the nearest towns is **Payyanur**, 50km north of Kannur. It's possible to catch the ferry from Kotti, from where KSWTD operates local ferries to the surrounding islands. It's five minutes' walk from Payyanur railway station. The 2½-hour trip (₹10) from Kotti takes you to the Ayitti Jetty, 8km from Payyanur, from where you can also catch the return ferry.

You can stay at the peaceful **Valiyaparamba Retreat** (0484-2371761; www.touristdesk.in/valiyaparambaretreat.htm; d incl meals ₹4000), a secluded homestay with simple rooms and stilted bungalows 15km north of Payyanur and 3km from Ayitti Jetty. Kochi's Tourist Desk (p981) also runs day trips on a traditional houseboat around the Valiyaparamba Backwaters.

Bekal Boat Stay (0467-2282633, 9447469747; www.bekalboatstay.com; Kottappuram, Nileshwar; 24hr cruise ₹6000-8000) is one of the few operators around here to offer overnight houseboat trips in the Valiyaparamba Backwaters. Day cruises (₹4000 for up to six people) are also available. It's around 22km south of Bekal and about 2km from Nileshwar – get off any bus between Kannur and Bekal and take an autorickshaw from there (₹30).

Bekal to both Kanhangad and Kasaragod (around ₹15, 20 minutes), from where you can pick up major trains to Mangaluru, Goa or south to Kochi. An autorickshaw from Bekal Junction to Kappil beach is around ₹80.

LAKSHADWEEP

POP 64,500

Comprising a string of 36 palm-covered, white-sand-skirted coral islands 300km off the coast of Kerala, Lakshadweep is as stunning as it is isolated. Only 10 of these islands are inhabited, mostly by Sunni Muslim fishermen, and foreigners are only allowed to stay on a few of these. With fishing and coir production the main sources of income, local life on the islands remains highly traditional, and a caste system divides the islanders between Koya (land owners), Malmi (sailors) and Melachery (farmers). Electricity is supplied by generator.

The real attraction of the islands lies under the water: the 4200 sq km of pristine archipelago lagoons, unspoilt coral reefs and warm waters are a magnet for scuba divers and snorkellers.

Lakshadweep can only be visited on a prearranged package trip. At the time of research, resorts on **Kadmat**, **Minicoy**, **Kavaratti** and **Bangaram** Islands were open to tourists - though most visits to the islands are boat-based packages that include a cruise from Kochi, island visits, water sports, diving and nights spent on board the boat. At the time of research foreigners were not permitted to stay on Agatti Island but can fly there and take a boat transfer to other islands. Packages include permits and meals, and can be arranged through SPORTS.

Sleeping & Eating

You can stay on the remote island of Minicoy, the second-largest island and the closest to the Maldives, in modern cottages or a 20-room guesthouse at **Minicoy Island Resort** (☎0484-2668387; www.lakshadweeptourism.com; s/d with AC from ₹5000/7000; ❄); book via SPORTS (p1001).

Kadmat Beach Resort (☎0484-4011134; www.kadmat.com; 2 night s/d incl meals from ₹11,450/16,050; ❄) on Kadmat Island has 28 modern, beach-facing cottages, reachable by overnight boat from Kochi or boat transfer from Agatti airport.

There are basic **cottages** (www.lakshadweeptourism.com; s/d ₹10,000/15,000) and Lakshadweep's most upmarket, newly reopened **Bangaram Island Resort** (☎0484-2397550; www.bangaram.org; s/d incl meals ₹11,150/16,900) on otherwise uninhabited Bangaram Island, reached by boat from Agatti.

DIVING LAKSHADWEEP

Lakshadweep is a scuba diver's dream, with excellent visibility and an embarrassment of marine life living on undisturbed coral reefs. The best time to dive is between November and mid-May when the seas are calm and visibility is 20m to 40m. There are dive centres on Bangaram, Kadmat, Kavaratti, Minicoy and Agatti islands (though the last was closed to foreigners at the time of research). SPORTS in Kochi can organise dive packages or courses.

Information

PERMITS

All visits require a special permit (one month's notice), which can be organised by tour operators or SPORTS in Kochi. At the time of research foreigners were allowed to stay at the government resorts on Kadmat, Minicoy, Kavaratti and Bangaram; enquire at SPORTS.

TOURIST INFORMATION

Mint Valley Travel (☎0484-2397550; www.mintvalley.com; Kochi) Reliable private tour operator.

SPORTS (Society for the Promotion of Recreational Tourism & Sports; ☎9495984001, 0484-2668387; www.lakshadweeptourism.com; PS Parameswaran Rd, Willingdon Island; ⏲10am-5pm Mon-Sat) In Kochi; the main organisation for tourist information and booking package tours.

Getting There & Away

Air India flies between Kochi and Agatti Island (from ₹9700 return) daily except Sunday. Boat transport between Agatti and Kadmat, Kavaratti and Bangaram is included in the package tours available.

Six passenger ships – MV *Kavaratti*, MV *Arabian Sea*, MV *Lakshadweep Sea*, MV *Bharat Seema*, MV *Amindivi* and MV *Minicoy* – operate between Kochi and Lakshadweep, taking 14 to 20 hours.

Cruise packages start from a weekend package (adult/child ₹7216/6185) to a five-day, three-island cruise from ₹25,000/18,000.

See the package tour section of www.lakshadweeptourism.com for more details.

Tamil Nadu & Chennai

Includes ➜

Best Places to Sleep

- ➜ Saratha Vilas (p1058)
- ➜ Les Hibiscus (p1041)
- ➜ Bungalow on the Beach (p1047)
- ➜ Visalam (p1058)
- ➜ 180º McIver (p1077)

Best Temples

- ➜ Meenakshi Amman Temple (p1059)
- ➜ Brihadishwara Temple (p1050)
- ➜ Arunachaleshwar Temple (p1034)
- ➜ Nataraja Temple (p1046)
- ➜ Sri Ranganathaswamy Temple (p1053)

Why Go?

Tamil Nadu is the homeland of one of humanity's living classical civilisations, stretching back uninterrupted for two millennia and very much alive today in the Tamils' language, dance, poetry and Hindu religion.

But this deep-South state, with its age-old trading vocation, is as dynamic as it is immersed in tradition. Fire-worshipping devotees who smear tikka on their brows in Tamil Nadu's famously spectacular temples might rush off to IT offices – and then unwind at a glitzy night-time haunt in rapidly modernising Chennai (Madras) or with sun salutations in bohemian Puducherry (Pondicherry).

When the hot chaos of Tamil temple towns overwhelms, escape to the southernmost tip of India where three seas mingle; to the splendid mansions sprinkled across arid Chettinadu; or up to the cool, forest-clad, wildlife-prowled Western Ghats. It's all packed into a state that remains proudly distinct from the rest of India, while also being among the most welcoming.

When to Go

Chennai

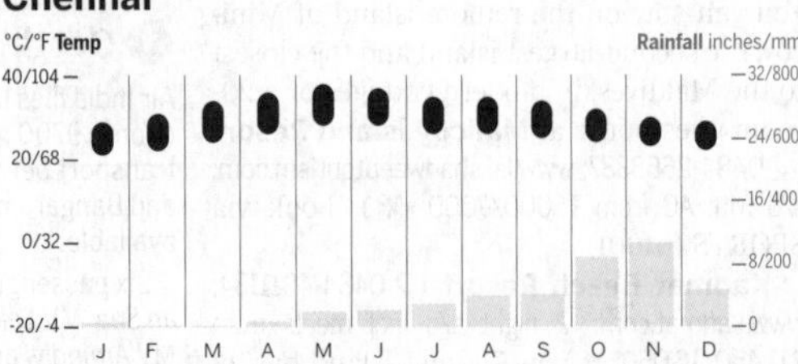

Jan–Mar The weather is at its (relative) coolest and the monsoon is over.

Jul–Sep Hit the hill stations after the crowded 'season' but while the weather is still good.

Nov–Dec The full-moon festival of lights.

Tamil Nadu & Chennai Highlights

1. **Puducherry** (p1037) Soaking up the unique Franco-Indian flair, boho boutiques and lively yoga scene.
2. **Hill Stations** (p1068) Escaping to the cool, mist-cloaked mountains and heritage hotels at Kodaikanal or Ooty.
3. **Thanjavur** (p1050) Admiring the Chola temple architecture of Brihadishwara Temple.
4. **Chettinadu** (p1057) Spending the night in an opulent mansion and feasting on fiery cuisine.
5. **Madurai** (p1059) Getting lost in the colourful chaos of Tamil temple life at Madurai's Meenakshi Amman Temple.
6. **Tranquebar** (p1047) Losing track of time at a quirky old Danish seaside colony.
7. **Mudumalai Tiger Reserve** (p1084) Tracking down rare exotic wildlife between mountain panoramas.
8. **Chennai** (p1005) Exploring the countless faces of Tamil Nadu's capital.

History

The Tamils consider themselves the standard bearers of Dravidian – pre-Aryan Indian – civilisation. Dravidians are defined as speakers of languages of the Dravidian family, the four most important of which are all rooted in South India – Tamil, Malayalam (Kerala), Telugu (Telangana and Andhra Pradesh) and Kannada (Karnataka). South Indian cultures and history are distinct from Aryan North India, and Tamils' ability to trace their identity back in an unbroken line to classical antiquity is a source of considerable pride.

Despite the Dravidians' long-standing southern location, elements of Dravidian culture – including a meditating god seated in the lotus position, possibly the world's first depiction of the yogi archetype – existed in the early Indus civilisations of northwest India some 4000 years ago. Whether Dravidian culture was widespread around India before Aryan cultures appeared in the north in the 2nd millennium BC, or whether the Dravidians only reached the south because the Aryans drove them from the north, is a matter of debate. But the cushion of distance has undoubtedly allowed South Indian cultures to develop with little interruption from northern influences or invasions for more than 2000 years.

The Tamil language was well established in Tamil Nadu by the 3rd century BC, the approximate start of the Sangam Age, when Tamil poets produced the body of classical literature known as Sangam literature. The Sangam period lasted until about AD 300, with three main Tamil dynasties arising in different parts of Tamil Nadu ('Tamil Country'): the early Cholas in the centre, the Cheras in the west and the Pandyas in the south.

By the 7th century the Pallavas, also Tamil, established an empire based at Kanchipuram extending from Tamil Nadu north into Andhra Pradesh. They take credit for the great stone carvings of Mamallapuram (Mahabalipuram) and constructed the region's first free-standing temples.

Next in power were the medieval Cholas (whose connection with the early Cholas is hazy). Based in the Cauvery valley of central Tamil Nadu, at their peak the Cholas ruled Sri Lanka and the Maldives plus much of South India, and extended their influence to Southeast Asia, spreading Tamil ideas of reincarnation, karma and yogic practice.

The Cholas raised Dravidian architecture to new heights with the magnificent towered temples at Thanjavur and Gangaikondacholapuram, and carried the art of bronze image casting to its peak, especially in their images of Shiva as Nataraja, the cosmic dancer. *Gopurams,* the tall temple gate towers characteristic of Tamil Nadu, made their appearance in late Chola times.

By the late 14th century much of Tamil Nadu was under the sway of the Vijayanagar empire based at Hampi (Karnataka). As the Vijayanagar state weakened in the 16th cen-

TOP STATE FESTIVALS

International Yoga Festival (p1041; 4–7 Jan, Puducherry) Shows, workshops and competitions.

Pongal (statewide; mid-Jan) Marks the end of the harvest season and is one of Tamil Nadu's most important festivals, named after a rice-and-lentil dish cooked in new clay pots. Animals, especially cows, are honoured for their contributions.

Thyagaraja Aradhana (p1052; Jan, Thiruvaiyaru) Carnatic music.

Teppam (Float) Festival (p1062; Jan/Feb, Madurai) Meenakshi temple deities are paraded around town.

Natyanjali Dance Festival (p1046; Feb/Mar, Chidambaram) Five days of professional classical dance.

Chithirai Festival (p1062; Apr/May, Madurai) Two-week event celebrating the marriage of Meenakshi to Sundareswarar (Shiva).

Karthikai Deepam Festival (p1035; Nov/Dec, statewide) Festival of lights.

Chennai Festival of Music & Dance (p1011; mid-Dec–mid-Jan, Chennai) A huge celebration of South Indian music and dance.

Mamallapuram Dance Festival (p1028; Dec–Jan, Mamallapuram) Four weeks of classical and folk dance from across India on open-air stages.

tury, some of their local governors, the Nayaks, set up strong independent kingdoms, notably at Madurai and Thanjavur. Vijayanagar and Nayak sculptors carved wonderfully detailed temple statues and reliefs.

Europeans first landed on Tamil shores in the 16th century, when the Portuguese settled at San Thome. The Dutch, British, French and Danes followed in the 17th century, striking deals with local rulers to set up coastal trading colonies. Eventually it came down to the British, based at Chennai (then Madras), against the French, based at Puducherry (then Pondicherry). The British won out in the three Carnatic Wars, fought between 1744 and 1763. By the end of the 18th century British dominance over most Tamil lands was assured.

The area governed by the British from Madras, the Madras Presidency, included parts of Andhra Pradesh, Kerala and Karnataka, an arrangement that continued (as Madras State) after Indian independence in 1947, until Kerala, Karnataka, Andhra Pradesh and present-day Tamil Nadu (130,058 sq km) were created on linguistic lines in the 1950s. It wasn't until 1968 that the current state (population 72.1 million) was officially named Tamil Nadu.

Tamil Nadu's political parties are often headed up by former film stars, most prominent among them controversial former Chief Minister and AIADMK (All India Anna Dravida Munnetra Kazhagam) leader Jayalalithaa Jayaram. Known as 'Amma' (mother), Jayalalithaa was worshipped with almost deity-like status across the state until her death on 5 December 2016.

CHENNAI (MADRAS)

☎044 / POP 8.7 MILLION

If you have time to explore Chennai (formerly Madras), this 400-sq-km conglomerate of urban villages and diverse neighbourhoods making up Tamil Nadu's capital will pleasantly surprise you. Its role is as keeper of South Indian artistic, religious and culinary traditions.

Among Chennai's greatest assets are its people, infectiously enthusiastic about their hometown; they won't hit you with a lot of hustle and hassle. Recent years have thrown in a new layer of cosmopolitan glamour: luxe hotels, sparkling boutiques, quirky cafes, smart contemporary restaurants and a sprinkling of swanky bars and clubs.

With its sweltering southern heat, roaring traffic and lack of outstanding sights, Chennai has often been seen as the dowdier sibling among India's four biggest cities. But even if you're just caught here between connections, it's well worth poking around the museums, exploring the temples, savouring deliciously authentic South Indian delicacies or taking a sunset saunter along Marina Beach.

History

The southern neighbourhood of Mylapore existed long before the rest of Chennai; there is evidence that it traded with Roman and even Chinese and Greek merchants. In 1523, the Portuguese established their nearby coastal settlement San Thome. Another century passed before Francis Day and the British East India Company rocked up in 1639, searching for a good southeast-Indian trading base, and struck a deal with the local Vijayanagar ruler to set up a fort-cum-trading-post at Madraspatnam fishing village. This was Fort St George, built from 1640 to 1653.

The three Carnatic Wars between 1744 and 1763 saw Britain and its colonialist rival France allying with competing South Indian princes in their efforts to get the upper hand over local rulers – and each other. The French occupied Fort St George from 1746 to 1749 but the British eventually triumphed, and the French withdrew to Pondicherry.

As capital of the Madras Presidency, one of the four major divisions of British-era India, Madras grew into an important naval and commercial centre. After Independence, it became capital of Madras State and its successor Tamil Nadu. The city was renamed Chennai in 1996. Today, it's a major IT hub, and is often called 'the Detroit of India' for its booming motor-vehicle industry.

Sights

Central Chennai

★Government Museum MUSEUM

(Map p1012; www.chennaimuseum.org; Pantheon Rd, Egmore; Indian/foreigner ₹15/250, camera/video ₹200/500; ⏲9.30am-5pm Sat-Thu) Housed across the striking British-built Pantheon Complex, this excellent museum is Chennai's best. The big highlight is building 3, the **Bronze Gallery**, with a superb collection of South Indian bronzes from the 7th-century Pallava era through to modern times (and English-language explanatory material).

It was from the 9th to 11th centuries, in the Chola period, that bronze sculpture

Chennai (Madras)

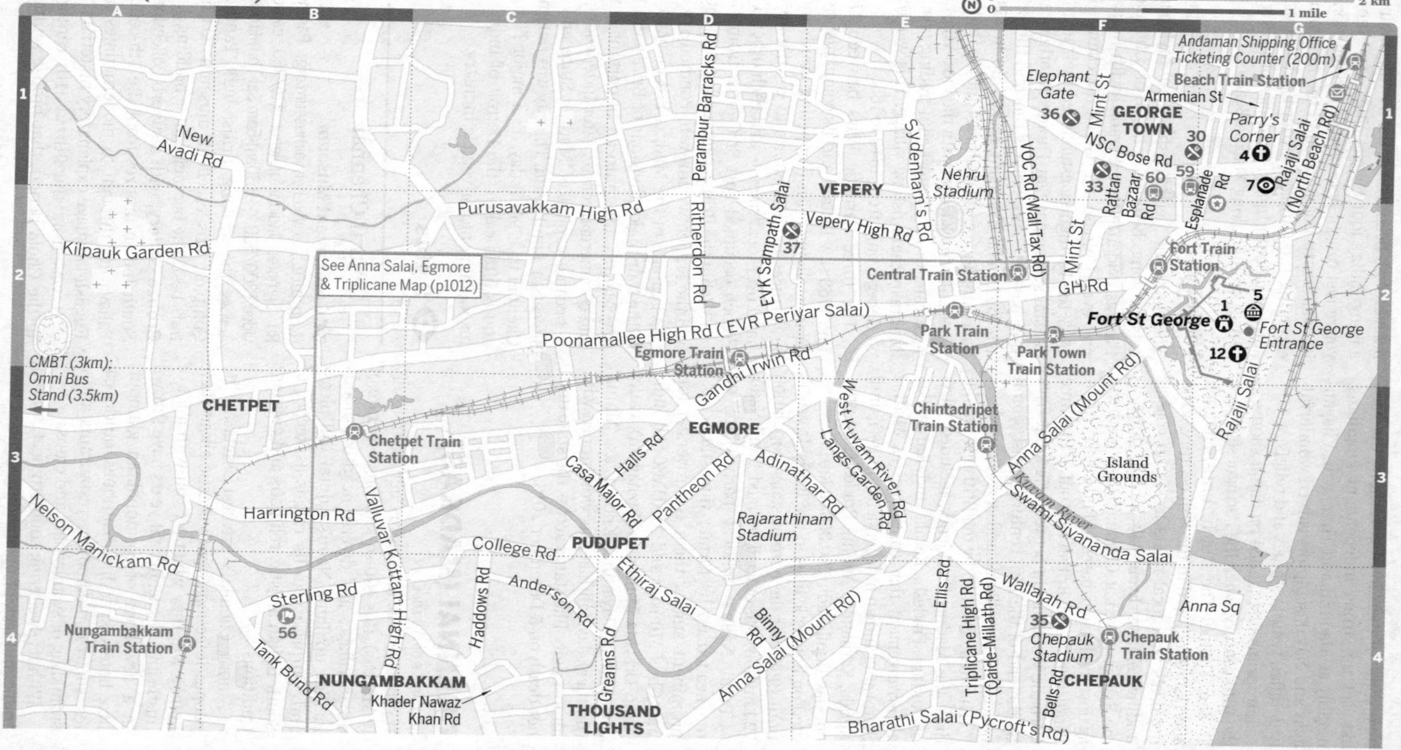

0 — 2 km
0 — 1 mile

A B C D E F G
1 2 3 4

Andaman Shipping Office Ticketing Counter (200m)
Beach Train Station
Armenian St
Elephant Gate
36
Mint St
GEORGE TOWN
Parry's Corner
4
30
NSC Bose Rd
Rajaji Salai (North Beach Rd)
33
Rattan Bazaar Rd
60
59
Esplanade Rd
7
New Avadi Rd
Nehru Stadium
Sydenham's Rd
VOC Rd (Wall Tax Rd)
Perambur Barracks Rd
VEPERY
Purusavakkam High Rd
Ritherdon Rd
EVK Sampath Salai
Vepery High Rd
37
Mint St
Kilpauk Garden Rd
Fort Train Station
See Anna Salai, Egmore & Triplicane Map (p1012)
Central Train Station
GH Rd
5
1
Fort St George
Fort St George Entrance
12
Poonamallee High Rd (EVR Periyar Salai)
Park Train Station
Park Town Train Station
Egmore Train Station
Gandhi Irwin Rd
CMBT (3km); Omni Bus Stand (3.5km)
CHETPET
West Kuvam River Rd
Chintadripet Train Station
Anna Salai (Mount Rd)
Rajaji Salai
EGMORE
Chetpet Train Station
Halls Rd
Island Grounds
Casa Major Rd
Pantheon Rd
Adinathar Rd
Langs Garden Rd
Kuvam River
Swami Sivananda Salai
Harrington Rd
Valluvar Kottam High Rd
Rajarathinam Stadium
Nelson Manickam Rd
College Rd
PUDUPET
Ethiraj Salai
Haddows Rd
Anderson Rd
Ellis Rd
Triplicane High Rd (Qaide-Millath Rd)
Wallajah Rd
Anna Sq
Sterling Rd
56
Binny Rd
Anna Salai (Mount Rd)
35
Chepauk Stadium
Chepauk Train Station
Nungambakkam Train Station
Tank Bund Rd
Greams Rd
NUNGAMBAKKAM
Khader Nawaz Khan Rd
THOUSAND LIGHTS
Bells Rd
CHEPAUK
Bharathi Salai (Pycroft's Rd)

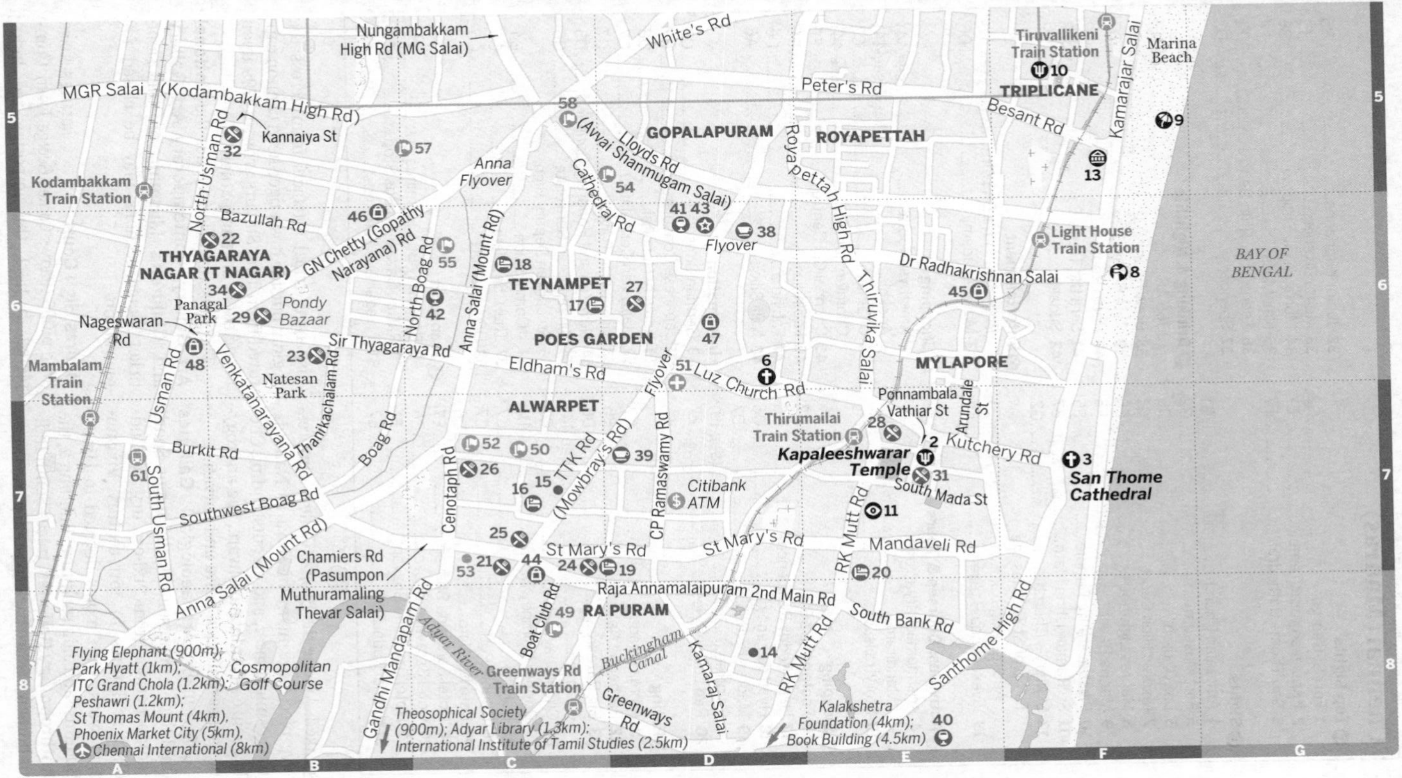

A
B
C
D
E
F
G
5
6
7
8
BAY OF BENGAL
Marina Beach
Kamarajar Salai
9
Tiruvallikeni Train Station
10
TRIPLICANE
13
Besant Rd
Light House Train Station
8
Dr Radhakrishnan Salai
45
MYLAPORE
Ponnambala Vathiar St
Arundale St
Kutchery Rd
3
San Thome Cathedral
2
Kapaleeshwarar Temple
31
South Mada St
28
Thirumailai Train Station
11
RK Mutt Rd
Mandaveli Rd
20
South Bank Rd
Santhome High Rd
40
Kalakshetra Foundation (4km); Book Building (4.5km)
RK Mutt Rd
14
Raja Annamalaipuram 2nd Main Rd
St Mary's Rd
Kamaraj Salai
Buckingham Canal
RA PURAM
Greenways Rd
Greenways Rd Train Station
Theosophical Society (900m); Adyar Library (1.3km); International Institute of Tamil Studies (2.5km)
Adyar River
Gandhi Mandapam Rd
Boat Club Rd
49
19
24
44
St Mary's Rd
Citibank ATM
CP Ramaswamy Rd
39
TTK Rd (Mowbray's Rd)
15
16
25
21
53
Cenotaph Rd
52
26
50
ALWARPET
Eldham's Rd
51
Flyover
Luz Church Rd
6
47
POES GARDEN
27
17
TEYNAMPET
18
Thiruvika Salai
Royapettah High Rd
ROYAPETTAH
Peter's Rd
38
41
43
Flyover
GOPALAPURAM
Lloyds Rd (Avvai Shanmugam Salai)
Cathedral Rd
54
58
White's Rd
Nungambakkam High Rd (MG Salai)
Anna Flyover
57
Anna Salai (Mount Rd)
55
North Boag Rd
42
46
GN Chetty (Gopathy Narayana) Rd
Sir Thyagaraya Rd
Boag Rd
Chamiers Rd
(Pasumpon Muthuramaling Thevar Salai)
Thanikachalam Rd
23
Natesan Park
Venkatanarayana Rd
Southwest Boag Rd
Anna Salai (Mount Rd)
Pondy Bazaar
29
34
22
THYAGARAYA NAGAR (T NAGAR)
Bazullah Rd
Kannaiya St
32
North Usman Rd
MGR Salai (Kodambakkam High Rd)
Kodambakkam Train Station
Panagal Park
Nageswaran Rd
48
Usman Rd
Burkit Rd
South Usman Rd
61
Mambalam Train Station
Flying Elephant (900m); Park Hyatt (1km); ITC Grand Chola (1.2km); Peshawri (1.2km); St Thomas Mount (4km); Phoenix Market City (5km); Chennai International (8km)
Cosmopolitan Golf Course

Chennai (Madras)

Top Sights
1 Fort St George G2
2 Kapaleeshwarar Temple E7
3 San Thome Cathedral F7

Sights
4 Armenian Church G1
5 Fort Museum G2
6 Luz Church D6
7 Madras High Court G1
8 Madras Lighthouse F6
9 Marina Beach F5
10 Parthasarathy Temple F5
11 Sri Ramakrishna Math E7
12 St Mary's Church G2
Tomb of St Thomas the Apostle .... (see 3)
13 Vivekananda House F5

Activities, Courses & Tours
14 Krishnamacharya Yoga Mandiram D8
15 Storytrails C7

Sleeping
16 Footprint B&B C7
17 Hanu Reddy Residences C6
18 Hyatt Regency C6
19 Madras B&B D7
Raintree .... (see 19)
20 Red Lollipop Hostel E7

Eating
21 Amma Naana C7
22 Barbeque Nation B6
23 Big Bazaar B6
Chamiers .... (see 44)
24 Chap Chay C7
Copper Chimney .... (see 41)
25 Dakshin C7
26 Double Roti C7
27 Enté Keralam D6
28 Hotel Saravana Bhavan E7
29 Hotel Saravana Bhavan B6
30 Hotel Saravana Bhavan F1
31 Jannal Kadai E7
32 Junior Kuppanna B5
33 Mehta Brothers F1
34 Murugan Idli Shop B6
35 Nair Mess F4
36 Seena Bhai Tiffin Centre F1
37 Spencer's D2

Drinking & Nightlife
365 AS .... (see 18)
38 Brew Room D6
39 Café Coffee Day D7
40 Radio Room E8
41 Sera the Tapas Bar D6
42 Sudaka C6

Entertainment
Bharatiya Vidya Bhavan .... (see 31)
43 Music Academy D6

Shopping
Amethyst Room .... (see 44)
Anokhi .... (see 44)
44 Chamiers C7
Chamiers for Men .... (see 44)
45 Chennai Citi Centre E6
46 Fabindia B6
47 Fabindia D6
48 Nalli Silks A6

Information
49 German Consulate C8
50 Japanese Consulate C7
51 Kauvery Hospital D6
52 Malaysian Consulate C7
53 Milesworth Travel C7
54 New Zealand Honorary Consul D5
55 Singaporean Consulate C6
56 Sri Lankan Deputy High Commission B4
57 Thai Consulate C5
58 US Consulate C5

Transport
59 Broadway Bus Terminus F1
60 Rattan Bazaar Rd Bus Stop F1
61 T Nagar Bus Terminus A7

peaked. Among the Bronze Gallery's impressive pieces are many of Shiva as Nataraja, the cosmic dancer, and an outstanding Chola bronze of Ardhanarishvara, the androgynous incarnation of Shiva and Parvati.

The main **Archaeological Galleries** (building 1) represent all the major South Indian periods from 2nd-century BC Buddhist sculptures to 16th-century Vijayanagar work, with rooms devoted to Hindu, Buddhist and Jain sculpture. Building 2, the **Anthropology Galleries**, traces South Indian human history back to prehistoric times, displaying tribal artefacts from across the region; outside it is a tiger-head cannon captured from Tipu Sultan's army in 1799 upon his defeat at Srirangapatnam.

The museum also includes the **National Art Gallery**, **Contemporary Art Gallery** and **Children's Museum**, on the same ticket. Some sections may be closed for renovation.

Madras High Court NOTABLE BUILDING

(Map p1006; Parry's Corner, George Town) Completed in 1892, this imposing red Indo-

Saracenic structure is said to be the world's largest judicial building after the Courts of London. The central tower was added in 1912. At research time, visitors were not permitted to wander the grounds, but if you fancy trying, take your passport.

★Fort St George FORT
(Map p1006; Rajaji Salai; ⌚10am-5pm) FREE Finished in 1653 by the British East India Company, the fort has undergone many facelifts. Inside the vast perimeter walls (the ramparts are 18th-century replacements) is now a precinct housing Tamil Nadu's Legislative Assembly & Secretariat, and a smattering of older buildings. The **Fort Museum** (Map p1006; Indian/foreigner ₹15/200; ⌚9am-5pm Sat-Thu) has displays on Chennai's origins and the fort, and interesting military memorabilia and artwork from colonial times. The 1st-floor portrait gallery of colonial-era VIPs includes a very assured-looking Robert Clive (Clive of India).

Also within the fort is **St Mary's Church** (Map p1006; ⌚10am-5pm Mon-Sat), completed in 1680, and India's oldest surviving British church, surrounded by even earlier gravestones; Clive was married here. To its right (west) is the neoclassical former **Admiralty House** (Clive's House).

Marina Beach BEACH
(Map p1006) Take an early morning or evening stroll (you don't want to roast here at any other time) along the 3km-long main stretch of Marina Beach and you'll pass cricket matches, flying kites, fortune-tellers, fish markets, corn-roasters and families enjoying the sea breeze. But don't swim: strong rips make it dangerous. At the southern end, the ridiculously popular **Madras Lighthouse** (Map p1006; adult/child ₹20/10, camera ₹25; ⌚10am-1pm & 3-5pm Tue-Sun) is India's only lighthouse with a lift; the panoramic city and beach views are fabulous.

Parthasarathy Temple HINDU TEMPLE
(Map p1006; Singarachari St, Triplicane; ⌚5.30am-noon & 4-9.30pm) Built under the 8th-century Pallavas and unusually dedicated to Krishna (a form of Vishnu) as the charioteer Parthasarathy, this is one of Chennai's oldest temples. Most of its elaborate carvings, however, date from its 16th-century Vijayanagar expansion, including the fine stone-carved colonnade fronting the entrance. It's special for its shrines dedicated to five of the incarnations of Vishnu.

Vivekananda House MUSEUM
(Vivekanandar Illam, Ice House; Map p1006; www.vivekanandahouse.org; Kamarajar Salai; adult/child ₹20/10; ⌚10am-12.15pm & 3-7.15pm Tue-Sat) The marshmallow-pink Vivekananda House is interesting not only for its displays on the famous 'wandering monk', Swami Vivekananda, but also for its semicircular form, built in 1842 to store ice imported from the USA. Vivekananda stayed here briefly in 1897, preaching his ascetic Hindu philosophy to adoring crowds. Displays include a photo exhibition on the swami's life, a 3D reproduction of Vivekananda's celebrated 1893 Chicago World's Parliament of Religions speech, and the room where he stayed, now used for meditation.

DRAVIDIAN PRIDE

Since before Indian independence in 1947, Tamil politicians have railed against caste (considered to favour light-skinned Brahmins) and the Hindi language (seen as North Indian cultural imperialism). The pre-Independence 'Self Respect' movement and Justice Party, influenced by Marxism, mixed South Indian communal values with class-war rhetoric, and spawned Tamil political parties that remain the major powers in Tamil Nadu today. In the early post-Independence decades there was even a movement for an independent Dravida Nadu nation comprising the four main South Indian peoples, but there was little solidarity between different groups. Today Dravidian politics is largely restricted to Tamil Nadu, where parties are often led by former film stars (who often have immense, passionate followings).

During the conflict in nearby Sri Lanka, many Indian Tamil politicians loudly defended the Tamil Tigers, the organisation that assassinated Rajiv Gandhi in Sriperumbudur near Chennai in 1991. There is still considerable prejudice among the generally tolerant Tamils towards anything Sinhalese. The most obvious sign of Tamil pride you'll see today is the white shirt and white *mundu* (sarong), worn by most Tamil public figures.

Southern Chennai

★Kapaleeshwarar Temple HINDU TEMPLE
(Map p1006; Ponnambala Vathiar St, Mylapore; ⏲6am-noon & 4-9.30pm) Mylapore is one of Chennai's most characterful and traditional neighbourhoods; it predated colonial Madras by several centuries. Its Kapaleeshwarar Temple is Chennai's most active and impressive, believed to have been built after the Portuguese destroyed the seaside original in 1566. It displays the main architectural elements of many a Tamil Nadu temple – a rainbow-coloured *gopuram*, pillared *mandapas* (pavilions), and a huge tank – and is dedicated to the state's most popular deity, Shiva.

Legend tells that in an angry fit Shiva turned his consort Parvati into a peacock, and commanded her to worship him here to regain her normal form. Parvati supposedly did so at a spot just outside the northeast corner of the temple's central block, where a shrine commemorates the event. Hence the name Mylapore, 'town of peacocks'. The story is depicted at the west end of the inner courtyard, on the exterior of the main sanctum.

The temple's colourful **Brahmotsavam festival** (March/April) sees the deities paraded around Mylapore's streets.

Sri Ramakrishna Math RELIGIOUS SITE
(Map p1006; www.chennaimath.org; 31 RK Mutt Rd, Mylapore; ⏲Universal Temple 4.30-11.45am & 3-9pm, evening prayers 6.30-7.30pm) The tranquil, flowery grounds of the Ramakrishna Math are a world away from Mylapore's chaos. Orange-robed monks glide around and there's a reverential feel. The Math is a monastic order following the teachings of the 19th-century sage Sri Ramakrishna, who preached the essential unity of all religions. Its Universal Temple is a handsome, modern, salmon-pink building incorporating architectural elements from different religions, and is open to all, to worship, pray or meditate.

★San Thome Cathedral CATHEDRAL
(Map p1006; Santhome High Rd, Mylapore; ⏲5.30am-8.30pm) This soaring Roman Catholic cathedral, a stone's throw from the beach, was founded by the Portuguese in 1523, then rebuilt by the British in neo-Gothic style in 1896, and is said to mark the final resting place of St Thomas the Apostle. It's believed 'Doubting Thomas' brought Christianity to the subcontinent in AD 52 and was killed at St Thomas Mount (p1011), Chennai, in AD 72. Behind the cathedral is the **tomb of St Thomas** (Map p1006; ⏲5.30am-8.30pm) FREE.

Although most of St Thomas' mortal remains now apparently lie in Italy, a cross on the tomb wall contains a tiny bone fragment marked 'Relic of St Thomas'. The museum above displays Thomas-related artefacts including the lancehead believed to have killed him.

St Thomas' Pole, at the beach end of the street on the cathedral's south side, is said to have miraculously saved the cathedral from the 2004 tsunami.

Theosophical Society GARDENS
(www.ts-adyar.org; south end of Thiru Vi Ka Bridge, Adyar; ⏲grounds 8.30-10am & 2-4pm Mon-Sat) FREE Between the Adyar River and the coast, the 100-hectare grounds of the Theosophical Society provide a peaceful, green, vehicle-free retreat from the city. Despite restricted opening hours, it's a lovely spot to wander, containing a church, mosque, Buddhist shrine, Zoroastrian temple and Hindu temple as well as a huge variety of native and introduced flora, including the offshoots of a 450-year-old banyan tree severely damaged by a storm in the 1980s.

The **Adyar Library** (www.ts-adyar.org; Theosophical Society, off Besant Ave Rd, Adyar; 1yr reader's card ₹50, deposit ₹250; ⏲9am-5pm Tue-Sun) here has an impressive collection of religion and philosophy books (some on display), from 1000-year-old Buddhist scrolls to handmade 19th-century Bibles.

Kalakshetra Foundation ARTS CENTRE
(☎044-24521169; www.kalakshetra.in; Muthulakshmi St, Thiruvanmiyur; Indian/foreigner incl craft centre ₹100/500; ⏲campus 8.30-11.30am Mon-Fri Jul-Feb, craft centre 9am-1pm & 2-5pm Mon-Sat, all closed 2nd & 4th Sat of month) Founded in 1936, Kalakshetra is a leading serious school of Tamil classical dance and music (sponsoring many students from disadvantaged backgrounds), set in beautiful, shady grounds in south Chennai. During morning class times visitors can (quietly) wander the complex and its **Rukmini Devi Museum**. Across the road is the **Kalakshetra Craft Centre**, where you can see Kanchipuram-style hand-loom weaving, textile block-printing and the fascinating, rare art of *kalamkari* (hand-painting on textiles with vegetable dyes). For upcoming performances, check the website.

The Thiruvanmiyur bus stand, terminus of many city bus routes, is 500m southwest of the Kalakshetra entrance.

CHENNAI'S OTHER CHURCHES

Armenian Church (Map p1006; Armenian St, George Town; ⌚9.30am-2.30pm, hours vary) A frangipani-scented haven in the midst of George Town, this 18th-century church is testament to the city's once-flourishing Armenian merchant community. Its courtyard displays ancient gravestones covered in Armenian script.

St Andrew's Church (St Andrew's Kirk; Map p1012; www.thekirk.in; 37 Poonamallee High Rd, Egmore; ⌚9.30am-5pm) This 1821 neoclassical Scottish Presbyterian church stands in leafy Egmore grounds. Inspired by London's St Martin-in-the-Fields, it has an exquisite columned portico, an unusual oval colonnade under a domed ceiling supported by Corinthian columns, and a slim multilevel spire.

Luz Church (Shrine of our Lady of Light; Map p1006; www.luzchurch.org; off Luz Church Rd, Mylapore; ⌚dawn-dusk) Styled with blue-and-white baroque elegance, palm-fringed 1516 Luz Church is Chennai's oldest European building.

Book Building GALLERY
(☎044-24426696; www.tarabooks.com; Plot 9, CGE Colony, Kuppam Beach Rd, Thiruvanmiyur; ⌚10am-7.30pm Mon-Sat) FREE Within this mural-covered space, Tara Books stages free exhibitions, author talks and workshops with visiting artists, and displays its own highly original handmade books. With prior notice, you can visit the workshop where the books are created (20 minutes' drive away).

St Thomas Mount RELIGIOUS SITE
(Parangi Malai; off Lawrence Rd, Guindy; ⌚6am-8pm) FREE The reputed site of St Thomas' martyrdom in AD 72 rises in the southwest of Chennai, 2.5km north of St Thomas Mount train station and metro station. The **Church of Our Lady of Expectation**, built atop the 'mount' by the Portuguese in 1523, contains what are supposedly a fragment of Thomas' finger bone and the 'Bleeding Cross' he carved. The city and airport views are wonderful.

Activities

Krishnamacharya Yoga Mandiram YOGA, MEDITATION
(KYM; Map p1006; ☎044-24937998; www.kym.org; 31 4th Cross St, RK Nagar; class US$30; ⌚8am-7pm) Highly regarded, serious two-week and month-long yoga courses, yoga therapy, and intensive teacher training.

Courses

Run by Storytrails, the four-hour Spice Trail (per person ₹2500) is a fascinating introduction to South Indian cooking, with hands-on, small-group cookathons.

Kalakshetra Foundation ART
(☎044-24525423; www.kalakshetra.in; Muthulakshmi St, Thiruvanmiyur; per day ₹500) Kalakshetra's crafts centre offers one-month to two-month courses in the intricate old art of *kalamkari*, which survives in only a handful of places. Courses run 10am to 1pm Monday to Friday.

International Institute of Tamil Studies LANGUAGE
(☎044-22542992, 9952448862; www.ulakaththamizh.org; CIT Campus, 2nd Main Rd, Tharamani; 3-/6-month course ₹5000/10,000) Intensive three-month and six-month Tamil-language courses.

Tours

Storytrails WALKING
(Map p1006; ☎044-45010202, 9940040215; www.storytrails.in; 21/2 1st Cross St, TTK Rd, Alwarpet; 3hr tour for up to 4 people from ₹4400) Entertaining neighbourhood walking tours on themes like dance, temples, jewellery and bazaars. Also runs popular food-tasting tours through George Town and in-house cooking classes.

Festivals & Events

Madras Week CULTURAL
(www.themadrasday.in; ⌚Aug) An inspired series of heritage walks, talks and exhibitions held across town to honour the 1639 founding of then-Madras.

Chennai Festival of Music & Dance MUSIC, DANCE
(Madras Music & Dance Season; ⌚mid-Dec–mid-Jan) One of the largest of its type in the world, this festival celebrates South Indian music and dance.

Sleeping

Hotels in Chennai are pricier than elsewhere in Tamil Nadu and don't offer particularly good value. The Triplicane High Rd area is

Anna Salai, Egmore & Triplicane

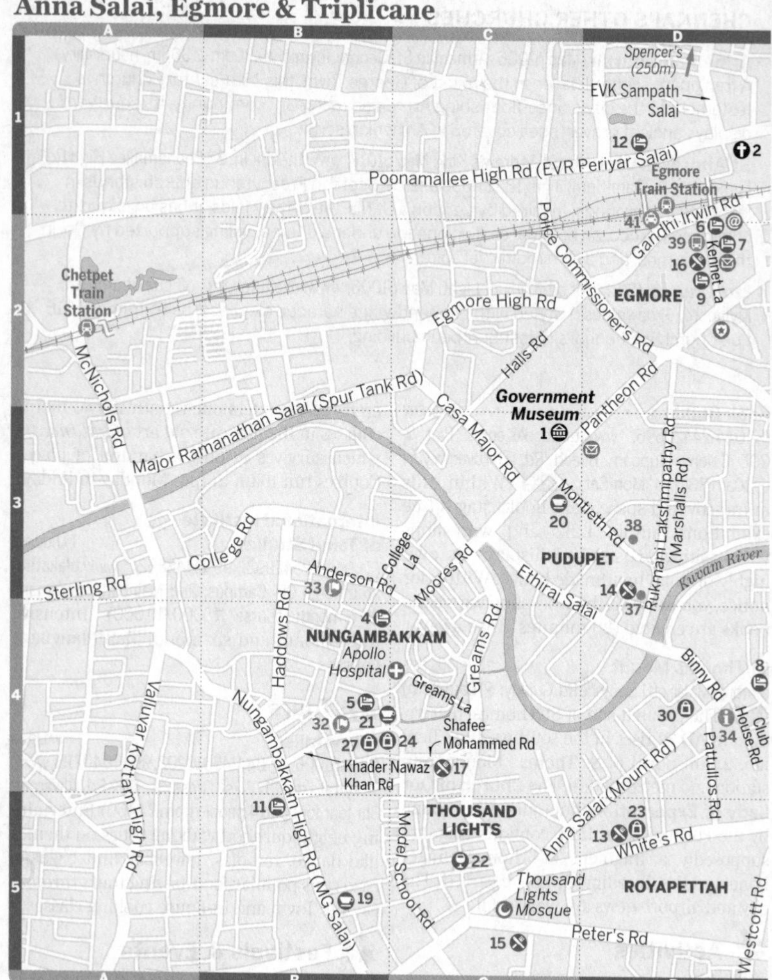

best for budget accommodation. There are some cheapies in Egmore, plus a few midrange options. You'll find upper-midrange B&Bs in Nungambakkam, Poes Garden and Alwarpet. Top-end hotels have become plentiful, especially in southern areas.

Many hotels have 24-hour checkout and fill up by noon; call ahead.

Egmore

New Lakshmi Lodge HOTEL **$**
(Map p1012; ☎044-28194576, 9840900343; 16 Kennet Lane; s/d ₹500/900, r with AC ₹1460-1580; ❄) With small and bare but spotless, pastel-walled rooms spread over four floors around a parking courtyard, this huge block is not a bad budget choice. Book ahead, as it's often full. Upper floors offer more privacy.

YWCA International Guest House GUESTHOUSE **$$**
(Map p1012; ☎044-25324234; http://ywcamadras.org/international-guest-house; 1086 Poonamallee High Rd; incl breakfast s ₹1760-2380, d ₹2170-2850, s/d without AC ₹1020/1560; ❄@📶) Chennai's YWCA guesthouse, set in shady grounds just north of Egmore station, offers excellent value combined with a calm atmosphere. Effi-

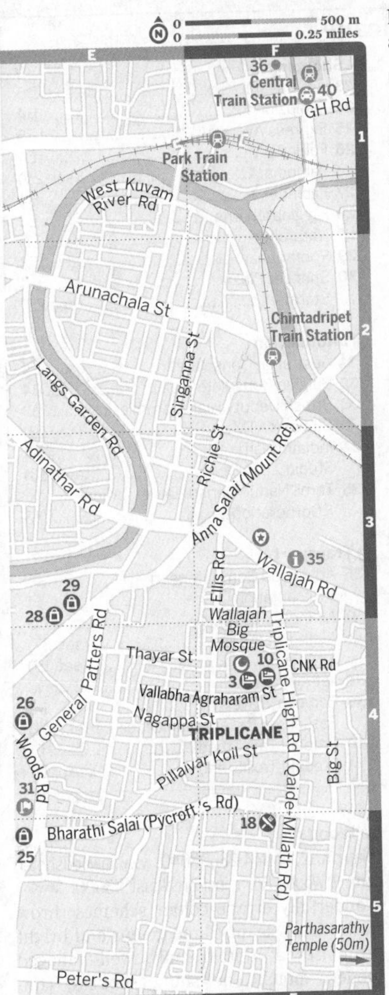

ciently run by helpful staff, it has good-sized, brilliantly clean rooms, spacious common areas and solid-value meals (veg/nonveg ₹225/330). Lobby-only wi-fi costs ₹150 per day.

Hotel Chandra Park HOTEL **$$**
(Map p1012; ☎044-40506060; www.hotelchandrapark.com; 9 Gandhi Irwin Rd; incl breakfast s ₹1580-2560, d ₹1820-3020; ❄📶) Chandra Park's prices remain mysteriously lower than most similar establishments. 'Standard' rooms are small and a bit dated but have air-con, clean towels and tight, white sheets. Throw in polite service, 24-hour checkout and free wi-fi, and this is good value by Egmore standards.

Hotel Victoria HOTEL **$$**
(Map p1012; ☎044-28193638; www.empeehotels.com; 3 Kennet Lane; incl breakfast s ₹2500-4300, d ₹2800-4700; ❄📶) Easily your smartest choice on hectic Kennet Lane. Rooms are clean and decent (with kettles, wi-fi and TVs), though not as exciting as the shiny lobby and cordial service suggest.

Nungambakkam & Around

Frangi House B&B **$$**
(Map p1012; ☎044-43084694; www.frangihouse.com; 6B Nawab Habibullah Ave, 1st St, off Anderson Rd; r incl breakfast ₹3940-4280; ❄📶) This elegant, immaculate retreat is tucked into a tranquil street in upmarket Nungambakkam, offering grassy gardens, comfy lounges and eight airy, all-different rooms. 'Boutique' rooms mix vintage four-poster beds with modern bathrooms sporting stylish square sinks. 'Old world' pads are styled in florals and pastels; the pick is blue-hued 'Dew', with its four-poster and shared balcony.

Hanu Reddy Residences B&B **$$**
(Map p1012; ☎9176869926, 044-43084563; www.hanureddyresidences.com; 6A/24 3rd St, Wallace Garden; incl breakfast s ₹3600-4200, d ₹4200-4800; ❄📶) Spread across two residential buildings engulfed by greenery in upscale Wallace Garden, this is exactly the kind of homey hideaway that central Chennai needs. The 13 unpretentious rooms come with air-con, free wi-fi, tea/coffee sets, splashes of colourful artwork – and anti-mosquito racquets! Terraces have bamboo lounging chairs. Service hits that ideal personal-yet-professional balance. There's another **branch** (Map p1006; ☎044-24661021; 41/19 Poes Garden; incl breakfast s ₹4200-5400, d ₹4800-7800; ❄📶) in exclusive Poes Garden.

Taj Coromandel HOTEL **$$$**
(Map p1012; ☎044-66002827; www.tajhotels.com; 37 Nungambakkam High Rd; r from ₹12,000; ❄📶🏊) Luxurious without going overly ostentatious, the glittering Coromandel offers a sensibly central top-end retreat from the city. Rooms flaunt a smart stripped-back style and there's a lovely palm-shaded pool. The marble-effect lobby hosts fine-dining South Indian restaurant **Southern Spice** (Map p1012; mains ₹550-900, thalis ₹1500-2200; ⏲12.30-2.45pm & 7-11pm), along with a busy cocktail bar.

Anna Salai, Egmore & Triplicane

Triplicane & Around

Paradise Guest House GUESTHOUSE **$**
(Map p1012; ☎044-28594252; www.paradiseguesthouse.co.in; 17/1 Vallabha Agraharam St; s/d ₹600/700, with AC ₹1000/1100; ❄📶) Paradise offers some of Triplicane's best-value digs: simple rooms with clean tiles, a breezy rooftop, friendly staff and hot water by the steaming bucket.

Broad Lands Lodge GUESTHOUSE **$**
(Map p1012; ☎044-28545573; broadlandshotel@yahoo.com; 18 Vallabha Agraharam St; s ₹400-750, d ₹450-800; 📶) In business since 1951, Broad Lands was a hippie-era stalwart. This laid-back colonial-era mansion, with leafy courtyards and rooms up rambling staircases, still has its devotees, who don't seem to mind the 44 bare-bones, idiosyncratic rooms, dank bathrooms, or high-volume muezzins of Wallajah Big Mosque. The cheapest rooms share bathrooms; wi-fi costs ₹50. The red-banistered back block has breezier rooms.

La Woods HOTEL **$$**
(Map p1012; ☎044-28608040; www.lawoodshotel.com; 1 Woods Rd; r incl breakfast ₹3600; ❄📶) Wonderfully erratic colour schemes throw fresh whites against lime greens and bright turquoises at this friendly, well-managed modern hotel. The shiny, spotless, contemporary rooms are perfectly comfy, with mountains of pillows, kettles, hairdryers and 'global' plug sockets.

Southern Chennai

Red Lollipop Hostel HOSTEL **$**
(Map p1006; ☎044-24629822; www.redlollipop.in; 129/68 RK Mutt Rd, Mandavelli; dm ₹650; ❄📶) Saving the day for Chennai's budget travellers, Red Lollipop is a genuine, sociable hostel, 700m south of Mylapore's temple. Boldly colourful walls are scrawled with inspirational messages. Each of the spotless, locker-equipped six- to 10-bed dorms (one women-only) has its own bathroom. There's

a rooftop terrace, plus a shared kitchen, a lounge, towel rental (₹30) and Chennai tips.

★ **Footprint B&B** B&B $$
(Map p1006; ☎9840037483; www.chennaibedandbreakfast.com; Gayatri Apartments, 16 South St, Alwarpet, behind Crowne Plaza Hotel; r incl breakfast ₹3900; ❄📶) A beautifully comfortable, relaxed base occupying three apartments on a quiet street in a leafy south-Chennai neighbourhood. Bowls of wild roses, organic Auroville soaps and old-Madras photos set the scene for nine cosy, pristine rooms with king-size or wide twin beds. Home-cooked breakfasts are generous, service is excellent, and the welcoming owners are full of Tamil Nadu tips. Book ahead.

Madras B&B B&B $$
(Map p1006; ☎9840037483; www.madrasbedandbreakfast.com; Flat 1/3, Nandini Apartments, 72/45 1st Main Rd, RA Puram; r incl breakfast ₹3040; ❄📶) Popular with yoga students, this multilocation operation offers good-sized, straightforward but comfy, stylish rooms in peaceful private apartments that feel like cosy self-service lodges, dotted around RA Puram and Alwarpet. Help yourself to fully equipped kitchens, washing machines, small libraries and relaxed communal lounges full of flower bowls. No walk-ins: book ahead.

★ **Raintree** HOTEL $$$
(Map p1006; ☎044-42252525; www.raintreehotels.com; 120 St Mary's Rd, Alwarpet; s/d ₹9590/10,790; ❄@📶🏊) 🍃 At this 'eco-sensitive' business-style hotel, floors are bamboo or rubber, water and electricity conservation hold pride of place, and AC-generated heat warms the bathroom water. Sleek, fresh, minimalist rooms are bright, comfy and stylish, with wonderful city vistas. A sea-view infinity pool (doubling as insulation) and an open-air bar-restaurant grace the rooftop. Downstairs is excellent pan-Asian restaurant **Chap Chay** (Map p1006; mains ₹500-900, set menu ₹1900; ⏲noon-3pm & 7-11pm).

Hyatt Regency HOTEL $$$
(Map p1006; ☎044-61001234; http://chennai.regency.hyatt.com; 365 Anna Salai, Teynampet; r ₹9720-15,800; ❄@📶🏊) Smart, swish and bang up to date, this towering, triangular hotel is the most central of Chennai's newer top-end offerings. Contemporary art surrounds the sun-flooded atrium, local chefs head up three good restaurants and an insanely popular bar (p1018), and glossy rooms have walk-through bathrooms and fabulous sea/city panoramas through massive picture windows. Flowers fringe the pool, and there's a luxury spa.

ITC Grand Chola HOTEL $$$
(☎044-22200000; www.itchotels.in; 63 Mount Rd, Guindy; r incl breakfast from ₹13,970; ❄📶🏊) 🍃 Chennai's most talked-about hotel is this ultraluxurious, 600-room, temple-inspired beauty in the city's southwest. A maze of sumptuous iPad-operated rooms, complete with soaking tubs and French press coffee kits, unfolds beyond the sweeping lantern-lit marble lobby. One corridor caters exclusively to women travellers. Also here are seven swish restaurants, two glitzy bars, three gyms, a spa and five pools.

Park Hyatt HOTEL $$$
(☎044-71771234; http://chennai.park.hyatt.com; 39 Velachery Rd, Guindy; s/d incl breakfast from ₹9720/10,940; ❄📶🏊) The gleaming, ultramodern Park Hyatt has swanky, straight-lined rooms kitted out with Nespresso machines, iPod docks and king-size beds; a divine spa; and a rooftop infinity pool overlooking Guindy National Park. The multi-floor **Flying Elephant** (☎044-71771234; per couple ₹3300 incl ₹2000 drink credit, women free; ⏲7pm-late Mon-Sat, noon-3pm & 7pm-late Sun) restaurant doubles as a popular party pad. It's a hike from central Chennai, but perfect if you're after a plush stay near the airport.

✕ Eating

Chennai is packed with inexpensive 'meals' joints ('messes'), serving lunch and dinner thalis (all you can eat meals), and tiffin (snacks) like *idlis* (spongy, round fermented rice cakes), *vadas* (doughnut-shaped deep-fried lentil savoury) and dosas (savoury crêpe). Hotel Saravana Bhavan (p1016) is always a quality veg choice. In the Muslim Triplicane High Rd area, you'll find great biryanis (fragrant, spiced steamed rice with meat and vegetables).

There's plenty of upmarket dining: classier Indian restaurants are on the rise, and international cuisines are soaring in popularity.

Useful, well-stocked supermarkets include **Spencer's** (Map p1006; 15 EVK Sampath Salai, Vepery; ⏲7.30am-10pm), near Egmore and Central stations, Big Bazaar at **T Nagar** (Map p1006; 34 Sir Thyagaraya Rd, Pondy Bazaar, T Nagar; ⏲10.30am-10pm) and **Express Avenue mall** (Map p1012; Express Avenue, White's Rd; ⏲10am-9.30pm Mon-Fri, to 10pm Sat & Sun),

Nilgiri's (Map p1012; 25 Shafee Mohammed Rd, Nungambakkam; ⏲7.30am-10pm) off Nungambakkam's Khader Nawaz Khan Rd and **Amma Naana** (Map p1006; www.ammanaana.com; 82/100 Chamiers Rd, Alwarpet; ⏲10am-9pm Mon-Sat) in Alwarpet.

Egmore

★Hotel Saravana Bhavan INDIAN $

(Map p1012; ☎044-28192055; www.saravanabhavan.com; 21 Kennet Lane; mains ₹70-140; ⏲6am-10.30pm) Dependably delish, Chennai's famous vegetarian chain doles out epically good South Indian thalis and breakfasts (*idlis* and *vadas* ₹15 to ₹35, dosas ₹20 to ₹40), filter coffee and other Indian vegetarian fare. This branch is handy for Egmore station. Others include **George Town** (Map p1006; ☎044-25387766; 209 NSC Bose Rd; mains ₹60-100, thalis ₹60-145; ⏲7am-10pm), **Mylapore** (Map p1006; ☎044-24611177; 70 North Mada St; mains ₹60-100, thalis ₹60-145; ⏲6am-10.30pm), **Pondy Bazaar** (Map p1006; ☎044-281576677; 102 Sir Thyagaraya Rd; mains ₹60-100, thalis ₹170-210; ⏲6am-11pm) and, more upscale with a ₹320 buffet, **Thousand Lights** (Map p1012; ☎044-28353377; 293 Peter's Rd; mains ₹100-180, thalis ₹60-150; ⏲8am-10.30pm), plus London, Paris and New York!

Annalakshmi INDIAN $$

(Map p1012; ☎044-28525109; www.annalakshmichennai.co.in; 1st fl, Sigapi Achi Bldg, 18/3 Rukmani Lakshmipathy Rd, Egmore; mains ₹180-280, set menus ₹700-1200, buffet weekday/weekend ₹420/470; ⏲noon-2.30pm & 7-9pm Tue-Sun) Very fine South and North Indian vegetarian fare, plus glorious fresh juices, in a beautiful dining room decorated with carvings and paintings, inside a high-rise behind the Air India building. Buffet lunches and dinners are served in another part of the same block. Annalakshmi is run by devotees of Swami Shanthanand Saraswathi; proceeds support medical programs for the poor.

Nungambakkam & Around

★Amethyst MULTICUISINE, CAFE $$$

(Map p1012; ☎044-45991633; www.amethystchennai.com; White's Rd, Royapettah; mains ₹250-470; ⏲10am-11.30pm; 📶) Set in an exquisitely converted warehouse with a wraparound verandah from which tables spill out into lush gardens, Amethyst is a nostalgically posh haven that's outrageously popular with expats and well-off Chennaiites. Well-executed European-flavoured dishes range over quiches, pastas, sandwiches, crepes, creative salads, all-day breakfasts and afternoon teas. Fight for your table, then check out the stunning Indian couture **boutique** (Map p1012; ⏲11am-7.30pm).

Triplicane & Around

Ratna Café SOUTH INDIAN $

(Map p1012; 255 Triplicane High Rd, Triplicane; dishes ₹70-110; ⏲6am-11pm) Often crowded and cramped, Ratna is famous for its scrumptious *idlis* accompanied by hearty doses of its signature *sambar* (soupy lentil dish with cubed vegetables). People have been sitting down to this ₹45 dish at all hours since 1948. There are also North Indian mains, and an air-con room out the back.

Nair Mess SOUTH INDIAN $

(Map p1006; 22 Mohammed Abdullah Sahib, 2nd St, Chepauk; meals ₹60-75; ⏲11.30am-3pm & 7-10pm) Big flavours are rustled up in a starkly simple setting at this no-nonsense, forever-busy meals spot, pocketed away in a lane opposite the Chepauk cricket stadium since 1961. Loaded banana-leaf thalis complemented by fish-fry dishes are the speciality.

Southern Chennai

Murugan Idli Shop SOUTH INDIAN $

(Map p1006; http://muruganidlishop.com; 77 GN Chetty Rd, T Nagar; dishes ₹50-85; ⏲7am-11.30pm) Those in the know generally agree that this particular branch of the small Madurai-born Murugan chain serves some of the best *idlis*, dosas, *uttapams* and South Indian meals in town.

Double Roti BURGERS $$

(Map p1006; ☎044-30853732; http://doubleroti.in; 4/27 1st St, Cenotaph Rd, Teynampet; mains ₹245-395; ⏲11am-11pm; 📶) 'Double roti' refers to burger buns – the semi-open kitchen at this always-packed industrial-chic cafe plates them up with fun, flair and buckets of flavour. Lemonades and milkshakes are served in jars; burgers arrive in mini-frying pans; buckets come filled with masala fries; and witty slogans are chalked up on boards. There's plenty for vegetarians too, including fantastic spicy-falafel burgers.

Junior Kuppanna SOUTH INDIAN $$

(Map p1006; ☎044-28340071; 4 Kannaiya St, North Usman Rd, T Nagar; mains ₹130-220, thalis ₹200; ⏲noon-4pm & 6.30-11.30pm) From an impeccably clean kitchen (which you're wel-

DON'T MISS

CHENNAI STREET FOOD

Chennai may not have the same killer street-food reputation as Mumbai, but there are some sensational South Indian street-side delicacies around, especially in Mylapore, George Town, Egmore and T Nagar, and along Marina Beach. **Storytrails** (p1011) runs George Town **food-tasting tours** (for one or two people ₹4000).

Mehta Brothers (Map p1006; 310 Mint St, George Town; dishes ₹15-25; ⏲7.30am-9.30pm Mon-Sat, to 2pm Sun) This tiny spot pulls in the crowds with the deep-fried delights of its signature Maharashtrian *vada pavs* – spiced potato fritters in buns, doused in garlicky chutney.

Seena Bhai Tiffin Centre (Map p1006; 111/1 NSC Bose Rd, George Town; idlis & uttapams ₹40; ⏲6pm-midnight) It's all about deliciously griddled, ghee-coated *idlis* and *uttapams* at this 37-year-old eatery in the thick of George Town.

Jannal Kadai (Map p1006; Ponnambala Vathiar St, Mylapore; items ₹20-30; ⏲8.30-10am & 5.30-8.30pm Mon-Sat) You take what you're given from the chap in the 'window shop', a fast-and-furious hole-in-the-wall famous for its hot crispy *bajjis* (vegetable fritters), *bondas* (battered potato balls) and *vadas*. Look for the blue windows opposite Pixel Service, just south of the Mylapore temple.

come to tour), come limitless, flavour-packed lunchtime thalis, dished up traditional-style on banana leaves. This typical, frenzied Chennai 'mess' also has a full menu. Carnivores tiring of the pure-veg lifestyle can seek solace in specialities like mutton brains and pan-fried seer fish. Arrive early: it's incredibly popular. Branches across Chennai.

Enté Keralam KERALAN **$$**

(Map p1006; ☎07604915091; http://entekeralam.in; 1 Kasturi Estate, 1st St, Poes Garden; mains ₹200-565; ⏲noon-3pm & 7-11pm) A calm ambience seeps through the four orange-toned, three- to four-table rooms of this elegant Keralan restaurant. Lightly spiced *pachakkari* vegetable stew is served with light, fluffy *appam* (rice pancake), the Alleppey curry is rich with mango, and there are plenty of fish dishes. Wind up with tender coconut ice cream. Set meals (veg/nonveg ₹795/1195) give a multidish miniformat taster.

Barbeque Nation INDIAN, BARBECUE **$$**

(Map p1006; ☎044-60600000; www.barbeque-nation.com; Shri Devi Park Hotel, 1 Hanumantha Rd, off North Usman Rd, T Nagar; veg/nonveg lunch ₹705/780, dinner ₹900/1050; ⏲12.30-4.30pm & 6.30-11.30pm) For an incredible-value red-hot BBQ blow-out, hunt down this busy-busy all-you-can-eat spot. The highlights are the spicy meat, seafood and veg (paneer, pineapple) skewers that you sizzle to personal taste on live-grills set into the middle of your table. And *then* there's a full-fledged pan-Indian buffet.

★**Peshawri** NORTH INDIAN **$$$**

(☎044-22200000; www.itchotels.in; ITC Grand Chola, 63 Mount Rd, Guindy; mains ₹870-1800, set meals ₹3240-4140; ⏲noon-3pm & 7-11.30pm) Perfect for a five-star splash-out, the ITC's signature Northwest Frontier restaurant serves inventive, flavour-popping creations at intimate booths alongside a glassed-in kitchen that gets you right in on the culinary action. Try huge hunks of pillowy chilli-grilled paneer, expertly spiced kebabs, or the deliciously rich house-special *dhal bukhara,* simmered overnight. There's an astounding international wine/cocktail list.

★**Copper Chimney** NORTH INDIAN **$$$**

(Map p1006; ☎044-28115770; 74 Cathedral Rd, Gopalapuram; mains ₹300-700; ⏲noon-3pm & 7-11.30pm) Meat-eaters will drool over the yummy North Indian tandoori dishes served in stylishly minimalist surroundings, but the veg food here is fantastic too. Jain specialities mingle with biryanis, chicken kebabs, chargrilled prawns and fluffy-fresh naan. The *machchi* tikka – skewers of tandoori-baked fish – is superb, as is the spiced paneer kebab.

Chamiers MULTICUISINE, CAFE **$$$**

(Map p1006; ☎044-42030734; www.chamiershop.com; 106 Chamiers Rd, RA Puram; mains ₹300-500; ⏲8.30am-11pm; 📶) This bubbly 1st-floor cafe feels a continent away from Chennai, except that Chennaiites love it too. Flowery wallpaper, printed cushions, wicker chairs, wi-fi (per hour ₹100), wonderful carrot cake, croissants and cappuccino, English breakfasts, American pancakes, pastas, quiches, quesadillas, salads...

Dakshin SOUTH INDIAN $$$

(Map p1006; ☎044-24994101; www.ihg.com; Crowne Plaza, 132 TTK Rd, Alwarpet; mains ₹690-1500, thalis ₹1800-2300; ⏰12.30-2.45pm & 7-11.15pm) Dakshin specialises in the cuisines of Kerala, Tamil Nadu, Andhra Pradesh, Telangana and Karnataka. Traditional sculptures, mirrored pillars and flute and tabla musicians set the temple-inspired scene. Food suggestion: the Andhra Pradesh fish curry – and perhaps a little something from the impressive whisky and wine list. Lunch revolves around fancy thalis.

Drinking & Nightlife

Chennai nightlife is on the up, with a smattering of lively new openings, but you'll need a full wallet for a night out here. Continental-style cafes are growing in number, and, yes, Starbucks has arrived.

Bars and clubs in five-star hotels serve alcohol 24 hours a day, seven days a week, so that's where most of the after-dark fun happens. Solo guys ('stags') can be turned away, and there's usually a hefty admission charge for couples and men. Dress codes are strict: no shorts or sandals.

Other hotel bars, mostly male-dominated, generally close by midnight. If you're buying your own alcohol, look for 'premium' or 'elite' government-run TASMAC liquor stores inside malls.

365 AS LOUNGE, CLUB

(Map p1006; ☎044-61001234; https://chennai.regency.hyatt.com; Hyatt Regency, 365 Anna Salai, Teynampet; drinks ₹400-700; ⏰3pm-2am) In the glamorous Hyatt Regency, Chennai's hottest party spot bursts into life on Friday and Saturday nights, when wild DJ sets kick off on the terrace. Otherwise, it's a swish, sultry lounge serving carefully crafted cocktails alongside Indian and international wines, beers and spirits. Dress code is smart casual (for guys, trousers and closed shoes).

Sera the Tapas Bar BAR

(Map p1006; ☎044-28111462; www.facebook.com/zaratapasbar; 71 Cathedral Rd, Gopalapuram; cocktails ₹400-500, tapas ₹220-330; ⏰12.30-11.30pm) Where else in the world can you find DJs playing club music beneath bullfight posters next to TVs showing cricket? Sera is packed most nights with a young, fashionable crowd sipping *sangría* and cocktails. It's a good idea to book. Tapas include garlic prawns, fried calamari and aubergine dips; the *tortilla española* (potato omelette) is authentically good.

Radio Room BAR

(Map p1006; ☎8500005672; www.facebook.com/radioroomchennai; Somerset Greenways, 94 Sathyadev Ave, MRC Nagar, RA Puram; cocktails ₹450-600, dishes ₹200-300; ⏰6-11.30pm Mon-Fri, 4-11.30pm Sat & Sun) From a keen young team comes this incredibly popular radio-themed bar in southeast Chennai. It's all about mismatched furniture, a bar made of speakers and carefully mixed, inspired cocktails and pitchers – some full of local flavour, like chai punch. Creative twists on Chennai's culinary favourites include mozzarella-stuffed *bajjis* (vegetable fritters) delivered in bicycle-shaped baskets.

Sudaka COCKTAIL BAR

(Map p1006; ☎044-42004355; www.facebook.com/besudaka; 37 North Boag Rd, T Nagar; cocktails ₹400-500, dishes ₹200-500; ⏰noon-3pm & 6pm-midnight Mon-Fri, noon-midnight Sat) A genuine, sassy cocktail bar where expertly concocted, wittily named liquid mixes are served in a moodily lit lounge alongside artful Latin American and international cooking. Just name your spirit and they'll whip up something special.

Plan B BAR

(Map p1012; https://holycowhospitality.com; 65/5 Murugesan Naicker Complex, Greams Rd; cocktails ₹320-400, dishes ₹230-350; ⏰noon-11pm) Like its student same-name Bengaluru (Bangalore) sibling, this easygoing, industrial-feel bar is a hit with young crowds for its reasonably priced cocktails, wines and beers (mugs, pints or 'towers'), pub-style food (burgers, nachos, chilli-cheese chips) and belting chart-toppers.

Brew Room CAFE

(Map p1006; www.saverahotel.com; Savera Hotel, Dr Radhakrishnan Salai; coffees ₹120-180, dishes ₹250-350; ⏰8am-10.30pm; 📶) Decked out in neo-rustic style, Brew Room does coffee like you've never had in Chennai, from double espresso and Italian cappuccino to Americano, French press and 'iceberg' coffee with ice cream. The contemporary Continental menu includes all-day breakfasts and brilliant vegetarian and vegan choices – even tofu!

Café Coffee Day CAFE

(Map p1012; www.cafecoffeeday.com; Ispahani Centre, 123 Nungambakkam High Rd, Nungambakkam;

drinks ₹60-120; ⏲10am-10pm Mon-Fri, to 11pm Sat & Sun) Reliably good hot and cold coffees and teas. Also at **Egmore** (Map p1012; Alsa Mall, Montieth Rd; drinks ₹60-120; ⏲11am-9pm), **Nungambakkam** (Map p1012; KNK Sq, Khader Nawaz Khan Rd; drinks ₹60-120; ⏲9am-11pm; 📶), **Express Avenue Mall** (Map p1012; 1st fl & 3rd fl, White's Rd; drinks ₹60-120; ⏲10am-9pm Mon-Fri, to 10pm Sat & Sun), **Alwarpet** (Map p1006; Ramakrishnan Towers, TTK Rd; drinks ₹60-120; ⏲10am-10pm) and **Phoenix Market City** (Basement, Phoenix Market City, Velachery; drinks ₹60-120; ⏲10am-11pm).

☆ Entertainment

There's *bharatanatyam* (Tamil classical dance) and/or a Carnatic music concert going on in Chennai almost every evening. Check listings in the *Hindu* or *Times of India*, or on www.timescity.com/chennai.

The **Music Academy** (Map p1006; ☎044-28112231; www.musicacademymadras.in; 168/306 TTK Rd, Royapettah) is the most popular venue. The Kalakshetra Foundation (p1010) and **Bharatiya Vidya Bhavan** (Map p1006; ☎044-24643420; www.bhavanchennai.org; East Mada St, Mylapore) also stage many events, often free.

Shopping

T Nagar has great shopping, especially at Pondy Bazaar and in the Panagal Park area. Many of Kanchipuram's finest silks turn up in Chennai, and the streets around Panagal Park are filled with silk shops; *this* is where you buy your sari.

Nungambakkam's shady Khader Nawaz Khan Rd is a lovely lane of increasingly upmarket designer boutiques, cafes and galleries.

Chennai's shopping malls are full of major international and Indian fashion chains. The best include **Express Avenue** (Map p1012; www.expressavenue.in; White's Rd, Royapettah; ⏲10am-10pm), **Chennai Citi Centre** (Map p1006; http://chennaiciticenter.com; 10 Dr Radhakrishnan Salai, Mylapore; ⏲10am-10pm), **Spencer Plaza** (Map p1012; 769 Anna Salai; ⏲10am-10pm) and the newer, glitzier **Phoenix Market City** (www.phoenixmarketcity.com; 142 Velachery Main Rd, Velachery; ⏲11am-10pm) in the city's south. Spencer Plaza is a bit downmarket, good for smaller craft and souvenir shops.

Central Chennai

★Higginbothams BOOKS
(Map p1012; higginbothams@vsnl.com; 116 Anna Salai; ⏲9am-8pm Mon-Sat, 10.30am-7.30pm Sun) Open since 1844, this grand white building is reckoned to be India's oldest bookshop. It has a brilliant English-language selection, including travel and fiction books, and a good range of maps.

Naturally Auroville ARTS & CRAFTS
(Map p1012; http://naturallyaurovillechennai.com; 8 Khader Nawaz Khan Rd, Nungambakkam; ⏲10.15am-9pm) Colourful handicrafts and home-decor trinkets, including bedspreads, cushions, incense, scented candles and handmade-paper notebooks, all from Auroville, near Puducherry.

Poompuhar ARTS & CRAFTS
(Map p1012; http://tnpoompuhar.org; 108 Anna Salai; ⏲10am-8pm Mon-Sat, 11am-7pm Sun) This large branch of the fixed-price state-government handicrafts chain is good for everything from cheap technicolour plaster deities to a ₹700,000 bronze Nataraja.

Evoluzione CLOTHING
(Map p1012; www.evoluzionestyle.com; 3 Khader Nawaz Khan Rd, Nungambakkam; ⏲10.30am-7.30pm Mon-Sat, 11am-6pm Sun) This sparkly high-end boutique showcases neotraditional creations by cutting-edge Indian designers. Great for browsing, even if your budget doesn't allow the fabulously glittery wedding gowns!

Southern Chennai

★Nalli Silks TEXTILES
(Map p1006; www.nallisilks.com; 9 Nageswaran Rd, T Nagar; ⏲9.30am-9.30pm) Set up in 1928, the enormous, supercolourful granddaddy of Chennai silk shops sparkles with wedding saris and rainbows of Kanchipuram silks, as well as silk dhotis (long loincloths) for men.

TRADITIONAL TRADERS

Even as Chennai expands relentlessly to the south, west and north, George Town, the local settlement that grew up near British Fort St George, remains the city's wholesale centre. Many of its narrow streets are entirely devoted to selling one particular product, as they have for hundreds of years – jewellery on NSC Bose Rd, paper goods in Anderson St. Even if you aren't buying, wander the maze-like streets to see Indian life flowing seamlessly from the past into the present.

Fabindia CLOTHING, HANDICRAFTS

(Map p1006; www.fabindia.com; 2nd fl, 35 TTK Rd, Alwarpet; 10.30am-8.30pm) This fair-trade, nationwide chain sells stylishly contemporary village-made clothes and crafts. Perfect for picking up a kurta (long shirt with short/no collar) to throw over trousers. This branch has incense, ceramics, table and bed linen, and natural beauty products too. Also at **Woods Road** (Map p1012; 3 Woods Rd; 10.30am-8.30pm), **Express Avenue** (Map p1012; 1st fl, White's Rd, Royapettah; 11.30am-9pm), **Nungambakkam** (Map p1012; 2nd fl, 9/15 Khader Nawaz Khan Rd; 10.30am-8.30pm), **T Nagar** (Map p1006; 44 GN Chetty Rd; 10.30am-8.30pm) and **Besant Nagar** (T-25, 7th Ave, Besant Nagar; 10.30am-8.30pm).

Chamiers CLOTHING, HANDICRAFTS

(Map p1006; http://chamiershop.com; 106 Chamiers Rd, RA Puram; 10.30am-7.30pm) On the ground floor of this popular cafe-and-boutique-complex, **Anokhi** (Map p1006; www.anokhi.com; 10.30am-7.30pm) has wonderful, East-meets-West hand-block-printed clothes, bedding, bags and accessories in floaty fabrics, at good prices. Elegant **Amethyst Room** (Map p1006; www.amethystchennai.com; 10.30am-7pm) next door takes things upmarket with beautiful Indian-design couture. Upstairs is **Chamiers for Men** (Map p1006; 10.30am-7.30pm).

Starmark BOOKS

(Map p1012; www.starmark.in; 2nd fl, Express Avenue, White's Rd, Royapettah; 10.30am-9.30pm Mon-Fri, 10am-10pm Sat & Sun) Smart bookshop with an excellent collection of English, Indian and Tamil fiction and nonfiction, India travel books and Lonely Planet guides. Also at Phoenix Market City (p1019).

Orientation

The old British Fort St George and George Town's jumble of narrow streets and bazaars constitute Chennai's historic hub. The two main train stations, Egmore and Central, sit inland (west) from the fort. Much of the best eating, drinking, shopping and accommodation lies in the city's leafier southern and southwestern suburbs such as Nungambakkam, T Nagar (Thyagaraya Nagar), Alwarpet, Guindy and Velachery. The hectic major thoroughfare linking northern with southern Chennai is Anna Salai (Mount Rd).

Information

INTERNET ACCESS

Many cafes and hotels have wi-fi. 'Browsing centres' (per hour ₹25 to ₹30) are everywhere; take your passport.

LEFT LUGGAGE

Egmore and Central train stations have left-luggage offices ('Cloakroom') for people with journey tickets. The airport also has left-luggage facilities.

MEDICAL SERVICES

Apollo Hospital (Map p1012; 044-28290200, emergency 044-28293333; www.apollohospitals.com; 21 Greams Lane, Nungambakkam; 24hr) State-of-the-art, expensive hospital, popular with 'medical tourists'.

Kauvery Hospital (Map p1006; 044-40006000; www.kauveryhospital.com; 199 Luz Church Rd, Mylapore; 24hr) Good, private, general hospital.

MONEY

Citibank ATMS are best for withdrawing large amounts of cash with foreign cards in Tamil Nadu. Axis Bank, Canara Bank, HDFC Bank, ICICI Bank and State Bank of India ATMs are other options.

NONSTOP DOMESTIC FLIGHTS FROM CHENNAI

DESTINATION	AIRLINES	TIME (HR)	DEPARTURES (DAILY)
Bengaluru	AI, SG, 6E, 9W	1	19
Delhi	AI, SG, 6E, 9W	2¾-3	23
Goa	AI, SG	1¼-2	2
Hyderabad	AI, G8, SG, 6E, 9W	1-1½	23
Kochi	AI, SG, 6E	1-1½	7
Kolkata	AI, SG, 6E	2-2¾	10
Mumbai	AI, G8, SG, 6E, 9W	2	22
Port Blair	AI, G8, SG, 6E, 9W	2-2¼	6
Trivandrum	AI, 6E	1-1½	3

Airline codes: AI – Air India, G8 – Go Air, SG – SpiceJet, 6E – IndiGo, 9W – Jet Airways

GOVERNMENT BUSES FROM CHENNAI'S CMBT

DESTINATION	FARE (₹)	TIME (HR)	DEPARTURES
Bengaluru	360-580	7-8	at least 40 daily
Coimbatore	40	11	11 daily
Ernakulam (Kochi)	590	12-16	3pm
Hyderabad	825-1500	14	5.30pm, 6.30pm, 7pm
Kodaikanal	380	10-13	5pm
Madurai	325	9-10	42 daily
Mamallapuram	40	2-2½	every 10min
Mysuru	550-900	10	7pm, 7.45pm, 8.40pm, 10.05pm
Ooty	435	12	4.30pm, 5.45pm, 7.15pm
Puducherry	125	4	36 daily
Thanjavur	250	8½	12 daily
Tirupati	150-320	4	every 30min
Trichy	235	6½-7	45 daily
Trivandrum	570	14	9 daily

POST

DHL (Map p1012; 044-42148886; www.dhl.com; 85 VVV Sq, Pantheon Rd, Egmore; 9am-9pm) Secure international parcel delivery; branches around town.

Main Post Office (Map p1006; Rajaji Salai, George Town; 8am-9pm Mon-Sat, 10am-4pm Sun)

TOURIST INFORMATION

Indiatourism (Map p1012; 044-28460285, 044-28461459; http://incredibleindia.org; 154 Anna Salai; 9.15am-5.45pm Mon-Fri) Helpful on all of India, as well as Chennai.

Tamil Nadu Tourism Development Corporation (TTDC; Map p1012; 044-25333333; www.tamilnadutourism.org; Tamil Nadu Tourism Complex, 2 Wallajah Rd, Triplicane; 24hr) The state tourism body's main office takes bookings for its own bus tours, answers questions and hands out leaflets. In the same building are state tourist offices from all over India, mostly open 10am to 6pm. The TTDC has a counter at Egmore station.

TRAVEL AGENCIES

Milesworth Travel (Map p1006; 044-24338664; http://milesworth.com; RM Towers, 108 Chamiers Rd, Alwarpet; 9.30am-6pm Mon-Fri, to 4pm Sat) Very professional, welcoming agency that will help with all your travel needs.

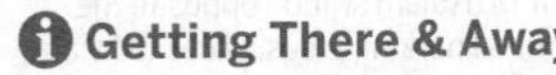

Getting There & Away

AIR

Chennai International Airport (044-22560551; Tirusulam) is in the far southwest of the city. The international terminal is 500m west of the domestic terminal; walkways link the two terminals.

There are direct flights to cities all over India, including Trichy (Tiruchirappalli), Madurai, Coimbatore and Thoothikudi (Tuticorin) within Tamil Nadu. Internationally, Chennai has many direct flights to/from Colombo, Singapore, Kuala Lumpur and the Gulf states. The best fares from Europe are often on Jet Airways (via Mumbai or Delhi), Qatar Airways (via Doha), Emirates (via Dubai) or Oman Air (via Muscat). Cathay Pacific flies to Hong Kong, and Maldivian to Male.

BOAT

Passenger ships sail from George Town harbour direct to Port Blair in the Andaman Islands once weekly. The **Andaman Shipping Office Ticketing Counter** (044-25226873; 2nd fl, Shipping Corporation of India, Jawahar Bldg, 17 Rajaji Salai, George Town; 10am-4pm Mon-Fri, to noon Sat) sells tickets (₹2500 to ₹6420) for the 60-hour trip. Book several days ahead, and take three copies each of your passport data page and Indian visa along with the original. It can be a long process.

BUS

Most government buses operate from the large but surprisingly orderly **CMBT** (Chennai Mofussil Bus Terminus; Jawaharlal Nehru Rd, Koyambedu), 6km west of the centre. The most comfortable and expensive are the air-con buses (best of these are Volvo AC services), followed by the UD ('Ultra Deluxe'); these can generally be reserved in advance. You can book up to 60 days ahead at the computerised reservation

MAJOR TRAINS FROM CHENNAI

DESTINATION	TRAIN NO & NAME	FARE (₹)	TIME (HR)	DEPARTURE
Agra	12615 Grand Trunk Exp	745/1960/2865 (C)	31½	7.15pm CC
Bengaluru	12007 Shatabdi Exp*	710/1435 (A)	5	6am CC
	12609 Bangalore Exp	150/540 (B)	6½	1.35pm CC
Coimbatore	12675 Kovai Express	180/660 (B)	7½	6.15am CC
	12671 Nilgiri Exp	315/810/1140 (C)	7¾	9.15pm CC
Delhi	12621 Tamil Nadu Exp	780/2040/2990 (C)	33	10pm CC
Goa	17311 Vasco Exp (Friday only)	475/1285/1865 (C)	21	3pm CC
Hyderabad	12759 Charminar Exp	425/1125/1605 (C)	13¾	6.10pm CC
Kochi	22639 Alleppey Exp	395/1045/1480 (C)	11½	8.45pm CC
Kolkata	12842 Coromandel Exp	665/1745/2540 (C)	27	8.45am CC
Madurai	12635 Vaigai Exp	180/660 (B)	7¾	1.30pm CE
	12637 Pandian Exp	315/810/1140 (C)	8¾	9.20pm CE
Mumbai	11042 Mumbai Exp	540/1450/2115 (C)	25¾	11.55am CC
Mysuru	12007 Shatabdi Exp*	930/1825 (A)	7	6am CC
	16021 Kaveri Exp	315/810/1140 (C)	9¾	9pm CC
Tirupati	16053 Tirupathi Exp	80/285 (B)	3½	2.15pm CC
Trichy	12635 Vaigai Exp	145/515 (B)	5	1.30pm CE
Trivandrum	12695 Trivandrum Exp	470/1240/1775 (C)	16	3.25pm CC

Departure Codes: CC – Chennai Central, CE – Chennai Egmore
*Daily except Wednesday
Fares: (A) chair/executive; (B) 2nd class/chair; (C) sleeper/3AC/2AC

centre at the left end of the main hall, or online (www.tnstc.in).

The **T Nagar Bus Terminus** (Map p1006; South Usman Rd, T Nagar) is handy for bus 599 to Mamallapuram (₹40, 1½ hours, hourly 5am to 7.30pm).

Private buses generally offer greater comfort than non-AC government buses, at up to double the price. Their main terminal is the **Omni Bus Stand** (off Kaliamman Koil St, Koyambedu), 500m west of the CMBT, but some companies also pick up and drop off elsewhere in the city. Service information is at www.redbus.in; tickets can be booked through travel agencies.

Parveen Travels (Map p1012; ☎044-28192577; www.parveentravels.com; 11/5 Kennet Lane, Egmore) Services to Bengaluru, Ernakulam (Kochi; Cochin), Kodaikanal, Madurai, Ooty (Udhagamandalam), Puducherry, Trichy and Thiruvananthapuram (Trivandrum) depart from its Egmore office.

CAR

Renting a car with a driver is the easiest form of transport and easily arranged through most travel agents, midrange or top-end hotels, or the airport's prepaid taxi desks. Sample rates for non-AC/AC cars are ₹700/900 for up to five hours and 50km, and ₹1400/1800 for up to 10 hours and 100km.

TRAIN

Interstate trains and those heading west generally depart from Central station, while trains heading south mostly leave from Egmore. The **Advanced Reservation Office** (Map p1012; 1st fl, Chennai Central suburban station; ⏱8am-2pm & 2.15-8pm Mon-Sat, 8am-2pm Sun), with its incredibly helpful Foreign Tourist Cell, is on the 1st floor in a separate 11-storey building just west of the main Central station building. Bring photocopies of your passport visa and photo pages. Egmore station has its own **Passenger Reservation Office** (Map p1012; 1st fl, Egmore station, Egmore; ⏱8am-2pm & 2.15-8pm Mon-Sat, 8am-2pm Sun).

ℹ Getting Around

TO/FROM THE AIRPORT

The cheapest airport transport are suburban trains to/from Tirusulam station opposite the domestic terminal parking areas, accessed via a signposted pedestrian subway under the highway. Trains run roughly every 15 minutes from 4.53am to 11.43pm to/from Chennai Beach station (₹10, 40 minutes); stops include Nungambakkam, Egmore, Chennai Park and Chennai Fort.

Prepaid taxi kiosks outside the airport's international terminal charge ₹550/600 for a non-AC/AC cab to Egmore, and ₹450/500 to T Nagar. Rates are slightly lower at prepaid taxi kiosks outside the domestic terminal. Both terminals have **Fast Track** (☎ 60006000) taxi booking counters.

The Chennai Metro Rail system provides cheap, easy transport between the airport and, at the time of writing, the CMBT only (₹50; possibly changing at Alandur). The metro station is between the two airport terminals. A metro branch connecting the airport with central Chennai isn't due until 2018.

From the CMBT, city buses 70 and 170 to Tambaram stop on the highway across from the airport (₹12 to ₹15, 30 to 40 minutes).

AUTORICKSHAW

Most autorickshaw drivers refuse to use their meters and quote astronomical fares. Avoid paying upfront, and always establish the price before getting into a rickshaw. Rates rise by up to 50% from 11pm to 5am.

There are prepaid autorickshaw booths outside the CMBT (₹125 to Egmore), and 24-hour prepaid stands on the south side of Central station and outside the north and south exits of Egmore station.

Tempting offers of ₹50 autorickshaw 'city tours' sound too good to be true. They are. You'll spend the day being dragged from one shop to another.

BUS

Chennai's city bus system is worth getting to know, although buses get packed to overflowing at busy times. Fares are between ₹3 and ₹14 (up to double for express and deluxe services, and multiplied by five for Volvo AC services). Route information is on www.mtcbus.org.

METRO RAIL

Chennai Metro Rail, a much-awaited, part-underground rapid transit system, partly opened in late 2016. At the time of writing, the only operational section was a part of Line 2 (Green) that runs from the CMBT south to St Thomas Mount and the airport. When completed, Line 2 will continue east from the CMBT to Egmore and Central train stations. Line 1 (Blue) goes from the airport to Teynampet, Thousand Lights, Central train station, the High Court and Washermanpet in northern Chennai, running beneath Anna Salai for several kilometres, but isn't due to be completed until 2018. Trains run from 5am to 10pm; tickets cost ₹10 to ₹50.

TAXI

Both airport terminals have prepaid taxi kiosks. There are prepaid taxi stands outside the south side of **Egmore** (Map p1012; Egmore station, Egmore; ⏰ 24hr) and **Central** (Map p1012; Central station; ⏰ 24hr) stations; a ride of 8km or 9km, such as to the CMBT, costs around ₹450.

CHENNAI BUS ROUTES

BUS NO	ROUTE
A1	Central–Anna Salai–RK Mutt Rd (Mylapore) –Theosophical Society–Thiruvanmiyur
1B	Parry's–Central–Anna Salai–Airport
10A	Parry's–Central–Egmore (S)–Pantheon Rd–T Nagar
11	Rattan–Central–Anna Salai–T Nagar
12	T Nagar–Pondy Bazaar–Eldham's Rd–Dr Radhakrishnan Salai–Vivekananda House
13	T Nagar–Royapettah–Triplicane
15B & 15F	Broadway–Central–CMBT
M27	CMBT–T Nagar
27B	CMBT–Egmore (S)–Bharathi Salai (Triplicane)
27D	Egmore (S)–Anna Salai–Cathedral Rd–Dr Radhakrishnan Salai–San Thome Cathedral
32A	Central–Vivekananda House
102	Broadway–Fort St George–Kamarajar Salai–San Thome Cathedral–Theosophical Society

Routes operate in both directions.

Broadway – Broadway Bus Terminus, George Town

Central – Central Station

Egmore (S) – Egmore station (south side)

Parry's – Parry's Corner

Rattan – Rattan Bazaar Rd Bus Stop

T Nagar – T Nagar Bus Terminus

HOLIDAY TRANSPORT

All kinds of transport in, to and from Tamil Nadu get booked up weeks in advance for periods around major celebrations, including Pongal, Karthikai Deepam, Gandhi Jayanti and Diwali. Plan ahead.

Relatively reliable **Fast Track** (p1023) taxis charge ₹100 for up to 4km, then ₹18 per kilometre (with a 25% hike in rates between 11pm and 5am); bookings by phone.

The Uber taxi app offers reliable, sensibly priced transport around town, as does the near-identical Ola Cabs app (for which you need an Indian mobile number).

TRAIN

Efficient, cheap suburban trains run from Beach station to Fort, Park (near Central station), Egmore, Chetpet, Nungambakkam, Kodambakkam, Mambalam, Saidapet, Guindy, St Thomas Mount, Tirusulam (for the airport), and on south to Tambaram. At Egmore station, the suburban platforms (10 and 11) and ticket office are on the station's north side. A second line branches south after Fort to Park Town, Chepauk, Tiruvallikeni (for Marina Beach), Light House and Thirumailai (near the Kapaleeshwarar Temple). Trains run several times hourly from 4am to midnight, costing ₹5 to ₹10.

NORTHERN TAMIL NADU

South of Chennai

Chennai's sprawl peters out after an hour or so heading south on the East Coast Rd (ECR), at which point Tamil Nadu becomes red dirt, blue skies, palm trees and green fields, sprinkled with towns and villages (or, if you take the 'IT Expressway' inland, enormous new buildings).

There are several worthwhile ECR stops if you're travelling between Chennai and Mamallapuram, 50km south. Among these is the low-key fishing-turned-surfing village of Kovalam (Covelong). Swimming along the coast is dangerous due to strong currents.

Sights

Cholamandal Artists' Village ARTIST COLONY, MUSEUM

(☎044-24490092; www.cholamandalartistvillage.com; Injambakkam; museum adult/child ₹20/5; ⊙museum 9.30am-6.30pm) There's a tropical bohemian groove floating around Injambakkam village, site of the Cholamandal Artists' Village, 10km south of Chennai's Adyar River. This 4-hectare artists' cooperative – founded in 1966 by artists of the Madras Movement, pioneers of modern art in South India – is a serene muse away from the world. The art in its museum is very much worth lingering over; look especially for work by KCS Paniker, SG Vasudev, M Senathipathi and S Nandagopal.

DakshinaChitra ARTS/CRAFTS CENTRE

(☎044-27472603; www.dakshinachitra.net; East Coast Rd, Muttukadu; adult/student Indian ₹100/50, foreign ₹250/70; ⊙10am-6pm Wed-Mon) DakshinaChitra, 22km south of Chennai's Adyar River, offers a fantastic insight into South India's traditional arts and crafts. Like a treasure chest of local art and architecture, this jumble of open-air museum, preserved village, artisan workshops (pottery, silk-weaving, basket-making) and galleries is strewn among an exquisite collection of real-deal traditional South Indian homes. You can see silk-weavers in action, have *mehndi* (ornate henna designs) applied and enjoy an array of shows.

Madras Crocodile Bank ZOO

(☎044-27472447; www.madrascrocodilebank.org; Vadanemmeli; adult/child ₹40/20; ⊙8.30am-5.30pm Tue-Sun) Just 6km south of Kovalam, this incredible conservation and research trust is a fascinating peek into the reptile world. Founded by croc/snake-expert Romulus Whitaker, the bank has thousands of reptiles, including 17 of the world's 23 species of crocodilian (crocodiles and similar creatures), and does crucial work in maintaining genetic reserves of these animals, several of which are endangered. There are openings for volunteers (minimum two weeks).

Tiger Cave HINDU SITE

(Saluvankuppam; ⊙6am-6pm) FREE The Tiger Cave, 5km north of Mamallapuram, is an unfinished but impressive rock-cut shrine, dedicated to Durga (a form of Devi, Shiva's wife) and probably dating from the 7th century. What's special is the 'necklace' of 11 monstrous tiger-like heads framing its central shrine-cavity, next to two elephant-carved heads. At the north end of the park-like complex is a same-era rock-cut **Shiva shrine**. Beyond the fence lies the **Subrahmanya Temple**: an 8th-century granite shrine built over a brick, Sangam-era Murugan temple.

Getting There & Away

To reach the ECR sights, take any Chennai–Mamallapuram bus, and hop off at the appropriate point(s). The **TTDC** (p1021) Chennai–Mamallapuram round-trip bus tour (₹625, 10 hours) visits several of these sights and Mamallapuram. A full-day taxi tour from Chennai costs ₹2500 to ₹3000.

Mamallapuram (Mahabalipuram)

044 / POP 15,170

Mamallapuram, 50km south of Chennai, was the major seaport of the ancient Pallava kingdom based at Kanchipuram. A wander round the town's magnificent, World Heritage–listed temples and carvings inflames the imagination, especially at sunset.

In addition to ancient archaeological wonders, salty air and coastal beauty, there's also the traveller hub of Othavadai and Othavadai Cross Sts, where restaurants serve pasta, pizza and pancakes, and shops sell Tibetan trinkets. The town's buzzing, growing surf scene is another attraction.

'Mahabs', as most call it, is less than two hours by bus from Chennai, and many travellers make a beeline straight here. It's small and laid-back, and sights can be explored on foot or by bicycle.

Sights

You can easily spend a full day exploring Mamallapuram's marvellous temples, caves and rock carvings. Most were carved from the rock during the 7th-century reign of Pallava king Narasimhavarman I, whose nickname Mamalla (Great Wrestler) gave the town its name. Official Archaeological Survey of India guides can be hired at sites.

★ Shore Temple HINDU TEMPLE

(Beach Rd; combined 1-day ticket with Five Rathas Indian/foreigner ₹30/500, video ₹25; 6am-6pm) Standing like a magnificent fist of rock-cut elegance overlooking the sea, surrounded by gardens and ruined courts, the two-towered Shore Temple symbolises the heights of Pallava architecture and the maritime ambitions of the Pallava kings. Its small size belies its excellent proportion and the supreme quality of the carvings, many now eroded into vaguely Impressionist embellishments. Built under Narasimhavarman II in the 8th century, it's the earliest significant free-standing stone temple in Tamil Nadu.

The two towers rise above shrines to Shiva and their original linga captured the sunrise and sunset. Between the Shiva shrines is one to Vishnu, shown sleeping. Rows of Nandi (Shiva's vehicle) statues frame the temple courtyard. A boulder-carved Durga sits on her lion-vehicle's knee on the temple's south side.

★ Five Rathas HINDU TEMPLE

(Pancha Ratha; Five Rathas Rd; combined 1-day ticket with Shore Temple Indian/foreigner ₹30/500, video ₹25; 6am-6pm) Huddled together at the southern end of Mamallapuram, the Five Rathas were, astonishingly, all carved from single large rocks. Each of these fine 7th-century temples was dedicated to a

DON'T MISS

SURF & SEA: KOVALAM (COVELONG)

Low-key fishing village **Kovalam** (Covelong), 30km south of Chennai, has sprung into the spotlight for having the best surfing waves in Tamil Nadu. It's now an increasingly popular travellers' hang-out, hosting the high-profile **Covelong Point Surf & Music Festival** (www.covelongpoint.com; Aug-Sep) and offering all kinds of water sports plus beachfront yoga.

For classes, head to 'social surfing school' **Covelong Point** (9840975916; www.covelongpoint.com; 10 Pearl Beach, Ansari Nagar; per hour board rental/surf class ₹300/500; hours vary), under the watch of Kovalam's original local surf pioneer Murthy. It also provides kayaking, diving, windsurfing and stand-up paddleboarding.

The same team runs stylish, surf-mad B&B **Surf Turf** (9884272572; www.surfturf.in; 10 Pearl Beach, Ansari Nagar; r incl breakfast ₹2810-4950; 2-person 'surf & stay' package from ₹9500;) and its breezy beach-facing cafe. The five tastefully unfussy rooms here have stripped-back contemporary decor, aqua-toned bedding and delicious sand-and-sea views from private balconies; 'standards' share a bathroom. Kovalam's luxury choice is beachside **Vivanta by Taj – Fisherman's Cove** (044-67413333; www.vivanta.tajhotels.com; Kovalam Beach; r incl breakfast ₹12,090-21,760;).

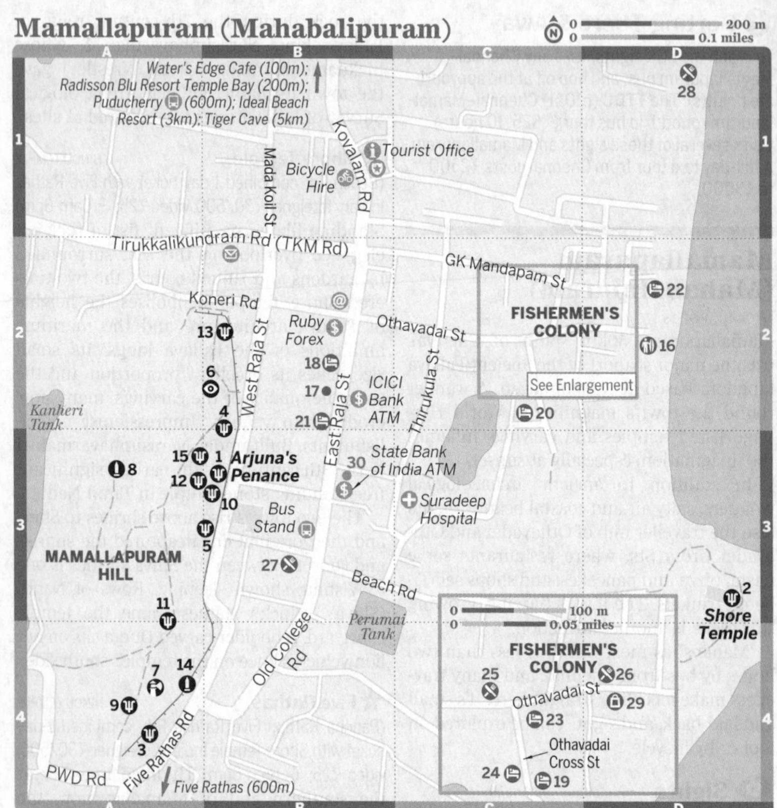

Hindu god and is now named after one or more of the Pandavas, the five hero-brothers of the epic Mahabharata, or their common wife, Draupadi. The *rathas* were hidden in the sand until excavated by the British 200 years ago.

Ratha is Sanskrit for 'chariot', and may refer to the temples' form or to their function as vehicles for the gods. It's thought they didn't originally serve as places of worship, but as architectural models.

The first *ratha* on the left after you enter is the **Draupadi Ratha**, in the form of a stylised South Indian hut. It's dedicated to the demon-fighting goddess Durga, who looks out from inside, standing on a lotus, and is depicted on the outside walls. Female guardians flank the entrance; a huge sculpted lion, Durga's mount, stands outside.

Next, on the same plinth, is the 'chariot' of the most important Pandava, the **Arjuna Ratha**, dedicated to Shiva. Its pilasters, miniature roof shrines, and small octagonal dome make it a precursor of many later South Indian temples. A huge Nandi stands behind. Shiva (leaning on Nandi, south side) and other gods are depicted on the temple's outer walls.

The barrel-roofed **Bhima Ratha** was never completed, as evidenced by the missing north-side colonnade; inside is a shrine to Vishnu. The **Dharmaraja Ratha**, tallest of the temples, is similar to the Arjuna Ratha but one storey higher, with lion pillars. The carvings on its outer walls mostly represent gods, including the androgynous Ardhanarishvara (half Shiva, half Parvati) on the east side. King Narasimhavarman I appears at the west end of the south side.

The **Nakula-Sahadeva Ratha** (named after two twin Pandavas) stands aside from the other four and is dedicated to Indra. The life-size stone elephant beside it is one of India's most perfectly sculpted elephants. Approaching from the gate to the north you

Mamallapuram (Mahabalipuram)

Top Sights
1 Arjuna's Penance B3
2 Shore Temple D3

Sights
3 Dharmaraja Cave Temple A4
4 Ganesh Ratha B2
5 Krishna Mandapa B3
6 Krishna's Butterball B2
7 Lighthouse A4
8 Lion Throne A3
9 Mahishamardini Mandapa A4
10 Panch Pandava Mandapa B3
11 Ramanuja Mandapa A3
12 Raya Gopura A3
13 Trimurti Cave Temple B2
14 Unfinished Relief Carving A4
15 Varaha Mandapa A3

Activities, Courses & Tours
16 Mumu Surf School D2
17 Travel XS B2

Sleeping
18 Butterball Bed 'n Breakfast B2
19 Greenwoods Beach Resort C4
20 Hotel Daphne C2
21 Hotel Mamalla Heritage B2
22 Sri Harul Guest House D2
23 Tina Blue View Lodge & Restaurant C4
24 Vinodhara Guesthouse C4

Eating
Burger Shack .... (see 18)
25 Gecko Restaurant C4
26 Le Yogi D4
27 Mamalla Bhavan B3
28 Wharf D1

Shopping
29 Apollo Books D4

Transport
30 Southern Railway Computerised Passenger Reservation Centre B3

see its back end first, hence its nickname Gajaprishthakara (elephant's backside).

★ **Arjuna's Penance** HINDU MONUMENT
(West Raja St; ⊙24hr) FREE The crowning masterpiece of Mamallapuram's stonework, this giant relief carving is one of India's greatest ancient artworks. Inscribed on two huge, adjacent boulders, the Penance bursts with scenes of Hindu myth and everyday South Indian life. In the centre, *nagas* (snake-beings) descend a once water-filled cleft, representing the Ganges. To the left Arjuna (hero of the Mahabharata) performs self-mortification (fasting on one leg), so that the four-armed Shiva will grant him his most powerful weapon, the god-slaying Pasupata.

Some scholars believe the carving actually shows the sage Bagiratha, who did severe penance to obtain Shiva's help in bringing the Ganges to earth. Shiva is attended by dwarves, and celestial beings fly across the carving's upper sections. Below Arjuna/Bagiratha is a temple to Vishnu (mythical ancestor of the Pallava kings), with sages, deer and a lion. The many wonderfully carved animals include a herd of elephants and – humour amid the holy – a cat mimicking Arjuna's penance to a crowd of mice.

South along the road from Arjuna's Penance are the unfinished **Panch Pandava Mandapa** (West Raja St; ⊙6am-6pm) FREE cave temple; the **Krishna Mandapa** (West Raja St; ⊙6am-6pm) FREE, which famously depicts Krishna lifting Govardhana Hill to protect cows and villagers from a storm sent by Indra; an **unfinished relief carving** (West Raja St; ⊙24hr) FREE of similar size to Arjuna's Penance; and the empty **Dharmaraja Cave Temple** (Five Rathas Rd; ⊙6am-6pm) FREE.

Activities

Beaches

The beach fronting the village isn't exactly pristine, but south of the Shore Temple it clears into finer sand. You'll also be further away from the leers of men who spend their days gawking at tourists. Like most of Tamil Nadu's coast, these beaches aren't great for swimming, due to dangerous rips.

Surfing

Mumu Surf School SURFING
(☎9789844191; http://mumusurfer.wixsite.com/indiasurfing; Othavadai St; 90min group/private class ₹750/1300; ⊙7.30am-6pm) Popular, well-organised school for all levels and board rental (per hour ₹250 to ₹300); also runs beach clean-ups and the relaxed Sandy Bottom cafe.

Yoga, Ayurveda & Massage

Numerous places offer massage (₹750 to ₹1500), yoga (₹300) and ayurvedic treatments, at similar rates.

Tours

Travel XS CYCLING, BIRDWATCHING
(044-27443260; www.travel-xs.com; 123 East Raja St; bicycle tour per person ₹500; 9.30am-6pm Mon-Fri, to 2pm Sat) Runs half-day bicycle tours (minimum two people) to nearby villages, visiting local potters and observing *kolam* drawing (elaborate chalk, rice-paste or coloured powder designs, also called *rangoli*), and organises day trips, including to Kanchipuram and (seasonally) Vedanthangal Bird Sanctuary.

Festivals & Events

Mamallapuram Dance Festival DANCE
(Jan-Feb) A four-week dance festival showcasing classical and folk dances from all over India, with many performances on an open-air stage. Dances include *bharatanatyam* (Tamil Nadu), Kuchipudi dance-drama (Andhra Pradesh) and Kathakali (Kerala drama).

Sleeping

Sri Harul Guest House GUESTHOUSE $
(9941070343; www.facebook.com/sriharulguesthouse; 181 Bajanai Koil St, Fishermen's Colony; r ₹800-1200) The beach sits right below your balcony if you land one of the half-dozen sea-view rooms at Sri Harul, one of Mamallapuram's better seafront budget deals. Rooms are basic, medium-sized and quite clean.

Vinodhara Guesthouse GUESTHOUSE $
(9444135118, 044-27442694; www.vinodhara.com; 9/4 Othavadai Cross St; s/d ₹600/700, r with AC ₹1200-1800;) An ever-growing collection of varied, clean-enough, no-frills rooms, from boxy fan-cooled singles to spacious, modernish air-con doubles, all under helpful management. Check out a few rooms first.

Greenwoods Beach Resort GUESTHOUSE $
(044-27442212, 9791145729; greenwoods_resort@yahoo.com; 7 Othavadai Cross St; r ₹700-900, with AC ₹1300-1700;) Perhaps the most char-

MAMALLAPURAM HILL

Many interesting monuments, mostly dating from the late 7th and early 8th centuries, are scattered across the rock-strewn hill on the west side of town. It takes about an hour to walk round the main ones. The hill is open from 6am to 6pm and has entrances on West Raja St and just off Five Rathas Rd.

Straight ahead inside the northernmost West Raja St entrance stands a huge, impossible-to-miss boulder with the inspired name of **Krishna's Butterball** (Mamallapuram Hill; 6am-6pm) FREE, immovable but apparently balancing precariously. Beyond the rocks north of here is the **Trimurti Cave Temple** (Mamallapuram Hill; 6am-6pm) FREE, honouring the Hindu 'trinity': Brahma (left), Shiva (centre) and Vishnu (right), flanked by guardians. On the back of this rock is a beautiful group of carved elephants.

South of Krishna's Butterball you reach the **Ganesh Ratha** (Mamallapuram Hill; 6am-6pm) FREE, carved from a single rock, with lion-shaped pillar bases. Once a Shiva temple, it became a shrine to Ganesh (Shiva's elephant-headed son) after the original lingam was removed. Southwest of here, the **Varaha Mandapa** (Mamallapuram Hill; 6am-6pm) FREE houses some of Mamallapuram's finest carvings, including columns with sitting lions. The left panel shows Vishnu's boar avatar, Varaha, lifting the earth out of the oceans. The outward-facing panels show Vishnu's consort Lakshmi (washed by elephants) and Durga, while the right-hand panel has Vishnu in his eight-armed giant form, Trivikrama, overcoming the demon king Bali.

A little further south, then east (up to the left), is the 16th-century **Raya Gopura** (Olakkanatha Temple; Mamallapuram Hill; 6am-6pm) FREE, probably an unfinished *gopuram* (gateway tower). West just up the hill is the finely carved **Lion Throne** (Mamallapuram Hill; 6am-6pm) FREE (depicted roaring). The main path continues south to the **Ramanuja Mandapa** (Mamallapuram Hill; 6am-6pm) FREE and up to Mamallapuram's **lighthouse** (Mamallapuram Hill; Indian/foreigner ₹10/25, camera/video ₹20/25; 10am-1pm & 2-5.30pm). Southwest of the lighthouse is the rock-carved **Mahishamardini Mandapa** (Mamallapuram Hill; 6am-6pm) FREE, with excellent scenes from the Puranas (Sanskrit stories from the 5th century AD). The left-side panel shows Vishnu sleeping on the coils of a snake; on the right, Durga bestrides her lion vehicle while killing the demon-buffalo Mahisha. Inside the central shrine, Murugan sits between his parents Shiva and Parvati.

acterful of the Othavadai Cross St cheapies and definitely not on the beach, Greenwoods is run by an enthusiastic family who put up backpackers in plain, cleanish rooms (some with balconies and/or outdoor showers) up staircases around a leafy courtyard.

Tina Blue View Lodge & Restaurant GUESTHOUSE $

(044-27442319; 48 Othavadai St; r ₹600-700, with AC ₹1200) Frayed and faded Tina is one of Mamallapuram's originals and looks it, but still remains deservedly popular for its whitewashed walls, blue flourishes, little porches and shady tropical garden, as well as tireless original owner Xavier.

Butterball Bed 'n Breakfast B&B $$

(9094792525; http://butterball-bnb.in; 9/26 East Raja St; s/d incl breakfast ₹1700/2000;) Smallish but pleasant, white-walled, spotlessly maintained rooms have old English prints, writing desks, big mirrors and blue-tiled bathrooms. There's a great view of the eponymous giant rock from the roof terrace, plus a lovely lawn, a massage centre, a little pool and daily yoga (₹300). Breakfast is in the attached **Burger Shack** (9094792525; http://butterball-bnb.in; 9/26 East Raja St; mains ₹120-300; 10am-10pm).

Hotel Daphne HOTEL $$

(9894282876; www.moonrakersrestaurants.com; 24 Othavadai Cross St; r without/with AC ₹900/1700;) Non-AC rooms are perfectly acceptable and clean if nothing fancy, but the Daphne's seven air-con rooms are great value (especially top-floor rooms 13 and 14), most with four-poster beds, balconies and cane swing chairs. The shaded fairy-lit courtyard, cordial staff and free wi-fi are other drawcards.

Hotel Mamalla Heritage HOTEL $$

(044-27442060; www.hotelmamallaheritage.com; 104 East Raja St; incl breakfast s ₹2920-3160, d ₹3160-3400;) King of tour-group packages, the Mamalla has 43 big, comfortable, forgettable rooms rising around a cool-blue pool, and a quality rooftop veg restaurant. 'Deluxe' rooms are more up-to-date than 'standards'.

Radisson Blu Resort Temple Bay RESORT $$$

(044-27443636; http://radissonblu.com/hotel-mamallapuram; 57 Kovalam Rd; r incl breakfast from ₹11,100;) The Radisson's luxurious chalets, villas and bungalows are strewn across manicured gardens stretching 500m to the beach. Somewhere in the middle is India's longest swimming pool (220m). Rooms range from large to enormous; the most expensive have private pools. The Radisson also offers Mamallapuram's finest (priciest) dining and a top-notch ayurvedic spa (massage ₹2500). It's ridiculously popular. Best rates online.

Ideal Beach Resort RESORT $$$

(044-27442240; www.idealresort.com; East Coast Rd; incl breakfast s ₹6600-13,200, d ₹7200-14,400;) With flowery landscaped gardens and its own stretch of beach, this laid-back resort, 3km north of town, is popular with weekending families and couples. Though dated in parts, it's quiet and secluded, there's a lovely poolside restaurant, and comfy rooms come with tea/coffee sets, hairdryers and, for some, open-air showers. Nonguest pool/beach day passes cost ₹500.

Eating

Restaurants on Othavadai and Othavadai Cross Sts provide semi-open-air settings, decent Continental mains and bland Indian curries. For real Indian food, try the cheap veg places near the bus stand.

Mamalla Bhavan SOUTH INDIAN $

(South Mada St; mains ₹65-80, meals ₹70-125; 6am-9.15pm) For an authentically good, wallet-friendly South Indian fill-up, swing by this simple, packed-out veg restaurant pumping out morning *idlis, vadas* and dosas, ₹18 filter coffee and banana-leaf lunchtime thalis. It's right beside the bus stand.

Le Yogi MULTICUISINE $$

(9840706340; 19 Othavadai St; mains ₹190-300; 7.30am-11pm;) Some of Mamallapuram's best Continental food. The pasta, pizza, sizzlers, crepes and *momos* (Tibetan dumplings) are genuine and tasty (if small), service is good, and the chilled-out setting, with bamboo posts, floor cushions and lamps dangling from a thatched roof, has a touch of the romantic.

Gecko Restaurant MULTICUISINE $$

(www.gecko-web.com; 37 Othavadai St; mains ₹180-320; 9am-9.30pm;) Two friendly brothers run this cute blue-and-yellow-walled spot sprinkled with colourful artwork and wood carvings, and with daily seafood specials chalked up on boards. The offerings and prices aren't that different from other tourist-oriented restaurants, but there's a little more love put into the cooking here and it's tastier.

Water's Edge Cafe MULTICUISINE $$$
(044-27443636; www.radissonblu.com/hotel-mamallapuram; Radisson Blu Resort Temple Bay, 57 Kovalam Rd; mains ₹545-800; 24hr) The Radisson's pool-side 'cafe' offers everything from American pancakes to grilled tofu, Indian veg dishes, pan-Asian cuisine and a fantastic breakfast buffet (₹1190). It's expensive, but smart and popular.

Wharf MULTICUISINE $$$
(044-27443636; www.radissonblu.com/hotel-mamallapuram; Radisson Blu Resort Temple Bay, 57 Kovalam Rd; mains ₹695-2575; noon-3pm & 7-11pm) Though it looks like a beach shack, the Wharf is actually the Radisson's gourmet multicuisine seaside restaurant, with a strong emphasis on fresh seafood.

Shopping

The roar of electric stone-grinders has just about replaced the tink-tink of chisels in Mamallapuram's stone-carving workshops, enabling sculptors to turn out ever more granite sculptures (of varying quality), from ₹100 pendants to ₹400,000 Ganesh. There are also some decent art galleries, tailors and antique shops.

Apollo Books BOOKS
(150 Fishermen's Colony; 9am-9.30pm) Good collection of books in several languages, to sell and swap.

Information

Suradeep Hospital (044-27442448; 15 Thirukula St; 24hr) Recommended by travellers.
Tourist Office (044-27442232; Kovalam Rd; 10am-5.45pm Mon-Fri)

Getting There & Away

From the **bus stand** (East Raja St), bus 599 heads to Chennai's T Nagar Bus Terminus (₹40, 1½ hours) every 30 minutes from 6.50am to 8.30pm; bus 118 runs to Chennai's CMBT (₹40, two hours) hourly, 4am to 8pm. For Chennai Airport take bus 515 to Tambaram (₹27, 1½ hours, every 30 minutes), then a taxi, autorickshaw or suburban train. There are also seven daily buses to Kanchipuram (₹42 to ₹45, two hours). Buses to Puducherry (₹90 to ₹150, two hours) stop roughly every 15 minutes at the junction of Kovalam Rd and the Mamallapuram bypass, 1km north of Mamallapuram centre.

You can make train reservations at the **Southern Railway Computerised Passenger Reservation Centre** (32 East Raja St, 1st fl; 8am-2pm).

Taxis are available from the bus stand, travel agents and hotels. It's ₹1500 to Chennai or the airport, or ₹2500 to Puducherry.

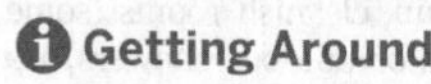

Getting Around

The easiest way to get around is by walking. **Bicycle hire** (per day ₹100; 8am-8pm) is available on Kovalam Rd.

Kanchipuram

044 / POP 164,384

Kanchipuram, 80km southwest of Chennai, was capital of the Pallava dynasty during the 6th to 8th centuries, when the Pallavas created the great stone monuments of Mamallapuram. Today a typically hectic modern Indian town, it's famous for its numerous important and vibrant temples (and their colourful festivals), some dating from Pallava, Chola or Vijayanagar times. It's also known for its high-quality silk saris, woven on hand looms by thousands of families in the town and nearby villages. Silk and sari shops are strung along Gandhi Rd, southeast of the centre, though their wares are generally no cheaper than at Chennai silk shops.

Kanchipuram is easily visited in a day trip from Mamallapuram or Chennai.

Sights

All temples have free admission, though you may have to pay small amounts for shoe-keeping and/or cameras. Ignore claims that there's an entrance fee for non-Hindus.

Kailasanatha Temple HINDU TEMPLE
(SVN Pillai St; 6am-6.30pm, inner sanctum 6am-noon & 4-6.30pm) Kanchipuram's oldest temple is its most impressive, not for its size but for its weight of historical presence and the intricacy of its stonework. As much monument as living temple, Kailasanatha is quieter than other temples in town, and has been heavily restored. Dedicated to Shiva, it was built in the 8th century by Pallava king Narasimhavarman II (Rajasimha), who also created Mamallapuram's Shore Temple.

The low-slung sandstone compound, in oleander-dotted grounds, has fascinating carvings, including many of the half-animal deities in vogue in early Dravidian architecture. It's framed by walls of subshrines topped by domed roofs and carved elephants and Nandis. Note the rearing lions on the outer walls and the large Nandi facing the compound from outside. The inner sanctum is centred on a large 16-sided lingam, which non-Hindus can view from about 8m away. The tower rising above is a precursor of the great *vimanas* of later Chola temples.

An autorickshaw from central Kanchipuram costs ₹50, but walking is nice.

Ekambareshwara Temple HINDU TEMPLE
(Ekambaranathar Temple; Ekambaranathar Sannidhi St; phone-camera/camera/video ₹10/20/100; ⊙6am-12.30pm & 4-8.30pm) Of South India's five Shiva temples associated with the five elements, this 12-hectare precinct is the shrine of earth. You enter beneath the 59m-high, unpainted south *gopuram,* whose lively carvings were chiselled in 1509 under Vijayanagar rule. Inside, a columned hall leads left into the central compound, which Nandi faces from the right. The inner sanctum (Hindus only) contains a lingam made of earth and a mirror chamber whose central Shiva image is reflected in endless repetition.

According to legend, the goddess Kamakshi (She Whose Eyes Awaken Desire; a form of Parvati, Shiva's consort) worshipped Shiva under a mango tree here, before the two were married on the same spot. In a courtyard behind the inner sanctum stands a mango tree said to be 2500 years old, with four branches representing the four Vedas (sacred Hindu texts). Also of note, in the temple's northwest corner, is the Sahasra Lingam, made of minilinga.

Kamakshi Amman Temple HINDU TEMPLE
(Kamakshi Amman Sannidhi St; ⊙5.30am-noon & 4-8pm) This imposing temple, dedicated to Kamakshi/Parvati, is one of India's most important places of *shakti* (female energy/deities) worship, said to mark the spot where Parvati's midriff fell to earth. It's thought to have been founded by the Pallavas. The entire main building, with its gold-topped sanctuary, is off imits to non-Hindus, but the small, square, 16th-century marriage hall, to the right inside the temple's southeast entrance, has wonderfully ornate pillars. No cameras allowed.

Vaikunta Perumal Temple HINDU TEMPLE
(Vaikundaperumal Koil St; ⊙6am-noon & 4-8pm) This 1200-year-old Vishnu temple is a Pallava creation. The passage around the central shrine has lion pillars and a wealth of weathered wall panels, some depicting historical events. The main shrine, uniquely spread over three levels and with jumping *yalis* (mythical lion creatures) on the exterior, contains images of Vishnu standing,

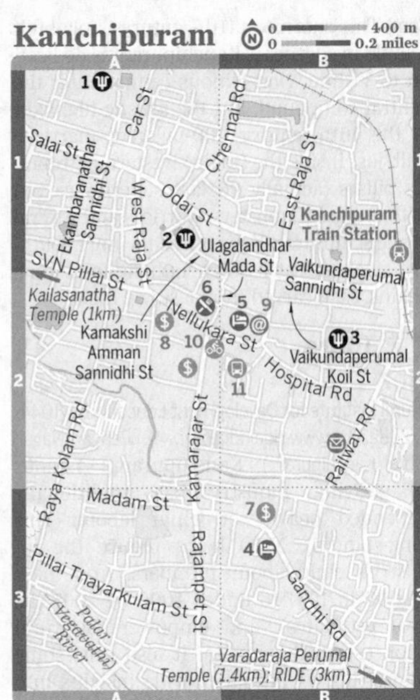

Kanchipuram

Sights
1 Ekambareshwara Temple A1
2 Kamakshi Amman Temple A1
3 Vaikunta Perumal Temple B2

Sleeping
4 GRT Regency B3
5 Sree Sakthi Residency B2

Eating
Dakshin .... (see 4)
Hotel Saravana Bhavan .... (see 4)
6 Hotel Saravana Bhavan A2
Upashana Veg Restaurant .... (see 5)

Information
7 Axis Bank ATM B3
8 State Bank of India ATM A2
9 State Bank of India ATM A2

Transport
10 Bicycle Hire A2
11 Bus Stand B2

sitting, reclining and riding his preferred mount, Garuda (half-eagle, half-man).

Varadaraja Perumal Temple HINDU TEMPLE
(Devarajaswami Temple; off Kanchipuram-Chengalpattu Rd, Little Kanchipuram; 100-pillared hall ₹1, camera/video ₹5/100; ⊙7.30am-12.30pm & 3.30-

8pm) This enormous 11th-century Chola-built temple in southeast Kanchipuram is dedicated to Vishnu. Non-Hindus cannot enter the central compound, but the artistic highlight is the 16th-century '100-pillared' marriage hall, just inside the (main) western entrance. Its pillars (actually 96) are superbly carved with animals, monsters, warriors and several erotic sculptures. *Yalis* frame its inner southern steps and at its corners hang four stone chains, each carved from a single rock.

Tours

RIDE CULTURAL

(Rural Institute for Development Education; ☎044-27268223; www.rideindia.org; 48 Periyar Nagar, Little Kanchipuram) Kanchipuram's famous silk-weaving industry has traditionally depended heavily on child labour. This long-standing NGO helps reduce the industry's child-labour numbers, from over 40,000 in 1997 to under 4000 by 2007 (its own estimates), and empower the rural poor, especially women. It also runs some interesting tours that provide insights into the lives of people working in the industry.

Sleeping & Eating

RIDE GUESTHOUSE $

(Rural Institute for Development Education; ☎044-27268223; www.rideindia.org; 48 Periyar Nagar, Little Kanchipuram; per person ₹750-1000; ❄) This NGO offers simple, clean rooms at its base in a residential area, 5km southeast of central Kanchipuram. If things are quiet, the friendly owners put you up in their own colourful home next door. Home-cooked breakfast (₹150), lunch (₹250) and dinner (₹250) available. Book a day ahead. It's signposted 1km east of the Varadaraja Perumal Temple.

GRT Regency HOTEL $$

(☎044-27225250; www.grthotels.com; 487 Gandhi Rd; incl breakfast s ₹2470-4010, d ₹4940; ❄📶) The cleanest, comfiest and most stylish rooms in Kanchi, boasting marble floors, tea/coffee makers and glass-partitioned showers. The GRT's smart-ish **Dakshin** (mains ₹300-550; ⏰7am-11pm; 📶) restaurant is overpriced, but offers a lengthy multicuisine menu of breakfast omelettes, South Indian favourites and tasty tandoori.

Sree Sakthi Residency HOTEL $$

(☎044-27233799; www.sreesakthiresidency.com; 71 Nellukara St; s ₹1820-2065, d ₹2190-2675; ❄📶) Simple blonde-wood furniture and in-room kettles make the clean 'standard' rooms perfectly comfy, while newer 'premiums' have hairdryers, glassed-in showers and more modern decor. The popular ground-floor **Upashana Veg Restaurant** (dishes ₹50-110; ⏰7am-10pm) does good vegetarian food, including thalis (₹90 to ₹175).

Hotel Saravana Bhavan SOUTH INDIAN $$

(☎044-27226877; www.saravanabhavan.com; 66 Nellukara St; mains ₹60-130, meals ₹95-125; ⏰6am-10.30pm) A reliably good pure-veg restaurant with delicious dosas, a few North Indian surprises, a welcome air-con hall, and thalis on the 1st floor. There's another (scruffier) **branch** (☎044-27222505; www.saravanabhavan.com; 504 Gandhi Rd; mains ₹60-130, meals ₹95-125; ⏰6am-10.30pm) just west off Gandhi Rd.

Getting There & Away

Suburban trains to Kanchipuram (₹25, 2½ hours) leave Chennai's Egmore station (platform 10 or 11) roughly hourly from 4.30am to 8.30pm. A full-day return taxi from Mamallapuram costs ₹2700. The busy **bus stand** (Kamarajar St) is in the town centre.

Getting Around

An autorickshaw for a half-day tour of the five main temples (around ₹500) will inevitably involve stopping at a silk shop.

Vellore

☎0416 / POP 185,800

For a dusty bazaar town, Vellore feels pretty cosmopolitan, thanks to a couple of ter-

BUSES FROM KANCHIPURAM

DESTINATION	FARE (₹)	TIME (HR)	DEPARTURES
Chennai	47	2	every 10min 3.30am-10.30pm
Mamallapuram	42	2	every 2hr 5.30am-8.30pm
Puducherry	68	3	every 30min 5.45am-9.20pm
Tiruvannamalai	63-72	3	every 30min 5.10am-9.30pm
Vellore	41	2	every 10min 3.30am-11pm

tiary institutions and the American-founded Christian Medical College (CMC), one of India's finest hospitals, which attracts both medical students and patients from across the country. On the main Chennai–Bengaluru road, Vellore is worth a visit mainly for its massive Vijayanagar fort and temple. Many Indians come to visit the golden Sripuram Temple, 10km southwest of town.

Central Vellore is bounded on the north by Arcot Rd (Ida Scudder Rd), home to the hospital and cheap hotels and restaurants; and on the west by Anna Salai (Officer's Line), with Vellore Fort on its west side.

Sights

Vellore Fort FORT
(off Anna Salai; 24hr) Vellore's splendid fort, with nearly 2km of moat-surrounded ramparts, was built in the 16th century and passed through Maratha and Mughal hands before the British occupied it in 1760. These days it houses, among other things, the magnificent Jalakantesvara Temple, two **museums** (9am-5pm Sat-Thu) FREE, two parade grounds, a **church** (7.30am-6pm Sun), government offices and a police recruiting school. A stroll around it is the most peaceful experience in town.

Jalakantesvara Temple HINDU TEMPLE
(Vellore Fort; 6.30am-1pm & 3-8.30pm) The Jalakantesvara Temple, a gem of late Vijayanagar architecture, dates from around 1566, and was once occupied as a garrison. Check out the small, beautifully detailed sculptures – especially the leaping *yali* – on the walls and columns of the **marriage hall** in the southwest corner.

Sleeping & Eating

Vellore's cheap hotels cluster along Ida Scudder Rd and in the busy, narrow streets just south. Many won't take foreigners; the better options fill up fast.

Vimal Lodge HOTEL $
(9500531686; 6/83 Babu Rao St; r ₹715, with AC ₹1090-1200;) Plain, clean budget rooms, neat sheets and a *relatively* helpful reception desk, in the busy bazaar area just south of Ida Scudder Rd.

Darling Residency HOTEL $$
(0416-2213001; www.darlingresidency.com; 11/8 Anna Salai; incl breakfast s ₹2670-2920, d ₹3040-3280;) It's no five-star property but the Darling has clean, comfortable, forgettable rooms (those at the back are quieter), as well as friendly reception and four in-house restaurants, including the breezy, multicuisine **Aaranya Roof Garden Restaurant** (mains ₹160-400; 11.30am-10.30pm). It's 1.5km south of Vellore Fort entrance.

GRT Regency Sameera HOTEL $$$
(0416-2206466; www.grthotels.com; 145 Green Circle, New Bypass Rd; incl breakfast s ₹4320-6790, d ₹5560-6790;) Mirrored cupboards, in-room tea/coffee sets and splashes of colour make the GRT's smart modern rooms pretty characterful for Vellore. The free wi-fi, upscale multicuisine **Gingee Restaurant** (mains ₹260-400; 7-10am, 12.30-3pm & 7-10.30pm) and 24-hour cafe are extra bonuses. It's 1.5km north of central Vellore, just off the Chennai–Bengaluru road (and surprisingly not too noisy).

Hotel Saravana Bhavan SOUTH INDIAN $
(0416-2217755; www.saravanabhavan.com; Sri Siva AVM Grande Hotel, 58/2 Katpadi Rd; dishes ₹60-125, meals ₹110-150; 6am-11pm) Tamil Nadu's favourite veg chain is a welcome addition, turning out delectably simple *idlis,* dosas, thalis and other South Indian staples. The air-con hall does North Indian fare, too. It's opposite the New Bus Stand. There's another **branch** (0416-2217433; www.saravanabhavan.com; 25B/25C Jeevarathnam Maaligai, Arcot Rd; dishes ₹60-140, meals ₹110-150; 10am-6pm) in town.

Information

Canara Bank ATM (Anna Salai) Opposite Vellore Fort entrance.

Getting There & Away

BUS

Buses use the **New Bus Stand** (Katpadi Rd), 1.5km north of central Vellore.

Bengaluru ₹156, five hours, every 30 minutes

Chennai AC Volvo buses ₹160, 2½ hours, noon & 2pm; other buses ₹81 to ₹105, three hours, every five minutes

Kanchipuram ₹40, two hours, every 10 minutes

Tiruvannamalai ₹37 to ₹40, three hours, every 10 minutes

TRAIN

Vellore's train station is 5km north at Katpadi. There are at least 22 daily superfast or express trains to/from Chennai Central (sleeper/3AC ₹170/540, two to three hours) and 10 to/from Bengaluru's Bangalore City station (₹170/490, three to five hours).

Buses 1 and 2 (₹4) shuttle between the train station and the **Town Bus Stand** (Anna Salai).

TAMIL NADU TEMPLES

Tamil Nadu is a gold mine for anyone wanting to explore Indian temple culture. It's home to some of the country's most spectacular temple architecture and sculpture, and few parts of India are as fervent in their worship of the Hindu gods as Tamil Nadu. Its 5000-odd temples are constantly abuzz with worshippers flocking in for *puja* (offering or prayer), and colourful temple festivals abound. Among the plethora of Hindu deities, Shiva has the most Tamil temples dedicated to him, in a multitude of forms including Nataraja, the cosmic dancer, who dances in a ring of fire with two of his four hands holding the flame of destruction and the drum of creation. Tamils also have a soft spot for Shiva's peacock-riding son Murugan (also Kartikeya or Skanda), who is intricately associated with their cultural identity.

The special significance of many Tamil temples makes them goals of countless Hindu pilgrims from all over India. The Pancha Sabhai Sthalangal are the five temples where Shiva is believed to have performed his cosmic dance (chief among them Chidambaram). Then there's the Pancha Bootha Sthalangal, the five temples where Shiva is worshipped as one of the five elements: Tiruvannamalai's Arunachaleshwar Temple (fire; p1034), Kanchipuram's Ekambareshwara Temple (earth; p1031), Chidambaram's Nataraja Temple (space; p1046), Trichy's Sri Jambukeshwara Temple (water; p1054) and, in Andhra Pradesh, Sri Kalahasteeswara Temple (air). Each of Kumbakonam's nine Navagraha temples is the abode of one of the nine celestial bodies of Hindu astronomy – key sites given the importance of astrology in Hindu faith.

Typical Tamil temple design features tall layered entrance towers *(gopurams)*, encrusted with often colourfully painted sculptures of gods and demons; halls of richly carved columns *(mandapas)*; a sacred water tank; and a series of compounds *(prakarams)*, one within the next, with the innermost containing the central sanctum where the temple's main deity resides. The earliest Tamil temples were small rock-cut shrines; the first free-standing temples were built in the 8th century AD; *gopurams* first appeared around the 12th century.

Admission to most temples is free, but non-Hindus are often not allowed inside inner sanctums. At other temples priests may invite you in and in no time you are doing *puja*, having an auspicious *tilak* mark daubed on your forehead and being hassled for a donation.

Temple touts can be a nuisance, but there are also many excellent guides; use your judgement and be on the lookout for badge-wearing official guides.

A South Indian Journey by Michael Wood and *Southern India: A Guide to Monuments, Sites & Museums* by George Michell are great reads if you're interested in Tamil temple culture. TempleNet (www.templenet.com) is one of the best online resources.

Tiruvannamalai

☎04175 / POP 145,280

There are temple towns, there are mountain towns, and then there are temple-mountain towns where God appears as a phallus of fire. Welcome to Tiruvannamalai, one of Tamil Nadu's holiest destinations.

Set below boulder-strewn Mt Arunachala, this is one of South India's five 'elemental' cities of Shiva; here the god is worshipped in his fire incarnation as Arunachaleshwar. At every full moon, 'Tiru' swells with thousands of pilgrims who circumnavigate Arunachala's base in a purifying ritual known as Girivalam; at any time you'll see Shaivite priests, sadhus (spiritual men) and devotees gathered around the Arunachaleshwar Temple.

Tiru's reputation for strong spiritual energies has produced numerous ashrams, and the town now attracts ever-growing numbers of spiritual-minded travellers.

Sights & Activities

Yoga, meditation and ayurveda sessions are advertised everywhere in the main ashram area.

★Arunachaleshwar Temple HINDU TEMPLE

(Annamalaiyar Temple; www.arunachaleswarartemple.tnhrce.in; 5.30am-12.30pm & 3.30-9.30pm) This 10-hectare temple is one of India's largest. Its oldest parts date to the 9th century, but the site was a place of worship long before that. Four huge, unpainted white *gopurams* mark the entrances; the main,

17th-century eastern one rises 13 storeys (an astonishing 66m), its sculpted passageway depicting dancers, dwarves and elephants. During festivals the Arunachaleshwar is awash with golden flames and the scent of burning ghee, as befits the fire incarnation of Shiva, Destroyer of the Universe.

Inside the complex are five more *gopurams*, a 17th-century 1000-pillared hall with impressive carvings, two tanks and a profusion of sub-temples and shrines. There's a helpful temple model inside the second *gopuram* from the east, where the temple elephant gives blessings. To reach the innermost sanctum, with its huge lingam, worshippers must pass through five surrounding *prakarams* (compounds).

Mt Arunachala MOUNTAIN

This 800m-high extinct volcano dominates Tiruvannamalai – and local conceptions of the element of fire, which supposedly finds its sacred abode in Arunachala's heart. Devout barefoot pilgrims, especially on full-moon and festival days, make the 14km (four-hour) circumambulation of the mountain, stopping at eight famous linga. The inner path was closed at research time, but it's possible to circle around on the main road, or climb the hill past two caves where Sri Ramana Maharshi lived and meditated (1899–1922).

The hot ascent to the top opens up superb views of Tiruvannamalai, and takes five or six hours round-trip: start early and take water. An unsigned path across the road from the northwest corner of the Arunachaleshwar Temple leads the way up past homes and the two caves, **Virupaksha** (about 20 minutes up) and **Skandasramam** (30 minutes). Women are advised not to hike alone.

If you aren't that devoted, buy a Giripradakshina map (₹15) from the bookshop at Sri Ramana Ashram (p1035), hire a bicycle on the roadside opposite (per hour/day ₹10/40) and ride around. Or make an autorickshaw circuit for about ₹300 (up to double at busy times).

Sri Ramana Ashram MEDITATION

(Sri Ramanasramam; ☎04175-237200; www.sriramanamaharshi.org; Chengam Rd; ⊙office 7.30am-12.30pm & 2-6.30pm) This tranquil ashram, 2km southwest of Tiruvannamalai centre amid green, peacock-filled grounds, draws devotees of Sri Ramana Maharshi, one of the first Hindu gurus to gain an international following; he died here in 1950 after half a century in contemplation. Visitors can meditate and attend daily *pujas* (prayers) and chantings, mostly in the **samadhi hall** where the guru's body is enshrined.

A limited amount of free accommodation (donations accepted) is available for *devotees only:* email a month ahead or write six weeks in advance.

Sri Seshadri Swamigal Ashram MEDITATION

(☎04175-236999; www.tiruvarunaimahan.org; Chengam Rd; ⊙6am-9.30pm) Dedicated to a contemporary and helper of Sri Ramana, with meditation platforms and some accommodation (by donation; book at least two weeks ahead). It's in the southwest of town next to Sri Ramana Ashram.

Sri Anantha Niketan MEDITATION

(☎9003480013; www.srianantbaniketan.com; Periya Paliyapattu village; by donation) A place for organised retreats rather than a permanent community, Sri Anantha Niketan has tree-shaded grounds, wonderful Arunachala views and homey rooms, and guests are welcome to join daily chanting in an attractive meditation hall. It's just off the Krishnagiri road, 7km west of Tiruvannamalai. Book at least three months ahead for December to February.

THE LINGAM OF FIRE

According to legend, Shiva appeared as the original lingam (phallic image of Shiva) of fire on Mt Arunachala to restore light to the world after his consort Parvati playfully plunged everything into darkness by closing his eyes. The **Karthikai Deepam Festival** (statewide; ⊙Nov/Dec) celebrates this legend throughout India but is particularly significant at Tiruvannamalai. The lighting of a huge fire atop Mt Arunachala on the full-moon night, from a 30m wick immersed in 3 tonnes of ghee, culminates a 10-day festival for which hundreds of thousands of people converge on Tiruvannamalai. Huge crowds scale the mountain or circumnavigate its base, chanting Shiva's name. The sun is relentless, the rocks are jagged and the journey is barefoot – none of which deters the thousands of pilgrims who joyfully make their way to the top.

Activities

Arunachala Animal Sanctuary VOLUNTEERING
(9442246108; www.arunachalasanctuary.com; Chengam Rd; 9am-5pm) Aimed at sterilisation, castration, rabies control, rehoming and affordable treatments, this nonprofit sanctuary, at the western end of Tiruvannamalai's ashram area, provides shelter to over 200 homeless and/or injured dogs, plus a few cats. Travellers can help with bathing, feeding, applying creams or simply playing with the animals – just show up. Possible openings for longer-term volunteers.

Sleeping & Eating

Rainbow Guest House GUESTHOUSE $
(9443886408, 04175-236408; rainbowguesthousetiru@gmail.com; 27/28 Lakshmanan Nagar, Perumbakkam Rd; s ₹450, d ₹900-1000;) A great-value, spick-and-span spot 800m southwest off Chengam Rd. Beyond the psychedelic exterior, wood-carved doors reveal simple, immaculate, fan-cooled rooms with hot water and tiled floors. Staff are gracious, cane chairs dangle along corridors and there are fantastic Mt Arunachala views from the spartan rooftop terrace.

Arunachala Ramana Home HOTEL $
(9626044492, 04175-236120; www.arunachalaramanahome.com; 70 Ramana Nagar; s/d ₹500/800, with AC r ₹1300;) Basic, clean and friendly, this popular place is down a lane south off Chengam Rd.

Sunshine Guest House GUESTHOUSE $$
(04175-235335; www.sunshineguesthouseindia.com; 5 Annamalai Nagar, Perumbakkam Rd; s/d ₹600/800, with AC ₹1400/1970;) In a blissfully quiet spot 1km southwest of the main ashram area, this colourful new building fronted by gardens offers excellent value. Tasteful, spotless rooms, each styled after a Hindu god, give the feel of an Indian trinkets shop: print-design sheets, sequined fabrics, cane swing-chairs and in-room water filters. The upstairs hall is perfect for yoga. Fresh breakfasts cost ₹150.

Hotel Arunachala HOTEL $$
(Arunachala Inn; 04175-228300; www.hotelarunachala.com; 5 Vada Sannathi St; r ₹990, with AC s/d ₹1125/1690, deluxe d ₹2250;) Right next to the Arunachaleshwar Temple's east entrance, Hotel Arunachala is clean and decent with pretensions to luxury in the marblesque floors, ugly furniture, keen management and lobby fish pond. The revamped 'deluxe' rooms are the best. Downstairs, pure-veg **Hotel Sri Arul Jothi** (dishes ₹40-80; 6am-10.30pm) provides good South Indian dishes (thalis ₹80 to ₹100).

★ **Dreaming Tree** CAFE $$
(8870057753; www.dreamingtree.in; Ramana Nagar; mains ₹150-250; 8.30am-10pm) Super-chilled Dreaming Tree dishes out huge portions of exquisite, health-focused veg fare, prepped with mostly organic ingredients, on a breezy thatched rooftop loaded with low-slung purple-cushioned booths. Expect fabulous 'hippie salads' and tofu stir-fries, luscious breakfasts, and all kinds of cakes, juices, lassis, lemonades and organic coffees. Signs lead the way (500m) across the road from Sri Ramana Ashram.

Shanti Café CAFE $$
(www.facebook.com/shanticafetiru; 115A Chengam Rd; dishes ₹60-200, drinks ₹30-80; 8.30am-8.30pm;) This popular and relaxed cafe with floor-cushion seating, up a lane off Chengam Rd, serves wonderful croissants, cakes, baguettes, pancakes, juices, coffees, teas, breakfasts and Indian meals with an extra-healthy twist. It's run by a delightful team and there's an **internet cafe** (www.shantionline.com; per hour ₹25; 8.30am-1.30pm & 3-7pm Mon-Sat, 8.30am-1.30pm Sun) downstairs.

Tasty Café CAFE $$
(Lakshmanan Nagar, Perumbakkam Rd; mains ₹100-210; 7am-10pm) In a peaceful, shady courtyard of plastic chairs and wooden ta-

BUSES FROM TIRUVANNAMALAI

DESTINATION	FARE (₹)	TIME (HR)	DEPARTURES
Chennai	120-140	5	every 10min
Kanchipuram	63	3	hourly
Puducherry	63	3	hourly
Trichy	123	5	every 45min
Vellore	37-50	2½	every 10min

bles, friendly Tasty Café does well-prepared Indian and Continental food, including pizza, pasta, pancakes and salads. It's 700m southwest off Chengam Rd.

Shopping

Shantimalai Handicrafts Development Society ARTS & CRAFTS
(www.smhds.org; 83/1 Chengam Rd; 9am-7pm) Beautiful bedspreads, bags, incense, candles, oils, bangles, scarves and cards, all made by local village women.

Getting There & Away

The **bus stand** (Polur Rd) is 800m north of the Arunachaleshwar Temple, and a ₹50 to ₹60 autorickshaw ride from the main ashram area. For Chennai, the best options are the hourly Ultra Deluxe services.

Gingee (Senji)

04145 / POP 27,000

Straddling the main Tiruvannamalai–Puducherry road, Gingee is mainly worth a visit for the fantastical ruins of 16th-century Gingee Fort, on the western edge of town.

Sights

Gingee Fort FORT
(04145-222072; Gingee; Indian/foreigner ₹15/200; 8am-5pm) With three separate hilltop citadels and a 6km perimeter of cliffs and thick walls, the ruins of enormous Gingee Fort rise out of the Tamil plain, 37km east of Tiruvannamalai, like castles misplaced by the Lord of the Rings. It was constructed mainly in the 16th century by the Vijayanagars and was later occupied by the Marathas, Mughals, French and British, then abandoned in the 19th century. The fort's sheer scale, dramatic beauty and peaceful setting make it a very worthwhile stop.

Today, few foreigners make it here, but Gingee is popular with domestic tourists for its starring role in various films. The main road between Tiruvannamalai and Puducherry slices through the fort, just west of Gingee town. Of the three citadels, the easiest to reach, **Krishnagiri**, rises north of the road. To the south are the highest of the three, **Rajagiri**, and the most distant and least interesting, **Chakklidurg** (which you can't climb). Ticket offices (with maps) are at the foot of Krishnagiri and Rajagiri.

Remains of numerous buildings stand in the site's lower parts, especially at the bottom of Rajagiri in the old palace area, where the main landmark is the white, restored, seven-storey **Kalyana Mahal** (Marriage Hall). Just east (outside) of the palace area is the 18th-century **Sadat Ullah Khan Mosque**; southeast of this lies the abandoned 16th-century **Venkataramana Temple**.

It's a one-hour round-trip hike up Krishnagiri and a two-hour round-trip hike for Rajagiri (more than 150m above the plain); allow at least half a day to cover both hills. Most visitors climb Rajagiri, which makes Krishnagiri quieter. Start early and bring water. Hill-climbing entry ends at 3pm.

Getting There & Away

A taxi between Tiruvannamalai and Puducherry with a two- to three-hour stop at Gingee costs around ₹3000.

Gingee is on the Tiruvannamalai–Puducherry bus route, with buses from Tiruvannamalai (₹25 to ₹35, one hour) every 10 minutes. Hop off at the fort to save a trip back out from Gingee town.

Puducherry (Pondicherry)

0413 / POP 244,380

The union territory of Puducherry (formerly Pondicherry; generally known as 'Pondy') was under French rule until 1954. Some people here still speak French (and English with French accents). Hotels, restaurants and 'lifestyle' shops sell a seductive vision of the French-subcontinental aesthetic, enhanced by Gallic creative types and Indian artists and designers. The internationally famous Sri Aurobindo Ashram and its offshoot just north of town, Auroville, draw large numbers of spiritually minded visitors. Thus Pondy's vibe: less faded colonial-era *ville*, more bohemian-chic, New Age–meets–Old World hang-out on the international travel trail.

The older 'French' part of town (where you'll probably spend most of your time) is full of quiet, clean streets, lined with bougainvillea-draped colonial-style townhouses numbered in an almost logical manner. Newer Pondy is typically, hectically South Indian.

Enjoy fabulous shopping, French food (hello steak!), beer (*au revoir* Tamil Nadu alcohol taxes), and plenty of yoga and meditation.

Puducherry is split from north to south by a partially covered canal. The 'French' part of town is on the east side (towards the sea). Nehru (JN) St and Rue Bussy (Lal Bahadur Shastri St) are the main east-west streets;

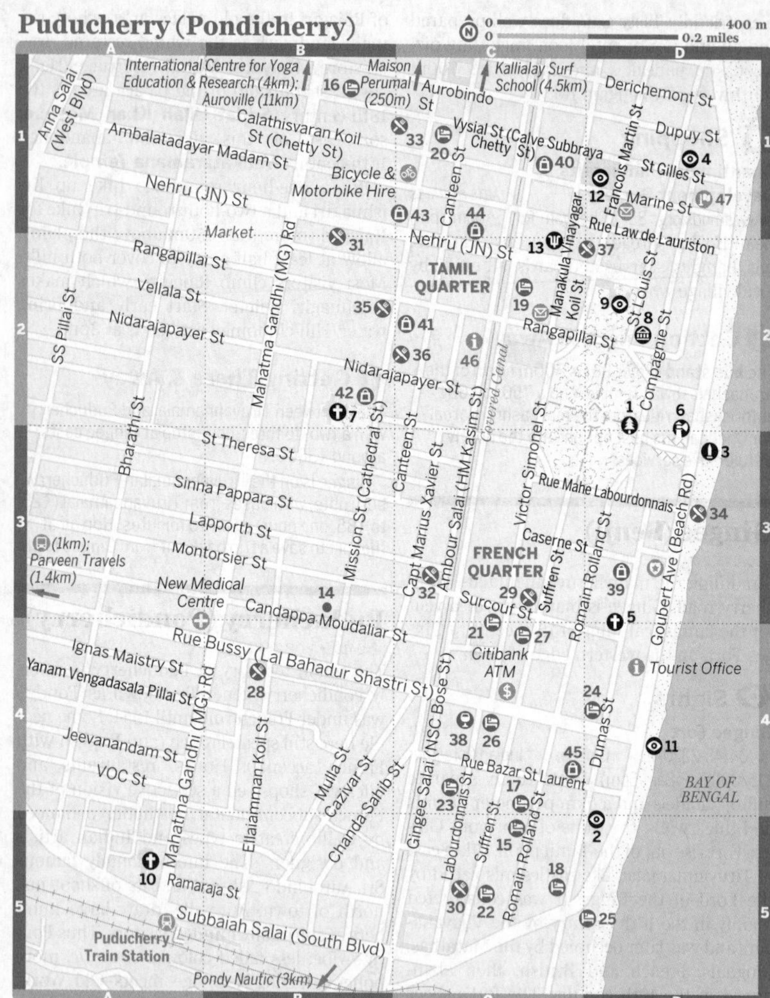

Mahatma Gandhi (MG) Rd and Mission St (Cathedral St) are the chief north–south thoroughfares. Many streets change names as they go along and often have English, French and Tamil names simultaneously.

Sights

Seafront WATERFRONT

(Goubert Ave) Pondy is a seaside town, but that doesn't make it a beach destination; the city's sand is a thin strip of dirty brown that slurps into a seawall of jagged rocks. But Goubert Ave (Beach Rd) is a killer stroll, especially at dawn and dusk when half the town takes a romantic wander. In a stroke of genius, authorities have banned traffic here from 6pm to 7.30am.

Sri Aurobindo Ashram ASHRAM

(0413-2233649; www.sriaurobindoashram.org; Marine St; 8am-noon & 2-6pm) FREE Founded in 1926 by Sri Aurobindo and a French-born woman, 'the Mother', this famous spiritual community has about 2000 members in its many departments. Aurobindo's teachings focus on 'integral yoga' that sees devotees work in the world, rather than retreat from it. Visits to the main, grey-walled ashram

Puducherry (Pondicherry)

Sights

1 Bharathi Park ... D2
2 École Française D'Extrême-Orient ... D5
3 Gandhi Memorial ... D3
4 Institut Français de Pondichéry ... D1
5 Notre Dame des Anges ... D3
6 Old Lighthouse ... D2
7 Our Lady of the Immaculate Conception Cathedral ... B2
8 Puducherry Museum ... D2
9 Raj Nivas ... D2
10 Sacred Heart Basilica ... A5
11 Seafront ... D4
12 Sri Aurobindo Ashram ... D1
13 Sri Manakula Vinayagar Temple ... C2

Activities, Courses & Tours

14 Sita ... B3

Sleeping

15 Coloniale Heritage Guest House ... C5
16 Dune Mansion Calvé ... B1
17 Gratitude ... C4
18 Hotel de Pondichéry ... C5
19 International Guest House ... C2
20 Kailash Guest House ... C1
21 La Villa ... C4
22 Les Hibiscus ... C5
23 Nila Home Stay ... C4
24 Palais de Mahé ... D4
25 Park Guest House ... D5
26 Villa Helena ... C4
27 Villa Shanti ... C4

Eating

28 Baker Street ... B4
29 Café des Arts ... C3
30 Domus ... C5
31 Indian Coffee House ... B2
32 Kasha Ki Aasha ... C3
33 La Pasta World ... C1
34 Le Café ... D3
Le Club ... (see 18)
35 Nilgiri's ... B2
Palais de Mahé ... (see 24)
36 Surguru ... C2
37 Surguru Spot ... D2
Villa Helena ... (see 26)
Villa Shanti ... (see 27)

Drinking & Nightlife

38 L'e-Space ... C4

Shopping

39 Anokhi ... D3
40 Auroshikha ... C1
41 Fabindia ... C2
42 Focus ... B2
43 Kalki ... C1
44 La Boutique d'Auroville ... C1
45 LivingArt Lifestyles ... C4

Information

46 Bureau Central ... C2
47 French Consulate ... D1
Shanti Travel ... (see 16)

building are cursory: you see the flower-festooned samadhi of Aurobindo and the Mother, then the bookshop. Ashram-accommodation guests can access other areas and activities. Evening meditation around the samadhi is for everyone.

There are daily weekday ashram tours (per person ₹50); enquire online (www.sriaurobindoautocare.com) or at the ashram's **Bureau Central** (☎0413-2233604; bureaucentral@sriaurobindoashram.org; Ambour Salai; ⏲6am-noon & 4-6pm).

Sri Manakula Vinayagar Temple HINDU TEMPLE
(www.manakulavinayagartemple.com; Manakula Vinayagar Koil St; ⏲5.45am-12.30pm & 4-9pm) Pondy may have more churches than most Indian towns, but the Hindu faith still reigns supreme. Pilgrims, tourists and the curious get a head pat from the temple elephant at this centuries-old temple dedicated to Ganesh, which contains around 40 skilfully painted friezes.

Puducherry Museum MUSEUM
(http://art.puducherry.gov.in/museum.html; St Louis St; Indian/foreigner ₹10/50; ⏲9am-6.30pm Tue-Sun) God knows how this converted late-18th-century villa keeps its artefacts from disintegrating, considering there's a whole floor of French-era furniture sitting in the South Indian humidity. On the ground floor look especially for Chola, Vijayanagar and Nayak bronzes, and pieces of ancient Greek and Spanish pottery and amphorae (storage vessels) excavated from Arikamedu, a once-major trading port just south of Puducherry. Upstairs is Governor Dupleix' bed.

Institut Français de Pondichéry LIBRARY
(☎0413-2231616; www.ifpindia.org; 11 St Louis St; ⏲9am-1pm & 2-5.30pm Mon-Fri) FREE This grand 19th-century neoclassical building is also a flourishing research institution devoted to Indian culture, history and ecology. Visitors can browse books in the beach-facing library.

French Quarter

Pocketed away just behind the seafront is a series of cobbled bougainvillea-wrapped streets and white-and-mustard buildings in various states of romantic *déshabillé*, otherwise known as Puducherry's French Quarter. A do-it-yourself heritage walk could start at the French consulate (p1185) near the north end of Goubert Ave, the seafront promenade (p1038). Head south, passing the 1836 **lighthouse** (Goubert Ave), then turn inland to shady, landscaped **Bharathi Park** (Compagnie St; 6am-7pm) FREE. The neoclassical governor's residence, **Raj Nivas** (Rangapillai St), faces the park's north side. Return to the seafront at the **Gandhi Memorial** (Goubert Ave), wander south past Notre Dame des Anges (p1040) church, and then potter south through the 'white town' – Dumas, Romain Rolland, Suffren and Labourdonnais Sts. Towards the southern end of Dumas St, pop into the beautiful **École Française d'Extrême-Orient** (www.efeo.fr; 16-19 Dumas St; 8.30am-12.30pm & 2.30-5.30pm Mon-Fri) FREE.

A lot of restoration has been happening in this area: if you're interested in Pondy's architectural heritage, check out INTACH Pondicherry (www.intachpondicherry.org). The tourist office (p1044) website details heritage walks.

PUDUCHERRY'S CATHEDRALS

Pondy hosts one of India's best collections of over-the-top cathedrals. *Merci*, French missionaries. **Our Lady of Immaculate Conception Cathedral** (Mission St; 7am-noon & 3-8.30pm), completed in 1791, is a sky-blue, hot-yellow and cloud-white typically Jesuit edifice in a Goa-like Portuguese style. The brown-and-white grandiosity of the **Sacred Heart Basilica** (Subbaiah Salai; 5.30am-1pm & 6-8pm) is set off by beautifully restored stained glass and a Gothic sense of proportion. The twin towers and dome of the mellow-pink-and-yellow **Notre Dame des Anges** (Dumas St; 6-10am & 4-7pm), built in the 1850s, look sublime in the late-afternoon light. Its smooth limestone interior was made using eggshell plaster; in the square opposite, there's a Joan of Arc statue.

Activities

Sita CULTURAL PROGRAMS
(0413-4200718; www.pondicherry-arts.com; 22 Candappa Moudaliar St; class ₹300-1200; 9am-1pm & 3-7.30pm) This energetic Franco-Indian cultural centre runs a host of activities, open to visitors (even for a single session): Indian cooking, *bharatanatyam* or Bollywood dance, *kolam* making, *mehndi* (henna 'tattoos'), yoga, pilates, ayurveda and sari 'workshops', plus brilliant cycling and photography tours.

Kallialay Surf School SURFING
(9442992874; www.surfschoolindia.com; Serenity Beach, Tandriankuppam; 1hr private class ₹1500, board rental per 90min ₹400-600; hours vary) Surfing continues to soar in popularity along Tamil Nadu's coast, and this long-standing, well-equipped, Spanish-run school, 5km north of Puducherry, offers everything from beginner sessions to intensive two-week courses.

Pondy Nautic BOATING
(8220125027; www.pondynautic.com; Thengaithittu; per person from ₹900; 9am-1pm & 3-7.30pm) One-hour speedboat jaunts whizz you across the Bay of Bengal, offering the unique chance of a 30-minute out-in-the-open swim; sailing tours head into the backwaters. Book tickets ahead through Sita.

Yoga & Ayurveda

You can practise and study yoga at Sri Aurobindo Ashram (p1038) and Auroville. Sita offers yoga, ayurvedic massages, and courses in practising ayurveda.

International Centre for Yoga Education & Research YOGA
(Ananda Ashram; 0413-2622902; www.icyer.com; 16A Mettu St, Chinnamudaliarchavady, Kottukuppam; 10am-2pm) Rigorous six-month yoga-teacher-training, and 10-lesson, one-to-one introductory courses (₹8000), these last at the **city-centre branch** (0413-2241561; 25 II Cross, Iyyanar Nagar; 9am-6pm).

Tours

A wonderful way to explore Pondy is on the Sita (p1040) popular early morning guided Wake Up Pondy bicycle tours (per person ₹1200), which include breakfast.

Shanti Travel (p1044) offers recommended two-hour walking tours (per person ₹500) of Puducherry with English- or French-speaking guides.

Festivals & Events

International Yoga Festival YOGA
(4-7 Jan) Puducherry's ashrams and yoga culture are put on show with workshops, demonstrations and competitions, attracting experts from across India and beyond.

Bastille Day PARADE
(14 Jul) Street parades, fireworks and French pomp and ceremony are part of the fun at this celebration.

Sleeping

If you've been saving for a splurge, this is the place: Puducherry's lodgings are as good as South India gets. Local heritage houses combine colonial-era romanticism with modern comfort and chic French-inspired styling, and there are some beautifully updated properties. Most of these rooms would cost five times as much in Europe. Book ahead for weekends.

Sri Aurobindo Ashram (p1038) runs several simple but clean guesthouses. They're primarily for ashram guests, but many accept other travellers who'll follow their rules: 10.30pm curfew and no smoking, alcohol or drugs. The ashram's Bureau Central (p1039) has a list.

Park Guest House ASHRAM GUESTHOUSE $
(0413-2233644; parkgh@sriaurobindoashram.org; 1 Goubert Ave; r without/with AC ₹900/1400;) Pondy's most sought-after ashram guesthouse thanks to its wonderful seafront position, with the best-value air-con rooms around, but no advance bookings. All front rooms face the sea and have a porch or balcony. There's a garden for yoga or meditation, plus vegetarian buffet lunches (₹125) and bicycle hire (per day ₹50).

International Guest House ASHRAM GUESTHOUSE $
(INGH; 0413-2336699; ingh@aurosociety.org; 47 NSC Bose St; s ₹450, d ₹550-700, with AC s ₹750, d ₹1300-1630;) The sparse, spotless rooms here, adorned with a single photo of the Mother, make for good-value ashram lodgings. It's very popular: book three weeks ahead.

Kailash Guest House GUESTHOUSE $
(0413-2224485; http://kailashguesthouse.in; 43 Vysial St; s/d ₹1000/1200, with AC ₹1500;) Good-value Kailash has simple, superclean rooms with well-mosquito-proofed windows, friendly management, and superb city views from top floors. It's geared to traveller needs, with loungey communal areas, clothes-drying facilities and a cafe-bar.

★ **Les Hibiscus** GUESTHOUSE $$
(9442066763, 0413-2227480; www.leshibiscus.in; 49 Suffren St; s/d incl breakfast ₹2725/2940;) A strong contender for our favourite Tamil Nadu hotel, mango-yellow Les Hibiscus has just a handful of fabulous high-ceilinged rooms with antique beds, coffee-makers and a mix of quaint Indian art and old-Pondy photos, at astoundingly reasonable prices. The whole place is immaculately styled, fresh breakfasts are fantastic and management is genuinely friendly and helpful. Book well ahead.

Gratitude GUESTHOUSE $$
(0413-2225029; www.gratitudeheritage.in; 52 Romain Rolland St; incl breakfast s ₹4200-6500, d ₹5000-7800;) A wonderfully tranquil 19th-century house (no shoes, no TVs, no children), sun-yellow Gratitude has been painstakingly restored to a state probably even more delightful than the original. Nine individually styled rooms sprawl across two floors around a tropically shaded courtyard, beside which delicious breakfasts are served. There's a roof terrace for yoga and massages.

Hotel de Pondichéry HERITAGE HOTEL $$
(0413-2227409; www.hoteldepondicherry.com; 38 Dumas St; incl breakfast s ₹2500, d ₹3000-5000;) A colourful heritage spot with 14 comfy, quiet, airy colonial-style rooms (some sporting semi-open bathrooms) and splashes of original modern art. The excellent restaurant, Le Club (p1043), takes up the charming front courtyard and staff are lovely.

Nila Home Stay GUESTHOUSE $$
(9994653006; www.nilahomestay.com; 18 Labourdonnais St; r ₹1300-1800, with AC ₹2000-3000;) A simple but brilliantly characterful and well-kept French Quarter guesthouse run by welcoming hosts, with a range of fresh, colourful, heritage-style rooms (some with kitchens and/or terraces), handy communal kitchens and a low-key lounge area.

Coloniale Heritage Guest House GUESTHOUSE $$
(0413-2224720; http://colonialeheritage.com; 54 Romain Rolland St; r incl breakfast ₹2900-3500;) This leafy colonial-era haven with six comfy rooms (some up steep stairs) is crammed with character thanks to the owner's impressive collection of gem-studded Tanjore paintings, Ravi Varma lithographs

and other 19th- and 20th-century South Indian art. One room has a swing, another its own balcony. Breakfast is laid out in the sunken garden-side patio.

★Villa Shanti HERITAGE HOTEL $$$
(☎0413-4200028; www.lavillashanti.com; 14 Suffren St; r incl breakfast ₹7960-12,500; ❄📶) Occupying a 100-year-old building revamped by two French architects, Villa Shanti puts an exquisitely contemporary twist on the French Quarter heritage hotel. Beautiful modern rooms combine superchic design with typically Tamil materials and colonial-style elegance: four-poster beds, Chettinadu tiles, walk-through bathrooms, Tamil-language murals. The sunken courtyard houses a hugely popular restaurant (p1043) and bar.

The owners are also behind uberchic top-end **La Villa** (☎0413-2338555; www.lavillapondicherry.com; 11 Surcouf St; r incl breakfast ₹15,960-19,380; ❄📶🏊).

Villa Helena HERITAGE HOTEL $$$
(☎0413-2226789; www.villa-helena-pondicherry.com; 13 Rue Bussy; incl breakfast s ₹4000, d ₹5500-7000; ❄📶) A smart revamp has infused this gorgeous 19th-century French-run mansion with contemporary character. Spread along plant-dotted galleries, freshly updated, soft-toned rooms are done up in tasteful minimalist style, with stripy bedding, printed cushions, vintage furniture and stylish modern bathrooms. There's wonderful Continental cooking in the romantic courtyard **restaurant** (☎0413-4210806; mains ₹350-520; ⏲noon-3pm & 7-10.30pm).

Dune Mansion Calvé HERITAGE HOTEL $$$
(☎0413-2656351; http://dunewellnessgroup.com; 44 Vysial St; r incl breakfast ₹6870-8180; ❄📶) 🍃 The old Tamil Quarter has almost as many mansions as the French Quarter but is off most tourists' radars. Reincarnated under environmentally friendly management, this 150-year-old heritage choice, on a quiet, tree-shaded street, mixes a soaring sense of space with a teak-columned atrium, Chettinadu-tiled floors, and 10 elegantly styled rooms featuring free-standing bathtubs and solar-powered hot-water systems.

Palais de Mahé HERITAGE HOTEL $$$
(☎0413-2345611; www.cghearth.com; 4 Rue Bussy; r incl breakfast ₹14,500-18,100; ❄📶🏊) Three colonnaded floors of swish soaring-ceilinged rooms with colonial-style wood furnishings and varnished-concrete floors rise around a seductive turquoise pool at this imposing heritage hotel. The first-rate rooftop **restaurant** (☎0413-2345611; www.cghearth.com; 4 Rue Bussy; mains ₹300-600; ⏲7.30-10.30am, 12.30-3pm & 7-11pm) serves impressive, creative fusion cuisine, including cooked-to-order breakfasts. Good value May to September, when rates drop by 30%.

Maison Perumal HERITAGE HOTEL $$$
(☎0413-2227519; www.cghearth.com; 44 Perumal Koil St; r incl breakfast ₹8360-10,450; ❄📶) Secluded rooms with colourful flourishes, antique beds and photos of original owners surround two pillared patios at this renovated 130-year-old home, pocketed away in Pondy's less touristic Tamil Quarter. The excellent Tamil/French **restaurant** (dinner ₹1200, lunch mains ₹350-550; ⏲12.30-3pm & 7.30-9.30pm) cooks everything to order from market-fresh ingredients. From May to September rates drop by 50%. Guests can use the pool at sister property Palais de Mahé.

Eating

Puducherry is a culinary highlight of Tamil Nadu. You can get great South Indian cooking, well-prepped French and Italian cuisine, and delicious fusion food. If you've been missing cheese or have a craving for croissants, you're in luck, and *everyone* in the French Quarter does good brewed coffee and crepes. There are some fabulous artsy cafes too.

Surguru SOUTH INDIAN $
(☎0413-4308083; www.hotelsurguru.com; 235 Mission St; mains ₹65-140; ⏲7am-10.40pm) Simple South Indian in a relatively posh setting. Surguru is the fix for thali (lunchtime only) and dosa addicts who like their veg with good strong AC. The *slightly* more refined **Surguru Spot branch** (☎0413-4308084; 12 Nehru St; mains ₹60-140; ⏲6.30am-11pm) is near the ashram.

Baker Street CAFE $
(123 Rue Bussy; dishes ₹40-200; ⏲7am-9pm; 📶) A popular upmarket French-style bakery that does delectable cakes, croissants and biscuits. The baguettes, brownies and quiches aren't bad either. Eat in or takeaway.

Indian Coffee House SOUTH INDIAN $
(125 Nehru St; dishes ₹30-55; ⏲6.30am-9.30pm) Snack to your heart's content on cheap, South Indian favourites – dosas, *vadas*, *uttapams* and ₹20 filter coffee – at this Pondy institution. It's also, incidentally, where Yann Martel's novel *Life of Pi* begins.

Nilgiri's SUPERMARKET $
(23 Rangapillai St; ⏲9.30am-9pm) Well-stocked, central air-con shop for groceries and toiletries.

★**Domus** CAFE, CONTINENTAL $$
(☎0413-4210807; www.facebook.com/domus-pondicherry-708267965970400; 59 Suffren St; dishes ₹210-350; ⏲10am-7pm; 📶) A laid-back, health-focused, all-veg hideaway cafe in the hushed garden of a zany design shop, where faded turquoise pillars clash beautifully against red walls. Dig into wholesome muesli breakfasts, build your own sandwich from a choice of breads, fillings and seasonings, or try the creative European-salad 'thalis', served traditional-style on stainless-steel dishes. Delicious espresso, smoothies and juices.

★**La Pasta World** ITALIAN $$
(☎9994670282; www.facebook.com/lapastaworld; 55 Vysial St; mains ₹295-355; ⏲10am-2pm & 5-10pm Thu-Sat, 5-10pm Sun-Wed) Pasta lovers should make a pilgrimage to this little Tamil Quarter spot with just a few check-cloth tables, where a real Italian concocts her own authentically yummy sauces and bubbles up her own perfect pasta in an open-plan kitchen as big as the dining area. No alcohol: it's all about the food.

Café des Arts CAFE $$
(www.facebook.com/café-des-arts-155637583166; 10 Suffren St; dishes ₹150-260; ⏲8.30am-7pm Wed-Mon; 📶) This bohemian cafe would look perfectly at home in Europe, but this is Pondy, so there's a cycle rickshaw in the garden. Refreshingly light dishes range from crisp salads to crepes, baguettes, omelettes and toasties. Coffees and fresh juices are great. The old-townhouse setting is lovely, with low tables and lounge chairs spilling out in front of a vintage boutique.

Kasha Ki Aasha CAFE $$
(www.kkapondy.com; 23 Surcouf St; mains ₹150-250; ⏲10am-8pm Thu-Tue; 📶) A friendly all-female team whips up great pancake breakfasts, lunches and cakes on the thatched rooftop of this colonial-era-house-turned-craft-shop-and-cafe, where fusion food includes 'European thalis' and 'Indian enchiladas'. The floaty fabrics and leather sandals downstairs come direct from their makers. Live music Saturday night.

Le Café CAFE $$
(☎0413-2334949; Goubert Ave; dishes ₹80-240; ⏲24hr) Pondy's only seafront cafe is good for croissants, cakes, salads, baguettes, breakfasts and organic South Indian coffee (hot or iced), plus welcome fresh breezes from the Bay of Bengal. It's popular, so you often have to wait for, or share, a table. But hey, it's all about the location.

★**Villa Shanti** CONTINENTAL, INDIAN $$$
(☎0413-4200028; www.lavillashanti.com; 14 Suffren St; mains ₹225-495; ⏲12.30-2.30pm & 7-10.30pm) Smart candlelit tables in a palm-dotted pillared courtyard attached to a colourful cocktail bar create a casually fancy vibe at this packed-out hotel restaurant, one of Pondy's hottest dining spots. The building's contemporary Franco-Indian flair runs right through the North Indian/European menu. While portions are small, flavours are exquisite, and there are some deliciously creative veg dishes. No bookings beyond 7.30pm.

Le Club CONTINENTAL, INDIAN $$$
(☎0413-2227409; www.leclubraj.com; 38 Dumas St; mains ₹200-530; ⏲11.45am-3pm & 6-10pm) The steaks (with sauces like blue cheese or Béarnaise), pizzas, pastas and crepes are all top-class at this romantically lit garden restaurant. Tempting local-themed options include creole prawn curry, veg-paneer kebabs and Malabar-style fish. There are plenty of wines, mojitos and margaritas to wash it all down.

Drinking & Nightlife

Although Pondy is one of the better places in Tamil Nadu to knock back beers, closing time is a strictly enforced 11pm. Despite low alcohol taxes, you'll only really find cheap beer in 'liquor shops' and their darkened bars. Hotel restaurants and bars make good drinking spots.

L'e-Space BAR
(2 Labourdonnais St; cocktails ₹200, dishes ₹150-300; ⏲5-11.30pm) A quirky little semi-open-air rooftop bar/cafe lounge that's friendly, laid-back and sociable, and does good cocktails (assuming the barman hasn't disappeared).

Shopping

With all the yogis congregating here, Pondy specialises in boutique-chic-meets-Indian-bazaar fashion and souvenirs. There's some beautiful and original stuff, a lot of it produced by Sri Aurobindo Ashram or Auroville. Nehru St and MG Rd are the shopping hot spots; boutiques line the French Quarter.

★ **Kalki** FASHION & ACCESSORIES
(www.maroma.com; 134 Mission St; ⏲10am-8.30pm) Dazzling, jewel-coloured silk and cotton fashion, as well as accessories, incense, oils, scented candles, handmade-paper trinkets and more, mostly made at Auroville, where there's another **branch** (visitors centre; ⏲9.30am-6pm).

Anokhi FASHION & ACCESSORIES
(www.anokhi.com; 1 Caserne St; ⏲10am-7.30pm) A sophisticated Jaipur-born boutique popular for its beautiful, bold block-printed garments with a traditional-turns-modern twist, and gorgeous colourful bedspreads, tablecloths, scarves, bags, homewares and accessories.

Auroshikha INCENSE
(www.auroshikha.com; 28 Marine St; ⏲9am-1pm & 3-7pm Tue-Sun) An endless array of incense, perfumed candles, essential oils and other scented trinkets, made by Sri Aurobindo Ashram.

Fabindia CLOTHING, TEXTILES
(www.fabindia.com; 223 Mission St; ⏲10.30am-8.30pm) Going strong since 1960, the Fabindia chain stocks stunning handmade, fair-trade products made by villagers using traditional craft techniques, and promotes rural employment. This branch has wonderful cotton and silk contemporary-Indian clothing, along with high-quality fabrics, tablecloths, beauty products and furniture.

La Boutique d'Auroville ARTS & CRAFTS
(www.auroville.com; 38 Nehru St; ⏲9.30am-8pm) Perfect for browsing through Auroville-made crafts: jewellery, pottery, clothing, shawls, handmade cards and herbal toiletries.

LivingArt Lifestyles FASHION & ACCESSORIES
(www.facebook.com/livingartlifestyles; 14 Rue Bazar St Laurent; ⏲10am-2pm & 3-8pm Tue-Sat) Breezy, boho-chic block-printed dresses, skirts, trousers and crop-tops in fun-but-fashionable geometric patterns (all handmade at Auroville) sit side-by-side with beautifully crafted saris from across India.

Focus BOOKS
(204 Mission St; ⏲9.30am-1.30pm & 3.30-9pm Mon-Sat) Good collection of India-related and other English-language books (including Lonely Planet guides).

ℹ Information

Rue Bussy between Bharathi St and MG Rd is packed with clinics and pharmacies.

New Medical Centre (☎0413-2225287; www.nmcpondy.com; 470 MG Rd; ⏲24hr) Recommended private clinic and hospital.

Shanti Travel (☎0413-4210401; www.shanti-travel.com; 44 Vysial St; ⏲10am-6pm) Professional agency offering walking tours, day trips and Chennai airport pick-ups.

Tourist Office (☎0413-2339497; www.pondytourism.in; 40 Goubert Ave; ⏲10am-5pm)

ℹ Getting There & Away

AIR

Puducherry's airport is 6km northwest of the centre, but has been in and out of action for several years. At the time of writing, it was scheduled to reopen in early 2017 with flights to Bengaluru via Trichy, plus, possibly, to other domestic destinations.

BUS

The **bus stand** (Maraimalai Adigal Salai) is 2km west of the French Quarter. Further services run from Villupuram (₹20, one hour, every 15 minutes), 38km west of Puducherry. Private bus companies, operating mostly overnight to various destinations, have offices along Maraimalai Adigal Salai west of the bus stand. **Parveen Travels** (☎0413-2201919; www.parveentravels.com; 288 Maraimalai Adigal Salai; ⏲24hr) runs an 11pm semi-sleeper service to Kodaikanal (₹650, eight hours).

TAXI

Air-conditioned taxis to/from Chennai airport cost ₹4000.

TRAIN

Puducherry train station has just a few services. Two daily trains go to Chennai Egmore, unreserved seating only (₹45 to ₹90, four to five hours). Connect at Villupuram for many more services. The station has a computerised booking office for trains throughout India.

ℹ Getting Around

Pondy's flat streets are great for getting around on foot. Autorickshaws are plentiful, but drivers usually refuse to use meters. A trip from the bus stand to the French Quarter costs ₹60.

A good way to explore Pondy and Auroville is by rented bicycle or motorbike from **outlets** (Mission St; per day bicycle ₹75, scooter or motorbike ₹250-400) on northern Mission St, between Nehru and Chetty Sts.

Auroville

☎0413 / POP 2570

Auroville, 'the City of Dawn', is a place that anyone with idealistic leanings will love:

an international community dedicated to peace, sustainability and 'divine consciousness', where people from across the globe, ignoring creed, colour and nationality, work together to build a universal, cash-free, non-religious township.

Outside opinions of Auroville's inhabitants range from admiration to accusations of self-indulgent escapism. Imagine over 100 small scattered countryside settlements, with 2500-odd residents of 52 nationalities. Nearly 60% of Aurovillians are foreign; most new members require more funds than most Indians may ever have. But the energy driving the place is palpable and, on a visit, you'll receive a positive vibe.

Some 12km northwest of Puducherry, Auroville was founded in 1968 by 'the Mother', cofounder of Puducherry's Sri Aurobindo Ashram. Aurovillians run a wide variety of projects, from schools and IT to organic farming, renewable energy and handicrafts production, employing 4000 to 5000 local villagers.

The Auroville website (www.auroville.org) is an encyclopedic resource.

Sights & Activities

Auroville isn't directly geared for tourism – most inhabitants are just busy getting on with their lives – but it does have a good **visitors centre** (☎0413-2622239; www.facebook.com/aurovillevisitorscentre; ⏲9.30am-1pm & 1.30-5pm) with information desks, exhibitions and Auroville products. You can buy a handbook and map (₹20), and watch a 10-minute video. Free passes for external viewing of the Matrimandir, Auroville's 'soul', a 1km woodland walk away, are handed out here.

Visitors are free to wander Auroville's 10-sq-km network of roads and tracks. With two million trees planted since Auroville's foundation, it's a lovely shaded space.

If you're interested in getting to know Auroville, authorities recommend you stay at least 10 days and join an introduction and orientation program. To get properly involved, you'll need to come as a volunteer for six to 12 months. Contact the **Auroville Guest Service** (☎0413-2622675; guestservice@auroville.org.in; Solar Kitchen Bldg, 2km east of visitors centre; ⏲9.30am-12.30pm & 1-4pm Mon-Fri, 9.30am-12.30pm Sat) for advice on active participation.

Matrimandir NOTABLE BUILDING
(1km east of visitors centre; ⏲passes issued 9.45am-1pm & 1.30-4.30pm Mon-Sat, 9.45am-12.30pm Sun) FREE The large, golden, almost spherical Matrimandir (Auroville's focal point) is often likened to a golf ball, on a bed of lotus petals. You might equally feel that its grand simplicity of form, surrounded by pristine green parkland, does indeed evoke the divine consciousness it's intended to represent. The main inner chamber, lined with white marble, houses a large glass crystal orb that suffuses a beam of sunlight around the space. It's conceived as a place for individual silent concentration.

If, after viewing the Matrimandir from the gardens, you want to meditate inside, you must reserve one to four days ahead at Auroville's **Matrimandir Access Office** (☎0413-2622239, 0413-2622204; mmconcentration@auroville.org.in; visitors centre; ⏲10-11am & 2-3pm Wed-Mon).

Sleeping

Auroville has over 80 guesthouses and homestays of hugely varied comfort levels and budgets, from ₹200 dorm beds to ₹5400 two-person cottages with pools. The **Guest Accommodation Service** (☎0413-2622704; www.aurovilleguesthouses.org; visitors centre; ⏲9.30am-12.30pm & 2-5pm) offers advice, but bookings are direct with individual guesthouses. For peak seasons (August, September and December to March) book three or four months ahead.

Getting There & Away

The main turning to Auroville from the East Coast Rd is at Periyar Mudaliarchavadi village, 6km north of Puducherry. From there it's 6km west to the visitors centre.

A one-way autorickshaw from Puducherry costs ₹270. Or you can take a Kottukuppam bus northbound from Puducherry's Ambour Salai to the Auroville turn-off (₹10 to ₹20, every 10 minutes), then an autorickshaw for ₹150. There are direct buses (₹10) from Puducherry bus station to Auroville visitors centre at 7.30am, 1.45pm and 4.30pm, returning at 8.15am, 2.20pm and 5.15pm.

Otherwise, rent a bicycle or motorcycle from **outlets** on northern Mission St in Puducherry.

CENTRAL TAMIL NADU

Chidambaram

☎04144 / POP 62,150

There's one reason to visit Chidambaram: the great temple complex of Nataraja, Shiva as the Dancer of the Universe. One of the holiest of all Shiva sites, this also happens to be a Dravidian architectural highlight. It's easily visited on a day trip from Puducherry, or en route between Puducherry and Tranquebar or Kumbakonam.

Most accommodation is near the temple or the bus stand (500m southeast of the temple). The train station is 1km further southeast.

Sights

★Nataraja Temple HINDU TEMPLE

(East Car St; inner compound 6am-noon & 4.30-10pm) According to legend, Shiva and Kali got into a dance-off judged by Vishnu. Shiva dropped an earring and picked it up with his foot, a move that Kali could not duplicate, so Shiva won the title Nataraja (Lord of the Dance). It's in this form that endless streams of people come to worship him at this great temple. It was built during Chola times (Chidambaram was a Chola capital), but the main shrines date to at least the 6th century.

The high-walled 22-hectare complex has four towering 12th-century *gopurams* decked out in schizophrenic Dravidian stone and stucco work. The main entrance is through the east (oldest) *gopuram*. The 108 sacred positions of classical Tamil dance are carved in its passageway. To your right through the *gopuram* are the 1000-pillared 12th-century **Raja Sabha** (King's Hall; open only festival days), with carved elephants, and the large **Sivaganga** tank.

You enter the central compound (no cameras) from the east. In its southern part (left from the entrance) is the 13th-century **Nritta Sabha** (Dance Hall), shaped like a chariot with 56 finely carved pillars. Some say this is the spot where Shiva out-danced Kali.

North of the Nritta Sabha, through a door, you enter the inner courtyard, where most temple rituals are performed. Right in front are the attached hut-like, golden-roofed **Kanaka Sabha** and **Chit Sabha** (Wisdom Hall). The Chit Sabha, the innermost sanctum, holds the temple's central bronze image of Nataraja – Shiva the cosmic dancer, ending one cycle of creation, beginning another and uniting all opposites. Shiva's invisible 'space' form is also worshipped here.

At *puja* times devotees crowd into the encircling pavilion to witness rites performed by the temple's hereditary Brahmin priests, the Dikshithars, who shave off some of their hair but grow the rest of it long (thus representing both Shiva and Parvati) and tie it into topknots.

On the south side of the two inner shrines is the **Govindaraja Shrine** with a reclining Vishnu. Overlooking the tank from the west, the **Shivakamasundari Shrine** displays fine ochre-and-white 17th-century Nayak ceiling murals.

Priests may offer to guide you around the temple for ₹200 to ₹300. Unusually for Tamil Nadu, this magnificent temple is privately funded and managed, so you may wish to support it by hiring one, but there are no official guides.

Festivals & Events

Chariot Festivals RELIGIOUS

(Jun-Jul & Dec-Jan) Of Chidambaram's many festivals, the two largest are the 10-day chariot festivals.

Natyanjali Dance Festival DANCE

(http://natyanjalichidambaram.com; Feb-Mar) Chidambaram's five-day dance festival attracts 300 to 400 classical dancers from all over India to the Nataraja Temple.

Sleeping & Eating

Many cheap pilgrims' lodges are clustered around the temple (some pretty grim). There are a couple of decent-ish lower-midrange hotels (with restaurants) nearby.

Hotel Saradharam HOTEL $$

(04144-221336; www.hotelsaradharam.co.in; 19 VGP St; r incl breakfast ₹1100, with AC ₹2200;) Opposite the bus stand, the busy,

BUSES FROM CHIDAMBARAM

DESTINATION	FARE (₹)	TIME (HR)	DEPARTURES
Chennai	140	6	every 10min
Kumbakonam	42	3	every 30min
Puducherry	75	2	every 10min
Thanjavur	60	3-4	every 30min
Tranquebar	75	2-3	every 30min

WORTH A TRIP

TRANQUIL TRANQUEBAR (THARANGAMBADI)

South of Chidambaram, the Cauvery River's many-armed delta stretches 180km along the coast and into the hinterland. The Cauvery is the beating heart of Tamil agriculture and its valley was the heartland of the Chola empire. Today the delta is one of Tamil Nadu's prettiest, poorest and most traditional areas.

The tiny seaside town of **Tharangambadi**, still known as Tranquebar, is easily the most appealing base. A great place to recharge from the crowded towns inland, this quiet former Danish colony is set right on a long sandy beach with fishing boats and delicious sea breezes. Denmark sold it to the British East India Company in 1845.

The old town inside the 1792 **Landporten Gate**, with its colonial-era buildings, has been significantly restored since the 2004 tsunami, which killed about 800 people here. INTACH Pondicherry (www.intachpondicherry.org) has a good downloadable map. The peach-hued, seafront Danish fort, **Dansborg** (Parade Ground, King's St; Indian/foreigner ₹5/50, camera/video ₹30/100; ⏰10am-5.45pm Sat-Thu), dates from 1624 and was occupied by the British in 1801; it now houses a small but fascinating museum. Among other notable buildings is the 1718 **New Jerusalem Church** (Tamil Evangelical Lutheran Church; King's St; ⏰dawn-dusk), in mixed Indian and European styles; it contains the tomb of German-born Bartholomäus Ziegenbalg, the first Lutheran missionary to arrive in South India and first ever translator of the New Testament into Tamil. Tranquebar's **post office** (Post Office St; ⏰8.30am-6pm Mon-Sat) has occupied the same dishevelled little building since 1884, while the 14th-century seafront **Masilamani Nathar Temple** (⏰6am-noon & 4-8pm, hours vary) is now painted in kaleidoscopic colours.

Most Tranquebar accommodation is run by the sea-fronting **Bungalow on the Beach** (☎04364-289036; http://neemranahotels.com; 24 King's St; r incl breakfast ₹6080-10,320; ❄📶🏊), in the exquisitely restored 17th-century former residence of the British administrator. There are 17 beautiful old-world rooms in the main building and two other heritage locations in town; book ahead. The main block has a good **restaurant** (☎04364-289036; http://neemranahotels.com; 24 King's St; mains ₹150-300; ⏰7.30-9.30am, 12.30-2.30pm, 7-9.30pm), a dreamy swimming pool and a fantastic wraparound terrace.

Tranquebar has regular (crowded) buses to/from Chidambaram (₹75, two hours, hourly) and Karaikal (₹12, 30 minutes, half-hourly). From Karaikal buses go to Kumbakonam (₹26 to ₹34, two hours, every two hours 4am to 10.15pm), Thanjavur (₹62, three hours, every two hours 4am to 10.15pm) and Puducherry (₹85, four hours, half-hourly 4.15am to midnight).

friendly Saradharam is as good as it gets. It's a bit worn and stuffy but comfortable enough, and a welcome respite from the town-centre frenzy. There's free wi-fi in the lobby, plus three restaurants – two vegetarian, and the good multicuisine, air-con **Anupallavi** (mains ₹150-225; ⏰7-10am, noon-3pm & 7-10pm).

ℹ Getting There & Away

BUS

Government buses depart from the **bus stand** (VGP St). **Universal Travels** (☎044-9842440926; VGP St; ⏰9am-10pm), opposite the bus stand, runs Volvo AC buses to Chennai (₹500, five hours) at 8am and 4.30pm.

TRAIN

Three or more daily trains head to Trichy (2nd class/3AC/2AC ₹80/490/695, 3½ hours) via Kumbakonam (₹55/490/695, 1½ hours) and Thanjavur (₹65/490/695, two hours), and seven to Chennai Egmore (₹105/490/695, 5½ hours).

Kumbakonam

☎0435 / POP 140,160

At first glance Kumbakonam is just another chaotic Indian junction town, but then you notice the dozens of colourful *gopurams* pointing skyward from its 18 temples – a reminder that this was once a seat of medieval South Indian power. With another two magnificent World Heritage–listed Chola temples (p1049) nearby, it's worth staying the night.

👁 Sights

Nageshwara Temple HINDU TEMPLE

(Nageswaran Koil St; ⏰6.30am-12.30pm & 4-8.30pm) Founded by the Cholas in 886, this is Kumbakonam's oldest temple, dedicated

Kumbakonam

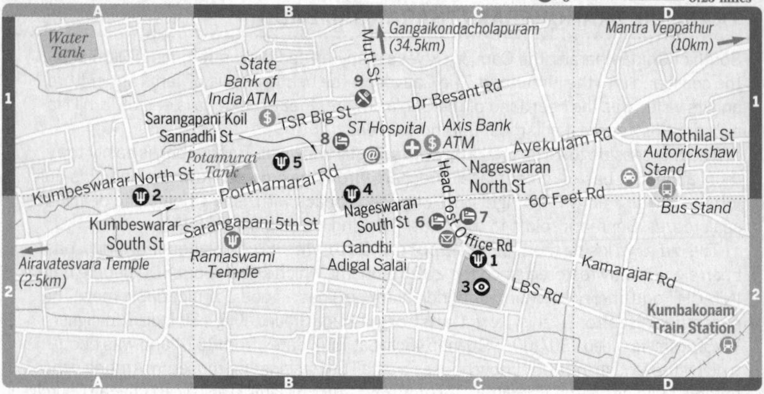

Kumbakonam

Sights

1 Kashivishvanatha Temple C2
2 Kumbeshwara Temple A2
3 Mahamaham Tank C2
4 Nageshwara Temple B1
5 Sarangapani Temple B1

Sleeping

6 Hotel Raya's C2
7 Hotel Raya's Annexe C2
8 Pandian Hotel B1

Eating

9 Hotel Sri Venkkatramana B1
Sathars Restaurant .... (see 6)

to Shiva as Nagaraja, the serpent king. On three days of the year (April or May) the sun's rays fall on the lingam. The elevated Nataraja shrine on the right in front of the inner sanctum is fashioned, in typical Chola style, like a horse-drawn chariot; colourful modern elephants stand beside it.

Sarangapani Temple HINDU TEMPLE
(Sarangapani Koil Sannadhi St; ⏲6.30am-12.30pm & 4-8.30pm) Sarangapani is Kumbakonam's largest Vishnu temple, with a 45m-high eastern *gopuram* embellished with low-level dancing panels as its main entrance. Past the temple cowshed (Krishna the cowherd is one of Vishnu's forms), another *gopuram* and a pillared hall, you reach the inner sanctuary, a 12th-century Chola creation styled like a chariot with big carved elephants, horses and wheels. Photography is not permitted inside.

Kumbeshwara Temple HINDU TEMPLE
(off Kumbeswarar East St; ⏲6.30am-12.30pm & 4-8.30pm) Kumbeshwara Temple, entered via a nine-storey *gopuram,* a small bazaar and a long porticoed *mandapa,* is Kumbakonam's biggest Shiva temple. It dates from the 17th and 18th centuries and contains a lingam said to have been made by Shiva himself when he mixed the nectar of immortality with sand.

Mahamaham Tank RELIGIOUS SITE
(LBS Rd) Surrounded by 16 pavilions, the huge Mahamaham Tank is one of Kumbakonam's most sacred sites. It's believed that every 12 years the waters of India's holiest rivers, including the Ganges, flow into it, and at this time a festival is held (next due: 2028). On the tank's north side, the **Kashivishvanatha Temple** (LBS Rd; ⏲6.30am-12.30pm & 4-8.30pm) contains an intriguing trio of river goddesses, the central of which embodies the Cauvery River.

Sleeping & Eating

Pandian Hotel HOTEL $
(☎0435-2430397; 52 Sarangapani Koil Sannadhi St; s/d ₹350/660, d with AC ₹990; ❄) It feels institutional, but you're generally getting fair value at this clean-enough budget standby.

Hotel Raya's HOTEL $$
(☎0435-2423170; www.hotelrayas.com; 18 Head Post Office Rd; r ₹1200, with AC ₹1560; ❄) Friendly service and spacious, spotless rooms make Raya's your top lodging option in town. Its newer **Hotel Raya's Annexe** (☎0435-2423270; 19 Head Post Office Rd; r ₹2000; ❄📶) has the best, brightest rooms, and a mural-lined lobby. The hotel runs a convenient

car service for out-of-town trips. **Sathars Restaurant** (☎0435-2423170; mains ₹120-240; ⏲11.30am-11.30pm) here does good veg and nonveg fare in clean surroundings.

Mantra Veppathur RESORT **$$$**
(☎0435-2462261; www.mantraveppathur.com; 536/537 A, 1 Bagavathapuram Main Rd Extension, Srisailapathipuram Village; incl breakfast s ₹8500-9720, d ₹9720-10,940;) Lost in the riverside jungle, 10km northeast of Kumbakonam, this is a wonderful retreat from temple-town chaos. Comfy modern-rustic rooms fronted by porches with rocking chairs have open-air showers and carved-teak doors; ayurveda is offered; there's rain-water harvesting; and the organic farm fuels the Indian-focused restaurant, where you can eat out on a turquoise-tiled verandah.

Hotel Sri Venkkatramana SOUTH INDIAN **$**
(TSR Big St; thalis ₹70-110; ⏲6am-10pm Mon-Sat) Good fresh veg food and an air-con hall; very popular with locals.

Getting There & Away

Government buses depart from the **bus stand** (60 Feet Rd).

Thirteen daily trains head to Thanjavur (2nd class/3AC/2AC ₹45/490/695, 30 minutes to one hour) and nine to Trichy (₹60/490/695, 1½ to 2½ hours). Five daily trains to/from Chennai

DON'T MISS

CHOLA TEMPLES NEAR KUMBAKONAM

Two of the three great monuments of Chola civilisation stand in villages just outside Kumbakonam: Darasuram's Airavatesvara Temple and the Gangaikondacholapuram temple. Unlike the also World Heritage–listed Brihadishwara Temple at Thanjavur, today these two temples receive relatively few worshippers (and visitors). They are wonderful both for their overall form (with pyramidal towers rising at the heart of rectangular walled compounds) and for the exquisite detail of their carved, unpainted stone.

From Kumbakonam bus stand (p1049), frequent buses to nearby villages will drop you at Darasuram; buses to Gangaikondacholapuram (₹20, 1½ hours) run every 15 minutes. A return autorickshaw to Darasuram costs about ₹150. A half-day car trip to both temples, through Kumbakonam's reliable Hotel Raya's (p1048), costs ₹1100 (₹1250 with AC).

Airavatesvara Temple (Darasuram; ⏲6am-8pm, inner shrine 6am-1pm & 4-8pm) Only 3km west of Kumbakonam, this late-Chola Shiva temple was constructed by Raja Raja II (1146–73). The steps of the **Rajagambhira Hall** are carved with vivid elephants and horses pulling chariots. This pavilion's 108 all-different pillars have detailed carvings including dancers, acrobats and the five-in-one beast *yali* (elephant's head, lion's body, goat's horns, pig's ears and a cow's backside). Inside the **main shrine** (flanked by guardians), you can honour the central lingam and get a *tilak* (auspicious forehead mark) for ₹10.

Gangaikondacholapuram Temple (Brihadishwara Temple; Gangaikondacholapuram; ⏲6am-noon & 4-8pm) The temple at Gangaikondacholapuram ('City of the Chola who Conquered the Ganges'), 35km north of Kumbakonam, is dedicated to Shiva. It was built by Rajendra I in the 11th century when he moved the Chola capital here from Thanjavur, and has many similarities to Thanjavur's earlier Brihadishwara Temple. Its beautiful 49m-tall tower, however, has a slightly concave curve, making it the 'feminine' counterpart to the mildly convex Thanjavur one. The artistic highlights are the wonderfully graceful sculptures around the tower's exterior.

A massive Nandi (Shiva's vehicle) faces the temple from the tranquil surrounding gardens; a lion stands guard nearby. The main shrine, beneath the tower, contains a huge lingam and is approached through a long 17th-century hall. The fine carvings on the tower's exterior include Shiva as the beggar Bhikshatana, immediately left of the southern steps; Ardhanarishvara (Shiva as half-man, half-woman), and Shiva as Nataraja, on the south side; Shiva with Ganga, Shiva emerging from the lingam, and Vishnu with Lakshmi and Bhudevi (southernmost three images on the west side); and Shiva with Parvati (northernmost image on the west side). Most famous is the masterful panel of Shiva garlanding the head of his follower, Chandesvara, beside the northern steps.

BUSES FROM KUMBAKONAM

DESTINATION	FARE (₹)	TIME (HR)	DEPARTURES
Chennai (AC)	300	8	1.50pm
Chidambaram	50	2½-3	every 30min
Karaikal	40	2¼	every 15min
Thanjavur	30	2	every 5min
Trichy	60	4	every 5min

Egmore include the overnight Mannai Express (sleeper/3AC/2AC/1AC ₹210/555/795/1325, 6½ hours) and the daytime Chennai Express/Trichy Express (₹210/555/795/1325, six to seven hours).

Thanjavur (Tanjore)

04362 / POP 222,940

Here are the ochre foundation blocks of perhaps the most remarkable civilisation of Dravidian history, one of the few kingdoms to expand Hinduism beyond India, a bedrock for aesthetic styles that spread from Madurai to the Mekong. A dizzying historical legacy was forged from Thanjavur, capital of the great Chola empire during its heyday. Today Thanjavur is a crowded, hectic, modern Indian town – but the past is still very much present. Every day thousands of people worship at the Cholas' grand Brihadishwara Temple, and the city's labyrinthine royal palace preserves memories of other, later powerful dynasties.

Sights

★Brihadishwara Temple HINDU TEMPLE

(Big Temple St; 6am-8.30pm, central shrine 8.30am-12.30pm & 4-8.30pm) Come here twice: in the morning, when the honey-hued granite begins to assert its dominance over the white dawn sunshine, and in the evening, when the rocks capture a hot palette of reds, oranges, yellows and pinks on the crowning glory of Chola temple architecture. The World Heritage–listed Brihadishwara Temple was built between 1003 and 1010 by Raja Raja I ('king of kings'). The outer fortifications were put up by Thanjavur's later Nayak and British regimes.

You enter through a Nayak gate, followed by two original *gopurams* with elaborate stucco sculptures. You might find the temple elephant under one of the *gopurams*. Several shrines are dotted around the extensive grassy areas of the walled temple compound, including one of India's largest statues of Nandi (Shiva's sacred bull), facing the main temple building. Cut from a single rock and framed by slim pillars, this 16th-century Nayak creation is 6m long.

A long, columned assembly hall leads to the **central shrine** with its 4m-high Shiva lingam, beneath the superb 61m-high *vimana* (tower). The assembly hall's southern steps are flanked by two huge *dvarapalas* (temple guardians). Many graceful deity images stand in niches around the *vimana's* lower outer levels, including Shiva emerging from the lingam (beside the southern steps); Shiva as the beggar Bhikshatana (first image, south side); Shiva as Nataraja, the cosmic dancer (west end of south wall); Harihara (half Shiva, half Vishnu) on the west wall; and Ardhanarishvara (Shiva as half-man, half-woman), leaning on Nandi, on the north side. Between the deity images are panels showing classical dance poses. On the *vimana's* upper east side is a later Maratha-period Shiva within three arches.

The compound also contains an interpretation centre along the south wall and, in the colonnade along the west and north walls, hundreds more linga. Both west and north walls are lined with exquisite lime-plaster Chola frescoes, for years buried under later Nayak-era murals. North of the temple compound, but still within the outer fortifications, are 18th-century neoclassical **Schwartz's Church** (dawn-dusk) and a park containing the **Sivaganga tank** (₹5, camera/video ₹10/25; dawn-dusk).

★Royal Palace PALACE

(East Main St; Indian/foreigner ₹50/200, camera ₹30/100; 9am-1pm & 1.30-5.30pm, Art Gallery 9am-1pm & 3-6pm, Sarawasti Mahal Library Museum closed Wed) Thanjavur's royal palace is a mixed bag of ruin and renovation, superb art and random royal paraphernalia. The maze-like complex was constructed partly by the Nayaks who took over Thanjavur in 1535, and partly by a local Maratha dynasty that ruled from 1676 to 1855. The two don't-

Thanjavur (Tanjore)

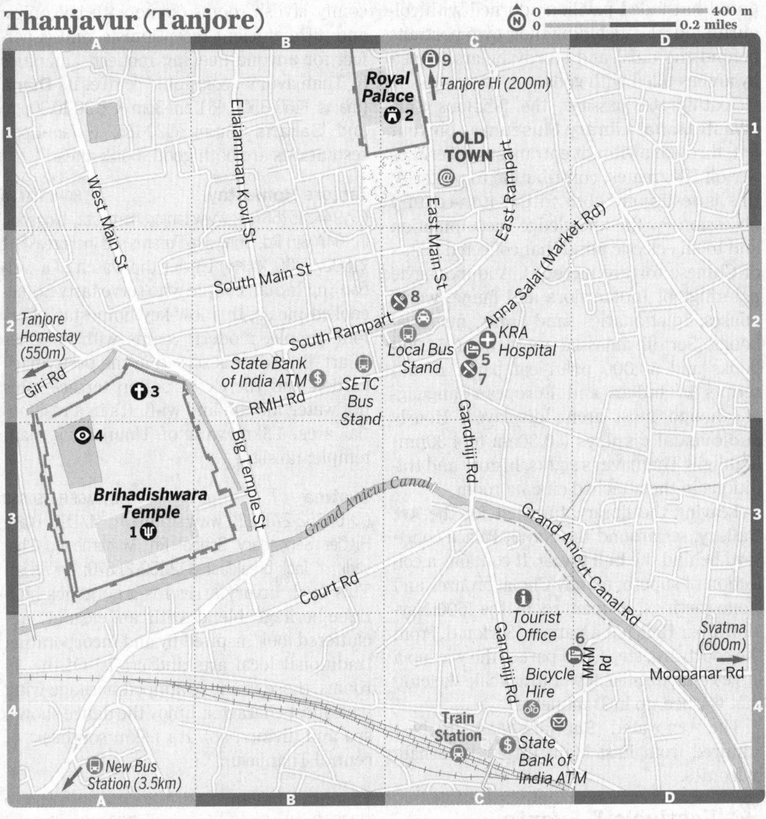

miss sections are the Saraswati Mahal Library Museum and the Art Gallery.

Seven different sections of the palace can be visited. 'Full' tickets include the Art Gallery and Saraswati Mahal Library Museum, along with the Mahratta Dharbar Hall, bell tower and Saarjah Madi; other sections require extra tickets. The main entrance is from the north, off East Main St. On the way in you'll come to the main ticket office, followed by the Maratha Palace complex.

Past the ticket office, a passage to the left leads to, first, the **Royal Palace Museum** (₹2), a small miscellany of sculptures, weaponry, elephant bells and rajas' headgears; second, the **Maharaja Serfoji Memorial Hall** (₹4), commemorating the enlightened Maratha scholar-king Serfoji II (1798–1832), with a better collection overlooking a once-splendid, now crumbling courtyard; and third, the **Mahratta Dharbar Hall**, where Maratha rulers gave audience in a

Thanjavur (Tanjore)

Top Sights
1 Brihadishwara Temple A3
2 Royal Palace C1

Sights
3 Schwartz's Church A2
4 Sivaganga Tank A3

Sleeping
5 Hotel Gnanam C2
6 Hotel Valli D4

Eating
Diana .... (see 5)
Sahana .... (see 5)
7 Sri Venkata Lodge C2
8 Vasanta Bhavan C2

Shopping
9 Kandiya Heritage C1

grand but faded pavilion adorned with colourful murals (including their own portraits behind the dais) and sturdy pillars topped by arches filled with gods.

Exiting the passage, the fabulous **Sarawasti Mahal Library Museum** is on your left, through a vibrant entranceway. Perhaps Serfoji II's greatest contribution to posterity, this is testimony both to the 19th-century obsession with knowledge accumulation and to an eclectic mind that collected prints of Chinese torture methods, Audubon-style paintings of Indian flora and fauna, world atlases, dictionaries and rare medieval books. Serfoji amassed more than 65,000 books and 50,000 palm-leaf paper manuscripts in Indian and European languages, though most aren't displayed. Hourly **audiovisual displays** (10.30am to 4.30pm) highlight Thanjavur's sights, history and traditions in the attached cinema room.

Leaving the library, turn left for the **Art Gallery**, set around the Nayak Palace courtyard behind the **bell tower**. It contains a collection of superb, mainly Chola, bronzes and stone carvings; its main room, the 1600 Nayak Durbar Hall, has a statue of Serfoji II. From the courtyard, steps lead part of the way up a large *gopuram*-like tower to a whale skeleton that washed up in Tranquebar.

The renovated **Saarjah Madi** is best admired from East Main Rd for its ornate balconies.

Festivals & Events

Thyagaraja Aradhana MUSIC
(Jan) At Thiruvaiyaru, 13km north of Thanjavur, this important five-day Carnatic music festival honours the saint and composer Thyagaraja.

Sleeping & Eating

Thanjavur has nondescript, cheap lodges opposite the SETC and local bus stands.

Hotel Valli HOTEL $
(04362-231584; www.hotelvalli.in; 2948 MKM Rd; s/d ₹610/770, r with AC ₹1090;) Near the train station, green-painted Valli offers good-value, spick-and-span rooms, friendly staff and a basic restaurant. It's in a reasonably peaceful leafy spot beyond a bunch of greasy backstreet workshops and a booze shop.

Hotel Gnanam HOTEL $$
(04362-278501; www.hotelgnanam.com; Anna Salai; s/d incl breakfast ₹2920/3280;) Easily the best value in town, the Gnanam has comfy, stylish rooms (some with balconies) and ultra-efficient receptionists, and is perfect for anyone needing modern amenities in Thanjavur's geographic centre. Its **Diana** (mains ₹160-350; 11am-3pm & 6.30-10.30pm) and **Sahana** (mains ₹120-185; 7am-11pm) restaurants are both good. Book ahead.

Tanjore Homestay HOMESTAY $$
(9443157667; www.tanjorehomestay.blogspot.in; 64A Giri Rd, Srinivasa Puram; s/d incl breakfast ₹1800/2300;) Under the watch of a welcoming Indian couple who serve tasty home-cooked meals, this low-key homestay offers four simple, modern rooms with splashes of art. Breakfast is served in the pretty back garden and there's a rooftop terrace, plus hot water, air-con and wi-fi. It's in a residential area, 1.5km west of Thanjavur's main temple; no sign.

Svatma HERITAGE HOTEL $$$
(04362-273222; www.svatma.in; 4/1116 Blake Higher Secondary School Rd, Maharnonbu Chavadi; r incl breakfast ₹12,150-21,870;) This fresh luxury arrival is a gorgeous boutique-heritage blend with an elegant, uncluttered look inspired by and incorporating traditional local arts and crafts. Of the 38 rooms, those in the revamped heritage wing have most character. Enjoy the dance shows, spa and divine pool. It's 1.5km southeast of central Thanjavur.

Vasanta Bhavan INDIAN $
(1338 South Rampart; mains ₹70-110; 6am-10.45pm) The busiest of several veg places facing the local bus stand, Vasanta Bhavan doles out biryanis and North Indian curries as well as smoothies, juices and your usual southern favourites.

Sri Venkata Lodge SOUTH INDIAN $
(Gandhiji Rd; thalis ₹60; 6.30am-9pm) A friendly, popular, veg-only place near the centre of everything, that does afternoon dosas and a nice thali.

Tanjore Hi MULTICUISINE $$
(04362-252111; www.duneecogroup.com; 464 East Main St; mains ₹230-360; 7.30-10am, 12.30-2.30pm & 7.30-10.30pm) On a boutique-hotel rooftop, this industrial-chic restaurant is a welcome surprise in traditional Thanjavur. The world-wandering menu is fuelled by fresh, organic ingredients grown at the hotel's sister property in Kodaikanal. Dine at terrace tables outside or in the glassed-in air-con room.

Shopping

Kandiya Heritage ANTIQUES, HANDICRAFTS
(634 East Main St; ⏲9.30am-8pm) Opposite the palace, Kandiya Heritage sells antiques, reproduction bronzes, brightly painted wooden horses and dolls, old European pottery and jewellery.

Information

Tourist Office (☎04362-230984; Hotel Tamil Nadu, Gandhiji Rd; ⏲10am-5.45pm Mon-Fri) One of Tamil Nadu's more helpful offices.

Getting There & Away

BUS

The downtown **SETC Bus Stand** (RMH Rd) has hourly express buses to Chennai (₹265, 8¼ hours) from 7.30am to 12.30pm and 8pm to 11pm. Buses for most other cities leave from the **New Bus Station** (Trichy Main Rd), 5km southwest of the centre. Many arriving buses will drop you off in the city centre on the way out there. Services from the New Bus Station:

Chidambaram ₹72, four hours, hourly
Kumbakonam ₹29, 1½ hours, every five minutes
Madurai ₹90, four hours, every 15 minutes
Trichy ₹31, 1½ hours, every five minutes

TRAIN

The train station is at the southern end of Gandhiji Rd. Five daily trains head to Chennai Egmore (seven hours) including the 10.45pm Mannai Express (sleeper/3AC/2AC/1AC ₹225/605/860/1445). Eighteen daily trains go to Trichy (2nd class/3AC/2AC ₹45/490/695, 1½ hours) and 12 to Kumbakonam (₹45/490/695, 30 minutes to 1¼ hours). Two go to Madurai (sleeper/3AC/2AC ₹160/490/695, four to five hours).

Getting Around

Bus 74 (₹6) shuttles between the New Bus Station and the central **local bus stand** (South Rampart); autorickshaws cost ₹120.

Trichy (Tiruchirappalli)

☎0431 / POP 847,390

Welcome to (more or less) the geographic centre of Tamil Nadu. Tiruchirappalli, universally called Trichy or Tiruchi, isn't just a travel junction: it also mixes up a heaving bazaar with some major temples. It's a huge, crowded, busy city, and the fact that most hotels are clumped together around the big bus station isn't exactly a plus point. But Trichy has a strong character and long history, and a way of overturning first impressions.

Trichy may have been a capital of the early Cholas in the 3rd century BC. It passed through the hands of the Pallavas, medieval Cholas, Pandyas, Delhi Sultanate and Vijayanagars before the Madurai Nayaks brought it to prominence, making it a capital in the 17th century and building its famous Rock Fort Temple. Under British control, it became an important railway hub known as Trichinopoly.

Trichy stretches a long way from north to south. Most of what's interesting to travellers is split into three distinct areas. The Trichy Junction, or Cantonment, area in the south has most of the hotels and restaurants and the main bus and train stations. The Rock Fort Temple and main bazaar are 4km north of here; the other important temples are on Srirangam island, a further 4km north, across the Cauvery River. Luckily, it's all connected by a good bus service.

Sights

★**Sri Ranganathaswamy Temple** HINDU TEMPLE
(Map p1054; Srirangam; camera/video ₹50/100; ⏲6am-9.30pm) So large it feels like a self-enclosed city, Sri Ranganathaswamy is quite possibly India's biggest temple. It has 49 separate Vishnu shrines, and reaching the inner sanctum from the south, as most worshippers do, requires passing through seven *gopurams*. The first (southernmost), the **Rajagopuram** (Map p1054), was added in 1987, and is one of Asia's tallest temple towers at 73m high. Non-Hindus cannot pass the sixth *gopuram* so won't see the innermost sanctum, where Vishnu as Ranganatha reclines on a five-headed snake.

You pass through streets with shops, restaurants, motorbikes and cars until you reach the temple proper at the fourth *gopuram*. Inside on the left is an information counter selling tickets for the **roof viewpoint** (₹20), which affords semi-panoramic views. Take no notice of would-be guides who spin stories to get hired. Also here, in the southwest corner, is the beautiful 16th-century **Venugopal Shrine**, adorned with superbly detailed Nayak-era carvings of preening *gopis* (milkmaids) and the flute-playing Krishna (Vishnu's eighth incarnation).

Turn right just before the fifth *gopuram* to the small **Art Museum** (Map p1054; ₹5; ⏲9am-1pm & 2-6pm), displaying fine bronzes,

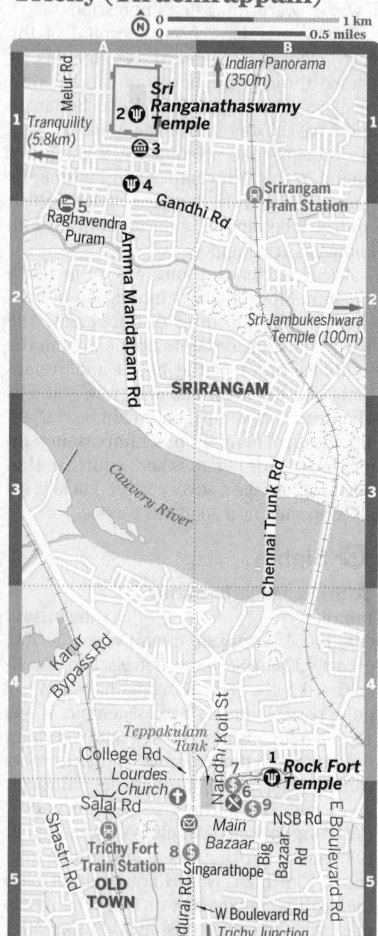

Trichy (Tiruchirappalli)

Top Sights

1 Rock Fort Temple B4
2 Sri Ranganathaswamy Temple A1

Sights

3 Art Museum A1
4 Rajagopuram A1

Sleeping

5 Home with a View A2

Eating

6 Vasanta Bhavan B5

Information

7 Canara Bank ATM B5
8 ICICI Bank ATM A5
9 State Bank of India ATM B5

tusks of bygone temple elephants, and a collection of exquisite 17th-century Nayak ivory figurines depicting gods, demons, and kings and queens (some in erotic poses). Continue left past the museum to the **Sesha Mandapa**, a 16th-century pillared hall with magnificently detailed monolithic Vijayanagar carvings of rearing battle horses and Vishnu's 10 incarnations sculpted on pillars. Immediately north is the **1000-pillared hall**, whose recently unearthed lower base is carved into dance positions.

Inside the fifth *gopuram* is the **Garuda Mandapa**, containing an enormous shrine to Vishnu's man-eagle vehicle and four remarkable sculptures of Nayak donors (with daggers on the hip).

Bus 1 to/from the Central Bus Station or the Rock Fort stops just south of the Rajagopuram.

Sri Jambukeshwara Temple HINDU TEMPLE
(Tiruvanakoil, Srirangam; ⏲5am-8pm) Of Tamil Nadu's five Shiva elemental temples, Sri Jambukeshwara is dedicated to Shiva, Parvati and the medium of water. The liquid theme is realised in the central shrine (closed to non-Hindus), whose Shiva lingam reputedly issues a nonstop trickle of water. In the north part of the complex is a shrine dedicated to Akilandeswari, Jambukeshwara's consort.

If you're taking bus 1, ask for 'Tiruvanakoil'; the temple is 350m east of the main road.

★**Rock Fort Temple** HINDU TEMPLE
(Map p1054; NSB Rd; ₹5, camera/video ₹20; ⏲6am-8pm) The Rock Fort Temple, perched 83m high on a massive outcrop, lords over Trichy with stony arrogance. The ancient rock was first hewn by the Pallavas and Pandyas, who cut small cave temples on its south side, but it was the war-savvy Nayaks who later made strategic use of the naturally fortified position. Reaching the top requires climbing over 400 stone-cut steps.

From NSB Rd on the south side, you pass between small shops and cross a street before entering the temple precinct itself, where there's a shoe stand. You might meet the **temple elephant** here. Then it's 180 steps up to the **Thayumanaswamy Temple**, the rock's biggest temple, on the left (closed to non-Hindus); a gold-topped tower rises over its sanctum. Further up, you pass the 6th-century Pallava **upper cave temple** on the left (usually railed off); on the left inside is a famous Gangadhara panel showing Shiva restraining the Ganges with a single strand of his hair. From here it's another 183 steps to the summit's small **Uchipillaiyar Temple**, dedicated to Ganesh. The views are wonderful, with eagles wheeling beneath and Trichy sprawling all around.

Back at the bottom, check out the 8th-century Pandya **lower rock-cut cave temple**, with particularly fine pillars (turn right as you exit the temple precinct, past five or six houses, then right again down a small lane).

The stone steps get scorching-hot in the midday sun and it's a barefoot climb, so time your visit carefully.

Railway Museum MUSEUM

(Bharatiyar Salai; adult/child ₹10/5, camera/video ₹20/40; 9.30am-5.30pm Tue-Sun) Trichy's Railway Museum is a fascinating jumble of disused train-related equipment (phones, clocks, control boards), British-era railway construction photos, old train-line maps (including a 1935 pre-Independence Indian Railway map) – and even modern-day London Underground tickets. It's 500m east of Trichy Junction.

Sleeping & Eating

Most hotels are near the Central Bus Station (p1057), a short walk north from Trichy Junction train station. There are also a few options in the Rock Fort area.

Hotel Abbirami HOTEL $

(Map p1056; 0431-2415001; 10 McDonald's Rd; r ₹770-990, with AC ₹1460-2430;) Most appealing are the 1st- and 4th-floor renovated rooms, with light wood and colourful glass panels. Older rooms are a bit worn, but still well kept. It's a busy, fair-value place with friendly staff.

Ashby Hotel HOTEL $

(Map p1056; 0431-2460652; 17A Rockins Rd; s ₹630-890, d ₹760-950, with AC s ₹1100-1380, d ₹1700-1930;) Wedged between the train station and the Central Bus Station, this long-running budget spot has a seedy location, but you could do worse at these prices. Behind a fiery-orange facade are plain, clean rooms around a patio.

Tranquility GUESTHOUSE $$

(9443157667; www.tranquilitytrichy.com; Anakkarai, Melur, Srirangam; s/d incl breakfast ₹3200/4000;) This charming rustic-chic guesthouse sits in a gloriously rural setting 6km west of Sri Ranganathaswamy Temple. Elegant, unfussy rooms are sprinkled with terracotta-horse statuettes, sparkly cushions, recycled wood-carved doors and custom-made furniture. Terrace swing-chairs overlook a sea of palms. Rates include bicycles and transfers. The knowledgeable owners also offer a thatched-roof homestay **room** (Map p1054; 43C Raghavendra Puram, Srirangam; r incl breakfast ₹2000;) just southwest of the temple's outermost wall.

Ramyas Hotel HOTEL $$

(Map p1056; 0431-2414646; www.ramyas.com; 13D/2 Williams Rd; incl breakfast s ₹2240-3020, d ₹2670-3630;) Comfortable rooms and good service and facilities make this business-oriented hotel excellent value, though 'business-class' rooms are ironically small. Turquoise-clad **Meridian** (Map p1056; mains ₹130-250; noon-3.30pm & 7-11.30pm) does tasty multicuisine fare, breakfast is a nice buffet and the breezy **Thendral** (Map p1056; mains ₹130-245; 7-10.30pm) roof-garden restaurant is brilliant.

Grand Gardenia HOTEL $$

(0431-4045000; www.grandgardenia.com; 22-25 Mannarpuram Junction; incl breakfast s ₹3020, d ₹3630-4840;) Elegant, modern rooms provide comfy beds and glassed-in showers at this corporate-style hotel, one of Trichy's smartest options. Nonveg **Kannappa** (mains ₹100-200; 11.30am-11.30pm) serves up excellent Chettinadu food; the rooftop terrace hosts a multicuisine **restaurant** (mains ₹120-240; 7-10.30am, 11.30am-3pm & 7-10.30pm). Comfort and amenities outweigh the uninspiring highway-side location, 1km south of Trichy Junction.

Femina Hotel HOTEL $$

(Map p1056; 0431-2414501; www.feminahotel.net; 109 Williams Rd; incl breakfast s ₹1690-4230, d ₹2240-4840;) From outside the enormous Femina looks 1950s, but renovations have turned parts of the interior quite contemporary. Facilities are good and staff helpful. Renovated deluxe rooms are cosy and modern; standard rooms are worn but spacious. There's an outdoor pool, plus a food court and supermarket.

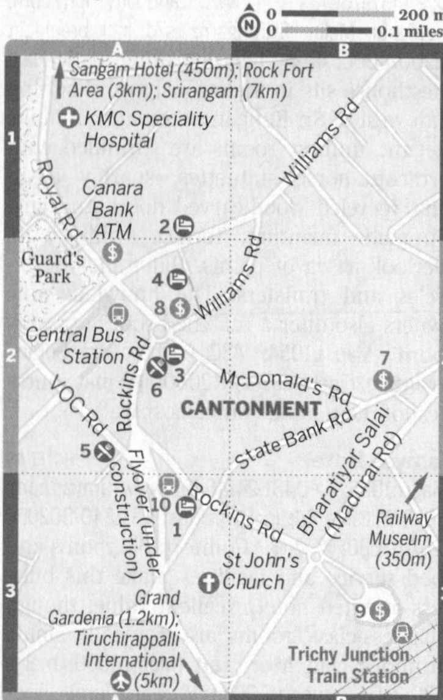

Trichy Junction Area

Sleeping

1 Ashby Hotel A3
2 Femina Hotel A1
3 Hotel Abbirami A2
4 Ramyas Hotel A2

Eating

Meridian .... (see 4)
5 Shri Sangeetas A2
Thendral .... (see 4)
6 Vasanta Bhavan A2

Information

7 State Bank of India ATM B2
8 State Bank of India ATM A2
9 State Bank of India ATM B3

Transport

Femina Travels .... (see 2)
10 Parveen Travels A3
SriLankan Airlines .... (see 2)

Sangam Hotel HOTEL **$$$**
(☎0431-2414700; www.sangamhotels.com; Collector's Office Rd; incl breakfast s ₹3950-6990, d ₹4740-7590, ste ₹11,540-18,230; ❄📶🏊) With its well-equipped rooms, smartly outfitted staff and guests-only pool, the Sangam offers a good upmarket-angled package. It's faded in parts, but service and facilities are good, including a 24-hour cafe, on-site bar and multicuisine restaurant. 'Deluxe' rooms are the most spacious and characterful, though they're all perfectly comfy.

Shri Sangeetas INDIAN **$**
(Map p1056; www.shrisangeetas.com; 2 VOC Rd; mains ₹95-130, thalis ₹85-150; ⏰5.30am-12.30am) Don't let the behind-the-bus-station address put you off. Super-popular Sangeetas has tables in a buzzing, fairy-lit courtyard (or inside in air-con comfort) and a tantalising menu of pure-veg North and South Indian favourites – everything from *idlis* and dosas to samosas, thalis and paneer tikka.

Vasanta Bhavan INDIAN **$**
(Map p1054; 3 NSB Rd; mains ₹40-90, thalis ₹70-150; ⏰8am-10pm) A great spot for a meal with views, near the Rock Fort. Tables on the outer gallery overlook the Teppakulam Tank, or there's an air-con hall. It's good for both North Indian veg food (of the paneer and naan genre) and South Indian. People crowd in for lunchtime thalis. There's another **branch** (Map p1056; Rockins Rd; mains ₹40-90, thalis ₹70-150; ⏰6am-11pm) in the Cantonment.

ℹ Information

Indian Panorama (☎0431-4226122; www.indianpanorama.in; 5 Annai Ave, Srirangam; ⏰10am-6pm) Trichy-based and covering all of India, this professional, reliable travel agency/tour operator is run by an Indian–New Zealander couple.

KMC Speciality Hospital (Kauvery Hospital; Map p1056; ☎0431-4077777; www.kauvery-hospital.com; 6 Royal Rd; ⏰24hr) Large, well-equipped, private hospital.

ℹ Getting There & Away

AIR

Trichy's airport is 6km southeast of Trichy Junction and the Central Bus Station.

AirAsia (www.airasia.com) Flies to Kuala Lumpur three times daily.

Air India Express (☎0431-2341744; www.airindiaexpress.in) Chennai, Dubai and Singapore daily.

Jet Airways (www.jetairways.com) Chennai three times daily; Abu Dhabi daily.

SriLankan Airlines (Map p1056; ☎0431-2460844; www.srilankan.com; 14C Williams Rd; ⏰9am-5.30pm Mon-Sat, to 1pm Sun) Colombo daily.

Tiger Air (www.tigerair.com) Singapore twice daily.

BUS

Government buses use the busy but orderly **Central Bus Station** (Map p1056; Rockins Rd). The best services for longer trips are the UD ('Ultra Deluxe') buses; there's a booking office for these in the southwest corner of the station. For Kodaikanal, you can also take a bus to Dindigul (₹57, two hours, every 15 minutes) and change there.

Private bus companies have offices near the Central Bus Station.

Parveen Travels (Map p1056; ☎0431-2419811; www.parveentravels.com; 12B Ashby Complex, Rockins Rd; ⊙24hr) AC buses to Chennai (₹815, six hours, five daily) and Trivandrum (₹1300, seven hours, 12.30am and 1.30am), plus non-AC semi-sleeper buses to Puducherry (₹535, four hours, 12.15am) and Kodaikanal (₹510, 4½ hours, 2.15am).

TAXI

Travel agencies and hotels provide cars with drivers. Reasonably priced **Femina Travels** (Map p1056; ☎0431-2418532; www.feminahotel.net; 109 Williams Rd; ⊙6.30am-9.30pm) charges ₹2000 for up to eight hours and 100km (AC car).

TRAIN

Trichy Junction station is on the main Chennai–Madurai line. Of the 17 daily express services to Chennai, the best daytime option is the 9.05am Vaigai Express (2nd/chair class ₹145/515, 5½ hours). The overnight Pandian Express (sleeper/3AC/2AC/1AC ₹245/625/875/1460, 6¼ hours) leaves at 11.10pm.

Thirteen daily trains to Madurai include the 7.15am Tirunelveli Express (2nd class/chair class ₹95/345, 2¼ hours) and the 1.20pm Guruvayur Express (2nd class/sleeper/3AC/2AC ₹80/140/490/695, 2¾ hours).

Eighteen trains head to Thanjavur (2nd class/sleeper/3AC ₹45/140/490, 40 minutes to 1½ hours).

ℹ Getting Around

Taxis between the airport and Central Bus Station area cost ₹300 and autorickshaws ₹200. From the Central Bus Station, Pudukkottai-bound buses will drop you at the airport.

Bus 1 from Rockins Rd outside the Central Bus Station goes every few minutes to the Sri Ranganathaswamy Temple (₹6) and back, stopping near the Rock Fort Temple and Sri Jambukeshwara Temple en route.

Autorickshaws from the Central Bus Station cost ₹170 to the Sri Ranganathaswamy Temple and ₹120 to the Rock Fort Temple.

SOUTHERN TAMIL NADU

Chettinadu

The Chettiars, a community of traders based around Karaikkudi (95km south of Trichy), hit the big time in the 19th century as financiers and entrepreneurs in colonial-era Sri Lanka and Southeast Asia. They lavished their fortunes on building 10,000 (maybe even 30,000) ridiculously opulent mansions in the 75 towns and villages of their arid rural homeland, Chettinadu. No expense was spared on finding the finest materials for these palatial homes: Burmese teak, Italian marble, Indian rosewood, English steel, and art and sculpture from everywhere.

After WWII, the Chettiars' businesses crashed. Many families left Chettinadu, and disused mansions decayed and were demolished or sold. Awareness of their value started to revive around the turn of the 21st century, with Chettinadu making it on to Unesco's tentative World Heritage list in

GOVERNMENT BUSES FROM TRICHY (TIRUCHIRAPPALLI)

DESTINATION	FARE (₹)	TIME (HR)	DEPARTURES
Bengaluru	380 (A)	8	20 UD daily
Chennai	188/260/325 (B)	6-7	15 UD, 2 AC daily
Coimbatore	116-155 (C)	4½-6	every 10min
Kodaikanal	116 (C)	5½	6.40am, 8.30am, 11am, 12.15pm
Madurai	80 (C)	2½	every 15min
Ooty	260 (A)	8½	UD 10.15pm
Rameswaram	170 (C)	6	hourly
Thanjavur	31 (C)	1½	every 5min
Trivandrum	365 (A)	8	UD 8am, 7.30pm, 9.30pm, 10.30pm

Fares: (A) Ultra Deluxe (UD), (B) regular/UD/AC, (C) regular

2014. Several mansions have now been converted into gorgeous heritage hotels that are some of Tamil Nadu's best.

Sights & Activities

Hotels give cooking demos or classes, and provide bicycles or bullock carts for rural rambles. They also arrange visits to sari-weavers, temples, mansions, Athangudi's tileworkers (producing the colourful handmade tiles you'll see in Chettiar mansions), and shrines of the popular pre-Hindu deity Ayyanar (identifiable by large terracotta horses, Ayyanar's vehicle).

Vijayalaya Cholisvaram HINDU TEMPLE
(Narthamalai; dawn-dusk) This small but stunning temple stands on a dramatically deserted rock slope 1km southwest of Narthamalai village (16km north of Pudukkottai). Reminiscent of the Shore Temple at Mamallapuram, without the crowds, it was probably built in the 8th or 9th century AD. Two (often locked) rock-cut shrines adorn the rock face behind, one with 12 impressively large reliefs of Vishnu. The Narthamalai turn-off is 7km south of Keeranur on the Trichy–Pudukkottai road; it's 2km west to Narthamalai itself.

Ellangudipatti SHRINE
(Namunasamudram; dawn-dusk) Just 8km southwest of Pudukkottai, this is an outstanding village shrine dedicated to the pre-Hindu guardian-god Ayyanar, worshipped only in rural Tamil Nadu and Sri Lanka. Hundreds of majestic terracotta horses and other beasts – offerings from local families, in various states of dishevelment – line a jungle-shrouded path leading to a modest altar.

Pudukkottai Museum MUSEUM
(Thirukokarnam, Pudukkottai; Indian/foreigner ₹5/100, camera/video ₹20/100; 9.30am-5pm Sat-Thu) The relics of Chettinadu's bygone days are on display at this wonderful museum, 4km north of Pudukkottai train station. Its eclectic collection includes musical instruments, stamps, jewellery, megalithic burial artefacts, and some remarkable paintings, sculptures and miniatures.

Sleeping & Eating

★ **Saratha Vilas** BOUTIQUE HOTEL $$$
(9884203175, 9884936158; www.sarathavilas.com; 832 Main Rd, Kothamangalam; r incl breakfast ₹7460-11,750;) A different Chettiar charm inhabits this stylishly renovated, French-run mansion from 1910, 6km east of Kanadukathan. Rooms combine traditional and contemporary with distinct French panache; the food is an exquisite mix of Chettiar and French; and there's a chic salt-water pool. Most furnishings were personally designed by the knowledgeable architect owners, hugely active players in the preservation of Chettinadu heritage.

They're also founders of local conservation NGO **ArcHeS** (www.arche-s.org; 832 Main Rd, Kothamangalam).

★ **Visalam** HERITAGE HOTEL $$$
(04565-273301; www.cghearth.com; Local Fund Rd, Kanadukathan; r incl breakfast ₹13,800-18,500;) Stunningly restored and professionally run by a Malayali hotel chain, Visalam is a relatively young Chettiar mansion, done in a fashionable 1930s art deco style. It's still decorated with the original owners' photos, furniture and paintings. The garden is exquisite, the 15 large rooms full of character, and the pool setting magical, with

CHETTINADU'S MANSIONS

Lakshmi House (Athangudi Periya Veedu; Athangudi Rd, Athangudi; ₹100; 9am-5pm) With perhaps the most exquisitely painted wood-carved ceilings in Chettinadu, Lakshmi House is a popular film set. Take in the especially fine materials (Belgian marble, English iron), Chettiar history panels, chequered floors, and curious statues of British colonials and Hindu gods looming above the entrance.

CVRMCT House (CVRMCT St, Kanadukathan; ₹50; 9am-5pm) Backed by the typical succession of pillar-lined courtyards, the impressive reception hall of this 'twin house' is shared by two branches of the same family. Don't miss the fabulous views over neighbouring mansions from the rooftop terrace.

VVRM House (CVRMCT St, Kanadukathan; 9am-5pm, hours vary) One of Chettinadu's oldest mansions, built in 1870 with distinctive egg-plaster walls, Burmese-teak columns, patterned tiled floors and intricate wood carvings. A ₹50 group 'donation' is expected.

overflowing bougainvillea and a low-key restaurant alongside.

★Bangala HERITAGE HOTEL $$$

(☎04565-220221; www.thebangala.com; Devakottai Rd, Karaikkudi; r incl breakfast ₹7050-8600; ❄📶🏊) Chettinadu's original heritage hotel, this lovingly revamped, efficiently managed whitewashed 'bungalow' isn't a typical mansion but has all the requisite charm: colour-crammed rooms, antique furniture, old family photos and a beautiful tile-fringed pool. It's famous for its food: banana-leaf 'meals' (veg/nonveg ₹850/1000) are actually Chettiar wedding feasts (12.30pm to 2.30pm and 8pm to 10pm; book two hours ahead).

Chettinadu Mansion HERITAGE HOTEL $$$

(☎04565-273080; www.chettinadmansion.com; SARM House, 11 AR St, Kanadukathan; s/d incl breakfast ₹6050/7950; ❄📶🏊) Slightly shabbier than Chettinadu's other heritage hotels, but friendly, well run and packed with character, this colourful century-old house is still owned (and lived in) by the original family. Of its 126 rooms, 12 are open to guests – all sizeable, with wacky colour schemes and private balconies gazing out over other mansions.

The owners also run nearby **Chettinadu Court** (☎04565-273080; www.deshadan.com; Raja's St, Kanadukathan; s/d incl breakfast ₹4250/5500; ❄📶🏊), which has eight heritage-inspired rooms. The two share an off-site pool.

ℹ Getting There & Around

Car is the best way to get to and around Chettinadu. Renting one with a driver from Trichy, Thanjavur or Madurai for two days costs around ₹5000.

From Trichy, buses run every five or 10 minutes to Pudukkottai (₹31, 1½ hours) and Karaikkudi (₹75, two hours); you can hop off and on along the way. From Madurai, buses run to Karaikkudi (₹80, two hours) every 30 minutes. There are also buses from Thanjavur and Rameswaram.

Three daily trains connect Chennai Egmore with Pudukkottai (sleeper/2AC/3AC ₹265/720/1030, six hours) and Karaikkudi (₹285/730/1025, 6¾ hours). One train connects Chennai with Chettinad Station, for Kanadukathan (₹275/740/1065, nine hours).

Madurai

☎0452 / POP 1.02 MILLION

Chennai may be the capital of Tamil Nadu, but Madurai claims its soul. Madurai is Tamil-born and Tamil-rooted, one of the oldest cities in India, a metropolis that traded with ancient Rome and was a great capital long before Chennai was even dreamed of.

Tourists, Indian and foreign, come here for the celebrated Meenakshi Amman Temple, a dazzling maze-like structure ranking among India's greatest temples. Otherwise, Madurai, perhaps appropriately given its age, captures many of India's glaring dichotomies: a centre dominated by a medieval temple and an economy increasingly driven by IT, all overlaid with the hustle, energy and excitement of a big Indian city and slotted into a much more manageable package than Chennai's sprawl.

History

Legend has it that Shiva showered drops of nectar *(madhuram)* from his locks on to the city, giving rise to the name Madurai – 'the City of Nectar'.

Ancient documents record the existence of Madurai from the 3rd century BC. It was a trading town, especially in spices, and according to legend was home to the third *sangam* (gathering of Tamil scholars and poets). Over the centuries Madurai came under the sway of the Cholas, Pandyas, local Muslim sultans, Hindu Vijayanagar kings and the Nayaks, who ruled until 1736 and set out the old city's lotus shape. Under Tirumalai Nayak (1623–59) the bulk of the Meenakshi Amman Temple was built, and Madurai became the hub of Tamil culture, playing an important role in the development of the Tamil language.

In 1840 the British East India Company razed Madurai's fort and filled in its moat. The four broad Veli streets were constructed on top and to this day define the old city's limits.

◉ Sights

★Meenakshi Amman Temple HINDU TEMPLE

(East Chitrai St; Indian/foreigner ₹5/50, phone camera ₹50; ⏲5am-noon & 4-9.30pm) The colourful abode of the triple-breasted warrior goddess Meenakshi ('fish-eyed' – an epithet for perfect eyes in classical Tamil poetry) is generally considered to be the peak of South Indian temple architecture, as vital to this region's aesthetic heritage as the Taj Mahal to North India. It's not so much a 17th-century temple as a 6-hectare complex with 12 tall *gopurams,* encrusted with a staggering array of gods, goddesses, demons and heroes (1511 on the 55m-high south *gopuram* alone).

Madurai

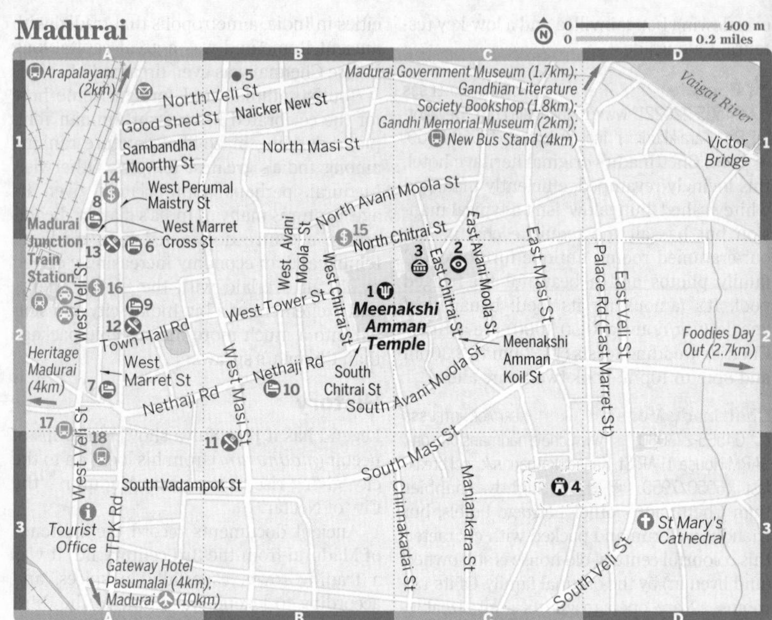

According to legend, the beautiful Meenakshi (a version of Parvati) was born with three breasts and this prophecy: her superfluous breast would melt away when she met her husband. This happened when she met Shiva and took her place as his consort. The existing temple was mostly built during the 17th-century reign of Tirumalai Nayak, but its origins go back 2000 years to when Madurai was a Pandyan capital.

The four streets surrounding the temple are pedestrian-only. Temple dress codes and security are airport-strict: no shoulders or legs (of either gender) may be exposed, and no bags or cameras are allowed inside (but you *can* use phone cameras). Despite this, the temple has a happier atmosphere than some of Tamil Nadu's more solemn shrines, and is adorned with especially vibrant ceiling and wall paintings. Every evening at 9pm, a frenetic, incense-clouded procession carries an icon of Sundareswarar (Shiva) to Meenakshi's shrine to spend the night; visitors can follow along.

Before or after entering the temple, look around the Pudhu Mandapa. The main temple entrance is through the eastern (oldest) *gopuram*. First, on the right, you'll come to the Thousand Pillared Hall, now housing the fascinating Temple Art Museum (p1060). Moving on into the temple, you'll reach a Nandi shrine surrounded by more beautifully carved columns. Ahead is the main Shiva shrine, flanked on each side by massive *dvarapalas,* and further ahead to the left in a separate enclosure is the main Meenakshi shrine, both off limits to non-Hindus. Anyone can however wander round the **Golden Lotus Tank**, where a small pavilion jutting out at the western end has ceiling murals depicting Sundareswarar and Meenakshi's marriage. Leave the temple via a hall of flower sellers and the arch-ceilinged **Ashta Shakti Mandapa** – lined with relief carvings of the goddess' eight attributes and displaying the loveliest of all the temple's elaborately painted ceilings, this is actually the temple entrance for most worshippers.

➡ Temple Art Museum

(East Chitrai St; Indian/foreigner ₹5/50, phone camera ₹50; ⏲6am-2pm & 3-9pm) Inside the Meenakshi Amman Temple's eastern *gopuram,* you'll find the Nayak-period Thousand Pillared Hall (with 985 columns) on your right. Now the Art Museum, it contains a Shiva shrine with a large bronze Nataraja at the end of a corridor of superbly carved pillars, plus many other fine bronzes and colourfully painted panels. Some of the best carvings, including Krishna with his flute and Ganesh

Madurai

Top Sights

1 Meenakshi Amman Temple B2

Sights

2 Pudhu Mandapa C2
3 Temple Art Museum C2
4 Tirumalai Nayak Palace C3

Activities, Courses & Tours

5 Storytrails B1

Sleeping

6 Berrys Boutique A2
7 Madurai Residency A2
8 Royal Court A1
9 TM Lodge A2
10 YMCA International Guest House B2

Eating

11 Murugan Idli Shop B3
12 Sri Sabareesh A2
13 Surya A2

Information

14 Canara Bank ATM A1
15 ICICI Bank ATM B1
16 State Bank of India ATM A2
Supreme Web ....(see 13)

Transport

17 Periyar Bus Stand A2
18 Shopping Complex Bus Stand A3

dancing with a woman on his knee, are immediately inside the museum entrance.

Pudhu Mandapa NOTABLE BUILDING
(East Chitrai St; dawn-dusk) FREE This 16th-century pillared hall stands outside the Meenakshi Amman Temple, opposite the eastern *gopuram*. It's crammed with colourful textile and crafts stalls and tailors at sewing machines, partly hiding some of the fine pillar sculptures, but it's easy to spot the triple-breasted Meenakshi near the southeast corner, facing Sundareswarar (opposite), and their marriage, accompanied by Vishnu, just inside the western entrance. A handsome pale-blue Nandi (Shiva's vehicle) sits outside the *mandapa's* eastern entrance.

Tirumalai Nayak Palace PALACE
(Palace Rd; Indian/foreigner ₹10/50, camera/video ₹30/100; 9am-1pm & 1.30-5pm) What Madurai's Meenakshi Amman Temple is to Nayak religious architecture, Tirumalai Nayak's crumbling palace is to the secular. It's said to be only a quarter of its original size, but its massive scale and hybrid Dravidian-Islamic style still testify to the lofty aspirations of its creator. From the east-side entrance, a large courtyard surrounded by tall, thick columns topped with fancy stucco work leads to the grand throne chamber with its 25m-high dome; two stone-carved horses frame the steps up.

Off the chamber's northwest corner is the Natakasala (Dance Hall), with a small archaeological collection.

Gandhi Memorial Museum MUSEUM
(www.gandhimmm.org; Gandhi Museum Rd; camera ₹50; 10am-1pm & 2-5.45pm) FREE Housed in a 17th-century Nayak queen's palace, this impressive museum contains a moving, comprehensive account of Gandhi's life and India's struggle for independence from 1757 to 1947; the English-language displays spare no detail about British rule. They include the blood-stained dhoti that Gandhi was wearing when he was assassinated in Delhi in 1948; it was here in Madurai, in 1921, that he first took up wearing the dhoti as a sign of native pride.

The small **Madurai Government Museum** (Indian/foreigner ₹5/100, camera ₹20; 9.30am-5pm Sat-Thu) is next door, and the **Gandhian Literature Society Bookshop** (10am-1pm & 2.30-5.45pm Mon-Sat) behind. Buses 3, 66, 75 and 700 from the **Periyar Bus Stand** (West Veli St) go to the Tamukkam bus stop on Alagarkoil Rd, 600m west of the museum.

Activities

Sivananda Vedanta Yoga Centre YOGA
(0452-2521170; http://sivananda.org.in; 444 KK Nagar, East 9th St; class ₹500; 6am-8.30pm Mon-Sat, 6.30am-5.30pm Sun) Offers daily drop-in yoga classes (6am, 10am, 4pm, 6pm; book a day ahead) and one-week programs. Also runs rigorous extended courses at its ashram, 22km north of Madurai.

Tours

Foodies Day Out FOOD & DRINK
(9840992340; www.foodiesdayout.com; 2nd fl, 393 Anna Nagar Main Rd; per person from ₹2000) The best way to delve into Madurai's famous foodie culture is on a fantastic evening tour with these local culinary enthusiasts. Vegetarian and vegan options available.

Storytrails WALKING
(7373675756; www.storytrails.in; 35 Krishnarayar Tank Rd; up to 4 people tour ₹4000) This Chennai-

born organisation runs highly rated story-based neighbourhood walking tours.

Festivals & Events

Teppam (Float) Festival RELIGIOUS
(Jan/Feb) A popular 12-day event held on the full moon of the Tamil month of Thai, when Meenakshi Amman Temple deities are paraded around town in elaborate procession and floated in a brightly lit 'minitemple' on the huge **Mariamman Teppakkulam Tank** (Kamarajar Rd), 3km east of the old city.

Chithirai Festival RELIGIOUS
(Apr/May) The highlight of Madurai's action-packed festival calendar is this two-week celebration of the marriage of Meenakshi to Sundareswarar (Shiva). The deities are wheeled around the Meenakshi Amman Temple in massive chariots forming part of long, colourful processions.

Sleeping

Budget hotels in central Madurai are mostly dreary and unloved, but there's a big choice of perfectly fine, near-identical midrange hotels along West Perumal Maistry St, near the train station. Higher-end hotels are outside the centre.

YMCA International Guest House GUESTHOUSE $
(0452-2346649; www.ymcamadurai.com; Main Guard Sq, Nethaji Rd; incl breakfast s/d ₹850/1110, with AC ₹1300/1450) Madurai's well-managed YMCA guesthouse offers sparse, clean, decent-value rooms. Proceeds help fund the organisation's charitable work.

TM Lodge HOTEL $
(0452-2341651; www.tmlodge.in; 50 West Perumal Maistry St; s/d ₹470/720, r with AC ₹1300;) The walls are a bit grubby, but the sheets are clean and TM is efficiently run.

Madurai Residency HOTEL $$
(0452-4380000; www.madurairesidency.com; 15 West Marret St; incl breakfast s ₹2640-3120, d ₹3000-3480;) The service is stellar and the rooms are comfy and fresh at this winner, which has a handy transport desk and one of the the highest rooftop restaurants in town. It's very popular, particularly with Indian businessmen: book at least a day ahead.

Berrys Boutique HOTEL $$
(0452-2340256; www.berrysboutique.in; 25 West Perumal Maistry St; incl breakfast s ₹2130-3220, d ₹2430-3220;) Just three months old at research time, Berrys' 15 smart, contemporary, minimalist fruit-named rooms are the most stylish on this hotel-packed street. There's a soothing atmosphere, plus a friendly welcome and in-house restaurant.

Royal Court HOTEL $$
(0452-4356666; www.royalcourtindia.com; 4 West Veli St; incl breakfast s ₹4110-4960, d ₹5080-5690;) The Royal Court blends a bit of white-sheeted, hardwood-floored colonial-style elegance with comfort, good eating options and friendly yet professional service. Rooms come with tea/coffee sets. It's an excellent, central choice for someone in need of a bit of a treat.

Gateway Hotel Pasumalai HERITAGE HOTEL $$$
(0452-6633000; www.gateway.tajhotels.com; 40 TPK Rd, Pasumalai; s ₹6260-12,710, d ₹7470-13,920; @) A stunning escape from the city scramble, the Taj-group Gateway sprawls across hilltop gardens 6km southwest of Madurai centre. The views, outdoor pool and 60 resident peacocks are wonderful, and rooms are luxuriously comfy and well equipped, with glassed-in showers and do-it-yourself yoga kits. The Garden All Day (p1063) restaurant is excellent.

Heritage Madurai HERITAGE HOTEL $$$
(0452-3244187; www.heritagemadurai.com; 11 Melakkal Main Rd, Kochadai; s ₹4030-8820, d ₹5370-11,600;) This leafy haven, 4km northwest of central Madurai, originally housed the old Madurai Club. It's been impeccably tarted up, with intricate Kerala-style woodwork, a sultry sunken pool and airy, terracotta-floored 'deluxe' rooms. Best are the 'villas' featuring private plunge pools. There's a good upscale North and South Indian **restaurant** (mains ₹200-450; 7am-10.30pm), along with a spa, bar and 24-hour cafe.

Eating

The hotel-rooftop restaurants along West Perumal Maistry St offer breezy night-time dining and temple views; most hotels also have air-con restaurants for breakfast and lunch. Keep an eye out for Madurai's famous summer drink *jigarthanda* (boiled milk, almond essence, rose syrup and vanilla ice cream).

★**Murugan Idli Shop** SOUTH INDIAN $
(http://muruganidlishop.com; 196 West Masi St; dishes ₹15-75; 7am-11pm) Though it now has multiple Chennai branches, Murugan is Madurai born and bred. Here you can put the fluffy signature *idlis* and chutneys to the

test, and feast on South Indian favourites like dosas, *vadas* and *uttapams*.

Sri Sabareesh INDIAN $
(49A West Perumal Maistry St; mains ₹65-90; ⏲6am-11pm) Decked with old-Madurai photos, Sri Sabareesh is a popular pure-veg cheapie that rustles up good South Indian thalis (₹80), dosas, *idlis, uttapams* and *vadas,* plus sturdy mains.

Surya MULTICUISINE $
(www.hotelsupreme.in; Hotel Supreme, 110 West Perumal Maistry St; mains ₹80-160; ⏲4pm-midnight) The Hotel Supreme's rooftop restaurant offers excellent service, good pure-veg food and superb city and temple views. The iced coffee might have been brewed by the gods when you sip it on a hot, dusty day.

Garden All Day MULTICUSINE $$$
(☎0452-6633000; www.gateway.tajhotels.com; Gateway Hotel Pasumalai, 40 TPK Rd, Pasumalai; mains ₹300-700; ⏲6.30am-11pm) If you're splashing out, the Gateway Hotel's panoramic all-day restaurant (6km southwest of central Madurai) works up an astounding array of delicious global dishes ranging from Chettinadu curries to fancy salads, pastas and burgers.

Shopping

Madurai teems with cloth stalls and tailors' shops, as you might notice upon being approached by tailor touts. Drivers, guides and touts will also be keen to lead you to the craft shops in North and West Chitrai Sts, offering to show you the rooftop temple view – the views are good, and so is the inevitable sales pitch.

Information

Tourist Office (☎0452-2334757; 1 West Veli St; ⏲10am-5.30pm Mon-Fri) Also branches at the airport and train station.

Getting There & Away

AIR

Madurai Airport is 12km south of town. **SpiceJet** (www.spicejet.com) flies once daily to Colombo, Dubai and Hyderabad, and four times daily to Chennai. **Jet Airways** (www.jetairways.com) has one daily flight to Bengaluru and five to Chennai. **Air India** (www.airindia.in) flies daily to Chennai and Mumbai.

BUS

Most government buses arrive and depart from the **New Bus Stand** (Melur Rd), 4km northeast of the centre. Services to Coimbatore, Kodaikanal, Ooty and Munnar go from the **Arapalayam Bus Stand** (Puttuthoppu Main Rd), 2km northwest of the old city. Tickets for more expensive (more comfortable) private buses are sold by agencies on the south side of the **Shopping Complex Bus Stand** (btwn West Veli St & TPK Rd); most travel overnight.

TRAIN

From Madurai Junction station, 12 daily trains head to Trichy and 10 to Chennai; fastest is the 7am Vaigai Express (Trichy 2nd/chair class ₹95/345, two hours; Chennai ₹180/660, 7¾ hours). A good overnight Chennai train is the 8.35pm Pandian Express (sleeper/3AC/2AC/1AC ₹315/810/1140/1930, nine hours). To Kanyakumari the only daily train departs at 1.30am (sleeper/3AC/2AC/1AC ₹210/540/740/1235, five hours); there's a later train some days.

GOVERNMENT BUSES FROM MADURAI

DESTINATION	FARE (₹)	TIME (HR)	DEPARTURES
Bengaluru	420-730	9-10	7am, 6pm, 8.30pm, 9pm, 9.15pm, 9.30pm, 9.35pm, 9.45pm
Chennai	325-420	9-10	every 15min, AC 9am, 8.30pm, 9pm
Kodaikanal	62	4	13 buses 1.30am-2.50pm, 5.50pm, 8.30pm
Coimbatore	125	5	every 10min
Ernakulam (Kochi)	325	9½	9am, 8pm, 9pm
Kanyakumari	200	6	every 30min
Munnar	115	6	5.55am, 8am, 10.40am
Mysuru	300-430	9-12	4.35pm, 6pm, 8pm, 9pm
Ooty	200	8	7.30am, 9.20pm
Puducherry	240-260	7½	9.05pm, 9.30pm
Rameswaram	150	4-5	every 30min
Trichy	90	2¼-3	every 5min

WORTH A TRIP

KATHADI WATER SPORTS

Launched by a team of Mumbaikar adventure-activity experts, laid-back water-sports centre **Kathadi North** (☎9820367412; www.quest-asia.com; Pirappan Valasai, off Madurai–Rameswaram Hwy; 2-day kitesurfing package incl accommodation ₹9250) offers kite-surfing, kayaking, windsurfing, snorkelling, stand-up paddleboarding, sailing, camping, beach clean-ups and after-dark wildlife walks. It's based on the mainland, 18km west of the Pamban Island bridge (which leads to Rameswaram). There's **accommodation** (☎9820367412; www.quest-asia.com; Pirappan Valasai, off Madurai–Rameswaram Hwy; s/d incl breakfast ₹3000/3500;) in four fan-cooled, beach-chic concrete huts with thatched roofs and open-air bathrooms, just inland from salt-white sands. Rainwater is harvested, power is solar, doors are recycled, palm fences use on-site materials, and the open kitchen serves communal meals (₹450).

On Pamban Island's southwest coast, budget-oriented branch **Kathadi South** (☎9820367412; www.quest-asia.com; off Old Dhanushkodhi Rd, Pamban Island; 2-day kitesurfing package incl accommodation ₹8250) has near-identical activities, plus simple shared-bathroom **huts** (☎9820367412; www.quest-asia.com; off Old Dhanushkodhi Rd, Pamban Island; s/d incl breakfast ₹1250/1500) and **tents** (single/double ₹650/1000).

Trivandrum (three daily; sleeper/3AC/2AC ₹205/545/775), Coimbatore (three daily; ₹235/590/825), Bengaluru (two daily; ₹1080/750/280) and Mumbai (one daily; ₹2540/1730/645) are other destinations.

Getting Around

Taxis cost ₹500 between the centre and the airport. Alternatively, bus 10 (₹13) runs to/from the Shopping Complex Bus Stand.

From the **New Bus Stand** (p1063), buses 3, 48 and 700 shuttle into the city; autorickshaws cost ₹120.

There's a fixed-rate taxi **stand** (Madurai Junction) outside Madurai Junction train station, with fare boards (one day around Madurai ₹1400 to ₹1800). Fast Track also has a **taxi booking counter** (☎0452-2888999; Madurai Junction; 24hr) here; rates are ₹90 for the first 3km, then ₹14 to ₹16 per kilometre.

Rameswaram

☎04573 / POP 44,860

Rameswaram was once the southernmost point of sacred India; leaving its boundaries meant abandoning caste and falling below the status of the lowliest skinner of sacred cows. Then Rama (incarnation of Vishnu, hero of the Ramayana) led a monkey-and-bear army across a monkey-built bridge to (Sri) Lanka, defeating the demon Ravana and rescuing his wife, Sita. Afterwards, prince and princess offered thanks to Shiva here. Today, millions of Hindus flock to the Ramanathaswamy Temple to worship where a god worshipped a god.

Otherwise, Rameswaram is a small, scruffy fishing town on conch-shaped Pamban Island, connected to the mainland by 2km-long bridges. If you aren't a pilgrim, the temple alone barely merits the journey here. But the island's eastern tip, Dhanushkodi, only 30km from Sri Lanka, has a magical natural beauty that adds to Rameswaram's appeal. And for activity-loving travellers, the island's western edge is buzzing as a low-key water-sports destination.

Most hotels and eateries are clustered around the Ramanathaswamy Temple, which is surrounded by North, East, South and West Car Sts.

Sights

Ramanathaswamy Temple HINDU TEMPLE

(East Car St; 5am-noon & 3-8.30pm) Housing the world's most sacred sand mound (a lingam said to have been created by Rama's wife Sita, so he could worship Shiva), this temple is one of India's holiest shrines. Dating mainly from the 16th to 18th centuries, it's notable for its lengthy 1000-pillar halls and 22 *theerthams* (temple tanks), in which pilgrims bathe before visiting the deity. Attendants tip pails of water over the (often fully dressed) faithful, who rush from *theertham* to *theertham*.

Sleeping & Eating

Most Rameswaram hotels are geared towards pilgrims. Some cheapies (mostly pretty grim) won't accept single travellers, but there are tolerable midrange hotels. Budgeteers can try the **rooms booking office** (East Car St; r ₹300-500; ⏲24hr).

Daiwik Hotel HOTEL **$$**
(☎04573-223222; www.daiwikhotels.com; Madurai–Rameswaram Hwy; r ₹4830-6040; ❄📶) Gleaming, comfy and welcoming, 'India's first four-star pilgrim hotel', 200m west of the bus station, is your classiest choice in Rameswaram. Airy rooms come smartly decked out with huge mirrors and local-life photos, there's a spa, and the pure-veg **Ahaan** (www.daiwikhotels.com; Daiwik Hotel, Madurai–Rameswaram Hwy; mains ₹145-270; ⏲7am-10pm) restaurant is good.

ℹ Getting There & Around

Rameswaram's **bus stand** (Madurai–Rameswaram Hwy) is 2.5km west of town. Buses run to Madurai (₹100, four hours) every five minutes and to Trichy (₹145, seven hours) every 30 minutes. 'Ultra Deluxe' (UD) services are scheduled to Chennai (₹435, 13 hours) at 4pm and 4.30pm, Kanyakumari (₹270, eight hours) at 7.15am and 7.30pm, and Bengaluru (₹580, 12 hours) at 4.30pm, but don't always run. There's also a 5pm AC bus to Chennai (₹565, 13 hours).

The train station is 1.5km southwest of the temple. Three daily trains to/from Madurai (₹35, four hours) have unreserved seating only. The Rameswaram–Chennai Express departs daily at 8.15pm (sleeper/3AC/2AC ₹360/945/1335, 11 hours) via Trichy (₹215/535/740, 4¾ hours). The Rameswaram–Kanyakumari Express leaves at 8.45pm Monday, Thursday and Saturday, reaching Kanyakumari (sleeper/3AC ₹275/710) at 4.05am.

Bus 1 (₹5) shuttles between the bus stand and East Car St. Autorickshaws into town from the bus stand or train station cost ₹50.

Kanyakumari (Cape Comorin)

☎04652 / POP 22,450

This is it, the end of India. There's a sense of accomplishment on making it to the tip of the subcontinent's 'V', past the final dramatic flourish of the Western Ghats and the green fields, glinting rice paddies and slow-looping wind turbines of India's deep south. Kanyakumari can feel surreal; at certain times of year you'll see the sun set and the moon rise over three seas (Bay of Bengal, Arabian Sea, Indian Ocean) simultaneously. The Temple of the Virgin Sea Goddess, Swami Vivekananda's legacy and the 'Land's End' symbolism draw crowds of pilgrims and tourists to Kanyakumari, but it remains a small-scale, refreshing respite from the hectic Indian road.

👁 Sights

Kumari Amman Temple HINDU TEMPLE
(Sannathi St; ⏲4.30am-noon & 4-8.30pm) The legends say the *kanya* (virgin) goddess Kumari, a manifestation of the Great Goddess Devi, single-handedly conquered demons and secured freedom for the world. At this temple

WORTH A TRIP

DHANUSHKODI

Pamban Island's promontory stretches 22km southeast from Rameswaram, narrowing to a thin strip of dunes halfway along. Near the southeasternmost tip stands the ghost town of **Dhanushkodi**. Once a thriving port, Dhanushkodi was washed away by a monster cyclone in 1964. The shells of its train station, church, post office and other ruins stand among fishers' shacks; Adam's Bridge (Rama's Bridge), the chain of reefs, sandbanks and islets that almost connects India with Sri Lanka, stretches away to the east. The atmosphere is at its most magical at sunrise, with pilgrims performing *pujas* (offerings).

Autorickshaws charge ₹500 round-trip (including waiting time) to Moonram Chattram, 14km southeast of Rameswaram. Buses run here from Rameswaram's bus stand every 30 minutes (₹12). From Moonram Chattram to Dhanushkodi it's a 4km walk, or a ₹180 to ₹200 two-hour round trip in a truck or minibus which departs when it fills up with 16 customers (6am to 6pm). You can also hire an entire bus/jeep (₹1500 to ₹2000 return). It's tempting to swim, but beware of strong rips.

At the time of writing, a new tarmac road traversing the once-wild dunes from Moonram Chattram to Dhanushkodi had been completed but not inaugurated. Visiting arrangements may change, and there are concerns that easy road access will ruin the ghost town's spectacularly secluded appeal.

Kanyakumari (Cape Comorin)

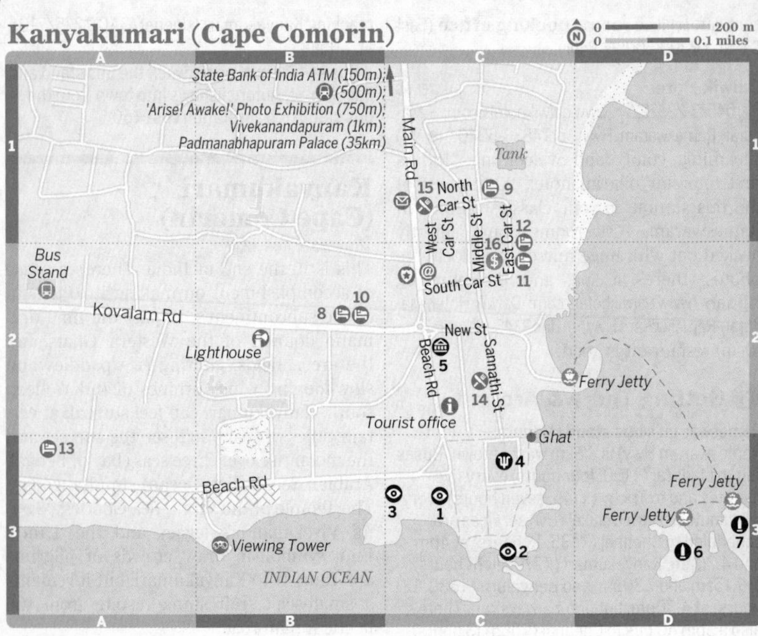

Kanyakumari (Cape Comorin)

Sights
1 Gandhi Memorial ... C3
2 Ghat ... C3
3 Kamaraj Memorial ... C3
4 Kumari Amman Temple ... C3
5 Swami Vivekananda Wandering Monk Exhibition ... C2
6 Thiruvalluvar Statue ... D3
7 Vivekananda Memorial ... D3

Sleeping
8 Hotel Narmadha ... B2
9 Hotel Sivamurugan ... C1
10 Hotel Tri Sea ... B2
11 Lakshmi Tourist Home ... C2
12 Seashore Hotel ... C2
13 Sparsa Resort ... A3

Eating
Auroma ... (see 13)
14 Hotel Anapoorna ... C2
15 Sangam Restaurant ... C1
Seashore Hotel ... (see 12)

Information
16 South Indian Bank ATM ... C2

on the tip of the subcontinent, pilgrims give her thanks in an intimately spaced, beautifully decorated temple, where the crash of waves from three seas can be heard beyond the twilight glow of oil fires clutched in vulva-shaped votive candles (referencing the sacred femininity of the goddess).

It's said that the temple's east-facing door stays locked to prevent the shimmer of the goddess' diamond nose-stud leading ships astray. From the main north-side gate, you'll be asked for a ₹10 donation to enter the 18th-century inner precinct, where men must remove their shirts, and cameras are forbidden.

The shoreline around the temple has a couple of tiny beaches, and bathing **ghats** where worshippers immerse themselves before visiting the temple. The *mandapa* just south of the temple is popular for sunset-watching and daytime shade.

Vivekananda Memorial MONUMENT
(₹20; 7.45am-4pm) Four hundred metres offshore is the rock where famous Hindu apostle Swami Vivekananda meditated from 25 to 27 December 1892, and decided to take his moral message beyond India's shores. A two-*mandapa* 1970 memorial to Vivekananda reflects temple architectural styles from

across India. The lower *mandapa* contains what's believed to be goddess Kumari's footprint. With the constant tourist crowds this brings, Vivekananda would no doubt choose somewhere else to meditate today. Ferries shuttle out to the rock (₹34 return).

Thiruvalluvar Statue MONUMENT
(⏲7.45am-4pm) FREE Looking like an Indian Colossus of Rhodes, the towering statue on the smaller island next to the Vivekananda Memorial is of the ancient Tamil poet Thiruvalluvar. The work of more than 5000 sculptors, it was erected in 2000 and honours the poet's 133-chapter work Thirukural – hence its height of exactly 133ft (40.5m). Tides permitting, Vivekananda Memorial ferries (₹34 return) continue to Thiruvalluvar.

Swami Vivekananda Wandering Monk Exhibition MUSEUM
(Beach Rd; ₹10; ⏲8am-noon & 4-8pm) In lovely leafy grounds, this excellent exhibition details Swami Vivekananda's wisdom, sayings and encounters with the mighty and the lowly during his five years as a wandering monk around India from 1888 to 1893. Tickets also cover the Vivekananda-inspired 'Arise! Awake!' exhibition in Vivekanandapuram, 1km north of town.

Gandhi Memorial MEMORIAL, MONUMENT
(Beach Rd; ⏲7am-7pm) FREE Poignantly placed at the end of the nation that Gandhi fathered, this cream-coloured memorial is designed in the form of an Odishan (Orissan) temple embellished by Hindu, Christian and Muslim architects. The central plinth stored some of the Mahatma's ashes before they were immersed in the sea; each year, on Gandhi's birthday (2 October), the sun's rays fall on the stone. The tower is also a popular sunset-gazing spot.

Kamaraj Memorial MEMORIAL, MONUMENT
(Beach Rd; ⏲7am-7pm) FREE This memorial near the shoreline commemorates K Kamaraj, the 'Gandhi of the South'. One of the most powerful and respected politicians of post-Independence India, Kamaraj held the chief ministership of both Madras State and its successor, Tamil Nadu. The dusty photos inside have English-language captions.

Vivekanandapuram ASHRAM
(☎04652-247012; www.vivekanandakendra.org; Vivekanandapuram; ⏲9am-8pm) Just 1km north of Kanyakumari, this peaceful ashram (offering a variety of yoga retreats) is the headquarters of spiritual organisation **Vivekananda Kendra**, devoted to carrying out Vivekananda's teachings. Its Vivekananda-focused **'Arise! Awake!'** (₹10; ⏲9am-1pm & 4-8pm Wed-Mon, 9am-1pm Tue) exhibition is worth a visit, and you can stroll to the sea past a beautiful lotus-pool-lined **memorial** to the swami.

Sleeping

Hotel Narmadha HOTEL $
(☎04652-246365; Kovalam Rd; r ₹500-700) This long, colourful concrete block conceals friendly staff, a back-up generator and a range of budget rooms, some of them cleaner and with less grim bathrooms than others. The cheapest are bucket-water only, but the ₹700 sea-view doubles with spearmint-stripe sheets are good value.

Lakshmi Tourist Home HOTEL $
(☎04652-246333; East Car St; r ₹1000, with AC ₹1500) Simple but well-kept, this relatively helpful family hotel is a decent town-centre deal. The better (pricier) rooms come with sea views and hot water, but most are neat and clean.

Hotel Tri Sea HOTEL $$
(☎04652-246586; www.hoteltrisea.in; Kovalam Rd; r ₹1170-2220, with AC ₹2340-2580; ❄📶🏊) You can't miss the high-rise Tri Sea, whose sea-view rooms are spacious, spotless and airy, with particularly hectic colour schemes. Reception is efficient and the rooftop pool, sunrise/sunset-viewing platforms and free in-room wi-fi are welcome bonuses.

Hotel Sivamurugan HOTEL $$
(☎04652-246862; www.hotelsivamurugan.com; 2/93 North Car St; r ₹1375, with AC ₹2280-2740; ❄📶) A welcoming, well-appointed hotel, with spacious, spotless, marble-floored rooms and lobby-only wi-fi. 'Super-deluxes' have sea glimpses past a couple of buildings. Rates stay fixed year-round (a novelty for Kanyakumari) and there's 24-hour hot water.

Sparsa Resort RESORT $$$
(☎04652-247041; www.sparsaresorts.com; 6/112B Beach Rd; r incl breakfast ₹4800-7200; ❄📶🏊) Away from the temple frenzy on the west edge of town, elegant Sparsa is a good few notches above Kanyakumari's other hotels. Fresh, orange-walled rooms with low darkwood beds, lounge chairs and mood-lighting make for a contemporary-oriental vibe, and there's a lovely pool surrounded by palms,

as well as good Indian cooking at **Auroma** (mains ₹150-400; ⏲7-10am, noon-3pm, 7-11pm).

Seashore Hotel HOTEL $$$
(☎04652-246704; www.theseashorehotel.com; East Car St; r ₹4140-7800; ❄📶) The fanciest town-centre hotel has shiny, roomy chambers with golden curtains and cushions, glassed-in showers and kettles. It's lost its original sparkle, but all rooms except the cheapest offer panoramic sea views, and the 7th-floor restaurant is one of Kanyakumari's best.

Eating

Hotel Anapoorna INDIAN $
(Sannathi St; mains ₹110-150, thalis ₹120-180; ⏲7am-9.30pm) A popular pan-Indian budget spot serving breakfast *idlis,* filter coffee and South Indian thalis alongside curries and biryanis, in a clean, friendly setting.

Seashore Hotel MULTICUISINE $$
(www.theseashorehotel.com; East Car St; mains ₹210-320; ⏲7-10am & 12.30-10pm) Amazingly, this spruced-up 7th-floor hotel restaurant is the only one in Kanyakumari with a proper sea view. There's great grilled fish and plenty of Indian veg and nonveg choices, plus the odd Continental creation. Service is spot-on and it's a good breakfast bet (buffet ₹270).

Sangam Restaurant INDIAN $$
(Main Rd; mains ₹95-300, thalis ₹100-135; ⏲7am-10.30pm) It's as if the Sangam started in Kashmir, trekked south across India, and stopped here to offer tasty veg and nonveg picks from every province along the way. The seats are soft and the food is good.

Information

Tourist office (☎04652-246276; Beach Rd; ⏲10am-5.30pm Mon-Fri)

Getting There & Away

BUS

Kanyakumari's sedate **bus stand** (Kovalam Rd) is a 10-minute walk west of the centre. Most comfortable are the 'Ultra Deluxe' (UD) buses.

TRAIN

The train station is 800m north of Kanyakumari's centre. One daily northbound train, the Kanyakumari Express, departs at 5.20pm for Chennai (sleeper/3AC/2AC/1AC ₹415/1095/1555/2630, 13½ hours) via Madurai (₹210/540/740/1235, 4½ hours) and Trichy (₹275/710/995/1670, seven hours). Two daily express trains depart at 6.40am and 10.30am for Trivandrum (sleeper/3AC/2AC ₹140/490/695, 2¼ hours), continuing to Kollam (Quilon; ₹140/490/695, 3½ hours) and Ernakulam (Kochi; ₹205/545/775, seven hours). More trains go from Nagercoil Junction, 20km northwest of Kanyakumari.

For real train buffs, the Vivek Express runs to Dibrugarh (Assam), 4236km and 80 hours – India's longest single train ride. It departs Kanyakumari at 11pm Thursday (₹1085/2830/4265).

THE WESTERN GHATS

Welcome to the lush Western Ghats, some of the most welcome heat relief in India. Rising like an impassable bulwark of evergreen and deciduous tangle from north of Mumbai to the tip of Tamil Nadu, the World Heritage–listed Ghats (with an average elevation of 915m) contain 27% of India's flowering plants and an incredible array of endemic wildlife. In Tamil Nadu they rise to over 2000m in the Palani Hills around Kodaikanal and the Nilgiris around Ooty. British influence lingers a little stronger up in these hills, where colonists built 'hill stations' to escape the sweltering plains and covered slopes in neatly trimmed tea plantations. It's not just the air and (relative) lack of pollution that's

BUSES FROM KANYAKUMARI

DESTINATION	FARE (₹)	TIME (HR)	DEPARTURES
Bengaluru (UD)	635	12-14	4.45pm, 5.30pm
Chennai (UD)	530	12-14	8 daily
Kodaikanal (UD)	310	10	8.15pm
Kovalam	120	3	6am, 2pm
Madurai	100, UD 210	8	9 daily; UD 2pm, 3pm
Rameswaram	250	8	7.30am, 7pm
Trivandrum	75-80	2½	9 daily

OFF THE BEATEN TRACK

PADMANABHAPURAM PALACE

With a forest's worth of intricately carved rosewood ceilings and polished-teak beams, labyrinthine **Padmanabhapuram Palace** (☎04651-250255; Padmanabhapuram; Indian/foreigner ₹35/300, camera/video ₹50/2000; ⏰9am-1pm & 2-4.30pm Tue-Sun), 35km northwest of Kanyakumari near the Kerala border, is considered the finest example of traditional Keralan architecture today. Asia's largest wooden palace complex, it was once capital of Travancore, an unstable princely state taking in parts of both Tamil Nadu and Kerala. Under successive rulers it expanded into a magnificent conglomeration of corridors, courtyards, gabled roofs and 14 palaces. The oldest sections date to 1550.

Direct buses leave from Kanyakumari's bus stand at 7.30am, 10.45am, 1.30pm and 3.20pm (₹25, two hours); buses also run every 20 minutes from Kanyakumari to Thuckalay (₹25), from where it's an autorickshaw ride or 15-minute walk to the palace. Return taxis from Kanyakumari cost ₹1200.

From Trivandrum (Thiruvananthapuram), take any bus towards Kanyakumari (₹70, three hours, four daily) and get off at Thuckalay. The Kerala Tourist Development Corporation (KTDC; p945) runs full-day Kanyakumari tours from Trivandrum covering Padmanabhapuram (₹700; minimum four people).

refreshing – there's a certain acceptance of quirkiness and eccentricity here. Expect organic farms, handlebar-moustached trekking guides and leopard-print earmuffs.

Kodaikanal (Kodai)

☎04542 / POP 36,500 / ELEV 2100M

There are few more refreshing Tamil Nadu moments than leaving the heat-soaked plains for the sharp pinch of a Kodaikanal night or morning. This misty hill station, 120km northwest of Madurai in the protected Palani Hills, is more relaxed and intimate than its big sister Ooty (Kodai is the 'Princess of Hill Stations', Ooty the Queen). It's not all cold either; days feel more like deep spring than early winter.

Centred on a beautiful star-shaped lake, Kodai rambles up and down hillsides with patches of *shola* (virgin forest), unique to South India's Western Ghats, and evergreen broadleaf trees like magnolia, mahogany, myrtle and rhododendron. Another plant speciality is the *kurinji* shrub, whose lilac-blue blossoms appear every 12 years (next due 2018).

Kodai is popular with honeymooners and groups, who flock to its spectacular viewpoints and waterfalls. The renowned Kodaikanal International School provides some cosmopolitan flair. Visit midweek for peace and quiet.

Sights & Activities

Sacred Heart Natural Science Museum MUSEUM

(Kodaikanal Museum; Sacred Heart College, Law's Ghat Rd; adult/child ₹20/10, camera ₹20; ⏰9am-6pm) In the grounds of a former Jesuit seminary 4km downhill east of town, this museum has a ghoulishly intriguing miscellany of flora and fauna put together over more than 100 years by priests and trainees. Displays range over bottled snakes, human embryos (!), giant moths and stuffed animal carcasses. You can also see pressed famous *kurinji* flowers *(Strobilanthes kunthiana)*.

Parks & Viewpoints

Several natural beauty spots around Kodai (crowded with souvenir and snack stalls) are very popular with Indian tourists. They're best visited by taxi; drivers offer three-hour 12-stop tours for ₹1500 to ₹1800. On clear days, **Green Valley View** (⏰dawn-dusk) FREE, 6km from the centre), **Pillar Rocks** (₹20; ⏰9am-4pm) FREE, 7km from the centre, and less-visited **Moir's Point** (₹10; ⏰10am-5pm), 13km from the centre, all along the same road west of town, have spectacular views to the plains below.

Bryant Park PARK

(off Lake Rd; adult/child ₹30/15, camera/video ₹50/100; ⏰9am-6pm) Landscaped and stocked by the British officer after whom it's named, pretty Bryant Park is usually full of tourists and canoodling couples.

Berijam Lake LAKE

(⏰9am-3pm) FREE Visiting forest-fringed Berijam Lake, 21km southwest of Kodaikanal, requires a Forest Department permit. Taxi drivers will organise this, if asked the day before, and do half-day 'forest tours' to Berijam, via other lookouts, for ₹1800.

Kodaikanal (Kodai)

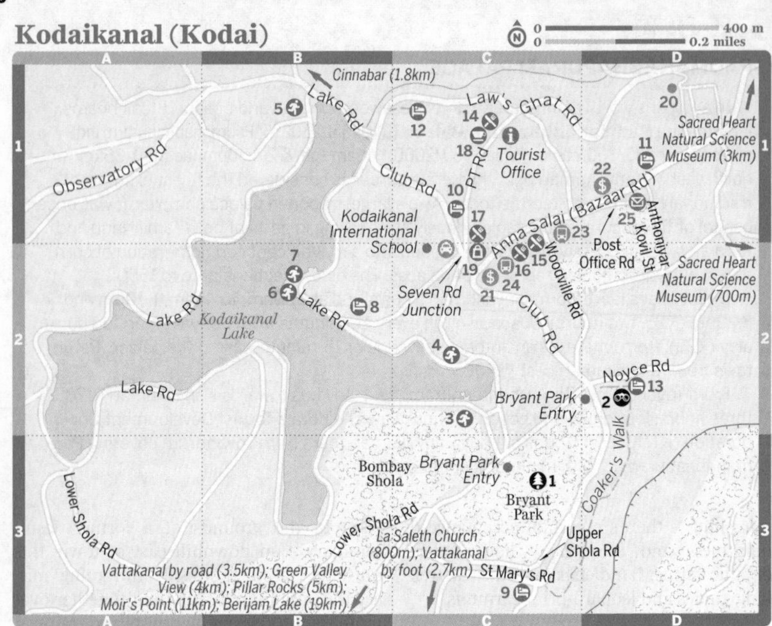

Walking

The 5km **Kodaikanal Lake circuit** is lovely in the early morning before the crowds roll in. A walk along Lower Shola Rd takes you through the **Bombay Shola**, the nearest surviving patch of *shola* to central Kodai.

Officially, you're free to hike anywhere within 19km of Kodai, but not beyond. Forest Department permits for more serious trekking routes in protected areas *may* be obtained with time, patience and luck; if you fancy trying, contact Kodai's **District Forest Office** (04542-241287; Muthaliarpuram; 10am-5.45pm Mon-Fri). The tourist office (p1073) and guesthouses like Greenlands Youth Hostel (p1070) can put you in touch with local guides, who help with permits and offer interesting off-road routes (₹600 to ₹1000 per half-day). The tourist office stocks a leaflet outlining 17 local treks.

A good trek, if you can organise it, is the two-day Kodai–Munnar route into Kerala via Top Station (involving some bus/rickshaw transport). Guides charge ₹5000 per person.

Coaker's Walk VIEWPOINT

(₹10; 7am-7pm) Assuming it isn't cloaked in opaque mist, the views from paved Coaker's Walk are beautiful, all the way down to the plains 2000m below. The stroll takes five minutes.

Trails & Tracks TREKKING

(9965524279; thenaturetrails@gmail.com; day walk per person per hr ₹200) A reliable, well-established trekking outfit run by very experienced local guide Vijay Kumar, offering day walks, longer hikes and overnight treks.

Boating & Cycling

If you're sappy in love like a bad Bollywood song, the thing to do in Kodai is rent a pedal boat, rowboat or Kashmiri *shikara* ('honeymoon boat') from the **Kodaikanal Boat & Rowing Club** (Lake Rd; per 30min pedal boat/rowboat ₹90/170, shikara incl boatman ₹480; 9am-6pm) or **TTDC Boat House** (Lake Rd; per hour pedal boat ₹180, rowboat/shikara incl boatman ₹640/970; 9am-5.30pm).

Bicycle-rental (per hour ₹50) stands are dotted around the lake.

Sleeping

Some hotels hike prices by up to 100% during the 'season' (April to June). There are some gorgeous heritage places, and good-value midrange options if you can live without colonial-era ambience. Most hotels have a 9am or 10am checkout April to June.

Greenlands Youth Hostel HOSTEL $

(04542-240899; www.greenlandskodaikanal.com; St Mary's Rd; dm ₹400, d ₹900-2500;)

Kodaikanal (Kodai)

This long-running, sociable budget favourite has a pretty garden and wonderful views. Accommodation is very bare and basic and hot water runs only from 8am to 10am. Dorms may be available, but are aimed at groups, while newer, comfier 'superdeluxes' and 'suites' have colourful decor and balconies.

Sri Vignesh Guest House GUESTHOUSE $
(☎9094972524; umaarkrishnan@gmail.com; Lake Rd; r ₹700-1200) Up a steep driveway, surrounded by neat flowery gardens with a swing, this simple but characterful Raj-era home is run by a friendly local couple, who welcome 'peaceful' guests (no packs of boys!). Rooms are clean and very basic; hot water until noon.

Snooze Inn HOTEL $
(☎04542-240837; www.jayarajgroup.com; Anna Salai; dm ₹330, r ₹880-1045;) Rooms don't have quite as much character as the exterior suggests, but this is a decent-value budget choice sporting clean bathrooms and plenty of blankets. There's also a 12-bed dorm with lockers and one shared bathroom.

Cinnabar HOMESTAY $$
(☎9842145220; www.cinnabar.in; Chettiar Rd; r incl half-board ₹6000;) Cinnabar's two elegant yet homey rooms offer a blissful escape, with 24-hour hot water, tea/coffee kits, glassed-in showers and lovely wooden floors and ceilings. Homemade cheese, bread, granola, jams and 'world' cuisine come courtesy of the clued-up owners, who recommend local hikes and source all ingredients for their organic fruit-and-veg garden out front. It's 2km north of town.

Villa Retreat HOTEL $$
(☎04542-240940; www.villaretreat.com; Club Rd; r incl breakfast ₹4740-7900;) Take in the fantastic Coaker's Walk views from your garden breakfast table at this lovely old stone-built hotel, right next to the walk's northern end. It's a friendly place with comfy, good-sized rooms and, when it's cold, a roaring fire in the dining room. Prices are steep, but service is attentive.

Hilltop Towers HOTEL $$
(☎04542-240413; www.hilltopgroup.in; Club Rd; r incl breakfast ₹2860-3440;) Although it's bland on the outside, rustic flourishes like polished-teak floors, plus keen staff, in-room tea/coffee sets and a central location make the Hilltop a good-value midranger.

★**Carlton** HERITAGE HOTEL $$$
(☎04542-240056; www.carlton-kodaikanal.com; Lake Rd; incl half-board s ₹10,350-11,630, d ₹11,820-12,880, cottage ₹17,430;) The cream of Kodai's hotels is a magnificent five-star colonial-era mansion overlooking the lake. Rooms are spacious with extra-comfy beds and, for some, huge private balconies. The grounds and common areas get the old hill-station ambience spot on: open-stone walls, billiards, evening bingo, fireplaces, a hot tub, and a bar that immediately makes you want to demand a Scotch.

WORTH A TRIP

DOLPHIN'S NOSE WALK

This is a lovely walk of 4.5km (each way) from central Kodai, passing through budget-traveller hang-out Vattakanal to reach the Dolphin's Nose, a narrow rock lookout overhanging a precipitous drop. You might spot gaur (bison) or giant squirrels in the forested bits.

From the south end of Coaker's Walk, follow St Mary's Rd west then southwest, passing 19th-century La Saleth Church after 1.2km. At a fork 400m after the church, go left downhill on what quickly becomes an unpaved track passing through the Pambar Shola forest. After 450m you emerge on a bridge above some falls. Across the bridge, stalls sell fruit, tea, coffee, bread omelettes and roasted corn with lime and masala. Follow the road 1km downhill, with panoramas opening up as you go, to Vattakanal village. Take the steep path down past Altaf's Cafe and in 15 minutes you'll reach the Dolphin's Nose.

Vattakanal

Little Vattakanal village ('Vatta'), 4.5km southwest of Kodai, is a wonderful rural retreat for budget travellers. It's very popular, particularly with groups of Indian and Israeli travellers, and there's a mellow party vibe when things gets busy.

Altaf's Cafe GUESTHOUSE $
(☎9487120846; www.altafscafe.com; Vattakanal; r ₹1200-2000) Popular little Middle Eastern–Italian Altaf's Cafe runs a few sizeable doubles and three-bed rooms for six people (sometimes more!) with private bathroom, scattered across Vattakanal's hillside.

Kodai Heaven GUESTHOUSE $$
(☎9865207207; www.kodaiheaven.com; 6 Dolphin's Nose Rd, Vattakanal; r ₹2000-3200; Wi-Fi) Simple hillside sharing rooms for two to six people, with splashes of colour and fabulous mountain views.

Eating & Drinking

PT Rd is the place for restaurants. Many Kodai eateries have organic and/or international tendencies, and you'll enjoy locally produced cheese, bread, coffee and avocados.

Pastry Corner BAKERY $
(3 Maratta Shopping Complex, Anna Salai; ⏲10.30am-2pm & 3-5.30pm) Pick up oven-fresh muffins, croissants, cakes, cinnamon swirls and sandwiches at this popular bakery, or squeeze on to the benches with a cuppa.

Tava INDIAN $
(PT Rd; mains ₹70-140; ⏲11.30am-8.45pm Thu-Tue) Cheap, fast and clean, pure-veg Tava has a wide all-Indian menu; try the spicy, cauliflower-stuffed *gobi paratha* or *sev puri* (crisp, puffy fried bread with potato and chutney).

Ten Degrees MULTICUISINE $$
(PT Rd; mains ₹200-360; ⏲noon-10pm) Honey-coloured wood and monochrome Kodai photos set the tone for tasty, elegantly prepared Indian and Continental food at this lively new PT Rd arrival. It does mouth-meltingly spicy wraps, homemade-bread sandwiches, burgers, salads, sizzlers, egg-based breakfasts and drinks served in jars.

Altaf's Cafe MULTICUISINE $$
(☎9487120846; www.altafscafe.com; Vattakanal; dishes ₹70-200; ⏲8am-8.30pm) This open-sided cafe whips up soulful Italian, Indian and Middle Eastern dishes including breakfasts and *sabich* (Israeli aubergine-and-egg pita sandwiches), plus teas, coffees, juices and lassis, for hungry travellers at Vattakanal.

Hotel Astoria INDIAN $$
(Anna Salai; mains ₹110-150, thalis ₹115-155; ⏲7am-10pm) This pure-veg restaurant is always packed with locals and tourists, especially at lunchtime when it serves fantastic all-you-can-eat thalis.

Cloud Street MULTICUISINE $$$
(www.cloudstreetcafe.com; PT Rd; mains ₹260-550; ⏲12.30-9pm Wed-Mon; Wi-Fi) Why yes, that is a real Italian-style wood-fire pizza oven. And yes, that's hummus and falafel on the menu, along with oven-baked pasta and homemade cakes. It's all great food in a simple, relaxed, family-run setting with scattered candles and a crackling fire on cold nights. Live music every other Saturday.

Carlton MULTICUISINE $$$
(Lake Rd; buffet ₹950; ⏲7.30-10.30am, 1-3pm & 7.30-10.30pm) Definitely the place to come for a splash-out buffet-dinner fill-up: a huge variety of excellent Indian and Continental dishes in limitless quantity. Lunch is à la carte.

★ **Cafe Cariappa** CAFE
(www.facebook.com/cafecariappa; PT Rd; coffees ₹80-100; ⏲10.30am-6.30pm Tue-Sun; 📶) A caffeine addict's dream, this rustic-chic wood-panelled shoe-box of a cafe crafts fantastic brews from its own locally grown organic coffee. It also does homemade carrot cake, crepes, sandwiches and fresh juices, and sells Kodai-made cheeses.

Shopping

Shops and stalls all over town sell homemade chocolates, spices, natural oils and handicrafts. Some also reflect a low-key but long-term commitment to social justice.

Re Shop ARTS & CRAFTS
(www.facebook.com/bluemangotrust; Seven Rd Junction; ⏲10am-7pm Mon-Sat) Stylish jewellery, fabrics, cards and more, at reasonable prices, made by and benefiting marginalised village women around Tamil Nadu.

Information

Tourist Office (☎04542-241675; PT Rd; ⏲10am-5.30pm Mon-Fri) Doesn't look too promising but it's helpful enough.

Getting There & Away

BUS

For most destinations, it's quickest and easiest to take a bus from Kodai's **bus stand** (Anna Salai).

Raja's Tours & Travels (http://rajastours.com; Anna Salai; ⏲8am-9pm) Runs 20-seat minibuses with push-back seats to Ooty (₹500, eight hours, 7.30pm), plus overnight AC sleeper and semisleeper buses to Chennai (₹650 to ₹950, 12 hours, 6pm and 6.30pm) and Bengaluru (₹650 to ₹850, 12 hours, 6.30pm).

TRAIN

The nearest train station is Kodai Rd, down in the plains 80km east of Kodaikanal. There are four daily trains to/from Chennai Egmore including the overnight Pandian Express (sleeper/3AC/2AC/1AC ₹295/765/1075/1815, 7½ hours), departing Chennai at 9.20pm and departing Kodai Rd northbound at 9.10pm. Kodai's post office has a **train booking office** (Post Office, Post Office Rd; ⏲9am-4pm Mon-Fri, to 2pm Sat).

Direct buses from Kodaikanal to Kodai Rd leave daily at 10.20am and 4.25pm (₹55, three hours); there are also plenty of buses between the train station and Batlagundu, on the Kodai–Madurai bus route. Taxis to/from the station cost ₹1200.

Getting Around

Central Kodaikanal is compact and easily walkable. There are no autorickshaws (believe it or not), but plenty of taxis. The minimum charge is ₹150 for up to 3km; to/from Vattakanal costs ₹300.

Around Kodaikanal

There are some lovely country retreats in the **Palani Hills** below Kodaikanal.

Elephant Valley FARMSTAY **$$**
(☎7867004398; www.duneecogroup.com; Ganesh Puram, Pethupari; r incl breakfast ₹4010-8750; 📶) Deep in the valley 22km northeast of Kodaikanal, off the Kodaikanal–Palani Rd, this ecofriendly French-run retreat sprawls across 48 hectares of mountain jungle and organic farm. Elephants, peacocks and bison wander through, and comfy local-material cottages, including a tree house, sit either side of a river. The French-Indian restaurant does wonderful meals packed with garden-fresh veg, and home-grown coffee.

Coimbatore

☎0422 / POP 1.05 MILLION

This big business and junction city – Tamil Nadu's second largest, often known as the Manchester of India for its textile industry – is friendly enough and increasingly cosmopolitan, but the lack of interesting sights means that for most travellers it's just a stepping stone towards Ooty or Kerala. There

GOVERNMENT BUSES FROM KODAIKANAL (KODAI)

DESTINATION	FARE (₹)	TIME (HR)	DEPARTURES
Bengaluru	560-760	12	5.30pm, 6pm
Chennai	480	12	6.30pm
Coimbatore	130	6	8.30am, 4.30pm
Madurai	65	4	15 daily
Trichy	120	6	1.30pm, 3.30pm, 5.40pm, 6pm

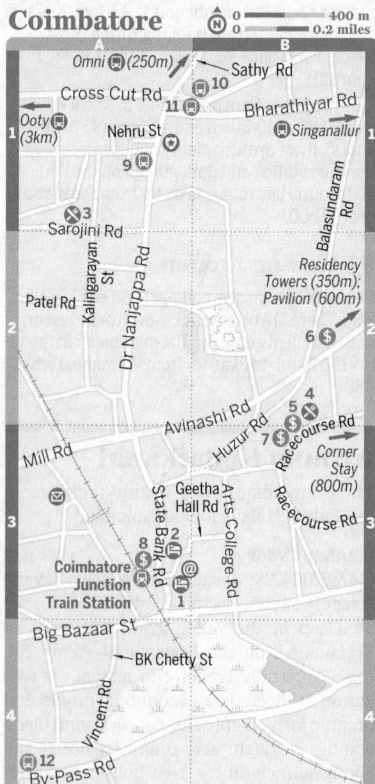

Coimbatore

Sleeping

1 Legend's Inn ... A3
2 Sree Subbu ... A3

Eating

3 Junior Kuppanna ... A1
4 On The Go ... B2

Information

5 HSBC ATM ... B2
6 State Bank of India ATM ... B2
7 State Bank of India ATM ... B3
8 State Bank of India ATM ... A3

Transport

9 Central Bus Stand ... A1
10 SETC Bus Stand ... B1
11 Town Bus Stand ... A1
12 Ukkadam Bus Stand ... A4

are plenty of accommodation and eating options if you're staying overnight.

Sleeping

Sree Subbu HOTEL $

(0422-2300006; Geetha Hall Rd; s/d ₹550/660) If price is the priority, Sree Subbu is a clean-enough, nonair-con budget spot.

Corner Stay GUESTHOUSE $$

(9842220742; www.cornerstay.in; 4/1 Abdul Rahim Rd, off Racecourse Rd; r ₹2000-3000;) On a quiet Racecourse-area lane, this homey guesthouse offers three impeccable, tastefully styled rooms with a communal lounge and balcony. Two share a kitchen, the other has its own, and there are home-cooked meals. It's 2km northeast of the train station.

Legend's Inn HOTEL $$

(0422-4350000; www.legendsinn.com; Geetha Hall Rd; r ₹1460, s/d with AC ₹1820/2070;) One of at least 10 places on this lane opposite the train station, this is a good-value midrange choice, with spacious, clean, comfortable rooms, 24-hour checkout and helpful receptionists. It gets busy: book ahead.

Residency Towers HOTEL $$$

(0422-2241414; www.theresidency.com; 1076 Avinashi Rd; s/d incl breakfast from ₹6800/7600;) Opening through a soaring lobby, the Residency is a top choice for its professional staff, well-equipped rooms, swimming pool, and excellent eating and drinking options, including great-value buffet meals at the **Pavilion** (www.theresidency.com; Residency Towers, 1076 Avinashi Rd; buffet breakfast/lunch/dinner ₹475/820/930; 7-10am, 12.30-3pm & 7pm-midnight). Check discounts online.

Eating

Junior Kuppanna SOUTH INDIAN $$

(0422-235773; www.hoteljuniorkuppanna.com; 177 Sarojini Rd, Ram Nagar; mains ₹160-200, thalis ₹170; noon-4pm & 6.30-11pm) Your favourite South Indian thalis come piled on to banana leaves with traditional flourish, and starving carnivores will love the long menu of famously nonveg southern specialities, all from a perfectly spotless kitchen. Three branches across town.

On The Go MULTICUISINE $$$

(0422-4520116; www.onthegocbe.com; 167 Racecourse Rd; mains ₹275-575; 12.30-2.45pm & 7-10.30pm) Colourful, contemporary, and filled with cartoons and turquoise sofas, this is a great place for tasty (if pricey) global fare from Italian and Middle Eastern to Sri Lankan and North Indian.

OFF THE BEATEN TRACK

ANAMALAI TIGER RESERVE

Anamalai Tiger Reserve (Indira Gandhi Wildlife Sanctuary & National Park; ₹30, camera/video ₹80/200; ⏲6am-noon & 3-5pm) is a 950-sq-km reserve of tropical jungle, *shola* forest and grassland rising to 2400m and spilling over the Western Ghats into Kerala between Kodaikanal and Coimbatore. A tiger reserve since 2007, it's home to all kinds of exotic endemic wildlife, much of it rare and endangered – including leopards and around 30 elusive tigers, plus lion-tailed macaques, peacocks, langurs, crocodiles, spotted deer and elephants.

The reserve's **Reception & Interpretation Centre** (☎04259-238360; Topslip; ⏲7am-6pm) at Topslip (35km southwest of Pollachi) runs official 45-minute **minibus safaris** (Topslip; per person from ₹130; ⏲7-10am & 3-5pm) and **guided treks** (Topslip; 2hr trek per person ₹500; ⏲7am-2pm). Topslip has simple **Forest Department accommodation** (☎bookings 04259-238360; Topslip; r ₹1500-4000); book ahead through Pollachi's **District Forest Office** (☎04259-225356, accommodation bookings 04259-238360; www.forests.tn.nic.in; 365/1 Meenkarai Rd, Pollachi; ⏲10am-5.45pm Mon-Fri).

Tiny tea-plantation town **Valparai**, on the reserve's fringes 65km south from Pollachi, makes a much more comfortable Anamalai base. Wonderful **Sinna Dorai's Bungalow** (☎7094739309; www.sinnadorai.com; Valparai; incl full-board s ₹7650-8650, d ₹9750-11,000; 📶) is exquisitely located on a rambling tea estate here, offering guided walks, after-dark wildlife-spotting drives, homemade meals and six huge rooms bursting with local early-20th-century history.

Buses connect Pollachi with Topslip (₹35, two hours, hourly) and Valparai (₹30, three hours, half-hourly). Buses to Pollachi (₹17 to ₹23, one hour, every five minutes) run from Coimbatore's Ukkadam Bus Stand, which also has one daily service to Valparai (₹65, four hours, 3pm). From Kodaikanal, buses serve Pollachi (₹110, six hours) at 8.30am and 4.30pm.

ℹ Getting There & Away

AIR

The airport is 10km east of town. Direct daily flights to domestic destinations include Bengaluru, Chennai, Delhi, Hyderabad and Mumbai on **Air India** (www.airindia.in), **IndiGo** (www.goindigo.in), **Jet Airways** (www.jetairways.com) or **SpiceJet** (www.spicejet.com). **SilkAir** (www.silkair.com) flies four times weekly to/from Singapore.

BUS

The **Ooty Bus Stand** (New Bus Stand; Mettupalayam (MTP) Rd), 5km northwest of the train station, has services to Ooty (₹53, four hours) via Mettupalayam (₹14 to ₹18, one hour) and Coonoor (₹40, three hours) every 10 minutes, plus half-hourly buses to Kotagiri (₹30, three hours), 28 buses daily to Mysuru (Mysore; ₹160 to ₹400, six hours) and 11 to Bengaluru (₹400 to ₹650, nine hours).

From **Singanallur Bus Stand** (Kamaraj Rd), 6km east of the centre, buses go to Trichy (₹116, five hours), Thanjavur (₹180, 7¼ hours) and Madurai (₹125, five hours) every 10 minutes. Bus 140 (₹11) shuttles between here and the **Town Bus Stand** (cnr Dr Nanjappa & Bharathiyar Rds), not to be confused with the **Central Bus Stand** (Dr Nanjappa Rd).

Ukkadam Bus Stand (NH Rd), 1.5km southwest of the train station, has buses to southern destinations including Pollachi (₹17 to ₹23, 1¼ hours, every five minutes), Kodaikanal (₹180, six hours, 10am) and Munnar (₹180, 6½ hours, 8.15am).

Express or superfast AC and Volvo government buses go from the **SETC Bus Stand** (Thiruvalluvar Bus Stand; Bharathiyar Rd).

Bengaluru ₹375 to ₹700, nine hours, 12 daily
Chennai ₹400 to ₹460, 11 hours, eight buses 5.30pm to 10.30pm
Ernakulam ₹170, 5½ hours, eight daily
Mysuru ₹160 to ₹400, six hours, 27 daily
Trivandrum ₹322, 10½ hours, seven daily

Private buses to destinations such as Bengaluru, Chennai, Ernakulam, Puducherry, Trichy and Trivandrum start from the **Omni Bus Stand** (Sathy Rd), 500m north of the Town Bus Stand, or from ticket-selling agencies on Sathy Rd.

TAXI

Taxis up to Ooty (three hours) cost ₹2500; Ooty buses often get so crowded that a taxi is worth considering.

TRAIN

Coimbatore Junction is on the main line between Chennai and Ernakulam (Kochi, Kerala), with at least 13 daily trains in each direction. The 5.15am Nilgiri Express to Mettupalayam (sleeper/2AC/3AC ₹170/535/740, one hour) connects with the miniature railway departure from Mettupalayam to Ooty at 7.10am. The whole trip to Ooty takes seven hours.

Getting Around

Buses 20A, 40, 41D or 44 (₹11) from the **Town Bus Stand** (p1075) drop you 1km from the airport. Taxis from the centre charge ₹300 to ₹400.

Many buses run between the train station and the **Town Bus Stand** (p1075). Autorickshaws charge ₹60 from the train station to the **Ukkadam Bus Station** (p1075), ₹80 to the **SETC** (p1075) or **Town Bus Stands** (p1075), and ₹150 to the **Ooty Bus Stand** (p1075).

Uber and Ola Cabs taxi apps work well here.

Around Coimbatore

The commercial town of **Mettupalayam**, 40km north of Coimbatore, is the starting point for the 7.10am miniature train to Ooty. If you need to stay the night, Mettupalayam has plenty of accommodation.

Coonoor

0423 / POP 45,490 / ELEV 1720M

Coonoor is one of the three Nilgiri hill stations – Ooty, Kotagiri and Coonoor – that sit high above the southern plains. Smaller and quieter than Ooty (20km northwest), it has some fantastic heritage hotels and guesthouses, from which you can do exactly the same things (hike, visit tea plantations, marvel at mountain views) you would do from bigger, busier Ooty. From upper Coonoor, 1km to 3km northeast (uphill) from the town centre, you can look down over a sea of red-tile rooftops to the slopes beyond and soak up the cool climate, quiet environment and beautiful scenery. But you get none of the above in lower (central) Coonoor, which is a bustling, honking mess.

Sights

The best way to see Coonoor's out-of-town sights is by autorickshaw (₹600) or taxi (₹800) tour.

Sim's Park PARK

(Upper Coonoor; adult/child ₹30/15, camera/video ₹50/100; 7am-6.30pm) Upper Coonoor's 12-hectare Sim's Park, established in 1874, is a peaceful oasis of sloping manicured lawns with more than 1000 plant species from several continents, including magnolia, tree ferns, roses and camellia. Kotagiri-bound buses drop you here.

Highfield Tea Estate PLANTATION

(Walker's Hill Rd; 8am-9pm) FREE This 50-year-old estate (2km northeast of upper Coonoor) is one of few working Nilgiri tea factories open to visitors. Guides jump in quickly, but you're perfectly welcome to watch the full tea-making process independently. You can also, of course, taste and buy.

Lamb's Rock VIEWPOINT

(Dolphin's Nose Rd; ₹10, camera/video ₹20/50; 8.30am-6.30pm) A favourite picnic spot in a patch of monkey-patrolled forest, Lamb's Rock has incredible views past glimmering tea and coffee plantations to the hazy plains below. It's 5km east of upper Coonoor – walkable, if you like.

Dolphin's Nose VIEWPOINT

(Dolphin's Nose Rd; ₹10, camera/video ₹20/50; 8.30am-6.30pm) About 10km west of town, this popular viewpoint exposes vast panoramas encompassing Catherine Falls (p1078) across the valley.

Sleeping & Eating

You'll need a rickshaw, car or great legs to reach Coonoor's best accommodation. Cheap South Indian restaurants cluster around the bus stand.

MAJOR TRAINS FROM COIMBATORE

DESTINATION	TRAIN NO & NAME	FARE (₹)	DURATION (HR)	DEPARTURE
Bengaluru	16525 Bangalore Exp	260/695/995 (B)	8½	10.55pm
Chennai Central	12676 Kovai Exp	180/660 (A)	7½	2.55pm
	22640 Chennai Exp	315/810/1140 (B)	7½	10.15pm
Ernakulam (Kochi)	12677 Ernakulam Exp	105/390 (A)	3¾	1.10pm
Madurai	16610 Nagercoil Exp	205/545 (C)	5½	8.30pm
Trivandrum	12695 Trivandrum Exp	285/730/1025 (B)	8½	11.10pm

Fares: (A) 2nd class/AC chair; (B) sleeper/3AC/2AC; (C) sleeper/3AC

THE NILGIRIS & THEIR TRIBES

The forest-clothed, waterfall-threaded **Nilgiris** (Blue Mountains) rise abruptly from the surrounding plains between the lowland towns of Mettupalayam (southeast) and Gudalur (northwest), ascended only by winding ghat roads and the famous Nilgiri Mountain Railway. The upland territory, a jumble of valleys and hills with more than 20 peaks above 2000m, is a botanist's dream, with over 2300 flowering plant species, although much of the native *shola* forest and grasslands have been displaced by tea, coffee, eucalyptus and cattle.

The Unesco-designated Nilgiri Biosphere Reserve is a larger, 5520-sq-km area that also includes parts of Kerala and Karnataka. One of the world's biodiversity hot spots, it contains several important tiger reserves, national parks and wildlife sanctuaries.

The Nilgiris' tribal inhabitants were left pretty much to themselves until the British arrived two centuries ago. Today, colonialism and migration have reduced many tribal cultures to the point of collapse, and some have assimilated to the point of invisibility. Others, however, continue at least a semitraditional lifestyle.

Best known, thanks to their proximity to Ooty, are the Toda (around 1500). Some still inhabit tiny villages *(munds)* of traditional barrel-shaped huts made of bamboo, cane and grass. Toda women style their hair in long, shoulder-length ringlets; both sexes wear distinctive black-and-red-embroidered shawls. Central to Toda life is the water buffalo, which provides milk and ghee. Traditionally, it is only at funerals that the strictly vegetarian Toda kill a buffalo, to accompany the deceased.

The 200,000-strong Badaga are thought to have migrated into the Nilgiris from Karnataka around 1600 AD. Their traditional dress is of white cloth with a border of narrow coloured stripes. They worship the mother goddess Hetti Amman, to whom their December/January Hettai Habba festival is dedicated.

The Kota, traditionally artisans, live in seven settlements in the Kotagiri area. They have adapted relatively well to modernity; a significant number hold government jobs.

The Kurumba, traditionally known for their sorcery, inhabit the thick forests of the south and are food-gatherers (particularly of wild honey), though many now work in agriculture. The Irula specialise in food gathering, too, and are botanical experts.

If you're interested in the Nilgiris' tribes, don't miss the **Tribal Research Centre Museum** (Muthorai Palada; Indian/foreigner ₹5/100; ⏲10am-1pm & 2-5pm Mon-Fri, hours vary), 10km southwest of Ooty. Organisations such as Kotagiri's **Keystone Foundation** (p1078) work to promote traditional crafts and activities.

YWCA Wyoming Guesthouse HERITAGE GUESTHOUSE **$**
(☎0423-2234426; http://ywcaagooty.com; Bedford; dm ₹220, s ₹600-720, d ₹1300) A ramshackle, 150-year-old gem, the good-value Wyoming is draughty and creaky but oozes colonial character with wooden terraces and serene town views through trees. Rooms are good and clean, with geysers, and simple meals are available on request.

★180° McIver HERITAGE HOTEL **$$**
(☎0423-2233323; http://serendipityo.com; Orange Grove Rd, Upper Coonoor; r incl breakfast ₹4560-7300; 📶) A classic 1900s British bungalow at the top of town has been transformed into something special. The six handsome, airy rooms sport antique furniture, working fireplaces and big fresh bathrooms. On-site restaurant **La Belle Vie** (mains ₹260-500; ⏲12.30-3.30pm & 7.30-10.30pm) has guests driving miles for its European-Indian food, and panoramas from the wraparound lawn (where you can dine) are fabulous.

Acres Wild FARMSTAY **$$**
(☎9443232621; www.acres-wild.com; 571 Upper Meanjee Estate, Kanni Mariamman Kovil St; r incl breakfast ₹3650-5460; 📶) 🍃 This beautifully positioned farm on Coonoor's southeast edge is sustainably run with solar heating, rainwater harvesting and cheese like you've never tasted in India from the milk of its own cows. The five large, stylish rooms, in three cottages, include kitchens and fireplaces. Your friendly Mumbaikar hosts are full of ideas for things to do away from the tourist crowds. Book ahead.

Gateway HERITAGE HOTEL **$$$**
(☎0423-2225400; https://gateway.tajhotels.com; Church Rd, Upper Coonoor; incl breakfast s ₹7120-14,930, d ₹7800-16,280; 📶) A colonial-era

priory turned gorgeous heritage hotel, the Taj-group Gateway has homey cream-coloured rooms immersed in greenery, most graced by working fireplaces. You get mountain views from those at the back. Evening bonfires are lit on the lawn, the good **Gateway All Day restaurant** (mains ₹400-600; ⌚7.30-10.30am, 12.30-3pm & 7.30-10.30pm) overlooks the gardens, and there's free yoga along with Keralan ayurvedic massages.

Shopping

Green Shop HANDICRAFTS, FOOD
(www.lastforest.in; Jograj Bldg, Bedford Circle; ⌚9.30am-7.30pm Mon-Sat) Beautiful fair-trade local tribal crafts, clothes, fabrics and notebooks, plus organic wild honey, nuts, chocolates, soaps and teas.

Getting There & Away

Coonoor's **bus stand** (Lower Coonoor) has services to/from Ooty (₹10, one hour) every 10 minutes. Buses to Kotagiri (₹12, 50 minutes) and Coimbatore (₹35, three hours) go every 30 minutes.

Coonoor is on the miniature train line between Mettupalayam (1st/2nd class ₹185/25, 2¼ to 3¼ hours) and Ooty (₹150/25, 1¼ hours), with three daily trains just to/from Ooty, as well as the daily Mettupalayam–Ooty–Mettupalayam service.

Taxis to/from Ooty cost ₹900.

Kotagiri

☎04266 / POP 28,200 / ELEV 1800M

The oldest and smallest of the three Nilgiri hill stations, Kotagiri lies 30km east of Ooty, beyond one of Tamil Nadu's highest passes. It's a quiet, unassuming place with a forgettable town centre – its appeal is the escape to red dirt tracks in the pines, the blue skies and the high green walls of the Nilgiris.

Sights

A half-day taxi tour encompassing **Catherine Falls** (Kotagiri–Mettupalayam Rd) and **Kodanad Viewpoint** (Kodanad; ⌚dawn-dusk) costs around ₹1200.

Sullivan Memorial MUSEUM
(☎9488771571; Kannerimukku; adult/child ₹20/10; ⌚10am-5pm Fri-Wed) Just 2km north of Kotagiri centre, the house built in 1819 by Ooty founder John Sullivan has been refurbished in bright red and filled with fascinating photos, newspaper cuttings and artefacts related to local tribal groups, European settlement and icons like the miniature train. Also here is the **Nilgiri Documentation Centre** (www.nilgiridocumentation.com), dedicated to preserving the region's beauty and heritage.

Volunteering

Keystone Foundation VOLUNTEERING
(☎04266-272277; http://keystone-foundation.org; Groves Hill Rd) This Kotagiri-based NGO works to improve environmental conditions in the Nilgiris while involving, and improving living standards for, indigenous communities. Occasional openings for volunteers.

Sleeping & Eating

La Maison HERITAGE HOTEL **$$$**
(☎9585857732; www.lamaison.in; Hadatharai; s ₹5630-7430, d ₹6750-8910;) Flower-draped, French-owned La Maison is a beautifully renovated 1890s Scottish bungalow superbly positioned on a hilltop surrounded by tea plantations, 5km southwest of Kotagiri. The design is all quirky French-chic: antique furniture, tribal handicrafts, old-Ooty paintings. Hike to waterfalls, visit tribal villages, tuck into home-cooked meals (₹800), or laze in the valley-facing hot tub.

Shopping

Green Shop FOOD, HANDICRAFTS
(http://lastforest.in; Johnstone Sq; ⌚9.30am-7pm) The ecofriendly Keystone Foundation's shop has goodies for picnics (local chocolates, wild honey) plus lovely tribal crafts.

Getting There & Away

Buses run half-hourly to/from Ooty (₹15, 1½ hours) and every 15 minutes to/from Coonoor (₹11, one hour) and Mettupalayam (₹16, 1½ hours). Buses to Coimbatore (₹34, 2½ hours) leave every 45 minutes. Taxis to/from Ooty cost ₹900.

Ooty (Udhagamandalam)

☎0423 / POP 88,430 / ELEV 2240M

Ooty may be a bit hectic, especially its messy centre, but it doesn't take long to escape into quieter, greener areas where tall pines rise above what could almost be English country lanes. Ooty, 'Queen of Hill Stations', mixes Indian bustle and Hindu temples with beautiful gardens, an international school and charming Raj-era bungalows (which provide its most atmospheric accommodation).

Memorably nicknamed 'Snooty Ooty', it was established by the British in the early

Nilgiri Hills

19th century as the summer headquarters of the Madras government. Development ploughed through a few decades ago, but old Ooty survives in patches – you just have to walk further out to find it.

The journey up here on the celebrated miniature train is romantic and the scenery stunning. Even the road up is impressive. During the April-to-June 'season', Ooty is a welcome relief from the steaming plains. Between October and March, overnight temperatures occasionally drop to 0°C.

The train and bus stations are at the west end of Ooty's racecourse, in almost the lowest part of town. To their west is the lake, while the streets of the town twist upwards all around. From the bus station it's a 20-minute walk east to Ooty's commercial centre, Charing Cross.

Sights

Botanical Gardens GARDENS

(Garden Rd; adult/child ₹30/15, camera/video ₹50/100; 7am-6.30pm) Established in 1848, these pretty 22-hectare gardens are a living gallery of the Nilgiris' natural flora. Keep an eye out for a typical Toda *mund* (village), a fossilised tree trunk believed to be 20 million years old and, on busy days, around 20 million Indian tourists.

St Stephen's Church CHURCH

(Church Hill Rd; 10am-6pm) Perched above Ooty's centre, immaculate pale-yellow St Stephen's, built in 1829, is the Nilgiris' oldest church. It has lovely stained glass, huge wooden beams hauled by elephant from the palace of Tipu Sultan 120km away, and slabs and plaques donated by colonial-era churchgoers. In the overgrown **cemetery** you'll find headstones commemorating many an Ooty Brit, including Ooty founder John Sullivan's wife and daughter.

Nilgiri Library LIBRARY

(0423-2441699; Hospital Rd; 10am-1pm & 2.30-6pm) This quaint little haven in a crumbling, earthy-red 1867 building houses more than 30,000 books, including rare titles on the Nilgiris and hill tribes and 19th-century British journals. Visitors can consult books in the reading room with a temporary one-month membership (₹500). Upstairs is a portrait of Queen Victoria presented to Ooty on her 1887 Golden Jubilee.

In 2016, the library hosted the first-ever **Ooty Literary Festival** (www.ootylitfest.com).

Doddabetta VIEWPOINT

(Ooty-Kotagiri Rd; ₹6, camera/video ₹10/50; 8am-5pm) About 7km east of Ooty, Doddabetta is the highest point (2633m) in the

Ooty (Udhagamandalam)

Nilgiris. On clear days, it's one of the best viewpoints around; go early for better chances of mist-free views. Kotagiri buses will drop you at the Doddabetta junction, then it's a steep 3km walk or a quick jeep ride. Taxis do return trips from Charing Cross (₹700).

Activities

Hiking & Trekking

The best of Ooty is out in the beautiful **Nilgiri Hills**. Most hotels can put you in touch with local guides who do half-day hikes for around ₹500 per person. You'll normally drive out of town and walk through hills, tribal villages and tea plantations.

More serious treks in the best forest areas with plenty of wildlife – such as beyond Avalanche to the southwest or Parsons Valley to the west, in Mukurthi National Park, or down to Walakkad and Sairandhri in Kerala's Silent Valley National Park – require Tamil Nadu Forest Department permits. At the time of research, the **Office of the Field Director** (0423-2444098, Mudumalai accommodation bookings 0423-2445971; fdmtr@tn.nic.in; Mount Stuart Hill; 10am-5.45pm Mon-Fri) was not issuing permits due to rising concerns about human–animal conflict in the region; in recent years there have been several elephant-related foreigner fatalities and multiple tiger attacks on local villagers (several fatal). But if you fancy trying, contact the Office of the Field Director in advance.

The **Nilgiri Wildlife & Environment Association** (0423-2447167; www.nwea.org.in; Mount Stuart Hill; 10am-1.30pm & 2-5pm Mon-Fri, 10am-1.30pm Sat), the **District Forest Office Nilgiris South Division** (0423-2444083; www.ootyavalanche.com; Mount Stuart Hill; 10am-5.45pm Mon-Fri) and the **District Forest Office Nilgiris North Division** (0423-2443968; dfonorth_ooty@yahoo.co.in; Mount Stuart Hill; 10am-5.45pm Mon-Fri) can help with trekking updates and advice.

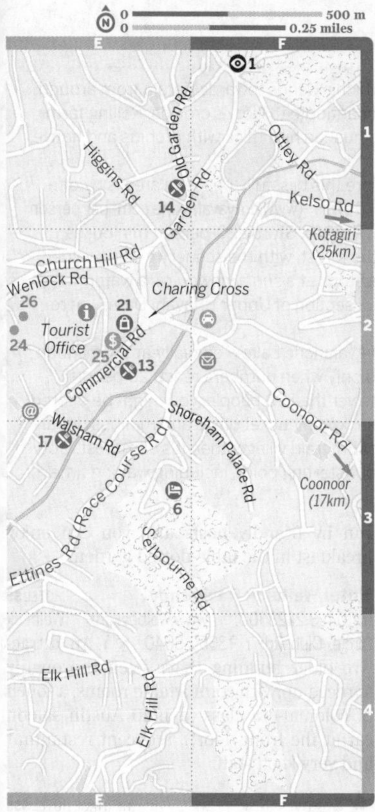

Ooty (Udhagamandalam)

Sights

1 Botanical Gardens ... F1
2 Nilgiri Library ... D2
3 St Stephen's Church ... D1
4 St Thomas' Church ... B4

Activities, Courses & Tours

5 Boathouse ... A3

Sleeping

6 Fortune Sullivan Court ... E3
7 Hotel Welbeck Residency ... C2
8 Lymond House ... B1
9 Reflections Guest House ... B4
10 Savoy ... B1
11 Wyoming ... D1
12 YWCA Anandagiri ... D4

Eating

13 Adyar Ananda Bhavan ... E2
14 Modern Stores ... E1
15 Place to Bee ... C2
Savoy ... (see 10)
16 Shinkow's Chinese Restaurant ... D2
17 Willy's Coffee Pub ... E3

Drinking & Nightlife

18 Café Coffee Day ... D2
Café Coffee Day ... (see 14)

Entertainment

19 Ooty Racecourse ... D4

Shopping

Green Shop ... (see 15)
20 Higginbothams ... D2
21 Higginbothams ... E2
22 K Mahaveer Chand ... C4

Information

23 Canara Bank ATM ... C4
24 District Forest Office Nilgiris North Division ... E2
District Forest Office Nilgiris South Division ... (see 24)
25 Indian Overseas Bank ATM ... E2
26 Nilgiri Wildlife & Environment Association ... E2
Office of the Field Director ... (see 26)
27 State Bank of India ATM ... D2

Boating

The **boathouse** (North Lake Rd; ₹12, camera/video ₹25/145; ⌚9am-6pm) by Ooty Lake rents rowboats and pedal boats. Prices start from ₹170 (plus ₹170 deposit) for a two-seater pedal boat (30 minutes).

Tours

Fixed taxi-tour rates are ₹1300 for four hours tootling around Ooty, ₹1400 to Coonoor (four hours) or ₹2500 to Mudumalai Tiger Reserve (full-day).

Sleeping

Ooty has some gorgeous colonial-era homes at the high end and some decent backpacker crashpads, but there isn't much in the lower midrange. During the 'season' (1 April to 15 June) hotels hike rates and checkout time is often 9am. Book well ahead for public holidays.

YWCA Anandagiri GUESTHOUSE $

(☎0423-2444262; www.ywcaagooty.com; Ettines Rd; dm ₹250, s ₹400-2240, d ₹800-2240) This former brewery and sprawling complex of cottages is dotted with flower gardens. With clean, characterful, freshly painted rooms, helpful staff, spacious common areas and a good restaurant (book ahead), you've got some excellent-value budget accommodation.

OFF THE BEATEN TRACK

AVALANCHE VALLEY

The serene, protected **Avalanche Valley** – which extends towards Kerala from around 20km southwest of Ooty – provides the perfect antidote to Ooty's crowds. Rolling farmlands and twinkling tea plantations give way to hushed hills thick with orchids and native *shola* (virgin forest).

Access is restricted, so the only way to explore this blissfully peaceful area is by official two-hour forest department **minibus 'ecotours'** (www.ootyavalanche.com; per person ₹150; ⌚9.30am-3pm) or private-hire jeep trips (₹1200). Sturdy 20-person minibuses trundle up semi-paved tracks southwest into the forest, with the scenery getting wilder and increasingly dramatic as you go. There are stops at a *shola* viewpoint, a waterfall-side Lakshmi temple and, finally, the Lakkidi section of Upper Bhavani Dam, where you get 30 minutes to stroll around.

Minibuses depart from the southern side of Avalanche Lake – officially at 10am, noon and 2pm, but more frequently on demand, and only when numbers reach 20 people (just show up 30 minutes ahead). If there are fewer than 20 people, you might be offered a jeep trip instead. The turn-off to the forest checkpoint, ticket office and minibus departure point is at hairpin bend 6/34, 1km south of Emerald village; then it's 5km west. Ooty taxi drivers charge ₹1600 (return) to the ecotour starting point, including waiting time.

The cheapest rooms have private bathrooms across the corridor. High ceilings can mean cold nights, but you can ask for extra blankets.

Reflections Guest House GUESTHOUSE $
(☎0423-2443834; reflectionsin@yahoo.co.in; 1B North Lake Rd; r ₹800-1200; 📶) A long-standing budget haunt, recently partly revamped, Reflections sits across the road from Ooty Lake. Most of its 12 spotless, good-value rooms have lake views; the best come with freshly updated bathrooms. The attentive owners serve snacks on request and can organise guided treks. Hot water is available once daily.

★**Lymond House** HERITAGE HOTEL $$
(☎9843149490; www.serendipityo.com; Sylks Rd; r incl breakfast ₹4200-5470; 📶) What is it about this 1855 British bungalow that gives it the edge over its peers? The cosy cottage set-up with garden-fresh flowers, four-poster beds, working fireplaces and antique-lined lounges? The contemporary fittings combined with rich, old-world style in the spacious, dramatic rooms? The good multicuisine food and beautiful gardens? All that, no doubt – plus informal yet efficient management.

Wyoming HERITAGE HOTEL $$
(☎0423-2452008; www.wyoming.in; 46 Sheddon Rd; r incl breakfast ₹3150-3680) Six simple, wonderfully spacious colonial-feel rooms open up to classic Nilgiri panoramas at this delightful sun-yellow heritage house high above Ooty. All have kettles, bottled water and pretty wood-panelled floors. It's well run by friendly hosts and you can enjoy breakfast in the table-dotted garden.

Hotel Welbeck Residency HOTEL $$
(☎0423-2223300; www.welbeck.in; Welbeck Circle, Club Rd; r ₹3650-5040; 📶) An attractive older building that's been thoroughly spruced up with comfortable rooms, a touch of colonial-era class (a 1920 Austin saloon car at the front door!), a decent restaurant and very keen staff.

★**Savoy** HERITAGE HOTEL $$$
(☎0423-2225500; www.gateway.tajhotels.com; 77 Sylks Rd; r incl breakfast from ₹7500; 📶) The Savoy is one of Ooty's oldest hotels, with parts dating back to 1829. Cottages and swing-chairs are set around a charming lawn and garden. Discreetly colonial-style rooms have huge marble-clad bathrooms, log fires, bay windows and hot-water bottles. Welcome touches include a cocktail bar, an ayurveda centre and an excellent multicuisine dining room. Compulsory half-board April to June.

King's Cliff HERITAGE HOTEL $$$
(☎0423-2244000; www.littlearth.in; Havelock Rd; r incl breakfast ₹4200-9410; 📶) Hidden away above Ooty on Strawberry Hill is this classic colonial-era house with wood panelling, antique furnishings, a snug lounge and good Indian/Continental cooking at **Earl's Secret** (☎0423-2452888; mains ₹340-600; ⌚8-10am, noon-3pm & 7-10pm; 📶), partly in a glassed-in conservatory. Cheaper rooms don't have the same old-world charm as the most expensive ones.

Fortune Sullivan Court HOTEL $$$
(☎0423-2441415; www.fortunehotels.in; 123 Selbourne Rd; incl breakfast s ₹6000-7200, d ₹6600-7800; 📶) In a quiet spot on the southern fringe of town, the Fortune is no Raj-era mansion, but twirling staircases around a grand lobby lead to comfy, colourful rooms with big beds, light woods and writing desks. Service is perfectly polished, and the hotel has its own bar, spa, small gym and multicuisine restaurant.

Eating & Drinking

Adyar Ananda Bhavan INDIAN $
(www.aabsweets.in; 58 Commercial Rd; mains ₹130-200, thalis ₹100-200; ⏰7.30-11.30am, noon-3.30pm & 6-10.30pm) This sparkly new Ooty favourite is constantly crammed with locals and tourists filling up on delicious, swiftly delivered South Indian staples (dosas, *vadas, idlis*), North Indian classics (try the paneer tikka), fresh juices, and thalis heaped onto plastic yellow trays.

Willy's Coffee Pub CAFE $
(KCR Arcade, Walsham Rd; dishes ₹40-90; ⏰10am-9.30pm; 📶) Climb the stairs and join Ooty's international students for board games, wifi, a lending library and well-priced pizzas, chips, toasties, cakes and cookies.

Modern Stores SUPERMARKET $
(144 Garden Rd; ⏰9.40am-9pm) Stocks all kinds of international foods, from muesli to marmalade, along with particularly good Western Ghats produce, such as breads, cheeses and chocolates.

Place to Bee ITALIAN $$
(☎0423-2449464; www.facebook.com/placet0bee; 176A Club Rd; mains ₹200-400; ⏰12.30-3pm & 6.30-9.30pm Wed-Mon) 🍃 Brush up on Nilgiri-bee facts over meals at this arty, fairy-lit restaurant tucked inside the Keystone Foundation's (p1078) little Bee Museum. It might sound bizarre, but the concept works, ingredients are locally sourced, and the divinely fresh dishes – many involving wild honey – don't disappoint. Choose from expertly executed pastas, Mediterranean-inspired salads and real-deal, build-your-own wood-fired pizzas.

Shinkow's Chinese Restaurant CHINESE $$
(38/83 Commissioner's Rd; mains ₹100-250; ⏰noon-3.45pm & 6.30-9.45pm) Shinkow's is an Ooty institution. The simple but tasty chicken, pork, beef, seafood, veg, noodle and rice dishes are reliably good and quick to arrive at your chequer-print table.

Savoy MULTICUISINE $$$
(☎0423-2225500; www.gateway.tajhotels.com; 77 Sylks Rd; mains ₹260-650; ⏰7.30-10am, 12.30-3pm & 7.30-10.30pm) All wood walls, intimate lighting, live piano and plush orange velvets, the Savoy's (p1082) candle-lit dining room dishes up fabulous contemporary Continental, Indian and pan-Asian cuisine – including all-day breakfasts, yummy salads, pastas and kebabs, and some unique tribal-inspired dishes.

Café Coffee Day CAFE
(www.cafecoffeeday.com; Garden Rd; drinks ₹60-120; ⏰9am-10pm) Reliably good coffee, tea and cakes. There's another **branch** (drinks ₹70-110; ⏰9am-10pm) on Church Hill Rd.

Shopping

K Mahaveer Chand JEWELLERY
(291 Main Bazaar Rd; ⏰10am-8pm) K Mahaveer Chand has been selling particularly beautiful Toda tribal and silver jewellery for 45 years.

Green Shop HANDICRAFTS, FOOD
(www.lastforest.in; Sargan Villa, off Club Rd; ⏰10am-7pm) 🍃 Run by Kotagiri's Keystone Foundation (p1078), this fair-trade, organic-oriented shop sells gorgeous tribal crafts and clothes (including Toda embroidery) and wild honey harvested by local indigenous farmers.

Higginbothams BOOKS
(Commercial Rd; ⏰9am-1pm & 3.30-7.30pm) Well-known outlet with a good stash of English-language books and another **branch** (Commissioner's Rd; ⏰9am-1pm & 2-6pm Mon-Sat) up the hill.

Information

Tourist Office (☎0423-2443977; Wenlock Rd; ⏰10am-5pm)

Getting There & Away

The fun way to arrive in Ooty is on the miniature train from Mettupalayam. Buses also run regularly up and down the mountain from across Tamil Nadu, from Kerala, and from Mysuru and Bengaluru in Karnataka.

BUS

The Tamil Nadu and Karnataka state bus companies have reservation offices at Ooty's busy **bus station**. For Kochi take a bus to Palakkad (₹96, six hours, 7am, 8am, 2pm) and change.

TAXI

Taxis cluster at stands around town. Fixed one-way fares include Coonoor (₹900), Kotagiri (₹900), Coimbatore (₹2000) and Mudumalai Tiger Reserve (₹1300).

TRAIN

The miniature ('toy') train from Mettupalayam to Ooty – one of the Mountain Railways of India given World Heritage status by Unesco – is the best way to get here. The **Nilgiri Mountain Railway** requires special cog wheels on the locomotive, meshing with a third, 'toothed' rail on the ground, to manage the exceptionally steep gradients. There are wonderful forest, waterfall, mountainside and tea-plantation views along the way. The section between Mettupalayam and Coonoor uses steam engines, which push, rather than pull, the train up the hill.

For high season, book several weeks ahead; at other times a few days ahead is advisable (though not always essential). The train departs Mettupalayam for Ooty at 7.10am daily (1st/2nd class ₹205/30, 4¾ hours). From Ooty to Mettupalayam the train leaves at 2pm (3½ hours). There are also three daily trains each way just between Ooty and Coonoor (₹150/25, 1¼ hours). Departures and arrivals at Mettupalayam connect with the Nilgiri Express to/from Chennai Central (sleeper/2AC/3AC ₹340/890/1250, 9¼ hours).

Ooty is often listed as Udhagamandalam in train timetables.

Getting Around

Autorickshaws and taxis are everywhere. You'll find taxi fare charts at Charing Cross and outside the bus station. Autorickshaw fare charts are posted outside the bus station and botanical gardens and elsewhere. An autorickshaw from the train or bus station to Charing Cross costs ₹60.

There are jeep taxi stands near the **bus station** (Avalanche Rd) and **municipal market** (Hobert Park Cross Rd); expect to pay about 1½ times the local taxi fares.

Mudumalai Tiger Reserve

0423

In the Nilgiris' foothills, the 321-sq-km **Mudumalai Tiger Reserve** (www.mudumalaitigerreserve.com; sometimes closed Apr, May or Jun) is like a classical Indian landscape painting given life: thin, spindly trees and light-slotted leaves concealing spotted chital deer and grunting wild boar. Also here are around 50 tigers, giving Mudumalai one of India's highest tiger population densities (though you'd be lucky to see one). Overall the reserve is Tamil Nadu's top wildlife-spotting place. You're most likely to see deer, peacocks, wild boar, langurs, jackals, Malabar giant squirrels, wild elephants (the park has several hundred) and gaur (Indian bison).

Along with Karnataka's Bandipur and Nagarhole, Kerala's Wayanad and Tamil Nadu's Sathyamangalam Tiger Reserve, Mudumalai forms part of an unbroken chain of reserves comprising an important wildlife refuge home to approximately 570 tigers – the world's single largest tiger population.

Mudumalai sometimes closes for fire risk in April, May or June. Rainy July and August are the least favourable months for visiting.

The reserve's **reception centre** (0423-2526235; Theppakadu; 6.30am-6pm), and some reserve-run accommodation, is at Theppakadu, on the main road between Ooty and Mysuru. The closest village to Theppakadu is Masinagudi, 7km east.

Sights & Activities

Hiking in the reserve is banned and private vehicles are only permitted on the main Ooty–Gudalur–Theppakadu–Mysuru road and the Theppakadu–Masinagudi and Masinagudi–Moyar River roads. Official minibus 'safaris' are the only way to get inside the reserve.

Some operators may offer hikes in the buffer zone around the reserve, but reserve authorities advise strongly against them; tourists have died from getting too close to wild elephants on illegal hikes. Expert-led jeep safaris organised through the better resorts are a safer option.

Elephant Camp LANDMARK
(Theppakadu; ₹15; 8.30-9am & 5.30-6pm) In the mornings and evenings, you can see the reserve's working elephants being fed at the

BUSES FROM OOTY (UDHAGAMANDALAM)

DESTINATION	FARE (₹)	TIME (HR)	DEPARTURES
Bengaluru	250-670	8	Volvo 10am, 11.15am, 5.45pm, 10.30pm
Chennai	450	14	4.30pm, 5.45pm, 6.30pm
Coimbatore	53	4	every 20min 5.50am-8.40pm
Coonoor	10	1	every 10min 5.30am-10pm
Kotagiri	15	1½	every 20min 6.30am-7pm, 7.40pm, 8.20pm
Mysuru	136-420	5	Volvo 10am, 11.15am, 5.45pm

elephant camp just east of Theppakadu's reception centre (p1084), where you'll need to buy tickets. Most elephants here are rescues or old timber-trade elephants unfit to return to the wild.

Minibus Safaris WILDLIFE-WATCHING
(per person ₹135; ⏲hourly 6-10am & 2-6pm) The only way to access the reserve is on official one-hour minibus 'safaris', which make a 15km loop in camouflage-striped 20- to 30-person minibuses. There's a good chance you'll spot some wildlife, though it's down to luck. Book at Theppakadu's reception centre (p1084) several hours ahead.

Sleeping & Eating

The reserve runs simple lodgings along a track just above the Moyar River at Theppakadu. Better accommodation is provided by numerous lodges and forest resorts outside the park's fringes, many of them welcoming, high-standard family-run businesses. Most of the best cluster at **Bokkapuram** village, 5km south of Masinagudi at the foot of the mountains.

Theppakadu

Reserve-run accommodation must be booked in advance; some may be available for booking online. For the rest, book ahead by phone or in person with Ooty's Office of the Field Director (p1080). The reception centre accepts walk-ins if there are vacancies.

Hotel Tamil Nadu LODGE $
(bookings 0423-2445971; www.mudumalaitigerreserve.com; Theppakadu; dm ₹2620) This government-run lodge provides basic, clean, new-build dorms with bathroom, for up to eight people, plus simple meals (₹80).

Theppakadu Log House LODGE $$
(bookings 0423-2445971; Theppakadu; d ₹2510) The best of Theppakadu's reserve-owned accommodation: well-maintained rooms, private bathrooms and ₹70 meals.

Bokkapuram & Around

Wilds at Northernhay LODGE $$
(9843149490; http://serendipityo.com; Singara; r incl breakfast ₹4800-5400;) A wonderful lodge 8km southwest of Masinagudi, in a converted coffee warehouse on a working coffee plantation filled with tall trees that give it a deep-in-the-forest feel. Seven cosy rooms (one up in the trees, another a tribal-inspired mud-house) and excellent meals complement jeep safaris, nature walks and birdwatching expeditions, on which you should see a good variety of wildlife.

Bamboo Banks Farm LODGE $$
(0423-2526211; www.bamboobanks.com; Masinagudi; full board d ₹7870;) This family-run operation has seven simple, comfy cottages tucked into its own patch of unkempt jungle, 2km south of Masinagudi. Geese waddle around; there's a peaceful pool area with hammocks, swing-chairs and a treetop viewing platform; meals are good Indian buffets; and the efficient owners organise biking and horse riding.

★ **Jungle Retreat** RESORT $$$
(0423-2526469; www.jungleretreat.com; Bokkapuram; dm ₹3800, r ₹5470-12,150;) Arguably Mudumalai's most stylish resort, with accommodation in lovingly built stone cottages, two tree houses or a dorm (minimum four people), all spread out for maximum seclusion. The bar, lounge and restaurant (three daily meals ₹2000) are great for meeting travellers, and staff are knowledgeable. The pool has a stunning setting – leopards and elephants often pop in for a drink.

Jungle Hut RESORT $$$
(0423-2526463; www.junglehut.in; Bokkapuram; full board r ₹7310-9730;) Along with ecofriendly touches (solar power, rainwater harvesting) and a sociable lounge, 30-year-old Jungle Hut has probably the best food in Bokkapuram (if you're visiting from another resort after dark, don't walk home alone!). Spacious rooms – the loveliest in semitented safari-style cottages – sprawl across large grounds, where 200-odd chital deer graze. Jeep safaris, treks and birdwatching can be arranged.

Getting There & Around

Taxi day trips to Mudumalai from Ooty cost ₹2000, usually via the alternative Sighur Ghat road with its spectacular 36-hairpin-bend hill. One-way taxis from Ooty to Theppakadu cost ₹1300.

Small buses that can handle the Sighur Ghat road run from Ooty to Masinagudi (₹17, 1½ hours, 12 daily 6.50am to 7.30pm), from where there are a few slow local buses daily to Theppakadu (₹5).

Shared jeeps also run between Masinagudi and Theppakadu for ₹10 per person (or you can have one to yourself for ₹120). Costs are similar for jeeps between Masinagudi and Bokkapuram.

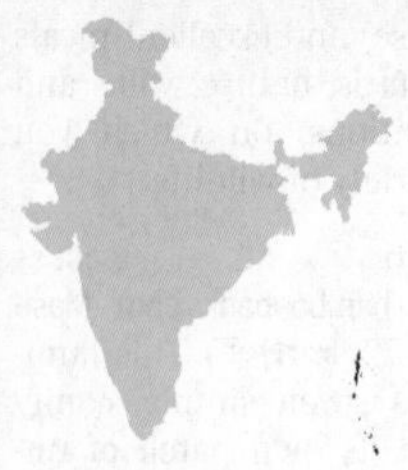

Andaman Islands

Includes ➡

Best Beaches

- ➡ Radhanagar (p1095)
- ➡ Merk Bay (p1102)
- ➡ Ross & Smith Islands (p1102)
- ➡ Butler Bay (p1104)
- ➡ Lalaji Bay (p1102)

Best Places to Sleep

- ➡ Barefoot at Havelock (p1097)
- ➡ Silversand (p1098)
- ➡ Pristine Beach Resort (p1103)
- ➡ Hotel Sinclairs Bayview (p1092)
- ➡ Blue View (p1104)

Why Go?

With breathtakingly beautiful coastline, lush forested interior, fantastic diving possibilities and a far-flung location, the Andaman Islands are a perfect place to ramble around or simply chill out on sun-toasted beaches.

Shimmering turquoise waters are surrounded by primeval jungle and mangrove forest, and its sugar-white beaches melt under glorious flame-and-purple sunsets. The population is a friendly mix of South and Southeast Asian settlers, as well as Negrito ethnic groups whose arrival here still has anthropologists somewhat baffled. Adding to the intrigue is its remote location, some 1370km from the Indian mainland, meaning the islands are geographically more Southeast Asia – just 150km from Indonesia and 190km from Myanmar.

Comprising 572 islands, only a dozen or so are open to tourists, Havelock by far being the most popular for its splendid beaches and diving. The Nicobar Islands are strictly off limits to tourists, as are the various patches of tribal areas.

When to Go

Port Blair

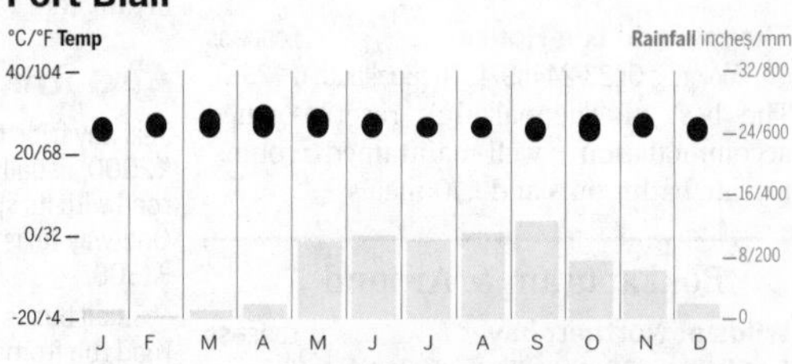

Dec–Mar Warm, sunny days, optimal diving conditions and turtle nesting.

Oct–Dec & Mar–mid-May Weather is a mixed bag, but fewer tourists and lower costs.

Feb–Aug Pumping waves on Little Andaman for experienced surfers.

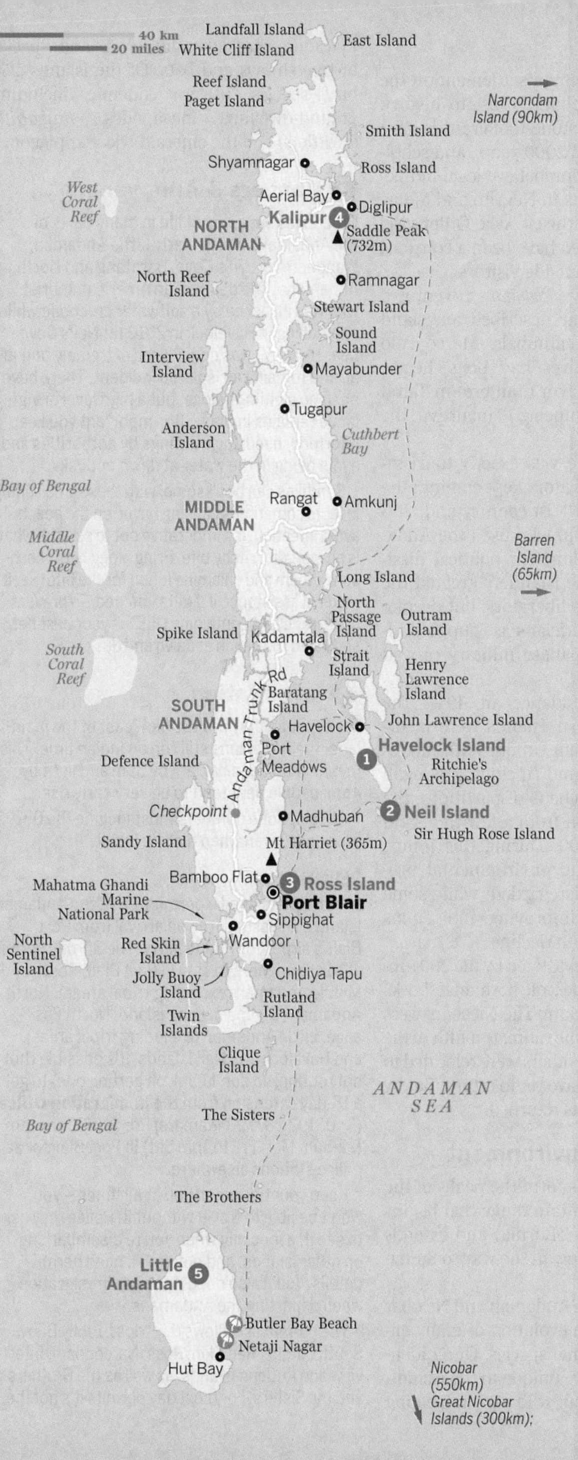

Andaman Islands Highlights

1. **Havelock Island** (p1095) Snorkelling, diving and socialising on this picturesque island.
2. **Neil Island** (p1099) Easing into a blissfully mellow pace of life.
3. **Ross Island** (p1092) Learning about Port Blair's colonial past.
4. **Kalipur** (p1102) Experiencing the wilds of northern Andaman while island-hopping to pristine beaches and coral reefs.
5. **Little Andaman** (p1103) Finding Butler Bay and a little piece of paradise.

History

The date of initial human settlement on the Andamans and Nicobars is lost to history. Anthropologists say stone-tool crafters have lived here for around 2000 years, and scholars of human migration believe local indigenous tribes have roots in Negrito and Malay ethnic groups in Southeast Asia. Otherwise, these specks in the sea have been a constant source of legend to outside visitors.

The 10th-century Persian adventurer Buzurg Ibn Shahriyar described an island chain inhabited by cannibals, Marco Polo added that the natives had dogs' heads, and tablets in Thanjavur (Tanjore) in Tamil Nadu named the archipelago Timaittivu: the Impure Islands.

None of the above was exactly tourism-brochure stuff, but visitors kept coming: the Marathas in the late 17th century and, 200 years later, the British, who used the Andamans as a penal colony for political dissidents. In WWII some islanders greeted the invading Japanese as liberators, but despite installing Indian politicians as (puppet) administrators, the Japanese military proved to be harsh occupiers.

Following Independence in 1947, the Andaman and Nicobar Islands were incorporated into the Indian Union. With migration from the mainland (including Bengali refugees fleeing the chaos of partition), the population has grown from a few thousand to more than 350,000. During this influx, tribal land rights and environmental protection were often disregarded; while some conditions are now improving, indigenous tribes remain largely in decline.

The islands were devastated by the 2004 Indian Ocean earthquake, offshore aftershocks and the resulting tsunami. The Nicobars were especially hard hit; some estimate a fifth of the population was killed, others were relocated to Port Blair and many have yet to return. But by and large normalcy has returned.

Geography & Environment

Incredibly, the islands form the peaks of the Arakan Yoma, a mountain range that begins in Western Myanmar (Burma) and extends into the ocean, running all the way to Sumatra in Indonesia.

The isolation of the Andaman and Nicobar Islands has led to the evolution of many endemic plant and animal species. Of 62 identified mammals, 32 are unique to the islands, including the Andaman wild pig, crab-eating macaque, masked palm civet, and species of tree shrews and bats. Of the islands' 250 bird species, 18 are endemic, including ground-dwelling megapodes, *hawabills* (swiftlets) and the emerald Nicobar pigeon.

Dangers & Annoyances

Crocodiles are a way of life in many parts of the Andamans, particularly Little Andaman, Wandoor, Corbyn's Cove, Baratang and North Andamans. The death of an American tourist who was attacked by a saltwater crocodile while snorkelling in Havelock in 2010 (at Neils Cove near Beach 7) was considered extremely unusual, and remains an isolated incident. There have been no sightings since, but a high level of vigilance remains in place. It's important you keep informed, heed any warnings by authorities and avoid being in the water at dawn or dusk.

Sandflies can be irksome, with these small biting insects sometimes causing havoc on the beach. To avoid infection, it's imperative not to scratch what is an incredibly itchy bite. Bring along hydrocortisone cream and calamine lotion for the bite. Seek medical assistance if it gets infected. To prevent bites, repellent containing DEET is your best bet, and avoid the beach at dawn and dusk.

Information

Even though they are 1000km east of the mainland, the Andamans still run on Indian time. This means that it can be dark by 5pm and light by 4am; people here tend to be very early risers.

All telephone numbers must include the 03192 area code, even when dialling locally.

PERMITS

All foreigners need a permit to visit the Andaman Islands; it's issued free on arrival from Port Blair's airport or Haddo Jetty. The 30-day permit allows foreigners to stay in Port Blair, South and Middle Andaman (excluding tribal areas), North Andaman (Diglipur), Long Island, North Passage, Little Andaman (excluding tribal areas), and Havelock and Neil Islands. It's possible (but not routine, so don't bank on getting one) to get a 15-day extension from the **Immigration Office** (☎03192-237793; Kamaraj Rd; ⏱8.30am-1pm & 2-5pm Mon-Fri, to 1pm Sat) in Port Blair, or at police stations elsewhere.

Keep your permit on you at all times – you won't be able to travel without it. Police may ask to see it, especially when you're disembarking on other islands, and hotels will need permit details. You'll also need it to pass immigration when departing the Andamans.

The permit also allows day trips to Jolly Buoy, South Cinque, Red Skin, Ross, Narcondam, Interview and Rutland Islands, as well as the Brothers and the Sisters. For most day permits it's not the hassle but the cost. For areas such as Mahatma Gandhi Marine National Park, and Ross and Smith Islands near Diglipur, the permits cost ₹50/500 for Indians/foreigners. Students with valid ID pay minimal entry fees, so bring your card.

The Nicobar Islands are off-limits to all except Indian nationals engaged in approved research, government business or trade.

Getting There & Away

AIR

There are daily flights to Port Blair from Delhi, Kolkata, Bengaluru, Mumbai and Chennai. Carriers that service Port Blair include, **Jet Airways** (☎03192-230545, 1800225522; www.jetairways.com), **Air India** (☎03192-233108; www.airindia.in), **SpiceJet** (☎0987-1803333; www.spicejet.com) and **GoAir** (☎reservations 092-23222111; www.goair.in). Round-trip fares vary in price depending on how early you book. A 15kg check-in luggage limit exists. There are no international flights from Port Blair.

BOAT

Depending on who you ask, the infamous boat to Port Blair is either the only *real* way to get to the Andamans or a hassle and a half. The truth lies somewhere in between. There are usually three to four sailings a month between Port Blair and Chennai (three days) and Kolkata (four to five days), plus a monthly ferry to Visakhapatnam (four days). All arrive at Haddo Jetty.

Take sailing times with a large grain of salt – travellers have reported sitting on the boat at Kolkata harbour for up to 12 hours, or waiting to dock near Port Blair for several hours. With hold-ups and variable weather and sea conditions, the trip can take a day or two extra.

Andaman Shipping Office (☎044-25226873; 2nd fl, Jawahar Bldg, 17 Rajaji Salai George Town, Chennai; ⏲10am-4pm Mon-Fri, to noon Sat) has boats from Chennai, **Shipping Corporation of India** (☎033-22482354; www.shipindia.com; Strand Rd, Kolkata; ⏲10am-1pm & 2-4pm Mon-Fri) departs from Kolkata, and **AV Bhanojirow, Garuda Pattabhiramayya & Co** (☎0891-2565597; ops@avbgpr.com; Harbour Approach Rd, next to NMDC, Port Area, Visakhapatnam; ⏲9am-5pm) from Visakhapatnam.

You can organise your return ticket at the **ferry booking office** (p1093) at Phoenix Bay. Bring three passport photos and a photocopy of your permit. Updated schedules and fares can be found at www.andamans.gov.in or www.shipindia.com. Otherwise enquire at Phoenix Bay's info office.

Classes vary slightly between boats, but the cheapest is bunk (₹2500), followed by 2nd-class (six beds, ₹6420), 1st class (four beds, ₹8080) and deluxe cabins (two beds, ₹9750). Higher-end tickets cost as much as, if not more than, a plane ticket. If you go bunk, prepare for little privacy and toilets that tend to get…unpleasant after three days at sea.

Food (tiffin for breakfast, thalis for lunch and dinner) costs around ₹150/200 per day for bunk/cabin class, though bring something (fruit in particular) to supplement your diet. Some bedding is supplied, but if you're travelling bunk class bring a sleeping sheet. Some travellers take a hammock to string up on deck.

There is no ferry between Port Blair and Thailand, but private yachts can usually get clearance. You can't legally get from the Andamans to Myanmar (Burma) by sea. Be aware you risk imprisonment or worse from the Indian and Burmese navies if you give this a go.

> **PERMIT COPIES**
>
> You need to produce a photocopy of your permit when booking ferry tickets. While you're not always asked to provide it, to avoid the hassle of having to re-queue, it's worth taking some copies before arriving at Port Blair's ferry office: you'll likely to need them later in your trip.

Getting Around

AIR

At the time of writing, inter-island sea planes were no longer operating and it was uncertain whether they would resume.

While the interisland helicopter service isn't generally for tourists, you can chance your luck by applying one day before at the **Directorate of Civil Aviation office** (☎03192-233601; Port Blair Helipad, VIP Rd) at the helipad near the airport. The 5kg baggage limit precludes most tourists from using this service.

BOAT

Most islands can only be reached by water. While this sounds romantic, ferry ticket offices can be utter chaos: expect hot waits, slow service, queue-jumping and a rugby scrum to the ticket window. Have your passport (for photo ID), permit and ticket handy. To hold your spot and advance in line, you need to be a little aggressive (but not a jerk) or be a woman; ladies' queues are a godsend, but they really only apply in Port Blair. You can buy tickets the day you travel by arriving at the appropriate jetty an hour beforehand, but this is risky, and normally one or two days in advance is recommended. You can't pre-book ferry tickets until you've been issued your island permit (p1088) upon arrival in the Andamans. Hotels can usually book ferry tickets for you.

Porters can be hired at jetties (expect to pay around ₹50 for an average-size bag), but if your

FERRY CANCELLATIONS

Bad weather can play havoc with your itinerary, with ferry services cancelled if the sea is too rough. It's wise to build in a few days' buffer to avoid being marooned and missing your flight.

luggage isn't too heavy it's not a long walk to/from jetties.

There are regular boat services to Havelock and Neil Islands (three to four per day), as well as Rangat, Mayabunder, Diglipur and Little Andaman. A schedule of interisland sailing times can be found at www.andamans.gov.in.

Several private ferry companies also run to Havelock and Neil Islands from Port Blair.

BUS

All roads – and ferries – lead to Port Blair, and you'll inevitably spend a night or two here booking onward travel. The main island group – South, Middle and North Andaman – is connected by road, with ferry crossings and bridges. Buses run south from Port Blair to Wandoor, and north to Baratang, Rangat, Mayabunder and finally to Diglipur.

CAR & MOTORCYCLE

A car with driver costs ₹550 per 35km, or around ₹10,000 for a return trip to Diglipur from Port Blair (including stopovers along the way). Motorbikes are available for hire from Port Blair and all the islands from around ₹300 to ₹400 per day. Due to restrictions in travel within tribal areas, it's not permitted for foreigners to drive their own vehicles to North and Middle Andaman.

Port Blair

POP 108,060

Surrounded by tropical forest and rugged coastline, lively Port Blair serves as the provincial capital of the Andamans. It's a vibrant mix of Indian Ocean inhabitants – Bengalis, Tamils, Telugus, Nicobarese and Burmese. Most travellers don't hang around any longer than necessary (usually one or two days while waiting to book onward travel in the islands, or returning for departure), but PB's fascinating history warrants extended exploration.

Sights

★Cellular Jail National Memorial HISTORIC BUILDING
(GB Pant Rd; ₹30, camera/video free/₹200, sound-and-light show adult/child ₹50/25; ⏲8.45am-12.30pm & 1.30-4.15pm) A former British prison, the Cellular Jail National Memorial now serves as a shrine to the political dissidents it once jailed. Construction began in 1896 and it was completed in 1906 – the original seven wings (several of which were destroyed by the Japanese during WWII) contained 698 cells radiating from a central tower. Like many political prisons, Cellular Jail became something of a university for freedom fighters, who exchanged books, ideas and debates despite walls and wardens.

Anthropological Museum MUSEUM
(MG Rd; ₹10, camera ₹20; ⏲9am-1pm & 1.30-4.30pm Tue-Sun) This museum provides a thorough and sympathetic portrait of the islands' indigenous tribal communities. The glass display cases may be a tad old school, but they don't feel anywhere near as ancient as the simple geometric patterns etched into a Jarawa chest guard, a skull left in a Sentinelese lean-to, or the totemic spirits represented by Nicobarese shamanic sculptures.

Samudrika Naval Marine Museum MUSEUM
(Haddo Rd; adult/child ₹50/25, camera/video ₹20/50; ⏲9am-1pm & 2-5pm Tue-Sun) Run by the Indian Navy, this museum has a diverse range of exhibits with informative coverage of the islands' ecosystem, tribal communities, plants, animals and marine life (including a small aquarium). Outside is a skeleton of a young blue whale washed ashore on the Nicobars.

Corbyn's Cove BEACH
No one comes to Port Blair for the beach, but if you need a break from town, Corbyn's Cove has a small curve of sand backed by palms. The coastal road here is a scenic journey, and passes several **Japanese WWII bunkers** along the way. Located 7km south of town, an autorickshaw costs ₹150, or you can rent a motorcycle. Crocodiles are occasionally spotted in the area.

Activities

Infinity Scuba DIVING
(☎03192-281183; www.infinityscubandamans.wordpress.com) Set up by Baath, an ex-Navy commander who has extensively dived in the Andamans, Infinity arranges diving and other day trips including fishing.

Sleeping

Homestays are an affordable alternative to standard accommodation options; the tourist office provides a list of approved Port Blair homestays (doubles ₹1000 to ₹2000).

Port Blair

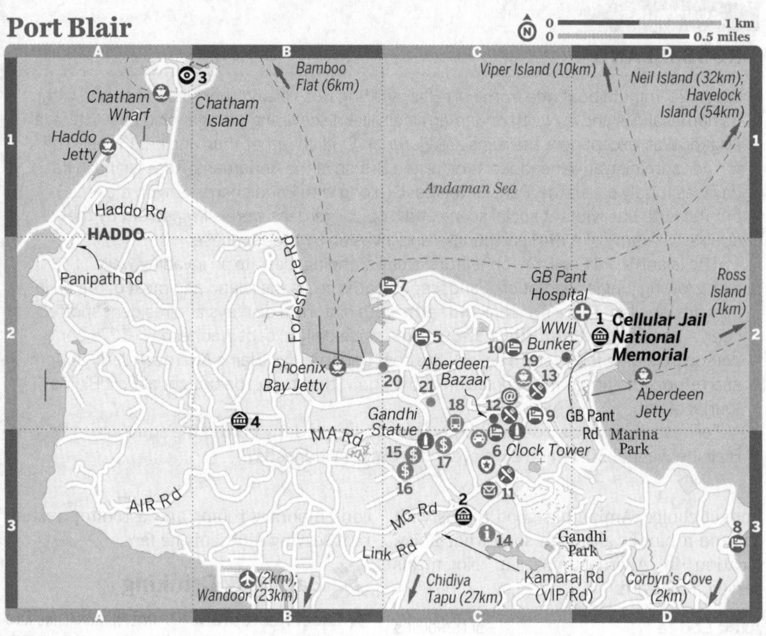

Port Blair

Top Sights

1 Cellular Jail National Memorial............ D2

Sights

2 Anthropological Museum C3
3 Chatham Saw Mill................................A1
4 Samudrika Naval Marine Museum....... B2

Sleeping

5 Aashiaanaa Rest Home....................... C2
Amina Lodge .... (see 6)
6 Azad Lodge C3
7 Fortune Resort – Bay Island C2
8 Hotel Sinclairs Bayview...................... D3
9 J Hotel... C2
10 Lalaji Bay View Hotel C2

Eating

11 Annapurna C3
Bayview .... (see 8)
Excel Restaurant .... (see 10)
12 Gagan Restaurant C2
13 Lighthouse Residency......................... C2

Drinking & Nightlife

Nico Bar .... (see 7)

Information

14 Andaman & Nicobar Tourism C3
Axis Bank ATM .... (see 9)
15 Axis Bank ATM C3
E-Cafe.. (see 12)
16 ICICI ATM.. C3
Immigration Office .... (see 14)
Island Travels .... (see 13)
17 State Bank of India............................. C3

Transport

18 Bus Stand C2
19 Coastal Cruise C2
20 Directorate of Shipping Information Office C2
Ferry Booking Office .... (see 20)
21 Saro Tours & Travels C2

Aashiaanaa Rest Home GUESTHOUSE $
(☎09474217008; shads_maria@hotmail.com; Marine Hill; r without bathroom ₹600, r ₹750, with AC from ₹1300; ❄📶) A reliable budget choice, Aashiaanaa has homely rooms and a convenient location uphill from Phoenix Bay jetty. Pricier rooms get you a balcony and air-con. Wi-fi is ₹60 per hour.

Amina Lodge GUESTHOUSE $
(☎9933258703; aminalodge@ymail.com; MA Rd, Aberdeen Bazaar; s/d ₹550/700; 📶) A popular

DON'T MISS

ROSS ISLAND

Just a 20-minute boat ride from Port Blair, visiting Ross Island (not to be confused with its namesake island in North Andaman) feels like discovering a jungle-clad Lost City, à la Angkor Wat, except here the ruins are Victorian English rather than ancient Khmer. The former administrative headquarters for the British in the Andamans, Ross Island in its day was fondly called the 'Paris of the East' (along with Pondicherry, Saigon etc etc…), but the cute title, vibrant social scene and tropical gardens were all wiped out by the double whammy of a 1941 earthquake and invasion by the Japanese.

The island's old English architecture is still standing, despite an invading wave of fast-growing jungle vegetation. Landscaped paths cross the island and most of the buildings are labelled. There's a small **museum** with historical displays and resident spotted deer. A good **sound-and-light show** takes place daily except Wednesday (₹275 per person including ferry return ticket); the boat departs Port Blair's Aberdeen Jetty at 4pm and returns at 7pm at the conclusion of the show; tickets can be bought at Port Blair's tourist office.

Ferries to Ross Island depart hourly from Aberdeen Jetty behind the aquarium in Port Blair, between 8.30am and 2pm every day except Wednesday.

budget choice, Amina has good rooms with TV and a handy, although somewhat noisy, location in Aberdeen Bazaar. No meals served. Free wi-fi.

Azad Lodge GUESTHOUSE **$**
(☎03192-242646; MA Rd, Aberdeen Bazaar; s/d without bathroom ₹400/500, d ₹700, with AC ₹900; ❄) Basic but adequately habitable rooms, some sporting colourful paint jobs, in a central location.

Lalaji Bay View Hotel GUESTHOUSE **$$**
(☎9476005820, 03192-233322; www.lalajibay-view.com; RP Rd; d from ₹800, with AC from ₹1200; ❄📶) This popular backpacker hotel has decent rooms, but it's the sociable rooftop restaurant-bar that makes the place tick.

★**Hotel Sinclairs Bayview** HOTEL **$$$**
(☎03192-227824; www.sinclairshotels.com/portblair; South Point; r incl breakfast from ₹12,000; ❄📶🏊) Located on the road to Corbyn's Cove, 2km outside town, Sinclairs' large modern rooms open right out to the water. There's a pleasant seaside garden, good multicuisine restaurant and a Japanese WWII bunker on-site.

Fortune Resort – Bay Island HOTEL **$$$**
(☎03192-234101; www.fortunehotels.in; Marine Hill; d incl breakfast from ₹9000; ❄📶🏊) One of PB's finest hotels, with panoramic bay views, pretty gardens, and modern rooms with polished floors; ask for one that's sea-facing.

J Hotel HOTEL **$$$**
(☎03192-246000; www.jhotel.in; r incl breakfast from ₹5000; ❄📶) A slick designer-esque hotel in the heart of Aberdeen Bazaar, with contemporary rooms and a rooftop restaurant serving multicuisine fare.

Eating & Drinking

★**Excel Restaurant** INTERNATIONAL, INDIAN **$**
(Lalaji Bay View Hotel, RP Rd; mains from ₹100; ⏰7am-11pm) This atmospheric bamboo-rooftop restaurant above Lalaji Bay View Hotel brings a 'Havelock' menu to the city, with grilled fish, burgers and more. A cool place to chill out over a beer.

Gagan Restaurant INDIAN **$**
(Clock Tower, Aberdeen Bazaar; mains from ₹100-200; ⏰7am-10pm) Popular with locals, this hole-in-the-wall Bengali restaurant serves great food at good prices, including Nicobari fish, crab curries and coconut chicken.

Annapurna INDIAN **$**
(MG Rd; mains ₹100-160; ⏰6.30am-10.30pm) A good veg option, that looks rather like a high-school cafeteria, serving delicious dosas and rich North Indian-style curries.

Lighthouse Residency SEAFOOD **$$**
(MA Rd; mains ₹150-800; ⏰11am-11pm) Select your meal from the display of red snapper, crab or tiger prawns to barbecue (served with rice and chips), and head to the rooftop for a cold Kingfisher beer.

Bayview MULTICUISINE **$$$**
(Hotel Sinclairs Bayview, South Point; mains ₹300-550; ⏰11am-11pm) Right on the water, with fine sea views, the Bayview is a relaxing place for an unhurried meal. The menu offers a good selection of multicuisine fare.

Nico Bar BAR
(Marine Hill; ⏲11am-11pm) The closest you'll get to the Nicobars, Fortune Bay Hotel's bar is the spot for sea breezes and scenic views (the picture on the ₹20 note is based on this spot). A pleasant place to while away an afternoon or balmy evening with a frosty cocktail.

ℹ Information

Port Blair is the only place in the Andamans where you can reliably change cash or travellers cheques and find enough ATMs. There are several ATMs around town including Axis Bank ones in **Aberdeen Bazaar** (Netaji Rd) and on **MG Rd**; **ICICI** (cnr Foreshore & MA Rds); and at the **State Bank of India** (MA Rd; ⏲9am-noon & 1-3pm Mon-Sat, 10am-noon Sat, closed 2nd & 4th Sat each month), where foreign currency can be changed.

Andaman & Nicobar Tourism (☎03192-232694; www.andamans.gov.in; Kamaraj Rd; ⏲8.30am-1pm & 2-5pm) The main island tourist office has brochures and is the place to book permits for areas around Port Blair.

GB Pant Hospital (☎03192-233473, emergency 03192-232102; GB Pant Rd) The premier public hospital in the Andamans.

Island Travels (☎03192-233358; www.islandtravelsandaman.com; MA Rd, Aberdeen Bazaar; ⏲10am-1pm & 2-6pm Mon-Sat) Come here to book flights, boat charters and guides.

Main Post Office (MG Rd; ⏲9am-5pm Mon-Sat)

ℹ Getting There & Away

BOAT

Most interisland ferries depart from Phoenix Bay Jetty. Tickets can be purchased from its **ferry booking office** (⏲9am-1pm & 2-4pm Mon-Fri, to noon Sat). Ferries can be pre-booked one to three days in advance; if they are sold out you can chance your luck with a same-day ticket issued an hour before departure from outside the ticket office. There's a **ferry information office** (☎03192-245555; Phoenix Bay Jetty; ⏲5.30am-6.30pm) outside the ticket office.

Ferries to Havelock (₹195, 2½ hours) depart daily at 6.20am, 11am, 1pm and 2pm, with several heading via Neil Island, all of which book out fast. Otherwise there are some private, pricier ferries. **Makruzz** (☎03192-212355; www.makruzz.com) has daily departures to Havelock (₹900 to ₹1250, two hours) at 6.15am and 2pm, which continue to Neil Island (₹700 to ₹1000, 1½ hours). **Coastal Cruise** (☎03192-230777; 13 RP Rd, Aberdeen Bazaar) heads to Neil Island (₹800 to ₹1100) via Havelock (₹700 to ₹1000) at 7.30am.

There are also daily boats to Little Andaman, which regularly sell out, and several boats a week to Diglipur and Long Island.

New arrivals should make the jetty their first port of call to book tickets. Hotels can usually book tickets, too, if you want to save time.

BUS

Government buses run all day from the **bus stand** (MA Rd) at Aberdeen Bazaar to Wandoor (₹20, one hour) and Chidiya Tapu (₹20, one hour). Buses to Diglipur run at 4am (to Aerial Bay) and 7am (₹270, 12 hours), and 9.30am for Mayabunder (₹200, 10 hours) all via Rangat (₹160, six hours) and Baratang (₹190, three hours). More comfortable, but pricier (around ₹50 to ₹100 extra), private buses have 'offices' (a guy with a ticket book) across from the main bus stand.

ℹ Getting Around

TO/FROM THE AIRPORT

A taxi or autorickshaw from Port Blair's airport to Aberdeen Bazaar costs around ₹100 for the 4km trip. There are also hourly buses (₹10) to/from the airport (100m outside the complex) to the main bus stand.

AUTORICKSHAW

An **autorickshaw** from Aberdeen Bazaar to Phoenix Bay Jetty is about ₹30, and to Haddo Jetty it's around ₹50.

MOTORCYCLE

You can hire a motorcycle from various spots in Port Blair for around ₹400 per day. One option is **Saro Tours & Travels** (☎9933291466; www.rentabikeandaman.com; Marine Rd, Aberdeen Bazaar).

Around Port Blair

Wandoor

Wandoor, a tiny speck of a village 29km southwest of Port Blair, is a good spot to see the interior of the island. It's best known as a jumping-off point for snorkelling at Mahatma Gandhi Marine National Park.

SLEEPING PRICE RANGES

The following price ranges refer to a double room with bathroom during high season (December to March).

$ less than ₹800

$$ ₹800 to ₹2500

$$$ more than ₹2500

WORTH A TRIP

CINQUE ISLAND

The uninhabited islands of North and South Cinque, connected by a sandbar, are part of the wildlife sanctuary south of Wandoor. Surrounded by coral reefs, the islands are among the Andamans' most beautiful. They're two hours by boat from Chidiya Tapu or 3½ hours from Wandoor.

Only day visits are allowed. Unless you're on one of the day trips occasionally organised by travel agencies, you'll need to get permission in advance from the Chief Wildlife Warden by purchasing the Mahatma Gandhi Marine National Park permit (p1088).

Activities

Wandoor has a nice beach, though at the time of research, swimming was prohibited due to crocodiles.

Mahatma Gandhi Marine National Park SNORKELLING
(permit Indian/foreigner ₹50/500, camera/video ₹25/500; Tue-Sun) The half-day snorkelling trips to Mahatma Gandhi Marine National Park are a fine option for those keen to get underwater while in Port Blair. The park comprises 15 islands of mangrove creeks, tropical rainforest and reefs supporting 50 types of coral and plenty of colourful fish. Boats depart at 9am and 10.30am from Wandoor Jetty, costing ₹750 in addition to the ₹500 permit which you need to pre-arrange from the tourist office in Port Blair.

Depending upon the time of year, the marine park's snorkelling sites alternate between Jolly Buoy and Red Skin, allowing the other to regenerate.

ANET VOLUNTEERING
(Andaman & Nicobar Environmental Team; 03192-280081; www.anetindia.org; North Wandoor) Led by an inspiring team of dynamic Indian ecologists, this is the place to gain a sense of the Andamans' wilderness as you learn about the mangroves, intertidal zones, snakes, crocs and much more. Call ahead for further details.

Sleeping

Sea Princess Beach Resort RESORT $$$
(03192-280002; www.seaprincessandaman.com; New Wandoor Beach; r incl breakfast ₹7000;) Just a short walk from the beach, Sea Princess' rooms are decked out in attractive wood tones and come in a range of categories with the beachfront suites being the pick of the bunch.

Anugama Resort RESORT $$$
(03192-280068; www.anugamaresort.com; r incl breakfast from ₹3400;) Anugama has basic but adequately comfortable cottages in a bucolic setting among forest and mud flats.

Getting There & Away

Catch the bus from Port Blair (₹20, one hour) or hire an autorickshaw for ₹200.

Chidiya Tapu

Chidiya Tapu, 30km south of Port Blair, is a tiny settlement fringed by beaches and mangroves, and famous for celestial sunsets. It also has **Munda Pahar Beach**, popular with day-trippers for its wonderfully natural setting but it's not so crash hot for swimming due to a rocky seabed.

Sights & Activities

Dive companies based in Chidiya Tapu can arrange trips to Cinque and Rutland Islands, known for their abundance of fish, colourful soft corals and excellent visibility.

Chidiya Tapu Biological Park ZOO
(Indian/foreigner ₹20/50; 9am-4pm Tue-Sun) A pleasant place to stroll in a forested setting with natural enclosures for indigenous species such as crab-eating macaques, Andaman wild pig and salt-water crocs.

Lacadives DIVING
(03192-281013; www.lacadives.com; Oct-May) Long-established dive company.

Reef Watch Marine Conservation VOLUNTEERING
(9867437640; www.reefwatchindia.org; Lacadives) NGO with a focus on marine conservation that accepts volunteers to be involved in beach clean ups, fish surveys and more; contact them directly to discuss possibilities that best match your skills with their needs.

Sleeping & Eating

Wild Grass Resort RESORT $$$
(011-65660202; www.wild-grass-resort-port-blair.hotelsgds.com; r incl breakfast ₹4250;) Unfussy double-storey cottages with an easygoing ambience and verdant jungle backdrop. It also has an atmospheric bamboo restaurant that's good for day-trippers.

Getting There & Away

Hourly buses head from Port Blair (₹20, one hour); the last bus back is at 6pm.

Havelock Island

POP 5500

With sublime silken beaches, twinkling teal shallows and some of the best diving in South Asia, Havelock has the well-deserved reputation of being a travellers paradise. Indeed for many, Havelock is *the* Andamans, and it's what lures most tourists across the Bay of Bengal, many of whom are content to stay here for the entirety of their trip.

Sights & Activities

Beaches

Radhanagar BEACH

(Beach 7) One of India's prettiest and most famous stretches of sand is the acclaimed Radhanagar. It's a beautiful curve of sugar fronted by perfectly spiraled waves, all backed by native forest. It's on the northwestern side of the island, about 12km from the jetty.

Late afternoon is the best time to visit to avoid the heat and crowds, as well as for its sunset. The further you walk from the main entry the more privacy you'll get.

Neils Cove BEACH

Northwest of Radhanagar is the gorgeous 'lagoon' at Neils Cove, a gem of sheltered sand and crystalline water. Swimming is prohibited at dusk and dawn; take heed of any warnings regarding crocodiles.

Beach 5 BEACH

On the north-eastern coast of the island, the palm-ringed Beach 5 has your more classic tropical vibe, with the bonus of shady patches and fewer sandflies. However, swimming is very difficult in low tide when the water becomes shallow for miles. Most of the island's accommodation is out this way.

Kalapathar BEACH

Hidden away 5km south of Beach 5, you'll find Kalapathar, a pristine beach. You may have to walk a bit to get away from throngs of package tourists.

Diving & Snorkelling

Havelock is the premier spot for diving in the Andamans. It's famed for its crystal-clear waters, deep-sea corals and kaleidoscope of marine life, including turtles. Diving here is suitable for all levels.

The main dive season is roughly November to April, but trips run year-round.

All companies offer fully equipped boat dives, and prices vary depending on the location, number of participants and duration of the course. Diving starts from around ₹5000 to ₹6000 for a two-tank dive, with options of PADI scuba diver (two dives ₹18,000), open-water (four dives ₹24,000) and advanced (five dives ₹19,500) courses.

While coral bleaching has been a major issue since 2010 (said to be linked to El Niño weather patterns), diving remains world-class. The shallows may not have particularly bright corals, but all the colourful fish are still here, and for depths beyond 16m, corals remain as vivid as ever. The Andamans recovered from a similar bleaching in 1998, and today things are, likewise, slowly repairing themselves.

Popular sites include **Dixon's Pinnacle** and **Pilot Reef** with colourful soft coral, **South Button** for macro dives (to see small critters) and rock formations, **Jackson Bar** or **Johnny's Gorge** for deeper dives with schools of snapper, sharks, rays and turtles, and **Minerva's Delight** for a bit of everything.

PROTECTING MARINE LIFE

If you plan on diving or snorkelling in the Andamans, play your part to protect its fragile marine ecosystem. Only snorkel when it's high tide: during low tide it's very easy to step on coral or sea sponges, which can irreparably damage them. In areas of reefs with very shallow water, avoid wearing flippers so as to protect marine life – even the gentle sweep of a flipper kick can result in damage to decades' worth of growth. Divers need to be extra cautious about descents near reefs; colliding with the coral at a strong pace with full gear can be environmentally disastrous. Choose ecologically responsible dive operators.

Avoid touching marine life, including coral, as doing so may not only cause stress and damage (some organisms have a protective coating that is rubbed off if touched, thus making them more vulnerable to parasites and disease), but they could also be toxic.

Finally, clear any rubbish you come across and refrain from taking souvenir shells or coral out of the ocean (it's ecologically detrimental but possibly also illegal).

Havelock Island

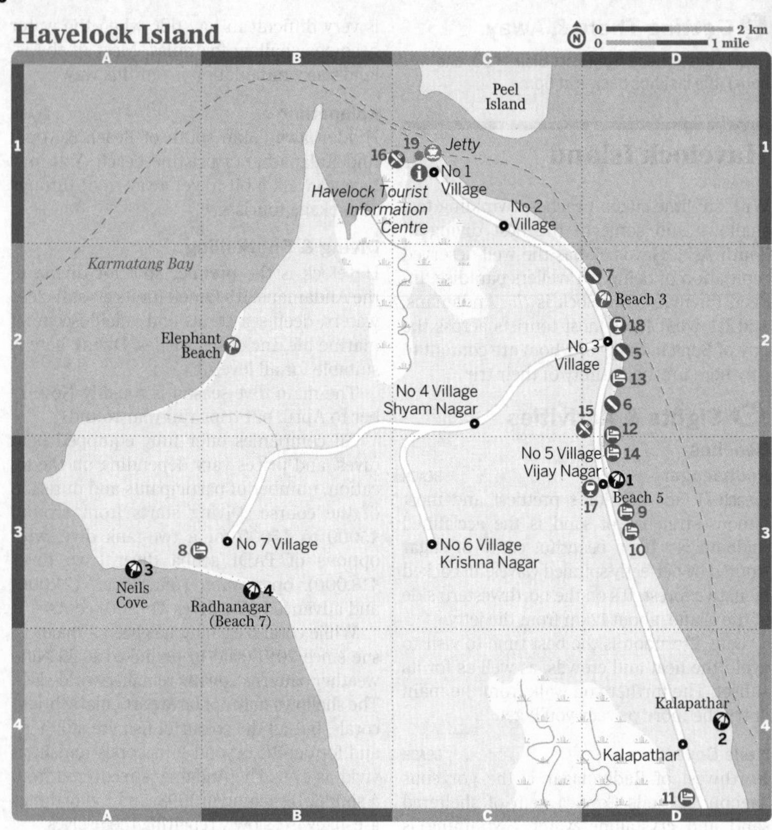

There's also a **wreck dive** to SS *Incheket,* a 1950s cargo carrier. Keep an eye out for trips further afield such as **Barren Island**, home to India's only active volcano, whose ash produces an eerie underwater spectacle for divers.

Dive companies arrange **snorkelling** trips, but it can be cheaper to organise a boat through your hotel or guesthouse. Snorkelling gear is widely available on Havelock but is generally mediocre quality, so consider bringing your own if you intend doing a lot of snorkelling.

Most boats head to **Elephant Beach** for snorkelling, which can also be reached by a 40-minute walk through a muddy elephant logging trail; it's well marked (off the cross-island road), but turns to bog if it has been raining. At high tide it's also impossible to reach – ask locally for more information. Lots of snorkelling charters come out this way, so be prepared as it can be a bit of a circus. If you head here around 6am, you'll have a better chance of getting the place to yourself.

Prices are standardised, so it's a matter of finding a dive operator you feel comfortable with.

Ocean Tribe DIVING
(☎03192-282255; www.ocean-tribe.com; No 3 Village) Run by legendary local Karen divers, including Dixon and Jackson, all who have had dive sites named after them.

Dive India DIVING
(☎03192-214247; www.diveindia.com; btwn No 3 & 5 Village; 1/2 dives ₹4500/₹6000) The original PADI company in Havelock, and still one of the best.

Barefoot Scuba DIVING
(☎9566088560; www.diveandamans.com; No 3 Village) Popular, long-established company with dive-and-accommodation packages.

Andaman Bubbles DIVING
(☎03192-282140; www.andamanbubbles.com; No 5 Village; 1hr dive ₹4500, 2-day 4-dive package

Havelock Island

₹10,500) Quality outfit with professional, personable staff.

Other Activities

Some resorts organise guided **jungle treks** for keen walkers or birdwatchers, though the forest floor turns to mush after rain. The inside rainforest is a spectacular, emerald-coloured hinterland cavern, and the **birdwatching** is rewarding (especially on the forest fringes); look out for the blue-black racket-tailed drongo or golden oriole.

High-season yoga lessons (per 1½ hours ₹300 to ₹500) are available at Flying Elephant (p1098).

Andaman Kayak Tours KAYAKING
(☎9933269653; www.andamanhomestay.com/kayak-and-snorkel; min 2 people 2½hr kayak ₹2500) Weather permitting, Andaman Kayak Tours explore Havelock's mangroves by sea kayak, and run memorable night trips gliding among bio-luminescence.

Sleeping

Pellicon Beach Resort BUNGALOW $
(☎9932081673; www.pelliconbeachresort.com; Beach 5; hut from ₹700; 📶) Attractive beachside bungalows as well as Nicobari huts with private porches on a peaceful plot of land close to the beach.

Coconut Grove Beach Resort GUESTHOUSE $
(☎9531835592; www.coconutgrovebeachresort.com; Beach 5; hut ₹600, without bathroom ₹300; 🍴) Particularly popular with Israeli travellers, Coconut Grove has an appealingly relaxed communal vibe with huts arranged in a circular outlay.

Sunrise Beach Resort BUNGALOW $
(☎9474206183; Beach 5; r ₹600-1000, with AC ₹5100) Offers the same thatched goodness as almost every other resort – what sets it apart is its budget A-frame huts with water views.

Emerald Gecko BUNGALOW $$
(☎9474286953; www.emerald-gecko.com; Beach 5; hut ₹1500-3000) Double-storey bungalows look to the water, while pricier rooms have ambient lighting and outdoor bathrooms constructed from bamboo rafts that have drifted ashore from Myanmar.

Orient Legend Resort GUESTHOUSE $$
(☎9434291008; www.havelockbeachresort.in; Beach 5; hut without bathroom ₹500, r ₹1200, with AC ₹2500) This popular place on Beach 5 covers most budgets, from doghouse A-frame huts and concrete rooms to double-storey cottages that offer a glimpse of the ocean.

Sea View Beach Resort BUNGALOW $$
(☎943429877; Beach 3; r ₹800-1000) Chilled-out beach bungalows, backing on to the Ocean Tribe (p1096) dive shop, a bit away from the crowds.

★ **Barefoot at Havelock** RESORT $$$
(☎03192-214534; www.barefootindia.com; Beach 7; tented cottage incl breakfast ₹9500, Nicobari cottage ₹13,500; ❄) 🍃 Thoughtfully designed, eco-conscious resort boasting elegantly comfortable timber and bamboo-thatched cottages just back from the famed Radhanagar Beach.

★ Silversand RESORT $$$
(☎03192-211073; www.silversandhavelock.com; Beach 5; r incl breakfast ₹12,000; ❄📶🏊) The highlight of this hotel is its location on a lovely stretch of beach, away from the crowds. Rooms are comfortable with the more expensive ones positioned closer to the sea. There's a good bar and restaurant.

Flying Elephant BUNGALOW $$$
(☎9474250821; www.flying-elephant.in; Kalapathar; r ₹4000) Hidden away on Kalapathar beach, in a pastoral setting among rice paddies and betel palms, this serene retreat has simple, earthy bamboo duplexes that feature landscaped outdoor stone-garden bathrooms.

Wild Orchid RESORT $$$
(☎03192-282472; www.wildorchidandaman.com; Beach 5; r incl breakfast from ₹6125; ❄📶) Modern Andamanese-style cottages, all set around a tropical garden a stone's throw from the beach.

Eating & Drinking

Most people eat at, or near, their hotel but there are *dhabas* (snack bars) near the jetty or you can head to the main bazaar (No 3 Village) for local meals.

Alcohol is available from a **store** (Beach 3; ⏱9am-noon & 3-8pm) next to the ATM at No 3 Village.

Fat Martin's INDIAN $
(Beach 5; mains ₹70-140; ⏱7.30am-10pm) Popular open-air cafe with a good selection of Indian dishes and some particularly impressive dosas including paneer tikka and nutella.

Anju-coco Resto INDIAN, CONTINENTAL $$
(Beach 5; mains ₹200-800; ⏱8am-10.30pm) One of Havelock's faves, down-to-earth Anju-coco offers a varied menu with standouts being its hearty breakfasts, yummy barbecue dishes and platters.

★ Red Snapper SEAFOOD $$$
(Wild Orchid Resort, Beach 5; mains ₹250-850; ⏱7.30-10am, noon-2.30pm & 6-9.30pm) This appealing thatched-roof restaurant with polished-bamboo decor exudes a romantic island ambience. Menu items include lavish seafood platters, pepper-crust tuna and handmade pasta. The outdoor deck seating is a good spot for a beer.

Full Moon Cafe MULTICUISINE $$$
(Dive India, Beach 5; mains ₹200-490) 🍃 Run by an Irish-Indian couple, this cool thatched-roof restaurant shares a site with Dive India on Beach 5. It does fabulous seafood and salads and a refreshing ginger-honey lemonade. Free water refills.

B3 – Barefoot Bayside & Brasserie MULTICUISINE $$$
(Village No 1; mains ₹350-500; ⏱noon-9.30pm) Come here for the best pizzas in Havelock or scrumptious handmade pasta. There's good gelato, too! Its breezy outside decking, with sea views, makes this a great place to wait for your ferry. Downstairs is **Dakshin** (mains ₹80-270; ⏱6.30am-10am & noon-3.30pm), specialising in South Indian cuisine.

Cicada LIVE MUSIC
(Beach 5; ⏱hours variable) Run by the team from Emerald Gecko, this live-music/hang-out venue has a groovy jungle location accessed down a path off the main road across from Beach 5.

Information

Satellite internet is insanely slow and pricey at around ₹300 per hour.

Havelock Tourist Information Centre
(☎03192-282117; next to jetty, Village No 1; ⏱8am-4.30pm) The official government tourist office provides brochures and information but does not book any tours.

Getting There & Away

Government ferries run from Havelock **jetty** at No 1 Village to Port Blair three times a day (₹420, 2½ hours) at 9am, 2.45pm and 4.30pm. It's best to book tickets from the **ferry ticket office** (⏱9.15am-noon & 2-4pm Mon-Fri, to noon Sat) at least two days in advance (most hotels can arrange this for a small fee). One to two ferries a day link Havelock with Neil Island (₹335, 1¼ hours), while four boats a week (9.30am on Monday, Wednesday, Friday, and Saturday) head to Long Island (₹335, two hours) en route to Rangat.

Private (more comfortable) ferries such as **Makruzz** (p1093) and **Coastal Cruise** (p1093) have daily services to Port Blair via Neil Island.

Getting Around

A local bus (₹10, 40 minutes) connects the jetty, villages and Radhanagar on a roughly hourly circuit from 10am until 5.30pm. Otherwise you can rent a scooter (per 24 hours from around ₹490) or bicycle (per day ₹100) – your guesthouse/hotel should be able to arrange this or point you in the right direction.

An autorickshaw from the jetty to No 3 Village is ₹50, to No 5 ₹90 and to No 7 ₹500.

Neil Island

Although its beaches are not as luxurious as its more famous island neighbour, Havelock, tranquil Neil has its own unique charm. There's a wonderfully unhurried pace of life here; cycling through picturesque little villages is a stellar way to soak up the island's character. The main bazaar has a mellow vibe and is a popular gathering spot in the early evening. On Neil Island you're about 40km from Port Blair, a short ferry ride from Havelock and several universes away from the bustle of life back home.

Sights & Activities

Beaches

Neil Island's five beaches (numbered one to five) all have their own personality, though they aren't necessarily great for swimming due to shallow, rocky sea floors.

Beach 1 BEACH

(Laxmanpur) Beach 1 is a long sweep of sandy coastline and mangrove, a 40-minute walk west of the jetty and village. There's a good sunset viewpoint out this way accessed via Pearl Park Beach Resort (p1099). Dugongs are sometime spotted here.

Beach 2 BEACH

On the north side of the island, Beach 2 has the Natural Bridge rock formation, accessible only at low tide by walking around the rocky cove. To get here by bicycle, take the side road that runs through the bazaar, then take a left where the road forks.

Beach 3 BEACH

(Ram Nagar) Beach 3 is a secluded rocky cove with powdery sand. There's also good snorkelling here.

Beach 4 BEACH

(Bharatpur) Beach 4 is Neil Island's best swimming beach, though its proximity to the jetty is a turn-off, as are rowdy day-trippers who descend upon the beach in motorised boats.

Beach 5 BEACH

(Sitapur) The more rugged Beach 5, 5km from the village on the eastern side of Neil, is a nice place to walk along the sand, with small limestone caves accessible at low tide.

Diving & Snorkelling

Neil offers some brilliant dive sites, with colourful fish, large schools of Jack, turtles, rays, and soft and hard corals. There are several dive operators on Neil Island and open-water courses, among others, are also available.

The island's best snorkelling is around the coral reef at the far (western) end of Beach 1 at high tide; if you're extremely lucky you may spot a dugong feeding in the shallows. Beach 3 also has good snorkelling. Gear costs around ₹200 to hire and is available from many guesthouses.

India Scuba Explorers DIVING

(9933271450; www.indiascubaexplorers.com; Beach 1; 1 dive ₹4500) Neil's first dive shop, set up by a husband-wife team, is popular for its personalised service.

Dive India DIVING

(8001122205; www.diveindia.com; per 1/2 dives ₹4500/6000) Established in Havelock, this professional company also has a branch in Neil. It's based just near the jetty.

Sleeping

Beach 1

Sunset Garden Guesthouse BUNGALOW $

(9933294573; hut ₹800, without bathroom ₹300) Ideal for those wanting to get away from it all, these basic bamboo huts have a secluded spot accessed via a 15-minute walk through rice fields.

Seashell RESORT $$$

(9933239625; www.seashellhotels.net; cottage incl breakfast ₹9000; ❄) Seashell has contemporary, well-appointed cottages that lead down to a mangrove-lined beach. Rooms have TVs and tea-and-coffee-making facilities.

Pearl Park Beach Resort BUNGALOW $$$

(9434260132; www.andamanpearlpark.com; r incl breakfast with fan from ₹3500, with AC from ₹5500; ❄📶) Comfortable bamboo huts arranged around a flower-filled garden.

Beach 3

★Kalapani BUNGALOW $

(9474274991; hut ₹600, without bathroom ₹300) Run by the lovely Prakash and Bina, laid-back Kalapani has simple bungalows. Motorbikes, bicycles and snorkelling gear are available for hire, and the owners have plenty of suggestions about things to do.

Breakwater Beach Resort BUNGALOW $

(9933292654; hut ₹500-1000, without bathroom ₹300) Easygoing ambience, acceptable rooms, attractive garden and delicious food.

Beach 5

Sunrise Beach Resort BUNGALOW $
(☎9933266900; r ₹400, without bathroom ₹300) Sunrise has simple thatched bungalows, a short walk from the beach. There's a sweet little restaurant among flowers serving up tasty dishes such as coconut fish masala (₹150).

Emerald Gecko BUNGALOW $$
(☎9474286953; www.emerald-gecko.com; r ₹2000-4000) Simple, eco-friendly bungalows, with ceiling fans and mosquito nets, set in a coconut plantation.

Neil Kendra

Silversand RESORT $$$
(☎03192-244914; www.silversandneil.com; r incl breakfast from ₹12,000;) One of Neil's most upmarket places to stay, Silversand has cosy contemporary cottages set among shady palms just a short walk from the water.

Eating

Garden View Restaurant INDIAN, CONTINENTAL $
(Beach 5; ₹50-130; 6am-10pm) Set in a cool garden, this is a relaxing little spot to drink Kingfisher beer (₹170 per bottle) or papaya lassi (₹60) and tuck into fish curry, prawn fried rice and much more.

Blue Sea SEAFOOD, INDIAN $$
(Beach 3; mains ₹120-300; 6am-11pm) Small, quirky beach shack with sandy floor, dangling beach curios and a blue whale skull centrepiece that serves simple, tasty Indian fare as well as some continental dishes. A path leads to, arguably, Neil's best beach. Come here for the unpretentious, chilled-out character and nearby beach.

Moonshine INTERNATIONAL, INDIAN $$
(Beach 1; mains ₹100-400; 8-11am, noon-1pm, 4-9.30pm) On the road to Beach 1, this backpacker favourite cooks up satiating homemade pasta and fish thalis. Cold beer can be arranged.

Information

There's no ATM or moneychanging facilities on Neil, so bring plenty of cash.

There's wi-fi access at **Pearl Park Beach Resort** (p1099) on Beach 1 (₹200 for two hours).

Getting There & Around

A ferry heads to Port Blair two or three times a day (₹400, two hours). There are also one or two daily ferries to Havelock (₹400, one hour), and three ferries a week to Long Island (₹400, five hours). **Makruzz** (p1093) and **Coastal Cruise** (p1093) also have ferries to/from Port Blair (from ₹875, one hour) and Havelock (from ₹710).

Hiring a bicycle (per day from ₹100) is the best way to get about; roads are flat and distances short. You'll be able to find one in the bazaar or at a guesthouse. An autorickshaw will take you from the jetty to Beach 1 or 3 for between ₹75 to ₹100.

Middle & North Andaman

The Andamans aren't just sun and sand. They are also jungle that feels as primeval as the Jurassic, a green tangle of ancient forest that could have been birthed in Mother Nature's subconscious. This wild, antediluvian side of the islands can be seen on a long, loping bus ride up the Andaman Trunk Rd (ATR), crossing tannin-red rivers prowled by saltwater crocodiles on roll-on, roll-off ferries.

But there's a negative side to riding the ATR: the road cuts through the homeland of the Jarawa (p1101) and has brought the tribe into incessant contact with the outside world. Modern India and tribal life do not seem able to coexist – every time Jarawa and settlers interact, misunderstandings have led to friction, confusion and, at worst, violent attacks and death. Indian anthropologists and indigenous rights groups such as Survival International have called for the ATR to be closed; its status continues to be under review. At present, vehicles are permitted to travel only in convoys at set times from 6am to 3pm. Photography is strictly prohibited, as is stopping or any other interaction with the Jarawa people who are becoming increasingly reliant on handouts from passing traffic.

The first point of interest north of Port Blair are the **limestone caves** (Baratang; Tue-Sun) at Baratang. It's a scenic 45-minute boat trip (₹450) from the jetty, through mangrove forest. A permit is required, and can be organised at the jetty.

Rangat & Around

Travelling north on the Andaman Trunk Rd, Rangat is the first main town in Middle Andaman after Baratang Island. It's primarily a transport hub with not much else going for it on the tourism front. The turtle breeding grounds at **Dhaninallah Mangrove** is the

ISLAND INDEGENES

The Andaman and Nicobar Islands' indigenous peoples constitute 12% of the population and, in most cases, their numbers are decreasing. The Onge, Sentinelese, Andamanese and Jarawa are all of Negrito ethnicity, and share a strong resemblance to people from Africa. Tragically, numerous groups have become extinct over the past century. In February 2010 the last speaker of the Bo language passed away, bringing an end to a culture and language that originated 65,000 years ago.

It's important to note that these tribal groups live in areas strictly off limits to foreigners – for their protection and dignity – and people have been arrested for trying to visit the regions.

Jarawa

The 300 or so remaining Jarawa occupy the 639-sq-km reserve on South and Middle Andaman Islands (p1100). In 1953 the chief commissioner requested that an armed sea plane bomb Jarawa settlements, and their territory has been consistently disrupted by the Andaman Trunk Rd, forest clearance and settler and tourist encroachment. In 2012, a video went viral showing an exchange between Jarawa and tourists, whereby a policeman orders them to dance in exchange for food. This resulted in a government inquest that saw to the end of the so-called 'human safari' tours.

Nicobarese

The 30,000 Nicobarese are the only indigenous people whose numbers are not decreasing. The majority have converted to Christianity and been partly assimilated into contemporary Indian society. Living in village units led by a head man, they farm pigs and cultivate coconuts, yams and bananas. The Nicobarese, who probably descended from people of Malaysia and Myanmar, inhabit a number of islands in the Nicobar group, centred on Car Nicobar, the region worst affected by the 2004 tsunami.

Onge

Two-thirds of Little Andaman's Onge Island was taken over by the Forest Department and 'settled' in 1977. The 100 or so remaining members of the Onge tribe live in a 25-sq-km reserve covering Dugong Creek and South Bay. Anthropologists say the Onge population has declined due to demoralisation through loss of territory.

Sentinelese

The Sentinelese, unlike the other tribes on these islands, have consistently repelled outside contact. For years, contact parties arrived on the beaches of North Sentinel Island, the last redoubt of the Sentinelese, with gifts of coconuts, bananas, pigs and plastic buckets, only to be showered with arrows, though some encounters have been a little less hostile. About 150 Sentinelese remain.

Andamanese

There were around 7000 Andamanese in the mid-19th century, but friendliness to colonisers was their undoing, and by 1971 all but 19 of the population had been wiped away by measles, syphilis and influenza epidemics. Their population now numbers only about 50 and they have been resettled on tiny Strait Island.

Shompen

Only about 250 Shompen remain in the forests on Great Nicobar. Seminomadic hunter-gatherers who live along the riverbanks, they have resisted integration and avoid areas occupied by Indian immigrants.

most popular sight, viewed early evening (mid-December to April) from the approximately 1km-long boardwalk, a 45-minute drive from Rangat.

Getting There & Away

Ferries depart for Long Island (₹11) from Yeratta Jetty, 8km from Rangat (accessed by local bus), at 9am and 3pm. Rangat Bay, 5km outside town, has ferries to/from Port Blair (₹378, six hours) and Havelock (₹378, two hours). A daily bus goes to Port Blair (₹145, seven hours) and Diglipur (₹65, four hours).

Long Island

With its friendly island community and deliciously slow pace of life, Long Island is perfect for those seeking to take the pace down a few more notches. Other than the odd motorcycle, there's no motorised vehicles on the island, and at certain times you may be the only tourist here.

Sights & Activities

Beaches

There's a lovely beach close to Blue Planet (p1102), a 15-minute walk from the jetty.

A 1½-hour trek (or cross-trail jog if you're feeling energetic) in the jungle will lead you to the secluded **Lalaji Bay**, a beautiful white-sand beach with good swimming and snorkelling; follow the red arrows from the jetty to get here. Hiring a boat (₹2500 return for two persons) is also an option. Inconveniently, you need a permit (free) from the Forest Office near the jetty to visit.

Diving & Snorkelling

Blue Planet has a dive shop (December to March) and hires snorkelling gear for around ₹100. Trips head to Campbell Shoal for its schools of trevally and barracuda.

You can also get a boat to North Passage Island for snorkelling at the stunning **Merk Bay** (₹3500 for two people) with blinding white sand and translucent waters.

There's terrific offshore **snorkelling** at Lalaji Bay with colourful corals out front from the rest huts. There's also good snorkelling at the beach near Blue Planet guesthouse, directly out from the blue Hindu temple; swim beyond the sea grass to get to the coral.

DON'T MISS

TURTLE NESTING IN KALIPUR

Reputedly the only beach in the world where leatherback, hawksbill, olive ridley marine and green turtles all nest along the same coastline, Kalipur is a fantastic place to observe this evening show from mid-December to April. Turtles can be witnessed most nights, and you may be able to assist with collecting eggs, or with the release of hatchlings. Contact Pristine Beach Resort for more information.

Sleeping & Eating

★Blue Planet GUESTHOUSE $$

(☎9474212180; www.blueplanetandamans.com; r from ₹1500, without bathroom from ₹500; @) An old favourite, Blue Planet has thatched-bamboo rooms and hammocks set around a Padauk tree. Food is delicious and there's free filtered water. It's a 15-minute walk from the jetty. They also have bamboo cottages (from ₹3200) at a nearby location.

Getting There & Away

There are four ferries a week to Havelock, Neil and Port Blair (₹195). If you can't get a ferry here from Port Blair, jump on a bus to Rangat to get the ferry from Yeratta, 8km from Rangat, from where two daily boats run to Long Island (₹11, one hour) at 9am and 3.30pm.

Diglipur & Around

Those who make it this far north are rewarded with some impressive attractions in the area. It's a giant outdoor adventure playground designed for nature lovers: home to a world-famous turtle nesting site, the Andamans' highest peak and a network of caves to go with white-sand beaches and some of the best snorkelling in the Andamans.

However, don't expect much of Diglipur (population 70,000), the second largest urban hub in the Andamans, a sprawling, gritty bazaar town. Instead head straight for the tranquil coastal village of **Kalipur**.

Activities

In season most people come to see the turtles.

★Ross & Smith Islands BEACH, SNORKELLING

Like lovely tropical counterweights, the twin islands of Smith and Ross are connected by a narrow sandbar of dazzling white sand, and are up there with the best in the Andamans for both swimming and snorkelling.

No permits are required for Smith Island, which is accessed by boat (₹2500 per boat, fits five people) from Aerial Bay. While theoretically you need a permit for Ross Island (₹500), as it's walkable from Smith, permits generally aren't checked. Enquire with Pristine Resort for more information.

Saddle Peak TREKKING

(Indian/foreigner ₹25/250) At 732m Saddle Peak is the Andamans' highest point. You

OFF THE BEATEN TRACK

MAYABUNDER & AROUND

In 'upper' Middle Andaman, Mayabunder is best known for its villages inhabited by Karen, members of a Burmese hill tribe who were relocated here during the British colonial period. It's a low-key destination, away from the crowds.

You can go on a range of day tours, with the highlight being jungle trekking at creepy **Interview Island** (boat hire ₹3000, fits six people), inhabited by a population of around 35 wild elephants, released after a logging company closed for business in the 1950s. Armed guards accompany you in case of elephant encounters. A permit (₹500) is required, which is best organised by emailing a copy of your arrival permit to Sea'n'Sand guesthouse. Other trips include **turtle nesting** at Dhaninallah Mangrove (December to March); **Forty One Caves**, where *hawabills* (swiftlets) make their highly prized edible nests; and snorkelling off **Avis Island** (boat hire ₹1500).

Sea'n'Sand (☎03192-273454; titusinseansand@yahoo.com; r from ₹850; ❄) is easily the best place to stay. Hosts Titus and Elizabeth (and their extended Karen family) are an excellent source for everything Mayabunder, and the food here is a treat.

Mayabunder, 71km north of Rangat (₹75, two hours), is linked by daily buses from Port Blair (₹200, 10 hours) and Diglipur (₹60, two hours) and by thrice-weekly ferries.

can trek through subtropical forest to the top and back from Kalipur in about six to seven hours; the views across the archipelago are incredible. It's a demanding trek, so bring plenty of water (around 4L). A permit (₹250) is required from the Forest Office at the trailhead, open 6am to 2pm.

A local guide (300₹) will make sure you don't get lost, but otherwise follow the red arrows marked on the trees.

Craggy Island SNORKELLING

A small island off Kalipur, Craggy is a good spot for snorkelling. Strong swimmers can make it across (flippers recommended), otherwise a motorised boat is available (₹3000 return).

Excelsior Island SNORKELLING

Excelsior has beautiful beaches, snorkelling plus resident spotted deer. Permits are required (₹500); boats cost ₹4500 and fit seven people.

Sleeping & Eating

★**Pristine Beach Resort** GUESTHOUSE $$$

(☎9474286787; www.andamanpristineresorts.com; Kalipur Beach; hut ₹1500, r ₹3500-4500; ❄@) Huddled among the palms between paddy fields and the beach, this relaxing resort has simple bamboo huts as well as more upmarket rooms. Its restaurant-bar serves delicious fish Nicobari.

Sion INDIAN $

(Kalipur Beach; mains ₹60-150; ⏲10am-10pm) This rooftop restaurant gets the thumbs up for its seafood dishes.

Getting There & Away

Diglipur, located about 80km north of Mayabunder, is served by daily buses to Port Blair (₹265, 12 hours) at 5am and 7am, plus a 10.40pm night bus. There are also buses to Mayabunder (₹55, 2½ hours) and Rangat (₹100, 4½ hours).

Ferries to Port Blair (seat/bunk ₹110/350, nine hours) depart three times a week (Tuesday, Thursday and Saturday).

Getting Around

Ferries and some buses arrive at Aerial Bay, from where it's 11km to Diglipur, and 8km to Kalipur in the other direction.

Buses run the 18km journey from Diglipur to Kalipur (₹15, 30 minutes) every 45 minutes; an autorickshaw costs ₹200.

Little Andaman

As far south as you can go in the islands, Little Andaman has an appealing end-of-the-world feel. It's a gorgeous fist of mangroves, jungle and teal, ringed by beaches as fresh as bread out of the oven. It rates highly as many travellers' favourite spot in the Andamans.

Badly hit by the 2004 tsunami, Little Andaman has slowly rebuilt itself. Located about 120km south of Port Blair, the main settlement here is **Hut Bay**, a pleasant small town.

Sights & Activities

Little Andaman Lighthouse LIGHTHOUSE

Located 14km east of Hut Bay, Little Andaman lighthouse makes for a worthwhile excursion. Standing 41m high, 200 steps spiral up to magnificent views over the coastline and forest. The easiest way to get here is by motorcycle. Otherwise take a sweaty bicycle journey or autorickshaw until the road becomes unpassable; from there, walk for an hour along the blissful stretch of deserted beach.

Beaches

Come prepared for sandflies; crocodiles also lurk about (seek local advice as to where crocs may be currently congregating).

Netaji Nagar BEACH

The sprawling and rugged Netaji Nagar, stretching 8km to 12km north of Hut Bay, is the beach where most accommodation is located.

Butler Bay BEACH

(₹20) Little Andaman's best beach is Butler Bay, a spectacular curved beach with lifeguards and good surf. It's located at the 14km mark.

Kalapathar BEACH

Located before Butler Bay is Kalapathar lagoon, a popular enclosed swimming area with shady patches of sand. Look for the cave in the cliff face that you can scramble through for stunning ocean views. It's accessed via a side road that runs past modern housing constructed after the 2004 tsunami.

Surfing

Intrepid surfing travellers have been whispering about Little Andaman since it first opened to foreigners some years back. The reef breaks are legendary, but best suited for more experienced surfers. The most accessible is **Jarawa Point**, a left reef break at the northern point of Butler Bay. Beginners should stick to beach breaks along Km8 to Km11. February to April generally bring the best waves.

Surfing Little Andaman SURFING

(☎9531877287; www.surfinglittleandaman.com; Hut Bay; 2hr lesson ₹1000) Here you can hire boards, arrange lessons and get the lowdown on everything about surfing in Little Andaman.

Waterfalls

Inland, the **White Surf** and **Whisper Wave** waterfalls offer a jungle experience for when you're done lazing on the beach. The latter involves a 4km forest trek and a guide is highly recommended. They are pleasant falls and you may be tempted to swim in the rock pools, but beware of crocodiles.

Sleeping & Eating

There are cheap and tasty thali places in Hut Bay.

Blue View BUNGALOW $

(☎9734480840; Km11.5, Netaji Nagar; r without bathroom from ₹300; ⏲Oct-May) With its relaxing atmosphere, Blue View's simple thatched bungalows are popular mainly for the warm hospitality of its hosts. Surfboards, bicycles and motorbikes can be hired.

Aastha Eco Resort BUNGALOW $

(Km10, Netaji Nagar; r ₹600) Set among betel and coconut palms, Aastha is a calm choice with its atmospheric Nicobari huts and thatched cottages.

Hawva Beach Resort BUNGALOW $

(☎9775181290; Km8, Netaji Nagar; r from ₹400) This laid-back family-run lodging has just a handful of simple cottages. Flavoursome home-cooked food is available.

Palm Groove INDIAN $

(Hut Bay; mains ₹60-140; ⏲7am-9pm) Set in a heritage-style bungalow, with an outdoor garden gazebo, Palm Grove dishes up a selection of tasty biriyanis and curries.

Information

There's an ATM in Hut Bay and village at 16Km.

Getting There & Away

Ferries land at Hut Bay Jetty. Buses (₹10, depart hourly) to Netaji Nagar usually coincide with ferry arrivals, but often leave before you clear immigration, leaving more pricey jeeps (per person ₹100) as the other option. An autorickshaw from the jetty to Netaji Nagar is around ₹250, or ₹80 to town. Motorbikes and bicycles are popular for getting around, and are available from most lodges; otherwise, shared jeeps (₹25) and buses are very handy.

Boats sail to Port Blair daily, alternating between afternoon and evening departures on vessels ranging from big ferries with four-/two-bed rooms (₹240/330, six to 8½ hours) to faster 5½-hour government boats (₹35); all have air-con. The ferry office is closed Sunday.

Understand India

India Today

With so many states, languages, religions, traditions, opinions and people jostling for space and attention, what is striking about India is not its problems, but how well things work considering these many obstacles. Despite challenges ranging from poverty and violence against women to religious tensions and military squabbles with its neighbours, India continues to thrive as the most successful nation in South Asia and the largest democracy in the world.

Best on Film

Fire (1996), **Earth** (1998) and **Water** (2005) Trilogy directed by Deepa Mehta.

Pather Panchali (1955) Haunting masterpiece from Satyajit Ray.

Pyaasa (Thirst; 1957) and **Kaagaz Ke Phool** (Paper Flowers; 1959) For a taste of nostalgia.

Gandhi (1982) The classic.

Lagaan (2001) Written and directed by Ashutosh Gowariker.

Best in Print

Midnight's Children Salman Rushdie's allegory about Independence and Partition.

A Fine Balance Rohinton Mistry's beautifully written, tragic tale set in Mumbai.

White Tiger Aravind Adiga's Man Booker-winning novel about class struggle in globalised India.

A Suitable Boy More than 1300 pages of romance, heartbreak, family secrets and political intrigue from Vikram Seth.

Shantaram Gregory David Roberts' vivid experiences of his life in India. A traveller favourite!

The Political Landscape

India's politics continues to be shaped – and in many cases, shaken – by the leadership of Prime Minister Narendra Modi, who surged to power in 2014, as the Bharatiya Janata Party scored a landslide victory over the ruling Indian National Congress and its dynastic leader Rahul Gandhi, great grandson of India's first prime minister, Jawaharlal Nehru. During the election campaign, Modi was painted as a religious fundamentalist and hawk by opponents, primarily because of lingering allegations of involvement in intercommunal violence in Gujarat in 2002, but his tenure has been more conciliatory than many feared.

Although some hardline causes have seen growing support – most significantly opposition to cow-slaughter, which has led to bans on the sale of beef and tragic attacks on people accused of killing cows – Modi's focus on neoliberal economics and the so-called Gujarat model of development has brought solid support from many sectors of the Indian population, regardless of religious background. In his first few years in government, Modi decreased welfare spending but lowered taxes, reduced red tape and increased investment by foreign companies, leading to growing opportunities for India's middle classes.

Perhaps Modi's bravest manoeuvre came on 8 November 2016, when the government, without warning, demonetised the nation's ₹500 and ₹1000 banknotes, in a shock move intended to drive tax-avoiders, corrupt officials and terrorism-funders out into the open. While criticised by many – including the International Monetary Fund, which downgraded India's economic forecast as a result of the ban – demonetisation did not lead to the predicted civil unrest, despite massive upheaval and vast queues at the nation's banks before new banknotes entered circulation.

Modi's progress on social issues has been less dynamic. Violence against women continues to be an issue that tarnishes India's reputation, following a string of high-profile rapes and murders, and mass assaults against women during New Year celebrations in Bengaluru in 2017. One unintended consequence of demonetisation has been the reduction in female control of wealth, as women have been forced to reveal personal savings and cede control of their money to male relatives. Nevertheless, there is some progress; the Modi government is debating a 33% quota for women workers in the public sector and a ban on the controversial practice of *talaq,* where Muslim men can divorce their wives by repeating the word *talaq* three times.

Plentiful People & Problematic Neighbours

Once a vassal of empire, India is fast emerging as a global superpower to rival Europe and the United States, but its greatest resource – its 1.27 billion people – is also perhaps its greatest challenge. India regularly ranks as the world's fastest-growing economy, but nearly a quarter of its vast and expanding population lives below the official poverty line, with less than US$1.90 of purchasing power parity per day. With the population continuing to grow by 1.2% – or 12.7 million people – per year, India faces an uphill struggle to ensure that the economic benefits of growth filter down to ordinary people.

Growing power has also placed India into conflict with its neighbours. The traditional divide between China and India – the impregnable line of the Himalaya – is becoming increasingly porous as China expands its influence in Nepal and Pakistan to check Indian power in the region. Plans for a railway connection directly across the world's highest mountains from Tibet may be positive for trade, but China's overtures to India's often hostile neighbours have left many Indians feeling threatened by the Sleeping Giant to the north.

India-Chinese relations are further complicated by the status of the Dalai Lama, the spiritual leader of Tibetan Buddhism, who lives in exile in McLeod Ganj near Dharamsala, along with members of the pre-1959 Tibetan Government. India's acceptance of Tibetan refugees is an ongoing source of tension with China, which disputes Indian ownership of parts of Arunachal Pradesh and Aksai Chin in Kashmir as part of its claim to Tibet. Chinese and Indian troops entered a tense standoff in Aksai Chin in 2013, before politicians negotiated an end to the dispute, and a subsequent incursion by Chinese forces into Arunachal Pradesh in 2016 has revived fears that China nurtures ambitions to claim the region it refers to as South Tibet.

POPULATION: **1.27 BILLION**

GDP: **US$2.3 TRILLION (2016)**

UNEMPLOYMENT RATE: **5% (2016)**

LITERACY RATE: **74.04% (65/82% FEMALE/MALE)**

GENDER RATIO: **940/1000 (FEMALE/MALE)**

if India were 100 people

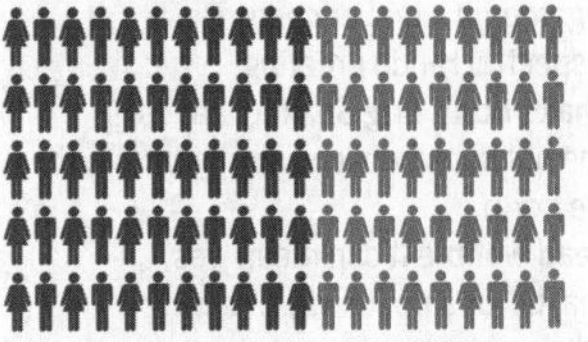

55 would speak one of 21 other official languages
41 would speak Hindi
4 would speak one of 400 other official languages

belief systems

(% of population)

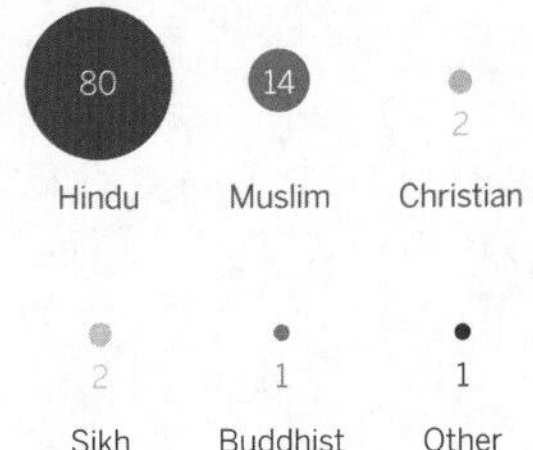

population per sq km

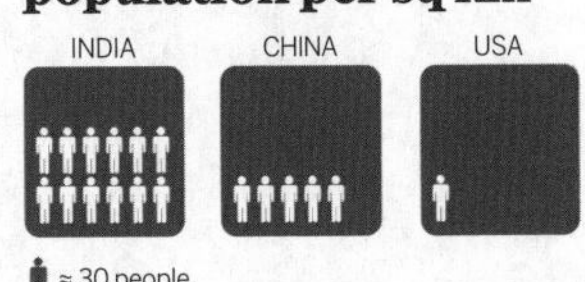

Dos & Don'ts

Dress modestly Avoid stares by avoiding tight, sheer and skimpy clothes.

Shoes It's polite to remove shoes before entering homes and places of worship.

Photos Best to ask before photographing people, ceremonies or sacred sites.

Bad vibes Avoid pointing soles of feet towards people or deities, or touching anyone with your feet.

Niceties

Namaste Saying *namaste* with hands together in a prayer gesture is a respectful Hindu greeting.

Shake don't hug Shaking hands is fine but hugs between strangers is not the norm.

Head wobble It can mean 'yes', 'maybe' or a polite way of saying 'I have no idea'.

Pure touch The right hand is for eating and shaking hands; the left hand is the 'toilet' hand.

China's ongoing supply of military equipment to Pakistan – including nuclear technology – is a further bone of contention. In 2015, China embarked on an ambitious plan to create the Pakistan China Economic Corridor, a network of road and rail links and gas and oil pipelines running through the Karakoram mountain range to the Pakistan seaboard, further cementing the impression that India is being hemmed in by its neighbour to the north.

The Kashmir Impasse

Decades of border skirmishes between India and Pakistan over the disputed territory of Kashmir show no signs of letting up, with a further upsurge in violence in 2016 following the killing of the Kashmiri militant commander Burhan Wani by Indian troops. In the subsequent protests, 85 people were killed and 13,000 injured, many blinded by pellets as the police tried to disperse rioters. The dispute over Kashmir has plagued India–Pakistan relations ever since the day of Partition in 1947, and the predominantly Muslim Kashmir Valley is still claimed in its entirety by both countries, with a separate movement for an independent Kashmiri state.

The dispute has led to three India–Pakistan wars – in 1947, 1965 and 1971 – and a string of incursions and firing incidents across the Line of Control that have killed tens of thousands of civilians on both sides of the divide. The dispute is also cited as the motivation for the bulk of the terrorist attacks carried out in India by Islamist militants. The government of Pakistan provides shelter – and, India alleges, financial, military and technical support – for armed groups who have carried out hundreds of attacks in India, including a series of deadly raids on Indian Army barracks close to the India–Pakistan border in 2016.

A lull in tensions in 2008 led to talks that might have created an autonomous region, but the situation deteriorated rapidly after militants killed at least 163 people during three days of coordinated bombings and shootings in Mumbai (Bombay). The one sniper caught alive, a Pakistani, had ties to Lashkar-e-Taiba, a militant group that formed to assist the Pakistani army in Kashmir in the 1990s and which has been implicated in dozens of attacks within India.

Despite brief meetings between Prime Minister Narendra Modi and Pakistani Prime Minister Nawaz Sharif in 2014 and 2015, tensions remain high, and the relationship deteriorated further following so-called surgical strikes against militants inside Pakistan-controlled Kashmir by the Indian Army in 2016. Since then, firing has continued across the Line of Control, and some 10,000 people have been evacuated from homes within shelling range of the border. The immediate future of Kashmir may depend as much on the diplomatic plans of new US president Donald Trump as on any changes in position by the governments of India or Pakistan.

History

Through invasions and empires, through the birth of religions and the collapse of civilisations, through great leaps forward and countless cataclysms, India has proved itself to be, in the words of its first prime minister, Jawaharlal Nehru, 'a bundle of contradictions held together by strong but invisible threads'. India's history is not just the history of a nation state, but the history of a veritable legion of communities and cultures who after centuries of strife found greater strength bonded together than apart. The resulting nation is a cultural patchwork quilt, stitched together from the ideas and attitudes of some of Asia's greatest civilisations.

Indus Valley Civilisation

The Indus Valley, straddling the modern India–Pakistan border, is the cradle of civilisation on the Indian subcontinent. The first inhabitants of this region were nomadic tribes who cultivated land and kept domestic animals. Over thousands of years, an urban culture began to emerge from these tribes, particularly from 3500 BC. By 2500 BC large cities were well established, the focal points of what became known as the Harappan culture, which would flourish for more than 1000 years.

The great cities of the Mature Harappan period were Moenjodaro and Harappa in present-day Pakistan, but the city of Lothal (p699) near Ahmedabad can still be visited, and from the precise, carefully laid-out street plan, some sense of the sophistication of this 4500-year-old civilisation can be gleaned. Harappan cities were astoundingly uniform, despite being spread across an enormous area. Even their brickwork and streets had a standard size. They often had a separate acropolis, suggesting a religious function, and great tanks which may have been used for ritual bathing purposes. The major Harappan cities were also notable for their size – estimates put the population of Moenjodaro at some 50,000 at its peak.

To learn more about the ancient Indus Valley civilisations, ramble around Harappa (www.harappa.com), which presents an accessible yet scholarly multimedia overview.

By the middle of the 3rd millennium BC, the Indus Valley culture was arguably the equal of other great civilisations emerging at the time. The Harappans traded with Mesopotamia, and developed a system of weights and measures, along with art in the form of terracotta and bronze figurines. Recovered relics, including models of bullock carts and jewellery, offer the

TIMELINE

10,000 BC

Stone Age paintings first made in the Bhimbetka rock shelters, in what is now Madhya Pradesh; the art continues here for many centuries. Settlements thought to exist across the subcontinent.

2600–1700 BC

The Indus Valley civilisation's heydey. Spanning parts of Rajasthan, Gujarat and Sindh province in present-day Pakistan, it takes shape around metropolises such as Harappa and Moenjodaro.

1500 BC

The Indo-Aryan civilisation takes root in the fertile plains of the Indo-Gangetic basin. Settlers speak an early form of Sanskrit, from which several Indian vernaculars, including Hindi, later evolve.

earliest evidence of a distinctive Indian culture. Indeed, many elements of Harappan culture would later become assimilated into Hinduism.

RK Narayan's 1973 *Ramayana* is a condensed and novelistic retelling of the 3rd century BC classic. The renowned novelist took on the Mahabharata in 1978.

Clay figurines found at Harappan sites suggest worship of a Mother goddess (later personified as Kali) and a male three-faced god sitting in the pose of a yogi (believed to be the historic Shiva) attended by four animals. Black stone pillars (associated with phallic worship of Shiva) and animal figures (the most prominent being the humped bull; later Shiva's mount, Nandi) have also been discovered. The 'dancing girl', a small bronze statuette of a young girl, whose insouciant gaze has endured over 4500 years, may be seen in the National Museum (p71) in Delhi, and indicates a highly developed society, both in its skilful sculpture and the indication of the opportunity for leisure pursuits.

Early Invasions & the Rise of Religions

The Harappan civilisation fell into decline from the beginning of the 2nd millennium BC. Some historians attribute the end of the empire to floods or decreased rainfall, which threatened the Harappans' agricultural base. Despite a lack of archaeological proof or written reports in the ancient Indian texts, an enduring, if contentious, theory is that an Aryan invasion put paid to the Harappans. A rival theory claims that it was the Aryans (from a Sanskrit word for 'noble') who were the original inhabitants of India. There's no clear evidence that the Aryans came from elsewhere, and it's even questionable whether the Aryans were a distinct race, so the 'invasion' could simply have been an invasion of new ideas from neighbouring cultures.

Mahavir and the Buddha were contemporaries, and their teachings overlapped. The Buddha lays out the discrepancies (and his critiques) in the *Sankha Sutta* and *Devadaha Sutta*, referring to Mahavir as Nigantha ('free from bonds') Nataputta. Read them at the Theravada resource, www.accesstoinsight.com.

Those who defend the traditional invasion theory believe that from around 1500 BC Aryan tribes from Afghanistan and Central Asia began to filter into northwest India. Despite their military superiority, their progress was gradual, with successive tribes fighting over territory and new arrivals pushing further east into the Ganges plain. Eventually these tribes controlled northern India as far as the Vindhya Hills. Many of the original inhabitants of northern India, the Dravidians, the theory goes, were pushed south.

What is certain is that the Aryans were responsible for the great Sanskrit literary tradition. The Hindu sacred scriptures, the Vedas, were written during this period of transition (1500–1200 BC), and the caste system became formalised. These compositions are of seminal importance in terms of India's spirituality and history.

As Aryan culture spread across the Ganges plain in the late 7th century BC, its followers were absorbed into 16 major kingdoms, which were, in turn, amalgamated into four large states. Out of these states arose the Nanda dynasty, which came to power in 364 BC, ruling over huge swaths of North India.

During this period, the Indian heartland narrowly avoided two invasions from the west which, if successful, could have significantly altered the path of Indian history. The first was by the Persian king Darius (521–

1500–1200 BC

The Rig-Veda, the first and longest of Hinduism's canonical texts, the Vedas, is written; three more books follow. Earliest forms of priestly Brahmanical Hinduism emerge.

599–528 BC

The life of Mahavir, the 24th and last *tirthankar* (enlightened teacher) who established Jainism. Like the Buddha, he preaches compassion and a path to enlightenment for all castes.

563–483 BC

The life of Siddhartha Gautama. The prince is born in modern-day Nepal and attains enlightenment beneath the Bodhi Tree in Bodhgaya (Bihar), thereby transforming into the Buddha (Awakened One).

400–321 BC

Nanda dynasty evolves from the wealthy region of Magadha (roughly, today's Bihar) and grows to encompass a huge area, from Bengal to Punjab. It falls to Maurya in 321 BC.

486 BC), who annexed Punjab and Sindh (on either side of the modern India–Pakistan border). Alexander the Great advanced to India from Greece in 326 BC, an achievement in itself, but he turned back in the Punjab, without ever extending his power deeper into India.

The period is also distinguished by the rise of two significant religions, Buddhism and Jainism, which arose around 500 BC in the northern plains. Both the Buddha and Jainism's Mahavir questioned the Vedas and were critical of the caste system, attracting many followers from the lower castes.

The Mauryan Empire & its Aftermath

If the Harappan culture was the cradle of Indian civilisation, Chandragupta Maurya was the founder of the first great Indian empire, probably the most extensive ever forged, stretching from Bengal to Afghanistan and Gujarat. He came to power in 321 BC, having seized control from the Nandas, and he soon expanded the empire to include the Indus Valley previously conquered by Alexander the Great.

From its capital at Pataliputra (modern-day Patna), with its many-pillared palace, the Mauryan empire encompassed much of North India and reached as far south as modern-day Karnataka. There is much documentation of this period in contemporary Jain and Buddhist texts, plus the intensely detailed depiction of Indian statecraft in the ancient text known as the *Arthasastra*. The empire reached its peak under emperor Ashoka, who converted to Buddhism and spread the faith across the subcontinent. Such was Ashoka's power to lead and unite that after his death in 232 BC, no one could be found to hold the disparate elements of the Mauryan empire together. The empire rapidly disintegrated, collapsing altogether in 184 BC.

None of the empires that immediately followed could match the stability or enduring historical legacy of the Mauryans, although the post-Ashokan era did produce at least one line of royalty whose patronage of the arts and ability to maintain a relatively high degree of social cohesion were substantial. The Satavahanas eventually controlled all of Maharashtra, Madhya Pradesh, Chhattisgarh, Karnataka and Andhra Pradesh. Under their rule, between 230 BC and AD 200, the arts, especially literature and philosophy, blossomed; the Buddha's teaching thrived; and the subcontinent enjoyed a period of considerable prosperity. South India may have lacked vast and fertile agricultural plains on the scale of North India, but it compensated by building strategic trade links via the Indian Ocean, and overland with the Roman Empire and China.

The Golden Age of the Guptas

The empires that followed the Mauryans may have claimed large areas of Indian territory as their own, but many secured only nominal power over their realms. Throughout the subcontinent, small tribes and kingdoms effectively controlled territory and dominated local affairs.

Mauryan Remains

Junagadh (Gujarat)

Allahabad Fort (Uttar Pradesh)

Sarnath (Uttar Pradesh)

Sanchi (Madhya Pradesh)

Bodhgaya (Bihar)

Vaishali (Bihar)

Amaravathi (Andhra Pradesh)

Emperor Ashoka's ability to rule was assisted by a standing army consisting of roughly 9000 elephants, 30,000 cavalry and 600,000 infantry.

326 BC
Alexander the Great invades India. He defeats King Porus in Punjab to enter the subcontinent, but a rebellion within his army keeps him from advancing beyond the Punjab.

321–185 BC
Rule of the Maurya kings. Founded by Chandragupta Maurya, this pan-Indian empire is ruled from Pataliputra (present-day Patna) and briefly adopts Buddhism during the reign of Emperor Ashoka.

c 300 BC
Buddhism spreads across the subcontinent and beyond via Ashoka's monastic ambassadors: monks travel to Sri Lanka and Southeast Asia. Amaravathi, Sanchi and other stupas are erected.

c 235 BC
Start of Early Chola reign in the south; it's unknown if they were related to the later Chola dynasty.

AN ENLIGHTENED EMPEROR

Apart from the Mughals and then the British many centuries later, no other power controlled more Indian territory than the Mauryan empire. It's therefore fitting that it provided India with one of its most important historical figures.

Emperor Ashoka's rule was characterised by flourishing art and sculpture, while his reputation as a philosopher-king was enhanced by the notably expressive rock-hewn edicts he used to both instruct his people, express remorse at the human suffering resulting from his battles, and delineate the enormous span of his territory. Some of these moral teachings can still be seen, particularly the Ashokan Edicts (p718) at Junagadh in Gujarat. Most of them mention and define the concept of dharma, variously as good behaviour, obedience, generosity and goodness.

Ashoka's reign also represented an undoubted historical high point for Buddhism: he embraced the Buddha's teaching in 262 BC, declaring it the state religion and cutting a radical swath through the spiritual and social body of Hinduism. The emperor also built thousands of stupas and monasteries across the region, the extant highlights of which are visible at Sarnath (p392) in Uttar Pradesh – on the spot where Buddha delivered his first sermon expounding the Noble Eightfold Path, or Middle Way to Enlightenment – and Sanchi (p650) in Madhya Pradesh. Ashoka also sent missions abroad, and he is revered in Sri Lanka because he sent his son and daughter to carry the Buddha's teaching to the island.

After his death and the empire's disintegration, his vision endured as an aspiration, if not a reality. One of this emperor's many legacies is the Indian national flag: its central design is the Ashoka Chakra, a wheel with 24 spokes.

In AD 319, Chandragupta I, the third king of one of these tribes, the little-known Guptas, came to prominence by a fortuitous marriage to the daughter of one of the most powerful tribes in the north, the Liccavis. The Gupta empire grew rapidly and under Chandragupta II (r 375–413) achieved its greatest extent. The Chinese pilgrim Fa-hsien, visiting India at the time, described a people 'rich and contented', ruled over by enlightened and just kings.

Poetry, literature, astronomy, medicine and the arts flourished, with some of the finest work done at Ajanta, Ellora, Sanchi and Sarnath. The Guptas were tolerant of, and even supported, Buddhist practice and art. Towards the end of the Gupta period, Hinduism became the dominant religious force, however, and its revival eclipsed Jainism and Buddhism; the latter in particular went into decline in India with the Hun invasion and would never again be India's dominant tradition.

The invasions of the Huns at the beginning of the 6th century signalled the end of this era, and in 510 the Gupta army was defeated by the Hun leader Toramana. Power in North India again devolved to a number of separate Hindu kingdoms.

The concepts of zero and infinity are widely believed to have been devised by eminent Indian mathematicians during the reign of the Guptas.

230 BC–AD 220

The Satavahana empire, of Andhra origin, rules over a huge central Indian area. Their interest in art and maritime trade influences artistic development regionally and in Southeast Asia.

AD 52

Possible arrival of St Thomas the Apostle on the coast of Kerala. Christianity thought to have been introduced to India with his preaching in Kerala and Tamil Nadu.

1st Century

International trade booms: the region's elaborate overland trade networks connect with ports linked to maritime routes. Trade to Africa, the Gulf, Socotra, Southeast Asia, China and even Rome thrives.

319–510

The golden era of the Gupta dynasty, the second of India's great empires after the Mauryas. The period is marked by a creative surge in literature and the arts.

The Hindu South

Southern India has always laid claim to its own unique history. Insulated by distance from the political developments in the north, a separate set of powerful kingdoms emerged, among them the Satavahanas – who, though predominantly Hindu, probably practised Buddhist meditation and patronised Buddhist art at Amaravathi and Sanchi – as well as the Kalingas and Vakatakas. But it was from the tribal territories on the fertile coastal plains that the greatest southern empires – the Cholas, Pandyas, Chalukyas, Cheras and Pallavas – came into their own.

The Chalukyas ruled mainly over the Deccan region of south-central India, although their power occasionally extended further north. In the far south, the Pallavas ruled from the 4th to 9th centuries and pioneered Dravidian architecture, with its exuberant, almost baroque, style. The surviving architectural high points of Pallava rule can be found across Tamil Nadu, including in the erstwhile Pallava capital at Kanchipuram (p1030).

The south's prosperity was based on long-established trading links with other civilisations, among them the Egyptians and Romans. In return for spices, pearls, ivory and silk, the Indians received Roman gold. Indian merchants also extended their influence to Southeast Asia. In 850, the Cholas rose to power and superseded the Pallavas. They soon set about turning the south's far-reaching trade influence into territorial conquest. Under the reign of Rajaraja Chola I (985–1014) they controlled almost the whole of South India, the Deccan plateau, Sri Lanka, parts of the Malay peninsula and the Sumatran-based Srivijaya kingdom.

Not all of their attention was focused overseas, however, and the Cholas left behind some of the finest examples of Dravidian architecture, most notably the sublime Brihadishwara Temple (p1050) in Thanjavur and Chidambaram's stunning Nataraja Temple (p1046). Throughout this period, Hinduism remained the bedrock of South Indian culture.

Architecture of the Deccan Sultanates

Citadel, Golgumbaz, Ibrahim Rouza, Jama Masjid (Bijapur)

Fort, Bahmani Tombs (Bidar)

Golconda Fort, Qutb Shahi Tombs, Charminar (Hyderabad)

The Muslim North

The first Muslims to reach India were some newly converted merchants crossing the Arabian Sea in the early 7th century who established communities in some southern ports, and some small Arabian forces in 663 from the north. Sporadic skirmishes took place over the ensuing centuries, but no major confrontations took place until the late 10th century. But at this point wave after wave of land assaults had begun convulsing the north.

At the vanguard of Islamic expansion was Mahmud of Ghazni. In the early 11th century, Mahmud turned Ghazni (in today's Afghanistan) into one of the world's most glorious capital cities, which he largely funded by plundering his neighbours' territories. From 1001 to 1025, Mahmud conducted 17 raids into India, most infamously on the famous Shiva Temple of Somnath (p713) in Gujarat. The Hindu force of 70,000 died trying to defend the temple, which eventually fell in early 1026. In the aftermath of his vic-

A History of South India from Prehistoric Times to the Fall of Vijayanagar by KA Nilakanta Sastri is arguably the most comprehensive (if heavy-going) history of this region.

4th–9th Centuries

The Pallavas, known for their temple architecture, enter the shifting landscape of southern power centres, establishing dominance in Andhra Pradesh and northern Tamil Nadu from their base in Kanchipuram.

500–600

The emergence of the Rajputs in Rajasthan. Hailing from three principal races supposedly of celestial origin, they form 36 clans which spread across the region to secure their own kingdoms.

610

Prophet Mohammed establishes Islam. He soon invites the people of Mecca to adopt the new religion under the command of God, and his call is met with eager response.

850

The Medieval Cholas, a Tamil dynasty, accreted power across South India, Sri Lanka and the Maldives in the 9th to 13th centuries.

tory, Mahmud transported a massive haul of gold and other booty back to his capital. These raids effectively shattered the balance of power in North India, allowing subsequent invaders to claim the territory for themselves.

Following Mahmud's death in 1033, Ghazni was seized by the Seljuqs and then fell to the Ghurs of western Afghanistan, who similarly had their eyes on the great Indian prize. In 1191, Mohammed of Ghur advanced into India in brutal fashion, before being defeated in a major battle against a confederacy of Hindu rulers. Undeterred, he returned the following year and routed his enemies. One of his generals, Qutb ud-din Aibak, captured Delhi and was appointed governor; it was during his reign that the great Delhi landmark, the Qutb Minar Complex (p101), containing India's first mosque, was built. A separate Islamic empire was established in Bengal, and within a short time almost the whole of North India was under Muslim control.

Following Mohammed's death in 1206, Qutb ud-din Aibak became the first sultan of Delhi. His successor, Iltutmish, brought Bengal back under central control and defended the empire from an attempted Mongol invasion. Ala-ud-din Khilji came to power in 1296 and pushed the borders of the empire inexorably south, while simultaneously fending off further attacks by Mongol hordes.

Pallava Architecture in Tamil Nadu

Shore Temple, Mamallapuram

Five Rathas, Mamallapuram

Temples, Kanchipuram

Rock Fort Temple, Trichy (Tiruchirappalli)

North Meets South

Ala-ud-din died in 1320, and Mohammed Tughlaq ascended the throne in 1324. In 1328, Tughlaq took the southern strongholds of the Hoysala empire, which had centres at Belur, Halebid and Somnathpur. However, while the empire of the pre-Mughal Muslims would achieve its greatest extent under Tughlaq's rule, his overreaching ambition also sowed the seeds of its disintegration. Unlike his forebears, Tughlaq dreamed not only of extending his indirect influence over South India, but of controlling it directly as part of his empire.

After a series of successful campaigns Tughlaq decided to move the capital from Delhi to a more central location. The new capital was called Daulatabad and was near Aurangabad in Maharashtra. Tughlaq sought to populate the new capital by forcefully marching the entire population of Delhi 1100km south, resulting in great loss of life. However, he soon realised that this left the north undefended, and so the entire capital was moved north again. The superb hilltop fortress of Daulatabad (p783) stands as the last surviving monument to his megalomanic vision.

The days of the Ghur empire were numbered. The last of the great sultans of Delhi, Firoz Shah, died in 1388, and the fate of the sultanate was sealed when Timur (Tamerlane) made a devastating raid from Samarkand (in Central Asia) into India in 1398. Timur's sacking of Delhi was truly merciless; some accounts say his soldiers slaughtered every Hindu inhabitant.

After Tughlaq's withdrawal from the south, several splinter kingdoms arose. The two most significant were the Islamic Bahmani sultanate,

In its 800-year history, the Qutb Minar has been damaged by two lightning strikes and one earthquake, and has been repaired or built up by four sultans, one British major and one governor general.

12th–19th Centuries

Africans are brought to the Konkan Coast as part of trade with the Gulf; the slaves become servants, dock workers and soldiers and are known as Siddis or Habshis.

1192

Prithviraj Chauhan loses Delhi to Mohammed of Ghori. The defeat effectively ends Hindu supremacy in the region, exposing the subcontinent to subsequent Muslim rulers marching in from the northwest.

1206

Ghori is murdered during prayer while returning to Ghazni from Lahore. In the absence of an heir, his kingdom is usurped by his generals. The Delhi Sultanate is born.

13th Century

The Pandyas, a Tamil dynasty dating to the 6th century BC, assumes control of Chola territory, expanding into Andhra Pradesh, Kalinga (Odisha [Orissa]) and Sri Lanka from their Madurai capital.

which emerged in 1345 with its capital at Gulbarga, and later Bidar, and the Hindu Vijayanagar empire, founded in 1336 with its capital at Hampi. The battles between the two were among the bloodiest communal violence in Indian history and ultimately resolved nothing in the two centuries before the Mughals ushered in a more enlightened age.

The Mughals

Even as Vijayanagar was experiencing its last days, the next great Indian empire was being founded. The Mughal empire was massive, at its height covering almost the entire subcontinent. Its significance, however, lay not only in its size. Mughal emperors presided over a golden age of arts and literature and had a passion for building that resulted in some of the finest architecture in India, including Shah Jahan's sublime Taj Mahal (p354).

The founder of the Mughal line, Babur (r 1526–30), was a descendant of both Genghis Khan and Timur (Tamerlane). In 1525, he marched into Punjab from his capital at Kabul. With technological superiority brought by firearms, and consummate skill in simultaneously employing artillery and cavalry, Babur defeated the larger armies of the sultan of Delhi at the Battle of Panipat in 1526.

Despite this initial success, Babur's son, Humayun (r 1530–56) was defeated by a powerful ruler of eastern India, Sher Shah, in 1539. Following Sher Shah's death in 1545, Humayun returned to claim his kingdom, eventually conquering Delhi in 1555. He died the following year and was succeeded by his young son Akbar (r 1556–1605) who, during his reign, managed to extend and consolidate the empire until he ruled over a mammoth area.

True to his name, Akbar (which means 'great' in Arabic) was probably the greatest of the Mughals: he not only had the military ability required of a ruler at that time, but was also a wise leader and a man of culture. He saw, as previous Muslim rulers had not, that the number of Hindus in India was too great to subjugate, and skillfully integrated Hindus into his empire, using them as advisers, generals and administrators.

Akbar also had a deep interest in religious matters; he spent many hours in discussion with religious experts of all persuasions, including Christians and Parsis. Nevertheless, Akbar's tolerance of other cultures was relative – massacres of Hindus and other minorities were commonplace during his reign.

Jehangir (r 1605–27) ascended to the throne following Akbar's death and kept his father's empire intact, despite several challenges to his authority. In periods of stability Jehangir spent time in his beloved Kashmir, eventually dying en route there in 1627. He was succeeded by his son, Shah Jahan (r 1627–58), who secured his position by executing all male relatives who stood in his way. During his reign, some of the most vivid and permanent reminders of the Mughals' glory were constructed;

Persian was the official language of several empires, from Mahmud of Ghazni to the Delhi Sultanate to the Mughals. Urdu, which combines Persian, Arabic and indigenous languages, evolved over hundreds of years and came into its own during Mughal reign.

Good History Reads

A Traveller's History of India, SinhaRaja Tammita-Delgoda

Empires of the Indus, Alice Albinia

India: a History, John Keay

1321

The Tughlaqs come to power in Delhi. Mohammed bin Tughlaq expands his empire but becomes known for inelegant schemes: moving the capital to Daulatabad and creating forgery-prone currency.

1336

Foundation of the mighty Vijayanagar empire, named after its capital city, the ruins of which can be seen today in the vicinity of Hampi (in Karnataka).

1345

Bahmani Sultanate is established in the Deccan following a revolt against the Tughlaqs of Delhi. The capital is set up at Gulbarga, in today's northern Karnataka, later shifting to Bidar.

1398

Timur (Tamerlane) invades Delhi, on the pretext that the Delhi Sultans are too tolerant with their Hindu subjects. He executes tens of thousands of Hindus before the battle for Delhi.

in addition to the Taj Mahal, he oversaw the construction of the mighty Red Fort (p60) in Delhi and converted the Agra Fort (p358) into a palace that would later become his prison.

The last of the great Mughals, Aurangzeb (r 1658–1707), imprisoned his father (Shah Jahan) and succeeded to the throne after a two-year struggle against his brothers. A religious zealot, Aurangzeb devoted his resources to extending the empire's boundaries, and thus fell into much the same trap as that of Mohammed Tughlaq some 300 years earlier. A combination of decaying court life and dissatisfaction among the Hindu population at inflated taxes and religious intolerance weakened the Mughal grip.

The empire was also facing serious challenges from the Marathas in central India and the British in Bengal. With Aurangzeb's death in 1707, the empire's fortunes rapidly declined, and Delhi was sacked by Persia's Nadir Shah in 1739. Mughal 'emperors' continued to rule right up until the First War of Independence in 1857, but they were emperors without an empire.

THE STRUGGLE FOR THE SOUL OF INDIA

Founded as an alliance of Hindu kingdoms banding together to counter the threat from the Muslims, the Vijayanagar empire rapidly grew into one of India's wealthiest and greatest Hindu empires. Under the rule of Bukka I (c 1343–79), the majority of South India was brought under its control.

The Vijayanagars and the Bahmani sultanate, which was also based in South India, were evenly matched. The Vijayanagar armies occasionally got the upper hand, but generally the Bahmanis inflicted the worst defeats. The atrocities committed by both sides almost defy belief. In 1366, Bukka I responded to a perceived slight by capturing the Muslim stronghold of Mudkal and slaughtering every inhabitant bar one, who managed to escape and carry news of the attack to Mohammad Shah, the sultan. Mohammad swore that he would not rest until he had killed 100,000 Hindus. Instead, according to the Muslim historian Firishtah, 500,000 'infidels' were killed in the ensuing campaign.

Somehow, Vijayanagar survived. In 1484, the Bahmani sultanate began to disintegrate, and five separate kingdoms, based on the major cities – Berar, Ahmadnagar, Bidar, Bijapur and Golconda – were formed. Bijapur and Bidar still bear exceptional traces of this period of Islamic rule. With little opposition from the north, the Hindu empire enjoyed a golden age of almost supreme power in the south. In 1520, the Vijayanagar king Krishnadevaraya even took Bijapur.

Like Bahmani, however, Vijayanagar's fault lines were soon laid bare. A series of uprisings divided the kingdom fatally, just at a time when the Muslim sultanates were beginning to form a new alliance. In 1565, Hampi was destroyed at the Battle of Talikota. Although the last of the Vijayanagar line escaped and the dynasty limped on for several years, real power passed to local Muslim rulers or Hindu chiefs once loyal to the Vijayanagar kings. One of India's grisliest periods came to an end when the Bahmani kingdoms fell to the Mughals.

1469

Guru Nanak, founder of the Sikh faith, which has millions of followers within and beyond India to the present day, is born in a village near Lahore (in modern-day Pakistan).

1484

Bahmani Sultanate begins to break up following independence movements; Berar is the first to revolt. By 1518 there are five Deccan sultanates: Berar, Ahmadnagar, Bidar, Bijapur and Golconda.

1498

Vasco da Gama discovers the sea route from Europe to India. The first European to reach India by sea, he engages in trade with the local nobility of Kerala.

1510

Portuguese forces capture Goa under the command of Alfonso de Albuquerque, whose initial attempt was thwarted by then-ruler, Sultan Adil Shah of Bijapur. He succeeds following Shah's death.

The Rajputs & the Marathas

Throughout the Mughal period, there remained strong Hindu powers, most notably the Rajputs, hereditary rulers of Rajasthan. The Rajputs were a proud warrior caste with a passionate belief in the dictates of chivalry, both in battle and state affairs. The Rajputs opposed every foreign incursion into their territory, but they were never united. When they weren't battling foreign oppression, they squandered their energies fighting one another. This eventually led to their territories becoming vassal states of the Mughal empire. Their prowess in battle, however, was acknowledged, and some of the best military men in the Mughal armies were Rajputs.

The Marathas were less picaresque but ultimately more effective. They first rose to prominence under their great leader Shivaji, also known as Chhatrapati Shivaji Maharaj, who gathered popular support by championing the Hindu cause against the Muslim rulers. Between 1646 and 1680 Shivaji performed heroic acts in confronting the Mughals across most of central India. Shivaji was captured by the Mughals and taken to Agra, but, naturally, he managed to escape and continue his adventures. Tales of his larger-than-life exploits are still popular with wandering storytellers. He is a particular hero in Maharashtra, where many of his wildest adventures took place. (Today, you'll see Shivaji's name all over Mumbai.) He's also revered for the fact that, as a lower-caste Shudra, he showed that great leaders don't have to be of the Kshatriya (soldier) caste.

Amar Chitra Katha, a hugely popular publisher of comic books about Indian folklore, mythology and history, has several books about Shivaji, including *Shivaji – The Great Maratha*, *Tales of Shivaji* and *Tanaji, the Maratha Lion*, about Shivaji's close friend and fellow warrior.

Shivaji's son was captured, blinded and executed by Aurangzeb, and his grandson wasn't made of the same sturdy stuff, so the Maratha empire continued under the Peshwas, hereditary government ministers who became the real rulers. They gradually took over more of the weakening Mughal empire's powers.

The expansion of Maratha power came to an abrupt halt in 1761 at Panipat. In the town where Babur had won the battle that established the Mughal empire more than 200 years earlier, the Marathas were defeated by Ahmad Shah Durrani from Afghanistan. Maratha expansion to the west was halted, and although they consolidated their control over central India, they were to fall to India's final imperial power – the British.

A Princess Remembers by Gayatri Devi and Santha Rama Rau is the captivating memoir of the former maharani of Jaipur, the glamorous Gayatri Devi (1919–2009).

The Rise of European Power

During the 15th century, the Portuguese sought a sea route to the Far East so they could trade directly in spices. They also hoped to find the kingdom of legendary Christian ruler Prester John, thought to contain the fountain of youth, but instead they found lucrative trading opportunities on the Indian coast, and unexpectedly, a thriving Syrian Christian community.

In 1498, Vasco da Gama arrived on the coast of modern-day Kerala, having sailed around the Cape of Good Hope. Pioneering this route gave the Portuguese a century-long monopoly over Indian and Far Eastern trade with

1526

Babur becomes the first Mughal emperor after conquering Delhi. He stuns Rajasthan by routing its confederate force, gaining an edge with the introduction of matchlock muskets in his army.

1542–45

St Francis Xavier's first mission to India. He preaches Catholicism in Goa, Tamil Nadu and Sri Lanka, returning in 1548–49 and 1552 in between travels in the Far East.

1560–1812

Portuguese Inquisition in Goa. Trials focus on converted Hindus and Muslims thought to have 'relapsed'. Thousands are tried and several dozen likely executed before it is abolished in 1812.

1600

Britain's Queen Elizabeth I grants the first trading charter to the East India Company, with the maiden voyage taking place in 1601 under the command of Sir James Lancaster.

Europe. In 1510, they captured Goa, followed by Diu in 1531; Goa was the last colony in India to be returned to the Indian people, following an Indian Army invasion in 1961. In its heyday, the trade flowing through 'Golden Goa' was said to rival that passing through Lisbon. However, the Portuguese didn't have the resources to maintain a worldwide empire and they were quickly eclipsed and isolated after the arrival of the British and French.

Plain Tales from the Raj by Charles Allen (ed) is a fascinating series of interviews with people who played a role in British India on both sides of the table.

In 1600, Queen Elizabeth I granted a charter to a London trading company that gave it a monopoly on British trade with India. In 1613, representatives of the East India Company established their first trading post at Surat in Gujarat. Further British trading posts, administered and governed by representatives of the company, were established at Madras (Chennai) in 1639, Bombay (Mumbai) in 1661 and Calcutta (Kolkata) in 1690. For nearly 250 years a commercial trading company and not the British government 'ruled' over British India.

By 1672, the French had established themselves at Pondicherry (Puducherry), an enclave they held even after the British departed and where architectural traces of the French era remain. The stage was set for more than a century of rivalry between the British and French for control of Indian trade. At one stage, the French appeared to hold the upper hand, but by the 1750s were no longer a serious influence on the subcontinent.

Serious French aspirations effectively ended in 1750 when the directors of the French East India Company decided that their representatives were playing too much politics and doing too little trading. Key representatives were sacked, and a settlement was made with the British. The decision effectively removed France as a serious influence on the subcontinent.

Britain's Surge to Power

White Mughals by William Dalrymple tells the true story of an East India Company soldier who married an Indian Muslim princess, a tragic love story interwoven with harem politics, intrigue and espionage.

The transformation of the British from traders to governors began almost by accident. Having been granted a licence to trade in Bengal by the Mughals, and following the establishment of a new trading post at Calcutta in 1690, business began to expand rapidly. Under the apprehensive gaze of the nawab (local ruler), British trading activities became extensive and the 'factories' took on an increasingly permanent (and fortified) appearance.

Eventually the nawab decided that British power had grown large enough. In June 1756, he attacked Calcutta and, having taken the city, locked his British prisoners in a tiny cell. The space was so cramped and airless that many were dead by the following morning.

Six months later, Robert Clive, an employee in the military service of the East India Company, led an expedition to retake Calcutta and entered into an agreement with one of the nawab's generals to overthrow the nawab himself. He did this in June 1757, at the Battle of Plassey (now called Palashi), and the general who had assisted him was placed on the throne. With the British effectively in control of Bengal, the company's agents engaged in a period of unbridled profiteering. When a subsequent nawab finally took up arms

1631

Construction of the Taj Mahal begins after Shah Jahan, overcome with grief following the death of his wife Mumtaz Mahal, vows to build the most beautiful mausoleum in the world.

1672

The French East India Company establishes an outpost at Pondicherry (Puducherry), which the French, Dutch and British fight over repeatedly in the coming century.

1674

Shivaji establishes the Maratha kingdom, spanning western India and parts of the Deccan and North India. He assumes the imperial title of Chhatrapati, which means 'Great Protector'.

1707

Death of Aurangzeb, the last of the Mughal greats. His demise triggers the gradual collapse of the Mughal empire, as anarchy and rebellion erupt across the country.

to protect his own interests, he was defeated at the Battle of Baksar in 1764, a victory that confirmed the British as the paramount power in east India.

In 1771, Warren Hastings was made governor in Bengal. During his tenure, the company greatly expanded its control. He was aided by the fact that India was experiencing a power vacuum created by the disintegration of the Mughal empire. The Marathas, the only real Indian power to step into this gap, were divided among themselves. Hastings concluded a series of treaties with local rulers, including one with the main Maratha leader. From 1784 onwards, the British government in London began to take a more direct role in supervising affairs in India, although the territory was still notionally administered by the East India Company until 1858.

In the south, the picture was confused by the strong British–French rivalry, and one ruler was played off against another. This was never clearer than in the series of Mysore wars in which Hyder Ali and his son, Tipu Sultan, waged a brave and determined campaign against the British. In the Fourth Mysore War (1789–99), Tipu Sultan was killed at Srirangapatnam, and British power took another step forward. The long-running struggle with the Marathas was concluded a few years later, leaving only Punjab (held by the Sikhs) outside British control. Punjab finally fell in 1849 after the two Sikh Wars.

By the early 19th century, India was effectively under British control, although there remained a patchwork of states, many nominally independent and governed by their own rulers, the maharajas (or similarly titled princes) and nawabs. While these 'princely states' administered their own territories, a system of central government was developed. British bureaucratic models were replicated in the Indian government and civil service – a legacy that still exists today.

Trade and profit continued to be the main focus of British rule in India, with far-reaching effects. Iron and coal mining were developed, and tea, coffee and cotton became key crops. A start was made on the vast rail network that's still in use today, irrigation projects were undertaken, and the Mughal-era zamindar (landowner) system was encouraged, further contributing to the development of an impoverished and landless peasantry.

The British also imposed English as the local language of administration. For them, this was critical in a country with so many different languages, but it also kept the new rulers at arm's length from the Indian populace.

The British brought many things to India but also took many things home with them, including dozens of Hindu words. Pajamas, shampoo, bandannas, dinghies, bangles and bungalows all have their origins in Hindi or Urdu.

Colonial-Era Architecture

Colaba and Kala Ghoda, Mumbai (British)

BBD Bagh and environs, Kolkata (British)

Old Goa and Panjim, Goa (Portuguese)

Puducherry, Tamil Nadu (French)

The Road to Independence

Opposition to the British increased at the turn of the 20th century, spearheaded by the Indian National Congress, the country's oldest political party, also known as the Congress Party and Congress.

It met for the first time in 1885 and soon began to push for participation in the government of India. A highly unpopular attempt by the British to partition Bengal in 1905 resulted in mass demonstrations and brought to

1757

The East India Company registers its first military victory on Indian soil. Siraj-ud-Daulah, nawab of Bengal, is defeated by Robert Clive in the Battle of Plassey.

1801

Ranjit Singh becomes maharaja (Great King) of the newly united Sikhs and forges a powerful new kingdom from his capital in Lahore (in present-day Pakistan).

1835–58

Life of Lakshmi Bai, Rani of Jhansi. The queen of the Maratha state led her army against the British, who seized Jhansi after her husband's death. She died in battle.

1857

The First War of Independence (Indian Uprising) against the British. With no national leader, freedom fighters coerce the Mughal king, Bahadur Shah Zafar, to proclaim himself emperor of India.

light Hindu opposition to the division; the Muslim community formed its own league and campaigned for protected rights in any future political settlement. As pressure rose, a split emerged in Hindu circles between moderates and radicals, the latter resorting to violence to publicise their aims.

With the outbreak of WWI, the political situation eased. India contributed hugely to the war: more than one million Indian volunteers were enlisted and sent overseas, suffering more than 100,000 casualties. The contribution was sanctioned by Congress leaders, largely with the expectation that it would be rewarded after the war. No such rewards transpired and disillusion followed. Disturbances were particularly persistent in Punjab, and in April 1919, following riots in Amritsar, a British army contingent was sent to quell the unrest. Under direct orders of the officer in charge, they ruthlessly fired into a crowd of unarmed protesters at Jallianwala Bagh (p213). News of the massacre spread rapidly throughout India, turning huge numbers of otherwise apolitical Indians into Congress supporters.

THE FIRST WAR OF INDEPENDENCE: THE INDIAN UPRISING

In 1857, half a century after having established firm control of India, the British suffered a serious setback. To this day, the causes of the Indian Uprising are the subject of debate. The key factors included the influx of cheap goods, such as textiles, from Britain that destroyed many livelihoods; the dispossession of territories from many rulers; and taxes imposed on landowners.

The incident that's popularly held to have sparked the Indian Uprising, however, took place at an army barracks in Meerut in Uttar Pradesh on 10 May 1857. A rumour leaked out that a new type of bullet was greased with what Hindus claimed was cow fat, while Muslims maintained that it came from pigs; pigs are considered unclean to Muslims, and cows are sacred to Hindus. Since loading a rifle involved biting the end off the waxed cartridge, these rumours provoked considerable unrest.

In Meerut, the situation was handled with a singular lack of judgement. The commanding officer lined up his soldiers and ordered them to bite off the ends of their issued bullets. Those who refused were immediately marched off to prison. The following morning, the soldiers of the garrison rebelled, shot their officers and marched to Delhi. Of the 74 Indian battalions of the Bengal army, seven (one of them Gurkhas) remained loyal, 20 were disarmed and the other 47 mutinied. The soldiers and peasants rallied around the ageing Mughal emperor in Delhi. They held Delhi for some months and besieged the British residency in Lucknow for five months before they were finally suppressed. The incident left festering wounds on both sides.

Almost immediately, the East India Company was wound up and direct control of the country was assumed by the British government, which announced its support for the existing rulers of the princely states, claiming they would not interfere in local matters as long as the states remained loyal to the British.

1858

British government assumes control over India – with power officially transferred from the East India Company to the Crown – beginning the period known as the British Raj.

1869

Opening of Suez Canal accelerates trade from Europe and makes Bombay (Mumbai) India's first port of call; trip from England changes from three months to three weeks.

1885

The Indian National Congress, India's first home-grown political organisation, is set up. It brings educated Indians together and plays a key role in India's enduring freedom struggle.

1919

The massacre, on 13 April, of unarmed Indian protesters at Jallianwala Bagh in Amritsar (Punjab). Gandhi responds with his programme of civil (nonviolent) disobedience against the British government.

At this time, the Congress movement found a new leader in Mohandas Gandhi, a British-educated lawyer who suggested a new route to Indian self-governance through *ahimsa* – nonviolent resistance to British rule. Not everyone involved in the struggle agreed with or followed Gandhi's policy of nonviolence, yet the Congress Party and Gandhi remained at the forefront of the push for independence.

As political power-sharing began to look more likely, and the mass movement led by Gandhi gained momentum, the Muslim reaction was to consider its own immediate future. The large Muslim minority realised that an independent India would be dominated by Hindus and that, while Gandhi's approach was fair-minded, others in the Congress Party might not be so willing to share power. By the 1930s Muslims were raising the possibility of a separate Islamic state.

Political events were partially disrupted by WWII, when large numbers of Congress supporters were jailed to prevent disruption to the war effort.

The Proudest Day – India's Long Road to Independence by Anthony Read and David Fisher is an engaging account of India's pre-Independence period.

Mahatma Gandhi

One of the great figures of the 20th century, Mohandas Karamchand Gandhi was born on 2 October 1869 in Porbandar, Gujarat. After studying in London (1888–91), he worked as a barrister in South Africa. Here, the young Gandhi became politicised, railing against the discrimination he encountered. He soon became the spokesperson for the Indian community and championed equality for all.

Gandhi returned to India in 1915 with the doctrine of *ahimsa* (nonviolence) central to his political plans, and committed to a simple and disciplined lifestyle. He set up the Sabarmati Ashram in Ahmedabad, which was innovative for its admission of Untouchables.

Within a year, Gandhi had won his first victory, defending farmers in Bihar from exploitation. This was when it's said he first received the title 'Mahatma' (Great Soul) from an admirer (often said to be Bengali poet Rabindranath Tagore). The passage of the discriminatory Rowlatt Acts in 1919, which allowed certain political cases to be tried without juries, spurred him to further action, and he organised a national protest. In the days that followed this *hartal* (strike), feelings ran high throughout the country. After the massacre of unarmed protesters in Amritsar, Gandhi began to organise his program of civil (nonviolent) disobedience against the British.

By 1920 Gandhi was a key figure in the Indian National Congress, and he coordinated a national campaign of noncooperation or *satyagraha* (nonviolent protest) to British rule, with the effect of raising nationalist feeling while earning the lasting enmity of the British. In early 1930, Gandhi captured the imagination of the country, and the world, when he led a march of several thousand followers from Ahmedabad to Dandi on the coast of Gujarat. On arrival, Gandhi ceremoniously made salt by evaporating sea water,

A golden oldie, *Gandhi*, directed by Richard Attenborough, is one of the few movies that adeptly captures the grand canvas that is India while tracing the country's rocky road to Independence.

1930

Salt Satyagraha begins on 12 March. Gandhi embarks on a 24-day walk from his Sabarmati Ashram near Ahmedabad to the coastal village of Dandi to protest the British salt tax.

1940

The Muslim League adopts its Lahore Resolution, which champions greater Muslim autonomy in India. Campaigns for the creation of a separate Islamic nation are spearheaded by Mohammed Ali Jinnah.

1942

Mahatma Gandhi launches the Quit India campaign, demanding that the British leave India without delay and allow the country to get on with the business of self-governance.

1947

India gains independence on 15 August. Pakistan is formed a day earlier. Partition is followed by mass cross-border exodus, as Hindus and Muslims migrate to their respective nations.

thus publicly defying the much-hated salt tax; not for the first time, he was imprisoned. Released in 1931 to represent the Indian National Congress at the second Round Table Conference in London, he won the hearts of many British people but failed to gain any real concessions from the government.

Disillusioned with politics, he resigned his parliamentary seat in 1934. He returned spectacularly to the fray in 1942 with the Quit India campaign, in which he urged the British to leave India immediately. His actions were deemed subversive, and he and most of the Congress leadership were imprisoned.

In the frantic independence bargaining that followed the end of WWII, Gandhi was largely excluded and watched helplessly as plans were made to partition the country – a dire tragedy in his eyes. Gandhi stood almost alone in urging tolerance and the preservation of a single India, and his work on behalf of members of all communities drew resentment from some Hindu hardliners. On his way to a prayer meeting in Delhi on 30 January 1948, he was assassinated by a Hindu zealot, Nathuram Godse.

Gandhian Sites

- *Raj Ghat, Delhi*
- *Gandhi Smriti, Delhi*
- *Anand Bhavan, Allahabad*
- *Sabarmati Ashram, Ahmedabad*
- *Kaba Gandhi No Delo, Rajkot*
- *Mani Bhavan, Mumbai*
- *Gandhi National Memorial, Pune*

Independence & the Partition of India

The Labour Party victory in the British elections in July 1945 dramatically altered the political landscape. For the first time, Indian independence was accepted as a legitimate goal. This new goodwill did not, however, translate into any new wisdom as to how to reconcile the divergent wishes of the two major Indian parties. Mohammed Ali Jinnah, the leader of the Muslim League, championed a separate Islamic state, while the Congress Party, led by Jawaharlal Nehru, campaigned for an independent greater India.

In early 1946, a British mission failed to bring the two sides together – indeed, there was evidence that the British deliberately fostered resentment on both sides to discourage a unified resistance – and the country slid closer towards civil war. A 'Direct Action Day', called by the Muslim League in August 1946, led to the slaughter of Hindus in Calcutta, which prompted reprisals against Muslims. In February 1947, the nervous British government made the momentous decision that Independence would come by June 1948. In the meantime, the viceroy, Lord Archibald Wavell, was replaced by Lord Louis Mountbatten.

The new viceroy encouraged the rival factions to agree upon a united India, but to no avail. A decision was made to divide the country, with Gandhi the only staunch opponent. Faced with increasing civil violence, Mountbatten made the precipitous decision to bring forward Independence to 15 August 1947.

Dividing the country into separate Hindu and Muslim territories was immensely tricky; the dividing line proved almost impossible to draw. Some areas were clearly Hindu or Muslim, but others had evenly mixed populations, and there were 'islands' of communities in areas predomi-

Our Moon has Blood Clots by Rahul Pandita, *Lost Rebellion* by Manoj Joshi, and *Curfewed Nights* by Basharat Peer are three excellent books bringing alive insider perspectives on the Kashmir conflict.

1947–48

First war between India and Pakistan takes place after the (procrastinating) maharaja of Kashmir signs the Instrument of Accession that cedes his state to India. Pakistan challenges the document's legality.

1948

Mahatma Gandhi is assassinated in New Delhi by Nathuram Godse on 30 January. Godse and his co-conspirator, Narayan Apte, are later tried, convicted and executed (by hanging).

1948

Asaf Jah VII, Hyderabad's last nizam, surrenders to the Indian government on 17 September. The Muslim dynasty was receiving support from Pakistan but had refused to join either new nation.

1948–56

Rajasthan takes shape, as the princely states form a beeline to sign the Instrument of Accession, giving up their territories which are incorporated into the newly formed Republic of India.

nantly settled by other religions. Moreover, the two overwhelmingly Muslim regions were on opposite sides of the country and, therefore, Pakistan would inevitably have an eastern and western half divided by a hostile India. The instability of this arrangement was self-evident, but it was 25 years before the split finally came and East Pakistan became Bangladesh.

An independent British referee was given the odious task of drawing the borders, well aware that the effects would be catastrophic for countless people. The decisions were fraught with impossible dilemmas. Calcutta, with its Hindu majority, port facilities and jute mills, was divided from East Bengal, which had a Muslim majority, large-scale jute

THE KASHMIR CONFLICT

Kashmir is the most enduring symbol of the turbulent partition of India. In the lead-up to Independence, the delicate task of drawing the India–Pakistan border was complicated by the fact that India's 'princely states' were nominally independent. As part of the settlement process, local rulers were asked which country they wished to belong to. Kashmir was a predominantly Muslim state with a Hindu maharaja, Hari Singh, who tried to delay his decision. A ragtag Pashtun (Pakistani) army crossed the border, intent on racing to Srinagar and annexing Kashmir for Pakistan. In the face of this advance, the maharaja panicked and requested armed assistance from India. The Indian army arrived only just in time to prevent the fall of Srinagar, and the maharaja signed the Instrument of Accession, tying Kashmir to India, in October 1947. The legality of the document was immediately disputed by Pakistan, and the two nations went to war, just two months after Independence.

In 1948, the fledgling UN Security Council called for a referendum (which remains a central plank of Pakistani policy) to decide the status of Kashmir, and a UN-brokered ceasefire in 1949 established a demarcation line between the two sides, called the Cease-Fire Line (later to become the Line of Control, or LOC). However, this did little to resolve the conflict. Two-thirds of Kashmir fell on the Indian side, while the remainder was left under Pakistani control, and both nations still claimed Kashmir in its entirety.

The Indian state of Jammu and Kashmir, as it has stood since that time, incorporates Ladakh (a majority Buddhist region with a small Muslim population), Jammu (with a Hindu majority) and the 130km-long, 55km-wide Kashmir Valley (with a Muslim majority and most of the state's inhabitants). On the Pakistani side, over three million Kashmiris live in Azad (Free) Kashmir, known to Indians as Pakistan Occupied Kashmir (POK). Since the frontier was drawn, incursions across the LOC have occurred with dangerous regularity.

In 1989–90, the majority of Kashmiri Pandits (*pandit* means scholar, usually referring to a particular Hindu community of Brahmins) fled their homes following persecution and murder by extremists among the Muslim majority. Up to 170,000 left, many settling in refugee camps around Jammu. In 2014, President Mukherjee, when outlining the Modi government's five-year programme, pledged the Pandits would be helped to return 'to the land of their ancestors with full dignity, security and assured livelihood'.

1949

The Constitution of India, drafted over two years by a 308-member Constituent Assembly, is adopted. The Assembly is chaired by BR Ambedkar and includes members from scheduled castes.

1950

Constitution goes into effect on 26 January, and India becomes a republic. The date commemorates the Declaration of Independence, put forth by the Indian National Congress in 1930.

1961

Indian troops annex Goa in a campaign lasting just 48 hours. The era of European colonialism in India is over.

1962

Border war (known as the Sino-Indian War) with China over the North-East Frontier Area and Ladakh. China successfully captures the disputed territory and ends the war with a unilateral ceasefire.

production, no mills and no port facilities. One million Bengalis became refugees in the mass movement across the new border.

China still claims parts of India as part of its historic claim to all lands formerly ruled by Tibet, including Aksai Chin in Kashmir, western Arunachal Pradesh, and a tiny strip of land in northern Sikkim known as 'The Finger'.

The problem was worse in Punjab, where intercommunity antagonisms were already running at fever pitch. Punjab, one of the most fertile and affluent regions of the country, had large Muslim, Hindu and Sikh communities. The Sikhs had already campaigned unsuccessfully for their own state and now saw their homeland divided down the middle. The new border ran straight between Punjab's two major cities, Lahore and Amritsar. Prior to Independence, Lahore's population of 1.2 million included approximately 500,000 Hindus and 100,000 Sikhs. When the dust had finally settled, roughly 1000 Hindus and Sikhs remained.

Punjab contained all the ingredients for an epic disaster, but the resulting bloodshed was far worse than anticipated. Huge population exchanges took place. Trains full of Muslims, fleeing westward, were held up and slaughtered by Hindu and Sikh mobs. Hindus and Sikhs fleeing to the east suffered the same fate at Muslim hands. The army that was sent to maintain order proved totally inadequate and, at times, all too ready to join the sectarian carnage. By the time the Punjab chaos had run its course, more than 10 million people had changed sides and at least 500,000 had been killed.

India and Pakistan became sovereign nations under the British Commonwealth in August 1947 as planned, but the violence, migrations and integration of a few states, especially Kashmir, continued. The Constitution of India was at last adopted in November 1949 and went into effect on 26 January 1950 and independent India officially became a Republic.

The word Pakistan was originally an acronym thought of by a group of Cambridge Muslims to define a homeland consisting of P(unjab), A(fghania), K(ashmir), I(ran), S(ind), T(urkharistan), A(fghanistan) and (Baluchia) N. It also conflates the terms *pak*, a Persian word meaning 'pure/clean', and *sthāna*, an Indo-Aryan term meaning 'place'.

Independent India

Jawaharlal Nehru tried to steer India towards a policy of nonalignment, balancing cordial relations with Britain and Commonwealth membership with moves towards the former USSR. The latter was due partly to conflicts with China, and US support for its arch-enemy Pakistan.

The 1960s and 1970s were tumultuous times for India. A border war with China in what was then known as the North-East Frontier Area (NEFA; now the Northeast States) and Ladakh, resulted in the loss of parts of Aksai Chin (Ladakh) and smaller NEFA areas. Wars with Pakistan in 1965 (over Kashmir) and 1971 (over Bangladesh) also contributed to a sense among many Indians of having enemies on all sides.

In the midst of it all, the hugely popular Nehru died in 1964 and his daughter Indira Gandhi (no relation to Mahatma Gandhi) was elected as prime minister in 1966. Indira Gandhi, like Nehru before her, loomed large over the country she governed. Unlike Nehru, however, she was always a profoundly controversial figure whose historical legacy remains disputed.

In 1975, facing serious opposition and unrest, she declared a state of emergency (which later became known as the Emergency). Freed of parliamentary constraints, Gandhi was able to boost the economy, control in-

1965

Skirmishes in Kashmir and Gujarat's disputed Rann of Kutch flare into the Second India-Pakistan War, which involve the biggest tank battles since WWII. The war ends with a UN-mandated ceasefire.

1966

Indira Gandhi, daughter of Jawaharlal Nehru, becomes prime minister of India, remembered today for her heavy-handed rule. She has been India's only female prime minister.

1971

East Pakistan champions independence from West Pakistan. India gets involved, sparking the Third India-Pakistan War. West Pakistan surrenders, losing sovereignty of East Pakistan, which becomes Bangladesh.

1972

The Simla Agreement between India and Pakistan attempts to normalise relations. The Kashmiri ceasefire line is formalised: the 'Line of Control' remains the de facto border between the two countries.

flation remarkably well and decisively increase efficiency. On the negative side, political opponents often found themselves in prison, India's judicial system was turned into a puppet theatre and the press was fettered.

Gandhi's government was bundled out of office in the 1977 elections, but the 1980 election brought Indira Gandhi back to power with a larger majority than ever before, firmly laying the foundation for the Nehru-Gandhi family dynasty that would continue to dominate Indian politics for decades. Indira Gandhi was assassinated in 1984 by one of her Sikh bodyguards after her decision to attack the Golden Temple which was being occupied by fundamentalist Sikh preacher, Sant Jarnail Singh Bhindranwale. Her son Rajiv took over and was subsequently killed in a suicide bomb attack in 1991. His widow, Sonia, later became president, with Manmohan Singh as prime minister. However, the Congress party lost popularity as the economy slowed, and has been accused of cronyism and corruption.

The 2014 Federal elections saw the unpopular Congress party suffer a humiliating defeat under the shaky leadership of Rahul Gandhi, Indira's grandson. The BJP, headed by Narendra Modi, swept to power in a landslide victory, promising to shake up Indian politics and usher in a new era of neoliberal economics. Modi was formerly chief minister of Gujarat, which was transformed into an economic powerhouse during his tenure, and his forceful, charismatic style was hugely popular with business leaders and the BJP's Hindu-nationalist traditionalists, as well as with the ordinary person on the street.

However, some continue to ask questions about Modi's role in the deadly riots in Gujarat in 2002, which killed nearly 1000 people, most of them Muslims. Despite an official inquiry in 2014 which cleared the prime minister of any wrong-doing, allegations still circulate that the Gujarat government was complicit in the violence, which was triggered by a deadly arson attack on a train carrying Hindu pilgrims from Ayodhya.

Nevertheless, as prime minister, Modi has thus far offered vision and hope, and a secular approach, which has appeased many of his critics. Despite an upsurge in support for Hindu nationalist causes – including bans on the slaughter of cattle in many states – Modi has pursued a broadly inclusive agenda, focusing on the economic situation rather than religious rivalries and slashing red tape to increase investment.

Narendra Modi's demonetisation of ₹500 and ₹1000 banknotes is just the latest twist in the long history of the rupee. The name rupee comes from the struck silver coins known as *rupa*, first mentioned in Sanskrit texts in the 6th century BC.

The results of the 2011 census found India's population had increased by 181 million over 10 years.

1975
In a questionable move, Prime Minister Indira Gandhi declares a state of emergency under Article 352 of the Indian Constitution, in response to growing civil unrest and political opposition.

1984
Indira Gandhi launches Operation Blue Star against Sikh separatists occupying the Golden Temple in Amritsar; four months later, she is assassinated by her Sikh bodyguards.

2014
Narendra Modi, born into a Gujarati grocery family, achieves a historic landslide victory for the BJP, routing the Congress Party.

2016
The Modi government demonetises ₹500 and ₹1000 banknotes in a clamp-down on tax evasion and corruption, leading to massive queues at banks as millions struggle to exchange old notes for legal tender.

The Way of Life

Spirituality and family lie at the heart of Indian society, with these two tenets often intertwining in various ceremonies to celebrate auspicious occasions and life's milestones. Despite the growing number of nuclear families – primarily in the more cosmopolitan cities such as Mumbai (Bombay), Bengaluru (Bangalore) and Delhi – the extended family still remains a cornerstone in both urban and rural India, with males – usually the main breadwinners – generally considered the head of the household.

Marriage, Birth & Death

Different religions practise different traditions, but for all communities, marriage, birth and death are important and marked with ceremonies according to the faith. Hindus are in the majority in India. Around 15% of the population is Muslim (at around 180 million, Indian Muslims almost match the population of Pakistan).

Marriage is an exceptionally auspicious event for Indians – for most Indians, the idea of being unmarried by their mid-30s is unpalatable. Although 'love marriages' have spiralled upwards in recent times (mainly in urban hubs), most Indian marriages are still arranged, be the family Hindu, Muslim, Sikh, Jain or Buddhist. Discreet enquiries are made within the community. If a suitable match is not found, the help of professional matchmakers may be sought, or advertisements may be placed in newspapers and/or on matrimonial websites. In Hindu families, the horoscopes of both potential partners are checked and, if propitious, there's a meeting between the two families.

The Wonder That Was India by AL Basham gives descriptions of Indian civilisations, major religions and social customs – a good thematic approach to weave the disparate strands together.

Dowry, although illegal, is still a key issue in more than a few arranged marriages (mostly in conservative communities), with some families plunging into debt to raise the required cash and merchandise (from cars and computers to refrigerators and televisions). Health workers claim that India's high rate of abortion of female foetuses (sex identification medical tests are banned in India, but they still clandestinely occur in some clinics) is predominantly due to the financial burden of providing a daughter's dowry. Muslim grooms have to pay what is called a *mehr* to the bride.

The Hindu wedding ceremony is officiated over by a priest and the marriage is formalised when the couple walk around a sacred fire seven times. Muslim ceremonies involve the reading of the Quran, and traditionally the husband and wife view each other via mirrors. Despite the existence of nuclear families, it's still the norm for a wife to live with her husband's family once married and assume the household duties outlined by her mother-in-law. Not surprisingly, the mother–daughter-in-law relationship can be a tricky one, as portrayed in various Indian TV soap operas.

Divorce and remarriage are becoming more common (primarily in bigger cities), but divorce is still not granted by courts as a matter of routine and is not looked upon very favourably by society. Among the higher castes, in more traditional areas, widows are expected not to remarry and are expected to wear white and live pious, celibate lives. It is still legal for Muslim males in India to obtain oral divorce according to Sharia law (by uttering the word *talaq,* meaning 'divorce', three times); however, members of the federal government and civil society are calling for this to be abolished so there is just one common law for all Indian citizens.

The birth of a child is another momentous occasion, with its own set of special ceremonies which take place at various auspicious times during the early years of childhood. For Hindus these include the casting of the child's first horoscope, name-giving, feeding the first solid food, and the first hair cutting.

Hindus cremate their dead, and funeral ceremonies are designed to purify and console both the living and the deceased. An important aspect of the proceedings is the *sharadda,* paying respect to one's ancestors by offering water and rice cakes. It's an observance that's repeated at each anniversary of the death. After the cremation, the ashes are collected and, 13 days after the death (when blood relatives are deemed ritually pure), a member of the family usually scatters them in a holy river such as the Ganges or in the ocean. Sikhs similarly wash then cremate their dead. Muslims also prepare their dead carefully, but bury them, while the minority Zoroastrian Parsi community place their dead in 'Towers of Silence' (stone towers) to be devoured by birds.

Matchmaking has inevitably gone online, with popular sites including www.shaadi.com, www.bharatmatrimony.com and, in a sign of the times, www.secondshaadi.com – for those seeking a partner again.

The Caste System

Although the Indian constitution does not recognise the caste system, caste still wields considerable influence, especially in rural India, where the caste you are born into largely determines your social standing in the community. It can also influence your vocational and marriage prospects. Castes are further divided into thousands of *jati,* groups of 'families' or social communities, which are sometimes but not always linked to occupation. Conservative Hindus will only marry someone of the same *jati,* and you'll often see caste as a criteria in matrimonial adverts: 'Mahar seeks Mahar' etc. In some traditional areas, young men and women who fall in love outside their caste have been murdered.

According to tradition, caste is the basic social structure of Hindu society. Living a righteous life and fulfilling your dharma (moral duty) raises your chances of being reborn into a higher caste and thus into better circumstances. Hindus are born into one of four varnas (castes): Brahmin (priests and scholars), Kshatriya (soldiers and administrators),

INDIAN ATTIRE

Widely worn by Indian women, the elegant sari comes in a single piece (between 5m and 9m long and 1m wide) and is ingeniously tucked and pleated into place without the need for pins or buttons. Worn with the sari is the choli (tight-fitting blouse) and a drawstring petticoat. The *palloo* is the part of the sari draped over the shoulder. Also commonly worn is the *salwar kameez,* a traditional dress-like tunic and trouser combination accompanied by a dupatta (long scarf). Saris and *salwar kameez* come in a wonderful range of fabrics, colours and designs.

Traditional attire for men includes the dhoti, and in the south, the lungi and the *mundu*. The dhoti is a loose, long loincloth pulled up between the legs. The lungi is more like a sarong, with its end usually sewn up like a tube. The *mundu* is like a lungi but is always white. A kurta (shirt) is a long tunic or shirt worn mainly by men, usually with no collar. Kurta pyjamas are a cotton shirt and trousers set, worn for relaxing or sleeping. *Churidar* are close-fitting trousers often worn under a kurta. A *sherwani* is a long coat-like men's garment, which originated as a fusion of the *salwar kameez* with the British frock coat.

There are regional and religious variations in costume – for example, you may see Muslim women wearing the all-enveloping burka.

Vaishya (merchants) and Shudra (labourers). The Brahmins were said to have emerged from the mouth of Lord Brahma at the moment of creation, Kshatriyas were said to have come from his arms, Vaishyas from his thighs and Shudras from his feet. Beneath the four main castes are the Dalits (formerly known as Untouchables), who hold menial jobs such as sweepers and latrine cleaners. Many of India's complex codes of ritual purity were devised to prevent physical contact between people of higher castes and Dalits. A less rigid system exists in Islamic communities in India, with society divided into *ashraf* (high born), *ajlaf* (low born) and *arzal* (equivalent to the Dalits).

If you want to learn more about India's caste system, these two books are a good start: *Interrogating Caste* by Dipankar Gupta and *Translating Caste* edited by Tapan Basu.

The word 'pariah' is derived from the name of a Tamil Dalit group, the Paraiyars. Some Dalit leaders, such as the renowned Dr BR Ambedkar (1891–1956), sought to change their status by adopting another faith; in his case it was Buddhism. At the bottom of the social heap are the Denotified Tribes. They were known as the Criminal Tribes until 1952, when a reforming law officially recognised 198 tribes and castes. Many are nomadic or seminomadic tribes, forced by the wider community to eke out a living on society's fringes.

To improve the Dalits' position, the government reserves a number of public-sector jobs, parliamentary seats and university places for them. Today these quotas account for almost 25% of government jobs and university (student) positions. The situation varies regionally, as different political leaders chase caste vote-banks by promising to include them in reservations. The reservation system, while generally regarded in a favourable light, has also been criticised for unfairly blocking tertiary and employment opportunities for those who would have otherwise got positions on merit. On the other hand, there are still examples of discrimination against Dalits in daily life – for example, higher castes denying them entry into certain temples.

Pilgrimage

Devout Hindus are expected to go on a *yatra* (pilgrimage) at least once a year. Pilgrimages are undertaken to implore the gods or goddesses to grant a wish, to take the ashes of a cremated relative to a holy river, or to gain spiritual merit. India has thousands of holy sites to which pilgrims travel; the elderly often make Varanasi their final one, as it's believed that dying in this sacred city releases a person from the cycle of rebirth. Sufi shrines in India attract thousands of Muslims to commemorate holy days, such as the birthday of a sufi saint, and many Muslims also make the hajj to Mecca in Saudi Arabia.

Most festivals in India are rooted in religion and are thus a magnet for throngs of pilgrims. As many festivals are spiritual occasions – even those that have a carnivalesque sheen – it's important for tourists to behave respectfully. Also be aware that there have been deaths at festivals because of stampedes, so be extra cautious in large crowds.

RANGOLIS

Rangolis, the strikingly intricate chalk, rice-paste or coloured powder designs (also called *kolams*) that adorn thresholds, especially in South India, are both auspicious and symbolic. *Rangolis* are traditionally drawn at sunrise and are sometimes made of rice-flour paste, which may be eaten by little creatures – symbolising a reverence for even the smallest living things. Deities are deemed to be attracted to a beautiful *rangoli,* which may also signal to sadhus (ascetics) that they will be offered food at a particular house. Some people believe that *rangolis* protect against the evil eye.

ADIVASIS

India's Adivasis (tribal communities; Adivasi translates to 'original inhabitant' in Sanskrit) have origins that precede the Vedic Aryans and the Dravidians of the south. These groups range from the Gondi of the central plains to the animist tribes of the Northeast States. Today, they constitute less than 10% of the population and are comprised of more than 300 different tribal groups. The literacy rate for Adivasis is significantly below the national average.

Historically, contact between Adivasis and Hindu villagers on the plains rarely led to friction as there was little or no competition for resources and land. However, in recent decades an increasing number of Adivasis have been dispossessed of their ancestral land and turned into impoverished labourers. Although they still have political representation thanks to a parliamentary quota system, the dispossession and exploitation of Adivasis has reportedly sometimes been with the connivance of officialdom.

Since coming to power, the Modi government has acknowledged that more must be done to protect Adivasis. His government has pledged to work towards greater social welfare initiatives, especially in the fields of development, education and health. He has said that under his government modern technology would be employed (such as underground mining) to lessen the impact on tribal settlements. Meanwhile, on the health front, the PM has called for measures to be taken to address the high rates of sickle-cell anaemia; 10% of tribals suffer from this affliction, with the highest numbers found in Jharkhand and Chhattisgarh. Time will tell if the government's tribal empowerment initiatives succeed.

Read more about Adivasis in *Archaeology and History: Early Settlements in the Andaman Islands* by Zarine Cooper, *The Tribals of India* by Sunil Janah and *Tribes of India: The Struggle for Survival* by Christoph von Fürer-Haimendorf.

Kumbh Mela

If crowds worry you, stay away. This one's big. Very big. Held four times every 12 years at four different locations across central and northern India, the Kumbh Mela is the largest religious congregation on the planet. This vast celebration attracts tens of millions of Hindu pilgrims, including mendicant *nagas* (naked sadhus, or holy men) from various Hindu monastic orders. The Kumbh Mela doesn't belong to any particular caste or creed – devotees from all branches of Hinduism come together to experience the electrifying sensation of mass belief and to take a ceremonial dip in the sacred Ganges, Shipra or Godavari Rivers.

The origins of the festival go back to the battle for supremacy between good and evil. In the Hindu creation myths, the gods and demons fought a great battle for a *kumbh* (pitcher) containing the nectar of immortality. Vishnu got hold of the container and spirited it away, but in flight four drops fell on the earth – at Allahabad, Haridwar, Nasik and Ujjain. Celebrations at each of these cities last for around six weeks but are centred on just a handful of auspicious bathing dates, normally six. The Allahabad event, known as the Maha (Great) Kumbh Mela, is even larger with even bigger crowds. Each location also holds an Ardh (Half) Mela every six years and a smaller, annual Magh Mela.

India has the world's biggest diaspora population (pegged at 16 million) according to a 2015 UN report.

Women in India

According to the most recent census, in 2011, India's population is comprised of 586 million women, with an estimated 68% of those working (mostly as labourers) in the agricultural sector.

Women in India are entitled to vote and own property. While the percentage of women in politics has risen over the past decade, they're still notably underrepresented in the national parliament, accounting for around 11% of parliamentary members.

Although the professions are male dominated, women are steadily making inroads, especially in urban centres. Kerala was India's first state to break societal norms by recruiting female police officers in 1938. It was also the first state to establish an all-female police station (1973). For village women it's much more difficult to get ahead, but groups such as the Self-Employed Women's Association (SEWA) in Gujarat have shown what's possible, organising socially disadvantaged women into unions and offering microfinance loans.

Read more about India's tribal communities at www.tribal.nic.in, a site maintained by the Indian government's Ministry of Tribal Affairs.

In low-income families, especially, girls can be regarded as a serious financial liability because at marriage a dowry might be demanded. For the urban middle-class woman, life is usually much more comfortable, but pressures still exist. Broadly speaking, she is far more likely to receive a tertiary education, but once married is still often expected to 'fit in' with her in-laws and be a homemaker above all else. Like her village counterpart, if she fails to live up to expectations – even if it's just not being able to produce a grandson – the consequences can sometimes be dire, as demonstrated by the extreme practice of 'bride burning', wherein a wife is doused with flammable liquid and set alight. A 2015 report stated there had been 24,771 dowry deaths in the preceding three years, most in Uttar Pradesh (7048 deaths) followed by Bihar (3830 deaths) and Madhya Pradesh (2252 deaths).

Although the constitution allows for divorcees (and widows) to remarry, relatively few reportedly do so, simply because divorcees are traditionally considered outcasts from society, most evidently so beyond big cities. Divorce rates in India are among the worlds' lowest (around 13 in 1000) although they are rising. Most divorces take place in urban centres and are deemed less socially unacceptable among those occupying the upper echelons of society.

Based on Rabindranath Tagore's novel, *Chokher Bali* (directed by Rituparno Ghosh) is a poignant film about a young widow living in early-20th-century Bengal who challenges the 'rules of widowhood' – something unthinkable in that era.

In October 2006, following women's civil rights campaigns, the Indian parliament passed a landmark bill (on top of existing legislation) which gives women who are suffering domestic violence increased protection and rights. Prior to this legislation, although women could lodge police complaints against abusive spouses, they weren't automatically entitled to a share of the marital property or to ongoing financial support. Critics claim that many women, especially those outside India's larger cities, are still reluctant to seek legal protection because of the social stigma involved.

India remains a conservative society, and despite the sexualised images of women churned out in Bollywood movies (although prolonged kissing is still rarely seen on screen), it's considered by many traditionally minded people that a woman is somehow wanton if she so much as goes out after dark or does not dress modestly.

According to India's National Crime Records Bureau (NCRB), reported incidences of rape have gone up over 50% in the last 10 years, but it's believed that only a small percentage of sexual assaults are reported, largely due to family pressure and/or shame, especially if the perpetrator is known to the family (which is true in many cases).

Following the highly publicised gang-rape and murder of a 23-year-old Indian physiotherapy student in Delhi in December 2012, tens of thousands of people protested in the capital and beyond, demanding swift government action to address the country's escalating gender-based violence. It took a further year before legal amendments were made to existing laws to address the problem of sexual assault, including harsher punishments such as life imprisonment and the death penalty. Despite this, sexual violence against women is still a major problem.

In 2015 the NCRB reported that there were 34,651 cases of rape across India, with women aged between 18 and 30 the most number of cases.

The statistics showed a decline in reported rape cases of 5.7% (down from a reported 36,735 in 2014), with gang-rape incidences also dropping from 2346 in 2014 to 2113 in 2015. Despite the marginal decrease in rape cases, the NCRB reported a slight increase of 2.5% in other sexual offences, with 2015 registering a total of 84,222 cases (up from 82,235 in 2014). The country's capital, Delhi, recorded India's highest incidence of crimes against women with 17,104 cases in 2015.

In a bid to address the sexual assault problem, the government is taking a number of measures. From 2017 it has made it mandatory for all mobile phones sold in India to have a panic button. In addition, there will be an increase in female police officers and the opening of centres for women who have been victims of violence; 660 centres have been earmarked for the coming years. Various public awareness programmes have also been launched. Although these moves are a step in the right direction, India still has a very long way to go.

Sport

Cricket has long been engraved on the nation's heart, with the first recorded match in 1721, and India's first test match victory in 1952 in Chennai (Madras) against England. It's not only a national sporting obsession, but a matter of enormous patriotism, especially evident whenever India plays against Pakistan. Matches between these South Asian neighbours – which have had rocky relations since Independence – attract especially passionate support, and the players of both sides are under immense pressure to do their respective countries proud. The most celebrated Indian cricketer of recent years is Sachin Tendulkar – fondly dubbed the 'Little Master' – who, in 2012, became the world's only player to score 100 international centuries, retiring on a high the following year. Cricket – especially the Twenty20 format (www.cricket20.com) – is big business in India, attracting lucrative sponsorship deals and celebrity status for its players. The sport has not been without its murky side though, with Indian cricketers among those embroiled in match-fixing scandals over past years. International games are played at various centres – see Indian newspapers or check online for details about matches that coincide with your visit. Keep your finger on the cricketing pulse at www.espncricinfo.com (rated most highly by many cricket aficionados) and www.cricbuzz.com.

The launch of the Indian Super League (ISL; www.indiansuperleague.com) in 2013 has achieved its aim of promoting football as a big-time, big-money sport. With games attracting huge crowds and international players, such as the legendary Juventus footballer Alessandro del Piero (who was signed for the Delhi Dynamos in 2014) or Marco Materazzi (of

HIJRAS

India's most visible nonheterosexual group is the *hijras*, a caste of transvestites and eunuchs who dress in women's clothing. Some are gay, some are intersex and some were unfortunate enough to be kidnapped and castrated. *Hijras* have long had a place in Indian culture, and in 2014 the Indian Supreme Court recognised *hijras* as a third gender and as a class entitled to reservation in education and jobs. Conversely, in 2013, homosexuality was ruled to be unlawful (having been legal since 2009). Section 377 of the Indian Penal Code, which harks back to 1861, makes homosexual sex legally punishable.

Hijras work mainly as uninvited entertainers at weddings and celebrations of the birth of male children, and possibly as prostitutes. In 2014, Padmini Prakash became India's first transgender daily TV news-show anchor, indicating a new level of acceptance.

Read more about *hijras* in *The Invisibles* by Zia Jaffrey and *Ardhanarishvara the Androgyne* by Dr Alka Pande.

World Cup headbutt fame) as trainer of Chennai, the ISL has become an international talking point. The first week of the ISL in 2014 had 170.6 million viewers – the figure for the first phase of the Indian Premier League cricket was 184 million, which gives a sense of football's growth in popularity. The I-League is the longer-running domestic league, but it has never attracted such media attention or funding.

Tap into India's hockey scene at Indian Hockey (www.indian-hockey.com) and Indian Field Hockey (www.bharatiyahockey.org).

The country is also known for its historical links to horse polo, which intermittently thrived on the subcontinent (especially among nobility) until Independence, after which patronage steeply declined due to dwindling funds. Today there's a renewed interest in polo thanks to beefed-up sponsorship and, although it still remains an elite sport, it's attracting more attention from the country's burgeoning upper middle class. The origins of polo are not completely clear. Believed to have its roots in Persia and China around 2000 years ago, on the subcontinent it's thought to have first been played in Baltistan (in present-day Pakistan). Some say that Emperor Akbar (who reigned in India from 1556 to 1605) first introduced rules to the game, but that polo, as it's played today, was largely influenced by a British cavalry regiment stationed in India during the 1870s. A set of international rules was implemented after WWI. The world's oldest surviving polo club, established in 1862, is in Kolkata (Calcutta Polo Club; www.calcuttapolo.com). Polo takes place during the cooler winter months in major cities, including Delhi, Jaipur, Mumbai and Kolkata. It is also occasionally played in Ladakh and Manipur.

Although officially the national sport, field hockey no longer enjoys the same fervent following it once did. During its golden era, between 1928 and 1956, India won six consecutive Olympic gold medals in hockey; it later bagged two further Olympic gold medals, one in 1964 and the other in 1980. Recent initiatives to ignite renewed interest in the game have had mixed results.

Cricket lovers are likely to be bowled over by *The Illustrated History of Indian Cricket* by Boria Majumdar and *The States of Indian Cricket* by Ramachandra Guha.

Kabaddi is another fairly popular competitive sport in the region. Two teams occupy two sides of a court. A raider runs into the opposing side, taking a breath and trying to tag one or more members of the opposite team. The raider chants *'kabaddi'* repeatedly to show that they have not taken a breath, returning to the home half before exhaling.

Other sports that are gaining ground in India include tennis (the country's star performers are Sania Mirza, Leander Paes and Mahesh Bhupathi – to delve deeper, see www.aitatennis.com) and horse racing, which is reasonably popular in larger cities such as Mumbai, Delhi, Kolkata and Bengaluru.

A record number of 118 athletes competed in the 2016 Rio Summer Olympics, but the results were disappointing, with India taking home just one silver and one bronze medal, finishing 67th on the final medal tally. At these games, Sakshi Malik became the first Indian woman wrestler to win an Olympic medal (with bronze in the women's freestyle 58kg category) while PV Sindhu (women's badminton) became the first Indian woman to win an Olympic silver.

Spiritual India

From elaborate city temples to simple village shrines, spirituality suffuses almost every facet of life in India. The nation's major faith, Hinduism, is practised by around 80% of the population and is one of the world's oldest extant religions, with roots extending beyond 1000 BC. Buddhism, Jainism and Zoroastrianism have a similarly historic pedigree. Indeed, in a land that has long embraced the sacred, no matter where you travel spiritual India is bound to be a constant companion.

Hinduism

Hinduism has no founder or central authority and it isn't a proselytising religion. Essentially, Hindus believe in Brahman, who is eternal, uncreated and infinite. Everything that exists emanates from Brahman and will ultimately return to it. The multitude of gods and goddesses are merely manifestations – knowable aspects of this formless phenomenon.

Hindus believe that earthly life is cyclical: you are born again and again (a process known as samsara), the quality of these rebirths being dependent upon your karma (conduct or action) in previous lives. Living a righteous life and fulfilling your dharma (moral code of behaviour; social duty) will enhance your chances of being born into a higher caste and better circumstances. Alternatively, if enough bad karma has accumulated, rebirth may take animal form. But it's only as a human that you can gain sufficient self-knowledge to escape the cycle of reincarnation and achieve moksha (liberation from samsara).

Unravelling the basic tenets of Hinduism are two books, both called *Hinduism: An Introduction* – one is by Shakunthala Jagannathan, the other by Dharam Vir Singh.

Gods & Goddesses

All Hindu deities are regarded as a manifestation of Brahman, who is often described as having three main representations, the Trimurti: Brahma, Vishnu and Shiva.

Brahman

The One; the ultimate reality. Brahman is formless, eternal and the source of all existence. Brahman is *nirguna* (without attributes), as opposed to all the other gods and goddesses, which are manifestations of Brahman and therefore *saguna* (with attributes).

Brahma

Only during the creation of the universe does Brahma play an active role. At other times he is in meditation. His consort is Saraswati, the goddess of learning, and his vehicle is a swan. He is sometimes shown sitting on a lotus that rises from Vishnu's navel, symbolising the interdependence of the gods. Brahma is generally depicted with four (crowned and bearded) heads, each turned towards a point of the compass. Worship of Brahma was eclipsed by the rise of groups devoted to Shiva and Vishnu. Today, India has few Brahma temples.

Vishnu

The preserver or sustainer, Vishnu is associated with 'right action'. He protects and sustains all that is good in the world. He is usually depicted

THE SACRED SEVEN

The number seven has special significance in Hinduism. There are seven sacred Indian cities, which are all major pilgrimage centres: Varanasi, associated with Shiva; Haridwar, where the Ganges enters the plains from the Himalaya; Ayodhya, birthplace of Rama; Dwarka, with the legendary capital of Krishna thought to be off the Gujarat coast; Mathura, birthplace of Krishna; Kanchipuram, site of the historic Shiva temples; and Ujjain, venue of the Kumbh Mela every 12 years.

There are also seven sacred rivers: the Ganges (Ganga), Saraswati (thought to be underground), Yamuna, Indus, Narmada, Godavari and Cauvery.

with four arms, holding a lotus, a conch shell (it can be blown like a trumpet so symbolises the cosmic vibration from which existence emanates), a discus and a mace. His consort is Lakshmi, the goddess of wealth, and his vehicle is Garuda, the man-bird creature. The Ganges is said to flow from his feet.

Shiva

Shiva is the destroyer – to deliver salvation – without whom creation couldn't occur. Shiva's creative role is phallically symbolised by his representation as the frequently worshipped lingam. With 1008 names, Shiva takes many forms, including Nataraja, lord of the *tandava* (cosmic victory dance), who paces out the creation and destruction of the cosmos.

Shiva is sometimes characterised as the lord of yoga, a Himalaya-dwelling ascetic with matted hair, an ash-smeared body, a penchant for chillum smoking, and a third eye symbolising wisdom.

Sometimes Shiva has snakes draped around his neck and is shown holding a trident (representative of the Trimurti) as a weapon while riding Nandi, his bull. Nandi symbolises power and potency, justice and moral order. Shiva's consort, Parvati, is capable of taking many forms.

Other Prominent Deities

Elephant-headed Ganesh is the god of good fortune, remover of obstacles, and patron of scribes (the broken tusk he holds was used to write sections of the Mahabharata). His animal vehicle is Mooshak (a rat-like creature). How Ganesh came to have an elephant's head is a story with several variations. One legend says that Ganesh was born to Parvati in the absence of his father Shiva, and so grew up not knowing him. One day, as Ganesh stood guard while his mother bathed, Shiva returned and asked to be let into Parvati's presence. Ganesh, who didn't recognise Shiva, refused. Enraged, Shiva lopped off Ganesh's head, only to later discover, much to his horror, that he had slaughtered his own son. He vowed to replace Ganesh's head with that of the first creature he came across, which happened to be an elephant.

Another prominent deity, Krishna is an incarnation of Vishnu sent to earth to fight for good and combat evil. His dalliances with the *gopis* (milkmaids) and his love for Radha have inspired countless paintings and songs. Depicted with blue-hued skin, Krishna is often seen playing the flute.

Did you know that blood-drinking Kali is another form of milk-giving Gauri? *Myth = Mithya: A Handbook of Hindu Mythology* by Devdutt Pattanaik sheds light on this and other Hindu beliefs.

Hanuman is the hero of the Ramayana and loyal ally of Rama. He embodies the concept of *bhakti* (devotion). He's the king of the monkeys, but is capable of taking on other forms.

Among Shaivites (followers of the Shiva movement), *shakti*, the divine creative power of women, is worshipped as a force in its own right. The concept of *shakti* is embodied in the ancient goddess Devi (divine mother), who is also manifested as Durga and, in a fiercer evil-destroying incarnation, Kali. Other widely worshipped goddesses include Lakshmi, the goddess of wealth, and Saraswati, the goddess of learning.

Sacred Texts

Hindu sacred texts fall into two categories: those believed to be the word of god (*shruti,* meaning 'heard') and those produced by people (*smriti,* meaning 'remembered'). The Vedas are regarded as *shruti* knowledge and are considered the authoritative basis for Hinduism. The oldest of the Vedic texts, the Rig-Veda, was compiled over 3000 years ago. Within its 1028 verses are prayers for prosperity and longevity, as well as an explanation of the universe's origins. The Upanishads, the last parts of the Vedas, reflect on the mystery of death and emphasise the oneness of the universe. The oldest of the Vedic texts were written in Vedic Sanskrit (related to Old Persian). Later texts were composed in classical Sanskrit, but many have been translated into the vernacular.

The Hindu pantheon is said to have a staggering 330 million deities; those worshipped are a matter of personal choice or tradition.

The *smriti* texts comprise a collection of literature spanning centuries and include expositions on the proper performance of domestic ceremonies as well as the proper pursuit of government, economics and religious law. Among its well-known works are the Ramayana and Mahabharata, as well as the Puranas, which expand on the epics and promote the notion of the Trimurti. Unlike the Vedas, reading the Puranas is not restricted to initiated higher-caste males.

The Mahabharata

Thought to have been composed around 1000 BC, the Mahabharata focuses on the exploits of Krishna. By about 500 BC, the text had evolved into a far more complex creation with substantial additions, including the Bhagavad Gita (where Krishna proffers advice to Arjuna before a battle).

The story centres on conflict between the heroic gods (Pandavas) and the demons (Kauravas). Overseeing events is Krishna, who has taken on human form. Krishna acts as charioteer for the Pandava hero Arjuna, who eventually triumphs in a great battle against the Kauravas.

The Ramayana

Composed around the 3rd or 2nd century BC, the Ramayana is believed to be largely the work of one person, the poet Valmiki. Like the Mahabharata, it centres on conflict between the gods and the demons.

The story goes that Dasharatha, the childless king of Ayodhya, called upon the gods to provide him with a son. His wife duly gave birth to a boy. But this child, named Rama, was in fact an incarnation of Vishnu, who had assumed human form to overthrow the demon king of Lanka (now Sri Lanka), Ravana.

As an adult, Rama, who won the hand of the princess Sita in a competition, was chosen by his father to inherit his kingdom. At the last minute Rama's stepmother intervened and demanded her son, Barathan, take Rama's place. Rama, Sita and Rama's brother, Lakshmana, were exiled and went off to the forests, where Rama and Lakshmana battled demons and other dark forces. Ravana's sister attempted to seduce Rama but she was rejected and, in revenge, Ravana captured Sita and spirited her away to his palace in Lanka.

Rama, assisted by an army of monkeys led by the loyal monkey god Hanuman, eventually found the palace, killed Ravana and rescued Sita. All returned victorious to Ayodhya, where Rama was welcomed and crowned king.

Sacred Flora & Fauna

Animals, particularly snakes and cows, have long been worshipped on the subcontinent. For Hindus, the cow represents fertility and nurturing, while snakes (especially cobras) are associated with fertility and welfare.

COMMUNAL CONFLICT

Religion-based conflict has, at times, been a bloody part of India's history. The post-Independence partition of the country into Hindu India and Muslim Pakistan resulted in horrendous carnage and epic displacement.

Later bouts of major sectarian violence in India include the Hindu–Sikh riots of 1984, which led to the assassination of then prime minister Indira Gandhi, and the politically fanned 1992 Ayodhya calamity, which sparked Hindu–Muslim clashes.

The ongoing dispute between India and Pakistan over Kashmir is also perilously entwined in religious conflict. Since Partition (1947), India and Pakistan have fought two major wars over Kashmir and have had subsequent artillery exchanges, coming dangerously close to full-blown war in 1999. The festering dispute over this landlocked territory continues to fuel Hindu–Muslim animosity on both sides of the border.

Naga stones (snake stones) serve the dual purpose of protecting humans from snakes and appeasing snake gods.

Plants can also have sacred associations, such as the banyan tree, which symbolises the Trimurti, while mango trees are symbolic of love – Shiva is believed to have married Parvati under one. Meanwhile, the lotus flower is said to have emerged from the primeval waters and is connected to the mythical centre of the earth through its stem. Often found in the most polluted of waters, the lotus has the remarkable ability to blossom above murky depths. The centre of the lotus corresponds to the centre of the universe, the navel of the earth: all is held together by the stem and the eternal waters. The fragile yet resolute lotus is an embodiment of beauty and strength and a reminder to Hindus of how their own lives should be. So revered has the lotus become that today it's India's national flower. The Rudraksha (meaning 'Shiva's eye') tree is said to have sprung from Shiva's tears, and its seeds are used as prayer beads.

A sadhu is someone who has surrendered all material possessions in pursuit of spirituality through meditation, the study of sacred texts, self-mortification and pilgrimage. Learn more in *Sadhus: India's Mystic Holy Men* by Dolf Hartsuiker.

Worship

Worship and ritual play a paramount role in Hinduism. In Hindu homes you'll often find a dedicated worship area, where members of the family pray to the deities of their choice. Beyond the home, Hindus worship at temples. *Puja* is a focal point of worship and ranges from silent prayer to elaborate ceremonies. Devotees leave the temple with a handful of *prasad* (temple-blessed food) which is shared among others. Other forms of worship include *aarti* (the auspicious lighting of lamps or candles) and the playing of *bhajans* (devotional songs).

Islam

Islam is India's largest minority religion, followed by approximately 13.4% of the population. It's believed that Islam was introduced to northern India by Muslim conquerors (in the 16th and 17th centuries the Mughal empire controlled much of North India) and to the south by Arab traders.

Islam was founded in Arabia by the Prophet Mohammed in the 7th century AD. The Arabic term *islam* means to surrender, and believers (Muslims) undertake to surrender to the will of Allah (God), which is revealed in the scriptures, the Quran. In this monotheistic religion, God's word is conveyed through prophets (messengers), of whom Mohammed was the most recent.

Following Mohammed's death, a succession dispute split the movement, and the legacy today is the Sunnis and the Shiites. Most Muslims in India are Sunnis. The Sunnis emphasise the 'well-trodden' path or the orthodox way. Shiites believe that only imams (exemplary leaders) can reveal the true meaning of the Quran. India also has a long tradition of Sufism, a mystical interpretation of Islam that dates back to the earliest days of the religion.

All Muslims, however, share a belief in the Five Pillars of Islam: the shahada (declaration of faith: 'There is no God but Allah; Mohammed is his prophet'); prayer (ideally five times a day); the zakat (tax), in the form of a charitable donation; fasting (during Ramadan) for all except the sick, young children, pregnant women, the elderly and those undertaking arduous journeys; and the hajj (pilgrimage) to Mecca, which every Muslim aspires to do at least once.

To grasp the intricacies of Sikhism, read *Volume One* (1469–1839) and *Volume Two* (1839–2004) of *A History of the Sikhs* by Khushwant Singh.

Sikhism

Sikhism, founded in Punjab by Guru Nanak in the 15th century, began as a reaction against the caste system and Brahmin domination of ritual. Sikhs believe in one god and although they reject the worship of idols, some keep pictures of the 10 gurus as a point of focus. The Sikhs' holy book, the Guru Granth Sahib, contains the teachings of the 10 Sikh gurus, several of whom were executed by the Mughals. Like Hindus and Buddhists, Sikhs believe in rebirth and karma. In Sikhism, there's no ascetic or monastic tradition ending the cycles of rebirth. Almost 2% of India's citizens are Sikhs, with most living in Punjab.

Born in present-day Pakistan, Guru Nanak (1469–1539) was largely dissatisfied with both Muslim and Hindu religious practices. He believed in family life and the value of hard work – he married, had two sons and worked as a farmer when not travelling around, preaching and singing self-composed *kirtan* (Sikh devotional songs) with his Muslim musician, Mardana. He is said to have performed miracles and he encouraged meditation on God's name as a prime path to enlightenment.

Nanak believed in equality centuries before it became socially fashionable and campaigned against the caste system. He was a practical guru: 'a person who makes an honest living and shares earnings with others

RELIGIOUS ETIQUETTE

Whenever visiting a sacred site in India, dress and behave respectfully – don't wear shorts or sleeveless tops (this applies to men and women) – and refrain from smoking. Loud and intrusive behaviour isn't appreciated, and neither are public displays of affection or kidding around.

Before entering a holy place, remove your shoes (tip the shoe-minder a few rupees when retrieving them) and check if photography is allowed. You're permitted to wear socks in most places of worship – often necessary during warmer months, when floors can be uncomfortably hot.

Religious etiquette advises against touching locals on the head, or directing the soles of your feet at a person, religious shrine or image of a deity. Protocol also advises against touching someone with your feet or touching a carving of a deity.

Head cover (for women and sometimes men) is required at some places of worship – especially gurdwaras (Sikh temples) and mosques – so carry a scarf just to be on the safe side. There are some sites that don't admit women and some that deny entry to nonadherents of their faith – enquire in advance. Women may be required to sit apart from men. Jain temples request the removal of leather items you may be wearing or carrying and may also request that menstruating women not enter. When walking around any Buddhist sacred site (chortens, stupas, temples, gompas) go clockwise. Don't touch them with your left hand. Turn prayer wheels clockwise, with your right hand.

Taking photos inside a shrine, at a funeral, at a religious ceremony or of people taking a holy dip can be offensive – ask first. Flash photography may be prohibited in certain areas of a shrine, or may not be permitted at all.

recognises the way to God'. He appointed his most talented disciple to be his successor, not one of his sons. His *kirtan* are still sung in gurdwaras (Sikh temples) today, and his picture is kept in millions of homes in and beyond the subcontinent.

Sikhs strive to follow the spiritual lead of the Khalsa, the five Sikh warriors anointed by Guru Gobind Singh as perfectly embodying the principles of the Sikh faith. Wearing a *dastar,* or turban, is mandatory for baptised Sikh men, and devout Sikhs uphold the 'Five Ks' – *kesh* (leaving hair uncut), *kanga* (carrying a wooden comb), *kara* (wearing an iron bracelet), *kacchera* (wearing cotton shorts) and *kirpan* (carrying a dagger or sword).

Buddhism

Less than 1% of the country's population is Buddhist. Bodhgaya, in the state of Bihar, where the Buddha achieved enlightenment, is one of Buddhism's most sacred sites, drawing pilgrims from across the world.

Buddhism's spiritual icon, the 14th Dalai Lama, resides in India as does the 17th Karmapa (the head of the Karma Kagyu sect of Tibetan Buddhism).

Scholars generally identify two predominant extant branches of Buddhism: Theravada (Doctrine of the Elders) and Mahayana (The Great Vehicle). Broadly speaking, followers of Theravada subscribe to the belief that attaining enlightenment – and thus liberating oneself from the cycle of birth and death – can be achieved by practising the Noble Eightfold Path (sometimes dubbed 'The Middle Way'). Theravada Buddhism focuses on the premise that self-effort is the path to enlightenment, with meditation playing a key role. Meanwhile, adherents of Mahayana believe Buddhahood (spiritual enlightenment as per Buddhist teachings) can be attained via the bodhisattva path – a state in which one deliberately stays in the cycle of rebirth to assist others achieve a state of awakening. Bodhisattvas are enlightened beings.

A sub-branch found in India is Tibetan Buddhism. Established in the 8th century AD, it incorporates teachings of Mahayana Buddhism as well as a range of rituals and spiritual practices (such as special mantras) derived from indigenous Tibetan religious beliefs. Supernatural beings are an important part of Tibetan Buddhism and come in the form of both benevolent and wrathful entities. India has notable Tibetan Buddhist communities that include Dharamsala (Himachal Pradesh), Tawang (Arunachal Pradesh), Rumtek (Sikkim) and Leh (Ladakh).

Buddhism emerged in the 6th century BC as a reaction against the strictures of Brahminical Hinduism. Buddha (Awakened One) is believed to have lived from about 563 to 483 BC. Formerly a prince (Siddhartha Gautama) from the Nepali plains, the Buddha, at the age of 29, embarked on a quest for emancipation from the world of suffering. He achieved nirvana (the state of full awareness) at Bodhgaya, aged 35. Critical of the caste system and the unthinking worship of gods, the Buddha urged his disciples to seek truth within their own experiences.

The Buddha taught that existence is based on Four Noble Truths: that life is rooted in suffering, that suffering is caused by craving, that one can

OM

The word 'Om' has significance for several religions, and is one of Hinduism's most venerated symbols. Pronounced 'aum', it's a highly propitious mantra (sacred word or syllable). The 'three' shape symbolises the creation, maintenance and destruction of the universe (and thus the holy Trimurti). The inverted *chandra* (crescent or half moon) represents the discursive mind and the *bindu* (dot) within it, Brahman.

Buddhists believe that if 'Om' is intoned often enough with complete concentration, it will lead to a state of blissful emptiness.

ANATOMY OF A GOMPA

Parts of India, such as Sikkim and Ladakh, are known for their ornate, colourful gompas (Tibetan-style Buddhist monasteries). The focal point of a gompa is the *dukhang* (prayer hall), where monks assemble to chant passages from the sacred scriptures (morning prayers are a particularly atmospheric time to visit gompas). The walls may be covered in vivid murals or *thangkas* (cloth paintings) of bodhisattvas (enlightened beings) and *dharmapalas* (protector deities). By the entrance to the *dukhang,* you'll usually find a mural depicting the Wheel of Life, a graphical representation of the core elements of Buddhist philosophy (see www.buddhanet.net/wheel1.htm for an interactive description of the Wheel of Life).

Most gompas hold *chaam* dances (ritual masked dances to celebrate the victory of good over evil) during major festivals. Dances to ward off evil feature masks of Mahakala, the Great Protector, usually dramatically adorned with a headdress of human skulls. The Durdag dance features skull masks depicting the Lords of the Cremation Grounds, while Shawa dancers wear masks of wild-eyed stags. These characters are often depicted with a third eye in the centre of their foreheads, signifying the need for inner reflection.

Another interesting activity at Buddhist monasteries is the production of butter sculptures, elaborate models made from coloured butter and dough. The sculptures are deliberately designed to decay, symbolising the impermanence of human existence. Many gompas also produce exquisite sand mandalas – geometric patterns made from sprinkled coloured sand, then destroyed to symbolise the futility of the physical plane.

find release from suffering by eliminating craving, and that the way to eliminate craving is by following the Noble Eightfold Path. This path consists of right understanding, right intention, right speech, right action, right livelihood, right effort, right awareness and right concentration. By successfully complying with these one can attain nirvana.

Buddhism had somewhat waned in parts of India by the turn of the 20th century. However, it saw a revival in the 1950s among intellectuals and Dalits who were disillusioned with the Hindu caste system. The number of followers has been further increased with the influx of Tibetan refugees.

Jainism

Jainism arose in the 6th century BC as a reaction against the caste restraints and rituals of Hinduism. It was founded by Mahavira, a contemporary of the Buddha.

Jains believe that liberation can be attained by achieving complete purity of the soul. Purity means shedding all *karman,* matter generated by one's actions that binds itself to the soul. By following various austerities (eg fasting and meditation), one can shed *karman* and purify the soul. Right conduct is essential, and fundamental to this is *ahimsa* (nonviolence) in thought and deed towards any living thing.

The religious disciplines of followers are less severe than for monks (some Jain monks go naked). The slightly less ascetic maintain a bare minimum of possessions, which include a broom to sweep the path before them to avoid stepping on any living creature, and a piece of cloth tied over their mouth to prevent the accidental inhalation of insects.

Today, around 0.4% of India's population is Jain, with the majority living in Gujarat and Mumbai. Some notable Jain holy sites include Sravanabelagola, Palitana, Ranakpur and the temples of Mt Abu.

Christianity

There are various theories circulating about Christ's link to the Indian subcontinent. Some, for instance, believe that Jesus spent his 'lost years' in India, while others say that Christianity came to South India with St

TRIBAL RELIGIONS

Tribal religions have so merged with Hinduism and other mainstream faiths that very few are now clearly identifiable. Some basic tenets of Hinduism are believed to have originated in tribal culture.

A considerable number of tribal groups in India are animist. They believe that certain objects, animals or places are inhabited by spiritual entities. Religious ideas are closely intertwined with nature – a stone, river, tree or mountain etc may be deemed to have a spirit form. One example is the Mizos of northeast India who may walk around with large stones, believing them to be the abode of spiritual forces. Meanwhile, the Naga tribes of northeast India believe the earth was created out of water by a series of quakes triggered by an earthquake god. It is the sons of the earthquake god who have watched over the world ever since and delivered punishment to those who do wrong. Also in the northeast exist tribes who follow Donyi-Polo (translated as 'Sun-Moon'), which is said to have emanated from Tibet's pre-Buddhist Bön religion. The sun and moon represent female and male energies – somewhat like the concept of yin and yang. Devotees believe in the oneness of all living creatures.

Thomas the Apostle, who allegedly died in Chennai in the 1st century AD. However, many scholars attest it's more likely Christianity is traced to around the 4th century with a Syrian merchant, Thomas Cana, who set out for Kerala with around 400 families. India's Christian community today stands at about 2.3% of the population, with the bulk residing in South India.

Catholicism established a strong presence in South India in the wake of Vasco da Gama's visit in 1498, and orders that have been active – not always welcomed – in the region include the Dominicans, Franciscans and Jesuits. Protestant missionaries are believed to have begun arriving – with a conversion agenda – from around the 18th century, particularly in India's tribal regions.

Zoroastrianism

Zoroastrianism, founded by Zoroaster (Zarathustra), had its inception in Persia in the 6th century BC and is based on the concept of dualism, whereby good and evil are locked in a continuous battle. Zoroastrianism isn't quite monotheistic: good and evil entities coexist, although believers are urged to honour only the good. Both body and soul are united in this struggle of good versus evil. Although humanity is mortal, it has components that are timeless, such as the soul. On the day of judgement the errant soul is not called to account for every misdemeanour – but a pleasant afterlife does depend on one's deeds, words and thoughts during earthly existence.

Zoroastrianism was eclipsed in Persia by the rise of Islam in the 7th century and its followers, many of whom openly resisted this, suffered persecution. Over the following centuries some immigrated to India, where they became known as Parsis. Historically, Parsis settled in Gujarat and became farmers; however, during British rule they moved into commerce, forming a prosperous community in Mumbai.

In recent decades the Parsi population has been spiralling downward; there are now believed to be less than 70,000 Parsis left in India, with most residing in Mumbai.

Delicious India

India's culinary terrain is deliciously diverse. From contemporary fusion dishes to traditional snacks, it's the sheer variety that makes eating your way through this country so rewarding. India has a particularly impressive array of vegetarian food, but carnivores won't be disappointed either, with plenty on offer – from hearty Mughal-inspired curries to succulent tandoori platters. Adding flair to the national smorgasbord are regional variations that make the most of locally sourced ingredients, be they native spices or fresh herbs.

A Culinary Carnival

India's culinary story is an ancient one, and the food you'll find here today reflects millennia of regional and global influences.

Land of Spices

Christopher Columbus was actually searching for the black pepper of Kerala's Malabar Coast when he stumbled upon America. The region still grows the finest quality of the world's favourite spice, and it's integral to most savoury Indian dishes.

Turmeric is the essence of the majority of Indian curries, but coriander seeds are the most widely used spice and lend flavour and body to just about every dish. Indian 'wet' dishes – commonly known as curries in the West – usually begin with the crackle of cumin seeds in hot oil. Tamarind is sometimes known as the 'Indian date' and is a popular souring agent in the south. The green cardamom of Kerala's Western Ghats is regarded as the world's best, and you'll find it in curries, desserts and warming chai (tea). Saffron, the dried stigmas of crocus flowers grown in Kashmir, is so light it takes more than 1500 hand-plucked flowers to yield just one gram.

Containing handy tips, including how to best store spices, Monisha Bharadwaj's *The Indian Spice Kitchen* is a slick cookbook with more than 200 traditional recipes.

Rice Paradise

Rice is a staple, especially in South India. Long-grain white rice varieties are the most popular, served hot with just about any 'wet' cooked dish. From Assam's sticky rice in the far northeast to Kerala's red grains in the extreme south, you'll find countless regional varieties that locals will claim to be the best in India, though this honour is usually conceded to basmati, a fragrant long-grain variety that is widely exported around the world. Rice is usually served after you have finished with the rotis (breads), often accompanied by curd to enrich the mix.

Spotlighting rice, *Finest Rice Recipes* by Sabina Sehgal Saikia shows just how versatile this humble grain is, with classy creations such as rice-crusted crab cakes.

Flippin' Fantastic Bread

While rice is paramount in the south, wheat is the mainstay in the north. Roti, the generic term for Indian-style bread, is a name used interchangeably with chapati to describe the most common variety, an irresistible unleavened round bread made with whole-wheat flour and cooked on a *tawa* (hotplate). It may be smothered with ghee (clarified butter) or oil. In some places, rotis are bigger and thicker than chapatis and sometimes cooked in a tandoor. *Paratha* is a layered pan-fried flat bread, that may

SOUTHERN BELLES

Savoury dosas (also spelt dosai), a family of large, crispy, papery rice-flour crêpes, usually served with a bowl of hot *sambar* (soupy lentil dish) and another bowl of cooling coconut *chatni* (chutney), are a South Indian breakfast speciality that can be eaten at any time of day. The most popular is the *masala dosa* (stuffed with spiced potatoes), but there are also other fantastic dosa varieties – the *rava* dosa (batter made with semolina), the Mysuru dosa (like *masala dosa* but with more vegetables and chilli in the filling), and the *pessarettu* dosa (batter made with mung-bean dhal) from Andhra Pradesh. Nowadays, dosas are readily found in almost every corner of South India, from Tamil Nadu to the Himalaya.

also be stuffed, and makes for a hearty and popular breakfast. *Puri* – puffy fried bread pillows – are another popular sauce soaker-upper. Naan is a larger, thicker bread, baked in a tandoor and usually eaten with meaty sauces or kebabs. In Punjab, look out for naan-like *kulcha*, flavoured with herbs and spices.

Dhal-icious!

The whole of India is united in its love for dhal (curried lentils or pulses). You may encounter up to 60 different pulses: the most common are *channa* (chickpeas); tiny yellow or green ovals called *moong* (mung beans); salmon-coloured *masoor* (red lentils); the ochre-coloured southern favourite, *tuvar* (yellow lentils; also known as *arhar*); *rajma* (kidney beans); *urad* (black gram or lentils); and *lobhia* (black-eyed peas).

Meaty Matters

Although India probably has more vegetarians than the rest of the world combined, it still has an extensive repertoire of carnivorous fare. Chicken, lamb and mutton (sometimes actually goat) are the mainstays; religious taboos make beef forbidden to devout Hindus and pork to Muslims.

The Anger of Aubergines: Stories of Women and Food by Bulbul Sharma is an amusing culinary analysis of social relationships interspersed with enticing recipes.

In northern India, you'll come across meat-dominated Mughlai cuisine, which includes rich curries, kebabs, koftas (meatballs) and biryanis (steamed rice with meat of vegetables). This spicy cuisine traces its history back to the (Islamic) Mughal empire that once reigned supreme. In the south, you'll find the meaty Chettinadu cuisine of Tamil Nadu, which is beautifully spiced without being too fiery.

Tandoori meat dishes are another North Indian favourite. The name is derived from the clay oven, or tandoor, in which the marinated meat is cooked.

Deep-Sea Delights

India has around 7500km of coastline, so it's no surprise that seafood is an important ingredient, especially on the west coast, from Mumbai down to Kerala. Kerala is the biggest fishing state, while Goa boasts particularly succulent prawns and fiery fish curries, and the fishing communities of the Konkan Coast – sandwiched between Goa and Mumbai – are renowned for their seafood recipes. Few main meals in Odisha (Orissa) exclude fish, and in West Bengal, puddled with ponds and lakes, fish is king. The far-flung Andaman Islands also won't disappoint seafood lovers with the day's catch featuring on many menus.

The Fruits (& Vegetables) of Mother Nature

Vegetables are usually served at each main meal across India, and *sabzi* (vegetables) is a word recognised in every Indian vernacular. They're generally cooked *sukhi* (dry) or *tari* (in a sauce), and within these two categories they can be fried, roasted, curried, stuffed, baked, mashed and combined (made into koftas) or dipped in chickpea-flour batter to make a deep-fried *pakora* (fritter).

Potatoes are ubiquitous and popularly cooked with various masalas (spice mixes), with other vegetables, or mashed and fried for the street snack *aloo tikki* (mashed-potato patties). Onions are fried with other vegetables, ground into a paste for cooking with meats, and served raw as relishes, but are avoided by Jains. Heads of cauliflower are usually cooked dry on their own, with potatoes to make *aloo gobi* (potato-and-cauliflower curry), or with other vegetables such as carrots and beans. Fresh green peas turn up stir-fried with other vegetables in pilaus and biryanis and in one of North India's signature dishes, the magnificent *mattar paneer* (unfermented cheese and pea curry). *Baigan* (eggplant/aubergine) can be curried or sliced and deep-fried. Also popular is *saag* (a generic term for leafy greens), which can include mustard, spinach and fenugreek. Something a little more unusual is the bumpy-skinned *karela* (bitter gourd) which, like the delectable *bhindi* (okra), is commonly prepared dry with spices.

The *Penguin Food Guide to India* by Charmaine O'Brien is an engrossing and evocative read.

India's fruit basket is also bountiful. Along the southern coast are super-luscious tropical fruits such as pineapples and papayas. Mangoes abound during summer (especially April and May), with India offering more than 500 varieties – the pick of the juicy bunch is the sweet Alphonso. Citrus fruit, such as oranges (often yellow-green in India), tangerines, pink and white grapefruits, kumquats and sweet limes are widely grown. Himachal Pradesh produces crisp apples in autumn, while plump strawberries are especially good in Kashmir during summer. You'll find fruit inventively fashioned into a *chatni* (chutney) or pickle, and also flavouring lassi, *kulfi* (flavoured firm-textured ice cream) and other sweet treats.

Technically speaking, there's no such thing as an Indian 'curry' – the word, an anglicised derivative of the Tamil word *kari* (sauce), was used by the British as a term for any spiced dish.

Vegetarians & Vegans

India is king when it comes to vegetarian fare. There's little understanding of veganism (the term 'pure vegetarian' means without eggs), and animal products such as milk, butter, ghee and curd are included in most Indian dishes. If you are vegan, your first problem is likely to be getting the cook to understand your requirements, though big hotels and larger cities are getting better at catering to vegans.

For further information, surf the web – try **Indian Vegan** (www.indianvegan.com) and **Vegan World Network** (www.vegansworldnetwork.org).

Pickles, Chutneys & Relishes

Pickles, chutneys and relishes are accompaniments that add zing to meals. A relish can be anything from a tiny pickled onion to a delicately crafted fusion of fruit, nuts and spices. One of the most popular side dishes is

PAAN

Meals are often rounded off with *paan,* a fragrant mixture of betel nut (also called areca nut), lime paste, spices and condiments wrapped in an edible, silky *paan* leaf. Peddled by *paan*-wallahs, who are usually strategically positioned outside busy restaurants, *paan* is eaten as a digestive and mouth-freshener. The betel nut is mildly narcotic and some aficionados eat *paan* the same way heavy smokers consume cigarettes – over the years these people's teeth can become rotted red and black. Usually the gloopy red juice is spat out, which is not always particularly sightly.

There are two basic types of *paan: mitha* (sweet) and *saadha* (with tobacco, which has similar health risks to other forms of tobacco use). A parcel of *mitha paan* is a splendid way to finish a meal. Pop the whole parcel in your mouth and chew slowly, allowing the juices to oooooooze.

yoghurt-based raita, which makes a tongue-cooling counter to spicy food. *Chatnis* can come in any number of varieties (sweet or savoury) and can be made from many different vegetables, fruits, herbs and spices.

Sweet at Heart

India has a colourful kaleidoscope of often-sticky and squishy *mithai* (Indian sweets), most of them sinfully sugary. The main categories are *barfi* (a fudgelike milk-based sweet), soft *halwa* (made with vegetables, cereals, lentils, nuts or fruit), *ladoos* (sweet balls made with gram flour and semolina), and those made from *chhana* (unpressed paneer), such as *rasgullas*. There are also simpler – but equally scrumptious – offerings such as crunchy *jalebis* (coils of deep-fried batter dunked in sugar syrup; served hot) that you'll see all over the country.

The Book of Indian Sweets by Satarupa Banerjee contains a jumble of regional sweet treats, from Bengali *rasgullas* to Goan *bebinca*.

Kheer (called *payasam* in the south) is one of the most popular after-meal desserts. It's a creamy rice pudding with a light, delicate flavour, enhanced with cardamom, saffron, pistachios, flaked almonds, chopped cashews or slivered dried fruit. Other favourites include hot *gulab jamuns* (deep-fried dough soaked in a rose flavoured syrup) and refreshing *kulfi*.

Each year, an estimated 14 tonnes of pure silver is converted into the edible foil that decorates many Indian sweets, especially during the Diwali festival.

Where to Fill Up

You can eat well in India everywhere from ramshackle street *dhabas* (eateries) to plush five-star hotels. Most midrange restaurants serve a few basic genres: South Indian (which usually means the vegetarian food of Tamil Nadu and Karnataka) and North Indian (which largely comprises Punjabi/Mughlai fare), and often Indian interpretations of Chinese dishes. You'll also find the cuisines of neighbouring regions and states. Indians frequently migrate in search of work and these restaurants cater to the large communities seeking the familiar tastes of home.

Ghee is made by melting butter and removing the water and milk solids – ghee is the clear butter fat that remains. It's better for high-heat cooking than butter and keeps for longer.

Not to be confused with burger joints and pizzerias, restaurants in the south advertising 'fast food' are some of India's best. They serve the whole gamut of tiffin (snack) items and often have separate sweet counters. Many upmarket hotels have outstanding restaurants, usually with pan-Indian menus so you can explore various regional cuisines. Meanwhile, the independent restaurant dining scene keeps mushrooming in India's larger cities, with every kind of cuisine available, from Mexican and Mediterranean to Japanese and Italian.

Dhabas are oases to millions of truck drivers, bus passengers and sundry travellers going anywhere by road. The original *dhabas* dot the North Indian landscape, but you'll find versions of them throughout the country. The rough-and-ready but satisfying food served in these happy-go-lucky shacks has become a genre of its own, known as '*dhaba* food'.

Street Food

Whatever the time of day, street food vendors are frying, boiling, roasting, peeling, simmering, mixing, juicing or baking different types of food

DEAR DAIRY

Milk and milk products make a staggering contribution to Indian cuisine: *dahi* (curd/yoghurt) is commonly served with meals and is great for subduing heat; paneer is a godsend for the vegetarian majority; lassi is one in a host of nourishing sweet and savoury beverages; ghee is the traditional and pure cooking medium; and some of the finest *mithai* (Indian sweets) are made with milk.

STREET FOOD TIPS

Tucking into street eats is a highlight of travelling in India, but to avoid tummy troubles:

- Give yourself a few days to adjust to the local cuisine, especially if you're unaccustomed to spicy food.
- If locals are avoiding a particular vendor, you should too. Also note the profile of the customers – any place popular with families will probably be your safest bet.
- Check how and where the vendor is cleaning the utensils, and how and where the food is covered. If the vendor is cooking in oil, take a peek to check it's clean. If the pots or surfaces are dirty, there are food scraps about or too many buzzing flies, don't be shy to make a hasty retreat.
- Don't be put off when you order some deep-fried snack and the cook throws it back into the wok. It's common practice to partly cook the snacks first and then finish them off once they've been ordered. Frying them hot again kills germs.
- Unless a place is reputable (and busy), it's best to avoid eating meat from the street.
- The hygiene standard at juice stalls varies, so exercise caution. Have the vendor press the juice in front of you and steer clear of anything stored in a jug or served in a glass (unless you're confident with the washing standards).
- Don't be tempted by glistening pre-sliced melon and other fruit, which keeps its luscious veneer with regular dousing of (often dubious) water.

and drink to lure peckish passers-by. Small operations usually have one special that they serve all day, while other vendors have different dishes for breakfast, lunch and dinner. The fare varies as you venture between neighbourhoods, towns and regions; it can be as simple as puffed rice or peanuts roasted in hot sand, or as complex as the riot of different flavours known as *chaat* (savoury snack). Fabulous calvalcades of taste include *chole bhature* (puffed bread served with spicy chickpeas and dipped in fragrant sauce) in North India, *aloo tikki* (spicy fried potato patties), which are renowned in Lucknow, *gol gappa/Panipuri/gup chup* (puffed spheres of bread with a spicy filling), all over India, and *idli sambar* (rice patties served with delectable sauce and chutney) in Chennai and the south.

Got the munchies? Grab *Street Foods of India* by Vimla and Deb Kumar Mukerji, which has recipes of much-loved Indian snacks, from samosas and *bhelpuri* to *jalebis* and *kulfi*.

Railway Snack Attack

One of the thrills of travelling by rail in India is the culinary circus that greets you at almost every station. Roving vendors accost arriving trains, yelling and scampering up and down the carriages; fruit, *namkin* (savoury nibbles), omelettes, nuts and sweets are offered through the grills on the windows; and platform cooks try to lure you from the train with the sizzle of spicy goodies such as samosas. Frequent rail travellers know which station is famous for which food item: Lonavla station in Maharashtra is known for *chikki* (rock-hard toffee-like confectionery), Agra for *peitha* (square sweet made from pumpkin and glucose, usually flavoured with rose water, coconut or saffron) and Dhaund near Delhi for biryani.

Daily Dining Habits

Three main meals a day is the norm in India. Breakfast is usually fairly light, maybe *idlis* (South Indian spongy fermented rice cake) and *sambar* in the south, and *parathas* in the north. Lunch can be substantial (perhaps a thali) or light, especially for time-strapped office workers. Dinner is usually the main meal of the day. It's generally comprised of a few different preparations – several curried vegetables (maybe also meat) dishes and dhal, accompanied by rice and/or chapatis. Dishes are served

FEASTING INDIAN-STYLE

Most people in India eat with their right hand. In the south, they use as much of the hand as is necessary, while elsewhere they use the tips of the fingers. The left hand is reserved for unsanitary actions such as removing shoes. You can use your left hand for holding drinks and serving yourself from a communal bowl, but it shouldn't be used for bringing food to your mouth. Before and after a meal, it's good manners to wash your hands.

Once your meal is served, mix the food with your fingers. If you are having dhal and *sabzi* (vegetables), only mix the dhal into your rice and have the *sabzi* in small scoops with each mouthful. If you are having fish or meat curry, mix the gravy into your rice. Scoop up lumps of the mix and, with your knuckles facing the dish, use your thumb to shovel the food into your mouth.

all at once rather than as courses. Desserts are optional and most prevalent during festivals or other special occasions. Fruit may wrap up a meal. In many Indian homes dinner can be a rather late affair (post-9pm) depending on personal preference and the season (eg late dinners during the warmer months). Restaurants usually spring to life after 9pm in the cities, but in smaller towns they're busy earlier.

Thali means 'plate' in Hindi, and is the name of a complete meal, a selection of dishes in small metal bowls served on a larger metal dish, plus bread, rice, chutneys and dessert. Unlimited thali means you get refills.

Spiritual Sustenance

For many in India, food is considered just as critical for fine-tuning the spirit as it is for sustaining the body. Broadly speaking, Hindus traditionally avoid foods that are thought to inhibit physical and spiritual development, although there are few hard-and-fast rules. The taboo on eating beef (the cow is holy to Hindus) is the most rigid restriction. Jains avoid foods such as garlic and onions, which, apart from harming insects in the ground when extracted, are thought to heat the blood and arouse sexual desire. You may come across vegetarian restaurants that make it a point to advertise the absence of onion and garlic in their dishes for this reason. Devout Hindus may also avoid garlic and onions. These items are also banned from many ashrams.

Some foods, such as dairy products, are considered innately pure and are eaten to cleanse the body, mind and spirit. Ayurveda, the ancient science of life, health and longevity, also influences food customs.

Pork is taboo for Muslims and stimulants such as alcohol are avoided by the most devout. Halal is the term for all permitted foods, and *haram* for those prohibited. Fasting is considered an opportunity to earn the approval of Allah, to wipe the sin-slate clean and to understand the suffering of the poor.

Food that is first offered to the gods at temples then shared among devotees is known as *prasad.*

Buddhists subscribe to the philosophy of *ahimsa* (nonviolence) and are mostly vegetarian. Jainism's central tenet is strict vegetarianism, and rigid restrictions are in place to avoid injury to any living creature. Vegetables that grow underground are considered *ananthkay* – one body containing many lives – and most Jains will avoid eating them because of the potential harm caused to insects during cultivation and harvesting.

India's Sikh, Christian and Parsi communities have few restrictions on what they can eat.

Drinks, Anyone?

Gujarat, Nagaland and Lakshadweep are India's only dry states, but there are drinking laws in place all over the country, and each state may have regular dry days when the sale of alcohol from liquor shops is banned. Kerala, where alcohol consumption was twice the national average, is moving towards complete prohibition by 2024, with hundreds of bars being closed down and alcohol only currently officially available at five-star hotels. On Gandhi's birthday (2 October), you'll find it hard to get an alcoholic drink anywhere. In Goa, because of the European influence, alcohol taxes are lower and the drinking culture less restricted.

You'll find excellent watering holes in most big cities, especially Mumbai, Bengaluru (the craft-beer capital of India), Kolkata and Delhi, which are usually at their liveliest on weekends. The more upmarket bars serve an impressive selection of domestic and imported drinks as well as draught beer. Many bars turn into music-thumping nightclubs anytime after 8pm, although there are quiet lounge-bars to be found in most large cities. In smaller towns, the bar scene can be a seedy, male-dominated affair – not the kind of place thirsty female travellers should venture into alone.

For India-wide restaurant reviews and recommendations, check out the excellent Zomato (zomato.com).

Wine-drinking is steadily on the rise, despite the domestic wine-producing industry still being relatively new. The favourable climate and soil conditions in certain areas – such as parts of Maharashtra and Karnataka – have spawned some decent Indian wineries, such as those of the Grover and Sula Vineyards.

Stringent licensing laws and religious restrictions mean some restaurants won't serve alcohol, but places that depend on the tourist rupee may covertly serve you beer in teapots and disguised glasses – however, don't assume anything, at the risk of causing offence.

Very few vegetarian restaurants serve alcohol.

Nonalcoholic Beverages

Chai (tea), the much-loved drink of the masses, is made with copious amounts of milk and sugar. A glass of steaming, frothy chai is the perfect antidote to the vicissitudes of life on the Indian road; the disembodied voice droning '*garam* chai, *garam* chai' (hot tea, hot tea) is likely to become one of the most familiar and welcome sounds of your trip. Masala chai adds cardamom, ginger and other spices.

While chai is the traditional choice of most of the nation, South Indians have long shared their loyalty with coffee. In recent years, though, the number of coffee-drinking North Indians has skyrocketed, with ever-multiplying branches of coffee chains.

Masala soda is the quintessentially Indian soft drink. It's a freshly opened bottle of fizzy soda, pepped up with lime, spices, salt and sugar. You can also plump for a plainer lime soda, which is soda with fresh lime, served sweet (with sugar) or salted as you prefer. Also refreshing is *jal jeera,* made of lime juice, cumin, mint and rock salt. Sweet and savoury lassi, a yoghurt-based drink, is especially popular nationwide and is another wonderfully cooling beverage.

Falooda is a rose-flavoured drink made with milk, cream, nuts and strands of vermicelli, while *badam* milk (served hot or cold) is flavoured with almonds and saffron.

Indian Recipes Online

www.recipesindian.com

www.thokalath.com/cuisine

www.indianfoodforever.com

The Booze Files

An estimated three-quarters of India's drinking population quaffs 'country liquor', such as the notorious arak (liquor distilled from coconut-palm sap, potatoes or rice) of the south. This is widely known as the poor-man's drink and millions are addicted to the stuff. Each year, many people are blinded or even killed by the methyl alcohol in illegal arak.

An interesting local drink is a clear spirit with a heady pungent flavour called *mahua,* distilled from the flower of the *mahua* tree. It's brewed in makeshift village stalls all over central India during March and April, when the trees bloom. *Mahua* is safe to drink as long as it comes from a trustworthy source. There have been cases of people being blinded after drinking *mahua* adulterated with methyl alcohol.

The subcontinent's wine industry is an ever-evolving one – take a cyber-sip of Indian wine at www.indianwines.info.

Rice beer is brewed all over east and northeast India, while in the Himalaya you'll find a grain alcohol called *raksi,* which is strong, has a mild charcoal flavour and tastes vaguely like Scotch whisky.

Toddy, the sap from the palm tree, is drunk in coastal areas, especially Kerala, while feni is the primo Indian spirit, and the preserve of laid-back Goa. Coconut feni is light and rather unexceptional but the more popular cashew feni – made from the fruit of the cashew tree – is worth a try.

Meanwhile, if you fancy sipping booze of the blue-blood ilk, traditional royal liqueurs of Rajasthan (once reserved for private consumption among nobility) are sold at some city liquor shops, especially in Delhi and Jaipur. Ingredients range from aniseed, cardamom and saffron to rose, dates and mint.

Menu Decoder

achar	pickle
aloo	potato; also alu
aloo tikki	mashed-potato patty
appam	South Indian rice pancake
arak	liquor distilled from coconut milk, potatoes or rice
baigan	eggplant/aubergine; also known as brinjal
barfi	fudge-like sweet made from milk
bebinca	Goan 16-layer cake
besan	chickpea flour
betel	nut of the betel tree; also called areca nut
bhajia	vegetable fritters
bhang lassi	blend of lassi and bhang (a derivative of marijuana)
bhelpuri	thin fried rounds of dough with rice, lentils, lemon juice, onion, herbs and chutney
bhindi	okra
biryani	fragrant spiced steamed rice with meat or vegetables
bonda	mashed-potato patty
chaat	savoury snack, may be seasoned with chaat masala
chach	buttermilk beverage
chai	tea
channa	spiced chickpeas
chapati	round unleavened Indian-style bread; also known as roti
chawal	rice
cheiku	small, sweet brown fruit
dahi	curd/yoghurt
dhal	spiced lentil dish
dhal makhani	black lentils and red kidney beans with cream and butter
dhansak	Parsi dish; meat, usually chicken or lamb, with curried lentils, pumpkin or gourd, and rice
dosa	large South Indian savoury crêpe
falooda	rose-flavoured drink made with milk, cream, nuts and vermicelli
faluda	long chickpea-flour noodles
feni	Goan liquor distilled from coconut milk or cashews
ghee	clarified butter
gobi	cauliflower

gulab jamun	deep-fried balls of dough soaked in rose-flavoured syrup
halwa	soft sweet made with vegetables, lentils, nuts or fruit
idli	South Indian spongy, round, fermented rice cake
imli	tamarind
jaggery	hard, brown, sugar-like sweetener made from palm sap
jalebi	orange-coloured coils of deep-fried batter dunked in sugar syrup; served hot
karela	bitter gourd
keema	spiced minced meat
kheer	creamy rice pudding
khichdi	blend of lightly spiced rice and lentils; also khichri
kofta	minced vegetables or meat; often ball-shaped
korma	curry-like braised dish
kulcha	soft leavened Indian-style bread
kulfi	flavoured (often with pistachio) firm-textured ice cream
ladoo	sweet ball made with gram flour and semolina; also ladu
lassi	yoghurt-and-iced-water drink
malai kofta	paneer cooked in a creamy sauce of cashews and tomato
masala dosa	large South Indian savoury crêpe (dosa) stuffed with spiced potatoes
mattar paneer	unfermented cheese and pea curry
methi	fenugreek
mishti doi	Bengali sweet; curd sweetened with jaggery
mithai	Indian sweets
momo	savoury Tibetan dumpling
naan	tandoor-cooked flat bread
namak	salt
namkin	savoury nibbles
noon chai	salt tea (Kashmir)
pakora	bite-sized vegetable pieces in batter
palak paneer	unfermented cheese chunks in a puréed spinach gravy
paneer	soft, unfermented cheese made from milk curd
pani	water
pappadam	thin, crispy lentil or chickpea-flour circle-shaped wafer; also pappad
paratha/parantha	flaky flatbread (thicker than chapati); often stuffed
phulka	a chapati that puffs up on an open flame
pilau	rice cooked in spiced stock; also pulau, pilao or pilaf
pudina	mint
puri	flat savoury dough that puffs up when deep-fried; also poori
raita	mildly spiced yoghurt, often containing shredded cucumber or diced pineapple
rasam	dhal-based broth flavoured with tamarind
rasgulla	cream-cheese balls flavoured with rose water
rogan josh	rich, spicy lamb curry
saag	leafy greens
sabzi	vegetables
sambar	South Indian soupy lentil dish with cubed vegetables
samosa	deep-fried pastry triangles filled with spiced vegetables (sometimes meat)

sonf	aniseed; used as a digestive and mouth-freshener; also saunf
tandoor	clay oven
tawa	flat hotplate/iron griddle
thali	all-you-can-eat meal; stainless steel (sometimes silver) compartmentalised plate
thukpa	Tibetan noodle soup
tiffin	snack; also refers to meal container often made of stainless steel
tikka	spiced, often marinated, chunks of chicken, paneer etc
toddy	alcoholic drink, tapped from palm trees
tsampa	Tibetan staple of roast-barley flour
upma	rava (semolina) cooked with onions, spices, chilli peppers and coconut
uttapam	thick savoury South Indian rice pancake with finely chopped onions, green chillies, coriander and coconut
vada	South Indian doughnut-shaped deep-fried lentil savoury
vindaloo	Goan dish; fiery curry in a marinade of vinegar and garlic
wazwan	traditional Kashmiri banquet

The Great Indian Bazaar

India's exuberant bazaars offer a treasure trove of goodies, including fabulously patterned textiles, finely crafted woodwork, chunky silver bangles, delicate gemstone jewellery and a tremendous mix of village creations. The array of arts and handicrafts is vast, with every region – sometimes every village – having its own unique traditions, some of them ancient. Indeed, the shopping opportunities you'll encounter on your journey are sure to be as inspiring and multifarious as the country itself.

Bronze Figures, Pottery, Stone Carving & Terracotta

In southern India and parts of the Himalaya, small images of deities are created by the age-old lost-wax process. A wax figure is made, a mould is formed around it, and the wax is melted, poured out and replaced with molten metal; the mould is then broken open to reveal the figure inside. Figures of Shiva as dancing Nataraja tend to be the most popular, but you can also find images of Buddha and numerous deities from the Hindu pantheon.

The West Bengalese also employ the lost-wax process to make Dokra tribal bell sculptures, while in Chhattisgarh's Bastar region, the Ghadwa Tribe has an interesting twist on the lost-wax process: a fine wax thread covers the metal mould, leaving a lattice-like design on the final product.

In Buddhist areas, you'll come across striking bronze statues of Buddha and the Tantric deities, finished off with exquisitely polished and painted faces.

In Mamallapuram (Tamil Nadu), craftsmen using local granite and soapstone have revived the ancient artistry of the Pallava sculptors; souvenirs range from tiny stone elephants to enormous deity statues weighing half a tonne. Tamil Nadu is also known for bronzeware from Thanjavur and Trichy (Tiruchirappalli).

A number of places produce attractive terracotta items, ranging from bowls and decorative flowerpots to images of deities, and children's toys.

Outside temples across India you can often buy small clay or plaster effigies of Hindu deities.

Carpets, Carpets, Carpets!

Carpet-making is a living craft in India, with workshops throughout producing top-notch wool and silk pieces. The finest carpets are produced in Kashmir, Ladakh, Himachal Pradesh, Sikkim and West Bengal. Carpet-making is also a major revenue earner for Tibetan refugees; most refugee settlements have cooperative carpet workshops. You can also find reproductions of tribal Turkmen and Afghan designs in states such as Uttar Pradesh. Antique carpets usually aren't antique – unless you buy from an internationally reputable dealer; stick to 'new' carpets.

In both Kashmir and Rajasthan, you'll find coarsely woven woollen *numdas* (or *namdas*), which are much cheaper than knotted carpets. Various regions manufacture flat-weave *dhurries* (kilim-like cotton rugs), including Kashmir, Himachal Pradesh, Rajasthan and Uttar Pradesh. Kashmiris also produce striking *gabbas* (rugs with appliqué), made from chain-stitched wool or silk.

Children have been employed as carpet weavers in the subcontinent for centuries. Child labour maintains a cycle of poverty, by driving down adult wages, reducing adult work opportunities and depriving children of their education. The carpets produced by Tibetan refugee cooperatives are almost always made by adults; government emporiums and charitable cooperatives are usually the best places to buy.

Throughout India you can find finely crafted gold and silver rings, anklets, earrings, toe rings, necklaces and bangles, and pieces can often be made to order.

Costs & Postage

The price of a carpet is determined by the number and the size of the hand-tied knots, the range of dyes and colours, the intricacy of the design and the material. Silk carpets cost more and look more luxurious, but wool carpets usually last longer. Expect to pay upwards of US$250 for a good-quality 90cm by 1.5m (or 90cm by 1.8m, depending on the region) wool carpet, and around US$2000 for a similar-sized carpet in silk. Tibetan carpets are cheaper, reflecting the relative simplicity of the designs; many refugee cooperatives sell the same size for around US$100.

Some people buy carpets thinking that they can be sold for a profit back home, but unless you really know your carpets, you're better off just buying a carpet because you love it. Many places can ship carpets home for a fee – although it may be safest to send things independently to avoid scams – or you can carry them in the plane's hold (allow 5kg to 10kg of your baggage allowance for a 90cm by 1.5m carpet, and check that your airline allows outsized baggage). Shipping to Europe for a carpet of this size would cost around ₹4000.

Jewellery

Virtually every town in India has at least one bangle shop selling a wide variety, ranging from colourful plastic and glass to brass and silver.

Heavy folk-art silver jewellery can be bought in various parts of the country, particularly in Rajasthan; Jaipur, Udaipur and Pushkar are par-

THE ART OF THE HAGGLE

Government emporiums, fair-trade cooperatives, department stores and modern shopping centres almost always charge fixed prices. Anywhere else you may need to bargain as prices can be highly inflated – shopkeepers in many tourist hubs are accustomed to travellers who have lots of money and little time to spend it, so you may end up being charged double or triple the going rate.

The first 'rule' to haggling is to never show too much interest in the item you've got your heart set upon. Second, resist purchasing the first thing that takes your fancy. Wander around several shops and price items, but don't make it too obvious: if you return to the first shop, the vendor will know it's because they are the cheapest (resulting in less haggling leeway).

Decide how much you would be happy paying, and then express a casual interest in buying. If you have absolutely no idea of the going rate, a common approach is to start by slashing the price by half. The vendor will, most likely, look aghast, but you can now work up and down respectively in small increments until you reach a mutually agreeable price. You'll find that many shopkeepers lower their so-called 'final price' if you head out of the store saying you'll 'think about it'.

Haggling is a way of life in India and is usually taken in good spirit. It should never turn ugly. Always keep in mind how much a rupee is worth in your own country's currency, and how much you'd pay for the item back home, to put things in perspective. If you're not sure of the 'right' price for an item, think about how much it is worth to you. If a vendor seems to be charging an unreasonably high price, look elsewhere.

ticularly good places to find silver jewellery pitched at foreign tastes. Jaipur is also renowned for its precious and semiprecious gems (and its gem scams). Chunky Tibetan jewellery made from silver (or white metal) and semiprecious stones is sold all over India. Many pieces feature Buddhist motifs and text in Tibetan script, including the famous mantra *Om Mani Padme Hum* (Hail to the Jewel in the Lotus). Some of the pieces sold in Tibetan centres, such as McLeod Ganj and Leh, are genuine antiques, but there's a huge industry in India, Nepal and China making artificially aged souvenirs. For creative types, loose beads of agate, turquoise, carnelian and silver are widely available. Buddhist meditation beaded strings made of gems or wood also make nice souvenirs.

Bidri, a method of damascening where silver wire is inlaid in gunmetal (a zinc alloy) and rubbed with soil from Bidar, Karnataka, is used to make jewellery, boxes and ornaments.

Pearls are produced by most Indian seaside states, but they're a speciality of Hyderabad. You'll find them at most state emporiums across the country. Prices vary depending on the colour and shape: you pay more for pure white pearls or rare colours like black, and perfectly round pearls are generally more expensive than misshapen or elongated pearls. A single strand of seeded pearls can cost as little as ₹500, but better-quality pearls are upwards of ₹1200.

Leatherwork

As cows are sacred in India, leatherwork is made from buffaloes, camels, goats or some other animal skin. Kanpur in Uttar Pradesh is the country's major leatherwork centre.

Most large cities offer a smart range of modern leather footwear at very reasonable prices, some stitched with zillions of sparkly sequins.

The states of Punjab and Rajasthan (especially Jaipur) are famed for *jootis* (traditional, often pointy-toed slip-on shoes).

Chappals, those wonderful (often curly-toed) leather sandals, are sold throughout India but are especially good in the Maharashtrian cities of Kolhapur, Pune and Matheran.

In Bikaner (Rajasthan), artisans decorate camel hide with gold to produce beautiful mirror frames, boxes and bottles, while in Indore in Madhya Pradesh, craftspeople stretch leather over wire-and-cloth frameworks to make cute toy animals.

Metal & Marble

You'll find copper and brassware throughout India. Candleholders, trays, bowls, tankards, figurines and ashtrays are popular buys. In Rajasthan and Uttar Pradesh, the brass is often inlaid with exquisite designs in red, green and blue enamel.

Cuttack in Odisha (Orissa) is famed for its lace-like silver-filigree ornaments known as *tarakasi*. A silver framework is made and then filled in with delicate curls and ribbons of silver.

Many Tibetan religious objects are created by inlaying silver in copper; prayer wheels, ceremonial horns and traditional document cases are all inexpensive buys. Resist the urge to buy *kangling* (Tibetan horns) and *kapala* (ceremonial bowls) made from inlaid human leg bones and skulls – they are illegal.

In all Indian towns you can find *kadhai* (Indian woks, also known as *balti*) and other cookware for incredibly low prices. Beaten-brass pots are particularly attractive, while steel storage vessels, copper-bottomed cooking pans and steel thali trays are also popular souvenirs. Ask if you can have your name engraved on them (usually free of charge).

The people of Bastar in Chhattisgarh use an iron-smelting technique similar to the one discovered 35,000 years ago to create abstract sculptures of spindly animal and human figures. These are often also made into functional items such as lamp stands and coat racks.

A sizeable cottage industry has sprung up in Agra reproducing the ancient Mughal art form of pietra dura (inlaying marble with semiprecious stones).

Musical Instruments

The best range of Indian musical instruments are available in the larger cities, especially Kolkata, Varanasi and Delhi. Prices vary according to the quality and sound of the instrument.

Be cautious when buying items that include international delivery, and avoid being led to shops by smooth-talking touts, but don't worry about too much else – except your luggage space!

Decent tabla sets (pair of drums) with a wooden tabla (tuned treble drum) and metal *dugi* or *bayan* (bass tone drums) cost upwards of ₹5000. Cheaper sets are generally heavier and often sound inferior.

Sitars range anywhere from ₹5000 to ₹25,000 (sometimes even more). The sound of each sitar will vary with the wood used and the shape of the gourd, so try a few. Note that some cheaper sitars can warp in colder or hotter climates. On any sitar, make sure the strings ring clearly and check the gourd carefully for damage. Spare string sets, sitar plectrums and a screw-in 'amplifier' gourd are sensible additions.

Other popular instruments include the *shehnai* (Indian flute), *sarod* (like an Indian lute), harmonium and *esraj* (similar to an upright violin). Conventional violins are great value – prices start at around ₹3500, while Kolkata is known for its quality acoustic guitars (from ₹2500).

Paintings

India is a major centre of contemporary art, and its larger cities are well stocked with independent galleries. Delhi, Mumbai and Kolkata are the best places to look for shops and galleries selling contemporary paintings by local artists.

Miniatures

Reproductions of Indian miniature paintings are widely available, but the quality varies: the cheaper ones have less detail and are made with inferior materials. Udaipur and Bikaner in Rajasthan have a particularly good range of shops specialising in modern reproductions on paper and silk, or you can browse Delhi's numerous state emporiums.

In regions such as Kerala and Tamil Nadu, you'll come across miniature paintings on leaf skeletons that portray domestic life, rural scenes and deities.

Folk Art

In Andhra Pradesh, *cheriyal* paintings, in bright, primary colours, were originally made as scrolls for travelling storytellers.

In Andhra Pradesh, intricately drawn, graphic cloth paintings called *kalamkari* depict deities and historic events.

The artists' community of Raghurajpur near Puri (Odisha) preserves the age-old art of *patachitra* (cloth) painting. Cotton or tassar (silk cloth) is covered with a mixture of gum and chalk; it's then polished, and images of deities and scenes from Hindu legends are painted on with exceedingly fine brushes. Odisha also produces *chitra pothi,* where images are etched onto dried palm-leaf sections with a fine stylus.

Bihar's unique folk art is Mithila (or Madhubani) painting, an ancient art form preserved by the women of Madhubani. These captivating paintings are most easily found in Patna, but are also sold in big city emporiums.

Thangkas

Exquisite *thangkas* (rectangular Tibetan paintings on cloth) of Tantric Buddhist deities and ceremonial mandalas are sold in Tibetan Buddhist areas, including Sikkim, parts of Himachal Pradesh and Ladakh. Some perfectly reproduce the glory of the murals in India's medieval gompas (Tibetan Buddhist monasteries); others are simpler. Prices vary, but bank on at least ₹4000 for a decent-quality *thangka* of A3 size, and a lot more (up to around ₹35,000) for large intricate *thangkas*. The selling of antique *thangkas* is illegal, and you would be unlikely to find the real thing anyway.

Textiles

Shawls

Indian shawls are famously warm and lightweight – they're often better than the best down jackets. It's worth buying one to use as a blanket on cold night journeys. Shawls are made from all sorts of wool, and many are embroidered with intricate designs.

The undisputed capital of the Indian shawl is the Kullu Valley in Himachal Pradesh, with dozens of women's cooperatives producing fine woollen pieces. These may be made from wool (the cheapest, from ₹700), angora (mohair – hairs from angora rabbit) or *pashmina* (the downy hair of the pashmina goat).

Ladakh and Kashmir are major centres for *pashmina* production – you'll pay at least ₹6000 for the authentic article. Be aware that many so-called *pashminas* are actually made from a mixture of wool and silk; however, these 'fake' pashminas are often very beautiful even so, and a lot less expensive, costing around ₹1200. Shawls from the Northeast States are famously warm, with bold geometric designs. In Sikkim and West Bengal, you may also find fantastically embroidered Bhutanese shawls. Gujarat's Kutch region produces some particularly distinctive woollen shawls, patterned with subtle embroidery and mirrorwork. Handmade shawls and tweeds can also be found in Ranikhet and Almora in Uttarakhand.

Be aware that it's illegal to buy *shahtoosh* shawls, as rare Tibetan antelopes are slaughtered to provide the wool. If you come across anyone selling these shawls, inform local authorities.

Saris

Saris are a very popular souvenir, especially given that they can be easily adapted to other purposes (from cushion covers to skirts). Real silk saris are the most expensive, and the silk usually needs to be washed before it becomes soft. The 'silk capital' of India is Kanchipuram in Tamil Nadu (Kanchipuram silk is also widely available in Chennai), but you can also find fine silk saris (and cheaper scarves) in centres including Varanasi, Mysuru and Kolkata. Assam is renowned for its muga, endi and pat silks (produced by different species of silkworms), which are widely available in Guwahati. You'll pay upwards of ₹3000 for a quality embroidered silk sari.

Patan in Gujarat is the centre for the ancient and laborious craft of *patola*-making. Every thread in these fine silk saris is individually hand-dyed before weaving, and patterned borders are woven with real gold. Slightly less involved versions are produced in Rajkot. Gold thread is also used in the famous *kota doria* saris of Kota in Rajasthan.

Aurangabad, in Maharashtra, is the traditional centre for the production of *himroo* shawls, sheets and saris, made from a blend of cotton, silk and silver thread. Silk and gold-thread saris produced at Paithan

GANDHI'S CLOTH

More than 80 years ago Mahatma Gandhi urged Indians to support the freedom movement by ditching their foreign-made clothing and turning to *khadi* – homespun cloth. *Khadi* became a symbol of Indian independence, and the fabric is still closely associated with politics. The government-run, nonprofit group Khadi and Village Industries Commission (www.kvic.org.in) serves to promote *khadi*, which is usually cotton, but can also be silk or wool.

Khadi outlets are simple, no-nonsense places where you can pick up genuine Indian clothing such as kurta pyjamas, headscarves, saris and, at some branches, assorted handicrafts – you'll find them all over India. Prices are reasonable and are often discounted in the period around Gandhi's birthday (2 October). A number of outlets also have a tailoring service.

PUTTING YOUR MONEY WHERE IT COUNTS

Overall, a comparatively small proportion of the money brought to India by tourism reaches people in rural areas. Travellers can make a greater contribution by shopping at community cooperatives set up to protect and promote traditional cottage industries and provide education, training and a sustainable livelihood at the grassroots level. Many of these projects focus on refugees, low-caste women, tribal people and others living on society's fringes.

The quality of products sold at cooperatives is high and the prices are usually fixed, which means you won't have to haggle. A share of the sales money is channelled directly into social projects such as schools, healthcare, training and other advocacy programs for socially disadvantaged groups. Shopping at the national network of Khadi and Village Industries Commission emporiums will also contribute to rural communities.

Wherever you travel, keep your eyes peeled for fair-trade cooperatives.

(near Aurangabad) are some of India's finest – prices range from around ₹7000 to a mind-blowing ₹300,000. Other regions famous for sari production include Madhya Pradesh for its cotton Maheshwari saris (from Maheshwar) and silk Chanderi saris (from Chanderi), and West Bengal, for its *baluchari* saris from Bishnupur, which employ a traditional form of weaving with untwisted silk thread.

Khadi & Embroidery

Textile production is India's major industry and around 40% takes place at the village level, where it's known as *khadi* (homespun cloth) – hence the government-backed *khadi* emporiums around the country. These inexpensive superstores sell all sorts of items made from *khadi*, including the popular Nehru jackets and kurta pyjamas (long shirt and loose-fitting trousers), with sales benefiting rural communities. *Khadi* has recently become increasingly chic, with India's designers referencing the fabrics in their collections.

Indian Textiles, by John Gillow and Nicholas Barnard, explores India's beautiful regional textiles and includes sections on tie-dye, weaving, beadwork, brocades and even camel girths.

You'll find a truly amazing variety of weaving and embroidery techniques around India. In tourist centres such as Goa, Rajasthan and Himachal Pradesh, textiles are stitched into popular items such as shoulder bags, wall hangings, cushion covers, bedspreads, clothes and much more. In Adivasi (tribal) areas of Gujarat and Rajasthan, small pieces of mirrored glass are embroidered onto fabric, creating eye-catching bags, cushion covers and wall hangings. The region of Kutch is particularly renowned for its embroidery.

Appliqué, Tie Dye & Block-Print

Appliqué is an ancient art in India, with most states producing their own version, often featuring abstract or anthropomorphic patterns. The traditional lampshades and *pandals* (tents) used in weddings and festivals are usually produced using the same technique.

Gujarat has a diversity of textile traditions: Jamnagar is famous for its vibrant *bandhani* (tie-dye work) used for saris and scarves, among other things, and Vadodara is renowned for block-printed fabrics, used for bedspreads and clothing. Ahmedabad is a good place to buy Gujarati textiles.

Block-printed and woven textiles are sold by fabric shops all over India: each region has its own speciality. The India-wide retail chainstores Fabindia (www.fabindia.com) and Anokhi (www.anokhi.com) are striving to preserve traditional patterns and fabrics, transforming them into home-decor items and Indian- and Western-style fashions. The latter has the Anokhi Museum of Hand Printing (p126), which demostrates the crafts.

Odisha has a reputation for bright appliqué and *ikat* (a Southeast Asian technique where thread is tie-dyed before weaving). The town of Pipli, between Bhubaneswar and Puri, produces striking appliqué work. The techniques used to create *kalamkari* cloth paintings in Andhra Pradesh (a centre for this ancient art is Sri Kalahasti) and Gujarat are also used to make lovely wall hangings and lampshades.

Woodcarving

Woodcarving is an ancient art form throughout India. In Kashmir, walnut wood is used to make finely carved wooden screens, tables, jewellery boxes and trays, inspired by the decorative trim of houseboats. Willow cricket bats are another Kashmiri speciality.

Wood inlay is one of Bihar's oldest crafts – you'll find lovely wooden wall hangings, tabletops, trays and boxes inlaid with metals and bone.

Sandalwood carvings of Hindu deities are one of Karnataka's specialities, but you'll pay a fair bit for the real thing – a 10cm-high Ganesh costs around ₹3000 in sandalwood, compared to roughly ₹300 in kadamb wood. However, the sandalwood will release fragrance for years.

In Udaipur in Rajasthan, you can buy brightly painted figures of Hindu deities carved from mango wood. In many parts of Rajasthan you can also find fabric printing blocks carved from teak wood.

Buddhist woodcarvings are a speciality of Sikkim, Ladakh, Arunachal Pradesh and all Tibetan refugee areas. You'll find wall plaques of the eight lucky signs, dragons and *chaam* masks, used for ritual dances. Most of the masks are cheap reproductions, but you can sometimes find genuine *chaam* masks made from lightweight whitewood or papier mâché from ₹3000 upwards.

Crafts aren't necessarily confined to their region of origin; artists migrate and are sometimes influenced by regional aesthetics, resulting in some interesting stylistic combinations. For example, you can visit a community of Rajasthani potters on the outskirts of Delhi.

Other Great Finds

It's little surprise that Indian spices are snapped up by tourists. Virtually all towns have shops and bazaars selling locally made spices at great prices. Karnataka, Kerala, Uttar Pradesh, Rajasthan and Tamil Nadu produce most of the spices that go into garam masala (the 'hot mix' used to flavour Indian dishes), while the Northeast States and Sikkim are known for black cardamom and cinnamon bark. Note that some countries, such as Australia, have stringent rules regarding the import of animal and plant products. Check with your country's embassy for details.

Attar (essential oil, mostly made from flowers) shops can be found around the country. Mysuru is famous for its sandalwood oil, while Mumbai is a major centre for the trade of traditional fragrances, including valuable *oud,* made from a rare mould that grows on the bark of the agarwood tree. In Tamil Nadu, Ooty and Kodaikanal produce aromatic and medicinal oils from herbs, flowers and eucalyptus.

Indian incense is exported worldwide, with Bengaluru and Mysuru, both in Karnataka, being major producers. Incense from Auroville in Tamil Nadu is also well regarded.

A speciality of Goa is *feni* (liquor distilled from coconut milk or cashews): a head-spinning spirit that often comes in decorative bottles.

Quality Indian tea is sold in Darjeeling and Kalimpong (both in West Bengal), Assam and Sikkim, as well as parts of South India, such as Munnar in Kerala and the Ooty area in Tamil Nadu's Western Ghats. There are also top tea retailers in Delhi and other urban hubs.

In Bhopal in Madhya Pradesh, colourful *jari* shoulder bags, embroidered with beads, are a speciality. Also on the portables front, the Northeast States are noted for their beautiful hand-woven baskets and wickerwork – each tribe has its own unique basket shape.

Jodhpur in Rajasthan, among other places, is famed for its antiques (though be aware that exporting antiques is prohibited).

Rajasthan is one of India's prime handicraft centres. Its capital, Jaipur, is renowned for block-printing and blue-glazed pottery sporting pretty floral and geometric motifs.

Artisans in Jammu and Kashmir have been producing lacquered papier mâché for centuries, and papier-mâché bowls, boxes, letter holders, coasters, trays and Christmas decorations are now sold across India, and make extremely inexpensive yet beautiful gifts (those with more intricate work command higher prices). In Rajasthan, look for colourful papier-mâché puppets, typically sold as a pair and often depicting a husband and wife, as well as beautiful little temples carved from mango wood, brightly painted with religious stories.

Fine-quality handmade paper – often fashioned into cards, boxes and notebooks – is worth seeking out. Puducherry in Tamil Nadu, Delhi, Jaipur and Mumbai are good places to start.

Hats are also popular: the Assamese make decorated reed-pith sun hats, and Tibetan refugees produce woollen hats, gloves and scarves, sold nationwide. Traditional caps worn by men and women of Himalayan tribes are available in many Himachal Pradesh towns.

India has a phenomenal range of books at very competitive prices, including leather-bound titles. Big city bookshops proffer the widest selections.

The Arts

India's magnificent artistic heritage is a reflection of the country's richly diverse ethnic groups and traditions. You'll encounter artful treasures around every corner: from the exquisite body art of *mehndi* (henna) to the soulful chants emanating from ancient temples to the vividly decorated trucks rumbling along dusty roads. The wealth of creative expression is a highlight of travelling here, with many of today's artists fusing ancient and contemporary techniques to produce works that are as evocative as they are edgy.

Dance

The ancient Indian art of dance is traditionally linked to mythology and classical literature. Dance can be divided into two main forms: classical and folk. Classical dance is based on well-defined traditional disciplines. Some classical dance styles:

Bharatanatyam (also spelt Bharata Natyam) Originated in Tamil Nadu, and has been embraced throughout India.

Kathak Has Hindu and Islamic influences and was particularly popular with the Mughals. Kathak suffered a period of notoriety when it moved from the courts into houses where *nautch* (dancing) girls tantalised audiences with renditions of the Krishna-and-Radha love story. It was restored as a serious art form in the early 20th century.

Kathakali Has its roots in Kerala; sometimes referred to as 'dance' but essentially is a kind of drama based on mythological subjects.

Kuchipudi A 17th-century dance-drama that originated in the Andhra Pradesh village from which it takes its name. The story centres on the envious wife of Krishna.

Odissi From Odisha (Orissa); thought to be India's oldest classical dance form. It was originally a temple art, and was later also performed at royal courts.

Manipuri Has a delicate, lyrical flavour; hails from Manipur. It attracted a wider audience in the 1920s when acclaimed Bengali writer Rabindranath Tagore invited one of its most revered exponents to teach at Shantiniketan (West Bengal).

Indian Classical Dance by Leela Venkataraman and Avinash Pasricha is a lavishly illustrated book covering various Indian dance forms, including *bharatanatyam*, Odissi, Kuchipudi and Kathakali.

India's second major dance form, folk, is widespread and varied. It ranges from the high-spirited bhangra dance of Punjab to the theatrical dummy-horse dances of Karnataka and Tamil Nadu, and the graceful fishers' dance of Odisha. In Gujarat, the colourful group dance known as *garba* is performed during Navratri (Hindu festival held in September or October).

Explore India's vibrant performing-arts scene – especially classical dance and music – at Art India (www.artindia.net).

Pioneers of modern dance forms in India include Uday Shankar (older brother of the late sitar master Ravi), who once partnered with Russian ballerina Anna Pavlova. Rabindranath Tagore was another innovator; in 1901 he set up a school at Shantiniketan in West Bengal that promoted the arts, including dance.

The dance you'll probably most commonly see, though, is in films. Dance has featured in Indian movies since the dawn of 'talkies' and often combines traditional, folk and contemporary choreography.

Music

Indian classical music traces its roots back to Vedic times, when religious poems chanted by priests were first collated in an anthology called the

Rig-Veda. Over the millennia classical music has been shaped by many influences, and the legacy today is Carnatic (characteristic of South India) and Hindustani (the classical style of North India) music. With common origins, they share a number of features. Both use the raga (the melodic shape of the music) and *tala* (the rhythmic meter characterised by the number of beats); *tintal*, for example, has a *tala* of 16 beats. The audience follows the *tala* by clapping at the appropriate beat, which in *tintal* is at beats one, five and 13. There's no clap at the beat of nine; that's the *khali* (empty section), which is indicated by a wave of the hand. Both the raga and the *tala* are used as a basis for composition and improvisation.

To tune into the melodious world of Hindustani classical music, including a glossary of musical terms, get a copy of *Nād: Understanding Raga Music* by Sandeep Bagchee.

Both Carnatic and Hindustani music are performed by small ensembles, generally comprising three to six musicians, and both have many instruments in common. There's no fixed pitch, but there are differences between the two styles. Hindustani has been more heavily influenced by Persian musical conventions (a result of Mughal rule); Carnatic music, as it developed in South India, cleaves more closely to theory. The most striking difference, at least for those unfamiliar with India's classical forms, is Carnatic's greater use of voice.

One of the best-known Indian instruments is the sitar (large stringed instrument), with which the soloist plays the raga. Other stringed instruments include the sarod (which is plucked) and the *sarangi* (which is played with a bow). Also popular is the tabla (twin drums), which provides the *tala*. The drone, which runs on two basic notes, is provided by the oboe-like *shehnai* or the stringed *tampura* (also spelt tamboura). The hand-pumped keyboard harmonium is used as a secondary melody instrument for vocal music.

Indian regional folk music is widespread and varied. Wandering musicians, magicians, snake charmers and storytellers often use song to entertain their audiences; the storyteller usually sings the tales from the great epics.

In North India you may come across *qawwali* (Sufi devotional singing), performed in mosques or at musical concerts. *Qawwali* concerts usually take the form of a *mehfil* (gathering) with a lead singer, a second singer, harmonium and tabla players, and a thunderous chorus of junior singers and clappers, all sitting cross-legged on the floor. The singers whip up the audience with lines of poetry, dramatic hand gestures and religious phrases as the two voices weave in and out, bouncing off each other to create an improvised, surging sound. On command the chorus dives in with a hypnotic and rhythmic refrain. Members of the audience often sway and shout out in ecstatic appreciation.

A completely different genre altogether, filmi (music from Bollywood films) includes modern, slower-paced love serenades, along with ebullient dance songs.

Get arty with *Indian Art* by Roy C Craven, *Contemporary Indian Art: Other Realities* edited by Yashodhara Dalmia, and *Indian Miniature Painting* by Dr Daljeet and Professor PC Jain.

Painting

Around 1500 years ago artists covered the walls and ceilings of the Ajanta caves in Maharashtra, western India, with scenes from the Buddha's past lives. The figures are endowed with an unusual freedom and grace, and contrast with the next major style that emerged from this part of India in the 11th century.

India's Jain community created some particularly lavish temple art. However, after the conquest of Gujarat by the Delhi Sultanate in 1299, the Jains turned their attention to illustrated manuscripts, which could be hidden away. These manuscripts are the only known form of Indian painting that survived the Islamic conquest of North India.

The Indo-Persian style – characterised by geometric design coupled with flowing form – developed from Islamic royal courts, although the

MEHNDI

Mehndi is the traditional art of painting a woman's hands (and sometimes feet) with intricate henna designs for auspicious ceremonies, such as marriage. If quality henna is used, the design, which is orange-brown, can last up to one month.

In touristy areas, *mehndi*-wallahs are adept at applying henna tattoo 'bands' on the arms, legs and lower back. If you get *mehndi* applied, allow at least a few hours for the design process and required drying time (during drying you can't use your hennaed hands).

It's always wise to request the artist to do a 'test' spot on your arm before proceeding: nowadays some dyes contain chemicals that can cause allergies. (Avoid 'black henna', which is mixed with some chemicals that may be harmful.) If good-quality henna is used, you should not feel any pain during or after the application.

depiction of the elongated eye is one convention that seems to have been retained from indigenous sources. The Persian influence blossomed when artisans fled to India following the 1507 Uzbek attack on Herat (in present-day Afghanistan), and with trade and gift-swapping between the Persian city of Shiraz, an established centre for miniature production, and Indian provincial sultans.

The 1526 victory by Babur at the Battle of Panipat ushered in the era of the Mughals in India. Although Babur and his son Humayun were both patrons of the arts, it's Humayun's son Akbar who is generally credited with developing the characteristic Mughal style. This painting style, often in colourful miniature form, largely depicts court life, architecture, nature, battle and hunting scenes, as well as detailed portraits. Akbar recruited artists from far and wide, and artistic endeavour first centred on the production of illustrated manuscripts (topics varied from history to mythology), but later broadened into portraiture and the glorification of everyday events. European painting styles influenced some artists, and this influence occasionally reveals itself in experiments with motifs and perspective.

Akbar's son Jehangir also patronised painting, but he preferred portraiture, and his fascination with natural science resulted in a vibrant legacy of paintings of flowers and animals. Under Jehangir's son Shah Jahan, the Mughal style became less fluid and, although the bright colouring was eye-catching, the paintings lacked the vigour of before.

Miniature painting flowered first at the Mughal court in the 16th century, as well as the Deccan sultanates (Golconda, Bijapur, Bidar etc). As Mughal power and wealth declined, many artists moved to Rajasthan where the Rajasthani school developed from the late 17th century. Later, artists from Rajasthan moved into the Himalayan foothills of Punjab, Himachal Pradesh and Uttarakhand, where the Pahari (Hill Country) school flourished in the 18th and early 19th centuries. The subject matter ranged from royal processions to shikhar (hunting expeditions), with many artists influenced by Mughal styles. The intense colours, still evident today in miniatures and frescoes in some Indian palaces, were often derived from crushed semiprecious stones, while the gold and silver colouring is finely pounded pure gold and silver leaf.

By the 19th century, painting in North India was notably influenced by Western styles (especially English watercolours), giving rise to what has been dubbed the Company School, which had its centre in Delhi. Meanwhile, in the south, painter Ravi Varma painted schmaltzy mythological scenes and portraits of women, which were hugely popular and gave Indian subjects a very Western treatment. Look out for the distinctive stylised works of Jamini Roy, depicting village life and culture.

The Madras Movement pioneered modern art in South India in the 1960s, and in the 21st century, paintings by modern and contemporary Indian artists have been selling at record numbers (and prices) around the world. One very successful online art auction house is Saffronart (www.saffronart.com). The larger cities, especially Delhi and Mumbai, are India's contemporary-art centres, with a range of galleries in which to view and/or buy art.

Literature

India has a long tradition of Sanskrit literature, although works in the vernacular have contributed to a particularly rich legacy. In fact, it's claimed there are as many literary traditions as there are written languages.

The brilliant writer and artist Rabindranath Tagore won the Nobel Prize in Literature in 1913 for *Gitanjali*. For a varied taste of Tagore's work, read *Selected Short Stories*.

Bengalis are traditionally credited with producing some of India's most celebrated literature, a movement often referred to as the Indian or Bengal Renaissance, which flourished from the 19th century with works by Bankim Chandra Chatterjee. But the man who to this day is mostly credited with first propelling India's cultural richness onto the world stage is the Bengali Rabindranath Tagore, with works such as *Gitanjali* (Song Offerings), *Gora* (Fair-Faced) and *Ghare-Baire* (The Home and the World).

One of the earliest Indian authors writing in English to receive an international audience, in the 1930s, was RK Narayan, whose deceptively simple writing about small-town life is subtly hilarious. Keralan Kamala Das (aka Kamala Suraiyya) wrote poetry, such as *Summer in Calcutta,* in English, and her memoir, *My Story,* in Malayalam, which she later translated to English; her frank approach to love and sexuality, especially in the 1960s and '70s, broke ground for women writers.

India has an ever-growing list of internationally acclaimed contemporary authors. Particularly prominent writers include Vikram Seth, best known for his epic novel *A Suitable Boy,* and Amitav Ghosh, who has won a number of accolades; his *Sea of Poppies* was shortlisted for the 2008 Man Booker Prize. A number of India-born authors have won the prestigious Man Booker Prize, the most recent being Aravind Adiga, who won in 2008 for his debut novel, *The White Tiger*. The prize went to Kiran Desai in 2006 for *The Inheritance of Loss;* Kiran Desai is the daughter of the award-winning Indian novelist Anita Desai, who has thrice been a Booker Prize nominee. In 1997 Arundhati Roy won the Booker Prize for her novel *The God of Small Things,* while Salman Rushdie took this coveted award in 1981 for *Midnight's Children*.

Hobnob with acclaimed local and international writers at Asia's biggest literary event, the Jaipur Literature Festival (www.jaipurliteraturefestival.org), held in January in Jaipur (Rajasthan).

Cinema

India's film industry was born in the late 19th century – the first major Indian-made motion picture, *Panorama of Calcutta,* was screened in 1899. India's first real feature film, *Raja Harishchandra,* was made during the silent era in 1913, and it's ultimately from this film that Indian cinema traces its lineage.

Today, India's film industry is the biggest in the world – twice as big as Hollywood. Mumbai, the Hindi-language film capital, aka Bollywood (p765), is the biggest, but India's other major film-producing cities – Chennai (Kollywood), Hyderabad (Tollywood) and Bengaluru (Sandalwood) – also have a considerable output. A number of other centres produce films, in their own regional vernaculars, too. Big-budget films are often partly or entirely shot abroad, with some countries vigorously wooing Indian production companies because of the potential spin-off tourism revenue these films generate.

Hundreds of feature films are produced annually throughout India. Apart from millions of local Bolly-, Tolly- and Kollywood buffs, there are also millions of Non-Resident Indian (NRI) fans, who have played a significant role in catapulting Indian cinema onto the international stage.

Broadly speaking, there are two categories of Indian films. Most prominent is the mainstream 'masala' movie – named for its 'spice mix' of elements. Designed to have something for every member of the family, these films encompass a blend of romance, action, slapstick humour and moral themes. Three hours and still running, these blockbusters are often tear-jerkers and are packed with dramatic twists interspersed with numerous song-and-dance performances. In Indian films made for the local market there is no explicit sex, and not even much kissing (although smooching has made its way into some Bollywood movies); however, lack of nudity is often compensated for by heroines dressed in skimpy or body-hugging attire, and the lack of overt eroticism is more than made up for with intense flirting and loaded innuendos.

Bengali director Satyajit Ray (1921–92) is considered the father of Indian art films, winning global awards for movies such as *Pather Panchali* and *Aparajito*.

The second Indian film genre is art house, which adopts Indian 'reality' as its base. Generally speaking, these films are socially and politically relevant. Usually made on infinitely smaller budgets than their commercial cousins, they are the ones that tend to win kudos at global film festivals and awards ceremonies. In 2013, *Dabba* (Lunchbox), a non-Bollywood romantic comedy written and directed by Ritesh Batra, won the Grand Rail d'Or at Cannes International Critics' Week.

Indian films that have made it to the final nomination list of the Academy Awards (Best Foreign Language Film category) are *Mother India* (directed by Mehboob Khan, 1957), *Salaam Bombay!* (directed by Mira Nair, 1988) and *Lagaan* (directed by Ashutosh Gowariker, 2001).

Sacred Architecture

India's remarkable assortment of historic and contemporary sacred architecture draws inspiration from an array of religious denominations. Although few of the wooden and occasionally brick temples built in early times have weathered the vagaries of nature, by the advent of the Guptas (4th to 6th centuries AD) of North India, sacred structures of a new type – better engineered to withstand the elements – were being constructed, and these largely set the standard for temples for several hundred years.

For Hindus, the square is a perfect shape, and complex rules govern the location, design and building of each temple, based on numerology, astrology, astronomy and religious principles. Essentially, a temple represents a map of the universe. At the centre is an unadorned space, the *garbhagriha* (inner sanctum), which is symbolic of the 'womb-cave'

Sri Meenakshi Temple

from which the universe is believed to have emerged. This provides a residence for the deity to which the temple is dedicated.

Above a Hindu temple's shrine rises a tower superstructure known as a *vimana* in South India, and a *sikhara* in North India. The *sikhara* is curvilinear and topped with a grooved disk, on which sits a pot-shaped finial, while the *vimana* is stepped, with the grooved disk being replaced by a solid dome. Some temples have a *mandapa* (forechamber) connected to the sanctum by vestibules. The *mandapa* may also contain *vimanas* or *sikharas*.

A *gopuram* is a soaring pyramidal gateway tower of a Dravidian temple. The towering *gopurams* of various South Indian temple complexes, such as the nine-storey *gopurams* of Madurai's Sri Meenakshi Temple, took ornamentation and monumentalism to new levels.

Commonly used for ritual bathing and religious ceremonies, as well as adding aesthetic appeal, temple tanks have long been a focal point of temple activity. These often-vast, angular, engineered reservoirs of water, sometimes fed by rain, sometimes fed – via a complicated drainage system – by rivers, serve both sacred and secular purposes. The waters of some temple tanks are believed to have healing properties, while others are said to have the power to wash away sins. Devotees (as well as travellers) may be required to wash their feet in a temple tank before entering a place of worship.

Discover more about India's diverse temple architecture (in addition to other temple-related information) at Temple Net (www.templenet.com).

Golden Temple

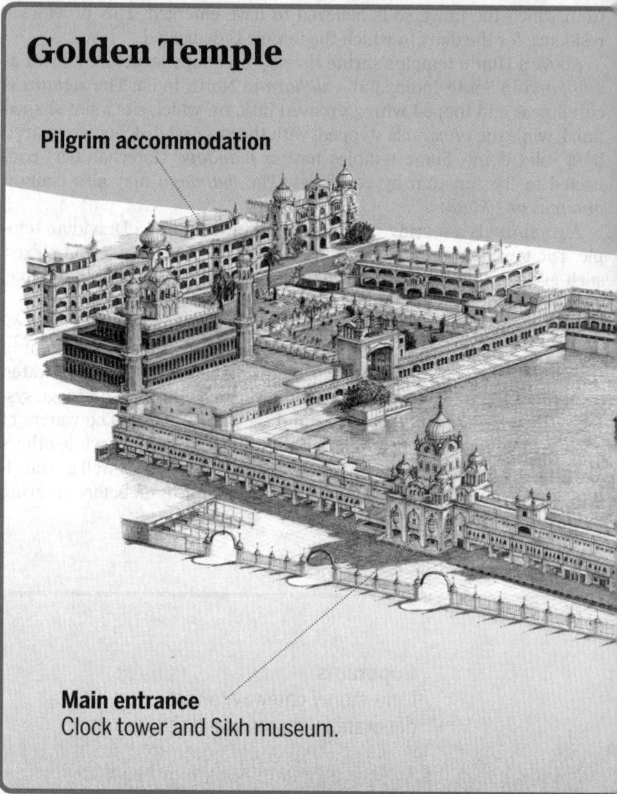

From the outside, Jain temples can resemble Hindu ones, but inside they're often a riot of sculptural ornamentation, the very opposite of ascetic austerity.

Buddhist shrines have their own unique features. Stupas, composed of a solid hemisphere topped by a spire, characterise Buddhist places of worship and essentially evolved from burial mounds. They served as repositories for relics of the Buddha and, later, other venerated souls. A further innovation is the addition of a *chaitya* (assembly hall) leading up to the stupa itself. Bodhgaya, where Siddhartha Gautama attained enlightenment and became the Buddha, has a collection of notable Buddhist monasteries and temples. The gompas (Tibetan Buddhist monasteries) found in places such as Ladakh and Sikkim are characterised by distinctly Tibetan motifs.

Masterpieces of Traditional Indian Architecture by Satish Grover and *The History of Architecture in India* by Christopher Tadgell give interesting insights into temple architecture.

In 262 BC, the Mauryan emperor Ashoka embraced Buddhism, and as a penance built the Great Stupa at Sanchi, in the central Indian state of Madhya Pradesh. It is among the oldest surviving Buddhist structures in the subcontinent.

India also has a rich collection of Islamic sacred sites, as its Muslim rulers contributed their own architectural conventions, including arched cloisters and domes. The Mughals uniquely melded Persian, Indian and provincial styles. Renowned examples include Humayun's Tomb in Delhi, Agra Fort, and the ancient fortified city of Fatehpur Sikri. Emperor

Shah Jahan was responsible for some of India's most spectacular architectural creations, most notably the Taj Mahal.

Islamic art eschews any hint of idolatry or portrayal of God, and it has evolved a vibrant heritage of calligraphic and decorative designs. In terms of mosque architecture, the basic design elements are similar worldwide. A large hall is dedicated to communal prayer and within the hall is a mihrab (niche) indicating the direction of Mecca. The faithful are called to prayer from minarets, placed at cardinal points. Delhi's formidable 17th-century Jama Masjid is India's biggest mosque, its courtyard able to hold 25,000 people.

The Sikh faith was founded by Guru Nanak, the first of 10 gurus, in the 15th century. Sikh temples, called gurdwaras, can usually be identified by their bud-like *gumbads* (domes) and *nishan sahib* (a flagpole flying a triangular flag with the Sikh insignia). Amritsar's stunning Golden Temple is Sikhism's holiest shrine.

The focal point of a gompa is the *dukhang* (prayer hall), where monks assemble to chant passages from sacred scriptures.

Jama Masjid

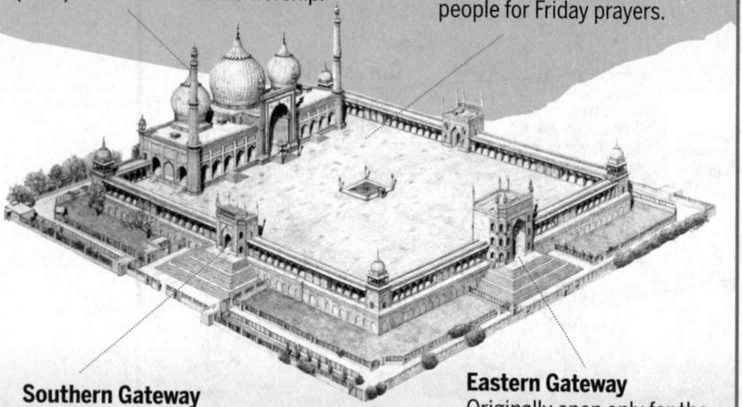

Minaret
Tower from which the muezzin (crier) calls the faithful to worship.

Central Courtyard
Holds up to 25,000 people for Friday prayers.

Southern Gateway
General public enter from here or the north.

Eastern Gateway
Originally open only for the emperor. Now open Fridays and Muslim festivals.

Sanchi

Great Stupa
Built by the emperor Ashoka in the 2nd century BC to enshrine relics of the Buddha.

Monastery Ruins
Accommodation surrounding a central courtyard.

Stupa Three
Contained the relics of two important disciples of the Buddha.

Processional path
Pilgrims circumambulated the stupa along this path.

India's Wildlife & Parks

The wildlife of India comprises a fascinating melting pot of animals from Europe, Asia and ancient Gondwanaland, all swirled together in a bewildering mix of habitats ranging from steamy mangrove forests and jungles to sandy deserts and icy alpine mountains. India is celebrated for its big, bold species – tigers, elephants, rhinos, leopards and bears. But there's much more, including a mesmerising collection of colourful birds and some of the world's most endangered and intriguing wildlife, such as the Ganges river dolphin and the Asiatic lion.

India's Iconic Species

If you had to pick India's most charismatic species, the list would inevitably include tigers, elephants and rhinos, all of which are scarce and in need of stringent protection.

Asian elephants – a thoroughly different species to the larger African elephant – are revered in Hindu custom and were able to be domesticated and put to work. Fortunately they've not been hunted into extinction (as they were in neighbouring China), and many still survive in the wild. Because they migrate long distances in search of food, these 3000kg animals require huge parks; interspecies conflicts often erupt when herds of elephants attempt to follow ancestral paths that are now occupied by villages and farms. Some of the best parks for elephant viewing are Corbett Tiger Reserve (p440) in Uttarakhand and Nagarhole National Park (p880) in Karnataka.

There are far fewer one-horned rhinos left and two-thirds (numbering 2401, according to a 2015 census) of the world's total population can be found in Kaziranga National Park (p567), where they wander lush alluvial grasslands at the base of the Himalaya. They may look sedate but rhinos are unpredictably dangerous, built like battering rams, covered in plates of armour-like skin and use their sharp teeth to tear off chunks of flesh when they attack – so let's just say that it's safest to watch them from a distance.

And then there's the tiger. This awesome, iconic animal is critically endangered but can be seen, if you're lucky, at tiger reserves around the country – your best chance of spotting one is in Madhya Pradesh.

India's national animal is the tiger, its national bird is the peacock and its national flower is the lotus. The national emblem of India is a column topped by three Asiatic lions.

Tourism & Conservation

Wildlife-watching has become one of India's prime tourist activities, and there are hundreds of national parks and wildlife sanctuaries offering opportunities to spot rare and unusual creatures. Your visit helps notify the government and local people that protecting endangered species and fragile ecosystems is important, and of economic value. So take some time to track down a rhino or spot a tiger on safari.

India has 270 species of snake, of which 60 are poisonous. Of the various species of cobra, the king cobra is the world's largest venomous snake, reaching a length of 5m.

Cats & Dogs

India is especially famed for its tigers, but is also home to 14 other species of cats.

Protection efforts have been successfully made on behalf of the Asiatic lion, a close relative of the more familiar African lion. A hundred years

PROJECT TIGER

When naturalist Jim Corbett first raised the alarm in the 1930s, no one believed that tigers would ever be threatened. At the time, it was believed there were 40,000 tigers in India, although no one had ever conducted a census. Then came Independence, which put guns into the hands of villagers who pushed into formerly off-limits hunting reserves seeking highly profitable tiger skins. By the time an official count was made in 1972, there were only 1800 tigers left, and the international outcry partly prompted Indira Gandhi to make the tiger the national symbol of India and set up Project Tiger (National Tiger Conservation Authority; http://projecttiger.nic.in). It has since established 47 tiger reserves totalling over 68,676 sq km that protect not only this top predator but all animals that share its habitat. After some initial successes against the practice, relentless poaching over the past decade has caused tiger numbers to plummet, from 3600 in 2002 to 1706 in 2011. Despite countless rupees and high-tech equipment devoted to saving this majestic animal, out of 63 wild tiger deaths in 2013, only one was from old age, while 48 were from poaching. Fortunately, the most recent tiger census results, from January 2015, show an encouraging rise in India's tiger population, to 2226. This census revealed that the country's highest number of tigers, in the age group of 1½ years and over, are in Karnataka, which has a total of 408 tigers. Karnataka is followed by Uttarakhand with 340 tigers. Other states with more than 100 tigers are Madhya Pradesh, Tamil Nadu, Maharashtra, Assam, Kerala and Uttar Pradesh.

ago there were only 20 of these lions left in the world but their population, an estimated 523 according to a May 2015 census, indicates that they now seem to be doing quite well in Gujarat's Sasan Gir National Park.

Up to 750 snow leopards exist in the alpine altitudes of Ladakh, Sikkim, Uttarakhand, Arunachal Pradesh and Himachal Pradesh – where it is the official state animal. This much-celebrated big cat is so elusive that many locals claim it can appear and disappear at will. Your chances of seeing one are small, but if you want to seek this ghost-like feline, try the Spiti region for starters.

Other wild cats include the clouded leopard and its smaller cousin, the marbled cat, both of which lurk in the jungles of northeast India. They are strikingly marked with rosettes and rings for camouflage in the dappled light of their forest homes.

The country is also home to about 3000 wild Indian wolves, which can best be seen in Gujarat's Blackbuck National Park. Jackals, foxes and dholes can be spotted in enclaves around the country. The rare, and most ancient, breed of wolf – the Spitian – howls over Spiti Valley.

Resources

Wildlife, conservation and environment awareness-raising at www.sanctuaryasia.com

Wildlife Trust of India news at www.wti.org.in

Top birdwatching information and photo galleries at www.birding.in

Indian Mammals

The most abundant forms of wildlife you'll see in India are deer (nine species), antelope (six species), goats and sheep (10 species), and primates (15 species). In the open grasslands of many parks look for the stocky nilgai, India's largest antelope, or elegantly horned blackbucks. If you're heading for the mountains keep your eyes open, in the Himalaya, for blue sheep – with partially curled horns – or the rare argali, with fully curled horns, found in Ladakh. The deserts of Rajasthan and Gujarat are home to arid land species such as chinkaras (Indian gazelles); while the mangrove swamps of the Sundarban Delta have chitals (spotted deer), who cope with their brackish environment by excreting salt from their nasal glands. Chitals are also the most prolific deer in central India's high-profile tiger reserves.

For memorable wildlife shots, a camera with a long lens – at least 300mm – is essential.

India's primates range from the extremely rare hoolock gibbon and golden langur of the northeast to species that are so common as to be pests – most notably the stocky and aggressive rhesus macaque and the grey langur. In the south, the cheeky monkeys that loiter around temples and tourist sites are bonnet macaques.

Endangered Species

Despite having amazing biodiversity, India faces a growing challenge from its burgeoning human population. Wildlife is severely threatened by poaching and habitat loss. One report suggested India had over 500 threatened species, including 247 species of plants, 53 species of mammals, 78 species of birds, 22 species of reptiles, 68 species of amphibians, 35 species of fish and 22 species of invertebrates. In 2012, the International Union for Conservation of Nature released a list of the 100 most threatened species in the world. It included four Indian species; a spider, a turtle and two birds – the great Indian bustard and white-bellied heron.

Even well-resourced conservation projects, such as Project Tiger, face ongoing challenges. Every good news story seems to be followed by yet another story of poaching gangs or tiger or leopard attacks on villagers. All of India's wild cats, from snow leopards to panthers and jungle cats, are facing extinction from habitat loss and poaching for the lucrative trade in skins and body parts for Chinese medicine (a whole tiger carcass can fetch upwards of UK£32,000). Still, conservation efforts are seeing some notable successes, with a particularly positive growth rate among the country's tiger population.

Even highly protected rhinos are poached for the medicine trade – rhino horn is highly valued as an aphrodisiac in China and as a material for making handles for daggers in the Gulf.

Elephants are widely poached for ivory. Although reliable statistics are difficult to find (due to the illegal nature of poaching), ivory poaching has reportedly been responsible for anywhere between 44% and 68% of all male elephant deaths in three Indian provinces; we implore you not to support this trade by buying ivory souvenirs.

Various species of deer are threatened by hunting for food and trophies, and the chiru, or Tibetan antelope, is nearly extinct because its hair is woven into wool for expensive *shahtoosh* shawls.

India's bear species remain under threat, although sloth bears are experiencing a reprieve with the recent demise of the dancing bear industry. In the rivers, India's famous freshwater dolphins are in dire straits from pollution, habitat alteration and direct human competition. The sea-turtle populations that nest on the Odisha coast also face environmental challenges.

Threatened primate species clinging on in rainforests in the south include lion-tailed macaques, glossy black Nilgiri langurs and the slender loris, an adept insect-catcher with huge eyes for nocturnal hunting.

Books about Wildlife

Mammals of India (Vivek Menon)

Treasures of Indian Wildlife (AS Kothari and BF Chappgar)

The Maneaters of Kumaon and *The Man-eating Leopard of Rudraprayag* (Jim Corbett)

ANIMAL ATTACKS

Human/animal conflict has been spiralling upwards across India in recent times, as wildlife habitat shrinks and human settlement expands.

There has been a rising number of reports of tigers taking up residence in inhabited areas, following hot on the heels of a huge increase in urban leopards, which have been spotted wandering around villages and even large towns. What is interesting is that the incomers are often tolerated by locals as a form of biological pest control. It has long been acknowledged that tiger attacks on humans are mainly carried out by elderly tigers who no longer have the vim to pursue their normal prey of boars, deer and other wildlife. The sense of symbiosis is striking: humans plant crops that attract boars, who in turn wreak havoc on said crops until tigers step in to restore the balance. At the same time, the presence of humans may deter prowling male tigers who might otherwise attack the female's cubs.

Nevertheless, authorities still advise caution, as annually there are around 100 people reportedly killed or injured by wild jungle cats. While such attacks tend to get lots of press coverage and cause panic, it's actually rare for tigers to turn into true maneaters; those that do are generally old, injured or both. In comparison, around 45,000 Indians die each year from snakebite, and an estimated 20,000 die from rabid dog bites.

Birds

With well over 1000 species of birds, India is a birdwatcher's dream. Many birds are thinly spread over this vast country, but wherever critical habitat has been preserved you might see phenomenal numbers of birds in one location. Winter can be a particularly good time, as wetlands throughout the country host northern migrants arriving to kick back in the lush subtropical warmth of the Indian peninsula. Throughout the year, wherever you may be travelling, look for colourful kingfishers, barbets, sunbirds, parakeets and magpies, or the blue flash of an Indian roller. Keen types will take a special trip into the Himalaya in search of one of India's (and the world's) mostly highly sought-after birds, the enigmatic ibisbill.

Located almost perfectly in the centre of the country, Bandhavgarh National Park is one dynamic example of what the original Indian landscape might have been like. Here you can explore meadows, forests and rocky ridges in a thrilling search for tigers, leopards and other big fauna.

Once considered the premier duck-hunting destination in the British Empire, when royal hunting parties would shoot 4000 ducks in a single day, the seasonal wetlands of Rajasthan's Keoladeo were elevated to national park status in 1982, and the park is rightly famous for its migratory avian visitors. Now whittled down to a relatively small pocket of habitat amid a sea of villages and agricultural fields, this is still one of the finest birdwatching destinations in the world. Even better, Keoladeo Ghana and its abundant birdlife are ridiculously easy to explore: just hop on a bike at the gate and tootle around the flat tracks that weave among the park's clearly defined ponds and marshes.

Plants

Once upon a time India was almost entirely covered in forest; now its total forest cover is estimated to be around 22%. Despite widespread clearing of native habitats, the country still boasts 49,219 plant species, of which some 5200 are endemic. Species on the southern peninsula show Malaysian ancestry, while desert plants in Rajasthan are more clearly allied with the Middle East, and the conifer forests of the Himalaya derive from European and Siberian origins. The Forest Survey of India has set an optimistic target of returning to 33% cover.

India has more than 16,000 species of flowering plants, constituting around 6.5% of the world's total plant species.

Outside of the mountain forests found in the Himalaya, nearly all the lowland forests of India are subtypes of tropical forest, with native sal forests forming the mainstay of the timber industry. Some of these tropical forests are true rainforest, staying green year-round – such as in the Western Ghats and in the northeast states – but most forests are deciduous; during the hot, dry months of April and May, many forests lose their canopies, as leaves wither and fall from the trees. This is often the best time to view wildlife, as the cover is thinner, and animals seek out scarce waterholes.

High-value trees such as Indian rosewood, Malabar kino and teak have been virtually cleared from the Western Ghats, and sandalwood is endangered across India due to illegal logging for the incense and woodcarving

PARKS & PEOPLE

While national parks and wildlife sanctuaries have been crucial to protecting the habitats of India's endangered species, their creation has had some tragic consequences. As a result of the Wildlife Protection Act of 1972, which banned people from living in parks, about 1.6 million Adivasis and other forest-dwellers were evicted from their traditional lands. Many were resettled into villages and forced to abandon their age-old ways of life, resulting in profound personal suffering and irreplaceable cultural losses. Today, the Forest Rights Act of 2006 forbids the displacement of forest-dwellers from national parks (except in so-called 'critical wildlife habitat'), and should protect the four million or so people who still live in them. It's still too early to tell how successful the law will be at helping tribes remain in parks – and how their continued presence will impact fragile wildlife habitat.

For more on the Forest Rights Act and 'people in parks', visit www.forestrightsact.com; also see the Traditional Cultures Project at www.traditionalculturesproject.org.

BIG & SMALL

India's largest contiguous protected area is the Nanda Devi Biosphere Reserve, in Uttarakhand, covering 2237 sq km. It includes India's second-highest peak (Nanda Devi – 7817m) and the famous Valley of Flowers. India's smallest national park is South Button Island, in the Andamans, at less than 5 sq km.

industries. A bigger threat to forested lands is firewood harvesting, often carried out by landless peasants who squat on gazetted government land.

Several trees have significant religious value in India, including the silk-cotton tree, a huge tree with spiny bark and large red flowers under which Pitamaha (Brahma), the god of creation, sat after his labours. Two well-known figs, the banyan and peepal, grow to immense size by dangling roots from their branches and fusing into massive multitrunked jungles of trunks and stems. It is said that Buddha achieved enlightenment while sitting under a peepal (also known as the Bodhi tree).

The foothills and slopes of the Himalaya preserve classic montane species, including blue pine and deodar (Himalayan cedar), and deciduous forests of apple, chestnut, birch, plum and cinnamon. Above the snowline, hardy plants such as anemones, edelweiss and gentians can be prolific, and one fabulous place to see such flowers is at the Valley of Flowers National Park in Uttarakhand.

India's hot deserts have their own unique species – the khejri tree and various strains of scrub acacia. The hardy sea-buckthorn bush is the main fruiting shrub in the high-altitude deserts of the Himalaya.

Top Parks North

- *Corbett Tiger Reserve*
- *Kaziranga National Park*
- *Keoladeo National Park*
- *Ranthambhore National Park*

National Parks & Wildlife Sanctuaries

Prior to 1972 India only had five national parks. The Wildlife Protection Act was introduced that year to set aside land for parks and stem the abuse of wildlife. The act was followed by a string of similar pieces of legislation with bold ambitions but few teeth with which to enforce them.

India now has 166 national parks and 515 wildlife sanctuaries, which constitute around 5% of India's territory. Additional parks have been authorised on paper but not yet implemented on the ground or only implemented to varying degrees. There are also 14 biosphere reserves, overlapping many of the national parks and sanctuaries, providing safe migration channels for wildlife and allowing scientists to monitor biodiversity.

We strongly recommend visiting at least one national park or sanctuary on your travels – the experience of coming face-to-face with a wild elephant, rhino or tiger will stay with you for a lifetime, while your visit adds momentum to efforts to protect India's natural resources. Wildlife reserves tend to be off the beaten track and infrastructure can be limited – book transport and accommodation in advance, and check opening times, permit requirements and entry fees before you visit. Many parks close to conduct a census of wildlife in the low season, and monsoon rains can make wildlife-viewing tracks inaccessible.

Almost all parks offer jeep/van tours, but you can also search for wildlife on guided treks, boat trips and elephant safaris. However, many animal welfare organisations advise against riding elephants because of the health implications for elephants, and because of the techniques used to train elephants to carry passengers. New rules introduced in 2012 put an end to 'tiger shows', whereby resting tigers became sitting ducks for tourists that were radioed in, taken off their jeep and put on elephants to get close to the, presumably peeved, resting tiger. Also, in many reserves, safari vehicle visits have been reduced and some tiger sanctuaries may be closed to safaris one day a week. These rules still are in flux, so do find out the latest situation before booking your safari.

Top Parks Central

- *Bandhavgarh National Park*
- *Kanha National Park*
- *Panna National Park*
- *Sunderbans Tiger Reserve*

Top Parks South

- *Mahatma Gandhi Marine National Park*
- *Nagarhole National Park*
- *Periyar Wildlife Sanctuary*

The Landscape

India's topography is stunningly diverse, with everything from steamy tropical jungles to expansive arid deserts to icy mountain peaks. At 3,287,263 sq km, it is the second-largest Asian country after China, and forms the vast bulk of the South Asian subcontinent – an ancient block of earth crust that carried a wealth of unique plants and animals like a lifeboat across a prehistoric ocean before slamming into Asia about 40 million years ago.

The Lie of the Land

Look for the three major geographic features that define modern-day India: Himalayan peaks and hills along the northern borders, the alluvial floodplains of the Indus and Ganges Rivers in the north, and the elevated Deccan Plateau that forms the core of India's triangular southern peninsula.

The Himalaya

As the world's highest mountains – with the highest peak in India (Khangchendzonga) reaching 8598m – the Himalaya create an almost impregnable boundary separating India from its neighbours to the north. These mountains formed when the Indian subcontinent broke away from Gondwanaland, a supercontinent in the southern hemisphere that included Africa, Antarctica, Australia and South America. All by itself, India drifted north and finally slammed slowly, but with immense force, into the Eurasian continent about 40 million years ago, buckling the ancient seafloor upward to form the Himalaya and many lesser ranges that stretch 2500km from Afghanistan to Myanmar (Burma).

Get the inside track on Indian environmental issues at Down to Earth (www.downtoearth.org.in), an online magazine that explores stories often overlooked by mainstream media.

When the Himalaya reached its great heights during the Pleistocene (less than 150,000 years ago), it blocked and altered weather systems, creating the monsoon climate that dominates India today, as well as forming a dry rainshadow to the north.

Although it looks like a continuous range on a map, the Himalaya is actually a series of interlocking ridges, separated by countless valleys. Until technology enabled roadbuilding into the Himalaya, many of these valleys were virtually isolated, creating a diverse array of mountain cultures.

The Indo-Gangetic

Noise pollution in major cities has been measured at over 90 decibels – more than 1½ times the recognised 'safe' limit.

Covering most of northern India, the vast alluvial plains of the sacred Ganges River are so flat that they drop a mere 200m between Delhi and the waterlogged wetlands of West Bengal, where the river joins forces with the Brahmaputra River from India's northeast, before dumping into the sea in Bangladesh. Vast quantities of eroded sediments from the neighbouring highlands accumulate on the plains to a depth of nearly 2km, creating fertile, well-watered agricultural land. This densely populated region was once extensively forested and rich in wildlife.

Gujarat in the far west of India is separated from Sindh (Pakistan) by the Rann of Kutch, a brackish marshland that becomes a huge inland sea during the wet season; the waters recede in the dry season, leaving isolated islands perched on an expansive plain.

The Deccan Plateau

South of the Indo-Gangetic (northern) plain, the land rises to the Deccan Plateau, marking the divide between the erstwhile Mughal heartlands of North India and the Dravidian civilisations of the south. The Deccan is bound on either side by the Western and Eastern Ghats, which come together in their southern reaches to form the Nilgiri Hills in Tamil Nadu.

On the Deccan's western border, the Western Ghats drop sharply down to a narrow coastal lowland, forming a luxuriant slope of rainforest.

The Islands

Offshore from India are a series of island groups, politically part of India but geographically linked to the landmasses of Southeast Asia and islands of the Indian Ocean. The Andaman and Nicobar Islands lie far out in the Bay of Bengal, while the coral atolls of Lakshadweep (300km west of Kerala) are a northerly extension of the Maldives islands, with a land area of just 32 sq km.

The Andaman and Nicobar Islands comprise 572 islands and are the peaks of a vast submerged mountain range extending almost 1000km between Myanmar (Burma) and Sumatra.

Environmental Issues

With well over a billion people, ever-expanding industrial and urban centres, and growth in chemical-intensive farming, India's environment is under considerable pressure. An estimated 65% of the land is degraded in some way, most of it seriously, and successive governments have been consistently falling short of the majority of their environmental protection goals. Many ongoing problems have been linked to the Green Revolution of the 1960s, when chemical fertilisers and pesticides enabled huge growth in agricultural output but at enormous cost to the environment.

Despite numerous environmental laws, corruption has continued to exacerbate environmental degradation – exemplified by the flagrant flouting of laws by some companies involved in hydroelectricity and mining. Usually, the people most affected are low-caste rural farmers and Adivasis (tribal people) who have limited political representation and few resources to fight big businesses.

Agricultural production has been reduced by soil degradation from over-farming, rising soil salinity, loss of tree cover and poor irrigation. The human cost is heart-rending, and lurking behind all these problems is a basic Malthusian truth: there are far too many people for India to support.

As anywhere, tourists tread a fine line between providing an incentive for change and making the problem worse. For example, many of the environmental problems in Goa are a direct result of irresponsible development for tourism. Always consider your environmental impact while travelling in India.

In 2016 the World Health Organization (WHO) reported that four Indian cities rank among the world's 10 most polluted, while 10 out of the top 20 are also in India.

STRADDLING THE FUTURE

India is grappling with a growing dilemma: how to develop, modernise and expand economically, without destroying what's left of its environment, or adding to the global climate problem. The government has come under criticism for some conflicting stances. On one hand, Prime Minister Modi has made it his personal mission to clean up the Ganges River by 2019, has launched the much-publicised Swachh Bharat campaign to reduce trash pollution nationwide, and supports large-scale solar power generation. His government is reportedly planning a US$3 billion package for the country's solar panel manufacturing industry and is aiming to increase renewable capacity to 175 gigawatts by around 2022. But his government faces challenges when it comes to domestic coal mining (a major source of greenhouse gas emissions). India is the world's third-largest producer of coal, but for electricity, despite domestic production having risen in recent decades, the rate of growth is not meeting demand, making India increasingly reliant on imported coal.

Climate Change

Changing climate patterns – linked to global carbon emissions – have been creating worrying extremes of weather in parts of India. While India's per-capita carbon emissions still rank far behind those of the USA, Australia and Europe, the sheer size of its population makes it a major polluter.

A UN study has predicted that by 2022 India will overtake China to become the world's most populous nation. Its estimated population in 2016 was 1.34 billion.

It has been estimated that by 2030, India will see a 30% increase in the severity of its floods and droughts. In the mountain deserts of Ladakh, increased rainfall is changing time-honoured farming patterns, while glaciers on nearby peaks are melting at alarming rates. In 2013, devastating flooding hit Uttarakhand – with unconfirmed estimates of between 6000 and 50,000 people killed over the course of a couple of days. In 2014, massive floods struck the Kashmir Valley, inundating Srinagar, wreaking widespread damage and loss of life. Conversely, other areas are experiencing reduced rainfall, causing drought and riots over access to water. Islands in the Lakshadweep group as well as the low-lying plains of the Ganges delta are being inundated by rising sea levels.

Deforestation

Since Independence, over 50,000 sq km of India's forests have been cleared for logging and farming, or destroyed by urban expansion, mining, industrialisation and river dams. Even in the well-funded, highly protected Project Tiger parks, the amount of forest cover classified as 'degraded' has tripled due to illegal logging. The number of mangrove forests has halved since the early 1990s, reducing the nursery grounds for the fish that stock the Indian Ocean and Bay of Bengal.

Between 2013 and 2015 India's forest cover increased by 5081 sq km, according to the India State Forest Report, with Mizoram having the highest forest cover at 88.9%.

India's first Five Year Plan in 1951 recognised the importance of forests for soil conservation, and various policies have been introduced to increase forest cover. This has yielded some success; however, many regulations have been ignored by officials or criminals and by ordinary people clearing forests for firewood and grazing. What can you do? Try to minimise the use of wood-burning stoves while you travel. Furthermore, you can support the numerous charities working with rural communities to encourage tree planting.

Water Resources

Arguably the biggest threat to public health in India is inadequate access to clean drinking water and proper sanitation. With the population marching upwards, agricultural, industrial and domestic water usage levels are all expected to soar, despite government policies designed to control water use. The World Health Organization (WHO) estimates that, out of more than 3000 cities and towns in India, less than a dozen have adequate waste-water treatment facilities. Many cities dump untreated sewage and partially cremated bodies directly into rivers, while open defecation is a simple fact of life in most rural (and many urban) areas.

India, 2.5% of the planet's landmass, is home to 18% of the world's population – making it one of the most densely populated countries in the world.

Rivers are also affected by run-off, industrial pollution and sewage contamination – the Sabarmati, Yamuna and Ganges are among the most polluted rivers on earth. At least 70% of the freshwater sources in India are now polluted in some way. Over recent years, drought has devastated parts of the subcontinent (particularly Rajasthan and Gujarat) and has been a driving force for rural-to-urban migration.

Water distribution is another volatile issue. Since 1947 an estimated 35 million people in India have been displaced by major dams, mostly built to provide hydroelectricity for this increasingly power-hungry nation. While hydroelectricity is one of the greener power sources, valleys across India are being sacrificed to create new power plants, and displaced people rarely receive adequate compensation.

Survival Guide

Scams

India has an unfortunately deserved reputation for scams, both classic and newfangled. Of course, most can be avoided with some common sense and an appropriate amount of caution. They tend to be more of a problem in the big cities of arrival (such as Delhi or Mumbai), or very touristy spots (such as Rajasthan), though in Goa and Kerala they are relatively rare. Chat with fellow travellers to keep abreast of the latest cons. Look at the India branch of Lonely Planet's Thorn Tree Travel Forum (www.lonelyplanet.com/thorntree), where travellers often post timely warnings about problems they've encountered on the road. Be aware there have been several cases where scammers who can speak the language target Japanese tourists.

Contaminated Food & Drink

➡ The late 1990s saw a scam in North India where travellers died after consuming food laced with dangerous bacteria from restaurants linked to dodgy medical clinics; we've heard no recent reports but the scam could resurface. In unrelated incidents, some clinics have also given more treatment than necessary to procure larger payments from insurance companies.

➡ Most bottled water is legit, but ensure the seal is intact and the bottom of the bottle hasn't been tampered with. While in transit, try and carry packed food if possible. If you eat at bus or train stations, follow the crowd and buy food only from fast-moving places

KEEPING SAFE

➡ A good travel-insurance policy is essential.

➡ Email copies of your passport identity page, visa and airline tickets to yourself, and keep copies on you.

➡ Keep your money and passport in a concealed money belt or a secure place under your shirt.

➡ Store at least US$100 separately from your main stash.

➡ Don't publicly display large wads of cash when paying for services or checking into hotels.

➡ Consider using your own padlock at cheaper hotels.

➡ If you can't lock your hotel room securely from the inside, stay somewhere else.

Credit-Card Con

Be careful when paying for souvenirs with a credit card. While government shops are usually legitimate, private souvenir shops have been known to surreptitiously run off extra copies of the credit-card imprint slip and use them for phoney transactions later. Ask the trader to process the transaction in front of you. Memorising the CVV/CVC2 number and scratching it off the card is also a good idea, to avoid misuse. In some restaurants, waiters will ask you for your PIN with the intention of taking your credit card to the machine – never give your PIN to anyone, and ask to use the machine in person.

Druggings

Occasionally, tourists (especially those travelling solo) have been drugged and robbed or apparently attacked. A spiked drink is the most commonly used method for sending them off to sleep – chocolates, chai from a co-conspiring vendor, 'homemade' Indian food and even bottled water are also known to be used.

Gem Scams

Smooth-talking con artists who promise foolproof 'get rich quick' schemes can be incredibly convincing, so watch out. In this scam, travellers are asked to carry or mail gems home and then sell them to the trader's (nonexistent) overseas representatives at a profit. Without exception, the goods – if they arrive at all – are worth a fraction of what you paid, and the 'representatives' never materialise.

Don't believe hard-luck stories about an inability to obtain an export licence, and don't believe the testimonials they show you from other travellers – they are all fake. Travellers have reported this con happening in Agra, Delhi, and Jaisalmer among other places, but it's particularly prevalent in Jaipur. Carpets, curios and *pashmina* woollens are other favourites for this con.

OTHER TOP SCAMS

- Gunk (dirt, paint, poo) suddenly appears on your shoes, only for a shoe cleaner to magically appear and offer to clean it off – for a price.
- Some shops are selling overpriced SIM cards and not activating them; it's best to buy your SIM from an official shop and check it works before leaving the area where you bought it (activation can take up to 24 hours).
- Shops, restaurants or tour guides 'borrow' the name of their more successful and popular competitor.
- Touts claim to be 'government-approved' guides or agents, and sting you for large sums of cash. Enquire at the local tourist office about licensed guides and ask to see identification from guides themselves.
- Artificial 'tourist offices' that are actually dodgy travel agencies whose aim is to sell you overpriced tours, tickets and tourist services.

Overpricing

Always agree on prices beforehand while availing services that don't have regulated tariffs. This particularly applies to friendly neighbourhood guides, snack bars at places of touristy interest, and autorickshaws and taxis without meters.

Photography

Use your instincts (better still, ask for permission) while photographing people. If you don't have permission, you may be asked to pay a fee.

Theft

- Theft is a risk in India, as anywhere else. Keep luggage locked and chained on buses and trains. Remember that snatchings often occur when a train is pulling out of the station, as it's too late for you to give chase.
- Take extra care in dormitories and never leave your valuables unattended.
- Remember to lock your door at night; it is not unknown for thieves to take things from hotel rooms while occupants are sleeping.

Touts & Commission Agents

- Cabbies and autorickshaw drivers will often try to coerce you to stay at a hotel of their choice, only to collect a commission (included within your room tariff) afterward.
- Wherever possible, prearrange hotel bookings (if only for the first night), and request a hotel pick-up. You'll often hear stories about hotels of your choice being 'full' or 'closed' – check things out yourself. Reconfirm and double-check your booking the day before you arrive.
- Be very sceptical of phrases like 'my brother's shop' and 'special deal at my friend's place'. Many fraudsters operate in collusion with souvenir stalls.
- Avoid friendly people and 'officials' in train and bus stations who offer unsolicited help, then guide you to a commission-paying travel agent. Look confident, and if anyone asks if this is your first trip to India, say you've been here several times. Telling touts that you have already prepaid your transfer/tour/onward journey may help dissuade them.

Transport Scams

- Upon arriving at train stations and airports, if you haven't prearranged a pick-up, call an Uber or go to the radio cab, prepaid taxi and airport shuttle bus counters. Never choose a loitering cabbie who offers you a cheap ride into town, especially at night.
- While booking multiday sightseeing tours, research your own itinerary, and be extremely wary of anyone in Delhi offering houseboat tours to Kashmir – we've received many complaints over the years about dodgy deals.
- When buying a bus, train or plane ticket anywhere other than the registered office of the transport company, make sure you're getting the ticket class you paid for. Use official online booking facilities where possible.
- Train station touts (even in uniform or with 'official' badges) may tell you that your intended train is cancelled/flooded/broken down or that your ticket is invalid or that you must pay to have your e-ticket validated on the platform. Do not respond to any approaches at train stations.

Women & Solo Travellers

Women Travellers

Reports of sexual assaults against women and girls are on the increase in India, despite tougher punishments being established following the notorious gang rape and murder of a local woman in 2012. There have been several instances of sexual attacks on tourists over the last few years, though it's worth bearing in mind that the vast majority of visits are trouble free.

Unwanted Attention

Unwanted attention from men is a common problem.

➡ Be prepared to be stared at; it's something you'll simply have to live with, so don't allow it to get the better of you.

➡ Refrain from returning male stares; this will be considered encouragement.

➡ Dark glasses, phones, books or electronic tablets are useful props for averting unwanted conversations.

➡ Wearing a wedding ring and saying you're married, and due to meet your husband shortly, is another way to ward off unwanted interest.

Clothing

Although in upper/middle-class Delhi, Mumbai and Chennai, you'll see local women dressing as they might in New York or London, elsewhere women are dressed traditionally. For travellers, culturally appropriate clothing will help reduce undesirable attention.

➡ Steer clear of sleeveless tops, shorts, short skirts (ankle-length skirts are recommended) and anything else that's skimpy, see-through, tight-fitting, or reveals too much skin.

➡ Wearing Indian-style clothes is viewed favourably.

➡ Draping a dupatta (long scarf) over T-shirts is another good way to avoid stares – it's also handy if you visit a shrine that requires your head to be covered.

➡ Wearing a *salwar kameez* (traditional dresslike tunic and trousers) will help you blend in; a smart alternative is a kurta (long shirt) worn over jeans or trousers.

➡ Avoid going out in public wearing a choli (sari blouse) or a sari petticoat (which some foreign women mistake for a skirt); it's like being half-dressed.

➡ Aside from at pools, many Indian women wear long shorts and a T-shirt when swimming in public view; it's wise to wear a sarong from the beach to your hotel.

Sexual Harassment

Many female travellers have reported sexual harassment while in India, most commonly lewd comments and groping.

➡ Women travellers have experienced provocative gestures, jeering, getting 'accidentally' bumped into on the street and being followed.

➡ Incidents are particularly common at exuberant (and crowded) public events such as the Holi festival. If a crowd is gathering, make yourself scarce or find a safer place overlooking the event so that you're away from wandering hands.

➡ Women travelling with a male partner will receive less hassle.

Staying Safe

The following tips will help you avoid uncomfortable or dangerous situations during your journey:

➡ Always be aware of your surroundings. If it feels wrong, trust your instincts. Tread with care. Don't be scared, but don't be reckless either.

➡ Keep conversations with unknown men short – getting involved in an inane conversation with someone you barely know can be misinterpreted.

➡ If you feel that a guy is encroaching on your space, he probably is. A firm request to keep away may well do the trick, especially if your tone is loud and curt enough to draw the attention of passers-by. The silent treatment can also be effective.

➡ Follow local women's cues and instead of shaking hands say *namaste* – the traditional, respectful Hindu greeting.

- Avoid wearing expensive-looking jewellery and carrying flashy accessories.
- Female filmgoers will lessen the chances of harassment by going to the cinema with a companion.
- At hotels, keep your door locked, as staff (particularly at budget and midrange places) could knock and walk in without waiting for your permission.
- Don't let anyone you don't know or have just met into your hotel room, even if they work for the tourist company with whom you're travelling and claim it's to discuss an aspect of your trip.
- Avoid wandering alone in isolated areas, even during daylight. Steer clear of *gallis* (narrow lanes), deserted roads, beaches and ruins.
- Act confidently in public; to avoid looking lost (and thus more vulnerable) consult maps at your hotel (or at a restaurant) rather than on the street.

Taxis & Public Transport

Being female has some advantages; women can usually queue-jump for buses and trains without consequence and on trains there are special ladies-only carriages. There are also women-only waiting rooms at some stations.

- Prearrange an airport pick-up from your hotel. This is essential if your flight is scheduled to arrive after dark.
- Avoid taking taxis alone late at night and never agree to have more than one man (the driver) in the car – ignore claims that this is 'just my brother' etc.
- Delhi and some other cities have licensed prepaid radio cab services such as Easycabs – they're more expensive than the regular prepaid taxis, but promote themselves as being safe, with drivers who have been vetted as part of their recruitment.
- Uber and Ola Taxis are also useful, as the rates are fixed and you get the driver's license plate in advance so you can check it's definitely the right taxi and pass details on to someone else if you want to be on the safe side.
- When taking rickshaws alone, pretend to call/text someone to indicate someone knows where you are.
- Don't organise your travel in such a way that means you're hanging out at bus/train stations or arriving late at night, or even after dark.
- Solo women have reported less hassle by opting for the more expensive classes on trains.
- If you're travelling overnight by train, the best option is the upper outer berth in 2AC; you're out of the way of wandering hands, but surrounded by plenty of other people and not locked in a four-person 1AC room (which might only have one other person in it).
- On public transport, don't hesitate to return any errant limbs, put an item of luggage between you and others, be vocal (attracting public attention), or simply find a new spot.

Health & Hygiene

- Sanitary pads are widely available but tampons are usually restricted to pharmacies.

Websites

Peruse personal experiences proffered by fellow female travellers at www.journeywoman.com and www.wanderlustandlipstick.com. Blogs such as Breathe, Dream, Go (breathedreamgo.com) and Hippie in Heels (hippie-inheels.com) are also full of tips.

Solo Travellers

Travelling solo in India may be great, because local people are often so friendly, helpful and interested. You're more likely to be 'adopted' by families, especially if you're commuting together on a long rail journey. It's a great opportunity to make friends and get a deeper understanding of local culture. If you're keen to hook up with fellow travellers, tourist hubs such as Delhi, Goa, Rajasthan, Kerala, Manali, McLeod Ganj, Leh, Agra and Varanasi are some popular places to do so. You may also be able to find travel companions on Lonely Planet's Thorn Tree Travel Forum (www.lonelyplanet.com/thorntree).

Cost

The most significant issue facing solo travellers is cost.

- Single-room accommodation rates are sometimes not much lower than double rates.
- Some midrange and top-end places don't even offer a single tariff.
- It's always worth trying to negotiate a lower rate for single occupancy.

Safety

Most solo travellers experience no major problems in India but, like anywhere else, it's wise to stay on your toes in unfamiliar surroundings.

- Some less honourable souls (locals and travellers alike) view lone tourists as an easy target for theft and sexual assault.
- Single men wandering around isolated areas have been mugged, even during the day.

Transport

- You'll save money if you find others to share taxis and autorickshaws, as well as when hiring a car for longer trips.
- Solo bus travellers may be able to get the 'co-pilot' (near the driver) seat on buses, which not only has a good view out front, but also handy if you've got a big bag.

Directory A–Z

Accommodation

Accommodation in India ranges from new-style hostels, with charging stations and soft pillows to opulent palaces with private plunge pools, and from dodgy dives with bucket showers to guesthouses with superlative home cooking. We've listed reviews first by price range and then by author preference.

Categories

Budget ($) covers everything from hostels, hotels and guesthouses in urban areas to traditional homestays in villages. Midrange hotels ($$) tend to offer extras such as cable/satellite TV and air-conditioning. Top-end places ($$$) stretch from luxury five-star chains to gorgeous heritage palaces.

Costs

Given that the cost of budget, midrange and top-end hotels varies so much across India, it would be misleading for us to provide a 'national' price strategy. Most establishments raise tariffs annually, so prices may have risen by the time you read this. Prices are highest in large cities (eg Delhi, Mumbai), lowest in rural areas (eg Bihar, Andhra Pradesh). Costs are also seasonal – hotel prices can drop by 20% to 50% outside of peak season. In areas such as Ladakh, Kashmir and Sikkim, you'll get a cheaper price as a walk in than booking ahead.

Price Icons

Lonely Planet price indicators refer to the cost of a double room, including private bathroom, unless otherwise noted.

Reservations

- It's a good idea to book ahead, especially when travelling to more popular destinations. Some hotels require a credit-card deposit at the time of booking.
- You can book hotels through Indian-based portals Goibibo (www.goibibo.com) or Oyo Rooms (www.oyorooms.com), which offer big discounts on mid- and upper-end hotels that are registered with them. However, these can be of variable quality.
- Some places may want a deposit at check-in – ask for a receipt and be wary of any request to sign a blank impression of your credit card. If the hotel insists, pay cash.
- Verify the check-out time when you check-in.
- Hotels often offer various packages: European Plan (EP; room only); Continental Plan (CP; includes breakfast); Modified American Plan (MAP; half-board, with breakfast and lunch/dinner); American Plan (AP; full board, with breakfast, lunch and dinner); and Jungle Plan (used at some jungle lodges – AP plus some safaris).

Seasons

- Rates given are full price in high season. High season usually coincides with the best weather for the area's sights and activities – normally spring and autumn in the mountains (March to May and September to November), and the cooler months in the plains (around November to mid-February).
- In areas popular with foreign tourists, there's an additional peak period over Christmas and New Year; make reservations well in advance.
- At other times you may find significant discounts; if the hotel seems quiet, ask for one.
- Some hotels in places like Goa close during the monsoon period, or in hill

SLEEPING PRICE RANGES

CATEGORY	MUMBAI	RAJASTHAN	SIKKIM
$ budget	<₹2500	<₹1500	<₹1500
$$ midrange	₹2500-6000	₹1500-5000	₹1500-5000
$$$ top end	>₹6000	>₹5000	>₹5000

stations such as Manali during winter.

➡ Many temple towns have additional peak seasons around major festivals and pilgrimages.

Taxes & Service Charges

➡ State governments slap a variety of taxes on hotel accommodation (except at the cheaper hotels charging less than around ₹1000), and these are added to the cost of your room.

➡ Taxes vary from state to state. Even within a state prices can vary, with more expensive hotels levying higher taxes.

➡ There's usually a 'luxury tax' of around 10 to 15%.

➡ Many upmarket hotels also add an additional 'service tax' (usually around 10%).

➡ They also levy nominal Krishi Kalyan Cess (a national agriculture initiative) and Swaccha Bharat Abhiyan Cess (a national sanitation and infrastructure initiative) charges of 0.05% each.

➡ Rates quoted in Lonely Planet listings include taxes.

➡ Note that India's new Goods & Service Tax (GST), due to come into force in 2017, may affect accommodation taxes and charges across the country.

Budget & Midrange Hotels

➡ Shared bathrooms (often with squat toilets) are usually only found at the cheapest lodgings.

➡ If you're staying in budget places, bring your own sheet or sleeping-bag liner, towel and soap.

➡ Insect repellent, a torch (flashlight) and padlock are essential accessories in many budget hotels.

➡ Sound pollution can be irksome (especially in urban hubs); pack earplugs and request a room that doesn't face a busy road.

BOOK YOUR STAY ONLINE

For more accommodation reviews by Lonely Planet authors, check out www.lonelyplanet.com/hotels. You'll find independent reviews, as well as recommendations on the best places to stay. Best of all, you can book online.

➡ It's wise to keep your door locked at all times, as some staff (particularly in budget hotels) may knock and walk in without awaiting your permission.

➡ Note that some hotels lock their doors at night. Let the hotel know in advance if you'll be arriving late at night or leaving early in the morning.

➡ Away from tourist areas, cheaper hotels may not take foreigners because they don't have the necessary foreigner-registration forms.

Camping & Holiday Parks

There are few official camping sites in India. On the other hand, wild camping is often the only accommodation option on trekking routes.

In some mountain or desert areas you'll also find summer-only tented camps, with accommodation in semipermanent 'Swiss tents' with attached bathrooms.

Hostels

There is an ever-increasing array of excellent backpacker hostels across India, notably in Delhi, Varanasi, Goa and Kerala, all high quality, with aircon dorms, cafe/bar, lockers, and free wifi, which are hugely popular with travellers wanting to connect with like-minded folk. They'll usually have mixed dorms, plus a female-only option. Impressive chains with branches dotted over India include **Stops** (www.gostops.com), **Backpacker Panda** (www.backpackerpanda.com), **Vedanta Wake Up!** (www.vedantawakeup.com), **Moustache** (http://www.moustachehostel.com), and **Zostel** (www.zostel.com).

A number of hotels have cheap dormitories, though these may be mixed gender and, in less touristy places, full of drunken males – not ideal conditions for women. The handful of hostels run by the YMCA, YWCA and Salvation Army or associated with HI or YHAI (Youth Hostels Association of India) are more traveller-friendly if a bit institutional.

Government Accommodation & Tourist Bungalows

The Indian government maintains a network of guesthouses for travelling officials and public workers, known variously as rest houses, dak bungalows, circuit houses, PWD (Public Works Department) bungalows and forest rest houses. These places may accept travellers if no government employees need the rooms, but permission is sometimes required from local officials.

'Tourist bungalows' are run by state governments – rooms are usually midpriced (some with cheap dorms) and have varying standards of cleanliness and service.

Some state governments also run chains of more expensive hotels, including some lovely heritage properties. Check with the local state tourism office.

Homestays

These family-run guesthouses will appeal to those seeking a small-scale, more homey setting with home-cooked meals.

Standards range from mud-and-stone village huts with hole-in-the-floor toilets to comfortable middle-class homes in cities.

In Ladakh and Kerala, homestays are the way to go but standards are fairly simple and prices can be relatively high.

Some hotels market themselves as 'homestays' but are run like hotels with little (or no) interaction with the family – reading up on your chosen place will get a view on whether it's a real homestay.

Contact the local tourist office for a full list of participating families.

Railway Retiring Rooms

Most large train stations have basic rooms for travellers holding an ongoing train ticket or Indrail Pass. Some are grim, others are surprisingly pleasant but suffer from the noise of passengers and trains.

They're useful for early-morning train departures and there's usually a choice of dormitories or private rooms (24-hour check-out) depending on the class you're travelling in.

Some smaller stations may have only waiting rooms (again divided by class).

Temples & Pilgrims' Rest Houses

Accommodation is available at some ashrams (spiritual retreats), *gurdwaras* (Sikh temples) and *dharamsalas* (pilgrims' guesthouses) for a donation or a nominal fee. Vegetarian meals are usually available at the refectories.

These places have been established for genuine pilgrims so please exercise judgement about the appropriateness of staying.

Always abide by any protocols. Smoking and drinking within the premises are a complete no-no.

Top-End & Heritage Hotels

India's top-end properties are stupendously fabulous, creating a cushioning bubble from the outside world, and ranging from wow-factor five-star chain hotels to historic palaces. In states such as Gujarat and Odisha, there are now increasing numbers of converted heritage properties.

You can browse members of the Indian Heritage Hotels Association on the tourist board website **Incredible India** (www.incredibleindia.org).

Customs Regulations

Technically you're supposed to declare Indian rupees in excess of ₹10,000, any amount of cash over US$5000, or total amount of currency over US$10,000 on arrival.

You're also prohibited from importing more than one laptop, two litres of alcohol, 100 cigarettes or equivalent, or gifts and souvenirs worth over ₹8000.

Electricity

230V/50Hz. Plugs have two round pins or, less commonly, three pins.

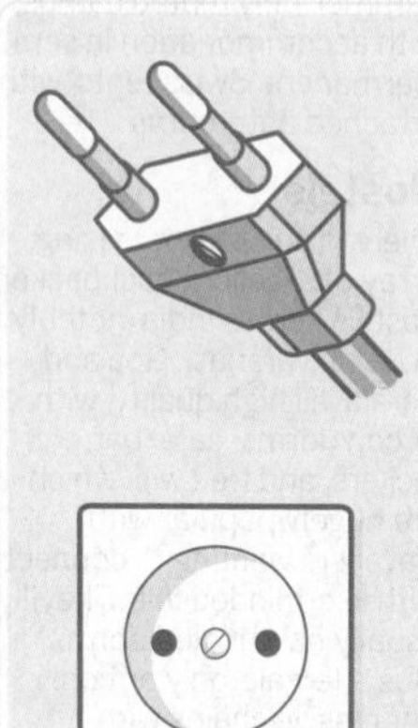

Type C
230V/50Hz

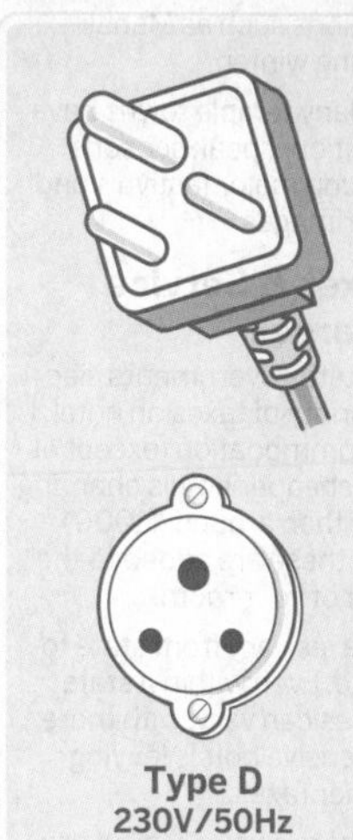

Type D
230V/50Hz

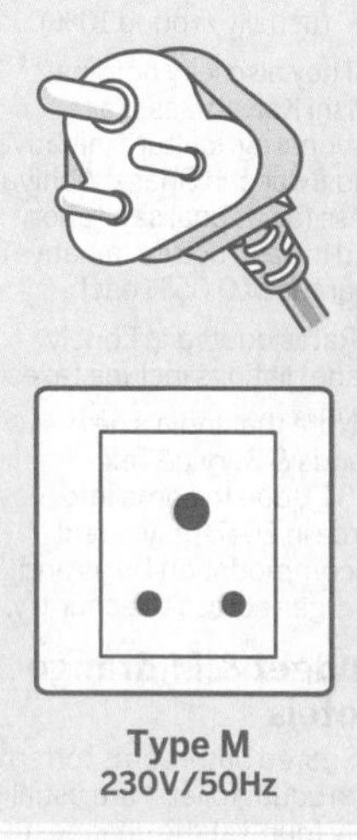

Type M
230V/50Hz

Embassies & Consulates

Most foreign diplomatic missions are based in Delhi, but there are various consulates in other Indian cities.

Australia: **Delhi** (Map p72; ☎011-41399900; www.india.highcommission.gov.au; 1/50G Shantipath, Chanakyapuri; Ⓜ Racecourse), **Mumbai**

(☎022-67574900; http://mumbai.consulate.gov.au; 10th fl, A Wing, Crescenzo Bldg, G Block, Plot C 38-39, Bandra Kurla Complex, Mumbai), **Chennai** (Map p1012;☎044-45921300; http://chennai.consulate.gov.au; 9th fl, Express Chambers, Express Avenue Estate, White's Rd, Royapettah; ⊙9am-5pm Mon-Fri)

Bangladesh: **Delhi** (Map p72;☎011-24121394; www.bdhcdelhi.org; EP39 Dr Radakrishnan Marg, Chanakyapuri; MChanakyapuri), **Kolkata** (☎033-40127500; 9 Circus Ave; ⊙visas 9-11am Mon-Fri)

Belgium Chennai (Map p1012; ☎044-40485500; http://india.diplomatie.belgium.be; Khader Nawaz Khan Rd, Nungambakkam; ⊙9.30am-12.30pm & 2.30-4.30pm)

Bhutan: **Delhi** (Map p72; ☎011-26889230; www.bhutan.gov.bt; Chandragupta Marg, Chanakyapuri; MChanakyapuri), **Kolkata** (Tivoli Court, Ballygunge Circular Rd; ⊙10am-4pm Mon-Fri)

Canada: **Delhi** (Map p72; ☎011-41782000; www.canadainternational.gc.ca/india-inde; 7/8 Shantipath, Chanakyapuri; ⊙consular services 9am-noon Mon-Fri), **Mumbai** (☎022-67494444; www.canadainternational.gc.ca; 21st fl, Tower 2, Indiabulls Finance Centre, Senapati Bapat Marg, Elphinstone Rd West, Mumbai)

China: **Delhi** (Map p72;☎011-26112345; in.china-embassy.org; 50-D Shantipath, Chanakyapuri; MChanakyapuri)

France: **Delhi** (Map p72; ☎011-24196100; http://ambafrance-in.org; 2/50E Shantipath, Chanakyapuri; MChanakyapuri), **Mumbai** (☎022-66694000; www.ambafrance-in.org/-Consulate-in-Bombay-; Wockhardt Towers, East Wing, 5th fl, Bandra Kurla Complex, Bandra East, Mumbai), **Puducherry** (Map p1038;☎0413-2231000; www.ambafrance-in.org; 2 Marine St; ⊙8am-5pm Mon-Fri)

Germany: **Delhi** (Map p72; ☎011-44199199; www.new-delhi.diplo.de; 6/50G Shantipath, Chanakyapuri; MChanakyapuri), **Kolkata** (☎033-24791141; 1 Hastings Park Rd, Alipore), **Mumbai** (☎022-22832422; www.india.diplo.de; 10th fl, Hoechst House, Nariman Point, Mumbai), **Chennai** (Map p1006; ☎044-24301600; www.india.diplo.de; 9 Boat Club Rd, RA Puram; ⊙7.30am-3.30pm Mon-Thu, to 1.30pm Fri),

Ireland: **Delhi** (Map p72; ☎011-24940 3200; www.dfa.ie/irish-embassy/india; C17 Malcha Marg, Chanakyapuri; MChanakyapuri)

Israel: **Delhi** (Map p72;☎011-30414500; embassies.gov.il/delhi; 3 Dr APJ Abdul Kalam Rd; ⊙9.30am-1pm Mon-Fri), **Mumbai** (☎022-61600500; http://embassies.gov.il/mumbai; Marathon Futurex, 1301, A Wing, N M Joshi Marg, Lower Parel, Mumbai)

Japan: **Delhi** (Map p72;☎011-26876581; www.in.emb-japan.go.jp; 50G Shantipath, Chanakyapuri; ⊙9am-1pm & 2-5.30pm Mon-Fri), **Mumbai** (☎022-23517101; www.mumbai.in.emb-japan.go.jp; 1 ML Dahanukar Marg, Cumballa Hill, Mumbai), **Chennai** (Map p1006;☎044-24323860; www.chennai.in.emb-japan.go.jp; 12/1 1st St, Cenotaph Rd, Teynampet; ⊙9am-5.45pm Mon-Fri)

Malaysia: **Delhi** (Map p72; ☎011-24159300; www.kln.gov.my/web/ind_new-delhi/home; 50M Satya Marg, Chanakyapuri; ⊙8.30am-4.30pm Mon-Fri), **Mumbai** (☎022-26455751; www.kln.gov.my/web/ind_mumbai/home; 5th fl, Notan Classic Bldg, off Turner Rd, Bandra West, Mumbai), **Chennai** (Map p1006;☎044-24334434; www.kln.gov.my; 7 1st St, Cenotaph Rd, Teynampet; ⊙9am-5pm Mon-Fri)

Maldives: **Delhi** (Map p76; ☎011-41435701; www.maldiveshigh com.in; B2 Anand Niketan)

Myanmar: **Delhi** (Map p72; ☎011-24678822; http://myanmedelhi.com; 3/50F Nyaya Marg; ⊙9.30am-4.30pm Mon-Fri), **Kolkata** (☎033-24851658; mcgkolcg@gmail.com; 57K Ballygunge Circular Rd; ⊙visas 9am-noon Mon-Fri)

Nepal: **Delhi** (Map p72;☎011-23476200; www.nepalembassy.in; Mandi House, Barakhamba Rd; ⊙9am-1pm & 2-5pm), **Kolkata** (☎033-24561224; 1 National Library Ave, Alipore)

Netherlands: **Delhi** (Map p72; ☎011-24197600; http://india.nlembassy.org; 6/50F Shantipath, Chanakyapuri; ⊙9am-5pm Mon-Fri), **Mumbai** (☎022-22194200; http://india.nlembassy.org; 1st fl, Forbes Bldg, Charanjit Rai Marg, Fort, Mumbai)

New Zealand: **Delhi** (Map p72; ☎011-46883170; www.nzembassy.com/india; Sir Edmund Hillary Marg, Chanakyapuri; ⊙8.30am-5pm Mon-Fri), **Mumbai** (☎022-61316666; https://www.mfat.govt.nz/en/countries-and-regions/south-asia/india/new-zealand-high-commission/new-zealand-consulate-general-mumbai-india; Lvl 2, Maker Maxity, 3 North Ave, Bandra Kurla Complex, Mumbai), **Chennai** (Map p1006;☎044-28112472; www.mfat.govt.nz; Rane Holdings Ltd, Maithri, 132 Cathedral Rd, Gopalapuram; ⊙9am-5.30pm Mon-Fri)

Pakistan: **Delhi** (Map p72; ☎011-26110601; pakhcnewdelhi.org.pk; 2/50G Shantipath, Chanakyapuri; ⊙9-11am Mon-Fri)

Singapore: **Delhi** (Map p72; ☎011-46000915; www.mfa.gov.sg/newdelhi; E6 Chandragupta Marg, Chanakyapuri; ⊙9am-1pm & 1.30-5pm Mon-Fri), **Mumbai** (☎022-22043209; https://www.mfa.gov.sg/content/mfa/overseasmission/mumbai.html; Maker Chambers IV, 10th fl, 222 Jamnalal Bajaj Rd, Nariman Point, Mumbai), **Chennai** (Map p1006;☎044-28158207; www.mfa.gov.sg; 17A North Boag Rd, T Nagar; ⊙9am-5pm Mon-Fri)

Sri Lanka: **Delhi** (Map p72; ☎011-23010201; 27 Kautilya Marg, Chanakyapuri; ⊙8.45am-5pm Mon-Fri), **Mumbai** (☎022-22045861; www.mumbai.mission.gov.lk; Mulla House, 34 Homi Modi St, Fort, Mumbai), **Chennai** (Map p1006; ☎044-28241896; www.sldhcchennai.org; 56 Sterling Rd, Nungambakkam; ⊙9am-5.15pm)

Thailand: **Delhi** (Map p76; ☎011-49774100; newdelhi.thaiembassy.org/en; D-1/3 Vasant Vihar; ⊙9am-5pm Mon-Fri), **Kolkata** (☎033-24407836; 18B Mandeville Gardens, Ballygunge), **Mumbai** (☎022-22823535; www.thaiembassy.org/mumbai/en/home; 12th fl, Express Towers, Barrister Rajni Patel Marg, Nariman Point, Mumbai), **Chennai** (Map p1006; ☎044-42300730; www.vfs-thailand.co.in; 3 1st Main Rd, Vidyodaya Colony, T Nagar; ⊙8am-noon & 1-3pm Mon-Fri)

UK: **Delhi** (Map p72; ☎011-24192100; Shantipath; Ⓜ Racecourse), **Kolkata** (☎033-22885172; 1A Ho Chi Minh Sarani), **Mumbai** (☎022-66502222; https://www.gov.uk/government/world/organisations/british-deputy-high-commission-mumbai; Naman Chambers, C/32 G Block Bandra Kurla Complex, Bandra East, Mumbai), **Chennai** (Map p1012; ☎044-42192151; www.gov.uk; 20 Anderson Rd, Nungambakkam; ⊙8.30am-4.30pm Mon-Thu, to 1.30pm Fri)

US: **Delhi** (Map p72; ☎011-24198000; http://newdelhi.usembassy.gov; Shantipath), **Kolkata** (☎033-39842400; http://kolkata.usconsulate.gov/; 5/1 Ho Chi Minh Sarani), **Mumbai**, (☎022-26724000; https://mumbai.usconsulate.gov; C49, G Block, Bandra Kurla Complex, Mumbai) **Chennai** (Map p1006; ☎044-28574000; http://in.usembassy.gov; 220 Anna Salai, Gemini Circle; ⊙8.30am-5pm Mon-Fri)

Insurance

- Comprehensive travel insurance to cover theft, loss and medical problems (as well as air evacuation) is strongly recommended.
- Some policies exclude potentially dangerous activities such as scuba diving, skiing, motorcycling, paragliding and even trekking: read the fine print.
- Some trekking agents may only accept customers who have cover for emergency helicopter evacuation.
- If you plan to hire a motorcycle in India, make sure the rental policy includes at least third-party insurance.
- Check in advance whether your insurance policy will pay doctors and hospitals directly or reimburse you later (keep all documentation for your claim).
- It's crucial to get a police report in India if you've had anything stolen; insurance companies may refuse to reimburse you without one.
- Worldwide travel insurance is available at www.lonelyplanet.com/bookings. You can buy, extend and claim online anytime – even if you're already on the road.

EATING PRICE RANGES

Prices in this book reflect the cost of a standard main meal (unless otherwise indicated). Reviews are listed by author preference within the following price categories.

$ budget less than ₹150

$$ midrange ₹150-300

$$$ top end more than ₹300

Internet Access

There are few internet cafes these days as wi-fi/3G/4G access is so widely available; wi-fi is usually free but some places charge. Many restaurants and cafes offer wi-fi, including Cafe Coffee Day branches.

Practicalities

- Internet charges vary regionally; hourly charges range from ₹15 to ₹100 (or as high as ₹500 in five-star hotels); often with a 15- to 30-minute minimum.
- Bandwidth load tends to be lowest in the early morning and early afternoon.
- Some places may ask to see your passport.

Security

Using online banking on any nonsecure system is unwise. If you have no choice but to do this, it's wise to change all passwords (email, netbanking, credit card 3D Secure code etc) when you get back home.

Laptops

- The simplest way to connect to the internet, when wi-fi is unavailable, is to use your smartphone as a personal wi-fi hotspot (use a local SIM to avoid roaming charges).
- Alternatively, companies that offer prepaid wireless 3G/4G modem sticks (dongles) include Reliance, Airtel, Tata Docomo and Vodafone. To connect you have to submit your proof of identity and address in India; activation can take up to 24 hours. At Vodafone, for example, the dongle costs ₹1500 plus ₹549 for the SIM. A 20GB recharge costs around ₹1999. Portable wi-fi is also available, a pocket-size modem (allow 10 people to connect). The device costs ₹2399 plus ₹549 for the SIM with the same recharge fees.
- Make sure your destinations are covered by your service provider.

➡ Consider purchasing a fuse-protected universal AC adaptor to protect your circuit board from power surges.

➡ Plug adaptors are widely available, but bring spare plug fuses from home.

Language Courses

There are a range of language courses across India, some requiring a minimum time commitment.

Delhi Hindi classes at Delhi's **Central Hindi Directorate** (Map p76; ☎011-26178454; http://hindinideshalaya.nic.in/english; West Block VII, RK Puram, Vivekanand Marg; 60hr basic course ₹6000). Hindu, Urdu and Sanskrit classes at **Zabaan** (http://zabaan.com/).

Himachal Pradesh Three-month courses in Tibetan at the **Library of Tibetan Works & Archives** (Map p320; ☎9218422467; www.ltwa.net; Gangchen Kyishong; ⏱9am-1pm & 2-5pm Mon-Sat, closed 2nd & 4th Sat), in McLeod Ganj. Several other places in McLeod Ganj offer courses in Tibetan and Hindi.

Mumbai (Bombay) Beginners' courses in Hindi, Marathi and Sanskrit at **Bharatiya Vidya Bhavan** (Map p746; ☎022-23631261; www.bhavans.info; 2nd fl, cnr KM Munshi Marg & Ramabai Rd, Girgaum; language per hr ₹500, music per month ₹900; ⏱4-8pm).

Tamil Nadu Tamil courses at **International Institute of Tamil Studies** (☎044-22542992, 9952448862; www.ulakaththamizh.org; CIT Campus, 2nd Main Rd, Tharamani; 3-/6-month course ₹5000/10,000), in Chennai.

Uttar Pradesh Hindi courses at **Pragati Hindi** (Map p384; ☎9335376488; www.pragati-hindi.com; B-7/176 Harar Bagh), in Varanasi.

Uttarakhand Hindi courses at the **Landour Language School** (☎0135-2631487; www.landourlanguageschool.com; Landour; per hr group/private ₹350/575; ⏱Feb-Dec), in Mussoorie.

West Bengal Tibetan courses at the **Manjushree Centre of Tibetan Culture** (Map p498; ☎0354-2252977; www.manjushreetibcentre.org; 12 Gandhi Rd; tuition per hr ₹200; ⏱mid-Mar–mid-Dec), in Darjeeling.

PRACTICALITIES

Newspapers & Magazines English-language daily newsapers include *Hindustan Times; Times of India; Indian Express; Hindu; Statesman; Telegraph; Daily News & Analysis* (DNA); and *Economic Times*.

Current-affairs magazines include *Frontline, India Today, Week, Open, Tehelka, Outlook* and *Motherland*.

Radio Government-controlled All India Radio (AIR), India's national broadcaster, has over 220 stations broadcasting local and international news. Dial-loads of FM stations include Private FM with music, current affairs, talkback and more and Mirchi FM.

TV The national (government) TV broadcaster is Doordarshan. More people watch satellite and cable TV; English-language channels include BBC, CNN, Star World, HBO, National Geographic and Discovery.

Weights & Measures Officially India is metric. Terms you're likely to hear are lakhs (one lakh = 100,000) and crores (one crore = 10 million).

Legal Matters

If you're in a sticky legal situation, contact your embassy immediately. However, be aware that all your embassy may be able to do is monitor your treatment in custody and arrange a lawyer. In the Indian justice system, the burden of proof can often be on the accused and stints in prison before trial are not unheard of.

Antisocial Behaviour

➡ Smoking in public places is illegal but this is rarely enforced; if caught you'll be fined ₹200, which could rise to ₹1000 if proposed changes go ahead.

➡ People can smoke inside their homes and in most open spaces such as streets (heed any signs stating otherwise).

➡ The status of e-cigarettes is in flux, but there are currently bans in Karnataka, and sale bans in Maharashtra and Punjab.

➡ Some Indian cities have banned spitting and littering, but this is also enforced irregularly.

Drugs

➡ Possession of any illegal drug is regarded as a criminal offence, which will result in a custodial sentence. This may be up to 10 years for possession, even for personal use, to 10 to 20 years if it's deemed the purpose was for sale or distribution. There's also usually a hefty fine on top.

➡ Cases can take months, even years, to appear before a court while the accused may have to wait in prison.

➡ Be aware that travellers have been targeted in sting operations in Manali, Goa and other backpacker enclaves.

➡ Marijuana grows wild in various areas, but consuming it is still an offence, except in towns

PROHIBITED EXPORTS

To protect India's cultural heritage, the export of certain antiques is prohibited, especially those which are verifiably more than 100 years old. Reputable antique dealers know the laws and can make arrangements for an export-clearance certificate for old items that are OK to export. Detailed information on prohibited items can be found on the Archaological Survey of India (ASI) website (http://asi.nic.in).

The Indian Wildlife Protection Act bans any form of wildlife trade. Don't buy any product that endangers threatened species and habitats – doing so can result in heavy fines and even imprisonment. This includes ivory, shahtoosh shawls (made from the down of chirus or rare Tibetan antelopes) and anything made from the fur, skin, horns or shell of any endangered species. Products made from certain rare plants are also banned.

where bhang is legally sold for religious rituals.

➡ Police are particularly tough on foreigners who use drugs, so you should take this risk seriously.

➡ Pharmaceutical drugs that are restricted at home may be available over the counter or via prescription. To take these without professional guidance can be dangerous.

Police

You should always carry your passport; police are entitled to ask you for identification at any time.

If you're arrested for an alleged offence and asked for a bribe, be aware that it is illegal to pay a bribe in India. Many people deal with an on-the-spot fine by just paying it to avoid trumped up charges. Corruption is rife so the less you have to do with local police the better; try to avoid all potentially risky situations.

LGBTI Travellers

Homosexuality was made illegal in India in 2013, after having only been decriminalised since 2009. Trans rights have fared better: in 2014, there was a ruling that gave legal recognition of a third gender in India, a step towards increased acceptance of the large yet marginalised transgender (hijra) population.

LGBTI visitors should be discreet in this conservative country. Public displays of affection are frowned upon for both homosexual and and heterosexual couples.

Despite the ban, there are gay scenes (and Gay Pride marches) in a number of cities including Mumbai, Delhi, Kolkata, Chennai and Bengaluru (Bangalore), as well as a holiday gay scene in Goa.

Websites & Publications

Bombay Dost (http://bombaydost.co.in) Annual LGBTQ India magazine, since 1990.

Gaysi Zine (http://gaysifamily.com) Thoughtful monthly magazine and website featuring gay writing and issues.

Indja Pink (www.indjapink.co.in) India's first 'gay travel boutique' founded by a well-known Indian fashion designer.

Pink Pages (https://pink-pages.co.in) A national gay magazine for nearly 10 years.

Queer Azaadi Mumbai (http://queerazaadi.wordpress.com) Mumbai's queer pride blog.

Queer Ink (www.queer-ink.com) Online bookstore specialising in gay- and lesbian-interest books from the subcontinent.

Salvation Star A Facebook community in Mumbai organising and promoting gay events and parties.

Orinam (orinam.net) Has helpful up-to-date info on LGBT support, events, pride marches, etc in Chennai and Tamil Nadu.

Support Groups

Gay Bombay (www.gaybombay.org) Lists gay events as well as offering support and advice.

Gay Delhi (www.gaydelhi.org) LGBT support group, also organises social events in Delhi.

Indian Dost (www.indiandost.com/gay.php) News and information including contact groups in India.

Maps

Maps available inside India are of variable quality. Throughout India, most state-government tourist offices stock basic local maps. These are some of the better map series. There's good GPS coverage in the main population centres.

Eicher Various state maps showing rail and road networks.

Leomann Maps Useful trekking maps for Jammu & Kashmir, Himachal Pradesh and Uttarakhand

Nelles (www.nelles-verlag.de)

Nest & Wings (www.nestwings.in)

Survey of India (www.surveyofindia.gov.in)

TTK (www.ttkmaps.com)

Money

There are ATMs in most towns; carry cash as backup. Mastercard and Visa are the most widely accepted credit cards.

ATMs & Eftpos

➡ ATMs are widespread.

➡ Visa, MasterCard, Cirrus, and Maestro are the most commonly accepted cards.

➡ ATMs at Axis Bank, Citibank, HDFC, HSBC, ICICI and State Bank of

India recognise foreign cards. Other banks may accept major cards (Visa, Mastercard etc).

➡ The limit you may withdraw in one transaction varies. It can be as low as ₹2000, up to a maximum of usually ₹10,000. The higher the amount you withdraw, the less charges you will incur. Citibank ATMs are often the best for withdrawing large amount of cash in one transation.

➡ Before your trip, check whether your card can access banking networks in India and ask for details of charges.

➡ Notify your bank that you'll be using your card in India to avoid having it blocked; take along your bank's phone number in case.

➡ Always keep the emergency lost-and-stolen numbers for your credit cards in a safe place, separate from your cards, and report any loss or theft immediately.

➡ Away from major towns, always carry cash (including a stock of rupees).

Black Market

Black-market moneychangers exist but legal moneychangers are so common that there's no reason to use illegal services, except perhaps to change small amounts of cash at land border crossings. If someone approaches you on the street and offers to change money, you're probably being set up for a scam.

Cash

➡ Major currencies such as US dollars, pounds sterling and euros are easy to change throughout India.

➡ Some banks also accept other currencies such as Australian and Canadian dollars, and Swiss francs.

➡ Private moneychangers deal with a wider range of currencies, but Pakistani, Nepali and Bangladeshi currency can be harder to change away from the border.

➡ When travelling off the beaten track, always carry an adequate stock of rupees.

➡ Whenever changing money, or receiving change, check every note. Don't accept any filthy, ripped or disintegrating notes, as these will be difficult to use.

➡ It can be tough getting change, so a stock of smaller currency (₹10, ₹20 and ₹50 notes) is invaluable.

➡ You can change any leftover rupees back into foreign currency most easily at the airport. You may have to present encashment certificates or credit-card/ATM receipts, and show your passport and airline ticket.

Credit & Debit Cards

➡ Credit cards are accepted at a growing number of shops, upmarket restaurants, and midrange and top-end hotels, and they can usually be used to pay for flights and train tickets.

➡ Cash advances on major credit cards are also possible at some banks.

➡ MasterCard and Visa are the most widely accepted cards.

Currency

The Indian rupee (₹) is divided into 100 paise, but only 50 paise coins are legal tender and these are rarely seen. Coins come in denominations of ₹1, ₹2, ₹5 and ₹10 (the 1s and 2s look almost identical); notes come in ₹5, ₹10, ₹20, ₹50, ₹100, ₹500 and ₹2000.

The Indian rupee is linked to a basket of currencies and has been subject to fluctuations in recent years.

Encashment Certificates

➡ Indian law states that all foreign currency must be changed at official moneychangers or banks.

➡ For every (official) foreign-exchange transaction, you'll receive an encashment certificate (receipt), which will allow you to change rupees back into foreign currency when departing India.

➡ Encashment certificates should cover the amount of rupees you intend to change back to foreign currency.

➡ Printed receipts from ATMs are also accepted as evidence of an international transaction at most banks.

International Transfers

If you run out of money, someone back home can wire you cash via moneychangers affiliated with **Western Union** (www.westernunion.com). A fee is added to the transaction.

To collect the cash, bring your passport and the name and reference number of the person who sent the funds.

Moneychangers

Private moneychangers are usually open for longer hours than banks and are found almost everywhere (many also double as internet cafes or travel agents).

Hotels may also change money, but their rates are usually not as competitive.

Tipping

➡ A service fee is often added to your bill at restaurants and hotels, in which case tipping is optional. Elsewhere, a tip is appreciated.

➡ Hotel bellboys and train/airport porters appreciate anything around ₹50; hotel staff should be given similar gratuities for services above and beyond the call of duty.

➡ It's not mandatory to tip taxi or rickshaw drivers, but it's good to tip drivers who are honest about the fare.

➡ If you hire a car with driver, a tip is recommended for good service.

➡ Baksheesh can loosely be defined as a 'tip'; it covers everything from alms for beggars to bribes.

➡ Many Indians implore tourists not to hand out

sweets, pens or money to children, as it encourages them to beg. To make a lasting difference, donate to a reputable school or charitable organisation.

➡ Except in fixed-price shops (such as government emporiums and fair-trade cooperatives), bargaining is the norm.

Opening Hours

Opening hours are year-round for banks, offices and restaurants; many sights keep summer and winter opening hours, and some places close in the low season.

Banks (nationalised) 10am–2pm/4pm Monday to Friday, to noon/1pm/4pm Saturday; closed second and fourth Saturday of month.

Restaurants 8am–10pm or lunch noon–3pm, dinner 7pm–10pm or 11pm

Bars & Clubs noon–12.30am

Shops 10am–7pm or 8pm, some closed Sunday

Markets 10am–7pm in major cities, usually with one closed day; rural markets may be once weekly, from early morning to lunchtime

Post Offices 9.30am–5pm Monday to Saturday

Post

India has a far-reaching postal service, with over 150,000 post offices. Mail and poste-restante services are good, although the speed of delivery will depend on the efficiency of any given office. Airmail is faster and more reliable than sea mail, although it's best to use courier services (such as DHL and TNT) to send and receive items of value – expect to pay around ₹3500 per kilogram to Europe, Australia or the USA. Smaller private couriers are often cheaper, but goods may be repacked into large packages to cut costs and things sometimes go missing.

Sending Mail

LETTERS

➡ Posting airmail letters/aerogrammes to anywhere overseas costs ₹25/15.

➡ International airmail postcards cost around ₹12.

➡ For postcards, stick on the stamps *before* writing on them, as post offices can give you as many as four stamps per card.

➡ Sending a letter overseas by registered post costs an extra ₹50.

PARCELS

➡ An airmail package (unregistered) costs ₹400 to ₹850 (up to 250g) and ₹50 to ₹150 per each additional 250g (up to a maximum of 2000g; charges change for higher weight).

➡ Parcel post has a maximum of 20kg to 30kg.

➡ Air/sea/SAL (sea and air) takes one to three weeks/two to four months/one month.

➡ Express mail service (EMS; delivery within three days) costs around 30% more than regular airmail.

➡ All parcels must be packed in white linen and wax sealed – agents outside the post office usually offer this service.

➡ Customs declaration forms, available from the post office, must be stitched or pasted to the parcel. No duty is payable by the recipient for gifts under the value of ₹1000.

➡ Carry a permanent marker to write on the parcel any information requested by the desk.

➡ You can send printed matter via surface mail 'Bulk Bag' for ₹350 (maximum 5kg, plus ₹100 for each additional kilogram). The parcel must have an opening for a customs check.

Receiving Mail

➡ To claim mail you'll need to show your passport.

➡ Ask senders to address letters to you with your surname in capital letters and underlined, followed by poste restante, GPO (main post office), and the city or town in question.

➡ Many 'lost' letters are simply misfiled under given/first names, so check under both your names and ask senders to provide a return address.

➡ Letters sent via poste restante are generally held for around one to two months before being returned.

➡ It's best to have any parcels sent to you by registered post.

Public Holidays

There are three official national public holidays – Republic and Independence Days and Gandhi's birthday (Gandhi Jayanti) – plus a lot of other holidays celebrated nationally or locally, many of them marking important days in various religions and falling on variable dates. The most important are the 18 'gazetted holidays' (listed) which are observed by central-government offices throughout India. On these days most businesses (offices, shops etc), banks and tourist sites close, but transport is usually unaffected. It's wise to make transport and hotel reservations well in advance if you intend visiting during major festivals.

Republic Day 26 January

Holi February/March

Ram Navami March/April

Mahavir Jayanti March/April

Good Friday March/April

Dr BL Ambedkar's Birthday 14 April

Mahavir Jayanti March/April

Buddha Purnima May

Eid al-Fitr June

Independence Day 15 August

Janmastami August/September

Eid al-Adha August/September

Dussehra September/October

Gandhi Jayanti 2 October

Muharram September/October

Diwali October/November

Guru Nanak Jayanti November

Eid-Milad-un-Nabi November/December

Christmas Day 25 December

Safe Travel

Travellers to India's major cities may fall prey to opportunistic crime, but many problems can be avoided with a bit of common sense and an appropriate amount of caution. Reports of sexual assaults have increased in recent years, so women should take care to avoid potentially risky situations.

Have a look at the India branch of Lonely Planet's Thorn Tree forum (www.lonelyplanet.com/thorntree), where travellers often post timely warnings about problems they've encountered on the road. Always check your government's travel advisory warnings.

Rebel Violence

- Due to ongoing terrorist threats, mobile phone use in Jammu & Kashmir, as well as Assam, is more strictly controlled.
- Roaming on foreign mobiles won't work in Jammu & Kashmir, nor will pay-as-you-go SIM cards purchased elsewhere in India. BSNL work best here. Coverage is scant in Ladakh and Kashmir once you're away from the main towns.
- AirTel and AirCell both offer pre-paid SIM cards; you'll need four or five photos, your passport, address (your hotel) and to wait at least 48 hours.
- Foreign mobile roaming won't work and domestic SIM cards are difficult to procure in Assam (except in Guwahati), but you can use a SIM card purchased elsewhere. Airtel and BSNL work best here, Vodaphone works best in Sikkim.

Telephone

- There are few payphones in India (apart from in airports), but private STD/ISD/PCO call booths do the same job, offering inexpensive local, interstate and international calls at lower prices than calls made from hotel rooms.
- These booths are found around the country. A digital meter displays how much the call is costing and usually provides a printed receipt when the call is finished.
- Costs vary depending on the operator and destination but can be from ₹1 per minute for local calls and around ₹10 for international calls.
- Some booths also offer a 'call-back' service – you ring home, provide the phone number of the booth and wait for people at home to call you back, for a fee of around ₹20 on top of the cost of the preliminary call.
- Getting a line can be difficult in remote country and mountain areas – an engaged signal may just mean that the exchange is overloaded or broken, so keep trying.
- Useful online resources include the **Yellow Pages** (www.yellowpages.in) and **Justdial** (www.justdial.com).

Mobile Phones

Roaming connections are excellent in urban areas, poor in the countryside and the Himalaya. Local prepaid SIMs are widely available; they involve some straightforward paperwork and sometimes a wait of up to 24 hours for activation.

GETTING CONNECTED

- Getting connected is inexpensive and straightforward in large cities or most tourist towns. It's wise to obtain a local SIM card when you arrive if you're flying into a large city.
- A SIM card or ISD package is usually only valid for a particular region, and once you leave it, it may function but you'll pay roaming charges, however, these are not particularly steep (eg ₹1 per minute within India rather than ₹0.10. There are no roaming charges for internet data packs.
- An ISD (international subscriber dialling) package can work out a good deal if you're phoning long-distance.
- Foreigners must supply between one and five passport photos, and

WARNING: BHANG LASSI

Although it's rarely printed in menus, some restaurants in popular tourist centres will clandestinely whip up bhang lassi, a yoghurt and iced-water beverage laced with cannabis (and occasionally other narcotics). Commonly dubbed 'special lassi', this often potent concoction can cause varying degrees of ecstasy, drawn-out delirium, hallucination, nausea and paranoia. Some travellers have been ill for several days, robbed or hurt in accidents after drinking this fickle brew. A few towns have legal (controlled) bhang outlets. While these legal bhang sellers are happy to sell to foreigners, the bhang is intended for religious purposes. For travellers, buying from a legal shop is not a protection against being arrested for possession.

photocopies of their passport identity and visa pages. Usually mobile shops can arrange all this for you. It's best to try to do this in tourist centres and cities, as in many regions – for example, Tamil Nadu, Andhra Pradesh, Telangana and most of Himachal Pradesh – it's a great deal more difficult.

➡ In some cases, you have to supply a residential address, which can be the address of your hotel. If you have to do this, the phone company will call your hotel (warn the hotel a call will come through) any time up to 24 hours after your application to verify that you are staying there, or sometimes you have to provide another mobile number.

➡ It's a good idea to obtain the SIM card somewhere where you're staying for a day or two so that you can return to the vendor if there's any problem. Only obtain your SIM card from a reputable branded phone store to avoid scams.

➡ Prepaid mobile phone kits (SIM card and phone number, plus an allocation of calls and texts) are available in most towns for ₹200 to ₹500 from a phone shop, local STD/ISD/PCO booth or grocery store.

➡ You must then purchase more credit, sold as direct credit. You pay the vendor and the credit is deposited straight into your account, minus some taxes and a service charge.

CHARGES

➡ Calls made within the state or city where you bought the SIM card may be around ₹0.10 a minute. You can call internationally for less than ₹10 a minute.

➡ International outgoing SMS messages cost ₹5. Incoming calls and messages are free.

➡ Unreliable signals and problems with international texting (messages or replies not coming through or being delayed) are not uncommon.

➡ The leading service providers are Airtel, Vodafone, Reliance, Idea and BSNL. Coverage varies from region to region – Airtel has wide coverage, for example, but BSNL is the only network that works in remote Himachal areas.

JAMMU & KASHMIR AND ASSAM

➡ Due to ongoing terrorist threats, mobile phone use in Jammu & Kashmir, as well as Assam, is more strictly controlled.

➡ Roaming on foreign mobiles won't work in Jammu & Kashmir, nor will pay-as-you-go SIM cards purchased elsewhere in India. BSNL work best here. Coverage is scant in Ladakh and Kashmir once you're away from the main towns.

➡ AirTel and AirCell both offer pre-paid SIM cards; you'll need four or five photos, your passport, address (your hotel) and to wait at least 48 hours.

➡ Foreign mobile roaming won't work and domestic SIM cards are difficult to procure in Assam (except in Guwahati), but you can use a SIM card purchased elsewhere. Airtel and BSNL work best here, Vodaphone works best in Sikkim.

Local Calls

Indian mobile phone numbers usually have 10 digits, mostly beginning with 9 (but sometimes also with 7 or 8).There's roaming coverage for international GSM phones in most cities and large towns.To avoid expensive roaming costs (often highest for incoming calls), get hooked up to the local mobile-phone network by applying for a local prepaid SIM card. Mobiles bought in some countries may be locked to a particular network; you'll have to get the phone unlocked or buy a local phone (available from ₹2000) to use an Indian SIM card.

Phonecards

➡ Calling India from abroad: dial your country's international access code, then 91 (India's country code), then the area code (without the initial zero), then the local number. For mobile phones, the area code and initial zero are not required.

➡ Calling internationally from India: dial 00 (the international access code),

GOVERNMENT TRAVEL ADVICE

The following government websites offer travel advice and information on current hotspots.

Australian Department of Foreign Affairs (www.smarttraveller.gov.au)

British Foreign Office (www.gov.uk/fco)

Canadian Department of Foreign Affairs (www.voyage.gc.ca)

German Foreign Office (www.auswaertiges-amt.de)

Japan Ministry of Foreign Affairs (www.mofa.go.jp)

Netherlands Ministry of Foreign Affairs (www.government.nl)

Swiss Department of Foreign Affairs (www.eda.admin.ch)

US State Department (http://travel.state.gov)

then the country code of the country you're calling, then the area code (without the initial zero) and the local number.

- Land-phone numbers have an area code followed by up to eight digits.
- Toll-free numbers begin with 1800.
- To make interstate calls to a mobile phone, add 0 before the 10-digit number.
- To call a land phone from a mobile phone, you always have to add the area code (with the initial zero).
- Some call centre numbers might require the initial zero (eg calling an airline ticketing service based in Delhi from Karnataka).
- A Home Country Direct service, which gives you access to the international operator in your home country, exists for the US (000 117) and the UK (000 4417).
- To access an international operator elsewhere, dial 000 127. The operator can place an international call and allow you to make collect calls.

Time

Indian Standard Time (GMT/UTC plus 5½ hours)

Toilets

Public toilets are most easily found in major cities and tourist sites; the cleanest (usually with sit-down and squat choices) are often at modern restaurants, shopping complexes and cinemas.

Beyond urban centres, toilets are of the squat variety and locals may use the 'hand-and-water' technique, which involves carrying out ablutions with a small jug of water and the left hand. It's always a good idea to carry your own toilet paper and hand sanitiser, just in case.

Tourist Information

In addition to Government of India tourist offices (also known as 'India Tourism'), each state maintains its own network of tourist offices. These vary in quality – some are run by enthusiastic souls who go out of their way to help, others have an air of torpor and are little more than a means of drumming up business for State Tourism Development Corporation tours.

The tourism website of the Government of India is **Incredible India** (www.incredibleindia.org).

Travellers with Disabilities

If you have a physical disability or are vision impaired, the difficulties of travel in India can be exacerbated. If your mobility is considerably restricted, you may like to ease the stress by travelling with an able-bodied companion. One way that India makes it easier to travel with a disability is the access to employed assistance – you could hire an assistant, or a car and driver to get around, for example.

Accommodation Wheelchair-friendly hotels are almost exclusively top-end. Make enquiries before travelling and book ground-floor rooms at hotels that lack adequate facilities.

Accessibility Some restaurants and offices have ramps but most tend to have at least one step. Staircases are often steep; lifts frequently stop at mezzanines between floors.

Footpaths Where pavements exist, they can be riddled with holes, littered with debris and crowded. If using crutches, bring along spare rubber caps.

Transport Hiring a car with driver will make moving around a lot easier; if you use a wheelchair, make sure the car-hire company can provide an appropriate vehicle.

The following organisations may proffer further information:

Accessible Journeys (www.disabilitytravel.com)

Access-Able Travel Source (www.access-able.com)

Enable Holidays (www.enableholidays.com)

Global Access News (www.globalaccessnews.com)

Mobility International USA (www.miusa.org)

Download Lonely Planet's free Accessible Travel guide from http://lptravel.to/AccessibleTravel.

Visas

Apart from citizens of Nepal, Bhutan and Maldives (Nepali citizens are, however, required to get a visa if they enter via China), everyone needs to apply for a visa before arriving in India. Over 100 nationalities can obtain a 30-day e-Tourist visa/Visa on Arrival, applying online prior to arrival; this is valid from the day you arrive. For longer trips, you'll need to obtain a six-month tourist visa, valid from the date of issue, not the date of arrival in India.

Entry Requirements

Visas are available at Indian missions worldwide, though in many countries, applications are processed by a separate private company.

- Student and business visas have strict conditions (consult the Indian embassy for details).
- A standard 180-day tourist visa permits multiple entry for most nationalities.
- Five- and 10-year tourist visas are available to US citizens *only* under a bilateral arrangement; however, you can still only stay in the country for up to 180 days continuously.
- Currently you are required to submit two digital photographs with your visa

application (format jpeg 10-300kb)

- An onward travel ticket is a requirement for some visas, but this isn't always enforced (check in advance).
- Visas are priced in the local currency and may have an added service fee.
- Extended visas are possible for those of Indian origin (excluding those in Pakistan and Bangladesh) who hold a non-Indian passport and live abroad.
- For visas lasting more than six months, you're supposed to register at the **Foreigners' Regional Registration Office** (FRRO; Map p76; ☎011-26711443; frrodil@nic.in; Level 2, East Block 8, Sector 1, Rama Krishna Puram, Delhi; ⏰9.30am-3pm Mon-Fri; Ⓜ Green Park) in Delhi within 14 days of arriving in India; enquire about these special conditions when you apply for your visa.
- Check with the Indian embassy in your home country for any special conditions that may exist for your nationality.

Re-entry Requirements

Most tourists are permitted to transit freely between India and its neighbouring countries. If you plan to fly out of India and don't have a visa covering re-entry to India already, it's a real hassle getting a new visa in Kathmandu. However, citizens of Afghanistan, China, Iran, Pakistan, Iraq, Sudan, foreigners of Pakistan and Stateless persons are barred from re-entering India within two months of the date of their previous exit.

E-Tourist Visa

Citizens from over 100 countries, from Albania to Zimbabwe, can apply for a 30-day e-Tourist visa online at indianvisaonline.gov.in a minimum of four and a maximum of 30 days before they are due to travel.

The fee is US$60, and it's necessary to upload a photograph as well as a copy of your passport, have at least six month's validity in your passport, and at least two pages blank. The facility is available at 16 airports, including Delhi, Mumbai, Bengaluru (Bangalore), Chennai, Kochi, Goa, Hyderabad, Kolkata and Thiruvanathapuram airports, though you can exit through any airport. You should also have a return or onward ticket, though proof of this is not usually requested.

If your application is approved, you will receive an attachment to an email, which you'll need to print out and take with you to the airport. You'll then have the e-Tourist visa stamped into your passport at the airport, hence the term 'Visa on Arrival', though you need to apply for it beforehand. It is valid from the date of arrival.

Visa Extensions

India is extremely stringent with visa extensions. At the time of writing, the government was granting extensions only in circumstances such as medical emergencies or theft of passport just before the applicant planned to leave the country (at the end of their visa).

If you do need to extend your visa due to any such exigency, you should contact the **Foreigners' Regional Registration Office** (FRRO; Map p76; ☎011-26711443; frrodil@nic.in; Level 2, East Block 8, Sector 1, Rama Krishna Puram, Delhi; ⏰9.30am-3pm Mon-Fri; Ⓜ Green Park) in Delhi. This is also the place to come for a replacement visa, and if you need your lost/stolen passport replaced (required before you can leave the country). Regional FRROs are even less likely to grant an extension.

Assuming you meet the stringent criteria, the FRRO is permitted to issue an extension of 14 days (free for nationals of most countries; enquire on application). You must bring one passport photo (take two, just in case), your passport (or emergency travel document, if your passport is missing), and a letter from the hospital where you're having treatment if it's a medical emergency. Note that this system is designed to get you out of the country promptly with the correct official stamps, not to give you two extra weeks of travel and leisure.

Travel Permits

Access to certain parts of India – particularly disputed border areas – is controlled by a system of permits that applies slightly differently to Indian citizens and foreigners.

A permit known as an Inner-Line Permit (ILP) or a Restricted Area Permit (RAP) is required to visit Arunachal Pradesh, Sikkim and certain parts of Himachal Pradesh, Ladakh and Uttarakhand that lie close to the disputed border with China/Tibet. Permits are also necessary for travel to the Andaman and Lakshadweep Islands, and some parts of Kutch in Gujarat.

Obtaining the ILP/RAP is usually a formality, but travel agents must apply on your behalf for certain areas, including many trekking routes passing close to the border.

Permits are issued by regional magistrates and district commissioners, either directly to travellers (for free) or through travel agents (for a fee). In some places you also need to pay an Environmental Tax of ₹300; ensure you keep the receipt.

In Odisha, permission is no longer required to visit tribal regions, and there's nothing to stop tourists from taking a bus or taxi to visit regional markets, but some villages are off-limits to visitors (due to potential Maoist activity), so seek local advice before setting out.

Double-check with tourism officials to see if permit requirements have undergone any changes before you head out to these areas.

Transport

GETTING THERE & AWAY

Plenty of international airlines service India, and overland routes to and from Nepal, Bangladesh, and Bhutan are all currently open. Flights, tours and other tickets can be booked online at www.lonelyplanet.com/bookings.

Entering India

Entering India by air or land is relatively straightforward, with standard immigration and customs procedures. A frustrating law barring re-entry into India within two months of the previous date of departure has been done away with (except for citizens of some Asian countries), thus allowing most travellers to combine their India tour with side trips to neighbouring countries.

Passports

To enter India you need a valid passport and an onward/return ticket, and a visa. Note that your passport needs to be valid for at least six months beyond your intended stay in India, with at least two blank pages. If your passport is lost or stolen, immediately contact your country's representative. Keep photocopies of your airline ticket and the identity and visa pages of your passport in case of emergency. Better yet, scan and email copies to yourself.

Air

Airports & Airlines

India has six main gateways for international flights; however, a number of other cities such as Goa, Kochi (Cochin), Lucknow, Trivandrum and Kunnar also service international carriers.

India's national carrier is **Air India** (☎1800-1801407; www.airindia.com), which operates international and domestic flights. Air travel in India has had a relatively decent safety record in recent years.

International airports include the following:

Bengaluru (☎18004254425; www.bengaluruairport.com)

Chennai (☎044-22560551; Tirusulam)

Delhi (☎01243376000; www.newdelhiairport.in)

Hyderabad (☎040-66546370; http://hyderabad.aero; Shamshabad)

Kolkata (NSCBIA (CCU); ☎033-25118036)

Mumbai (Map p750; ☎022-66851010; www.csia.in)

Kerala (☎0484-2610115; http://cial.aero)

Departure Tax

Departure tax and other charges are included in airline tickets. You are required to show a copy of your ticket and your passport in order to enter the airport, whether flying internationally or within India.

CLIMATE CHANGE & TRAVEL

Every form of transport that relies on carbon-based fuel generates CO_2, the main cause of human-induced climate change. Modern travel is dependent on aeroplanes, which might use less fuel per kilometre per person than most cars but travel much greater distances. The altitude at which aircraft emit gases (including CO_2) and particles also contributes to their climate change impact. Many websites offer 'carbon calculators' that allow people to estimate the carbon emissions generated by their journey and, for those who wish to do so, to offset the impact of the greenhouse gases emitted with contributions to portfolios of climate-friendly initiatives throughout the world. Lonely Planet offsets the carbon footprint of all staff and author travel.

Sea

Passenger ships sail from Chennai to Port Blair in the Andaman Islands once weekly (₹2500 to ₹6420; 60 hours).

Land

Although most visitors fly into India, it is possible to travel overland between India and Bangladesh, Bhutan, Nepal, Pakistan and Myanmar. The overland route from Nepal is the most popular. For more on these routes, check for up-to-date information on Lonely Planet's Thorntree forum (www.lonelyplanet.com/thorntree) or see the 'Europe to India overland' section on www.seat61.com/India.htm.

Border Crossings

If you enter India by bus or train, you'll be required to disembark at the border for standard immigration and customs checks.

You *must* have a valid Indian visa in advance, as no visas are available at the border.

Drivers of cars and motorbikes will need the vehicle's registration papers, liability insurance and an international drivers' permit in addition to their domestic licence. You'll also need a *Carnet de Passage en Douane*, which acts as a temporary waiver of import duty on the vehicle.

For travellers wishing to visit Tibet from India, the only way to do so is to exit to Nepal and then enter Tibet through the border crossing at Kodari as part of an organised tour. Alternately, you could fly to Lhasa from Kathmandu.

To find out the latest requirements for the paperwork and other important driving information, contact your local automobile association.

BANGLADESH

Foreigners can use four land crossings between Bangladesh and India, all in West Bengal or the Northeast States.

Heading from Bangladesh to India, you have to prepay the exit tax, which can be done at a Sonali Bank branch (either in Dhaka, another big city or at the closest branch to the border).

Exiting Bangladesh overland is complicated by red tape – if you enter the country by air, you require a road permit (or 'change of route' permit) to leave by land.

To apply for visa extensions and change of route permits you will need to visit the **Immigration and Passport Office** (☎01733393323; Agargaon Rd, Dhaka, Bangladesh; ⏰Sat-Thu) in Dhaka.

Some travellers have reported problems exiting Bangladesh overland with the visa issued on arrival at Dhaka airport.

BHUTAN

Phuentsholing is the main entry and exit point between India and Bhutan, although the eastern checkpost at Samdrup Jongkhar is also used.

As entry requirements need advance planning and are subject to change, we recommend you consult a travel agent or Bhutanese embassy for up-to-the-minute details. Travellers need to organise a tour with a Bhutanese travel agent and pay

OVERLAND TO/FROM BANGLADESH

ROUTE/BORDER TOWNS	TRANSPORT	VISAS	MORE INFORMATION
Kolkata–Dhaka/Petrapole (India) & Benapole (Bangladesh)	Regular daily Kolkata–Dhaka buses; twice-weekly train via Darsana border post.	Obtain in advance. To buy a train ticket, Darsana must be marked on your Bangladesh visa.	p480
Siliguri–Chengrabandha/Chengrabandha (India) & Burimari (Bangladesh)	Regular direct Siliguri–Chengrabandha buses; then bus to Rangpur, Bogra & Dhaka.	Obtain in advance.	p494
Shillong–Sylhet/Dawki (India) & Tamabil (Bangladesh)	Jeeps run from Shillong to Dawki. From Dawki walk (1.5km) or take a taxi to Tamabil bus station for regular buses to Sylhet.	Obtain in advance.	p592
Agartala–Dhaka/Agartala, 3km from border along Akhaura Rd (India) & Akhaura, 5km from border (Bangladesh)	Akhaura is on Dhaka–Comilla train line. Dhaka–Sylhet trains run from Ajampur train station, 3km further north.	Obtain in advance.	p586

OVERLAND TO/FROM BHUTAN

ROUTE/BORDER TOWNS	TRANSPORT	VISAS	MORE INFORMATION
Siliguri–Kolkata–Phuentsholing/Jaigon (India) & Phuentsholing (Bhutan)	From Kolkata, direct bus at 7pm thrice weekly. From Siliguri daily buses and possibly shared jeeps to Jaigon/Phuentsholing.	Non-Indian nationals need visa & tour booking with registered operator.	p480, p494

a fixed daily fee in order to obtain a Bhutanese visa. Also see www.tourism.gov.bt and Lonely Planet's *Bhutan*.

NEPAL

Political and weather conditions permitting, there are five land border crossings between India and Nepal. Check the current security status before crossing into Nepal; local newspapers and websites are good sources of information.

Multiple-entry visas (15/30/90 days US$25/40/100 – US dollars cash, not rupees) are available at the Nepal immigration post (you need two passport photos). You can now save time by applying online at http://online.nepalimmigration.gov.np/tourist-visa. Your receipt, which you must produce at the border within 15 days of your application, outlines border procedures.

Travellers have reported being harassed crossing into India at the Sunauli border and having to pay inflated prices for bus and train tickets. Consider taking a taxi to Gorakpur and getting a train or bus from there.

PAKISTAN

Given the rocky relationship between India and Pakistan, crossing by land depends on the current state of relations between the two countries – check locally.

If the crossings are open, you can reach Pakistan from Delhi, Amritsar (Punjab) and Rajasthan by bus or train. The 'Karvan-e-Aman' (Caravan of Peace) bus route from Srinagar to Pakistan-administered Kashmir is only open to Indian citizens.

You must have a visa to enter Pakistan. It's easiest to obtain this from the Pakistan mission in your home country. At the time of writing, the **Pakistan Embassy** (☎011-26110601; www.mofa.gov.pk; 2/50G Shantipath, Chanakyapuri) in Delhi was not issuing tourist visas for most nationalities, but this could change.

GETTING AROUND

Transport in India is frequent and inexpensive, though prone to overcrowding and delays. Trains, buses and shared jeeps run almost everywhere, at all times of day and night, though working out the time you will actually arrive at your destination after all the delays, traffic jams and mechancial faults can be a challenge. To save time, consider domestic flights over long-distance buses and trains. Urban transport is cheap and frequent, and you'll never struggle to find a taxi, rickshaw or autorickshaw.

Air

Airlines in India

Transporting vast numbers of passengers annually, India has a very competitive domestic airline industry. Major carriers include Air India, IndiGo, Spice Jet and Jet Airways.

Apart from airline sites, bookings can be made through portals such as **Cleartrip** (www.cleartrip.com), **Make My Trip** (www.

OVERLAND TO/FROM PAKISTAN

Assuming the border is open, the Lahore Bus Service departs from Delhi (6am daily, ₹ 2400) for Lahore, the journey takes 12 hours, with four stops. Advance bookings are essential.

Current government advice warns foreigners against using trains within Pakistan for security reasons. There are twice weekly trains between Lahore and Attari (on the Indian side of the border), where there is a customs and immigration stop. There are buses from Amritsar to Attari. Check the border is open before you leave; usual hours are 8.30am to 2.30pm mid-April to mid-October, and 9.30am to 3pm mid-October to mid-April; arrive at least an hour before closure. From Wagah there are buses and taxis on to Lahore.

The Thar Express, a Jodhpur–Karachi train leaves every Saturday at 1am (Friday in the opposite direction). Advance booking only (but not possible online). Customs/immigration is at Munabao (Indian border), where you physically change trains. Expect extremely tight security.

makemytrip.com) and **Yatra** (www.yatra.com).

Security norms require you to produce your ticket and your passport at the time of entering an airport. Every item of cabin baggage needs a label, which must be stamped as part of the security check (collect tags at the check-in counter). Flights to sensitive destinations, such as Srinagar and Ladakh, have extra security restrictions. You may also have to allow for a spot-check of your cabin baggage on the tarmac before you board.

Keeping peak hour congestion in mind, the recommended check-in time for domestic flights is two hours before departure – the deadline is 45 minutes. The usual baggage allowance is 20kg (10kg for smaller aircraft) in economy class.

Bicycle

There are no restrictions on bringing a bicycle into the country. However, bicycles sent by sea can take a few weeks to clear customs in India, so it's better to fly them in. It may be cheaper – and less hassle – to hire or buy a bicycle locally. Read up on bicycle touring before you travel: Rob Van Der Plas' *Bicycle Touring Manual* and Stephen Lord's *Adventure Cycle-Touring Handbook* and Laura Stone's *Himalaya by Bike* are good places to start. The **Cycling Federation of India** (☎011-23753528; www.cyclingfederationofindia.org) can provide local information.

Hire

➡ Tourist centres and traveller hang-outs are the easiest spots to find bicycles for hire – enquire locally.

➡ Prices vary: from around ₹40 to ₹150 per day for a roadworthy, Indian-made bicycle; mountain bikes, where available, are usually ₹400 to ₹800 per day.

➡ Hire places may require a cash security deposit (it may be stating the obvious,

OVERLAND TO/FROM NEPAL

BORDER CROSSING	TRANSPORT	VISAS	MORE INFORMATION
Sunauli (India)–Bhairawa/Siddharthanagar (Nepal)	Trains from Delhi to Gorakhpur, then half-hourly buses to border. There are direct AC buses now from Varanasi to Kathmandu (via Sunauli), departing nightly 10pm, for Rs1370. Buses & jeeps from Bhairawa (Siddharthanagar) to Pokhara, Kathmandu and central Nepal.	Nepali visas only available at border (6am-10pm)	p396
Raxaul Bazaar (India)–Birganj (Nepal)	Daily buses from Patna & Kolkata to Raxaul Bazaar. Mithila Express train daily from Kolkata. Regular day/night buses from Birganj to Kathmandu & Pokhara.	As above. (6am-6pm)	p524
Panitanki (India)–Kakarbhitta (Nepal)	Jeeps run to Panitanki from Siliguri, Darjeeling & Kalimpong. Regular buses from Kakarbhitta to Kathmandu (17hr) & other destinations. Bhadrapur airport (23km away) has flights to Kathmandu.	As above. (7am-7pm)	p494
Rupaidiha Bazaar/Jamunaha (India) – Nepalganj (Nepal)	Slow buses from Lucknow to Rupaidha Bazaar, then rickshaw to Jamunaha. Nepalganj has buses to Kathmandu & Pokhara, flights to Kathmandu.	As above.	
Banbassa (India)–Bhimdatta/Mahendranangar (Nepal)	Buses from Haldwani & Pithoragarh to Banbassa then rickshaw to border. From Bhimdatta (Mahendranagar) there are daily buses to Kathmadu and one daily service to Pokhara.	As above. (6am-6pm)	p447
Gauriphanta (India)–Dhangadhi (Nepal)	Daily buses run from Lucknow to Gauriphanta. Dhangadi is served by buses and flights from Kathmandu.	As above. (8am-5pm)	

but avoid leaving your airline ticket or passport).

Practicalities

- Mountain bikes with off-road tyres give the best protection against India's puncture-inducing roads.
- Roadside cycle mechanics abound but you should still bring spare tyres, brake cables, lubricating oil, chain repair kit and plenty of puncture-repair patches.
- Bikes can often be carried for free, or for a small luggage fee, on the roof of public buses – handy for uphill stretches.
- Contact your airline for information about transporting your bike and customs formalities in your home country.

Buying a Bike

- Delhi's **Jhandewalan Cycle Market** (Map p64; approx 10am-8pm) has imported and domestic, new and second-hand bikes, and spare parts.
- Mountain bikes with reputable brands that include **Hero** and **Atlas** generally start at around ₹6000.
- Reselling is usually fairly easy – ask at local cycle shops or put up an advert on travel noticeboards. If you purchased a new bike and it's still in reasonable condition, you should be able to recoup around 50% of what you originally paid.

Road Rules

- Vehicles drive on the left in India but otherwise road rules are not generally followed.
- Cities and national highways can be hazardous places to cycle so, where possible, stick to back roads.
- Be conservative about the distance you expect to cover – an experienced cyclist can manage around 60km to 100km a day on the plains, 40km to 60km on all-weather mountain roads and 40km or less on dirt roads.

Bike by Train

For long hauls, transporting your bike or motorbike by train can be a convenient option. Buy a standard train ticket for the journey, then take your bike to the station parcel office with your passport, registration papers, driver's licence and insurance documents. If you're transporting a motorbike, you need to empty the petrol tank beforehand. Packing-wallahs will wrap your bike in protective sacking for around ₹100 to ₹200 and you must fill out various forms and pay the shipping fee, which varies according to the route and train type – plus an insurance fee of 1% of the declared value of the bike. Bring the same paperwork to collect your bike from the goods office at the other end. If the bike is left waiting at the destination for more than 24 hours, you'll pay a storage fee of around ₹100 per day.

Boat

Scheduled ferries connect mainland India to the Andaman Islands, with departures to Port Blair from Chennai, Kolkata and Visakhapatnam; see www.andamans.gov.in.

Between October and May, there are cruise packages from Kochi (Kerala) to the Lakshadweep islands. There's also a popular day-long canal ferry between Kollam and Alleppey.

There are also numerous shorter ferry services across rivers, from chain pontoons to coracles and various boat cruises.

Bus

Buses go almost everywhere in India and are the only way to get around many mountainous areas. They tend to be the cheapest way to travel. Services are fast and frequent.

Roads in mountainous or curvy terrain can be perilous; buses are often driven with wilful abandon, and accidents are always a risk.

Avoid night buses unless there's no alternative: driving conditions are more hazardous and drivers may be inebriated or overtired.

All buses make snack and toilet stops (some more frequently than others), providing a break but possibly adding hours to journey times.

Shared jeeps complement the bus service in many mountain areas.

Classes

State-owned and private bus companies both offer several types of buses, graded loosely as 'ordinary', 'semi-deluxe', 'deluxe' or 'super deluxe'. These are usually open to interpretation, and the exact grade of luxury offered in a particular class varies.

Ordinary buses tend to be ageing rattletraps while the deluxe grades range from less decrepit versions of ordinary buses to flashy Volvo buses with air-con and reclining seating.

Buses run by the state government are usually more reliable (if there's a breakdown, another bus will be sent to pick up passengers), and seats can usually be booked up to a month in advance. Many state governments now operate super-deluxe buses.

Travel agencies in many tourist towns offer relatively expensive private two-by-two buses, which tend to leave and terminate at conveniently central stops.

On any bus, try to sit upfront to minimise the bumpy effect of potholes. Never sit directly above the wheels. Earplugs are invaluable on long-distance trips.

Costs

The cheapest buses are 'ordinary' government buses.

but prices vary from state to state.

Add around 50% to the ordinary fare for deluxe services, double the fare for air-conditioning, and triple or quadruple the fare for a two-by-two super-deluxe service.

Rajasthan Roadways offer discounts for female travellers.

Luggage

Luggage is stored in compartments underneath the bus (sometimes for a small fee) or carried on the roof.

Arrive at least an hour before departure time – some buses cover roof-stored bags with a canvas sheet, making last-minute additions inconvenient/impossible.

If your bags go on the roof, make sure they're securely locked, and tied to the metal baggage rack – unsecured bags can fall off on rough roads.

Theft is a (minor) risk: watch your bags at snack and toilet stops. Never leave day-packs or valuables unattended inside the bus.

Reservations

Most deluxe buses can be booked in advance at the bus station, travel agencies, and online at the portals **Cleartrip** (www.cleartrip.com), **Makemytrip** (www.makemytrip.com), and **Redbus** (www.redbus.in).

Reservations are rarely possible on 'ordinary' buses; travellers can be left behind in the mad rush for a seat.

To secure a seat, send a travelling companion ahead to claim some space, or pass a book or article of clothing through an open window to bag an empty seat.

If you board a bus midway through its journey, you may have to stand until a seat becomes free.

Many buses only depart when full – passengers might suddenly leave yours to join one that looks nearer to departing.

Many bus stations have a separate women's queue (not always obvious when signs are in Hindi and men join the melee), but women also have an unspoken right to elbow their way to the front of any bus queue.

Car

Few people bother with self-drive car hire – not only because of the hair-raising driving conditions, but also because hiring a car with driver is potentially affordable in India, particularly if several people share the cost. **Hertz** (www.hertz.com) is one of the few international companies with representatives in India.

Hiring a Car & Driver

Most towns have taxi stands or car-hire companies where you can arrange short or long tours.

Not all hire cars are licensed to travel beyond their home state. Those that are will pay extra state taxes, which are added to the hire charge.

Ask for a driver who speaks some English and knows the region you intend visiting. Try to see the car and meet the driver before paying anything.

A wide range of cars now ply as taxis. From a proletarian Tata Indica hatchback to a comfy Toyota Innova SUV, there's a model to suit every pocket.

Hire charges for multiday trips cover the driver's meals and accommodation, and drivers should make their own sleeping and eating arrangements.

It's essential to set the ground rules from day one; politely but firmly let the driver know that you're boss to avoid difficulties later.

Costs

Car hire costs depend on the distance and the terrain (driving on mountain roads uses more petrol, hence the higher cost).

One-way trips usually cost the same as return ones (to cover the petrol and driver charges for getting back).

Hire charges vary from state to state. Some taxi unions set a maximum time limit or a maximum kilometre distance for day trips – if you go over, you'll have to pay extra. Prices also vary according to the make and model of the taxi.

To avoid misunderstandings, get *in writing* what you've been promised (quotes should include petrol, sightseeing stops, all your chosen destinations, and meals and accommodation for the driver). If a driver asks you for money for petrol en route because he is short of cash, get receipts for reimbursement later. If you're travelling by the kilometre, check the odometer reading

THE POETIC SIGNAGE OF THE BRO

In Ladakh, Himachal Pradesh, Arunachal Pradesh and Sikkim, the Border Roads Organisation (BRO) builds 'roads in the sky', including some of the world's highest passes accessible by car. Risking life and limb to keep the roads open, the BRO has a bewitching turn of phrase when it comes to driver warnings, including:

- Life is short, don't make it shorter.
- It is not a rally, enjoy the valley.
- After whisky, driving risky.
- Be gentle on my curves.
- Better to be late than to be the late Mr.

before you set out so as to avoid confusions later.

For sightseeing day trips around a single city, expect to pay upwards of ₹1400/1800 for a non-air-con/air-con car with an eight-hour, 80km limit per day (extra charges apply for longer trips). For multiday trips, operators usually peg a 250km minimum running distance per day and charge around ₹8/10 per km for a non-air-con/air-con car, for anything over this.

A tip is customary at the end of your journey; at least ₹150 to ₹200 per day is fair.

Hitching

Hitching is never entirely safe, and not recommended. Travellers who hitch should understand that they are taking a small but serious risk. However, for a negotiable fee, truck drivers supplement the bus service in some remote areas. As drivers rarely speak English, you may have difficulty explaining where you wish to go, and working out a fair price to pay. Be aware that truck drivers have a reputation for driving under the influence of alcohol. Women are strongly advised against hitching. Always use your instincts.

Local Transport

Buses, cycle-rickshaws, autorickshaws, taxis, boats and urban trains provide transport around India's cities.

Costs for public transport vary from town to town.

For any transport without a fixed fare, agree on the price *before* you start your journey and make sure that it covers your luggage and every passenger.

Even where meters exist, drivers may refuse to use them, demanding an elevated 'fixed' fare; bargain hard. Fares usually increase at night (by up to 100%) and some drivers charge a few rupees extra for luggage.

Carry plenty of small bills for taxi and rickshaw fares as drivers rarely have change.

In some places, taxi/autorickshaw drivers are involved in the commission racket.

Apps such as Uber and Ola Cabs have transformed local transport, as if you have a smartphone you can call a taxi or auto and the fare is electronically calculated – no arguments.

Autorickshaw, Tempo & Vikram

AUTORICKSHAW

Similar to the tuk-tuks of Southeast Asia, the Indian autorickshaw is a three-wheeled motorised contraption with a tin or canvas roof and sides, usually with room for two passengers (although you'll often see many more squeezed in) and limited luggage.

They are also referred to as autos, scooters and riks.

Autorickshaws are mostly cheaper than taxis and usually have a meter, although getting it turned on can be a challenge. You can call autos via the Ola Taxi and Auto app (www.olacabs.com), which electronically calculates your fare when you finish the journey – no more haggling! Flagfall is around ₹25, then it's ₹8 to ₹14 per km.

Travelling by auto is great fun but, thanks to the open windows, can be noisy and hot (or severely cold!).

In some cities there are larger electric rickshaws, which are shared and thus cheaper but you'll have to be going in the same direction as the other passengers.

TEMPO & VIKRAM

Tempos and vikrams (large tempos) are outsized autorickshaws with room for more passengers, shuttling on fixed routes for a fixed fare.

In country areas, you may also see the fearsome-looking 'three-wheeler' – a crude tractor-like tempo with a front wheel on an articulated arm – or the Magic, a cute minivan that can take in up to a dozen passengers.

Boat

Various kinds of local boats offer transport across and down rivers in India, from big car ferries to wooden canoes and wicker coracles. Most of the larger boats carry bicycles and motorcycles for a fee.

Bus

Urban buses range from fume-belching, human-stuffed mechanical monsters that travel at breakneck speed to sanitised air-conditioned vehicles with comfortable seating and smoother ride quality. In any case, it's usually far more convenient to opt for an autorickshaw or taxi, as they are quicker and more frequent.

Cycle-Rickshaw

A cycle-rickshaw is a pedal cycle with two rear wheels, supporting a bench seat for passengers. Most have a canopy that can be raised in wet weather or lowered to provide extra space for luggage.

Fares must be agreed upon in advance – speak to locals to get an idea of what is a fair price for the distance you intend to travel.

Kolkata is the last bastion of the hand-pulled rickshaw, known as the *tana* rickshaw. This is a hand-cart on two wheels pulled directly by the rickshaw-wallah.

Taxi

Most towns have taxis, and these are usually metered, however, getting drivers to use the meter can be a hassle. To avoid fare-setting shenanigans, use prepaid taxis where possible. Apps such as Uber and Ola, or radio cabs, are the most efficient option in larger cities.

MANNING THE METER

Getting a metered ride is only half the battle. Meters are almost always outdated, so fares are calculated using a combination of the meter reading and a complicated 'fare adjustment card'. Predictably, this system is open to abuse. To get a rough estimate of fares in advance, try the portal www.taxiautofare.com.

PREPAID TAXIS

Major Indian airports and train stations have prepaid-taxi and radio-cab booths. Here, you can book a taxi, even long distance, for a fixed price (which will include baggage) and thus avoid commission scams. Hold onto your receipt until you reach your destination, as proof of payment.

Radio cabs cost marginally more than prepaid taxis, but are air-conditioned and manned by the company's chauffeurs. Cabs have electronic, receipt-generating fare meters and are fitted with GPS units, so the company can monitor the vehicle's movement around town. These minimise chances of errant driving or unreasonable demands for extra cash by the driver afterward.

Smaller airports and stations may have prepaid autorickshaw booths instead.

Other Local Transport

In some towns, *tongas* (horse-drawn two-wheelers) and *victorias* (horse-drawn carriages) still operate. Kolkata has a tram network, and Mumbai, Delhi, Kolkata and Chennai, among other centres, have suburban trains that leave from ordinary train stations.

Motorcycle

Long-distance motorcycle touring is hugely popular in India. However, it can be quite an undertaking; there are some popular motorcycle tours for those who don't want the rigmarole of going it alone.

The most preferred starting point for motorcycle tours is Delhi, as well as Manali, and popular destinations include Rajasthan, South India and Ladakh. Weather is an important factor and you should check for the best times to visit different areas. To cross from neighbouring countries, check the latest regulations and paperwork requirements from the relevant diplomatic mission.

Driving Licence

To hire a motorcycle in India, technically you're required to have a valid international drivers' permit in addition to your domestic licence. In tourist areas, some places may rent out a motorcycle without asking for a driving permit/licence, but you won't be covered by insurance in the event of an accident, and may also face a fine.

Hire

The classic way to motorcycle around India is on a Royal Enfield, built to both vintage and modern specs. Fully manual, these are easy to repair (parts can be found almost everywhere in India). On the other hand, Enfields are often less reliable than many of the newer, Japanese-designed bikes.

Plenty of places rent out motorcycles for local trips and longer tours. Japanese- and Indian-made bikes in the 100cc to 150cc range are cheaper than the big 350cc to 500cc Enfields.

As security, you'll need to leave a large cash deposit (ensure you get a receipt that stipulates the refundable amount) or your passport/air ticket. We strongly advise not leaving these documents, in particular your passport, which you need for hotel check-ins and if stopped by the police.

For three weeks' hire, a 500cc Enfield costs from ₹25,000 to ₹28,000; a 350cc costs ₹18,000 to ₹22,000. The price will include accessories, spare parts, tolls required for the journey and an invaluable free maintenance course.

As for accessories, helmets are available for ₹1000 to ₹5500, with the best Indian brand 'Studs' coming in many different models. Extras (panniers, luggage racks, protection bars, rear-view mirrors, lockable fuel caps, petrol filters, extra tools) are also easy to come by.

The following dealers come recommended:

Lalli Motorbike Exports (Map p64; ☎011-28750869; www.lallisingh.com; 1740-A/55 Hari Singh Nalwa St, Abdul Aziz Rd; ⏰10am-7pm Tue-Sun; Ⓜ Karol Bagh) Run by the knowledgeable Lalli Singh, this Delhi-based outfit sells and rents out Enfields and parts, and buyers get a crash course in running and maintaining these lovable but temperamental machines. Lalli can also recommend other reputable dealers in the area.

Anu Auto Works (Royal Moto Touring; Map p310; ☎9816163378; www.royalmototouring.com; Vashisht Rd; ⏰office 9am-9pm or later, approx Jun-Sep) Manali-based; rents Enfields and takes tours over high Himalayan passes to Ladakh and Spiti from June to September. Typical Enfield rental rates are ₹1400 to ₹1500 per day for a 500cc, ₹1200 to ₹1300 per day for 350cc. Discounts usually available for rentals of about 18 days or more.

Allibhai Premji Tyrewalla (Map p746; ☎022-23099417, 022-23099313; www.premjis.com; 205/20 Dr D Bhadkamkar (Lamington) Rd; ⏰10am-7pm

Mon-Sat) Sells new and second-hand motorcycles with a buy-back optioni in Mumbai.

Rajasthan Auto Centre (Map p108; ☎0141-2568074, 9829188064; www.royalenfieldsalim.com; Sanganeri Gate, Sanjay Bazaar; ⏲10am-8pm Mon-Sat, to 2pm Sun) Comes recommended as a place for hiring, fixing or purchasing a motorcycle in Jaipur.

Kerala Bike Tours (☎0484-2356652, 9388476817; www.keralabiketours.com; Kirushupaly Rd, Ravipuram) Organises motorcycle tours around Kerala and the Western Ghats and hires out touring quality Enfield Bullets (from US$155 per week) for serious riders with unlimited mileage, full insurance and free recovery/maintenance options.

Purchase

For longer tours, purchasing a new motorcycle may sound like a great idea. However, selling motor vehicles to foreigners comes with reams of complicated paperwork, foreigners are not allowed to register vehicles in their names, and in many situations, procuring a motorcycle might not be possible or feasible at all.

Second-hand bikes are widely available, though, and paperwork is simpler than for a new machine. All privately owned vehicles over 15 years old are banned from Delhi roads.

To find a second-hand motorcycle, check travellers' noticeboards and ask motorcycle mechanics and other bikers.

A well looked-after second-hand 350cc Enfield costs ₹65,000 to ₹115,000. A good condition 500cc with UCI Engine ranges between ₹95,000 to ₹140,000. You will also have to pay for insurance.

OWNERSHIP PAPERS

There's plenty of paperwork associated with owning a motorcycle. The process is complicated and time-consuming, so it's wise to seek advice from the agent selling the bike.

Registration papers are signed by the local registration authority when the bike is first sold; you need these when you buy a second-hand bike.

Foreign nationals cannot change the name on the registration but you must fill out forms for change of ownership and transfer of insurance.

A new registration lasts for 15 years, after which it may be renewed for ₹5000 for five years; make absolutely sure that it states the 'road-worthiness' of the vehicle, and that there are no outstanding debts or criminal proceedings associated with the bike. The office of the state transport department where the bike was registered can provide this information.

Insurance

Only hire a bike that has insurance – if you hit someone without insurance the consequences will be very costly. Reputable companies will include third-party cover in their policies; those that don't probably aren't trustworthy.

You must also arrange insurance if you buy a motorcycle (usually you can organise this through the person selling the bike).

Comprehensive insurance for a new Royal Enfield can cost ₹4000 to ₹5000 per year. Insurance for second-hand Royal Enfield may cost from ₹800 to ₹4000, depending on the age of the vehicle.

Fuel, Spare Parts & Extras

Petrol and engine oil are widely available in the plains, but petrol stations are rarer in the mountains. If travelling to remote regions, carry enough extra fuel (seek local advice about fuel availability before setting off). At the time of writing, petrol cost around ₹67 per litre in Delhi, but could cost to to three times that in different regions.

Get your machine serviced regularly (particularly older ones). Indian roads and engine vibration work things loose quite quickly.

Check the engine and gearbox oil level regularly (at least every 500km) and clean the oil filter every few thousand kilometres.

Given the road conditions, the chances are you'll make at least a couple of visits to a puncture-wallah – start your trip with new tyres and carry spanners to remove your own wheels.

It's a good idea to bring your own protective equipment (jackets, gloves etc).

Road Conditions

Given the varied road conditions, India can be challenging for novice riders. Hazards range from cows and chickens crossing the carriageway to broken-down trucks, unruly traffic, pedestrians on the road, and ubiquitous potholes and unmarked speed humps. Rural roads sometimes have grain crops strewn across them to be threshed by passing vehicles – a serious sliding hazard for bikers.

Try not to cover too much territory in one day and never ride in the dark – many vehicles drive without lights, and dynamo-powered motorcycle headlamps are useless at low revs while negotiating around potholes.

On busy national highways, expect to average 40 to 50km/h without stops; on winding back roads and dirt tracks this can drop to 10km/h.

Organised Motorcycle Tours

Dozens of companies offer organised motorcycle tours around India with a support vehicle, mechanic and guide. Here are a few well-established companies:

Lalli Singh Tours (www.lallisingh.com)

Blazing Trails (☎05603-666788; www.blazingtrailstours.com)

World on Wheels (www.worldonwheels.tours)

H-C Travel (www.hctravel.com)

Himalayan Roadrunners (www.ridehigh.com)

Indian Motorcycle Adventure (www.indianmotorcycleadventures.com)

Moto Discovery (www.motodiscovery.com)

Royal Expeditions (☎011-26238545; http://royalexpeditions.com)

Shared Jeep

In mountain areas shared jeeps supplement the bus services, charging similar fixed fares.

Although nominally designed for five to six passengers, most shared jeeps squeeze in more. The seats beside and immediately behind the driver are more expensive than the cramped bench seats at the rear.

Jeeps only leave when full; people often bail out of a half-full jeep and pile into one with more passengers that's ready to depart. Drivers will leave immediately if you pay for all the empty seats and 'reserve' a vehicle for yourself.

Jeeps run from jeep stands and 'passenger stations' at the junctions of major roads; ask locals to point you in the right direction.

In some states, jeeps are known as 'sumos' after the Tata Sumo, a popular vehicle.

Travel sickness, particularly on winding mountain roads, may mean you are asked to give up your window seat to queasy fellow passengers.

Train

Travelling by train is a quintessential Indian experience. Trains offer a smoother ride than buses and are especially recommended for long journeys that include overnight travel. India's rail network is one of the largest and busiest in the world and Indian Railways is the largest utility employer on earth, with roughly 1.5 million workers. There are almost 7000 train stations scattered across the country.

We've listed useful trains but there are hundreds more. The best way of sourcing updated railway information is to use relevant internet sites such as **Indian Railways** (rbs.indianrail.gov.in) and the excellent **India Rail Info** (http://indiarailinfo.com), with added offline browsing support, as well as the user-friendly **Erail** (erail.in). There's also *Trains at a Glance* (₹45), available at many train station bookstands and better bookshops/newsstands, however, it's published annually so it's not as up to date as websites. Nevertheless, it offers comprehensive timetables covering all the main lines.

Booking Tickets in India

You can book through a travel agency or hotel (for a commission), or in person at the train station. Another hopefully straightforward way is to book online through **IRCTC** (www.irctc.co.in; accepts Mastercard & Visa), the e-ticketing division of Indian Railways, or portals such as **Cleartrip** (www.cleartrip.com), **Make My Trip** (www.makemytrip.com), **Yatra** (www.yatra.com) and **Redbus** (bus only; www.redbus.com) are also useful; you'll usually need an Indian mobile number, though you may be able to enter a random number then use an email. **The Man in Seat 61** (www.seat61.com) has lots of good information, and explains in detail how to register an IRCTC account if you don't have an Indian mobile number.

However, online booking of train tickets has its share of glitches: travellers have reported problems with registering themselves on some portals and using credit cards. Big stations often have English-speaking staff who can help with reservations. At smaller stations, the stationmaster and his deputy usually speak English. It's also worth approaching tourist-office staff if you need advice.

You can only book six train tickets online per calendar month, and after that you can only buy them in person. If you book online and accept a waitlisted ticket and it isn't confirmed before the train leaves its destination, the money is refunded to the

EXPRESS TRAIN FARES IN RUPEES

DISTANCE (KM)	1AC	2AC	3AC	FIRST CLASS	CHAIR CAR (CC)	SECOND (II)
100	1047	613	428	262	205	48
200	1047	613	428	412	282	73
300	1047	613	561	558	378	103
400	1460	843	591	690	467	128
500	1794	1058	733	843	577	151
1000	2940	1708	1352	1371	931	258
1500	3787	2188	1487	1753	1189	334
2000	4620	2659	1797	2127	1443	412

credit card and the ticket is worthless.

AT THE STATION

Get a reservation slip from the information window, fill in the name of the departure station, destination station, the class you want to travel and the name and number of the train. Join the long queue for the ticket window where your ticket will be printed. Women should take advantage of the separate women's queue – if there isn't one, go to the front of the regular queue.

TOURIST RESERVATION BUREAU

Larger cities and major tourist centres have an International Tourist Bureau, which sells tourist quota seats on certain classes of train, and allows you to book tickets in relative peace.

Reservations

Bookings open up to 120 days before departure and you must make a reservation for chair-car, executive-chair-car, sleeper, 1AC, 2AC and 3AC carriages. No reservations are required for general (2nd class) compartments; you have to grab seats here the moment the train pulls in.

Trains are always busy so it's wise to book as far in advance as possible, especially for overnight journeys. There may be additional services to certain destinations during major festivals but it's still worth booking well in advance.

Reserved tickets show your seat/berth and carriage number. Carriage numbers are written on the side of the train (station staff and porters can point you in the right direction). A list of names and berths is posted on the side of each reserved carriage.

Refunds are available on any ticket, even after departure, with a penalty – rules are complicated, check when you book.

Trains can be delayed at any stage of the journey; to avoid stress, factor some leeway into your plans.

TOURIST QUOTA

A special (albeit small) tourist quota is set aside for foreign tourists travelling between popular stations. These seats can only be booked at dedicated reservation offices in major cities, and you need to show your passport and visa as ID. Tickets can be paid for in rupees (some offices may ask to see foreign exchange certificates – ATM receipts will suffice).

TATKAL TICKETS

Indian Railways holds back a small number of tickets on key trains and releases them at 10am one day before the train is due to depart. A charge of ₹10 to ₹500 is added to each ticket price. First AC tickets are excluded from the scheme.

RESERVATION AGAINST CANCELLATION (RAC)

Even when a train is fully booked, Indian Railways sells a handful of seats in each class as 'Reservation Against Cancellation' (RAC). This means that if you have an RAC ticket and someone cancels before the departure date, you will get his or her seat (or berth). You'll have to check the reservation list at the station on the day of travel to see if you've been allocated a confirmed seat/berth. Even if no one cancels, you can still board the train as an RAC ticket holder and travel without a seat.

WAITLIST (WL)

If the RAC quota is maxed out as well, you will be handed a waitlisted ticket (marked WL). This means that if there are enough cancellations, you may eventually move up the order to land a confirmed berth, or at least an RAC seat. Check your booking status at rbs.indianrail.gov.in/pnr_Enq.html by entering your ticket's PNR number. You can't board the train on a waitlisted ticket, but a refund is available – ask the ticket office about your chances.

Costs

Fares are calculated by distance and class of travel; Rajdhani and Shatabdi trains are slightly more expensive, but the price includes meals. Most air-conditioned carriages have a catering service (meals are brought to your seat). In unreserved classes it's a good idea to carry portable snacks. Male/female seniors (those over 60/58) get 40/50% off all fares in all classes on all types of train. Children below the age of six travel free, those aged between six and 12 are charged half price, up to 300km.

FARE FINDER

Go to www.indiarailinfo.com or erail.in and type in the name of the two destinations. You'll promptly get a list of every train (with the name, number, arrival/departure times and journey details) plying the route, as well as fares for each available class.

Health

There is huge geographical variation in India, so in different areas, heat, cold and altitude can cause health problems. Hygiene is poor in most regions so food and water-borne illnesses are common. A number of insect-borne diseases are present, particularly in tropical areas. Medical care is basic in various areas (especially beyond the larger cities) so it's essential to be well prepared.

Pre-existing medical conditions and accidental injury (especially traffic accidents) account for most life-threatening problems. Becoming ill in some way, however, is common. Fortunately, most travellers' illnesses can be prevented with some common-sense behaviour or treated with a well-stocked travellers' medical kit – however, never hesitate to consult a doctor while on the road, as self-diagnosis can be hazardous.

BEFORE YOU GO

You can buy many medications over the counter in India without a doctor's prescription, but it can be difficult to find some of the newer drugs, particularly the latest antidepressant drugs, blood-pressure medications and contraceptive pills. Be circumspect about self-medicating, as travellers mixing the wrong drugs or overdosing has on occasion ended in tragedy. Bring the following:

- medications in their original, labelled containers
- a signed, dated letter from your physician describing your medical conditions and medications, including generic names
- a physician's letter documenting the medical necessity of any syringes you bring
- if you have a heart condition, a copy of your ECG taken just prior to travelling
- any regular medication (double your ordinary needs).

Insurance

Don't travel without health insurance. Emergency evacuation is expensive. There are various factors to consider when choosing insurance. Read the small print.

- You may require extra cover for adventure activities such as rock climbing and scuba diving.
- In India, doctors usually require immediate payment in cash. Your insurance plan may make payments directly to providers or it will reimburse you later for overseas health expenditures. If you do have to claim later, make sure you keep all relevant documentation.
- Some policies ask that you telephone back (reverse charges) to a centre in your home country where an immediate assessment of your problem will be made.

Vaccinations

Specialised travel-medicine clinics are your best source of up-to-date information; they stock all available vaccines and can give specific recommendations for your trip. Most vaccines don't give immunity until *at least* two weeks after they're given, so visit a doctor well before departure. Ask your doctor for an International Certificate of Vaccination (sometimes known as the 'yellow booklet'), which will list all the vaccinations you've received.

Medical Checklist

Recommended items for a personal medical kit:

- Antifungal cream, eg clotrimazole
- Antibacterial cream, eg mupirocin
- Antibiotic for skin infections, eg amoxicillin/clavulanate or cephalexin
- Antihistamine – there are many options, eg cetrizine for daytime and promethazine for night
- Antiseptic, eg Betadine
- Antispasmodic for stomach cramps, eg Buscopam
- Contraceptive

- Decongestant, eg pseudoephedrine
- DEET-based insect repellent
- Diarrhoea medication – consider an oral rehydration solution (eg Gastrolyte), diarrhoea 'stopper' (eg loperamide) and antinausea medication (eg prochlorperazine). Antibiotics for diarrhoea include ciprofloxacin; for bacterial diarrhoea azithromycin; for giardia or amoebic dysentery tinidazole
- First-aid items such as scissors, elastoplasts, bandages, gauze, thermometer (but not mercury), sterile needles and syringes, safety pins and tweezers
- Ibuprofen or another anti-inflammatory
- Iodine tablets (unless you are pregnant or have a thyroid problem) to purify water
- Migraine medication if you suffer from migraines
- Paracetamol
- Pyrethrin to impregnate clothing and mosquito nets
- Steroid cream for allergic or itchy rashes, eg 1% to 2% hydrocortisone
- High-factor sunscreen
- Throat lozenges
- Thrush (vaginal yeast infection) treatment, eg

REQUIRED & RECOMMENDED VACCINATIONS

The only vaccine required by international regulations is **yellow fever**. Proof of vaccination will only be required if you have visited a country in the yellow-fever zone within the six days prior to entering India. If you are travelling to India from Africa or South America, you should check to see if you require proof of vaccination.

The World Health Organization (WHO) recommends the following vaccinations for travellers going to India (as well as being up to date with measles, mumps and rubella vaccinations):

Adult diphtheria & tetanus Single booster recommended if none in the previous 10 years. Side effects include sore arm and fever.

Hepatitis A Provides almost 100% protection for up to a year; a booster after 12 months provides at least another 20 years' protection. Mild side effects such as headache and sore arm occur in 5% to 10% of people.

Hepatitis B Now considered routine for most travellers. Given as three shots over six months. A rapid schedule is also available, as is a combined vaccination with hepatitis A. Side effects are mild and uncommon, usually headache and a sore arm. In 95% of people lifetime protection results.

Polio Only one booster is required as an adult for lifetime protection. Inactivated polio vaccine is safe during pregnancy.

Typhoid Recommended for all travellers to India, even those only visiting urban areas. The vaccine offers around 70% protection, lasts for two to three years and comes as a single shot. Tablets are also available, but the injection is usually recommended as it has fewer side effects. Sore arm and fever may occur.

Varicella If you haven't had chickenpox, discuss this vaccination with your doctor.

These immunisations are recommended for long-term travellers (more than one month) or those at special risk (seek further advice from your doctor):

Japanese B encephalitis Three injections in all. Booster recommended after two years. Sore arm and headache are the most common side effects. In rare cases, an allergic reaction comprising hives and swelling can occur up to 10 days after any of the three doses.

Meningitis Single injection. There are two types of vaccination: the quadravalent vaccine gives two to three years' protection; meningitis group C vaccine gives around 10 years' protection. Recommended for long-term backpackers aged under 25.

Rabies Three injections in all. A booster after one year will then provide 10 years' protection. Side effects are rare – occasionally headache and sore arm.

Tuberculosis (TB) A complex issue. Adult long-term travellers are usually recommended to have a TB skin test before and after travel, rather than vaccination. Only one vaccine given in a lifetime.

clotrimazole pessaries or Diflucan tablet

- Ural or equivalent if prone to urine infections

Websites

There is a wealth of travel-health advice on the internet; www.lonelyplanet.com is a good place to start. Some other suggestions:

Centers for Disease Control and Prevention (CDC; www.cdc.gov) Good general information.

MD Travel Health (www.mdtravelhealth.com) Provides complete travel-health recommendations for every country; updated daily.

World Health Organization (WHO; www.who.int/ith) Its superb book *International Travel & Health* is revised annually and is available online

Further Reading

Recommended references include *Travellers' Health* by Dr Richard Dawood and *Travelling Well* by Dr Deborah Mills, which is now also available as an app; check out the website (www.travellingwell.com.au) too.

IN INDIA

Availability & Cost of Health Care

Medical care is hugely variable in India. Some cities now have clinics catering specifically to travellers and expatriates; these clinics are usually more expensive than local medical facilities, and offer a higher standard of care. Additionally, they know the local system, including reputable local hospitals and specialists. They may also liaise with insurance companies should you require evacuation. It is usually difficult to find reliable medical care in rural areas.

Self-treatment may be appropriate if your problem is minor (eg traveller's diarrhoea), you are carrying the relevant medication, and you cannot attend a recommended clinic. If you suspect a serious disease, especially malaria, travel to the nearest quality facility.

Before buying medication over the counter, check the use-by date, and ensure the packet is sealed and properly stored (eg not exposed to the sunshine).

Infectious Diseases

Malaria

This is a serious and potentially deadly disease. Before you travel, seek expert advice according to your itinerary (rural areas are especially risky) and on medication and side effects.

Malaria is caused by a parasite transmitted by the bite of an infected mosquito. The most important symptom of malaria is fever, but general symptoms, such as headache, diarrhoea, cough or chills, may also occur. Diagnosis can only be properly made by taking a blood sample.

Two strategies should be combined to prevent malaria: mosquito avoidance and antimalarial medications. Most people who catch malaria are taking inadequate or no antimalarial medication.

Travellers are advised to prevent mosquito bites by taking these steps:

- Use a DEET-based insect repellent on exposed skin. Wash this off at night – as long as you are sleeping under a mosquito net. Natural repellents such as citronella can be effective, but must be applied more frequently than products containing DEET.
- Sleep under a mosquito net impregnated with pyrethrin.
- Choose accommodation with proper screens and fans (if not air-conditioned).
- Impregnate clothing with pyrethrin in high-risk areas.
- Wear long sleeves and trousers in light colours.
- Use mosquito coils.
- Spray your room with insect repellent before going out for your evening meal.

There are a variety of medications available:

Chloroquine & Paludrine combination Limited effectiveness in many parts of South Asia. Common side effects include nausea (40% of people) and mouth ulcers.

Doxycycline (daily tablet) A broad-spectrum antibiotic that helps prevent a variety of tropical diseases, including leptospirosis, tick-borne disease and typhus. Potential side effects include photosensitivity (a tendency to sunburn), thrush (in women), indigestion, heartburn, nausea and interference with the contraceptive pill. More serious side effects include ulceration of the oesophagus – take your tablet with a meal and a large glass of water, and never lie down within half an hour of taking it.

HEALTH ADVISORIES

It's a good idea to consult your government's travel-health website before departure, if one is available:

Australia (www.smartraveller.gov.au)

Canada (www.travelhealth.gc.ca)

New Zealand (safetravel.govt.nz/health-and-travel)

UK (www.fco.gov.uk/en/travelling-and-living-overseas)

US (www.cdc.gov/travel)

It must be taken for four weeks after leaving the risk area.

Lariam (mefloquine) This weekly tablet suits many people. Serious side effects are rare but include depression, anxiety, psychosis and seizures. Anyone with a history of depression, anxiety, other psychological disorders or epilepsy should not take Lariam. It is considered safe in the second and third trimesters of pregnancy. Tablets must be taken for four weeks after leaving the risk area.

Malarone A combination of atovaquone and proguanil. Side effects are uncommon and mild, most commonly nausea and headache. It is the best tablet for scuba divers and for those on short trips to high-risk areas. It must be taken for one week after leaving the risk area.

Other Diseases

Avian flu 'Bird flu' or Influenza A (H5N1) is a subtype of the type A influenza virus. Contact with dead or sick birds is the principal source of infection and bird-to-human transmission does not easily occur. Symptoms include high fever and flu-like symptoms with rapid deterioration, leading to respiratory failure and death in many cases. Immediate medical care should be sought if bird flu is suspected. Check www.who.int/en/or www.avianinfluenza.com.au.

Cholera There are occasional outbreaks of cholera in India. This acute gastrointestinal infection is transmitted through contaminated water and food, including raw or undercooked fish and shellfish. Cases are rare among travellers, but those who are travelling to an area of active transmission should consult with their healthcare practitioner regarding vaccination.

Dengue fever This mosquito-borne disease is becomingly increasingly problematic, especially in the cities. As there is no vaccine available it can only be prevented by avoiding mosquito bites at all times. Symptoms include high fever, severe headache and body ache and sometimes a rash and diarrhoea. Treatment is rest and paracetamol – do not take aspirin or ibuprofen as it increases the likelihood of haemorrhaging. Make sure you see a doctor to be diagnosed and monitored.

Hepatitis A This food- and water-borne virus infects the liver, causing jaundice (yellow skin and eyes), nausea and lethargy. There is no specific treatment for hepatitis A, you just need to allow time for the liver to heal. All travellers to India should be vaccinated against hepatitis A.

Hepatitis B This sexually transmitted disease is spread by body fluids and can be prevented by vaccination. The long-term consequences can include liver cancer and cirrhosis.

Hepatitis E Transmitted through contaminated food and water, hepatitis E has similar symptoms to hepatitis A, but is far less common. It is a severe problem in pregnant women and can result in the death of both mother and baby. There is no commercially available vaccine, and prevention is by following safe eating and drinking guidelines.

HIV Spread via contaminated body fluids. Avoid unsafe sex, unsterile needles (including in medical facilities) and procedures such as tattoos. The growth rate of HIV in India is one of the highest in the world.

Influenza Present year-round in the tropics, influenza (flu) symptoms include fever, muscle aches, a runny nose, cough and sore throat. It can be severe in people over the age of 65 or in those with medical conditions such as heart disease or diabetes – vaccination is recommended for these individuals. There is no specific treatment, just rest and paracetamol.

Japanese B encephalitis This viral disease is transmitted by mosquitoes and is rare in travellers. Most cases occur in rural areas and vaccination is recommended for travellers spending more than one month outside of cities. There is no treatment, and it may result in permanent brain damage or death. Ask your doctor for further details.

Rabies This fatal disease is spread by the bite or possibly even the lick of an infected animal – most commonly a dog or monkey. You should seek medical advice immediately after any animal bite and commence postexposure treatment. Having pretravel vaccination means the postbite treatment is greatly simplified. If an animal bites you, gently wash the wound with soap and water, and apply iodine-based antiseptic. If you are not prevaccinated you will need to receive rabies immunoglobulin as soon as possible, and this is very difficult to obtain in much of India.

Tuberculosis While TB is rare in travellers, those who have significant contact with the local population (such as medical and aid workers and long-term travellers) should take precautions. Vaccination is usually only given to children under the age of five, but adults at risk are recommended to have pre- and post-travel TB testing. The main symptoms are fever, cough, weight loss, night sweats and fatigue.

Typhoid This serious bacterial infection is also spread via food and water. It gives a high and slowly progressive fever and headache, and may be accompanied by a dry cough and stomach pain. It is diagnosed by blood tests and treated with antibiotics. Vaccination is recommended for all travellers who are spending more than a week in India. Be aware that vaccination is not 100% effective, so you must still be careful with what you eat and drink.

Traveller's Diarrhoea

This is by far the most common problem affecting travellers in India – between 30% and 70% of people will suffer from it within two weeks of starting their trip. It's usually caused by a bacteria, and thus responds promptly to treatment with antibiotics.

Traveller's diarrhoea is defined as the passage of more

than three watery bowel actions within 24 hours, plus at least one other symptom, such as fever, cramps, nausea, vomiting or feeling generally unwell.

Treatment consists of staying well hydrated; rehydration solutions like Gastrolyte are the best for this. Antibiotics such as ciprofloxacin or azithromycin should kill the bacteria quickly. Seek medical attention quickly if you do not respond to an appropriate antibiotic.

Loperamide is just a 'stopper' and doesn't get to the cause of the problem. It can be helpful, though (eg if you have to go on a long bus ride). Don't take loperamide if you have a fever or blood in your stools.

Amoebic dysentery Amoebic dysentery is very rare in travellers but is quite often misdiagnosed by poor-quality labs. Symptoms are similar to bacterial diarrhoea: fever, bloody diarrhoea and generally feeling unwell. You should always seek reliable medical care if you have blood in your diarrhoea. Treatment involves two drugs: tinidazole or metronidazole to kill the parasite in your gut and then a second drug to kill the cysts. If left untreated complications such as liver or gut abscesses can occur.

Giardiasis Giardia is a parasite that is relatively common in travellers. Symptoms include nausea, bloating, excess gas, fatigue and intermittent diarrhoea. The parasite will eventually go away if left untreated but this can take months; the best advice is to seek medical treatment. The treatment of choice is tinidazole, with metronidazole being a second-line option.

Environmental Hazards

Air Pollution

Air pollution, particularly vehicle pollution, is an increasing problem in most of India's urban hubs. If you have severe respiratory problems, speak with your doctor before travelling to India. All travellers are advised to listen to advisories on pollution levels from the press or government officials (if the Air Quality Index measures 100 or above in any of its eight pollutant categories, this is poor). It's worth taking a disposable face mask if you are affected by air quality.

Diving & Surfing

Divers and surfers should seek specialised advice before they travel to ensure their medical kit contains treatment for coral cuts and tropical ear infections. Divers should ensure their insurance covers them for decompression illness – get specialised dive insurance through an organisation such as Divers Alert Network (www.danasiapacific.org). Certain medical conditions are incompatible with diving; check with your doctor.

Food

Dining out brings with it the possibility of contracting diarrhoea. Ways to help avoid food-related illness:

- eat only freshly cooked food
- avoid shellfish and buffets
- peel fruit
- cook vegetables
- soak salads in iodine water for at least 20 minutes
- eat in busy restaurants with a high turnover of customers.

Heat

Many parts of India, especially down south, are hot and humid throughout the year. For most visitors it takes around two weeks to comfortably adapt to the hot climate. Swelling of the feet and ankles is common, as are muscle cramps caused by excessive sweating. Prevent these by avoiding dehydration and excessive activity in the heat. Don't eat salt tablets (they aggravate the gut); drinking rehydration solution or eating salty food helps. Treat cramps by resting, rehydrating with double-strength rehydration solution and gently stretching.

Dehydration is the main contributor to heat exhaustion. Recovery is usually rapid and it is common to feel weak for some days afterwards. Symptoms include:

- feeling weak
- headache
- irritability
- nausea or vomiting
- sweaty skin
- a fast, weak pulse
- normal or slightly elevated body temperature.

Treatment:

- get out of the heat
- fan the sufferer
- apply cool, wet cloths to the skin
- lay the sufferer flat with their legs raised
- rehydrate with water containing one-quarter teaspoon of salt per litre.

CARBON-MONOXIDE POISONING

Some mountain areas rely on charcoal burners for warmth, but these should be avoided due to the risk of fatal carbon-monoxide poisoning. The thick, mattress-like blankets used in many mountain areas are amazingly warm once you get beneath the covers. If you're still cold, improvise a hot-water bottle by filling your drinking-water bottle with boiled water and covering it with a sock.

Heatstroke is a serious medical emergency. Symptoms include:

- weakness
- nausea
- a hot, dry body
- temperature of over 41°C
- dizziness
- confusion
- loss of coordination
- seizures
- eventual collapse.

Treatment:

- get out of the heat
- fan the sufferer
- apply cool, wet cloths to the skin or ice to the body, especially to the groin and armpits.

Prickly heat is a common skin rash in the tropics, caused by sweat trapped under the skin. Treat it by moving out of the heat for a few hours and by having cool showers. Creams and ointments clog the skin so they should be avoided. Locally bought prickly-heat powder can be helpful.

Altitude Sickness

If you are going to altitudes above 3000m, acute mountain sickness (AMS) is an issue. The biggest risk factor is going too high too quickly – follow a conservative acclimatisation schedule found in good trekking guides, and *never* go to a higher altitude when you have any symptoms that could be altitude related. There is no way to predict who will get altitude sickness and it is quite often the younger, fitter members of a group who succumb.

Symptoms usually develop during the first 24 hours at altitude but may be delayed up to three weeks. Mild symptoms include:

- headache
- lethargy
- dizziness
- difficulty sleeping
- loss of appetite.

AMS may become more severe without warning and can be fatal. Severe symptoms include:

- breathlessness
- a dry, irritative cough (which may progress to the production of pink, frothy sputum)
- severe headache
- lack of coordination and balance
- confusion
- irrational behaviour
- vomiting
- drowsiness
- unconsciousness.

Treat mild symptoms by resting at the same altitude until recovery, which usually takes a day or two. Paracetamol or aspirin can be taken for headaches. If symptoms persist or become worse, immediate descent is necessary; even 500m can help. Drug treatments should never be used to avoid descent or to enable further ascent.

The drugs acetazolamide and dexamethasone are recommended by some doctors for the prevention of AMS; however, their use is controversial. They can reduce the symptoms, but they may also mask warning signs; severe and fatal AMS has occurred in people taking these drugs.

To prevent AMS:

- ascend slowly – have frequent rest days, spending two to three nights at each rise of 1000m
- sleep at a lower altitude than the greatest height reached during the day, if possible. Above 3000m, don't increase sleeping altitude by more than 300m daily
- drink extra fluids
- eat light, high-carbohydrate meals
- avoid alcohol and sedatives.

Insect Bites & Stings

Bedbugs Don't carry disease but their bites can be itchy. You can treat the itch with an antihistamine.

Lice Most commonly appear on the head and pubic areas. You may need numerous applications of an antilice shampoo such as pyrethrin.

Ticks Contracted walking in rural areas. Ticks are commonly found behind the ears, on the belly and in armpits. If you have had a tick bite and have a rash at the site of the bite or elsewhere, fever or muscle aches, see a doctor.

DRINKING WATER

- Never drink tap water.
- Bottled water is generally safe – check the seal is intact at purchase.
- Avoid ice unless you know it has been made hygienically.
- Be careful of fresh juices served at street stalls in particular – they may have been watered down or may be served in unhygienic jugs/glasses.
- Boiling water is usually the most efficient method of purifying it.
- The best chemical purifier is iodine. It should not be used by pregnant women or those with thyroid problems.
- Water filters should also filter out most viruses. Ensure your filter has a chemical barrier such as iodine and a small pore size (less than four microns).

Doxycycline prevents tick-borne diseases.

Leeches Found in humid rainforest areas. They do not transmit any disease but their bites are often itchy for weeks and can easily become infected. Apply an iodine-based antiseptic to any leech bite to help prevent infection.

Bee and wasp stings Anyone with a serious bee or wasp allergy should carry an injection of adrenalin (eg an Epipen).

Skin Problems

Fungal rashes There are two common fungal rashes that affect travellers. The first occurs in moist areas, such as the groin, armpits and between the toes. It starts as a red patch that slowly spreads and is usually itchy. Treatment involves keeping the skin dry, avoiding chafing and using an antifungal cream such as clotrimazole or Lamisil. The second, *Tinea versicolor*, causes light-coloured patches, most commonly on the back, chest and shoulders. Consult a doctor.

Cuts and scratches These become easily infected in humid climates. Immediately wash all wounds in clean water and apply antiseptic. If you develop signs of infection (increasing pain and redness), see a doctor.

Sunburn

Even on a cloudy day sunburn can occur rapidly.

➡ Use a strong sunscreen (factor 50+) and reapply after a swim.

➡ Wear a wide-brimmed hat and sunglasses.

➡ Avoid lying in the sun during the hottest part of the day (10am to 2pm).

➡ Be vigilant above 3000m – you can get burnt very easily at altitude.

If you become sunburnt, stay out of the sun until you have recovered, apply cool compresses and, if necessary, take painkillers for the discomfort. One per cent hydrocortisone cream applied twice daily is also helpful.

Women's Health

For gynaecological health issues, seek out a female doctor.

Birth control Bring adequate supplies of your own form of contraception.

Sanitary products Pads, but rarely tampons, are readily available.

Thrush Heat, humidity and antibiotics can all contribute to thrush. Treatment is with antifungal creams and pessaries such as clotrimazole. A practical alternative is a single tablet of fluconazole (Diflucan).

Urinary-tract infections These can be precipitated by dehydration or long bus journeys without toilet stops; bring suitable antibiotics.

Language

The number of languages spoken in India helps explain why English is still widely spoken here, and why it's still in official use. Another 22 languages are recognised in the constitution, and more than 1600 minor languages are spoken throughout the country.

Major efforts have been made to promote Hindi as the national language of India and to gradually phase out English. However, English remains popular, and while Hindi is the predominant language in the north, it bears little relation to the Dravidian languages of the south such as Tamil. Consequently, very few people in the south speak Hindi.

Many educated Indians speak English as virtually their first language and for a large number of Indians it's their second tongue. Although you'll find it easy to get around India with English, it's always good to know a little of the local language.

HINDI

Hindi has about 600 million speakers worldwide, of which 180 million are in India. It developed from Classical Sanskrit, and is written in the Devanagari script. In 1947 it was granted official status along with English.

Most Hindi sounds are similar to their English counterparts. The main difference is that Hindi has both 'aspirated' consonants (pronounced with a puff of air, like saying 'h' after the sound) and unaspirated ones, as well as 'retroflex' (pronounced with the tongue bent backwards) and nonretroflex consonants. Our simplified pronunciation guides don't include these distinctions – read them as if they were English and you'll be understood.

Pronouncing the vowels correctly is important, especially their length (eg a and aa). The consonant combination ng after a vowel indicates nasalisation (ie the vowel is pronounced 'through the nose'). Note also that au is pronounced as the 'ow' in 'how'. Word stress is very light – we've indicated the stressed syllables with italics.

WANT MORE?

For in-depth language information and handy phrases, check out Lonely Planet's *Hindi, Urdu & Bengali Phrasebook* and *India Phrasebook*. You'll find them at **shop.lonelyplanet.com**, or you can buy Lonely Planet's iPhone phrasebooks at the Apple App Store.

Basics

Hindi verbs change form depending on the gender of the speaker (or the subject of the sentence in general), so it's the verbs, not the pronouns 'he' or 'she' (as is the case in English) which show whether the subject of the sentence is masculine or feminine. In these phrases we include the options for male and female speakers, marked 'm' and 'f' respectively.

Hello./Goodbye.	नमस्ते ।	na·ma·*ste*
Yes.	जी हाँ ।	jee haang
No.	जी नहीश् ।	jee na·*heeng*
Excuse me.	सुनिये ।	su·ni·*ye*
Sorry.	माफ़ कीजिये ।	maaf *kee*·ji·ye
Please ...	कृपया ...	kri·pa·*yaa* ...
Thank you.	थैश्क्यू ।	*thayn*·kyoo
You're welcome.	कोई बात नहीश् ।	*ko*·ee baat na·*heeng*

How are you?
आप कैसे/कैसी हैश्? — aap *kay*·se/*kay*·see hayng (m/f)

Fine. And you?
मैश् ठीक हूँ । आप सुनाइये । — mayng teek hoong aap su·*naa*·i·ye

NUMBERS – HINDI

1	१	एक	ek
2	२	दो	do
3	३	तीन	teen
4	४	चार	chaar
5	५	पाँच	paanch
6	६	छह	chay
7	७	सात	saat
8	८	आठ	aat
9	९	नौ	nau
10	१०	दस	das
20	२०	बीस	bees
30	३०	तीस	tees
40	४०	चालीस	*chaa*·lees
50	५०	पचास	pa·*chaas*
60	६०	साठ	saat
70	७०	सत्तर	*sat*·tar
80	८०	अस्सी	*as*·see
90	९०	नब्बे	*nab*·be
100	१००	सौ	sau
1000	१०००	एक हज़ार	ek ha·*zaar*

What's your name?
आप का नाम क्या है? — aap kaa naam kyaa hay

My name is ...
मेरा नाम ... है। — *me*·raa naam ... hay

Do you speak English?
क्या आपको अंग्रेज़ी आती है? — kyaa aap ko an·*gre*·zee *aa*·tee hay

I don't understand.
मैं नहीं समझा/समझी। — mayng na·*heeng* sam·jaa/ *sam*·jee (m/f)

Accommodation

Where's a ...?	... कहाँ है?	... ka·*haang* hay
guesthouse	गेस्ट हाउस	gest *haa*·us
hotel	होटल	*ho*·tal
youth hostel	यूथ हास्टल	yoot *haas*·tal

Do you have a ... room?	क्या ... कमरा है?	kyaa ... *kam*·raa hay
single	सिंगल	*sin*·gal
double	डबल	da·*bal*

How much is it per ...?	... के लिये कितने पैसे लगते हैं?	... ke li·*ye* *kit*·ne *pay*·se *lag*·te hayng
night	एक रात	ek raat
person	हर व्यक्ति	har *vyak*·ti

air-con	ए॰ सी॰	e see
bathroom	बाथरूम	*baat*·room
hot water	गर्म पानी	garm *paa*·nee
mosquito net	मसहरी	*mas*·ha·ree
washerman	धोबी	do·*bee*
window	खिड़की	*kir*·kee

Directions

Where's ...?
... कहाँ है? — ... ka·*haang* hay

How far is it?
वह कितनी दूर है? — voh *kit*·nee door hay

What's the address?
पता क्या है? — pa·*taa* kyaa hay

Can you show me (on the map)?
(नक्शे में) दिखा सकते हैं? — (*nak*·she meng) di·*kaa* *sak*·te hayng

Turn left/right.
लेफ़्ट/राइट मुड़िये। — left/*raa*·it mu·ri·*ye*

at the corner	कोने पर	*ko*·ne par
at the traffic lights	सिगनल पर	*sig*·nal par
behind ...	... के पीछे	... ke *pee*·che
in front of ...	... के सामन	... ke *saam*·ne
near ...	... के पास	... ke paas
opposite ...	... के सामने	... ke *saam*·ne
straight ahead	सीधे	*see*·de

Eating & Drinking

What would you recommend?
आपके ख़्याल में क्या अच्छा होगा? — aap ke kyaal meng kyaa *ach*·chaa *ho*·gaa

Do you have vegetarian food?
क्या आप का खाना शाकाहारी है? — kyaa aap kaa *kaa*·naa shaa·kaa·*haa*·ree hay

I don't eat (meat).
मैं (गोश्त) नहीं खाता/खाती। — mayng (gosht) na·*heeng* *kaa*·taa/*kaa*·tee (m/f)

I'll have ...
मुझे ... दीजिये। — mu·*je* ... *dee*·ji·ye

That was delicious.
बहुत मज़ेदार हुआ। — ba·*hut* ma·ze·*daar* hu·aa

Please bring the menu/bill.
मेन्यू/बिल लाइये। — *men*·yoo/bil *laa*·i·ye

Key Words

bottle	बोतल	*bo*·tal
bowl	कटोरी	ka·*to*·ree
breakfast	नाश्ता	*naash*·taa
dessert	मीठा	*mee*·taa
dinner	रात का खाना	raat kaa *kaa*·naa
drinks	पीने की चीज़ें	*pee*·ne kee *chee*·zeng
food	खाना	*kaa*·naa
fork	काँटा	*kaan*·taa
glass	गिलास	glaas
knife	चाकू	*chaa*·koo
local eatery	ढाबा	*daa*·baa
lunch	दिन का खाना	din kaa *kaa*·naa
market	बाज़ार	*baa*·zaar
plate	प्लेट	plet
restaurant	रेस्टोरेन्ट	*res*·to·rent
set meal	थाली	*taa*·lee
snack	नाश्ता	*naash*·taa
spoon	चम्मच	*cham*·mach

Meat & Fish

beef	गाय का गोश्त	gaai kaa gosht
chicken	मुर्ग़ी	*mur*·gee
duck	बतख़	ba·*tak*
fish	मछली	*mach*·lee
goat	बकरा	*bak*·raa
lobster	बड़ी झींगा	ba·*ree jeeng*·gaa
meat	गोश्त	gosht
meatballs	कोफ़्ता	*kof*·taa
pork	सुअर का गोश्त	*su*·ar kaa gosht
prawn	झींगी मछली	*jeeng*·gee *mach*·lee
seafood	मछली	*mach*·lee

Fruit & Vegetables

apple	सेब	seb
apricot	खुबानी	ku·*baa*·nee
banana	केला	*ke*·laa
capsicum	मिर्च	mirch
carrot	गाजर	*gaa*·jar
cauliflower	फूल गोभी	pool go·*bee*
corn	मक्का	*mak*·kaa
cucumber	ककड़ी	*kak*·ree
date	खजूर	ka·*joor*
eggplant	बैंगन	*bayng*·gan
fruit	फल	pal
garlic	लहसुन	*leh*·sun
grape	अंगूर	*an*·goor
grapefruit	चकोतरा	cha·*kot*·raa
lemon	निम्बू	*nim*·boo
lentils	दाल	daal
mandarin	सन्तरा	*san*·ta·raa
mango	आम	aam
mushroom	खुम्भी	*kum*·bee
nuts	मेवे	*me*·ve
orange	नारंगी	naa·*ran*·gee
papaya	पपीता	pa·*pee*·taa
peach	आड़ू	*aa*·roo
peas	मटर	ma·*tar*
pineapple	अनन्नास	a·*nan*·naas
potato	आलू	*aa*·loo
pumpkin	कद्दू	*kad*·doo
spinach	पालक	*paa*·lak
vegetables	सब्ज़ी	*sab*·zee
watermelon	तरबूज़	*tar*·booz

Other

bread	चपाती/नान/रोटी	cha·*paa*·tee/naan/*ro*·tee
butter	मक्खन	*mak*·kan
chilli	मिर्च	mirch
chutney	चटनी	*chat*·nee
egg	अण्डे	*an*·de
honey	मधु	*ma*·dhu
ice	बर्फ़	barf
ice cream	कुल्फ़ी	*kul*·fee
pappadams	पपड़	pa·*par*
pepper	काली मिर्च	*kaa*·lee mirch
relish	अचार	a·*chaar*
rice	चावल	*chaa*·val
salt	नमक	na·*mak*
spices	मिर्च मसाला	mirch ma·*saa*·laa
sugar	चीनी	*chee*·nee
tofu	टोफू	to·*foo*

Drinks

beer	बियर	bi·*yar*
coffee	काफ़ी	*kaa*·fee
(sugarcane) juice	(गन्ने का) रस	(*gan*·ne kaa) ras
milk	दूध	dood
red wine	लाल शराब	laal sha·*raab*
sweet fruit drink	शरबत	*shar*·bat
tea	चाय	chaai
water	पानी	*paa*·nee
white wine	सफ़ेद शराब	sa·*fed* sha·*raab*
yoghurt	लस्सी	*las*·see

Emergencies

Help!	
मदद कीजिये!	ma·*dad* *kee*·ji·ye
Go away!	
जाओ!	*jaa*·o
I'm lost.	
मैश्न रास्ता भूल गया/गयी हूँ।	mayng *raas*·taa bool ga·*yaa*/ga·*yee* hoong (m/f)
Call a doctor!	
डॉक्टर को बुलाओ!	*daak*·tar ko bu·*laa*·o
Call the police!	
पुलिस को बुलाओ!	pu·*lis* ko bu·*laa*·o
I'm ill.	
मैश्न बीमार हूँ।	mayng *bee*·maar hoong
Where is the toilet?	
टॉइलेट कहाँ है?	*taa*·i·let ka·*haang* hay

Shopping & Services

I'd like to buy ...	
मुझे ... चाहिये।	mu·*je* ... *chaa*·hi·ye
I'm just looking.	
सिर्फ़ देखने आया/आयी हूँ।	sirf *dek*·ne *aa*·yaa/ *aa*·yee hoong (m/f)
Can I look at it?	
दिखाइये।	di·*kaa*·i·ye
How much is it?	
कितने का है?	*kit*·ne kaa hay
It's too expensive.	
यह बहुत महश्नगा/महश्नगी है।	yeh ba·*hut* ma·*han*·gaa/ ma·*han*·gee hay (m/f)
There's a mistake in the bill.	
बिल मेश्न गलती है।	bil meng *gal*·tee hay

bank	बैश्नक	baynk
post office	डाक ख़ाना	daak *kaa*·naa
public phone	सार्वजनिक फ़ोन	*saar*·va·ja·nik fon
tourist office	पर्यटन ऑफ़िस	*par*·ya·tan *aa*·fis

Time & Dates

What time is it?	
टाइम क्या है?	*taa*·im kyaa hay
It's (10) o'clock.	
(दस) बजे हैश्न।	(das) ba·*je* hayng
Half past (10).	
साढ़े (दस)।	*saa*·re (das)

morning	सुबह	su·*bah*
afternoon	दोपहर	*do*·pa·har
evening	शाम	shaam
Monday	सोमवार	*som*·vaar
Tuesday	मश्नगलवार	man·*gal*·vaar
Wednesday	बुधवार	*bud*·vaar
Thursday	गुरुवार	gu·ru·*vaar*
Friday	शुक्रवार	*shuk*·ra·vaar
Saturday	शनिवार	sha·ni·*vaar*
Sunday	रविवार	ra·vi·*vaar*

Transport

When's the ... (bus)?	... (बस) कब जाती है?	... (bas) kab *jaa*·tee hay
first	पहली	*peh*·lee
last	आख़िरी	*aa*·ki·ree

bicycle rickshaw	साइकिल रिक्शा	*saa*·i·kil *rik*·shaa
boat	जहाज़	ja·*haaz*
bus	बस	bas
plane	हवाई जहाज़	ha·*vaa*·ee ja·*haaz*
train	ट्रेन	tren

a ... ticket	के लिये ... टिकट दीजिये।	ke li·*ye* ... ti·*kat* *dee*·ji·ye
one-way	एक तरफ़ा	ek ta·ra·*faa*
return	आने जाने का	*aa*·ne *jaa*·ne kaa

bus stop	बस स्टॉप	bas *is*·taap
ticket office	टिकटघर	ti·*kat*·gar
timetable	समय सारणी	sa·*mai* *saa*·ra·nee
train station	स्टेशन	*ste*·shan

Does it stop at ...?	
क्या ... मेश्न रुकती है?	kyaa ... meng *ruk*·tee hay
Please tell me when we get to ...	
जब ... आता है, मुझे बताइये।	jab ... *aa*·taa hay mu·*je* ba·*taa*·i·ye
Please go straight to this address.	
इसी जगह को फ़ौरन जाइए।	*is*·ee *ja*·gah ko *fau*·ran *jaa*·i·ye
Please stop here.	
यहाँ रुकिये।	ya·*haang* ru·ki·*ye*

TAMIL

Tamil is the official language in the South Indian state of Tamil Nadu. It's one of the major Dravidian languages of South India, with records of its existence going back more than 2000 years. Tamil has about 62 million speakers in India.

Like Hindi, the Tamil sound system includes a number of 'retroflex' consonants (pronounced with the tongue bent backwards). Unlike Hindi, however, Tamil has no 'aspirated' sounds (pronounced with a puff of air). Our simplified pronunciation guides don't distinguish the retroflex consonants from their nonretroflex counterparts – just read the guides as if they were English and you'll be understood. Note that aw is pronounced as in 'law' and ow as in 'how'. The stressed syllables are indicated with italics.

Basics

Hello.	வணக்கம்.	va·*nak*·kam
Goodbye.	போய் வருகிறேன்.	*po*·i va·*ru*·ki·reyn
Yes./No.	ஆமாம்./இல்லை.	*aa*·maam/*il*·lai
Excuse me.	தயவு செய்து.	ta·ya·*vu* sei·*du*
Sorry.	மன்னிக்கவும.	*man*·nik·ka·vum
Please.	தயவு செய்து.	ta·ya·*vu* chey·*tu*
Thank you.	நன்றி.	*nan*·dri

Do you speak English?
நீங்கள் ஆங்கிலம் பேசுவீரகளா? — *neeng*·kal *aang*·ki·lam pey·chu·*veer*·ka·la

I don't understand.
எனக்கு விளங்கவில்லை. — e·*nak*·ku vi·*lang*·ka·vil·*lai*

Accommodation

Where's a ... nearby?	அருகே ஒரு ... எங்கே உள்ளது?	a·ru·*ke* o·*ru* ... eng·ke *ul*·la·tu
guesthouse	விருந்தினர் இல்லம	vi·*run*·ti·nar *il*·lam
hotel	ஹோட்டல	*hot*·tal
Do you have a ... room?	உங்களிடம் ஓர் ... அறை உள்ளதா?	*ung*·ka·li·tam awr ... a·*rai* *ul*·la·taa
single	தன	ta·*ni*
double	இரட்டை	i·rat·*tai*
How much is it per ...?	ஓர் ... என்னவிலை?	awr ... *en*·na·vi·lai
night	இரவுக்கு	i·ra·*vuk*·ku
person	ஒருவருக்கு	o·ru·va·*ruk*·ku

NUMBERS – TAMIL

1	ஒன்று	on·*dru*
2	இரண்டு	i·*ran*·tu
3	மூன்று	*moon*·dru
4	நான்கு	naan·*ku*
5	ஐந்து	ain·*tu*
6	ஆறு	*aa*·ru
7	ஏழு	*ey*·zu
8	எட்டு	et·*tu*
9	ஒன்பது	on·pa·*tu*
10	பத்து	pat·*tu*
20	இருபது	i·ru·pa·*tu*
30	முப்பது	mup·pa·*tu*
40	நாற்பது	naar·pa·*tu*
50	ஐம்பது	aim·pa·*tu*
60	அறுபது	a·ru·pa·*tu*
70	எழுபது	e·zu·pa·*tu*
80	எண்பது	en·pa·*tu*
90	தொன்னூறு	ton·noo·*ru*
100	நூறு	noo·*ru*
1000	ஓராயிரம்	*aw*·raa·yi·ram

air-conditioned	குளிர்சாதன வசதியுடையது	ku·*lir*·chaa·ta·na va·*cha*·ti·yu·*tai*·ya·tu
bathroom	குளியலறை	ku·li·*ya*·la·rai
bed	படுக்கை	pa·*tuk*·kai
window	சன்னல	*chan*·nal

Eating & Drinking

Can you recommend a ...?	நீங்கள் ஒரு ... பரிந்துரைக்க முடியுமா?	*neeng*·kal o·*ru* ... pa·rin·tu·*raik*·ka mu·ti·*yu*·maa
bar	பார்	paar
dish	உணவு வகை	u·na·*vu* va·*kai*
place to eat	உணவகம்	u·na·va·*ham*
I'd like (a/the) ..., please.	எனக்கு தயவு செய்து ... கொடுங்கள்.	e·*nak*·ku ta·ya·*vu* chey·*tu* ... ko·*tung*·kal
bill	விலைச்சீட்டு	vi·*laich*·cheet·tu
menu	உணவுப்– பட்டியல்	u·na·*vup*·pat·ti·yal
that dish	அந்த உணவு வகை	*an*·ta u·na·*vu* va·*hai*

Do you have vegetarian food?
உங்களிடம சைவ உணவு உள்ளதா? — *ung*·ka·li·tam *chai*·va u·na·*vu* *ul*·la·taa

Emergencies

Help!	உதவ!	u·ta·*vi*
Go away!	போய் விடு!	*pow*·i *vi*·tu

Call a doctor!
ஐ அழைக்கவும் ஒரு மருத்துவர்! — i a·*zai*·ka·vum o·*ru* ma·*rut*·tu·var

Call the police!
ஐ அழைக்கவும் போலிஸ! — i a·*zai*·ka·vum pow·*lees*

I'm lost.
நான் வழி தவறி போய்விட்டேன். — naan va·*zi* ta·va·*ri* pow·i·*vit*·teyn

Where are the toilets?
கழிவறைகள் எங்கே? — ka·*zi*·va·rai·kal *eng*·key

Shopping & Services

Where's the market?
எங்கே சந்தை இருக்கிறது? — *eng*·key *chan*·tai i·*ruk*·ki·ra·tu

Can I look at it?
நான் இதைப் பார்க்கலாமா? — naan i·*taip* *paark*·ka·laa·maa

How much is it?
இது என்ன விலை? — i·*tu* *en*·na vi·*lai*

That's too expensive.
அது அதிக விலையாக இருக்கிறது. — a·*tu* a·*ti*·ka vi·*lai*·yaa·ka i·*ruk*·ki·ra·tu

bank	வங்கி	*vang*·ki
internet	இணையம்	i·nai·*yam*
post office	தபால் நிலையம்	ta·*paal* ni·*lai*·yam
tourist office	சுற்றுப்பயண அலுவலகம்	chut·*rup*·pa·ya·na a·lu·va·la·*kam*

Time & Dates

What time is it?
மணி என்ன? — ma·*ni* *en*·na

It's (two) o'clock.
மணி (இரண்டு). — ma·*ni* (i·*ran*·tu)

Half past (two).
(இரண்டு) முப்பது. — (i·*ran*·tu) mup·pa·*tu*

yesterday	நேற்று	*neyt*·tru
today	இன்று	in·*dru*
tomorrow	நாளை	*naa*·lai
morning	காலை	kaa·*lai*
evening	மாலை	maa·*lai*
night	இரவு	i·ra·*vu*
Monday	திங்கள்	*ting*·kal
Tuesday	செவ்வாய்	chev·*vai*
Wednesday	புதன்	pu·*tan*
Thursday	வியாழன்	vi·*yaa*·zan
Friday	வெள்ளி	vel·*li*
Saturday	சனி	cha·*ni*
Sunday	ஞாயிறு	*nyaa*·yi·ru

Transport & Directions

Where's the ...?
... எங்கே இருக்கிறது? — ... *eng*·key i·*ruk*·ki·ra·tu

What's the address?
விலாசம் என்ன? — vi·*laa*·cham *en*·na

Can you show me (on the map)?
எனக்கு (வரைபடத்தில்) காட்ட முடியுமா? — e·*nak*·ku (va·*rai*·pa·*tat*·til) *kaat*·ta mu·ti·yu·*maa*

Is this the ... to (New Delhi)?	இது தானா (புது– டில்லிக்குப்) புறப்படும் ...?	i·*tu* taa·*naa* (pu·*tu* til·lik·*kup*) pu·*rap*·pa·tum ...
bus	பஸ்	pas
plane	விமானம்	vi·*maa*·nam
train	இரயில்	i·ra·*yil*

One ... ticket (to Madurai), please.	(மதுரைக்கு) தயவு செய்து ... டிக்கட் கொடுங்கள்.	(ma·tu·raik·*ku*) ta·ya·*vu* chey·*tu* ... tik·*kat* ko·tung·*kal*
one-way	ஒரு வழிப்பயண	o·*ru* va·*zip*·pa·ya·na
return	இரு வழிப்பயண	i·*ru* va·*zip*·pa·ya·na

bicycle	சைக்கிள்	*chaik*·kil
boat	படகு	pa·ta·*ku*
bus stop	பஸ் நிறுத்தும்	pas ni·*rut*·tum
economy class	சிக்கன வகுப்பு	*chik*·ka·na va·*kup*·pu
first class	முதல் வகுப்பு	mu·*tal* va·*kup*·pu
motorcycle	மோட்டார் சைக்கிள்	*mowt*·taar *chaik*·kil
train station	நிலையம்	ni·*lai*·yam

What time's the first/last bus?
எத்தனை மணிக்கு முதல்/இறுதி பஸ் வரும்? — *et*·ta·nai ma·*nik*·ku mu·*tal*/i·ru·*ti* pas va·*rum*

How long does the trip take?
பயணம் எவ்வளவு நேரம் எடுக்கும்? — pa·ya·*nam* ev·*va*·la·vu ney·*ram* e·*tuk*·kum

GLOSSARY

Adivasis – tribal people

Ardhanarishvara – *Shiva*'s half-male, half-female form

Arjuna – Mahabharata hero and military commander; he had the *Bhagavad Gita* related to him by *Krishna*.

Aryan – Sanskrit for 'noble'; those who migrated from Persia and settled in northern India

ashram – spiritual community or retreat

ASI – Archaeological Survey of India; an organisation involved in monument preservation

autorickshaw – noisy, three-wheeled, motorised contraption for transporting passengers, livestock etc for short distances; found throughout the country, they are cheaper than taxis

Avalokitesvara – in Mahayana Buddhism, the *bodhisattva* of compassion

avatar – incarnation, usually of a deity

ayurveda – ancient and complex science of Indian herbal medicine and holistic healing

azad – Urdu for 'free', as in Azad Jammu and Kashmir

Baba – religious master or father; term of respect

bagh – garden

bahadur – brave or chivalrous; an honorific title

baksheesh – tip, donation (alms) or bribe

banyan – Indian fig tree; spiritual to many Indians

baoli – see *baori*

baori – well, particularly a step-well with landings and galleries; in Gujarat it is more commonly referred to as a *baoli*

barasingha – deer

basti – slum

bearer – like a butler

Bhagavad Gita – Hindu Song of the Divine One; Krishna's lessons to *Arjuna*, the main thrust of which was to emphasise the philosophy of *bhakti*; it is part of the Mahabharata

bhajan – devotional song

bhakti – surrendering to the gods; faith, devotion

bhang – dried leaves and flowering shoots of the marijuana plant

bhangra – rhythmic Punjabi music/dance

Bharat – Hindi for India

bhavan – house, building; also spelt bhawan

Bhima – Mahabharata hero; the brother of Hanuman, husband of Hadimba, father of Ghatotkach, and renowned for his great strength

bindi – forehead mark (often dot-shaped) made from *kumkum*, worn by women

BJP – Bharatiya Janata Party

Bodhi Tree – tree under which *Buddha* sat when he attained enlightenment

bodhisattva – enlightened beings

Bollywood – India's answer to Hollywood; the film industry of Mumbai (Bombay)

Brahma – Hindu god; worshipped as the creator in the Trimurti

Brahmanism – early form of Hinduism that evolved from Vedism (see *Vedas*); named after *Brahmin* priests and *Brahma*

Brahmin – member of the priest/scholar caste, the highest Hindu caste

Buddha – Awakened One; the originator of *Buddhism*; also regarded by Hindus as the ninth incarnation of *Vishnu*

Buddhism – see *Early Buddhism*

cantonment – administrative and military area of a Raj-era town

Carnatic music – classical music of South India

caste – a Hindu's hereditary station (social standing) in life; there are four main castes: Brahmin, Kshatriya, Vaishya and Shudra

chaam – ritual masked dance performed by some Buddhist monks in gompas to celebrate the victory of good over evil and of Buddhism over preexisting religions

chaitya – prayer room; assembly hall

chakra – focus of one's spiritual power; disc-like weapon of *Vishnu*

Chamunda – form of Durga; armed with a scimitar, noose and mace, and clothed in elephant hide, her mission was to kill the demons Chanda and Munda

chandra – moon, or the moon as a god

Chandragupta – Indian ruler in the 3rd century BC

chappals – sandals or leather thonglike footwear; flip-flops

char dham – four pilgrimage destinations of Badrinath, Kedarnath, Yamunotri and Gangotri

charas – resin of the marijuana plant; also referred to as hashish

charbagh – formal Persian garden, divided into quarters (literally 'four gardens')

chedi – see *chaitya*

chhatri – cenotaph (literally 'umbrella'), or pavilion

chikan – embroidered cloth (speciality of Lucknow)

chillum – pipe of a hookah; commonly used to describe the pipes used for smoking ganja (marijuana)

chinkara – gazelle

chital – spotted deer

chogyal – king

choli – sari blouse

chorten – Tibetan for stupa

choultry – pilgrim's rest house; also called dharamsala

chowk – town square, intersection or marketplace

Cong (I) – Congress Party of India; also known as Congress (I)

coracle – a small, traditional keel-less boat, often round or oval in shape, comprising a wickerwork or lath frame over which greased cloth or hide is stretched

dagoba – see *stupa*

Dalit – preferred term for India's Untouchable caste; see also *Harijan*

dargah – shrine or place of burial of a Muslim saint

darshan – offering or audience with a deity
deul – temple sanctuary
Devi – *Shiva*'s wife; goddess
dhaba – basic restaurant or snack bar
dham – holiest pilgrimage places of India
dharamsala – pilgrim's rest house
dharma – for Hindus, the moral code of behaviour or social duty; for Buddhists, following the law of nature, or path, as taught by Buddha
dhobi – person who washes clothes; commonly referred to as dhobi-wallah
dhobi ghat – place where clothes are washed
dhoti – long loincloth worn by men; like a lungi, but the ankle-length cloth is then pulled up between the legs
Digambara – 'Sky-Clad'; Jain group that demonstrates disdain for worldly goods by going naked
diwan – principal officer in a princely state; royal court or council
Diwan-i-Am – hall of public audience
Diwan-i-Khas – hall of private audience
dowry – money and/or goods given by a bride's parents to their son-in-law's family; it's illegal but still widely exists in many arranged marriages
Draupadi – wife of the five Pandava princes in the *Mahabharata*
Dravidian – general term for the cultures and languages of the deep south of India, including Tamil, Malayalam, Telugu and Kannada
dukhang – Tibetan prayer hall
dun – valley
dupatta – long scarf for women often worn with the *salwar kameez*
durbar – royal court; also a government
Durga – the Inaccessible; a form of *Shiva*'s wife, Devi, a beautiful, fierce woman riding a tiger/lion; a major goddess of the *Shakti* order
Early Buddhism – any of the schools of Buddhism established directly after Buddha's death and before the advent of Mahayana; a modern form is the Theravada (Teaching of the Elders) practised in Sri Lanka and Southeast Asia; Early Buddhism differed from the Mahayana in that it did not teach the *bodhisattva* ideal

gabba – appliquéd Kashmiri rug
gali – lane or alleyway
Ganesh – Hindu god of good fortune; elephant-headed son of *Shiva* and Parvati, he is also known as Ganpati and his vehicle is Mooshak (a ratlike creature)
Ganga – Hindu goddess representing the sacred Ganges River; said to flow from *Vishnu*'s toe
ganj – market
gaon – village
garh – fort
Garuda – man-bird vehicle of *Vishnu*
gaur – Indian bison
Gayatri – sacred verse of Rig-Veda repeated mentally by Brahmins twice a day
geyser – hot-water unit found in many bathrooms
ghat – steps or landing on a river; a range of hills or a road up hills
giri – hill
gompa – Tibetan Buddhist monastery
Gopala – see *Govinda*
gopi – milkmaid; Krishna was fond of them
gopuram – soaring pyramidal gateway tower of Dravidian temples
Govinda – Krishna as a cowherd; also just cowherd
gumbad – dome on an Islamic tomb or mosque
gurdwara – Sikh temple
guru – holy teacher; in Sanskrit literally 'goe' (darkness) and 'roe' (to dispel)
Guru Granth Sahib – Sikh holy book

haat – village market
haj – Muslim pilgrimage to Mecca
haji – Muslim who has made the haj
hammam – Turkish bath; public bathhouse
Hanuman – Hindu monkey god, prominent in the Ramayana, and a follower of Rama
Hari – another name for *Vishnu*
Harijan – name (no longer considered acceptable) given by Mahatma Gandhi to India's Untouchable caste, meaning 'children of god'
hashish – see *charas*
hathi – elephant
haveli – traditional, often ornately decorated, residences, particularly those found in Rajasthan and Gujarat
hijab – headscarf used by Muslim women
hijra – eunuch, transvestite
hookah – water pipe used for smoking marijuana or strong tobacco
howdah – seat for carrying people on an elephant's back

ikat – fabric made with thread which is tie-dyed before weaving
imam – Muslim religious leader
imambara – tomb dedicated to a Shiite Muslim holy man
Indo-Saracenic – style of colonial architecture that integrated Western designs with Islamic, Hindu and Jain influences
Indra – significant and prestigious Vedic god; god of rain, thunder, lightning and war

jagamohan – assembly hall
Jagannath – Lord of the Universe; a form of Krishna
jali – carved lattice (often marble) screen; also refers to the holes or spaces produced through carving timber or stone
Jataka – tale from Buddha's various lives
jauhar – ritual mass suicide by immolation, traditionally performed by Rajput women at times of military defeat to avoid being dishonoured by their captors
jhula – bridge
ji – honorific that can be added to the end of almost anything as

a form of respect; thus 'Babaji', 'Gandhiji'
jooti – traditional, often pointy-toed, slip-in shoes; commonly found in North India
juggernaut – huge, extravagantly decorated temple 'car' dragged through the streets during certain Hindu festivals
jyoti linga – naturally occurring lingam believed to derive currents of *Shakti*

kabaddi – traditional game (similar to tag)
Kailasa – sacred Himalayan mountain; home of *Shiva*
Kali – ominous-looking evil-destroying form of Devi; commonly depicted with dark skin, dripping with blood, and wearing a necklace of skulls
Kama – Hindu god of love
Kama Sutra – ancient Sanskrit text largely covering the subjects of love and sexuality
kameez – woman's shirtlike tunic; see also *salwar kameez*
karma – Hindu, Buddhist and Sikh principle of retributive justice for past deeds
khadi – homespun cloth; Mahatma Gandhi encouraged people to spin this rather than buy English cloth
Khalsa – Sikh brotherhood
Khan – Muslim honorific title
khur – Asiatic wild ass
kirtan – Sikh devotional singing
koil – Hindu temple
kolam – see *rangoli*
kot – fort
kothi – residence or mansion
kotwali – police station
Krishna – *Vishnu*'s eighth incarnation, often coloured blue; he revealed the *Bhagavad Gita* to *Arjuna*
kumkum – coloured powder used for *bindi* dots
kund – lake or tank; Toda village
kurta – long shirt with either short collar or no collar

Lakshmana – half-brother and aide of Rama in the Ramayana
Lakshmi – *Vishnu*'s consort, Hindu goddess of wealth; she sprang forth from the ocean holding a lotus
lama – Tibetan Buddhist priest or monk
Laxmi – see *Lakshmi*
lingam – phallic symbol; auspicious symbol of *Shiva*; plural 'linga'
lok – people
Lok Sabha – lower house in the Indian parliament (House of the People)
Losar – Tibetan New Year
lungi – worn by men, this loose, coloured garment (similar to a sarong) is pleated by the wearer at the waist to fit

madrasa – Islamic seminary
maha – prefix meaning 'great'
Mahabharata – Great Hindu Vedic epic poem of the Bharata dynasty; containing approximately 10,000 verses describing the battle between the Pandavas and the Kauravas
Mahakala – Great Time; *Shiva* and one of 12 jyoti linga (sacred shrines)
mahal – house or palace
maharaja – literally 'great king'; princely ruler
maharana – see *maharaja*
maharani – wife of a princely ruler or a ruler in her own right
maharao – see *maharaja*
maharawal – see *maharaja*
mahatma – literally 'great soul'
Mahavir – last tirthankar
Mahayana – the 'greater-vehicle' of Buddhism; a later adaptation of the teaching that lays emphasis on the *bodhisattva* ideal, teaching the renunciation of nirvana in order to help other beings along the way to enlightenment
maidan – open (often grassed) area; parade ground
Maitreya – future Buddha
mandal – shrine
mandala – circle; symbol used in Hindu and Buddhist art to symbolise the universe
mandapa – pillared pavilion, temple forechamber
mandi – market
mandir – temple
mani stone – stone carved with the Tibetan-Buddhist mantra 'Om mani padme hum' ('Hail the jewel in the lotus')
mani walls – Tibetan stone walls with sacred inscriptions
mantra – sacred word or syllable used by Buddhists and Hindus to aid concentration; metrical psalms of praise found in the *Vedas*
Maratha – central Indian people who controlled much of India at various times and fought the Mughals and Rajputs
marg – road
masjid – mosque
mata – mother
math – monastery
maya – illusion
mehndi – henna; ornate henna designs on women's hands (and often feet), traditionally for certain festivals or ceremonies (eg marriage)
mela – fair or festival
mithuna – pairs of men and women; often seen in temple sculpture
Moghul – see *Mughal*
monsoon – rainy season
muezzin – one who calls Muslims to prayer, traditionally from the minaret of a mosque
Mughal – Muslim dynasty of subcontinental emperors from Babur to Aurangzeb
Mumbaikar – resident of Mumbai (Bombay)

namaste – traditional Hindu greeting (hello or goodbye), often accompanied by a respectful small bow with the hands together at the chest or head level
Nanda – cowherd who raised Krishna
Nandi – bull, vehicle of *Shiva*
Narayan – incarnation of *Vishnu* the creator
Nataraja – *Shiva* as the cosmic dancer
nawab – Muslim ruling prince or powerful landowner
Naxalites – ultra-leftist political movement begun in West Bengal as a peasant rebellion; characterised by violence
nilgai – antelope

nirvana – ultimate aim of Buddhists and the final release from the cycle of existence
niwas – house, building
nizam – hereditary title of the rulers of Hyderabad
nullah – ditch or small stream

Om – sacred invocation representing the essence of the divine principle; for Buddhists, if repeated often enough with complete concentration, it leads to a state of emptiness
Osho – the late Bhagwan Shree Rajneesh, a popular, controversial guru

paan – mixture of betel nut and leaves for chewing
padma – lotus; another name for the Hindu goddess Lakshmi
pagoda – see *stupa*
paise – the Indian rupee is divided into 100 paise
palanquin – boxlike enclosure carried on poles on four bearer's shoulders; the occupant sits inside on a seat
Pali – the language, related to Sanskrit, in which the Buddhist scriptures were recorded; scholars still refer to the original Pali texts
pandal – marquee; temple shrine
Parsi – adherent of the Zoroastrian faith
Partition – formal division of British India in 1947 into two separate countries, India and Pakistan
Parvati – another form of Devi
pashmina – fine woollen shawl
PCO – Public Call Office, from where you can make local, interstate and international phone calls
peepul – fig tree, especially a bo tree
peon – lowest-grade clerical worker
pietra dura – marble inlay work characteristic of the Taj Mahal
pradesh – state
pranayama – study of breath control; meditative practice
prasad – temple-blessed food offering
puja – literally 'respect'; offering or prayers
pukka – proper; a Raj-era term
punka – cloth fan, swung by pulling a cord
Puranas – set of 18 encyclopaedic Sanskrit stories, written in verse, relating to the three gods, dating from the 5th century AD
purdah – custom among some conservative Muslims (also adopted by some Hindus, especially the Rajputs) of keeping women in seclusion; veiled
Purnima – full moon; considered to be an auspicious time

qawwali – Islamic devotional singing
qila – fort
Quran – the holy book of Islam, also spelt Koran

Radha – Krishna's consort and the most revered of the gopis
raga – any of several conventional patterns of melody and rhythm that form the basis for freely interpreted compositions
railhead – station or town at the end of a railway line; termination point
raj – rule or sovereignty; British Raj (sometimes just Raj) refers to British rule
raja – king; sometimes rana
rajkumar – prince
Rajput – Hindu warrior caste, former rulers of northwestern India
Rama – seventh incarnation of *Vishnu*
Ramadan – Islamic holy month of sunrise-to-sunset fasting (no eating, drinking or smoking); also referred to as Ramazan
Ramayana – story of Rama and Sita and their conflict with Ravana; one of India's best-known epics
rana – king; sometimes raja
rangoli – elaborate chalk, rice-paste or coloured powder design; also known as kolam
rani – female ruler or wife of a king
ranns – deserts
rath – temple chariot or car used in religious festivals
rathas – rock-cut Dravidian temples
Ravana – demon king of Lanka who abducted Sita; the titanic battle between him and Rama is told in the Ramayana
rickshaw – small, two- or three-wheeled passenger vehicle
Rig-Veda – original and longest of the four main *Vedas*
rishi – any poet, philosopher, saint or sage; originally a sage to whom the hymns of the *Vedas* were revealed
Road – railway town that serves as a communication point to a larger town off the line, eg Mt Abu and Abu Road
Rukmani – wife of Krishna; died on his funeral pyre

sadar – main
sadhu – ascetic, holy person, one who is trying to achieve enlightenment; often addressed as 'swamiji' or 'babaji'
sagar – lake, reservoir
sahib – respectful title applied to a gentleman
salai – road
salwar – trousers usually worn with a kameez
salwar kameez – traditional dresslike tunic and trouser combination for women
samadhi – in Hinduism, ecstatic state, sometimes defined as 'ecstasy, trance, communion with God'; in Buddhism, concentration; also a place where a holy man has been cremated/buried, usually venerated as a shrine
sambar – deer
samsara – Buddhists, Hindus and Sikhs believe earthly life is cyclical; you are born again and again, the quality of these rebirths being dependent upon your karma in previous lives
sangha – community of Buddhist monks and nuns
Saraswati – wife of Brahma, goddess of learning; sits on a white swan, holding a veena (a type of string instrument)
Sat Sri Akal – Sikh greeting
Sati – wife of *Shiva*; became a sati ('honourable woman') by immolating herself; although banned more than a century

ago, the act of sati is still (very) occasionally performed

satra – Hindu Vaishnavaite monastery and centre for art

satyagraha – nonviolent protest involving a hunger strike, popularised by Mahatma Gandhi; from Sanskrit, literally meaning 'insistence on truth'

Scheduled Castes – official term used for the Untouchable or Dalit caste

Shaivism – worship of *Shiva*

Shaivite – follower of *Shiva*

shakti – creative energies perceived as female deities; devotees follow Shaktism order

sheesha – see *hookah*

shikara – gondola-like boat used on lakes in Srinagar (Kashmir)

shikhar – hunting expedition

Shiva – Destroyer; also the Creator, in which form he is worshipped as a lingam

shola – virgin forest

shree – see *shri*

shri – honorific male prefix; Indian equivalent of 'Respected Sir'

Shudra – caste of labourers

sikhara – Hindu temple-spire or temple

Singh – literally 'lion'; a surname adopted by Sikhs

Sita – Hindu goddess of agriculture; more commonly associated with the Ramayana

sitar – Indian stringed instrument

Siva – see *Shiva*

sree – see *shri*

sri – see *shri*

stupa – Buddhist religious monument composed of a solid hemisphere topped by a spire, containing relics of Buddha; also known as a *dagoba* or *pagoda*

Subhadra – Krishna's incestuous sister

Sufi – Muslim mystic

Sufism – Islamic mysticism

Surya – the sun; a major deity in the *Vedas*

sutra – string; list of rules expressed in verse

swami – title of respect meaning 'lord of the self'; given to initiated Hindu monks

tabla – twin drums

tal – lake

tank – reservoir; pool or large receptacle of holy water found at some temples

tantric Buddhism – Tibetan Buddhism with strong sexual and occult overtones

tempo – noisy three-wheeler public transport vehicle, bigger than an *autorickshaw*; see *Vikram*

thakur – nobleman

thangka – Tibetan cloth painting

theertham – temple tank

Theravada – orthodox form of Buddhism practised in Sri Lanka and Southeast Asia that is characterised by its adherence to the Pali canon; literally 'dwelling'

tikka – mark Hindus put on their foreheads

tirthankars – the 24 great Jain teachers

tonga – two-wheeled horse or pony carriage

torana – architrave over a temple entrance

trekkers – jeeps; hikers

Trimurti – triple form or three-faced; the Hindu triad of *Brahma*, *Shiva* and *Vishnu*

Untouchable – lowest caste or 'casteless', for whom the most menial tasks are reserved; the name derives from the belief that higher castes risk defilement if they touch one; formerly known as *Harijan*, now *Dalit*

Upanishads – esoteric doctrine; ancient texts forming part of the *Vedas*; delving into weighty matters such as the nature of the universe and soul

urs – death anniversary of a revered Muslim; festival in memory of a Muslim saint

Valmiki – author of the Ramayana

Vedas – Hindu sacred books; collection of hymns composed in preclassical Sanskrit during the second millennium BC and divided into four books: Rig-Veda, Yajur-Veda, Sama-Veda and Atharva-Veda

vihara – Buddhist monastery, generally with central court or hall off which open residential cells, usually with a Buddha shrine at one end; resting place

vikram – tempo or a larger version of the standard tempo

vimana – principal part of Hindu temple; a tower over the sanctum

vipassana – insight meditation technique of Theravada Buddhism in which mind and body are closely examined as changing phenomena

Vishnu – part of the Trimurti; Vishnu is the Preserver and Restorer who so far has nine *avatars*: the fish Matsya; the tortoise Kurma; the wild boar Naraha; Narasimha; Vamana; Parasurama; Rama; Krishna; and Buddha

wallah – man; added onto almost anything, eg dhobi-wallah, chai-wallah, taxi-wallah

yakshi – maiden

yali – mythical lion creature

yatra – pilgrimage

yatri – pilgrim

yogini – female goddess attendants

yoni – female fertility symbol; female genitalia

zenana – area of an upperclass home where women are secluded; women's quarters

Behind the Scenes

SEND US YOUR FEEDBACK

We love to hear from travellers – your comments keep us on our toes and help make our books better. Our well-travelled team reads every word on what you loved or loathed about this book. Although we cannot reply individually to your submissions, we always guarantee that your feedback goes straight to the appropriate authors, in time for the next edition. Each person who sends us information is thanked in the next edition – the most useful submissions are rewarded with a selection of digital PDF chapters.

Visit **lonelyplanet.com/contact** to submit your updates and suggestions or to ask for help. Our award-winning website also features inspirational travel stories, news and discussions.

Note: We may edit, reproduce and incorporate your comments in Lonely Planet products such as guidebooks, websites and digital products, so let us know if you don't want your comments reproduced or your name acknowledged. For a copy of our privacy policy visit lonelyplanet.com/privacy.

OUR READERS

Many thanks to the travellers who used the last edition and wrote to us with helpful hints, useful advice and interesting anecdotes:

A Adeline Bouchery, Amanda Larson-Mekler, Amber Richardson, Andy Foster, Ansuya Patel-Yorke, Anthony Naylon, Arpita Singh **B** Bernd Scholz, Borja Ramirez, Brett Leighton **C** Callum McQueen, Carolina Echenique, Chimmy Vyas, Chris Vaughan, Cindy Gray **D** Daniel Scott, David Wilson, Deanna D'Onofrio, Deep Grewal **E** Emanuela Milo, Erica Wijarnako **G** Gabriele Marangon, Gail Bruk-Jackson, Glenn Riddell, Grant Szuveges **H** Harry Smith, Henk Hilkmann, Hugh Connolly **I** Igor De Ruitz, Isabel Barrientos **J** James Freeborn, James Gannon, James Huxley, Jane McNab, Jessica Killaspy, Joe Morley, Josée Arsenault, Julian Trummer **K** Kai Xue, Katya Burns, Kevin Pomplun, Kirit Mehta **L** Les Sutherland, Lidor Cohen, Lisa Worthington, Lorenzo Facinelli, Lucas Almendra, Lynnell Mickelsen **M** Manish Jain, Marie Grif, Mario Tarallo, Martin Davis, Michael Bridger, Michael Hornsby, Michael Yon, Mrinal Kamat **N** Nasreen Singh, Nicholas cooper, Nick Brock, Nikola Smith, Nina Bee **O** Ofelia Diaz **P** Patricia Keith, Paul Wiegmann, Pratibha Sahu **R** Rachel Ross, Rolf Wrelf, Ronin Pierre, Rosemary O'Donnell, Roz Green **S** Sam Ewalt, Samantha Spiro, Santosh Mohanty, Sean McHugh, Shane Hussey, Stephen Grinter, Steve Hughes **T** Thomas Janssens, Tom Stuart, Tony Wheeler, Tricia Bergman **V** Van Cauwenberghe, Vanessa Bulhões, Víctor Castro, Vincent Robitaille **Z** Zachary Nowak, Zoe Evans

WRITER THANKS

Abigail Blasi

Thanks to all the people who helped me in Delhi, including my Delhi family Jyoti and Niranjan Desai, to Danish Abbas, Nicholas Thompson, Sarah Fotheringham, Toby Sinclair and the Delhi Walla himself, Mayank Austen Soofi. Special gratitude to Joe Bindloss and to all the other India authors for their help and knowledge. Huge thanks to my Mum, Ant & Luca for looking after everyone at home.

Lindsay Brown

I am very grateful for the help and encouragement provided by Satinder, Karan & Ritu and Dicky & Kavita in Jaipur, Anoop in Pushkhar, Usha in Ranthambhore, Harsh in Bikaner, Siddharth in Jaisalmer, Ramesh Jangid in Nawalgarh, Laxmi Kant Jangid in Jhunjhunu and many many others who helped out along the road. Last but not least, thanks to Jenny.

Anirban Mahapatra

My sincerest thanks above all to the amazing people of Punjab, Haryana, Kolkata, West Bengal and the Northeast States for their splendid warmth and hospitality. To Raja, Gina, Ashish, Samita, Joyita, Krishno, Sukanya, Jone, Rajib, Mamli, Oken, Sum, Richard, Kanno, Omak, Souvik, Madhuparna, George, Sheila, Mahesh, Vikas, John, Tatu, Punyo and many other wonderful souls for sharing their local knowledge and experience, inviting me into their homes, throwing me their car keys and cooking me some delicious meals along the way. Thanks to everyone at Lonely

Planet who made working on this title a breeze – cheers to all of you!

Isabella Noble

Thanks to everyone in Tamil Nadu, Ashish and Rucha Gupta and Shoshana Treichel in Chennai, Bernard Dragon and Michel Adment in Chettinadu, Raja Balasubramanian in Trichy, Junaid Sait and team in Ooty, Vijay Kumar in Kodai, and Mr Krishnamurthi on the Kanyakumari–Puducherry Express. In Madhya Pradesh, huge thanks to Belinda Wright and Saptarishi Saigal. Thanks to the dream India co-author team, especially John Noble for laughs, tips and tiger safaris. At home, extra-special thanks to Jack, Andrew and Sarah.

John Noble

So many fantastic people in India gave me help, smiles and fellowship. Extra special thanks to Balvinder, Shubhda Chaturvedi, the Dhami family, Mark Elliott, Gilbert Gillou and family, Nitesh Jaiswal, Puneetinder Kaur Sidhu, Kristina Lauer, Vaneet Rana, Saptarishi Saigal, Sagnik Sengupta, Reggie Singh, Ankit Sood, Panki Sood, Praveen Sood, Sumit Raj Vashisht and Belinda Wright. Also to Joe Bindloss for steering the ship so expertly, and above all to Isabella Noble with whom I shared the entire experience!

Kevin Raub

Thanks to my wife, Adriana Schmidt Raub, Joe Bindloss, Sarina Singh, John Noble, Izzy Noble, Paul Harding and all my partners-in-crime at LP. On the road, Anil Wadwa, Amit Arora, Dhanya Pilo, Sarita Hedge Roy, Tanvi Maidkaker, Roshnee Desai, Greg Kroitzsh, Rishupreet Oberoi, Bindu Panicker, Aditya Dhanwatay, Ashok T Kadam, Abha Lambah, Karina Aggarwal and Pankil Shah.

Michael Benanav

Huge thanks to Michael Schmid at Brown Bread Bakery in Varanasi for being incredibly helpful to many travellers, including myself, when the 'cash crisis' of 2016 struck. Thanks also to Shikha Tripathi, Sindhu Shah, Mukti Datta, John Noble, Monika Agarwal, Karan Singh, Praveen Kaushal and Mohan Rayal. As always, I'm ever grateful to Kelly and Luke for taking care of the animals and each other while I was on the road.

Mark Elliott

Enormous thanks to Rouf John & family, Tundup & Gurmet, Mikka, Darren Clarkson-King, Najum, Meraj, Shubham & Pranav, Manon, Maunil Vora, Abhishek & Pranav, Wasil Nawaz Khan, Namgyal & Sani, Christina & Tashi, Peter & Wendy, Veena & Maruti, Nittish & Sri, Tashi Tsering, Thinley, Sonam, Jamie McG, Yanin & Mushtaq, Linda, Marie & Claire. In Sikkim thanks so much to Smriti and Sartaj, Nukul, Rinjong, OT Lepcha, Karma Dorje & Minla Zaymu, Wangdi, Sonam Bhutia, Pema at Mama's, Tom, Kheli & Gili, Anuj & Sonali, Edu, Jacky, Monika & Stina, Chundip, Champala & Thendup at Gangyak, Passang, Guus, Pala, Farid Belhadj, Michael.

Paul Harding

Thanks to all my dear friends in Goa and Kerala who helped out with company, advice and friendship – you all know who you are. Thanks also to new people, travellers and locals, I met on this trip. The biggest thanks goes to Hannah and my worldly young daughter Layla for accompanying me at least part of the way and putting up with my absences at other times.

Anna Kaminski

Thank you to Joe for entrusting me with Gujarat and Odisha, and to all who've assisted me along the way, including: Abigail, Michael, Kevin, Iain (fellow scribes), Abhay, Rajiv, Saiyed, Mohammed and Anil in Ahmedabad, Jehan, Katie and Salim in Bhuj, the Singhs in Wankaner, Mustak in Jamnagar, the good people of Desia and Chandoori Sai in Odisha's tribal country, Bubu in Puri; also Debjit, Sangarmitha, the Raja of Aul and everyone who helped me during the demonetisation crisis.

Bradley Mayhew

Thanks to Norden and Thinley at Holumba Haven for their many tips and to Jigme Tshering and Bunty for showing me around Kalimpong. Tash delek to Norbu and Sangay-la in Darjeeling. Thanks also to Mithun Das in Madarihat and Gatty in Darjeeling.

Sarina Singh

Thank you to everyone who worked on this edition, with special thanks to Joe for being such a fab DE. Gratitude, also, to the many readers who took the time to send in their feedback and travel experiences – much appreciated indeed. Finally, warm thanks to my wise and wonderful parents who have always encouraged me to walk my own path.

Iain Stewart

Thanks to Trent Holden and John Noble for tips and contacts, and Joe Bindloss and the LP team in London and Melbourne. On the road I was helped by Jonty in Hyderabad, Poornima Dasharathi in Bengaluru, the teams at Golden Mist in Kodagu and Uramma in Hampi, Prakash in Vijapura, Oliver the yogi in Gokarna and Vijay in Vizag.

ACKNOWLEDGEMENTS

Climate map data adapted from Peel MC, Finlayson BL & McMahon TA (2007) 'Updated World Map of the Köppen-Geiger Climate Classification', Hydrology and Earth System Sciences, 11, 1633-44.

Illustrations pp1164–5, pp1166–7, p1168 by Kelli Hamblet; pp372–3, pp870–1 by Michael Weldon, pp62–3, pp356–7, pp638–9 by Javier Zarracina.

Cover photograph: Woman covered in coloured *gulal* (powder) celebrating Holi/THEPALMER/Getty Images©

THIS BOOK

This 17th edition of Lonely Planet's *India* guidebook was curated by Abigail Blasi, Lindsay Brown, Anirban Mahapatra, Isabella Noble, John Noble and Kevin Raub, who also researched and wrote it along with Michael Benanav, Mark Elliott, Paul Harding, Anna Kaminski, Bradley Mayhew, Sarina Singh and Iain Stewart. This guidebook was produced by the following:

Destination Editor Joe Bindloss

Product Editor Kathryn Rowan

Cartographers Lonely Planet Cartography

Book Designer Michael Buick

Assisting Editors Sarah Bailey, Judith Bamber, Imogen Bannister, Bridget Blair, Nigel Chin, Melanie Dankel, Sam Forge, Carly Hall, Helen Koehne, Kellie Langdon, Ali Lemer, Anne Mulvaney, Rosie Nicholson, Lauren O'Connell, Kristin Odijk, Ross Taylor, Saralinda Turner

Cover Researcher Naomi Parker

Thanks to Will Allen, Michelle Bennett, Hannah Cartmel, Kate Chapman, Joel Cotterell, Sasha Drew, Daniel Fahey, Gemma Graham, Shona Gray, Liz Heynes, Kate Kiely, Virginia Moreno, Catherine Naghten, Martine Power, Kirsten Rawlings, Alison Ridgway, Wibowo Rusli, Tom Stainer, Tracy Whitmey

Index

C

Map Pages **000**
Photo Pages **000**

Map Pages **000**
Photo Pages **000**

Map Pages **000**
Photo Pages **000**

I

J

Map Pages **000**
Photo Pages **000**

N

Map Pages **000**
Photo Pages **000**

Q

R

S

T

U

Map Pages **000**
Photo Pages **000**

Map Legend

Sights
- Beach
- Bird Sanctuary
- Buddhist
- Castle/Palace
- Christian
- Confucian
- Hindu
- Islamic
- Jain
- Jewish
- Monument
- Museum/Gallery/Historic Building
- Ruin
- Shinto
- Sikh
- Taoist
- Winery/Vineyard
- Zoo/Wildlife Sanctuary
- Other Sight

Activities, Courses & Tours
- Bodysurfing
- Diving
- Canoeing/Kayaking
- Course/Tour
- Sento Hot Baths/Onsen
- Skiing
- Snorkelling
- Surfing
- Swimming/Pool
- Walking
- Windsurfing
- Other Activity

Sleeping
- Sleeping
- Camping

Eating
- Eating

Drinking & Nightlife
- Drinking & Nightlife
- Cafe

Entertainment
- Entertainment

Shopping
- Shopping

Information
- Bank
- Embassy/Consulate
- Hospital/Medical
- Internet
- Police
- Post Office
- Telephone
- Toilet
- Tourist Information
- Other Information

Geographic
- Beach
- Hut/Shelter
- Lighthouse
- Lookout
- Mountain/Volcano
- Oasis
- Park
- Pass
- Picnic Area
- Waterfall

Population
- Capital (National)
- Capital (State/Province)
- City/Large Town
- Town/Village

Transport
- Airport
- Border crossing
- Bus
- Cable car/Funicular
- Cycling
- Ferry
- Metro station
- Monorail
- Parking
- Petrol station
- Subway station
- Taxi
- Train station/Railway
- Tram
- Underground station
- Other Transport

Note: Not all symbols displayed above appear on the maps in this book

Routes
- Tollway
- Freeway
- Primary
- Secondary
- Tertiary
- Lane
- Unsealed road
- Road under construction
- Plaza/Mall
- Steps
- Tunnel
- Pedestrian overpass
- Walking Tour
- Walking Tour detour
- Path/Walking Trail

Boundaries
- International
- State/Province
- Disputed
- Regional/Suburb
- Marine Park
- Cliff
- Wall

Hydrography
- River, Creek
- Intermittent River
- Canal
- Water
- Dry/Salt/Intermittent Lake
- Reef

Areas
- Airport/Runway
- Beach/Desert
- Cemetery (Christian)
- Cemetery (Other)
- Glacier
- Mudflat
- Park/Forest
- Sight (Building)
- Sportsground
- Swamp/Mangrove

Anna Kaminski

Odisha, Gujarat For as long as Anna has been travelling in India, she's been enchanted and exasperated by the country in equal measure, and never ever bored. This trip was no exception. Cons? The demonetisation crisis. Pros? Exploring two vastly different corners of the country. Highlights included the ancient architecture of Ahmedabad, spending time in traditional villages in Odisha's tribal country, lion-spotting in Sasan Gir National Park and witnessing first-hand the centuries-old craft kept alive in the villages of Kachchh.

Bradley Mayhew

Bihar & Jharkhand, West Bengal & Darjeeling Bradley has been writing guidebooks for 20 years now. He started travelling while studying Chinese at Oxford University, and has since focused his expertise on China, Tibet, the Himalaya and Central Asia. He is the co-author of Lonely Planet guides to Tibet, Nepal, Trekking in the Nepal Himalaya, Bhutan, Central Asia and many others. Bradley has also fronted two TV series for Arte and SWR, one retracing the route of Marco Polo via Turkey, Iran, Afghanistan, Central Asia and China, and the other trekking Europe's ten most scenic long-distance trails.

Iain Stewart

Karnataka, Telangana & Andhra Pradesh Iain's trained as a journalist and worked as reporter and restaurant critic in London in the 1990s. He started writing guidebooks in 1997 and has penned more than 60 titles for destinations as diverse as Ibiza and Cambodia. For Lonely Planet, Iain's worked on books including Mexico, Indonesia, Croatia, Vietnam, India, Sri Lanka and Central America. Other passions include tennis, scuba and freediving. He'll consider working anywhere there's a palm tree or two and a beach of a generally sandy persuasion. Home is Brighton, UK, within firing range of the city's south-facing horizon. He tweets at @iaintravel.

Contributing Writer Joe Bindloss wrote the History and India Today chapters.

John Noble

Himachal Pradesh, Madhya Pradesh & Chattisgarh John has been travelling since his teens and doing so as a Lonely Planet writer since the 1980s. The number of LP titles he's written or co-written is well into three figures, covering a somewhat random selection of countries scattered across the globe, predominantly ones where Spanish, Russian or English are spoken (usually alongside numerous local languages). He still gets as excited as ever about heading out on the road to unfamiliar experiences, people and destinations, especially remote, off-the-beaten-track ones. Above all, he loves mountains, from the English Lake District to the Himalaya. See his pics on Instagram: @johnnoble11.

Kevin Raub

Mumbai, Maharashtra Kevin Raub grew up in Atlanta and started his career as a music journalist in New York, working for *Men's Journal* and *Rolling Stone* magazines. Being a pursuer of hops himself, he was all too happy to put Kingfisher in his rearview drinking mirror and immerse himself in Mumbai's exploding craft beer scene for this edition of the India guide. This is Kevin's 40th Lonely Planet guide. Follow him on Twitter and Instagram (@RaubOnTheRoad). To learn more about Kevin, check out www.lonelyplanet.com/members/kraub.

Sarina Singh

Andaman Islands, Plan & Understand sections After finishing a business degree in her hometown of Melbourne, Sarina went to India to pursue a corporate traineeship before working as a journalist. After five years she returned to Australia and completed postgraduate journalism qualifications before authoring Lonely Planet's first edition of *Rajasthan*. Apart from numerous Lonely Planet books she has written for a raft of other publications and has been a scriptwriter and expert commentator. Sarina is also the author of *Polo in India* as well as *India: Essential Encounters*. Her award-nominated documentary premiered at the prestigious Melbourne International Film Festival before screening internationally.

Michael Benanav

Uttar Pradesh, Uttarakhand When Michael was young, his father made the mistake of handing him a biography of Lawrence of Arabia, along with adventure novels like *Around the World in 80 Days*. Something was sparked as this bookwormish boy over-identified with the main characters in these tales. Today, he is a veteran traveller, writer, and photographer, who loves exploring places far from beaten tourist trails. He's authored three non-fiction books (set on three different continents) and writes and shoots for major publications. He also founded Traditional Cultures Project, which documents indigenous cultures around the world. To see some of his work, visit www.michaelbenanav.com.

Mark Elliott

Jammu & Kashmir (including Ladakh), Sikkim British-born travel writer Mark Elliott has lived and worked on five continents, authoring or contributing to more than 60 books. He has been visiting the subcontinent since a 1982 trip which lined his stomach for all eventualities. While delighting in India's full rainbow of cultures, he's especially drawn to the cool air, magnificent mountains and spiritual warmth of the Himalayan regions whether sharing sufi secrets in Srinagar, mumbling mantras in Ladakh or being dazzled by Sikkim's larger than life mega-temples/statues.

Paul Harding

Goa, Kerala As a writer and photographer, Paul has been travelling the globe for the best part of two decades, with an interest in remote and offbeat places and cultures. He's an author and contributor to more than 50 Lonely Planet guides to countries and regions as diverse as India, Iceland, Belize, Vanuatu, Iran, Indonesia, New Zealand, Finland and – his home patch – Australia.

OUR STORY

A beat-up old car, a few dollars in the pocket and a sense of adventure. In 1972 that's all Tony and Maureen Wheeler needed for the trip of a lifetime – across Europe and Asia overland to Australia. It took several months, and at the end – broke but inspired – they sat at their kitchen table writing and stapling together their first travel guide, *Across Asia on the Cheap*. Within a week they'd sold 1500 copies. Lonely Planet was born.

Today, Lonely Planet has offices in Franklin, London, Melbourne, Oakland, Dublin, Beijing and Delhi, with more than 600 staff and writers. We share Tony's belief that 'a great guidebook should do three things: inform, educate and amuse'.

OUR WRITERS

Abigail Blasi

Delhi, Plan & Survival sections A freelance travel writer, Abigail has lived and worked in London, Rome, Hong Kong, and Copenhagen. Lonely Planet have sent her to India, Egypt, Tunisia, Mauritania, Mali, Italy, Portugal, Malta and around Britain. She writes regularly for newspapers and magazines, such as the *Independent*, the *Telegraph*, and *Lonely Planet Traveller*. She has three children and they often come along for the ride. Follow her on Twitter and Instagram: @abiwhere

Lindsay Brown

Rajasthan Lindsay started travelling as a young bushwalker exploring the Blue Mountains west of Sydney. Then as a marine biologist he dived the coastal and island waters of southeastern Australia. He continued travelling whenever he could while employed at Lonely Planet as an editor and publishing manager. On becoming a freelance writer and photographer he has co-authored more than 30 Lonely Planet guides to Australia, Bhutan, India, Nepal, Pakistan and Papua New Guinea.

Anirban Mahapatra

Punjab & Haryana, Kolkata, West Bengal & Darjeeling, Northeast States Ever since he gave up his journalist day job in 2009, Anirban Mahapatra has been travelling across the farthest extents of India on professional assignments as a travel writer and documentary filmmaker. A Lonely Planet writer since 2007, he has so far worked on five consecutive editions of the India guidebook, mostly specialising in destinations in east and northeast India. When not socialising with tribal chiefs over rice beer in Meghalaya or hiking along jungle trails in primeval Arunachal Pradesh, he cools his heels at his studio in Kolkata, conveniently located near some of the city's choicest pubs and restaurants.

Isabella Noble

Tamil Nadu English-Australian on paper but Spanish at heart, Isabella has been wandering the globe since her first round-the-world trip as a one-year-old. Having grown up in a whitewashed Andalucian village, she is a Spain specialist travel journalist, but also writes extensively about India, Thailand, the UK and beyond for Lonely Planet, the *Daily Telegraph* and others. Isabella has co-written Lonely Planet guides to Spain and Andalucía, and contributed to *India, South India, Thailand, Thailand's Islands & Beaches, Southeast Asia on a Shoestring* and *Great Britain*, and authored *Pocket Phuket*. Find Isabella on Twitter and Instagram (@isabellamnoble).

OVER PAGE MORE WRITERS

Published by Lonely Planet Global Limited
CRN 554153
17th edition – October 2017
ISBN 978 1 78657 144 1

10 9 8 7 6 5 4 3 2 1
Printed in Singapore